List of Elements with Their Symbols and Atomic Masses

Element	Symbol	Atomic Number	Atomic Mass	Element	Symbol	Atomic Number	Atomic Mass
Actinium	Ac	89	227.03[a]	Meitnerium	Mt	109	268.14[a]
Aluminum	Al	13	26.98	Mendelevium	Md	101	258.10[a]
Americium	Am	95	243.06[a]	Mercury	Hg	80	200.59
Antimony	Sb	51	121.76	Molybdenum	Mo	42	95.96
Argon	Ar	18	39.95	Neodymium	Nd	60	144.24
Arsenic	As	33	74.92	Neon	Ne	10	20.18
Astatine	At	85	209.99[a]	Neptunium	Np	93	237.05[a]
Barium	Ba	56	137.33	Nickel	Ni	28	58.69
Berkelium	Bk	97	247.07[a]	Niobium	Nb	41	92.91
Beryllium	Be	4	9.012	Nitrogen	N	7	14.01
Bismuth	Bi	83	208.98	Nobelium	No	102	259.10[a]
Bohrium	Bh	107	264.12[a]	Osmium	Os	76	190.23
Boron	B	5	10.81	Oxygen	O	8	16.00
Bromine	Br	35	79.90	Palladium	Pd	46	106.42
Cadmium	Cd	48	112.41	Phosphorus	P	15	30.97
Calcium	Ca	20	40.08	Platinum	Pt	78	195.08
Californium	Cf	98	251.08[a]	Plutonium	Pu	94	244.06[a]
Carbon	C	6	12.01	Polonium	Po	84	208.98[a]
Cerium	Ce	58	140.12	Potassium	K	19	39.10
Cesium	Cs	55	132.91	Praseodymium	Pr	59	140.91
Chlorine	Cl	17	35.45	Promethium	Pm	61	145[a]
Chromium	Cr	24	52.00	Protactinium	Pa	91	231.04
Cotalt	Co	27	58.93	Radium	Ra	88	226.03[a]
Copernicium	Cn	112	285[a]	Radon	Rn	86	222.02[a]
Copper	Cu	29	63.55	Rhenium	Re	75	186.21
Curium	Cm	96	247.07[a]	Rhodium	Rh	45	102.91
Darmstadtium	Ds	110	271[a]	Roentgenium	Rg	111	272[a]
Dubnium	Db	105	262.11[a]	Rubidium	Rb	37	85.47
Dysprosium	Dy	66	162.50	Ruthenium	Ru	44	101.07
Einsteinium	Es	99	252.08[a]	Rutherfordium	Rf	104	261.11[a]
Erbium	Er	68	167.26	Samarium	Sm	62	150.36
Europium	Eu	63	151.96	Scandium	Sc	21	44.96
Fermium	Fm	100	257.10[a]	Seaborgium	Sg	106	266.12[a]
Flerovium	Fl	114	289[a]	Selenium	Se	34	78.96
Fluorine	F	9	19.00	Silicon	Si	14	28.09
Francium	Fr	87	223.02[a]	Silver	Ag	47	107.87
Gadolinium	Gd	64	157.25	Sodium	Na	11	22.99
Gallium	Ga	31	69.72	Strontium	Sr	38	87.62
Germanium	Ge	32	72.63	Sulfur	S	16	32.06
Gold	Au	79	196.97	Tantalum	Ta	73	180.95
Hafnium	Hf	72	178.49	Technetium	Tc	43	98[a]
Hassium	Hs	108	269.13[a]	Tellurium	Te	52	127.60
Helium	He	2	4.003	Terbium	Tb	65	158.93
Holmium	Ho	67	164.93	Thallium	Tl	81	204.38
Hydrogen	H	1	1.008	Thorium	Th	90	232.04
Indium	In	49	114.82	Thulium	Tm	69	168.93
Iodine	I	53	126.90	Tin	Sn	50	118.71
Iridium	Ir	77	192.22	Titanium	Ti	22	47.87
Iron	Fe	26	55.85	Tungsten	W	74	183.84
Krypton	Kr	36	83.80	Uranium	U	92	238.03
Lanthanum	La	57	138.91	Vanadium	V	23	50.94
Lawrencium	Lr	103	262.11[a]	Xenon	Xe	54	131.293
Lead	Pb	82	207.2	Ytterbium	Yb	70	173.05
Lithium	Li	3	6.94	Yttrium	Y	39	88.91
Livermorium	Lv	116	292[a]	Zinc	Zn	30	65.38
Lutetium	Lu	71	174.97	Zirconium	Zr	40	91.22
Magnesium	Mg	12	24.31	*[b]		113	284[a]
Manganese	Mn	25	54.94	*[b]		115	288[a]

[a]Mass of longest-lived or most important isotope.
[b]The names of these elements have not yet been decided.

PEARSON　　　　　ALWAYS LEARNING

Nivaldo J. Tro

Chemistry
A Molecular Approach

Custom Edition for Washington State University

Taken from:
Chemistry: A Molecular Approach, Third Edition
by Nivaldo J. Tro

Cover Art: Courtesy of Pearson Learning Solutions.

Taken from:

Chemistry: A Molecular Approach, Third Edition
by Nivaldo J. Tro
Copyright © 2014, 2011, 2008 by Pearson Education, Inc.
Upper Saddle River, New Jersey 07458

This special edition published in cooperation with Pearson Learning Solutions.

Pearson Learning Solutions, 501 Boylston Street, Suite 900, Boston, MA 02116
A Pearson Education Company
www.pearsoned.com

Printed in the United States of America

1 2 3 4 5 6 7 8 9 10 V0CR 17 16 15 14

000200010271890773

SL

ISBN 10: 1-269-93260-8
ISBN 13: 978-1-269-93260-8

To Michael, Ali, Kyle, and Kaden

About the Author

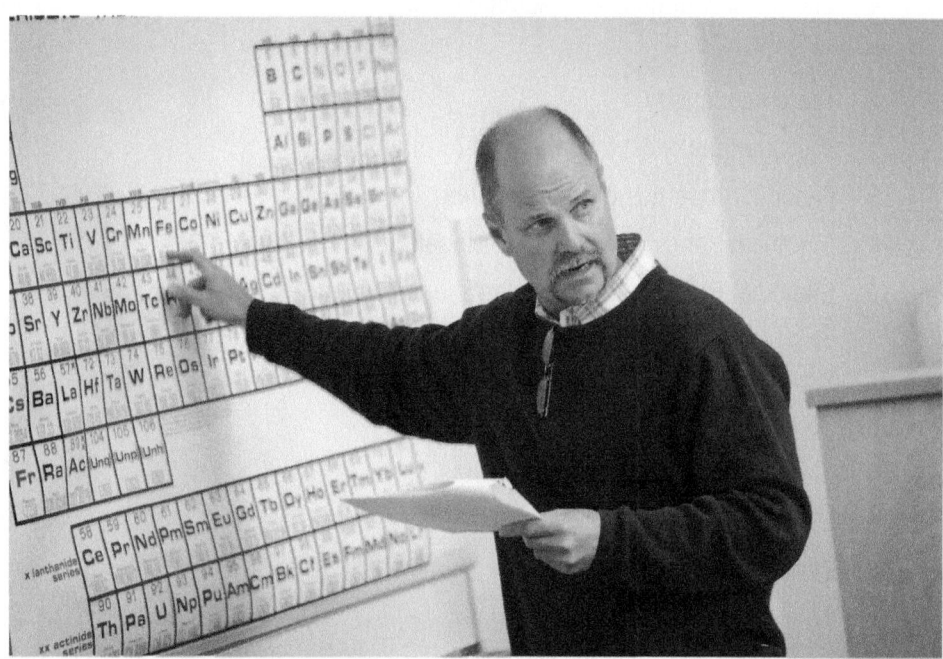

NIVALDO TRO is a professor of chemistry at Westmont College in Santa Barbara, California, where he has been a faculty member since 1990. He received his Ph.D. in chemistry from Stanford University for work on developing and using optical techniques to study the adsorption and desorption of molecules to and from surfaces in ultrahigh vacuum. He then went on to the University of California at Berkeley, where he did postdoctoral research on ultrafast reaction dynamics in solution. Since coming to Westmont, Professor Tro has been awarded grants from the American Chemical Society Petroleum Research Fund, from Research Corporation, and from the National Science Foundation to study the dynamics of various processes occurring in thin adlayer films adsorbed on dielectric surfaces. He has been honored as Westmont's outstanding teacher of the year three times and has also received the college's outstanding researcher of the year award. Professor Tro lives in Santa Barbara with his wife, Ann, and their four children, Michael, Ali, Kyle, and Kaden. In his leisure time, Professor Tro enjoys mountain biking, surfing, reading to his children, and being outdoors with his family.

Brief Contents

Contents

3   Molecules, Compounds, and Chemical Equations   86

4   Chemical Quantities and Aqueous Reactions   138

5 Gases   194

8 Periodic Properties of the Elements   334

9 Chemical Bonding I: The Lewis Model   380

10 Chemical Bonding II: Molecular Shapes, Valence Bond Theory, and Molecular Orbital Theory   424

11 Liquids, Solids, and Intermolecular Forces   482

12 Solutions   **544**

17 Free Energy and Thermodynamics 812

18 Electrochemistry 860

19   Radioactivity and Nuclear Chemistry   **910**

24 Transition Metals and Coordination Compounds 1098

Preface

To the Student

As you begin this course, I invite you to think about your reasons for enrolling in it. Why are you taking general chemistry? More generally, why are you pursuing a college education? If you are like most college students taking general chemistry, part of your answer is probably that this course is required for your major and that you are pursuing a college education so you can get a good job some day. While these are good reasons, I would like to suggest a better one. I think the primary reason for your education is to prepare you to *live a good life*. You should understand chemistry—not for what it can *get* you—but for what it can *do* to you. Understanding chemistry, I believe, is an important source of happiness and fulfillment. Let me explain.

Understanding chemistry helps you to live life to its fullest for two basic reasons. The first is *intrinsic*: through an understanding of chemistry, you gain a powerful appreciation for just how rich and extraordinary the world really is. The second reason is *extrinsic*: understanding chemistry makes you a more informed citizen—it allows you to engage with many of the issues of our day. In other words, understanding chemistry makes *you* a deeper and richer person and makes your country and the world a better place to live. These reasons have been the foundation of education from the very beginnings of civilization.

How does chemistry help prepare you for a rich life and conscientious citizenship? Let me explain with two examples. My first one comes from the very first page of Chapter 1 of this book. There, I ask the following question: What is the most important idea in all of scientific knowledge? My answer to that question is this: **the behavior of matter is determined by the properties of molecules and atoms**. That simple statement is the reason I love chemistry. We humans have been able to study the substances that compose the world around us and explain their behavior by reference to particles so small that they can hardly be imagined. If you have never realized the remarkable sensitivity of the world we *can* see to the world we *cannot*, you have missed out on a fundamental truth about our universe. To have never encountered this truth is like never having read a play by Shakespeare or seen a sculpture by Michelangelo—or, for that matter, like never having discovered that the world is round. It robs you of an amazing and unforgettable experience of the world and the human ability to understand it.

My second example demonstrates how science literacy helps you to be a better citizen. Although I am largely sympathetic to the environmental movement, a lack of science literacy within some sectors of that movement, and the resulting anti-environmental backlash, creates confusion that impedes real progress and opens the door to what could be misinformed policies. For example, I have heard conservative pundits say that volcanoes emit more carbon dioxide—the most significant greenhouse gas—than does petroleum combustion. I have also heard a liberal environmentalist say that we have to stop using hairspray because it is causing holes in the ozone layer that will lead to global warming. Well, the claim about volcanoes emitting more carbon dioxide than petroleum combustion can be refuted by the basic tools you will learn to use in Chapter 4 of this book. We can easily show that volcanoes emit only 1/50th as much carbon dioxide as petroleum combustion. As for hairspray depleting the ozone layer and thereby leading to global warming, the chlorofluorocarbons that deplete ozone have been banned from hairspray since 1978, and ozone depletion has nothing to do with global warming anyway. People with special interests or axes to grind can conveniently distort the truth before an ill-informed public, which is why we all need to be knowledgeable.

So this is why I think you should take this course. Not just to satisfy the requirement for your major, and not just to get a good job some day, but to help you to lead a fuller life and to make the world a little better for everyone. I wish you the best as you embark on the journey to understand the world around you at the molecular level. The rewards are well worth the effort.

To the Professor

First and foremost, thanks to all of you who adopted this book in its first and second editions. You helped to make this book one of the most popular general chemistry textbooks in the world. I am grateful beyond words. Second, I have listened carefully to your feedback on the previous edition. The changes you see in this edition are the direct result of your input, as well as my own experience using the book in my general chemistry courses. If you have acted as a reviewer or have contacted me directly, you will likely see your suggestions reflected in the changes I have made. Thank you.

In spite of the changes I just mentioned, the goal of the book remains the same: *to present a rigorous and accessible treatment of general chemistry in the context of relevance.* Teaching general chemistry would be much easier if all of our students had exactly the same level of preparation and ability. But alas, that is not the case. Even though I teach at a relatively selective institution, my courses are populated with students with a range of backgrounds and abilities in chemistry. The challenge of successful teaching, in my opinion, is therefore figuring out how to instruct and challenge the best students while not losing those with lesser backgrounds and abilities. My strategy has always been to set the bar relatively high, while at the same time providing the motivation and support necessary to reach the high bar. That is exactly the philosophy of this book. We do not have to compromise away rigor in order to make chemistry accessible to our students. In this book, I have worked hard to combine rigor with accessibility—to create a book that does not dilute the content, yet can be used and understood by any student willing to put in the necessary effort.

Chemistry: A Molecular Approach is first and foremost a *student-oriented book*. My main goal is to motivate students and get them to achieve at the highest possible level. As we all

Acknowledgments

The book you hold in your hands bears my name on the cover, but I am really only one member of a large team that carefully crafted the first edition, the second edition, and now the third edition of this book. Most importantly, I thank my new editor on this edition, Terry Haugen. Terry is a great editor and friend. He gives me the right balance of freedom and direction and always supports me in my endeavors. Thanks Terry for all you have done for me and for general chemistry courses throughout the world. I am just as grateful for my project editor, Jennifer Hart, who has now worked with me on multiple editions of several books. Jennifer, your guidance, organizational skills, and wisdom are central to the success of my projects, and I am eternally grateful. New to this edition is Jessica Moro. Although we have only worked together a short while, I am already indebted to her helpfulness. I am also grateful to Erin Kneuer, who helped with organizing reviews, as well as numerous other tasks associated with keeping the team running smoothly. I also thank Erin Mulligan, who has now worked with me on several projects. Erin is an outstanding developmental editor who not only worked with me on crafting and thinking through every word, but also became a friend and fellow foodie in the process. I am also grateful to Adam Jaworski. His skills and competence have led the chemistry team since he took over as editor-in-chief. And of course, I am continually grateful for Paul Corey, with whom I have now worked for over 12 years and 9 projects. Paul is a man of incredible energy and vision, and it is my great privilege to work with him. Paul told me many years ago (when he first signed me on to the Pearson team) to dream big, and then he provided the resources I needed to make those dreams come true. *Thanks, Paul.* I would also like to thank my first editor at Pearson, Kent Porter-Hamann. Kent and I spent many good years together writing books, and I continue to miss her presence in my work.

New to the team is my marketing manager, Jonathan Cottrell, and although we have worked together for only a short while, I am already impressed by his energy in marketing this book. I continue to owe a special word of thanks to Glenn and Meg Turner of Burrston House, ideal collaborators whose contributions to the first edition of the book were extremely important and much appreciated. Quade and Emiko Paul, who make my ideas come alive with their art, have been with us from the beginning, and I owe a special debt of gratitude to them. I am also grateful to Mark Ong and Emily Friel for their creativity and hard work in crafting the design of this text; to Michelle Durgerian, Shari Toron, and Gina Cheselka, whose skill and diligence gave this book its physical existence; and to Connie Long who managed the extensive art program. Finally, I would like to thank my copyeditor and proofreader from the GEX Publishing Services editorial team for their dedication and professionalism, and Erin Schrader for his exemplary photo research. The team at Pearson is a first-class operation—this text has benefited immeasurably from their talents and hard work.

I acknowledge the great work of my colleague Mary Beth Kramer from the Chemistry Department at University of Delaware, who has been a co-author on the solutions manual for this book. Mary Beth Kramer worked tirelessly to ensure that the solutions manual was accurate and useful to students. Sadly, Professor Kramer passed away shortly before this book went to press. We will all miss her and her excellent work. A special thank you to Kathleen Thrush Shaginaw for all her hard work in order to complete the Solutions Manual on time.

I acknowledge the help of my colleagues Allan Nishimura, Kristi Lazar, David Marten, Stephen Contakes, Michael Everest, and Carrie Hill who have supported me in my department while I worked on this book. I am also grateful to Gayle Beebe, the president of Westmont College, who has allowed me the time and space to work on my books. Thank you, Gayle, for allowing me to pursue my gifts and my vision. I am also grateful to those who have supported me personally. First on that list is my wife, Ann. Her patience and love for me are beyond description, and without her, this book would never have been written. I am also indebted to my children, Michael, Ali, Kyle, and Kaden, whose smiling faces and love of life always inspire me. I come from a large Cuban family whose closeness and support most people would envy. Thanks to my parents, Nivaldo and Sara; my siblings, Sarita, Mary, and Jorge; my siblings-in-law, Jeff, Nachy, Karen, and John; my nephews and nieces, Germain, Danny, Lisette, Sara, and Kenny. These are the people with whom I celebrate life.

I would like to thank all of the general chemistry students who have been in my classes throughout my 22 years as a professor at Westmont College. You have taught me much about teaching that is now in this book. I am especially grateful to Michael Tro who put in many hours proofreading my manuscript, working problems and quiz questions, and organizing art codes and appendices. Michael, you are an amazing kid—it is my privilege to have you work with me on this project. I would also like to express my appreciation to Josh Alamillo, Catherine Olson, Hannah Sievers, and Rose Corcoran, who were a tremendous help with the new self assessment quizzes.

I would like to thank Brian Woodfield from Brigham Young University, the students at the University of Kentucky, and the Pearson Student Advisory Board for helping me create the interactive worked examples.

Lastly, I am indebted to the many reviewers, listed on the following pages, whose ideas are imbedded throughout this book. They have corrected me, inspired me, and sharpened my thinking on how best to teach this subject we call chemistry. I deeply appreciate their commitment to this project. I am particularly grateful to Bob Boikess for his important contributions to the book. Thanks also to Frank Lambert for his review of the entropy sections in the first edition of the book, and to Diane K. Smith for her review of and input on the electrochemistry chapter. Last but by no means least, I would like to thank Nancy Lee for her suggestions on the origin of elements box, and Alyse Dilts, Tracey Knowles, Gary Mines, and Alison Soult for their help in reviewing page proofs.

Reviewers

Michael R. Adams, *Xavier University of Louisiana*
Patricia G. Amateis, *Virginia Tech*
Margaret R. Asirvatham, *University of Colorado*
Paul Badger, *Robert Morris University*
Monica H. Baloga, *Florida Institute of Technology*
Rebecca Barlag, *Ohio University*
Mufeed M. Basti, *North Carolina Agricultural & Technological State University*
Amy E. Beilstein, *Centre College*
Maria Benavides, *University of Houston, Downtown*
Kyle A. Beran, *University of Texas of the Permian Basin*
Thomas Bertolini, *University of Southern California*
Christine V. Bilicki, *Pasadena City College*

Silas C. Blackstock, *University of Alabama*
Robert E. Blake, *Texas Tech University*
Angela E. Boerger, *Loyola University*
Robert S. Boikess, *Rutgers University*
Paul Brandt, *North Central College*
Michelle M. Brooks, *College of Charleston*
Joseph H. Bularzik, *Purdue University, Calumet*
Cindy M. Burkhardt, *Radford University*
Andrew E. Burns, *Kent State University, Stark Campus*
Kim C. Calvo, *University of Akron*
Stephen C. Carlson, *Lansing Community College*
David A. Carter, *Angelo State University*
Eric G. Chesloff, *Villanova University*
William M. Cleaver, *University of Vermont*
Charles T. Cox, Jr., *Georgia Institute of Technology*
J. Ricky Cox, *Murray State University*
Samuel R. Cron, *Arkansas State*
Darwin B. Dahl, *Western Kentucky University*
Robert F. Dias, *Old Dominion University*
Daniel S. Domin, *Tennessee State University*
Alan D. Earhart, *Southeast Community College*
Amina K. El-Ashmawy, *Collin County Community College*
Joseph P. Ellison, *United States Military Academy, West Point*
Joseph M. Eridon, *Albuquerque TVI*
Deborah B. Exton, *University of Oregon*
William A. Faber, *Grand Rapids Community College*
Michael Ferguson, *University of Hawaii*
Maria C. Fermin-Ennis, *Gordon College*
Oscar Navarro Fernandez, *University of Hawaii*
Jan Florian, *Loyola University*
Andy Frazer, *University of Central Florida*
Candice E. Fulton, *Midwestern State*
Ron Garber, *California State University Long Beach*
Carlos D. Garcia, *University of Texas, San Antonio*
Eric S. Goll, *Brookdale Community College*
Robert A. Gossage, *Acadia University*
Pierre Y. Goueth, *Santa Monica College*
Thomas J. Greenbowe, *Iowa State*
Victoria Guarisco, *Macon State College*
Christin Gustafson, *Illinois Central College*
Jason A. Halfen, *University of Wisconsin, Eau Claire*
Nathan Hammer, *University of Mississippi*
Michael D. Hampton, *University of Central Florida*
Tamara Hanna, *Texas Tech University*
Lois Hansen-Polcar, *Cuyahoga Community College West*
Tony Hascall, *Northern Arizona University*
Monte L. Helm, *Fort Lewis College*
David E. Henderson, *Trinity College*
Susan K. Henderson, *Quinnipiac University*
Peter M. Hierl, *University of Kansas*
Paula Hjorth-Gustin, *San Diego Mesa College*
Angela Hoffman, *University of Portland*
Todd A. Hopkins, *Butler University*
Byron E. Howell, *Tyler Junior College*
Ralph Isovitsch, *Xavier University of Louisiana*
Kenneth C. Janda, *University of California, Irvine*
Milt Johnston, *University of South Florida*
Jason A. Kautz, *University of Nebraska, Lincoln*
Catherine A. Keenan, *Chaffey College*
Steven W. Keller, *University of Missouri, Columbia*
Resa Kelly, *San Jose State University*
Chulsung Kim, *Georgia Gwinnett College*
Louis J. Kirschenbaum, *University of Rhode Island*
Mark Knecht, *University of Kentucky*
Bette Kreuz, *University of Michigan, Dearborn*
Tim Krieder
Sergiy Kryatov, *Tufts University*
Richard H. Langley, *Stephen F. Austin State University*
Clifford B. Lemaster, *Boise State University*
Robley Light, *Florida State University*
Adam List, *Vanderbilt University*
Christopher Lovallo, *Mount Royal College*
Eric Malina, *University of Nebraska, Lincoln*
Benjamin R. Martin, *Texas State*
Lydia J. Martinez-Rivera, *University of Texas, San Antonio*
Marcus T. McEllistrem, *University of Wisconsin, Eau Claire*
Danny G. McGuire, *Cameron University*
Charles W. McLaughlin, *University of Nebraska, Lincoln*
Curt L. McLendon, *Saddleback College*
Robert C. McWilliams, *United States Military Academy*
David H. Metcalf, *University of Virginia*
Ray Mohseni, *East Tennessee State University*
Elisabeth A. Morlino, *University of the Science, Philadelphia*
James E. Murphy, *Santa Monica College*
Maria C. Nagan, *Truman State University*
Edward J. Neth, *University of Connecticut*
Aric Opdahl, *University of Wisconsin La Crosse*
Kenneth S. Overway, *Bates College*

Greg Owens, *University of Utah*
Naresh Pandya, *University of Hawaii*
Gerard Parkin, *Columbia University*
Jessica Parr, *University of Southern California*
Yasmin Patell, *Kansas State University*
Tom Pentecost, *Grand Valley State University*
Glenn A. Petrie, *Central Missouri State*
Norbert J. Pienta, *University of Iowa*
Louis H. Pignolet, *University of Minnesota*
Valerie Reeves, *University of New Brunswick*
Dawn J. Richardson, *Colin College*
Thomas G. Richmond, *University of Utah*
Dana L. Richter-Egger, *University of Nebraska*
Jason Ritchie, *University of Mississippi*
Christopher P. Roy, *Duke University*
A. Timothy Royappa, *University of West Florida*
Stephen P. Ruis, *American River College*
Alan E. Sadurski, *Ohio Northern University*
Thomas W. Schleich, *University of California, Santa Cruz*
Rod Schoonover, *CA Polytechnic State University*
Tom Selegue, *Pima Community College, West*
Anju H. Sharma, *Stevens Institute of Technology*
Sherril A. Soman, *Grand Valley State University*
Michael S. Sommer, *University of Wyoming*
Jie S. Song, *University of Michigan, Flint*
Mary Kay Sorenson, *University of Wisconsin, Milwaukee*
Stacy E. Sparks, *University of Texas, Austin*
Richard Spinney, *Ohio State University*
William H. Steel, *York College of Pennsylvania*
Vinodhkumar Subramaniam, *East Carolina University*
Jerry Suits, *University of Northern Colorado*
Tamar Y. Susskind, *Oakland Community College*
Uma Swamy, *Florida International University*
Ryan Sweeder, *Michigan State University*
Dennis Taylor, *Clemson University*
Jacquelyn Thomas, *Southwestern College*
Kathleen Thrush Shaginaw, *Villanova University*
Lydia Tien, *Monroe Community College*
David Livingstone Toppen, *California State University Northridge*
Marcy Towns, *Purdue University*
Harold Trimm, *Broome Community College*
Laura VanDorn, *University of Arizona*
Susan Varkey, *Mount Royal College*
Ramaiyer Venkatraman, *Jackson State University*
John B. Vincent, *University of Alabama, Tuscaloosa*
Kent S. Voelkner, *Lake Superior College*
Sheryl K. Wallace, *South Plains College*
Wayne E. Wesolowski, *University of Arizona*
Sarah E. West, *Notre Dame University*
John Wiginton, *University of Mississippi*
Kurt J. Winkelmann, *Florida Institute of Technology*
Troy D. Wood, *University of Buffalo*
Servet M. Yatin, *Quincy College*
Kazushige Yokoyama, *SUNY Geneseo*
Lin Zhu, *IUPUI*

Focus Group Participants

We would like to thank the following professors for contributing their valuable time to meet with the author and the publishing team in order to provide a meaningful perspective on the most important challenges they face in teaching general chemistry and give us insight into creating a new general chemistry text that successfully responds to those challenges.

Focus Group 1

Michael R. Abraham, *University of Oklahoma*
Steven W. Keller, *University of Missouri, Columbia*
Roy A. Lacey, *State University of New York, Stony Brook*
Norbert J. Pienta, *University of Iowa*
Cathrine E. Reck, *Indiana University*
Reva A. Savkar, *Northern Virginia Community College*

Focus Group 2

Amina K. El-Ashmawy, *Collin County Community College*
Steven W. Keller, *University of Missouri, Columbia*
Joseph L. March, *University of Alabama, Birmingham*
Norbert J. Pienta, *University of Iowa*

Focus Group 3

James A. Armstrong, *City College of San Francisco*
Roberto A. Bogomolni, *University of California, Santa Cruz*

Taking your students further

DR. TRO'S hallmark problem-solving approach is reinforced through interactive media that incorporates worked examples accessible on mobile devices via QR code on the back cover of your textbook, via links within the eText, and also in the study area of MasteringChemistry.® He makes chemistry relevant to your everyday life, your future career, and the world around you through expanded coverage on the latest developments in chemistry.

Telling the Story of Chemistry with

Chemistry is **relevant to every process** occurring around us, at every second. Niva Tro helps you understand this connection by weaving specific, vivid examples throughout the text that tell the story of chemistry. Every chapter begins with a brief story showing chemistry is relevant to all people, at every moment.

Relevant Stories and Examples

Tro opens each chapter by giving a specific example of the concept to grab students' attention, stepping back to make a more general and relatable analogy, and then going back into specifics. This style is reinforced by both his own classroom experiences and other successful science writers.

Problem Solving Reinforced by

A consistent **step-by-step framework** encourages thinking logically through the problem-solving process rather than simply memorizing formulas.

NEW! 40 Interactive Worked Examples have been created for viewing on mobile devices. Interactive examples instruct you in breaking down problems with Tro's proven 'Sort, Strategize, Solve, and Check" technique and include questions asking students to predict the outcome.

The **left column** explains how the problem is solved.

A four-part structure ("Sort, Strategize, Solve, Check") provides you with a framework for analyzing and solving problems.

Every Worked Example is followed by "For Practice" Problems that you can try to solve on your own. Answers to "For Practice" Problems are in Appendix IV.

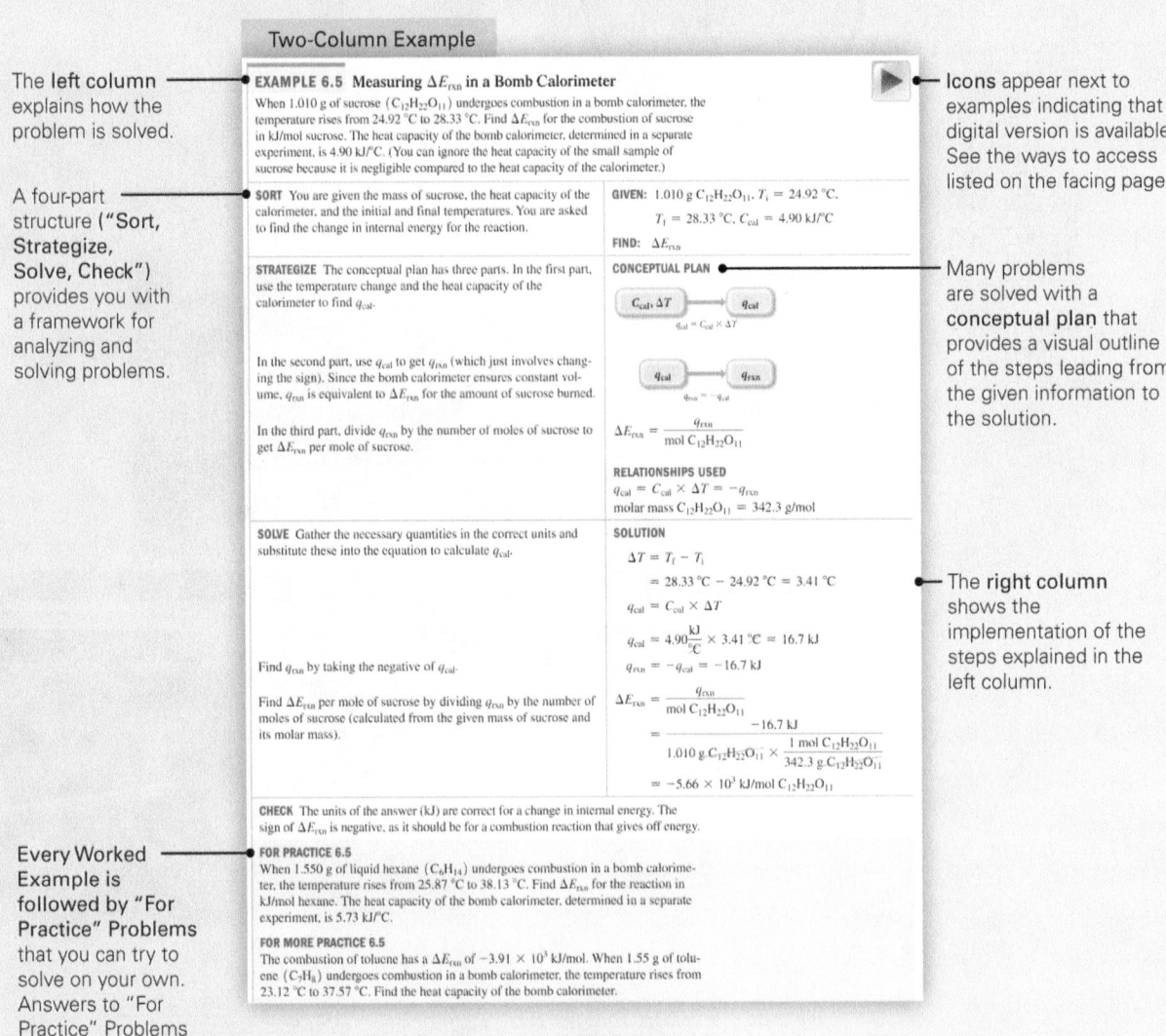

Two-Column Example

EXAMPLE 6.5 Measuring ΔE_{rxn} in a Bomb Calorimeter

When 1.010 g of sucrose ($C_{12}H_{22}O_{11}$) undergoes combustion in a bomb calorimeter, the temperature rises from 24.92 °C to 28.33 °C. Find ΔE_{rxn} for the combustion of sucrose in kJ/mol sucrose. The heat capacity of the bomb calorimeter, determined in a separate experiment, is 4.90 kJ/°C. (You can ignore the heat capacity of the small sample of sucrose because it is negligible compared to the heat capacity of the calorimeter.)

SORT You are given the mass of sucrose, the heat capacity of the calorimeter, and the initial and final temperatures. You are asked to find the change in internal energy for the reaction.

GIVEN: 1.010 g $C_{12}H_{22}O_{11}$, $T_i = 24.92$ °C.
$T_f = 28.33$ °C, $C_{cal} = 4.90$ kJ/°C

FIND: ΔE_{rxn}

STRATEGIZE The conceptual plan has three parts. In the first part, use the temperature change and the heat capacity of the calorimeter to find q_{cal}.

In the second part, use q_{cal} to get q_{rxn} (which just involves changing the sign). Since the bomb calorimeter ensures constant volume, q_{rxn} is equivalent to ΔE_{rxn} for the amount of sucrose burned.

In the third part, divide q_{rxn} by the number of moles of sucrose to get ΔE_{rxn} per mole of sucrose.

CONCEPTUAL PLAN

$$C_{cal}, \Delta T \longrightarrow q_{cal}$$
$$q_{cal} = C_{cal} \times \Delta T$$

$$q_{cal} \longrightarrow q_{rxn}$$
$$q_{rxn} = -q_{cal}$$

$$\Delta E_{rxn} = \frac{q_{rxn}}{\text{mol } C_{12}H_{22}O_{11}}$$

RELATIONSHIPS USED
$q_{cal} = C_{cal} \times \Delta T = -q_{rxn}$
molar mass $C_{12}H_{22}O_{11} = 342.3$ g/mol

SOLVE Gather the necessary quantities in the correct units and substitute these into the equation to calculate q_{cal}.

Find q_{rxn} by taking the negative of q_{cal}.

Find ΔE_{rxn} per mole of sucrose by dividing q_{rxn} by the number of moles of sucrose (calculated from the given mass of sucrose and its molar mass).

SOLUTION

$$\Delta T = T_f - T_i$$
$$= 28.33\ °C - 24.92\ °C = 3.41\ °C$$

$$q_{cal} = C_{cal} \times \Delta T$$

$$q_{cal} = 4.90\frac{kJ}{°C} \times 3.41\ °C = 16.7\ kJ$$

$$q_{rxn} = -q_{cal} = -16.7\ kJ$$

$$\Delta E_{rxn} = \frac{q_{rxn}}{\text{mol } C_{12}H_{22}O_{11}}$$

$$= \frac{-16.7\ kJ}{1.010\ g\ C_{12}H_{22}O_{11} \times \frac{1\ mol\ C_{12}H_{22}O_{11}}{342.3\ g\ C_{12}H_{22}O_{11}}}$$

$$= -5.66 \times 10^3\ kJ/mol\ C_{12}H_{22}O_{11}$$

CHECK The units of the answer (kJ) are correct for a change in internal energy. The sign of ΔE_{rxn} is negative, as it should be for a combustion reaction that gives off energy.

FOR PRACTICE 6.5
When 1.550 g of liquid hexane (C_6H_{14}) undergoes combustion in a bomb calorimeter, the temperature rises from 25.87 °C to 38.13 °C. Find ΔE_{rxn} for the reaction in kJ/mol hexane. The heat capacity of the bomb calorimeter, determined in a separate experiment, is 5.73 kJ/°C.

FOR MORE PRACTICE 6.5
The combustion of toluene has a ΔE_{rxn} of -3.91×10^3 kJ/mol. When 1.55 g of toluene (C_7H_8) undergoes combustion in a bomb calorimeter, the temperature rises from 23.12 °C to 37.57 °C. Find the heat capacity of the bomb calorimeter.

Icons appear next to examples indicating that a digital version is available. See the ways to access listed on the facing page.

Many problems are solved with a **conceptual plan** that provides a visual outline of the steps leading from the given information to the solution.

The **right column** shows the implementation of the steps explained in the left column.

Interactive Worked Examples

Four Ways for Students to Access Digital Worked Examples!

- **Via QR code** on the back cover of your textbook
- **Located in the Study Area** in MasteringChemistry®
- **Instructors can access these via the Instructor Resource DVD** (IR-DVD) and Instructor Resource Center for in-class use (www.pearsonhighered.com/irc)
- **Via links within the eText**

Example 1.9 Unit Conversions Involving Units Raised to a Power

$$L \longrightarrow mL \longrightarrow cm^3 \longrightarrow in^3$$

$$\frac{1\ mL}{10^{-3}\ L} \qquad \frac{1\ cm^3}{1\ mL} \qquad \frac{(1\ in)^3}{(2.54\ cm)^3}$$

$$5.70\ L \times \frac{1\ mL}{10^{-3}\ L} \times \frac{1\ cm^3}{1\ mL} \times \frac{(1\ in)^3}{(2.54\ cm)^3} = 347.835\ in^3$$

Scan this QR code (located on the back cover of the textbook) with your smartphone to access the Digital Worked Examples.

A Consistent Problem-solving Strategy

A **consistent approach to problem solving** is used throughout the book and helps students understand the logic and purpose of each step in the problem-solving process.

Problem-solving Procedure Boxes for important categories of problems enable you to see how the same reasoning applies to different problems.

The **general procedure** is shown in the left column.

Two Worked Examples, side by side, make it easy to see how differences are handled.

Three-Column Example

PROCEDURE FOR... Predicting Molecular Geometries	EXAMPLE 10.2 Predicting Molecular Geometries Predict the geometry and bond angles of PCl_3.	EXAMPLE 10.3 Predicting Molecular Geometries Predict the geometry and bond angles of ICl_4^-.
1. **Draw the Lewis structure for the molecule.**	PCl_3 has 26 valence electrons.	ICl_4^- has 36 valence electrons.
2. **Determine the total number of electron groups around the central atom.** Lone pairs, single bonds, double bonds, triple bonds, and single electrons each count as one group.	The central atom (P) has four electron groups.	The central atom (I) has six electron groups.
3. **Determine the number of bonding groups and the number of lone pairs around the central atom.** These should sum to your result from step 2. Bonding groups include single bonds, double bonds, and triple bonds.	Lone pair. Three of the four electron groups around P are bonding groups and one is a lone pair.	Lone pairs. Four of the six electron groups around I are bonding groups and two are lone pairs.
4. **Refer to Table 10.1 to determine the electron geometry and molecular geometry.** If no lone pairs are present around the central atom, the bond angles will be that of the ideal geometry. If lone pairs are present, the bond angles may be smaller than the ideal geometry.	The electron geometry is tetrahedral (four electron groups) and the molecular geometry—the shape of the molecule—is *trigonal pyramidal* (three bonding groups and one lone pair). Because of the presence of a lone pair, the bond angles are less than 109.5°. <109.5° Trigonal pyramidal	The electron geometry is octahedral (six electron groups) and the molecular geometry—the shape of the molecule—is *square planar* (four bonding groups and two lone pairs). Even though lone pairs are present, the bond angles are 90° because the lone pairs are symmetrically arranged and do not compress the I—Cl bond angles. 90° Square planar
	FOR PRACTICE 10.2 Predict the molecular geometry and bond angle of ClNO.	**FOR PRACTICE 10.3** Predict the molecular geometry of I_3^-.

Conceptual Connections are strategically placed to reinforce conceptual understanding of the most complex concepts.

Conceptual Connection 1.3 Chemical and Physical Changes

The diagram on the left represents liquid water molecules in a pan. Which of the three diagrams (a, b or c) best represents the water molecules after they have been vaporized by the boiling of liquid water?

(a)   (b)   (c)

Each chapter includes several Conceptual Connections, in which students are asked to think about concepts and solve problems without doing any math.

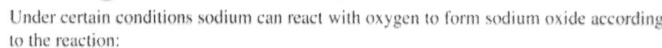

Conceptual Connection 4.1 Stoichiometry

Under certain conditions sodium can react with oxygen to form sodium oxide according to the reaction:

$$4 \, Na(s) + O_2(g) \rightarrow 2 \, Na_2O(s)$$

A flask contains the amount of oxygen represented by the diagram at left.

Which image below best represents the amount of sodium required to completely react with all of the oxygen in the flask according to the equation?

(a)   (b)   (c)   (d)

Conceptual Connection 5.5 Pressure and Number of Moles

Nitrogen and hydrogen react to form ammonia according to the following equation:

$$N_2(g) + 3 \, H_2(g) \rightleftharpoons 2 \, NH_3(g)$$

Consider the following representations of the initial mixture of reactants and the resulting mixture after the reaction has been allowed to react for some time:

If the volume is kept constant, and nothing is added to the reaction mixture, what happens to the total pressure during the course of the reaction?

(a) the pressure increases

(b) the pressure decreases

(c) the pressure does not change

NEW! Approximately 50 Conceptual Connections have been added, including many that involve visualization and drawing.

MasteringChemistry® **for Students**
www.masteringchemistry.com

MasteringChemistry tutorials guide students through the most challenging topics while helping them make connections between related chemical concepts. Immediate feedback and tutorial assistance help students understand and master concepts and skills in chemistry—allowing them to retain more knowledge and perform better in this course and beyond.

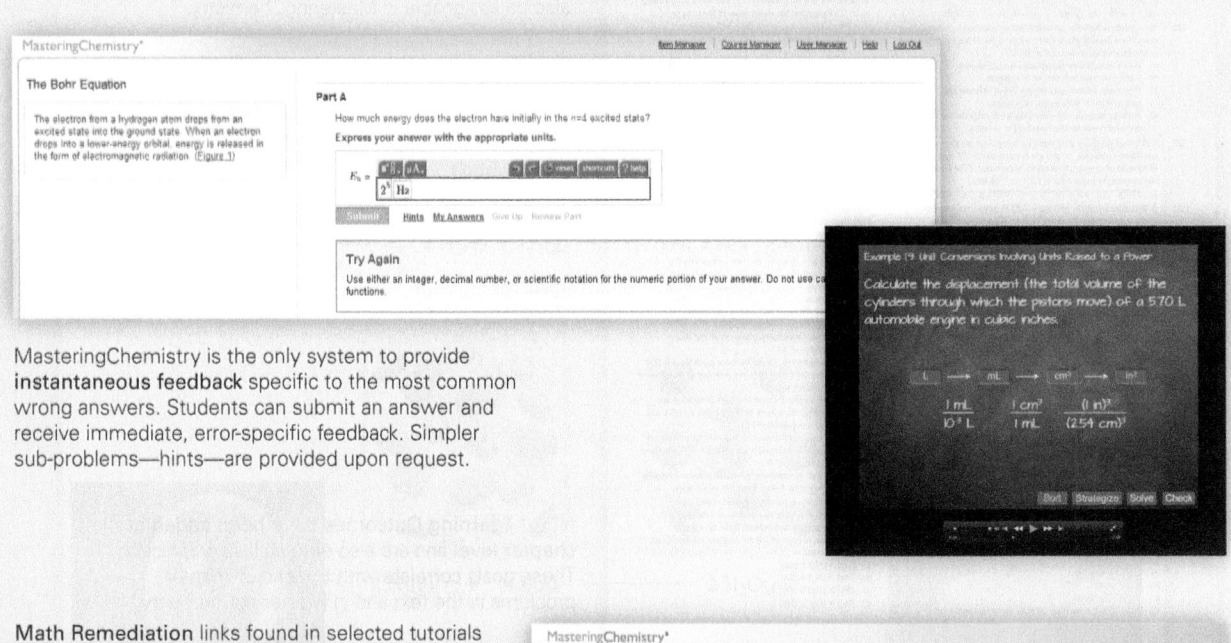

MasteringChemistry is the only system to provide **instantaneous feedback** specific to the most common wrong answers. Students can submit an answer and receive immediate, error-specific feedback. Simpler sub-problems—hints—are provided upon request.

Math Remediation links found in selected tutorials launch algorithmically generated math exercises that give students unlimited opportunity for practice and mastery of math skills. Math Remediation exercises provide additional practice and free up class and office-hour time to focus on the chemistry. Exercises include guided solutions, sample problems, and learning aids for extra help, and offer helpful feedback when students enter incorrect answers.

MasteringChemistry brings chemistry to life by illustrating key topics in general chemistry.

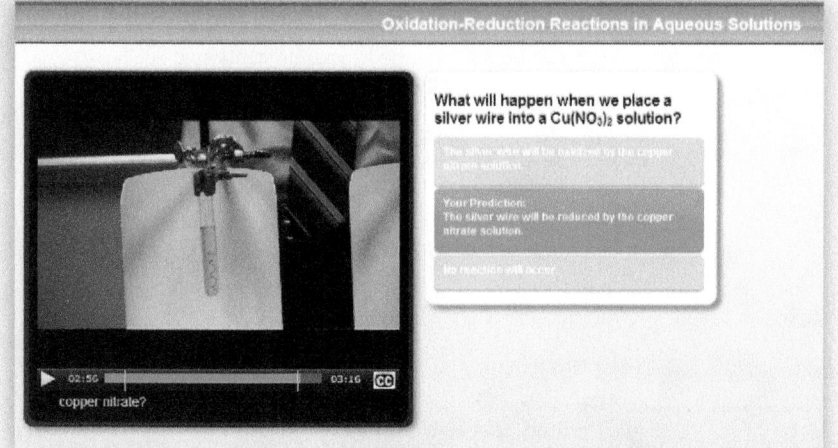

NEW! 15 Pause and Predict Video Quizzes ask students to predict the outcome of experiments and demonstrations as they watch the videos; a set of multiple-choice questions challenges students to apply the concepts from the video to related scenarios. These videos are also available in web and mobile-friendly formats through the Study Area of MasteringChemistry and in the Pearson eText.

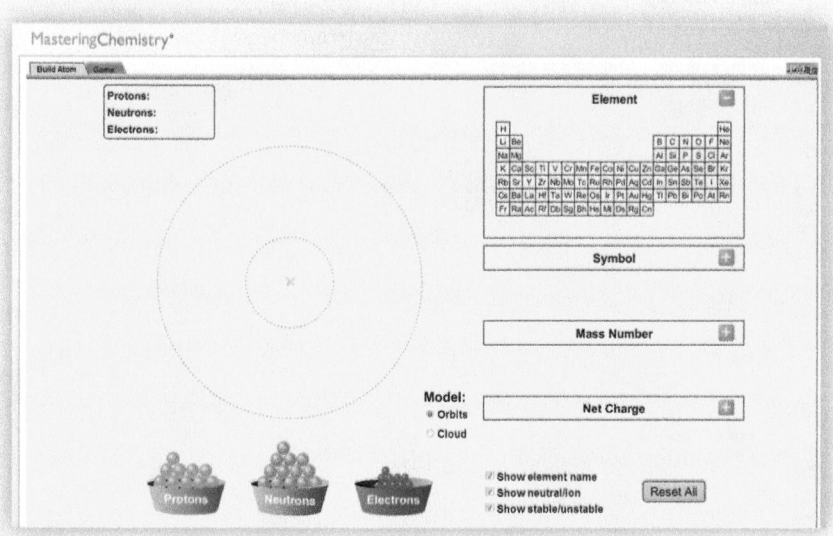

NEW! 15 Simulations, assignable in MasteringChemistry, include those developed by the PhET Chemistry Group, and the leading authors in the simulation development covering some of the most difficult chemistry concepts.

MasteringChemistry® for Instructors
www.masteringchemistry.com

The Mastering platform was developed **by scientists** for science students and instructors. Mastering has been refined from data-driven insights derived from over a decade of real-world use by faculty and students.

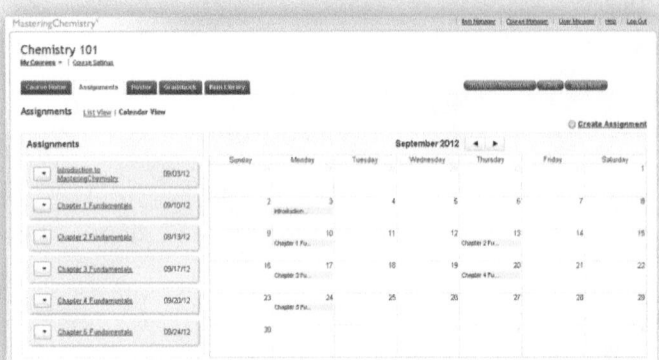

NEW! Calendar Features

The Course Home default page now features a **Calendar View** displaying upcoming assignments and due dates.

- Instructors can schedule assignments by dragging and dropping the assignment onto a date in the calendar. If the due date of an assignment needs to change, instructors can drag the assignment to the new due date and change the "available from and to dates" accordingly.

- The calendar view gives students a syllabus-style overview of due dates, making it easy to see all assignments due in a given month.

Gradebook

Every assignment is automatically graded. Shades of red highlight struggling students and challenging assignments.

Gradebook Diagnostics

This screen provides you with your favorite diagnostics. With a single click, charts summarize the most difficult problems, vulnerable students, grade distribution, and even score improvement over the course.

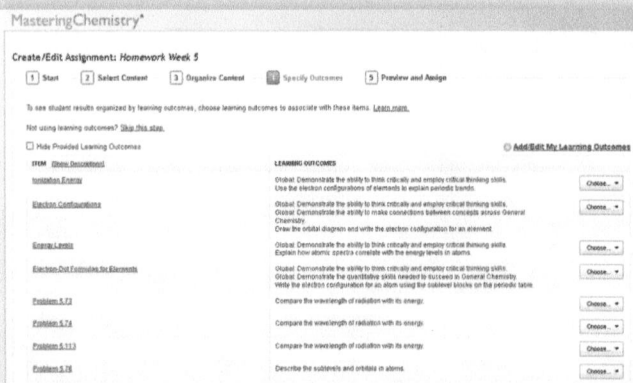

NEW! Learning Outcomes

Let Mastering do the work in tracking student performance against your learning outcomes:

- Add your own or use the publisher provided learning outcomes.

- View class performance against the specified learning outcomes.

- Export results to a spreadsheet that you can further customize and share with your chair, dean, administrator, or accreditation board.

CHEMISTRY

1

Matter, Measurement, and Problem Solving

The most incomprehensible thing about the universe is that it is comprehensible.

—Albert Einstein (1879–1955)

WHAT DO YOU THINK is the most important idea in all of human knowledge? There are, of course, many possible answers to this question—some practical, some philosophical, and some scientific. If we limit ourselves only to scientific answers, mine would be this: **the properties of matter are determined by the properties of atoms and molecules.** Atoms and molecules determine how matter behaves—if they were different, matter would be different. The properties of water molecules determine how water behaves, the properties of sugar molecules determine how sugar behaves, and the properties of the molecules that compose our bodies determine how our bodies behave. The understanding of matter at the molecular level gives us unprecedented control over that matter. For example, our understanding of the details of the molecules that compose living organisms has revolutionized biology over the last 50 years.

Hemoglobin (depicted in blue and green) is the oxygen-carrying protein in blood. Hemoglobin normally binds oxygen, but it can also bind carbon monoxide molecules (the linked red and black spheres).

1.1 Atoms and Molecules

The air over most U.S. cities, including my own, contains at least some pollution. A significant component of that pollution is carbon monoxide, a colorless gas emitted in the exhaust of cars and trucks. Carbon monoxide gas is composed of carbon monoxide molecules, each of which contains a carbon *atom* and an oxygen *atom* held together by a chemical bond. **Atoms** are the submicroscopic particles that constitute the fundamental building blocks of ordinary matter. Free atoms are rare in nature; instead they bind together in specific geometrical arrangements to form **molecules**.

The properties of the substances around us depend on the atoms and molecules that compose the substances, so the properties of carbon monoxide *gas* depend on the properties of carbon monoxide *molecules*. Carbon monoxide molecules happen to be just the right size and shape, and happen to have just the right chemical properties, to fit neatly into cavities within hemoglobin molecules in blood that normally carry oxygen molecules (Figure 1.1 ▶). Consequently, carbon monoxide diminishes the oxygen-carrying capacity of blood. Breathing air containing too much carbon monoxide (greater than 0.04% by volume) can lead to unconsciousness and even death because not enough

Carbon monoxide molecule

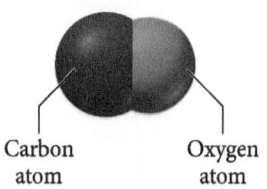

Carbon   Oxygen
atom   atom

1

Hemoglobin, the oxygen-carrying molecule in red blood cells

Carbon monoxide can bind to the site on hemoglobin that normally carries oxygen.

▲ FIGURE 1.1 **Binding of Oxygen and Carbon Monoxide to Hemoglobin**   Hemoglobin, a large protein molecule, is the oxygen carrier in red blood cells. Each subunit of the hemoglobin molecule contains an iron atom to which oxygen binds. Carbon monoxide molecules can take the place of oxygen, thus reducing the amount of oxygen reaching the body's tissues.

oxygen reaches the brain. Carbon monoxide deaths can occur as a result of running an automobile in a closed garage or using a propane burner in an enclosed space for too long. In smaller amounts, carbon monoxide causes the heart and lungs to work harder and can result in headaches, dizziness, weakness, and confusion.

Cars and trucks emit another closely related molecule, called carbon dioxide, in far greater quantities than carbon monoxide. The only difference between carbon dioxide and carbon monoxide is that carbon dioxide molecules contain two oxygen atoms instead of just one. However, this extra oxygen atom dramatically affects the properties of the gas. We breathe much more carbon dioxide—which composes 0.04% of air, and is a product of our own respiration as well—than carbon monoxide, yet it does not kill us. Why? Because the presence of the second oxygen atom prevents carbon dioxide from binding to the oxygen-carrying site in hemoglobin, making it far less toxic. Although high levels of carbon dioxide (greater than 10% of air) can be hazardous for other reasons, lower levels can enter the bloodstream with no adverse effects. Such is the molecular world. Any differences between molecules—such as the extra oxygen atom in carbon monoxide—results in differences between the substances that the molecules compose.

As another example, consider two other closely related molecules, water and hydrogen peroxide:

Carbon dioxide molecule

Oxygen atom   Oxygen atom

Carbon atom

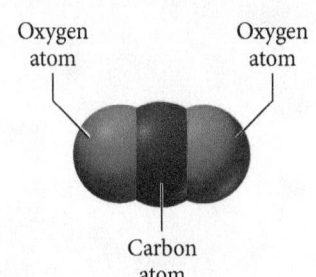

In the study of chemistry, atoms are often portrayed as colored spheres, with each color representing a different kind of atom. For example, a black sphere represents a carbon atom, a red sphere represents an oxygen atom, and a white sphere represents a hydrogen atom. For a complete color code of atoms, see Appendix IIA.

Water molecule

Oxygen atom

Hydrogen atoms

Hydrogen peroxide molecule

Oxygen atoms

Hydrogen atoms

A water molecule is composed of *one* oxygen atom and two hydrogen atoms. A hydrogen peroxide molecule is composed of *two* oxygen atoms and two hydrogen atoms. This seemingly small molecular difference results in a huge difference in the properties of water and hydrogen peroxide. Water is the familiar and stable liquid we all drink and bathe in. Hydrogen peroxide, in contrast, is an unstable liquid that, in its pure form, burns the skin on contact and is used in rocket fuel. When you pour water onto your hair, your hair simply becomes wet. However, if you put diluted hydrogen peroxide on your hair—which you may have done if you have ever bleached your hair—a chemical reaction occurs that strips your hair of its color.

The hydrogen peroxide we use as an antiseptic or bleaching agent is considerably diluted.

The details of how specific atoms bond to form a molecule—in a straight line, at a particular angle, in a ring, or in some other pattern—as well as the type of atoms in the molecule, determine everything about the substance that the molecule composes. If we want to understand the substances around us, we must understand the atoms and molecules that compose them—this is the central goal of chemistry. A good simple definition of **chemistry** is

> **Chemistry—the science that seeks to understand the behavior of matter by studying the behavior of atoms and molecules**.

The term *atoms* in this definition can be interpreted loosely to include atoms that have lost or gained electrons.

1.2 The Scientific Approach to Knowledge

Throughout history, humans have approached knowledge about the physical world in different ways. For example, the Greek philosopher Plato (427–347 B.C.) thought that the best way to learn about reality was not through the senses, but through reason. He believed that the physical world was an imperfect representation of a perfect and transcendent world (a world beyond space and time). For him, true knowledge came not through observing the real physical world, but through reasoning and thinking about the ideal one.

Although some Greek philosophers, such as Aristotle, did use observation to attain knowledge, they did not emphasize experiment and measurement to the extent that modern science does.

The *scientific* approach to knowledge, however, is exactly the opposite of Plato's. Scientific knowledge is empirical—it is based on *observation* and *experiment*. Scientists observe and perform experiments on the physical world to learn about it. Some observations and experiments are qualitative (noting or describing how a process happens), but many are quantitative (measuring or quantifying something about the process). For example, Antoine Lavoisier (1743–1794), a French chemist who studied combustion (or burning), made careful measurements of the mass of objects before and after burning them in closed containers. He noticed that there was no change in the total mass of material within the container during combustion. In doing so, Lavoisier made an important *observation* about the physical world.

Observations often lead scientists to formulate a **hypothesis**, a tentative interpretation or explanation of the observations. For example, Lavoisier explained his observations on combustion by hypothesizing that when a substance burns, it combines with a component of air. A good hypothesis is *falsifiable*, which means that it makes predictions that can be confirmed or refuted by further observations. Scientists test hypotheses by **experiments**, highly controlled procedures designed to generate observations that may confirm or refute a hypothesis. The results of an experiment may support a hypothesis or prove it wrong—in which case the scientist must modify or discard the hypothesis.

In some cases, a series of similar observations leads to the development of a **scientific law**, a brief statement that summarizes past observations and predicts future ones. Lavoisier summarized his observations on combustion with the **law of conservation of mass**, which states, "In a chemical reaction, matter is neither created nor destroyed." This statement summarized his observations on chemical reactions and predicted the outcome of future observations on reactions. Laws, like hypotheses, are also subject to experiments, which can support them or prove them wrong.

Scientific laws are not *laws* in the same sense as civil or governmental laws. Nature does not follow laws in the way that we obey the laws against speeding or running a stop sign. Rather, scientific laws *describe* how nature behaves—they are generalizations about what nature does. For that reason, some people find it more appropriate to refer to them as *principles* rather than *laws*.

One or more well-established hypotheses may form the basis for a scientific **theory**. A scientific theory is a model for the way nature is and tries to explain not merely what nature does but why. As such, well-established theories are the pinnacle of scientific knowledge, often predicting behavior far beyond the observations or laws from which they were developed. A good example of a theory is the **atomic theory** proposed by English chemist John Dalton (1766–1844). Dalton explained the law of conservation of mass, as well as other laws and observations of the time, by proposing that matter is composed of small, indestructible particles called atoms. Since these particles are merely rearranged in chemical changes (and not created or destroyed), the total amount of mass remains the same. Dalton's theory is a model for the physical world—it gives us insight into how nature works and, therefore, *explains* our laws and observations.

▲ A painting of the French chemist Antoine Lavoisier with his wife, Marie, who helped him in his work by illustrating his experiments and translating scientific articles from English. Lavoisier, who also made significant contributions to agriculture, industry, education, and government administration, was executed during the French Revolution. (The Metropolitan Museum of Art)

In Dalton's time, people thought atoms were indestructible. Today, because of nuclear reactions, we know that atoms can be broken apart into their smaller components.

The Scientific Method

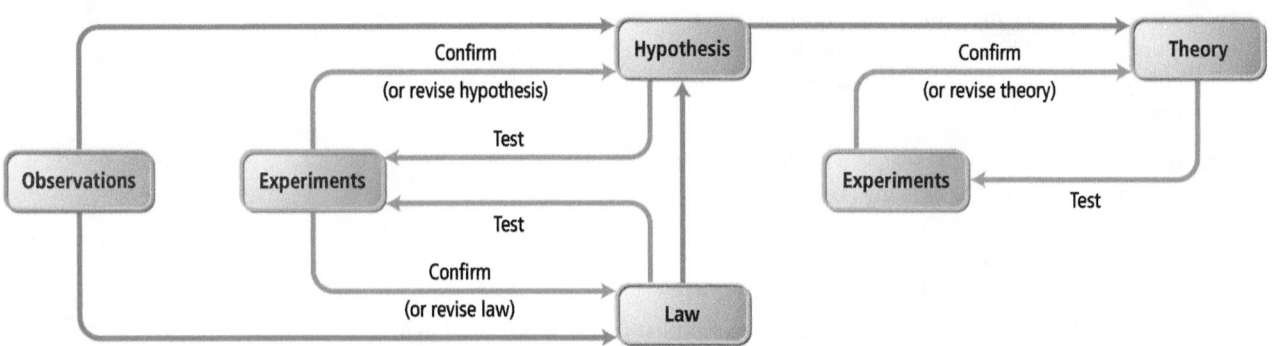

▲ FIGURE 1.2 The Scientific Approach to Knowledge

Finally, the scientific approach returns to observation to test theories. For example, scientists can test the atomic theory by trying to isolate single atoms or by trying to image them (both of which, by the way, have already been accomplished). Theories are validated by experiments; however, theories can never be conclusively proven because some new observation or experiment always has the potential to reveal a flaw. Notice that the scientific approach to knowledge begins with observation and ends with observation. An experiment is in essence a highly controlled procedure for generating critical observations designed to test a theory or hypothesis. Each new set of observations has the potential to refine the original model. Figure 1.2 ▲ summarizes one way to map the scientific approach to knowledge. Scientific laws, hypotheses, and theories are all subject to continued experimentation. If a law, hypothesis, or theory is proved wrong by an experiment, it must be revised and tested with new experiments. Over time, the scientific community eliminates or corrects poor theories and laws, and valid theories and laws—those consistent with experimental results—remain.

Established theories with strong experimental support are the most powerful pieces of scientific knowledge. You may have heard the phrase "That is just a theory," as if theories are easily dismissible. Such a statement reveals a deep misunderstanding of the nature of a scientific theory. Well-established theories are as close to truth as we get in science. The idea that all matter is made of atoms is "just a theory," but it has over 200 years of experimental evidence to support it. It is a powerful piece of scientific knowledge on which many other scientific ideas have been built.

One last word about the scientific approach to knowledge: some people wrongly imagine science to be a strict set of rules and procedures that automatically lead to inarguable, objective facts. This is not the case. Even our diagram of the scientific approach to knowledge is only an idealization of real science, useful to help us see the key distinctions of science. Real science requires hard work, care, creativity, and even a bit of luck. Scientific theories do not just arise out of data—men and women of great genius and creativity craft theories. A great theory is not unlike a master painting, and many see a similar kind of beauty in both. (For more on this aspect of science, see the box entitled *Thomas S. Kuhn and Scientific Revolutions.*)

Conceptual Connection 1.1 Laws and Theories

Which statement best explains the difference between a law and a theory?

(a) A law is truth; a theory is mere speculation.

(b) A law summarizes a series of related observations; a theory gives the underlying reasons for them.

(c) A theory describes *what* nature does; a law describes *why* nature does it.

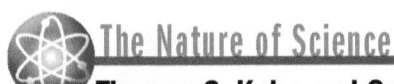

The Nature of Science

Thomas S. Kuhn and Scientific Revolutions

When scientists talk about science, they often talk in ways that imply that their theories are "true." Further, they talk as if they arrive at theories in logical and unbiased ways. For example, a theory central to chemistry that we have discussed in this chapter is John Dalton's atomic theory—the idea that all matter is composed of atoms. Is this theory "true"? Was it reached in logical, unbiased ways? Will this theory still be around in 200 years?

The answers to these questions depend on how we view science and its development. One way to view science—let's call it the *traditional view*—is as the continual accumulation of knowledge and the building of increasingly precise theories. In this view, a scientific theory is a model of the world that reflects what is *actually in* nature. New observations and experiments result in gradual adjustments to theories. Over time, theories get better, giving us a more accurate picture of the physical world.

In the twentieth century, a different view of scientific knowledge began to develop. A book by Thomas Kuhn, published in 1964 and entitled *The Structure of Scientific Revolutions*, challenged the traditional view. Kuhn's ideas came from his study of the history of science, which, he argued, does not support the idea that science progresses in a smooth cumulative way. According to Kuhn, science goes through fairly quiet periods that he called *normal science*. In these periods, scientists make their data fit the reigning theory, or paradigm. Small inconsistencies are swept aside during periods of normal science. However, when too many inconsistencies and anomalies develop, a crisis emerges. The crisis brings about a *revolution* and a new reigning theory. According to Kuhn, the new theory is usually quite different from the old one; it not only helps us to make sense of new or anomalous information, but also enables us to see accumulated data from the past in a dramatically new way.

Kuhn further contended that theories are held for reasons that are not always logical or unbiased, and that theories are not *true* models—in the sense of a one-to-one mapping—of the physical world. Because new theories are often so different from the ones they replace, he argued, and because old theories always make good sense to those holding them, they must not be "True" with a capital *T*; otherwise "truth" would be constantly changing.

Kuhn's ideas created a controversy among scientists and science historians that continues to this day. Some, especially postmodern philosophers of science, have taken Kuhn's ideas one step further. They argue that scientific knowledge is *completely* biased and lacks any objectivity. Most scientists, including Kuhn, would disagree. Although Kuhn pointed out that scientific knowledge has *arbitrary elements*, he also said, "*Observation ... can and must drastically restrict the range of admissible scientific belief, else there would be no science.*" In other words, saying that science contains arbitrary elements is quite different from saying that science itself is arbitrary.

Question

In his book, Kuhn stated, "*A new theory ... is seldom or never just an increment to what is already known.*" Can you think of any examples that support Kuhn's statement from your knowledge of the history of science? Do you know of any instances in which a new theory or model was drastically different from the one it replaced?

1.3 The Classification of Matter

Matter is anything that occupies space and has mass. This book, your desk, your chair, and even your body are all composed of matter. Less obviously, the air around you is also matter—it too occupies space and has mass. We call a specific instance of matter—such as air, water, or sand—a **substance**. We can classify matter according to its **state** (its physical form) and its **composition** (the basic components that make it up).

The States of Matter: Solid, Liquid, and Gas

Matter can exist in three different states: **solid**, **liquid**, and **gas**. In *solid matter*, atoms or molecules pack close to each other in fixed locations. Although the atoms and molecules in a solid vibrate, they do not move around or past each other. Consequently, a solid has a fixed volume and rigid shape. Ice, aluminum, and diamond are good examples of solids. Solid matter may be **crystalline**, in which case its atoms or molecules are in patterns with long-range, repeating order (Figure 1.3 ▶), or it may be **amorphous**, in which case its atoms or molecules do not have any long-range order. Table salt and diamond are examples of *crystalline* solids; the well-ordered geometric shapes of salt and diamond crystals reflect the well-ordered geometric arrangement of their atoms (although this is not the case for *all* crystalline solids). Examples of *amorphous* solids include glass and plastic. In *liquid matter*, atoms or molecules pack about as closely as they do in solid

The state of matter changes from solid to liquid to gas with increasing temperature.

Glass and other amorphous solids can be thought of, from one point of view, as intermediate between solids and liquids. Their atoms are fixed in position at room temperature, but they have no long-range structure and do not have distinct melting points.

▶ In a solid, the atoms or molecules are fixed in place and can only vibrate. In a liquid, although the atoms or molecules are closely packed, they can move past one another, allowing the liquid to flow and assume the shape of its container. In a gas, the atoms or molecules are widely spaced, making gases compressible as well as fluid (able to flow).

Solid matter

Liquid matter

Gaseous matter

Crystalline Solid:
Regular
three-dimensional pattern

Diamond
C (*s*, diamond)

▲ FIGURE 1.3 **Crystalline Solid**
Diamond is a crystalline solid composed of carbon atoms arranged in a regular, repeating pattern.

▶ FIGURE 1.4 **The Compressibility of Gases**   Gases can be compressed—squeezed into a smaller volume—because there is so much empty space between atoms or molecules in the gaseous state.

matter, but they are free to move relative to each other, giving liquids a fixed volume but not a fixed shape. Liquids assume the shape of their container. Water, alcohol, and gasoline are all substances that are liquids at room temperature.

In *gaseous matter*, atoms or molecules have a lot of space between them and are free to move relative to one another, making gases *compressible* (Figure 1.4▼). When you squeeze a balloon or sit down on an air mattress, you force the atoms and molecules into a smaller space so that they are closer together. Gases always assume the shape *and* volume of their container. Substances that are gases at room temperature include helium, nitrogen (the main component of air), and carbon dioxide.

Solid—not compressible

Gas—compressible

Classifying Matter according to Its Composition: Elements, Compounds, and Mixtures

In addition to classifying matter according to its state, we can classify it according to its composition, as shown in the following chart:

Helium

Pure water

Wet sand

Tea with sugar

The first division in the classification of matter is between a *pure substance* and a *mixture*. A **pure substance** is made up of only one component and its composition is invariant (it does not vary from one sample to another). The *components* of a pure substance can be individual atoms or groups of atoms joined together. For example, helium, water, and table salt (sodium chloride) are all pure substances. Each of these substances is made up of only one component: helium is made up of helium atoms, water is made up of water molecules, and sodium chloride is made up of sodium chloride units. The composition of a pure sample of any one of these is always exactly the same (because you can't vary the composition of a substance made up of only one component).

A **mixture**, by contrast, is composed of two or more components in proportions that can vary from one sample to another. For example, sweetened tea, composed primarily of water molecules and sugar molecules (with a few other substances mixed in), is a mixture. We can make tea slightly sweet (a small proportion of sugar to water) or very sweet (a large proportion of sugar to water) or any level of sweetness in between.

We can categorize pure substances themselves into two types—*elements* and *compounds*—depending on whether or not they can be broken down (or decomposed) into simpler substances. Helium, which we just noted is a pure substance, is also a good example of an **element**, a substance that cannot be chemically broken down into simpler substances. Water, also a pure substance, is a good example of a **compound**, a substance composed of two or more elements (in this case hydrogen and oxygen) in a fixed, definite proportion. On Earth, compounds are more common than pure elements because most elements combine with other elements to form compounds.

We can also categorize mixtures into two types—heterogeneous and homogeneous—depending on how *uniformly* the substances within them mix. Wet sand is a **heterogeneous mixture**, one in which the composition varies from one region of the mixture to another.

Physical Change versus Chemical Change

Dry ice subliming:

$$CO_2(s) \longrightarrow CO_2(g)$$

Chemical composition unaltered
Physical change

CO$_2$(g)
Gaseous carbon dioxide

CO$_2$(s)
Solid carbon dioxide (dry ice)

(a)

Sugar dissolving:

$$C_{12}H_{22}O_{11}(s) \longrightarrow C_{12}H_{22}O_{11}(aq)$$

Chemical composition unaltered
Physical change

C$_{12}$H$_{22}$O$_{11}$(s)
Solid sugar

C$_{12}$H$_{22}$O$_{11}$(aq)
Dissolved sugar

(b)

Propane gas burning:

$$C_3H_8(g) + 5\,O_2(g) \longrightarrow$$
$$3\,CO_2(g) + 4\,H_2O(g)$$

Chemical composition altered
Chemical change

CO$_2$(g), H$_2$O(g)
Carbon dioxide and water

C$_3$H$_8$(g)
Propane

(c)

▲ **FIGURE 1.9 Physical and Chemical Changes**   (a) The sublimation (the state change from a solid to a gas) of dry ice (solid CO$_2$) is a physical change. (b) The dissolution of sugar is a physical change. (c) The burning of propane is a chemical change.

The differences between physical and chemical changes are not always apparent. Only chemical examination can confirm whether any particular change is physical or chemical. In many cases, however, we can identify chemical and physical changes based on what we know about the changes. Changes in the state of matter, such as melting or boiling, or changes in the physical condition of matter, such as those that result from cutting or crushing, are typically physical changes. Changes involving chemical reactions—often evidenced by temperature or color changes—are chemical changes.

EXAMPLE 1.1   Physical and Chemical Changes and Properties

Determine whether each change is physical or chemical. What kind of property (chemical or physical) is demonstrated in each case?

(a) the evaporation of rubbing alcohol

(b) the burning of lamp oil

(c) the bleaching of hair with hydrogen peroxide

(d) the forming of frost on a cold night

SOLUTION

(a) When rubbing alcohol evaporates, it changes from liquid to gas, but it remains alcohol—this is a physical change. The volatility (the ability to evaporate easily) of alcohol is a therefore a physical property.

(b) Lamp oil burns because it reacts with oxygen in air to form carbon dioxide and water—this is a chemical change. The flammability of lamp oil is therefore a chemical property.

(c) Applying hydrogen peroxide to hair changes pigment molecules in hair that give it color—this is a chemical change. The susceptibility of hair to bleaching is therefore a chemical property.

(d) Frost forms on a cold night because water vapor in air changes its state to form solid ice—this is a physical change. The temperature at which water freezes is therefore a physical property.

FOR PRACTICE 1.1

Determine whether each change is physical or chemical. What kind of property (chemical or physical) is demonstrated in each case?

(a) A copper wire is hammered flat.

(b) A nickel dissolves in acid to form a blue-green solution.

(c) Dry ice sublimes without melting.

(d) A match ignites when struck on a flint.

Answers to For Practice and For More Practice problems can be found in Appendix IV.

Conceptual Connection 1.3 **Chemical and Physical Changes**

The diagram on the left represents liquid water molecules in a pan. Which of the three diagrams (a, b, or c) best represents the water molecules after they have been vaporized by the boiling of liquid water?

(a)

(b)

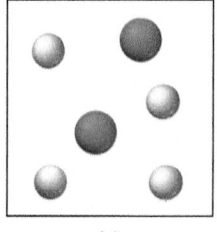

(c)

1.5 Energy: A Fundamental Part of Physical and Chemical Change

The physical and chemical changes discussed in Section 1.4 are usually accompanied by energy changes. For example, when water evaporates from your skin (a physical change), the water molecules absorb energy from your body, making you feel cooler. When you burn natural gas on the stove (a chemical change), energy is released, heating the food you are cooking. Understanding the physical and chemical changes of matter—that is, understanding chemistry—requires that we understand energy changes and energy flow.

Force acts through distance; work is done.

—10 kg   High potential energy (unstable)

Kinetic energy

Low potential energy (stable)

Heat

▲ FIGURE 1.10 **Energy Conversions**
Gravitational potential energy is converted into kinetic energy when the weight is dropped. The kinetic energy is converted mostly to thermal energy when the weight strikes the ground.

In Chapter 19 we will discuss how energy conservation is actually part of a more general law that allows for the interconvertibility of mass and energy.

The scientific definition of **energy** is *the capacity to do work*. **Work** is defined as the action of a force through a distance. For instance, when you push a box across the floor or pedal your bicycle across the street, you have done work.

The *total energy* of an object is a sum of its **kinetic energy** (the energy associated with its motion) and its **potential energy** (the energy associated with its position or composition). For example, a weight held several meters above the ground has potential energy due to its position within Earth's gravitational field (Figure 1.10 ◀). If you drop the weight, it accelerates, and its potential energy is converted to kinetic energy. When the weight hits the ground, its kinetic energy is converted primarily to **thermal energy**, the energy associated with the temperature of an object. Thermal energy is actually a type of kinetic energy because it is associated with the motion of the individual atoms or molecules that make up an object. When the weight hits the ground its kinetic energy is essentially transferred to the atoms and molecules that compose the ground, raising the temperature of the ground ever so slightly.

The first principle to note about how energy changes as the weight falls to the ground is that *energy is neither created nor destroyed*. The potential energy of the weight becomes kinetic energy as the weight accelerates toward the ground. The kinetic energy then becomes thermal energy when the weight hits the ground. The total amount of thermal energy that is released through the process is exactly equal to the initial potential energy of the weight. The idea that energy is neither created nor destroyed is known as the **law of conservation of energy**. Although energy can change from one type into another, and although it can flow from one object to another, the *total quantity* of energy does not change—it remains constant.

The second principle to note about the raised weight and its fall is *the tendency of systems with high potential energy to change in a way that lowers their potential energy*. For this reason, objects or systems with high potential energy tend to be *unstable*. The weight lifted several meters from the ground is unstable because it contains a significant amount of potential energy. Unless restrained, the weight will naturally fall, lowering its potential energy. We can harness some of the raised weight's potential energy to do work. For example, we can attach the weight to a rope that turns a paddle wheel or spins a drill as the weight falls. After the weight falls to the ground, it contains less potential energy—it has become more *stable*.

Molecules in
gasoline (unstable)

Molecules in
exhaust (stable)

Some of released energy
harnessed to do work

Car moves forward

◀ FIGURE 1.11 **Using Chemical Energy to Do Work** The compounds produced when gasoline burns have less chemical potential energy than the gasoline molecules.

Some chemical substances are like the raised weight just described. For example, the molecules that compose gasoline have a relatively high potential energy—energy is concentrated in them just as energy is concentrated in the raised weight. The molecules in the gasoline tend to undergo chemical changes (specifically combustion) that lower their potential energy. As the energy of the molecules is released, some of it can be harnessed to do work, such as moving a car forward (Figure 1.11 ▲). The molecules that result from the chemical change have less potential energy than the original molecules in gasoline and are more stable.

Chemical potential energy, such as the energy contained in the molecules that compose gasoline, arises primarily from electrostatic forces between the electrically charged particles (protons and electrons) that compose atoms and molecules. We will learn more about those particles, as well as the properties of electrical charge, in Chapter 2, but for now, know that molecules contain specific, usually complex, arrangements of these charged particles. Some of these arrangements—such as the one within the molecules that compose gasoline—have a much higher potential energy than others. When gasoline undergoes combustion the arrangement of these particles changes, creating molecules with much lower potential energy and transferring a great deal of energy (mostly in the form of heat) to the surroundings.

Summarizing Energy:

▶ Energy is always conserved in a physical or chemical change; it is neither created nor destroyed.

▶ Systems with high potential energy tend to change in a direction that lowers their potential energy, releasing energy into the surroundings.

1.6 The Units of Measurement

In 1999, NASA lost the $125 million *Mars Climate Orbiter*. The chairman of the commission that investigated the disaster concluded, "The root cause of the loss of the spacecraft was a failed translation of English units into metric units." As a result, the orbiter—which was supposed to monitor weather on Mars—descended too far into the Martian atmosphere and burned up. In chemistry as in space exploration, **units**—standard quantities used to specify measurements—are critical. If we get them wrong, the consequences can be disastrous.

The two most common unit systems are the **metric system**, used in most of the world, and the **English system**, used in the United States. Scientists use the **International System of Units (SI)**, which is based on the metric system.

▲ The $125 million *Mars Climate Orbiter* was lost in the Martian atmosphere in 1999 because two groups of engineers failed to communicate to each other the units that they used in their calculations.

The Standard Units

Table 1.1 shows the standard SI base units. For now, we focus on the first four of these units: the *meter*, the standard unit of length; the *kilogram*, the standard unit of mass; the *second*, the standard unit of time; and the *kelvin*, the standard unit of temperature.

The abbreviation *SI* comes from the French, *Système International d'Unités.*

The Celsius Temperature Scale

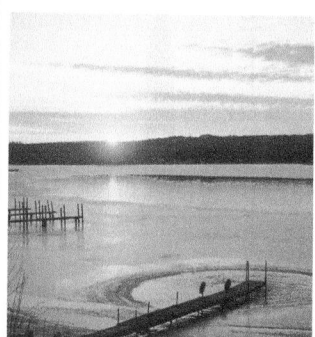

0 °C – Water freezes

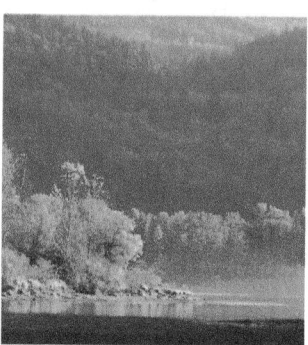

10 °C – Brisk fall day

22 °C – Room temperature

45 °C – Summer day in Death Valley

Celsius degree—the only difference is the temperature that each scale designates as zero. You can convert between the temperature scales with these formulas:

$$°C = \frac{(°F - 32)}{1.8}$$

$$K = °C + 273.15$$

> Note that we give Kelvin temperatures in kelvins (*not* "degrees Kelvin") or K (*not* °K).

Throughout this book we provide examples worked out in formats that are designed to help you develop problem-solving skills. The most common format uses two columns to guide you through the worked example. The left column describes the thought processes and steps used in solving the problem while the right column shows the implementation. Example 1.2 follows this two-column format.

EXAMPLE 1.2   Converting between Temperature Scales

A sick child has a temperature of 40.00 °C. What is the child's temperature in **(a)** K and **(b)** °F?

SOLUTION

(a) Begin by finding the equation that relates the quantity that is given (°C) and the quantity you are trying to find (K).	$K = °C + 273.15$
Since this equation gives the temperature in K directly, substitute in the correct value for the temperature in °C and calculate the answer.	$K = °C + 273.15$ $K = 40.00 + 273.15 = 313.15$ K
(b) To convert from °C to °F, first find the equation that relates these two quantities.	$°C = \dfrac{(°F - 32)}{1.8}$
Since this equation expresses °C in terms of °F, solve the equation for °F.	$°C = \dfrac{(°F - 32)}{1.8}$ $1.8(°C) = (°F - 32)$ $°F = 1.8(°C) + 32$
Now substitute °C into the equation and calculate the answer. *Note: The number of digits reported in this answer follows significant figure conventions, covered in Section 1.7.*	$°F = 1.8(°C) + 32$ $°F = 1.8(40.00 °C) + 32 = 104.00$ °F

FOR PRACTICE 1.2

Gallium is a solid metal at room temperature but will melt to a liquid in your hand. The melting point of gallium is 85.6 °F. What is this temperature on (a) the Celsius scale and (b) the Kelvin scale?

Prefix Multipliers

Scientific notation (see Appendix IA) allows us to express very large or very small quantities in a compact manner by using exponents. For example, the diameter of a hydrogen atom can be written as 1.06×10^{-10} m. The International System of Units uses the **prefix multipliers** shown in Table 1.2 with the standard units. These multipliers change the value of the unit by powers of 10 (just like an exponent does in scientific notation). For example, the kilometer has the prefix *kilo* meaning 1000 or 10^3. Therefore,

$$1 \text{ kilometer} = 1000 \text{ meters} = 10^3 \text{ meters}$$

Similarly, the millimeter has the prefix *milli* meaning 0.001 or 10^{-3}.

$$1 \text{ millimeter} = 0.001 \text{ meters} = 10^{-3} \text{ meters}$$

TABLE 1.2 SI Prefix Multipliers

Prefix	Symbol	Multiplier	
exa	E	1,000,000,000,000,000,000	(10^{18})
peta	P	1,000,000,000,000,000	(10^{15})
tera	T	1,000,000,000,000	(10^{12})
giga	G	1,000,000,000	(10^{9})
mega	M	1,000,000	(10^{6})
kilo	k	1000	(10^{3})
deci	d	0.1	(10^{-1})
centi	c	0.01	(10^{-2})
milli	m	0.001	(10^{-3})
micro	μ	0.000001	(10^{-6})
nano	n	0.000000001	(10^{-9})
pico	p	0.000000000001	(10^{-12})
femto	f	0.000000000000001	(10^{-15})
atto	a	0.000000000000000001	(10^{-18})

When reporting a measurement, choose a prefix multiplier close to the size of the quantity you are measuring. For example, to state the diameter of a hydrogen atom, which is 1.06×10^{-10} m, use picometers (106 pm) or nanometers (0.106 nm) rather than micrometers or millimeters. Choose the prefix multiplier that is most convenient for a particular number.

Conceptual Connection 1.5 Prefix Multipliers

What prefix multiplier is appropriate for reporting a measurement of 5.57×10^{-5} m?

Derived Units: Volume and Density

A **derived unit** is a combination of other units. For example, the SI unit for speed is meters per second (m/s), a derived unit. Notice that this unit is formed from two other SI units— meters and seconds—put together. You are probably more familiar with speed in miles/ hour or kilometers/hour—these are also examples of derived units. Two other common derived units are those for volume (SI base unit is m^3) and density (SI base unit is kg/m^3).

Volume **Volume** is a measure of space. Any unit of length, when cubed (raised to the third power), becomes a unit of volume. The cubic meter (m^3), cubic centimeter (cm^3), and cubic millimeter (mm^3) are all units of volume. The cubic nature of volume is not

Relationship between Length and Volume

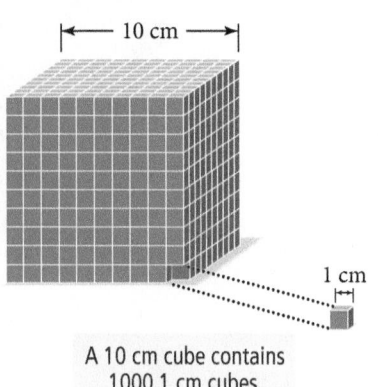

A 10 cm cube contains 1000 1 cm cubes.

▲ FIGURE 1.13 **The Relationship between Length and Volume**

always intuitive, and studies have shown that our brains are not naturally wired to think abstractly, which we need to do in order to think about volume. For example, consider this question: how many small cubes measuring 1 cm on each side are required to construct a large cube measuring 10 cm (or 1 dm) on a side?

The answer to this question, as you can see by carefully examining the unit cube in Figure 1.13 ◂, is 1000 small cubes. When we go from a linear, one-dimensional distance to three-dimensional volume, we must raise both the linear dimension *and* its unit to the third power (not multiply by 3). Thus the volume of a cube is equal to the length of its edge cubed:

$$\text{volume of cube} = (\text{edge length})^3$$

A cube with a 10 cm edge length has a volume of $(10\,\text{cm})^3$ or $1000\,\text{cm}^3$, and a cube with a 100 cm edge length has a volume of $(100\,\text{cm})^3 = 1{,}000{,}000\,\text{cm}^3$.

Other common units of volume in chemistry are the **liter (L)** and the **milliliter (mL)**. One milliliter ($10^{-3}\,\text{L}$) is equal to $1\,\text{cm}^3$. A gallon of gasoline contains 3.785 L. Table 1.3 lists some common units—for volume and other quantities—and their equivalents.

TABLE 1.3 Some Common Units and Their Equivalents

Length	Mass	Volume
1 kilometer (km) = 0.6214 mile (mi)	1 kilogram (kg) = 2.205 pounds (lb)	1 liter (L) = 1000 mL = 1000 cm³
1 meter (m) = 39.37 inches (in) = 1.094 yards (yd)	1 pound (lb) = 453.59 grams (g)	1 liter (L) = 1.057 quarts (qt)
1 foot (ft) = 30.48 centimeters (cm)	1 ounce (oz) = 28.35 grams (g)	1 U.S. gallon (gal) = 3.785 liters (L)
1 inch (in) = 2.54 centimeter (cm) (exact)		

The *m* in the equation for density is in italic type, meaning that it stands for mass rather than for meters. In general, the symbols for units such as meters (m), seconds (s), or kelvins (K) appear in regular type while those for variables such as mass (*m*), volume (*V*), and time (*t*) appear in italics.

Density An old riddle asks, "Which weighs more, a ton of bricks or a ton of feathers?" The answer, of course, is neither—they both weigh the same (1 ton). If you answered bricks, you confused weight with density. The **density** (*d*) of a substance is the ratio of its mass (*m*) to its volume (*V*):

$$\text{Density} = \frac{\text{mass}}{\text{volume}} \quad \text{or} \quad d = \frac{m}{V}$$

Density is a characteristic physical property of substances (see Table 1.4) that depends on temperature. Density is an example of an **intensive property**, one that is *independent* of the amount of the substance. The density of aluminum, for example, is the same whether you have a gram or a kilogram. Intensive properties are often used to identify substances because these properties depend only on the type of substance, not on the amount of it. For example, from Table 1.4 on the next page you can see that pure gold has a density of $19.3\,\text{g/cm}^3$. One way to determine whether a substance is pure gold is to determine its density and compare it to $19.3\,\text{g/cm}^3$. Mass, in contrast, is an **extensive property**, one that depends on the amount of the substance. If you know only the mass of a sample of gold, that information alone will not allow you to identify it as gold.

The units of density are those of mass divided by volume. Although the SI derived unit for density is kg/m^3, the density of liquids and solids is most often expressed in g/cm^3 or g/mL. (Remember that cm^3 and mL are equivalent units: $1\,\text{cm}^3 = 1\,\text{mL}$.) Aluminum is one of the least dense structural metals with a density of $2.7\,\text{g/cm}^3$, while platinum is one of the densest metals with a density of $21.4\,\text{g/cm}^3$.

Calculating Density

We can calculate the density of a substance by dividing the mass of a given amount of the substance by its volume. For example, suppose a small nugget we suspect to be gold has a mass of 22.5 g and a volume of 2.38 cm³. To find its density, we divide the mass by the volume:

$$d = \frac{m}{V} = \frac{22.5\,\text{g}}{2.38\,\text{cm}^3} = 9.45\,\text{g/cm}^3$$

In this case, the density reveals that the nugget is not pure gold because the density of gold is 19.3 g/cm³.

TABLE 1.4 The Density of Some Common Substances at 20 °C

Substance	Density (g/cm³)
Charcoal (from oak)	0.57
Ethanol	0.789
Ice	0.917 (at 0 °C)
Water	1.00 (at 4 °C)
Sugar (sucrose)	1.58
Table salt (sodium chloride)	2.16
Glass	2.6
Aluminum	2.70
Titanium	4.51
Iron	7.86
Copper	8.96
Lead	11.4
Mercury	13.55
Gold	19.3
Platinum	21.4

EXAMPLE 1.3   Calculating Density

A man receives a platinum ring from his fiancée. Before the wedding, he notices that the ring feels a little light for its size and decides to determine its density. He places the ring on a balance and finds that it has a mass of 3.15 grams. He then finds that the ring displaces 0.233 cm³ of water. Is the ring made of platinum ? (Note: The volume of irregularly shaped objects is often measured by the displacement of water. To use this method, the object is placed in water and the change in volume of the water is measured. This increase in the total volume represents the volume of water *displaced* by the object and is equal to the volume of the object.)

Set up the problem by writing the important information that is *given* as well as the information that you are asked to *find*. In this case, we are to find the density of the ring and compare it to that of platinum *Note: This standardized way of setting up problems is discussed in detail in Section 1.8.*	**GIVEN:** $m = 3.15$ g $V = 0.233$ cm³ **FIND:** Density in g/cm³
Next, write down the equation that defines density.	**EQUATION:** $d = \dfrac{m}{V}$
Solve the problem by substituting the correct values of mass and volume into the expression for density.	**SOLUTION:** $d = \dfrac{m}{V} = \dfrac{3.15\,\text{g}}{0.233\,\text{cm}^3} = 13.5\,\text{g/cm}^3$

The density of the ring is much too low to be platinum (platinum density is 21.4 g/cm³), and the ring is therefore a fake.

FOR PRACTICE 1.3

The woman in this example is shocked that the ring is fake and returns it. She buys a new ring that has a mass of 4.53 g and a volume of 0.212 cm³. Is the new ring genuine?

FOR MORE PRACTICE 1.3

A metal cube has an edge length of 11.4 mm and a mass of 6.67 g. Calculate the density of the metal and use Table 1.4 to determine the likely identity of the metal.

Conceptual Connection 1.6 Density

The density of copper decreases as temperature increases (as does the density of most substances). Which statement accurately describes the changes in a sample of copper when it is warmed from room temperature to 95 °C?

(a) The sample will become lighter.

(b) The sample will become heavier.

(c) The sample will expand.

(d) The sample will contract.

Chemistry and Medicine

Bone Density

Osteoporosis—which means *porous bone*—is a condition in which bone density becomes too low. The healthy bones of a young adult have a density of about 1.0 g/cm³. Patients suffering from osteoporosis, however, can have bone densities as low as 0.22 g/cm³. These low densities indicate that the bones have deteriorated and weakened, resulting in increased susceptibility to fractures, especially hip fractures. Patients suffering from osteoporosis can also experience height loss and disfiguration such as dowager's hump, a condition in which the patient becomes hunched over due to compression of the vertebrae. Osteoporosis is most common in postmenopausal women, but it can also occur in people (including men) who have certain diseases, such as insulin-dependent diabetes, or who take certain medications, such as prednisone. Osteoporosis is usually diagnosed and monitored with hip X-rays. Low-density bones absorb less of the X-rays than do high-density bones, producing characteristic differences in the X-ray image. Treatments for osteoporosis include calcium and vitamin D supplements, drugs that prevent bone weakening, exercise and strength training, and, in extreme cases, hip-replacement surgery.

Question

Suppose you find a large animal bone in the woods, too large to fit in a beaker or flask. How might you approximate its density?

▲ Top: Severe osteoporosis can necessitate surgery to implant an artificial hip joint, seen above in this X-ray image. Bottom: Views of the bone matrix in a normal bone (left) and one weakened by osteoporosis (right).

1.7 The Reliability of a Measurement

Recall from Section 1.1 that carbon monoxide is a colorless gas emitted by motor vehicles and found in polluted air. The table below shows carbon monoxide concentrations in Los Angeles County as reported by the U.S. Environmental Protection Agency (EPA) over the period 1990–2010:

Year	Carbon Monoxide Concentration (ppm)*
1990	8.9
1995	6.2
2000	4.8
2005	3.1
2010	2.1

*Second maximum, 8 hour average; ppm = *parts per million*, defined as mL pollutant per million mL of air. (Long Beach Site 060374002)

The first thing you should notice about these values is that they decrease over time. For this decrease, we can thank the Clean Air Act and its amendments, which have resulted in more efficient engines and specially blended fuels and consequently in cleaner air in all major U.S. cities over the last 30 years. The second thing you might notice is the number of digits to which the measurements are reported. The number of digits in a reported measurement indicates the certainty associated with that measurement. A less certain measurement of carbon monoxide levels might be reported as follows:

Year	Carbon Monoxide Concentration (ppm)
1990	9
1995	6
2000	5
2005	3
2010	2

Notice that the first set of data is reported to the nearest 0.1 ppm while the second set is reported to the nearest 1 ppm. Scientists report measured quantities in an agreed-upon standard way. The number of reported digits reflects the certainty in the measurement: more digits, more certainty; fewer digits, less certainty. Numbers are usually written so that the uncertainty is in the last reported digit. (We assume that uncertainty to be ± 1 in the last digit unless otherwise indicated.) By reporting the 2010 carbon monoxide concentration as 2.1 ppm, the scientists mean 2.1 ± 0.1 ppm. The carbon monoxide concentration is between 2.0 and 2.2 ppm—it might be 2.2 ppm, for example, but it could not be 3.0 ppm. In contrast, if the reported value was 2 ppm (as in the second set of measurements), this would mean 2 ± 1 ppm, or between 1 and 3 ppm. In general,

Scientific measurements are reported so that every digit is certain except the last, which is estimated.

For example, consider the following reported number:

$$5.21\underset{\text{estimated}}{3}$$

certain   estimated

The first three digits are certain; the last digit is estimated.

The number of digits reported in a measurement depends on the measuring device. Consider weighing a pistachio nut on two different balances (Figure 1.14 ▶). The balance on the top has marks every 1 gram, while the balance on the bottom has marks every 0.1 gram. For the balance on the top, we mentally divide the space between the 1- and 2-gram marks into ten equal spaces and estimate that the pointer is at about 1.2 grams. We then write the measurement as 1.2 grams, indicating that we are sure of the "1" but have estimated the ".2." The balance on the bottom, with marks every *tenth* of a gram, requires that we write the result with more digits. The pointer is between the 1.2-gram mark and the 1.3-gram mark. We again divide the space between the two marks into ten equal spaces and estimate the third digit. For the figure shown, we report 1.27 g.

Estimation in Weighing

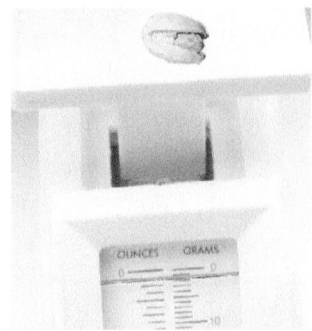

(a)

Markings every 1 g
Estimated reading 1.2 g

(b)

Markings every 0.1 g
Estimated reading 1.27 g

▲ FIGURE 1.14 **Estimation in Weighing** (a) This scale has markings every 1 g, so we mentally divide the space into ten equal spaces to estimate the last digit. This reading is 1.2 g. (b) Because this balance has markings every 0.1 g, we estimate to the hundredths place. This reading is 1.27 g.

EXAMPLE 1.4   Reporting the Correct Number of Digits

The graduated cylinder shown at the right has markings every 0.1 mL. Report the volume (which is read at the bottom of the meniscus) to the correct number of digits. (Note: The meniscus is the crescent-shaped surface at the top of a column of liquid.)

SOLUTION

Since the bottom of the meniscus is between the 4.5 and 4.6 mL markings, mentally divide the space between the markings into ten equal spaces and estimate the next digit. In this case, you should report the result as 4.57 mL.

What if you estimated a little differently and wrote 4.56 mL? In general, one unit difference in the last digit is acceptable because the last digit is estimated and different people might estimate it slightly differently. However, if you wrote 4.63 mL, you would have misreported the measurement.

FOR PRACTICE 1.4

Record the temperature on the thermometer shown at the right to the correct number of digits.

Meniscus

Counting Significant Figures

The precision of a measurement—which depends on the instrument used to make the measurement—must be preserved, not only when recording the measurement, but also when performing calculations that use the measurement. We can accomplish the preservation of this precision by using *significant figures*. In any reported measurement, the non-place-holding digits—those that are not simply marking the decimal place—are called **significant figures** (or **significant digits**). *The greater the number of significant figures, the greater the certainty of the measurement.* For example, the number 23.5 has three significant figures while the number 23.56 has four. To determine the number of significant figures in a number containing zeroes, we must distinguish between zeroes that are significant and those that simply mark the decimal place. For example, in the number 0.0008, the leading zeroes (zeroes to the left of the first non-zero digit) mark the decimal place but *do not* add to the certainty of the measurement and are therefore not significant; this number has only one significant figure. In contrast, the trailing zeroes (zeroes at the end of a number) in the number 0.000800 *do add* to the certainty of the measurement and are therefore counted as significant; this number has three significant figures.

To determine the number of significant figures in a number, follow these rules. (See the examples on the right).

Significant Figure Rules	Examples	
1. All nonzero digits are significant.	28.03	0.0540
2. Interior zeroes (zeroes between two nonzero digits) are significant.	408	7.0301
3. Leading zeroes (zeroes to the left of the first nonzero digit) are not significant. They only serve to locate the decimal point.	0.0032	0.00006
	↑	↑
		not significant
4. Trailing zeroes (zeroes at the end of a number) are categorized as follows:		
• Trailing zeroes after a decimal point are always significant.	45.000	3.5600
• Trailing zeroes before a decimal point (and after a nonzero number) are always significant.	140.00	2500.55
• Trailing zeroes before an *implied* decimal point are ambiguous and should be avoided by using scientific notation.	1200 1.2×10^3 1.20×10^3 1.200×10^3	ambiguous 2 significant figures 3 significant figures 4 significant figures
• Some textbooks put a decimal point after one or more trailing zeroes if the zeroes are to be considered significant. We avoid that practice in this book, but you should be aware of it.	1200.	4 significant figures (common in some textbooks)

Exact Numbers

Exact numbers have no uncertainty and thus do not limit the number of significant figures in any calculation. We can regard an exact number as having an unlimited number of significant figures. Exact numbers originate from three sources:

• From the accurate counting of discrete objects. For example, 3 atoms means 3.00000.... atoms.

• From defined quantities, such as the number of centimeters in 1 m. Because 100 cm is defined as 1 m,

$$100 \text{ cm} = 1 \text{ m means } 100.00000 \ldots \text{ cm} = 1.0000000 \ldots \text{ m}$$

• From integral numbers that are part of an equation. For example, in the equation $radius = \dfrac{diameter}{2}$, the number 2 is exact and therefore has an unlimited number of significant figures.

EXAMPLE 1.5   Determining the Number of Significant Figures in a Number

How many significant figures are in each number?

(a) 0.04450 m   (b) 5.0003 km
(c) 10 dm = 1 m   (d) 1.000×10^5 s
(e) 0.00002 mm   (f) 10,000 m

SOLUTION

(a) 0.04450 m	*Four significant figures.* The two 4s and the 5 are significant (Rule 1). The trailing zero is after a decimal point and is therefore significant (Rule 4). The leading zeroes only mark the decimal place and are therefore not significant (Rule 3).
(b) 5.0003 km	*Five significant figures.* The 5 and 3 are significant (Rule 1), as are the three interior zeroes (Rule 2).
(c) 10 dm = 1 m	*Unlimited significant figures.* Defined quantities have an unlimited number of significant figures.
(d) 1.000×10^5 s	*Four significant figures.* The 1 is significant (Rule 1). The trailing zeroes are after a decimal point and therefore significant (Rule 4).
(e) 0.00002 mm	*One significant figure.* The 2 is significant (Rule 1). The leading zeroes only mark the decimal place and are therefore not significant (Rule 3).
(f) 10,000 m	*Ambiguous.* The 1 is significant (Rule 1) but the trailing zeroes occur before an implied decimal point and are therefore ambiguous (Rule 4). Without more information, we would assume one significant figure. It is better to write this as 1×10^5 to indicate one significant figure or as 1.0000×10^5 to indicate five (Rule 4).

FOR PRACTICE 1.5

How many significant figures are in each number?

(a) 554 km   (b) 7 pennies
(c) 1.01×10^5 m   (d) 0.00099 s
(e) 1.4500 km   (f) 21,000 m

Significant Figures in Calculations

When we use measured quantities in calculations, the results of the calculation must reflect the precision of the measured quantities. We should not lose or gain precision during mathematical operations. Follow these rules when carrying significant figures through calculations.

Rules for Calculations   **Examples**

1. In multiplication or division, the result carries the same number of significant figures as the factor with the fewest significant figures.

$$1.052 \times 12.504 \times 0.53 = 6.7208 = 6.7$$
(4 sig. figures) (5 sig. figures) (2 sig. figures)   (2 sig. figures)

$$2.0035 \div 3.20 = 0.626094 = 0.626$$
(5 sig. figures) (3 sig. figures)   (3 sig. figures)

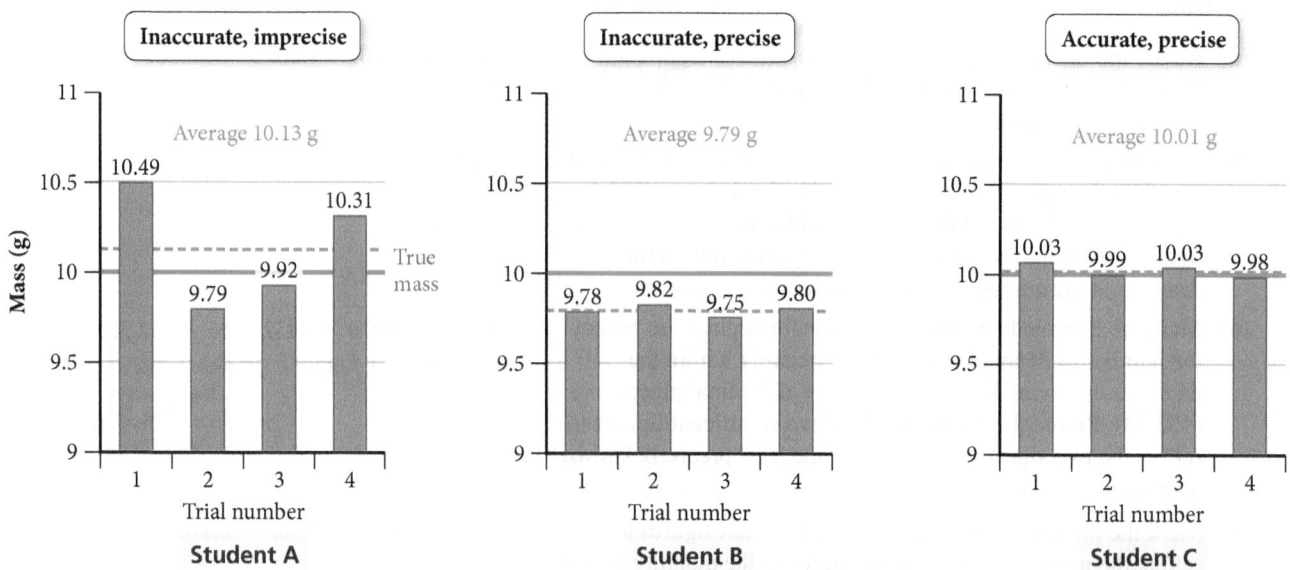

▲ Measurements are said to be precise if they are consistent with one another, but they are accurate only if they are close to the actual value.

- The results of student B are precise (close to one another in value) but inaccurate. The inaccuracy is the result of **systematic error**, error that tends toward being either too high or too low. In contrast to random error, systematic error does not average out with repeated trials. For instance, if a balance is not properly calibrated, it may systematically read too high or too low.

- The results of student C display little systematic error or random error—they are both accurate and precise.

 ## Chemistry in Your Day

Integrity in Data Gathering

Most scientists spend many hours collecting data in the laboratory. Often, the data do not turn out exactly as the scientist had expected (or hoped). A scientist may then be tempted to "fudge" the results. For example, suppose you are expecting a particular set of measurements to follow a certain pattern. After working hard over several days or weeks to make the measurements, you notice that a few of them do not quite fit the pattern that you anticipated. You might find yourself wishing that you could simply change or omit the "faulty" measurements. Altering data in this way is considered highly unethical in the scientific community and, when discovered, is usually punished severely.

In 2004, Dr. Hwang Woo Suk, a stem cell researcher at the Seoul National University in Korea, published a research paper in *Science* (a highly respected research journal) claiming that he and his colleagues had cloned human embryonic stem cells. As part of his evidence, he showed photographs of the cells. The paper was hailed as an incredible breakthrough, and Dr. Hwang traveled the world lecturing on his work. *Time* magazine even included him on its "people that matter" list for 2004. Several months later, however, one of his co-workers revealed that the photographs were fraudulent. According to the co-worker, the photographs came from a computer data bank of stem cell photographs, not from a cloning experiment. A university panel investigated the results and confirmed that the photographs and other data had indeed been faked. Dr. Hwang was forced to resign his prestigious post at the university.

Although not common, incidents like this do occur from time to time. They are damaging to a community that is largely built on trust. A scientist's peers (other researchers in similar fields) review all published research papers, but usually they are judging whether the data support the conclusion—they assume that the experimental measurements are authentic. The pressure to succeed sometimes leads researchers to betray that trust. However, over time, the tendency of scientists to reproduce and build upon one another's work results in the discovery of the fraudulent data. When that happens, the researchers at fault are usually banished from the community and their careers are ruined.

1.8 Solving Chemical Problems

Learning to solve problems is one of the most important skills you will acquire in this course. No one succeeds in chemistry—or in life, really—without the ability to solve problems. Although no simple formula applies to every chemistry problem, you can learn problem-solving strategies and begin to develop some chemical intuition. Many of the problems you will solve in this course are *unit conversion problems*, where you are given one or more quantities and asked to convert them into different units. Other problems require that you use *specific equations* to get to the information you are trying to find. In the sections that follow, you will find strategies to help you solve both of these types of problems. Of course, many problems contain both conversions and equations, requiring the combination of these strategies, and some problems may require an altogether different approach.

Converting from One Unit to Another

In Section 1.6, we learned the SI unit system, the prefix multipliers, and a few other units. Knowing how to work with and manipulate these units in calculations is central to solving chemical problems. In calculations, units help to determine correctness. Using units as a guide to solving problems is called **dimensional analysis**. Units should always be included in calculations; they are multiplied, divided, and canceled like any other algebraic quantity.

Consider converting 12.5 inches (in) to centimeters (cm). We know from Table 1.3 that 1 in = 2.54 cm (exact), so we can use this quantity in the calculation:

$$12.5 \ \cancel{\text{in}} \times \frac{2.54 \ \text{cm}}{1 \ \cancel{\text{in}}} = 31.8 \ \text{cm}$$

The unit, in, cancels and we are left with cm as our final unit. The quantity $\frac{2.54 \ \text{cm}}{1 \ \text{in}}$ is a **conversion factor**—a fractional quantity with the units we are *converting from* on the bottom and the units we are *converting to* on the top. Conversion factors are constructed from any two equivalent quantities. In this example, 2.54 cm = 1 in, so we construct the conversion factor by dividing both sides of the equality by 1 in and canceling the units:

$$2.54 \ \text{cm} = 1 \ \text{in}$$

$$\frac{2.54 \ \text{cm}}{1 \ \text{in}} = \frac{1 \ \cancel{\text{in}}}{1 \ \cancel{\text{in}}}$$

$$\frac{2.54 \ \text{cm}}{1 \ \text{in}} = 1$$

Because the quantity $\frac{2.54 \ \text{cm}}{1 \ \text{in}}$ is equivalent to 1, multiplying by the conversion factor affects only the units, not the actual quantity. To convert the other way, from centimeters to inches, we must—using units as a guide—use a different form of the conversion factor. If you accidentally use the same form, you will get the wrong result, indicated by erroneous units. For example, suppose that we want to convert 31.8 cm to inches:

$$31.8 \ \text{cm} \times \frac{2.54 \ \text{cm}}{1 \ \text{in}} = \frac{80.8 \ \text{cm}^2}{\text{in}}$$

The units in the answer (cm^2/in), as well as the value of the answer, are obviously wrong. When you solve a problem, always look at the final units. Are they the desired units? Always look at the magnitude of the numerical answer as well. Does it make sense? In this case, our mistake was the form of the conversion factor. It should have been inverted so that the units cancel as follows:

$$31.8 \ \cancel{\text{cm}} \times \frac{1 \ \text{in}}{2.54 \ \cancel{\text{cm}}} = 12.5 \ \text{in}$$

Conversion factors can be inverted because they are equal to 1 and the inverse of 1 is 1. Therefore,

$$\frac{2.54 \ \text{cm}}{1 \ \text{in}} = 1 = \frac{1 \ \text{in}}{2.54 \ \text{cm}}$$

Most unit conversion problems take the following form:

Information given × conversion factor(s) = information sought

$$\cancel{\text{Given unit}} \times \frac{\text{desired unit}}{\cancel{\text{given unit}}} = \text{desired unit}$$

In this book, we diagram problem solutions using a *conceptual plan*. A conceptual plan is a visual outline that helps you to see the general flow of the problem solution. For unit conversions, the conceptual plan focuses on units and the conversion from one unit to another. The conceptual plan for converting in to cm is

The conceptual plan for converting the other way, from cm to in, is just the reverse, with the reciprocal conversion factor:

Each arrow in a conceptual plan for a unit conversion has an associated conversion factor with the units of the previous step in the denominator and the units of the following step in the numerator. In the following section, we incorporate the idea of a conceptual plan into an overall approach to solving numerical chemical problems.

General Problem-Solving Strategy

In this book, we use a standard problem-solving procedure that can be adapted to many of the problems encountered in general chemistry and beyond. To solve any problem, you need to assess the information given in the problem and devise a way to get to the information asked for. In other words, you must

- Identify the starting point (the *given* information).
- Identify the end point (what you must *find*).
- Devise a way to get from the starting point to the end point using what is given as well as what you already know or can look up. (As we just discussed, we call this the *conceptual plan*.)

In graphic form, we can represent this progression as

Given → Conceptual Plan → Find

One of the main difficulties beginning students encounter when trying to solve problems in general chemistry is not knowing where to begin. While no problem-solving procedure is applicable to all problems, the following four-step procedure can be helpful in working through many of the numerical problems you will encounter in this book.

1. **Sort.** Begin by sorting the information in the problem. *Given* information is the basic data provided by the problem—often one or more numbers with their associated units. *Find* indicates what information you will need for your answer.

2. **Strategize.** This is usually the most challenging part of solving a problem. In this process, you must develop a *conceptual plan*—a series of steps that will get you from the given information to the information you are trying to find. You have already seen conceptual plans for simple unit conversion problems. Each arrow in a conceptual plan represents a computational step. On the left side of the arrow is the quantity you had before the step, on the right side of the arrow is the quantity you will have after the step, and below the arrow is the information you need to get from one to the other—the relationship between the quantities.

Often such relationships take the form of conversion factors or equations. These may be given in the problem, in which case you will have written them down under "Given" in step 1. Usually, however, you will need other information—which may include physical constants, formulas, or conversion factors—to help get you from what you are given to what you must find. This information comes from what you have learned or can look up in the chapter or in tables within the book.

In some cases, you may get stuck at the strategize step. If you cannot figure out how to get from the given information to the information you are asked to find, you might try working backward. For example, you can look at the units of the quantity you are trying

Most problems can be solved in more than one way. The solutions we derive in this book will tend to be the most straightforward but certainly are not the only way to solve the problem.

to find and attempt to find conversion factors to get to the units of the given quantity. You may even try a combination of strategies; work forward, backward, or some of both. If you persist, you will develop a strategy to solve the problem.

3. **Solve.** This is the easiest part of solving a problem. Once you set up the problem properly and devise a conceptual plan, you simply follow the plan to solve the problem. Carry out any mathematical operations (paying attention to the rules for significant figures in calculations) and cancel units as needed.

4. **Check.** This is the step beginning students most often overlook. Experienced problem solvers always ask, "Does this answer make sense? Are the units correct? Is the number of significant figures correct?" When solving multistep problems, errors easily creep into the solution. You can catch most of these errors by simply checking the answer. For example, suppose you are calculating the number of atoms in a gold coin and end up with an answer of 1.1×10^{-6} atoms. Could the gold coin really be composed of one-millionth of one atom?

In Examples 1.7 and 1.8, we apply this problem-solving procedure to unit conversion problems. The procedure is summarized in the left column and two examples of applying the procedure are provided in the middle and right columns. This three-column format will be used in selected examples throughout this text. It allows you to see how you can apply a particular procedure to two different problems. Work through one problem first (from top to bottom) and then see how you can apply the same procedure to the other problem. Recognizing the commonalities and differences between problems is a key part of developing problem-solving skills.

PROCEDURE FOR... **Solving Unit Conversion Problems**	EXAMPLE 1.7 **Unit Conversion** Convert 1.76 yards to centimeters.	EXAMPLE 1.8 **Unit Conversion** Convert 1.8 quarts to cubic centimeters.
SORT Begin by sorting the information in the problem into *given* and *find*.	**GIVEN:** 1.76 yd **FIND:** cm	**GIVEN:** 1.8 qt **FIND:** cm^3
STRATEGIZE Devise a *conceptual plan* for the problem. Begin with the *given* quantity and symbolize each conversion step with an arrow. Below each arrow, write the appropriate conversion factor for that step. Focus on the units. The conceptual plan should end at the *find* quantity and its units. In these examples, the other information needed consists of relationships between the various units as shown.	**CONCEPTUAL PLAN** $$\text{yd} \rightarrow \text{m} \rightarrow \text{cm}$$ $$\frac{1 \text{ m}}{1.094 \text{ yd}} \qquad \frac{1 \text{ cm}}{10^{-2} \text{ m}}$$ **RELATIONSHIPS USED** $1.094 \text{ yd} = 1 \text{ m}$ $1 \text{ cm} = 10^{-2} \text{ cm}$ (These conversion factors are from Tables 1.2 and 1.3.)	**CONCEPTUAL PLAN** $$\text{qt} \rightarrow \text{L} \rightarrow \text{mL} \rightarrow \text{cm}^3$$ $$\frac{1 \text{ L}}{1.057 \text{ qt}} \quad \frac{1 \text{ mL}}{10^{-3} \text{ L}} \quad \frac{1 \text{ cm}^3}{1 \text{ mL}}$$ **RELATIONSHIPS USED** $1.057 \text{ qt} = 1 \text{ L}$ $1 \text{ mL} = 10^{-3} \text{ L}$ $1 \text{ mL} = 1 \text{ cm}^3$ (These conversion factors are from Tables 1.2 and 1.3.)
SOLVE Follow the conceptual plan. Begin with the *given* quantity and its units. Multiply by the appropriate conversion factor(s), canceling units, to arrive at the *find* quantity. Round the answer to the correct number of significant figures following the rules in Section 1.7. Remember that exact conversion factors do not limit significant figures.	**SOLUTION** $$1.76 \text{ yd} \times \frac{1 \text{ m}}{1.094 \text{ yd}} \times \frac{1 \text{ cm}}{10^{-2} \text{ m}}$$ $$= 160.8775 \text{ cm}$$ $160.8775 \text{ cm} = 161 \text{ cm}$	**SOLUTION** $$1.8 \text{ qt} \times \frac{1 \text{ L}}{1.057 \text{ qt}} \times \frac{1 \text{ mL}}{10^{-3} \text{ L}} \times \frac{1 \text{ cm}^3}{1 \text{ mL}}$$ $$= 1.70293 \times 10^3 \text{ cm}^3$$ $1.70293 \times 10^3 \text{ cm}^3 = 1.7 \times 10^3 \text{ cm}^3$
CHECK Check your answer. Are the units correct? Does the answer make sense?	The units (cm) are correct. The magnitude of the answer (161) makes sense because a centimeter is a much smaller unit than a yard.	The units (cm^3) are correct. The magnitude of the answer (1700) makes sense because a cubic centimeter is a much smaller unit than a quart.
	FOR PRACTICE 1.7 Convert 288 cm to yards.	**FOR PRACTICE 1.8** Convert 9255 cm^3 to gallons.

Units Raised to a Power

When building conversion factors for units raised to a power, remember to raise both the number and the unit to the power. For example, to convert from in^2 to cm^2, we construct the conversion factor as follows:

$$2.54 \text{ cm} = 1 \text{ in}$$
$$(2.54 \text{ cm})^2 = (1 \text{ in})^2$$
$$(2.54)^2 \text{ cm}^2 = 1^2 \text{ in}^2$$
$$6.45 \text{ cm}^2 = 1 \text{ in}^2$$
$$\frac{6.45 \text{ cm}^2}{1 \text{ in}^2} = 1$$

Example 1.9 demonstrates how to use conversion factors involving units raised to a power.

EXAMPLE 1.9 Unit Conversions Involving Units Raised to a Power

Calculate the displacement (the total volume of the cylinders through which the pistons move) of a 5.70 L automobile engine in cubic inches.

SORT Sort the information in the problem into *given* and *find*.	**GIVEN:** 5.70 L **FIND:** in^3
STRATEGIZE Write a conceptual plan. Begin with the given information and devise a path to the information that you are asked to find. Notice that for cubic units, you must cube the conversion factors.	**CONCEPTUAL PLAN** $\boxed{L} \longrightarrow \boxed{mL} \longrightarrow \boxed{cm^3} \longrightarrow \boxed{in^3}$ $\quad\quad \dfrac{1 \text{ mL}}{10^{-3} \text{ L}} \quad\quad \dfrac{1 \text{ cm}^3}{1 \text{ mL}} \quad\quad \dfrac{(1 \text{ in})^3}{(2.54 \text{ cm})^3}$ **RELATIONSHIPS USED** $1 \text{ mL} = 10^{-3} \text{ L}$ $1 \text{ mL} = 1 \text{ cm}^3$ $2.54 \text{ cm} = 1 \text{ in}$ (These conversion factors are from Tables 1.2 and 1.3)
SOLVE Follow the conceptual plan to solve the problem. Round the answer to three significant figures to reflect the three significant figures in the least precisely known quantity (5.70 L). These conversion factors are all exact and therefore do not limit the number of significant figures.	**SOLUTION** $5.70 \text{ L} \times \dfrac{1 \text{ mL}}{10^{-3} \text{ L}} \times \dfrac{1 \text{ cm}^3}{1 \text{ mL}} \times \dfrac{(1 \text{ in})^3}{(2.54 \text{ cm})^3} = 347.835 \text{ in}^3$ $\quad\quad\quad\quad\quad\quad\quad\quad\quad\quad\quad\quad\quad\quad\quad\quad\quad = 348 \text{ in}^3$

CHECK The units of the answer are correct, and the magnitude makes sense. The unit cubic inches is smaller than liters, so the volume in cubic inches should be larger than the volume in liters.

FOR PRACTICE 1.9

How many cubic centimeters are there in 2.11 yd^3?

FOR MORE PRACTICE 1.9

A vineyard has 145 acres of Chardonnay grapes. A particular soil supplement requires 5.50 grams for every square meter of vineyard. How many kilograms of the soil supplement are required for the entire vineyard? ($1 \text{ km}^2 = 247 \text{ acres}$)

EXAMPLE 1.10 Density as a Conversion Factor

The mass of fuel in a jet must be calculated before each flight to ensure that the jet is not too heavy to fly. A 747 is fueled with 173,231 L of jet fuel. If the density of the fuel is 0.768 g/cm³, what is the mass of the fuel in kilograms?

SORT Begin by sorting the information in the problem into *given* and *find*.	**GIVEN:** fuel volume = 173,231 L density of fuel = 0.768 g/cm³ **FIND:** mass in kg
STRATEGIZE Draw the conceptual plan by beginning with the given quantity—in this case the volume in liters (L). The overall goal of this problem is to find the mass. You can convert between volume and mass using density (g/cm³). However, you must first convert the volume to cm³. Once you have converted the volume to cm³, use the density to convert to g. Finally, convert g to kg.	**CONCEPTUAL PLAN** **RELATIONSHIPS USED** $1 \text{ mL} = 10^{-3} \text{ L}$ $1 \text{ mL} = 1 \text{ cm}^3$ $d = 0.768 \text{ g/cm}^3$ $1000 \text{ g} = 1 \text{ kg}$ (These conversion factors are from Tables 1.2 and 1.3.)
SOLVE Follow the conceptual plan to solve the problem. Round the answer to three significant figures to reflect the three significant figures in the density.	**SOLUTION** $173{,}231 \text{ L} \times \dfrac{1 \text{ mL}}{10^{-3} \text{ L}} \times \dfrac{1 \text{ cm}^3}{1 \text{ mL}} \times \dfrac{0.768 \text{ g}}{1 \text{ cm}^3} \times \dfrac{1 \text{ kg}}{1000 \text{ g}} = 1.33 \times 10^5 \text{ kg}$

CHECK The units of the answer (kg) are correct. The magnitude makes sense because the mass (1.33×10^5 kg) is similar in magnitude to the given volume (173,231 L or 1.73231×10^5 L), as expected for a density close to 1 (0.768 g/cm³).

FOR PRACTICE 1.10

Backpackers often use canisters of white gas to fuel a cooking stove's burner. If one canister contains 1.45 L of white gas, and the density of the gas is 0.710 g/cm³, what is the mass of the fuel in kilograms?

FOR MORE PRACTICE 1.10

A drop of gasoline has a mass of 22 mg and a density of 0.754 g/cm³. What is its volume in cubic centimeters?

Order-of-Magnitude Estimations

Calculation is an integral part of chemical problem solving. But precise numerical calculation is not always necessary, or even possible. Sometimes data are only approximate; other times we may not need a high degree of precision—a rough estimate or a simplified "back of the envelope" calculation is enough. We can also use approximate calculations to get an initial feel for a problem or as a quick check to see whether our solution is "in the right ballpark."

One way to make such estimates is to simplify the numbers so that they can be manipulated easily. The technique known as *order-of-magnitude estimation* is based on focusing only on the exponential part of numbers written in scientific notation, according to these guidelines:

- If the decimal part of the number is less than 5, just drop it. Thus, 4.36×10^5 becomes 10^5 and 2.7×10^{-3} becomes 10^{-3}.

- If the decimal part is 5 or more, round it up to 10 and rewrite the number as a power of 10. Thus, 5.982×10^7 becomes $10 \times 10^7 = 10^8$, and 6.1101×10^{-3} becomes $10 \times 10^{-3} = 10^{-2}$.

When we make these approximations, we are left with powers of 10, which are easier to multiply and divide. Of course our answer is only as reliable as the numbers used to get it, so we should not assume that the results of an order-of-magnitude calculation are accurate to more than an order of magnitude.

Suppose, for example, that we want to estimate the number of atoms that an immortal being could have counted in the 14 billion (1.4×10^{10}) years that the universe has been in existence, assuming a counting rate of ten atoms per second. Since a year has 3.2×10^7 seconds, we can approximate the number of atoms counted as follows:

$$10^{10} \text{ years} \quad \times \quad 10^7 \frac{\text{seconds}}{\text{year}} \quad \times \quad 10^1 \frac{\text{atoms}}{\text{second}} \quad \approx 10^{18} \text{ atoms}$$

| (number of years) | (number of seconds per year) | (number of atoms counted per second) |

A million trillion atoms (10^{18}) may seem like a lot, but as we discuss in Chapter 2, a speck of matter made up of a million trillion atoms is nearly impossible to see without a microscope.

In our general problem-solving procedure, the last step is to check whether the results seem reasonable. Order-of-magnitude estimations can often help us catch the kinds of mistakes that may happen in a detailed calculation, such as entering an incorrect exponent or sign into a calculator, or multiplying when we should have divided.

Problems Involving an Equation

Problems involving equations can be solved in much the same way as problems involving conversions. Usually, in problems involving equations, we must find one of the variables in the equation, given the others. The *conceptual plan* concept outlined earlier can be used for problems involving equations. For example, suppose we are given the mass (*m*) and volume (*V*) of a sample and asked to calculate its density. The conceptual plan shows how the *equation* takes us from the *given* quantities to the *find* quantity.

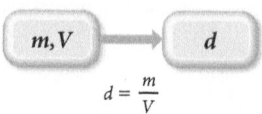

$$d = \frac{m}{V}$$

Here, instead of a conversion factor under the arrow, this conceptual plan has an equation. The equation shows the *relationship* between the quantities on the left of the arrow and the quantities on the right. Note that at this point the equation need not be solved for the quantity on the right (although in this particular case it is). The procedure that follows, as well as the two examples, will guide you in developing a strategy to solve problems involving equations. We again use the three-column format. Work through one problem from top to bottom and then see how you can apply the same general procedure to the second problem.

PROCEDURE FOR... **Solving Problems Involving Equations**	**EXAMPLE 1.11** **Problems with Equations** Find the radius (r) in centimeters of a spherical water droplet with a volume (V) of 0.058 cm^3. For a sphere, $V = (4/3)\,\pi r^3$.	**EXAMPLE 1.12** **Problems with Equations** Find the density (in g/cm^3) of a metal cylinder with a mass (m) of 8.3 g, a length (l) of 1.94 cm, and a radius (r) of 0.55 cm. For a cylinder, $V = \pi r^2 l$.
SORT Begin by sorting the information in the problem into *given* and *find*.	**GIVEN:** $V = 0.058$ cm^3 **FIND:** r in cm	**GIVEN:** $m = 8.3$ g $\quad\quad\; l = 1.94$ cm $\quad\quad\; r = 0.55$ cm **FIND:** d in g/cm^3
STRATEGIZE Write a conceptual plan for the problem. Focus on the equation(s). The conceptual plan shows how the equation takes you from the *given* quantity (or quantities) to the *find* quantity. The conceptual plan may have several parts, involving other equations or required conversions. In these examples, you use the geometrical relationships given in the problem statements as well as the definition of density, $d = m/V$, which you learned in this chapter.	**CONCEPTUAL PLAN** $$\boxed{V} \longrightarrow \boxed{r}$$ $$V = \frac{4}{3}\,\pi\,r^3$$ **RELATIONSHIPS USED** $$V = \frac{4}{3}\,\pi\,r^3$$	**CONCEPTUAL PLAN** $$\boxed{l,r} \longrightarrow \boxed{V}$$ $$V = \pi r^2 l$$ $$\boxed{m,V} \longrightarrow \boxed{d}$$ $$d = m/V$$ **RELATIONSHIPS USED** $$V = \pi r^2 l$$ $$d = \frac{m}{V}$$
SOLVE Follow the conceptual plan. Solve the equation(s) for the *find* quantity (if it is not already). Gather each of the quantities that must go into the equation in the correct units. (Convert to the correct units if necessary.) Substitute the numerical values and their units into the equation(s) and calculate the answer. Round the answer to the correct number of significant figures.	**SOLUTION** $$V = \frac{4}{3}\,\pi\,r^3$$ $$r^3 = \frac{3}{4\pi}V$$ $$r = \left(\frac{3}{4\pi}V\right)^{1/3}$$ $$= \left(\frac{3}{4\pi}0.058 \text{ cm}^3\right)^{1/3}$$ $$= 0.24013 \text{ cm}$$ 0.24013 cm = 0.24 cm	**SOLUTION** $$V = \pi r^2 l$$ $$= \pi(0.55 \text{ cm})^2 (1.94 \text{ cm})$$ $$= 1.\underline{8}436 \text{ cm}^3$$ $$d = \frac{m}{V}$$ $$= \frac{8.3 \text{ g}}{1.\underline{8}436 \text{ cm}^3} = 4.50195 \text{ g/cm}^3$$ 4.50195 g/cm^3 = 4.5 g/cm^3
CHECK Check your answer. Are the units correct? Does the answer make sense?	The units (cm) are correct and the magnitude makes sense.	The units (g/cm^3) are correct. The magnitude of the answer seems correct for one of the lighter metals (see Table 1.4).
	FOR PRACTICE 1.11 Find the radius (r) of an aluminum cylinder that is 2.00 cm long and has a mass of 12.4 g. For a cylinder, $V = \pi r^2 l$.	**FOR PRACTICE 1.12** Find the density, in g/cm^3, of a metal cube with a mass of 50.3 g and an edge length (l) of 2.65 cm. For a cube, $V = l^3$.

CHAPTER IN REVIEW

Self Assessment Quiz

Q1. A chemist mixes sodium with water and witnesses a violent reaction between the metal and water. This is best classified as
a) an observation.   b) a law.
c) a hypothesis.   d) a theory.

Q2. This image represents a particulate view of a sample of matter. Classify the sample according to its composition.

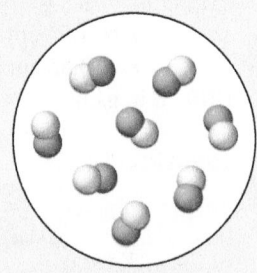

a) The sample is a pure element.
b) The sample is a homogeneous mixture.
c) The sample is a compound.
d) The sample is a heterogeneous mixture.

Q3. Which change is a physical change?
a) wood burning
b) iron rusting
c) dynamite exploding
d) gasoline evaporating

Q4. Which property of rubbing alcohol is a chemical property?
a) its density (0.786 g/cm^3)
b) its flammability
c) its boiling point (82.5 °C)
d) its melting point (−89 °C)

Q5. Convert 85.0 °F to K.
a) 181.1 K   b) 358 K
c) 29.4 K   d) 302.6 K

Q6. Express the quantity 33.2×10^{-4} m in mm.
a) 33.2 mm
b) 3.32 mm
c) 0.332 mm
d) 3.32×10^{-6} mm

Q7. What is the mass of a 1.75 L sample of a liquid that has a density of 0.921 g/mL?
a) 1.61×10^3 g   b) 1.61×10^{-3} g
c) 1.90×10^3 g   d) 1.90×10^{-3} g

Q8. Perform the calculation to the correct number of significant figures.
$$(43.998 \times 0.00552)/2.002$$
a) 0.121   b) 0.12
c) 0.12131   d) 0.1213

Q9. Perform the calculation to the correct number of significant figures.
$$(8.01 - 7.50)/3.002$$
a) 0.1698867   b) 0.17
c) 0.170   d) 0.1700

Q10. Convert 1285 cm^2 to m^2.
a) 1.285×10^7 m^2 b) 12.85 m^2
c) 0.1285 m^2 d) 1.285×10^5 m^2

Q11. The first diagram depicts a compound in its liquid state. Which of the other diagrams best depicts the compound after it has evaporated into a gas?

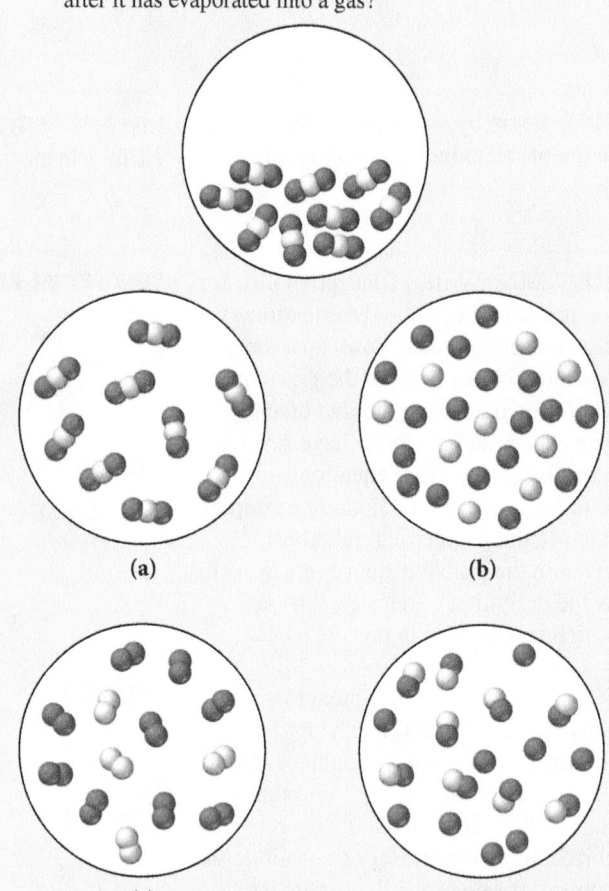

(a)   (b)

(c)   (d)

Q12. Three samples, each of a different substance, are weighed and their volume is measured. The results are tabulated below. List the substances in order of decreasing density.

	Mass	Volume
Substance I	10.0 g	10.0 mL
Substance II	10.0 kg	12.0 L
Substance III	12.0 mg	10.0 µL

a) III > II > I   b) I > II > III
c) III > I > II   d) II > I > III

Q13. A solid metal sphere has a radius of 3.53 cm and a mass of 1.796 kg. What is the density of the metal in g/cm^3? (The volume of sphere is $V = \frac{4}{3}\pi r^3$.)
a) 34.4 g/cm^3 b) 0.103 g/cm^3
c) 121 g/cm^3 d) 9.75 g/cm^3

Q14. A German automobile gets a gas mileage of 22 km/L. Convert this quantity to miles per gallon.
a) 9.4 mi/gal   b) 1.3×10^2 mi/gal
c) 52 mi/gal   d) 3.6 mi/gal

Q15. A wooden block has a volume of 18.5 in^3. Express the volume of the cube in cm^3.
a) 303 cm^3 b) 47.0 cm^3
c) 1.13 cm^3 d) 7.28 cm^3

Answers: 1. (a) **2.** (c) **3.** (d) **4.** (b) **5.** (d) **6.** (b) **7.** (a) **8.** (a) **9.** (b) **10.** (c) **11.** (a) **12.** (c) **13.** (d) **14.** (c) **15.** (a)

Key Terms

Section 1.1
atoms (1)
molecules (1)
chemistry (3)

Section 1.2
hypothesis (3)
experiment (3)
scientific law (3)
law of conservation
of mass (3)
theory (3)
atomic theory (3)

Section 1.3
matter (5)
substance (5)
state (5)
composition (5)
solid (5)
liquid (5)
gas (5)
crystalline (5)
amorphous (5)
pure substance (7)
mixture (7)
element (7)
compound (7)

heterogeneous mixture (7)
homogeneous mixture (8)
decanting (8)
distillation (8)
volatile (8)
filtration (8)

Section 1.4
physical change (9)
chemical change (9)
physical property (9)
chemical property (9)

Section 1.5
energy (12)
work (12)
kinetic energy (12)
potential energy (12)
thermal energy (12)
law of conservation
of energy (12)

Section 1.6
units (13)
English system (13)
metric system (13)
International System of Units (SI) (13)
meter (m) (14)
kilogram (kg) (14)

mass (14)
second (s) (14)
kelvin (K) (15)
temperature (15)
Fahrenheit (°F) scale (15)
Celsius (°C) scale (15)
Kelvin scale (15)
prefix multipliers (17)
derived unit (17)
volume (17)
liter (L) (18)
milliliter (mL) (18)
density (d) (18)
intensive property (18)
extensive property (18)

Section 1.7
significant figures
(significant digits) (22)
exact numbers (22)
accuracy (25)
precision (25)
random error (25)
systematic error (26)

Section 1.8
dimensional analysis (27)
conversion factor (27)

Key Concepts

Atoms and Molecules (1.1)

▶ All matter is composed of atoms and molecules.
▶ Chemistry is the science that investigates the properties of matter by examining the atoms and molecules that compose it.

The Scientific Approach to Knowledge (1.2)

▶ Science begins with the observation of the physical world. A number of related observations can often be summarized in a statement or generalization called a scientific law.
▶ A hypothesis is a tentative interpretation or explanation of observations. One or more well-established hypotheses may prompt the development of a scientific theory, a model for nature that explains the underlying reasons for observations and laws.
▶ Laws, hypotheses, and theories all give rise to predictions that can be tested by experiments, carefully controlled procedures designed to produce critical new observations. If scientists cannot confirm the predictions, they must modify or replace the law, hypothesis, or theory.

The Classification of Matter (1.3)

▶ We classify matter according to its state (solid, liquid, or gas) or according to its composition (pure substance or mixture).
▶ A pure substance can either be an element, which cannot be chemically broken down into simpler substances, or a compound, which is composed of two or more elements in fixed proportions.
▶ A mixture can be either homogeneous, with the same composition throughout, or heterogeneous, with different compositions in different regions.

The Properties of Matter (1.4)

▶ We can classify the properties of matter into two types: physical and chemical. Matter displays its physical properties without changing its composition.
▶ Changes in matter in which composition does not change are physical changes. Changes in matter in which composition does change are chemical changes.

Energy (1.5)

▶ In chemical and physical changes, matter often exchanges energy with its surroundings. In these exchanges, the total energy is always conserved; energy is neither created nor destroyed.
▶ Systems with high potential energy tend to change in the direction of lower potential energy, releasing energy into the surroundings.

The Units of Measurement and Significant Figures (1.6, 1.7)

▶ Scientists use primarily SI units, which are based on the metric system. The SI base units include the meter (m) for length, the kilogram (kg) for mass, the second (s) for time, and the kelvin (K) for temperature.
▶ Derived units are those formed from a combination of other units. Common derived units include those for volume (cm^3 or m^3) and density (g/cm^3).
▶ Measured quantities are reported so that the number of digits reflects the uncertainty in the measurement. Significant figures are the non-place-holding digits in a reported number.

Key Equations and Relationships

Relationship between Kelvin (K) and Celsius (°C) Temperature Scales (1.6)

$$K = °C + 273.15$$

Relationship between Celsius (°C) and Fahrenheit (°F) Temperature Scales (1.6)

$$°C = \frac{(°F - 32)}{1.8}$$

Relationship between Density (*d*), Mass (*m*), and Volume (*V*) (1.6)

$$d = \frac{m}{V}$$

Key Learning Outcomes

Chapter Objectives		Assessment
Determining Physical and Chemical Changes and Properties (1.4)		Example 1.1 For Practice 1.1 Exercises 43–50
Converting between the Temperature Scales: Fahrenheit, Celsius, and Kelvin (1.6)		Example 1.2 For Practice 1.2 Exercises 51–54
Calculating the Density of a Substance (1.6)		Example 1.3 For Practice 1.3 For More Practice 1.3 Exercises 65–68
Reporting Scientific Measurements to the Correct Digit of Uncertainty (1.7)		Example 1.4 For Practice 1.4 Exercises 73, 74
Working with Significant Figures (1.7)		Examples 1.5, 1.6 For Practice 1.5, 1.6 Exercises 77, 78, 80, 83–88
Using Conversion Factors (1.8)		Examples 1.7, 1.8, 1.9, 1.10 For Practice 1.7, 1.8, 1.9, 1.10 For More Practice 1.9, 1.10 Exercises 91, 92, 96–99, 101, 102
Solving Problems Involving Equations (1.8)		Examples 1.11, 1.12 For Practice 1.11, 1.12 Exercises 117, 118

EXERCISES

Review Questions

1. Explain this statement in your own words and give an example. *The properties of the substances around us depend on the atoms and molecules that compose them.*

2. Explain the main goal of chemistry.

3. Describe the scientific approach to knowledge. How does it differ from other approaches?

4. Explain the differences between a hypothesis, a law, and a theory.

5. What observations did Antoine Lavoisier make? What law did he formulate?

6. What theory did John Dalton formulate?

7. What is wrong with the expression "That is just a theory," if by *theory* the speaker is referring to a scientific theory?

8. What are two different ways to classify matter?

9. How do solids, liquids, and gases differ?

10. What is the difference between a crystalline solid and an amorphous solid?

11. Explain the difference between a pure substance and a mixture.

12. Explain the difference between an element and a compound.

13. Explain the difference between a homogeneous and a heterogeneous mixture.

14. What kind of mixtures can be separated by filtration?

15. Explain how distillation is used to separate mixtures.

16. What is the difference between a physical property and a chemical property?

17. What is the difference between a physical change and a chemical change? List some examples of each.

18. Explain the significance of the law of conservation of energy.

19. What kind of energy is chemical energy? In what way is an elevated weight similar to a tank of gasoline?

20. What are the standard SI base units of length, mass, time, and temperature?

21. What are the three common temperature scales? Does the size of a degree differ among them?

22. What are prefix multipliers? List some examples.

23. What is a derived unit? List an example.

24. Explain the difference between density and mass.

25. Explain the difference between *intensive* and *extensive* properties.

26. What is the meaning of the number of digits reported in a measured quantity?

27. When multiplying or dividing measured quantities, what determines the number of significant figures in the result?

28. When adding or subtracting measured quantities, what determines the number of significant figures in the result?

29. What are the rules for rounding off the results of calculations?

30. Explain the difference between precision and accuracy.

31. Explain the difference between random error and systematic error.

32. What is dimensional analysis?

Problems by Topic

Note: Answers to all odd-numbered Problems, numbered in blue, can be found in Appendix III. Exercises in the Problems by Topic section are paired, with each odd-numbered problem followed by a similar even-numbered problem. Exercises in the Cumulative Problems section are also paired, but more loosely. Challenge Problems and Conceptual Problems, because of their nature, are unpaired.

The Scientific Approach to Knowledge

33. Classify each statement as an observation, a law, or a theory.
    a. All matter is made of tiny, indestructible particles called atoms.
    b. When iron rusts in a closed container, the mass of the container and its contents does not change.
    c. In chemical reactions, matter is neither created nor destroyed.
    d. When a match burns, heat is released.

34. Classify each statement as an observation, a law, or a theory.
    a. Chlorine is a highly reactive gas.
    b. If elements are listed in order of increasing mass of their atoms, their chemical reactivity follows a repeating pattern.
    c. Neon is an inert (or nonreactive) gas.
    d. The reactivity of elements depends on the arrangement of their electrons.

35. A chemist decomposes several samples of carbon monoxide into carbon and oxygen and weighs the resultant elements. The results are shown in the table.

Sample	Mass of Carbon (g)	Mass of Oxygen (g)
1	6	8
2	12	16
3	18	24

a. Do you notice a pattern in these results?
Next, the chemist decomposes several samples of hydrogen peroxide into hydrogen and oxygen. The results are shown in the table:

Sample	Mass of Hydrogen (g)	Mass of Oxygen (g)
1	0.5	8
2	1	16
3	1.5	24

b. Do you notice a similarity between these results and those for carbon monoxide in part a?
c. Can you formulate a law from the observations in a and b?
d. Can you formulate a hypothesis that might explain your law in c?

36. When astronomers observe distant galaxies, they can tell that most of them are moving away from one another. In addition, the more distant the galaxies, the more rapidly they are likely to be moving away from each other. Can you devise a hypothesis to explain these observations?

The Classification and Properties of Matter

37. Classify each substance as a pure substance or a mixture. If it is a pure substance, classify it as an element or a compound. If it is a mixture, classify it as homogeneous or heterogeneous.
    a. sweat
    b. carbon dioxide
    c. aluminum
    d. vegetable soup

38. Classify each substance as a pure substance or a mixture. If it is a pure substance, classify it as an element or a compound. If it is a mixture, classify it as homogeneous or heterogeneous.
a. wine
b. beef stew
c. iron
d. carbon monoxide

39. Complete the table.

Substance	Pure or mixture	Type
aluminum	pure	element
apple juice	_____	_____
hydrogen peroxide	_____	_____
chicken soup	_____	_____

40. Complete the table.

Substance	Pure or mixture	Type
water	pure	compound
coffee	_____	_____
ice	_____	_____
carbon	_____	_____

41. Determine whether each molecular diagram represents a pure substance or a mixture. If it represents a pure substance, classify the substance as an element or a compound. If it represents a mixture, classify the mixture as homogeneous or heterogeneous.

(a)   (b)

(c)   (d)

42. Determine whether each molecular diagram represents a pure substance or a mixture. If it represents a pure substance, classify the substance as an element or a compound. If it represents a mixture, classify the mixture as homogeneous or heterogeneous.

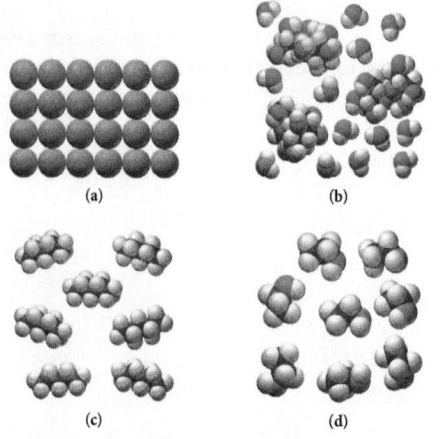

(a)   (b)

(c)   (d)

43. Classify each of the listed properties of isopropyl alcohol (also known as rubbing alcohol) as physical or chemical.
a. colorless
b. flammable
c. liquid at room temperature
d. density = 0.79 g/mL
e. mixes with water

44. Classify each of the listed properties of ozone (a pollutant in the lower atmosphere but part of a protective shield against UV light in the upper atmosphere) as physical or chemical.
a. bluish color
b. pungent odor
c. very reactive
d. decomposes on exposure to ultraviolet light
e. gas at room temperature

45. Classify each property as physical or chemical.
a. the tendency of ethyl alcohol to burn
b. the shine on silver
c. the odor of paint thinner
d. the flammability of propane gas

46. Classify each property as physical or chemical.
a. the boiling point of ethyl alcohol
b. the temperature at which dry ice evaporates
c. the tendency of iron to rust
d. the color of gold

47. Classify each change as physical or chemical.
a. Natural gas burns in a stove.
b. The liquid propane in a gas grill evaporates because the valve was left open.
c. The liquid propane in a gas grill burns in a flame.
d. A bicycle frame rusts on repeated exposure to air and water.

48. Classify each change as physical or chemical.
a. Sugar burns when heated in a skillet.
b. Sugar dissolves in water.
c. A platinum ring becomes dull because of continued abrasion.
d. A silver surface becomes tarnished after exposure to air for a long period of time.

49. Based on the molecular diagram, classify each change as physical or chemical.

(a)

(b)

(c)

50. Based on the molecular diagram, classify each change as physical or chemical.

(a)

(b)

(c)

Units in Measurement

51. Convert each temperature.
   a. 32 °F to °C (temperature at which water freezes)
   b. 77 K to °F (temperature of liquid nitrogen)
   c. −109 °F to °C (temperature of dry ice)
   d. 98.6 °F to K (body temperature)

52. Convert each temperature.
   a. 212 °F to °C (temperature of boiling water at sea level)
   b. 22 °C to K (approximate room temperature)
   c. 0.00 K to °F (coldest temperature possible, also known as absolute zero)
   d. 2.735 K to °C (average temperature of the universe as measured from background black body radiation)

53. The coldest temperature ever measured in the United States is −80 °F on January 23, 1971, in Prospect Creek, Alaska. Convert that temperature to °C and K. (Assume that −80 °F is precise to two significant figures.)

54. The warmest temperature ever measured in the United States is 134 °F on July 10, 1913, in Death Valley, California. Convert that temperature to °C and K.

55. Use the prefix multipliers to express each measurement without any exponents.
   a. 1.2×10^{-9} m   **b.** 22×10^{-15} s
   c. 1.5×10^9 g   **d.** 3.5×10^6 L

56. Use prefix multipliers to express each measurement without any exponents.
   a. 38.8×10^5 g   **b.** 55.2×10^{-10} s
   c. 23.4×10^{11} m   **d.** 87.9×10^{-7} L

57. Use scientific notation to express each quantity with only the base units (no prefix multipliers).
   a. 4.5 ns
   b. 18 fs
   c. 128 pm
   d. 35 μm

58. Use scientific notation to express each quantity with only the base units (no prefix multipliers).
   a. 35 μL   **b.** 225 Mm   **c.** 133 Tg   **d.** 1.5 cg

59. Complete the table.

a. 1245 kg	1.245×10^6 g	1.245×10^9 mg
b. 515 km	_____dm	_____cm
c. 122.355 s	_____ms	_____ks
d. 3.345 kJ	_____J	_____mJ

60. Complete the table.

a. 355 km/s	_____cm/s	_____m/ms
b. 1228 g/L	_____g/mL	_____kg/ML
c. 554 mK/s	_____K/s	_____μK/ms
d. 2.554 mg/mL	_____g/L	_____μg/mL

61. Express the quantity 254,998 m in each unit.
   a. km   **b.** Mm   **c.** mm   **d.** cm

62. Express the quantity 556.2×10^{-12} s in each unit.
   a. ms   **b.** ns   **c.** ps   **d.** fs

63. How many 1 cm squares would it take to construct a square that is 1 m on each side?

64. How many 1 cm cubes would it take to construct a cube that is 4 cm on edge?

Density

65. A new penny has a mass of 2.49 g and a volume of 0.349 cm³. Is the penny made of pure copper? Explain.

66. A titanium bicycle frame displaces 0.314 L of water and has a mass of 1.41 kg. What is the density of the titanium in g/cm³?

67. Glycerol is a syrupy liquid often used in cosmetics and soaps. A 3.25 L sample of pure glycerol has a mass of 4.10×10^3 g. What is the density of glycerol in g/cm³?

68. A supposedly gold nugget is tested to determine its density. It is found to displace 19.3 mL of water and has a mass of 371 grams. Could the nugget be made of gold?

69. Ethylene glycol (antifreeze) has a density of 1.11 g/cm³.
   a. What is the mass in g of 417 mL of this liquid?
   b. What is the volume in L of 4.1 kg of this liquid?

70. Acetone (nail polish remover) has a density of 0.7857 g/cm³.
   a. What is the mass, in g, of 28.56 mL of acetone?
   b. What is the volume, in mL, of 6.54 g of acetone?

71. A small airplane takes on 245 L of fuel. If the density of the fuel is 0.821 g/mL, what mass of fuel has the airplane taken on?

72. Human fat has a density of 0.918 g/cm³. How much volume (in cm³) is gained by a person who gains 10.0 lb of pure fat?

The Reliability of a Measurement and Significant Figures

73. Read each measurement to the correct number of significant figures. Laboratory glassware should always be read from the bottom of the meniscus.

(a)   (b)   (c)

74. Read each measurement to the correct number of significant figures. Laboratory glassware should always be read from the bottom of the meniscus. Digital balances normally display mass to the correct number of significant figures for that particular balance.

(a)   (b)   (c)

75. For each number, underline the zeroes that are significant and draw an **x** through the zeroes that are not.
   a. 1,050,501 km   **b.** 0.0020 m
   c. 0.000000000000002 s   **d.** 0.001090 cm

76. For each number, underline the zeroes that are significant and draw an **x** through the zeroes that are not.
   a. 180,701 mi   **b.** 0.001040 m
   c. 0.005710 km   **d.** 90,201 m

77. How many significant figures are in each number?
   a. 0.000312 m   **b.** 312,000 s
   c. 3.12×10^5 km   **d.** 13,127 s
   e. 2000

78. How many significant figures are in each number?
   a. 0.1111 s   **b.** 0.007 m
   c. 108,700 km   **d.** 1.563300×10^{11} m
   e. 30,800

79. Which numbers are exact (and therefore have an unlimited number of significant figures)?
   a. $\pi = 3.14$
   b. 12 inches = 1 foot
   c. EPA gas mileage rating of 26 miles per gallon
   d. 1 gross = 144

80. Indicate the number of significant figures in each number. If the number is an exact number, indicate an unlimited number of significant figures.
   a. 305,435,087 (2008 U.S. population)
   b. 2.54 cm = 1 in
   c. 11.4 g/cm³ (density of lead)
   d. 12 = 1 dozen

81. Round each number to four significant figures.
   a. 156.852   **b.** 156.842
   c. 156.849   **d.** 156.899

82. Round each number to three significant figures.
   a. 79,845.82   **b.** 1.548937×10^7
   c. 2.3499999995   **d.** 0.000045389

Significant Figures in Calculations

83. Calculate to the correct number of significant figures.
   a. $9.15 \div 4.970$
   b. $1.54 \times 0.03060 \times 0.69$
   c. $27.5 \times 1.82 \div 100.04$
   d. $(2.290 \times 10^6) \div (6.7 \times 10^4)$

84. Calculate to the correct number of significant figures.
   a. $89.3 \times 77.0 \times 0.08$
   b. $(5.01 \times 10^5) \div (7.8 \times 10^2)$
   c. $4.005 \times 74 \times 0.007$
   d. $453 \div 2.031$

85. Calculate to the correct number of significant figures.
   a. $43.7 - 2.341$
   b. $17.6 + 2.838 + 2.3 + 110.77$
   c. $19.6 + 58.33 - 4.974$
   d. $5.99 - 5.572$

86. Calculate to the correct number of significant figures.
   a. $0.004 + 0.09879$ **b.** $1239.3 + 9.73 + 3.42$
   c. $2.4 - 1.777$ **d.** $532 + 7.3 - 48.523$

87. Calculate to the correct number of significant figures.
   a. $(24.6681 \times 2.38) + 332.58$
   b. $(85.3 - 21.489) \div 0.0059$
   c. $(512 \div 986.7) + 5.44$
   d. $[(28.7 \times 10^5) \div 48.533] + 144.99$

88. Calculate to the correct number of significant figures.
   a. $[(1.7 \times 10^6) \div (2.63 \times 10^5)] + 7.33$
   b. $(568.99 - 232.1) \div 5.3$
   c. $(9443 + 45 - 9.9) \times 8.1 \times 10^6$
   d. $(3.14 \times 2.4367) - 2.34$

Unit Conversions

89. Perform each unit conversion.
   a. 27.8 L to cm³   **b.** 1898 mg to kg
   c. 198 km to cm

90. Perform each unit conversion.
   a. 28.9 nm to μm   **b.** 1432 cm³ to L
   c. 1211 Tm to Gm

91. Perform each unit conversion.
   a. 154 cm to in   **b.** 3.14 kg to g
   c. 3.5 L to qt   **d.** 109 mm to in

92. Perform each unit conversion.
   a. 1.4 in to mm   **b.** 116 ft to cm
   c. 1845 kg to lb   **d.** 815 yd to km

93. A runner wants to run 10.0 km. She knows that her running pace is 7.5 miles per hour. How many minutes must she run?

94. A cyclist rides at an average speed of 18 miles per hour. If she wants to bike 212 km, how long (in hours) must she ride?

95. A European automobile has a gas mileage of 17 km/L. What is the gas mileage in miles per gallon?

96. A gas can holds 5.0 gallons of gasoline. Express this quantity in cm³.

97. A house has an area of 195 m². What is its area in each unit?
   a. km²   **b.** dm²   **c.** cm²

98. A bedroom has a volume of 115 m³. What is its volume in each unit?
   a. km³   **b.** dm³   **c.** cm³

99. The average U.S. farm occupies 435 acres. How many square miles is this? (1 acre = 43,560 ft², 1 mile = 5280 ft)

100. Total U.S. farmland occupies 954 million acres. How many square miles is this? (1 acre = 43,560 ft², 1 mile = 5280 ft). Total U.S. land area is 3.537 million square miles. What percentage of U.S. land is farmland?

101. An acetaminophen suspension for infants contains 80 mg/0.80 mL suspension. The recommended dose is 15 mg/kg body weight. How many mL of this suspension should be given to an infant weighing 14 lb? (Assume two significant figures.)

102. An ibuprofen suspension for infants contains 100 mg/5.0 mL suspension. The recommended dose is 10 mg/kg body weight. How many mL of this suspension should be given to an infant weighing 18 lb? (Assume two significant figures.)

Cumulative Problems

103. There are exactly 60 seconds in a minute, there are exactly 60 minutes in an hour, there are exactly 24 hours in a mean solar day, and there are 365.24 solar days in a solar year. How many seconds are in a solar year? Be sure to give your answer with the correct number of significant figures.

104. Determine the number of picoseconds in 2.0 hours.

105. Classify each property as intensive or extensive.
    a. volume   b. boiling point
    c. temperature   d. electrical conductivity
    e. energy

106. At what temperatures are the readings on the Fahrenheit and Celsius thermometers the same?

107. Suppose you design a new thermometer called the X thermometer. On the X scale the boiling point of water is 130 °X and the freezing point of water is 10 °X. At what temperature will the readings on the Fahrenheit and X thermometers be the same?

108. On a new Jekyll temperature scale, water freezes at 17 °J and boils at 97 °J. On another new temperature scale, the Hyde scale, water freezes at 0 °H and boils at 120 °H. If methyl alcohol boils at 84 °H, what is its boiling point on the Jekyll scale?

109. Force is defined as mass times acceleration. Starting with SI base units, derive a unit for force. Using SI prefixes, suggest a convenient unit for the force resulting from a collision with a 10-ton trailer truck moving at 55 miles per hour and for the force resulting from the collision of a molecule of mass around 10^{-20} kg moving almost at the speed of light (3×10^8 m/s) with the wall of its container. (Assume a 1-second deceleration time for both collisions.)

110. A temperature measurement of 25 °C has three significant figures, while a temperature measurement of −196 °C has only two significant figures. Explain.

111. Do each calculation without using your calculator and give the answers to the correct number of significant figures.
    a. $1.76 \times 10^{-3}/8.0 \times 10^2$
    b. $1.87 \times 10^{-2} + 2 \times 10^{-4} - 3.0 \times 10^{-3}$
    c. $[(1.36 \times 10^5)(0.000322)/0.082](129.2)$

112. The value of the Euro was recently $1.35 U.S. and the price of 1 liter of gasoline in France is 1.42 Euro. What is the price of 1 gallon of gasoline in U.S. dollars in France?

113. A thief uses a can of sand to replace a solid gold cylinder that sits on a weight-sensitive, alarmed pedestal. The can of sand and the gold cylinder have exactly the same dimensions (length = 22 cm and radius = 3.8 cm).
    a. Calculate the mass of each cylinder (ignore the mass of the can itself). (density of gold = 19.3 g/cm³, density of sand = 3.00 g/cm³)
    b. Did the thief set off the alarm? Explain.

114. The proton has a radius of approximately 1.0×10^{-13} cm and a mass of 1.7×10^{-24} g. Determine the density of a proton for a sphere $V = (4/3)\pi r^3$.

115. The density of titanium is 4.51 g/cm³. What is the volume (in cubic inches) of 3.5 lb of titanium?

116. The density of iron is 7.86 g/cm³. What is its density in pounds per cubic inch (lb/in³)?

117. A steel cylinder has a length of 2.16 in, a radius of 0.22 in, and a mass of 41 g. What is the density of the steel in g/cm³?

118. A solid aluminum sphere has a mass of 85 g. Use the density of aluminum to find the radius of the sphere in inches.

119. A backyard swimming pool holds 185 cubic yards (yd³) of water. What is the mass of the water in pounds?

120. An iceberg has a volume of 7655 cubic feet. What is the mass of the ice (in kg) composing the iceberg (at 0 °C)?

121. The Toyota Prius, a hybrid electric vehicle, has an EPA gas mileage rating of 52 mi/gal in the city. How many kilometers can the Prius travel on 15 liters of gasoline?

122. The Honda Insight, a hybrid electric vehicle, has an EPA gas mileage rating of 57 mi/gal in the city. How many kilometers can the Insight travel on the amount of gasoline that would fit in a soda can? The volume of a soda can is 355 mL.

123. The single proton that forms the nucleus of the hydrogen atom has a radius of approximately 1.0×10^{-13} cm. The hydrogen atom itself has a radius of approximately 52.9 pm. What fraction of the space within the atom is occupied by the nucleus?

124. A sample of gaseous neon atoms at atmospheric pressure and 0 °C contains 2.69×10^{22} atoms per liter. The atomic radius of neon is 69 pm. What fraction of the space is occupied by the atoms themselves? What does this reveal about the separation between atoms in the gaseous phase?

125. The diameter of a hydrogen atom is 212 pm. Find the length in kilometers of a row of 6.02×10^{23} hydrogen atoms. The diameter of a ping pong ball is 4.0 cm. Find the length in kilometers of a row of 6.02×10^{23} ping pong balls.

126. The world's record in the 100 m dash is 9.69 s, and in the 100 yard dash it is 9.21 s. Find the speed in miles/hr of the runners who set these records. (Assume three significant figures for 100 m and 100 yards.)

127. Table salt contains 39.33 g of sodium per 100 g of salt. The U.S. Food and Drug Administration (FDA) recommends that adults consume less than 2.40 g of sodium per day. A particular snack mix contains 1.25 g of salt per 100 g of the mix. What mass of the snack mix can an adult consume and still be within the FDA limit? (Assume three significant figures for 100 g.)

128. Lead metal can be extracted from a mineral called galena, which contains 86.6% lead by mass. A particular ore contains 68.5% galena by mass. If the lead can be extracted with 92.5% efficiency, what mass of ore is required to make a lead sphere with a 5.00 cm radius?

129. A length of #8 copper wire (radius = 1.63 mm) has a mass of 24.0 kg and a resistance of 2.061 ohm per km (Ω/km). What is the overall resistance of the wire?

130. Rolls of aluminum foil are 304 mm wide and 0.016 mm thick. What maximum length of aluminum foil can be made from 1.10 kg of aluminum?

131. Liquid nitrogen has a density of 0.808 g/mL and boils at 77 K. Researchers often purchase liquid nitrogen in insulated 175 L tanks. The liquid vaporizes quickly to gaseous nitrogen (which has a density of 1.15 g/L at room temperature and atmospheric pressure) when the liquid is removed from the tank. Suppose that all 175 L of liquid nitrogen in a tank accidentally vaporized in a lab that measured 10.00 m × 10.00 m × 2.50 m. What maximum fraction of the air in the room could be displaced by the gaseous nitrogen?

132. Mercury is often used in thermometers. The mercury sits in a bulb on the bottom of the thermometer and rises up a thin capillary as the temperature rises. Suppose a mercury thermometer contains 3.380 g of mercury and has a capillary that is 0.200 mm in diameter. How far does the mercury rise in the capillary when the temperature changes from 0.0 °C to 25.0 °C? The density of mercury at these temperatures is 13.596 g/cm³ and 13.534 g/cm³, respectively.

Challenge Problems

133. A force of 2.31×10^4 N is applied to a diver's face mask that has an area of 125 cm^2. Find the pressure in atm on the face mask.

134. The SI unit of force is the Newton, derived from the base units by using the definition of force, $F = ma$. The dyne is a non-SI unit of force in which mass is measured in grams and time is measured in seconds. The relationship between the two units is 1 dyne $= 10^{-5}$ N. Find the unit of length used to define the dyne.

135. Kinetic energy can be defined as $1/2 \, mv^2$ or as $3/2 \, PV$. Show that the derived SI units of each of these terms are those of energy. (Pressure is force/area and force is mass $\times$ acceleration.)

136. In 1999, scientists discovered a new class of black holes with masses 100 to 10,000 times the mass of our sun that occupy less space than our moon. Suppose that one of these black holes has a mass of 1×10^3 suns and a radius equal to one-half the radius of our moon. What is the density of the black hole in g/cm^3? The radius of our sun is 7.0×10^5 km and it has an average density of 1.4×10^3 kg/m^3. The diameter of the moon is 2.16×10^3 miles.

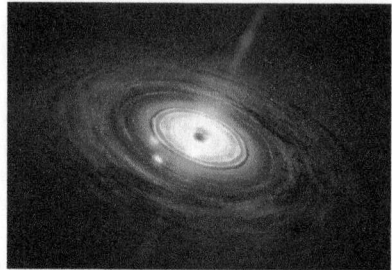

137. Suppose that polluted air has carbon monoxide (CO) levels of 15.0 ppm. An average human inhales about 0.50 L of air per breath and takes about 20 breaths per minute. How many milligrams of carbon monoxide does the average person inhale in an 8-hour period at this level of carbon monoxide pollution? Assume that the carbon monoxide has a density of 1.2 g/L. (Hint: 15.0 ppm CO means 15.0 L CO per 10^6 L air.)

138. Nanotechnology, the field of building ultrasmall structures one atom at a time, has progressed in recent years. One potential application of nanotechnology is the construction of artificial cells. The simplest cells would probably mimic red blood cells, the body's oxygen transporters. Nanocontainers, perhaps constructed of carbon, could be pumped full of oxygen and injected into a person's bloodstream. If the person needed additional oxygen—due to a heart attack perhaps, or for the purpose of space travel—these containers could slowly release oxygen into the blood, allowing tissues that would otherwise die to remain alive. Suppose that the nanocontainers were cubic and had an edge length of 25 nanometers.
   a. What is the volume of one nanocontainer? (Ignore the thickness of the nanocontainer's wall.)
   b. Suppose that each nanocontainer could contain pure oxygen pressurized to a density of 85 g/L. How many grams of oxygen could be contained by each nanocontainer?
   c. Air typically contains about 0.28 g of oxygen per liter. An average human inhales about 0.50 L of air per breath and takes about 20 breaths per minute. How many grams of oxygen does a human inhale per hour? (Assume two significant figures.)
   d. What is the minimum number of nanocontainers that a person would need in his or her bloodstream to provide 1 hour's worth of oxygen?
   e. What is the minimum volume occupied by the number of nanocontainers calculated in part d? Is such a volume feasible, given that total blood volume in an adult is about 5 liters?

139. Approximate the percent increase in waist size that occurs when a 155 lb person gains 40.0 lb of fat. Assume that the volume of the person can be modeled by a cylinder that is 4.0 feet tall. The average density of a human is about 1.0 g/cm^3, and the density of fat is 0.918 g/cm^3.

140. A box contains a mixture of small copper spheres and small lead spheres. The total volume of both metals is measured by the displacement of water to be 427 cm^3, and the total mass is 4.36 kg. What percentage of the spheres are copper?

Conceptual Problems

141. A volatile liquid (one that easily evaporates) is put into a jar and the jar is then sealed. Does the mass of the sealed jar and its contents change upon the vaporization of the liquid?

142. The diagram shown first represents solid carbon dioxide, also known as dry ice. Which of the other diagrams best represents the dry ice after it has sublimed into a gas?

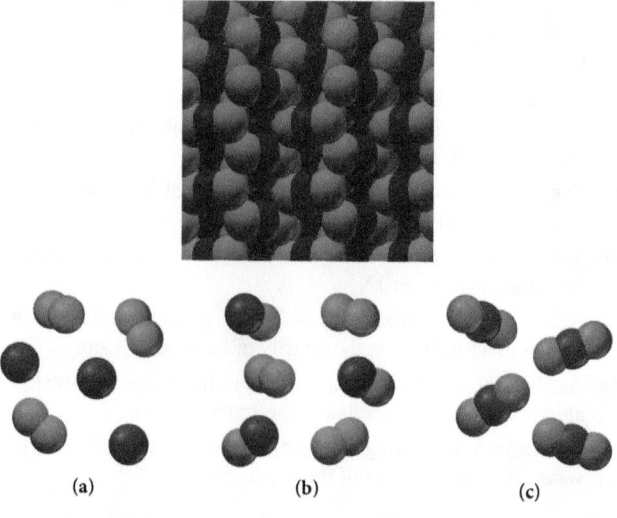

(a)   (b)   (c)

143. A cube has an edge length of 7 cm. If it is divided up into 1 cm cubes, how many 1 cm cubes are there?

144. Substance A has density of 1.7 g/cm^3. Substance B has a density of 1.7 kg/m^3. Without doing any calculations, determine which substance is most dense.

145. For each box, examine the blocks attached to the balances. Based on their positions and sizes, determine which block is more dense (the dark block or the lighter-colored block), or if the relative densities cannot be determined. (Think carefully about the information being shown.)

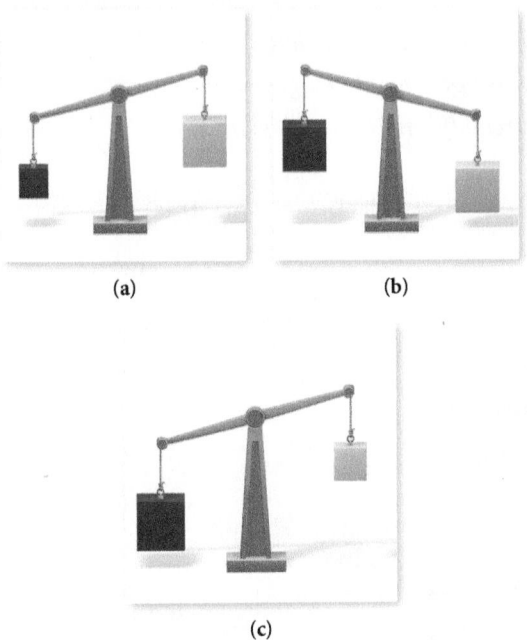

(a)   (b)

(c)

146. Let a triangle represent atoms of element A and a circle represent atoms of element B.
  a. Draw an atomic level view of a homogenous mixture of elements A and B.
  b. Draw an atomic view of the compound AB in a liquid state (molecules close together).
  c. Draw an atomic view of the compound AB after it has undergone a physical change (such as evaporation).
  d. Draw an atomic view of the compound after it has undergone a chemical change (such as decomposition of AB into A and B).

147. Identify each statement as being most like an observation, a law, or a theory.
  a. All coastal areas experience two high tides and two low tides each day.
  b. The tides in Earth's oceans are caused mainly by the gravitational attraction of the moon.
  c. Yesterday, high tide in San Francisco Bay occurred at 2:43 A.M. and 3:07 P.M.
  d. Tides are higher at the full moon and new moon than at other times of the month.

Answers to Conceptual Connections

Laws and Theories

1.1 (b) A law only summarizes a series of related observations; a theory gives the underlying reasons for them.

Pure Substances and Mixtures

1.2

    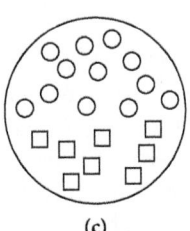

(a)   (b)   (c)

Chemical and Physical Changes

1.3 View (a) best represents the water after vaporization. Vaporization is a physical change, so the molecules must remain the same before and after the change.

The Mass of a Gas

1.4 No, the mass does not change. The water vaporizes and becomes a gas, but the water molecules are still present within the flask and have the same mass.

Prefix Multipliers

1.5 The prefix micro (10^{-6}) is appropriate. The measurement would be reported as 55.7 μm.

Density

1.6 (c) The copper sample expands. However, because its mass remains constant while its volume increases, its density decreases.

2 Atoms and Elements

*These observations have tacitly led to the conclusion which
seems universally adopted, that all bodies of sensible magnitude . . .
are constituted of a vast number of extremely small particles, or atoms
of matter . . . .*

—John Dalton (1766–1844)

I F YOU CUT A PIECE OF GRAPHITE from the tip of a pencil into smaller and smaller pieces, how far could you go? Could you divide it forever? Would you eventually run into some basic particles that were no longer divisible, not because of their sheer smallness, but because of the nature of matter? This fundamental question about the nature of matter has been asked by thinkers for over two millennia. The answers they reached, however, have varied over time. On the scale of everyday objects, matter appears continuous, or infinitely divisible. Until about 200 years ago, many scientists thought that matter was indeed continuous—but they were proven wrong. If you were to divide the graphite from your pencil tip into smaller and smaller pieces (far smaller than the eye could see), you would eventually end up with individual carbon atoms. The word *atom* comes from the Greek *atomos*, meaning "indivisible." You cannot divide a carbon atom into smaller pieces and still have carbon. Atoms compose all ordinary matter—if you want to understand matter, you must begin by understanding atoms.

2.1 Imaging and Moving Individual Atoms

On March 16, 1981, Gerd Binnig and Heinrich Rohrer worked late into the night in their laboratory at IBM in Zurich, Switzerland. They were measuring how an electrical current—flowing between a sharp metal tip and a flat metal surface—depended on the separation between the tip and the surface. The results of that night's experiment and subsequent results over the next several months won Binnig and Rohrer a share of the 1986 Nobel Prize in Physics. Their work also led to the development of *scanning tunneling microscopy (STM)*, a technique that can image, and even move, individual atoms and molecules.

A scanning tunneling microscope works by moving an extremely sharp *electrode* (an electrical conductor) over a surface and measuring the resulting *tunneling current*, the electrical current that flows between the tip of the electrode and the surface even though the two are not in physical contact (Figure 2.1 ▶).

The tunneling current, as Binnig and Rohrer discovered that night in their laboratory at IBM, is extremely sensitive to distance, making it possible to maintain a precise separation between the tip and the surface by moving the tip up or down to compensate

The tip of a scanning tunneling microscope (STM) moves across an atomic surface.

▶ FIGURE 2.1 **Scanning Tunneling Microscopy** In this technique, an atomically sharp tip is scanned across a surface. The tip is kept at a fixed distance from the surface by moving it up and down so as to maintain a constant tunneling current. The motion of the tip is recorded to create an image of the surface with atomic resolution.

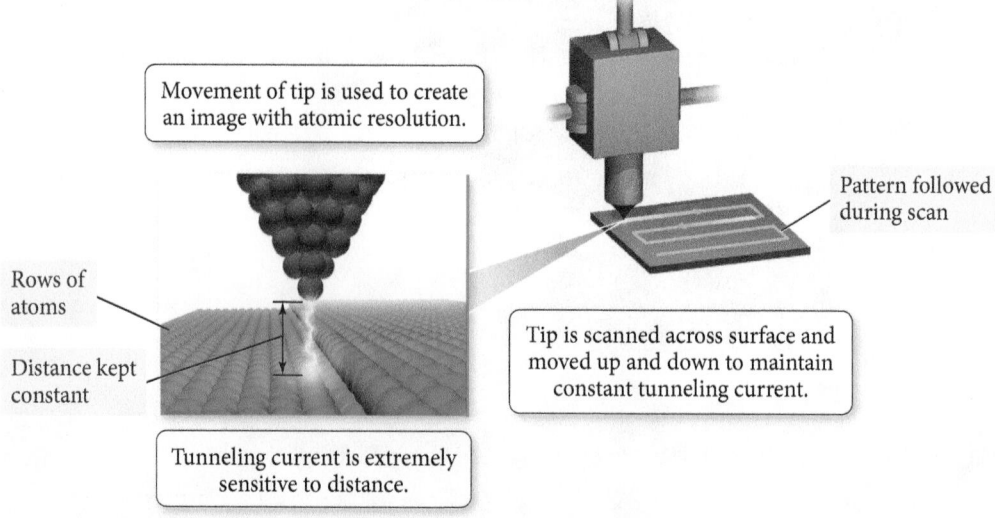

Movement of tip is used to create an image with atomic resolution.

Pattern followed during scan

Rows of atoms

Distance kept constant

Tip is scanned across surface and moved up and down to maintain constant tunneling current.

Tunneling current is extremely sensitive to distance.

for changes in current. As the tip goes over an atom, therefore, the tip moves up away from the surface to maintain constant current. As the tip goes over a gap between atoms, it moves down toward the surface to maintain constant current. By measuring the up-and-down movement of the tip as it scans a surface, the microscope creates an image that shows the location of individual atoms on that surface (see Figure 2.2 (a) ▼).

In other words, Binnig and Rohrer developed a type of microscope that could "see" atoms. When I was a child taking science in elementary school, my teachers always told me that, although scientists were certain that matter was made of atoms, we could not see them, even with the most powerful microscopes (and probably never would) because they were too small. Today, with STM, we can form incredible images of atoms and molecules. Later work by other scientists showed that STM can also be used to *pick up and move* individual atoms or molecules, allowing structures and patterns to be made one atom at a time. Figure 2.2 (b), for example, shows the Kanji characters for the word "atom" written with individual iron atoms on top of a copper surface. If all of the words in the books in the Library of Congress—35 million books occupying 840 miles of shelves—were written in letters the size of these Kanji characters, they would fit into an area of about 5 square millimeters.

As we discussed in Chapter 1, it was only 200 years ago that John Dalton proposed his atomic theory. Today we can image atoms, move them, and even build tiny machines out of just a few dozen atoms (an area of research called nanotechnology). These atomic machines, and the atoms that compose them, are almost unimaginably small.

▶ FIGURE 2.2 **Imaging Atoms** (a) A scanning tunneling microscope image of iodine atoms (green) on a platinum surface (blue). (b) The Japanese Kanji characters for "atom" written with iron atoms (red) on a copper surface (blue). The copper atoms are not as distinct as the iron atoms, but they appear as blue ripples in the background.

(a)

(b)

To get an idea of the size of an atom, imagine picking up a grain of sand at a beach. That grain contains more atoms than you could count in a lifetime. In fact, the number of atoms in one sand grain far exceeds the number of grains on an entire beach.

In spite of their small size, atoms are the key to connecting the macroscopic and microscopic worlds. An *atom* is the smallest identifiable unit of an *element*. There are about 91 different naturally occurring elements. In addition, scientists have succeeded in making over 20 synthetic elements (elements not found in nature). In this chapter, we learn about atoms: what they are made of, how they differ from one another, and how they are structured. We also learn about the elements that are composed of these different kinds of atoms, and about some of their characteristic properties. We will also discuss how the elements can be organized in a way that reveals patterns in their properties and helps us to understand what underlies those properties.

> The exact number of naturally occurring elements is controversial because some elements that were first discovered when they were synthesized are believed to also be present in trace amounts in nature.

2.2 Early Ideas about the Building Blocks of Matter

The first people to propose that matter was composed of small, indestructible particles were Leucippus (fifth century B.C., exact dates unknown) and his student Democritus (460–370 B.C.). These Greek philosophers theorized that matter was ultimately composed of small, indivisible particles they named *atomos*. Democritus wrote, "Nothing exists except atoms and empty space; everything else is opinion." Leucippus and Democritus proposed that many different kinds of atoms existed, each different in shape and size, and that they moved randomly through empty space. Other influential Greek thinkers of the time, such as Plato and Aristotle, did not embrace the atomic ideas of Leucippus and Democritus. Instead, they held that matter had no smallest parts and that different substances were composed of various proportions of fire, air, earth, and water. Since there was no experimental way to test the relative merits of the competing ideas, Aristotle's view prevailed, largely because he was so influential. The idea that matter was composed of atoms took a back seat in intellectual thought for nearly 2000 years.

In the sixteenth century modern science began to emerge. A greater emphasis on observation led Nicolaus Copernicus (1473–1543) to publish *On the Revolution of the Heavenly Orbs* in 1543. The publication of that book—which proposed that the sun, not Earth, was at the center of the universe—marks the beginning of what we now call the *scientific revolution*. The next 200 years—and the work of scientists such as Francis Bacon (1561–1626), Johannes Kepler (1571–1630), Galileo Galilei (1564–1642), Robert Boyle (1627–1691), and Isaac Newton (1642–1727)—brought rapid advancement as the scientific approach became the established way to learn about the physical world. By the early 1800s certain observations led the English chemist John Dalton (1766–1844) to offer convincing evidence that supported the early atomic ideas of Leucippus and Democritus.

2.3 Modern Atomic Theory and the Laws That Led to It

Recall the discussion of the scientific approach to knowledge from Chapter 1. The theory that all matter is composed of atoms grew out of observations and laws. The three most important laws that led to the development and acceptance of the atomic theory are the law of conservation of mass, the law of definite proportions, and the law of multiple proportions.

The Law of Conservation of Mass

In 1789, as we saw in Chapter 1, Antoine Lavoisier formulated the **law of conservation of mass**, which states:

In a chemical reaction, matter is neither created nor destroyed.

We will see in Chapter 19 that this law is a slight oversimplification. However, the changes in mass in ordinary chemical processes are so minute that they can be ignored for all practical purposes.

In other words, when a chemical reaction occurs, the total mass of the substances involved in the reaction does not change. For example, consider the reaction between sodium and chlorine to form sodium chloride.

Na(s)   Cl₂(g)   NaCl(s)

7.7 g Na   11.9 g Cl₂   19.6 g NaCl

Total mass = 19.6 g

Mass of reactants = Mass of product

The combined mass of the sodium and chlorine that react (the reactants) exactly equals the mass of the sodium chloride that forms (the product). This law is consistent with the idea that matter is composed of small, indestructible particles. The particles rearrange during a chemical reaction, but the amount of matter is conserved because the particles themselves are indestructible (at least by chemical means).

Conceptual Connection 2.1 The Law of Conservation of Mass

When a small log completely burns in a campfire, the mass of the ash is much less than the mass of the log. What happens to the matter that composed the log?

The Law of Definite Proportions

In 1797, a French chemist named Joseph Proust (1754–1826) made observations on the composition of compounds. He found that the elements composing a given compound always occur in fixed (or definite) proportions in all samples of the compound. In contrast, the components of a mixture can be present in any proportions whatsoever. He summarized his observations in the **law of definite proportions:**

The law of definite proportions is sometimes called the law of constant composition.

> **All samples of a given compound, regardless of their source or how they were prepared, have the same proportions of their constituent elements.**

For example, the decomposition of 18.0 g of water results in 16.0 g of oxygen and 2.0 g of hydrogen, or an oxygen-to-hydrogen mass ratio of

$$\text{Mass ratio} = \frac{16.0 \text{ g O}}{2.0 \text{ g H}} = 8.0 \text{ or } 8{:}1$$

This ratio holds for any sample of pure water, regardless of its origin. The law of definite proportions applies to every compound. Consider ammonia, a compound composed of nitrogen and hydrogen. Ammonia contains 14.0 g of nitrogen for every 3.0 g of hydrogen, resulting in a nitrogen-to-hydrogen mass ratio of 4.7:

$$\text{Mass ratio} = \frac{14.0 \text{ g N}}{3.0 \text{ g H}} = 4.7 \text{ or } 4.7{:}1$$

Again, this ratio is the same for every sample of ammonia. The law of definite proportions also hints at the idea that matter is composed of atoms. Compounds have definite proportions of their constituent elements because the atoms that compose them, each with its own specific mass, occur in a definite ratio. Since the ratio of atoms is the same for all samples of a particular compound, the ratio of masses is also the same.

EXAMPLE 2.1 Law of Definite Proportions

Two samples of carbon dioxide are decomposed into their constituent elements. One sample produces 25.6 g of oxygen and 9.60 g of carbon, and the other produces 21.6 g of oxygen and 8.10 g of carbon. Show that these results are consistent with the law of definite proportions.

SOLUTION

To show this, calculate the mass ratio of one element to the other for both samples by dividing the mass of one element by the mass of the other. For convenience, divide the larger mass by the smaller one.	For the first sample: $\dfrac{\text{Mass oxygen}}{\text{Mass carbon}} = \dfrac{25.6}{9.60} = 2.67 \text{ or } 2.67{:}1$ For the second sample: $\dfrac{\text{Mass oxygen}}{\text{Mass carbon}} = \dfrac{21.6}{8.10} = 2.67 \text{ or } 2.67{:}1$

The ratios are the same for the two samples, so these results are consistent with the law of definite proportions.

FOR PRACTICE 2.1

Two samples of carbon monoxide are decomposed into their constituent elements. One sample produces 17.2 g of oxygen and 12.9 g of carbon, and the other sample produces 10.5 g of oxygen and 7.88 g of carbon. Show that these results are consistent with the law of definite proportions.

Answers to For Practice and For More Practice Problems can be found in Appendix IV.

The Law of Multiple Proportions

In 1804, John Dalton published his **law of multiple proportions:**

> **When two elements (call them A and B) form two different compounds, the masses of element B that combine with 1 g of element A can be expressed as a ratio of small whole numbers.**

Dalton already suspected that matter was composed of atoms, so that when two elements A and B combine to form more than one compound, an atom of A combines with either one, two, three, or more atoms of B (AB_1, AB_2, AB_3, etc.). Therefore, the masses of B that react with a fixed mass of A are always related to one another as small whole-number ratios. Consider the compounds carbon monoxide and carbon dioxide, which we discussed in the opening section of Chapter 1. Carbon monoxide and carbon dioxide are two compounds composed of the same two elements: carbon and oxygen. We saw in Example 2.1 that the mass ratio of oxygen to carbon in carbon dioxide is 2.67:1; therefore, 2.67 g of oxygen reacts with 1 g of carbon. In carbon monoxide, however, the mass ratio of oxygen to carbon is 1.33:1, or 1.33 g of oxygen to every 1 g of carbon.

Carbon dioxide — Mass oxygen that combines with 1 g carbon = 2.67 g

Carbon monoxide — Mass oxygen that combines with 1 g carbon = 1.33 g

The ratio of these two masses is itself a small whole number.

$$\frac{\text{Mass oxygen to 1 g carbon in carbon dioxide}}{\text{Mass oxygen to 1 g carbon in carbon monoxide}} = \frac{2.67}{1.33} = 2$$

With the help of the molecular models, we can see why the ratio is 2:1—carbon dioxide contains two oxygen atoms to every carbon atom, while carbon monoxide contains only one. Of course, neither John Dalton nor Joseph Proust had access to any kind of modern instrumentation that could detect individual atoms—Dalton supported his atomic ideas primarily by using the *masses* of samples.

EXAMPLE 2.2 Law of Multiple Proportions

Nitrogen forms several compounds with oxygen, including nitrogen dioxide and dinitrogen monoxide. Nitrogen dioxide contains 2.28 g oxygen to every 1.00 g nitrogen, while dinitrogen monoxide contains 0.570 g oxygen to every 1.00 g nitrogen. Show that these results are consistent with the law of multiple proportions.

SOLUTION

To show this, calculate the ratio of the mass of oxygen from one compound to the mass of oxygen in the other. Always divide the larger of the two masses by the smaller one.	$$\frac{\text{Mass oxygen to 1 g nitrogen in nitrogen dioxide}}{\text{Mass oxygen to 1 g nitrogen in dinitrogen monoxide}} = \frac{2.28}{0.570} = 4.00$$

The ratio is a small whole number (4); these results are consistent with the law of multiple proportions.

FOR PRACTICE 2.2

Hydrogen and oxygen form both water and hydrogen peroxide. The decomposition of a sample of water forms 0.125 g hydrogen to every 1.00 g oxygen. The decomposition of a sample of hydrogen peroxide forms 0.250 g hydrogen to every 1.00 g oxygen. Show that these results are consistent with the law of multiple proportions.

Conceptual Connection 2.2 **The Laws of Definite and Multiple Proportions**

Explain the difference between the law of definite proportions and the law of multiple proportions.

John Dalton and the Atomic Theory

In 1808, John Dalton explained the laws just discussed with his **atomic theory**:

1. Each element is composed of tiny, indestructible particles called atoms.
2. All atoms of a given element have the same mass and other properties that distinguish them from the atoms of other elements.

In Section 2.6, we will see that, contrary to Dalton's theory, all atoms of a given element do not have exactly the same mass.

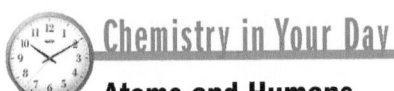

Chemistry in Your Day

Atoms and Humans

You and I are composed of atoms. We get those atoms from the food we eat. Yesterday's cheeseburger contributes to today's skin, muscle, and hair. Not only are we made of atoms, but we are made of *recycled* atoms. The carbon atoms that compose our bodies were used by other living organisms before we got them. And they will be used by still others when we are done with them. In fact, it is likely that at this moment, your body contains some carbon atoms (over one trillion[*]) that were at one time part of your chemistry professor.

The idea that humans are composed of atoms acting in accord with the laws of chemistry and physics has significant implications and raises important questions. If atoms compose our brains, for example, do those atoms determine our thoughts and emotions? Are our feelings caused by atoms acting according to the laws of chemistry and physics?

[*]This calculation assumes that all of the carbon atoms metabolized by your professor over the last 40 years have been uniformly distributed into atmospheric carbon dioxide, and subsequently incorporated into the plants that you have eaten.

Richard Feynman (1918–1988), a Nobel Prize–winning physicist, said that "The most important hypothesis in all of biology is that everything that animals do, atoms do. In other words, there is nothing that living things do that cannot be understood from the point of view that they are made of atoms acting according to the laws of physics." Indeed, biology has undergone a revolution in the last 50 years, mostly through the investigation of the atomic and molecular basis for life. Some people have seen the atomic view of life as a devaluation of human life. We have always wanted to distinguish ourselves from everything else, and the idea that we are made of the same basic particles as all other matter takes something away from that distinction . . . or does it?

Questions

Do you find the idea that you are made of recycled atoms disturbing? Why or why not? *Reductionism* is the idea that complex systems can be understood by understanding their parts. Is reductionism a good way to understand humans? Is it the only way?

---

3. Atoms combine in simple, whole-number ratios to form compounds.
4. Atoms of one element cannot change into atoms of another element. In a chemical reaction, atoms only change the way that they are *bound together* with other atoms.

Today, the evidence for the atomic theory is overwhelming. Matter is indeed composed of atoms.

2.4 The Discovery of the Electron

By the end of the nineteenth century, scientists were convinced that matter is made up of atoms, the permanent, supposedly indestructible building blocks that compose everything. However, further experiments revealed that the atom itself is composed of even smaller, more fundamental particles.

Cathode Rays

In the late 1800s an English physicist named J. J. Thomson (1856–1940), working at Cambridge University, performed experiments to probe the properties of **cathode rays.** Thomson constructed a partially evacuated glass tube called a **cathode ray tube**, shown in Figure 2.3 ▼. Thomson then applied a high electrical voltage between two electrodes at

Cathode — Cathode rays — Anode

+

−

Partially evacuated glass tube

High voltage

◄ FIGURE 2.3 **Cathode Ray Tube**

Properties of Electrical Charge

Positive (red) and negative (yellow) electrical charges attract one another.

Positive charges repel one another. Negative charges repel one another.

+1 + (−1) = 0

Positive and negative charges of exactly the same magnitude sum to zero when combined.

For a full explanation of electrical voltage, see Chapter 18.

The coulomb (C) is the SI unit for charge.

either end of the tube. He found that a beam of particles, called cathode rays, traveled from the negatively charged electrode (which is called the cathode) to the positively charged one (which is called the anode).

Thomson found that the particles that compose the cathode ray have the following properties: they travel in straight lines, they are independent of the composition of the material from which they originate (the cathode), and they carry a negative **electrical charge.** Electrical charge is a fundamental property of some of the particles that compose atoms and results in attractive and repulsive forces—called *electrostatic forces*—between those particles. The area around a charged particle where these forces exist is called an *electric field.* The characteristics of electrical charge are summarized in the figure in the margin. You have probably experienced excess electrical charge when brushing your hair on a dry day. The brushing action causes the accumulation of charged particles in your hair, which repel each other, making your hair stand on end.

J. J. Thomson measured the charge-to-mass ratio of the cathode ray particles by deflecting them using electric and magnetic fields, as shown in Figure 2.4 ▼. The value he measured, -1.76×10^8 coulombs (C) per gram, implied that the cathode ray particle was about 2000 times lighter (less massive) than hydrogen, the lightest known atom. These results were incredible—the indestructible atom could apparently be chipped!

J. J. Thomson had discovered the **electron**, a negatively charged, low mass particle present within all atoms. He wrote, "We have in the cathode rays matter in a new state, a state in which the subdivision of matter is carried very much further . . . a state in which all matter . . . is of one and the same kind; this matter being the substance from which all the chemical elements are built up."

Millikan's Oil Drop Experiment: The Charge of the Electron

In 1909, American physicist Robert Millikan (1868–1953), working at the University of Chicago, performed his now famous oil drop experiment in which he deduced the charge of a single electron. The apparatus for the oil drop experiment is shown in Figure 2.5 ▶.

In his experiment, Millikan sprayed oil into fine droplets using an atomizer. The droplets were allowed to fall under the influence of gravity through a small hole into the lower portion of the apparatus where Millikan viewed them with the aid of a light source and a viewing microscope. During their fall, the drops acquired electrons that had been produced by bombarding the air in the chamber with ionizing radiation (a kind of energy described in Chapter 7). The electrons imparted a negative charge to the drops. In the lower portion of the apparatus, Millikan could create an electric field between two

Charge-to-Mass Ratio of the Electron

▲ FIGURE 2.4 **Thomson's Measurement of the Charge-to-Mass Ratio of the Electron**   J. J. Thomson used electric and magnetic fields to deflect the electron beam in a cathode ray tube. By measuring the strengths at which the effects of the two fields (electric and magnetic) canceled exactly, leaving the beam undeflected, he was able to calculate the charge-to-mass ratio of the electron.

◀ **FIGURE 2.5 Millikan's Measurement of the Electron's Charge** Millikan calculated the charge on oil droplets falling in an electric field. He found that it was always a whole-number multiple of -1.60×10^{-19} C, the charge of a single electron.

Labels in figure: Atomizer; Positively charged plate; Ionizing radiation; Light source; Negatively charged plate; Viewing microscope; Charged oil droplets are suspended in electric field.

metal plates. Since the lower plate was negatively charged, and since Millikan could vary the strength of the electric field, he could slow or even reverse the free fall of the negatively charged drops. (Remember that like charges repel each other.)

By measuring the strength of the electric field required to halt the free fall of the drops, and by figuring out the masses of the drops themselves (determined from their radii and density), Millikan calculated the charge of each drop. He then reasoned that, since each drop must contain an integral (or whole) number of electrons, the charge of each drop must be a whole-number multiple of the electron's charge. Indeed, Millikan was correct; the measured charge on any drop was always a whole-number multiple of -1.60×10^{-19} C, the fundamental charge of a single electron.

With this number in hand, and knowing Thomson's mass-to-charge ratio for electrons, we can deduce the mass of an electron:

$$\text{Charge} \times \frac{\text{mass}}{\text{charge}} = \text{mass}$$

$$-1.60 \times 10^{-19} \, \cancel{C} \times \frac{\text{g}}{-1.76 \times 10^{8} \, \cancel{C}} = 9.10 \times 10^{-28} \, \text{g}$$

As Thomson had correctly determined, this mass is about 2000 times lighter than hydrogen, the lightest atom.

Why did scientists work so hard to measure the charge of the electron? Since the electron is a fundamental building block of matter, scientists want to know its properties, including its charge. The magnitude of the charge of the electron is of tremendous importance because it determines how strongly an atom holds its electrons. Imagine how matter would be different if electrons had a much smaller charge, so that atoms held them more loosely. Many atoms might not even be stable. On the other hand, imagine how matter would be different if electrons had a much greater charge, so that atoms held them more tightly. Since atoms form compounds by exchanging and sharing electrons (more on this in Chapter 3), there could be fewer compounds or maybe even none. Without the abundant diversity of compounds, life would not be possible. So, the magnitude of the charge of the electron—even though it may seem like an insignificantly small number—has great importance.

Conceptual Connection 2.3 The Millikan Oil Drop Experiment

Suppose that one of Millikan's oil drops has a charge of -4.8×10^{-19} C. How many excess electrons does the drop contain?

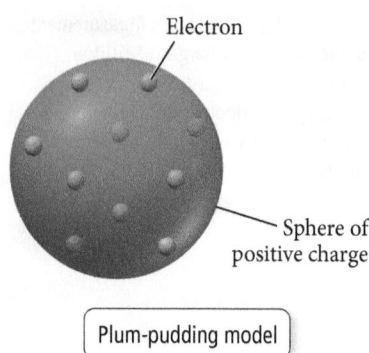

Electron

Sphere of
positive charge

Plum-pudding model

2.5 The Structure of the Atom

The discovery of negatively charged particles within atoms raised a new question. Since atoms are charge-neutral, they must contain a positive charge that neutralizes the negative charge of the electrons—but how do the positive and negative charges fit together? Are atoms just a jumble of even more fundamental particles? Are they solid spheres? Do they have some internal structure? J. J. Thomson proposed that the negatively charged electrons were small particles held within a positively charged sphere, as shown at left.

This model, the most popular of the time, became known as the plum-pudding model. The model suggested by Thomson, to those of us not familiar with plum pudding (an English dessert), was like a blueberry muffin, where the blueberries are the electrons and the muffin is the positively charged sphere.

The discovery of **radioactivity**—the emission of small energetic particles from the core of certain unstable atoms—by scientists Henri Becquerel (1852–1908) and Marie Curie (1867–1934) at the end of the nineteenth century allowed researchers to experimentally probe the structure of the atom. At the time, scientists had identified three different types of radioactivity: alpha (α) particles, beta (β) particles, and gamma (γ) rays. We will discuss these and other types of radioactivity in more detail in Chapter 19. For now, just know that α particles are positively charged and that they are by far the most massive of the three.

In 1909, Ernest Rutherford (1871–1937), who had worked under Thomson and subscribed to his plum-pudding model, performed an experiment in an attempt to confirm Thomson's model. Rutherford's experiment, which employed α particles, proved it wrong instead. In the experiment, Rutherford directed the positively charged α particles at an ultrathin sheet of gold foil, as shown in Figure 2.6 ▼.

These particles were to act as probes of the gold atoms' structure. If the gold atoms were indeed like blueberry muffins or plum pudding—with their mass and charge spread throughout the entire volume of the atom—these speeding probes would pass right through the gold foil with minimum deflection.

Rutherford and his coworkers performed the experiment, but the results were not what they expected. The majority of the particles did pass directly through the foil, but some particles were deflected, and some (approximately 1 in 20,000) even bounced back. The results puzzled Rutherford, who wrote that they were "about as credible as if you had fired a 15-inch shell at a piece of tissue paper and it came back and hit you." What sort of atomic structure could explain this odd behavior?

Rutherford created a new model—a modern version of which is shown in Figure 2.7 ▶ alongside the plum-pudding model—to explain his results.

Rutherford's Gold Foil Experiment

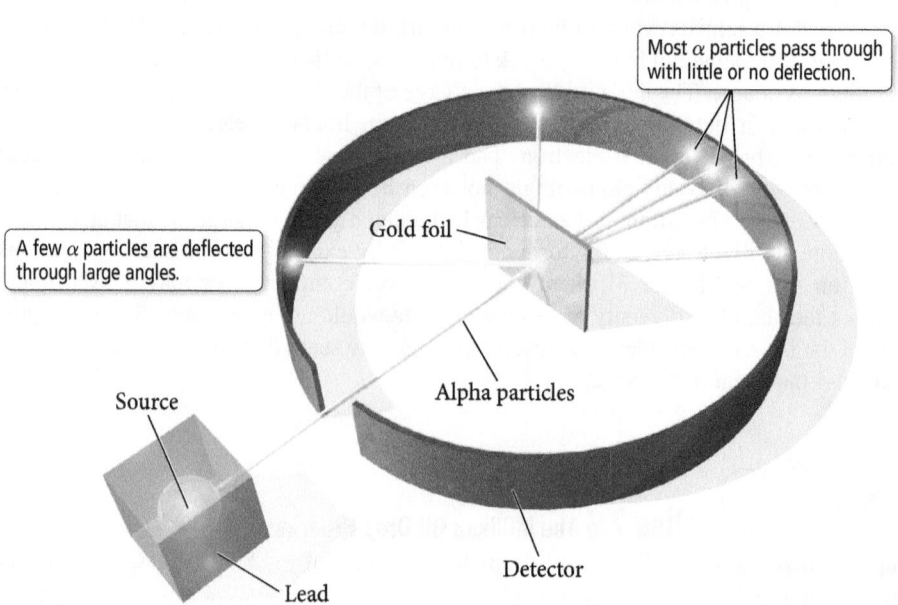

Most α particles pass through
with little or no deflection.

A few α particles are deflected
through large angles.

Gold foil

Source

Alpha particles

Detector

Lead

▶ **FIGURE 2.6 Rutherford's Gold Foil
Experiment** Alpha particles were
directed at a thin sheet of gold foil.
Most of the particles passed
through the foil, but a small fraction
were deflected, and a few even
bounced backward.

Predicted Result

Alpha particles

Plum-pudding model

Actual Result

Nucleus   Electron cloud   ● Proton
● Neutron

Nuclear model

◀ **FIGURE 2.7 The Nuclear Atom**
Rutherford's results could not be
explained by the plum-pudding
model. Instead, they suggested
that the atom has a small,
dense nucleus.

Rutherford realized that to account for the deflections he observed, the mass and positive charge of an atom must be concentrated in a space much smaller than the size of the atom itself. He concluded that, in contrast to the plum-pudding model, matter must not be as uniform as it appears. It must contain large regions of empty space dotted with small regions of very dense matter. Building on this idea, he proposed the **nuclear theory** of the atom, with three basic parts:

1. Most of the atom's mass and all of its positive charge are contained in a small core called the **nucleus**.
2. Most of the volume of the atom is empty space, throughout which tiny, negatively charged electrons are dispersed.
3. There are as many negatively charged electrons outside the nucleus as there are positively charged particles (named **protons**) within the nucleus, so the atom is electrically neutral.

Although Rutherford's model was highly successful, scientists realized that it was incomplete. For example, hydrogen atoms contain one proton, and helium atoms contain two, yet a hydrogen atom has only one-fourth the mass of a helium atom. Why? The helium atom must contain some additional mass. Later work by Rutherford and one of his students, British scientist James Chadwick (1891–1974), demonstrated that the previously unaccounted for mass was due to **neutrons**, neutral particles within the nucleus. The mass of a neutron is similar to that of a proton, but a neutron has no electrical charge. The helium atom is four times as massive as the hydrogen atom because it contains two protons *and two neutrons* (while hydrogen contains only one proton and no neutrons).

The dense nucleus contains over 99.9% of the mass of the atom but occupies very little of its volume. For now, we can think of the electrons that surround the nucleus in analogy to the water droplets that make up a cloud—although their mass is almost negligibly small, they are dispersed over a very large volume. Consequently, an atom, like a cloud, is mostly empty space.

Rutherford's nuclear theory was a success and is still valid today. The revolutionary part of this theory is the idea that matter—at its core—is much less uniform than it appears. If the nucleus of the atom were the size of the period at the end of this sentence, the average electron would be about 10 meters away. Yet the period would contain nearly all of the atom's mass. Imagine what matter would be like if atomic structure were different. What if matter were composed of atomic nuclei piled on top of each other like marbles in a box? Such matter would be incredibly dense; a single grain of sand composed of solid atomic nuclei would have a mass of 5 million kilograms (or a weight of about 11 million pounds). Astronomers believe there are some objects in the universe composed of such matter—neutron stars.

If matter really is mostly empty space, as Rutherford suggested, then why does it appear so solid? Why can we tap our knuckles on a table and feel a solid thump? Matter appears solid because the variation in its density is on such a small scale that our eyes cannot see it. Imagine a scaffolding 100 stories high and the size of a football field as shown at right. The volume of the scaffolding is mostly empty space. Yet if you viewed it from an airplane, it would appear as a solid mass. Matter is similar. When you tap your knuckle on the table, it is much like one giant scaffolding (your finger) crashing into another (the table). Even though they are both primarily empty space, one does not fall into the other.

2.6 Subatomic Particles: Protons, Neutrons, and Electrons in Atoms

All atoms are composed of the same subatomic particles: protons, neutrons, and electrons. Protons and neutrons, as we saw earlier, have nearly identical masses. In SI units, the mass of the proton is 1.67262×10^{-27} kg, and the mass of the neutron is 1.67493×10^{-27} kg. A more common unit to express these masses is the **atomic mass unit (amu)**, defined as 1/12 the mass of a carbon atom containing six protons and six neutrons. The mass of a proton or neutron is approximately 1 amu. Electrons, by contrast, have an almost negligible mass of 0.00091×10^{-27} kg or 0.00055 amu.

The proton and the electron both have electrical *charge*. We know from Millikan's oil drop experiment that the electron has a charge of -1.60×10^{-19} C. In atomic (or relative) units, the electron is assigned a charge of −1 and the proton is assigned a charge of +1. *The charge of the proton and the electron are equal in magnitude but opposite in sign*, so that when the two particles are paired, the charges sum to zero. The neutron has no charge.

Matter is usually charge-neutral (it has no overall charge) because protons and electrons are normally present in equal numbers. When matter does acquire charge imbalances, these imbalances usually equalize quickly, often in dramatic ways. For example, the shock you receive when touching a doorknob during dry weather is the equalization of a charge imbalance that developed as you walked across the carpet. Lightning is an equalization of charge imbalances that develop during electrical storms as shown at left.

A sample of matter—even a tiny sample, such as a sand grain—composed of only protons or only electrons, would have extraordinary repulsive forces inherent within it and would be unstable. Luckily, matter is not that way. Table 2.1 summarizes the properties of protons, neutrons, and electrons.

If a proton had the mass of a baseball, an electron would have the mass of a rice grain.

Negative charge builds up on clouds.

Electrical discharge equalizes charge imbalance.

Positive charge builds up on ground.

▲ When the normal charge balance of matter is disturbed, as happens during an electrical storm, it quickly equalizes, often in dramatic ways.

TABLE 2.1   Subatomic Particles

	Mass (kg)	Mass (amu)	Charge (relative)	Charge (C)
Proton	1.67262×10^{-27}	1.00727	+1	$+1.60218 \times 10^{-19}$
Neutron	1.67493×10^{-27}	1.00866	0	0
Electron	0.00091×10^{-27}	0.00055	−1	-1.60218×10^{-19}

Elements: Defined by Their Numbers of Protons

If all atoms are composed of the same subatomic particles, what makes the atoms of one element different from those of another? The answer is the *number* of these particles. The most important number to the *identity* of an atom is the number of protons in its nucleus. *The number of protons defines the element.* For example, an atom with 2 protons in its nucleus is a helium atom, an atom with 6 protons in its nucleus is a carbon atom (Figure 2.8 ▶), and an atom with 92 protons in its nucleus is a uranium atom. The number of protons in an atom's nucleus is its **atomic number** and is given the symbol Z. The atomic numbers of known elements range from 1 to 116 (although additional elements may still be discovered), as shown in the periodic table of the elements (Figure 2.9 ▶). In the periodic table, described in more detail in Section 2.7, the elements are arranged so that those with similar properties are in the same column.

Each element, identified by its unique atomic number, is represented with a unique **chemical symbol**, a one- or two-letter abbreviation listed directly below its atomic

The Number of Protons Defines the Element

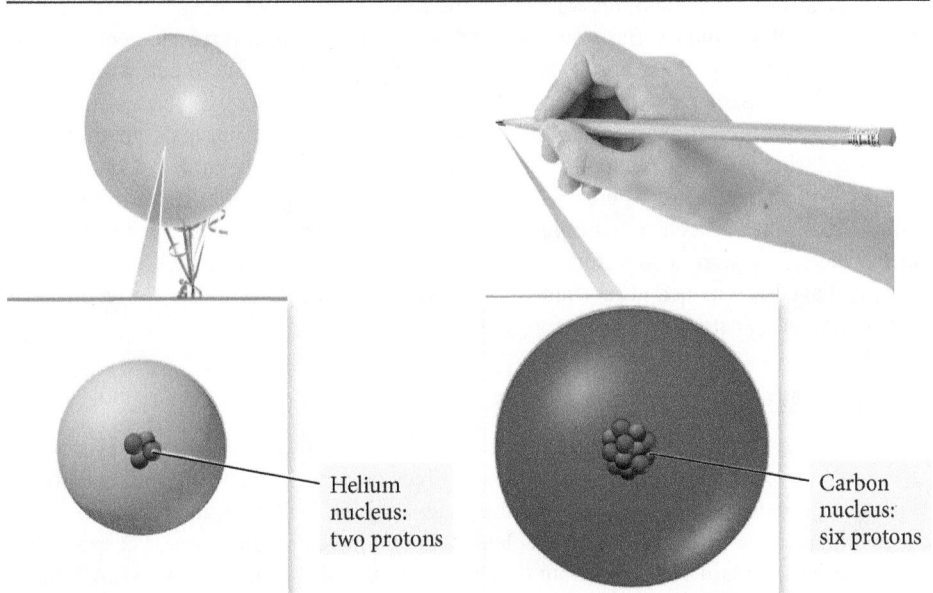

Helium nucleus: two protons

Carbon nucleus: six protons

◀ **FIGURE 2.8 How Elements Differ** Each element is defined by a unique atomic number (Z), the number of protons in the nucleus of every atom of that element.

number on the periodic table. The chemical symbol for helium is He; for carbon, it is C; and for uranium, it is U. The chemical symbol and the atomic number always go together. If the atomic number is 2, the chemical symbol *must be* He. If the atomic number is 6, the chemical symbol *must be* C. This is another way of saying that the number of protons defines the element.

Most chemical symbols are based on the English name of the element. For example, the symbol for sulfur is S; for oxygen, O; and for chlorine, Cl. Several of the oldest

▼ **FIGURE 2.9 The Periodic Table** Each element is represented by its symbol and atomic number. Elements in the same column have similar properties.

The Periodic Table

Atomic number (Z)

4
Be
beryllium

Chemical symbol

Name

1 **H** hydrogen																	2 **He** helium
3 **Li** lithium	4 **Be** beryllium											5 **B** boron	6 **C** carbon	7 **N** nitrogen	8 **O** oxygen	9 **F** fluorine	10 **Ne** neon
11 **Na** sodium	12 **Mg** magnesium											13 **Al** aluminum	14 **Si** silicon	15 **P** phosphorus	16 **S** sulfur	17 **Cl** chlorine	18 **Ar** argon
19 **K** potassium	20 **Ca** calcium	21 **Sc** scandium	22 **Ti** titanium	23 **V** vanadium	24 **Cr** chromium	25 **Mn** manganese	26 **Fe** iron	27 **Co** cobalt	28 **Ni** nickel	29 **Cu** copper	30 **Zn** zinc	31 **Ga** gallium	32 **Ge** germanium	33 **As** arsenic	34 **Se** selenium	35 **Br** bromine	36 **Kr** krypton
37 **Rb** rubidium	38 **Sr** strontium	39 **Y** yttrium	40 **Zr** zirconium	41 **Nb** niobium	42 **Mo** molybdenum	43 **Tc** technetium	44 **Ru** ruthenium	45 **Rh** rhodium	46 **Pd** palladium	47 **Ag** silver	48 **Cd** cadmium	49 **In** indium	50 **Sn** tin	51 **Sb** antimony	52 **Te** tellurium	53 **I** iodine	54 **Xe** xenon
55 **Cs** cesium	56 **Ba** barium	57 **La** lanthanum	72 **Hf** hafnium	73 **Ta** tantalum	74 **W** tungsten	75 **Re** rhenium	76 **Os** osmium	77 **Ir** iridium	78 **Pt** platinum	79 **Au** gold	80 **Hg** mercury	81 **Tl** thallium	82 **Pb** lead	83 **Bi** bismuth	84 **Po** polonium	85 **At** astatine	86 **Rn** radon
87 **Fr** francium	88 **Ra** radium	89 **Ac** actinium	104 **Rf** rutherfordium	105 **Db** dubnium	106 **Sg** seaborgium	107 **Bh** bohrium	108 **Hs** hassium	109 **Mt** meitnerium	110 **Ds** darmstadtium	111 **Rg** roentgenium	112 **Cn** copernicium	113 **	114 **Fl** flerovium	115 **	116 **Lv** livermorium	117 **	118 **

58 **Ce** cerium	59 **Pr** praseodymium	60 **Nd** neodymium	61 **Pm** promethium	62 **Sm** samarium	63 **Eu** europium	64 **Gd** gadolinium	65 **Tb** terbium	66 **Dy** dysprosium	67 **Ho** holmium	68 **Er** erbium	69 **Tm** thulium	70 **Yb** ytterbium	71 **Lu** lutetium
90 **Th** thorium	91 **Pa** protactinium	92 **U** uranium	93 **Np** neptunium	94 **Pu** plutonium	95 **Am** americium	96 **Cm** curium	97 **Bk** berkelium	98 **Cf** californium	99 **Es** einsteinium	100 **Fm** fermium	101 **Md** mendelevium	102 **No** nobelium	103 **Lr** lawrencium

96
Cm
Curium

▲ Element 96 is named curium, after Marie Curie, co-discoverer of radioactivity.

known elements, however, have symbols based on their original Latin names. For example, the symbol for sodium is Na from the Latin *natrium*, and the symbol for tin is Sn from the Latin *stannum*. Early scientists often gave newly discovered elements names that reflect their properties. For example, argon originates from the Greek word *argos* meaning inactive, referring to argon's chemical inertness (it does not react with other elements). Chlorine originates from the Greek word *chloros* meaning pale green, referring to chlorine's pale green color. Other elements, including helium, selenium, and mercury, are named after figures from Greek or Roman mythology or astronomical bodies. Still others (such as europium, polonium, and berkelium) are named for the places where they were discovered or where their discoverers were born. More recently, elements have been named after scientists; for example, curium for Marie Curie, einsteinium for Albert Einstein, and rutherfordium for Ernest Rutherford.

Isotopes: When the Number of Neutrons Varies

All atoms of a given element have the same number of protons; however, they do not necessarily have the same number of neutrons. Since neutrons have nearly the same mass as protons (1 amu), this means that—contrary to what John Dalton originally proposed in his atomic theory—all atoms of a given element *do not* have the same mass. For example, all neon atoms contain 10 protons, but they may contain 10, 11, or 12 neutrons. All three types of neon atoms exist, and each has a slightly different mass. Atoms with the same number of protons but different numbers of neutrons are called **isotopes**. Some elements, such as beryllium (Be) and aluminum (Al), have only one naturally occurring isotope, while other elements, such as neon (Ne) and chlorine (Cl), have two or more.

The relative amount of each different isotope in a naturally occurring sample of a given element is roughly constant. For example, in any natural sample of neon atoms, 90.48% of them are the isotope with 10 neutrons, 0.27% are the isotope with 11 neutrons, and 9.25% are the isotope with 12 neutrons. These percentages are called the **natural abundance** of the isotopes. Each element has its own characteristic natural abundance of isotopes. However, advances in mass spectrometry (see Section 2.8) have allowed accurate measurements that reveal small but significant variations in the natural abundance of isotopes for many elements.

The sum of the number of neutrons and protons in an atom is its **mass number** and is represented by the symbol A:

$$A = \text{number of protons (p)} + \text{number of neutrons (n)}$$

For neon, with 10 protons, the mass numbers of the three different naturally occurring isotopes are 20, 21, and 22, corresponding to 10, 11, and 12 neutrons, respectively.

We symbolize isotopes using the notation:

Mass number ⟶ $^{A}_{Z}X$ ⟵ Chemical symbol
Atomic number ⟶

where X is the chemical symbol, A is the mass number, and Z is the atomic number. Therefore, the symbols for the neon isotopes are:

$$^{20}_{10}\text{Ne} \quad ^{21}_{10}\text{Ne} \quad ^{22}_{10}\text{Ne}$$

Notice that the chemical symbol, Ne, and the atomic number, 10, are redundant: if the atomic number is 10, the symbol must be Ne. The mass numbers, however, are different for the different isotopes, reflecting the different number of neutrons in each one.

A second common notation for isotopes is the chemical symbol (or chemical name) followed by a dash and the mass number of the isotope.

Chemical symbol or name ⟶ X-A ⟵ Mass number

In this notation, the neon isotopes are

Ne-20	Ne-21	Ne-22
neon-20	neon-21	neon-22

We summarize what we have learned about the neon isotopes in the following table:

Symbol	Number of Protons	Number of Neutrons	A (Mass Number)	Natural Abundance (%)
Ne−20 or $^{20}_{10}$Ne	10	10	20	90.48
Ne−21 or $^{21}_{10}$Ne	10	11	21	0.27
Ne−22 or $^{22}_{10}$Ne	10	12	22	9.25

Notice that all isotopes of a given element have the same number of protons (otherwise they would be different elements). Notice also that the mass number is the *sum* of the number of protons and the number of neutrons. The number of neutrons in an isotope is therefore the difference between the mass number and the atomic number (A–Z). The different isotopes of an element generally exhibit the same chemical behavior—the three isotopes of neon, for example, all exhibit chemical inertness.

EXAMPLE 2.3 Atomic Numbers, Mass Numbers, and Isotope Symbols

(a) What are the atomic number (Z), mass number (A), and symbol of the chlorine isotope with 18 neutrons?

(b) How many protons, electrons, and neutrons are present in an atom of $^{52}_{24}$Cr?

SOLUTION

(a) Look up the atomic number (Z) for chlorine on the periodic table. The atomic number specifies the number of protons.	$Z = 17$, so chlorine has 17 protons.
The mass number (A) for an isotope is the sum of the number of protons and the number of neutrons.	A = number of protons + number of neutrons = 17 + 18 = 35
The symbol for an isotope is its two-letter abbreviation with the atomic number (Z) in the lower left corner and the mass number (A) in the upper left corner.	$^{35}_{17}$Cl
(b) For any isotope (in this case $^{52}_{24}$Cr) the number of protons is indicated by the atomic number located at the lower left. Since this is a neutral atom, the number of electrons equals the number of protons.	Number of protons = Z = 24 Number of electrons = 24 (neutral atom)
The number of neutrons is equal to the mass number (upper left) minus the atomic number (lower left).	Number of neutrons = 52 − 24 = 28

FOR PRACTICE 2.3

(a) What are the atomic number, mass number, and symbol for the carbon isotope with seven neutrons?

(b) How many protons and neutrons are present in an atom of $^{39}_{19}$K?

Conceptual Connection 2.4 Isotopes

Carbon has two naturally occurring isotopes: C-12 (natural abundance is 98.93%) and C-13 (natural abundance is 1.07%). Using circles to represent protons and squares to represent neutrons, draw the nucleus of each isotope. How many C-13 atoms are present, on average, in a 10,000-atom sample of carbon?

Ions: Losing and Gaining Electrons

The number of electrons in a neutral atom is equal to the number of protons in its nucleus (designated by its atomic number Z). During chemical changes, however, atoms can lose or gain electrons and become charged particles called **ions**. For example, neutral lithium

Chemistry in Your Day

Where Did Elements Come From?

We find ourselves on a planet containing many different kinds of elements. If it were otherwise, we would not exist and would not be here to reflect on why. Where did these elements come from? The story of element formation is as old as the universe itself, and we have to go back to the very beginning to tell the story.

The birth of the universe is described by the big bang theory, which asserts that the universe began as a hot, dense collection of matter and energy that expanded rapidly. As it expanded, it cooled, and within the first several hours, subatomic particles formed the first atomic nuclei: hydrogen and helium. These two elements were (and continue to be) the most abundant in the universe. As the universe continued expanding, some of the hydrogen and helium clumped together under the influence of gravity to form nebulae (clouds of gas) that eventually gave birth to stars and galaxies. These stars and galaxies became the nurseries where all other elements formed.

Stars are fueled by nuclear fusion, which we discuss in more detail in Chapter 19. Under the conditions within the core of a star, hydrogen nuclei can combine (or fuse) to form helium. Fusion gives off enormous quantities of energy, which is why stars emit so much heat and light. The fusion of hydrogen to helium can fuel a star for billions of years.

After it burns through large quantities of hydrogen, if a star is large enough, the helium that builds up in its core can in turn fuse to form carbon. The carbon then builds up in the core and (again, if the star is large enough) can fuse to form even heavier elements. The fusion process ends with iron, which has a highly stable nucleus. By the time iron is formed, however, the star is near the end of its existence and may enter a phase of expansion, transforming into a supernova. Within a supernova, which is in essence a large exploding star, a shower of neutrons allows the lighter elements (which formed during the lifetime of the star through the fusion processes just described) to capture extra neutrons. These neutrons can transform into protons (through processes that we discuss in Chapter 19), contributing ultimately to the formation of elements heavier than iron, all the way up to uranium. As the supernova continues to expand, the elements present within it are blown out into space, where they can incorporate into other nebulae and perhaps even eventually form planets that orbit stars like our own sun.

▲ Stars are born in nebulae such as the Eagle Nebula (also known as M16). This image was taken by the Hubble Space Telescope and shows a gaseous pillar in a star-forming region of the Eagle Nebula.

(Li) atoms contain three protons and three electrons; however, in many chemical reactions lithium atoms lose one electron (e^-) to form Li^+ ions.

$$Li \rightarrow Li^+ + 1\ e^-$$

The charge of an ion is indicated in the upper right corner of the chemical symbol. Since the Li^+ *ion* contains three protons and only two electrons, its charge is 1+ (ion charges are written as the magnitude first followed by the sign of the charge; for a charge of 1+, the 1 is usually dropped and the charge is written as simply +).

Ions can also be negatively charged. For example, neutral fluorine (F) atoms contain nine protons and nine electrons; however, in many chemical reactions fluorine atoms gain one electron to form F^- ions.

$$F + 1\ e^- \rightarrow F^-$$

The F⁻ *ion* contains nine protons and ten electrons, resulting in a charge of 1− (written simply as −). For many elements, such as lithium and fluorine, the ion is much more common than the neutral atom. In fact, lithium and fluorine occur in nature mostly as ions.

Positively charged ions, such as Li^+, are called **cations**, and negatively charged ions, such as F^-, are called **anions**. Ions behave quite differently than their corresponding atoms. Neutral sodium atoms, for example, are extremely unstable, reacting violently with most things they contact. Sodium cations (Na^+), by contrast, are relatively inert— we eat them all the time in sodium chloride (table salt). In ordinary matter, cations and anions always occur together so that matter is charge neutral overall.

Conceptual Connection 2.5 The Nuclear Atom, Isotopes, and Ions

In light of the nuclear model for the atom, which statement is true?

(**a**) For a given element, the size of an isotope with more neutrons is larger than one with fewer neutrons.

(**b**) For a given element, the size of an atom is the same for all of the element's isotopes.

2.7 Finding Patterns: The Periodic Law and the Periodic Table

The modern periodic table grew out of the work of Dmitri Mendeleev (1834–1907), a nineteenth-century Russian chemistry professor. In his time, scientists had discovered about 65 different elements, and chemists had identified many of the properties of these elements—such as their relative masses, their chemical activity, and some of their physical properties. However, no one had developed any systematic way of organizing them.

▲ Many of the elements that we know today were discovered during Mendeleev's lifetime.

▶ **FIGURE 2.10** **Recurring Properties**
These elements are listed in order of increasing atomic number. Elements with similar properties are represented with the same color. Notice that the colors form a repeating pattern, much like musical notes form a repeating pattern on a piano keyboard.

To be periodic means to exhibit a repeating pattern.

Eka means "the one beyond" or "the next one in a family of elements". So, eka-silicon means the element beyond silicon in the same family as silicon.

▲ Dmitri Mendeleev, a Russian chemistry professor who proposed the periodic law and arranged early versions of the periodic table, was honored on a Soviet postage stamp.

▶ **FIGURE 2.11** **Making a Periodic Table**
We can arrange the elements in Figure 2.10 in a table in which atomic number increases from left to right and elements with similar properties (as represented by the different colors) are aligned in columns.

The Periodic Law

Elements with similar properties recur in a regular pattern.

In 1869, Mendeleev noticed that certain groups of elements had similar properties. He also found that when he listed elements in order of increasing mass, these similar properties recurred in a periodic pattern (Figure 2.10 ▲).

Mendeleev summarized these observations in the **periodic law:**

When the elements are arranged in order of increasing mass, certain sets of properties recur periodically.

Mendeleev organized the known elements in a table consisting of a series of rows in which mass increases from left to right. He arranged the rows so that elements with similar properties fall in the same vertical columns (Figure 2.11 ▼).

Since many elements had not yet been discovered, Mendeleev's table contained some gaps, which allowed him to predict the existence (and even the properties) of yet undiscovered elements. For example, Mendeleev predicted the existence of an element he called eka-silicon, which fell below silicon on the table and between gallium and arsenic. In 1886, eka-silicon was discovered by German chemist Clemens Winkler (1838–1904), who named it germanium, after his home country.

Mendeleev's original listing evolved into the modern periodic table shown in Figure 2.12 ▶. In the modern table, elements are listed in order of increasing atomic number rather than increasing relative mass. The modern periodic table also contains more elements than Mendeleev's original table because more have been discovered since his time. Mendeleev's periodic law was based on observation. Like all scientific laws, the periodic law summarizes many observations but does not give the underlying reason for the observations—only theories do that. For now, we accept the periodic law as it is, but in Chapters 7 and 8 we will examine a powerful theory—called quantum mechanics—that explains the law and gives the underlying reasons for it.

We can broadly classify the elements in the periodic table as metals, nonmetals, or metalloids, as shown in Figure 2.12. **Metals** lie on the lower left side and middle of the periodic table and share some common properties: they are good conductors of heat and electricity, they can be pounded into flat sheets (malleability), they can be drawn into wires (ductility), they are often shiny, and they tend to lose electrons when they undergo chemical changes. Chromium, copper, strontium, and lead are typical metals.

Nonmetals lie on the upper right side of the periodic table. The dividing line between metals and nonmetals is the zigzag diagonal line running from boron to astatine. Nonmetals have varied properties—some are solids at room temperature, others are

A Simple Periodic Table

1 H								2 He
3 Li	4 Be	5 B	6 C	7 N	8 O	9 F	10 Ne
11 Na	12 Mg	13 Al	14 Si	15 P	16 S	17 Cl	18 Ar
19 K	20 Ca						

Elements with similar properties fall into columns.

Major Divisions of the Periodic Table

▲ **FIGURE 2.12 Metals, Nonmetals, and Metalloids** The elements in the periodic table fall into these three broad classes.

liquids or gases—but as a whole they tend to be poor conductors of heat and electricity and they all tend to gain electrons when they undergo chemical changes. Oxygen, carbon, sulfur, bromine, and iodine are nonmetals.

Many of the elements that lie along the zigzag diagonal line that divides metals and nonmetals are **metalloids** and exhibit mixed properties. Several metalloids are also classified as **semiconductors** because of their intermediate (and highly temperature-dependent) electrical conductivity. Our ability to change and control the conductivity of semiconductors makes them useful to us in the manufacture of the electronic chips and circuits central to computers, cellular telephones, and many other modern devices. Good examples of metalloids include silicon, arsenic, and antimony.

| Metalloids are sometimes called semimetals.

The periodic table, as shown in Figure 2.13 ▶, can also be divided into **main-group elements**, whose properties tend to be largely predictable based on their position in the periodic table, and **transition elements or transition metals**, whose properties tend to be less predictable based simply on their position in the periodic table. Main-group elements are in columns labeled with a number and the letter A. Transition elements are in columns labeled with a number and the letter B. An alternative numbering system does not use letters, but only the numbers 1–18. Both numbering systems are shown in most of the periodic tables in this book. Each column within the main-group regions of the periodic table is a **family or group** of elements.

The elements within a group usually have similar properties. For example, the group 8A elements, called the **noble gases**, are mostly unreactive. The most familiar noble gas is probably helium, used to fill buoyant balloons. Helium is chemically stable—it does not combine with other elements to form compounds—and is therefore safe to put into balloons. Other noble gases are neon (often used in electronic signs), argon (a small component of our atmosphere), krypton, and xenon.

Main-group elements			Transition elements											Main-group elements					

Periods

1A 1	Group number																			8A 18
1 **H**	2A 2											3A 13	4A 14	5A 15	6A 16	7A 17				2 **He**
3 **Li**	4 **Be**												5 **B**	6 **C**	7 **N**	8 **O**	9 **F**	10 **Ne**
11 **Na**	12 **Mg**	3B 3	4B 4	5B 5	6B 6	7B 7	8	8B 9	10	1B 11	2B 12	13 **Al**	14 **Si**	15 **P**	16 **S**	17 **Cl**	18 **Ar**
19 **K**	20 **Ca**	21 **Sc**	22 **Ti**	23 **V**	24 **Cr**	25 **Mn**	26 **Fe**	27 **Co**	28 **Ni**	29 **Cu**	30 **Zn**	31 **Ga**	32 **Ge**	33 **As**	34 **Se**	35 **Br**	36 **Kr**
37 **Rb**	38 **Sr**	39 **Y**	40 **Zr**	41 **Nb**	42 **Mo**	43 **Tc**	44 **Ru**	45 **Rh**	46 **Pd**	47 **Ag**	48 **Cd**	49 **In**	50 **Sn**	51 **Sb**	52 **Te**	53 **I**	54 **Xe**
55 **Cs**	56 **Ba**	57 **La**	72 **Hf**	73 **Ta**	74 **W**	75 **Re**	76 **Os**	77 **Ir**	78 **Pt**	79 **Au**	80 **Hg**	81 **Tl**	82 **Pb**	83 **Bi**	84 **Po**	85 **At**	86 **Rn**
87 **Fr**	88 **Ra**	89 **Ac**	104 **Rf**	105 **Db**	106 **Sg**	107 **Bh**	108 **Hs**	109 **Mt**	110 **Ds**	111 **Rg**	112 **Cn**	113	114 **Fl**	115	116 **Lv**	117	118

▲ **FIGURE 2.13 The Periodic Table: Main-Group and Transition Elements**   The elements in the periodic table fall into columns. The two columns at the left and the six columns at the right comprise the main-group elements. Each of these eight columns is a group or family. The properties of main-group elements can generally be predicted from their position in the periodic table. The properties of the elements in the middle of the table, known as transition elements, are less predictable.

Alkali metals

Halogens

The group 1A elements, called the **alkali metals**, are all reactive metals. A marble-sized piece of sodium explodes violently when dropped into water. Lithium, potassium, and rubidium are also alkali metals.

The group 2A elements, called the **alkaline earth metals**, are also fairly reactive, although not quite as reactive as the alkali metals. Calcium, for example, reacts fairly vigorously when dropped into water but does not explode as dramatically as sodium. Other alkaline earth metals include magnesium (a common low-density structural metal), strontium, and barium.

The group 7A elements, the **halogens**, are very reactive nonmetals. One of the most familiar halogens is chlorine, a greenish-yellow gas with a pungent odor. Because of its reactivity, chlorine is used as a sterilizing and disinfecting agent. Other halogens include bromine, a red-brown liquid that easily evaporates into a gas; iodine, a purple solid; and fluorine, a pale-yellow gas.

Ions and the Periodic Table

We have learned that, in chemical reactions, metals tend to lose electrons (forming cations) and nonmetals tend to gain them (forming anions). The number of electrons lost or gained, and therefore the charge of the resulting ion, is often predictable for a given element, especially main-group elements. Main-group elements tend to form ions that have the same number of electrons as the nearest noble gas (i.e., the noble gas that has the number of electrons closest to that of the element).

- **A main-group metal tends to lose electrons, forming a cation with the same number of electrons as the nearest noble gas.**

- **A main-group nonmetal tends to gain electrons, forming an anion with the same number of electrons as the nearest noble gas.**

For example, lithium, a metal with 3 electrons, tends to lose 1 electron, forming a 1+ cation that has the same number of electrons (2) as helium. Chlorine, a nonmetal with 17 electrons, tends to gain 1 electron, forming a 1− anion that has the same number of electrons (18) as argon.

Elements That Form Ions with Predictable Charges

1A																7A	8A
H^+	2A											3A	4A	5A	6A	H^-	N
Li^+														N^{3-}	O^{2-}	F^-	o b
Na^+	Mg^{2+}				Transition metals							Al^{3+}			S^{2-}	Cl^-	l e
K^+	Ca^{2+}														Se^{2-}	Br^-	G a
Rb^+	Sr^{2+}														Te^{2-}	I^-	s e
Cs^+	Ba^{2+}																s

▲ FIGURE 2.14 Elements That Form Ions with Predictable Charges

In general, the alkali metals (group 1A) tend to lose one electron and form 1+ ions. The alkaline earth metals (group 2A) tend to lose two electrons and form 2+ ions. The halogens (group 7A) tend to gain one electron and form 1− ions. The oxygen family nonmetals (group 6A) tend to gain two electrons and form 2− ions. More generally, for the main-group elements that form cations with predictable charge, the charge is equal to the group number. For main-group elements that form anions with predictable charge, the charge is equal to the group number minus eight. Transition elements may form various different ions with different charges. Figure 2.14 ▲ shows the ions formed by the main-group elements that form ions with predictable charges. In Chapters 7 and 8, we will introduce quantum-mechanical theory, which more fully explains *why* these groups form ions as they do.

EXAMPLE 2.4 Predicting the Charge of Ions

Predict the charges of the monoatomic (single atom) ions formed by these main-group elements.

(a) Al

(b) S

SOLUTION

(a) Aluminum is a main-group metal and tends to lose electrons to form a cation with the same number of electrons as the nearest noble gas. Aluminum atoms have 13 electrons and the nearest noble gas is neon, which has 10 electrons. Aluminum therefore loses 3 electrons to form a cation with a 3+ charge (Al^{3+}).

(b) Sulfur is a nonmetal and tends to gain electrons to form an anion with the same number of electrons as the nearest noble gas. Sulfur atoms have 16 electrons and the nearest noble gas is argon, which has 18 electrons. Sulfur therefore gains 2 electrons to form an anion with a 2− charge (S^{2-}).

FOR PRACTICE 2.4

Predict the charges of the monoatomic ions formed by these main-group elements.

(a) N

(b) Rb

Chemistry and Medicine

The Elements of Life

What kind of atoms compose us? In terms of mass, our bodies are 65% oxygen (because of the large amount of water), 18% carbon, and 10% hydrogen, with a few other elements present in smaller quantities, as shown in Figure 2.15 ▶ and Table 2.2. Because the atoms of different elements have different masses (more on this in Sections 2.8 and 2.9), if we consider number of atoms (instead of mass), hydrogen comes in first (because hydrogen atoms are so light), with oxygen second and carbon third.

TABLE 2.2 Approximate Percent Elemental Composition of Humans

Element	% by Mass	% by Number of Atoms
Oxygen	65	26.4
Carbon	18	9.2
Hydrogen	10	62.3
Nitrogen	3	1.4
Calcium	1.5	0.2
Phosphorus	1	0.3
Other	1.5	0.2

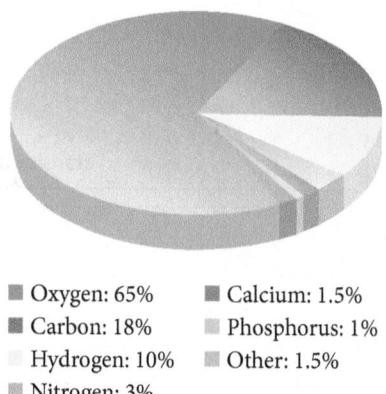

- Oxygen: 65%
- Carbon: 18%
- Hydrogen: 10%
- Nitrogen: 3%
- Calcium: 1.5%
- Phosphorus: 1%
- Other: 1.5%

▲ FIGURE 2.15 Elemental Composition of Humans (by Mass)

Much of the *chemistry* of life revolves not around oxygen or hydrogen but around the chemistry of carbon, an element that forms a disproportionately large number of compounds with a few other elements such as hydrogen, oxygen, and nitrogen. We will explore the chemistry of carbon—called organic chemistry—briefly in Chapter 3 and in more detail in Chapter 20.

2.8 Atomic Mass: The Average Mass of an Element's Atoms

An important part of Dalton's atomic theory is that all atoms of a given element have the same mass. In Section 2.6, we learned that because of isotopes, the atoms of a given element often have different masses, so Dalton was not completely correct. We can, however, calculate an average mass—called the **atomic mass**—for each element.

The atomic mass of each element is directly beneath the element's symbol in the periodic table and represents the average mass of the isotopes that compose that element, *weighted according to the natural abundance of each isotope.* For example, the periodic table lists the atomic mass of chlorine as 35.45 amu. Naturally occurring chlorine consists of 75.77% chlorine-35 atoms (mass 34.97 amu) and 24.23% chlorine-37 atoms (mass 36.97 amu). We can calculate its atomic mass:

$$\text{Atomic mass} = 0.7577(34.97 \text{ amu}) + 0.2423(36.97 \text{ amu}) = 35.45 \text{ amu}$$

Notice that the atomic mass of chlorine is closer to 35 than 37. Naturally occurring chlorine contains more chlorine-35 atoms than chlorine-37 atoms, so the weighted average mass of chlorine is closer to 35 amu than to 37 amu.

In general, we calculate the atomic mass with the equation

$$\text{Atomic mass} = \sum_n (\text{fraction of isotope } n) \times (\text{mass of isotope } n)$$

$$= (\text{fraction of isotope 1} \times \text{mass of isotope 1})$$
$$+ (\text{fraction of isotope 2} \times \text{mass of isotope 2})$$
$$+ (\text{fraction of isotope 3} \times \text{mass of isotope 3}) + \dots$$

where the fractions of each isotope are the percent natural abundances converted to their decimal values. The concept of atomic mass is useful because it allows us to assign a characteristic mass to each element and, as we will see shortly, it allows us to quantify the number of atoms in a sample of that element.

Atomic mass is sometimes called *atomic weight* or *standard atomic weight.*

17
Cl
35.45
chlorine

In this book, we use the atomic masses recommended by IUPAC for users needing an atomic mass value for an unspecified sample. Detailed studies of the atomic masses of many samples, however, have shown that atomic masses are not constants of nature because the exact isotopic abundances in any given sample depend on the history of the sample (See the Chemistry in Your Day box later in this section).

When percentages are used in calculations, we convert them to their decimal value by dividing by 100.

EXAMPLE 2.5 Atomic Mass

Copper has two naturally occurring isotopes: Cu-63 with a mass of 62.9396 amu and a natural abundance of 69.17%, and Cu-65 with a mass of 64.9278 amu and a natural abundance of 30.83%. Calculate the atomic mass of copper.

SOLUTION

Convert the percent natural abundances into decimal form by dividing by 100.	Fraction Cu-63 $= \dfrac{69.17}{100} = 0.6917$
	Fraction Cu-65 $= \dfrac{30.83}{100} = 0.3083$
Calculate the atomic mass using the equation given in the text.	Atomic mass $= 0.6917(62.9396 \text{ amu}) + 0.3083(64.9278 \text{ amu})$ $= 43.5353 \text{ amu} + 20.0172 \text{ amu} = 63.5525 = 63.55 \text{ amu}$

FOR PRACTICE 2.5

Magnesium has three naturally occurring isotopes with masses of 23.99 amu, 24.99 amu, and 25.98 amu and natural abundances of 78.99%, 10.00%, and 11.01%, respectively. Calculate the atomic mass of magnesium.

FOR MORE PRACTICE 2.5

Gallium has two naturally occurring isotopes: Ga-69 with a mass of 68.9256 amu and a natural abundance of 60.11%, and Ga-71. Use the atomic mass of gallium from the periodic table to find the mass of Ga-71.

Conceptual Connection 2.6 Atomic Mass

Recall from Conceptual Connection 2.4 that carbon has two naturally occurring isotopes: C-12 (natural abundance is 98.93%; mass is 12.0000 amu) and C-13 (natural abundance is 1.07%; mass is 13.0034 amu). Without doing any calculations, determine which mass is closest to the atomic mass of carbon.

(a) 12.00 amu   (b) 12.50 amu   (c) 13.00 amu

Mass Spectrometry: Measuring the Mass of Atoms and Molecules

The masses of atoms and the percent abundances of isotopes of elements are measured using **mass spectrometry**, a technique that separates particles according to their mass. In a mass spectrometer, such as the one in Figure 2.16 ▼, the sample (containing the

▼ FIGURE 2.16 **The Mass Spectrometer** Atoms are converted to positively charged ions, accelerated, and passed through a magnetic field that deflects their path. The heaviest ions undergo the least deflection.

Mass Spectrometer

Heater vaporizes sample

Electron beam ionizes sample

Electrically charged plates

Magnets   Lightest particles

Detector

Sample

Beam of charged particles

Electric field accelerates particles

Heaviest particles

Magnetic field separates particles based on ratio of mass to charge.

▲ **FIGURE 2.17 The Mass Spectrum of Chlorine** The position of each peak on the *x*-axis indicates the mass of the isotope. The intensity (or height) of the peak indicates the relative abundance of the isotope. The intensity of the highest peak is usually set to 100% and the intensity of all other peaks is reported relative to the most intense one.

atoms whose mass is to be measured) is injected into the instrument and vaporized. The vaporized atoms are ionized by an electron beam—the electrons in the beam collide with the atoms, removing electrons and creating positively charged ions. The ions are then accelerated into a magnetic field. When ions drift through a magnetic field, they experience a force that bends their trajectory. The amount of bending depends on the mass of the ions—the trajectories of lighter ions are bent more than those of heavier ones.

In the right side of the spectrometer shown in Figure 2.16, you can see three different paths, each corresponding to ions of different mass. Finally, the ions strike a detector and produce an electrical signal that is recorded. The result is the separation of the ions according to their mass, producing a mass spectrum such as the one in Figure 2.17 ◄. The *position* of each peak on the *x*-axis indicates the *mass of the isotope* that was ionized, and the *intensity* (indicated by the height of the peak) indicates the *relative abundance of that isotope.*

The mass spectrum of an elemental sample can be used to determine the atomic mass of that sample of the element. For example, consider the mass spectrum of a naturally occurring sample of silver.

The two peaks correspond to the two naturally occurring isotopes of silver. We can determine the percent abundance of each isotope from the intensity of each line. However, the *total* intensity must be *normalized*—it must be made to equal 100%. We can accomplish this by dividing the intensity of each peak by the total intensity:

$$\text{Abundance of Ag-107} = \frac{100.0\%}{100.0\% + 92.90\%} \times 100\% = 51.84\%$$

$$\text{Abundance of Ag-109} = \frac{92.90\%}{100.0\% + 92.90\%} \times 100\% = 48.16\%$$

Then we can calculate the atomic mass of silver.

Ag atomic mass $= 0.5184\,(106.905\text{ amu}) + 0.4816\,(108.904\text{ amu})$

$= 55.4195\text{ amu} + 52.4482\text{ amu} = 107.8677 = 107.87\text{ amu}$

Mass spectrometry can also be used on molecules. Because molecules often fragment (break apart) during ionization, the mass spectrum of a molecule usually contains many peaks representing the masses of different parts of the molecule, as well as a peak representing the mass of the molecule as a whole. The fragments that form upon ionization, and therefore the corresponding peaks that appear in the mass spectrum, are specific to the molecule, so a mass spectrum is like a molecular fingerprint. Mass spectroscopy can be used to identify an unknown molecule and to determine how much of it is present in a particular sample. For example, mass spectrometry has been used to detect organic (carbon-containing) compounds present in meteorites, a puzzling observation that some scientists speculate may be evidence of life outside of our planet. Most scientists think that the carbon compounds in meteorites probably formed in the same way as the first organic molecules on Earth, indicating that the formation of organic molecules may be common in the universe.

Since the early 1990s, researchers have also successfully applied mass spectrometry to biological molecules, including proteins (the workhorse molecules in cells) and nucleic acids (the molecules that carry genetic information). For a long time, these molecules could not be analyzed by mass spectrometry because they were difficult to vaporize and ionize without being destroyed but modern techniques have overcome this problem. A tumor, for example, can now be instantly analyzed by mass spectrometry to determine whether it contains specific proteins associated with cancer.

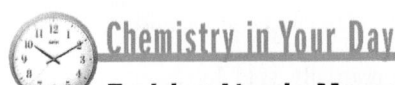

Chemistry in Your Day

Evolving Atomic Masses

At the beginning of 2011, IUPAC (International Union of Pure and Applied Chemistry) published a new periodic table with atomic masses that looked different from previous IUPAC periodic tables. For the first time, instead of listing a single atomic mass for each element, IUPAC listed upper and lower bounds for the atomic masses of several elements (see the following periodic table). For example, previous IUPAC periodic tables reported the atomic mass of O (rounded to four significant figures) as 16.00. However, the new periodic table reports the atomic mass as [15.99, 16.00] denoting the upper and lower bounds for the possible atomic masses of terrestrial oxygen.

Why did this happen? The changes were necessary because developments in mass spectrometry have increasingly demonstrated that the atomic masses of several elements are not constant from one sample to another because the isotopic composition is not constant from one sample to another. In other words, the isotopic composition of a sample of a given element can vary depending on

the source of the sample. For example, the lower bound for the atomic mass of oxygen (15.99 amu) comes from measurements of oxygen from Antarctic precipitation and the upper bound (16.00 amu) comes from measurements of oxygen in marine N_2O (dinitrogen monoxide). Although we have long treated atomic masses as *constants of nature*, they are not, and the new periodic table reflects this.

So what do we do if we need an atomic mass for an element of unknown or unspecified origin? IUPAC has recommended values that apply to most samples found on Earth. The values are rounded so that atomic mass variations in samples found on Earth are plus or minus one in the last digit (just like accepted significant figure conventions). These values are adopted throughout all of the periodic tables in this book except the one shown here, which displays the upper and lower bound for those elements in which variation occurs. For further reading see IUPAC. *Pure Appl. Chem.* **2011**, 83(2), 359–396.

IUPAC Periodic Table of the Elements

Key:
atomic number
Symbol
name
standard atomic weight

1 H hydrogen [1.007, 1.009]																	2 He helium 4.003
3 Li lithium [6.938; 6.997]	4 Be beryllium 9.012											5 B boron [10.80; 10.83]	6 C carbon [12.00; 12.02]	7 N nitrogen [14.00; 14.01]	8 O oxygen [15.99; 16.00]	9 F fluorine 19.00	10 Ne neon 20.18
11 Na sodium 22.99	12 Mg magnesium 24.31											13 Al aluminium 26.98	14 Si silicon [28.08; 28.09]	15 P phosphorus 30.97	16 S sulfur [32.05; 32.08]	17 Cl chlorine [35.44; 35.46]	18 Ar argon 39.95
19 K potassium 39.10	20 Ca calcium 40.08	21 Sc scandium 44.96	22 Ti titanium 47.87	23 V vanadium 50.94	24 Cr chromium 52.00	25 Mn manganese 54.94	26 Fe iron 55.85	27 Co cobalt 58.93	28 Ni nickel 58.69	29 Cu copper 63.55	30 Zn zinc 65.38(2)	31 Ga gallium 69.72	32 Ge germanium 72.63	33 As arsenic 74.92	34 Se selenium 78.96(3)	35 Br bromine 79.90	36 Kr krypton 83.80
37 Rb rubidium 85.47	38 Sr strontium 87.62	39 Y yttrium 88.91	40 Zr zirconium 91.22	41 Nb niobium 92.91	42 Mo molybdenum 95.96(2)	43 Tc technetium	44 Ru ruthenium 101.1	45 Rh rhodium 102.9	46 Pd palladium 106.4	47 Ag silver 107.8	48 Cd cadmium 112.4	49 In indium 114.8	50 Sn tin 118.7	51 Sb antimony 121.8	52 Te tellurium 127.6	53 I iodine 126.9	54 Xe xenon 131.3
55 Cs caesium 132.9	56 Ba barium 137.3	57-71 lanthanoids	72 Hf hafnium 178.5	73 Ta tantalum 180.9	74 W tungsten 183.8	75 Re rhenium 186.2	76 Os osmium 190.2	77 Ir iridium 192.2	78 Pt platinum 195.1	79 Au gold 197.0	80 Hg mercury 200.6	81 Tl thallium [204.3; 204.4]	82 Pb lead 207.2	83 Bi bismuth 209.0	84 Po polonium	85 At astatine	86 Rn radon
87 Fr francium	88 Ra radium	89-103 actinoids	104 Rf rutherfordium	105 Db dubnium	106 Sg seaborgium	107 Bh bohrium	108 Hs hassium	109 Mt meitnerium	110 Ds darmstadtium	111 Rg roentgenium	112 Cn copernicium		114 Fl flerovium		116 Lv livermorium		

57 La lanthanum 138.9	58 Ce cerium 140.1	59 Pr praseodymium 140.9	60 Nd neodymium 144.2	61 Pm promethium	62 Sm samarium 150.4	63 Eu europium 152.0	64 Gd gadolinium 157.3	65 Tb terbium 158.9	66 Dy dysprosium 162.5	67 Ho holmium 164.9	68 Er erbium 167.3	69 Tm thulium 168.9	70 Yb ytterbium 173.1	71 Lu lutetium 175.0
89 Ac actinium	90 Th thorium 232.0	91 Pa protactinium 231.0	92 U uranium 238.0	93 Np neptunium	94 Pu plutonium	95 Am americium	96 Cm curium	97 Bk berkelium	98 Cf californium	99 Es einsteinium	100 Fm fermium	101 Md mendelevium	102 No nobelium	103 Lr lawrencium

Notes

- IUPAC 2009 Standard atomic weights abridged to four significant digits (Table 4 published in *Pure Appl. Chem.* 83, 359-396 (2011); doi:10.1351/PAC-REP-10-09-14). The uncertainty in the last digit of the standard atomic weight value is listed in parentheses following the value. In the absence of parentheses, the uncertainty is one in that last digit. An interval in square brackets provides the lower and upper bounds of the standard atomic weight for that element. No values are listed for elements which lack isotopes with a characteristic isotopic abundance in natural terrestrial samples. See PAC for more details.

- "Aluminum" and "cesium" are commonly used alternative spellings for "aluminium" and "caesium."

- Claims for the discovery of all the remaining elements in the last row of the table, namely elements with atomic numbers 113, 115, 117 and 118, and for which no assignments have yet been made, are being considered by a IUPAC and IUPAP Joint Working Party.

For updates to this table, see iupac.org/reports/periodic_table/. This version is dated 1 June 2012.
Copyright © 2012 IUPAC, the International Union of Pure and Applied Chemistry.

INTERNATIONAL UNION OF
PURE AND APPLIED CHEMISTRY

2.9 Molar Mass: Counting Atoms by Weighing Them

Have you ever bought shrimp by *count*? Shrimp is normally sold by count, which indicates the number of shrimp per pound. For example, 41–50 count shrimp means that there are between 41 and 50 shrimp per pound. The smaller the count, the larger the shrimp. Big tiger prawns have counts as low as 10–15, which means that each shrimp can weigh up to 1/10 of a pound. One advantage of categorizing shrimp in this way is that we can count the shrimp by weighing them. For example, two pounds of 41–50 count shrimp contains between 82 and 100 shrimp.

A similar (but more precise) concept exists for atoms. Counting atoms is much more difficult than counting shrimp, yet as chemists we often need to know the number of atoms in a sample of a given mass. Why? *Because chemical processes happen between particles.* For elements, those particles are atoms. For example, when hydrogen and oxygen combine to form water, two hydrogen atoms combine with one oxygen atom to form one water molecule. If we want to know how much hydrogen to react with a given mass of oxygen to form water, we need to know the number of atoms in the given mass of oxygen. We also need to know the mass of hydrogen that contains exactly twice that number of atoms.

As another example consider intravenous fluids—fluids that are delivered to patients by directly dripping them into veins. These fluids are saline (sodium chloride) solutions that must have a specific number of sodium and chloride ions per liter of fluid. The number of particles in the fluid directly influences the properties of the fluid. Administering an intravenous fluid with the wrong number of sodium and chloride ions could be fatal.

Atoms are far too small to count by any ordinary means. As we saw earlier, even if you could somehow count atoms, and counted them 24 hours a day for as long as you lived, you would barely begin to count the number of atoms in something as small as a sand grain. Therefore, if we want to know the number of atoms in anything of ordinary size, we count them by weighing.

Twenty-two copper pennies contain approximately 1 mol of copper atoms.

Before 1982, when they became almost all zinc with only a copper coating, pennies were mostly copper.

The Mole: A Chemist's "Dozen"

When we count large numbers of objects, we often use units such as a dozen (12 objects) or a gross (144 objects) to organize our counting and to keep our numbers more manageable. With atoms, quadrillions of which may be in a speck of dust, we need a much larger number for this purpose. The chemist's "dozen" is the **mole** (abbreviated mol). A mole is the *amount* of material containing 6.02214×10^{23} particles.

$$1 \text{ mol} = 6.02214 \times 10^{23} \text{ particles}$$

This number is **Avogadro's number**, named after Italian physicist Amedeo Avogadro (1776–1856), and is a convenient number to use when working with atoms, molecules, and ions. In this book, we usually round Avogadro's number to four significant figures or 6.022×10^{23}. Notice that the definition of the mole is an *amount* of a substance. We will often refer to the number of moles of substance as the *amount* of the substance.

The first thing to understand about the mole is that it can specify Avogadro's number of anything. For example, 1 mol of marbles corresponds to 6.022×10^{23} marbles, and 1 mol of sand grains corresponds to 6.022×10^{23} sand grains. *One mole of anything is 6.022×10^{23} units of that thing.* One mole of atoms, ions, or molecules, however, makes up objects of everyday sizes. Twenty-two copper pennies, for example, contain approximately 1 mol of copper atoms and 1 tablespoon of water contains approximately 1 mol of water molecules.

The second, and more fundamental, thing to understand about the mole is how it gets its specific value.

One tablespoon of water contains approximately 1 mole of water molecules.

One tablespoon is approximately 15 mL; 1 mole of water occupies 18 mL.

The value of the mole is equal to the number of atoms in exactly 12 grams of pure carbon-12 (12 g C = 1 mol C atoms = 6.022×10^{23} C atoms).

The definition of the mole gives us a relationship between mass (grams of carbon) and number of atoms (Avogadro's number). This relationship, as we will see shortly, allows us to count atoms by weighing them.

Converting between Number of Moles and Number of Atoms

Converting between number of moles and number of atoms is similar to converting between dozens of eggs and number of eggs. For eggs, you use the conversion factor 1 dozen eggs = 12 eggs. For atoms, you use the conversion factor 1 mol atoms = 6.022×10^{23} atoms. The conversion factors take the following forms:

$$\frac{1 \text{ mol atoms}}{6.022 \times 10^{23} \text{ atoms}} \quad \text{or} \quad \frac{6.022 \times 10^{23} \text{ atoms}}{1 \text{ mol atoms}}$$

Example 2.6 demonstrates how to use these conversion factors in calculations.

EXAMPLE 2.6 Converting between Number of Moles and Number of Atoms

Calculate the number of copper atoms in 2.45 mol of copper.

SORT You are given the amount of copper in moles and asked to find the number of copper atoms.	**GIVEN:** 2.45 mol Cu **FIND:** Cu atoms
STRATEGIZE Convert between number of moles and number of atoms by using Avogadro's number as a conversion factor.	**CONCEPTUAL PLAN** $\boxed{\text{mol Cu}} \longrightarrow \boxed{\text{Cu atoms}}$ $\dfrac{6.022 \times 10^{23} \text{ Cu atoms}}{1 \text{ mol Cu}}$ **RELATIONSHIPS USED** $6.022 \times 10^{23} = 1$ mol (Avogadro's number)
SOLVE Follow the conceptual plan to solve the problem. Begin with 2.45 mol Cu and multiply by Avogadro's number to get to the number of Cu atoms.	**SOLUTION** $2.45 \text{ mol Cu} \times \dfrac{6.022 \times 10^{23} \text{ Cu atoms}}{1 \text{ mol Cu}} = 1.48 \times 10^{24} \text{ Cu atoms}$

CHECK Since atoms are small, it makes sense that the answer is large. The given number of moles of copper is almost 2.5, so the number of atoms is almost 2.5 times Avogadro's number.

FOR PRACTICE 2.6

A pure silver ring contains 2.80×10^{22} silver atoms. How many moles of silver atoms does it contain?

Converting between Mass and Amount (Number of Moles)

To count atoms by weighing them, we need one other conversion factor—the mass of 1 mol of atoms. For the isotope carbon-12, we know that the mass of 1 mol of atoms is exactly 12 grams, which is numerically equivalent to carbon-12's atomic mass in atomic mass units. Since the masses of all other elements are defined relative to carbon-12, the same relationship holds for all elements.

The mass of 1 mol of atoms of an element is the **molar mass**.

An element's molar mass in grams per mole is numerically equal to the element's atomic mass in atomic mass units.

For example, copper has an atomic mass of 63.55 amu and a molar mass of 63.55 g/mol. One mole of copper atoms therefore has a mass of 63.55 g. Just as the count for shrimp depends on the size of the shrimp, so the mass of 1 mol of atoms depends on the element: 1 mol of aluminum atoms (which are lighter than copper atoms) has a mass of 26.98 g, 1 mol of carbon atoms (which are even lighter than aluminum atoms) has a mass of 12.01 g, and 1 mol of helium atoms (lighter yet) has a mass of 4.003 g.

$$26.98 \text{ g aluminum} = 1 \text{ mol aluminum} = 6.022 \times 10^{23} \text{ Al atoms}$$

$$12.01 \text{ g carbon} = 1 \text{ mol carbon} = 6.022 \times 10^{23} \text{ C atoms}$$

$$4.003 \text{ g helium} = 1 \text{ mol helium} = 6.022 \times 10^{23} \text{ He atoms}$$

Al

C

He

The lighter the atom, the less mass in 1 mol of atoms.

1 dozen peas

1 dozen marbles

▶ The two dishes contain the same number of objects (12), but the masses are different because peas are less massive than marbles. Similarly, a mole of light atoms will have less mass than a mole of heavier atoms.

The molar mass of any element is the conversion factor between the mass (in grams) of that element and the amount (in moles) of that element. For carbon,

$$12.01 \text{ g C} = 1 \text{ mol C} \text{ or } \frac{12.01 \text{ g C}}{\text{mol C}} \text{ or } \frac{1 \text{ mol C}}{12.01 \text{ g C}}$$

Example 2.7 demonstrates how to use these conversion factors.

EXAMPLE 2.7 Converting between Mass and Amount (Number of Moles)

Calculate the amount of carbon (in moles) contained in a 0.0265 g pencil "lead." (Assume that the pencil lead is made of pure graphite, a form of carbon.)

SORT You are given the mass of carbon and asked to find the amount of carbon in moles.	GIVEN: 0.0265 g C FIND: mol C
STRATEGIZE Convert between mass and amount (in moles) of an element by using the molar mass of the element.	CONCEPTUAL PLAN g C → mol C $\frac{1 \text{ mol}}{12.01 \text{ g}}$ RELATIONSHIPS USED 12.01 g C = 1 mol C (carbon molar mass)

SOLVE Follow the conceptual plan to solve the problem.	**SOLUTION** $0.0265 \text{ g C} \times \dfrac{1 \text{ mol C}}{12.01 \text{ g C}} = 2.21 \times 10^{-3} \text{ mol C}$

CHECK The given mass of carbon is much less than the molar mass of carbon, so it makes sense that the answer (the amount in moles) is much less than 1 mol of carbon.

FOR PRACTICE 2.7
Calculate the amount of copper (in moles) in a 35.8 g pure copper sheet.

FOR MORE PRACTICE 2.7
Calculate the mass (in grams) of 0.473 mol of titanium.

We now have all the tools to count the number of atoms in a sample of an element by weighing it. First, we obtain the mass of the sample. Then we convert it to amount in moles using the element's molar mass. Finally, we convert to number of atoms using Avogadro's number. The conceptual plan for these kinds of calculations takes the following form:

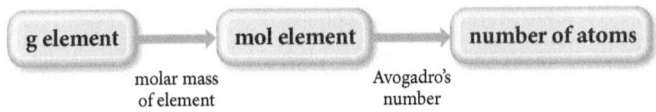

g element → mol element → number of atoms
molar mass of element   Avogadro's number

Examples 2.8 and 2.9 demonstrate these conversions.

EXAMPLE 2.8   The Mole Concept—Converting between Mass and Number of Atoms

How many copper atoms are in a copper penny with a mass of 3.10 g? (Assume that the penny is composed of pure copper.)

SORT You are given the mass of copper and asked to find the number of copper atoms.	**GIVEN:** 3.10 g Cu **FIND:** Cu atoms
STRATEGIZE Convert between the mass of an element in grams and the number of atoms of the element by first converting to moles (using the molar mass of the element) and then to number of atoms (using Avogadro's number).	**CONCEPTUAL PLAN** g Cu → mol Cu → number of Cu atoms $\dfrac{1 \text{ mol Cu}}{63.55 \text{ g Cu}}$ $\dfrac{6.022 \times 10^{23} \text{ Cu atoms}}{1 \text{ mol Cu}}$ **RELATIONSHIPS USED** 63.55 g Cu = 1 mol Cu (molar mass of copper) 6.022×10^{23} = 1 mol (Avogadro's number)
SOLVE Follow the conceptual plan to solve the problem. Begin with 3.10 g Cu and multiply by the appropriate conversion factors to arrive at the number of Cu atoms.	**SOLUTION** $3.10 \text{ g Cu} \times \dfrac{1 \text{ mol Cu}}{63.55 \text{ g Cu}} \times \dfrac{6.022 \times 10^{23} \text{ Cu atoms}}{1 \text{ mol Cu}} = 2.94 \times 10^{22} \text{ Cu atoms}$

CHECK The answer (the number of copper atoms) is less than 6.022×10^{23} (1 mole). This is consistent with the given mass of copper atoms, which is less than the molar mass of copper.

FOR PRACTICE 2.8
How many carbon atoms are there in a 1.3-carat diamond? Diamonds are a form of pure carbon. (1 carat = 0.20 grams)

FOR MORE PRACTICE 2.8
Calculate the mass of 2.25×10^{22} tungsten atoms.

Notice that numbers with large exponents, such as 6.022×10^{23}, are almost unbe-lievably large. Twenty-two copper pennies contain 6.022×10^{23} or 1 mol of copper atoms, but 6.022×10^{23} pennies would cover Earth's entire surface to a depth of 300 m. Even objects small by everyday standards occupy a huge space when we have a mole of them. For example, a grain of sand has a mass of less than 1 mg and a diameter of less than 0.1 mm, yet 1 mol of sand grains would cover the state of Texas to a depth of several feet. For every increase of 1 in the exponent of a number, the number increases by a factor of 10, so 10^{23} is incredibly large. Of course 1 mole has to be a large number if it is to have practical value, because atoms are so small.

EXAMPLE 2.9 The Mole Concept

An aluminum sphere contains 8.55×10^{22} aluminum atoms. What is the sphere's radius in centimeters? The density of aluminum is $2.70 \ \text{g/cm}^3$.

SORT You are given the number of aluminum atoms in a sphere and the density of aluminum. You are asked to find the radius of the sphere.	**GIVEN:** 8.55×10^{22} Al atoms $\qquad d = 2.70 \ \text{g/cm}^3$ **FIND:** radius (r) of sphere

STRATEGIZE The heart of this problem is density, which relates mass to volume; though you aren't given the mass directly, you are given the number of atoms, which you can use to find mass.

1. Convert from number of atoms to number of moles using Avogadro's number as a conversion factor.
2. Convert from number of moles to mass using molar mass as a conversion factor.
3. Convert from mass to volume (in cm³) using density as a conversion factor.
4. Once you calculate the volume, find the radius from the volume using the formula for the volume of a sphere.

CONCEPTUAL PLAN

$$V = \frac{4}{3}\pi r^3$$

RELATIONSHIPS AND EQUATIONS USED

$6.022 \times 10^{23} = 1 \ \text{mol}$ (Avogadro's number)
$26.98 \ \text{g Al} = 1 \ \text{mol Al}$ (molar mass of aluminum)
$2.70 \ \text{g/cm}^3$ (density of aluminum)
$V = \dfrac{4}{3}\pi r^3$ (volume of a sphere)

SOLVE

Finally, follow the conceptual plan to solve the problem. Begin with 8.55×10^{22} Al atoms and multiply by the appropriate conversion factors to arrive at volume in cm³.

Then solve the equation for the volume of a sphere for r and substitute the volume to calculate r.

SOLUTION

$$8.55 \times 10^{22} \ \cancel{\text{Al atoms}} \times \frac{1 \ \cancel{\text{mol Al}}}{6.022 \times 10^{23} \ \cancel{\text{Al atoms}}}$$

$$\times \frac{26.98 \ \cancel{\text{g Al}}}{1 \ \cancel{\text{mol Al}}} \times \frac{1 \ \text{cm}^3}{2.70 \ \cancel{\text{g Al}}} = \underline{1.4187} \ \text{cm}^3$$

$$V = \frac{4}{3}\pi r^3$$

$$r = \sqrt[3]{\frac{3V}{4\pi}} = \sqrt[3]{\frac{3(\underline{1.4187} \ \text{cm}^3)}{4\pi}} = 0.697 \ \text{cm}$$

CHECK The units of the answer (cm) are correct. The magnitude cannot be estimated accurately, but a radius of about one-half of a centimeter is reasonable for just over one-tenth of a mole of aluminum atoms.

FOR PRACTICE 2.9

A titanium cube contains 2.86×10^{23} atoms. What is the edge length of the cube? The density of titanium is 4.50 g/cm^3.

FOR MORE PRACTICE 2.9

Find the number of atoms in a copper rod with a length of 9.85 cm and a radius of 1.05 cm. The density of copper is 8.96 g/cm^3.

Conceptual Connection 2.7 Avogadro's Number

Why is Avogadro's number defined as 6.022×10^{23} and not a simpler round number such as 1.00×10^{23}?

Conceptual Connection 2.8 The Mole

Without doing any calculations, determine which sample contains the most atoms.

(a) a 1 g sample of copper   (b) a 1 g sample of carbon   (c) a 10 g sample of uranium

CHAPTER IN REVIEW

Self Assessment Quiz

Q1. Two samples of a compound containing elements A and B were decomposed. The first sample produced 15 g of A and 35 g of B. The second sample produced 25 g of A and what mass of B?
  a) 11 g
  b) 58 g
  c) 21 g
  d) 45 g

Q2. A compound containing only carbon and hydrogen has a carbon-to-hydrogen mass ratio of 11.89. Which carbon-to-hydrogen mass ratio is possible for another compound composed only of carbon and hydrogen?
  a) 2.50
  b) 3.97
  c) 4.66
  d) 7.89

Q3. Which idea came out of Rutherford's gold foil experiment?
  a) Atoms contain protons and neutrons.
  b) Matter is composed of atoms.
  c) Elements have isotopes.
  d) Atoms are mostly empty space.

Q4. A student re-creates the Millikan oil drop experiment and tabulates the relative charges of the oil drops in terms of a constant, α.

Drop #1	α
Drop #2	$\frac{3}{2}\alpha$
Drop #3	$\frac{5}{2}\alpha$
Drop #4	3α

What charge for the electron (in terms of α) is consistent with this data?
  a) $\frac{1}{2}\alpha$
  b) α
  c) $\frac{3}{2}\alpha$
  d) 2α

Q5. Determine the number of protons and neutrons in the isotope Fe-58.
a) 26 protons and 58 neutrons
b) 32 protons and 26 neutrons
c) 26 protons and 32 neutrons
d) 58 protons and 58 neutrons

Q6. An isotope of an element contains 82 protons and 122 neutrons. What is the symbol for the isotope?
a) $^{204}_{82}\text{Pb}$ b) $^{122}_{82}\text{Pb}$ c) $^{122}_{40}\text{Zr}$ d) $^{204}_{40}\text{Zr}$

Q7. Determine the number of electrons in the Cr^{3+} ion.
a) 24 electrons   b) 27 electrons
c) 3 electrons   d) 21 electrons

Q8. Which pair of elements do you expect to be most similar in their chemical properties?
a) K and Fe   b) O and Si
c) Ne and N   d) Br and I

Q9. Which element is *not* a main-group element?
a) Se   b) Mo   c) Sr   d) Ba

Q10. What is the charge of the ion most commonly formed by S?
a) 2+   b) +   c) −   d) 2−

Q11. A naturally occurring sample of an element contains only two isotopes. The first isotope has a mass of 68.9255 amu and a natural abundance of 60.11%. The second isotope has a mass of 70.9247 amu. Find the atomic mass of the element.
a) 70.13 amu   b) 69.72 amu
c) 84.06 amu   d) 69.93 amu

Q12. Which sample contains the greatest number of atoms?
a) 14 g C
b) 49 g Cr
c) 102 g Ag
d) 202 g Pb

Q13. Determine the number of atoms in 1.85 mL of mercury. (The density of mercury is 13.5 g/mL.)
a) 3.02×10^{27} atoms
b) 4.11×10^{20} atoms
c) 7.50×10^{22} atoms
d) 1.50×10^{25} atoms

Q14. A 20.0 g sample of an element contains 4.95×10^{23} atoms. Identify the element.
a) Cr   b) O   c) Mg   d) Fe

Q15. Copper has two naturally occurring isotopes with masses 62.94 amu and 64.93 amu and has an atomic mass of 63.55 amu. Which mass spectrum is most likely to correspond to a naturally occurring sample of copper?

(a)

(b)

(c)

(d)

Answers: 1. (b)   **2.** (b)   **3.** (d)   **4.** (a)   **5.** (c)   **6.** (a)   **7.** (d)   **8.** (d)   **9.** (b)   **10.** (d)   **11.** (b)   **12.** (a)   **13.** (c)   **14.** (c)   **15.** (a)

Key Terms

Section 2.3
law of conservation of mass (47)
law of definite proportions (48)
law of multiple proportions (49)
atomic theory (50)

Section 2.4
cathode rays (51)
cathode ray tube (51)
electrical charge (52)
electron (52)

Section 2.5
radioactivity (54)
nuclear theory (55)
nucleus (55)
proton (55)
neutron (55)

Section 2.6
atomic mass unit (amu) (56)
atomic number (Z) (56)
chemical symbol (57)
isotope (58)
natural abundance (58)
mass number (A) (58)

ion (59)
cation (61)
anion (61)

Section 2.7
periodic law (62)
metal (62)
nonmetal (62)
metalloid (63)
semiconductor (63)
main-group elements (63)
transition elements (transition metals) (63)
family (group) (63)

noble gases (63)
alkali metals (64)
alkaline earth metals (64)
halogens (64)

Section 2.8
atomic mass (66)
mass spectrometry (67)

Section 2.9
mole (mol) (70)
Avogadro's number (70)
molar mass (71)

Key Concepts

Imaging and Moving Individual Atoms (2.1)

▶ Although it was only 200 years ago that John Dalton proposed his atomic theory, technology has since progressed to the level where individual atoms can be imaged and moved by techniques such as *scanning tunneling microscopy* (STM).

The Atomic Theory (2.2, 2.3)

▶ Each element is composed of indestructible particles called atoms.
▶ All atoms of a given element have the same mass and other properties.
▶ Atoms combine in simple, whole-number ratios to form compounds.
▶ Atoms of one element cannot change into atoms of another element. In a chemical reaction, atoms change the way that they are bound together with other atoms to form a new substance.

The Electron (2.4)

▶ J. J. Thomson discovered the electron in the late 1800s through experiments with cathode rays. He deduced that electrons are negatively charged, and he measured their charge-to-mass ratio.
▶ Robert Millikan measured the charge of the electron, which—in conjunction with Thomson's results—led to the calculation of the mass of an electron.

The Nuclear Atom (2.5)

▶ In 1909, Ernest Rutherford probed the inner structure of the atom by working with a form of radioactivity called alpha radiation and developed the nuclear theory of the atom.
▶ Nuclear theory states that the atom is mainly empty space, with most of its mass concentrated in a tiny region called the nucleus and most of its volume occupied by relatively light electrons.

Subatomic Particles (2.6)

▶ Atoms are composed of three fundamental particles: the proton (1 amu, +1 charge), the neutron (1 amu, 0 charge), and the electron (~0 amu, −1 charge).

▶ The number of protons in the nucleus of the atom is its atomic number (Z) and defines the element.
▶ The sum of the number of protons and neutrons is the mass number (A).
▶ Atoms of an element that have different numbers of neutrons (and therefore different mass numbers) are isotopes.
▶ Atoms that lose or gain electrons become charged and are called ions. Cations are positively charged and anions are negatively charged.

The Periodic Table (2.7)

▶ The periodic table tabulates all known elements in order of increasing atomic number.
▶ The periodic table is arranged so that similar elements are grouped together in columns.
▶ Elements on the left side and in the center of the periodic table are metals and tend to lose electrons in chemical changes.
▶ Elements on the upper right side of the periodic table are nonmetals and tend to gain electrons in chemical changes.
▶ Elements located on the boundary between metals and nonmetals are metalloids.

Atomic Mass and the Mole (2.8, 2.9)

▶ The atomic mass of an element, listed directly below its symbol in the periodic table, is a weighted average of the masses of the naturally occurring isotopes of the element.
▶ One mole of an element is the amount of that element that contains Avogadro's number (6.022×10^{23}) of atoms.
▶ Any sample of an element with a mass (in grams) that equals its atomic mass contains 1 mole of the element. For example, the atomic mass of carbon is 12.011 amu; therefore, 12.011 grams of carbon contains 1 mol of carbon atoms.

Key Equations and Relationships

Relationship between Mass Number (A), Number of Protons (p), and Number of Neutrons (n) (2.6)

$$A = \text{number of protons (p)} + \text{number of neutrons (n)}$$

Atomic Mass (2.8)

$$\text{Atomic mass} = \sum_n (\text{fraction of isotope } n) \times (\text{mass of isotope } n)$$

Avogadro's Number (2.9)

$$1 \text{ mol} = 6.0221421 \times 10^{23} \text{ particles}$$

Key Learning Outcomes

Chapter Objectives	Assessment		
Using the Law of Definite Proportions (2.3)	Example 2.1	For Practice 2.1	Exercises 31, 32
Using the Law of Multiple Proportions (2.3)	Example 2.2	For Practice 2.2	Exercises 35–38

Key Learning Outcomes, *continued*

Working with Atomic Numbers, Mass Numbers, and Isotope Symbols (2.6)

Example 2.3 For Practice 2.3 Exercises 51–58

Predicting the Charge of Ions (2.7)

Example 2.4 For Practice 2.4 Exercises 59–62

Calculating Atomic Mass (2.8)

Example 2.5 For Practice 2.5 For More Practice 2.5
Exercises 71, 72, 74–77

Converting between Moles and Number of Atoms (2.9)

Example 2.6 For Practice 2.6 Exercises 81, 82

Converting between Mass and Amount (in Moles) (2.9)

Example 2.7 For Practice 2.7 For More Practice 2.7
Exercises 83, 84

Using the Mole Concept (2.9)

Examples 2.8, 2.9 For Practice 2.8, 2.9 For More Practice 2.8, 2.9
Exercises 85–94, 112, 113

EXERCISES

Review Questions

1. What is scanning tunneling microscopy? How does it work?
2. Summarize the history of the atomic idea. How was Dalton able to convince others to accept an idea that had been controversial for 2000 years?
3. State and explain the law of conservation of mass.
4. State and explain the law of definite proportions.
5. State and explain the law of multiple proportions. How is the law of multiple proportions different from the law of definite proportions?
6. What are the main ideas in Dalton's atomic theory? How do they help explain the laws of conservation of mass, of constant composition, and of definite proportions?
7. How and by whom was the electron discovered? What basic properties of the electron were reported with its discovery?
8. Explain Millikan's oil drop experiment and how it led to the measurement of the electron's charge. Why is the magnitude of the charge of the electron so important?
9. Describe the plum-pudding model of the atom.

10. Describe Rutherford's gold foil experiment. How did the experiment prove that the plum-pudding model of the atom was wrong?

11. Describe Rutherford's nuclear model of the atom. What was revolutionary about his model?

12. If matter is mostly empty space, as suggested by Rutherford, then why does it appear so solid?

13. List the three subatomic particles that compose atoms and give the basic properties (mass and charge) of each.

14. What defines an element?

15. Explain the difference between Z (the atomic number) and A (the mass number).

16. Where do elements get their names?

17. What are isotopes? What is percent natural abundance of isotopes?

18. Describe the two different notations used to specify isotopes and give an example of each.

19. What is an ion? A cation? An anion?

20. State the periodic law. How did the periodic law lead to the periodic table?

21. What are the characteristic properties of metals, nonmetals, and metalloids?

22. What are the characteristic properties of each group?
    a. noble gases
    b. alkali metals
    c. alkaline earth metals
    d. halogens

23. How do you predict the charges of ions formed by main-group elements?

24. What is atomic mass? How is it calculated?

25. Explain how a mass spectrometer works.

26. What kind of information can be determined from a mass spectrum?

27. What is a mole? How is the mole concept useful in chemical calculations?

28. Why is the mass corresponding to a mole of one element different from the mass corresponding to a mole of another element?

Problems by Topic

Note: Answers to all odd-numbered Problems, numbered in blue, can be found in Appendix III. Exercises in the Problems by Topic section are paired, with each odd-numbered problem followed by a similar even-numbered problem. Exercises in the Cumulative Problems section are also paired, but somewhat more loosely. (Challenge Problems and Conceptual Problems, because of their nature, are unpaired.)

The Laws of Conservation of Mass, Definite Proportions, and Multiple Proportions

29. A hydrogen-filled balloon was ignited and 1.50 g of hydrogen reacted with 12.0 g of oxygen. How many grams of water vapor formed? (Assume that water vapor is the only product.)

30. An automobile gasoline tank holds 21 kg of gasoline. When the gasoline burns, 84 kg of oxygen is consumed, and carbon dioxide and water are produced. What is the total combined mass of carbon dioxide and water that is produced?

31. Two samples of carbon tetrachloride were decomposed into their constituent elements. One sample produced 38.9 g of carbon and 448 g of chlorine, and the other sample produced 14.8 g of carbon and 134 g of chlorine. Are these results consistent with the law of definite proportions? Show why or why not.

32. Two samples of sodium chloride were decomposed into their constituent elements. One sample produced 6.98 g of sodium and 10.7 g of chlorine, and the other sample produced 11.2 g of sodium and 17.3 g of chlorine. Are these results consistent with the law of definite proportions? Explain your answer.

33. The mass ratio of sodium to fluorine in sodium fluoride is 1.21:1. A sample of sodium fluoride produces 28.8 g of sodium upon decomposition. How much fluorine (in grams) is formed?

34. Upon decomposition, one sample of magnesium fluoride produced 1.65 kg of magnesium and 2.57 kg of fluorine. A second sample produced 1.32 kg of magnesium. How much fluorine (in grams) did the second sample produce?

35. Two different compounds containing osmium and oxygen have the following masses of oxygen per gram of osmium: 0.168 and 0.3369 g. Show that these amounts are consistent with the law of multiple proportions.

36. Palladium forms three different compounds with sulfur. The mass of sulfur per gram of palladium in each compound is listed below. Show that these masses are consistent with the law of multiple proportions.

Compound	Grams S per Gram Pd
A	0.603
B	0.301
C	0.151

37. Sulfur and oxygen form both sulfur dioxide and sulfur trioxide. When samples of these were decomposed the sulfur dioxide produced 3.49 g oxygen and 3.50 g sulfur, while the sulfur trioxide produced 6.75 g oxygen and 4.50 g sulfur. Calculate the mass of oxygen per gram of sulfur for each sample and show that these results are consistent with the law of multiple proportions.

38. Sulfur and fluorine form several different compounds including sulfur hexafluoride and sulfur tetrafluoride. Decomposition of a sample of sulfur hexafluoride produces 4.45 g of fluorine and 1.25 g of sulfur, while decomposition of a sample of sulfur tetrafluoride produces 4.43 g of fluorine and 1.87 g of sulfur. Calculate the mass of fluorine per gram of sulfur for each sample and show that these results are consistent with the law of multiple proportions.

Atomic Theory, Nuclear Theory, and Subatomic Particles

39. Which statements are *consistent* with Dalton's atomic theory as it was originally stated? Why?
    a. Sulfur and oxygen atoms have the same mass.
    b. All cobalt atoms are identical.
    c. Potassium and chlorine atoms combine in a 1:1 ratio to form potassium chloride.
    d. Lead atoms can be converted into gold.

40. Which statements are *inconsistent* with Dalton's atomic theory as it was originally stated? Why?
  a. All carbon atoms are identical.
  b. An oxygen atom combines with 1.5 hydrogen atoms to form a water molecule.
  c. Two oxygen atoms combine with a carbon atom to form a carbon dioxide molecule.
  d. The formation of a compound often involves the destruction of one or more atoms.

41. Which statements are *consistent* with Rutherford's nuclear theory as it was originally stated? Why?
  a. The volume of an atom is mostly empty space.
  b. The nucleus of an atom is small compared to the size of the atom.
  c. Neutral lithium atoms contain more neutrons than protons.
  d. Neutral lithium atoms contain more protons than electrons.

42. Which statements are *inconsistent* with Rutherford's nuclear theory as it was originally stated? Why?
  a. Since electrons are smaller than protons, and since a hydrogen atom contains only 1 proton and 1 electron, it must follow that the volume of a hydrogen atom is mostly due to the proton.
  b. A nitrogen atom has 7 protons in its nucleus and 7 electrons outside of its nucleus.
  c. A phosphorus atom has 15 protons in its nucleus and 150 electrons outside of its nucleus.
  d. The majority of the mass of a fluorine atom is due to its 9 electrons.

43. A chemist in an imaginary universe, where electrons have a different charge than they do in our universe, performs the Millikan oil drop experiment to measure the electron's charge. The charges of several drops are recorded here. What is the charge of the electron in this imaginary universe?

Drop #	Charge
A	-6.9×10^{-19} C
B	-9.2×10^{-19} C
C	-11.5×10^{-19} C
D	-4.6×10^{-19} C

44. Imagine a unit of charge called the zorg. A chemist performs the oil drop experiment and measures the charge of each drop in zorgs. Based on the results shown here, what is the charge of the electron in zorgs (z)? How many electrons are in each drop?

Drop #	Charge
A	-4.8×10^{-9} z
B	-9.6×10^{-9} z
C	-6.4×10^{-9} z
D	-12.8×10^{-9} z

45. On a dry day, your body can accumulate static charge from walking across a carpet or from brushing your hair. If your body develops a charge of $-15\,\mu C$ (microcoulombs), how many excess electrons has it acquired? What is their collective mass?

46. How many electrons are necessary to produce a charge of -1.0 C? What is the mass of this many electrons?

47. Which statements about subatomic particles are true?
  a. If an atom has an equal number of protons and electrons, it will be charge-neutral.
  b. Electrons are attracted to protons.
  c. Electrons are much lighter than neutrons.
  d. Protons have twice the mass of neutrons.

48. Which statements about subatomic particles are false?
  a. Protons and electrons have charges of the same magnitude but opposite signs.
  b. Protons have about the same mass as neutrons.
  c. Some atoms don't have any protons.
  d. Protons and neutrons have charges of the same magnitude but opposite signs.

49. How many electrons would it take to equal the mass of a proton?

50. A helium nucleus has two protons and two neutrons. How many electrons would it take to equal the mass of a helium nucleus?

Isotopes and Ions

51. Write isotopic symbols in the form X-*A* (e.g., C-13) for each isotope.
  a. the silver isotope with 60 neutrons
  b. the silver isotope with 62 neutrons
  c. the uranium isotope with 146 neutrons
  d. the hydrogen isotope with 1 neutron

52. Write isotopic symbols in the form $^{A}_{Z}X$ for each isotope.
  a. the copper isotope with 34 neutrons
  b. the copper isotope with 36 neutrons
  c. the potassium isotope with 21 neutrons
  d. the argon isotope with 22 neutrons

53. Determine the number of protons and the number of neutrons in each isotope.
  a. $^{14}_{7}N$
  b. $^{23}_{11}Na$
  c. $^{222}_{86}Rn$
  d. $^{208}_{82}Pb$

54. Determine the number of protons and the number of neutrons in each isotope.
  a. $^{40}_{19}K$
  b. $^{226}_{88}Ra$
  c. $^{99}_{43}Tc$
  d. $^{33}_{15}P$

55. The amount of carbon-14 in ancient artifacts and fossils is often used to establish their age. Determine the number of protons and the number of neutrons in a carbon-14 isotope and write its symbol in the form $^{A}_{Z}X$.

56. Uranium-235 is used in nuclear fission. Determine the number of protons and the number of neutrons in uranium-235 and write its symbol in the form $^{A}_{Z}X$.

57. Determine the number of protons and the number of electrons in each ion.
  a. Ni^{2+} **b.** S^{2-} **c.** Br^{-} **d.** Cr^{3+}

58. Determine the number of protons and the number of electrons in each ion.
  a. Al^{3+} **b.** Se^{2-} **c.** Ga^{3+} **d.** Sr^{2+}

59. Predict the charge of the ion formed by each element.
  a. O   **b.** K   **c.** Al   **d.** Rb

60. Predict the charge of the ion formed by each element.
  a. Mg   **b.** N   **c.** F   **d.** Na

61. Fill in the blanks to complete the table.

Symbol	Ion Formed	Number of Electrons in Ion	Number of Protons in Ion
Ca	Ca²⁺	___	___
___	Be²⁺	2	___
Se	___	___	34
In	___	___	49

62. Fill in the blanks to complete the table.

Symbol	Ion Formed	Number of Electrons in Ion	Number of Protons in Ion
Cl	___	___	17
Te	___	54	___
Br	Br⁻	___	___
___	Sr²⁺	___	38

The Periodic Table and Atomic Mass

63. Write the name of each element and classify it as a metal, nonmetal, or metalloid.
  a. K   **b.** Ba   **c.** I   **d.** O   **e.** Sb

64. Write the symbol for each element and classify it as a metal, nonmetal, or metalloid.
  a. gold   **b.** fluorine   **c.** sodium
  d. tin   **e.** argon

65. Determine whether or not each element is a main-group element.
  a. tellurium   **b.** potassium
  c. vanadium   **d.** manganese

66. Determine whether or not each element is a transition element.
  a. Cr   **b.** Br   **c.** Mo   **d.** Cs

67. Classify each element as an alkali metal, alkaline earth metal, halogen, or noble gas.
  a. sodium   **b.** iodine   **c.** calcium
  d. barium   **e.** krypton

68. Classify each element as an alkali metal, alkaline earth metal, halogen, or noble gas.
  a. F   **b.** Sr   **c.** K   **d.** Ne   **e.** At

69. Which pair of elements do you expect to be most similar? Why?
  a. N and Ni   **b.** Mo and Sn
  c. Na and Mg   **d.** Cl and F
  e. Si and P

70. Which pair of elements do you expect to be most similar? Why?
  a. nitrogen and oxygen   **b.** titanium and gallium
  c. lithium and sodium   **d.** germanium and arsenic
  e. argon and bromine

71. Gallium has two naturally occurring isotopes with the following masses and natural abundances:

Isotope	Mass (amu)	Abundance (%)
Ga-69	68.92558	60.108
Ga-71	70.92470	39.892

Sketch the mass spectrum of Gallium.

72. Magnesium has three naturally occurring isotopes with the following masses and natural abundances:

Isotope	Mass (amu)	Abundance (%)
Mg-24	23.9850	78.99
Mg-25	24.9858	10.00
Mg-26	25.9826	11.01

Sketch the mass spectrum of magnesium.

73. The atomic mass of fluorine is 18.998 amu and its mass spectrum shows a large peak at this mass. The atomic mass of chlorine is 35.45 amu, yet the mass spectrum of chlorine does not show a peak at this mass. Explain the difference.

74. The atomic mass of copper is 63.546 amu. Do any copper isotopes have a mass of 63.546 amu? Explain.

75. An element has two naturally occurring isotopes. Isotope 1 has a mass of 120.9038 amu and a relative abundance of 57.4%, and isotope 2 has a mass of 122.9042 amu. Find the atomic mass of this element and identify it.

76. An element has four naturally occurring isotopes with the masses and natural abundances given here. Find the atomic mass of the element and identify it.

Isotope	Mass (amu)	Abundance (%)
1	135.90714	0.19
2	137.90599	0.25
3	139.90543	88.43
4	141.90924	11.13

77. Bromine has two naturally occurring isotopes (Br-79 and Br-81) and has an atomic mass of 79.904 amu. The mass of Br-81 is 80.9163 amu, and its natural abundance is 49.31%. Calculate the mass and natural abundance of Br-79.

78. Silicon has three naturally occurring isotopes (Si-28, Si-29, and Si-30). The mass and natural abundance of Si-28 are 27.9769 amu and 92.2%, respectively. The mass and natural abundance of Si-29 are 28.9765 amu and 4.67%, respectively. Find the mass and natural abundance of Si-30.

79. Use the mass spectrum of europium to determine the atomic mass of europium.

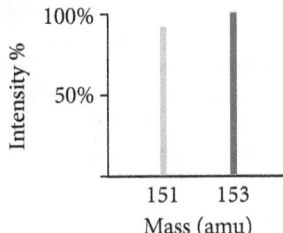

80. Use the mass spectrum of rubidium to determine the atomic mass of rubidium.

The Mole Concept

81. How many sulfur atoms are there in 5.52 mol of sulfur?

82. How many moles of aluminum do 3.7×10^{24} aluminum atoms represent?

83. What is the amount, in moles, of each elemental sample?
    a. 11.8 g Ar
    b. 3.55 g Zn
    c. 26.1 g Ta
    d. 0.211 g Li

84. What is the mass, in grams, of each elemental sample?
    a. 2.3×10^{-3} mol Sb
    b. 0.0355 mol Ba
    c. 43.9 mol Xe
    d. 1.3 mol W

85. How many silver atoms are there in 3.78 g of silver?

86. What is the mass of 4.91×10^{21} platinum atoms?

87. Calculate the number of atoms in each sample.
    a. 5.18 g P
    b. 2.26 g Hg
    c. 1.87 g Bi
    d. 0.082 g Sr

88. Calculate the number of atoms in each sample.
    a. 14.955 g Cr
    b. 39.733 g S
    c. 12.899 g Pt
    d. 97.552 g Sn

89. Calculate the mass, in grams, of each sample.
    a. 1.1×10^{23} gold atoms
    b. 2.82×10^{22} helium atoms
    c. 1.8×10^{23} lead atoms
    d. 7.9×10^{21} uranium atoms

90. Calculate the mass, in kg, of each sample.
    a. 7.55×10^{26} cadmium atoms
    b. 8.15×10^{27} nickel atoms
    c. 1.22×10^{27} manganese atoms
    d. 5.48×10^{29} lithium atoms

91. How many carbon atoms are there in a diamond (pure carbon) with a mass of 52 mg?

92. How many helium atoms are there in a helium blimp containing 536 kg of helium?

93. Calculate the average mass, in grams, of one platinum atom.

94. Using scanning tunneling microscopy, scientists at IBM wrote the initials of their company with 35 individual xenon atoms (as shown below). Calculate the total mass of these letters in grams.

Cumulative Problems

95. A 7.83 g sample of HCN contains 0.290 g of H and 4.06 g of N. Find the mass of carbon in a sample of HCN with a mass of 3.37 g.

96. The ratio of sulfur to oxygen by mass in SO_2 is 1.0:1.0.
    a. Find the ratio of sulfur to oxygen by mass in SO_3.
    b. Find the ratio of sulfur to oxygen by mass in S_2O.

97. The ratio of oxygen to carbon by mass in carbon monoxide is 1.33:1.00. Find the formula of an oxide of carbon in which the ratio by mass of oxygen to carbon is 2.00:1.00.

98. The ratio of the mass of a nitrogen atom to the mass of an atom of ^{12}C is 7:6 and the ratio of the mass of nitrogen to oxygen in N_2O is 7:4. Find the mass of 1 mol of oxygen atoms.

99. An α particle, $^4He^{2+}$, has a mass of 4.00151 amu. Find the value of its charge-to-mass ratio in C/kg.

100. Naturally occurring iodine has an atomic mass of 126.9045. A 12.3849 g sample of iodine is accidentally contaminated with an additional 1.00070 g of ^{129}I, a synthetic radioisotope of iodine used in the treatment of certain diseases of the thyroid gland. The mass of ^{129}I is 128.9050 amu. Find the apparent "atomic mass" of the contaminated iodine.

101. Use the mass spectrum of lead to estimate the atomic mass of lead. Estimate the mass and percent intensity values from the graph to three significant figures.

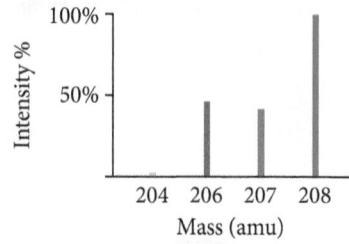

102. Use the mass spectrum of mercury to estimate the atomic mass of mercury. Estimate the masses and percent intensity values from the graph to three significant figures.

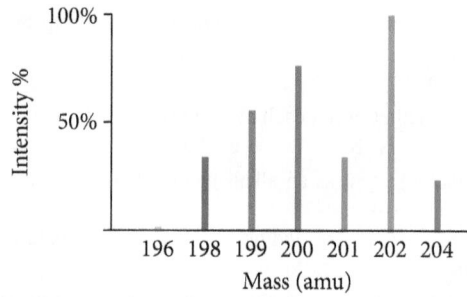

103. Nuclei with the same number of *neutrons* but different mass numbers are called *isotones*. Write the symbols of four isotones of ^{236}Th.

104. Fill in the blanks to complete the table.

Symbol	Z	A	Number of p	Number of e^-	Number of n	Charge
Si	14	___	___	14	14	___
S^{2-}	___	32	___	___	___	2−
Cu^{2+}	___	___	___	___	34	2+
___	15	___	___	15	16	___

105. Fill in the blanks to complete the table.

Symbol	Z	A	Number of p	Number of e⁻	Number of n	Charge
____	8	____	____	____	8	2−
Ca^{2+}	20	____	____	____	20	____
Mg^{2+}	____	25	____	____	13	2+
N^{3-}	____	14	____	10	____	____

106. Neutron stars are composed of solid nuclear matter, primarily neutrons. Assume the radius of a neutron is approximately 1.0×10^{-13} cm. Calculate the density of a neutron. [*Hint:* For a sphere $V = (4/3)\pi r^3$.] Assuming that a neutron star has the same density as a neutron, calculate the mass (in kg) of a small piece of a neutron star the size of a spherical pebble with a radius of 0.10 mm.

107. Carbon-12 contains six protons and six neutrons. The radius of the nucleus is approximately 2.7 fm (femtometers) and the radius of the atom is approximately 70 pm (picometers). Calculate the volume of the nucleus and the volume of the atom. What percentage of the carbon atom's volume is occupied by the nucleus? (Assume two significant figures.)

108. A penny has a thickness of approximately 1.0 mm. If you stacked Avogadro's number of pennies one on top of the other on Earth's surface, how far would the stack extend (in km)? [For comparison, the sun is about 150 million km from Earth and the nearest star (Proxima Centauri) is about 40 trillion km from Earth.]

109. Consider the stack of pennies in the previous problem. How much money (in dollars) would this represent? If this money were equally distributed among the world's population of 6.5 billion people, how much would each person receive? Would each person be a millionaire? Billionaire? Trillionaire?

110. The mass of an average blueberry is 0.75 g and the mass of an automobile is 2.0×10^3 kg. Find the number of automobiles whose total mass is the same as 1.0 mol of blueberries.

111. Suppose that atomic masses were based on the assignment of a mass of 12.000 g to 1 mol of carbon, rather than 1 mol of ^{12}C. What would the atomic mass of oxygen be? (The atomic masses of carbon and oxygen based on the assignment of 12.000 g to 1 mol of ^{12}C are 12.011 amu and 15.9994 amu, respectively.)

112. A pure titanium cube has an edge length of 2.78 in. How many titanium atoms does it contain? Titanium has a density of 4.50 g/cm³.

113. A pure copper sphere has a radius of 0.935 in. How many copper atoms does it contain? [The volume of a sphere is $(4/3)\pi r^3$ and the density of copper is 8.96 g/cm³.]

114. Boron has only two naturally occurring isotopes. The mass of boron-10 is 10.01294 amu and the mass of boron-11 is 11.00931 amu. Calculate the relative abundances of the two isotopes.

115. Lithium has only two naturally occurring isotopes. The mass of lithium-6 is 6.01512 amu and the mass of lithium-7 is 7.01601 amu. Calculate the relative abundances of the two isotopes.

116. Common brass is a copper and zinc alloy containing 37.0% zinc by mass and having a density of 8.48 g/cm³. A fitting composed of common brass has a total volume of 112.5 cm³. How many atoms (copper and zinc) does the fitting contain?

117. A 67.2 g sample of a gold and palladium alloy contains 2.49×10^{23} atoms. What is the composition (by mass) of the alloy?

118. Naturally occurring chlorine is composed of two isotopes: 75.76% Cl-35 (mass 34.9688 amu) and 24.24% Cl-37 (mass 36.9659 amu). Naturally occurring oxygen is composed of three isotopes: 99.757% O-16 (mass 15.9949 amu), 0.038% O-17 (mass 16.9991 amu), and 0.205% O-18 (mass 17.9991 amu). The compound dichlorine monoxide is composed of two chlorine atoms and one oxygen atom bonded together to form the Cl_2O molecule. How many Cl_2O molecules of different masses naturally exist? Give the masses of the three most abundant Cl_2O molecules.

119. Silver is composed of two naturally occurring isotopes: Ag-107 (51.839%) and Ag-109. The ratio of the masses of the two isotopes is 1.0187. What is the mass of Ag-107?

120. The U.S. Environmental Protection Agency (EPA) sets limits on healthful levels of air pollutants. The maximum level that the EPA considers safe for lead air pollution is 1.5 μg/m³. If your lungs were filled with air containing this level of lead, how many lead atoms would be in your lungs? (Assume a total lung volume of 5.50 L.)

121. Pure gold is usually too soft for jewelry, so it is often alloyed with other metals. How many gold atoms are in an 0.255 ounce, 18 K gold bracelet? (18 K gold is 75% gold by mass.)

Challenge Problems

122. In Section 2.9, it was stated that 1 mol of sand grains would cover the state of Texas to several feet. Estimate how many feet by assuming that the sand grains are roughly cube-shaped, each one with an edge length of 0.10 mm. Texas has a land area of 268,601 square miles.

123. Use the concepts in this chapter to obtain an estimate for the number of atoms in the universe. Make the following assumptions: **(a)** All of the atoms in the universe are hydrogen atoms in stars. (This is not a ridiculous assumption because over three-fourths of the atoms in the universe are in fact hydrogen. Gas and dust between the stars represent only about 15% of the visible matter of our galaxy, and planets compose a far tinier fraction.) **(b)** The sun is a typical star composed of pure hydrogen with a density of 1.4 g/cm³ and a radius of 7×10^8 m.

(c) Each of the roughly 100 billion stars in the Milky Way galaxy contains the same number of atoms as our sun. **(d)** Each of the 10 billion galaxies in the visible universe contains the same number of atoms as our Milky Way galaxy.

124. On the previous page is a representation of 50 atoms of a fictitious element called westmontium (Wt). The red spheres represent Wt-296, the blue spheres Wt-297, and the green spheres Wt-298.

  a. Assuming that the sample is statistically representative of a naturally occurring sample, calculate the percent natural abundance of each Wt isotope.

  b. Draw the mass spectrum for a naturally occurring sample of Wt.

  c. The mass of each Wt isotope is measured relative to C-12 and tabulated next. Use the mass of C-12 to convert each of the masses to amu and calculate the atomic mass of Wt.

Isotope	Mass
Wt-296	$24.6630 \times \text{Mass}(^{12}C)$
Wt-297	$24.7490 \times \text{Mass}(^{12}C)$
Wt-298	$24.8312 \times \text{Mass}(^{12}C)$

125. The ratio of oxygen to nitrogen by mass in NO_2 is 2.29. The ratio of fluorine to nitrogen by mass in NF_3 is 4.07. Find the ratio of oxygen to fluorine by mass in OF_2.

126. Naturally occurring cobalt consists of only one isotope, ^{59}Co, whose relative atomic mass is 58.9332. A synthetic radioactive isotope of cobalt, ^{60}Co, has a relative atomic mass of 59.9338 and is used in radiation therapy for cancer. A 1.5886 g sample of cobalt has an apparent "atomic mass" of 58.9901. Find the mass of ^{60}Co in this sample.

127. A 7.36 g sample of copper is contaminated with an additional 0.51 g of zinc. Suppose an atomic mass measurement was performed on this sample. What would be the measured atomic mass?

128. The ratio of the mass of O to the mass of N in N_2O_3 is 12:7. Another binary compound of nitrogen has a ratio of O to N of 16:7. What is its formula? What is the ratio of O to N in the next member of this series of compounds?

129. Naturally occurring magnesium has an atomic mass of 24.312 and consists of three isotopes. The major isotope is ^{24}Mg, natural abundance 78.99%, relative atomic mass 23.98504. The next most abundant isotope is ^{26}Mg, relative atomic mass 25.98259. The third most abundant isotope is ^{25}Mg, whose natural abundance is in the ratio of 0.9083 to that of ^{26}Mg. Find the relative atomic mass of ^{25}Mg.

Conceptual Problems

130. Which is an example of the law of multiple proportions? Explain.

  a. Two different samples of water are found to have the same ratio of hydrogen to oxygen.

  b. When hydrogen and oxygen react, the mass of water formed is exactly equal to the mass of hydrogen and oxygen that reacted.

  c. The mass ratio of oxygen to hydrogen in water is 8:1. The mass ratio of oxygen to hydrogen in hydrogen peroxide (a compound that only contains hydrogen and oxygen) is 16:1.

131. Lithium has two naturally occurring isotopes: Li-6 (natural abundance 7.5%) and Li-7 (natural abundance 92.5%). Using circles to represent protons and squares to represent neutrons, draw the nucleus of each isotope. How many Li-6 atoms would be present, on average, in a 1000-atom sample of lithium?

132. As we saw in the previous problem, lithium has two naturally occurring isotopes: Li-6 (natural abundance 7.5%; mass 6.0151 amu) and Li-7 (natural abundance 92.5%; mass 7.0160 amu). Without doing any calculations, determine which mass is closest to the atomic mass of Li.

  a. 6.00 amu   **b.** 6.50 amu   **c.** 7.00 amu

133. The mole is defined as the amount of a substance containing the same number of particles as exactly 12 grams of C-12. The amu is defined as 1/12 of the mass of an atom of C-12. Why is it important that both of these definitions reference the same isotope? What would be the result, for example, of defining the mole with respect to C-12, but the amu with respect to Ne-20?

134. Without doing any calculations, determine which of the samples contains the greatest amount of the element in moles. Which contains the greatest mass of the element?

  a. 55.0 g Cr

  b. 45.0 g Ti

  c. 60.0 g Zn

135. The atomic radii of the isotopes of an element are identical to one another. However, the atomic radii of the ions of an element are significantly different from the atomic radii of the neutral atom of the element. Explain.

Answers to Conceptual Connections

The Law of Conservation of Mass

2.1 Most of the matter that composed the log undergoes a chemical change by reacting with oxygen molecules in the air. The products of the reaction (mostly carbon dioxide and water) are released as gases into the air.

The Laws of Definite and Multiple Proportions

2.2 The law of definite proportions applies to two or more samples of the *same compound* and states that the ratio of one element to the other is always the same. The law of multiple proportions applies to two *different compounds* containing the same two elements (A and B) and states that the masses of B that combine with 1 g of A are always related to each other as a small whole-number ratio.

The Millikan Oil Drop Experiment

2.3 The drop contains three excess electrons ($3 \times (-1.6 \times 10^{-19} \text{ C})$ $= -4.8 \times 10^{-19} \text{ C}$).

Isotopes

2.4

C-12 nucleus   C-13 nucleus

A 10,000-atom sample of carbon, on average, contains 107 C-13 atoms.

The Nuclear Atom, Isotopes, and Ions

2.5 **(b)** The number of neutrons in the nucleus of an atom does not affect the atom's size because the nucleus is miniscule compared to the atom itself.

Atomic Mass

2.6 **(a)** Since 98.93% of the atoms are C-12, we would expect the atomic mass to be very close to the mass of the C-12 isotope.

Avogadro's Number

2.7 Avogadro's number is defined with respect to carbon-12—it is the number equal to the number of atoms in exactly 12 g of carbon-12. If Avogadro's number was defined as 1.00×10^{23} (a nice round number), it would correspond to 1.99 g of carbon-12 atoms (an inconvenient number). Avogadro's number is defined with respect to carbon-12 because, as you recall from Section 2.6, the amu (the basic mass unit used for all atoms) is defined relative to carbon-12. Therefore, the mass in grams of 1 mol of *any* element is equal to its atomic mass. As we have seen, these two definitions together make it possible to determine the number of atoms in a known mass of any element.

The Mole

2.8 **(b)** The carbon sample contains more atoms than the copper sample because carbon has a lower molar mass than copper. Carbon atoms are lighter than copper atoms, so a 1 g sample of carbon contains more atoms than a 1 g sample of copper. The carbon sample also contains more atoms than the uranium sample because even though the uranium sample has 10 times the mass of the carbon sample, a uranium atom is more than 10 times as massive (238 g/mol for uranium versus 12 g/mol for carbon).

3

Molecules, Compounds, and Chemical Equations

Almost all aspects of life are engineered at the molecular level, and without understanding molecules we can only have a very sketchy understanding of life itself.

—Francis Harry Compton Crick (1916–2004)

OW MANY DIFFERENT SUBSTANCES EXIST? Recall from Chapter 2 that about 91 different elements exist in nature, so there are at least 91 different substances. However, the world would be dull—not to mention lifeless—with only 91 different substances. Fortunately, elements combine with each other to form *compounds*. Just as combinations of only 26 letters in our English alphabet allow for an almost limitless number of words, each with its own specific meaning, combinations of the 91 naturally occurring elements allow for an almost limitless number of compounds, each with its own specific properties. The great diversity of substances that we find in nature is a direct result of the ability of elements to form compounds. Life, for example, could not exist with just 91 different elements. It takes compounds, in all of their diversity, to make life possible.

3.1 Hydrogen, Oxygen, and Water

Hydrogen (H_2) is an explosive gas used as a fuel in rocket engines. Oxygen (O_2), also a gas, is a natural component of the air on Earth. Oxygen itself is not flammable but must be present for combustion (burning) to occur. Hydrogen and oxygen both have extremely low boiling points, as you can see from the following table. When hydrogen and oxygen combine to form the compound water (H_2O), however, a dramatically different substance results.

When a balloon filled with H_2 and O_2 is ignited, the two elements react violently to form H_2O.

Selected Properties	Hydrogen	Oxygen	Water
Boiling Point	−253 °C	−183 °C	100 °C
State at Room Temperature	Gas	Gas	Liquid
Flammability	Explosive	Necessary for combustion	Used to extinguish flame

First of all, water is a liquid rather than a gas at room temperature, and its boiling point is hundreds of degrees higher than the boiling points of hydrogen and oxygen. Second, instead of being flammable (like hydrogen gas) or supporting combustion (like oxygen gas), water actually smothers flames. Water is nothing like the hydrogen and oxygen from which it forms. The dramatic difference between the elements hydrogen and oxygen and the compound water is typical of the differences between elements and the compounds that they form. *When two or more elements combine to form a compound, an entirely new substance results.*

Mixtures and Compounds

> **Hydrogen and Oxygen Mixture**
> This can have any ratio of
> hydrogen to oxygen.

> **Water (A Compound)**
> Water molecules have a fixed ratio of
> hydrogen (two atoms) to oxygen (one atom).

▲ FIGURE 3.1 **Mixtures and Compounds**   The balloon in this illustration is filled with a mixture of hydrogen gas and oxygen gas. The proportions of hydrogen and oxygen are variable. The glass is filled with water, a compound of hydrogen and oxygen. The ratio of hydrogen to oxygen in water is fixed: water molecules always have two hydrogen atoms for each oxygen atom.

Consider as another example common table salt, a highly stable compound composed of sodium and chlorine. Elemental sodium, by contrast, is a highly reactive, silvery metal that can explode on contact with water. Elemental chlorine is a corrosive, greenish-yellow gas that can be fatal if inhaled. Yet the compound formed from the combination of these two elements is sodium chloride (or table salt), a flavor enhancer that tastes great on steak.

Although some of the substances that we encounter in everyday life are elements, most are compounds. As we discussed in Chapter 1, a compound is different from a mixture of elements. In a compound, elements combine in fixed, definite proportions; in a mixture, elements can mix in any proportions whatsoever. Consider the difference between a hydrogen–oxygen mixture and water as shown in Figure 3.1 ▲. A hydrogen–oxygen mixture can have any proportions of hydrogen and oxygen gas. Water, by contrast, is composed of water molecules that always contain two hydrogen atoms to every one oxygen atom. Water has a definite proportion of hydrogen to oxygen.

In this chapter you will learn about compounds: how to represent them, how to name them, how to distinguish between their different types, and how to write chemical equations showing how they form and change. You will also learn how to quantify the elemental composition of a compound. This is important in determining how much of a particular element is contained within a particular compound. For example, patients with high blood pressure (hypertension) often have to reduce their sodium ion intake. Since the sodium ion is normally consumed in the form of sodium chloride, a hypertension patient needs to know how much sodium is present in a given amount of sodium chloride. Similarly, an iron-mining company needs to know how much iron it can recover from a given amount of iron ore. This chapter provides the tools to understand and answer these kinds of questions.

3.2 Chemical Bonds

Compounds are composed of atoms held together by *chemical bonds*. Chemical bonds result from the attractions between the charged particles (the electrons and protons) that compose atoms. We discuss these interactions more thoroughly in Chapter 9 (see Section 9.2). For now, remember that, as we discussed in Section 2.4, charged particles exert forces on one another: like charges repel and opposite charges attract. These electrostatic forces are responsible for chemical bonding.

We can broadly classify most chemical bonds into two types: ionic and covalent. *Ionic bonds*—which occur between metals and nonmetals—involve the *transfer* of electrons from one atom to another. *Covalent bonds*—which occur between two or more nonmetals—involve the *sharing* of electrons between two atoms.

Ionic Bonds

Recall from Chapter 2 that metals have a tendency to lose electrons and that nonmetals have a tendency to gain them. Therefore, when a metal interacts with a nonmetal, it can transfer one or more of its electrons to the nonmetal. The metal atom then becomes a *cation* (a positively charged ion), and the nonmetal atom becomes an *anion* (a negatively charged ion) as shown in Figure 3.2 ▼. These oppositely charged ions attract one another by electrostatic forces and form an **ionic bond**. The result is an ionic compound, which in the solid phase is composed of a lattice—a regular three-dimensional array—of alternating cations and anions.

Covalent Bonds

When a nonmetal bonds with another nonmetal, neither atom transfers its electron to the other. Instead the bonding atoms *share* some of their electrons. The shared electrons have lower potential energy than they would in the isolated atoms because they interact with

The Formation of an Ionic Compound

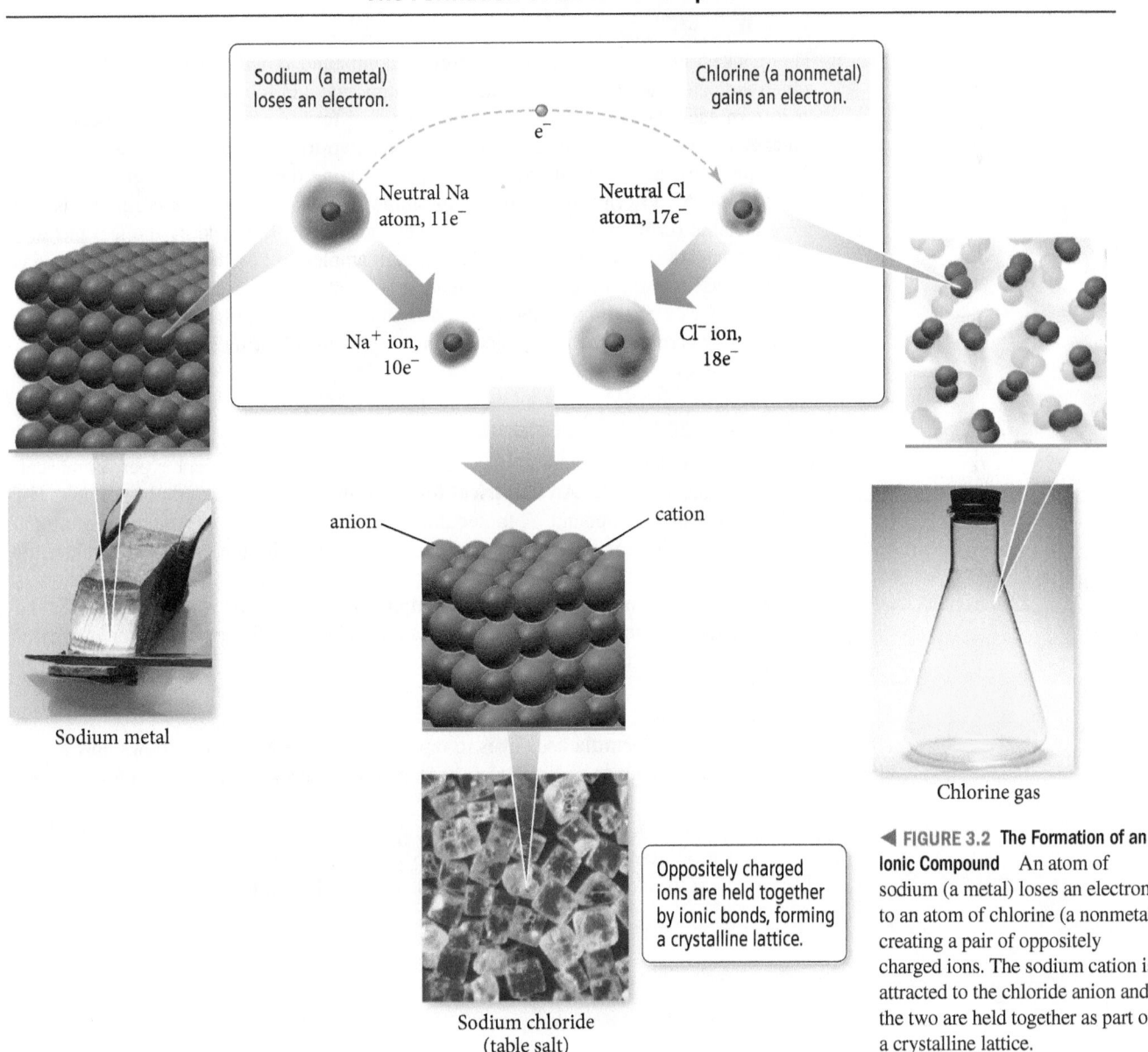

Sodium (a metal) loses an electron.

Chlorine (a nonmetal) gains an electron.

e^-

Neutral Na atom, $11e^-$

Neutral Cl atom, $17e^-$

Na^+ ion, $10e^-$

Cl^- ion, $18e^-$

Sodium metal

anion

cation

Oppositely charged ions are held together by ionic bonds, forming a crystalline lattice.

Sodium chloride (table salt)

Chlorine gas

◀ FIGURE 3.2 **The Formation of an Ionic Compound** An atom of sodium (a metal) loses an electron to an atom of chlorine (a nonmetal), creating a pair of oppositely charged ions. The sodium cation is attracted to the chloride anion and the two are held together as part of a crystalline lattice.

▶ FIGURE 3.3 **The Stability of a Covalent Bond**   The potential energy of a negative charge interacting with two positive charges is lowest when the negative charge is between the two positive charges.

Lowest potential energy (most stable)

the nuclei of both atoms. The bond is called a **covalent bond** and the covalently bound atoms compose a *molecule*. Each molecule is independent of the others—the molecules are themselves not covalently bound to one another. Therefore, we call covalently bonded compounds *molecular compounds*.

We can begin to understand the stability of a covalent bond by considering the most stable (or lowest potential energy) configuration of a negative charge interacting with two positive charges (which are separated by some small distance). Figure 3.3 ▲ shows that the lowest potential energy occurs when the negative charge lies *between* the two positive charges because in this arrangement the negative charge can interact with *both positive charges*. Similarly, shared electrons in a covalent chemical bond hold the bonding atoms together by attracting the positively charged nuclei of both bonding atoms.

3.3 Representing Compounds: Chemical Formulas and Molecular Models

The quickest and easiest way to represent a compound is with its **chemical formula**, which indicates the elements present in the compound and the relative number of atoms or ions of each. For example, H_2O is the chemical formula for water—it indicates that water consists of hydrogen and oxygen atoms in a two-to-one ratio. The formula contains the symbol for each element and a subscript indicating the relative number of atoms of the element. A subscript of 1 is typically omitted. Chemical formulas normally list the more metallic (or more positively charged) elements first, followed by the less metallic (or more negatively charged) elements. Other examples of common chemical formulas include NaCl for sodium chloride, indicating sodium and chloride ions in a one-to-one ratio; CO_2 for carbon dioxide, indicating carbon and oxygen atoms in a one-to-two ratio; and CCl_4 for carbon tetrachloride, indicating carbon and chlorine in a one-to-four ratio.

Types of Chemical Formulas

Chemical formulas can generally be categorized into three different types: empirical, molecular, and structural. An **empirical formula** gives the *relative* number of atoms of each element in a compound. A **molecular formula** gives the *actual* number of atoms of each element in a molecule of a compound. For example, the empirical formula for hydrogen peroxide is HO, but its molecular formula is H_2O_2. The molecular formula is always a whole-number multiple of the empirical formula. For some compounds, the empirical formula and the molecular formula are identical. For example, the empirical and molecular formula for water is H_2O because water molecules contain two hydrogen atoms and one oxygen atom, and no simpler whole-number ratio can express the relative number of hydrogen atoms to oxygen atoms.

A **structural formula** uses lines to represent covalent bonds and shows how atoms in a molecule are connected or bonded to each other. The structural formula for H_2O_2 is:

$$H—O—O—H$$

Structural formulas may also be written to give a sense of the molecule's geometry. The structural formula for hydrogen peroxide can also be written as:

$$
\begin{array}{c}
H \\
\diagdown \\
O—O \\
\hphantom{O—}\diagdown \\
\hphantom{O—O}H
\end{array}
$$

This version of the formula represents the approximate angles between bonds, giving a sense of the molecule's shape. Structural formulas can also depict the different types of bonds that occur within molecules. For example, consider the structural formula for carbon dioxide:

$$O=C=O$$

The two lines between each carbon and oxygen atom represent a double bond, which is generally stronger and shorter than a single bond (represented by a single line). A single bond corresponds to one shared electron pair, while a double bond corresponds to two shared electron pairs. We will learn more about single, double, and even triple bonds in Chapter 9.

The type of formula we use depends on how much we know about the compound and how much we want to communicate. A structural formula communicates the most information, while an empirical formula communicates the least.

Conceptual Connection 3.1 Structural Formulas

Write a structural formula for water.

EXAMPLE 3.1 Molecular and Empirical Formulas

Write empirical formulas for the compounds represented by the molecular formulas.

(a) C_4H_8 **(b)** B_2H_6 **(c)** CCl_4

SOLUTION

To determine the empirical formula from a molecular formula, divide the subscripts by the greatest common factor (the largest number that divides exactly into all of the subscripts).

(a) For C_4H_8, the greatest common factor is 4. The empirical formula is therefore CH_2.

(b) For B_2H_6, the greatest common factor is 2. The empirical formula is therefore BH_3.

(c) For CCl_4, the only common factor is 1, so the empirical formula and the molecular formula are identical.

FOR PRACTICE 3.1

Write the empirical formula for the compounds represented by the molecular formulas.

(a) C_5H_{12} **(b)** Hg_2Cl_2 **(c)** $C_2H_4O_2$

Answers to For Practice and For More Practice problems can be found in Appendix IV.

Molecular Models

A *molecular model* is a more accurate and complete way to specify a compound. A **ball-and-stick molecular model** represents atoms as balls and chemical bonds as sticks; how the two connect reflects a molecule's shape. The balls are typically color-coded to specific elements. For example, carbon is customarily black, hydrogen is white, nitrogen is blue, and oxygen is red. (For a complete list of colors of elements in the molecular models used in this book, see Appendix IIA.)

In a **space-filling molecular model**, atoms fill the space between each other to more closely represent our best estimates for how a molecule might appear if scaled to visible size. Consider the following ways to represent a molecule of methane, the main component of natural gas:

Hydrogen

Carbon

Nitrogen

Oxygen

Fluorine

Phosphorus

Sulfur

Chlorine

CH_4

H—C—H with H above and below

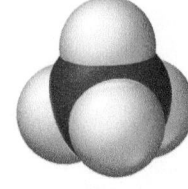

Molecular formula   Structural formula   Ball-and-stick model   Space-filling model

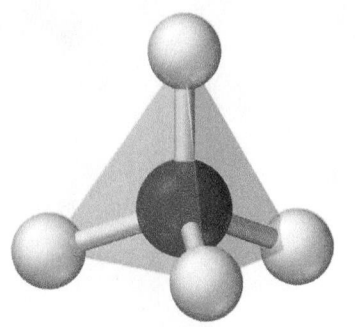

▲ A tetrahedron is a three-dimensional geometrical shape characterized by four equivalent triangular faces.

The molecular formula of methane indicates the number and type of each atom in the molecule: one carbon atom and four hydrogen atoms. The structural formula indicates how the atoms are connected: the carbon atom is bonded to the four hydrogen atoms. The ball-and-stick model clearly portrays the geometry of the molecule: the carbon atom sits in the center of a *tetrahedron* formed by the four hydrogen atoms. And finally, the space-filling model gives the best sense of the relative sizes of the atoms and how they merge together in bonding.

Throughout this book, you will see molecules represented in all of these ways. As you look at these representations, keep in mind what you learned in Chapter 1: the details about a molecule—the atoms that compose it, the lengths of the bonds between atoms, the angles of the bonds between atoms, and its overall shape—determine the properties of the substance that the molecule composes. Change any of these details and those properties change. Table 3.1 shows various compounds represented in the different ways we have just discussed.

Conceptual Connection 3.2 Representing Molecules

Based on what you learned in Chapter 2 about atoms, what part of the atom do you think the spheres in the molecular space-filling models shown in Table 3.1 represent? If you were to superimpose a nucleus on one of these spheres, how big would you draw it?

TABLE 3.1 Benzene, Acetylene, Glucose, and Ammonia

Name of Compound	Empirical Formula	Molecular Formula	Structural Formula	Ball-and-Stick Model	Space-Filling Model
Benzene	CH	C_6H_6			
Acetylene	CH	C_2H_2	$H-C\equiv C-H$		
Glucose	CH_2O	$C_6H_{12}O_6$			
Ammonia	NH_3	NH_3			

3.4 An Atomic-Level View of Elements and Compounds

Recall from Chapter 1 that we can categorize pure substances as either elements or compounds. We can subcategorize elements and compounds according to the basic units that compose them, as shown in Figure 3.4 ▼. Elements may be either atomic or molecular. Compounds may be either molecular or ionic.

▼ FIGURE 3.4 A Molecular View of Elements and Compounds

Classification of Elements and Compounds

Example: Ne   Example: O$_2$ Example: H$_2$O   Example: NaCl

NaCl formula unit

Atomic elements exist in nature with single atoms as their basic units. Most elements fall into this category. For example, helium is composed of helium atoms, aluminum is composed of aluminum atoms, and iron is composed of iron atoms. **Molecular elements** do not normally exist in nature with single atoms as their basic units; instead, they exist as molecules—two or more atoms of the element bonded together. Most molecular elements exist as *diatomic* molecules. For example, hydrogen is composed of H$_2$ molecules, nitrogen is composed of N$_2$ molecules, and chlorine is composed of Cl$_2$ molecules. A few molecular elements exist as *polyatomic molecules*. Phosphorus exists as P$_4$, and sulfur exists as S$_8$. Figure 3.5 ▼ shows the elements that exist primarily as diatomic or polyatomic molecules.

Diatomic chlorine molecules

▲ The basic units that compose chlorine gas are diatomic chlorine molecules.

Molecular Elements

◄ FIGURE 3.5 Molecular Elements
The highlighted elements exist primarily as diatomic molecules (yellow) or polyatomic molecules (red).

A Molecular Compound

(a)

An Ionic Compound

(b)

▲ **FIGURE 3.6 Molecular and Ionic Compounds** (a) Propane is an example of a molecular compound. The basic units that compose propane gas are propane (C_3H_8) molecules. (b) Table salt (NaCl) is an ionic compound. Its formula unit is the simplest charge-neutral collection of ions: one Na^+ ion and one Cl^- ion.

Some ionic compounds, such as K_2NaPO_4, contain more than one type of metal ion.

People occasionally refer to formula units as molecules, but this is *not* correct since ionic compounds do not contain distinct molecules.

▲ Polyatomic ions are common in household products such as bleach, which contains sodium hypochlorite (NaClO).

Molecular compounds are usually composed of two or more covalently bonded nonmetals. The basic units of molecular compounds are molecules composed of the constituent atoms. For example, water is composed of H_2O molecules, dry ice is composed of CO_2 molecules, and propane (often used as a fuel for grills) is composed of C_3H_8 molecules as shown in Figure 3.6(a) ▲.

Ionic compounds are composed of cations (usually a metal) and anions (usually one or more nonmetals) bound together by ionic bonds. The basic unit of an ionic compound is the **formula unit**, the smallest, electrically neutral collection of ions. A formula unit is not a molecule—it does not usually exist as a discrete entity but rather as part of a larger lattice. For example, the ionic compound table salt, with the formula unit NaCl, is composed of Na^+ and Cl^- ions in a one-to-one ratio. In table salt, Na^+ and Cl^- ions exist in a three-dimensional alternating array. Because ionic bonds are not directional, no one Na^+ ion pairs with a specific Cl^- ion. Rather, as you can see in Figure 3.6(b) ▲, any one Na^+ cation is surrounded by Cl^- anions and vice versa.

Many common ionic compounds contain ions that are themselves composed of a group of covalently bonded atoms with an overall charge. For example, the active ingredient in household bleach is sodium hypochlorite, which acts to chemically alter color-causing molecules in clothes (bleaching action) and to kill bacteria (disinfection). Hypochlorite is a **polyatomic ion**—an ion composed of two or more atoms—with the formula ClO^-. (Note that the charge on the hypochlorite ion is a property of the whole ion, not just the oxygen atom; this is true for all polyatomic ions.) The hypochlorite ion is often found as a unit in other compounds as well [such as KClO and $Mg(ClO)_2$]. Other common compounds that contain polyatomic ions include sodium bicarbonate ($NaHCO_3$), also known as baking soda, sodium nitrite ($NaNO_2$), an inhibitor of bacterial growth in packaged meats, and calcium carbonate ($CaCO_3$), the active ingredient in antacids such as Tums.

Conceptual Connection 3.3 A Molecular View of Elements and Compounds

Suppose that the two elements A (represented by triangles) and B (represented by squares) form a molecular compound with the molecular formula A_2B, and that two other elements, C (represented by circles) and D (represented by diamonds) form an ionic compound with the formula CD. Draw a molecular level view of each compound.

EXAMPLE 3.2 Classifying Substances as Atomic Elements, Molecular Elements, Molecular Compounds, or Ionic Compounds

Classify each of the substances as an atomic element, molecular element, molecular compound, or ionic compound.

(a) xenon   **(b)** $NiCl_2$ **(c)** bromine   **(d)** NO_2 **(e)** $NaNO_3$

SOLUTION

(a) Xenon is an element. It is not a molecular element (see Figure 3.5); therefore, it is an atomic element.

(b) $NiCl_2$ is a compound composed of a metal (left side of the periodic table) and nonmetal (right side of the periodic table); therefore, it is an ionic compound.

(c) Bromine is one of the elements that exists as a diatomic molecule (see Figure 3.5); therefore, it is a molecular element.

(d) NO_2 is a compound composed of a nonmetal and a nonmetal; therefore, it is a molecular compound.

(e) $NaNO_3$ is a compound composed of a metal and a polyatomic ion; therefore, it is an ionic compound.

FOR PRACTICE 3.2

Classify each of the substances as an atomic element, molecular element, molecular compound, or ionic compound.

(a) fluorine   **(b)** N_2O **(c)** silver   **(d)** K_2O **(e)** Fe_2O_3

Conceptual Connection 3.4 Ionic and Molecular Compounds

Which statement best summarizes the difference between ionic and molecular compounds?

(a) Molecular compounds contain highly directional covalent bonds, which results in the formation of molecules—discrete particles that do not covalently bond to each other. Ionic compounds contain non-directional ionic bonds, which results (in the solid phase) in the formation of ionic lattices—extended networks of alternating cations and anions.

(b) Molecular compounds contain covalent bonds in which one of the atoms shares an electron with the other one, resulting in a new force that holds the atoms together in a covalent molecule. Ionic compounds contain ionic bonds in which one atom donates an electron to the other, resulting in a new force that holds the ions together in pairs (in the solid phase).

(c) The key difference between ionic and covalent compounds is the types of elements that compose them, not the way that the atoms bond together.

(d) A molecular compound is composed of covalently bonded molecules. An ionic compound is composed of ionically bonded molecules (in the solid phase).

▲ Ionic compounds are common in food and consumer products such as light salt (a mixture of NaCl and KCl) and Tums ($CaCO_3$).

3.5 Ionic Compounds: Formulas and Names

Ionic compounds occur throughout Earth's crust as minerals. Examples include limestone ($CaCO_3$), a type of sedimentary rock; gibbsite [$Al(OH)_3$], an aluminum-containing mineral; and soda ash (Na_2CO_3), a natural deposit. We can also find ionic compounds in the foods that we eat. Examples include sodium chloride (NaCl), which is table salt; calcium carbonate ($CaCO_3$), a source of calcium necessary for bone health; and potassium chloride (KCl), a source of potassium necessary for fluid balance and muscle function. Ionic compounds are generally very stable because the attractions between cations and anions within ionic compounds are strong and because each ion interacts with several oppositely charged ions in the crystalline lattice.

▶ Calcite (left) is the main component of limestone, marble, and other forms of calcium carbonate ($CaCO_3$) commonly found in Earth's crust. Trona (right) is a crystalline form of hydrated sodium carbonate ($Na_3H(CO_3)_2 \cdot 2H_2O$).

Writing Formulas for Ionic Compounds

Since ionic compounds are charge-neutral, and since many elements form only one type of ion with a predictable charge, we can deduce the formulas for many ionic compounds from their constituent elements. For example, the formula for the ionic compound composed of sodium and chlorine must be NaCl because in compounds Na always forms 1+ cations and Cl always forms 1– anions. In order for the compound to be charge-neutral, it must contain one Na^+ cation to every one Cl^- anion. The formula for the ionic compound composed of *calcium* and chlorine, however, is $CaCl_2$ because Ca always forms 2+ cations and Cl always forms 1– anions. In order for this compound to be charge-neutral, it must contain one Ca^{2+} cation for every two Cl^- anions.

Summarizing Ionic Compound Formulas:

▶ Ionic compounds always contain positive and negative ions.

▶ In a chemical formula, the sum of the charges of the positive ions (cations) must equal the sum of the charges of the negative ions (anions).

▶ The formula of an ionic compound reflects the smallest whole-number ratio of ions.

See Figure 2.14 to review the elements that form ions with a predictable charge.

To write the formula for an ionic compound, follow the procedure in the left column below. Two examples of how to apply the procedure are provided in the center and right columns.

PROCEDURE FOR... **Writing Formulas for Ionic Compounds**	**EXAMPLE 3.3** **Writing Formulas for Ionic Compounds** Write the formula for the ionic compound that forms between aluminum and oxygen.	**EXAMPLE 3.4** **Writing Formulas for Ionic Compounds** Write the formula for the ionic compound that forms between calcium and oxygen.
1. Write the symbol for the metal cation and its charge followed by the symbol for the nonmetal anion and its charge. Determine charges from the element's group number in the periodic table (refer to Figure 2.14).	Al^{3+} O^{2-}	Ca^{2+} O^{2-}
2. Adjust the subscript on each cation and anion to balance the overall charge.	Al^{3+} O^{2-} ↓ Al_2O_3	Ca^{2+} O^{2-} ↓ CaO
3. Check that the sum of the charges of the cations equals the sum of the charges of the anions.	cations: $2(3+) = 6+$ anions: $3(2-) = 6-$ The charges cancel.	cations: 2+ anions: 2– The charges cancel.

FOR PRACTICE 3.3	**FOR PRACTICE 3.4**
Write the formula for the compound formed between potassium and sulfur.	Write the formula for the compound formed between aluminum and nitrogen.

Naming Ionic Compounds

Some ionic compounds—such as NaCl (table salt) and NaHCO₃ (baking soda)—have **common names**, which are nicknames of sorts learned by familiarity. However, chemists have developed **systematic names** for different types of compounds including ionic ones. Even if you are not familiar with a compound, you can determine its systematic name from its chemical formula. Conversely, you can deduce the formula of a compound from its systematic name.

The first step in naming an ionic compound is to identify it as one. Remember, *ionic compounds are usually composed of metals and nonmetals*; any time you see a metal and one or more nonmetals together in a chemical formula, assume that you have an ionic compound. Ionic compounds can be categorized into two types, depending on the metal in the compound. The first type contains a metal whose charge is invariant from one compound to another. Whenever the metal in this first type of compound forms an ion, the ion always has the same charge.

TABLE 3.2 Metals Whose Charge Is Invariant from One Compound to Another

Metal	Ion	Name	Group Number
Li	Li$^+$	Lithium	1A
Na	Na$^+$	Sodium	1A
K	K$^+$	Potassium	1A
Rb	Rb$^+$	Rubidium	1A
Cs	Cs$^+$	Cesium	1A
Be	Be^{2+}	Beryllium	2A
Mg	Mg^{2+}	Magnesium	2A
Ca	Ca^{2+}	Calcium	2A
Sr	Sr^{2+}	Strontium	2A
Ba	Ba^{2+}	Barium	2A
Al	Al^{3+}	Aluminum	3A
Zn	Zn^{2+}	Zinc	*
Sc	Sc^{3+}	Scandium	*
Ag**	Ag$^+$	Silver	*

*The charge of these metals cannot be inferred from their group number.

**Silver sometimes forms compounds with other charges, but these are rare.

Since the charge of the metal in this first type of ionic compound is always the same, it need not be specified in the name of the compound. Sodium, for instance, has a 1+ charge in all of its compounds. Table 3.2 lists some examples of these types of metals; the charges of these metals can be inferred from their group number in the periodic table.

The second type of ionic compound contains a metal with a charge that can differ in different compounds. In other words, the metal in this second type of ionic compound can form more than one kind of cation (depending on the compound), and its charge must therefore be specified for a given compound. Iron, for instance, forms a 2+ cation in some of its compounds and a 3+ cation in others. Metals of this type are often *transition metals* (Figure 3.7 ▶). However, some transition metals, such as Zn and Ag, form cations with the same charge in all of their compounds (as shown in Table 3.2), and some main group metals, such as Pb and Sn, form more than one type of cation.

▲ FIGURE 3.7 **Transition Metals** Metals that can have different charges in different compounds are usually (but not always) transition metals.

Naming Binary Ionic Compounds Containing a Metal That Forms Only One Type of Cation

Binary compounds contain only two different elements. The names of binary ionic compounds take the form:

name of cation (metal)	base name of anion (nonmetal) + -ide

For example, the name for KCl consists of the name of the cation, *potassium*, followed by the base name of the anion, *chlor*, with the ending *-ide*. Its full name is *potassium chloride*.

KCl   potassium chloride

TABLE 3.3 Some Common Monoatomic Anions

Nonmetal	Symbol for Ion	Base Name	Anion Name
Fluorine	F^-	fluor	Fluoride
Chlorine	Cl^-	chlor	Chloride
Bromine	Br^-	brom	Bromide
Iodine	I^-	iod	Iodide
Oxygen	O^{2-}	ox	Oxide
Sulfur	S^{2-}	sulf	Sulfide
Nitrogen	N^{3-}	nitr	Nitride
Phosphorus	P^{3-}	phosph	Phosphide

The name for CaO consists of the name of the cation, *calcium*, followed by the base name of the anion, *ox*, with the ending *-ide*. Its full name is *calcium oxide*.

$$CaO \quad \text{calcium oxide}$$

The base names for various nonmetals, and their most common charges in ionic compounds, are shown in Table 3.3.

EXAMPLE 3.5 Naming Ionic Compounds Containing a Metal That Forms Only One Type of Cation

Name the compound $CaBr_2$.

SOLUTION

The cation is *calcium*. The anion is from bromine, which becomes *bromide*. The correct name is *calcium bromide*.

FOR PRACTICE 3.5

Name the compound Ag_3N.

FOR MORE PRACTICE 3.5

Write the formula for rubidium sulfide.

Naming Binary Ionic Compounds Containing a Metal That Forms More Than One Kind of Cation

Note that there is no space between the name of the cation and the parenthetical number indicating its charge.

For these types of metals, the name of the cation is followed by a roman numeral (in parentheses) that indicates the charge of the metal in that particular compound. For example, we distinguish between Fe^{2+} and Fe^{3+} as follows:

$$Fe^{2+} \quad \text{iron(II)}$$

$$Fe^{3+} \quad \text{iron(III)}$$

The full names for compounds containing metals that form more than one kind of cation have the form:

TABLE 3.4 Some Metals That Form Cations with Different Charges

Metal	Ion	Name	Older Name*
Chromium	Cr^{2+}	Chromium(II)	Chromous
	Cr^{3+}	Chromium(III)	Chromic
Iron	Fe^{2+}	Iron(II)	Ferrous
	Fe^{3+}	Iron(III)	Ferric
Cobalt	Co^{2+}	Cobalt(II)	Cobaltous
	Co^{3+}	Cobalt(III)	Cobaltic
Copper	Cu^+	Copper(I)	Cuprous
	Cu^{2+}	Copper(II)	Cupric
Tin	Sn^{2+}	Tin(II)	Stannous
	Sn^{4+}	Tin(IV)	Stannic
Mercury	Hg_2^{2+}	Mercury(I)	Mercurous
	Hg^{2+}	Mercury(II)	Mercuric
Lead	Pb^{2+}	Lead(II)	Plumbous
	Pb^{4+}	Lead(IV)	Plumbic

*An older naming system substitutes the names found in this column for the name of the metal and its charge. Under this system, chromium(II) oxide is named chromous oxide. Additionally, the suffix *-ous* indicates the ion with the lesser charge and *-ic* indicates the ion with the greater charge. We will *not* use the older system in this text.

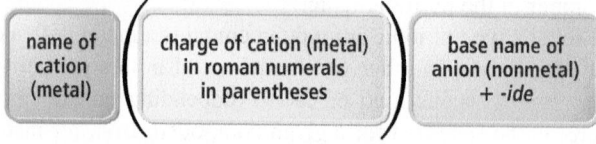

You can determine the charge of the metal cation by inference from the sum of the charges of the nonmetal anions—remember that the sum of all the charges in the compound must be zero. Table 3.4 shows some of the metals that form more than one cation and their most common charges. For example, in $CrBr_3$, the charge of chromium must be 3+ in order for the compound to be charge-neutral with three Br^- anions. The cation is named

$$Cr^{3+} \quad \text{chromium(III)}$$

The full name of the compound is

$$CrBr_3 \quad \text{chromium(III) bromide}$$

Similarly, in CuO the charge of copper must be 2+ in order for the compound to be charge-neutral with one O^{2-} anion. The cation is therefore named

$$Cu^{2+} \quad \text{copper(II)}$$

The full name of the compound is

$$CuO \quad \text{copper(II) oxide}$$

3.6 Molecular Compounds: Formulas and Names

In contrast to ionic compounds, the formula for a molecular compound *cannot* readily be determined from its constituent elements because the same combination of elements may form many different molecular compounds, each with a different formula. Recall from Chapter 1, for example, that carbon and oxygen form both CO and CO_2, and that hydrogen and oxygen form both H_2O and H_2O_2. Nitrogen and oxygen form all of the following unique molecular compounds: NO, NO_2, N_2O, N_2O_3, N_2O_4, and N_2O_5. In Chapter 9, you will learn how to understand the stability of these various combinations of the same elements. For now, we focus on naming a molecular compound based on its formula and writing its formula based on its name.

Naming Molecular Compounds

Like ionic compounds, many molecular compounds have common names. For example, H_2O and NH_3 have the common names *water* and *ammonia*. However, the sheer number of existing molecular compounds—numbering in the millions—necessitates a systematic approach to naming them.

The first step in naming a molecular compound is identifying it as one. Remember, *molecular compounds are composed of two or more nonmetals*. In this section, you learn how to name binary (two-element) molecular compounds. Their names have the form

| prefix | name of 1st element | prefix | base name of 2nd element + -ide |

When writing the name of a molecular compound, as when writing the formula, the first element is the more metal-like one (toward the left and bottom of the periodic table). Generally, write the name of the element with the smallest group number first. If the two elements lie in the same group, then write the element with the greatest row number first. The prefixes given to each element indicate the number of atoms present:

mono = 1		hexa = 6	
di = 2		hepta = 7	
tri = 3		octa = 8	
tetra = 4		nona = 9	
penta = 5		deca = 10	

These prefixes are the same as those used in naming hydrates.

If there is only one atom of the *first element* in the formula, the prefix *mono-* is normally omitted. For example, we name NO_2 according to the first element, *nitrogen*, with no prefix because *mono-* is omitted for the first element, followed by the prefix *di*, to indicate two oxygen atoms, and the base name of the second element, *ox*, with the ending *-ide*. Its full name is *nitrogen dioxide*.

NO_2 nitrogen dioxide

We name the compound N_2O, sometimes called laughing gas, similarly except that we use the prefix *di-* before nitrogen to indicate two nitrogen atoms and the prefix *mono-* before oxide to indicate one oxygen atom. Its full name is *dinitrogen monoxide*.

N_2O dinitrogen monoxide

When a prefix ends with "o" and the base name begins with "o," the first "o" is often dropped. So mono-oxide becomes *monoxide*.

EXAMPLE 3.8 Naming Molecular Compounds

Name each compound.

(a) NI_3 (b) PCl_5 (c) P_4S_{10}

SOLUTION

(a) The name of the compound is the name of the first element, *nitrogen*, followed by the base name of the second element, *iod*, prefixed by *tri-* to indicate three and given the suffix *-ide*.

$$NI_3 \qquad \text{nitrogen triiodide}$$

(b) The name of the compound is the name of the first element, *phosphorus*, followed by the base name of the second element, *chlor*, prefixed by *penta-* to indicate five and given the suffix *-ide*.

$$PCl_5 \qquad \text{phosphorus pentachloride}$$

(c) The name of the compound is the name of the first element, *phosphorus*, prefixed by *tetra-* to indicate four, followed by the base name of the second element, *sulf*, prefixed by *deca* to indicate ten and given the suffix *-ide*.

$$P_4S_{10} \qquad \text{tetraphosphorus decasulfide}$$

FOR PRACTICE 3.8

Name the compound N_2O_5.

FOR MORE PRACTICE 3.8

Write the formula for phosphorus tribromide.

Conceptual Connection 3.5 Nomenclature

The compound NCl_3 is nitrogen trichloride, but $AlCl_3$ is simply aluminum chloride. Why?

Naming Acids

We can define acids in a number of ways, as we will discuss in Chapter 15. For now we define **acids** as molecular compounds that release hydrogen ions (H^+) when dissolved in water. Acids are composed of hydrogen, usually written first in their formula, and one or more nonmetals, written second. For example, HCl is a molecular compound that, when dissolved in water, forms $H^+(aq)$ and $Cl^-(aq)$ ions, where *aqueous (aq)* means *dissolved in water*. Therefore, HCl is an acid when dissolved in water. To distinguish between gaseous HCl (which is named hydrogen chloride because it is a molecular compound) and HCl in solution (which is named hydrochloric acid because it is an acid), we write the former as HCl(*g*) and the latter as HCl(*aq*).

▲ Many fruits are acidic and have the characteristically sour taste of acids.

Acids are characterized by their sour taste and their ability to dissolve many metals. For example, hydrochloric acid is present in stomach fluids, and its sour taste becomes painfully obvious during vomiting. Hydrochloric acid also dissolves some metals. For example, if you put a strip of zinc into a test tube of hydrochloric acid, it slowly dissolves as the $H^+(aq)$ ions convert the zinc metal into $Zn^{2+}(aq)$ cations (Figure 3.9 ▶).

Acids are present in foods such as lemons and limes and are used in household products such as toilet bowl cleaner and Lime-A-Way. In this section, we discuss how

Acids Dissolve Many Metals

Zn atoms

Zn metal

H$_2$ gas

HCl solution

Zn^{2+} H$_3$O$^+$ Cl$^-$ H$_2$O

◄ **FIGURE 3.9 Hydrochloric Acid Dissolving Zinc Metal**   The zinc atoms are ionized to zinc ions, which dissolve in the water. The HCl forms H$_2$ gas, which is responsible for the bubbles you can see in the test tube.

to name them; in Chapter 15 you will learn more about their properties. Acids can be categorized into two types: binary acids and oxyacids.

```
            ┌──────────────────┐
            │      ACIDS       │
            │ Formula has H as │
            │  first element.  │
            └──────────────────┘
              ┌───────┴───────┐
              ▼               ▼
    ┌──────────────┐  ┌──────────────┐
    │ Binary acids │  │   Oxyacids   │
    │contain only two│ │contain oxygen.│
    │   elements.  │  │              │
    └──────────────┘  └──────────────┘
```

Naming Binary Acids

Binary acids are composed of hydrogen and a nonmetal. Names for binary acids have the form:

hydro | base name of nonmetal + -ic | acid

For example, HCl(*aq*) is hydro*chlor*ic acid and HBr(*aq*) is hydro*brom*ic acid.

HCl(*aq*) hydrochloric acid   HBr(*aq*)   hydrobromic acid

EXAMPLE 3.9 Naming Binary Acids

Name HI(*aq*).

SOLUTION

The base name of I is *iod*, so HI(*aq*) is hydroiodic acid.

HI(*aq*)   hydroiodic acid

FOR PRACTICE 3.9

Name HF(*aq*).

Naming Oxyacids

Oxyacids contain hydrogen and an oxyanion (an anion containing a nonmetal and oxygen). The common oxyanions are listed in the table of polyatomic ions (Table 3.5). For example, $HNO_3(aq)$ contains the nitrate (NO_3^-) ion, $H_2SO_3(aq)$ contains the sulfite (SO_3^{2-}) ion, and $H_2SO_4(aq)$ contains the sulfate (SO_4^{2-}) ion. Oxyacids are a combination of one or more H^+ ions with an oxyanion. The number of H^+ ions depends on the charge of the oxyanion; the formula is always charge-neutral. The names of oxyacids depend on the ending of the oxyanion and take the following forms:

oxyanions ending with -*ate*   base name of oxyanion + -*ic*   acid

oxyanions ending with -*ite*   base name of oxyanion + -*ous*   acid

So $HNO_3(aq)$ is nitric acid (oxyanion is nitrate), and $H_2SO_3(aq)$ is sulfurous acid (oxyanion is sulfite).

$HNO_3(aq)$ nitric acid $H_2SO_3(aq)$ sulfurous acid

Chemistry in the Environment
Acid Rain

Certain pollutants—such as NO, NO_2, and SO_2—form acids when mixed with water. NO and NO_2, primarily emitted in vehicular exhaust, combine with atmospheric oxygen and water to form nitric acid, $HNO_3(aq)$. SO_2, emitted primarily from coal-powered electricity generation, combines with atmospheric oxygen and water to form sulfuric acid, $H_2SO_4(aq)$. Both $HNO_3(aq)$ and $H_2SO_4(aq)$ result in acidic rainwater. The problem is greatest in the northeastern United States where pollutants from midwestern electrical power plants combine with rainwater to produce rain that is up to ten times more acidic than normal.

Acid rain can fall or flow into lakes and streams, making these bodies of water more acidic. Some species of aquatic animals—such as trout, bass, snails, salamanders, and clams—cannot tolerate the increased acidity and die. This in turn disturbs the ecosystem of the lake, resulting in imbalances that may lead to the death of other aquatic species. Acid rain also weakens trees by dissolving and washing away

nutrients in the soil and by damaging leaves. Appalachian red spruce trees have been the hardest hit, with many forests showing significant acid rain damage.

In addition, acid rain degrades building materials because acids dissolve iron, the main component of steel, and $CaCO_3$ (limestone), a main component of marble and concrete. Consequently, acid rain has damaged many statues, buildings, and bridges in the northeastern United States.

Acid rain has been a problem for many years but legislation passed toward the end of the last century has begun to address this issue. In 1990, Congress passed several amendments to the Clean Air Act that included provisions requiring electrical utilities to lower SO_2 emissions. Since then, SO_2 emissions have decreased and rain in the northeastern United States has become somewhat less acidic. With time, and with continued enforcement of the acid rain regulation, lakes, streams, and forests damaged by acid rain should recover.

Question

Name each compound given here as formulas: NO, NO_2, SO_2, H_2SO_4, HNO_3, $CaCO_3$.

▼ A forest damaged by acid rain.

► Acid rain damages building materials such as the limestone that composes many statues.

EXAMPLE 3.10 Naming Oxyacids

Name $HC_2H_3O_2(aq)$.

SOLUTION

The oxyanion is acetate, which ends in *-ate*; therefore, the name of the acid is *acetic acid*.

$$HC_2H_3O_2(aq) \qquad \text{acetic acid}$$

FOR PRACTICE 3.10

Name $HNO_2(aq)$.

FOR MORE PRACTICE 3.10

Write the formula for perchloric acid.

3.7 Summary of Inorganic Nomenclature

In the previous two sections, we discussed naming inorganic compounds, specifically ionic compounds, molecular compounds, and acids. However, we often have to name a compound without initially knowing the category into which it falls. In other words, real life nomenclature is a bit messier than the categorized nomenclature we just worked through. Figure 3.10 ▼ summarizes inorganic nomenclature in a flow chart that will help you to tackle nomenclature from beginning to end.

To use the flow chart, begin by determining what type of compound you are trying to name. For example, to name the compound $MgCl_2$, you need to decide if the

Inorganic Nomenclature Flow Chart

▲ **FIGURE 3.10 Inorganic Nomenclature Flow Chart** The chart summarizes how to name inorganic compounds. Begin by determining if the compound to be named is ionic, molecular, or an acid. Then follow the flow chart for that category from top to bottom until you arrive at a name for the compound.

*Acids must be in aqueous solution.

MgCl₂

Magnesium chloride

▲ FIGURE 3.11 **Flow Chart Path for MgCl₂**

compound is ionic, molecular, or an acid. In this case, since $MgCl_2$ is composed of a metal and nonmetal, it is ionic. Therefore, you begin at the box labeled "IONIC" at the far left side of the flow chart.

Next, determine whether the metal in the compound forms only one type of ion or more than one type. You can decide this by looking for the metal (in this case magnesium) in Table 3.2. Since magnesium is listed in the table, it forms only one type of ion; therefore, you take the left branch in the flow chart as shown in Figure 3.11 ◄.

Finally, name the compound according to the blocks at the end of the path in the flow chart. In this case, write the name of the cation (the metal) followed by the base name of the anion (the nonmetal) appended with the ending *-ide*. Its full name is magnesium chloride.

EXAMPLE 3.11 Using the Nomenclature Flow Chart to Name Compounds

Use the flow chart in Figure 3.10 to name each compound.

(a) SO_2 **(b)** $HClO_4(aq)$ **(c)** CoF_2

SOLUTION

(a) SO_2 Begin by determining whether the compound is ionic, molecular, or an acid. Since SO_2 contains only nonmetals, it is molecular. Name the compound as the name of the first element, *sulfur* (no prefix since the prefix is dropped for mono), followed by the base name of the second element, *ox*, prefixed by *di* to indicate two, and given the suffix *-ide*.	 Sulfur dioxide
(b) $HClO_4(aq)$ Begin by determining whether the compound is ionic, molecular, or an acid. Since $HClO_4(aq)$ contains H and one more nonmetal and is designated as aqueous, it is an acid. Next determine whether the acid contains oxygen. Since $HClO_4$ contains oxygen, it is an oxyacid. Then determine whether the name of the oxyanion ends in *-ate* or *-ite*. Since the oxyanion is perchlor*ate*, it ends in *-ate*. Finally, name the acid as the base name of the oxyanion, *perchlor*, with the ending *-ic*, followed by the word *acid*.	 Perchloric acid
(c) CoF_2 Begin by determining whether the compound is ionic, molecular, or an acid. Since CoF_2 contains a metal and a nonmetal, it is ionic. Next refer to Table 3.2 to determine whether the metal forms one type of ion or more than one type. Since Co is not listed in Table 3.2, it must form more than one type of ion. Name the compound as the name of the cation, *cobalt*, followed by the charge of the cation in parentheses *(II)*, and the base name of the anion, *fluor*, with the ending *-ide*.	 Cobalt(II) fluoride

FOR PRACTICE 3.11

Use the flow chart in Figure 3.10 to name $H_2SO_3(aq)$.

3.8 Formula Mass and the Mole Concept for Compounds

In Chapter 2, we defined the average mass of an atom of an element as its *atomic mass*. Similarly, we now define the average mass of a molecule (or a formula unit) of a compound as its **formula mass**. (The terms *molecular mass* or *molecular weight* are synonymous with formula mass and are also common.) For any compound, the formula mass is the sum of the atomic masses of all the atoms in its chemical formula.

$$\text{Formula mass} = \left(\begin{array}{c} \text{Number of atoms} \\ \text{of 1st element in} \\ \text{chemical formula} \end{array} \times \begin{array}{c} \text{Atomic mass} \\ \text{of} \\ \text{1st element} \end{array} \right) + \left(\begin{array}{c} \text{Number of atoms} \\ \text{of 2nd element in} \\ \text{chemical formula} \end{array} \times \begin{array}{c} \text{Atomic mass} \\ \text{of} \\ \text{2nd element} \end{array} \right) + \ldots$$

For example, the formula mass of carbon dioxide, CO_2, is

Multiply by 2 because formula has two oxygen atoms.

$$\begin{aligned} \text{Formula mass} &= 12.01 \text{ amu } + 2(16.00 \text{ amu}) \\ &= 44.01 \text{ amu} \end{aligned}$$

and that of sodium oxide, Na_2O, is

Multiply by 2 because formula has two sodium atoms.

$$\begin{aligned} \text{Formula mass} &= 2(22.99 \text{ amu}) + 16.00 \text{ amu} \\ &= 61.98 \text{ amu} \end{aligned}$$

EXAMPLE 3.12 Calculating Formula Mass

Calculate the formula mass of glucose, $C_6H_{12}O_6$.

SOLUTION

To find the formula mass, add the atomic masses of each atom in the chemical formula:

$$\begin{aligned} \text{Formula mass} &= 6 \times (\text{atomic mass C}) + 12 \times (\text{atomic mass H}) + 6 \times (\text{atomic mass O}) \\ &= 6(12.01 \text{ amu}) \qquad + 12(1.008 \text{ amu}) \qquad + 6(16.00 \text{ amu}) \\ &= 180.16 \text{ amu} \end{aligned}$$

FOR PRACTICE 3.12

Calculate the formula mass of calcium nitrate.

Molar Mass of a Compound

In Chapter 2 (Section 2.9), we saw that an element's molar mass—the mass in grams of one mole of its atoms—is numerically equivalent to its atomic mass. We then used the molar mass in combination with Avogadro's number to determine the number of atoms in a given mass of the element. The same concept applies to compounds. The *molar mass of a compound*—the mass in grams of 1 mol of its molecules or formula units—is numerically equivalent to its formula mass. For example, we just calculated the formula mass of CO_2 to be 44.01 amu. The molar mass is, therefore:

$$CO_2 \text{ molar mass} = 44.01 \text{ g/mol}$$

> Remember, ionic compounds do not contain individual molecules. In casual language, the smallest electrically neutral collection of ions is sometimes called a molecule but is more correctly called a formula unit.

Using Molar Mass to Count Molecules by Weighing

The molar mass of CO_2 is a conversion factor between mass (in grams) and amount (in moles) of CO_2. Suppose we want to find the number of CO_2 molecules in a sample of dry ice (solid CO_2) with a mass of 10.8 g. This calculation is analogous to Example 2.8, where we found the number of atoms in a sample of copper of a given mass. We begin with the mass of 10.8 g and use the molar mass to convert to the amount in moles. Then we use Avogadro's number to convert to number of molecules. The conceptual plan is as follows:

Conceptual Plan

$$\boxed{\text{g } CO_2} \longrightarrow \boxed{\text{mol } CO_2} \longrightarrow \boxed{CO_2 \text{ molecules}}$$

$$\frac{1 \text{ mol } CO_2}{44.01 \text{ g } CO_2} \qquad \frac{6.022 \times 10^{23} \text{ } CO_2 \text{ molecules}}{1 \text{ mol } CO_2}$$

To solve the problem, we follow the conceptual plan, beginning with 10.8 g CO_2, converting to moles, and then to molecules.

Solution

$$10.8 \text{ g } \cancel{CO_2} \times \frac{1 \text{ mol } \cancel{CO_2}}{44.01 \text{ g } \cancel{CO_2}} \times \frac{6.022 \times 10^{23} \text{ } CO_2 \text{ molecules}}{1 \text{ mol } \cancel{CO_2}} = 1.48 \times 10^{23} \text{ } CO_2 \text{ molecules}$$

EXAMPLE 3.13 The Mole Concept—Converting between Mass and Number of Molecules

An aspirin tablet contains 325 mg of acetylsalicylic acid ($C_9H_8O_4$). How many acetylsalicylic acid molecules does it contain?

SORT You are given the mass of acetylsalicylic acid and asked to find the number of molecules.	**GIVEN:** 325 mg $C_9H_8O_4$ **FIND:** number of $C_9H_8O_4$ molecules
STRATEGIZE First convert to moles (using the molar mass of the compound) and then to number of molecules (using Avogadro's number). You will need both the molar mass of acetylsalicylic acid and Avogadro's number as conversion factors. You will also need the conversion factor between g and mg.	**CONCEPTUAL PLAN** **RELATIONSHIPS USED** $C_9H_8O_4$ molar mass = 9(12.01) + 8(1.008) + 4(16.00) = 180.15 g/mol 6.022×10^{23} = 1 mol 1 mg = 10^{-3} g
SOLVE Follow the conceptual plan to solve the problem.	**SOLUTION** $325 \text{ mg } \cancel{C_9H_8O_4} \times \dfrac{10^{-3} \cancel{g}}{1 \cancel{mg}} \times \dfrac{1 \text{ mol } \cancel{C_9H_8O_4}}{180.15 \cancel{g} \cancel{C_9H_8O_4}} \times$ $\dfrac{6.022 \times 10^{23} \text{ } C_9H_8O_4 \text{ molecules}}{1 \text{ mol } \cancel{C_9H_8O_4}} = 1.09 \times 10^{21} \text{ } C_9H_8O_4 \text{ molecules}$

CHECK The units of the answer, $C_9H_8O_4$ molecules, are correct. The magnitude is smaller than Avogadro's number, as expected, since you have less than 1 molar mass of acetylsalicylic acid.

FOR PRACTICE 3.13

Find the number of ibuprofen molecules in a tablet containing 200.0 mg of ibuprofen ($C_{13}H_{18}O_2$).

FOR MORE PRACTICE 3.13

What is the mass of a sample of water containing 3.55×10^{22} H_2O molecules?

Conceptual **Connection 3.6   Molecular Models and the Size of Molecules**

Throughout this book, we use space-filling molecular models to represent molecules. Which number is the best estimate for the scaling factor used in these models? In other words, by approximately what number would you have to multiply the radius of an actual oxygen atom to get the radius of the sphere used to represent the oxygen atom in the water molecule shown at right.

(a) 10   **(b)** 10^4 **(c)** 10^8 **(d)** 10^{16}

3.9 Composition of Compounds

A chemical formula, in combination with the molar masses of its constituent elements, indicates the relative quantities of each element in a compound, which is extremely useful information. For example, about 30 years ago, scientists began to suspect that synthetic compounds known as chlorofluorocarbons (or CFCs) were destroying ozone (O_3) in Earth's upper atmosphere. Upper atmospheric ozone is important because it acts as a shield, protecting life on Earth from the sun's harmful ultraviolet light.

CFCs are chemically inert compounds that were used primarily as refrigerants and industrial solvents. Over time, CFCs accumulated in the atmosphere. In the upper atmosphere, sunlight breaks bonds within CFCs, releasing chlorine atoms. The chlorine atoms then react with ozone, converting it into O_2. So the harmful part of CFCs is the chlorine atoms that they carry. How can we determine the mass of chlorine in a given mass of a CFC?

▲ The chlorine in chlorofluorocarbons caused the ozone hole over Antarctica. The dark blue color indicates depressed ozone levels.

One way to express how much of an element is in a given compound is to use the element's mass percent composition for that compound. The **mass percent composition** or **mass percent** of an element is that element's percentage of the compound's total mass. We can calculate the mass percent of element X in a compound from the chemical formula as follows:

$$\text{Mass percent of element X} = \frac{\text{mass of element X in 1 mol of compound}}{\text{mass of 1 mol of the compound}} \times 100\%$$

Suppose, for example, that we want to calculate the mass percent composition of Cl in the chlorofluorocarbon CCl_2F_2. The mass percent Cl is given by:

CCl_2F_2 ● ●

$$\text{Mass percent Cl} = \frac{2 \times \text{molar mass Cl}}{\text{molar mass } CCl_2F_2} \times 100\%$$

We multiply the molar mass of Cl by 2 because the chemical formula has a subscript of 2 for Cl, indicating that 1 mol of CCl_2F_2 contains 2 mol of Cl atoms. We calculate the molar mass of CCl_2F_2 as follows:

$$\text{Molar mass} = 12.01 \text{ g/mol} + 2(35.45 \text{ g/mol}) + 2(19.00 \text{ g/mol})$$

$$= 120.91 \text{ g/mol}$$

So the mass percent of Cl in CCl_2F_2 is:

$$\text{Mass percent Cl} = \frac{2 \times \text{molar mass Cl}}{\text{molar mass } CCl_2F_2} \times 100\%$$

$$= \frac{2 \times 35.45 \text{ g/mol}}{120.91 \text{ g/mol}} \times 100\%$$

$$= 58.64\%$$

EXAMPLE 3.14 Mass Percent Composition

Calculate the mass percent of Cl in Freon-112 ($C_2Cl_4F_2$), a CFC refrigerant.

SORT You are given the molecular formula of Freon-112 and asked to find the mass percent of Cl.	**GIVEN:** $C_2Cl_4F_2$ **FIND:** mass percent Cl
STRATEGIZE The molecular formula tells you that there are 4 mol of Cl in each mole of Freon-112. Find the mass percent composition from the chemical formula by using the equation that defines mass percent. The conceptual plan shows you how to use the mass of Cl in 1 mol of $C_2Cl_4F_2$ and the molar mass of $C_2Cl_4F_2$ to find the mass percent of Cl.	**CONCEPTUAL PLAN** $$\text{Mass \% Cl} = \frac{4 \times \text{molar mass Cl}}{\text{molar mass } C_2Cl_4F_2} \times 100\%$$ **RELATIONSHIPS USED** $$\text{Mass percent of element X} = \frac{\text{mass of element X in 1 mol of compound}}{\text{mass of 1 mol of compound}} \times 100\%$$
SOLVE Calculate the necessary parts of the equation and substitute the values into the equation to find mass percent Cl.	**SOLUTION** $4 \times$ molar mass Cl $= 4(35.45 \text{ g/mol}) = 141.8 \text{ g/mol}$ Molar mass $C_2Cl_4F_2 = 2(12.01 \text{ g/mol}) + 4(35.45 \text{ g/mol}) + 2(19.00 \text{ g/mol})$ $\quad\quad = 24.02 \text{ g/mol} + 141.8 \text{ g/mol} + 38.00 \text{ g/mol} = 203.8 \text{ g/mol}$ $$\text{Mass \% Cl} = \frac{4 \times \text{molar mass Cl}}{\text{molar mass } C_2Cl_4F_2} \times 100\%$$ $$= \frac{141.8 \text{ g/mol}}{203.8 \text{ g/mol}} \times 100\%$$ $$= 69.58\%$$

CHECK The units of the answer (%) are correct, and the magnitude is reasonable because (a) it is between 0 and 100% and (b) chlorine is the heaviest atom in the molecule and there are four atoms of it.

FOR PRACTICE 3.14

Acetic acid ($C_2H_4O_2$) is the active ingredient in vinegar. Calculate the mass percent composition of oxygen in acetic acid.

FOR MORE PRACTICE 3.14

Calculate the mass percent composition of sodium in sodium oxide.

Conceptual Connection 3.7 Chemical Formula and Mass Percent Composition

Without doing any calculations, list the elements in C_6H_6O in order of decreasing mass percent composition.

Mass Percent Composition as a Conversion Factor

The mass percent composition of an element in a compound is a conversion factor between mass of the element and mass of the compound. For example, we saw that the mass percent composition of Cl in CCl_2F_2 is 58.64%. Since percent means *per hundred*, there are 58.64 g Cl *per hundred* grams CCl_2F_2, which can be expressed as the ratio:

$$58.64 \text{ g Cl} : 100 \text{ g } CCl_2F_2$$

or, in fractional form:

$$\frac{58.64 \text{ g Cl}}{100 \text{ g } CCl_2F_2} \quad \text{or} \quad \frac{100 \text{ g } CCl_2F_2}{58.64 \text{ g Cl}}$$

These ratios can function as conversion factors between grams of Cl and grams of CCl_2F_2. For example, to calculate the mass of Cl in 1.00 kg CCl_2F_2, we use the following conceptual plan:

Conceptual Plan

$$\boxed{\text{kg } CCl_2F_2} \longrightarrow \boxed{\text{g } CCl_2F_2} \longrightarrow \boxed{\text{g Cl}}$$

$$\frac{1000 \text{ g}}{1 \text{ kg}} \qquad \frac{58.64 \text{ g Cl}}{100 \text{ g } CCl_2F_2}$$

Notice that the mass percent composition acts as a conversion factor between grams of the compound and grams of the constituent element. To calculate grams Cl, we follow the conceptual plan.

Solution

$$1.00 \text{ kg } CCl_2F_2 \times \frac{1000 \text{ g}}{1 \text{ kg}} \times \frac{58.64 \text{ g Cl}}{100 \text{ g } CCl_2F_2} = 5.86 \times 10^2 \text{ g Cl}$$

EXAMPLE 3.15 Using Mass Percent Composition as a Conversion Factor

The U.S. Food and Drug Administration (FDA) recommends that a person consume less than 2.4 g of sodium per day. What mass of sodium chloride (in grams) can you consume and still be within the FDA guidelines? Sodium chloride is 39% sodium by mass.

SORT You are given a mass of sodium and the mass percent of sodium in sodium chloride. You are asked to find the mass of NaCl that contains the given mass of sodium.	**GIVEN:** 2.4 g Na **FIND:** g NaCl
STRATEGIZE Convert between mass of a constituent element and mass of a compound by using mass percent composition as a conversion factor.	**CONCEPTUAL PLAN** $\boxed{\text{g Na}} \longrightarrow \boxed{\text{g NaCl}}$ $\frac{100 \text{ g NaCl}}{39 \text{ g Na}}$ **RELATIONSHIPS USED** 39 g Na: 100 g NaCl
SOLVE Follow the conceptual plan to solve the problem.	**SOLUTION** $2.4 \text{ g Na} \times \dfrac{100 \text{ g NaCl}}{39 \text{ g Na}} = 6.2 \text{ g NaCl}$ You can consume 6.2 g NaCl and still be within the FDA guidelines.

CHECK The units of the answer are correct. The magnitude seems reasonable because it is larger than the amount of sodium, as expected, because sodium is only one of the elements in NaCl.

FOR PRACTICE 3.15

What mass (in grams) of iron(III) oxide contains 58.7 grams of iron? Iron(III) oxide is 69.94% iron by mass.

FOR MORE PRACTICE 3.15

If someone consumes 22 g of sodium chloride per day, what mass (in grams) of sodium does that person consume? Sodium chloride is 39% sodium by mass.

▲ 12.5 packets of salt contain 6.2 g of NaCl.

Conversion Factors from Chemical Formulas

Mass percent composition is one way to understand how much chlorine is in a particular chlorofluorocarbon or, more generally, how much of a constituent element is present in a given mass of any compound. However, we can also approach this type of problem in a different way. Chemical formulas contain within them inherent relationships between atoms (or moles of atoms) and molecules (or moles of molecules). For example, the formula for CCl_2F_2 tells us that 1 mol of CCl_2F_2 contains 2 mol of Cl atoms. We write the ratio as:

$$1 \text{ mol } CCl_2F_2 : 2 \text{ mol } Cl$$

With ratios such as these—which come from the chemical formula—we can directly determine the amounts of the constituent elements present in a given amount of a compound without having to calculate mass percent composition. For example, we calculate the number of moles of Cl in 38.5 mol of CCl_2F_2 as follows:

Conceptual Plan

Solution

$$38.5 \text{ mol } CCl_2F_2 \times \frac{2 \text{ mol Cl}}{1 \text{ mol } CCl_2F_2} = 77.0 \text{ mol Cl}$$

As we have seen, however, we often want to know, not the *amount in moles* of an element in a certain number of moles of compound, but the *mass in grams* (or other units) of a constituent element in a given *mass* of the compound. Suppose we want to know the mass (in grams) of Cl contained in 25.0 g CCl_2F_2. The relationship inherent in the chemical formula (2 mol Cl : 1 mol CCl_2F_2) applies to the amount in moles, not to mass. Therefore, we first convert the mass of CCl_2F_2 to moles CCl_2F_2. *Then* we use the conversion factor from the chemical formula to convert to moles Cl. Finally, we use the molar mass of Cl to convert to grams Cl.

Conceptual Plan

$$g\ CCl_2F_2 \longrightarrow mol\ CCl_2F_2 \longrightarrow mol\ Cl \longrightarrow g\ Cl$$

$$\frac{1 \text{ mol } CCl_2F_2}{120.91 \text{ g } CCl_2F_2} \qquad \frac{2 \text{ mol Cl}}{1 \text{ mol } CCl_2F_2} \qquad \frac{35.45 \text{ g Cl}}{1 \text{ mol Cl}}$$

Solution

$$25.0 \text{ g } CCl_2F_2 \times \frac{1 \text{ mol } CCl_2F_2}{120.91 \text{ g } CCl_2F_2} \times \frac{2 \text{ mol Cl}}{1 \text{ mol } CCl_2F_2} \times \frac{35.45 \text{ g Cl}}{1 \text{ mol Cl}} = 14.7 \text{ g Cl}$$

Notice that we must convert from g CCl_2F_2 to mol CCl_2F_2 *before* we can use the chemical formula as a conversion factor. *Always remember that the chemical formula gives us a relationship between the amounts (in moles) of substances, not between the masses (in grams) of them.*

The general form for solving problems in which we are asked to find the mass of an element present in a given mass of a compound is

Mass compound → moles compound → moles element → mass element

We use the atomic or molar mass to convert between mass and moles, and we use relationships inherent in the chemical to convert between moles and moles.

EXAMPLE 3.16 Chemical Formulas as Conversion Factors

Hydrogen may potentially be used in the future to replace gasoline as a fuel. Most major automobile companies are developing vehicles that run on hydrogen. These cars are environmentally friendly because their only emission is water vapor. One way to obtain hydrogen for fuel is to use an emission-free energy source such as wind power to form elemental hydrogen from water. What mass of hydrogen (in grams) is contained in 1.00 gallon of water? (The density of water is 1.00 g/mL.)

SORT You are given a volume of water and asked to find the mass of hydrogen it contains. You are also given the density of water.	GIVEN: 1.00 gal H_2O $d_{H_2O} = 1.00$ g/mL FIND: g H
STRATEGIZE The first part of the conceptual plan shows how to convert the units of volume from gallons to liters and then to mL. It also shows how you can then use the density to convert mL to g. The second part of the conceptual plan is the basic sequence of mass → moles → moles → mass. Convert between moles and mass using the appropriate molar masses, and convert from mol H_2O to mol H using the conversion factor derived from the molecular formula.	CONCEPTUAL PLAN RELATIONSHIPS USED 3.785 L = 1 gal (Table 1.3) 1000 mL = 1 L 1.00 g H_2O = 1 mL H_2O (density of H_2O) Molar mass H_2O = 2(1.008) + 16.00 = 18.02 g/mol 2 mol H : 1 mol H_2O 1.008 g H = 1 mol H
SOLVE Follow the conceptual plan to solve the problem.	SOLUTION $1.00 \text{ gal } H_2O \times \dfrac{3.785 \text{ L}}{1 \text{ gal}} \times \dfrac{1000 \text{ mL}}{1 \text{ L}} \times \dfrac{1.0 \text{ g}}{\text{mL}} = 3.785 \times 10^3 \text{ g } H_2O$ $3.785 \times 10^3 \text{ g } H_2O \times \dfrac{1 \text{ mol } H_2O}{18.02 \text{ g } H_2O} \times \dfrac{2 \text{ mol } H}{1 \text{ mol } H_2O}$ $\times \dfrac{1.008 \text{ g } H}{1 \text{ mol } H} = 4.23 \times 10^2 \text{ g } H$

CHECK The units of the answer (g H) are correct. Since a gallon of water is about 3.8 L, its mass is about 3.8 kg. H is a light atom, so its mass should be significantly less than 3.8 kg, as it is in the answer.

FOR PRACTICE 3.16
Determine the mass of oxygen in a 7.2 g sample of $Al_2(SO_4)_3$.

FOR MORE PRACTICE 3.16
Butane (C_4H_{10}) is the liquid fuel in lighters. How many grams of carbon are present within a lighter containing 7.25 mL of butane? (The density of liquid butane is 0.601 g/mL.)

Conceptual Connection 3.8 Chemical Formulas and Elemental Composition

The molecular formula for water is H_2O. Which ratio can be correctly derived from this formula? Explain.

(a) 2 g H : 1 g H_2O **(b)** 2 mL H : 1 mL H_2O **(c)** 2 mol H : 1 mol H_2O

Chemistry and Medicine

Methylmercury in Fish

In the last decade, the U.S. Environmental Protection Agency (EPA) has grown increasingly concerned about mercury levels in fish. Mercury—which is present in fish as methylmercury—affects the central nervous system of humans who eat the fish, especially in children and developing fetuses. In a developing fetus, excessive mercury exposure can result in slowed mental development and even retardation. Some lakes now have warnings about eating too much fish caught in the lake.

Recent regulations force many fish vendors to alert customers about the dangers of eating too much of certain kinds of commercial fish, including shark, tuna, and mackerel. These fish tend to contain high levels of methylmercury and therefore should be eaten in moderation, especially by children and pregnant women. The U.S. Food and Drug Administration (FDA) action level—the level below which the FDA claims the food has no adverse health effects—for methylmercury in fish is 1.0 ppm or 1.0 g of methylmercury per million grams of fish. However, a number of environmental advocacy groups, including the EPA, have suggested that, while this level may be safe for adults, it is too high for children and pregnant women. Consequently, the FDA suggests that pregnant women limit their intake of fish to 12 ounces per week.

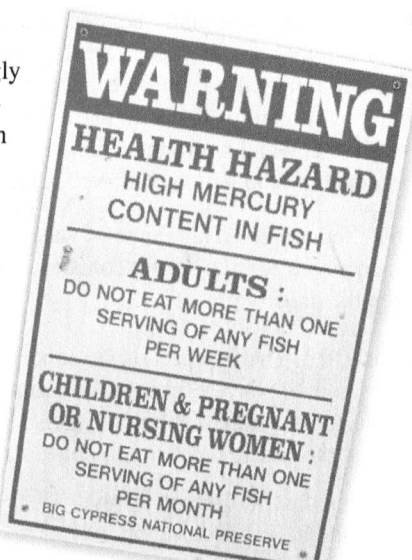

▲ Lakes containing mercury—either from natural sources or from pollution—often have posted limits for the number of fish from the lake that can be eaten safely.

Question

The levels of methylmercury in fish are normally tested by laboratory techniques that measure only the mercury (Hg). Suppose a lab analyzes a 14.5 g sample of fish and finds that it contains 1.03×10^{-5} g of mercury. How much methylmercury ($HgCH_3Cl$) is in the fish in parts per million (ppm)? Is this above the FDA action level?

3.10 Determining a Chemical Formula from Experimental Data

In Section 3.8, we calculated mass percent composition from a chemical formula. Can we also do the reverse? Can we calculate a chemical formula from mass percent composition? This question is important because many laboratory analyses of compounds give the relative masses of each element present in the compound. For example, if we decompose water into hydrogen and oxygen in the laboratory, we can measure the masses of hydrogen and oxygen produced. Can we get a chemical formula from this kind of data? The answer is a qualified yes. We can determine a chemical formula, but it is an empirical formula (not a molecular formula). To get a molecular formula, we need additional information, such as the molar mass of the compound.

Suppose we decompose a sample of water in the laboratory and find that it produces 0.857 g of hydrogen and 6.86 g of oxygen. How do we determine an empirical formula from these data? We know that an empirical formula represents a ratio of atoms or a ratio of moles of atoms, *not a ratio of masses*. So the first thing we must do is convert our data from mass (in grams) to amount (in moles). How many moles of each element are present in the sample? To convert to moles, we divide each mass by the molar mass of that element:

$$\text{Moles H} = 0.857 \text{ g H} \times \frac{1 \text{ mol H}}{1.01 \text{ g H}} = 0.849 \text{ mol H}$$

$$\text{Moles O} = 6.86 \text{ g O} \times \frac{1 \text{ mol O}}{16.00 \text{ g O}} = 0.429 \text{ mol O}$$

From these data, we know there are 0.849 mol H for every 0.429 mol O. We can now write a pseudoformula for water:

$$H_{0.849}O_{0.429}$$

To get the smallest whole-number subscripts in our formula, we divide all the subscripts by the smallest one, in this case 0.429:

$$H_{\frac{0.849}{0.429}}O_{\frac{0.429}{0.429}} = H_{1.98}O = H_2O$$

Our empirical formula for water, which also happens to be the molecular formula, is H_2O. You can use the procedure shown below to obtain the empirical formula of any compound from experimental data giving the relative masses of the constituent elements. The left column outlines the procedure, and the center and right columns contain two examples of how to apply the procedure.

PROCEDURE FOR...	EXAMPLE 3.17	EXAMPLE 3.18
Obtaining an Empirical Formula from Experimental Data	**Obtaining an Empirical Formula from Experimental Data**	**Obtaining an Empirical Formula from Experimental Data**
	A compound containing nitrogen and oxygen is decomposed in the laboratory and produces 24.5 g nitrogen and 70.0 g oxygen. Calculate the empirical formula of the compound.	A laboratory analysis of aspirin determined the following mass percent composition: C 60.00% H 4.48% O 35.52% Find the empirical formula.
1. Write down (or calculate) as *given* the masses of each element present in a sample of the compound. If you are given mass percent composition, assume a 100 g sample and calculate the masses of each element from the given percentages.	**GIVEN:** 24.5 g N, 70.0 g O **FIND:** empirical formula	**GIVEN:** In a 100 g sample: 60.00 g C, 4.48 g H, 35.52 g O **FIND:** empirical formula
2. Convert each of the masses in step 1 to moles by using the appropriate molar mass for each element as a conversion factor.	$24.5 \text{ g N} \times \dfrac{1 \text{ mol N}}{14.01 \text{ g N}} = 1.75 \text{ mol N}$ $70.0 \text{ g O} \times \dfrac{1 \text{ mol O}}{16.00 \text{ g O}} = 4.38 \text{ mol O}$	$60.00 \text{ g C} \times \dfrac{1 \text{ mol C}}{12.01 \text{ g C}} = 4.996 \text{ mol C}$ $4.48 \text{ g H} \times \dfrac{1 \text{ mol H}}{1.008 \text{ g H}} = 4.44 \text{ mol H}$ $35.52 \text{ g O} \times \dfrac{1 \text{ mol O}}{16.00 \text{ g O}} = 2.220 \text{ mol O}$
3. Write down a pseudoformula for the compound using the number of moles of each element (from step 2) as subscripts.	$N_{1.75}O_{4.38}$	$C_{4.996}H_{4.44}O_{2.220}$
4. Divide all the subscripts in the formula by the smallest subscript.	$N_{\frac{1.75}{1.75}}O_{\frac{4.38}{1.75}} \longrightarrow N_1O_{2.5}$	$C_{\frac{4.996}{2.220}}H_{\frac{4.44}{2.220}}O_{\frac{2.220}{2.220}} \longrightarrow C_{2.25}H_2O_1$
5. If the subscripts are not whole numbers, multiply all the subscripts by a small whole number (see table) to get whole-number subscripts.	$N_1O_{2.5} \times 2 \longrightarrow N_2O_5$ The correct empirical formula is N_2O_5.	$C_{2.25}H_2O_1 \times 4 \longrightarrow C_9H_8O_4$ The correct empirical formula is $C_9H_8O_4$.

Fractional Subscript	Multiply by This
0.20	5
0.25	4
0.33	3
0.40	5
0.50	2
0.66	3
0.75	4
0.80	5

FOR PRACTICE 3.17

A sample of a compound is decomposed in the laboratory and produces 165 g carbon, 27.8 g hydrogen, and 220.2 g oxygen. Calculate the empirical formula of the compound.

FOR PRACTICE 3.18

Ibuprofen has the following mass percent composition:
    C 75.69%, H 8.80%, O 15.51%.
What is the empirical formula of ibuprofen?

Calculating Molecular Formulas for Compounds

We can find the molecular formula of a compound from the empirical formula if we also know the molar mass of the compound. Recall from Section 3.3 that the molecular formula is always a whole-number multiple of the empirical formula:

$$\text{Molecular formula} = \text{empirical formula} \times n, \text{ where } n = 1, 2, 3,...$$

Suppose we want to find the molecular formula for fructose (a sugar found in fruit) from its empirical formula, CH_2O, and its molar mass, 180.2 g/mol. We know that the molecular formula is a whole-number multiple of CH_2O:

$$\text{Molecular formula} = (CH_2O) \times n$$
$$= C_nH_{2n}O_n$$

We also know that the molar mass is a whole-number multiple of the **empirical formula molar mass**, the sum of the masses of all the atoms in the empirical formula.

$$\text{Molar mass} = \text{empirical formula molar mass} \times n$$

For a particular compound, the value of n in both cases is the same. Therefore, we can find n by calculating the ratio of the molar mass to the empirical formula molar mass:

$$n = \frac{\text{molar mass}}{\text{empirical formula molar mass}}$$

For fructose, the empirical formula molar mass is:

Empirical formula molar mass

$$= 12.01 \text{ g/mol} + 2(1.01 \text{ g/mol}) + 16.00 \text{ g/mol} = 30.03 \text{ g/mol}$$

Therefore, n is

$$n = \frac{180.2 \text{ g/mol}}{30.03 \text{ g/mol}} = 6$$

We can then use this value of n to find the molecular formula:

$$\text{Molecular formula} = (CH_2O) \times 6 = C_6H_{12}O_6$$

EXAMPLE 3.19 Calculating a Molecular Formula from an Empirical Formula and Molar Mass

Butanedione—a main component responsible for the smell and taste of butter and cheese—contains the elements carbon, hydrogen, and oxygen. The empirical formula of butanedione is C_2H_3O, and its molar mass is 86.09 g/mol. Find its molecular formula.

SORT You are given the empirical formula and molar mass of butanedione and asked to find the molecular formula.	**GIVEN:** Empirical formula = C_2H_3O molar mass = 86.09 g/mol **FIND:** molecular formula
STRATEGIZE A molecular formula is always a whole-number multiple of the empirical formula. Divide the molar mass by the empirical formula mass to get the whole number.	Molecular formula = empirical formula $\times n$ $n = \dfrac{\text{molar mass}}{\text{empirical formula mass}}$
SOLVE Calculate the empirical formula mass.	Empirical formula molar mass $= 2(12.01 \text{ g/mol}) + 3(1.008 \text{ g/mol}) + 16.00 \text{ g/mol} = 43.04 \text{ g/mol}$
Divide the molar mass by the empirical formula mass to find n.	$n = \dfrac{\text{molar mass}}{\text{empirical formula mass}} = \dfrac{86.09 \text{ g/mol}}{43.04 \text{ g/mol}} = 2$
Multiply the empirical formula by n to obtain the molecular formula.	Molecular formula = $C_2H_3O \times 2$ $= C_4H_6O_2$

CHECK Check the answer by calculating the molar mass of the formula as follows:

$$4(12.01 \text{ g/mol}) + 6(1.008 \text{ g/mol}) + 2(16.00 \text{ g/mol}) = 86.09 \text{ g/mol}$$

The calculated molar mass is in agreement with the given molar mass.

FOR PRACTICE 3.19

A compound has the empirical formula CH and a molar mass of 78.11 g/mol. What is its molecular formula?

FOR MORE PRACTICE 3.19

A compound with the percent composition shown next has a molar mass of 60.10 g/mol. Determine its molecular formula.

C, 39.97%

H, 13.41%

N, 46.62%

Combustion Analysis

In the previous section, we discussed how to determine the empirical formula of a compound from the relative masses of its constituent elements. Another common (and related) way to obtain empirical formulas for unknown compounds, especially those containing carbon and hydrogen, is **combustion analysis**. In combustion analysis, the unknown compound undergoes combustion (or burning) in the presence of pure oxygen, as shown in Figure 3.12 ▼. When the sample is burned, all of the carbon in the sample is converted to CO_2, and all of the hydrogen is converted to H_2O. The CO_2 and H_2O produced are weighed. With these masses, we can use the numerical relationships between moles inherent in the formulas for CO_2 and H_2O (1 mol CO_2 : 1 mol C and 1 mol H_2O : 2 mol H) to determine the amounts of C and H in the original sample. The amounts of any other elemental constituents, such as O, Cl, or N, can be determined by subtracting the sum of the masses of C and H from the original mass of the sample. Examples 20 and 21 show how to perform these calculations for a sample containing only C and H and for a sample containing C, H, and O.

Combustion is a type of *chemical reaction.* We discuss chemical reactions and their representation in Section 3.11.

Combustion Analysis

Unknown compound is burned in oxygen.

Water and carbon dioxide produced are isolated and weighed.

Oxygen

Furnace with sample

Other substances not absorbed

H_2O absorber

CO_2 absorber

▲ **FIGURE 3.12 Combustion Analysis Apparatus** The sample to be analyzed is placed in a furnace and burned in oxygen. The water and carbon dioxide produced are absorbed into separate containers and weighed.

PROCEDURE FOR... Obtaining an Empirical Formula from Combustion Analysis	EXAMPLE 3.20 Determining an Empirical Formula from Combustion Analysis	EXAMPLE 3.21 Determining an Empirical Formula from Combustion Analysis
	Upon combustion, a compound containing only carbon and hydrogen produces 1.83 g CO_2 and 0.901 g H_2O. Find the empirical formula of the compound.	Upon combustion, a 0.8233 g sample of a compound containing only carbon, hydrogen, and oxygen produces 2.445 g CO_2 and 0.6003 g H_2O. Find the empirical formula of the compound.
1. Write down as *given* the masses of each combustion product and the mass of the sample (if given).	**GIVEN:** 1.83 g CO_2, 0.901 g H_2O **FIND:** empirical formula	**GIVEN:** 0.8233g sample, 2.445 g CO_2, 0.6003 g H_2O **FIND:** empirical formula
2. Convert the masses of CO_2 and H_2O from step 1 to moles by using the appropriate molar mass for each compound as a conversion factor.	$1.83 \text{ g } CO_2 \times \dfrac{1 \text{ mol } CO_2}{44.01 \text{ g } CO_2}$ $= 0.0416 \text{ mol } CO_2$ $0.901 \text{ g } H_2O \times \dfrac{1 \text{ mol } H_2O}{18.02 \text{ g } H_2O}$ $= 0.0500 \text{ mol } H_2O$	$2.445 \text{ g } CO_2 \times \dfrac{1 \text{ mol } CO_2}{44.01 \text{ g } CO_2}$ $= 0.05556 \text{ mol } CO_2$ $0.6003 \text{ g } H_2O \times \dfrac{1 \text{ mol } H_2O}{18.01 \text{ g } H_2O}$ $= 0.03331 \text{ mol } H_2O$
3. Convert the moles of CO_2 and moles of H_2O from step 2 to moles of C and moles of H using the conversion factors inherent in the chemical formulas of CO_2 and H_2O.	$0.0416 \text{ mol } CO_2 \times \dfrac{1 \text{ mol C}}{1 \text{ mol } CO_2}$ $= 0.0416 \text{ mol C}$ $0.0500 \text{ mol } H_2O \times \dfrac{2 \text{ mol H}}{1 \text{ mol } H_2O}$ $= 0.100 \text{ mol H}$	$0.05556 \text{ mol } CO_2 \times \dfrac{1 \text{ mol C}}{1 \text{ mol } CO_2}$ $= 0.05556 \text{ mol C}$ $0.03331 \text{ mol } H_2O \times \dfrac{2 \text{ mol H}}{1 \text{ mol } H_2O}$ $= 0.06662 \text{ mol H}$
4. If the compound contains an element other than C and H, find the mass of the other element by subtracting the sum of the masses of C and H (obtained in step 3) from the mass of the sample. Finally, convert the mass of the other element to moles.	The sample contains no elements other than C and H, so proceed to the next step.	$\text{Mass C} = 0.05556 \text{ mol C} \times \dfrac{12.01 \text{ g C}}{\text{mol C}}$ $= 0.6673 \text{ g C}$ $\text{Mass H} = 0.06662 \text{ mol H} \times \dfrac{1.008 \text{ g H}}{\text{mol H}}$ $= 0.06715 \text{ g H}$ $\text{Mass O} = 0.8233 \text{ g}$ $\quad\quad -(0.6673 \text{ g} + 0.06715 \text{ g})$ $= 0.0889 \text{ g}$ $\text{Mol O} = 0.0889 \text{ g O} \times \dfrac{\text{mol O}}{16.00 \text{ g O}}$ $= 0.00556 \text{ mol O}$
5. Write down a pseudoformula for the compound using the number of moles of each element (from steps 3 and 4) as subscripts.	$C_{0.0416}H_{0.100}$	$C_{0.05556}H_{0.06662}O_{0.00556}$
6. Divide all the subscripts in the formula by the smallest subscript. (Round all subscripts that are within 0.1 of a whole number.)	$C_{\frac{0.0416}{0.0416}}H_{\frac{0.100}{0.0416}} \longrightarrow C_1H_{2.4}$	$C_{\frac{0.05556}{0.00556}}H_{\frac{0.06662}{0.00556}}O_{\frac{0.00556}{0.00556}} \longrightarrow C_{10}H_{12}O_1$

7. If the subscripts are not whole numbers, multiply all the subscripts by a small whole number to get whole-number subscripts.	$C_1H_{2.4} \times 5 \longrightarrow C_5H_{12}$ The correct empirical formula is C_5H_{12}.	The subscripts are whole numbers; no additional multiplication is needed. The correct empirical formula is $C_{10}H_{12}O$.
	FOR PRACTICE 3.20 Upon combustion, a compound containing only carbon and hydrogen produced 1.60 g CO_2 and 0.819 g H_2O. Find the empirical formula of the compound.	**FOR PRACTICE 3.21** Upon combustion, a 0.8009 g sample of a compound containing only carbon, hydrogen, and oxygen produced 1.6004 g CO_2 and 0.6551 g H_2O. Find the empirical formula of the compound.

3.11 Writing and Balancing Chemical Equations

Combustion analysis (which we just examined in Section 3.10) employs a **chemical reaction**, a process in which one or more substances are converted into one or more different ones. Compounds form and change through chemical reactions. As we have seen, water can be made by the reaction of hydrogen with oxygen. A **combustion reaction** is a particular type of chemical reaction in which a substance combines with oxygen to form one or more oxygen-containing compounds. Combustion reactions also emit heat. The heat produced in a number of combustion reactions is critical to supplying our society's energy needs. For example, the heat from the combustion of gasoline expands the gaseous combustion products in a car engine's cylinders, which push the pistons and propel the car. We use the heat released by the combustion of *natural gas* to cook food and to heat our homes.

We represent a chemical reaction with a **chemical equation**. For example, we represent the combustion of natural gas with the equation

$$CH_4 + O_2 \longrightarrow CO_2 + H_2O$$
reactants   products

The substances on the left side of the equation are the **reactants** and the substances on the right side are the **products**. We often specify the states of each reactant or product in parentheses next to the formula as follows:

$$CH_4(g) + O_2(g) \longrightarrow CO_2(g) + H_2O(g)$$

The (*g*) indicates that these substances are gases in the reaction. Table 3.6 summarizes the common states of reactants and products and their symbols used in chemical equations.

The equation just presented for the combustion of natural gas is not complete, however. If you look closely, you should immediately spot a problem.

$$CH_4(g) + O_2(g) \longrightarrow CO_2(g) + H_2O(g)$$

2 O atoms   2 O atoms + 1 O atom =
3 O atoms

The left side of the equation has two oxygen atoms while the right side has three. The reaction as written, therefore, violates the law of conservation of mass because an oxygen atom formed out of nothing. Notice also that the left side has four hydrogen atoms while the right side has only two.

$$CH_4(g) + O_2(g) \longrightarrow CO_2(g) + H_2O(g)$$

4 H atoms   2 H atoms

Two hydrogen atoms have vanished, again violating mass conservation. To correct these problems—that is, to write an equation that more closely represents *what actually happens*—we must **balance** the equation. We need to change the coefficients (the numbers *in front of* the chemical formulas), not the subscripts (the numbers within the

TABLE 3.6 States of Reactants and Products in Chemical Equations

Abbreviation	State
(*g*)	Gas
(*l*)	Liquid
(*s*)	Solid
(*aq*)	Aqueous (water solution)

The reason that you cannot change the subscripts when balancing a chemical equation is that changing the subscripts changes the substance itself, while changing the coefficients changes the number of molecules of the substance. For example, 2 H_2O is simply two water molecules, but H_2O_2 is hydrogen peroxide, a drastically different compound.

chemical formulas), to ensure that the number of each type of atom on the left side of the equation is equal to the number on the right side. New atoms do not form during a reaction, nor do atoms vanish—matter must be conserved.

When we add coefficients to the reactants and products to balance an equation, we change the number of molecules in the equation but not the *kind of* molecules. To balance the equation for the combustion of methane, we put the coefficient 2 before O_2 in the reactants, and the coefficient 2 before H_2O in the products.

$$CH_4(g) + 2\,O_2(g) \longrightarrow CO_2(g) + 2\,H_2O(g)$$

The equation is now balanced because the numbers of each type of atom on either side of the equation are equal. The balanced equation tells us that one CH_4 molecule reacts with two O_2 molecules to form one CO_2 molecule and two H_2O molecules. We verify that the equation is balanced by summing the number of each type of atom on each side of the equation.

$$CH_4(g) + 2\,O_2(g) \rightarrow CO_2(g) + 2\,H_2O(g)$$

Reactants	Products
1 C atom (1 × CH_4)	1 C atom (1 × CO_2)
4 H atoms (1 × CH_4)	4 H atoms (2 × H_2O)
4 O atoms (2 × O_2)	4 O atoms (1 × CO_2 + 2 × H_2O)

The number of each type of atom on both sides of the equation is now equal—the equation is balanced.

How to Write Balanced Chemical Equations

We can balance many chemical equations simply by trial and error. However, some guidelines are useful. For example, balancing the atoms in the most complex substances first and the atoms in the simplest substances (such as pure elements) last often makes the process shorter. The following illustrations of how to balance chemical equations are presented in a two- or three-column format. The general guidelines are shown on the left, with examples of how to apply them on the right. This procedure is meant only as a flexible guide, not a rigid set of steps.

PROCEDURE FOR... **Balancing Chemical Equations**	EXAMPLE 3.22 **Balancing Chemical Equations**	EXAMPLE 3.23 **Balancing Chemical Equations**
	Write a balanced equation for the reaction between solid cobalt(III) oxide and solid carbon to produce solid cobalt and carbon dioxide gas.	Write a balanced equation for the combustion of gaseous butane (C_4H_{10}), a fuel used in portable stoves and grills, in which it combines with gaseous oxygen to form gaseous carbon dioxide and gaseous water.
1. Write a skeletal equation by writing chemical formulas for each of the reactants and products. Review Sections 3.5 and 3.6 for nomenclature rules. (If a skeletal equation is provided, go to step 2.)	$Co_2O_3(s) + C(s) \longrightarrow$ $Co(s) + CO_2(g)$	$C_4H_{10}(g) + O_2(g) \longrightarrow$ $CO_2(g) + H_2O(g)$

2. Balance atoms that occur in more complex substances first. Always balance atoms in compounds before atoms in pure elements.	**Begin with O:** $Co_2O_3(s) + C(s) \longrightarrow Co(s) + CO_2(g)$ 3 O atoms → 2 O atoms To balance O, put a 2 before $Co_2O_3(s)$ and a 3 before $CO_2(g)$. $2\,Co_2O_3(s) + C(s) \longrightarrow Co(s) + 3\,CO_2(g)$ 6 O atoms → 6 O atoms	**Begin with C:** $C_4H_{10}(g) + O_2(g) \longrightarrow CO_2(g) + H_2O(g)$ 4 C atoms → 1 C atom To balance C, put a 4 before $CO_2(g)$. $C_4H_{10}(g) + O_2(g) \longrightarrow 4\,CO_2(g) + H_2O(g)$ 4 C atoms → 4 C atoms **Balance H:** $C_4H_{10}(g) + O_2(g) \longrightarrow 4\,CO_2(g) + H_2O(g)$ 10 H atoms → 2 H atoms To balance H, put a 5 before $H_2O(g)$: $C_4H_{10}(g) + O_2(g) \longrightarrow 4\,CO_2(g) + 5\,H_2O(g)$ 10 H atoms → 10 H atoms
3. Balance atoms that occur as free elements on either side of the equation last. Always balance free elements by adjusting the coefficient on the free element.	**Balance Co:** $2\,Co_2O_3(s) + C(s) \longrightarrow Co(s) + 3\,CO_2(g)$ 4 Co atoms → 1 Co atom To balance Co, put a 4 before $Co(s)$. $2\,Co_2O_3(s) + C(s) \longrightarrow 4\,Co(s) + 3\,CO_2(g)$ 4 Co atoms → 4 Co atoms **Balance C:** $2\,Co_2O_3(s) + C(s) \longrightarrow 4\,Co(s) + 3\,CO_2(g)$ 1 C atom → 3 C atoms To balance C, put a 3 before $C(s)$. $2\,Co_2O_3(s) + 3\,C(s) \longrightarrow 4\,Co(s) + 3\,CO_2(g)$	**Balance O:** $C_4H_{10}(g) + O_2(g) \longrightarrow 4\,CO_2(g) + 5\,H_2O(g)$ 2 O atoms → 8 O + 5 O = 13 O atoms To balance O, put a 13/2 before $O_2(g)$: $C_4H_{10}(g) + 13/2\,O_2(g) \longrightarrow 4\,CO_2(g) + 5\,H_2O(g)$ 13 O atoms → 13 O atoms
4. If the balanced equation contains coefficient fractions, clear these by multiplying the entire equation by the denominator of the fraction.	This step is not necessary in this example. Proceed to step 5.	$[C_4H_{10}(g) + 13/2\,O_2(g) \longrightarrow 4\,CO_2(g) + 5\,H_2O(g)] \times 2$ $2\,C_4H_{10}(g) + 13\,O_2(g) \longrightarrow 8\,CO_2(g) + 10\,H_2O(g)$
5. Check to make certain the equation is balanced by summing the total number of each type of atom on both sides of the equation.	$2\,Co_2O_3(s) + 3\,C(s) \longrightarrow 4\,Co(s) + 3\,CO_2(g)$ Left / Right 4 Co atoms / 4 Co atoms 6 O atoms / 6 O atoms 3 C atoms / 3 C atoms The equation is balanced.	$2\,C_4H_{10}(g) + 13\,O_2(g) \longrightarrow 8\,CO_2(g) + 10\,H_2O(g)$ Left / Right 8 C atoms / 8 C atoms 20 H atoms / 20 H atoms 26 O atoms / 26 O atoms The equation is balanced.

FOR PRACTICE 3.22
Write a balanced equation for the reaction between solid silicon dioxide and solid carbon to produce solid silicon carbide and carbon monoxide gas.

FOR PRACTICE 3.23
Write a balanced equation for the combustion of gaseous ethane (C_2H_6), a minority component of natural gas, in which it combines with gaseous oxygen to form gaseous carbon dioxide and gaseous water.

Conceptual Connection 3.9 Balanced Chemical Equations

Which quantity or quantities must always be the same on both sides of a chemical equation?

(a) the number of atoms of each kind

(b) the number of molecules of each kind

(c) the number of moles of each kind of molecule

(d) the sum of the masses of all substances involved

EXAMPLE 3.24 Balancing Chemical Equations Containing Ionic Compounds with Polyatomic Ions

Write a balanced equation for the reaction between aqueous strontium chloride and aqueous lithium phosphate to form solid strontium phosphate and aqueous lithium chloride.

SOLUTION

1. Write a skeletal equation by writing chemical formulas for each of the reactants and products. Review Sections 3.5 and 3.6 for naming rules. (If a skeletal equation is provided, go to step 2.)	$SrCl_2(aq) + Li_3PO_4(aq) \rightarrow Sr_3(PO_4)_2(s) + LiCl(aq)$
2. Balance metal ions (cations) first. If a polyatomic cation exists on both sides of the equation, balance it as a unit.	**Begin with Sr^{2+}:** $SrCl_2(aq) + Li_3PO_4(aq) \rightarrow Sr_3(PO_4)_2(s) + LiCl(aq)$ $1\ Sr^{2+}\ \text{ion} \rightarrow 3\ Sr^{2+}\ \text{ions}$ To balance Sr^{2+}, put a 3 before $SrCl_2(aq)$. $3\ SrCl_2(aq) + Li_3PO_4(aq) \rightarrow Sr_3(PO_4)_2(s) + LiCl(aq)$ $3\ Sr^{2+}\ \text{ion} \rightarrow 3\ Sr^{2+}\ \text{ions}$ **Balance Li^+:** $3\ SrCl_2(aq) + Li_3PO_4(aq) \rightarrow Sr_3(PO_4)_2(s) + LiCl(aq)$ $3\ Li^+\ \text{ions} \rightarrow 1\ Li^+\ \text{ion}$ To balance Li^+, put a 3 before $LiCl(aq)$. $3\ SrCl_2(aq) + Li_3PO_4(aq) \rightarrow Sr_3(PO_4)_2(s) + 3\ LiCl(aq)$ $3\ Li^+\ \text{ions} \rightarrow 3\ Li^+\ \text{ions}$
3. Balance nonmetal ions (anions) second. If a polyatomic anion exists on both sides of the equation, balance it as a unit.	**Balance PO_4^{3-}:** $3\ SrCl_2(aq) + Li_3PO_4(aq) \rightarrow Sr_3(PO_4)_2(s) + 3\ LiCl(aq)$ $1\ PO_4^{3-}\ \text{ion} \rightarrow 2\ PO_4^{3-}\ \text{ions}$ To balance PO_4^{3-}, put a 2 before $Li_3PO_4(aq)$. $3\ SrCl_2(aq) + 2\ Li_3PO_4(aq) \rightarrow Sr_3(PO_4)_2(s) + 3\ LiCl(aq)$ $2\ PO_4^{3-}\ \text{ion} \rightarrow 2\ PO_4^{3-}\ \text{ions}$ **Balance Cl^-:** $3\ SrCl_2(aq) + 2\ Li_3PO_4(aq) \rightarrow Sr_3(PO_4)_2(s) + 3\ LiCl(aq)$ $6\ Cl^-\ \text{ions} \rightarrow 3\ Cl^-\ \text{ion}$ To balance Cl^-, replace the 3 before $LiCl(aq)$ with a 6. This also corrects the balance for Li^+, which was thrown off in the previous step. $3\ SrCl_2(aq) + 2\ Li_3PO_4(aq) \rightarrow Sr_3(PO_4)_2(s) + 6\ LiCl(aq)$ $6\ Cl^-\ \text{ions} \rightarrow 6\ Cl^-\ \text{ions}$

| Check to make certain the equation is balanced by summing the total number of each type of ion on both sides of the equation. | $3\,SrCl_2(aq) + 2\,Li_3PO_4(aq) \rightarrow Sr_3(PO_4)_2(s) + 6\,LiCl(aq)$ |

Left	Right
$3\,Sr^{2+}$ ions	$3\,Sr^{2+}$ ions
$6\,Li^+$ ions	$6\,Li^+$ ions
$2\,PO_4^{3-}$ ions	$2\,PO_4^{3-}$ ions
$6\,Cl^-$ ions	$6\,Cl^-$ ions

The equation is balanced.

FOR PRACTICE 3.24

Write a balanced equation for the reaction between aqueous lead(II) nitrate and aqueous potassium chloride to form solid lead(II) chloride and aqueous potassium nitrate.

3.12 Organic Compounds

Early chemists divided compounds into two types: organic and inorganic. They designated organic compounds as those that originate from living things. Sugar—from sugarcane or the sugar beet—is a common example of an organic compound. Inorganic compounds, on the other hand, originate from the earth. Salt—mined from the ground or from the ocean—is a common example of an inorganic compound.

Not only did early chemists view organic and inorganic compounds as different in their origin, they also recognized them to be different in their properties. Organic compounds are easily decomposed. Inorganic compounds, however, are typically more difficult to decompose. Eighteenth-century chemists could synthesize inorganic compounds in the laboratory, but not organic compounds, so this was considered another great difference between the two different types of compounds. Today, chemists can synthesize both organic and inorganic compounds, and even though organic chemistry is a subfield of chemistry, the differences between organic and inorganic compounds are now viewed as primarily organizational (not fundamental).

Organic compounds are common in everyday substances. Many smells—such as those in perfumes, spices, and foods—are caused by organic compounds. When you sprinkle cinnamon onto your French toast, some cinnamaldehyde—an organic compound present in cinnamon—evaporates into the air. As you inhale cinnamaldehyde molecules, you experience the unique smell of cinnamon. Organic compounds are the major components of living organisms. They are also the main components of most of our fuels, such as gasoline, oil, and natural gas, and they are the active ingredients in most pharmaceuticals, such as aspirin and ibuprofen.

Organic compounds are composed of carbon and hydrogen and a few other elements, including nitrogen, oxygen, and sulfur. The key element in organic chemistry, however, is carbon. In its compounds, carbon always forms four bonds. The simplest organic compound is methane, or CH_4.

The chemistry of carbon is unique and complex because carbon frequently bonds to itself to form chain, branched, and ring structures:

▲ The organic compound cinnamaldehyde is largely responsible for the taste and smell of cinnamon.

Structural formula   Space-filling model

Methane, CH_4

Propane (C_3H_8) Isobutane (C_4H_{10}) Cyclohexane (C_6H_{12})

Carbon can also form double bonds and triple bonds with itself and with other elements.

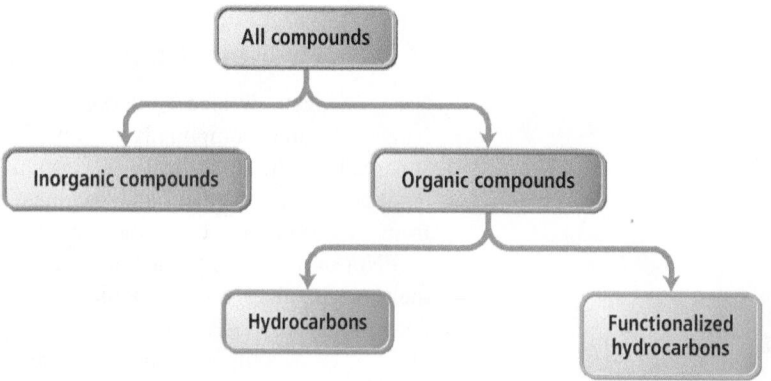

Ethene (C_2H_4)   Ethyne (C_2H_2)   Acetic acid (CH_3COOH)

This versatility allows carbon to serve as the backbone of millions of different chemical compounds, which is why a general survey of organic chemistry is a yearlong course.

Hydrocarbons

We can begin to scratch the surface of organic chemistry by categorizing organic compounds into types: hydrocarbons and functionalized hydrocarbons.

▲ Gasoline is composed mostly of hydrocarbons.

Hydrocarbons are organic compounds that contain only carbon and hydrogen. Hydrocarbons compose common fuels such as oil, gasoline, liquid propane gas, and natural gas.

Hydrocarbons containing only single bonds are called **alkanes**, while those containing double or triple bonds are **alkenes** and **alkynes**, respectively. The names of simple, straight-chain hydrocarbons consist of a base name, which is determined by the number of carbon atoms in the chain, and a suffix, determined by whether the hydrocarbon is an alkane (*-ane*), alkene (*-ene*), or alkyne (*-yne*).

Base name determined by number of C atoms	Suffix determined by presence of multiple bonds

The base names for a number of hydrocarbons are listed here:

meth = 1	hex = 6
eth = 2	hept = 7
prop = 3	oct = 8
but = 4	non = 9
pent = 5	dec = 10

Table 3.7 lists some common hydrocarbons, their names, and their uses.

The term *functional group* derives from the functionality or chemical character that a specific atom or group of atoms imparts to an organic compound. Even a carbon–carbon double bond can justifiably be called a "functional group."

Functionalized Hydrocarbons

Functionalized hydrocarbons can be thought of as hydrocarbons in which a **functional group**—a characteristic atom or group of atoms—is incorporated into the hydrocarbon. For example, **alcohols** are organic compounds that have an –OH functional group. We designate

TABLE 3.7 Common Hydrocarbons

Name	Molecular Formula	Structural Formula	Space-filling Model	Common Uses
Methane	CH_4			Primary component of natural gas
Propane	C_3H_8			LP gas for grills and outdoor stoves
n-Butane*	C_4H_{10}			Common fuel for lighters
n-Pentane*	C_5H_{12}			Component of gasoline
Ethene	C_2H_4			Ripening agent in fruit
Ethyne	C_2H_2			Fuel for welding torches

*The "n" in the names of these hydrocarbons stands for "normal", which means straight chain.

the hydrocarbon portion of a molecule as "R," so the general formula for an alcohol can be written R—OH. Some examples of alcohols include methanol (also known as methyl alcohol or wood alcohol) and isopropanol (also known as isopropyl alcohol or rubbing alcohol):

Hydrocarbon (R) group → CH_3OH ← OH functional group
Methanol

$$CH_3$$
Hydrocarbon (R) group → CH_3CHOH ← OH functional group
Isopropanol
(2-propanol)

A group of organic compounds with the same functional group forms a **family**. Methanol and isopropyl alcohol are both members of the alcohol family of compounds.

The addition of a functional group to a hydrocarbon usually alters the properties of the compound significantly. Take *methanol*, which can be thought of as methane with an –OH group substituted for one of the hydrogen atoms. It is a liquid at room temperature,

▲ Rubbing alcohol is isopropyl alcohol.

while *methane* is a gas. While each member of a family is unique, the common functional group bestows some chemical similarities on members of the same family. The names of functional groups have suffixes or endings unique to that functional group. Alcohols, for example, always have names that end in *-ol*. Table 3.8 provides examples of some common functional groups, their general formulas, and their characteristic suffixes or endings.

TABLE 3.8 Families of Organic Compunds

Family	Name Ending	General Formula	Example	Name	Occurrence/Use
Alcohols	-ol	R—OH	CH_3CH_2—OH	Ethanol (ethyl alcohol)	Alcohol in fermented beverages
Ethers	ether	R—O—R'	CH_3CH_2—O—CH_2CH_3	Diethyl ether	Anesthetic; laboratory solvent
Aldehydes	-al	R—C(=O)—H	H_3C—C(=O)—H	Ethanal (acetaldehyde)	Perfumes; flavors
Ketones	-one	R—C(=O)—R'	H_3C—C(=O)—CH_3	Propanone (acetone)	Fingernail polish remover
Carboxylic acids	acid	R—C(=O)—OH	H_3C—C(=O)—OH	Acetic acid	Vinegar
Esters	-ate	R—C(=O)—OR'	H_3C—C(=O)—OCH_3	Methyl acetate	Laboratory solvent
Amines	amine	RNH_2	CH_3CH_2—N(H)—H	Ethyl amine	Smell of rotten fish

CHAPTER IN REVIEW

Self Assessment Quiz

Q1. What is the empirical formula of a compound with the molecular formula $C_{10}H_8$?
a) C_5H_3
b) C_2H_4
c) C_5H_4
d) CH

Q2. Which substance is an ionic compound?
a) SrI_2
b) N_2O_4
c) He
d) CCl_4

Q3. What is the correct formula for the compound formed between calcium and sulfur?
a) CaS
b) Ca_2S
c) CaS_2
d) CaS_3

Q4. Name the compound SrI_2.
a) strontium iodide
b) strontium diiodide
c) strontium(II) iodide
d) strontium(II) diiodide

Q5. What is the formula for manganese(IV) oxide?
   a) Mn_4O
   b) MnO_4
   c) Mn_2O
   d) MnO_2

Q6. Name the compound $Pb(C_2H_3O_2)_2$.
   a) lead(II) carbonate
   b) lead(II) acetate
   c) lead bicarbonate
   d) lead diacetate

Q7. Name the compound P_2I_4.
   a) phosphorus iodide
   b) phosphorus diiodide
   c) phosphorus(II) iodide
   d) diphosphorus tetraiodide

Q8. Name the compound $HNO_2(aq)$.
   a) hydrogen nitrogen dioxide
   b) hydrogen nitrate
   c) nitric acid
   d) nitrous acid

Q9. Determine the number of CH_2Cl_2 molecules in 25.0 g CH_2Cl_2.
   a) 0.294 molecules
   b) 1.77×10^{23} molecules
   c) 1.28×10^{27} molecules
   d) 1.51×10^{25} molecules

Q10. List the elements in the compound CF_2Cl_2 in order of decreasing mass percent composition.
   a) $C > F > Cl$
   b) $F > Cl > C$
   c) $Cl > C > F$
   d) $Cl > F > C$

Q11. Determine the mass of potassium in 35.5 g of KBr.
   a) 17.4 g
   b) 0.298 g
   c) 11.7 g
   d) 32.9 g

Q12. A compound is 52.14% C, 13.13% H, and 34.73% O by mass. What is the empirical formula of the compound?
   a) $C_2H_8O_3$
   b) C_2H_6O
   c) C_4HO_3
   d) C_3HO_6

Q13. A compound has the empirical formula CH_2O and a formula mass of 120.10 amu. What is the molecular formula of the compound?
   a) CH_2O
   b) $C_2H_4O_2$
   c) $C_3H_6O_3$
   d) $C_4H_8O_4$

Q14. Combustion of 30.42 g of a compound containing only carbon, hydrogen, and oxygen produces 35.21 g CO_2 and 14.42 g H_2O. What is the empirical formula of the compound?
   a) $C_4H_8O_6$
   b) $C_2H_4O_3$
   c) $C_2H_2O_3$
   d) C_6HO_{12}

Q15. What are the correct coefficients (reading from left to right) when the chemical equation is balanced?

   $$\_PCl_3(l) + \_H_2O(l) \rightarrow \_H_3PO_3(aq) + \_HCl(aq)$$

   a) 1, 3, 1, 3
   b) 1, 2, 1, 1
   c) 1, 3, 2, 1
   d) 3, 6, 1, 9

Answers: 1. (c) **2.** (a) **3.** (a) **4.** (a) **5.** (d) **6.** (b) **7.** (d) **8.** (d) **9.** (b) **10.** (d) **11.** (c) **12.** (b) **13.** (d) **14.** (b) **15.** (a)

Key Terms

Section 3.2
ionic bond (89)
covalent bond (90)

Section 3.3
chemical formula (90)
empirical formula (90)
molecular formula (90)
structural formula (90)
ball-and-stick molecular model (91)
space-filling molecular model (91)

Section 3.4
atomic element (93)
molecular element (93)
molecular compound (94)

ionic compound (94)
formula unit (94)
polyatomic ion (94)

Section 3.5
common name (97)
systematic name (97)
binary compound (97)
oxyanion (100)
hydrate (100)

Section 3.6
acid (102)
binary acid (103)
oxyacid (104)

Section 3.8
formula mass (107)

Section 3.9
mass percent composition (mass percent) (109)

Section 3.10
empirical formula molar mass (116)
combustion analysis (117)

Section 3.11
chemical reaction (119)
combustion reaction (119)
chemical equation (119)
reactants (119)
products (119)
balanced chemical equation (119)

Section 3.12
organic compound (123)
hydrocarbon (124)
alkane (124)
alkene (124)
alkyne (124)
functional group (124)
alcohol (124)
family (125)

Key Concepts

Chemical Bonds (3.2)

▶ Chemical bonds, the forces that hold atoms together in compounds, arise from the interactions between nuclei and electrons in atoms.

▶ In an ionic bond, one or more electrons are *transferred* from one atom to another, forming a cation (positively charged) and an anion (negatively charged). The two ions are then drawn together by the attraction between the opposite charges.

▶ In a covalent bond, one or more electrons are *shared* between two atoms. The atoms are held together by the attraction between their nuclei and the shared electrons.

Representing Molecules and Compounds (3.3, 3.4)

▶ A compound is represented with a chemical formula, which indicates the elements present and the number of atoms of each.

▶ An empirical formula gives only the *relative* number of atoms, while a molecular formula gives the *actual* number of atoms present in the molecule.

▶ Structural formulas show how the atoms are bonded together, while molecular models portray the geometry of the molecule.

▶ Compounds can be divided into two types: molecular compounds, formed between two or more covalently bonded nonmetals, and ionic compounds, usually formed between a metal ionically bonded to one or more nonmetals. The smallest identifiable unit of a molecular compound is a molecule, and the smallest identifiable unit of an ionic compound is a formula unit: the smallest electrically neutral collection of ions.

▶ Elements can also be divided into two types: molecular elements, which occur as (mostly diatomic) molecules, and atomic elements, which occur as individual atoms.

Naming Inorganic Ionic and Molecular Compounds and Acids (3.5–3.7)

▶ A flowchart for naming simple inorganic compounds is provided in Section 3.7.

Formula Mass and Mole Concept for Compounds (3.8)

▶ The formula mass of a compound is the sum of the atomic masses of all the atoms in the chemical formula. Like the atomic masses of elements, the formula mass characterizes the average mass of a molecule (or a formula unit).

▶ The mass of 1 mole of a compound is called the molar mass and equals its formula mass (in grams).

Chemical Composition (3.9, 3.10)

▶ The mass percent composition of a compound indicates each element's percentage of the total compound's mass. The mass percent composition can be determined from the compound's chemical formula and the molar masses of its elements.

▶ The chemical formula of a compound provides the relative number of atoms (or moles) of each element in a compound and can therefore be used to determine numerical relationships between moles of the compound and moles of its constituent elements. This relationship can be extended to mass by using the molar masses of the compound and its constituent elements.

▶ If the mass percent composition and molar mass of a compound are known, its empirical and molecular formulas can be determined.

Writing and Balancing Chemical Equations (3.11)

▶ In chemistry, we represent chemical reactions with chemical equations. The substances on the left-hand side of a chemical equation are the reactants, and the substances on the right-hand side are the products.

▶ Chemical equations are balanced when the number of each type of atom on the left side of the equation is equal to the number on the right side.

Organic Compounds (3.12)

▶ Organic compounds are composed of carbon, hydrogen, and a few other elements such as nitrogen, oxygen, and sulfur.

▶ The simplest organic compounds are hydrocarbons, compounds composed of only carbon and hydrogen.

▶ Hydrocarbons can be categorized into three types based on the bonds they contain: alkanes contain single bonds, alkenes contain double bonds, and alkynes contain triple bonds.

▶ All other organic compounds can be thought of as hydrocarbons with one or more functional groups—characteristic atoms or groups of atoms.

▶ Common functionalized hydrocarbons include alcohols, ethers, aldehydes, ketones, carboxylic acids, esters, and amines.

Key Equations and Relationships

Formula Mass (3.8)

$$\left(\begin{array}{c}\text{\# atoms of 1st element}\\ \text{in chemical formula}\end{array} \times \begin{array}{c}\text{atomic mass}\\ \text{of 1st element}\end{array}\right) + \left(\begin{array}{c}\text{\# atoms of 2nd element}\\ \text{in chemical formula}\end{array} \times \begin{array}{c}\text{atomic mass}\\ \text{of 2nd element}\end{array}\right) + \cdots$$

Mass Percent Composition (3.9)

$$\text{Mass \% of element X} = \frac{\text{mass of X in 1 mol compound}}{\text{mass of 1 mol compound}} \times 100\%$$

Empirical Formula Molar Mass (3.10)

$$\text{Molecular formula} = n \times (\text{empirical formula})$$

$$n = \frac{\text{molar mass}}{\text{empirical formula molar mass}}$$

Key Learning Outcomes

Chapter Objectives	Assessment
Writing Molecular and Empirical Formulas (3.3)	Example 3.1 For Practice 3.1 Exercises 4, 23–26
Classifying Substances as Atomic Elements, Molecular Elements, Molecular Compounds, or Ionic Compounds (3.4)	Example 3.2 For Practice 3.2 Exercises 27–32
Writing Formulas for Ionic Compounds (3.5)	Examples 3.3, 3.4 For Practice 3.3, 3.4 Exercises 33–36, 43, 44
Naming Ionic Compounds (3.5)	Examples 3.5, 3.6 For Practice 3.5, 3.6 For More Practice 3.5, 3.6 Exercises 37–40
Naming Ionic Compounds Containing Polyatomic Ions (3.5)	Example 3.7 For Practice 3.7 For More Practice 3.7 Exercises 41–44
Naming Molecular Compounds (3.6)	Example 3.8 For Practice 3.8 For More Practice 3.8 Exercises 47–50
Naming Acids (3.6)	Examples 3.9, 3.10 For Practice 3.9, 3.10 For More Practice 3.10 Exercises 51–54
Naming Uncategorized Inorganic Compounds (3.7)	Example 3.11 For Practice 3.11 Exercises 55–58
Calculating Formula Mass (3.8)	Example 3.12 For Practice 3.12 Exercises 59, 60
Using Formula Mass to Count Molecules by Weighing (3.8)	Example 3.13 For Practice 3.13 For More Practice 3.13 Exercises 65–70
Calculating Mass Percent Composition (3.9)	Example 3.14 For Practice 3.14 For More Practice 3.14 Exercises 71–76
Using Mass Percent Composition as a Conversion Factor (3.9)	Example 3.15 For Practice 3.15 For More Practice 3.15 Exercises 77, 78
Using Chemical Formulas as Conversion Factors (3.9)	Example 3.16 For Practice 3.16 For More Practice 3.16 Exercises 83, 84
Obtaining an Empirical Formula from Experimental Data (3.10)	Examples 3.17, 3.18 For Practice 3.17, 3.18 Exercises 85–92
Calculating a Molecular Formula from an Empirical Formula and Molar Mass (3.10)	Example 3.19 For Practice 3.19 For More Practice 3.19 Exercises 93–94
Obtaining an Empirical Formula from Combustion Analysis (3.10)	Examples 3.20, 3.21 For Practice 3.20, 3.21 Exercises 95–98
Balancing Chemical Equations (3.11)	Examples 3.22, 3.23, 3.24 For Practice 3.22, 3.23, 3.24 Exercises 99–110

EXERCISES

Review Questions

1. How do the properties of compounds compare to the properties of the elements from which they are composed?

2. What is a chemical bond? Explain the difference between an ionic bond and a covalent bond.

3. Explain the different ways to represent compounds. Why are there so many?

4. What is the difference between an empirical formula and a molecular formula?

5. Define and provide an example for each of the following: atomic element, molecular element, ionic compound, molecular compound.

6. Explain how to write a formula for an ionic compound given the names of the metal and nonmetal (or polyatomic ion) in the compound.

7. Explain how to name binary ionic compounds. How do you name an ionic compound if it contains a polyatomic ion?

8. Why do the names of some ionic compounds include the charge of the metal ion while others do not?

9. Explain how to name molecular inorganic compounds.

10. How many atoms are specified by these prefixes: *mono-, di-, tri-, tetra-, penta-, hexa-*?

11. Explain how to name binary and oxy acids.

12. What is the formula mass for a compound? Why is it useful?

13. Explain how the information in a chemical formula can be used to determine how much of a particular element is present in a given amount of a compound. Provide some examples of why this might be important.

14. What is mass percent composition? Why is it useful?

15. What kinds of conversion factors are inherent in chemical formulas? Provide an example.

16. What kind of chemical formula can be obtained from experimental data showing the relative masses of the elements in a compound?

17. How can a molecular formula be obtained from an empirical formula? What additional information is required?

18. What is combustion analysis? What is it used for?

19. Which elements are normally present in organic compounds?

20. What is the difference between an alkane, an alkene, and an alkyne?

21. What are functionalized hydrocarbons? Give an example of a functionalized hydrocarbon.

22. Write a generic formula for each of the families of organic compounds.
   a. alcohols   **b.** ethers
   c. aldehydes   **d.** ketones
   e. carboxylic acids **f.** esters
   g. amines

Problems by Topic

Note: Answers to all odd-numbered Problems, numbered in blue, can be found in Appendix III. Exercises in the Problems by Topic section are paired, with each odd-numbered problem followed by a similar even-numbered problem. Exercises in the Cumulative Problems section are also paired, but somewhat more loosely. (Challenge Problems and Conceptual Problems, because of their nature, are unpaired.)

Chemical Formulas and Molecular View of Elements and Compounds

23. Determine the number of each type of atom in each formula:
   a. $Mg_3(PO_4)_2$ **b.** $BaCl_2$
   c. $Fe(NO_2)_2$ **d.** $Ca(OH)_2$

24. Determine the number of each type of atom in each formula:
   a. $Ca(NO_2)_2$ **b.** $CuSO_4$
   c. $Al(NO_3)_3$ **d.** $Mg(HCO_3)_2$

25. Write a chemical formula for each molecular model. (See Appendix IIA for color codes.)

(a)   (b)   (c)

26. Write a chemical formula for each molecular model. (See Appendix IIA for color codes.)

(a)   (b)   (c)

27. Classify each element as atomic or molecular.
   a. neon   **b.** fluorine
   c. potassium   **d.** nitrogen

28. Identify the elements that have molecules as their basic units.
   a. hydrogen   **b.** iodine
   c. lead   **d.** oxygen

29. Classify each compound as ionic or molecular.
   a. CO_2 **b.** $NiCl_2$ **c.** NaI **d.** PCl_3

30. Classify each compound as ionic or molecular.
   a. CF_2Cl_2 **b.** CCl_4 **c.** PtO_2 **d.** SO_3

31. Based on the molecular views, classify each substance as an atomic element, a molecular element, an ionic compound, or a molecular compound.

(a)   (b)

(c)

32. Based on the molecular views, classify each substance as an atomic element, a molecular element, an ionic compound, or a molecular compound.

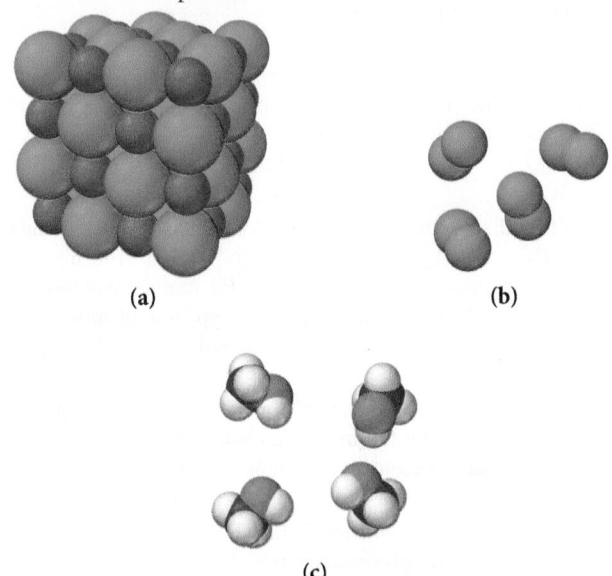

(a)   (b)

(c)

Formulas and Names for Ionic Compounds

33. Write a formula for the ionic compound that forms between each pair of elements.
  a. calcium and oxygen   **b.** zinc and sulfur
  c. rubidium and bromine   **d.** aluminum and oxygen

34. Write a formula for the ionic compound that forms between each pair of elements.
  a. silver and chlorine   **b.** sodium and sulfur
  c. aluminum and sulfur   **d.** potassium and chlorine

35. Write a formula for the compound that forms between calcium and each polyatomic ion.
  a. hydroxide **b.** chromate **c.** phosphate **d.** cyanide

36. Write a formula for the compound that forms between potassium and each polyatomic ion.
  a. carbonate   **b.** phosphate
  c. hydrogen phosphate   **d.** acetate

37. Name each ionic compound.
  a. Mg_3N_2 **b.** KF   **c.** Na_2O
  d. Li_2S **e.** CsF   **f.** KI

38. Name each ionic compound.
  a. $SnCl_4$ **b.** PbI_2 **c.** Fe_2O_3
  d. CuI_2 **e.** $HgBr_2$ **f.** $CrCl_2$

39. Give each ionic compound an appropriate name.
  a. SnO   **b.** Cr_2S_3 **c.** RbI   **d.** $BaBr_2$

40. Give each ionic compound an appropriate name.
  a. BaS   **b.** $FeCl_3$ **c.** PbI_4 **d.** $SrBr_2$

41. Name each ionic compound containing a polyatomic ion.
  a. $CuNO_2$ **b.** $Mg(C_2H_3O_2)_2$
  c. $Ba(NO_3)_2$ **d.** $Pb(C_2H_3O_2)_2$

42. Name each ionic compound containing a polyatomic ion.
  a. $Ba(OH)_2$ **b.** NH_4I **c.** $NaBrO_4$ **d.** $Fe(OH)_3$

43. Write a formula for each ionic compound.
  a. sodium hydrogen sulfite
  b. lithium permanganate
  c. silver nitrate
  d. potassium sulfate
  e. rubidium hydrogen sulfate
  f. potassium hydrogen carbonate

44. Write a formula for each ionic compound.
  a. copper(II) chloride
  b. copper(I) iodate
  c. lead(II) chromate
  d. calcium fluoride
  e. potassium hydroxide
  f. iron(II) phosphate

45. Write the name from the formula or the formula from the name for each hydrated ionic compound.
  a. $CoSO_4 \cdot 7H_2O$
  b. iridium(III) bromide tetrahydrate
  c. $Mg(BrO_3)_2 \cdot 6H_2O$
  d. potassium carbonate dihydrate

46. Write the name from the formula or the formula from the name for each hydrated ionic compound.
  a. cobalt(II) phosphate octahydrate
  b. $BeCl_2 \cdot 2H_2O$
  c. chromium(III) phosphate trihydrate
  d. $LiNO_2 \cdot H_2O$

Formulas and Names for Molecular Compounds and Acids

47. Name each molecular compound.
  a. CO   **b.** NI_3
  c. $SiCl_4$ **d.** N_4Se_4

48. Name each molecular compound.
  a. SO_3 **b.** SO_2
  c. BrF_5 **d.** NO

49. Write a formula for each molecular compound.
  a. phosphorus trichloride
  b. chlorine monoxide
  c. disulfur tetrafluoride
  d. phosphorus pentafluoride

50. Write a formula for each molecular compound.
  a. boron tribromide
  b. dichlorine monoxide
  c. xenon tetrafluoride
  d. carbon tetrabromide

51. Name each acid.
  a. HI(aq)   **b.** $HNO_3(aq)$ **c.** $H_2CO_3(aq)$

52. Name each acid.
  a. HCl(aq)   **b.** $HClO_2(aq)$ **c.** $H_2SO_4(aq)$

53. Write formulas for each acid.
  a. hydrofluoric acid
  b. hydrobromic acid
  c. sulfurous acid

54. Write formulas for each acid.
  a. phosphoric acid
  b. hydrocyanic acid
  c. chlorous acid

Using the Nomenclature Flow Chart

55. Use the nomenclature flow chart (Figure 3.10) to name each compound.
  a. $SrCl_2$ **b.** SnO_2
  c. P_2S_5 **d.** $HC_2H_3O_2(aq)$

56. Use the nomenclature flow chart (Figure 3.10) to name each compound.
  a. $HNO_2(aq)$ **b.** B_2Cl_2
  c. $BaCl_2$ **d.** $CrCl_3$

57. Use the nomenclature flow chart (Figure 3.10) to name each compound.
    a. $KClO_3$ b. I_2O_5 c. $PbSO_4$

58. Use the nomenclature flow chart (Figure 3.10) to name each compound.
    a. XeO_3 b. $KClO$ c. $CoSO_4$

Formula Mass and the Mole Concept for Compounds

59. Calculate the formula mass for each compound.
    a. NO_2 b. C_4H_{10}
    c. $C_6H_{12}O_6$ d. $Cr(NO_3)_3$

60. Calculate the formula mass for each compound.
    a. $MgBr_2$ b. HNO_2
    c. CBr_4 d. $Ca(NO_3)_2$

61. Calculate the number of moles in each sample.
    a. 72.5 g CCl_4
    b. 12.4 g $C_{12}H_{22}O_{11}$
    c. 25.2 kg C_2H_2
    d. 12.3 g of dinitrogen monoxide

62. Calculate the mass of each sample.
    a. 15.7 mol HNO_3
    b. 1.04×10^{-3} mol H_2O_2
    c. 72.1 mmol SO_2
    d. 1.23 mol xenon difluoride

63. Determine the number of moles (of molecules or formula units) in each sample.
    a. 25.5 g NO_2
    b. 1.25 kg CO_2
    c. 38.2 g KNO_3
    d. 155.2 kg Na_2SO_4

64. Determine the number of moles (of molecules or formula units) in each sample.
    a. 55.98 g CF_2Cl_2
    b. 23.6 kg $Fe(NO_3)_2$
    c. 0.1187 g C_8H_{18}
    d. 195 kg CaO

65. How many molecules are in each sample?
    a. 6.5 g H_2O
    b. 389 g CBr_4
    c. 22.1 g O_2
    d. 19.3 g C_8H_{10}

66. How many molecules (or formula units) are in each sample?
    a 85.26 g CCl_4
    b. 55.93 kg $NaHCO_3$
    c. 119.78 g C_4H_{10}
    d. 4.59×10^5 g Na_3PO_4

67. Calculate the mass (in g) of each sample.
    a. 5.94×10^{20} SO_3 molecules
    b. 2.8×10^{22} H_2O molecules
    c. 1 glucose molecule ($C_6H_{12}O_6$)

68. Calculate the mass (in g) of each sample.
    a. 4.5×10^{25} O_3 molecules
    b. 9.85×10^{19} CCl_2F_2 molecules
    c. 1 water molecule

69. A sugar crystal contains approximately 1.8×10^{17} sucrose ($C_{12}H_{22}O_{11}$) molecules. What is its mass in mg?

70. A salt crystal has a mass of 0.12 mg. How many NaCl formula units does it contain?

Composition of Compounds

71. Calculate the mass percent composition of carbon in each carbon-containing compound.
    a. CH_4 b. C_2H_6
    c. C_2H_2 d. C_2H_5Cl

72. Calculate the mass percent composition of nitrogen in each nitrogen-containing compound.
    a. N_2O b. NO
    c. NO_2 d. HNO_3

73. Most fertilizers consist of nitrogen-containing compounds such as NH_3, $CO(NH_2)_2$, NH_4NO_3, and $(NH_4)_2SO_4$. The nitrogen content in these compounds is used for protein synthesis by plants. Calculate the mass percent composition of nitrogen in each of the fertilizers named. Which fertilizer has the highest nitrogen content?

74. Iron in the earth is in the form of iron ore. Common ores include Fe_2O_3 (hematite), Fe_3O_4 (magnetite), and $FeCO_3$ (siderite). Calculate the mass percent composition of iron for each of these iron ores. Which ore has the highest iron content?

75. Copper(II) fluoride contains 37.42% F by mass. Calculate the mass of fluorine (in g) contained in 55.5 g of copper(II) fluoride.

76. Silver chloride, often used in silver plating, contains 75.27% Ag by mass. Calculate the mass of silver chloride required to plate 155 mg of pure silver.

77. The iodide ion is a dietary mineral essential to good nutrition. In countries where potassium iodide is added to salt, iodine deficiency (or goiter) has been almost completely eliminated. The recommended daily allowance (RDA) for iodine is 150 μg/day. How much potassium iodide (76.45% I) should you consume if you want to meet the RDA?

78. The American Dental Association recommends that an adult female should consume 3.0 mg of fluoride (F^-) per day to prevent tooth decay. If the fluoride is consumed in the form of sodium fluoride (45.24% F), what amount of sodium fluoride contains the recommended amount of fluoride?

79. Write a ratio showing the relationship between the molar amounts of each element for each compound. (See Appendix IIA for color codes.)

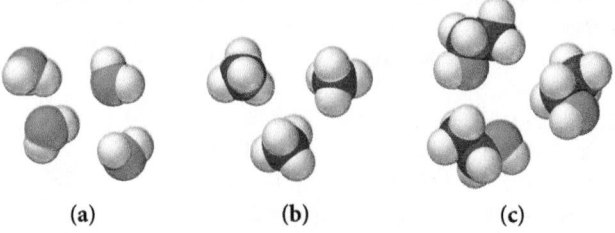

(a)   (b)   (c)

80. Write a ratio showing the relationship between the molar amounts of each element for each compound. (See Appendix IIA for color codes.)

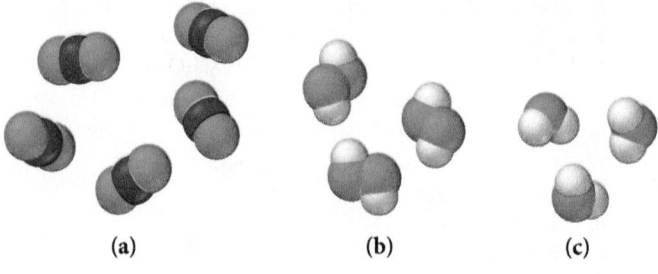

(a)   (b)   (c)

81. Determine the number of moles of hydrogen atoms in each sample.
    a. 0.0885 mol C_4H_{10}
    b. 1.3 mol CH_4
    c. 2.4 mol C_6H_{12}
    d. 1.87 mol C_8H_{18}

82. Determine the number of moles of oxygen atoms in each sample.
    a. 4.88 mol H_2O_2
    b. 2.15 mol N_2O
    c. 0.0237 mol H_2CO_3
    d. 24.1 mol CO_2

83. Calculate mass (in grams) of sodium in 8.5 g of each sodium-containing food additive.
    a. NaCl (table salt)
    b. Na_3PO_4 (sodium phosphate)
    c. $NaC_7H_5O_2$ (sodium benzoate)
    d. $Na_2C_6H_6O_7$ (sodium hydrogen citrate)

84. Calculate the mass (in kilograms) of chlorine in 25 kg of each chlorofluorocarbon (CFC).
    a. CF_2Cl_2
    b. $CFCl_3$
    c. $C_2F_3Cl_3$
    d. CF_3Cl

Chemical Formulas from Experimental Data

85. A chemist decomposes samples of several compounds; the masses of their constituent elements are shown below. Calculate the empirical formula for each compound.
    a. 1.651 g Ag, 0.1224 g O
    b. 0.672 g Co, 0.569 g As, 0.486 g O
    c. 1.443 g Se, 5.841 g Br

86. A chemist decomposes samples of several compounds; the masses of their constituent elements are shown below. Calculate the empirical formula for each compound.
    a. 1.245 g Ni, 5.381 g I
    b. 2.677 g Ba, 3.115 g Br
    c. 2.128 g Be, 7.557 g S, 15.107 g O

87. Calculate the empirical formula for each stimulant based on its elemental mass percent composition.
    a. nicotine (found in tobacco leaves): C 74.03%, H 8.70%, N 17.27%
    b. caffeine (found in coffee beans): C 49.48%, H 5.19%, N 28.85%, O 16.48%

88. Calculate the empirical formula for each natural flavor based on its elemental mass percent composition.
    a. methyl butyrate (component of apple taste and smell): C 58.80%, H 9.87%, O 31.33%
    b. vanillin (responsible for the taste and smell of vanilla): C 63.15%, H 5.30%, O 31.55%

89. The elemental mass percent composition of ibuprofen (an aspirin substitute) is 75.69% C, 8.80% H, and 15.51% O. Determine the empirical formula of ibuprofen.

90. The elemental mass percent composition of ascorbic acid (vitamin C) is 40.92% C, 4.58% H, and 54.50% O. Determine the empirical formula of ascorbic acid.

91. A 0.77 mg sample of nitrogen reacts with chlorine to form 6.61 mg of the chloride. Determine the empirical formula of nitrogen chloride.

92. A 45.2 mg sample of phosphorus reacts with selenium to form 131.6 mg of the selenide. Determine the empirical formula of phosphorus selenide.

93. The empirical formula and molar mass of several compounds are listed next. Find the molecular formula of each compound.
    a. C_6H_7N, 186.24 g/mol
    b. C_2HCl, 181.44 g/mol
    c. $C_5H_{10}NS_2$, 296.54 g/mol

94. The molar mass and empirical formula of several compounds are listed next. Find the molecular formula of each compound.
    a. C_4H_9, 114.22 g/mol
    b. CCl, 284.77 g/mol
    c. C_3H_2N, 312.29 g/mol

95. Combustion analysis of a hydrocarbon produced 33.01 g CO_2 and 13.51 g H_2O. Calculate the empirical formula of the hydrocarbon.

96. Combustion analysis of naphthalene, a hydrocarbon used in mothballs, produced 8.80 g CO_2 and 1.44 g H_2O. Calculate the empirical formula for naphthalene.

97. The foul odor of rancid butter is due largely to butyric acid, a compound containing carbon, hydrogen, and oxygen. Combustion analysis of a 4.30 g sample of butyric acid produced 8.59 g CO_2 and 3.52 g H_2O. Determine the empirical formula for butyric acid.

98. Tartaric acid is the white, powdery substance that coats tart candies such as Sour Patch Kids. Combustion analysis of a 12.01 g sample of tartaric acid—which contains only carbon, hydrogen, and oxygen—produced 14.08 g CO_2 and 4.32 g H_2O. Determine the empirical formula for tartaric acid.

Writing and Balancing Chemical Equations

99. Sulfuric acid is a component of acid rain formed when gaseous sulfur dioxide pollutant reacts with gaseous oxygen and liquid water to form aqueous sulfuric acid. Write a balanced chemical equation for this reaction. (Note: this is a simplified representation of this reaction.)

100. Nitric acid is a component of acid rain that forms when gaseous nitrogen dioxide pollutant reacts with gaseous oxygen and liquid water to form aqueous nitric acid. Write a balanced chemical equation for this reaction. (Note: this is a simplified representation of this reaction.)

101. In a popular classroom demonstration, solid sodium is added to liquid water and reacts to produce hydrogen gas and aqueous sodium hydroxide. Write a balanced chemical equation for this reaction.

102. When iron rusts, solid iron reacts with gaseous oxygen to form solid iron(III) oxide. Write a balanced chemical equation for this reaction.

103. Write a balanced chemical equation for the fermentation of sucrose ($C_{12}H_{22}O_{11}$) by yeasts in which the aqueous sugar reacts with water to form aqueous ethyl alcohol (C_2H_5OH) and carbon dioxide gas.

104. Write a balanced equation for the photosynthesis reaction in which gaseous carbon dioxide and liquid water react in the presence of chlorophyll to produce aqueous glucose ($C_6H_{12}O_6$) and oxygen gas.

105. Write a balanced chemical equation for each reaction.

   a. Solid lead(II) sulfide reacts with aqueous hydrobromic acid to form solid lead(II) bromide and dihydrogen monosulfide gas.

   b. Gaseous carbon monoxide reacts with hydrogen gas to form gaseous methane (CH_4) and liquid water.

   c. Aqueous hydrochloric acid reacts with solid manganese(IV) oxide to form aqueous manganese(II) chloride, liquid water, and chlorine gas.

   d. Liquid pentane (C_5H_{12}) reacts with gaseous oxygen to form carbon dioxide and liquid water.

106. Write a balanced chemical equation for each reaction.

   a. Solid copper reacts with solid sulfur to form solid copper(I) sulfide.

   b. Solid iron(III) oxide reacts with hydrogen gas to form solid iron and liquid water.

   c. Sulfur dioxide gas reacts with oxygen gas to form sulfur trioxide gas.

   d. Gaseous ammonia (NH_3) reacts with gaseous oxygen to form gaseous nitrogen monoxide and gaseous water.

107. Write a balanced chemical equation for the reaction of aqueous sodium carbonate with aqueous copper(II) chloride to form solid copper(II) carbonate and aqueous sodium chloride.

108. Write a balanced chemical equation for the reaction of aqueous potassium hydroxide with aqueous iron(III) chloride to form solid iron(III) hydroxide and aqueous potassium chloride

109. Balance each chemical equation.

   a. $CO_2(g) + CaSiO_3(s) + H_2O(l) \longrightarrow$
$$SiO_2(s) + Ca(HCO_3)_2(aq)$$

   b. $Co(NO_3)_3(aq) + (NH_4)_2S(aq) \longrightarrow$
$$Co_2S_3(s) + NH_4NO_3(aq)$$

   c. $Cu_2O(s) + C(s) \longrightarrow Cu(s) + CO(g)$

   d. $H_2(g) + Cl_2(g) \longrightarrow HCl(g)$

110. Balance each chemical equation.

   a. $Na_2S(aq) + Cu(NO_3)_2(aq) \longrightarrow NaNO_3(aq) + CuS(s)$

   b. $N_2H_4(l) \longrightarrow NH_3(g) + N_2(g)$

   c. $HCl(aq) + O_2(g) \longrightarrow H_2O(l) + Cl_2(g)$

   d. $FeS(s) + HCl(aq) \longrightarrow FeCl_2(aq) + H_2S(g)$

Organic Compounds

111. Classify each compound as organic or inorganic.

   a. $CaCO_3$ **b.** C_4H_8

   c. $C_4H_6O_6$ **d.** LiF

112. Classify each compound as organic or inorganic.

   a. C_8H_{18} **b.** CH_3NH_2

   c. CaO   **d.** $FeCO_3$

113. Classify each hydrocarbon as an alkane, alkene, or alkyne.

   a. $H_2C{=}CH{-}CH_3$

   b. $H_3C{-}CH_2{-}CH_3$

   c. $HC{\equiv}C{-}CH_3$

   d. $H_3C{-}CH_2{-}CH_2{-}CH_3$

114. Classify each hydrocarbon as an alkane, alkene, or alkyne.

   a. $HC{\equiv}CH$

   b. $H_3C{-}CH{=}C{-}CH_3$

   c.
$$\overset{\displaystyle CH_3}{\underset{\displaystyle |}{}}$$
$$H_3C{-}\overset{|}{C}H{-}CH_3$$

   d. $H_3C{-}C{\equiv}C{-}CH_3$

115. Write a formula based on the name, or a name based on the formula, for each hydrocarbon.

   a. propane

   b. $CH_3CH_2CH_3$

   c. octane

   d. $CH_3CH_2CH_2CH_2CH_3$

116. Write a formula based on the name, or a name based on the formula, for each hydrocarbon:

   a. CH_3CH_3

   b. pentane

   c. $CH_3CH_2CH_2CH_2CH_2CH_3$

   d. heptane

117. Classify each organic compound as a hydrocarbon or a functionalized hydrocarbon. For functionalized hydrocarbons, identify the family to which the compound belongs.

   a. $H_3C{-}CH_2OH$

   b. $H_3C{-}CH_3$

   c.
$$H_3C{-}\overset{\displaystyle O}{\overset{\displaystyle \|}{C}}{-}CH_2{-}CH_3$$

   d. $H_3C{-}NH_2$

118. Classify each organic compound as a hydrocarbon or a functionalized hydrocarbon. For functionalized hydrocarbons, identify the family to which the compound belongs.

   a.
$$H_3C{-}CH_2{-}\overset{\displaystyle O}{\overset{\displaystyle \|}{C}}{-}OH$$

   b.
$$H_3C{-}\overset{\displaystyle O}{\overset{\displaystyle \|}{C}}H$$

   c.
$$H_3C{-}\overset{\displaystyle CH_3}{\underset{\displaystyle CH_3}{\overset{\displaystyle |}{\underset{\displaystyle |}{C}}}}{-}CH_3$$

   d. $H_3C{-}CH_2{-}O{-}CH_3$

Cumulative Problems

119. How many molecules of ethanol (C_2H_5OH) (the alcohol in alcoholic beverages) are present in 145 mL of ethanol? The density of ethanol is 0.789 g/cm^3.

120. A drop of water has a volume of approximately 0.05 mL. How many water molecules does it contain? The density of water is 1.0 g/cm^3.

121. Determine the chemical formula of each compound and then use it to calculate the mass percent composition of each constituent element.

   a. potassium chromate   **b.** lead(II) phosphate

   c. sulfurous acid   **d.** cobalt(II) bromide

122. Determine the chemical formula of each compound and then use it to calculate the mass percent composition of each constituent element.

   a. perchloric acid

   b. phosphorus pentachloride

   c. nitrogen triiodide

   d. carbon dioxide

123. A Freon leak in the air-conditioning system of an old car releases 25 g of CF_2Cl_2 per month. What mass of chlorine does this car emit into the atmosphere each year?

124. A Freon leak in the air-conditioning system of a large building releases 12 kg of CHF_2Cl per month. If the leak is allowed to continue, how many kilograms of Cl are emitted into the atmosphere each year?

125. A metal (M) forms a compound with the formula MCl_3. If the compound contains 65.57% Cl by mass, what is the identity of the metal?

126. A metal (M) forms an oxide with the formula M_2O. If the oxide contains 16.99% O by mass, what is the identity of the metal?

127. Estradiol is a female sexual hormone that causes maturation and maintenance of the female reproductive system. Elemental analysis of estradiol gives the following mass percent composition: C 79.37%, H 8.88%, O 11.75%. The molar mass of estradiol is 272.37 g/mol. Find the molecular formula of estradiol.

128. Fructose is a common sugar found in fruit. Elemental analysis of fructose gives the following mass percent composition: C 40.00%, H 6.72%, O 53.28%. The molar mass of fructose is 180.16 g/mol. Find the molecular formula of fructose.

129. Combustion analysis of a 13.42 g sample of equilin (which contains only carbon, hydrogen, and oxygen) produces 39.61 g CO_2 and 9.01 g H_2O. The molar mass of equilin is 268.34 g/mol. Find its molecular formula.

130. Estrone, which contains only carbon, hydrogen, and oxygen, is a female sexual hormone that occurs in the urine of pregnant women. Combustion analysis of a 1.893 g sample of estrone produces 5.545 g of CO_2 and 1.388 g H_2O. The molar mass of estrone is 270.36 g/mol. Find its molecular formula.

131. Epsom salts is a hydrated ionic compound with the following formula: $MgSO_4 \cdot xH_2O$. A 4.93 g sample of Epsom salts was heated to drive off the water of hydration. The mass of the sample after complete dehydration was 2.41 g. Find the number of waters of hydration (x) in Epsom salts.

132. A hydrate of copper(II) chloride has the following formula: $CuCl_2 \cdot xH_2O$. The water in a 3.41 g sample of the hydrate was driven off by heating. The remaining sample had a mass of 2.69 g. Find the number of waters of hydration (x) in the hydrate.

133. A compound of molar mass 177 g/mol contains only carbon, hydrogen, bromine, and oxygen. Analysis reveals that the compound contains 8 times as much carbon as hydrogen by mass. Find the molecular formula.

134. Researchers obtained the following data from experiments to find the molecular formula of benzocaine, a local anesthetic, which contains only carbon, hydrogen, nitrogen, and oxygen. Complete combustion of a 3.54 g sample of benzocaine with excess O_2 formed 8.49 g of CO_2 and 2.14 g H_2O.

Another sample of mass 2.35 g was found to contain 0.199 g of N. The molar mass of benzocaine was found to be 165 g/mol. Find the molar formula of benzocaine.

135. Find the total number of atoms in a sample of cocaine hydrochloride, $C_{17}H_{22}ClNO_4$, of mass 23.5 mg.

136. Vanadium forms four different oxides in which the percent by mass of vanadium is respectively (a) 76%, (b) 68%, (c) 61%, and (d) 56%. Determine the formula and the name of each one of these oxides.

137. The chloride of an unknown metal is believed to have the formula MCl_3. A 2.395 g sample of the compound is found to contain 3.606×10^{-2} mol Cl. Find the atomic mass of M.

138. Write the structural formulas of three different compounds that each have the molecular formula C_5H_{12}.

139. A chromium-containing compound has the formula $Fe_xCr_yO_4$ and is 28.59% oxygen by mass. Find x and y.

140. A phosphorus compound that contains 34.00% phosphorus by mass has the formula X_3P_2. Identify the element X.

141. A particular brand of beef jerky contains 0.0552% sodium nitrite by mass and is sold in an 8.00 oz bag. What mass of sodium does the sodium nitrite contribute to sodium content of the bag of beef jerky?

142. Phosphorus is obtained primarily from ores containing calcium phosphate. If a particular ore contains 57.8% calcium phosphate, what minimum mass of the ore must be processed to obtain 1.00 kg of phosphorus?

Challenge Problems

143. A mixture of NaCl and NaBr has a mass of 2.00 g and contains 0.75 g of Na. What is the mass of NaBr in the mixture?

144. Three pure compounds form when 1.00 g samples of element X combine with, respectively, 0.472 g, 0.630 g, and 0.789 g of element Z. The first compound has the formula X_2Z_3. Find the empirical formulas of the other two compounds.

145. A mixture of $CaCO_3$ and $(NH_4)_2CO_3$ is 61.9% CO_3 by mass. Find the mass percent of $CaCO_3$ in the mixture.

146. A mixture of 50.0 g of S and 1.00×10^2 g of Cl_2 reacts completely to form S_2Cl_2 and SCl_2. Find the mass of S_2Cl_2 formed.

147. Because of increasing evidence of damage to the ozone layer, chlorofluorocarbon (CFC) production was banned in 1996. However, there are about 100 million auto air conditioners in operation that still use CFC-12 (CF_2Cl_2). These air conditioners are recharged from stockpiled supplies of CFC-12. If each of the 100 million automobiles contains 1.1 kg of CFC-12 and leaks 25% of its CFC-12 into the atmosphere per year, how much chlorine, in kg, is added to the atmosphere each year due to auto air conditioners? (Assume two significant figures in your calculations.)

148. A particular coal contains 2.55% sulfur by mass. When the coal is burned, it produces SO_2 emissions, which combine with rainwater to produce sulfuric acid. Use the formula of sulfuric acid to calculate the mass percent of S in sulfuric acid. Then determine how much sulfuric acid (in metric tons) is produced by the combustion of 1.0 metric ton of this coal. (A metric ton is 1000 kg.)

149. Lead is found in Earth's crust as several different lead ores. Suppose a certain rock is 38.0% PbS (galena), 25.0% $PbCO_3$ (cerussite), and 17.4% $PbSO_4$ (anglesite). The remainder of the rock is composed of substances containing no lead. How much of this rock (in kg) must be processed to obtain 5.0 metric tons of lead? (A metric ton is 1000 kg.)

150. A 2.52 g sample of a compound containing only carbon, hydrogen, nitrogen, oxygen, and sulfur was burned in excess O to yield 4.23 g of CO_2 and 1.01 g of H_2O. Another sample of the same compound, of mass 4.14 g, yielded 2.11 g of SO_3. A third sample, of mass 5.66 g, yielded 2.27 g of HNO_3. Calculate the empirical formula of the compound.

151. A compound of molar mass 229 contains only carbon, hydrogen, iodine, and sulfur. Analysis shows that a sample of the compound contains 6 times as much carbon as hydrogen, by mass. Calculate the molecular formula of the compound.

152. The elements X and Y form a compound that is 40% X and 60% Y by mass. The atomic mass of X is twice that of Y. What is the empirical formula of the compound?

153. A compound of X and Y is $\frac{1}{3}$ X by mass. The atomic mass of element X is $\frac{1}{3}$ the atomic mass of element Y. Find the empirical formula of the compound.

154. A mixture of carbon and sulfur has a mass of 9.0 g. Complete combustion with excess O_2 gives 23.3 g of a mixture of CO_2 and SO_2. Find the mass of sulfur in the original mixture.

Conceptual Problems

155. When molecules are represented by molecular models, what does each sphere represent? How big is the nucleus of an atom in comparison to the sphere used to represent an atom in a molecular model?

156. Without doing any calculations, determine which element in each of the compounds will have the highest mass percent composition.
    a. CO
    b. N_2O
    c. $C_6H_{12}O_6$
    d. NH_3

157. Explain the problem with the following statement and correct it. "The chemical formula for ammonia (NH_3) indicates that ammonia contains three grams of hydrogen to each gram of nitrogen."

158. Explain the problem with the following statement and correct it. "When a chemical equation is balanced, the number of molecules of each type on both sides of the equation will be equal."

159. Without doing any calculations, arrange the elements in H_2SO_4 in order of decreasing mass percent composition.

160. Element A is an atomic element and element B is a diatomic molecular element. Using circles to represent atoms of A and squares to represent atoms of B, draw molecular level views of each element.

Answers to Conceptual Connections

Structural Formulas
3.1 H—O—H

Representing Molecules
3.2 The spheres represent the electron cloud of the atom. It would be nearly impossible to draw a nucleus to scale on any of the space-filling molecular models in this book—on this scale, the nucleus would be too small to see.

A Molecular View of Elements and Compounds
3.3

A_2B

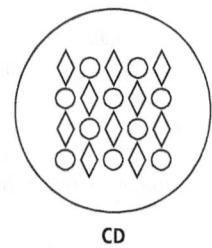
CD

Ionic and Molecular Compounds
3.4 Choice **(a)** best describes the difference between ionic and molecular compounds. The **(b)** answer is incorrect because there are no "new" forces in bonding (just rearrangements that result in lower potential energy) and because ions do not group together in pairs in the solid phase. The **(c)** answer is incorrect because the main difference between ionic and molecular compounds is

the way that the atoms bond. The **(d)** answer is incorrect because ionic compounds do not contain molecules.

Nomenclature
3.5 This conceptual connection addresses one of the main errors you can make in nomenclature: the failure to correctly categorize the compound. Remember that you must first determine whether the compound is an ionic compound, a molecular compound, or an acid, and then you must name it accordingly. NCl_3 is a molecular compound (two or more nonmetals), and therefore in its name prefixes indicate the number of each type of atom—so NCl_3 is nitrogen trichloride. The compound $AlCl_3$, however, is an ionic compound (metal and nonmetal), and therefore does not require prefixes—so $AlCl_3$ is aluminum chloride.

Molecular Models and the Size of Molecules
3.6 (c) Atomic radii range in the hundreds of picometers, while the spheres in these models have radii of less than a centimeter. The scaling factor is therefore about 10^8 (100 million).

Chemical Formula and Mass Percent Composition
3.7 C > O > H Since carbon and oxygen differ in atomic mass by only 4 amu, and since there are six carbon atoms in the formula, we can conclude that carbon constitutes the greatest fraction of the mass. Oxygen is next because its mass is 16 times that of hydrogen and there are only six hydrogen atoms to every one oxygen atom.

Chemical Formulas and Elemental Composition

3.8 (c) The chemical formula for a compound gives relationships between *atoms* or *moles of atoms*. The chemical formula for water states that water molecules contain two H atoms to every one O atom or 2 mol H to every 1 mol H_2O. This *does not* imply a two-to-one relationship between *masses* of hydrogen and oxygen because these atoms have different masses. It also does not imply a two-to-one relationship between volumes.

Balanced Chemical Equations

3.9 Both (a) and (d) are correct. When the number of atoms of each type is balanced, the sum of the masses of the substances involved will be the same on both sides of the equation. Since molecules change during a chemical reaction, their number is not the same on both sides, nor is the number of moles necessarily the same.

4
Chemical Quantities and Aqueous Reactions

I feel sorry for people who don't understand anything about chemistry.
They are missing an important source of happiness.

—Linus Pauling (1901–1994)

THE AMOUNT OF PRODUCT FORMED IN A CHEMICAL REACTION is related to the amount of reactant that reacts. This concept makes sense intuitively, but how can we describe and understand this relationship more fully? The first half of this chapter focuses on chemical stoichiometry—the numerical relationships between the amounts of reactants and products in chemical reactions. In Chapter 3, you learned how to write balanced chemical equations for chemical reactions. Here we will examine more closely the meaning of those balanced equations. In the second half of this chapter, we turn to describing chemical reactions that occur in water. You have probably witnessed many of these types of reactions in your daily life because they are so common. Have you ever mixed baking soda with vinegar and observed the subsequent bubbling or noticed the hard water deposits that form on plumbing fixtures? These reactions—and many others, including those that occur within the watery environment of living cells—are aqueous chemical reactions, the subject of the second half of this chapter.

The following handwritten notes appear in the figure:

$9 CO_2$

World's petroleum combustion

$\frac{1\ mol\ C_8H_{18}}{114.22g\ C_8H_{18}} \times \frac{16\ mol\ CO_2}{2\ mol\ C_8H_{18}} \times \frac{44.01g\ CO_2}{1\ mol\ CO_2} = 1.0 \times 10$

Volcanoes $= 2.0 \times 10^{11}$ ... $\times 10^{13}$ g CO_2 $(1.0 \times 10^{13}$ kg$)$ per year

Volcanoes emit only 2.0% as much CO_2 ... year

$\frac{2.0 \times 10^{11}\ kg}{1.0 \times 10^{13}\ kg} \times 100\% = $

per year as petroleum

$$2\ C_8H_{18}\ (\ell) + 25\ O_2\ (g) \longrightarrow 16\ CO_2\ (g) + 18\ H_2O$$

GREENHOUSE

4.1 Climate Change and the Combustion of Fossil Fuels

The temperature outside my office today is a cool 48 °F, lower than normal for this time of year on the California coast. However, today's "chill" pales in comparison with how cold it would be without the presence of *greenhouse gases* in the atmosphere. These gases act like the glass of a greenhouse, allowing sunlight to enter the atmosphere and warm Earth's surface but preventing some of the heat generated by the sunlight from escaping, as shown in Figure 4.1 ▶. The balance between incoming and outgoing energy from the sun determines Earth's average temperature.

If the greenhouse gases in the atmosphere were not present, more heat energy would escape, and Earth's average temperature would be about 60 °F colder than it currently is. The temperature outside of my office today would be below 0 °F, and even the sunniest U.S. cities would most likely be covered with snow. However, if the concentration of greenhouse gases in the atmosphere were to increase, Earth's average temperature would rise.

The molecular models on this balance represent the reactants and products in the combustion of octane, a component of petroleum. One of the products, carbon dioxide, is the main greenhouse gas implicated in global climate change.

The extremely cold temperatures of Mars are as much a result of its lack of atmosphere as its greater distance from the sun than Earth. Conversely, Venus is an inferno partly because its thick atmosphere is rich in greenhouse gases.

▶ FIGURE 4.1 **The Greenhouse Effect** Greenhouse gases in the atmosphere act as a one-way filter. They allow visible light to pass through and warm Earth's surface, but they prevent heat energy from radiating back out into space.

The Greenhouse Effect

Sunlight passes through atmosphere and warms Earth's surface.

Greenhouse gases

Some of the heat radiated from Earth's surface is trapped by greenhouse gases.

Earth

In recent years scientists have become increasingly concerned because the quantity of atmospheric carbon dioxide (CO_2)—Earth's most significant greenhouse gas—is rising. More CO_2 enhances the atmosphere's ability to hold heat and is believed to lead to *global warming,* an increase in Earth's average temperature. Since 1860, atmospheric CO_2 levels have risen by 38% (Figure 4.2 ▼), and Earth's average temperature has risen by 0.7 °C (about 1.2 °F), as shown in Figure 4.3 ▼.

Most scientists believe that the primary cause of rising atmospheric CO_2 concentration is the burning of fossil fuels (natural gas, petroleum, and coal), which provide 90% of our society's energy. Some people, however, have suggested that fossil fuel combustion does not significantly contribute to global warming and climate change. They argue that the amount of carbon dioxide emitted into the atmosphere by natural sources, such as volcanic eruptions, far exceeds that from fossil fuel combustion. Which group is right? We can judge the validity of the naysayers' argument by calculating how much carbon dioxide is emitted by fossil fuel combustion and comparing that amount to the amount released by volcanic eruptions.

4.2 Reaction Stoichiometry: How Much Carbon Dioxide?

The balanced chemical equations for fossil-fuel combustion reactions provide the exact relationships between the amount of fossil fuel burned and the amount of carbon dioxide emitted. In this discussion, we use octane (a component of gasoline) as a representative fossil fuel. The balanced equation for the combustion of octane is:

$$2\,C_8H_{18}(l) + 25\,O_2(g) \rightarrow 16\,CO_2(g) + 18\,H_2O(g)$$

Atmospheric Carbon Dioxide

▲ FIGURE 4.2 **Carbon Dioxide Concentrations in the Atmosphere** The rise in carbon dioxide levels is due largely to fossil fuel combustion.

Global Temperature

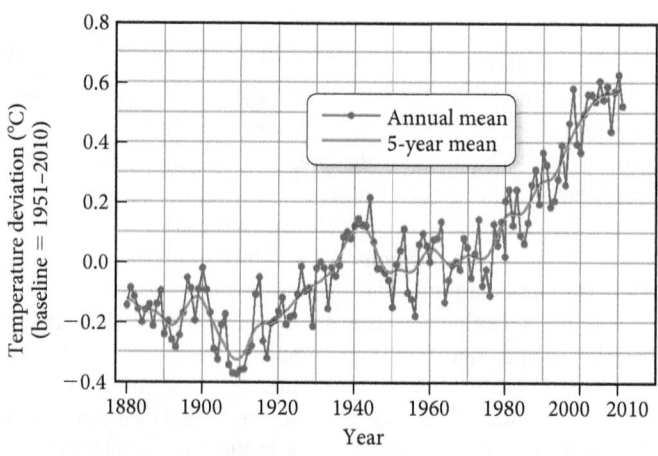

▲ FIGURE 4.3 **Global Temperature** Average temperatures worldwide have risen by about 0.7 °C since 1880.

The balanced equation shows that 16 CO_2 molecules are produced for every 2 molecules of octane burned. We can extend this numerical relationship between molecules to the amounts in moles as follows:

> **The coefficients in a chemical equation specify the relative amounts in moles of each of the substances involved in the reaction**.

In other words, from the equation, we know that 16 *moles* of CO_2 are produced for every 2 *moles* of octane burned. The numerical relationships between chemical amounts in a balanced chemical equation are called reaction **stoichiometry**. Stoichiometry allows us to predict the amounts of products that will form in a chemical reaction based on the amounts of reactants that react. Stoichiometry also allows us to determine the amount of reactants necessary to form a given amount of product. These calculations are central to chemistry, allowing chemists to plan and carry out chemical reactions to obtain products in the desired quantities.

| Stoichiometry is pronounced stoy-kee-AHM-e-tree.

Making Pizza: The Relationships among Ingredients

The concepts of stoichiometry are similar to those in a cooking recipe. Calculating the amount of carbon dioxide produced by the combustion of a given amount of a fossil fuel is analogous to calculating the number of pizzas that can be made from a given amount of cheese. For example, suppose we use the following pizza recipe:

$$1 \text{ crust } + \text{ 5 ounces tomato sauce } + \text{ 2 cups cheese } \rightarrow 1 \text{ pizza}$$

The recipe contains the numerical relationships between the pizza ingredients. It says that if we have 2 cups of cheese—and enough of everything else—we can make 1 pizza. We can write this relationship as a ratio between the cheese and the pizza:

$$2 \text{ cups cheese : 1 pizza}$$

What if we have 6 cups of cheese? Assuming that we have enough of everything else, we can use the ratio as a conversion factor to calculate the number of pizzas:

$$6 \text{ cups cheese } \times \frac{1 \text{ pizza}}{2 \text{ cups cheese}} = 3 \text{ pizzas}$$

Six cups of cheese are sufficient to make 3 pizzas. The pizza recipe contains numerical ratios between other ingredients as well, including the crust and the tomato sauce:

$$1 \text{ crust : 1 pizza}$$

$$5 \text{ ounces tomato sauce : 1 pizza}$$

Making Molecules: Mole-to-Mole Conversions

In a balanced chemical equation, we have a "recipe" for how reactants combine to form products. From our balanced equation for the combustion of octane, for example, we can write the following stoichiometric ratio:

$$2 \text{ mol } C_8H_{18} : 16 \text{ mol } CO_2$$

We can use this ratio to determine how many moles of CO_2 form when a given number of moles of C_8H_{18} burns. Suppose that we burn 22.0 moles of C_8H_{18}; how many moles of CO_2 form? We use the ratio from the balanced chemical equation in the same way that we used the ratio from the pizza recipe. The ratio acts as a conversion factor between the amount in moles of the reactant (C_8H_{18}) and the amount in moles of the product (CO_2):

$$22.0 \text{ mol } C_8H_{18} \times \frac{16 \text{ mol } CO_2}{2 \text{ mol } C_8H_{18}} = 176 \text{ mol } CO_2$$

The combustion of 22.0 moles of C_8H_{18} adds 176 moles of CO_2 to the atmosphere.

Making Molecules: Mass-to-Mass Conversions

According to the U.S. Department of Energy, the world burned 3.1×10^{10} barrels of petroleum in 2010, the equivalent of approximately 3.5×10^{15} g of gasoline. We can estimate the mass of CO_2 emitted into the atmosphere from burning this much gasoline using the combustion of 3.5×10^{15} g octane as the representative reaction. This calculation is similar to the one we just did, except that we are now given the *mass* of octane instead of the *amount* of octane in moles. Consequently, we must first convert the mass (in grams) to the amount (in moles). The general conceptual plan for calculations in which we are given the mass of a reactant or product in a chemical reaction and asked to find the mass of a different reactant or product takes the form:

where A and B are two different substances involved in the reaction. We use the molar mass of A to convert from the mass of A to the amount of A (in moles). We use the appropriate ratio from the balanced chemical equation to convert from the amount of A (in moles) to the amount of B (in moles). And finally, we use the molar mass of B to convert from the amount of B (in moles) to the mass of B. To calculate the mass of CO_2 emitted upon the combustion of 3.5×10^{15} g of octane, we use the following conceptual plan:

Conceptual Plan

$$\boxed{\text{g } C_8H_{18}} \longrightarrow \boxed{\text{mol } C_8H_{18}} \longrightarrow \boxed{\text{mol } CO_2} \longrightarrow \boxed{\text{g } CO_2}$$

$$\frac{1 \text{ mol } C_8H_{18}}{114.22 \text{ g } C_8H_{18}} \qquad \frac{16 \text{ mol } CO_2}{2 \text{ mol } C_8H_{18}} \qquad \frac{44.01 \text{ g } CO_2}{1 \text{ mol } CO_2}$$

Relationships Used

2 mol C_8H_{18} : 16 mol CO_2 (from the chemical equation)

molar mass C_8H_{18} = 114.22 g/mol

molar mass CO_2 = 44.01 g/mol

Solution

We follow the conceptual plan to solve the problem, beginning with g C_8H_{18} and canceling units to arrive at g CO_2:

$$3.5 \times 10^{15} \text{ g } C_8H_{18} \times \frac{1 \text{ mol } C_8H_{18}}{114.22 \text{ g } C_8H_{18}} \times$$

$$\frac{16 \text{ mol } CO_2}{2 \text{ mol } C_8H_{18}} \times \frac{44.01 \text{ g } CO_2}{1 \text{ mol } CO_2} = 1.1 \times 10^{16} \text{ g } CO_2$$

The world's petroleum combustion produces 1.1×10^{16} g CO_2 (1.1×10^{13} kg) per year. In comparison, volcanoes produce about 2×10^{11} kg CO_2 per year.[*] In other words, volcanoes emit only $\frac{2.0 \times 10^{11} \text{ kg}}{1.1 \times 10^{13} \text{ kg}} \times 100\% = 1.8\%$ as much CO_2 per year as petroleum combustion. The argument that volcanoes emit more carbon dioxide than fossil fuel combustion is clearly mistaken. Additional examples of stoichiometric calculations follow.

The percentage of CO_2 emitted by volcanoes relative to all fossil fuels is even less than 2% because the combustion of coal and natural gas also emits CO_2.

[*]Gerlach, T. M., Present-day CO_2 emissions from volcanoes. *Eos, Transactions, American Geophysical Union.* **1991** *72*, 249, 254–255.

EXAMPLE 4.1 Stoichiometry

In photosynthesis, plants convert carbon dioxide and water into glucose ($C_6H_{12}O_6$)
according to the reaction:

$$6\ CO_2(g) + 6\ H_2O(l) \xrightarrow{\text{sunlight}} 6\ O_2(g) + C_6H_{12}O_6(aq)$$

Suppose you determine that a particular plant consumes 37.8 g of CO_2 in one week.
Assuming that there is more than enough water present to react with all of the CO_2,
what mass of glucose (in grams) can the plant synthesize from the CO_2?

SORT The problem gives the mass of carbon dioxide and asks you to find the mass of glucose that can be produced.	**GIVEN:** 37.8 g CO_2 **FIND:** g $C_6H_{12}O_6$

STRATEGIZE The conceptual plan follows the general pattern of mass A → amount A (in moles) → amount B (in moles) → mass B. From the chemical equation, deduce the relationship between moles of carbon dioxide and moles of glucose. Use the molar masses to convert between grams and moles.	**CONCEPTUAL PLAN** **RELATIONSHIPS USED** molar mass CO_2 = 44.01 g/mol 6 mol CO_2 : 1 mol $C_6H_{12}O_6$ molar mass $C_6H_{12}O_6$ = 180.2 g/mol

SOLVE Follow the conceptual plan to solve the problem. Begin with g CO_2 and use the conversion factors to arrive at g $C_6H_{12}O_6$.	**SOLUTION** $37.8\ \text{g } CO_2 \times \dfrac{1\ \text{mol } CO_2}{44.01\ \text{g } CO_2} \times \dfrac{1\ \text{mol } C_6H_{12}O_6}{6\ \text{mol } CO_2} \times \dfrac{180.2\ \text{g } C_6H_{12}O_6}{1\ \text{mol } C_6H_{12}O_6} = 25.8\ \text{g } C_6H_{12}O_6$

CHECK The units of the answer are correct. The magnitude of the answer (25.8 g) is
less than the initial mass of CO_2 (37.8 g). This is reasonable because each carbon in
CO_2 has two oxygen atoms associated with it, while in $C_6H_{12}O_6$ each carbon has
only one oxygen atom associated with it and two hydrogen atoms, which are much
lighter than oxygen. Therefore, the mass of glucose produced should be less than the
mass of carbon dioxide for this reaction.

FOR PRACTICE 4.1
Magnesium hydroxide, the active ingredient in milk of magnesia, neutralizes
stomach acid, primarily HCl, according to the reaction:

$$Mg(OH)_2(aq) + 2\ HCl(aq) \rightarrow 2\ H_2O(l) + MgCl_2(aq)$$

What mass of HCl, in grams, is neutralized by a dose of milk of magnesia containing
3.26 g $Mg(OH)_2$?

EXAMPLE 4.2 Stoichiometry

Sulfuric acid (H_2SO_4) is a component of acid rain that forms when SO_2, a pollutant,
reacts with oxygen and water according to the simplified reaction:

$$2\ SO_2(g) + O_2(g) + 2\ H_2O(l) \rightarrow 2\ H_2SO_4(aq)$$

The generation of the electricity used by a medium-sized home produces about 25 kg
of SO_2 per year. Assuming that there is more than enough O_2 and H_2O, what mass of
H_2SO_4, in kg, can form from this much SO_2?

... problem gives the mass of ...dioxide and asks you to find ...mass of sulfuric acid.	**GIVEN:** 25 kg SO_2 **FIND:** kg H_2SO_4

| **STRATEGIZE** The conceptual plan follows the standard format of mass → amount (in moles) → amount (in moles) → mass. Since the original quantity of SO_2 is given in kg, you must first convert to grams. You can deduce the relationship between moles of sulfur dioxide and moles of sulfuric acid from the chemical equation. Since the final quantity is requested in kg, convert to kg at the end. | **CONCEPTUAL PLAN**
 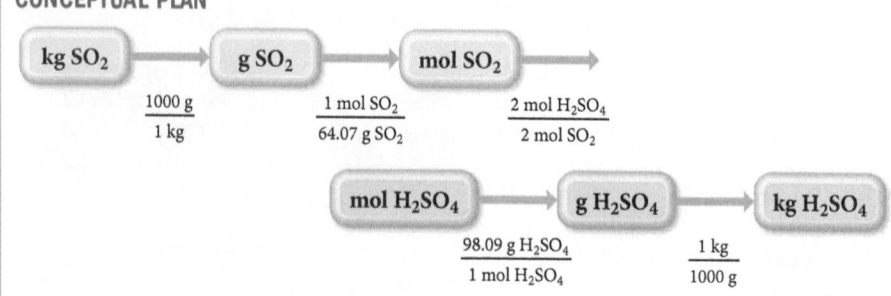

 RELATIONSHIPS USED
 1 kg = 1000 g   2 mol SO_2 : 2 mol H_2SO_4
 molar mass SO_2 = 64.07 g/mol   molar mass H_2SO_4 = 98.09 g/mol |

| **SOLVE** Follow the conceptual plan to solve the problem. Begin with the given amount of SO_2 in kilograms and use the conversion factors to arrive at kg H_2SO_4. | **SOLUTION**
 $$25 \text{ kg } SO_2 \times \frac{1000 \text{ g}}{1 \text{ kg}} \times \frac{1 \text{ mol } SO_2}{64.07 \text{ g } SO_2} \times \frac{2 \text{ mol } H_2SO_4}{2 \text{ mol } SO_2}$$
 $$\times \frac{98.09 \text{ g } H_2SO_4}{1 \text{ mol } H_2SO_4} \times \frac{1 \text{ kg}}{1000 \text{ g}} = 38 \text{ kg } H_2SO_4$$ |

CHECK The units of the final answer are correct. The magnitude of the final answer (38 kg H_2SO_4) is larger than the amount of SO_2 given (25 kg). This is reasonable because in the reaction each SO_2 molecule "gains weight" by reacting with O_2 and H_2O.

FOR PRACTICE 4.2

Another component of acid rain is nitric acid, which forms when NO_2, also a pollutant, reacts with oxygen and water according to the simplified equation:

$$4 NO_2(g) + O_2(g) + 2 H_2O(l) \rightarrow 4 HNO_3(aq)$$

The generation of the electricity used by a medium-sized home produces about 16 kg of NO_2 per year. Assuming that there is adequate O_2 and H_2O, what mass of HNO_3, in kg, can form from this amount of NO_2 pollutant?

Conceptual Connection 4.1 Stoichiometry

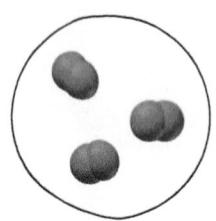

Under certain conditions sodium can react with oxygen to form sodium oxide according to the reaction:

$$4 Na(s) + O_2(g) \rightarrow 2 Na_2O(s)$$

A flask contains the amount of oxygen represented by the diagram at left.

Which image below best represents the amount of sodium required to completely react with all of the oxygen in the flask according to the equation?

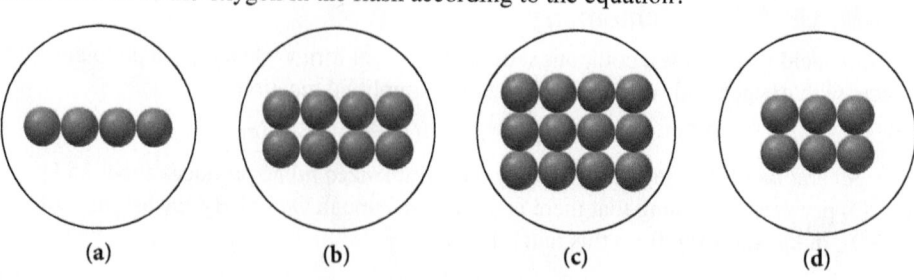

(a)   (b)   (c)   (d)

Conceptual Connection 4.2 Stoichiometry II

Consider the generic chemical equation A + 3B → 2C. Let circles represent molecules of A, squares represent molecules of B, and triangles represent molecules of C. If the diagram at right represents the amount of B available for reaction, draw similar diagrams showing (a) the amount of A necessary to completely react with B, and (b) the amount of C that forms if B completely reacts.

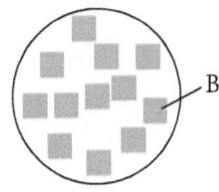

B

4.3 Limiting Reactant, Theoretical Yield, and Percent Yield

Let's return to our pizza analogy to understand three more important concepts in reaction stoichiometry: *limiting reactant, theoretical yield,* and *percent yield.* Recall our pizza recipe from Section 4.2:

$$1 \text{ crust } + \text{ 5 ounces tomato sauce } + \text{ 2 cups cheese} \rightarrow 1 \text{ pizza}$$

Suppose that we have 4 crusts, 10 cups of cheese, and 15 ounces of tomato sauce. How many pizzas can we make?

We have enough crusts to make:

$$4 \text{ crusts} \times \frac{1 \text{ pizza}}{1 \text{ crust}} = 4 \text{ pizzas}$$

We have enough cheese to make:

$$10 \text{ cups cheese} \times \frac{1 \text{ pizza}}{2 \text{ cups cheese}} = 5 \text{ pizzas}$$

We have enough tomato sauce to make:

$$15 \text{ ounces tomato sauce} \times \frac{1 \text{ pizza}}{5 \text{ ounces tomato sauce}} = 3 \text{ pizzas}$$

Limiting reactant

Smallest number of pizzas

We have enough crusts for four pizzas and enough cheese for five pizzas, but enough tomato sauce for only three pizzas. Consequently, unless we get more ingredients, we can make only three pizzas. The tomato sauce *limits* how many pizzas we can make. If the pizza recipe were a chemical reaction, the tomato sauce would be the **limiting reactant,** the reactant that limits the amount of product in a chemical reaction. Notice that the limiting reactant is the reactant that makes *the least amount of product.* The reactants that *do not* limit the amount of product—such as the crusts and the cheese in this example—are said to be *in excess.* If this were a chemical reaction, three pizzas would be the **theoretical yield,** the maximum amount of product that can be made in a chemical reaction based on the amount of limiting reactant.

The term *limiting reagent* is sometimes used in place of *limiting reactant.*

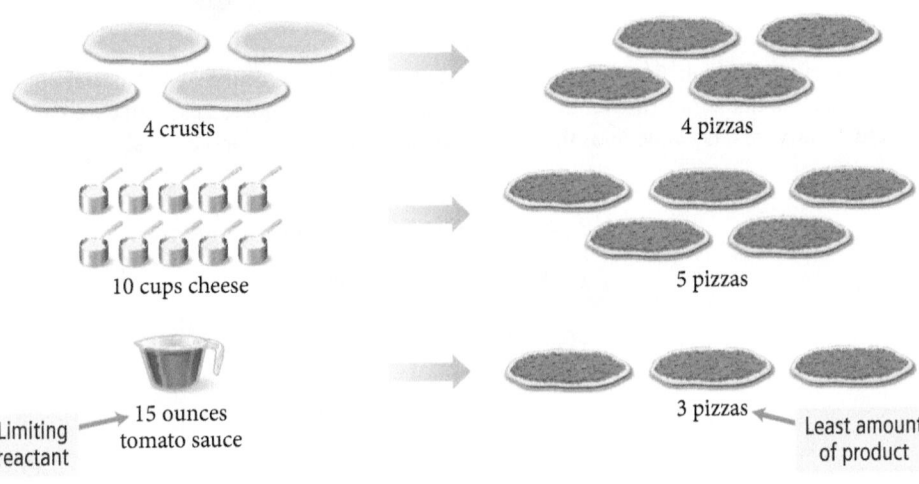

4 crusts → 4 pizzas

10 cups cheese → 5 pizzas

Limiting reactant → 15 ounces tomato sauce → 3 pizzas ← Least amount of product

◀ The ingredient that makes the least amount of pizza determines how many pizzas you can make.

Let us carry this analogy one step further. Suppose we go on to cook our pizzas and accidentally burn one of them. Even though we theoretically have enough ingredients for three pizzas, we end up with only two. If this were a chemical reaction, the two pizzas would be our **actual yield**, the amount of product actually produced by a chemical reaction. (The actual yield is always equal to or less than the theoretical yield because a small amount of product is usually lost to other reactions or does not form during a reaction.) Finally, our **percent yield**, the percentage of the theoretical yield that was actually attained, is calculated as the ratio of the actual yield to the theoretical yield:

Actual yield

$$\% \text{ yield } = \frac{2 \text{ pizzas}}{3 \text{ pizzas}} \times 100\% = 67\%$$

Theoretical yield

Since one of our pizzas burned, our percent yield for pizzas is 67%.

Summarizing Limiting Reactant and Yield:

▶ **The limiting reactant** (or **limiting reagent**) is the reactant that is completely consumed in a chemical reaction and limits the amount of product.

▶ **The reactant in excess** is any reactant that occurs in a quantity greater than is required to completely react with the limiting reactant.

▶ **The theoretical yield** is the amount of product that can be made in a chemical reaction based on the amount of limiting reactant.

▶ **The actual yield** is the amount of product actually produced by a chemical reaction.

▶ **The percent yield** is calculated as $\dfrac{\text{actual yield}}{\text{theoretical yield}} \times 100\%$.

We can apply these concepts to a chemical reaction. Recall from Section 3.11 our balanced equation for the combustion of methane:

$$CH_4(g) + 2\,O_2(g) \longrightarrow CO_2(g) + 2\,H_2O(l)$$

If we start out with five CH_4 molecules and eight O_2 molecules, what is our limiting reactant? What is our theoretical yield of carbon dioxide molecules? First we calculate the number of CO_2 molecules that can be made from five CH_4 molecules:

$$5\,CH_4 \times \frac{1\,CO_2}{1\,CH_4} = 5\,CO_2$$

We then calculate the number of CO_2 molecules that can be made from eight O_2 molecules:

$$8 \; O_2 \times \frac{1 \; CO_2}{2 \; O_2} = 4 \; CO_2$$

Limiting
reactant

Least amount
of product

We have enough CH_4 to make five CO_2 molecules and enough O_2 to make four CO_2 molecules; therefore, O_2 is the limiting reactant, and four CO_2 molecules is the theoretical yield. The CH_4 is in excess.

An alternative way to calculate the limiting reactant (which we mention here but do not use in this book) is to pick any reactant and determine how much of the *other reactant* is necessary to completely react with it. For the reaction we just examined, we have five CH_4 molecules and eight O_2 molecules. Let's pick the five CH_4 molecules and determine how many O_2 molecules are necessary to completely react with them:

$$5 \; CH_4 \times \frac{2 \; O_2}{1 \; CH_4} = 10 \; O_2$$

Since we need ten O_2 molecules to completely react with the five CH_4 molecules, and since we have only eight O_2 molecules, we know that the O_2 is the limiting reactant. The same method can be applied by comparing the amounts of reactants in moles.

Conceptual Connection 4.3 Limiting Reactant and Theoretical Yield

Nitrogen and hydrogen gas react to form ammonia according to the reaction:

$$N_2(g) + 3H_2(g) \rightarrow 2 \; NH_3(g)$$

If a flask contains a mixture of reactants represented by the image at right, which image below best represents the mixture in the flask after the reactants have reacted as completely as possible? What is the limiting reactant? Which reactant is in excess?

(a)   (b)   (c)

Limiting Reactant, Theoretical Yield, and Percent Yield from Initial Reactant Masses

When working in the laboratory, we normally measure the initial quantities of reactants in grams, not in number of molecules. To find the limiting reactant and theoretical yield from initial masses, we must first convert the masses to amounts in moles. Consider the reaction:

$$2 \; Mg(s) + O_2(g) \rightarrow 2 \; MgO(s)$$

A reaction mixture contains 42.5 g Mg and 33.8 g O_2; what is the limiting reactant and theoretical yield?

To solve this problem, we must determine which of the reactants makes the least amount of product.

Conceptual Plan

We can find the limiting reactant by calculating how much product can be made from each reactant. However, we are given the initial quantities in grams, and stoichiometric relationships are between moles, so we must first convert to moles. We then convert from moles of the reactant to moles of product. The reactant that makes the *least amount of product* is the limiting reactant. The conceptual plan is:

In this conceptual plan, we compare the number of moles of MgO made by each reactant and convert only the smaller amount to grams. (Alternatively, we can convert both quantities to grams and determine the limiting reactant based on the mass of the product.)

Relationships Used

   molar mass Mg $= 24.31$ g Mg

   molar mass $O_2 = 32.00$ g O_2

   2 mol Mg : 2 mol MgO

   1 mol O_2 : 2 mol MgO

   molar mass MgO $= 40.31$ g MgO

Solution

Beginning with the masses of each reactant, we follow the conceptual plan to calculate how much product can be made from each:

$$42.5 \text{ g Mg} \times \frac{1 \text{ mol Mg}}{24.31 \text{ g Mg}} \times \frac{2 \text{ mol MgO}}{2 \text{ mol Mg}} = 1.7483 \text{ mol MgO}$$

Limiting reactant

Least amount of product

$$33.8 \text{ g O}_2 \times \frac{1 \text{ mol O}_2}{32.00 \text{ g O}_2} \times \frac{2 \text{ mol MgO}}{1 \text{ mol O}_2} = 2.1125 \text{ mol MgO}$$

$$1.7483 \text{ mol MgO} \times \frac{40.31 \text{ g MgO}}{1 \text{ mol MgO}} = 70.5 \text{ g MgO}$$

Since Mg makes the least amount of product, it is the limiting reactant, and O_2 is in excess. Notice that the limiting reactant is not necessarily the reactant with the least mass. In this case, the mass of O_2 is less than the mass of Mg, yet Mg is the limiting reactant because it makes the least amount of MgO. The theoretical yield is 70.5 g of MgO, the mass of product possible based on the limiting reactant.

Suppose that after the synthesis, the actual yield of MgO is 55.9 g. What is the percent yield? We calculate the percent yield as follows:

$$\% \text{ yield} = \frac{\text{actual yield}}{\text{theoretical yield}} \times 100\% = \frac{55.9 \text{ g}}{70.5 \text{ g}} \times 100\% = 79.3\%$$

EXAMPLE 4.3 Limiting Reactant and Theoretical Yield

Ammonia, NH_3, can be synthesized by the reaction:

$$2 NO(g) + 5 H_2(g) \rightarrow 2 NH_3(g) + 2 H_2O(g)$$

Starting with 86.3 g NO and 25.6 g H_2, find the theoretical yield of ammonia in grams.

SORT You are given the mass of each reactant in grams and asked to find the theoretical yield of a product.	**GIVEN:** 86.3 g NO, 25.6 g H_2 **FIND:** theoretical yield of $NH_3(g)$

STRATEGIZE Determine which reactant makes the least amount of product by converting from grams of each reactant to moles of the reactant to moles of the product. Use molar masses to convert between grams and moles and use the stoichiometric relationships (deduced from the chemical equation) to convert between moles of reactant and moles of product. Remember that the reactant that makes *the least amount of product* is the limiting reactant. Convert the number of moles of product obtained using the limiting reactant to grams of product.	**CONCEPTUAL PLAN** 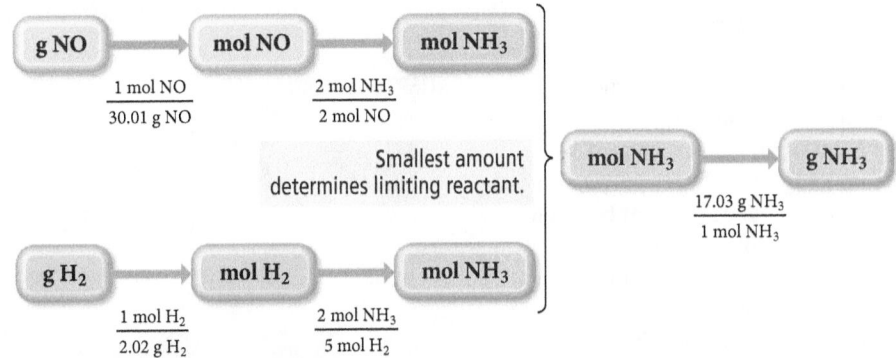 **RELATIONSHIPS USED** molar mass NO = 30.01 g/mol molar mass H_2 = 2.02 g/mol 2 mol NO : 2 mol NH_3 (from chemical equation) 5 mol H_2 : 2 mol NH_3 (from chemical equation) molar mass NH_3 = 17.03 g/mol

SOLVE Beginning with the given mass of each reactant, calculate the amount of product that can be made in moles. Convert the amount of product made by the limiting reactant to grams—this is the theoretical yield.	**SOLUTION** $86.3 \text{ g NO} \times \dfrac{1 \text{ mol NO}}{30.01 \text{ g NO}} \times \dfrac{2 \text{ mol NH}_3}{2 \text{ mol NO}} = 2.8757 \text{ mol NH}_3$ ↑ Limiting reactant Least amount of product $2.8757 \text{ mol NH}_3 \times \dfrac{17.03 \text{ g NH}_3}{\text{mol NH}_3} = 49.0 \text{ g NH}_3$ $25.6 \text{ g H}_2 \times \dfrac{1 \text{ mol H}_2}{2.02 \text{ g H}_2} \times \dfrac{2 \text{ mol NH}_3}{5 \text{ mol H}_2} = 5.0693 \text{ mol NH}_3$ Since NO makes the least amount of product, it is the limiting reactant, and the theoretical yield of ammonia is 49.0 g.

CHECK The units of the answer (g NH_3) are correct. The magnitude (49.0 g) seems reasonable given that 86.3 g NO is the limiting reactant. NO contains one oxygen atom per nitrogen atom and NH_3 contains three hydrogen atoms per nitrogen atom. Since three hydrogen atoms have less mass than one oxygen atom, it is reasonable that the mass of NH_3 obtained is less than the mass of NO.

FOR PRACTICE 4.3

Ammonia can also be synthesized by the reaction:

$$3 H_2(g) + N_2(g) \rightarrow 2 NH_3(g)$$

What is the theoretical yield of ammonia, in kg, that we can synthesize from 5.22 kg of H_2 and 31.5 kg of N_2?

EXAMPLE 4.4 Limiting Reactant and Theoretical Yield

We can obtain titanium metal from its oxide according to the following balanced equation:

$$TiO_2(s) + 2\,C(s) \rightarrow Ti(s) + 2\,CO(g)$$

When 28.6 kg of C reacts with 88.2 kg of TiO_2, 42.8 kg of Ti is produced. Find the limiting reactant, theoretical yield (in kg), and percent yield.

SORT You are given the mass of each reactant and the mass of product formed. You are asked to find the limiting reactant, theoretical yield, and percent yield.	**GIVEN:** 28.6 kg C, 88.2 kg TiO_2, 42.8 kg Ti produced **FIND:** limiting reactant, theoretical yield, % yield
STRATEGIZE Determine which of the reactants makes the least amount of product by converting from kilograms of each reactant to moles of product. Convert between grams and moles using molar mass. Convert between moles of reactant and moles of product using the stoichiometric relationships derived from the chemical equation. Remember that the reactant that makes the *least amount of product* is the limiting reactant. Determine the theoretical yield (in kg) by converting the number of moles of product obtained with the limiting reactant to kilograms of product.	**CONCEPTUAL PLAN** 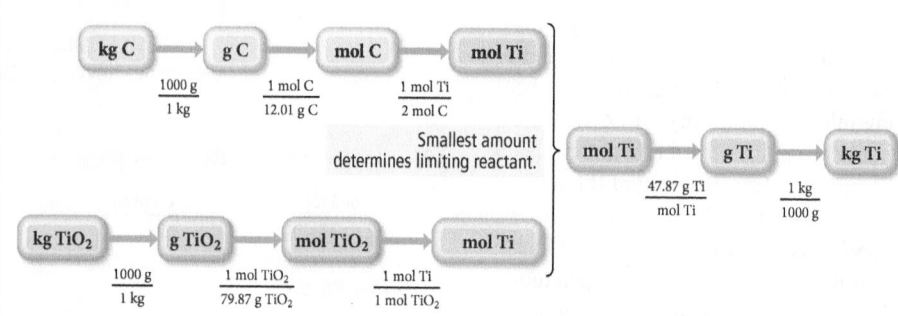 **RELATIONSHIPS USED** 1000 g = 1 kg molar mass of C = 12.01 g/mol molar mass of TiO_2 = 79.87 g/mol 1 mol TiO_2 : 1 mol Ti 2 mol C : 1 mol Ti molar mass of Ti = 47.87 g/mol
SOLVE Beginning with the actual amount of each reactant, calculate the amount of product that can be made in moles. Convert the amount of product made by the limiting reactant to kilograms—this is the theoretical yield.	**SOLUTION** $$28.6\ \text{kg C} \times \frac{1000\ \text{g}}{1\ \text{kg}} \times \frac{1\ \text{mol C}}{12.01\ \text{g C}} \times \frac{1\ \text{mol Ti}}{2\ \text{mol C}} = 1.1907 \times 10^3\ \text{mol Ti}$$ Limiting reactant / Least amount of product $$88.2\ \text{kg TiO}_2 \times \frac{1000\ \text{g}}{1\ \text{kg}} \times \frac{1\ \text{mol TiO}_2}{79.87\ \text{g TiO}_2} \times \frac{1\ \text{mol Ti}}{1\ \text{mol TiO}_2} = 1.1043 \times 10^3\ \text{mol Ti}$$ $$1.1043 \times 10^3\ \text{mol Ti} \times \frac{47.87\ \text{g Ti}}{1\ \text{mol Ti}} \times \frac{1\ \text{kg}}{1000\ \text{g}} = 52.9\ \text{kg Ti}$$
Calculate the percent yield by dividing the actual yield (42.8 kg Ti) by the theoretical yield.	Since TiO_2 makes the least amount of product, it is the limiting reactant, and 52.9 kg Ti is the theoretical yield. $$\%\ \text{yield} = \frac{\text{actual yield}}{\text{theoretical yield}} \times 100\% = \frac{42.8\ \text{g}}{52.9\ \text{g}} \times 100\% = 80.9\%$$

CHECK The theoretical yield has the correct units (kg Ti) and has a reasonable magnitude compared to the mass of TiO_2. Since Ti has a lower molar mass than TiO_2, the amount of Ti made from TiO_2 should have a lower mass. The percent yield is reasonable (under 100% as it should be).

FOR PRACTICE 4.4

Mining companies use this reaction to obtain iron from iron ore:

$$Fe_2O_3(s) + 3\,CO(g) \rightarrow 2\,Fe(s) + 3\,CO_2(g)$$

The reaction of 167 g Fe_2O_3 with 85.8 g CO produces 72.3 g Fe. Determine the limiting reactant, theoretical yield, and percent yield.

Conceptual Connection 4.4 Reactant in Excess

Nitrogen dioxide reacts with water to form nitric acid and nitrogen monoxide according to the equation:

$$3\,NO_2(g) + H_2O(l) \rightarrow 2\,HNO_3(l) + NO(g)$$

Suppose that 5 mol NO_2 and 1 mol H_2O combine and react completely. How many moles of the reactant in excess are present after the reaction has completed?

Chemistry in the Environment
MTBE in Gasoline

We have seen the balanced chemical equation for the combustion of octane, a component of gasoline, is:

$$2\,C_8H_{18}(l) + 25\,O_2(g) \rightarrow 16\,CO_2(g) + 18\,H_2O(g)$$

The equation shows that 25 moles of O_2 are required to completely react with 2 moles of C_8H_{18}. What if there is not enough O_2 in an automobile cylinder to fully react with the amount of octane that is present? For many reactions, a shortage of one reactant means that less product forms—so, in the reaction shown here, oxygen would become the limiting reactant. However, for some reactions, a shortage of one reactant causes side reactions to occur along with the desired reaction. In the case of octane and the other major components of gasoline, those side reactions produce pollutants such as carbon monoxide (CO) and unburned hydrocarbon fragments that lead to the formation of ozone (O_3).

In 1990, the U.S. Congress, in efforts to lower air pollution, passed amendments to the Clean Air Act requiring oil companies to add substances to gasoline that prevent these side reactions. Because these additives increase the amount of oxygen present during combustion, the resulting gasoline is called an oxygenated fuel. The additive of choice among oil companies was a compound called MTBE (methyl tertiary butyl ether).

◀ MTBE, a gasoline additive that promotes complete combustion.

The immediate results of adding MTBE to gasoline were positive. Carbon monoxide and ozone levels in many major cities decreased significantly.

Over time, however, MTBE—a compound that does not readily biodegrade (naturally break down in the environment)—began to appear in drinking water across the nation. MTBE entered the drinking water supply via gasoline spills at gas stations, from boat motors, and from leaking underground storage tanks. MTBE, even at low levels, imparts a turpentine-like odor and foul taste to drinking water. It is also a suspected carcinogen.

Public response was swift and dramatic. Several class action lawsuits were filed against the manufacturers of MTBE, against gas stations suspected of leaking it, and against the oil companies that put it into gasoline. Many states banned MTBE from gasoline, and the oil industry stopped adding it to gasoline (because of liability concerns). This raises a question, however. MTBE was added to gasoline as a way to meet the requirements of the 1990 Clean Air Act amendments. If MTBE is no longer an option, and the oil companies are not able to comply with the law, should the government remove the requirements, weakening the Clean Air Act? One potential solution is substituting ethanol for MTBE. Ethanol, made from the fermentation of grains, has many of the same pollution-reducing effects without the associated health hazards.

Question

How many kilograms of oxygen (O_2) are required to completely react with 48 kg of octane (approximate capacity of a 15-gallon automobile gasoline tank)?

▶ Oxygenated fuel contains compounds that increase the amount of oxygen available for combustion, reducing the formation of by-products such as carbon monoxide and hydrocarbon fragments.

4.4 Solution Concentration and Solution Stoichiometry

Chemical reactions involving reactants dissolved in water are among the most common and important. The reactions that occur in lakes, streams, and oceans, as well as the reactions that occur in every cell within our bodies, take place in water. A homogeneous mixture of two substances—such as salt and water—is a **solution**. The majority component of the mixture is the **solvent**, and the minority component is the **solute**. An **aqueous solution** is one in which water acts as the solvent. In this section, we first examine how to quantify the concentration of a solution (the amount of solute relative to solvent) and then turn to applying the principles of stoichiometry, which we discussed in the previous section, to reactions occurring in solution.

Concentrated and Dilute Solutions

Concentrated solution   Dilute solution

▲ FIGURE 4.4 **Concentrated and Dilute Solutions** A concentrated solution contains a relatively large amount of solute relative to solvent. A dilute solution contains a relatively small amount of solute relative to solvent.

Solution Concentration

The amount of solute in a solution is variable. For example, we can add just a little salt to water to make a **dilute solution**, one that contains a small amount of solute relative to the solvent, or we can add a lot of salt to water to make a **concentrated solution**, one that contains a large amount of solute relative to the solvent (Figure 4.4 ◄). A common way to express solution concentration is **molarity (M)**, the amount of solute (in moles) divided by the volume of solution (in liters):

$$\text{Molarity (M)} = \frac{\text{amount of solute (in mol)}}{\text{volume of solution (in L)}}$$

Notice that molarity is a ratio of the amount of solute per liter of *solution*, not per liter of solvent. To make an aqueous solution of a specified molarity, we usually put the solute into a flask and then add water to reach the desired volume of solution. For example, to make 1 L of a 1 M NaCl solution, we add 1 mol of NaCl to a flask and then add enough water to make 1 L of solution (Figure 4.5 ▼). We *do not* combine 1 mol of NaCl with 1 L of water, because the resulting solution would have a total volume different from 1 L and therefore a molarity different than 1 M. To calculate molarity, divide the amount of the solute in moles by the volume of the solution (solute *and* solvent) in liters, as shown in Example 4.5.

Preparing a Solution of Specified Concentration

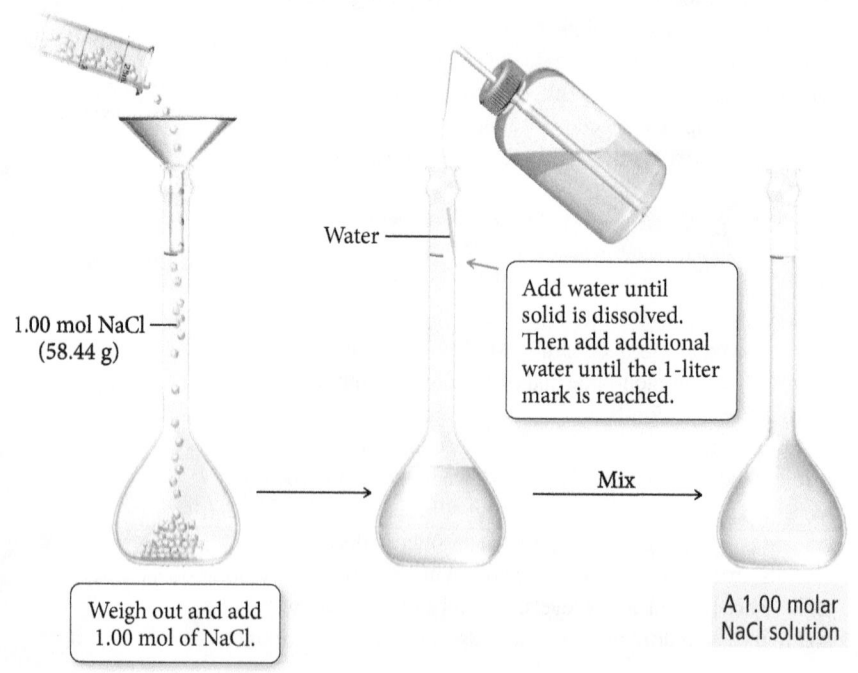

1.00 mol NaCl
(58.44 g)

Water

Add water until solid is dissolved. Then add additional water until the 1-liter mark is reached.

Mix

A 1.00 molar NaCl solution

Weigh out and add 1.00 mol of NaCl.

▶ FIGURE 4.5 **Preparing a 1-Molar NaCl Solution**

EXAMPLE 4.5 Calculating Solution Concentration

If you dissolve 25.5 g KBr in enough water to make 1.75 L of solution, what is the molarity of the solution?

SORT You are given the mass of KBr and the volume of a solution and asked to find its molarity.	**GIVEN:** 25.5 g KBr, 1.75 L of solution **FIND:** molarity (M)
STRATEGIZE When formulating the conceptual plan, think about the definition of molarity, the amount of solute *in moles* per liter of solution. You are given the mass of KBr, so first use the molar mass of KBr to convert from g KBr to mol KBr. Then use the number of moles of KBr and liters of solution to find the molarity.	**CONCEPTUAL PLAN** $$\text{Molarity (M)} = \frac{\text{amount of solute (in mol)}}{\text{volume of solution (in L)}}$$ **RELATIONSHIPS USED** molar mass of KBr = 119.00 g/mol
SOLVE Follow the conceptual plan. Begin with g KBr and convert to mol KBr; then use mol KBr and L solution to calculate molarity.	**SOLUTION** $$25.5 \text{ g KBr} \times \frac{1 \text{ mol KBr}}{119.00 \text{ g KBr}} = 0.21\underline{4}29 \text{ mol KBr}$$ $$\text{molarity (M)} = \frac{\text{amount of solute (in mol)}}{\text{volume of solution (in L)}}$$ $$= \frac{0.21\underline{4}29 \text{ mol KBr}}{1.75 \text{ L solution}}$$ $$= 0.122 \text{ M}$$

CHECK The units of the answer (M) are correct. The magnitude is reasonable since common solutions range in concentration from 0 to about 18 M. Concentrations significantly above 18 M are suspect and should be double-checked.

FOR PRACTICE 4.5

Calculate the molarity of a solution made by adding 45.4 g of $NaNO_3$ to a flask and dissolving it with water to create a total volume of 2.50 L.

FOR MORE PRACTICE 4.5

What mass of KBr (in grams) do you need to make 250.0 mL of a 1.50 M KBr solution?

Using Molarity in Calculations

We can use the molarity of a solution as a conversion factor between moles of the solute and liters of the solution. For example, a 0.500 M NaCl solution contains 0.500 mol NaCl for every liter of solution:

$$\frac{0.500 \text{ mol NaCl}}{\text{L solution}}$$ *converts* L solution → mol NaCl

This conversion factor converts from L solution to mol NaCl. If we want to go the other way, we invert the conversion factor:

$$\frac{\text{L solution}}{0.500 \text{ mol NaCl}}$$ *converts* mol NaCl → L solution

Example 4.6 illustrates how to use molarity in this way.

EXAMPLE 4.6 Using Molarity in Calculations

How many liters of a 0.125 M NaOH solution contain 0.255 mol of NaOH?

SORT You are given the concentration of a NaOH solution. You are asked to find the volume of the solution that contains a given amount (in moles) of NaOH.	**GIVEN:** 0.125 M NaOH solution, 0.255 mol NaOH **FIND:** volume of NaOH solution (in L)
STRATEGIZE The conceptual plan begins with mol NaOH and shows the conversion to L of solution using molarity as a conversion factor.	**CONCEPTUAL PLAN** mol NaOH $\longrightarrow$ L solution $\dfrac{\text{1 L solution}}{\text{0.125 mol NaOH}}$ **RELATIONSHIPS USED** 0.125 M NaOH = $\dfrac{0.125 \text{ mol NaOH}}{1 \text{ L solution}}$
SOLVE Follow the conceptual plan. Begin with mol NaOH and convert to L solution.	**SOLUTION** $0.255 \text{ mol NaOH} \times \dfrac{1 \text{ L solution}}{0.125 \text{ mol NaOH}} = 2.04 \text{ L solution}$

CHECK   The units of the answer (L) are correct. The magnitude is reasonable because the solution contains 0.125 mol per liter. Therefore, roughly 2 L contains the given amount of moles (0.255 mol).

FOR PRACTICE 4.6

How many grams of sucrose ($C_{12}H_{22}O_{11}$) are in 1.55 L of 0.758 M sucrose solution?

FOR MORE PRACTICE 4.6

How many mL of a 0.155 M KCl solution contain 2.55 g KCl?

Conceptual Connection 4.5 Solutions

If we dissolve 25 grams of salt in 251 grams of water, what is the mass of the resulting solution?

(a) 251 g   **(b)** 276 g   **(c)** 226 g

Solution Dilution

> When diluting acids, always add the concentrated acid to the water. Never add water to concentrated acid solutions, as the heat generated may cause the concentrated acid to splatter and burn your skin.

To save space in storerooms, laboratories often store solutions in concentrated forms called **stock solutions.** For example, hydrochloric acid is frequently stored as a 12 M stock solution. However, many lab procedures call for much less concentrated hydrochloric acid solutions, so we must dilute the stock solution to the required concentration. How do we know how much of the stock solution to use? The easiest way to solve dilution problems is to use the following dilution equation:

$$M_1 V_1 = M_2 V_2 \quad\quad\quad [4.1]$$

where M_1 and V_1 are the molarity and volume of the initial concentrated solution, and M_2 and V_2 are the molarity and volume of the final diluted solution. This equation works because the molarity multiplied by the volume gives the number of moles of solute, which is the same in both solutions.

$$M_1 V_1 = M_2 V_2$$
$$\text{mol}_1 = \text{mol}_2$$

In other words, the number of moles of solute does not change when we dilute a solution.

Diluting a Solution

Measure 0.150 L of 10.0 M stock solution.

Dilute with water to total volume of 3.00 L.

0.150 L of 10.0 M stock solution

0.500 M $CaCl_2$

$$M_1V_1 = M_2V_2$$

$$\frac{10.0 \text{ mol}}{\cancel{L}} \times 0.150\cancel{L} = \frac{0.500 \text{ mol}}{\cancel{L}} \times 3.00\cancel{L}$$

$$1.50 \text{ mol} = 1.50 \text{ mol}$$

▲ FIGURE 4.6 **Preparing 3.00 L of 0.500 M CaCl$_2$ from a 10.0 M Stock Solution**

For example, suppose a laboratory procedure calls for 3.00 L of a 0.500 M $CaCl_2$ solution. How should we prepare this solution from a 10.0 M stock solution? We solve Equation 4.1 for V_1, the volume of the stock solution required for the dilution, and then substitute in the correct values to calculate it.

$$M_1V_1 = M_2V_2$$

$$V_1 = \frac{M_2V_2}{M_1}$$

$$= \frac{0.500 \text{ mol/L} \times 3.00 \text{ L}}{10.0 \text{ mol/L}}$$

$$= 0.150 \text{ L}$$

Consequently, we make the solution by diluting 0.150 L of the stock solution to a total volume of 3.00 L (V_2). The resulting solution will be 0.500 M in $CaCl_2$ (Figure 4.6 ▲).

EXAMPLE 4.7 Solution Dilution

To what volume should you dilute 0.200 L of a 15.0 M NaOH solution to obtain a
3.00 M NaOH solution?

SORT You are given the initial volume, initial concentration, and final concentration of a solution, and you need to determine the final volume.	**GIVEN:** $V_1 = 0.200$ L $M_1 = 15.0$ M $M_2 = 3.00$ M **FIND:** V_2
STRATEGIZE Equation 4.1 relates the initial and final volumes and concentrations for solution dilution problems. You are asked to find V_2. The other quantities (V_1, M_1, and M_2) are all given in the problem.	**CONCEPTUAL PLAN** $M_1V_1 = M_2V_2$ **RELATIONSHIPS USED** $M_1V_1 = M_2V_2$
SOLVE Begin with the solution dilution equation and solve it for V_2. Substitute in the required quantities and calculate V_2. Make the solution by diluting 0.200 L of the stock solution to a total volume of 1.00 L (V_2). The resulting solution will have a concentration of 3.00 M.	**SOLUTION** $M_1V_1 = M_2V_2$ $V_2 = \dfrac{M_1V_1}{M_2}$ $= \dfrac{15.0 \; \cancel{\text{mol/L}} \times 0.200 \text{ L}}{3.00 \; \cancel{\text{mol/L}}}$ $= 1.00$ L

CHECK The final units (L) are correct. The magnitude of the answer is
reasonable because the solution is diluted from 15.0 M to 3.00 M, a factor
of five. Therefore the volume should increase by a factor of five.

FOR PRACTICE 4.7
To what volume (in mL) should you dilute 100.0 mL of a 5.00 M $CaCl_2$
solution to obtain a 0.750 M $CaCl_2$ solution?

FOR MORE PRACTICE 4.7
What volume of a 6.00 M $NaNO_3$ solution should you use to make 0.525 L of
a 1.20 M $NaNO_3$ solution?

Conceptual Connection 4.6 Solution Dilution

The image at left represents a small volume within 500 mL of aqueous ethanol
(CH_3CH_2OH) solution. (The water molecules have been omitted for clarity.)
 Which image below best represents the same volume of the solution after we add an
additional 500 mL of water?

(a)   (b)   (c)

Solution Stoichiometry

In Section 4.2 we discussed how the coefficients in chemical equations are used as conversion factors between the amounts of reactants (in moles) and the amounts of products
(in moles). In aqueous reactions, quantities of reactants and products are often specified

in terms of volumes and concentrations. We can use the volume and concentration of a reactant or product to calculate its amount in moles. We can then use the stoichiometric coefficients in the chemical equation to convert to the amount of another reactant or product in moles. The general conceptual plan for these kinds of calculations begins with the volume of a reactant or product:

We make the conversions between solution volumes and amounts of solute in moles using the molarities of the solutions. We make the conversions between amounts in moles of A and B using the stoichiometric coefficients from the balanced chemical equation. Example 4.8 demonstrates solution stoichiometry.

EXAMPLE 4.8 Solution Stoichiometry

What volume (in L) of 0.150 M KCl solution will completely react with 0.150 L of a 0.175 M $Pb(NO_3)_2$ solution according to the following balanced chemical equation?

$$2 KCl(aq) + Pb(NO_3)_2(aq) \rightarrow PbCl_2(s) + 2 KNO_3(aq)$$

SORT You are given the volume and concentration of a $Pb(NO_3)_2$ solution. You are asked to find the volume of KCl solution (of a given concentration) required to react with it.	**GIVEN:** 0.150 L of $Pb(NO_3)_2$ solution, 0.175 M $Pb(NO_3)_2$ solution, 0.150 M KCl solution **FIND:** volume KCl solution (in L)
STRATEGIZE The conceptual plan has the form: volume A → amount A (in moles) → amount B (in moles) → volume B. Use the molar concentrations of the KCl and $Pb(NO_3)_2$ solutions as conversion factors between the number of moles of reactants in these solutions and their volumes. Use the stoichiometric coefficients from the balanced equation to convert between number of moles of $Pb(NO_3)_2$ and number of moles of KCl.	**CONCEPTUAL PLAN** **RELATIONSHIPS USED** $$M\ Pb(NO_3)_2 = \frac{0.175\ mol\ Pb(NO_3)_2}{1\ L\ Pb(NO_3)_2\ solution}$$ $$2\ mol\ KCl : 1\ mol\ Pb(NO_3)_2$$ $$M\ KCl = \frac{0.150\ mol\ KCl}{1\ L\ KCl\ solution}$$
SOLVE Begin with L $Pb(NO_3)_2$ solution and follow the conceptual plan to arrive at L KCl solution.	**SOLUTION** $0.150\ L\ Pb(NO_3)_2\ solution \times \dfrac{0.175\ mol\ Pb(NO_3)_2}{1\ L\ Pb(NO_3)_2\ solution}$ $\times \dfrac{2\ mol\ KCl}{1\ mol\ Pb(NO_3)_2} \times \dfrac{1\ L\ KCl\ solution}{0.150\ mol\ KCl} = 0.350\ L\ KCl\ solution$

CHECK The final units (L KCl solution) are correct. The magnitude (0.350 L) is reasonable because the reaction stoichiometry requires 2 mol of KCl per mole of $Pb(NO_3)_2$. Since the concentrations of the two solutions are not very different (0.150 M compared to 0.175 M), the volume of KCl required is roughly two times the 0.150 L of $Pb(NO_3)_2$ given in the problem.

FOR PRACTICE 4.8

What volume (in mL) of a 0.150 M HNO_3 solution will completely react with 35.7 mL of a 0.108 M Na_2CO_3 solution according to the following balanced chemical equation?

$$Na_2CO_3(aq) + 2\,HNO_3(aq) \rightarrow 2\,NaNO_3(aq) + CO_2(g) + H_2O(l)$$

FOR MORE PRACTICE 4.8

In the previous reaction, what mass (in grams) of carbon dioxide forms?

Solute and Solvent Interactions

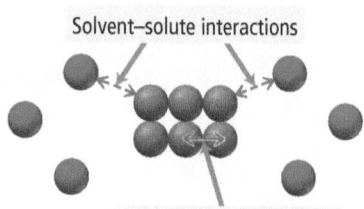

▲ **FIGURE 4.7 Solute and Solvent Interactions** When a solid is put into a solvent, the interactions between solvent and solute particles compete with the interactions between the solute particles themselves.

▲ **FIGURE 4.8 Charge Distribution in a Water Molecule** An uneven distribution of electrons within the water molecule causes the oxygen side of the molecule to have a partial negative charge and the hydrogen side to have a partial positive charge.

4.5 Types of Aqueous Solutions and Solubility

Consider two familiar aqueous solutions: salt water and sugar water. Salt water is a homogeneous mixture of NaCl and H_2O, and sugar water is a homogeneous mixture of $C_{12}H_{22}O_{11}$ and H_2O. You may have made these solutions yourself by adding table salt or sugar to water. As you stir either of these two substances into the water, it seems to disappear. However, you know that the original substance is still present because you can taste saltiness or sweetness in the water. How do solids such as salt and sugar dissolve in water?

When a solid is put into a liquid solvent, the attractive forces that hold the solid together (the solute–solute interactions) compete with the attractive forces between the solvent molecules and the particles that compose the solid (the solvent–solute interactions), as shown in Figure 4.7 ◄. For example, when sodium chloride is put into water, there is a competition between the attraction of Na^+ cations and Cl^- anions to each other (due to their opposite charges) and the attraction of Na^+ and Cl^- to water molecules. The attraction of Na^+ and Cl^- to water is based on the *polar nature* of the water molecule. For reasons we discuss later in this book (Section 9.6), the oxygen atom in water is electron-rich, giving it a partial negative charge (δ^-), as shown in Figure 4.8 ◄. The hydrogen atoms, in contrast, are electron-poor, giving them a partial positive charge (δ^+). As a result, the positively charged sodium ions are strongly attracted to the oxygen side of the water molecule (which has a partial negative charge), and the negatively charged chloride ions are attracted to the hydrogen side of the water molecule (which has a partial positive charge), as shown in Figure 4.9 ▼. In the case of NaCl, the attraction between the separated ions and the water molecules overcomes the attraction of sodium and chloride ions to each other, and the sodium chloride dissolves in the water (Figure 4.10 ▼).

Dissolution of an Ionic Compound

Interactions in a Sodium Chloride Solution

▲ **FIGURE 4.9 Solute and Solvent Interactions in a Sodium Chloride Solution** When sodium chloride is put into water, the attraction of Na^+ and Cl^- ions to water molecules competes with the attraction between the oppositely charged ions themselves.

▲ **FIGURE 4.10 Sodium Chloride Dissolving in Water** The attraction between water molecules and the ions of sodium chloride causes NaCl to dissolve in the water.

Electrolyte and Nonelectrolyte Solutions

Salt

Battery   Battery

Sugar

Salt
solution

Sugar
solution

Conducts current

Does not conduct current

◀ **FIGURE 4.11 Electrolyte and Nonelectrolyte Solutions** A solution of salt (an electrolyte) conducts electrical current. A solution of sugar (a nonelectrolyte) does not.

Electrolyte and Nonelectrolyte Solutions

As Figure 4.11 ▲ shows, a salt solution conducts electricity while a sugar solution does not. The difference between the way that salt (an ionic compound) and sugar (a molecular compound) dissolve in water illustrates a fundamental difference between types of solutions. Ionic compounds such as the sodium chloride in the previous example dissociate into their component ions when they dissolve in water. An NaCl solution, represented as $NaCl(aq)$, does not contain any NaCl units, but rather dissolved Na^+ ions and Cl^- ions. The dissolved ions act as charge carriers, allowing the solution to conduct electricity. Substances that dissolve in water to form solutions that conduct electricity are **electrolytes**. Substances such as sodium chloride that completely dissociate into ions when they dissolve in water are **strong electrolytes**, and the resulting solutions are strong electrolyte solutions.

In contrast to sodium chloride, sugar is a molecular compound. Most molecular compounds—with the important exception of acids, which we discuss shortly—dissolve in water as intact molecules. Sugar dissolves because the attraction between sugar molecules and water molecules (shown in Figure 4.12 ▼) overcomes the attraction of sugar

Cl^-
Na^+

$NaCl(aq)$

Strong
electrolyte

Interactions between Sugar and Water Molecules

sugar molecule
(sucrose)

Solute–solvent
interactions

◀ **FIGURE 4.12 Sugar and Water Interactions** Partial charges on sugar molecules and water molecules (discussed more fully in Chapter 11) result in attractions between the sugar molecules and water molecules.

Sugar Solution

▲ **FIGURE 4.13 A Sugar Solution** Sugar dissolves because the attractions between sugar molecules and water molecules, which both contain a distribution of electrons that results in partial positive and partial negative charges, overcome the attractions between sugar molecules to each other.

Unlike soluble ionic compounds, which contain ions and therefore *dissociate* in water, acids are molecular compounds that *ionize* in water.

HC$_2$H$_3$O$_2$(aq)

Weak acid

▲ AgCl does not dissolve in water; it remains as a white powder at the bottom of the beaker.

molecules to each other (Figure 4.13 ◄). So unlike a sodium chloride solution (which is composed of dissociated ions), a sugar solution is composed of intact C$_{12}$H$_{22}$O$_{11}$ molecules homogeneously mixed with the water molecules. Compounds such as sugar that do not dissociate into ions when dissolved in water are called **nonelectrolytes**, and the resulting solutions—called *nonelectrolyte solutions*—do not conduct electricity.

Acids, first encountered in Section 3.6, are molecular compounds, but they do ionize—form ions—when they dissolve in water. Hydrochloric acid (HCl) is a molecular compound that ionizes into H$^+$ and Cl$^-$ when it dissolves in water. HCl is an example of a **strong acid**, one that completely ionizes in solution. Since strong acids completely ionize in solution, they are also strong electrolytes. We represent the complete ionization of a strong acid with a single reaction arrow between the acid and its ionized form:

HCl(aq)

Strong acid

$$HCl(aq) \rightarrow H^+(aq) + Cl^-(aq)$$

Many acids are **weak acids**; they do not completely ionize in water. For example, acetic acid (HC$_2$H$_3$O$_2$), the acid in vinegar, is a weak acid. A solution of a weak acid is composed mostly of the nonionized acid—only a small percentage of the acid molecules ionize. We represent the partial ionization of a weak acid with opposing half arrows between the reactants and products:

$$HC_2H_3O_2(aq) \rightleftharpoons H^+(aq) + C_2H_3O_2^-(aq)$$

Weak acids are classified as **weak electrolytes,** and the resulting solutions—called *weak electrolyte solutions*—conduct electricity only weakly. Figure 4.14 ▶ summarizes the electrolytic properties of solutions.

The Solubility of Ionic Compounds

As we have just discussed, when an ionic compound dissolves in water, the resulting solution contains not the intact ionic compound itself, but its component ions dissolved in water. However, not all ionic compounds dissolve in water. If we add AgCl to water, for example, it remains solid and appears as a white powder at the bottom of the water.

In general, a compound is termed **soluble** if it dissolves in water and **insoluble** if it does not. However, these classifications are a bit of an oversimplification. (In reality, solubility is a continuum and even "insoluble" compounds dissolve to some extent, though usually orders of magnitude less than soluble compounds.) For example, silver nitrate is soluble. If we mix solid AgNO$_3$ with water, it dissolves and forms a strong electrolyte solution. Silver chloride, on the other hand, is almost completely insoluble. If we mix solid AgCl with water, virtually all of it remains as a solid within the liquid water.

AgCl(s)

Insoluble

AgNO$_3$(aq)

Soluble

Electrolytic Properties of Solutions

$C_{12}H_{22}O_{11}(aq)$ $HC_2H_3O_2(aq)$ $NaCl(aq)$

Nonelectrolyte   Weak electrolyte   Strong electrolyte

▲ FIGURE 4.14 **Electrolytic Properties of Solutions**

Whether a particular compound is soluble or insoluble depends on several factors. In Section 12.3, we will examine more closely the energy changes associated with solution formation. For now, we can follow a set of empirical rules that chemists have inferred from observations on many ionic compounds. These *solubility rules* are summarized in Table 4.1.

TABLE 4.1 Solubility Rules for Ionic Compounds in Water

Compounds Containing the Following Ions Are Generally Soluble	Exceptions
Li^+, Na^+, K^+, and NH_4^+	None
NO_3^- and $C_2H_3O_2^-$	None
Cl^-, Br^-, and I^-	When these ions pair with Ag^+, Hg_2^{2+}, or Pb^{2+}, the resulting compounds are insoluble.
SO_4^{2-}	When SO_4^{2-} pairs with Sr^{2+}, Ba^{2+}, Pb^{2+}, Ag^+, or Ca^{2+}, the resulting compound is insoluble.
Compounds Containing the Following Ions Are Generally Insoluble	**Exceptions**
OH^- and S^{2-}	When these ions pair with Li^+, Na^+, K^+, or NH_4^+, the resulting compounds are soluble.
	When S^{2-} pairs with Ca^{2+}, Sr^{2+}, or Ba^{2+}, the resulting compound is soluble.
	When OH^- pairs with Ca^{2+}, Sr^{2+}, or Ba^{2+}, the resulting compound is slightly soluble.
CO_3^{2-} and PO_4^{3-}	When these ions pair with Li^+, Na^+, K^+, or NH_4^+, the resulting compounds are soluble.

The solubility rules state that compounds containing the sodium ion are soluble. That means that compounds such as NaBr, $NaNO_3$, Na_2SO_4, NaOH, and Na_2CO_3 all dissolve in water to form strong electrolyte solutions. Similarly, the solubility rules state that compounds containing the NO_3^- ion are soluble. That means that compounds such as $AgNO_3$, $Pb(NO_3)_2$, $NaNO_3$, $Ca(NO_3)_2$, and $Sr(NO_3)_2$ all dissolve in water to form strong electrolyte solutions.

Notice that when compounds containing polyatomic ions such as NO_3^- dissolve, the polyatomic ions dissolve as intact units.

The solubility rules also state that, with some exceptions, compounds containing the CO_3^{2-} ion are insoluble. Therefore, compounds such as $CuCO_3$, $CaCO_3$, $SrCO_3$, and $FeCO_3$ do not dissolve in water. Note that the solubility rules contain many exceptions. For example, compounds containing CO_3^{2-} *are* soluble when paired with Li^+, Na^+, K^+, or NH_4^+. Thus Li_2CO_3, Na_2CO_3, K_2CO_3, and $(NH_4)_2CO_3$ are all soluble.

EXAMPLE 4.9 Predicting whether an Ionic Compound Is Soluble

Predict whether each compound is soluble or insoluble.

(a) $PbCl_2$ **(b)** $CuCl_2$ **(c)** $Ca(NO_3)_2$ **(d)** $BaSO_4$

SOLUTION

(a) Insoluble. Compounds containing Cl^- are normally soluble, but Pb^{2+} is an exception.

(b) Soluble. Compounds containing Cl^- are normally soluble and Cu^{2+} is not an exception.

(c) Soluble. Compounds containing NO_3^- are always soluble.

(d) Insoluble. Compounds containing SO_4^{2-} are normally soluble, but Ba^{2+} is an exception.

FOR PRACTICE 4.9

Predict whether each compound is soluble or insoluble.

(a) NiS   **(b)** $Mg_3(PO_4)_2$ **(c)** Li_2CO_3 **(d)** NH_4Cl

---

4.6 Precipitation Reactions

Have you ever taken a bath in hard water? Hard water contains dissolved ions such as Ca^{2+} and Mg^{2+} that diminish the effectiveness of soap. These ions react with soap to form a gray curd that may appear as "bathtub ring" after you drain the tub. Hard water is particularly troublesome when washing clothes. Consider how your white shirt would look covered with the gray curd from the bathtub and you can understand the problem. Consequently, most laundry detergents include substances designed to remove Ca^{2+} and Mg^{2+} from the laundry mixture. The most common substance used for this purpose is sodium carbonate, which dissolves in water to form sodium cations (Na^+) and carbonate (CO_3^{2-}) anions:

$$Na_2CO_3(aq) \rightarrow 2\,Na^+(aq) \;+\; CO_3^{2-}(aq)$$

Sodium carbonate is soluble, but calcium carbonate and magnesium carbonate are not (see the solubility rules in Table 4.1). Consequently, the carbonate anions react with dissolved Mg^{2+} and Ca^{2+} ions in hard water to form solids that *precipitate* from (or come out of) solution:

$$Mg^{2+}(aq) + CO_3^{2-}(aq) \rightarrow MgCO_3(s)$$
$$Ca^{2+}(aq) + CO_3^{2-}(aq) \rightarrow CaCO_3(s)$$

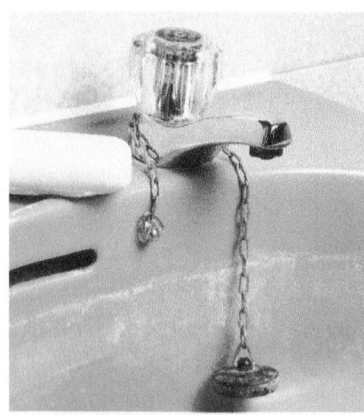

▲ The reaction of ions in hard water with soap produces a gray curd you can see after you drain the bathwater.

The precipitation of these ions prevents their reaction with the soap, eliminating curd and preventing white shirts from turning gray.

The reactions between CO_3^{2-} and Mg^{2+} and Ca^{2+} are examples of **precipitation reactions**, reactions in which a solid or **precipitate** forms when we mix two solutions. Precipitation reactions are common in chemistry. As another example, consider potassium iodide and lead(II) nitrate, which form colorless, strong electrolyte solutions when

Precipitation Reaction

$$2\ KI(aq) + Pb(NO_3)_2(aq) \longrightarrow 2\ KNO_3(aq) + PbI_2(s)$$
(soluble)   (soluble)   (soluble)   (insoluble)

When a potassium iodide solution is mixed with a lead(II) nitrate solution, a yellow lead(II) iodide precipitate forms.

2 KI(aq)
(soluble)

+

Pb(NO$_3$)$_2$(aq)
(soluble)

2 KNO$_3$(aq)
(soluble)

+

PbI$_2$(s)
(insoluble)

▲ FIGURE 4.15 **Precipitation of Lead(II) Iodide** When a potassium iodide solution is mixed with a lead(II) nitrate solution, a yellow lead(II) iodide precipitate forms.

dissolved in water separately. When the two solutions are combined, however, a brilliant yellow precipitate forms (Figure 4.15 ▲). We can describe this precipitation reaction with the following chemical equation:

$$2\ KI(aq) + Pb(NO_3)_2(aq) \rightarrow PbI_2(s) + 2\ KNO_3(aq)$$

Precipitation reactions do not always occur when two aqueous solutions are mixed. For example, if we combine solutions of KI(aq) and NaCl(aq), nothing happens (Figure 4.16 ▶):

$$KI(aq) + NaCl(aq) \rightarrow NO\ REACTION$$

The key to predicting precipitation reactions is to understand that *only insoluble compounds form precipitates*. In a precipitation reaction, two solutions containing soluble compounds combine and an insoluble compound precipitates. Consider the precipitation reaction described previously:

$$2\ KI(aq) + Pb(NO_3)_2(aq) \rightarrow PbI_2(s) + 2\ KNO_3(aq)$$
soluble   soluble   insoluble   soluble

No Reaction

KI(*aq*)

+

NaCl(*aq*)

No reaction

▶ FIGURE 4.16 **No Precipitation**
When a potassium iodide solution is
mixed with a sodium chloride solution,
no reaction occurs.

KI and Pb(NO$_3$)$_2$ are both soluble, but the precipitate, PbI$_2$, is insoluble. Before mixing,
KI(*aq*) and Pb(NO$_3$)$_2$(*aq*) are both dissociated in their respective solutions:

KI(*aq*)   Pb(NO$_3$)$_2$(*aq*)

The instant that the solutions come into contact, all four ions are present:

Pb^{2+}
K^+
NO_3^-
I^-

KI(aq) and Pb(NO$_3$)$_2$(aq)

Now, new compounds—one or both of which might be insoluble—are possible. Specifically, the cation from either compound can pair with the anion from the other to form possibly insoluble products:

Original compounds

K   I

Pb   (NO$_3$)$_2$

Possible products

KNO$_3$

PbI$_2$

If the possible products are both soluble, no reaction occurs and no precipitate forms. If one or both of the possible products are insoluble, a precipitation reaction occurs. In this case, KNO$_3$ is soluble, but PbI$_2$ is insoluble. Consequently, PbI$_2$ precipitates.

To predict whether a precipitation reaction will occur when two solutions are mixed and to write an equation for the reaction, we use the procedure that follows. The steps are outlined in the left column, and two examples illustrating how to apply the procedure are shown in the center and right columns.

K^+
NO_3^-
PbI$_2$

PbI$_2$(s) and KNO$_3$(aq)

PROCEDURE FOR... **Writing Equations for Precipitation Reactions**	**EXAMPLE 4.10** **Writing Equations for Precipitation Reactions** Write an equation for the precipitation reaction that occurs (if any) when solutions of potassium carbonate and nickel(II) chloride are mixed.	**EXAMPLE 4.11** **Writing Equations for Precipitation Reactions** Write an equation for the precipitation reaction that occurs (if any) when solutions of sodium nitrate and lithium sulfate are mixed.
1. Write the formulas of the two compounds being mixed as reactants in a chemical equation.	K$_2$CO$_3$(aq) + NiCl$_2$(aq) →	NaNO$_3$(aq) + Li$_2$SO$_4$(aq) →
2. Below the equation, write the formulas of the products that could form from the reactants. Obtain these by combining the cation from each reactant with the anion from the other. Make sure to write correct formulas for these ionic compounds using the procedure demonstrated in Section 3.5.	K$_2$CO$_3$(aq) + NiCl$_2$(aq) ⟶ Possible products KCl NiCO$_3$	NaNO$_3$(aq) + Li$_2$SO$_4$(aq) ⟶ Possible products LiNO$_3$ Na$_2$SO$_4$
3. Refer to the solubility rules to determine whether any of the possible products are insoluble.	KCl is soluble. (Compounds containing Cl$^-$ are usually soluble and K$^+$ is not an exception.) NiCO$_3$ is insoluble. (Compounds containing CO$_3^{2-}$ are usually insoluble and Ni^{2+} is not an exception.)	LiNO$_3$ is soluble. (Compounds containing NO$_3^-$ are soluble and Li$^+$ is not an exception.) Na$_2$SO$_4$ is soluble. (Compounds containing SO$_4^{2-}$ are generally soluble and Na$^+$ is not an exception.)

4. If all of the possible products are soluble, there will be no precipitate. Write "NO REACTION" after the arrow.	Since this example has an insoluble product, we proceed to the next step.	Since this example has no insoluble product, there is no reaction. $NaNO_3(aq) + Li_2SO_4(aq) \rightarrow$ NO REACTION
5. If any of the possible products are insoluble, write their formulas as the products of the reaction, using (s) to indicate solid. Write any soluble products with (aq) to indicate aqueous.	$K_2CO_3(aq) + NiCl_2(aq) \rightarrow$ $NiCO_3(s) + KCl(aq)$	
6. Balance the equation. Remember to adjust only coefficients, not subscripts.	$K_2CO_3(aq) + NiCl_2(aq) \rightarrow$ $NiCO_3(s) + 2KCl(aq)$	
	FOR PRACTICE 4.10 Write an equation for the precipitation reaction that occurs (if any) when solutions of ammonium chloride and iron(III) nitrate are mixed.	**FOR PRACTICE 4.11** Write an equation for the precipitation reaction that occurs (if any) when solutions of sodium hydroxide and copper(II) bromide are mixed.

Conceptual Connection 4.7 Precipitation Reactions

Consider the generic ionic compounds with the formulas AX and BY and the following solubility rules:

AX soluble; BY soluble; AY soluble; BX insoluble

Let A^+ ions be represented by circles; B^+ ions be represented by squares; X^- ions be represented by triangles; and Y^- ions be represented by diamonds. Solutions of the two compounds (AX and BY) can be represented as follows:

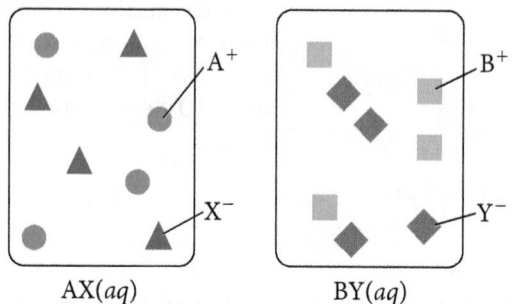

Draw a molecular level representation showing the result of mixing the two solutions and write an equation to represent the reaction.

4.7 Representing Aqueous Reactions: Molecular, Ionic, and Complete Ionic Equations

Consider the following equation for a precipitation reaction:

$$Pb(NO_3)_2(aq) + 2KCl(aq) \rightarrow PbCl_2(s) + 2KNO_3(aq)$$

This equation is a **molecular equation**, an equation showing the complete neutral formulas for each compound in the reaction as if they existed as molecules. In actual solutions of soluble ionic compounds, dissolved substances are present as ions. We can write equations for reactions occurring in aqueous solution in a way that better shows the dissociated nature of dissolved ionic compounds. For example, we can rewrite the previous equation as:

$$Pb^{2+}(aq) + 2NO_3^-(aq) + 2K^+(aq) + 2Cl^-(aq) \rightarrow$$
$$PbCl_2(s) + 2K^+(aq) + 2NO_3^-(aq)$$

Equations such as this, which list all of the ions present as either reactants or products in a chemical reaction, are **complete ionic equations**. Strong electrolytes are always represented as their component ions in ionic equations—weak electrolytes are not.

Notice that in the complete ionic equation, some of the ions in solution appear unchanged on both sides of the equation. These ions are called **spectator ions** because they do not participate in the reaction.

$$Pb^{2+}(aq) + 2NO_3^-(aq) + 2K^+(aq) + 2Cl^-(aq) \longrightarrow$$
$$PbCl_2(s) + 2K^+(aq) + 2NO_3^-(aq)$$

Spectator ions

To simplify the equation, and to show more clearly what is happening, we can omit spectator ions:

$$Pb^{2+}(aq) + 2Cl^-(aq) \rightarrow PbCl_2(s)$$

Equations that show only the species that actually change during the reaction are **net ionic equations**.

As another example, consider the reaction between $HCl(aq)$ and $KOH(aq)$:

$$HCl(aq) + KOH(aq) \rightarrow H_2O(l) + KCl(aq)$$

Since HCl, KOH, and KCl all exist in solution primarily as independent ions, the complete ionic equation is:

$$H^+(aq) + Cl^-(aq) + K^+(aq) + OH^-(aq) \rightarrow H_2O(l) + K^+(aq) + Cl^-(aq)$$

To write the net ionic equation, we remove the spectator ions, those that are unchanged on both sides of the equation:

$$H^+(aq) + Cl^-(aq) + K^+(aq) + OH^-(aq) \longrightarrow H_2O(l) + K^+(aq) + Cl^-(aq)$$

Spectator ions

The net ionic equation is $H^+(aq) + OH^-(aq) \rightarrow H_2O(l)$.

Summarizing Aqueous Equations:

▶ A **molecular equation** is a chemical equation showing the complete, neutral formulas for every compound in a reaction.

▶ A **complete ionic equation** is a chemical equation showing all of the species as they are actually present in solution.

▶ A **net ionic equation** is an equation showing only the species that actually change during the reaction.

EXAMPLE 4.12 Writing Complete Ionic and Net Ionic Equations

Write complete ionic and net ionic equations for each reaction.

(a) $3\ SrCl_2(aq)\ +\ 2\ Li_3PO_4(aq) \rightarrow Sr_3(PO_4)_2(s)\ +\ 6\ LiCl(aq)$

(b) $HC_2H_3O_2(aq)\ +\ KOH(aq) \rightarrow H_2O(l)\ +\ KC_2H_3O_2(aq)$

SOLUTION	
(a) Write the complete ionic equation by separating aqueous ionic compounds into their constituent ions. The $Sr_3(PO_4)_2(s)$, precipitating as a solid, remains as one unit. Write the net ionic equation by eliminating the spectator ions, those that do not change from one side of the reaction to the other.	**Complete ionic equation:** $3\ Sr^{2+}(aq)\ +\ 6\ Cl^-(aq)\ +\ 6\ Li^+(aq)\ +\ 2\ PO_4{}^{3-}(aq) \rightarrow$ $Sr_3(PO_4)_2(s)\ +\ 6\ Li^+(aq)\ +\ 6\ Cl^-(aq)$ **Net ionic equation:** $3\ Sr^{2+}(aq)\ +\ 2\ PO_4{}^{3-}(aq) \rightarrow Sr_3(PO_4)_2(s)$
(b) Write the complete ionic equation by separating aqueous ionic compounds into their constituent ions. Do not separate $HC_2H_3O_2(aq)$ because it is a weak electrolyte. Write the net ionic equation by eliminating the spectator ions.	**Complete ionic equation:** $HC_2H_3O_2(aq)\ +\ K^+(aq)\ +\ OH^-(aq) \rightarrow$ $H_2O(l)\ +\ K^+(aq)\ +\ C_2H_3O_2{}^-(aq)$ **Net ionic equation:** $HC_2H_3O_2(aq)\ +\ OH^-(aq) \rightarrow H_2O(l)\ +\ C_2H_3O_2{}^-(aq)$

FOR PRACTICE 4.12

Consider the following reaction occurring in aqueous solution:

$$2\ HI(aq)\ +\ Ba(OH)_2(aq) \rightarrow 2\ H_2O(l)\ +\ BaI_2(aq)$$

Write the complete ionic equation and net ionic equation for this reaction.

4.8 Acid–Base and Gas-Evolution Reactions

Two other important classes of reactions that occur in aqueous solution are acid–base reactions and gas-evolution reactions. In an **acid–base reaction** (also called a **neutralization reaction**), an acid reacts with a base and the two neutralize each other, producing water (or in some cases a weak electrolyte). In a **gas-evolution reaction**, a gas forms, resulting in bubbling. In both cases, as in precipitation reactions, the reactions occur when the anion from one reactant combines with the cation of the other. Many gas-evolution reactions are also acid–base reactions.

Acid–Base Reactions

Our stomachs contain hydrochloric acid, which acts in the digestion of food. Certain foods or stress, however, can increase the stomach's acidity to uncomfortable levels, causing acid stomach or heartburn. Antacids are over-the-counter medicines that work by reacting with and neutralizing stomach acid. Antacids employ different *bases*—substances that produce hydroxide (OH^-) ions in water—as neutralizing agents. Milk of magnesia, for example, contains $Mg(OH)_2$ and Mylanta contains $Al(OH)_3$. All antacids, regardless of the base they employ, have the same effect of neutralizing stomach acid and relieving heartburn through *acid–base reactions*.

Recall from Chapter 3 that an acid forms H^+ ions in solution, and we saw earlier that a base is a substance that produces OH^- ions in solution. More formally:

▲ Gas-evolution reactions, such as the reaction of hydrochloric acid with limestone ($CaCO_3$), typically produce CO_2; bubbling occurs as the gas is released.

- Acid: Substance that produces H^+ ions in aqueous solution
- Base: Substance that produces OH^- ions in aqueous solution

These definitions of acids and bases, called the **Arrhenius definitions**, are named after Swedish chemist Svante Arrhenius (1859–1927). In Chapter 15, we will learn more general definitions of acids and bases, but these definitions are sufficient to describe neutralization reactions.

According to the Arrhenius definition, HCl is an acid because it produces H^+ ions in solution:

$$HCl(aq) \rightarrow H^+(aq) + Cl^-(aq)$$

An H^+ ion is a bare proton. In solution bare protons normally associate with water molecules to form **hydronium ions** (Figure 4.17 ▶):

$$H^+(aq) + H_2O(l) \rightarrow H_3O^+(aq)$$

Chemists use $H^+(aq)$ and $H_3O^+(aq)$ interchangeably to mean the same thing—a hydronium ion. The chemical equation for the ionization of HCl and other acids is often written to show the association of the proton with a water molecule to form the hydronium ion:

$$HCl(aq) + H_2O(l) \rightarrow H_3O^+(aq) + Cl^-(aq)$$

Some acids—called **polyprotic acids**—contain more than one ionizable proton and release them sequentially. For example, sulfuric acid, H_2SO_4, is a **diprotic acid**. It is strong in its first ionizable proton, but weak in its second:

$$H_2SO_4(aq) \rightarrow H^+(aq) + HSO_4^-(aq)$$
$$HSO_4^-(aq) \rightleftharpoons H^+(aq) + SO_4^{2-}(aq)$$

According to the Arrhenius definition, NaOH is a base because it produces OH^- ions in solution:

$$NaOH(aq) \rightarrow Na^+(aq) + OH^-(aq)$$

In analogy to diprotic acids, some bases, such as $Sr(OH)_2$, produce two moles of OH^- per mole of the base:

$$Sr(OH)_2(aq) \rightarrow Sr^{2+}(aq) + 2\,OH^-(aq)$$

Table 4.2 lists common acids and bases. You can find acids and bases in many everyday substances. Foods such as citrus fruits and vinegar contain acids. Soap, baking soda, and milk of magnesia all contain bases.

When we mix an acid and a base, the $H^+(aq)$ from the acid—whether it is weak or strong—combines with the $OH^-(aq)$ from the base to form $H_2O(l)$ (Figure 4.18 ▶). Consider the reaction between hydrochloric acid and sodium hydroxide:

$$\underset{\text{Acid}}{HCl(aq)} + \underset{\text{Base}}{NaOH(aq)} \longrightarrow \underset{\text{Water}}{H_2O(l)} + \underset{\text{Salt}}{NaCl(aq)}$$

▲ **FIGURE 4.17 The Hydronium Ion** Protons normally associate with water molecules in solution to form H_3O^+ ions, which in turn interact with other water molecules.

▲ Lemons, oranges, and vinegar contain acids. Vitamin C and aspirin are acids.

TABLE 4.2 Some Common Acids and Bases

Name of Acid	Formula	Name of Base	Formula
Hydrochloric acid	HCl	Sodium hydroxide	NaOH
Hydrobromic acid	HBr	Lithium hydroxide	LiOH
Hydroiodic acid	HI	Potassium hydroxide	KOH
Nitric acid	HNO_3	Calcium hydroxide	$Ca(OH)_2$
Sulfuric acid	H_2SO_4	Barium hydroxide	$Ba(OH)_2$
Perchloric acid	$HClO_4$	Ammonia*	NH_3 (weak base)
Acetic acid	$HC_2H_3O_2$ (weak acid)		
Hydrofluoric acid	HF (weak acid)		

*Ammonia does not contain OH^-, but it produces OH^- in a reaction with water that occurs only to a small extent: $NH_3(aq) + H_2O(l) \rightleftharpoons NH_4^+(aq) + OH^-(aq)$.

▲ Many common household products contain bases.

Acid–Base Reaction

$$\text{HCl}(aq) + \text{NaOH}(aq) \longrightarrow \text{H}_2\text{O}(l) + \text{NaCl}(aq)$$

The reaction between hydrochloric acid and sodium hydroxide forms water and a salt, sodium chloride, which remains dissolved in the solution.

$\text{HCl}(aq)$

$+$

$\text{NaOH}(aq)$

$\text{H}_2\text{O}(l)$

$+$

$\text{NaCl}(aq)$

▲ **FIGURE 4.18 Acid–Base Reaction** The reaction between hydrochloric acid and sodium hydroxide forms water and a salt, sodium chloride, which remains dissolved in the solution.

The word *salt* in this sense applies to any ionic compound and is therefore more general than the common usage, which refers only to table salt (NaCl).

Acid–base reactions generally form water and an ionic compound—called a **salt**—that usually remains dissolved in the solution. The net ionic equation for many acid–base reactions is:

$$\text{H}^+(aq) + \text{OH}^-(aq) \rightarrow \text{H}_2\text{O}(l)$$

Another example of an acid–base reaction is the reaction between sulfuric acid and potassium hydroxide:

$$\underset{\text{acid}}{H_2SO_4(aq)} + \underset{\text{base}}{2\,KOH(aq)} \rightarrow \underset{\text{water}}{2\,H_2O(l)} + \underset{\text{salt}}{K_2SO_4(aq)}$$

Again, notice the pattern of acid and base reacting to form water and a salt.

$$\textbf{Acid} + \textbf{Base} \rightarrow \textbf{Water} + \textbf{Salt} \quad \text{(acid–base reactions)}$$

When writing equations for acid–base reactions, write the formula of the salt using the procedure for writing formulas of ionic compounds demonstrated in Section 3.5.

EXAMPLE 4.13 Writing Equations for Acid–Base Reactions

Write a molecular and net ionic equation for the reaction between aqueous HI and aqueous $Ba(OH)_2$.

SOLUTION First identify these substances as an acid and a base. Begin by writing the unbalanced equation in which the acid and the base combine to form water and a salt.	$\underset{\text{acid}}{HI(aq)} + \underset{\text{base}}{Ba(OH)_2(aq)} \rightarrow \underset{\text{water}}{H_2O(l)} + \underset{\text{salt}}{BaI_2(aq)}$
Next, balance the equation; this is the molecular equation.	$2\,HI(aq) + Ba(OH)_2(aq) \rightarrow 2\,H_2O(l) + BaI_2(aq)$
Write the net ionic equation by removing the spectator ions.	$2\,H^+(aq) + 2\,OH^-(aq) \rightarrow 2\,H_2O(l)$ or simply $H^+(aq) + OH^-(aq) \rightarrow H_2O(l)$

FOR PRACTICE 4.13

Write a molecular and a net ionic equation for the reaction that occurs between aqueous H_2SO_4 and aqueous LiOH.

Acid–Base Titrations We can apply the principles of acid–base neutralization and stoichiometry to a common laboratory procedure called a *titration*. In a **titration**, a substance in a solution of known concentration is reacted with another substance in a solution of unknown concentration. For example, consider the following acid–base reaction:

$$HCl(aq) + NaOH(aq) \rightarrow H_2O(l) + NaCl(aq)$$

The net ionic equation for this reaction eliminates the spectator ions:

$$H^+(aq) + OH^-(aq) \rightarrow H_2O(l)$$

Suppose we have an HCl solution represented by the molecular diagram at right (we have omitted the Cl^- ions and the H_2O molecules not involved in the reaction from this representation for clarity).

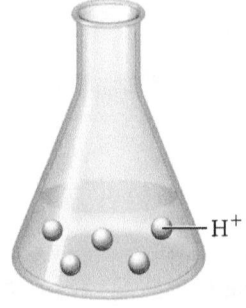

In titrating this sample, we slowly add a solution of known OH^- concentration, as shown in the molecular diagrams in Figure 4.19 ▶. As the OH^- is added, it reacts with and neutralizes the H^+, forming water. At the **equivalence point**—the point in the titration when the number of moles of OH^- added equals the number of moles of H^+ initially in solution—the titration is complete. The equivalence point is typically signaled by an **indicator**, a dye whose color depends on the acidity or basicity of the solution (Figure 4.20 ▶).

We cover acid–base titrations and indicators in more detail in Chapter 16. In most laboratory titrations, the concentration of one of the reactant solutions is unknown, and the concentration of the other is precisely known. By carefully measuring the volume of each solution required to reach the equivalence point, we can determine the concentration of the unknown solution, as demonstrated in Example 4.14.

▶ FIGURE 4.19 **Acid–Base Titration**

Acid–Base Titration

$OH^-(aq)$

$H^+(aq)$

$H^+(aq) + OH^-(aq) \longrightarrow H_2O(l)$

Beginning of titration

Equivalence point

▶ FIGURE 4.20 **Titration** In this titration, NaOH is added to a dilute HCl solution. When the NaOH and HCl reach stoichiometric proportions (the equivalence point), the phenolphthalein indicator changes color to pink.

Indicator in Titration

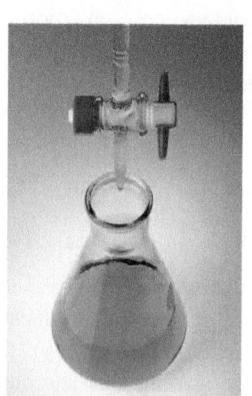

EXAMPLE 4.14 Acid–Base Titration

The titration of a 10.00 mL sample of an HCl solution of unknown concentration requires 12.54 mL of a 0.100 M NaOH solution to reach the equivalence point. What is the concentration of the unknown HCl solution in M?

SORT You are given the volume and concentration of NaOH solution required to titrate a given volume of HCl solution. You are asked to find the concentration of the HCl solution.	**GIVEN:** 12.54 mL of NaOH solution, 0.100 M NaOH solution, 10.00 mL of HCl solution
	FIND: concentration of HCl solution

STRATEGIZE Since this problem involves an acid–base neutralization reaction between HCl and NaOH, you start by writing the balanced equation, using the techniques covered earlier in this section.

The first part of the conceptual plan has the form volume A → moles A → moles B. The concentration of the NaOH solution is a conversion factor between moles and volume of NaOH. The balanced equation provides the relationship between number of moles of NaOH and number of moles of HCl.

$$HCl(aq) + NaOH(aq) \rightarrow H_2O(l) + NaCl(aq)$$

CONCEPTUAL PLAN

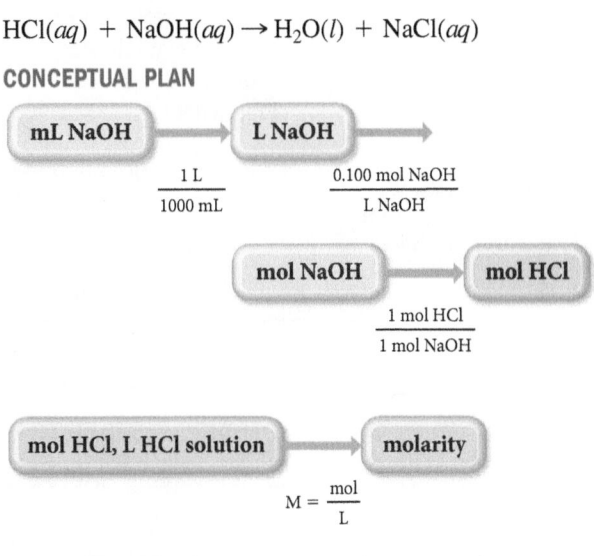

In the second part of the conceptual plan, use the number of moles of HCl (from the first part) and the volume of HCl solution (given) to calculate the molarity of the HCl solution.

RELATIONSHIPS USED

$1 \text{ L} = 1000 \text{ mL}$

$$M \text{ (NaOH)} = \frac{0.100 \text{ mol NaOH}}{\text{L NaOH}}$$

$1 \text{ mol HCl} : 1 \text{ mol NaOH}$

$$\text{Molarity (M)} = \frac{\text{moles of solute (mol)}}{\text{volume of solution (L)}}$$

SOLVE In the first part of the solution, determine the number of moles of HCl in the unknown solution.

SOLUTION

$$12.54 \text{ mL NaOH} \times \frac{1 \text{ L}}{1000 \text{ mL}} \times \frac{0.100 \text{ mol NaOH}}{\text{L NaOH}}$$

$$\times \frac{1 \text{ mol HCl}}{1 \text{ mol NaOH}} = 1.25 \times 10^{-3} \text{ mol HCl}$$

In the second part of the solution, divide the number of moles of HCl by the volume of the HCl solution in L. 10.00 mL is equivalent to 0.01000 L.

$$\text{Molarity} = \frac{1.25 \times 10^{-3} \text{ mol HCl}}{0.01000 \text{ L}} = 0.125 \text{ M HCl}$$

CHECK The units of the answer (M HCl) are correct. The magnitude of the answer (0.125 M) is reasonable because it is similar to the molarity of the NaOH solution, as expected from the reaction stoichiometry (1 mol HCl reacts with 1 mol NaOH) and the similar volumes of NaOH and HCl.

FOR PRACTICE 4.14

The titration of a 20.0 mL sample of an H_2SO_4 solution of unknown concentration requires 22.87 mL of a 0.158 M KOH solution to reach the equivalence point. What is the concentration of the unknown H_2SO_4 solution?

FOR MORE PRACTICE 4.14

What volume (in mL) of 0.200 M NaOH do we need to titrate 35.00 mL of 0.140 M HBr to the equivalence point?

Gas-Evolution Reactions

In a *gas-evolution reaction*, two aqueous solutions mix to form a gaseous product that bubbles out of solution. Some gas-evolution reactions form a gaseous product directly when the cation of one reactant combines with the anion of the other. For example, when sulfuric acid reacts with lithium sulfide, dihydrogen sulfide gas forms:

$$H_2SO_4(aq) + Li_2S(aq) \rightarrow \underset{\text{gas}}{H_2S(g)} + Li_2SO_4(aq)$$

Other gas-evolution reactions often form an intermediate product that then decomposes (breaks down into simpler substances) to form a gas. For example, when aqueous hydrochloric acid is mixed with aqueous sodium bicarbonate, the following reaction occurs (Figure 4.21 ▼):

Many gas-evolution reactions such as this one are also acid–base reactions. In Chapter 15 we will learn how ions such as CO_3^{2-} act as bases in aqueous solution.

$$HCl(aq) + NaHCO_3(aq) \rightarrow \underset{\text{intermediate product}}{H_2CO_3(aq)} + NaCl(aq) \rightarrow H_2O(l) + \underset{\text{gas}}{CO_2(g)} + NaCl(aq)$$

Gas-Evolution Reaction

$$NaHCO_3(aq) + HCl(aq) \longrightarrow H_2O(l) + NaCl(aq) + CO_2(g)$$

When aqueous sodium bicarbonate is mixed with aqueous hydrochloric acid, gaseous CO_2 bubbles are the result of the reaction.

▶ FIGURE 4.21 **Gas-Evolution Reaction** When aqueous hydrochloric acid is mixed with aqueous sodium bicarbonate, gaseous CO_2 bubbles out of the reaction mixture.

$NaHCO_3(aq)$

+

$HCl(aq)$

$H_2O(l)$

+

$NaCl(aq)$

+

$CO_2(g)$

TABLE 4.3 Types of Compounds That Undergo Gas-Evolution Reactions

Reactant Type	Intermediate Product	Gas Evolved	Example
Sulfides	None	H_2S	$2\ HCl(aq) + K_2S(aq) \rightarrow H_2S(g) + 2\ KCl(aq)$
Carbonates and bicarbonates	H_2CO_3	CO_2	$2\ HCl(aq) + K_2CO_3(aq) \rightarrow H_2O(l) + CO_2(g) + 2\ KCl(aq)$
Sulfites and bisulfites	H_2SO_3	SO_2	$2\ HCl(aq) + K_2SO_3(aq) \rightarrow H_2O(l) + SO_2(g) + 2\ KCl(aq)$
Ammonium	NH_4OH	NH_3	$NH_4Cl(aq) + KOH(aq) \rightarrow H_2O(l) + NH_3(g) + KCl(aq)$

The intermediate product, H_2CO_3, is not stable and decomposes into H_2O and gaseous CO_2. Other important gas-evolution reactions form either H_2SO_3 or NH_4OH as intermediate products:

$$HCl(aq) + NaHSO_3(aq) \rightarrow \underset{\text{intermediate product}}{H_2SO_3(aq)} + NaCl(aq) \rightarrow H_2O(l) + \underset{\text{gas}}{SO_2(g)} + NaCl(aq)$$

$$NH_4Cl(aq) + NaOH(aq) \rightarrow \underset{\text{intermediate product}}{NH_4OH(aq)} + NaCl(aq) \rightarrow H_2O(l) + \underset{\text{gas}}{NH_3(g)} + NaCl(aq)$$

The intermediate product NH_4OH provides a convenient way to think about this reaction, but the extent to which it actually forms is debatable.

Table 4.3 lists the main types of compounds that form gases in aqueous reactions, as well as the gases formed.

EXAMPLE 4.15 Writing Equations for Gas-Evolution Reactions

Write a molecular equation for the gas-evolution reaction that occurs when you mix aqueous nitric acid and aqueous sodium carbonate.

Begin by writing an unbalanced equation in which the cation of each reactant combines with the anion of the other.	$HNO_3(aq) + Na_2CO_3(aq) \longrightarrow$ $ H_2CO_3(aq) + NaNO_3(aq)$
You must then recognize that $H_2CO_3(aq)$ decomposes into $H_2O(l)$ and $CO_2(g)$ and write these products into the equation.	$HNO_3(aq) + Na_2CO_3(aq) \rightarrow H_2O(l) + CO_2(g) + NaNO_3(aq)$
Finally, balance the equation.	$2\ HNO_3(aq) + Na_2CO_3(aq) \rightarrow H_2O(l) + CO_2(g) + 2\ NaNO_3(aq)$

FOR PRACTICE 4.15

Write a molecular equation for the gas-evolution reaction that occurs when you mix aqueous hydrobromic acid and aqueous potassium sulfite.

FOR MORE PRACTICE 4.15

Write a net ionic equation for the reaction that occurs when you mix hydroiodic acid with calcium sulfide.

4.9 Oxidation–Reduction Reactions

Oxidation–reduction reactions or **redox reactions** are reactions in which electrons transfer from one reactant to the other. The rusting of iron, the bleaching of hair, and the production of electricity in batteries involve redox reactions. Many redox reactions involve the reaction of a substance with oxygen (Figure 4.22 ▶):

Oxidation-reduction reactions are covered in more detail in Chapter 18.

$$4\ Fe(s) + 3\ O_2(g) \rightarrow 2\ Fe_2O_3(s) \qquad \text{(rusting of iron)}$$

$$2\ C_8H_{18}(l) + 25\ O_2(g) \rightarrow 16\ CO_2(g) + 18\ H_2O(g) \qquad \text{(combustion of octane)}$$

$$2\ H_2(g) + O_2(g) \rightarrow 2\ H_2O(g) \qquad \text{(combustion of hydrogen)}$$

Oxidation–Reduction Reaction

▶ FIGURE 4.22 **Oxidation–Reduction Reaction** The hydrogen in the balloon reacts with oxygen upon ignition to form gaseous water (which is dispersed in the flame).

$$2\ H_2(g) + O_2(g) \longrightarrow 2\ H_2O(g)$$

Hydrogen and oxygen react to form gaseous water.

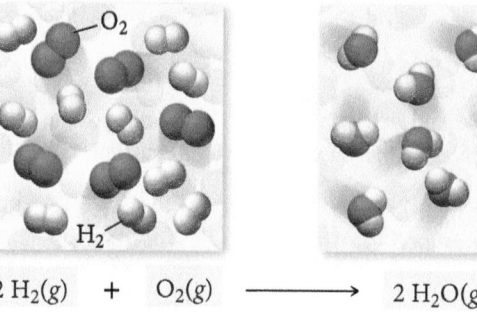

$$2\ H_2(g) + O_2(g) \longrightarrow 2\ H_2O(g)$$

However, redox reactions need not involve oxygen. Consider, for example, the reaction between sodium and chlorine to form sodium chloride (NaCl), depicted in Figure 4.24 ▶:

$$2\ Na(s) + Cl_2(g) \rightarrow 2\ NaCl(s)$$

This reaction is similar to the reaction between sodium and oxygen, which forms sodium oxide:

$$4\ Na(s) + O_2(g) \rightarrow 2\ Na_2O(s)$$

In both cases, a metal (which has a tendency to lose electrons) reacts with a nonmetal (which has a tendency to gain electrons). In both cases, metal atoms lose electrons to nonmetal atoms. A fundamental definition of **oxidation** is the loss of electrons, and a fundamental definition of **reduction** is the gain of electrons.

The transfer of electrons does not need to be a *complete* transfer (as occurs in the formation of an ionic compound) for the reaction to qualify as oxidation–reduction. For example, consider the reaction between hydrogen gas and chlorine gas:

$$H_2(g) + Cl_2(g) \rightarrow 2\ HCl(g)$$

Even though hydrogen chloride is a molecular compound with a covalent bond, and even though the hydrogen has not completely transferred its electron to chlorine during the reaction, you can see from the electron density diagrams (Figure 4.23 ◀) that hydrogen has lost some of its electron density—it has *partially* transferred its electron to chlorine. In the reaction, hydrogen is oxidized and chlorine is reduced and, therefore, this is a redox reaction.

| The reaction between sodium and oxygen forms other oxides as well.

| Helpful Mnemonic: O I L R I G—**O**xidation **I**s **L**oss; **R**eduction **I**s **G**ain.

| The ability of an element to attract electrons in a chemical bond is called electronegativity. We cover electronegativity in more detail in Section 8.6.

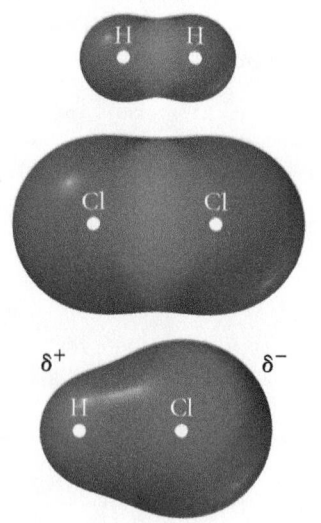

Hydrogen loses electron density (oxidation) and chlorine gains electron density (reduction).

▲ FIGURE 4.23 **Redox with Partial Electron Transfer** When hydrogen bonds to chlorine, the electrons are unevenly shared, resulting in an increase of electron density (reduction) for chlorine and a decrease in electron density (oxidation) for hydrogen.

Oxidation States

Identifying whether or not a reaction between a metal and a nonmetal is a redox reaction is fairly straightforward because of ion formation. But how do we identify redox reactions that occur between nonmetals? Chemists have devised a scheme to track electrons before and after a chemical reaction. In this scheme—which is like bookkeeping for electrons—each shared electron is assigned to the atom that attracts the electrons most strongly. Then a number, called the **oxidation state** or **oxidation number**, is given to each atom based on the electron assignments. In other words, the oxidation number of an atom in a compound is the "charge" it would have if all shared electrons were assigned to the atom with the greatest attraction for those electrons.

For example, consider HCl. Since chlorine attracts electrons more strongly than hydrogen, we assign the two shared electrons in the bond to chlorine; then H (which has lost an electron in our assignment) has an oxidation state of +1, and Cl (which has gained

Oxidation–Reduction Reaction without Oxygen

$$2\,Na(s) + Cl_2(g) \longrightarrow 2\,NaCl(s)$$

Electrons are transferred from sodium to chlorine, forming sodium chloride.
Sodium is oxidized and chlorine is reduced.

Na(s)

Electron
transfer

+

Cl_2

$Cl_2(g)$

Na
Cl

NaCl(s)

▲ FIGURE 4.24 **Oxidation-Reduction
without Oxygen** When sodium reacts
with chlorine, electrons transfer from
the sodium to the chlorine, resulting
in the formation of sodium chloride.
In this redox reaction, sodium is
oxidized and chlorine is reduced.

one electron in our assignment) has an oxidation state of -1. Notice that in contrast to ionic charges, which are usually written with the sign of the charge *after* the magnitude ($1+$ and $1-$, for example), oxidation states are written with the sign of the charge *before* the magnitude ($+1$ and -1, for example). You can use the following rules to assign oxidation states to atoms in elements, ions, and compounds.

Rules for Assigning Oxidation States

(These rules are hierarchical. If any two rules conflict, follow the rule that is higher on the list.)

Examples

1. The oxidation state of an atom in a free element is 0.

$$\underset{\text{0 ox state}}{Cu} \quad \underset{\text{0 ox state}}{Cl_2}$$

2. The oxidation state of a monoatomic ion is equal to its charge.

$$\underset{\text{+2 ox state}}{Ca^{2+}} \quad \underset{\text{-1 ox state}}{Cl^-}$$

> Do not confuse oxidation state with ionic charge. Unlike ionic charge–which is a real property of an ion–the oxidation state of an atom is merely a theoretical (but useful) construct.

3. The sum of the oxidation states of all atoms in:

  • A neutral molecule or formula unit is 0.

$$\underset{\text{2(H ox state) + 1(O ox state) = 0}}{H_2O}$$

  • An ion is equal to the charge of the ion.

$$\underset{\text{1(N ox sate) + 3(O ox state) = -1}}{NO_3^-}$$

4. In their compounds, metals have positive oxidation states.

  • Group 1A metals *always* have an oxidation state of $+1$.

$$\underset{\text{+1 ox state}}{NaCl}$$

  • Group 2A metals *always* have an oxidation state of $+2$.

$$\underset{\text{+2 ox state}}{CaF_2}$$

5. In their compounds, nonmetals are assigned oxidation states according to the table at right. Entries at the top of the table take precedence over entries at the bottom of the table.

Nonmetal	Oxidation State	Example
Fluorine	-1	MgF_2 -1 ox state
Hydrogen	$+1$	H_2O $+1$ ox state
Oxygen	-2	CO_2 -2 ox state
Group 7A	-1	CCl_4 -1 ox state
Group 6A	-2	H_2S -2 ox state
Group 5A	-3	NH_3 -3 ox state

When assigning oxidation states, keep these points in mind:

- The oxidation state of any given element generally depends on what other elements are present in the compound. (The exceptions are the group 1A and 2A metals, which are *always* +1 and +2, respectively.)
- Rule 3 must always be followed. Therefore, when following the hierarchy shown in rule 5, give priority to the element(s) highest on the list and then assign the oxidation state of the element lowest on the list using rule 3.
- When assigning oxidation states to elements that are not covered by rules 4 and 5 (such as carbon), use rule 3 to deduce their oxidation state once all other oxidation states have been assigned.

EXAMPLE 4.16 Assigning Oxidation States

Assign an oxidation state to each atom in each element, ion, or compound.

(a) Cl_2 **(b)** Na^+ **(c)** KF   **(d)** CO_2 **(e)** SO_4^{2-} **(f)** K_2O_2

SOLUTION

Since Cl_2 is a free element, the oxidation state of both Cl atoms is 0 (rule 1).	**(a)** Cl_2 ClCl 0 0
Since Na^+ is a monoatomic ion, the oxidation state of the Na^+ ion is +1 (rule 2).	**(b)** Na^+ Na^+ +1
The oxidation state of K is +1 (rule 4). The oxidation state of F is −1 (rule 5). Since this is a neutral compound, the sum of the oxidation states is 0.	**(c)** KF KF +1 −1 sum: +1−1=0
The oxidation state of oxygen is −2 (rule 5). The oxidation state of carbon must be deduced using rule 3, which says that the sum of the oxidation states of all the atoms must be 0.	**(d)** CO_2 (C ox state) + 2(O ox state) = 0 (C ox state) + 2(−2) = 0 C ox state = +4 CO_2 +4 −2 sum: +4+2(−2)=0
The oxidation state of oxygen is −2 (rule 5). We would ordinarily expect the oxidation state of S to be −2 (rule 5). However, if that were the case, the sum of the oxidation states would not equal the charge of the ion. Since O is higher on the list than S, it takes priority and we compute the oxidation state of sulfur by setting the *sum* of all of the oxidation states equal to −2 (the charge of the ion).	**(e)** SO_4^{2-} (S ox state) + 4(O ox state) = −2 (S ox state) + 4(−2) = −2 S ox state = +6 SO_4^{2-} +6 −2 sum: +6+4(−2)=−2
The oxidation state of potassium is +1 (rule 4). We would ordinarily expect the oxidation state of O to be −2 (rule 5), but rule 4 takes priority, and we deduce the oxidation state of O by setting the sum of all of the oxidation states equal to 0.	**(f)** K_2O_2 2(K ox state) + 2(O ox state) = 0 2(+1) + 2(O ox state) = 0 O ox state = −1 K_2O_2 +1 −1 sum: 2(+1)+2(−1)=0

FOR PRACTICE 4.16

Assign an oxidation state to each atom in each element, ion, or compound.

(a) Cr   **(b)** Cr^{3+} **(c)** CCl_4 **(d)** $SrBr_2$ **(e)** SO_3 **(f)** NO_3^-

In most cases, oxidation states are positive or negative integers; however, on occasion an atom within a compound can have a fractional oxidation state. Consider KO_2. The oxidation states are assigned as follows:

$$KO_2$$
$$+1 \; -\frac{1}{2}$$
$$\text{sum: } +1 + 2\left(-\frac{1}{2}\right) = 0$$

In KO_2, oxygen has a $-\frac{1}{2}$ oxidation state. Although this seems unusual, it is accepted because oxidation states are merely an imposed electron bookkeeping scheme, not an actual physical quantity.

Conceptual Connection 4.8 Oxidation Numbers in Polyatomic Ions

Which statement best describes the *difference* between the *charge* of a polyatomic ion and the *oxidation states* of its constituent atoms? (For example, the charge of NO_3^- is 1−, and the oxidation states of its atoms are +5 for the nitrogen atom and −2 for each oxygen atom.)

(a) The charge of a polyatomic ion is a property of the entire ion, while the oxidation states are assigned to each individual atom.

(b) The oxidation state of the ion is the same as its charge.

(c) The charge of a polyatomic ion is not a real physical property, while the oxidation states of atoms are actual physical properties.

Identifying Redox Reactions

We can use oxidation states to identify redox reactions, even between nonmetals. For example, is the following reaction between carbon and sulfur a redox reaction?

$$C + 2\,S \rightarrow CS_2$$

If so, what element is oxidized? What element is reduced? We can use the oxidation state rules to assign oxidation states to all elements on both sides of the equation.

$$C + 2\,S \longrightarrow CS_2$$

Oxidation states: 0   0   +4 −2

Reduction

Oxidation

Carbon changes from an oxidation state of 0 to an oxidation state of +4. In terms of our electron bookkeeping scheme (the assigned oxidation state), carbon *loses electrons* and is *oxidized*. Sulfur changes from an oxidation state of 0 to an oxidation state of −2. In terms of our electron bookkeeping scheme, sulfur *gains electrons* and is *reduced*. In terms of oxidation states, oxidation and reduction are defined as follows:

- Oxidation: An increase in oxidation state
- Reduction: A decrease in oxidation state

Remember that a reduction is a *reduction* in oxidation state.

EXAMPLE 4.17 Using Oxidation States to Identify Oxidation and Reduction

Use oxidation states to identify the element that is oxidized and the element that is reduced in the following redox reaction.

$$Mg(s) + 2\,H_2O(l) \rightarrow Mg(OH)_2(aq) + H_2(g)$$

SOLUTION

Begin by assigning oxidation states to each atom in the reaction.

$$Mg(s) + 2\,H_2O(l) \longrightarrow Mg(OH)_2(aq) + H_2(g)$$

Oxidation states: 0   +1 −2   +2 −2 +1   0

Reduction

Oxidation

Since Mg increased in oxidation state, it was oxidized. Since H decreased in oxidation state, it was reduced.

FOR PRACTICE 4.17

Use oxidation states to identify the element that is oxidized and the element that is reduced in the following redox reaction.

$$Sn(s) + 4\,HNO_3(aq) \rightarrow SnO_2(s) + 4\,NO_2(g) + 2\,H_2O(g)$$

FOR MORE PRACTICE 4.17

Determine whether or not each reaction is a redox reaction. If the reaction is a redox reaction, identify which element is oxidized and which is reduced.

(a) $Hg_2(NO_3)_2(aq) + 2\,KBr(aq) \rightarrow Hg_2Br_2(s) + 2\,KNO_3(aq)$

(b) $4\,Al(s) + 3\,O_2(g) \rightarrow 2\,Al_2O_3(s)$

(c) $CaO(s) + CO_2(g) \rightarrow CaCO_3(s)$

Notice that *oxidation and reduction must occur together.* If one substance loses electrons (oxidation) then another substance must gain electrons (reduction). A substance that causes the oxidation of another substance is an **oxidizing agent**. Oxygen, for example, is an excellent oxidizing agent. In a redox reaction, *the oxidizing agent is always reduced.* A substance that causes the reduction of another substance is a **reducing agent**. Hydrogen, for example, as well as the group 1A and group 2A metals (because of their tendency to lose electrons) are excellent reducing agents. In a redox reaction, *the reducing agent is always oxidized.*

In Section 18.2 you will learn more about redox reactions, including how to balance them. For now, you need to be able to identify redox reactions, as well as oxidizing and reducing agents, according to the following guidelines.

Redox reactions:

- Any reaction in which there is a change in the oxidation states of atoms in going from reactants to products.

In a redox reaction:

- The oxidizing agent oxidizes another substance (and is itself reduced).
- The reducing agent reduces another substance (and is itself oxidized).

EXAMPLE 4.18 Identifying Redox Reactions, Oxidizing Agents, and Reducing Agents

Determine whether each reaction is an oxidation–reduction reaction. For each oxidation–reduction reaction, identify the oxidizing agent and the reducing agent.

(a) $2\,Mg(s) + O_2(g) \rightarrow 2\,MgO(s)$

(b) $2\,HBr(aq) + Ca(OH)_2(aq) \rightarrow 2\,H_2O(l) + CaBr_2(aq)$

(c) $Zn(s) + Fe^{2+}(aq) \rightarrow Zn^{2+}(aq) + Fe(s)$

SOLUTION

This is a redox reaction because magnesium increases in oxidation number (oxidation) and oxygen decreases in oxidation number (reduction).	**(a)** $2\,Mg(s) + O_2(g) \longrightarrow 2\,MgO(s)$ $\quad\quad\;\; 0 \quad\quad\; 0 \quad\quad\quad\;\; +2\;-2$ Reduction Oxidation Oxidizing agent: O_2 Reducing agent: Mg

This is not a redox reaction because none of the atoms undergo a change in oxidation number.	**(b)** $\begin{array}{c} 2\ \text{HBr}(aq)\ +\ \text{Ca(OH)}_2(aq) \rightarrow 2\text{H}_2\text{O}(l)\ +\ \text{CaBr}_2(aq) \\ {\scriptstyle +1-1} \qquad {\scriptstyle +2-2+1} \qquad\quad {\scriptstyle +1-2} \qquad {\scriptstyle +2-1} \end{array}$
This is a redox reaction because zinc increases in oxidation number (oxidation) and iron decreases in oxidation number (reduction).	**(c)** $\text{Zn}(s)\ +\ \text{Fe}^{2+}(aq) \longrightarrow \text{Zn}^{2+}(aq)\ +\ \text{Fe}(s)$ $\qquad 0 \qquad\ +2 \qquad\qquad\quad +2 \qquad\quad 0$ Reduction Oxidation Oxidizing agent: Fe^{2+} Reducing agent: Zn

FOR PRACTICE 4.18

Determine whether or not each reaction is a redox reaction. For all redox reactions, identify the oxidizing agent and the reducing agent.

(a) $2\ \text{Li}(s)\ +\ \text{Cl}_2(g) \rightarrow 2\ \text{LiCl}(s)$

(b) $2\ \text{Al}(s)\ +\ 3\ \text{Sn}^{2+}(aq) \rightarrow 2\ \text{Al}^{3+}(aq)\ +\ 3\ \text{Sn}(s)$

(c) $\text{Pb(NO}_3)_2(aq)\ +\ 2\ \text{LiCl}(aq) \rightarrow \text{PbCl}_2(s)\ +\ 2\ \text{LiNO}_3(aq)$

(d) $\text{C}(s)\ +\ \text{O}_2(g) \rightarrow \text{CO}_2(g)$

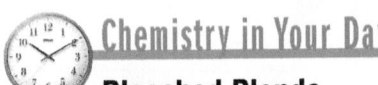

Conceptual Connection 4.9 Oxidation and Reduction

Which statement is true?

(a) A redox reaction involves *either* the transfer of an electron *or* a change in the oxidation state of an element.

(b) If any of the reactants or products in a reaction contain oxygen, the reaction is a redox reaction.

(c) In a reaction, oxidation can occur independently of reduction.

(d) In a redox reaction, any increase in the oxidation state of a reactant must be accompanied by a decrease in the oxidation state of a reactant.

Chemistry in Your Day

Bleached Blonde

Have you ever bleached your hair? Most home kits for hair bleaching contain hydrogen peroxide (H_2O_2), an excellent oxidizing agent. When applied to hair, hydrogen peroxide oxidizes melanin, the dark pigment that gives hair its color. Once melanin is oxidized, it no longer imparts a dark color, leaving the hair with the familiar bleached look. Hydrogen peroxide also oxidizes other components of hair. For example, protein molecules in hair contain —SH groups called thiols. Hydrogen peroxide oxidizes these thiol groups to sulfonic acid groups, —SO_3H. The oxidation of thiol groups to sulfonic acid groups causes changes in the proteins that compose hair, making the hair more brittle and more likely to tangle. Consequently, people with heavily bleached hair generally use conditioners, which contain compounds that form thin,

lubricating coatings on individual hair shafts. These coatings prevent tangling and make hair softer and more manageable.

Question

The following is a reaction of hydrogen peroxide with an alkene:

$$\text{H}_2\text{O}_2\ +\ \text{C}_2\text{H}_4 \rightarrow \text{C}_2\text{H}_4\text{O}\ +\ \text{H}_2\text{O}$$

Can you see why this reaction is a redox reaction? Can you identify the oxidizing and reducing agents?

▲ The bleaching of hair involves a redox reaction in which melanin—the main pigment in hair— is oxidized.

Combustion Reactions

We encountered combustion reactions, a type of redox reaction, in the opening section of this chapter. Combustion reactions are important because most of our society's energy is derived from them (Figure 4.25 ◀).

As you learned in Section 4.1, *combustion reactions* are characterized by the reaction of a substance with O_2 to form one or more oxygen-containing compounds, often including water. Combustion reactions also emit heat. For example, as you saw earlier in this chapter, natural gas (CH_4) reacts with oxygen to form carbon dioxide and water:

$$CH_4(g) + 2\,O_2(g) \rightarrow CO_2(g) + 2\,H_2O(g)$$
$$\text{Oxidation state:} \quad -4+1 \qquad\quad 0 \qquad\quad +4\,-2 \qquad +1\,-2$$

In this reaction, carbon is oxidized and oxygen is reduced. Ethanol, the alcohol in alcoholic beverages, also reacts with oxygen in a combustion reaction to form carbon dioxide and water:

$$C_2H_5OH(l) + 3\,O_2(g) \rightarrow 2\,CO_2(g) + 3\,H_2O(g)$$

Compounds containing carbon and hydrogen—or carbon, hydrogen, and oxygen—always form carbon dioxide and water upon complete combustion. Other combustion reactions include the reaction of carbon with oxygen to form carbon dioxide:

$$C(s) + O_2(g) \rightarrow CO_2(g)$$

and the reaction of hydrogen with oxygen to form water:

$$2\,H_2(g) + O_2(g) \rightarrow 2\,H_2O(g)$$

▼ **FIGURE 4.25 U.S. Energy Consumption**
About 82% of the energy the United States uses is produced by combustion reactions. Source: U.S. Energy Information Administration. *Annual Energy Review.* 2012. (Numbers may not sum to 100% because of independent rounding.)

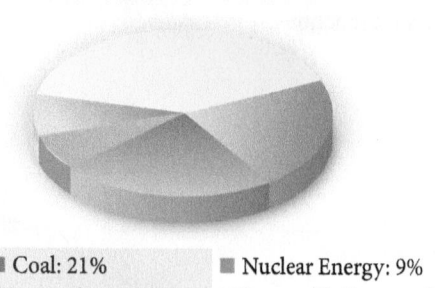

U.S. Energy Use by Source, 2010

Fossil fuel combustion {
■ Coal: 21%
■ Natural gas: 25%
■ Petroleum: 37%

■ Nuclear Energy: 9%
■ Renewable Energy: 8%

EXAMPLE 4.19 Writing Equations for Combustion Reactions

Write a balanced equation for the combustion of liquid methyl alcohol (CH_3OH).

SOLUTION

Begin by writing an unbalanced equation showing the reaction of CH_3OH with O_2 to form CO_2 and H_2O.	$CH_3OH(l) + O_2(g) \rightarrow CO_2(g) + H_2O(g)$
Balance the equation using the guidelines in Section 3.10.	$2\,CH_3OH(l) + 3\,O_2(g) \rightarrow 2\,CO_2(g) + 4\,H_2O(g)$

FOR PRACTICE 4.19
Write a balanced equation for the complete combustion of liquid C_2H_5SH.

CHAPTER IN REVIEW

Self Assessment Quiz

Q1. Manganese(IV) oxide reacts with aluminum to form elemental manganese and aluminum oxide:

$$3\,MnO_2 + 4\,Al \rightarrow 3\,Mn + 2\,Al_2O_3$$

What mass of Al is required to completely react with 25.0 g MnO_2?
a) 7.76 g Al
b) 5.82 g Al
c) 33.3 g Al
d) 10.3 g Al

Q2. Sodium and chlorine react to form sodium chloride:

$$2\,Na(s) + Cl_2(g) \rightarrow 2\,NaCl(s)$$

What is the theoretical yield of sodium chloride for the reaction of 55.0 g Na with 67.2 g Cl_2?
a) 1.40×10^2 g NaCl
b) 111 g NaCl
c) 55.4 g NaCl
d) 222 g NaCl

Q3. Sulfur and fluorine react to form sulfur hexafluoride:

$$S(s) + 3 F_2(g) \rightarrow SF_6(g)$$

If 50.0 g S is allowed to react as completely as possible with 105.0 g $F_2(g)$, what mass of the excess reactant is left?

a) 20.5 g S   c) 45.7 g F_2
c) 15.0 g S   d) 36.3 g F_2

Q4. A reaction has a theoretical yield of 45.8 g. When the reaction is carried out, 37.2 g of the product is obtained. What is the percent yield?

a) 55.1%   b) 44.8%
c) 123%   d) 81.2%

Q5. What is the molarity of a solution containing 55.8 g of $MgCl_2$ dissolved in 1.00 L of solution?

a) 55.8 M   b) 1.71 M
c) 0.586 M   d) 0.558 M

Q6. What mass (in grams) of $Mg(NO_3)_2$ is present in 145 mL of a 0.150 M solution of $Mg(NO_3)_2$?

a) 3.23 g   b) 0.022 g
c) 1.88 g   d) 143 g

Q7. What volume of a 1.50 M HCl solution should you use to prepare 2.00 L of a 0.100 M HCl solution?

a) 0.300 L   b) 0.133 L
c) 30.0 L   d) 2.00 L

Q8. Potassium iodide reacts with lead(II) nitrate in the following precipitation reaction:

$$2 KI(aq) + Pb(NO_3)_2(aq) \rightarrow 2 KNO_3(aq) + PbI_2(s)$$

What minimum volume of 0.200 M potassium iodide solution is required to completely precipitate all of the lead in 155.0 mL of a 0.112 M lead(II) nitrate solution?

a) 348 mL   b) 86.8 mL
c) 174 mL   d) 43.4 mL

Q9. Which solution will form a precipitate when mixed with a solution of aqueous Na_2CO_3?

a) $KNO_3(aq)$
b) $NaBr(aq)$
c) $NH_4Cl(aq)$
d) $CuCl_2(aq)$

Q10. What is the net ionic equation for the reaction that occurs when aqueous solutions of KOH and $SrCl_2$ are mixed?

a) $K^+(aq) + Cl^-(aq) \rightarrow KCl(s)$
b) $Sr^{2+}(aq) + 2 OH^-(aq) \rightarrow Sr(OH)_2(s)$
c) $H^+(aq) + OH^-(aq) \rightarrow H_2O(l)$
d) None of the above because no reaction occurs

Q11. What is the net ionic equation for the reaction that occurs when aqueous solutions of KOH and HNO_3 are mixed?

a) $K^+(aq) + NO_3^-(aq) \rightarrow KNO_3(s)$
b) $NO_3^-(aq) + OH^-(aq) \rightarrow NO_3OH(s)$
c) $H^+(aq) + OH^-(aq) \rightarrow H_2O(l)$
d) None of the above because no reaction occurs.

Q12. What is the net ionic equation for the reaction that occurs when aqueous solutions of $KHCO_3$ and HBr are mixed?

a) $K^+(aq) + C_2H_3O_2^-(aq) \rightarrow KC_2H_3O_2(s)$
b) $H^+(aq) + HCO_3^-(aq) \rightarrow CO_2(g) + H_2O(l)$
c) $H^+(aq) + OH^-(aq) \rightarrow H_2O(l)$
d) None of the above because no reaction occurs.

Q13. What is the oxidation state of carbon in CO_3^{2-}?

a) +4
b) +3
c) −3
d) −2

Q14. Sodium reacts with water according to the reaction:

$$2 Na(s) + 2 H_2O(l) \rightarrow 2 NaOH(aq) + H_2(g)$$

Identify the oxidizing agent.

a) $Na(s)$
b) $H_2O(l)$
c) $NaOH(aq)$
d) $H_2(aq)$

Q15. Identify the correct balanced equation for the combustion of propane (C_3H_8).

a) $C_3H_8(g) \rightarrow 4 H_2(g) + 3 C(s)$
b) $C_3H_8(g) + 5 O_2(g) \rightarrow 4 H_2O(g) + 3 CO_2(g)$
c) $C_3H_8(g) + 3 O_2(g) \rightarrow 4 H_2O(g) + 3 CO_2(g)$
d) $2 C_3H_8(g) + 9 O_2(g) \rightarrow 6 H_2CO_3(g) + 2 H_2(g)$

Answers: 1. (d) **2.** (b) **3.** (a) **4.** (d) **5.** (c) **6.** (a) **7.** (b) **8.** (c) **9.** (d) **10.** (b) **11.** (c) **12.** (b) **13.** (a) **14.** (b) **15.** (b)

Key Terms

Section 4.2
stoichiometry (141)

Section 4.3
limiting reactant (145)
theoretical yield (145)
actual yield (146)
percent yield (146)

Section 4.4
solution (152)
solvent (152)
solute (152)
aqueous solution (152)
dilute solution (152)
concentrated solution (152)

molarity (M) (152)
stock solution (154)

Section 4.5
electrolyte (159)
strong electrolyte (159)
nonelectrolyte (160)
strong acid (160)
weak acid (160)
weak electrolyte (160)
soluble (160)
insoluble (160)

Section 4.6
precipitation reaction (162)
precipitate (162)

Section 4.7
molecular equation (166)
complete ionic equation (167)
spectator ion (167)
net ionic equation (167)

Section 4.8
acid–base reaction
  (neutralization reaction)
  (168)
gas-evolution reaction (168)
Arrhenius definitions (169)
hydronium ion (169)
polyprotic acid (169)
diprotic acid (169)
salt (170)

titration (171)
equivalence point (171)
indicator (171)

Section 4.9
oxidation–reduction (redox)
  reaction (175)
oxidation (176)
reduction (176)
oxidation state (oxidation
  number) (176)
oxidizing agent (180)
reducing agent (180)

Key Concepts

Climate Change and the Combustion of Fossil Fuels (4.1)

▶ Greenhouse gases warm Earth by trapping some of the sunlight that penetrates Earth's atmosphere. Global warming, resulting from rising atmospheric carbon dioxide levels, is potentially harmful.

▶ The largest atmospheric carbon dioxide source is the burning of fossil fuels. This can be verified by reaction stoichiometry.

Reaction Stoichiometry (4.2)

▶ Reaction stoichiometry refers to the numerical relationships between the reactants and products in a balanced chemical equation.

▶ Reaction stoichiometry allows us to predict, for example, the amount of product that can be formed for a given amount of reactant, or how much of one reactant is required to react with a given amount of another.

Limiting Reactant, Theoretical Yield, and Percent Yield (4.3)

▶ When a chemical reaction actually occurs, the reactants are usually not present in the exact stoichiometric ratios specified by the balanced chemical equation. The limiting reactant is the one that is available in the smallest stoichiometric quantity—it will be completely consumed in the reaction and it limits the amount of product that can be made.

▶ Any reactant that does not limit the amount of product is said to be in excess.

▶ The amount of product that can be made from the limiting reactant is the theoretical yield.

▶ The actual yield—always equal to or less than the theoretical yield—is the amount of product that is actually made when the reaction is carried out.

▶ The percentage of the theoretical yield that is actually produced is the percent yield.

Solution Concentration and Stoichiometry (4.4)

▶ An aqueous solution is a homogeneous mixture of water (the solvent) with another substance (the solute).

▶ We often express the concentration of a solution in molarity, the number of moles of solute per liter of solution.

▶ We can use the molarities and volumes of reactant solutions to predict the amount of product that will form in an aqueous reaction.

Aqueous Solutions and Precipitation Reactions (4.5, 4.6)

▶ Solutes that completely dissociate (or completely ionize in the case of the acids) to ions in solution are strong electrolytes and their *solutions* are good conductors of electricity.

▶ Solutes that only partially dissociate (or partially ionize) are weak electrolytes.

▶ Solutes that do not dissociate (or ionize) are nonelectrolytes.

▶ A substance that dissolves in water to form a solution is soluble.

▶ In a precipitation reaction, we mix two aqueous solutions and a solid—or precipitate—forms.

▶ The solubility rules are an empirical set of guidelines that help predict the solubilities of ionic compounds; these rules are especially useful when determining whether or not a precipitate will form.

Equations for Aqueous Reactions (4.7)

▶ We can represent an aqueous reaction with a molecular equation, which shows the complete neutral formula for each compound in the reaction.

▶ We can also represent an aqueous reaction with a complete ionic equation, which shows the dissociated nature of the aqueous ionic compounds.

▶ A third representation of an aqueous reaction is the net ionic equation, in which the spectator ions—those that do not change in the course of the reaction—are left out of the equation.

Acid–Base and Gas-Evolution Reactions (4.8)

▶ In an acid–base reaction, an acid, a substance that produces H^+ in solution, reacts with a base, a substance that produces OH^- in solution, and the two neutralize each other, producing water (or in some cases a weak electrolyte).

▶ An acid–base titration is a laboratory procedure in which a reaction is carried to its equivalence point—the point at which the reactants are in exact stoichiometric proportions; titrations are useful in determining the concentrations of unknown solutions.

▶ In gas-evolution reactions, two aqueous solutions combine and a gas is produced.

Oxidation–Reduction Reactions (4.9)

▶ In oxidation–reduction reactions, one substance transfers electrons to another substance.

▶ The substance that loses electrons is oxidized and the substance that gains them is reduced.

▶ An oxidation state is a fictitious charge given to each atom in a redox reaction by assigning all shared electrons to the atom with the greater attraction for those electrons. Oxidation states are an imposed electronic bookkeeping scheme, not an actual physical state.

▶ The oxidation state of an atom increases upon oxidation and decreases upon reduction.

▶ A combustion reaction is a specific type of oxidation–reduction reaction in which a substance reacts with oxygen, emitting heat and forming one or more oxygen-containing products.

Key Equations and Relationships

Mass-to-Mass Conversion: Stoichiometry (4.2)

mass A $\rightarrow$ amount A (in moles) $\rightarrow$ amount B (in moles) $\rightarrow$ mass B

Percent Yield (4.3)

$$\% \text{ yield} = \frac{\text{actual yield}}{\text{theoretical yield}} \times 100\%$$

Molarity (M): Solution Concentration (4.4)

$$M = \frac{\text{amount of solute (in mol)}}{\text{volume of solution (in L)}}$$

Solution Dilution (4.4)

$$M_1 V_1 = M_2 V_2$$

Solution Stoichiometry (4.4)

volume A $\rightarrow$ amount A (in moles) $\rightarrow$
amount B (in moles) $\rightarrow$ volume B

Key Learning Outcomes

Chapter Objectives	Assessment
Calculations Involving the Stoichiometry of a Reaction (4.2)	Example 4.1, 4.2 For Practice 4.1, 4.2 Exercises 31–36
Determining the Limiting Reactant and Calculating Theoretical and Percent Yield (4.3)	Example 4.3, 4.4 For Practice 4.3, 4.4 Exercises 41–51
Calculating and Using Molarity as a Conversion Factor (4.4)	Example 4.5, 4.6 For Practice 4.5, 4.6 For More Practice 4.5, 4.6 Exercises 53–60
Determining Solution Dilutions (4.4)	Example 4.7 For Practice 4.7 For More Practice 4.7 Exercises 63, 64
Using Solution Stoichiometry to Find Volumes and Amounts (4.4)	Example 4.8 For Practice 4.8 For More Practice 4.8 Exercises 65–67
Predicting Whether a Compound Is Soluble (4.5)	Example 4.9 For Practice 4.9 Exercises 73, 74
Writing Equations for Precipitation Reactions (4.6)	Example 4.10, 4.11 For Practice 4.10, 4.11 Exercises 75–78
Writing Complete Ionic and Net Ionic Equations (4.7)	Example 4.12 For Practice 4.12 For More Practice 4.12 Exercises 79, 80
Writing Equations for Acid–Base Reactions (4.8)	Example 4.13 For Practice 4.13 Exercises 83, 84
Calculations Involving Acid–Base Titrations (4.8)	Example 4.14 For Practice 4.14 For More Practice 4.14 Exercises 87, 88
Writing Equations for Gas-Evolution Reactions (4.8)	Example 4.15 For Practice 4.15 For More Practice 4.15 Exercises 89, 90
Assigning Oxidation States (4.9)	Example 4.16 For Practice 4.16 Exercises 91–94
Identifying Redox Reactions, Oxidizing Agents, and Reducing Agents Using Oxidation States (4.9)	Example 4.17, 4.18 For Practice 4.17, 4.18 For More Practice 4.17 Exercises 95, 96
Writing Equations for Combustion Reactions (4.9)	Example 4.19 For Practice 4.19 Exercises 97, 98

EXERCISES

Review Questions

1. What is reaction stoichiometry? What is the significance of the coefficients in a balanced chemical equation?

2. In a chemical reaction, what is the limiting reactant? The theoretical yield? The percent yield? What do we mean when we say a reactant is in excess?

3. We typically calculate the percent yield using the actual yield and theoretical yield in units of mass (g or kg). Would the percent yield be different if the actual yield and theoretical yield were in units of amount (moles)?

4. What is an aqueous solution? What is the difference between the solute and the solvent?

5. What is molarity? How is it useful?

6. Explain how a strong electrolyte, a weak electrolyte, and a nonelectrolyte differ.

7. Explain the difference between a strong acid and a weak acid.

8. What does it mean for a compound to be soluble? Insoluble?

9. What are the solubility rules? How are they useful?

10. What are the cations and anions whose compounds are usually soluble? What are the exceptions? What are the anions whose compounds are mostly insoluble? What are the exceptions?

11. What is a precipitation reaction? Give an example.

12. How can you predict whether a precipitation reaction will occur upon mixing two aqueous solutions?

13. Explain how a molecular equation, a complete ionic equation, and a net ionic equation differ.

14. What is the Arrhenius definition of an acid? A base?

15. What is an acid–base reaction? Give an example.

16. Explain the principles behind an acid–base titration. What is an indicator?

17. What is a gas-evolution reaction? Give an example.

18. What reactant types give rise to gas-evolution reactions?

19. What is an oxidation–reduction reaction? Give an example.

20. What are oxidation states?

21. How can oxidation states be used to identify redox reactions?

22. What happens to a substance when it becomes oxidized? Reduced?

23. In a redox reaction, which reactant is the oxidizing agent? The reducing agent?

24. What is a combustion reaction? Why are they important? Give an example.

Problems by Topic

Reaction Stoichiometry

25. Consider the unbalanced equation for the combustion of hexane:

$$C_6H_{14}(g) + O_2(g) \rightarrow CO_2(g) + H_2O(g)$$

Balance the equation and determine how many moles of O_2 are required to react completely with 7.2 moles of C_6H_{14}.

26. Consider the unbalanced equation for the neutralization of acetic acid:

$$HC_2H_3O_2(aq) + Ba(OH)_2(aq) \rightarrow H_2O(l) + Ba(C_2H_3O_2)_2(aq)$$

Balance the equation and determine how many moles of $Ba(OH)_2$ are required to completely neutralize 0.461 mole of $HC_2H_3O_2$.

27. Calculate how many moles of NO_2 form when each quantity of reactant completely reacts.

$$2 N_2O_5(g) \rightarrow 4 NO_2(g) + O_2(g)$$

a. 2.5 mol N_2O_5
b. 6.8 mol N_2O_5
c. 15.2 g N_2O_5
d. 2.87 kg N_2O_5

28. Calculate how many moles of NH_3 form when each quantity of reactant completely reacts.

$$3 N_2H_4(l) \rightarrow 4 NH_3(g) + N_2(g)$$

a. 2.6 mol N_2H_4
b. 3.55 mol N_2H_4
c. 65.3 g N_2H_4
d. 4.88 kg N_2H_4

29. Consider the balanced equation:

$$SiO_2(s) + 3 C(s) \rightarrow SiC(s) + 2 CO(g)$$

Complete the table showing the appropriate number of moles of reactants and products. If the number of moles of a *reactant* is provided, fill in the required amount of the other reactant, as well as the moles of each product that forms. If the number of moles of a *product* is provided, fill in the required amount of each reactant to make that amount of product, as well as the amount of the other product that is made.

Mol SiO$_2$	Mol C	Mol SiC	Mol CO
3	___	___	___
___	6	___	___
___	___	___	10
2.8	___	___	___
___	1.55	___	___

30. Consider the balanced equation

$$2 N_2H_4(g) + N_2O_4(g) \rightarrow 3 N_2(g) + 4 H_2O(g)$$

Complete the table showing the appropriate number of moles of reactants and products. If the number of moles of a *reactant* is provided, fill in the required amount of the other reactant, as well as the moles of each product that forms. If the number of moles of a *product* is provided, fill in the required amount of each reactant to make that amount of product, as well as the amount of the other product that is made.

Mol N$_2$H$_4$	Mol N$_2$O$_4$	Mol N$_2$	Mol H$_2$O
2	___	___	___
___	5	___	___
___	___	___	10
2.5	___	___	___
___	4.2	___	___
___	___	11.8	___

31. Hydrobromic acid dissolves solid iron according to the reaction:

$$Fe(s) + 2\,HBr(aq) \rightarrow FeBr_2(aq) + H_2(g)$$

What mass of HBr (in g) do you need to dissolve a 3.2 g pure iron bar on a padlock? What mass of H_2 would the complete reaction of the iron bar produce?

32. Sulfuric acid dissolves aluminum metal according to the reaction:

$$2\,Al(s) + 3\,H_2SO_4(aq) \rightarrow Al_2(SO_4)_3(aq) + 3\,H_2(g)$$

Suppose you want to dissolve an aluminum block with a mass of 15.2 g. What minimum mass of H_2SO_4 (in g) do you need? What mass of H_2 gas (in g) does the complete reaction of the aluminum block produce?

33. For each of the reactions, calculate the mass (in grams) of the product that forms when 3.67 g of the underlined reactant completely reacts. Assume that there is more than enough of the other reactant.

a. <u>Ba</u>(s) + $Cl_2(g) \rightarrow BaCl_2(s)$
b. <u>CaO</u>(s) + $CO_2(g) \rightarrow CaCO_3(s)$
c. 2 <u>Mg</u>(s) + $O_2(g) \rightarrow 2\,MgO(s)$
d. 4 <u>Al</u>(s) + $3\,O_2(g) \rightarrow 2\,Al_2O_3(s)$

34. For each of the reactions, calculate the mass (in grams) of the product that forms when 15.39 g of the underlined reactant completely reacts. Assume that there is more than enough of the other reactant.

a. $2\,K(s)$ + <u>$Cl_2(g)$</u> $\rightarrow 2\,KCl(s)$
b. $2\,K(s)$ + <u>$Br_2(l)$</u> $\rightarrow 2\,KBr(s)$
c. $4\,Cr(s)$ + <u>$3\,O_2(g)$</u> $\rightarrow 2\,Cr_2O_3(s)$
d. 2 <u>Sr</u>(s) + $O_2(g) \rightarrow 2\,SrO(s)$

35. For each of the acid–base reactions, calculate the mass (in grams) of each acid necessary to completely react with and neutralize 4.85 g of the base.

a. $HCl(aq) + NaOH(aq) \rightarrow H_2O(l) + NaCl(aq)$
b. $2\,HNO_3(aq) + Ca(OH)_2(aq) \rightarrow$
$$2\,H_2O(l) + Ca(NO_3)_2(aq)$$
c. $H_2SO_4(aq) + 2\,KOH(aq) \rightarrow 2\,H_2O(l) + K_2SO_4(aq)$

36. For each precipitation reaction, calculate how many grams of the first reactant are necessary to completely react with 55.8 g of the second reactant.

a. $2\,KI(aq) + Pb(NO_3)_2(aq) \rightarrow PbI_2(s) + 2\,KNO_3(aq)$
b. $Na_2CO_3(aq) + CuCl_2(aq) \rightarrow CuCO_3(s) + 2\,NaCl(aq)$
c. $K_2SO_4(aq) + Sr(NO_3)_2(aq) \rightarrow$
$$SrSO_4(s) + 2\,KNO_3(aq)$$

Limiting Reactant, Theoretical Yield, and Percent Yield

37. For the following reaction, determine the limiting reactant for each of the initial amounts of reactants.

$$2\,Na(s) + Br_2(g) \rightarrow 2\,NaBr(s)$$

a. 2 mol Na, 2 mol Br_2
b. 1.8 mol Na, 1.4 mol Br_2
c. 2.5 mol Na, 1 mol Br_2
d. 12.6 mol Na, 6.9 mol Br_2

38. Find the limiting reactant for each initial amount of reactants.

$$4\,Al(s) + 3\,O_2(g) \rightarrow 2\,Al_2O_3(s)$$

a. 1 mol Al, 1 mol O_2 **b.** 4 mol Al, 2.6 mol O_2
c. 16 mol Al, 13 mol O_2 **d.** 7.4 mol Al, 6.5 mol O_2

39. Consider the reaction:

$$4\,HCl(g) + O_2(g) \rightarrow 2\,H_2O(g) + 2\,Cl_2(g)$$

Each molecular diagram represents an initial mixture of the reactants. How many molecules of Cl_2 would be formed from the reaction mixture that produces the greatest amount of products?

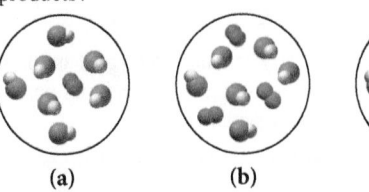

(a)   (b)   (c)

40. Consider the reaction:

$$2\,CH_3OH(g) + 3\,O_2(g) \rightarrow 2\,CO_2(g) + 4\,H_2O(g)$$

Each of the molecular diagrams represents an initial mixture of the reactants. How many CO_2 molecules would be formed from the reaction mixture that produces the greatest amount of products?

(a)   (b)   (c)

41. Calculate the theoretical yield of the product (in moles) for each initial amount of reactants.

$$Ti(s) + 2\,Cl_2(g) \rightarrow TiCl_4(s)$$

a. 4 mol Ti, 4 mol Cl_2 **b.** 7 mol Ti, 17 mol Cl_2
c. 12.4 mol Ti, 18.8 mol Cl_2

42. Calculate the theoretical yield of product (in moles) for each initial amount of reactants.

$$3\,Mn(s) + 2\,O_2(g) \rightarrow Mn^3O_4(s)$$

a. 3 mol Mn, 3 mol O_2 **b.** 4 mol Mn, 7 mol O_2
c. 27.5 mol Mn, 43.8 mol O_2

43. Zinc(II) sulfide reacts with oxygen according to the reaction:

$$2\,ZnS(s) + 3\,O_2(g) \rightarrow 2\,ZnO(s) + 2\,SO_2(g)$$

A reaction mixture initially contains 4.2 mol ZnS and 6.8 mol O_2. Once the reaction has occurred as completely as possible, what amount (in moles) of the excess reactant is left?

44. Iron(II) sulfide reacts with hydrochloric acid according to the reaction:

$$FeS(s) + 2\,HCl(aq) \rightarrow FeCl_2(s) + H_2S(g)$$

A reaction mixture initially contains 0.223 mol FeS and 0.652 mol HCl. Once the reaction has occurred as completely as possible, what amount (in moles) of the excess reactant is left?

45. For the reaction shown, calculate the theoretical yield of product (in grams) for each initial amount of reactants.

$$2\,Al(s) + 3\,Cl_2(g) \rightarrow 2\,AlCl_3(s)$$

a. 2.0 g Al, 2.0 g Cl_2 **b.** 7.5 g Al, 24.8 g Cl_2
c. 0.235 g Al, 1.15 g Cl_2

46. For the reaction shown, calculate the theoretical yield of the product (in grams) for each initial amount of reactants.

$$Ti(s) + 2\,F_2(g) \rightarrow TiF_4(s)$$

a. 5.0 g Ti, 5.0 g F_2 **b.** 2.4 g Ti, 1.6 g F_2
c. 0.233 g Ti, 0.288 g F_2

47. Iron(III) sulfide reacts with carbon monoxide according to the equation:

$$Fe_2O_3(s) + 3\,CO(g) \rightarrow 2\,Fe(s) + 3\,CO_2(g)$$

A reaction mixture initially contains 22.55 g Fe_2O_3 and 14.78 g CO. Once the reaction has occurred as completely as possible, what mass (in g) of the excess reactant is left?

48. Elemental phosphorus reacts with chlorine gas according to the equation:

$$P_4(s) + 6\,Cl_2(g) \rightarrow 4\,PCl_3(l)$$

A reaction mixture initially contains 45.69 g P_4 and 131.3 g Cl_2. Once the reaction has occurred as completely as possible, what mass (in g) of the excess reactant is left?

49. Lead ions can be precipitated from solution with KCl according to the reaction:

$$Pb^{2+}(aq) + 2\,KCl(aq) \rightarrow PbCl_2(s) + 2\,K^+(aq)$$

When 28.5 g KCl is added to a solution containing 25.7 g Pb^{2+}, a $PbCl_2$ precipitate forms. The precipitate is filtered and dried and found to have a mass of 29.4 g. Determine the limiting reactant, theoretical yield of $PbCl_2$, and percent yield for the reaction.

50. Magnesium oxide can be made by heating magnesium metal in the presence of oxygen. The balanced equation for the reaction is

$$2\,Mg(s) + O_2(g) \rightarrow 2\,MgO(s)$$

When 10.1 g of Mg reacts with 10.5 g O_2, 11.9 g MgO is collected. Determine the limiting reactant, theoretical yield, and percent yield for the reaction.

51. Urea (CH_4N_2O) is a common fertilizer that is synthesized by the reaction of ammonia (NH_3) with carbon dioxide:

$$2\,NH_3(aq) + CO_2(aq) \rightarrow CH_4N_2O(aq) + H_2O(l)$$

In an industrial synthesis of urea, a chemist combines 136.4 kg of ammonia with 211.4 kg of carbon dioxide and obtains 168.4 kg of urea. Determine the limiting reactant, theoretical yield of urea, and percent yield for the reaction.

52. Many computer chips are manufactured from silicon, which occurs in nature as SiO_2. When SiO_2 is heated to melting, it reacts with solid carbon to form liquid silicon and carbon monoxide gas. In an industrial preparation of silicon, 155.8 kg of SiO_2 reacts with 78.3 kg of carbon to produce 66.1 kg of silicon. Determine the limiting reactant, theoretical yield, and percent yield for the reaction.

Solution Concentration and Solution Stoichiometry

53. Calculate the molarity of each solution.
a. 3.25 mol of LiCl in 2.78 L solution
b. 28.33 g $C_6H_{12}O_6$ in 1.28 L of solution
c. 32.4 mg NaCl in 122.4 mL of solution

54. Calculate the molarity of each solution.
a. 0.38 mol of $LiNO_3$ in 6.14 L of solution
b. 72.8 g C_2H_6O in 2.34 L of solution
c. 12.87 mg KI in 112.4 mL of solution

55. What is the molarity of NO_3^- in each solution?
a. 0.150 M KNO_3 **b.** 0.150 M $Ca(NO_3)_2$
c. 0.150 M $Al(NO_3)_3$

56. What is the molarity of Cl^- in each solution?
a. 0.200 M NaCl   **b.** 0.150 M $SrCl_2$
c. 0.100 M $AlCl_3$

57. How many moles of KCl are contained in each solution?
a. 0.556 L of a 2.3 M KCl solution
b. 1.8 L of a 0.85 M KCl solution
c. 114 mL of a 1.85 M KCl solution

58. What volume of 0.200 M ethanol solution contains each amount in moles of ethanol?
a. 0.45 mol ethanol   **b.** 1.22 mol ethanol
c. 1.2×10^{-2} mol ethanol

59. A laboratory procedure calls for making 400.0 mL of a 1.1 M $NaNO_3$ solution. What mass of $NaNO_3$ (in g) is needed?

60. A chemist wants to make 5.5 L of a 0.300 M $CaCl_2$ solution. What mass of $CaCl_2$ (in g) should the chemist use?

61. If 123 mL of a 1.1 M glucose solution is diluted to 500.0 mL, what is the molarity of the diluted solution?

62. If 3.5 L of a 4.8 M $SrCl_2$ solution is diluted to 45 L, what is the molarity of the diluted solution?

63. To what volume should you dilute 50.0 mL of a 12 M stock HNO_3 solution to obtain a 0.100 M HNO_3 solution?

64. To what volume should you dilute 25 mL of a 10.0 M H_2SO_4 solution to obtain a 0.150 M H_2SO_4 solution?

65. Consider the precipitation reaction:

$$2\,Na_3PO_4(aq) + 3\,CuCl_2(aq) \rightarrow Cu_3(PO_4)_2(s) + 6\,NaCl(aq)$$

What volume of 0.175 M Na_3PO_4 solution is necessary to completely react with 95.4 mL of 0.102 M $CuCl_2$?

66. Consider the reaction:

$$Li_2S(aq) + Co(NO_3)_2(aq) \rightarrow 2\,LiNO_3(aq) + CoS(s)$$

What volume of 0.150 M Li_2S solution is required to completely react with 125 mL of 0.150 M $Co(NO_3)_2$?

67. What is the minimum amount of 6.0 M H_2SO_4 necessary to produce 25.0 g of $H_2(g)$ according to the reaction between aluminum and sulfuric acid?

$$2\,Al(s) + 3\,H_2SO_4(aq) \rightarrow Al_2(SO_4)_3(aq) + 3\,H_2(g)$$

68. What is the molarity of $ZnCl_2$ that forms when 25.0 g of zinc completely reacts with $CuCl_2$ according to the following reaction? Assume a final volume of 275 mL.

$$Zn(s) + CuCl_2(aq) \rightarrow ZnCl_2(aq) + Cu(s)$$

69. A 25.0 mL sample of a 1.20 M potassium chloride solution is mixed with 15.0 mL of a 0.900 M barium nitrate solution and this precipitation reaction occurs:

$$2\,KCl(aq) + Ba(NO_3)_2(aq) \rightarrow BaCl_2(s) + 2\,KNO_3(aq)$$

The solid $BaCl_2$ is collected, dried, and found to have a mass of 2.45 g. Determine the limiting reactant, the theoretical yield, and the percent yield.

70. A 55.0 mL sample of a 0.102 M potassium sulfate solution is mixed with 35.0 mL of a 0.114 M lead(II) acetate solution and this precipitation reaction occurs:

$$K_2SO_4(aq) + Pb(C_2H_3O_2)_2(aq) \rightarrow 2\,KC_2H_3O_2(aq) + PbSO_4(s)$$

The solid $PbSO_4$ is collected, dried, and found to have a mass of 1.01 g. Determine the limiting reactant, the theoretical yield, and the percent yield.

Types of Aqueous Solutions and Solubility

71. For each compound (all water soluble), would you expect the resulting aqueous solution to conduct electrical current?
a. CsCl   **b.** CH_3OH **c.** $Ca(NO_2)_2$ **d.** $C_6H_{12}O_6$

72. Classify each compound as a strong electrolyte or nonelectrolyte.
a. $MgBr_2$ **b.** $C_{12}H_{22}O_{11}$ **c.** Na_2CO_3 **d.** KOH

73. Determine whether each compound is soluble or insoluble. If the compound is soluble, list the ions present in solution.
a. $AgNO_3$ **b.** $Pb(C_2H_3O_2)_2$ **c.** KNO_3 **d.** $(NH_4)_2S$

74. Determine whether each compound is soluble or insoluble. For the soluble compounds, list the ions present in solution.
a. AgI   **b.** $Cu_3(PO_4)_2$ **c.** $CoCO_3$ **d.** K_3PO_4

Precipitation Reactions

75. Complete and balance each equation. If no reaction occurs, write "NO REACTION."
  a. $LiI(aq) + BaS(aq) \rightarrow$
  b. $KCl(aq) + CaS(aq) \rightarrow$
  c. $CrBr_2(aq) + Na_2CO_3(aq) \rightarrow$
  d. $NaOH(aq) + FeCl_3(aq) \rightarrow$

76. Complete and balance each equation. If no reaction occurs, write "NO REACTION."
  a. $NaNO_3(aq) + KCl(aq) \rightarrow$
  b. $NaCl(aq) + Hg_2(C_2H_3O_2)_2(aq) \rightarrow$
  c. $(NH_4)_2SO_4(aq) + SrCl_2(aq) \rightarrow$
  d. $NH_4Cl(aq) + AgNO_3(aq) \rightarrow$

77. Write a molecular equation for the precipitation reaction that occurs (if any) when each pair of aqueous solutions is mixed. If no reaction occurs, write "NO REACTION."
  a. potassium carbonate and lead(II) nitrate
  b. lithium sulfate and lead(II) acetate
  c. copper(II) nitrate and magnesium sulfide
  d. strontium nitrate and potassium iodide

78. Write a molecular equation for the precipitation reaction that occurs (if any) when each pair of aqueous solutions is mixed. If no reaction occurs, write "NO REACTION."
  a. sodium chloride and lead(II) acetate
  b. potassium sulfate and strontium iodide
  c. cesium chloride and calcium sulfide
  d. chromium(III) nitrate and sodium phosphate

Ionic and Net Ionic Equations

79. Write balanced complete ionic and net ionic equations for each reaction.
  a. $HCl(aq) + LiOH(aq) \rightarrow H_2O(l) + LiCl(aq)$
  b. $MgS(aq) + CuCl_2(aq) \rightarrow CuS(s) + MgCl_2(aq)$
  c. $NaOH(aq) + HC_2H_3O_2(aq) \rightarrow H_2O(l) + NaC_2H_3O_2(aq)$
  d. $Na_3PO_4(aq) + NiCl_2(aq) \rightarrow Ni_3(PO_4)_2(s) + NaCl(aq)$

80. Write balanced complete ionic and net ionic equations for each reaction.
  a. $K_2SO_4(aq) + CaI_2(aq) \rightarrow CaSO_4(s) + KI(aq)$
  b. $NH_4Cl(aq) + NaOH(aq) \rightarrow$
      $H_2O(l) + NH_3(g) + NaCl(aq)$
  c. $AgNO_3(aq) + NaCl(aq) \rightarrow AgCl(s) + NaNO_3(aq)$
  d. $HC_2H_3O_2(aq) + K_2CO_3(aq) \rightarrow$
      $H_2O(l) + CO_2(g) + KC_2H_3O_2(aq)$

81. Mercury(I) ions (Hg_2^{2+}) can be removed from solution by precipitation with Cl^-. Suppose that a solution contains aqueous $Hg_2(NO_3)_2$. Write complete ionic and net ionic equations to show the reaction of aqueous $Hg_2(NO_3)_2$ with aqueous sodium chloride to form solid Hg_2Cl_2 and aqueous sodium nitrate.

82. Lead(II) ions can be removed from solution by precipitation with sulfate ions. Suppose that a solution contains lead(II) nitrate. Write complete ionic and net ionic equations to show the reaction of aqueous lead(II) nitrate with aqueous potassium sulfate to form solid lead(II) sulfate and aqueous potassium nitrate.

Acid–Base and Gas-Evolution Reactions

83. Write balanced molecular and net ionic equations for the reaction between hydrobromic acid and potassium hydroxide.

84. Write balanced molecular and net ionic equations for the reaction between nitric acid and calcium hydroxide.

85. Complete and balance each acid–base equation.
  a. $H_2SO_4(aq) + Ca(OH)_2(aq) \rightarrow$
  b. $HClO_4(aq) + KOH(aq) \rightarrow$
  c. $H_2SO_4(aq) + NaOH(aq) \rightarrow$

86. Complete and balance each acid–base equation.
  a. $HI(aq) + LiOH(aq) \rightarrow$
  b. $HC_2H_3O_2(aq) + Ca(OH)_2(aq) \rightarrow$
  c. $HCl(aq) + Ba(OH)_2(aq) \rightarrow$

87. A 25.00 mL sample of an unknown $HClO_4$ solution requires titration with 22.62 mL of 0.2000 M NaOH to reach the equivalence point. What is the concentration of the unknown $HClO_4$ solution? The neutralization reaction is
$$HClO_4(aq) + NaOH(aq) \rightarrow H_2O(l) + NaClO_4(aq)$$

88. A 30.00 mL sample of an unknown H_3PO_4 solution is titrated with a 0.100 M NaOH solution. The equivalence point is reached when 26.38 mL of NaOH solution is added. What is the concentration of the unknown H_3PO_4 solution? The neutralization reaction is
$$H_3PO_4(aq) + 3\ NaOH(aq) \rightarrow 3\ H_2O(l) + Na_3PO_4(aq)$$

89. Complete and balance each gas-evolution equation.
  a. $HBr(aq) + NiS(s) \rightarrow$
  b. $NH_4I(aq) + NaOH(aq) \rightarrow$
  c. $HBr(aq) + Na_2S(aq) \rightarrow$
  d. $HClO_4(aq) + Li_2CO_3(aq) \rightarrow$

90. Complete and balance each gas-evolution equation.
  a. $HNO_3(aq) + Na_2SO_3(aq) \rightarrow$
  b. $HCl(aq) + KHCO_3(aq) \rightarrow$
  c. $HC_2H_3O_2(aq) + NaHSO_3(aq) \rightarrow$
  d. $(NH_4)_2SO_4(aq) + Ca(OH)_2(aq) \rightarrow$

Oxidation–Reduction and Combustion

91. Assign oxidation states to each atom in each element, ion, or compound.
  a. Ag   **b.** Ag^+ **c.** CaF_2
  d. H_2S **e.** CO_3^{2-} **f.** CrO_4^{2-}

92. Assign oxidation states to each atom in each element, ion, or compound.
  a. Cl_2 **b.** Fe^{3+} **c.** $CuCl_2$
  d. CH_4 **e.** $Cr_2O_7^{2-}$ **f.** HSO_4^-

93. What is the oxidation state of Cr in each compound?
  a. CrO   **b.** CrO_3 **c.** Cr_2O_3

94. What is the oxidation state of Cl in each ion?
  a. ClO^- **b.** ClO_2^- **c.** ClO_3^- **d.** ClO_4^-

95. Determine whether each reaction is a redox reaction. For each redox reaction, identify the oxidizing agent and the reducing agent.
  a. $4\ Li(s) + O_2(g) \rightarrow 2\ Li_2O(s)$
  b. $Mg(s) + Fe^{2+}(aq) \rightarrow Mg^{2+}(aq) + Fe(s)$
  c. $Pb(NO_3)_2(aq) + Na_2SO_4(aq) \rightarrow PbSO_4(s) + 2\ NaNO_3(aq)$
  d. $HBr(aq) + KOH(aq) \rightarrow H_2O(l) + KBr(aq)$

96. Determine whether each reaction is a redox reaction. For each redox reaction, identify the oxidizing agent and the reducing agent.
  a. $Al(s) + 3\ Ag^+(aq) \rightarrow Al^{3+}(aq) + 3\ Ag(s)$
  b. $SO_3(g) + H_2O(l) \rightarrow H_2SO_4(aq)$
  c. $Ba(s) + Cl_2(g) \rightarrow BaCl_2(s)$
  d. $Mg(s) + Br_2(l) \rightarrow MgBr_2(s)$

97. Complete and balance each combustion reaction equation.
 a. $S(s) + O_2(g) \rightarrow$ **b.** $C_3H_6(g) + O_2(g) \rightarrow$
 c. $Ca(s) + O_2(g) \rightarrow$ **d.** $C_5H_{12}S(l) + O_2(g) \rightarrow$

98. Complete and balance each combustion reaction equation:
 a. $C_4H_6(g) + O_2(g) \rightarrow$ **b.** $C(s) + O_2(g) \rightarrow$
 c. $CS_2(s) + O_2(g) \rightarrow$ **d.** $C_3H_8O(l) + O_2(g) \rightarrow$

Cumulative Problems

99. The density of a 20.0% by mass ethylene glycol ($C_2H_6O_2$) solution in water is 1.03 g/mL. Find the molarity of the solution.

100. Find the percent by mass of sodium chloride in a 1.35 M NaCl solution. The density of the solution is 1.05 g/mL.

101. People often use sodium bicarbonate as an antacid to neutralize excess hydrochloric acid in an upset stomach. What mass of hydrochloric acid (in grams) can 2.5 g of sodium bicarbonate neutralize? (Hint: Begin by writing a balanced equation for the reaction between aqueous sodium bicarbonate and aqueous hydrochloric acid.)

102. Toilet bowl cleaners often contain hydrochloric acid, which dissolves the calcium carbonate deposits that accumulate within a toilet bowl. What mass of calcium carbonate (in grams) can 3.8 g of HCl dissolve? (Hint: Begin by writing a balanced equation for the reaction between hydrochloric acid and calcium carbonate.)

103. The combustion of gasoline produces carbon dioxide and water. Assume gasoline to be pure octane (C_8H_{18}) and calculate the mass (in kg) of carbon dioxide that is added to the atmosphere per 1.0 kg of octane burned. (Hint: Begin by writing a balanced equation for the combustion reaction.)

104. Many home barbeques are fueled with propane gas (C_3H_8). What mass of carbon dioxide (in kg) is produced upon the complete combustion of 18.9 L of propane (approximate contents of one 5-gallon tank)? Assume that the density of the liquid propane in the tank is 0.621 g/mL. (Hint: Begin by writing a balanced equation for the combustion reaction.)

105. Aspirin can be made in the laboratory by reacting acetic anhydride ($C_4H_6O_3$) with salicylic acid ($C_7H_6O_3$) to form aspirin ($C_9H_8O_4$) and acetic acid ($C_2H_4O_2$). The balanced equation is

$$C_4H_6O_3 + C_7H_6O_3 \rightarrow C_9H_8O_4 + C_2H_4O_2$$

In a laboratory synthesis, a student begins with 3.00 mL of acetic anhydride (density = 1.08 g/mL) and 1.25 g of salicylic acid. Once the reaction is complete, the student collects 1.22 g of aspirin. Determine the limiting reactant, theoretical yield of aspirin, and percent yield for the reaction.

106. The combustion of liquid ethanol (C_2H_5OH) produces carbon dioxide and water. After 4.62 mL of ethanol (density = 0.789 g/mL) is allowed to burn in the presence of 15.55 g of oxygen gas, 3.72 mL of water (density = 1.00 g/mL) is collected. Determine the limiting reactant, theoretical yield of H_2O, and percent yield for the reaction. (Hint: Write a balanced equation for the combustion of ethanol.)

107. A loud classroom demonstration involves igniting a hydrogen-filled balloon. The hydrogen within the balloon reacts explosively with oxygen in the air to form water. If the balloon is filled with a mixture of hydrogen and oxygen, the explosion is even louder than if the balloon is filled only with hydrogen—the intensity of the explosion depends on the relative amounts of oxygen and hydrogen within the balloon. Look at the molecular views representing different amounts of hydrogen and oxygen in four different balloons. Based on the balanced

chemical equation, which balloon will make the loudest explosion?

(a)   (b)

(c)   (d)

108. A hydrochloric acid solution will neutralize a sodium hydroxide solution. Look at the molecular views showing one beaker of HCl and four beakers of NaOH. Which NaOH beaker will just neutralize the HCl beaker? Begin by writing a balanced chemical equation for the neutralization reaction.

(a)   (b)   (c)   (d)

109. Predict the products and write a balanced molecular equation for each reaction. If no reaction occurs, write "NO REACTION."
 a. $HCl(aq) + Hg_2(NO_3)_2(aq) \rightarrow$
 b. $KHSO_3(aq) + HNO_3(aq) \rightarrow$
 c. aqueous ammonium chloride and aqueous lead(II) nitrate
 d. aqueous ammonium chloride and aqueous calcium hydroxide

110. Predict the products and write a balanced molecular equation for each reaction. If no reaction occurs, write "NO REACTION."
 a. $H_2SO_4(aq) + HNO_3(aq) \rightarrow$
 b. $Cr(NO_3)_3(aq) + LiOH(aq) \rightarrow$
 c. liquid pentanol ($C_5H_{12}O$) and gaseous oxygen
 d. aqueous strontium sulfide and aqueous copper(II) sulfate

111. Hard water often contains dissolved Ca^{2+} and Mg^{2+} ions. One way to soften water is to add phosphates. The phosphate ion forms insoluble precipitates with calcium and magnesium ions, removing them from solution. A solution is 0.050 M in calcium chloride and 0.085 M in magnesium nitrate. What mass of sodium phosphate would have to be added to 1.5 L of this solution to completely eliminate the hard water ions? Assume complete reaction.

112. An acid solution is 0.100 M in HCl and 0.200 M in H_2SO_4. What volume of a 0.150 M KOH solution would completely neutralize all the acid in 500.0 mL of this solution?

113. Find the mass of barium metal (in grams) that must react with O_2 to produce enough barium oxide to prepare 1.0 L of a 0.10 M solution of OH^-.

114. A solution contains Cr^{3+} ion and Mg^{2+} ion. The addition of 1.00 L of 1.51 M NaF solution causes the complete precipitation of these ions as $CrF_3(s)$ and $MgF_2(s)$. The total mass of the precipitate is 49.6 g. Find the mass of Cr^{3+} in the original solution.

115. The nitrogen in sodium nitrate and in ammonium sulfate is available to plants as fertilizer. Which is the more economical source of nitrogen, a fertilizer containing 30.0% sodium nitrate by weight and costing $9.00 per 100 lb or one containing 20.0% ammonium sulfate by weight and costing $8.10 per 100 lb?

116. Find the volume of 0.110 M hydrochloric acid necessary to react completely with 1.52 g $Al(OH)_3$.

117. Treatment of gold metal with BrF_3 and KF produces Br_2 and $KAuF_4$, a salt of gold. Identify the oxidizing agent and the reducing agent in this reaction. Find the mass of the gold salt that forms when a 73.5 g mixture of equal masses of all three reactants is prepared.

118. We prepare a solution by mixing 0.10 L of 0.12 M sodium chloride with 0.23 L of a 0.18 M $MgCl_2$ solution. What volume of a 0.20 M silver nitrate solution do we need to precipitate all the Cl^- ion in the solution as AgCl?

119. A solution contains one or more of the following ions: Ag^+, Ca^{2+}, and Cu^{2+}. When you add sodium chloride to the solution, no precipitate forms. When you add sodium sulfate to the solution, a white precipitate forms. You filter off the precipitate and add sodium carbonate to the remaining solution, producing another precipitate. Which ions were present in the original solution? Write net ionic equations for the formation of each of the precipitates observed.

120. A solution contains one or more of the following ions: Hg_2^{2+}, Ba^{2+}, and Fe^{2+}. When potassium chloride is added to the solution, a precipitate forms. The precipitate is filtered off, and potassium sulfate is added to the remaining solution, producing no precipitate. When potassium carbonate is added to the remaining solution, a precipitate forms. Which ions were present in the original solution? Write net ionic equations for the formation of each of the precipitates observed.

121. The reaction of NH_3 and O_2 forms NO and water. The NO can be used to convert P_4 to P_4O_6, forming N_2 in the process. The P_4O_6 can be treated with water to form H_3PO_3, which forms PH_3 and H_3PO_4 when heated. Find the mass of PH_3 that forms from the reaction of 1.00 g NH_3.

122. An important reaction that takes place in a blast furnace during the production of iron is the formation of iron metal and CO_2 from Fe_2O_3 and CO. Determine the mass of Fe_2O_3 required to form 910 kg of iron. Determine the amount of CO_2 that forms in this process.

123. A liquid fuel mixture contains 30.35% hexane (C_6H_{14}), 15.85% heptane (C_7H_{16}), and the rest octane (C_8H_{18}). What maximum mass of carbon dioxide is produced by the complete combustion of 10.0 kg of this fuel mixture?

124. Titanium occurs in the magnetic mineral ilmenite ($FeTiO_3$), which is often found mixed up with sand. The ilmenite can be separated from the sand with magnets. The titanium can then be extracted from the ilmenite by the following set of reactions:

$FeTiO_3(s) + 3 Cl_2(g) + 3 C(s) \rightarrow$
$$3 CO(g) + FeCl_2(s) + TiCl_4(g)$$
$$TiCl_4(g) + 2 Mg(s) \rightarrow 2 MgCl_2(l) + Ti(s)$$

Suppose that an ilmenite–sand mixture contains 22.8% ilmenite by mass and that the first reaction is carried out with a 90.8% yield. If the second reaction is carried out with an 85.9% yield, what mass of titanium can be obtained from 1.00 kg of the ilmenite–sand mixture?

Challenge Problems

125. A mixture of C_3H_8 and C_2H_2 has a mass of 2.0 g. It is burned in excess O_2 to form a mixture of water and carbon dioxide that contains 1.5 times as many moles of CO_2 as of water. Find the mass of C_2H_2 in the original mixture.

126. A mixture of 20.6 g of P and 79.4 g Cl_2 reacts completely to form PCl_3 and PCl_5 as the only products. Find the mass of PCl_3 that forms.

127. A solution contains Ag^+ and Hg^{2+} ions. The addition of 0.100 L of 1.22 M NaI solution is just enough to precipitate all the ions as AgI and HgI_2. The total mass of the precipitate is 28.1 g. Find the mass of AgI in the precipitate.

128. The water in lakes that have been acidified by acid rain (HNO_3 and H_2SO_4) can be neutralized by a process called liming, in which limestone ($CaCO_3$) is added to the acidified water. What mass of limestone (in kg) would completely neutralize a 15.2 billion-liter lake that is 1.8×10^{-5} M in H_2SO_4 and 8.7×10^{-6} M in HNO_3?

129. Recall from Section 4.6 that sodium carbonate is often added to laundry detergents to soften hard water and make the detergent more effective. Suppose that a particular detergent mixture is designed to soften hard water that is 3.5×10^{-3} M in Ca^{2+} and 1.1×10^{-3} M in Mg^{2+} and that the average capacity of a washing machine is 19.5 gallons of water. If the detergent requires using 0.65 kg detergent per load of laundry, what percentage (by mass) of the detergent should be sodium carbonate in order to completely precipitate all of the calcium and magnesium ions in an average load of laundry water?

130. Lead poisoning is a serious condition resulting from the ingestion of lead in food, water, or other environmental sources. It affects the central nervous system, leading to a variety of symptoms such as distractibility, lethargy, and loss of motor coordination. Lead poisoning is treated with chelating agents, substances that bind to metal ions, allowing them to be eliminated in the urine. A modern chelating agent used for this purpose is succimer ($C_4H_6O_4S_2$). Suppose you are trying to determine the appropriate dose for succimer treatment of lead poisoning. What minimum mass of succimer (in mg) is needed to bind all of the lead in a patient's bloodstream? Assume that patient blood lead levels are 45 $\mu g/dL$, that total blood volume is 5.0 L, and that 1 mole of succimer binds 1 mole of lead.

131. A particular kind of emergency breathing apparatus—often placed in mines, caves, or other places where oxygen might become depleted or where the air might become poisoned—works via the following chemical reaction:

$$4 KO_2(s) + 2 CO_2(g) \rightarrow 2 K_2CO_3(s) + 3 O_2(g)$$

Notice that the reaction produces O_2, which can be breathed, and absorbs CO_2, a product of respiration. Suppose you work for a company interested in producing a self-rescue breathing apparatus (based on the given reaction) that would allow the user to survive for 10 minutes in an emergency situation. What are the important chemical considerations in designing such a unit? Estimate how much KO_2 would be required for the apparatus. (Find any necessary additional information—such as human breathing rates—from appropriate sources. Assume that normal air is 20% oxygen.)

Conceptual Problems

134. Consider the reaction:

$$4 \text{ K}(s) + O_2(g) \rightarrow 2 \text{ K}_2O(s)$$

The molar mass of K is 39.09 g/mol and that of O_2 is 32.00 g/mol. Without doing any calculations, pick the conditions under which potassium is the limiting reactant and explain your reasoning.
a. 170 g K, 31 g O_2 **b.** 16 g K, 2.5 g O_2
c. 165 kg K, 28 kg O_2 **d.** 1.5 g K, 0.38 g O_2

135. Consider the reaction:

$$2 \text{ NO}(g) + 5 \text{ H}_2(g) \rightarrow 2 \text{ NH}_3(g) + 2 \text{ H}_2O(g)$$

A reaction mixture initially contains 5 moles of NO and 10 moles of H_2. Without doing any calculations, determine which set of amounts best represents the mixture after the reactants have reacted as completely as possible. Explain your reasoning.
a. 1 mol NO, 0 mol H_2, 4 mol NH_3, 4 mol H_2O
b. 0 mol NO, 1 mol H_2, 5 mol NH_3, 5 mol H_2O
c. 3 mol NO, 5 mol H_2, 2 mol NH_3, 2 mol H_2O
d. 0 mol NO, 0 mol H_2, 4 mol NH_3, 4 mol H_2O

136. The following circle represents 1.0 liter of a solution with a solute concentration of 1 M:

Explain what you would add (the amount of solute or volume of solvent) to the solution to obtain a solution represented by each diagram:

  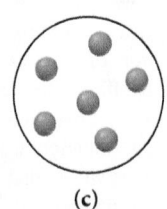

(a)   (b)   (c)

137. Consider the reaction:

$$2 \text{ N}_2H_4(g) + N_2O_4(g) \rightarrow 3 \text{ N}_2(g) + 4 \text{ H}_2O(g)$$

Consider also this representation of an initial mixture of N_2H_4 and N_2O_4:

132. Metallic aluminum reacts with MnO_2 at elevated temperatures to form manganese metal and aluminum oxide. A mixture of the two reactants is 67.2% mole percent Al. Find the theoretical yield (in grams) of manganese from the reaction of 250 g of this mixture.

133. Hydrolysis of the compound B_5H_9 forms boric acid, H_3BO_3. Fusion of boric acid with sodium oxide forms a borate salt, $Na_2B_4O_7$. Without writing complete equations, find the mass (in grams) of B_5H_9 required to form 151 g of the borate salt by this reaction sequence.

Which diagram best represents the reaction mixture after the reactants have reacted as completely as possible?

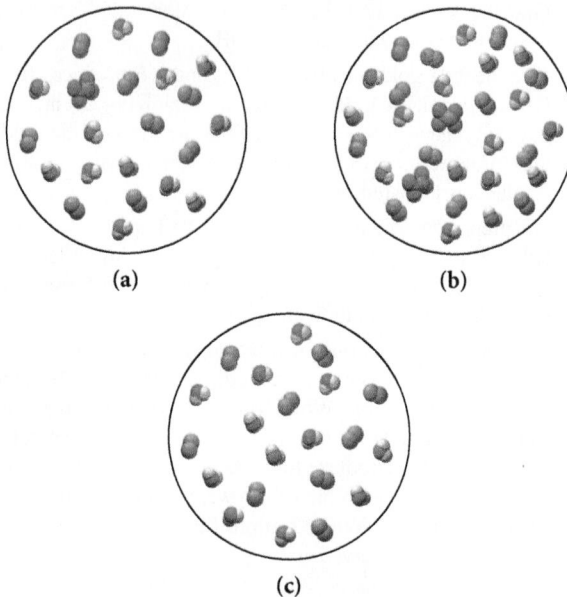

(a)   (b)

(c)

138. Consider the generic ionic compounds with the formulas A_2X and BY_2 and the following solubility rules:

A_2X soluble; BY_2 soluble; AY insoluble; BX soluble.

Let A^+ ions be represented by circles, B^{2+} ions be represented by squares, X^{2-} ions be represented by triangles, and Y^- ions be represented by diamonds. Solutions of the two compounds (A_2X and BY_2) can be represented as follows:

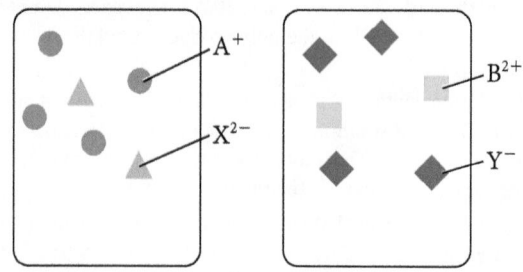

Draw a molecular level representation showing the result of mixing the two solutions given and write an equation to represent the reaction.

Answers to Conceptual Connections

Stoichiometry

4.1 (c) Since each O_2 molecule reacts with 4 Na atoms, 12 Na atoms are required to react with 3 O_2 molecules.

Stoichiometry II

4.2

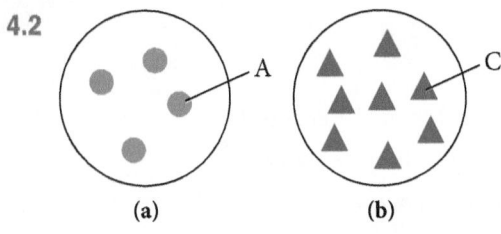

(a)   (b)

Limiting Reactant and Theoretical Yield

4.3 (c) Nitrogen is the limiting reactant, and there is enough nitrogen to make four NH_3 molecules. Hydrogen is in excess, and two hydrogen molecules remain after the reactants have reacted as completely as possible.

Reactant in Excess

4.4 The limiting reactant is the 1 mol H_2O, which is completely consumed. The 1 mol of H_2O requires 3 mol of NO_2 to completely react; therefore, 2 mol NO_2 remain after the reaction is complete.

Solutions

4.5 (b) The mass of a solution is equal to the mass of the solute plus the mass of the solvent. Although the solute seems to disappear, it really does not, and its mass becomes part of the mass of the solution, in accordance with the law of mass conservation.

Solution Dilution

4.6 (c) Since the volume has doubled, the concentration is halved, so the same volume should contain half as many solute molecules.

Precipitation Reactions

4.7

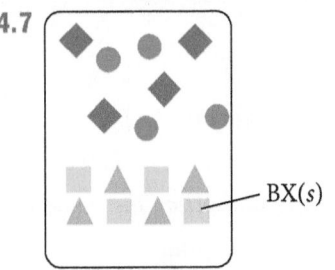

$$AX(aq) \ + \ BY(aq) \rightarrow BX(s) \ + \ AY(aq)$$

Oxidation Numbers in Polyatomic Ions

4.8 (a) The charge of a polyatomic ion is the charge associated with the ion *as a whole*. The oxidation states of the individual atoms must sum to the charge of the ion, but they are assigned to *the individual atoms themselves*. Answer (**b**) is incorrect because oxidation state and charge *are not identical*, even though the charge of a *monoatomic* ion is equal to its oxidation state. Answer (**c**) is incorrect because charge *is* a physical property of ions. Conversely, the oxidation states of atoms are *not* real physical properties, but an imposed electron bookkeeping scheme.

Oxidation and Reduction

4.9 (d) Since oxidation and reduction must occur together, an increase in the oxidation state of a reactant is always accompanied by a decrease in the oxidation state of a reactant.

5

Gases

So many of the properties of matter, especially when in the gaseous form, can be deduced from the hypothesis that their minute parts are in rapid motion, the velocity increasing with the temperature, that the precise nature of this motion becomes a subject of rational curiosity.

—James Clerk Maxwell (1831–1879)

W E CAN SURVIVE FOR WEEKS without food, days without water, but only minutes without air. Fortunately, we live at the bottom of a vast ocean of air, held to Earth by gravity. We inhale a lungful of this air every few seconds, keep some of the molecules for our own uses, add some molecules that our bodies no longer need, and exhale the mixture back into the surrounding air. The air around us is matter in the gaseous state. What are the fundamental properties of these gases? What laws describe their behavior? What theory explains these properties and laws? Recall that the scientific approach (see Section 1.2) proceeds in this way—from observations to laws to theories—exactly the way we will proceed in this chapter. The gaseous state is the simplest and best-understood state of matter. In this chapter, we examine that state.

5.1 Breathing: Putting Pressure to Work

Every day, without even thinking about it, you move approximately 8500 liters of air into and out of your lungs. The total mass of this air is about 11 kg (or 25 pounds). How do you do it? The simple answer is *pressure*. You rely on your body's ability to create pressure differences in order to breathe. **Pressure** is the force exerted per unit area by gas molecules as they strike the surfaces around them (Figure 5.1 ▶). Just as a ball exerts a force when it bounces against a wall, so a gaseous atom or molecule exerts a force when it collides with a surface. The result of many of these molecular collisions is pressure— a constant force on the surfaces exposed to any gas. The total pressure exerted by a gas depends on several factors, including the concentration of gas molecules in the sample; the higher the concentration, the greater the pressure.

When you inhale, the muscles that surround your chest cavity expand the volume of your lungs. The expanded volume results in a lower concentration of gas molecules (the number of molecules does not change, but since the volume increases, the *concentration*

The buildup of pressure, which results from the constant collisions of gas molecules with the surfaces around them, expels the cork in a bottle of champagne.

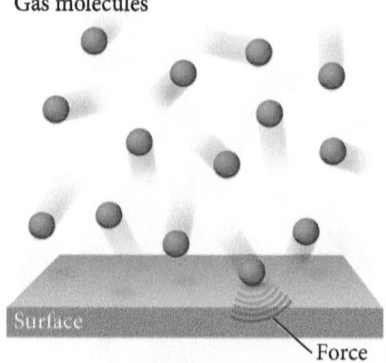

Gas molecules

Surface

Force

Collisions with surfaces create pressure.

▲ FIGURE 5.1 **Gas Pressure** Pressure is the force per unit area exerted by gas molecules colliding with the surfaces around them.

goes down). This in turn results in fewer molecular collisions, which results in lower pressure. The external pressure (the pressure outside of your lungs) remains relatively constant, and when you inhale it is higher than the pressure within your lungs. As a result, gaseous molecules flow into your lungs, from the region of higher pressure to the region of lower pressure. When you exhale, the process is reversed. Your chest cavity muscles relax, which *decreases* your lung volume, increasing the pressure within your lungs and forcing air back out. In this way, within the course of your lifetime, you will take about half a billion breaths and move about 250 million liters of air through your lungs. With each breath, you create pressure differences that allow you to obtain the oxygen you need to live.

5.2 Pressure: The Result of Molecular Collisions

Air can hold up a jumbo jet or knock down a building. How? As we just discussed, air contains gaseous atoms and molecules in constant motion. The particles collide with each other and with the surfaces around them. Each collision exerts only a small force, but when the forces of the many particles are summed, they quickly add up. The result of the constant collisions between the atoms or molecules in a gas and the surfaces around them is *pressure*. Because of pressure, we can drink from straws, inflate basketballs, and breathe. Variation in pressure in Earth's atmosphere creates wind, and changes in pressure help us to predict weather. Pressure is all around us and inside of us. The pressure that a gas sample exerts is the *force* that results from the collisions of gas particles divided by the *area* of the surface with which they collide:

$$\text{Pressure} = \frac{\text{force}}{\text{area}} = \frac{F}{A} \qquad [5.1]$$

▶ Pressure variations in Earth's atmosphere create wind and weather. The H's in this map indicate regions of high pressure, usually associated with clear weather. The L's indicate regions of low pressure, usually associated with unstable weather. The map shows a typhoon off the northeast coast of Japan. The isobars, or lines of constant pressure, are labeled in hectopascals (100 Pa).

The pressure exerted by a gas sample, therefore, depends on the number of gas particles in a given volume—the fewer the gas particles, the lower the force per unit area and the lower the pressure (Figure 5.2 ◀). Since the number of gas particles in a given volume generally decreases with increasing altitude, *pressure decreases with increasing altitude.* Above 30,000 ft, for example, where most commercial airplanes fly, the pressure is so low that a person could pass out due to a lack of oxygen. For this reason, most airplane cabins are artificially pressurized.

You may sometimes feel the effect of a drop in pressure as a brief pain in your ears. This pain arises within the air-containing cavities in your ear (Figure 5.3 ▶). When you ascend a mountain, the external pressure (the pressure that surrounds you) drops, while the pressure within your ear cavities (the internal pressure) remains the same. This creates an imbalance—the greater internal pressure forces your eardrum to bulge outward, causing pain. With time, and with the help of a yawn or two, the excess air within your ear's cavities escapes, equalizing the internal and external pressure and relieving the pain.

Pressure and Density

Lower pressure   Higher pressure

▲ FIGURE 5.2 **Pressure and Particle Density** A low density of gas particles results in low pressure. A high density of gas particles results in high pressure.

Pressure Imbalance

Eardrum

Reduced external pressure

Normal pressure

Eardrum bulges outward, causing pain.

◄ **FIGURE 5.3 Pressure Imbalance** The discomfort you may feel in your ears upon ascending a mountain is caused by a pressure imbalance between the cavities in your ears and the outside air.

Pressure Units

Pressure is measured in several different units. A common unit of pressure, the **millimeter of mercury (mmHg)**, originates from how pressure is measured with a **barometer** (Figure 5.4 ►). A barometer is an evacuated glass tube, the tip of which is submerged in a pool of mercury. The liquid mercury is forced upward into the evacuated tube by atmospheric pressure on the liquid's surface. Because mercury is so dense (13.5 times more dense than water), atmospheric pressure can support a column of Hg that is only about 0.760 m or 760 mm (about 30 in) tall. (By contrast, atmospheric pressure can support a column of water that is about 10.3 m tall.) This makes a column of mercury a convenient way to measure pressure.

In a barometer, when the atmospheric pressure rises, the height of the mercury column rises as well. Similarly, when atmospheric pressure falls, the height of the column falls. The unit *millimeter of mercury* is often called a **torr**, after the Italian physicist Evangelista Torricelli (1608–1647) who invented the barometer.

$$1 \text{ mmHg} = 1 \text{ torr}$$

A second unit of pressure is the **atmosphere (atm)**, the average pressure at sea level. Since one atmosphere of pressure pushes a column of mercury to a height of 760 mm, 1 atm and 760 mmHg are equal:

$$1 \text{ atm} = 760 \text{ mmHg}$$

A fully inflated mountain bike tire has a pressure of about 6 atm, and the pressure at the top of Mt. Everest is about 0.31 atm.

The SI unit of pressure is the **pascal (Pa)**, defined as 1 newton (N) per square meter:

$$1 \text{ Pa} = 1 \text{ N/m}^2$$

The pascal is a much smaller unit of pressure than the atmosphere:

$$1 \text{ atm} = 101,325 \text{ Pa}$$

Other common units of pressure include inches of mercury (in Hg) and pounds per square inch (psi).

$$1 \text{ atm} = 29.92 \text{ in Hg} \qquad 1 \text{ atm} = 14.7 \text{ psi}$$

Table 5.1 summarizes these units.

The Mercury Barometer

Vacuum

Glass tube

Atmospheric pressure

760 mm (29.92 in)

Mercury

▲ **FIGURE 5.4 The Mercury Barometer** Average atmospheric pressure at sea level can support a column of mercury 760 mm in height.

TABLE 5.1 Common Units of Pressure

Unit	Abbreviation	Average Air Pressure at Sea Level
Pascal (1 N/m²)	Pa	101,325 Pa
Pounds per square inch	psi	14.7 psi
Torr (1 mmHg)	torr	760 torr (exact)
Inches of mercury	in Hg	29.92 in Hg
Atmosphere	atm	1 atm

EXAMPLE 5.1 Converting between Pressure Units

A high-performance road bicycle tire is inflated to a total pressure of 132 psi. What is this pressure in mmHg?

SORT The problem gives a pressure in psi and asks you to convert the units to mmHg.	**GIVEN:** 132 psi **FIND:** mmHg
STRATEGIZE Since Table 5.1 does not have a direct conversion factor between psi and mmHg but does provide relationships between both of these units and atmospheres, convert to atm as an intermediate step.	**CONCEPTUAL PLAN** **RELATIONSHIPS USED** $1 \text{ atm} = 14.7 \text{ psi}$ $760 \text{ mmHg} = 1 \text{ atm}$ (both from Table 5.1)
SOLVE Follow the conceptual plan to solve the problem. Begin with 132 psi and use the conversion factors to arrive at the pressure in mmHg.	**SOLUTION** $132 \text{ psi} \times \dfrac{1 \text{ atm}}{14.7 \text{ psi}} \times \dfrac{760 \text{ mmHg}}{1 \text{ atm}} = 6.82 \times 10^3 \text{ mmHg}$

CHECK The units of the answer are correct. The magnitude of the answer $(6.82 \times 10^3 \text{ mmHg})$ is greater than the given pressure in psi. This is reasonable since mmHg is a much smaller unit than psi.

FOR PRACTICE 5.1

Your local weather report announces that the barometric pressure is 30.44 in Hg. Convert this pressure to psi.

FOR MORE PRACTICE 5.1

Convert a pressure of 23.8 in Hg to kPa.

The Manometer

▲ **FIGURE 5.5 The Manometer**
A manometer measures the pressure exerted by a sample of gas.

The Manometer: A Way to Measure Pressure in the Laboratory

We can measure the pressure of a gas sample in the laboratory with a **manometer**. A manometer is a U-shaped tube containing a dense liquid, usually mercury, as shown in Figure 5.5 ◄. In this manometer, one end of the tube is open to atmospheric pressure and the other is attached to a flask containing the gas sample. If the pressure of the gas sample is exactly equal to atmospheric pressure, then the mercury levels on both sides of the tube are the same. If the pressure of the sample is *greater than* atmospheric pressure, the mercury level on the left side of the tube is *higher than* the level on the right. If the pressure of the sample is *less than* atmospheric pressure, the mercury level on the left side is *lower than* the level on the right. This type of manometer always measures the pressure of the gas sample relative to atmospheric pressure. The difference in height between the two levels is equal to the difference between the sample's pressure and atmospheric pressure. To accurately calculate the absolute pressure of the sample, we also need a barometer to measure atmospheric pressure (which can vary from day to day).

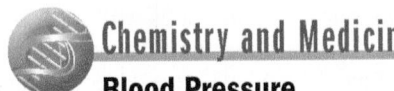
Chemistry and Medicine
Blood Pressure

Blood pressure is the force within arteries that drives the circulation of blood throughout the body. Blood pressure in the body is analogous to water pressure in a plumbing system. Just as water pressure pushes water through the pipes to faucets and fixtures throughout a house, blood pressure pushes blood to muscles and other tissues throughout the body. However, unlike the water pressure in a plumbing system—which is typically nearly constant—our blood pressure varies with each heartbeat. When the heart muscle contracts, blood pressure increases; between contractions it decreases. Systolic blood pressure is the peak pressure during a contraction, and diastolic blood pressure is the lowest pressure between contractions. Just as excessively high water pressure in a plumbing system can damage pipes, so too high blood pressure in a circulatory system can damage the heart and arteries, resulting in increased risk of stroke and heart attack.

Medical professionals usually measure blood pressure with an instrument called a sphygmomanometer—an inflatable cuff equipped with a pressure gauge—and a stethoscope. The cuff is wrapped around the patient's arm and inflated with air. As air is pumped into the cuff, the pressure in the cuff increases. The cuff tightens around the arm and compresses the artery, momentarily stopping blood flow. The person measuring the blood pressure listens to the artery through the stethoscope while slowly releasing the air pressure in the cuff. When the air pressure in the cuff equals the systolic blood pressure (the peak pressure), a pulse is heard through the stethoscope. The pulse is the sound of blood getting through the compressed artery during a contraction of the heart. The pressure reading at that exact moment is the systolic blood pressure. As the pressure in the cuff continues to decrease, the blood can flow through the compressed artery even between contractions, so the pulsing sound stops. The pressure reading when the pulsing sound stops is the diastolic blood pressure (the lowest pressure).

A blood pressure measurement is usually reported as two pressures, in mmHg, separated by a slash. For example, a blood pressure measurement of 122/84 indicates that the systolic blood pressure is 122 mmHg and the diastolic blood pressure is 84 mmHg. Although the value of blood pressure can vary throughout the day, a healthy (or normal) value is usually considered to be below 120 mmHg for systolic and below 80 mmHg for diastolic (Table 5.2). High blood pressure, also called hypertension, entails the health risks mentioned previously.

Risk factors for hypertension include obesity, high salt (sodium) intake, high alcohol intake, lack of exercise, stress, a family history of high blood pressure, and age (blood pressure tends to increase as we get older). Mild hypertension can be managed with diet and exercise. Moderate to severe cases require doctor-prescribed medication.

▲ A doctor or a nurse measures blood pressure with an inflatable cuff that compresses the main artery in the arm. A stethoscope is used to listen for blood flowing through the artery with each heartbeat.

TABLE 5.2 Blood Pressure Ranges

Blood Pressure	Systolic (mmHg)	Diastolic (mmHg)
Hypotension	<100	<60
Normal	100–119	60–79
Prehypertension	120–139	80–89
Hypertension Stage 1	140–159	90–99
Hypertension Stage 2	>160	>100

5.3 The Simple Gas Laws: Boyle's Law, Charles's Law, and Avogadro's Law

We have learned about pressure and its characteristics. We now broaden our discussion to include the four basic properties of a gas sample: pressure (P), volume (V), temperature (T), and amount in moles (n). These properties are interrelated—when one changes, it affects the others. The *simple gas laws* describe the relationships between pairs of these properties. For example, one simple gas law describes how *volume* varies with *pressure* at constant temperature and amount of gas; another law describes how volume varies with *temperature* at constant pressure and amount of gas. These laws were deduced from observations in which two of the four basic properties were held constant in order to elucidate the relationship between the other two.

Boyle's Law: Volume and Pressure

In the early 1660s, the pioneering English scientist Robert Boyle (1627–1691) and his assistant Robert Hooke (1635–1703) used a J-tube (Figure 5.6 ▼) to measure the volume of a sample of gas at different pressures. They trapped a sample of air in the J-tube and added mercury to increase the pressure on the gas. Boyle and Hook observed an *inverse relationship* between volume and pressure—an increase in one causes a decrease in the other—as shown in Figure 5.7 ▼. This relationship is now known as **Boyle's law**.

> Boyle's law assumes constant temperature and constant amount of gas.

$$\text{Boyle's law:} \quad V \propto \frac{1}{P} \quad (\text{constant } T \text{ and } n)$$

Boyle's law follows from the idea that pressure results from the collisions of the gas particles with the walls of their container. If the volume of a gas sample is decreased, the same number of gas particles is crowded into a smaller volume, resulting in more collisions with the walls and therefore an increase in the pressure (Figure 5.8 ▶).

Scuba divers learn about Boyle's law during certification because it explains why a diver should not ascend toward the surface without continuous breathing. For every 10 m of depth that a diver descends in water, she experiences an additional 1 atm of pressure due to the weight of the water above her (Figure 5.9 ▶). The pressure regulator used in scuba diving delivers air into the diver's lungs at a pressure that matches the external pressure; otherwise the diver could not inhale the air (see *Chemistry in Your Day: Extra-Long Snorkels* on page 203). For example, when a diver is 20 m below the surface, the regulator delivers air at a pressure of 3 atm to match the 3 atm of pressure around the diver (1 atm due to normal atmospheric pressure and 2 additional atmospheres due to the weight of the water at 20 m). Suppose that a diver inhaled a lungful of air at a pressure of 3 atm and swam quickly to the surface (where the pressure is 1 atm) while holding her breath. What would happen to the volume of air in her lungs? Since the pressure decreases by a factor of 3, the volume of the air in her lungs would increase by a factor of 3—a dangerous situation. Of course, the volume increase in the diver's lungs would be

The J-Tube

▲ FIGURE 5.6 **The J-Tube**   In a J-tube, a column of mercury traps a sample of gas. The pressure on the gas can be increased by increasing the height (*h*) of mercury in the column.

▲ FIGURE 5.7 **Volume versus Pressure**   A plot of the volume of a gas sample—as measured in a J-tube—versus pressure. The plot shows that volume and pressure are inversely related.

Volume versus Pressure: A Molecular View

◀ **FIGURE 5.8 Molecular Interpretation of Boyle's Law** As the volume of a gas sample is decreased, gas molecules collide with surrounding surfaces more frequently, resulting in greater pressure.

$P = 1$ atm

$V = 1$ L

$P = 2$ atm

$V = 0.5$ L

so great that she would not be able to hold her breath all the way to the surface—the air would force itself out of her mouth but probably not before the expanded air severely damaged her lungs, possibly killing her. Consequently, the most important rule in diving is *never hold your breath*. To avoid such catastrophic results, divers must ascend slowly and breathe continuously, allowing the regulator to bring the air pressure in their lungs back to 1 atm by the time they reach the surface.

We can use Boyle's law to calculate the volume of a gas following a pressure change or the pressure of a gas following a volume change *as long as the temperature and the amount of gas remain constant*. For these types of calculations, we write Boyle's law in a slightly different way.

$$\text{Since } V \propto \frac{1}{P}, \quad \text{then} \quad V = (\text{constant}) \times \frac{1}{P} \quad \text{or} \quad V = \frac{(\text{constant})}{P}$$

If two quantities are proportional, then one is equal to the other multiplied by a constant.

If we multiply both sides by P, we find that the product of P and V is equal to a constant:

$$PV = \text{constant}$$

Depth $= 0$ m
$P = 1$ atm

Depth $= 20$ m
$P = 3$ atm

◀ **FIGURE 5.9 Increase in Pressure with Depth** For every 10 m of depth, a diver experiences approximately one additional atmosphere of pressure due to the weight of the surrounding water. At 20 m, for example, the diver experiences approximately 3 atm of pressure (1 atm of normal atmospheric pressure plus an additional 2 atm due to the weight of the water).

This relationship indicates that if the pressure increases, the volume decreases, but the product $P \times V$ always equals the same constant. For two different sets of conditions, we can say that:

$$P_1V_1 = \text{constant} = P_2V_2$$

or

$$P_1V_1 = P_2V_2 \qquad [5.2]$$

where P_1 and V_1 are the initial pressure and volume of the gas and P_2 and V_2 are the final volume and pressure.

EXAMPLE 5.2 Boyle's Law

As discussed in the opening section of this chapter, you inhale by increasing your lung volume. A woman has an initial lung volume of 2.75 L, which is filled with air at an atmospheric pressure of 1.02 atm. If she increases her lung volume to 3.25 L without inhaling any additional air, what is the pressure in her lungs?

| To solve the problem, first solve Boyle's law (Equation 5.2) for P_2 and then substitute the given quantities to calculate P_2. | **SOLUTION** $P_1V_1 = P_2V_2$ $$P_2 = \frac{V_1}{V_2}P_1$$ $$= \frac{2.75\ \cancel{L}}{3.25\ \cancel{L}}\,1.02\ \text{atm}$$ $$= 0.863\ \text{atm}$$ |

FOR PRACTICE 5.2

A snorkeler takes a syringe filled with 16 mL of air from the surface, where the pressure is 1.0 atm, to an unknown depth. The volume of the air in the syringe at this depth is 7.5 mL. What is the pressure at this depth? If the pressure increases by 1 atm for every additional 10 m of depth, how deep is the snorkeler?

Charles's Law: Volume and Temperature

Suppose we keep the pressure of a gas sample constant and measure its volume at a number of different temperatures. Figure 5.10 ▼ shows the results of several such measurements. From the plot we can see a relationship between volume and temperature: the volume

▶ FIGURE 5.10 **Volume versus Temperature** The volume of a fixed amount of gas at a constant pressure increases linearly with increasing temperature in kelvins. (The extrapolated lines cannot be measured experimentally because all gases condense into liquids before −273.15 °C is reached.)

Chemistry in Your Day

Extra-Long Snorkels

Several episodes of *The Flintstones* cartoon featured Fred Flintstone and Barney Rubble snorkeling. Their snorkels, however, were not the modern kind, but long reeds that stretched from the surface of the water down to many meters of depth. Fred and Barney swam around in deep water while breathing air provided to them by these extra-long snorkels. Would this work? Why do people bother with scuba diving equipment if they could instead simply use 10 m snorkels as Fred and Barney did?

As we saw in Section 5.1, when we breathe, we expand the volume of our chest cavity, reducing the pressure in our lungs to less than 1 atm (Boyle's law). Because of this pressure, differential air from outside our lungs flows into them. Extra-long snorkels do not work because the pressure exerted by water at depth is too great. A diver at 10 m experiences an external pressure of 2 atm. This is more than the muscles of the chest cavity can overcome. Instead, the chest cavity and lungs are compressed, resulting in an air pressure within them of more than 1 atm. If the diver had a snorkel that went to the surface—where the air pressure is 1 atm—air would flow out of his lungs (*from* greater pressure *to* less pressure), not into them. It would be impossible for the diver to breathe.

▲ In the popular cartoon *The Flintstones*, cavemen used long reeds to breathe surface air while swimming at depth. This would not work because the increased pressure at depth would force air out of their lungs; the pressure would not allow them to inhale.

▲ If two balloons were joined by a long tube and one end was submerged in water, what would happen to the volumes of the two balloons?

Question

A diver takes a balloon with a volume of 2.5 L from the surface, where the pressure is 1.0 atm, to a depth of 20 m, where the pressure is 3.0 atm. What happens to the volume of the balloon? What if the end of the submerged balloon is on a long pipe that goes to the surface and is attached to another balloon? Which way would air flow as the diver descended?

---

of a gas increases with increasing temperature. Looking at the plot more closely reveals more—volume and temperature are *linearly related*. If two variables are linearly related, then plotting one against the other produces a straight line.

Another interesting feature emerges if we extend or *extrapolate* the line in the plot in Figure 5.10 backward from the lowest measured temperature. The dotted extrapolated line shows that the gas should have a zero volume at −273.15 °C. Recall from Chapter 1 that −273.15 °C corresponds to 0 K (zero on the Kelvin scale), the coldest possible temperature. The extrapolated line indicates that below −273.15 °C, the gas would have a negative volume, which is physically impossible. For this reason, we refer to 0 K as *absolute zero*—colder temperatures do not exist.

The first person to carefully quantify the relationship between the volume of a gas and its temperature was J. A. C. Charles (1746–1823), a French mathematician and physicist. Charles was interested in gases and was among the first people to ascend in a hydrogen-filled balloon. The direct proportionality between volume and temperature is named **Charles's law** after him.

$$\text{Charles's law:} \quad V \propto T \quad (\text{constant } P \text{ and } n)$$

Charles's law assumes constant pressure and constant amount of gas.

When the temperature of a gas sample increases, the gas particles move faster; collisions with the walls are more frequent, and the force exerted with each collision is greater. The only way for the pressure (the force per unit area) to remain constant is for

Volume versus Temperature: A Molecular View

Low kinetic energy

High kinetic energy

Ice water

Boiling water

▲ **FIGURE 5.11 Molecular Interpretation of Charles's Law** If we move a balloon from an ice water bath to a boiling water bath, its volume expands as the gas particles within the balloon move faster (due to the increased temperature) and collectively occupy more space.

▲ A hot-air balloon floats because the hot air is less dense than the surrounding cold air.

▲ If we place a balloon into liquid nitrogen (77 K), it shrivels up as the air within it cools and occupies less volume at the same external pressure.

the gas to occupy a larger volume so that collisions become less frequent and occur over a larger area (Figure 5.11 ▲).

Charles's law explains why the second floor of a house is usually warmer than the ground floor. According to Charles's law, when air is heated, its volume increases, resulting in a lower density. The warm, less dense air tends to rise in a room filled with colder, denser air. Similarly, Charles's law explains why a hot-air balloon can take flight. The gas that fills a hot-air balloon is warmed with a burner, increasing its volume, lowering its density, and causing it to float in the colder, denser surrounding air.

You can experience Charles's law directly by holding a partially inflated balloon over a warm toaster. As the air in the balloon warms, you can feel the balloon expanding. Alternatively, you can a put an inflated balloon into liquid nitrogen and watch it become smaller as it cools.

We can use Charles's law to calculate the volume of a gas following a temperature change or the temperature of a gas following a volume change *as long as the pressure and the amount of gas are constant*. For these calculations, we rearrange Charles's law as follows:

$$\text{Since } V \propto T, \quad \text{then } V = \text{constant} \times T$$

If we divide both sides by T, we find that V/T is equal to a constant:

$$V/T = \text{constant}$$

If the temperature increases, the volume increases in direct proportion so that the quotient, V/T, is always equal to the same constant. So, for two different measurements, we can say that:

$$V_1/T_1 = \text{constant} = V_2/T_2$$

or

$$\frac{V_1}{T_1} = \frac{V_2}{T_2} \qquad\qquad [5.3]$$

where V_1 and T_1 are the initial volume and temperature of the gas and V_2 and T_2 are the final volume and temperature. *The temperatures must always be expressed in kelvins (K)*, because, as shown in Figure 5.10, the volume of a gas is directly proportional to its absolute temperature, not its temperature in °C. For example, doubling the temperature of a gas sample from 1 °C to 2 °C does not double its volume, but doubling the temperature from 200 K to 400 K does.

EXAMPLE 5.3 Charles's Law

A sample of gas has a volume of 2.80 L at an unknown temperature. When the sample is submerged in ice water at $T = 0.00\,°C$, its volume decreases to 2.57 L. What was its initial temperature (in K and in °C)?

	SOLUTION
To solve the problem, first solve Charles's law for T_1.	$$\frac{V_1}{T_1} = \frac{V_2}{T_2}$$ $$T_1 = \frac{V_1}{V_2}T_2$$
Before you substitute the numerical values to calculate T_1, convert the temperature to kelvins (K). *Remember, gas law problems must always be worked with Kelvin temperatures.*	$T_2\,(K) = 0.00 + 273.15 = 273.15\,K$
Substitute T_2 and the other given quantities to calculate T_1.	$$T_1 = \frac{V_1}{V_2}T_2$$ $$= \frac{2.80\ \cancel{L}}{2.57\ \cancel{L}}\,273.15\ K$$ $$= 297.6\ K$$
Calculate T_1 in °C by subtracting 273 from the value in kelvins.	$T_1\,(°C) = 297.6 - 273.15 = 24\,°C$

FOR PRACTICE 5.3

A gas in a cylinder with a moveable piston has an initial volume of 88.2 mL. If we heat the gas from 35 °C to 155 °C, what is its final volume (in mL)?

Conceptual Connection 5.1 Boyle's Law and Charles's Law

The pressure exerted on a sample of a fixed amount of gas is doubled at constant temperature, and then the temperature of the gas in kelvins is doubled at constant pressure. What is the final volume of the gas?

(a) The final volume is twice the initial volume.
(b) The final volume of the gas is four times the initial volume.
(c) The final volume of the gas is one-half the initial volume.
(d) The final volume of the gas is one-fourth the initial volume.
(e) The final volume of the gas is the same as the initial volume.

Avogadro's Law: Volume and Amount (in Moles)

So far, we have discussed the relationships between volume and pressure, and volume and temperature, but we have considered only a constant amount of a gas. What happens when the amount of gas changes? The volume of a gas sample (at constant temperature and pressure) as a function of the amount of gas (in moles) in the sample is shown in Figure 5.12 ▶. We can see that the relationship between volume and amount is linear. As we might expect, extrapolation to zero moles shows zero volume. This relationship, first stated formally by Amadeo Avogadro, is **Avogadro's law**.

$$\text{Avogadro's law:}\quad V \propto n \quad (\text{constant } T \text{ and } P)$$

When the amount of gas in a sample increases at constant temperature and pressure, its volume increases in direct proportion because the greater number of gas particles fill more space.

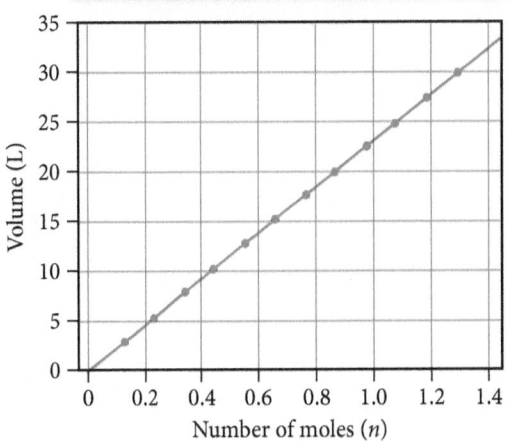

▲ **FIGURE 5.12 Volume versus Number of Moles** The volume of a gas sample increases linearly with the number of moles of gas in the sample.

You experience Avogadro's law when you inflate a balloon. With each exhaled breath, you add more gas particles to the inside of the balloon, increasing its volume. We can use Avogadro's law to calculate the volume of a gas following a change in the amount of the gas *as long as the pressure and temperature of the gas are constant*. For these types of calculations, we express Avogadro's law as:

> Avogadro's law assumes constant temperature and constant pressure and is independent of the nature of the gas.

$$\frac{V_1}{n_1} = \frac{V_2}{n_2}$$ [5.4]

where V_1 and n_1 are the initial volume and number of moles of the gas and V_2 and n_2 are the final volume and number of moles. In calculations, we use Avogadro's law in a manner similar to the other gas laws, as demonstrated in Example 5.4.

EXAMPLE 5.4 Avogadro's Law

A male athlete in a kinesiology research study has a lung volume of 6.15 L during a deep inhalation. At this volume, his lungs contain 0.254 moles of air. During exhalation, his lung volume decreases to 2.55 L. How many moles of gas did the athlete exhale? Assume constant temperature and pressure.

To solve the problem, first solve Avogadro's law for the number of moles of gas left in the athlete's lungs after exhalation, n_2. Then substitute the given quantities to calculate n_2.	**SOLUTION** $$\frac{V_1}{n_1} = \frac{V_2}{n_2}$$ $$n_2 = \frac{V_2}{V_1} n_1$$
Since the lungs initially contained 0.254 mol of air, calculate the amount of air exhaled by subtracting the result from 0.254 mol. (In Chapter 1, we introduced the practice of underlining the least (rightmost) significant digit of intermediate answers but not rounding the final answer until the very end of the calculation. We continue that practice throughout the book. However, in order to avoid unnecessary notation, we will not carry additional digits in cases, such as this one, where doing so does not affect the final answer.)	$$= \frac{2.55 \, \cancel{L}}{6.15 \, \cancel{L}} 0.254 \, mol$$ $$= 0.105 \, mol$$ $$\text{moles exhaled} = 0.254 \, mol - 0.105 \, mol$$ $$= 0.149 \, mol$$

FOR PRACTICE 5.4

A chemical reaction occurring in a cylinder equipped with a moveable piston produces 0.621 mol of a gaseous product. If the cylinder contained 0.120 mol of gas before the reaction and had an initial volume of 2.18 L, what was its volume after the reaction? (Assume constant pressure and temperature and that the initial amount of gas completely reacts.)

5.4 The Ideal Gas Law

The relationships that we have discussed so far can be combined into a single law that encompasses all of them. So far, we have shown that:

$$V \propto \frac{1}{P} \qquad \text{(Boyle's law)}$$

$$V \propto T \qquad \text{(Charles's law)}$$

$$V \propto n \qquad \text{(Avogadro's law)}$$

Combining these three expressions, we find that V is proportional to nT/P:

$$V \propto \frac{nT}{P}$$

The volume of a gas is directly proportional to the number of moles of gas and to the temperature of the gas, but is inversely proportional to the pressure of the gas. We can replace the proportionality sign with an equals sign by incorporating R, a proportionality constant called the *ideal gas constant*:

$$V = \frac{RnT}{P}$$

Rearranging, we get the equation:

$$PV = nRT \qquad [5.5]$$

This equation is the **ideal gas law**, and a hypothetical gas that exactly follows this law is an **ideal gas**. The value of R, the **ideal gas constant**, is the same for all gases and has the value:

$$R = 0.08206 \frac{\text{L} \cdot \text{atm}}{\text{mol} \cdot \text{K}}$$

L = liters
atm = atmospheres
mol = moles
K = kelvins

The ideal gas law contains within it the simple gas laws that we have discussed. For example, recall that Boyle's law states that $V \propto 1/P$ when the amount of gas (n) and the temperature of the gas (T) are kept constant. We can rearrange the ideal gas law as follows:

$$PV = nRT$$

First, divide both sides by P:

$$V = \frac{nRT}{P}$$

Then put the variables that are constant, along with R, in parentheses:

$$V = (nRT)\frac{1}{P}$$

Since n and T are constant in this case, and since R is always a constant, we can write:

$$V \propto (\text{constant}) \times \frac{1}{P}$$

which means that $V \propto 1/P$.

The ideal gas law also shows how other pairs of variables are related. For example, from Charles's law we know that $V \propto T$ at constant pressure and constant number of moles. But what if we heat a sample of gas at constant *volume* and constant number of moles? This question applies to the warning labels on aerosol cans such as hair spray or deodorants. These labels warn against excessive heating or incineration of the can, even after the contents are used up. Why? An "empty" aerosol can is not really empty but contains a fixed amount of gas trapped in a fixed volume. What would happen if we were to heat the can? We can rearrange the ideal gas law to clearly see the relationship between pressure and temperature at constant volume and constant number of moles:

$$PV = nRT$$

$$P = \frac{nRT}{V} = \left(\frac{nRT}{V}\right)T$$

Since n and V are constant and since R is always a constant:

$$P = (\text{constant}) \times T$$

This relationship between pressure and temperature is also known as *Gay-Lussac's law*. As the temperature of a fixed amount of gas in a fixed volume increases, the pressure increases. In an aerosol can, this pressure increase can blow the can apart, which is why aerosol cans should not be heated or incinerated. They might explode.

We can use the ideal gas law to determine the value of any one of the four variables (P, V, n, or T) given the other three. To do so, we must express each of the quantities in the ideal gas law in the units within R:

- pressure (P) in atm
- volume (V) in L
- moles (n) in mol
- temperature (T) in K

Ideal Gas Law

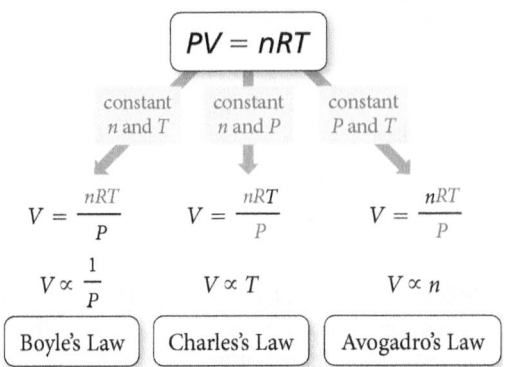

$$PV = nRT$$

constant n and T	constant n and P	constant P and T
$V = \dfrac{nRT}{P}$	$V = \dfrac{nRT}{P}$	$V = \dfrac{nRT}{P}$
$V \propto \dfrac{1}{P}$	$V \propto T$	$V \propto n$
Boyle's Law	Charles's Law	Avogadro's Law

▲ The ideal gas law contains the simple gas laws within it.

Divide both sides by V.

▲ The labels on most aerosol cans warn against incineration. Since the volume of the can is constant, an increase in temperature causes an increase in pressure and possibly an explosion.

EXAMPLE 5.5 Ideal Gas Law I

Calculate the volume occupied by 0.845 mol of nitrogen gas at a pressure of 1.37 atm and a temperature of 315 K.

SORT The problem gives you the number of moles of nitrogen gas, the pressure, and the temperature. You are asked to find the volume.	**GIVEN:** $n = 0.845\,\text{mol}$, $\quad P = 1.37\,\text{atm},\ T = 315\,\text{K}$ **FIND:** V
STRATEGIZE You are given three of the four variables $(P, T,$ and $n)$ in the ideal gas law and asked to find the fourth (V). The conceptual plan shows how the ideal gas law provides the relationship between the known quantities and the unknown quantity.	**CONCEPTUAL PLAN** **RELATIONSHIPS USED** $PV = nRT$ (ideal gas law)
SOLVE To solve the problem, first solve the ideal gas law for V. Then substitute the given quantities to calculate V.	**SOLUTION** $PV = nRT$ $V = \dfrac{nRT}{P}$ $V = \dfrac{0.845\,\text{mol} \times 0.08206\dfrac{\text{L}\cdot\text{atm}}{\text{mol}\cdot\text{K}} \times 315\,\text{K}}{1.37\,\text{atm}}$ $= 15.9\,\text{L}$

CHECK The units of the answer are correct. The magnitude of the answer (15.9 L) makes sense because, as you will see in the next section, one mole of an ideal gas under standard temperature and pressure (273 K and 1 atm) occupies 22.4 L. Although this is not standard temperature and pressure, the conditions are close enough for a ballpark check of the answer. Since this gas sample contains 0.845 mol, a volume of 15.9 L is reasonable.

FOR PRACTICE 5.5

An 8.50 L tire contains 0.552 mol of gas at a temperature of 305 K. What is the pressure (in atm and psi) of the gas in the tire?

EXAMPLE 5.6 Ideal Gas Law II

Calculate the number of moles of gas in a 3.24 L basketball inflated to a *total pressure* of 24.3 psi at 25 °C. (Note: The *total pressure* is not the same as the pressure read on a pressure gauge such as the type used for checking a car or bicycle tire. That pressure, called the *gauge pressure*, is the *difference* between the total pressure and atmospheric pressure. In this case, if atmospheric pressure is 14.7 psi, the gauge pressure would be 9.6 psi. However, for calculations involving the ideal gas law, you must use the *total pressure* of 24.3 psi.)

SORT The problem gives you the pressure, the volume, and the temperature. You are asked to find the number of moles of gas.	**GIVEN:** $P = 24.3\,\text{psi},\ V = 3.24\ \text{L},\ T(°\text{C}) = 25\,°\text{C}$ **FIND:** n
STRATEGIZE The conceptual plan shows how the ideal gas law provides the relationship between the given quantities and the quantity to be found.	**CONCEPTUAL PLAN** **RELATIONSHIPS USED** $PV = nRT$ (ideal gas law)

SOLVE To solve the problem, first solve the ideal gas law for n.	**SOLUTION** $$PV = nRT$$ $$n = \frac{PV}{RT}$$
Before substituting into the equation, convert P and T into the correct units.	$$P = 24.3 \text{ psi} \times \frac{1 \text{ atm}}{14.7 \text{ psi}} = 1.6\underline{5}31 \text{ atm}$$ (Since rounding the intermediate answer would result in a slightly different final answer, we mark the least significant digit in the intermediate answer but don't round until the end.)
Finally, substitute into the equation and calculate n.	$$T \text{ (K)} = 25 + 273 = 298 \text{ K}$$ $$n = \frac{1.6\underline{5}31 \text{ atm} \times 3.24 \text{ L}}{0.08206 \frac{\text{L} \cdot \text{atm}}{\text{mol} \cdot \text{K}} \times 298 \text{ K}} = 0.219 \text{ mol}$$

CHECK The units of the answer are correct. The magnitude of the answer (0.219 mol) makes sense because, as you will see in the next section, one mole of an ideal gas under standard temperature and pressure (273 K and 1 atm) occupies 22.4 L. At a pressure that is 65% higher than standard pressure, the volume of 1 mol of gas would be proportionally lower. Since this gas sample occupies 3.24 L, the answer of 0.219 mol is reasonable.

FOR PRACTICE 5.6
What volume does 0.556 mol of gas occupy at a pressure of 715 mmHg and a temperature of 58 °C?

FOR MORE PRACTICE 5.6
Determine the pressure in mmHg of a 0.133 g sample of helium gas in a 648 mL container at a temperature of 32 °C.

5.5 Applications of the Ideal Gas Law: Molar Volume, Density, and Molar Mass of a Gas

We just examined how we can use the ideal gas law to calculate one of the variables (P, V, T, or n) given the other three. We now turn to three other applications of the ideal gas law: molar volume, density, and molar mass.

Molar Volume at Standard Temperature and Pressure

The volume occupied by one mole of a substance is its **molar volume**. For gases, we often specify the molar volume under conditions known as **standard temperature** ($T = 0$ °C or 273 K) **and pressure** ($P = 1.00$ atm), abbreviated as **STP**. Using the ideal gas law, we can determine that the molar volume of an ideal gas at STP is:

$$V = \frac{nRT}{P}$$

$$= \frac{1.00 \text{ mol} \times 0.08206 \frac{\text{L} \cdot \text{atm}}{\text{mol} \cdot \text{K}} \times 273 \text{ K}}{1.00 \text{ atm}}$$

$$= 22.4 \text{ L}$$

The molar volume of 22.4 L only applies at STP.

22.4 L | 22.4 L | 22.4 L

1 mol He(g) at STP | 1 mol Xe(g) at STP | 1 mol CH$_4$(g) at STP

▲ One mole of any gas occupies approximately 22.4 L at standard temperature (273 K) and pressure (1.0 atm).

The molar volume of an ideal gas at STP is useful because—as we saw in the *Check* steps of Examples 5.5 and 5.6—it gives us a way to approximate the volume of an ideal gas under conditions that are close to STP.

Conceptual Connection 5.2 Molar Volume

Assuming ideal behavior, which of these gas samples will have the greatest volume at STP?

(a) 1 g of H_2 **(b)** 1 g of O_2 **(c)** 1 g of Ar

Density of a Gas

Since one mole of an ideal gas occupies 22.4 L under standard temperature and pressure, we can readily calculate the density of an ideal gas under these conditions. Since density is mass/volume, and since the mass of one mole of a gas is simply its molar mass, the *density of a gas* is its molar mass divided by its molar volume:

$$\text{Density} = \frac{\text{molar mass}}{\text{molar volume}}$$

We can calculate the density of a gas at STP by using 22.4 L as the molar volume. For example, the densities of helium and nitrogen gas at STP are:

$$d_{He} = \frac{4.00 \text{ g/mol}}{22.4 \text{ L/mol}} = 0.179 \text{ g/L} \qquad d_{N_2} = \frac{28.02 \text{ g/mol}}{22.4 \text{ L/mol}} = 1.25 \text{ g/L}$$

Notice that *the density of a gas is directly proportional to its molar mass*. The greater the molar mass of a gas, the more dense the gas. For this reason, a gas with a molar mass lower than that of air tends to rise in air. For example, both helium and hydrogen gas (molar masses of 4.00 and 2.01 g/mol, respectively) have molar masses that are lower than the average molar mass of air (approximately 28.8 g/mol). Therefore, a balloon filled with either helium or hydrogen gas floats in air.

The primary components of air are nitrogen (about four-fifths) and oxygen (about one-fifth). We will discuss the detailed composition of air in Section 5.6.

We can calculate the density of a gas more generally (under any conditions) by using the ideal gas law. To do so, we can arrange the ideal gas law as:

$$PV = nRT$$

$$\frac{n}{V} = \frac{P}{RT}$$

Since the left-hand side of this equation has units of moles/liter, it represents the *molar density*. We can obtain the density in grams/liter from the molar density by multiplying by the molar mass ($\mathcal{M}$):

$$\underbrace{\frac{\text{moles}}{\text{liter}}}_{\text{Molar density}} \times \underbrace{\frac{\text{grams}}{\text{mole}}}_{\text{Molar mass}} = \underbrace{\frac{\text{grams}}{\text{liter}}}_{\substack{\text{Density in} \\ \text{grams/liter}}}$$

Therefore,

$$d = \frac{P\mathcal{M}}{RT} \tag{5.6}$$

Density
$$\underbrace{\frac{n}{V}}_{\text{Molar density}} \; \underbrace{\mathcal{M}}_{\text{Molar mass}} = \frac{P\mathcal{M}}{RT}$$

$$d = \frac{P\mathcal{M}}{RT}$$

Notice that, as expected, density increases with increasing molar mass. Notice also that as we discussed in Section 5.3, density decreases with increasing temperature.

EXAMPLE 5.7 Density

Calculate the density of nitrogen gas at 125 °C and a pressure of 755 mmHg.

SORT The problem gives you the temperature and pressure of a gas and asks you to find its density. The problem states that the gas is nitrogen.	**GIVEN:** $T(°C) = 125 °C$, $P = 755$ mmHg **FIND:** d
STRATEGIZE Equation 5.6 provides the relationship between the density of a gas and its temperature, pressure, and molar mass. The temperature and pressure are given. You can calculate the molar mass from the formula of the gas, which we know is N_2.	**CONCEPTUAL PLAN** 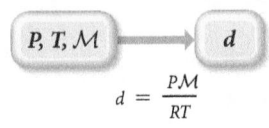 $$d = \frac{P\mathcal{M}}{RT}$$ **RELATIONSHIPS USED** $d = \dfrac{P\mathcal{M}}{RT}$ (density of a gas) Molar mass $N_2 = 28.02$ g/mol
SOLVE To solve the problem, gather each of the required quantities in the correct units. Convert the temperature to kelvins and the pressure to atmospheres. Substitute the quantities into the equation to calculate density.	**SOLUTION** $T(K) = 125 + 273 = 398$ K $P = 755 \text{ mmHg} \times \dfrac{1 \text{ atm}}{760 \text{ mmHg}} = 0.99342 \text{ atm}$ $d = \dfrac{P\mathcal{M}}{RT}$ $= \dfrac{0.99342 \text{ atm}\left(28.02 \dfrac{\text{g}}{\text{mol}}\right)}{0.08206 \dfrac{\text{L} \cdot \text{atm}}{\text{mol} \cdot \text{K}}(398 \text{ K})}$ $= 0.852$ g/L

CHECK The units of the answer are correct. The magnitude of the answer (0.852 g/L) makes sense because earlier we calculated the density of nitrogen gas at STP as 1.25 g/L. Since the temperature is higher than standard temperature, it follows that the density is lower.

FOR PRACTICE 5.7
Calculate the density of xenon gas at a pressure of 742 mmHg and a temperature of 45 °C.

FOR MORE PRACTICE 5.7
A gas has a density of 1.43 g/L at a temperature of 23 °C and a pressure of 0.789 atm. Calculate its molar mass.

Conceptual Connection 5.3 Density of a Gas

Arrange the following gases in order of increasing density at STP: Ne, Cl_2, F_2, and O_2.

Molar Mass of a Gas

We can use the ideal gas law in combination with mass measurements to calculate the molar mass of an unknown gas. First we measure the mass and volume of an unknown gas under conditions of known pressure and temperature. Then, we determine the amount of the gas in moles from the ideal gas law. Finally, we calculate the molar mass by dividing the mass (in grams) by the amount (in moles) as shown in Example 5.8.

EXAMPLE 5.8 Molar Mass of a Gas

A sample of gas has a mass of 0.311 g. Its volume is 0.225 L at a temperature of 55 °C and a pressure of 886 mmHg. Find its molar mass.

SORT The problem gives you the mass of a gas sample, along with its volume, temperature, and pressure. You are asked to find the molar mass.	**GIVEN:** $m = 0.331$ g, $V = 0.225$ L, $T (°C) = 55 °C$, $P = 886$ mmHg **FIND:** molar mass (g/mol)
STRATEGIZE The conceptual plan has two parts. In the first part, use the ideal gas law to find the number of moles of gas. In the second part, use the definition of molar mass to find the molar mass.	**CONCEPTUAL PLAN** $PV = nRT$ $\text{molar mass} = \dfrac{\text{mass } (m)}{\text{moles } (n)}$ **RELATIONSHIPS USED** $PV = nRT$ $\text{Molar mass} = \dfrac{\text{mass } (m)}{\text{moles } (n)}$
SOLVE To find the number of moles, first solve the ideal gas law for n. Before substituting into the equation for n, convert the pressure to atm and the temperature to K. Then substitute into the equation and calculate n, the number of moles. Finally, use the number of moles (n) and the given mass (m) to find the molar mass.	**SOLUTION** $PV = nRT$ $n = \dfrac{PV}{RT}$ $P = 886 \text{ mmHg} \times \dfrac{1 \text{ atm}}{760 \text{ mmHg}} = 1.1658 \text{ atm}$ $T(K) = 55 + 273 = 328 \text{ K}$ $n = \dfrac{1.1658 \text{ atm} \times 0.225 \text{ L}}{0.08206 \dfrac{\text{L} \cdot \text{atm}}{\text{mol} \cdot \text{K}} \times 328 \text{ K}}$ $= 9.7454 \times 10^{-3} \text{ mol}$ $\text{molar mass} = \dfrac{\text{mass } (m)}{\text{moles } (n)}$ $= \dfrac{0.311 \text{ g}}{9.7454 \times 10^{-3} \text{ mol}}$ $= 31.9 \text{ g/mol}$

CHECK The units of the answer are correct. The magnitude of the answer (31.9 g/mol) is a reasonable number for a molar mass. If you calculated a very small number (such as any number smaller than 1) or a very large number, you solved the problem incorrectly. Most gases have molar masses between one and several hundred grams per mole.

FOR PRACTICE 5.8

A sample of gas has a mass of 827 mg. Its volume is 0.270 L at a temperature of 88 °C and a pressure of 975 mmHg. Find its molar mass.

5.6 Mixtures of Gases and Partial Pressures

Many gas samples are not pure, but are mixtures of gases. Dry air, for example, is a mixture containing nitrogen, oxygen, argon, carbon dioxide, and a few other gases in trace amounts (Table 5.3).

Because the molecules in an ideal gas do not interact (as we will discuss further in Section 5.8), each of the components in an ideal gas mixture acts independently of the others. For example, the nitrogen molecules in air exert a certain pressure—78% of the total pressure—that is independent of the other gases in the mixture. Likewise, the oxygen molecules in air exert a certain pressure—21% of the total pressure—that is also independent of the other gases in the mixture. The pressure due to any individual component in a gas mixture is its **partial pressure** (P_n). We can calculate partial pressure from the ideal gas law by assuming that each gas component acts independently.

$$P_n = n_n \frac{RT}{V}$$

For a multicomponent gas mixture, we calculate the partial pressure of each component from the ideal gas law and the number of moles of that component (n_n) as follows:

$$P_a = n_a \frac{RT}{V}; \quad P_b = n_b \frac{RT}{V}; \quad P_c = n_c \frac{RT}{V}; \dots \qquad [5.7]$$

The sum of the partial pressures of the components in a gas mixture equals the total pressure:

$$P_{total} = P_a + P_b + P_c + \dots \qquad [5.8]$$

where P_{total} is the total pressure and P_a, P_b, P_c, ... are the partial pressures of the components. This relationship is known as **Dalton's law of partial pressures**.

Combining Equations 5.7 and 5.8, we get:

$$P_{total} = P_a + P_b + P_c + \dots$$

$$= n_a \frac{RT}{V} + n_b \frac{RT}{V} + n_c \frac{RT}{V} + \dots \qquad [5.9]$$

$$= (n_a + n_b + n_c + \dots) \frac{RT}{V}$$

$$= (n_{total}) \frac{RT}{V}$$

The total number of moles in the mixture, when substituted into the ideal gas law, indicates the total pressure of the sample.

If we divide Equation 5.7 by Equation 5.9, we get:

$$\frac{P_a}{P_{total}} = \frac{n_a(RT/V)}{n_{total}(RT/V)} = \frac{n_a}{n_{total}} \qquad [5.10]$$

The quantity n_a/n_{total}, the number of moles of a component in a mixture divided by the total number of moles in the mixture, is the **mole fraction** (χ_a):

$$\chi_a = \frac{n_a}{n_{total}} \qquad [5.11]$$

Rearranging Equation 5.10 and substituting the definition of mole fraction gives:

$$\frac{P_a}{P_{total}} = \frac{n_a}{n_{total}}$$

$$P_a = \frac{n_a}{n_{total}} P_{total} = \chi_a P_{total}$$

or simply

$$P_a = \chi_a P_{total} \qquad [5.12]$$

TABLE 5.3 Composition of Dry Air

Gas	Percent by Volume (%)
Nitrogen (N_2)	78
Oxygen (O_2)	21
Argon (Ar)	0.9
Carbon dioxide (CO_2)	0.04

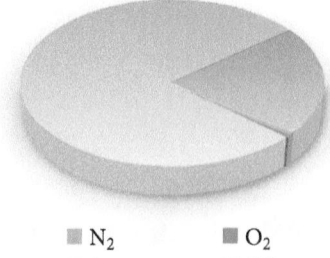

■ N_2 ■ O_2
■ Ar ■ CO_2

The partial pressure of a component in a gaseous mixture is its mole fraction multiplied by the total pressure. For gases, the mole fraction of a component is equivalent to its percent by volume divided by 100%. Therefore, based on Table 5.3, we calculate the partial pressure of nitrogen (P_{N_2}) in air at 1.00 atm as:

$$P_{N_2} = 0.78 \times 1.00 \text{ atm}$$
$$= 0.78 \text{ atm}$$

Likewise, the partial pressure of oxygen in air at 1.00 atm is 0.21 atm and the partial pressure of Ar in air is 0.01 atm. Applying Dalton's law of partial pressures to air at 1.00 atm, we can find the total pressure:

For these purposes, we can ignore the contribution of the CO_2 and other trace gases because they are so small.

$$P_{total} = P_{N_2} + P_{O_2} + P_{Ar}$$
$$P_{total} = 0.78 \text{ atm} + 0.21 \text{ atm} + 0.01 \text{ atm}$$
$$= 1.00 \text{ atm}$$

Conceptual Connection 5.4 Partial Pressures

A gas mixture contains an equal number of moles of He and Ne. The total pressure of the mixture is 3.0 atm. What are the partial pressures of He and Ne?

EXAMPLE 5.9 Total Pressure and Partial Pressures

A 1.00 L mixture of helium, neon, and argon has a total pressure of 662 mmHg at 298 K. If the partial pressure of helium is 341 mmHg and the partial pressure of neon is 112 mmHg, what mass of argon is present in the mixture?

SORT The problem gives you the partial pressures of two of the three components in a gas mixture, along with the total pressure, the volume, and the temperature, and asks you to find the mass of the third component.	**GIVEN:** $P_{He} = 341$ mmHg, $P_{Ne} = 112$ mmHg, $P_{total} = 662$ mmHg, $V = 1.00$ L, $T = 298$ K **FIND:** m_{Ar}
STRATEGIZE You can find the mass of argon from the number of moles of argon, which you can calculate from the partial pressure of argon and the ideal gas law. Begin by using Dalton's law to determine the partial pressure of argon. Then use the partial pressure of argon together with the volume of the sample and the temperature to find the number of moles of argon. Finally, use the molar mass of argon to calculate the mass of argon from the number of moles of argon.	**CONCEPTUAL PLAN** $P_{tot}, P_{He}, P_{Ne} \rightarrow P_{Ar}$ $P_{tot} = P_{He} + P_{Ne} + P_{Ar}$ $P_{Ar}, V, T \rightarrow n_{Ar}$ $PV = nRT$ $n_{Ar} \rightarrow m_{Ar}$ $\dfrac{39.95 \text{ g Ar}}{1 \text{ mol Ar}}$ **RELATIONSHIPS USED** $P_{total} = P_{He} + P_{Ne} + P_{Ar}$ (Dalton's law) $PV = nRT$ (ideal gas law) molar mass Ar = 39.95 g/mol
SOLVE Follow the conceptual plan. To find the partial pressure of argon, solve the equation for P_{Ar} and substitute the values of the other partial pressures to calculate P_{Ar}.	**SOLUTION** $P_{total} = P_{He} + P_{Ne} + P_{Ar}$ $P_{Ar} = P_{total} - P_{He} - P_{Ne}$ $= 662$ mmHg $- 341$ mmHg $- 112$ mmHg $= 209$ mmHg

Convert the partial pressure from mmHg to atm and use it in the ideal gas law to calculate the amount of argon in moles.	$209 \ \text{mmHg} \times \dfrac{1 \ \text{atm}}{760 \ \text{mmHg}} = 0.275 \ \text{atm}$
	$n = \dfrac{PV}{RT} = \dfrac{0.275 \ \text{atm} \, (1.00 \ \text{L})}{0.08206 \ \dfrac{\text{L} \cdot \text{atm}}{\text{mol} \cdot \text{K}} (298 \ \text{K})} = 1.1\underline{2}5 \times 10^{-2} \ \text{mol Ar}$
Use the molar mass of argon to convert from amount of argon in moles to mass of argon.	$1.1\underline{2}5 \times 10^{-2} \ \text{mol Ar} \times \dfrac{39.95 \ \text{g Ar}}{1 \ \text{mol Ar}} = 0.449 \ \text{g Ar}$

CHECK The units of the answer are correct. The magnitude of the answer makes sense because the volume is 1.0 L, which at STP would contain about 1/22 mol. Since the partial pressure of argon in the mixture is about 1/3 of the total pressure, we roughly estimate about 1/66 of one molar mass of argon, which is fairly close to the answer we got.

FOR PRACTICE 5.9
A sample of hydrogen gas is mixed with water vapor. The mixture has a total pressure of 755 torr and the water vapor has a partial pressure of 24 torr. What amount (in moles) of hydrogen gas is contained in 1.55 L of this mixture at 298 K?

Deep-Sea Diving and Partial Pressures

Our lungs have evolved to breathe oxygen at a partial pressure of $P_{O_2} = 0.21$ atm. If the total pressure decreases—when we climb a mountain, for example—the partial pressure of oxygen also decreases. On top of Mt. Everest, where the total pressure is 0.311 atm, the partial pressure of oxygen is only 0.065 atm. Low oxygen levels produce a physiological condition called **hypoxia** or oxygen starvation (Figure 5.13 ▶). Mild hypoxia causes dizziness, headache, and shortness of breath. Severe hypoxia, which occurs when (P_{O_2}) drops below 0.1 atm, may result in unconsciousness or even death. For this reason, climbers hoping to make the summit of Mt. Everest usually carry oxygen to breathe.

While not as dangerous as a lack of oxygen, too much oxygen can also cause physiological problems. Recall from Section 5.3 that scuba divers breathe pressurized air. At 30 m, a scuba diver breathes air at a total pressure of 4.0 atm, making P_{O_2} about 0.84 atm. This elevated partial pressure of oxygen raises the density of oxygen molecules in the lungs, resulting in a higher concentration of oxygen in body tissues. When P_{O_2} increases beyond 1.4 atm, the increased oxygen concentration in body tissues causes a condition called **oxygen toxicity**, which results in muscle twitching, tunnel vision, and convulsions. Divers who venture too deep without proper precautions have drowned because of oxygen toxicity. A second problem associated with breathing pressurized air is the increase of nitrogen in the lungs. At 30 m, a scuba diver breathes nitrogen at $P_{N_2} = 3.12$ atm, which increases the nitrogen concentration in body tissues and fluids. When P_{N_2} increases beyond about 4 atm, a condition called **nitrogen narcosis** or *rapture of the deep* results. Divers describe this condition as feeling inebriated or drunk. A diver breathing compressed air at 60 m feels as if he has consumed too much wine.

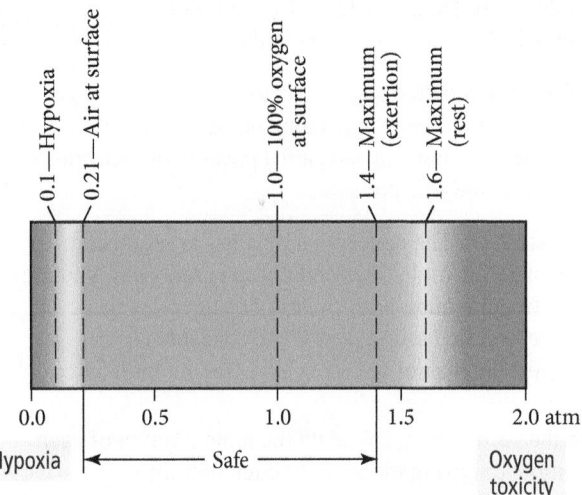

▲ **FIGURE 5.13 Oxygen Partial Pressure Limits** The partial pressure of oxygen in air at sea level is 0.21 atm. Partial pressures of oxygen below 0.1 atm and above 1.4 atm are dangerous to humans.

Surface	**30 m**
P_{tot} = 1 atm	P_{tot} = 4 atm
P_{N_2} = 0.78 atm	P_{N_2} = 3.12 atm
P_{O_2} = 0.21 atm	P_{O_2} = 0.84 atm

▶ When a diver breathes compressed air, the abnormally high partial pressure of oxygen in the lungs leads to an elevated concentration of oxygen in body tissues.

To avoid oxygen toxicity and nitrogen narcosis, deep-sea divers—those who descend beyond 50 m—breathe specialized mixtures of gases. One common mixture is heliox, a mixture of helium and oxygen. These mixtures usually contain a smaller percentage of oxygen than would be found in air, thereby lowering the risk of oxygen toxicity. Heliox also contains helium instead of nitrogen, eliminating the risk of nitrogen narcosis.

EXAMPLE 5.10 Partial Pressures and Mole Fractions

A 12.5 L scuba diving tank contains a helium–oxygen (heliox) mixture made up of 24.2 g of He and 4.32 g of O_2 at 298 K. Calculate the mole fraction and partial pressure of each component in the mixture and the total pressure of the mixture.

SORT The problem gives the masses of two gases in a mixture and the volume and temperature of the mixture. You are to find the mole fraction and partial pressure of each component, as well as the total pressure.	**GIVEN:** m_{He} = 24.2 g, m_{O_2} = 4.32 g, V = 12.5 L, T = 298 K **FIND:** χ_{He}, χ_{O_2}, P_{He}, P_{O_2}, P_{total}
STRATEGIZE The conceptual plan has several parts. To calculate the mole fraction of each component, you must first find the number of moles of each component. Therefore, in the first part of the conceptual plan, convert the masses to moles using the molar masses. In the second part, calculate the mole fraction of each component using the mole fraction definition. To calculate *partial pressures* calculate the *total pressure* and then use the mole fractions from the previous part to calculate the partial pressures. Calculate the total pressure from the sum of the moles of both components. (Alternatively, you can calculate the partial pressures of the components individually, using the number of moles of each component. Then you can sum them to obtain the total pressure.) Last, use the mole fractions of each component and the total pressure to calculate the partial pressure of each component.	**CONCEPTUAL PLAN** $m_{He} \longrightarrow n_{He}$ $\dfrac{1 \text{ mol He}}{4.00 \text{ g He}}$ $m_{O_2} \longrightarrow n_{O_2}$ $\dfrac{1 \text{ mol } O_2}{32.00 \text{ g } O_2}$ $\chi_{He} = \dfrac{n_{He}}{n_{He} + n_{O_2}}$; $\chi_{O_2} = \dfrac{n_{O_2}}{n_{He} + n_{O_2}}$ $P_{total} = \dfrac{(n_{He} + n_{O_2})RT}{V}$ $P_{He} = \chi_{He}P_{total}$; $P_{O_2} = \chi_{O_2}P_{total}$ **RELATIONSHIPS USED** $\chi_a = n_a/n_{total}$ (mole fraction definition) $P_{total}V = n_{total}RT$ $P_a = \chi_a P_{total}$

SOLVE Follow the plan to solve the problem. Begin by converting each of the masses to amounts in moles.	**SOLUTION** $24.2 \text{ g He} \times \dfrac{1 \text{ mol He}}{4.00 \text{ g He}} = 6.05 \text{ mol He}$ $4.32 \text{ g O}_2 \times \dfrac{1 \text{ mol O}_2}{32.00 \text{ g O}_2} = 0.135 \text{ mol O}_2$
Calculate each of the mole fractions.	$\chi_{He} = \dfrac{n_{He}}{n_{He} + n_{O_2}} = \dfrac{6.05}{6.05 + 0.135} = 0.97\underline{8}17$ $\chi_{O_2} = \dfrac{n_{O_2}}{n_{He} + n_{O_2}} = \dfrac{0.135}{6.05 + 0.135} = 0.0218\underline{2}7$
Calculate the total pressure.	$P_{total} = \dfrac{\left(n_{He} + n_{O_2}\right)RT}{V}$ $= \dfrac{(6.05 \text{ mol} + 0.135 \text{ mol})\left(0.08206\dfrac{L \cdot atm}{mol \cdot K}\right)(298 \text{ K})}{12.5 \text{ L}}$ $= 12.0\underline{9}9 \text{ atm}$
Finally, calculate the partial pressure of each component.	$P_{He} = \chi_{He}\, P_{total} = 0.97\underline{8}17 \times 12.0\underline{9}9 \text{ atm}$ $= 11.8 \text{ atm}$ $P_{O_2} = \chi_{O_2} P_{total} = 0.0218\underline{2}7 \times 12.0\underline{9}9 \text{ atm}$ $= 0.264 \text{ atm}$

CHECK The units of the answers are correct and the magnitudes are reasonable.

FOR PRACTICE 5.10

A diver breathes a heliox mixture with an oxygen mole fraction of 0.050. What must the total pressure be for the partial pressure of oxygen to be 0.21 atm?

Collecting Gases over Water

When the desired product of a chemical reaction is a gas, the gas is often collected by the displacement of water. For example, suppose we use the reaction of zinc with hydrochloric acid as a source of hydrogen gas:

$$Zn(s) + 2\,HCl(aq) \rightarrow ZnCl_2(aq) + H_2(g)$$

To collect the gas, we can set up an apparatus like the one shown in Figure 5.14 ▶. As the hydrogen gas forms, it bubbles through the water and gathers in the collection flask. The hydrogen gas collected in this way is not pure, however, but mixed with water vapor because some water molecules evaporate and mix with the hydrogen molecules.

▶ FIGURE 5.14 **Collecting a Gas over Water**   When the gaseous product of a chemical reaction is collected over water, the product molecules (in this case H_2) are mixed with water molecules. The pressure of water in the final mixture is equal to the vapor pressure of water at the temperature at which the gas is collected. The partial pressure of the product is the total pressure minus the partial pressure of water.

Collecting a Gas over Water

Hydrogen plus water vapor

H_2

Zn

HCl

H_2O

Appendix IIE includes a more complete table of the vapor pressure of water versus temperature.

TABLE 5.4 Vapor Pressure of Water versus Temperature

Temperature (°C)	Pressure (mmHg)	Temperature (°C)	Pressure (mmHg)
0	4.58	55	118.2
5	6.54	60	149.6
10	9.21	65	187.5
15	12.79	70	233.7
20	17.55	75	289.1
25	23.78	80	355.1
30	31.86	85	433.6
35	42.23	90	525.8
40	55.40	95	633.9
45	71.97	100	760.0
50	92.6		

The partial pressure of water in the mixture, called its **vapor pressure**, depends on temperature (Table 5.4). Vapor pressure increases with increasing temperature because higher temperatures cause more water molecules to evaporate. We discuss vapor pressure more thoroughly in Chapter 11.

Suppose we collect the hydrogen gas over water at a total pressure of 758.2 mmHg and a temperature of 25 °C. What is the partial pressure of the hydrogen gas? We know that the total pressure is 758.2 mmHg and that the partial pressure of water is 23.78 mmHg (its vapor pressure at 25 °C):

$$P_{total} = P_{H_2} + P_{H_2O}$$

$$758.2 \text{ mmHg} = P_{H_2} + 23.78 \text{ mmHg}$$

Therefore,

$$P_{H_2} = 758.2 \text{ mmHg} - 23.78 \text{ mmHg}$$

$$= 734.4 \text{ mmHg}$$

The partial pressure of the hydrogen in the mixture is 734.4 mmHg.

EXAMPLE 5.11 Collecting Gases over Water

In order to determine the rate of photosynthesis, the oxygen gas emitted by an aquatic plant is collected over water at a temperature of 293 K and a total pressure of 755.2 mmHg. Over a specific time period, a total of 1.02 L of gas is collected. What mass of oxygen gas (in grams) is formed?

SORT The problem gives the volume of gas collected over water as well as the temperature and the pressure. You are to find the mass in grams of oxygen that forms.	**GIVEN:** $V = 1.02$ L, $P_{total} = 755.2$ mmHg, $T = 293$ K **FIND:** g O_2

STRATEGIZE You can determine the mass of oxygen from the amount of oxygen in moles, which you can calculate from the ideal gas law if you know the partial pressure of oxygen. Since the oxygen is mixed with water vapor, you find the partial pressure of oxygen in the mixture by subtracting the partial pressure of water at 293 K (20 °C) from the total pressure.

Next, use the ideal gas law to determine the number of moles of oxygen from its partial pressure, volume, and temperature.

Finally, use the molar mass of oxygen to convert the number of moles to grams.

CONCEPTUAL PLAN

$$P_{O_2} = P_{total} - P_{H_2O} \ (20 °C)$$

$$P_{O_2}V = n_{O_2}RT$$

n_{O_2} ⟶ $g \, O_2$
$$\frac{32.00 \text{ g } O_2}{\text{mol } O_2}$$

RELATIONSHIPS USED

$$P_{total} = P_a + P_b + P_c + \ldots \ \text{(Dalton's law)}$$
$$PV = nRT \ \text{(ideal gas law)}$$

SOLVE Follow the conceptual plan to solve the problem. Begin by calculating the partial pressure of oxygen in the oxygen/water mixture. You can find the partial pressure of water at 20 °C in Table 5.4.

Next, solve the ideal gas law for number of moles.

Before substituting into the ideal gas law, convert the partial pressure of oxygen from mmHg to atm.

Substitute into the ideal gas law to find the number of moles of oxygen.

Finally, use the molar mass of oxygen to convert to grams of oxygen.

SOLUTION

$$P_{O_2} = P_{total} - P_{H_2O} \ (20 °C)$$
$$= 755.2 \text{ mmHg} - 17.55 \text{ mmHg}$$
$$= 737.65 \text{ mmHg}$$

$$n_{O_2} = \frac{P_{O_2}V}{RT}$$

$$737.65 \text{ mmHg} \times \frac{1 \text{ atm}}{760 \text{ mmHg}} = 0.97059 \text{ atm}$$

$$n_{O_2} = \frac{P_{O_2}V}{RT} = \frac{0.97059 \text{ atm} \ (1.02 \text{ L})}{0.08206 \dfrac{\text{L} \cdot \text{atm}}{\text{mol} \cdot \text{K}} \ (293 \text{ K})}$$

$$= 4.1175 \times 10^{-2} \text{ mol}$$

$$4.1175 \times 10^{-2} \text{ mol } O_2 \times \frac{32.00 \text{ g } O_2}{1 \text{ mol } O_2} = 1.32 \text{ g } O_2$$

CHECK The answer is in the correct units. You can quickly check the magnitude of the answer by using molar volume. Under STP one liter is about 1/22 of one mole. Therefore the answer should be about 1/22 the molar mass of oxygen ($1/22 \times 32 = 1.45$). The magnitude of the answer seems reasonable.

FOR PRACTICE 5.11

A common way to make hydrogen gas in the laboratory is to place a metal such as zinc in hydrochloric acid. The hydrochloric acid reacts with the metal to produce hydrogen gas, which is then collected over water. Suppose a student carries out this reaction and collects a total of 154.4 mL of gas at a pressure of 742 mmHg and a temperature of 25 °C. What mass of hydrogen gas (in mg) does the student collect?

5.7 Gases in Chemical Reactions: Stoichiometry Revisited

In Chapter 4, we discussed how to use the coefficients in chemical equations as conversion factors between number of moles of reactants and number of moles of products in a chemical reaction. We can use these conversion factors to determine, for example, the mass of product obtained in a chemical reaction based on a given mass of reactant, or the mass of one reactant needed to react completely with a given mass of another reactant. The general conceptual plan for these kinds of calculations is:

where A and B are two different substances involved in the reaction and the conversion factor between amounts (in moles) of each comes from the stoichiometric coefficients in the balanced chemical equation.

In reactions involving *gaseous* reactant or products, we often specify the quantity of a gas in terms of its volume at a given temperature and pressure. As we have seen, stoichiometry involves relationships between amounts in moles. For stoichiometric calculations involving gases, we can use the ideal gas law to determine the amounts in moles from the volumes, or to determine the volumes from the amounts in moles.

$$n = \frac{PV}{RT} \qquad V = \frac{nRT}{P}$$

The pressures here could also be partial pressures.

The general conceptual plan for these kinds of calculations is:

Examples 5.12 and 5.13 demonstrate this kind of calculation.

EXAMPLE 5.12   Gases in Chemical Reactions

Methanol (CH_3OH) can be synthesized by the reaction:

$$CO(g) + 2\,H_2(g) \rightarrow CH_3OH(g)$$

What volume (in liters) of hydrogen gas, at a temperature of 355 K and a pressure of 738 mmHg, do we need to synthesize 35.7 g of methanol?

SORT You are given the mass of methanol, the product of a chemical reaction. You are asked to find the required volume of one of the reactants (hydrogen gas) at a specified temperature and pressure.	**GIVEN:** 35.7 g CH_3OH, $T = 355$ K, $P = 738$ mmHg **FIND:** V_{H_2}
STRATEGIZE You can calculate the required volume of hydrogen gas from the number of moles of hydrogen gas, which you can obtain from the number of moles of methanol via the stoichiometry of the reaction. First, find the number of moles of methanol from its mass by using the molar mass. Then use the stoichiometric relationship from the balanced chemical equation to find the number of moles of hydrogen you need to form that quantity of methanol. Finally, substitute the number of moles of hydrogen together with the pressure and temperature into the ideal gas law to find the volume of hydrogen.	**CONCEPTUAL PLAN**
	RELATIONSHIPS USED $PV = nRT$ (ideal gas law) 2 mol H_2 : 1 mol CH_3OH (from balanced chemical equation) molar mass $CH_3OH = 32.04$ g/mol

SOLVE Follow the conceptual plan to solve the problem. Begin by using the mass of methanol to determine the number of moles of methanol.

Next, convert the number of moles of methanol to moles of hydrogen.

Finally, use the ideal gas law to find the volume of hydrogen. Before substituting into the equation, you need to convert the pressure to atmospheres.

SOLUTION

$$35.7 \text{ g } CH_3OH \times \frac{1 \text{ mol } CH_3OH}{32.04 \text{ g } CH_3OH} = 1.1142 \text{ mol } CH_3OH$$

$$1.1142 \text{ mol } CH_3OH \times \frac{2 \text{ mol } H_2}{1 \text{ mol } CH_3OH} = 2.2284 \text{ mol } H_2$$

$$V_{H_2} = \frac{n_{H_2}RT}{P}$$

$$P = 738 \text{ mmHg} \times \frac{1 \text{ atm}}{760 \text{ mmHg}} = 0.97105 \text{ atm}$$

$$V_{H_2} = \frac{(2.2284 \text{ mol})\left(0.08206\frac{L \cdot atm}{mol \cdot K}\right)(355 \text{ K})}{0.97105 \text{ atm}}$$

$$= 66.9 \text{ L}$$

CHECK The units of the answer are correct. The magnitude of the answer (66.9 L) seems reasonable. You are given slightly more than one molar mass of methanol, which is therefore slightly more than one mole of methanol. From the equation you can see that you need 2 mol hydrogen to make 1 mol methanol so the answer must be slightly greater than 2 mol hydrogen. Under standard temperature and pressure, slightly more than 2 mol hydrogen occupies slightly more than $2 \times 22.4 \text{ L} = 44.8 \text{ L}$. At a temperature greater than standard temperature, the volume would be even greater; therefore, this answer is reasonable.

FOR PRACTICE 5.12

In the following reaction, 4.58 L of O_2 was formed at P = 745 mmHg and T = 308 K. How many grams of Ag_2O decomposed?

$$2 Ag_2O(s) \rightarrow 4 Ag(s) + O_2(g)$$

FOR MORE PRACTICE 5.12

In the previous reaction, what mass of $Ag_2O(s)$ (in grams) is required to form 388 mL of oxygen gas at P = 734 mmHg and 25.0 °C?

Molar Volume and Stoichiometry

In Section 5.5 we saw that under standard temperature and pressure, 1 mol of an ideal gas occupies 22.4 L. Consequently, if a reaction occurs at or near standard temperature and pressure, we can use 1 mol = 22.4 L as a conversion factor in stoichiometric calculations, as shown in Example 5.13.

EXAMPLE 5.13 Using Molar Volume in Gas Stoichiometric Calculations

How many grams of water form when 1.24 L of H_2 gas at STP completely reacts with O_2?

$$2 H_2(g) + O_2(g) \rightarrow 2 H_2O(g)$$

SORT You are given the volume of hydrogen gas (a reactant) at STP and asked to determine the mass of water that forms upon complete reaction.

GIVEN: 1.24 L H_2

FIND: g H_2O

STRATEGIZE Since the reaction occurs under standard temperature and pressure, you can convert directly from the volume (in L) of hydrogen gas to the amount in moles. Then use the stoichiometric relationship from the balanced equation to find the number of moles of water formed. Finally, use the molar mass of water to obtain the mass of water formed.

CONCEPTUAL PLAN

$$\boxed{\text{L } H_2} \longrightarrow \boxed{\text{mol } H_2} \longrightarrow \boxed{\text{mol } H_2O} \longrightarrow \boxed{\text{g } H_2O}$$

$$\dfrac{1 \text{ mol } H_2}{22.4 \text{ L } H_2} \qquad \dfrac{2 \text{ mol } H_2O}{2 \text{ mol } H_2} \qquad \dfrac{18.02 \text{ g}}{1 \text{ mol}}$$

RELATIONSHIPS USED
1 mol = 22.4 L (at STP)
2 mol H_2 : 2 mol H_2O (from balanced equation)
molar mass H_2O = 18.02 g/mol

SOLVE Follow the conceptual plan to solve the problem.

$$1.24 \text{ L } H_2 \times \frac{1 \text{ mol } H_2}{22.4 \text{ L } H_2} \times \frac{2 \text{ mol } H_2O}{2 \text{ mol } H_2O} \times \frac{18.02 \text{ g } H_2O}{1 \text{ mol } H_2O} = 0.998 \text{ g } H_2O$$

CHECK The units of the answer are correct. The magnitude of the answer (0.998 g) is about 1/18 of the molar mass of water, roughly equivalent to the approximately 1/22 of a mole of hydrogen gas given, as expected for the 1:1 stoichiometric relationship between number of moles of hydrogen and number of moles of water.

FOR PRACTICE 5.13
How many liters of oxygen (at STP) are required to form 10.5 g of H_2O?
$$2 H_2(g) + O_2(g) \rightarrow 2 H_2O(g)$$

Conceptual Connection 5.5 **Pressure and Number of Moles**

Nitrogen and hydrogen react to form ammonia according to the following equation:

$$N_2(g) + 3 H_2(g) \rightleftharpoons 2 NH_3(g)$$

Consider the following representations of the initial mixture of reactants and the resulting mixture after the reaction has been allowed to react for some time:

Kinetic Molecular Theory

▲ **FIGURE 5.15 A Model for Gas Behavior** In the kinetic molecular theory of gases, a gas sample is modeled as a collection of particles in constant straight-line motion. The size of each particle is negligibly small, and the particles' collisions are elastic.

If the volume is kept constant, and nothing is added to the reaction mixture, what happens to the total pressure during the course of the reaction?

(a) the pressure increases
(b) the pressure decreases
(c) the pressure does not change

5.8 Kinetic Molecular Theory: A Model for Gases

In Chapter 1, we discussed how the scientific approach proceeds from observations to laws and eventually to theories. Remember that laws summarize behavior—for example, Charles's law summarizes *how* the volume of a gas depends on temperature—while theories give the underlying reasons for the behavior. A theory of gas behavior explains, for example, *why* the volume of a gas increases with increasing temperature.

The simplest model for the behavior of gases is the **kinetic molecular theory**. In this theory, a gas is modeled as a collection of particles (either molecules or atoms, depending on the gas) in constant motion (Figure 5.15 ◄). A single particle moves in a straight line until it collides with another particle (or with the wall of the container). The basic postulates (or assumptions) of kinetic molecular theory are listed here:

1. **The size of a particle is negligibly small.** Kinetic molecular theory assumes that the particles themselves occupy no volume, even though they have mass. This postulate is justified because, under normal pressures, the space between atoms or molecules in a gas is very large compared to the size of the atoms or molecule themselves. For example, in a sample of argon gas at STP, only about 0.01% of the volume is occupied by atoms, and the average distance from one argon atom to another is 3.3 nm. In comparison, the atomic radius of argon is 97 pm. If an argon atom were the size of a golf ball, its nearest neighbor would be, on average, just over 4 ft away at STP.

2. **The average kinetic energy of a particle is proportional to the temperature in kelvins.** The motion of atoms or molecules in a gas is due to thermal energy, which distributes itself among the particles in the gas. At any given moment, some particles are moving faster than others—there is a distribution of velocities—but the higher the temperature, the faster the overall motion and the greater the average kinetic energy. Notice that *kinetic energy* $(\frac{1}{2}mv^2)$—not *velocity*—is proportional to temperature. The atoms in a sample of helium and a sample of argon at the same temperature have the same average *kinetic energy* but not the same average *velocity*. Since the helium atoms are lighter, they must move faster to have the same kinetic energy as argon atoms.

3. **The collision of one particle with another (or with the walls of its container) is completely elastic.** This means that when two particles collide, they may *exchange energy*, but there is no overall *loss of energy*. Any kinetic energy lost by one particle is completely gained by the other. In other words, the particles have no "stickiness," and they are not deformed by the collision. An encounter between two particles in kinetic molecular theory is more like the collision between two billiard balls than the collision between two lumps of clay (Figure 5.16 ▼). Between collisions, the particles do not exert any forces on one another.

If we start with the postulates of kinetic molecular theory, we can mathematically derive the ideal gas law (as we will show later). In other words, the ideal gas law follows directly from kinetic molecular theory, which gives us confidence that the assumptions of the theory are valid, at least under conditions where the ideal gas law applies. Let's see how the concept of pressure as well as each of the gas laws we have examined in this chapter follow conceptually from kinetic molecular theory.

The Nature of Pressure In Section 5.2, we defined pressure as force divided by area:

$$P = \frac{F}{A}$$

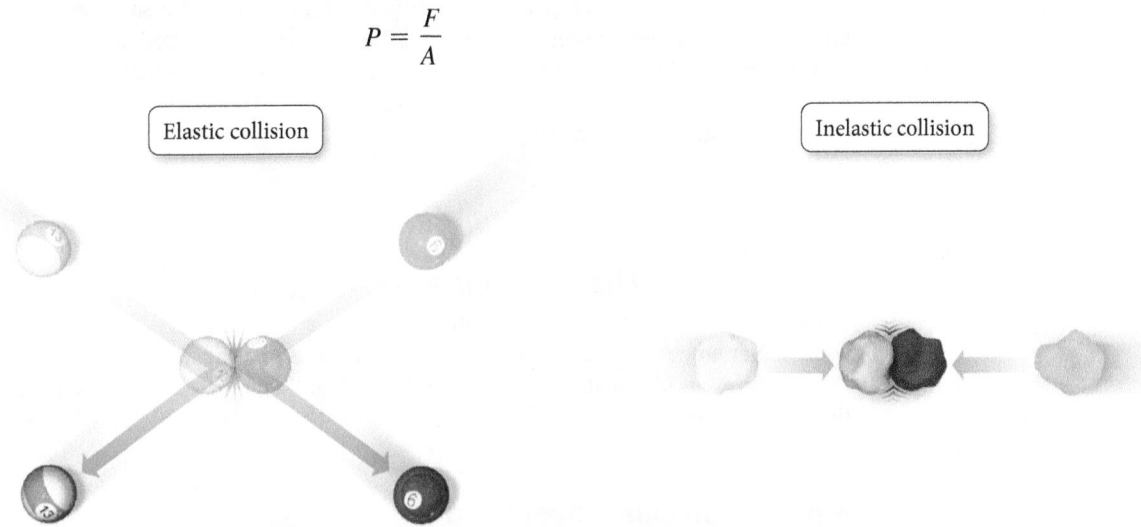

▲ **FIGURE 5.16 Elastic versus Inelastic Collisions** When two billiard balls collide, the collision is elastic—the total kinetic energy of the colliding bodies is the same before and after the collision. When two lumps of clay collide, the collision is inelastic—the kinetic energy of the colliding bodies dissipates in the form of heat during the collision.

The force (F) associated with an individual collision is given by $F = ma$, where m is the mass of the particle and a is its acceleration as it changes its direction of travel due to the collision.

According to kinetic molecular theory, a gas is a collection of particles in constant motion. The motion results in collisions between the particles and the surfaces around them. As each particle collides with a surface, it exerts a force upon that surface. The result of many particles in a gas sample exerting forces on the surfaces around them is a constant pressure.

Boyle's Law Boyle's law states that for a constant number of particles at constant temperature, the volume of a gas is inversely proportional to its pressure. According to kinetic molecular theory, if you decrease the volume of a gas, you force the gas particles to occupy a smaller space. As long as the temperature remains the same, the number of collisions with the surrounding surfaces (per unit surface area) must necessarily increase, resulting in a greater pressure.

Charles's Law Charles's law states that for a constant number of particles at constant pressure, the volume of a gas is proportional to its temperature. According to kinetic molecular theory, when we increase the temperature of a gas, the average speed, and thus the average kinetic energy, of the particles increases. Since this greater kinetic energy results in more frequent collisions and more force per collision, the pressure of the gas increases if its volume is held constant (Gay-Lussac's law). The only way for the pressure to remain constant is for the volume to increase. The greater volume spreads the collisions out over a greater surface area so that the pressure (defined as force per unit area) is unchanged.

Avogadro's Law Avogadro's law states that at constant temperature and pressure, the volume of a gas is proportional to the number of particles. According to kinetic molecular theory, when we increase the number of particles in a gas sample, the number of collisions with the surrounding surfaces increases. The greater number of collisions results in a greater overall force on surrounding surfaces; the only way for the pressure to remain constant is for the volume to increase so that the number of particles per unit volume (and thus the number of collisions) remains constant.

Dalton's Law Dalton's law states that the total pressure of a gas mixture is the sum of the partial pressures of its components. In other words, according to Dalton's law, the components in a gas mixture act identically to, and independently of, one another. According to kinetic molecular theory, the particles have negligible size and they do not interact. Consequently, the only property that would distinguish one type of particle from another is its mass. However, even particles of different masses have the same average kinetic energy at a given temperature, so they exert the same force upon collision with a surface. Consequently, adding components to a gas mixture—even different *kinds* of gases— has the same effect as simply adding more particles. The partial pressures of all the components sum to the overall pressure.

Conceptual Connection 5.6 Kinetic Molecular Theory I

Draw a depiction, as described by kinetic molecular theory, of a gas sample containing equal molar amounts of argon and xenon. Use red dots to represent argon atoms and blue dots to represent xenon atoms. Give each atom a "tail" to represent its velocity relative to the others in the mixture.

Kinetic Molecular Theory and the Ideal Gas Law

We have just seen how each of the gas laws conceptually follows from kinetic molecular theory. We can also *derive* the ideal gas law from the postulates of kinetic molecular theory. In other words, the kinetic molecular theory is a quantitative model that *implies* $PV = nRT$. Let's now explore this derivation.

Calculating Gas Pressure: A Molecular View

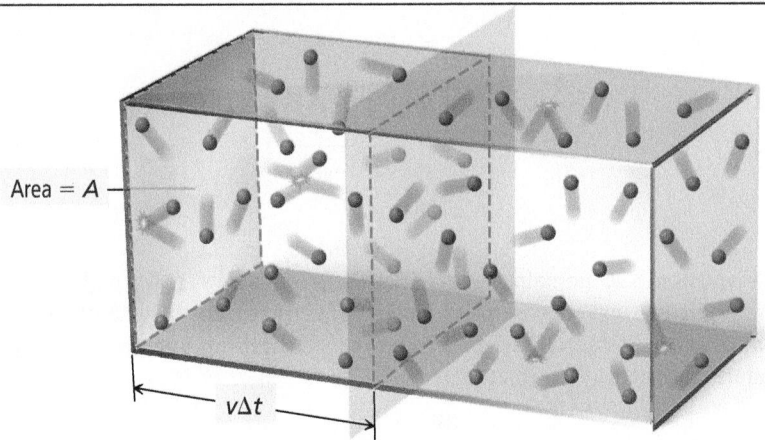

◀ **FIGURE 5.17 The Pressure on the Wall of a Container** The pressure on the wall of a container can be calculated by determining the total force due to collisions of the particles with the wall.

The pressure on a wall of a container (Figure 5.17 ▲) occupied by particles in constant motion is the total force on the wall (due to the collisions) divided by the area of the wall.

$$P = \frac{F_{total}}{A} \qquad [5.13]$$

From Newton's second law, the force (F) associated with an individual collision is given by $F = ma$, where m is the mass of the particle and a is its acceleration as it changes its direction of travel due to the collision. The acceleration for each collision is the change in velocity (Δv) divided by the time interval (Δt), so the force imparted for each collision is:

$$F_{collision} = m\frac{\Delta v}{\Delta t} \qquad [5.14]$$

If a particle collides elastically with the wall, it bounces off the wall with no loss of energy. For a straight-line collision, the change in velocity is $2v$ (the particle's velocity was v before the collision and $-v$ after the collision; therefore, the change is $2v$). The force per collision is given by:

$$F_{collision} = m\frac{2v}{\Delta t} \qquad [5.15]$$

The total number of collisions in the time interval Δt on a wall of surface area A is proportional to the number of particles that can reach the wall in this time interval—in other words, all particles within a distance of $v\Delta t$ of the wall. These particles occupy a volume given by $v\,\Delta t \times A$, and their total number is equal to this volume multiplied by the density of particles in the container (n/V):

$$\text{Number of collisions} \propto \text{number of particles within } v\,\Delta t$$

$$\propto \underset{\text{Volume}}{\underbrace{v\,\Delta t \times A}} \times \underset{\substack{\text{Density of}\\\text{particles}}}{\underbrace{\frac{n}{V}}} \qquad [5.16]$$

The *total force* on the wall is equal to the force per collision multiplied by the number of collisions:

$$F_{total} = F_{collision} \times \text{number of collisions}$$

$$\propto m\frac{2v}{\Delta t} \times v\,\Delta t \times A \times \frac{n}{V} \qquad [5.17]$$

$$\propto mv^2 \times A \times \frac{n}{V}$$

The pressure on the wall is equal to the total force divided by the surface area of the wall:

$$P = \frac{F_{\text{total}}}{A}$$

$$\propto \frac{mv^2 \times \cancel{A} \times \frac{n}{V}}{\cancel{A}}$$

$$P \propto mv^2 \times \frac{n}{V} \qquad [5.18]$$

Notice that Equation 5.18 contains within it Boyle's law ($P \propto 1/V$) and Avogadro's law ($V \propto n$). We can get the complete ideal gas law from postulate 2 of the kinetic molecular theory, which states that the average kinetic energy ($\frac{1}{2}mv^2$) is proportional to the temperature in kelvins (T):

$$mv^2 \propto T \qquad [5.19]$$

By combining Equations 5.18 and 5.19, we get:

$$P \propto \frac{T \times n}{V}$$

$$PV \propto nT \qquad [5.20]$$

The proportionality can be replaced by an equals sign if we provide the correct constant, R:

$$PV = nRT \qquad [5.21]$$

In other words, the kinetic molecular theory (a model for how gases behave) predicts behavior that is consistent with our observations and measurements of gases—the theory agrees with the experiment. Recall from Chapter 1 that a scientific theory is the most powerful kind of scientific knowledge. In the kinetic molecular theory, we have a model for what a gas is like. Although the model is not perfect—indeed, it breaks down under certain conditions, as we shall see later in this chapter—it predicts a great deal about the behavior of gases. Therefore, the model is a good approximation of what a gas is actually like. A careful examination of the conditions under which the model breaks down (see Section 5.10) gives us even more insight into the behavior of gases.

Temperature and Molecular Velocities

According to kinetic molecular theory, particles of different masses have the same average kinetic energy at a given temperature. The kinetic energy of a particle depends on its mass and velocity according to the equation:

$$KE = \frac{1}{2}mv^2$$

The only way for particles of different masses to have the same kinetic energy is for them to have different velocities as we saw in Conceptual Connection 5.6.

In a gas mixture at a given temperature, lighter particles travel faster (on average) than heavier ones.

In kinetic molecular theory, we define the root mean square velocity (u_{rms}) of a particle as:

$$u_{\text{rms}} = \sqrt{\overline{u^2}} \qquad [5.22]$$

where $\overline{u^2}$ is the average of the squares of the particle velocities. Even though the root mean square velocity of a collection of particles is not identical to the average velocity, the two are close in value and conceptually similar. Root mean square velocity is a special *type* of average. The average kinetic energy of one mole of gas particles is given by the equation:

$$KE_{\text{avg}} = \frac{1}{2}N_A m \overline{u^2} \qquad [5.23]$$

where N_A is Avogadro's number.

Postulate 2 of the kinetic molecular theory states that the average kinetic energy is proportional to the temperature in kelvins. The constant of proportionality in this relationship is $(3/2)R$:

$$\text{KE}_{avg} = (3/2)RT \qquad [5.24]$$

where R is the gas constant, but in different units ($R = 8.314$ J/mol · K) than those we use in the ideal gas law. If we combine Equations 5.23 and 5.24, and solve for $\overline{u^2}$, we get:

$$(1/2)\,N_A m\overline{u^2} = (3/2)RT$$

$$\overline{u^2} = \frac{(3/2)RT}{(1/2)N_A m} = \frac{3RT}{N_A m}$$

> The $(3/2)R$ proportionality constant comes from a derivation that is beyond the current scope of this textbook.

Taking the square root of both sides we get:

$$\sqrt{\overline{u^2}} = u_{rms} = \sqrt{\frac{3RT}{N_A m}} \qquad [5.25]$$

> The joule (J) is a unit of energy that we will discuss in more detail in Section 6.2.
> $$\left(1\text{ J} = 1\text{ kg}\,\frac{\text{m}^2}{\text{s}^2}\right)$$

In Equation 5.25, m is the mass of a particle in kg and N_A is Avogadro's number. The product $N_A m$, then, is the molar mass in kg/mol. If we call this quantity $\mathcal{M}$, then the expression for mean square velocity as a function of temperature becomes the following important result:

$$u_{rms} = \sqrt{\frac{3RT}{\mathcal{M}}} \qquad [5.26]$$

The root mean square velocity of a collection of gas particles is proportional to the square root of the temperature in kelvins and inversely proportional to the square root of the molar mass of the particles (which because of the units of R must be in kilograms per mole). The root mean square velocity of nitrogen molecules at 25 °C, for example, is 515 m/s (1152 mi hr). The root mean square velocity of hydrogen molecules at room temperature is 1920 m/s (4295 mi/hr). Notice that the lighter molecules move much faster at a given temperature.

The root mean square velocity, as we have seen, is a kind of average velocity. Some particles are moving faster and some are moving slower than this average. The velocities of all the particles in a gas sample form distributions like those shown in Figure 5.18 ▼. We can see from these distributions that some particles are indeed traveling at the root mean square velocity. However, many particles are traveling faster and many slower than the root mean square velocity. For lighter particles, such as helium and hydrogen, the velocity distribution is shifted toward higher velocities and the curve becomes broader, indicating a wider range of velocities. The velocity distribution for nitrogen at different temperatures is shown in Figure 5.19 ►. As the temperature increases, the root mean square velocity increases and the distribution becomes broader.

> ▼ **FIGURE 5.19 Velocity Distribution for Nitrogen at Several Temperatures** As the temperature of a gas sample increases, the velocity distribution of the molecules shifts toward higher velocity and becomes less sharply peaked.

Variation of Velocity Distribution with Temperature

Variation of Velocity Distribution with Molar Mass

▲ **FIGURE 5.18 Velocity Distribution for Several Gases at 25 °C**   At a given temperature, there is a distribution of velocities among the particles in a sample of gas. The exact shape and peak of the distribution varies with the molar mass of the gas.

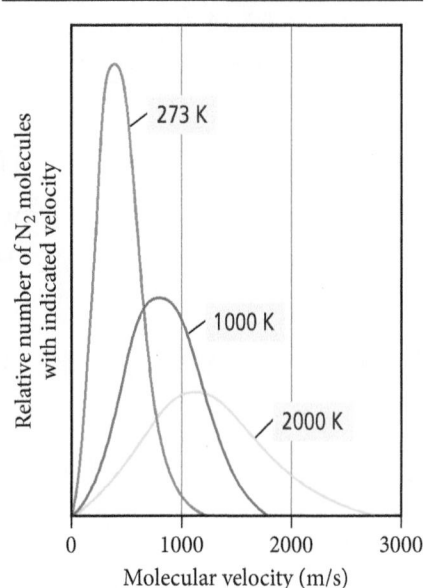

EXAMPLE 5.14   Root Mean Square Velocity

Calculate the root mean square velocity of oxygen molecules at 25 °C.

SORT You are given the kind of molecule and the temperature and asked to find the root mean square velocity.	**GIVEN:** $O_2, t = 25$ °C **FIND:** u_{rms}
STRATEGIZE The conceptual plan for this problem shows how you can use the molar mass of oxygen and the temperature (in kelvins) with the equation that defines the root mean square velocity to calculate root mean square velocity.	**CONCEPTUAL PLAN** **RELATIONSHIP USED** $$u_{rms} = \sqrt{\frac{3RT}{M}}$$ $u_{rms} = \sqrt{\frac{3RT}{M}}$ (Equation 5.26)
SOLVE First gather the required quantities in the correct units. Note that molar mass must be in kg/mol. Substitute the quantities into the equation to calculate root mean square velocity. Note that $1 \text{ J} = 1 \text{ kg} \cdot \text{m}^2/\text{s}^2$.	**SOLUTION** $T = 25 + 273 = 298$ K $$M = \frac{32.00 \text{ g } O_2}{1 \text{ mol } O_2} \times \frac{1 \text{ kg}}{1000 \text{ g}} = \frac{32.00 \times 10^{-3} \text{ kg } O_2}{1 \text{ mol } O_2}$$ $$u_{rms} = \sqrt{\frac{3RT}{M}}$$ $$= \sqrt{\frac{3\left(8.314 \dfrac{J}{mol \cdot K}\right)(298 \text{ K})}{\dfrac{32.00 \times 10^{-3} \text{ kg } O_2}{1 \text{ mol } O_2}}}$$ $$= \sqrt{2.32 \times 10^5 \frac{J}{kg}}$$ $$= \sqrt{2.32 \times 10^5 \frac{\dfrac{kg \cdot m^2}{s^2}}{kg}} = 482 \text{ m/s}$$

CHECK The units of the answer (m/s) are correct. The magnitude of the answer seems reasonable because oxygen is slightly heavier than nitrogen and should therefore have a slightly lower root mean square velocity at the same temperature. Recall that earlier we stated that the root mean square velocity of nitrogen is 515 m/s at 25 °C.

FOR PRACTICE 5.14

Calculate the root mean square velocity of gaseous xenon atoms at 25 °C.

Conceptual Connection 5.7   **Kinetic Molecular Theory II**

Which sample of an ideal gas has the greatest pressure? Assume that the mass of each particle is proportional to its size and that all the gas samples are at the same temperature.

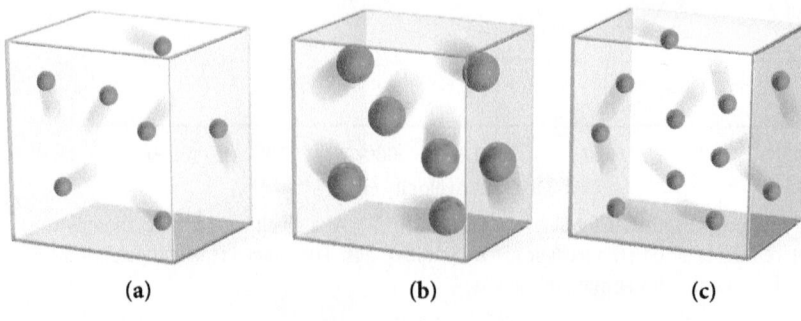

              (a)   (b)   (c)

5.9 Mean Free Path, Diffusion, and Effusion of Gases

We have just seen that the root mean square velocity of gas molecules at room temperature is in the range of hundreds of meters per second. However, suppose that your roommate just put on too much perfume in the bathroom only 2 m away. Why does it take a minute or two before you can smell the fragrance? Although most molecules in a perfume bottle have higher molar masses than nitrogen, their velocities are still hundreds of meters per second, so why the delay? The answer is that even though gaseous particles travel at tremendous speeds, they also travel in haphazard paths (Figure 5.20 ▶). To a perfume molecule, the path from the perfume bottle in the bathroom to your nose 2 m away is much like a bargain hunter's path through a busy shopping mall during a clearance sale. The molecule travels only a short distance before it collides with another molecule and changes direction, only to collide again, and so on. In fact, at room temperature and atmospheric pressure, a molecule in the air experiences several billion collisions per second. The average distance that a molecule travels between collisions is its **mean free path**. At room temperature and atmospheric pressure, the mean free path of a nitrogen molecule with a molecular diameter of 300 pm (four times the covalent radius) is 93 nm, or about 310 molecular diameters. If the nitrogen molecule were the size of a golf ball, it would travel about 40 ft between collisions. Mean free path increases with *decreasing* pressure. Under conditions of ultrahigh vacuum (10^{-10} torr), the mean free path of a nitrogen molecule is hundreds of kilometers.

The process by which gas molecules spread out in response to a concentration gradient is **diffusion**, and even though the particles undergo many collisions, the root mean square velocity still influences the rate of diffusion. Heavier molecules diffuse more slowly than lighter ones, so the first molecules you smell from a perfume mixture (in a room with no air currents) are the lighter ones.

A process related to diffusion is **effusion**, the process by which a gas escapes from a container into a vacuum through a small hole (Figure 5.21 ▼). The rate of effusion is also related to root mean square velocity—heavier molecules effuse more slowly than lighter ones. The rate of effusion—the amount of gas that effuses in a given time—is inversely proportional to the square root of the molar mass of the gas as follows:

$$\text{rate} \propto \frac{1}{\sqrt{\mathcal{M}}}$$

The ratio of effusion rates of two different gases is given by **Graham's law of effusion**, named after Thomas Graham (1805–1869):

$$\frac{\text{rate}_A}{\text{rate}_B} = \sqrt{\frac{\mathcal{M}_B}{\mathcal{M}_A}} \qquad [5.27]$$

In this expression, rate_A and rate_B are the effusion rates of gases A and B, and $\mathcal{M}_A$ and $\mathcal{M}_B$ are their molar masses.

Graham's law explains, in part, why helium balloons only float for a day or so. Since helium has such a low molar mass, it escapes from the balloon quite quickly. A balloon filled with air, by contrast, remains inflated longer.

Typical Gas Molecule Path

The average distance between collisions is the mean free path.

▲ FIGURE 5.20 **Mean Free Path** A molecule in a volume of gas follows a haphazard path, involving many collisions with other molecules.

In a ventilated room, air currents also enhance the transport of gas molecules.

▼ FIGURE 5.21 **Effusion** Effusion is the escape of a gas from a container into a vacuum through a small hole.

Effusion

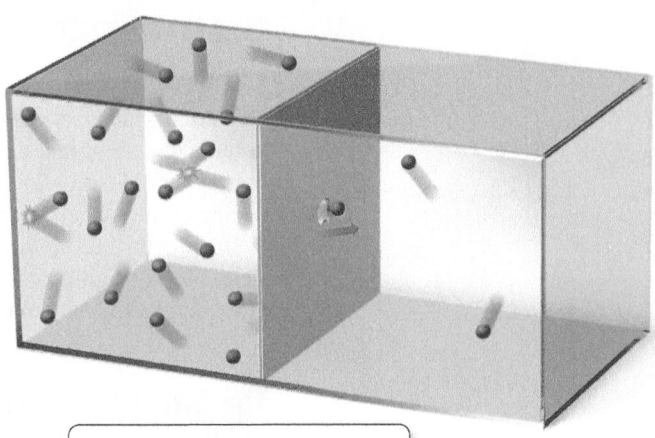

Gas escapes from container into a vacuum through a small hole

---

EXAMPLE 5.15 Graham's Law of Effusion

An unknown gas effuses at a rate that is 0.462 times that of nitrogen gas (at the same temperature). Calculate the molar mass of the unknown gas in g/mol.

SORT You are given the ratio of effusion rates for the unknown gas and nitrogen and asked to find the molar mass of the unknown gas.	**GIVEN:** $\dfrac{\text{Rate}_{unk}}{\text{Rate}_{N_2}} = 0.462$ **FIND:** $\mathcal{M}_{unk}$
STRATEGIZE The conceptual plan uses Graham's law of effusion. You are given the ratio of rates and you know the molar mass of the nitrogen. You can use Graham's law to determine the molar mass of the unknown gas.	**CONCEPTUAL PLAN** 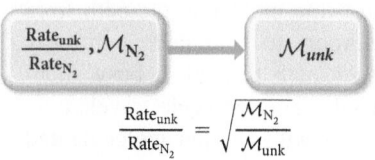 $\dfrac{\text{Rate}_{unk}}{\text{Rate}_{N_2}} = \sqrt{\dfrac{\mathcal{M}_{N_2}}{\mathcal{M}_{unk}}}$ **RELATIONSHIPS USED** $\dfrac{\text{rate}_A}{\text{rate}_B} = \sqrt{\dfrac{\mathcal{M}_B}{\mathcal{M}_A}}$ (Graham's law)
SOLVE Solve the equation for $\mathcal{M}_{unk}$ and substitute the correct values and calculate.	**SOLUTION** $\dfrac{\text{rate}_{unk}}{\text{rate}_{N_2}} = \sqrt{\dfrac{\mathcal{M}_{N_2}}{\mathcal{M}_{unk}}}$ $\mathcal{M}_{unk} = \dfrac{\mathcal{M}_{N_2}}{\left(\dfrac{\text{rate}_{unk}}{\text{rate}_{N_2}}\right)^2}$ $= \dfrac{28.02 \text{ g/mol}}{(0.462)^2}$ $= 131 \text{ g/mol}$

CHECK The units of the answer are correct. The magnitude of the answer seems reasonable for the molar mass of a gas. In fact, from the answer you can even conclude that the gas is probably xenon, which has a molar mass of 131.29 g/mol.

FOR PRACTICE 5.15

Find the ratio of effusion rates of hydrogen gas and krypton gas.

5.10 Real Gases: The Effects of Size and Intermolecular Forces

One mole of an ideal gas has a volume of 22.41 L at STP. Figure 5.22 ▶ shows the molar volume of several real gases at STP. As you can see, most of these gases have a volume that is very close to 22.41 L, meaning that they act very nearly as ideal gases. Gases behave ideally when both of the following are true: (a) the volume of the gas particles is small compared to the space between them, and (b) the forces between the gas particles are not significant. At STP, these assumptions are valid for most common gases. However, these assumptions break down at higher pressures or lower temperatures.

The Effect of the Finite Volume of Gas Particles

The finite volume of gas particles—that is, their actual *size*—becomes important at high pressure because the volume of the particles themselves occupies a significant portion of the total gas volume (Figure 5.23 ▶). We can see the effect of particle volume by

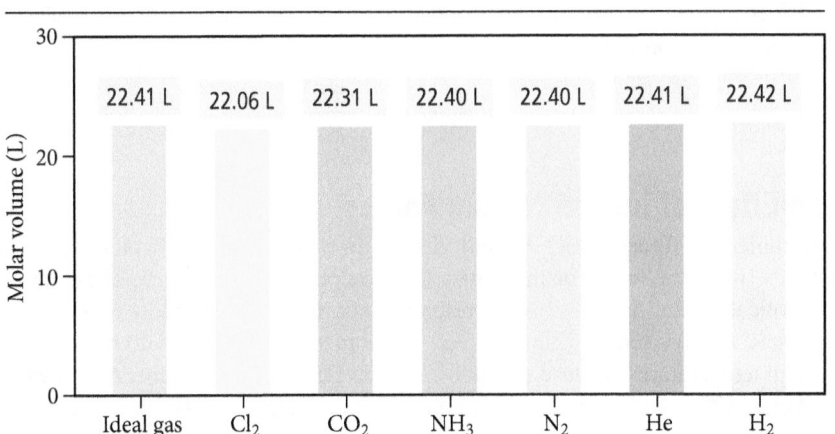

Molar Volume

◀ **FIGURE 5.22 Molar Volumes of Real Gases**   The molar volumes of several gases at STP are all close to 22.414 L, indicating that their departures from ideal behavior are small.

comparing the molar volume of argon to the molar volume of an ideal gas as a function of pressure at 500 K as shown in Figure 5.24 ▼. At low pressures, the molar volume of argon is nearly identical to that of an ideal gas. But as the pressure increases, the molar volume of argon becomes *greater than* that of an ideal gas. At the higher pressures, the argon atoms themselves occupy a significant portion of the gas volume, making the actual volume greater than that predicted by the ideal gas law.

In 1873, Johannes van der Waals (1837–1923) modified the ideal gas equation to fit the behavior of real gases. From the graph for argon in Figure 5.24 we can see that the ideal gas law predicts a volume that is too small. Van der Waals suggested a small correction factor that accounts for the volume of the gas particles themselves:

▲ **FIGURE 5.23 Particle Volume and Ideal Behavior**   As a gas is compressed the gas particles themselves begin to occupy a significant portion of the total gas volume, leading to deviations from ideal behavior.

Ideal behavior
$$V = \frac{nRT}{P}$$

Corrected for volume of gas particles $V = \dfrac{nRT}{P} + nb$ [5.28]

Nonideal Behavior: The effect of particle volume

◀ **FIGURE 5.24 The Effect of Particle Volume**   At high pressures, 1 mol of argon occupies a larger volume than 1 mol of an ideal gas because of the volume of the argon atoms themselves. (This example was chosen to minimize the effects of intermolecular forces, which are very small in argon at 500 K, thereby isolating the effect of particle volume.)

TABLE 5.5 Van der Waals Constants for Common Gases

Gas	$a\,(L^2 \cdot atm/mol^2)$	$b\,(L/mol)$
He	0.0342	0.02370
Ne	0.211	0.0171
Ar	1.35	0.0322
Kr	2.32	0.0398
Xe	4.19	0.0511
H_2	0.244	0.0266
N_2	1.39	0.0391
O_2	1.36	0.0318
Cl_2	6.49	0.0562
H_2O	5.46	0.0305
CH_4	2.25	0.0428
CO_2	3.59	0.0427
CCl_4	20.4	0.1383

The correction adds the quantity nb to the volume, where n is the number of moles and b is a constant that depends on the gas (see Table 5.5). We can rearrange the corrected equation as follows:

$$(V - nb) = \frac{nRT}{P} \qquad [5.29]$$

The Effect of Intermolecular Forces

Intermolecular forces, which we will discuss in more detail in Chapter 11, are attractions between the atoms or molecules that compose any substance. These attractions are typically small in gases and therefore do not matter much at low pressure because the molecules are too far apart to "feel" the attractions. They also do not matter much at high temperatures because the molecules have a lot of kinetic energy and when two particles with high kinetic energies collide, a weak attraction between them does not affect the collision much. At lower temperatures, however, the collisions occur with less kinetic energy, and weak attractions can affect the collisions. We can understand this difference with an analogy to billiard balls. Imagine two billiard balls that are coated with a substance that makes them slightly sticky. If they collide when moving at high velocities, the stickiness will not have much of an effect—the balls bounce off one another as if the sticky substance was not even there. However, if the two billiard balls collide when moving very slowly (say barely rolling) the sticky substance would have an effect—the billiard balls might even stick together and not bounce off one another.

The effect of these weak attractions between particles is a decrease in the number of collisions with the surfaces of the container and a corresponding decrease in the pressure compared to that of an ideal gas. We can see the effect of intermolecular forces when we compare the pressure of 1.0 mol of xenon gas to the pressure of 1.0 mol of an ideal gas as a function of temperature and at a fixed volume of 1.0 L, as shown in Figure 5.25 ▼. At high temperature, the pressure of the xenon gas is nearly identical to that of an ideal gas. But at lower temperatures, the pressure of xenon is *less than* that of an ideal gas. At the lower temperatures, the xenon atoms spend more time interacting with each other and less time colliding with the walls, making the actual pressure less than that predicted by the ideal gas law.

From the graph for xenon shown in Figure 5.25 we can see that the ideal gas law predicts a pressure that is too large at low temperatures. Van der Waals suggested a small correction factor that accounts for the intermolecular forces between gas particles:

Ideal behavior $$P = \frac{nRT}{V}$$

Corrected for intermolecular forces $$P = \frac{nRT}{V} - a\left(\frac{n}{V}\right)^2 \qquad [5.30]$$

◀ **FIGURE 5.25 The Effect of Intermolecular Forces** At low temperatures, the pressure of xenon is less than an ideal gas exerts because interactions among xenon molecules reduce the number of collisions with the walls of the container.

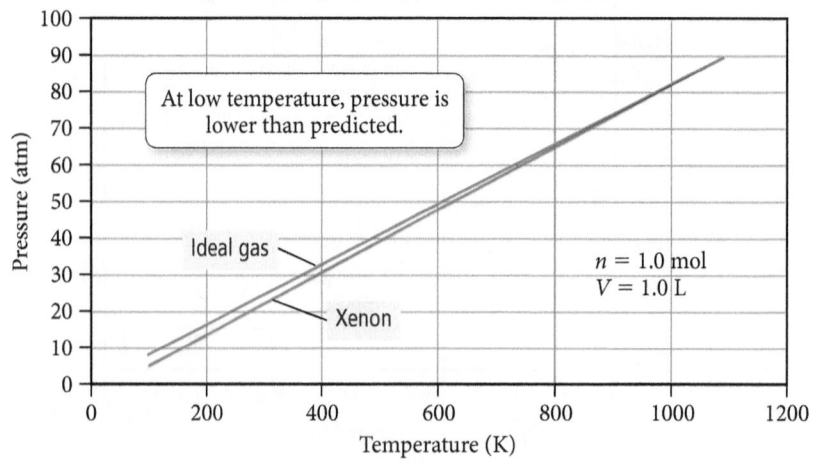

Nonideal Behavior: The effect of intermolecular forces

At low temperature, pressure is lower than predicted.

Ideal gas

Xenon

$n = 1.0$ mol
$V = 1.0$ L

The correction subtracts the quantity $a(n/V)^2$ from the pressure, where n is the number of moles, V is the volume, and a is a constant that depends on the gas (see Table 5.5). Notice that the correction factor increases as n/V (the number of moles of particles per unit volume) increases because a greater concentration of particles makes it more likely that they will interact with one another. We can rearrange the corrected equation as:

$$P + a\left(\frac{n}{V}\right)^2 = \frac{nRT}{V} \qquad [5.31]$$

Van der Waals Equation

We can now combine the effects of particle volume (Equation 5.29) and particle intermolecular forces (Equation 5.31) into one equation that describes nonideal gas behavior:

$$[P + a(\tfrac{n}{V})^2] \times [V - nb] = nRT$$

Correction for intermolecular forces   Correction for particle volume

This equation is called the **van der Waals equation** and can be used to calculate the properties of a gas under nonideal conditions.

Real Gases

We can see the combined effects of particle volume and intermolecular forces by examining a plot of PV/RT versus P for 1 mol of a number of real gases (Figure 5.26 ▼). For an ideal gas, $PV/RT = n$, the number of moles of gas. Therefore, for 1 mol of an ideal gas, PV/RT is equal to 1, as shown in the plot. For real gases, PV/RT deviates from 1, but the deviations are not uniform. For example, water displays a large negative deviation from PV/RT because, for water, the effect of intermolecular forces on lowering the pressure (relative to an ideal gas) is far greater than the effect of particle size on increasing the volume. Notice from Table 5.5 that water has a high value of a, the

The Behavior of Real Gases

▲ **FIGURE 5.26 Real versus Ideal Behavior** For 1 mol of an ideal gas, PV/RT is equal to 1. The combined effects of the volume of gas particles and the interactions among them cause each real gas to deviate from ideal behavior in a slightly different way. These curves were calculated at a temperature of 500 K.

constant that corrects for intermolecular forces, but a moderate value of b, the constant that corrects for particle size. Therefore PV/RT is lower than predicted from the ideal gas law for water.

By contrast, consider the behavior of helium, which displays a positive deviation from the ideal behavior. This is because helium has very weak intermolecular forces and their effect on lowering the pressure (relative to ideal gas) is small compared to the effect of particle size on increasing the volume. Therefore PV/RT is greater than predicted from the ideal gas law for helium.

Conceptual Connection 5.8 Real Gases

The graph below shows PV/RT for carbon dioxide at three different temperatures. Rank the curves in order of increasing temperature.

CHAPTER IN REVIEW

Self Assessment Quiz

Q1. A gas sample has an initial pressure of 547 mmHg and an initial volume of 0.500 L. What is the pressure (in atm) when the volume of the sample is decreased to 225 mL? (Assume constant temperature and constant number of moles of gas.)
a) 1.60×10^{-3} atm   b) 1.60 atm
c) 0.324 atm   d) 1.22 atm

Q2. A gas sample has a volume of 178 mL at 0.00 °C. The temperature is raised (at constant pressure) until the volume reaches 211 mL. What is the temperature of the gas sample in °C at this volume?
a) 0.00 °C   b) 324 °C
c) −43 °C   d) 51 °C

Q3. What is the pressure of 1.78 g of nitrogen gas confined to a volume of 0.118 L at 25 °C?
a) 13.2 atm   b) 369 atm
c) 1.10 atm   d) 26.3 atm

Q4. What is the density of a sample of argon gas at 55 °C and 765 mmHg?
a) 2.99 g/L   b) 1.13×10^3 g/L
c) 1.49 g/L   d) 8.91 g/L

Q5. Which gas sample has the greatest volume at STP?
a) 10.0 g Ar
b) 10.0 g Kr
c) 10.0 g Xe
d) None of the above (They all have the same volume.)

Q6. A 1.25 g gas sample occupies 663 mL at 25 °C and 1.00 atm. What is the molar mass of the gas?
a) 0.258 g/mol   b) 0.0461 g/mol
c) 3.87 g/mol   d) 46.1 g/mol

Q7. A 255 mL gas sample contains argon and nitrogen at a temperature of 65 °C. The total pressure of the sample is 725 mmHg and the partial pressure of argon is 231 mmHg. What mass of nitrogen is present in the sample?
a) 0.324 g nitrogen   b) 0.167 g nitrogen
c) 0.0837 g nitrogen   d) 0.870 g nitrogen

Q8. A gas mixture in a 1.55 L at 298 K container contains 10.0 g of Ne and 10.0 g of Ar. Calculate the partial pressure (in atm) of Ne and Ar in the container.
a) $P_{Ne} = 10.5$ atm, $P_{Ar} = 5.29$ atm
b) $P_{Ne} = 5.83$ atm, $P_{Ar} = 2.95$ atm
c) $P_{Ne} = 5.88$ atm, $P_{Ar} = 5.88$ atm
d) $P_{Ne} = 7.82$ atm, $P_{Ar} = 3.95$ atm

Q9. A gas sample at STP contains 1.15 g oxygen and 1.55 g nitrogen. What is the volume of the gas sample?
a) 1.26 L   b) 2.04 L
c) 4.08 L   d) 61.0 L

Q10. Aluminum reacts with chlorine gas to form aluminum chloride.

$$2\,Al(s)\ +\ 3\,Cl_2(g) \rightarrow 2\,AlCl_3(s)$$

What minimum volume of chlorine gas (at 298 K and 225 mmHg) is required to completely react with 7.85 g of aluminum?

a) 36.0 L   b) 24.0 L
c) 0.0474 L   d) 16.0 L

Q11. Calculate the root mean square velocity of $I_2(g)$ at 373 K.

a) 19.0 m/s   b) 191 m/s
c) 6.05 m/s   d) 99.1 m/s

Q12. Which gas has the greatest kinetic energy at STP?

a) He
b) Ne
c) Ar
d) None of the above (All have the same kinetic energy.)

Q13. A sample of Xe takes 75 seconds to effuse out of a container. An unknown gas takes 37 seconds to effuse out of the identical container under identical conditions. What is the most likely identity of the unknown gas?

a) He   b) O_2 c) Br_2 d) Kr

Q14. Consider the generic reaction: $2\,A(g) + B(g) \rightarrow 2\,C(g)$. If a flask initially contains 1.0 atm of A and 1.0 atm of B, what will be the pressure in the flask if the reaction proceeds to completion? (Assume constant volume and temperature.)

a) 1.0 atm   b) 1.5 atm
c) 2.0 atm   d) 3.0 atm

Q15. Rank the gases Ar, N_2, CH_4, and C_2H_6 in order of increasing density at STP.

a) $CH_4 < C_2H_6 < N_2 < Ar$
b) $CH_4 < N_2 < Ar < C_2H_6$
c) $Ar < C_2H_6 < N_2 < CH_4$
d) $CH_4 < N_2 < C_2H_6 < Ar$

Answers: 1. (b) 2. (d) 3. (a) 4. (c) 5. (a) 6. (d) 7. (b) 8. (d) 9. (b) 10. (a) 11. (b) 12. (d) 13. (b) 14. (b) 15. (d)

Key Terms

Section 5.1
pressure (195)

Section 5.2
millimeter of mercury (mmHg) (197)
barometer (197)
torr (197)
atmosphere (atm) (197)
pascal (Pa) (197)
manometer (198)

Section 5.3
Boyle's law (200)

Charles's law (203)
Avogadro's law (205)

Section 5.4
ideal gas law (207)
ideal gas (207)
ideal gas constant (207)

Section 5.5
molar volume (209)
standard temperature and pressure (STP) (209)

Section 5.6
partial pressure (213)
Dalton's law of partial pressures (213)
mole fraction (χ_a) (213)
hypoxia (215)
oxygen toxicity (215)
nitrogen narcosis (215)
vapor pressure (218)

Section 5.8
kinetic molecular theory (222)

Section 5.9
mean free path (229)
diffusion (229)
effusion (229)
Graham's law of effusion (229)

Section 5.10
van der Waals equation (233)

Key Concepts

Pressure (5.1, 5.2)

▶ Gas pressure is the force per unit area that results from gas particles colliding with the surfaces around them. Pressure is measured in a number of units including mmHg, torr, Pa, psi, in Hg, and atm.

The Simple Gas Laws (5.3)

▶ The simple gas laws express relationships between pairs of variables when other variables are held constant.
▶ Boyle's law states that the volume of a gas is inversely proportional to its pressure.
▶ Charles's law states that the volume of a gas is directly proportional to its temperature.
▶ Avogadro's law states that the volume of a gas is directly proportional to the amount (in moles).

The Ideal Gas Law and Its Applications (5.4, 5.5)

▶ The ideal gas law, $PV = nRT$, gives the relationship among all four gas variables and contains the simple gas laws within it.

▶ We can use the ideal gas law to find one of the four variables given the other three. We can use it to calculate the molar volume of an ideal gas, which is 22.4 L at STP, and to calculate the density and molar mass of a gas.

Mixtures of Gases and Partial Pressures (5.6)

▶ In a mixture of gases, each gas acts independently of the others so that any overall property of the mixture is the sum of the properties of the individual components.
▶ The pressure of any individual component is its partial pressure.

Gas Stoichiometry (5.7)

▶ In reactions involving gaseous reactants and products, we often report quantities in volumes at specified pressures and temperatures. We can convert these quantities to amounts (in moles) using the ideal gas law. Then we can use the stoichiometric coefficients from the balanced equation to determine the stoichiometric amounts of other reactants or products.

▶ The general form for these types of calculations is often: volume A → amount A (in moles) → amount B (in moles) → quantity of B (in desired units).

▶ In cases where the reaction is carried out at STP, we can use the molar volume at STP ($22.4 \, \text{L} = 1 \, \text{mol}$) to convert between volume in liters and amount in moles.

Kinetic Molecular Theory and Its Applications (5.8, 5.9)

▶ Kinetic molecular theory is a quantitative model for gases. The theory has three main assumptions: (1) the gas particles are negligibly small, (2) the average kinetic energy of a gas particle is proportional to the temperature in kelvins, and (3) the collision of one gas particle with another is completely elastic (the particles do not stick together). The gas laws all follow from the kinetic molecular theory.

▶ We can use kinetic molecular theory to derive the expression for the root mean square velocity of gas particles. This velocity is inversely proportional to the molar mass of the gas, and therefore—at a given temperature—smaller gas particles are (on average) moving more quickly than larger ones.

▶ The kinetic molecular theory also allows us to predict the mean free path of a gas particle (the distance it travels between collisions) and relative rates of diffusion or effusion.

Real Gases (5.10)

▶ Real gases differ from ideal gases to the extent that they do not always fit the assumptions of kinetic molecular theory.

▶ These assumptions tend to break down at high pressures where the volume is higher than predicted for an ideal gas because the particles are no longer negligibly small compared to the space between them.

▶ The assumptions also break down at low temperatures where the pressure is lower than predicted because the attraction between molecules combined with low kinetic energies causes partially inelastic collisions.

▶ The Van der Waals equation predicts gas properties under nonideal conditions.

Key Equations and Relationships

Relationship between Pressure (P), Force (F), and Area (A) (5.2)

$$P = \frac{F}{A}$$

Boyle's Law: Relationship between Pressure (P) and Volume (V) (5.3)

$$V \propto \frac{1}{P}$$

$$P_1 V_1 = P_2 V_2$$

Charles's Law: Relationship between Volume (V) and Temperature (T) (5.3)

$$V \propto T \quad (\text{in K})$$

$$\frac{V_1}{T_1} = \frac{V_2}{T_2}$$

Avogadro's Law: Relationship between Volume (V) and Amount in Moles (n) (5.3)

$$V \propto n$$

$$\frac{V_1}{n_1} = \frac{V_2}{n_2}$$

Ideal Gas Law: Relationship between Volume (V), Pressure (P), Temperature (T), and Amount (n) (5.4)

$$PV = nRT$$

Dalton's Law: Relationship between Partial Pressures P_n in Mixture of Gases and Total Pressure (P_{total}) (5.6)

$$P_{\text{total}} = P_a + P_b + P_c + \ldots$$

$$P_a = \frac{n_a RT}{V} \quad P_b = \frac{n_b RT}{V} \quad P_c = \frac{n_c RT}{V}$$

Mole Fraction (χ_a) (5.6)

$$\chi_a = \frac{n_a}{n_{\text{total}}}$$

$$P_a = \chi_a P_{\text{total}}$$

Average Kinetic Energy (KE_{avg}) (5.8)

$$KE_{\text{avg}} = \frac{3}{2}RT$$

Relationship between Root Mean Square Velocity (u_{rms}) and Temperature (T) (5.8)

$$u_{\text{rms}} = \sqrt{\frac{3RT}{M}}$$

Relationship of Effusion Rates of Two Different Gases (5.9)

$$\frac{\text{rate A}}{\text{rate B}} = \sqrt{\frac{M_B}{M_A}}$$

Van der Waals Equation: The Effects of Volume and Intermolecular Forces on Nonideal Gas Behavior (5.10)

$$\left[P + a\left(\frac{n}{V}\right)^2 \right] \times (V - nb) = nRT$$

Key Learning Outcomes

Chapter Objectives	Assessment
Converting between Pressure Units (5.2)	Example 5.1 For Practice 5.1 For More Practice 5.1 Exercises 25–28
Relating Volume and Pressure: Boyle's Law (5.3)	Example 5.2 For Practice 5.2 Exercises 31, 32
Relating Volume and Temperature: Charles's Law (5.3)	Example 5.3 For Practice 5.3 Exercises 33, 34
Relating Volume and Moles: Avogadro's Law (5.3)	Example 5.4 For Practice 5.4 Exercises 35, 36
Determining P, V, n, or T using the Ideal Gas Law (5.4)	Examples 5.5, 5.6 For Practice 5.5, 5.6 For More Practice 5.6 Exercises 37–46, 51, 52
Relating the Density of a Gas to Its Molar Mass (5.5)	Example 5.7 For Practice 5.7 For More Practice 5.7 Exercises 55, 56
Calculating the Molar Mass of a Gas with the Ideal Gas Law (5.5)	Example 5.8 For Practice 5.8 Exercises 57–60
Calculating Total Pressure, Partial Pressures, and Mole Fractions of Gases in a Mixture (5.6)	Examples 5.9, 5.10, 5.11 For Practice 5.9, 5.10, 5.11 Exercises 61, 62, 65, 67, 68, 70
Relating the Amounts of Reactants and Products in Gaseous Reactions: Stoichiometry (5.7)	Examples 5.12, 5.13 For Practice 5.12, 5.13 For More Practice 5.12 Exercises 71–77
Calculating the Root Mean Square Velocity of a Gas (5.8)	Example 5.14 For Practice 5.14 Exercises 83, 84
Calculating the Effusion Rate or the Ratio of Effusion Rates of Two Gases (5.9)	Example 5.15 For Practice 5.15 Exercises 85–88

EXERCISES

Review Questions

1. What is pressure? What causes pressure?
2. Explain what happens when you inhale. What forces air into your lungs?
3. Explain what happens when you exhale. What forces air out of your lungs?
4. What are the common units of pressure? List them in order of smallest to largest unit.
5. What is a manometer? How does it measure the pressure of a sample of gas?
6. Summarize each of the simple gas laws (Boyle's law, Charles's law, and Avogadro's law). For each law, explain the relationship between the two variables and also state which variables must be kept constant.
7. Explain the source of ear pain experienced due to a rapid change in altitude.
8. Explain why scuba divers should never hold their breath as they ascend to the surface.
9. Why is it impossible to breathe air through an extra-long snorkel (greater than a couple of meters) while swimming under water?
10. Explain why hot air balloons float above the ground and why the second story of a two-story home is often warmer than the ground story.
11. What is the ideal gas law? Why is it useful?
12. Explain how the ideal gas law contains within it the simple gas laws (show an example).
13. Define molar volume and give its value for a gas at STP.

14. How does the density of a gas depend on temperature? Pressure? How does it depend on the molar mass of the gas?
15. What is partial pressure? What is the relationship between the partial pressures of each gas in a sample and the total pressure of gas in the sample?
16. Why do deep-sea divers breathe a mixture of helium and oxygen?
17. When a gas is collected over water, is the gas pure? Why or why not? How can the partial pressure of the collected gas be determined?
18. If a reaction occurs in the gas phase at STP, the mass of a product can be determined from the volumes of reactants. Explain.
19. What are the basic postulates of kinetic molecular theory? How does the concept of pressure follow from kinetic molecular theory?
20. Explain how Boyle's law, Charles's law, Avogadro's law, and Dalton's law all follow from kinetic molecular theory.
21. How is the kinetic energy of a gas related to temperature? How is the root mean square velocity of a gas related to its molar mass?
22. Describe how the molecules in a perfume bottle travel from the bottle to your nose. What is mean free path?
23. Explain the difference between diffusion and effusion. How is the effusion rate of a gas related to its molar mass?
24. Deviations from the ideal gas law are often observed at high pressure and low temperature. Explain this in light of kinetic molecular theory.

Problems by Topic

Converting between Pressure Units

25. The pressure in Denver, Colorado (elevation 5280 ft), averages about 24.9 in Hg. Convert this pressure to each indicated unit.
    a. atm
    b. mmHg
    c. psi
    d. Pa
26. The pressure on top of Mt. Everest averages about 235 mmHg. Convert this pressure to each indicated unit.
    a. torr
    b. psi
    c. in Hg
    d. atm
27. The North American record for highest recorded barometric pressure is 31.85 in Hg, set in 1989 in Northway, Alaska. Convert this pressure to each indicated unit.
    a. mmHg
    b. atm
    c. torr
    d. kPa (kilopascals)
28. The world record for lowest pressure (at sea level) was 652.5 mmHg recorded inside Typhoon Tip on October 12, 1979, in the western Pacific Ocean. Convert this pressure to each indicated unit.
    a. torr
    b. atm
    c. in Hg
    d. psi

29. Given a barometric pressure of 762.4 mmHg, calculate the pressure of each gas sample as indicated by the manometer.

109. Gaseous ammonia is injected into the exhaust stream of a coal-burning power plant to reduce the pollutant NO to N_2 according to the reaction:

$$4\,NH_3(g) + 4\,NO(g) + O_2(g) \rightarrow 4\,N_2(g) + 6\,H_2O(g)$$

Suppose that the exhaust stream of a power plant has a flow rate of 335 L/s at a temperature of 955 K, and that the exhaust contains a partial pressure of NO of 22.4 torr. What should be the flow rate of ammonia delivered at 755 torr and 298 K into the stream to react completely with the NO if the ammonia is 65.2% pure (by volume)?

110. The emission of NO_2 by fossil fuel combustion can be prevented by injecting gaseous urea into the combustion mixture. The urea reduces NO (which oxidizes in air to form NO_2) according to the reaction:

$$2\,CO(NH_2)_2(g) + 4\,NO(g) + O_2(g) \rightarrow 4\,N_2(g)$$
$$+ 2\,CO_2(g) + 4\,H_2O(g)$$

Suppose that the exhaust stream of an automobile has a flow rate of 2.55 L/s at 655 K and contains a partial pressure of NO of 12.4 torr. What total mass of urea is necessary to react completely with the NO formed during 8.0 hours of driving?

111. An ordinary gasoline can measuring 30.0 cm by 20.0 cm by 15.0 cm is evacuated with a vacuum pump. Assuming that virtually all of the air can be removed from inside the can, and that atmospheric pressure is 14.7 psi, what is the total force (in pounds) on the surface of the can? Do you think that the can could withstand the force?

112. Twenty-five milliliters of liquid nitrogen (density = 0.807 g/mL) is poured into a cylindrical container with a radius of 10.0 cm and a length of 20.0 cm. The container initially contains only air at a pressure of 760.0 mmHg (atmospheric pressure) and a temperature of 298 K. If the liquid nitrogen completely vaporizes, what is the total force (in lb) on the interior of the container at 298 K?

113. A 160.0 L helium tank contains pure helium at a pressure of 1855 psi and a temperature of 298 K. How many 3.5 L helium balloons will the helium in the tank fill? (Assume an atmospheric pressure of 1.0 atm and a temperature of 298 K.)

114. An 11.5 mL sample of liquid butane (density = 0.573 g/mL) is evaporated in an otherwise empty container at a temperature of 28.5 °C. The pressure in the container following evaporation is 892 torr. What is the volume of the container?

115. A scuba diver creates a spherical bubble with a radius of 2.5 cm at a depth of 30.0 m where the total pressure (including atmospheric pressure) is 4.00 atm. What is the radius of the bubble when it reaches the surface of the water? (Assume that the atmospheric pressure is 1.00 atm and the temperature is 298 K.)

116. A particular balloon can be stretched to a maximum surface area of 1257 cm^2. The balloon is filled with 3.0 L of helium gas at a pressure of 755 torr and a temperature of 298 K. The balloon is then allowed to rise in the atmosphere. If the atmospheric temperature is 273 K, at what pressure will the balloon burst? (Assume the balloon to be in the shape of a sphere.)

117. A catalytic converter in an automobile uses a palladium or platinum catalyst (a substance that increases the rate of a reaction

without being consumed by the reaction) to convert carbon monoxide gas to carbon dioxide according to the reaction:

$$2\,CO(g) + O_2(g) \rightarrow 2\,CO_2(g)$$

A chemist researching the effectiveness of a new catalyst combines a 2.0:1.0 mole ratio mixture of carbon monoxide and oxygen gas (respectively) over the catalyst in a 2.45 L flask at a total pressure of 745 torr and a temperature of 552 °C. When the reaction is complete, the pressure in the flask has dropped to 552 torr. What percentage of the carbon monoxide was converted to carbon dioxide?

118. A quantity of N_2 occupies a volume of 1.0 L at 300 K and 1.0 atm. The gas expands to a volume of 3.0 L as the result of a change in both temperature and pressure. Find the density of the gas at these new conditions.

119. A mixture of $CO(g)$ and $O_2(g)$ in a 1.0 L container at 1.0×10^3 K has a total pressure of 2.2 atm. After some time the total pressure falls to 1.9 atm as the result of the formation of CO_2. Determine the mass (in grams) of CO_2 that forms.

120. The radius of a xenon atom is 1.3×10^{-8} cm. A 100 mL flask is filled with Xe at a pressure of 1.0 atm and a temperature of 273 K. Calculate the fraction of the volume that is occupied by Xe atoms. (Hint: The atoms are spheres.)

121. A natural gas storage tank is a cylinder with a moveable top whose volume can change only as its height changes. Its radius remains fixed. The height of the cylinder is 22.6 m on a day when the temperature is 22 °C. The next day the height of the cylinder increases to 23.8 m when the gas expands because of a heat wave. Find the temperature on the second day, assuming that the pressure and amount of gas in the storage tank have not changed.

122. A mixture of 8.0 g CH_4 and 8.0 g Xe is placed in a container and the total pressure is found to be 0.44 atm. Determine the partial pressure of CH_4.

123. A steel container of volume 0.35 L can withstand pressures up to 88 atm before exploding. What mass of helium can be stored in this container at 299 K?

124. Binary compounds of alkali metals and hydrogen react with water to liberate $H_2(g)$. The H_2 from the reaction of a sample of NaH with an excess of water fills a volume of 0.490 L above the water. The temperature of the gas is 35 °C and the total pressure is 758 mmHg. Determine the mass of H_2 liberated and the mass of NaH that reacted.

125. In a given diffusion apparatus, 15.0 mL of HBr gas diffused in 1.0 min. In the same apparatus and under the same conditions, 20.3 mL of an unknown gas diffused in 1.0 min. The unknown gas is a hydrocarbon. Find its molecular formula.

126. A sample of $N_2O_3(g)$ has a pressure of 0.017 atm. The temperature (in K) is then doubled and the N_2O_3 undergoes complete decomposition to $NO_2(g)$ and $NO(g)$. Find the total pressure of the mixture of gases assuming constant volume and no additional temperature change.

127. When 0.583 g of neon is added to an 800 cm^3 bulb containing a sample of argon, the total pressure of the gases is 1.17 atm at a temperature of 295 K. Find the mass of the argon in the bulb.

128. A gas mixture composed of helium and argon has a density of 0.670 g/L at a 755 mmHg and 298 K. What is the composition of the mixture by volume?

129. A gas mixture contains 75.2% nitrogen and 24.8% krypton by mass. What is the partial pressure of krypton in the mixture if the total pressure is 745 mmHg?

Challenge Problems

130. A 10-liter container is filled with 0.10 mol of $H_2(g)$ and heated to 3000 K, causing some of the $H_2(g)$ to decompose into $H(g)$. The pressure is found to be 3.0 atm. Find the partial pressure of the $H(g)$ that forms from H_2 at this temperature. (Assume two significant figures for the temperature.)

131. A mixture of $NH_3(g)$ and $N_2H_4(g)$ is placed in a sealed container at 300 K. The total pressure is 0.50 atm. The container is heated to 1200 K at which time both substances decompose completely according to the equations $2\,NH_3(g) \rightarrow N_2(g) + 3\,H_2(g)$; $N_2H_4(g) \rightarrow N_2(g) + 2\,H_2(g)$. After decomposition is complete the total pressure at 1200 K is found to be 4.5 atm. Find the percent of $N_2H_4(g)$ in the original mixture. (Assume two significant figures for the temperature.)

132. A quantity of CO gas occupies a volume of 0.48 L at 1.0 atm and 275 K. The pressure of the gas is lowered and its temperature is raised until its volume is 1.3 L. Determine the density of the CO under the new conditions.

133. When $CO_2(g)$ is put in a sealed container at 701 K and a pressure of 10.0 atm and is heated to 1401 K, the pressure rises to 22.5 atm. Some of the CO_2 decomposes to CO and O_2. Calculate the mole percent of CO_2 that decomposes.

134. The world burns approximately 3.5×10^{12} kg of fossil fuel per year. Use the combustion of octane as the representative reaction and determine the mass of carbon dioxide (the most significant greenhouse gas) formed per year. The current concentration of carbon dioxide in the atmosphere is approximately 387 ppm (by volume). By what percentage does the concentration increase each year due to fossil fuel combustion? Approximate the average properties of the entire atmosphere by assuming that the atmosphere extends from sea level to 15 km and that it has an average pressure of 381 torr and average temperature of 275 K. Assume Earth is a perfect sphere with a radius of 6371 km.

135. The atmosphere slowly oxidizes hydrocarbons in a number of steps that eventually convert the hydrocarbon into carbon dioxide and water. The overall reaction of a number of such steps for methane gas is

$$CH_4(g) + 5\,O_2(g) + 5\,NO(g) \rightarrow CO_2(g) + H_2O(g)$$
$$+ 5\,NO_2(g) + 2\,OH(g)$$

Suppose that an atmospheric chemist combines 155 mL of methane at STP, 885 mL of oxygen at STP, and 55.5 mL of NO at STP in a 2.0 L flask. The flask is allowed to stand for several weeks at 275 K. If the reaction reaches 90.0% of completion (90.0% of the limiting reactant is consumed), what is the partial pressure of each of the reactants and products in the flask at 275 K? What is the total pressure in the flask?

136. Two identical balloons are filled to the same volume, one with air and one with helium. The next day, the volume of the air-filled balloon has decreased by 5.0%. By what percent has the volume of the helium-filled balloon decreased? (Assume that the air is four-fifths nitrogen and one-fifth oxygen and that the temperature did not change.)

137. A mixture of $CH_4(g)$ and $C_2H_6(g)$ has a total pressure of 0.53 atm. Just enough $O_2(g)$ is added to the mixture to bring about its complete combustion to $CO_2(g)$ and $H_2O(g)$. The total pressure of the two product gases is found to be 2.2 atm. Assuming constant volume and temperature, find the mole fraction of CH_4 in the mixture.

138. A sample of $C_2H_2(g)$ has a pressure of 7.8 kPa. After some time a portion of it reacts to form $C_6H_6(g)$. The total pressure of the mixture of gases is then 3.9 kPa. Assume the volume and the temperature do not change. What fraction of $C_2H_2(g)$ has undergone reaction?

Conceptual Problems

139. When the driver of an automobile applies the brakes, the passengers are pushed toward the front of the car, but a helium balloon is pushed toward the back of the car. Upon forward acceleration, the passengers are pushed toward the back of the car, but the helium balloon is pushed toward the front of the car. Why?

140. Suppose that a liquid is ten times denser than water. If you were to sip this liquid at sea level using a straw, what is the maximum length your straw can be?

141. The reaction occurs in a closed container:

$$A(g) + 2\,B(g) \rightarrow 2\,C(g)$$

A reaction mixture initially contains 1.5 L of A and 2.0 L of B. Assuming that the volume and temperature of the reaction mixture remain constant, what is the percent change in pressure if the reaction goes to completion?

142. One mole of nitrogen and one mole of neon are combined in a closed container at STP. How big is the container?

143. Exactly equal amounts (in moles) of gas A and gas B are combined in a 1 L container at room temperature. Gas B has a molar mass that is twice that of gas A. Which statement is true for the mixture of gases and why?

a. The molecules of gas B have greater kinetic energy than those of gas A.

b. Gas B has a greater partial pressure than gas A.

c. The molecules of gas B have a greater average velocity than those of gas A.

d. Gas B makes a greater contribution to the average density of the mixture than gas A.

144. Which gas would you expect to deviate most from ideal behavior under conditions of low temperature: F_2, Cl_2, or Br_2? Explain.

145. The volume of a sample of a fixed amount of gas is decreased from 2.0 L to 1.0 L. The temperature of the gas in kelvins is then doubled. What is the final pressure of the gas in terms of the initial pressure?

146. Which gas sample has the greatest volume at STP?
a. 10.0 g Kr   **b.** 10.0 g Xe   **c.** 10.0 g He

147. Draw a depiction of a gas sample, as described by kinetic molecular theory, containing equal molar amounts of helium, neon, and krypton. Use different color dots to represent each element. Give each atom a "tail" to represent its velocity relative to the others in the mixture.

Answers to Conceptual Connections

Boyle's Law and Charles's Law

5.1 **(e)** The final volume of the gas is the same as the initial volume because doubling the pressure *decreases* the volume by a factor of two, but doubling the temperature *increases* the volume by a factor of two. The two changes in volume are equal in magnitude but opposite in sign, resulting in a final volume that is equal to the initial volume.

Molar Volume

5.2 **(a)** Since 1 g of H_2 contains the greatest number of moles (due to H_2 having the lowest molar mass of the listed gases), and since one mole of *any* ideal gas occupies the same volume, the H_2 will occupy the greatest volume.

Density of a Gas

5.3 $Ne < O_2 < F_2 < Cl_2$

Partial Pressures

5.4 $P_{He} = 1.5$ atm; $P_{Ne} = 1.5$ atm. Since the number of moles of each gas are equal, the mole fraction of each gas is 0.50 and the partial pressure of each gas is simply $0.50 \times P_{tot}$.

Pressure and Number of Moles

5.5 **(b)** Since the total number of gas molecules decreases, the total pressure—the sum of all the partial pressures—must also decrease.

Kinetic Molecular Theory I

5.6 Although the velocity "tails" have different lengths, the average length of the tails on the argon atoms in your drawing should be longer than the average length of the tails on the xenon atoms.

Since the argon atoms are lighter, they must on average move faster than the xenon atoms to have the same kinetic energy.

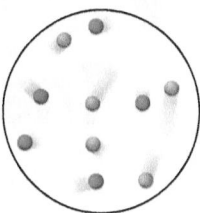

Kinetic Molecular Theory II

5.7 **(c)** Since the temperature and the volume are both constant, the ideal gas law tells us that the pressure depends solely on the number of particles. Sample **(c)** has the greatest number of particles per unit volume, and therefore has the greatest pressure. The pressures of samples **(a)** and **(b)** at a given temperature are identical. Even though the particles in **(b)** are more massive than those in **(a)**, they have the same average kinetic energy at a given temperature. The particles in **(b)** move more slowly than those in **(a)**, and so exert the same pressure as the particles in **(a)**.

Real Gases

5.8 $A < B < C$. Curve A is the lowest temperature curve because it deviates the most from ideality. The tendency for the intermolecular forces in carbon dioxide to lower the pressure (relative to that of an ideal gas) is greatest at low temperature (because the molecules are moving more slowly and are therefore less able to overcome the intermolecular forces). As a result, the curve that dips the lowest must correspond to the lowest temperature.

6

Thermochemistry

There is a fact, or if you wish, a law, governing all natural phenomena that are known to date. There is no exception to this law—it is exact as far as we know. The law is called the conservation of energy. It states that there is a certain quantity, which we call energy, that does not change in the manifold changes which nature undergoes.

—Richard P. Feynman (1918–1988)

WE HAVE SPENT THE FIRST FEW CHAPTERS of this book examining one of the two major components of our universe—matter. We now turn our attention to the other major component—energy. As far as we know, matter and energy—which can be interchanged but not destroyed—make up the physical universe. Unlike matter, energy is not something we can touch or hold in our hand, but we experience it in many ways. The warmth of sunlight, the feel of wind on our faces, and the force that presses us back when a car accelerates are all manifestations of energy and its interconversions. And of course energy is critical to society and to the world. The standard of living around the globe is strongly correlated with the access to and use of energy resources. Most of those resources, as we shall see, are chemical ones, and we can understand their advantages as well as their drawbacks in terms of chemistry.

6.1 Chemical Hand Warmers

My family loves to snowboard. However, my wife hates being cold (with a passion), especially in her hands and toes. Her solution is the chemical hand warmer, a small pouch that comes sealed in a plastic package. She opens the package and places the pouch in her glove or boot. The pouch slowly warms up and keeps her hand (or foot) warm all day long.

Warming your hands with chemical hand warmers involves many of the principles of **thermochemistry**, the study of the relationships between chemistry and energy. When you open the package that contains the hand warmer, the contents are exposed to air, and an *exothermic reaction* occurs. Most hand warmers use the oxidation of iron as the exothermic reaction:

$$4\,Fe(s) \ + \ 3\,O_2(g) \rightarrow 2\,Fe_2O_3(s) \ + \ heat$$

A chemical hand warmer contains substances that react to emit heat.

(a)

(b)

(c)

▲ **(a)** A rolling billiard ball has energy due to its motion. **(b)** When the ball collides with a second ball it does work, transferring energy to the second ball. **(c)** The second ball now has energy as it rolls away from the collision.

▼ **FIGURE 6.1 The Different Manifestations of Energy**

```
Energy: Capacity to Do Work
    ├── Kinetic Energy:
    │   Due to Motion
    │       └── Thermal Energy:
    │           Associated with
    │           Temperature
    └── Potential Energy: Due to
        Position or Composition
            └── Chemical Energy:
                Associated with Positions
                of Electrons and Nuclei
```

Einstein showed that it is mass-energy that is conserved; one can be converted into the other. This equivalence becomes important in nuclear reactions, discussed in Chapter 19. In ordinary chemical reactions, however, the interconversion of mass and energy is not a significant factor, and we can regard mass and energy as independently conserved.

The useful product of this reaction is not a substance—it is *heat*. We'll define heat more carefully later, but heat is what you feel when you touch something that is warmer than your hand (in this case, the hot hand warmer). Although some of the heat is lost through the minute openings in your gloves (which is why my wife prefers mittens), most of it is transferred to your hands and to the pocket of air surrounding your hands, resulting in a temperature increase. The magnitude of the temperature increase depends on the size of the hand warmer and the size of your glove (as well as some other details). But in general, the size of the temperature increase is proportional to the amount of heat released by the reaction.

In this chapter, we examine the relationship between chemical reactions and energy. Specifically, we look at how chemical reactions can *exchange* energy with their surroundings and how we can quantify the magnitude of those exchanges. These kinds of calculations are important, not only for chemical hand warmers, but also for many other important processes such as the heating of homes and the production of energy.

6.2 The Nature of Energy: Key Definitions

Recall that we briefly examined energy in Section 1.5. At that point, we defined **energy** as the capacity to do work and defined **work** as the result of a force acting through a distance. When you push a box across the floor, you have done work. Consider another example of work: a billiard ball rolling across a billiard table and colliding straight on with a second, stationary billiard ball. The rolling ball has *energy* due to its motion. When it collides with another ball it does *work,* resulting in the *transfer* of energy from one ball to the other. The second billiard ball absorbs the energy and begins to roll across the table.

As we just saw with chemical hand warmers, energy can also be transferred through **heat**, the flow of energy caused by a temperature difference. For example, if you hold a cup of coffee in your hand, energy is transferred, in the form of heat, from the hot coffee to your cooler hand. Think of *energy* as something that an object or set of objects possesses. Think of *heat* and *work* as ways that objects or sets of objects *exchange* energy.

The energy contained in a rolling billiard ball is an example of **kinetic energy**, the energy associated with the *motion* of an object. The energy contained in a hot cup of coffee is **thermal energy**, the energy associated with the *temperature* of an object. Thermal energy is actually a type of kinetic energy because it arises from the motions of atoms or molecules within a substance. If you raise a billiard ball off the table, you increase its **potential energy**, the energy associated with the *position* or *composition* of an object. The potential energy of the billiard ball, for example, is a result of its position in Earth's gravitational field. Raising the ball off the table, against Earth's gravitational pull, gives it more potential energy. Another example of potential energy is the energy contained in a compressed spring. When you compress a spring, you push against the forces that tend to maintain the spring's uncompressed shape, storing energy as potential energy. **Chemical energy**, the energy associated with the relative positions of electrons and nuclei in atoms and molecules, is also a form of potential energy. Some chemical compounds, such as the methane in natural gas or the iron in a chemical hand warmer, are like a compressed spring—they contain potential energy, and a chemical reaction can release that potential energy. Figure 6.1 ◀ summarizes these different kinds of energy.

The **law of conservation of energy** states that *energy can be neither created nor destroyed*. However, energy can be transferred from one object to another, and it can assume different forms. For example, if you drop a raised billiard ball, some of its potential energy becomes kinetic energy as the ball falls toward the table, as shown in Figure 6.2 ▶. If you release a compressed spring, the potential energy becomes kinetic energy as the spring expands outward, as shown in Figure 6.3 ▶. When iron reacts with oxygen within a chemical hand warmer, the chemical energy of the iron and oxygen becomes thermal energy that increases the temperature of your hand and glove.

Energy Transformation I

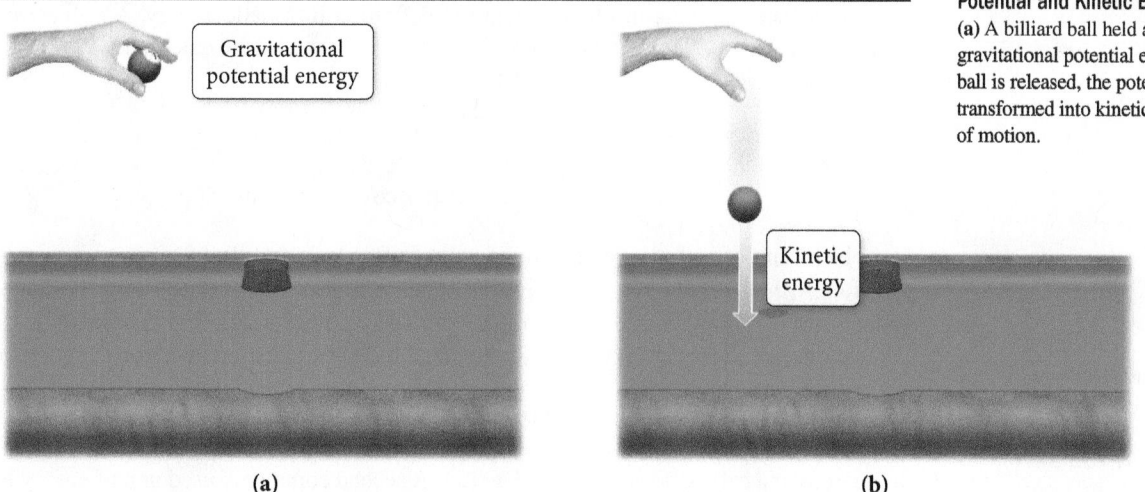

(a)   (b)

◀ FIGURE 6.2 **Energy Transformation: Potential and Kinetic Energy I** (a) A billiard ball held above the ground has gravitational potential energy. (b) When the ball is released, the potential energy is transformed into kinetic energy, the energy of motion.

A good way to understand and track energy changes is to define the **system** under investigation. For example, the system may be the chemicals in a beaker, or it may be the iron reacting in a hand warmer. The system's **surroundings** are everything with which the system can exchange energy. If we define the chemicals in a beaker as the system, the surroundings may include the water in which the chemicals are dissolved (for aqueous solutions), the beaker itself, the lab bench on which the beaker sits, the air in the room, and so on. For the iron in the hand warmer, the surroundings include your hand, your glove, the air in the glove, and even the air outside of the glove.

In an energy exchange, energy is transferred between the system and the surroundings, as shown in Figure 6.4 ▼. If the system loses energy, the surroundings gain the same exact amount of energy, and vice versa. When the iron within the chemical hand warmer reacts, the system loses energy to the surroundings, producing the desired temperature increase within your gloves.

Energy Transformation II

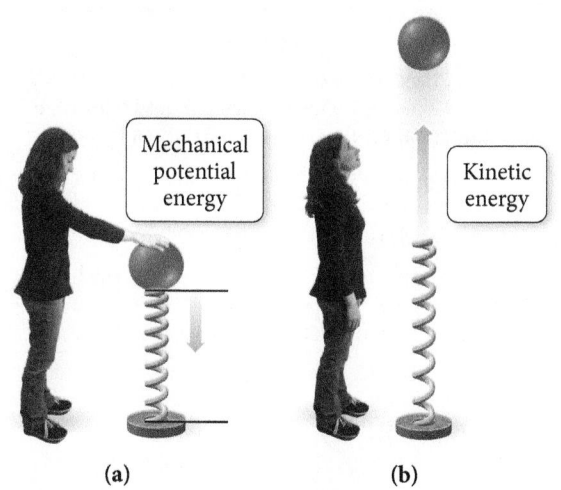

(a)   (b)

▲ FIGURE 6.3 **Energy Transformation: Potential and Kinetic Energy II** (a) A compressed spring has potential energy. (b) When the spring is released, the potential energy is transformed into kinetic energy.

Energy Transfer

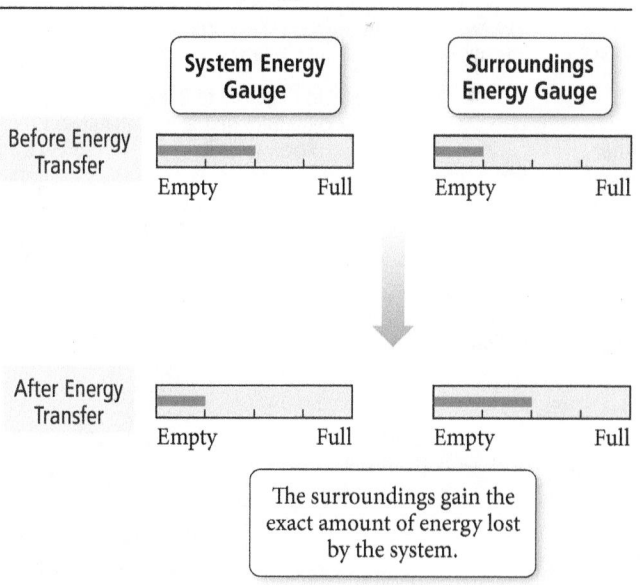

The surroundings gain the exact amount of energy lost by the system.

▲ FIGURE 6.4 **Energy Transfer** If a system and surroundings had energy gauges (which would measure energy content in the way a fuel gauge measures fuel content), an energy transfer in which the system transfers energy to the surroundings would result in a decrease in the energy content of the system and an increase in the energy content of the surroundings. The total amount of energy, however, must be conserved.

3.6 × 10⁵ J or 0.10 kWh
used in 1 hour

▲ A watt (W) is 1 J/s, so a 100 W lightbulb uses 100 J every second or 3.6×10^5 J every hour.

The "calorie" referred to on all nutritional labels (regardless of the capitalization) is always the capital C Calorie.

Units of Energy

We can deduce the units of energy from the definition of kinetic energy. An object of mass m, moving at velocity v, has a kinetic energy KE given by the equation:

$$KE = \frac{1}{2}mv^2$$

$$\underset{\text{kg}}{} \quad \underset{\text{m/s}}{}$$

[6.1]

The SI unit of mass is the kg and the unit of velocity is m/s. The SI unit of energy is therefore $\text{kg} \cdot \text{m}^2/\text{s}^2$, defined as the **joule (J)**, named after the English scientist James Joule (1818–1889).

$$1 \text{ kg}\frac{\text{m}^2}{\text{s}^2} = 1 \text{ J}$$

One joule is a relatively small amount of energy—for example, a 100-watt lightbulb uses 3.6×10^5 J in 1 hour. Therefore, we often use the kilojoule (kJ) in our energy discussions and calculations (1 kJ = 1000 J). A second commonly used unit of energy is the **calorie (cal)**, originally defined as the amount of energy required to raise the temperature of 1 g of water by 1 °C. The current definition is 1 cal = 4.184 J (exact); a calorie is a larger unit than a joule. A related energy unit is the nutritional, or uppercase "C" **Calorie (Cal)**, equivalent to 1000 lowercase "c" calories. The Calorie is the same as a kilocalorie (kcal): 1 Cal = 1 kcal = 1000 cal. Electricity bills typically are based on another, even larger, energy unit, the **kilowatt-hour (kWh)**: 1 kWh = 3.60×10^6 J. Electricity costs $0.08–$0.15 per kWh. Table 6.1 lists various energy units and their conversion factors. Table 6.2 shows the amount of energy required for various processes.

TABLE 6.1 Energy Conversion Factors*

1 calorie (cal)	= 4.184 joules (J)
1 Calorie (Cal) or kilocalorie (kcal)	= 1000 cal = 4184 J
1 kilowatt-hour (kWh)	= 3.60×10^6 J

*All conversion factors in this table are exact.

TABLE 6.2 Energy Uses in Various Units

Unit	Amount Required to Raise Temperature of 1 g of Water by 1 °C	Amount Required to Light 100 W Bulb for 1 Hour	Amount Used by Human Body in Running 1 Mile (Approximate)	Amount Used by Average U.S. Citizen in 1 Day
joule (J)	4.18	3.60×10^5	4.2×10^5	9.0×10^8
calorie (cal)	1.00	8.60×10^4	1.0×10^5	2.2×10^8
Calorie (Cal)	0.00100	86.0	100	2.2×10^5
kilowatt-hour (KWh)	1.16×10^{-6}	0.100	0.12	2.5×10^2

6.3 The First Law of Thermodynamics: There Is No Free Lunch

Thermodynamics is the general study of energy and its interconversions. The laws of thermodynamics are among the most fundamental in all of science, governing virtually every process that involves change. The **first law of thermodynamics** is the law of energy conservation, which we state as follows:

The total energy of the universe is constant.

In other words, since energy is neither created nor destroyed, and since the universe does not exchange energy with anything else, its energy content does not change. The first law has many implications: the most important one is that with energy, you cannot get

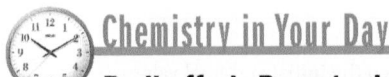
Chemistry in Your Day

Redheffer's Perpetual Motion Machine

In 1812, a man named Charles Redheffer appeared in Philadelphia with a machine that he claimed could run forever without any energy input—a perpetual motion machine. He set up the machine on the edge of town and charged admission to view it. He also appealed to the city for money to build a larger version of the machine. When city commissioners came out to inspect the machine, Redheffer did his best to keep them from viewing it too closely. Nonetheless, one of the commissioners noticed something suspicious: the gears that supposedly ran to an external driveshaft were cut in the wrong direction. The driveshaft that the machine was allegedly powering was instead powering the machine. The city commissioners hired a local engineer and clockmaker named Isaiah Lukens to make a similar machine to expose Redheffer's deception. Lukens's machine was even more ingenious than Redheffer's, and Redheffer left Philadelphia exposed as a fraud.

Redheffer was persistent, however, and took his machine to New York. In 1813, during a public display of the machine, the famous mechanical engineer Robert Fulton—who 6 years earlier had demonstrated the first successful steamboat—noticed a rhythm to the machine's motion. It seemed to speed up and slow down at regular intervals. Fulton knew that such rhythmic motion is indicative of motion generated by a manual crank. He knocked away some boards in a wall next to the machine and discovered a long belt that led to an enclosed room where, indeed, an old man sat turning a crank. Redheffer's machine—like many other perpetual motion machines throughout history—was again exposed as a hoax.

Question

Can you think of any recent claims of perpetual motion or limitless free energy?

---

something for nothing. The best you can do with energy is break even—there is no free lunch. According to the first law, a device that would continually produce energy with no energy input, sometimes known as a *perpetual motion machine*, cannot exist. Occasionally, the media report or speculate on the discovery of a machine that can produce energy without the need for energy input. For example, you may have heard someone propose an electric car that recharges itself while driving, or a new motor that can create additional usable electricity as well as the electricity to power itself. Although some hybrid (electric and gasoline powered) vehicles can capture energy from braking and use that energy to recharge their batteries, they could never run indefinitely without additional fuel. As for the motor that powers an external load as well as itself—no such thing exists. Our society has a continual need for energy, and as our current energy resources dwindle, new energy sources will be required. But those sources, whatever they may be, must follow the first law of thermodynamics—energy is always conserved.

Internal Energy

The **internal energy** (**E**) of a system is *the sum of the kinetic and potential energies of all of the particles that compose the system*. Internal energy is a **state function**, which means that its value depends *only on the state of the system*, not on how the system arrived at that state. The state of a chemical system is specified by parameters such as temperature, pressure, concentration, and physical state (solid, liquid, or gas). Consider the mountain-climbing analogy depicted in Figure 6.5 ▶. The elevation at any point during a mountain climb is analogous to a state function. For example, when we reach 10,000 ft, our elevation is 10,000 ft, no matter how we got there. The distance we traveled to get there, by contrast, is not a state function; we could have climbed the mountain by any number of routes, each requiring us to cover a different distance.

Since state functions depend only on the state of the system, the value of a *change* in a state function is always the difference between its final and initial values. If we start climbing a mountain at an elevation of 3000 ft and reach the summit at 10,000 feet, then our elevation change is 7000 ft (10,000 ft − 3000 ft), regardless of what path we took.

▶ FIGURE 6.5 **Altitude as a State Function** The change in altitude during a climb depends only on the difference between the final and initial altitudes, not on the route traveled.

A State Function
Change in altitude depends only on the difference between the initial and final values, not on the path taken.

Like an altitude change, an internal energy change (ΔE) is determined by the difference in internal energy between the final and initial states:

$$\Delta E = E_{final} - E_{initial}$$

In a chemical system, the reactants constitute the initial state and the products constitute the final state. So ΔE is the difference in internal energy between the products and the reactants:

$$\Delta E = E_{products} - E_{reactants} \qquad [6.2]$$

For example, consider the reaction between carbon and oxygen to form carbon dioxide:

$$C(s) + O_2(g) \longrightarrow CO_2(g)$$

Just as we can portray the changes that occur when climbing a mountain with an *altitude* diagram that depicts the *altitude* before and after the climb (see Figure 6.5), so we can portray the energy changes that occur during a reaction with an *energy* diagram, which compares the *internal energy* of the reactants and the products:

Internal energy

$C(s), O_2(g)$ (reactants)

$\Delta E < 0$ (negative)

$CO_2(g)$ (product)

The vertical axis of the diagram is internal *energy*, which increases as we move up on the diagram. For this reaction, the reactants are *higher* on the diagram than the products because they have higher internal energy. As the reaction occurs, the reactants become products, which have lower internal energy. Therefore, energy is given off by the reaction and ΔE (that is, $E_{products} - E_{reactants}$) is *negative*.

Where does the energy lost by the reactants (as they transform to products) go? If we define the thermodynamic *system* as the reactants and products of the reaction, then energy flows *out of the system* and *into the surroundings*.

System → Surroundings
Energy flow

$\Delta E_{sys} < 0$ (negative) $\Delta E_{surr} > 0$ (positive)

According to the first law, energy must be conserved. Therefore, the amount of energy lost by the system must exactly equal the amount gained by the surroundings.

$$\Delta E_{sys} = -\Delta E_{surr} \qquad [6.3]$$

Now, suppose the reaction is reversed:

$$CO_2(g) \longrightarrow C(s) + O_2(g)$$

The energy level diagram is nearly identical, with one important difference: $CO_2(g)$ is now the reactant and $C(s)$ and $O_2(g)$ are the products. Instead of decreasing in energy as the reaction occurs, the system increases in energy:

In this reversed reaction ΔE is *positive* and energy flows *into the system* and *out of the surroundings*.

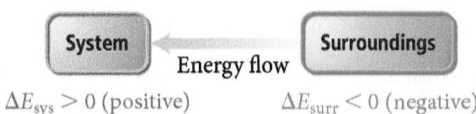

Summarizing Energy Flow:

▶ If the reactants have a higher internal energy than the products, ΔE_{sys} is negative and energy flows out of the system into the surroundings.

▶ If the reactants have a lower internal energy than the products, ΔE_{sys} is positive and energy flows into the system from the surroundings.

You can think of the internal energy of the system in the same way you think about the balance in a checking account. Energy flowing *out of* the system is like a withdrawal and therefore carries a negative sign. Energy flowing *into* the system is like a deposit and carries a positive sign.

Conceptual Connection 6.1 System and Surroundings

Consider these fictitious internal energy gauges for a chemical system and its surroundings:

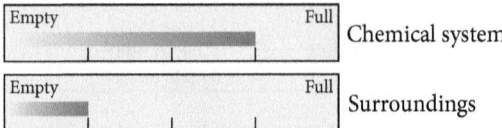

Which diagram best represents the energy gauges for the same system and surroundings following an energy exchange in which ΔE_{sys} is negative?

TABLE 6.3 Sign Conventions for q, w, and ΔE

q (heat)	+ system *gains* thermal energy	− system *loses* thermal energy
w (work)	+ work done *on* the system	− work done *by* the system
ΔE (change in internal energy)	+ energy flows *into* the system	− energy flows *out* of the system

As we saw earlier, a system can exchange energy with its surroundings through *heat* and *work*:

According to the first law of thermodynamics, the change in the internal energy of the system (ΔE) is the sum of the heat transferred (q) and the work done (w):

$$\Delta E = q + w \qquad [6.4]$$

In Equation 6.4, and from this point forward, we follow the standard convention that ΔE (with no subscript) refers to the internal energy change of the *system*. As shown in Table 6.3, energy entering the system through heat or work carries a positive sign, and energy leaving the system through heat or work carries a negative sign. Again, recall the checking account analogy. The system is like the checking account—withdrawals are negative and deposits are positive.

We can define our system as the previously discussed billiard ball rolling across a pool table. The rolling ball has a certain initial amount of kinetic energy. When it reaches the other end of the table, the rolling ball collides head-on with a second ball. Assume that the first ball loses all of its kinetic energy so that it remains completely still (it has no kinetic energy) at the point of collision. The total change in internal energy (ΔE) for the first ball is the difference between its initial kinetic energy and its final kinetic energy (which is zero); the first billiard ball lost all of its energy. What happened to that energy? According to the first law, it must have been transferred to the surroundings. In fact, the energy lost by the system must *exactly equal* the amount gained by the surroundings.

The surroundings include both the pool table and the second ball. The pool table absorbs some of the ball's kinetic energy as the ball rolls down the table. Minute bumps on the table surface cause friction, which slows the ball down by converting kinetic energy to heat (q). The second ball absorbs some of the ball's kinetic energy in the form of work (w) upon collision.

Although it is always the case that $\Delta E_{sys} = -\Delta E_{surr}$, the exact amount of *work* done on the second ball depends on the quality of the billiard table. On a smooth, high-quality billiard table, the amount of energy lost to friction is relatively small, as shown in Figure 6.6(a) ▶. The speed of the first ball is not reduced by much as it travels across the table and a great deal of its original kinetic energy is available to perform work when it collides with the second ball. In contrast, on a rough, poor-quality table, the ball loses much of its initial kinetic energy as heat, leaving only a relatively small amount available for work, as shown in Figure 6.6(b) ▶.

Notice that the respective amounts of energy converted to heat and work depend on the details of the pool table and the path taken, while the change in internal energy of the rolling ball does not. In other words, since internal energy is a state function, the value of ΔE for the process in which the ball moves across the table and collides with another ball depends only on the ball's initial and final kinetic energy. Work and heat, however, are *not*

(a) Smooth table

(b) Rough table

▲ FIGURE 6.6 **Energy, Work, and Heat**   (a) On a smooth table, most of the first billiard ball's initial kinetic energy is transferred to the second ball as work. Only a small amount is lost to heat. (b) On a rough table, most of the first billiard ball's initial kinetic energy is lost to heat. Only a small amount is left to do work on the second billiard ball.

state functions; therefore, the values of q and w depend on the details of the ball's journey across the table. On the smooth table, w is greater in magnitude than q; on the rough table, q is greater in magnitude than w. However, ΔE (the sum of q and w) is constant.

Conceptual Connection 6.2 **Heat and Work**

Identify each energy exchange as heat or work and determine whether the sign of heat or work (relative to the system) is positive or negative.

(a) An ice cube melts and cools the surrounding beverage. (The ice cube is the system.)

(b) A metal cylinder is rolled up a ramp. (The metal cylinder is the system.)

(c) Steam condenses on skin, causing a burn. (The condensing steam is the system.)

EXAMPLE 6.1 Internal Energy, Heat, and Work

The firing of a potato cannon provides a good example of the heat and work associated with a chemical reaction. A potato is stuffed into a long cylinder that is capped on one end and open at the other. Some kind of fuel is introduced under the potato at the capped end—usually through a small hole—and ignited. The potato then shoots out of the cannon, sometimes flying hundreds of feet, and the cannon emits heat to the surroundings. If the burning of the fuel performs 855 J of work on the potato and produces 1422 J of heat, what is ΔE for the burning of the fuel? (Note: A potato cannon can be dangerous and should not be constructed without proper training and experience.)

SOLUTION To solve the problem, substitute the values of q and w into the equation for ΔE. Since work is done by the system on the surroundings, w is negative. Similarly, since heat is released by the system to the surroundings, q is also negative.

$$\Delta E = q + w$$
$$= -1422 \text{ J} - 855 \text{ J}$$
$$= -2277 \text{ J}$$

FOR PRACTICE 6.1

A cylinder and piston assembly (defined as the system) is warmed by an external flame. The contents of the cylinder expand, doing work on the surroundings by pushing the piston outward against the external pressure. If the system absorbs 559 J of heat and does 488 J of work during the expansion, what is the value of ΔE?

6.4 Quantifying Heat and Work

In the previous section, we calculated ΔE based on *given values of q and w*. We now turn to *calculating q (heat) and w (work)* based on changes in temperature and volume.

Heat

Recall from Section 6.2 that *heat* is the exchange of thermal energy between a system and its surroundings caused by a temperature difference. Notice the distinction between heat and temperature. Temperature is a *measure* of the thermal energy within a sample of matter. Heat is the *transfer* of thermal energy. Thermal energy always flows from matter at higher temperatures to matter at lower temperatures. For example, a hot cup of coffee transfers thermal energy—as heat—to the lower temperature surroundings as it cools down. Imagine a world where the cooler surroundings actually got colder as they transferred thermal energy to the hot coffee, which got hotter. Such a world exists only in our imaginations (or in the minds of science fiction writers), because the spontaneous transfer of heat from a hotter object to a colder one is a fundamental principle of our universe—no exception has ever been observed. The thermal energy in the molecules that compose the hot coffee distributes itself to the molecules in the surroundings. The heat transfer from the coffee to the surroundings stops when the two reach the same temperature, a condition called **thermal equilibrium**. At thermal equilibrium, there is no additional net transfer of heat.

The reason for this one-way transfer is related to the second law of thermodynamics, which we will discuss in Chapter 17.

Temperature Changes and Heat Capacity When a system absorbs heat (q), its temperature changes by ΔT:

Experiments show that the heat absorbed by a system and its corresponding temperature change are directly proportional: $q \propto \Delta T$. The constant of proportionality between q and ΔT is the system's *heat capacity* (C), a measure of the system's ability to absorb thermal energy without undergoing a large change in temperature.

$$q = C \times \Delta T$$

Heat capacity

[6.5]

Notice that the higher the heat capacity of a system, the smaller the change in temperature for a given amount of absorbed heat. We define the **heat capacity (C)** of a system as the quantity of heat required to change its temperature by 1 °C. As we can see by solving Equation 6.5 for heat capacity, the units of heat capacity are those of heat (typically J) divided by those of temperature (typically °C).

$$C = \frac{q}{\Delta T} = \frac{J}{°C}$$

In order to understand two important concepts related to heat capacity, consider putting a steel saucepan on a kitchen flame. The saucepan's temperature rises rapidly as it absorbs heat from the flame. However, if you add some water to the saucepan, the temperature rises more slowly. Why? The first reason is that when you add the water, the same amount of heat must now warm more matter, so the temperature rises more slowly. In other words, heat capacity is an extensive property—*it depends on the amount of matter being heated* (see Section 1.6). The second (and more fundamental) reason is that *water is more resistant to temperature change than steel*—water has an intrinsically higher capacity to absorb heat without undergoing a large temperature change. The measure of the *intrinsic capacity* of a substance to absorb heat is its **specific heat capacity (C_s)**, the amount of heat required to raise the temperature of *1 gram* of the substance by 1 °C. The units of specific heat capacity (also called *specific heat*) are J/g·°C. Table 6.4 lists the values of the specific heat capacity for several substances. Heat capacity is sometimes reported as **molar heat capacity**, the amount of heat required to raise the temperature of *1 mole* of a substance by 1 °C. The units of molar heat capacity are J/mol·°C. You can see from these definitions that *specific* heat capacity and *molar* heat capacity are intensive properties—they depend on the *kind* of substance being heated, not on the amount.

Notice that water has the highest specific heat capacity of all the substances in Table 6.4—changing the temperature of water requires a lot of heat. If you have ever experienced the drop in temperature that occurs when traveling from an inland region to the coast during the summer, you have experienced the effects of water's high specific heat capacity. On a summer's day in California, for example, the temperature difference between Sacramento (an inland city) and San Francisco (a coastal city) can be 18 °C (30 °F)—San Francisco enjoys a cool 20 °C (68 °F), while Sacramento bakes at nearly 38 °C (100 °F). Yet the intensity of sunlight falling on these two cities is the same. Why the large temperature difference? San Francisco sits on a peninsula, surrounded by the water of the Pacific Ocean. Water, with its high heat capacity, absorbs much of the sun's heat without undergoing a large increase in temperature, keeping San Francisco cool. Sacramento, by contrast, is about 160 km (100 mi) inland. The land surrounding Sacramento, with its low heat capacity, undergoes a large increase in temperature as it absorbs a similar amount of heat.

Similarly, only two U.S. states have never recorded a temperature above 100 °F. One of them is obvious: Alaska. It is too far north to get that hot. The other one, however, may come as a surprise. It is Hawaii. The high heat capacity of the water that surrounds the only island state moderates the temperature, preventing Hawaii from ever getting too hot.

The specific heat capacity of a substance can be used to quantify the relationship between the amount of heat added to a given amount of the substance and the corresponding temperature increase. The following equation relates these quantities:

Heat (J) $\longrightarrow$ $q = m \times C_s \times \Delta T \longleftarrow$ Temperature change (°C)

                      Mass (g)   Specific heat capacity J/g·°C

[6.6]

where q is the amount of heat in J, m is the mass of the substance in g, C_s is the specific heat capacity in J/g·°C, and ΔT is the temperature change in °C. Example 6.2 demonstrates the use of this equation.

TABLE 6.4 Specific Heat Capacities of Some Common Substances

Substance	Specific Heat Capacity, C_s(J/g·°C)*
Elements	
Lead	0.128
Gold	0.128
Silver	0.235
Copper	0.385
Iron	0.449
Aluminum	0.903
Compounds	
Ethanol	2.42
Water	4.18
Materials	
Glass (Pyrex)	0.75
Granite	0.79
Sand	0.84

*At 298 K.

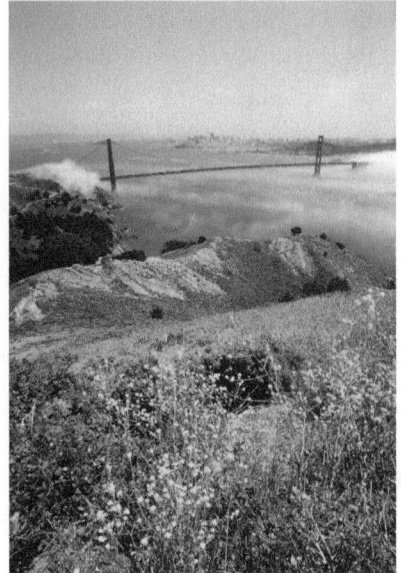

▲ The high heat capacity of the water surrounding San Francisco results in relatively cool summer temperatures.

ΔT in °C is equal to ΔT in K, but not equal to ΔT in °F (Section 1.6).

EXAMPLE 6.2 Temperature Changes and Heat Capacity

Suppose you find a penny (minted before 1982, when pennies were almost entirely copper) in the snow. How much heat is absorbed by the penny as it warms from the temperature of the snow, which is −8.0 °C, to the temperature of your body, 37.0 °C? Assume the penny is pure copper and has a mass of 3.10 g.

SORT You are given the mass of copper as well as its initial and final temperature. You are asked to find the heat required for the given temperature change.	**GIVEN:** $m = 3.10$ g copper $T_i = -8.0\,°C$ $T_f = 37.0\,°C$ **FIND:** q
STRATEGIZE The equation $q = m \times C_s \times \Delta T$ gives the relationship between the amount of heat (q) and the temperature change (ΔT).	**CONCEPTUAL PLAN** $\boxed{C_s, m, \Delta T} \longrightarrow \boxed{q}$ $\quad\quad q = m \times C_s \times \Delta T$ **RELATIONSHIPS USED** $q = m \times C_s \times \Delta T$ (Equation 6.6) $C_s = 0.385$ J/g · °C (Table 6.4)
SOLVE Gather the necessary quantities for the equation in the correct units and substitute these into the equation to calculate q.	**SOLUTION** $\Delta T = T_f - T_i = 37.0\,°C - (-8.0\,°C) = 45.0\,°C$ $q = m \times C_s \times \Delta T$ $\quad = 3.10\,\cancel{g} \times 0.385\,\dfrac{J}{\cancel{g} \cdot \cancel{°C}} \times 45.0\,\cancel{°C} = 53.7$ J

CHECK The units (J) are correct for heat. The sign of q is *positive*, as it should be since the penny *absorbed* heat from the surroundings.

FOR PRACTICE 6.2

To determine whether a shiny gold-colored rock is actually gold, a chemistry student decides to measure its heat capacity. She first weighs the rock and finds it has a mass of 4.7 g. She then finds that upon absorption of 57.2 J of heat, the temperature of the rock rises from 25 °C to 57 °C. Find the specific heat capacity of the substance composing the rock and determine whether the value is consistent with the rock being pure gold.

FOR MORE PRACTICE 6.2

A 55.0 g aluminum block initially at 27.5 °C absorbs 725 J of heat. What is the final temperature of the aluminum?

Conceptual Connection 6.3 The Heat Capacity of Water

Suppose you are cold-weather camping and decide to heat some objects to bring into your sleeping bag for added warmth. You place a large water jug and a rock of equal mass near the fire. Over time, both the rock and the water jug warm to about 38 °C (100 °F). If you could bring only one into your sleeping bag, which one should you choose to keep you the warmest? Why?

Thermal Energy Transfer As we noted earlier, when two substances of different temperature are combined, thermal energy flows as heat from the hotter substance to the cooler one. If we assume that the two substances are thermally isolated from everything else, then the heat lost by one substance exactly equals the heat gained by the other (according to the law of energy conservation). If we define one substance as the system and the other as the surroundings, we can quantify the heat exchange as:

$$q_{sys} = -q_{surr}$$

Suppose a block of metal initially at 55 °C is submerged into water initially at 25 °C. Thermal energy transfers as heat from the metal to the water:

$q_{metal} = -q_{water}$

The metal will get colder and the water will get warmer until the two substances reach the same temperature (thermal equilibrium). The exact temperature change that occurs depends on the masses of the metal and the water and on their specific heat capacities. Since $q = m \times C_s \times \Delta T$ we can arrive at the following relationship:

$$q_{metal} = -q_{water}$$
$$m_{metal} \times C_{s, metal} \times \Delta T_{metal} = -m_{water} \times C_{s, water} \times \Delta T_{water}$$

Example 6.3 shows how to work with thermal energy transfer.

EXAMPLE 6.3   Thermal Energy Transfer

A 32.5 g cube of aluminum initially at 45.8 °C is submerged into 105.3 g of water at 15.4 °C. What is the final temperature of both substances at thermal equilibrium? (Assume that the aluminum and the water are thermally isolated from everything else.)

SORT You are given the masses of aluminum and water and their initial temperatures. You are asked to find the final temperature.	**GIVEN:** $m_{Al} = 32.5$ g $m_{H_2O} = 105.3$ g $T_{i, Al} = 45.8$ °C; $T_{i, H_2O} = 15.4$ °C **FIND:** T_f
STRATEGIZE The heat lost by the aluminum (q_{Al}) equals the heat gained by the water (q_{H_2O}). Use the relationship between q and ΔT and the given variables to find a relationship between ΔT_{Al} and ΔT_{H_2O}. Use the relationship between ΔT_{A_1} and ΔT_{H_2O} (that you just found) along with the initial temperatures of the aluminum and the water to determine the final temperature. Note that at thermal equilibrium, the final temperature of the aluminum and the water is the same, that is, $T_{f, Al} = T_{f, H_2O} = T_f$.	**CONCEPTUAL PLAN** $q_{Al} = -q_{H_2O}$ $\boxed{m_{Al}, C_{s, Al}, m_{H_2O}, C_{s, H_2O}} \longrightarrow \boxed{\Delta T_{Al} = \text{constant} \times \Delta T_{H_2O}}$ $m_{Al} \times C_{s, Al} \times \Delta T_{Al} = -m_{H_2O} \times C_{s, H_2O} \times \Delta T_{H_2O}$ $\boxed{T_{l, Al}, T_{i, H_2O}} \longrightarrow \boxed{T_f}$ $\Delta T_{Al} = \text{constant} \times \Delta T_{H_2O}$ **RELATIONSHIPS USED** $C_{s, H_2O} = 4.18$ J/g·°C; $C_{s,Al} = 0.903$ J/g·°C (Table 6.4) $q = m \times C_s \times \Delta T$ (Equation 6.6)
SOLVE Write the equation for the relationship between the heat lost by the aluminum (q_{Al}) and the heat gained by the water (q_{H_2O}) and substitute $q = m \times C_s \times \Delta T$ for each substance. Substitute the values of m (given) and C_s (from Table 6.4) for each substance and solve the equation for ΔT_{Al}. (Alternatively, you can solve the equation for ΔT_{H_2O}.) Substitute the initial temperatures of aluminum and water into the relationship from the previous step and solve the expression for the final temperature (T_f). Remember that the final temperature for both substances will be the same.	**SOLUTION** $q_{Al} = -q_{H_2O}$ $m_{Al} \times C_{s, Al} \times \Delta T_{Al} = -m_{H_2O} \times C_{s,H_2O} \times \Delta T_{H_2O}$ $32.5 \text{ g} \times \dfrac{0.903 \text{ J}}{\text{g} \cdot {}^{\circ}\text{C}} \cdot \Delta T_{Al} = -105.3 \text{ g} \times \dfrac{4.18 \text{ J}}{\text{g} \cdot {}^{\circ}\text{C}} \cdot \Delta T_{H_2O}$ $29.348 \cdot \Delta T_{Al} = -440.15 \cdot \Delta T_{H_2O}$ $\Delta T_{Al} = -14.998 \cdot \Delta T_{H_2O}$ $T_f - T_{i, Al} = -14.998 \, (T_f - T_{i, H_2O})$ $T_f = -14.998 \cdot T_f + 14.998 \cdot T_{i, H_2O} + T_{i, Al}$ $T_f + 14.998 \cdot T_f = 14.998 \cdot T_{i, H_2O} + T_{i, Al}$ $15.998 \cdot T_f = 14.998 \cdot T_{i, H_2O} + T_{i, Al}$ $T_f = \dfrac{14.998 \cdot T_{i, H_2O} + T_{i, Al}}{15.998} = \dfrac{14.998 \cdot 15.4 \, {}^{\circ}\text{C} + 45.8 \, {}^{\circ}\text{C}}{15.998}$ $= 17.3 \, {}^{\circ}\text{C}$

CHECK The units °C are correct. The final temperature of the mixture is closer to the initial temperature of the *water* than the *aluminum*. This makes sense for two reasons: (1) water has a higher specific heat capacity than aluminum, and (2) there is more water than aluminum. Since the aluminum loses the same amount of heat that is gained by the water, the greater mass and specific heat capacity of the water make the temperature change in the water *less than* the temperature change in the aluminum.

FOR PRACTICE 6.3

A block of copper of unknown mass has an initial temperature of 65.4 °C. The copper is immersed in a beaker containing 95.7 g of water at 22.7 °C. When the two substances reach thermal equilibrium, the final temperature is 24.2 °C. What is the mass of the copper block?

Conceptual Connection 6.4 Thermal Energy Transfer

Substances A and B, initially at different temperatures, come in contact with each other and reach thermal equilibrium. The mass of substance A is twice the mass of substance B. The specific heat capacity of substance B is twice the specific heat capacity of substance A. Which statement is true about the final temperature of the two substances once thermal equilibrium is reached?

(a) The final temperature will be closer to the initial temperature of substance A than substance B.

(b) The final temperature will be closer to the initial temperature of substance B than substance A.

(c) The final temperature will be exactly midway between the initial temperatures of substances A and B.

Work: Pressure–Volume Work

We have seen that energy transfer between a system and its surroundings can occur via heat (*q*) or work (*w*). We just saw how to calculate the *heat* associated with an observed *temperature* change. We now turn to calculating the *work* associated with an observed *volume* change. Although a chemical reaction can do several different types of work, for now we limit our discussion to **pressure–volume work**. We have already defined work as a force acting through a distance. Pressure–volume work occurs when the force is caused by a volume change against an external pressure. For example, pressure–volume work occurs in the cylinder of an automobile engine. The combustion of gasoline causes gases within the cylinders to expand, pushing the piston outward and ultimately moving the wheels of the car.

—Combustion

▲ The combustion of gasoline within an engine's cylinders does pressure–volume work that ultimately results in the motion of the car.

We can derive an equation for the value of pressure–volume work from the definition of work as a force (*F*) acting through a distance (*D*):

$$w = F \times D \qquad [6.7]$$

When the volume of a cylinder increases (Figure 6.7 ▶), it pushes against an external force. That external force is pressure (*P*), which is defined as force (*F*) divided by area (*A*):

> The force in this equation must be a constant force.

$$P = \frac{F}{A} \quad \text{or} \quad F = P \times A$$

If we substitute this expression for force into the definition of work given in Equation 6.7, we arrive at the expression:

$$w = F \times D$$
$$= P \times A \times D$$

The distance through which the force acts is the change in the height of the piston as it moves during the expansion (Δh). Substituting Δh for D, we get:

$$w = P \times A \times \Delta h$$

Since the volume of a cylinder is the area of its base times its height, then $A \times \Delta h$ is actually the change in volume (ΔV) that occurs during the expansion. Thus, the expression for work becomes the product of the pressure times the change in volume:

$$w = P \, \Delta V$$

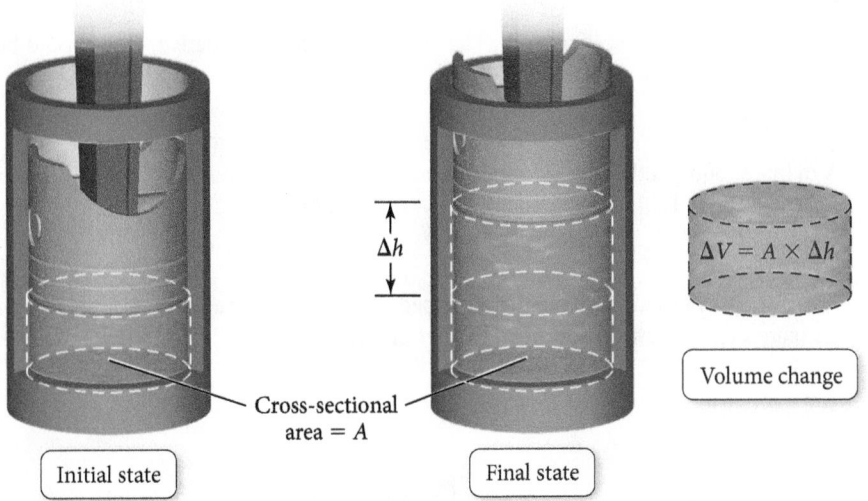

Volume change

▲ FIGURE 6.7 Piston Moving within a Cylinder against an External Pressure

Still missing from the equation is the *sign* of the work done by the expanding gases. As the volume of the cylinder increases, work is done *on* the surroundings *by* the system, so w should be negative. However, upon expansion, V_2 (the final volume) is greater than V_1 (the initial volume) so ΔV is positive. In order for w to be negative for a positive expansion, we need to add a negative sign to our equation. In other words, w and ΔV must be opposite in sign.

$$w = -P \, \Delta V \qquad\qquad [6.8]$$

So the work caused by an expansion of volume is the negative of the pressure that the volume expands against multiplied by the change in volume that occurs during the expansion. The units of the work obtained by using this equation are those of pressure (usually atm) multiplied by those of volume (usually L). To convert between L · atm and J, use the conversion factor 101.3 J = 1 L · atm.

EXAMPLE 6.4 Pressure–Volume Work

To inflate a balloon you must do pressure–volume work on the surroundings. If you inflate a balloon from a volume of 0.100 L to 1.85 L against an external pressure of 1.00 atm, how much work is done (in joules)?

SORT You know the initial and final volumes of the balloon and the pressure against which it expands. The balloon and its contents are the system.	**GIVEN:** $V_1 = 0.100$ L, $V_2 = 1.85$ L, $P = 1.00$ atm **FIND:** w
STRATEGIZE The equation $w = -P \, \Delta V$ specifies the amount of work done during a volume change against an external pressure.	**CONCEPTUAL PLAN** $\boxed{P, \Delta V} \longrightarrow \boxed{w}$ $w = -P\,\Delta V$
SOLVE To solve the problem, calculate the value of ΔV and substitute it, together with P, into the equation.	**SOLUTION** $\Delta V = V_2 - V_1$ $\quad\quad = 1.85\text{ L} - 0.100\text{ L}$ $\quad\quad = 1.75\text{ L}$ $w = -P \, \Delta V$ $\quad = -1.00\text{ atm} \times 1.75\text{ L}$ $\quad = -1.75\text{ L} \cdot \text{atm}$
Convert the units of the answer (L · atm) to joules using 101.3 J = 1 L · atm.	$-1.75\ \text{L} \cdot \text{atm} \times \dfrac{101.3\text{ J}}{1\ \text{L} \cdot \text{atm}} = -177\text{ J}$

CHECK

The units (J) are correct for work. The sign of the work is negative, as it should be for an expansion: work is done on the surroundings by the expanding balloon.

FOR PRACTICE 6.4

A cylinder equipped with a piston expands against an external pressure of 1.58 atm. If the initial volume is 0.485 L and the final volume is 1.245 L, how much work (in J) is done?

FOR MORE PRACTICE 6.4

When fuel is burned in a cylinder equipped with a piston, the volume expands from 0.255 L to 1.45 L against an external pressure of 1.02 atm. In addition, 875 J is emitted as heat. What is ΔE for the burning of the fuel?

6.5 Measuring ΔE for Chemical Reactions: Constant-Volume Calorimetry

We now have a complete picture of how a system exchanges energy with its surroundings via heat and pressure–volume work:

$$\text{System} \xleftrightarrow[\text{Work } (w) = -P \Delta V]{\text{Heat } (q) = m \times C_\text{s} \times \Delta T} \text{Surroundings}$$

Recall from Section 6.3 that the change in internal energy that occurs during a chemical reaction (ΔE) is a measure of *all of the energy* (heat and work) exchanged with the surroundings ($\Delta E = q + w$). Therefore, we can measure the changes in temperature (to calculate heat) and the changes in volume (to calculate work) that occur during a chemical reaction, and then sum them together to calculate ΔE. However, an easier way to obtain the value of ΔE for a chemical reaction is to force all of the energy change associated with a reaction to manifest itself as heat rather than work. We can then measure the temperature change caused by the heat flow.

Recall that $\Delta E = q + w$ and that $w = -P \Delta V$. If a reaction is carried out at constant volume, then $\Delta V = 0$ and $w = 0$. The heat evolved (or given off), called the *heat at constant volume* (q_v), is then equal to ΔE_rxn.

$$\Delta E_\text{rxn} = q_\text{v} + w \overset{\diagup \text{Equals zero}}{\underset{\text{at constant volume}}{}}$$

$$\Delta E_\text{rxn} = q_\text{v} \qquad [6.9]$$

We can measure the heat evolved in a chemical reaction using *calorimetry*. In **calorimetry**, we measure the thermal energy exchanged between the reaction (defined as the system) and the surroundings by observing the change in temperature of the surroundings.

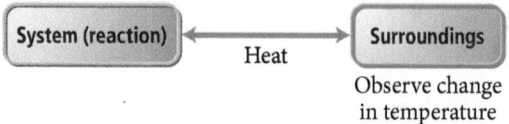

$$\text{System (reaction)} \xleftrightarrow[\text{Heat}]{} \text{Surroundings}$$

Observe change in temperature

The magnitude of the temperature change in the surroundings depends on the magnitude of ΔE for the reaction and on the heat capacity of the surroundings.

Figure 6.8 ▸ shows a **bomb calorimeter**, a piece of equipment designed to measure ΔE for combustion reactions. In a bomb calorimeter, the reaction occurs in a sealed

The Bomb Calorimeter

Thermometer

Ignition wire

Stirrer

Water

Tightly sealed "bomb"

Sample

Oxygen

◄ FIGURE 6.8 The Bomb Calorimeter
A bomb calorimeter measures changes in internal energy for combustion reactions.

container called a *bomb*, which ensures that the reaction occurs at constant volume. To use a bomb calorimeter, we put the sample to be burned (of known mass) into a cup equipped with an ignition wire. We then seal the cup into the bomb, which is filled with oxygen gas, and place the bomb in a water-filled, insulated container. The container is equipped with a stirrer and a thermometer. Finally, we ignite the sample with a wire coil and monitor the temperature with the thermometer. The temperature change (ΔT) is related to the heat absorbed by the entire calorimeter assembly (q_{cal}) by the equation:

$$q_{cal} = C_{cal} \times \Delta T \qquad [6.10]$$

where C_{cal} is the heat capacity of the entire calorimeter assembly (which is usually determined in a separate measurement involving the burning of a substance that gives off a known amount of heat). If no heat escapes from the calorimeter, the amount of heat *gained by* the calorimeter exactly equals that *released by* the reaction (the two are equal in magnitude but opposite in sign):

$$q_{cal} = -q_{rxn} \qquad [6.11]$$

The heat capacity of the calorimeter, C_{cal}, has units of energy over temperature; its value accounts for all of the heat absorbed by all of the components within the calorimeter (including the water).

Since the reaction occurs under conditions of constant volume, $q_{rxn} = q_v = \Delta E_{rxn}$. This measured quantity is the change in the internal energy of the reaction for the specific amount of reactant burned. To get ΔE_{rxn} per mole of a particular reactant—a more general quantity—we divide by the number of moles that actually reacted, as shown in Example 6.5.

EXAMPLE 6.5 Measuring ΔE_{rxn} in a Bomb Calorimeter

When 1.010 g of sucrose $(C_{12}H_{22}O_{11})$ undergoes combustion in a bomb calorimeter, the temperature rises from 24.92 °C to 28.33 °C. Find ΔE_{rxn} for the combustion of sucrose in kJ/mol sucrose. The heat capacity of the bomb calorimeter, determined in a separate experiment, is 4.90 kJ/°C. (You can ignore the heat capacity of the small sample of sucrose because it is negligible compared to the heat capacity of the calorimeter.)

SORT You are given the mass of sucrose, the heat capacity of the calorimeter, and the initial and final temperatures. You are asked to find the change in internal energy for the reaction.	**GIVEN:** 1.010 g $C_{12}H_{22}O_{11}$, $T_i = 24.92$ °C, $T_f = 28.33$ °C, $C_{cal} = 4.90$ kJ/°C **FIND:** ΔE_{rxn}
STRATEGIZE The conceptual plan has three parts. In the first part, use the temperature change and the heat capacity of the calorimeter to find q_{cal}.	**CONCEPTUAL PLAN** $\boxed{C_{cal}, \Delta T} \longrightarrow \boxed{q_{cal}}$ $q_{cal} = C_{cal} \times \Delta T$
In the second part, use q_{cal} to get q_{rxn} (which just involves changing the sign). Since the bomb calorimeter ensures constant volume, q_{rxn} is equivalent to ΔE_{rxn} for the amount of sucrose burned.	$\boxed{q_{cal}} \longrightarrow \boxed{q_{rxn}}$ $q_{rxn} = -q_{cal}$
In the third part, divide q_{rxn} by the number of moles of sucrose to get ΔE_{rxn} per mole of sucrose.	$\Delta E_{rxn} = \dfrac{q_{rxn}}{mol\ C_{12}H_{22}O_{11}}$ **RELATIONSHIPS USED** $q_{cal} = C_{cal} \times \Delta T = -q_{rxn}$ molar mass $C_{12}H_{22}O_{11} = 342.3$ g/mol
SOLVE Gather the necessary quantities in the correct units and substitute these into the equation to calculate q_{cal}.	**SOLUTION** $\Delta T = T_f - T_i$ $\quad = 28.33\ °C - 24.92\ °C = 3.41\ °C$ $q_{cal} = C_{cal} \times \Delta T$ $q_{cal} = 4.90\dfrac{kJ}{°C} \times 3.41\ °C = 16.7$ kJ
Find q_{rxn} by taking the negative of q_{cal}.	$q_{rxn} = -q_{cal} = -16.7$ kJ
Find ΔE_{rxn} per mole of sucrose by dividing q_{rxn} by the number of moles of sucrose (calculated from the given mass of sucrose and its molar mass).	$\Delta E_{rxn} = \dfrac{q_{rxn}}{mol\ C_{12}H_{22}O_{11}}$ $\quad = \dfrac{-16.7\ kJ}{1.010\ \cancel{g\ C_{12}H_{22}O_{11}} \times \dfrac{1\ mol\ C_{12}H_{22}O_{11}}{342.3\ \cancel{g\ C_{12}H_{22}O_{11}}}}$ $\quad = -5.66 \times 10^3$ kJ/mol $C_{12}H_{22}O_{11}$

CHECK The units of the answer (kJ) are correct for a change in internal energy. The sign of ΔE_{rxn} is negative, as it should be for a combustion reaction that gives off energy.

FOR PRACTICE 6.5
When 1.550 g of liquid hexane (C_6H_{14}) undergoes combustion in a bomb calorimeter, the temperature rises from 25.87 °C to 38.13 °C. Find ΔE_{rxn} for the reaction in kJ/mol hexane. The heat capacity of the bomb calorimeter, determined in a separate experiment, is 5.73 kJ/°C.

FOR MORE PRACTICE 6.5
The combustion of toluene has a ΔE_{rxn} of -3.91×10^3 kJ/mol. When 1.55 g of toluene (C_7H_8) undergoes combustion in a bomb calorimeter, the temperature rises from 23.12 °C to 37.57 °C. Find the heat capacity of the bomb calorimeter.

6.6 Enthalpy: The Heat Evolved in a Chemical Reaction at Constant Pressure

We have just seen that when a chemical reaction occurs in a sealed container under conditions of constant volume, the energy evolves only as heat. However, when a chemical reaction occurs open to the atmosphere under conditions of constant pressure—for example, a reaction occurring in an open beaker or the burning of natural gas on a stove—the energy can evolve as both heat and work. As we have also seen, ΔE_{rxn} is a measure of the *total energy change* (both heat and work) that occurs during the reaction. However, in many cases, we are interested only in the heat exchanged, not the work done. For example, when we burn natural gas on a stove to cook food, we do not really care how much work the combustion reaction does on the atmosphere by expanding against it—we just want to know how much heat is given off to cook the food. Under conditions of constant pressure, a thermodynamic quantity called *enthalpy* represents exactly this.

We define the **enthalpy (H)** of a system as the sum of its internal energy and the product of its pressure and volume:

$$H = E + PV \qquad [6.12]$$

Since internal energy, pressure, and volume are all state functions, enthalpy is also a state function. The *change in enthalpy* (ΔH) for any process occurring under constant pressure is given by the expression:

$$\Delta H = \Delta E + P\,\Delta V \qquad [6.13]$$

To better understand this expression, we can interpret the two terms on the right with the help of relationships already familiar to us. We saw previously that $\Delta E = q + w$. If we represent the heat at constant pressure as q_p, then the change in internal energy at constant pressure is $\Delta E = q_p + w$. In addition, from our definition of pressure–volume work, we know that $P\,\Delta V = -w$. Substituting these expressions into the expression for ΔH gives us the following expression:

$$
\begin{aligned}
\Delta H &= \Delta E + P\,\Delta V \\
&= (q_p + w) + P\,\Delta V \qquad [6.14] \\
&= q_p + w - w \\
\Delta H &= q_p
\end{aligned}
$$

We can see that ΔH is equal to q_p, the heat at constant pressure.

Conceptually (and often numerically), ΔH and ΔE are similar: they both represent changes in a state function for the system. However, ΔE is a measure of *all of the energy* (heat and work) exchanged with the surroundings, while ΔH is a measure of only the heat exchanged under conditions of constant pressure. For chemical reactions that do not exchange much work with the surroundings—that is, those that do not cause a large change in reaction volume as they occur—ΔH and ΔE are nearly identical in value. For chemical reactions that produce or consume large amounts of gas, and therefore result in large volume changes, ΔH and ΔE can be slightly different in value.

Conceptual Connection 6.5 The Difference between ΔH and ΔE

Lighters are usually fueled by butane (C_4H_{10}). When 1 mole of butane burns at constant pressure, it produces 2658 kJ of heat and does 3 kJ of work. What are the values of ΔH and ΔE for the combustion of one mole of butane?

The signs of ΔH and ΔE follow the same conventions. A positive ΔH indicates that heat flows into the system as the reaction occurs. A chemical reaction with a positive ΔH, called an **endothermic reaction**, absorbs heat from its surroundings. A chemical cold pack, often used to ice athletic injuries, is a good example of an endothermic reaction. When a barrier separating the reactants in a chemical cold pack is broken, the substances mix, react, and absorb heat from the surroundings. The surroundings—including, say, your bruised wrist—get *colder* because they *lose* energy as the cold pack absorbs it.

Heat

Surroundings

Endothermic

Surroundings

Heat

Exothermic

▲ The reaction that occurs in a chemical cold pack is endothermic—it absorbs energy from the surroundings. The combustion of natural gas is an exothermic reaction—it releases energy to the surroundings.

A chemical reaction with a negative ΔH, called an **exothermic reaction**, gives off heat to its surroundings. The reaction occurring in the chemical hand warmer discussed in Section 6.1 is a good example of an exothermic reaction. As the reaction occurs, heat is given off into the surroundings (including your hand and glove), making them warmer. The burning of natural gas is another example of an exothermic reaction. As the gas burns, it gives off energy, raising the temperature of its surroundings.

Summarizing Enthalpy:

▶ The value of ΔH for a chemical reaction is the amount of heat absorbed or evolved in the reaction under conditions of constant pressure.

▶ An endothermic reaction has a *positive* ΔH and absorbs heat from the surroundings. An endothermic reaction feels cold to the touch.

▶ An exothermic reaction has a *negative* ΔH and gives off heat to the surroundings. An exothermic reaction feels warm to the touch.

EXAMPLE 6.6 Exothermic and Endothermic Processes

Identify each process as endothermic or exothermic and indicate the sign of ΔH.

(a) sweat evaporating from skin

(b) water freezing in a freezer

(c) wood burning in a fire

SOLUTION

(a) Sweat evaporating from skin cools the skin and is therefore endothermic, with a positive ΔH. The skin must supply heat to the perspiration in order for it to continue to evaporate.

(b) Water freezing in a freezer releases heat and is therefore exothermic, with a negative ΔH. The refrigeration system in the freezer must remove this heat for the water to continue to freeze.

(c) Wood burning in a fire releases heat and is therefore exothermic, with a negative ΔH.

FOR PRACTICE 6.6

Identify each process as endothermic or exothermic and indicate the sign of ΔH.

(a) an ice cube melting

(b) nail polish remover quickly evaporating after it is accidentally spilled on the skin

(c) gasoline burning within the cylinder of an automobile engine

Exothermic and Endothermic Processes: A Molecular View

When a chemical system undergoes a change in enthalpy, where does the energy come from or go to? For example, we just saw that an exothermic chemical reaction gives off *thermal energy*—what is the source of that energy?

First, we know that the emitted thermal energy *does not* come from the original thermal energy of the system. Recall from Section 6.2 that the thermal energy of a system is the total kinetic energy of the atoms and molecules that compose the system. This kinetic energy *cannot* be the source of the energy given off in an exothermic reaction because if the atoms and molecules that compose the system were to lose kinetic energy, their temperature would necessarily fall—the system would get colder. Yet we know that in exothermic reactions, the temperature of the system and the surroundings rises. So there must be some other source of energy.

Recall also from Section 6.2 that the internal energy of a chemical system is the sum of its kinetic energy and its *potential energy*. This potential energy is the source in an exothermic chemical reaction. Under normal circumstances, chemical potential energy (or simply chemical energy) arises primarily from the electrostatic forces between the protons and electrons that compose the atoms and molecules within the system. In an exothermic reaction, some bonds break and new ones form, and the nuclei and electrons reorganize into an arrangement with lower potential energy. As the molecules rearrange, their potential energy converts into thermal energy, the heat emitted in the reaction. In an endothermic reaction, the opposite happens: as some bonds break and others form, the nuclei and electrons reorganize into an arrangement with higher potential energy, absorbing thermal energy in the process.

Conceptual Connection 6.6 Exothermic and Endothermic Reactions

If an endothermic reaction absorbs heat, then why does it feel cold to the touch?

Stoichiometry Involving ΔH: Thermochemical Equations

The enthalpy change for a chemical reaction, abbreviated ΔH_{rxn}, is also called the **enthalpy of reaction** or **heat of reaction** and is an extensive property, one that depends on the amount of material undergoing the reaction. In other words, the amount of heat generated or absorbed when a chemical reaction occurs depends on the *amounts* of reactants that actually react. We usually specify ΔH_{rxn} in combination with the balanced chemical equation for the reaction. *The magnitude of ΔH_{rxn} is for the stoichiometric amounts of reactants and products for the reaction as written.* For example, consider the balanced equation and ΔH_{rxn} for the combustion of propane, the main component of LP gas:

$$C_3H_8(g) \ + \ 5\,O_2(g) \longrightarrow 3\,CO_2(g) + 4\,H_2O(g) \quad \Delta H_{rxn} \ = \ -2044\ kJ$$

The equation tells us that when 1 mol of C_3H_8 reacts with 5 mol of O_2 to form 3 mol of CO_2 and 4 mol of H_2O, 2044 kJ of heat is emitted. We can write these relationships in the same way that we expressed stoichiometric relationships in Chapter 4, as ratios between two quantities. For example, for the reactants, we write the following ratios:

$$1\ mol\ C_3H_8 : -2044\ kJ \qquad or \qquad 5\ mol\ O_2 : -2044\ kJ$$

The ratios indicate that 2044 kJ of heat evolves when 1 mol of C_3H_8 and 5 mol of O_2 completely react. We can use these ratios to construct conversion factors between amounts of reactants or products and the quantity of heat emitted (for exothermic reactions) or absorbed (for endothermic reactions). To find out how much heat is emitted upon the combustion of a certain mass in grams of C_3H_8, we use the following conceptual plan:

We use the molar mass to convert between grams and moles, and the stoichiometric relationship between moles of C_3H_8 and the heat of reaction to convert between moles and kilojoules, as shown in Example 6.7.

EXAMPLE 6.7 Stoichiometry Involving ΔH

An LP gas tank in a home barbeque contains 13.2 kg of propane, C_3H_8. Calculate the heat (in kJ) associated with the complete combustion of all of the propane in the tank.

$$C_3H_8(g) + 5\,O_2(g) \rightarrow 3\,CO_2(g) + 4\,H_2O(g) \qquad \Delta H_{rxn} = -2044 \text{ kJ}$$

SORT You are given the mass of propane and asked to find the heat evolved in its combustion.	**GIVEN:** 13.2 kg C_3H_8 **FIND:** q
STRATEGIZE Starting with kg C_3H_8, convert to g C_3H_8 and then use the molar mass of C_3H_8 to find the number of moles. Next, use the stoichiometric relationship between mol C_3H_8 and kJ to determine the heat evolved.	**CONCEPTUAL PLAN** kg C_3H_8 → g C_3H_8 → mol C_3H_8 → kJ $\dfrac{1000 \text{ g}}{1 \text{ kg}}$ $\dfrac{1 \text{ mol } C_3H_8}{44.09 \text{ g } C_3H_8}$ $\dfrac{-2044 \text{ kJ}}{1 \text{ mol } C_3H_8}$ **RELATIONSHIPS USED** 1000 g = 1 kg molar mass C_3H_8 = 44.09 g/mol 1 mol C_3H_8 : -2044 kJ (from balanced equation)
SOLVE Follow the conceptual plan to solve the problem. Begin with 13.2 kg C_3H_8 and multiply by the appropriate conversion factors to arrive at kJ.	**SOLUTION** $13.2 \text{ kg } C_3H_8 \times \dfrac{1000 \text{ g}}{1 \text{ kg}} \times \dfrac{1 \text{ mol } C_3H_8}{44.09 \text{ g } C_3H_8} \times \dfrac{-2044 \text{ kJ}}{1 \text{ mol } C_3H_8}$ $= -6.12 \times 10^5 \text{ kJ}$

CHECK The units of the answer (kJ) are correct for energy. The answer is negative, as it should be for heat evolved by the reaction.

FOR PRACTICE 6.7
Ammonia reacts with oxygen according to the equation:

$$4\,NH_3(g) + 5\,O_2(g) \rightarrow 4\,NO(g) + 6\,H_2O(g) \qquad \Delta H_{rxn} = -906 \text{ kJ}$$

Calculate the heat (in kJ) associated with the complete reaction of 155 g of NH_3.

FOR MORE PRACTICE 6.7
What mass of butane in grams is necessary to produce 1.5×10^3 kJ of heat? What mass of CO_2 is produced?

$$C_4H_{10}(g) + 13/2\,O_2(g) \rightarrow 4\,CO_2(g) + 5\,H_2O(g) \qquad \Delta H_{rxn} = -2658 \text{ kJ}$$

6.7 Constant-Pressure Calorimetry: Measuring ΔH_{rxn}

For many aqueous reactions, we can measure ΔH_{rxn} fairly simply using a **coffee-cup calorimeter** shown in Figure 6.9 ▸. The calorimeter consists of two Styrofoam coffee cups, one inserted into the other, to provide insulation from the laboratory environment. The calorimeter is equipped with a thermometer and a stirrer. The reaction occurs in a specifically measured quantity of solution within the calorimeter, so that the mass of the solution is known. During the reaction, the heat evolved (or absorbed) causes a temperature change in the solution, which the thermometer measures. If we know the specific heat capacity of the solution, normally assumed to be that of water, we can calculate q_{soln}, the heat absorbed by or lost from the solution (which is acting as the surroundings) using the equation:

$$q_{soln} = m_{soln} \times C_{s,\,soln} \times \Delta T$$

The insulated calorimeter prevents heat from escaping, so we assume that the heat gained by the solution equals that lost by the reaction (or vice versa):

$$q_{rxn} = -q_{soln}$$

Since the reaction happens under conditions of constant pressure (open to the atmosphere), $q_{rxn} = q_p = \Delta H_{rxn}$. This measured quantity is the heat of reaction for the specific amount (which is measured ahead of time) of reactants that reacted. To get ΔH_{rxn} per mole of a particular reactant—a more general quantity—we divide by the number of moles that actually reacted, as shown in Example 6.8.

Summarizing Calorimetry:

▸ Bomb calorimetry occurs at constant *volume* and measures ΔE for a reaction.

▸ Coffee-cup calorimetry occurs at constant *pressure* and measures ΔH for a reaction.

The Coffee-Cup Calorimeter

—— Thermometer

—— Glass stirrer

—— Cork lid (loose fitting)

—— Two nested Styrofoam® cups containing reactants in solution

▲ FIGURE 6.9 **The Coffee-Cup Calorimeter**   A coffee-cup calorimeter measures enthalpy changes for chemical reactions in solution.

> This equation assumes that no heat is lost to the calorimeter itself. If heat absorbed by the calorimeter is accounted for, the equation becomes $q_{rxn} = +(q_{soln} + q_{cal})$.

EXAMPLE 6.8 Measuring ΔH_{rxn} in a Coffee-Cup Calorimeter

Magnesium metal reacts with hydrochloric acid according to the balanced equation:

$$Mg(s) + 2\,HCl(aq) \rightarrow MgCl_2(aq) + H_2(g)$$

In an experiment to determine the enthalpy change for this reaction, 0.158 g of Mg metal is combined with enough HCl to make 100.0 mL of solution in a coffee-cup calorimeter. The HCl is sufficiently concentrated so that the Mg completely reacts. The temperature of the solution rises from 25.6 °C to 32.8 °C as a result of the reaction. Find ΔH_{rxn} for the reaction as written. Use 1.00 g/mL as the density of the solution and $C_{s,soln} = 4.18$ J/g · °C as the specific heat capacity of the solution.

SORT You are given the mass of magnesium, the volume of solution, the initial and final temperatures, the density of the solution, and the heat capacity of the solution. You are asked to find the change in enthalpy for the reaction.	**GIVEN:** 0.158 g Mg 100.0 mL soln $T_i = 25.6\,°C$ $T_f = 32.8\,°C$ $d = 1.00$ g/mL, $C_{s,\,soln} = 4.18$ J/g · °C **FIND:** ΔH_{rxn}

STRATEGIZE The conceptual plan has three parts. In the first part, use the temperature change and the other given quantities, together with the equation $q = m \times C_s \times \Delta T$, to find q_{soln}.

In the second part, use q_{soln} to get q_{rxn} (which simply involves changing the sign). Because the pressure is constant, q_{rxn} is equivalent to ΔH_{rxn} for the amount of magnesium that reacts.

In the third part, divide q_{rxn} by the number of moles of magnesium to get ΔH_{rxn} per mole of magnesium.

CONCEPTUAL PLAN

$$C_{s,\,soln}, m_{soln}, \Delta T \longrightarrow q_{soln}$$
$$q = m \times C_s \times \Delta T$$

$$q_{soln} \longrightarrow q_{rxn}$$
$$q_{rxn} = -q_{soln}$$

$$\Delta H_{rxn} = \frac{q_{rxn}}{\text{mol Mg}}$$

RELATIONSHIPS USED
$$q = m \times C_s \times \Delta T$$
$$q_{rxn} = -q_{soln}$$

SOLVE Gather the necessary quantities in the correct units for the equation $q = m \times C_s \times \Delta T$ and substitute these into the equation to calculate q_{soln}. Notice that the sign of q_{soln} is positive, meaning that the solution absorbed heat from the reaction.

SOLUTION

$$C_{s,soln} = 4.18 \text{ J/g} \cdot {}^\circ\text{C}$$

$$m_{soln} = 100.0 \text{ mL soln} \times \frac{1.00 \text{ g}}{1 \text{ mL soln}} = 1.00 \times 10^2 \text{ g}$$

$$\Delta T = T_f - T_i$$
$$= 32.8 \,{}^\circ\text{C} - 25.6 \,{}^\circ\text{C} = 7.2 \,{}^\circ\text{C}$$

$$q_{soln} = m_{soln} \times C_{s,\,soln} \times \Delta T$$
$$= 1.00 \times 10^2 \text{ g} \times 4.18 \frac{\text{J}}{\text{g} \cdot {}^\circ\text{C}} \times 7.2 \,{}^\circ\text{C} = 3.0 \times 10^3 \text{ J}$$

Find q_{rxn} by taking the negative of q_{soln}. Notice that q_{rxn} is negative, as expected for an exothermic reaction.

$$q_{rxn} = -q_{soln} = -3.0 \times 10^3 \text{ J}$$

Finally, find ΔH_{rxn} per mole of magnesium by dividing q_{rxn} by the number of moles of magnesium that reacts. Find the number of moles of magnesium from the given mass of magnesium and its molar mass.

$$\Delta H_{rxn} = \frac{q_{rxn}}{\text{mol Mg}}$$

$$= \frac{-3.0 \times 10^3 \text{ J}}{0.158 \text{ g Mg} \times \dfrac{1 \text{ mol Mg}}{24.31 \text{ g Mg}}}$$

$$= -4.6 \times 10^5 \text{ J/mol Mg}$$

Since the stoichiometric coefficient for magnesium in the balanced chemical equation is 1, the calculated value represents ΔH_{rxn} for the reaction as written.

$$\text{Mg}(s) + 2\,\text{HCl}(aq) \rightarrow \text{MgCl}_2(aq) + \text{H}_2(g)$$
$$\Delta H_{rxn} = -4.6 \times 10^5 \text{ J}$$

CHECK The units of the answer (J) are correct for the change in enthalpy of a reaction. The sign is negative, as expected for an exothermic reaction.

FOR PRACTICE 6.8
The addition of hydrochloric acid to a silver nitrate solution precipitates silver chloride according to the reaction:

$$\text{AgNO}_3(aq) + \text{HCl}(aq) \rightarrow \text{AgCl}(s) + \text{HNO}_3(aq)$$

When 50.0 mL of 0.100 M AgNO_3 is combined with 50.0 mL of 0.100 M HCl in a coffee-cup calorimeter, the temperature changes from 23.40 °C to 24.21 °C. Calculate ΔH_{rxn} for the reaction as written. Use 1.00 g/mL as the density of the solution and $C = 4.18$ J/g · °C as the specific heat capacity.

Conceptual Connection 6.7 Constant-Pressure versus Constant-Volume Calorimetry

The same reaction, with exactly the same amount of reactant, is conducted in a bomb calorimeter and in a coffee-cup calorimeter. In one measurement, $q_{rxn} = -12.5$ kJ and in the other $q_{rxn} = -11.8$ kJ. Which value was obtained in the bomb calorimeter? (Assume that the reaction has a positive ΔV in the coffee-cup calorimeter.)

6.8 Relationships Involving ΔH_{rxn}

The change in enthalpy for a reaction is always associated with a *particular* reaction. If we change the reaction in well-defined ways, then ΔH_{rxn} also changes in well-defined ways. We now turn our attention to three quantitative relationships between a chemical equation and ΔH_{rxn}.

1. **If a chemical equation is multiplied by some factor, then ΔH_{rxn} is also multiplied by the same factor.**

Recall from Section 6.6 that ΔH_{rxn} is an extensive property; it depends on the quantity of reactants undergoing reaction. Recall also that ΔH_{rxn} is usually reported for a reaction involving stoichiometric amounts of reactants. For example, for a reaction A + 2 B $\longrightarrow$ C, ΔH_{rxn} is typically reported as the amount of heat emitted or absorbed when 1 mol A reacts with 2 mol B to form 1 mol C. Therefore, if a chemical equation is multiplied by a factor, then ΔH_{rxn} is also multiplied by the same factor. For example,

$$A + 2B \longrightarrow C \qquad \Delta H_1$$
$$2A + 4B \longrightarrow 2C \qquad \Delta H_2 = 2 \times \Delta H_1$$

2. **If a chemical equation is reversed, then ΔH_{rxn} changes sign.**

Recall from Section 6.6 that ΔH_{rxn} is a state function, which means that its value depends only on the initial and final states of the system.

$$\Delta H = H_{final} - H_{initial}$$

When a reaction is reversed, the final state becomes the initial state and vice versa. Consequently, ΔH_{rxn} changes sign:

$$A + 2B \longrightarrow C \qquad \Delta H_1$$
$$C \longrightarrow A + 2B \qquad \Delta H_2 = -\Delta H_1$$

3. **If a chemical equation can be expressed as the sum of a series of steps, then ΔH_{rxn} for the overall equation is the sum of the heats of reactions for each step.**

This last relationship, known as **Hess's law**, also follows from the enthalpy of reaction being a state function. Since ΔH_{rxn} is dependent only on the initial and final states, and not on the pathway the reaction follows, ΔH obtained from summing the individual steps that lead to an overall reaction must be the same as ΔH for that overall reaction. For example,

$$A + 2B \longrightarrow C \qquad \Delta H_1$$
$$C \longrightarrow 2D \qquad \Delta H_2$$
$$\overline{A + 2B \longrightarrow 2D \qquad \Delta H_3 = \Delta H_1 + \Delta H_2}$$

We illustrate Hess's law with the energy level diagram shown in Figure 6.10 ▶.

These three quantitative relationships make it possible to determine ΔH for a reaction without directly measuring it in the laboratory. (For some reactions, direct measurement can be difficult.) If we can find

> **Hess's Law**
> The change in enthalpy for a stepwise process is the sum of the enthalpy changes of the steps.

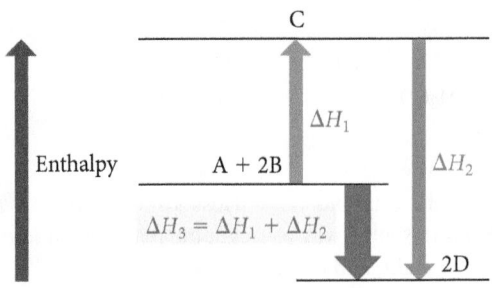

▲ **FIGURE 6.10 Hess's Law** The change in enthalpy for a stepwise process is the sum of the enthalpy changes of the steps.

related reactions (with known ΔH's) that sum to the reaction of interest, we can find ΔH for the reaction of interest. For example, the following reaction between $C(s)$ and $H_2O(g)$ is an industrially important method of generating hydrogen gas:

$$C(s) + H_2O(g) \longrightarrow CO(g) + H_2(g) \qquad \Delta H_{rxn} = ?$$

We can find ΔH_{rxn} from the following reactions with known ΔH's:

$$C(s) + O_2(g) \longrightarrow CO_2(g) \qquad \Delta H = -393.5 \text{ kJ}$$
$$2\,CO(g) + O_2(g) \longrightarrow 2\,CO_2(g) \qquad \Delta H = -566.0 \text{ kJ}$$
$$2\,H_2(g) + O_2(g) \longrightarrow 2\,H_2O(g) \qquad \Delta H = -483.6 \text{ kJ}$$

We just have to determine how to sum these reactions to get the overall reaction of interest. We do this by manipulating the reactions with known ΔH's in such a way as to get the reactants of interest on the left, the products of interest on the right, and other species to cancel.

Since the first reaction has $C(s)$ as a reactant, and the reaction of interest also has $C(s)$ as a reactant, we write the first reaction unchanged.

$$C(s) + O_2(g) \rightarrow CO_2(g) \quad \Delta H = -393.5 \text{ kJ}$$

The second reaction has 2 mol of $CO(g)$ as a reactant. However, the reaction of interest has 1 mol of $CO(g)$ as a product. Therefore, we reverse the second reaction, change the sign of ΔH, and multiply the reaction and ΔH by $^1/_2$.

$$^1/_2 \times [2\,CO_2(g) \rightarrow 2\,CO(g) + O_2(g)]$$
$$\Delta H = {}^1/_2 \times (+566.0 \text{ kJ})$$

The third reaction has $H_2(g)$ as a reactant. In the reaction of interest, however, $H_2(g)$ is a product. Therefore, we reverse the equation and change the sign of ΔH. In addition, to obtain coefficients that match the reaction of interest, and to cancel O_2, we must multiply the reaction and ΔH by $^1/_2$.

$$^1/_2 \times [2\,H_2O(g) \rightarrow 2\,H_2(g) + O_2(g)]$$
$$\Delta H = {}^1/_2 \times (+483.6 \text{ kJ})$$

Lastly, we rewrite the three reactions after multiplying through by the indicated factors and show how they sum to the reaction of interest. ΔH for the reaction of interest is then just the sum of the ΔH's for the steps.

$$
\begin{array}{ll}
C(s) + \cancel{O_2(g)} \rightarrow \cancel{CO_2(g)} & \Delta H = -393.5 \text{ kJ} \\
\cancel{CO_2(g)} \rightarrow CO(g) + {}^1/_2\,\cancel{O_2(g)} & \Delta H = +283.0 \text{ kJ} \\
H_2O(g) \rightarrow H_2(g) + {}^1/_2\,\cancel{O_2(g)} & \Delta H = +241.8 \text{ kJ} \\
\hline
C(s) + H_2O(g) \rightarrow CO(g) + H_2(g)\ \Delta H_{rxn} & = +131.3 \text{ kJ}
\end{array}
$$

EXAMPLE 6.9 Hess's Law

Find ΔH_{rxn} for the reaction:

$$3\,C(s) + 4\,H_2(g) \longrightarrow C_3H_8(g)$$

Use these reactions with known ΔH's:

$$C_3H_8(g) + 5\,O_2(g) \longrightarrow 3\,CO_2(g) + 4\,H_2O(g) \qquad \Delta H = -2043 \text{ kJ}$$
$$C(s) + O_2(g) \longrightarrow CO_2(g) \qquad \Delta H = -393.5 \text{ kJ}$$
$$2\,H_2(g) + O_2(g) \longrightarrow 2\,H_2O(g) \qquad \Delta H = -483.6 \text{ kJ}$$

SOLUTION

To work this and other Hess's law problems, manipulate the reactions with known ΔH's in such a way as to get the reactants of interest on the left, the products of interest on the right, and other species to cancel.

The first reaction has C_3H_8 as a reactant, and the reaction of interest has C_3H_8 as a product, so you can reverse the first reaction and change the sign of ΔH.	$3\,CO_2(g) + 4\,H_2O(g) \rightarrow C_3H_8(g) + 5\,O_2(g) \quad \Delta H = +2043 \text{ kJ}$

The second reaction has C as a reactant and CO_2 as a product, just as required in the reaction of interest. However, the coefficient for C is 1, and in the reaction of interest, the coefficient for C is 3. You need to multiply this equation and its ΔH by 3.	$3 \times [C(s) + O_2(g) \rightarrow CO_2(g)] \quad \Delta H = 3 \times (-393.5 \text{ kJ})$
The third reaction has $H_2(g)$ as a reactant, as required. However, the coefficient for H_2 is 2, and in the reaction of interest, the coefficient for H_2 is 4. Multiply this reaction and its ΔH by 2.	$2 \times [2 H_2(g) + O_2(g) \rightarrow 2 H_2O(g)] \quad \Delta H = 2 \times (-483.6 \text{ kJ})$
Lastly, rewrite the three reactions after multiplying through by the indicated factors and show how they sum to the reaction of interest. ΔH for the reaction of interest is the sum of the ΔH's for the steps.	$3\,CO_2(g) + 4\,H_2O(g) \rightarrow C_3H_8(g) + 5\,O_2(g) \qquad \Delta H = +2043 \text{ kJ}$ $3\,C(s) + 3\,O_2(g) \rightarrow 3\,CO_2(g) \qquad \Delta H = -1181 \text{ kJ}$ $4\,H_2(g) + 2\,O_2(g) \rightarrow 4\,H_2O(g) \qquad \Delta H = -967.2 \text{ kJ}$ $3\,C(s) + 4\,H_2(g) \rightarrow C_3H_8(g) \qquad \Delta H_{rxn} = -105 \text{ kJ}$

FOR PRACTICE 6.9

Find ΔH_{rxn} for the reaction:

$$N_2O(g) + NO_2(g) \longrightarrow 3 NO(g)$$

Use these reactions with known ΔH's:

$$2 NO(g) + O_2(g) \longrightarrow 2 NO_2(g) \qquad \Delta H = -113.1 \text{ kJ}$$
$$N_2(g) + O_2(g) \longrightarrow 2 NO(g) \qquad \Delta H = +182.6 \text{ kJ}$$
$$2 N_2O(g) \longrightarrow 2 N_2(g) + O_2(g) \qquad \Delta H = -163.2 \text{ kJ}$$

FOR MORE PRACTICE 6.9

Find ΔH_{rxn} for the reaction:

$$3 H_2(g) + O_3(g) \rightarrow 3 H_2O(g)$$

Use these reactions with known ΔH's:

$$2 H_2(g) + O_2(g) \longrightarrow 2 H_2O(g) \qquad \Delta H = -483.6 \text{ kJ}$$
$$3 O_2(g) \longrightarrow 2 O_3(g) \qquad \Delta H = +285.4 \text{ kJ}$$

6.9 Determining Enthalpies of Reaction from Standard Enthalpies of Formation

We have examined two ways to determine ΔH for a chemical reaction: experimentally through calorimetry and inferentially through Hess's law. We now turn to a third and more convenient way to determine ΔH for a large number of chemical reactions: from tabulated *standard enthalpies of formation*.

Standard States and Standard Enthalpy Changes

Recall that ΔH is the *change* in enthalpy for a chemical reaction—the difference in enthalpy between the products and the reactants. Since we are interested in changes in enthalpy (and not in absolute values of enthalpy itself), we are free to define the *zero* of enthalpy as conveniently as possible. Returning to our mountain-climbing analogy, a change in altitude (like a change in enthalpy) is an absolute quantity. Altitude itself (like enthalpy), however, is a relative quantity, defined relative to some standard (such as sea level in the case of altitude). We must define a similar, albeit slightly more complex, standard for enthalpy. This standard has three parts: the **standard state**, the **standard enthalpy change** ($\Delta H°$), and the **standard enthalpy of formation** ($\Delta H_f°$).

The standard state was changed in 1997 to a pressure of 1 bar, which is very close to 1 atm (1 atm = 1.013 bar). Both standards are now in common use.

1. **Standard State**
   - *For a Gas:* The standard state for a gas is the pure gas at a pressure of exactly 1 atmosphere.
   - *For a Liquid or Solid:* The standard state for a liquid or solid is the pure substance in its most stable form at a pressure of 1 atm and at the temperature of interest (often taken to be 25 °C).
   - *For a Substance in Solution:* The standard state for a substance in solution is a concentration of exactly 1 M.

2. **Standard Enthalpy Change ($\Delta H°$)**
   - The change in enthalpy for a process when all reactants and products are in their standard states. The degree sign indicates standard states.

3. **Standard Enthalpy of Formation ($\Delta H_f°$)**
   - *For a Pure Compound:* The change in enthalpy when one mole of the compound forms from its constituent elements in their standard states.
   - *For a Pure Element in Its Standard State:* $\Delta H_f° = 0$.

The standard enthalpy of formation is also called the **standard heat of formation**.

Assigning the value of zero to the standard enthalpy of formation for an element in its standard state is the equivalent of assigning an altitude of zero to sea level. Once we assume sea level is zero, we can then measure all subsequent changes in altitude relative to sea level. Similarly, we can measure all changes in enthalpy relative to those of pure elements in their standard states. For example, consider the standard enthalpy of formation of methane gas at 25 °C:

The carbon in this equation must be graphite (the most stable form of carbon at 1 atm and 25 °C).

$$C(s, \text{graphite}) + 2\,H_2(g) \rightarrow CH_4(g) \qquad \Delta H_f° = -74.6 \text{ kJ/mol}$$

For methane, as with most compounds, $\Delta H_f°$ is negative. Continuing our analogy, if we think of pure elements in their standard states as being at *sea level*, then most compounds lie *below sea level*. The chemical equation for the enthalpy of formation of a compound is always written to form one mole of the compound, so $\Delta H_f°$ has the units of kJ/mol. Table 6.5 lists $\Delta H_f°$ values for some selected compounds. A more complete list can be found in Appendix IIB.

TABLE 6.5 Standard Enthalpies (or Heats) of Formation, $\Delta H_f°$, at 298 K

Formula	$\Delta H_f°$ (kJ/mol)	Formula	$\Delta H_f°$ (kJ/mol)	Formula	$\Delta H_f°$ (kJ/mol)
Bromine		C_3H_8O(*l*, isopropanol)	−318.1	*Oxygen*	
Br(*g*)	111.9	C_6H_6(*l*)	49.1	O_2(*g*)	0
Br_2(*l*)	0	$C_6H_{12}O_6$(*s*, glucose)	−1273.3	O_3(*g*)	142.7
HBr(*g*)	−36.3	$C_{12}H_{22}O_{11}$(*s*, sucrose)	−2226.1	H_2O(*g*)	−241.8
Calcium		*Chlorine*		H_2O(*l*)	−285.8
Ca(*s*)	0	Cl(*g*)	121.3	*Silver*	
CaO(*s*)	−634.9	Cl_2(*g*)	0	Ag(*s*)	0
$CaCO_3$(*s*)	−1207.6	HCl(*g*)	−92.3	AgCl(*s*)	−127.0
Carbon		*Fluorine*		*Sodium*	
C(*s*, graphite)	0	F(*g*)	79.38	Na(*s*)	0
C(*s*, diamond)	1.88	F_2(*g*)	0	Na(*g*)	107.5
CO(*g*)	−110.5	HF(*g*)	−273.3	NaCl(*s*)	−411.2
CO_2(*g*)	−393.5	*Hydrogen*		Na_2CO_3(*s*)	−1130.7
CH_4(*g*)	−74.6	H(*g*)	218.0	$NaHCO_3$(*s*)	−950.8
CH_3OH(*l*)	−238.6	H_2(*g*)	0	*Sulfur*	
C_2H_2(*g*)	227.4	*Nitrogen*		S_8(*s*, rhombic)	0
C_2H_4(*g*)	52.4	N_2(*g*)	0	S_8(*s*, monoclinic)	0.3
C_2H_6(*g*	−84.68	NH_3(*g*)	−45.9	SO_2(*g*)	−296.8
C_2H_5OH(*l*)	−277.6	NH_4NO_3(*s*)	−365.6	SO_3(*g*)	−395.7
C_3H_8(*g*)	−103.85	NO(*g*)	91.3	H_2SO_4(*l*)	−814.0
C_3H_6O(*l*, acetone)	−248.4	N_2O(*g*)	81.6		

EXAMPLE 6.10 Standard Enthalpies of Formation

Write equations for the formation of (a) $MgCO_3(s)$ and (b) $C_6H_{12}O_6(s)$ from their respective elements in their standard states. Include the value of ΔH_f° for each equation.

SOLUTION

a. $MgCO_3(s)$

Write the equation with the elements in $MgCO_3$ in their standard states as the reactants and 1 mol of $MgCO_3$ as the product.

$$Mg(s) + C(s, \text{graphite}) + O_2(g) \rightarrow MgCO_3(s)$$

Balance the equation and look up ΔH_f° in Appendix IIB. (Use fractional coefficients so that the product of the reaction is 1 mol of $MgCO_3$.)

$$Mg(s) + C(s, \text{graphite}) + \frac{3}{2}O_2(g) \rightarrow MgCO_3(s)$$
$$\Delta H_f^\circ = -1095.8 \text{ kJ/mol}$$

b. $C_6H_{12}O_6(s)$

Write the equation with the elements in $C_6H_{12}O_6$ in their standard states as the reactants and 1 mol of $C_6H_{12}O_6$ as the product.

$$C(s, \text{graphite}) + H_2(g) + O_2(g) \rightarrow C_6H_{12}O_6(s)$$

Balance the equation and look up ΔH_f° in Appendix IIB.

$$6\,C(s, \text{graphite}) + 6\,H_2(g) + 3\,O_2(g) \rightarrow C_6H_{12}O_6(s)$$
$$\Delta H_f^\circ = -1273.3 \text{ kJ/mol}$$

FOR PRACTICE 6.10

Write equations for the formation of (a) $NaCl(s)$ and (b) $Pb(NO_3)_2(s)$ from their respective elements in their standard states. Include the value of ΔH_f° for each equation.

Calculating the Standard Enthalpy Change for a Reaction

We have just seen that the standard enthalpy of formation corresponds to the *formation* of a compound from its constituent elements in their standard states:

$$\text{elements} \rightarrow \text{compound} \quad \Delta H_f^\circ$$

Therefore, the *negative* of the standard enthalpy of formation corresponds to the *decomposition* of a compound into its constituent elements in their standard states:

$$\text{compound} \rightarrow \text{elements} \quad -\Delta H_f^\circ$$

We can use these two concepts—the decomposition of a compound into its elements and the formation of a compound from its elements—to calculate the enthalpy change of any reaction by mentally taking the reactants through two steps. In the first step we *decompose the reactants* into their constituent elements in their standard states; in the second step we *form the products* from the constituent elements in their standard states.

$$\begin{aligned} \text{reactants} \rightarrow \text{elements} \quad & \Delta H_1 = -\Sigma\,\Delta H_f^\circ(\text{reactants}) \\ \text{elements} \rightarrow \text{products} \quad & \Delta H_2 = +\Sigma\,\Delta H_f^\circ(\text{products}) \\ \hline \text{reactants} \rightarrow \text{products} \quad & \Delta H_{rxn}^\circ = \Delta H_1 + \Delta H_2 \end{aligned}$$

In these equations, Σ means "the sum of" so that ΔH_1 is the sum of the negatives of the heats of formation of the reactants and ΔH_2 is the sum of the heats of formation of the products.

We can demonstrate this procedure by calculating the standard enthalpy change (ΔH_{rxn}°) for the combustion of methane:

$$CH_4(g) + 2\,O_2(g) \rightarrow CO_2(g) + 2\,H_2O(g) \quad \Delta H_{rxn}^\circ = ?$$

The energy changes associated with the decomposition of the reactants and the formation of the products are shown in Figure 6.11 ▶. The first step (1) is the decomposition of 1 mol of methane into its constituent elements in their standard states. We can obtain the

EXAMPLE 6.12 ΔH_{rxn}° and Standard Enthalpies of Formation

A city of 100,000 people uses approximately 1.0×10^{11} kJ of energy per day. Suppose all of that energy comes from the combustion of liquid octane (C_8H_{18}) to form gaseous water and gaseous carbon dioxide. Use standard enthalpies of formation to calculate ΔH_{rxn}° for the combustion of octane and then determine how many kilograms of octane would be necessary to provide this amount of energy.

SORT You are given the amount of energy used and asked to find the mass of octane required to produce the energy.	**GIVEN:** 1.0×10^{11} kJ **FIND:** kg C_8H_{18}

STRATEGIZE The conceptual plan has three parts. In the first part, write a balanced equation for the combustion of octane.

In the second part, calculate ΔH_{rxn}° from the ΔH_f°'s of the reactants and products.

In the third part, convert from kilojoules of energy to moles of octane using the conversion factor found in step 2, and then convert from moles of octane to mass of octane using the molar mass.

CONCEPTUAL PLAN

(1) Write the balanced equation.

(2)

$$\boxed{\Delta H_f^{\circ}\text{'s}} \longrightarrow \boxed{\Delta H_{rxn}^{\circ}}$$

$$\Delta H_{rxn}^{\circ} = \Sigma\, n_p \Delta H_f^{\circ}\,(\text{products})\; -\; \Sigma\, n_r \Delta H_f^{\circ}\,(\text{reactants})$$

(3)

$$\boxed{\text{kJ}} \longrightarrow \boxed{\text{mol } C_8H_{18}} \longrightarrow \boxed{\text{g } C_8H_{18}} \longrightarrow \boxed{\text{kg } C_8H_{18}}$$

$$\frac{114.22 \text{ g } C_8H_{18}}{\text{mol } C_8H_{18}} \qquad \frac{1 \text{ kg}}{1000 \text{ g}}$$

Conversion factor to be determined from steps 1 and 2

RELATIONSHIPS USED

molar mass C_8H_{18} = 114.22 g/mol

1 kg = 1000 g

SOLVE Begin by writing the balanced equation for the combustion of octane. For convenience, do not clear the 25/2 fraction in order to keep the coefficient on octane as 1.

SOLUTION STEP 1

$$C_8H_{18}(l) + \frac{25}{2} O_2(g) \longrightarrow 8\,CO_2(g) + 9\,H_2O(g)$$

SOLUTION STEP 2

Reactant or product	ΔH_f° (kJ/mol from Appendix IIB)
$C_8H_{18}(l)$	−250.1
$O_2(g)$	0.0
$CO_2(g)$	−393.5
$H_2O(g)$	−241.8

Look up (in Appendix IIB) the standard enthalpy of formation for each reactant and product and then calculate ΔH_{rxn}°.

$$\Delta H_{rxn}^{\circ} = \Sigma\, n_p \Delta H_f^{\circ}\,(\text{products}) - \Sigma\, n_r \Delta H_f^{\circ}\,(\text{reactants})$$

$$= \left[8\,(\Delta H_{f,\,CO_2(g)}^{\circ}) + 9\,(\Delta H_{f,\,H_2O(g)}^{\circ})\right]$$

$$-\left[1\,(\Delta H_{f,\,C_8H_{18}(l)}^{\circ}) + \frac{25}{2}\,(\Delta H_{f,\,O_2(g)}^{\circ})\right]$$

$$= [8(-393.5 \text{ kJ}) + 9(-241.8 \text{ kJ})] - \left[1(-250.1 \text{ kJ}) + \frac{25}{2}(0.0 \text{ kJ})\right]$$

$$= -5324.2 \text{ kJ} - (-250.1 \text{ kJ})$$

$$= -5074.1 \text{ kJ}$$

From steps 1 and 2 build a conversion factor between mol C_8H_{18} and kJ.	**SOLUTION STEP 3**
	1 mol C_8H_{18} : -5074.1 kJ
Follow step 3 of the conceptual plan. Begin with -1.0×10^{11} kJ (since the city uses this much energy, the reaction must emit it, and therefore the sign is negative) and follow the steps to determine kg octane.	$-1.0 \times 10^{11} \text{ kJ} \times \dfrac{1 \text{ mol } C_8H_{18}}{-5074.1 \text{ kJ}} \times \dfrac{114.22 \text{ g } C_8H_{18}}{1 \text{ mol } C_8H_{18}}$ $\times \dfrac{1 \text{ kg}}{1000 \text{ g}} = 2.3 \times 10^6 \text{ kg } C_8H_{18}$

CHECK

The units of the answer (kg C_8H_{18}) are correct. The answer is positive, as it should be for mass. The magnitude is fairly large, as you would expect since this amount of octane is supposed to provide the energy for an entire city.

FOR PRACTICE 6.12

The chemical hand warmers described in Section 6.1 produce heat when they are removed from their airtight plastic wrappers. Recall that they utilize the oxidation of iron to form iron oxide according to the reaction $4 \text{ Fe}(s) + 3 \text{ O}_2(g) \longrightarrow 2 \text{ Fe}_2\text{O}_3(s)$. Calculate ΔH°_{rxn} for this reaction and calculate how much heat is produced from a hand warmer containing 15.0 g of iron powder.

6.10 Energy Use and the Environment

In this chapter, we have learned about the relationship between chemical reactions and energy changes. As noted earlier, our society derives the majority of its energy from the energy changes associated with burning fossil fuels. Fossil fuels have traditionally been regarded as convenient sources of energy due to their abundance and portability and because they undergo combustion reactions that have large negative enthalpies of reaction (the reactions are highly exothermic). However, the burning of fossil fuels also has some serious environmental impacts.

Energy Consumption

According to the U.S. Department of Energy, the United States currently consumes close to 100 quads (1 quad = 1 quadrillion British thermal units = 1.06×10^{18} J) of energy per year in the categories shown in this chart.

This corresponds to over 100,000 kWh of energy use per person per year. If we used physical laborers to do the equivalent amount of work, we would need about 120 people. In other words, the average American employs the work output of 120 people, day and night, all year long! For this reason, Americans enjoy one of the highest standards of living in the world. However, as we learned earlier in the chapter, when it comes to energy, there is no free lunch. Our consumption of energy has significant environmental consequences.

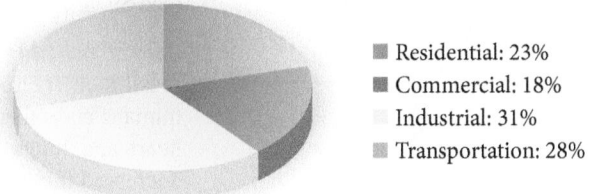

■ Residential: 23%
■ Commercial: 18%
■ Industrial: 31%
■ Transportation: 28%

Source: U.S. Energy Information Administration. *Annual Energy Review.* 2010.

Most U.S. energy comes from the combustion of fossil fuels, as shown in Figure 6.12 ▶. Fossil fuels include petroleum, natural gas, and coal, all of which have been considered convenient fuels because they are relatively abundant in Earth's crust (and therefore are relatively inexpensive), they are easily transportable, and their combustion is highly exothermic. The reactions for the combustion of the main or representative components of several fossil fuels, and the associated enthalpies of reaction, are:

Coal: $C(s) + O_2(g) \longrightarrow CO_2(g)$ $\qquad\qquad\qquad\qquad \Delta H^\circ_{rxn} = -393.5$ kJ

Natural gas: $CH_4(g) + 2 O_2(g) \longrightarrow CO_2(g) + 2 H_2O(g)$ $\qquad \Delta H^\circ_{rxn} = -802.3$ kJ

Petroleum: $C_8H_{18}(l) + 25/2 O_2(g) \longrightarrow 8 CO_2(g) + 9 H_2O(g)$ $\quad \Delta H^\circ_{rxn} = -5074.1$ kJ

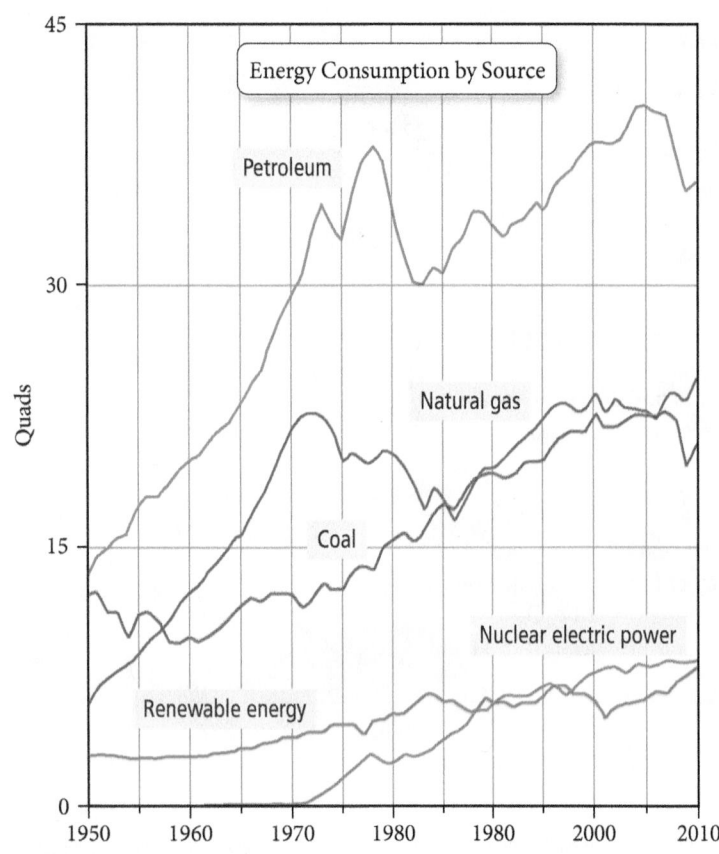

▲ FIGURE 6.12 Energy Consumption by Source

Source: U.S. Energy Information Administration. *Annual Energy Review*. 2010.

Environmental Problems Associated with Fossil Fuel Use

One of the main problems associated with the burning of fossil fuels is that even though they are abundant in Earth's crust, they are also finite. Fossil fuels originate from ancient plant and animal life and are a nonrenewable energy source—once they are all burned, they cannot be replenished. At current rates of consumption, oil and natural gas supplies will be depleted in 50 to 100 years. While there is enough coal to last much longer, it is a dirtier fuel (it produces more pollution) and, because it is a solid, is less convenient (more difficult to transport and use) than petroleum and natural gas.

The other major problems associated with fossil fuel use stem from the products of combustion. The chemical equations shown for fossil fuel combustion all produce carbon dioxide and water. However, these equations represent the reactions under ideal conditions and do not account for impurities in the fuel, side reactions, and incomplete combustion. When these are taken into account, we can identify three major environmental problems associated with the emissions of fossil fuel combustion: air pollution, acid rain, and global climate change. We discussed acid rain in Chapter 3 (see *Chemistry in the Environment: Acid Rain* in Section 3.6). Here we will address air pollution and global climate change, which we first touched on in Section 4.1.

Air Pollution

The air in all major cities in the world is polluted. Pollution comes from a number of sources including electricity generation, motor vehicle emissions, and industrial waste. There are many different kinds of air pollutants.

Sulfur Oxides (SO_x) Sulfur oxides include SO_2 and SO_3, produced primarily during coal-fired electricity generation and industrial metal refining. The sulfur oxides are lung and eye irritants that affect the respiratory system and are the main precursors of acid rain (see Section 3.6).

Carbon Monoxide (CO) Carbon monoxide is formed during the incomplete combustion of fossil fuels (petroleum, natural gas, and coal). It is emitted mainly by motor vehicles. In humans and other animals, carbon monoxide displaces oxygen in the blood, forcing the heart and lungs to work harder. At high levels, CO can cause sensory impairment, decreased thinking ability, unconsciousness, and even death.

Nitrogen Oxides (NO_x) The nitrogen oxides include NO and NO_2, emitted by motor vehicles, fossil fuel–based electricity generation plants, and any high-temperature combustion process occurring in air. Nitrogen dioxide is an orange-brown gas that causes the dark haze over polluted cities. Nitrogen oxides are eye and lung irritants and precursors of acid rain.

Ozone (O_3) Ozone is produced when some of the products of fossil fuel combustion, especially nitrogen oxides and unburned volatile organic compounds (VOCs), react in the presence of sunlight. The products of this reaction, which include ozone, are called *photochemical smog*. Ozone produced in this way—sometimes called ground-level ozone—should not be confused with upper atmospheric or *stratospheric* ozone. Although ozone is always the same molecule (O_3), stratospheric ozone is a natural part of our environment that protects Earth from harmful ultraviolet light. Stratospheric ozone does not harm us because we are not directly exposed to it. Ground-level ozone, on the other hand, is a pollutant to which we are directly exposed; it is an eye and lung irritant, and prolonged exposure can cause permanent lung damage.

In the United States, the U.S. Environmental Protection Agency (EPA) has established limits on these pollutants. Beginning in the 1970s, the U.S. Congress passed the Clean Air Act and its amendments, requiring U.S. cities to reduce their pollution and maintain levels below the standards set by the EPA. As a result of this legislation, pollutant levels in U.S. cities have decreased over the last 30 years, even as the number of vehicles has increased. For example, according to the EPA's 2010 National Air Quality and Emissions Trends Report, the levels of the major pollutants in the air of U.S. cities have decreased significantly during the period 1980–2010 as shown in Table 6.6.

Although the levels of pollutants (especially ozone) in some cities are still above what the EPA considers safe, real progress has been made. These trends demonstrate that legislation can improve our environment.

TABLE 6.6 Changes in National Average Pollutant Levels, 1980–2010

Pollutant	Change (%) in Average Level
SO_2	−76
CO	−82
NO_2	−52
O_3	−28

*Source: EPA's 2010 National Air Quality and Emissions Trends Report.

Global Climate Change

One of the main products of fossil fuel combustion is carbon dioxide. Carbon dioxide is a greenhouse gas; it allows visible light from the sun to enter Earth's atmosphere but prevents heat (in the form of infrared light) from escaping. In doing so, carbon dioxide acts as a blanket, keeping Earth warm, which, in moderation, is a very good thing and allows life as we know it to exist on our planet. However, because of fossil fuel combustion, carbon dioxide levels in the atmosphere have been steadily increasing, as shown in Figure 6.13 ▶. This increase is expected to change the global climate and raise Earth's average temperature. Current observations suggest that Earth has already warmed by about 0.7 °C in the last century due to an approximately 38% increase in atmospheric carbon dioxide. Computer models suggest that the warming could worsen if carbon dioxide emissions are not curbed. The possible effects of this warming include heightened storm severity, increasing numbers of floods and droughts, major shifts in agricultural zones, rising sea levels and coastal flooding, and profound changes in habitats that could result in the extinction of some plant and animal species.

Atmospheric Carbon Dioxide

▲ FIGURE 6.13 **The Rise in Atmospheric Carbon Dioxide** Atmospheric carbon dioxide levels have been steadily increasing as a result of fossil fuel combustion.

EXAMPLE 6.13 Fossil Fuels and Climate Change

One way to evaluate fuels with respect to global warming is to determine how much heat they release during combustion relative to how much CO_2 they produce. The greater the heat relative to the amount of CO_2, the better the fuel. Use the combustion reactions of carbon, natural gas, and octane, in combination with the enthalpy of combustion for each reaction (all given earlier), to calculate the heat (in kJ) released by each fuel per 1.00 kg of CO_2 produced.

SORT You are given the mass of CO_2 emitted and asked to find the energy output for three different fuels.	**GIVEN:** 1.00 kg CO_2 **FIND:** kJ
STRATEGIZE You must first write the thermochemical equations for the combustion of each fuel given in Section 6.10.	$C(s) + O_2(g) \longrightarrow CO_2(g)$ $\Delta H^{\circ}_{rxn} = -393.5 \text{ kJ}$ $CH_4(g) + 2\,O_2(g) \longrightarrow CO_2(g) + 2\,H_2O(g)$ $\Delta H^{\circ}_{rxn} = -802.3 \text{ kJ}$ $C_8H_{18}(l) + 25/2\,O_2(g) \longrightarrow 8\,CO_2(g) + 9\,H_2O(g)$ $\Delta H^{\circ}_{rxn} = -5074.1 \text{ kJ}$

The conceptual plan has two parts. In the first part, use the molar mass of CO_2 to convert from mass of CO_2 to moles of CO_2. This step is the same for each fuel.

CONCEPTUAL PLAN

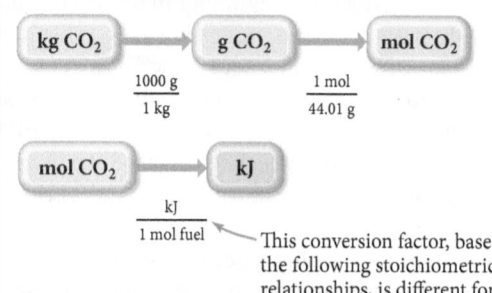

In the second part, use the stoichiometric relationship between moles of CO_2 produced and kilojoules of energy released to calculate the energy output. Repeat the second part for each fuel using the appropriate stoichiometric relationship from the balanced equations.

This conversion factor, based on the following stoichiometric relationships, is different for each fuel.

STOICHIOMETRIC RELATIONSHIPS

For C: 1 mol CO_2 : -393.5 kJ
For CH_4:   1 mol CO_2 : -802.3 kJ
For C_8H_{18}: 8 mol CO_2 : -5074.1 kJ

OTHER RELATIONSHIPS USED

1 kg = 1000 g
molar mass CO_2 = 44.01 g/mol

SOLVE Begin by converting kg CO_2 to mol CO_2.

SOLUTION

$$1.00 \text{ kg } CO_2 \times \frac{1000 \text{ g}}{1 \text{ kg}} \times \frac{1 \text{ mol } CO_2}{44.01 \text{ g } CO_2} = 22.72 \text{ mol } CO_2$$

Then, for each fuel, convert mol CO_2 to kJ.

For C:

$$22.72 \text{ mol } CO_2 \times \frac{-393.5 \text{ kJ}}{1 \text{ mol } CO_2} = -8.94 \times 10^3 \text{ kJ}$$

For CH_4:

$$22.72 \text{ mol } CO_2 \times \frac{-802.3 \text{ kJ}}{1 \text{ mol } CO_2} = -1.82 \times 10^4 \text{ kJ}$$

For C_8H_{18}:

As you can see from the heat released in the production of 1 kg CO_2, natural gas, CH_4, provides the most energy per kg CO_2; therefore, it is the best fuel with respect to climate change.

$$22.72 \text{ mol } CO_2 \times \frac{-5074.1 \text{ kJ}}{8 \text{ mol } CO_2} = -1.44 \times 10^4 \text{ kJ}$$

CHECK Each answer is in kJ, as it should be for heat produced. Each answer is negative, as expected for exothermic combustion reactions.

FOR PRACTICE 6.13
What mass of CO_2 (in kg) does the combustion of a 15-gallon tank of gasoline release into the atmosphere? Assume the gasoline is pure octane (C_8H_{18}) and that it has a density of 0.70 g /mL.

Chemistry in the Environment
Renewable Energy

Because of their finite supply and environmental impacts, fossil fuels will not be our major source of energy in the future. What will replace them? Although the answer is not clear, several alternative energy technologies are beginning to emerge. Unlike fossil fuels, these technologies are renewable, and we can use them indefinitely.

Our planet's greatest source of renewable energy is the sun. If we could capture and harness just a small fraction of the total sunlight falling on Earth, we could meet our energy needs several times over. The main problem with solar energy, however, is diffuseness—the sun's

▲ Honda's 2009 FCX Clarity, a fuel cell vehicle that runs on hydrogen gas and produces only water as exhaust.

energy falls over an enormous area. How do we concentrate and store it? In California, some of the state's electricity is generated by parabolic troughs, solar power towers, and dish/engines.

These devices use reflective surfaces to focus the sun's energy and produce enough heat to generate electricity. Although the direct cost of generating electricity this way is higher than using fossil fuels, the benefits to the environment are obvious. In addition, with time, the costs are expected to fall.

Another way to capture the sun's energy is in chemical bonds. For example, solar energy could be used to drive the decomposition of water:

$$H_2O(l) \longrightarrow H_2(g) + {}^1\!/_2\,O_2(g) \quad \Delta H^\circ_{rxn} = +285.8\ kJ$$

The hydrogen gas produced could be stored until needed to provide energy by re-forming water in the reverse reaction:

$$H_2(g) + {}^1\!/_2\,O_2(g) \longrightarrow H_2O(l) \quad \Delta H^\circ_{rxn} = -285.8\ kJ$$

This reaction can be carried out in an electrochemical device called a fuel cell. In a fuel cell, hydrogen and oxygen gases combine to form water and produce electricity. In 2007, Honda introduced the FCX, a fuel cell four-passenger vehicle with a 240-mile range and a top speed of 100 mph. The automobile is selectively available for lease, primarily in Southern California. The main challenge for the FCX and other fuel cell vehicles is refueling. The FCX requires hydrogen fuel, which can only be obtained at a small number of refueling stations. Other automakers have similar proto-type models in development.

Other renewable energy sources are hydroelectric power and wind power. Hydroelectric power plants—which generate approximately 8% of U.S. electricity—harness the gravitational potential energy of water held behind a dam. Water is released at a controlled rate. As it falls, it acquires kinetic energy that is used to spin a turbine, generating electricity. Wind power plants—which produce about 2% of U.S. electricity—consist of hundreds of turbines that are spun by the wind to generate electricity. Both of these technologies are cost competitive with fossil fuels, have no emissions, and are completely renewable.

Our energy future will probably involve a combination of these technologies and some new ones, combined with a focus on greater efficiency and conservation. One thing, however, is clear—the future of fossil fuels is limited.

▲ Wind turbines such as these generate about 2% of U.S. electricity.

| Parabolic troughs | Solar power tower | Dish/engine |

▲ The sun's energy, concentrated by reflective surfaces in various arrangements, can produce enough heat to generate electricity.

CHAPTER IN REVIEW

Self Assessment Quiz

Q1. A chemical system produces 155 kJ of heat and does 22 kJ of work. What is ΔE for the *surroundings*?
a) 177 kJ
b) −177 kJ
c) 133 kJ
d) −133 kJ

Q2. Which sample is most likely to undergo the smallest change in temperature upon the absorption of 100 kJ of heat?
a) 15 g water
b) 15 g lead
c) 50 g water
d) 50 g lead

Q3. How much heat must be absorbed by a 15.0 g sample of water to raise its temperature from 25.0 °C to 55.0 °C? (For water, $C_s = 4.18\ J/g\ °C$.)
a) 1.57 kJ
b) 1.88 kJ
c) 3.45 kJ
d) 107 J

Q4. A 12.5 g sample of granite initially at 82.0 °C is immersed into 25.0 g of water initially at 22.0 °C. What is the final temperature of both substances when they reach thermal equilibrium? (For water, $C_s = 4.18\ J/g\ °C$ and for granite, $C_s = 0.790\ J/g\ °C$.)
a) 52.0 °C
b) 1.55×10^3 °C
c) 15.7 °C
d) 27.2 °C

Q5. A cylinder with a moving piston expands from an initial volume of 0.250 L against an external pressure of 2.00 atm. The expansion does 288 J of work on the surroundings. What is the final volume of the cylinder?
a) 1.42 L
b) 1.17 L
c) 144 L
d) 1.67 L

Q6. When a 3.80 g sample of liquid octane (C_8H_{18}) is burned in a bomb calorimeter, the temperature of the calorimeter rises by 27.3 °C. The heat capacity of the calorimeter, measured in a separate experiment, is 6.18 kJ/ °C. Determine the enthalpy of combustion for octane in units of kJ/mol octane.
a) -5.07×10^3 kJ/mol
b) 5.07×10^3 kJ/mol
c) -44.4×10^3 kJ/mol
d) -16.7×10^3 kJ/mol

Q7. Hydrogen gas reacts with oxygen to form water.

$$2\,H_2(g) + O_2(g) \longrightarrow 2\,H_2O(g) \qquad \Delta H = -483.5 \text{ kJ}$$

Determine the minimum mass of hydrogen gas required to produce 226 kJ of heat.
a) 8.63 g
b) 1.88 g
c) 0.942 g
d) 0.935 g

Q8. Manganese reacts with hydrochloric acid to produce manganese(II) chloride and hydrogen gas.

$$Mn(s) + 2\,HCl(aq) \longrightarrow MnCl_2(aq) + H_2(g)$$

When 0.625 g Mn is combined with enough hydrochloric acid to make 100.0 mL of solution in a coffee-cup calorimeter, all of the Mn reacts, raising the temperature of the solution from 23.5 °C to 28.8 °C. Find ΔH_{rxn} for the reaction as written. (Assume that the specific heat capacity of the solution is 4.18 J/g °C and the density is 1.00 g/mL.)
a) -195 kJ
b) -3.54 kJ
c) -1.22 kJ
d) -2.21 kJ

Q9. Consider the reactions:

$$A \longrightarrow 2\,B \qquad \Delta H_1$$
$$A \longrightarrow 3\,C \qquad \Delta H_2$$

What is ΔH for the reaction $2\,B \longrightarrow 3\,C$?
a) $\Delta H_1 + \Delta H_2$
b) $\Delta H_1 - \Delta H_2$
c) $\Delta H_2 - \Delta H_1$
d) $2 \times (\Delta H_1 + \Delta H_2)$

Q10. Use standard enthalpies of formation to determine ΔH°_{rxn} for the reaction:

$$Fe_2O_3(s) + 3\,CO(g) \longrightarrow 2\,Fe(s) + 3\,CO_2(g)$$

a) -541.2 kJ
b) -2336 kJ
c) -541.2 kJ
d) -24.8 kJ

Q11. Two substances, A and B, of equal mass but at different temperatures come into thermal contact. The specific heat capacity of substance A is twice the specific heat capacity of substance B. Which statement is true of the temperature of the two substances when they reach thermal equilibrium? (Assume no heat loss other than the thermal transfer between the substances.)
a) The final temperature of both substances will be closer to the initial temperature of substance A than the initial temperature of substance B.
b) The final temperature of both substances will be closer to the initial temperature of substance B than the initial temperature of substance A.
c) The final temperature of both substances will be exactly midway between the initial temperatures of substance A and substance B.
d) The final temperature of substance B will be greater than the final temperature of substance A.

Q12. Which process is endothermic?
a) The evaporation of water from the skin.
b) The burning of candle wax.
c) The oxidation of iron in a chemical hand warmer.
d) The combustion of natural gas in a stove.

Q13. Which fuel is not a fossil fuel?
a) coal
b) hydrogen
c) natural gas
d) petroleum

Q14. The standard enthalpy of formation for glucose [$C_6H_{12}O_6(s)$] is -1273.3 kJ/mol. What is the correct formation equation corresponding to this ΔH°_f?
a) $6C(s, \text{graphite}) + 6H_2O(g) \longrightarrow C_6H_{12}O_6(s, \text{glucose})$
b) $6C(s, \text{graphite}) + 6H_2O(l) \rightarrow C_6H_{12}O_6(s, \text{glucose})$
c) $6C(s, \text{graphite}) + 6H_2(l) + 3O_2(l) \longrightarrow$
$$C_6H_{12}O_6(s, \text{glucose})$$
d) $6C(s, \text{graphite}) + 6H_2(g) + 3O_2(g) \longrightarrow$
$$C_6H_{12}O_6(s, \text{glucose})$$

Q15. Natural gas burns in air to form carbon dioxide and water, releasing heat.

$$CH_4(g) + O_2(g) \longrightarrow CO_2(g) + H_2O(g)$$
$$\Delta H^\circ_{rxn} = -802.3 \text{ kJ}$$

What minimum mass of CH_4 is required to heat 55 g of water by 25 °C? (Assume 100% heating efficiency.)
a) 0.115 g
b) 2.25×10^3 g
c) 115 g
d) 8.70 g

Answers: 1. (a) 2. (c) 3. (b) 4. (d) 5. (d) 6. (a) 7. (b) 8. (a) 9. (c) 10. (d) 11. (a) 12. (a) 13. (b) 14. (d) 15. (a)

Key Terms

Section 6.1
thermochemistry (247)

Section 6.2
energy (248)
work (248)
heat (248)

kinetic energy (248)
thermal energy (248)
potential energy (248)
chemical energy (248)
law of conservation of energy (248)

system (249)
surroundings (249)
joule (J) (250)
calorie (cal) (250)
Calorie (Cal) (250)
kilowatt-hour (kWh) (250)

Section 6.3
first law of thermodynamics (250)
internal energy (E) (251)
state function (251)

Key Concepts

The Nature of Energy and Thermodynamics (6.2, 6.3)

▶ Energy, which is measured in the SI unit of joules (J), is the capacity to do work.

▶ Work is the result of a force acting through a distance.

▶ Many different kinds of energy exist, including kinetic energy, thermal energy, potential energy, and chemical energy, a type of potential energy associated with the relative positions of electrons and nuclei in atoms and molecules.

▶ The first law of thermodynamics states that energy can be converted from one form to another, but the total amount of energy is always conserved.

▶ The internal energy (E) of a system is the sum of all of its kinetic and potential energy. Internal energy is a state function, which means that it depends only on the state of the system and not on the pathway by which it got to that state.

▶ A chemical system exchanges energy with its surroundings through heat (the transfer of thermal energy caused by a temperature difference) or work. The total change in internal energy is the sum of these two quantities.

Heat and Work (6.4)

▶ We quantify heat with the equation $q = m \times C_s \times \Delta T$. In this expression, C_s is the specific heat capacity, the amount of heat required to change the temperature of 1 g of the substance by 1 °C. Compared to most substances, water has a very high heat capacity—it takes a lot of heat to change its temperature.

▶ The type of work most characteristic of chemical reactions is pressure–volume work, which occurs when a gas expands against an external pressure. Pressure–volume work can be quantified with the equation $w = -P\Delta V$.

▶ The change in internal energy (ΔE) that occurs during a chemical reaction is the sum of the heat (q) exchanged and the work (w) done: $\Delta E = q + w$

Enthalpy (6.6)

▶ The heat evolved in a chemical reaction occurring at constant pressure is the change in enthalpy (ΔH) for the reaction. Like internal energy, enthalpy is a state function.

▶ An endothermic reaction has a positive enthalpy of reaction; an exothermic reaction has a negative enthalpy of reaction.

▶ The enthalpy of reaction can be used to determine stoichiometrically the heat evolved when a specific amount of reactant reacts.

Calorimetry (6.5, 6.7)

▶ Calorimetry is a method of measuring ΔE or ΔH for a reaction.

▶ In bomb calorimetry, the reaction is carried out under conditions of constant volume, so $\Delta E = q_v$. The temperature change of the calorimeter can therefore be used to calculate ΔE for the reaction.

▶ When a reaction takes place at constant pressure, energy may be released both as heat and as work.

▶ In coffee-cup calorimetry, a reaction is carried out under atmospheric pressure in a solution, so $q = \Delta H$. The temperature change of the solution is then used to calculate ΔH for the reaction.

Calculating ΔH_{rxn} (6.8, 6.9)

▶ The enthalpy of reaction (ΔH_{rxn}) can be calculated from known thermochemical data using the following relationships: (a) when a reaction is multiplied by a factor, ΔH_{rxn} is multiplied by the same factor; (b) when a reaction is reversed, ΔH_{rxn} changes sign; and (c) if a chemical reaction can be expressed as a sum of two or more steps, ΔH_{rxn} is the sum of the ΔH's for the individual steps (Hess's law). Together, these relationships can be used to determine the enthalpy change of an unknown reaction from reactions with known enthalpy changes.

▶ A second method to calculate ΔH_{rxn} from known thermochemical data involves using tabulated standard enthalpies of formation for the reactants and products of the reaction. These are usually tabulated for substances in their standard states, and the enthalpy of reaction is called the standard enthalpy of reaction ($\Delta H_{rxn}°$). For any reaction, ($\Delta H_{rxn}°$) is obtained by subtracting the sum of the enthalpies of formation of the reactants multiplied by their stoichiometric coefficients from the sum of the enthalpies of formation of the products multiplied by their stoichiometric coefficients.

Environmental Problems Associated with Fossil Fuel Use (6.10)

▶ Fossil fuels are nonrenewable fuels; once they are consumed, they cannot be replaced.

▶ At current rates of consumption, natural gas and petroleum reserves will be depleted in 50–100 years.

▶ In addition to their limited supply, the products of the combustion of fossil fuels—directly or indirectly formed—contribute to environmental problems including air pollution, acid rain, and global climate change, which involves an increase in Earth's average temperature caused by CO_2 emission.

Key Equations and Relationships

Kinetic Energy (6.2)

$$KE = \frac{1}{2}mv^2$$

Change in Internal Energy (ΔE) of a Chemical System (6.3)

$$\Delta E = E_{products} - E_{reactants}$$

Energy Flow between System and Surroundings (6.3)

$$\Delta E_{system} = -\Delta E_{surroundings}$$

Relationship between Internal Energy (ΔE), Heat (q), and Work (w) (6.3)

$$\Delta E = q + w$$

Relationship between Heat (q), Temperature (T), and Heat Capacity (C) (**6.4**)

$$q = C \times \Delta T$$

Relationship between Heat (q), Mass (m), Temperature (T), and Specific Heat Capacity of a Substance (C_s) (**6.4**)

$$q = m \times C_s \times \Delta T$$

Relationship between Work (w), Force (F), and Distance (D) (**6.4**)

$$w = F \times D$$

Relationship between Work (w), Pressure (P), and Change in Volume (ΔV) (**6.4**)

$$w = -P \Delta V$$

Change in Internal Energy (ΔE) of System at Constant Volume (**6.5**)

$$\Delta E = q_v$$

Heat of a Bomb Calorimeter (q_{cal}) (**6.5**)

$$q_{cal} = C_{cal} \times \Delta T$$

Heat Exchange between a Calorimeter and a Reaction (**6.5**)

$$q_{cal} = -q_{rxn}$$

Relationship between Enthalpy (ΔH), Internal Energy (ΔE), Pressure (P), and Volume (V) (**6.6**)

$$\Delta H = \Delta E + P \Delta V$$
$$\Delta H = q_p$$

Relationship between Enthalpy of a Reaction (ΔH°_{rxn}) and the Heats of Formation (ΔH°_f) (**6.9**)

$$\Delta H^\circ_{rxn} = \sum n_p \Delta H^\circ_f (\text{products}) - \sum n_r \Delta H^\circ_f (\text{reactants})$$

Key Learning Outcomes

Chapter Objectives	Assessment
Calculating Internal Energy from Heat and Work (**6.3**)	Example 6.1 For Practice 6.1 Exercises 41–44
Finding Heat from Temperature Changes (**6.4**)	Example 6.2 For Practice 6.2 For More Practice 6.2 Exercises 47–50
Determining Quantities in Thermal Energy Transfer (**6.4**)	Example 6.3 For Practice 6.3 Exercises 65–70
Finding Work from Volume Changes (**6.4**)	Example 6.4 For Practice 6.4 For More Practice 6.4 Exercises 51, 52
Using Bomb Calorimetry to Calculate ΔE_{rxn} (**6.5**)	Example 6.5 For Practice 6.5 For More Practice 6.5 Exercises 53, 54
Predicting Endothermic and Exothermic Processes (**6.6**)	Example 6.6 For Practice 6.6 Exercises 57, 58
Determining Heat from ΔH and Stoichiometry (**6.6**)	Examples 6.7, 6.13 For Practice 6.7, 6.13 For More Practice 6.7 Exercises 59–64
Finding ΔH_{rxn} Using Calorimetry (**6.7**)	Example 6.8 For Practice 6.8 Exercises 75, 76
Finding ΔH_{rxn} Using Hess's Law (**6.8**)	Example 6.9 For Practice 6.9 For More Practice 6.9 Exercises 79–82
Finding ΔH°_{rxn} Using Standard Enthalpies of Formation (**6.9**)	Examples 6.10, 6.11, 6.12 For Practice 6.10, 6.11, 6.12 Exercises 83–92

EXERCISES

Review Questions

1. What is thermochemistry? Why is it important?
2. What is energy? What is work? List some examples of each.
3. What is kinetic energy? What is potential energy? List some examples of each.
4. What is the law of conservation of energy? How does it relate to energy exchanges between a thermodynamic system and its surroundings?
5. What is the SI unit of energy? List some other common units of energy.
6. What is the first law of thermodynamics? What are its implications?
7. A friend claims to have constructed a machine that creates electricity but requires no energy input. Explain why you should be suspicious of your friend's claim.
8. What is a state function? List some examples of state functions.
9. What is internal energy? Is internal energy a state function?
10. If energy flows out of a chemical system and into the surroundings, what is the sign of ΔE_{system}?
11. If the internal energy of the products of a reaction is higher than the internal energy of the reactants, what is the sign of ΔE for the reaction? In which direction does energy flow?
12. What is heat? Explain the difference between heat and temperature.
13. How is the change in internal energy of a system related to heat and work?
14. Explain how the sum of heat and work can be a state function, even though heat and work are themselves not state functions.
15. What is heat capacity? Explain the difference between heat capacity and specific heat capacity.
16. Explain how the high specific heat capacity of water can affect the weather in coastal regions.
17. If two objects, A and B, of different temperature come into direct contact, what is the relationship between the heat lost by one object and the heat gained by the other? What is the relationship between the temperature changes of the two objects? (Assume that the two objects do not lose any heat to anything else.)

18. What is pressure–volume work? How is it calculated?
19. What is calorimetry? Explain the difference between a coffee-cup calorimeter and a bomb calorimeter. What is each designed to measure?
20. What is the change in enthalpy (ΔH) for a chemical reaction? How is ΔH different from ΔE?
21. Explain the difference between an exothermic and an endothermic reaction. Give the sign of ΔH for each type of reaction.
22. From a molecular viewpoint, where does the energy emitted in an exothermic chemical reaction come from? Why does the reaction mixture undergo an increase in temperature even though energy is emitted?
23. From a molecular viewpoint, where does the energy absorbed in an endothermic chemical reaction go? Why does the reaction mixture undergo a decrease in temperature even though energy is absorbed?
24. Is the change in enthalpy for a reaction an extensive property? Explain the relationship between ΔH for a reaction and the amounts of reactants and products that undergo reaction.
25. Explain how the value of ΔH for a reaction changes upon each operation:
    a. multiplying the reaction by a factor.
    b. reversing the reaction.
    Why do these relationships hold?
26. What is Hess's law? Why is it useful?
27. What is a standard state? What is the standard enthalpy change for a reaction?
28. What is the standard enthalpy of formation for a compound? For a pure element in its standard state?
29. How do you calculate ΔH^0_{rxn} from tabulated standard enthalpies of formation?
30. What are the main sources of the energy consumed in the United States?
31. What are the main environmental problems associated with fossil fuel use?
32. Explain global climate change. What causes global warming? What is the evidence that global warming is occurring?

Problems by Topic

Energy Units

33. Convert between energy units:
    a. 534 kWh to J
    b. 215 kJ to Cal
    c. 567 Cal to J
    d. 2.85×10^3 J to cal
34. Convert between energy units:
    a. 231 cal to kJ
    b. 132×10^4 kJ to kcal
    c. 4.99×10^3 kJ to kWh
    d. 2.88×10^4 J to Cal
35. Suppose that a person eats 2387 Calories per day. Convert this amount of energy into each unit:
    a. J
    b. kJ
    c. kWh
36. A particular frost-free refrigerator uses about 745 kWh of electrical energy per year. Express this amount of energy in each unit:
    a. J
    b. kJ
    c. Cal

Internal Energy, Heat, and Work

37. Which statement is true of the internal energy of a system and its surroundings during an energy exchange with a negative ΔE_{sys}?
    a. The internal energy of the system increases and the internal energy of the surroundings decreases.
    b. The internal energy of both the system and the surroundings increases.
    c. The internal energy of both the system and the surroundings decreases.
    d. The internal energy of the system decreases and the internal energy of the surroundings increases.
38. During an energy exchange, a chemical system absorbs energy from its surroundings. What is the sign of ΔE_{sys} for this process? Explain.

39. Identify each energy exchange as primarily heat or work and determine whether the sign of ΔE is positive or negative for the system.
    a. Sweat evaporates from skin, cooling the skin. (The evaporating sweat is the system.)
    b. A balloon expands against an external pressure. (The contents of the balloon is the system.)
    c. An aqueous chemical reaction mixture is warmed with an external flame. (The reaction mixture is the system.)

40. Identify each energy exchange as primarily heat or work and determine whether the sign of ΔE is positive or negative for the system.
    a. A rolling billiard ball collides with another billiard ball. The first billiard ball (defined as the system) stops rolling after the collision.
    b. A book is dropped to the floor. (The book is the system).
    c. A father pushes his daughter on a swing. (The daughter and the swing are the system).

41. A system releases 622 kJ of heat and does 105 kJ of work on the surroundings. What is the change in internal energy of the system?

42. A system absorbs 196 kJ of heat and the surroundings do 117 kJ of work on the system. What is the change in internal energy of the system?

43. The gas in a piston (defined as the system) warms and absorbs 655 J of heat. The expansion performs 344 J of work on the surroundings. What is the change in internal energy for the system?

44. The air in an inflated balloon (defined as the system) warms over a toaster and absorbs 115 J of heat. As it expands, it does 77 kJ of work. What is the change in internal energy for the system?

Heat, Heat Capacity, and Work

45. We pack two identical coolers for a picnic, placing twenty-four 12-ounce soft drinks and 5 pounds of ice in each. However, the drinks that we put into cooler A were refrigerated for several hours before they were packed in the cooler, while the drinks that we put into cooler B were at room temperature. When we open the two coolers 3 hours later, most of the ice in cooler A is still present, while nearly all of the ice in cooler B has melted. Explain this difference.

46. A kilogram of aluminum metal and a kilogram of water are each warmed to 75 °C and placed in two identical insulated containers. One hour later, the two containers are opened and the temperature of each substance is measured. The aluminum has cooled to 35 °C while the water has cooled only to 66 °C. Explain this difference.

47. How much heat is required to warm 1.50 L of water from 25.0 °C to 100.0 °C? (Assume a density of 1.0 g/mL for the water.)

48. How much heat is required to warm 1.50 kg of sand from 25.0 °C to 100.0 °C?

49. Suppose that 25 g of each substance is initially at 27.0 °C. What is the final temperature of each substance upon absorbing 2.35 kJ of heat?
    a. gold   b. silver
    c. aluminum   d. water

50. An unknown mass of each substance, initially at 23.0 °C, absorbs 1.95×10^3 J of heat. The final temperature is recorded as indicated. Find the mass of each substance.
    a. Pyrex glass ($T_f = 55.4$ °C)
    b. sand ($T_f = 62.1$ °C)
    c. ethanol ($T_f = 44.2$ °C)
    d. water ($T_f = 32.4$ °C)

51. How much work (in J) is required to expand the volume of a pump from 0.0 L to 2.5 L against an external pressure of 1.1 atm?

52. The average human lung expands by about 0.50 L during each breath. If this expansion occurs against an external pressure of 1.0 atm, how much work (in J) is done during the expansion?

53. The air within a piston equipped with a cylinder absorbs 565 J of heat and expands from an initial volume of 0.10 L to a final volume of 0.85 L against an external pressure of 1.0 atm. What is the change in internal energy of the air within the piston?

54. A gas is compressed from an initial volume of 5.55 L to a final volume of 1.22 L by an external pressure of 1.00 atm. During the compression the gas releases 124 J of heat. What is the change in internal energy of the gas?

Enthalpy and Thermochemical Stoichiometry

55. When 1 mol of a fuel burns at constant pressure, it produces 3452 kJ of heat and does 11 kJ of work. What are ΔE and ΔH for the combustion of the fuel?

56. The change in internal energy for the combustion of 1.0 mol of octane at a pressure of 1.0 atm is 5084.3 kJ. If the change in enthalpy is 5074.1 kJ, how much work is done during the combustion?

57. Determine whether each process is exothermic or endothermic and indicate the sign of ΔH.
    a. natural gas burning on a stove
    b. isopropyl alcohol evaporating from skin
    c. water condensing from steam

58. Determine whether each process is exothermic or endothermic and indicate the sign of ΔH.
    a. dry ice evaporating
    b. a sparkler burning
    c. the reaction that occurs in a chemical cold pack used to ice athletic injuries

59. Consider the thermochemical equation for the combustion of acetone (C_3H_6O), the main ingredient in nail polish remover.

    $$C_3H_6O(l) + 4\,O_2(g) \longrightarrow 3\,CO_2(g) + 3\,H_2O(g)$$
    $$\Delta H^{\circ}_{rxn} = -1790 \text{ kJ}$$

    If a bottle of nail polish remover contains 177 mL of acetone, how much heat is released by its complete combustion? The density of acetone is 0.788 g/mL.

60. What mass of natural gas (CH_4) must burn to emit 267 kJ of heat?

    $$CH_4(g) + 2\,O_2(g) \longrightarrow CO_2(g) + 2\,H_2O(g)$$
    $$\Delta H^{\circ}_{rxn} = -802.3 \text{ kJ}$$

61. Nitromethane (CH_3NO_2) burns in air to produce significant amounts of heat.

    $$2\,CH_3NO_2(l) + \tfrac{3}{2}\,O_2(g) \longrightarrow 2\,CO_2(g) + 3\,H_2O(l) + N_2(g)$$
    $$\Delta H^{\circ}_{rxn} = -1418 \text{ kJ}$$

    How much heat is produced by the complete reaction of 5.56 kg of nitromethane?

62. Titanium reacts with iodine to form titanium(III) iodide, emitting heat.

    $$2\,Ti(s) + 3\,I_2(g) \longrightarrow 2\,TiI_3(s) \qquad \Delta H^{\circ}_{rxn} = -839 \text{ kJ}$$

    Determine the masses of titanium and iodine that react if 1.55×10^3 kJ of heat is emitted by the reaction.

63. The propane fuel (C_3H_8) used in gas barbeques burns according to the thermochemical equation:

    $$C_3H_8(g) + 5\,O_2(g) \longrightarrow 3\,CO_2(g) + 4\,H_2O(g)$$
    $$\Delta H^{\circ}_{rxn} = -2217 \text{ kJ}$$

If a pork roast must absorb 1.6×10^3 kJ to fully cook, and if only 10% of the heat produced by the barbeque is actually absorbed by the roast, what mass of CO_2 is emitted into the atmosphere during the grilling of the pork roast?

64. Charcoal is primarily carbon. Determine the mass of CO_2 produced by burning enough carbon (in the form of charcoal) to produce 5.00×10^2 kJ of heat.

$$C(s) + O_2(g) \longrightarrow CO_2(g) \qquad \Delta H^\circ_{rxn} = -393.5 \text{ kJ}$$

Thermal Energy Transfer

65. A silver block, initially at 58.5 °C, is submerged into 100.0 g of water at 24.8 °C, in an insulated container. The final temperature of the mixture upon reaching thermal equilibrium is 26.2 °C. What is the mass of the silver block?

66. A 32.5 g iron rod, initially at 22.7 °C, is submerged into an unknown mass of water at 63.2 °C, in an insulated container. The final temperature of the mixture upon reaching thermal equilibrium is 59.5 °C. What is the mass of the water?

67. A 31.1 g wafer of pure gold, initially at 69.3 °C, is submerged into 64.2 g of water at 27.8 °C in an insulated container. What is the final temperature of both substances at thermal equilibrium?

68. A 2.85 g lead weight, initially at 10.3 °C, is submerged in 7.55 g of water at 52.3 °C in an insulated container. What is the final temperature of both substances at thermal equilibrium?

69. Two substances, A and B, initially at different temperatures, come into contact and reach thermal equilibrium. The mass of substance A is 6.15 g and its initial temperature is 20.5 °C. The mass of substance B is 25.2 g and its initial temperature is 52.7 °C. The final temperature of both substances at thermal equilibrium is 46.7 °C. If the specific heat capacity of substance B is 1.17 J/g · °C, what is the specific heat capacity of substance A?

70. A 2.74 g sample of a substance suspected of being pure gold is warmed to 72.1 °C and submerged into 15.2 g of water initially at 24.7 °C. The final temperature of the mixture is 26.3 °C. What is the heat capacity of the unknown substance? Could the substance be pure gold?

Calorimetry

71. Exactly 1.5 g of a fuel burns under conditions of constant pressure and then again under conditions of constant volume. In measurement A the reaction produces 25.9 kJ of heat, and in measurement B the reaction produces 23.3 kJ of heat. Which measurement (A or B) corresponds to conditions of constant pressure? Which one corresponds to conditions of constant volume? Explain.

72. In order to obtain the largest possible amount of heat from a chemical reaction in which there is a large increase in the number of moles of gas, should you carry out the reaction under conditions of constant volume or constant pressure? Explain.

73. When 0.514 g of biphenyl ($C_{12}H_{10}$) undergoes combustion in a bomb calorimeter, the temperature rises from 25.8 °C to 29.4 °C. Find ΔE_{rxn} for the combustion of biphenyl in kJ/mol biphenyl. The heat capacity of the bomb calorimeter, determined in a separate experiment, is 5.86 kJ/°C.

74. Mothballs are composed primarily of the hydrocarbon naphthalene ($C_{10}H_8$). When 1.025 g of naphthalene burns in a bomb calorimeter, the temperature rises from 24.25 °C to 32.33 °C. Find ΔE_{rxn} for the combustion of naphthalene. The heat capacity of the calorimeter, determined in a separate experiment, is 5.11 kJ/°C.

75. Zinc metal reacts with hydrochloric acid according to the balanced equation:

$$Zn(s) + 2 \, HCl(aq) \longrightarrow ZnCl_2(aq) + H_2(g)$$

When 0.103 g of $Zn(s)$ is combined with enough HCl to make 50.0 mL of solution in a coffee-cup calorimeter, all of the zinc reacts, raising the temperature of the solution from 22.5 °C to 23.7 °C. Find ΔH_{rxn} for this reaction as written. (Use 1.0 g/mL for the density of the solution and 4.18 J/g · °C as the specific heat capacity.)

76. Instant cold packs used to ice athletic injuries on the field contain ammonium nitrate and water separated by a thin plastic divider. When the divider is broken, the ammonium nitrate dissolves according to the endothermic reaction:

$$NH_4NO_3(s) \longrightarrow NH_4^+(aq) + NO_3^-(aq)$$

In order to measure the enthalpy change for this reaction, 1.25 g of NH_4NO_3 is dissolved in enough water to make 25.0 mL of solution. The initial temperature is 25.8 °C and the final temperature (after the solid dissolves) is 21.9 °C. Calculate the change in enthalpy for the reaction in kJ. (Use 1.0 g/mL as the density of the solution and 4.18 J/g · °C as the specific heat capacity.)

Quantitative Relationships Involving ΔH and Hess's Law

77. For each generic reaction, determine the value of ΔH_2 in terms of ΔH_1.

a. $A + B \longrightarrow 2 \, C \qquad \Delta H_1$
$2 \, C \longrightarrow A + B \qquad \Delta H_2 = ?$

b. $A + \frac{1}{2} B \longrightarrow C \qquad \Delta H_1$
$2 \, A + B \longrightarrow 2 \, C \qquad \Delta H_2 = ?$

c. $A \longrightarrow B + 2 \, C \qquad \Delta H_1$
$\frac{1}{2} B + C \longrightarrow \frac{1}{2} A \qquad \Delta H_2 = ?$

78. Consider the generic reaction:

$$A + 2 \, B \longrightarrow C + 3 \, D \qquad \Delta H = 155 \text{ kJ}$$

Determine the value of ΔH for each related reaction:

a. $3 \, A + 6 \, B \longrightarrow 3 \, C + 9 \, D$
b. $C + 3 \, D \longrightarrow A + 2 \, B$
c. $\frac{1}{2} C + \frac{3}{2} D \longrightarrow \frac{1}{2} A + B$

79. Calculate ΔH_{rxn} for the reaction:

$$Fe_2O_3(s) + 3 \, CO(g) \longrightarrow 2 \, Fe(s) + 3 \, CO_2(g)$$

Use the following reactions and given ΔH's.

$2 \, Fe(s) + \frac{3}{2} O_2(g) \longrightarrow Fe_2O_3(s) \qquad \Delta H = -824.2 \text{ kJ}$
$CO(g) + \frac{1}{2} O_2(g) \longrightarrow CO_2(g) \qquad \Delta H = -282.7 \text{ kJ}$

80. Calculate ΔH_{rxn} for the reaction:

$$CaO(s) + CO_2(g) \longrightarrow CaCO_3(s)$$

Use the following reactions and given ΔH's.

$Ca(s) + CO_2(g) + \frac{1}{2} O_2(g) \longrightarrow CaCO_3(s)$
$\qquad\qquad\qquad\qquad\qquad \Delta H = -812.8 \text{ kJ}$
$2 \, Ca(s) + O_2(g) \longrightarrow 2 \, CaO(s) \qquad \Delta H = -1269.8 \text{ kJ}$

81. Calculate ΔH_{rxn} for the reaction:

$$5 \, C(s) + 6 \, H_2(g) \longrightarrow C_5H_{12}(l)$$

Use the following reactions and given ΔH's.

$C_5H_{12}(l) + 8 \, O_2(g) \longrightarrow 5 \, CO_2(g) + 6 \, H_2O(g)$
$\qquad\qquad\qquad\qquad\qquad \Delta H = -3244.8 \text{ kJ}$
$C(s) + O_2(g) \longrightarrow CO_2(g) \qquad \Delta H = -393.5 \text{ kJ}$
$2 \, H_2(g) + O_2(g) \longrightarrow 2 \, H_2O(g) \qquad \Delta H = -483.5 \text{ kJ}$

82. Calculate ΔH_{rxn} for the reaction:

$$CH_4(g) + 4\,Cl_2(g) \longrightarrow CCl_4(g) + 4\,HCl(g)$$

Use the following reactions and given ΔH's.

$$
\begin{array}{ll}
C(s) + 2\,H_2(g) \longrightarrow CH_4(g) & \Delta H = -74.6\ \text{kJ} \\
C(s) + 2\,Cl_2(g) \longrightarrow CCl_4(g) & \Delta H = -95.7\ \text{kJ} \\
H_2(g) + Cl_2(g) \longrightarrow 2\,HCl(g) & \Delta H = -92.3\ \text{kJ}
\end{array}
$$

Enthalpies of Formation and ΔH

83. Write an equation for the formation of each compound from its elements in their standard states, and find ΔH_f° for each from Appendix IIB.
   a. $NH_3(g)$ **b.** $CO_2(g)$ **c.** $Fe_2O_3(s)$ **d.** $CH_4(g)$

84. Write an equation for the formation of each compound from its elements in their standard states, and find ΔH_{rxn}° for each from Appendix IIB.
   a. $NO_2(g)$ **b.** $MgCO_3(s)$
   c. $C_2H_4(g)$ **d.** $CH_3OH(l)$

85. Hydrazine (N_2H_4) is a fuel used by some spacecraft. It is normally oxidized by N_2O_4 according to the equation:

$$N_2H_4(l) + N_2O_4(g) \longrightarrow 2\,N_2O(g) + 2\,H_2O(g)$$

Calculate ΔH_{rxn}° for this reaction using standard enthalpies of formation.

86. Pentane (C_5H_{12}) is a component of gasoline that burns according to the following balanced equation:

$$C_5H_{12}(l) + 8\,O_2(g) \longrightarrow 5\,CO_2(g) + 6\,H_2O(g)$$

Calculate ΔH_{rxn}° for this reaction using standard enthalpies of formation. (The standard enthalpy of formation of liquid pentane is -146.8 kJ/mol.)

87. Use standard enthalpies of formation to calculate ΔH_{rxn}° for each reaction:
   a. $C_2H_4(g) + H_2(g) \longrightarrow C_2H_6(g)$
   b. $CO(g) + H_2O(g) \longrightarrow H_2(g) + CO_2(g)$
   c. $3\,NO_2(g) + H_2O(l) \longrightarrow 2\,HNO_3(aq) + NO(g)$
   d. $Cr_2O_3(s) + 3\,CO(g) \longrightarrow 2\,Cr(s) + 3\,CO_2(g)$

88. Use standard enthalpies of formation to calculate ΔH_{rxn}° for each reaction:
   a. $2\,H_2S(g) + 3\,O_2(g) \longrightarrow 2\,H_2O(l) + 2\,SO_2(g)$
   b. $SO_2(g) + {}^1\!/_2\,O_2(g) \longrightarrow SO_3(g)$
   c. $C(s) + H_2O(g) \longrightarrow CO(g) + H_2(g)$
   d. $N_2O_4(g) + 4\,H_2(g) \longrightarrow N_2(g) + 4\,H_2O(g)$

89. During photosynthesis, plants use energy from sunlight to form glucose ($C_6H_{12}O_6$) and oxygen from carbon dioxide and water. Write a balanced equation for photosynthesis and calculate ΔH_{rxn}°.

90. Ethanol (C_2H_5OH) can be made from the fermentation of crops and has been used as a fuel additive to gasoline. Write a balanced equation for the combustion of ethanol and calculate ΔH_{rxn}°.

91. Top fuel dragsters and funny cars burn nitromethane as fuel according to the balanced combustion equation:

$$2\,CH_3NO_2(l) + {}^3\!/_2\,O_2(g) \longrightarrow 2\,CO_2(g) + 3\,H_2O(l) + N_2(g)$$
$$\Delta H_{rxn}^\circ = -1418\ \text{kJ}$$

The enthalpy of combustion for nitromethane is -709.2 kJ/mol. Calculate the standard enthalpy of formation (ΔH_f°) for nitromethane.

92. The explosive nitroglycerin ($C_3H_5N_3O_9$) decomposes rapidly upon ignition or sudden impact according to the balanced equation:

$$4\,C_3H_5N_3O_9(l) \longrightarrow 12\,CO_2(g) + 10\,H_2O(g)$$
$$+ 6\,N_2(g) + O_2(g) \quad \Delta H_{rxn}^\circ = -5678\ \text{kJ}$$

Calculate the standard enthalpy of formation (ΔH_f°) for nitroglycerin.

Energy Use and the Environment

93. Determine the mass of CO_2 produced by burning enough of each of the following fuels to produce 1.00×10^2 kJ of heat. Which fuel contributes least to global warming per kJ of heat produced?
   a. $CH_4(g) + 2\,O_2(g) \longrightarrow CO_2(g) + 2\,H_2O(g)$
   $$\Delta H_{rxn}^\circ = -802.3\ \text{kJ}$$
   b. $C_3H_8(g) + 5\,O_2(g) \longrightarrow 3\,CO_2(g) + 4\,H_2O(g)$
   $$\Delta H_{rxn}^\circ = -2043\ \text{kJ}$$
   c. $C_8H_{18}(l) + {}^{25}\!/_2\,O_2(g) \longrightarrow 8\,CO_2(g) + 9\,H_2O(g)$
   $$\Delta H_{rxn}^\circ = -5074.1\ \text{kJ}$$

94. Methanol (CH_3OH) has been suggested as a fuel to replace gasoline. Write a balanced equation for the combustion of methanol, find ΔH_{rxn}°, and determine the mass of carbon dioxide emitted per kJ of heat produced. Use the information from the previous exercise to calculate the same quantity for octane, C_8H_{18}. How does methanol compare to octane with respect to global warming?

95. The citizens of the world burn the fossil fuel equivalent of 7×10^{12} kg of petroleum per year. Assume that all of this petroleum is in the form of octane (C_8H_{18}) and calculate how much CO_2 (in kg) is produced by world fossil fuel combustion per year. (Hint: Begin by writing a balanced equation for the combustion of octane.) If the atmosphere currently contains approximately 3×10^{15} kg of CO_2, how long will it take for the world's fossil fuel combustion to double the amount of atmospheric carbon dioxide?

96. In a sunny location, sunlight has a power density of about 1 kW/m^2. Photovoltaic solar cells can convert this power into electricity with 15% efficiency. If a typical home uses 385 kWh of electricity per month, how many square meters of solar cells would be required to meet its energy requirements? Assume that electricity can be generated from the sunlight for 8 hours per day.

▲ What area of solar cells do you need to power a home?

Cumulative Problems

97. The kinetic energy of a rolling billiard ball is given by $KE = \frac{1}{2}mv^2$. Suppose a 0.17 kg billiard ball is rolling down a pool table with an initial speed of 4.5 m/s. As it travels, it loses some of its energy as heat. The ball slows down to 3.8 m/s and then collides head-on with a second billiard ball of equal mass. The first billiard ball completely stops and the second one rolls away with a velocity of 3.8 m/s. Assume the first billiard ball is the system and calculate w, q, and ΔE for the process.

98. A 100 W lightbulb is placed in a cylinder equipped with a moveable piston. The lightbulb is turned on for 0.015 hour, and the assembly expands from an initial volume of 0.85 L to a final volume of 5.88 L against an external pressure of 1.0 atm. Use the wattage of the lightbulb and the time it is on to calculate ΔE in joules (assume that the cylinder and lightbulb assembly is the system and assume two significant figures). Calculate w and q.

99. Evaporating sweat cools the body because evaporation is an endothermic process:

$$H_2O(l) \longrightarrow H_2O(g) \qquad \Delta H^\circ_{rxn} = +44.01 \text{ kJ}$$

Estimate the mass of water that must evaporate from the skin to cool the body by 0.50 °C. Assume a body mass of 95 kg and assume that the specific heat capacity of the body is 4.0 J/g · °C.

100. LP gas burns according to the exothermic reaction:

$$C_3H_8(g) + 5\,O_2(g) \longrightarrow 3\,CO_2(g) + 4\,H_2O(g)$$
$$\Delta H^\circ_{rxn} = -2044 \text{ kJ}$$

What mass of LP gas is necessary to heat 1.5 L of water from room temperature (25.0 °C) to boiling (100.0 °C)? Assume that during heating, 15% of the heat emitted by the LP gas combustion goes to heat the water. The rest is lost as heat to the surroundings.

101. Use standard enthalpies of formation to calculate the standard change in enthalpy for the melting of ice. (The ΔH°_f for $H_2O(s)$ is –291.8 kJ/mol.) Use this value to calculate the mass of ice required to cool 355 mL of a beverage from room temperature (25.0 °C) to 0.0 °C. Assume that the specific heat capacity and density of the beverage are the same as those of water.

102. Dry ice is solid carbon dioxide. Instead of melting, solid carbon dioxide sublimes according to the equation:

$$CO_2(s) \longrightarrow CO_2(g)$$

When carbon dioxide sublimes, the gaseous CO_2 is cold enough to cause water vapor in the air to condense, forming fog.

When dry ice is added to warm water, heat from the water causes the dry ice to sublime more quickly. The evaporating carbon dioxide produces a dense fog often used to create special effects. In a simple dry ice fog machine, dry ice is added to warm water in a Styrofoam cooler. The dry ice produces fog until it evaporates away, or until the water gets too cold to sublime the dry ice quickly enough. Suppose that a small Styrofoam cooler holds 15.0 liters of water heated to 85 °C. Use standard enthalpies of formation to calculate the change in enthalpy for dry ice sublimation, and calculate the mass of dry ice that should be added to the water so that the dry ice completely sublimes away when the water reaches 25 °C. Assume no heat loss to the surroundings. [The ΔH°_f for $CO_2(s)$ is –427.4 kJ/mol.]

103. A 25.5 g aluminum block is warmed to 65.4 °C and plunged into an insulated beaker containing 55.2 g water initially at 22.2 °C. The aluminum and the water are allowed to come to thermal equilibrium. Assuming that no heat is lost, what is the final temperature of the water and aluminum?

104. If 50.0 mL of ethanol (density = 0.789 g/mL) initially at 7.0 °C is mixed with 50.0 mL of water (density = 1.0 g/mL) initially at 28.4 °C in an insulated beaker, and assuming that no heat is lost, what is the final temperature of the mixture?

105. Palmitic acid $(C_{16}H_{32}O_2)$ is a dietary fat found in beef and butter. The caloric content of palmitic acid is typical of fats in general. Write a balanced equation for the complete combustion of palmitic acid and calculate the standard enthalpy of combustion. What is the caloric content of palmitic acid in Cal/g? Do the same calculation for table sugar (sucrose, $C_{12}H_{22}O_{11}$). Which dietary substance (sugar or fat) contains more Calories per gram? The standard enthalpy of formation of palmitic acid is −208 kJ/mol and that of sucrose is −2226.1 kJ/mol. [Use $H_2O(l)$ in the balanced chemical equations because the metabolism of these compounds produces liquid water.]

106. Hydrogen and methanol have both been proposed as alternatives to hydrocarbon fuels. Write balanced reactions for the complete combustion of hydrogen and methanol and use standard enthalpies of formation to calculate the amount of heat released per kilogram of the fuel. Which fuel contains the most energy in the least mass? How does the energy of these fuels compare to that of octane (C_8H_{18})?

107. Derive a relationship between ΔH and ΔE for a process in which the temperature of a fixed amount of an ideal gas changes.

108. Under certain nonstandard conditions, oxidation by $O_2(g)$ of 1 mol of $SO_2(g)$ to $SO_3(g)$ absorbs 89.5 kJ. The enthalpy of formation of $SO_3(g)$ is −204.2 kJ under these conditions. Find the enthalpy of formation of $SO_2(g)$.

109. One tablespoon of peanut butter has a mass of 16 g. It is combusted in a calorimeter whose heat capacity is 120.0 kJ/°C. The temperature of the calorimeter rises from 22.2 °C to 25.4 °C. Find the food caloric content of peanut butter.

110. A mixture of 2.0 mol of $H_2(g)$ and 1.0 mol of $O_2(g)$ is placed in a sealed evacuated container made of a perfect insulating material at 25 °C. The mixture is ignited with a spark and reacts to form liquid water. Determine the temperature of the water.

111. A 20.0 L volume of an ideal gas in a cylinder with a piston is at a pressure of 3.0 atm. Enough weight is suddenly removed from the piston to lower the external pressure to 1.5 atm. The gas then expands at constant temperature until its pressure is 1.5 atm. Find ΔE, ΔH, q, and w for this change in state.

112. When 10.00 g of phosphorus is burned in $O_2(g)$ to form $P_4O_{10}(s)$, enough heat is generated to raise the temperature of 2950 g of water from 18.0 °C to 38.0 °C. Calculate the enthalpy of formation of $P_4O_{10}(s)$ under these conditions.

113. The ΔH for the oxidation of S in the gas phase to SO_3 is −204 kJ/mol and for the oxidation of SO_2 to SO_3 is 89.5 kJ/mol. Find the enthalpy of formation of SO_2 under these conditions.

114. The ΔH_f° of $TiI_3(s)$ is –328 kJ/mol and the ΔH° for the reaction $2\ Ti(s) + 3\ I_2(g) \longrightarrow 2\ TiI_3(s)$ is –839 kJ. Calculate the ΔH of sublimation of $I_2(s)$, which is a solid at 25 °C.

115. A gaseous fuel mixture contains 25.3% methane (CH_4), 38.2% ethane (C_2H_6), and the rest propane (C_3H_8) by volume. When the fuel mixture contained in a 1.55 L tank, stored at 755 mmHg and 298 K, undergoes complete combustion, how much heat is emitted? (Assume that the water produced by the combustion is in the gaseous state.)

116. A gaseous fuel mixture stored at 745 mmHg and 298 K contains only methane (CH_4) and propane (C_3H_8). When 11.7 L of this fuel mixture is burned, it produces 769 kJ of heat. What is the mole fraction of methane in the mixture? (Assume that the water produced by the combustion is in the gaseous state.)

117. A copper cube measuring 1.55 cm on edge and an aluminum cube measuring 1.62 cm on edge are both heated to 55.0 °C and submerged in 100.0 mL of water at 22.2 °C. What is the final temperature of the water when equilibrium is reached? (Assume a density of 0.998 g/mL for water.)

118. A pure gold ring and a pure silver ring have a total mass of 14.9 g. The two rings are heated to 62.0 °C and dropped into 15.0 mL of water at 23.5 °C. When equilibrium is reached, the temperature of the water is 25.0 °C. What is the mass of each ring? (Assume a density of 0.998 g/mL for water.)

Challenge Problems

119. A typical frostless refrigerator uses 655 kWh of energy per year in the form of electricity. Suppose that all of this electricity is generated at a power plant that burns coal containing 3.2% sulfur by mass and that all of the sulfur is emitted as SO_2 when the coal is burned. If all of the SO_2 goes on to react with rainwater to form H_2SO_4, what mass of H_2SO_4 does the annual operation of the refrigerator produce? (Hint: Assume that the remaining percentage of the coal is carbon and begin by calculating ΔH_{rxn}° for the combustion of carbon.)

120. A large sport utility vehicle has a mass of 2.5×10^3 kg. Calculate the mass of CO_2 emitted into the atmosphere upon accelerating the SUV from 0.0 mph to 65.0 mph. Assume that the required energy comes from the combustion of octane with 30% efficiency. (Hint: Use $KE = \frac{1}{2}mv^2$ to calculate the kinetic energy required for the acceleration.)

121. Combustion of natural gas (primarily methane) occurs in most household heaters. The heat given off in this reaction is used to raise the temperature of the air in the house. Assuming that all the energy given off in the reaction goes to heating up only the air in the house, determine the mass of methane required to heat the air in a house by 10.0 °C. Assume that the house dimensions are 30.0 m × 30.0 m × 3.0 m, specific heat capacity of air is 30 J/K · mol, and 1.00 mol of air occupies 22.4 L for all temperatures concerned.

122. When backpacking in the wilderness, hikers often boil water to sterilize it for drinking. Suppose that you are planning a backpacking trip and will need to boil 35 L of water for your group. What volume of fuel should you bring? Assume that the fuel has an average formula of C_7H_{16}, 15% of the heat generated from combustion goes to heat the water (the rest is lost to the surroundings), the density of the fuel is 0.78 g/mL, the initial temperature of the water is 25.0 °C, and the standard enthalpy of formation of C_7H_{16} is –224.4 kJ/mol.

123. An ice cube of mass 9.0 g is added to a cup of coffee. The coffee's initial temperature is 90.0 °C and the cup contains 120.0 g of liquid. Assume the specific heat capacity of the coffee is the same as that of water. The heat of fusion of ice (the heat associated with ice melting) is 6.0 kJ/mol. Find the temperature of the coffee after the ice melts.

124. Find ΔH, ΔE, q, and w for the freezing of water at –10.0 °C. The specific heat capacity of ice is 2.04 J/g · °C and its heat of fusion (the quantity of heat associated with melting) is –332 J/g.

125. Starting from the relationship between temperature and kinetic energy for an ideal gas, find the value of the molar heat capacity of an ideal gas when its temperature is changed at constant volume. Find its molar heat capacity when its temperature is changed at constant pressure.

126. An amount of an ideal gas expands from 12.0 L to 24.0 L at a constant pressure of 1.0 atm. Then the gas is cooled at a constant volume of 24.0 L back to its original temperature. Then it contracts back to its original volume. Find the total heat flow for the entire process.

127. The heat of vaporization of water at 373 K is 40.7 kJ/mol. Find q, w, ΔE, and ΔH for the evaporation of 454 g of water at this temperature at 1 atm.

128. Find ΔE, ΔH, q, and w for the change in state of 1.0 mol $H_2O(l)$ at 80 °C to $H_2O(g)$ at 110 °C. The heat capacity of $H_2O(l)$ = 75.3 J/mol K, heat capacity of $H_2O(g)$ = 25.0 J/mol K, and the heat of vaporization of H_2O is 40.7×10^3 J/mol at 100 °C.

129. The heat of combustion of liquid octane (C_8H_{18}) to carbon dioxide and liquid water at 298 K is –1303 kJ/mol. Find ΔE for this reaction.

130. Find ΔH for the combustion of ethanol (C_2H_6O) to carbon dioxide and liquid water from the following data. The heat capacity of the bomb calorimeter is 34.65 kJ/K and the combustion of 1.765 g of ethanol raises the temperature of the calorimeter from 294.33 K to 295.84 K.

Conceptual Problems

131. Which statement is true of the internal energy of the system and its surroundings following a process in which $\Delta E_{sys} = +65$ kJ? Explain.
    a. The system and the surroundings both lose 65 kJ of energy.
    b. The system and the surroundings both gain 65 kJ of energy.
    c. The system loses 65 kJ of energy and the surroundings gain 65 kJ of energy.
    d. The system gains 65 kJ of energy and the surroundings lose 65 kJ of energy.

132. The internal energy of an ideal gas depends only on its temperature. Which statement is true of an isothermal (constant-temperature) expansion of an ideal gas against a constant external pressure? Explain.
    a. ΔE is positive
    b. w is positive
    c. q is positive
    d. ΔE is negative

133. Which expression describes the heat evolved in a chemical reaction when the reaction is carried out at constant pressure? Explain.
    a. $\Delta E - w$ b. ΔE c. $\Delta E - q$

134. Two identical refrigerators are plugged in for the first time. Refrigerator A is empty (except for air) and refrigerator B is filled with jugs of water. The compressors of both refrigerators immediately turn on and begin cooling the interiors of the refrigerators. After 2 hours, the compressor of refrigerator A turns off while the compressor of refrigerator B continues to run. The next day, the compressor of refrigerator A can be heard turning on and off every few minutes, while the compressor of refrigerator B turns off and on every hour or so (and stays on longer each time). Explain these observations.

135. A 1 kg cylinder of aluminum and 1 kg jug of water, both at room temperature, are put into a refrigerator. After 1 hour, the temperature of each object is measured. One of the objects is much cooler than the other. Which one is cooler and why?

136. Two substances A and B, initially at different temperatures, are thermally isolated from their surroundings and allowed to come into thermal contact. The mass of substance A is twice the mass of substance B, but the specific heat capacity of substance B is four times the specific heat capacity of substance A. Which substance will undergo a larger change in temperature?

137. When 1 mol of a gas burns at constant pressure, it produces 2418 J of heat and does 5 J of work. Determine ΔE, ΔH, q, and w for the process.

138. In an exothermic reaction, the reactants lose energy and the reaction feels hot to the touch. Explain why the reaction feels hot even though the reactants are losing energy. Where does the energy come from?

139. Which statement is true of a reaction in which ΔV is positive? Explain.
    a. $\Delta H = \Delta E$ b. $\Delta H > \Delta E$ c. $\Delta H < \Delta E$

Answers to Conceptual Connections

System and Surroundings

6.1 The correct answer is (a). When ΔE_{sys} is negative, energy flows out of the system and into the surroundings. The energy increase in the surroundings must exactly match the decrease in the system.

Heat and Work

6.2 (a) heat, sign is positive (b) work, sign is positive (c) heat, sign is negative

The Heat Capacity of Water

6.3 Bring the water; it has the higher heat capacity and will therefore release more heat as it cools.

Thermal Energy Transfer

6.4 (c) The specific heat capacity of substance B is twice that of A, but since the mass of B is half that of A, the quantity $m \times C_s$ will be identical for both substances so that the final temperature is exactly midway between the two initial temperatures.

The Difference between ΔH and ΔE

6.5 ΔH represents only the heat exchanged; therefore, $\Delta H = -2658$ kJ. ΔE represents the heat *and work* exchanged; therefore, $\Delta E = -2661$ kJ. The signs of both ΔH and ΔE are negative because heat and work are flowing out of the system and into the surroundings. Notice that the values of ΔH and ΔE are similar in magnitude, as is the case in many chemical reactions.

Exothermic and Endothermic Reactions

6.6 An endothermic reaction feels cold to the touch because the reaction (acting here as the system) absorbs heat from the surroundings. When you touch the vessel in which the reaction occurs, you, being part of the surroundings, lose heat to the system (the reaction), which makes you feel cold. The heat absorbed by the reaction (from your body, in this case) does not increase its temperature, but rather becomes potential energy stored in chemical bonds.

Constant-Pressure versus Constant-Volume Calorimetry

6.7 The value of q_{rxn} with the greater magnitude (-12.5 kJ) must have come from the bomb calorimeter. Recall that $\Delta E_{rxn} = q_{rxn} + w_{rxn}$. In a bomb calorimeter, the energy change that occurs in the course of the reaction all takes the form of heat (q). In a coffee-cup calorimeter, the amount of energy released as heat may be smaller because some of the energy may be used to do work (w).

7 The Quantum-Mechanical Model of the Atom

Anyone who is not shocked by quantum mechanics has not understood it.

—Niels Bohr (1885–1962)

THE EARLY PART OF THE TWENTIETH century brought changes that revolutionized how we think about physical reality, especially in the atomic realm. Before that time, all descriptions of the behavior of matter had been deterministic—the present set of conditions completely determining the future. Quantum mechanics changed that. This new theory suggested that for subatomic particles—electrons, neutrons, and protons—the present does NOT completely determine the future. For example, if you shoot one electron down a path and measure where it lands, a second electron shot down the same path under the same conditions will most likely land in a different place! Quantum-mechanical theory was developed by several unusually gifted scientists including Albert Einstein, Niels Bohr, Louis de Broglie, Max Planck, Werner Heisenberg, P. A. M. Dirac, and Erwin Schrödinger. These scientists did not necessarily feel comfortable with their own theory. Bohr said, "Anyone who is not shocked by quantum mechanics has not understood it." Schrödinger wrote, "I don't like it, and I'm sorry I ever had anything to do with it." Albert Einstein disbelieved the very theory he helped create, stating, "God does not play dice with the universe." In fact, Einstein attempted to disprove quantum mechanics—without success—until he died. But quantum mechanics is able to account for fundamental observations, including the very stability of atoms, which could not be understood within the framework of classical physics. Today, quantum mechanics forms the foundation of chemistry—explaining the periodic table and the behavior of the elements in chemical bonding—as well as providing the practical basis for lasers, computers, and countless other applications.

On the chalkboard:

Schrödinger's Cat

$$\Delta x \times m \Delta v \geq \frac{h}{4\pi}$$

7.1 Schrödinger's Cat

Atoms and the particles that compose them are unimaginably small. Electrons have a mass of less than a trillionth of a trillionth of a gram, and a size so small that it is immeasurable. A single speck of dust contains more electrons than the number of people that have existed on Earth over all the centuries of time. Electrons are *small* in the absolute sense of the word—they are among the smallest particles that make up matter. And yet, as we have seen, an atom's electrons determine many of its chemical and physical properties. If we are to understand these properties, we must try to understand electrons.

In the early twentieth century, scientists discovered that the *absolutely small* (or *quantum*) world of the electron behaves differently than the *large* (or *macroscopic*) world that we are used to observing. Chief among these differences is the idea that, when unobserved, *absolutely small particles like electrons can be in two different states at the same time.* For example, through a process called radioactive decay (see Chapter 19) an atom can emit small (that is, *absolutely* small) energetic particles from its nucleus. In the macroscopic world, something either emits an energetic particle or it doesn't. In the quantum world, however, the unobserved atom can be in a state in which it is doing both—emitting the particle and not emitting the particle—simultaneously. At first, this seems absurd.

The thought experiment known as Schrödinger's cat is intended to show that the strangeness of the quantum world does not transfer to the macroscopic world.

The absurdity resolves itself, however, upon observation. When we set out to measure the emitted particle, the act of measurement actually forces the atom into one state or other.

Early twentieth century physicists struggled with this idea. Austrian physicist Erwin Schrödinger (1887–1961), in an attempt to demonstrate that this quantum strangeness could never transfer itself to the macroscopic world, published a paper in 1935 that contained a thought experiment about a cat, now known as Schrödinger's cat. In the thought experiment, the cat is put into a steel chamber that contains radioactive atoms such as the atom described in the previous paragraph. The chamber is equipped with a mechanism that, upon the emission of an energetic particle by one of the radioactive atoms, causes a hammer to break a flask of hydrocyanic acid, a poison. If the flask breaks, the poison is released and the cat dies.

Now here comes the absurdity: if the steel chamber is closed, the whole system remains unobserved, and the radioactive atom is in a state in which it has emitted the particle and not emitted the particle (with equal probability). Therefore, the cat is both dead and undead. Schrödinger put it this way: "[the steel chamber would have] *in it the living and dead cat (pardon the expression) mixed or smeared out in equal parts.*" When the chamber is opened, the act of observation forces the entire system into one state or the other: the cat is either dead or alive, not both. However, while unobserved, the cat is both dead and alive. The absurdity of the both dead and undead cat in Schrödinger's thought experiment was meant to demonstrate how quantum strangeness does not transfer to the macroscopic world.

In this chapter, we examine the **quantum-mechanical model** of the atom, a model that explains the strange behavior of electrons. In particular, we focus on how the model describes electrons as they exist within atoms, and how those electrons determine the chemical and physical properties of elements. You have already learned much about those properties. You know, for example, that some elements are metals and that others are nonmetals. You know that the noble gases are chemically inert and that the alkali metals are chemically reactive. You know that sodium tends to form 1+ ions and that fluorine tends to form 1− ions. But we have not explored *why*. The quantum-mechanical model explains why. In doing so, it explains the modern periodic table and provides the basis for our understanding of chemical bonding.

7.2 The Nature of Light

Before we explore electrons and their behavior within the atom, we must understand some of the properties of light. As quantum mechanics developed, light was (surprisingly) found to have many characteristics in common with electrons. Chief among these is the *wave–particle duality* of light. Certain properties of light are best described by thinking of it as a wave, while other properties are best described by thinking of it as a particle. In this section, we will first explore the wave behavior of light, and then its particle behavior. We will then turn to electrons to see how they also display the same wave–particle duality.

The Wave Nature of Light

Light is **electromagnetic radiation**, a type of energy embodied in oscillating electric and magnetic fields. A *magnetic field* is a region of space where a magnetic particle experiences a force (think of the space around a magnet). An *electric field* is a region of space where an electrically charged particle experiences a force. A proton, for example, has an electric field around it. If you bring another charged particle into that field, that particle will experience a force.

Electromagnetic radiation can be described as a wave composed of oscillating, mutually perpendicular electric and magnetic fields propagating through space, as shown in Figure 7.1 ▶. In a vacuum, these waves move at a constant speed of 3.00×10^8 m/s (186,000 mi/s)—fast enough to circle the Earth in one-seventh of a second. This great speed is the reason for the delay between the moment when you see a firework in the sky and the moment when you hear the sound of its explosion. The light from the exploding firework reaches your eye almost instantaneously. The sound, traveling much more slowly

Electromagnetic Radiation

Electric field component

Magnetic field component

Direction of travel

◀ FIGURE 7.1 **Electromagnetic Radiation** Electromagnetic radiation can be described as a wave composed of oscillating electric and magnetic fields. The fields oscillate in perpendicular planes.

(340 m/s), takes longer. The same thing happens in a thunderstorm—you see the flash of lightening immediately, but the sound of thunder takes a few seconds to reach you (The sound of thunder is delayed by 5 seconds for each mile between you and its origin.)

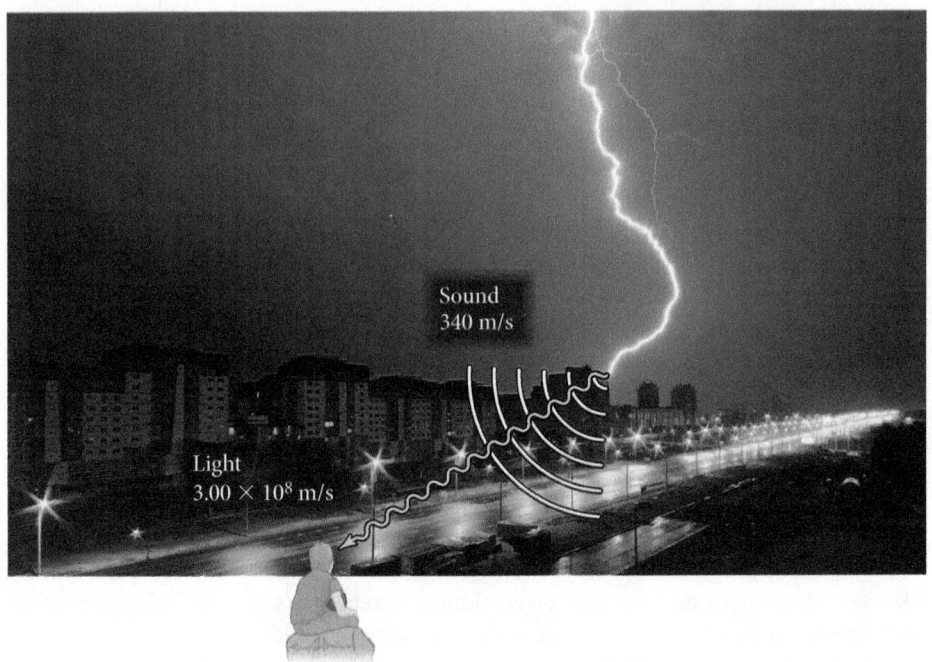

Sound
340 m/s

Light
3.00×10^8 m/s

◀ Because light travels nearly a million times faster than sound, the flash of lightning reaches your eyes before the roll of thunder reaches your ears.

We can characterize a wave by its *amplitude* and its *wavelength*. In the graphical representation shown below, the **amplitude** of the wave is the vertical height of a crest (or depth of a trough). The amplitude of the electric and magnetic field waves in light determines the light's *intensity* or brightness—the greater the amplitude, the greater the intensity. The **wavelength** (λ) of the wave is the distance between adjacent crests (or any two analogous points) and is measured in units such as meters, micrometers, or nanometers.

The symbol λ is the Greek letter lambda, pronounced "lamb-duh."

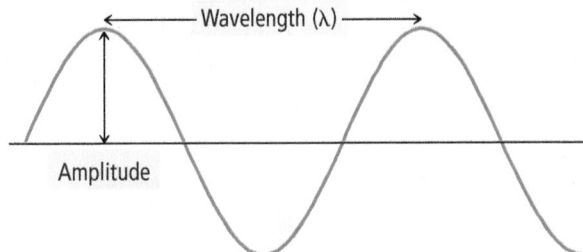

Wavelength (λ)

Amplitude

Wavelength and amplitude are both related to the quantity of energy carried by a wave. Imagine trying to swim out from a shore pounded by waves. Waves of greater amplitude (higher waves) or shorter wavelength (more closely spaced, and thus steeper, waves) will make the swim more difficult. Notice also that amplitude and wavelength

▶ **FIGURE 7.2 Wavelength and Amplitude** Wavelength and amplitude are independent properties. The wavelength of light determines its color. The amplitude, or intensity, determines its brightness.

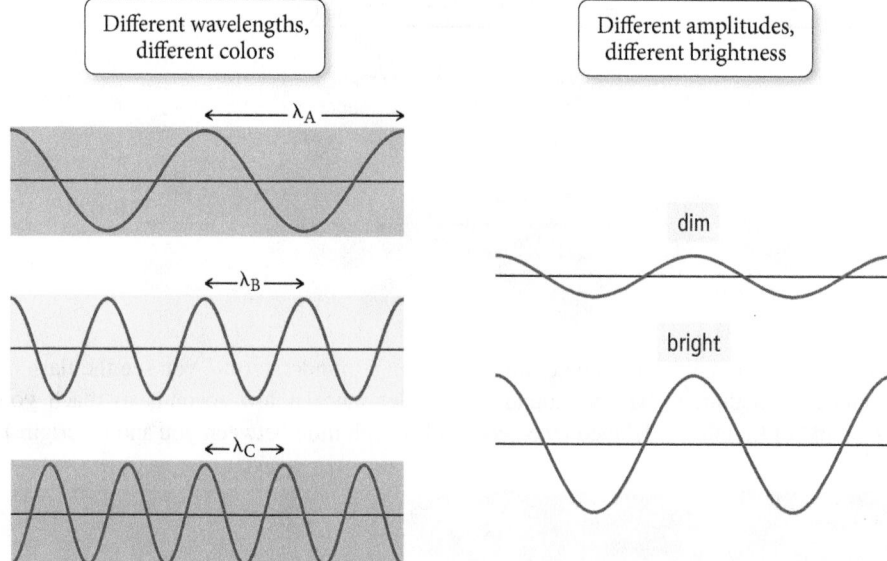

Different wavelengths, different colors

Different amplitudes, different brightness

λ_A

λ_B

λ_C

dim

bright

The symbol ν is the Greek letter nu, pronounced "noo."

nano $= 10^{-9}$

can vary independently of one another, as shown in Figure 7.2 ▲. A wave can have a large amplitude and a long wavelength, or a small amplitude and a short wavelength. The most energetic waves have large amplitudes and short wavelengths.

Like all waves, light is also characterized by its **frequency** (ν), the number of cycles (or wave crests) that pass through a stationary point in a given period of time. The units of frequency are cycles per second (cycle/s) or simply s^{-1}. An equivalent unit of frequency is the hertz (Hz), defined as 1 cycle/s. The frequency of a wave is directly proportional to the speed at which the wave is traveling—the faster the wave, the more crests will pass a fixed location per unit time. Frequency is also *inversely* proportional to the wavelength (λ)—the farther apart the crests, the fewer that will pass a fixed location per unit time. For light, therefore, we can write the equation:

$$\nu = \frac{c}{\lambda} \qquad [7.1]$$

where the speed of light, c, and the wavelength, λ, are both expressed in the same unit of distance. Wavelength and frequency represent different ways of specifying the same information—if we know one, we can readily calculate the other.

For *visible light*—light that can be seen by the human eye—wavelength (or, alternatively, frequency) determines color. White light, produced by the sun or by a lightbulb, contains a spectrum of wavelengths and therefore a spectrum of colors. We can see these colors—red, orange, yellow, green, blue, indigo, and violet—in a rainbow or when white light is passed through a prism (Figure 7.3 ▼). Red light, with a wavelength of about 750 nanometers (nm), has the longest wavelength of visible light; violet light, with a wavelength of about 400 nm, has the shortest. The presence of a variety of wavelengths in white light is responsible for the way we perceive colors in objects. When a substance absorbs some colors while reflecting others, it appears colored. For example, a red shirt appears red because it reflects predominantly red light while absorbing most other colors (Figure 7.4 ▼). Our eyes see only the reflected light, making the shirt appear red.

▶ **FIGURE 7.3 Components of White Light** We can pass white light through a prism and decompose it into its constituent colors, each with a different wavelength. The array of colors makes up the spectrum of visible light.

◀ **FIGURE 7.4 The Color of an Object** A red shirt is red because it reflects predominantly red light while absorbing most other colors.

EXAMPLE 7.1 Wavelength and Frequency

Calculate the wavelength (in nm) of the red light emitted by a barcode scanner that has a frequency of $4.62 \times 10^{14}\,s^{-1}$.

SOLUTION

You are given the frequency of the light and asked to find its wavelength. Use Equation 7.1, which relates frequency to wavelength. You can convert the wavelength from meters to nanometers by using the conversion factor between the two ($1\,nm = 10^{-9}\,m$).

$$v = \frac{c}{\lambda}$$

$$\lambda = \frac{c}{v} = \frac{3.00 \times 10^8\,m/s}{4.62 \times 10^{14}/s}$$

$$= 6.49 \times 10^{-7}\,m$$

$$= 6.49 \times 10^{-7}\,m \times \frac{1\,nm}{10^{-9}\,m} = 649\,mm$$

FOR PRACTICE 7.1

A laser dazzles the audience in a rock concert by emitting green light with a wavelength of 515 nm. Calculate the frequency of the light.

The Electromagnetic Spectrum

Visible light makes up only a tiny portion of the entire **electromagnetic spectrum**, which includes all wavelengths of electromagnetic radiation. Figure 7.5 ▼ shows the main regions of the electromagnetic spectrum, ranging in wavelength from 10^{-15} m (gamma rays) to 10^5 m (radio waves). In Figure 7.5, short-wavelength, high-frequency radiation is on the right and long-wavelength, low-frequency radiation is on the left. As you can see, visible light constitutes only a small region in the middle.

Recall that short-wavelength light inherently has greater energy than long-wavelength light. The most energetic forms of electromagnetic radiation have the shortest wavelengths. The form of electromagnetic radiation with the shortest wavelength is the **gamma (γ) ray**. Gamma rays are produced by the sun, other stars, and certain unstable atomic nuclei on Earth. Excessive exposure to gamma rays is dangerous to humans because the high energy of gamma rays can damage biological molecules.

We will discuss gamma rays in more detail in Chapter 19.

Next on the electromagnetic spectrum, with longer wavelengths than gamma rays, are **X-rays**, familiar to us from their medical use. X-rays pass through many substances that

The Electromagnetic Spectrum

▲ **FIGURE 7.5 The Electromagnetic Spectrum** The right side of the spectrum consists of high-energy, high-frequency, short-wavelength radiation. The left side consists of low-energy, low-frequency, long-wavelength radiation. Visible light constitutes a small segment in the middle.

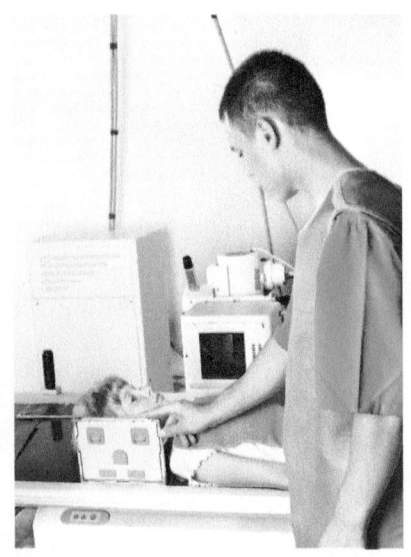

▲ To produce a medical X-ray, the patient is exposed to short-wavelength electromagnetic radiation that can pass through the skin to create an image of bones and internal organs.

block visible light and are therefore used to image bones and internal organs. Like gamma rays, X-rays are sufficiently energetic to damage biological molecules. While several annual exposures to X-rays are relatively harmless, too much exposure to X-rays increases cancer risk.

Sandwiched between X-rays and visible light in the electromagnetic spectrum is **ultraviolet (UV) radiation**, most familiar to us as the component of sunlight that produces a sunburn or suntan. While not as energetic as gamma rays or X-rays, ultraviolet light still carries enough energy to damage biological molecules. Excessive exposure to ultraviolet light increases the risk of skin cancer and cataracts and causes premature wrinkling of the skin.

Next on the spectrum is **visible light**, ranging from violet (shorter wavelength, higher energy) to red (longer wavelength, lower energy). Visible light—at low to moderate intensity—does not carry enough energy to damage biological molecules. It does, however, cause certain molecules in our eyes to change their shape, sending a signal to our brains that results in our ability to see.

Beyond visible light lies **infrared (IR) radiation**. The heat you feel when you place your hand near a hot object is infrared radiation. All warm objects, including human bodies, emit infrared light. Although infrared light is invisible to our eyes, infrared sensors can detect it and are often employed in night vision technology to help people "see" in the dark.

 ## Chemistry and Medicine

Radiation Treatment for Cancer

X-rays and gamma rays are sometimes called ionizing radiation because their short wavelengths correspond to high energies that can ionize atoms and molecules. When ionizing radiation interacts with biological molecules, it can permanently change or even destroy them. Consequently, we normally try to limit our exposure to ionizing radiation. However, doctors use ionizing radiation to destroy molecules within unwanted cells such as cancer cells.

In radiation therapy (also called radiotherapy) doctors aim X-ray or gamma-ray beams at cancerous tumors (groups of cells that divide uncontrollably and invade surrounding healthy tissue). The ionizing radiation damages the molecules within the tumor's cells that carry genetic information—information necessary for the cell to grow and divide. Consequently, the cell dies or stops dividing. Ionizing radiation also damages molecules in healthy cells, but cancerous cells divide more quickly than normal cells, making them more susceptible to genetic damage. Nonetheless, harm to healthy tissues during treatments can result in side effects such as fatigue, skin lesions, hair loss, and organ damage. Medical workers try to reduce such effects by appropriate shielding (of healthy tissue) and by targeting the tumor from multiple directions, minimizing the exposure of healthy cells while maximizing the exposure of cancerous cells.

Another side effect of exposing healthy cells to radiation is that they too may become cancerous. If a treatment for cancer may cause cancer, why do we continue to use it? In radiation therapy, as in most other disease therapies, there is an associated risk. We take risks all the time, many of them for lesser reasons. For example, every time we fly in an airplane or drive in a car, we risk injury or even death. Why? Because we perceive the benefit—the convenience of being able to travel a significant distance in a short time—to be worth the relatively small risk. The situation is similar in cancer therapy, or any other medical therapy for that matter. The benefit of cancer therapy (possibly curing a cancer that might otherwise kill you) is worth the risk (a slight increase in the chance of developing a future cancer).

▲ During radiation therapy, a tumor is targeted from multiple directions in order to minimize the exposure of healthy cells while maximizing the exposure of cancerous cells.

▲ In radiation therapy, highly energetic gamma rays are aimed at cancerous tumors.

Question

Why is visible light (by itself) not used to destroy cancerous tumors?

Beyond infrared light, at longer wavelengths still, are **microwaves**, used for radar and in microwave ovens. Although microwave radiation has longer wavelengths and therefore lower energies than visible or infrared light, it is efficiently absorbed by water and can therefore heat substances that contain water. The longest wavelengths are those of **radio waves**, which are used to transmit the signals responsible for AM and FM radio, cellular telephone, television, and other forms of communication.

▲ Warm objects emit infrared light, which is invisible to the eye but can be captured on film or by detectors to produce an infrared photograph.

Interference and Diffraction

Waves, including electromagnetic waves, interact with each other in a characteristic way called **interference**: they cancel each other out or build each other up, depending on their alignment upon interaction. For example, if two waves of equal amplitude are *in phase* when they interact—that is, they align with overlapping crests—a wave with twice the amplitude results. This is called **constructive interference**.

Waves in phase → Constructive interference

Understanding interference in waves is critical to understanding the wave nature of the electron, as we will soon see.

On the other hand, if two waves are completely *out of phase* when they interact—that is, they align so that the crest from one source overlaps with the trough from the other source—the waves cancel by **destructive interference**.

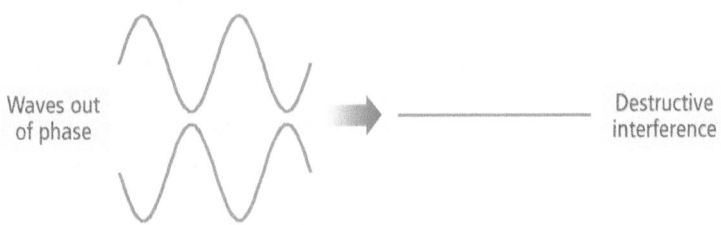

Waves out of phase → Destructive interference

▲ When a reflected wave meets an incoming wave near the shore, the two waves interfere constructively for an instant, producing a large amplitude spike.

Waves also exhibit a characteristic behavior called **diffraction** (Figure 7.6 ▼). When a wave encounters an obstacle or a slit that is comparable in size to its wavelength, it bends (or *diffracts*) around it. The diffraction of light through two slits separated by a distance comparable to the wavelength of the light, coupled with interference, results in

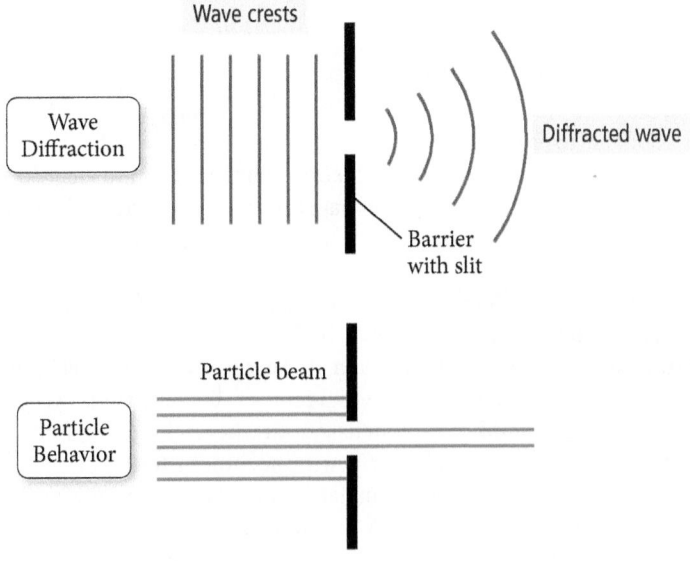

Wave crests

Wave Diffraction

Diffracted wave

Barrier with slit

Particle beam

Particle Behavior

◀ FIGURE 7.6 **Diffraction** In this view from above, we can see how waves bend, or diffract, when they encounter an obstacle or slit with a size comparable to their wavelength. When a wave passes through a small opening, it spreads out. Particles, by contrast, do not diffract; they simply pass through the opening.

Interference from Two Slits

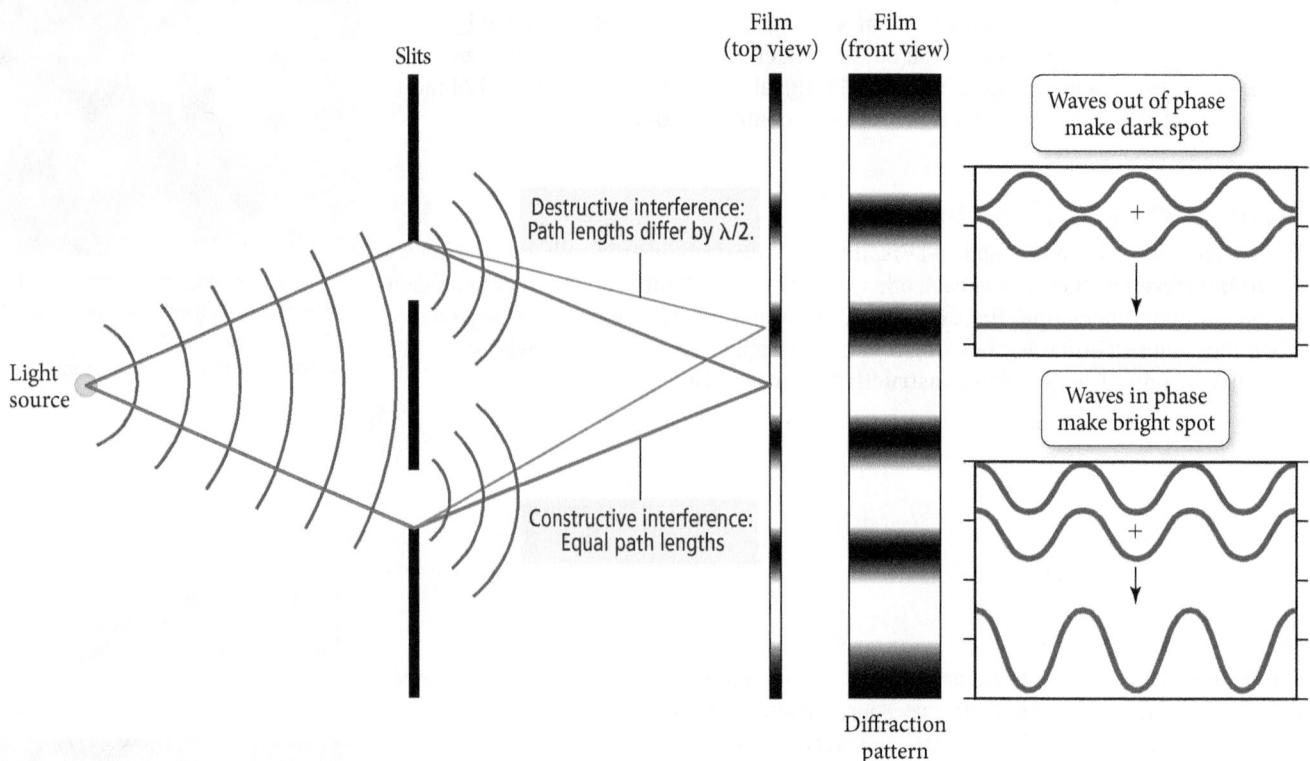

▲ **FIGURE 7.7 Interference from Two Slits** When a beam of light passes through two small slits, the two resulting waves interfere with each other. Whether the interference is constructive or destructive at any given point depends on the difference in the path lengths traveled by the waves. The resulting interference pattern appears as a series of bright and dark lines on a screen.

an *interference pattern*, as shown in Figure 7.7 ▲. Each slit acts as a new wave source, and the two new waves interfere with each other. The resulting pattern is a series of bright and dark lines that can be viewed on a screen (or recorded on a film) placed a short distance behind the slits. At the center of the screen, the two waves travel equal distances and interfere constructively to produce a bright line. A small distance away from the center in either direction, the two waves travel slightly different distances, so they are out of phase. At the point where the difference in distance is one-half of one wavelength, the interference is destructive and a dark line appears on the screen. Moving a bit further away from the center produces constructive interference again because the difference between the paths is one whole wavelength. The end result is the interference pattern shown by the light and dark bars in Figure 7.7. Notice that interference results from the ability of a wave to diffract through two slits—an inherent property of waves.

The Particle Nature of Light

Prior to the early 1900s, and especially after the discovery of the diffraction of light, light was thought to be purely a wave phenomenon. Its behavior was described adequately by classical electromagnetic theory, which treated the electric and magnetic fields that constitute light as waves propagating through space. However, a number of discoveries brought the classical view into question. Chief among these was the *photoelectric effect.*

The **photoelectric effect** is the observation that many metals emit electrons when light shines upon them, as shown in Figure 7.8 ▶. Classical electromagnetic theory attributed this effect to the transfer of energy from the light to an electron in the metal, which resulted in the dislodgment of the electron. According to this explanation, only the amplitude (intensity) of the light affects the emission of electrons, not the wavelength. In other words, according to the classical description, the rate at which electrons leave the metal due to the photoelectric effect increases with increasing intensity of the light. A dim light was expected to result in a *lag time* between the initial shining of the light and the subsequent emission of an electron.

The term *classical*, as in classical electromagnetic theory or classical mechanics, refers to descriptions of matter and energy before the advent of quantum mechanics.

The Photoelectric Effect

(a)   (b)

▲ **FIGURE 7.8 The Photoelectric Effect** (a) When sufficiently energetic light shines on a metal surface, the surface emits electrons. (b) The emitted electrons can be measured as an electrical current.

The lag time would be the minimum amount of time required for the dim light to transfer sufficient energy to the electron to dislodge it.

The experimental results, however, did not support the classical prediction. Scientists found that a high-frequency, low-intensity light produces electrons *without* the predicted lag time. Furthermore, the light used to dislodge electrons in the photoelectric effect exhibits a *threshold frequency,* below which no electrons are emitted from the metal, no matter how long the light shines on the metal. Figure 7.9 ▶ is a graph of the rate of electron ejection from the metal versus the frequency of light used. Notice that increasing the intensity of the light does not change the threshold frequency. In other words, low-frequency (long-wavelength) light *does not* eject electrons from a metal regardless of its intensity or its duration. But high-frequency (short-wavelength) light *does* eject electrons, even if its intensity is low. What could explain this odd behavior?

In 1905, Albert Einstein proposed a bold explanation for the photoelectric effect: *light energy must come in packets.* According to Einstein, the amount of energy (*E*) in a light packet depends on its frequency (*ν*) according to the following equation:

$$E = h\nu \qquad [7.2]$$

where *h*, called *Planck's constant,* has the value $h = 6.626 \times 10^{-34}\,\text{J}\cdot\text{s}$. A *packet* of light is called a **photon** or a **quantum** of light. Since $\nu = c/\lambda$, the energy of a photon can also be expressed in terms of wavelength as follows:

$$E = \frac{hc}{\lambda} \qquad [7.3]$$

Unlike classical electromagnetic theory, in which light was viewed purely as a wave whose intensity was *continuously variable,* Einstein suggested that light was *lumpy.* From this perspective, a beam of light is *not* a wave propagating through space, but a shower of particles (photons), each with energy *hν*.

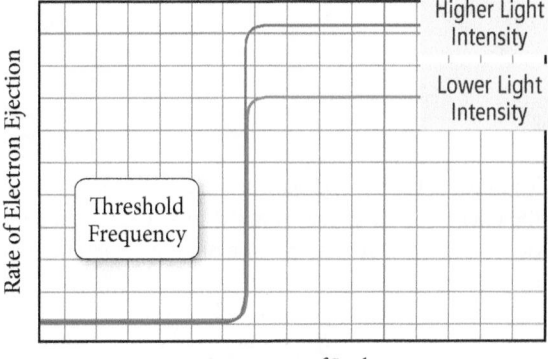

Frequency of Light

▲ **FIGURE 7.9 The Photoelectric Effect** A plot of the electron ejection rate versus frequency of light for the photoelectric effect. Electrons are only ejected when the energy of a photon exceeds the energy with which an electron is held to the metal. The frequency at which this occurs is called the *threshold frequency.*

Einstein was not the first to suggest that energy was quantized. Max Planck used the idea in 1900 to account for certain characteristics of radiation from hot bodies. However, he did not suggest that light actually traveled in discrete packets.

The energy of a photon is directly proportional to its frequency and inversely proportional to its wavelength.

EXAMPLE 7.2 Photon Energy

A nitrogen gas laser pulse with a wavelength of 337 nm contains 3.83 mJ of energy.
How many photons does it contain?

SORT You are given the wavelength and total energy of a light pulse and asked to find the number of photons it contains.	**GIVEN:** $E_{pulse} = 3.83$ mJ $\lambda = 337$ nm **FIND:** number of photons
STRATEGIZE In the first part of the conceptual plan, calculate the energy of an individual photon from its wavelength.	**CONCEPTUAL PLAN** $$E = \frac{hc}{\lambda}$$
In the second part, divide the total energy of the pulse by the energy of a photon to get the number of photons in the pulse.	$$\frac{E_{pulse}}{E_{photon}} = \text{number of photons}$$ **RELATIONSHIPS USED** $E = hc/\lambda$ (Equation 7.3)
SOLVE To execute the first part of the conceptual plan, convert the wavelength to meters and substitute it into the equation to calculate the energy of a 337 nm photon.	**SOLUTION** $\lambda = 337 \text{ nm} \times \dfrac{10^{-9} \text{ m}}{1 \text{ nm}} = 3.37 \times 10^{-7} \text{ m}$ $E_{photon} = \dfrac{hc}{\lambda} = \dfrac{(6.626 \times 10^{-34} \text{ J} \cdot \text{s})\left(3.00 \times 10^8 \dfrac{\text{m}}{\text{s}}\right)}{3.37 \times 10^{-7} \text{ m}}$ $= 5.8985 \times 10^{-19} \text{ J}$
To execute the second part of the conceptual plan, convert the energy of the pulse from mJ to J. Then divide the energy of the pulse by the energy of a photon to obtain the number of photons.	$3.83 \text{ mJ} \times \dfrac{10^{-3} \text{ J}}{1 \text{ mJ}} = 3.83 \times 10^{-3} \text{ J}$ $\text{number of photons} = \dfrac{E_{pulse}}{E_{photon}} = \dfrac{3.83 \times 10^{-3} \text{ J}}{5.8985 \times 10^{-19} \text{ J}}$ $= 6.49 \times 10^{15} \text{ photons}$

CHECK The units of the answer, photons, are correct. The magnitude of the answer (10^{15}) is reasonable. Photons are small particles and any macroscopic collection should contain a large number of them.

FOR PRACTICE 7.2

A 100-watt lightbulb radiates energy at a rate of 100 J/s (The watt, a unit of power, or energy over time, is defined as 1 J/s.) If all of the light emitted has a wavelength of 525 nm, how many photons are emitted per second? (Assume three significant figures in this calculation.)

FOR MORE PRACTICE 7.2

The energy required to dislodge electrons from sodium metal via the photoelectric effect is 275 kJ/mol. What wavelength in nm of light has sufficient energy per photon to dislodge an electron from the surface of sodium?

EXAMPLE 7.3 Wavelength, Energy, and Frequency

Arrange the three types of electromagnetic radiation—visible light, X-rays, and microwaves—in order of increasing

(a) wavelength.   (b) frequency.   (c) energy per photon.

SOLUTION:

Examine Figure 7.5 and note that X-rays have the shortest wavelength, followed by visible light and then microwaves.	(a) wavelength X rays < visible < microwaves
Since frequency and wavelength are inversely proportional—the longer the wavelength the shorter the frequency—the ordering with respect to frequency is the reverse of the ordering with respect to wavelength.	(b) frequency microwaves < visible < X rays
Energy per photon decreases with increasing wavelength but increases with increasing frequency; therefore, the ordering with respect to energy per photon is the same as for frequency.	(c) energy per photon microwaves < visible < X rays

FOR PRACTICE 7.3

Arrange these three colors of visible light—green, red, and blue—in order of increasing

(a) wavelength.   (b) frequency.   (c) energy per photon.

Einstein's idea that light is quantized elegantly explains the photoelectric effect. The emission of electrons from the metal depends on whether or not a single photon has sufficient energy (as given by $h\nu$) to dislodge a single electron. For an electron bound to the metal with binding energy ϕ, the threshold frequency is reached when the energy of the photon is equal to ϕ.

> The symbol ϕ is the Greek letter phi, pronounced "fi."

Threshold frequency condition

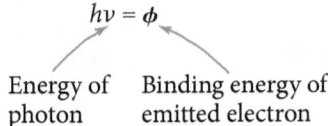

$$h\nu = \phi$$

Energy of   Binding energy of
photon   emitted electron

Low-frequency light does not eject electrons because no single photon has the minimum energy necessary to dislodge the electron. We can draw an analogy between a photon ejecting an electron from a metal surface and a ball breaking a glass window. In this analogy, low-frequency photons are like ping-pong balls—a ping-pong ball thrown at glass window does not break it (just as a low-frequency photon does not eject an electron). Increasing the *intensity* of low-frequency light is like increasing the number of ping-pong balls thrown at the window—doing so simply increases the number of low-energy photons but does not produce any single photon with sufficient energy. In contrast, increasing the *frequency* of the light, even at low intensity, *increases the energy of each photon*. In our analogy, a high-frequency photon is like a baseball—a baseball thrown at a glass window breaks it (just as a high frequency photon dislodges an electron with no lag time).

As the frequency of the light is increased past the threshold frequency, the excess energy of the photon (beyond what is needed to dislodge the electron) is transferred to the electron in the form of kinetic energy. The kinetic energy (KE) of the ejected electron, therefore, is the difference between the energy of the photon ($h\nu$) and the binding energy of the electron, as given by the equation:

$$KE = h\nu - \phi$$

Although the quantization of light explained the photoelectric effect, the wave explanation of light continued to have explanatory power as well, depending on the circumstances of the particular observation. So the principle that slowly emerged (albeit with some measure of resistance) is what we now call the *wave–particle duality of light.* Sometimes light appears to behave like a wave, at other times like a particle. Which behavior you observe depends on the particular experiment.

Conceptual Connection 7.1 The Photoelectric Effect

Light of three different wavelengths—325 nm, 455 nm, and 632 nm—is shined on a metal surface. The observations for each wavelength, labeled A, B, and C, is as follows:

> Observation A: No photoelectrons were observed.
> Observation B: Photoelectrons with a kinetic energy of 155 kJ/mol were observed.
> Observation C: Photoelectrons with a kinetic energy of 51 kJ/mol were observed.

Which observation corresponds to which wavelength of light?

7.3 Atomic Spectroscopy and the Bohr Model

The discovery of the particle nature of light began to break down the division that existed in nineteenth-century physics between electromagnetic radiation, which was thought of as a wave phenomenon, and the small particles (protons, neutrons, and electrons) that compose atoms, which were thought to follow Newton's laws of motion. Just as the photoelectric effect suggested the particle nature of light, so certain observations about atoms began to suggest a wave nature for particles. The most important of these came from *atomic spectroscopy,* the study of the electromagnetic radiation absorbed and emitted by atoms.

When an atom absorbs energy—in the form of heat, light, or electricity—it often re-emits that energy as light. For example, a neon sign is composed of one or more glass tubes filled with neon gas. When an electric current is passed through the tube, the neon atoms absorb some of the electrical energy and re-emit it as the familiar red light of a neon sign. If the atoms in the tube are different (that is, not neon), they emit light of a different color. In other words, atoms of each element emit light of a characteristic color. Mercury atoms, for example, emit light that appears blue, helium atoms emit light that appears violet, and hydrogen atoms emit light that appears reddish (Figure 7.10 ◄).

Remember that the color of visible light is determined by its wavelength. Closer inspection of the light emitted by various atoms reveals that it contains several distinct wavelengths. We can separate the light emitted by a single element in a glass tube into its constituent wavelengths by passing it through a prism (just like we separate the white light from a lightbulb), as shown in Figure 7.11 ►. The result is a series of bright lines called an **emission spectrum**. The emission spectrum of a particular element is always the same—it consists of the same bright lines at the same characteristic wavelengths—and can be used to identify the element. For example, light arriving from a distant star contains the emission spectra of the elements that compose the star. Analysis of the light allows us to identify the elements present in the star.

Notice the differences between a white light spectrum and the emission spectra of hydrogen, helium, and barium (shown in Figure 7.11). The white light spectrum is *continuous,* meaning that there are no sudden interruptions in the intensity of the light as a function of wavelength—the spectrum consists of light of all wavelengths. The emission spectra of hydrogen, helium, and barium, however, are not continuous—they consist of bright lines at specific wavelengths, with complete darkness in between. That is, only certain discrete wavelengths of light are present. Classical physics could not explain why these spectra consisted of discrete lines. In fact, according to classical physics, an atom composed of an electron orbiting a nucleus should emit a continuous white light spectrum. Even more problematic, the electron should lose energy as it emits the light and spiral into the nucleus. According to classical physics, an atom should not even be stable.

▲ The familiar red light from a neon sign is emitted by neon atoms that have absorbed electrical energy, which they re-emit as visible radiation.

▲ **FIGURE 7.10 Mercury, Helium, and Hydrogen** Each element emits a characteristic color.

Emission Spectra

Prism separates component wavelengths

Slit

Hydrogen lamp

Photographic film

Hydrogen spectrum

(a)

Helium spectrum

Barium spectrum

White light spectrum

(b)

◀ FIGURE 7.11 **Emission Spectra**
(a) The light emitted from a hydrogen, helium, or barium lamp consists of specific wavelengths that can be separated by passing the light through a prism. **(b)** The resulting bright lines constitute an emission spectrum characteristic of the element that produced it.

Johannes Rydberg, a Swedish mathematician, analyzed many atomic spectra and developed an equation that predicts the wavelengths of the hydrogen emission spectrum. However, his equation (shown in the margin) gives little insight into *why* atomic spectra are discrete, *why* atoms are stable, or *why* his equation works.

The Rydberg equation is
$1/\lambda = R(1/m^2 - 1/n^2)$, where R is the Rydberg constant ($1.097 \times 10^7 \, m^{-1}$), and m and n are integers.

The Danish physicist Niels Bohr (1885–1962) attempted to develop a model for the atom that explained atomic spectra. In his model, electrons travel around the nucleus in circular orbits (analogous to those of the planets around the sun). However, in contrast to planetary orbits—which can theoretically exist at any distance from the sun—Bohr's orbits exist only at specific, fixed distances from the nucleus. The energy of each Bohr orbit is also fixed, or *quantized*. Bohr called these orbits *stationary states* and suggested that, although they obey the laws of classical mechanics, they also posses "a peculiar, mechanically unexplainable, stability." We now know that the stationary states were really manifestations of the wave nature of the electron, which we will expand upon shortly. Bohr further proposed that, in contradiction to classical electromagnetic theory, no radiation is emitted by an electron orbiting the nucleus in a stationary state. It is only when an electron jumps, or makes a *transition*, from one stationary state to another that radiation is emitted or absorbed (Figure 7.12 ▶).

The transitions between stationary states in a hydrogen atom are quite unlike any transitions

The Bohr Model and Emission Spectra

434 nm Violet

486 nm Blue-green

657 nm Red

$n = 5$
$n = 4$
$n = 3$
$n = 2$
$n = 1$

e^-

▲ FIGURE 7.12 **The Bohr Model and Emission Spectra** According to the Bohr model, each spectral line is produced when an electron falls from one stable orbit, or stationary state, to another of lower energy.

Chemistry in Your Day

Atomic Spectroscopy, a Bar Code for Atoms

When you check out of the grocery store, a laser scanner reads the bar code on the items that you buy. Each item has a unique code that identifies the item and its price. Similarly, each element in the periodic table has a spectrum unlike that of any other element. For example, Figure 7.13 ▼ shows the emission spectra of oxygen and neon. (In Figure 7.11, we saw the emission spectra of hydrogen, helium, and barium.) Notice that each spectrum is unique and, as such, can be used to identify the substance.

The presence of intense lines in the spectra of a number of metals is the basis for *flame tests*, simple tests used to identify elements in ionic compounds in the absence of a precise analysis of a compound's spectrum. For example, the emission spectrum of sodium features two closely spaced, bright yellow lines. When a crystal of a sodium salt (or a drop of a solution containing a sodium salt) is put into a flame, the flame glows bright yellow (Figure 7.14 ▶). As Figure 7.14 shows, other metals exhibit similarly characteristic colors in flame tests. Each color represents an especially bright spectral emission line (or a combination of two or more such lines). Similar emissions form the basis of the colors seen in fireworks.

▲ Fireworks typically contain the salts of such metals as sodium, calcium, strontium, barium, and copper. Emissions from these elements produce the brilliant colors of pyrotechnic displays.

Although the *emission* of light from elements is easier to detect, the *absorption* of light by elements is even more commonly used for purposes of identification. Whereas emission spectra consist of bright lines on a dark background, absorption spectra consist of dark lines on a bright background (Figure 7.15 ▶). An absorption spectrum is measured by passing white light through a

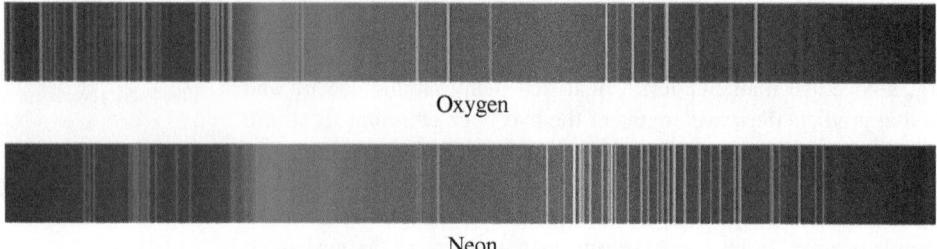

Oxygen

Neon

▲ **FIGURE 7.13 Emission Spectra of Oxygen and Neon**   The emission spectrum of each element is unique and we can use it to identify the element.

that you might be familiar with in the macroscopic world. The electron is *never* observed *between states*; it is observed only in one state or another. The emission spectrum of an atom consists of discrete lines because the stationary states exist only at specific, fixed energies. The energy of the photon emitted when an electron makes a transition from one stationary state to another is the energy difference between the two stationary states. Transitions between stationary states that are closer together, therefore, produce light of lower energy (longer wavelength) than transitions between stationary states that are farther apart.

In spite of its initial success in explaining the line spectrum of hydrogen, the Bohr model left many unanswered questions. It did, however, serve as an intermediate model between a classical view of the electron and a fully quantum-mechanical view, and therefore has great historical and conceptual importance. Nonetheless, it was ultimately replaced by a more complete quantum-mechanical theory that fully incorporated the wave nature of the electron.

◀ FIGURE 7.14 **Flame Tests (from left to right) for Sodium, Potassium, Lithium, and Barium** We can identify elements by the characteristic color of the light they produce when heated. The colors derive from especially bright lines in their emission spectra.

sample and observing what wavelengths are *missing* due to absorption by the sample. Notice that, in the spectrum of mercury shown in Figure 7.15, the absorption lines are at the same wavelengths as the emission lines. This is because the processes that produce them are mirror images. In emission, an electron makes a transition from a higher energy level to a lower energy one. In absorption, the transition is between the same two energy levels, but from the lower level to the higher one.

Absorption spectrometers, found in most chemistry laboratories, typically plot the intensity of absorption as a function of wavelength. Such plots are useful both for identifying substances (qualitative analysis) and for determining the concentration of substances (quantitative analysis). Quantitative analysis is possible because the amount of light absorbed by a sample depends on the concentration of the absorbing substance within the sample. For example, the concentration of Ca^{2+} in a hard water sample can be determined by measuring the quantity of light absorbed by the calcium ion at its characteristic wavelength.

◀ FIGURE 7.15 **Emission and Absorption Spectrum of Mercury** Elements absorb light of the same wavelengths that they radiate when heated. When these wavelengths are subtracted from a beam of white light, the result is a pattern of dark lines corresponding to an absorption spectrum.

7.4 The Wave Nature of Matter: The de Broglie Wavelength, the Uncertainty Principle, and Indeterminacy

The heart of the quantum-mechanical theory that replaced Bohr's model is the wave nature of the electron, first proposed by Louis de Broglie (1892–1987) in 1924 and later confirmed by experiments in 1927. It seemed incredible at the time, but electrons—which were then thought of only as particles and known to have mass—also have a wave nature. The wave nature of the electron is seen most clearly in its diffraction. If an electron beam is aimed at two closely spaced slits, and a series (or array) of detectors is arranged to detect the electrons after they pass through the slits, an interference pattern similar to that observed for light is recorded behind the slits (Figure 7.16(a) ▶). The detectors at the center of the array (midway between the two slits) detect a large number of electrons—exactly the opposite of what you would expect for particles (Figure 7.16(b) ▶). Moving outward from this center spot, the detectors alternately detect small numbers of electrons and then large numbers again and so on, forming an interference pattern characteristic of waves.

The first evidence of electron wave properties was provided by the Davisson–Germer experiment of 1927, in which electrons were observed to undergo diffraction by a metal crystal.

▶ **FIGURE 7.16 Electron Diffraction**
When a beam of electrons goes through two closely spaced slits (**a**), an interference pattern is created, as if the electrons were waves. By contrast, a beam of particles passing through two slits (**b**) produces two smaller beams of particles. Notice that particle beams produce two bright stripes with darkness in between but waves produce the brightest strip directly in the center of the screen.

Actual electron behavior

Interference pattern

Electron source

(a)

Expected behavior for particles

Particle beam

Bright spot

Bright spot

(b)

For interference to occur, the spacing of the slits has to be on the order of atomic dimensions.

Counter to what might be our initial intuition about electron interference, the interference pattern is *not caused by pairs of electrons interfering with each other, but rather by single electrons interfering with themselves.* If the electron source is turned down to a very low level, so that electrons come out only one at a time, *the interference pattern remains.* In other words, we can design an experiment in which electrons come out of the source singly. We can then record where each electron strikes the detector after it has passed through the slits. If we record the positions of thousands of electrons over a long period of time, we find the same interference pattern shown in Figure 7.16(a). This leads us to an important conclusion: *the wave nature of the electron is an inherent property of individual electrons.* Recall from Section 7.1 that unobserved electrons can simultaneously occupy two different states. In this case, the unobserved electron goes through both slits—it exists in two states simultaneously, just like Schrödinger's cat—and interferes with itself. As it turns out, this wave nature explains the existence of stationary states (in the Bohr model) and prevents the electrons in an atom from crashing into the nucleus as predicted by classical physics. We now turn to three important manifestations of the electron's wave nature: the de Broglie wavelength, the uncertainty principle, and indeterminacy.

The de Broglie Wavelength

As we have seen, a single electron traveling through space has a wave nature; its wavelength is related to its kinetic energy (the energy associated with its motion). The faster the electron is moving, the higher its kinetic energy and the shorter its wavelength.

The wavelength (λ) of an electron of mass m moving at velocity v is given by the **de Broglie relation**:

$$\lambda = \frac{h}{mv} \qquad \text{de Broglie relation} \qquad [7.4]$$

where h is Planck's constant. *Notice that the velocity of a moving electron is related to its wavelength—knowing one is equivalent to knowing the other.*

> The mass of an object (m) times its velocity (v) is its momentum. Therefore, the wavelength of an electron is inversely proportional to its momentum.

EXAMPLE 7.4   De Broglie Wavelength

Calculate the wavelength of an electron traveling with a speed of 2.65×10^6 m/s.

SORT You are given the speed of an electron and asked to calculate its wavelength.	**GIVEN:** $v = 2.65 \times 10^6$ m/s **FIND:** λ
STRATEGIZE The conceptual plan shows how the de Broglie relation relates the wavelength of an electron to its mass and velocity.	**CONCEPTUAL PLAN** $$v \longrightarrow \lambda$$ $$\lambda = \frac{h}{mv}$$ **RELATIONSHIPS USED** $\lambda = h/mv$ (de Broglie relation, Equation 7.4)
SOLVE Substitute the velocity, Planck's constant, and the mass of an electron to calculate the electron's wavelength. To correctly cancel the units, break down the J in Planck's constant into its SI base units $(1 \text{ J} = 1 \text{ kg} \cdot \text{m}^2/\text{s}^2)$.	**SOLUTION** $$\lambda = \frac{h}{mv} = \frac{6.626 \times 10^{-34} \frac{\text{kg} \cdot \text{m}^2}{\text{s}^2} \text{s}}{(9.11 \times 10^{-31} \text{ kg})\left(2.65 \times 10^6 \frac{\text{m}}{\text{s}}\right)}$$ $$= 2.74 \times 10^{-10} \text{ m}$$

CHECK The units of the answer (m) are correct. The magnitude of the answer is very small, as expected for the wavelength of an electron.

FOR PRACTICE 7.4

What is the velocity of an electron that has a de Broglie wavelength approximately the length of a chemical bond? Assume this length to be 1.2×10^{-10} m.

Conceptual Connection 7.2   The de Broglie Wavelength of Macroscopic Objects

Since quantum-mechanical theory is universal, it applies to all objects, regardless of size. Therefore, according to the de Broglie relation, a thrown baseball should also exhibit wave properties. Why don't we observe such properties at the ballpark?

The Uncertainty Principle

The wave nature of the electron is difficult to reconcile with its particle nature. How can a single entity behave as both a wave and a particle? We can begin to address this question by returning to the single-electron diffraction experiment. How does a single electron aimed at a double slit produce an interference pattern? We saw previously that the electron travels through both slits and interferes with itself. This idea is testable. We simply have to observe the single electron as it travels through both of the slits.

If it travels through both slits simultaneously, our hypothesis is correct. But here is where nature gets tricky.

Any experiment designed to observe the electron as it travels through the slits results in the detection of an electron "particle" traveling through a single slit and no interference pattern. Recall from Section 7.1 that an *unobserved* electron can occupy two different states; however, the act of observation forces it into one state or the other. Similarly, the act of observing the electron as it travels through both slits forces it to go through only one slit. The following electron diffraction experiment is designed to observe which slit the electron travels through by using a laser beam placed directly behind the slits.

An electron that crosses the laser beam produces a tiny "flash" when a single photon is scattered at the point of crossing. If a flash shows up behind a particular slit, that indicates an electron is passing through that slit. When the experiment is performed, the flash always originates either from one slit *or* the other, but *never* from both at once. Furthermore, the interference pattern, which was present without the laser, is now absent. With the laser on, the electrons hit positions directly behind each slit, as if they were ordinary particles; their wavelike behavior is no longer manifested.

As it turns out, no matter how hard we try or whatever method we set up, *we can never both see the interference pattern and simultaneously determine which hole the electron goes through.* It has never been done, and most scientists agree that it never will. In the words of P. A. M. Dirac,

> There is a limit to the fineness of our powers of observation and the smallness of the accompanying disturbance—a limit which is inherent in the nature of things and can never be surpassed by improved technique or increased skill on the part of the observer.

The single electron diffraction experiment demonstrates that we cannot simultaneously observe both the wave nature and the particle nature of the electron. When we try to observe which hole the electron goes through (associated with the particle nature of the electron) we lose the interference pattern (associated with the wave nature of the electron). When we try to observe the interference pattern, we cannot determine which hole the electron goes through. The wave nature and particle nature of the electron are said to be **complementary properties**. Complementary properties exclude one another—the more we know about one, the less we know about the other. Which of two complementary properties we observe depends on the experiment we perform—in quantum mechanics, the observation of an event affects its outcome.

As we just saw in the de Broglie relation, the *velocity* of an electron is related to its *wave nature*. The *position* of an electron, however, is related to its *particle nature*. (Particles have well-defined position, but waves do not.) Consequently, our inability to observe the electron simultaneously as both a particle and a wave means that *we cannot simultaneously measure its position and its velocity*. Werner Heisenberg formalized this idea with the equation:

$$\Delta x \times m \, \Delta v \geq \frac{h}{4\pi} \text{ Heisenberg's uncertainty principle} \qquad [7.5]$$

where Δx is the uncertainty in the position, Δv is the uncertainty in the velocity, m is the mass of the particle, and h is Planck's constant. **Heisenberg's uncertainty principle** states that the product of Δx and $m\Delta v$ must be greater than or equal to a finite number $(h/4\pi)$. In other words, the more accurately you know the position of an electron (the smaller Δx) the less accurately you can know its velocity (the bigger Δv) and vice versa. The complementarity of the wave nature and particle nature of the electron results in the complementarity of velocity and position.

Although Heisenberg's uncertainty principle may seem puzzling, it actually solves a great puzzle. Without the uncertainty principle, we are left with a paradox: how can something be *both* a particle and a wave? Saying that an object is both a particle and a wave is like saying that an object is both a circle and a square, a contradiction. Heisenberg solved the contradiction by introducing complementarity—an electron is observed as *either* a particle or a wave, but never both at once. This idea was captured by Schrodinger's thought experiment about the cat: when observed, the cat is either dead or alive, not both.

▲ Werner Heisenberg (1901–1976)

Indeterminacy and Probability Distribution Maps

According to classical physics, and in particular Newton's laws of motion, particles move in a *trajectory* (or path) that is determined by the particle's velocity (the speed and direction of travel), its position, and the forces acting on it. Even if you are not familiar with Newton's laws, you probably have an intuitive sense of them. For example, when you chase a baseball in the outfield, you visually predict where the ball will land by observing its path. You do this by noting its initial position and velocity, watching how these are affected by the forces acting on it (gravity, air resistance, wind), and then inferring its trajectory, as shown in Figure 7.17 ▼. If you knew only the ball's velocity, or only its position (imagine a still photo of the baseball in the air), you could not predict its landing spot. In classical mechanics, both position and velocity are required to predict a trajectory.

Newton's laws of motion are **deterministic**—the present *determines* the future. This means that if two baseballs are hit consecutively with the same velocity from the same

Remember that velocity includes speed as well as direction of travel.

The Classical Concept of Trajectory

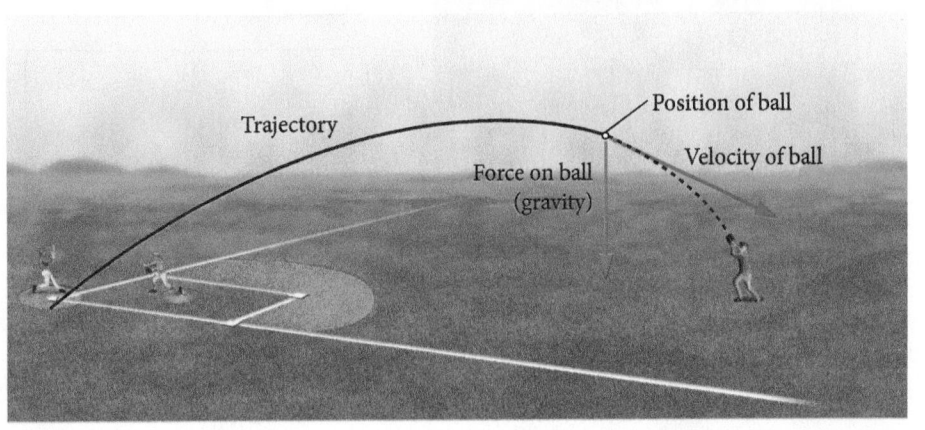

◀ **FIGURE 7.17 The Concept of Trajectory** In classical mechanics, the position and velocity of a particle determine its future trajectory, or path. Thus, an outfielder can catch a baseball by observing its position and velocity, allowing for the effects of forces acting on it, such as gravity, and estimating its trajectory. (For simplicity, air resistance and wind are not shown.)

Classical trajectory

Quantum-mechanical probability distribution map

▲ **FIGURE 7.18 Trajectory versus Probability** In quantum mechanics, we cannot calculate deterministic trajectories. Instead, it is necessary to think in terms of probability maps: statistical pictures of where a quantum-mechanical particle, such as an electron, is most likely to be found. In this hypothetical map, darker shading indicates greater probability.

position under identical conditions, they will land in exactly the same place. The same is not true of electrons. We have just seen that we cannot simultaneously know the position and velocity of an electron; therefore, we cannot know its trajectory. In quantum mechanics, trajectories are replaced with *probability distribution maps,* as shown in Figure 7.18 ▲. A probability distribution map is a statistical map that shows where an electron is likely to be found under a given set of conditions.

To understand the concept of a probability distribution map, let us return to baseball. Imagine a baseball thrown from the pitcher's mound to a catcher behind home plate (Figure 7.19 ◄.) The catcher can watch the baseball's path, predict exactly where it will cross home plate, and place his mitt in the correct place to catch it. As we have seen, the same predictions cannot be made for an electron. If an electron were thrown from the pitcher's mound to home plate, it would land in a different place every time, even if it were thrown in exactly the same way. This behavior is called **indeterminacy**. Unlike a baseball, whose future path is *determined* by its position and velocity when it leaves the pitcher's hand, the future path of an electron is indeterminate, and can only be described statistically.

In the quantum-mechanical world of the electron, the catcher cannot know exactly where the electron will cross the plate for any given throw. However, if he were to record hundreds of identical electron throws, the catcher would observe a reproducible, *statistical pattern* of where the electron crosses the plate. He could even draw a map of the strike zone showing the probability of an electron crossing a certain area, as shown in Figure 7.20 ▼. This would be a probability distribution map. In the sections that follow, we discuss quantum-mechanical electron *orbitals*, which are essentially probability distribution maps for electrons as they exist within atoms.

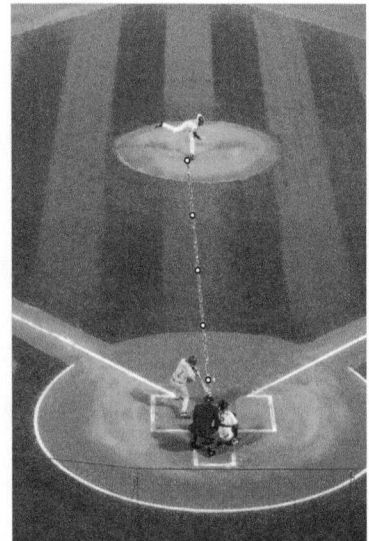

▲ **FIGURE 7.19 Trajectory of a Macroscopic Object** A baseball follows a well-defined trajectory from the hand of the pitcher to the mitt of the catcher.

20%

10%

70%

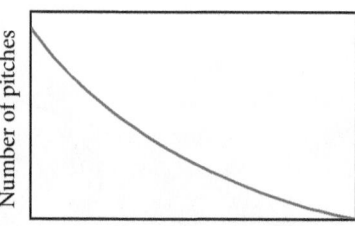

The Quantum-Mechanical Strike Zone

Number of pitches

Distance from center of strike zone

▲ **FIGURE 7.20 The Quantum-Mechanical Strike Zone** An electron does not have a well-defined trajectory. However, we can construct a probability distribution map to show the relative probability of it crossing home plate at different points.

7.5 Quantum Mechanics and the Atom

As we have seen, the position and velocity of the electron are complementary properties—if we know one accurately, the other becomes indeterminate. Since velocity is directly related to energy (recall that kinetic energy equals $\frac{1}{2}mv^2$), position and *energy* are also complementary properties—the more we know about one, the less we know about the other. Many of the properties of an element, however, depend on the energies of its electrons. For example, whether an electron is transferred from one atom to another to form an ionic bond depends in part on the relative energies of the electron in the two atoms. In the following paragraphs, we describe the probability distribution maps for electron states in which the electron has well-defined energy, but not well-defined position. In other words, for each of these states, we can specify the *energy* of the electron precisely, but not its location at a given instant. Instead, the electron's position is described in terms of an **orbital**, a probability distribution map showing where the electron is likely to be found. Since chemical bonding often involves the sharing of electrons between atoms to form covalent bonds, the spatial distribution of atomic electrons is important to bonding.

The mathematical derivation of energies and orbitals for electrons in atoms comes from solving the *Schrödinger* equation for the atom of interest. The general form of the Schrödinger equation is:

$$\mathcal{H}\psi = E\psi \qquad [7.6]$$

The symbol $\mathcal{H}$ stands for the Hamiltonian operator, a set of mathematical operations that represent the total energy (kinetic and potential) of the electron within the atom. The symbol E is the actual energy of the electron. The symbol ψ is the **wave function**, a mathematical function that describes the wavelike nature of the electron. A plot of the wave function squared (ψ^2) represents an orbital, a position probability distribution map of the electron.

| These states are known as energy *eigenstates*.

| An operator is different from a normal algebraic entity. In general, an operator transforms a mathematical function into another mathematical function. For example, d/dx is an operator that means "take the derivative of." When d/dx operates on a function (such as x^2) it returns another function ($2x$).

| The symbol ψ is the Greek letter psi, pronounced "sigh."

Solutions to the Schrödinger Equation for the Hydrogen Atom

When the Schrödinger equation is solved, it yields many solutions—many possible wave functions. The wave functions themselves are fairly complicated mathematical functions, and we do not examine them in detail in this book. Instead, we will introduce graphical representations (or plots) of the orbitals that correspond to the wave functions. Each orbital is specified by three interrelated **quantum numbers**: n, the **principal quantum number**; l, the **angular momentum quantum number** (sometimes called the *azimuthal quantum number*); and m_l, the **magnetic quantum number**. These quantum numbers all have integer values, as had been hinted at by both the Rydberg equation and Bohr's model. A fourth quantum number, $\mathbf{m_s}$, the **spin quantum number**, specifies the orientation of the spin of the electron. We examine each of these quantum numbers individually.

The Principal Quantum Number (n) The principal quantum number is an integer that determines the overall size and energy of an orbital. Its possible values are $n = 1, 2, 3, \ldots$ and so on. For the hydrogen atom, the energy of an electron in an orbital with quantum number n is given by the equation:

$$E_n = -2.18 \times 10^{-18} \text{ J} \left(\frac{1}{n^2}\right) \qquad (n = 1, 2, 3, \ldots) \qquad [7.7]$$

The energy is negative because the electron's energy is lowered (made more negative) by its interaction with the nucleus (see the description of Coulomb's law in Section 8.3). The constant, 2.18×10^{-18} J, is known as the Rydberg constant for hydrogen (R_H). Notice that orbitals with higher values of n have greater (less negative) energies, as shown in the energy level diagram at right. Notice also that, as n increases, the spacing between the energy levels becomes smaller.

The Angular Momentum Quantum Number (l) The angular momentum quantum number is an integer that determines the shape of the orbital. We will consider these shapes in Section 7.6. The possible values of l are $0, 1, 2, \ldots, (n-1)$. In other words, for a given value of n, l can be any integer (including 0) up to $n-1$.

Energy

$n = 4$ ———— $E_4 = -1.36 \times 10^{-19}$ J
$n = 3$ ———— $E_3 = -2.42 \times 10^{-19}$ J

$n = 2$ ———— $E_2 = -5.45 \times 10^{-19}$ J

$n = 1$ ———— $E_1 = -2.18 \times 10^{-18}$ J

For example, if $n = 1$, then the only possible value of l is 0; if $n = 2$, the possible values of l are 0 and 1. To avoid confusion between n and l, values of l are often assigned letters as follows:

The values of l beyond 3 are designated with letters in alphabetical order so that $l = 4$ is designated g, $l = 5$ is designated h, and so on.

Value of l	Letter Designation
$l = 0$	s
$l = 1$	p
$l = 2$	d
$l = 3$	f

Conceptual Connection 7.3 The Relationship between n and l.

What values of l are possible for $n = 3$?

(a) 0 (or s)

(b) 0 and 1 (or s and p)

(c) 0, 1, and 2 (or s, p, and d)

(d) 0, 1, 2, and 3 (or s, p, d, and f)

The Magnetic Quantum Number (m_l) The magnetic quantum number is an integer that specifies the orientation of the orbital. We will consider these orientations in Section 7.6. The possible values of m_l are the integer values (including zero) ranging from $-l$ to $+l$. For example, if $l = 0$ then the only possible value of m_l is 0; if $l = 1$, the possible values of m_l are -1, 0, and $+1$.

Conceptual Connection 7.4 The Relationship between l and m_l.

What values of m_l are possible for $l = 2$?

(a) 0, 1, and 2

(b) 0

(c) $-1, 0$ and $+1$

(d) $-2, -1, 0, +1$, and $+2$

The idea of a "spinning" electron is something of a metaphor. A more correct way to express the same idea is to say that an electron has inherent angular momentum.

The Spin Quantum Number (m_s) The spin quantum number specifies the orientation of the *spin* of the electron. Electron spin is a fundamental property of an electron (like its negative charge). One electron does not have more or less spin than another—all electrons have the same amount of spin. The orientation of the electron's spin is quantized, with only two possibilities: that we can call spin up ($m_s = +1/2$) and spin down ($m_s = -1/2$). The spin quantum number becomes important in Section 8.3 when we begin to consider how electrons occupy orbitals. For now, we will focus on the first three quantum numbers.

Each specific combination of the first three quantum numbers (n, l, and m_l) specifies one atomic orbital. For example, the orbital with $n = 1$, $l = 0$, and $m_l = 0$ is known as the 1s orbital. The 1 in 1s is the value of n and the s specifies that $l = 0$. There is only one 1s orbital in an atom, and its m_l value is zero. Orbitals with the same value of n are said to be in the same **principal level (or principal shell)**. Orbitals with the same value of n and l are said to be in the same **sublevel (or subshell)**.

The following diagram shows all of the orbitals (each represented by a small square) in the first three principal levels.

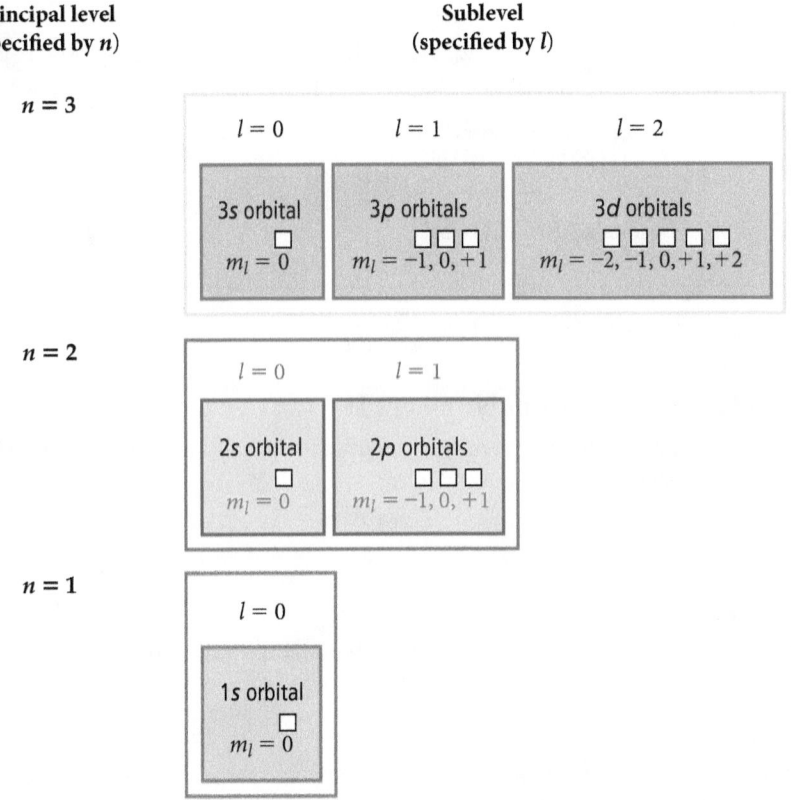

| Principal level (specified by n) | Sublevel (specified by l) |

For example, the $n = 2$ level contains the $l = 0$ and $l = 1$ sublevels. Within the $n = 2$ level, the $l = 0$ sublevel—called the $2s$ sublevel—contains only one orbital (the $2s$ orbital), with $m_l = 0$. The $l = 1$ sublevel—called the $2p$ sublevel—contains three $2p$ orbitals, with $m_l = -1, 0, +1$.

In general, notice the following:

• The number of sublevels in any level is equal to n, the principal quantum number. Therefore, the $n = 1$ level has one sublevel, the $n = 2$ level has two sublevels, etc.

• The number of orbitals in any sublevel is equal to $2l + 1$. Therefore, the s sublevel ($l = 0$) has one orbital, the p sublevel ($l = 1$) has three orbitals, the d sublevel ($l = 2$) has five orbitals, etc.

• The number of orbitals in a level is equal to n^2. Therefore, the $n = 1$ level has one orbital, the $n = 2$ level has four orbitals, the $n = 3$ level has nine orbitals, etc.

EXAMPLE 7.5   Quantum Numbers I

What are the quantum numbers and names (for example, $2s$, $2p$) of the orbitals in the $n = 4$ principal level? How many $n = 4$ orbitals exist?

SOLUTION

First determine the possible values of l (from the given value of n). For a given value of n, the possible values of l are $0, 1, 2, \ldots, (n - 1)$.	$n = 4$; therefore, $l = 0, 1, 2$, and 3

Next, determine the the possible values of m_l for each value of l. For a given value of l, the possible values of m_l are the integer values including zero ranging from $-l$ to $+l$. The name of an orbital is its principal quantum number (n) followed by the letter corresponding to the value l. The total number of orbitals is given by n^2.

l	Possible m_l Values	Orbital name
0	0	$4s$ (1 orbital)
1	$-1, 0, +1$	$4p$ (3 orbitals)
2	$-2, -1, 0, +1, +2$	$4d$ (5 orbitals)
3	$-3, -2, -1, 0, +1, +2, +3$	$4f$ (7 orbitals)

Total number of orbitals $= 4^2 = 16$

FOR PRACTICE 7.5

List the quantum numbers associated with all of the $5d$ orbitals. How many $5d$ orbitals exist?

EXAMPLE 7.6 Quantum Numbers II

These sets of quantum numbers are each supposed to specify an orbital. One set, however, is erroneous. Which one and why?

(a) $n = 3; l = 0; m_l = 0$ (b) $n = 2; l = 1; m_l = -1$
(c) $n = 1; l = 0; m_l = 0$ (d) $n = 4; l = 1; m_l = -2$

SOLUTION

Choice (d) is erroneous because for $l = 1$, the possible values of m_l are only -1, 0, and $+1$.

FOR PRACTICE 7.6

Each set of quantum numbers is supposed to specify an orbital. However, each set contains one quantum number that is not allowed. Replace the quantum number that is not allowed with one that is allowed.

(a) $n = 3;\ l = 3;\ m_l = +2$
(b) $n = 2;\ l = 1;\ m_l = -2$
(c) $n = 1;\ l = 1;\ m_l = 0$

Atomic Spectroscopy Explained

Quantum theory explains the atomic spectra of atoms discussed in Section 7.3. Each wavelength in the emission spectrum of an atom corresponds to an electron *transition* between quantum-mechanical orbitals. When an atom absorbs energy, an electron in a lower energy orbital is *excited* or promoted to a higher energy orbital, as shown in Figure 7.21 ▼. In this new configuration, however, the atom is unstable, and the

Excitation and Radiation

▶ **FIGURE 7.21 Excitation and Radiation** When an atom absorbs energy, an electron can be excited from an orbital in a lower energy level to an orbital in a higher energy level. The electron in this "excited state" is unstable, however, and relaxes to a lower energy level, releasing energy in the form of electromagnetic radiation.

electron quickly falls back or *relaxes* to a lower energy orbital. As it does so, it releases a photon of light containing an amount of energy precisely equal to the energy difference between the two energy levels. We saw previously (see Equation 7.7) that the energy of an orbital in a hydrogen atom with principal quantum number n is given by $E_n = -2.18 \times 10^{-18}$ J$(1/n^2)$, where $n = 1, 2, 3, \ldots$ Therefore, the *difference* in energy between two levels $n_{initial}$ and n_{final} is given by $\Delta E = E_{final} - E_{initial}$. If we substitute the expression for E_n into the expression for ΔE, we get the following important expression for the change in energy that occurs in a hydrogen atom when an electron changes energy levels:

$$\Delta E = E_{final} - E_{initial}$$

$$= -2.18 \times 10^{-18} \text{ J}\left(\frac{1}{n_f^2}\right) - \left[-2.18 \times 10^{-18} \text{ J}\left(\frac{1}{n_i^2}\right)\right]$$

$$\Delta E = -2.18 \times 10^{-18} \text{ J}\left(\frac{1}{n_f^2} - \frac{1}{n_i^2}\right) \qquad [7.8]$$

For example, suppose that an electron in a hydrogen atom relaxes from an orbital in the $n = 3$ level to an orbital in the $n = 2$ level. Then ΔE, the energy difference corresponding to the transition from $n = 3$ to $n = 2$, is determined as follows:

$$\Delta E_{atom} = E_2 - E_3$$

$$= -2.18 \times 10^{-18} \text{ J}\left(\frac{1}{2^2}\right) - \left[-2.18 \times 10^{-18} \text{ J}\left(\frac{1}{3^2}\right)\right]$$

$$= -2.18 \times 10^{-18} \text{ J}\left(\frac{1}{2^2} - \frac{1}{3^2}\right)$$

$$= -3.03 \times 10^{-19} \text{ J}$$

> The Rydberg equation, $1/\lambda = R\,(1/m^2 - 1/n^2)$, can be derived from the relationships just covered. We leave this derivation to an exercise (see Problem 7.96).

The energy carries a negative sign because the atom *emits* the energy as it relaxes from $n = 3$ to $n = 2$. Since energy must be conserved, the exact amount of energy emitted by the atom is carried away by the photon:

$$\Delta E_{atom} = -E_{photon}$$

This energy then determines the frequency and wavelength of the photon. Since the wavelength of the photon is related to its energy as $E = hc/\lambda$, we calculate the wavelength of the photon as:

$$\lambda = \frac{hc}{E}$$

$$= \frac{(6.626 \times 10^{-34} \text{ J} \cdot \text{s})(3.00 \times 10^8 \text{ m/s})}{3.03 \times 10^{-19} \text{ J}}$$

$$= 6.56 \times 10^{-7} \text{ m} \quad \text{or} \quad 656 \text{ nm}$$

Consequently, the light emitted by an excited hydrogen atom as it relaxes from an orbital in the $n = 3$ level to an orbital in the $n = 2$ level has a wavelength of 656 nm (red). Similarly, we can calculate the light emitted due to a transition from $n = 4$ to $n = 2$ to be 486 nm (green). Notice that transitions between orbitals that are further apart in energy produce light that is higher in energy, and therefore shorter in wavelength, than transitions between orbitals that are closer together. Figure 7.22 ▶ shows several of the transitions in the hydrogen atom and their corresponding wavelengths.

▶ FIGURE 7.22 **Hydrogen Energy Transitions and Radiation** An atomic energy level diagram for hydrogen, showing some possible electron transitions between levels and the corresponding wavelengths of emitted light.

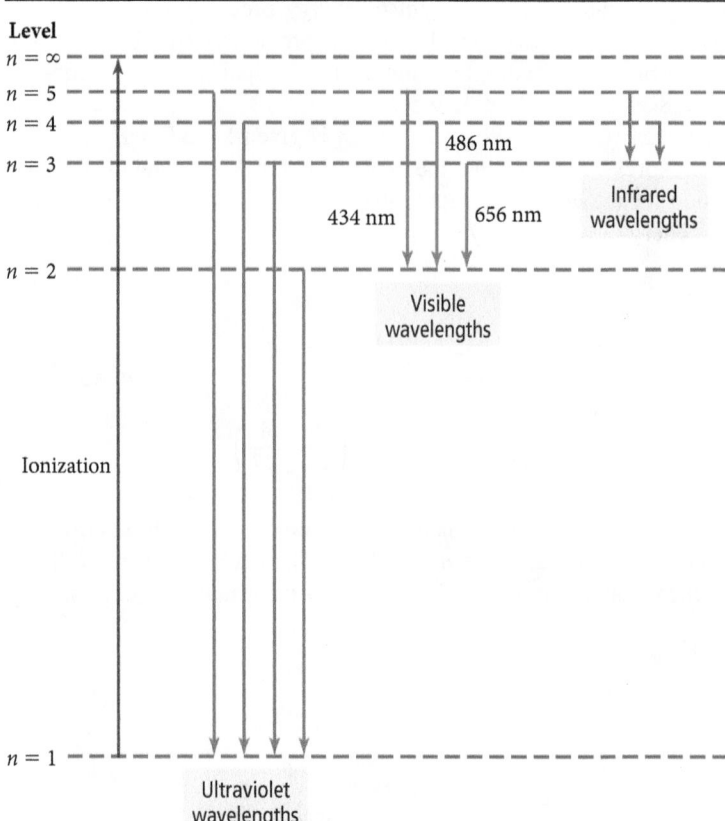

Hydrogen Energy Transitions and Radiation

Level
$n = \infty$
$n = 5$
$n = 4$
$n = 3$

486 nm

434 nm   656 nm

Infrared wavelengths

$n = 2$

Visible wavelengths

Ionization

$n = 1$

Ultraviolet wavelengths

Conceptual Connection 7.5 **Emission Spectra**

Which transition results in emitted light with the shortest wavelength?

(a) $n = 5 \longrightarrow n = 4$ **(b)** $n = 4 \longrightarrow n = 3$ **(c)** $n = 3 \longrightarrow n = 2$

EXAMPLE 7.7 Wavelength of Light for a Transition in the Hydrogen Atom

Determine the wavelength of light emitted when an electron in a hydrogen atom makes a transition from an orbital in $n = 6$ to an orbital in $n = 5$.

SORT You are given the energy levels of an atomic transition and asked to find the wavelength of emitted light.	**GIVEN:** $n = 6 \longrightarrow n = 5$ **FIND:** λ
STRATEGIZE In the first part of the conceptual plan, calculate the energy of the electron in the $n = 6$ and $n = 5$ orbitals using Equation 7.7 and subtract to find ΔE_{atom}.	**CONCEPTUAL PLAN** $n = 5, n = 6 \longrightarrow \Delta E_{atom}$ $\Delta E = E_5 - E_6$
In the second part, find E_{photon} by taking the negative of ΔE_{atom} and then calculate the wavelength corresponding to a photon of this energy using Equation 7.3. (The difference in sign between E_{photon} and ΔE_{atom} applies only to emission. *The energy of a photon must always be positive.*)	$\Delta E_{atom} \longrightarrow E_{photon} \longrightarrow \lambda$ $\Delta E_{atom} = -E_{photon}$ $E = \dfrac{hc}{\lambda}$ **RELATIONSHIPS USED** $E_n = -2.18 \times 10^{-18} \text{ J} (1/n^2)$ $E = hc/\lambda$

SOLVE Follow the conceptual plan. Begin by calculating ΔE_{atom}.	SOLUTION $\Delta E_{atom} = E_5 - E_6$ $= -2.18 \times 10^{-18}J\left(\frac{1}{5^2}\right) - \left[-2.18 \times 10^{-18}J\left(\frac{1}{6^2}\right)\right]$ $= -2.18 \times 10^{-18}J\left(\frac{1}{5^2} - \frac{1}{6^2}\right)$ $= -2.6644 \times 10^{-20} \text{ J}$
Calculate E_{photon} by changing the sign of ΔE_{atom}.	$E_{photon} = -\Delta E_{atom} = +2.6644 \times 10^{-20} \text{ J}$
Solve the equation relating the energy of a photon to its wavelength for λ. Substitute the energy of the photon and calculate λ.	$E = \frac{hc}{\lambda}$ $\lambda = \frac{hc}{E}$ $= \frac{(6.626 \times 10^{-34} \text{ J} \cdot \text{s})(3.00 \times 10^8 \text{ m/s})}{2.6644 \times 10^{-20} \text{ J}}$ $= 7.46 \times 10^{-6} \text{ m or 7460 nm}$

CHECK The units of the answer (m) are correct for wavelength. The magnitude is reasonable because 10^{-6} m is in the infrared region of the electromagnetic spectrum. We know that transitions from $n = 3$ or $n = 4$ to $n = 2$ lie in the visible region, so it makes sense that a transition between levels of higher n value (which are energetically closer to one another) would result in light of longer wavelength.

FOR PRACTICE 7.7
Determine the wavelength of the light absorbed when an electron in a hydrogen atom makes a transition from an orbital in which $n = 2$ to an orbital in which $n = 7$.

FOR MORE PRACTICE 7.7
An electron in the $n = 6$ level of the hydrogen atom relaxes to a lower energy level, emitting light of $\lambda = 93.8$ nm. Find the principal level to which the electron relaxed.

7.6 The Shapes of Atomic Orbitals

As we noted previously, the shapes of atomic orbitals are important because covalent chemical bonds depend on the sharing of the electrons that occupy these orbitals. In one model of chemical bonding, for example, a bond consists of the overlap of atomic orbitals on adjacent atoms. The shapes of the overlapping orbitals determine the shape of the molecule. Although we limit ourselves in this chapter to the orbitals of the hydrogen atom, we will see in Chapter 8 that the orbitals of all atoms can be approximated as being hydrogen-like and therefore having very similar shapes to those of hydrogen.

The shape of an atomic orbital is determined primarily by l, the angular momentum quantum number. Recall that each value of l is assigned a letter that corresponds to particular orbitals. For example, the orbitals with $l = 0$ are called s orbitals; those with $l = 1$, p orbitals; those with $l = 2$, d orbitals, etc. We now examine the shape of each of these orbitals.

s Orbitals ($l = 0$)

The lowest energy orbital is the spherically symmetrical $1s$ orbital shown in Figure 7.23(a) ▶. This image is actually a three-dimensional plot of the wave function

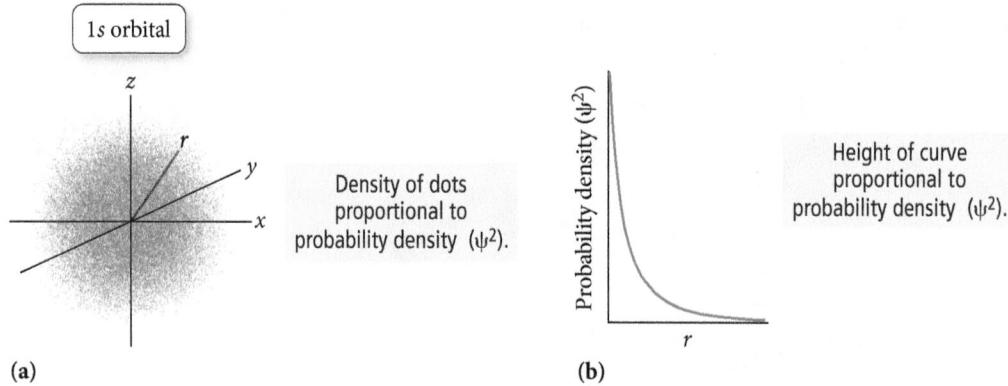

▲ **FIGURE 7.23 The 1s Orbital: Two Representations** In **(a)** the dot density is proportional to the electron probability density. In **(b)**, the height of the curve is proportional to the electron probability density. The x-axis is r, the distance from the nucleus.

squared (ψ^2), which represents **probability density**, the probability (per unit volume) of finding the electron at a point in space.

$$\psi^2 = \text{probability density} = \frac{\text{probability}}{\text{unit volume}}$$

The magnitude of ψ^2 in this plot is proportional to the density of the dots shown in the image. The high dot density near the nucleus (at the very center of the plot) indicates a higher probability density for the electron there. As you move away from the nucleus, the probability density decreases. Figure 7.23(b) ▲ shows a plot of probability density (ψ^2) versus r, the distance from the nucleus. The plot represents a slice through the three-dimensional plot of ψ^2 and shows how the probability density decreases as r increases.

We can understand probability density with the help of a thought experiment. Imagine an electron in the 1s orbital located within the volume surrounding the nucleus. Imagine also taking a photograph of the electron every second for 10 or 15 minutes. In one photograph, the electron is very close to the nucleus, in another it is farther away, and so on. Each photo has a dot showing the electron's position relative to the nucleus when the photo was taken. Remember that you can never predict where the electron will be for any one photo. However, if you took hundreds of photos and superimposed all of them, you would have a plot similar to Figure 7.23(a)—a statistical representation of how likely the electron is to be found at each point.

The thought experiment we just examined can result in a possible misunderstanding: that the electron is moving around (like a moth near a flame) between photographs. However, in the quantum-mechanical model, that is not the case. Between photographs, the location of the electron is uncertain—in a sense its location is spread out over the entire volume of the orbital. Only when the photograph is taken (that is, when a measurement of its location is made) does the location of the electron become localized to one spot. Between measurements, the electron has no single location. Recall from Section 7.1 that the measurement affects the outcome of any quantum system.

An atomic orbital can also be represented by a geometrical shape that encompasses the volume where the electron is likely to be found most frequently—typically, 90% of the time. For example, the 1s orbital can be represented as the three-dimensional sphere shown in Figure 7.24 ◄. If we were to superimpose the dot-density representation of the 1s orbital on the shape representation, 90% of the dots would be within the sphere, meaning that when the electron is in the 1s orbital it has a 90% chance of being found within the sphere.

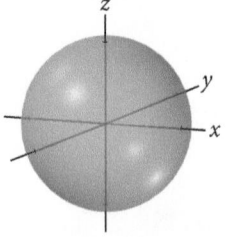

▲ **FIGURE 7.24 The 1s Orbital Surface** In this representation, the surface of the sphere encompasses the volume where the electron is found 90% of the time when the electron is in the 1s orbital.

The plots we have just seen represent probability *density*. However, they are a bit misleading because they seem to imply that the electron is most likely to be found *at the nucleus.* To get a better idea of where the electron is most likely to be found, we can use a plot called the **radial distribution function**, shown in Figure 7.25 ▶ for the 1s orbital. The radial distribution function represents the *total probability of finding the electron within a thin spherical shell at a distance r from the nucleus.*

$$\text{Total radial probability (at a given } r) = \frac{\text{probability}}{\text{unit volume}} \times \text{volume of shell at } r$$

The radial distribution function represents, not probability density *at a point r,* but total probability *at a radius r.* In contrast to probability density, which has a maximum at the nucleus, the radial distribution function has a value of *zero* at the nucleus. It increases to a maximum at 52.9 pm and then decreases again with increasing r.

The shape of the radial distribution function is the result of multiplying together two functions with opposite trends in r:

1. The probability density function (ψ^2), which is the probability per unit volume, has a maximum at the nucleus, and decreases with increasing r.
2. The volume of the thin shell, which is zero at the nucleus and increases with increasing r.

At the nucleus ($r = 0$), for example, the probability *density* is at a maximum; however, the volume of a thin spherical shell is zero, so the radial distribution function is zero. As r increases, the volume of the thin spherical shell increases. We can understand this by making an analogy to an onion. A spherical shell at a distance r from the nucleus is like a layer in an onion at a distance r from its center. If the layers of the onion all have the same thickness, then the volume of any one layer—think of this as the total amount of onion in the layer—is greater as r increases. Similarly, the volume of any one spherical shell in the radial distribution function increases with increasing distance from the nucleus, resulting in a greater total probability of finding the electron within that shell. Close to the nucleus, this increase in volume with increasing r outpaces the decrease in probability density, producing a maximum at 52.9 pm. Farther out, however, the density tapers off faster than the volume increases.

The maximum in the radial distribution function, 52.9 pm, turns out to be the very same radius that Bohr had predicted for the innermost orbit of the hydrogen atom. However, there is a significant conceptual difference between the two radii. In the Bohr model, every time you probe the atom (in its lowest energy state), you would find the electron at a radius of 52.9 pm. In the quantum-mechanical model, you would generally find the electron at various radii, with 52.9 pm having the greatest probability.

The probability densities and radial distribution functions for the 2s and 3s orbitals are shown in Figure 7.26 ▶. Like the 1s orbital, these orbitals are spherically symmetric. These orbitals are larger in size than the 1s orbital, and, unlike the 1s orbital, they contain at least one *node.* A **node** is a point where the wave function (ψ), and therefore the probability density (ψ^2) and radial distribution function, all go through zero. A node in a wave function is much like a node in a standing wave on a vibrating string. We can see nodes in an orbital most clearly by looking at a slice through the orbital. Plots of probability density and the radial distribution function as a function of r both reveal the presence of nodes. The probability of finding the electron at a node is zero.

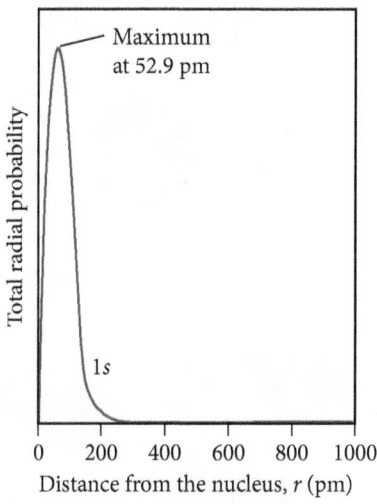

1s Radial Distribution Function

Maximum at 52.9 pm

1s

0   200   400   600   800   1000
Distance from the nucleus, r (pm)

Total radial probability

▲ **FIGURE 7.25 The Radial Distribution Function for the 1s Orbital** The curve shows the total probability of finding the electron within a thin shell at a distance r from the nucleus.

$|\ 1\ \text{pm} = 10^{-12}\ m$

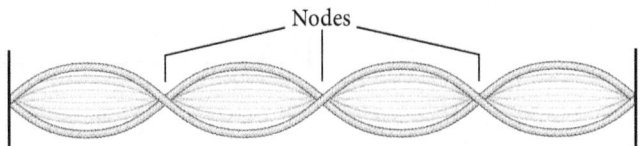

Nodes

▲ The nodes in quantum-mechanical atomic orbitals are three-dimensional analogs of the nodes on a vibrating string.

The 2s and 3s Orbitals

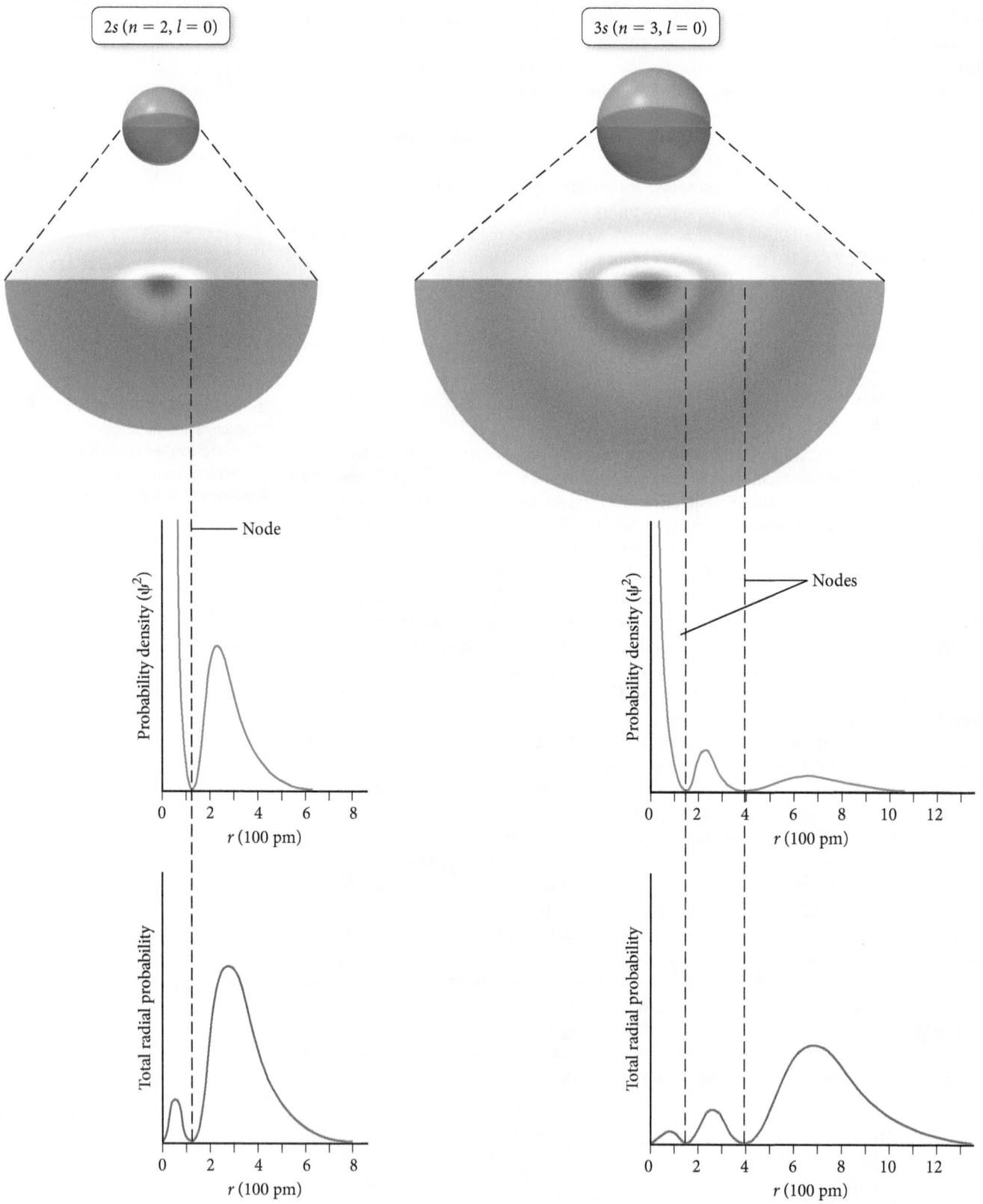

▲ FIGURE 7.26 Probability Densities and Radial Distribution Functions for the 2s and 3s Orbitals.

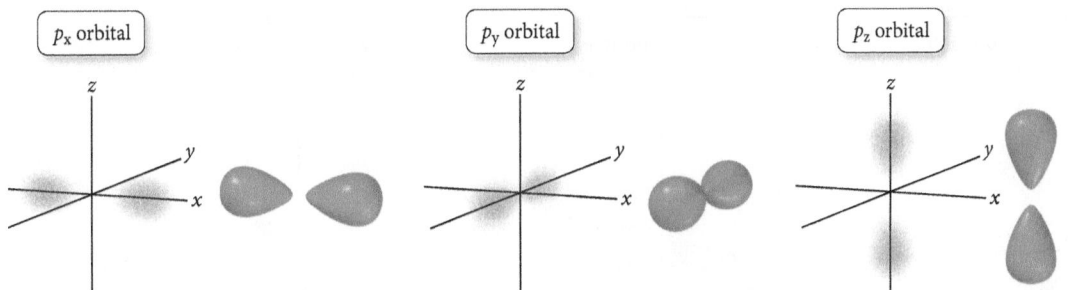

▲ **FIGURE 7.27 The 2p Orbitals and Their Radial Distribution Function**   The radial distribution function is the same for all three 2p orbitals when the x-axis of the graph is taken as the axis containing the lobes of the orbital.

p Orbitals (*l* = 1)

Each principal level with $n = 2$ or greater contains three p orbitals ($m_l = -1, 0, +1$). The three 2p orbitals and their radial distribution functions are shown in Figure 7.27 ▲. The p orbitals are not spherically symmetric like the s orbitals, but they have two *lobes* of electron density on either side of the nucleus and a node located at the nucleus. The three p orbitals differ only in their orientation and are orthogonal (mutually perpendicular) to one another. It is convenient to define an x, y, and z axis system and then label each p orbital as p_x, p_y and p_z. The 3p, 4p, 5p, and higher p orbitals are all similar in shape to the 2p orbitals, but they contain additional nodes (like the higher s orbitals) and are progressively larger in size.

d Orbitals (*l* = 2)

Each principal level with $n = 3$ or greater contains five d orbitals ($m_l = -2, -1, 0, +1, +2$). The five 3d orbitals are shown in Figure 7.28 ▼. Four of these orbitals have a cloverleaf shape, with four lobes of electron density around the nucleus and two perpendicular nodal planes. The d_{xy}, d_{xz}, and d_{yz} orbitals are oriented along the xy, xz, and yz planes, respectively, and their lobes are oriented *between* the corresponding axes. The four lobes of the $d_{x^2-y^2}$ orbital are oriented along the x- and y-axes. The d_{z^2} orbital is different in shape from the other four, having two lobes oriented along the z-axis and a donut-shaped ring along the xy plane. The 4d, 5d, 6d, etc., orbitals are all similar in shape to the 3d orbitals, but they contain additional nodes and are progressively larger in size.

A nodal plane is a plane where the electron probability density is zero. For example, in the d_{xy} orbitals, the nodal planes lie in the xz and yz planes.

▼ **FIGURE 7.28 The 3d Orbitals.**

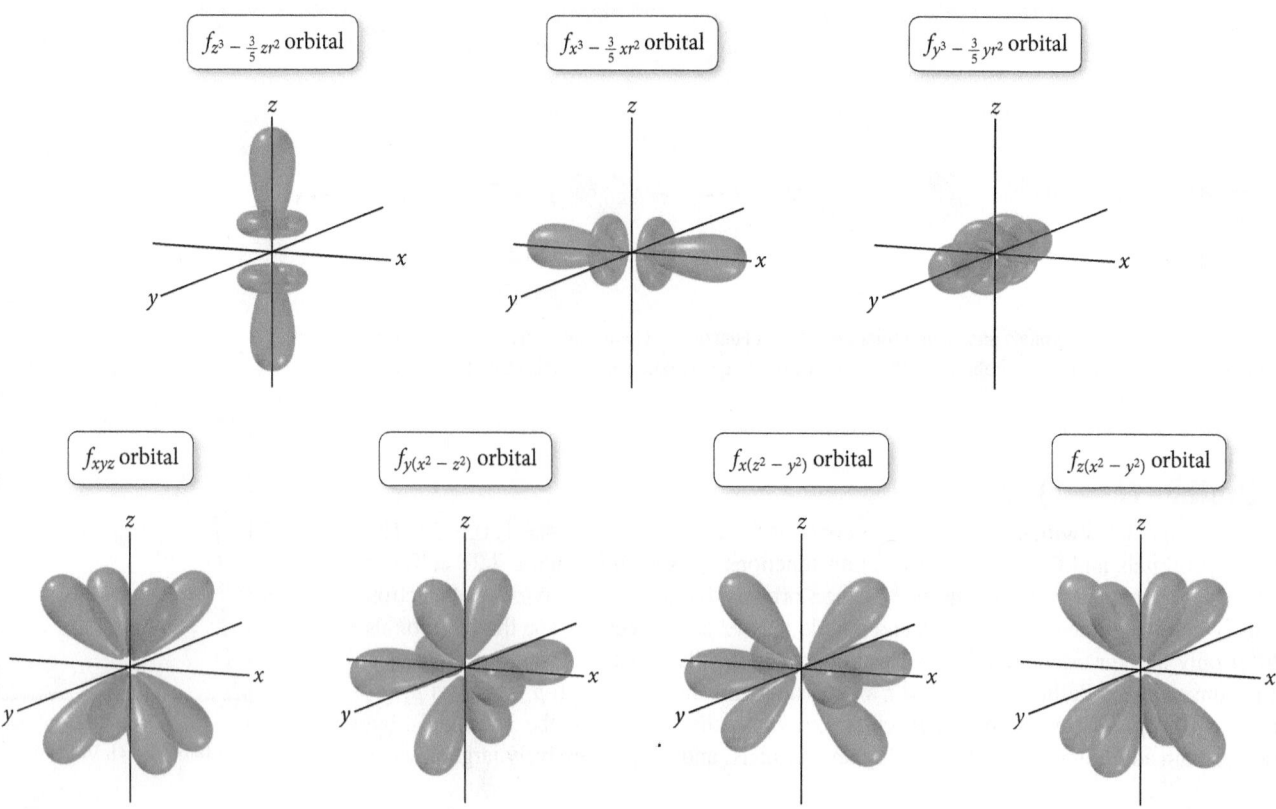

▲ FIGURE 7.29 The 4f Orbitals.

f Orbitals (l = 3)

Each principal level with $n = 4$ or greater contains seven f orbitals ($m_l = -3$, $-2, -1, 0, +1, +2, +3$), as shown in Figure 7.29 ▲. These f orbitals have more lobes and nodes than d orbitals.

The Phase of Orbitals

The orbitals we have just shown are three-dimensional waves. We can understand an important property of these orbitals by analogy to one-dimensional waves. Consider the following one-dimensional waves:

The wave on the left has a positive amplitude over its entire length, while the wave on the right has a positive amplitude over half of its length and a negative amplitude over the other half. The sign of the amplitude of a wave—positive or negative—is known as its **phase**. In these images, blue indicates positive phase and red indicates negative phase. The phase of a wave determines how it interferes with another wave as we saw in Section 7.2.

Just as a one-dimensional wave has a phase, so does a three-dimensional wave. We often represent the phase of a quantum-mechanical orbital with color. For example, the phase of a 1s and 2p orbital can be represented as follows:

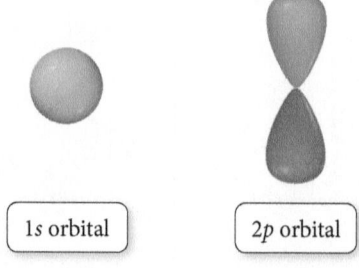

1s orbital   2p orbital

In these depictions, blue represents positive phase and red represents negative phase. The 1s orbital is all one phase, while the 2p orbital exhibits two different phases. The phase of quantum-mechanical orbitals is important in bonding, as we shall see in Chapter 10.

The Shape of Atoms

If some orbitals are shaped like dumbbells and three-dimensional cloverleafs, and if most of the volume of an atom is empty space diffusely occupied by electrons in these orbitals, then why do we often depict atoms as spheres? Atoms are usually drawn as spheres because most atoms contain many electrons occupying a number of different orbitals. Therefore, the shape of an atom is obtained by superimposing all of its orbitals. If we superimpose the s, p, and d orbitals we get a roughly spherical shape, as shown in Figure 7.30 ▸.

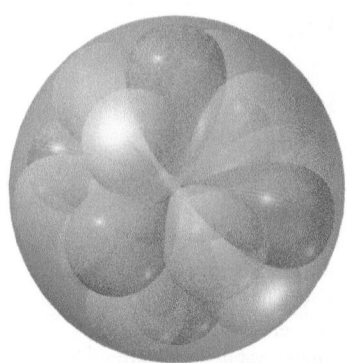

▲ **FIGURE 7.30 Why Atoms Are Spherical** Atoms are depicted as roughly spherical because all the orbitals together make up a roughly spherical shape.

CHAPTER IN REVIEW

Self Assessment Quiz

Q1. Which wavelength of light has the highest frequency?
 a) 10 nm
 b) 10 mm
 c) 1 nm
 d) 1 mm

Q2. Which kind of electromagnetic radiation contains the greatest energy per photon?
 a) microwaves
 b) gamma rays
 c) X-rays
 d) visible light

Q3. How much energy (in J) is contained in 1.00 mole of 552 nm photons?
 a) 3.60×10^{-19} J
 b) 2.17×10^{5} J
 c) 3.60×10^{-28} J
 d) 5.98×10^{-43} J

Q4. Light from three different lasers (A, B, and C), each with a different wavelength, was shined onto the same metal surface. Laser A produced no photoelectrons. Lasers B and C both produced photoelectrons, but the photoelectrons produced by laser B had a greater velocity than those produced by laser C. Arrange the lasers in order of increasing wavelength.
 a) $A < B < C$
 b) $B < C < A$
 c) $C < B < A$
 d) $A < C < B$

Q5. Calculate the wavelength of an electron traveling at 1.85×10^7 m/s.
 a) 2.54×10^{13} m
 b) 3.93×10^{-14} m
 c) 2.54×10^{10} m
 d) 3.93×10^{-11} m

Q6. Which set of three quantum numbers *does not* specify an orbital in the hydrogen atom?
 a) $n = 2; l = 1; m_l = -1$
 b) $n = 3; l = 3; m_l = -2$
 c) $n = 2; l = 0; m_l = 0$
 d) $n = 3; l = 2; m_l = 2$

Q7. Calculate the wavelength of light emitted when an electron in the hydrogen atom makes a transition from an orbital with n = 5 to an orbital with n = 3.
 a) 1.28×10^{-6} m
 b) 6.04×10^{-7} m
 c) 2.28×10^{-6} m
 d) 1.55×10^{-19} m

Q8. Which electron transition produces light of the highest frequency in the hydrogen atom?
 a) $5p \longrightarrow 1s$
 b) $4p \longrightarrow 1s$
 c) $3p \longrightarrow 1s$
 d) $2p \longrightarrow 1s$

Q9. How much time (in seconds) does it take light to travel 1.00 billion km?
 a) 3.00×10^{17} s
 b) 3.33 s
 c) 3.33×10^{3} s
 d) 3.00×10^{20} s

Q10. Which orbital is a *d* orbital?

 a)

 b)

 c)
 d) None of the above

Key Terms

Key Concepts

The Realm of Quantum Mechanics (7.1)

▶ The theory of quantum mechanics explains the behavior of particles, such as photons (particles of light) and electrons, in the atomic and subatomic realms.

▶ Since the electrons of an atom determine many of its chemical and physical properties, quantum mechanics is foundational to understanding chemistry.

The Nature of Light (7.2)

▶ Light is a type of electromagnetic radiation—a form of energy embodied in oscillating electric and magnetic fields that travels though space at 3.00×10^8 m/s.

▶ The wave nature of light is characterized by its wavelength—the distance between wave crests—and its ability to experience interference (constructive or destructive) and diffraction.

▶ The particle nature of light is characterized by the specific quantity of energy carried in each photon.

▶ The electromagnetic spectrum includes all wavelengths of electromagnetic radiation from gamma rays (high energy per photon, short wavelength) to radio waves (low energy per photon, long wavelength). Visible light is a tiny sliver in the middle of the electromagnetic spectrum.

Atomic Spectroscopy (7.3)

▶ Atomic spectroscopy is the study of the light absorbed and emitted by atoms when an electron makes a transition from one energy level to another.

▶ The wavelengths absorbed or emitted depend on the energy differences between the levels involved in the transition; large energy differences result in short wavelengths and small energy differences result in long wavelengths.

The Wave Nature of Matter (7.4)

▶ Electrons have a wave nature with an associated wavelength, as quantified by the de Broglie relation.

▶ The wave nature and particle nature of matter are complementary—the more we know of one, the less we know of the other.

▶ The wave–particle duality of electrons is quantified in Heisenberg's uncertainty principle, which states that there is a limit to how well we can know both the position of an electron (associated with the electron's particle nature) and the velocity times the mass of an electron (associated with the electron's wave nature)—the more accurately one is measured, the greater the uncertainty in measurement of the other.

▶ The inability to simultaneously know both the position and the velocity of an electron results in indeterminacy, the inability to predict a trajectory for an electron. Consequently, electron behavior is described differently than the behavior of everyday-sized particles.

▶ The trajectory we normally associate with macroscopic objects is replaced, for electrons, with statistical descriptions that show not the electron's path, but the region where it is most likely to be found.

The Quantum-Mechanical Model of the Atom (7.5, 7.6)

▶ The most common way to describe electrons in atoms according to quantum mechanics is to solve the Schrödinger equation for the energy states of the electrons within the atom. When the electron is in these states, its energy is well-defined but its position is not. The position of an electron is described by a probability distribution map called an orbital.

▶ The solutions to the Schrödinger equation (including the energies and orbitals) are characterized by four quantum numbers: n, l, m_l, and m_s.

▶ The principal quantum number (n) determines the energy of the electron and the size of the orbital, the angular momentum quantum number (l) determines the shape of the orbital, the magnetic quantum number (m_l) determines the orientation of the orbital, and the spin quantum number (m_s) specifies the orientation of the spin of the electron.

Key Equations and Relationships

Relationship between Frequency (v), Wavelength (λ), and the Speed of Light (c) (**7.2**)

$$\nu = \frac{c}{\lambda}$$

Relationship between Energy (E), Frequency (v), Wavelength (λ), and Planck's Constant (h) (**7.2**)

$$E = h\nu$$

$$E = \frac{hc}{\lambda}$$

De Broglie Relation: Relationship between Wavelength (λ), Mass (m), and Velocity (v) of a Particle (**7.4**)

$$\lambda = \frac{h}{mv}$$

Heisenberg's Uncertainty Principle: Relationship between a Particle's Uncertainty in Position (Δx) and Uncertainty in Velocity (Δv) (**7.4**)

$$\Delta x \times m\Delta v \geq \frac{h}{4\pi}$$

Energy of an Electron in an Orbital with Quantum Number n in a Hydrogen Atom (**7.5**)

$$E_n = -2.18 \times 10^{-18} \text{ J}\left(\frac{1}{n^2}\right) \quad (n = 1, 2, 3, \ldots)$$

Change in Energy That Occurs in an Atom When It Undergoes a Transition between Levels n_{initial} and n_{final} (**7.5**)

$$\Delta E = -2.18 \times 10^{-18} \text{ J}\left(\frac{1}{n_f^2} - \frac{1}{n_i^2}\right)$$

Key Learning Outcomes

Chapter Objectives	Assessment
Calculating the Wavelength and Frequency of Light (**7.2**)	Example 7.1 For Practice 7.1 Exercises 39, 40
Calculating the Energy of a Photon (**7.2**)	Example 7.2 For Practice 7.2 For More Practice 7.4 Exercises 41–46
Relating Wavelength, Energy, and Frequency to the Electromagnetic Spectrum (**7.2**)	Example 7.3 For Practice 7.3 Exercises 37, 42
Using the de Broglie Relation to Calculate Wavelength (**7.4**)	Example 7.4 For Practice 7.4 Exercises 49–54
Relating Quantum Numbers to One Another and to Their Corresponding Orbitals (**7.5**)	Examples 7.5, 7.6 For Practice 7.5, 7.6 Exercises 59–62
Relating the Wavelength of Light to Transitions in the Hydrogen Atom (**7.5**)	Example 7.7 For Practice 7.7 For More Practice 7.7 Exercises 69–72

EXERCISES

Review Questions

1. Why is the quantum-mechanical model of the atom important for understanding chemistry?

2. What is light? How fast does it travel in a vacuum?

3. Define the wavelength and amplitude of a wave. How are these related to the energy of the wave?

4. Define the frequency of electromagnetic radiation. How is frequency related to wavelength?

5. What determines the color of light? Describe the difference between red light and blue light.

6. What determines the color of a colored object? Explain why grass appears green.

7. Give an approximate range of wavelengths for each type of electromagnetic radiation and summarize the characteristics and/or the uses of each.

   a. gamma rays   **b.** X-rays
   c. ultraviolet radiation   **d.** visible light
   e. infrared radiation   **f.** microwave radiation
   g. radio waves

8. Explain the wave behavior known as interference. Explain the difference between constructive and destructive interference.

9. Explain the wave behavior known as diffraction. Draw the diffraction pattern that occurs when light travels through two slits comparable in size and separation to the light's wavelength.

10. Describe the photoelectric effect. How did experimental observations of this phenomenon differ from the predictions of classical electromagnetic theory?

11. How did the photoelectric effect lead Einstein to propose that light is quantized?

12. What is a photon? How is the energy of a photon related to its wavelength? Its frequency?

13. What is an emission spectrum? How does an emission spectrum of a gas in a discharge tube differ from a white light spectrum?

14. Describe the Bohr model for the atom. How did the Bohr model account for the emission spectra of atoms?

15. Explain electron diffraction.

16. What is the de Broglie wavelength of an electron? What determines the value of the de Broglie wavelength for an electron?

17. What are complementary properties? How does electron diffraction demonstrate the complementarity of the wave nature and particle nature of the electron?

18. Explain Heisenberg's uncertainty principle. What paradox is at least partially solved by the uncertainty principle?

19. What is a trajectory? What kind of information do you need to predict the trajectory of a particle?

20. Why does the uncertainty principle make it impossible to predict a trajectory for the electron?

21. Newton's laws of motion are *deterministic*. Explain this statement.

22. An electron behaves in ways that are at least partially indeterminate. Explain this statement.

23. What is a probability distribution map?

24. For each solution to the Schrödinger equation, what can be precisely specified: the electron's energy or its position? Explain.

25. What is a quantum-mechanical orbital?

26. What is the Schrödinger equation? What is a wave function? How is a wave function related to an orbital?

27. What are the possible values of the principal quantum number n? What does the principal quantum number determine?

28. What are the possible values of the angular momentum quantum number l? What does the angular momentum quantum number determine?

29. What are the possible values of the magnetic quantum number m_l? What does the magnetic quantum number determine?

30. List all the orbitals in each principal level. Specify the three quantum numbers for each orbital.
    a. $n = 1$ b. $n = 2$
    c. $n = 3$ d. $n = 4$

31. Explain the difference between a plot showing the probability density for an orbital and one showing the radial distribution function.

32. Make sketches of the general shapes of the s, p, and d orbitals.

33. List the four different sublevels. Given that only a maximum of two electrons can occupy an orbital, determine the maximum number of electrons that can exist in each sublevel.

34. Why are atoms usually portrayed as spheres when most orbitals are not spherically shaped?

Problems by Topic

Electromagnetic Radiation

35. The distance from the sun to Earth is 1.496×10^8 km. How long does it take light to travel from the sun to Earth?

36. The nearest star to our sun is Proxima Centauri, at a distance of 4.3 light-years from the sun. A light-year is the distance that light travels in one year (365 days). How far away, in km, is Proxima Centauri from the sun?

37. List these types of electromagnetic radiation in order of (i) increasing wavelength and (ii) increasing energy per photon:
    a. radio waves   b. microwaves
    c. infrared radiation   d. ultraviolet radiation

38. List these types of electromagnetic radiation in order of (i) increasing frequency and (ii) decreasing energy per photon:
    a. gamma rays   b. radio waves
    c. microwaves   d. visible light

39. Calculate the frequency of each wavelength of electromagnetic radiation:
    a. 632.8 nm (wavelength of red light from helium–neon laser)
    b. 503 nm (wavelength of maximum solar radiation)
    c. 0.052 nm (a wavelength contained in medical X-rays)

40. Calculate the wavelength of each frequency of electromagnetic radiation:
    a. 100.2 MHz (typical frequency for FM radio broadcasting)
    b. 1070 kHz (typical frequency for AM radio broadcasting) (assume four significant figures)
    c. 835.6 MHz (common frequency used for cell phone communication)

41. Calculate the energy of a photon of electromagnetic radiation at each of the wavelengths indicated in Problem 39.

42. Calculate the energy of a photon of electromagnetic radiation at each of the frequencies indicated in Problem 40.

43. A laser pulse with wavelength 532 nm contains 3.85 mJ of energy. How many photons are in the laser pulse?

44. A heat lamp produces 32.8 watts of power at a wavelength of $6.5 \mu m$. How many photons are emitted per second? (1 watt = 1 J/s)

45. Determine the energy of 1 mol of photons for each kind of light. (Assume three significant figures.)
    a. infrared radiation (1500 nm)
    b. visible light (500 nm)
    c. ultraviolet radiation (150 nm)

46. How much energy is contained in 1 mol of each?
    a. X-ray photons with a wavelength of 0.135 nm
    b. γ-ray photons with a wavelength of 2.15×10^{-5} nm.

The Wave Nature of Matter and the Uncertainty Principle

47. Sketch the interference pattern that results from the diffraction of electrons passing through two closely spaced slits.

48. What happens to the interference pattern described in Problem 47 if the rate of electrons going through the slits is decreased to one electron per hour? What happens to the pattern if we try to determine which slit the electron goes through by using a laser placed directly behind the slits?

49. The resolution limit of a microscope is roughly equal to the wavelength of light used in producing the image. Electron microscopes use an electron beam (in place of photons) to produce much higher resolution images, about 0.20 nm in modern instruments. Assuming that the resolution of an electron microscope is equal to the de Broglie wavelength of the electrons used, to what speed must the electrons be accelerated to obtain a resolution of 0.20 nm?

50. The smallest atoms can themselves exhibit quantum-mechanical behavior. Calculate the de Broglie wavelength (in pm) of a hydrogen atom traveling at 475 m/s.

51. What is the de Broglie wavelength of an electron traveling at 1.35×10^5 m/s?

52. A proton in a linear accelerator has a de Broglie wavelength of 122 pm. What is the speed of the proton?

53. Calculate the de Broglie wavelength of a 143 g baseball traveling at 95 mph. Why is the wave nature of matter not important for a baseball?

54. A 0.22-caliber handgun fires a 27 g bullet at a velocity of 765 m/s. Calculate the de Broglie wavelength of the bullet. Is the wave nature of matter significant for bullets?

55. An electron has an uncertainty in its position of 552 pm. What is the uncertainty in its velocity?

56. An electron traveling at 3.7×10^5 m/s has an uncertainty in its velocity of 1.88×10^5 m/s. What is the uncertainty in its position?

Orbitals and Quantum Numbers

57. Which electron is, on average, closer to the nucleus: an electron in a 2s orbital or an electron in a 3s orbital?

58. Which electron is, on average, further from the nucleus: an electron in a 3p orbital or an electron in a 4p orbital?

59. What are the possible values of l for each value of n?
  a. 1   **b.** 2   **c.** 3   **d.** 4

60. What are the possible values of m_l for each value of l?
  a. 0   **b.** 1   **c.** 2   **d.** 3

61. Which set of quantum numbers *cannot* occur together to specify an orbital?
  a. $n = 2, l = 1, m_l = -1$
  b. $n = 3, l = 2, m_l = 0$
  c. $n = 3, l = 3, m_l = 2$
  d. $n = 4, l = 3, m_l = 0$

62. Which combinations of n and l represent real orbitals and which do not exist?
  a. 1s   **b.** 2p   **c.** 4s   **d.** 2d

63. Sketch the 1s and 2p orbitals. How would the 2s and 3p orbitals differ from the 1s and 2p orbitals?

64. Sketch the 3d orbitals. How would the 4d orbitals differ from the 3d orbitals?

Atomic Spectroscopy

65. An electron in a hydrogen atom is excited with electrical energy to an excited state with $n = 2$. The atom then emits a photon. What is the value of n for the electron following the emission?

66. Determine whether each transition in the hydrogen atom corresponds to absorption or emission of energy.
  a. $n = 3 \longrightarrow n = 1$
  b. $n = 2 \longrightarrow n = 4$
  c. $n = 4 \longrightarrow n = 3$

67. According to the quantum-mechanical model for the hydrogen atom, which electron transitions would produce light with the longer wavelength: $2p \longrightarrow 1s$ or $3p \longrightarrow 1s$?

68. According to the quantum-mechanical model for the hydrogen atom, which electron transition would produce light with the longer wavelength: $3p \longrightarrow 2s$ or $4p \longrightarrow 3p$?

69. Calculate the wavelength of the light emitted when an electron in a hydrogen atom makes each transition and indicate the region of the electromagnetic spectrum (infrared, visible, ultraviolet, etc.) where the light is found.
  a. $n = 2 \longrightarrow n = 1$ **b.** $n = 3 \longrightarrow n = 1$
  c. $n = 4 \longrightarrow n = 2$ **d.** $n = 5 \longrightarrow n = 2$

70. Calculate the frequency of the light emitted when an electron in a hydrogen atom makes each transition:
  a. $n = 4 \longrightarrow n = 3$ **b.** $n = 5 \longrightarrow n = 1$
  c. $n = 5 \longrightarrow n = 4$ **d.** $n = 6 \longrightarrow n = 5$

71. An electron in the $n = 7$ level of the hydrogen atom relaxes to a lower energy level, emitting light of 397 nm. What is the value of n for the level to which the electron relaxed?

72. An electron in a hydrogen atom relaxes to the $n = 4$ level, emitting light of 114 THz. What is the value of n for the level in which the electron originated?

Cumulative Problems

73. Ultraviolet radiation and radiation of shorter wavelengths can damage biological molecules because they carry enough energy to break bonds within the molecules. A typical carbon–carbon bond requires 348 kJ/mol to break. What is the longest wavelength of radiation with enough energy to break carbon–carbon bonds?

74. The human eye contains a molecule called 11-*cis*-retinal that changes shape when struck with light of sufficient energy. The change in shape triggers a series of events that results in an electrical signal being sent to the brain. The minimum energy required to change the conformation of 11-*cis*-retinal within the eye is about 164 kJ/mol. Calculate the longest wavelength visible to the human eye.

75. An argon ion laser puts out 5.0 W of continuous power at a wavelength of 532 nm. The diameter of the laser beam is 5.5 mm. If the laser is pointed toward a pinhole with a diameter of 1.2 mm, how many photons will travel through the pinhole per second? Assume that the light intensity is equally distributed throughout the entire cross-sectional area of the beam. (1 W = 1 J/s)

76. A green leaf has a surface area of 2.50 cm^2. If solar radiation is 1000 W/m^2, how many photons strike the leaf every second? Assume three significant figures and an average wavelength of 504 nm for solar radiation.

77. In a technique used for surface analysis called Auger electron spectroscopy (AES), electrons are accelerated toward a metal surface. These electrons cause the emissions of secondary electrons—called auger electrons—from the metal surface. The kinetic energy of the auger electrons depends on the composition of the surface. The presence of oxygen atoms on the surface results in auger electrons with a kinetic energy of approximately 506 eV. What is the de Broglie wavelength of one of these electrons?

$$\left[KE = \tfrac{1}{2}mv^2; \text{1 electron volt (eV)} = 1.602 \times 10^{-19} \text{ J} \right]$$

78. An X-ray photon of wavelength 0.989 nm strikes a surface. The emitted electron has a kinetic energy of 969 eV. What is the binding energy of the electron in kJ/mol?

$$\left[KE = \tfrac{1}{2}mv^2; \text{1 electron volt (eV)} = 1.602 \times 10^{-19} \text{ J} \right]$$

79. Ionization involves completely removing an electron from an atom. How much energy is required to ionize a hydrogen atom in its ground (or lowest energy) state? What wavelength of light contains enough energy in a single photon to ionize a hydrogen atom?

80. The energy required to ionize sodium is 496 kJ/mol. What minimum frequency of light is required to ionize sodium?

81. Suppose that in an alternate universe, the possible values of l were the integer values from 0 to n (instead of 0 to $n - 1$). Assuming no other differences between this imaginary universe and ours, how many orbitals would exist in each level?
    a. $n = 1$ b. $n = 2$ c. $n = 3$

82. Suppose that, in an alternate universe, the possible values of m_l are the integer values including 0 ranging from $-l - 1$ to $l + 1$ (instead of simply $-l$ to $+l$). How many orbitals exist in each sublevel?
    a. s sublevel   b. p sublevel   c. d sublevel

83. An atomic emission spectrum of hydrogen shows three wavelengths: 1875 nm, 1282 nm, and 1093 nm. Assign these wavelengths to transitions in the hydrogen atom.

84. An atomic emission spectrum of hydrogen shows three wavelengths: 121.5 nm, 102.6 nm, and 97.23 nm. Assign these wavelengths to transitions in the hydrogen atom.

85. The binding energy of electrons in a metal is 193 kJ/mol. Find the threshold frequency of the metal.

86. In order for a thermonuclear fusion reaction of two deuterons ($^2_1H^+$) to take place, the deuterons must collide each with a velocity of about 1×10^6 m/s. Find the wavelength of such a deuteron.

87. The speed of sound in air is 344 m/s at room temperature. The lowest frequency of a large organ pipe is 30 s^{-1} and the highest frequency of a piccolo is 1.5×10^4 s^{-1}. Find the difference in wavelength between these two sounds.

88. The distance from Earth to the sun is 1.5×10^8 km. Find the number of crests in a light wave of frequency 1.0×10^{14} s^{-1} traveling from the sun to the Earth.

89. The iodine molecule can be photodissociated into iodine atoms in the gas phase with light of wavelengths shorter than about 792 nm. A 100.0 mL glass tube contains 55.7 mtorr of gaseous iodine at 25.0 °C. What minimum amount of light energy must be absorbed by the iodine in the tube to dissociate 15.0% of the molecules?

90. A 5.00 mL ampule of a 0.100 M solution of naphthalene in hexane is excited with a flash of light. The naphthalene emits 15.5 J of energy at an average wavelength of 349 nm. What percentage of the naphthalene molecules emitted a photon?

91. A laser produces 20.0 mW of red light. In 1.00 hr, the laser emits 2.29×10^{20} photons. What is the wavelength of the laser?

92. A particular laser consumes 150.0 watts of electrical power and produces a stream of 1.33×10^{19} 1064 nm photons per second. What is the percent efficiency of the laser in converting electrical power to light?

Challenge Problems

93. An electron confined to a one-dimensional box has energy levels given by the equation

$$E_n = n^2 h^2 / 8 \, mL^2$$

where n is a quantum number with possible values of 1, 2, 3, . . . , m is the mass of the particle, and L is the length of the box.
    a. Calculate the energies of the $n = 1$, $n = 2$, and $n = 3$ levels for an electron in a box with a length of 155 pm.
    b. Calculate the wavelength of light required to make a transition from $n = 1 \longrightarrow n = 2$ and from $n = 2 \longrightarrow n = 3$. In what region of the electromagnetic spectrum do these wavelengths lie?

94. The energy of a vibrating molecule is quantized much like the energy of an electron in the hydrogen atom. The energy levels of a vibrating molecule are given by the equation

$$E_n = \left(n + \frac{1}{2} \right) h\nu$$

where n is a quantum number with possible values of 1, 2, . . . , and ν is the frequency of vibration. The vibration frequency of HCl is approximately 8.85×10^{13} s^{-1}. What minimum energy is required to excite a vibration in HCl? What wavelength of light is required to excite this vibration?

95. The wave functions for the 1s and 2s orbitals are as follows:

1s $\quad \psi = (1/\pi)^{1/2} (1/a_0^{3/2}) \exp(-r/a_0)$

2s $\quad \psi = (1/32\pi)^{1/2} (1/a_0^{3/2}) (2 - r/a_0) \exp(-r/a_0)$

where a_0 is a constant ($a_0 = 53$ pm) and r is the distance from the nucleus. Use a spreadsheet to make a plot of each of these wave functions for values of r ranging from 0 pm to 200 pm. Describe the differences in the plots and identify the node in the 2s wave function.

96. Before quantum mechanics was developed, Johannes Rydberg developed an equation that predicted the wavelengths (λ) in the atomic spectrum of hydrogen:

$$1/\lambda = R(1/m^2 - 1/n^2)$$

In this equation R is a constant and m and n are integers. Use the quantum-mechanical model for the hydrogen atom to derive the Rydberg equation.

97. Find the velocity of an electron emitted by a metal whose threshold frequency is 2.25×10^{14} s^{-1} when it is exposed to visible light of wavelength 5.00×10^{-7} m.

98. Water is exposed to infrared radiation of wavelength 2.8×10^{-4} cm. Assume that all the radiation is absorbed and converted to heat. How many photons are required to raise the temperature of 2.0 g of water by 2.0 K?

99. The 2005 Nobel Prize in physics was given, in part, to scientists who had made ultrashort pulses of light. These pulses are important in making measurements involving very short time periods. One challenge in making such pulses is the uncertainty principle, which can be stated with respect to energy and time as $\Delta E \cdot \Delta t \geq h/4\pi$. What is the energy uncertainty (ΔE) associated with a short pulse of laser light that lasts for only 5.0 femtoseconds (fs)? Suppose the low energy end of the pulse had a wavelength of 722 nm. What is the wavelength of the high energy end of the pulse that is limited only by the uncertainty principle?

100. A metal whose threshold frequency is $6.71 \times 10^{14}\,s^{-1}$ emits an electron with a velocity of 6.95×10^5 m/s when radiation of $1.01 \times 10^{15}\,s^{-1}$ strikes the metal. Calculate the mass of the electron.

101. Find the longest wavelength of a wave that can travel around in a circular orbit of radius 1.8 m.

102. The heat of fusion of ice is 6.00 kJ/mol. Find the number of photons of wavelength $= 6.42 \times 10^{-6}$ m that must be absorbed to melt 1.00 g of ice.

Conceptual Problems

103. Explain the difference between the Bohr model for the hydrogen atom and the quantum-mechanical model. Is the Bohr model consistent with Heisenberg's uncertainty principle?

104. The light emitted from one of the following electronic transitions ($n = 4 \longrightarrow n = 3$ or $n = 3 \longrightarrow n = 2$) in the hydrogen atom causes the photoelectric effect in a particular metal while light from the other transition does not. Which transition causes the photoelectric effect and why?

105. Determine whether an interference pattern is observed on the other side of the slits in each experiment.
   a. An electron beam is aimed at two closely spaced slits. The beam is attenuated to produce only one electron per minute.
   b. An electron beam is aimed at two closely spaced slits. A light beam is placed at each slit to determine when an electron goes through the slit.

   c. A high-intensity light beam is aimed at two closely spaced slits.
   d. A gun is fired at a solid wall containing two closely spaced slits. (Will the bullets that pass through the slits form an interference pattern on the other side of the solid wall?)

106. Which transition in the hydrogen atom will result in emitted light with the longest wavelength?
   a. $n = 4 \longrightarrow n = 3$
   b. $n = 2 \longrightarrow n = 1$
   c. $n = 3 \longrightarrow n = 2$

Answers to Conceptual Connections

The Photoelectric Effect

7.1 Observation A corresponds to 632 nm, observation B corresponds to 325 nm, and observation C corresponds to 455 nm. The shortest wavelength of light (highest energy per photon) must correspond to the photoelectrons with the greatest kinetic energy. The longest wavelength of light (lowest energy per photon) must correspond to the instance in which no photoelectrons were observed.

The de Broglie Wavelength of Macroscopic Objects

7.2 Because of the baseball's large mass, its de Broglie wavelength is minuscule. (For a 150 g baseball, λ is on the order of 10^{-34} m.) This minuscule wavelength is insignificant compared to the size of the baseball itself, and therefore its effects are not observable.

The Relationship between n and l

7.3 (c) Since l can have a maximum value of $n - 1$, and since $n = 3$, then l can have a maximum value of 2.

The Relationship between l and m_l.

7.4 (d) Since m_l can have the integer values (including 0) between $-l$ and $+l$, and since $l = 2$, the possible values of m_l are $-2, -1, 0, +1,$ and $+2$.

Emission Spectra

7.5 (c) The energy difference between $n = 3$ and $n = 2$ is greatest because the energy differences get closer together with increasing n. The greater energy difference results in an emitted photon of greater energy and therefore shorter wavelength.

8

Periodic Properties of the Elements

Beginning students of chemistry often think of the science as a mere collection of disconnected data to be memorized by brute force. Not at all! Just look at it properly and everything hangs together and makes sense.

—Isaac Asimov (1920–1992)

G REAT ADVANCES IN SCIENCE occur not only when a scientist sees something new, but also when a scientist sees what everyone else has seen in a new way. In other words, great scientists often see patterns where others have seen only disjointed facts. Such was the case in 1869 when Dmitri Mendeleev, a Russian chemistry professor, saw a pattern in the properties of elements. Mendeleev's insight led to the periodic table, arguably the single most important tool for chemists. Recall that scientists devise theories that explain the underlying reasons for observations. If we think of Mendeleev's periodic table as a compact way to summarize a large number of observations, then quantum mechanics (covered in Chapter 7) is the theory that explains the underlying reasons for the periodic table. Quantum mechanics explains how electrons are arranged in atoms, which in turn determines the element's properties. Since the periodic table is organized according to those properties, quantum mechanics beautifully accounts for Mendeleev's periodic table. In this chapter, we see a continuation of the theme we have been developing since page one of this book—the properties of macroscopic substances (in this case, the elements in the periodic table) are explained by the properties of the particles that compose them (in this case, atoms and their electrons).

8.1 Nerve Signal Transmission

As you sit reading this book, tiny pumps in the membranes of your cells are working hard to transport ions—especially sodium (Na$^+$) and potassium (K$^+$)—through those membranes. Amazingly, the ions are pumped in opposite directions. Sodium ions are pumped *out of cells*, while potassium ions are pumped *into cells*. The result is a *chemical gradient* for each ion: the concentration of sodium is higher outside the cell than within, while just the opposite is true for potassium. These ion pumps are analogous to the water pumps in a high-rise building that pump water against the force of gravity to a tank on the roof. Other structures within the membrane, called ion channels, are like the building's faucets. When these open, sodium and potassium ions flow back down their gradients—sodium flowing in and potassium flowing out. This movement of ions is the basis for the transmission of nerve signals in the brain and throughout the body. Every move you make, every thought you have, and every sensation you experience is mediated by these ion movements.

How do the pumps and channels differentiate between sodium and potassium ions to selectively move one out of the cell and the other into the cell? To answer this question, we must examine the ions more closely. Both ions are cations of group 1A metals. All group 1A

In order for a nerve cell to transmit a signal, sodium and potassium ions must flow in opposite directions through specific ion channels in the cell membrane.

3
Li
6.94

11
Na
22.99

19
K
39.10

37
Rb
85.47

55
Cs
132.91

87
Fr
(223.02)

▲ The group 1A metals. Potassium is directly beneath sodium in the periodic table.

metals tend to lose one electron to form cations with a 1+ charge, so that cannot be the decisive factor. Potassium (atomic number 19) lies directly below sodium in the periodic table (atomic number 11), indicating that it has more protons, neutrons, and electrons than sodium. How do these additional subatomic particles affect the properties of potassium? As we will see in this chapter, although a higher atomic number does not always result in a larger ion (or atom), it does in the case of potassium (relative to sodium). The potassium ion has a radius of 133 pm while the sodium ion has a radius of 95 pm. (Recall that 1 pm $= 10^{-12}$ m.) The pumps and channels within cell membranes are so sensitive that they distinguish between the sizes of these two ions and selectively allow only one or the other to pass.

$r = 95$ pm $r = 133$ pm

The relative size of sodium and potassium ions is an example of a **periodic property**: one that is predictable based on an element's position within the periodic table. In this chapter, we examine several periodic properties of elements, including atomic radius, ionization energy, and electron affinity. We will see that these properties, as well as the overall arrangement of the periodic table, are explained by quantum-mechanical theory, which we examined in Chapter 7. The arrangement of elements in the periodic table—originally based on similarities in the properties of the elements—reflects how electrons fill quantum-mechanical orbitals.

8.2 The Development of the Periodic Table

Prior to the 1700s, the number of known elements was relatively small, consisting mostly of the metals that had long been used for coinage, jewelry, and weapons. From the early 1700s to the mid-1800s, however, chemists discovered over 50 new elements. The first attempt to organize these elements according to similarities in their properties was made by the German chemist Johann Döbereiner (1780–1849), who grouped elements into *triads*: three elements with similar properties. For example, Döbereiner formed a triad out of barium, calcium, and strontium, three fairly reactive metals. About 50 years later, English chemist John Newlands (1837–1898) organized elements into *octaves*, in analogy to musical notes. When arranged this way, the properties of every eighth element were similar, much as every eighth note in the musical scale is similar. Newlands endured some ridicule for drawing an analogy between chemistry and music, including the derisive comments of one colleague who asked Newlands if he had ever tried ordering the elements according to the first letters of their names.

The modern periodic table is credited primarily to the Russian chemist Dmitri Mendeleev (1834–1907), even though a similar organization had been suggested by the German chemist Julius Lothar Meyer (1830–1895). Recall from Chapter 2 that Mendeleev's table is based on the periodic law, which states that when elements are arranged in order of increasing mass, certain properties recur periodically. Mendeleev arranged the elements in a table in which mass increases from left to right and elements with similar properties fall in the same columns.

Mendeleev's arrangement was a huge success, allowing him to predict the existence and properties of yet undiscovered elements such as eka-aluminum (later discovered and named gallium) and eka-silicon (later discovered and named germanium). The properties of these two elements are summarized in Figure 8.1 ▶. (As noted in Chapter 2, *eka* means "the one beyond" or "the next one" in a family of elements.) However, Mendeleev did encounter some difficulties. For example, according to accepted values of atomic masses, tellurium (with higher mass) should come *after* iodine. But based on their properties, Mendeleev placed tellurium *before* iodine and suggested that the mass of tellurium was erroneous. The mass was correct; later work by the English physicist Henry Moseley (1887–1915) showed that listing elements according to *atomic number*, rather than atomic mass, resolved this problem and resulted in even better correlation with elemental properties.

▲ Dmitri Mendeleev is credited with the arrangement of the periodic table.

Gallium (eka-aluminum)

	Mendeleev's predicted properties	Actual properties
Atomic mass	About 68 amu	69.72 amu
Melting point	Low	29.8 °C
Density	5.9 g/cm^3	5.90 g/cm^3
Formula of oxide	X$_2$O$_3$	Ga$_2$O$_3$
Formula of chloride	XCl$_3$	GaCl$_3$

Germanium (eka-silicon)

	Mendeleev's predicted properties	Actual properties
Atomic mass	About 72 amu	72.64 amu
Density	5.5 g/cm^3	5.35 g/cm^3
Formula of oxide	XO$_2$	GeO$_2$
Formula of chloride	XCl$_4$	GeCl$_4$

▲ **FIGURE 8.1 Eka-aluminum and Eka-silicon** Mendeleev's arrangement of elements in the periodic table allowed him to predict the existence of these elements, now known as gallium and germanium, and anticipate their properties.

Notice the scientific approach in practice in the history of the periodic table. A number of related observations led to a scientific law—the periodic law. Mendeleev's table, an expression of the periodic law, had predictive power, as laws usually do. However, it did not explain *why* the properties of elements recurred, or *why* certain elements had similar properties. Recall from Chapter 1 that laws *summarize* behavior while theories *explain* behavior. The theory that explains the reasons behind the periodic law is quantum-mechanical theory. In this chapter, we turn to exploring the connection between the periodic table and quantum-mechanical theory.

8.3 Electron Configurations: How Electrons Occupy Orbitals

Quantum-mechanical theory describes the behavior of electrons in atoms. Since chemical bonding involves the transfer or sharing of electrons, quantum-mechanical theory helps us understand and describe chemical behavior. As we saw in Chapter 7, electrons in atoms exist within orbitals. An **electron configuration** for an atom shows the particular orbitals that electrons occupy for that atom. For example, consider the **ground state**—or lowest energy state—electron configuration for a hydrogen atom:

$$\text{H} \qquad 1s^1 \leftarrow \text{Number of electrons in orbital}$$
$$\underset{\text{Orbital}}{\nearrow}$$

The electron configuration indicates that hydrogen's one electron is in the $1s$ orbital. Electrons generally occupy the lowest energy orbitals available. Since the $1s$ orbital is the lowest energy orbital in hydrogen (see Section 7.5), hydrogen's electron occupies that orbital. If we could write electron configurations for all the elements, we could see how the arrangements of the electrons within their atoms correlate with the element's chemical properties. However, the Schrödinger equation solutions (the atomic orbitals and their energies) that we described in Chapter 7 are for the hydrogen atom. What do the atomic orbitals of *other atoms* look like? What are their relative energies?

The Schrödinger equation for multielectron atoms has terms to account for the interactions of the electrons with one another that make it too complicated to solve exactly. However, approximate solutions indicate that the orbitals in multielectron atoms are hydrogen-like—they are similar to the s, p, d, and f orbitals that we examined in Chapter 7. In order to see how the electrons in multielectron atoms occupy these hydrogen-like orbitals, we must examine two additional concepts: *the effects of electron spin*, a fundamental property of all electrons that affects the number of electrons allowed in any one orbital; and *sublevel energy splitting*, which determines the order of orbital filling within a level.

Electron Spin and the Pauli Exclusion Principle

We can represent the electron configuration of hydrogen ($1s^1$) in a slightly different way with an **orbital diagram**, which gives similar information but symbolizes the electron as an arrow and the orbital as a box. The orbital diagram for a hydrogen atom is:

H   [↑]
     $1s$

In an orbital diagram, the direction of the arrow (pointing up or pointing down) represents the orientation of the *electron's spin*. Recall from Section 7.5 that the orientation of the electron's spin is quantized, with only two possibilities—spin up $\left(m_s = +\frac{1}{2}\right)$ and spin down $\left(m_s = -\frac{1}{2}\right)$. In an orbital diagram, $m_s = +\frac{1}{2}$ is represented with a half-arrow pointing up (↑) and $m_s = -\frac{1}{2}$ is represented with a half-arrow pointing down (↓). In a collection of hydrogen atoms, the electrons in about half of the atoms are spin up and the electrons in the other half are spin down. Since no additional electrons are present within the hydrogen atom, we conventionally represent the hydrogen atom electron configuration with its one electron as spin up.

Helium is the first element on the periodic table that contains two electrons. Its two electrons occupy the $1s$ orbital.

He $1s^2$

How do the spins of the two electrons in helium align relative to each other? The answer to this question is addressed by the **Pauli exclusion principle**, formulated by Wolfgang Pauli in 1925.

> **Pauli exclusion principle: no two electrons in an atom can have the same four quantum numbers.**

Since two electrons occupying the same orbital have three identical quantum numbers (n, l, and m_l), they must have different spin quantum numbers. Since there are only two possible spin quantum numbers $\left(+\frac{1}{2} \text{ and } -\frac{1}{2}\right)$, the Pauli exclusion principle implies that *each orbital can have a maximum of only two electrons, with opposing spins*. By applying the exclusion principle, we can write an electron configuration and orbital diagram for helium as follows:

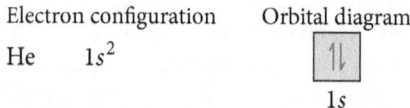

The following table shows the four quantum numbers for each of the two electrons in helium.

n	l	m_l	m_s
1	0	0	$+\dfrac{1}{2}$
1	0	0	$-\dfrac{1}{2}$

The two electrons have three quantum numbers in common (because they are in the same orbital) but have different spin quantum numbers (as indicated by the opposing half-arrows in the orbital diagram).

Sublevel Energy Splitting in Multielectron Atoms

A major difference in the (approximate) solutions to the Schrödinger equation for multielectron atoms compared to the solutions for the hydrogen atom is the energy ordering of the orbitals. In the hydrogen atom, the energy of an orbital depends only on n, the principal quantum number. For example, the $3s$, $3p$, and $3d$ orbitals (which are empty for hydrogen in its lowest energy state) all have the same energy—they are **degenerate**. The orbitals within a principal level of a *multielectron atom*, in contrast, are not degenerate—their energy depends on the value of *l*. We say that the energies of the sublevels are *split*. In general, the lower the value of *l within a principal level*, the lower the energy (*E*) of the corresponding orbital. Thus, for a given value of *n*:

$$E(s \text{ orbital}) < E(p \text{ orbital}) < E(d \text{ orbital}) < E(f \text{ orbital})$$

In order to understand why the sublevels split in this way, we must examine three key concepts associated with the energy of an electron in the vicinity of a nucleus: (1) Coulomb's law, which describes the interactions between charged particles; (2) shielding, which describes how one electron can shield another electron from the full charge of the nucleus; and (3) penetration, which describes how one atomic orbital can overlap spatially with another, thus penetrating into a region that is close to the nucleus (and therefore less shielded from nuclear charge). We will then examine how these concepts, together with the spatial distributions of electron probability for each orbital, result in the energy ordering that we just saw.

Coulomb's Law The attractions and repulsions between charged particles, first introduced in Section 2.4, are described by **Coulomb's law**, which states that the potential energy (*E*) of two charged particles depends on their charges (q_1 and q_2) and on their separation (*r*):

$$E = \frac{1}{4\pi\varepsilon_0} \frac{q_1 q_2}{r} \qquad [8.1]$$

In this equation, ε_0 is a constant ($\varepsilon_0 = 8.85 \times 10^{-12} \text{ C}^2/\text{J}\cdot\text{m}$). The potential energy is positive for charges of the same sign (plus $\times$ plus, or minus $\times$ minus) and negative for charges of opposite sign (plus $\times$ minus, or minus $\times$ plus). The *magnitude* of the potential energy depends inversely on the separation between the charged particles. We can draw three important conclusions from Coulomb's law:

- For like charges, the potential energy (*E*) is positive and decreases as the particles get *farther apart* (as *r* increases). Since systems tend toward lower potential energy, like charges repel each other (in much the same way that like poles of two magnets repel each other).

- For opposite charges, the potential energy is negative and becomes more negative as the particles get *closer together* (as *r* decreases). Therefore, opposite charges (like opposite poles on a magnet) *attract each other.*

- The *magnitude* of the interaction between charged particles increases as the charges of the particles increases. Consequently, an electron with a charge of 1− is more strongly attracted to a nucleus with a charge of 2+ than it would be to a nucleus with a charge of 1+.

Conceptual Connection 8.1 Coulomb's Law

According to Coulomb's law, what happens to the potential energy of two oppositely charged particles as they get closer together?

(a) Their potential energy decreases.

(b) Their potential energy increases.

(c) Their potential energy does not change.

Shielding For multielectron atoms, any one electron experiences both the positive charge of the nucleus (which is attractive) and the negative charges of the other electrons (which are repulsive). We can think of the repulsion of one electron by other electrons as *screening* or **shielding** that electron from the full effects of the nuclear charge. For example, consider a lithium ion (Li^+). Since the lithium ion contains two electrons, its electron configuration is identical to that of helium:

$$Li^+ \qquad 1s^2$$

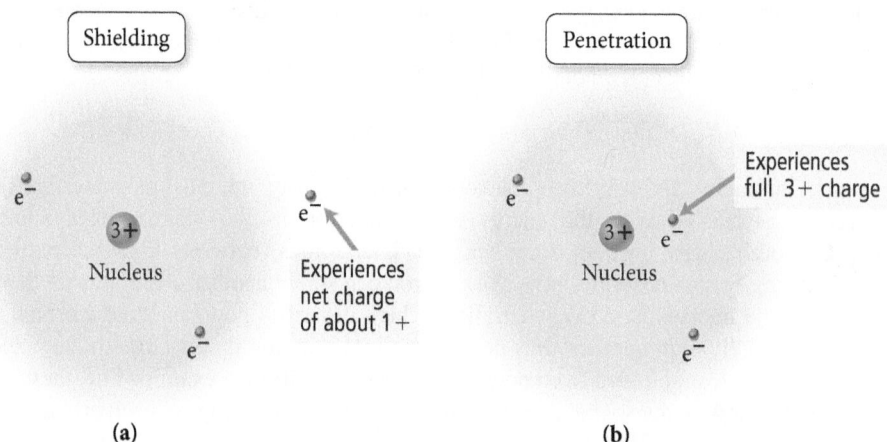

▲ **FIGURE 8.2 Shielding and Penetration**   (a) An electron far from the nucleus is partly shielded by the electrons in the 1s orbital, reducing the effective net nuclear charge that it experiences. (b) An electron that penetrates the electron cloud of the 1s orbital experiences more of the nuclear charge.

Now imagine bringing a third electron toward the lithium ion. When the third electron is far from the nucleus, it experiences the 3+ charge of the nucleus through the *screen* or *shield* of the 2− charge of the two 1s electrons, as shown in Figure 8.2a ▲. We can think of the third electron as experiencing an **effective nuclear charge (Z$_{eff}$)** of approximately 1+ (3+ from the nucleus and 2− from the electrons, for a net charge of 1+). The inner electrons in effect *shield* the outer electron from the full nuclear charge.

Penetration   Now imagine allowing this third electron to come closer to the nucleus. As the electron *penetrates* the electron cloud of the 1s electrons it begins to experience the 3+ charge of the nucleus more fully because it is less shielded by the intervening electrons. If the electron could somehow get closer to the nucleus than the 1s electrons, it would experience the full 3+ charge, as shown in Figure 8.2b. In other words, as the outer electron undergoes **penetration** into the region occupied by the inner electrons, it experiences a greater nuclear charge and therefore (according to Coulomb's law) a lower energy.

Electron Spatial Distributions and Sublevel Splitting   We now have examined the concepts we need to understand the energy splitting of the sublevels within a principal level. The splitting is a result of the spatial distributions of electrons within a sublevel. Recall from Section 7.6 that the radial distribution function for an atomic orbital shows the total probability of finding the electron within a thin spherical shell at a distance r from the nucleus. Figure 8.3 ◄ shows the radial distribution functions of the 2s and 2p orbitals superimposed on one another (the radial distribution function of the 1s orbital is also shown). Notice that, in general, an electron in a 2p orbital has a greater probability of being found closer to the nucleus than an electron in a 2s orbital. We might initially expect, therefore, that the 2p orbital would be lower in energy. However, exactly the opposite is true—the 2s orbital is actually lower in energy, *but only when the 1s orbital is occupied.* (When the 1s orbital is empty, the 2s and 2p orbitals are degenerate.) Why? The reason is the bump near $r = 0$ (near the nucleus) for the 2s orbital. This bump represents a significant probability of the electron being found very close to the nucleus. Even more importantly, this area of the probability penetrates into the 1s orbital—it gets into the region where shielding by the 1s electrons is less effective. In contrast, most of the probability in the radial distribution function of the 2p orbital lies *outside* the radial distribution function of the 1s orbital. Consequently, almost all of the 2p orbital is shielded from nuclear charge by the 1s orbital. The end result is that the 2s orbital—since it experiences more of the nuclear charge due to its greater *penetration*—is lower in energy than the 2p orbital. The results

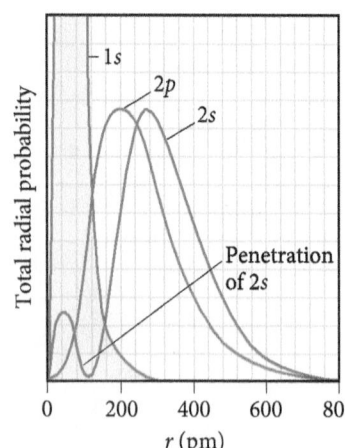

▲ **FIGURE 8.3 Radial Distribution Functions for the 1s, 2s, and 2p Orbitals.**

▲ **FIGURE 8.4 Radial Distribution Functions for the 3s, 3p, and 3d Orbitals**   The 3s electrons penetrate most deeply into the inner orbitals, are least shielded, and experience the greatest effective nuclear charge. The 3d electrons penetrate least. This accounts for the energy ordering of the sublevels: $s < p < d$.

are similar when we compare the 3s, 3p, and 3d orbitals. The s orbitals penetrate more fully than the p orbitals, which in turn penetrate more fully than the d orbitals, as shown in Figure 8.4 ▲.

Figure 8.5 ▼ shows the energy ordering of a number of orbitals in multielectron atoms. Notice these features of Figure 8.5:

- Because of penetration, the sublevels of each principal level are *not* degenerate for multielectron atoms.

- In the fourth and fifth principal levels, the effects of penetration become so important that the 4s orbital lies lower in energy than the 3d orbitals and the 5s orbital lies lower in energy than the 4d orbitals.

- The energy separations between one set of orbitals and the next become smaller for 4s orbitals and beyond, and the relative energy ordering of these orbitals can actually vary among elements. These variations result in irregularities in the electron configurations of the transition metals and their ions (as we shall see later).

General Energy Ordering of Orbitals for Multielectron Atoms

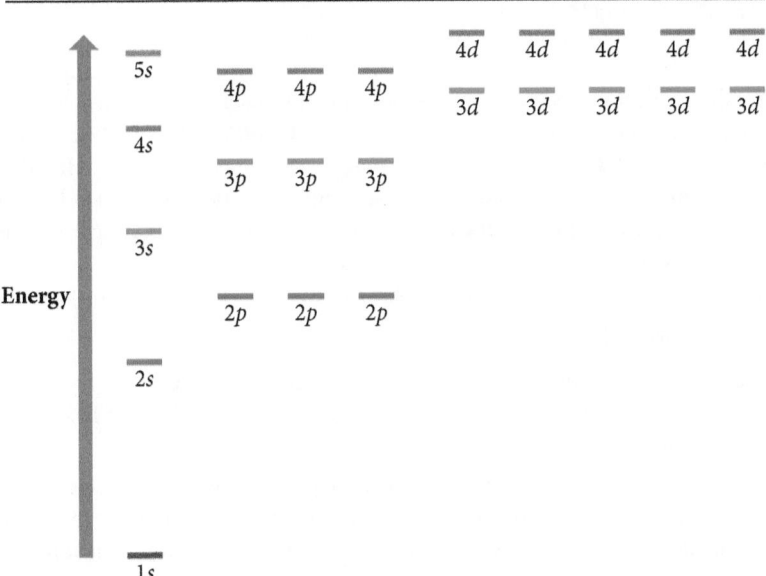

▲ **FIGURE 8.5 General Energy Ordering of Orbitals for Multielectron Atoms.**

Conceptual Connection 8.2 Penetration and Shielding

Which statement is true?

(a) An orbital that penetrates into the region occupied by core electrons is more shielded from nuclear charge than an orbital that does not penetrate and will therefore have a higher energy.

(b) An orbital that penetrates into the region occupied by core electrons is less shielded from nuclear charge than an orbital that does not penetrate and will therefore have a higher energy.

(c) An orbital that penetrates into the region occupied by core electrons is less shielded from nuclear charge than an orbital that does not penetrate and will therefore have a lower energy.

(d) An orbital that penetrates into the region occupied by core electrons is more shielded from nuclear charge than an orbital that does not penetrate and will therefore have a lower energy.

Electron Configurations for Multielectron Atoms

> *Unless otherwise specified, we will use the term electron configuration to mean the ground state (or lowest energy) configuration.*

Now that we know the energy ordering of orbitals in multielectron atoms, we can determine ground state electron configurations for the rest of the elements. Since we know that electrons occupy the lowest energy orbitals available when the atom is in its ground state and that only two electrons (with opposing spins) are allowed in each orbital, we can systematically build up the electron configurations for the elements. This pattern of orbital filling is known as the **aufbau principle** (the German word *aufbau* means "build up"). For lithium, with three electrons, the electron configuration and orbital diagram are:

> *Remember that the number of electrons in a neutral atom is equal to its atomic number.*

Electron configuration   Orbital diagram

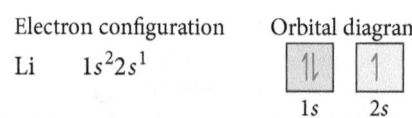

Li $1s^2 2s^1$

For carbon, which has six electrons, the electron configuration and orbital diagram are:

> *Electrons with parallel spins have correlated motion that minimizes their mutual repulsion.*

Electron configuration   Orbital diagram

C $1s^2 2s^2 2p^2$

Notice that the $2p$ electrons occupy the p orbitals (of equal energy) singly, rather than pairing in one orbital. This way of filling orbitals is known as **Hund's rule**, which states that *when filling degenerate orbitals, electrons fill them singly first, with parallel spins*. Hund's rule is a result of an atom's tendency to find the lowest energy state possible. When two electrons occupy separate orbitals of equal energy, the repulsive interaction between them is lower than when they occupy the same orbital because the electrons are spread out over a larger region of space. By convention we denote these parallel spins with half arrows pointing up.

Summarizing Orbital Filling:

▶ Electrons occupy orbitals so as to minimize the energy of the atom; therefore, lower energy orbitals fill before higher energy orbitals. Orbitals fill in the following order: $1s\ 2s\ 2p\ 3s\ 3p\ 4s\ 3d\ 4p\ 5s\ 4d\ 5p\ 6s$.

▶ Orbitals can hold no more than two electrons each. When two electrons occupy the same orbital, their spins are opposite. This is another way of expressing the Pauli exclusion principle (no two electrons in one atom can have the same four quantum numbers).

▶ When orbitals of identical energy are available, electrons first occupy these orbitals singly with parallel spins rather than in pairs. Once the orbitals of equal energy are half full, the electrons start to pair (Hund's rule).

Consider the electron configurations and orbital diagrams for elements with atomic numbers 3–10.

Symbol	Number of electrons	Electron configuration	Orbital diagram
Li	3	$1s^2 2s^1$	$\boxed{\uparrow\downarrow}$ $\boxed{\uparrow}$ $1s$ $\quad 2s$
Be	4	$1s^2 2s^2$	$\boxed{\uparrow\downarrow}$ $\boxed{\uparrow\downarrow}$ $1s$ $\quad 2s$
B	5	$1s^2 2s^2 2p^1$	$\boxed{\uparrow\downarrow}$ $\boxed{\uparrow\downarrow}$ $\boxed{\uparrow\,|\,|\,}$ $1s$ $\quad 2s$ $\qquad 2p$
C	6	$1s^2 2s^2 2p^2$	$\boxed{\uparrow\downarrow}$ $\boxed{\uparrow\downarrow}$ $\boxed{\uparrow\,|\,\uparrow\,|\,}$ $1s$ $\quad 2s$ $\qquad 2p$

Notice that, as a result of Hund's rule, the p orbitals fill with single electrons before the electrons pair.

N	7	$1s^2 2s^2 2p^3$	$\boxed{\uparrow\downarrow}$ $\boxed{\uparrow\downarrow}$ $\boxed{\uparrow\,|\,\uparrow\,|\,\uparrow}$ $1s$ $\quad 2s$ $\qquad 2p$
O	8	$1s^2 2s^2 2p^4$	$\boxed{\uparrow\downarrow}$ $\boxed{\uparrow\downarrow}$ $\boxed{\uparrow\downarrow\,|\,\uparrow\,|\,\uparrow}$ $1s$ $\quad 2s$ $\qquad 2p$
F	9	$1s^2 2s^2 2p^5$	$\boxed{\uparrow\downarrow}$ $\boxed{\uparrow\downarrow}$ $\boxed{\uparrow\downarrow\,|\,\uparrow\downarrow\,|\,\uparrow}$ $1s$ $\quad 2s$ $\qquad 2p$
Ne	10	$1s^2 2s^2 2p^6$	$\boxed{\uparrow\downarrow}$ $\boxed{\uparrow\downarrow}$ $\boxed{\uparrow\downarrow\,|\,\uparrow\downarrow\,|\,\uparrow\downarrow}$ $1s$ $\quad 2s$ $\qquad 2p$

The electron configuration of neon represents the complete filling of the $n = 2$ principal level. When writing electron configurations for elements beyond neon, or beyond any other noble gas, we can abbreviate the electron configuration of the previous noble gas—sometimes called the *inner electron configuration*—by the symbol for the noble gas in square brackets. For example, the electron configuration of sodium is:

$$\text{Na} \qquad 1s^2 2s^2 2p^6 3s^1$$

We can write this configuration more compactly by using [Ne] to represent the inner electrons:

$$\text{Na} \qquad [\text{Ne}] \, 3s^1$$

[Ne] represents $1s^2 2s^2 2p^6$, the electron configuration for neon.

To write an electron configuration for an element, first find its atomic number from the periodic table—this number equals the number of electrons. Then use the order of filling to distribute the electrons in the appropriate orbitals. Remember that each orbital can hold a maximum of 2 electrons. Consequently,

- the s sublevel has only one orbital and can therefore hold only 2 electrons.
- the p sublevel has three orbitals and can hold 6 electrons.
- the d sublevel has five orbitals and can hold 10 electrons.
- the f sublevel has seven orbitals and can hold 14 electrons.

EXAMPLE 8.1 Electron Configurations

Write electron configurations for each element.

(a) Mg   (b) P   (c) Br   (d) Al

SOLUTION

(a) Mg Magnesium has 12 electrons. Distribute 2 of these into the $1s$ orbital, 2 into the $2s$ orbital, 6 into the $2p$ orbitals, and 2 into the $3s$ orbital.	Mg $1s^2 2s^2 2p^6 3s^2$ or $[\text{Ne}] 3s^2$
(b) P Phosphorus has 15 electrons. Distribute 2 of these into the $1s$ orbital, 2 into the $2s$ orbital, 6 into the $2p$ orbitals, 2 into the $3s$ orbital, and 3 into the $3p$ orbitals.	P $1s^2 2s^2 2p^6 3s^2 3p^3$ or $[\text{Ne}] 3s^2 3p^3$
(c) Br Bromine has 35 electrons. Distribute 2 of these into the $1s$ orbital, 2 into the $2s$ orbital, 6 into the $2p$ orbitals, 2 into the $3s$ orbital, 6 into the $3p$ orbitals, 2 into the $4s$ orbital, 10 into the $3d$ orbitals, and 5 into the $4p$ orbitals.	Br $1s^2 2s^2 2p^6 3s^2 3p^6 4s^2 3d^{10} 4p^5$ or $[\text{Ar}] 4s^2 3d^{10} 4p^5$
(d) Al Aluminum has 13 electrons. Distribute 2 of these into the $1s$ orbital, 2 into the $2s$ orbital, 6 into the $2p$ orbitals, 2 into the $3s$ orbital, and 1 into the $3p$ orbital.	Al $1s^2 2s^2 2p^6 3s^2 3p^1$ or $[\text{Ne}] 3s^2 3p^1$

FOR PRACTICE 8.1

Write electron configurations for each element.

(a) Cl   (b) Si   (c) Sr   (d) O

EXAMPLE 8.2 Writing Orbital Diagrams

Write the orbital diagram for sulfur and determine the number of unpaired electrons.

SOLUTION

Since sulfur's atomic number is 16, it has 16 electrons and the electron configuration $1s^2 2s^2 2p^6 3s^2 3p^4$. Draw a box for each orbital, putting the lowest energy orbital ($1s$) on the far left and proceeding to orbitals of higher energy to the right.	$\square$ $\square$ $\square\square\square$ $\square$ $\square\square\square$ $1s$ $2s$ $2p$ $3s$ $3p$
Distribute the 16 electrons into the boxes representing the orbitals, allowing a maximum of 2 electrons per orbital and remembering Hund's rule. You can see from the diagram that sulfur has two unpaired electrons.	[↑↓] [↑↓] [↑↓][↑↓][↑↓] [↑↓] [↑↓][↑][↑] $1s$ $2s$ $2p$ $3s$ $3p$ Two unpaired electrons

FOR PRACTICE 8.2

Write the orbital diagram for Ar and determine the number of unpaired electrons.

Conceptual **Connection 8.3 Electron Configurations and Quantum Numbers**

What are the four quantum numbers for each of the two electrons in a $4s$ orbital?

8.4 Electron Configurations, Valence Electrons, and the Periodic Table

Recall that Mendeleev arranged the periodic table so that elements with similar chemical properties lie in the same column. We can begin to make the connection between an element's properties and its electron configuration by superimposing the electron configurations of the first 18 elements onto a partial periodic table, as shown in Figure 8.6 ▶. As we move to the right across a row, the orbitals fill in the correct order. With each subsequent row, the highest principal quantum number increases by one. Notice that as we move down a column, *the number of electrons in the outermost principal energy level (highest n value) remains the same.* The key connection between the macroscopic world (an element's chemical properties) and the atomic world (an atom's electronic structure) lies in these outermost electrons.

An atom's **valence electrons** are those that are important in chemical bonding. *For main-group elements, the valence electrons are those in the outermost principal energy level.* For transition elements, we also count the outermost *d* electrons among the valence electrons (even though they are not in an outermost principal energy level). The chemical properties of an element depend on its valence electrons, which are instrumental in bonding because they are held most loosely (and are therefore the easiest to lose or share). We can now see *why* the elements in a column of the periodic table have similar chemical properties: *they have the same number of valence electrons.*

Valence electrons are distinguished from all the other electrons in an atom, which are called **core electrons**. The core electrons are those in *complete* principal energy levels and those in *complete d* and *f* sublevels. For example, silicon, with the electron configuration $1s^2 2s^2 2p^6 3s^2 3p^2$, has four valence electrons (those in the $n = 3$ principal level) and ten core electrons as shown at right.

Outer Electron Configurations of Elements 1–18

1A							8A
1 **H** $1s^1$	2A	3A	4A	5A	6A	7A	2 **He** $1s^2$
3 **Li** $2s^1$	4 **Be** $2s^2$	5 **B** $2s^2 2p^1$	6 **C** $2s^2 2p^2$	7 **N** $2s^2 2p^3$	8 **O** $2s^2 2p^4$	9 **F** $2s^2 2p^5$	10 **Ne** $2s^2 2p^6$
11 **Na** $3s^1$	12 **Mg** $3s^2$	13 **Al** $3s^2 3p^1$	14 **Si** $3s^2 3p^2$	15 **P** $3s^2 3p^3$	16 **S** $3s^2 3p^4$	17 **Cl** $3s^2 3p^5$	18 **Ar** $3s^2 3p^6$

▲ **FIGURE 8.6 Outer Electron Configurations of the First 18 Elements in the Periodic Table.**

Si $1s^2 2s^2 2p^6 3s^2 3p^2$

Core electrons   Valence electrons

EXAMPLE 8.3 Valence Electrons and Core Electrons

Write the electron configuration for Ge. Identify the valence electrons and the core electrons.

SOLUTION

Write the electron configuration for Ge by determining the total number of electrons from germanium's atomic number (32) and then distributing them into the appropriate orbitals.	Ge $1s^2 2s^2 2p^6 3s^2 3p^6 4s^2 3d^{10} 4p^2$
Since germanium is a main-group element, its valence electrons are those in the outermost principal energy level. For germanium, the $n = 1, 2,$ and 3 principal levels are complete (or full) and the $n = 4$ principal level is outermost. Consequently, the $n = 4$ electrons are valence electrons and the rest are core electrons.	4 valence electrons Ge $1s^2 2s^2 2p^6 3s^2 3p^6 4s^2 3d^{10} 4p^2$ 28 core electrons

Note: In this book, we write electron configurations with the orbitals in the order *of filling. However, electron configurations are sometimes written in* order *of increasing principal quantum number. The electron configuration of germanium written in order of increasing principal quantum number is*
Ge $1s^2 2s^2 2p^6 3s^2 3p^6 3d^{10} 4s^2 4p^2$.

FOR PRACTICE 8.3
Write an electron configuration for phosphorus. Identify the valence electrons and core electrons.

Orbital Blocks in the Periodic Table

A pattern similar to what we just saw for the first 18 elements exists for the entire periodic table, as shown in Figure 8.7 ▼. Note that because of the filling order of orbitals, the periodic table can be divided into blocks representing the filling of particular sublevels. The first two columns on the left side of the periodic table comprise the s block, with outer electron configurations of ns^1 (the alkali metals) and ns^2 (the alkaline earth metals). The six columns on the right side of the periodic table comprise the p block, with outer electron configurations of $ns^2 np^1$, $ns^2 np^2$, $ns^2 np^3$, $ns^2 np^4$, $ns^2 np^5$ (halogens), and $ns^2 np^6$ (noble gases). The transition elements comprise the d block, and the lanthanides and actinides (also called the inner transition elements) comprise the f block. (For compactness, the f block is normally printed below the d block instead of being imbedded within it.)

You can see that *the number of columns in a block corresponds to the maximum number of electrons that can occupy the particular sublevel of that block.* The s block has 2 columns (corresponding to one s orbital holding a maximum of two electrons); the p block has 6 columns (corresponding to three p orbitals with two electrons each); the d block has 10 columns (corresponding to five d orbitals with two electrons each); and the f block has 14 columns (corresponding to seven f orbitals with two electrons each).

Notice also that, except for helium, *the number of valence electrons for any main-group element is equal to its lettered group number.* We can tell that chlorine has seven valence electrons because it is in group number 7A.

> Helium is an exception. Even though it lies in the column with an outer electron configuration of $ns^2 np^6$, its electron configuration is simply $1s^2$.

Orbital Blocks of the Periodic Table

▲ FIGURE 8.7 The s, p, d, and f Blocks of the Periodic Table.

Lastly, note that, for main-group elements, *the row number in the periodic table is equal to the number (or n value) of the highest principal level*. For example, because chlorine is in row 3, its highest principal level is the $n = 3$ level.

Recall from Chapter 2 that main-group elements are those in the two far left columns (groups 1A, 2A) and the six far right columns (groups 3A–8A) of the periodic table.

Summarizing Periodic Table Organization:

▶ The periodic table is divisible into four blocks corresponding to the filling of the four quantum sublevels (*s*, *p*, *d*, and *f*).

▶ The group number of a main-group element is equal to the number of valence electrons for that element.

▶ The row number of a main-group element is equal to the highest principal quantum number of that element.

Writing an Electron Configuration for an Element from Its Position in the Periodic Table

The organization of the periodic table allows us to write the electron configuration for any element based on its position in the periodic table. For example, suppose we want to write an electron configuration for Cl. The *inner electron configuration* of Cl is that of the noble gas that precedes it in the periodic table, Ne. So we can represent the inner electron configuration with [Ne]. The *outer electron configuration*—the configuration of the electrons beyond the previous noble gas—is obtained by tracing the elements between Ne and Cl and assigning electrons to the appropriate orbitals, as shown here. Remember that the highest *n* value is indicated by the row number (3 for chlorine).

So, we begin with [Ne], then add in the two 3*s* electrons as we trace across the *s* block, followed by five 3*p* electrons as we trace across the *p* block to Cl, which is in the fifth column of the *p* block. The electron configuration is:

$$\text{Cl} \quad [\text{Ne}]\, 3s^2 3p^5$$

Notice that Cl is in column 7A and therefore has seven valence electrons and an outer electron configuration of $ns^2 np^5$.

EXAMPLE 8.4 Writing Electron Configurations from the Periodic Table

Use the periodic table to write the electron configuration for selenium (Se).

SOLUTION

The atomic number of Se is 34. The noble gas that precedes Se in the periodic table is argon, so the inner electron configuration is [Ar]. Obtain the outer electron configuration by tracing the elements between Ar and Se and assigning electrons to the appropriate orbitals. Begin with [Ar]. Because Se is in row 4, add two 4s electrons as you trace across the s block (n = row number). Next, add ten 3d electrons as you trace across the d block (n = row number − 1). Lastly, add four 4p electrons as you trace across the p block to Se, which is in the fourth column of the p block (n = row number).

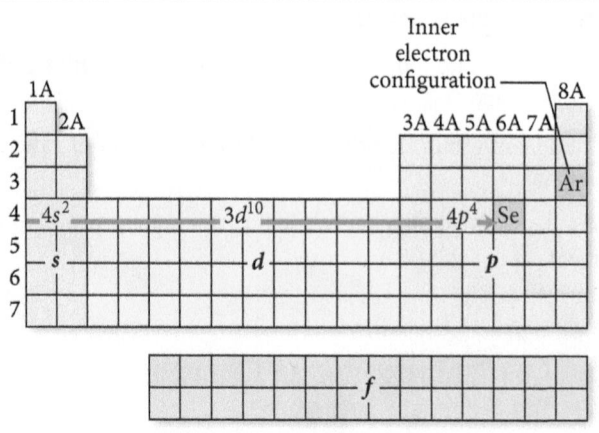

Se [Ar] $4s^2 3d^{10} 4p^4$

FOR PRACTICE 8.4
Use the periodic table to determine the electron configuration of bismuth (Bi).

FOR MORE PRACTICE 8.4
Use the periodic table to write the electron configuration for iodine (I).

The Transition and Inner Transition Elements

The electron configurations of the transition elements (d block) and inner transition elements (f block) exhibit trends that differ somewhat from those of the main-group elements. As we move to the right across a row in the d block, the d orbitals fill as shown here:

21 Sc $4s^2 3d^1$	22 Ti $4s^2 3d^2$	23 V $4s^2 3d^3$	24 Cr $4s^1 3d^5$	25 Mn $4s^2 3d^5$	26 Fe $4s^2 3d^6$	27 Co $4s^2 3d^7$	28 Ni $4s^2 3d^8$	29 Cu $4s^1 3d^{10}$	30 Zn $4s^2 3d^{10}$
39 Y $5s^2 4d^1$	40 Zr $5s^2 4d^2$	41 Nb $5s^1 4d^4$	42 Mo $5s^1 4d^5$	43 Tc $5s^2 4d^5$	44 Ru $5s^1 4d^7$	45 Rh $5s^1 4d^8$	46 Pd $4d^{10}$	47 Ag $5s^1 4d^{10}$	48 Cd $5s^2 4d^{10}$

However, *the principal quantum number of the d orbitals that fill across each row in the transition series is equal to the row number minus one.* In the fourth row, the 3d orbitals fill, and in the fifth row, the 4d orbitals fill, and so on. This happens because, as we discussed in Section 8.3, the 4s orbital is generally lower in energy than the 3d orbital (because it more efficiently penetrates into the region occupied by the core electrons). The result is that the 4s orbital fills before the 3d orbital, even though its principal quantum number (n = 4) is higher.

Keep in mind, however, that the 4s and the 3d orbitals are extremely close to each other in energy so their relative energy ordering depends on the exact species under consideration; this causes some irregular behavior in the transition metals. For example, in the first transition series of the d block, the outer configuration is

$4s^2 3d^x$ with two exceptions: Cr is $4s^1 3d^5$ and Cu is $4s^1 3d^{10}$. This behavior is related to the closely spaced $3d$ and $4s$ energy levels and the stability associated with a half-filled (as in Cr) or completely filled (as in Cu) sublevel. Actual electron configurations are definitively determined experimentally (through spectroscopy) and do not always conform to the general pattern. Nonetheless, the patterns we have described allow us to accurately predict electron configurations for most of the elements in the periodic table.

As we move across the f block (the inner transition series), the f orbitals fill. For these elements, the principal quantum number of the f orbitals that fill across each row is the row number *minus two*. (In the sixth row, the $4f$ orbitals fill, and in the seventh row, the $5f$ orbitals fill.) In addition, within the inner transition series, the close energy spacing of the $5d$ and $4f$ orbitals sometimes causes an electron to enter a $5d$ orbital instead of the expected $4f$ orbital. For example, the electron configuration of gadolinium is $[\text{Xe}]\, 6s^2 4f^7 5d^1$ (instead of the expected $[\text{Xe}]\, 6s^2 4f^8$).

8.5 The Explanatory Power of the Quantum-Mechanical Model

We can now see how the quantum-mechanical model accounts for the chemical properties of the elements, such as the inertness of helium or the reactivity of hydrogen, and (more generally) how it accounts for the periodic law. *The chemical properties of elements are largely determined by the number of valence electrons they contain.* Their properties are periodic because the number of valence electrons is periodic.

Since elements within a column in the periodic table have the same number of valence electrons, they also have similar chemical properties. The noble gases, for example, all have eight valence electrons, except for helium, which has two. Although we do not cover the quantitative (or numerical) aspects of the quantum-mechanical model in this book, calculations of the overall energy of the electrons within atoms with eight valence electrons (or two, in the case of helium) show that they are particularly stable. In other words, when a quantum level is completely full, the overall energy of the electrons that occupy that level is particularly low. Therefore, those electrons *cannot* lower their energy by reacting with other atoms or molecules, so the corresponding atom is relatively unreactive or inert. The noble gases are the most chemically stable and relatively unreactive family in the periodic table.

Elements with electron configurations *close* to those of the noble gases are the most reactive because they can attain noble gas electron configurations by losing or gaining a small number of electrons. For example, alkali metals (group 1A) are among the most reactive metals because their outer electron configuration (ns^1) is one electron beyond a noble gas configuration. They readily react to lose the ns^1 electron, obtaining a noble gas configuration. This explains why—as we saw in Chapter 2— the group 1A metals tend to form 1+ cations. Similarly, alkaline earth metals, with an outer electron configuration of ns^2, also tend to be reactive metals, losing their ns^2 electrons to form 2+ cations. This does not mean that forming an ion with a noble gas configuration is in itself energetically favorable. In fact, forming cations always *requires energy*. But when the cation formed has a noble gas configuration, the energy cost of forming the cation is often less than the energy payback that occurs when that cation forms ionic bonds with anions, as we shall see in Chapter 9.

On the right side of the periodic table, halogens are among the most reactive nonmetals because of their $ns^2 np^5$ electron configurations. They are only one electron short of a noble gas configuration and tend to react to gain that one electron, forming 1− ions. Figure 8.8 ▶, first introduced in Chapter 2, shows the elements that form predictable ions. The charges of these ions reflect their electron configurations—in their reactions, these elements form ions with noble gas electron configurations.

8A

| 2 |
| He |
| $1s^2$ |
| 10 |
| Ne |
| $2s^2 2p^6$ |
| 18 |
| Ar |
| $3s^2 3p^6$ |
| 36 |
| Kr |
| $4s^2 4p^6$ |
| 54 |
| Xe |
| $5s^2 5p^6$ |
| 86 |
| Rn |
| $6s^2 6p^6$ |

Noble gases

◀ The noble gases all have eight valence electrons except for helium, which has two. They have full outer energy levels and are particularly stable and unreactive.

▶ The alkali metals all have one valence electron. Each is one electron beyond a stable electron configuration, and they tend to lose that electron in their reactions.

1A

| 3 |
| Li |
| $2s^1$ |
| 11 |
| Na |
| $3s^1$ |
| 19 |
| K |
| $4s^1$ |
| 37 |
| Rb |
| $5s^1$ |
| 55 |
| Cs |
| $6s^1$ |
| 87 |
| Fr |
| $7s^1$ |

Alkali metals

2A

| 4 |
| Be |
| $2s^2$ |
| 12 |
| Mg |
| $3s^2$ |
| 20 |
| Ca |
| $4s^2$ |
| 38 |
| Sr |
| $5s^2$ |
| 56 |
| Ba |
| $6s^2$ |
| 88 |
| Ra |
| $7s^2$ |

Alkaline earth metals

◀ The alkaline earth metals all have two valence electrons. Each is two electrons beyond a stable electron configuration, and they tend to lose those electrons in their reactions.

7A

9
F
$2s^2 2p^5$

17
Cl
$3s^2 3p^5$

35
Br
$4s^2 4p^5$

53
I
$5s^2 5p^5$

85
At
$6s^2 6p^5$

Halogens

▲ The halogens all have seven valence electrons. Each is one electron short of a stable electron configuration, and they tend to gain one electron in their reactions.

Elements That Form Ions with Predictable Charges

	1A	2A	3B	4B	5B	6B	7B	⌐8B⌐	1B	2B	3A	4A	5A	6A	7A	8A
1	Li^+													N^{3-}	O^{2-}	F^-	
2	Na^+	Mg^{2+}										Al^{3+}			S^{2-}	Cl^-	
3	K^+	Ca^{2+}													Se^{2-}	Br^-	
4	Rb^+	Sr^{2+}													Te^{2-}	I^-	
5	Cs^+	Ba^{2+}															

▲ **FIGURE 8.8 Elements That Form Ions with Predictable Charges** Notice that each ion has a noble gas electron configuration.

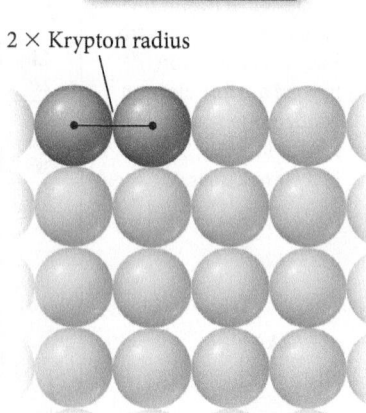

van der Waals radius

2 × Krypton radius

Krypton solid

▲ The van der Waals radius of an atom is one-half the distance between adjacent nuclei in the atomic solid.

Covalent radius

Br   Br

228 pm

Br radius = $\dfrac{228 \text{ pm}}{2}$ = 114 pm

▲ The covalent radius of bromine is one-half the distance between two bonded bromine atoms.

8.6 Periodic Trends in the Size of Atoms and Effective Nuclear Charge

In previous chapters, we saw that the volume of an atom is taken up primarily by its electrons (Chapter 2) occupying quantum-mechanical orbitals (Chapter 7). We also saw that these orbitals do not have a definite boundary but represent only a statistical probability distribution for where the electron is found. So how do we define the size of an atom? One way to define atomic radii is to consider the distance between *non-bonding* atoms that are in direct contact. For example, krypton can be frozen into a solid in which the krypton atoms are touching each other but are not bonded together. The distance between the centers of adjacent krypton atoms—which can be determined from the solid's density—is then twice the radius of a krypton atom. An atomic radius determined in this way is called the **nonbonding atomic radius** or the **van der Waals radius**. The van der Waals radius represents the radius of an atom when it is not bonded to another atom.

Another way to define the size of an atom, called the **bonding atomic radius** or **covalent radius**, is defined differently for nonmetals and metals, as follows:

Nonmetals: one-half the distance between two of the atoms bonded together

Metals: one-half the distance between two of the atoms next to each other in a crystal of the metal

For example, the distance between Br atoms in Br_2 is 228 pm; therefore, the Br covalent radius is assigned to be one-half of 228 pm or 114 pm.

Using this method, we can assign radii to all elements in the periodic table that form chemical bonds or form metallic crystals. A more general term, the **atomic radius**, refers to a set of average bonding radii determined from measurements on a large number of elements and compounds. The atomic radius represents the radius of an atom when it is bonded to another atom and is always smaller than the van der Waals radius. The approximate bond length of any two covalently bonded atoms is the sum of their atomic radii. For example, the approximate bond length for ICl is iodine's atomic radius (133 pm) plus chlorine's atomic radius (99 pm), for a bond length of 232 pm. (The actual experimentally measured bond length in ICl is 232.07 pm.)

Figure 8.9 ▶ shows the atomic radius plotted as a function of atomic number for the first 57 elements in the periodic table. Notice the periodic trend in the radii. Atomic radii peak with each alkali metal. Figure 8.10 ▶ is a relief map of atomic radii for most of the elements in the periodic table. The general trends in the atomic radii of main-group elements, which are the same as trends observed in van der Waals radii, are:

Atomic Radii

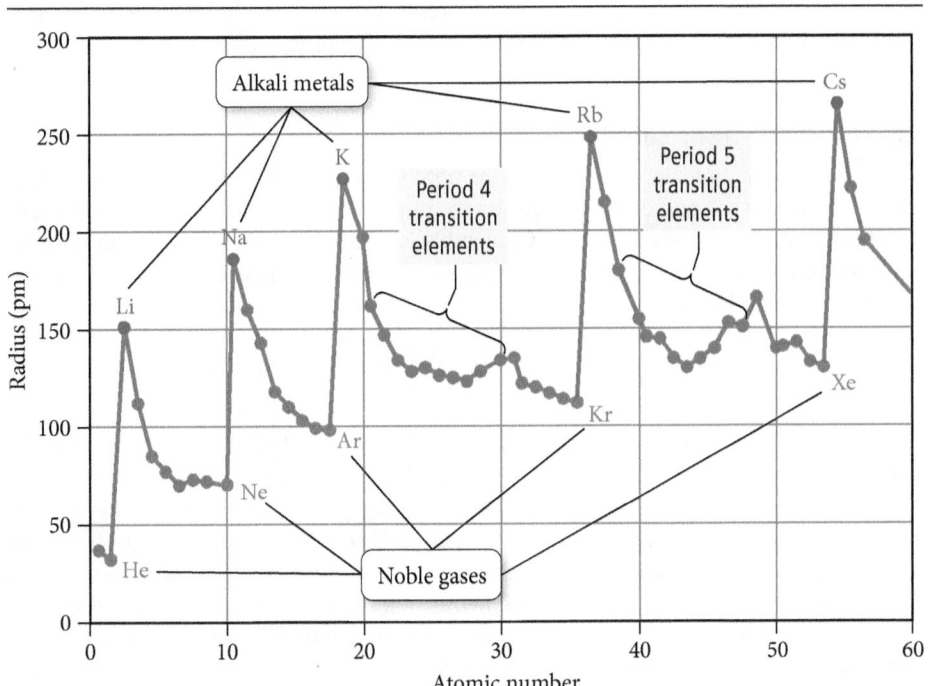

◀ FIGURE 8.9 **Atomic Radius versus Atomic Number** Notice the periodic trend in atomic radius, starting at a peak with each alkali metal and falling to a minimum with each noble gas.

1. As we move down a column (or family) in the periodic table, atomic radius increases.
2. As we move to the right across a period (or row) in the periodic table, atomic radius decreases.

We can understand the observed trend in radius as we move down a column based on the trends in the sizes of atomic orbitals. The atomic radius is largely determined by the valence electrons, the electrons farthest from the nucleus. As we move down a column in the periodic table, the highest principal quantum number (n) of the valence electrons increases. Consequently, the valence electrons occupy larger orbitals, resulting in larger atoms.

The bonding radii of some elements, such as helium and neon, must be approximated since they do not form either chemical bonds or metallic crystals.

Trends in Atomic Radius

▲ FIGURE 8.10 **Trends in Atomic Radius** In general, atomic radii increase as we move down a column and decrease as we move to the right across a period in the periodic table.

The observed trend in atomic radius as we move to the right across a row, however, is a bit more complex. To understand this trend, we must revisit some concepts from Section 8.3, including effective nuclear charge and shielding.

Effective Nuclear Charge

The trend in atomic radius as we move to the right across a row in the periodic table is determined by the inward pull of the nucleus on the electrons in the outermost principal energy level (highest n value). According to Coulomb's law, the attraction between a nucleus and an electron increases with increasing magnitude of nuclear charge. For example, compare the H atom to the He^+ ion:

$$H \quad 1s^1$$
$$He^+ \quad 1s^1$$

It takes 1312 kJ/mol of energy to remove the $1s$ electron from hydrogen but 5251 kJ/mol of energy to remove it from He^+. Why? Although each electron is in a $1s$ orbital, the electron in the helium ion is attracted to the nucleus by a $2+$ charge, while the electron in the hydrogen atom is attracted to the nucleus by only a $1+$ charge. Therefore, the electron in the helium ion is held more tightly (it has lower potential energy according to Coulomb's law), making it more difficult to remove and making the helium ion smaller than the hydrogen atom.

As we saw in Section 8.3, any one electron in a multielectron atom experiences both the positive charge of the nucleus (which is attractive) and the negative charges of the other electrons (which are repulsive). Consider again the outermost electron in the lithium atom:

$$Li \quad 1s^2 2s^1$$

Even though the $2s$ orbital penetrates into the $1s$ orbital to some degree, the majority of the $2s$ orbital is outside of the $1s$ orbital. Therefore the electron in the $2s$ orbital is partially *screened* or *shielded* from the $3+$ charge of the nucleus by the $2-$ charge of the $1s$ (or core) electrons, reducing the net charge experienced by the $2s$ electron as shown in Figure 8.11 ▼.

As we have seen, we can define the average or net charge experienced by an electron as the *effective nuclear charge*. The effective nuclear charge experienced by a particular electron in an atom is the *actual nuclear charge (Z)* minus *the charge shielded by other electrons (S)*:

$$Z_{eff} = Z - S$$

Effective nuclear charge   Charge screened by other electrons

Actual nuclear charge

Screening and Effective Nuclear Charge

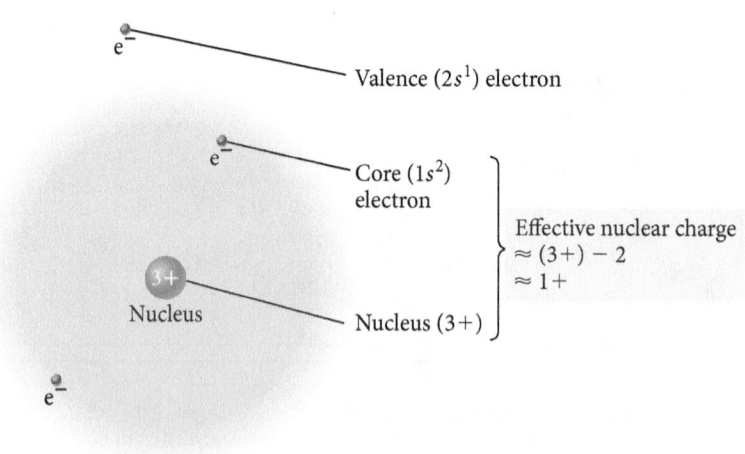

e^- Valence ($2s^1$) electron

e^- Core ($1s^2$) electron

Nucleus   Nucleus ($3+$)

Effective nuclear charge
$\approx (3+) - 2$
$\approx 1+$

Lithium

▶ FIGURE 8.11 **Screening and Effective Nuclear Charge** The valence electron in lithium experiences the $3+$ charge of the nucleus through the screen of the $2-$ charge of the core electrons. The effective nuclear charge acting on the valence electron is approximately $1+$.

For lithium, we estimate that the two core electrons shield the valence electron from the nuclear charge with high efficiency (S is nearly 2). The effective nuclear charge experienced by lithium's valence electron is therefore slightly greater than $1+$.

Now consider the valence electrons in beryllium (Be), with atomic number 4. Its electron configuration is:

$$\text{Be} \quad 1s^2 2s^2$$

To estimate the effective nuclear charge experienced by the $2s$ electrons in beryllium, we must distinguish between two different types of shielding: (1) the shielding of the outermost electrons by the core electrons and (2) the shielding of the outermost electrons by *each other*. The key to understanding the trend in atomic radius is the difference between these two types of shielding.

> **Core electrons efficiently shield electrons in the outermost principal energy level from nuclear charge, but outermost electrons do not efficiently shield one another from nuclear charge.**

For example, the two outermost electrons in beryllium experience the $4+$ charge of the nucleus through the shield of the two $1s$ core electrons without shielding each other from that charge very much. We estimate that the shielding (S) experienced by any one of the outermost electrons due to the core electrons is nearly 2, but that the shielding due to the other outermost electron is nearly zero. The effective nuclear charge experienced by beryllium's outermost electrons is therefore slightly greater than $2+$.

The effective nuclear charge experienced by *beryllium's* outermost electrons is greater than that experienced by *lithium's* outermost electron. Consequently, beryllium's outermost electrons are held more tightly than lithium's, resulting in a smaller atomic radius for beryllium. The effective nuclear charge experienced by an atom's outermost electrons continues to become more positive as we move to the right across the rest of the second row in the periodic table, resulting in successively smaller atomic radii. The same trend is generally observed in all main-group elements.

Summarizing Atomic Radii for Main-Group Elements:

▶ As we move down a column in the periodic table, the principal quantum number (n) of the electrons in the outermost principal energy level increases, resulting in larger orbitals and therefore larger atomic radii.

▶ As we move to the right across a row in the periodic table, the effective nuclear charge (Z_{eff}) experienced by the electrons in the outermost principal energy level increases, resulting in a stronger attraction between the outermost electrons and the nucleus, and smaller atomic radii.

Conceptual Connection 8.4 Effective Nuclear Charge

Which electrons experience the greatest effective nuclear charge?

(a) The valence electrons in Mg

(b) The valence electrons in Al

(c) The valence electrons in S

Atomic Radii and the Transition Elements

In Figure 8.10, we can see that as we move down the first two rows of a column within the transition metals, the elements follow the same general trend in atomic radii as the main-group elements (the radii get larger). However, with the exception of the first couple of elements in each transition series, the atomic radii of the transition elements *do not* follow the same trend as the main-group elements as we move to the right across a row. Instead of decreasing in size, *the radii of transition elements stay roughly constant across each row*. Why? The difference is that, across a row of transition elements, the number of electrons in the outermost principal energy level (highest n value) is nearly constant (recall from Section 8.3, for example, that the $4s$ orbital fills before the $3d$). As another proton is added to the nucleus of each successive element, another electron is added as well, but the electron goes into an $n_{highest} - 1$ orbital. The number of outermost electrons stays constant, and they experience a roughly constant effective nuclear charge, keeping the radius approximately constant.

EXAMPLE 8.5 Atomic Size

On the basis of periodic trends, choose the larger atom in each pair (if possible). Explain your choices.

(a) N or F   **(b)** C or Ge   **(c)** N or Al   **(d)** Al or Ge

SOLUTION

(a) N atoms are larger than F atoms because as you trace the path between N and F on the periodic table, you move to the right within the same period. As you move to the right across a period, the effective nuclear charge experienced by the outermost electrons increases, resulting in a smaller radius.

(b) Ge atoms are larger than C atoms because as you trace the path between C and Ge on the periodic table, you move down a column. Atomic size increases as you move down a column because the outermost electrons occupy orbitals with a higher principal quantum number that are therefore larger, resulting in a larger atom.

(c) Al atoms are larger than N atoms because as you trace the path between N and Al on the periodic table, you move down a column (atomic size increases) and then to the left across a period (atomic size increases). These effects add together for an overall increase.

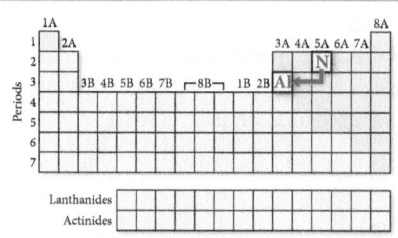

(d) Based on periodic trends alone, you cannot tell which atom is larger, because as you trace the path between Al and Ge you go to the right across a period (atomic size decreases) and then down a column (atomic size increases). These effects tend to counter each other, and it is not easy to tell which will predominate.

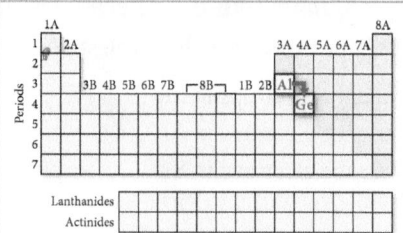

FOR PRACTICE 8.5

On the basis of periodic trends, choose the larger atom in each pair (if possible):

(a) Sn or I   **(b)** Ge or Po   **(c)** Cr or W   **(d)** F or Se

FOR MORE PRACTICE 8.5

Arrange the elements in order of decreasing radius: S, Ca, F, Rb, Si.

8.7 Ions: Electron Configurations, Magnetic Properties, Ionic Radii, and Ionization Energy

Recall that ions are simply atoms (or groups of atoms) that have lost or gained electrons. In this section, we examine periodic trends in ionic electron configurations, magnetic properties, ionic radii, and ionization energies.

Electron Configurations and Magnetic Properties of Ions

We can deduce the electron configuration of a main-group monoatomic ion from the electron configuration of the neutral atom and the charge of the ion. For anions, we *add* the number of electrons indicated by the magnitude of the charge of the anion. For example, the electron configuration of fluorine (F) is $1s^2 2s^2 2p^5$ and that of the fluoride ion (F^-) is $1s^2 2s^2 2p^6$.

We determine the electron configuration of cations by *subtracting* the number of electrons indicated by the magnitude of the charge. For example, the electron configuration of lithium (Li) is $1s^2 2s^1$ and that of the lithium ion (Li^+) is $1s^2 2s^0$ (or simply $1s^2$). For main-group cations, we remove the required number of electrons in the reverse order of filling. However for transition metal cations, the trend is different. When writing the electron configuration of a transition metal cation, we *remove the electrons in the highest n-value orbitals first, even if this does not correspond to the reverse order of filling.* For example, the electron configuration of vanadium is:

$$V \quad [Ar]\, 4s^2 3d^3$$

The V^{2+} ion, however, has the following electron configuration:

$$V^{2+} \quad [Ar]\, 4s^0 3d^3$$

In other words, for transition metal cations, the order in which electrons are removed upon ionization is *not* the reverse of the filling order. During filling, the $4s$ orbital normally fills before the $3d$ orbital. When a fourth period transition metal ionizes, however, it normally loses its $4s$ electrons before its $3d$ electrons. Why this unexpected behavior? The full answer to this question is beyond our scope, but the following two factors contribute to this phenomenon.

- As discussed previously, the ns and $(n-1)d$ orbitals are extremely close in energy and, depending on the exact configuration, can vary in relative energy ordering.
- As the $(n-1)d$ orbitals begin to fill in the first transition series, the increasing nuclear charge stabilizes the $(n-1)d$ orbitals relative to the ns orbitals. This happens because the $(n-1)d$ orbitals are not the outermost (or highest n) orbitals and are therefore not effectively shielded from the increasing nuclear charge by the ns orbitals.

The bottom-line experimental observation is that an $ns^0(n-1)d^x$ configuration is lower in energy than an $ns^2(n-1)d^{x-2}$ configuration for transition metal ions. Therefore, we remove the ns electrons before the $(n-1)d$ electrons when writing electron configurations for transition metal ions.

The magnetic properties of transition metal ions support these assignments. Recall from Section 8.3 that an unpaired electron generates a magnetic field due to its spin. Consequently, an atom or ion that contains unpaired electrons is attracted to an external magnetic field, and we say that the atom or ion is **paramagnetic**. For example, consider the electron configuration of silver:

$$Ag \quad [Kr]\, 5s^1 4d^{10}$$

Silver's unpaired $5s$ electron causes silver to be paramagnetic. In fact, an early demonstration of electron spin—called the Stern–Gerlach experiment—involved the interaction of a beam of silver atoms with a magnetic field. An atom or ion in which all electrons are paired is not attracted to an external magnetic field—it is instead slightly repelled—and we say that the atom or ion is **diamagnetic**. The zinc atom is diamagnetic.

$$\text{Zn} \quad [\text{Ar}] \quad 4s^2 3d^{10}$$

The magnetic properties of the zinc ion provide confirmation that the $4s$ electrons are indeed lost before $3d$ electrons in the ionization of zinc. If zinc lost two $3d$ electrons upon ionization, then the Zn^{2+} would become paramagnetic (because the two electrons would come out of two different filled d orbitals, leaving each of them with one unpaired electron). But the zinc ion, like the zinc atom, is diamagnetic because the $4s$ electrons are lost instead.

$$Zn^{2+} \quad [\text{Ar}] \quad 4s^0 3d^{10}$$

Observations in other transition metals confirm that the ns electrons are lost before the $(n-1)d$ electrons upon ionization.

EXAMPLE 8.6 Electron Configurations and Magnetic Properties for Ions

Write the electron configuration and orbital diagram for each ion and determine whether each is diamagnetic or paramagnetic.

(a) Al^{3+} (b) S^{2-} (c) Fe^{3+}

SOLUTION

(a) Al^{3+}	
Begin by writing the electron configuration of the neutral atom.	Al [Ne] $3s^2 3p^1$
Since this ion has a 3+ charge, remove three electrons to write the electron configuration of the ion. Write the orbital diagram by drawing half-arrows to represent each electron in boxes representing the orbitals. Because there are no unpaired electrons, Al^{3+} is diamagnetic.	Al^{3+} [Ne] or [He] $2s^2 2p^6$ Al^{3+} [He] Diamagnetic
(b) S^{2-}	
Begin by writing the electron configuration of the neutral atom.	S [Ne] $3s^2 3p^4$
Since this ion has a 2− charge, add two electrons to write the electron configuration of the ion. Write the orbital diagram by drawing half-arrows to represent each electron in boxes representing the orbitals. Because there are no unpaired electrons, S^{2-} is diamagnetic.	S^{2-} [Ne] $3s^2 3p^6$ S^{2-} [Ne] Diamagnetic
(c) Fe^{3+}	
Begin by writing the electron configuration of the neutral atom.	Fe [Ar] $4s^2 3d^6$
Since this ion has a 3+ charge, remove three electrons to write the electron configuration of the ion. Since it is a transition metal, remove the electrons from the $4s$ orbital before removing electrons from the $3d$ orbitals. Write the orbital diagram by drawing half-arrows to represent each electron in boxes representing the orbitals. There are unpaired electrons, so Fe^{3+} is paramagnetic.	Fe^{3+} [Ar] $4s^0 3d^5$ Fe^{3+} [Ar] Paramagnetic

FOR PRACTICE 8.6

Write the electron configuration and orbital diagram for each ion and predict whether each will be paramagnetic or diamagnetic.

(a) Co^{2+} (b) N^{3-} (c) Ca^{2+}

Ionic Radii

What happens to the radius of an atom when it becomes a cation? An anion? Consider, for example, the difference between the Na atom and the Na^+ ion. Their electron configurations are:

$$Na \quad [Ne]\,3s^1$$
$$Na^+ \quad [Ne]\,3s^0$$

The sodium atom has an outer $3s$ electron and a neon core. Since the $3s$ electron is the outermost electron, and since it is shielded from the nuclear charge by the core electrons, it contributes greatly to the size of the sodium atom. The sodium cation, having lost the outermost $3s$ electron, has only the neon core and carries a charge of $1+$. Without the $3s$ electron, the sodium cation (ionic radius = 95 pm) becomes much smaller than the sodium atom (covalent radius = 186 pm). The trend is the same with all cations and their atoms, as shown in Figure 8.12 ▼.

Cations are much smaller than their corresponding atoms.

Radii of Atoms and Their Cations (pm)

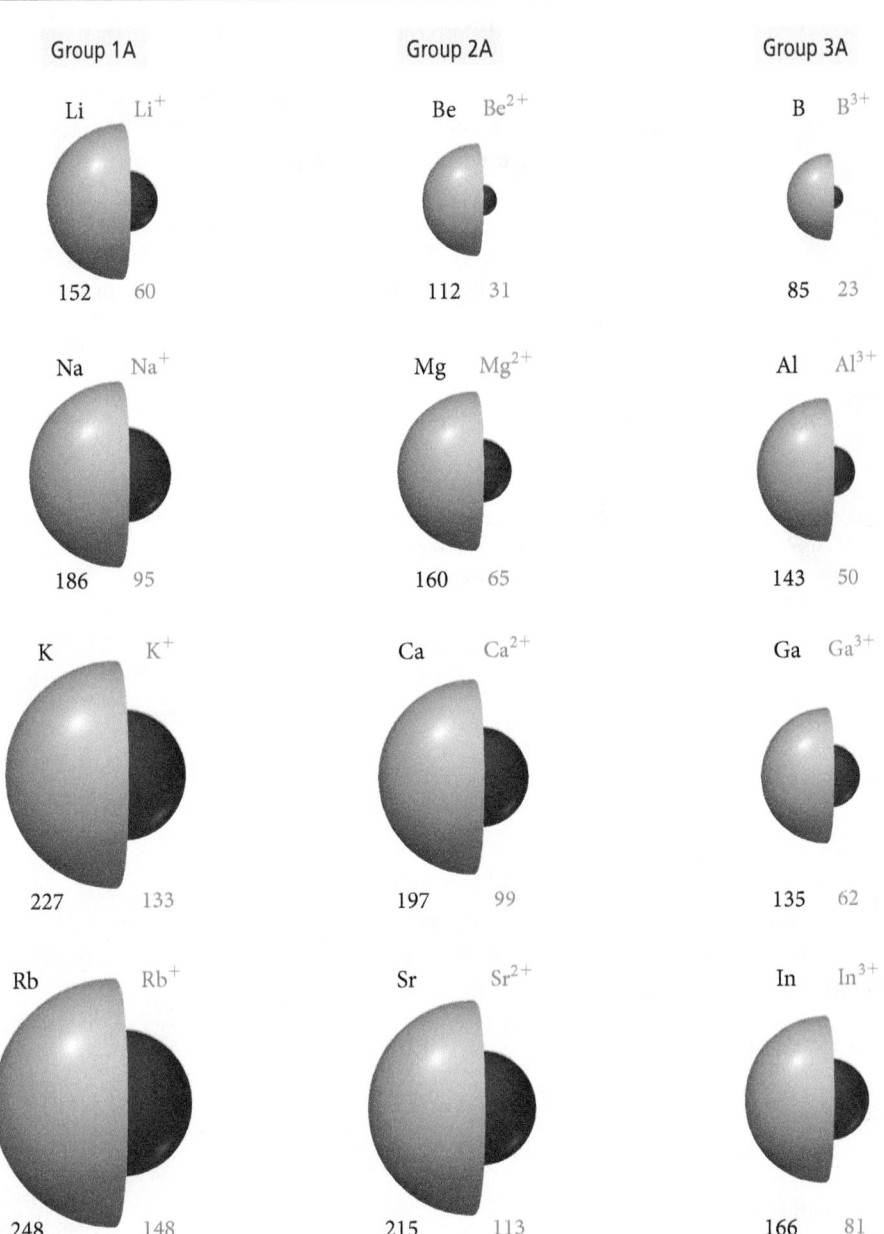

<table>
<tr><td>Group 1A</td><td>Group 2A</td><td>Group 3A</td></tr>
<tr><td>Li   Li$^+$
152   60</td><td>Be   Be^{2+}
112   31</td><td>B   B^{3+}
85   23</td></tr>
<tr><td>Na   Na$^+$
186   95</td><td>Mg   Mg^{2+}
160   65</td><td>Al   Al^{3+}
143   50</td></tr>
<tr><td>K   K$^+$
227   133</td><td>Ca   Ca^{2+}
197   99</td><td>Ga   Ga^{3+}
135   62</td></tr>
<tr><td>Rb   Rb$^+$
248   148</td><td>Sr   Sr^{2+}
215   113</td><td>In   In^{3+}
166   81</td></tr>
</table>

◀ **FIGURE 8.12 Sizes of Atoms and Their Cations** Atomic and ionic radii (pm) for the first three columns of main-group elements.

Radii of Atoms and Their Anions (pm)

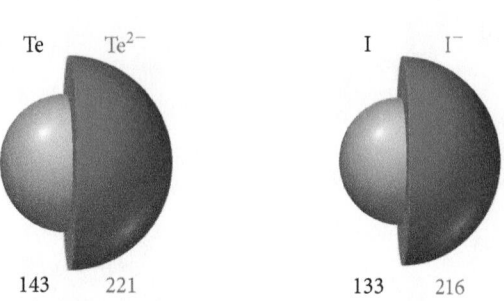

Group 6A		Group 7A	
O O^{2-}		F F^-	
73 140		72 136	
S S^{2-}		Cl Cl^-	
103 184		99 181	
Se Se^{2-}		Br Br^-	
117 198		114 195	
Te Te^{2-}		I I^-	
143 221		133 216	

What about anions? Consider, for example, the difference between Cl and Cl^-. Their electron configurations are:

$$Cl \quad [Ne]\, 3s^2 3p^5$$
$$Cl^- \quad [Ne]\, 3s^2 3p^6$$

The chlorine anion has one additional outermost electron but no additional proton to increase the nuclear charge. The extra electron increases the repulsions among the outermost electrons, resulting in a chloride anion that is larger than the chlorine atom. The trend is the same with all anions and their atoms, as shown in Figure 8.13 ◄.

Anions are much larger than their corresponding atoms.

We can observe an interesting trend in ionic size by examining the radii of an *isoelectronic* series of ions—ions with the same number of electrons. Consider the following ions and their radii:

S^{2-} (184 pm)	Cl^- (181 pm)	K^+ (133 pm)	Ca^{2+} (99 pm)
18 electrons	18 electrons	18 electrons	18 electrons
16 protons	17 protons	19 protons	20 protons

All of these ions have 18 electrons in exactly the same orbitals, but the radius of each ion gets successively smaller. Why? The reason is the progressively greater number of protons. The S^{2-} ion has 16 protons and therefore a charge of 16+ pulling on 18 electrons. The Ca^{2+} ion, however, has 20 protons, and therefore a charge of 20+ pulling on the same 18 electrons. The result is a much smaller radius. For a given number of electrons, a greater nuclear charge results in a smaller atom or ion.

◄ **FIGURE 8.13 Sizes of Atoms and Their Anions** Atomic and ionic radii for groups 6A and 7A in the periodic table.

EXAMPLE 8.7 Ion Size

Choose the larger atom or ion from each pair.
(a) S or S^{2-} (b) Ca or Ca^{2+} (c) Br^- or Kr

SOLUTION

(a) The S^{2-} ion is larger than an S atom because anions are larger than the atoms from which they are formed.

(b) A Ca atom is larger than Ca^{2+} because cations are smaller than the atoms from which they are formed.

(c) A Br^- ion is larger than a Kr atom because, although they are isoelectronic, Br^- has one fewer proton than Kr, resulting in a lesser pull on the electrons and therefore a larger radius.

FOR PRACTICE 8.7

Choose the larger atom or ion from each pair.
(a) K or K^+ (b) F or F^- (c) Ca^{2+} or Cl^-

FOR MORE PRACTICE 8.7

Arrange the following in order of decreasing radius: Ca^{2+}, Ar, Cl^-.

Conceptual Connection 8.5 Ions, Isotopes, and Atomic Size

In the previous sections, we have seen how the number of electrons and the number of protons affects the size of an atom or ion. However, we have not considered how the number of neutrons affects the size of an atom. Why not? Would you expect isotopes—for example, C-12 and C-13—to have different atomic radii?

Ionization Energy

The **ionization energy (IE)** of an atom or ion is the energy required to remove an electron from the atom or ion in the gaseous state. Ionization energy is always positive because removing an electron always takes energy. (The process is similar to an endothermic reaction, which absorbs heat and therefore has a positive ΔH.) The energy required to remove the first electron is called the *first ionization energy (IE₁)*. For example, we represent the first ionization of sodium with the equation:

$$Na(g) \rightarrow Na^+(g) + 1\,e^- \qquad IE_1 = 496 \text{ kJ/mol}$$

The energy required to remove the second electron is the *second ionization energy (IE₂)*, the energy required to remove the third electron is the *third ionization energy (IE₃)*, and so on. We represent the second ionization energy of sodium as:

$$Na^+(g) \rightarrow Na^{2+}(g) + 1\,e^- \qquad IE_2 = 4560 \text{ kJ/mol}$$

Notice that the second ionization energy is not the energy required to remove *two* electrons from sodium (that quantity is the sum of IE_1 and IE_2), but rather the energy required to remove one electron from Na^+. We look at trends in IE_1 and IE_2 separately.

Trends in First Ionization Energy

The first ionization energies of the elements through Xe are shown in Figure 8.14 ▼. Notice the periodic trend in ionization energy, peaking at each noble gas and bottoming at each alkali metal. Based on what we have learned about electron configurations and effective nuclear charge, how can we account for the observed trend? As we have seen,

First Ionization Energies

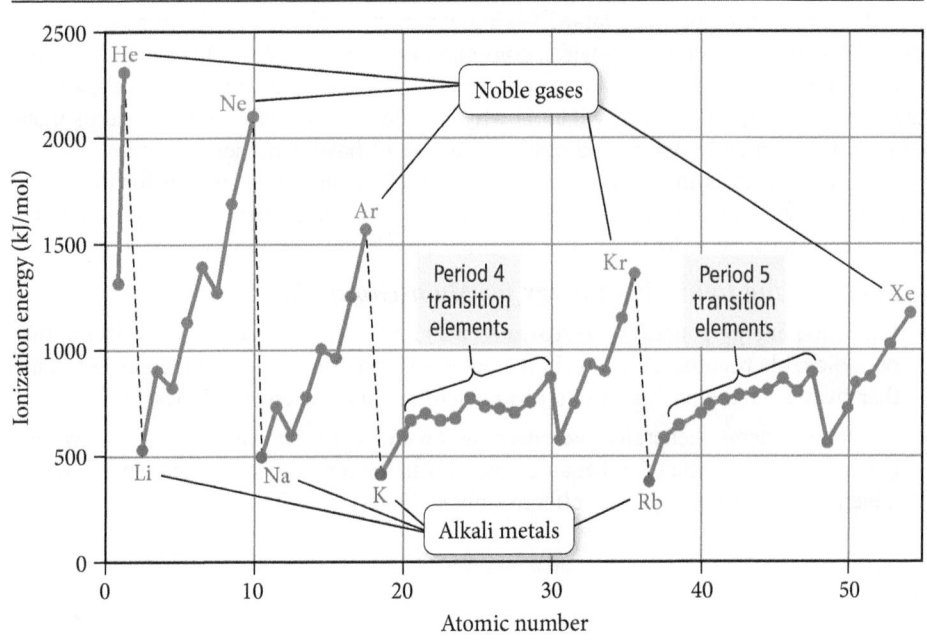

◄ **FIGURE 8.14 First Ionization Energy versus Atomic Number for the Elements through Xenon**   Ionization starts at a minimum with each alkali metal and rises to a peak with each noble gas.

Trends in First Ionization Energy

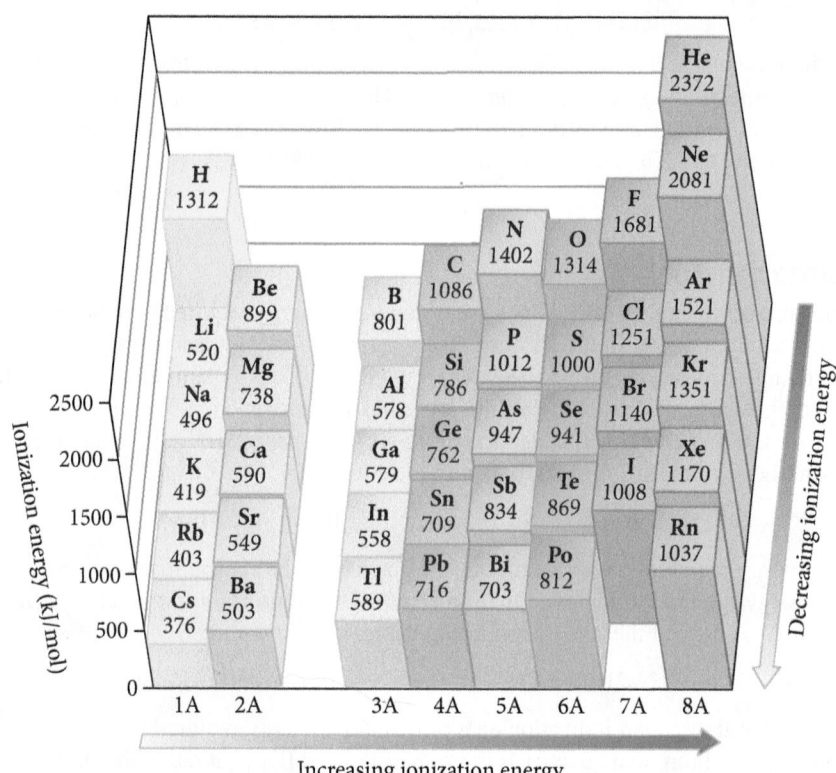

▲ FIGURE 8.15 **Trends in Ionization Energy** Ionization energy increases as we move to the right across a period and decreases as we move down a column in the periodic table.

the principal quantum number, n, increases as we move down a column. Within a given sublevel, orbitals with higher principal quantum numbers are larger than orbitals with smaller principal quantum numbers. Consequently, electrons in the outermost principal level are farther away from the positively charged nucleus—and are therefore held less tightly—as we move down a column. This results in a lower ionization energy as we move down a column, as shown in Figure 8.15 ▲.

What about the trend as we move to the right across a row? For example, would it take more energy to remove an electron from Na or from Cl, two elements on either end of the third row in the periodic table? We know that Na has an outer electron configuration of $3s^1$ and Cl has an outer electron configuration of $3s^2 3p^5$. As discussed previously, the outermost electrons in chlorine experience a higher effective nuclear charge than the outermost electrons in sodium (which is why chlorine has a smaller atomic radius than sodium). Consequently, we would expect chlorine to have a higher ionization energy than sodium, which is indeed the case. We can make a similar argument for the other main-group elements: ionization energy generally increases as we move to the right across a row in the periodic table, as shown in Figure 8.15.

Summarizing Ionization Energy for Main-Group Elements:

▶ Ionization energy generally *decreases* as we move down a column (or family) in the periodic table because electrons in the outermost principal level are increasingly farther away from the positively charged nucleus and are therefore held less tightly.

▶ Ionization energy generally *increases* as we move to the right across a row (or period) in the periodic table because electrons in the outermost principal energy level generally experience a greater effective nuclear charge (Z_{eff}).

EXAMPLE 8.8 Ionization Energy

On the basis of periodic trends, determine which element in each pair has the higher first ionization energy (if possible).

(a) Al or S

(b) As or Sb

(c) N or Si

(d) O or Cl

SOLUTION

(a) Al or S

S has a higher ionization energy than Al because as you trace the path between Al and S on the periodic table, you move to the right within the same row. Ionization energy increases as you go to the right due to increasing effective nuclear charge.

(b) As or Sb

As has a higher ionization energy than Sb because as you trace the path between As and Sb on the periodic table, you move down a column. Ionization energy decreases as you go down a column as a result of the increasing size of orbitals with increasing n.

(c) N or Si

N has a higher ionization energy than Si because as you trace the path between N and Si on the periodic table, you move down a column (ionization energy decreases) and then to the left across a row (ionization energy decreases). These effects sum together for an overall decrease.

(d) O or Cl

Based on periodic trends alone, it is impossible to tell which has a higher ionization energy because, as you trace the path between O and Cl, you go to the right across a row (ionization energy increases) and then down a column (ionization energy decreases). These effects tend to counter each other, and it is not obvious which will dominate.

FOR PRACTICE 8.8

On the basis of periodic trends, determine the element in each pair with the higher first ionization energy (if possible).

(a) Sn or I

(b) Ca or Sr

(c) C or P

(d) F or S

FOR MORE PRACTICE 8.8

Arrange the following elements in order of decreasing first ionization energy: S, Ca, F, Rb, Si.

Exceptions to Trends in First Ionization Energy

If we carefully examine Figure 8.15, we can see some exceptions to the trends in first ionization energies. For example, boron has a smaller ionization energy than beryllium, even though it lies to the right of beryllium in the same row. This exception is caused by the change in going from the *s* block to the *p* block. Recall from Section 8.3 that the $2p$ orbital penetrates into the nuclear region *less than* the $2s$ orbital. Consequently, the $1s$ electrons shield the electron in the $2p$ orbital from nuclear charge more than they shield the electrons in the $2s$ orbital. The result, as we saw in Section 8.3, is that the $2p$ orbitals are higher in energy, and therefore the electron is easier to remove (it has a lower ionization energy). Similar exceptions occur for aluminum and gallium, both directly below boron in group 3A.

Another exception occurs between nitrogen and oxygen. Although oxygen is to the right of nitrogen in the same row, it has a lower ionization energy. This exception is caused by the repulsion between electrons when they occupy the same orbital. Examine the electron configurations and orbital diagrams of nitrogen and oxygen shown here.

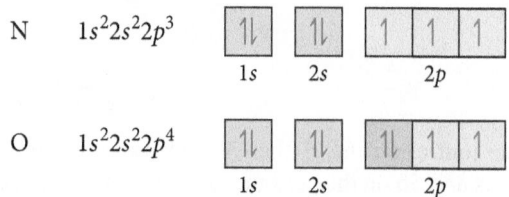

Nitrogen has three electrons in three *p* orbitals, while oxygen has four. In nitrogen, the $2p$ orbitals are half-filled (which makes the configuration particularly stable). Oxygen's fourth electron must pair with another electron, making it easier to remove (and less stable). Exceptions for similar reasons occur for S and Se, directly below oxygen in group 6A.

Trends in Second and Successive Ionization Energies

Notice the trends in the first, second, and third ionization energies of sodium (group 1A) and magnesium (group 2A), as shown at left.

For sodium, there is a huge jump between the first and second ionization energies. For magnesium, the ionization energy roughly doubles from the first to the second, but then a huge jump occurs between the second and third ionization energies. What is the reason for these jumps?

We can understand these trends by examining the electron configurations of sodium and magnesium:

$$\text{Na} \quad [\text{Ne}]\, 3s^1$$
$$\text{Mg} \quad [\text{Ne}]\, 3s^2$$

The first ionization of sodium involves removing the valence electron in the $3s$ orbital. Recall that these valence electrons are held more loosely than the core electrons, and that the resulting ion has a noble gas configuration, which is particularly stable. Consequently, the first ionization energy is fairly low. The second ionization of sodium, however, involves removing a core electron from an ion with a noble gas configuration. This requires a tremendous amount of energy, making the value of IE_2 very high.

As with sodium, the first ionization of magnesium involves removing a valence electron in the $3s$ orbital. This requires a bit more energy than the corresponding ionization of sodium because of the trends in Z_{eff} that we discussed earlier (Z_{eff} increases as we move to the right across a row). The second ionization of magnesium also involves removing an outer electron in the $3s$ orbital, but this time from an ion with a 1+ charge (instead of from a neutral atom). This requires roughly twice the energy as removing the electron from the neutral atom. The third ionization of magnesium is analogous to the

TABLE 8.1 Successive Values of Ionization Energies for the Elements Sodium through Argon (kJ/mol)

Element	IE_1	IE_2	IE_3	IE_4	IE_5	IE_6	IE_7
Na	496	4560			Core electrons		
Mg	738	1450	7730				
Al	578	1820	2750	11,600			
Si	786	1580	3230	4360	16,100		
P	1012	1900	2910	4960	6270	22,200	
S	1000	2250	3360	4560	7010	8500	27,100
Cl	1251	2300	3820	5160	6540	9460	11,000
Ar	1521	2670	3930	5770	7240	8780	12,000

second ionization of sodium—it requires removing a core electron from an ion with a noble gas configuration. This requires a tremendous amount of energy, making the value of IE_3 very high.

As shown in Table 8.1, similar trends exist for the successive ionization energies of many elements. The ionization energy increases fairly uniformly with each successive removal of an outermost electron, but then takes a large jump with the removal of the first core electron.

Conceptual Connection 8.6 Ionization Energies and Chemical Bonding

Based on what you just learned about ionization energies, explain why valence electrons are more important than core electrons in determining the reactivity and bonding in atoms.

8.8 Electron Affinities and Metallic Character

Electron affinity and metallic character also exhibit periodic trends. Electron affinity is a measure of how easily an atom will accept an additional electron and is crucial to chemical bonding because bonding involves the transfer or sharing of electrons. Metallic character is important because of the high proportion of metals in the periodic table and the large role they play in our lives. Of the roughly 110 elements, 87 are metals. We examine each of these periodic properties individually in this section.

Electron Affinity

The **electron affinity (EA)** of an atom or ion is the energy change associated with the gaining of an electron by the atom in the gaseous state. Electron affinity is usually—though not always—negative because an atom or ion usually releases energy when it gains an electron. (The process is analogous to an exothermic reaction, which releases heat and therefore has a negative ΔH.) In other words, the coulombic attraction between the nucleus of an atom and the incoming electron usually results in the release of energy as the electron is gained. For example, we can represent the electron affinity of chlorine with the equation:

$$Cl(g) + 1\,e^- \rightarrow Cl^-(g) \quad EA = -349 \text{ kJ/mol}$$

Figure 8.16 ▶ displays the electron affinities for a number of main-group elements. As you can see from this figure, the trends in electron affinity are not as regular as trends in other properties we have examined. For instance, we might expect electron affinities to

Electron Affinities (kJ/mol)

1A								8A
H −73	2A	3A	4A	5A	6A	7A		He >0
Li −60	Be >0		B −27	C −122	N >0	O −141	F −328	Ne >0
Na −53	Mg >0		Al −43	Si −134	P −72	S −200	Cl −349	Ar >0
K −48	Ca −2		Ga −30	Ge −119	As −78	Se −195	Br −325	Kr >0
Rb −47	Sr −5		In −30	Sn −107	Sb −103	Te −190	I −295	Xe >0

▲ FIGURE 8.16 **Electron Affinities of Selected Main-Group Elements.**

become relatively more positive (so that the addition of an electron is less exothermic) as we move down a column because the electron is entering orbitals with successively higher principal quantum numbers and will therefore be farther from the nucleus. This trend applies to the group 1A metals but does not hold for the other columns in the periodic table.

A more regular trend in electron affinity occurs as we move to the right across a row, however. Based on the periodic properties we have learned so far, would you expect more energy to be released by Na or Cl when an electron is gained? We know that Na has an outer electron configuration of $3s^1$ and Cl has an outer electron configuration of $3s^2 3p^5$. Since adding an electron to chlorine gives it a noble gas configuration and adding an electron to sodium does not, and since the outermost electrons in chlorine experience a higher Z_{eff} than the outermost electrons in sodium, we would expect chlorine to have a more negative electron affinity—the process should be more exothermic for chlorine. This is in fact the case. For main-group elements, electron affinity generally becomes more negative (more exothermic) as we move to the right across a row in the periodic table. The halogens (group 7A) therefore have the most negative electron affinities. But exceptions do occur. For example, notice that nitrogen and the other group 5A elements do not follow the general trend. These elements have $ns^2 np^3$ outer electron configurations. When an electron is added to this configuration, it must pair with another electron in an already occupied p orbital. The repulsion between two electrons occupying the same orbital causes the electron affinity to be more positive than for elements in the previous column.

Summarizing Electron Affinity for Main-Group Elements:

▶ Most groups (columns) of the periodic table do not exhibit any definite trend in electron affinity. Among the group 1A metals, however, electron affinity becomes more positive as we move down the column (adding an electron becomes less exothermic).

▶ Electron affinity generally becomes more negative (adding an electron becomes more exothermic) as we move to the right across a period (row) in the periodic table.

Metallic Character

As we discussed in Chapter 2, metals are good conductors of heat and electricity: they can be pounded into flat sheets (malleability), they can be drawn into wires (ductility), they are often shiny, and they tend to lose electrons in chemical reactions. Nonmetals, in contrast, have more varied physical properties; some are solids at room temperature, others are gases, but in general nonmetals are typically poor conductors of heat and electricity, and they all tend to gain electrons in chemical reactions. As we move to the right across a row in the periodic table, ionization energy increases and electron affinity becomes more negative; therefore, elements on the left side of the periodic table are more likely to lose electrons than elements on the right side of the periodic table (which are more likely to gain them). The other properties associated with metals follow the same general trend (even though we do not quantify them here). Consequently, as shown in Figure 8.17 ▶:

As we move to the right across a row (or period) in the periodic table, metallic character decreases.

As we move down a column in the periodic table, ionization energy decreases, making electrons more likely to be lost in chemical reactions. Therefore,

As we move down a column (or family) in the periodic table, metallic character increases.

Trends in Metallic Character

Metallic character decreases →

Metallic character increases ↓

Periods

| 1A 1 | 2A 2 | | | | | | | | | | | 3A 13 | 4A 14 | 5A 15 | 6A 16 | 7A 17 | 8A 18 |

□ Metals   □ Metalloids   □ Nonmetals

◀ **FIGURE 8.17** Trends in Metallic Character I   Metallic character decreases as we move to the right across a period and increases as we move down a column in the periodic table.

These trends, based on the quantum-mechanical model, explain the distribution of metals and nonmetals in the periodic table discussed in Chapter 2. Metals are found on the left side and toward the center and nonmetals on the upper right side. The change in chemical behavior from metallic to nonmetallic can be seen most clearly as we proceed to the right across period 3, or down along group 5A as can be seen in Figure 8.18 ▼.

▼ **FIGURE 8.18** Trends in Metallic Character II   As we move down group 5A in the periodic table, metallic character increases. As we move across period 3, metallic character decreases.

Trends in Metallic Character

Metallic character decreases →

EXAMPLE 8.9 Metallic Character

On the basis of periodic trends, choose the more metallic element from each pair (if possible).

(a) Sn or Te   **(b)** P or Sb   **(c)** Ge or In   **(d)** S or Br

SOLUTION

(a) Sn or Te

Sn is more metallic than Te because as you trace the path between Sn and Te on the periodic table, you move to the right within the same period. Metallic character decreases as we go to the right.

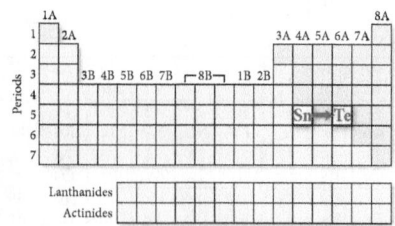

(b) P or Sb

Sb is more metallic than P because as you trace the path between P and Sb on the periodic table, you move down a column. Metallic character increases as we go down a column.

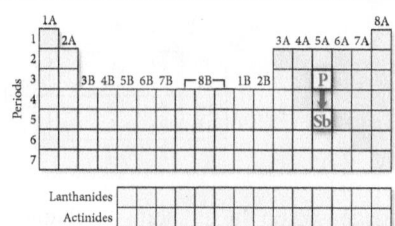

(c) Ge or In

In is more metallic than Ge because as you trace the path between Ge and In on the periodic table, you move down a column (metallic character increases) and then to the left across a period (metallic character increases). These effects add together for an overall increase.

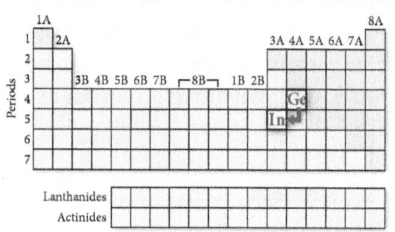

(d) S or Br

Based on periodic trends alone, we cannot tell which is more metallic because as you trace the path between S and Br, you go to the right across a period (metallic character decreases) and then down a column (metallic character increases). These effects tend to counter each other, and it is not easy to tell which will predominate.

FOR PRACTICE 8.9

On the basis of periodic trends, choose the more metallic element from each pair (if possible).

(a) Ge or Sn   **(b)** Ga or Sn   **(c)** P or Bi   **(d)** B or N

FOR MORE PRACTICE 8.9

Arrange the following elements in order of increasing metallic character: Si, Cl, Na, Rb.

Conceptual Connection 8.7 Periodic Trends

Use the trends in ionization energy and electron affinity to explain why sodium chloride has the formula NaCl and not Na_2Cl or $NaCl_2$.

8.9 Some Examples of Periodic Chemical Behavior: The Alkali Metals, the Halogens, and the Noble Gases

In this section, we explore some of the properties and chemical reactions of three families in the periodic table: the alkali metals, the halogens, and the noble gases. These families exemplify the connection between chemical behavior and electron configuration. The alkali metals (group 1A) have ns^1 outer electron configurations. The single valence electron that keeps these metals from having noble gas configurations is easily removed (the metals have low ionization energies), making these elements the most active metals in the periodic table. The halogens (group 7A) have $ns^2 np^5$ outer electron configurations. The one electron needed to attain noble gas configurations is easily acquired (the halogens have highly negative electron affinities), making these elements among the most active nonmetals in the periodic table. The noble gases (group 8A) have electron configurations with full outer principal quantum levels ($ns^2 np^6$) and so are the most chemically inert family in the periodic table. We will examine the properties of each of these groups separately. (Even though hydrogen is often listed in group 1A, it behaves like a nonmetal because of its high ionization energy: 1312 kJ/mol. We therefore do not include hydrogen in our discussion of the group 1A metals.)

The Alkali Metals (Group 1A)

Table 8.2 lists some selected properties of the alkali metals. Notice that, in general, the properties of the alkali metals vary fairly regularly as we proceed down the column. As expected from periodic trends, the atomic radius increases steadily while the first ionization energy decreases steadily.

With the exception of potassium, density increases as we move down the column. This is a general trend that occurs in other columns within the periodic table. As we move down a column, the increase in mass (due to the additional protons and neutrons) outpaces the increase in volume caused by greater atomic radius. The result is successively greater densities. The melting points of the alkali metals as a group are anomalously low for metals, and they steadily decrease as we move down the column. (This is not a general trend for the rest of the periodic table, which shows more irregular patterns in melting points.)

Because of their generally low ionization energies, the alkali metals are excellent reducing agents—they are readily oxidized, losing electrons to other substances. Consequently, the alkali metals exist naturally in their oxidized state, either in compounds or as dissolved ions in seawater. Since ionization energy *decreases* as we go down the column, the relative reactivities of the alkali metals tend to *increase* as we move down the column. In other words, the lower the ionization energy of an alkali metal, the greater tendency it will have to lose its electron and the more reactive it is.

The reactions of the alkali metals with nonmetals are vigorous. For example, the alkali metals (M) react with halogens (X) according to the reaction:

$$2\,M + X_2 \longrightarrow 2\,MX$$

The reaction of sodium and chlorine to form sodium chloride is typical:

$$2\,Na(s) + Cl_2(g) \longrightarrow 2\,NaCl(s)$$

This reaction emits heat and sparks as it occurs (Figure 8.19 ▶). Each successive alkali metal reacts even more vigorously with chlorine. The alkali metals also react with water to form the dissolved alkali metal ion, the hydroxide ion, and hydrogen gas:

$$2\,M(s) + 2\,H_2O(l) \longrightarrow 2\,M^+(aq) + 2\,OH^-(aq) + H_2(g)$$

▲ FIGURE 8.19 **Reaction of Sodium and Chlorine to Form Sodium Chloride.**

TABLE 8.2 Properties of the Alkali Metals*

Element	Electron Configuration	Atomic Radius (pm)	IE$_1$ (kJ/mol)	Density at 25 °C (g/cm^3)	Melting Point (°C)
Li	[He] $2s^1$	152	520	0.535	181
Na	[Ne] $3s^1$	186	496	0.968	102
K	[Ar] $4s^1$	227	419	0.856	98
Rb	[Kr] $5s^1$	248	403	1.532	39
Cs	[Xe] $6s^1$	265	376	1.879	29

*Francium is omitted because it has no stable isotopes.

Reactions of the Alkali Metals with Water

Lithium   Sodium   Potassium

▲ **FIGURE 8.20 Reactions of the Alkali Metals with Water** The reactions become progressively more vigorous as we move down the group.

The reaction is highly exothermic and can be explosive because the heat from the reaction can ignite the hydrogen gas. The reaction becomes more explosive as we move down the column from one metal to the next, as shown in Figure 8.20 ▲.[*]

The Halogens (Group 7A)

Table 8.3 lists selected properties of the first four halogens. Notice that the properties of the halogens, like those of the alkali metals, vary fairly regularly as we proceed down the column. As expected from periodic trends, the atomic radius and the density increase for each successive halogen. We can see from the melting and boiling points that fluorine and chlorine are both gases at room temperature, bromine is a liquid, and iodine is a solid.

All of the halogens are powerful oxidizing agents—they are readily reduced, gaining electrons from other substances in their reactions. Fluorine is the most powerful oxidizing agent of the group—reacting with almost everything, including the heavier noble gases—and iodine is the least. The halogens all react with metals to form *metal halides* according to the equation:

$$2\,M + n\,X_2 \longrightarrow 2\,MX_n$$

where M is the metal, X is the halogen, and MX_n is the metal halide. For example, chlorine reacts with iron according to the equation:

$$2\,Fe(s) + 3\,Cl_2(g) \longrightarrow 2\,FeCl_3(s)$$

TABLE 8.3 Properties of the Halogens*

Element	Electron Configuration	Atomic Radius (pm)	EA (kJ/mol)	Melting Point (°C)	Boiling Point (°C)	Density of Liquid (g/cm³)
F	[He] $2s^2\,2p^5$	72	−328	−219	−188	1.51
Cl	[Ne] $3s^2\,3p^5$	99	−349	−101	−34	2.03
Br	[Ar] $4s^2\,4p^5$	114	−325	−7	59	3.19
I	[Kr] $5s^2\,5p^5$	133	−295	114	184	3.96

*At is omitted because it is rare and radioactive.

[*]The rate of the alkali metal reaction with water, and therefore its vigor, is enhanced by the successively lower melting points of the alkali metals as we move down the column. The low melting points of the heavier metals allow the emitted heat to actually melt the metal, increasing the reaction rate.

Since metals tend to lose electrons and the halogens tend to gain them, the metal halides—like all compounds that form between metals and nonmetals—contain ionic bonds.

The halogens also react with hydrogen to form *hydrogen halides* according to the equation:

$$H_2(g) + X_2 \longrightarrow 2\,HX(g)$$

The hydrogen halides—like all compounds that form between two nonmetals— contain covalent bonds. All of the hydrogen halides form acidic solutions when combined with water.

The halogens also react with each other to form *interhalogen compounds*. For example, bromine reacts with fluorine according to the equation:

$$Br_2(l) + F_2(g) \longrightarrow 2\,BrF(g)$$

Again, like all compounds that form between two nonmetals, the interhalogen compounds contain covalent bonds.

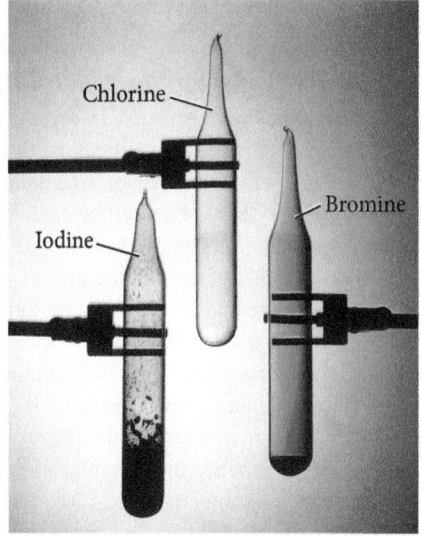

EXAMPLE 8.10 Alkali Metal and Halogen Reactions

Write a balanced chemical equation for each reaction.
(a) the reaction between potassium metal and bromine gas
(b) the reaction between rubidium metal and liquid water
(c) the reaction between gaseous chlorine and solid iodine

SOLUTION

(a) Alkali metals react with halogens to form metal halides. Write the formulas for the reactants and the metal halide product (making sure to write the correct ionic chemical formula for the metal halide, as outlined in Section 3.5), and then balance the equation.	$2\,K(s) + Br_2(g) \longrightarrow 2\,KBr(s)$
(b) Alkali metals react with water to form the dissolved metal ion, the hydroxide ion, and hydrogen gas. Write the skeletal equation including each of these and then balance it.	$2\,Rb(s) + 2\,H_2O(l) \longrightarrow 2\,Rb^+(aq) + 2\,OH^-(aq) + H_2(g)$
(c) Halogens react with each other to form interhalogen compounds. Write the skeletal equation with each of the halogens as the reactants and the interhalogen compound as the product and balance the equation.	$Cl_2(g) + I_2(s) \longrightarrow 2\,ICl(g)$

FOR PRACTICE 8.10
Write a balanced chemical equation for each reaction.
(a) the reaction between aluminum metal and chlorine gas
(b) the reaction between lithium metal and liquid water
(c) the reaction between gaseous hydrogen and liquid bromine

Chemistry and Medicine

Potassium Iodide in Radiation Emergencies

Since the attack on the World Trade Center on September 11, 2001, the United States has been concerned about the threat of additional terrorist strikes, including the possibility of nuclear attack. One danger of such an attack is radiation from the decay of radioisotopes released by a nuclear device—especially a so-called dirty bomb. This radiation can produce elevated rates of many cancers for years following exposure. The risk of developing thyroid cancer after ingesting radioactive isotopes of iodine, for example, is particularly high, especially in children. The number of thyroid cancers among children and adolescents in Belarus and Ukraine (areas affected by the radioactive plume from the 1986 nuclear accident at Chernobyl in the former Soviet Union) is 30–100 times higher than in the normal population.

The U.S. Food and Drug Administration (FDA), in cooperation with other federal agencies, recommends the administration of potassium iodide (KI) to citizens in the event of a nuclear radiation emergency. The 2011 nuclear accident at the Fukushima Daiichi Nuclear Power Plant in Japan caused panicked buying of KI, even in the United States. Although KI does not prevent exposure to radiation, it does decrease the risk of thyroid cancer that follows the intake of radioactive isotopes, particularly I-131. The chief function of the thyroid gland is to synthesize and release the hormone thyroxine, which regulates many aspects of human metabolism. In order to produce thyroxine, which contains iodine, the thyroid normally accumulates iodine in concentrations far greater than those found elsewhere in the body.

When potassium iodide is taken in the recommended doses, it floods the thyroid with nonradioactive iodine, preventing the thyroid from absorbing the cancer-causing radioactive iodine, which is then excreted in the urine.

In the United States, the FDA prioritizes KI treatment in the event of a nuclear emergency based on age. Infants, children, and pregnant females are at highest risk and are therefore treated at the lowest threshold exposure levels. Adults aged 18 to 40 are treated at slightly higher exposure levels, and those over 40 are only treated if the exposure level is actually high enough to destroy the thyroid.

The federal government has purchased stockpiles of potassium iodide for all states with nuclear reactors. Potassium iodide, also available over the counter, works best if taken 3–4 hours after exposure. Because of the increased threat of terrorist attacks after 9/11, potassium iodide pills have been distributed to residents, schools, and businesses within a 10-mile radius of a nuclear reactor. In the event of a terrorist attack on a nuclear reactor, residents are advised to take the potassium iodide pill and evacuate the area as soon as possible.

▲ The U.S. Food and Drug Administration recommends taking potassium iodide pills in the event of a nuclear emergency.

▲ Each molecule of thyroxine, a thyroid hormone that plays a key role in metabolism, contains four iodine atoms.

The Noble Gases (Group 8A)

Table 8.4 lists selected properties of the noble gases. Notice that the properties of the noble gases, like those of the alkali metals and halogens, vary fairly regularly as we proceed down the column. As expected from periodic trends, the atomic radius and the density increase for each successive noble gas, and the ionization energy decreases. As their boiling points indicate, all of the noble gases are gases at room temperature and must be cooled to extremely low temperatures before they liquefy. For this reason some noble gases can be cryogenic liquids—liquids used to cool other substances to low temperatures. For example, researchers often submerse samples of interest in boiling liquid helium to cool them down to 4.2 K (or lower) and study their properties at this extremely low temperature.

The high ionization energies of the noble gases and their completely full outer quantum levels make them exceptionally unreactive. In fact, before the 1960s, no noble gas compounds were known. Since then, two of the noble gases have been shown to react

▲ Liquid helium, a cryogenic liquid, cools substances to temperatures as low as 1.2 K.

TABLE 8.4 Properties of the Noble Gases*

Element	Electron Configuration	Atomic Radius (pm)**	IE_1 (kJ/mol)	Boiling Point (K)	Density of Gas (g/L at STP)
He	$1s^2$	32	2372	4.2	0.18
Ne	$[He]2s^2 2p^6$	70	2081	27.1	0.90
Ar	$[Ne]3s^2 3p^6$	98	1521	87.3	1.78
Kr	$[Ar]4s^2 4p^6$	112	1351	119.9	3.74
Xe	$[Kr]5s^2 5p^6$	130	1170	165.1	5.86

*Radon is omitted because it is radioactive.

**Since only the heavier noble gases form compounds, covalent radii for the smaller noble gases are estimated.

with fluorine (the most reactive nonmetal on the periodic table) under fairly extreme conditions. Krypton reacts with fluorine to form KrF_2:

$$Kr + F_2 \rightarrow KrF_2$$

Similarly, Xe reacts with fluorine to form three different xenon fluorides:

$$Xe + F_2 \rightarrow XeF_2$$
$$Xe + 2 F_2 \rightarrow XeF_4$$
$$Xe + 3 F_2 \rightarrow XeF_6$$

Xenon can also be forced to react with oxygen to form XeO_3 and XeO_4.

The inertness of the noble gases has led to their use in situations where reactions are undesirable. For example, argon is used in lightbulbs to prevent the hot tungsten filament from oxidizing, and helium is part of the mixture breathed by deep-sea divers to prevent the toxicity caused by too much oxygen and nitrogen under high pressures. (The helium replaces some of the oxygen and nitrogen in the tank, lowering the concentrations of oxygen and nitrogen in the blood.)

CHAPTER IN REVIEW

Self Assessment Quiz

Q1. According to Coulomb's law, if the separation between two particles of the same charge is doubled, the potential energy of the two particles:
a) becomes twice as high as it was before the distance separation.
b) becomes one-half as high as it was before the separation.
c) does not change.
d) becomes one-fourth as high as it was before the separation.

Q2. Which electron in sulfur is most shielded from nuclear charge?
a) An electron in the $1s$ orbital
b) An electron in a $2p$ orbital
c) An electron in a $3p$ orbital
d) none of the above (All of these electrons are equally shielded from nuclear charge.)

Q3. Choose the correct electron configuration for Se.
a) $1s^2 2s^2 2p^6 3s^2 3p^4$
b) $1s^2 2s^2 2p^6 3s^2 3p^6 4s^2 3d^{10} 4p^4$
c) $1s^2 2s^2 2p^6 3s^2 3p^6 4s^2 4p^4$
d) $1s^2 2s^2 2p^6 3s^2 3p^6 4s^2 3d^4$

Q4. Choose the correct orbital diagram for vanadium.

a) [Ar] $\boxed{\uparrow\downarrow}$ $_{4s}$ $\boxed{\uparrow\downarrow}\boxed{\uparrow}\boxed{}\boxed{}\boxed{}$ $_{3d}$

b) [Ar] $\boxed{}$ $_{4s}$ $\boxed{\uparrow}\boxed{\uparrow}\boxed{\uparrow}\boxed{\uparrow}\boxed{\uparrow}$ $_{3d}$

c) [Ar] $\boxed{\uparrow}$ $_{4s}$ $\boxed{\uparrow}\boxed{\uparrow}\boxed{\uparrow}\boxed{\uparrow}$ $_{3d}$

d) [Ar] $\boxed{\uparrow\downarrow}$ $_{4s}$ $\boxed{\uparrow}\boxed{\uparrow}\boxed{\uparrow}$ $_{3d}$

Q5. Which set of four quantum numbers corresponds to an electron in a $4p$ orbital?
a) $n = 4, l = 1, m_l = 0, m_s = \frac{1}{2}$
b) $n = 4, l = 3, m_l = 3, m_s = -\frac{1}{2}$
c) $n = 4, l = 2, m_l = 0, m_s = \frac{1}{2}$
d) $n = 4, l = 4, m_l = 3, m_s = -\frac{1}{2}$

Q6. Which element has the smallest atomic radius?
- a) C
- b) Si
- c) Be
- d) F

Q7. Which statement is true about electron shielding of nuclear charge?
- a) Outermost electrons efficiently shield one another from nuclear charge.
- b) Core electrons efficiently shield one another from nuclear charge.
- c) Outermost electrons efficiently shield core electrons from nuclear charge.
- d) Core electrons efficiently shield outermost electrons from nuclear charge.

Q8. Which statement is true about effective nuclear charge?
- a) Effective nuclear charge *increases* as you move to the right across a row in the periodic table and *increases* as you move down a column.
- b) Effective nuclear charge *increases* as you move to the right across a row in the periodic table and *decreases* as you move down a column.
- c) Effective nuclear charge *decreases* as you move to the right across a row in the periodic table and *decreases* as you move down a column.
- d) Effective nuclear charge *decreases* as you move to the right across a row in the periodic table and *increases* as you move down a column.

Q9. What is the electron configuration for Fe^{2+}?
- a) $[Ar]4s^2 3d^6$
- b) $[Ar]4s^2 3d^4$
- c) $[Ar]4s^0 3d^6$
- d) $[Ar]4s^2 3d^8$

Q10. Which species is diamagnetic?
- a) Cr^{2+}
- b) Zn
- c) Mn
- d) C

Q11. Arrange these atoms and ions in order of increasing radius: Cs^+, Xe, I^-.
- a) $I^- < Xe < Cs^+$
- b) $Cs^+ < Xe < I^-$
- c) $Xe < Cs^+ < I^-$
- d) $I^- < Cs^+ < Xe$

Q12. Arrange these elements in order of increasing first ionization energy: Cl, Sn, Si.
- a) $Cl < Si < Sn$
- b) $Sn < Si < Cl$
- c) $Si < Cl < Sn$
- d) $Sn < Cl < Si$

Q13. The ionization energies of an unknown third period element are shown below. Identify the element.

$IE_1 = 786$ kJ/mol; $IE_2 = 1580$ kJ/mol; $IE_3 = 3230$ kJ/mol; $IE_4 = 4360$ kJ/mol; $IE_5 = 16,100$ kJ/mol
- a) Mg
- b) Al
- c) Si
- d) P

Q14. Which statement is true about trends in metallic character?
- a) Metallic character *increases* as you go to the right across a row in the periodic table and *increases* as you go down a column.
- b) Metallic character *decreases* as you go to the right across a row in the periodic table and *increases* as you go down a column.
- c) Metallic character *decreases* as you go to the right across a row in the periodic table and *decreases* as you go down a column.
- d) Metallic character *decreases* as you go to the right across a row in the periodic table and *increases* as you go down a column.

Q15. For which element is the gaining of an electron most exothermic?
- a) Li
- b) N
- c) F
- d) B

Answers: 1. (b) **2.** (c) **3.** (b) **4.** (d) **5.** (a) **6.** (d) **7.** (d) **8.** (b) **9.** (c) **10.** (b) **11.** (b) **12.** (b) **13.** (c) **14.** (b) **15.** (c).

Key Terms

Section 8.1
periodic property (336)

Section 8.3
electron configuration (337)
ground state (337)
orbital diagram (338)
Pauli exclusion principle (338)
degenerate (338)

Coulomb's law (339)
shielding (339)
effective nuclear
  charge (Z_{eff}) (340)
penetration (340)
aufbau principle (342)
Hund's rule (342)

Section 8.4
valence electrons (345)

core electrons (345)

Section 8.6
van der Waals radius
  (nonbonding
  atomic radius) (350)
covalent radius (bonding
  atomic radius) (350)
atomic radius (350)

Section 8.7
paramagnetic (355)
diamagnetic (356)
ionization energy (IE) (359)

Section 8.8
electron affinity (EA) (363)

Key Concepts

Periodic Properties and the Development of the Periodic Table (8.1, 8.2)

▶ The periodic table was primarily developed by Dmitri Mendeleev in the nineteenth century. Mendeleev arranged the elements in a table so that atomic mass increased from left to right in a row and elements with similar properties fell in the same columns.

▶ Periodic properties are predictable based on an element's position within the periodic table. Periodic properties include atomic radius, ionization energy, electron affinity, density, and metallic character.

▶ Quantum mechanics explains the periodic table by explaining how electrons fill the quantum-mechanical orbitals within the atoms that compose the elements.

Electron Configurations (8.3)

▶ An electron configuration for an atom shows which quantum-mechanical orbitals are occupied by the atom's electrons. For example, the electron configuration of helium ($1s^2$) indicates that helium's two electrons exist within the $1s$ orbital.

▶ The order of filling quantum-mechanical orbitals in multielectron atoms is $1s\ 2s\ 2p\ 3s\ 3p\ 4s\ 3d\ 4p\ 5s\ 4d\ 5p\ 6s$.

▶ According to the Pauli exclusion principle, each orbital can hold a maximum of two electrons with opposing spins.

▶ According to Hund's rule, orbitals of the same energy first fill singly with electrons with parallel spins before pairing.

Electron Configurations and the Periodic Table (8.4, 8.5)

▶ Because quantum-mechanical orbitals fill sequentially with increasing atomic number, we can infer the electron configuration of an element from its position in the periodic table.

▶ The most stable configurations are those with completely full principal energy levels. Therefore, the most stable and unreactive elements—those with the lowest energy electron configurations—are the noble gases.

▶ Elements with one or two valence electrons are among the most active metals, readily losing their valence electrons to attain noble gas configurations.

▶ Elements with six or seven valence electrons are among the most active nonmetals, readily gaining enough electrons to attain a noble gas configuration.

Effective Nuclear Charge and Periodic Trends in Atomic Size (8.6)

▶ The size of an atom is largely determined by its outermost electrons. As we move down a column in the periodic table, the principal quantum number (n) of the outermost electrons increases, resulting in successively larger orbitals and therefore larger atomic radii.

▶ As we move across a row in the periodic table, atomic radii decrease because the effective nuclear charge—the net or average charge experienced by the atom's outermost electrons—increases.

▶ The atomic radii of the transition elements stay roughly constant as we move across each row because electrons are added to the $n_{highest} - 1$ orbitals while the number of highest n electrons stays roughly constant.

Ion Properties (8.7)

▶ We can determine the electron configuration of an ion by adding or subtracting the corresponding number of electrons to the electron configuration of the neutral atom.

▶ For main-group ions, the order of removing electrons is the same as the order in which they are added in building up the electron configuration.

▶ For transition metal atoms, the ns electrons are removed before the $(n - 1)d$ electrons.

▶ The radius of a cation is much *smaller* than that of the corresponding atom, and the radius of an anion is much *larger* than that of the corresponding atom.

▶ The ionization energy—the energy required to remove an electron from an atom in the gaseous state—generally decreases as we move down a column in the periodic table and increases when we move to the right across a row.

▶ Successive ionization energies increase smoothly from one valence electron to the next, but the ionization energy increases dramatically for the first core electron.

Electron Affinities and Metallic Character (8.8)

▶ Electron affinity—the energy associated with an element in its gaseous state gaining an electron—does not show a general trend as we move down a column in the periodic table, but it generally becomes more negative (more exothermic) to the right across a row.

▶ Metallic character—the tendency to lose electrons in a chemical reaction—generally increases down a column in the periodic table and decreases to the right across a row.

The Alkali Metals, Halogens, and Noble Gases (8.9)

▶ The most active metals are the alkali metals (group 1A), and the most active nonmetals are the halogens (group 7A).

▶ The alkali metals are powerful reducing agents, reacting with many nonmetals—including the halogens and water—to form ionic compounds.

▶ The halogens are powerful oxidizing agents, reacting with many metals to form ionic compounds. The halogens also react with many nonmetals to form covalent compounds.

▶ The noble gases are relatively unreactive; only krypton and xenon form compounds, typically only with fluorine, the most reactive element in the periodic table.

Key Equations and Relationships

Order of Filling Quantum-Mechanical Orbitals (8.3)

$$1s\ 2s\ 2p\ 3s\ 3p\ 4s\ 3d\ 4p\ 5s\ 4d\ 5p\ 6s$$

Key Learning Outcomes

Chapter Objectives	Assessment
Writing Electron Configurations (8.3)	Example 8.1 For Practice 8.1 Exercises 41, 42
Writing Orbital Diagrams (8.3)	Example 8.2 For Practice 8.2 Exercises 43, 44
Valence Electrons and Core Electrons (8.4)	Example 8.3 For Practice 8.3 Exercises 51, 52
Electron Configurations from the Periodic Table (8.4)	Example 8.4 For Practice 8.4 For More Practice 8.4 Exercises 45, 46

Key Learning Outcomes, *continued*

Using Periodic Trends to Predict Atomic Size (8.6)		Example 8.5 For Practice 8.5 For More Practice 8.5 Exercises 61–64
Writing Electron Configurations for Ions (8.7)		Example 8.6 For Practice 8.6 Exercises 65, 66
Using Periodic Trends to Predict Ion Size (8.7)		Example 8.7 For Practice 8.7 For More Practice 8.7 Exercises 69–72
Using Periodic Trends to Predict Relative Ionization Energies (8.7)		Example 8.8 For Practice 8.8 For More Practice 8.8 Exercises 73–76
Predicting Metallic Character Based on Periodic Trends (8.8)		Example 8.9 For Practice 8.9 For More Practice 8.9 Exercises 81–84
Writing Reactions for Alkali Metal and Halogen Reactions (8.9)		Example 8.10 For Practice 8.10 Exercises 85–90

EXERCISES

Review Questions

1. What are periodic properties?

2. Which periodic property is particularly important to nerve signal transmission? Why?

3. Explain the contributions of Johann Döbereiner and John Newlands to the organization of elements according to their properties.

4. Who is credited with arranging the periodic table? How were elements arranged in this table?

5. Explain the contributions of Meyer and Moseley to the periodic table.

6. The periodic table is a result of the periodic law. What observations led to the periodic law? What theory explains the underlying reasons for the periodic law?

7. What is an electron configuration? Give an example.

8. What is Coulomb's law? Explain how the potential energy of two charged particles depends on the distance between the charged particles and on the magnitude and sign of their charges.

9. What is shielding? In an atom, which electrons tend to do the most shielding (core electrons or valence electrons)?

10. What is penetration? How does the penetration of an orbital into the region occupied by core electrons affect the energy of an electron in that orbital?

11. Why are the sublevels within a principal level split into different energies for multielectron atoms but not for the hydrogen atom?

12. What is an orbital diagram? Provide an example.

13. Why is electron spin important when writing electron configurations? Explain in terms of the Pauli exclusion principle.

14. What are degenerate orbitals? According to Hund's rule, how are degenerate orbitals occupied?

15. List all orbitals from 1s through 5s according to increasing energy for multielectron atoms.

16. What are valence electrons? Why are they important?

17. Copy this blank periodic table onto a sheet of paper and label each of the blocks within the table: s block, p block, d block, and f block.

18. Explain why the s block in the periodic table has only two columns while the p block has six.

19. Why do the rows in the periodic table get progressively longer as you move down the table? For example, the first row contains 2 elements, the second and third rows each contain 8 elements, and the fourth and fifth rows each contain 18 elements. Explain.

20. Explain the relationship between a main-group element's lettered group number (the number of the element's column) and its valence electrons.

21. Explain the relationship between an element's row number in the periodic table and the highest principal quantum number in the element's electron configuration. How does this relationship differ for main-group elements, transition elements, and inner transition elements?

22. Which of the transition elements in the first transition series have anomalous electron configurations?

23. Explain how to write the electron configuration for an element based on its position in the periodic table.

24. Explain the relationship between the properties of an element and the number of valence electrons that it contains.

25. List the number of valence electrons for each family in the periodic table, and explain the relationship between the number of valence electrons and the resulting chemistry of the elements in the family.
    a. alkali metals   b. alkaline earth metals
    c. halogens   d. oxygen family

26. Define atomic radius. For main-group elements, give the observed trends in atomic radius as you
    a. move across a period in the periodic table.
    b. move down a column in the periodic table.

27. What is effective nuclear charge? What is shielding?

28. Use the concepts of effective nuclear charge, shielding, and n value of the valence orbital to explain the trend in atomic radius as you move across a period in the periodic table.

29. For transition elements, give the trends in atomic radius as you
    a. move across a period in the periodic table.
    b. move down a column in the periodic table.
    Explain the reasons for the trends described in parts a and b.

30. How is the electron configuration of an anion different from that of the corresponding neutral atom? How is the electron configuration of a cation different?

31. Explain how to write an electron configuration for a transition metal cation. Is the order of electron removal upon ionization simply the reverse of electron addition upon filling? Why or why not?

32. Describe the relationship between
    a. the radius of a cation and that of the atom from which it is formed.
    b. the radius of an anion and that of the atom from which it is formed.

33. What is ionization energy? What is the difference between first ionization energy and second ionization energy?

34. What is the general trend in ionization energy as you move down a column in the periodic table? As you move across a row?

35. What are the exceptions to the periodic trends in ionization energy? Why do they occur?

36. Examination of the first few successive ionization energies for a given element usually reveals a large jump between two ionization energies. For example, the successive ionization energies of magnesium show a large jump between IE_2 and IE_3. The successive ionization energies of aluminum show a large jump between IE_3 and IE_4. Explain why these jumps occur and how you might predict them.

37. What is electron affinity? What are the observed periodic trends in electron affinity?

38. What is metallic character? What are the observed periodic trends in metallic character?

39. Write a general equation for the reaction of an alkali metal with
    a. a halogen.
    b. water.

40. Write a general equation for the reaction of a halogen with
    a. a metal.
    b. hydrogen.
    c. another halogen.

Problems by Topic

Electron Configurations

41. Write the full electron configuration for each element.
    a. Si   b. O   c. K   d. Ne

42. Write the full electron configuration for each element.
    a. C   b. P   c. Ar   d. Na

43. Write the full orbital diagram for each element.
    a. N   b. F   c. Mg   d. Al

44. Write the full orbital diagram for each element.
    a. S   b. Ca   c. Ne   d. He

45. Use the periodic table to write an electron configuration for each element. Represent core electrons with the symbol of the previous noble gas in brackets.
    a. P   b. Ge   c. Zr   d. I

46. Use the periodic table to determine the element corresponding to each electron configuration.
    a. [Ar] $4s^2 3d^{10} 4p^6$ b. [Ar] $4s^2 3d^2$
    c. [Kr] $5s^2 4d^{10} 5p^2$ d. [Kr] $5s^2$

47. Use the periodic table to determine each quantity.
    a. The number of $2s$ electrons in Li
    b. The number of $3d$ electrons in Cu
    c. The number of $4p$ electrons in Br
    d. The number of $4d$ electrons in Zr

48. Use the periodic table to determine each quantity.
    a. The number of $3s$ electrons in Mg
    b. The number of $3d$ electrons in Cr
    c. The number of $4d$ electrons in Y
    d. The number of $6p$ electrons in Pb

49. Name an element in the fourth period (row) of the periodic table with
    a. five valence electrons.   b. four $4p$ electrons.
    c. three $3d$ electrons.   d. a complete outer shell.

50. Name an element in the third period (row) of the periodic table with
    a. three valence electrons.
    b. four $3p$ electrons.
    c. six $3p$ electrons.
    d. two $3s$ electrons and no $3p$ electrons.

Valence Electrons and Simple Chemical Behavior from the Periodic Table

51. Determine the number of valence electrons in each element.
    a. Ba   b. Cs   c. Ni   d. S

52. Determine the number of valence electrons in each element. Which elements do you expect to lose electrons in their chemical reactions? Which do you expect to gain electrons?
    a. Al   b. Sn   c. Br   d. Se

53. Which outer electron configuration would you expect to belong to a reactive metal? To a reactive nonmetal?
    a. ns^2
    b. ns^2np^6
    c. ns^2np^5
    d. ns^2np^2

54. Which outer electron configurations would you expect to belong to a noble gas? To a metalloid?
    a. ns^2
    b. ns^2np^6
    c. ns^2np^5
    d. ns^2np^2

Coulomb's Law and Effective Nuclear Charge

55. According to Coulomb's Law, which pair of charged particles has the lowest potential energy?
    a. a particle with a 1− charge separated by 150 pm from a particle with a 2+ charge
    b. a particle with a 1− charge separated by 150 pm from a particle with a 1+ charge
    c. a particle with a 1− charge separated by 100 pm from a particle with a 3+ charge

56. According to Coulomb's law, rank the interactions between charged particles from lowest potential energy to highest potential energy.
    a. a 1+ charge and a 1− charge separated by 100 pm
    b. a 2+ charge and a 1− charge separated by 100 pm
    c. a 1+ charge and a 1+ charge separated by 100 pm
    d. a 1+ charge and a 1− charge separated by 200 pm

57. Which electrons experience a greater effective nuclear charge: the valence electrons in beryllium or the valence electrons in nitrogen? Why?

58. Arrange the atoms according to decreasing effective nuclear charge experienced by their valence electrons: S, Mg, Al, Si.

59. If core electrons completely shielded valence electrons from nuclear charge (i.e., if each core electron reduced nuclear charge by 1 unit) and if valence electrons did not shield one another from nuclear charge at all, what would be the effective nuclear charge experienced by the valence electrons of each atom?
    a. K
    b. Ca
    c. O
    d. C

60. In Section 8.6, we estimated the effective nuclear charge on beryllium's valence electrons to be slightly greater than 2+. What would a similar treatment predict for the effective nuclear charge on boron's valence electrons? Would you expect the effective nuclear charge to be different for boron's $2s$ electrons compared to its $2p$ electron? In what way? (Hint: Consider the shape of the $2p$ orbital compared to that of the $2s$ orbital.)

Atomic Radius

61. Choose the larger atom from each pair.
    a. Al or In
    b. Si or N
    c. P or Pb
    d. C or F

62. Choose the larger atom from each pair.
    a. Sn or Si
    b. Br or Ga
    c. Sn or Bi
    d. Se or Sn

63. Arrange these elements in order of increasing atomic radius: Ca, Rb, S, Si, Ge, F.

64. Arrange these elements in order of decreasing atomic radius: Cs, Sb, S, Pb, Se.

Ionic Electron Configurations, Ionic Radii, Magnetic Properties, and Ionization Energy

65. Write the electron configuration for each ion.
    a. O^{2-}
    b. Br^-
    c. Sr^{2+}
    d. Co^{3+}
    e. Cu^{2+}

66. Write the electron configuration for each ion.
    a. Cl^-
    b. P^{3-}
    c. K^+
    d. Mo^{3+}
    e. V^{3+}

67. Write orbital diagrams for each ion and determine if the ion is diamagnetic or paramagnetic.
    a. V^{5+}
    b. Cr^{3+}
    c. Ni^{2+}
    d. Fe^{3+}

68. Write orbital diagrams for each ion and determine if the ion is diamagnetic or paramagnetic.
    a. Cd^{2+}
    b. Au^+
    c. Mo^{3+}
    d. Zr^{2+}

69. Which is the larger species in each pair?
    a. Li or Li^+
    b. I^- or Cs^+
    c. Cr or Cr^{3+}
    d. O or O^{2-}

70. Which is the larger species in each pair?
    a. Sr or Sr^{2+}
    b. N or N^{3-}
    c. Ni or Ni^{2+}
    d. S^{2-} or Ca^{2+}

71. Arrange this isoelectronic series in order of decreasing radius: F^-, Ne, O^{2-}, Mg^{2+}, Na^+.

72. Arrange this isoelectronic series in order of increasing atomic radius: Se^{2-}, Kr, Sr^{2+}, Rb^+, Br^-.

73. Choose the element with the higher first ionization energy from each pair.
    a. Br or Bi
    b. Na or Rb
    c. As or At
    d. P or Sn

74. Choose the element with the higher first ionization energy from each pair.
    a. P or I
    b. Si or Cl
    c. P or Sb
    d. Ga or Ge

75. Arrange these elements in order of increasing first ionization energy: Si, F, In, N.

76. Arrange these elements in order of decreasing first ionization energy: Cl, S, Sn, Pb.

77. For each element, predict where the "jump" occurs for successive ionization energies. (For example, does the jump occur between the first and second ionization energies, the second and third, or the third and fourth?)
    a. Be
    b. N
    c. O
    d. Li

78. Consider this set of successive ionization energies:

$$IE_1 = 578 \text{ kJ/mol}$$
$$IE_2 = 1820 \text{ kJ/mol}$$
$$IE_3 = 2750 \text{ kJ/mol}$$
$$IE_4 = 11,600 \text{ kJ/mol}$$

To which third-period element do these ionization values belong?

Electron Affinities and Metallic Character

79. Choose the element with the more negative (more exothermic) electron affinity from each pair.
    a. Na or Rb
    b. B or S
    c. C or N
    d. Li or F

80. Choose the element with the more negative (more exothermic) electron affinity from each pair.
    a. Mg or S
    b. K or Cs
    c. Si or P
    d. Ga or Br

81. Choose the more metallic element from each pair.
    a. Sr or Sb
    b. As or Bi
    c. Cl or O
    d. S or As

82. Choose the more metallic element from each pair.
    a. Sb or Pb
    b. K or Ge
    c. Ge or Sb
    d. As or Sn

83. Arrange these elements in order of increasing metallic character: Fr, Sb, In, S, Ba, Se.

84. Arrange these elements in order of decreasing metallic character: Sr, N, Si, P, Ga, Al.

Chemical Behavior of the Alkali Metals and the Halogens

85. Write a balanced chemical equation for the reaction of solid strontium with iodine gas.

86. Based on the ionization energies of the alkali metals, which alkali metal would you expect to undergo the most exothermic reaction with chlorine gas? Write a balanced chemical equation for the reaction.

87. Write a balanced chemical equation for the reaction of solid lithium with liquid water.

88. Write a balanced chemical equation for the reaction of solid potassium with liquid water.

89. Write a balanced equation for the reaction of hydrogen gas with bromine gas.

90. Write a balanced equation for the reaction of chlorine gas with fluorine gas.

Cumulative Problems

91. Bromine is a highly reactive liquid while krypton is an inert gas. Explain the difference based on their electron configurations.

92. Potassium is a highly reactive metal while argon is an inert gas. Explain the difference based on their electron configurations.

93. Both vanadium and its 3+ ion are paramagnetic. Use electron configurations to explain this statement.

94. Use electron configurations to explain why copper is paramagnetic while its 1+ ion is not.

95. Suppose you were trying to find a substitute for K^+ in nerve signal transmission. Where would you begin your search? What ions would be most like K^+? For each ion you propose, explain the ways in which it would be similar to K^+ and the ways it would be different. Refer to periodic trends in your discussion.

96. Suppose you were trying to find a substitute for Na^+ in nerve signal transmission. Where would you begin your search? What ions would be most like Na^+? For each ion you propose, explain the ways in which it would be similar to Na^+ and the ways it would be different. Use periodic trends in your discussion.

97. Life on Earth evolved based on the element carbon. Based on periodic properties, what two or three elements would you expect to be most like carbon?

98. Which pair of elements would you expect to have the most similar atomic radii, and why?
a. Si and Ga   **b.** Si and Ge   **c.** Si and As

99. Consider these elements: N, Mg, O, F, Al.
a. Write the electron configuration for each element.
b. Arrange the elements in order of decreasing atomic radius.
c. Arrange the elements in order of increasing ionization energy.
d. Use the electron configurations in part a to explain the differences between your answers to parts b and c.

100. Consider these elements: P, Ca, Si, S, Ga.
a. Write the electron configuration for each element.
b. Arrange the elements in order of decreasing atomic radius.
c. Arrange the elements in order of increasing ionization energy.
d. Use the electron configurations in part a to explain the differences between your answers to parts b and c.

101. Explain why atomic radius decreases as we move to the right across a period for main-group elements but not for transition elements.

102. Explain why vanadium (radius = 134 pm) and copper (radius = 128 pm) have nearly identical atomic radii, even though the atomic number of copper is about 25% higher than that of vanadium. What would you predict about the relative densities of these two metals? Look up the densities in a reference book, periodic table, or on the Web. Are your predictions correct?

103. The lightest noble gases, such as helium and neon, are completely inert—they do not form any chemical compounds whatsoever. The heavier noble gases, in contrast, do form a limited number of compounds. Explain this difference in terms of trends in fundamental periodic properties.

104. The lightest halogen is also the most chemically reactive, and reactivity generally decreases as we move down the column of halogens in the periodic table. Explain this trend in terms of periodic properties.

105. Write general outer electron configurations ($ns^x np^y$) for groups 6A and 7A in the periodic table. The electron affinity of each group 7A element is more negative than that of each corresponding group 6A element. Use the electron configurations to explain why this is so.

106. The electron affinity of each group 5A element is more positive than that of each corresponding group 4A element. Use the outer electron configurations for these columns to suggest a reason for this behavior.

107. The elements with atomic numbers 35 and 53 have similar chemical properties. Based on their electronic configurations, predict the atomic number of a heavier element that also should have these chemical properties.

108. Write the electronic configurations of the six cations that form from sulfur by the loss of one to six electrons. For those cations that have unpaired electrons, write orbital diagrams.

109. You have cracked a secret code that uses elemental symbols to spell words. The code uses numbers to designate the elemental symbols. Each number is the sum of the atomic number and the highest principal quantum number of the highest occupied orbital of the element whose symbol is to be used. The message may be written forward or backward. Decode the following messages:
a. 10, 12, 58, 11, 7, 44, 63, 66
b. 9, 99, 30, 95, 19, 47, 79

110. The electron affinity of sodium is lower than that of lithium, while the electron affinity of chlorine is higher than that of fluorine. Suggest an explanation for this observation.

111. Use Coulomb's law to calculate the ionization energy in kJ/mol of an atom composed of a proton and an electron separated by 100.00 pm. What wavelength of light would have sufficient energy to ionize the atom?

112. The first ionization energy of sodium is 496 kJ/mol. Use Coulomb's law to estimate the average distance between the sodium nucleus and the 3s electron. How does this distance compare to the atomic radius of sodium? Explain the difference.

Challenge Problems

113. Consider the densities and atomic radii of the noble gases at 25 °C:

Element	Atomic Radius (pm)	Density (g/L)
He	32	0.18
Ne	70	0.90
Ar	98	–
Kr	112	3.75
Xe	130	–
Rn	–	9.73

    a. Estimate the densities of argon and xenon by interpolation from the data.

    b. Provide an estimate of the density of the yet undiscovered element with atomic number 118 by extrapolation from the data.

    c. Use the molar mass of neon to estimate the mass of a neon atom. Then use the atomic radius of neon to calculate the average density of a neon atom. How does this density compare to the density of neon gas? What does this comparison suggest about the nature of neon gas?

    d. Use the densities and molar masses of krypton and neon to calculate the number of atoms of each element found in a volume of 1.0 L. Use these values to estimate the number of atoms that occur in 1.0 L of Ar. Now use the molar mass of argon to estimate the density of Ar. How does this estimate compare to that in part a?

114. As you have seen, the periodic table is a result of empirical observation (i.e., the periodic law), but quantum-mechanical theory explains *why* the table is so arranged. Suppose that, in another universe, quantum theory was such that there were one s orbital but only two p orbitals (instead of three) and only three d orbitals (instead of five). Draw out the first four periods of the periodic table in this alternative universe. Which elements would be the equivalent of the noble gases? Halogens? Alkali metals?

115. Consider the metals in the first transition series. Use periodic trends to predict a trend in density as you move to the right across the series.

116. Imagine a universe in which the value of m_s can be $+\frac{1}{2}, 0,$ and $-\frac{1}{2}$. Assuming that all the other quantum numbers can take only the values possible in our world and that the Pauli exclusion principle applies, determine

    a. the new electronic configuration of neon.

    b. the atomic number of the element with a completed $n = 2$ shell.

    c. the number of unpaired electrons in fluorine.

117. A carbon atom can absorb radiation of various wavelengths with resulting changes in its electronic configuration. Write orbital diagrams for the electronic configuration of carbon that would result from absorption of the three longest wavelengths of radiation it can absorb.

118. Only trace amounts of the synthetic element darmstadtium, atomic number 110, have been obtained. The element is so highly unstable that no observations of its properties have been possible. Based on its position in the periodic table, propose three different reasonable valence electron configurations for this element.

119. What is the atomic number of the as yet undiscovered element in which the 8s and 8p electron energy levels fill? Predict the chemical behavior of this element.

120. The trend in second ionization energy for the elements from lithium to fluorine is not a regular one. Predict which of these elements has the highest second ionization energy and which has the lowest and explain. Of the elements N, O, and F, O has the highest and N the lowest second ionization energy. Explain.

121. Unlike the elements in groups 1A and 2A, those in group 3A do not show a regular decrease in first ionization energy in going down the column. Explain the irregularities.

122. Using the data in Figures 8.15 and 8.16, calculate ΔE for the reaction $Na(g) + Cl(g) \rightarrow Na^+(g) + Cl^-(g)$.

123. Even though adding two electrons to O or S forms an ion with a noble gas electron configuration, the second electron affinity of both of these elements is positive. Explain.

124. In Section 2.7 we discussed the metalloids, which form a diagonal band separating the metals from the nonmetals. There are other instances in which elements such as lithium and magnesium that are diagonal to each other have comparable metallic character. Suggest an explanation for this observation.

125. The heaviest known alkaline earth metal is radium, atomic number 88. Find the atomic numbers of the as yet undiscovered next two members of the series.

126. Predict the electronic configurations of the first two excited states (next higher energy states beyond the ground state) of Pd.

127. Table 8.2 does not include francium because none of its isotopes are stable. Predict the values of the entries for Fr in Table 8.2. Predict the nature of the products of the reaction of Fr with (a) water, (b) oxygen, and (c) chlorine.

128. From its electronic configuration, predict which of the first ten elements would be most similar in chemical behavior to the as yet undiscovered element 165.

Conceptual Problems

129. Imagine that in another universe atoms and elements are identical to ours, except that atoms with six valence electrons have particular stability (in contrast to our universe where atoms with eight valence electrons have particular stability). Give an example of an element in the alternative universe that corresponds to
  a. a noble gas. **b.** a reactive nonmetal.
  c. a reactive metal.

130. The outermost valence electron in atom A experiences an effective nuclear charge of 2+ and is on average 225 pm from the nucleus. The outermost valence electron in atom B experiences an effective nuclear charge of 1+ and is on average 175 pm from the nucleus. Which atom (A or B) has the highest first ionization energy? Explain.

131. Determine whether each statement regarding penetration and shielding is true or false. (Assume that all lower energy orbitals are fully occupied.)
  a. An electron in a 3s orbital is more shielded than an electron in a 2s orbital.
  b. An electron in a 3s orbital penetrates into the region occupied by core electrons more than electrons in a 3p orbital.
  c. An electron in an orbital that penetrates closer to the nucleus will always experience more shielding than an electron in an orbital that does not penetrate as far.
  d. An electron in an orbital that penetrates close to the nucleus will tend to experience a higher effective nuclear charge than one that does not.

132. Give a combination of four quantum numbers that could be assigned to an electron occupying a 5p orbital. Do the same for an electron occupying a 6d orbital.

133. Use the trends in ionization energy and electron affinity to explain why calcium fluoride has the formula CaF_2 and not Ca_2F or CaF.

Answers to Conceptual Connections

Coulomb's Law

8.1 (a) Since the charges are opposite, the potential energy of the interaction is negative. As the charges get closer together, r becomes smaller and the potential energy decreases (becomes more negative).

Penetration and Shielding

8.2 (c) Penetration results in less shielding from nuclear charge and therefore lower energy.

Electron Configurations and Quantum Numbers

8.3 $n = 4, l = 0, m_l = 0, m_s = +\frac{1}{2}; n = 4, l = 0, m_l = 0, m_s = -\frac{1}{2}$

Effective Nuclear Charge

8.4 (c) Since Z_{eff} increases from left to right across a row in the periodic table, the valence electrons in S experience a greater effective nuclear charge than the valence electrons in Al or in Mg.

Ions, Isotopes, and Atomic Size

8.5 The isotopes of an element all have the same radii for two reasons: (1) neutrons are negligibly small compared to the size of an atom and therefore extra neutrons do not increase atomic size, and (2) neutrons have no charge and therefore do not attract electrons in the way that protons do.

Ionization Energies and Chemical Bonding

8.6 As you can see from the successive ionization energies of any element, valence electrons are held most loosely and can therefore be transferred or shared most easily. Core electrons, on the other hand, are held tightly and are not easily transferred or shared. Consequently, valence electrons are most important to chemical bonding.

Periodic Trends

8.7 The 3s electron in sodium has a relatively low ionization energy (496 kJ/mol) because it is a valence electron. The energetic cost for sodium to lose a second electron is extraordinarily high (4560 kJ/mol) because the next electron to be lost is a core electron (2p). Similarly, the electron affinity of chlorine to gain one electron (−349 kJ/mol) is highly exothermic since the added electron completes chlorine's valence shell. The gain of a second electron by the negatively charged chlorine anion would not be so favorable. Therefore, we would expect sodium and chlorine to combine in a 1:1 ratio.

9

Chemical Bonding I: The Lewis Model

Theories are nets cast to catch what we call 'the world': to rationalize, to explain, and to master it. We endeavor to make the mesh ever finer and finer.
—Karl Popper (1902–1994)

CHEMICAL BONDING IS AT THE HEART of chemistry. The bonding theories that we are about to examine are—as Karl Popper, a philosopher of science, eloquently states in the chapter-opening quote—nets cast to understand the world. In the next two chapters, we will examine three theories with successively finer "meshes." The first is the Lewis model, a simple model of chemical bonding, which can be carried out on the back of an envelope. With just a few dots, dashes, and chemical symbols, the Lewis model can help us to understand and predict a myriad of chemical observations. The second is valence bond theory, which treats electrons in a more quantum-mechanical manner but stops short of viewing them as belonging to the entire molecule. The third is molecular orbital theory, essentially a full quantum-mechanical treatment of the molecule and its electrons as a whole. Molecular orbital theory has great predictive power, but at the expense of great complexity and intensive computational requirements. Which theory is "correct"? Remember that theories are models that help us understand and predict behavior. All three of these theories are extremely useful, depending on exactly what aspect of chemical bonding we want to predict or understand.

The AIDS drug Indinavir—shown here as the missing piece in a puzzle depicting the protein HIV-protease—was developed with the help of chemical bonding theories.

9.1 Bonding Models and AIDS Drugs

In 1989, researchers using X-ray crystallography—a technique in which X-rays are scattered from crystals of the molecule of interest—determined the structure of a molecule called HIV-protease. HIV-protease is a protein (a class of large biological molecules) synthesized by the human immunodeficiency virus (HIV). This particular protein is crucial to the virus's ability to multiply and cause acquired immune deficiency syndrome, or AIDS. Without HIV-protease, HIV cannot spread in the human body because the virus cannot replicate. In other words, without HIV-protease, AIDS can't develop.

With knowledge of the HIV-protease structure, pharmaceutical companies set out to create a molecule that would disable HIV-protease by attaching to the working part of the molecule, called the active site. To design such a molecule, researchers used *bonding theories*—models that predict how atoms bond together to form molecules—to simulate the shape of potential drug molecules and determine how they would interact with the protease molecule. By the early 1990s, pharmaceutical companies had developed several

We will discuss X-ray crystallography in more detail in Section 11.10.

We will discuss proteins in more detail in Chapter 21.

▲ G. N. Lewis

drug molecules that seemed to work. Since these molecules inhibit the action of HIV-protease, they were named *protease inhibitors*. Protease inhibitors, when given in combination with other drugs, decrease the viral count in HIV-infected individuals to undetectable levels. Although protease inhibitors do not cure AIDS, many AIDS patients are still alive today because of these drugs.

Bonding theories are central to chemistry because they explain how atoms bond together to form molecules. They explain why some combinations of atoms are stable and others are not. For example, bonding theories explain why table salt is NaCl and not $NaCl_2$ and why water is H_2O and not H_3O. Bonding theories also predict the shapes of molecules—a topic in the next chapter—which in turn determine many of the physical and chemical properties of compounds. The bonding model we examine in this chapter is called the **Lewis model**, named after the American chemist G. N. Lewis (1875–1946). In the Lewis model, valence electrons are represented as dots, and we draw **Lewis electron-dot structures** (or simply **Lewis structures**) to depict molecules. These structures, which are fairly simple to draw, have tremendous predictive power. With minimal computation, the Lewis model can be used to predict whether a particular set of atoms will form a stable molecule and what that molecule might look like. Although we will also examine more advanced theories in the following chapter, the Lewis model remains the simplest model for making quick, everyday predictions about most molecules.

9.2 Types of Chemical Bonds

We begin our discussion of chemical bonding by asking why bonds form in the first place. This seemingly simple question is vitally important. Imagine our universe without chemical bonding. Such a universe would contain only 91 different kinds of substances (the 91 naturally occurring elements). With such a poor diversity of substances, life would be impossible, and we would not be around to wonder why. The *answer* to the question of why bonds form, however, is not simple and involves not only quantum mechanics but also some thermodynamics that we will not introduce until Chapter 17. Nonetheless, we can address an important *aspect* of the answer now: *chemical bonds form because they lower the potential energy between the charged particles that compose atoms.*

As you already know, atoms are composed of particles with positive charges (the protons in the nucleus) and negative charges (the electrons). When two atoms approach each other, the electrons of one atom are attracted to the nucleus of the other according to Coulomb's law (see Section 8.3) and vice versa. However, at the same time, the electrons of each atom repel the electrons of the other, and the nucleus of each atom repels the nucleus of the other. The result is a complex set of interactions among a potentially large number of charged particles. If these interactions lead to an overall net reduction of energy between the charged particles, a chemical bond forms. Bonding theories help us to predict the circumstances under which bonds form and also the properties of the resultant molecules.

We can broadly classify chemical bonds into three types depending on the kind of atoms involved in the bonding (Figure 9.1 ▶).

Types of Atoms	Type of Bond	Characteristic of Bond
Metal and nonmetal	Ionic	Electrons transferred
Nonmetal and nonmetal	Covalent	Electrons shared
Metal and metal	Metallic	Electrons pooled

In Chapter 8 we discussed that metals tend to have low ionization energies (their electrons are relatively easy to remove) and that nonmetals tend to have negative electron affinities (they readily gain electrons). When a metal bonds with a nonmetal, it transfers one or more electrons to the nonmetal. The metal atom becomes a cation and the nonmetal atom an anion. These oppositely charged ions then attract one another, lowering their overall potential energy as described by Coulomb's law. The resulting bond is an **ionic bond**.

We also discussed in Chapter 8 that nonmetals tend to have high ionization energies (their electrons are relatively difficult to remove). Therefore when a nonmetal bonds with another nonmetal, neither atom transfers electrons to the other. Instead, the two atoms

Ionic bonding

Covalent bonding

Na^+ Cl^-

Table salt, NaCl(*s*)

H_2O molecules

Ice, $H_2O(s)$

Metallic bonding

e^- sea

Na^+

Sodium metal, Na(*s*)

▲ FIGURE 9.1 Ionic, Covalent, and Metallic Bonding

share some electrons. The shared electrons interact with the nuclei of both of the bonding atoms, lowering their potential energy in accordance with Coulomb's law. The resulting bond is a **covalent bond.**

Recall from Section 3.2 that we can understand the stability of a covalent bond by considering the most stable arrangement (the one with the lowest potential energy) of two positively charged particles separated by a small distance and a negatively charged particle. As you can see in Figure 9.2 ▼, the arrangement in which the negatively charged particle lies *between* the two positively charged ones has the lowest potential energy because in this arrangement, the negatively charged particle interacts most strongly with *both of the positively charged ones.* In a sense, the negatively charged particle holds the two positively charged ones together. Similarly, shared electrons in a covalent chemical bond *hold* the bonding atoms together by attracting the positive charges of their nuclei.

A third type of bonding, **metallic bonding,** occurs in metals. Since metals have low ionization energies, they tend to lose electrons easily. In the simplest model for metallic bonding—called the *electron sea* model—all of the atoms in a metal lattice pool their valence electrons. These pooled electrons are no longer localized on a single atom, but delocalized over the entire metal. The positively charged metal atoms are then attracted to the sea of electrons, holding the metal together. We discuss metallic bonding in more detail in Section 9.11.

Lowest potential energy
(most stable)

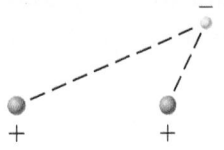

◄ FIGURE 9.2 Possible Configurations of One Negatively Charged Particle and Two Positively Charged Ones

9.3 Representing Valence Electrons with Dots

Remember, the number of valence electrons
for any main group is equal to the group
number of the element (except for helium,
which is in group 8A but has only two
valence electrons).

In Chapter 8, we saw that, for main-group elements, valence electrons are those electrons in the outermost principal energy level. Since valence electrons are held most loosely, and since chemical bonding involves the transfer or sharing of electrons between two or more atoms, valence electrons are most important in bonding, so the Lewis model focuses on these. In a **Lewis symbol,** we represent the valence electrons of main-group elements as dots surrounding the abbreviation for the element. For example, the electron configuration of O is:

$$1s^2 2s^2 2p^4$$
6 valence electrons

And the Lewis symbol is:

$\cdot \ddot{O} \colon$ 6 dots representing valence electrons

While the exact location of dots is not
critical, in this book we will first place dots
singly before pairing (except for helium,
which always has two paired dots signifying
its duet).

Each dot represents a valence electron. The dots are placed around the element's symbol with a maximum of two dots per side. The Lewis symbols for all of the period 2 elements are drawn in a similar way:

$$\text{Li} \cdot \quad \cdot \text{Be} \cdot \quad \cdot \dot{\text{B}} \cdot \quad \cdot \dot{\text{C}} \cdot \quad \cdot \ddot{\text{N}} \colon \quad \cdot \ddot{\text{O}} \colon \quad \colon \ddot{\text{F}} \colon \quad \colon \ddot{\text{Ne}} \colon$$

Lewis symbols provide a simple way to visualize the number of valence electrons in a main-group atom. Notice that atoms with eight valence electrons—which are particularly stable because they have a full outer level—are easily identified because they have eight dots, an **octet.**

Helium is somewhat of an exception. Its electron configuration and Lewis symbol are:

$$1s^2 \quad \text{He} \colon$$

The Lewis symbol of helium contains only two dots (a **duet**). For helium, a duet represents a stable electron configuration because the $n = 1$ quantum level fills with only two electrons.

In the Lewis model, a **chemical bond** is the sharing or transfer of electrons to attain stable electron configurations for the bonding atoms. If electrons are transferred, as occurs between a metal and a nonmetal, the bond is an *ionic bond*. If the electrons are shared, as occurs between two nonmetals, the bond is a *covalent bond*. In either case, the bonding atoms obtain stable electron configurations; since the stable configuration is usually eight electrons in the outermost shell, this is known as the **octet rule**. When applying the Lewis model we do not try to calculate the energies associated with the attractions and repulsions between electrons and nuclei on neighboring atoms. The energy changes that occur because of these interactions are central to chemical bonding (as we saw in Section 9.2), yet the Lewis model ignores them because calculating these energy changes is extremely complicated. Instead the Lewis model uses the simple octet rule, a practical approach that accurately predicts what we see in nature for a large number of compounds—hence the success and longevity of the Lewis model.

9.4 Ionic Bonding: Lewis Symbols and Lattice Energies

Although the Lewis model's strength is in modeling covalent bonding, it can also be applied to ionic bonding. To represent ionic bonding, we move electron dots from the Lewis symbol of the metal to the Lewis symbol of the nonmetal and then allow the resultant ions to form a crystalline lattice composed of alternating cations and anions.

Ionic Bonding and Electron Transfer

Consider potassium and chlorine, which have the following Lewis symbols:

$$\text{K} \cdot \quad \colon \ddot{\text{Cl}} \colon$$

When these atoms bond, potassium transfers its valence electron to chlorine:

$$K\cdot \; + \; :\ddot{\underset{\cdot}{Cl}}: \; \longrightarrow \; K^+ \left[:\ddot{\underset{\cdot\cdot}{Cl}}: \right]^-$$

The transfer of the electron gives chlorine an octet (shown as eight dots around chlorine) and leaves potassium without any valence electrons but with an octet in the *previous* principal energy level (which is now the outermost level).

$$K \quad 1s^2 2s^2 2p^6 3s^2 3p^6 4s^1$$
$$K^+ \quad 1s^2 2s^2 2p^6 \underbrace{3s^2 3p^6}_{} 4s^0$$
$$\text{Octet in previous level}$$

The potassium, because it has lost an electron, becomes positively charged (a cation), while the chlorine, which has gained an electron, becomes negatively charged (an anion). The Lewis symbol of an anion is usually written within brackets with the charge in the upper right-hand corner, outside the brackets. The positive and negative charges attract one another, resulting in the compound KCl.

So we can use the Lewis model to predict the correct chemical formulas for ionic compounds. For the compound that forms between K and Cl, for example, the Lewis model predicts a ratio of one potassium cation to every one chloride anion, KCl. In nature, when we examine the compound formed between potassium and chlorine, we indeed find one potassium ion to every chloride ion. As another example, consider the ionic compound formed between sodium and sulfur. The Lewis symbols for sodium and sulfur are:

$$Na\cdot \qquad \cdot\ddot{\underset{\cdot\cdot}{S}}:$$

Sodium must lose its one valence electron in order to have an octet (in the previous principal shell), while sulfur must gain two electrons to get an octet. Consequently, the compound that forms between sodium and sulfur requires a ratio of two sodium atoms to every one sulfur atom.

$$2\,Na^+ \left[:\ddot{\underset{\cdot\cdot}{S}}: \right]^{2-}$$

The two sodium atoms each lose their one valence electron while the sulfur atom gains two electrons and gets an octet. The Lewis model predicts that the correct chemical formula is Na_2S, exactly what we see in nature.

> Recall that solid ionic compounds do not contain distinct molecules; they are composed of alternating positive and negative ions in a three-dimensional crystalline array.

EXAMPLE 9.1 Using Lewis Symbols to Predict the Chemical Formula of an Ionic Compound

Use Lewis symbols to predict the formula for the compound that forms between calcium and chlorine.

SOLUTION

Draw Lewis symbols for calcium and chlorine based on their number of valence electrons, obtained from their group number in the periodic table.	$\cdot Ca\cdot \qquad \cdot\ddot{\underset{\cdot\cdot}{Cl}}:$
Calcium must lose its two valence electrons (to be left with an octet in its previous principal shell), while chlorine only needs to gain one electron to get an octet. Draw two chlorine anions, each with an octet and a 1− charge, and one calcium cation with a 2+ charge. Place brackets around the chlorine anions and indicate the charges on each ion.	$Ca^{2+} \; 2\left[:\ddot{\underset{\cdot\cdot}{Cl}}: \right]^-$
Finally, write the formula with subscripts to indicate the number of atoms.	$CaCl_2$

FOR PRACTICE 9.1

Use Lewis symbols to predict the formula for the compound that forms between magnesium and nitrogen.

Lattice Energy: The Rest of the Story

The formation of an ionic compound from its constituent elements is usually quite exothermic. For example, when sodium chloride (table salt) forms from elemental sodium and chlorine, 411 kJ of heat is evolved in the following violent reaction:

$$Na(s) + {}^1/_2\, Cl_2(g) \longrightarrow NaCl(s) \qquad \Delta H_f^\circ = -411 \text{ kJ/mol}$$

Where does this energy come from? You might think that it comes solely from the tendency of metals to lose electrons and nonmetals to gain electrons—but it does not. In fact, the transfer of an electron from sodium to chlorine—by itself—actually *absorbs* energy. The first ionization energy of sodium is +496 kJ/mol, and the electron affinity of Cl is only −349 kJ/mol. Based only on these energies, the reaction should be *endothermic* by +147 kJ/mol. So why is the reaction so *exothermic*?

The answer lies in the **lattice energy**—the energy associated with the formation of a crystalline lattice of alternating cations and anions from the gaseous ions. Since the sodium ions are positively charged and the chlorine ions are negatively charged, the potential energy decreases—as prescribed by Coulomb's law—when these ions come together to form a lattice. That energy is emitted as heat when the lattice forms, as shown in Figure 9.3 ▼. The exact value of the lattice energy, however, is not simple to determine because it involves a large number of interactions among many charged particles in a lattice. The easiest way to calculate lattice energy is with the *Born–Haber cycle*.

Lattice Energy of an Ionic Compound

—Na$^+$

Gaseous ions coalesce.
Heat is emitted.

—Cl$^-$

▶ FIGURE 9.3 **Lattice Energy** The lattice energy of an ionic compound is the energy associated with the formation of a crystalline lattice of the compound from the gaseous ions.

$$Na^+(g) \quad + \quad Cl^-(g) \quad \longrightarrow \quad NaCl(s) \qquad \Delta H^\circ = \text{lattice energy}$$

The Born–Haber Cycle

The **Born–Haber cycle** is a hypothetical series of steps that represents the formation of an ionic compound from its constituent elements. The steps are chosen so that the change in enthalpy of each step is known except for the last one, which is the lattice energy. The change in enthalpy for the overall process is also known. Using Hess's law (see Section 6.8), we can therefore determine the enthalpy change for the unknown last step, the lattice energy.

Recall that Hess's law states that the change in the overall enthalpy of a stepwise process is the sum of the enthalpy changes of the steps.

Consider the formation of NaCl from its constituent elements in their standard states. The enthalpy change for the overall reaction is simply the standard enthalpy of formation of NaCl(s):

$$Na(s) + {}^1/_2\, Cl_2(g) \longrightarrow NaCl(s) \qquad \Delta H_f^\circ = -411 \text{ kJ/mol}$$

Now consider the following set of steps—the Born–Haber cycle—from which NaCl(s) can also be made from Na(s) and $Cl_2(g)$:

- The first step is the formation of gaseous sodium from solid sodium.

$$Na(s) \longrightarrow Na(g) \qquad \Delta H^\circ_{step\ 1} \text{(sublimation energy of Na)} = +108 \text{ kJ}$$

- The second step is the formation of a chlorine atom from a chlorine molecule.

$$^1/_2 \ Cl_2(g) \longrightarrow Cl(g) \qquad \Delta H^\circ_{step\ 2} \text{(bond energy of } Cl_2 \times \ ^1/_2) = +122 \text{ kJ}$$

- The third step is the ionization of gaseous sodium. The enthalpy change for this step is the ionization energy of sodium.

$$Na(g) \longrightarrow Na^+(g) + e^- \qquad \Delta H^\circ_{step\ 3} \text{(ionization energy of Na)} = +496 \text{ kJ}$$

- The fourth step is the addition of an electron to gaseous chlorine. The enthalpy change for this step is the electron affinity of chlorine.

$$Cl(g) + e^- \longrightarrow Cl^-(g) \qquad \Delta H^\circ_{step\ 4} \text{(electron affinity of Cl)} = -349 \text{ kJ}$$

- The fifth and final step is the formation of the crystalline solid from the gaseous ions. The enthalpy change for this step is the lattice energy, the unknown quantity.

$$Na^+(g) + Cl^-(g) \longrightarrow NaCl(s) \qquad \Delta H^\circ_{step\ 5} = \Delta H^\circ_{lattice} = ?$$

Figure 9.4 ▼ illustrates the entire Born–Haber cycle for NaCl.

Born–Haber Cycle for Production of NaCl from Na(s) and $Cl_2(g)$

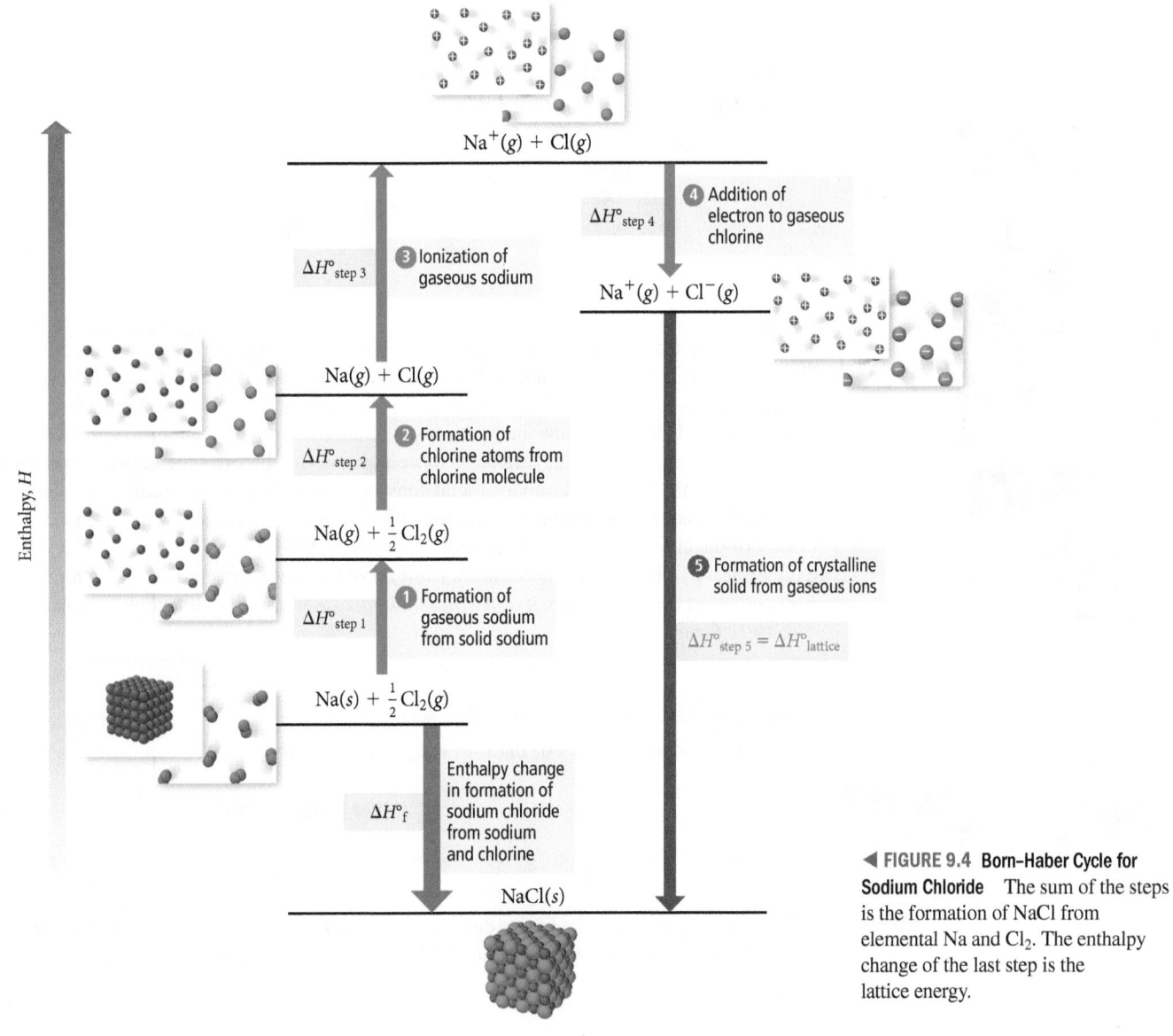

◀ FIGURE 9.4 **Born–Haber Cycle for Sodium Chloride** The sum of the steps is the formation of NaCl from elemental Na and Cl_2. The enthalpy change of the last step is the lattice energy.

Since the overall reaction obtained by summing the steps in the Born–Haber cycle is equivalent to the formation of NaCl from its constituent elements, we use Hess's law to set the overall enthalpy of formation for NaCl(s) equal to the sum of the steps in the Born–Haber cycle:

Lattice energy

$$\Delta H_f^\circ = \Delta H_{\text{step 1}}^\circ + \Delta H_{\text{step 2}}^\circ + \Delta H_{\text{step 3}}^\circ + \Delta H_{\text{step 4}}^\circ + \Delta H_{\text{step 5}}^\circ$$

We then solve this equation for $\Delta H_{\text{step 5}}^\circ$, which is $\Delta H_{\text{lattice}}^\circ$, and substitute the appropriate values to calculate the lattice energy.

$$
\begin{aligned}
\Delta H_{\text{lattice}}^\circ = \Delta H_{\text{step 5}}^\circ &= \Delta H_f^\circ - (\Delta H_{\text{step 1}}^\circ + \Delta H_{\text{step 2}}^\circ + \Delta H_{\text{step 3}}^\circ + \Delta H_{\text{step 4}}^\circ) \\
&= -411 \text{ kJ} - (+108 \text{ kJ} + 122 \text{ kJ} + 496 \text{ kJ} - 349 \text{ kJ}) \\
&= -788 \text{ kJ}
\end{aligned}
$$

Some books define the lattice energy as the energy associated with *separating* one mole of an ionic lattice into its gaseous constituents, which makes the sign of the lattice energy positive instead of negative.

The value of the lattice energy is a large negative number. The formation of the crystalline NaCl lattice from sodium cations and chloride anions is highly exothermic and more than compensates for the endothermicity of the electron transfer process. In other words, the formation of ionic compounds is not exothermic because sodium "wants" to lose electrons and chlorine "wants" to gain them; rather, it is exothermic because of the large amount of heat released when sodium and chlorine ions coalesce to form a crystalline lattice.

Trends in Lattice Energies: Ion Size

Consider the lattice energies of the following alkali metal chlorides:

Metal Chloride	Lattice Energy kJ/mol
LiCl	−834
NaCl	−788
KCl	−701
CsCl	−657

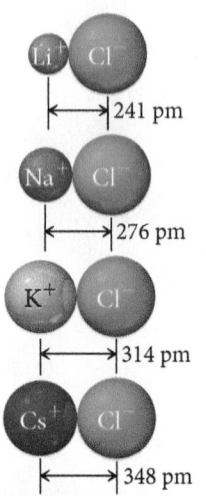

▲ Bond lengths of the group 1A metal chlorides.

Why does the magnitude of the lattice energy decrease as we move down the column? We know from the periodic trends discussed in Chapter 8 that ionic radius increases as we move down a column in the periodic table (see Section 8.7). We also know, from our discussion of Coulomb's law in Section 8.3, that the potential energy of oppositely charged ions becomes less negative (or more positive) as the distance between the ions increases. As the size of the alkali metal ions increases down the column, so does the distance between the metal cations and the chloride anions. The magnitude of the lattice energy of the chlorides decreases accordingly, making the formation of the chlorides less exothermic. In other words, *as the ionic radii increase as we move down the column, the ions cannot get as close to each other and therefore do not release as much energy when the lattice forms.*

Trends in Lattice Energies: Ion Charge

Consider the lattice energies of the following two compounds:

Compound	Lattice Energy (kJ/mol)
NaF	−910
CaO	−3414

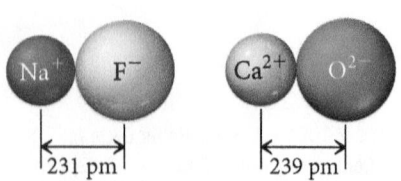

Why is the magnitude of the lattice energy of CaO so much greater than the lattice energy of NaF? Na^+ has a radius of 95 pm and F^- has a radius of 136 pm, resulting in a distance between ions of 231 pm. Ca^{2+} has a radius of 99 pm and O^{2-} has a radius of 140 pm, resulting in a distance between ions of 239 pm. Even though the separation between the calcium and oxygen is slightly greater (which would tend to lower the lattice energy), the lattice energy for CaO is almost four times *greater*. The explanation lies in the charges of the ions. Recall from Coulomb's law that the magnitude of the potential energy of two interacting charges depends not only on the distance between the charges, but also on the product of the charges:

$$E = \frac{1}{4\pi\varepsilon_0}\frac{q_1 q_2}{r}$$

For NaF, E is proportional to $(1+)(1-) = 1-$, while for CaO, E is proportional to $(2+)(2-) = 4-$, so the relative stabilization for CaO relative to NaF is roughly four times greater, as observed in the lattice energy.

Summarizing Trends in Lattice Energies:

▶ *Lattice energies become less exothermic (less negative) with increasing ionic radius.*

▶ *Lattice energies become more exothermic (more negative) with increasing magnitude of ionic charge.*

EXAMPLE 9.2 Predicting Relative Lattice Energies

Arrange these ionic compounds in order of increasing *magnitude* of lattice energy: CaO, KBr, KCl, SrO.

SOLUTION

KBr and KCl should have lattice energies of smaller magnitude than CaO and SrO because of their lower ionic charges (1+, 1− compared to 2+, 2−.) When you compare KBr and KCl, you expect KBr to have a lattice energy of lower magnitude due to the larger ionic radius of the bromide ion relative to the chloride ion. Between CaO and SrO, you expect SrO to have a lattice energy of lower magnitude due to the larger ionic radius of the strontium ion relative to the calcium ion.

Order of increasing *magnitude* of lattice energy:

KBr < KCl < SrO < CaO

Actual lattice energy values:

Compound	Lattice Energy (kJ/mol)
KBr	−671
KCl	−701
SrO	−3217
CaO	−3414

FOR PRACTICE 9.2

Arrange the following in order of increasing magnitude of lattice energy: LiBr, KI, and CaO.

FOR MORE PRACTICE 9.2

Which compound has a lattice energy of higher magnitude, NaCl or $MgCl_2$?

Ionic Bonding: Models and Reality

In this section, we have developed a model for ionic bonding. The value of a model is in how well it accounts for what we see in nature (through experiments). Does our ionic bonding model explain the properties of ionic compounds, including their high melting and boiling points, their tendency *not to conduct* electricity as solids, and their tendency *to conduct* electricity when dissolved in water?

We modeled an ionic solid as a lattice of individual ions held together by coulombic forces that are *nondirectional* (which means that, as you move away from the center of an ion, the forces are equally strong in all directions). To melt the solid, these forces must be overcome, which requires a significant amount of heat. Therefore, our model accounts for the high melting points of ionic solids. In the model, electrons are transferred from the metal to the nonmetal, but the transferred electrons remain localized on one atom. In other words, our model does not include any free electrons that might conduct electricity

▶ The melting of solid ionic compounds such as sodium chloride requires enough heat to overcome the electrical forces holding the anions and cations together in a lattice. Thus, the melting points of ionic compounds are relatively high.

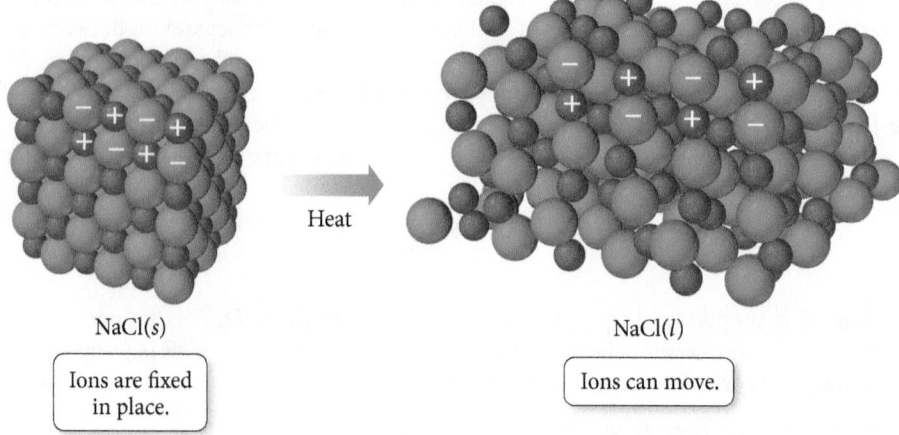

NaCl(*s*)

Ions are fixed
in place.

Heat

NaCl(*l*)

Ions can move.

(the movement or flow of electrons or other charged particles in response to an electric potential, or voltage, is electrical current). In addition, the ions themselves are fixed in place; therefore, our model accounts for the nonconductivity of ionic solids. When our idealized ionic solid dissolves in water, however, the cations and anions dissociate, forming free ions in solution. These ions can move in response to electrical forces, creating an electrical current. Thus, our model predicts that solutions of ionic compounds conduct electricity (which in fact they do).

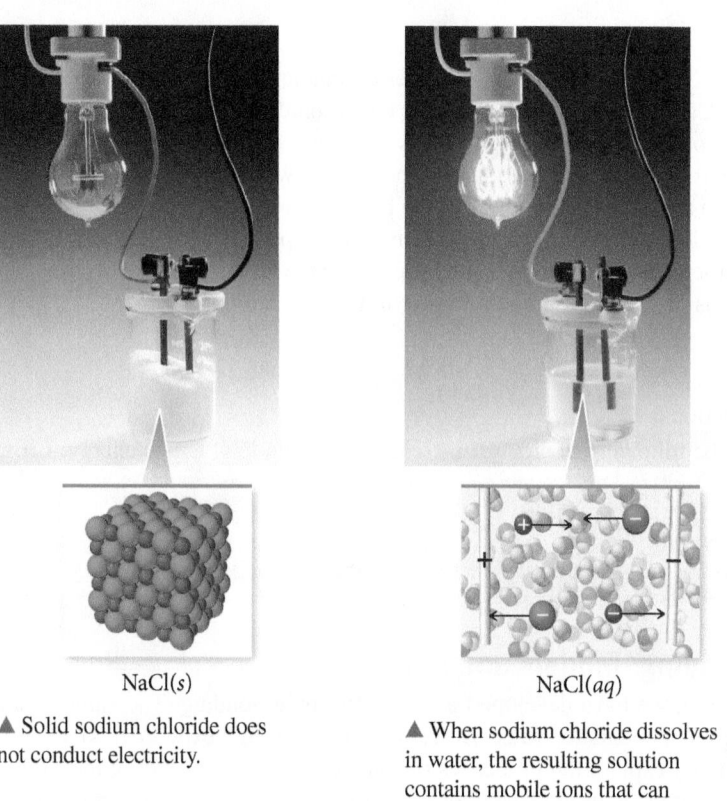

NaCl(*s*)

▲ Solid sodium chloride does not conduct electricity.

NaCl(*aq*)

▲ When sodium chloride dissolves in water, the resulting solution contains mobile ions that can create an electric current.

Conceptual Connection 9.1 Melting Points of Ionic Solids

Use the ionic bonding model to determine which has the higher melting point, NaCl or MgO. Explain the relative ordering.

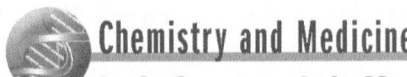

Chemistry and Medicine

Ionic Compounds in Medicine

Although most drugs are molecular compounds, a number of ionic compounds have medical uses. Consider the following partial list of ionic compounds used in medicine. Notice that many of these compounds contain polyatomic ions. The bonding between a metal and a polyatomic ion is ionic. However, the bonding within a polyatomic ion is covalent, the topic of our next section.

Formula	Name	Medical Use
$AgNO_3$	Silver nitrate	Topical anti-infective agent; in solution, used to treat and prevent eye infection, especially in newborn infants
$BaSO_4$	Barium sulfate	Given as a contrast medium—or image enhancer—in X-rays
$CaSO_4$	Calcium sulfate	Used to make plaster casts
$KMnO_4$	Potassium permanganate	Topical anti-infective agent; often used to treat fungal infections on the feet
KI	Potassium iodide	Antiseptic and disinfectant; given orally to prevent radiation sickness
Li_2CO_3	Lithium carbonate	Used to treat bipolar (manic–depressive) disorders
$MgSO_4$	Magnesium sulfate	Used to treat eclampsia (a condition that can occur during pregnancy in which elevated blood pressure leads to convulsions)
$Mg(OH)_2$	Magnesium hydroxide	Antacid and mild laxative
$NaHCO_3$	Sodium bicarbonate	Oral antacid used to treat heartburn and acid stomach; injected into blood to treat severe acidosis (acidification of the blood)
NaF	Sodium fluoride	Used to strengthen teeth
ZnO	Zinc oxide	Used as protection from ultraviolet light in sun

9.5 Covalent Bonding: Lewis Structures

The Lewis model provides us with a simple and useful model for covalent bonding. In this model, we represent molecular compounds with a *Lewis structure*, which depicts neighboring atoms as sharing some (or all) of their valence electrons in order to attain octets (or duets for hydrogen).

Single Covalent Bonds

To see how covalent bonding is conceived in terms of the Lewis model, consider hydrogen and oxygen, which have the following Lewis symbols:

$$\text{H}\cdot \qquad \cdot\ddot{\ddot{\text{O}}}\colon$$

In water, these atoms share their unpaired valence electrons so that each hydrogen atom gets a duet and the oxygen atom gets an octet as represented with this Lewis structure:

$$\text{H}\colon\!\ddot{\ddot{\text{O}}}\!\colon\text{H}$$

The shared electrons—those that appear in the space between the two atoms—count toward the octets (or duets) of *both of the atoms*.

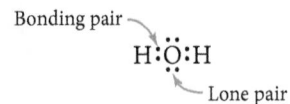

A shared pair of electrons is called a **bonding pair**, while a pair that is associated with only one atom—and therefore not involved in bonding—is called a **lone pair**. Lone pair electrons are also called **nonbonding electrons**.

Bonding pair $\rightharpoonup$

$$\text{H}\colon\!\ddot{\ddot{\text{O}}}\!\colon\text{H}$$

$\rightharpoonup$ Lone pair

We often represent a bonding pair of electrons by a dash to emphasize that it constitutes a chemical bond.

$$H - \overset{..}{\underset{..}{O}} - H$$

The Lewis model also shows why the halogens form diatomic molecules. Consider the Lewis symbol for chlorine:

$$:\overset{..}{\underset{..}{Cl}}\cdot$$

If two Cl atoms pair together, they can each get an octet:

$$:\overset{..}{\underset{..}{Cl}}:\overset{..}{\underset{..}{Cl}}: \quad or \quad :\overset{..}{\underset{..}{Cl}} - \overset{..}{\underset{..}{Cl}}:$$

Elemental chlorine does indeed exist as a diatomic molecule in nature, just as the Lewis model predicts. The same is true for the other halogens.

Similarly, the Lewis model predicts that hydrogen, which has the Lewis symbol

$$H\cdot$$

should exist as H_2. When two hydrogen atoms share their valence electrons, each gets a duet, a stable configuration for hydrogen.

$$H:H \quad or \quad H - H$$

Again, the Lewis model is correct. In nature, elemental hydrogen exists as H_2 molecules.

Double and Triple Covalent Bonds

In the Lewis model, two atoms may share more than one electron pair to get octets. For example, if we pair two oxygen atoms together, they share two electron pairs in order for each oxygen atom to have an octet.

$$\cdot\overset{..}{O}: + \cdot\overset{..}{O}:$$
$$\downarrow$$

Keep in mind that one dash always stands for *two* electrons (a single bonding pair).

$$:\overset{..}{O}::\overset{..}{O}: \quad or \quad :\overset{..}{O} = \overset{..}{O}: \qquad \text{Octet} \overset{\frown}{\quad} \boxed{:O::O:} \overset{\frown}{\quad} \text{Octet}$$

Each oxygen atom now has an octet because *the additional bonding pair counts toward the octet of both oxygen atoms*. When two electron pairs are shared between two atoms, the resulting bond is a **double bond**. In general, double bonds are shorter and stronger than single bonds. Atoms can also share three electron pairs. Consider the Lewis structure of N_2. Since each N atom has five valence electrons, the Lewis structure for N_2 has 10 electrons. Both nitrogen atoms attain octets by sharing three electron pairs:

We will explore the characteristics of multiple bonds more fully in Section 9.10.

$$:N:::N: \quad or \quad :N \equiv N:$$

The bond is a **triple bond**. Triple bonds are even shorter and stronger than double bonds. When we examine nitrogen in nature, we find that it exists as a diatomic molecule with a very strong bond between the two nitrogen atoms. The bond is so strong that it is difficult to break, making N_2 a relatively unreactive molecule.

Covalent Bonding: Models and Reality

The Lewis model predicts the properties of molecular compounds in many ways. First, it accounts for why particular combinations of atoms form molecules and others do not. For example, why is water H_2O and not H_3O? We can write a good Lewis structure for H_2O, but not for H_3O.

$$H - \overset{..}{\underset{..}{O}} - H \qquad\qquad H - \overset{\overset{\displaystyle H}{|}}{\underset{..}{O}} - H$$

Oxygen has nine electrons (one electron beyond an octet)

In this way, the Lewis model predicts that H_2O should be stable, while H_3O should not be, and that is in fact the case. However, if we remove an electron from H_3O, we get H_3O^+, which should be stable (according to the Lewis model) because, when we remove the extra electron, oxygen gets an octet.

$$\left[\begin{array}{c} H \\ | \\ H-\underset{\cdot\cdot}{O}-H \end{array}\right]^+$$

This ion, called the hydronium ion, is in fact stable in aqueous solutions (see Section 4.8). The Lewis model predicts other possible combinations for hydrogen and oxygen as well. For example, we can write a Lewis structure for H_2O_2 as follows:

$$H-\underset{\cdot\cdot}{\overset{\cdot\cdot}{O}}-\underset{\cdot\cdot}{\overset{\cdot\cdot}{O}}-H$$

Indeed, H_2O_2, or hydrogen peroxide, exists and is often used as a disinfectant and a bleach.

The Lewis model also accounts for why covalent bonds are highly *directional*. The attraction between two covalently bonded atoms is due to the sharing of one or more electron pairs in the space between them. Thus, each bond links just one specific pair of atoms—*in contrast to ionic bonds, which are nondirectional and hold together an entire array of ions.* As a result, the fundamental units of covalently bonded compounds are individual molecules. These molecules can interact with one another in a number of different ways that we cover in Chapter 11. However, in covalently bonded molecular compounds the interactions *between* molecules (intermolecular forces) are generally much weaker than the bonding interactions within a molecule (intramolecular forces), as shown in Figure 9.5 ▼. When a molecular compound melts or boils, the molecules themselves remain intact—only the relatively weak interactions between molecules must be overcome. Consequently, molecular compounds tend to have lower melting and boiling points than ionic compounds.

Molecular Compound

Strong covalent bonds *within* molecules

Weaker intermolecular forces *between* molecules

▲ FIGURE 9.5 **Intermolecular and Intramolecular Forces** The covalent bonds between atoms of a molecule are much stronger than the interactions between molecules. To boil a molecular substance, you simply have to overcome the relatively weak intermolecular forces, so molecular compounds generally have low boiling points.

Conceptual Connection 9.2 **Energy and the Octet Rule**

What is wrong with the following statement? *Atoms form bonds in order to satisfy the octet rule.*

9.6 Electronegativity and Bond Polarity

We know from Chapter 7 that representing electrons with dots, as we do in the Lewis model, is a drastic oversimplification. As we have already discussed, this does not invalidate the Lewis model—which is an extremely useful theory—but we must recognize and compensate for its inherent limitations. One limitation of representing electrons as dots, and covalent bonds as two dots shared between two atoms, is that the shared electrons always appear to be *equally* shared. Such is not the case. For example, consider the Lewis structure of hydrogen fluoride:

$$H:\ddot{\ddot{F}}:$$

The two shared electron dots sitting between the H and the F atoms appear to be equally shared between hydrogen and fluorine. However, based on laboratory measurements, we know they are not. When HF is put in an electric field, the molecules orient as shown in Figure 9.6 ▼. From this observation, we know that the hydrogen side of the molecule must have a slight positive charge and the fluorine side of the molecule must have a slight negative charge. We represent this partial separation of charge as follows:

$$\overset{+\longrightarrow}{H-F} \quad or \quad \overset{\delta^+ \quad \delta^-}{H-F}$$

The red arrow on the left, with a positive sign on the tail, indicates that the left side of the molecule has a partial positive charge and that the right side of the molecule (the side the arrow is pointing *toward*) has a partial negative charge. Similarly, the $\delta+$ (delta plus) represents a partial positive charge and the $\delta-$ (delta minus) represents a partial negative charge. Does this make the bond ionic? No. In an ionic bond, the electron is essentially *transferred* from one atom to another. In HF, the electron is *unequally shared*. In other words, even though the Lewis structure of HF portrays the bonding electrons as residing *between* the two atoms, in reality the electron density is greater on the fluorine atom than on the hydrogen atom (Figure 9.7 ▼). The bond is said to be *polar*—having a positive pole and a negative pole. A **polar covalent bond** is intermediate in nature between a pure covalent bond and an ionic bond. In fact, the categories of pure covalent and ionic are really two extremes within a broad continuum. Most covalent bonds between dissimilar atoms are actually *polar covalent*, somewhere between the two extremes.

▶ **FIGURE 9.6 Orientation of Gaseous Hydrogen Fluoride in an Electric Field** Because one side of the HF molecule has a slight positive charge and the other side a slight negative charge, the molecules align themselves with an external electric field.

HF molecules align with an electric field.

○H ○F

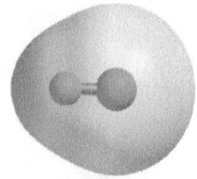

▲ **FIGURE 9.7 Electrostatic Potential Map for the HF Molecule** The F end of the molecule, with its partial negative charge, is yellow/pink; the H end, with its partial positive charge, is blue.

Electronegativity

The ability of an atom to attract electrons to itself in a chemical bond (which results in polar and ionic bonds) is called **electronegativity**. We say that fluorine is more *electronegative* than hydrogen because it takes a greater share of the electron density in HF.

Electronegativity was quantified by the American chemist Linus Pauling in his classic book, *The Nature of the Chemical Bond*. Pauling compared the bond energy—the energy required to break a bond—of a heteronuclear diatomic molecule such as HF with the bond energies of its homonuclear counterparts, in this case H_2 and F_2. The bond energies of H_2 and F_2 are 436 kJ/mol and 155 kJ/mol, respectively. Pauling reasoned that if the HF bond

Trends in Electronegativity

▲ FIGURE 9.8 **Electronegativities of the Elements** Electronegativity generally increases as we move across a row in the periodic table and decreases as we move down a column.

were purely covalent—that is, if the electrons were shared exactly equally—the bond energy of HF should simply be an average of the bond energies of H_2 and F_2, which would be 296 kJ/mol. However, the bond energy of HF is experimentally measured to be 565 kJ/mol. Pauling suggested that the additional bond energy was due to the *ionic character* of the bond. Based on many such comparisons of bond energies, and by arbitrarily assigning an electronegativity of 4.0 to fluorine (the most electronegative element on the periodic table), Pauling developed the electronegativity values shown in Figure 9.8 ▲.

For main-group elements, notice the following periodic trends in electronegativity from Figure 9.8:

- Electronegativity generally increases across a period in the periodic table.
- Electronegativity generally decreases down a column in the periodic table.
- Fluorine is the most electronegative element.
- Francium is the least electronegative element (sometimes called the most *electropositive*).

The periodic trends in electronegativity are consistent with other periodic trends we have seen. In general, electronegativity is inversely related to atomic size—the larger the atom, the less ability it has to attract electrons to itself in a chemical bond.

> We cover the concept of bond energy in more detail in Section 9.10.

> Pauling's "average" bond energy was actually calculated a little bit differently than the normal average shown here. He took the square root of the product of the bond energies of the homonuclear counterparts as the "average."

Conceptual Connection 9.3 **Periodic Trends in Electronegativity**

Arrange these elements in order of decreasing electronegativity: P, Na, N, Al.

Bond Polarity, Dipole Moment, and Percent Ionic Character

The degree of polarity in a chemical bond depends on the electronegativity difference (sometimes abbreviated ΔEN) between the two bonding atoms. The greater the electronegativity difference, the more polar the bond. If two atoms with identical electronegativities form a covalent bond, they share the electrons equally, and the bond is purely covalent or *nonpolar*. For example, the chlorine molecule, composed of two chlorine atoms (which necessarily have identical electronegativities), has a covalent bond in which electrons are evenly shared.

If there is a large electronegativity difference between the two atoms in a bond, such as normally occurs between a metal and a nonmetal, the electron from the metal is almost completely transferred to the nonmetal, and the bond is ionic. For example, sodium and chlorine form an ionic bond.

If there is an intermediate electronegativity difference between the two atoms, such as between two different nonmetals, then the bond is polar covalent. For example, HCl has a polar covalent bond.

While all attempts to divide the bond polarity continuum into specific regions are necessarily arbitrary, it is helpful to classify bonds as covalent, polar covalent, and ionic, based on the electronegativity difference between the bonding atoms as shown in Table 9.1 and Figure 9.9 ▼.

TABLE 9.1 The Effect of Electronegativity Difference on Bond Type

Electronegativity Difference (ΔEN)	Bond Type	Example
Small (0–0.4)	Covalent	Cl_2
Intermediate (0.4–2.0)	Polar covalent	HCl
Large (2.0+)	Ionic	NaCl

▶ FIGURE 9.9 Electronegativity Difference (ΔEN) and Bond Type

We quantify the polarity of a bond by the size of its dipole moment. A **dipole moment** (μ) occurs any time there is a separation of positive and negative charge. The magnitude of a dipole moment created by separating two particles of equal but opposite charges of magnitude q by a distance r is given by the equation:

$$\mu = qr \qquad [9.1]$$

We can get a sense for the dipole moment of a completely ionic bond by calculating the dipole moment that results from separating a proton and an electron ($q = 1.6 \times 10^{-19}$ C) by a distance of $r = 130$ pm (the approximate length of a short chemical bond).

$$\mu = qr$$
$$= (1.6 \times 10^{-19}\text{ C})(130 \times 10^{-12}\text{ m})$$
$$= 2.1 \times 10^{-29}\text{ C} \cdot \text{m}$$
$$= 6.2\text{ D}$$

The debye (D) is the unit commonly used for reporting dipole moments (1 D $= 3.34 \times 10^{-30}$ C·m). Based on this calculation, we would expect the dipole moment of completely ionic bonds with bond lengths close to 130 pm to be about 6 D. The smaller the magnitude of the charge separation, and the smaller the distance between the charges, the smaller the dipole moment. Table 9.2 lists the dipole moments of several molecules along with the electronegativity differences of their atoms.

By comparing the *actual* dipole moment of a bond to what the dipole moment would be if the electron were completely transferred from one atom to the other, we can get a sense of the degree to which the electron is transferred (or the degree to which the bond is ionic). A quantity called the **percent ionic character** is the ratio of a bond's actual dipole moment to the dipole moment it would have if the electron were completely transferred from one atom to the other, multiplied by 100%:

$$\text{Percent ionic character} = \frac{\text{measured dipole moment of bond}}{\text{dipole moment if electron were completely transferred}} \times 100\%$$

For example, suppose a diatomic molecule with a bond length of 130 pm has a dipole moment of 3.5 D. We previously calculated that separating a proton and an electron by 130 pm results in a dipole moment of 6.2 D. Therefore, the percent ionic character of the bond is 56%:

$$\text{Percent ionic character} = \frac{3.5 \text{ D}}{6.2 \text{ D}} \times 100\%$$

$$= 56\%$$

A bond in which an electron is completely transferred from one atom to another would have 100% ionic character (although even the most ionic bonds do not reach this ideal). Figure 9.10 ▼ shows the percent ionic character of a number of diatomic gas-phase molecules plotted against the electronegativity difference between the bonding atoms. As expected, the percent ionic character generally increases as the electronegativity difference increases. However, as we can see, no bond is 100% ionic. In general, bonds with greater than 50% ionic character are referred to as ionic bonds.

TABLE 9.2 Dipole Moments of Several Molecules in the Gas Phase

Molecule	ΔEN	Dipole Moment (D)
Cl_2	0	0
ClF	1.0	0.88
HF	1.9	1.82
LiF	3.0	6.33

◀ **FIGURE 9.10** Percent Ionic Character versus Electronegativity Difference for Some Compounds

EXAMPLE 9.3 Classifying Bonds as Pure Covalent, Polar Covalent, or Ionic

Determine whether the bond formed between each pair of atoms is covalent, polar covalent, or ionic.

(a) Sr and F   **(b)** N and Cl   **(c)** N and O

SOLUTION

(a) In Figure 9.8, find the electronegativity of Sr (1.0) and of F (4.0). The electronegativity difference (ΔEN) is $\Delta EN = 4.0 - 1.0 = 3.0$. Using Table 9.1, classify this bond as ionic.

(b) In Figure 9.8, find the electronegativity of N (3.0) and of Cl (3.0). The electronegativity difference (ΔEN) is $\Delta EN = 3.0 - 3.0 = 0$. Using Table 9.1, classify this bond as covalent.

(c) In Figure 9.8, find the electronegativity of N (3.0) and of O (3.5). The electronegativity difference (ΔEN) is $\Delta EN = 3.5 - 3.0 = 0.5$. Using Table 9.1, classify this bond as polar covalent.

FOR PRACTICE 9.3

Determine whether the bond formed between each pair of atoms is pure covalent, polar covalent, or ionic.

(a) I and I   **(b)** Cs and Br   **(c)** P and O

Conceptual **Connection 9.4   Percent Ionic Character**

The $HCl(g)$ molecule has a bond length of 127 pm and a dipole moment of 1.08 D. Without doing detailed calculations, determine the best estimate for its percent ionic character.

(a) 5%   **(b)** 15%   **(c)** 50%   **(d)** 80%

9.7 Lewis Structures of Molecular Compounds and Polyatomic Ions

We now turn to the basic sequence of steps involved in actually writing Lewis structures for given combinations of atoms.

Writing Lewis Structures for Molecular Compounds

To write a Lewis structure for a molecular compound, follow these steps:

1. **Write the correct skeletal structure for the molecule.** The Lewis structure of a molecule must have the atoms in the correct positions. For example, you could not write a Lewis structure for water if you started with the hydrogen atoms next to each other and the oxygen atom at the end (H H O). In nature, oxygen is the central atom and the hydrogen atoms are *terminal* (at the ends). The correct skeletal structure is H O H. The only way to determine the skeletal structure of a molecule with absolute certainty is to examine its structure experimentally. However, you can write likely skeletal structures by remembering two guidelines. First, *hydrogen atoms are always terminal*. Hydrogen does not ordinarily occur as a central atom because central atoms must form at least two bonds, and hydrogen, which has only a single valence electron to share and requires only a duet, can form just one. Second, *put the more electronegative elements in terminal positions* and the less electronegative elements (other than hydrogen) in the central position. Later in this section, you will learn how to distinguish between competing skeletal structures by applying the concept of formal charge.

2. **Calculate the total number of electrons for the Lewis structure by summing the valence electrons of each atom in the molecule.** Remember that the number of valence

Often, chemical formulas are written in a way that provides clues to how the atoms are bonded together. For example, CH_3OH indicates that three hydrogen atoms and the oxygen atom are bonded to the carbon atom, but the fourth hydrogen atom is bonded to the oxygen atom.

There are a few exceptions to this rule, such as diborane (B_2H_6), which contains *bridging hydrogens*, but these are rare and cannot be adequately addressed by the Lewis model.

electrons for any main-group element is equal to its group number in the periodic table. *If you are writing a Lewis structure for a polyatomic ion, you must consider the charge of the ion when calculating the total number of electrons.* Add one electron for each negative charge and subtract one electron for each positive charge. Don't worry about which electron comes from which atom—only the total number is important.

3. **Distribute the electrons among the atoms, giving octets (or duets in the case of hydrogen) to as many atoms as possible.** Begin by placing two electrons between every two atoms. These represent the minimum number of bonding electrons. Then distribute the remaining electrons as lone pairs, first to terminal atoms, and then to the central atom, giving octets (or duets for hydrogen) to as many atoms as possible.

4. **If any atoms lack an octet, form double or triple bonds as necessary to give them octets.** Do this by moving lone electron pairs from terminal atoms into the bonding region with the central atom.

> Sometimes distributing all the remaining electrons to the central atom results in more than an octet. This is called an expanded octet and is covered in Section 9.9.

The left column that follows contains an abbreviated version of the procedure for writing Lewis structures; the center and right columns contain two examples of applying the procedure.

PROCEDURE FOR... **Writing Lewis Structures for Covalent Compounds**	**EXAMPLE 9.4** **Writing Lewis Structures** Write the Lewis Structure for CO_2.	**EXAMPLE 9.5** **Writing Lewis Structures** Write the Lewis Structure for NH_3.
1. Write the correct skeletal structure for the molecule.	**SOLUTION** Because carbon is the less electronegative atom, put it in the central position. O C O	**SOLUTION** Since hydrogen is always terminal, put nitrogen in the central position. H N H H
2. Calculate the total number of electrons for the Lewis structure by summing the valence electrons of each atom in the molecule.	Total number of electrons for Lewis structure = $\left(\begin{array}{c}\text{number of}\\\text{valence}\\e^- \text{ for C}\end{array}\right) + 2\left(\begin{array}{c}\text{number of}\\\text{valence}\\e^- \text{ for O}\end{array}\right)$ $= 4 + 2(6) = 16$	Total number of electrons for Lewis structure = $\left(\begin{array}{c}\text{number of}\\\text{valence}\\e^- \text{ for N}\end{array}\right) + 3\left(\begin{array}{c}\text{number of}\\\text{valence}\\e^- \text{ for H}\end{array}\right)$ $= 5 + 3(1) = 8$
3. Distribute the electrons among the atoms, giving octets (or duets for hydrogen) to as many atoms as possible. Begin with the bonding electrons, and then proceed to lone pairs on terminal atoms, and finally to lone pairs on the central atom.	Bonding electrons are first. O:C:O (4 of 16 electrons used) Lone pairs on terminal atoms are next. :Ö:C:Ö: (16 of 16 electrons used)	Bonding electrons are first. H:N:H H (6 of 8 electrons used) Lone pairs on terminal atoms are next, but none is needed on hydrogen. Lone pairs on central atom are last. H—N̈—H | H (8 of 8 electrons used)
4. If any atom lacks an octet, form double or triple bonds as necessary to give them octets.	Since carbon lacks an octet, move lone pairs from the oxygen atoms to bonding regions to form double bonds. :Ö:C:Ö: ↓ :O̤=C̈=O̤:	Since all of the atoms have octets (or duets for hydrogen), the Lewis structure for NH_3 is complete as shown in the previous step.
	FOR PRACTICE 9.4 Write the Lewis structure for CO.	**FOR PRACTICE 9.5** Write the Lewis structure for H_2CO.

Writing Lewis Structures for Polyatomic Ions

Write Lewis structures for polyatomic ions by following the same procedure, but pay special attention to the charge of the ion when calculating the number of electrons for the Lewis structure. Add one electron for each negative charge and subtract one electron for each positive charge. The Lewis structure for a polyatomic ion is usually written within brackets with the charge of the ion in the upper right-hand corner, outside the bracket.

EXAMPLE 9.6   Writing Lewis Structures for Polyatomic Ions

Write the Lewis structure for the NH_4^+ ion.

SOLUTION

Begin by writing the skeletal structure. Since hydrogen is always terminal, put the nitrogen atom in the central position.	H H N H H
Calculate the total number of electrons for the Lewis structure by summing the number of valence electrons for each atom and subtracting 1 for the 1+ charge.	Total number of electrons for Lewis structure = (number of valence e⁻ in N) + (number of valence e⁻ in H) − 1 = 5 + 4(1) − 1 = 8 Subtract 1 e⁻ to account for 1⁺ charge of ion.
Place two bonding electrons between every two atoms. Since all of the atoms have complete octets, no double bonds are necessary.	H H:N:H H (8 of 8 electrons used)
Lastly, write the Lewis structure in brackets with the charge of the ion in the upper right-hand corner.	$\left[\begin{array}{c} H \\ | \\ H-N-H \\ | \\ H \end{array}\right]^+$

FOR PRACTICE 9.6
Write the Lewis structure for the hypochlorite ion, ClO⁻.

9.8 Resonance and Formal Charge

We need two additional concepts to write the best possible Lewis structures for a large number of compounds. The concepts are *resonance,* used when two or more valid Lewis structures can be drawn for the same compound, and *formal charge,* an electron book-keeping system that allows us to discriminate between alternative Lewis structures.

Resonance

When writing Lewis structures, we may find that, for some molecules, we can write more than one valid Lewis structure. For example, consider writing a Lewis structure for O_3. The following two Lewis structures, with the double bond on alternate sides, are equally correct:

$$:\ddot{O}=\ddot{O}-\ddot{O}:\quad\quad:\ddot{O}-\ddot{O}=\ddot{O}:$$

In cases such as this—where there are two or more valid Lewis structures for the same molecule—we find that, in nature, the molecule exists as an *average* of the two Lewis structures. Both of the two Lewis structures for O_3 predict that O_3 contains two different bonds (one double bond and one single bond). However, when we experimentally examine the structure of O_3, we find that the bonds in the O_3 molecule are equivalent and each is intermediate in strength and length between a double bond and single bond. We account for this by representing the molecule with both structures, called **resonance structures**, with a double-headed arrow between them:

$$\ddot{\text{:}}\ddot{\text{O}}=\ddot{\text{O}}-\ddot{\ddot{\text{O}}}\text{:} \quad \longleftrightarrow \quad \ddot{\text{:}}\ddot{\ddot{\text{O}}}-\ddot{\text{O}}=\ddot{\text{O}}\text{:}$$

A resonance structure is one of two or more Lewis structures that have the same skeletal formula (the atoms are in the same locations), but different electron arrangements. The actual structure of the molecule is intermediate between the two (or more) resonance structures and is called a **resonance hybrid**. The term *hybrid* comes from breeding and means the offspring of two animals or plants of different varieties or breeds. If we breed a Labrador retriever with a German shepherd, we get a *hybrid* that is intermediate between the two breeds (Figure 9.11(a) ▼). Similarly, the actual structure of a resonance hybrid is intermediate between the two resonance structures (Figure 9.11(b)). The only structure that actually exists is the hybrid structure—the individual resonance structures do not exist and are merely a convenient way to describe the actual structure. Notice that the actual structure of ozone has two equivalent bonds and a bent geometry (we will discuss molecular geometries in Chapter 10).

The concept of resonance is an adaptation of the Lewis model that helps account for the complexity of actual molecules. In the Lewis model, electrons are *localized* either on one atom (lone pair) or between atoms (bonding pair). However, in nature, the electrons in molecules are often *delocalized* over several atoms or bonds. The delocalization of electrons lowers their energy; it stabilizes them (for reasons that are beyond the scope of this book). Resonance depicts two or more structures with the electrons in different places in an attempt to more accurately reflect the delocalization of electrons. In the real hybrid structure, an average between the resonance structures, the electrons are more spread out (or delocalized) than in any of the resonance structures. The resulting stabilization of the electrons (that is, the lowering of their potential energy due to delocalization) is sometimes called *resonance stabilization*. Resonance stabilization makes an important contribution to the stability of many molecules.

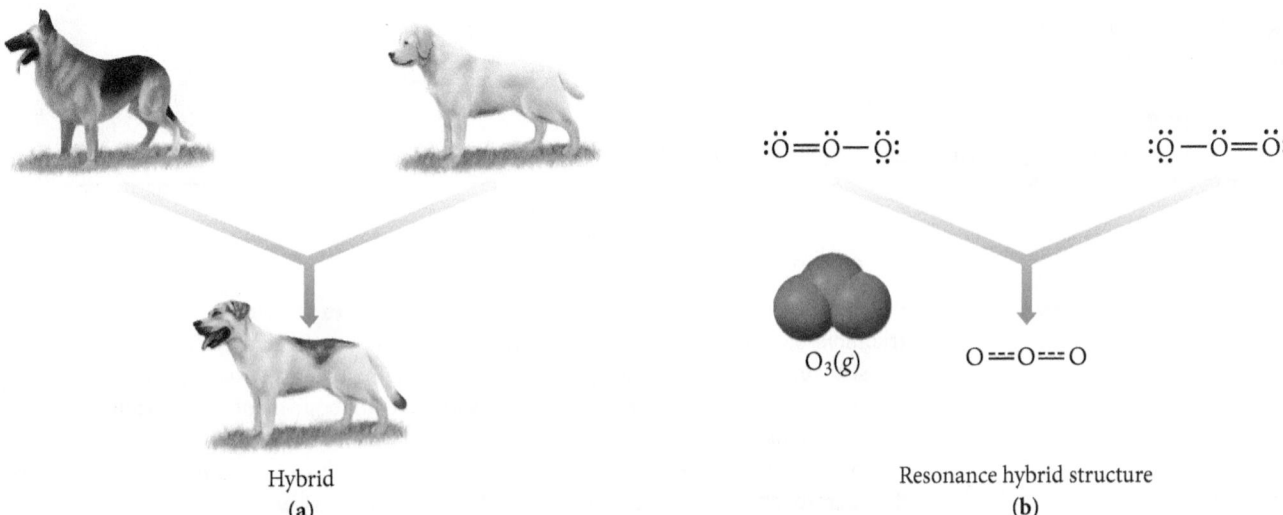

Hybrid
(a)

Resonance hybrid structure
(b)

▲ **FIGURE 9.11 Hybridization**   Just as the offspring of two different dog breeds is a hybrid that is intermediate between the two breeds (a), the structure of a resonance hybrid is intermediate between that of the contributing resonance structures (b).

EXAMPLE 9.7   Writing Resonance Structures

Write a Lewis structure for the NO_3^- ion. Include resonance structures.

SOLUTION

Begin by writing the skeletal structure. Since nitrogen is the least electronegative atom, put it in the central position.	O O N O
Calculate the total number of electrons for the Lewis structure by summing the number of valence electrons for each atom and adding 1 for the 1− charge.	Total number of electrons for Lewis structure = (number of valence e⁻ in N) + 3 (number of valence e⁻ in O) + 1 = 5 + 3(6) + 1 = 24 Add 1 e⁻ to account for 1− charge of ion.
Place two bonding electrons between each pair of atoms.	O O:N̈:O (6 of 24 electrons used)
Distribute the remaining electrons, first to terminal atoms. There are not enough electrons to complete the octet on the central atom.	:Ö: :Ö:N:Ö: (24 of 24 electrons used)
Form a double bond by moving a lone pair from one of the oxygen atoms into the bonding region with nitrogen. Enclose the structure in brackets and include the charge.	$\left[\begin{array}{c} :\ddot{O}: \\ :\ddot{O}:N::\ddot{O}: \end{array}\right]^-$ *or* $\left[\begin{array}{c} :\ddot{O}: \\ \| \\ :\ddot{O}-N=\ddot{O}: \end{array}\right]^-$
Since the double bond can form equally well with any of the three oxygen atoms, write all three structures as resonance structures. (The actual space filling model of NO_3^- is shown here for comparison. Note that all three bonds are equal in length.)	$\left[\begin{array}{c} :\ddot{O}: \\ \| \\ :\ddot{O}-N=\ddot{O}: \end{array}\right]^- \longleftrightarrow \left[\begin{array}{c} :O: \\ \| \\ :\ddot{O}-N-\ddot{O}: \end{array}\right]^- \longleftrightarrow \left[\begin{array}{c} :\ddot{O}: \\ \| \\ :\ddot{O}=N-\ddot{O}: \end{array}\right]^-$ NO_3-

FOR PRACTICE 9.7

Write a Lewis structure for the NO_2^- ion. Include resonance structures.

In the examples of resonance hybrids that we have examined so far, the contributing structures have been equivalent (or equally valid) Lewis structures. In these cases, the true structure is an equally weighted average of the resonance structures. In some cases, however, we can write resonance structures that are not equivalent. For reasons we cover in the material that follows—such as formal charge—one possible resonance structure may be somewhat better than another. In such cases, the true structure is still an average of the resonance structures, but the better resonance structure contributes more to the true structure. In other words, multiple nonequivalent resonance structures may be weighted differently in their contributions to the true overall structure of a molecule (see Example 9.8).

Formal Charge

Formal charge is a fictitious charge assigned to each atom in a Lewis structure that helps us to distinguish among competing Lewis structures. The **formal charge** of an atom in a Lewis structure is *the charge it would have if all bonding electrons were shared equally between the bonded atoms*. In other words, formal charge is the calculated charge for an atom if we completely ignore the effects of electronegativity. For example, we know that because fluorine is more electronegative than hydrogen, HF has a dipole moment— the hydrogen atom has a slight positive charge and the fluorine atom has a slight negative charge. However, the *formal charges* of hydrogen and fluorine in HF (the calculated charges if we ignore their differences in electronegativity) are both zero.

$$H \!:\! \ddot{\ddot{F}}\!:$$

Formal charge = 0   Formal charge = 0

We can calculate the formal charge on any atom as the difference between the number of valence electrons in the atom and the number of electrons that it "owns" in a Lewis structure. An atom in a Lewis structure can be thought of as "owning" all of its nonbonding electrons and one-half of its bonding electrons.

Formal charge = number of valence electrons −

(number of nonbonding electrons + $\frac{1}{2}$ number of bonding electrons)

So the formal charge of hydrogen in HF is 0:

$$\text{Formal charge} = 1 - [0 + \tfrac{1}{2}(2)] = 0$$

Number of valence electrons for H   Number of electrons that H "owns" in the Lewis structure

Similarly, we calculate the formal charge of fluorine in HF as 0:

$$\text{Formal charge} = 7 - [6 + \tfrac{1}{2}(2)] = 0$$

Number of valence electrons for F   Number of electrons that F "owns" in the Lewis structure

The concept of formal charge is useful because it can help us distinguish between competing skeletal structures or competing resonance structures. In general, these four rules apply:

1. The sum of all formal charges in a neutral molecule must be zero.
2. The sum of all formal charges in an ion must equal the charge of the ion.
3. Small (or zero) formal charges on individual atoms are better than large ones.
4. When formal charge cannot be avoided, negative formal charge should reside on the most electronegative atom.

We can use formal charge to determine which of the competing skeletal structures for hydrogen cyanide shown here is best (or most stable). Notice that both skeletal structures satisfy the octet rule equally. The formal charge of each atom in the structure is calculated below it.

	Structure A			Structure B		
	H —	C ≡	N:	H —	N ≡	C:
number of valence e⁻	1	4	5	1	5	4
− number of nonbonding e⁻	−0	−0	−2	−0	−0	−2
− ½ (number of bonding e⁻)	−½(2)	−½(8)	−½(6)	−½(2)	−½(8)	−½(6)
Formal charge	**0**	**0**	**0**	**0**	**+1**	**−1**

As required, the sum of the formal charges for each of these structures is zero (as it always must be for neutral molecules). However, structure B has formal charges on both the N atom and the C atom, while structure A has no formal charges on any atom. Furthermore, in structure B, the negative formal charge is not on the most electronegative element (nitrogen is more electronegative than carbon). Consequently, structure A is the best Lewis structure. Since atoms in the middle of a molecule tend to have more bonding electrons and fewer nonbonding electrons, they also tend to have more positive formal charges. Consequently, the best skeletal structure usually has the least electronegative atom in the central position, as we learned in step 1 of our procedure for writing Lewis structures.

| Both HCN and HNC exist, but—as predicted by formal charge—HCN is more stable than HNC.

EXAMPLE 9.8 Assigning Formal Charges

Assign formal charges to each atom in the resonance forms of the cyanate ion (OCN^-). Which resonance form is likely to contribute most to the correct structure of OCN^-?

A	B	C
$[:\ddot{O}-C\equiv N:]^-$	$[:\ddot{O}=C=\ddot{N}:]^-$	$[:O\equiv C-\ddot{N}:]^-$

SOLUTION

Calculate the formal charge on each atom by finding the number of valence electrons and subtracting the number of nonbonding electrons and one-half the number of bonding electrons.		A $[:\ddot{O}-C\equiv N:]^-$			B $[:\ddot{O}=C=\ddot{N}:]^-$			C $[:O\equiv C-\ddot{N}:]^-$		
	Number of valence e⁻	6	4	5	6	4	5	6	4	5
	−number of nonbonding e⁻	−6	−0	−2	−4	−0	−4	−2	−0	−6
	$-^1/_2$ (number of bond e⁻)	−1	−4	−3	−2	−4	−2	−3	−4	−1
	Formal charge	**−1**	**0**	**0**	**0**	**0**	**−1**	**+1**	**0**	**−2**

The sum of all formal charges for each structure is −1, as it should be for a 1− ion. Structures A and B have the least amount of formal charge and are therefore to be preferred over structure C. Structure A is preferable to B because it has the negative formal charge on the more electronegative atom. You therefore expect structure A to make the biggest contribution to the resonance forms of the cyanate ion.

FOR PRACTICE 9.8

Assign formal charges to each atom in the resonance forms of N_2O. Which resonance form is likely to contribute most to the correct structure of N_2O?

A	B	C
$\ddot{N}=N=\ddot{O}:$	$:N\equiv N-\ddot{O}:$	$:\ddot{N}-N\equiv O:$

FOR MORE PRACTICE 9.8

Assign formal charges to each of the atoms in the nitrate ion (NO_3^-). The Lewis structure for the nitrate ion is shown in Example 9.7.

EXAMPLE 9.9 Drawing Resonance Structures and Assigning Formal Charge for Organic Compounds

Draw the Lewis structure (including resonance structures) for nitromethane (CH_3NO_2). For each resonance structure, assign formal charges to all atoms that have formal charge.

SOLUTION

Begin by writing the skeletal structure. For organic compounds, the condensed structural formula (in this case CH_3NO_2) indicates how the atoms are connected.	$\begin{array}{cccc} H & O & & \\ H & C & N & O \\ H & & & \end{array}$
Calculate the total number of electrons for the Lewis structure by summing the number of valence electrons for each atom.	Total number of electrons for Lewis structure $= (\text{\# valence e}^- \text{ in C}) + 3(\text{\# valence e}^- \text{ in H}) + (\text{\# valence e}^- \text{ in N})$ $+ 2(\text{\# valence e}^- \text{ in O})$ $= 4 + 3(1) + 5 + 2(6)$ $= 24$
Place a dash between each pair of atoms to indicate a bond. Each dash counts for two electrons.	$\begin{array}{ccccc} & H & & O & \\ & \| & & \| & \\ H & - C & - N & - O \\ & \| & & & \\ & H & & & \end{array}$ (12 of 24 electrons used)
Distribute the remaining electrons, first to terminal atoms then to interior atoms.	$\begin{array}{ccccc} & H & & :\ddot{O}: & \\ & \| & & \| & \\ H & - C & - N & - \ddot{O}: \\ & \| & & & \\ & H & & & \end{array}$ (24 of 24 electrons used)
If there are not enough electrons to complete the octets on the interior atoms, form double bonds by moving lone pair electrons from terminal atoms into the bonding region with interior atoms.	$\begin{array}{ccccc} & H & & :\ddot{O} & \\ & \| & & \|\| & \\ H & - C & - N & - \ddot{O}: \\ & \| & & & \\ & H & & & \end{array}$
Draw any necessary resonance structures by moving only electron dots. (In this case, you can form a double bond between the nitrogen atom and the other oxygen atom.)	$\begin{array}{ccc} H \quad :\ddot{O}: & & H \quad :\ddot{O} \\ \| \qquad \| & & \| \qquad \|\| \\ H - C - N = \ddot{O}: & \longleftrightarrow & H - C - N - \ddot{O}: \\ \| & & \| \\ H & & H \end{array}$
Assign formal charges (FC) to each atom. $\text{FC} = \text{\# valence e}^- - (\text{\# nonbonding e}^- + \frac{1}{2}\,\text{\# bonding e}^-)$	$\begin{array}{ccc} H \quad :\ddot{O}:^{-1} & & H \quad :\ddot{O} \\ \| \qquad \|^{+1} & & \| \qquad \|\|^{+1} \\ H - C - N = \ddot{O}: & \longleftrightarrow & H - C - N - \ddot{O}:^{-1} \\ \| & & \| \\ H & & H \end{array}$ Carbon, hydrogen, and the doubly-bonded oxygen atoms have no formal charge. Nitrogen has a +1 formal charge $[5 - \frac{1}{2}(8)]$ and the singly bonded oxygen atom in each resonance structure has a −1 formal charge $[6 - (6 + \frac{1}{2}(2))]$.

FOR PRACTICE 9.9

Draw the Lewis structure (including resonance structures) for diazomethane (CH_2N_2). For each resonance structure, assign formal charges to all atoms that have formal charge.

9.9 Exceptions to the Octet Rule: Odd-Electron Species, Incomplete Octets, and Expanded Octets

The octet rule in the Lewis model has some exceptions, which we examine in this section of the chapter. They include (1) *odd-electron species,* molecules or ions with an odd number of electrons; (2) *incomplete octets,* molecules or ions with *fewer than eight electrons* around an atom; and (3) *expanded octets,* molecules or ions with *more than eight electrons* around an atom.

Odd-Electron Species

Molecules and ions with an odd number of electrons in their Lewis structures are called **free radicals** (or simply *radicals*). For example, nitrogen monoxide—a pollutant found in motor vehicle exhaust—has 11 electrons. If we try to write a Lewis structure for nitrogen monoxide, we can't achieve octets for both atoms:

$$:\overset{\cdot}{N}::\overset{\cdot\cdot}{O}: \qquad or \qquad :\overset{\cdot}{N}=\overset{\cdot\cdot}{O}:$$

> The unpaired electron in nitrogen monoxide is put on the nitrogen rather than the oxygen in order to minimize formal charges.

The nitrogen atom does not have an octet, so this Lewis structure does not satisfy the octet rule. Yet, nitrogen monoxide exists, especially in polluted air. Why? As with any simple theory, the Lewis model is not sophisticated enough to handle every single case. It is impossible to write good Lewis structures for free radicals, nevertheless, some of these molecules exist in nature. Perhaps it is a testament to the Lewis model, however, that *relatively few* such molecules exist and that, in general, they tend to be somewhat unstable and reactive. NO, for example, reacts with oxygen in the air to form NO_2, another odd-electron molecule represented with the following 17-electron resonance structures:

$$:\overset{\cdot\cdot}{O}=\overset{\cdot}{N}-\overset{\cdot\cdot}{\underset{\cdot\cdot}{O}}: \leftrightarrow :\overset{\cdot\cdot}{\underset{\cdot\cdot}{O}}-\overset{\cdot}{N}=\overset{\cdot\cdot}{O}:$$

In turn, NO_2 reacts with water to form nitric acid (a component of acid rain) and also reacts with other atmospheric pollutants to form peroxyacetylnitrate (PAN), an active component of photochemical smog. For free radicals, such as NO and NO_2, we simply write the best Lewis structure that we can.

Conceptual Connection 9.5 Odd-Electron Species

Which molecule would you expect to be a free radical?

(a) CO **(b)** CO_2 **(c)** N_2O **(d)** NO_2

Incomplete Octets

Another significant exception to the octet rule involves those elements that tend to form *incomplete octets.* The most important of these is boron, which forms compounds with only six electrons around B, rather than eight. For example, BF_3 and BH_3 lack an octet for B.

Beryllium compounds, such as BeH_2, also have incomplete octets.

You might be wondering why we don't just form double bonds to increase the number of electrons around B. For BH_3, of course, we can't, because there are no additional electrons to move into the bonding region. For BF_3, however, we could attempt to give B an octet by moving a lone pair from an F atom into the bonding region with B.

$$:\overset{\cdot\cdot}{\underset{\cdot\cdot}{F}}-B=\overset{\overset{\cdot\cdot}{F}}{\|}-:\overset{\cdot\cdot}{\underset{\cdot\cdot}{F}}:$$

Chemistry in the Environment
Free Radicals and the Atmospheric Vacuum Cleaner

Free radicals play a key role in much of the chemistry of the atmosphere. The free radical that is most important to atmospheric reactions is the hydroxyl radical:

$$:\ddot{O}-H$$

NO$_2$(g)

▲ NO$_2$(g) is a pollutant found in urban air.

Many free radical structures are abbreviated by writing a single dot with the formula. Thus, the hydroxyl radical is often abbreviated as:

$$\cdot OH$$

In the atmosphere, the hydroxyl radical forms when excited oxygen atoms—formed from the photodecomposition of ozone—react with water vapor.

$$O_3 \xrightarrow{\text{uv light}} O_2 + O^*$$
$$O^* + H_2O \longrightarrow 2 \cdot OH$$

The * next to the O indicates that the oxygen atom has excess energy.

The resulting hydroxyl radical reacts with a wide variety of molecules from both natural sources and from air pollution that are present in the atmosphere. For example, the hydroxyl radical reacts with carbon monoxide, an atmospheric pollutant that we first encountered in Chapter 1, in the following two-step process:

$$CO + \cdot OH \longrightarrow HOCO \cdot$$
$$HOCO \cdot + O_2 \longrightarrow CO_2 + HOO \cdot$$

We can see from this reaction that the hydroxyl radical converts toxic CO into relatively nontoxic CO$_2$.

The HOO · free radical generated by the second reaction is converted back into the hydroxyl radical when it reacts with other atmospheric substances, and the process repeats itself. Therefore, a single hydroxyl radical can convert a lot of CO into CO$_2$.

Do you ever wonder what happens to the hydrocarbons you accidentally spill when filling your car's gas tank or to the natural gas that is released into the atmosphere as you light your kitchen stove? Hydrocarbons released into the atmosphere are converted to CO$_2$ and H$_2$O in a series of steps initiated by the hydroxyl free radical. Consider the following representative reaction of methane, the main hydrocarbon in natural gas:

$$CH_4 + 5\,O_2 + NO\cdot + 2\cdot OH \xrightarrow{\text{UV light}}$$
$$CO_2 + H_2O + NO_2\cdot + 4\,HOO\cdot$$

Notice the similarity between this reaction and the direct combustion (or burning) of methane:

$$CH_4 + 2\,O_2 \longrightarrow CO_2 + 2\,H_2O$$

As you can see, the free radical reaction initiates a slow "burning" of CH$_4$ in a series of steps that produce carbon dioxide and water and some additional free radicals. The hydroxyl radical initiates similar reactions with other pollutants as well as undesirable naturally occurring atmospheric gases. Without the hydroxyl free radical—sometimes called *the atmospheric vacuum cleaner*—our atmosphere would be a much dirtier place.

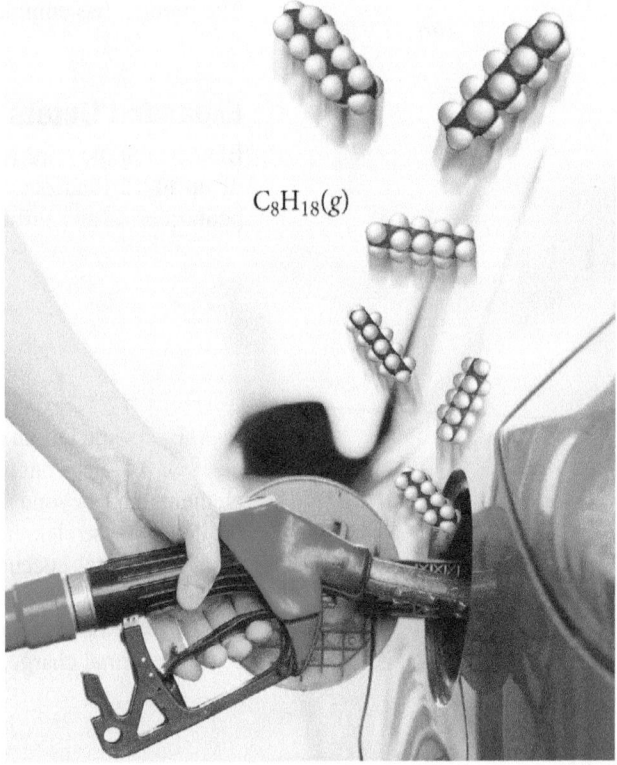

C$_8$H$_{18}$(g)

▲ Hydrocarbons such as octane evaporate into the atmosphere when a motor vehicle is fueled. What happens to them?

Question
Draw the best possible Lewis structures for the free radicals important in atmospheric chemistry: NO, NO$_2$, HOO, OH, CH$_3$.

This Lewis structure has octets for all atoms, including boron. However, when we assign formal charges to this structure, we get a negative formal charge on B and a positive formal charge on F:

$$_0 :\ddot{F}-\overset{\overset{+1 \ddot{F}:}{\|}}{\underset{-1}{B}}-\ddot{F}:^0$$

The positive formal charge on fluorine—the most electronegative element in the periodic table—makes this an unfavorable structure. This leaves us with some questions. Do we complete the octet on B at the expense of giving fluorine a positive formal charge? Or do we leave B without an octet in order to avoid the positive formal charge on fluorine? The answers to these kinds of questions are not always clear because we are pushing the limits of the Lewis model. In the case of boron, we usually accept the incomplete octet as the better Lewis structure. However, doing so does not rule out the possibility that the doubly bonded Lewis structure might be a minor contributing resonance structure. The ultimate answers to these kinds of questions must be determined from experiments. Experimental measurements of the B—F bond length in BF_3 suggest that the bond may be slightly shorter than expected for a single B—F bond, indicating that it may indeed have a small amount of double-bond character.

BF_3 can complete its octet in another way—via a chemical reaction. The Lewis model predicts that BF_3 might react in ways that would complete its octet, and indeed it does. For example, BF_3 reacts with NH_3 as follows:

When nitrogen bonds to boron, the nitrogen atom provides both of the electrons. This kind of bond is called a *coordinate covalent bond*, which we will discuss in Chapter 24.

$$\ddot{F}-B-\ddot{F}: + H-\ddot{N}-H \longrightarrow \ddot{F}-B-N-H$$

The product has complete octets for all atoms in the structure.

Expanded Octets

Elements in the third row of the periodic table and beyond often exhibit *expanded octets* of up to 12 (and occasionally 14) electrons. Consider the Lewis structures of arsenic pentafluoride and sulfur hexafluoride.

In AsF_5 arsenic has an expanded octet of 10 electrons, and in SF_6 sulfur has an expanded octet of 12 electrons. Both of these compounds exist and are stable. In third-period elements and beyond, 10 and 12-electron expanded octets are common because the d orbitals in these elements are energetically accessible (they are not much higher in energy than the orbitals occupied by the valence electrons) and can accommodate the extra electrons (see Section 8.3). Expanded octets *never* occur in second-period elements.

In some Lewis structures, we must decide whether or not to expand an octet in order to lower formal charge. For example, consider the Lewis structure of H_2SO_4:

Notice that both of the oxygen atoms have a -1 formal charge and that sulfur has a $+2$ formal charge. While this amount of formal charge is acceptable, especially since the negative formal charge resides on the more electronegative atom, it is possible to eliminate the formal charge by expanding the octet on sulfur:

$$
\begin{array}{c}
\text{H} \\
| \\
\text{:O:} \\
| \\
\text{:O}\!\!=\!\!\text{S}\!\!-\!\!\text{O}\!\!-\!\!\text{H} \\
\| \\
\text{:O:}
\end{array}
$$

Which of these two Lewis structures for H_2SO_4 is better? Again, the answer is not straightforward. Experiments show that the sulfur–oxygen bond lengths in the two sulfur–oxygen bonds without the hydrogen atoms are shorter than expected for sulfur–oxygen single bonds, indicating that the double-bonded Lewis structure plays an important role in describing the bonding in H_2SO_4. In general, we expand octets in third-row (or beyond) elements in order to lower formal charge. However, we should *never* expand the octets of second-row elements. Second-row elements do not have energetically accessible *d* orbitals and therefore never exhibit expanded octets.

EXAMPLE 9.10 Writing Lewis Structures for Compounds Having Expanded Octets

Write the Lewis structure for XeF_2.

SOLUTION

Begin by writing the skeletal structure. Since xenon is the less electronegative atom, put it in the central position.	F Xe F
Calculate the total number of electrons for the Lewis structure by summing the number of valence electrons for each atom.	Total number of electrons for Lewis structure = (number of valence e⁻ in Xe) + 2(number of valence e⁻ in F) = 8 + 2(7) = 22
Place two bonding electrons between the atoms of each pair of atoms.	F:Xe:F (4 of 22 electrons used)
Distribute the remaining electrons to give octets to as many atoms as possible, beginning with terminal atoms and finishing with the central atom. Arrange additional electrons around the central atom, giving it an expanded octet of up to 12 electrons.	:F: Xe :F: (16 of 22 electrons used) :F:Xe:F: or :F:—Xe—:F: (22 of 22 electrons used)

FOR PRACTICE 9.10

Write the Lewis structure for XeF_4.

FOR MORE PRACTICE 9.10

Write the Lewis structure for H_3PO_4. If necessary, expand the octet on any appropriate atoms to lower formal charge.

Conceptual Connection 9.6 Expanded Octets

Which molecule could have an expanded octet?

(a) H_2CO_3 **(b)** H_3PO_4 **(c)** HNO_2

9.10 Bond Energies and Bond Lengths

In Chapter 6, we discussed how to calculate the standard enthalpy change for a chemical reaction (ΔH°_{rxn}) from tabulated standard enthalpies of formation. However, sometimes we may not easily find standard enthalpies of formation for all of the reactants and products of a reaction. In such cases, we can use individual *bond energies* to estimate enthalpy changes of reaction. In this section, we examine the concept of bond energy and how we can use bond energies to calculate enthalpy changes of reaction. We also look at average bond lengths for a number of commonly encountered bonds.

Bond Energy

Bond energy is also called bond enthalpy or bond dissociation energy.

The **bond energy** of a chemical bond is the energy required to break 1 mole of the bond in the gas phase. For example, the bond energy of the Cl—Cl bond in Cl_2 is 243 kJ/mol.

$$Cl_2(g) \longrightarrow 2\,Cl(g) \quad \Delta H = 243\ kJ$$

The bond energy of HCl is 431 kJ/mol.

$$HCl(g) \longrightarrow H(g) + Cl(g) \quad \Delta H = 431\ kJ$$

Bond energies are always positive, because it always takes energy to break a bond. We say that the HCl bond is *stronger* than the Cl_2 bond because it requires more energy to break it. In general, compounds with stronger bonds tend to be more chemically stable, and therefore less chemically reactive, than compounds with weaker bonds. The triple bond in N_2 has a bond energy of 946 kJ/mol.

$$N_2(g) \longrightarrow N(g) + N(g) \quad \Delta H = 946\ kJ$$

It is a very strong and stable bond, which explains nitrogen's relative inertness.

The bond energy of a particular bond in a polyatomic molecule is a little more difficult to determine because a particular type of bond can have different bond energies in different molecules. For example, consider the C—H bond. In CH_4, the energy required to break one C—H bond is 438 kJ/mol.

$$H_3C-H(g) \longrightarrow H_3C(g) + H(g) \quad \Delta H = 438\ kJ$$

However, the energy required to break a C—H bond in other molecules varies slightly, as shown here:

$$F_3C-H(g) \longrightarrow F_3C(g) + H(g) \quad \Delta H = 446\ kJ$$

$$Br_3C-H(g) \longrightarrow Br_3C(g) + H(g) \quad \Delta H = 402\ kJ$$

$$Cl_3C-H(g) \longrightarrow Cl_3C(g) + H(g) \quad \Delta H = 401\ kJ$$

We can calculate an *average bond energy* for a chemical bond, which is an average of the bond energies for that bond in a large number of compounds. For the limited number of compounds listed, we calculate an average C—H bond energy of 422 kJ/mol. Table 9.3 lists average bond energies for a number of common chemical bonds averaged over a large number of compounds. Notice that the C—H bond energy listed is 414 kJ/mol, which is not too different from the value we calculated from our limited number of compounds. Notice also that bond energies depend, not only on the kind of atoms involved in the bond, but also on the type of bond: single, double, or triple. In general, for a given pair of atoms, triple bonds are stronger than double bonds, which are, in turn, stronger than single bonds. For example, consider the bond energies of carbon–carbon triple, double, and single bonds listed in Table 9.3 (middle of left column).

TABLE 9.3 Average Bond Energies

Bond	Bond Energy (kJ/mol)	Bond	Bond Energy (kJ/mol)	Bond	Bond Energy (kJ/mol)
H—H	436	N—N	163	Br—F	237
H—C	414	N=N	418	Br—Cl	218
H—N	389	N≡N	946	Br—Br	193
H—O	464	N—O	222	I—Cl	208
H—S	368	N=O	590	I—Br	175
H—F	565	N—F	272	I—I	151
H—Cl	431	N—Cl	200	Si—H	323
H—Br	364	N—Br	243	Si—Si	226
H—I	297	N—I	159	Si—C	301
C—C	347	O—O	142	S—O	265
C=C	611	O=O	498	Si=O	368
C≡C	837	O—F	190	S=O	523
C—N	305	O—Cl	203	Si—Cl	464
C=N	615	O—I	234	S=S	418
C≡N	891	F—F	159	S—F	327
C—O	360	Cl—F	253	S—Cl	253
C=O	736*	Cl—Cl	243	S—Br	218
C≡O	1072			S—S	266
C—Cl	339				

*799 in CO_2.

TABLE 9.4 Average Bond Lengths

Bond	Bond Length (pm)	Bond	Bond Length (pm)	Bond	Bond Length (pm)
H—H	74	C—C	154	N—N	145
H—C	110	C=C	134	N=N	123
H—N	100	C≡C	120	N≡N	110
H—O	97	C—N	147	N—O	136
H—S	132	C=N	128	N=O	120
H—F	92	C≡N	116	O—O	145
H—Cl	127	C—O	143	O=O	121
H—Br	141	C=O	120	F—F	143
H—I	161	C—Cl	178	Cl—Cl	199
				Br—Br	228
				I—I	266

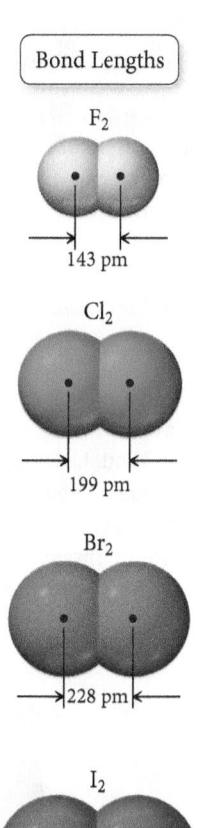

Bond Lengths

F_2

143 pm

Cl_2

199 pm

Br_2

228 pm

I_2

266 pm

▲ Bond lengths in the diatomic halogen molecules.

length of a bond between two particular atoms in a large number of compounds. Like bond energies, bond lengths depend not only on the kind of atoms involved in the bond, but also on the type of bond: single, double, or triple. In general, for a particular pair of atoms, triple bonds are shorter than double bonds, which are in turn shorter than single bonds. For example, consider the bond lengths (shown here with bond strengths) of carbon–carbon triple, double, and single bonds:

Bond	Bond Length (pm)	Bond Strength (kJ/mol)
C≡C	120 pm	837 kJ/mol
C=C	134 pm	611 kJ/mol
C—C	154 pm	347 kJ/mol

Notice that, as the bond gets longer, it also becomes weaker. This relationship between the length of a bond and the strength of a bond does not necessarily hold true for all bonds. Consider the following series of nitrogen–halogen single bonds:

Bond	Bond Length (pm)	Bond Strength (kJ/mol)
N—F	139	272
N—Cl	191	200
N—Br	214	243
N—I	222	159

Although the bonds generally get weaker as they get longer, the trend is not a smooth one.

9.11 Bonding in Metals: The Electron Sea Model

So far, we have developed simple models for bonding between a metal and a nonmetal (ionic bonding) and for bonding between two nonmetals (covalent bonding). We have seen how these models account for and predict the properties of ionic and molecular compounds. The last type of bonding that we examine in this chapter is metallic bonding, which occurs between metals.

As we have already discussed, metals have a tendency to lose electrons, which means that they have relatively low ionization energies. When metal atoms bond together to form a solid, each metal atom donates one or more electrons to an *electron sea.* For example, we can think of sodium metal as an array of positively charged Na^+ ions immersed in a sea of negatively charged electrons (e^-), as shown in Figure 9.13 ▶.

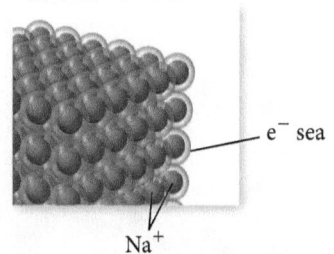

e^- sea

Na^+

▲ FIGURE 9.13 The Electron Sea Model for Sodium In this model of metallic bonding, Na^+ ions are immersed in a "sea" of electrons.

Chemistry in the Environment

The Lewis Structure of Ozone

Ozone is a form of oxygen in which three oxygen atoms bond together. Its Lewis structure consists of the following resonance structures:

$$:\ddot{O}=\ddot{O}-\ddot{O}: \longleftrightarrow :\ddot{O}-\ddot{O}=\ddot{O}:$$

Compare the Lewis structure of ozone to the Lewis structure of O_2:

$$:\ddot{O}=\ddot{O}:$$

Since double bonds are stronger and shorter than single bonds, O_2 must have a stronger bond because it is a double bond. O_3, on the other hand, has bonds that are intermediate between single and double, which are weaker bonds. The effects of this are significant. As we discussed in Section 6.10, O_3 absorbs harmful ultraviolet light entering Earth's atmosphere. Ozone is ideally suited to do this because photons at wavelengths of 280–320 nm (the most harmful components of sunlight) are just strong enough to break the bonds in the O_3 molecule:

$$:\ddot{O}=\ddot{O}-\ddot{O}: + \text{UV light} \longrightarrow :\ddot{O}=\ddot{O}: + \cdot\ddot{O}:$$

In this process, the photon is absorbed. O_2 and O then recombine to re-form O_3, which can in turn absorb more UV light. The same wavelengths of UV light, however, do not have sufficient energy to break the stronger double bond of O_2. No other molecules in our atmosphere can do the job that ozone does. Consequently, we should continue, and even strengthen, the ban on ozone-depleting compounds.

Question

Calculate the average bond energy of one O_3 bond. What wavelength of light has just the right amount of energy to break this bond?

▲ Ozone protects life on Earth from harmful ultraviolet light.

▲ Copper can easily be drawn into fine strands like those used in household electrical cords.

Each sodium atom donates its one valence electron to the "sea" and becomes a sodium ion. The sodium cations are held together by their attraction to the sea of electrons.

Although this model is simple, it accounts for many of the properties of metals. For example, metals conduct electricity because—in contrast to ionic solids, in which electrons are localized on an ion—the electrons in a metal are free to move. The movement or flow of electrons in response to an electric potential (or voltage) is an electric current. Metals are also excellent conductors of heat, again because of the highly mobile electrons, which help to disperse thermal energy throughout the metal.

The electron sea model also accounts for the *malleability* of metals (their capacity to be pounded into sheets) and the *ductility* of metals (their capacity to be drawn into wires). Since there are no localized or specific "bonds" in a metal, we can deform it relatively easily by forcing the metal ions to slide past one another. The electron sea easily accommodates deformations by flowing into the new shape.

CHAPTER IN REVIEW

Self Assessment Quiz

Q1. Which pair of elements is most likely to form an ionic bond?
a) nitrogen and oxygen
b) carbon and hydrogen
c) sulfur and oxygen
d) calcium and oxygen

Q2. Which set of elements is arranged in order of increasing electronegativity?
a) $O < S < As < Ge$
b) $Ge < As < S < O$
c) $S < O < As < Ge$
d) $As < O < Ge < S$

Q3. Which is the correct Lewis structure for magnesium bromide?

a) $2 \, Mg^{2+} \left[:\ddot{Br}: \right]^{-}$

b) $Mg \! :\! \ddot{Br}:$

c) $Mg^{2+} \, 2 \left[:\ddot{Br}: \right]^{-}$

d) $:\ddot{Mg} \! :\! \ddot{Br}:$

Q4. Which compound is likely to have an incomplete octet?
a) NH_3 b) SO_3 c) N_2O d) BH_3

Q5. Which compound has the highest magnitude of lattice energy?
a) MgS   b) CaS   c) SrS   d) BaS

Q6. Which set of compounds is arranged in order of increasing magnitude of lattice energy?
a) $CsI < NaCl < MgS$
b) $NaCl < CsI < MgS$
c) $MgS < NaCl < CsI$
d) $CsI < MgS < NaCl$

Q7. Which pair of atoms forms the most polar bond?
a) N and O   b) C and O
c) C and F   d) N and F

Q8. Which pair of atoms forms a nonpolar covalent bond?
a) C and S   b) C and O
c) B and O   d) Na and Cl

Q9. Which is the correct Lewis structure for nitrogen trifluoride?

a) $:\ddot{F}=\ddot{N}—\ddot{F}:$
    $\overset{|}{:\ddot{F}:}$

b) $:\ddot{F}—N—\ddot{F}:$
    $\overset{|}{:\ddot{F}:}$

c) $:\ddot{F}—\ddot{N}—\ddot{F}:$
    $\overset{|}{:\ddot{F}:}$

d) $:\ddot{F}—\ddot{N}—\ddot{F}—\ddot{F}:$

Q10. Which is the correct Lewis structure for CO_3^{2-}?

a) $\left[\overset{\displaystyle :\ddot{O}}{\underset{}{\overset{\|}{:\ddot{O}=C=\ddot{O}:}}} \right]^{2-}$

b) $\left[\overset{:\ddot{O}}{\underset{:\ddot{O}—C—\ddot{O}:}{\|}} \right]^{2-} \longleftrightarrow \left[\overset{:\ddot{O}:}{\underset{:\ddot{O}=C—\ddot{O}:}{|}} \right]^{2-} \longleftrightarrow \left[\overset{:\ddot{O}:}{\underset{:\ddot{O}—C=\ddot{O}:}{|}} \right]^{2-}$

c) $\left[\overset{:\ddot{O}:}{\underset{:\ddot{O}—C—\ddot{O}:}{|}} \right]^{2-}$

d) $\left[:\ddot{O}—\ddot{C}=\ddot{O}—\ddot{O}: \right]^{2-}$

Q11. Determine the formal charge of nitrogen in this structure.

$$H—\overset{\displaystyle H}{\underset{\displaystyle H}{\overset{|}{\underset{|}{C}}}}—\overset{\displaystyle \ddot{O}:}{\overset{\|}{N}}—\ddot{O}:$$

a) +1   b) +2   c) −1   d) −2

Q12. A Lewis structure for the acetate ion is shown here:

$$\left[H—\overset{\displaystyle H}{\underset{\displaystyle H}{\overset{|}{\underset{|}{C}}}}—\overset{\displaystyle :\ddot{O}}{\overset{\|}{C}}—\ddot{O}: \right]^{-}$$

Which structure is the best resonance structure for the acetate ion?

a) $\left[H—\overset{\displaystyle H}{\underset{\displaystyle H}{\overset{|}{\underset{|}{C}}}}—\ddot{C}—\ddot{O}—\ddot{O}: \right]^{-}$

b) $\left[H—\overset{\displaystyle H}{\underset{\displaystyle H}{\overset{|}{\underset{|}{C}}}}=\overset{:\ddot{O}:}{\overset{}{C}}—\ddot{O}: \right]^{-}$

c) $\left[H—\overset{\displaystyle :\ddot{O}—H}{\underset{\displaystyle H}{\overset{}{\underset{|}{C}}}}—\ddot{C}—\ddot{O}: \right]^{-}$

d) $\left[H—\overset{\displaystyle H}{\underset{\displaystyle H}{\overset{|}{\underset{|}{C}}}}—\overset{:\ddot{O}:}{\overset{|}{C}}=\ddot{O}: \right]^{-}$

Q13. Use formal charge to choose the best Lewis structure for CH_3SOCH_3.

a)

b)

c)

d)

Q14. Use bond energies to determine ΔH_{rxn} for the reaction between ethanol and hydrogen chloride.

$$CH_3CH_2OH(g) + HCl(g) \longrightarrow CH_3CH_2Cl(g) + H_2O(g)$$

a) −1549 kJ
b) 1549 kJ
c) −12 kJ
d) 12 kJ

Q15. Consider the halogenation of ethene, where X is a generic halogen:

$$H_2C = CH_2(g) + X_2(g) \longrightarrow H_2XC - CH_2X(g)$$

Use bond energies to determine which halogen produces the most exothermic halogenation reaction with ethene. The C—F, C—Br, and C—I bond energies are 552 kJ/mol, 280 kJ/mol, and 209 kJ/mol, respectively. Find all other necessary bond energies in Table 9.3.
a) fluorine
b) chlorine
c) bromine
d) iodine

Answers: 1. (d) **2.** (b) **3.** (c) **4.** (d) **5.** (a) **6.** (a) **7.** (c) **8.** (a) **9.** (c) **10.** (b) **11.** (a) **12.** (d) **13.** (b) **14.** (c) **15.** (a)

Key Terms

Section 9.1
Lewis model (382)
Lewis electron-dot structures (Lewis structures) (382)

Section 9.2
ionic bond (382)
covalent bond (383)
metallic bonding (383)

Section 9.3
Lewis symbol (384)
octet (384)
duet (384)
chemical bond (384)
octet rule (384)

Section 9.4
lattice energy (386)
Born–Haber cycle (386)

Section 9.5
bonding pair (391)
lone pair (391)
nonbonding electrons (391)
double bond (392)
triple bond (392)

Section 9.6
polar covalent bond (394)
electronegativity (394)
dipole moment (μ) (397)
percent ionic character (397)

Section 9.8
resonance structures (401)
resonance hybrid (401)
formal charge (403)

Section 9.9
free radical (406)

Section 9.10
bond energy (410)
bond length (412)

Key Concepts

Bonding Models and AIDS Drugs (9.1)

▶ Theories that predict how and why atoms bond together are central to chemistry because they explain compound stability and molecule shape.

▶ Bonding theories have been useful in combating HIV because they help in the design of molecules that bind to the active site of a protein crucial for the development of AIDS.

Types of Chemical Bonds (9.2)

▶ We can divide chemical bonds into three general types: ionic bonds, which occur between a metal and a nonmetal; covalent bonds, which occur between two nonmetals; and metallic bonds, which occur within metals.

▶ In an ionic bond, an electron transfers from the metal to the nonmetal and the resultant ions attract each other by coulombic forces.

- In a covalent bond, nonmetals share electrons that interact with the nuclei of both atoms via coulombic forces, holding the atoms together.
- In a metallic bond, the atoms form a lattice in which each metal loses electrons to an "electron sea." The attraction of the positively charged metal ions to the electron sea holds the metal together.

The Lewis Model and Electron Dots (9.3)

- In the Lewis model, chemical bonds are formed when atoms transfer (ionic bonding) or share (covalent bonding) valence electrons to attain noble gas electron configurations.
- The Lewis model represents valence electrons as dots surrounding the symbol for an element. When two or more elements bond together, the dots are transferred or shared so that every atom gets eight dots, an octet (or two dots, a duet, in the case of hydrogen).

Ionic Lewis Structures and Lattice Energy (9.4)

- In an ionic Lewis structure involving main-group metals, the metal transfers its valence electrons (dots) to the nonmetal.
- The formation of most ionic compounds is exothermic because of lattice energy, the energy released when metal cations and nonmetal anions coalesce to form the solid; the smaller the radius of the ions and the greater their charge, the more exothermic the lattice energy.

Covalent Lewis Structures, Electronegativity, and Polarity (9.5, 9.6, 9.7)

- In a covalent Lewis structure, neighboring atoms share valence electrons to attain octets (or duets).
- A single shared electron pair constitutes a single bond, while two or three shared pairs constitute double or triple bonds, respectively.
- The shared electrons in a covalent bond are not always *equally* shared; when two dissimilar nonmetals form a covalent bond, the electron density is greater on the more electronegative element. The result is a polar bond, with one element carrying a partial positive charge and the other a partial negative charge.
- Electronegativity—the ability of an atom to attract electrons to itself in chemical bonding—increases as we move to the right across a period in the periodic table and decreases as we move down a column.
- Elements with very dissimilar electronegativities form ionic bonds, those with very similar electronegativities form nonpolar covalent bonds, and those with intermediate electronegativity differences form polar covalent bonds.

Resonance and Formal Charge (9.8)

- Some molecules are best represented not by a single Lewis structure, but by two or more resonance structures. The actual structure of these molecules is a resonance hybrid: a combination or average of the contributing structures.
- The formal charge of an atom in a Lewis structure is the charge the atom would have if all bonding electrons were shared equally between bonding atoms.
- In general, the best Lewis structures will have the fewest atoms with formal charge and any negative formal charge will be on the most electronegative atom.

Exceptions to the Octet Rule (9.9)

- Although the octet rule is normally used in drawing Lewis structures, some exceptions occur.
- These exceptions include odd-electron species, which necessarily have Lewis structures with only seven electrons around an atom. Such molecules, called free radicals, tend to be unstable and chemically reactive.
- Other exceptions to the octet rule include molecules with incomplete octets—usually totaling 6 electrons (especially important in compounds containing boron)—and molecules with expanded octets—usually 10 or 12 electrons (which can occur in compounds containing elements from the third row of the periodic table and below). Expanded octets never occur in second-period elements.

Bond Energies and Bond Lengths (9.10)

- The bond energy of a chemical bond is the energy required to break 1 mole of the bond in the gas phase.
- Average bond energies for a number of different bonds are tabulated and can be used to calculate enthalpies of reaction.
- Average bond lengths are also tabulated.
- In general, triple bonds are shorter and stronger than double bonds, which are in turn shorter and stronger than single bonds.

Bonding in Metals (9.11)

- When metal atoms bond together to form a solid, each metal atom donates one or more electrons to an *electron sea*. The metal cations are then held together by their attraction to the sea of electrons.
- The *electron sea* model accounts for the electrical conductivity, thermal conductivity, malleability, and ductility of metals.

Key Equations and Relationships

Dipole Moment (μ): Separation of Two Particles of Equal but Opposite Charges of Magnitude q by a Distance r (9.6)

$$\mu = qr$$

Percent Ionic Character (9.6)

Percent ionic character =

$$\frac{\text{measured dipole moment of bond}}{\text{dipole moment if electron were completely transferred}} \times 100\%$$

Formal Charge (9.8)

Formal charge = number of valence electrons $-$

(number of nonbonding electrons $+ \frac{1}{2}$ number of shared electrons)

Enthalpy Change of a Reaction (ΔH_{rxn}): Relationship of Bond Energies (9.10)

$$\Delta H_{rxn} = \Sigma (\Delta H\text{'s bonds broken}) + \Sigma (\Delta H\text{'s bonds formed})$$

Key Learning Outcomes

Chapter Objectives	Assessment
Predicting Chemical Formulas of an Ionic Compound (9.4)	Example 9.1 For Practice 9.1 Exercises 41–42
Predicting Relative Lattice Energies (9.4)	Example 9.2 For Practice 9.2 For More Practice 9.2 Exercise 46
Classifying Bonds: Pure Covalent, Polar Covalent, or Ionic (9.6)	Example 9.3 For Practice 9.3 Exercises 55–56
Writing Lewis Structures for Covalent Compounds (9.7)	Example 9.4–9.5 For Practice 9.4–9.5 Exercises 51–52
Writing Lewis Structures for Polyatomic Ions (9.7)	Example 9.6 For Practice 9.6 Exercises 59–64
Writing Resonance Lewis Structures (9.8)	Example 9.7 For Practice 9.7 Exercises 63–64
Assigning Formal Charges to Assess Competing Resonance Structures (9.8)	Example 9.8 For Practice 9.8 For More Practice 9.8 Exercises 65–66
Drawing Resonance Structures and Assigning Formal Charge for Organic Compounds (9.8)	Example 9.9 For Practice 9.9 Exercises 69–72
Writing Lewis Structures for Compounds Having Expanded Octets (9.9)	Example 9.9 For Practice 9.9 For More Practice 9.9 Exercises 77–78
Calculating ΔH_{rxn} from Bond Energies (9.10)	Example 9.10 For Practice 9.10 For More Practice 9.10 Exercises 81–83

EXERCISES

Review Questions

1. Why are bonding theories important? Provide some examples of what bonding theories can predict.

2. Why do chemical bonds form? What basic forces are involved in bonding?

3. What are the three basic types of chemical bonds? What happens to electrons in the bonding atoms in each type?

4. How do you determine how many dots to put around the Lewis symbol of an element?

5. Describe the octet rule in the Lewis model.

6. According to the Lewis model, what is a chemical bond?

7. How do you draw an ionic Lewis structure?

8. How can Lewis structures be used to determine the formula of ionic compounds? Give an example.

9. What is lattice energy?

10. Why is the formation of solid sodium chloride from solid sodium and gaseous chlorine exothermic, even though it takes more energy to form the Na^+ ion than the amount of energy released upon formation of Cl^-?

11. What is the Born–Haber cycle? List each of the steps in the cycle and show how the cycle is used to calculate lattice energy.

12. How does lattice energy relate to ionic radii? To ion charge?

13. How does the ionic bonding model explain the relatively high melting points of ionic compounds?

14. How does the ionic bonding model explain the nonconductivity of ionic solids, and at the same time the conductivity of ionic solutions?

15. Within a covalent Lewis structure, what is the difference between lone pair and bonding pair electrons?

16. In what ways are double and triple covalent bonds different from single covalent bonds?

17. How does the Lewis model for covalent bonding account for why certain combinations of atoms are stable while others are not?

18. How does the Lewis model for covalent bonding account for the relatively low melting and boiling points of molecular compounds (compared to ionic compounds)?

19. What is electronegativity? What are the periodic trends in electronegativity?

20. Explain the difference between a pure covalent bond, a polar covalent bond, and an ionic bond.

21. Explain what is meant by the percent ionic character of a bond. Do any bonds have 100% ionic character?

22. What is a dipole moment?

23. What is the magnitude of the dipole moment formed by separating a proton and an electron by 100 pm? 200 pm?

24. What is the basic procedure for writing a covalent Lewis structure?

25. How do you determine the number of electrons that go into the Lewis structure of a molecule? A polyatomic ion?

26. What are resonance structures? What is a resonance hybrid?

27. Do resonance structures always contribute equally to the overall structure of a molecule? Explain.

28. What is formal charge? How is formal charge calculated? How is it helpful?

29. Why does the octet rule have exceptions? Give the three major categories of exceptions and an example of each.

30. What elements can have expanded octets? What elements should never have expanded octets?

31. What is bond energy? How can you use average bond energies to calculate enthalpies of reaction?

32. Explain the difference between endothermic reactions and exothermic reactions with respect to the bond energies of the bonds broken and formed.

33. What is the electron sea model for bonding in metals?

34. How does the electron sea model explain the conductivity of metals? The malleability and ductility of metals?

Problems by Topic

Valence Electrons and Dot Structures

35. Write an electron configuration for N. Then write a Lewis symbol for N and show which electrons from the electron configuration are included in the Lewis symbol.

36. Write an electron configuration for Ne. Then write a Lewis symbol for Ne and show which electrons from the electron configuration are included in the Lewis symbol.

37. Write a Lewis symbol for each atom or ion.
    a. Al   **b.** Na^+ **c.** Cl   **d.** Cl^-

38. Write a Lewis symbol for each atom or ion.
    a. S^{2-} **b.** Mg   **c.** Mg^{2+} **d.** P

Ionic Lewis Symbols and Lattice Energy

39. Write the Lewis symbols that represent the ions in each ionic compound.
    a. NaF   **b.** CaO   **c.** $SrBr_2$ **d.** K_2O

40. Write the Lewis symbols that represent the ions in each ionic compound.
    a. SrO   **b.** Li_2S **c.** CaI_2 **d.** RbF

41. Use Lewis symbols to determine the formula for the compound that forms between each pair of elements.
    a. Sr and Se   **b.** Ba and Cl
    c. Na and S   **d.** Al and O

42. Use Lewis symbols to determine the formula for the compound that forms between each pair of elements:
    a. Ca and N   **b.** Mg and I
    c. Ca and S   **d.** Cs and F

43. Explain the trend in the lattice energies of the alkaline earth metal oxides.

Metal Oxide	Lattice Energy (kJ/mol)
MgO	−3795
CaO	−3414
SrO	−3217
BaO	−3029

44. Rubidium iodide has a lattice energy of −617 kJ/mol, while potassium bromide has a lattice energy of −671 kJ/mol. Why is the lattice energy of potassium bromide more exothermic than the lattice energy of rubidium iodide?

45. The lattice energy of CsF is −744 kJ/mol, whereas that of BaO is −3029 kJ/mol. Explain this large difference in lattice energy.

46. Arrange these compounds in order of increasing magnitude of lattice energy: KCl, SrO, RbBr, CaO.

47. Use the Born–Haber cycle and data from Appendix IIB, and Chapter 8 and this chapter to calculate the lattice energy of KCl. (ΔH_{sub} for potassium is 89.0 kJ/mol.)

48. Use the Born–Haber cycle and data from Appendix IIB and Table 9.3 to calculate the lattice energy of CaO. (ΔH_{sub} for calcium is 178 kJ/mol; IE_1 and IE_2 for calcium are 590 kJ/mol and 1145 kJ/mol, respectively; EA_1 and EA_2 for O are −141 kJ/mol and 744 kJ/mol, respectively.)

Simple Covalent Lewis Structures, Electronegativity, and Bond Polarity

49. Use covalent Lewis structures to explain why each element (or family of elements) occurs as diatomic molecules.
    a. hydrogen   **b.** the halogens
    c. oxygen   **d.** nitrogen

50. Use covalent Lewis structures to explain why the compound that forms between nitrogen and hydrogen has the formula NH_3. Show why NH_2 and NH_4 are not stable.

51. Write the Lewis structure for each molecule.
    a. PH_3 **b.** SCl_2 **c.** HI   **d.** CH_4

52. Write the Lewis structure for each molecule.
    a. NF_3 **b.** HBr   **c.** SBr_2 **d.** CCl_4

53. Write the Lewis structure for each molecule.
    a. SF_2
    b. SiH_4
    c. HCOOH (both O bonded to C)
    d. CH_3SH (C and S central)

54. Write the Lewis structure for each molecule.
  a. CH_2O
  b. C_2Cl_4
  c. CH_3NH_2
  d. $CFCl_3$ (C central)

55. Determine whether a bond between each pair of atoms would be pure covalent, polar covalent, or ionic.
  a. Br and Br
  b. C and Cl
  c. C and S
  d. Sr and O

56. Determine whether a bond between each pair of atoms would be pure covalent, polar covalent, or ionic.
  a. C and N
  b. N and S
  c. K and F
  d. N and N

57. Draw the Lewis structure for CO with an arrow representing the dipole moment. Use Figure 9.10 to estimate the percent ionic character of the CO bond.

58. Draw the Lewis structure for BrF with an arrow representing the dipole moment. Use Figure 9.10 to estimate the percent ionic character of the BrF bond.

Covalent Lewis Structures, Resonance, and Formal Charge

59. Write the Lewis structure for each molecule or ion.
  a. CI_4
  b. N_2O
  c. SiH_4
  d. Cl_2CO

60. Write the Lewis structure for each molecule or ion.
  a. H_3COH
  b. OH^-
  c. BrO^-
  d. O_2^{2-}

61. Write the Lewis structure for each molecule or ion.
  a. N_2H_2
  b. N_2H_4
  c. C_2H_2
  d. C_2H_4

62. Write the Lewis structure for each molecule or ion.
  a. H_3COCH_3
  b. CN^-
  c. NO_2^-
  d. ClO^-

63. Write a Lewis structure that obeys the octet rule for each molecule or ion. Include resonance structures if necessary and assign formal charges to each atom.
  a. SeO_2
  b. CO_3^{2-}
  c. ClO^-
  d. NO_2^-

64. Write a Lewis structure that obeys the octet rule for each ion. Include resonance structures if necessary and assign formal charges to each atom.
  a. ClO_3^-
  b. ClO_4^-
  c. NO_3^-
  d. NH_4^+

65. Use formal charge to determine which Lewis structure is better:

66. Use formal charge to determine which Lewis structure is better:

67. How important is this resonance structure to the overall structure of carbon dioxide? Explain.

68. In N_2O, nitrogen is the central atom and the oxygen atom is terminal. In OF_2, however, oxygen is the central atom. Use formal charges to explain why.

69. Draw the Lewis structure (including resonance structures) for the acetate ion (CH_3COO^-). For each resonance structure, assign formal charges to all atoms that have formal charge.

70. Draw the Lewis structure (including resonance structures) for methyl azide (CH_3N_3). For each resonance structure, assign formal charges to all atoms that have formal charge.

71. What are the formal charges of the atoms shown in red?

72. What are the formal charges of the atoms shown in red?

Odd-Electron Species, Incomplete Octets, and Expanded Octets

73. Write the Lewis structure for each molecule (octet rule not followed).
  a. BCl_3
  b. NO_2
  c. BH_3

74. Write the Lewis structure for each molecule (octet rule not followed).
  a. BBr_3
  b. NO
  c. ClO_2

75. Write the Lewis structure for each ion. Include resonance structures if necessary and assign formal charges to all atoms. If necessary, expand the octet on the central atom to lower formal charge.
  a. PO_4^{3-}
  b. CN^-
  c. SO_3^{2-}
  d. ClO_2^-

76. Write Lewis structures for each molecule or ion. Include resonance structures if necessary and assign formal charges to all atoms. If necessary, expand the octet on the central atom to lower formal charge.
  a. SO_4^{2-}
  b. HSO_4^-
  c. SO_3
  d. BrO_2^-

77. Write Lewis structures for each molecule or ion. Use expanded octets as necessary.
  a. PF_5
  b. I_3^-
  c. SF_4
  d. GeF_4

78. Write Lewis structures for each molecule or ion. Use expanded octets as necessary.
  a. ClF_5
  b. AsF_6^-
  c. Cl_3PO
  d. IF_5

Bond Energies and Bond Lengths

79. Order these compounds in order of increasing carbon–carbon bond strength and in order of decreasing carbon–carbon bond length: HCCH, H_2CCH_2, H_3CCH_3.

80. Which of these compounds has the stronger nitrogen–nitrogen bond? The shorter nitrogen–nitrogen bond?

$$H_2NNH_2, \quad HNNH$$

81. Hydrogenation reactions are used to add hydrogen across double bonds in hydrocarbons and other organic compounds. Use average bond energies to calculate ΔH_{rxn} for the hydrogenation reaction.

$$H_2C{=}CH_2(g) + H_2(g) \longrightarrow H_3C{-}CH_3(g)$$

82. Ethanol is a possible fuel. Use average bond energies to calculate ΔH_{rxn} for the combustion of ethanol.

$$CH_3CH_2OH(g) + 3\ O_2(g) \longrightarrow 2\ CO_2(g) + 3\ H_2O(g)$$

83. Hydrogen, a potential future fuel, can be produced from carbon (from coal) and steam by this reaction:

$$C(s) + 2 H_2O(g) \longrightarrow 2 H_2(g) + CO_2(g)$$

Use average bond energies to calculate ΔH_{rxn} for the reaction.

84. In the *Chemistry and the Environment* box on free radicals in this chapter, we discussed the importance of the hydroxyl radical in reacting with and eliminating many atmospheric pollutants.

However, the hydroxyl radical does not clean up everything. For example, chlorofluorocarbons—which destroy stratospheric ozone—are not attacked by the hydroxyl radical. Consider the hypothetical reaction by which the hydroxyl radical might react with a chlorofluorocarbon:

$$OH(g) + CF_2Cl_2(g) \longrightarrow HOF(g) + CFCl_2(g)$$

Use bond energies to explain why this reaction is improbable.

Cumulative Problems

85. Write an appropriate Lewis structure for each compound. Make certain to distinguish between ionic and molecular compounds.
    a. BI_3 **b.** K_2S **c.** HCFO   **d.** PBr_3

86. Write an appropriate Lewis structure for each compound. Make certain to distinguish between ionic and molecular compounds.
    a. Al_2O_3 **b.** ClF_5 **c.** MgI_2 **d.** XeO_4

87. Each compound contains both ionic and covalent bonds. Write ionic Lewis structures for each of them, including the covalent structure for the ion in brackets. Write resonance structures if necessary.
    a. $BaCO_3$ **b.** $Ca(OH)_2$
    c. KNO_3 **d.** LiIO

88. Each compound contains both ionic and covalent bonds. Write ionic Lewis structures for each of them, including the covalent structure for the ion in brackets. Write resonance structures if necessary.
    a. $RbIO_2$ **b.** NH_4Cl **c.** KOH   **d.** $Sr(CN)_2$

89. Carbon ring structures are common in organic chemistry. Draw a Lewis structure for each carbon ring structure, including any necessary resonance structures.
    a. C_4H_8 **b.** C_4H_4 **c.** C_6H_{12} **d.** C_6H_6

90. Amino acids are the building blocks of proteins. The simplest amino acid is glycine (H_2NCH_2COOH). Draw a Lewis structure for glycine. (Hint: the central atoms in the skeletal structure are nitrogen bonded to carbon, which is bonded to another carbon. The two oxygen atoms are bonded directly to the rightmost carbon atom.)

91. Formic acid is responsible for the sting of ant bites. By mass, formic acid is 26.10% C, 4.38% H, and 69.52% O. The molar mass of formic acid is 46.02 g/mol. Find the molecular formula of formic acid and draw its Lewis structure.

92. Diazomethane is a highly poisonous, explosive compound because it readily evolves N_2. Diazomethane has the following composition by mass: 28.57% C; 4.80% H; and 66.64% N. The molar mass of diazomethane is 42.04 g/mol. Find the molecular formula of diazomethane, draw its Lewis structure, and assign formal charges to each atom. Why is diazomethane not very stable? Explain.

93. The reaction of $Fe_2O_3(s)$ with $Al(s)$ to form $Al_2O_3(s)$ and $Fe(s)$ is called the thermite reaction and is highly exothermic. What role does lattice energy play in the exothermicity of the reaction?

94. NaCl has a lattice energy of -787 kJ/mol. Consider a hypothetical salt XY. X^{3+} has the same radius of Na^+ and Y^{3-} has the same radius as Cl^-. Estimate the lattice energy of XY.

95. Draw the Lewis structure for nitric acid (the hydrogen atom is attached to one of the oxygen atoms). Include all three resonance structures by alternating the double bond among the three oxygen atoms. Use formal charge to determine which of the resonance structures is most important to the structure of nitric acid.

96. Phosgene (Cl_2CO) is a poisonous gas used as a chemical weapon during World War I. It is a potential agent for chemical terrorism today. Draw the Lewis structure of phosgene. Include all three resonance forms by alternating the double bond among the three terminal atoms. Which resonance structure is the best?

97. The cyanate ion (OCN^-) and the fulminate ion (CNO^-) share the same three atoms but have vastly different properties. The cyanate ion is stable, while the fulminate ion is unstable and forms explosive compounds. The resonance structures of the cyanate ion were explored in Example 9.8. Draw Lewis structures for the fulminate ion—including possible resonance forms—and use formal charge to explain why the fulminate ion is less stable (and therefore more reactive) than the cyanate ion.

98. Draw the Lewis structure for each organic compound from its condensed structural formula.
    a. C_3H_8 **b.** CH_3OCH_3
    c. CH_3COCH_3 **d.** CH_3COOH
    e. CH_3CHO

99. Draw the Lewis structure for each organic compound from its condensed structural formula.
    a. C_2H_4 **b.** CH_3NH_2
    c. HCHO   **d.** CH_3CH_2OH
    e. HCOOH

100. Use Lewis structures to explain why Br_3^- and I_3^- are stable, while F_3^- is not.

101. Draw the Lewis structure for $HCSNH_2$. (The carbon and nitrogen atoms are bonded together and the sulfur atom is bonded to the carbon atom.) Label each bond in the molecule as polar or nonpolar.

102. Draw the Lewis structure for urea, H_2NCONH_2, one of the compounds responsible for the smell of urine. (The central carbon atom is bonded to both nitrogen atoms and to the oxygen atom.) Does urea contain polar bonds? Which bond in urea is most polar?

103. Some theories of aging suggest that free radicals cause certain diseases and perhaps aging in general. As you know from the Lewis model, such molecules are not chemically stable and will quickly react with other molecules. According to certain theories, free radicals may attack molecules within the cell, such as DNA, changing them and causing cancer or other diseases. Free radicals may also attack molecules on the surfaces of cells, making them appear foreign to the body's immune system. The immune system then attacks the cells and destroys them, weak-

ening the body. Draw Lewis structures for each free radical implicated in this theory of aging.

a. O_2^-

b. O^-

c. OH

d. CH_3OO (unpaired electron on terminal oxygen)

104. Free radicals are important in many environmentally significant reactions (see the *Chemistry in the Environment* box on free radicals in this chapter). For example, photochemical smog—smog that results from the action of sunlight on air pollutants—forms in part by these two steps:

$$NO_2 \xrightarrow{\text{UV light}} NO + O$$

$$O + O_2 \longrightarrow O_3$$

The product of this reaction, ozone, is a pollutant in the lower atmosphere. (Upper atmospheric ozone is a natural part of the atmosphere that protects life on Earth from ultraviolet light.) Ozone is an eye and lung irritant and also accelerates the weathering of rubber products. Rewrite the given reactions using the Lewis structure of each reactant and product. Identify the free radicals.

105. If hydrogen were used as a fuel, it could be burned according to this reaction:

$$H_2(g) + {}^1/_2 O_2(g) \longrightarrow H_2O(g)$$

Use average bond energies to calculate ΔH_{rxn} for this reaction and also for the combustion of methane (CH_4). Which fuel yields more energy per mole? Per gram?

106. Calculate ΔH_{rxn} for the combustion of octane (C_8H_{18}), a component of gasoline, by using average bond energies and then

calculate it using enthalpies of formation from Appendix IIB. What is the percent difference between your results? Which result would you expect to be more accurate?

107. Draw Lewis structures for each compound.

a. Cl_2O_7 (no Cl—Cl bond)   b. H_3PO_3 (two OH bonds)

c. H_3AsO_4

108. The azide ion, N_3^-, is a symmetrical ion, all of whose contributing resonance structures have formal charges. Draw three important contributing structures for this ion.

109. List the following gas-phase ion pairs in order of the quantity of energy released when they form from separated gas-phase ions. Start with the pair that releases the least energy. Na^+F^-, $Mg^{2+}F^-$, Na^+O^{2-}, $Mg^{2+}O^{2-}$, $Al^{3+}O^{2-}$.

110. Calculate $\Delta H°$ for the reaction $H_2(g) + Br_2(g) \longrightarrow 2\,HBr(g)$ using the bond energy values. The $\Delta H_f°$ of $HBr(g)$ is not equal to one-half of the value calculated. Account for the difference.

111. The heat of atomization is the heat required to convert a molecule in the gas phase into its constituent atoms in the gas phase. The heat of atomization is used to calculate average bond energies. Without using any tabulated bond energies, calculate the average C—Cl bond energy from the following data: the heat of atomization of CH_4 is 1660 kJ/mol and of CH_2Cl_2 is 1495 kJ/mol.

112. Calculate the heat of atomization (see previous problem) of C_2H_3Cl, using the average bond energies in Table 9.3.

113. A compound composed of only carbon and hydrogen is 7.743% hydrogen by mass. Propose a Lewis structure for the compound.

114. A compound composed of only carbon and chlorine is 85.5% chlorine by mass. Propose a Lewis structure for the compound.

Challenge Problems

115. The main component of acid rain (H_2SO_4) forms from SO_2 pollutant in the atmosphere via these steps:

$SO_2 + OH \cdot \longrightarrow HSO_3 \cdot$

$HSO_3 \cdot + O_2 \longrightarrow SO_3 + HOO \cdot$

$SO_3 + H_2O \longrightarrow H_2SO_4$

Draw the Lewis structure for each of the species in these steps and use bond energies and Hess's law to estimate ΔH_{rxn} for the overall process. (Use 265 kJ/mol for the S—O single bond energy.)

116. A 0.167 g sample of an unknown acid requires 27.8 mL of 0.100 M NaOH to titrate to the equivalence point. Elemental analysis of the acid gives the following percentages by mass: 40.00% C, 6.71% H, 53.29% O. Determine the molecular formula, molar mass, and Lewis structure of the unknown acid.

117. Use the dipole moments of HF and HCl (given at the end of the problem) together with the percent ionic character of each bond (Figure 9.10) to estimate the bond length in each molecule. How well does your estimated bond length agree with the bond length in Table 9.4?

$$HCl\ \mu = 1.08\ D$$

$$HF\ \mu = 1.82\ D$$

118. Use average bond energies together with the standard enthalpy of formation of C(g) (718.4 kJ/mol) to estimate the standard enthalpy of formation of gaseous benzene, $C_6H_6(g)$. (Remember that average bond energies apply to the gas phase only.) Compare the value you obtain using average bond energies to the actual standard enthalpy of formation of gaseous benzene, 82.9 kJ/mol. What does the difference between these two values tell you about the stability of benzene?

119. The standard state of phosphorus at 25°C is P_4. This molecule has four equivalent P atoms, no double or triple bonds, and no expanded octets. Draw its Lewis structure.

120. The standard heat of formation of $CaBr_2$ is −675 kJ/mol. The first ionization energy of Ca is 590 kJ/mol and its second ionization energy is 1145 kJ/mol. The heat of sublimation of Ca[Ca(s) $\longrightarrow$ Ca(g)] is 178 kJ/mol. The bond energy of Br_2 is 193 kJ/mol, the heat of vaporization of $Br_2(l)$ is 31 kJ/mol, and the electron affinity of Br is −325 kJ/mol. Calculate the lattice energy of $CaBr_2$.

121. The standard heat of formation of $PI_3(s)$ is −24.7 kJ/mol and the PI bond energy in this molecule is 184 kJ/mol. The standard heat of formation of P(g) is 334 kJ/mol and that of $I_2(g)$ is 62 kJ/mol. The I_2 bond energy is 151 kJ/mol. Calculate the heat of sublimation of $PI_3[PI_3(s) \longrightarrow PI_3(g)]$.

122. A compound has the formula C_8H_8 and does not contain any double or triple bonds. All the carbon atoms are chemically identical and all the hydrogen atoms are chemically identical. Draw the Lewis structure for this molecule.

123. Find the oxidation number of each sulfur in the molecule H_2S_4, which has a linear arrangement of its atoms.

124. Ionic solids of the O^- and O^{3-} anions do not exist, while ionic solids of the O^{2-} anion are common. Explain.

125. The standard state of sulfur is solid rhombic sulfur. Use the appropriate standard heats of formation given in Appendix II to find the average bond energy of the $S=O$ in SO_2.

Conceptual Problems

126. Which statement is true of an endothermic reaction?

  a. Strong bonds break and weak bonds form.

  b. Weak bonds break and strong bonds form.

  c. The bonds that break and those that form are of approximately the same strength.

127. When a firecracker explodes, energy is obviously released. The compounds in the firecracker can be viewed as being "energy rich." What does this mean? Explain the source of the energy in terms of chemical bonds.

128. A fundamental difference between compounds containing ionic bonds and those containing covalent bonds is the existence of molecules. Explain why molecules exist in solid covalent compounds but do not exist in solid ionic compounds.

129. In the very first chapter of this book, we described the scientific approach and put a special emphasis on scientific models or theories. In this chapter, we looked carefully at a model for chemical bonding (the Lewis model). Why is this theory successful? What are some of the limitations of the theory?

Answers to Conceptual Connections

Melting Points of Ionic Solids

9.1 You would expect MgO to have the higher melting point because, in our bonding model, the magnesium and oxygen ions are held together in a crystalline lattice by charges of 2+ for magnesium and 2− for oxygen. In contrast, the NaCl lattice is held together by charges of 1+ for sodium and 1− for chlorine. The experimentally measured melting points of these compounds are 801 °C for NaCl and 2852 °C for MgO, in accordance with our model.

Energy and the Octet Rule

9.2 The reasons that atoms form bonds are complex. One contributing factor is the lowering of their potential energy. The octet rule is just a handy way to predict the combinations of atoms that will have a lower potential energy when they bond together.

Periodic Trends in Electronegativity

9.3 $N > P > Al > Na$

Percent Ionic Character

9.4 (b) You are given that the dipole moment of the HCl bond is about 1 D and that the bond length is 127 pm. Previously we calculated the dipole moment for a 130 pm bond that is 100% ionic to be about 6.2 D. You can therefore estimate the bond's ionic character as $1/6 \times 100$, which is closest to 15%.

Odd-Electron Species

9.5 (d) NO_2 because the sum of the valence electrons of its atoms is an odd number.

Expanded Octets

9.6 (b) The only molecule in this group that could have an expanded octet is H_3PO_4 because phosphorus is a third-period element. Expanded octets *never* occur in second-period elements such as carbon and nitrogen.

Bond Energies and ΔH_{rxn}

9.7 (b) In a highly exothermic reaction, the energy needed to break bonds is less than the energy released when the new bonds form, resulting in a net release of energy.

10 Chemical Bonding II: Molecular Shapes, Valence Bond Theory, and Molecular Orbital Theory

No theory ever solves all the puzzles with which it is confronted at a given time; nor are the solutions already achieved often perfect.

—Thomas Kuhn (1922–1996)

I N CHAPTER 9, WE EXAMINED a simple model for chemical bonding called the Lewis model. We saw how this model helps us to explain and predict the combinations of atoms that form stable molecules. When we combine the Lewis model with the idea that valence electron groups repel one another—the basis of an approach known as VSEPR theory—we can predict the general shape of a molecule from its Lewis structure. We address molecular shapes and their importance in the first part of this chapter. We then move on to explore two additional bonding theories—called valence bond theory and molecular orbital theory—that are progressively more sophisticated, but at the cost of being more complex, than the Lewis model. As you work through this chapter, our second on chemical bonding, keep in mind the importance of this topic. In our universe, elements join together to form compounds, and that makes many things possible, including our own existence.

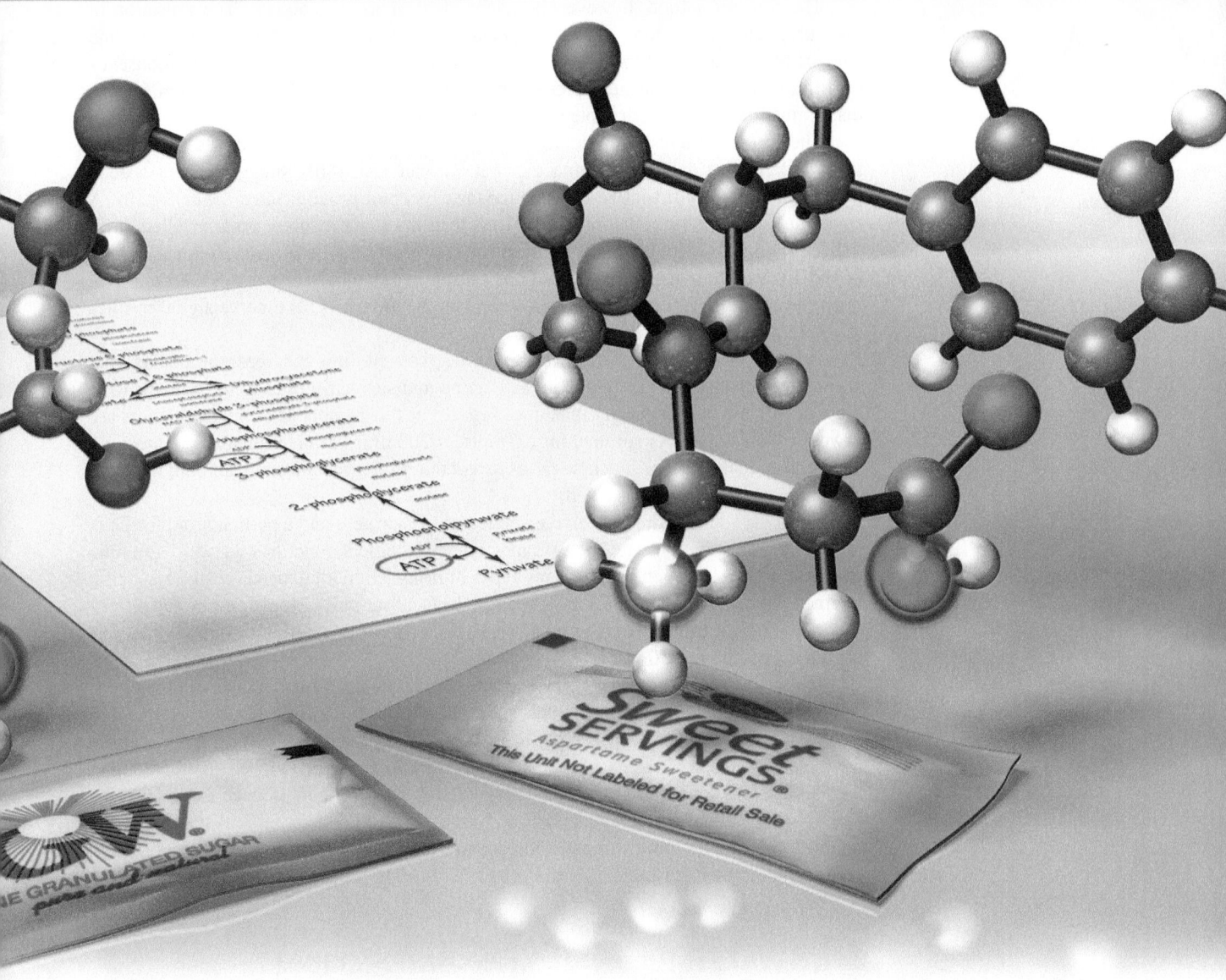

Similarities in the shape of sucrose and aspartame give both molecules the ability to stimulate a sweet taste sensation.

10.1 Artificial Sweeteners: Fooled by Molecular Shape

Artificial sweeteners, such as aspartame (NutraSweet), taste sweet but have few or no calories. Why? *Because taste and caloric value are independent properties of foods.* The caloric value of a food depends on the amount of energy released when the food is metabolized. For example, sucrose (table sugar) is metabolized by oxidation to carbon dioxide and water:

$$C_{12}H_{22}O_{11} + 12\ O_2 \longrightarrow 12\ CO_2 + 11\ H_2O \qquad \Delta H^\circ_{rxn} = -5644\ kJ$$

When your body metabolizes a mole of sucrose, it obtains 5644 kJ of energy. Some artificial sweeteners, such as saccharin, for example, are not metabolized at all—they just pass through the body unchanged—and therefore have no caloric value. Other artificial sweeteners, such as aspartame, are metabolized but have a much lower caloric content (for a given amount of sweetness) than sucrose.

The *taste* of a food, however, is independent of its metabolism. The sensation of taste originates in the tongue, where specialized taste cells act as highly sensitive and specific molecular detectors. These cells can discern sugar molecules from the thousands of different types of molecules present in a mouthful of food. The main factors for this discrimination are the sugar molecule's shape and charge distribution.

The surface of a taste cell contains specialized protein molecules called taste receptors. A particular *tastant*—a molecule that we can taste—fits snuggly into a special pocket (just as a key fits into a lock) on the taste receptor protein called the *active site*. A sugar molecule precisely fits into the active site of the sugar receptor protein called T1r3. When the sugar molecule (the key) enters the active site (the lock), the different subunits of the T1r3 protein split apart. This split causes ion channels in the cell membrane to open, resulting in nerve signal transmission (see Section 8.1). The nerve signal reaches the brain and registers a sweet taste.

Artificial sweeteners taste sweet because they fit into the receptor pocket that normally binds sucrose. In fact, both aspartame and saccharin bind to the active site in the T1r3 protein more strongly than does sugar! For this reason, artificial sweeteners are "sweeter than sugar." Aspartame, for example, is 200 times sweeter than sugar, meaning that it takes 200 times as much sugar as aspartame to trigger the same amount of nerve signal transmission from taste cells.

The lock-and-key fit between the active site of a protein and a particular molecule is important not only to taste but to many other biological functions as well. Immune response, the sense of smell, and many types of drug action all depend on shape-specific interactions between molecules and proteins. In fact, our ability to determine the shapes of key biological molecules is largely responsible for the revolution in biology that has occurred over the last 50 years.

In this chapter, we look at ways to predict and account for the shapes of molecules. The molecules we examine are much smaller than the protein molecules we just discussed, but the same principles apply to both. The simple model we examine to account for molecular shape is called *valence shell electron pair repulsion* (VSEPR) theory, and we will use it in conjunction with the Lewis model. We will then proceed to explore two additional bonding theories: valence bond theory and molecular orbital theory. These bonding theories are more complex, but also more powerful, than the Lewis model. They predict and account for molecular shape as well as other properties of molecules.

10.2 VSEPR Theory: The Five Basic Shapes

Valence shell electron pair repulsion (VSEPR) theory is based on the simple idea that **electron groups**—which we define as lone pairs, single bonds, multiple bonds, and even single electrons—repel one another through coulombic forces. The electron groups, of course, are also attracted to the nucleus (otherwise the molecule would fall apart), but VSEPR theory focuses on the repulsions. According to VSEPR theory, the repulsions between electron groups on *interior atoms* of a molecule determine the geometry of the molecule (Figure 10.1 ◄). The preferred geometry of a molecule is the one in which the electron groups have the maximum separation (and therefore the minimum energy) possible. Consequently, for molecules having just one interior atom (the central atom), molecular geometry depends on (a) the number of electron groups around the central atom and (b) how many of those electron groups are bonding groups and how many are lone pairs. We first look at the molecular geometries associated with two to six electron groups around the central atom when all of those groups are bonding groups (single or multiple bonds). The resulting geometries constitute the five basic shapes of molecules. We will then consider how these basic shapes are modified if one or more of the electron groups are lone pairs.

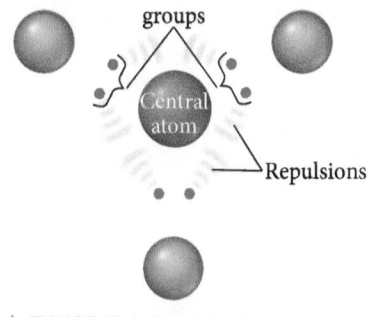

▲ FIGURE 10.1 **Repulsion between Electron Groups** The basic idea of VSEPR theory is that repulsions between electron groups determine molecular geometry.

Two Electron Groups: Linear Geometry

Beryllium often forms incomplete octets, as it does in this structure.

Consider the Lewis structure of $BeCl_2$, which has two electron groups (two single bonds) about the central atom:

According to VSEPR theory, the geometry of $BeCl_2$ is determined by the repulsion between these two electron groups, which maximize their separation by assuming a 180° bond angle or a **linear geometry**. Experimental measurements of the geometry of $BeCl_2$ indicate that the molecule is indeed linear, as predicted by the theory.

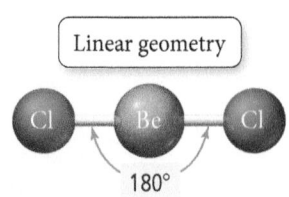

Molecules that form only two single bonds, with no lone pairs, are rare because they do not follow the octet rule. However, the same geometry is observed in all molecules that have two electron groups (and no lone pairs). Consider the Lewis structure of CO_2, which has two electron groups (the double bonds) around the central carbon atom:

| A double bond counts as one electron group.

$$:\ddot{O}{=}C{=}\ddot{O}:$$

According to VSEPR theory, the two double bonds repel each other (just as the two single bonds in $BeCl_2$ repel each other), resulting in a linear geometry for CO_2. Experimental observations confirm that CO_2 is indeed a linear molecule.

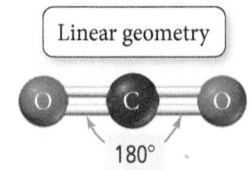

Three Electron Groups: Trigonal Planar Geometry

The Lewis structure of BF_3 (another molecule with an incomplete octet) has three electron groups around the central atom:

$$\begin{array}{c} :\ddot{F}: \\ :\ddot{F}:B:\ddot{F}: \end{array}$$

These three electron groups can maximize their separation by assuming 120° bond angles in a plane—a **trigonal planar geometry**. Experimental observations of the structure of BF_3 again confirm the predictions of VSEPR theory.

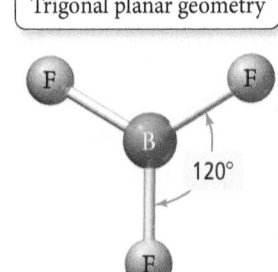

Another molecule with three electron groups, formaldehyde, has one double bond and two single bonds around the central atom:

$$\begin{array}{c} :O: \\ \| \\ H{-}C{-}H \end{array}$$

Since formaldehyde has three electron groups around the central atom, we initially predict that the bond angles should also be 120°. However, experimental observations show that the HCO bond angles are 121.9° and the HCH bond angle is 116.2°. These bond angles are close to the idealized 120° that we originally predicted, but the HCO bond angles are slightly greater than the HCH bond angle because the double bond contains more electron density than the single bond and therefore exerts a slightly greater repulsion on the single bonds. In general, *different types of electron groups exert slightly different repulsions—the resulting bond angles reflect these differences.*

Conceptual Connection 10.1 Electron Groups and Molecular Geometry

In determining electron geometry, why do we consider only the electron groups on the central atom? In other words, why don't we consider electron groups on terminal atoms?

Four Electron Groups: Tetrahedral Geometry

The VSEPR geometries of molecules with two or three electron groups around the central atom are two-dimensional and therefore easily visualized and represented on paper. For molecules with four or more electron groups around the central atom, the geometries are three-dimensional and therefore more difficult to imagine and draw. One common way to help visualize these basic shapes is by analogy to balloons tied together. In this analogy, each electron group around a central atom is like a balloon tied to a central point. The bulkiness of

(a) Linear geometry

(b) Trigonal planar geometry

▲ **FIGURE 10.2 Representing Electron Geometry with Balloons**   (a) The bulkiness of balloons causes them to assume a linear arrangement when two of them are tied together. Similarly, the repulsion between two electron groups produces a linear geometry. (b) Like three balloons tied together, three electron groups adopt a trigonal planar geometry.

the balloons causes them to spread out as much as possible, much as the repulsion between electron groups causes them to position themselves as far apart as possible. For example, if you tie two balloons together, they assume a roughly linear arrangement, as shown in Figure 10.2a ▲, analogous to the linear geometry of $BeCl_2$ that we just examined. Notice that the balloons do not represent atoms, but *electron groups*. Similarly, if you tie three balloons together—in analogy to three electron groups—they assume a trigonal planar geometry, as shown in Figure 10.2b ▲, much like the BF_3 molecule. If you tie *four* balloons together, however, they assume a three-dimensional **tetrahedral geometry** with 109.5° angles between the balloons. That is, the balloons point toward the vertices of a *tetrahedron*—a geometrical shape with four identical faces, each an equilateral triangle, as shown here.

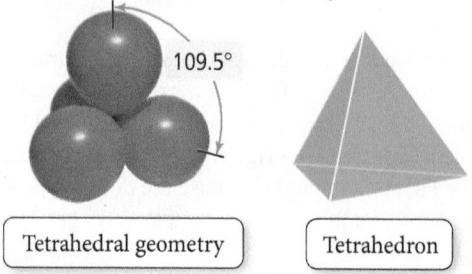

Tetrahedral geometry

Tetrahedron

Methane is an example of a molecule with four electron groups around the central atom:

Tetrahedral geometry

For four electron groups, the tetrahedron is the three-dimensional shape that allows the maximum separation among the groups. The repulsions among the four electron groups in the C—H bonds cause the molecule to assume the tetrahedral shape. When we write the Lewis structure of CH_4 on paper, it may seem that the molecule should be square planar, with bond angles of 90°. However, in three dimensions, the electron groups can get farther away from each other by forming the tetrahedral geometry, as shown by our balloon analogy.

Conceptual Connection 10.2 Molecular Geometry

What is the geometry of the HCN molecule? The Lewis structure of HCN is $H\text{—}C\equiv N$.

(a) linear   **(b)** trigonal planar   **(c)** tetrahedral

Five Electron Groups: Trigonal Bipyramidal Geometry

Five electron groups around a central atom assume a **trigonal bipyramidal geometry**, like that of five balloons tied together. In this structure, three of the groups lie in a single plane, as in the trigonal planar configuration, while the other two are positioned above and below this plane. The angles in the trigonal bipyramidal structure are not all the same. The angles between the *equatorial positions* (the three bonds in the trigonal plane) are 120°, while the angle between the *axial positions* (the two bonds on either side of the trigonal plane) and the trigonal plane is 90°. As an example of a molecule with five electron groups around the central atom, consider PCl_5:

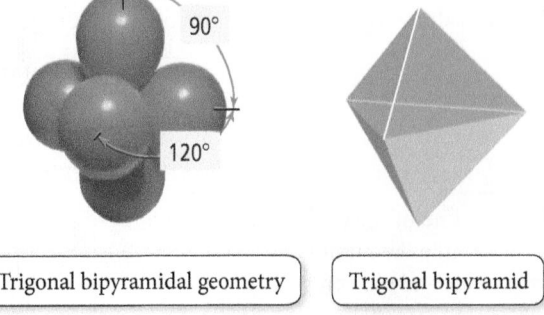

Trigonal bipyramidal geometry   Trigonal bipyramid

Trigonal bipyramidal geometry

The three equatorial chlorine atoms are separated by 120° bond angles and the two axial chlorine atoms are separated from the equatorial atoms by 90° bond angles.

Six Electron Groups: Octahedral Geometry

Six electron groups around a central atom assume an **octahedral geometry**, like that of six balloons tied together. In this structure—named after the eight-sided geometrical shape called the octahedron—four of the groups lie in a single plane, with a fifth group above the plane and another below it. The angles in this geometry are all 90°. As an example of a molecule with six electron groups around the central atom, consider SF_6:

Octahedral geometry   Octahedron

Octahedral geometry

The structure of this molecule is highly symmetrical; all six bonds are equivalent.

EXAMPLE 10.1   VSEPR Theory and the Basic Shapes

Determine the molecular geometry of NO_3^-.

SOLUTION

The molecular geometry of NO_3^- is determined by the number of electron groups around the central atom (N). Begin by drawing a Lewis structure of NO_3^-.	NO_3^- has $5 + 3(6) + 1 = 24$ valence electrons. The Lewis structure has three resonance structures: $$\left[:\ddot{O}-N-\ddot{O}:\right]^- \longleftrightarrow \left[\ddot{O}=N-\ddot{O}:\right]^- \longleftrightarrow \left[:\ddot{O}-N=\ddot{O}\right]^-$$ $$\begin{matrix} \\ :O: \end{matrix} \qquad \begin{matrix} \\ :O: \end{matrix} \qquad \begin{matrix} \\ :O: \end{matrix}$$ The hybrid structure is intermediate between these three and has three equivalent bonds.
Use any one of the resonance structures to determine the number of electron groups around the central atom.	$$\left[:\ddot{O}-N-\ddot{O}:\right]^-$$ $$:O:$$ The nitrogen atom has three electron groups.
Based on the number of electron groups, determine the geometry that minimizes the repulsions between the groups.	The electron geometry that minimizes the repulsions between three electron groups is trigonal planar. 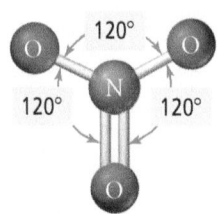 Since the three bonds are equivalent (because of the resonance structures), they each exert the same repulsion on the other two and the molecule has three equal bond angles of 120°.

FOR PRACTICE 10.1
Determine the molecular geometry of CCl_4.

10.3 VSEPR Theory: The Effect of Lone Pairs

Each of the examples we have just seen has only bonding electron groups around the central atom. What happens in molecules that have lone pairs around the central atom as well? The lone pairs also repel other electron groups, as we see in the examples that follow.

Four Electron Groups with Lone Pairs

Consider the Lewis structure of ammonia:

$$\begin{matrix} & H & \\ & | & \\ H - & \underset{\cdot\cdot}{N} & - H \end{matrix}$$

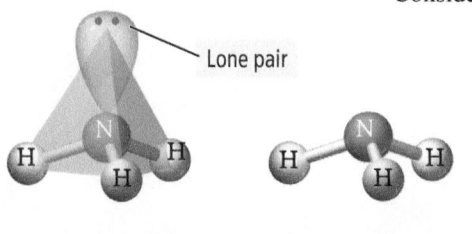

Lone pair

Electron geometry: tetrahedral

Molecular geometry: trigonal pyramidal

The central nitrogen atom has four electron groups (one lone pair and three bonding pairs) that repel one another. If we do not distinguish between bonding electron groups and lone pairs, we find that the **electron geometry**—the geometrical arrangement of the *electron groups*—is still tetrahedral, as we expect for four electron groups. However, the **molecular geometry**—the geometrical arrangement of the atoms—is **trigonal pyramidal**, as shown at left.

Notice that although the electron geometry and the molecular geometry are different, *the electron geometry is relevant to the molecular geometry.* The lone pair exerts its influence on the bonding pairs.

As we noted previously, different kinds of electron groups generally result in different amounts of repulsion. Lone pair electrons generally exert slightly greater repulsions than bonding electrons. If all four electron groups in NH_3 exerted equal repulsions on one another, the bond angles in the molecule would all be the ideal tetrahedral angle, 109.5°. However, the actual angle between N—H bonds in ammonia is slightly smaller, 107°. A lone electron pair is more spread out in space than a bonding electron pair because a lone pair is attracted to only one nucleus while a bonding pair is attracted to two (Figure 10.3 ▼). The lone pair occupies more of the angular space around a nucleus, exerting a greater repulsive force on neighboring electrons and compressing the N—H bond angles.

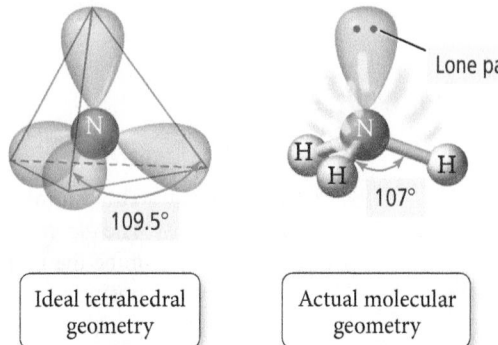

Ideal tetrahedral geometry   Actual molecular geometry

▲ FIGURE 10.3 **Nonbonding versus Bonding Electron Pairs**   A lone electron pair occupies more space than a bonding pair.

A water molecule's Lewis structure is:

$$H - \overset{\cdot\cdot}{\underset{\cdot\cdot}{O}} - H$$

Since it has four electron groups (two bonding pairs and two lone pairs), its *electron geometry* is also tetrahedral, but its *molecular geometry* is **bent**, as shown at right. As in NH_3, the bond angles in H_2O are smaller (104.5°) than the ideal tetrahedral bond angles because of the greater repulsion exerted by the lone pair electrons. The bond angle in H_2O is even smaller than in NH_3 because H_2O has *two* lone pairs of electrons on the central oxygen atom. These lone pairs compress the H_2O bond angle to a greater extent than in NH_3. In general, electron group repulsions vary as follows:

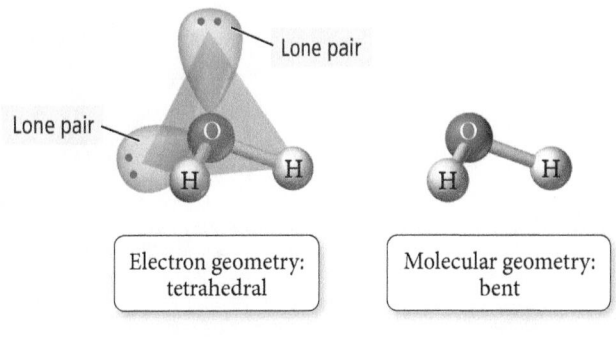

Electron geometry: tetrahedral   Molecular geometry: bent

Lone pair–lone pair > Lone pair–bonding pair > Bonding pair–bonding pair

Most repulsive   Least repulsive

We see the effects of this ordering in the progressively smaller bond angles of CH_4, NH_3, and H_2O, as shown in Figure 10.4 ▼. The relative ordering of repulsions also helps to determine the geometry of molecules with five and six electron groups when one or more of those groups are lone pairs.

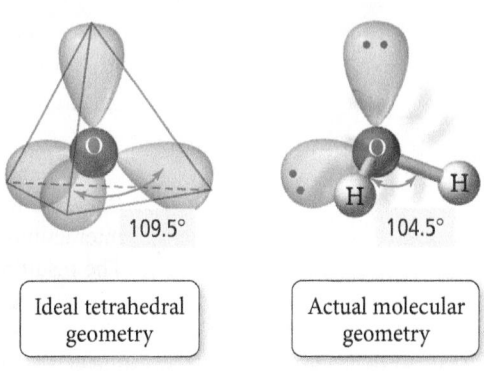

Ideal tetrahedral geometry   Actual molecular geometry

Effect of Lone Pairs on Molecular Geometry

No lone pairs   One lone pair   Two lone pairs

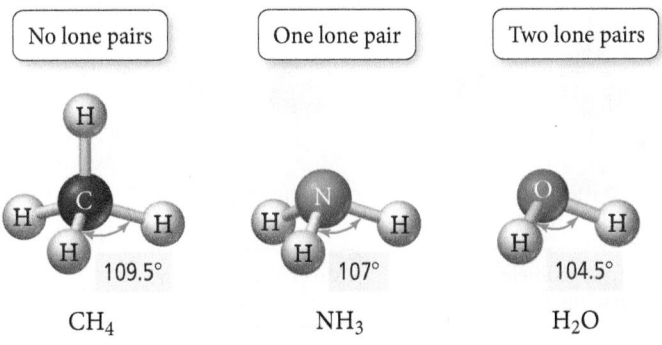

◀ FIGURE 10.4 **The Effect of Lone Pairs on Molecular Geometry**   The bond angles get progressively smaller as the number of lone pairs on the central atom increases from zero in CH_4 to one in NH_3 to two in H_2O.

Five Electron Groups with Lone Pairs

Consider the Lewis structure of SF_4:

$$\ddot{:F:}$$
$$|$$
$$:\ddot{F}-\overset{..}{S}-\ddot{F}:$$
$$|$$
$$:\ddot{F}:$$

The central sulfur atom has five electron groups (one lone pair and four bonding pairs). The *electron geometry*, due to the five electron groups, is trigonal bipyramidal. To determine the molecular geometry, notice that the lone pair could occupy either an equatorial position or an axial position within the trigonal bipyramidal electron geometry. Which position is most favorable? To answer this question, we must consider that, as we have just seen, lone pair–bonding pair repulsions are greater than bonding pair–bonding pair repulsions. Therefore, the lone pair occupies the position that minimizes its interaction with the bonding pairs. If the lone pair were in an axial position, it would have three 90° interactions with bonding pairs. In an equatorial position, however, it has only two 90° interactions. Consequently, the lone pair occupies an equatorial position. The resulting molecular geometry is called **seesaw** because it resembles a seesaw (or teeter-totter).

The seesaw molecular geometry is sometimes called an *irregular tetrahedron*.

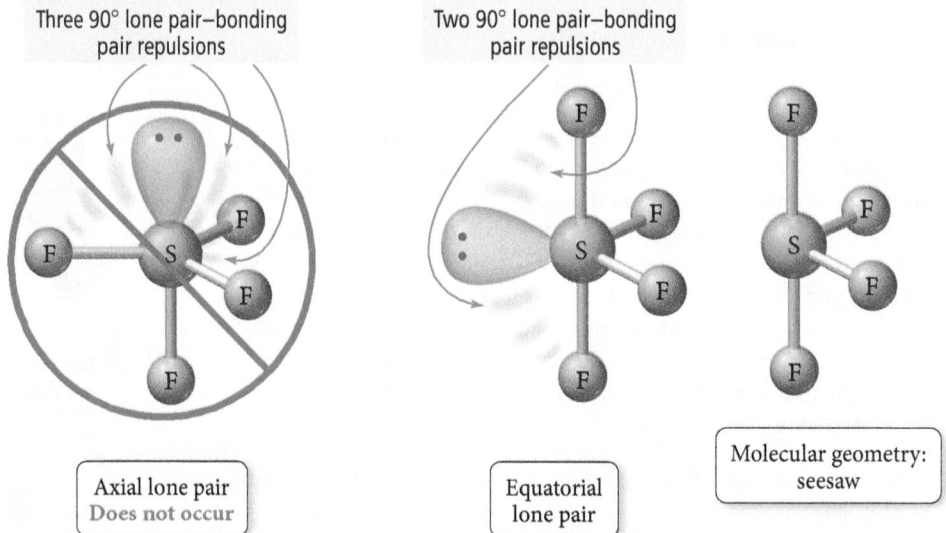

Three 90° lone pair–bonding pair repulsions

Two 90° lone pair–bonding pair repulsions

| Axial lone pair
Does not occur | Equatorial lone pair | Molecular geometry:
seesaw |

When two of the five electron groups around the central atom are lone pairs, as in BrF_3, the lone pairs occupy two of the three equatorial positions—again minimizing 90° interactions with bonding pairs and also avoiding a lone pair–lone pair 90° repulsion. The resulting molecular geometry is **T-shaped**.

| Electron geometry:
trigonal bipyramidal | Molecular geometry:
T-shaped |

When three of the five electron groups around the central atom are lone pairs, as in XeF_2, the lone pairs occupy all three of the equatorial positions, and the resulting molecular geometry is linear.

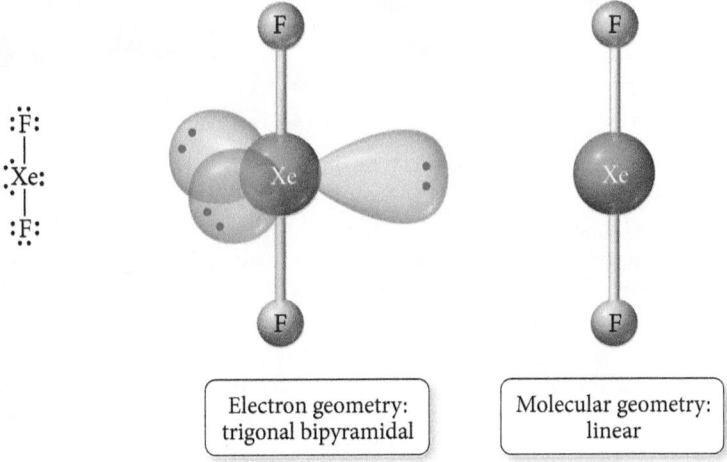

Electron geometry:
trigonal bipyramidal

Molecular geometry:
linear

Six Electron Groups with Lone Pairs

The Lewis structure of BrF_5, is shown next. The central bromine atom has six electron groups (one lone pair and five bonding pairs). The electron geometry, due to the six electron groups, is octahedral. Since all six positions in the octahedral geometry are equivalent, the lone pair can be situated in any one of these positions. The resulting molecular geometry is **square pyramidal**.

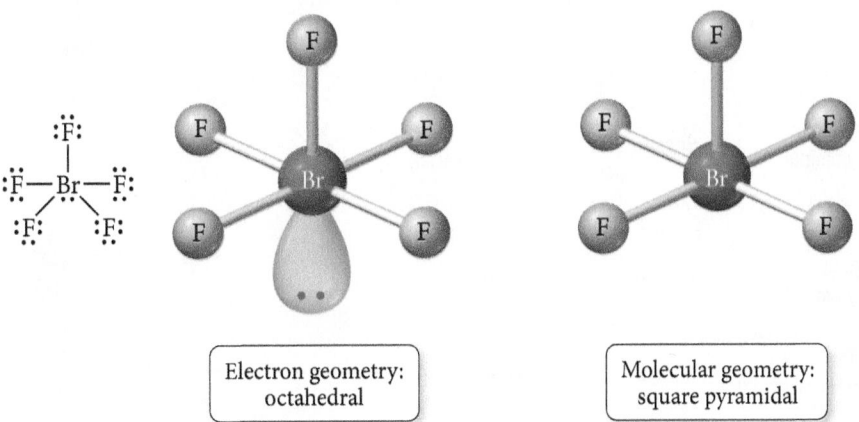

Electron geometry:
octahedral

Molecular geometry:
square pyramidal

When two of the six electron groups around the central atom are lone pairs, as in XeF_4, the lone pairs occupy positions across from one another (to minimize lone pair–lone pair repulsions), and the resulting molecular geometry is **square planar**.

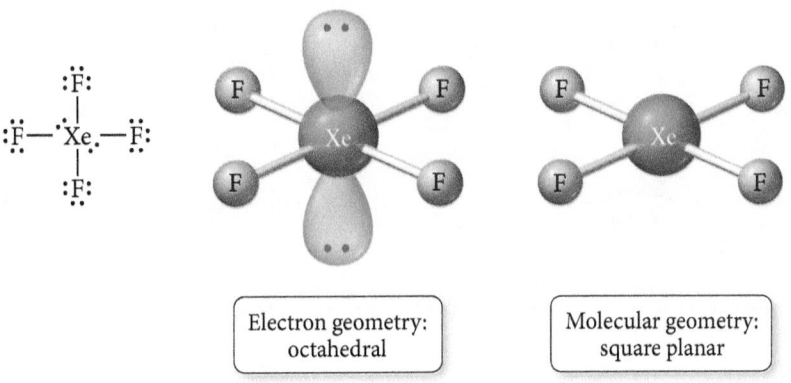

Electron geometry:
octahedral

Molecular geometry:
square planar

TABLE 10.1 Electron and Molecular Geometries

Electron Groups*	Bonding Groups	Lone Pairs	Electron Geometry	Molecular Geometry	Approximate Bond Angles	Example
2	2	0	Linear	Linear	180°	$\ddot{O}=C=\ddot{O}$
3	3	0	Trigonal planar	Trigonal planar	120°	$F-B-F$ with F above
3	2	1	Trigonal planar	Bent	<120°	$\ddot{O}=\ddot{S}-\ddot{O}$
4	4	0	Tetrahedral	Tetrahedral	109.5°	$H-C-H$ (methane)
4	3	1	Tetrahedral	Trigonal pyramidal	<109.5°	$H-N-H$ (ammonia)
4	2	2	Tetrahedral	Bent	<109.5°	$H-\ddot{O}-H$
5	5	0	Trigonal bipyramidal	Trigonal bipyramidal	120° (equatorial) 90° (axial)	PCl_5
5	4	1	Trigonal bipyramidal	Seesaw	<120° (equatorial) <90° (axial)	SF_4
5	3	2	Trigonal bipyramidal	T-shaped	<90°	BrF_3
5	2	3	Trigonal bipyramidal	Linear	180°	$\ddot{F}-Xe-\ddot{F}$
6	6	0	Octahedral	Octahedral	90°	SF_6
6	5	1	Octahedral	Square pyramidal	<90°	BrF_5
6	4	2	Octahedral	Square planar	90°	XeF_4

*Count only electron groups around the central atom. Each of the following is considered one electron group: a lone pair, a single bond, a double bond, a triple bond, or a single electron.

Conceptual Connection 10.3 Lone Pair Electrons and Molecular Geometry

Suppose that a molecule with six electron groups were confined to two dimensions and therefore had a hexagonal planar electron geometry. If two of the six groups were lone pairs, where would they be located?

(a) positions 1 and 2   **(b)** positions 1 and 3   **(c)** positions 1 and 4

Summarizing VSEPR Theory:

▶ The geometry of a molecule is determined by the number of electron groups on the central atom (or on all interior atoms, if there is more than one).

▶ The number of electron groups is determined from the Lewis structure of the molecule. If the Lewis structure contains resonance structures, use any one of the resonance structures to determine the number of electron groups.

▶ Each of the following counts as a single electron group: a lone pair, a single bond, a double bond, a triple bond, or a single electron (as in a free radical).

▶ The geometry of the electron groups is determined by their repulsions as summarized in Table 10.1. In general, electron group repulsions vary as follows:

Lone pair–lone pair > lone pair–bonding pair > bonding pair–bonding pair

▶ Bond angles can vary from the idealized angles because double and triple bonds occupy more space than single bonds (they are bulkier even though they are shorter), and lone pairs occupy more space than bonding groups. The presence of lone pairs usually makes bond angles smaller than the ideal angle for the particular geometry.

Conceptual Connection 10.4 Molecular Geometry and Electron Group Repulsions

Which statement is *always* true according to VSEPR theory?

(a) The shape of a molecule is determined only by repulsions among bonding electron groups.
(b) The shape of a molecule is determined only by repulsions among nonbonding electron groups.
(c) The shape of a molecule is determined by the polarity of its bonds.
(d) The shape of a molecule is determined by repulsions among all electron groups on the central atom (or interior atoms, if there is more than one).

10.4 VSEPR Theory: Predicting Molecular Geometries

To determine the geometry of a molecule, follow the procedure presented here. As in other examples, we provide the steps in the left column and provide two examples of applying the steps in the center and right columns.

PROCEDURE FOR... Predicting Molecular Geometries	EXAMPLE 10.2 **Predicting Molecular Geometries** Predict the geometry and bond angles of PCl_3.	EXAMPLE 10.3 **Predicting Molecular Geometries** Predict the geometry and bond angles of ICl_4^-.
1. **Draw the Lewis structure for the molecule.**	PCl_3 has 26 valence electrons. :Cl: | :Cl—P—Cl:	ICl_4^- has 36 valence electrons. [:Cl: | :Cl—I—Cl: | :Cl:]$^-$
2. **Determine the total number of electron groups around the central atom.** Lone pairs, single bonds, double bonds, triple bonds, and single electrons each count as one group.	The central atom (P) has four electron groups.	The central atom (I) has six electron groups.
3. **Determine the number of bonding groups and the number of lone pairs around the central atom.** These should sum to your result from step 2. Bonding groups include single bonds, double bonds, and triple bonds.	:Cl: | :Cl—P—Cl: Lone pair Three of the four electron groups around P are bonding groups and one is a lone pair.	Lone pairs [:Cl: | :Cl—I—Cl: | :Cl:]$^-$ Four of the six electron groups around I are bonding groups and two are lone pairs.
4. **Refer to Table 10.1 to determine the electron geometry and molecular geometry.** If no lone pairs are present around the central atom, the bond angles will be that of the ideal geometry. If lone pairs are present, the bond angles may be smaller than the ideal geometry.	The electron geometry is tetrahedral (four electron groups) and the molecular geometry—the shape of the molecule—is *trigonal pyramidal* (three bonding groups and one lone pair). Because of the presence of a lone pair, the bond angles are less than 109.5°. Trigonal pyramidal	The electron geometry is octahedral (six electron groups) and the molecular geometry—the shape of the molecule—is *square planar* (four bonding groups and two lone pairs). Even though lone pairs are present, the bond angles are 90° because the lone pairs are symmetrically arranged and do not compress the I—Cl bond angles. Square planar
	FOR PRACTICE 10.2 Predict the molecular geometry and bond angle of $ClNO$.	**FOR PRACTICE 10.3** Predict the molecular geometry of I_3^-.

Representing Molecular Geometries on Paper

Since molecular geometries are three-dimensional, they are often difficult to represent on two-dimensional paper. Many chemists use the notation shown here for bonds to indicate three-dimensional structures on two-dimensional paper.

Straight line	*Hatched wedge*	*Solid wedge*
Bond in plane of paper	Bond going into the page	Bond coming out of the page

Some examples of the molecular geometries used in this book are shown below using this notation.

Linear

Trigonal planar

Bent

Tetrahedral

Trigonal pyramidal

Trigonal bipyramidal

Seesaw

Octahedral

Square planar

Predicting the Shapes of Larger Molecules

Larger molecules may have two or more *interior* atoms. When predicting the shapes of these molecules, we apply the principles we just covered to each interior atom. Consider glycine, an amino acid found in many proteins (such as those involved in taste discussed in Section 10.1). Glycine, shown at right, contains four interior atoms: one nitrogen atom, two carbon atoms, and an oxygen atom. To determine the shape of glycine, we determine the geometry about each interior atom as follows:

Four interior atoms

Glycine

Atom	Number of Electron Groups	Number of Lone Pairs	Molecular Geometry
Nitrogen	4	1	Trigonal pyramidal
Leftmost carbon	4	0	Tetrahedral
Rightmost carbon	3	0	Trigonal planar
Oxygen	4	2	Bent

Using the geometries of each of these, we can determine the entire three-dimensional shape of the molecule as shown at right.

EXAMPLE 10.4 **Predicting the Shape of Larger Molecules**

Predict the geometry about each interior atom in methanol (CH_3OH) and make a sketch of the molecule.

SOLUTION

Begin by drawing the Lewis structure of CH_3OH. CH_3OH contains two interior atoms: one carbon atom and one oxygen atom. To determine the shape of methanol, determine the geometry about each interior atom as follows:

Atom	Number of Electron Groups	Number of Lone Pairs	Molecular Geometry
Carbon	4	0	Tetrahedral
Oxygen	4	2	Bent

Using the geometries of each of these, draw a three-dimensional sketch of the molecule as shown here:

FOR PRACTICE 10.4

Predict the geometry about each interior atom in acetic acid (H_3C—$\overset{\overset{\displaystyle O}{\|}}{C}$—OH) and make a sketch of the molecule.

10.5 Molecular Shape and Polarity

In Chapter 9, we discussed polar bonds. Entire molecules can also be polar, depending on their shape and the nature of their bonds. For example, if a diatomic molecule has a polar bond, the molecule as a whole will be polar:

The figure on the right is an electrostatic potential map of HCl. In these maps, red areas indicate electron rich regions in the molecule and the blue areas indicate electron poor regions. Yellow indicates moderate electron density. Notice that the region around the more electronegative atom (chlorine) is more electron rich than the region around the hydrogen atom. Thus the molecule itself is polar. If the bond in a diatomic molecule is *nonpolar*, the molecule as a whole will be *nonpolar*.

In polyatomic molecules, the presence of polar bonds may or may not result in a polar molecule, depending on the molecular geometry. If the molecular geometry is such that the dipole moments of individual polar bonds sum together to a net dipole moment, then the molecule will be polar. But, if the molecular geometry is such that the dipole moments of the individual polar bonds cancel each other (that is, sum to zero), then the molecule will be nonpolar. It all depends on the geometry of the molecule. Consider carbon dioxide:

$$:\overset{..}{O}=C=\overset{..}{O}:$$

Each $C=O$ bond in CO_2 is polar because oxygen and carbon have significantly different electronegativities (3.5 and 2.5, respectively). However, since CO_2 is a linear molecule, the polar bonds directly oppose one another and the dipole moment of one bond exactly opposes the dipole moment of the other—the two dipole moments sum to zero and the *molecule* is nonpolar. Dipole moments cancel each other because they are *vector quantities*; they have both a magnitude and a direction. Think of each polar bond as a vector, pointing in the direction of the more electronegative atom. The length of the vector is proportional to the electronegativity difference between the bonding atoms. In CO_2, we have two identical vectors pointing in exactly opposite directions—the vectors sum to zero, much as $+1$ and -1 sum to zero:

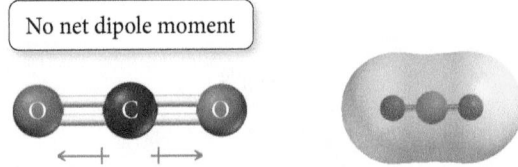

Notice that the electrostatic potential map shows regions of moderately high electron density (yellow with slight red) positioned symmetrically on either end of the molecule with a region of low electron density (blue) located in the middle.

In contrast, consider water:

$$H-\overset{..}{\underset{..}{O}}-H$$

The O—H bonds in water are also polar; oxygen and hydrogen have electronegativities of 3.5 and 2.1, respectively. However, the water molecule is not linear but bent, so the two dipole moments do not sum to zero. If we imagine each bond as a vector pointing toward oxygen (the more electronegative atom) we see that, because of the angle between the vectors, they do not cancel, but sum to an overall vector or a net dipole moment (shown by the dashed arrow).

See the box on p. 440 for an explanation of how to add vectors.

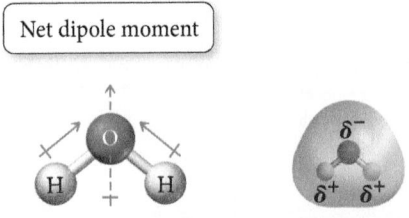

The electrostatic potential map shows an electron rich region at the oxygen end of the molecule. Consequently, water is a polar molecule. Table 10.2 summarizes common geometries and molecular polarity.

Summarizing Molecular Shape and Polarity:

▶ **Draw the Lewis structure for the molecule and determine its molecular geometry.**

▶ **Determine if the molecule contains polar bonds.** A bond is polar if the two bonding atoms have sufficiently different electronegativities (see Figure 9.8). If the molecule contains polar bonds, superimpose a vector, pointing toward the more electronegative atom, on each bond. Make the length of the vector proportional to the electronegativity difference between the bonding atoms.

▶ **Determine if the polar bonds add together to form a net dipole moment.** Sum the vectors corresponding to the polar bonds together. If the vectors sum to zero, the molecule is nonpolar. If the vectors sum to a net vector, the molecule is polar.

Vector Addition

As discussed previously, we can determine whether a molecule is polar by summing the vectors associated with the dipole moments of all the polar bonds in the molecule. If the vectors sum to zero, the molecule will be nonpolar. If they sum to a net vector, the molecule will be polar. In this box, we demonstrate how to add vectors together in one dimension and in two or more dimensions.

One Dimension

To add two vectors that lie on the same line, assign one direction as positive. Vectors pointing in that direction have positive magnitudes. Consider vectors pointing in the opposite direction to have negative magnitudes. Then sum the vectors (always remembering to include their signs), as shown in Examples 1 and 2.

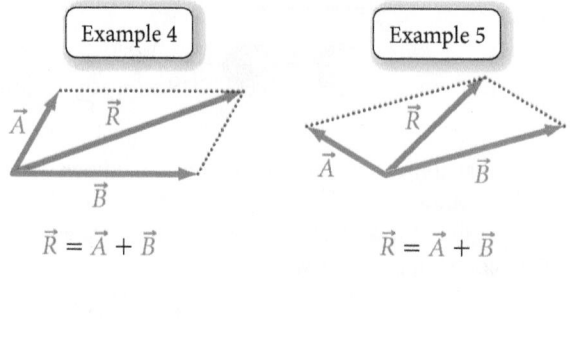

Two or More Dimensions

To add two vectors, draw a parallelogram in which the two vectors form two adjacent sides. Draw the other two sides of the parallelogram parallel to and the same length as the two original vectors. Draw the resultant vector beginning at the origin and extending to the far corner of the parallelogram.

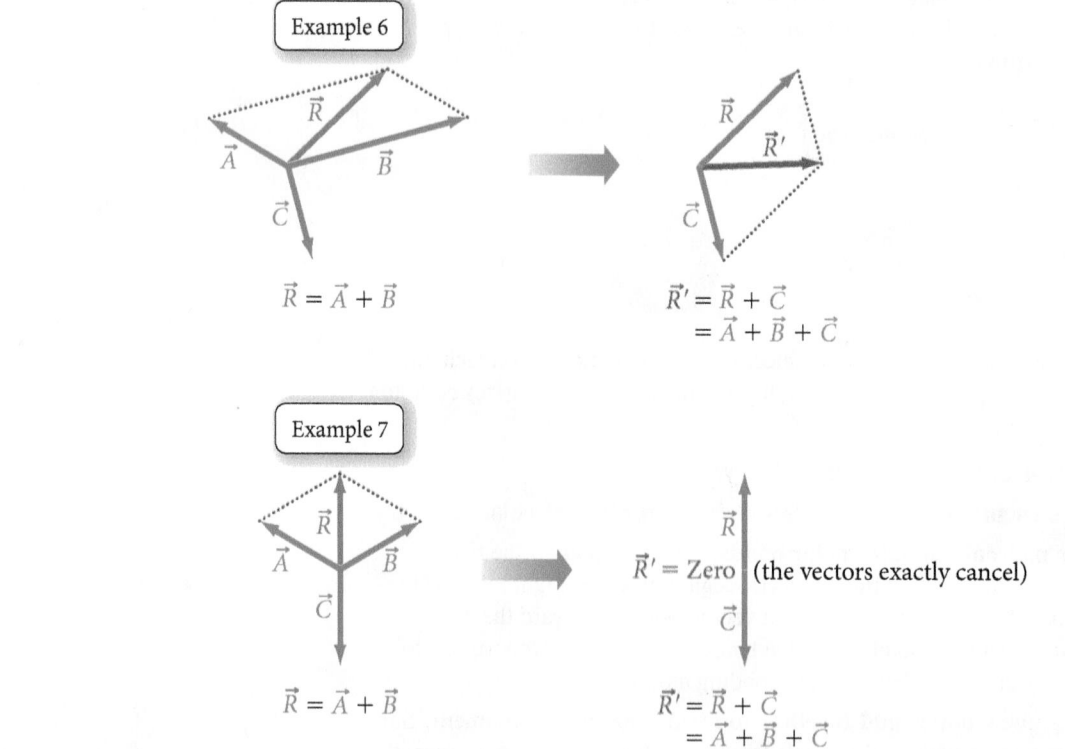

To add three or more vectors, add two of them together first, and then add the third vector to the result.

TABLE 10.2 **Common Cases of Adding Dipole Moments to Determine whether a Molecule Is Polar**

Bent

Linear

Nonpolar

Polar

The dipole moments of two identical polar bonds pointing in opposite directions will cancel. The molecule is nonpolar.

The dipole moments of two polar bonds with an angle of less than 180° between them will not cancel. The resultant dipole moment vector is shown in red. The molecule is polar.

Trigonal planar

Tetrahedral

Nonpolar

Nonpolar

The dipole moments of three identical polar bonds at 120° from each other will cancel. The molecule is nonpolar.

The dipole moments of four identical polar bonds in a tetrahedral arrangement (109.5° from each other) will cancel. The molecule is nonpolar.

Trigonal pyramidal

Polar

The dipole moments of three polar bonds in a trigonal pyramidal arrangement (109.5° from each other) will not cancel. The resultant dipole moment vector is shown in red. The molecule is polar.

Note: In all cases in which the dipoles of two or more polar bonds cancel, the bonds are assumed to be identical. If one or more of the bonds are different from the other(s), the dipoles will not cancel and the molecule will be polar.

EXAMPLE 10.5 Determining if a Molecule Is Polar

Determine if NH_3 is polar.

SOLUTION

Draw the Lewis structure for the molecule and determine its molecular geometry.	H | H—N—H ‥ The Lewis structure has three bonding groups and one lone pair about the central atom. Therefore the molecular geometry is trigonal pyramidal.
Determine if the molecule contains polar bonds. Sketch the molecule and superimpose a vector for each polar bond. The relative length of each vector should be proportional to the electronegativity difference between the atoms forming each bond. The vector should point in the direction of the more electronegative atom.	The electronegativities of nitrogen and hydrogen are 3.0 and 2.1, respectively. Therefore, the bonds are polar.
Determine if the polar bonds add together to form a net dipole moment. Examine the symmetry of the vectors (representing dipole moments) and determine if they cancel each other or sum to a net dipole moment.	 The three dipole moments sum to a net dipole moment. The molecule is polar.

FOR PRACTICE 10.5

Determine if CF_4 is polar.

Polar and nonpolar molecules have different properties. Water and oil do not mix, for example, because water molecules are polar and the molecules that compose oil are generally nonpolar. Polar molecules interact strongly with other polar molecules because the positive end of one molecule is attracted to the negative end of another, just as the south pole of a magnet is attracted to the north pole of another magnet (Figure 10.5 ◄). A mixture of polar and nonpolar molecules is similar to a mixture of small magnetic particles and nonmagnetic ones. The magnetic particles (which are like polar molecules) clump together, excluding the nonmagnetic particles (which are like nonpolar molecules) and separating into distinct regions.

Opposite magnetic poles attract one another.

N S ····· N S

Opposite partial charges on molecules attract one another.

▲ **FIGURE 10.5 Interaction of Polar Molecules** The north pole of one magnet attracts the south pole of another magnet. In an analogous way, the positively charged end of one molecule attracts the negatively charged end of another (although the forces involved are different). As a result of this electrical attraction, polar molecules interact strongly with one another.

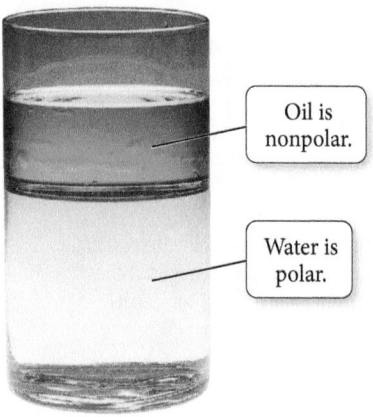

Oil is nonpolar.

Water is polar.

▲ Oil and water do not mix, because water molecules are polar and the molecules that compose oil are nonpolar.

▲ A mixture of polar and nonpolar molecules is analogous to a mixture of magnetic marbles (opaque) and nonmagnetic marbles (transparent). As with the magnetic marbles, mutual attraction causes polar molecules to clump together, excluding the nonpolar molecules.

Chemistry in Your Day

How Soap Works

Imagine eating a greasy cheeseburger with both hands and without a napkin. By the end of the meal, your hands are coated with grease and oil. If you try to wash them with only water, they remain greasy. However, if you add a little soap, the grease washes away. Why? As we just learned, water molecules are polar and the molecules that compose grease and oil are nonpolar. As a result, water and grease do not mix.

The molecules that compose soap, however, have a special structure that allows them to interact strongly with both water and grease. One end of a soap molecule is polar while the other end is nonpolar.

The nonpolar end is a long hydrocarbon chain. Hydrocarbons are always nonpolar because the electronegativity difference between carbon and hydrogen is small and because the tetrahedral arrangement about each carbon atom tends to cancel any small dipole moments of individual bonds. The polar head of a soap molecule—usually, though not always, ionic—strongly attracts water molecules, while the nonpolar tail interacts more strongly with grease and oil molecules (we will examine the nature of these interactions in Chapter 11). Thus, soap acts as a sort of molecular liaison, one end interacting with water and the other end interacting with grease. Soap allows water and grease to mix, removing the grease from your hands and washing it down the drain.

Polar head attracts water.

Nonpolar tail interacts with grease.

Question

Consider the detergent molecule shown here. Which end do you think is polar? Which end is nonpolar?

$CH_3(CH_2)_{11}OCH_2CH_2OH$

10.6 Valence Bond Theory: Orbital Overlap as a Chemical Bond

In the Lewis model, we use "dots" to represent electrons as they are transferred or shared between bonding atoms. We know from quantum-mechanical theory, however, that such a treatment is an oversimplification. More advanced bonding theories treat electrons in a quantum-mechanical manner. These theories are actually extensions of quantum mechanics, applied to molecules. Although a detailed quantitative treatment of these theories is beyond the scope of this book, we introduce them in a *qualitative* manner in the sections that follow. Keep in mind, however, that modern *quantitative* approaches to chemical bonding using these theories accurately predict many of the properties of molecules— such as bond lengths, bond strengths, molecular geometries, and dipole moments—that we have been discussing in this book.

The simpler of the two more advanced bonding theories is called **valence bond theory**. According to valence bond theory, electrons reside in quantum-mechanical orbitals localized on individual atoms. In many cases, these orbitals are simply the standard *s*, *p*, *d*, and *f* atomic orbitals that we learned about in Chapter 7. In other cases, these orbitals are *hybridized atomic orbitals*, a kind of blend or combination of two or more standard atomic orbitals.

When two atoms approach each other, the electrons and nucleus of one atom interact with the electrons and nucleus of the other atom. In valence bond theory, we calculate the effect of these interactions on the energies of the electrons in the atomic orbitals. If the energy of the system is lowered because of the interactions, then a chemical bond forms. If the energy of the system is raised by the interactions, then a chemical bond does not form.

The interaction energy is usually calculated as a function of the internuclear distance between the two bonding atoms. For example, Figure 10.6 ▾ shows the calculated interaction energy between two hydrogen atoms as a function of the distance between them. The *y*-axis of the graph is the potential energy of the interaction between the electron and nucleus of one hydrogen atom and the electron and nucleus of the other. The *x*-axis is the separation (or internuclear distance) between the two atoms. As we can see from the graph, when the atoms are far apart (right side of the graph), the interaction energy is nearly zero because the two atoms do not interact to any significant extent. As the atoms get closer, the interaction energy becomes negative. This is a net stabilization that attracts

> Valence bond theory is an application of a general quantum-mechanical approximation method called *perturbation theory*. In perturbation theory, a complex system (such as a molecule) is viewed as a simpler system (such as two atoms) that is slightly altered or perturbed by some additional force or interaction (such as the interaction between the two atoms).

Interaction Energy of Two Hydrogen Atoms

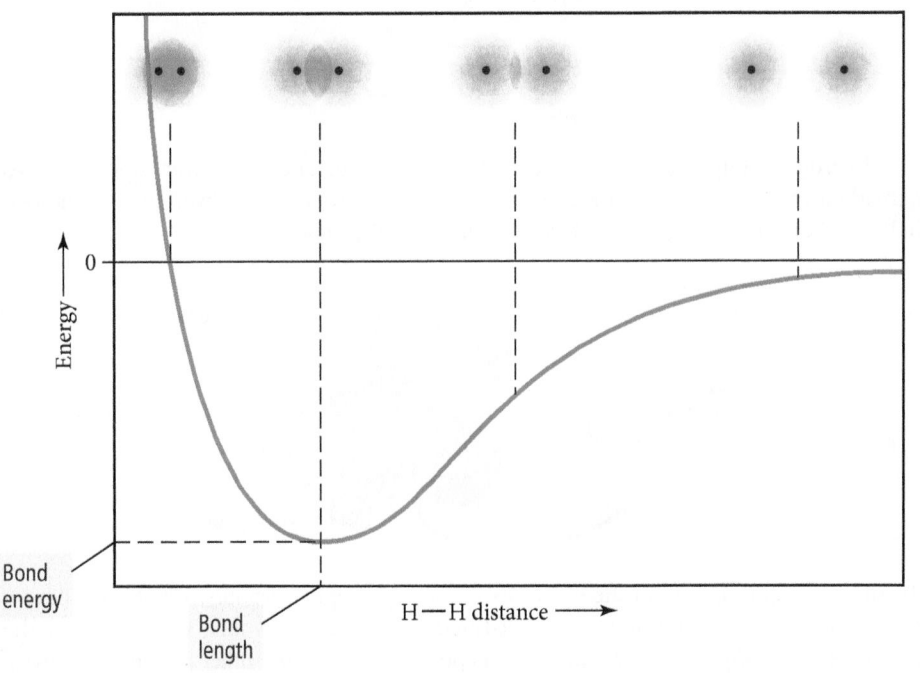

◀ FIGURE 10.6 **Interaction Energy Diagram for H_2** The potential energy of two hydrogen atoms is lowest when they are separated by a distance that allows their 1*s* orbitals a substantial degree of overlap without too much repulsion between their nuclei. This distance, at which the system is most stable, is the bond length of the H_2 molecule.

one hydrogen atom to the other. If the atoms get too close, however, the interaction energy begins to rise, primarily because of the mutual repulsion of the two positively charged nuclei. The most stable point on the curve occurs at the minimum of the interaction energy—this is the equilibrium bond length. At this distance, the two atomic $1s$ orbitals have a significant amount of overlap and the electrons spend time in the internuclear region where they can interact with both nuclei. The value of the interaction energy at the equilibrium bond distance is the bond energy.

When we apply valence bond theory to a number of atoms and their corresponding molecules, we arrive at the following general observation: *the interaction energy is usually negative (or stabilizing) when the interacting atomic orbitals contain a total of two electrons that can spin-pair (orient with opposing spins).* Most commonly, the two electrons come from two half-filled orbitals, but in some cases, the two electrons come from one filled orbital overlapping with a completely empty orbital (this is called a coordinate covalent bond and we will cover it in more detail in Chapter 24). In other words, when two atoms with half-filled orbitals approach each other, the half-filled orbitals *overlap*—parts of the orbitals occupy the same space—and the electrons occupying them align with opposite spins. This results in a net energy stabilization that constitutes a covalent chemical bond. The resulting geometry of the molecule emerges from the geometry of the overlapping orbitals.

| When *completely filled* orbitals overlap, the interaction energy is positive (or destabilizing) and no bond forms.

Summarizing Valence Bond Theory:

▶ The valence electrons of the atoms in a molecule reside in quantum-mechanical atomic orbitals. The orbitals can be the standard s, p, d, and f orbitals or they may be hybrid combinations of these.

▶ A chemical bond results from the overlap of two half-filled orbitals with spin-pairing of the two valence electrons (or less commonly the overlap of a completely filled orbital with an empty orbital).

▶ The geometry of the overlapping orbitals determines the shape of the molecule.

We can apply the general concepts of valence bond theory to explain bonding in hydrogen sulfide, H_2S. The valence electron configurations of the atoms in the molecule are as follows:

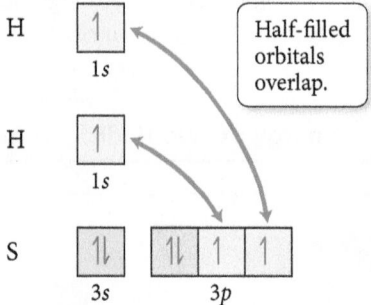

The hydrogen atoms each have one half-filled orbital, and the sulfur atom has two half-filled orbitals. The half-filled orbitals on each hydrogen atom overlap with the two half-filled orbitals on the sulfur atom, forming two chemical bonds:

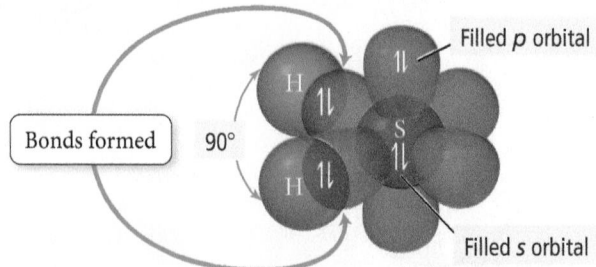

To show the spin-pairing of the electrons in the overlapping orbitals, we superimpose a half-arrow for each electron in each half-filled orbital and show that, within a bond, the electrons are spin-paired (one half-arrow is pointing up and the other is pointing down).

We also superimpose paired half-arrows in the filled sulfur s and p orbitals to represent the lone pair electrons in those orbitals. (Since those orbitals are full, they are not involved in bonding.)

A quantitative calculation of H_2S using valence bond theory yields bond energies, bond lengths, and bond angles. In our qualitative treatment, we simply show how orbital overlap leads to bonding and make a rough sketch of the molecule based on the overlapping orbitals. Notice that, because the overlapping orbitals on the central atom (sulfur) are p orbitals, and because p orbitals are oriented at 90° to one another, the predicted bond angle is 90°. The actual bond angle in H_2S is 92°. In the case of H_2S, a simple valence bond treatment matches well with the experimentally measured bond angle (in contrast to VSEPR theory, which predicts a bond angle of less than 109.5°).

Conceptual Connection 10.5 What Is a Chemical Bond? Part I

The answer to the question "What is a chemical bond?" depends on the bonding model. Answer these three questions:

(a) What is a covalent chemical bond according to the Lewis model?
(b) What is a covalent chemical bond according to valence bond theory?
(c) Why are the answers different?

10.7 Valence Bond Theory: Hybridization of Atomic Orbitals

Although the overlap of half-filled *standard* atomic orbitals adequately explains the bonding in H_2S, it cannot adequately explain the bonding in many other molecules. For example, suppose we try to explain the bonding between hydrogen and carbon using the same approach. The valence electron configurations of H and C are as follows:

H   ⬜ 1
          1s

C   ⬜ 1⬇   ⬜ 1   1   ⬜
          2s   2p

Carbon has only two half-filled orbitals and should therefore form only two bonds with two hydrogen atoms. We would therefore predict that carbon and hydrogen should form a molecule with the formula CH_2 and with a bond angle of 90° (corresponding to the angle between any two p orbitals).

However, from experiments, we know that the stable compound formed from carbon and hydrogen is CH_4 (methane), with bond angles of 109.5°. The experimental reality is different from our simple prediction in two ways. First, carbon forms bonds to four hydrogen atoms, not two. Second, the bond angles are much larger than the angle between two p orbitals. Valence bond theory accounts for the bonding in CH_4 and many other polyatomic molecules by incorporating an additional concept called *orbital hybridization*.

So far, we have assumed that the overlapping orbitals that form chemical bonds are simply the standard s, p, or d atomic orbitals. Valence bond theory treats the electrons in a molecule as if they occupied these standard atomic orbitals, but this is a major oversimplification. The concept of hybridization in valence bond theory is essentially a step toward recognizing that *the orbitals in a molecule are not necessarily the same as the orbitals in an atom*. **Hybridization** is a mathematical procedure in which the standard atomic orbitals are combined to form new atomic orbitals called **hybrid orbitals** that

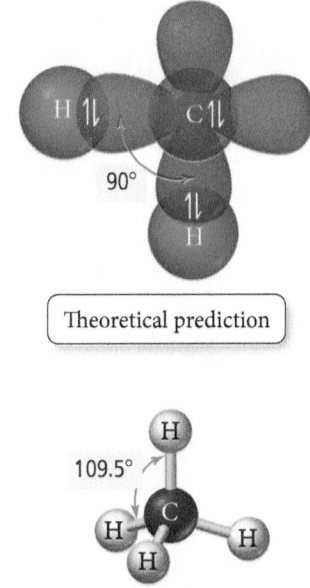

Theoretical prediction

109.5°

Observed reality

In Section 10.8, we examine another theory called *molecular orbital theory*, which treats electrons in a molecule as occupying orbitals that belong to the molecule as a whole.

correspond more closely to the actual distribution of electrons in chemically bonded atoms. Hybrid orbitals are still localized on individual atoms, but they have different shapes and energies from those of standard atomic orbitals.

Why do we hypothesize that electrons in some molecules occupy hybrid orbitals? In valence bond theory, a chemical bond is the overlap of two orbitals that together contain two electrons. The greater the overlap, the stronger the bond and the lower the energy. In hybrid orbitals, the electron probability density is more concentrated in a single directional lobe, allowing greater overlap with the orbitals of other atoms. Hybrid orbitals *minimize* the energy of the molecule by *maximizing* the orbital overlap in a bond.

Hybridization, however, is not a free lunch—in most cases it actually costs some energy. So hybridization occurs only to the degree that the energy payback through bond formation is large. In general, therefore, the more bonds that an atom forms, the greater the tendency of its orbitals to hybridize. Central or interior atoms, which form the most bonds, have the greatest tendency to hybridize. Terminal atoms, which form the fewest bonds, have the least tendency to hybridize. *In this book, we focus on the hybridization of interior atoms and assume that all terminal atoms—those bonding to only one other atom—are unhybridized.* Hybridization is particularly important in carbon, which tends to form four bonds in its compounds and therefore always hybridizes.

Although we cannot examine the procedure for obtaining hybrid orbitals in mathematical detail here, we can make the following general statements regarding hybridization:

▶ The *number of standard atomic orbitals* added together always equals the *number of hybrid orbitals* formed. The total number of orbitals is conserved.

▶ The *particular combinations* of standard atomic orbitals added together determines the *shapes and energies* of the hybrid orbitals formed.

▶ The *particular type of hybridization that occurs* is the one that yields the *lowest overall energy for the molecule*. Since actual energy calculations are beyond the scope of this book, we use electron geometries as determined by VSEPR theory to predict the type of hybridization.

sp^3 Hybridization

We can account for the tetrahedral geometry in CH_4 by the hybridization of the one $2s$ orbital and the three $2p$ orbitals on the carbon atom. The four new orbitals that result, called sp^3 hybrids, are shown in the following energy diagram:

The notation "sp^3" indicates that the hybrid orbitals are mixtures of one s orbital and three p orbitals. Notice that the hybrid orbitals all have the same energy—they are degenerate. The shapes of the sp^3 hybrid orbitals are shown in Figure 10.7 ▶. The four hybrid orbitals are arranged in a tetrahedral geometry with 109.5° angles between them.

We can write an orbital diagram for carbon using these hybrid orbitals:

Formation of *sp³* Hybrid Orbitals

One *s* orbital and three *p* orbitals combine to form four *sp³* orbitals.

s orbital

p$_x$ orbital

+

p$_y$ orbital

p$_z$ orbital

Unhybridized atomic orbitals

Hybridization →

sp^3

sp^3

sp^3

sp^3

sp³ hybrid orbitals (shown separately)

sp^3

sp^3

sp^3

sp^3

109.5°

sp³ hybrid orbitals (shown together)

▲ FIGURE 10.7 *sp³* **Hybridization** One *s* orbital and three *p* orbitals combine to form four *sp³* hybrid orbitals.

Carbon's four valence electrons occupy the orbitals singly with parallel spins as dictated by Hund's rule. With this electron configuration, carbon has four half-filled orbitals and can form four bonds with four hydrogen atoms:

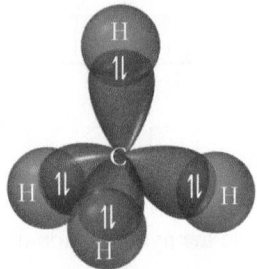

The geometry of the *overlapping orbitals* (the hybrids) is tetrahedral, with angles of 109.5° between the orbitals, so the *resulting geometry of the molecule* is tetrahedral, with 109.5° bond angles, in agreement with the experimentally measured geometry of CH_4 and with the predicted VSEPR geometry.

Hybridized orbitals readily form chemical bonds because they tend to maximize overlap with other orbitals. However, if the central atom of a molecule contains lone pairs, hybrid orbitals can also accommodate them. For example, the nitrogen orbitals in ammonia are sp^3 hybrids. Three of the hybrids are involved in bonding with three hydrogen atoms, but the fourth hybrid contains a lone pair. The presence of the lone pair lowers the tendency of nitrogen's orbitals to hybridize. (Remember that the tendency to hybridize increases with the number of bonds formed.) Therefore the bond angle in NH_3 is 107°, a bit closer to the unhybridized p orbital bond angle of 90°.

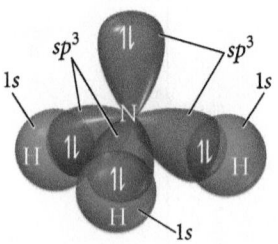

sp^2 Hybridization and Double Bonds

Hybridization of one s and two p orbitals results in three sp^2 hybrids and one leftover unhybridized p orbital.

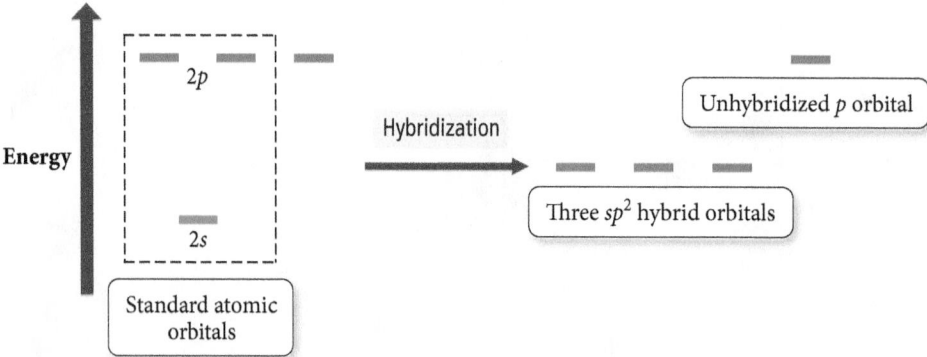

The notation "sp^2" indicates that the hybrids are mixtures of one s orbital and two p orbitals. The shapes of the sp^2 hybrid orbitals are shown in Figure 10.8 ▶. Notice that the three hybrid orbitals have a trigonal planar geometry with 120° angles between them. The unhybridized p orbital is oriented perpendicular to the three hybridized orbitals.

As an example of a molecule with sp^2 hybrid orbitals, consider H_2CO. The unhybridized valence electron configurations of each of the atoms are as follows:

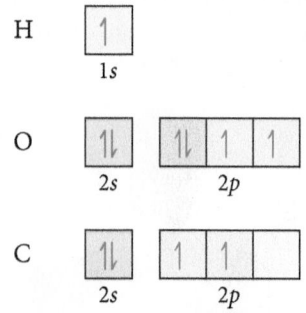

Carbon is the central atom and the hybridization of its orbitals is sp^2:

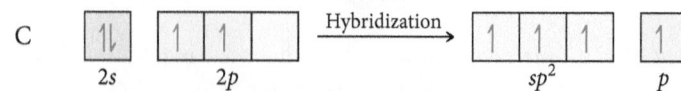

Formation of sp^2 Hybrid Orbitals

One s orbital and two p orbitals combine to form three sp^2 orbitals.

s orbital + p_x orbital + p_y orbital → **Hybridization** → sp^2 hybrid orbitals (shown together)

Unhybridized atomic orbitals

sp^2 hybrid orbitals (shown separately)

▲ **FIGURE 10.8 sp^2 Hybridization** One s orbital and two p orbitals combine to form three sp^2 hybrid orbitals. One p orbital (not shown) remains unhybridized.

Each of the sp^2 orbitals is half filled. The remaining electron occupies the leftover p orbital, even though it is slightly higher in energy. We can now see that the carbon atom has four half-filled orbitals and can therefore form four bonds: two with two hydrogen atoms and two (a double bond) with the oxygen atom. We draw the molecule and the overlapping orbitals as follows:

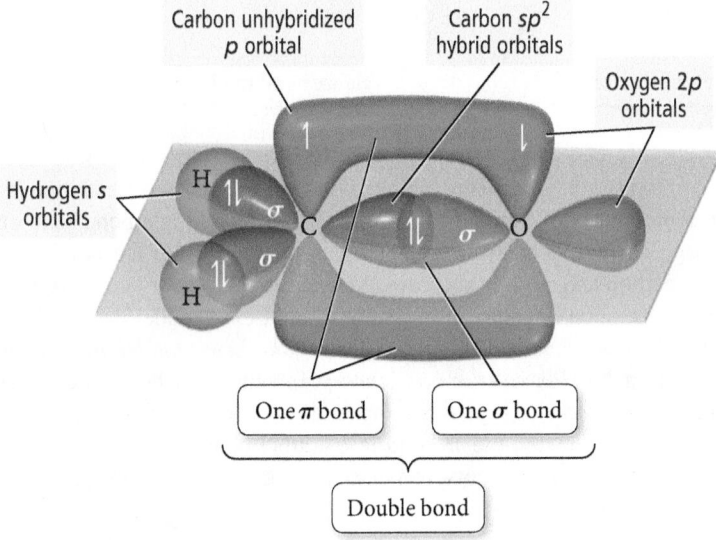

Carbon unhybridized p orbital

Carbon sp^2 hybrid orbitals

Oxygen $2p$ orbitals

Hydrogen s orbitals

One π bond

One σ bond

Double bond

▶ **FIGURE 10.9 Sigma and
Pi Bonding** When orbitals overlap
side-by-side, the result is a pi (π)
bond. When orbitals overlap end-
to-end, they form a sigma (σ) bond.
Two atoms can form only one sigma
bond. A single bond is a sigma bond, a
double bond consists of a sigma bond
and a pi bond, a triple bond consists of
a sigma bond and two pi bonds.

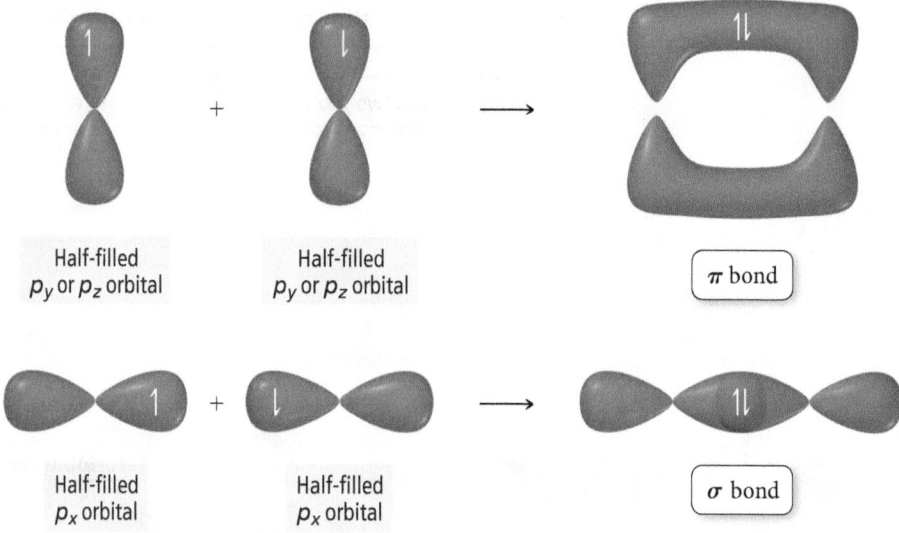

Half-filled
p_y or p_z orbital

Half-filled
p_y or p_z orbital

π bond

Half-filled
p_x orbital

Half-filled
p_x orbital

σ bond

Notice the overlap between the half-filled p orbitals on the carbon and oxygen atoms.
When p orbitals overlap this way (side by side) the resulting bond is a **pi (π) bond**, and
the electron density is above and below the internuclear axis. When orbitals overlap end-
to-end, as in all of the rest of the bonds in the molecule, the resulting bond is a **sigma (σ)
bond** (Figure 10.9 ▲). Even though we represent the two electrons in a π bond as two
half arrows in the upper lobe, they are actually spread out over both the upper and lower
lobes (this is one of the limitations we encounter when we try to represent electrons with
arrows). We can label all the bonds in the molecule using a notation that specifies the
type of bond (σ or π) as well as the type of overlapping orbitals. We have included this
notation, as well as the Lewis structure of H_2CO for comparison, in the bonding diagram
for H_2CO:

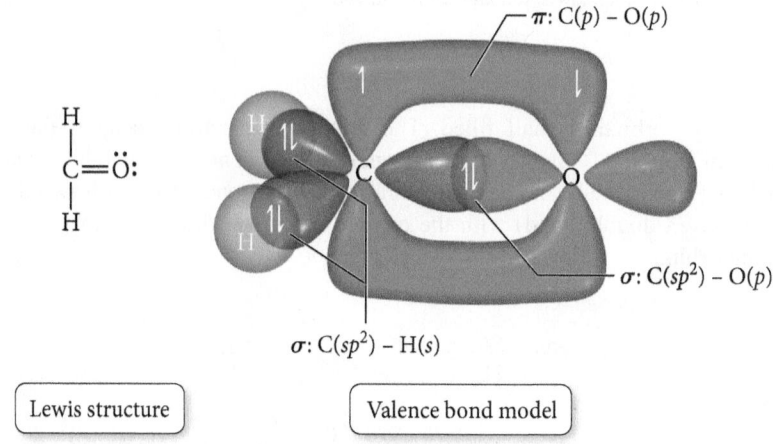

π: C(p) – O(p)

σ: C(sp^2) – O(p)

σ: C(sp^2) – H(s)

Lewis structure

Valence bond model

Notice the correspondence between valence bond theory and the Lewis model. In both
models, the central carbon atom is forming four bonds: two single bonds and one double
bond. However, valence bond theory gives us more insight into the bonds. The double
bond between carbon and oxygen according to valence bond theory consists of two different kinds of bonds—one σ and one π—while in the Lewis model the two bonds within
the double bond appear identical. *A double bond in the Lewis model always corresponds
to one σ and one π bond in valence bond theory.* In general, π bonds are weaker than σ
bonds because the side-to-side orbital overlap tends to be less efficient than the end-to-end
orbital overlap. Consequently, the π bond in a double bond is generally easier to break
than the σ bond. Valence bond theory, as you can see, gives us more insight into the nature
of a double bond than the Lewis model.

One—and only one—σ bond forms between
any two atoms. Additional bonds must be
π bonds.

Valence bond theory allows us to see why the rotation about a double bond is severely restricted. Because of the side-by-side overlap of the p orbitals, the π bond must essentially break for rotation to occur (see Chemistry in Your Day: *The Chemistry of Vision*). Valence bond theory shows us the types of orbitals involved in the bonding and their shapes. In H_2CO, the sp^2 hybrid orbitals on the central atom are trigonal planar with $120°$ angles between them, so the resulting predicted geometry of the molecule is trigonal planar with $120°$ bond angles. The experimentally measured bond angles in H_2CO, as discussed previously, are $121.9°$ for the HCO bond and $116.2°$ for the HCH bond angle, close to the predicted values.

Although rotation about a double bond is highly restricted, rotation about a single bond is relatively unrestricted. Consider, for example, the structures of two chlorinated hydrocarbons, 1,2-dichloroethane and 1,2-dichloroethene.

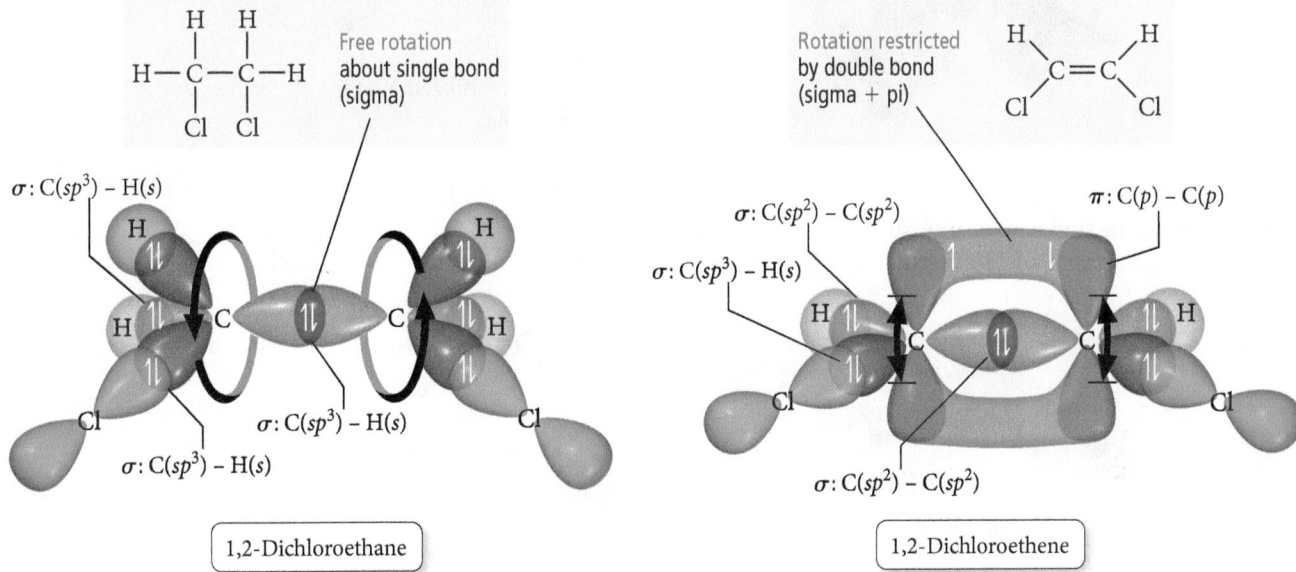

1,2-Dichloroethane

1,2-Dichloroethene

The hybridization of the carbon atoms in 1,2-dichloroethane is sp^3, resulting in relatively free rotation about the sigma single bond. Consequently, there is no difference between the following two structures at room temperature, because they quickly interconvert:

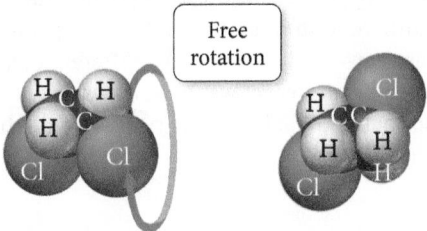

In contrast, rotation about the double bond (sigma + pi) in 1,2-dichloroethene is restricted, so that, at room temperature, 1,2-dichloroethene exists in two forms:

cis-1,2-Dichloroethene   *trans*-1,2-Dichloroethene

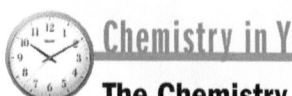
Chemistry in Your Day

The Chemistry of Vision

In the human eye, light is detected by a chemical switch involving the breaking and re-forming of a π bond. The back portion of the eye, the retina, is coated with millions of light-sensitive cells called rods and cones. Each of these cells contains proteins that bind a compound called 11-*cis*-retinal, which has the following structure:

11-*cis*-Retinal

When a photon of sufficient energy strikes a rod or cone, it causes the isomerization of 11-*cis*-retinal to all-*trans*-retinal:

all-*trans*-Retinal

The isomerization occurs because visible light contains enough energy to break the π bond between the eleventh and twelfth carbon atom in 11-*cis*-retinal. The σ bond, which is stronger, does not break, allowing the molecule to freely rotate about that bond. The π bond then re-forms with the molecule in the *trans* conformation. The different shape of the resultant all-*trans*-retinal causes conformational changes in the protein to which it is bound. These changes cause an electrical signal to be transmitted to the brain.

Question

What is the hybridization of the eleventh and twelfth carbon atoms in retinal?

These two forms of 1,2-dichloroethene are indeed different compounds with different properties. We distinguish between them with the designations *cis* (meaning "same side") and *trans* (meaning "opposite sides"). Compounds such as these, with the same molecular formula but different structures or different spatial arrangement of atoms, are called *isomers*. Nature can—and does—make different compounds out of the same atoms by arranging the atoms in different ways. Isomerism is common throughout chemistry and especially important in organic chemistry, as we will discuss in Chapter 20.

Conceptual Connection 10.6 Single and Double Bonds

In Section 9.10 we learned that double bonds are stronger and shorter than single bonds. For example, a C—C single bond has an average bond energy of 347 kJ/mole while a C=C double bond has an average bond energy of 611 kJ/mole. Use valence bond theory to explain why a double bond is *not* simply twice as strong as a single bond.

sp Hybridization and Triple Bonds

Hybridization of one *s* and one *p* orbital results in two *sp* hybrid orbitals and two leftover unhybridized *p* orbitals.

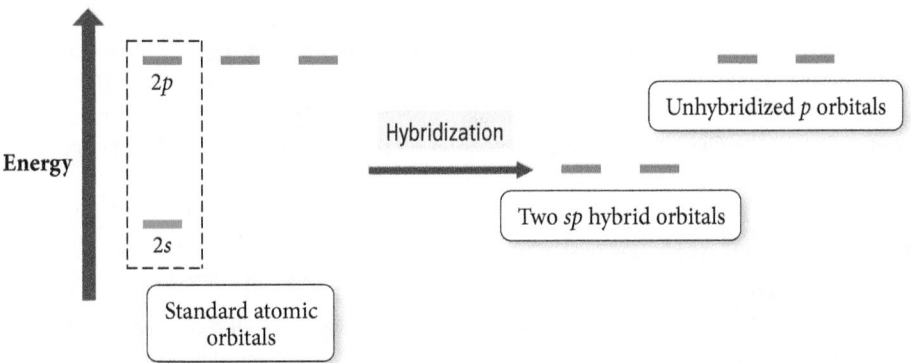

The shapes of the *sp* hybrid orbitals are shown in Figure 10.10 ▼. Notice that the two *sp* hybrid orbitals are arranged in a linear geometry with a 180° angle between them. The unhybridized *p* orbitals are oriented in the plane that is perpendicular to the hybridized *sp* orbitals.

Formation of *sp* Hybrid Orbitals

◄ **FIGURE 10.10 *sp* Hybridization**   One *s* orbital and one *p* orbital combine to form two *sp* hybrid orbitals. Two *p* orbitals (not shown) remain unhybridized.

The acetylene molecule, HC≡CH, has *sp* hybrid orbitals. The four valence electrons of carbon can distribute themselves among the two *sp* hybrid orbitals and the two *p* orbitals:

Each carbon atom then has four half-filled orbitals and can form four bonds: one with a hydrogen atom and three (a triple bond) with the other carbon atom. We draw the molecule and the overlapping orbitals as follows:

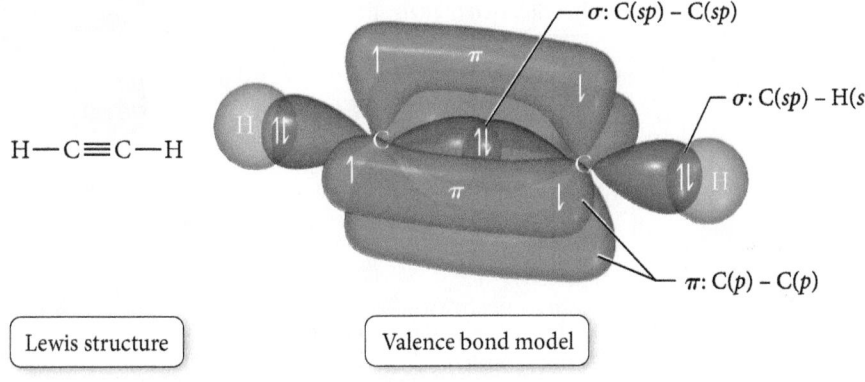

Notice that the triple bond between the two carbon atoms consists of two π bonds (overlapping p orbitals) and one σ bond (overlapping sp orbitals). The sp orbitals on the carbon atoms are linear with 180° between them, so the resulting geometry of the molecule is linear with 180° bond angles, in agreement with the experimentally measured geometry of HC≡CH, and also in agreement with the prediction of VSEPR theory.

sp^3d and sp^3d^2 Hybridization

Recall that, according to the Lewis model, elements occurring in the third row of the periodic table (or below) can exhibit expanded octets (see Section 9.9). The equivalent concept in valence bond theory is hybridization involving the d orbitals. For third-period elements, the $3d$ orbitals are involved in hybridization because their energies are close to the energies of the $3s$ and $3p$ orbitals. The hybridization of one s orbital, three p orbitals, and one d orbital results in sp^3d hybrid orbitals, as shown in Figure 10.11a ▼. The five sp^3d hybrid orbitals have a trigonal bipyramidal arrangement, as shown in Figure 10.11b ▼. As an example of sp^3d hybridization, consider arsenic pentafluoride, AsF$_5$. The arsenic atom bonds to five fluorine atoms by overlap between the sp^3d hybrid orbitals on arsenic and p orbitals on the fluorine atoms, as shown here:

Lewis structure   Valence bond model

The sp^3d orbitals on the arsenic atom are trigonal bipyramidal, so the molecular geometry is trigonal bipyramidal.

(a)   (b)

▲ FIGURE 10.11 **sp^3d Hybridization**   One s orbital, three p orbitals, and one d orbital combine to form five sp^3d hybrid orbitals.

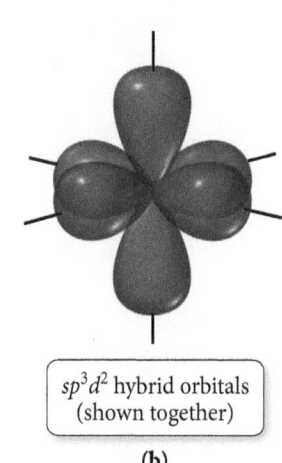

sp^3d^2 hybrid orbitals (shown together)

(b)

▲ **FIGURE 10.12** sp^3d^2 **Hybridization**   One s orbital, three p orbitals, and two d orbitals combine to form six sp^3d^2 hybrid orbitals.

The hybridization of one s orbital, three p orbitals, and *two* d orbitals results in sp^3d^2 hybrid orbitals, as shown in Figure 10.12a ▲. The six sp^3d^2 hybrid orbitals have an octahedral geometry, shown in Figure 10.12b ▲. As an example of sp^3d^2 hybridization, consider sulfur hexafluoride, SF_6. The sulfur atom bonds to six fluorine atoms by overlap between the sp^3d^2 hybrid orbitals on sulfur and p orbitals on the fluorine atoms:

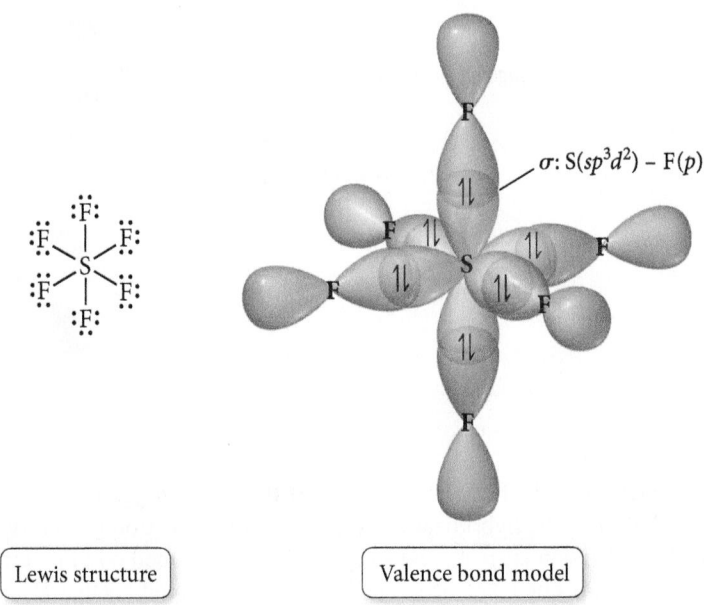

Lewis structure

Valence bond model

The sp^3d^2 orbitals on the sulfur atom are octahedral, so the molecular geometry is octahedral, again in agreement with VSEPR theory and with the experimentally observed geometry.

Writing Hybridization and Bonding Schemes

We have now studied examples of the five main types of atomic orbital hybridization. *But how do we know which hybridization scheme best describes the orbitals of a specific atom in a specific molecule?* In computational valence bond theory, the energy of the molecule is calculated using a computer; the degree of hybridization as well as the type of hybridization are varied to find the combination that gives the molecule the lowest overall energy. For our purposes, we can assign a hybridization scheme from the electron geometry—determined using VSEPR theory—of the central atom (or interior atoms) of the molecule. The five VSEPR electron geometries and the corresponding hybridization

TABLE 10.3 Hybridization Scheme from Electron Geometry

Number of Electron Groups	Electron Geometry (from VSEPR Theory)	Hybridization Scheme	
2	Linear	sp	
3	Trigonal planar	sp^2	120°
4	Tetrahedral	sp^3	109.5°
5	Trigonal bipyramidal	sp^3d	90° / 120°
6	Octahedral	sp^3d^2	90° / 90°

schemes are shown in Table 10.3. For example, if the electron geometry of the central atom is tetrahedral, then the hybridization is sp^3, and if the electron geometry is octahedral, then the hybridization is sp^3d^2, and so on. Although this method of determining the hybridization scheme is not 100% accurate (for example, it predicts that H_2S should be sp^3 when in fact H_2S is largely unhybridized) it is the best we can do without more complex computer-based calculations.

We are now ready to put the Lewis model and valence bond theory together to describe bonding in molecules. In the procedure and examples that follow, you will learn how to write a *hybridization and bonding scheme* for a molecule. This involves drawing the Lewis structure for the molecule, determining its geometry using VSEPR theory, determining the hybridization of the interior atoms, drawing the molecule with its overlapping orbitals, and labeling each bond with the σ and π notation followed by the type of overlapping orbitals. As you can see, this procedure involves virtually everything you have learned about bonding in this chapter and Chapter 9. The procedure for writing a hybridization and bonding scheme is shown in the left column, with two examples of how to apply the procedure in the columns to the right.

PROCEDURE FOR...	EXAMPLE 10.6	EXAMPLE 10.7
Hybridization and Bonding Scheme	**Hybridization and Bonding Scheme** Write a hybridization and bonding scheme for bromine trifluoride, BrF_3.	**Hybridization and Bonding Scheme** Write a hybridization and bonding scheme for acetaldehyde,
1. **Write the Lewis structure for the molecule.**	**SOLUTION** BrF_3 has 28 valence electrons and the following Lewis structure: 	**SOLUTION** Acetaldehyde has 18 valence electrons and the following Lewis structure:
2. **Use VSEPR theory to predict the electron geometry about the central atom (or interior atoms).**	The bromine atom has five electron groups and therefore has a trigonal bipyramidal electron geometry.	The leftmost carbon atom has four electron groups and a tetrahedral electron geometry. The rightmost carbon atom has three electron groups and a trigonal planar geometry.
3. **Select the correct hybridization for the central atom (or interior atoms) based on the electron geometry (see Table 10.3).**	A trigonal bipyramidal electron geometry corresponds to sp^3d hybridization.	The leftmost carbon atom is sp^3 hybridized, and the rightmost carbon atom is sp^2 hybridized.
4. **Sketch the molecule, beginning with the central atom and its orbitals. Show overlap with the appropriate orbitals on the terminal atoms.**		
5. **Label all bonds using the σ or π notation followed by the type of overlapping orbitals.**	σ: $Br(sp^3d)$ – $F(p)$ Lone pairs in sp^3d orbitals	σ: $C(sp^3)$ – $H(s)$ π: $C(p)$ – $O(p)$ σ: $C(sp^2)$ – $H(s)$ σ: $C(sp^3)$ – $C(sp^2)$ σ: $C(sp^2)$ – $O(p)$
	FOR PRACTICE 10.6 Write a hybridization and bonding scheme for XeF_4.	**FOR PRACTICE 10.7** Write a hybridization and bonding scheme for HCN.

EXAMPLE 10.8 Hybridization and Bonding Scheme

Use valence bond theory to write a hybridization and bonding scheme for ethene,
$H_2C=CH_2$

SOLUTION

1. Write the Lewis structure for the molecule.	$$\begin{array}{c} \quad\; H \quad\; H \\ \quad\; \vert \quad\quad \vert \\ H-C=C-H \end{array}$$
2. Apply VSEPR theory to predict the electron geometry about the central atom (or interior atoms).	The molecule has two interior atoms. Since each atom has three electron groups (one double bond and two single bonds), the electron geometry about each atom is trigonal planar.
3. Select the correct hybridization for the central atom (or interior atoms) based on the electron geometry (see Table 10.3).	A trigonal planar geometry corresponds to sp^2 hybridization.
4. Sketch the molecule, beginning with the central atom and its orbitals. Show overlap with the appropriate orbitals on the terminal atoms.	
5. Label all bonds using the σ or π notation followed by the type of overlapping orbitals.	π: C(p) – C(p) σ: C(sp^2) – C(sp^2) σ: C(sp^2) – H(s)

FOR PRACTICE 10.8

Use valence bond theory to write a hybridization and bonding scheme for CO_2.

FOR MORE PRACTICE 10.8

What is the hybridization of the central iodine atom in I_3^-?

10.8 Molecular Orbital Theory: Electron Delocalization

Valence bond theory can explain many aspects of chemical bonding—such as the rigidity of a double bond—but it also has limitations. In valence bond theory, we treat electrons as if they reside in the quantum-mechanical orbitals that we calculated *for atoms*. This is a significant oversimplification that we partially compensate for by hybridization. Nevertheless, we can do better.

In Chapter 7, we learned that the mathematical derivation of energies and orbitals for electrons *in atoms* comes from solving the Schrödinger equation for the atom of interest. For a molecule, we can theoretically do the same thing. The resulting orbitals would be the actual *molecular* orbitals of the molecule as a whole (in contrast to valence bond theory, in which the orbitals are those of individual atoms). As it turns out, however, solving the Schrödinger equation exactly for even the simplest molecules is impossible without making some approximations.

In **molecular orbital (MO) theory**, we do not actually solve the Schrödinger equation for a molecule directly. Instead, we use a trial function, an "educated guess" as to what the solution might be. In other words, rather than mathematically solving the Schrödinger equation, which would give us a mathematical function describing an orbital, we start with a trial mathematical function for the orbital. We then test the trial function to see how well it "works."

We can understand this process by analogy to solving an algebraic equation. Suppose we want to know x in the equation $4x + 5 = 70$ without actually solving the equation. For an easy equation like this one, we might first estimate that $x = 16$. We can then determine how well our estimate works by substituting $x = 16$ into the equation. If the estimate did not work, we could try again until we found the right value of x. (In this case, we can quickly see that x must be a little more than 16.)

In molecular orbital theory, the estimating procedure is analogous. However, we need to add one more important concept to get at the heart of molecular orbital theory. In order to determine how well a trial function for an orbital "works" in molecular orbital theory, we calculate its energy. No matter how good our trial function, *we can never do better than nature at minimizing the energy of the orbital*. In other words, we can devise any trial function for an orbital in a molecule and calculate its energy. The energy we calculate for the devised orbital will always be greater than or (at best) equal to the energy of the actual orbital.

How does this help us? The best possible orbital will therefore be the one with the minimum energy. In modern molecular orbital theory, computer programs are designed to try many different variations of a guessed orbital and compare the energies of each one. The variation with the lowest energy is the best approximation for the actual molecular orbital.

> Molecular orbital theory is a specific application of a more general quantum-mechanical approximation technique called the variational method. In the variational method, the energy of a trial function within the Schrödinger equation is minimized.

> We calculate the energy of an estimated orbital by substituting it into the Schrödinger equation and solving for the energy.

Linear Combination of Atomic Orbitals (LCAO)

The simplest trial functions that work reasonably well in molecular orbital theory turn out to be linear combinations of atomic orbitals, or LCAOs. An LCAO molecular orbital is a *weighted linear sum—analogous to a weighted average—of the valence atomic orbitals* of the atoms in the molecule. At first glance, this concept might seem very similar to that of hybridization in valence bond theory. However, in valence bond theory, hybrid orbitals are weighted linear sums of the valence atomic orbitals of a *particular atom*, and the hybrid orbitals remain *localized* on that atom. In molecular orbital theory, the molecular orbitals are weighted linear sums of the valence atomic orbitals of *all the atoms* in a molecule, and many of the molecular orbitals are *delocalized* over the entire molecule.

Consider the H_2 molecule. One of the molecular orbitals for H_2 is simply an equally weighted sum of the $1s$ orbital from one atom and the $1s$ orbital from the other. We can represent this pictorially and energetically as follows:

> When molecular orbitals are calculated mathematically, it is actually the *wave functions* corresponding to the orbitals that are combined.

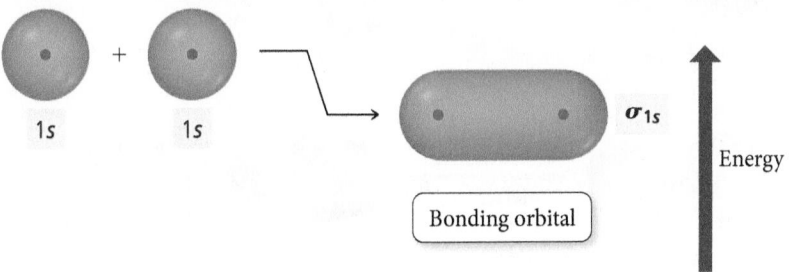

$1s$ $+$ $1s$ σ_{1s} Energy

Bonding orbital

The name of this molecular orbital is σ_{1s}. The σ comes from the shape of the orbital, which looks like a σ bond in valence bond theory, and the $1s$ comes from its formation by a linear sum of $1s$ orbitals. The σ_{1s} orbital is lower in energy than either of the two $1s$ atomic orbitals from which it was formed. For this reason, this orbital is called a **bonding orbital**. When electrons occupy bonding molecular orbitals, the energy of the electrons is lower than it would be if they were occupying atomic orbitals.

We can think of a molecular orbital in a molecule in much the same way that we think about an atomic orbital in an atom. Electrons will seek the lowest energy molecular orbital available, but just as an atom has more than one atomic orbital (and some may be empty), a molecule has more than one molecular orbital (and some may be empty). The next molecular orbital of H_2 is approximated by summing the $1s$ orbital on one hydrogen atom with the *negative* (opposite phase) of the $1s$ orbital on the other hydrogen atom.

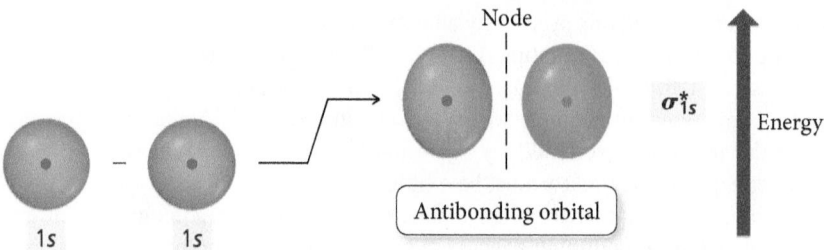

The different phases of the orbitals result in *destructive* interference between them. The resulting molecular orbital therefore has a node between the two atoms. The different colors (red and blue) on either side of the node represent the different phases of the orbital (see Section 7.6). The name of this molecular orbital is σ_{1s}^*. The star indicates that this orbital is an **antibonding orbital**. Electrons in antibonding orbitals have higher energies than they did in their respective atomic orbitals and therefore tend to raise the energy of the system (relative to the unbonded atoms).

In general, when two atomic orbitals are added together to form molecular orbitals, one of the resultant molecular orbitals will be lower in energy (the bonding orbital) than the atomic orbitals and the other will be higher in energy (the antibonding orbital). Remember that electrons in orbitals behave like waves. The bonding molecular orbital arises out of constructive interference between the overlapping atomic orbitals because both orbitals have the same phase. The antibonding orbital arises out of destructive interference between the overlapping atomic orbitals because *subtracting* one from the other means the two interacting orbitals have opposite phases (Figure 10.13 ▼).

For this reason, the bonding orbital has an increased electron density in the internuclear region while the antibonding orbital has a node in the internuclear region. Bonding orbitals have greater electron density in the internuclear region, thereby lowering their energy compared to the orbitals in nonbonded atoms. Antibonding orbitals have less electron density in the internuclear region, and their energies are generally higher than in the orbitals of nonbonded atoms.

▶ **FIGURE 10.13 Formation of Bonding and Antibonding Orbitals** Constructive interference between two atomic orbitals gives rise to a molecular orbital that is lower in energy than the atomic orbitals. This is the bonding orbital. Destructive interference between two atomic orbitals gives rise to a molecular orbital that is higher in energy than the atomic orbitals. This is the antibonding orbital.

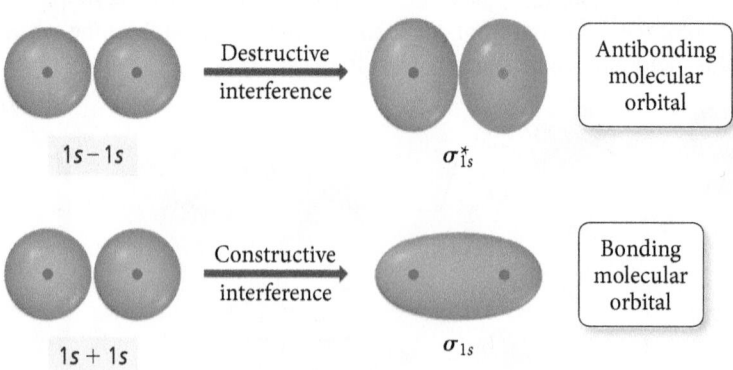

We put all of this together in the molecular orbital energy diagram for H_2:

The molecular orbital (MO) diagram shows that two hydrogen atoms can lower their overall energy by forming H_2 because the electrons can move from higher energy atomic orbitals into the lower energy σ_{1s} bonding molecular orbital. In molecular orbital theory, we define the **bond order** of a diatomic molecule such as H_2 as follows:

$$\text{Bond order} = \frac{\text{(number of electrons in bonding MOs)} \; - \; \text{(number of electrons in antibonding MOs)}}{2}$$

For H_2, the bond order is 1:

$$H_2 \text{ bond order } = \frac{2 - 0}{2} = 1$$

A positive bond order means that there are more electrons in bonding molecular orbitals than in antibonding molecular orbitals. The electrons will therefore have lower energy than they did in the orbitals of the isolated atoms, and a chemical bond will form. In general, the higher the bond order, the stronger the bond. A negative or zero bond order indicates that a bond will *not* form between the atoms. For example, consider the MO diagram for He_2:

Notice that the two additional electrons must go into the higher energy antibonding orbital. There is no net stabilization by joining two helium atoms to form a helium molecule, as indicated by the bond order:

$$He_2 \text{ bond order } = \frac{2 - 2}{2} = 0$$

So according to MO theory, He_2 should not exist as a stable molecule, and indeed it does not. Another interesting case is the helium–helium ion, He_2^+, with the following MO diagram:

The bond order is $\frac{1}{2}$, indicating that He_2^+ should exist, and indeed it does.

Summarizing LCAO–MO Theory:

▶ We can approximate molecular orbitals (MOs) as a linear combination of atomic orbitals (AOs). The total number of MOs formed from a particular set of AOs always equals the number of AOs in the set.

▶ When two AOs combine to form two MOs, one MO is lower in energy (the bonding MO) and the other is higher in energy (the antibonding MO).

▶ When assigning the electrons of a molecule to MOs, fill the lowest energy MOs first with a maximum of two spin-paired electrons per orbital.

▶ When assigning electrons to two MOs of the same energy, follow Hund's rule—fill the orbitals singly first, with parallel spins, before pairing.

▶ The bond order in a diatomic molecule is the number of electrons in bonding MOs minus the number in antibonding MOs divided by two. Stable bonds require a positive bond order (more electrons in bonding MOs than in antibonding MOs).

Notice the power of the molecular orbital approach. Every electron that enters a bonding molecular orbital stabilizes the molecule or polyatomic ion, and every electron that enters an antibonding molecular orbital destabilizes it. The emphasis on electron pairs has been removed. One electron in a bonding molecular orbital stabilizes half as much as two, so a bond order of one-half is nothing mysterious.

EXAMPLE 10.9 Bond Order

Use molecular orbital theory to predict the bond order in H_2^-. Is the H_2^- bond a stronger or weaker bond than the H_2 bond?

SOLUTION

The H_2^- ion has three electrons. Assign the three electrons to the molecular orbitals, filling lower energy orbitals first and proceeding to higher energy orbitals.	
Calculate the bond order by subtracting the number of electrons in antibonding orbitals from the number in bonding orbitals and dividing the result by two.	H_2^- bond order $= \dfrac{2-1}{2} = +\frac{1}{2}$

Since the bond order is positive, H_2^- should be stable. However, the bond order of H_2^- is lower than the bond order of H_2 (which is 1); therefore, the bond in H_2^- is weaker than in H_2.

FOR PRACTICE 10.9
Use molecular orbital theory to predict the bond order in H_2^+. Is the H_2^+ bond a stronger or weaker bond than the H_2 bond?

Period Two Homonuclear Diatomic Molecules

Homonuclear diatomic molecules (molecules made up of two atoms of the same kind) formed from second-period elements have between 2 and 16 valence electrons. To explain bonding in these molecules, we must consider the next set of higher energy molecular orbitals, which can be approximated by linear combinations of the valence atomic orbitals of the period 2 elements.

The core electrons can be ignored (as they are in other models for bonding), because these electrons do not contribute significantly to chemical bonding.

We begin with Li_2. Even though lithium is normally a metal, we can use MO theory to predict whether or not the Li_2 molecule should exist in the gas phase. We approximate the molecular orbitals in Li_2 as linear combinations of the $2s$ atomic orbitals. The resulting molecular orbitals look much like those of the H_2 molecule. The MO diagram for Li_2 therefore looks a lot like the MO diagram for H_2:

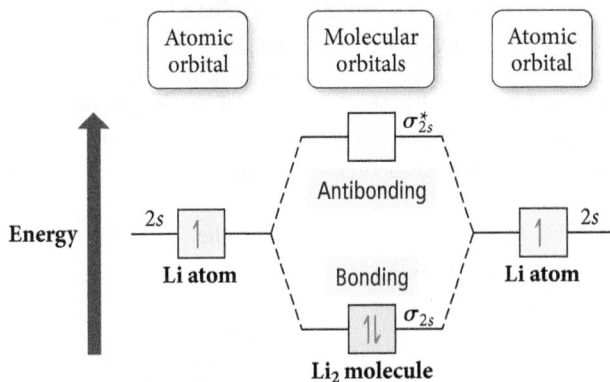

The two valence electrons of Li_2 occupy a bonding molecular orbital. We would predict that the Li_2 molecule is stable with a bond order of 1. Experiments confirm this prediction. In contrast, consider the MO diagram for Be_2:

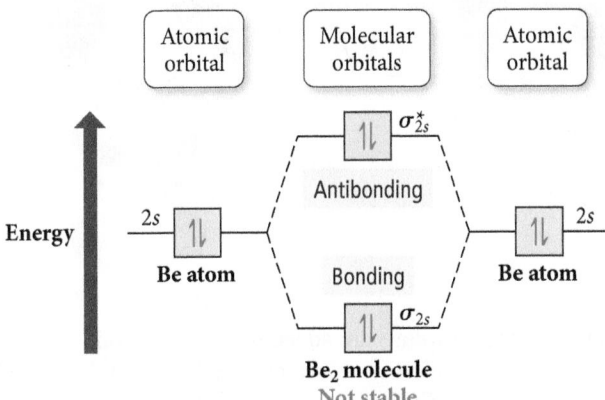

The four valence electrons of Be_2 occupy one bonding MO and one antibonding MO. The bond order is 0 and we predict that Be_2 should not be stable, again consistent with experimental findings.

The next homonuclear molecule composed of second row elements is B_2, which has six total valence electrons to accommodate. We can approximate the next higher energy molecular orbitals for B_2 and the rest of the period 2 diatomic molecules as linear combinations of the 2*p* orbitals taken pairwise. Since the three 2*p* orbitals orient along three orthogonal axes, we must assign similar axes to the molecule. In this book, we assign the internuclear axis to be the *x* direction. Then the LCAO–MOs that result from combining the $2p_x$ orbitals—the ones that lie along the internuclear axis—from each atom are represented pictorially as follows:

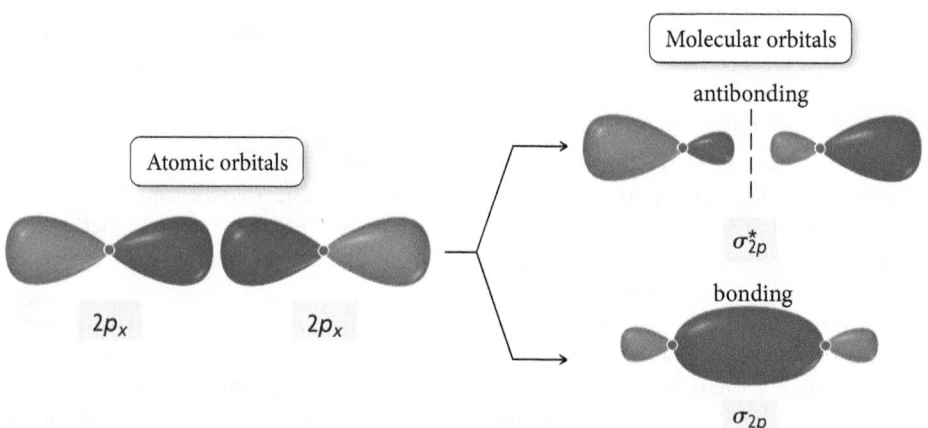

The bonding MO in this pair looks something like candy in a wrapper, with increased electron density in the internuclear region due to constructive interference between the two 2*p* atomic orbitals. It has the characteristic σ shape (it is cylindrically symmetric about the bond axis) and is therefore called the σ_{2p} bonding orbital. The antibonding orbital, called σ^*_{2p}, has a node between the two nuclei (due to destructive interference between the two 2*p* orbitals) and is higher in energy than either of the $2p_x$ orbitals.

The LCAO–MOs that result from combining the $2p_z$ orbitals from each atom are represented pictorially as follows:

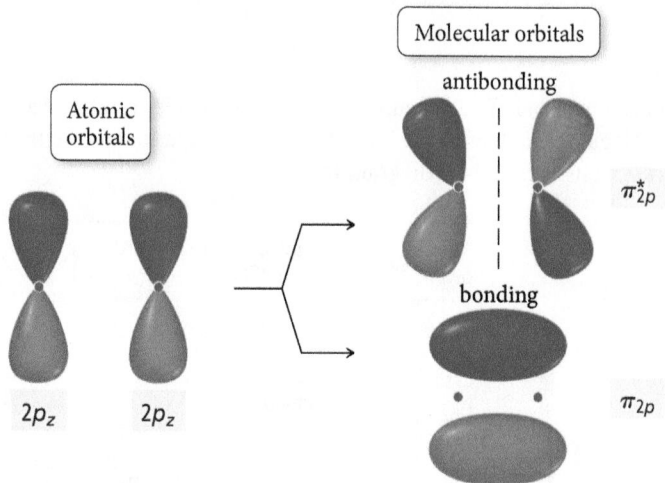

Notice that in this case the *p* orbitals are added together in a side-by-side orientation (in contrast to the $2p_x$ orbitals, which were oriented end to end). The resultant molecular orbitals consequently have a different shape. The electron density in the bonding molecular orbital is above and below the internuclear axis with a nodal plane that includes the internuclear axis. This orbital resembles the electron density distribution of a π bond in valence bond theory. We call this orbital the π_{2p} orbital. The corresponding antibonding orbital has an additional node *between* the nuclei (perpendicular to the internuclear axis) and is called the π^*_{2p} orbital.

The LCAO–MOs that result from combining the $2p_y$ orbitals from each atom are represented pictorially as follows:

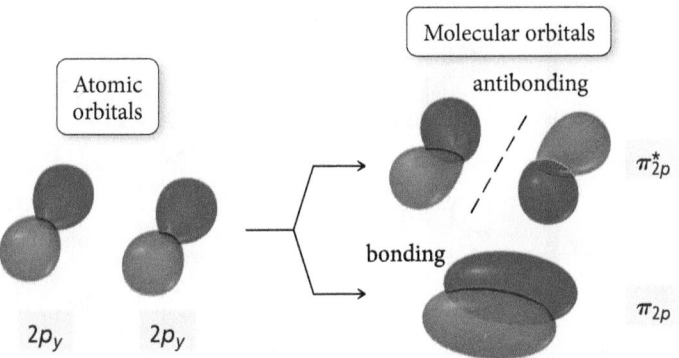

The only difference between the $2p_y$ and the $2p_z$ atomic orbitals is a 90° rotation about the internuclear axis. Consequently, the only difference between the resulting MOs is a 90° rotation about the internuclear axis. The energies and the names of the bonding and antibonding MOs obtained from the combination of the $2p_y$ AOs are identical to those obtained from the combination of the $2p_z$ AOs.

Before we can draw MO diagrams for B_2 and the other second-period diatomic molecules, we must determine the relative energy ordering of the MOs obtained from the $2p$ AO combinations. This is not a simple task. The relative ordering of MOs obtained from LCAO–MO theory is usually determined computationally. There is no single order that works for all molecules. For second-period diatomic molecules, computations reveal that the energy ordering for B_2, C_2, and N_2 is slightly different than that for O_2, F_2, and Ne_2 as follows:

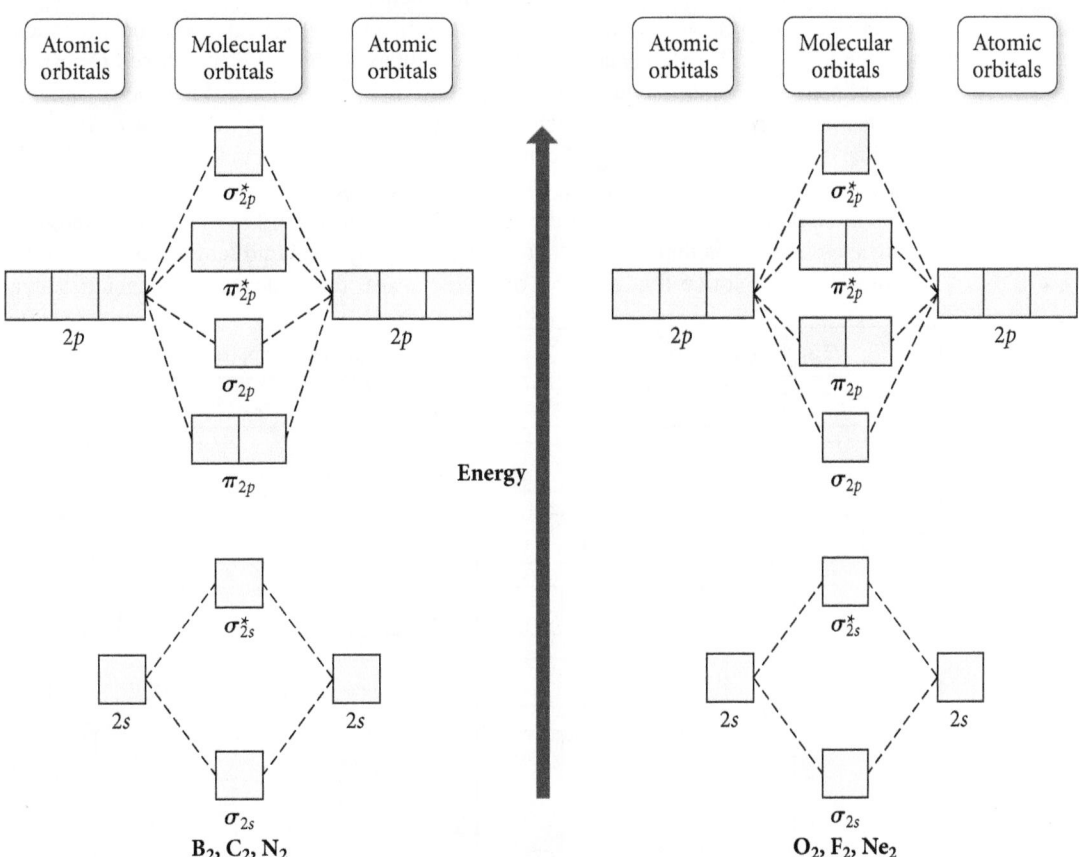

▲ Molecular orbital energy diagrams for second-period diatomic molecules show that the energy ordering of the π_{2p} and σ_{2p} molecular orbitals can vary.

▶ **FIGURE 10.14 The Effects of 2s–2p Mixing** The degree of mixing between two orbitals decreases with increasing energy difference between them. Mixing of the $2s$ and $2p_x$ orbitals is therefore greater in B_2, C_2, and N_2 than in O_2, F_2, and Ne_2 because in B, C, and N the energy levels of the atomic orbitals are more closely spaced than in O, F, and Ne. This mixing produces a change in energy ordering for the π_{2p} and σ_{2p} molecular orbitals.

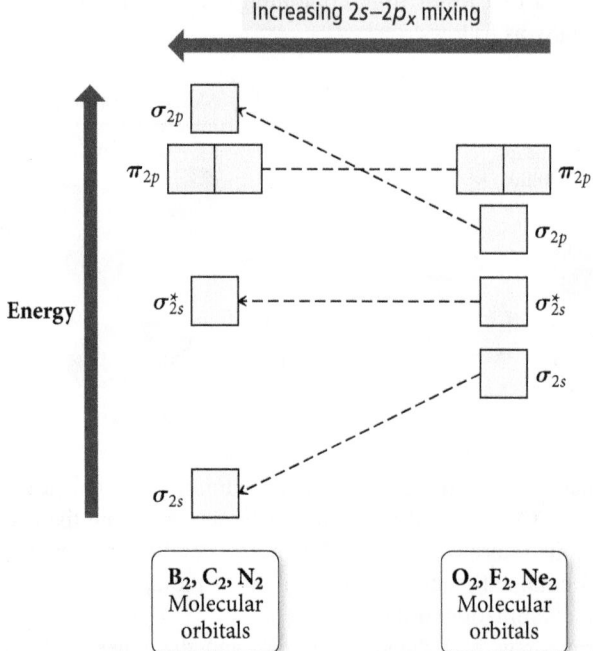

The reason for the difference in energy ordering can only be explained by going back to our LCAO–MO model. In our simplified treatment, we assumed that the MOs that result from the second-period AOs could be calculated pairwise. In other words, we took the linear combination of a $2s$ from one atom with the $2s$ from another, a $2p_x$ from one atom with a $2p_x$ from the other and so on. However, in a more comprehensive treatment, the MOs are formed from linear combinations that include all of the AOs that are relatively close to each other in energy and of the correct symmetry. Specifically, in a more detailed treatment, the two $2s$ orbitals and the two $2p_x$ orbitals should all be combined to form a total of four molecular orbitals. The extent to which you include this type of mixing affects the energy levels of the corresponding MOs, as shown in Figure 10.14 ▲. The bottom line is that s–p mixing is significant in B_2, C_2, and N_2 but not in O_2, F_2, and Ne_2. The result is a different energy ordering, depending on the specific molecule.

The MO energy diagrams for the rest of the second-period homonuclear diatomic molecules, as well as their bond orders, bond energies, and bond lengths, are shown in Figure 10.15 ▼. Notice that as bond order increases, the bond gets stronger (greater

	Large 2s–2p_x interaction			Small 2s–2p_x interaction		
	B_2	C_2	N_2	O_2	F_2	Ne_2
σ_{2p}^*	☐	☐	☐	σ_{2p}^* ☐	☐	⇅
π_{2p}^*	☐ ☐	☐ ☐	☐ ☐	π_{2p}^* ↑ ↑	⇅ ⇅	⇅ ⇅
σ_{2p}	☐	☐	⇅	π_{2p} ⇅ ⇅	⇅ ⇅	⇅ ⇅
π_{2p}	↑ ↑	⇅ ⇅	⇅ ⇅	σ_{2p} ⇅	⇅	⇅
σ_{2s}^*	⇅	⇅	⇅	σ_{2s}^* ⇅	⇅	⇅
σ_{2s}	⇅	⇅	⇅	σ_{2s} ⇅	⇅	⇅
Bond order	1	2	3	2	1	0
Bond energy (kJ/mol)	290	620	946	498	159	—
Bond length (pm)	159	131	110	121	143	—

▲ **FIGURE 10.15 Molecular Orbital Energy Diagrams for Second-Row p-block Homonuclear Diatomic Molecules** bond energy) and shorter (smaller bond length). For B_2, with six electrons, the bond order is 1. For C_2, the bond order is 2, and for N_2, the bond order reaches a maximum with a value of 3. Recall that the Lewis structure for N_2 has a triple bond, so both the Lewis model and molecular orbital theory predict a strong bond for N_2, which is experimentally observed.

In O_2, the two additional electrons occupy antibonding orbitals and the bond order is 2. These two electrons are unpaired—they occupy the π_{2p}^* orbitals *singly with parallel spins*, as indicated by Hund's rule. The presence of unpaired electrons in the molecular orbital diagram of oxygen is significant because oxygen is known from experiment to be *paramagnetic* (see Section 8.7)—it is attracted to a magnetic field. The paramagnetism of oxygen can be demonstrated by suspending liquid oxygen between the poles of a magnet. This magnetic property is the direct result of *unpaired electrons,* whose spin and movement around the nucleus (more accurately known as orbital angular momentum) generate tiny magnetic fields. When a paramagnetic substance is placed in an external magnetic field, the magnetic fields of each atom or molecule align with the external field, creating the attraction (much as two magnets attract each other when properly oriented). In contrast, when the electrons in an atom or molecule are all *paired*, the magnetic fields caused by electron spin and orbital angular momentum tend to cancel each other, resulting in diamagnetism. A **diamagnetic** substance is not attracted to a magnetic field (and is, in fact, slightly repelled).

▲ Liquid oxygen can be suspended between the poles of a magnet because it is paramagnetic. It contains unpaired electrons (depicted here in the inset) that generate tiny magnetic fields, which align with and interact with the external field.

In the Lewis structure of O_2, as well as in the valence bond model of O_2, all of the electrons seem to be paired:

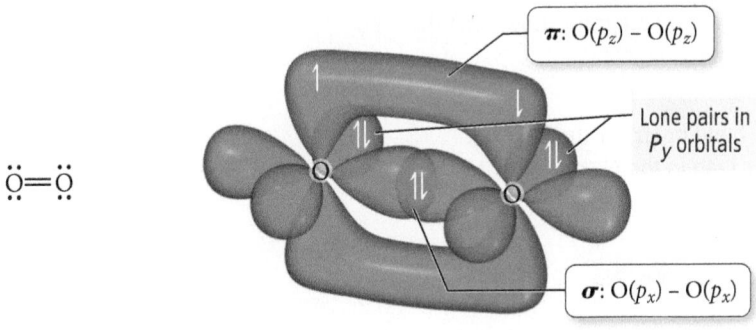

The s orbital on each O atom contains two electrons, but for clarity neither the s orbitals nor the electrons that occupy them are shown.

In the MO diagram for O_2, however, we can see the unpaired electrons. Molecular orbital theory is the more powerful theory in that it can account for the paramagnetism of O_2—it gives us a picture of bonding that more closely corresponds to what we see in experiments. Continuing along the second-row homonuclear diatomic molecules we see that F_2 has a bond order of 1 and Ne_2 has a bond order of 0, again consistent with experiment since F_2 exists and Ne_2 does not.

EXAMPLE 10.10 Molecular Orbital Theory

Draw an MO energy diagram and determine the bond order for the N_2^- ion. Do you expect the bond to be stronger or weaker than in the N_2 molecule? Is N_2^- diamagnetic or paramagnetic?

SOLUTION

Write an energy level diagram for the molecular orbitals in N_2^-. Use the energy ordering for N_2.	□ σ_{2p}^* □□ π_{2p}^* □ σ_{2p} □□ π_{2p} □ σ_{2s}^* □ σ_{2s}
The N_2^- ion has 11 valence electrons (5 for each nitrogen atom plus 1 for the negative charge). Assign the electrons to the molecular orbitals beginning with the lowest energy orbitals and following Hund's rule.	□ σ_{2p}^* $\uparrow$ □ π_{2p}^* $\uparrow\downarrow$ σ_{2p} $\uparrow\downarrow$ $\uparrow\downarrow$ π_{2p} $\uparrow\downarrow$ σ_{2s}^* $\uparrow\downarrow$ σ_{2s}
Calculate the bond order by subtracting the number of electrons in antibonding orbitals from the number in bonding orbitals and dividing the result by two.	N_2^- bond order $= \dfrac{8-3}{2} = +2.5$

The bond order is 2.5, which is a lower bond order than in the N_2 molecule (bond order = 3); therefore, the bond is weaker. The MO diagram shows that the N_2^- ion has one unpaired electron and is therefore paramagnetic.

FOR PRACTICE 10.10
Draw an MO energy diagram and determine the bond order for the N_2^+ ion. Do you expect the bond to be stronger or weaker than in the N_2 molecule? Is N_2^+ diamagnetic or paramagnetic?

FOR MORE PRACTICE 10.10
Use molecular orbital theory to determine the bond order of Ne_2.

Second-Period Heteronuclear Diatomic Molecules

We can also apply molecular orbital theory to heteronuclear diatomic molecules (two different atoms). For example, we can draw an MO diagram for NO as follows:

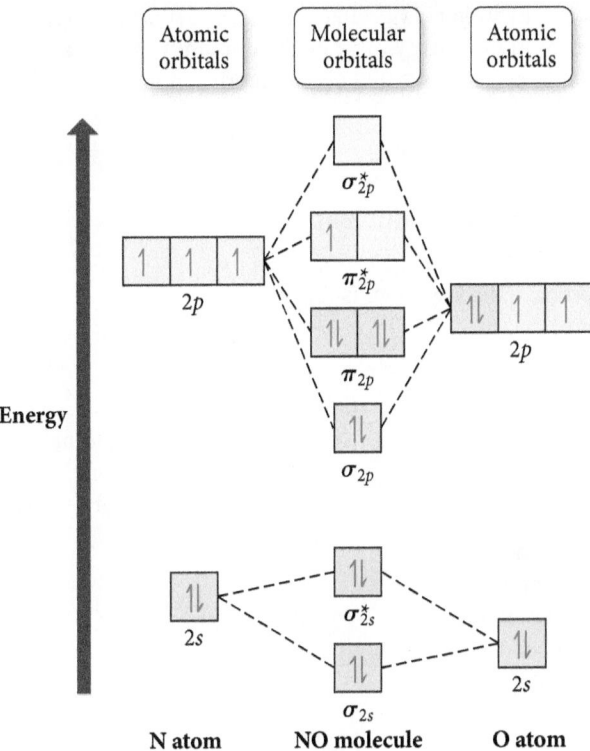

Oxygen is more electronegative than nitrogen, so its atomic orbitals are lower in energy than nitrogen's atomic orbitals. When two atomic orbitals are identical and of equal energy, the weighting of each orbital in forming a molecular orbital is identical. However, when two atomic orbitals are different, the weighting of each orbital in forming a molecular orbital may be different. More specifically, when a molecular orbital is approximated as a linear combination of atomic orbitals of different energies, the lower energy atomic orbital makes a greater contribution to the bonding molecular orbital and the higher energy atomic orbital makes a greater contribution to the antibonding molecular orbital. For example, notice that the σ_{2s} bonding orbital is closer in energy to the oxygen $2s$ orbital than to the nitrogen $2s$ orbital. We can also see this unequal weighting in the shape of the resultant molecular orbital, in which the electron density is concentrated on the oxygen atom, as shown in Figure 10.16 ►.

As another example of a heteronuclear diatomic molecule, consider the MO diagram for HF:

A given orbital will have lower energy in a more electronegative atom. For this reason, electronegative atoms have the ability to attract electrons to themselves.

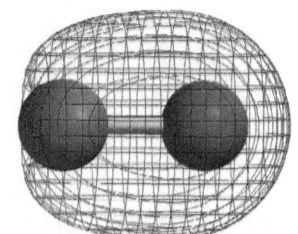

▲ FIGURE 10.16 **Shape of σ_{2s} bonding orbital in NO** The molecular orbital shows more electron density at the oxygen end of the molecule because the atomic orbitals of oxygen, the more electronegative element, are lower in energy than those of nitrogen. They therefore contribute more to the bonding molecular orbital.

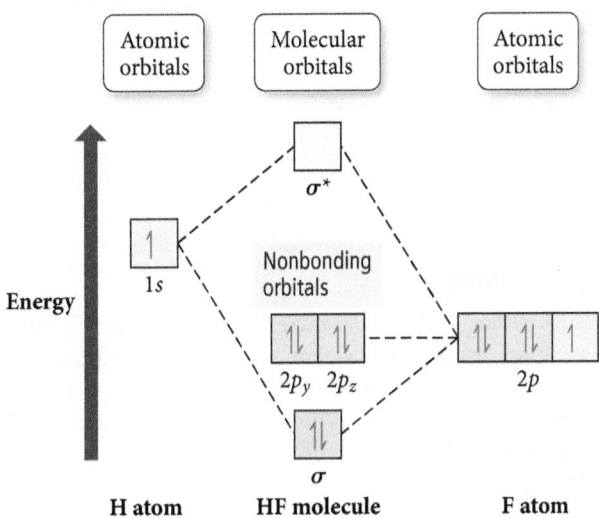

Fluorine is so electronegative that all of its atomic orbitals are lower in energy than hydrogen's atomic orbitals. In fact, fluorine's $2s$ orbital is so low in energy compared to hydrogen's $1s$ orbital that it does not contribute appreciably to the molecular orbitals. The molecular orbitals in HF are approximated by the linear combination of the fluorine $2p_x$ orbital and the hydrogen $1s$ orbital. The other $2p$ orbitals remain localized on the fluorine and appear in the energy diagram as **nonbonding orbitals**. The electrons in the nonbonding orbitals remain localized on the fluorine atom.

EXAMPLE 10.11   Molecular Orbital Theory for Heteronuclear Diatomic Molecules and Ions

Use molecular orbital theory to determine the bond order of the CN^- ion. Is the ion paramagnetic or diamagnetic?

SOLUTION

Determine the number of valence electrons in the molecule or ion.	Number of valence electrons $= 4$ (from C) $+ 5$ (from N) $+ 1$ (from negative charge) $= 10$
Write an energy level diagram using Figure 10.15 as a guide. Fill the orbitals beginning with the lowest energy orbital and progressing upward until all electrons have been assigned to an orbital. Remember to allow no more than two electrons (with paired spins) per orbital and to fill degenerate orbitals with single electrons (with parallel spins) before pairing.	σ_{2p}^* π_{2p}^* σ_{2p} ($\uparrow\downarrow$) π_{2p} ($\uparrow\downarrow$ $\uparrow\downarrow$) σ_{2s}^* ($\uparrow\downarrow$) σ_{2s} ($\uparrow\downarrow$)
Calculate the bond order using the appropriate formula: Bond order = $\frac{\text{(number of } e^- \text{ in bonding MOs)} - \text{(number of } e^- \text{ in antibonding MOs)}}{2}$	CN^- bond order $= \frac{8-2}{2} = +3$
If the MO diagram has unpaired electrons, the molecule or ion is paramagnetic. If the electrons are all paired, the molecule or ion is diamagnetic.	Since the MO diagram has no unpaired electrons, the ion is diamagnetic.

FOR PRACTICE 10.11
Use molecular orbital theory to determine the bond order of NO. (Use the energy ordering of O_2.) Is the molecule paramagnetic or diamagnetic?

Polyatomic Molecules

With the aid of computers, molecular orbital theory can be applied to polyatomic molecules and ions, yielding results that correlate very well with experimental measurements. These applications are beyond the scope of this text. However, the delocalization of electrons over an entire molecule is an important contribution of molecular orbital theory to our basic understanding of chemical bonding. For example, consider the Lewis structure and valence bond diagram of ozone:

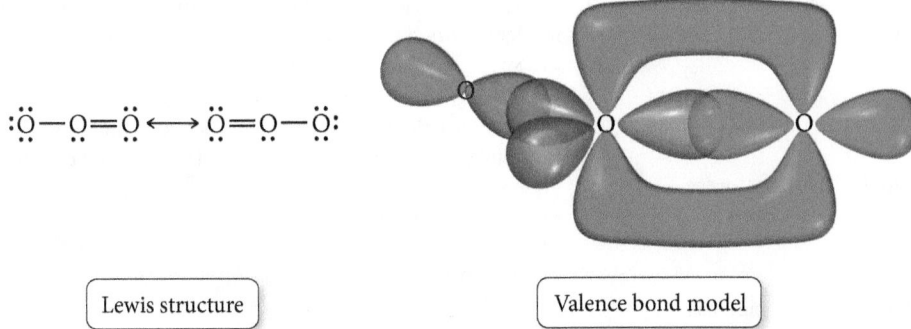

:Ö—O=Ö: ⟷ :Ö=O—Ö:

| Lewis structure | Valence bond model |

In the Lewis model, we use resonance forms to represent the two equivalent bonds. In valence bond theory, it appears that the two oxygen–oxygen bonds should be different. In molecular orbital theory, however, the π molecular orbitals in ozone are formed from a linear combination of the three oxygen 2p orbitals and are delocalized over the entire molecule. The lowest energy π bonding molecular orbital is shown here.

When we examine ozone in nature, we indeed find two equivalent bonds. A similar situation occurs with benzene (C_6H_6). In the Lewis model, we represent the structure with two resonance forms:

In molecular orbital theory, the π molecular orbitals in benzene are formed from a linear combination of the six carbon 2p orbitals and are delocalized over the entire molecule. The lowest energy π bonding molecular orbital is shown here.

Benzene is in fact a highly symmetric molecule with six identical carbon–carbon bonds. The best picture of the π electrons in benzene is one in which the electrons occupy roughly circular-shaped orbitals above and below the plane of the molecule, as depicted in the molecular orbital theory approach.

Conceptual Connection 10.7 What Is a Chemical Bond? Part II

We have learned that the Lewis model portrays a chemical bond as the transfer or sharing of electrons represented as dots. Valence bond theory portrays a chemical bond as the overlap of two half-filled atomic orbitals. What is a chemical bond according to molecular orbital theory?

CHAPTER IN REVIEW

Self Assessment Quiz

Q1. Determine the molecular geometry of CBr_4.
a) linear
b) trigonal planar
c) tetrahedral
d) trigonal pyramidal

Q2. Determine the molecular geometry of SeF_4.
a) tetrahedral
b) trigonal bipyramidal
c) T-shaped
d) seesaw

Q3. Predict the relative bond angles in BF_3 and SO_2.
a) BF_3 bond angles > SO_2 bond angle
b) SO_2 bond angle > BF_3 bond angles
c) BF_3 bond angles = SO_2 bond angle
d) Relative bond angles cannot be predicted.

Q4. Predict the molecular geometry about N in the molecule CH_3NHCH_3.
a) linear
b) trigonal planar
c) trigonal pyramidal
d) bent

Q5. Which molecule is polar?
a) SF_2
b) BH_3
c) PF_5
d) CS_2

Q6. Determine the hybridization about O in CH_3OH.
a) sp
b) sp^2
c) sp^3
d) sp^3d

Q7. Determine the hybridization about C in H_2CO.
a) sp
b) sp^2
c) sp^3
d) sp^3d

Q8. According to valence bond theory, which kind of orbitals overlap to form the P—Cl bonds in PCl_5?
a) $P(sp^3)$ - $Cl(p)$
b) $P(sp^3d)$ - $Cl(s)$
c) $P(sp^3)$ - $Cl(s)$
d) $P(sp^3d)$ - $Cl(p)$

Q9. Use molecular orbital theory to determine the bond order in C_2.
a) 0
b) 1
c) 2
d) 3

Q10. Use molecular orbital theory to predict which species has the strongest bond.
a) N_2
b) N_2^-
c) N_2^+
d) All bonds are equivalent according to molecular orbital theory.

Q11. Use molecular orbital theory to determine which molecule is diamagnetic.
a) CO
b) B_2
c) O_2
d) None of the above (all are paramagnetic)

Q12. Which hybridization scheme occurs about nitrogen when nitrogen forms a double bond?
a) sp
b) sp^2
c) sp^3
d) sp^3d

Q13. Which molecule geometry results when a central atom has five total electron groups, with three of those being bonding groups and two being lone pairs?
a) trigonal bipyramidal
b) seesaw
c) T-shaped
d) bent

Q14. Determine the correct molecular geometry (from left to right) about each interior atom in CH_3CH_2OH.
a) 1st C tetrahedral; 2nd C trigonal planar; O linear
b) 1st C trigonal planar; 2nd C bent; O linear
c) 1st C trigonal planar; 2nd C trigonal pyramidal; O bent
d) 1st C tetrahedral; 2nd C tetrahedral; O bent

Q15. The central atom in a molecule has a bent molecular geometry. Determine the hybridization of the orbitals in the atom.
a) sp
b) sp^2
c) sp^3
d) Hybridization cannot be determine from information given.

Answers: 1. (c) **2.** (d) **3.** (a) **4.** (c) **5.** (a) **6.** (c) **7.** (b) **8.** (d) **9.** (c) **10.** (a) **11.** (a) **12.** (b) **13.** (c) **14.** (d) **15.** (d)

Key Terms

Section 10.2
valence shell electron pair repulsion (VSEPR) theory (426)
electron groups (426)
linear geometry (427)
trigonal planar geometry (427)
tetrahedral geometry (428)
trigonal bipyramidal geometry (429)

octahedral geometry (429)

Section 10.3
electron geometry (430)
molecular geometry (430)
trigonal pyramidal geometry (430)
bent geometry (431)
seesaw geometry (432)

T-shaped geometry (432)
square pyramidal geometry (433)
square planar geometry (433)

Section 10.6
valence bond theory (443)

Section 10.7
hybridization (445)
hybrid orbitals (445)

pi (π) bond (450)
sigma (σ) bond (450)

Section 10.8
molecular orbital theory (459)
bonding orbital (460)
antibonding orbital (460)
bond order (461)
diamagnetic (467)
nonbonding orbitals (470)

Key Concepts

Molecular Shape and VSEPR Theory (10.1–10.4)

▶ The properties of molecules are directly related to their shapes. In VSEPR theory, molecular geometries are determined by the repulsions between electron groups on the central atom. An electron group can be a single bond, double bond, triple bond, lone pair, or even a single electron.

▶ The five basic molecular shapes are linear (two electron groups), trigonal planar (three electron groups), tetrahedral (four electron groups), trigonal bipyramidal (five electron groups), and octahedral (six electron groups).

▶ When lone pairs are present on the central atom, the *electron* geometry is still one of the five basic shapes, but one or more positions are occupied by lone pairs. The *molecular* geometry is therefore different from the electron geometry. Lone pairs are positioned so as to minimize repulsions with other lone pairs and with bonding pairs.

Polarity (10.5)

▶ The polarity of a polyatomic molecule containing polar bonds depends on its geometry. If the dipole moments of the polar bonds are aligned in such a way that they cancel one another, the molecule will not be polar. If they are aligned in such a way as to sum together, the molecule will be polar.

▶ Highly symmetric molecules tend to be nonpolar, while asymmetric molecules containing polar bonds tend to be polar. The polarity of a molecule dramatically affects its properties.

Valence Bond Theory (10.6–10.7)

▶ In contrast to the Lewis model, in which a covalent chemical bond is the sharing of electrons represented by dots, in valence bond theory a chemical bond is the overlap of half-filled atomic orbitals (or in some cases the overlap between a completely filled orbital and an empty one).

▶ The overlapping orbitals may be the standard atomic orbitals, such as $1s$ or $2p$ or they may be hybridized atomic orbitals, which are mathematical combinations of the standard orbitals on a single atom. The basic hybridized orbitals are sp, sp^2, sp^3, sp^3d, and sp^3d^2.

▶ The geometry of the molecule is determined by the geometry of the overlapping orbitals.

▶ In our treatment of valence bond theory, we use the molecular geometry determined by VSEPR theory to determine the correct hybridization scheme.

▶ In valence bond theory, we distinguish between two types of bonds, σ (sigma) and π (pi). In a σ bond, the orbital overlap occurs in the region that lies directly between the two bonding atoms. In a π bond, formed from the side-by-side overlap of p orbitals, the overlap occurs above and below the region that lies directly between the two bonding atoms.

▶ Rotation about a σ bond is relatively free, while rotation about a π bond is restricted.

Molecular Orbital Theory (10.8)

▶ The simplest molecular orbitals are linear combinations of atomic orbitals (LCAOs), weighted averages of the atomic orbitals of the different atoms in the molecule.

▶ When two atomic orbitals combine to form molecular orbitals, they will form one molecular orbital of lower energy (the bonding orbital) and one of higher energy (the antibonding orbital).

▶ A set of molecular orbitals are filled in much the same way as atomic orbitals.

▶ The stability of the molecule and the strength of the bond depend on the number of electrons in bonding orbitals compared to the number in antibonding orbitals.

Key Equations and Relationships

Bond Order of a Diatomic Molecule (10.8)

$$\text{Bond order} = \frac{(\text{number of electron in bonding MOs}) - (\text{number of electrons in antibonding MOs})}{2}$$

Key Learning Outcomes

Chapter Objectives	Assessment
Using VSEPR Theory to Predict the Basic Shapes of Molecules (10.2)	Example 10.1 For Practice 10.1 Exercises 31–32
Predicting Molecular Geometries Using VSEPR Theory and the Effects of Lone Pairs (10.4)	Examples 10.2–10.3 For Practice 10.2–10.3 Exercises 35–36
Predicting the Shapes of Larger Molecules (10.4)	Example 10.4 For Practice 10.4 Exercises 41–42, 45–46
Using Molecular Shape to Determine Polarity of a Molecule (10.5)	Example 10.5 For Practice 10.5 Exercises 49–52
Writing Hybridization and Bonding Schemes Using Valence Bond Theory (10.7)	Examples 10.6–10.8 For Practice 10.6–10.8 For More Practice 10.8 Exercises 61–66
Drawing Molecular Orbital Diagrams to Predict Bond Order and Magnetism of a Diatomic Molecule (10.8)	Examples 10.9–10.11 For Practice 10.9–10.11 For More Practice 10.10 Exercises 71–72, 75–78, 81–82

EXERCISES

Review Questions

1. Why is molecular geometry important? Cite some examples.
2. According to VSEPR theory, what determines the geometry of a molecule?
3. Name and sketch the five basic electron geometries, and state the number of electron groups corresponding to each. What constitutes an *electron group?*
4. Explain the difference between electron geometry and molecular geometry. Under what circumstances are they not the same?
5. Give the correct electron and molecular geometries that correspond to each set of electron groups around the central atom of a molecule.
   a. four electron groups overall; three bonding groups and one lone pair
   b. four electron groups overall; two bonding groups and two lone pairs
   c. five electron groups overall; four bonding groups and one lone pair
   d. five electron groups overall; three bonding groups and two lone pairs
   e. five electron groups overall; two bonding groups and three lone pairs
   f. six electron groups overall; five bonding groups and one lone pair
   g. six electron groups overall; four bonding groups and two lone pairs
6. How do you apply VSEPR theory to predict the shape of a molecule with more than one interior atom?
7. How do you determine if a molecule is polar? Why is polarity important?
8. What is a chemical bond according to valence bond theory?
9. In valence bond theory, what determines the geometry of a molecule?
10. In valence bond theory, the interaction energy between the electrons and nucleus of one atom with the electrons and nucleus of another atom is usually negative (stabilizing) when
   _____.
11. What is hybridization? Why is hybridization necessary in valence bond theory?
12. How does hybridization of the atomic orbitals in the central atom of a molecule help lower the overall energy of the molecule?
13. How is the *number* of hybrid orbitals related to the number of standard atomic orbitals that are hybridized?
14. Sketch each hybrid orbital:
   a. sp
   b. sp^2
   c. sp^3
   d. sp^3d
   e. sp^3d^2

15. In the Lewis model, the two bonds in a double bond look identical. However, valence bond theory shows that they are not. Describe a double bond according to valence bond theory. Explain why rotation is restricted about a double bond, but not about a single bond.
16. Name the hybridization scheme that corresponds to each electron geometry:
   a. linear
   b. trigonal planar
   c. tetrahedral
   d. trigonal bipyramidal
   e. octahedral
17. What is a chemical bond according to molecular orbital theory?
18. Explain the difference between hybrid atomic orbitals in valence bond theory and LCAO molecular orbitals in molecular orbital theory.
19. What is a bonding molecular orbital?
20. What is an antibonding molecular orbital?
21. What is the role of wave interference in determining whether a molecular orbital is bonding or antibonding?
22. In molecular orbital theory, what is bond order? Why is it important?
23. How is the number of molecular orbitals approximated by a linear combination of atomic orbitals related to the number of atomic orbitals used in the approximation?
24. Sketch each molecular orbital.
   a. σ_{2s}
   b. σ_{2s}^*
   c. σ_{2p}
   d. σ_{2p}^*
   e. π_{2p}
   f. π_{2p}^*
25. Draw an energy diagram for the molecular orbitals of period 2 diatomic molecules. Show the difference in ordering for B_2, C_2, and N_2 compared to O_2, F_2, and Ne_2.
26. Why does the energy ordering of the molecular orbitals of the period 2 diatomic molecules change in going from N_2 to O_2?
27. Explain the difference between a paramagnetic species and a diamagnetic one.
28. When applying molecular orbital theory to heteronuclear diatomic molecules, the atomic orbitals used may be of different energies. If two atomic orbitals of different energies make two molecular orbitals, how are the energies of the molecular orbitals related to the energies of the atomic orbitals? How is the shape of the resultant molecular orbitals related to the shapes of the atomic orbitals?
29. In molecular orbital theory, what is a nonbonding orbital?
30. Write a short paragraph describing chemical bonding according to the Lewis model, valence bond theory, and molecular orbital theory. Indicate how the theories differ in their description of a chemical bond and indicate the strengths and weaknesses of each theory. Which theory is correct?

Problems by Topic

VSEPR Theory and Molecular Geometry

31. A molecule with the formula AB_3 has a trigonal pyramidal geometry. How many electron groups are on the central atom (A)?

32. A molecule with the formula AB_3 has a trigonal planar geometry. How many electron groups are on the central atom?

33. For each molecular geometry, list the number of total electron groups, the number of bonding groups, and the number of lone pairs on the central atom.

(a)   (b)   (c)

34. For each molecular geometry, list the number of total electron groups, the number of bonding groups, and the number of lone pairs on the central atom.

(a)   (b)   (c)

35. Determine the electron geometry, molecular geometry, and idealized bond angles for each molecule. In which cases do you expect deviations from the idealized bond angle?
a. PF_3
b. SBr_2
c. $CHCl_3$
d. CS_2

36. Determine the electron geometry, molecular geometry, and idealized bond angles for each molecule. In which cases do you expect deviations from the idealized bond angle?
a. CF_4
b. NF_3
c. OF_2
d. H_2S

37. Which species has the smaller bond angle, H_3O^+ or H_2O? Explain.

38. Which species has the smaller bond angle, ClO_4^- or ClO_3^-? Explain.

39. Determine the molecular geometry and sketch each molecule or ion using the bond conventions shown in the "Representing Molecular Geometries on Paper" box in Section 10.4.
a. SF_4
b. ClF_3
c. IF_2^-
d. IBr_4^-

40. Determine the molecular geometry and sketch each molecule or ion, using the bond conventions shown in the "Representing Molecular Geometries on Paper" Box in Section 10.4.
a. BrF_5
b. SCl_6
c. PF_5
d. IF_4^+

41. Determine the molecular geometry about each interior atom and sketch each molecule.
a. C_2H_2 (skeletal structure HCCH)
b. C_2H_4 (skeletal structure H_2CCH_2)
c. C_2H_6 (skeletal structure H_3CCH_3)

42. Determine the molecular geometry about each interior atom and sketch each molecule.
a. N_2
b. N_2H_2 (skeletal structure HNNH)
c. N_2H_4 (skeletal structure H_2NNH_2)

43. Each ball-and-stick model shows the electron and molecular geometry of a generic molecule. Explain what is wrong with each molecular geometry and provide the correct molecular geometry, given the number of lone pairs and bonding groups on the central atom.

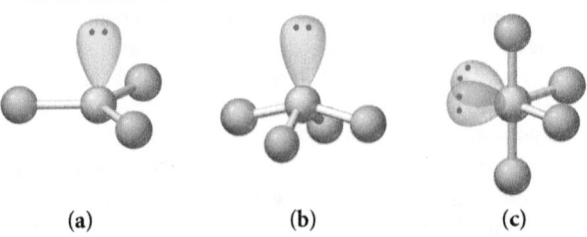

(a)   (b)   (c)

44. Each ball-and-stick model shows the electron and molecular geometry of a generic molecule. Explain what is wrong with each molecular geometry and provide the correct molecular geometry, given the number of lone pairs and bonding groups on the central atom.

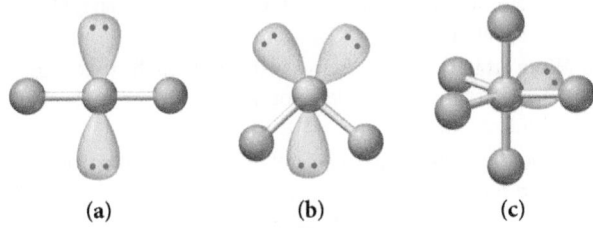

(a)   (b)   (c)

45. Determine the geometry about each interior atom in each molecule and sketch the molecule. (Skeletal structure is indicated in parentheses.)
a. CH_3OH (H_3COH)
b. CH_3OCH_3 (H_3COCH_3)
c. H_2O_2 (HOOH)

46. Determine the geometry about each interior atom in each molecule and sketch the molecule. (Skeletal structure is indicated in parentheses.)
a. CH_3NH_2 (H_3CNH_2)
b. $CH_3CO_2CH_3$ ($H_3CCOOCH_3$ both O atoms attached to second C)
c. NH_2CO_2H (H_2NCOOH both O atoms attached to C)

Molecular Shape and Polarity

47. Explain why CO_2 and CCl_4 are both nonpolar even though they contain polar bonds.

48. CH_3F is a polar molecule, even though the tetrahedral geometry often leads to nonpolar molecules. Explain.

49. Determine whether each molecule in Exercise 35 is polar or nonpolar.

50. Determine whether each molecule in Exercise 36 is polar or nonpolar.

51. Determine whether each molecule is polar or nonpolar.
a. ClO_3^- b. SCl_2 c. SCl_4 d. $BrCl_5$

52. Determine whether each molecule is polar or nonpolar.
a. $SiCl_4$ b. CF_2Cl_2 c. SeF_6 d. IF_5

Valence Bond Theory

53. The valence electron configurations of several atoms are shown next. How many bonds can each atom make without hybridization?
a. Be $2s^2$ b. P $3s^23p^3$ c. F $2s^22p^5$

54. The valence electron configurations of several atoms are shown next. How many bonds can each atom make without hybridization?
a. B $2s^22p^1$ b. N $2s^22p^3$ c. O $2s^22p^4$

55. Write orbital diagrams (boxes with arrows in them) to represent the electron configurations—without hybridization—for all the atoms in PH_3. Circle the electrons involved in bonding. Draw a three-dimensional sketch of the molecule and show orbital overlap. What bond angle do you expect from the unhybridized orbitals? How well does valence bond theory agree with the experimentally measured bond angle of 93.3°?

56. Write orbital diagrams (boxes with arrows in them) to represent the electron configurations—without hybridization—for all the atoms in SF_2. Circle the electrons involved in bonding. Draw a three-dimensional sketch of the molecule and show orbital overlap. What bond angle do you expect from the unhybridized orbitals? How well does valence bond theory agree with the experimentally measured bond angle of 98.2°?

57. Write orbital diagrams (boxes with arrows in them) to represent the electron configuration of carbon before and after sp^3 hybridization.

58. Write orbital diagrams (boxes with arrows in them) to represent the electron configurations of carbon before and after sp hybridization.

59. Which hybridization scheme allows the formation of at least one π bond?

$$sp^3,\ sp^2,\ sp^3d^2$$

60. Which hybridization scheme allows the central atom to form more than four bonds?

$$sp^3, sp^3d, sp^2$$

61. Write a hybridization and bonding scheme for each molecule. Sketch the molecule, including overlapping orbitals, and label all bonds using the notation shown in Examples 10.6 and 10.7.
   a. CCl_4 b. NH_3
   c. OF_2 d. CO_2

62. Write a hybridization and bonding scheme for each molecule. Sketch the molecule, including overlapping orbitals, and label all bonds using the notation shown in Examples 10.6 and 10.7.
   a. CH_2Br_2 b. SO_2
   c. NF_3 d. BF_3

63. Write a hybridization and bonding scheme for each molecule or ion. Sketch the structure, including overlapping orbitals, and label all bonds using the notation shown in Examples 10.6 and 10.7.
   a. $COCl_2$ (carbon is the central atom)
   b. BrF_5
   c. XeF_2
   d. I_3^-.

64. Write a hybridization and bonding scheme for each molecule or ion. Sketch the structure, including overlapping orbitals, and label all bonds using the notation shown in Examples 10.6 and 10.7.
   a. SO_3^{2-} b. PF_6^- c. BrF_3 d. HCN

65. Write a hybridization and bonding scheme for each molecule that contains more than one interior atom. Indicate the hybridization about each interior atom. Sketch the structure, including overlapping orbitals, and label all bonds using the notation shown in Examples 10.6 and 10.7.
   a. N_2H_2 (skeletal structure HNNH)
   b. N_2H_4 (skeletal structure H_2NNH_2)
   c. CH_3NH_2 (skeletal structure H_3CNH_2)

66. Write a hybridization and bonding scheme for each molecule that contains more than one interior atom. Indicate the hybridization about each interior atom. Sketch the structure, including

overlapping orbitals, and label all bonds using the notation shown in Examples 10.6 and 10.7.
   a. C_2H_2 (skeletal structure HCCH)
   b. C_2H_4 (skeletal structure H_2CCH_2)
   c. C_2H_6 (skeletal structure H_3CCH_3)

67. Consider the structure of the amino acid alanine. Indicate the hybridization about each interior atom.

68. Consider the structure of the amino acid aspartic acid. Indicate the hybridization about each interior atom.

Molecular Orbital Theory

69. Sketch the bonding molecular orbital that results from the linear combination of two $1s$ orbitals. Indicate the region where interference occurs and state the kind of interference (constructive or destructive).

70. Sketch the antibonding molecular orbital that results from the linear combination of two $1s$ orbitals. Indicate the region where interference occurs and state the kind of interference (constructive or destructive).

71. Draw an MO energy diagram and predict the bond order of Be_2^+ and Be_2^-. Do you expect these molecules to exist in the gas phase?

72. Draw an MO energy diagram and predict the bond order of Li_2^+ and Li_2^-. Do you expect these molecules to exist in the gas phase?

73. Sketch the bonding and antibonding molecular orbitals that result from linear combinations of the $2p_x$ atomic orbitals in a homonuclear diatomic molecule. (The $2p_x$ orbitals are those whose lobes are oriented along the bonding axis.)

74. Sketch the bonding and antibonding molecular orbitals that result from linear combinations of the $2p_z$ atomic orbitals in a homonuclear diatomic molecule. (The $2p_z$ orbitals are those whose lobes are oriented perpendicular to the bonding axis.) How do these molecular orbitals differ from those obtained from linear combinations of the $2p_y$ atomic orbitals? (The $2p_y$ orbitals are also oriented perpendicular to the bonding axis, but also perpendicular to the $2p_z$ orbitals.)

75. Using the molecular orbital energy ordering for second-row homonuclear diatomic molecules in which the π_{2p} orbitals lie at *lower* energy than the σ_{2p}, draw MO energy diagrams and predict the bond order in a molecule or ion with each number of total valence electrons. Will the molecule or ion be diamagnetic or paramagnetic?
    a. 4   b. 6   c. 8   d. 9

76. Using the molecular orbital energy ordering for second-row homonuclear diatomic molecules in which the π_{2p} orbitals lie at *higher* energy than the σ_{2p}, draw MO energy diagrams and predict the bond order in a molecule or ion with each number of total valence electrons. Will the molecule or ion be diamagnetic or paramagnetic?
    a. 10   b. 12   c. 13   d. 14

77. Use molecular orbital theory to predict if each molecule or ion exists in a relatively stable form.
    a. H_2^{2-} b. Ne_2 c. He_2^{2+} d. F_2^{2-}

78. Use molecular orbital theory to predict if each molecule or ion exists in a relatively stable form.
    a. C_2^{2+} b. Li_2 c. Be_2^{2+} d. Li_2^{2-}

79. According to MO theory, which molecule or ion has the highest bond order? Highest bond energy? Shortest bond length?

$$C_2, C_2^+, C_2^-$$

80. According to MO theory, which molecule or ion has the highest bond order? Highest bond energy? Shortest bond length?

$$O_2, O_2^-, O_2^{2-}$$

81. Draw an MO energy diagram for CO. (Use the energy ordering of O_2.) Predict the bond order and make a sketch of the lowest energy bonding molecular orbital.

82. Draw an energy diagram for HCl. Predict the bond order and make a sketch of the lowest energy bonding molecular orbital.

Cumulative Problems

83. For each compound, draw the Lewis structure, determine the geometry using VSEPR theory, determine whether the molecule is polar, identify the hybridization of all interior atoms, and make a sketch of the molecule, according to valence bond theory, showing orbital overlap.
    a. COF_2 (carbon is the central atom)
    b. S_2Cl_2 (ClSSCl)
    c. SF_4

84. For each compound, draw the Lewis structure, determine the geometry using VSEPR theory, determine whether the molecule is polar, identify the hybridization of all interior atoms, and make a sketch of the molecule, according to valence bond theory, showing orbital overlap.
    a. IF_5 b. CH_2CHCH_3 c. CH_3SH

85. Amino acids are biological compounds that link together to form proteins, the workhorse molecules in living organisms. The skeletal structures of several simple amino acids are shown here. For each skeletal structure, complete the Lewis structure, determine the geometry and hybridization about each interior atom, and make a sketch of the molecule, using the bond conventions of Section 10.4.

(a) serine

(b) asparagine

(c) cysteine

86. The genetic code is based on four different bases with the structures shown here. Assign a geometry and hybridization to each interior atom in these four bases.
    a. cytosine   b. adenine   c. thymine   d. guanine

(a)   (b)

(c)   (d)

87. The structure of caffeine, present in coffee and many soft drinks, is shown here. How many pi bonds are present in caffeine? How many sigma bonds? Insert the lone pairs in the molecule. What kinds of orbitals do the lone pairs occupy?

88. The structure of acetylsalicylic acid (aspirin) is shown here. How many pi bonds are present in acetylsalicylic acid? How many sigma bonds? What parts of the molecule are free to rotate? What parts are rigid?

89. Most vitamins can be classified either as fat soluble, which results in their tendency to accumulate in the body (so that taking too much can be harmful), or water soluble, which results in their tendency to be quickly eliminated from the body in urine. Examine the structural formulas and space-filling models of these vitamins and determine whether each one is fat soluble (mostly nonpolar) or water soluble (mostly polar).

(a) vitamin C

(b) vitamin A

(c) niacin (vitamin B$_3$)

(d) vitamin E

90. Water does not easily remove grease from dishes or hands, because grease is nonpolar and water is polar. The addition of soap to water, however, allows the grease to dissolve. Study the structure of sodium stearate (a soap) and describe how it works.

$$CH_3(CH_2)_{16}\overset{\overset{\displaystyle O}{\|}}{C}-O^-Na^+$$

91. Draw a molecular orbital energy diagram for ClF. (Assume that the σ_p orbitals are lower in energy than the π orbitals.) What is the bond order in ClF?

92. Draw Lewis structures and MO diagrams for CN$^+$, CN, and CN$^-$. According to the Lewis model, which species is most stable? According to MO theory, which species is most stable? Do the two theories agree?

93. Bromine can form compounds or ions with any number of fluorine atoms from one to five. Write the formulas of all five of these species, assign a hybridization, and describe their electron and molecular geometry.

94. The compound C$_3$H$_4$ has two double bonds. Describe its bonding and geometry, using a valence bond approach.

95. Draw the structure of a molecule with the formula C$_4$H$_6$Cl$_2$ that has a dipole moment of 0.

96. Draw the structures of two compounds that have the composition CH$_3$NO$_2$ and have all three H atoms bonded to the C. Predict which compound has the larger ONO bond angle.

97. How many hybrid orbitals do we use to describe each molecule?
   a. N$_2$O$_5$
   b. C$_2$H$_5$NO (four C — H bonds and one O — H bond)
   c. BrCN (no formal charges)

98. Indicate which orbitals overlap to form the σ bonds in the following.
   a. BeBr$_2$ **b.** HgCl$_2$ **c.** ICN

Challenge Problems

99. In VSEPR theory, which uses the Lewis model to determine molecular geometry, the trend of decreasing bond angle in CH_4, NH_3, and H_2O is accounted for by the greater repulsion of lone pair electrons compared to bonding pair electrons. How would this trend be accounted for in valence bond theory?

100. The results of a molecular orbital calculation for H_2O are shown here. Examine each of the orbitals and classify them as bonding, antibonding, or nonbonding. Assign the correct number of electrons to the energy diagram. According to this energy diagram, is H_2O stable? Explain.

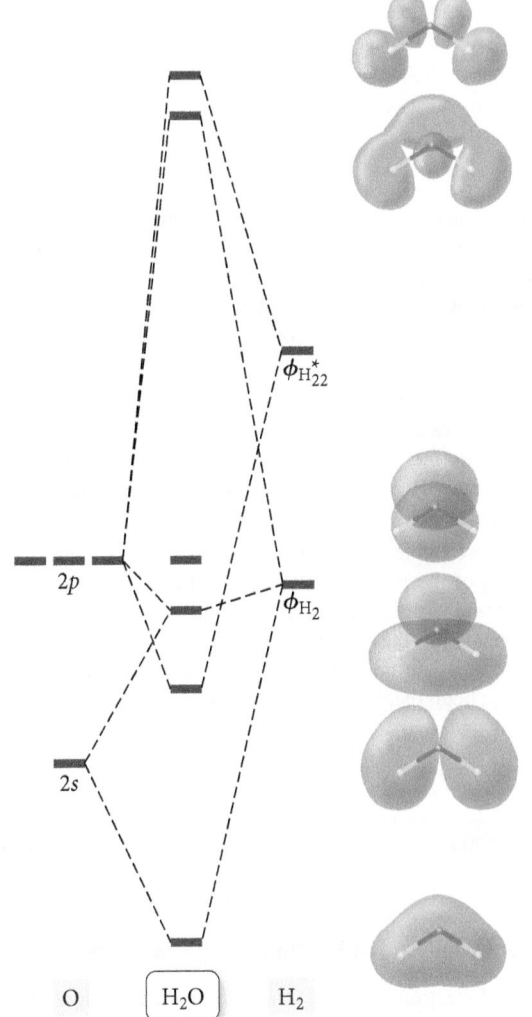

101. The results of a molecular orbital calculation for NH_3 are shown here. Examine each of the orbitals and classify them as bonding, antibonding, or nonbonding. Assign the correct number of electrons to the energy diagram. According to this energy diagram, is NH_3 stable? Explain.

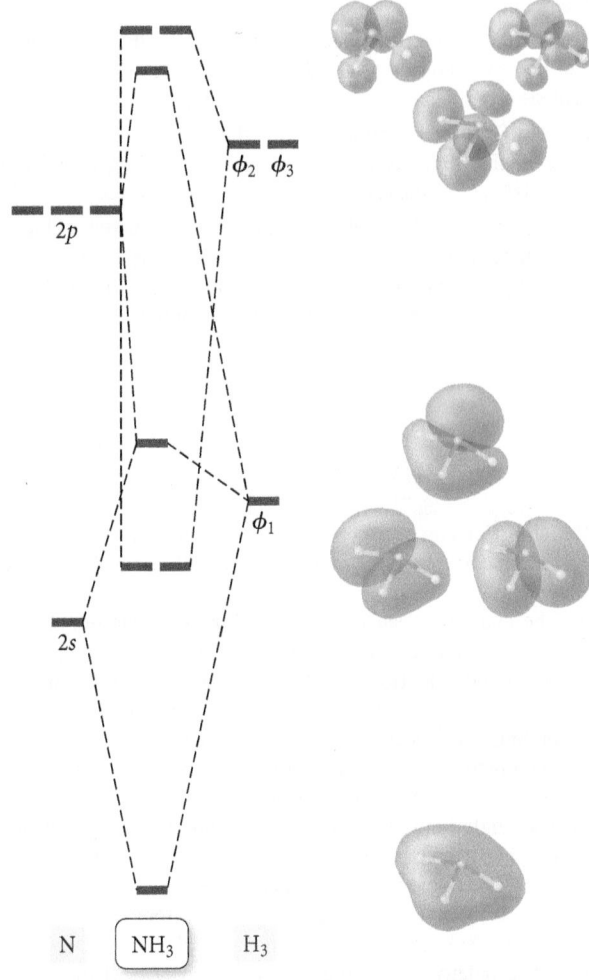

102. *cis*-2-Butene isomerizes to *trans*-2-butene via the reaction

a. If isomerization requires breaking the π bond, what minimum energy is required for isomerization in J/mol? In J/molecule?

b. If the energy for isomerization came from light, what minimum frequency of light would be required? In what portion of the electromagnetic spectrum does this frequency lie?

103. The species NO_2, NO_2^+, and NO_2^- in which N is the central atom, have very different bond angles. Predict what these bond angles might be with respect to the ideal angles and justify your prediction.

104. The bond angles increase steadily in the series PF_3, PCl_3, PBr_3, and PI_3. After consulting the data on atomic radii in Chapter 8, provide an explanation for this observation.

105. The ion CH_5^+ can form under very special high-energy conditions in the vapor phase in a mass spectrometer. Propose a hybridization for the carbon atom and predict the geometry.

106. Neither the VSEPR model nor the hybridization model is able to account for the experimental observation that the F — Ba — F bond angle in gaseous BaF_2 is 108° rather than the predicted 180°. Suggest some possible explanations for this observation.

107. Draw the Lewis structure for acetamide (CH_3CONH_2), an organic compound, and determine the geometry about each interior atom. Experiments show that the geometry about the nitrogen atom in acetamide is nearly planar. What resonance structure can account for the planar geometry about the nitrogen atom?

108. Use VSEPR to predict the geometry (including bond angles) about each interior atom of methyl azide (CH_3N_3), and make a sketch of the molecule. Would you expect the bond angle between the two interior nitrogen atoms to be the same or different? Would you expect the two nitrogen–nitrogen bond lengths to be the same or different?

Conceptual Problems

109. Which statement best captures the fundamental idea behind VSEPR theory? Explain what is wrong with each of the other statements.

   a. The angle between two or more bonds is determined primarily by the repulsions between the electrons within those bonds and other (lone pair) electrons on the central atom of a molecule. Each of these electron groups (bonding electrons or lone pair electrons) will lower its potential energy by maximizing its separation from other electron groups, thus determining the geometry of the molecule.

   b. The angle between two or more bonds is determined primarily by the repulsions between the electrons within those bonds. Each of these bonding electrons will lower its potential energy by maximizing its separation from other electron groups, thus determining the geometry of the molecule.

   c. The geometry of a molecule is determined by the shapes of the overlapping orbitals that form the chemical bonds. Therefore, to determine the geometry of a molecule, you must determine the shapes of the orbitals involved in bonding.

110. Suppose that a molecule has four bonding groups and one lone pair on the central atom. Suppose further that the molecule is confined to two dimensions (this is a purely hypothetical assumption for the sake of understanding the principles behind VSEPR theory). Make a sketch of the molecule and estimate the bond angles.

111. How does each of the three major bonding theories (the Lewis model, valence bond theory, and molecular orbital theory) define a single chemical bond? A double bond? A triple bond? How are these definitions similar? How are they different?

112. The most stable forms of the nonmetals in groups 4A, 5A, and 6A of the first period are molecules with multiple bonds. Beginning with the second period, the most stable forms of the nonmetals of these groups are molecules without multiple bonds. Propose an explanation for this observation based on valence bond theory.

Answers to Conceptual Connections

Electron Groups and Molecular Geometry

10.1   The geometry of a molecule is determined by how the terminal atoms are arranged around the central atom, which is in turn determined by how the electron groups are arranged around the *central* atom. The electron groups on the terminal atoms do not affect this arrangement.

Molecular Geometry

10.2   Linear. HCN has two electron groups (the single bond and the triple bond) resulting in a linear geometry.

Lone Pair Electrons and Molecular Geometry

10.3   (c) Positions 1 and 4 would put the greatest distance between the lone pairs and minimize lone pair–lone pair repulsions.

Molecular Geometry and Electron Group Repulsions

10.4   (d) All electron groups on the central atom (or interior atoms, if there is more than one) determine the shape of a molecule according to VSEPR theory.

What Is a Chemical Bond? Part I

10.5   (a) In the Lewis model, a covalent chemical bond is the sharing of electrons (represented by dots). (b) In valence bond theory, a covalent chemical bond is the overlap of half-filled atomic orbitals. (c) The answers are different because the Lewis model and valence bond theory are different models for chemical bonding. They both make useful and often similar predictions, but the assumptions of each model are different, and so are their respective descriptions of a chemical bond.

Single and Double Bonds

10.6 Applying valence bond theory, we see that a double bond is actually composed of two different kinds of bonds, one σ and one π. The orbital overlap in the π bond is side-to-side between two p orbitals and consequently different than the end-to-end overlap in a σ bond. Since the bonds are different types, the bond energy of the double bond is not just twice the bond energy of the single bond.

What Is a Chemical Bond? Part II

10.7 In MO theory, atoms will join together (or bond) when the electrons in the atoms can lower their energy by occupying the molecular orbitals of the resultant molecule. Unlike the Lewis model or valence bond theory, the chemical "bonds" in MO theory are not localized between atoms, but spread throughout the entire molecule.

11 Liquids, Solids, and Intermolecular Forces

It's a wild dance floor there at the molecular level.
—Roald Hoffmann (1937–)

RECALL FROM CHAPTER 1 that matter exists primarily in three states (or phases): solid, liquid, and gas. In Chapter 5, we examined the gas state. In this chapter we turn to the solid and liquid states, known collectively as the *condensed* states. The solid and liquid states are more similar to each other than they are to the gas state. In the gas state, constituent particles—atoms or molecules—are separated by large distances and do not interact with each other very much. In the condensed states, constituent particles are close together and exert moderate to strong attractive forces on one another. Whether a substance is a solid, liquid, or gas depends on the structure of the particles that compose the substance. Remember the theme we have emphasized since Chapter 1 of this book: the properties of matter are determined by the properties of molecules and atoms. In this chapter, we will see how the structure of a particular atom or molecule determine the state in which it will exist at a given temperature.

11.1 Climbing Geckos and Intermolecular Forces

The gecko shown here can run up a polished glass window in seconds or even walk across a ceiling. It can support its entire weight by a single toe in contact with a surface. How? Research by several scientists points to *intermolecular forces*—attractive forces that exist *between* all

Intermolecular
forces

Research suggest that the gecko's remarkable ability to climb walls and adhere to surfaces depends on intermolecular forces.

molecules and atoms—as the reason that the gecko can perform its gravity-defying feats. Intermolecular forces are the forces that hold many liquids and solids—such as water and ice, for example—together.

The key to the gecko's sticky feet lies in the millions of microhairs, called *setae,* that line its toes. Each seta is between 30 and 130 μm long and branches out to end in several hundred flattened tips called *spatulae,* as you can see in the photo at right. This unique structure allows the gecko's toes to have unusually close contact with the surfaces it climbs. The close contact allows intermolecular forces—which are significant only at short distances—to hold the gecko to the wall.

All living organisms depend on intermolecular forces, not for adhesion to walls, but for many physiological processes. For example, in Chapter 21 we will examine how intermolecular forces help determine the shapes of protein molecules (the workhorse molecules in living organisms). Later in this chapter, we discuss how intermolecular forces are central to the structure of DNA, the inheritable molecule that carries the blueprints for life. (See the *Chemistry and Medicine* box in Section 11.3.)

More generally, intermolecular forces are responsible for the very existence of condensed states. The state of a sample of matter—solid, liquid, or gas—depends on the magnitude of intermolecular forces between the constituent particles relative to the amount

▲ Each of the millions of microhairs on a gecko's feet branches out to end in flattened tips called *spatulae.*

483

of thermal energy in the sample. Recall from Chapter 6 that the molecules and atoms composing matter are in constant random motion that increases with increasing temperature. The energy associated with this motion is *thermal energy*. When thermal energy is high relative to intermolecular forces, matter tends to be gaseous. When thermal energy is low relative to intermolecular forces, matter tends to be liquid or solid.

11.2 Solids, Liquids, and Gases: A Molecular Comparison

We are all familiar with solids and liquids. Water, gasoline, rubbing alcohol, and nail polish remover are common liquids that you have probably encountered. Ice, dry ice, and diamond are familiar solids. To begin to understand the differences between the three common states of matter, examine Table 11.1, which shows the density and molar volume of water in its three different states, along with molecular representations of each state. Notice that the densities of the solid and liquid states are much greater than the density of the gas state. Notice also that the solid and liquid states are more similar in density and molar volume to one another than they are to the gas state. The molecular representations show the reason for these differences. The molecules in liquid water and ice are in close contact with one another—essentially touching—while those in gaseous water are separated by large distances. The molecular representation of gaseous water in Table 11.1 is actually out of proportion—the water molecules in the figure should be much farther apart for their size. (Only a fraction of a molecule could be included in the figure if it were drawn to scale.) From the molar volumes, we know that 18.0 mL of liquid water (slightly more than a tablespoon) occupies 30.5 L when converted to gas at 100 °C (at atmospheric pressure). The low density of gaseous water is a direct result of this large separation between molecules.

Notice also that, for water, the solid is slightly less dense than the liquid. This is *atypical* behavior. Most solids are slightly denser than their corresponding liquids because the molecules move closer together upon freezing. As we will discuss in Section 11.9, ice is less dense than liquid water because the unique crystal structure of ice results in water molecules moving slightly farther apart upon freezing.

A major difference between liquids and solids is the freedom of movement of the constituent molecules or atoms. Even though the atoms or molecules in a liquid are in close contact, thermal energy partially overcomes the attractions between them, allowing them to move around one another. This is not the case in solids; the atoms or molecules

TABLE 11.1 The Three States of Water

Phase	Temperature (°C)	Density (g/cm³, at 1 atm)	Molar Volume	Molecular View
Gas (steam)	100	5.90×10^{-4}	30.5 L	
Liquid (water)	20	0.998	18.0 mL	
Solid (ice)	0	0.917	19.6 mL	

TABLE 11.2 Properties of the States of Matter

State	Density	Shape	Volume	Strength of Intermolecular Forces (Relative to Thermal Energy)
Gas	Low	Indefinite	Indefinite	Weak
Liquid	High	Indefinite	Definite	Moderate
Solid	High	Definite	Definite	Strong

in a solid are virtually locked in their positions, only vibrating back and forth about a fixed point. Table 11.2 summarizes the properties of liquids and solids, as well as the properties of gases for comparison.

Liquids assume the shape of their containers because the atoms or molecules that compose liquids are free to flow (or move around one another). When we pour water into a beaker, the water flows and assumes the shape of the beaker (Figure 11.1 ▶). Liquids are not easily compressed because the molecules or atoms that compose them are already in close contact—they cannot be pushed much closer together. The molecules in a gas, by contrast, have a great deal of space between them and are easily forced into a smaller volume by an increase in external pressure (Figure 11.2 ▼).

Solids have a definite shape because, in contrast to liquids and gases, the molecules or atoms that compose solids are fixed in place—each molecule or atom merely vibrates about a fixed point. Like liquids, solids have a definite volume and generally cannot be compressed because the molecules or atoms composing them are already in close contact.

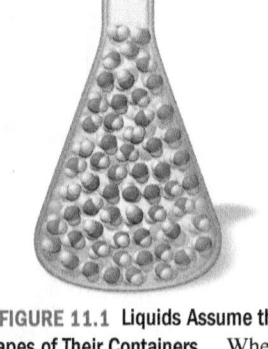

▲ FIGURE 11.1 **Liquids Assume the Shapes of Their Containers** When we pour water into a flask, it assumes the shape of the flask because water molecules are free to flow.

Molecules closely spaced — not easily compressible

Molecules widely spaced — highly compressible

Liquid

Gas

▲ FIGURE 11.2 **Gases Are Compressible** Molecules in a liquid are closely spaced and are not easily compressed. Molecules in a gas have a great deal of space between them, making gases compressible.

Solids may be **crystalline**, in which case the atoms or molecules that compose them are arranged in a well-ordered three-dimensional array, or they may be **amorphous**, in which case the atoms or molecules that compose them have no long-range order (Figure 11.3 ▼).

According to some definitions, an amorphous solid is considered a unique state, different from the normal solid state because it lacks any long-range order.

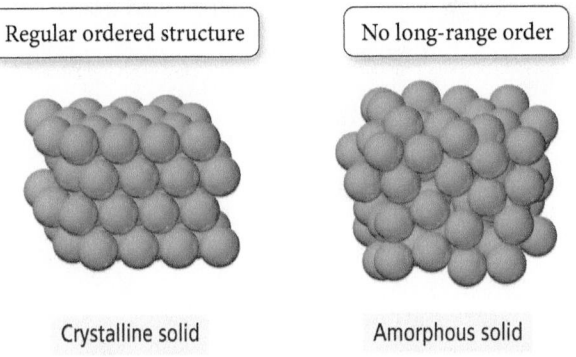

Regular ordered structure

No long-range order

Crystalline solid

Amorphous solid

◀ FIGURE 11.3 **Crystalline and Amorphous Solids** In a crystalline solid, the arrangement of the particles displays long-range order. In an amorphous solid, the arrangement of the particles has no long-range order.

Changes between States

We can transform one state of matter to another by changing the temperature, pressure, or both. For example, we can convert solid ice to liquid water by heating, and liquid water to solid ice by cooling. The following diagram shows the three states of matter and the changes in conditions that commonly induce transitions between the states.

Solid   Liquid   Gas

C_3H_8 (g)

C_3H_8 (l)

▲ The propane in an LP gas tank is in the liquid state. When you open the tank, some propane vaporizes and escapes as a gas.

We can induce a transition between the liquid and gas state, not only by heating and cooling, but also through changing the pressure. In general, increases in pressure favor the denser state, so increasing the pressure of a gas sample results in a transition to the liquid state. The most familiar example of this phenomenon occurs in the LP (liquefied petroleum) gas used as a fuel for outdoor grills and lanterns. LP gas is composed primarily of propane, a gas at room temperature and atmospheric pressure. However, it liquefies at pressures exceeding about 2.7 atm. The propane you buy in a tank is under pressure and therefore in the liquid form. When you open the tank, some of the propane escapes as a gas, lowering the pressure in the tank for a brief moment. Immediately, however, some of the liquid propane evaporates, replacing the gas that escaped. Storing gases like propane as liquids is efficient because, in their liquid form, they occupy much less space.

Conceptual Connection 11.1 State Changes

This molecular diagram shows a sample of liquid water.

Which of the diagrams below best depicts the vapor emitted from a pot of boiling water?

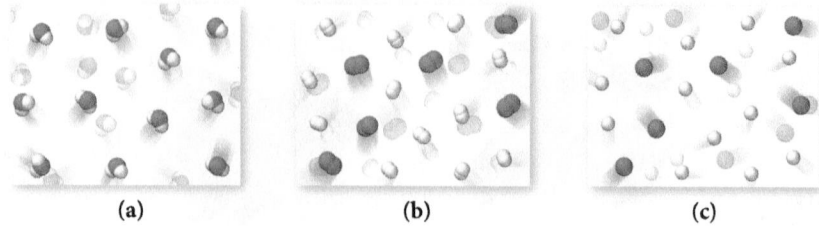

(a)   (b)   (c)

11.3 Intermolecular Forces: The Forces That Hold Condensed States Together

The structure of the particles that compose a substance determine the strength of the intermolecular forces that hold the substance together, which in turn determine whether the substance is a solid, liquid, or gas at a given temperature. At room temperature, moderate to strong intermolecular forces tend to result in liquids and solids (high melting and boiling points) and weak intermolecular forces tend to result in gases (low melting and boiling points).

Intermolecular forces originate from the interactions between charges, partial charges, and temporary charges on molecules (or atoms and ions), much as bonding forces originate from interactions between charged particles in atoms. Recall from Section 8.3 that according to Coulomb's law, the potential energy (E) of two oppositely charged particles (with charges q_1 and q_2) decreases (becomes more negative) with increasing magnitude of charge and with decreasing separation (r):

$$E = \frac{1}{4\pi\varepsilon_0} \frac{q_1 q_2}{r} \quad \text{(When } q_1 \text{ and } q_2 \text{ are opposite in sign, } E \text{ is negative.)}$$

Therefore, as we have seen, protons and electrons are attracted to each other because their potential energy decreases as they get closer together. Similarly, molecules with partial or temporary charges are attracted to each other because *their* potential energy decreases as they get closer together. However, intermolecular forces, even the strongest ones, are generally *much weaker* than bonding forces.

The reason for the relative weakness of intermolecular forces compared to bonding forces is also related to Coulomb's law. Bonding forces are the result of large charges (the charges on protons and electrons) interacting at very close distances. Intermolecular forces are the result of smaller charges (as we shall see in the following discussion) interacting at greater distances. For example, consider the interaction between two water molecules in liquid water:

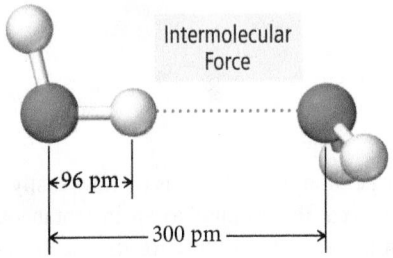

The length of an O—H bond in liquid water is 96 pm; however, the average distance between water molecules in liquid water is about 300 pm. The larger distances between molecules, as well as the smaller charges involved (the partial charges on the hydrogen and oxygen atoms), result in weaker forces. To break the O—H bonds in water, we have to heat the water to thousands of degrees Celsius. However, to completely overcome the intermolecular forces *between* water molecules, we have to heat water only to its boiling point, 100 °C (at sea level).

In this section we examine several different types of intermolecular forces, including dispersion forces, dipole–dipole forces, hydrogen bonding, and ion–dipole forces. The first three of these can potentially occur in all substances; the last one occurs only in mixtures.

Dispersion Force

The one intermolecular force present in all molecules and atoms is the **dispersion force** (also called the London force). Dispersion forces are the result of fluctuations in the electron distribution within molecules or atoms. Since all atoms and molecules have electrons, they all exhibit dispersion forces. The electrons in an atom or molecule may,

The nature of dispersion forces was first recognized by Fritz W. London (1900–1954), a German-American physicist.

at any one instant, be unevenly distributed. Imagine a frame-by-frame movie of a helium atom in which each "frame" captures the position of the helium atom's two electrons.

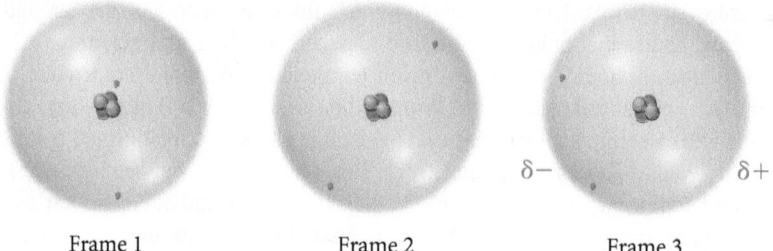

Frame 1   Frame 2   Frame 3

In any one frame, the electrons may not be symmetrically arranged around the nucleus. In frame 3, for example, helium's two electrons are on the left side of the helium atom. At that instant, the left side will have a slightly negative charge ($\delta-$). The right side of the atom, which temporarily has no electrons, will have a slightly positive charge ($\delta+$) because of the charge of the nucleus. This fleeting charge separation is called an *instantaneous dipole* or a *temporary dipole.* As shown in Figure 11.4 ▼, an instantaneous dipole on one helium atom induces an instantaneous dipole on its neighboring atoms because the positive end of the instantaneous dipole attracts electrons in the neighboring atoms. The neighboring atoms then attract one another—the positive end of one instantaneous dipole attracting the negative end of another. This attraction is the dispersion force.

▶ **FIGURE 11.4 Dispersion Interactions**
The temporary dipole in one helium atom induces a temporary dipole in its neighbor. The resulting attraction between the positive and negative charges creates the dispersion force.

Dispersion Force

> An instantaneous dipole on any one helium atom induces instantaneous dipoles on neighboring atoms, which then attract one another.

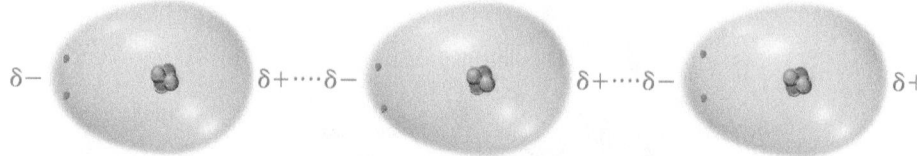

| To polarize means to form a dipole moment (see Section 9.6).

The *magnitude* of the dispersion force depends on how easily the electrons in the atom or molecule can move or *polarize* in response to an instantaneous dipole, which in turn depends on the size (or volume) of the electron cloud. A larger electron cloud results in a greater dispersion force because the electrons are held less tightly by the nucleus and therefore polarize more easily. If all other variables are constant, the dispersion force increases with increasing molar mass because molecules or atoms of higher molar mass generally have more electrons dispersed over a greater volume. For example, consider the boiling points of the noble gases displayed in Table 11.3 ◀. As the molar masses and electron cloud volumes of the noble gases increase, the greater dispersion forces result in increasing boiling points (because the molecules are more strongly attracted to one another).

Molar mass alone, however, does not determine the magnitude of the dispersion force. Compare the molar masses and boiling points of *n*-pentane and neopentane:

TABLE 11.3 Boiling Points of the Noble Gases

Noble Gas		Molar Mass (g/mol)	Boiling Point (K)
He	●	4.00	4.2
Ne	●	20.18	27
Ar	●	39.95	87
Kr	●	83.80	120
Xe	●	131.30	165

n-Pentane
molar mass = 72.15 g/mol
boiling point = 36.1 °C

Neopentane
molar mass = 72.15 g/mol
boiling point = 9.5 °C

(a) *n*-Pentane   (b) Neopentane

▲ **FIGURE 11.5 Dispersion Force and Molecular Shape**   (a) The straight shape of *n*-pentane molecules allows them to interact with one another along the entire length of the molecules. (b) The nearly spherical shape of neopentane molecules allows for only a small area of interaction. Thus, dispersion forces are weaker in neopentane than in *n*-pentane, resulting in a lower boiling point.

These molecules have identical molar masses, but *n*-pentane has a higher boiling point than neopentane. Why? Because the two molecules have different shapes. The *n*-pentane molecules are long and can interact with one another along their entire length, as shown in Figure 11.5a ▲. In contrast, the bulky, round shape of neopentane molecules results in a smaller area of interaction between neighboring molecules, as shown in Figure 11.5b ▲. The result is a lower boiling point for neopentane.

Although molecular shape and other factors must always be considered in determining the magnitude of dispersion forces, molar mass can act as a guide when comparing dispersion forces within a family of similar elements or compounds as shown in Figure 11.6 ▼.

▲ **FIGURE 11.6 Boiling Points of the *n*-Alkanes**   The boiling points of the *n*-alkanes rise with increasing molar mass and the consequent stronger dispersion forces.

Conceptual Connection 11.2 Dispersion Forces

Which halogen has the highest boiling point?

(a) Cl_2 (b) Br_2 (c) I_2

See Section 9.6 to review how to determine if a molecule is polar.

Dipole–Dipole Force

The **dipole–dipole force** exists in all molecules that are polar. Polar molecules have electron-rich regions (which have a partial negative charge) and electron deficient regions (which have a partial positive charge). For example, consider acetone:

Structural formula   Space-filling model   Electrostatic potential map

The image on the right is an electrostatic potential map of acetone; these kinds of maps were first introduced in Sections 9.6 and 10.5. Recall that the red areas indicate electron-rich regions in the molecule and that the blue areas indicate electron poor regions. Notice that acetone has an electron-rich region surrounding the oxygen atom (because oxygen is more electronegative than the rest of the molecule) and electron-poorer regions surrounding the carbon and hydrogen atoms. The result is that acetone has a **permanent dipole** that can interact with other acetone molecules as shown in Figure 11.7 ▼. The positive end of one permanent dipole attracts the negative end of another; this attraction is the dipole–dipole force. Polar molecules, therefore, have higher melting and boiling points than nonpolar molecules of similar molar mass. Remember that all molecules (including polar ones) have dispersion forces. Polar molecules have, *in addition,* dipole–dipole forces. This additional attractive force raises their melting and boiling points relative to nonpolar molecules of similar molar mass. For example, consider formaldehyde and ethane:

Name	Formula	Molar Mass (amu)	Structure		bp (°C)	mp (°C)
Formaldehyde	CH_2O	30.03			−19.5	−92
Ethane	C_2H_6	30.07			−88	−172

▶ **FIGURE 11.7 Dipole–Dipole Interaction** Molecules with permanent dipoles, such as acetone, are attracted to one another via dipole–dipole interactions.

Dipole–Dipole Interaction

The positive end of a polar molecule is attracted to the negative end of its neighbor.

Space-filling model   Electrostatic potential map

▲ **FIGURE 11.8 Dipole Moment and Boiling Point** The molecules shown here all have similar molar masses but different dipole moments. The boiling points increase with increasing dipole moment.

Formaldehyde is polar, and has a higher melting point and boiling point than nonpolar ethane, even though the two compounds have the same molar mass. Figure 11.8 ▲ shows the boiling points of a series of molecules with similar molar mass but progressively greater dipole moments. Notice that the boiling points increase with increasing dipole moment.

The polarity of molecules is also important in determining the **miscibility**—the ability to mix without separating into two states—of liquids. In general, polar liquids are miscible with other polar liquids but are not miscible with nonpolar liquids. For example, water, a polar liquid, is not miscible with pentane (C_5H_{12}), a nonpolar liquid (Figure 11.9 ▼). Similarly, water and oil (also nonpolar) do not mix. Consequently, oily hands or oily stains on clothes cannot be washed with plain water (see *Chemistry in Your Day*: *How Soap Works* in Section 10.5).

$C_5H_{12}(l)$

$H_2O(l)$

▲ **FIGURE 11.9 Polar and Nonpolar Compounds** Water and pentane do not mix because water molecules are polar and pentane molecules are nonpolar.

EXAMPLE 11.1 Dipole–Dipole Forces

Which of these molecules have dipole–dipole forces?

(a) CO_2 (b) CH_2Cl_2 (c) CH_4

SOLUTION

A molecule has dipole–dipole forces if it is polar. To determine if a molecule is polar, (1) *determine if the molecule contains polar bonds* and (2) *determine if the polar bonds add together to form a net dipole moment* (Section 9.6).

(a) CO_2 (1) Since the electronegativity of carbon is 2.5 and that of oxygen is 3.5 (Figure 9.8), CO_2 has polar bonds. (2) The geometry of CO_2 is linear. Consequently, the dipoles of the polar bonds cancel, so the molecule is *not polar* and does not have dipole–dipole forces.	 $O=C=O$ No dipole forces present
(b) CH_2Cl_2 (1) The electronegativity of C is 2.5, that of H is 2.1, and that of Cl is 3.0. Consequently, CH_2Cl_2 has two polar bonds (C—Cl) and two bonds that are nearly nonpolar (C—H). (2) The geometry of CH_2Cl_2 is tetrahedral. Since the C—Cl bonds and the C—H bonds are different, their dipoles do not cancel but sum to a net dipole moment. The molecule is polar and has dipole–dipole forces.	CH_2Cl_2 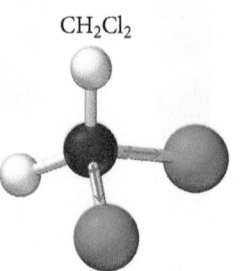 Dipole forces present
(c) CH_4 (1) Since the electronegativity of C is 2.5 and that of hydrogen is 2.1, the C—H bonds are nearly nonpolar. (2) In addition, since the geometry of the molecule is tetrahedral, any slight polarities that the bonds might have will cancel. CH_4 is therefore nonpolar and does not have dipole–dipole forces.	CH_4 No dipole forces present

FOR PRACTICE 11.1

Which molecules have dipole–dipole forces?

(a) CI_4 (b) CH_3Cl (c) HCl

Conceptual Connection 11.3 Dipole-Dipole Interaction

An electrostatic potential map for acetonitrile (CH_3CN), which is polar, is shown at left. From this map, determine the geometry for how two acetonitrile molecules would interact with each other. Draw structural formulas, using the three-dimensional bond notation introduced in Section 10.4, to illustrate the geometry of the interaction.

Hydrogen Bonding

Polar molecules containing hydrogen atoms bonded directly to small electronegative atoms—most importantly fluorine, oxygen, or nitrogen—exhibit an intermolecular force called **hydrogen bonding**. HF, NH_3, and H_2O, for example, all undergo hydrogen bonding. The hydrogen bond is a sort of *super* dipole–dipole force. The large electronegativity difference

Hydrogen Bonding

When H bonds directly to F, O, or N, the bonding atoms acquire relatively large partial charges, giving rise to strong dipole–dipole attractions between neighboring molecules.

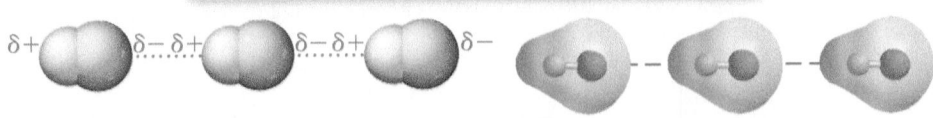

$\delta+$ $\delta-$ $\delta+$ $\delta-$ $\delta+$ $\delta-$

Space-filling model   Electrostatic potential map

◀ **FIGURE 11.10** Hydrogen Bonding in HF The hydrogen of one HF molecule, with its partial positive charge, is attracted to the fluorine of its neighbor, with its partial negative charge. This dipole–dipole interaction is an example of a hydrogen bond.

between hydrogen and any of these electronegative elements causes the hydrogen atom to have a fairly large partial positive charge ($\delta+$) within the bond, while the F, O, or N atom has a fairly large partial negative charge ($\delta-$). In addition, since these atoms are all quite small, the H atom on one molecule can approach the F, O, or N atom on an adjacent molecule very closely. The result is a strong attraction between the H atom on one molecule and the F, O, or N on its neighbor—an attraction called a **hydrogen bond**. For example, in HF, the hydrogen atom in one molecule is strongly attracted to the fluorine atom on a neighboring molecule (Figure 11.10 ▲). The electrostatic potential maps in Figure 11.10 show the large differences in electron density that result in unusually large partial charges.

Hydrogen bonds should not be confused with chemical bonds. Chemical bonds occur *between individual atoms within a molecule,* whereas hydrogen bonds—like dispersion forces and dipole–dipole forces—are intermolecular forces that occur *between molecules.* A typical hydrogen bond is only 2–5% as strong as a typical covalent chemical bond. Hydrogen bonds are, however, the strongest of the three *intermolecular* forces we have discussed so far. Substances composed of molecules that form hydrogen bonds have higher melting and boiling points than comparable substances composed of molecules that do not form hydrogen bonds. For example, consider ethanol and dimethyl ether:

Hydrogen Bonding in Ethanol

The partially positive charge on H is strongly attracted to the partial negative charge on O.

— Hydrogen Bond —

Space-filling model   Electrostatic potential map

▲ **FIGURE 11.11** Hydrogen Bonding in Ethanol The left side shows the space-filling models, and the right side shows the electrostatic potential maps.

Name	Formula		Molar Mass (amu)	Structure	bp (°C)	mp (°C)
Ethanol	C_2H_6O		46.07	CH_3CH_2OH	78.3	−114.1
Dimethyl Ether	C_2H_6O		46.07	CH_3OCH_3	−22.0	−138.5

Since ethanol contains hydrogen bonded directly to oxygen, ethanol molecules form hydrogen bonds with each other as shown in Figure 11.11 ▶. The hydrogen that is directly bonded to oxygen in an individual ethanol molecule is also strongly attracted to the oxygen on neighboring molecules. This strong attraction makes the boiling point of ethanol 78.3 °C. Consequently, ethanol is a liquid at room temperature. In contrast, dimethyl ether has an identical molar mass to ethanol but does not exhibit hydrogen bonding because in the dimethyl ether molecule, the oxygen atom is not bonded directly to hydrogen; this results in lower boiling and melting points, and dimethyl ether is a gas at room temperature.

Water is another good example of a molecule with hydrogen bonding (Figure 11.12 ▶). Figure 11.13 ▶ shows the boiling points of the simple hydrogen compounds of the group 4A and group 6A elements. In general, boiling points increase with increasing molar mass, as expected based on increasing dispersion forces. However, because of hydrogen bonding, the boiling point of water (100 °C) is much higher than expected based on its molar mass (18.0 g/mol). Without hydrogen bonding, all the water on our planet would be gaseous.

Hydrogen Bonding in Water

Hydrogen Bonds

▲ **FIGURE 11.12** Hydrogen Bonding in Water

▶ **FIGURE 11.13 Boiling Points of Group 4A and 6A Compounds** Because of hydrogen bonding, the boiling point of water is anomalous compared to the boiling points of other hydrogen-containing compounds.

EXAMPLE 11.2 Hydrogen Bonding

One of these compounds is a liquid at room temperature. Which one and why?

O‖   H
H—C—H   H—C—F   H—O—O—H
         H

Formaldehyde   Fluoromethane   Hydrogen peroxide

SOLUTION

The three compounds have similar molar masses:

Formaldehyde	30.03 g/mol
Fluoromethane	34.03 g/mol
Hydrogen peroxide	34.02 g/mol

So the strengths of their dispersion forces are similar. All three compounds are also polar, so they have dipole–dipole forces. Hydrogen peroxide, however, is the only one of these compounds that also contains H bonded directly to F, O, or N. Therefore, it also has hydrogen bonding and is likely to have the highest boiling point of the three. Since the example stated that only one of the compounds was a liquid, you can safely assume that hydrogen peroxide is the liquid. Note that, although fluoromethane *contains* both H and F, H is not *directly bonded* to F, so fluoromethane does not have hydrogen bonding as an intermolecular force. Similarly, formaldehyde *contains* both H and O, but H is not *directly bonded* to O, so formaldehyde does not have hydrogen bonding either.

FOR PRACTICE 11.2

Which has the higher boiling point, HF or HCl? Why?

Ion–Dipole Force

The **ion–dipole force** occurs when an ionic compound is mixed with a polar compound; it is especially important in aqueous solutions of ionic compounds. For example, when sodium chloride is mixed with water, the sodium and chloride ions interact with water molecules via ion–dipole forces, as shown in Figure 11.14 ▶. The positive sodium ions interact with the negative poles of water molecules, while the negative chloride ions interact with the positive poles. Ion–dipole forces are the strongest of the types of intermolecular forces discussed and are responsible for the ability of ionic substances to form solutions with water. We will discuss aqueous solutions more thoroughly in Chapter 12.

Summarizing Intermolecular Forces (as shown in Table 11.4):

▶ Dispersion forces are present in all molecules and atoms and increase with increasing molar mass. These forces are always weak in small molecules but can be significant in molecules with high molar masses.

▶ Dipole–dipole forces are present in polar molecules.

▶ Hydrogen bonds, the strongest of the intermolecular forces that can occur in pure substances (second only to ion–dipole forces in general), are present in molecules containing hydrogen bonded directly to fluorine, oxygen, or nitrogen.

▶ Ion–dipole forces are present in mixtures of ionic compounds and polar compounds. These forces are very strong and are especially important in aqueous solutions of ionic compounds.

Ion–Dipole Forces

The positively charged end of a polar molecule such as H_2O is attracted to negative ions and the negatively charged end of the molecule is attracted to positive ions.

▲ FIGURE 11.14 Ion-Dipole Forces Ion–dipole forces exist between Na^+ and the negative ends of H_2O molecules and between Cl^- and the positive ends of H_2O molecules.

TABLE 11.4   Types of Intermolecular Forces

Type	Present in	Molecular perspective	Strength
Dispersion	All molecules and atoms		
Dipole-dipole	Polar molecules		
Hydrogen bonding	Molecules containing H bonded to F, O, or N		
Ion-dipole	Mixtures of ionic compounds and polar compounds		

Conceptual Connection 11.4 Intermolecular Forces and Boiling Point

Which substance has the highest boiling point?

(a) CH_3OH (b) CO (c) N_2

Chemistry and Medicine

Hydrogen Bonding in DNA

DNA is a long, chainlike molecule that acts as a blueprint for each living organism. Copies of DNA are passed from parent to offspring, which is how we inherit traits from our parents. A DNA molecule is composed of thousands of repeating units called *nucleotides* (Figure 11.15 ▼). Each nucleotide contains one of four different *organic bases:* adenine, thymine, cytosine, and guanine (abbreviated A, T, C, and G). The sequence of these bases along DNA encodes the information that determines the nature of the proteins that are made in the body (proteins are the molecules that do most of the work in living organisms). Our proteins in turn determine many of our characteristics, including how we look, what diseases we are at risk of developing, and even our behavior.

▶ **FIGURE 11.16 Complementary Base Pairing via Hydrogen Bonds** The individual bases in DNA interact with one another via specific hydrogen bonds that form between A and T and between C and G.

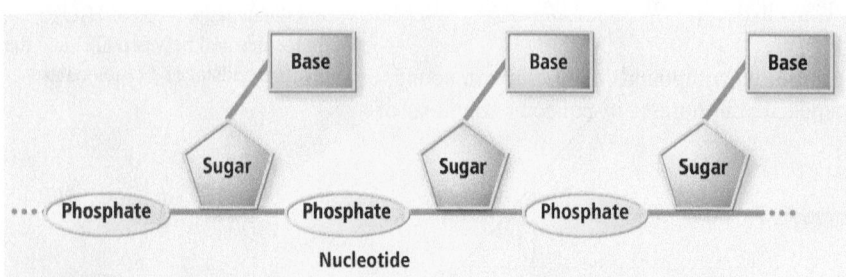

▲ **FIGURE 11.15 Nucleotides** The individual units in a DNA polymer are nucleotides. Each nucleotide contains one of four bases: adenine, thymine, cytosine, and guanine (abbreviated A, T, C, and G).

The replicating mechanism of DNA is related to its structure, which was discovered in 1953 by James Watson and Francis Crick. DNA consists of two *complementary* strands wrapped around each other in the now famous double helix and linked by hydrogen bonds between the bases on each strand. Each base (A, T, C, and G) has a complementary partner with which it forms hydrogen bonds (Figure 11.16 ▲): adenine (A) with thymine (T) and cytosine (C) with guanine (G). The hydrogen

bonding is so specific that each base will pair only with its complementary partner. When a cell is going to divide, enzymes unzip the DNA molecule across the hydrogen bonds that join its two strands (Figure 11.17 ▼). Then new bases, complementary to the bases in each strand, are added along each of the original strands, forming hydrogen bonds with their complements. The result is two identical copies of the original DNA.

Question

Why would dispersion forces not work as a way to hold the two strands of DNA together? Why would covalent bonds not work?

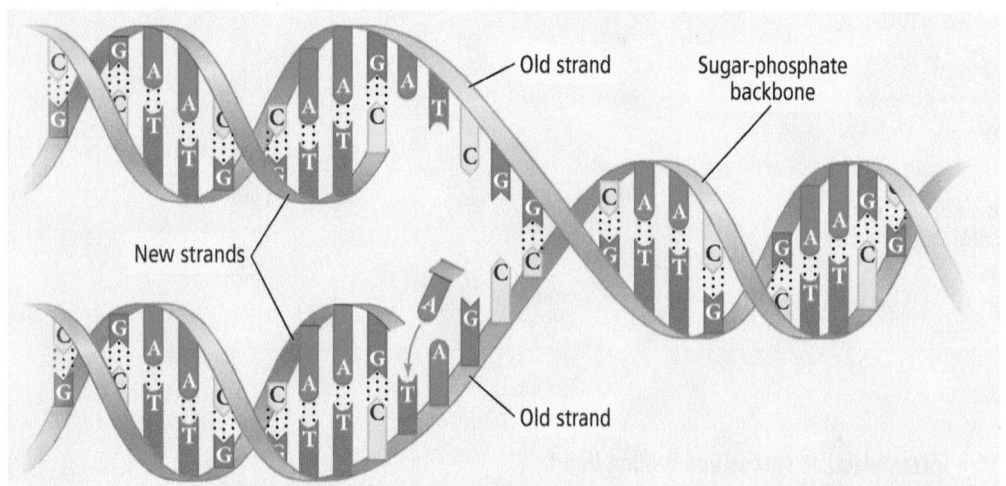

◀ **FIGURE 11.17 Copying DNA** The two strands of the DNA molecule "unzip" by breaking the hydrogen bonds that join the base pairs. New bases complementary to the bases of each strand are assembled and joined together. The result is two molecules, each identical to the original one.

11.4 Intermolecular Forces in Action: Surface Tension, Viscosity, and Capillary Action

The most important manifestation of intermolecular forces is the very existence of liquids and solids. In liquids, we also observe several other manifestations of intermolecular forces including surface tension, viscosity, and capillary action.

Surface Tension

A fly fisherman delicately casts a small fishing fly (a metal hook with a few feathers and strings attached to make it look like an insect) onto the surface of a moving stream. The fly floats on the surface of the water—even though the metal composing the hook is denser than water—and attracts trout. Why? The hook floats because of *surface tension*, the tendency of liquids to minimize their surface area.

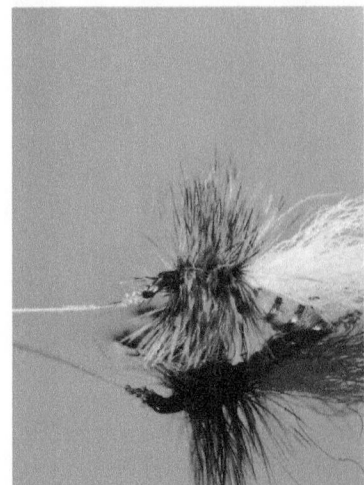

▲ A trout fly can float on water because of surface tension.

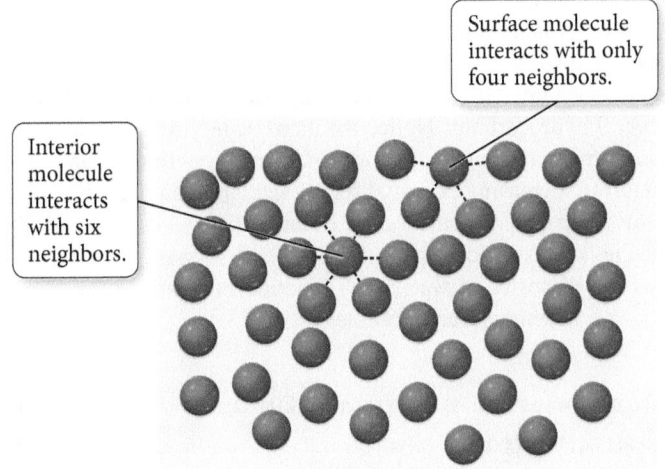

Surface molecule interacts with only four neighbors.

Interior molecule interacts with six neighbors.

◀ **FIGURE 11.18 The Origin of Surface Tension**   Molecules at the liquid surface have a higher potential energy than those in the interior. As a result, a liquid tends to minimize its surface area; its surface behaves like a "skin."

Figure 11.18 ▲ depicts the intermolecular forces experienced by a molecule at the surface of the liquid compared to those experienced by a molecule in the interior. Notice that a molecule at the surface has relatively fewer neighbors with which to interact, and it is therefore inherently less stable—it has higher potential energy—than those in the interior. (Remember that attractive interactions with other molecules lower potential energy.) In order to increase the surface area of the liquid, molecules from the interior have to be moved to the surface, and, because molecules at the surface have a higher potential energy than those in the interior, this movement requires energy. Therefore, liquids tend to minimize their surface area. The **surface tension** of a liquid is the energy required to increase the surface area by a unit amount. For example, at room temperature, water has a surface tension of 72.8 mJ/m^2—it takes 72.8 mJ to increase the surface area of water by one square meter.

Why does surface tension allow the fly fisherman's hook to float on water? The tendency for liquids to minimize their surface creates a kind of skin at the surface that resists penetration. For the fisherman's hook to sink into the water, the water's surface area must increase slightly—an increase that is resisted by the surface tension. We can observe surface tension by carefully placing a paper clip on the surface of water (Figure 11.19 ▶). The paper clip, even though it is denser than water, floats on the surface of the water. A slight tap on the clip provides the energy necessary to overcome the surface tension and causes the clip to sink.

Surface tension decreases as intermolecular forces decrease. You can't float a paper clip on benzene, for example, because the dispersion forces among the molecules composing benzene are significantly weaker than the hydrogen bonds among water molecules. The surface tension of benzene is only 28 mJ/m^2—just 40% that of water.

Recall from Section 11.3 that the interactions between molecules lower their potential energy in much the same way that the interaction between protons and electrons lowers their potential energy, in accordance with Coulomb's law.

▲ **FIGURE 11.19 Surface Tension in Action**   A paper clip floats on water because of surface tension.

▲ **FIGURE 11.20 Spherical Water Droplets** On the space shuttle in orbit, under weightless conditions, collections of water molecules coalesce into nearly perfect spheres held together by intermolecular forces between molecules.

Surface tension is also the reason that small water droplets (those not large enough to be distorted by gravity) form nearly perfect spheres. On the space shuttle, the complete absence of gravity allows even large samples of water to form nearly perfect spheres (Figure 11.20 ◄). Why? Just as gravity pulls the matter of a planet or star inward to form a sphere, so intermolecular forces among water molecules pull the water into a sphere. A sphere is the geometrical shape with the smallest surface area to volume ratio; the formation of a sphere minimizes the number of molecules at the surface, thus minimizing the potential energy of the system.

Viscosity

Another manifestation of intermolecular forces is **viscosity**, the resistance of a liquid to flow. Motor oil, for example, is more viscous than gasoline, and maple syrup is more viscous than water. Viscosity is measured in a unit called the poise (P), defined as $1 \, g/cm \cdot s$. The viscosity of water at room temperature is approximately one centipoise (cP). Viscosity is greater in substances with stronger intermolecular forces because if molecules are more strongly attracted to each other, they do not flow around each other as freely. Viscosity also depends on molecular shape, increasing in longer molecules that can interact over a greater area and possibly become entangled. Table 11.5 lists the viscosity of several hydrocarbons. Notice the increase in viscosity with increasing molar mass (and therefore increasing magnitude of dispersion forces) and with increasing length (and therefore increasing potential for molecular entanglement).

Viscosity also depends on temperature because thermal energy partially overcomes the intermolecular forces, allowing molecules to flow past each other more easily. Table 11.6 lists the viscosity of water as a function of temperature. Nearly all liquids become less viscous as temperature increases.

TABLE 11.6 Viscosity of Liquid Water at Several Temperatures

Temperature (°C)	Viscosity (cP)
20	1.002
40	0.653
60	0.467
80	0.355
100	0.282

TABLE 11.5 Viscosity of Several Hydrocarbons at 20 °C

Hydrocarbon	Molar Mass (g/mol)	Formula	Viscosity (cP)
n-Pentane	72.15	$CH_3CH_2CH_2CH_2CH_3$	0.240
n-Hexane	86.17	$CH_3CH_2CH_2CH_2CH_2CH_3$	0.326
n-Heptane	100.2	$CH_3CH_2CH_2CH_2CH_2CH_2CH_3$	0.409
n-Octane	114.2	$CH_3CH_2CH_2CH_2CH_2CH_2CH_2CH_3$	0.542
n-Nonane	128.3	$CH_3CH_2CH_2CH_2CH_2CH_2CH_2CH_2CH_3$	0.711

Chemistry in Your Day

Viscosity and Motor Oil

Viscosity is an important property of the motor oil you put into your car. The oil must be thick enough to adequately coat engine surfaces to lubricate them, but also thin enough to be pumped easily into all the required engine compartments. Motor oil viscosity is usually reported on a scale called the SAE scale (named after the Society of Automotive Engineers). The higher the SAE rating, the more viscous the oil. The thinnest motor oils have SAE ratings of 5 or 10, while the thickest have SAE ratings of up to 50.

Before the 1950s, most automobile owners changed the oil in their engine to accommodate seasonal changes in weather—a higher SAE rating was required in the summer months and a lower rating in the winter. Today, the advent of multigrade oils allows car owners in many climates to keep the same oil all year long. Multigrade oils, such as the 10W-40 oil shown at right, contain polymers (long molecules made up of repeating structural units) that coil at low temperatures but unwind at high temperatures. At low temperatures, the coiled polymers—because of their compact shape—do not contribute very much to the oil's viscosity. As the temperature increases, however, the molecules unwind and their long shape results in intermolecular forces and molecular entanglements that prevent the viscosity from decreasing as much as it would normally. The result is an oil whose viscosity is less temperature-dependent than it would be otherwise, allowing the same oil to be used over a wider range of temperatures. The 10W-40 designation indicates that the oil has an SAE rating of 10 at low temperatures and 40 at high temperatures.

Capillary Action

Medical technicians take advantage of **capillary action**—the ability of a liquid to flow against gravity up a narrow tube—when taking a blood sample. The technician pokes the patient's finger with a pin, squeezes some blood out of the puncture, and then collects the blood with a thin tube. When the tube's tip comes into contact with the blood, the blood is drawn into the tube by capillary action. The same force helps trees and plants draw water from the soil.

Capillary action results from a combination of two forces: the attraction between molecules in a liquid, called *cohesive forces,* and the attraction between these molecules and the surface of the tube, called *adhesive forces.* The adhesive forces cause the liquid to spread out over the surface of the tube, while the cohesive forces cause the liquid to stay together. If the adhesive forces are greater than the cohesive forces (as is the case for water in a glass tube), the attraction to the surface draws the liquid up the tube and the cohesive forces pull along those molecules not in direct contact with the tube walls (Figure 11.21 ▶). The water rises up the tube until the force of gravity balances the capillary action—the thinner the tube, the higher the rise. If the adhesive forces are smaller than the cohesive forces (as is the case for liquid mercury), the liquid does not rise up the tube at all (and in fact will drop to a level below the level of the surrounding liquid).

We can see the result of the differences in the relative magnitudes of cohesive and adhesive forces by comparing the meniscus of water to the meniscus of mercury (Figure 11.22 ▶). (The meniscus is the curved shape of a liquid surface within a tube.) The meniscus of water is concave (rounded inward) because the *adhesive forces* are greater than the cohesive forces, causing the edges of the water to creep up the sides of the tube a bit, forming the familiar cupped shape. The meniscus of mercury is convex (rounded outward) because the *cohesive forces*—due to metallic bonding between the atoms—are greater than the adhesive forces. The mercury atoms crowd toward the interior of the liquid to maximize their interactions with each other, resulting in the upward bulge at the center of the surface.

▲ Blood is drawn into a capillary tube by capillary action.

▲ **FIGURE 11.21 Capillary Action** The attraction of water molecules to the glass surface draws the liquid around the edge of the tube up the walls. The water in the rest of the column is pulled along by the attraction of water molecules to one another. As can be seen in this figure, the narrower the tube, the higher the liquid will rise.

11.5 Vaporization and Vapor Pressure

We now turn our attention to vaporization, the process by which thermal energy can overcome intermolecular forces and produce a state change from liquid to gas. We first discuss the process of vaporization itself, then the energetics of vaporization, and finally the concepts of vapor pressure, dynamic equilibrium, and critical point. Vaporization is a common occurrence that we experience every day and even depend on to maintain proper body temperature.

The Process of Vaporization

Imagine water molecules in a beaker at room temperature and open to the atmosphere (Figure 11.23 ▶). The molecules are in constant motion due to thermal energy. If we could actually see the molecules at the surface, we would witness what Roald Hoffmann described as a "wild dance floor" (see the chapter-opening quote) because of all the vibrating, jostling, and molecular movement. *The higher the temperature, the greater the average energy of the collection of molecules.* However, at any one time, some molecules have more thermal energy than the average and some have less.

The distributions of thermal energies for the molecules in a sample of water at two different temperatures

$H_2O(g)$

$H_2O(l)$

▲ **FIGURE 11.22 Meniscuses of Water and Mercury** The meniscus of water is concave because water molecules are more strongly attracted to the glass wall than to one another. The meniscus of mercury is convex because mercury atoms are more strongly attracted to one another than to the glass walls.

◀ **FIGURE 11.23 Vaporization of Water** Some molecules in an open beaker have enough kinetic energy to vaporize from the surface of the liquid.

► **FIGURE 11.24 Distribution of Thermal Energy**   The thermal energies of the molecules in a liquid are distributed over a range. The peak energy increases with increasing temperature.

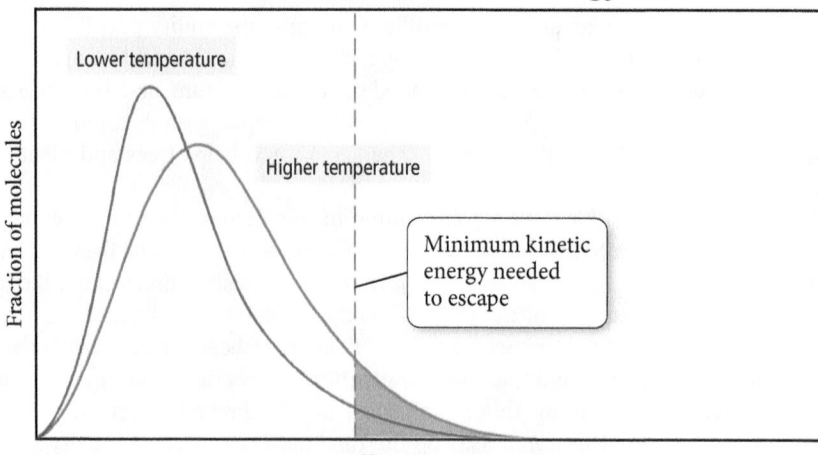

Distribution of Thermal Energy

Lower temperature

Higher temperature

Minimum kinetic energy needed to escape

Fraction of molecules

Kinetic energy

are shown in Figure 11.24 ▲. The molecules at the high end of the distribution curve have enough energy to break free from the surface—where molecules are held less tightly than in the interior due to fewer neighbor–neighbor interactions—and into the gas state. This transition, from liquid to gas, is called **vaporization**. Some of the water molecules in the gas state, at the low end of the energy distribution curve for the gaseous molecules, plunge back into the water and are captured by intermolecular forces. This transition, from gas to liquid, is the opposite of vaporization and is called **condensation**.

Although both evaporation and condensation occur in a beaker open to the atmosphere, under normal conditions evaporation takes place at a greater rate because most of the newly evaporated molecules escape into the surrounding atmosphere and never come back. The result is a noticeable decrease in the water level within the beaker over time (usually several days).

What happens if we increase the temperature of the water within the beaker? Because of the shift in the energy distribution to higher energies (see Figure 11.24), more molecules now have enough energy to break free and evaporate, so vaporization occurs more quickly. What happens if we spill the water on the table or floor? The same amount of water is now spread over a wider area, resulting in more molecules at the surface of the liquid. Since molecules at the surface have the greatest tendency to evaporate—because they are held less tightly—vaporization also occurs more quickly in this case. You probably know from experience that water in a beaker or glass may take many days to evaporate completely, while the same amount of water spilled on a table or floor typically evaporates within a few hours (depending on the exact conditions).

What happens if the liquid in the beaker is not water, but some other substance with weaker intermolecular forces, such as acetone (the main component in nail polish remover)? The weaker intermolecular forces allow more molecules to evaporate at a given temperature, increasing the rate of vaporization. We call liquids that vaporize easily **volatile,** and those that do not vaporize easily **nonvolatile**. Acetone is more volatile than water. Motor oil is virtually nonvolatile at room temperature.

Summarizing the Process of Vaporization:

► The rate of vaporization increases with increasing temperature.

► The rate of vaporization increases with increasing surface area.

► The rate of vaporization increases with decreasing strength of intermolecular forces.

The Energetics of Vaporization

To understand the energetics of vaporization, consider again a beaker of water from the molecular point of view, except now imagine that the beaker is thermally insulated so that heat from the surroundings cannot enter the beaker. What happens to the temperature of the water left in the beaker as molecules evaporate? To answer this question, think about the energy distribution curve again (see Figure 11.24). The molecules that leave the beaker are the ones at the high end of the energy curve—the most energetic. If no additional heat enters the beaker, the average energy of the entire collection of molecules decreases—much as the class average on an exam goes down if you eliminate the highest-scoring students. So vaporization is an *endothermic* process; it takes energy to vaporize the molecules in a liquid. Another way to understand the endothermicity of vaporization is to remember that vaporization requires overcoming the intermolecular forces that hold liquids together. Since energy is needed to pull the molecules away from one another, the process is endothermic.

Our bodies use the endothermic nature of vaporization for cooling. When we over-heat, we sweat, causing our skin to be covered with liquid water. As this water evaporates, it absorbs heat from the body, cooling the skin. A fan makes us feel cooler because it blows newly vaporized water away from our skin, allowing more sweat to vaporize and causing even more cooling. High humidity, on the other hand, slows down the net rate of evaporation, preventing cooling. When the air already contains large amounts of water vapor, the sweat evaporates more slowly, making the body's cooling system less efficient.

Condensation, the opposite of vaporization, is exothermic—heat is released when a gas condenses to a liquid. If you have ever accidentally put your hand above a steaming kettle or opened a bag of microwaved popcorn too soon, you may have experienced a *steam burn*. As the steam condenses to a liquid on your skin, it releases a lot of heat, causing the burn. The condensation of water vapor is also the reason that winter overnight temperatures in coastal regions, which tend to have water vapor in the air, do not get as low as in deserts, which tend to have dry air. As the air temperature in a coastal area drops, water condenses out of the air, releasing heat and preventing the temperature from dropping further. In deserts, the air contains almost no moisture to condense, so the temperature drop is more extreme.

Heat of Vaporization The amount of heat required to vaporize one mole of a liquid to gas is its **heat (or enthalpy) of vaporization (ΔH_{vap}).** The heat of vaporization of water at its normal boiling point of 100 °C is +40.7 kJ/mol:

$$H_2O(l) \longrightarrow H_2O(g) \quad \Delta H_{vap} = +40.7 \text{ kJ/mol}$$

The heat of vaporization is always positive because the process is endothermic—energy must be absorbed to vaporize a substance. The heat of vaporization is somewhat temperature dependent. For example, at 25 °C the heat of vaporization of water is +44.0 kJ/mol, slightly more than at 100 °C because the water contains less thermal energy at 25 °C. Table 11.7 lists the heats of vaporization of several liquids at their boiling points and at 25 °C.

When a substance condenses from a gas to a liquid, the same amount of heat is involved, but the heat is emitted rather than absorbed:

$$H_2O(g) \longrightarrow H_2O(l) \quad \Delta H = -\Delta H_{vap} = -40.7 \text{ kJ (at 100 °C)}$$

When one mole of water condenses, it releases 40.7 kJ of heat. The sign of ΔH in this case is negative because the process is exothermic.

We can use the heat of vaporization of a liquid to calculate the amount of energy required to vaporize a given mass of the liquid (or the amount of heat given off by the condensation of a given mass of liquid), using concepts similar to those covered in Section 6.6 (stoichiometry of ΔH). The heat of vaporization is like a conversion factor between number of moles of a liquid and the amount of heat required to vaporize it (or the amount of heat emitted when it condenses), as demonstrated in Example 11.3.

See Chapter 6 to review endothermic and exothermic processes.

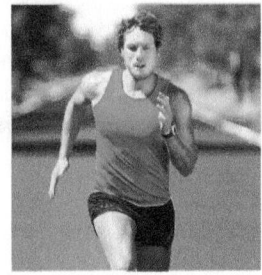

▲ When we sweat, water evaporates from the skin. Since evaporation is endothermic, the result is a cooling effect.

The sign conventions of ΔH were introduced in Chapter 6.

TABLE 11.7 Heats of Vaporization of Several Liquids at Their Boiling Points and at 25 °C

Liquid	Chemical Formula	Normal Boiling Point (°C)	ΔH_{vap} (kJ/mol) at Boiling Point	ΔH_{vap} (kJ/mol) at 25 °C
Water	H_2O	100	40.7	44.0
Rubbing alcohol (isopropyl alcohol)	C_3H_8O	82.3	39.9	45.4
Acetone	C_3H_6O	56.1	29.1	31.0
Diethyl ether	$C_4H_{10}O$	34.6	26.5	27.1

EXAMPLE 11.3 Using the Heat of Vaporization in Calculations

Calculate the mass of water (in g) that can be vaporized at its boiling point with 155 kJ of heat.

SORT You are given a certain amount of heat in kilojoules and asked to find the mass of water that can be vaporized.	**GIVEN:** 155 kJ **FIND:** g H_2O
STRATEGIZE The heat of vaporization gives the relationship between heat absorbed and moles of water vaporized. Begin with the given amount of heat (in kJ) and convert to moles of water that can be vaporized. Then use the molar mass as a conversion factor to convert from moles of water to mass of water.	**CONCEPTUAL PLAN** kJ → mol H_2O → g H_2O $\dfrac{1 \text{ mol } H_2O}{40.7 \text{ kJ}}$ $\dfrac{18.02 \text{ g } H_2O}{1 \text{ mol } H_2O}$ **RELATIONSHIPS USED** $\Delta H_{vap} = 40.7$ kJ/mol (at 100° C) 18.02 g H_2O = 1 mol H_2O
SOLVE Follow the conceptual plan to solve the problem.	**SOLUTION** $155 \text{ kJ} \times \dfrac{1 \text{ mol } H_2O}{40.7 \text{ kJ}} \times \dfrac{18.02 \text{ g } H_2O}{1 \text{ mol } H_2O} = 68.6 \text{ g } H_2O$

FOR PRACTICE 11.3

Calculate the amount of heat (in kJ) required to vaporize 2.58 kg of water at its boiling point.

FOR MORE PRACTICE 11.3

Suppose that 0.48 g of water at 25 °C condenses on the surface of a 55 g block of aluminum that is initially at 25 °C. If the heat released during condensation goes only toward heating the metal, what is the final temperature (in °C) of the metal block? (The specific heat capacity of aluminum is 0.903 J/g °C.)

Vapor Pressure and Dynamic Equilibrium

We have already seen that if a container of water is left uncovered at room temperature, the water slowly evaporates away. But what happens if the container is sealed? Imagine a sealed evacuated flask—one from which the air has been removed—containing liquid water, as shown in Figure 11.25 ▼. Initially, the water molecules evaporate, as they did in the open beaker. However, because of the seal, the evaporated molecules cannot escape

Dynamic equilibrium:
Rate of evaporation =
rate of condensation

▶ FIGURE 11.25 Vaporization in a Sealed Flask (a) When water is in a sealed container, water molecules begin to vaporize. (b) As water molecules build up in the gas state, they begin to recondense into the liquid. (c) When the rate of evaporation equals the rate of condensation, dynamic equilibrium is reached.

(a)   (b)   (c)

into the atmosphere. As water molecules enter the gas state, some start condensing back into the liquid. As the concentration (or partial pressure) of gaseous water molecules increases, the rate of condensation also increases. However, as long as the water remains at a constant temperature, the rate of evaporation remains constant. Eventually the rate of condensation and the rate of vaporization become equal—**dynamic equilibrium** has been reached (Figure 11.26 ▶). Condensation and vaporization continue at equal rates and the concentration of water vapor above the liquid is constant.

The pressure of a gas in dynamic equilibrium with its liquid is called its **vapor pressure**. The vapor pressure of a particular liquid depends on the intermolecular forces present in the liquid and the temperature. Weak intermolecular forces result in volatile substances with high vapor pressures because the intermolecular forces are easily overcome by thermal energy. Strong intermolecular forces result in nonvolatile substances with low vapor pressures.

A liquid in dynamic equilibrium with its vapor is a balanced system that tends to return to equilibrium if disturbed. For example, consider a sample of *n*-pentane (a component of gasoline) at 25 °C in a cylinder equipped with a moveable piston (Figure 11.27a ▼). The cylinder contains no other gases except *n*-pentane vapor in dynamic equilibrium with the liquid. Since the vapor pressure of *n*-pentane at 25 °C is 510 mmHg, the pressure in the cylinder is 510 mmHg. Now, what happens when the piston is moved upward to expand the volume within the cylinder? Initially, the pressure in the cylinder drops below 510 mmHg, in accordance with Boyle's law. Then, however, more liquid vaporizes until equilibrium is reached once again (Figure 11.27b). If the volume of the cylinder is expanded again, the same thing happens—the pressure initially drops and more *n*-pentane vaporizes to bring the system back into equilibrium. Further expansion will cause the same result *as long as some liquid n-pentane remains in the cylinder.*

Conversely, what happens if the piston is lowered, decreasing the volume in the cylinder? Initially, the pressure in the cylinder rises above 510 mmHg, but then some of the gas condenses into liquid until equilibrium is reached again (Figure 11.27c).

We can describe the tendency of a system in dynamic equilibrium to return to equilibrium with the following general statement:

> **When a system in dynamic equilibrium is disturbed, the system responds so as to minimize the disturbance and return to a state of equilibrium.**

If the pressure above a liquid–vapor system in equilibrium decreases, some of the liquid evaporates, restoring the equilibrium pressure. If the pressure increases, some of the vapor condenses, bringing the pressure back down to the equilibrium pressure. This basic principle—Le Châtelier's principle—is applicable to any chemical system in equilibrium, as we shall see in Chapter 14.

▲ **FIGURE 11.26 Dynamic Equilibrium** Dynamic equilibrium occurs when the rate of condensation is equal to the rate of evaporation.

| Boyle's law is discussed in Section 5.3.

(a)   (b)   (c)

◀ **FIGURE 11.27 Dynamic Equilibrium in n-Pentane** (a) Liquid *n*-pentane is in dynamic equilibrium with its vapor. (b) When the volume is increased, the pressure drops and some liquid is converted to gas to bring the pressure back up. (c) When the volume is decreased, the pressure increases and some gas is converted to liquid to bring the pressure back down.

Conceptual Connection 11.5 Vapor Pressure

What happens to the vapor pressure of a substance when its surface area is increased at constant temperature?

(a) The vapor pressure increases.

(b) The vapor pressure remains the same.

(c) The vapor pressure decreases.

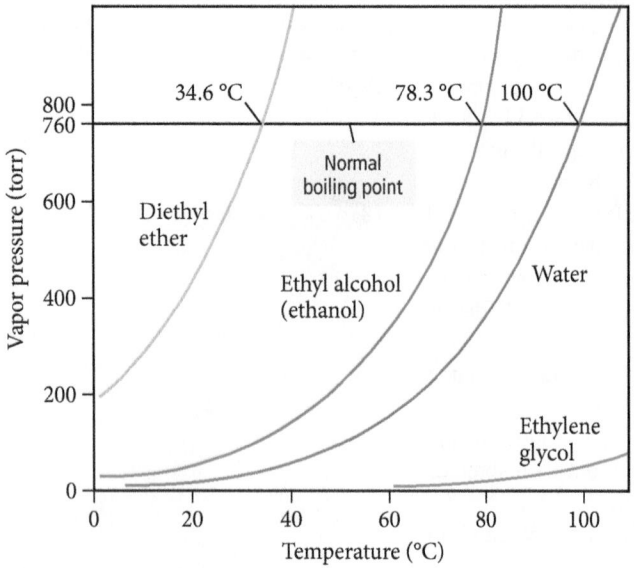

▲ **FIGURE 11.28 Vapor Pressure of Several Liquids at Different Temperatures**
At higher temperatures, more molecules have enough thermal energy to escape into the gas state, so vapor pressure increases with increasing temperature.

Sometimes you see bubbles begin to form in hot water below 100 °C. These bubbles are dissolved air—not gaseous water—leaving the liquid. Dissolved air comes out of water as you heat it because the solubility of a gas in a liquid decreases with increasing temperature (as we will see in Chapter 12).

Temperature Dependence of Vapor Pressure and Boiling Point
When the temperature of a liquid increases, its vapor pressure rises because the higher thermal energy increases the number of molecules that have enough energy to vaporize (see Figure 11.24). Because of the shape of the thermal energy distribution curve, a small change in temperature makes a large difference in the number of molecules that have enough energy to vaporize, which results in a large increase in vapor pressure. For example, the vapor pressure of water at 25 °C is 23.3 torr, while at 60 °C the vapor pressure is 149.4 torr. Figure 11.28 ◄ shows the vapor pressure of water and several other liquids as a function of temperature.

The **boiling point** of a liquid is *the temperature at which the liquid's vapor pressure equals the external pressure.* When a liquid reaches its boiling point, the thermal energy is enough for molecules in the interior of the liquid (not just those at the surface) to break free of their neighbors and enter the gas state (Figure 11.29 ▼). The bubbles in boiling water are pockets of gaseous water that have formed within the liquid water. The bubbles float to the surface and leave as gaseous water or steam.

The **normal boiling point** of a liquid is *the temperature at which its vapor pressure equals 1 atm.* The normal boiling point of pure water is 100 °C. However, at a lower pressure, water boils at a lower temperature. In Denver, Colorado, where the altitude is around 1600 meters (5200 feet) above sea level, for example, the average atmospheric pressure is about 83% of what it is at sea level, and water boils at approximately 94 °C. For this reason, it takes slightly longer to cook food in boiling water in Denver than in San Francisco (which is at sea level). Table 11.8 shows the boiling point of water at several locations of varied altitudes.

Once the boiling point of a liquid is reached, additional heating only causes more rapid boiling; it does not raise the temperature of the liquid above its boiling point, as

► **FIGURE 11.29 Boiling**   A liquid boils when thermal energy is high enough to cause molecules in the interior of the liquid to become gaseous, forming bubbles that rise to the surface.

TABLE 11.8 Boiling Points of Water at Several Locations of Varied Altitudes

Location	Elevation (ft)	Approximate Pressure (atm)*	Approximate Boiling Point of Water (°C)
Mt. Everest, Tibet (highest mountain peak on Earth)	29,035	0.32	78
Mt. McKinley (Denali), Alaska (highest mountain peak in North America)	20,320	0.46	83
Mt. Whitney, California (highest mountain peak in 48 contiguous U.S. states)	14,495	0.60	87
Denver, Colorado (mile high city)	5,280	0.83	94
Boston, Massachusetts (sea level)	20	1.0	100

*The atmospheric pressure in each of these locations is subject to weather conditions and can vary significantly from these values.

shown in the *heating curve* in Figure 11.30 ▶. Therefore, at 1 atm, boiling water always has a temperature of 100 °C. *As long as liquid water is present, its temperature cannot rise above its boiling point.* After all the water has been converted to steam, the temperature of the steam can continue to rise beyond 100 °C.

The Clausius–Clapeyron Equation Now, let's return our attention to Figure 11.28. As we can see from the graph, the vapor pressure of a liquid increases with increasing temperature. However, *the relationship is not linear.* In other words, doubling the temperature results in more than a doubling of the vapor pressure. The relationship between vapor pressure and temperature is exponential, and can be expressed as follows:

$$P_{vap} = \beta \exp\left(\frac{-\Delta H_{vap}}{RT}\right) \qquad [11.1]$$

In this expression P_{vap} is the vapor pressure, β is a constant that depends on the gas, ΔH_{vap} is the heat of vaporization, R is the gas constant (8.314 J/mol·K), and T is the temperature in kelvins. We can rearrange Equation 11.1 by taking the natural logarithm of both sides:

$$\ln P_{vap} = \ln\left[\beta \exp\left(\frac{-\Delta H_{vap}}{RT}\right)\right] \qquad [11.2]$$

Because $\ln AB = \ln A + \ln B$, we can rearrange the right side of Equation 11.2:

$$\ln P_{vap} = \ln \beta + \ln\left[\exp\left(\frac{-\Delta H_{vap}}{RT}\right)\right] \qquad [11.3]$$

Because $\ln e^x = x$ (see Appendix IB), we can simplify Equation 11.3:

$$\ln P_{vap} = \ln \beta + \frac{-\Delta H_{vap}}{RT} \qquad [11.4]$$

A slight additional rearrangement gives the following important result:

$$\ln P_{vap} = \frac{-\Delta H_{vap}}{R}\left(\frac{1}{T}\right) + \ln \beta \qquad \text{Clausius–Clapeyron equation}$$

$$y = m(x) + b \qquad \text{(equation for a line)}$$

Notice the parallel relationship between the **Clausius–Clapeyron equation** and the equation for a straight line. Just as a plot of *y* versus *x* yields a straight line with slope *m* and intercept *b*, so a plot of $\ln P_{vap}$ (equivalent to *y*) versus $1/T$ (equivalent to *x*) gives a straight line with slope $-\Delta H_{vap}/R$ (equivalent to *m*) and y-intercept $\ln \beta$ (equivalent to *b*), as shown in Figure 11.31 ▶. The Clausius–Clapeyron equation gives a linear relationship—not between the vapor pressure and the temperature (which have an

▲ **FIGURE 11.30 The Temperature during Boiling** The temperature of water during boiling remains at 100 °C.

Using the Clausius–Clapeyron equation in this way ignores the relatively small temperature dependence of ΔH_{vap}.

► FIGURE 11.31 A Clausius–Clapeyron Plot for Diethyl Ether ($CH_3CH_2OCH_2CH_3$) A plot of the natural log of the vapor pressure versus the inverse of the temperature in K yields a straight line with slope $-\Delta H_{vap}/R$.

A Clausius–Clapeyron Plot

Slope $= -3478$ K
$= -\Delta H_{vap}/R$
$\Delta H_{vap} = -\text{slope} \times R$
$= 3478 \text{ K} \times 8.314 \text{ J/mol·K}$
$= 28.92 \times 10^3 \text{ J/mol}$

exponential relationship)—but between the *natural log* of the vapor pressure and the *inverse* of temperature. This is a common technique in the analysis of chemical data. If two variables are not linearly related, it is often convenient to find ways to graph *functions of those variables* that are linearly related.

The Clausius–Clapeyron equation leads to a convenient way to measure the heat of vaporization in the laboratory. We simply measure the vapor pressure of a liquid as a function of temperature and create a plot of the natural log of the vapor pressure versus the inverse of the temperature. We can then determine the slope of the line to find the heat of vaporization, as shown in Example 11.4.

EXAMPLE 11.4 Using the Clausius–Clapeyron Equation to Determine Heat of Vaporization from Experimental Measurements of Vapor Pressure

The vapor pressure of dichloromethane was measured as a function of temperature, and the following results were obtained:

Temperature (K)	Vapor Pressure (torr)
200	0.8
220	4.5
240	21
260	71
280	197
300	391

Determine the heat of vaporization of dichloromethane.

SOLUTION

To find the heat of vaporization, use an Excel spreadsheet or a graphing calculator to make a plot of the natural log of vapor pressure ($\ln P$) as a function of the inverse of the temperature in kelvins ($1/T$). Then fit the points to a line and determine the slope of the line. The slope of the best-fitting line is -3773 K. Since the slope equals $-\Delta H_{vap}/R$, we find the heat of vaporization as follows:

$$\text{slope} = -\Delta H_{vap}/R$$
$$\Delta H_{vap} = -\text{slope} \times R$$
$$= -(-3773 \text{ K})(8.314 \text{ J/mol} \cdot \text{K})$$
$$= 3.14 \times 10^4 \text{ J/mol}$$
$$= 31.4 \text{ kJ/mol}$$

$y = -3773x + 18.8$

FOR PRACTICE 11.4

The vapor pressure of carbon tetrachloride was measured as a function of the temperature, and the following results were obtained:

Temperature (K)	Vapor Pressure (torr)
255	11.3
265	21.0
275	36.8
285	61.5
295	99.0
300	123.8

Determine the heat of vaporization of carbon tetrachloride.

The Clausius–Clapeyron equation can also be expressed in a two-point form that we can use with just two measurements of vapor pressure and temperature to determine the heat of vaporization.

$$\ln \frac{P_2}{P_1} = \frac{-\Delta H_{vap}}{R}\left(\frac{1}{T_2} - \frac{1}{T_1}\right)$$ Clausius–Clapeyron equation (two-point form)

We can use this form of the equation to predict the vapor pressure of a liquid at any temperature if we know the enthalpy of vaporization and the normal boiling point (or the vapor pressure at some other temperature), as shown in Example 11.5.

The two-point method is generally inferior to plotting multiple points because fewer data points result in more chance for error.

EXAMPLE 11.5 Using the Two-Point Form of the Clausius–Clapeyron Equation to Predict the Vapor Pressure at a Given Temperature

Methanol has a normal boiling point of 64.6 °C and a heat of vaporization (ΔH_{vap}) of 35.2 kJ/mol. What is the vapor pressure of methanol at 12.0 °C?

SORT You are given the normal boiling point of methanol (the temperature at which the vapor pressure is 760 mmHg) and the heat of vaporization. You are asked to find the vapor pressure at a specified temperature that is also given.	**GIVEN:** $T_1(°C) = 64.6\ °C$ $\qquad P_1 = 760$ torr $\qquad \Delta H_{vap} = 35.2$ kJ/mol $\qquad T_2(°C) = 12.0\ °C$ **FIND:** P_2
STRATEGIZE The conceptual plan is essentially the Clausius–Clapeyron equation, which relates the given and find quantities.	**CONCEPTUAL PLAN** $\ln \dfrac{P_2}{P_1} = \dfrac{-\Delta H_{vap}}{R}\left(\dfrac{1}{T_2} - \dfrac{1}{T_1}\right)$ (Clausius–Clapeyron equation, two-point form)
SOLVE First, convert T_1 and T_2 from °C to K.	**SOLUTION** $T_1(K) = T_1(°C) + 273.15$ $\qquad = 64.6 + 273.15$ $\qquad = 337.8$ K $T_2(K) = T_2(°C) + 273.15$ $\qquad = 12.0 + 273.15$ $\qquad = 285.2$ K

| Then, substitute the required values into the Clausius–Clapeyron equation and solve for P_2. | $$\ln \frac{P_2}{P_1} = \frac{-\Delta H_{vap}}{R}\left(\frac{1}{T_2} - \frac{1}{T_1}\right)$$ $$\ln \frac{P_2}{P_1} = \frac{-35.2 \times 10^3 \frac{J}{mol}}{8.314 \frac{J}{mol \cdot K}}\left(\frac{1}{285.2\ K} - \frac{1}{337.8\ K}\right)$$ $$= -2.31$$ $$\frac{P_2}{P_1} = e^{-2.31}$$ $$P_2 = P_1(e^{-2.31})$$ $$= 760\ torr(0.0993)$$ $$= 75.4\ torr$$ |

CHECK The units of the answer are correct. The magnitude of the answer makes sense because vapor pressure should be significantly lower at the lower temperature.

FOR PRACTICE 11.5
Propane has a normal boiling point of $-42.0\ °C$ and a heat of vaporization (ΔH_{vap}) of $19.04\ kJ/mol$. What is the vapor pressure of propane at $25.0\ °C$?

The Critical Point: The Transition to an Unusual State of Matter

We have considered the vaporization of a liquid in a container open to the atmosphere with and without heating, and the vaporization of a liquid in a *sealed* container without heating. We now examine the vaporization of a liquid in a *sealed* container *during heating*. Consider liquid *n*-pentane in equilibrium with its vapor in a sealed container initially at 25 °C. At this temperature, the vapor pressure of *n*-pentane is 0.67 atm. What happens if we heat the liquid? As the temperature rises, more *n*-pentane vaporizes and the pressure within the container increases. At 100 °C, the pressure is 5.5 atm, and at 190 °C the pressure is 29 atm. As the temperature and pressure increase, more and more gaseous *n*-pentane is forced into the same amount of space, and the density of the *gas* gets higher and higher. At the same time, the increasing temperature causes the density of the *liquid* to become lower and lower. At 197 °C, the meniscus between the liquid and gaseous *n*-pentane disappears and the gas and liquid states commingle to form a *supercritical fluid* (Figure 11.32 ▼). For any substance, the *temperature* at which this transition occurs is the **critical temperature** (T_c). The liquid cannot exist (regardless of pressure) above this temperature. The *pressure* at which this transition occurs is the **critical pressure** (P_c).

▲ **FIGURE 11.32 Critical Point Transition** As *n*-pentane is heated in a sealed container, it undergoes a transition to a supercritical fluid. At the critical point, the meniscus separating the liquid and gas disappears, and the fluid becomes supercritical—neither a liquid nor a gas.

Researchers are interested in supercritical fluids because of their unique properties. A supercritical fluid has properties of both liquids and gases—it is in some sense intermediate between the two. Supercritical fluids can act as good solvents, selectively dissolving a number of compounds. For example, supercritical carbon dioxide is used as a solvent to extract caffeine from coffee beans. The caffeine dissolves in the supercritical carbon dioxide, but other substances—such as those responsible for the flavor of coffee—do not. Consequently, the caffeine is removed without substantially altering the coffee's flavor. The supercritical carbon dioxide is easily removed from the mixture by simply lowering the pressure below the critical pressure, at which point the carbon dioxide evaporates, leaving no residue.

11.6 Sublimation and Fusion

In Section 11.5, we examined a beaker of liquid water at room temperature from the molecular viewpoint. Now, let's examine a block of ice at $-10\,°C$ from the same molecular perspective, paying close attention to two common processes: sublimation and fusion.

Sublimation

Even though a block of ice is solid, the water molecules have thermal energy, which causes each one to vibrate about a fixed point. The motion is much less vigorous than in a liquid, but it is significant nonetheless. As in liquids, at any instant some molecules in the block of ice have more thermal energy than the average and some have less. The molecules with high enough thermal energy can break free from the ice surface—where, as in liquids, molecules are held less tightly than in the interior due to fewer neighbor–neighbor interactions—and go directly into the gas state (Figure 11.33 ►). This process is **sublimation**, the transition from solid to gas. Some of the water molecules in the gas state (those at the low end of the energy distribution curve for the gaseous molecules) collide with the surface of the ice and are captured by the intermolecular forces with other molecules. This process—the opposite of sublimation—is **deposition**, the transition from gas to solid. As is the case with liquids, the pressure of a gas in dynamic equilibrium with its solid is the vapor pressure of the solid.

Although both sublimation and deposition occur on the surface of an ice block open to the atmosphere at $-10\,°C$, sublimation usually occurs at a greater rate because most of the newly sublimed molecules escape into the surrounding atmosphere and never come back. The result is a noticeable decrease in the size of the ice block over time (even though the temperature is below the melting point).

If you live in a cold climate, you may have noticed the disappearance of ice and snow from the ground even though the temperature remains below $0\,°C$. Similarly, ice cubes left in the freezer for a long time slowly shrink, even though the freezer is always below $0\,°C$. In both cases, the ice is *subliming,* turning directly into water vapor. Ice also sublimes out of frozen foods. You may have noticed, for example, the gradual growth of ice crystals on the *inside* of airtight plastic food-storage bags in a freezer. The ice crystals are composed of water that has sublimed out of the food and redeposited on the surface of the bag or on the surface of the food. For this reason, food that remains frozen for too long becomes dried out. Such dehydration can be avoided to some degree by freezing foods to colder temperatures, a process called deep-freezing. The colder temperature lowers the vapor pressure of ice and preserves the food longer. Freezer burn on meats is another common manifestation of sublimation. When you improperly store meat (for example, in a container that is not airtight) sublimation continues unabated. The result is the dehydration of the surface of the meat, which becomes discolored and loses flavor and texture.

A substance commonly associated with sublimation is solid carbon dioxide or dry ice, which does not melt under atmospheric pressure no matter what the temperature is. However, at $-78\,°C$ the CO_2 molecules have enough energy to leave the surface of the dry ice and become gaseous through sublimation.

▲ **FIGURE 11.33 The Sublimation of Ice** The water molecules at the surface of an ice cube can sublime directly into the gas state.

▲ Dry ice (solid CO_2) sublimes but does not melt at atmospheric pressure.

Fusion

Let's return to our ice block and examine what happens at the molecular level as we increase its temperature. The increasing thermal energy causes the water molecules to vibrate faster and faster. At the **melting point** (0 °C for water), the molecules have enough thermal energy to overcome the intermolecular forces that hold the molecules at their stationary points, and the solid turns into a liquid. This process is **melting** or **fusion**, the transition from solid to liquid. The opposite of melting is **freezing**, the transition from liquid to solid. Once the melting point of a solid is reached, additional heating only causes more rapid melting; it does not raise the temperature of the solid above its melting point (Figure 11.34). Only after all of the ice has melted will additional heating raise the temperature of the liquid water past 0 °C. A mixture of water *and* ice always has a temperature of 0 °C (at 1 atm pressure).

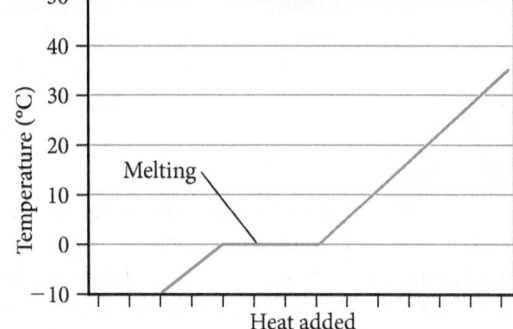

▶ **FIGURE 11.34 Temperature during Melting** The temperature of water during melting remains at 0.0 °C as long as both solid and liquid water remain.

Energetics of Melting and Freezing

The most common way to cool a beverage quickly is to drop several ice cubes into it. As the ice melts, the drink cools because melting is endothermic—the melting ice absorbs heat from the liquid. The amount of heat required to melt 1 mol of a solid is called the **heat of fusion** (ΔH_{fus}). The heat of fusion for water is 6.02 kJ/mol:

$$H_2O(s) \longrightarrow H_2O(l) \quad \Delta H_{fus} = 6.02 \text{ kJ/mol}$$

The heat of fusion is positive because melting is endothermic.

Freezing, the opposite of melting, is exothermic—heat is released when a liquid freezes into a solid. For example, as water in the freezer turns into ice, it releases heat, which must be removed by the refrigeration system of the freezer. If the refrigeration system did not remove the heat, the water would not completely freeze into ice. The heat released as the water began to freeze would warm the freezer, preventing further freezing. The change in enthalpy for freezing has the same magnitude as the heat of fusion but the opposite sign:

$$H_2O(l) \longrightarrow H_2O(s) \quad \Delta H = -\Delta H_{fus} = -6.02 \text{ kJ/mol}$$

Different substances have different heats of fusion as shown in Table 11.9.

TABLE 11.9 Heats of Fusion of Several Substances

Liquid	Chemical Formula	Melting Point (°C)	ΔH_{fus}(kJ/mol)
Water	H_2O	0.00	6.02
Rubbing alcohol (isopropyl alcohol)	C_3H_8O	−89.5	5.37
Acetone	C_3H_6O	−94.8	5.69
Diethyl ether	$C_3H_{10}O$	−116.3	7.27

In general, the heat of fusion for a substance is significantly less than its heat of vaporization, as shown in Figure 11.35 ▶. We have already seen that the solid and liquid states are closer to each other in many ways than they are to the gas state. It takes less energy to melt 1 mol of ice into liquid than it does to vaporize 1 mol of liquid water into gas because vaporization requires complete separation of molecules from one another, so the intermolecular forces must be completely overcome. Melting, however, requires that intermolecular forces be only partially overcome, allowing molecules to move around one another while still remaining in contact.

11.7 Heating Curve for Water

We can combine and build on the concepts from the Sections 11.5 and 11.6 by examining the *heating curve* for 1.00 mol of water at 1.00 atm pressure shown in Figure 11.36 ▼. The *y*-axis of the heating curve represents the temperature of the water sample. The *x*-axis represents the amount of heat added (in kilojoules) during heating. In the diagram, we divide the process into five segments: (1) ice warming; (2) ice melting into liquid water; (3) liquid water warming; (4) liquid water vaporizing into steam; and (5) steam warming.

In two of these segments (2 and 4) the temperature is constant as heat is added because the added heat goes into producing the transition between states, not into increasing the temperature. The two states are in equilibrium during the transition and the temperature remains constant. The amount of heat required to achieve the state change is given by $q = n\Delta H$.

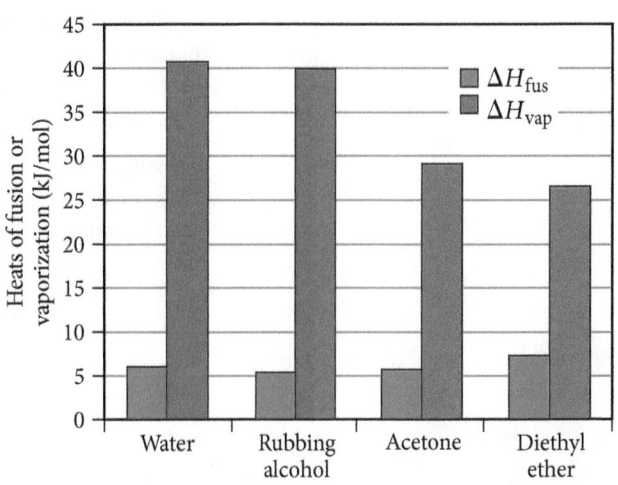

▲ FIGURE 11.35 **Heat of Fusion and Heat of Vaporization** Typical heats of fusion are significantly less than heats of vaporization.

1. Ice warming
   0.941 kJ/mol
2. Ice melting to liquid
   6.02 kJ/mol
3. Liquid water warming
   7.52 kJ/mol
4. Liquid water vaporizing to steam
   40.7 kJ/mol
5. Steam warming
   0.904 kJ/mol

▲ FIGURE 11.36 **Heating Curve for Water**

In the other three segments (1, 3, and 5), temperature increases linearly. These segments represent the heating of a single state in which the deposited heat raises the temperature in accordance with the substance's heat capacity ($q = mC_s \Delta T$). We examine each of these segments individually.

Segment 1 In segment 1, solid ice is warmed from $-25\,°C$ to $0\,°C$. Since no transition between states occurs here, the amount of heat required to heat the solid ice is given by $q = mC_s \Delta T$ (see Section 6.4), where C_s is the specific heat capacity of ice ($C_{s,\,ice} = 2.09$ J/g·°C). For 1.00 mol of water (18.0 g), we calculate the amount of heat as follows:

$$q = mC_{s,\,ice}\ \Delta T$$
$$= 18.0\ \cancel{g}\left(2.09\frac{J}{\cancel{g}\cdot\cancel{°C}}\right)[0.0\ \cancel{°C} - (-25.0\ \cancel{°C})]$$
$$= 941\ J\ =\ 0.941\ kJ$$

So in segment 1, 0.941 kJ of heat is added to the ice, warming it from $-25°$ C to 0 °C.

Segment 2 In segment 2, the added heat does not change the temperature of the ice and water mixture because the heat is absorbed by the transition from solid to liquid. The amount of heat required to convert the ice to liquid water is given by $q = n\,\Delta H_{fus}$, where n is the number of moles of water and ΔH_{fus} is the heat of fusion (see Section 11.6):

$$q = n\,\Delta H_{fus}$$
$$= 1.00\ \cancel{mol}\left(\frac{6.02\ kJ}{\cancel{mol}}\right)$$
$$= 6.02\ kJ$$

In segment 2, 6.02 kJ is added to the ice, melting it into liquid water. Notice that the temperature does not change during melting. The liquid and solid coexist at 0 °C as the melting occurs.

Segment 3 In segment 3, the liquid water is warmed from 0 °C to 100 °C. Since no transition between states occurs here, the amount of heat required to heat the liquid water is given by $q = mC_s\,\Delta T$, as in segment 1. However, now we must use the heat capacity of liquid water (not ice) for the calculation. For 1.00 mol of water (18.0 g), we calculate the amount of heat as follows:

$$q = mC_{s,\,liq}\ \Delta T$$
$$= 18.0\ \cancel{g}\left(4.18\frac{J}{\cancel{g}\cdot\cancel{°C}}\right)(100.0\ \cancel{°C} - 0.0\ \cancel{°C})$$
$$= 7.52\times 10^3\ J = 7.52\ kJ$$

So in segment 3, 7.52 kJ of heat is added to the liquid water, warming it from 0 °C to 100 °C.

Segment 4 In segment 4, the water undergoes a second transition between states, this time from liquid to gas. The amount of heat required to convert the liquid to gas is given by $q = n\,\Delta H_{vap}$, where n is the number of moles and ΔH_{vap} is the heat of vaporization (see Section 11.5):

$$q = n\,\Delta H_{vap}$$
$$= 1.00\ \cancel{mol}\left(\frac{40.7\ kJ}{\cancel{mol}}\right)$$
$$= 40.7\ kJ$$

Thus, in segment 4, 40.7 kJ is added to the water, vaporizing it into steam. Notice that the temperature does not change during boiling. The liquid and gas coexist at 100 °C as the boiling occurs.

Segment 5 In segment 5, the steam is warmed from 100 °C to 125 °C. Since no transition between states occurs here, the amount of heat required to heat the steam is given by

$q = mC_s \Delta T$ (as in segments 1 and 3) except that we must use the heat capacity of steam $(2.01\ \text{J/g}\cdot{}^\circ\text{C})$:

$$q = mC_{s,\,steam} \Delta T$$

$$= 18.0\ \text{g}\left(2.01\frac{\text{J}}{\cancel{\text{g}}\cdot{}^\circ\cancel{\text{C}}}\right)(125.0\ {}^\circ\cancel{\text{C}} - 100.0\ {}^\circ\cancel{\text{C}})$$

$$= 904 = 0.904\ \text{kJ}$$

So in segment 5, 0.904 kJ of heat is added to the steam, warming it from 100 °C to 125 °C.

Conceptual Connection 11.6 Cooling of Water with Ice

You just saw that the heat capacity of ice is $C_{s,\,ice} = 2.09\ \text{J/g}\cdot{}^\circ\text{C}$ and that the heat of fusion of ice is 6.02 kJ/mol. When a small ice cube at $-10\ {}^\circ\text{C}$ is put into a cup of water at room temperature, which of the following plays a greater role in cooling the liquid water: the warming of the ice from $-10\ {}^\circ\text{C}$ to $0\ {}^\circ\text{C}$, or the melting of the ice?

11.8 Phase Diagrams

Throughout most of this chapter, we have examined how the state of a substance changes with temperature and pressure. We can combine both the temperature dependence and pressure dependence of the state of a particular substance in a graph called a *phase diagram*. A **phase diagram** is a map of the state or *phase* of a substance as a function of pressure (on the *y*-axis) and temperature (on the *x*-axis). We first examine the major features of a phase diagram, then turn to navigating within a phase diagram, and finally examine and compare the phase diagrams of selected substances.

The Major Features of a Phase Diagram

We can introduce the major features of a phase diagram by examining the phase diagram for water as an example (Figure 11.37 ▼). The *y*-axis displays the pressure in torr and the *x*-axis displays the temperature in degrees Celsius. We categorize the main features of the phase diagram as regions, lines, and points.

Phase Diagram for Water

◀ FIGURE 11.37 **Phase Diagram for Water**

Regions *Any of the three main regions—solid, liquid, and gas—in the phase diagram represent conditions where that particular state is stable.* For example, under any of the temperatures and pressures within the liquid region in the phase diagram of water, the liquid is the stable state. Notice that the point 25 °C and 760 torr falls within the liquid region, as we know from everyday experience. In general, low temperature and high pressure favor the solid state, high temperature and low pressure favor the gas state, and intermediate conditions favor the liquid state. A sample of matter that is not in the state indicated by its phase diagram for a given set of conditions converts to that state when those conditions are imposed. For example, steam that is cooled to room temperature at 1 atm condenses to liquid.

Lines *Each of the lines (or curves) in the phase diagram represents a set of temperatures and pressures at which the substance is in equilibrium between the two states on either side of the line.* In the phase diagram for water, consider the curved line beginning just beyond 0 °C separating the liquid from the gas. This line is the vaporization curve (also called the vapor pressure curve) for water that we examined in Section 11.5. At any of the temperatures and pressures that fall along this line, the liquid and gas states of water are equally stable and in equilibrium. For example, at 100 °C and 760 torr pressure, water and its vapor are in equilibrium—they are equally stable and will coexist. The other two major lines in a phase diagram are the sublimation curve (separating the solid and the gas) and the fusion curve (separating the solid and the liquid).

> The triple point of a substance such as water can be reproduced anywhere to calibrate a thermometer or pressure gauge with a known temperature and pressure.

The Triple Point *The **triple point** in a phase diagram represents the unique set of conditions at which the three states are equally stable and in equilibrium.* In the phase diagram for water, the triple point occurs at 0.0098 °C and 4.58 torr. Under these unique conditions (and only under these conditions), the solid, liquid, and gas states of water are equally stable and will coexist in equilibrium.

The Critical Point As we discussed in Section 11.5, at the critical temperature and pressure, the liquid and gas states coalesce into a *supercritical fluid.* The **critical point** *in a phase diagram represents the temperature and pressure above which a supercritical fluid exists.*

Navigation within a Phase Diagram

We can represent changes in the temperature or pressure of a sample of water as movement within the phase diagram. For example, suppose we heat a block of ice initially at 1.0 atm and −25 °C. We represent the change in temperature at constant pressure as movement along the line marked A in Figure 11.38 ▼. As the temperature rises, we move to the right along the

Navigation within a Phase Diagram

▶ FIGURE 11.38 **Navigation on the Phase Diagram for Water**

line. At the fusion curve, the temperature stops rising and melting occurs until the solid ice is completely converted to liquid water. Crossing the fusion curve requires the complete transition from solid to liquid. Once the ice has completely melted, the temperature of the liquid water can begin to rise until the vaporization curve is reached. At this point, the temperature again stops rising and boiling occurs until all the liquid is converted to gas.

We can represent a change in pressure with a vertical line on the phase diagram. For example, suppose we lower the pressure above a sample of water initially at 1.0 atm and 25 °C. We represent the change in pressure at constant temperature as movement along the line marked B in Figure 11.38. As the pressure drops, we move down the line and approach the vaporization curve. At the vaporization curve, the pressure stops dropping and vaporization occurs until the liquid is completely converted to vapor. Crossing the vaporization curve requires the complete transition from liquid to gas. Only after the liquid has all vaporized can the pressure continue to drop.

The Phase Diagrams of Other Substances

Examine the phase diagrams of iodine and carbon dioxide, shown in Figure 11.39 ▼. The phase diagrams are similar to that of water in most of their general features, but some significant differences exist.

The fusion curves for both carbon dioxide and iodine have a positive slope—as the temperature increases the pressure also increases—in contrast to the fusion curve for water, which has a negative slope. The behavior of water is atypical. The fusion curve within the phase diagrams for most substances has a positive slope because increasing pressure favors the denser state, which for most substances is the solid state. For example, suppose we increase the pressure on a sample of iodine from 1 atm to 100 atm at 184 °C, as shown by line A in Figure 11.39(a). Notice that this change crosses the fusion curve, converting the liquid into a solid. In contrast, a pressure increase from 1 atm to 100 atm at −0.1 °C in water causes a state transition from solid to liquid. Unlike most substances, the liquid state of water is actually denser than the solid state.

Both water and iodine have stable solid, liquid, and gaseous states at a pressure of 1 atm. However, notice that carbon dioxide has no stable liquid state at a pressure of 1 atm. If we increase the temperature of a block of solid carbon dioxide (dry ice) at 1 atm, as indicated by line B in Figure 11.39(b), we cross the sublimation curve at −78.5 °C. At this temperature, the solid sublimes to a gas, which is one reason that dry ice is useful (it does not melt into a liquid at atmospheric pressure). Carbon dioxide will form a liquid only above pressures of 5.1 atm.

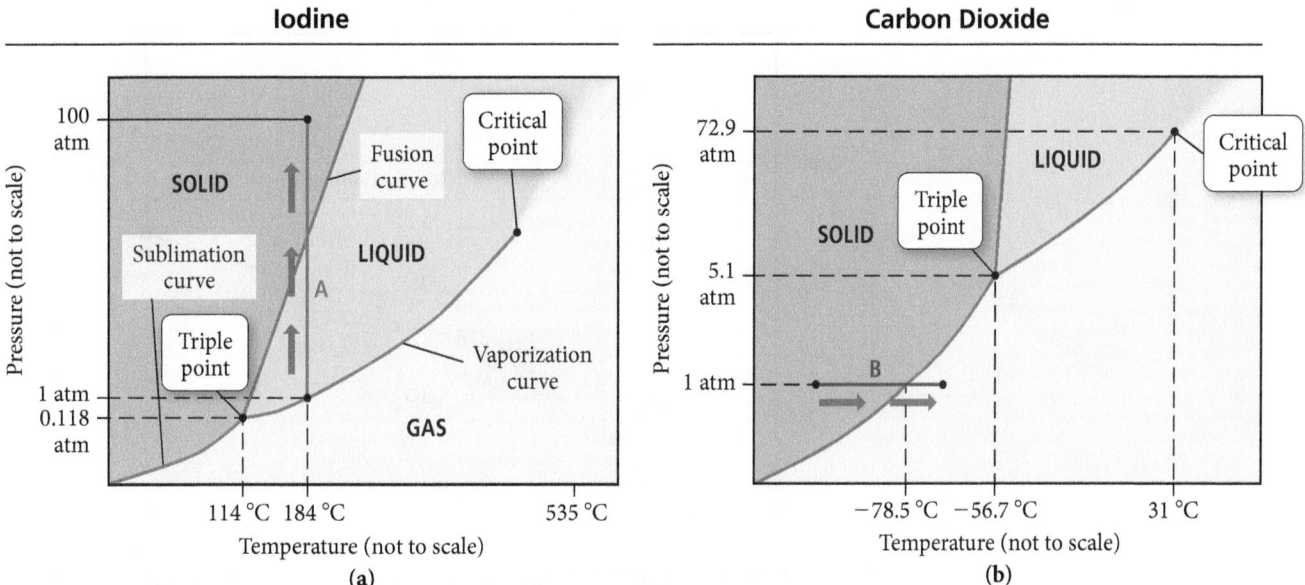

▲ **FIGURE 11.39 Phase Diagrams for Other Substances** (a) Iodine, (b) Carbon dioxide.

Conceptual Connection 11.7 Phase Diagrams

A substance has a triple point at −24.5 °C and 225 mm Hg. What is most likely to happen to a solid sample of the substance as it is warmed from −35 °C to 0 °C at a pressure of 220 mm Hg?

(a) The solid will melt into a liquid.

(b) The solid will sublime into a gas.

(c) Nothing (the solid will remain as a solid).

11.9 Water: An Extraordinary Substance

▲ The *Phoenix Mars Lander* is looking for evidence of life in frozen water that lies below the surface of Mars's north polar region.

Water is the most common and important liquid on Earth. It fills our oceans, lakes, and streams. In its solid form, it caps our mountains, and in its gaseous form, it humidifies our air. We drink water, we sweat water, and we excrete bodily wastes dissolved in water. Indeed, the majority of our body mass *is* water. Life is impossible without water, and in most places on Earth where liquid water exists, life exists. Recent evidence for the past existence of water on Mars has fueled hopes of finding life or evidence of past life there. And though it may not be obvious to us (because we take water for granted), this familiar substance has many remarkable properties.

Among liquids, water is unique. It has a low molar mass (18.02 g/mol), yet it is a liquid at room temperature. Other main-group hydrides have higher molar masses but lower boiling points, as shown in Figure 11.40 ▼. No other substance of similar molar mass (except for HF) comes close to being a liquid at room temperature. We can understand water's high boiling point (in spite of its low molar mass) by examining its molecular structure. The bent geometry of the water molecule and the highly polar nature of the O—H bonds result in a molecule with a significant dipole moment. Water's two O—H bonds (hydrogen directly bonded to oxygen) allow a water molecule to form strong hydrogen bonds with four other water molecules (Figure 11.41 ▶), resulting in a relatively high boiling point. Water's high polarity also allows it to dissolve many other polar and ionic compounds and even a number of nonpolar gases such as oxygen and carbon dioxide (by inducing a dipole moment in their molecules). Consequently, water is the main solvent within living organisms, transporting nutrients and other important compounds throughout the body. Water is the main solvent in our environment as well, allowing aquatic animals, for example, to survive by breathing dissolved oxygen and allowing aquatic plants to survive by using dissolved carbon dioxide for photosynthesis.

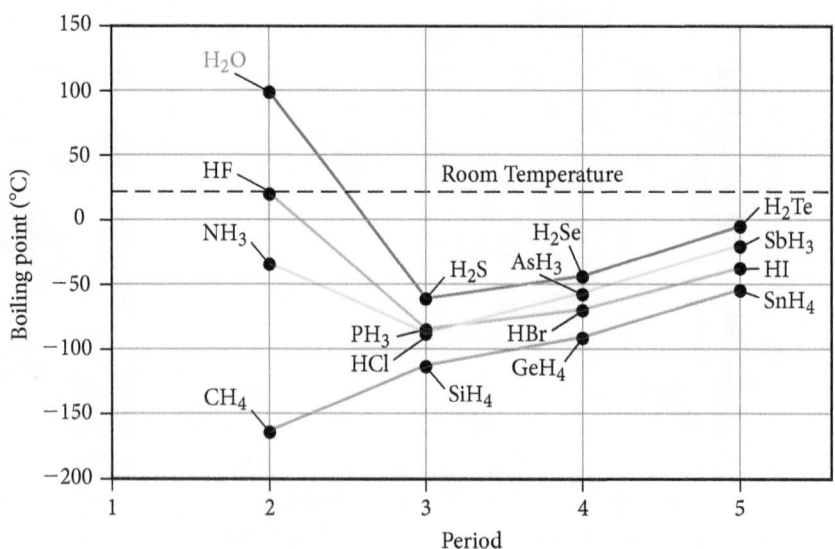

▲ **FIGURE 11.40 Boiling Points of Main Group Hydrides** Water is the only common main-group hydride that is a liquid at room temperature.

We have already seen in Section 6.4 that water has an exceptionally high specific heat capacity, which has a moderating effect on the climate of coastal cities. In some cities, such as San Francisco, for example, the daily fluctuation in temperature can be less than 10 °C. This same moderating effect occurs over the entire planet, two-thirds of which is covered by water. Without water, the daily temperature fluctuations on our planet might be more like those on Mars, where temperature fluctuations of 63 °C (113 °F) occur between midday and early morning. Imagine awakening to below freezing temperatures, only to bake at summer desert temperatures in the afternoon! The presence of water on Earth and water's uniquely high specific heat capacity are largely responsible for our planet's much smaller daily fluctuations.

As we have seen, the way water freezes is also unique. Unlike other substances, which contract upon freezing, water expands upon freezing. Consequently, ice is less dense than liquid water, which is why ice floats. This seemingly trivial property has significant consequences. The frozen layer of ice at the surface of a winter lake insulates the water in the lake from further freezing. If this ice layer sank, it would kill bottom-dwelling aquatic life and possibly allow the lake to freeze solid, eliminating virtually all life in the lake.

The expansion of water upon freezing, however, is one reason that most organisms do not survive freezing. When the water within a cell freezes, it expands and often ruptures the cell, just as water freezing within a pipe bursts the pipe. Many foods, especially those with high water content, do not survive freezing very well either. Have you ever tried, for example, to freeze your own vegetables? If you put lettuce or spinach in the freezer, it will be limp and damaged upon thawing. The frozen-food industry gets around this problem by *flash freezing* vegetables and other foods. In this process, foods are frozen nearly instantaneously, which prevents water molecules from settling into their preferred crystalline structure. Consequently, the water does not expand very much and the food remains largely undamaged.

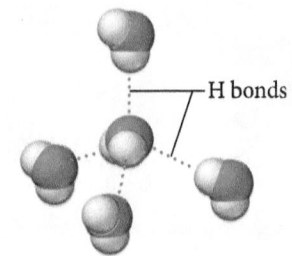

▲ FIGURE 11.41 **Hydrogen Bonding in Water** A water molecule can form four strong hydrogen bonds with four other water molecules.

▲ When lettuce freezes, the water within its cells expands, rupturing them.

Chemistry in the Environment
Water Pollution

Water quality is critical to human health. Many human diseases—especially in developing nations—are caused by poor water quality. Several kinds of pollutants, including biological and chemical contaminants, can enter water supplies.

▲ Uncontaminated, sanitary water supplies are critical to human health.

Biological contaminants are microorganisms that cause diseases such as hepatitis, cholera, dysentery, and typhoid. They get into drinking water primarily when human or animal waste is dumped into bodies of water. Drinking water in developed nations is usually chemically treated to kill microorganisms. Water containing biological contaminants poses an immediate danger to human health and should not be consumed. Boiling eliminates most biological contaminants from untreated water.

Chemical contaminants enter drinking water supplies as a result of industrial dumping, pesticide and fertilizer use, and household dumping. These contaminants include organic compounds, such as carbon tetrachloride and dioxin, and inorganic elements and compounds, such as mercury, lead, and nitrates. Since many chemical contaminants are neither volatile nor alive (like biological contaminants are), they are usually *not* eliminated through boiling.

The U.S. Environmental Protection Agency (EPA), under the Safe Drinking Water Act of 1974 and its amendments, sets standards that specify the maximum contamination level (MCL) of nearly 100 biological and chemical contaminants in water. Water providers that serve more than 25 people must periodically test the water they deliver to their consumers for these contaminants. If levels exceed the standards set by the EPA, the water provider must notify consumers and take appropriate measures to remove the contaminant from the water. According to the EPA, water from providers that serve more than 25 people should be safe to consume over a lifetime. If it is not safe to drink for a short period of time, providers must notify consumers.

Question
Why doesn't boiling eliminate nonvolatile contaminants such as lead?

▲ The well-defined angles and smooth faces of crystalline solids reflect the underlying order of the atoms composing them.

▲ The hexagonal shape of a snowflake derives from the hexagonal arrangement of water molecules in crystalline ice.

11.10 Crystalline Solids: Determining Their Structure by X-Ray Crystallography

Recall that crystalline solids are composed of atoms or molecules arranged in structures with long-range order (see Section 11.2). If you have ever visited the mineral section of a natural history museum and seen crystals with smooth faces and well-defined angles between them, or if you have carefully observed the hexagonal shapes of snowflakes, you have witnessed some of the effects of the underlying order in crystalline solids. The often beautiful geometric shapes that you see on the macroscopic scale are the result of specific structural patterns on the molecular and atomic scales. But how do we study these patterns? How do we look into the atomic and molecular world to determine the arrangement of the atoms and measure the distances between them? In this section, we examine **X-ray diffraction**, a powerful laboratory technique that enables us to do exactly that.

In Section 7.2 we saw that electromagnetic (or light) waves interact with each other in a characteristic way called *interference:* they can cancel each other out or reinforce each other, depending on the alignment of their crests and troughs. *Constructive interference* occurs when two waves interact with their crests and troughs in alignment. *Destructive interference* occurs when two waves interact with the crests of one aligning with the troughs of the other. Recall also that when light encounters two slits separated by a distance comparable to the wavelength of the light, constructive and destructive interference between the resulting beams produces a characteristic *interference pattern*, consisting of alternating bright and dark lines.

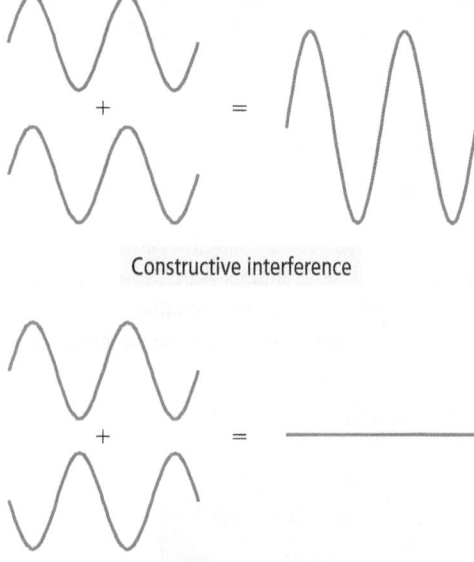

Constructive interference

Destructive interference

Atoms within crystal structures have spacings between them on the order of 10^2 pm, so light of similar wavelength (which happens to fall in the X-ray region of the electromagnetic spectrum) forms interference patterns or *diffraction patterns* when it interacts with those atoms. The exact pattern of diffraction reveals the spacings between planes of atoms. Consider two planes of atoms within a crystalline lattice separated by a distance *d*, as shown in Figure 11.42 ▶. If two rays of light with wavelength λ that are initially in phase (that is, the crests of one wave are aligned with the crests of the other) diffract from the two planes, the diffracted rays may interfere with each other constructively or destructively, depending on the difference between the path lengths traveled by each ray. If the difference between the two path lengths (2*a*) is an integral number (*n*) of wavelengths, then the interference will be constructive:

$$n\lambda = 2a \quad \text{(criterion for constructive interference)} \qquad [11.5]$$

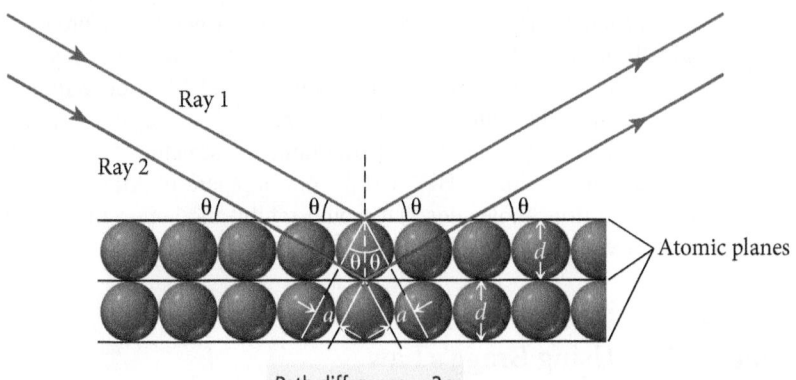

Path difference = 2*a*

Using trigonometry, we can see that the angle of reflection (θ) is related to the distance a and the separation between layers (d) by the following relation:

$$\sin \theta = \frac{a}{d} \qquad [11.6]$$

Rearranging, we get:

$$a = d \sin \theta \qquad [11.7]$$

By substituting Equation 11.7 into Equation 11.5, we arrive at the following important relationship:

$$n\lambda = 2d \sin \theta \qquad \text{Bragg's law}$$

This equation is known as *Bragg's law*. For a given wavelength of light incident on atoms arranged in layers, we can measure the angle that produces constructive interference (which appears as a bright spot on the X-ray diffraction pattern) and then calculate d, the distance between the atomic layers:

$$d = \frac{n\lambda}{2 \sin \theta} \qquad [11.8]$$

In a modern X-ray diffractometer (Figure 11.43 ▼), the diffraction pattern from a crystal is collected and analyzed by a computer. By rotating the crystal and collecting the resulting diffraction patterns at different angles, the distances between various crystalline planes can be measured, eventually yielding the entire crystalline structure. This process is called X-ray crystallography. Researchers use X-ray crystallography to determine not only the structures of simple atomic lattices, but also the structures of proteins, DNA, and other biologically important molecules. For example, the famous X-ray diffraction photograph shown at left, obtained by Rosalind Franklin and Maurice Wilkins, helped Watson and Crick determine the double-helical structure of DNA. Recall from Section 9.1 that researchers also used X-ray diffraction to determine the structure of HIV protease, a protein critical to the reproduction of HIV and the development of AIDS. That structure was then used to design drug molecules that would inhibit the action of HIV protease, thus halting the advance of the disease.

EXAMPLE 11.6   Using Bragg's Law

When an X-ray beam of $\lambda = 154$ pm was incident on the surface of an iron crystal, it produced a maximum reflection at an angle of $\theta = 32.6°$. Assuming $n = 1$, calculate the separation between layers of iron atoms in the crystal.

SOLUTION

To solve this problem, use Bragg's law in the form given by Equation 11.8. The distance, d, is the separation between layers in the crystal.

$$d = \frac{n\lambda}{2 \sin \theta}$$

$$= \frac{154 \text{ pm}}{2 \sin(32.6°)}$$

$$= 143 \text{ pm}$$

FOR PRACTICE 11.6

The spacing between layers of molybdenum atoms is 157 pm. Calculate the angle at which 154 pm X-rays produces a maximum reflection for $n = 1$.

11.11 Crystalline Solids: Unit Cells and Basic Structures

Simple cubic

$l = 2r$

▲ In the simple cubic lattice, the atoms touch along each edge so that the edge length is $2r$.

X-Ray crystallography allows us to determine the regular arrangements of atoms within a crystalline solid. This arrangement is called the **crystalline lattice**. The crystalline lattice of any solid is nature's way of aggregating the particles to minimize their energy. We can represent the crystalline lattice with a small collection of atoms, ions, or molecules called the **unit cell**. When the unit cell is repeated over and over—like the tiles of a floor or the pattern in a wallpaper design, but in three dimensions—the entire lattice is reproduced. For example, consider the two-dimensional crystalline lattice shown at left. The unit cell for this lattice is the dark-colored square. Each circle represents a *lattice point,* a point in space occupied by an atom, ion, or molecule. Repeating the pattern in the square throughout the two-dimensional space generates the entire lattice.

Many different unit cells exist, and we often classify unit cells by their symmetry. In this book, we focus primarily on *cubic unit cells* (although we look at one hexagonal unit cell). Cubic unit cells are characterized by equal edge lengths and 90° angles at their corners. The three cubic unit cells—simple cubic, body-centered cubic, and face-centered cubic—along with some of their basic characteristics, are presented in Figure 11.44 ▶. There are two colors in this figure to help you visualize the different positions of the atoms; the colors *do not* represent different *kinds* of atoms. For these unit cells, *each atom in any one structure is identical to the other atoms in that structure.*

The **simple cubic** unit cell (Figure 11.45 ▶) consists of a cube with one atom at each corner. The atoms touch along each edge of the cube, so the edge length is twice the radius of the atoms ($l = 2r$). Even though it may seem like the unit cell contains eight atoms, it actually contains only one. Each corner atom is shared by eight other unit cells. In other words, any one unit cell actually contains only one-eighth of each of the eight atoms at its corners, for a total of only one atom per unit cell.

Cubic Cell Name	Atoms per Unit Cell	Structure	Coordination Number	Edge Length in terms of r	Packing Efficiency (fraction of volume occupied)
Simple Cubic	1		6	$2r$	52%
Body-Centered Cubic	2		8	$\dfrac{4r}{\sqrt{3}}$	68%
Face-Centered Cubic	4		12	$2\sqrt{2}r$	74%

▲ FIGURE 11.44 **The Cubic Crystalline Lattices** The different colors used for the atoms in this figure are for clarity only. All atoms within each structure are identical.

A characteristic feature of any unit cell is the **coordination number**, the number of atoms with which each atom is in *direct contact*. The coordination number is the number of atoms with which a particular atom can strongly interact. The simple cubic unit cell has a coordination number of 6; any one atom touches only six others, as you can see in Figure 11.45. A quantity closely related to the coordination number is the **packing efficiency**, the percentage of the volume of the unit cell occupied by the spheres. The higher the coordination number, the greater the packing efficiency. The simple cubic unit cell has a packing efficiency of 52%—the simple cubic unit cell contains a lot of empty space.

The **body-centered cubic** unit cell (Figure 11.46 ▶) consists of a cube with one atom at each corner and one atom (of the same kind) in the very center of the cube. Note that in the body-centered unit cell, the atoms *do not* touch along each edge of the cube, but instead along the diagonal line that runs from one corner, through the middle of the cube, to the

Unit cells, such as the cubic ones shown here, are customarily portrayed with "whole" atoms, even though only a part of the whole atom may actually be in the unit cell.

▼ FIGURE 11.45 **Simple Cubic Crystal Structure**

Simple Cubic Unit Cell

Coordination number = 6

Atoms per unit cell=
$\dfrac{1}{8} \times 8 = 1$

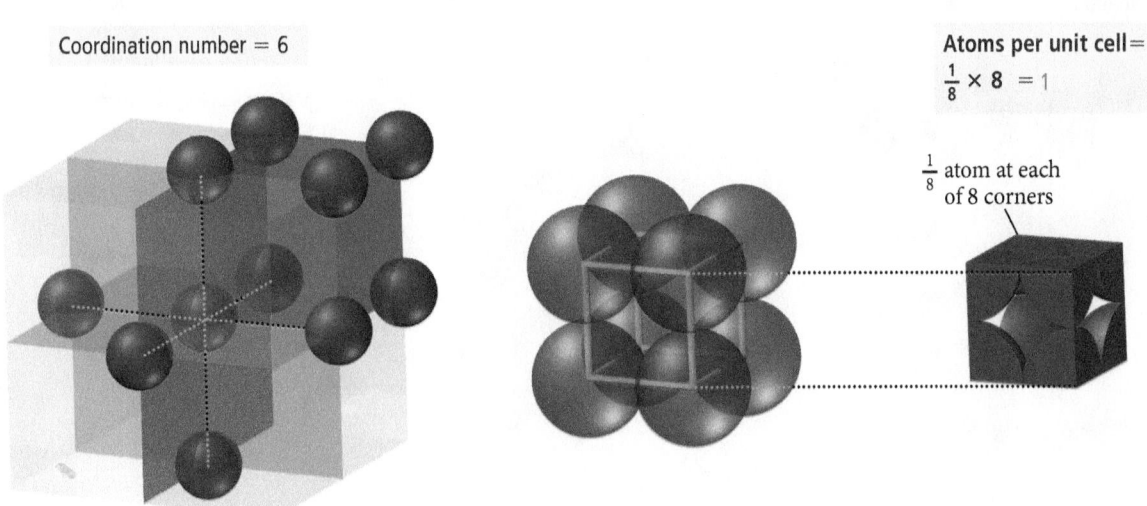

$\dfrac{1}{8}$ atom at each of 8 corners

Body-Centered Cubic Unit Cell

Coordination number = 8

Atoms per unit cell=
$$\left(\frac{1}{8} \times 8\right) + 1 = 2$$

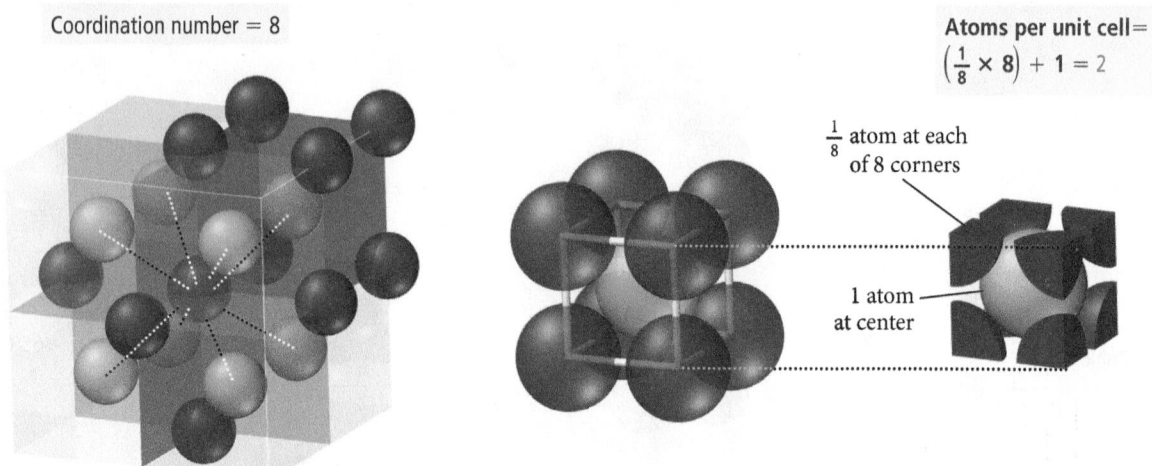

$\frac{1}{8}$ atom at each of 8 corners

1 atom at center

▲ **FIGURE 11.46 Body-Centered Cubic Crystal Structure** The different colors used for the atoms in this figure are for clarity only. All atoms within the structure are identical.

Body-centered cubic

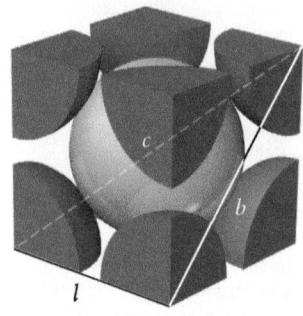

$$c^2 = b^2 + l^2 \qquad b^2 = l^2 + l^2$$
$$c = 4r \qquad b^2 = 2l^2$$
$$(4r)^2 = 2l^2 + l^2$$
$$(4r)^2 = 3l^2$$
$$l^2 = \frac{(4r)^2}{3}$$
$$l = \frac{4r}{\sqrt{3}}$$

▲ In the body-centered cubic lattice, the atoms touch only along the cube diagonal. The edge length is $4r/\sqrt{3}$.

opposite corner. The edge length in terms of the atomic radius is therefore $l = 4r/\sqrt{3}$ as shown in the diagram at left. The body-centered unit cell contains two atoms per unit cell because the center atom is not shared with any other neighboring cells. The coordination number of the body-centered cubic unit cell is 8, which we can see by examining the atom in the very center of the cube, which touches eight atoms at the corners. The packing efficiency is 68%, significantly higher than for the simple cubic unit cell. Each atom in this structure strongly interacts with more atoms than each atom in the simple cubic unit cell.

The **face-centered cubic** unit cell (Figure 11.47 ▼) is a cube with one atom at each corner and one atom (of the same kind) in the center of each cube face. Note

Face-Centered Cubic Unit Cell

Face-centered cubic: extended structure
Coordination number = 12

Face-centered cubic: unit cell
Atoms/unit $= \left(\frac{1}{8} \times 8\right) + \left(\frac{1}{2} \times 6\right) = 4$

$\frac{1}{8}$ atom at 8 corners

$\frac{1}{2}$ atom at 6 faces

▲ **FIGURE 11.47 Face-Centered Cubic Crystal Structure** The different colors used on the atoms in this figure are for clarity only. All atoms within the structure are identical.

that in the face-centered unit cell (like the body-centered unit cell), the atoms *do not* touch along each edge of the cube. Instead, the atoms touch *along the diagonal face.* The edge length in terms of the atomic radius is therefore $l = 2\sqrt{2}r$, as shown in the figure at right. The face-centered unit cell contains four atoms per unit cell because the center atoms on each of the six faces are shared between two unit cells. There are $\frac{1}{2} \times 6 = 3$ face-centered atoms plus $1/8 \times 8 = 1$ corner atoms, for a total of four atoms per unit cell. The coordination number of the face-centered cubic unit cell is 12 and its packing efficiency is 74%. In this structure, any one atom strongly interacts with more atoms than in either the simple cubic unit cell or the body-centered cubic unit cell.

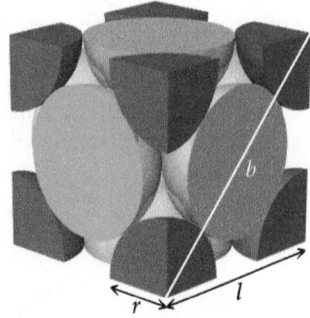

Face-centered cubic

$$b^2 = l^2 + l^2 = 2l^2$$
$$b = 4r$$
$$(4r)^2 = 2l^2$$
$$l^2 = \frac{(4r)^2}{2}$$
$$l = \frac{4r}{\sqrt{2}}$$
$$= 2\sqrt{2}r$$

▲ In the face-centered cubic lattice, the atoms touch along a face diagonal. The edge length is $2\sqrt{2}r$.

EXAMPLE 11.7 Relating Density to Crystal Structure

Aluminum crystallizes with a face-centered cubic unit cell. The radius of an aluminum atom is 143 pm. Calculate the density of solid crystalline aluminum in g/cm³.

SORT You are given the radius of an aluminum atom and its crystal structure. You are asked to find the density of solid aluminum.	**GIVEN:** $r = 143$ pm, face-centered cubic **FIND:** d

STRATEGIZE The conceptual plan is based on the definition of density.
 	
 Since the unit cell has the physical properties of the entire crystal, you can find the mass and volume of the unit cell and use these to calculate its density.
	CONCEPTUAL PLAN
	
	 $d = m/V$
	
	 m = mass of unit cell
	     = number of atoms in unit cell $\times$ mass of each atom
	
	 V = volume of unit cell
	     = (edge length)³

SOLVE Begin by finding the mass of the unit cell. Determine the mass of an aluminum atom from its molar mass. Since the face-centered cubic unit cell contains four atoms per unit cell, multiply the mass of aluminum by 4 to get the mass of a unit cell.	**SOLUTION** $m(\text{Al atom}) = 26.98\dfrac{\text{g}}{\text{mol}} \times \dfrac{1 \text{ mol}}{6.022 \times 10^{23} \text{ atoms}}$ $\qquad\qquad = 4.480 \times 10^{-23}$ g/atom $m(\text{unit cell}) = 4 \text{ atoms}(4.480 \times 10^{-23} \text{ g/atoms})$ $\qquad\qquad = 1.792 \times 10^{-22}$ g
Next, calculate the edge length (l) of the unit cell (in m) from the atomic radius of aluminum. For the face-centered cubic structure, $l = 2\sqrt{2}r$.	$l = 2\sqrt{2}r$ $\quad = 2\sqrt{2}(143 \text{ pm})$ $\quad = 2\sqrt{2}(143 \times 10^{-12} \text{ m})$ $\quad = 4.0\underline{4}5 \times 10^{-10} \text{ m}$
Calculate the volume of the unit cell (in cm) by converting the edge length to cm and cubing the edge length. (Use centimeters because you will want to report the density in units of g/cm³.)	$V = l^3$ $\quad = \left(4.0\underline{4}5 \times 10^{-10} \text{ m} \times \dfrac{1 \text{ cm}}{10^{-2} \text{ m}}\right)^3$ $\quad = 6.6\underline{1}8 \times 10^{-23} \text{ cm}^3$
Finally, calculate the density by dividing the mass of the unit cell by the volume of the unit cell.	$d = \dfrac{m}{V} = \dfrac{1.792 \times 10^{-22} \text{ g}}{6.6\underline{1}8 \times 10^{-23} \text{ cm}^3}$ $\quad = 2.71 \text{ g/cm}^3$

CHECK

The units of the answer are correct. The magnitude of the answer is reasonable because the density is greater than 1 g/cm³ (as you would expect for metals), but still not too high (because aluminum is a low-density metal).

FOR PRACTICE 11.7

Chromium crystallizes with a body-centered cubic unit cell. The radius of a chromium atom is 125 pm. Calculate the density of solid crystalline chromium in g/cm³.

Closest-Packed Structures

Another way to envision crystal structures, especially useful in metals where bonds are not usually directional, is to think of the atoms as stacking in layers, much as fruit is stacked at the grocery store. For example, the simple cubic structure can be envisioned as one layer of atoms arranged in a square pattern with the next layer stacking directly over the first, so that the atoms in one layer align exactly on top of the atoms in the layer beneath it, as shown here:

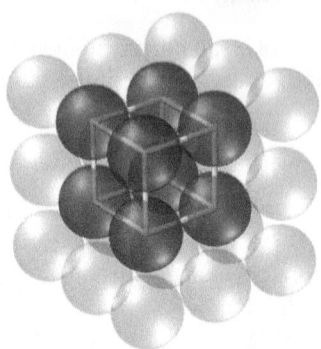

As we saw previously, this crystal structure has a great deal of empty space—only 52% of the volume is occupied by the spheres, and the coordination number is 6.

More space-efficient packing can be achieved by aligning neighboring rows of atoms in a pattern with one row offset from the next by one-half a sphere, as shown here:

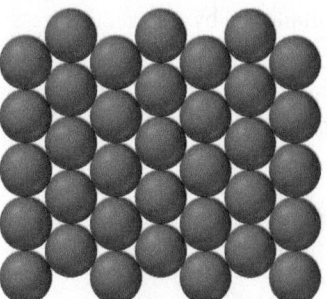

In this way, the atoms pack more closely to each other in any one layer. We can further increase the packing efficiency by placing the next layer *not directly on top of the first,* but again offset so that any one atom actually sits in the indentation formed by three atoms in the layer beneath it, as shown here:

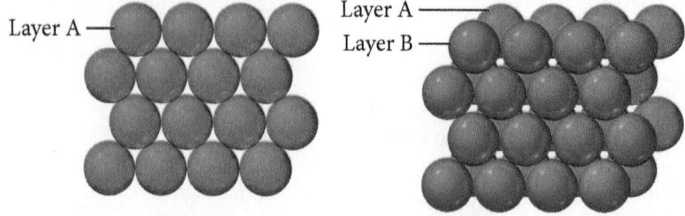

Layer A

Layer A
Layer B

This kind of packing leads to two different crystal structures called *closest-packed structures*, both of which have a packing efficiency of 74% and a coordination number of 12. In the first of these two closest-packed structures—called **hexagonal closest packing**—the third layer of atoms aligns exactly on top of the first, as shown here:

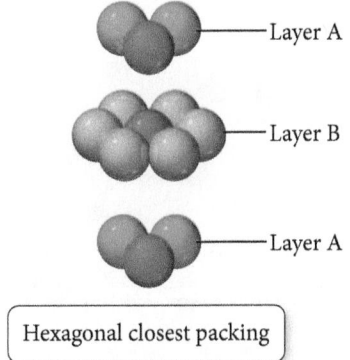

Hexagonal closest packing

The pattern from one layer to the next is ABAB, with the third layer aligning exactly above the first. Notice that the central atom in layer B of this structure is touching six atoms in its own layer, three atoms in the layer above it, and three atoms in the layer below, for a coordination number of 12. The unit cell for this crystal structure is not a cubic unit cell, but a hexagonal one, as shown in Figure 11.48 ▼.

Hexagonal Closest Packing

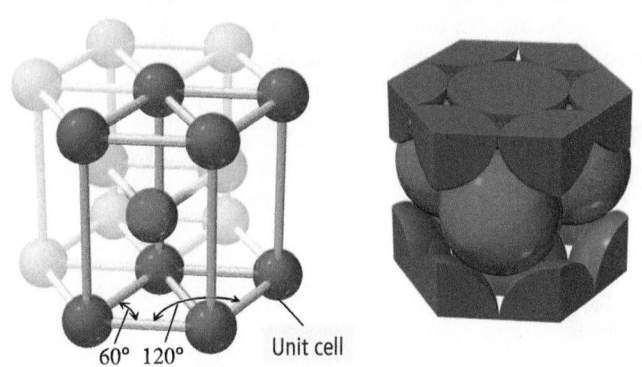

60° 120°   Unit cell

◀ FIGURE 11.48 **Hexagonal Closest Packing Crystal Structure**   The unit cell is outlined in bold.

In the second of the two closest-packed structures—called **cubic closest packing**—the third layer of atoms is offset from the first, as shown here:

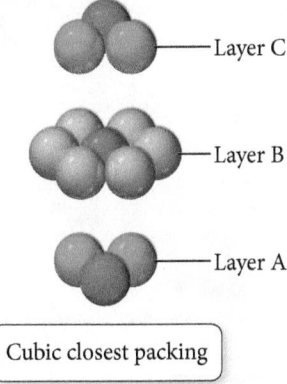

Cubic closest packing

The pattern from one layer to the next is ABCABC, with every fourth layer aligning with the first. Although not simple to visualize, the unit cell for cubic closest packing is the face-centered cubic unit cell, as shown in Figure 11.49 ▶. The cubic closest-packed structure is identical to the face-centered cubic unit cell structure.

▶ **FIGURE 11.49 Cubic Closest-Packing Crystal Structure** The unit cell of the cubic closest-packed structure is face-centered cubic.

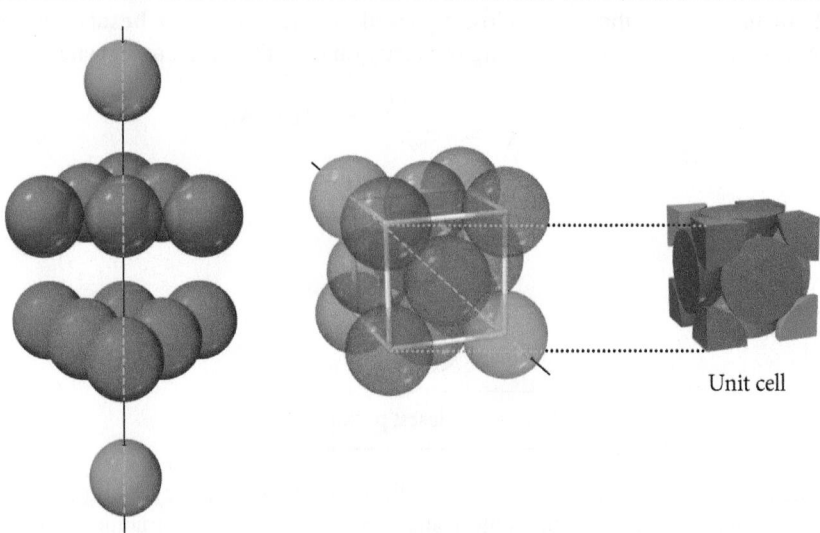

Cubic Closest Packed = Face-Centered Cubic

Unit cell

11.12 Crystalline Solids: The Fundamental Types

As we discussed in Section 11.2, solids may be crystalline (comprising a well-ordered array of atoms or molecules) or amorphous (having no long-range order). We can classify crystalline solids into three categories—molecular, ionic, and atomic—based on the individual units that compose the solid. Atomic solids can themselves be classified into three categories—nonbonded, metallic, and network covalent—depending on the types of interactions between atoms within the solid. Figure 11.50 ▼ shows the different categories of crystalline solids.

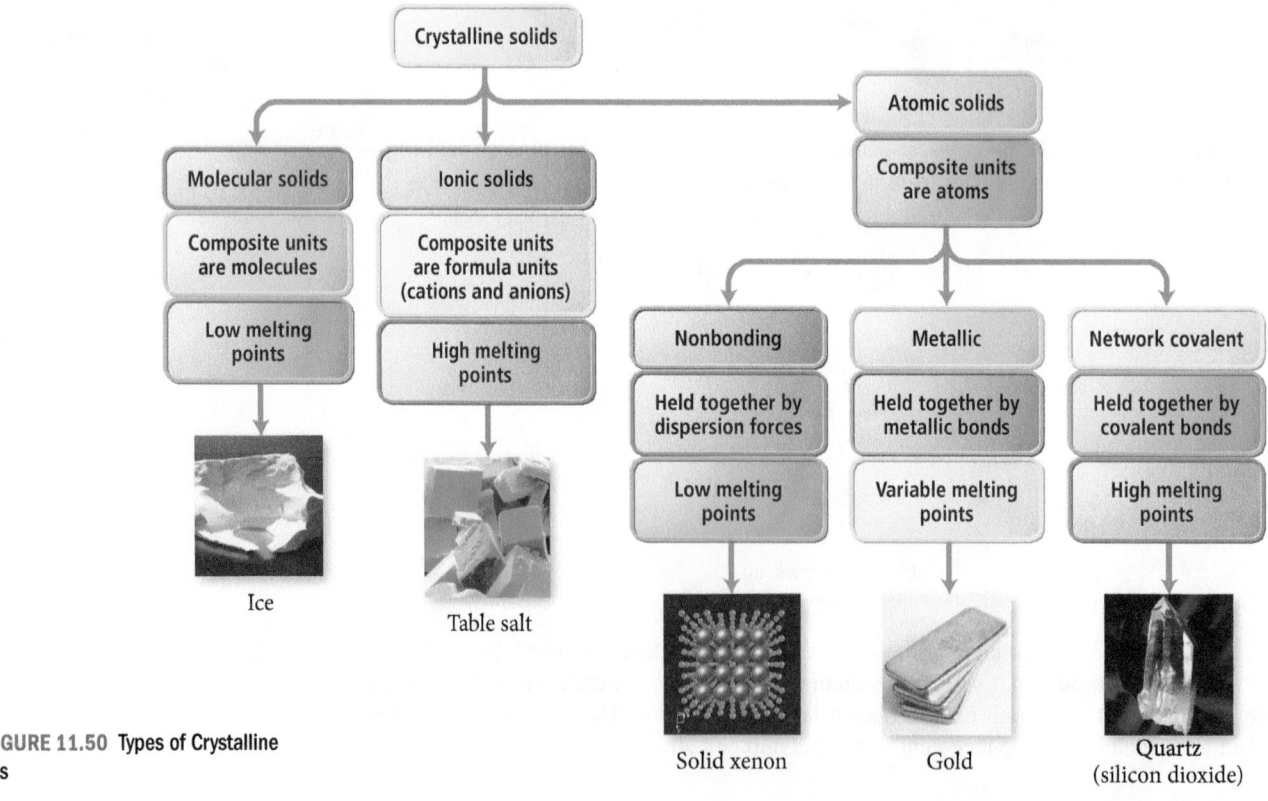

▶ **FIGURE 11.50 Types of Crystalline Solids**

Molecular Solids

Molecular solids are solids whose composite units are *molecules*. The lattice sites in a crystalline molecular solid are therefore occupied by molecules. Ice (solid H_2O) and dry ice (solid CO_2) are examples of molecular solids. Molecular solids are held together by the kinds of intermolecular forces—dispersion forces, dipole–dipole forces, and hydrogen bonding—discussed earlier in this chapter. Molecular solids as a whole tend to have low to moderately low melting points. However, strong intermolecular forces (such as the hydrogen bonds in water) can increase the melting points of some molecular solids.

Ionic Solids

Ionic solids are solids whose composite units are ions. Table salt (NaCl) and calcium fluoride (CaF_2) are examples of ionic solids. Ionic solids are held together by the coulombic interactions that occur between the cations and anions occupying the lattice sites in the crystal. The coordination number of the unit cell for an ionic compound, therefore, represents the number of close cation–anion interactions. Since these interactions lower potential energy, the crystal structure of a particular ionic compound is the one that maximizes the coordination number while accommodating both charge neutrality (each unit cell must be charge neutral) and the different sizes of the cations and anions that compose the particular compound. In general, the more similar the radii of the cation and the anion, the higher the coordination number.

Cesium chloride (CsCl) is a good example of an ionic compound with cations and anions of similar size (Cs^+ radius = 167 pm; Cl^- radius = 181 pm). In the cesium chloride structure, the chloride ions occupy the lattice sites of a simple cubic cell and one cesium ion lies in the very center of the cell, as shown in Figure 11.51 ▶. (In this and subsequent figures of ionic crystal structures, the different colored spheres represent different ions.) The coordination number for cesium chloride is 8, meaning that each cesium ion is in direct contact with eight chloride ions (and vice versa). The cesium chloride unit cell contains one chloride anion ($8 \times 1/8 = 1$) and one cesium cation for a ratio of Cs to Cl of 1:1, as the formula for the compound indicates. (Note that complete chloride ions are shown in Figure 11.51 even though only $1/8$ of each ion is in the unit cell.) Calcium sulfide (CaS) has the same structure as cesium chloride.

The crystal structure of sodium chloride must accommodate the more disproportionate sizes of Na^+ (radius = 97 pm) and Cl^- (radius = 181 pm). If ion size were the only consideration, the larger chloride anion could theoretically fit many of the smaller sodium cations around it, but charge neutrality requires that each sodium cation be surrounded by an equal number of chloride anions. Therefore, the coordination number is limited by the number of chloride anions that can fit around the relatively small sodium cation. The structure that minimizes the energy is shown in Figure 11.52 ▶ and has a coordination number of 6 (each chloride anion is surrounded by six sodium cations and vice versa). We can visualize this structure, called the *rock salt* structure, as chloride anions occupying the lattice sites of a face-centered cubic structure with the smaller sodium cations occupying the holes between the anions. (Alternatively, we can visualize this structure as the *sodium cations* occupying the lattice sites of a face-centered cubic structure with the *larger chloride anions* occupying the spaces between the cations.) Each unit cell contains four chloride anions $[(8 \times \frac{1}{8}) + (6 \times \frac{1}{2}) = 4]$ and four sodium cations $[(12 \times \frac{1}{4}) + 1 = 4]$, resulting in a ratio of 1:1, as the formula of the compound specifies. Other compounds exhibiting the sodium chloride structure include LiF, KCl, KBr, AgCl, MgO, and CaO.

A greater disproportion between the sizes of the cations and anions in a compound makes a coordination number of even 6 physically impossible. For example, in ZnS (Zn^{2+} radius = 74 pm; S^{2-} radius = 184 pm) the crystal structure, shown in Figure 11.53 ▶, has a coordination number of only 4. We can visualize this structure, called the *zinc blende* structure, as sulfide anions occupying the lattice sites of a face-centered cubic structure with the smaller zinc cations occupying four of the eight tetrahedral holes located directly beneath each corner atom. A tetrahedral hole is the

Cesium chloride (CsCl)

▲ **FIGURE 11.51 Cesium Chloride Unit Cell** The different colored spheres in this figure represent the different ions in the compound.

Sodium chloride (NaCl)

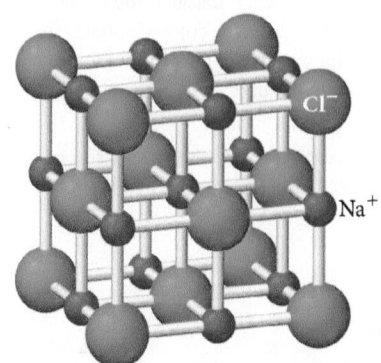

▲ **FIGURE 11.52 Sodium Chloride Unit Cell** The different colored spheres in this figure represent the different ions in the compound.

Zinc blende (ZnS)

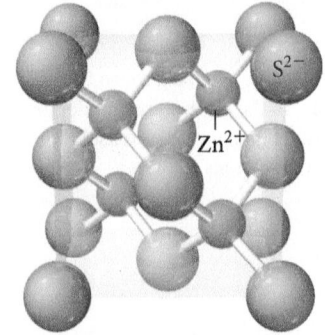

▲ **FIGURE 11.53 Zinc Sulfide (Zinc Blende) Unit Cell** The different colored spheres in this figure represent the different ions in the compound.

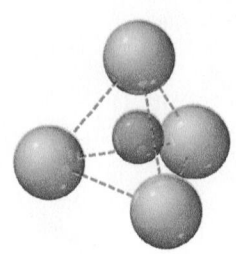

▲ A tetrahedral hole

Calcium fluoride (CaF$_2$)

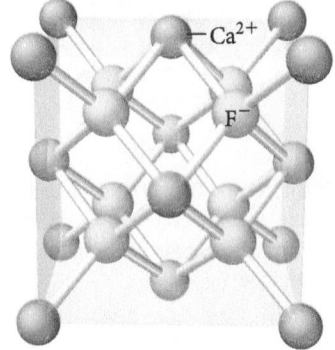

—Ca^{2+}

F$^-$

▲ FIGURE 11.54 Calcium Fluoride Unit Cell   The different colored spheres in this figure represent the different ions in the compound.

We examine a more sophisticated model for bonding in metals in Section 11.13.

▲ FIGURE 11.55 The Electron Sea Model   In the electron sea model for metals, the metal cations exist in a "sea" of electrons.

▶ FIGURE 11.56 Closest-Packed Crystal Structures in Metals   Nickel crystallizes in the cubic closest-packed structure. Zinc crystallizes in the hexagonal closest-packed structure.

empty space that lies in the center of a tetrahedral arrangement of four atoms, as shown at left. Each unit cell contains four sulfide anions $[(8 \times \frac{1}{8}) + (6 \times \frac{1}{2} = 4)]$ and four zinc cations (each of the four zinc cations is completely contained within the unit cell), resulting in a ratio of 1:1, just as the formula of the compound indicates. Other compounds exhibiting the zinc blende structure include CuCl, AgI, and CdS.

When the ratio of cations to anions is not 1:1, the crystal structure must accommodate the unequal number of cations and anions. Many compounds that contain a cation to anion ratio of 1:2 adopt the *fluorite (CaF$_2$) structure* shown in Figure 11.54 ◀. We can visualize this structure as calcium cations occupying the lattice sites of a face-centered cubic structure with the larger fluoride anions occupying all eight of the tetrahedral holes located directly beneath each corner atom. Each unit cell contains four calcium cations $[(8 \times \frac{1}{8}) + (6 \times \frac{1}{2}) = 4]$ and eight fluoride anions (each of the eight fluoride anions is completely contained within the unit cell), resulting in a cation to anion ratio of 1:2, just as in the formula of the compound. Other compounds exhibiting the fluorite structure include PbF$_2$, SrF$_2$, and BaCl$_2$. Compounds with a cation to anion ratio of 2:1 often exhibit the *antifluorite structure,* in which the anions occupy the lattice sites of a face-centered cubic structure and the cations occupy the tetrahedral holes beneath each corner atom.

The forces holding ionic solids together are strong coulombic forces (or ionic bonds), and since these forces are much stronger than the intermolecular forces, ionic solids tend to have much higher melting points than molecular solids. For example, sodium chloride melts at 801 °C, while carbon disulfide (CS$_2$)—a molecular solid with a higher molar mass—melts at −110 °C.

Atomic Solids

Solids whose composite units are individual atoms are **atomic solids**. Solid xenon (Xe), iron (Fe), and silicon dioxide (SiO$_2$) are examples of atomic solids. We can classify atomic solids themselves into three categories—*nonbonding atomic solids, metallic atomic solids, and network covalent atomic solids*—each held together by a different kind of force.

Nonbonding atomic solids are held together by relatively weak dispersion forces. In order to maximize these interactions, nonbonding atomic solids form closest-packed structures, maximizing their coordination numbers and minimizing the distance between them. Nonbonding atomic solids have very low melting points that increase uniformly with molar mass. The only nonbonding atomic solids are noble gases in their solid form. Argon, for example, has a melting point of −189 °C and xenon has a melting point of −112 °C.

Metallic atomic solids, such as iron or gold, are held together by *metallic bonds,* which in the simplest model are represented by the interaction of metal cations with the sea of electrons that surround them, as described in Section 9.11 (Figure 11.55 ◀).

Since metallic bonds are not directional, metals also tend to form closest-packed crystal structures. For example, nickel crystallizes in the cubic closest-packed structure and zinc crystallizes in the hexagonal closest-packed structure (Figure 11.56 ▼). Metallic

Nickel (Ni)   Zinc (Zn)

(a) Diamond   (b) Graphite

▲ FIGURE 11.57 **Network Covalent Atomic Solids**   (a) In diamond, each carbon atom forms four covalent bonds to four other carbon atoms in a tetrahedral geometry. (b) In graphite, carbon atoms are arranged in sheets. Within each sheet, the atoms are covalently bonded to one another by a network of sigma and pi bonds. Neighboring sheets are held together by dispersion forces.

bonds have varying strengths. Some metals, such as mercury, have melting points below room temperature, whereas other metals, such as iron, have relatively high melting points (iron melts at 1809 °C).

Network covalent atomic solids, such as diamond, graphite, and silicon dioxide, are held together by covalent bonds. The crystal structures of these solids are more restricted by the geometrical constraints of the covalent bonds (which tend to be more directional than intermolecular forces, ionic bonds, or metallic bonds) so they *do not* tend to form closest-packed structures.

In diamond (Figure 11.57a ▲), each carbon atom forms four covalent bonds to four other carbon atoms in a tetrahedral geometry. This structure extends throughout the entire crystal, so that a diamond crystal can be thought of as a giant molecule, held together by these covalent bonds. Since covalent bonds are very strong, covalent atomic solids have high melting points. Diamond is estimated to melt at about 3800 °C. The electrons in diamond are confined to the covalent bonds and are not free to flow. Therefore, diamond does not conduct electricity.

In graphite (Figure 11.57b), carbon atoms are arranged in sheets. Within each sheet, carbon atoms are covalently bonded to each other by a network of sigma and pi bonds, similar to those in benzene. Just as the electrons within the pi bonds in benzene are delocalized over the entire molecule, so the pi bonds in graphite are delocalized over the entire sheet, making graphite a good electrical conductor along the sheets. The bond length between carbon atoms *within a sheet* is 142 pm. However, the forces *between* sheets are much different. The separation between sheets is 341 pm. There are no covalent bonds between sheets, only relatively weak dispersion forces. Consequently, the sheets slide past each other relatively easily, which explains the slippery feel of graphite and its extensive use as a lubricant.

The silicates (extended arrays of silicon and oxygen) are the most common network covalent atomic solids. Geologists estimate that 90% of Earth's crust is composed of silicates; we will cover these in more detail in Chapter 22. The basic silicon oxygen compound is silica (SiO_2), which in its most common crystalline form is called quartz. The structure of quartz consists of an array of SiO_4 tetrahedra with shared oxygen atoms, as shown in Figure 11.58a ▶. The strong silicon–oxygen covalent bonds that hold quartz together result in its high melting point of about 1600 °C. Common glass is also composed of SiO_2, but in its amorphous form (Figure 11.58b).

Sigma and pi bonds were discussed in Section 10.7.

(a)

(b)

▲ FIGURE 11.58 **The Structure of Quartz** (a) Quartz consists of an array of SiO_4 tetrahedra with shared oxygen atoms. (b) Glass is amorphous SiO_2.

11.13 Crystalline Solids: Band Theory

In Section 9.11, we explored a model for bonding in metals called the *electron sea model*. We now turn to a model for bonding in solids that is both more sophisticated and more broadly applicable—it applies to both metallic solids and covalent solids. The model is **band theory** and it grows out of molecular orbital theory, first discussed in Section 10.8.

Recall that in molecular orbital theory, we combine the atomic orbitals of the atoms within a molecule to form molecular orbitals. These molecular orbitals are not localized on individual atoms, but *delocalized over the entire molecule.* Similarly, in band theory, we combine the atomic orbitals of the atoms within a solid crystal to form orbitals that are not localized on individual atoms, but delocalized over the entire *crystal.* In some sense then, the crystal is like a very large molecule, and its valence electrons occupy the molecular orbitals formed from the atomic orbitals of each atom in the crystal.

Consider a series of molecules constructed from individual lithium atoms. The energy levels of the atomic orbitals and resulting molecular orbitals for Li, Li_2, Li_3, Li_4, and Li_N (where N is a large number on the order of 10^{23}) are shown in Figure 11.59 ▼. The lithium atom has a single electron in a single $2s$ atomic orbital. The Li_2 molecule contains two electrons and two molecular orbitals. The electrons occupy the lower energy bonding orbital—the higher energy, or antibonding, molecular orbital is empty. The Li_4 molecule contains four electrons and four molecular orbitals. The electrons occupy the two bonding molecular orbitals—the two antibonding orbitals are completely empty.

The Li_N molecule contains N electrons and N molecular orbitals. However, because there are so many molecular orbitals, the energy spacings between them are infinitesimally small; they are no longer discrete energy levels, but rather they form a *band* of energy levels. One half of the orbitals in the band ($N/2$) are bonding molecular orbitals and (at 0 K) contain the N valence electrons. The other $N/2$ molecular orbitals are antibonding and (at 0 K) are completely empty. If the atoms composing a solid have p orbitals available, then the same process leads to another band of orbitals at higher energies.

▶ FIGURE 11.59 **Energy Levels of Molecular Orbitals in Lithium Molecules** When many Li atoms are present, the energy levels of the molecular orbitals are so closely spaced that they fuse to form a band. Half of the orbitals are bonding orbitals and contain valence electrons; the other half are antibonding orbitals and are empty.

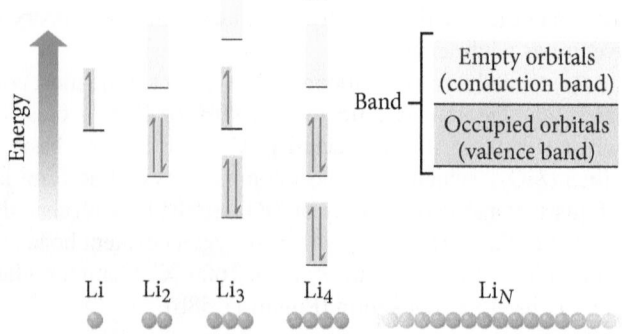

In band theory, electrons become mobile when they make a transition from the highest occupied molecular orbital into higher energy empty molecular orbitals. For this reason, we call the occupied molecular orbitals the *valence band* and the unoccupied orbitals the *conduction band.* In lithium metal, the highest occupied molecular orbital lies in the middle of a band of orbitals, and the energy difference between it and the next higher energy orbital is infinitesimally small. Therefore, above 0 K, electrons can easily make the transition from the valence band to the conduction band. Since electrons in the conduction band are mobile, lithium, like all metals, is a good electrical conductor. Mobile electrons in the conduction band are also responsible for the thermal conductivity of metals. When a metal is heated, electrons are excited to higher energy molecular orbitals. These electrons can then quickly transport the thermal energy throughout the crystal lattice.

In metals, the valence band and conduction band are energetically continuous—the energy difference between the top of the valence band and the bottom of the conduction band is infinitesimally small. In semiconductors and insulators, however, an energy gap, called the **band gap**, exists between the valence band and conduction band as shown in Figure 11.60 ▼. In insulators, the band gap is large, and electrons are not promoted into the conduction band at ordinary temperatures, resulting in no electrical conductivity. In semiconductors, the band gap is small, allowing some electrons to be promoted at ordinary temperatures and resulting in limited conductivity. However, the conductivity of semiconductors can be increased in a controlled way by adding minute amounts of other substances, called *dopants*, to the semiconductor.

Doping: Controlling the Conductivity of Semiconductors

Doped semiconductors contain minute amounts of impurities that result in additional electrons in the conduction band or electron "holes" in the valence band. For example, silicon is a group 4A semiconductor. Its valence electrons just fill its valence band. The band gap in silicon is large enough that only a few electrons are promoted into the conduction band at room temperature; therefore, silicon is a poor electrical conductor. However, silicon can be doped with phosphorus, a group 5A element with five valence electrons, to increase its conductivity. The phosphorus atoms are incorporated into the silicon crystal structure, and each phosphorus atom brings with it one additional electron. Since the valence band is completely full, the additional electrons must go into the conduction band. These electrons are then mobile and can conduct electrical current. This type of semiconductor is called an **n-type semiconductor** because the charge carriers are negatively charged electrons in the conduction band.

Silicon can also be doped with a group 3A element, such as gallium, which has only three valence electrons. When gallium is incorporated into the silicon crystal structure, it results in electron "holes," or empty molecular orbitals, in the valence band. The presence of holes also allows for the movement of electrical current because electrons in the valence band can move between holes. In this way, the holes move in the opposite direction as the electrons. This type of semiconductor is called a **p-type semiconductor** because each hole acts as a positive charge.

The heart of most modern electronic devices are silicon chips containing millions of **p–n junctions**, tiny spots that are p-type on one side and n-type on the other. These junctions can serve a number of functions including acting as **diodes** (circuit elements that allow the flow of electrical current in only one direction) or amplifiers (elements that amplify a small electrical current into a larger one).

◀ FIGURE 11.60 **Band Gap** In a conductor, there is no energy gap between the valence band and the conduction band. In semiconductors there is a small energy gap, and in insulators there is a large energy gap.

CHAPTER IN REVIEW

Self Assessment Quiz

Q1. Which state of matter is compressible?
a) gas
b) liquid
c) solid
d) none of the above

Q2. Liquid nitrogen boils at 77 K. The image shown below depicts a sample of liquid nitrogen.

Which image best depicts the nitrgogen after it has boiled?

a)

b)

c)

d)
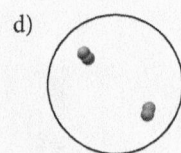

Q3. Based on the expected intermolecular forces, which halogen has the highest boiling point?
a) F_2
b) Cl_2
c) Br_2
d) I_2

Q4. Which substance has dipole–dipole forces?
a) CCl_4
b) NF_3
c) CS_2
d) SO_3

Q5. One of these substances is a liquid at room temperature. Which one?
a) CH_3OH
b) CF_4
c) SiH_4
d) CO_2

Q6. Which property of a liquid increases with increasing temperature?
a) surface tension
b) viscosity
c) vapor pressure
d) none of the above

Q7. Determine the amount of heat (in kJ) required to vaporize 1.55 kg of water at its boiling point. For water, $\Delta H_{vap} = 40.7$ kJ/mol (at 100 °C).
a) 3.50×10^3 kJ
b) 1.14×10^6 kJ
c) 2.11 kJ
d) 686 kJ

Q8. The vapor pressure of a substance is measured over a range of temperatures. A plot of the natural log of the vapor pressure versus the inverse of the temperature (in Kelvin) produces a straight line with a slope of -3.46×10^3 K. Find the enthalpy of vaporization of the substance.
a) 2.40×10^{-3} kJ/mol
b) 28.8 kJ/mol
c) 0.416 kJ/mol
d) 3.22 kJ/mol

Q9. Acetic acid has a normal boiling point of 118 °C and a ΔH_{vap} of 23.4 kJ/mol. What is the vapor pressure (in mmHg) of acetic acid at 25 °C?
a) 2.92×10^{-39} mmHg
b) 7.16×10^3 mmHg
c) 758 mmHg
d) 80.6 mmHg

Q10. Consider the phase diagram shown below. A sample of the substance in the phase diagram is initially at 175 °C and 925 mmHg. What phase transition occurs when the pressure is decreased to 760 mmHg at constant temperature?

a) solid to liquid
b) liquid to gas
c) solid to gas
d) liquid to solid

Q11. How many atoms are in the body-centered cubic unit cell?
a) 1
b) 2
c) 4
d) 5

Q12. Rhodium crystallizes in a face-centered cubic unit cell. The radius of a rhodium atom is 135 pm. Determine the density of rhodium in g/cm^3.
 a) 3.07 g/cm^3
 b) 12.4 g/cm^3
 c) 278 g/cm^3
 d) 0.337 g/cm^3

Q13. A mixture containing 21.4 g of ice (at exactly 0.00 °C) and 75.3 g of water (at 55.3 °C) is placed in an insulated container. Assuming no loss of heat to the surroundings, what is the final temperature of the mixture?
 a) 22.5 °C
 b) 25.4 °C
 c) 32.6 °C
 d) 41.9 °C

Q14. Which type of solid is dry ice (solid carbon dioxide)?
 a) ionic
 b) molecular
 c) atomic
 d) none of the above

Q15. Which process *releases* the greatest amount of heat?
 a) the condensation of 10 g of gaseous water
 b) the freezing of 10 g of liquid water
 c) the boiling of 10 g of liquid water
 d) the melting of 10 g of ice

Answers: 1. (a) 2. (d) 3. (d) 4. (b) 5. (a) 6. (c) 7. (a) 8. (b) 9. (d) 10. (b) 11. (b) 12. (b) 13. (b) 14. (b) 15. (a)

Key Terms

Section 11.2
crystalline (485)
amorphous (485)

Section 11.3
dispersion force (487)
dipole–dipole force (490)
permanent dipole (490)
miscibility (491)
hydrogen bonding (492)
hydrogen bond (493)
ion–dipole force (495)

Section 11.4
surface tension (497)
viscosity (498)
capillary action (499)

Section 11.5
vaporization (500)
condensation (500)

volatile (500)
nonvolatile (500)
heat of vaporization
 (ΔH_{vap}) (501)
dynamic equilibrium (503)
vapor pressure (503)
boiling point (504)
normal boiling point (504)
Clausius–Clapeyron
 equation (505)
critical temperature (T_c) (508)
critical pressure (P_c) (508)

Section 11.6
sublimation (509)
deposition (509)
melting point (510)
melting (fusion) (510)
freezing (510)
heat of fusion (ΔH_{fus}) (510)

Section 11.8
phase diagram (513)
triple point (514)
critical point (514)

Section 11.10
X-ray diffraction (518)

Section 11.11
crystalline lattice (520)
unit cell (520)
simple cubic (520)
coordination number (521)
packing efficiency (521)
body-centered cubic (521)
face-centered cubic (522)
hexagonal closest
 packing (525)
cubic closest packing (525)

Section 11.12
molecular solids (527)
ionic solids (527)
atomic solids (528)
nonbonding atomic
 solids (528)
metallic atomic solids (528)
network covalent atomic
 solids (528)

Section 11.13
band theory (530)
band gap (531)
n-type semiconductor (531)
p-type semiconductor (531)
p–n junctions (531)
diodes (531)

Key Concepts

Solids, Liquids, and Intermolecular Forces (11.1, 11.2, 11.3)

▶ The forces that hold molecules or atoms together in a liquid or solid are intermolecular forces. The strength of the intermolecular forces in a substance determines its state.

▶ Dispersion forces are present in all elements and compounds; they arise from the fluctuations in electron distribution within atoms and molecules. These are the weakest intermolecular forces, but they are significant in molecules with high molar masses.

▶ Dipole–dipole forces, generally stronger than dispersion forces, are present in all polar molecules.

▶ Hydrogen bonding occurs in polar molecules that contain hydrogen atoms bonded directly to fluorine, oxygen, or nitrogen. These are the strongest intermolecular forces.

▶ Ion–dipole forces occur when ionic compounds are mixed with polar compounds, and they are especially important in aqueous solutions.

Surface Tension, Viscosity, and Capillary Action (11.4)

▶ Surface tension results from the tendency of liquids to minimize their surface area in order to maximize the interactions between their constituent particles, thus lowering potential energy. Surface tension causes water droplets to form spheres and allows insects and paper clips to "float" on the surface of water.

▶ Viscosity is the resistance of a liquid to flow. Viscosity increases with increasing strength of intermolecular forces and decreases with increasing temperature.

▶ Capillary action is the ability of a liquid to flow against gravity up a narrow tube. It is the result of adhesive forces, the attraction between the molecules and the surface of the tube, and cohesive forces, the attraction between the molecules in the liquid.

Vaporization and Vapor Pressure (11.5, 11.7)

▶ Vaporization, the transition from liquid to gas, occurs when thermal energy overcomes the intermolecular forces present in a liquid. The opposite process is condensation. Vaporization is endothermic and condensation is exothermic.

▶ The rate of vaporization increases with increasing temperature, increasing surface area, and decreasing strength of intermolecular forces.

▶ The heat of vaporization (ΔH_{vap}) is the heat required to vaporize one mole of a liquid.

▶ In a sealed container, a solution and its vapor come into dynamic equilibrium, at which point the rate of vaporization equals the rate of condensation. The pressure of a gas that is in dynamic equilibrium with its liquid is its vapor pressure.

▶ The vapor pressure of a substance increases with increasing temperature and with decreasing strength of its intermolecular forces.

▶ The boiling point of a liquid is the temperature at which its vapor pressure equals the external pressure.

▶ The Clausius–Clapeyron equation expresses the relationship between the vapor pressure of a substance and its temperature and can be used to calculate the heat of vaporization from experimental measurements.

▶ When a liquid is heated in a sealed container it eventually forms a supercritical fluid, which has properties intermediate between a liquid and a gas. This occurs at critical temperature and critical pressure.

Fusion and Sublimation (11.6, 11.7)

▶ Sublimation is the transition from solid to gas. The opposite process is deposition.

▶ Fusion, or melting, is the transition from solid to liquid. The opposite process is freezing.

▶ The heat of fusion (ΔH_{fus}) is the amount of heat required to melt one mole of a solid. Fusion is endothermic.

▶ The heat of fusion is generally less than the heat of vaporization because intermolecular forces do not have to be completely overcome for melting to occur.

Phase Diagrams (11.8)

▶ A phase diagram is a map of the states of a substance as a function of its pressure (y-axis) and temperature (x-axis).

▶ The regions in a phase diagram represent conditions under which a single stable state (solid, liquid, gas) exists.

▶ The lines represent conditions under which two states are in equilibrium.

▶ The triple point represents the conditions under which all three states coexist.

▶ The critical point is the temperature and pressure above which a supercritical fluid exists.

The Uniqueness of Water (11.9)

▶ Water is a liquid at room temperature despite its low molar mass. Water forms strong hydrogen bonds, resulting in its high boiling point.

▶ The polarity of water enables it to dissolve many polar and ionic compounds and even nonpolar gases.

▶ Water expands upon freezing, so ice is less dense than liquid water. Water is critical both to the existence of life and to human health.

Crystalline Structures (11.10–11.13)

▶ X-ray crystallography uses the diffraction pattern of X-rays to determine the crystal structure of solids.

▶ The crystal lattice is represented by a unit cell, a structure that reproduces the entire lattice when repeated in all three dimensions.

▶ Three basic cubic unit cells are the simple cubic, the body-centered cubic, and the face-centered cubic.

▶ Some crystal lattices can also be depicted as closest-packed structures, including the hexagonal closest-packing structure (not cubic) and the cubic closest-packing structure (which has a face-centered cubic unit cell).

▶ The basic types of crystal solids are molecular, ionic, and atomic solids. We divide atomic solids into three different types: nonbonded, metallic, and covalent.

▶ Band theory is a model for bonding in solids in which the atomic orbitals of the atoms are combined and delocalized over the entire crystal solid.

Key Equations and Relationships

Clausius–Clapeyron Equation: Relationship between Vapor Pressure (P_{vap}), the Heat of Vaporization (ΔH_{vap}), and Temperature (T) (11.5)

$$\ln P_{vap} = \frac{-\Delta H_{vap}}{RT} + \ln \beta \quad (\beta \text{ is a constant})$$

$$\ln \frac{P_2}{P_1} = \frac{-\Delta H_{vap}}{R}\left(\frac{1}{T_2} - \frac{1}{T_1}\right)$$

Bragg's Law: Relationship between Light Wavelength (λ), Angle of Reflection (θ), and Distance (d) between the Atomic Layers (11.10)

$$n\lambda = 2d \sin \theta \quad (n = \text{integer})$$

Key Learning Outcomes

Chapter Objectives		Assessment
Determining Whether a Molecule Has Dipole-Dipole Forces (11.3)		Example 11.1 For Practice 11.1 Exercises 49–60

Key Learning Outcomes, *continued*

Determining Whether a Molecule Displays Hydrogen Bonding (**11.3**)	Example 11.2 For Practice 11.2 Exercises 49–60
Using the Heat of Vaporization in Calculations (**11.5**)	Example 11.3 For Practice 11.3 For More Practice 11.3 Exercises 71–74
Using the Clausius–Clapeyron Equation (**11.5**)	Examples 11.4, 11.5 For Practice 11.4, 11.5 Exercises 75–78
Using Bragg's Law in X-Ray Diffraction Calculations (**11.10**)	Example 11.6 For Practice 11.6 Exercises 95, 96
Relating Density to Crystal Structure (**11.11**)	Example 11.7 For Practice 11.7 Exercises 99–102

EXERCISES

Review Questions

1. Explain how a gecko is able to walk on a polished glass surface.

2. Why are intermolecular forces important?

3. What are the main properties of liquids (in contrast to gases and solids)?

4. What are the main properties of solids (in contrast to liquids and gases)?

5. What is the fundamental difference between an amorphous solid and a crystalline solid?

6. What factors cause transitions between the solid and liquid state? The liquid and gas state?

7. Describe the relationship between the state of a substance, its temperature, and the strength of its intermolecular forces.

8. From what kinds of interactions do intermolecular forces originate?

9. Why are intermolecular forces generally much weaker than bonding forces?

10. What is the dispersion force? What does the magnitude of the dispersion force depend on? How can you predict the magnitude of the dispersion force for closely related elements or compounds?

11. What is the dipole–dipole force? How can you predict the presence of dipole–dipole forces in a compound?

12. How is the miscibility of two liquids related to their polarity?

13. What is hydrogen bonding? How can you predict the presence of hydrogen bonding in a compound?

14. What is the ion–dipole force? Why is it important?

15. What is surface tension? How does surface tension result from intermolecular forces? How is it related to the strength of intermolecular forces?

16. What is viscosity? How does viscosity depend on intermolecular forces? What other factors affect viscosity?

17. What is capillary action? How does it depend on the relative strengths of adhesive and cohesive forces?

18. Explain what happens in the processes of vaporization and condensation. Why does the rate of vaporization increase with increasing temperature and surface area?

19. Why is vaporization endothermic? Why is condensation exothermic?

20. How is the volatility of a substance related to the intermolecular forces present within the substance?

21. What is the heat of vaporization for a liquid and why is it useful?

22. Explain the process of dynamic equilibrium. How is dynamic equilibrium related to vapor pressure?

23. What happens to a system in dynamic equilibrium when it is disturbed in some way?

24. How is vapor pressure related to temperature? What happens to the vapor pressure of a substance when the temperature is increased? Decreased?

25. Define the terms *boiling point* and *normal boiling point.*

26. What is the Clausius–Clapeyron equation and why is it important?

27. Explain what happens to a substance when it is heated in a closed container to its critical temperature.

28. What is sublimation? Give a common example of sublimation.

29. What is fusion? Is fusion exothermic or endothermic? Why?

30. What is the heat of fusion and why is it important?

31. Examine the heating curve for water in Section 11.7 (Figure 11.36). Explain why the curve has two segments in which heat is added to the water but the temperature does not rise.

32. Examine the heating curve for water in Section 11.7 (Figure 11.36). Explain the significance of the slopes of each of the three rising segments. Why are the slopes different?

33. What is a phase diagram? Draw a generic phase diagram and label its important features.

34. What is the significance of crossing a line in a phase diagram?

35. How do the properties of water differ from those of most other substances?

36. Explain the basic principles involved in X-ray crystallography. Include Bragg's law in your explanation.

37. What is a crystalline lattice? How is the lattice represented with the unit cell?

38. Make a drawing of each unit cell: simple cubic, body-centered cubic, and face-centered cubic.

39. For each of the cubic cells in the previous problem, give the coordination number, edge length in terms of *r*, and number of atoms per unit cell.

40. What is the difference between hexagonal closest packing and cubic closest packing? What are the unit cells for each of these structures?

41. What are the three basic types of solids and the composite units of each? What types of forces hold each type of solid together?

42. In an ionic compound, how are the relative sizes of the cation and anion related to the coordination number of the crystal structure?

43. Show how the cesium chloride, sodium chloride, and zinc blende unit cells each contain a cation-to-anion ratio of 1:1.

44. Show how the fluorite structure accommodates a cation-to-anion ratio of 1:2.

45. What are the three basic subtypes of atomic solids? What kinds of forces hold each of these subtypes together?

46. In band theory of bonding for solids, what is a *band?* What is the difference between the *valence band* and the *conduction band?*

47. In band theory of bonding for solids, what is a band gap? How does the band gap differ in metals, semiconductors, and insulators?

48. Explain how doping can increase the conductivity of a semiconductor. What is the difference between an n-type semiconductor and a p-type semiconductor?

Problems by Topic

Intermolecular Forces

49. Determine the kinds of intermolecular forces that are present in each element or compound.
a. N_2
b. NH_3
c. CO
d. CCl_4

50. Determine the kinds of intermolecular forces that are present in each element or compound.
a. Kr
b. NCl_3
c. SiH_4
d. HF

51. Determine the kinds of intermolecular forces that are present in each element or compound.
a. HCl
b. H_2O
c. Br_2
d. He

52. Determine the kinds of intermolecular forces that are present in each element or compound.
a. PH_3
b. HBr
c. CH_3OH
d. I_2

53. Arrange these compounds in order of increasing boiling point. Explain your reasoning.
a. CH_4
b. CH_3CH_3
c. CH_3CH_2Cl
d. CH_3CH_2OH

54. Arrange these compounds in order of increasing boiling point. Explain your reasoning.
a. H_2S
b. H_2Se
c. H_2O

55. In each pair of compounds, pick the one with the highest boiling point. Explain your reasoning.
a. CH_3OH or CH_3SH
b. CH_3OCH_3 or CH_3CH_2OH
c. CH_4 or CH_3CH_3

56. In each pair of compounds, pick the one with the higher boiling point. Explain your reasoning.
a. NH_3 or CH_4
b. CS_2 or CO_2
c. CO_2 or NO_2

57. In each pair of compounds, pick the one with the higher vapor pressure at a given temperature. Explain your reasoning.
a. Br_2 or I_2
b. H_2S or H_2O
c. NH_3 or PH_3

58. In each pair of compounds, pick the one with the higher vapor pressure at a given temperature. Explain your reasoning.
a. CH_4 or CH_3Cl
b. $CH_3CH_2CH_2OH$ or CH_3OH
c. CH_3OH or H_2CO

59. Determine if each pair of compounds forms a homogeneous solution when combined. For those that form homogeneous solutions, indicate the type of forces that are involved.
a. CCl_4 and H_2O
b. KCl and H_2O
c. Br_2 and CCl_4
d. CH_3CH_2OH and H_2O

60. Determine if each pair of compounds forms a homogeneous solution when combined. For those that form homogeneous solutions, indicate the type of forces that are involved.
  a. $CH_3CH_2CH_2CH_2CH_3$ and $CH_3CH_2CH_2CH_2CH_2CH_3$
  b. CBr_4 and H_2O
  c. $LiNO_3$ and H_2O
  d. CH_3OH and $CH_3CH_2CH_2CH_2CH_3$

Surface Tension, Viscosity, and Capillary Action

61. Which compound would you expect to have greater surface tension: acetone $[(CH_3)_2CO]$ or water (H_2O)? Explain.

62. Water (a) "wets" some surfaces and beads up on others. Mercury (b), in contrast, beads up on almost all surfaces. Explain this difference.

  (a)   **(b)**

63. The structures of two isomers of heptane are shown below. Which of these two compounds would you expect to have the greater viscosity?

Compound A

Compound B

64. Explain why the viscosity of multigrade motor oils is less temperature-dependent than that of single-grade motor oils.

65. Water in a glass tube that contains grease or oil residue displays a flat meniscus (left), whereas water in a clean glass tube displays a concave meniscus (right). Explain this observation.

66. When a thin glass tube is put into water, the water rises 1.4 cm. When the same tube is put into hexane, the hexane rises only 0.4 cm. Explain.

Vaporization and Vapor Pressure

67. Which evaporates more quickly: 55 mL of water in a beaker with a diameter of 4.5 cm, or 55 mL of water in a dish with a diameter of 12 cm? Is the vapor pressure of the water different in the two containers? Explain.

68. Which evaporates more quickly: 55 mL of water (H_2O) in a beaker or 55 mL of acetone $[(CH_3)_2CO]$ in an identical beaker under identical conditions? Is the vapor pressure of the two substances different? Explain.

69. Spilling room-temperature water over your skin on a hot day cools you down. Spilling room-temperature vegetable oil over your skin on a hot day does not. Explain the difference.

70. Why is the heat of vaporization of water greater at room temperature than it is at its boiling point?

71. The human body obtains 915 kJ of energy from a candy bar. If this energy were used to vaporize water at 100.0 °C, how much water (in liters) could be vaporized? (Assume the density of water is 1.00 g/mL.)

72. A 100.0 mL sample of water is heated to its boiling point. How much heat (in kJ) is required to vaporize it? (Assume a density of 1.00 g/mL.)

73. Suppose that 0.95 g of water condenses on a 75.0 g block of iron that is initially at 22 °C. If the heat released during condensation goes only to warming the iron block, what is the final temperature (in °C) of the iron block? (Assume a constant enthalpy of vaporization for water of 44.0 kJ/mol.)

74. Suppose that 1.15 g of rubbing alcohol (C_3H_8O) evaporates from a 65.0 g aluminum block. If the aluminum block is initially at 25 °C, what is the final temperature of the block after the evaporation of the alcohol? Assume that the heat required for the vaporization of the alcohol comes only from the aluminum block and that the alcohol vaporizes at 25 °C.

75. This table displays the vapor pressure of ammonia at several different temperatures. Use the data to determine the heat of vaporization and normal boiling point of ammonia.

Temperature (K)	Pressure (torr)
200	65.3
210	134.3
220	255.7
230	456.0
235	597.0

76. This table displays the vapor pressure of nitrogen at several different temperatures. Use the data to determine the heat of vaporization and normal boiling point of nitrogen.

Temperature (K)	Pressure (torr)
65	130.5
70	289.5
75	570.8
80	1028
85	1718

77. Ethanol has a heat of vaporization of 38.56 kJ/mol and a normal boiling point of 78.4 °C. What is the vapor pressure of ethanol at 15 °C?

78. Benzene has a heat of vaporization of 30.72 kJ/mol and a normal boiling point of 80.1 °C. At what temperature does benzene boil when the external pressure is 445 torr?

Sublimation and Fusion

79. How much energy is released when 65.8 g of water freezes?

80. Calculate the amount of heat required to completely sublime 50.0 g of solid dry ice (CO_2) at its sublimation temperature. The heat of sublimation for carbon dioxide is 32.3 kJ/mol.

81. An 8.5 g ice cube is placed into 255 g of water. Calculate the temperature change in the water upon the complete melting of the ice. Assume that all of the energy required to melt the ice comes from the water.

82. How much ice (in grams) would have to melt to lower the temperature of 352 mL of water from 25 °C to 5 °C? (Assume the density of water is 1.0 g/ml.)

83. How much heat (in kJ) is required to warm 10.0 g of ice, initially at −10.0 °C, to steam at 110.0 °C? The heat capacity of ice is 2.09 J/g · °C, and that of steam is 2.01 J/g · °C.

84. How much heat (in kJ) is evolved in converting 1.00 mol of steam at 145 °C to ice at −50 °C? The heat capacity of steam is 2.01 J/g · °C, and that of ice is 2.09 J/g · °C.

Phase Diagrams

85. Consider the phase diagram shown here. Identify the states present at points *a* through *g*.

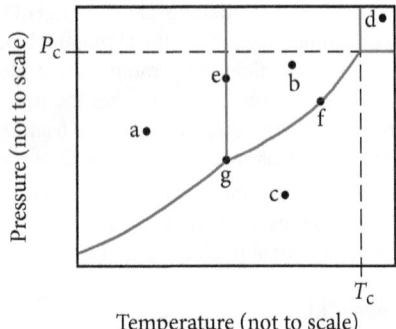

Temperature (not to scale)

86. Consider the phase diagram for iodine shown here.
   a. What is the normal boiling point for iodine?
   b. What is the melting point for iodine at 1 atm?
   c. What state is present at room temperature and normal atmospheric pressure?
   d. What state is present at 186 °C and 1.0 atm?

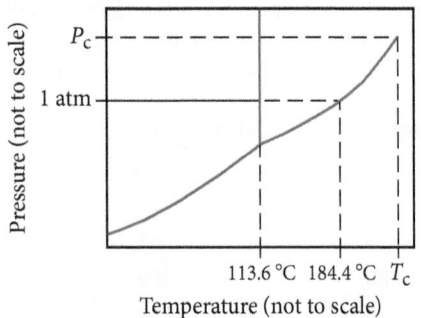

Temperature (not to scale)

87. Nitrogen has a normal boiling point of 77.3 K and a melting point (at 1 atm) of 63.1 K. Its critical temperature is 126.2 K and critical pressure is 2.55×10^4 torr. It has a triple point at 63.1 K and 94.0 torr. Sketch the phase diagram for nitrogen. Does nitrogen have a stable liquid state at 1 atm?

88. Argon has a normal boiling point of 87.2 K and a melting point (at 1 atm) of 84.1 K. Its critical temperature is 150.8 K and critical pressure is 48.3 atm. It has a triple point at 83.7 K and 0.68 atm. Sketch the phase diagram for argon. Which has the greater density, solid argon or liquid argon?

89. The phase diagram for sulfur is shown here. The rhombic and monoclinic states are two solid states with different structures.
   a. Below what pressure does solid sulfur sublime?
   b. Which of the two solid states of sulfur is most dense?

Temperature

90. The high-pressure phase diagram of ice is shown here. Notice that, under high pressure, ice can exist in several different solid forms. What three forms of ice are present at the triple point marked O? What is the density of ice II compared to ice I (the familiar form of ice)? Would ice III sink or float in liquid water?

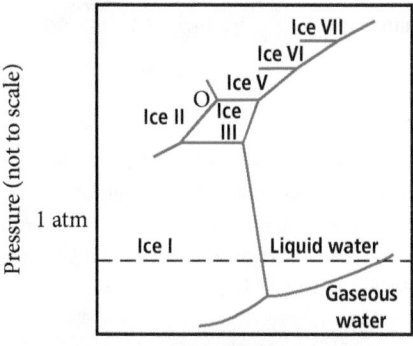

Temperature (not to scale)

The Uniqueness of Water

91. Water has a high boiling point given its relatively low molar mass. Why?

92. Water is a good solvent for many substances. What is the molecular basis for this property and why is it significant?

93. Explain the role of water in moderating Earth's climate.

94. How is the density of solid water compared to that of liquid water atypical among substances? Why is this significant?

Types of Solids and Their Structures

95. An X-ray beam with $\lambda = 154$ incident on the surface of a crystal produced a maximum reflection at an angle of $\theta = 28.3°$. Assuming $n = 1$, calculate the separation between layers of atoms in the crystal.

96. An X-ray beam of unknown wavelength is diffracted from a NaCl surface. If the interplanar distance in the crystal is 286 pm, and the angle of maximum reflection is found to be 7.23°, what is the wavelength of the X-ray beam? (Assume $n = 1$.)

97. Determine the number of atoms per unit cell for each metal.

(a) Polonium   **(b)** Tungsten

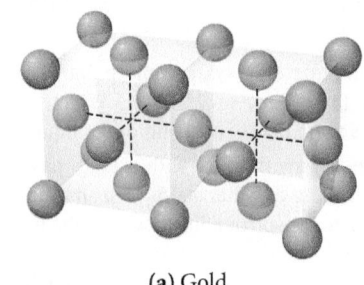

(c) Nickel

98. Determine the coordination number for each structure.

(a) Gold

(b) Ruthenium

(c) Chromium

99. Platinum crystallizes with the face-centered cubic unit cell. The radius of a platinum atom is 139 pm. Calculate the edge length of the unit cell and the density of platinum in g/cm^3.

100. Molybdenum crystallizes with the body-centered unit cell. The radius of a molybdenum atom is 136 pm. Calculate the edge length of the unit cell and the density of molybdenum.

101. Rhodium has a density of 12.41 g/cm^3 and crystallizes with the face-centered cubic unit cell. Calculate the radius of a rhodium atom.

102. Barium has a density of 3.59 g/cm^3 and crystallizes with the body-centered cubic unit cell. Calculate the radius of a barium atom.

103. Polonium crystallizes with a simple cubic structure. It has a density of 9.3 g/cm^3, a radius of 167 pm, and a molar mass of 209 g/mol. Use this data to estimate Avogadro's number (the number of atoms in one mole).

104. Palladium crystallizes with a face-centered cubic structure. It has a density of 12.0 g/cm^3, a radius of 138 pm, and a molar mass of 106.42 g/mol. Use this data to estimate Avogadro's number.

105. Identify each solid as molecular, ionic, or atomic.
   a. $Ar(s)$ **b.** $H_2O(s)$
   c. $K_2O(s)$ **d.** $Fe(s)$

106. Identify each solid as molecular, ionic, or atomic.
   a. $CaCl_2(s)$ **b.** $CO_2(s)$
   c. $Ni(s)$ **d.** $I_2(s)$

107. Which solid has the highest melting point? Why?

$$Ar(s), CCl_4(s), LiCl(s), CH_3OH(s)$$

108. Which solid has the highest melting point? Why?

$$C(s, diamond), Kr(s), NaCl(s), H_2O(s)$$

109. Which solid in each pair has the higher melting point and why?
   a. $TiO_2(s)$ or $HOOH(s)$ **b.** $CCl_4(s)$ or $SiCl_4(s)$
   c. $Kr(s)$ or $Xe(s)$ **d.** $NaCl(s)$ or $CaO(s)$

110. Which solid in each pair has the higher melting point and why?
   a. $Fe(s)$ or $CCl_4(s)$ **b.** $KCl(s)$ or $HCl(s)$
   c. $Ti(s)$ or $Ne(s)$ **d.** $H_2O(s)$ or $H_2S(s)$

111. An oxide of titanium crystallizes with the unit cell shown here (titanium = gray; oxygen = red) What is the formula of the oxide?

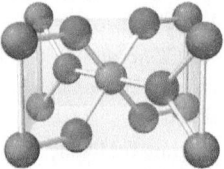

112. An oxide of rhenium crystallizes with the unit cell shown here (rhenium = gray; oxygen = red) . What is the formula of the oxide?

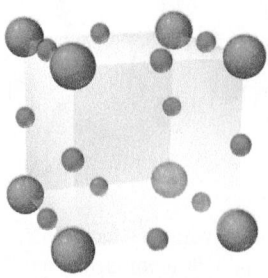

113. The unit cells for cesium chloride and barium(II) chloride are shown here. Show that the ratio of cations to anions in each unit cell corresponds to the ratio of cations to anions in the formula of each compound.

Cesium chloride   Barium(II) chloride

114. The unit cells for lithium oxide and silver iodide are shown here. Show that the ratio of cations to anions in each unit cell corresponds to the ratio of cations to anions in the formula of each compound.

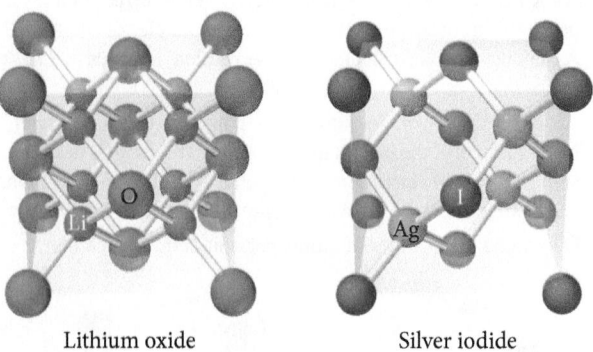

Lithium oxide   Silver iodide

Band Theory

115. Which solid would you expect to have little or no band gap?
  a. Zn(s)   **b.** Si(s)   **c.** As(s)

116. How many molecular orbitals are present in the valence band of a sodium crystal with a mass of 5.45 g?

117. Indicate if each solid would form an n-type or a p-type semiconductor.
  a. germanium doped with gallium
  b. silicon doped with arsenic

118. Indicate if each solid would form an n-type or a p-type semiconductor.
  a. silicon doped with gallium
  b. germanium doped with antimony

Cumulative Problems

119. Explain the observed trend in the melting points of the hydrogen halides.

HI	−50.8 °C
HBr	−88.5 °C
HCl	−114.8 °C
HF	−83.1 °C

120. Explain the observed trend in the boiling points of these compounds.

H_2Te	−2 °C
H_2Se	−41.5 °C
H_2S	−60.7 °C
H_2O	−100 °C

121. The vapor pressure of water at 25 °C is 23.76 torr. If 1.25 g of water is enclosed in a 1.5 L container, will any liquid be present? If so, what mass of liquid?

122. The vapor pressure of CCl_3F at 300 K is 856 torr. If 11.5 g of CCl_3F is enclosed in a 1.0 L container, will any liquid be present? If so, what mass of liquid?

123. Examine the phase diagram for iodine shown in Figure 11.39(a). What state transitions occur as we uniformly increase the pressure on a gaseous sample of iodine from 0.010 atm at 185 °C to 100 atm at 185 °C? Make a graph, analogous to the heating curve for water shown in Figure 11.36. Plot pressure versus time during the pressure increase.

124. Carbon tetrachloride displays a triple point at 249.0 K and a melting point (at 1 atm) of 250.3 K. Which state of carbon tetrachloride is more dense, the solid or the liquid? Explain.

125. Four ice cubes at exactly 0 °C with a total mass of 53.5 g are combined with 115 g of water at 75 °C in an insulated container. If no heat is lost to the surroundings, what is the final temperature of the mixture?

126. A sample of steam with a mass of 0.552 g and at a temperature of 100 °C condenses into an insulated container holding 4.25 g of water at 5.0 °C. Assuming that no heat is lost to the surroundings, what is the final temperature of the mixture?

127. Draw a heating curve (such as the one in Figure 11.36) for 1 mole of methanol beginning at 170 K and ending at 350 K. Assume that the values given here are constant over the relevant temperature ranges.

Melting point	176 K
Boiling point	338 K
ΔH_{fus}	2.2 kJ/mol
ΔH_{vap}	35.2 kJ/mol
$C_{s,solid}$	105 J/mol · K
$C_{s,liquid}$	81.3 J/mol · K
$C_{s,gas}$	48 J/mol · K

128. Draw a heating curve (such as the one in Figure 11.36) for 1 mole of benzene beginning at 0 °C and ending at 100 °C. Assume that the values given here are constant over the relevant temperature ranges.

Melting point	5.4 °C
Boiling point	90.1 °C
ΔH_{fus}	9.9 kJ/mol
ΔH_{vap}	30.7 kJ/mol
$C_{s,solid}$	118 J/mol · K
$C_{s,liquid}$	135 J/mol · K
$C_{s,gas}$	104 J/mol · K

129. Air conditioners not only cool air, but dry it as well. A room in a home measures 6.0 m × 10.0 m × 2.2 m. If the outdoor temperature is 30 °C and the vapor pressure of water in the air is 85% of the vapor pressure of water at this temperature, what mass of water must be removed from the air each time the volume of air in the room is cycled through the air conditioner? The vapor pressure for water at 30 °C is 31.8 torr.

130. A sealed flask contains 0.55 g of water at 28 °C. The vapor pressure of water at this temperature is 28.36 mmHg. What is the minimum volume of the flask in order that no liquid water be present in the flask?

131. Silver iodide crystallizes in the zinc blende structure. The separation between nearest neighbor cations and anions is approximately 325 pm, and the melting point is 558 °C. Cesium chloride, by contrast, crystallizes in the cesium chloride structure shown in Figure 11.51. Even though the separation between nearest neighbor cations and anions is greater (348 pm), the melting point of cesium chloride is higher (645 °C). Explain.

132. Copper iodide crystallizes in the zinc blende structure. The separation between nearest neighbor cations and anions is approximately 311 pm, and the melting point is 606 °C. Potassium chloride, by contrast, crystallizes in the rock salt structure. Even though the separation between nearest neighbor cations and anions is greater (319 pm), the melting point of potassium chloride is higher (776 °C). Explain.

133. Consider the face-centered cubic structure shown here:

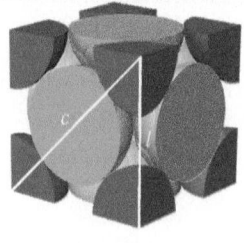

a. What is the length of the line (labeled *c*) that runs diagonally across one of the faces of the cube in terms of *r* (the atomic radius)?

b. Use the answer to part a and the Pythagorean theorem to derive the expression for the edge length (*l*) in terms of *r*.

134. Consider the body-centered cubic structure shown here:

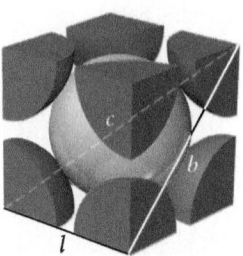

a. What is the length of the line (labeled *c*) that runs from one corner of the cube diagonally through the center of the cube to the other corner in terms of *r* (the atomic radius)?

b. Use the Pythagorean theorem to derive an expression for the length of the line (labeled *b*) that runs diagonally across one of the faces of the cube in terms of the edge length (*l*).

c. Use the answer to parts (a) and (b) along with the Pythagorean theorem to derive the expression for the edge length (*l*) in terms of *r*.

135. The unit cell in a crystal of diamond belongs to a crystal system different from any we discussed in this chapter. The volume of a unit cell of diamond is 0.0454 nm^3 and the density of diamond is 3.52 g/cm^3. Find the number of carbon atoms in a unit cell of diamond.

136. The density of an unknown metal is 12.3 g/cm^3 and its atomic radius is 0.134 nm. It has a face-centered cubic lattice. Find the atomic mass of this metal.

137. Based on the phase diagram of CO_2 shown in Figure 11.39(b), describe the state changes that occur when the temperature of CO_2 is increased from 190 K to 350 K at a constant pressure of (a) 1 atm, (b) 5.1 atm, (c) 10 atm, (d) 100 atm.

138. Consider a planet where the pressure of the atmosphere at sea level is 2500 mmHg. Does water behave in a way that can sustain life on the planet?

139. An unknown metal is found to have a density of 7.8748 g/cm^3 and to crystallize in a body-centered cubic lattice. The edge of the unit cell is 0.28664 nm. Calculate the atomic mass of the metal.

140. When spheres of radius *r* are packed in a body-centered cubic arrangement, they occupy 68.0% of the available volume. Use the fraction of occupied volume to calculate the value of *a*, the length of the edge of the cube, in terms of *r*.

Challenge Problems

141. Potassium chloride crystallizes in the rock salt structure. Estimate the density of potassium chloride using the ionic radii provided in Chapter 8.

142. Butane (C_4H_{10}) has a heat of vaporization of 22.44 kJ/mol and a normal boiling point of −0.4 °C. A 250 mL sealed flask contains 0.55 g of butane at −22 °C. How much butane is present as a liquid? If the butane is warmed to 25 °C, how much is present as a liquid?

143. Liquid nitrogen can be used as a cryogenic substance to obtain low temperatures. Under atmospheric pressure, liquid nitrogen boils at 77 K, allowing low temperatures to be reached. However, if the nitrogen is placed in a sealed, insulated container connected to a vacuum pump, even lower temperatures can be reached. Why? If the vacuum pump has sufficient capacity and is left on for an extended period of time, the liquid nitrogen will start to freeze. Explain.

144. Calculate the fraction of empty space in cubic closest packing to five significant figures.

145. A tetrahedral site in a closest-packed lattice is formed by four spheres at the corners of a regular tetrahedron. This is equivalent to placing the spheres at alternate corners of a cube. In such a closest-packed arrangement the spheres are in contact, and if the spheres have a radius r, the diagonal of the face of the cube is $2r$. The tetrahedral hole is inside the middle of the cube. Find the length of the body diagonal of this cube and then find the radius of the tetrahedral hole.

146. Given that the heat of fusion of water is -6.02 kJ/mol, the heat capacity of $H_2O(l)$ is 75.2 J/mol·K, and the heat capacity of $H_2O(s)$ is 37.7 J/mol·K, calculate the heat of fusion of water at $-10\ ^\circ C$.

147. The heat of combustion of CH_4 is 890.4 kJ/mol and the heat capacity of H_2O is 75.2 J/mol·K. Find the volume of methane measured at 298 K and 1.00 atm required to convert 1.00 L of water at 298 K to water vapor at 373 K.

148. Two liquids, A and B, have vapor pressures at a given temperature of 24 mmHg and 36 mmHg, respectively. We prepare solutions of A and B at a given temperature and measure the total pressures above the solutions. We obtain this data:

Solution	Amt A (mol)	Amt B (mol)	P (mmHg)
1	1	1	30
2	2	1	28
3	1	2	32
4	1	3	33

Predict the total pressure above a solution of 5 mol A and 1 mol B.

149. Three 1.0 L flasks, maintained at 308 K, are connected to each other with stopcocks. Initially the stopcocks are closed. One of the flasks contains 1.0 atm of N_2; the second, 2.0 g of H_2O; and the third, 0.50 g of ethanol, C_2H_6O. The vapor pressure of H_2O at 308 K is 42 mmHg and that of ethanol is 102 mmHg. The stopcocks are then opened and the contents mix freely. What is the pressure?

Conceptual Problems

150. One prediction of global warming is the melting of global ice, which may result in coastal flooding. A criticism of this prediction is that the melting of icebergs does not increase ocean levels any more than the melting of ice in a glass of water increases the level of liquid in the glass. Is this a valid criticism? Does the melting of an ice cube in a cup of water raise the level of the liquid in the cup? Why or why not? In response to this criticism, scientists have asserted that they are not worried about melting icebergs, but rather the melting of ice sheets that sit on the continent of Antarctica. Would the melting of this ice increase ocean levels? Why or why not?

151. The rate of vaporization depends on the surface area of the liquid. However, the vapor pressure of a liquid does not depend on the surface area. Explain.

152. Substance A has a smaller heat of vaporization than substance B. Which of the two substances will undergo a larger change in vapor pressure for a given change in temperature?

153. The density of a substance is greater in its solid state than in its liquid state. If the triple point in the phase diagram of the substance is below 1.0 atm, which will necessarily be at a lower temperature, the triple point or the normal melting point?

154. A substance has a heat of vaporization of ΔH_{vap} and heat of fusion of ΔH_{fus}. Express the heat of sublimation in terms of ΔH_{vap} and ΔH_{fus}.

155. Examine the heating curve for water in Section 11.7 (Figure 11.36). If heat is added to the water at a constant rate, which of the three segments in which temperature is rising will have the least steep slope? Why?

156. A root cellar is an underground chamber used to store fruits, vegetables, and even meats. In extreme cold, farmers put large vats of water into the root cellar to prevent the fruits and vegetables from freezing. Explain why this works.

157. Suggest an explanation for the observation that the heat of fusion of a substance is always smaller than its heat of vaporization.

158. Refer to Figure 11.36 to answer each question.

    a. A sample of steam begins on the line segment labeled 5 on the graph. Is heat absorbed or released in moving from the line segment labeled 5 to the line segment labeled 3? What is the sign of q for this change?

    b. In moving from left to right along the line segment labeled 2 on the graph, heat is absorbed, but the temperature remains constant. Where does the heat go?

    c. How would the graph change if it were for another substance (other than water)?

159. The following image is an electrostatic potential map for ethylene oxide, $(CH_2)_2O$, a polar molecule. Use the electrostatic potential map to predict the geometry for how one ethylene oxide molecule interacts with another. Draw structural formulas, using the 3D bond notation introduced in Section 10.4, to show the geometry of the interaction.

Answers to Conceptual Connections

State Changes

11.1 (a) When water boils, it simply changes state from liquid to gas. Water molecules do not decompose during boiling.

Dispersion Forces

11.2 (c) I_2 has the highest boiling point because it has the highest molar mass. Since the halogens are all similar in other ways, we expect I_2 to have the greatest dispersion forces and therefore the highest boiling point (and in fact it does).

Dispersion Forces

11.3

Inter Molecular Forces and Boiling Point

11.4 (a) CH_3OH. The compounds all have similar molar masses, so the dispersion forces are similar in all three. CO is polar, but because CH_3OH contains H directly bonded to O, it has hydrogen bonding, resulting in the highest boiling point.

Vapor Pressure

11.5 (b) Although the *rate of vaporization* increases with increasing surface area, the *vapor pressure* of a liquid is independent of surface area. An increase in surface area increases both the rate of vaporization and the rate of condensation—the effects exactly cancel and the vapor pressure does not change.

Cooling of Water with Ice

11.6 The warming of the ice from $-10\,°C$ to $0\,°C$ absorbs only 20.9 J/g of ice. The melting of the ice, however, absorbs about 334 J/g of ice. (You can obtain this value by dividing the heat of fusion of water by its molar mass.) Therefore, the melting of the ice produces a larger temperature decrease in the water than does the warming of the ice.

Phase Diagrams

11.7 (b) The solid will sublime into a gas. Since the pressure is below the triple point, the liquid state is not stable.

12 Solutions

One molecule of nonsaline substance (held in the solvent) dissolved in 100 molecules of any volatile liquid decreases the vapor pressure of this liquid by a nearly constant fraction, nearly 0.0105.

—François-Marie Raoult (1830–1901)

WE LEARNED IN Chapter 1 that most of the matter we encounter is in the form of mixtures. In this chapter, we focus on homogeneous mixtures, known as solutions. Solutions are mixtures in which atoms and molecules intermingle on the molecular and atomic scale. Common examples of solutions include ocean water, gasoline, and air. Why do solutions form? How are their properties different from the properties of the pure substances that compose them? As you read this chapter, keep in mind the large number of solutions that surround you at every moment, including those that exist within your own body.

12.1 Thirsty Solutions: Why You Shouldn't Drink Seawater

In the popular novel *Life of Pi* by Yann Martel, the main character (whose name is Pi) is stranded on a lifeboat with a Bengal tiger in the middle of the Pacific Ocean for 227 days. He survives in part by rigging a solar still to distill seawater for drinking. However, in the first three days of his

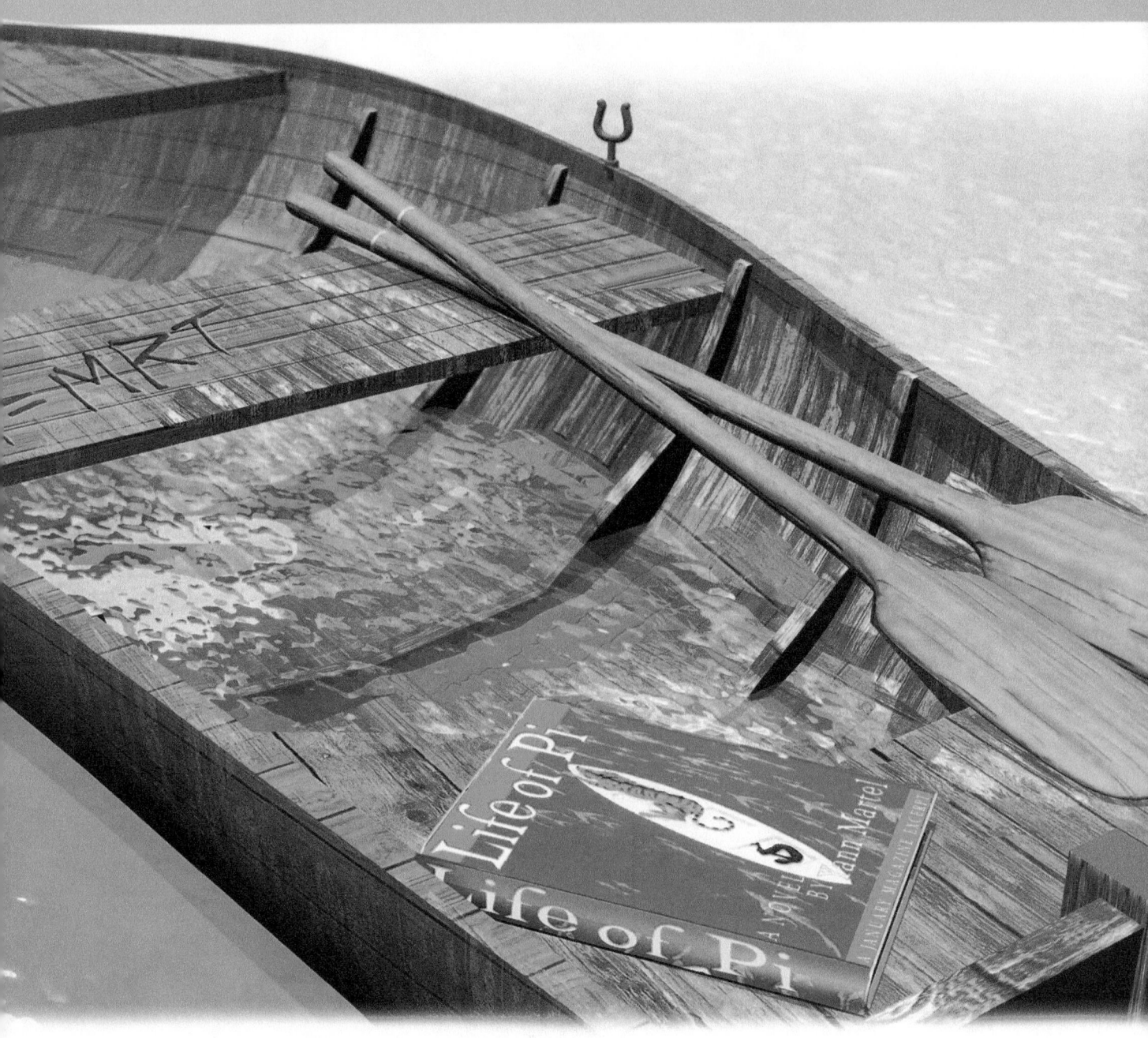

predicament (before he rigs the still) he becomes severely dehydrated from lack of water. He is surrounded by seawater, but drinking *that* water would only have made his condition worse. Why? Seawater actually draws water *out of the body* as it passes through the stomach and intestines, resulting in diarrhea and further dehydration. We can think of seawater as a *thirsty solution*—one that draws more water to itself. Consequently, seawater should never be consumed as drinking water.

Seawater is a **solution**, a homogeneous mixture of two or more substances or components as shown in Figure 12.1 ▶. The majority component is typically called the **solvent** and the minority component is called the **solute**. In seawater, water is the solvent and sodium chloride is the primary solute. Solutions form in part because of the intermolecular forces we discussed in Chapter 11. In most solutions, the particles of the solute interact with the particles of the solvent through intermolecular forces.

The reason that seawater draws water to itself is related to nature's tendency toward spontaneous mixing, which we discuss in more detail later in this chapter and in Chapter 17. For now, we simply observe that, unless it is highly unfavorable energetically,

Drinking seawater causes dehydration because seawater draws water out of body tissues.

In some cases, the concepts of solute and solvent are not useful. For example, a homogeneous mixture of water and ethanol can contain equal amounts of both components and neither component can then be identified as the solvent.

▶ **FIGURE 12.1 A Typical Solution** In seawater, sodium chloride is the primary solute. Water is the solvent.

H₂O
Solvent

Na⁺
Cl⁻ **Solute**

substances tend to combine into uniform mixtures, not separate into pure substances. For example, suppose pure water and a sodium chloride solution are in separate compartments with a removable barrier between them, as shown in Figure 12.2(a) ▶. If we remove the barrier, the two liquids spontaneously mix, eventually forming a more dilute sodium chloride solution of uniform concentration, as shown in Figure 12.2(b). The tendency toward mixing results in a uniform concentration of the final solution.

Seawater is a *thirsty* solution because of this tendency toward mixing. As seawater moves through the intestine, it flows past cells that line the digestive tract. These cells consist of largely fluid interiors surrounded by membranes. Cellular fluids themselves contain dissolved ions, including sodium and chloride, but the fluids in the cells are more dilute than seawater. Nature's tendency toward mixing (which tends to produce solutions of uniform concentration), together with the selective permeability of the cell membranes (which allows water to flow in and out, but restricts the flow of dissolved solids), cause a *flow of solvent out of the body's cells into the seawater*. In this way, the two solutions become more similar in concentration (as though they had mixed)—the solution in the intestine becomes somewhat more dilute than it was and the solution in the cells becomes somewhat more concentrated. The accumulation of extra fluid in the intestines causes diarrhea, and the decreased fluid in the cells causes dehydration. If Pi had drunk the seawater instead of constructing the solar still, neither he nor his companion, the large Bengal tiger, would have survived his ordeal.

▶ Seawater is a more concentrated solution than the fluids in body cells. As a result, when seawater flows through the digestive tract, it draws water out of the surrounding tissues.

Interior of body cells
–dilute solution

Seawater in intestinal tract
–concentrated solution

Direction of water flow

CO₂   H₂O

▲ Club soda is a solution of carbon dioxide and water.

12.2 Types of Solutions and Solubility

A solution may be composed of a solid and a liquid (such as the salt and water that are the primary components of seawater), but it may also be composed of a gas and a liquid, two different liquids, or other combinations (see Table 12.1). In **aqueous solutions**, water is the solvent, and a solid, liquid, or gas is the solute. For example, sugar water and salt water are both aqueous solutions. Similarly, ethyl alcohol—the alcohol in alcoholic beverages—readily mixes with water to form a solution, and carbon dioxide dissolves in water to form the aqueous solution that we know as club soda.

Spontaneous Mixing

When the barrier is removed, spontaneous mixing occurs, producing a solution of uniform concentration.

Concentration difference | Uniform concentration

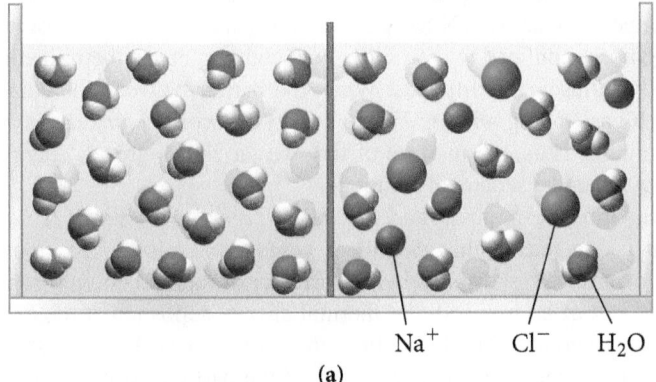

Na⁺ Cl⁻ H₂O
(a)

(b)

▲ **FIGURE 12.2 The Tendency to Mix** (**a**) Pure water and a sodium chloride solution are separated by a barrier. (**b**) When the barrier is removed, the two liquids spontaneously mix, producing a single solution of uniform concentration.

TABLE 12.1 Common Types of Solutions

Solution Phase	Solute Phase	Solvent Phase	Example
Gaseous solution	Gas	Gas	Air (mainly oxygen and nitrogen)
Liquid solution	Gas	Liquid	Club soda (CO_2 and water)
	Liquid	Liquid	Vodka (ethanol and water)
	Solid	Liquid	Seawater (salt and water)
Solid solution	Solid	Solid	Brass (copper and zinc) and other alloys

The general solubilities of a number of ionic compounds are described by the solubility rules in Section 4.5.

You probably know from experience that a particular solvent, such as water, does not dissolve all possible solutes. For example, you cannot clean your greasy hands with just water because the water does not dissolve the grease. However, another solvent, such as paint thinner, can easily dissolve the grease. The grease is *insoluble* in water but *soluble* in the paint thinner. The **solubility** of a substance is the amount of the substance that will dissolve in a given amount of solvent. The solubility of sodium chloride in water at 25 °C is 36 g NaCl per 100 g water, while the solubility of grease in water is nearly zero. The solubility of one substance in another depends both on the tendency toward mixing that we discussed in Section 12.1 and on the types of intermolecular forces that we discussed in Chapter 11.

Nature's Tendency toward Mixing: Entropy

So far in this book, we have seen that many physical systems tend toward lower *potential energy*. For example, two particles with opposite charges (such as a proton and an electron or a cation and an anion) move toward each other because their potential energy decreases as their separation decreases according to Coulomb's law. The formation of a solution, however, *does not necessarily* lower the potential energy of its constituent particles. The clearest example of this phenomenon is the formation of a homogeneous mixture (a *solution*) of two ideal gases. Suppose that we enclose neon and argon in a container with a removable barrier between them, as shown in Figure 12.3(a) ▶. As soon as we remove the barrier, the neon and argon mix together to form a solution, as shown in Figure 12.3(b). *Why?*

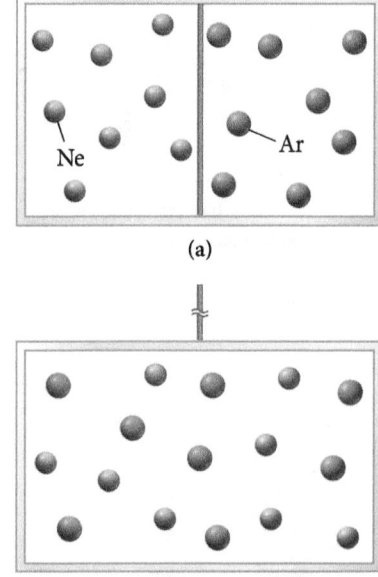

Ne   Ar
(a)

(b)

▲ FIGURE 12.3 **Spontaneous Mixing of Two Ideal Gases** (**a**) Neon and argon are separated by a barrier. (**b**) When the barrier is removed, the two gases spontaneously mix to form a uniform solution.

At low pressures and moderate temperatures both neon and argon behave as ideal gases—they do not interact with each other in any way (that is, there are no significant intermolecular forces between their constituent particles). When the barrier is removed, the two gases mix, but their potential energy remains unchanged. In other words, *we cannot think of the mixing of two ideal gases as lowering their potential energy.* Rather, the tendency to mix is related to a concept called *entropy*.

Entropy is a measure of *energy randomization* or *energy dispersal* in a system. Recall that a gas at any temperature above 0 K has kinetic energy due to the motion of its atoms. When neon and argon are confined to their individual compartments, their kinetic energies are also confined to those compartments. When the barrier between the compartments is removed, each gas—along with its kinetic energy—becomes *spread out* or *dispersed* over a larger volume. Thus, the mixture of the two gases has greater energy dispersal, or greater *entropy*, than the separated components.

The pervasive tendency for energy to spread out, or disperse, whenever it is not restrained from doing so is the reason that two ideal gases mix. Another common example of the tendency toward energy dispersal is the transfer of thermal energy from hot to cold. If we heat one end of an iron rod, the thermal energy deposited at the end of the rod will spontaneously spread along the entire length of the rod. In contrast to the mixing of two ideal gases—where the kinetic energy of the particles becomes dispersed over a larger volume because the particles themselves become dispersed—the thermal energy in the rod, initially concentrated in relatively fewer particles, becomes dispersed by being distributed over a larger number of particles. The tendency for energy to disperse is why thermal energy flows from the hot end of the rod to the cold one, and not the other way around. Imagine a metal rod that became spontaneously hotter on one end and ice cold on the other—this does not happen because energy does not spontaneously concentrate itself. In Chapter 17, we will see that the dispersal of energy is actually the fundamental criterion that ultimately determines the spontaneity of any process.

The Effect of Intermolecular Forces

We have just seen that, in the absence of intermolecular forces, two substances spontaneously mix to form a homogeneous solution. We know from Chapter 11, however, that solids and liquids exhibit a number of different types of intermolecular forces including dispersion forces, dipole–dipole forces, hydrogen bonding, and ion–dipole forces (Figure 12.4) ▼. These forces may promote the formation of a solution or prevent it, depending on the nature of the forces in the particular combination of solute and solvent.

▼ FIGURE 12.4 Intermolecular Forces Involved in Solutions

Intermolecular Forces

These forces may contribute to or oppose the formation of a solution.

| Dispersion | Dipole–dipole | Hydrogen bond | Ion–dipole |

Heptane (C_7H_{16})
Pentane (C_5H_{12})

Acetone (C_3H_6O)
Chloroform $(CHCl_3)$

Ethanol (C_2H_5OH)
H_2O

Na^+

TABLE 12.2 Relative Interactions and Solution Formation

Solvent-solute interactions	>	Solvent-solvent and solute-solute interactions	Solution forms
Solvent-solute interactions	=	Solvent-solvent and solute-solute interactions	Solution forms
Solvent-solute interactions	<	Solvent-solvent and solute-solute interactions	Solution may or may not form, depending on relative disparity

Intermolecular forces exist between (a) the solvent and solute particles, (b) the solvent particles themselves, and (c) the solute particles themselves, as shown in Figure 12.5 ▾.

Solvent–solute interactions: The interactions between a solvent particle and a solute particle.

Solvent–solvent interactions: The interactions between a solvent particle and another solvent particle.

Solute–solute interactions: The interactions between a solute particle and another solute particle.

As shown in Table 12.2, a solution always forms if the solvent–solute interactions are comparable to, or stronger than, the solvent–solvent interactions and the solute–solute interactions. For example, consider mixing the hydrocarbons pentane (C_5H_{12}) and heptane (C_7H_{16}). The intermolecular forces present within both pentane and heptane are dispersion forces. Similarly, the intermolecular forces present *between* heptane and pentane are also dispersion forces. All three interactions are of similar magnitude so the two substances are soluble in each other in all proportions—they are said to be **miscible**. The formation of the solution is driven by the tendency toward mixing, or toward greater entropy, that we just discussed.

If solvent–solute interactions are weaker than solvent–solvent and solute–solute interactions—in other words, if solvent molecules and solute molecules each interact more strongly with molecules of their own kind than with molecules of the other kind—then a solution may still form, depending on the relative disparities between the interactions. If the disparity is small, the tendency to mix results in the formation of a solution even though the process is energetically uphill. If the disparity is large, however, a solution does not form. For example, consider mixing hexane and water. The water molecules have strong hydrogen-bonding attractions to each other but cannot form hydrogen bonds with hexane. The energy required to pull water molecules away from one another is too

Solution Interactions

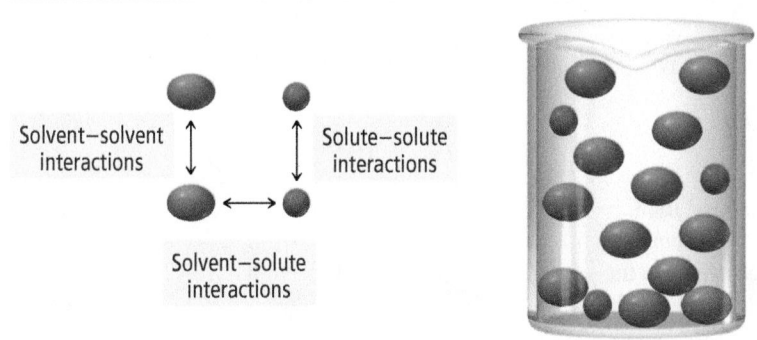

▲ FIGURE 12.5 **Forces in a Solution**   The relative strengths of these three interactions determine whether a solution will form.

TABLE 12.3 Common Laboratory Solvents

Common Polar Solvents	Common Nonpolar Solvents
Water (H_2O)	Hexane (C_6H_{14})
Acetone (CH_3COCH_3)	Diethyl ether ($CH_3CH_2OCH_2CH_3$)*
Methanol (CH_3OH)	Toluene (C_7H_8)
Ethanol (CH_3CH_2OH)	Carbon tetrachloride (CCl_4)

*Diethyl ether has a small dipole moment and can be considered intermediate between polar and nonpolar.

great, and too little energy is returned when the water molecules interact with hexane molecules. As a result, a solution does not form when hexane and water are mixed. Although the tendency to mix is strong, it cannot overcome the large energy disparity between the powerful solvent–solvent interactions and the weak solvent–solute interactions.

In general, we can use the rule of thumb that *like dissolves like* when predicting the formation of solutions. Polar solvents, such as water, tend to dissolve many polar or ionic solutes, and nonpolar solvents, such as hexane, tend to dissolve many nonpolar solutes. Similar kinds of solvents dissolve similar kinds of solutes. Table 12.3 lists some common polar and nonpolar laboratory solvents.

EXAMPLE 12.1 Solubility

Vitamins are often categorized as either fat soluble or water soluble. Water-soluble vitamins dissolve in body fluids and are easily eliminated in the urine, so there is little danger of overconsumption. Fat-soluble vitamins, on the other hand, can accumulate in the body's fatty deposits. Overconsumption of a fat-soluble vitamin can be dangerous to your health. Examine the structure of each vitamin shown here and classify it as either fat soluble or water soluble.

(a) Vitamin C

(b) Vitamin K_3

(c) Vitamin A

(d) Vitamin B_5

SOLUTION

(a) The four —OH bonds in vitamin C make it highly polar and allow it to hydrogen bond with water. Vitamin C is water soluble.	
(b) The C—C bonds in vitamin K_3 are nonpolar and the C—H bonds are nearly so. The C=O bonds are polar, but the bond dipoles oppose and largely cancel each other, so the molecule is dominated by the nonpolar bonds. Vitamin K_3 is fat soluble.	

(c) The C—C bonds in vitamin A are nonpolar and the C—H bonds are nearly so. The one polar —OH bond may increase its water solubility slightly, but overall vitamin A is nonpolar and therefore fat soluble.

(d) The three —OH bonds and one —NH bond in vitamin B_5 make it highly polar and allow it to hydrogen bond with water. Vitamin B_5 is water soluble.

FOR PRACTICE 12.1

Determine whether each compound is soluble in hexane.

(a) water (H_2O)

(b) propane ($CH_3CH_2CH_3$)

(c) ammonia (NH_3)

(d) hydrogen chloride (HCl)

Conceptual Connection 12.1 Solubility

Consider the table listing the solubilities of several alcohols in water and in hexane. Explain the observed trend in terms of intermolecular forces.

Alcohol	Space-Filling Model	Solubility in H_2O (mol alcohol/100 g H_2O)	Solubility in Hexane (C_6H_{14}) (mol alcohol/100 g C_6H_{14})
Methanol (CH_3OH)		Miscible	0.12
Ethanol (CH_3CH_2OH)		Miscible	Miscible
Propanol ($CH_3CH_2CH_2OH$)		Miscible	Miscible
Butanol ($CH_3CH_2CH_2CH_2OH$)		0.11	Miscible
Pentanol ($CH_3CH_2CH_2CH_2CH_2OH$)		0.030	Miscible

12.3 Energetics of Solution Formation

In Chapter 6, we examined the energy changes associated with chemical reactions. Similar energy changes can occur when a solution forms, depending on the magnitude of the interactions between the solute and solvent particles. For example, when we dissolve sodium hydroxide in water, heat is evolved—the solution process is *exothermic*. In contrast, when we dissolve ammonium nitrate (NH_4NO_3) in water, heat is absorbed—this solution process is *endothermic*. Other solutions, such as sodium chloride in water, barely absorb or evolve heat upon formation. What causes these different behaviors?

We can understand the energy changes associated with solution formation by envisioning the process as occurring in three steps, each with an associated change in enthalpy:

1. Separating the solute into its constituent particles.

This step is always endothermic (positive ΔH) because energy is required to overcome the forces that hold the solute particles together.

2. Separating the solvent particles from each other to make room for the solute particles.

This step is also endothermic because energy is required to overcome the intermolecular forces among the solvent particles.

3. Mixing the solute particles with the solvent particles.

This step is exothermic because energy is released as the solute particles interact (through intermolecular forces) with the solvent particles.

According to Hess's law, the overall enthalpy change upon solution formation, called the **enthalpy of solution** (ΔH_{soln}) is the sum of the changes in enthalpy for each step:

$$\Delta H_{soln} = \underset{\text{endothermic (+)}}{\Delta H_{solute}} + \underset{\text{endothermic (+)}}{\Delta H_{solvent}} + \underset{\text{exothermic (−)}}{\Delta H_{mix}}$$

Since the first two terms are endothermic (positive ΔH) and the third term is exothermic (negative ΔH), the overall sign of ΔH_{soln} depends on the magnitudes of the individual terms, as shown in Figure 12.6 ▶.

1. *If the sum of the endothermic terms is approximately equal in magnitude to the exothermic term, then ΔH_{soln} is about zero.* The increasing entropy upon mixing drives the formation of a solution while the overall energy of the system remains nearly constant.

2. *If the sum of the endothermic terms is smaller in magnitude than the exothermic term, then ΔH_{soln} is negative and the solution process is exothermic.* In this case, both the tendency toward lower energy and the tendency toward greater entropy drive the formation of a solution.

3. *If the sum of the endothermic terms is greater in magnitude than the exothermic term, then ΔH_{soln} is positive and the solution process is endothermic.* In this case, as long as ΔH_{soln} is not too large, the tendency toward greater entropy still drives the formation of a solution. If, on the other hand, ΔH_{soln} is too large, a solution does not form.

Energetics of Solution Formation

Solvent
separated

Solute
separated

❷ Separating
solvent $\Delta H_{\text{solvent}}$
particles

Solvent   Solute
aggregated   separated

❶ Separating
solute ΔH_{solute} ❸ Mixing solute and ΔH_{mix}
particles   solvent particles

Solvent   Solute
aggregated   aggregated

Net
exothermic $\Delta H_{\text{solution}}$ Solution
process

(a) Exothermic

Solvent
separated

Solute
separated

❷ Separating
solvent $\Delta H_{\text{solvent}}$
particles

Solvent   Solute
aggregated   separated

❶ Separating
solute ΔH_{solute} ❸ Mixing solute and ΔH_{mix}
particles   solvent particles

Solution

Solvent   Solute
aggregated   aggregated   Net
                              $\Delta H_{\text{solution}}$ endothermic
                                                              process

(b) Endothermic

▲ FIGURE 12.6 **Energetics of the
Solution Process** **(a)** When ΔH_{mix} is
greater in magnitude than the sum of
ΔH_{solute} and $\Delta H_{\text{solvent}}$, the heat of
solution is negative (exothermic).
(b) When ΔH_{mix} is smaller in
magnitude than the sum of ΔH_{solute}
and $\Delta H_{\text{solvent}}$, the heat of solution is
positive (endothermic).

Aqueous Solutions and Heats of Hydration

Many common solutions, such as the seawater mentioned in the opening example of this
chapter, contain an ionic compound dissolved in water. In these aqueous solutions, $\Delta H_{\text{solvent}}$
and ΔH_{mix} can be combined into a single term called the **heat of hydration** ($\Delta H_{\text{hydration}}$)
(Figure 12.7 ▼). The heat of hydration is the enthalpy change that occurs when 1 mol of the

Heat of Hydration

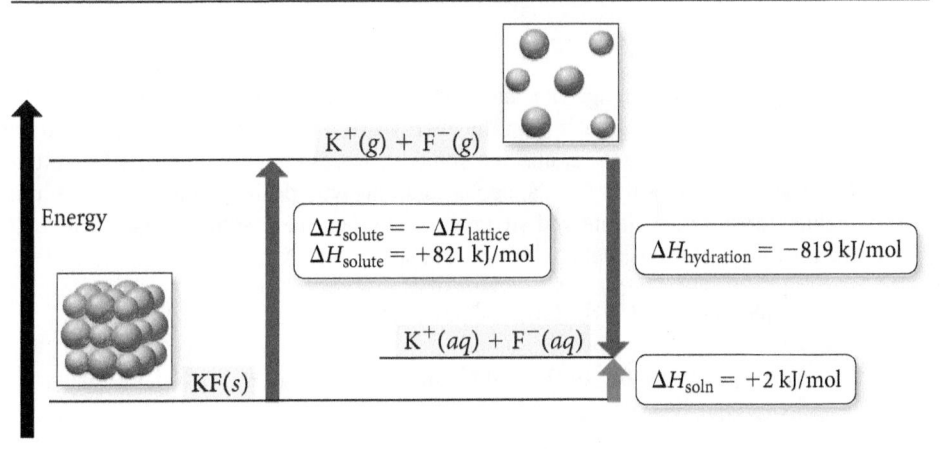

Energy

$K^+(g) + F^-(g)$

$\Delta H_{\text{solute}} = -\Delta H_{\text{lattice}}$
$\Delta H_{\text{solute}} = +821 \text{ kJ/mol}$

$\Delta H_{\text{hydration}} = -819 \text{ kJ/mol}$

$K^+(aq) + F^-(aq)$

$KF(s)$

$\Delta H_{\text{soln}} = +2 \text{ kJ/mol}$

◀ FIGURE 12.7 **Heat of Hydration and
Heat of Solution** The heat of hydration
is the heat emitted when 1 mol of
gaseous solute ions is dissolved in
water. The sum of the negative of the
lattice energy (which is ΔH_{solute})
and the heat of hydration is the heat
of solution.

▶ **FIGURE 12.8 Ion–Dipole Interactions** Ion–dipole interactions such as those between potassium ions, fluoride ions, and water molecules cause the heat of hydration to be largely negative (exothermic).

Ion–Dipole Interactions

KF solution

gaseous solute ions is dissolved in water. Because the ion–dipole interactions that occur between a dissolved ion and the surrounding water molecules (Figure 12.8 ▲) are much stronger than the hydrogen bonds in water, $\Delta H_{hydration}$ is always largely negative (exothermic) for ionic compounds. Using the heat of hydration, we can write the enthalpy of solution as a sum of just two terms, one endothermic and one exothermic:

$$\Delta H_{soln} = \Delta H_{solute} + \underbrace{\Delta H_{solvent} + \Delta H_{mix}}$$

$$\Delta H_{soln} = \underset{\substack{\text{endothermic}\\\text{(positive)}}}{\Delta H_{solute}} + \underset{\substack{\text{exothermic}\\\text{(negative)}}}{\Delta H_{hydration}}$$

For ionic compounds, ΔH_{solute}, the energy required to separate the solute into its constituent particles, is the negative of the solute's lattice energy ($\Delta H_{solute} = -\Delta H_{lattice}$), discussed in Section 9.4. For ionic aqueous solutions, then, the overall enthalpy of solution depends on the relative magnitudes of ΔH_{solute} and $\Delta H_{hydration}$, with three possible scenarios (in each case we refer to the *magnitude (absolute value)* of ΔH):

1. $|\Delta H_{\textbf{solute}}| < |\Delta H_{\textbf{hydration}}|$. The amount of energy required to separate the solute into its constituent ions is less than the energy given off when the ions are hydrated. ΔH_{soln} is therefore negative, and the solution process is exothermic. Solutes with negative enthalpies of solution include lithium bromide and potassium hydroxide. When these solutes dissolve in water, the resulting solutions feel warm to the touch.

$$\text{LiBr}(s) \xrightarrow{\text{H}_2\text{O}} \text{Li}^+(aq) + \text{Br}^-(aq) \quad \Delta H_{soln} = -48.78 \text{ kJ/mol}$$

$$\text{KOH}(s) \xrightarrow{\text{H}_2\text{O}} \text{K}^+(aq) + \text{OH}^-(aq) \quad \Delta H_{soln} = -57.56 \text{ kJ/mol}$$

2. $|\Delta H_{\textbf{solute}}| > |\Delta H_{\textbf{hydration}}|$. The amount of energy required to separate the solute into its constituent ions is greater than the energy given off when the ions are hydrated. ΔH_{soln} is therefore positive, and the solution process is endothermic (if a solution forms at all). Solutes that form aqueous solutions with positive enthalpies of solution include ammonium nitrate and silver nitrate. When these solutes dissolve in water, the resulting solutions feel cool to the touch.

$$\text{NH}_4\text{NO}_3(s) \xrightarrow{\text{H}_2\text{O}} \text{NH}_4^+(aq) + \text{NO}_3^-(aq) \quad \Delta H_{soln} = +25.67 \text{ kJ/mol}$$

$$\text{AgNO}_3(s) \xrightarrow{\text{H}_2\text{O}} \text{Ag}^+(aq) + \text{NO}_3^-(aq) \quad \Delta H_{soln} = +36.91 \text{ kJ/mol}$$

3. $|\Delta H_{\text{solute}}| \approx |\Delta H_{\text{hydration}}|$. The amount of energy required to separate the solute into its constituent ions is roughly equal to the energy given off when the ions are hydrated. ΔH_{soln} is therefore approximately zero, and the solution process is neither appreciably exothermic nor appreciably endothermic. Solutes with enthalpies of solution near zero include sodium chloride and sodium fluoride. When these solutes dissolve in water, the resulting solutions do not undergo a noticeable change in temperature.

$$NaCl(s) \xrightarrow{\text{H}_2\text{O}} Na^+(aq) + Cl^-(aq) \quad \Delta H_{\text{soln}} = +3.88 \text{ kJ/mol}$$

$$NaF(s) \xrightarrow{\text{H}_2\text{O}} Na^+(aq) + F^-(aq) \quad \Delta H_{\text{soln}} = +0.91 \text{ kJ/mol}$$

Conceptual Connection 12.2 Energetics of Aqueous Solution Formation

The enthalpy of solution for cesium fluoride is -36.8 kJ/mol. What can you conclude about the relative magnitudes of ΔH_{solute} and $\Delta H_{\text{hydration}}$?

12.4 Solution Equilibrium and Factors Affecting Solubility

The dissolution of a solute in a solvent is an equilibrium process similar to the equilibrium process associated with a phase change (discussed in Chapter 11). Imagine, from a molecular viewpoint, the dissolution of a solid solute such as sodium chloride in a liquid solvent such as water (Figure 12.9 ▼). Initially, water molecules rapidly solvate sodium cations and chloride anions, resulting in a noticeable decrease in the amount of solid sodium chloride in the water. Over time, however, the concentration of dissolved

▼ FIGURE 12.9 **Dissolution of NaCl** (a) When sodium chloride is first added to water, sodium and chloride ions dissolve into the water. (b) As the solution becomes more concentrated, some of the sodium and chloride ions recrystallize as solid sodium chloride. (c) When the rate of dissolution equals the rate of recrystallization, dynamic equilibrium is reached.

Solution Equilibrium

NaCl(s)	$NaCl(s) \longrightarrow Na^+(aq) + Cl^-(aq)$	$NaCl(s) \rightleftharpoons Na^+(aq) + Cl^-(aq)$
When sodium chloride is first added to water, sodium and chloride ions begin to dissolve into the water.	As the solution becomes more concentrated, some of the sodium and chloride ions can begin to recrystallize as solid sodium chloride.	When the rate of dissolution equals the rate of recrystallization, dynamic equilibrium has been reached.

(a) **Initial**

Rate of dissolution > Rate of recrystallization
(b) **Dissolving**

Rate of dissolution = Rate of recrystallization
(c) **Dynamic equilibrium**

▶ **FIGURE 12.10 Precipitation from a Supersaturated Solution**   When a small piece of solid sodium acetate is added to a supersaturated sodium acetate solution, the excess solid precipitates out of the solution.

sodium chloride in the solution increases. This dissolved sodium chloride then begins to recrystallize as solid sodium chloride. Initially the rate of dissolution far exceeds the rate of recrystallization, but as the concentration of dissolved sodium chloride increases, the rate of recrystallization also increases. Eventually the rates of dissolution and recrystallization become equal—**dynamic equilibrium** has been reached.

$$NaCl(s) \rightleftharpoons Na^+(aq) + Cl^-(aq)$$

A solution in which the dissolved solute is in dynamic equilibrium with the solid (undissolved) solute is a **saturated solution**. *If you add additional solute to a saturated solution, it will not dissolve.* A solution containing less than the equilibrium amount of solute is an **unsaturated solution**. *If you add additional solute to an unsaturated solution, it will dissolve.*

Under certain circumstances, a **supersaturated solution**—one containing more than the equilibrium amount of solute—may form. Supersaturated solutions are unstable and the excess solute normally precipitates out of the solution. However, in some cases, if left undisturbed, a supersaturated solution can exist for an extended period of time. For example, in a common classroom demonstration a tiny piece of solid sodium acetate is added to a supersaturated solution of sodium acetate. This triggers the precipitation of the solute, which crystallizes out of solution in a dramatic and often beautiful way (Figure 12.10 ▲).

The Temperature Dependence of the Solubility of Solids

In the case of sugar dissolving in water, the higher temperature increases both *how fast* the sugar dissolves and *how much* sugar dissolves.

The solubility of solids in water can be highly dependent on temperature. Have you ever noticed how much more sugar you can dissolve in hot tea than in cold tea? Although exceptions exist, *the solubility of most solids in water increases with increasing temperature,* as shown in Figure 12.11 ▼. For example, the solubility of potassium

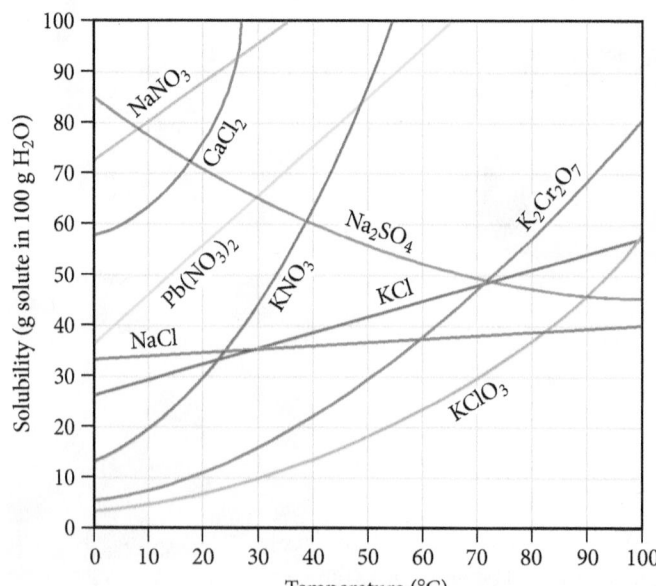

▶ **FIGURE 12.11 Solubility and Temperature**   The solubility of most solids increases with increasing temperature.

nitrate (KNO_3) at room temperature is about 37 g KNO_3 per 100 g of water. At 50 °C, the solubility rises to 88 g KNO_3 per 100 g of water.

A common way to purify a solid is a technique called **recrystallization**. In this technique, enough solid is added to water (or some other solvent) to create a saturated solution at an elevated temperature. As the solution cools, it becomes supersaturated and the excess solid precipitates out of solution. If the solution cools slowly, the solid forms crystals as it comes out of solution. The crystalline structure tends to reject impurities, resulting in a purer solid.

You can use the temperature dependence of the solubility of solids to make rock candy. Prepare a saturated sucrose (table sugar) solution at an elevated temperature, and allow a string or stick to dangle into the solution for several days. As the solution cools and the solvent evaporates, the solution becomes supersaturated and sugar crystals grow on the string or stick. After several days, beautiful edible crystals or "rocks" of sugar cover the string.

▲ Rock candy is formed by the recrystallization of sugar.

Factors Affecting the Solubility of Gases in Water

Solutions of gases dissolved in water are common. Club soda, for example, is a solution of carbon dioxide and water, and most liquids exposed to air contain dissolved gases from air. Fish depend on the oxygen dissolved in lake or ocean water for life, and our blood contains dissolved nitrogen, oxygen, and carbon dioxide. Even tap water contains dissolved gases. The solubility of a gas in a liquid is affected by both temperature and pressure.

The Effect of Temperature You can observe the effect of temperature on the solubility of a gas in water by heating ordinary tap water on a stove. Before the water reaches its boiling point, small bubbles develop in the water. These bubbles are the dissolved air (mostly nitrogen and oxygen) coming out of solution. (Once the water boils, the bubbling becomes more vigorous—these larger bubbles are composed of water vapor.) The dissolved air comes out of the heated solution because—unlike solids, whose solubility generally increases with increasing temperature—*the solubility of gases in liquids decreases with increasing temperature.*

The inverse relationship between gas solubility and temperature is the reason that warm soda pop bubbles more than cold soda pop when you open it and warm beer goes flat faster than cold beer. More carbon dioxide comes out of these solutions at room temperature than at a lower temperature because the gas is less soluble at room temperature. The decreasing solubility of gases with increasing temperature is also the reason that fish don't bite much in a warm lake. The warm temperature results in a lower oxygen concentration. With lower oxygen levels, the fish become lethargic and do not strike as aggressively at the lure or bait you cast their way.

Cold soda pop   Warm soda pop

▲ Warm soda pop bubbles more than cold soda pop because carbon dioxide is less soluble in the warm solution.

Conceptual Connection 12.3 Solubility and Temperature

A solution is saturated in both nitrogen gas and potassium bromide at 75 °C. When the solution is cooled to room temperature, what is most likely to happen?

a) Some nitrogen gas bubbles out of solution.

b) Some potassium bromide precipitates out of solution.

c) Some nitrogen gas bubbles out of solution *and* some potassium bromide precipitates out of solution.

d) Nothing happens.

The Effect of Pressure The solubility of gases also depends on pressure. The higher the pressure of a gas above a liquid, the more soluble the gas is in the liquid. In a sealed can of soda pop, for example, the carbon dioxide is maintained in solution by a high pressure of carbon dioxide within the can. When the can is opened, this pressure is released and the solubility of carbon dioxide decreases, resulting in bubbling (Figure 12.12 ▶).

CO₂ pressure released

CO₂ under pressure

CO₂ bubbles out of solution

CO₂ dissolved in solution

The increased solubility of a gas in a liquid can be understood by considering cylinders containing water and carbon dioxide gas.

Equilibrium | Pressure is increased. More CO₂ dissolves. | Equilibrium is restored.

The first cylinder represents an equilibrium between gaseous and dissolved carbon dioxide—the rate of carbon dioxide molecules entering solution exactly equals the rate of molecules leaving the solution. Now imagine decreasing the volume, as shown in the second cylinder. The pressure of carbon dioxide increases, causing the rate of molecules entering the solution to rise. The number of molecules in solution increases until equilibrium is established again, as shown in the third cylinder. However, the amount of carbon dioxide in solution is now greater.

We can quantify the solubility of gases with increasing pressure with **Henry's law**:

$$S_{gas} = k_H P_{gas}$$

where S_{gas} is the solubility of the gas (usually in M), k_H is a constant of proportionality (called the *Henry's law constant*) that depends on the specific solute and solvent and also on temperature, and P_{gas} is the partial pressure of the gas (usually in atm). The equation shows that the solubility of a gas in a liquid is directly proportional to the pressure of the gas above the liquid. Table 12.4 lists the Henry's law constants for several common gases.

TABLE 12.4 Henry's Law Constants for Several Gases in Water at 25 °C

Gas	k_H (M/atm)
O₂	1.3×10^{-3}
N₂	6.1×10^{-4}
CO₂	3.4×10^{-2}
NH₃	5.8×10^{1}
He	3.7×10^{-4}

Conceptual Connection 12.4 Henry's Law

Examine the Henry's law constants in Table 12.4. Why is the constant for ammonia bigger than the others?

EXAMPLE 12.2 Henry's Law

What pressure of carbon dioxide is required to keep the carbon dioxide concentration in a bottle of club soda at 0.12 M at 25 °C?

SORT You are given the desired solubility of carbon dioxide and asked to find the pressure required to achieve this solubility.	**GIVEN:** $S_{CO_2} = 0.12$ M **FIND:** P_{CO_2}
STRATEGIZE Use Henry's law to find the required pressure from the solubility. You will need the Henry's law constant for carbon dioxide, which is listed in Table 12.4.	**CONCEPTUAL PLAN** $\boxed{S_{CO_2}} \longrightarrow \boxed{P_{CO_2}}$ $\quad\quad S_{CO_2} = k_{H, CO_2}P_{CO_2}$ **RELATIONSHIPS USED** $S_{gas} = k_H P_{gas}$ (Henry's law) $k_{H, CO_2} = 3.4 \times 10^{-2}$ M/atm (from Table 12.4)
SOLVE Solve the Henry's law equation for P_{CO_2} and substitute the other quantities to calculate it.	**SOLUTION** $S_{CO_2} = k_{H, CO_2}P_{CO_2}$ $P_{CO_2} = \dfrac{S_{CO_2}}{k_{H, CO_2}}$ $\quad\quad = \dfrac{0.12 \text{ M}}{3.4 \times 10^{-2}\dfrac{\text{M}}{\text{atm}}}$ $\quad\quad = 3.5$ atm

CHECK The answer is in the correct units and seems reasonable. A small answer (for example, less than 1 atm) would be suspect because you know that the soda is under a pressure greater than atmospheric pressure when you open it. A very large answer (for example, over 100 atm) would be suspect because an ordinary can or bottle probably could not sustain such high pressures without bursting.

FOR PRACTICE 12.2
Determine the solubility of oxygen in water at 25 °C exposed to air at 1.0 atm. Assume a partial pressure for oxygen of 0.21 atm.

12.5 Expressing Solution Concentration

As we have seen, the amount of solute in a solution is an important property of the solution. For example, the amount of sodium chloride in a solution determines whether or not the solution will cause dehydration if consumed. A **dilute solution** contains small quantities of solute relative to the amount of solvent. Drinking a dilute sodium chloride solution will not cause dehydration. A **concentrated solution** contains large quantities of solute relative to the amount of solvent. Drinking a concentrated sodium chloride solution will cause dehydration. Common ways of reporting solution concentration include molarity, molality, parts by mass, parts by volume, mole fraction, and mole

Chemistry in the Environment

Lake Nyos

Most people living near Lake Nyos in Cameroon, West Africa, began August 22, 1986, like any other day. Unfortunately, the day ended in tragedy. On that evening, a large cloud of carbon dioxide gas burped up from the depths of Lake Nyos, killing over 1700 people and about 3000 cattle. Two years before, a similar tragedy had occurred in Lake Monoun, just 60 miles away, killing 37 people. Today, scientists have taken steps to prevent these lakes from accumulating the carbon dioxide that caused the disasters.

◄ Lake Nyos, in Cameroon, has a deceptively peaceful appearance; in the summer of 1986, more than 1700 people died around its shores.

Lake Nyos is a water-filled volcanic crater. Some 50 miles beneath the surface of the lake, molten volcanic rock (magma) produces carbon dioxide gas that seeps into the lake. The

carbon dioxide forms a solution with the lake water. The high pressure at the bottom of the deep lake allows the solution to become highly concentrated in carbon dioxide. The 1986 disaster occurred because over time—either because of the high concentration itself or because of some other natural trigger such as a landslide or small earthquake—some gaseous carbon dioxide escaped. The rising bubbles disrupted the stratified layers of lake water, causing water at the bottom of the lake to rise to a region of lower pressure. The drop in pressure decreased the solubility of the carbon dioxide, so more carbon dioxide bubbles formed. This in turn caused more churning and still more carbon dioxide release. The result was a massive cloud of carbon dioxide gas that escaped from the lake. Since carbon dioxide is heavier than air, the carbon dioxide traveled down the sides of the volcano and into the nearby valley, displacing air and asphyxiating many of the local residents.

In an effort to keep these events from recurring, scientists have constructed a piping system that slowly vents carbon dioxide from the lake bottom, preventing the buildup that led to the tragedy.

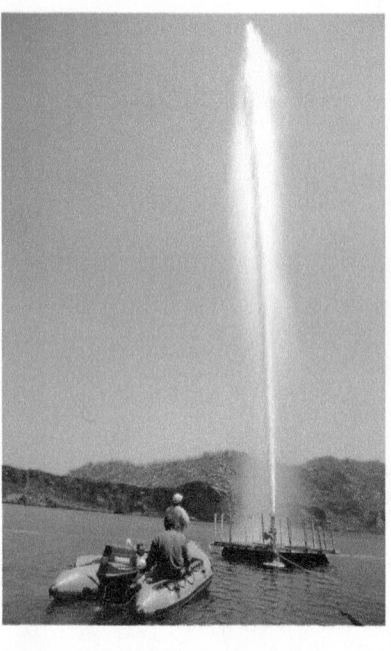

◄ A plumbing system slowly vents carbon dioxide from Lake Nyos.

Question

Suppose that the water pressure at the bottom of Lake Nyos is 25 atm. What is the solubility of carbon dioxide at that depth?

---

percent, as summarized in Table 12.5. We have seen two of these units before: molarity in Section 4.4, and mole fraction in Section 5.6. In the following section, we review the terms we have already covered and introduce the new ones.

Molarity

The **molarity (M)** of a solution is the amount of solute (in moles) divided by the volume of solution (in liters).

$$\text{Molarity (M)} = \frac{\text{amount solute (in mol)}}{\text{volume solution (in L)}}$$

TABLE 12.5 Solution Concentration Terms

Unit	Definition	Units
Molarity (M)	$\dfrac{\text{amount solute (in mol)}}{\text{volume solution (in L)}}$	$\dfrac{\text{mol}}{\text{L}}$
Molality (*m*)	$\dfrac{\text{amount solute (in mol)}}{\text{mass solvent (in kg)}}$	$\dfrac{\text{mol}}{\text{kg}}$
Mole fraction (χ)	$\dfrac{\text{amount solute (in mol)}}{\text{total amount of solute and solvent (in mol)}}$	None
Mole percent (mol %)	$\dfrac{\text{amount solute (in mol)}}{\text{total amount of solute and solvent (in mol)}} \times 100\%$	%
Parts by mass	$\dfrac{\text{mass solute}}{\text{mass solution}} \times \text{multiplication factor}$	
Percent by mass (%)	Multiplication factor = 100	%
Parts per million by mass (ppm)	Multiplication factor = 10^6	ppm
Parts per billion by mass (ppb)	Multiplication factor = 10^9	ppb
Parts by volume (%, ppm, ppb)	$\dfrac{\text{volume solute}}{\text{volume solution}} \times \text{multiplication factor}$ *	

*Multiplication factors for parts by volume are identical to those for parts by mass.

Note that molarity is moles of solute per liter of *solution*, not per liter of solvent. To make a solution of a specified molarity, we usually put the solute into a flask and then add water (or another solvent) to the desired volume of solution, as shown in Figure 12.13 ▼. Molarity is a convenient unit to use when making, diluting, and transferring solutions because it specifies the amount of solute per unit of solution.

Weigh out 1.00 mol NaCl (58.44 g).

Add water until solid is dissolved. Then add additional water until the 1 L mark is reached.

Mix

A 1.00 molar NaCl solution

▲ **FIGURE 12.13 Preparing a Solution of Known Concentration**   To make a 1 M NaCl solution, we add 1 mol of the solid to a flask and dilute with water to make 1 L of solution.

Molarity depends on volume, and because volume varies with temperature, molarity also varies with temperature. For example, a 1 M aqueous solution at room temperature will be slightly less than 1 M at an elevated temperature because the volume of the solution is greater at the elevated temperature.

Molality

A concentration unit that is independent of temperature is **molality (*m*)**, the amount of solute (in moles) divided by the mass of solvent (in kilograms).

$$\text{Molality }(m) = \frac{\text{amount solute (in mol)}}{\text{mass solvent (in kg)}}$$

Notice that molality is defined with respect to kilograms *solvent,* not kilograms solution. Molality is particularly useful when we need to compare concentrations over a range of different temperatures.

Parts by Mass and Parts by Volume

It is often convenient to report a concentration as a ratio of masses. A **parts by mass** concentration is the ratio of the mass of the solute to the mass of the solution, all multiplied by a multiplication factor:

$$\frac{\text{Mass solute}}{\text{Mass solution}} \times \text{multiplication factor}$$

The particular parts by mass unit we use, which determines the size of the multiplication factor, depends on the concentration of the solution. For example, for **percent by mass** the multiplication factor is 100:

$$\text{Percent by mass} = \frac{\text{mass solute}}{\text{mass solution}} \times 100\%$$

Percent means *per hundred*; a solution with a concentration of 14% by mass contains 14 g of solute per 100 g of solution.

For more dilute solutions, we might use **parts per million (ppm)**, which has a multiplication factor of 10^6, or **parts per billion (ppb)**, which has a multiplication factor of 10^9.

$$\text{ppm} = \frac{\text{mass solute}}{\text{mass solution}} \times 10^6$$

$$\text{ppb} = \frac{\text{mass solute}}{\text{mass solution}} \times 10^9$$

A solution with a concentration of 15 ppm by mass, for example, contains 15 g of solute per 10^6 g of solution.

Sometimes, we report concentrations as a ratio of volumes, especially for solutions in which both the solute and solvent are liquids. A **parts by volume** concentration is usually the ratio of the volume of the solute to the volume of the solution, all multiplied by a multiplication factor.

$$\frac{\text{Volume solute}}{\text{Volume solution}} \times \text{multiplication factor}$$

The multiplication factors are identical to those just described for parts by mass concentrations. For example, a 22% ethanol solution by volume contains 22 mL of ethanol for every 100 mL of solution.

Using Parts by Mass (or Parts by Volume) in Calculations We can use the parts by mass (or parts by volume) concentration of a solution as a conversion factor between mass (or volume) of the solute and mass (or volume) of the solution. For example, for a solution containing 3.5% sodium chloride by mass, we write the following conversion factor:

$$\frac{3.5 \text{ g NaCl}}{100 \text{ g solution}}$$ converts   g solution → g NaCl

This conversion factor converts from grams solution to grams NaCl. To convert the other way, we simply invert the conversion factor:

$$\frac{100 \text{ g solution}}{3.5 \text{ g NaCl}}$$ converts $\boxed{\text{g NaCl}} \longrightarrow \boxed{\text{g solution}}$

EXAMPLE 12.3 Using Parts by Mass in Calculations

What volume (in mL) of a soft drink that is 10.5% sucrose ($C_{12}H_{22}O_{11}$) by mass contains 78.5 g of sucrose? (The density of the solution is 1.04 g/mL.)

SORT You are given a mass of sucrose and the concentration and density of a sucrose solution, and you are asked to find the volume of solution containing the given mass.	**GIVEN:** 78.5 g $C_{12}H_{22}O_{11}$ 10.5% $C_{12}H_{22}O_{11}$ by mass density = 1.04 g/mL **FIND:** mL
STRATEGIZE Begin with the mass of sucrose in grams. Use the mass percent concentration of the solution (written as a ratio, as shown under relationships used) to find the number of grams of solution containing this quantity of sucrose. Then use the density of the solution to convert grams to milliliters of solution.	**CONCEPTUAL PLAN** $\dfrac{100 \text{ g soln}}{10.5 \text{ g } C_{12}H_{22}O_{11}}$ $\dfrac{1 \text{ mL}}{1.04 \text{ g}}$ **RELATIONSHIPS USED** $\dfrac{10.5 \text{ g } C_{12}H_{22}O_{11}}{100 \text{ g soln}}$ (percent by mass written as ratio) $\dfrac{1 \text{ mL}}{1.04 \text{ g}}$ (given density of the solution)
SOLVE Begin with 78.5 g $C_{12}H_{22}O_{11}$ and multiply by the conversion factors to arrive at the volume of solution.	**SOLUTION** $78.5 \text{ g } \cancel{C_{12}H_{22}O_{11}} \times \dfrac{100 \text{ g soln}}{10.5 \text{ g } \cancel{C_{12}H_{22}O_{11}}} \times \dfrac{1 \text{ mL}}{1.04 \text{ g}} = 719 \text{ mL soln}$

CHECK The units of the answer are correct. The magnitude seems correct because the solution is approximately 10% sucrose by mass. Since the density of the solution is approximately 1 g/mL, the volume containing 78.5 g sucrose should be roughly 10 times larger, as calculated ($719 \approx 10 \times 78.5$).

FOR PRACTICE 12.3
What mass of sucrose ($C_{12}H_{22}O_{11}$), in g, is contained in 355 mL (12 ounces) of a soft drink that is 11.5% sucrose by mass? (Assume a density of 1.04 g/mL.)

FOR MORE PRACTICE 12.3
A water sample is found to contain the pollutant chlorobenzene with a concentration of 15 ppb (by mass). What volume of this water contains 5.00×10^2 mg of chlorobenzene? (Assume a density of 1.00 g/mL.)

Mole Fraction and Mole Percent

For some applications, especially those in which the ratio of solute to solvent can vary widely, the most useful way to express concentration is the amount of solute (in moles) divided by the total amount of solute and solvent (in moles). This ratio is the **mole fraction** (χ_{solute}):

> The mole fraction can also be defined for the solvent:
> $$\chi_{solvent} = \frac{n_{solvent}}{n_{solute} + n_{solvent}}$$

$$\chi_{solute} = \frac{\text{amount solute (in mol)}}{\text{total amount of solute and solvent (in mol)}} = \frac{n_{solute}}{n_{solute} + n_{solvent}}$$

Also in common use is the **mole percent (mol %)**, which is simply the mole fraction × 100 percent.

$$\text{mol \%} = \chi_{solute} \times 100\%$$

Chemistry in the Environment
The Dirty Dozen

A number of potentially harmful chemicals—such as DDT, dioxin, and polychlorinated biphenyls (PCBs)—can make their way into water sources from industrial dumping, atmospheric emissions, agricultural use, and household dumping. Since crops, livestock, and fish consume water, they too can accumulate these chemicals. Human consumption of food or water contaminated with harmful chemicals can lead to a number of diseases and adverse health effects such as increased cancer risk, liver damage, and central nervous system damage. Governments around the world have joined forces to ban the production of a number of these kinds of chemicals—called persistent organic pollutants or POPs. The original treaty targeted 12 such substances referred to as the "dirty dozen" (Table 12.6).

TABLE 12.6 The Dirty Dozen

1. Aldrin—insecticide	7. Furan—industrial by-product
2. Chlordane—insecticide	8. Heptachlor—insecticide
3. DDT—insecticide	9. Hexachlorobenzene—fungicide, industrial by-product
4. Dieldrin—insecticide	10. Mirex—insecticide, fire retardant
5. Dioxin—industrial by-product	11. Polychlorinated biphenyls (PCBs)—electrical insulators
6. Eldrin—insecticide	12. Toxaphene—insecticide

One problem common to all of these chemicals is their persistence in the environment. These compounds are fairly stable and do not break down under normal environmental conditions. Once they get into the environment, they stay there for a long time. A second problem with these chemicals is their contribution to a process called *bioamplification*. Because they are nonpolar, these chemicals are stored and concentrated in the fatty tissues of the organisms that consume them. As larger organisms eat smaller ones they consume more of the stored chemicals. The result is an increase in the concentrations of these chemicals as they move up the food chain.

Nearly all intentional production of these chemicals has been banned. In the United States, the presence of these contaminants in water supplies is monitored by the Environmental Protection Agency (EPA). The EPA has set limits, called maximum contaminant levels (MCLs), for each of these contaminants in food and drinking water. Table 12.7 lists some MCLs for selected compounds in water supplies. Notice the units that the EPA uses to express the concentration of the contaminants, mg/L. This unit is a conversion factor between liters of water consumed and the mass (in mg) of the pollutant. According to the EPA, as long as the contaminant concentrations are below these levels, the water is safe to drink.

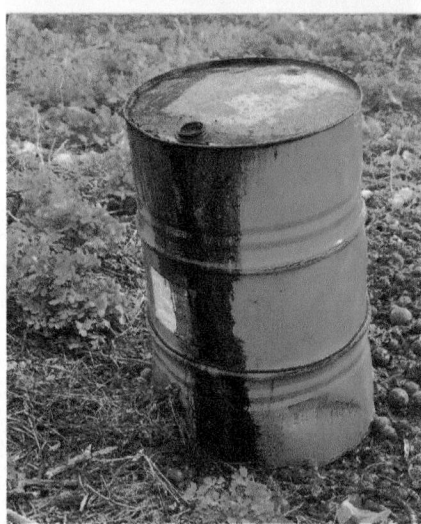

▲ Potentially harmful chemicals make their way into water sources in many ways.

TABLE 12.7 EPA Maximum Contaminant Level (MCL) for Several "Dirty Dozen" Chemicals

Chlordane	0.002 mg/L
Dioxin	0.00000003 mg/L
Heptachlor	0.0004 mg/L
Hexachlorobenzene	0.001 mg/L

Question
Calculate how much of each of the chemicals in Table 12.7 at the MCL is present in 715 L of water, the approximate amount of water consumed by an adult in 1 year.

EXAMPLE 12.4 Calculating Concentrations

A solution is prepared by dissolving 17.2 g of ethylene glycol $(C_2H_6O_2)$ in 0.500 kg of water. The final volume of the solution is 515 mL. For this solution, calculate the concentration in each unit.

(a) molarity (b) molality (c) percent by mass

(d) mole fraction (e) mole percent

SOLUTION

(a) To calculate molarity, first find the amount of ethylene glycol in moles from the mass and molar mass. Then divide the amount in moles by the volume of the solution in liters.	$\text{mol } C_2H_6O_2 = 17.2 \text{ g } C_2H_6O_2 \times \dfrac{1 \text{ mol g } C_2H_6O_2}{62.07\text{g } C_2H_6O_2} = 0.2771 \text{ mol } C_2H_6O_2$ $\text{Molarity (M)} = \dfrac{\text{amount solute (in mol)}}{\text{volume solution (in L)}}$ $= \dfrac{0.2771 \text{ mol } C_2H_6O}{0.515 \text{ L solution}}$ $= 0.538 \text{ M}$
(b) To calculate molality, use the amount of ethylene glycol in moles from part (a), and divide by the mass of the water in kilograms.	$\text{Molality } (m) = \dfrac{\text{amount solute (in mol)}}{\text{mass solvent (in kg)}}$ $= \dfrac{0.2771 \text{ mol } C_2H_6O}{0.500 \text{ kg } H_2O}$ $= 0.554 \ m$
(c) To calculate percent by mass, divide the mass of the solute by the sum of the masses of the solute and solvent and multiply the ratio by 100%.	$\text{Percent by mass} = \dfrac{\text{mass solute}}{\text{mass solution}} \times 100\%$ $= \dfrac{17.2 \text{ g}}{17.2 \text{ g} + 5.00 \times 10^2 \text{ g}} \times 100\%$ $= 3.33\%$
(d) To calculate mole fraction, first determine the amount of water in moles from the mass of water and its molar mass. Then divide the amount of ethylene glycol in moles (from part (a)) by the total number of moles.	$\text{mol } H_2O = 5.00 \times 10^2 \text{ g } H_2O \times \dfrac{1 \text{ mol } H_2O}{18.02 \text{ g } H_2O} = 27.75 \text{ mol } H_2O$ $\chi_{\text{solute}} = \dfrac{n_{\text{solute}}}{n_{\text{solute}} + n_{\text{solvent}}}$ $= \dfrac{0.2771 \text{ mol}}{0.2771 \text{ mol} + 27.75 \text{ mol}}$ $= 9.89 \times 10^{-3}$
(e) To calculate mole percent, multiply the mole fraction by 100%.	$\text{mol } \% = \chi_{\text{solute}} \times 100\%$ $= 0.989\%$

FOR PRACTICE 12.4

A solution is prepared by dissolving 50.4 g sucrose $(C_{12}H_{22}O_{11})$ in 0.332 kg of water. The final volume of the solution is 355 mL. Calculate the concentration of the solution in each unit.

(a) molarity (b) molality (c) percent by mass

(d) mole fraction (e) mole percent

EXAMPLE 12.5 Converting between Concentration Units

What is the molarity of a 6.56% by mass glucose ($C_6H_{12}O_6$) solution? (The density of the solution is 1.03 g/mL.)

SORT You are given the concentration of a glucose solution in percent by mass and the density of the solution. Find the concentration of the solution in molarity.	**GIVEN:** 6.56% $C_6H_{12}O_6$ density = 1.03 g/mL **FIND:** M
STRATEGIZE Begin with the mass percent concentration of the solution written as a ratio, and separate the numerator from the denominator. Convert the numerator from g $C_6H_{12}O_6$ to mol $C_6H_{12}O_6$. Convert the denominator from g soln to mL of solution and then to L solution. Then divide the numerator (now in mol) by the denominator (now in L) to obtain molarity.	**CONCEPTUAL PLAN** 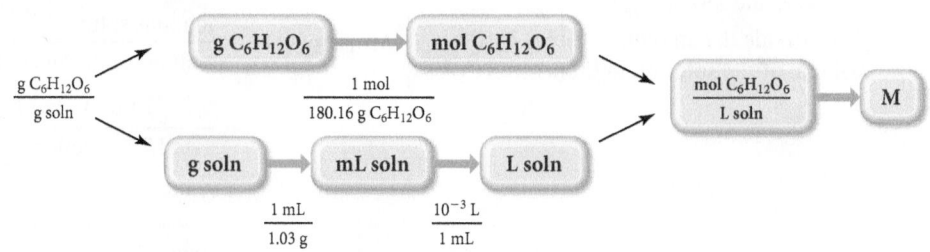 **RELATIONSHIPS USED** $\dfrac{6.56\,\text{g}\,C_6H_{12}O_6}{100\,\text{g soln}}$ (percent by mass written as ratio) $\dfrac{1\,\text{mol}}{180.16\,\text{g}\,C_6H_{12}O_6}$ (from molar mass of glucose) $\dfrac{1\,\text{mL}}{1.03\,\text{g}}$ (from given density of the solution)
SOLVE Begin with the numerator (6.56 g $C_6H_{12}O_6$) and use the molar mass to convert to mol $C_6H_{12}O_6$. Convert the denominator (100 g solution) into mL of solution (using the density) and then to L of solution. Finally, divide mol $C_6H_{12}O_6$ by L solution to arrive at molarity.	**SOLUTION** $6.56\,\cancel{\text{g}\,C_6H_{12}O_6} \times \dfrac{1\,\text{mol}\,C_6H_{12}O_6}{180.16\,\cancel{\text{g}\,C_6H_{12}O_6}} = 0.036\underline{4}12\,\text{mol}\,C_6H_{12}O_6$ $100\,\cancel{\text{g soln}} \times \dfrac{1\,\cancel{\text{mL}}}{1.03\,\cancel{\text{g}}} \times \dfrac{10^{-3}\,\text{L}}{\cancel{\text{mL}}} = 0.097\underline{0}87\,\text{L soln}$ $\dfrac{0.036\underline{4}12\,\text{mol}\,C_6H_{12}O_6}{0.097\underline{0}87\,\text{L soln}} = 0.375\,\text{M}\,C_6H_{12}O_6$

CHECK The units of the answer are correct. The magnitude seems correct. Very high molarities (especially above 25 M) should immediately appear suspect. One liter of water contains about 55 moles of water molecules, so molarities higher than 55 M are physically impossible.

FOR PRACTICE 12.5

What is the molarity of a 10.5% by mass glucose ($C_6H_{12}O_6$) solution? (The density of the solution is 1.03 g/mL.)

FOR MORE PRACTICE 12.5

What is the molality of a 10.5% by mass glucose ($C_6H_{12}O_6$) solution? (The density of the solution is 1.03 g/mL.)

12.6 Colligative Properties: Vapor Pressure Lowering, Freezing Point Depression, Boiling Point Elevation, and Osmotic Pressure

Have you ever wondered why you add salt to the ice in an ice-cream maker? Or why salt is scattered on icy roads in cold climates? Salt lowers the temperature at which a salt water solution freezes. A salt and water solution will remain liquid even below 0 °C. When salt is added to ice in the ice-cream maker, an ice/water/salt mixture forms that can reach a temperature of about −10 °C, at which point the cream freezes. On the winter road, the salt allows the ice to melt when the ambient temperature is below freezing.

▲ In winter, salt is often applied to roads so that the ice will melt at lower temperatures.

The depression of the freezing point of water by salt is an example of a **colligative property**, a property that depends on the number of particles dissolved in solution, not on the type of particle. In this section, we examine four colligative properties: vapor pressure lowering, freezing point depression, boiling point elevation, and osmotic pressure. Since these properties depend on the *number* of dissolved particles, nonelectrolytes are treated slightly differently than electrolytes when determining colligative properties. When 1 mol of a nonelectrolyte dissolves in water, it forms 1 mol of dissolved particles. When 1 mol of an electrolyte dissolves in water, however, it normally forms more than 1 mol of dissolved particles (as shown in Figure 12.14 ▶). For example, when 1 mol of NaCl dissolves in water, it forms 1 mol of dissolved Na^+ ions and 1 mol of dissolved Cl^- ions. Therefore, the resulting solution has 2 mol of dissolved particles. The colligative properties of electrolyte solutions reflect this higher concentration of dissolved particles. In this section we examine colligative properties of nonelectrolyte solutions; we then expand the concept to include electrolyte solutions in Section 12.7.

Cl^- Na^+

4 formula units

8 ions

◀ **FIGURE 12.14** When sodium chloride is dissolved in water, each mole of NaCl produces 2 mol of particles: 1 mol of Na^+ cations and 1 mol of Cl^- anions.

Vapor Pressure Lowering

Recall from Section 11.5 that the vapor pressure of a liquid is the pressure of the gas above the liquid when the two are in dynamic equilibrium (that is, when the rate of vaporization equals the rate of condensation). What is the effect of a nonvolatile nonelectrolyte solute on the vapor pressure of the liquid into which it dissolves? The basic answer to this question is that *the vapor pressure of the solution is lower than the vapor pressure of the pure solvent*. We can understand why this happens in two different ways.

The simplest explanation for why the vapor pressure of a solution is lower than that of the pure solvent is related to the concept of dynamic equilibrium itself. Consider the following representation of a liquid in dynamic equilibrium with its vapor. Here the rate of vaporization is equal to the rate of condensation.

Dynamic equilibrium

When a nonvolatile solute is added, however, the solute particles (shown in red) interfere with the ability of the solvent particles (blue) to vaporize. The rate of vaporization is thus diminished compared to that of the pure solvent.

Rate of vaporization reduced by solute

The change in the rate of vaporization creates an imbalance in the rates; the rate of condensation is now *greater* than the rate of vaporization. The net effect is that some of the molecules that were in the gas state condense into the liquid state. As they condense, the reduced number of molecules in the gas state causes the rate of condensation to decrease. Eventually the two rates become equal again, but only after the concentration of solvent molecules in the gas state has decreased.

Equilibrium reestablished but with fewer molecules in gas phase

The result is a lower vapor pressure for the solution compared to the pure solvent.

A more fundamental explanation of why the vapor pressure of a solution is lower than that of the pure solvent is related to the tendency toward mixing (toward greater entropy) that we discussed in Sections 12.1 and 12.2. Recall that a concentrated solution is a *thirsty* solution—it has the ability to draw solvent to itself. We can see a dramatic demonstration of this tendency by placing a concentrated solution of a nonvolatile solute and a beaker of the pure solvent in a sealed container. Over time, the level of the pure solvent will drop and the level of the solution will rise as molecules vaporize out of the pure solvent and condense into the solution. Notice the similarity between this process

Pure solvent   Concentrated solution

Level of pure solvent drops   Level of solution rises

and the dehydration caused by drinking seawater. In both cases, a concentrated solution has the ability to draw solvent to itself. The reason is nature's tendency to mix. If a pure solvent and concentrated solution are combined in a beaker, they naturally form a mixture in which the concentrated solution becomes less concentrated than it was initially. Similarly, if a pure solvent and concentrated solution are combined in a sealed container—even though they are in separate beakers—the two mix so that the concentrated solution becomes less concentrated.

The net transfer of solvent from the beaker containing pure solvent to the one containing the solution shows that the vapor pressure of the solution is lower than that of the pure solvent. As solvent molecules vaporize, the vapor pressure in the sealed container rises. Before dynamic equilibrium can be attained, however, the pressure exceeds the vapor pressure of the solution, causing molecules to condense into the solution (the beaker on the right). Therefore, molecules constantly vaporize from the pure solvent, but the solvent's vapor pressure is never reached because molecules are constantly condensing into the solution. The result is a continuous transfer of solvent molecules from the pure solvent to the solution.

We can quantify the vapor pressure of a solution with **Raoult's law**:

$$P_{solution} = \chi_{solvent} P^{\circ}_{solvent}$$

In this equation, $P_{solution}$ is the vapor pressure of the solution, $\chi_{solvent}$ is the mole fraction of the solvent, and $P^{\circ}_{solvent}$ is the vapor pressure of the pure solvent at the same temperature. For example, suppose a water sample at 25 °C contains 0.90 mol of water and 0.10 mol of a nonvolatile solute such as sucrose. The pure water has a vapor pressure of 23.8 torr. We calculate the vapor pressure of the solution by substituting into Raoult's law:

$$
\begin{aligned}
P_{solution} &= \chi_{H_2O} P^{\circ}_{H_2O} \\
&= 0.90(23.8 \text{ torr}) \\
&= 21.4 \text{ torr}
\end{aligned}
$$

Notice that the vapor pressure of the solution is directly proportional to the amount of the solvent in the solution. Since the solvent particles compose 90% of all of the particles in the solution, the vapor pressure of the solution is 90% of the vapor pressure of the pure solvent.

To arrive at an equation that shows how much the vapor pressure is lowered by a solute, we define the **vapor pressure lowering (ΔP)** as the difference in vapor pressure between the pure solvent and the solution.

$$\Delta P = P^{\circ}_{solvent} - P_{solution}$$

Then, for a two-component solution, we can substitute $\chi_{solvent} = 1 - \chi_{solute}$ into Raoult's law.

$$
\begin{aligned}
P_{solution} &= \chi_{solvent} P^{\circ}_{solvent} \\
P_{solution} &= (1 - \chi_{solute}) P^{\circ}_{solvent} \\
P^{\circ}_{solvent} - P_{solution} &= \chi_{solute} P^{\circ}_{solvent} \\
\Delta P &= \chi_{solute} P^{\circ}_{solvent}
\end{aligned}
$$

This last equation indicates that the lowering of the vapor pressure is directly proportional to the mole fraction of the solute.

EXAMPLE 12.6 Calculating the Vapor Pressure of a Solution Containing a Nonelectrolyte and Nonvolatile Solute

Calculate the vapor pressure at 25 °C of a solution containing 99.5 g sucrose ($C_{12}H_{22}O_{11}$) and 300.0 mL water. The vapor pressure of pure water at 25 °C is 23.8 torr. Assume the density of water to be 1.00 g/mL.

SORT You are given the mass of sucrose and volume of water in a solution. You are also given the vapor pressure and density of pure water and asked to find the vapor pressure of the solution.	**GIVEN:** 99.5g $C_{12}H_{22}O_{11}$ 300.0 mL H_2O $P^\circ_{H_2O} = 23.8$ torr at 25 °C $d_{H_2O} = 1.00$ g/ml **FIND:** $P_{solution}$
STRATEGIZE Raoult's law relates the vapor pressure of a solution to the mole fraction of the solvent and the vapor pressure of the pure solvent. Begin by calculating the amount in moles of sucrose and water.	**CONCEPTUAL PLAN**
Calculate the mole fraction of the solvent from the calculated amounts of solute and solvent.	$$mol\ C_{12}H_{22}O_{11},\ mol\ H_2O \longrightarrow \chi_{H_2O}$$ $$\chi_{H_2O} = \frac{n_{H_2O}}{n_{H_2O} + n_{C_{12}H_{22}O_{11}}}$$
Then use Raoult's law to calculate the vapor pressure of the solution.	 $$P_{solution} = \chi_{H_2O} P^\circ_{H_2O}$$
SOLVE Calculate the number of moles of each solution component.	**SOLUTION** $99.5\ g\ C_{12}H_{22}O_{11} \times \dfrac{1\ mol\ C_{12}H_{22}O_{11}}{342.30\ g\ C_{12}H_{22}O_{11}} = 0.2907\ mol\ C_{12}H_{22}O_{11}$ $300.0\ mL\ H_2O \times \dfrac{1.00\ g}{1\ mL} \times \dfrac{1\ mol\ H_2O}{18.02\ g\ H_2O} = 16.65\ mol\ H_2O$
Use the number of moles of each component to calculate the mole fraction of the solvent (H_2O).	$\chi_{H_2O} = \dfrac{n_{H_2O}}{n_{C_{12}H_{22}O_{11}} + n_{H_2O}}$ $= \dfrac{16.65\ mol}{0.2907\ mol + 16.65\ mol}$ $= 0.9828$
Use the mole fraction of water and the vapor pressure of pure water to calculate the vapor pressure of the solution.	$P_{solution} = \chi_{H_2O} P^\circ_{H_2O}$ $= 0.9828\ (23.8\ torr)$ $= 23.4\ torr$

CHECK The units of the answer are correct. The magnitude of the answer seems right because the calculated vapor pressure of the solution is just below that of the pure liquid, as you would expect for a solution with a large mole fraction of solvent.

FOR PRACTICE 12.6
Calculate the vapor pressure at 25 °C of a solution containing 55.3 g ethylene glycol ($HOCH_2CH_2CH_2OH$) and 285.2 g water. The vapor pressure of pure water at 25 °C is 23.8 torr.

FOR MORE PRACTICE 12.6
A solution containing ethylene glycol and water has a vapor pressure of 7.88 torr at 10 °C. Pure water has a vapor pressure of 9.21 torr at 10 °C. What is the mole fraction of ethylene glycol in the solution?

Vapor Pressures of Solutions Containing a Volatile (Nonelectrolyte) Solute

Some solutions contain not only a volatile solvent, but also a volatile *solute*. In this case, *both* the solvent and the solute contribute to the overall vapor pressure of the solution. A solution like this may be an **ideal solution** (in which case its behavior follows Raoult's law at all concentrations for both the solvent and the solute) or it may be nonideal (in which case it does not follow Raoult's law). An ideal solution is similar in concept to an ideal gas. Just as an ideal gas follows the ideal gas law exactly, so an ideal solution follows Raoult's law exactly. In an ideal solution, the solute–solvent interactions are similar in magnitude to the solute–solute and solvent–solvent interactions. In this type of solution, the solute simply dilutes the solvent and ideal behavior is observed. The vapor pressure of each of the solution components is described by Raoult's law throughout the entire composition range of the solution. For a two-component solution containing liquids A and B, we can write:

$$P_A = \chi_A P°_A$$
$$P_B = \chi_B P°_B$$

The total pressure above such a solution is the sum of the partial pressures of the components:

$$P_{tot} = P_A + P_B$$

Figure 12.15(a) ▼ is a plot of vapor pressure versus solution composition for an ideal two-component solution.

In a nonideal solution, the solute–solvent interactions are either stronger or weaker than the solvent–solvent interactions. If the solute–solvent interactions are stronger, then the solute tends to prevent the solvent from vaporizing as readily as it would otherwise. If the solution is sufficiently dilute, then the effect will be small and Raoult's law works as an approximation. However, if the solution is not dilute, the effect will be significant and the vapor pressure of the solution will be *less than* that predicted by Raoult's law, as shown in Figure 12.15(b).

> Over a complete range of composition of a solution, it no longer makes sense to designate a solvent and solute, so we simply label the two components A and B.

Deviations from Raoult's Law

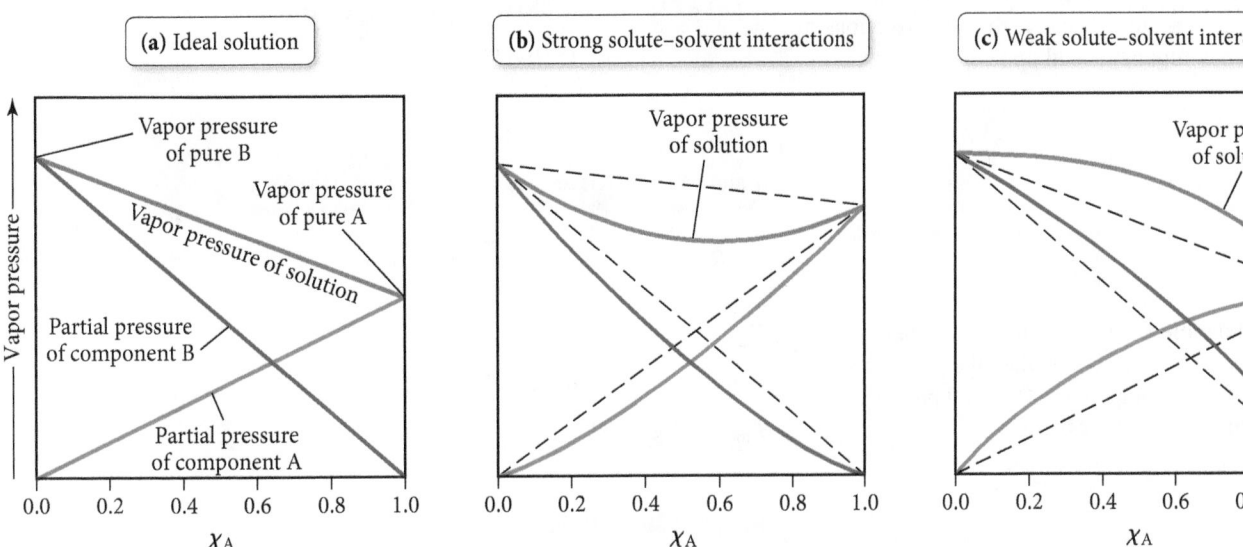

▲ **FIGURE 12.15 Behavior of Ideal and Nonideal Solutions** **(a)** An ideal solution follows Raoult's law for both components. **(b)** A solution with particularly strong solute–solvent interactions displays negative deviations from Raoult's law. **(c)** A solution with particularly weak solute–solvent interactions displays positive deviations from Raoult's law. (The dashed lines in parts b and c represent ideal behavior.)

If, on the other hand, the solute–solvent interactions are weaker than solvent–solvent interactions, then the solute tends to allow more vaporization than would occur with just the solvent. If the solution is not dilute, the effect will be significant and the vapor pressure of the solution will be *greater than* predicted by Raoult's law, as shown in Figure 12.15(c).

EXAMPLE 12.7   Calculating the Vapor Pressure of a Two-Component Solution

A solution contains 3.95 g of carbon disulfide (CS_2) and 2.43 g of acetone (CH_3COCH_3). The vapor pressures at 35 °C of pure carbon disulfide and pure acetone are 515 torr and 332 torr, respectively. Assuming ideal behavior, calculate the vapor pressures of each of the components and the total vapor pressure above the solution. The experimentally measured total vapor pressure of the solution at 35 °C is 645 torr. Is the solution ideal? If not, what can you say about the relative strength of carbon disulfide–acetone interactions compared to the acetone–acetone and carbon disulfide–carbon disulfide interactions?

SORT You are given the masses and vapor pressures of carbon disulfide and acetone and are asked to find the vapor pressures of each component in the mixture and the total pressure assuming ideal behavior.	**GIVEN:** 3.95 g CS_2 2.43 g CH_3COCH_3 $P°_{CS_2}$ = 515 torr (at 35 °C) $P°_{CH_3COCH_3}$ = 332 torr (at 35 °C) $P_{tot}(exp)$ = 645 torr (at 35 °C) **FIND:** P_{CS_2}, $P_{CH_3COCH_3}$, $P_{tot}(ideal)$

STRATEGIZE This problem requires the use of Raoult's law to calculate the partial pressures of each component. In order to use Raoult's law, you must first calculate the mole fractions of the two components. Convert the masses of each component to moles and then use the definition of mole fraction to calculate the mole fraction of carbon disulfide. You can then find the mole fraction of acetone because the mole fractions of the two components add up to 1.	**CONCEPTUAL PLAN**
	
	 ```3.95 g CS_2``` ⟶ ```mol CS_2```
	 $\dfrac{1\ \text{mol } CS_2}{76.15\ \text{g } CS_2}$
	
	 ```2.43 g CH_3COCH_3``` ⟶ ```mol CH_3COCH_3```
	 $\dfrac{1\ \text{mol } CH_3COCH_3}{58.08\ \text{g } CH_3COCH_3}$
	
	 ```mol CS_2, mol CH_3OCH_3``` ⟶ ```χ_{CS_2}, χ_{CH_3COCH_3}```
	 $\chi_{CS_2} = \dfrac{n_{CS_2}}{n_{CS_2} + n_{CH_3COCH_3}}$

Use the mole fraction of each component along with Raoult's law to calculate the partial pressure of each component. The total pressure is the sum of the partial pressures.	$P_{CS_2} = \chi_{CS_2} P°_{CS_2}$ $P_{CH_3COCH_3} = \chi_{CH_3COCH_3} P°_{CH_3COCH_3}$ $P_{tot} = P_{CS_2} + P_{CH_3COCH_3}$ **RELATIONSHIPS USED** $\chi_A = \dfrac{n_A}{n_A + n_B}$ (mole fraction definition) $P_A = \chi_A P°_A$ (Raoult's law)

SOLVE Begin by converting the mass of each component to the amounts in moles.	**SOLUTION** $$3.95 \text{ g CS}_2 \times \frac{1 \text{ mol CS}_2}{76.15 \text{ g CS}_2} = 0.05187 \text{ mol CS}_2$$ $$2.43 \text{ g CH}_3\text{COCH}_3 \times \frac{1 \text{ mol CH}_3\text{COCH}_3}{58.08 \text{ g CH}_3\text{COCH}_3} = 0.04184 \text{ mol CH}_3\text{COCH}_3$$
Then calculate the mole fraction of carbon disulfide.	$$\chi_{CS_2} = \frac{n_{CS_2}}{n_{CS_2} + n_{CH_3COCH_3}}$$ $$= \frac{0.05187 \text{ mol}}{0.05187 \text{ mol} + 0.04184 \text{ mol}}$$ $$= 0.5535$$
Calculate the mole fraction of acetone by subtracting the mole fraction of carbon disulfide from 1.	$$\chi_{CH_3COCH_3} = 1 - 0.5535$$ $$= 0.4465$$
Calculate the partial pressures of carbon disulfide and acetone by using Raoult's law and the given values of the vapor pressures of the pure substances.	$$P_{CS_2} = \chi_{CS_2} P^{\circ}_{CS_2}$$ $$= 0.5535 \,(515 \text{ torr})$$ $$= 285 \text{ torr}$$ $$P_{CH_3COCH_3} = \chi_{CH_3COCH_3} P^{\circ}_{CH_3COCH_3}$$ $$= 0.4465 \,(332 \text{ torr})$$ $$= 148 \text{ torr}$$
Calculate the total pressure by summing the partial pressures.	$$P_{tot}(\text{ideal}) = 285 \text{ torr} + 148 \text{ torr}$$ $$= 433 \text{ torr}$$
Lastly, compare the calculated total pressure for the ideal case to the experimentally measured total pressure. Since the experimentally measured pressure is greater than the calculated pressure, we can conclude that the interactions between the two components are weaker than the interactions between the components themselves.	$$P_{tot}(\text{exp}) = 645 \text{ torr}$$ $$P_{tot}(\text{exp}) > P_{tot}(\text{ideal})$$ The solution is not ideal and shows positive deviations from Raoult's law. Therefore, carbon disulfide–acetone interactions must be weaker than acetone–acetone and carbon disulfide–carbon disulfide interactions.

CHECK The units of the answer (torr) are correct. The magnitude seems reasonable given the partial pressures of the pure substances.

FOR PRACTICE 12.7
A solution of benzene (C_6H_6) and toluene (C_7H_8) is 25.0% benzene by mass. The vapor pressures of pure benzene and pure toluene at 25 °C are 94.2 torr and 28.4 torr, respectively. Assuming ideal behavior, calculate the following:
(a) The vapor pressure of each of the solution components in the mixture.
(b) The total pressure above the solution.
(c) The composition of the vapor in mass percent.

Why is the composition of the vapor different from the composition of the solution?

Conceptual Connection 12.5 **Raoult's Law**

A solution contains equal amounts (in moles) of liquid components A and B. The vapor pressure of pure A is 100 mmHg and that of pure B is 200 mmHg. The experimentally measured vapor pressure of the solution is 120 mmHg. What are the relative strengths of the solute–solute, solute–solvent, and solvent–solvent interactions in this solution?

Freezing Point Depression and Boiling Point Elevation

Vapor pressure lowering occurs at all temperatures. We can see the effect of vapor pressure lowering over a range of temperatures by comparing the phase diagrams for a pure solvent and for a solution containing a nonvolatile solute:

▶ A nonvolatile solute lowers the vapor pressure of a solution, resulting in a lower freezing point and an elevated boiling point.

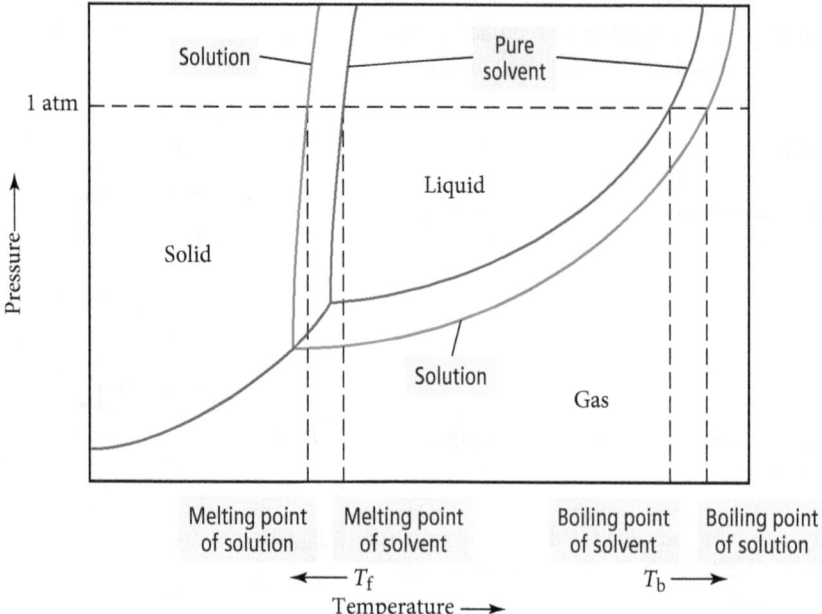

Notice that the vapor pressure for the solution is shifted downward compared to that of the pure solvent. Consequently, the vapor pressure curve intersects the solid–gas curve at a lower temperature. The net effect is that the solution has a *lower melting point* and a *higher boiling point* than the pure solvent. These effects are called **freezing point depression** and **boiling point elevation**, both of which are colligative properties (like vapor pressure lowering).

The freezing point of a solution containing a nonvolatile solute is lower than the freezing point of the pure solvent. For example, antifreeze, used to prevent the freezing of engine blocks in cold climates, is an aqueous solution of ethylene glycol $(C_2H_6O_2)$. The more concentrated the solution, the lower the freezing point becomes.

The amount that the freezing point decreases is given by the following equation:

$$\Delta T_f = m \times K_f$$

where

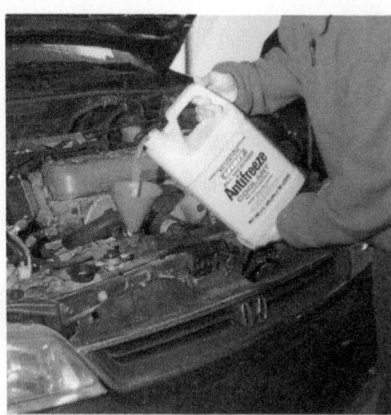

▲ Antifreeze is an aqueous solution of ethylene glycol. The solution has a lower freezing point and higher boiling point than pure water.

- ΔT_f is the change in temperature of the freezing point in Celsius degrees (relative to the freezing point of the pure solvent), usually reported as a positive number;
- m is the molality of the solution in moles solute per kilogram solvent;
- K_f is the freezing point depression constant for the solvent.

For water,

$$K_f = 1.86 \, °C/m$$

When an aqueous solution containing a dissolved solid solute freezes slowly, the ice that forms does not normally contain much of the solute. For example, when ice forms in ocean

TABLE 12.8 Freezing Point Depression and Boiling Point Elevation Constants for Several Liquid Solvents

Solvent	Normal Freezing Point (°C)	K_f (°C/m)	Normal Boiling Point (°C)	K_b (°C/m)
Benzene (C_6H_6)	5.5	5.12	80.1	2.53
Carbon tetrachloride (CCl_4)	− 22.9	29.9	76.7	5.03
Chloroform ($CHCl_3$)	− 63.5	4.70	61.2	3.63
Ethanol (C_2H_5OH)	− 114.1	1.99	78.3	1.22
Diethyl ether ($C_4H_{10}O$)	− 116.3	1.79	34.6	2.02
Water (H_2O)	0.00	1.86	100.0	0.512

water, the ice is not salt water, but freshwater. As the ice forms, the crystal structure of the ice tends to exclude the solute particles. You can verify this yourself by partially freezing a salt water solution in the freezer. Take out the newly formed ice, rinse it several times, and taste it. Compare its taste to the taste of the original solution. The ice is much less salty.

Table 12.8 provides freezing point depression and boiling point elevation constants for several liquids. Calculating the freezing point of a solution involves substituting into the freezing point depression equation as Example 12.8 demonstrates.

EXAMPLE 12.8 Freezing Point Depression

Calculate the freezing point of a 1.7 m aqueous ethylene glycol solution

SORT You are given the molality of a solution and asked to find its freezing point.	**GIVEN:** 1.7 m solution **FIND:** freezing point (from ΔT_f)
STRATEGIZE To solve this problem, use the freezing point depression equation.	**CONCEPTUAL PLAN** $\boxed{m} \longrightarrow \boxed{\Delta T_f}$ $\Delta T_f = m \times K_f$
SOLVE Substitute into the equation to calculate ΔT_f. The actual freezing point is the freezing point of pure water (0.00 °C) − ΔT_f.	**SOLUTION** $\Delta T_f = m \times K_f$ $\quad = 1.7\,m \times 1.86\ °C/m$ $\quad = 3.2\ °C$ Freezing point = 0.00 °C − 3.2 °C $\quad\quad\quad\quad\quad\quad = -3.2\ °C$

CHECK The units of the answer are correct. The magnitude seems about right. The expected range for freezing points of an aqueous solution is anywhere from −10 °C to just below 0 °C. Any answers out of this range would be suspect.

FOR PRACTICE 12.8

Calculate the freezing point of a 2.6 m aqueous sucrose solution.

The boiling point of a solution containing a nonvolatile solute is higher than the boiling point of the pure solvent. In automobiles, antifreeze not only prevents the freezing of water within engine blocks in cold climates, it also prevents the boiling of water within engine blocks in hot climates. The amount that the boiling point rises in solutions is given by the equation:

$$\Delta T_b = m \times K_b$$

where

- ΔT_b is the change in temperature of the boiling point in Celsius degrees (relative to the boiling point of the pure solvent);

• m is the molality of the solution in moles solute per kilogram solvent;
• K_b is the boiling point elevation constant for the solvent.

For water,

$$K_b = 0.512 \,°C/m$$

Calculating the boiling point of a solution involves substituting into the boiling-point elevation equation, as Example 12.9 demonstrates.

Conceptual Connection 12.6 Boiling Point Elevation

Solution A is a 1.0 M solution with a nonionic solute and water as the solvent. Solution B is a 1.0 M solution with the same nonionic solute and ethanol as the solvent. Which solution has the greatest increase in its boiling point (relative to the pure solvent)?

EXAMPLE 12.9 Boiling Point Elevation

What mass of ethylene glycol $(C_2H_6O_2)$, in grams, must be added to 1.0 kg of water to produce a solution that boils at 105.0 °C?

SORT You are given the desired boiling point of an ethylene glycol solution containing 1.0 kg of water and asked to find the mass of ethylene glycol you need to add to achieve the boiling point.

GIVEN: $\Delta T_b = 5.0\,°C$, 1.0 kg H_2O

FIND: g $C_2H_6O_2$

STRATEGIZE To solve this problem, use the boiling-point elevation equation to calculate the desired molality of the solution from ΔT_b.

CONCEPTUAL PLAN

$$\Delta T_b = m \times K_b$$

Then use that molality to determine how many moles of ethylene glycol are needed per kilogram of water. Finally, calculate the molar mass of ethylene glycol and use it to convert from moles of ethylene glycol to mass of ethylene glycol.

From first step

RELATIONSHIPS USED $C_2H_6O_2$ molar mass $= 62.07\,g/mol$
$$\Delta T_b = m \times K_b \,(\text{boiling point elevation})$$

SOLVE Begin by solving the boiling point elevation equation for molality and substituting the required quantities to calculate m.

SOLUTION

$$\Delta T_b = m \times K_b$$

$$m = \frac{\Delta T_b}{K_b} = \frac{5.0\,°C}{0.512\,\frac{°C}{m}} = 9.\underline{77}m$$

$$1.0\,\text{kg}\,H_2O \times \frac{9.\underline{77}\,\text{mol}\,C_2H_6O_2}{\text{kg}\,H_2O} \times \frac{62.07\,\text{g}\,C_2H_6O_2}{1\,\text{mol}\,C_2H_6O_2} = 6.1 \times 10^2\,\text{g}\,C_2H_6O_2$$

CHECK The units of the answer are correct. The magnitude might seem a little high initially, but the boiling point elevation constant is so small that a lot of solute is required to raise the boiling point by a small amount.

FOR PRACTICE 12.9
Calculate the boiling point of a 3.60 m aqueous sucrose solution.

Chemistry in Your Day

Antifreeze in Frogs

Wood frogs (*Rana sylvatica*) look like most other frogs. They are a few inches long and have characteristic greenish-brown skin. However, wood frogs survive cold winters in a remarkable way—they partially freeze. In its partially frozen state, a wood frog has no heartbeat, no blood circulation, no breathing, and no brain activity. Within 1–2 hours of thawing, however, these vital functions return and the frog hops off to find food. How does the wood frog do this?

Most cold-blooded animals cannot survive freezing temperatures because the water within their cells freezes. As we learned in Section 11.9, when water freezes, it expands, irreversibly damaging cells. When the wood frog hibernates for the winter, however, it produces large amounts of glucose that is secreted into its bloodstream and fills the interior of its cells. When the temperature drops below freezing, extracellular body fluids, such as those in the frog's abdominal cavity, freeze solid. Fluids within cells, however, remain liquid because the high glucose concentration lowers their freezing point. In other words, the concentrated glucose solution within the frog's cells acts as antifreeze, preventing the water within the cells from freezing and allowing the frog to survive.

Question

The wood frog can survive at body temperatures as low as -8.0 °C. Calculate the molality of a glucose solution $(C_6H_{12}O_6)$ required to lower the freezing point of water to -8.0 °C.

▲ The wood frog survives winter by partially freezing. It protects its cells by flooding them with glucose, which acts as an antifreeze.

Osmotic Pressure

The process by which seawater causes dehydration (discussed in the opening section of this chapter) is *osmosis*. **Osmosis** is the flow of solvent from a solution of lower solute concentration to one of higher solute concentration. Concentrated solutions draw solvent from more dilute solutions because of nature's tendency to mix.

Figure 12.16 ▼ illustrates an osmosis cell. The left side of the cell contains a concentrated saltwater solution and the right side of the cell contains pure water. A **semipermeable membrane**—a membrane that selectively allows some substances to pass through but not

Osmosis and Osmotic Pressure

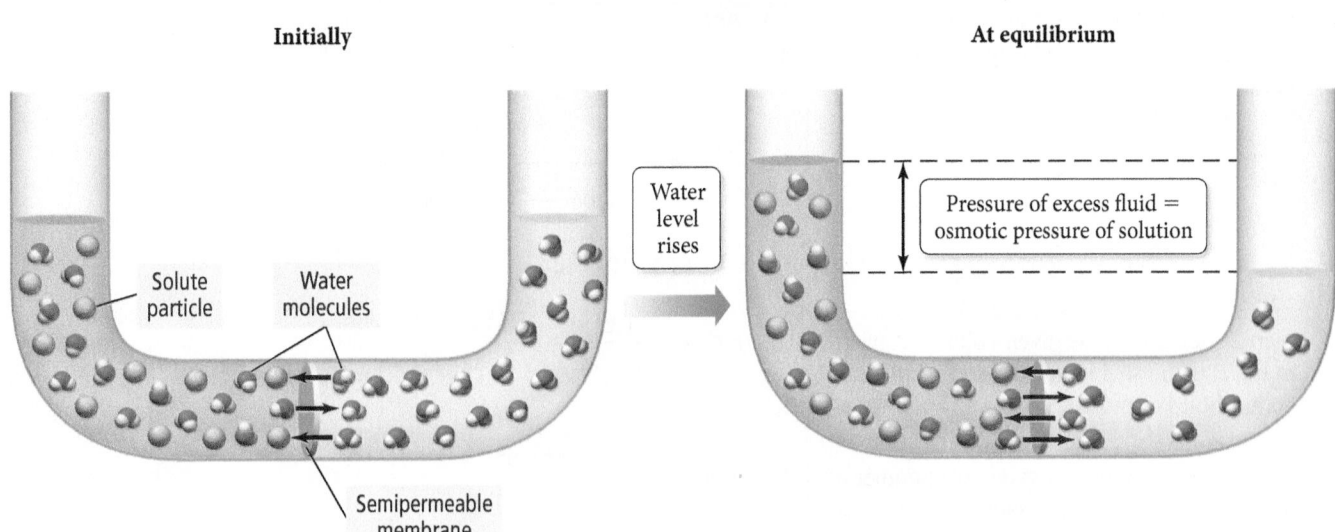

Initially

At equilibrium

Water level rises

Pressure of excess fluid = osmotic pressure of solution

Solute particle   Water molecules

Semipermeable membrane

▲ **FIGURE 12.16 An Osmosis Cell**   In an osmosis cell, water flows from the pure-water side of the cell through the semipermeable membrane to the salt water side.

others—separates the two halves of the cell. Water flows by osmosis from the pure-water side of the cell through the semipermeable membrane and into the saltwater side. Over time, the water level on the left side of the cell rises, while the water level on the right side of the cell falls. If external pressure is applied to the water in the left cell, this process can be opposed and even stopped. The pressure required to stop the osmotic flow, called the **osmotic pressure**, is given by the following equation:

$$\Pi = MRT$$

where M is the molarity of the solution, T is the temperature (in Kelvin), and R is the ideal gas constant (0.08206 L · atm/mol · K).

EXAMPLE 12.10 Osmotic Pressure

The osmotic pressure of a solution containing 5.87 mg of an unknown protein per 10.0 mL of solution is 2.45 torr at 25 °C. Find the molar mass of the unknown protein.

SORT You are given that a solution of an unknown protein contains 5.87 mg of the protein per 10.0 mL of solution. You are also given the osmotic pressure of the solution at a particular temperature and asked to find the molar mass of the unknown protein.	**GIVEN:** 5.87 mg protein 10.0 mL solution $\Pi = 2.45$ torr $T = 25$ °C **FIND:** molar mass of protein (g/mol)
STRATEGIZE Step 1: Use the given osmotic pressure and temperature to find the molarity of the protein solution.	**CONCEPTUAL PLAN** $\Pi = MRT$
Step 2: Use the molarity calculated in step 1 to find the number of moles of protein in 10 mL of solution.	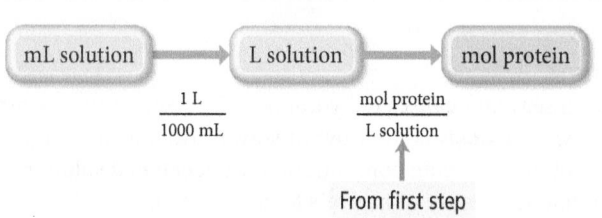 From first step
Step 3: Finally, use the number of moles of the protein calculated in step 2 and the given mass of the protein in 10.0 mL of solution to find the molar mass	Molar mass $= \dfrac{\text{mass protein}}{\text{moles protein}}$ **RELATIONSHIPS USED** $\Pi = MRT$ (osmotic pressure equation)
SOLVE Step 1: Begin by solving the osmotic pressure equation for molarity and substituting in the required quantities in the correct units to calculate M.	**SOLUTION** $\Pi = MRT$ $M = \dfrac{\Pi}{RT} = \dfrac{2.45 \text{ torr} \times \dfrac{1 \text{ atm}}{760 \text{ torr}}}{0.08206 \dfrac{\text{L} \cdot \text{atm}}{\text{mol} \cdot \text{K}} (298 \text{ K})}$ $= 1.3\underline{1}8 \times 10^{-4}$ M
Step 2: Begin with the given volume, convert to liters, then use the molarity to find the number of moles of protein.	$10.0 \text{ mL} \times \dfrac{1 \text{ L}}{1000 \text{ mL}} \times \dfrac{1.3\underline{1}8 \times 10^{-4} \text{ mol}}{\text{L}}$ $= 1.3\underline{1}8 \times 10^{-6}$ mol
Step 3: Use the given mass and the number of moles from step 2 to calculate the molar mass of the protein.	Molar mass $= \dfrac{\text{mass protein}}{\text{moles protein}}$ $= \dfrac{5.87 \times 10^{-3} \text{ g}}{1.3\underline{1}8 \times 10^{-6} \text{ mol}} = 4.45 \times 10^{3}$ g/mol

CHECK The units of the answer are correct. The magnitude might seem a little high initially, but proteins are large molecules and therefore have high molar masses.

FOR PRACTICE 12.10

Calculate the osmotic pressure (in atm) of a solution containing 1.50 g ethylene glycol ($C_2H_6O_2$) in 50.0 mL of solution at 25 °C.

12.7 Colligative Properties of Strong Electrolyte Solutions

At the beginning of Section 12.6, we saw that colligative properties depend on the number of dissolved particles and that electrolytes must therefore be treated slightly differently than nonelectrolytes when determining colligative properties. For example, the freezing point depression of a 0.10 m sucrose solution is $\Delta T_f = 0.186$ °C. However, the freezing point depression of a 0.10 m sodium chloride solution is nearly twice this large. Why? Because 1 mol of sodium chloride dissociates into nearly 2 mol of ions in solution. The ratio of moles of particles in solution to moles of formula units dissolved is called the **van't Hoff factor** (i):

$$i = \frac{\text{moles of particles in solution}}{\text{moles of fomula units dissolved}}$$

TABLE 12.9 Van't Hoff Factors at 0.05 m Concentration in Aqueous Solution

Solute	i Expected	i Measured
Nonelectrolyte	1	1
NaCl	2	1.9
MgSO$_4$	2	1.3
MgCl$_2$	3	2.7
K$_2$SO$_4$	3	2.6
FeCl$_3$	4	3.4

Since 1 mol of NaCl produces 2 mol of particles in solution, we expect the van't Hoff factor for NaCl to be exactly 2. In reality, this expected factor only occurs in very dilute solutions. For example, the van't Hoff factor for a 0.10 m NaCl solution is 1.87 and that for a 0.010 m NaCl solution is 1.94. The van't Hoff factor approaches the expected value at infinite dilution (as the concentration approaches zero). Table 12.9 lists the actual and expected van't Hoff factors for a number of solutes.

The reason that van't Hoff factors do not exactly equal expected values is that some ions effectively pair in solution. We expect the dissociation of an ionic compound to be complete in solution. In reality, however, the dissociation is not complete— at any moment, some cations pair with anions (Figure 12.17 ▶), slightly reducing the number of particles in solution.

Ion pairing

◀ **FIGURE 12.17 Ion Pairing** Hydrated anions and cations may get close enough together to effectively pair, lowering the concentration of particles below what would be expected.

To calculate freezing point depression, boiling point elevation, and osmotic pressure of ionic solutions we use the van't Hoff factor in each equation as follows:

$$\Delta T_f = im \times K_f \text{ (freezing point depression)}$$
$$\Delta T_b = im \times K_b \text{ (boiling point elevation)}$$
$$\Pi = iMRT \text{ (osmotic pressure)}$$

Conceptual Connection 12.7 Colligative Properties

Which solution has the highest boiling point?

(a) 0.50 M $C_{12}H_{22}O_{11}$
(b) 0.50 M NaCl
(c) 0.50 M MgCl$_2$

EXAMPLE 12.11   Van't Hoff Factor and Freezing Point Depression

The freezing point of an aqueous 0.050 m $CaCl_2$ solution is -0.27 °C. What is the van't Hoff factor (i) for $CaCl_2$ at this concentration? How does it compare to the expected value of i?

SORT You are given the molality of a solution and its freezing point. You are asked to find the value of i, the van't Hoff factor, and compare it to the expected value.	**GIVEN:** 0.050 m $CaCl_2$ solution, $$\Delta T_f = 0.27 \text{ °C}$$ **FIND:** i
STRATEGIZE To solve this problem, use the freezing point depression equation including the van't Hoff factor.	**CONCEPTUAL PLAN** $$\Delta T_f = im \times K_f$$
SOLVE Solve the freezing point depression equation for i, substituting in the given quantities to calculate its value. The expected value of i for $CaCl_2$ is 3 because calcium chloride forms 3 mol of ions for each mole of calcium chloride that dissolves. The experimental value is slightly less than 3, probably because of ion pairing.	**SOLUTION** $$\Delta T_f = im \times K_f$$ $$i = \frac{\Delta T_f}{m \times K_f}$$ $$= \frac{0.27 \text{ °C}}{0.050 \text{ }m \times \dfrac{1.86 \text{ °C}}{m}}$$ $$= 2.9$$

CHECK The answer has no units, as expected since i is a ratio. The magnitude is about right since it is close to the value you would expect upon complete dissociation of $CaCl_2$.

FOR PRACTICE 12.11
Calculate the freezing point of an aqueous 0.10 m $FeCl_3$ solution using a van't Hoff factor of 3.2.

Strong Electrolytes and Vapor Pressure

Just as the freezing point depression of a solution containing an electrolyte solute is greater than that of a solution containing the same concentration of a nonelectrolyte solute, so the vapor pressure lowering is greater (for the same reasons). The vapor pressure for a sodium chloride solution, for example, is lowered about twice as much as it is for a nonelectrolyte solution of the same concentration. To calculate the vapor pressure of a solution containing an ionic solute, we need to account for the dissociation of the solute when we calculate the mole fraction of the solvent, as shown in Example 12.12.

EXAMPLE 12.12   Calculating the Vapor Pressure of a Solution Containing an Ionic Solute

A solution contains 0.102 mol $Ca(NO_3)_2$ and 0.927 mol H_2O. Calculate the vapor pressure of the solution at 55 °C. The vapor pressure of pure water at 55 °C is 118.1 torr. (Assume that the solute completely dissociates.)

SORT You are given the number of moles of each component of a solution and asked to find the vapor pressure of the solution. You are also given the vapor pressure of pure water at the appropriate temperature.	**GIVEN:** 0.102 mol $Ca(NO_3)_2$ 0.927 mol H_2O $P^\circ_{H_2O} = 118.1$ torr (at 55 °C) **FIND:** $P_{solution}$
STRATEGIZE To solve this problem, use Raoult's law as you did in Example 12.6. Calculate $\chi_{solvent}$ from the given amounts of solute and solvent.	**CONCEPTUAL PLAN** $$\boxed{\chi_{H_2O}, P^\circ_{H_2O}} \longrightarrow \boxed{P_{solution}}$$ $$P_{solution} = \chi_{H_2O} P^\circ_{H_2O}$$

SOLVE The key to this problem is to understand the dissociation of calcium nitrate. Write an equation showing the dissociation.	**SOLUTION** $Ca(NO_3)_2(s) \longrightarrow Ca^{2+}(aq) + 2\,NO_3^-(aq)$
Since 1 mol of calcium nitrate dissociates into 3 mol of dissolved particles, the number of moles of calcium nitrate must be multiplied by 3 when computing the mole fraction.	$\chi_{H_2O} = \dfrac{n_{H_2O}}{3 \times n_{Ca(NO_3)_2} + n_{H_2O}}$ $= \dfrac{0.927 \text{ mol}}{3\,(0.102)\text{ mol} + 0.927\text{mol}}$ $= 0.7518$
Use the mole fraction of water and the vapor pressure of pure water to calculate the vapor pressure of the solution.	$P_{solution} = \chi_{H_2O}P^\circ_{H_2O}$ $= 0.7518\,(118.1 \text{ torr})$ $= 88.8 \text{ torr}$

CHECK The units of the answer are correct. The magnitude also seems right because the calculated vapor pressure of the solution is significantly less than that of the pure solvent, as you would expect for a solution with a significant amount of solute.

FOR PRACTICE 12.12
A solution contains 0.115 mol H_2O and an unknown number of moles of sodium chloride. The vapor pressure of the solution at 30 °C is 25.7 torr. The vapor pressure of pure water at 30 °C is 31.8 torr. Calculate the number of moles of sodium chloride in the solution.

Colligative Properties and Medical Solutions

Doctors and others healthcare workers often administer solutions to patients. The osmotic pressure of these solutions is controlled for the desired effect on the patient. Solutions having osmotic pressures greater than those of body fluids are called *hyperosmotic*. These solutions take water out of cells and tissues. When a human cell is placed in a hyperosmotic solution, it tends to shrivel as it loses water to the surrounding solution (Figure 12.18b ▼). Solutions having osmotic pressures less than those of body fluids are called *hyposmotic*. These solutions pump water into cells. When a human cell is placed in a hyposmotic solution—such as pure water, for example—water enters the cell, sometimes causing it to burst (Figure 12.18c).

Isosmotic solution	Hyperosmotic solution	Hyposmotic solution

(a) Normal red blood cells   (b) Shriveled red blood cells   (c) Swollen red blood cells

▲ **FIGURE 12.18 Red Blood Cells and Osmosis** (a) In an isosmotic solution, red blood cells have the normal shape shown here. In a hyperosmotic solution (b), they lose water and shrivel. In a hyposmotic solution (c), they swell up and may burst as water flows into the cell.

Intravenous solutions—those that are administered directly into a patient's veins—must have osmotic pressures equal to those of body fluids. These solutions are called *isosmotic* (or *isotonic*). When a patient is given an IV in a hospital, the majority of the fluid is usually an isosmotic saline solution—a solution containing 0.9 g NaCl per 100 mL of solution. In medicine and in other health-related fields, solution concentrations are often reported in units that indicate the mass of the solute per given volume of solution. Also common is *percent mass to volume*—which is the mass of the solute in grams divided by the volume of the solution in milliliters times 100%. In these units, the concentration of an isotonic saline solution is 0.9% mass/volume.

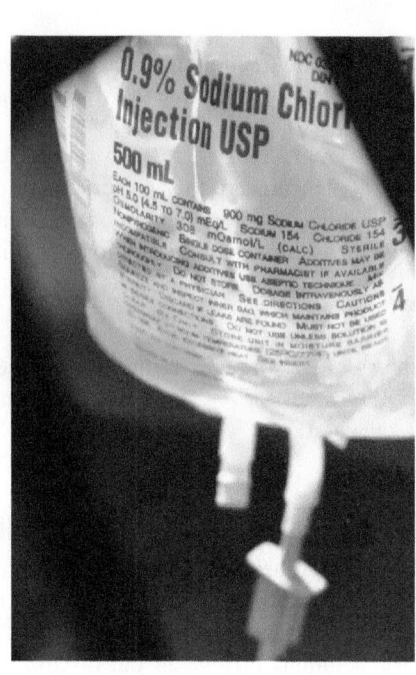

▶ Fluids used for intravenous transfusion must be isosmotic with bodily fluids—that is, they must have the same osmotic pressure.

12.8 Colloids

When you mix water and soap together, the resulting mixture has a distinctive haze (Figure 12.19 ◀). Soapy water is hazy because soap and water form a *colloidal dispersion,* rather than a true solution. A **colloidal dispersion,** or more simply a **colloid,** is a mixture in which a dispersed substance (which is solute-like) is finely divided in a dispersing medium (which is solvent-like). Examples of colloids including fog, smoke, whipped cream, and milk are listed in Table 12.10

Whether or not a mixture is a colloid is determined by the size of the particles it contains. If the particles are small (for example, individual small molecules), then the mixture is a solution. If the particles have a diameter greater than 1 μm (for example, grains of sand), then the mixture is a heterogeneous mixture. Sand stirred into water will slowly settle out of the water. *If the particles are between 1 nm and 1000 nm in size, the mixture is a colloid.* Colloidal particles are small enough that they stay dispersed throughout the dispersing medium by collisions with other molecules or atoms. When you view a colloidal particle dispersed in a liquid under a microscope, you can witness its jittery motion, which proceeds along a random path, as shown in Figure 12.20 ▶. This motion, called Brownian motion, is caused by collisions with molecules in the liquid. In the beginning of the twentieth century, Brownian motion was a decisive factor in confirming the molecular and atomic nature of matter.

Soap forms a colloid because of its unique structure, shown in Figure 12.21 ▶. One end of the molecule is ionic and therefore interacts strongly with water molecules via ion–dipole interactions. However, the other end of the soap molecule is a long, nonpolar,

▲ FIGURE 12.19 **A Colloid** Soapy water is an example of a colloidal dispersion. The haze is due to the scattering of light by the colloidal particles.

TABLE 12.10 Types of Colloidal Dispersions

Classification	Dispersing Substance (Solute-like)	Dispersing Medium (Solvent-like)		Example
Aerosol	Liquid	Gas		Fog (water droplets in air)
Solid aerosol	Solid	Gas		Smoke (ash in air)
Foam	Gas	Liquid		Whipped cream (air bubbles in butterfat)
Emulsion	Liquid	Liquid		Milk (milk fat globules in water)
Solid emulsion	Liquid	Solid		Opal (water in silica glass)

▲ **FIGURE 12.20 Brownian Motion** A colloidal particle exhibits Brownian motion, moving in a jerky, haphazard path as it undergoes collisions with molecules in the liquid.

hydrocarbon tail. When enough soap is added to water, the soap molecules aggregate in structures called *micelles* (Figure 12.22 ▼). In a micelle, the nonpolar hydrocarbon tails crowd into the center of a sphere to maximize their interactions with one another. The ionic heads orient toward the surface of the sphere where they can interact with water molecules. The micelle structures are responsible for the haze seen in soapy water—they are too small to be seen by the naked eye, but they still scatter light (as particles in other

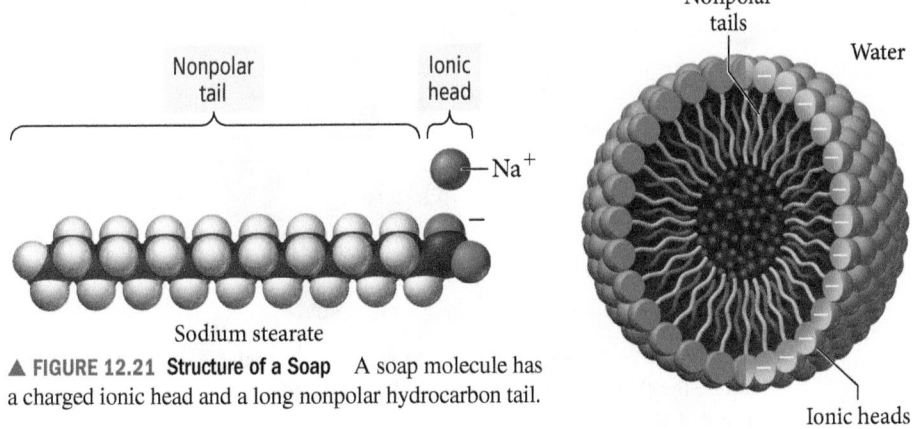

▲ **FIGURE 12.21 Structure of a Soap** A soap molecule has a charged ionic head and a long nonpolar hydrocarbon tail.

◄ **FIGURE 12.22 Micelle Structure** In a micelle, the nonpolar tails of soap molecules (or of other molecules that have properties that are similar to soap) are oriented inward (where they can interact with one another), and the ionic heads are oriented outward (where they can interact with the polar water molecules).

▲ **FIGURE 12.23 The Tyndall Effect**   When a light beam passes through a colloidal suspension (left), it is visible because the colloid particles scatter some of the light. The beam is not visible in pure water (right), nor would it be visible in a noncolloidal solution.

▲ Light beams are invisible when they are not scattered by colloidally dispersed particles such as dust or mist in the air.

types of colloids do). This scattering of light by a colloidal dispersion is known as the **Tyndall effect** (Figure 12.23 ▲). You can observe the Tyndall effect in other colloids such as fog (water droplets dispersed in air) or dusty air. In fact, you can use the Tyndall effect as a test to determine whether a mixture is a solution or a colloid, since solutions contain completely dissolved solute molecules that are too small to scatter light.

Colloidal suspensions of micelles are kept stable by electrostatic repulsions that occur at their surfaces. For example, in soap, the ionic heads of the soap molecules compose the surface of the spherical particle (Figure 12.24 ▼). These ionic heads interact strongly with water molecules but repel other colloid particles. Heating a colloid composed of micelles can destroy the micelles because collisions occur with enough force to overcome the electrostatic repulsions and allow the molecules within the micelles to coalesce with those in other micelles. Similarly, adding an electrolyte to a colloidal suspension of micelles can also disrupt the electrostatic repulsions that occur between the particles and thus destroy the colloid. For this reason, soap does not work well in a salt water solution.

The particles in a colloid need not be clusters of molecules. Some colloids, such as many protein solutions, contain dispersed macromolecules. For example, blood contains dispersed hemoglobin. The hemoglobin molecules are so large that they scatter light; thus, blood is considered a colloid.

▲ **FIGURE 12.24 Micelle Repulsions**   Micelles do not coalesce, because the charged surface of one micelle repels the charged surface of another.

CHAPTER IN REVIEW

Self Assessment Quiz

Q1. Which compound do you expect to be soluble in octane (C_8H_{18})?
 a) CH_3OH b) CBr_4 c) H_2O d) NH_3

Q2. An aqueous solution is saturated in both potassium chlorate and carbon dioxide gas at room temperature. What happens when the solution is warmed to 85 °C?
 a) Potassium chlorate precipitates out of solution.
 b) Carbon dioxide bubbles out of solution.
 c) Potassium chlorate precipitates out of solution and carbon dioxide bubbles out of solution.
 d) Nothing happens; all of the potassium chloride and the carbon dioxide remain dissolved in solution.

Q3. A 500.0 ml sample of pure water is allowed to come to equilibrium with pure oxygen gas at a pressure of 755 mmHg. What mass of oxygen gas dissolves in the water? (The Henry's law constant for oxygen gas is 1.3×10^{-3} M/atm.)
 a) 15.7 g   b) 6.5×10^{-3} g   c) 0.041 g   d) 0.021 g

Q4. A potassium bromide solution is 7.55 % potassium bromide by mass and its density is 1.03 g/mL. What mass of potassium bromide is contained in 35.8 mL of the solution?
 a) 2.78 g   b) 2.70 g   c) 4.88 g   d) 2.62 g

Q5. A solution contains 22.4 g glucose ($C_6H_{12}O_6$) dissolved in 0.500 L of water. What is the molality of the solution? (Assume a density of 1.00 g/mL for water.)
 a) 0.238 m b) 44.8 m c) 0.249 m d) 4.03 m

Q6. A sodium nitrate solution is 12.5% $NaNO_3$ by mass and has a density of 1.02 g/mL. Calculate the molarity of the solution.
 a) 1.44 M   b) 12.8 M   c) 6.67 M   d) 1.50 M

Q7. Determine the vapor pressure of an aqueous ethylene glycol ($C_2H_6O_2$) solution that is 14.8 % $C_2H_6O_2$ by mass. The vapor pressure of pure water at 25 °C is 23.8 torr.
 a) 3.52 torr   b) 22.7 torr   c) 1.14 torr   d) 20.3 torr

Q8. A solution contains a mixture of substance A and substance B, both of which are volatile. The mole fraction of substance A is 0.35. At 32 °C the vapor pressure of pure A is 87 mmHg and the vapor pressure of pure B is 122 mmHg. What is the total vapor pressure of the solution at this temperature?
 a) 110 mmHg   b) 209 mmHg
 c) 99.3 mmHg   d) 73.2 mmHg

Q9. What mass of glucose ($C_6H_{12}O_6$) should be dissolved in 10.0 kg of water to obtain a solution with a freezing point of −4.2 °C?
 a) 0.023 kg   b) 4.1 kg   c) 0.41 kg   d) 14.1 kg

Q10. Which of these aqueous solutions has the highest boiling point?
 a) 1.25 M $C_6H_{12}O_6$
 b) 1.25 M KNO_3
 c) 1.25 M $Ca(NO_3)_2$
 d) None of the above (they all have the same boiling point)

Q11. The osmotic pressure of a solution containing 22.7 mg of an unknown protein in 50.0 mL of solution is 2.88 mmHg at 25 °C. Determine the molar mass of the protein.
 a) 246 g/mol   b) 3.85 g/mol
 c) 2.93×10^3 g/mol   d) 147 g/mol

Q12. The enthalpy of solution for NaOH is −44.46 kJ/mol. What can you conclude about the relative magnitudes of the absolute values of ΔH_{solute} and $\Delta H_{hydration}$, where ΔH_{solute} is the heat associated with separating the solute particles and $\Delta H_{hydration}$ is the heat associated with dissolving the solute particles in water?
 a) $|\Delta H_{solute}| > |\Delta H_{hydration}|$
 b) $|\Delta H_{solute}| < |\Delta H_{hydration}|$
 c) $|\Delta H_{solute}| = |\Delta H_{hydration}|$
 d) None of the above (nothing can be concluded about the relative magnitudes)

Q13. A 2.4 m aqueous solution of an ionic compound with the formula MX_2 has a boiling point of 103.4 °C. Calculate the van't Hoff factor (i) for MX_2 at this concentration.
 a) 2.8   b) 83   c) 0.73   d) 1.0

Q14. A solution is an equimolar mixture of two volatile components A and B. Pure A has a vapor pressure of 50 torr and pure B has a vapor pressure of 100 torr. The vapor pressure of the mixture is 85 torr. What can you conclude about the relative strengths of the intermolecular forces between particles of A and B (relative to those between particles of A and those between particles of B)?
 a) The intermolecular forces between particles A and B are *weaker* than those between particles of A and those between particles of B.
 b) The intermolecular forces between particles A and B are *stronger* than those between particles of A and those between particles of B.
 c) The intermolecular forces between particles A and B are *the same as* those between particles of A and those between particles of B.
 d) Nothing can be concluded about the relative strengths of intermolecular forces from this observation.

Q15. An aqueous solution is in equilibrium with a gaseous mixture containing an equal number of moles of oxygen, nitrogen, and helium. Rank the relative concentrations of each gas in the aqueous solution from highest to lowest.
 a) $[O_2] > [N_2] > [He]$
 b) $[He] > [N_2] > [O_2]$
 c) $[N_2] > [He] > [O_2]$
 d) $[N_2] > [O_2] > [He]$

Answers: 1. (b) 2. (b) 3. (d) 4. (a) 5. (c) 6. (d) 7. (b) 8. (a) 9. (b) 10. (c) 11. (c) 12. (b) 13. (a) 14. (a) 15. (a)

Key Terms

Section 12.1
solution (545)
solvent (545)
solute (545)

Section 12.2
aqueous solution (546)
solubility (547)
entropy (548)
miscible (549)

Section 12.3
enthalpy of solution
(ΔH_{soln}) (552)
heat of hydration
($\Delta H_{hydration}$) (553)

Section 12.4
dynamic equilibrium (556)
saturated solution (556)
unsaturated solution (556)
supersaturated solution (556)
recrystallization (557)
Henry's law (558)

Section 12.5
dilute solution (559)
concentrated solution (559)
molarity (M) (560)
molality (m) (562)
parts by mass (562)
percent by mass (562)
parts per million (ppm) (562)
parts per billion (ppb) (562)

parts by volume (562)
mole fraction (χ_{solute}) (563)
mole percent (mol %) (563)

Section 12.6
colligative property (567)
Raoult's law (569)
vapor pressure lowering
(ΔP) (569)
ideal solution (571)
freezing point depression (574)
boiling point elevation (574)
osmosis (577)
semipermeable membrane (577)
osmotic pressure (578)

Section 12.7
van't Hoff factor (i) (579)

Section 12.8
colloidal dispersion
(colloid) (582)
Tyndall effect (584)

Key Concepts

Solutions (12.1, 12.2)

▶ A solution is a homogeneous mixture of two or more substances. In a solution, the majority component is the solvent and the minority component is the solute.

▶ The tendency toward greater entropy (or greater energy dispersal) is the driving force for solution formation.

▶ In aqueous solutions, water is a solvent, and a solid, liquid, or gas is the solute.

Solubility and Energetics of Solution Formation (12.2, 12.3)

▶ The solubility of a substance is the amount of the substance that will dissolve in a given amount of solvent. The solubility of one substance in another depends on the types of intermolecular forces that exist *between* the substances as well as *within* each substance.

▶ We can determine the overall enthalpy change upon solution formation by adding the enthalpy changes for the three steps of solution formation: (1) separation of the solute particles, (2) separation of the solvent particles, and (3) mixing of the solute and solvent particles. The first two steps are both endothermic, while the last is exothermic.

▶ In aqueous solutions of an ionic compound, the change in enthalpy for steps 2 and 3 can be combined as the heat of hydration ($\Delta H_{hydration}$), which is always negative.

Solution Equilibrium (12.4)

▶ Dynamic equilibrium in a solution occurs when the rates of dissolution and recrystallization in a solution are equal. A solution in this state is said to be saturated. Solutions containing less than or more than the equilibrium amount of solute are unsaturated or supersaturated, respectively.

▶ The solubility of most solids in water increases with increasing temperature.

▶ The solubility of gases in liquids generally decreases with increasing temperature, but it increases with increasing pressure.

Concentration Units (12.5)

▶ Common units used to express solution concentration include molarity (M), molality (m), mole fraction (χ), mole percent (mol %), percent (%) by mass or volume, parts per million (ppm) by mass or volume, and parts per billion (ppb) by mass or volume. These units are summarized in Table 12.5.

Vapor Pressure Lowering, Freezing Point Depression, Boiling Point Elevation, and Osmosis (12.6, 12.7)

▶ The presence of a nonvolatile solute in a liquid results in a lower vapor pressure of the solution relative to the vapor pressure of the pure liquid. This lower vapor pressure is predicted by Raoult's law for an ideal solution.

▶ If the solute–solvent interactions are particularly strong, the actual vapor pressure is lower than that predicted by Raoult's law.

▶ If the solute–solvent interactions are particularly weak, the actual vapor pressure is higher than that predicted by Raoult's law.

▶ The addition of a nonvolatile solute to a liquid will result in a solution with a lower freezing point and a higher boiling point than those of the pure solvent.

▶ The flow of solvent from a solution of lower concentration to a solution of higher concentration is called osmosis.

▶ All of these phenomena are colligative properties and depend only on the number of solute particles added, not the type of solute particles.

▶ Electrolyte solutes have a greater effect on these properties than the corresponding amount of a nonelectrolyte solute as specified by the van't Hoff factor.

Colloids (12.8)

▶ A colloid is a mixture in which a substance is finely divided in a dispersing medium.

▶ Colloidal mixtures occur when the dispersed substance ranges in size from 1 nm to 1000 nm.

▶ One way to identify colloidal mixtures is by their tendency to scatter light, known as the Tyndall effect.

Key Equations and Relationships

Henry's Law: Solubility of Gases with Increasing Pressure (**12.4**)

$$S_{gas} = k_H P_{gas} \ (k_H \text{ is Henry's law constant})$$

Molarity (M) of a Solution (**12.5**)

$$(M) = \frac{\text{amount solute (in mol)}}{\text{volume solution (in L)}}$$

Molality (*m*) of a Solution (**12.5**)

$$(m) = \frac{\text{amount solute (in mol)}}{\text{mass solvent (in kg)}}$$

Concentration of a Solution in Parts by Mass and Parts by Volume (**12.5**)

$$\text{Percent by mass} = \frac{\text{mass solute} \times 100\%}{\text{mass solution}}$$

$$\text{Parts per million (ppm)} = \frac{\text{mass solute} \times 10^6}{\text{mass solution}}$$

$$\text{Parts per billion (ppb)} = \frac{\text{mass solute} \times 10^9}{\text{mass solution}}$$

$$\text{Parts by volume} = \frac{\text{volume solute} \times \text{multiplication factor}}{\text{volume solution}}$$

Concentration of a Solution in Mole Fraction (χ) and Mole Percent (**12.5**)

$$\chi_{solute} = \frac{n_{solute}}{n_{solute} + n_{solvent}}$$

$$\text{Mol } \% = \chi \times 100\%$$

Raoult's Law: Relationship between the Vapor Pressure of a Solution ($P_{solution}$), the Mole Fraction of the Solvent ($\chi_{solvent}$), and the Vapor Pressure of the Pure Solvent ($P^\circ_{solvent}$) (**12.6**)

$$P_{solution} = \chi_{solvent} P^\circ_{solvent}$$

The Vapor Pressure of a Solution Containing Two Volatile Components (**12.6**)

$$P_A = \chi_A P^\circ_A$$

$$P_B = \chi_B P^\circ_B$$

$$P_{tot} = P_A + P_B$$

Relationship between Freezing Point Depression (ΔT_f), molality (*m*), and Freezing Point Depression Constant (K_f) (**12.6**)

$$\Delta T_f = m \times K_f$$

Relationship between Boiling Point Elevation (ΔT_b), Molality (*m*), and Boiling Point Elevation Constant (K_b) (**12.6**)

$$\Delta T_b = m \times K_b$$

Relationship between Osmotic Pressure (Π), Molarity (M), the Ideal Gas Constant (*R*), and Temperature (*T*, in K) (**12.6**)

$$\Pi = MRT \quad (R = 0.08206 \text{ L} \cdot \text{atm/mol} \cdot \text{K})$$

van't Hoff Factor (*i*): Ratio of Moles of Particles in Solution to Moles of Formula Units Dissolved (**12.7**)

$$i = \frac{\text{moles of particles in solution}}{\text{moles of formula units dissolved}}$$

Key Learning Outcomes

Chapter Objectives	Assessment
Determining Whether a Solute Is Soluble in a Solvent (**12.2**)	Example 12.1 For Practice 12.1 Exercises 31–34
Using Henry's Law to Predict the Solubility of Gases with Increasing Pressure (**12.4**)	Example 12.2 For Practice 12.2 Exercises 49, 50
Calculating Concentrations of Solutions (**12.5**)	Example 12.3, 12.4 For Practice 12.3, 12.4 For More Practice 12.3 Exercises 51–56, 63, 64
Converting between Concentration Units (**12.5**) $\frac{3.5 \text{ g NaCl}}{100 \text{ g solution}}$ converts [g solution] → [g NaCl]	Example 12.5 For Practice 12.5 Exercises 65–68
Determining the Vapor Pressure of a Solution Containing a Nonelectrolyte and Nonvolatile Solute (**12.6**)	Example 12.6 For Practice 12.6 For More Practice 12.6 Exercises 71, 72
Determining the Vapor Pressure of a Two-Component Solution (**12.6**)	Example 12.7 For Practice 12.7 Exercises 73–76
Calculating Freezing Point Depression (**12.6**)	Example 12.8 For Practice 12.8 Exercises 77–82, 87, 88
Calculating Boiling Point Elevation (**12.6**)	Example 12.9 For Practice 12.9 Exercises 77, 78, 87, 88
Determining the Osmotic Pressure (**12.6**)	Example 12.10 For Practice 12.10 Exercises 83–86

Key Learning Outcomes, *continued*

Determining and Using the van't Hoff Factor (**12.7**)	Example 12.11 For Practice 12.11 Exercises 91–96
Determining the Vapor Pressure of a Solution Containing an Ionic Solute (**12.7**)	Example 12.12 For Practice 12.12 Exercises 97, 98

EXERCISES

Review Questions

1. Explain why drinking seawater results in dehydration.
2. What is a solution? What are the solute and solvent?
3. What does it mean to say that a substance is soluble in another substance? Which units are used in reporting solubility?
4. Why do two ideal gases thoroughly mix when combined? What drives the mixing?
5. What is entropy? Why is entropy important in discussing the formation of solutions?
6. What kinds of intermolecular forces are involved in solution formation?
7. Explain how the relative strengths of solute–solute interactions, solvent–solvent interactions, and solvent–solute interactions affect solution formation.
8. What does the statement *like dissolves like* mean with respect to solution formation?
9. What are three steps involved in evaluating the enthalpy changes associated with solution formation?
10. What is the heat of hydration ($\Delta H_{hydration}$)? How does the enthalpy of solution depend on the relative magnitudes of ΔH_{solute} and $\Delta H_{hydration}$?
11. Explain dynamic equilibrium with respect to solution formation. What is a saturated solution? An unsaturated solution? A supersaturated solution?
12. How does the solubility of a solid in a liquid depend on temperature? How is this temperature dependence exploited to purify solids through recrystallization?
13. How does the solubility of a gas in a liquid depend on temperature? How does this temperature dependence affect the amount of oxygen available for fish and other aquatic animals?
14. How does the solubility of a gas in a liquid depend on pressure? How does this pressure dependence account for the bubbling that occurs upon opening a can of soda?
15. What is Henry's law? For what kinds of calculations is Henry's law useful?
16. What are the common units for expressing solution concentration?
17. How are parts by mass and parts by volume used in calculations?
18. What is the effect of a nonvolatile solute on the vapor pressure of a liquid? Why is the vapor pressure of a solution different from the vapor pressure of the pure liquid solvent?
19. What is Raoult's law? For what kind of calculations is Raoult's law useful?
20. Explain the difference between an ideal and a nonideal solution.
21. What is the effect on vapor pressure of a solution with particularly *strong* solute–solvent interactions? With particularly *weak* solute–solvent interactions?
22. Explain why the lower vapor pressure for a solution containing a nonvolatile solute results in a higher boiling point and lower melting point compared to the pure solvent.
23. What are colligative properties?
24. What is osmosis? What is osmotic pressure?
25. Explain the meaning of the van't Hoff factor and its role in determining the colligative properties of solutions containing ionic solutes.
26. Describe a colloidal dispersion. What is the difference between a colloidal dispersion and a true solution?
27. What is the Tyndall effect and how can it be used to help identify colloidal dispersions?
28. What keeps the particles in a colloidal dispersion from coalescing?

Problems by Topic

Solubility

29. Pick an appropriate solvent from Table 12.3 to dissolve each substance. State the kind of intermolecular forces that would occur between the solute and solvent in each case.
    a. motor oil (nonpolar)
    b. ethanol (polar, contains an OH group)
    c. lard (nonpolar)
    d. potassium chloride (ionic)

30. Pick an appropriate solvent from Table 12.3 to dissolve each substance. State the kind of intermolecular forces that would occur between the solute and solvent in each case.
    a. isopropyl alcohol (polar, contains an OH group)
    b. sodium chloride (ionic)
    c. vegetable oil (nonpolar)
    d. sodium nitrate (ionic)

31. Which molecule would you expect to be more soluble in water, $CH_3CH_2CH_2OH$ or $HOCH_2CH_2CH_2OH$?

32. Which molecule would you expect to be more soluble in water, CCl_4 or CH_2Cl_2?

33. For each compound, would you expect greater solubility in water or in hexane? Indicate the kinds of intermolecular forces that occur between the solute and the solvent in which the molecule is most soluble.

a. glucose

b. naphthalene

c. dimethyl ether

d. alanine (an amino acid)

34. For each compound, would you expect greater solubility in water or in hexane? Indicate the kinds of intermolecular forces that would occur between the solute and the solvent in which the molecule is most soluble.

a. toluene

b. sucrose (table sugar)

c. isobutene

d. ethylene glycol

Energetics of Solution Formation

35. When ammonium chloride (NH_4Cl) is dissolved in water, the solution becomes colder.
   a. Is the dissolution of ammonium chloride endothermic or exothermic?
   b. What can you conclude about the relative magnitudes of the lattice energy of ammonium chloride and its heat of hydration?
   c. Sketch a qualitative energy diagram similar to Figure 12.7 for the dissolution of NH_4Cl.
   d. Why does the solution form? What drives the process?

36. When lithium iodide (LiI) is dissolved in water, the solution becomes hotter.
   a. Is the dissolution of lithium iodide endothermic or exothermic?
   b. What can you conclude about the relative magnitudes of the lattice energy of lithium iodide and its heat of hydration?
   c. Sketch a qualitative energy diagram similar to Figure 12.7 for the dissolution of LiI.
   d. Why does the solution form? What drives the process?

37. Silver nitrate has a lattice energy of -820 kJ/mol and a heat of solution of -22.6 kJ/mol. Calculate the heat of hydration for silver nitrate.

38. Use the data to calculate the heats of hydration of lithium chloride and sodium chloride. Which of the two cations, lithium or sodium, has stronger ion–dipole interactions with water? Why?

Compound	Lattice Energy (kJ/mol)	ΔH_{soln} (kJ/mol)
LiCl	-834	-37.0
NaCl	-769	$+3.88$

39. Lithium iodide has a lattice energy of -7.3×10^2 kJ/mol and a heat of hydration of -793 kJ/mol. Find the heat of solution for lithium iodide and determine how much heat is evolved or absorbed when 15.0 g of lithium iodide completely dissolves in water.

40. Potassium nitrate has a lattice energy of -163.8 kcal/mol and a heat of hydration of -155.5 kcal/mol. How much potassium nitrate has to dissolve in water to absorb 1.00×10^2 kJ of heat?

Solution Equilibrium and Factors Affecting Solubility

41. A solution contains 25 g of NaCl per 100.0 g of water at 25 °C. Is the solution unsaturated, saturated, or supersaturated? (Use Figure 12.11.)

42. A solution contains 32 g of KNO_3 per 100.0 g of water at 25 °C. Is the solution unsaturated, saturated, or supersaturated? (Use Figure 12.11.)

43. A KNO_3 solution containing 45 g of KNO_3 per 100.0 g of water is cooled from 40 °C to 0 °C. What happens during cooling? (Use Figure 12.11.)

44. A KCl solution containing 42 g of KCl per 100.0 g of water is cooled from 60 °C to 0 °C. What happens during cooling? (Use Figure 12.11.)

45. Some laboratory procedures involving oxygen-sensitive reactants or products call for using water that has been boiled (and then cooled). Explain.

46. A person preparing a fish tank fills the tank with water that has been boiled (and then cooled). When the person puts fish into the tank, they die. Explain.

47. Scuba divers breathing air at increased pressure can suffer from nitrogen narcosis—a condition resembling drunkenness—when the partial pressure of nitrogen exceeds about 4 atm. What property of gas/water solutions causes this to happen? How can a diver reverse this effect?

48. Scuba divers breathing air at increased pressure can suffer from oxygen toxicity—too much oxygen in their bloodstream—when the partial pressure of oxygen exceeds about 1.4 atm. What happens to the amount of oxygen in a diver's bloodstream when he or she breathes oxygen at elevated pressures? How can this be reversed?

49. Calculate the mass of nitrogen dissolved at room temperature in an 80.0 L home aquarium. Assume a total pressure of 1.0 atm and a mole fraction for nitrogen of 0.78.

50. Use Henry's law to determine the molar solubility of helium at a pressure of 1.0 atm and 25 °C.

Concentrations of Solutions

51. An aqueous NaCl solution is made using 112 g of NaCl diluted to a total solution volume of 1.00 L. Calculate the molarity, molality, and mass percent of the solution. (Assume a density of 1.08 g/mL for the solution.)

52. An aqueous KNO_3 solution is made using 72.5 g of KNO_3 diluted to a total solution volume of 2.00 L. Calculate the molarity, molality, and mass percent of the solution. (Assume a density of 1.05 g/mL for the solution.)

53. To what volume should you dilute 50.0 mL of a 5.00 M KI solution so that 25.0 mL of the diluted solution contains 3.05 g of KI?

54. To what volume should you dilute 125 mL of an 8.00 M $CuCl_2$ solution so that 50.0 mL of the diluted solution contains 4.67 g $CuCl_2$?

55. Silver nitrate solutions are often used to plate silver onto other metals. What is the maximum amount of silver (in grams) that can be plated out of 4.8 L of an $AgNO_3$ solution containing 3.4% Ag by mass? Assume that the density of the solution is 1.01 g/mL.

56. A dioxin-contaminated water source contains 0.085% dioxin by mass. How much dioxin is present in 2.5 L of this water? Assume a density of 1.00 g/mL.

57. A hard water sample contains 0.0085% Ca by mass (in the form of Ca^{2+} ions). How much water (in grams) contains 1.2 g of Ca? (1.2 g of Ca is the recommended daily allowance of calcium for those between 19 and 24 years old.)

58. Lead is a toxic metal that affects the central nervous system. A Pb-contaminated water sample contains 0.0011% Pb by mass. How much of the water (in mL) contains 150 mg of Pb? (Assume a density of 1.0 g/mL.)

59. You can purchase nitric acid in a concentrated form that is 70.3% HNO_3 by mass and has a density of 1.41 g/mL. Describe exactly how you would prepare 1.15 L of 0.100 M HNO_3 from the concentrated solution.

60. You can purchase hydrochloric acid in a concentrated form that is 37.0% HCl by mass and that has a density of 1.20 g/mL. Describe exactly how to prepare 2.85 L of 0.500 M HCl from the concentrated solution.

61. Describe how to prepare each solution from the dry solute and the solvent.
    a. 1.00×10^2 mL of 0.500 M KCl
    b. 1.00×10^2 g of 0.500 m KCl
    c. 1.00×10^2 g of 5.0% KCl solution by mass

62. Describe how to prepare each solution from the dry solute and the solvent.
    a. 125 mL of 0.100 M $NaNO_3$
    b. 125 g of 0.100 m $NaNO_3$
    c. 125 g of 1.0% $NaNO_3$ solution by mass

63. A solution is prepared by dissolving 28.4 g of glucose ($C_6H_{12}O_6$) in 355 g of water. The final volume of the solution is 378 mL. For this solution, calculate the concentration in each unit.
    a. molarity
    b. molality
    c. percent by mass
    d. mole fraction
    e. mole percent

64. A solution is prepared by dissolving 20.2 mL of methanol (CH_3OH) in 100.0 mL of water at 25 °C. The final volume of the solution is 118 mL. The densities of methanol and water at this temperature are 0.782 g/mL and 1.00 g/mL, respectively. For this solution, calculate the concentration in each unit.
    a. molarity
    b. molality
    c. percent by mass
    d. mole fraction
    e. mole percent

65. Household hydrogen peroxide is an aqueous solution containing 3.0% hydrogen peroxide by mass. What is the molarity of this solution? (Assume a density of 1.01 g/mL.)

66. One brand of laundry bleach is an aqueous solution containing 4.55% sodium hypochlorite (NaOCl) by mass. What is the molarity of this solution? (Assume a density of 1.02 g/mL.)

67. An aqueous solution contains 36% HCl by mass. Calculate the molality and mole fraction of the solution.

68. An aqueous solution contains 5.0% NaCl by mass. Calculate the molality and mole fraction of the solution.

Vapor Pressure of Solutions

69. A beaker contains 100.0 mL of pure water. A second beaker contains 100.0 mL of seawater. The two beakers are left side by side on a lab bench for 1 week. At the end of the week, the liquid level in both beakers has decreased. However, the level has decreased more in one of the beakers than in the other. Which one and why?

70. Which solution has the highest vapor pressure?
    a. 20.0 g of glucose ($C_6H_{12}O_6$) in 100.0 mL of water
    b. 20.0 g of sucrose ($C_{12}H_{22}O_{11}$) in 100.0 mL of water
    c. 10.0 g of potassium acetate $KC_2H_3O_2$ in 100.0 mL of water

71. Calculate the vapor pressure of a solution containing 24.5 g of glycerin ($C_3H_8O_3$) in 135 mL of water at 30.0 °C. The vapor pressure of pure water at this temperature is 31.8 torr. Assume that glycerin is not volatile and dissolves molecularly (i.e., it is not ionic), and use a density of 1.00 g/mL for the water.

72. A solution contains naphthalene ($C_{10}H_8$) dissolved in hexane (C_6H_{14}) at a concentration of 12.35% naphthalene by mass. Calculate the vapor pressure at 25 °C of hexane above the solution. The vapor pressure of pure hexane at 25 °C is 151 torr.

73. A solution contains 50.0 g of heptane (C_7H_{16}) and 50.0 g of octane (C_8H_{18}) at 25 °C. The vapor pressures of pure heptane and pure octane at 25 °C are 45.8 torr and 10.9 torr, respectively. Assuming ideal behavior, answer the following:
    a. What is the vapor pressure of each of the solution components in the mixture?
    b. What is the total pressure above the solution?
    c. What is the composition of the vapor in mass percent?
    d. Why is the composition of the vapor different from the composition of the solution?

74. A solution contains a mixture of pentane and hexane at room temperature. The solution has a vapor pressure of 258 torr. Pure pentane and hexane have vapor pressures of 425 torr and 151 torr, respectively, at room temperature. What is the mole fraction composition of the mixture? (Assume ideal behavior.)

75. A solution contains 4.08 g of chloroform ($CHCl_3$) and 9.29 g of acetone (CH_3COCH_3). The vapor pressures at 35 °C of pure chloroform and pure acetone are 295 torr and 332 torr, respectively. Assuming ideal behavior, calculate the vapor pressures of each of the components and the total vapor pressure above the solution. The experimentally measured total vapor pressure of the solution at 35 °C was 312 torr. Is the solution ideal? If not, what can you say about the relative strength of chloroform–acetone interactions compared to the acetone–acetone and chloroform–chloroform interactions?

76. A solution of methanol and water has a mole fraction of water of 0.312 and a total vapor pressure of 211 torr at 39.9 °C. The vapor pressures of pure methanol and pure water at this temperature are 256 torr and 55.3 torr, respectively. Is the solution ideal? If not, what can you say about the relative strengths of the solute–solvent interactions compared to the solute–solute and solvent–solvent interactions?

Freezing Point Depression, Boiling Point Elevation, and Osmosis

77. A glucose solution contains 55.8 g of glucose ($C_6H_{12}O_6$) in 455 g of water. Determine the freezing point and boiling point of the solution.

78. An ethylene glycol solution contains 21.2 g of ethylene glycol ($C_2H_6O_2$) in 85.4 mL of water. Determine the freezing point and boiling point of the solution. (Assume a density of 1.00 g/mL for water.)

79. Calculate the freezing point and melting point of a solution containing 10.0 g of naphthalene ($C_{10}H_8$) in 100.0 mL of benzene. Benzene has a density of 0.877 g/cm³.

80. Calculate the freezing point and melting point of a solution containing 7.55 g of ethylene glycol ($C_2H_6O_2$) in 85.7 mL of ethanol. Ethanol has a density of 0.789 g/cm³.

81. An aqueous solution containing 17.5 g of an unknown molecular (nonelectrolyte) compound in 100.0 g of water has a freezing point of −1.8 °C. Calculate the molar mass of the unknown compound.

82. An aqueous solution containing 35.9 g of an unknown molecular (nonelectrolyte) compound in 150.0 g of water has a freezing point of −1.3 °C. Calculate the molar mass of the unknown compound.

83. Calculate the osmotic pressure of a solution containing 24.6 g of glycerin ($C_3H_8O_3$) in 250.0 mL of solution at 298 K.

84. What mass of sucrose ($C_{12}H_{22}O_{11}$) would you combine with 5.00×10^2 g of water to make a solution with an osmotic pressure of 8.55 atm at 298 K? (Assume a density of 1.0 g/mL for the solution.)

85. A solution containing 27.55 mg of an unknown protein per 25.0 mL solution was found to have an osmotic pressure of 3.22 torr at 25 °C. What is the molar mass of the protein?

86. Calculate the osmotic pressure of a solution containing 18.75 mg of hemoglobin in 15.0 mL of solution at 25 °C. The molar mass of hemoglobin is 6.5×10^4 g/mol.

87. Calculate the freezing point and boiling point of each aqueous solution, assuming complete dissociation of the solute.
   a. 0.100 *m* K_2S
   b. 21.5 g of $CuCl_2$ in 4.50×10^2 g water
   c. 5.5% $NaNO_3$ by mass (in water)

88. Calculate the freezing point and boiling point in each solution, assuming complete dissociation of the solute.
   a. 10.5 g $FeCl_3$ in 1.50×10^2 g water
   b. 3.5% KCl by mass (in water)
   c. 0.150 *m* MgF_2

89. What mass of salt (NaCl) should you add to 1.00 L of water in an ice cream maker to make a solution that freezes at −10.0 °C? Assume complete dissociation of the NaCl and density of 1.00 g/mL for water.

90. Determine the required concentration (in percent by mass) for an aqueous ethylene glycol ($C_2H_6O_2$) solution to have a boiling point of 104.0 °C.

91. Use the van't Hoff factors in Table 12.9 to calculate each colligative property:
   a. the melting point of a 0.100 *m* iron(III) chloride solution
   b. the osmotic pressure of a 0.085 M potassium sulfate solution at 298 K
   c. the boiling point of a 1.22% by mass magnesium chloride solution

92. Assuming the van't Hoff factors in Table 12.9, calculate the mass of solute required to make each aqueous solution:
   a. a sodium chloride solution containing 1.50×10^2 g of water that has a melting point of −1.0 °C
   b. 2.50×10^2 mL of a magnesium sulfate solution that has an osmotic pressure of 3.82 atm at 298 K
   c. an iron(III) chloride solution containing 2.50×10^2 g of water that has a boiling point of 102 °C

93. A 1.2 *m* aqueous solution of an ionic compound with the formula MX_2 has a boiling point of 101.4 °C. Calculate the van't Hoff factor (*i*) for MX_2 at this concentration.

94. A 0.95 m aqueous solution of an ionic compound with the formula MX has a freezing point of −3.0 °C. Calculate the van't Hoff factor (*i*) for MX at this concentration.

95. A 0.100 M ionic solution has an osmotic pressure of 8.3 atm at 25 °C. Calculate the van't Hoff factor (*i*) for this solution.

96. A solution contains 8.92 g of KBr in 500.0 mL of solution and has an osmotic pressure of 6.97 atm at 25 °C. Calculate the van't Hoff factor (*i*) for KBr at this concentration.

97. Calculate the vapor pressure at 25 °C of an aqueous solution that is 5.50% NaCl by mass. (Assume complete dissociation of the solute.)

98. An aqueous $CaCl_2$ solution has a vapor pressure of 81.6 mmHg at 50 °C. The vapor pressure of pure water at this temperature is 92.6 mmHg. What is the concentration of $CaCl_2$ in mass percent? (Assume complete dissociation of the solute.)

Cumulative Problems

99. The solubility of carbon tetrachloride (CCl_4) in water at 25 °C is 1.2 g/L. The solubility of chloroform ($CHCl_3$) at the same temperature is 10.1 g/L. Why is chloroform almost ten times more soluble in water than carbon tetrachloride?

100. The solubility of phenol in water at 25 °C is 8.7 g/L. The solubility of naphthol at the same temperature is only 0.074 g/L. Examine the structures of phenol and naphthol shown here and explain why phenol is so much more soluble than naphthol.

Phenol   Naphthol

101. Potassium perchlorate ($KClO_4$) has a lattice energy of −599 kJ/mol and a heat of hydration of −548 kJ/mol. Find the heat of solution for potassium perchlorate and determine the temperature change that occurs when 10.0 g of potassium perchlorate is dissolved with enough water to make 100.0 mL of solution. (Assume a heat capacity of 4.05 J/g · °C for the solution and a density of 1.05 g/mL.)

102. Sodium hydroxide (NaOH) has a lattice energy of −887 kJ/mol and a heat of hydration of −932 kJ/mol. How much solution could be heated to boiling by the heat evolved by the dissolution of 25.0 g of NaOH? (For the solution, assume a heat capacity of 4.0 J/g · °C, an initial temperature of 25.0 °C, a boiling point of 100.0 °C, and a density of 1.05 g/mL.)

103. A saturated solution forms when 0.0537 L of argon, at a pressure of 1.0 atm and temperature of 25 °C, is dissolved in 1.0 L of water. Calculate the Henry's law constant for argon.

104. A gas has a Henry's law constant of 0.112 M/atm. What total volume of solution is needed to completely dissolve 1.65 L of the gas at a pressure of 725 torr and a temperature of 25 °C?

105. The Safe Drinking Water Act (SDWA) sets a limit for mercury—a toxin to the central nervous system—at 0.0020 ppm by mass. Water suppliers must periodically test their water to ensure that mercury levels do not exceed this limit. Suppose water becomes contaminated with mercury at twice the legal limit (0.0040 ppm). How much of this water would a person have to consume to ingest 50.0 mg of mercury?

106. Water softeners often replace calcium ions in hard water with sodium ions. Since sodium compounds are soluble, the presence of sodium ions in water does not cause the white, scaly residues caused by calcium ions. However, calcium is more beneficial to human health than sodium because calcium is a necessary part of the human diet, while high levels of sodium intake are linked to increases in blood pressure. The U.S. Food and Drug Administration (FDA) recommends that adults ingest less than 2.4 g of sodium per day. How many liters of softened water, containing a sodium concentration of 0.050% sodium by mass, would a person have to consume to exceed the FDA recommendation? (Assume a water density of 1.0 g/mL.)

107. An aqueous solution contains 12.5% NaCl by mass. What mass of water (in grams) is contained in 2.5 L of the vapor above this solution at 55 °C? The vapor pressure of pure water at 55 °C is 118 torr. (Assume complete dissociation of NaCl.)

108. The vapor above an aqueous solution contains 19.5 mg water per liter at 25 °C. Assuming ideal behavior, what is the concentration of the solute within the solution in mole percent?

109. What is the freezing point of an aqueous solution that boils at 106.5 °C?

110. What is the boiling point of an aqueous solution that has a vapor pressure of 20.5 torr at 25 °C? (Assume a nonvolatile solute.)

111. An isotonic solution contains 0.90% NaCl mass to volume. Calculate the percent mass to volume for isotonic solutions containing each solute at 25 °C. Assume a van't Hoff factor of 1.9 for all *ionic* solutes.
    a. KCl
    b. NaBr
    c. glucose ($C_6H_{12}O_6$)

112. Magnesium citrate, $Mg_3(C_6H_5O_7)_2$ belongs to a class of laxatives called *hyperosmotics*, which cause rapid emptying of the bowel. When a concentrated solution of magnesium citrate is consumed, it passes through the intestines, drawing water and promoting diarrhea, usually within 6 hours. Calculate the osmotic pressure of a magnesium citrate laxative solution containing 28.5 g of magnesium citrate in 235 mL of solution at 37 °C (approximate body temperature). Assume complete dissociation of the ionic compound.

113. A solution is prepared from 4.5701 g of magnesium chloride and 43.238 g of water. The vapor pressure of water above this solution is 0.3624 atm at 348.0 K. The vapor pressure of pure water at this temperature is 0.3804 atm. Find the value of the van't Hoff factor (*i*) for magnesium chloride in this solution.

114. When HNO_2 is dissolved in water it partially dissociates according to the equation $HNO_2 \rightleftharpoons H^- + NO_2^-$. A solution is prepared that contains 7.050 g of HNO_2 in 1.000 kg of water. Its freezing point is 20.2929 °C. Calculate the fraction of HNO_2 that has dissociated.

115. A solution of a nonvolatile solute in water has a boiling point of 375.3 K. Calculate the vapor pressure of water above this solution at 338 K. The vapor pressure of pure water at this temperature is 0.2467 atm.

116. The density of a 0.438 M solution of potassium chromate (K_2CrO_4) at 298 K is 1.063 g/mL. Calculate the vapor pressure of water above the solution. The vapor pressure of pure water at this temperature is 0.0313 atm. (Assume complete dissociation of the solute.)

117. The vapor pressure of carbon tetrachloride, CCl_4, is 0.354 atm and the vapor pressure of chloroform, $CHCl_3$, is 0.526 atm at 316 K. A solution is prepared from equal masses of these two compounds at this temperature. Calculate the mole fraction of the chloroform in the vapor above the solution. If the vapor above the original solution is condensed and isolated into a separate flask, what would the vapor pressure of chloroform be above this new solution?

118. Distillation is a method of purification based on successive separations and recondensations of vapor above a solution. Use the result of the previous problem to calculate the mole fraction of chloroform in the vapor above a solution obtained by three successive separations and condensations of the vapors above the original solution of carbon tetrachloride and chloroform. Show how this result explains the use of distillation as a separation method.

119. A solution of 49.0% H_2SO_4 by mass has a density of 1.39 g/cm^3 at 293 K. A 25.0 cm^3 sample of this solution is mixed with enough water to increase the volume of the solution to 99.8 cm^3. Find the molarity of sulfuric acid in this solution.

120. Find the mass of urea (CH_4N_2O) needed to prepare 50.0 g of a solution in water in which the mole fraction of urea is 0.0770.

121. A solution contains 10.05 g of unknown compound dissolved in 50.0 mL of water. (Assume a density of 1.00 g/mL for water.) The freezing point of the solution is −3.16 °C. The mass percent composition of the compound is 60.97% C, 11.94% H, and the rest is O. What is the molecular formula of the compound?

122. The osmotic pressure of a solution containing 2.10 g of an unknown compound dissolved in 175.0 mL of solution at 25 °C is 1.93 atm. The combustion of 24.02 g of the unknown compound produced 28.16 g CO_2 and 8.64 g H_2O. What is the molecular formula of the compound (which contains only carbon, hydrogen, and oxygen)?

123. A 100.0 mL aqueous sodium chloride solution is 13.5% NaCl by mass and has a density of 1.12 g/mL. What would you add (solute or solvent) and what mass of it to make the boiling point of the solution 104.4 °C? (Use $i = 1.8$ for NaCl.)

124. A 50.0 mL solution is initially 1.55% $MgCl_2$ by mass and has a density of 1.05 g/mL. What is the freezing point of the solution after you add an additional 1.35 g $MgCl_2$? (Use $i = 2.5$ for $MgCl_2$.)

Challenge Problems

125. The small bubbles that form on the bottom of a water pot that is being heated (before boiling) are due to dissolved air coming out of solution. Use Henry's law and the solubilities given to calculate the total volume of nitrogen and oxygen gas that should bubble out of 1.5 L of water upon warming from 25 °C to 50 °C. Assume that the water is initially saturated with nitrogen and oxygen gas at 25 °C and a total pressure of 1.0 atm. Assume that the gas bubbles out at a temperature of 50 °C. The solubility of oxygen gas at 50 °C is 27.8 mg/L at an oxygen pressure of 1.00 atm. The solubility of nitrogen gas at 50 °C is 14.6 mg/L at a nitrogen pressure of 1.00 atm. Assume that the air above the water contains an oxygen partial pressure of 0.21 atm and a nitrogen partial pressure of 0.78 atm.

126. The vapor above a mixture of pentane and hexane at room temperature contains 35.5% pentane by mass. What is the mass percent composition of the solution? Pure pentane and hexane have vapor pressures of 425 torr and 151 torr, respectively, at room temperature.

127. A 1.10 g sample contains only glucose ($C_6H_{12}O_6$) and sucrose ($C_{12}H_{22}O_{11}$). When the sample is dissolved in water to a total solution volume of 25.0 mL, the osmotic pressure of the solution is 3.78 atm at 298 K. What is the mass percent composition of glucose and sucrose in the sample?

128. A solution is prepared by mixing 631 mL of methanol with 501 mL of water. The molarity of methanol in the resulting solution is 14.29 M. The density of methanol at this temperature is 0.792 g/mL. Calculate the difference in volume between this solution and the total volume of water and methanol that were mixed to prepare the solution.

129. Two alcohols, isopropyl alcohol and propyl alcohol, have the same molecular formula, C_3H_8O. A solution of the two that is two-thirds by mass isopropyl alcohol has a vapor pressure of 0.110 atm at 313 K. A solution that is one-third by mass isopropyl alcohol has a vapor pressure of 0.089 atm at 313 K. Calculate the vapor pressure of each pure alcohol at this temperature. Explain the difference given that the formula of propyl alcohol is $CH_3CH_2CH_2OH$ and that of isopropyl alcohol is $(CH_3)_2CHOH$.

130. A metal, M, of atomic mass 96 amu reacts with fluorine to form a salt that can be represented as MF_x. In order to determine x and therefore the formula of the salt, a boiling point elevation experiment is performed. A 9.18 g sample of the salt is dissolved in 100.0 g of water and the boiling point of the solution is found to be 374.38 K. Find the formula of the salt. (Assume complete dissociation of the salt in solution.)

131. Sulfuric acid in water dissociates completely into H^+ and HSO_4^- ions. The HSO_4^- ion dissociates to a limited extent into H^+ and SO_4^{2-}. The freezing point of a 0.1000 m solution of sulfuric acid in water is 272.76 K. Calculate the molality of SO_4^{2-} in the solution, assuming ideal solution behavior.

132. A solution of 75.0 g of benzene (C_6H_6) and 75.0 g of toluene (C_7H_8) has a total vapor pressure of 80.9 mmHg at 303 K. Another solution of 100.0 g benzene and 50.0 g toluene has a total vapor pressure of 93.9 mmHg at this temperature. Find the vapor pressure of pure benzene and pure toluene at 303 K.

133. A solution is prepared by dissolving 11.60 g of a mixture of sodium carbonate and sodium bicarbonate in 1.00 L of water. A 300.0 cm^3 sample of the solution is treated with excess HNO_3 and boiled to remove all the dissolved gas. A total of 0.940 L of dry CO_2 is collected at 298 K and 0.972 atm. Find the molarity of the carbonate and bicarbonate in the solution.

Conceptual Problems

134. Substance A is a nonpolar liquid and has only dispersion forces among its constituent particles. Substance B is also a nonpolar liquid and has about the same magnitude of dispersion forces among its constituent particles as substance A. When substance A and B are combined, they spontaneously mix.
  a. Why do the two substances mix?
  b. Predict the sign and magnitude of ΔH_{soln}.
  c. Determine the signs and relative magnitudes of ΔH_{solute}, $\Delta H_{solvent}$, and ΔH_{mix}.

135. A power plant built on a river uses river water as a coolant. The water is warmed as it is used in heat exchangers within the plant. Should the warm water be immediately cycled back into the river? Why or why not?

136. The vapor pressure of a 1 M ionic solution is different from the vapor pressure of a 1 M nonelectrolyte solution. In both cases, the solute is nonvolatile. Which set of diagrams best represents the differences between the two solutions and their vapors?

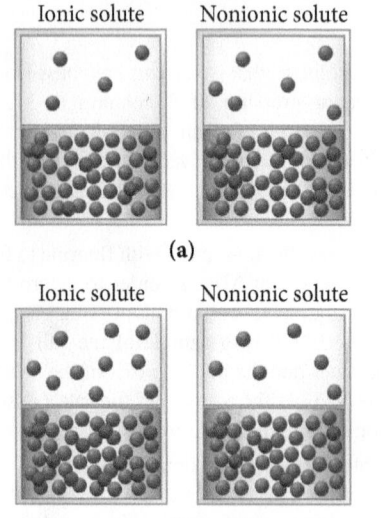

Ionic solute   Nonionic solute

● Solvent particles

● Solute particles

(a)

Ionic solute   Nonionic solute

(b)

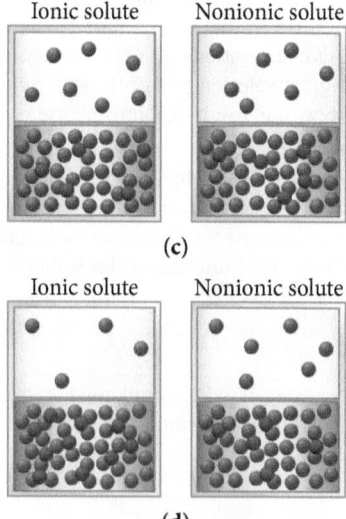

Ionic solute   Nonionic solute

(c)

Ionic solute   Nonionic solute

(d)

137. If each substance listed here costs the same amount per kilogram, which would be most cost-effective as a way to lower the freezing point of water? (Assume complete dissociation for all ionic compounds.) Explain.
  a. $HOCH_2CH_2OH$
  b. $NaCl$
  c. KCl
  d. $MgCl_2$
  e. $SrCl_2$

138. A helium balloon inflated on one day will fall to the ground by the next day. The volume of the balloon decreases somewhat overnight but not by enough to explain why it no longer floats. (If you inflate a new balloon with helium to the same size as the balloon that fell to the ground, the newly inflated balloon floats.) Explain.

Answers to Conceptual Problems

Solubility

12.1 The first alcohol on the list is methanol, which is highly polar and forms hydrogen bonds with water. It is miscible in water and has only limited solubility in hexane, which is nonpolar. However, as the carbon chain gets longer in the series of alcohols, the OH group becomes less important relative to the growing nonpolar carbon chain. Therefore, the alcohols become progressively less soluble in water and more soluble in hexane. This table demonstrates the rule of thumb *like dissolves like*. Methanol is like water and therefore dissolves in water. It is unlike hexane and therefore has limited solubility in hexane. As you move down the list, the alcohols become increasingly like hexane and increasingly unlike water and therefore become increasingly soluble in hexane and increasingly insoluble in water.

Energetics of Aqueous Solution Formation

12.2 You can conclude that $|\Delta H_{solute}| < |\Delta H_{hydration}|$. Since ΔH_{soln} is negative, the absolute value of the negative term ($\Delta H_{hydration}$) must be greater than the absolute value of the positive term (ΔH_{solute}).

Solubility and Temperature

12.3 **(b)** Some potassium bromide precipitates out of solution. The solubility of most solids decreases with decreasing temperature. However, the solubility of gases increases with decreasing temperature. Therefore, the nitrogen becomes more soluble and will not bubble out of solution.

Henry's Law

12.4 Ammonia is the only compound on the list that is polar, so we would expect its solubility in water to be greater than those of the other gases (which are all nonpolar).

Raoult's Law

12.5 The solute–solvent interactions must be stronger than the solute–solute and solvent–solvent interactions. The stronger interactions lower the vapor pressure from the expected ideal value of 150 mmHg.

Boiling Point Elevation

12.6 Solution B because K_b for ethanol is greater than K_b for water.

Colligative Properties

12.7 **(c)** The 0.50 M $MgCl_2$ solution has the highest boiling point because it has the highest concentration of particles. We expect 1 mol of $MgCl_2$ to form 3 mol of particles in solution (although it effectively forms slightly fewer).

13

Chemical Kinetics

Nobody, I suppose, could devote many years to the study of chemical kinetics without being deeply conscious of the fascination of time and change: this is something that goes outside science into poetry. . . .

—Sir Cyril N. Hinshelwood (1897–1967)

I N THE PASSAGE QUOTED above, Oxford chemistry professor Sir Cyril Hinshelwood calls attention to an aspect of chemistry often overlooked by the casual observer—the mystery of change with time. Since the opening chapter of this book, you have learned that the goal of chemistry is to understand the macroscopic world by examining the molecular one. In this chapter, we focus on understanding how this molecular world changes with time, an area of study called chemical kinetics. The molecular world is anything but static. Thermal energy produces constant molecular motion, causing molecules to repeatedly collide with one another. In a tiny fraction of these collisions, something extraordinary happens—the electrons on one molecule or atom are attracted to the nuclei of another. Some bonds weaken and new bonds form—a chemical reaction occurs. Chemical kinetics is the study of how these kinds of changes occur in time.

13.1 Catching Lizards

The children who live in my neighborhood (including my own kids) have a unique way of catching lizards. Armed with cups of ice water, they chase one of these cold-blooded reptiles into a corner, and then take aim and pour the cold water directly onto the lizard's body. The lizard's body temperature drops and it becomes virtually immobilized—easy prey for little hands. The kids scoop up the lizard and place it in a tub filled with sand and leaves. They then watch as the lizard warms back up and becomes active again. They usually release the lizard back into the yard within hours. I guess you could call them catch-and-release lizard hunters.

Unlike mammals, which actively regulate their body temperature through metabolic activity, lizards are *ectotherms*—their body temperature depends on their surroundings. When splashed with cold water, a lizard's body simply gets colder. The drop in body temperature immobilizes the lizard because its movement depends on chemical reactions that occur within its muscles, and the *rates* of those reactions—how fast they occur—are highly sensitive to temperature. In other words, when the temperature drops, the reactions that produce movement in the lizard occur more slowly; therefore, the movement itself slows down. When reptiles get cold, they become lethargic, unable to move very quickly. For this reason, reptiles try to maintain their body temperature within a narrow range by moving between sun and shade.

The rates of chemical reactions, and especially the ability to *control* those rates, are important not just in reptile movement but in many other phenomena as well. For example, a successful rocket launch depends on the rate at which fuel burns—too quickly and the rocket can explode, too slowly and it will not leave the ground. Chemists must always consider reaction rates when synthesizing compounds. No matter how stable a compound might be, its synthesis is impossible if the rate at which it forms is too slow. As we have seen with reptiles, reaction rates are important to life. In fact, the human body's ability to switch a specific reaction on or off at a specific time is achieved largely by controlling the rate of that reaction through the use of enzymes (biological molecules that we explore more fully in Section 13.7).

The first person to measure the rate of a chemical reaction carefully was Ludwig Wilhelmy. In 1850, he measured how fast sucrose, upon treatment with acid, hydrolyzed into glucose and fructose. This reaction occurred over several hours, and Wilhelmy was able to show how the rate depended on the initial amount of sugar present—the greater the initial amount, the faster the initial rate. Today we can measure the rates of reactions that occur in times as short as several femtoseconds (femto = 10^{-15}). The knowledge of reaction rates is not only practically important—giving us the ability to control how fast a reaction occurs—but also theoretically important. As you will see in Section 13.6, the rate of a reaction can tell us much about how the reaction occurs on the molecular scale.

13.2 The Rate of a Chemical Reaction

The rate of a chemical reaction is a measure of how fast the reaction occurs, as shown in Figure 13.1 ▶. If a chemical reaction has a fast rate, a large fraction of molecules react to form products in a given period of time. If a chemical reaction has a slow rate, only a relatively small fraction of molecules react to form products in a given period of time.

When we measure how fast something occurs, or more specifically the *rate* at which it occurs, we usually express the measurement as a change in some quantity per unit of time. For example, we measure the speed of a car—the rate at which it travels—in *miles per hour*, and we might measure how fast people lose weight in *pounds per week*. We report these rates in units that represent the change in what we are measuring (distance or weight) divided by the change in time.

$$\text{Speed} = \frac{\text{change in distance}}{\text{change in time}} = \frac{\Delta x}{\Delta t} \qquad \text{Weight loss} = \frac{\text{change in weight}}{\text{change in time}} = \frac{\Delta \text{ weight}}{\Delta t}$$

Similarly, the rate of a chemical reaction is measured as a change in the amounts of reactants or products (usually in concentration units) divided by the change in time. For example, consider the gas-phase reaction between $H_2(g)$ and $I_2(g)$:

$$H_2(g) + I_2(g) \longrightarrow 2\,HI(g)$$

We can define the rate of this reaction in the time interval t_1 to t_2 as follows:

Recall that [A] means the concentration of A in M (mol/L).

$$\text{Rate} = -\frac{\Delta[H_2]}{\Delta t} = -\frac{[H_2]_{t_2} - [H_2]_{t_1}}{t_2 - t_1} \qquad [13.1]$$

In this expression, $[H_2]_{t_2}$ is the hydrogen concentration at time t_2 and $[H_2]_{t_1}$ is the hydrogen concentration at time t_1. The reaction rate is defined as *the negative* of the change in concentration of a reactant divided by the change in time. The negative sign is usually part of the definition when the reaction rate is defined in terms of a reactant because reactant concentrations decrease as a reaction proceeds; therefore, *the change in the concentration of a reactant is negative*. The negative sign thus makes the overall *rate* positive. (By convention, reaction rates are reported as positive quantities.)

The reaction rate can also be defined in terms of the other reactant as follows:

$$\text{Rate} = -\frac{\Delta[I_2]}{\Delta t} \qquad [13.2]$$

A reaction with a fast rate

A reaction with a slow rate

$A + B \longrightarrow C$

$X + Y \longrightarrow Z$

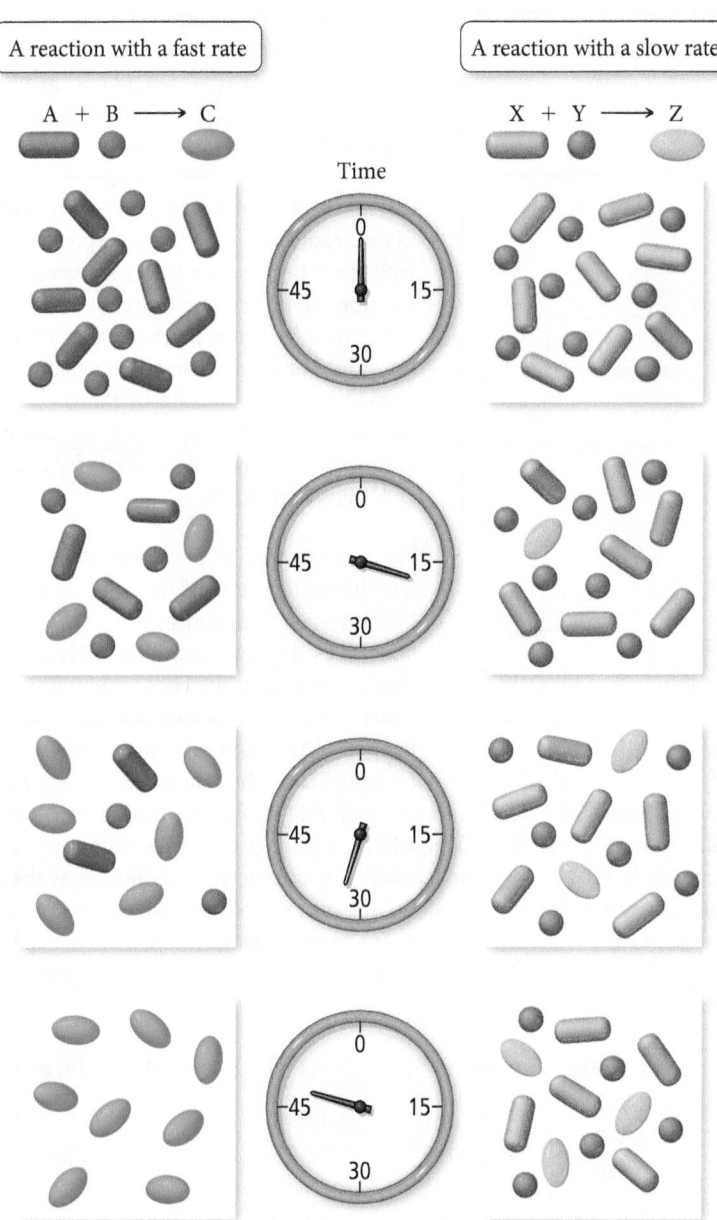

Time

Since 1 mol of H_2 reacts with 1 mol of I_2, the rates are defined in the same way. The rate can also be defined with respect to the *product* of the reaction as follows:

$$\text{Rate} = +\frac{1}{2}\frac{\Delta[\text{HI}]}{\Delta t} \qquad [13.3]$$

Because product concentrations *increase* as the reaction proceeds, the change in concentration of a product is positive. Therefore, when the rate is defined with respect to a product, we do not include a negative sign in the definition—the rate is naturally positive. The factor of $\frac{1}{2}$ in this definition is related to the stoichiometry of the reaction. In order to have a single rate for the entire reaction, the definition of the rate with respect to each reactant and product must reflect the stoichiometric coefficients of the reaction. For this particular reaction, 2 mol of HI is produced from 1 mol of H_2 and 1 mol of I_2.

The concentration of HI increases at twice the rate that the concentration of H_2 or I_2 decreases. In other words, if 100 I_2 molecules react per second, then 200 HI molecules form per second. In order for the overall rate to have the same value when defined with respect to any of the reactants or products, the change in HI concentration must be multiplied by a factor of one-half.

▲ **FIGURE 13.2 Reactant and Product Concentrations as a Function of Time** The graph shows the concentration of one of the reactants (H_2) and the product (HI) as a function of time. The other reactant (I_2) is omitted for clarity.

Consider the graph shown in Figure 13.2 ◄, which represents the changes in concentration for H_2 (one of the reactants) and HI (the product) versus time. Let's examine several features of this graph individually.

Change in Reactant and Product Concentrations

The reactant concentration, as expected, *decreases* with time because reactants are consumed in a reaction. The product concentration *increases* with time because products are formed in a reaction. The increase in HI concentration occurs at exactly twice the rate of the decrease in H_2 concentration because of the stoichiometry of the reaction: 2 mol of HI form for every 1 mol of H_2 consumed.

The Average Rate of the Reaction

We can calculate the average rate of the reaction for any time interval using Equation 13.1 for H_2. The following table lists H_2 concentration ($[H_2]$) at various times, the change in H_2 concentration for each interval ($\Delta[H_2]$), the change in time for each interval (Δt), and the rate for each interval ($-\Delta[H_2]/\Delta t$). The rate is the average rate within the given time interval. For example, the average rate of the reaction in the time interval between 10 and 20 seconds is 0.0149 M/s, while the average rate in the time interval between 20 and 30 seconds is 0.0121 M/s. Notice that the average rate *decreases* as the reaction progresses. In other words, the reaction slows down as it proceeds. We discuss this further in the next section, where we will see that, for most reactions, the rate depends on the concentrations of the reactants. As the reactants transform to products, their concentrations decrease, and the reaction slows down.

Time (s)	$[H_2]$ (M)	$\Delta[H_2]$ (M)	Δt (s)	Rate $= -\Delta[H_2]/\Delta t$ (M/s)
0.000	1.000			
		−0.181	10.000	0.0181
10.000	0.819			
		−0.149	10.000	0.0149
20.000	0.670			
		−0.121	10.000	0.0121
30.000	0.549			
		−0.100	10.000	0.0100
40.000	0.449			
		−0.081	10.000	0.0081
50.000	0.368			
		−0.067	10.000	0.0067
60.000	0.301			
		−0.054	10.000	0.0054
70.000	0.247			
		−0.045	10.000	0.0045
80.000	0.202			
		−0.037	10.000	0.0037
90.000	0.165			
		−0.030	10.000	0.0030
100.000	0.135			

The Instantaneous Rate of the Reaction

The instantaneous rate of the reaction is the rate at any one point in time and is represented by the instantaneous slope of the curve at that point. We can determine the instantaneous rate by calculating the slope of the tangent to the curve at the point of interest. In Figure 13.2, we have drawn the tangent lines for both $[H_2]$ and [HI] at 50 seconds. We calculate the instantaneous rate at 50 seconds as follows:

Using $[H_2]$

$$\text{Instantaneous rate (at 50 s)} = -\frac{\Delta[H_2]}{\Delta t} = -\frac{-0.28 \text{ M}}{40 \text{ s}} = 0.0070 \text{ M/s}$$

Using

$$\text{Instantaneous rate (at 50 s)} = +\frac{1}{2}\frac{\Delta[\text{HI}]}{\Delta t} = +\frac{1}{2}\frac{0.56 \text{ M}}{40 \text{ s}} = 0.0070 \text{ M/s}$$

As we would expect, the rate is the same whether we use one of the reactants or the product for the calculation. Notice that the instantaneous rate at 50 seconds (0.0070 M/s) is between the average rates calculated for the 10-second intervals just before and just after 50 seconds.

We can generalize our definition of reaction rate for the generic reaction:

$$aA + bB \longrightarrow cC + dD \qquad [13.4]$$

where A and B are reactants, C and D are products, and a, b, c, and d are the stoichiometric coefficients. We define the rate of the reaction as follows:

$$\text{Rate} = -\frac{1}{a}\frac{\Delta[A]}{\Delta t} = -\frac{1}{b}\frac{\Delta[B]}{\Delta t} = +\frac{1}{c}\frac{\Delta[C]}{\Delta t} = +\frac{1}{d}\frac{\Delta[D]}{\Delta t} \qquad [13.5]$$

From the definition, we can see that knowing the rate of change in the concentration of any one reactant or product at a point in time allows us to determine the rate of change in the concentration of any other reactant or product at that point in time (from the balanced equation). *However, predicting the rate at some future time is not possible from just the balanced equation.*

EXAMPLE 13.1 Expressing Reaction Rates

Consider this balanced chemical equation:

$$H_2O_2(aq) + 3\,I^-(aq) + 2\,H^+(aq) \longrightarrow I_3^-(aq) + 2\,H_2O(l)$$

In the first 10.0 seconds of the reaction, the concentration of I^- dropped from 1.000 M to 0.868 M.

(a) Calculate the average rate of this reaction in this time interval.

(b) Determine the rate of change in the concentration of H^+ (that is, $\Delta[H^+]/\Delta t$) during this time interval.

SOLUTION

(a) Use Equation 13.5 to calculate the average rate of the reaction.	$\text{Rate} = -\dfrac{1}{3}\dfrac{\Delta[I^-]}{\Delta t}$ $= -\dfrac{1}{3}\dfrac{(0.868\text{ M} - 1.000\text{ M})}{10.0\text{ s}}$ $= 4.40 \times 10^{-3}\text{ M/s}$
(b) Use Equation 13.5 again for the relationship between the rate of the reaction and $\Delta[H^+]/\Delta t$. After solving for $\Delta[H^+]/\Delta t$, substitute the calculated rate from part (a) and calculate $\Delta[H^+]/\Delta t$.	$\text{Rate} = -\dfrac{1}{2}\dfrac{\Delta[H^+]}{\Delta t}$ $\dfrac{\Delta[H^+]}{\Delta t} = -2(\text{rate})$ $= -2(4.40 \times 10^{-3}\text{ M/s})$ $= -8.80 \times 10^{-3}\text{ M/s}$

FOR PRACTICE 13.1

For the reaction shown in Example 13.1, predict the rate of change in concentration of H_2O_2 ($\Delta[H_2O_2]/\Delta t$) and I_3^- ($\Delta[I_3^-]/\Delta t$) during this time interval.

Conceptual Connection 13.1 Reaction Rates

For the reaction A + 2B $\longrightarrow$ C under a given set of conditions, the initial rate is 0.100 M/s. What is $\Delta[B]/\Delta t$ under the same conditions?

(a) −0.0500 M/s   **(b)** −0.100 M/s   **(c)** −0.200 M/s

Measuring Reaction Rates

In order to study the kinetics of a reaction, we must have an experimental way to measure the concentration of at least one of the reactants or products as a function of time. For example, Ludwig Wilhelmy, whose experiment on the rate of the conversion of sucrose to glucose and fructose we discussed briefly in Section 13.1, took advantage of sucrose's ability to rotate polarized light. (Polarized light is light with an electric field oriented along one plane.) When a beam of polarized light is passed through a sucrose solution, the polarization of the light is rotated clockwise. In contrast, the products of the reaction (glucose and fructose) rotate polarized light counter clockwise. By measuring the degree of polarization of light passing through a reacting solution—a technique known as polarimetry—Wilhelmy was able to determine the relative concentrations of the reactants and products as a function of time.

Perhaps the most common way to study the kinetics of a reaction is through spectroscopy (see Section 7.3). For example, the reaction of H_2 and I_2 to form HI can be followed spectroscopically because I_2 is violet and H_2 and HI are colorless. As I_2 reacts with H_2 to form HI, the violet color of the reaction mixture fades. The fading color can be monitored with a spectrometer, a device that passes light through a sample and measures how strongly the light is absorbed (Figure 13.3 ▼). If the sample contains the reacting mixture, the intensity of the light absorption will decrease as the reaction proceeds, providing a direct measure of the concentration of I_2 as a function of time. Because light travels so fast and because experimental techniques can produce very short pulses of light, spectroscopy can be used to measure reactions that happen on time scales as short as several femtoseconds.

Reactions in which the number of moles of gaseous reactants and products changes as the reaction proceeds can be readily monitored by measuring changes in pressure. Consider the reaction in which dinitrogen monoxide reacts to form nitrogen and oxygen gas:

$$2\,N_2O(g) \longrightarrow 2\,N_2(g) + O_2(g)$$

For every 2 mol of N_2O that reacts, the reaction vessel will contain one additional mole of gas. As the reaction proceeds and the amount of gas increases, the pressure steadily rises. We can use the rise in pressure to determine the relative concentrations of reactants and products as a function of time.

The three techniques mentioned here—polarimetry, spectroscopy, and pressure measurement—can all be used to monitor a reaction as it occurs in a reaction vessel. Some reactions occur slowly enough that samples, or *aliquots*, can be periodically withdrawn from the reaction vessel and analyzed to determine the progress of the reaction. Instrumental techniques such as gas chromatography (Figure 13.4 ▶) or mass spectrometry, as well as wet chemical techniques such as titration, can be used to measure the relative amounts of reactants or products in the aliquot. By taking aliquots at regular time intervals, we can determine the relative amounts of reactants and products as a function of time.

| Source | Slit | Monochromator | Sample | Detector | Computer |

▲ FIGURE 13.3 **The Spectrometer** In a spectrometer, light of a specific wavelength is passed through the sample and the intensity of the transmitted light—which depends on how much light is absorbed by the sample—is measured and recorded.

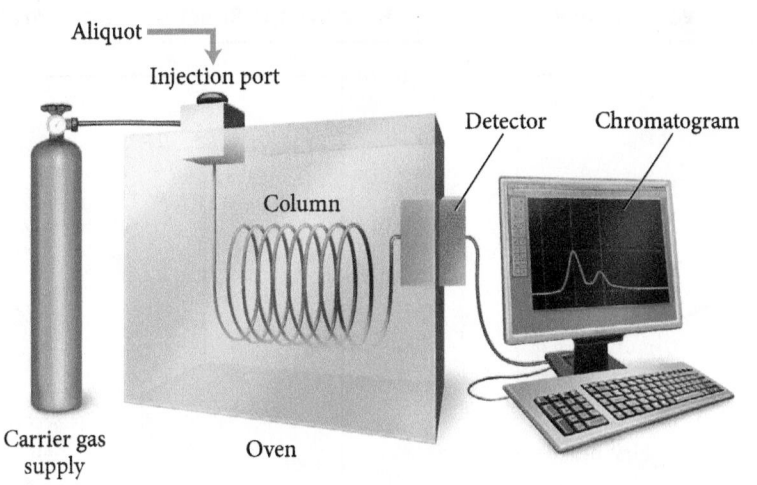

Aliquot

Injection port

Detector   Chromatogram

Column

Carrier gas supply

Oven

◀ **FIGURE 13.4 The Gas Chromatograph** In a gas chromatograph (GC), a sample of the reaction mixture, or aliquot, is injected into a specially constructed column. Because of their characteristic physical and chemical properties, different components of the mixture pass through the column at different rates and thus exit at different times. As each component leaves the column, it is identified electronically and a chromatogram is recorded. The area under each peak in the chromatogram is proportional to the amount of one particular component in the sample mixture.

13.3 The Rate Law: The Effect of Concentration on Reaction Rate

The rate of a reaction often depends on the concentration of one or more of the reactants. Wilhelmy noticed this effect in 1850 for the hydrolysis of sucrose. For simplicity, let's consider a reaction in which a single reactant, A, decomposes into products:

$$A \longrightarrow products$$

As long as the rate of the reverse reaction (in which the products return to reactants) is negligibly slow, we can express the relationship between the rate of the reaction and the concentration of the reactant—called the **rate law**—as follows:

$$Rate = k[A]^n \qquad [13.6]$$

where k is a constant of proportionality called the **rate constant** and n is the **reaction order**. The value of n (usually an integer) determines how the rate depends on the concentration of the reactant.

- If $n = 0$, the reaction is *zero order* and the rate is independent of the concentration of A.
- If $n = 1$, the reaction is *first order* and the rate is directly proportional to the concentration of A.
- If $n = 2$, the reaction is *second order* and the rate is proportional to the square of the concentration of A.

By definition, $[A]^0 = 1$, so the rate is equal to k regardless of [A].

Although other orders are possible, including noninteger (or fractional) orders, these three are the most common.

Figure 13.5 ▶ shows three plots illustrating how the *concentration of A changes with time* for the three common reaction orders with identical numerical values for the rate constant (k) and identical initial concentrations. Figure 13.6 ▶ has three plots showing the *rate of the reaction* (the slope of the lines in Figure 13.5) *as a function of the reactant concentration* for each reaction order.

Zero-Order Reaction In a zero-order reaction, the rate of the reaction is independent of the concentration of the reactant.

$$Rate = k[A]^0 = k \qquad [13.7]$$

Consequently, for a zero-order reaction, the concentration of the reactant decreases linearly with time, as shown in Figure 13.5. The slope of the line is constant, indicating a constant rate. The rate is constant because the reaction does not slow down as the concentration of A decreases. The graph in Figure 13.6 shows that the rate of a zero-order reaction is the same at any concentration of A. Zero-order reactions occur under conditions where the amount of reactant actually *available for reaction* is unaffected by changes in the *overall quantity of reactant*. For example, sublimation is normally zero order because only molecules at the surface can sublime, and their concentration does not change as the amount of subliming substance decreases (Figure 13.7 ▶).

Reactant Concentration versus Time

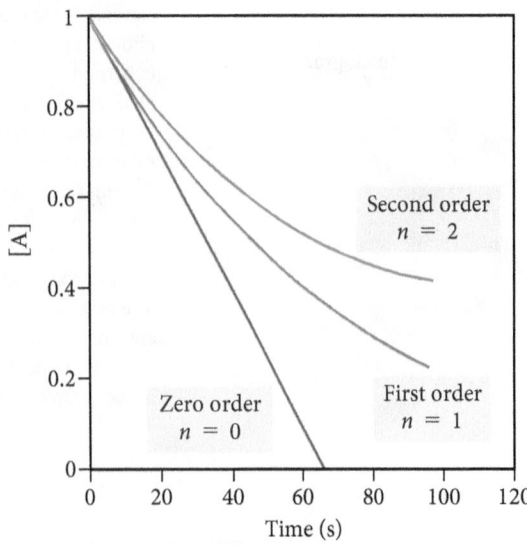

▲ FIGURE 13.5 Reactant Concentration as a Function of Time for Different Reaction Orders

Rate versus Reactant Concentration

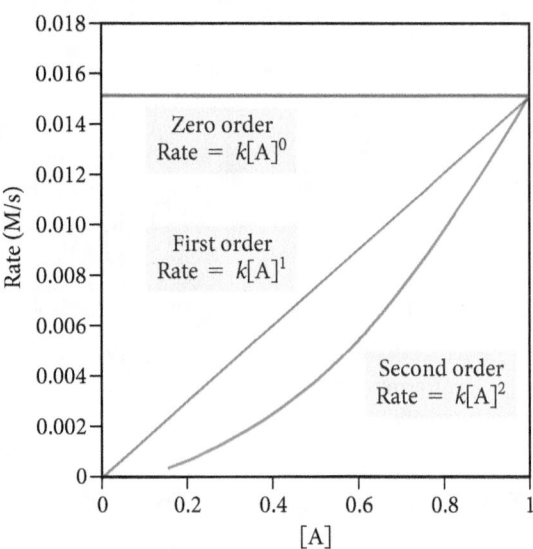

▲ FIGURE 13.6 Reaction Rate as a Function of Reactant Concentration for Different Reaction Orders

Sublimation Is Zero-Order

Ice in glass tube

When one layer of particles sublimes, the next layer is exposed. The number of particles available to sublime remains constant.

▲ FIGURE 13.7 Sublimation When a layer of particles sublimes, another identical layer is just below it. Consequently, the number of particles available to sublime at any one time does not change with the total number of particles in the sample, and the process is zero order.

First-Order Reaction In a first-order reaction, the rate of the reaction is directly proportional to the concentration of the reactant.

$$\text{Rate} = k[A]^1 \qquad [13.8]$$

For a first-order reaction the rate slows down as the reaction proceeds because the concentration of the reactant decreases. You can see this in Figure 13.5—the slope of the curve (the rate) becomes less steep (slower) with time. Figure 13.6 shows the rate as a function of the concentration of A. Notice the linear relationship—the rate is directly proportional to the concentration.

Second-Order Reaction In a second-order reaction, the rate of the reaction is proportional to the square of the concentration of the reactant.

$$\text{Rate} = k[A]^2 \qquad [13.9]$$

Consequently, for a second-order reaction, the rate is even more sensitive to the reactant concentration. You can see this in Figure 13.5—the slope of the curve (the rate) flattens out more quickly than it does for a first-order reaction. Figure 13.6 shows the rate as a function of the concentration of A. Notice the quadratic relationship—the rate is proportional to the square of the concentration.

Determining the Order of a Reaction

The order of a reaction can be determined only by experiment. A common way to determine reaction order is the *method of initial rates*. In this method, the initial rate—the rate for a short period of time at the beginning of the reaction—is measured by running the reaction several times with different initial reactant concentrations to determine the effect of the concentration on the rate. For example, let's return to our simple reaction in which a single reactant, A, decomposes into products:

$$A \longrightarrow \text{products}$$

In an experiment, the initial rate is measured at several different initial concentrations with the following results:

[A] (M)	Initial Rate (M/s)
0.10	0.015
0.20	0.030
0.40	0.060

In this data set, when the concentration of A doubles, the rate doubles—the initial rate is directly proportional to the initial concentration. The reaction is therefore first order in A, and the rate law takes the first-order form:

$$\text{Rate} = k[A]^1$$

We can determine the value of the rate constant, k, by solving the rate law for k and substituting the concentration and the initial rate from any one of the three measurements (here we use the first measurement).

$$\text{Rate} = k[A]^1$$

$$k = \frac{\text{rate}}{[A]} = \frac{0.015 \text{ M/s}}{0.10 \text{ M}} = 0.15 \text{ s}^{-1}$$

Notice that the rate constant for a first-order reaction has units of s^{-1}.

The following two data sets show how measured initial rates are different for zero-order and for second-order reactions having the same initial rate at $[A] = 0.10$ M:

Zero Order ($n = 0$)		Second Order ($n = 2$)	
[A] (M)	Initial Rate (M/s)	[A] (M)	Initial Rate (M/s)
0.10	0.015	0.10	0.015
0.20	0.015	0.20	0.060
0.40	0.015	0.40	0.240

For a zero-order reaction, the initial rate is independent of the reactant concentration—the rate is the same at all measured initial concentrations. For a second-order reaction, the initial rate quadruples for a doubling of the reactant concentration—the relationship between concentration and rate is quadratic. If we are unsure about how the initial rate is changing with the initial reactant concentration, or if the numbers are not as obvious as they are in these examples, we can substitute any two initial concentrations and the corresponding initial rates into a ratio of the rate laws to determine the order (n):

$$\frac{\text{rate 2}}{\text{rate 1}} = \frac{k[A]_2^n}{k[A]_1^n}$$

For example, we can substitute the last two measurements in the data set just given for the second-order reaction as follows:

$$\frac{0.240 \text{ M/s}}{0.060 \text{ M/s}} = \frac{k(0.40 \text{ M})^n}{k(0.20 \text{ M})^n}$$

$$4.0 = \left(\frac{0.40}{0.20}\right)^n = 2^n$$

$$\log 4.0 = \log(2^n)$$

$$= n \log 2$$

$$n = \frac{\log 4}{\log 2}$$

$$= 2$$

| Remember that $\frac{x^n}{y^n} = \left(\frac{x}{y}\right)^n$

| Remember that $\log x^n = n \log x$.

The rate constants for zero- and second-order reactions have different units than for first-order reactions. The rate constant for a zero-order reaction has units of $M \cdot s^{-1}$, and the rate constant for a second-order reaction has units of $M^{-1} \cdot s^{-1}$.

Conceptual Connection 13.2 Order of Reaction

The reaction A $\rightarrow$ B has been experimentally determined to be second order. The initial rate is 0.0100 M/s at an initial concentration of A of 0.100 M. What is the initial rate at $[A] = 0.500$ M?

(a) 0.00200 M/s   (b) 0.0100 M/s   (c) 0.0500 M/s   (d) 0.250 M/s

Reaction Order for Multiple Reactants

So far, we have considered a simple reaction with only one reactant. How is the rate law defined for reactions with more than one reactant? Consider the generic reaction:

$$a\text{A} + b\text{B} \longrightarrow c\text{C} + d\text{D}$$

As long as the reverse reaction is negligibly slow, the rate law is proportional to the concentration of [A] raised to the m power multiplied by the concentration of [B] raised to the n power:

$$\text{Rate} = k[\text{A}]^m[\text{B}]^n \qquad [13.10]$$

where m is the reaction order with respect to A and n is the reaction order with respect to B. The **overall order** is the sum of the exponents $(m + n)$. For example, the reaction between hydrogen and iodine has been experimentally determined to be first order with respect to hydrogen, first order with respect to iodine, and thus second order overall.

$$\text{H}_2(g) + \text{I}_2(g) \longrightarrow 2\,\text{HI}(g) \quad \text{Rate} = k[\text{H}_2]^1[\text{I}_2]^1$$

Similarly, the reaction between hydrogen and nitrogen monoxide has been experimentally determined to be first order with respect to hydrogen, second order with respect to nitrogen monoxide, and thus third order overall.

$$2\,\text{H}_2(g) + 2\,\text{NO}(g) \longrightarrow \text{N}_2(g) + 2\,\text{H}_2\text{O}(g) \quad \text{Rate} = k[\text{H}_2]^1[\text{NO}]^2$$

The rate law for any reaction must always be determined by experiment, often by the method of initial rates described previously. There is no way to simply look at a chemical equation and determine the rate law for the reaction. When the reaction has two or more reactants, the concentration of each reactant is usually varied independently of the others to determine the dependence of the rate on the concentration of that reactant. Example 13.2 shows how to use the method of initial rates to determine the order of a reaction with multiple reactants.

EXAMPLE 13.2 Determining the Order and Rate Constant of a Reaction

Consider the reaction between nitrogen dioxide and carbon monoxide:

$$\text{NO}_2(g) + \text{CO}(g) \longrightarrow \text{NO}(g) + \text{CO}_2(g)$$

The initial rate of the reaction is measured at several different concentrations of the reactants with the accompanied results. From the data, determine:

(a) the rate law for the reaction

(b) the rate constant (k) for the reaction

$[\text{NO}_2]$ (M)	[CO] (M)	Initial Rate (M/s)
0.10	0.10	0.0021
0.20	0.10	0.0082
0.20	0.20	0.0083
0.40	0.10	0.033

SOLUTION

(a) Begin by examining how the rate changes for each change in concentration. Between the first two experiments, the concentration of NO_2 doubles, the concentration of CO stays constant, and the rate quadruples, suggesting that the reaction is second order in NO_2.

Between the second and third experiments, the concentration of NO_2 stays constant, the concentration of CO doubles, and the rate remains constant (the small change in the least significant figure is simply experimental error), suggesting that the reaction is zero order in CO.

Between the third and fourth experiments, the concentration of NO_2 again doubles and the concentration of CO halves, yet the rate quadruples again, confirming that the reaction is second order in NO_2 and zero order in CO.

$[\text{NO}_2]$	[CO]	Initial Rate (M/s)
0.10 M	0.10 M	0.0021
$\downarrow \times 2$	$\downarrow$ constant	$\downarrow \times 4$
0.20 M	0.10 M	0.0082 M
$\downarrow$ constant	$\downarrow \times 2$	$\downarrow \times 1$
0.20 M	0.20 M	0.0083 M
$\downarrow \times 2$	$\downarrow \times \frac{1}{2}$	$\downarrow \times 4$
0.40 M	0.10 M	0.033 M

Write the overall rate expression.	Rate $= k[NO_2]^2[CO]^0 = k[NO_2]^2$
(b) To determine the rate constant for the reaction, solve the rate law for k and substitute the concentration and the initial rate from any one of the four measurements. In this case, we use the first measurement.	Rate $= k[NO_2]^2$ $k = \dfrac{\text{rate}}{[NO_2]^2} = \dfrac{0.0021 \text{ M/s}}{(0.10 \text{ M})^2} = 0.21 \text{ M}^{-1} \cdot \text{s}^{-1}$

FOR PRACTICE 13.2

Consider the equation:

$$CHCl_3(g) + Cl_2(g) \longrightarrow CCl_4(g) + HCl(g)$$

The initial rate of reaction is measured at several different concentrations of the reactants with the following results:

[CHCl₃] (M)	[Cl₂] (M)	Initial Rate (M/s)
0.010	0.010	0.0035
0.020	0.010	0.0069
0.020	0.020	0.0098
0.040	0.040	0.027

From the data, determine:

(a) the rate law for the reaction   **(b)** the rate constant (k) for the reaction

Conceptual Connection 13.3 Rate and Concentration

This reaction was experimentally determined to be first order with respect to O_2 and second order with respect to NO.

$$O_2(g) + 2 NO(g) \longrightarrow 2 NO_2(g)$$

These diagrams represent reaction mixtures in which the number of each type of molecule represents its relative initial concentration. Which mixture has the fastest initial rate?

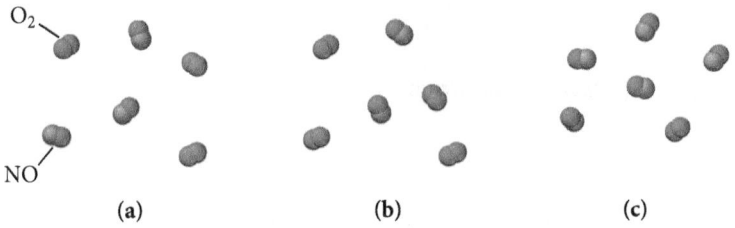

(a)   (b)   (c)

13.4 The Integrated Rate Law: The Dependence of Concentration on Time

The rate laws we have examined so far show the relationship between *the rate of a reaction and the concentration of a reactant*. But we often want to know the relationship between *the concentration of a reactant and time*. For example, the presence of chlorofluorocarbons (CFCs) in the atmosphere threatens the ozone layer. One of the reasons that CFCs pose such a significant threat is that the reactions that consume them are so slow (see Table 13.1). Legislation has significantly reduced CFC emissions, but even if we were to completely stop adding CFCs to the atmosphere, their concentration would decrease only very slowly. Nonetheless, we would like to know how their concentration changes with time. How much will be left in 20 years? In 50 years?

TABLE 13.1   Atmospheric Lifetimes of Several CFCs

CFC Name	Structure	Atmospheric Lifetime*
CFC-11 (CCl_3F) Trichlorofluoromethane		45 years
CFC-12 (CCl_2F_2) Dichlorodifluoromethane		100 years
CFC-113 ($C_2F_3Cl_3$) 1,1,2-Trichloro-1,2,2-trifluoroethane		85 years
CFC-114 ($C_2F_4Cl_2$) 1,2-Dichlorotetrafluoroethane		300 years
CFC-115 (C_2F_5Cl) Monochloropentafluoroethane		1700 years

*Data taken from EPA site (under section 602 of Clean Air Act).

The **integrated rate law** for a chemical reaction is a relationship between the concentrations of the reactants and time. For simplicity, we return to a single reactant decomposing into products:

$$A \longrightarrow \text{products}$$

The integrated rate law for this reaction depends on the order of the reaction; let's examine each of the common reaction orders individually.

First-Order Integrated Rate Law If our simple reaction is first order, the rate is directly proportional to the concentration of A:

$$\text{Rate} = k[A]$$

Since Rate $= -\Delta[A]/\Delta t$, we can write:

$$-\frac{\Delta[A]}{\Delta t} = k[A] \qquad [13.11]$$

In this form, the rate law is also known as the *differential rate law*.

Although we do not show the steps here, we can use calculus (see End-of-Chapter Exercise 112) to integrate the differential rate law and obtain the first-order *integrated rate law*:

$$\ln[A]_t = -kt + \ln[A]_0 \qquad [13.12]$$

or

$$\ln\frac{[A]_t}{[A]_0} = -kt \qquad [13.13]$$

$\ln[A]_t = -kt + \ln[A]_0$

$\ln[A]_t - \ln[A]_0 = -kt$

$\ln\dfrac{[A]_t}{[A]_0} = -kt$

Remember that $\ln A - \ln B = \ln(A/B)$.

where $[A]_t$ is the concentration of A at any time t, k is the rate constant, and $[A]_0$ is the initial concentration of A. These two forms of the equation are equivalent, as shown in the margin.

Notice that the integrated rate law shown in Equation 13.12 has the form of an equation for a straight line.

$$\ln[A]_t = -kt + \ln[A]_0$$
$$y = mx + b$$

For a first-order reaction, a plot of the natural log of the reactant concentration as a function of time yields a straight line with a slope of $-k$ and a y-intercept of $\ln[A]_0$, as shown in Figure 13.8 ▸. (Note that the slope is negative but that the rate constant is always positive.)

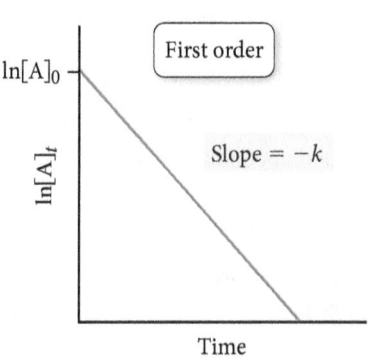

▲ FIGURE 13.8 **First-Order Integrated Rate Law** For a first-order reaction, a plot of the natural log of the reactant concentration as a function of time yields a straight line. The slope of the line is equal to $-k$ and the y-intercept is $\ln[A]_0$.

EXAMPLE 13.3 The First-Order Integrated Rate Law: Using Graphical Analysis of Reaction Data

Consider the equation for the decomposition of SO_2Cl_2:

$$SO_2Cl_2(g) \longrightarrow SO_2(g) + Cl_2(g)$$

The concentration of SO_2Cl_2 was monitored at a fixed temperature as a function of time during the decomposition reaction, and the following data were tabulated:

Time (s)	[SO₂Cl₂] (M)	Time (s)	[SO₂Cl₂] (M)
0	0.100	800	0.0793
100	0.0971	900	0.0770
200	0.0944	1000	0.0748
300	0.0917	1100	0.0727
400	0.0890	1200	0.0706
500	0.0865	1300	0.0686
600	0.0840	1400	0.0666
700	0.0816	1500	0.0647

Show that the reaction is first order, and determine the rate constant for the reaction.

SOLUTION

In order to show that the reaction is first order, prepare a graph of $\ln[SO_2Cl_2]$ versus time as shown.

The plot is linear, confirming that the reaction is indeed first order. To obtain the rate constant, fit the data to a line. The slope of the line will be equal to $-k$. Since the slope of the best fitting line (which is most easily determined on a graphing calculator or with spreadsheet software such as Microsoft Excel) is $-2.90 \times 10^{-4}\,s^{-1}$, the rate constant is therefore $+2.90 \times 10^{-4}\,s^{-1}$.

FOR PRACTICE 13.3

Use the graph and the best fitting line in Example 13.3 to predict the concentration of SO_2Cl_2 at 1900 s.

EXAMPLE 13.4 The First-Order Integrated Rate Law: Determining the Concentration of a Reactant at a Given Time

In Example 13.3, you determined that the decomposition of SO_2Cl_2 (under the given reaction conditions) is first order and has a rate constant of $+2.90 \times 10^{-4} s^{-1}$. If the reaction is carried out at the same temperature, and the initial concentration of SO_2Cl_2 is 0.0225 M, what will the SO_2Cl_2 concentration be after 865 s?

SORT You are given the rate constant of a first-order reaction and the initial concentration of the reactant and asked to find the concentration at 865 seconds.	**GIVEN:** $k = +2.90 \times 10^{-4} s^{-1}$ $[SO_2Cl_2]_0 = 0.0225$ M **FIND:** $[SO_2Cl_2]$ at $t = 865$ s
STRATEGIZE Refer to the first-order integrated rate law to determine the information you are asked to find.	**EQUATION** $\ln[A]_t = -kt + \ln[A]_0$
SOLVE Substitute the rate constant, the initial concentration, and the time into the integrated rate law. Solve the integrated rate law for the concentration of $[SOCl_2]_t$.	**SOLUTION** $\ln[SO_2Cl_2]_t = -kt + \ln[SO_2Cl_2]_0$ $\ln[SO_2Cl_2]_t = -(2.90 \times 10^{-4} s^{-1})865 \, s + \ln(0.0225)$ $\ln[SO_2Cl_2]_t = -0.251 - 3.79$ $[SO_2Cl_2]_t = e^{-4.04}$ $= 0.0175$ M

CHECK The concentration is smaller than the original concentration as expected. If the concentration were larger than the initial concentration, this would indicate a mistake in the signs of one of the quantities on the right-hand side of the equation.

FOR PRACTICE 13.4

Cyclopropane rearranges to form propene in the gas phase.

$$\underset{H_2C-CH_2}{\overset{CH_2}{\triangle}} \longrightarrow CH_3-CH=CH_2$$

The reaction is first order in cyclopropane and has a measured rate constant of $3.36 \times 10^{-5} s^{-1}$ at 720 K. If the initial cyclopropane concentration is 0.0445 M, what will the cyclopropane concentration be after 235.0 minutes?

Second-Order Integrated Rate Law If our simple reaction (A ⟶ products) is second order, the rate is proportional to the square of the concentration of A:

$$\text{Rate} = k[A]^2$$

Since Rate $= -\Delta[A]/\Delta t$, we can write:

$$-\frac{\Delta[A]}{\Delta t} = k[A]^2 \tag{13.14}$$

Again, although we do not show the steps here, this differential rate law can be integrated to obtain the *second-order integrated rate law*:

$$\frac{1}{[A]_t} = kt + \frac{1}{[A]_0} \tag{13.15}$$

The second-order integrated rate law is also in the form of an equation for a straight line:

$$\frac{1}{[A]_t} = kt + \frac{1}{[A]_0}$$
$$y = mx + b$$

However, you must plot the inverse of the concentration of the reactant as a function of time. The plot yields a straight line with a slope of k and an intercept of $1/[A]_0$ as shown in Figure 13.9 ▶.

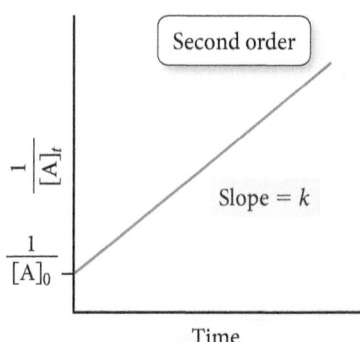

▲ **FIGURE 13.9 Second-Order Integrated Rate Law**   For a second-order reaction, a plot of the inverse of the reactant concentration as a function of time yields a straight line. The slope of the line is equal to k and the y-intercept is $1/[A]_0$.

EXAMPLE 13.5 The Second-Order Integrated Rate Law: Using Graphical Analysis of Reaction Data

Consider the equation for the decomposition of NO_2:

$$NO_2(g) \longrightarrow NO(g) + O(g)$$

The concentration of NO_2 is monitored at a fixed temperature as a function of time during the decomposition reaction and the data tabulated in the margin at right. Show by graphical analysis that the reaction is not first order and that it is second order. Determine the rate constant for the reaction.

SOLUTION

In order to show that the reaction is *not* first order, prepare a graph of $\ln[NO_2]$ versus time as shown.

The plot is *not* linear (the straight line does not fit the data points), confirming that the reaction is not first order. In order to show that the reaction is second order, prepare a graph of $1/[NO_2]$ versus time as shown.

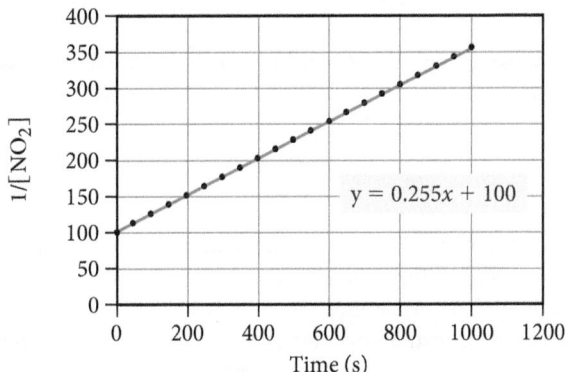

This graph is linear (the data points fit well to a straight line), confirming that the reaction is indeed second order. To obtain the rate constant, determine the slope of the best fitting line. The slope is $0.255 \text{ M}^{-1} \cdot \text{s}^{-1}$; therefore, the rate constant is $0.255 \text{ M}^{-1} \cdot \text{s}^{-1}$.

FOR PRACTICE 13.5

Use the graph and the best fitting line in Example 13.5 to predict the concentration of NO_2 at 2000 s.

Time (s)	[NO₂] (M)
0	0.01000
50	0.00887
100	0.00797
150	0.00723
200	0.00662
250	0.00611
300	0.00567
350	0.00528
400	0.00495
450	0.00466
500	0.00440
550	0.00416
600	0.00395
650	0.00376
700	0.00359
750	0.00343
800	0.00329
850	0.00316
900	0.00303
950	0.00292
1000	0.00282

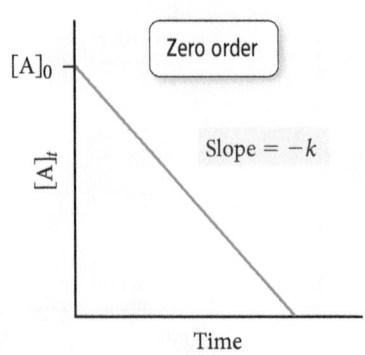

$[A]_0$

$[A]_t$

Zero order

Slope $= -k$

Time

▲ FIGURE 13.10 **Zero-Order Integrated Rate Law**   For a zero-order reaction, a plot of the reactant concentration as a function of time yields a straight line. The slope of the line is equal to $-k$ and the y-intercept is $[A]_0$.

Zero-Order Integrated Rate Law   If our simple reaction is zero order, the rate is proportional to a constant:

$$Rate = k[A]^0 = k$$

Since $Rate = -\Delta[A]/\Delta t$, we can write:

$$-\frac{\Delta[A]}{\Delta t} = k \qquad [13.16]$$

We can integrate this differential rate law to obtain the *zero-order integrated rate law*:

$$[A]_t = -kt + [A]_0 \qquad [13.17]$$

The zero-order integrated rate law in Equation 13.17 is also in the form of an equation for a straight line. A plot of the concentration of the reactant as a function of time yields a straight line with a slope of $-k$ and an intercept of $[A]_0$, as shown in Figure 13.10 ◄.

The Half-Life of a Reaction

The **half-life** ($t_{1/2}$) of a reaction is the time required for the concentration of a reactant to fall to one-half of its initial value. For example, if a reaction has a half-life of 100 seconds, and if the initial concentration of the reactant is 1.0 M, the concentration will fall to 0.50 M in 100 s. The half-life expression—which defines the dependence of half-life on the rate constant and the initial concentration—is different for different reaction orders.

First-Order Reaction Half-Life   From the definition of half-life, and from the integrated rate law, we can derive an expression for the half-life. For a first-order reaction, the integrated rate law is:

$$\ln \frac{[A]_t}{[A]_0} = -kt$$

At a time equal to the half-life ($t = t_{1/2}$), the concentration is exactly half of the initial concentration: ($[A]_t = \frac{1}{2}[A]_0$). Therefore, when $t = t_{1/2}$ we can write the following expression:

$$\ln \frac{\frac{1}{2}[A]_0}{[A]_0} = \ln \frac{1}{2} = -kt_{1/2} \qquad [13.18]$$

Solving for $t_{1/2}$, and substituting -0.693 for $\ln \frac{1}{2}$, we arrive at the expression for the half-life of a first-order reaction:

$$t_{1/2} = \frac{0.693}{k} \qquad [13.19]$$

Notice that, for a first-order reaction, $t_{1/2}$ *is independent of the initial concentration.* For example, if $t_{1/2}$ is 100 s, and if the initial concentration is 1.0 M, the concentration falls to 0.50 M in 100 s, to 0.25 M in another 100 s, to 0.125 M in another 100 s, and so on (Figure 13.11 ►). Even though the concentration is changing as the reaction proceeds, the half-life (how long it takes for the concentration to halve) is constant. A constant half-life is unique to first-order reactions, making the concept of half-life particularly useful for first-order reactions.

Half-Life for a First-Order Reaction

At t_0

For a first-order reaction, the half-life is constant and independent of concentration.

After 1 half-life

After 2 half-lives

After 3 half-lives

◀ **FIGURE 13.11 Half-Life: Concentration versus Time for a First-Order Reaction**   For this reaction, the concentration decreases by one-half every 100 seconds ($t_{1/2} = 100$ s). The blue spheres represent reactant molecules (the products are omitted for clarity).

EXAMPLE 13.6 Half-Life

Molecular iodine dissociates at 625 K with a first-order rate constant of 0.271 s^{-1}. What is the half-life of this reaction?

SOLUTION

Because the reaction is first order, the half-life is given by Equation 13.19. Substitute the value of k into the expression and calculate $t_{1/2}$.

$$t_{1/2} = \frac{0.693}{k}$$

$$= \frac{0.693}{0.271/s} = 2.56 \text{ s}$$

FOR PRACTICE 13.6

A first-order reaction has a half-life of 26.4 seconds. How long does it take for the concentration of the reactant in the reaction to fall to one-eighth of its initial value?

Second-Order Reaction Half-Life For a second-order reaction, the integrated rate law is:

$$\frac{1}{[A]_t} = kt + \frac{1}{[A]_0}$$

At a time equal to the half-life ($t = t_{1/2}$), the concentration is exactly one-half of the initial concentration ($[A]_t = \frac{1}{2}[A]_0$). We can therefore write the following expression at $t = t_{1/2}$:

$$\frac{1}{\frac{1}{2}[A]_0} = kt_{1/2} + \frac{1}{[A]_0} \qquad [13.20]$$

And then solve for $t_{1/2}$:

$$kt_{1/2} = \frac{1}{\frac{1}{2}[A]_0} - \frac{1}{[A]_0}$$

$$kt_{1/2} = \frac{2}{[A]_0} - \frac{1}{[A]_0}$$

$$t_{1/2} = \frac{1}{k[A]_0} \qquad [13.21]$$

Notice that, for a second-order reaction, the half-life depends on the initial concentration. So if the initial concentration of a reactant in a second-order reaction is 1.0 M, and the half-life is 100 s, the concentration falls to 0.50 M in 100 s. However, the time it takes for the concentration to fall to 0.25 M is now *longer than 100 s* because the initial concentration has decreased. Thus, the half-life continues to get longer as the concentration decreases.

Zero-Order Reaction Half-Life For a zero-order reaction, the integrated rate law is:

$$[A]_t = -kt + [A]_0$$

Making the substitutions ($t = t_{1/2}$; $[A]_t = \frac{1}{2}[A]_0$), we can write the expression at $t = t_{1/2}$:

$$\tfrac{1}{2}[A]_0 = -kt_{1/2} + [A]_0 \qquad [13.22]$$

We then solve for $t_{1/2}$:

$$t_{1/2} = \frac{[A]_0}{2k} \qquad [13.23]$$

Notice that, for a zero-order reaction, the half-life also depends on the initial concentration; however, unlike in the second order case, the two are directly proportional—the half-life gets *shorter* as the concentration decreases.

Summarizing Basic Kinetic Relationships (see Table 13.2):

▶ The reaction order and rate law must be determined experimentally.

▶ The rate law relates the *rate* of the reaction to the *concentration* of the reactant(s).

▶ The integrated rate law (which is mathematically derived from the rate law) relates the *concentration* of the reactant(s) to *time*.

▶ The half-life is the time it takes for the concentration of a reactant to fall to one-half of its initial value.

▶ The half-life of a first-order reaction is independent of the initial concentration.

▶ The half-lives of zero-order and second-order reactions depend on the initial concentration.

Conceptual Connection 13.4 Rate Law and Integrated Rate Law

A decomposition reaction, with a rate that is observed to slow down as the reaction proceeds, is found to have a half-life that depends on the initial concentration of the reactant. Which statement is most likely true for this reaction?

(a) A plot of the natural log of the concentration of the reactant as a function of time is linear.

(b) The half-life of the reaction increases as the initial concentration increases.

(c) A doubling of the initial concentration of the reactant results in a quadrupling of the rate.

TABLE 13.2 Rate Law Summary Table

Order	Rate Law	Units of k	Integrated Rate Law	Straight-Line Plot	Half-Life Expression
0	Rate $= k[A]^0$	$M \cdot s^{-1}$	$[A]_t = -kt + [A]_0$		$t_{1/2} = \dfrac{[A]_0}{2k} = \dfrac{1}{k}\dfrac{[A]_0}{2}$
1	Rate $= k[A]^1$	s^{-1}	$\ln[A]_t = -kt + \ln[A]_0$ $\ln\dfrac{[A]_t}{[A]_0} = -kt$		$t_{1/2} = \dfrac{0.693}{k} = \dfrac{1}{k}(0.693)$
2	Rate $= k[A]^2$	$M^{-1} \cdot s^{-1}$	$\dfrac{1}{[A]_t} = kt + \dfrac{1}{[A]_0}$		$t_{1/2} = \dfrac{1}{k[A]_0} = \dfrac{1}{k}\dfrac{1}{[A]_0}$

13.5 The Effect of Temperature on Reaction Rate

In the opening section of this chapter, you learned that lizards become lethargic when their body temperature drops because the chemical reactions that control their muscle movement slow down at lower temperatures. The rates of chemical reactions are, in general, highly sensitive to temperature. For example, at around room temperature, a 10 °C increase in temperature increases the rate of a typical biological reaction by two or three times. How do we explain this highly sensitive temperature dependence?

Recall that the rate law for a reaction is Rate $= k[A]^n$. *The temperature dependence of the reaction rate is contained in the rate constant, k* (which is actually a constant only when the temperature remains constant). An increase in temperature generally results in an increase in k, which results in a faster rate. In 1889, Swedish chemist Svante Arrhenius wrote a paper quantifying the temperature dependence of the rate constant. The modern form of the **Arrhenius equation** shows the relationship between the rate constant (k) and the temperature in kelvin (T):

$$k = Ae^{\frac{-E_a}{RT}}$$

Activation energy (pointing to $-E_a$)
Frequency factor (pointing to A)
Exponential factor (pointing to $e^{\frac{-E_a}{RT}}$)

[13.24]

In this equation, R is the gas constant ($8.314 \text{ J/mol} \cdot \text{K}$), A is a constant called the *frequency factor* (or the *pre-exponential factor*), and E_a is the *activation energy* (or *activation barrier*).

► FIGURE 13.12 The Activation Energy
Barrier Even though the reaction is
energetically favorable (the energy of
the products is lower than that of the
reactants), an input of energy is needed
for the reaction to take place.

Activation Energy

$$2\,H_2(g) + O_2(g) \rightleftharpoons 2\,H_2O(g)$$

► FIGURE 13.12 The Activation Energy
Barrier Even though the reaction is
energetically favorable (the energy of
the products is lower than that of the
reactants), an input of energy is needed
for the reaction to take place.

The **activation energy E_a** is an energy barrier or hump that must be surmounted for the reactants to be transformed into products (Figure 13.12 ▲). We examine the frequency factor more closely in the next section; for now, we can think of the **frequency factor (A)** as the number of times that the reactants approach the activation barrier per unit time.

To understand each of these quantities better, consider the simple reaction in which CH_3NC (methyl isonitrile) rearranges to form CH_3CN (acetonitrile):

$$CH_3-N{\equiv}C \longrightarrow CH_3-C{\equiv}N$$

Let's examine the physical meaning of the activation energy, frequency factor, and exponential factor for this reaction.

The Activation Energy Figure 13.13 ▼ shows the energy of a molecule as the reaction proceeds. The x-axis represents the progress of the reaction from left (reactant) to right (product). To get from the reactant to the product, the molecule must go through a high-energy intermediate state called the **activated complex** or **transition state**. Even though the overall reaction is energetically downhill (exothermic), it must first go uphill to reach

► FIGURE 13.13 The Activated
Complex The reaction pathway
includes a transitional state—the
activated complex—that has a higher
energy than either the reactant or
the product.

the activated complex because energy is required to initially weaken the H_3C-N bond and allow the NC group to begin to rotate:

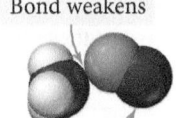

Bond weakens

NC group begins to rotate

The energy required to reach the activated complex is the *activation energy. The higher the activation energy, the slower the reaction rate (at a given temperature).*

The Frequency Factor Recall that the frequency factor represents the number of approaches to the activation barrier per unit time. Any time that it begins to rotate, the NC group approaches the activation barrier. For this reaction, the frequency factor represents the rate at which the NC part of the molecule wags (vibrates side-to-side). With each wag, the reactant approaches the activation barrier. However, approaching the activation barrier is not equivalent to surmounting it. Most of the approaches do not have enough total energy to make it over the activation barrier.

The Exponential Factor The **exponential factor** is a number between 0 and 1 that represents the fraction of molecules that have enough energy to make it over the activation barrier on a given approach. The exponential factor is the fraction of approaches that are actually successful and result in the product. For example, if the frequency factor is $10^9/s$ and the exponential factor is 10^{-7} at a certain temperature, then the overall rate constant at that temperature is $10^9/s \times 10^{-7} = 10^2/s$. In this case, the CN group is wagging at a rate of $10^9/s$. With each wag, the activation barrier is approached. However, for a given wag only 1 in 10^7 molecules has sufficient energy to actually make it over the activation barrier.

The exponential factor depends on both the temperature (T) and the activation energy (E_a) of the reaction.

$$\text{Exponential factor} = e^{-E_a/RT}$$

A low activation energy and a high temperature make the negative exponent small, so the exponential factor approaches one. For example, if the activation energy is zero, then the exponent is zero, and the exponential factor is exactly one ($e^{-0} = 1$)—every approach to the activation barrier is successful. By contrast, a large activation energy and a low temperature make the exponent a very large negative number, so the exponential factor becomes very small. For example, as the temperature approaches 0 K, the exponent approaches an infinitely large number, and the exponential factor approaches zero ($e^{-\infty} = 0$).

As the temperature increases, the number of molecules having enough thermal energy to surmount the activation barrier increases. At any given temperature, a sample of molecules will have a distribution of energies, as shown in Figure 13.14 ▶. Under common circumstances, only a small fraction of the molecules have enough energy to make it over the activation barrier. Because of the shape of the energy distribution curve, however, a small change in temperature results in a large difference in the number of molecules having enough energy to surmount the activation barrier. This explains the sensitivity of reaction rates to temperature.

Summarizing Temperature and Reaction Rate:

▶ The frequency factor is the number of times that the reactants approach the activation barrier per unit time.

▶ The exponential factor is the fraction of the approaches that are successful in surmounting the activation barrier and forming products.

▶ The exponential factor increases with increasing temperature but decreases with increasing activation energy.

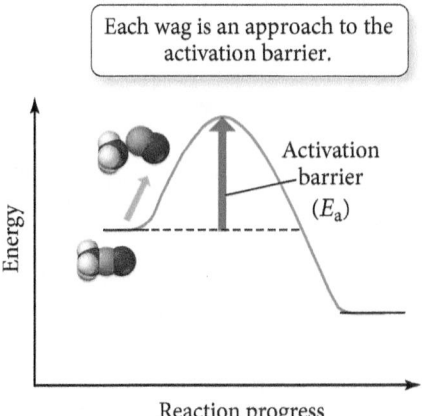

Each wag is an approach to the activation barrier.

Activation barrier (E_a)

Energy

Reaction progress

Thermal Energy Distribution

As temperature increases, the fraction of molecules with enough energy to surmount the activation energy barrier also increases.

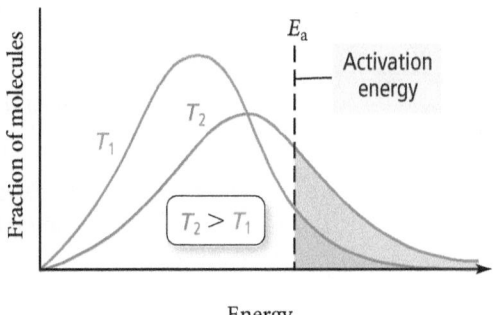

Fraction of molecules

E_a

Activation energy

T_1

T_2

$T_2 > T_1$

Energy

▲ **FIGURE 13.14 Thermal Energy Distribution**   At any given temperature, the atoms or molecules in a gas sample have a range of energies. The higher the temperature, the wider the energy distribution and the greater the average energy. The fraction of molecules with enough energy to surmount the activation energy barrier and react (shaded regions) increases sharply as the temperature rises.

Arrhenius Plots: Experimental Measurements of the Frequency Factor and the Activation Energy

The frequency factor and activation energy are important quantities in understanding the kinetics of any reaction. To see how we measure these factors in the laboratory, consider again Equation 13.24: $k = Ae^{-E_a/RT}$. Taking the natural log of both sides of this equation, we get the following result:

$\ln k = \ln\left(Ae^{-E_a/RT}\right)$	[13.25]

$$\ln k = \ln A + \ln e^{-E_a/RT}$$

$$\ln k = \ln A - \frac{E_a}{RT}$$

$\ln k = -\frac{E_a}{R}\left(\frac{1}{T}\right) + \ln A$	[13.26]

$$\underset{y\;=}{}\quad\underset{mx}{}\quad\underset{+\;\;b}{}$$

> Remember that $\ln(AB) = \ln A + \ln B$.

> Remember that $\ln e^x = x$.

> In an Arrhenius analysis, the pre-exponential factor (A) is assumed to be independent of temperature. Although the pre-exponential factor does depend on temperature to some degree, its temperature dependence is much less than that of the exponential factor and is often ignored.

Equation 13.26 is in the form of a straight line. *A plot of the natural log of the rate constant (ln k) versus the inverse of the temperature in kelvins (1/T) yields a straight line with a slope of* $-E_a/R$ *and a y-intercept of ln A.* Such a plot is called an **Arrhenius plot** and is commonly used in the analysis of kinetic data, as shown in Example 13.7.

EXAMPLE 13.7   Using an Arrhenius Plot to Determine Kinetic Parameters

The decomposition of ozone shown here is important to many atmospheric reactions.

$$O_3(g) \longrightarrow O_2(g) + O(g)$$

A study of the kinetics of the reaction results in the following data:

Temperature (K)	Rate Constant ($M^{-1} \cdot s^{-1}$)	Temperature (K)	Rate Constant ($M^{-1} \cdot s^{-1}$)
600	3.37×10^3	1300	7.83×10^7
700	4.85×10^4	1400	1.45×10^8
800	3.58×10^5	1500	2.46×10^8
900	1.70×10^6	1600	3.93×10^8
1000	5.90×10^6	1700	5.93×10^8
1100	1.63×10^7	1800	8.55×10^8
1200	3.81×10^7	1900	1.19×10^9

Determine the value of the frequency factor and activation energy for the reaction.

SOLUTION

To determine the frequency factor and activation energy, prepare a graph of the natural log of the rate constant (ln k) versus the inverse of the temperature ($1/T$).

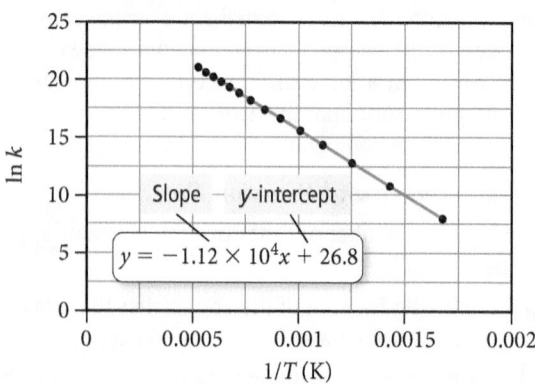

The plot is linear, as expected for Arrhenius behavior. The line that fits best has a slope of -1.12×10^4 K and a y-intercept of 26.8. Calculate the activation energy from the slope by setting the slope equal to $-E_a/R$ and solving for E_a:

$$-1.12 \times 10^4 \text{ K} = \frac{-E_a}{R}$$

$$E_a = 1.12 \times 10^4 \text{ K} \left(8.314 \frac{\text{J}}{\text{mol} \cdot \text{K}} \right)$$

$$= 9.31 \times 10^4 \text{ J/mol}$$

$$= 93.1 \text{ kJ/mol}$$

Calculate the frequency factor (A) by setting the intercept equal to $\ln A$.

$$26.8 = \ln A$$

$$A = e^{26.8}$$

$$= 4.36 \times 10^{11}$$

Since the rate constants are measured in units of $M^{-1} \cdot s^{-1}$, the frequency factor is in the same units. Consequently, we can conclude that the reaction has an activation energy of 93.1 kJ/mol and a frequency factor of $4.36 \times 10^{11} \ M^{-1} \cdot s^{-1}$.

FOR PRACTICE 13.7

For the decomposition of ozone reaction in Example 13.7, use the results of the Arrhenius analysis to predict the rate constant at 298 K.

In some cases, when either data are limited or plotting capabilities are absent, we can calculate the activation energy if we know the rate constant at just two different temperatures. We can apply the Arrhenius expression in Equation 13.26 to the two different temperatures as follows:

$$\ln k_2 = -\frac{E_a}{R}\left(\frac{1}{T_2}\right) + \ln A \qquad \ln k_1 = -\frac{E_a}{R}\left(\frac{1}{T_1}\right) + \ln A$$

We can then subtract $\ln k_1$ from $\ln k_2$:

$$\ln k_2 - \ln k_1 = \left[-\frac{E_a}{R}\left(\frac{1}{T_2}\right) + \ln A \right] - \left[-\frac{E_a}{R}\left(\frac{1}{T_1}\right) + \ln A \right]$$

Rearranging, we get the two-point form of the Arrhenius equation:

$$\ln \frac{k_2}{k_1} = \frac{E_a}{R}\left(\frac{1}{T_1} - \frac{1}{T_2}\right) \qquad\qquad [13.27]$$

Example 13.8 shows how you can use this equation to calculate the activation energy from experimental measurements of the rate constant at two different temperatures.

EXAMPLE 13.8 Using the Two-Point Form of the Arrhenius Equation

Consider the reaction between nitrogen dioxide and carbon monoxide.

$$NO_2(g) + CO(g) \longrightarrow NO(g) + CO_2(g)$$

The rate constant at 701 K is measured as $2.57 \ M^{-1} \cdot s^{-1}$ and that at 895 K is measured as $567 \ M^{-1} \cdot s^{-1}$. Find the activation energy for the reaction in kJ/mol.

SORT You are given the rate constant of a reaction at two different temperatures and asked to find the activation energy.	**GIVEN:** $T_1 = 701$ K, $k_1 = 2.57$ $M^{-1} \cdot s^{-1}$ $T_2 = 895$ K, $k_2 = 567$ $M^{-1} \cdot s^{-1}$ **FIND:** E_a
STRATEGIZE Use the two-point form of the Arrhenius equation, which relates the activation energy to the given information and R (a constant).	**EQUATION** $\ln \dfrac{k_2}{k_1} = \dfrac{E_a}{R}\left(\dfrac{1}{T_1} - \dfrac{1}{T_2}\right)$
SOLVE Substitute the two rate constants and the two temperatures into the equation. Solve the equation for E_a, the activation energy, and convert to kJ/mol.	**SOLUTION** $\ln \dfrac{567\ \cancel{M^{-1} \cdot s^{-1}}}{2.57\ \cancel{M^{-1} \cdot s^{-1}}} = \dfrac{E_a}{R}\left(\dfrac{1}{701\ \text{K}} - \dfrac{1}{895\ \text{K}}\right)$ $5.40 = \dfrac{E_a}{R}\left(\dfrac{3.09 \times 10^{-4}}{\text{K}}\right)$ $E_a = 5.40\left(\dfrac{\text{K}}{3.09 \times 10^{-4}}\right)R$ $= 5.40\left(\dfrac{\text{K}}{3.09 \times 10^{-4}}\right)8.314\ \dfrac{\text{J}}{\text{mol} \cdot \text{K}}$ $= 1.45 \times 10^5$ J/mol $= 145$ kJ/mol

CHECK The magnitude of the answer is reasonable. Activation energies for most reactions range from tens to hundreds of kilojoules per mole.

FOR PRACTICE 13.8

Use the results from Example 13.8 and the given rate constant of the reaction at either of the two temperatures to predict the rate constant for this reaction at 525 K.

Conceptual Connection 13.5 Temperature Dependence of Reaction Rate

Reaction A and reaction B have identical frequency factors. However, reaction B has a higher activation energy than reaction A. Which reaction has a greater rate constant at room temperature?

The Collision Model: A Closer Look at the Frequency Factor

We saw previously that the frequency factor in the Arrhenius equation represents the number of approaches to the activation barrier per unit time. Let's now refine that idea for a reaction involving two gas-phase reactants:

$$A(g) + B(g) \longrightarrow \text{products}$$

In the **collision model**, a chemical reaction occurs after a sufficiently energetic collision between two reactant molecules (Figure 13.15 ◄). In collision theory, therefore, each approach to the activation barrier is a collision between the reactant molecules. Consequently, the value of the frequency factor should simply be the number of collisions that occur per second. However, the frequency factors of most (though not all) gas-phase chemical reactions tend to be smaller than the number of collisions that occur per second. Why?

In the collision model, we can separate the frequency factor into two distinct parts, as shown in the following equations:

$$k = Ae^{\frac{-E_a}{RT}}$$
$$= pze^{\frac{-E_a}{RT}}$$

Orientation factor   Collision frequency

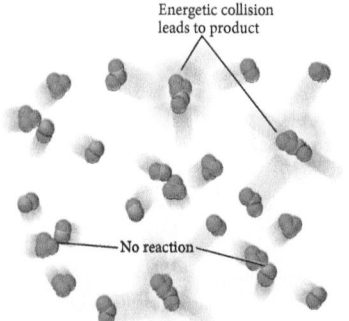

Energetic collision leads to product

No reaction

▲ **FIGURE 13.15 The Collision Model** In the collision model, two molecules react after a sufficiently energetic collision with the correct orientation brings the reacting groups together.

where p is the **orientation factor** and z is the **collision frequency**. The collision frequency is the number of collisions that occur per unit time, which we can calculate for a gas-phase reaction from the pressure of the gases and the temperature of the reaction mixture. Under typical conditions, a single molecule undergoes on the order of 10^9 collisions every second. The orientation factor is a number, usually between 0 and 1, which represents the fraction of collisions with an orientation that allows the reaction to occur.

To better understand the orientation factor, consider the reaction represented by the following equation:

$$NOCl(g) + NOCl(g) \longrightarrow 2\,NO(g) + Cl_2(g)$$

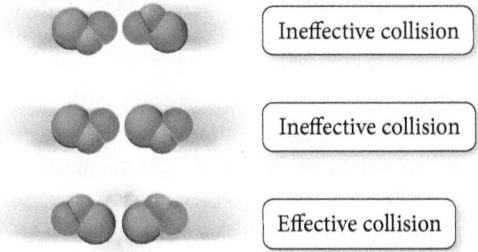

In order for the reaction to occur, two NOCl molecules must collide with sufficient energy. However, not all collisions with sufficient energy will lead to products, because the reactant molecules must also be properly oriented. Consider the three possible collision orientations of the reactant molecules shown below. The first two collisions, even if they occur with sufficient energy, will not result in a reaction, because the reactant molecules are not oriented in a way that allows the chlorine atoms to bond. In other words, if two molecules are to react with each other, they must collide in such a way that allows the necessary bonds to break and form. For the reaction of NOCl(g), the orientation factor is $p = 0.16$. This means that only 16 out of 100 sufficiently energetic collisions are actually successful in forming the products.

Ineffective collision

Ineffective collision

Effective collision

Some reactions have orientation factors that are much smaller than one. Consider the reaction between hydrogen and ethene:

$$H_2(g) + CH_2{=}CH_2(g) \longrightarrow CH_3{-}CH_3(g)$$

The orientation factor for this reaction is 1.7×10^{-6}, which means that fewer than two out of each million sufficiently energetic collisions actually form products. The small orientation factor indicates that the orientational requirements for this reaction are very stringent—the molecules must be aligned in a *very specific way* for the reaction to occur.

Reactions between *individual atoms* usually have orientation factors of approximately 1 because atoms are spherically symmetric and thus any orientation can lead to the formation of products. A few reactions have orientation factors greater than one. Consider the reaction between potassium and bromine:

$$K(g) + Br_2(g) \longrightarrow KBr(g) + Br(g)$$

This reaction has an orientation factor of $p = 4.8$. In other words, there are more reactions than collisions—the reactants do not even have to collide to react! Apparently, through a process dubbed *the harpoon mechanism,* a potassium atom can actually transfer an electron to a bromine molecule without a collision. The resulting positive charge on the potassium and the negative charge on the bromine cause the two species to attract each other and form a bond. The potassium atom essentially *harpoons* a passing bromine molecule with an electron and *reels it in* through the coulombic attraction between unlike charges.

We can picture a sample of reactive gases as a frenzy of collisions between the reacting atoms or molecules. At normal temperatures, the vast majority of these collisions do not have sufficient energy to overcome the activation barrier, and the atoms or molecules simply bounce off one another. Of the collisions having sufficient energy to overcome the activation barrier, most do not have the proper orientation for the reaction to occur (for the majority of common reactions). When two molecules with sufficient energy *and* the correct orientation collide, something extraordinary happens. The electrons on one of the atoms or molecules are attracted to the nuclei of the other; some bonds begin to weaken while other bonds begin to form and, if all goes well, the reactants go through the transition state and are transformed into the products. This is how a chemical reaction occurs.

Conceptual Connection 13.6 Collision Theory

Which reaction would you expect to have the smallest orientation factor?

(a) $H(g) + I(g) \longrightarrow HI(g)$

(b) $H_2(g) + I_2(g) \longrightarrow 2 HI(g)$

(c) $HCl(g) + HCl(g) \longrightarrow H_2(g) + Cl_2(g)$

13.6 Reaction Mechanisms

Most chemical reactions do not occur in a single step, but over the course of several steps. When we write a chemical equation to represent a chemical reaction, *we usually represent the overall reaction, not the series of individual steps by which the reaction occurs.* Consider the reaction in which hydrogen gas reacts with iodine monochloride:

$$H_2(g) + 2 ICl(g) \longrightarrow 2 HCl(g) + I_2(g)$$

The overall equation just shows the substances present at the beginning of the reaction and the substances formed by the reaction—it does not show the intermediate steps. The **reaction mechanism** is the series of individual chemical steps by which an overall chemical reaction occurs. For example, the proposed mechanism for the reaction between hydrogen and iodine monochloride contains two steps:

$$\textit{Step 1}\quad H_2(g) + ICl(g) \longrightarrow HI(g) + HCl(g)$$
$$\textit{Step 2}\quad HI(g) + ICl(g) \longrightarrow HCl(g) + I_2(g)$$

In the first step, an H_2 molecule collides with an ICl molecule and forms an HI molecule and an HCl molecule. In the second step, the HI molecule formed in the first step collides with a second ICl molecule to form another HCl molecule and an I_2 molecule. Each step in a reaction mechanism is an **elementary step**. Elementary steps cannot be broken down into simpler steps—they occur as they are written (they represent the exact species that are colliding in the reaction).

> An elementary step represents an actual interaction between the reactant molecules in the step. An overall reaction equation shows only the starting substances and the ending substances, not the path between them.

One of the requirements for a valid reaction mechanism is that the individual steps in the mechanism add to the overall reaction. For example, the mechanism just shown sums to the overall reaction as shown here:

$$H_2(g) + ICl(g) \longrightarrow \cancel{HI}(g) + HCl(g)$$
$$\underline{\cancel{HI}(g) + ICl(g) \longrightarrow HCl(g) + I_2(g)}$$
$$H_2(g) + 2 ICl(g) \longrightarrow 2 HCl(g) + I_2(g)$$

Notice that the HI molecule appears in the reaction mechanism but not in the overall reaction equation. We call species such as HI *reaction intermediates*. A **reaction intermediate** forms in one elementary step and is consumed in another. The reaction mechanism is a complete, detailed description of the reaction at the molecular level—it specifies the individual collisions and reactions that result in the overall reaction. As such, reaction mechanisms are highly sought-after pieces of chemical knowledge.

How do we determine reaction mechanisms? Recall from the opening section of this chapter that chemical kinetics are not only practically important (because they allow us to control the rate of a particular reaction), but also theoretically important because they can help us determine the mechanism of the reaction. We can piece together possible reaction mechanisms by measuring the kinetics of the overall reaction and working backward to write a mechanism consistent with the measured kinetics.

Rate Laws for Elementary Steps

We characterize elementary steps by their **molecularity**, the number of reactant particles involved in the step. The most common molecularities are unimolecular and bimolecular:

$$A \longrightarrow products \qquad \textbf{Unimolecular}$$

$$A + A \longrightarrow products \qquad \textbf{Bimolecular}$$

$$A + B \longrightarrow products \qquad \textbf{Bimolecular}$$

Elementary steps in which three reactant particles collide, called **termolecular** steps, are very rare because the probability of three particles simultaneously colliding is small.

Although we cannot deduce the rate law for an *overall chemical reaction* from the balanced chemical equation, we can deduce the rate law for an *elementary step* from its equation. Since we know that an elementary step occurs through the collision of the reactant particles, the rate is proportional to the product of the concentrations of those particles. For example, the rate for the bimolecular elementary step in which A reacts with B is proportional to the concentration of A multiplied by the concentration of B:

$$A + B \longrightarrow products \qquad Rate = k[A][B]$$

Similarly, the rate law for the bimolecular step in which A reacts with A is proportional to the square of the concentration of A:

$$A + A \longrightarrow products \qquad Rate = k[A]^2$$

Table 13.3 summarizes the rate laws for the common elementary steps, as well as those for the rare termolecular step. Notice that the molecularity of the elementary step is equal to the overall order of the step.

TABLE 13.3 Rate Laws for Elementary Steps

Elementary Step	Molecularity	Rate Law
A $\longrightarrow$ products	1	Rate = $k[A]$
A + A $\longrightarrow$ products	2	Rate = $k[A]^2$
A + B $\longrightarrow$ products	2	Rate = $k[A][B]$
A + A + A $\longrightarrow$ products	3 (rare)	Rate = $k[A]^3$
A + A + B $\longrightarrow$ products	3 (rare)	Rate = $k[A]^2[B]$
A + B + C $\longrightarrow$ products	3 (rare)	Rate = $k[A][B][C]$

Rate-Determining Steps and Overall Reaction Rate Laws

In most chemical reactions, one of the elementary steps—called the **rate-determining step**—is much slower than the others. The rate-determining step in a chemical reaction is analogous to the narrowest section on a freeway. If a section of a freeway narrows from four lanes to two lanes, for even a short distance, the rate at which cars travel along the freeway is limited by the rate at which they can travel through the narrow section (even though the rate might be much faster along the four-lane section). Similarly, the rate-determining step in a reaction mechanism limits the overall rate of the reaction (even though the other steps occur much faster) and therefore determines *the rate law for the overall reaction*.

▶ The rate-limiting step in a reaction mechanism limits the overall rate of the reaction just as the narrowest section of a highway limits the rate at which traffic can pass.

Rate-limiting section

As an example, consider the reaction between nitrogen dioxide gas and carbon monoxide gas:

$$NO_2(g) + CO(g) \longrightarrow NO(g) + CO_2(g)$$

The experimentally determined rate law for this reaction is Rate $= k[NO_2]^2$. We can see from this rate law that the reaction must not be a single-step reaction—otherwise the rate law would be Rate $= k[NO_2][CO]$. A possible mechanism for this reaction involves two steps:

$$NO_2(g) + NO_2(g) \longrightarrow NO_3(g) + NO(g) \quad \text{Slow}$$

$$NO_3(g) + CO(g) \longrightarrow NO_2(g) + CO_2(g) \quad \text{Fast}$$

Figure 13.16 ▼ shows the energy diagram for this mechanism. The first step has a much larger activation energy than the second step. This greater activation energy results in a much smaller rate constant for the first step compared to the second step. The first step determines the overall rate of the reaction, and the predicted *overall* rate law is therefore Rate $= k[NO_2]^2$, which is consistent with the observed experimental rate law.

For a proposed reaction mechanism, such as the one shown here for NO_2 and CO, to be *valid* (mechanisms can only be validated, not proven), two conditions must be met:

1. **The elementary steps in the mechanism must sum to the overall reaction**.

2. **The rate law predicted by the mechanism must be consistent with the experimentally observed rate law**.

Energy Diagram for a Two-Step Mechanism

Because E_a for Step 1 > E_a for Step 2, Step 1 has the smaller rate constant and is rate limiting.

Transition states

- Step 1 has higher activation energy.

- Step 1 has smaller rate constant.

- Step 1 determines overall rate.

E_{a1}

E_{a2}

Energy

Reactants

ΔH_{rxn}

Products

Step 1 Step 2

Reaction progress

▶ FIGURE 13.16 Energy Diagram for a Two-Step Mechanism

We have already seen that the rate law predicted by the earlier mechanism is consistent with the experimentally observed rate law. We can check whether the elementary steps sum to the overall reaction by adding them together:

$$NO_2(g) + \cancel{NO_2}(g) \longrightarrow \cancel{NO_3}(g) + NO(g) \quad \text{Slow}$$

$$\underline{\cancel{NO_3}(g) + CO(g) \longrightarrow \cancel{NO_2}(g) + CO_2(g)} \quad \text{Fast}$$

$$NO_2(g) + CO(g) \longrightarrow NO(g) + CO_2(g) \quad \text{Overall}$$

The mechanism fulfills both of the given requirements and is therefore valid. A valid mechanism is not a *proven* mechanism (because other mechanisms may also fulfill both of the given requirements). We can only say that a given mechanism is consistent with kinetic observations of the reaction and therefore possible. Other types of data—such as the experimental evidence for a proposed intermediate—are necessary to further strengthen the validity of a proposed mechanism.

Mechanisms with a Fast Initial Step

When the proposed mechanism for a reaction has a slow initial step—like the one shown previously for the reaction between NO_2 and CO—the rate law predicted by the mechanism normally contains only reactants involved in the overall reaction. However, when a mechanism begins with a fast initial step, some other subsequent step in the mechanism is the rate-limiting step. In these cases, the rate law predicted by the rate-limiting step may contain reaction intermediates. Since reaction intermediates do not appear in the overall reaction equation, a rate law containing intermediates cannot generally correspond to the experimental rate law. Fortunately, however, we can often express the concentration of intermediates in terms of the concentrations of the reactants of the overall reaction.

In a multistep mechanism where the first step is fast, the products of the first step may build up, because the rate at which they are consumed is limited by some slower step further down the line. As those products build up, they can begin to react with one another to re-form the reactants. As long as the first step is fast enough compared to the rate-limiting step, the first-step reaction will reach equilibrium. We indicate equilibrium as follows:

$$\text{Reactants} \underset{k_{-1}}{\overset{k_1}{\rightleftharpoons}} \text{products}$$

The double arrows indicate that both the forward reaction and the reverse reaction occur. If equilibrium is reached, then the rate of the forward reaction equals the rate of the reverse reaction.

As an example, consider the reaction by which hydrogen reacts with nitrogen monoxide to form water and nitrogen gas:

$$2 H_2(g) + 2 NO(g) \longrightarrow 2 H_2O(g) + N_2(g)$$

The experimentally observed rate law is Rate $= k[H_2][NO]^2$. The reaction is first order in hydrogen and second order in nitrogen monoxide. The proposed mechanism has a slow second step:

$$2 NO(g) \underset{k_{-1}}{\overset{k_1}{\rightleftharpoons}} N_2O_2(g) \quad \text{Fast}$$

$$H_2(g) + N_2O_2(g) \overset{k_2}{\longrightarrow} H_2O(g) + N_2O(g) \quad \text{Slow (rate limiting)}$$

$$\underline{N_2O(g) + H_2(g) \overset{k_3}{\longrightarrow} N_2(g) + H_2O(g)} \quad \text{Fast}$$

$$2 H_2(g) + 2 NO(g) \longrightarrow 2 H_2O(g) + N_2(g) \quad \text{Overall}$$

To determine whether the mechanism is valid, we must determine whether the two conditions described previously are met. As you can see, the steps do indeed sum to the overall reaction, so the first condition is met.

The second condition is that the rate law predicted by the mechanism must be consistent with the experimentally observed rate law. Since the second step is rate limiting, we write the following expression for the rate law:

$$\text{Rate} = k_2[\text{H}_2][\text{N}_2\text{O}_2] \qquad [13.28]$$

This rate law contains an intermediate (N_2O_2) and can therefore not be consistent with the experimentally observed rate law (which does not contain intermediates). Because of the equilibrium in the first step, however, *we can express the concentration of the intermediate in terms of the reactants of the overall equation*. Since the first step reaches equilibrium, the rate of the forward reaction in the first step equals the rate of the reverse reaction:

$$\text{Rate (forward)} = \text{Rate (reverse)}$$

The rate of the forward reaction is given by the rate law:

$$\text{Rate} = k_1[\text{NO}]^2$$

The rate of the reverse reaction is given by the rate law:

$$\text{Rate} = k_{-1}[\text{N}_2\text{O}_2]$$

Since these two rates are equal at equilibrium, we write the expression:

$$k_1[\text{NO}]^2 = k_{-1}[\text{N}_2\text{O}_2]$$

Rearranging, we get:

$$[\text{N}_2\text{O}_2] = \frac{k_1}{k_{-1}}[\text{NO}]^2$$

We can now substitute this expression into Equation 13.28, the rate law obtained from the slow step:

$$\text{Rate} = k_2[\text{H}_2][\text{N}_2\text{O}_2]$$

$$= k_2[\text{H}_2]\frac{k_1}{k_{-1}}[\text{NO}]^2$$

$$= \frac{k_2k_1}{k_{-1}}[\text{H}_2][\text{NO}]^2$$

If we combine the individual rate constants into one overall rate constant, we get the predicted rate law:

$$\text{Rate} = k[\text{H}_2][\text{NO}]^2 \qquad [13.29]$$

Since this rate law is consistent with the experimentally observed rate law, condition 2 is met and the proposed mechanism is valid.

EXAMPLE 13.9 Reaction Mechanisms

Ozone naturally decomposes to oxygen by this reaction:

$$2\,\text{O}_3(g) \longrightarrow 3\,\text{O}_2(g)$$

The experimentally observed rate law for this reaction is:

$$\text{Rate} = k[\text{O}_3]^2[\text{O}_2]^{-1}$$

Show that this proposed mechanism is consistent with the experimentally observed rate law.

$$\text{O}_3(g) \underset{k_{-1}}{\overset{k_1}{\rightleftharpoons}} \text{O}_2(g) + \text{O}(g) \qquad \text{Fast}$$

$$\text{O}_3(g) + \text{O}(g) \xrightarrow{k_2} 2\,\text{O}_2(g) \qquad \text{Slow}$$

SOLUTION

To determine whether the mechanism is valid, you must first determine whether the steps sum to the overall reaction. Since the steps do indeed sum to the overall reaction, the first condition is met.	$O_3(g) \underset{k_{-1}}{\overset{k_1}{\rightleftharpoons}} O_2(g) + O(g)$ $O_3(g) + O(g) \xrightarrow{k_2} 2\,O_2(g)$ ——————————————— $2\,O_3(g) \longrightarrow 3\,O_2(g)$
The second condition is that the rate law predicted by the mechanism must be consistent with the experimentally observed rate law. Because the second step is rate limiting, write the rate law based on the second step.	Rate $= k_2[O_3][O]$
Because the rate law contains an intermediate (O), you must express the concentration of the intermediate in terms of the concentrations of the reactants of the overall reaction. To do this, set the rates of the forward reaction and the reverse reaction of the first step equal to each other. Solve the expression from the previous step for [O], the concentration of the intermediate.	Rate (forward) $=$ Rate (backward) $k_1[O_3] = k_{-1}[O_2][O]$ $[O] = \dfrac{k_1[O_3]}{k_{-1}[O_2]}$
Finally, substitute [O] into the rate law predicted by the slow step.	Rate $= k_2[O_3][O]$ $= k_2[O_3]\dfrac{k_1[O_3]}{k_{-1}[O_2]}$ $= k_2\dfrac{k_1}{k_{-1}}\dfrac{[O_3]^2}{[O_2]}$ $= k[O_3]^2[O_2]^{-1}$

CHECK Because the two steps in the proposed mechanism sum to the overall reaction, and because the rate law obtained from the proposed mechanism is consistent with the experimentally observed rate law, the proposed mechanism is valid. The -1 reaction order with respect to $[O_2]$ indicates that the rate slows down as the concentration of oxygen increases—oxygen inhibits, or slows down, the reaction.

FOR PRACTICE 13.9

Predict the overall reaction and rate law that results from the following two-step mechanism.

$$2\,A \longrightarrow A_2 \qquad \text{Slow}$$
$$A_2 + B \longrightarrow A_2B \qquad \text{Fast}$$

13.7 Catalysis

Throughout this chapter, we have learned about ways to control the rates of chemical reactions. We can speed up the rate of a reaction by increasing the concentration of the reactants or by increasing the temperature. However, these approaches are not always feasible. There are limits to how concentrated we can make a reaction mixture, and increases in temperature may allow unwanted reactions—such as the decomposition of a reactant—to occur.

Alternatively, reaction rates can be increased by using a **catalyst**, a substance that increases the rate of a chemical reaction but is not consumed by the reaction. A catalyst works by providing an alternative mechanism for the reaction—one in which the rate-determining step has a lower activation energy. For example, consider the noncatalytic destruction of ozone in the upper atmosphere, discussed in Section 6.10, which happens according to this reaction:

$$O_3(g) + O(g) \longrightarrow 2\,O_2(g)$$

▶ FIGURE 13.17 **Catalyzed and Uncatalyzed Decomposition of Ozone** In the catalytic destruction of ozone (red), the activation barrier for the rate-limiting step is much lower than in the uncatalyzed process (blue).

Energy Diagram for Catalyzed and Uncatalyzed Pathways

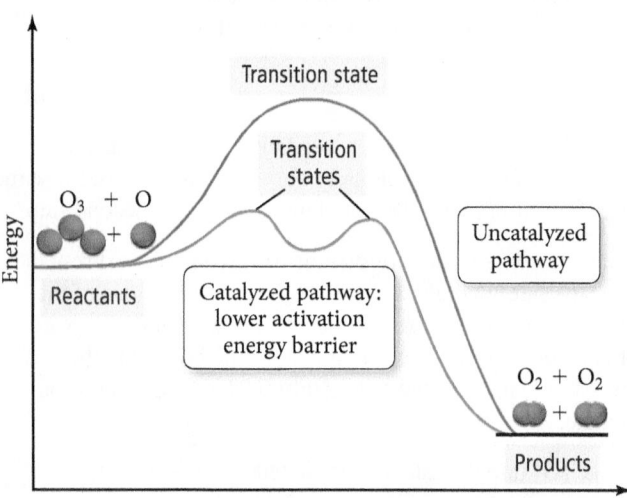

Reaction progress

Photodissociation means *light-induced* dissociation. The energy from a photon of light can break chemical bonds and therefore dissociate, or break apart, a molecule.

In this reaction, an ozone molecule collides with an oxygen atom to form two oxygen molecules in a single elementary step. The reason that Earth has a protective ozone layer in the upper atmosphere is that the activation energy for this reaction is fairly high and the reaction, therefore, proceeds at a fairly slow rate; the ozone layer does not rapidly decompose into O_2. However, the addition of Cl atoms (which come from the photodissociation of man-made chlorofluorocarbons) to the upper atmosphere makes available another pathway by which O_3 can be destroyed. The first step in this pathway—called the catalytic destruction of ozone—is the reaction of Cl with O_3 to form ClO and O_2:

$$Cl + O_3 \longrightarrow ClO + O_2$$

This is followed by a second step in which ClO reacts with O, regenerating Cl:

$$ClO + O \longrightarrow Cl + O_2$$

If we add the two reactions, the overall reaction is identical to the noncatalytic reaction:

$$\begin{aligned} \cancel{Cl} + O_3 &\longrightarrow \cancel{ClO} + O_2 \\ \cancel{ClO} + O &\longrightarrow \cancel{Cl} + O_2 \\ \hline O_3 + O &\longrightarrow 2\,O_2 \end{aligned}$$

However, the activation energy for the rate-limiting step in this pathway is much smaller than for the first, uncatalyzed pathway (as shown in Figure 13.17 ▲), and therefore the reaction occurs at a much faster rate. Note that the Cl is not consumed in the overall reaction—this is characteristic of a catalyst.

In the case of the catalytic destruction of ozone, the catalyst speeds up a reaction that we *do not* want to happen. Most of the time, however, catalysts are used to speed up reactions that we *do* want to happen. For example, your car most likely has a catalytic converter in its exhaust system. The catalytic converter contains solid catalysts, such as platinum, rhodium, or palladium, dispersed on an underlying high-surface-area ceramic structure. These catalysts convert exhaust pollutants such as nitrogen monoxide and carbon monoxide into less harmful substances:

$$2\,NO(g) + 2\,CO(g) \xrightarrow{\text{catalyst}} N_2(g) + 2\,CO_2(g)$$

The catalytic converter also promotes the complete combustion of any fuel fragments present in the exhaust:

$$CH_3CH_2CH_3(g) + 5\,O_2(g) \xrightarrow{\text{catalyst}} 3\,CO_2(g) + 4\,H_2O(g)$$

↑
Fuel fragment

◄ The catalytic converter in the exhaust system of a car helps eliminate pollutants in the exhaust.

Fuel fragments in exhaust are harmful because they lead to the formation of ozone. Recall from Section 6.10 that although ozone is a natural part of our *upper* atmosphere that protects us from excess exposure to ultraviolet light, it is a pollutant in the *lower* atmosphere, interfering with cardiovascular function and acting as an eye and lung irritant. The use of catalytic converters in motor vehicles has resulted in lower levels of these pollutants over most U.S. cities in the last 30 years even though the number of cars on the roadways has dramatically increased (see Table 13.4).

TABLE 13.4 Change in Pollutant Levels

Pollutant	Change 1980–2010
NO_2	−52%
O_3	−28%
CO	−82%

Source: *U.S. Environmental Protection Agency, Our Nation's Air: Status and Trends through 2010.*

Homogeneous and Heterogeneous Catalysis

Catalysis can be categorized into two types: homogeneous and heterogeneous (Figure 13.18 ▼). In **homogeneous catalysis**, the catalyst exists in the same phase (or state) as the reactants. The catalytic destruction of ozone by Cl is an example of homogeneous catalysis—the chlorine atoms exist in the gas phase with the gas-phase reactants. In **heterogeneous catalysis**, the catalyst exists in a different phase than the reactants. The solid catalysts used in catalytic converters are examples of heterogeneous catalysts—they are solids while the reactants are gases. The use of solid catalysts with gas-phase or solution-phase reactants is the most common type of heterogeneous catalysis.

Research has shown that heterogeneous catalysis is most likely responsible for the annual formation of an ozone hole over Antarctica. After the discovery of the Antarctic ozone hole in 1985, scientists wondered why there was such a dramatic drop in ozone over Antarctica but not over the rest of the planet. After all, the chlorine from chlorofluorocarbons that catalyzes ozone destruction is evenly distributed throughout the entire atmosphere.

As it turns out, most of the chlorine that enters the atmosphere from chlorofluorocarbons gets bound up in chlorine reservoirs, substances such as $ClONO_2$ that hold chlorine and prevent it from catalyzing ozone destruction. The unique conditions over Antarctica—especially the cold isolated air mass that exists during the long dark winter—result in clouds that contain solid ice particles. These unique clouds are called

▲ Polar stratospheric clouds contain ice particles that catalyze reactions by which chlorine is released from its atmospheric chemical reservoirs.

Homogeneous catalysis

Heterogeneous catalysis

Product

Reactant

Catalyst in same phase as reactants

Catalyst in different phase than reactants

◄ **FIGURE 13.18 Homogeneous and Heterogeneous Catalysis**
A homogeneous catalyst exists in the same phase as the reactants. A heterogeneous catalyst exists in a different phase than the reactants. Often a heterogeneous catalyst provides a solid surface on which the reaction can take place.

▶ FIGURE 13.19 **Ozone Depletion in the Antarctic Spring** The concentration of ozone over Antarctica drops sharply during the months of September and October due to the catalyzed destruction of ozone by chlorine. The image at the left shows the average ozone levels in May 2011 while the image at the right shows the average levels from September 2011. (The lowest ozone levels are represented in purple.) Source: NASA Ozone Watch, OMI instrument (KNMI/NASA) onboard the Aura satellite.

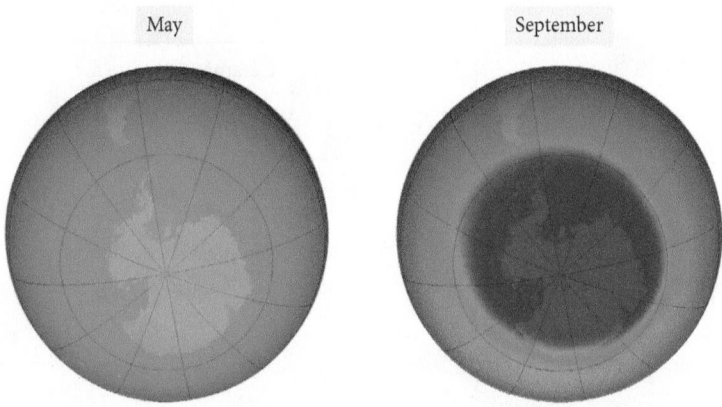

May   September

polar stratospheric clouds (or PSCs), and the surfaces of the ice particles within these clouds appear to catalyze the release of chlorine from their reservoirs:

$$ClONO_2 + HCl \xrightarrow{\text{PSCs}} Cl_2 + HNO_3$$

When the sun rises in the Antarctic spring, the sunlight dissociates the chlorine molecules into chlorine atoms:

$$Cl_2 \xrightarrow{\text{light}} 2\,Cl$$

The chlorine atoms then catalyze the destruction of ozone by the mechanism discussed previously. This continues until the sun melts the stratospheric clouds, allowing chlorine atoms to be reincorporated into their reservoirs. The result is an ozone hole that forms every spring and lasts about 6–8 weeks (Figure 13.19 ▲).

A second example of heterogeneous catalysis involves the **hydrogenation** of double bonds within alkenes. Consider the reaction between ethene and hydrogen, which is relatively slow at normal temperatures:

$$H_2C{=}CH_2(g) + H_2(g) \longrightarrow H_3C{-}CH_3(g) \quad \text{Slow at room temperature}$$

However, in the presence of finely divided platinum, palladium, or nickel, the reaction happens rapidly. The catalysis occurs by the four-step process depicted in Figure 13.20 ▼.

Heterogeneous Catalysis

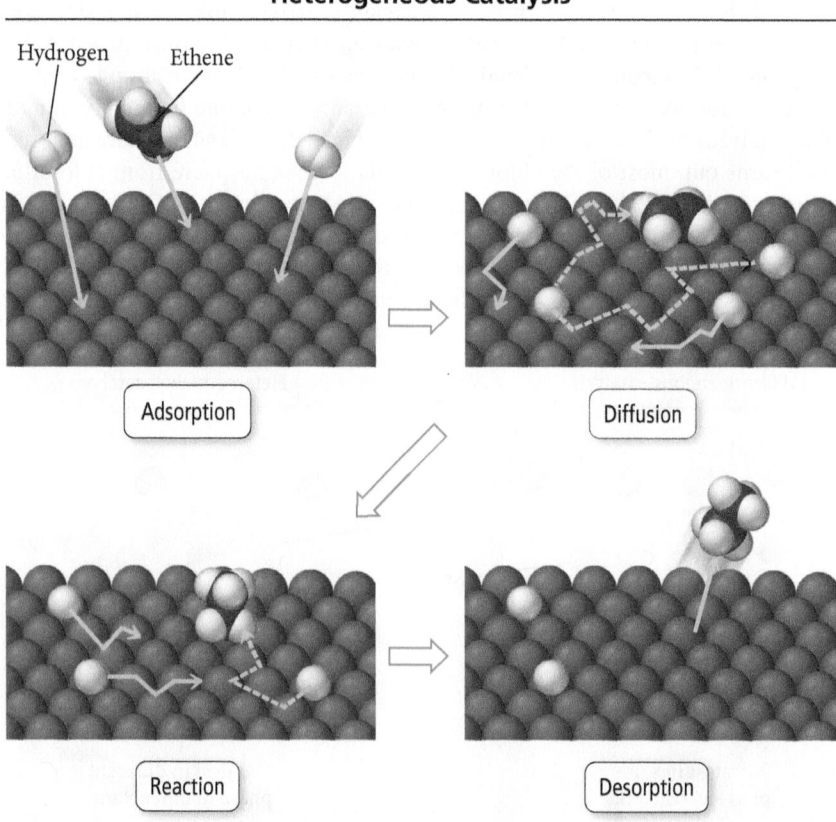

Hydrogen   Ethene

Adsorption   Diffusion

Reaction   Desorption

▶ FIGURE 13.20 **Catalytic Hydrogenation of Ethene**

1. Adsorption: the reactants are adsorbed onto the metal surface.
2. Diffusion: the reactants diffuse on the surface until they approach each other.
3. Reaction: the reactants react to form the products.
4. Desorption: the products desorb from the surface into the gas phase.

The large activation energy of the hydrogenation reaction—due primarily to the strength of the hydrogen–hydrogen bond in H_2—is greatly lowered when the reactants adsorb onto the surface.

Enzymes: Biological Catalysts

We find perhaps the best example of chemical catalysis in living organisms. Most of the thousands of reactions that must occur for an organism to survive are too slow at normal temperatures. So living organisms rely on **enzymes**, biological catalysts that increase the rates of biochemical reactions. Enzymes are usually large protein molecules with complex three-dimensional structures. Within each enzyme's structure is a specific area called the **active site**. The properties and shape of the active site are just right to bind the reactant molecule, usually called the **substrate**. The substrate fits into the active site in a manner that is analogous to a key fitting into a lock (Figure 13.21 ▼). When the substrate binds to the active site of the enzyme—through intermolecular forces such as hydrogen bonding and dispersion forces, or even covalent bonds—the activation energy of the reaction is greatly lowered, allowing the reaction to occur at a much faster rate. The general mechanism by which an enzyme (E) binds a substrate (S) and then reacts to form the products (P) is:

$$E + S \rightleftharpoons ES \qquad \text{Fast}$$
$$ES \longrightarrow E + P \qquad \text{Slow, rate limiting}$$

Sucrase is an enzyme that catalyzes the breaking up of sucrose (table sugar) into glucose and fructose within the body. At body temperature, sucrose does not break into glucose and fructose because the activation energy is high, resulting in a slow reaction rate. However,

> The strategies used to speed up chemical reactions in the laboratory—high temperatures, high pressures, strongly acidic or alkaline conditions—are not available to living organisms, since they would be fatal to cells.

Glucose part of molecule   Fructose part of molecule

Bond to be broken

$$C_{12}H_{22}O_{11} + H_2O \longrightarrow C_6H_{12}O_6 + C_6H_{12}O_6$$
Sucrose   Glucose   Fructose

◀ Sucrose breaks up into glucose and fructose during digestion.

Enzyme–Substrate Binding

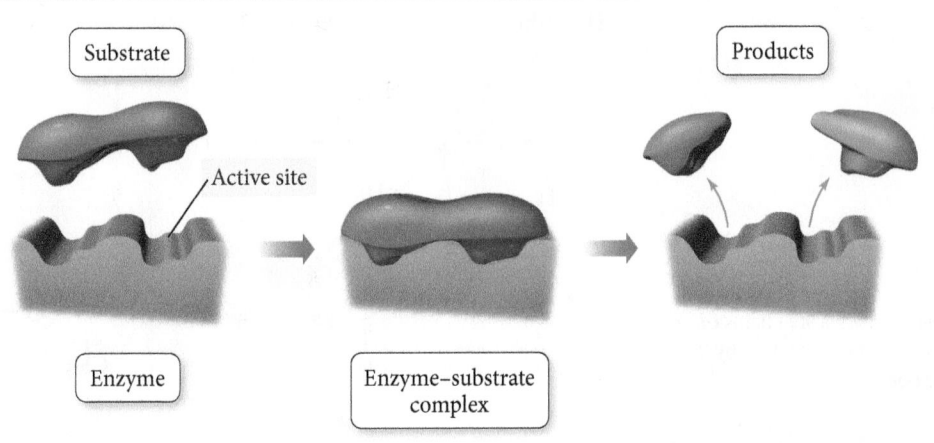

Substrate

Active site

Enzyme

Enzyme–substrate complex

Products

◀ **FIGURE 13.21 Enzyme-Substrate Binding** A substrate (or reactant) fits into the active site of an enzyme much as a key fits into a lock. It is held in place by intermolecular forces and forms an enzyme–substrate complex. (Sometimes temporary covalent bonding may also be involved.) After the reaction occurs, the products are released from the active site.

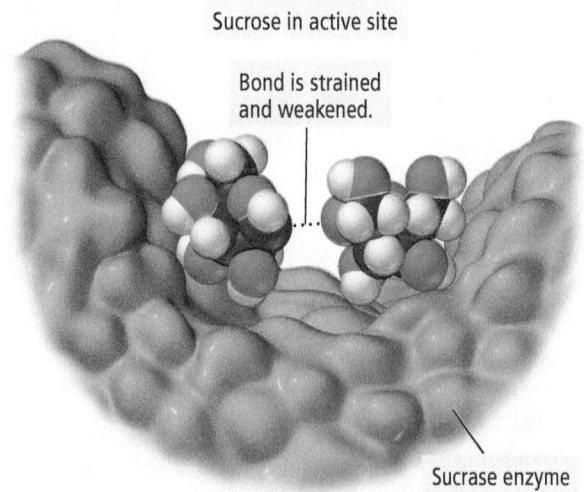

Sucrose in active site

Bond is strained
and weakened.

Sucrase enzyme

▲ FIGURE 13.22 **An Enzyme-Catalyzed Reaction**   Sucrase catalyzes the conversion of sucrose into glucose and fructose by weakening the bond that joins the two rings.

when a sucrose molecule binds to the active site within sucrase, the bond between the glucose and fructose units weakens because glucose is forced into a geometry that stresses the bond (Figure 13.22 ◄). Weakening of this bond lowers the activation energy for the reaction, increasing the reaction rate. The reaction can then proceed toward equilibrium—which favors the products—at a much lower temperature.

By allowing otherwise slow reactions to occur at reasonable rates, enzymes give living organisms tremendous control over which reactions occur and when they occur. Enzymes are extremely specific (each enzyme catalyzes only a single reaction) and efficient, speeding up reaction rates by factors of as much as a billion. To turn a particular reaction on, a living organism produces or activates the correct enzyme to catalyze that reaction. Because organisms are so dependent on the reactions enzymes catalyze, many substances that inhibit the action of enzymes are highly toxic. Locking up a single enzyme molecule can stop the reaction of billions of substrates, much as one motorist stalled at a tollbooth can paralyze an entire highway full of cars. (For another example of enzyme action, see the *Chemistry and Medicine* box on the role of chymotrypsin in digestion.)

 Chemistry and Medicine

Enzyme Catalysis and the Role of Chymotrypsin in Digestion

When we eat foods containing proteins—such as meats, eggs, beans, and nuts—the proteins must be digested. Proteins are large biological molecules composed of individual units called amino acids. (We will discuss the structure of proteins and other biologically important molecules more fully in Chapter 21.) The amino acids in proteins are linked together via peptide bonds, as shown in Figure 13.23 ▼. During digestion, the protein must be broken up into individual amino acids (Figure 13.24 ►), which can pass through the walls of the small intestine and into the bloodstream. However, the peptide bonds that link amino acids together are relatively stable, and under ordinary conditions the reaction is slow.

The pancreas secretes an enzyme called chymotrypsin (Figure 13.25 ►) into the small intestine. Like many enzymes, chymotrypsin is highly selective in its action—it operates

Amino acids

Digestion

◄ FIGURE 13.24 **Protein Digestion**   During digestion, a protein is broken down into its component amino acids.

only on peptide bonds between certain kinds of amino acids. When a protein molecule containing such a pair of amino acids is attached to the active site of chymotrypsin, the peptide bond between them is weakened as the chymotrypsin forms a covalent bond with the carbon in the peptide bond. A water molecule can then come in and cleave the bond, with an —OH from the water binding to the carbon atom and the remaining —H bonding to the nitrogen (Figure 13.26 ►).

Amino acids

Protein chain

Peptide bond

◄ FIGURE 13.23 **The Structure of a Protein**   Proteins are chains of amino acids linked together by peptide bonds.

▲ FIGURE 13.25 **Chymotrypsin, a Digestive Enzyme** This model of chymotrypsin shows a section of a protein substrate in the active site.

The amino acid chain is thus clipped at the peptide bond. The products of the reaction leave the active site, another protein binds to the chymotrypsin, and the process is repeated. Other digestive enzymes cleave protein chains between other pairs of amino acids. Together, these enzymes eventually reduce the entire protein to its constituent amino acids.

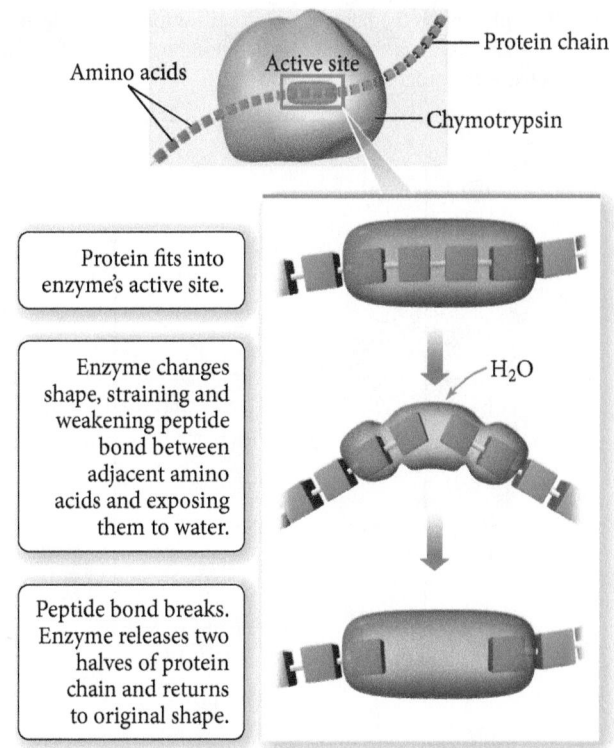

Protein fits into enzyme's active site.

Enzyme changes shape, straining and weakening peptide bond between adjacent amino acids and exposing them to water.

Peptide bond breaks. Enzyme releases two halves of protein chain and returns to original shape.

▲ FIGURE 13.26 **The Action of Chymotrypsin**

CHAPTER IN REVIEW

Self Assessment Quiz

Q1. This graph shows the concentration of the reactant A in the reaction A → B. Determine the average rate of the reaction between 0 and 10 seconds.

a) 0.07 M/s b) 0.007 M/s
c) 0.86 M/s d) 0.014 M/s

Q2. Dinitrogen monoxide decomposes into nitrogen and oxygen when heated. The initial rate of the reaction is 0.022 M/s. What is the initial rate of change of the concentration of N_2O (that is, $\Delta[N_2O]/\Delta t$)?

$$2\,N_2O(g) \rightarrow 2\,N_2(g) + O_2(g)$$

a) −0.022 M/s
b) −0.011 M/s
c) −0.044 M/s
d) +0.022 M/s

Q3. This plot shows the rate of the decomposition of SO_2Cl_2 into SO_2 and Cl_2 as a function of the concentration of SO_2Cl_2. What is the order of the reaction?

a) first order
b) second order
c) zero order
d) Order cannot be determined without more information.

Q4. For the reaction $2A + B \rightarrow C$, the initial rate was measured at several different reactant concentrations. From the tabulated data, determine the rate law for the reaction.

[A] (M)	[B] (M)	Initial Rate (M/s)
0.05	0.05	0.035
0.10	0.05	0.070
0.20	0.10	0.56

a) Rate $= k[A][B]$ b) Rate $= k[A]^2[B]$
c) Rate $= k[A][B]^2$ d) Rate $= k[A]^2[B]^2$

Q5. What is the rate constant for the reaction in Question 4?
a) $2.8 \times 10^2 \text{ M}^{-2} \cdot \text{s}^{-1}$ b) $14 \text{ M}^{-2} \cdot \text{s}^{-1}$
c) $1.4 \times 10^2 \text{ M}^{-2} \cdot \text{s}^{-1}$ d) $1.4 \times 10^3 \text{ M}^{-2} \cdot \text{s}^{-1}$

Q6. The decomposition of Br_2 was followed as a function of time; two different plots of the data are shown here. Determine the order and rate constant for the reaction.

Q7. The reaction $X \rightarrow$ products is second order in X and has a rate constant of $0.035 \text{ M}^{-1}\text{s}^{-1}$. If a reaction mixture is initially 0.45 M in X, what is the concentration of X after 155 seconds?
a) 7.6 M
b) 2.0×10^{-3} M
c) 0.13 M
d) 0.00 M

Q8. A decomposition reaction has a half-life that does not depend on the initial concentration of the reactant. What is the order of the reaction?
a) zero order
b) first order
c) second order
d) Order cannot be determined without more information.

Q9. The rate constant of a reaction is measured at different temperatures. A plot of the natural log of the rate constant as a function of the inverse of the temperature (in kelvins) yields a straight line with a slope of $-8.55 \times 10^3 \text{ K}^{-1}$. What is the activation energy (E_a) for the reaction?
a) -71 kJ   b) 71 kJ
c) 1.0 kJ   d) -1.0 kJ

Q10. The rate constant for a reaction at $25.0 \,^\circ\text{C}$ is 0.010 s^{-1}, and its activation energy is 35.8 kJ. Find the rate constant at $50.0 \,^\circ\text{C}$.
a) 0.021 s^{-1} b) 0.010 s^{-1}
c) 0.0033 s^{-1} d) 0.031 s^{-1}

Q11. The mechanism shown here is proposed for the gas phase reaction, $2 \text{ N}_2\text{O}_5 \rightarrow 2 \text{ NO}_2 + \text{O}_2$. What rate law does the mechanism predict?

$$\text{N}_2\text{O}_5 \underset{k_{-1}}{\overset{k_1}{\rightleftharpoons}} \text{NO}_2 + \text{NO}_3 \qquad \text{Fast}$$
$$\text{NO}_2 + \text{NO}_3 \rightarrow \text{NO}_2 + \text{O}_2 + \text{NO} \qquad \text{Slow}$$
$$\text{NO} + \text{N}_2\text{O}_5 \rightarrow 3 \text{ NO}_2 \qquad \text{Fast}$$

a) Rate $= k[\text{N}_2\text{O}_5]$ b) Rate $= k[\text{N}_2\text{O}_5]^2$
c) Rate $= k[\text{N}_2\text{O}_5]^0$ d) Rate $= k[\text{NO}_2][\text{NO}_3]$

Q12. Which statement is true regarding the function of a catalyst in a chemical reaction?
a) A catalyst increases the rate of a reaction.
b) A catalyst provides an alternate mechanism for the reaction.
c) A catalyst is not consumed by the reaction.
d) All of the above are true.

Q13. These images represent the first order reaction A → B initially and at some later time. The rate law for the reaction is Rate = 0.010 s⁻¹ [A]. How much time has passed between the two images?

 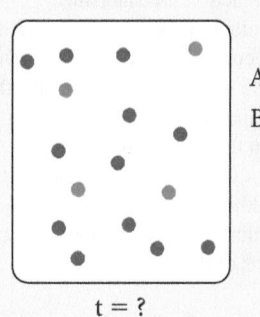

A ●
B ●

| Initial | t = ? |

a) 69 s   b) 139 s
c) 60 s   d) 12.5 s

Q14. Pick the single-step reaction that, according to collision theory, has the smallest orientation factor.
a) $H + H \rightarrow H_2$
b) $I + HI \rightarrow I_2 + H$
c) $H_2 + H_2C{=}CH_2 \rightarrow H_3C{-}CH_3$
d) All of these reactions have the same orientation factor.

Q15. Carbon monoxide and chlorine gas react to form phosgene (COCl₂) according to the equation:

$$CO(g) + Cl_2(g) \rightarrow COCl_2(g)$$

The rate law for the reaction is rate $= k[Cl_2]^{3/2}[CO]$. Which mixture of chlorine gas and carbon monoxide gas has the fastest initial rate?

(a)   (b)

 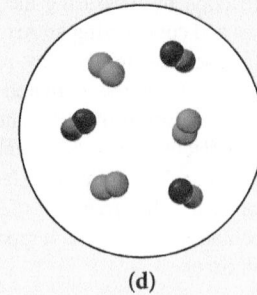

(c)   (d)

Answers: 1. (d) 2. (c) 3. (a) 4. (c) 5. (a) 6. (a) 7. (c) 8. (b) 9. (b) 10. (d) 11. (a) 12. (d) 13. (b) 14. (c) 15. (b)

Key Terms

Section 13.3
rate law (603)
rate constant (k) (603)
reaction order (n) (603)
overall order (606)

Section 13.4
integrated rate law (608)
half-life ($t_{1/2}$) (612)

Section 13.5
Arrhenius equation (615)
activation energy (E_a) (616)
frequency factor (A) (616)
activated complex (transition state) (616)
exponential factor (617)
Arrhenius plot (618)
collision model (620)
orientation factor (621)
collision frequency (621)

Section 13.6
reaction mechanism (622)
elementary step (622)
reaction intermediates (622)
molecularity (623)
unimolecular (623)
bimolecular (623)
termolecular (623)
rate-determining step (623)

Section 13.7
catalyst (627)
homogeneous catalysis (629)
heterogeneous catalysis (629)
hydrogenation (630)
enzyme (631)
active site (631)
substrate (631)

Key Concepts

Reaction Rates, Orders, and Rate Laws (13.1–13.3)

▶ The rate of a chemical reaction is a measure of how fast a reaction occurs. The rate reflects the change in the concentration of a reactant or product per unit time and is usually reported in units of M/s.

▶ Reaction rates generally depend on the concentration of the reactants. The rate of a first-order reaction is directly proportional to the concentration of the reactant, the rate of a second-order reaction is proportional to the square of the concentration of the reactant, and the rate of a zero-order reaction is independent of the concentration of the reactant.

▶ For a reaction with more than one reactant, the order with respect to each reactant is, in general, independent of the order with respect to other reactants. The rate law shows the relationship between the rate and the concentrations of each reactant and must be determined experimentally.

Integrated Rate Laws and Half-Life (13.4)

▶ The rate law for a reaction describes the relationship between the rate of the reaction and the concentrations of the reactants.

▶ The integrated rate law for a reaction describes the relationship between the concentration of a reactant and time.

▶ The integrated rate law for a zero-order reaction shows that the concentration of the reactant varies linearly with time. For a first-order reaction, the *natural log* of the concentration of the reactant varies linearly with time, and for a second-order reaction, the *inverse* of the concentration of the reactant varies linearly with time.

▶ The half-life of a reaction can be derived from the integrated rate law and represents the time required for the concentration of a reactant to fall to one-half of its initial value. The half-life of a first-order reaction is *independent* of initial concentration of the reactant. The half-life of a zero-order or second-order reaction *depends* on the initial concentration of reactant.

The Effect of Temperature on Reaction Rate (13.5)

▶ The rate constant of a reaction generally depends on temperature and can be expressed by the Arrhenius equation, which consists of a frequency factor and an exponential factor.

▶ The frequency factor represents the number of times that the reactants approach the activation barrier per unit time. The exponential factor is the fraction of approaches that are successful in surmounting the activation barrier and forming products.

▶ The exponential factor depends on both the temperature and the activation energy, a barrier that the reactants must overcome to become products. The exponential factor increases with increasing temperature but decreases with increasing activation energy.

▶ We can determine the frequency factor and activation energy for a reaction by measuring the rate constant at different temperatures and constructing an Arrhenius plot.

▶ For reactions in the gas phase, Arrhenius behavior can be modeled with the collision model. In this model, reactions occur as a result of sufficiently energetic collisions. The colliding molecules must be oriented in such a way that the reaction can occur. The frequency factor contains two terms: p, which represents the fraction of collisions that have the proper orientation, and z, which represents the number of collisions per unit time.

Reaction Mechanisms (13.6)

▶ Most chemical reactions occur not in a single step, but in several steps. The series of individual steps by which a reaction occurs is the reaction mechanism.

▶ In order for a proposed reaction mechanism to be valid, it must fulfill two conditions: (a) the steps must sum to the overall reaction, and (b) the mechanism must predict the experimentally observed rate law.

▶ For mechanisms with a slow initial step, we derive the rate law from the slow step.

▶ For mechanisms with a fast initial step, we first write the rate law based on the slow step but then assume that the fast steps reach equilibrium, so we can write concentrations of intermediates in terms of the reactants.

Catalysis (13.7)

▶ A catalyst is a substance that increases the rate of a chemical reaction by providing an alternative mechanism that has a lower activation energy for the rate-determining step.

▶ Catalysts can be homogeneous or heterogeneous. A homogeneous catalyst exists in the same phase as the reactants and forms a homogeneous mixture with them. A heterogeneous catalyst generally exists in a different phase than the reactants.

▶ Enzymes are biological catalysts capable of increasing the rate of specific biochemical reactions by many orders of magnitude.

Key Equations and Relationships

The Rate of Reaction (13.2)

For a reaction, $aA + bB \longrightarrow cC + dD$, the rate is defined as

$$\text{Rate} = -\frac{1}{a}\frac{\Delta[A]}{\Delta t} = -\frac{1}{b}\frac{\Delta[B]}{\Delta t} = +\frac{1}{c}\frac{\Delta[C]}{\Delta t} = +\frac{1}{d}\frac{\Delta[D]}{\Delta t}$$

The Rate Law (13.3)

$$\text{Rate} = k[A]^n \qquad \text{(single reactant)}$$
$$\text{Rate} = k[A]^m[B]^n \qquad \text{(multiple reactants)}$$

Integrated Rate Laws and Half-Life (13.4)

Reaction Order	Integrated Rate Law	Units of k	Half-Life Expression
0	$[A]_t = -kt + [A]_0$	$M \cdot s^{-1}$	$t_{1/2} = \dfrac{[A]_0}{2k}$
1	$\ln[A]_t = -kt + \ln[A]_0$	s^{-1}	$t_{1/2} = \dfrac{0.693}{k}$
2	$\dfrac{1}{[A]_t} = kt + \dfrac{1}{[A]_0}$	$M^{-1} \cdot s^{-1}$	$t_{1/2} = \dfrac{1}{k[A]_0}$

Arrhenius Equation (13.5)

$$k = Ae^{-E_a/RT}$$

$$\ln k = -\frac{E_a}{R}\left(\frac{1}{T}\right) + \ln A \qquad \text{(linearized form)}$$

$$\ln\frac{k_2}{k_1} = \frac{E_a}{R}\left(\frac{1}{T_1} - \frac{1}{T_2}\right) \qquad \text{(two-point form)}$$

$$k = pze^{-E_a/RT} \qquad \text{(collision theory)}$$

Rate Laws for Elementary Steps (13.6)

Elementary Step	Molecularity	Rate Law
$A \longrightarrow$ products	1	Rate $= k[A]$
$A + A \longrightarrow$ products	2	Rate $= k[A]^2$
$A + B \longrightarrow$ products	2	Rate $= k[A][B]$
$A + A + A \longrightarrow$ products	3 (rare)	Rate $= k[A]^3$
$A + A + B \longrightarrow$ products	3 (rare)	Rate $= k[A]^2[B]$
$A + B + C \longrightarrow$ products	3 (rare)	Rate $= k[A][B][C]$

Key Learning Outcomes

Chapter Objectives	Assessment
Expressing Reaction Rates (13.2)	Example 13.1 For Practice 13.1 Exercises 25–34

Key Learning Outcomes, *continued*

Determining the Order, Rate Law, and Rate Constant of a Reaction (**13.3**)	Example 13.2 For Practice 13.2 Exercises 41–44
Using Graphical Analysis of Reaction Data to Determine Reaction Order and Rate Constants (**13.4**)	Examples 13.3, 13.5 For Practice 13.3, 13.5 Exercises 47–52
Determining the Concentration of a Reactant at a Given Time (**13.4**)	Example 13.4 For Practice 13.4 Exercises 51–54
Working with the Half-Life of a Reaction (**13.4**)	Example 13.6 For Practice 13.6 Exercises 53–56
Using the Arrhenius Equation to Determine Kinetic Parameters (**13.5**)	Examples 13.7, 13.8 For Practice 13.7, 13.8 Exercises 59–70
Determining whether a Reaction Mechanism Is Valid (**13.6**)	Example 13.9 For Practice 13.9 Exercises 73–76

EXERCISES

Review Questions

1. Explain why lizards become sluggish in cold weather. How is this phenomenon related to chemistry?

2. Why are reaction rates important (both practically and theoretically)?

3. What units are typically used to express the rate of a reaction?

4. Why is the reaction rate for reactants defined as the *negative* of the change in reactant concentration with respect to time, whereas for products it is defined as the change in reactant concentration with respect to time (with a positive sign)?

5. Explain the difference between the average rate of reaction and the instantaneous rate of reaction.

6. Consider a simple reaction in which a reactant A forms products:

$$A \longrightarrow products$$

What is the rate law if the reaction is zero order with respect to A? First order? Second order? For each case, explain how a doubling of the concentration of A would affect the rate of reaction.

7. How is the order of a reaction generally determined?

8. For a reaction with multiple reactants, how is the overall order of the reaction defined?

9. Explain the difference between the rate law for a reaction and the integrated rate law for a reaction. What relationship does each kind of rate law express?

10. Write integrated rate laws for zero-order, first-order, and second-order reactions of the form A $\longrightarrow$ products.

11. What does the term *half-life* mean? Write the expressions for the half-lives of zero-order, first-order, and second-order reactions.

12. How do reaction rates typically depend on temperature? What part of the rate law is temperature dependent?

13. Explain the meaning of each term within the Arrhenius equation: activation energy, frequency factor, and exponential factor. Use these terms and the Arrhenius equation to explain why small changes in temperature can result in large changes in reaction rates.

14. What is an Arrhenius plot? Explain the significance of the slope and intercept of an Arrhenius plot.

15. Explain how a chemical reaction occurs according to the collision model. Explain the meaning of the orientation factor in this model.

16. Explain the difference between a normal chemical equation for a chemical reaction and the mechanism of that reaction.

17. In a reaction mechanism, what is an elementary step? Write down the three most common elementary steps and the corresponding rate law for each one.

18. What are the two requirements for a proposed mechanism to be valid for a given reaction?

19. What is an intermediate within a reaction mechanism?

20. What is a catalyst? How does a catalyst increase the rate of a chemical reaction?

21. Explain the difference between homogeneous catalysis and heterogeneous catalysis.

22. What are the four basic steps involved in heterogeneous catalysis?

23. What are enzymes? What is the active site of an enzyme? What is a substrate?

24. What is the general two-step mechanism by which most enzymes work?

Problems by Topic

Reaction Rates

25. Consider the reaction:

$$2 \, HBr(g) \longrightarrow H_2(g) + Br_2(g)$$

   a. Express the rate of the reaction in terms of the change in concentration of each of the reactants and products.
   b. In the first 25.0 s of this reaction, the concentration of HBr dropped from 0.600 M to 0.512 M. Calculate the average rate of the reaction during this time interval.
   c. If the volume of the reaction vessel in part b was 1.50 L, what amount of Br_2 (in moles) was formed during the first 15.0 s of the reaction?

26. Consider the reaction:

$$2 \, N_2O(g) \longrightarrow 2 \, N_2(g) + O_2(g)$$

   a. Express the rate of the reaction in terms of the change in concentration of each of the reactants and products.
   b. In the first 15.0 s of the reaction, 0.015 mol of O_2 is produced in a reaction vessel with a volume of 0.500 L. What is the average rate of the reaction during this time interval?
   c. Predict the rate of change in the concentration of N_2O during this time interval. In other words, what is $\Delta[N_2O]/\Delta t$?

27. For the reaction $2 \, A(g) + B(g) \longrightarrow 3 \, C(g)$,
   a. determine the expression for the rate of the reaction in terms of the change in concentration of each of the reactants and products.
   b. when A is decreasing at a rate of 0.100 M/s, how fast is B decreasing? How fast is C increasing?

28. For the reaction $A(g) + \frac{1}{2} B(g) \longrightarrow 2 \, C(g)$,
   a. determine the expression for the rate of the reaction in terms of the change in concentration of each of the reactants and products.
   b. when C is increasing at a rate of 0.025 M/s, how fast is B decreasing? How fast is A decreasing?

29. Consider the reaction:

$$Cl_2(g) + 3 \, F_2(g) \longrightarrow 2 \, ClF_3(g)$$

Complete the table.

$\Delta[Cl_2]/\Delta t$	$\Delta[F_2]/\Delta t$	$\Delta[ClF_3]/\Delta t$	Rate
−0.012 M/s			

30. Consider the reaction:

$$8 \, H_2S(g) + 4 \, O_2(g) \longrightarrow 8 \, H_2O(g) + S_8(g)$$

Complete the table.

$\Delta[H_2S]/\Delta t$	$\Delta[O_2]/\Delta t$	$\Delta[H_2O]/\Delta t$	$\Delta[S_8]/\Delta t$	Rate
−0.080 M/s				

31. Consider the reaction:

$$C_4H_8(g) \longrightarrow 2 \, C_2H_4(g)$$

The tabulated data were collected for the concentration of C_4H_8 as a function of time:

Time (s)	$[C_4H_8]$ (M)
0	1.000
10	0.913
20	0.835
30	0.763
40	0.697
50	0.637

   a. What is the average rate of the reaction between 0 and 10 s? Between 40 and 50 s?
   b. What is the rate of formation of C_2H_4 between 20 and 30 s?

32. Consider the reaction:

$$NO_2(g) \longrightarrow NO(g) + \frac{1}{2} O_2(g)$$

The tabulated data were collected for the concentration of NO_2 as a function of time:

Time (s)	$[NO_2]$ (M)
0	1.000
10	0.951
20	0.904
30	0.860
40	0.818
50	0.778
60	0.740
70	0.704
80	0.670
90	0.637
100	0.606

   a. What is the average rate of the reaction between 10 and 20 s? Between 50 and 60 s?
   b. What is the rate of formation of O_2 between 50 and 60 s?

33. Consider the reaction:

$$H_2(g) + Br_2(g) \longrightarrow 2 \, HBr(g)$$

The graph shows the concentration of Br_2 as a function of time.

a. Use the graph to calculate each quantity:
   (i) the average rate of the reaction between 0 and 25 s
   (ii) the instantaneous rate of the reaction at 25 s
   (iii) the instantaneous rate of formation of HBr at 50 s
b. Make a rough sketch of a curve representing the concentration of HBr as a function of time. Assume that the initial concentration of HBr is zero.

34. Consider the reaction:

$$2 H_2O_2(aq) \longrightarrow 2 H_2O(l) + O_2(g)$$

The graph below shows the concentration of H_2O_2 as a function of time.

Use the graph to calculate each quantity:
a. the average rate of the reaction between 10 and 20 s
b. the instantaneous rate of the reaction at 30 s
c. the instantaneous rate of formation of O_2 at 50 s
d. If the initial volume of the H_2O_2 is 1.5 L, what total amount of O_2 (in moles) is formed in the first 50 s of reaction?

The Rate Law and Reaction Orders

35. This graph shows a plot of the rate of a reaction versus the concentration of the reactant A for the reaction A $\longrightarrow$ products.

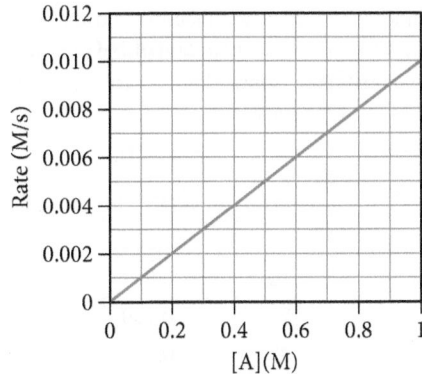

a. What is the order of the reaction with respect to A?
b. Make a rough sketch of a plot of [A] versus *time*.
c. Write a rate law for the reaction including an estimate for the value of k.

36. This graph shows a plot of the rate of a reaction versus the concentration of the reactant.

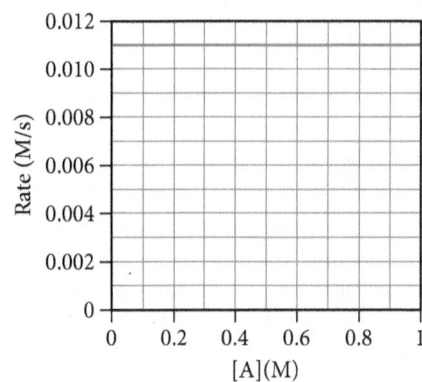

a. What is the order of the reaction with respect to A?
b. Make a rough sketch of a plot of [A] versus *time*.
c. Write a rate law for the reaction including the value of k.

37. What are the units of k for each type of reaction?
a. first-order reaction
b. second-order reaction
c. zero-order reaction

38. This reaction is first order in N_2O_5:

$$N_2O_5(g) \longrightarrow NO_3(g) + NO_2(g)$$

The rate constant for the reaction at a certain temperature is 0.053/s.
a. Calculate the rate of the reaction when $[N_2O_5] = 0.055$ M.
b. What would the rate of the reaction be at the concentration indicated in part a if the reaction were second order? Zero order? (Assume the same *numerical* value for the rate constant with the appropriate units.)

39. A reaction in which A, B, and C react to form products is first order in A, second order in B, and zero order in C.
a. Write a rate law for the reaction.
b. What is the overall order of the reaction?
c. By what factor does the reaction rate change if [A] is doubled (and the other reactant concentrations are held constant)?
d. By what factor does the reaction rate change if [B] is doubled (and the other reactant concentrations are held constant)?
e. By what factor does the reaction rate change if [C] is doubled (and the other reactant concentrations are held constant)?
f. By what factor does the reaction rate change if the concentrations of all three reactants are doubled?

40. A reaction in which A, B, and C react to form products is zero order in A, one-half order in B, and second order in C.
a. Write a rate law for the reaction.
b. What is the overall order of the reaction?
c. By what factor does the reaction rate change if [A] is doubled (and the other reactant concentrations are held constant)?
d. By what factor does the reaction rate change if [B] is doubled (and the other reactant concentrations are held constant)?
e. By what factor does the reaction rate change if [C] is doubled (and the other reactant concentrations are held constant)?
f. By what factor does the reaction rate change if the concentrations of all three reactants are doubled?

41. Consider the data showing the initial rate of a reaction (A $\longrightarrow$ products) at several different concentrations of A. What is the order of the reaction? Write a rate law for the reaction including the value of the rate constant, k.

[A] (M)	Initial Rate (M/s)
0.100	0.053
0.200	0.210
0.300	0.473

42. Consider the data showing the initial rate of a reaction (A $\longrightarrow$ products) at several different concentrations of A. What is the order of the reaction? Write a rate law for the reaction including the value of the rate constant, k.

[A] (M)	Initial Rate (M/s)
0.15	0.008
0.30	0.016
0.60	0.032

43. The tabulated data were collected for this reaction:

$$2\,NO_2(g) + F_2(g) \longrightarrow 2\,NO_2F(g)$$

[NO$_2$] (M)	[F$_2$] (M)	Initial Rate (M/s)
0.100	0.100	0.026
0.200	0.100	0.051
0.200	0.200	0.103
0.400	0.400	0.411

Write an expression for the reaction rate law and calculate the value of the rate constant, k. What is the overall order of the reaction?

44. The tabulated data were collected for this reaction:

$$CH_3Cl(g) + 3\,Cl_2(g) \longrightarrow CCl_4(g) + 3\,HCl(g)$$

[CH$_3$Cl] (M)	[Cl$_2$] (M)	Initial Rate (M/s)
0.050	0.050	0.014
0.100	0.050	0.029
0.100	0.100	0.041
0.200	0.200	0.115

Write an expression for the reaction rate law and calculate the value of the rate constant, k. What is the overall order of the reaction?

The Integrated Rate Law and Half-Life

45. Indicate the order of reaction consistent with each observation.
   a. A plot of the concentration of the reactant versus time yields a straight line.
   b. The reaction has a half-life that is independent of initial concentration.
   c. A plot of the inverse of the concentration versus time yields a straight line.

46. Indicate the order of reaction consistent with each observation.
   a. The half-life of the reaction gets shorter as the initial concentration is increased.
   b. A plot of the natural log of the concentration of the reactant versus time yields a straight line.
   c. The half-life of the reaction gets longer as the initial concentration is increased.

47. The tabulated data show the concentration of AB versus time for this reaction:

$$AB(g) \longrightarrow A(g) + B(g)$$

Time (s)	[AB] (M)
0	0.950
50	0.459
100	0.302
150	0.225
200	0.180
250	0.149
300	0.128
350	0.112
400	0.0994
450	0.0894
500	0.0812

Determine the order of the reaction and the value of the rate constant. Predict the concentration of AB at 25 s.

48. The tabulated data show the concentration of N$_2$O$_5$ versus time for this reaction:

$$N_2O_5(g) \longrightarrow NO_3(g) + NO_2(g)$$

Time (s)	[N$_2$O$_5$] (M)
0	1.000
25	0.822
50	0.677
75	0.557
100	0.458
125	0.377
150	0.310
175	0.255
200	0.210

Determine the order of the reaction and the value of the rate constant. Predict the concentration of N$_2$O$_5$ at 250 s.

49. The tabulated data show the concentration of cyclobutane (C$_4$H$_8$) versus time for this reaction:

$$C_4H_8 \longrightarrow 2\,C_2H_4$$

Time (s)	[C$_4$H$_8$] (M)
0	1.000
10	0.894
20	0.799
30	0.714
40	0.638
50	0.571
60	0.510
70	0.456
80	0.408
90	0.364
100	0.326

Determine the order of the reaction and the value of the rate constant. What is the rate of reaction when [C$_4$H$_8$] = 0.25 M?

50. A reaction in which A $\longrightarrow$ products was monitored as a function of time. The results are shown here.

Time (s)	[A] (M)
0	1.000
25	0.914
50	0.829
75	0.744
100	0.659
125	0.573
150	0.488
175	0.403
200	0.318

Determine the order of the reaction and the value of the rate constant. What is the rate of reaction when [A] = 0.10 M?

51. This reaction was monitored as a function of time:

$$A \longrightarrow B + C$$

A plot of ln[A] versus time yields a straight line with slope −0.0045/s.

  a. What is the value of the rate constant (k) for this reaction at this temperature?
  b. Write the rate law for the reaction.
  c. What is the half-life?
  d. If the initial concentration of A is 0.250 M, what is the concentration after 225 s?

52. This reaction was monitored as a function of time:

$$AB \longrightarrow A + B$$

A plot of 1/[AB] versus time yields a straight line with a slope of +0.55/M · s.

  a. What is the value of the rate constant (k) for this reaction at this temperature?
  b. Write the rate law for the reaction.
  c. What is the half-life when the initial concentration is 0.55 M?
  d. If the initial concentration of AB is 0.250 M, and the reaction mixture initially contains no products, what are the concentrations of A and B after 75 s?

53. The decomposition of SO_2Cl_2 is first order in SO_2Cl_2 and has a rate constant of $1.42 \times 10^{-4}\,s^{-1}$ at a certain temperature.

  a. What is the half-life for this reaction?
  b. How long will it take for the concentration of SO_2Cl_2 to decrease to 25% of its initial concentration?
  c. If the initial concentration of SO_2Cl_2 is 1.00 M, how long will it take for the concentration to decrease to 0.78 M?
  d. If the initial concentration of SO_2Cl_2 is 0.150 M, what is the concentration of SO_2Cl_2 after 2.00×10^2 s? After 5.00×10^2 s?

54. The decomposition of XY is second order in XY and has a rate constant of $7.02 \times 10^{-3}\,M^{-1} \cdot s^{-1}$ at a certain temperature.

  a. What is the half-life for this reaction at an initial concentration of 0.100 M?
  b. How long will it take for the concentration of XY to decrease to 12.5% of its initial concentration when the initial concentration is 0.100 M? When the initial concentration is 0.200 M?

  c. If the initial concentration of XY is 0.150 M, how long will it take for the concentration to decrease to 0.062 M?
  d. If the initial concentration of XY is 0.050 M, what is the concentration of XY after 5.0×10^1 s? After 5.50×10^2 s?

55. The half-life for the radioactive decay of U-238 is 4.5 billion years and is independent of initial concentration. How long will it take for 10% of the U-238 atoms in a sample of U-238 to decay? If a sample of U-238 initially contained 1.5×10^{18} atoms when the universe was formed 13.8 billion years ago, how many U-238 atoms does it contain today?

56. The half-life for the radioactive decay of C-14 is 5730 years and is independent of the initial concentration. How long does it take for 25% of the C-14 atoms in a sample of C-14 to decay? If a sample of C-14 initially contains 1.5 mmol of C-14, how many millimoles are left after 2255 years?

The Effect of Temperature and the Collision Model

57. The diagram shows the energy of a reaction as the reaction progresses. Label each blank box in the diagram.

  a. reactants
  b. products
  c. activation energy (E_a)
  d. enthalpy of reaction (ΔH_{rxn})

58. A chemical reaction is endothermic and has an activation energy that is twice the value of the enthalpy change of the reaction. Draw a diagram depicting the energy of the reaction as it progresses. Label the position of the reactants and products and indicate the activation energy and enthalpy of reaction.

59. The activation energy of a reaction is 56.8 kJ/mol and the frequency factor is 1.5×10^{11}/s. Calculate the rate constant of the reaction at 25 °C.

60. The rate constant of a reaction at 32 °C is 0.055/s. If the frequency factor is 1.2×10^{13}/s, what is the activation barrier?

61. The rate constant (k) for a reaction was measured as a function of temperature. A plot of ln k versus $1/T$ (in K) is linear and has a slope of −7445 K. Calculate the activation energy for the reaction.

62. The rate constant (k) for a reaction was measured as a function of temperature. A plot of ln k versus $1/T$ (in K) is linear and has a slope of -1.01×10^4 K. Calculate the activation energy for the reaction.

63. The data shown here were collected for the first-order reaction:

$$N_2O(g) \longrightarrow N_2(g) + O(g)$$

Use an Arrhenius plot to determine the activation barrier and frequency factor for the reaction.

Temperature (K)	Rate Constant (1/s)
800	3.24×10^{-5}
900	0.00214
1000	0.0614
1100	0.955

64. The tabulated data show the rate constant of a reaction measured at several different temperatures. Use an Arrhenius plot to determine the activation barrier and frequency factor for the reaction.

Temperature (K)	Rate Constant (1/s)
300	0.0134
310	0.0407
320	0.114
330	0.303
340	0.757

65. The tabulated data were collected for the second-order reaction:

$$Cl(g) + H_2(g) \longrightarrow HCl(g) + H(g)$$

Use an Arrhenius plot to determine the activation barrier and frequency factor for the reaction.

Temperature (K)	Rate Constant (L/mol · s)
90	0.00357
100	0.0773
110	0.956
120	7.781

66. The tabulated data show the rate constant of a reaction measured at several different temperatures. Use an Arrhenius plot to determine the activation barrier and frequency factor for the reaction.

Temperature (K)	Rate Constant (1/s)
310	0.00434
320	0.0140
330	0.0421
340	0.118
350	0.316

67. A reaction has a rate constant of 0.0117/s at 400.0 K and 0.689/s at 450.0 K.
a. Determine the activation barrier for the reaction.
b. What is the value of the rate constant at 425 K?

68. A reaction has a rate constant of 0.000122/s at 27 °C and 0.228/s at 77 °C.
a. Determine the activation barrier for the reaction.
b. What is the value of the rate constant at 17 °C?

69. If a temperature increase from 10.0 °C to 20.0 °C doubles the rate constant for a reaction, what is the value of the activation barrier for the reaction?

70. If a temperature increase from 20.0 °C to 35.0 °C triples the rate constant for a reaction, what is the value of the activation barrier for the reaction?

71. Consider these two gas-phase reactions:
a. $AA(g) + BB(g) \longrightarrow 2\,AB(g)$
b. $AB(g) + CD(g) \longrightarrow AC(g) + BD(g)$

If the reactions have identical activation barriers and are carried out under the same conditions, which one would you expect to have the faster rate?

72. Which of these two reactions would you expect to have the smaller orientation factor? Explain.
a. $O(g) + N_2(g) \longrightarrow NO(g) + N(g)$
b. $NO(g) + Cl_2(g) \longrightarrow NOCl(g) + Cl(g)$

Reaction Mechanisms

73. Consider this overall reaction, which is experimentally observed to be second order in AB and zero order in C:

$$AB + C \longrightarrow A + BC$$

Is the following mechanism valid for this reaction?

$$AB + AB \xrightarrow{k_1} AB_2 + A \qquad \text{Slow}$$

$$AB_2 + C \xrightarrow{k_2} AB + BC \qquad \text{Fast}$$

74. Consider this overall reaction, which is experimentally observed to be second order in X and first order in Y:

$$X + Y \longrightarrow XY$$

a. Does the reaction occur in a single step in which X and Y collide?
b. Is this two-step mechanism valid?

$$2\,X \underset{k_2}{\overset{k_1}{\rightleftharpoons}} X_2 \qquad\qquad \text{Fast}$$

$$X_2 + Y \xrightarrow{k_3} XY + X \qquad \text{Slow}$$

75. Consider this three-step mechanism for a reaction:

$$Cl_2(g) \underset{k_2}{\overset{k_1}{\rightleftharpoons}} 2\,Cl(g) \qquad\qquad\qquad \text{Fast}$$

$$Cl(g) + CHCl_3(g) \xrightarrow{k_3} HCl(g) + CCl_3(g) \qquad \text{Slow}$$

$$Cl(g) + CCl_3(g) \xrightarrow{k_4} CCl_4(g) \qquad\qquad \text{Fast}$$

a. What is the overall reaction?
b. Identify the intermediates in the mechanism.
c. What is the predicted rate law?

76. Consider this two-step mechanism for a reaction:

$$NO_2(g) + Cl_2(g) \xrightarrow{k_1} ClNO_2(g) + Cl(g) \qquad \text{Slow}$$

$$NO_2(g) + Cl(g) \xrightarrow{k_2} ClNO_2(g) \qquad\qquad \text{Fast}$$

a. What is the overall reaction?
b. Identify the intermediates in the mechanism.
c. What is the predicted rate law?

Catalysis

77. Many heterogeneous catalysts are deposited on high surface-area supports. Why?

78. Suppose that the reaction A $\longrightarrow$ products is exothermic and has an activation barrier of 75 kJ/mol. Sketch an energy diagram showing the energy of the reaction as a function of the progress of the reaction. Draw a second energy curve showing the effect of a catalyst.

79. Suppose that a catalyst lowers the activation barrier of a reaction from 125 kJ/mol to 55 kJ/mol. By what factor would you expect the reaction rate to increase at 25 °C? (Assume that the frequency factors for the catalyzed and uncatalyzed reactions are identical.)

80. The activation barrier for the hydrolysis of sucrose into glucose and fructose is 108 kJ/mol. If an enzyme increases the rate of the hydrolysis reaction by a factor of 1 million, how much lower must the activation barrier be when sucrose is in the active site of the enzyme? (Assume that the frequency factors for the catalyzed and uncatalyzed reactions are identical and a temperature of 25 °C.)

Cumulative Problems

81. The tabulated data were collected for this reaction at 500 °C:

$$CH_3CN(g) \longrightarrow CH_3NC(g)$$

Time (h)	[CH$_3$CN] (M)
0.0	1.000
5.0	0.794
10.0	0.631
15.0	0.501
20.0	0.398
25.0	0.316

a. Determine the order of the reaction and the value of the rate constant at this temperature.
b. What is the half-life for this reaction (at the initial concentration)?
c. How long will it take for 90% of the CH_3CN to convert to CH_3NC?

82. The tabulated data were collected for this reaction at a certain temperature:

$$X_2Y \longrightarrow 2X + Y$$

Time (h)	[X$_2$Y] (M)
0.0	0.100
1.0	0.0856
2.0	0.0748
3.0	0.0664
4.0	0.0598
5.0	0.0543

a. Determine the order of the reaction and the value of the rate constant at this temperature.
b. What is the half-life for this reaction (at the initial concentration)?
c. What is the concentration of X after 10.0 hours?

83. Consider the reaction:

$$A + B + C \longrightarrow D$$

The rate law for this reaction is:

$$Rate = k \frac{[A][C]^2}{[B]^{1/2}}$$

Suppose the rate of the reaction at certain initial concentrations of A, B, and C is 0.0115 M/s. What is the rate of the reaction if the concentrations of A and C are doubled and the concentration of B is tripled?

84. Consider the reaction:

$$2 O_3(g) \longrightarrow 3 O_2(g)$$

The rate law for this reaction is:

$$Rate = k \frac{[O_3]^2}{[O_2]}$$

Suppose that a 1.0 L reaction vessel initially contains 1.0 mol of O_3 and 1.0 mol of O_2. What fraction of the O_3 will have reacted when the rate falls to one-half of its initial value?

85. At 700 K acetaldehyde decomposes in the gas phase to methane and carbon monoxide. The reaction is:

$$CH_3CHO(g) \longrightarrow CH_4(g) + CO(g)$$

A sample of CH_3CHO is heated to 700 K and the pressure is measured as 0.22 atm before any reaction takes place. The kinetics of the reaction are followed by measurements of total pressure and these data are obtained:

t (s)	0	1000	3000	7000
P_{Total} (atm)	0.22	0.24	0.27	0.31

Find the rate law, the rate constant and the total pressure after 2.00×10^4 s.

86. At 400 K oxalic acid decomposes according to the reaction:

$$H_2C_2O_4(g) \longrightarrow CO_2(g) + HCOOH(g)$$

In three separate experiments, the initial pressure of oxalic acid and final total pressure after 20,000 s are measured.

Experiment	1	2	3
$P_{H_2C_2O_4}$ at $t = 0$	65.8	92.1	111
P_{Total} at $t = 20,000$ s	94.6	132	160

Find the rate law of the reaction and its specific rate constant.

87. Dinitrogen pentoxide decomposes in the gas phase to form nitrogen dioxide and oxygen gas. The reaction is first order in dinitrogen pentoxide and has a half-life of 2.81 h at 25 °C. If a 1.5 L reaction vessel initially contains 745 torr of N_2O_5 at 25 °C, what partial pressure of O_2 is present in the vessel after 215 minutes?

88. Cyclopropane (C_3H_6) reacts to form propene (C_3H_6) in the gas phase. The reaction is first order in cyclopropane and has a rate constant of 5.87×10^{-4}/s at 485 °C. If a 2.5 L reaction vessel initially contains 722 torr of cyclopropane at 485 °C, how long will it take for the partial pressure of cyclopropane to drop to below 1.00×10^2 torr?

89. Iodine atoms combine to form I_2 in liquid hexane solvent with a rate constant of 1.5×10^{10} L/mol · s. The reaction is second order in I. Since the reaction occurs so quickly, the only way to study the reaction is to create iodine atoms almost instantaneously, usually by photochemical decomposition of I_2. Suppose a flash of light creates an initial [I] concentration of 0.0100 M. How long will it take for 95% of the newly created iodine atoms to recombine to form I_2?

90. The hydrolysis of sucrose ($C_{12}H_{22}O_{11}$) into glucose and fructose in acidic water has a rate constant of $1.8 \times 10^{-4}\,s^{-1}$ at 25 °C. Assuming the reaction is first order in sucrose, determine the mass of sucrose that is hydrolyzed when 2.55 L of a 0.150 M sucrose solution is allowed to react for 195 minutes.

91. The reaction $AB(aq) \longrightarrow A(g) + B(g)$ is second order in AB and has a rate constant of $0.0118\,M^{-1} \cdot s^{-1}$ at 25.0 °C. A reaction vessel initially contains 250.0 mL of 0.100 M AB that is allowed to react to form the gaseous product. The product is collected over water at 25.0 °C. How much time is required to produce 200.0 mL of the products at a barometric pressure of 755.1 mmHg? (The vapor pressure of water at this temperature is 23.8 mmHg.)

92. The reaction $2\,H_2O_2(aq) \longrightarrow 2\,H_2O(l) + O_2(g)$ is first order in H_2O_2 and under certain conditions has a rate constant of $0.00752\,s^{-1}$ at 20.0 °C. A reaction vessel initially contains 150.0 mL of 30.0% H_2O_2 by mass solution (the density of the solution is 1.11 g/mL). The gaseous oxygen is collected over water at 20.0 °C as it forms. What volume of O_2 forms in 85.0 seconds at a barometric pressure of 742.5 mmHg? (The vapor pressure of water at this temperature is 17.5 mmHg.)

93. Consider this energy diagram:

a. How many elementary steps are involved in this reaction?
b. Label the reactants, products, and intermediates.
c. Which step is rate limiting?
d. Is the overall reaction endothermic or exothermic?

94. Consider the reaction in which HCl adds across the double bond of ethene:

$$HCl + H_2C{=}CH_2 \longrightarrow H_3C{-}CH_2Cl$$

The following mechanism, with the accompanying energy diagram, has been suggested for this reaction:

Step 1 $HCl + H_2C{=}CH_2 \longrightarrow H_3C{=}CH_2{}^+ + Cl^-$

Step 2 $H_3C{=}CH_2^+ + Cl^- \longrightarrow H_3C{-}CH_2Cl$

a. Based on the energy diagram, determine which step is rate limiting.
b. What is the expected order of the reaction based on the proposed mechanism?
c. Is the overall reaction exothermic or endothermic?

95. The desorption of a single molecular layer of *n*-butane from a single crystal of aluminum oxide is found to be first order with a rate constant of 0.128/s at 150 K.
a. What is the half-life of the desorption reaction?
b. If the surface is initially completely covered with *n*-butane at 150 K, how long will it take for 25% of the molecules to desorb? For 50% to desorb?
c. If the surface is initially completely covered, what fraction will remain covered after 10 s? After 20 s?

96. The evaporation of a 120 nm film of *n*-pentane from a single crystal of aluminum oxide is zero order with a rate constant of 1.92×10^{13} molecules/$cm^2 \cdot s$ at 120 K.
a. If the initial surface coverage is 8.9×10^{16} molecules/cm^2, how long will it take for one-half of the film to evaporate?
b. What fraction of the film is left after 10 s? Assume the same initial coverage as in part a.

97. The kinetics of this reaction were studied as a function of temperature. (The reaction is first order in each reactant and second order overall.)

$$C_2H_5Br(aq) + OH^-(aq) \longrightarrow C_2H_5OH(l) + Br^-(aq)$$

Temperature (°C)	k(L/mol · s)
25	8.81×10^{-5}
35	0.000285
45	0.000854
55	0.00239
65	0.00633

a. Determine the activation energy and frequency factor for the reaction.
b. Determine the rate constant at 15 °C.
c. If a reaction mixture is 0.155 M in C_2H_5Br and 0.250 M in OH^-, what is the initial rate of the reaction at 75 °C?

98. The reaction $2\,N_2O_5 \longrightarrow 2\,N_2O_4 + O_2$ takes place at around room temperature in solvents such as CCl_4. The rate constant at 293 K is found to be $2.35 \times 10^{-4}\,s^{-1}$, and at 303 K the rate constant is found to be $9.15 \times 10^{-4}\,s^{-1}$. Calculate the frequency factor for the reaction.

99. This reaction has an activation energy of zero in the gas phase:

$$CH_3 + CH_3 \longrightarrow C_2H_6$$

a. Would you expect the rate of this reaction to change very much with temperature?
b. Why might the activation energy be zero?
c. What other types of reactions would you expect to have little or no activation energy?

100. Consider the two reactions:

$$O + N_2 \longrightarrow NO + N \quad E_a = 315\ kJ/mol$$
$$Cl + H_2 \longrightarrow HCl + H \quad E_a = 23\ kJ/mol$$

a. Why is the activation barrier for the first reaction so much higher than that for the second?
b. The frequency factors for these two reactions are very close to each other in value. Assuming that they are the same, calculate the ratio of the reaction rate constants for these two reactions at 25 °C.

101. Anthropologists can estimate the age of a bone or other sample of organic matter by its carbon-14 content. The carbon-14 in a living organism is constant until the organism dies, after which carbon-14 decays with first-order kinetics and a half-life of 5730 years. Suppose a bone from an ancient human contains 19.5% of the C-14 found in living organisms. How old is the bone?

102. Geologists can estimate the age of rocks by their uranium-238 content. The uranium is incorporated in the rock as it hardens and then decays with first-order kinetics and a half-life of 4.5 billion years. A rock contains 83.2% of the amount of uranium-238 that it contained when it was formed. (The amount that the rock contained when it was formed can be deduced from the presence of the decay products of U-238.) How old is the rock?

103. Consider the gas-phase reaction:

$$H_2(g) + I_2(g) \longrightarrow 2\,HI(g)$$

The reaction was experimentally determined to be first order in H_2 and first order in I_2. Consider the proposed mechanisms.

Proposed mechanism I:

$$H_2(g) + I_2(g) \longrightarrow 2\,HI(g) \qquad \text{Single step}$$

Proposed mechanism II:

$$I_2(g) \underset{k_{-1}}{\overset{k_1}{\rightleftharpoons}} 2\,I(g) \qquad \text{Fast}$$

$$H_2(g) + 2\,I(g) \overset{k_2}{\longrightarrow} 2\,HI(g) \qquad \text{Slow}$$

a. Show that both of the proposed mechanisms are valid.

b. What kind of experimental evidence might lead you to favor mechanism II over mechanism I?

104. Consider the reaction:

$$2\,NH_3(aq) + OCl^-(aq) \longrightarrow N_2H_4(aq) + H_2O(l) + Cl^-(aq)$$

This three-step mechanism is proposed:

$$NH_3(aq)\,OCl^-(aq) \underset{k_2}{\overset{k_1}{\rightleftharpoons}} NH_2Cl(aq) + OH^-(aq) \qquad \text{Fast}$$

$$NH_2Cl(aq) + NH_3(aq) \overset{}{\underset{k_3}{\longrightarrow}} N_2H_5^+(aq) + Cl^-(aq) \qquad \text{Slow}$$

$$N_2H_5^+(aq) + OH^-(aq) \overset{}{\underset{k_4}{\longrightarrow}} N_2H_4(aq) + H_2O(l) \qquad \text{Fast}$$

a. Show that the mechanism sums to the overall reaction.

b. What is the rate law predicted by this mechanism?

105. The proposed mechanism for the formation of hydrogen bromide can be written in a simplified form as:

$$Br_2(g) \underset{k_{-1}}{\overset{k_1}{\rightleftharpoons}} 2\,Br(g) \qquad \text{Fast}$$

$$Br(g) + H_2(g) \overset{k_2}{\longrightarrow} HBr(g) + H(g) \qquad \text{Slow}$$

$$H(g) + Br_2(g) \overset{k_3}{\longrightarrow} HBr(g) + Br(g) \qquad \text{Fast}$$

What rate law corresponds to this mechanism?

106. A proposed mechanism for the formation of hydrogen iodide can be written in simplified form as

$$I_2 \underset{k_{-1}}{\overset{k_1}{\rightleftharpoons}} 2\,I \qquad \text{Fast}$$

$$I + H_2 \underset{k_{-2}}{\overset{k_2}{\rightleftharpoons}} H_2I \qquad \text{Fast}$$

$$H_2I + I \underset{k_3}{\longrightarrow} 2\,HI \qquad \text{Slow}$$

What rate law corresponds to this mechanism?

107. A certain substance X decomposes. Fifty percent of X remains after 100 minutes. How much X remains after 200 minutes if the reaction order with respect to X is (a) zero order, (b) first order, (c) second order?

108. The half-life for radioactive decay (a first-order process) of plutonium-239 is 24,000 years. How many years does it take for one mole of this radioactive material to decay until just one atom remains?

109. The energy of activation for the decomposition of 2 mol of HI to H_2 and I_2 in the gas phase is 185 kJ. The heat of formation of $HI(g)$ from $H_2(g)$ and $I_2(g)$ is -5.65 kJ/mol. Find the energy of activation for the reaction of 1 mol of H_2 and 1 mol of I_2 to form 2 mol of HI in the gas phase.

110. Ethyl chloride vapor decomposes by the first-order reaction:

$$C_2H_5Cl \longrightarrow C_2H_4 + HCl$$

The activation energy is 249 kJ/mol, and the frequency factor is $1.6 \times 10^{14}\,s^{-1}$. Find the value of the specific rate constant at 710 K. What fraction of the ethyl chloride decomposes in 15 minutes at this temperature? Find the temperature at which the rate of the reaction would be twice as fast.

Challenge Problems

111. In this chapter we have seen a number of reactions in which a single reactant forms products. For example, consider the following first-order reaction:

$$CH_3NC(g) \longrightarrow CH_3CN(g)$$

However, we also learned that gas-phase reactions occur through collisions.

a. One possible explanation is that two molecules of CH_3NC collide with each other and form two molecules of the product in a single elementary step. If that were the case, what reaction order would you expect?

b. Another possibility is that the reaction occurs through more than one step. For example, a possible mechanism involves one step in which the two CH_3NC molecules collide, resulting in the "activation" of one of them. In a second step, the activated molecule goes on to form the product. Write down this mechanism and determine which step must be rate determining in order for the kinetics of the reaction to be first order. Show explicitly how the mechanism predicts first-order kinetics.

112. The first-order *integrated* rate law for a reaction A ⟶ products is derived from the rate law using calculus:

$$\text{Rate} = k[A] \text{ (first-order rate law)}$$

$$\text{Rate} = -\frac{d[A]}{dt}$$

$$\frac{d[A]}{dt} = -k[A]$$

The equation just given is a first-order, separable differential equation that can be solved by separating the variables and integrating:

$$\frac{d[A]}{[A]} = -kdt$$

$$\int_{[A]_0}^{[A]} \frac{d[A]}{[A]} = -\int_0^t kdt$$

In the integral just given, $[A]_0$ is the initial concentration of A. We then evaluate the integral:

$$[\ln[A]]_{[A]_0}^{[A]} = -k[t]_0^t$$

$$\ln[A] - \ln[A]_0 = -kt$$

$$\ln[A] = -kt + \ln[A]_0 \text{ (integrated rate law)}$$

a. Use a procedure similar to the one just to derive an integrated rate law for a reaction A ⟶ products, which is one-half order in the concentration of A (that is, Rate = $k[A]^{1/2}$).

b. Use the result from part a to derive an expression for the half-life of a one-half-order reaction.

113. The previous exercise shows how the first-order integrated rate law is derived from the first-order differential rate law. Begin with the second-order differential rate law and derive the second-order integrated rate law.

114. The rate constant for the first-order decomposition of $N_2O_5(g)$ to $NO_2(g)$ and $O_2(g)$ is $7.48 \times 10^{-3}\ s^{-1}$ at a given temperature.
   a. Find the length of time required for the total pressure in a system containing N_2O_5 at an initial pressure of 0.100 atm to rise to 0.145 atm.
   b. To 0.200 atm.
   c. Find the total pressure after 100 s of reaction.

115. Phosgene (Cl_2CO), a poison gas used in World War I, is formed by the reaction of Cl_2 and CO. The proposed mechanism for the reaction is:

$Cl_2 \rightleftharpoons 2\ Cl$	(fast, equilibrium)
$Cl + CO \rightleftharpoons ClCO$	(fast, equilibrium)
$ClCO + Cl_2 \longrightarrow Cl_2CO + Cl$	(slow)

What rate law is consistent with this mechanism?

116. The rate of decomposition of $N_2O_3(g)$ to $NO_2(g)$ and $NO(g)$ is followed by measuring $[NO_2]$ at different times. The following data are obtained.

$[NO_2]$ (mol/L)	0	0.193	0.316	0.427	0.784
t (s)	0	884	1610	2460	50,000

The reaction follows a first-order rate law. Calculate the rate constant. Assume that after 50,000 s all the $N_2O_3(g)$ had decomposed.

117. At 473 K, for the elementary reaction $2\ NOCl(g) \underset{k_{-1}}{\overset{k_1}{\rightleftharpoons}} 2\ NO(g) + Cl_2(g)$

$$k_1 = 7.8 \times 10^{-2}\ L/mol\ s \quad \text{and}$$

$$k_{-1} = 4.7 \times 10^2\ L^2/mol^2\ s$$

A sample of NOCl is placed in a container and heated to 473 K. When the system comes to equilibrium, [NOCl] is found to be 0.12 mol/L. What are the concentrations of NO and Cl_2?

Conceptual Problems

118. Consider the reaction:

$$CHCl_3(g) + Cl_2(g) \longrightarrow CCl_4(g) + HCl(g)$$

The reaction is first order in $CHCl_3$ and one-half order in Cl_2. Which reaction mixture would you expect to have the fastest initial rate?

(a)   (b)

(c)

119. The accompanying graph shows the concentration of a reactant as a function of time for two different reactions. One of the reactions is first order and the other is second order. Which of the two reactions is first order? Second order? How would you change each plot to make it linear?

120. A particular reaction, A $\longrightarrow$ products, has a rate that slows down as the reaction proceeds. The half-life of the reaction is found to depend on the initial concentration of A. Determine whether each statement is likely to be true or false for this reaction.

a. A doubling of the concentration of A doubles the rate of the reaction.

b. A plot of 1/[A] versus time is linear.

c. The half-life of the reaction gets longer as the initial concentration of A increases.

d. A plot of the concentration of A versus time has a constant slope.

Answers to Conceptual Connections

Reaction Rates

13.1 (**c**) The rate at which B changes is twice the rate of the reaction because its coefficient is 2, and it is negative because B is a reactant.

Order of Reaction

13.2 (**d**) Since the reaction is second order, increasing the concentration of A by a factor of 5 causes the rate to increase by 5^2 or 25.

Rate and Concentration

13.3 All three mixtures have the same total number of molecules, but mixture (**c**) has the greatest number of NO molecules. Since the reaction is second order in NO and only first order in O_2, mixture (**c**) has the fastest initial rate.

Rate Law and Integrated Rate Law

13.4 (**c**) The reaction is most likely second order because its rate depends on the concentration (therefore it cannot be zero order), and its half-life depends on the initial concentration (therefore it cannot be first order). For a second-order reaction, a doubling of the initial concentration results in the quadrupling of the rate.

Temperature Dependence of Reaction Rate

13.5 Reaction A has a faster rate because it has a lower activation energy; therefore, the exponential factor is larger at a given temperature, making the rate constant larger. (With a larger rate constant and the same initial concentration, the rate will be faster).

Collision Theory

13.6 (**c**) Since the reactants in part (**a**) are atoms, the orientation factor should be about one. The reactants in parts (**b**) and (**c**) are both molecules, so we expect orientation factors of less than one. Since the reactants in (**b**) are symmetrical, we would not expect the collision to have as specific an orientation requirement as in (**c**), where the reactants are asymmetrical and must therefore collide in such way that a hydrogen atom is in close proximity to another hydrogen atom. Therefore, we expect (**c**) to have the smallest orientation factor.

14 Chemical Equilibrium

*Every system in chemical equilibrium, under the influence of
a change of any one of the factors of equilibrium, undergoes a
transformation . . . [that produces a change] . . . in the opposite
direction of the factor in question.*

—Henri Le Châtelier (1850–1936)

I N CHAPTER 13, we examined *how fast* a chemical reaction occurs. In this chapter we examine
how far a chemical reaction goes. The *speed* of a chemical reaction is determined by kinetics.
The *extent* of a chemical reaction is determined by thermodynamics. In this chapter, we focus
on describing and quantifying how far a chemical reaction goes based on an experimentally
measurable quantity called *the equilibrium constant*. A reaction with a large equilibrium constant
proceeds nearly to completion—nearly all the reactants react to form products. A reaction with
a small equilibrium constant barely proceeds at all—nearly all the reactants remain as reactants,
hardly forming any products. In this chapter we simply accept the equilibrium constant as
an experimentally measurable quantity and learn how to use it to predict and quantify the
extent of a reaction. In Chapter 17, we will explore the reasons underlying the magnitude of
equilibrium constants.

A developing fetus gets oxygen from the mother's blood because the reaction between oxygen and fetal hemoglobin has a larger equilibrium constant than the reaction between oxygen and maternal hemoglobin.

14.1 Fetal Hemoglobin and Equilibrium

Have you ever wondered how a baby in the womb gets oxygen? Unlike you and me, a fetus does not breathe air. Yet, like you and me, a fetus needs oxygen. Where does that oxygen come from? After we are born, we inhale air into our lungs and that air diffuses into capillaries, where it comes into contact with our blood. Within our red blood cells, a protein called hemoglobin (Hb) reacts with oxygen according to the chemical equation:

$$Hb + O_2 \rightleftharpoons HbO_2$$

The double arrows in this equation indicate that the reaction can occur in both the forward and reverse directions and can reach chemical *equilibrium*. We encountered this term in Chapters 11 and 12, and we define it more carefully in the next section.

649

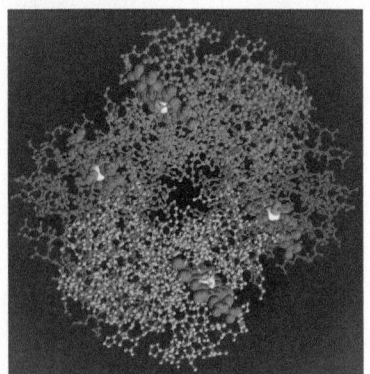

▲ Hemoglobin is the oxygen-carrying protein in red blood cells. Oxygen binds to iron atoms, which are depicted here in white.

For now, understand that the concentrations of the reactants and products in a reaction at equilibrium are described by the *equilibrium constant, K.* A large value of *K* means that the reaction lies far to the right at equilibrium—a high concentration of products and a low concentration of reactants. A small value of *K* means that the reaction lies far to the left at equilibrium—a high concentration of reactants and a low concentration of products. In other words, the value of *K* is a measure of how far a reaction proceeds—the larger the value of *K*, the more the reaction proceeds toward the products.

The equilibrium constant for the reaction between hemoglobin and oxygen is such that hemoglobin efficiently binds oxygen at typical lung oxygen concentrations, but it can also release oxygen under the appropriate conditions. Any system at equilibrium, including the hemoglobin–oxygen system, responds to changes in ways that maintain equilibrium. If any of the concentrations of the reactants or products change, the reaction shifts to counteract that change. For the hemoglobin system, as blood flows through the lungs where oxygen concentrations are high, the equilibrium shifts to the right—hemoglobin binds oxygen:

Lungs:
high $[O_2]$

$$Hb + O_2 \rightleftharpoons HbO_2$$

Reaction shifts right.

As blood flows out of the lungs and into muscles and organs where oxygen concentrations have been depleted (because muscles and organs use oxygen), the equilibrium shifts to the left—hemoglobin releases oxygen:

Muscles:
low $[O_2]$

$$Hb + O_2 \rightleftharpoons HbO_2$$

Reaction shifts left.

In other words, in order to maintain equilibrium, *hemoglobin binds oxygen when the surrounding oxygen concentration is high,* but *it releases oxygen when the surrounding oxygen concentration is low.* In this way, hemoglobin transports oxygen from the lungs to all parts of the body that use oxygen.

A fetus has its own circulatory system. The mother's blood never flows into the fetus's body, and the fetus cannot get any air in the womb. How, then, does the fetus get oxygen? The answer lies in the properties of fetal hemoglobin (HbF), which is slightly different from adult hemoglobin. Like adult hemoglobin, fetal hemoglobin is in equilibrium with oxygen:

$$HbF + O_2 \rightleftharpoons HbFO_2$$

However, the equilibrium constant for fetal hemoglobin is larger than the equilibrium constant for adult hemoglobin, meaning that the reaction tends to go farther in the direction of the product. Consequently, fetal hemoglobin loads oxygen at a lower oxygen concentration than does adult hemoglobin. In the placenta, fetal blood flows in close proximity to maternal blood. Although the two never mix, because of the different equilibrium constants, the maternal hemoglobin releases oxygen that the fetal hemoglobin then binds and carries into its own circulatory system (Figure 14.1 ▶). Nature has evolved a chemical system through which the mother's hemoglobin can in effect *hand off* oxygen to the hemoglobin of the fetus.

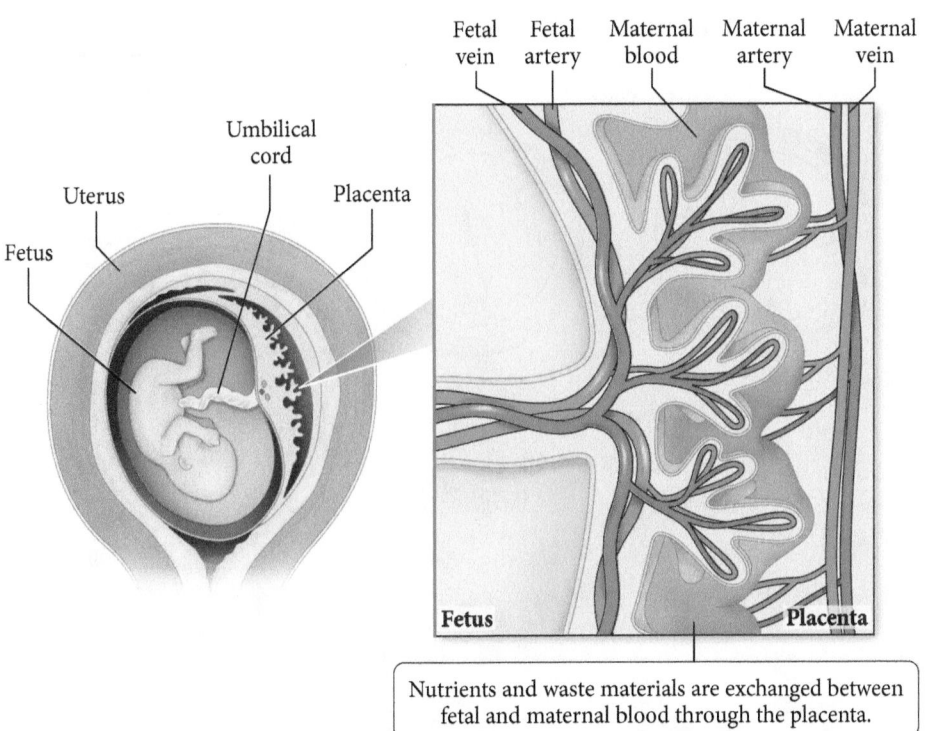

Fetal vein   Fetal artery   Maternal blood   Maternal artery   Maternal vein

Umbilical cord

Uterus   Placenta

Fetus

Fetus   **Placenta**

Nutrients and waste materials are exchanged between fetal and maternal blood through the placenta.

◀ **FIGURE 14.1 Oxygen Exchange between the Maternal and Fetal Circulation** In the placenta, the blood of the fetus comes into close proximity with that of the mother, although the two do not mix directly. Because the reaction of fetal hemoglobin with oxygen has a larger equilibrium constant than the reaction of maternal hemoglobin with oxygen, the fetus receives oxygen from the mother's blood.

14.2 The Concept of Dynamic Equilibrium

Recall from the previous chapter that reaction rates generally increase with increasing concentration of the reactants (unless the reaction order is zero) and decrease with decreasing concentration of the reactants. With this in mind, consider the reaction between hydrogen and iodine:

$$H_2(g) + I_2(g) \rightleftharpoons 2\ HI(g)$$

In this reaction, H_2 and I_2 react to form 2 HI molecules, but the 2 HI molecules can also react to re-form H_2 and I_2. A reaction such as this one—that can proceed in both the forward and reverse directions—is said to be **reversible.** Suppose we begin with only H_2 and I_2 in a container (Figure 14.2a ▶). What happens? Initially H_2 and I_2 begin to react to form HI (Figure 14.2b). However, as H_2 and I_2 react, their concentrations decrease, which in turn *decreases the rate of the forward reaction*. At the same time, HI begins to form. As the concentration of HI increases, the reverse reaction begins to occur at a faster and faster rate. Eventually the rate of the reverse reaction (which has been increasing) equals the rate of the forward reaction (which has been decreasing). At that point, **dynamic equilibrium** is reached (Figure 14.2c, d).

> **Dynamic equilibrium for a chemical reaction is the condition in which the rate of the forward reaction equals the rate of the reverse reaction.**

Dynamic equilibrium is called "dynamic" because the forward and reverse reactions are still occurring; however, they are occurring at the same rate. When dynamic equilibrium is reached, the concentrations of H_2, I_2, and HI no longer change. They remain constant because the reactants and products form at the same rate that they are depleted. Note that just because the concentrations of reactants and products no longer change at equilibrium *does not mean that the concentrations of reactants and products are equal to one another* at equilibrium. Some reactions reach equilibrium only after most of the reactants have formed products. Others reach equilibrium when only a small fraction of the reactants have formed products. It depends on the reaction.

Nearly all chemical reactions are at least theoretically reversible. In many cases, however, the reversibility is so small that it can be ignored.

Dynamic Equilibrium

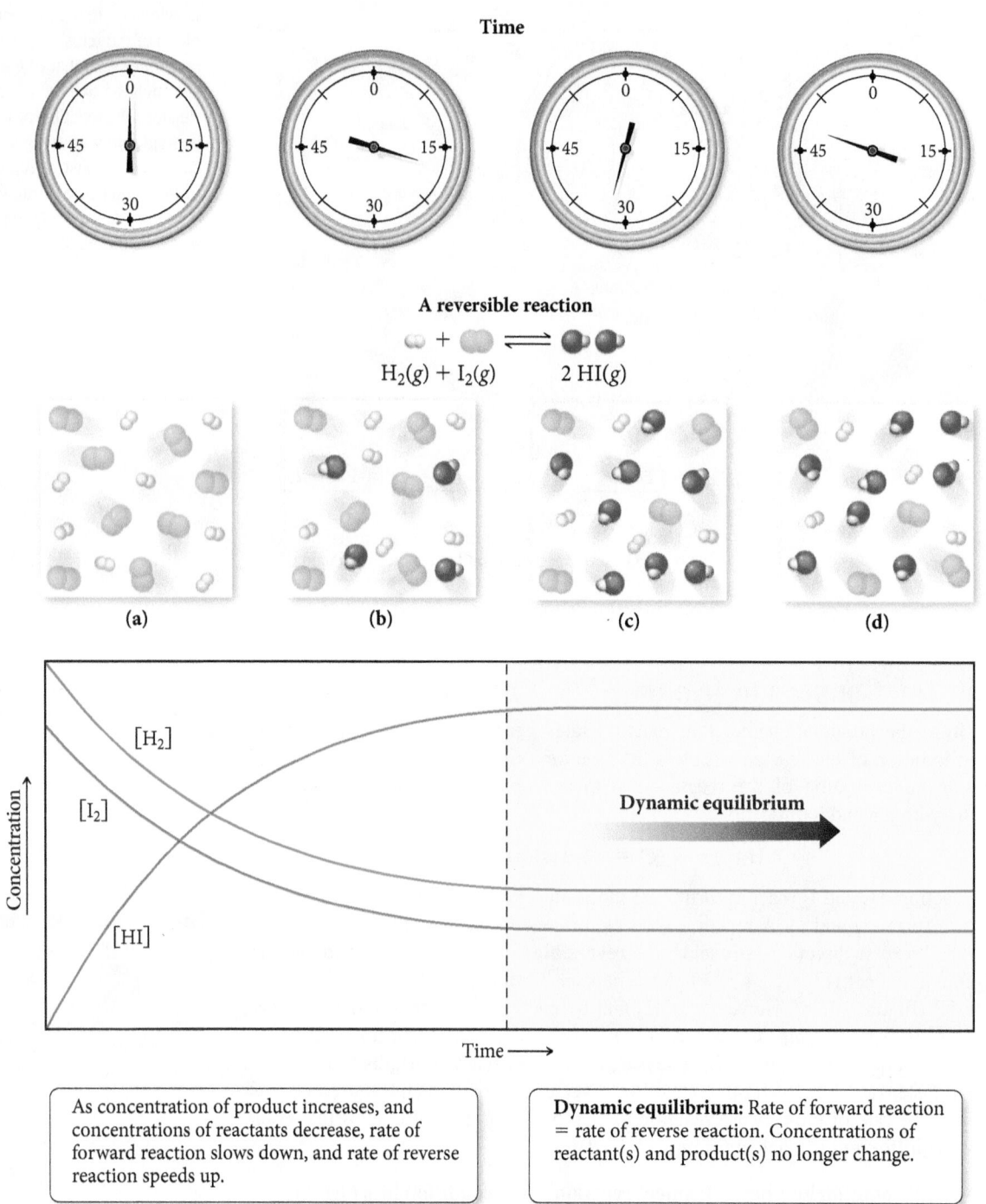

▲ FIGURE 14.2 Dynamic Equilibrium Equilibrium is reached in a chemical reaction when the concentrations of the reactants and products no longer change. The molecular images depict the progress of the reaction $H_2(g) + I_2(g) \rightleftharpoons 2\,HI(g)$. The graph shows the concentrations of H_2, I_2, and HI as a function of time. When equilibrium is reached, both the forward and reverse reactions continue, but at equal rates, so the concentrations of the reactants and products remain constant.

We can better understand dynamic equilibrium with a simple analogy. Imagine two neighboring countries (A and B) with a closed border between them (Figure 14.3 ▶). Country A is overpopulated and Country B is underpopulated. One day, the border between the two countries opens, and people immediately begin to leave Country A for Country B.

$$\text{Country A} \longrightarrow \text{Country B}$$

Dynamic Equilibrium: An Analogy

Initial
Net movement from A to B

Equilibrium
Equal movement in both directions

◀ **FIGURE 14.3 A Population Analogy for Chemical Equilibrium** Because Country A is initially overpopulated, people migrate from Country A to Country B. As the population of Country A falls and that of Country B rises, the rate of migration from Country A to Country B decreases and the rate of migration from Country B to Country A increases. Eventually the two rates become equal. Equilibrium has been reached.

The population of Country A goes down as the population of Country B goes up. As people leave Country A, however, the *rate* at which they leave slows down, because as Country A becomes less populated, the pool of potential emigrants gets smaller. (In other words, the rate of emigration is directly proportional to the population—as the population decreases, the emigration rate goes down.) On the other hand, as people move into Country B, it gets more crowded and some people begin to move from Country B to Country A.

$$\text{Country A} \longleftarrow \text{Country B}$$

As the population of Country B continues to grow, the rate of people moving out of Country B gets faster. Eventually the *rate* of people moving out of Country A (which has been slowing down as people leave) equals the *rate* of people moving out of Country B (which has been increasing as Country B gets more crowded). Dynamic equilibrium has been reached.

$$\text{Country A} \rightleftharpoons \text{Country B}$$

Notice that when the two countries reach dynamic equilibrium, their populations no longer change, because the number of people moving out of either country equals the number of people moving in. However, one country—because of its charm or the availability of good jobs or lower taxes, or for whatever other reason—may have a higher population than the other country, even when dynamic equilibrium is reached.

Similarly, when a chemical reaction reaches dynamic equilibrium, the rate of the forward reaction equals the rate of the reverse reaction, and the relative concentrations of reactants and products become *constant*. But the concentrations of reactants and products will not necessarily be *equal* at equilibrium, just as the populations of the two countries are not necessarily equal at equilibrium.

14.3 The Equilibrium Constant (*K*)

We have just seen that the *concentrations of reactants and products* are not equal at equilibrium—rather, the *rates of the forward and reverse reactions* are equal. So what about the concentrations? The *equilibrium constant* is a way to quantify the concentrations of the reactants and products at equilibrium.

Consider the general chemical equation:

$$aA + bB \rightleftharpoons cC + dD$$

where A and B are reactants, C and D are products, and a, b, c, and d are the respective stoichiometric coefficients in the chemical equation. The **equilibrium constant (K)** for the reaction is defined as the ratio—*at equilibrium*—of the concentrations of the products raised to their stoichiometric coefficients divided by the concentrations of the reactants raised to their stoichiometric coefficients.

Law of Mass Action

$$K = \frac{[C]^c[D]^d}{[A]^a[B]^b}$$

Products

Reactants

In this notation, [A] represents the molar concentration of A. The equilibrium constant quantifies the relative concentrations of reactants and products *at equilibrium*. The relationship between the balanced chemical equation and the expression of the equilibrium constant is known as the **law of mass action.**

Expressing Equilibrium Constants for Chemical Reactions

To express an equilibrium constant for a chemical reaction, we examine the balanced chemical equation and apply the law of mass action. For example, suppose we want to express the equilibrium constant for the reaction:

$$2\,N_2O_5(g) \rightleftharpoons 4\,NO_2(g) + O_2(g)$$

The equilibrium constant is $[NO_2]$ raised to the fourth power multiplied by $[O_2]$ raised to the first power divided by $[N_2O_5]$ raised to the second power:

$$K = \frac{[NO_2]^4[O_2]}{[N_2O_5]^2}$$

Notice that the *coefficients* in the chemical equation become the *exponents* in the expression of the equilibrium constant.

EXAMPLE 14.1 Expressing Equilibrium Constants for Chemical Equations

Express the equilibrium constant for the chemical equation:

$$CH_3OH(g) \rightleftharpoons CO(g) + 2\,H_2(g)$$

SOLUTION

The equilibrium constant is the equilibrium concentrations of the products raised to their stoichiometric coefficients divided by the equilibrium concentrations of the reactants raised to their stoichiometric coefficients.

$$K = \frac{[CO][H_2]^2}{[CH_3OH]}$$

FOR PRACTICE 14.1

Express the equilibrium constant for the combustion of propane as shown by the balanced chemical equation:

$$C_3H_8(g) + 5\,O_2(g) \rightleftharpoons 3\,CO_2(g) + 4\,H_2O(g)$$

The Significance of the Equilibrium Constant

You now know how to express the equilibrium constant, but what does it mean? What, for example, does a large equilibrium constant $(K \gg 1)$ imply about a reaction? A large equilibrium constant indicates that the numerator (which specifies the amounts of products at equilibrium) is larger than the denominator (which specifies the amounts of reactants at equilibrium). Therefore, when the equilibrium constant is large, the forward reaction is favored. For example, consider the reaction:

$$H_2(g) + Br_2(g) \rightleftharpoons 2\,HBr(g) \qquad K = 1.9 \times 10^{19} \text{ (at 25 °C)}$$

The equilibrium constant is large, indicating that the equilibrium point for the reaction lies far to the right—high concentrations of products, low concentrations of reactants (Figure 14.4 ▼). Remember that the equilibrium constant says nothing about *how fast* a reaction reaches equilibrium, only *how far* the reaction has proceeded once equilibrium is reached. A reaction with a large equilibrium constant may be kinetically very slow and take a long time to reach equilibrium.

$$H_2(g) + Br_2(g) \rightleftharpoons 2\,HBr(g)$$

$$K = \frac{[HBr]^2}{[H_2][Br_2]} = \text{large number}$$

◀ **FIGURE 14.4 The Meaning of a Large Equilibrium Constant** If the equilibrium constant for a reaction is large, the equilibrium point of the reaction lies far to the right—the concentration of products is large and the concentration of reactants is small.

Conversely, what does a *small* equilibrium constant $(K \ll 1)$ mean? It indicates that the reverse reaction is favored and that there will be more reactants than products when equilibrium is reached. For example, consider the reaction:

$$N_2(g) + O_2(g) \rightleftharpoons 2\,NO(g) \qquad K = 4.1 \times 10^{-31} \text{ (at 25 °C)}$$

The equilibrium constant is very small, indicating that the equilibrium point for the reaction lies far to the left—high concentrations of reactants, low concentrations of products (Figure 14.5 ▼). This is fortunate because N_2 and O_2 are the main components of air. If this equilibrium constant were large, much of the N_2 and O_2 in air would react to form NO, a toxic gas.

Summarizing the Significance of the Equilibrium Constant:

▶ $K \ll 1$ Reverse reaction is favored; forward reaction does not proceed very far.

▶ $K \approx 1$ Neither direction is favored; forward reaction proceeds about halfway.

▶ $K \gg 1$ Forward reaction is favored; forward reaction proceeds essentially to completion.

$$N_2(g) + O_2(g) \rightleftharpoons 2\,NO(g)$$

$$K = \frac{[NO]^2}{[N_2][O_2]} = \text{small number}$$

◀ **FIGURE 14.5 The Meaning of a Small Equilibrium Constant** If the equilibrium constant for a reaction is small, the equilibrium point of the reaction lies far to the left—the concentration of products is small and the concentration of reactants is large.

Conceptual Connection 14.1 Equilibrium Constants

The equilibrium constant for the reaction $A(g) \rightleftharpoons B(g)$ is 10. A reaction mixture initially contains $[A] = 1.1$ M and $[B] = 0.0$ M. Which statement is true at equilibrium?

(a) The reaction mixture will contain $[A] = 1.0$ M and $[B] = 0.1$ M.

(b) The reaction mixture will contain $[A] = 0.1$ M and $[B] = 1.0$ M.

(c) The reaction mixture will contain equal concentrations of A and B.

Relationships between the Equilibrium Constant and the Chemical Equation

If a chemical equation is modified in some way, then the equilibrium constant for the equation changes because of the modification. The three modifications discussed here are common.

1. **If you reverse the equation, invert the equilibrium constant.** For example, consider this equilibrium equation:

$$A + 2\,B \rightleftharpoons 3\,C$$

The expression for the equilibrium constant of this reaction is:

$$K_{\text{forward}} = \frac{[C]^3}{[A][B]^2}$$

Chemistry and Medicine

Life and Equilibrium

Have you ever tried to define life? If you have, you probably know that a definition is elusive. How are living things different from nonliving things? You may try to define living things as those things that can move. But of course many living things do not move (most plants, for example), and some nonliving things, such as glaciers and Earth itself, do move. So motion is neither unique to nor definitive of life. You may try to define living things as those things that can reproduce. But again, many living things, such as mules or sterile humans, cannot reproduce; yet they are alive. In addition, some nonliving things, such as crystals, for example, reproduce (in some sense). So what is unique about living things?

One definition of life involves the concept of equilibrium—living things *are not* in equilibrium with their surroundings. Our body temperature, for example, is not the same as the temperature of our surroundings. If we jump into a

◄ What makes these cells alive?

swimming pool, the acidity of our blood does not become the same as the acidity of the surrounding water. Living things, even the simplest ones, maintain some measure of *disequilibrium* with their environment.

We must add one more concept, however, to complete our definition of life with respect to equilibrium. A cup of hot water is in disequilibrium with its environment with respect to temperature, yet it is not alive. The cup of hot water has no control over its disequilibrium, however, and will slowly come to equilibrium with its environment. In contrast, living things—as long as they are alive—maintain and *control* their disequilibrium. Your body temperature, for example, is not *only* in disequilibrium with your surroundings—it is in *controlled disequilibrium.* Your body maintains your temperature within a specific range that is not in equilibrium with the surrounding temperature.

So, one criterion for life is that living things are in *controlled disequilibrium* with their environment. Maintaining disequilibrium is a main activity of living organisms, requiring energy obtained from their environment. Plants derive that energy from sunlight; animals eat plants (or other animals that have eaten plants), and thus they too ultimately derive their energy from the sun. A living thing comes into equilibrium with its surroundings only after it dies.

If we reverse the equation:

$$3\,C \rightleftharpoons A + 2\,B$$

then, according to the law of mass action, the expression for the equilibrium constant becomes:

$$K_{reverse} = \frac{[A][B]^2}{[C]^3} = \frac{1}{K_{forward}}$$

2. **If you multiply the coefficients in the equation by a factor, raise the equilibrium constant to the same factor.** Consider again this chemical equation and corresponding expression for the equilibrium constant:

$$A + 2\,B \rightleftharpoons 3\,C \qquad K = \frac{[C]^3}{[A][B]^2}$$

If we multiply the equation by n, we get:

$$n\,A + 2n\,B \rightleftharpoons 3n\,C$$

Applying the law of mass action, the expression for the equilibrium constant becomes:

$$K' = \frac{[C]^{3n}}{[A]^n[B]^{2n}} = \left(\frac{[C]^3}{[A][B]^2}\right)^n = K^n$$

> If n is a fractional quantity, raise K to the same fractional quantity.

3. **If you add two or more individual chemical equations to obtain an overall equation, multiply the corresponding equilibrium constants by each other to obtain the overall equilibrium constant.** Consider these two chemical equations and their corresponding equilibrium constant expressions:

> Remember that $(x^a)^b = x^{ab}$.

$$A \rightleftharpoons 2\,B \qquad K_1 = \frac{[B]^2}{[A]}$$

$$2\,B \rightleftharpoons 3\,C \qquad K_2 = \frac{[C]^3}{[B]^2}$$

The two equations sum as follows:

$$A \rightleftharpoons \cancel{2\,B}$$
$$\cancel{2\,B} \rightleftharpoons 3\,C$$
$$\overline{A \rightleftharpoons 3\,C}$$

According to the law of mass action, the equilibrium constant for this overall equation is then:

$$K_{overall} = \frac{[C]^3}{[A]}$$

Notice that $K_{overall}$ is the product of K_1 and K_2:

$$K_{overall} = K_1 \times K_2$$

$$= \frac{\cancel{[B]^2}}{[A]} \times \frac{[C]^3}{\cancel{[B]^2}}$$

$$= \frac{[C]^3}{[A]}$$

Conceptual Connection 14.2 The Equilibrium Constant and the Chemical Equation

The reaction $A(g) \rightleftharpoons 2\,B(g)$ has an equilibrium constant of $K = 0.010$. What is the equilibrium constant for the reaction $B(g) \rightleftharpoons \frac{1}{2}A(g)$?

(a) 1   **(b)** 10   **(c)** 100   **(d)** 0.0010

EXAMPLE 14.2 Manipulating the Equilibrium Constant to Reflect Changes in the Chemical Equation

Consider the chemical equation and equilibrium constant for the synthesis of ammonia at 25 °C:

$$N_2(g) + 3\,H_2(g) \rightleftharpoons 2\,NH_3(g) \qquad K = 5.6 \times 10^5$$

Calculate the equilibrium constant for the following reaction at 25 °C:

$$NH_3(g) \rightleftharpoons \tfrac{1}{2}N_2(g) + \tfrac{3}{2}H_2(g) \qquad K' = ?$$

SOLUTION

You want to manipulate the given reaction and value of K to obtain the desired reaction and value of K. You can see that the given reaction is the reverse of the desired reaction, and its coefficients are twice those of the desired reaction.

Begin by reversing the given reaction and taking the inverse of the value of K.	$N_2(g) + 3\,H_2(g) \rightleftharpoons 2\,NH_3(g) \qquad K = 5.6 \times 10^5$ $2\,NH_3(g) \rightleftharpoons N_2(g) + 3\,H_2(g) \qquad K_{reverse} = \dfrac{1}{5.6 \times 10^5}$
Next, multiply the reaction by $\tfrac{1}{2}$ and raise the equilibrium constant to the $\tfrac{1}{2}$ power.	$NH_3(g) \rightleftharpoons \tfrac{1}{2}N_2(g) + \tfrac{3}{2}H_2(g)$ $K' = K_{reverse}^{1/2} = \left(\dfrac{1}{5.6 \times 10^5}\right)^{1/2}$
Calculate the value of K'.	$K' = 1.3 \times 10^{-3}$

FOR PRACTICE 14.2

Consider the following chemical equation and equilibrium constant at 25 °C:

$$2\,COF_2(g) \rightleftharpoons CO_2(g) + CF_4(g) \qquad K = 2.2 \times 10^6$$

Calculate the equilibrium constant for the following reaction at 25 °C:

$$2\,CO_2(g) + 2\,CF_4(g) \rightleftharpoons 4\,COF_2(g) \qquad K' = ?$$

FOR MORE PRACTICE 14.2

Predict the equilibrium constant for the first reaction shown here given the equilibrium constants for the second and third reactions:

$$CO_2(g) + 3\,H_2(g) \rightleftharpoons CH_3OH(g) + H_2O(g) \qquad K_1 = ?$$
$$CO(g) + H_2O(g) \rightleftharpoons CO_2(g) + H_2(g) \qquad K_2 = 1.0 \times 10^5$$
$$CO(g) + 2\,H_2(g) \rightleftharpoons CH_3OH(g) \qquad K_3 = 1.4 \times 10^7$$

14.4 Expressing the Equilibrium Constant in Terms of Pressure

So far, we have expressed the equilibrium constant only in terms of the *concentrations* of the reactants and products. For gaseous reactions, the partial pressure of a particular gas is proportional to its concentration. Therefore, we can also express the equilibrium constant in terms of the *partial pressures* of the reactants and products. Consider the gaseous reaction:

$$2\,SO_3(g) \rightleftharpoons 2\,SO_2(g) + O_2(g)$$

From this point on, we designate K_c as the equilibrium constant with respect to concentration in molarity. For the reaction just given, K_c is expressed using the law of mass action:

$$K_c = \frac{[SO_2]^2[O_2]}{[SO_3]^2}$$

We now designate K_p as the equilibrium constant with respect to partial pressures in atmospheres. *The expression for K_p takes the form of the expression for K_c, except that we use the partial pressure of each gas in place of its concentration.* For the SO_3 reaction, we write K_p as:

$$K_p = \frac{(P_{SO_2})^2 P_{O_2}}{(P_{SO_3})^2}$$

where P_A is simply the partial pressure of gas A in units of atmospheres.

Since the partial pressure of a gas in atmospheres is not the same as its concentration in molarity, the value of K_p for a reaction is not necessarily equal to the value of K_c. However, as long as the gases are behaving ideally, we can derive a relationship between the two constants. The concentration of an ideal gas A is the number of moles of A (n_A) divided by its volume (V) in liters:

$$[A] = \frac{n_A}{V}$$

From the ideal gas law, we can relate the quantity n_A/V to the partial pressure of A as follows:

$$P_A V = n_A R T$$

$$P_A = \frac{n_A}{V} R T$$

Since $[A] = n_A/V$, we can write:

$$P_A = [A]RT \qquad \text{or} \qquad [A] = \frac{P_A}{RT} \qquad\qquad [14.1]$$

Now consider the following general equilibrium chemical equation:

$$aA + bB \rightleftharpoons cC + dD$$

According to the law of mass action, we write K_c as follows:

$$K_c = \frac{[C]^c[D]^d}{[A]^a[B]^b}$$

Substituting $[X] = P_X/RT$ for each concentration term, we get:

$$K_c = \frac{\left(\dfrac{P_C}{RT}\right)^c\left(\dfrac{P_D}{RT}\right)^d}{\left(\dfrac{P_A}{RT}\right)^a\left(\dfrac{P_B}{RT}\right)^b} = \frac{P_C^c P_D^d \left(\dfrac{1}{RT}\right)^{c+d}}{P_A^a P_B^b \left(\dfrac{1}{RT}\right)^{a+b}} = \frac{P_C^c P_D^d}{P_A^a P_B^b}\left(\frac{1}{RT}\right)^{c+d-(a+b)}$$

$$= K_p\left(\frac{1}{RT}\right)^{c+d-(a+b)}$$

Rearranging,

$$K_p = K_c(RT)^{c+d-(a+b)}$$

Finally, if we let $\Delta n = c + d - (a + b)$, which is the sum of the stoichiometric coefficients of the gaseous products minus the sum of the stoichiometric coefficients of the gaseous reactants, we get the following general result:

$$K_p = K_c(RT)^{\Delta n} \qquad\qquad [14.2]$$

Notice that if the total number of moles of gas is the same after the reaction as before, then $\Delta n = 0$, and K_p is equal to K_c.

In the equation $K_p = K_c(RT)^{\Delta n}$, the quantity Δn represents the difference between the number of moles of gaseous products and gaseous reactants.

EXAMPLE 14.3 Relating K_p and K_c

Nitrogen monoxide, a pollutant in automobile exhaust, is oxidized to nitrogen dioxide in the atmosphere according to the equation:

$$2 \, NO(g) + O_2(g) \rightleftharpoons 2 \, NO_2(g) \qquad K_p = 2.2 \times 10^{12} \text{ at } 25 \,°C$$

Find K_c for this reaction.

SORT You are given K_p for the reaction and asked to find K_c.	**GIVEN:** $K_p = 2.2 \times 10^{12}$ **FIND:** K_c
STRATEGIZE Use Equation 14.2 to relate K_p and K_c.	**EQUATION** $K_p = K_c (RT)^{\Delta n}$
SOLVE Solve the equation for K_c.	**SOLUTION** $$K_c = \dfrac{K_p}{(RT)^{\Delta n}}$$
Calculate Δn.	$\Delta n = 2 - 3 = -1$
Substitute the required quantities to calculate K_c. The temperature must be in kelvins. The units are dropped when reporting K_c as described previously.	$$K_c = \dfrac{2.2 \times 10^{12}}{\left(0.08206 \, \dfrac{L \cdot atm}{mol \cdot K} \times 298 \text{ K}\right)^{-1}}$$ $= 5.4 \times 10^{13}$

CHECK The easiest way to check this answer is to substitute it back into Equation 14.2 and confirm that you get the original value for K_p.

$$K_p = K_c (RT)^{\Delta n}$$

$$= 5.4 \times 10^{13} \left(0.08206 \, \frac{L \cdot atm}{mol \cdot K} \times 298 \text{ K}\right)^{-1}$$

$$= 2.2 \times 10^{12}$$

FOR PRACTICE 14.3

Consider the following reaction and corresponding value of K_c:

$$H_2(g) + I_2(g) \rightleftharpoons 2 \, HI(g) \qquad K_c = 6.2 \times 10^2 \text{ at } 25 \,°C$$

What is the value of K_p at this temperature?

Units of K

Throughout this book, we express concentrations and partial pressures within the equilibrium constant expression in units of molarity and atmospheres, respectively. When expressing the value of the equilibrium constant, however, we have not included the units. Formally, the values of concentration or partial pressure that we substitute into the equilibrium constant expression are ratios of the concentration or pressure to a reference concentration (exactly 1 M) or a reference pressure (exactly 1 atm). For example, within the equilibrium constant expression, a pressure of 1.5 atm becomes

$$\frac{1.5 \text{ atm}}{1 \text{ atm}} = 1.5$$

Similarly, a concentration of 1.5 M becomes

$$\frac{1.5 \text{ M}}{1 \text{ M}} = 1.5$$

As long as concentration units are expressed in molarity for K_c and pressure units are expressed in atmospheres for K_p, we can skip this formality and enter the quantities directly into the equilibrium expression, dropping their corresponding units.

Conceptual Connection 14.3 The Relationship between K_p and K_c

Under which circumstances are K_p and K_c equal for the reaction
$a\text{A}(g) + b\text{B}(g) \rightleftharpoons c\text{C}(g) + d\text{D}(g)$?

(a) If $a + b = c + d$.

(b) If the reaction is reversible.

(c) If the equilibrium constant is small.

14.5 Heterogeneous Equilibria: Reactions Involving Solids and Liquids

Many chemical reactions involve pure solids or pure liquids as reactants or products. Consider, for example, the reaction:

$$2\,\text{CO}(g) \rightleftharpoons \text{CO}_2(g) + \text{C}(s)$$

We might expect the expression for the equilibrium constant to be:

$$K_c = \frac{[\text{CO}_2][\text{C}]}{[\text{CO}]^2} \quad \text{(incorrect)}$$

However, since carbon is a solid, its concentration is constant (if you double the amount of carbon its *concentration* remains the same). The concentration of a solid does not change, because a solid does not expand to fill its container. Its concentration, therefore, depends only on its density, which is constant as long as *some* solid is present (Figure 14.6 ▼). Consequently, pure solids—those reactants or products labeled in the chemical equation with an (*s*)—are not included in the equilibrium expression (because their constant value is incorporated into the value of *K*). The correct equilibrium expression for this reaction is therefore:

$$K_c = \frac{[\text{CO}_2]}{[\text{CO}]^2}$$

Similarly, the concentration of a pure liquid does not change. So, pure liquids—reactants or products labeled in the chemical equation with an (ℓ)—are also excluded from the equilibrium expression. For example, consider the equilibrium expression for the reaction between carbon dioxide and water:

$$\text{CO}_2(g) + \text{H}_2\text{O}(\ell) \rightleftharpoons \text{H}^+(aq) + \text{HCO}_3^-(aq)$$

Since $\text{H}_2\text{O}(\ell)$ is pure liquid, it is omitted from the equilibrium expression:

$$K_c = \frac{[\text{H}^+][\text{HCO}_3^-]}{[\text{CO}_2]}$$

A Heterogeneous Equilibrium

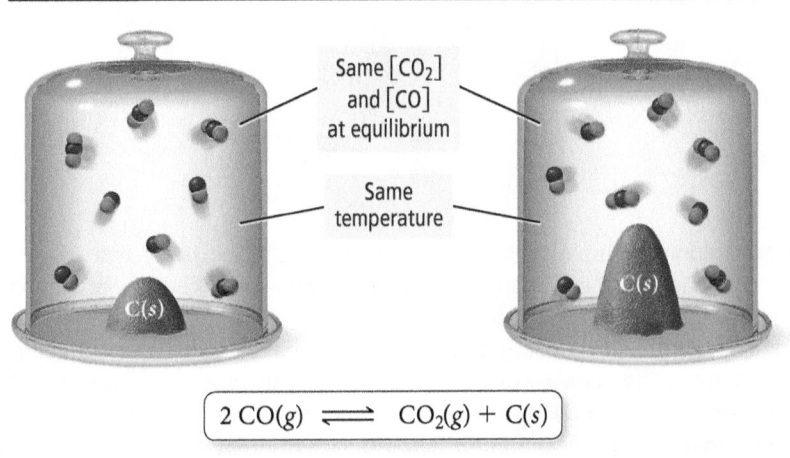

Same $[\text{CO}_2]$ and $[\text{CO}]$ at equilibrium

Same temperature

C(s)

C(s)

$$2\,\text{CO}(g) \rightleftharpoons \text{CO}_2(g) + \text{C}(s)$$

◄ **FIGURE 14.6 Heterogeneous Equilibrium** The concentration of solid carbon (the number of atoms per unit volume) is constant as long as some solid carbon is present. The same is true for pure liquids. For this reason, the concentrations of solids and pure liquids are not included in equilibrium constant expressions.

EXAMPLE 14.4 Writing Equilibrium Expressions for Reactions Involving a Solid or a Liquid

Write an expression for the equilibrium constant (K_c) for this chemical equation:

$$CaCO_3(s) \rightleftharpoons CaO(s) + CO_2(g)$$

SOLUTION

Since $CaCO_3(s)$ and $CaO(s)$ are both solids, omit them from the equilibrium expression.	$K_c = [CO_2]$

FOR PRACTICE 14.4

Write an equilibrium expression (K_c) for the equation:

$$4 HCl(g) + O_2(g) \rightleftharpoons 2 H_2O(\ell) + 2 Cl_2(g)$$

Conceptual Connection 14.4 Heterogeneous Equilibria, K_p and K_c

For which reaction does $K_p = K_c$?

(a) $2 Na_2O_2(s) + 2 CO_2(g) \rightleftharpoons 2 Na_2CO_3(s) + O_2(g)$

(b) $Fe_2O_3(s) + 3 CO(g) \rightleftharpoons 2 Fe(s) + 3 CO_2(g)$

(c) $NH_4NO_3(s) \rightleftharpoons N_2O(g) + 2 H_2O(g)$

14.6 Calculating the Equilibrium Constant from Measured Equilibrium Concentrations

The most direct way to obtain an experimental value for the equilibrium constant of a reaction is to measure the concentrations of the reactants and products in a reaction mixture at equilibrium. Consider the following reaction:

$$H_2(g) + I_2(g) \rightleftharpoons 2 HI(g)$$

Suppose a mixture of H_2 and I_2 is allowed to come to equilibrium at 445 °C. The measured equilibrium concentrations are $[H_2] = 0.11$ M, $[I_2] = 0.11$ M, and $[HI] = 0.78$ M. What is the value of the equilibrium constant at this temperature? We can write the expression for K_c from the balanced equation:

$$K_c = \frac{[HI]^2}{[H_2][I_2]}$$

To calculate the value of K_c, we substitute the correct equilibrium concentrations into the expression for K_c:

$$K_c = \frac{[HI]^2}{[H_2][I_2]}$$

$$= \frac{(0.78)^2}{(0.11)(0.11)}$$

$$= 5.0 \times 10^1$$

The concentrations within K_c should always be written in moles per liter (M); however, as noted in Section 14.4, we do not normally include the units when expressing the value of the equilibrium constant, so K_c is unitless.

For any reaction, the equilibrium *concentrations* of the reactants and products depend on the initial concentrations (and in general vary from one set of initial concentrations to another). However, the equilibrium *constant* is always the same at a given temperature, regardless of the initial concentrations. For example, Table 14.1

Since equilibrium constants depend on temperature, many equilibrium problems state the temperature even though it has no formal part in the calculation.

TABLE 14.1   Initial and Equilibrium Concentrations for the Reaction
$H_2(g) + I_2(g) \rightleftharpoons 2\,HI(g)$ at 445 °C

Initial Concentrations			Equilibrium Concentrations			Equilibrium Constant
$[H_2]$	$[I_2]$	$[HI]$	$[H_2]$	$[I_2]$	$[HI]$	$K_c = \dfrac{[HI^2]}{[H_2][I_2]}$
0.50	0.50	0.0	0.11	0.11	0.78	$\dfrac{(0.78)^2}{(0.11)(0.11)} = 50$
0.0	0.0	0.50	0.055	0.055	0.39	$\dfrac{(0.39)^2}{(0.055)(0.055)} = 50$
0.50	0.50	0.50	0.165	0.165	1.17	$\dfrac{(1.17)^2}{(0.165)(0.165)} = 50$
1.0	0.50	0.0	0.53	0.033	0.934	$\dfrac{(0.934)^2}{(0.53)(0.033)} = 50$
0.50	1.0	0.0	0.033	0.53	0.934	$\dfrac{(0.934)^2}{(0.033)(0.53)} = 50$

shows several different equilibrium concentrations of H_2, I_2, and HI, each from a different set of initial concentrations. Notice that the equilibrium constant is always the same, regardless of the initial concentrations. Whether you start with only reactants or only products, the reaction reaches equilibrium concentrations at which the equilibrium constant is the same. No matter what the initial concentrations are, the reaction always goes in a direction that ensures that the equilibrium concentrations—when substituted into the equilibrium expression—give the same constant, K.

So far, we have calculated equilibrium constants from values of the equilibrium concentrations of all the reactants and products. In most cases, however, we need only know the initial concentrations of the reactant(s) and the equilibrium concentration of any *one* reactant or product. We can deduce the other equilibrium concentrations from the stoichiometry of the reaction. For example, consider the simple reaction:

$$A(g) \rightleftharpoons 2\,B(g)$$

Suppose that we have a reaction mixture in which the initial concentration of A is 1.00 M and the initial concentration of B is 0.00 M. When equilibrium is reached, the concentration of A is 0.75 M. Since [A] has changed by -0.25 M, we can deduce (based on the stoichiometry) that [B] must have changed by $2 \times (+0.25$ M) or $+0.50$ M. We summarize the initial conditions, the changes, and the equilibrium conditions in the following table:

	[A]	[B]
Initial	1.00	0.00
Change	−0.25	+0.50
Equilibrium	0.75	0.50

This type of table is often referred to as an ICE table (I = initial, C = change, E = equilibrium). To calculate the equilibrium constant, we use the balanced equation to write an expression for the equilibrium constant and then substitute the equilibrium concentrations from the ICE table:

$$K = \frac{[B]^2}{[A]} = \frac{(0.50)^2}{(0.75)} = 0.33$$

In Example 14.5 and 14.6, we show the general procedure for solving these kinds of equilibrium problems in the left column and work two examples exemplifying the procedure in the center and right columns.

PROCEDURE FOR...

Finding Equilibrium Constants from Experimental Concentration Measurements

To solve these types of problems, follow the given procedure.

EXAMPLE 14.5

Finding Equilibrium Constants from Experimental Concentration Measurements

Consider the following reaction:

$$CO(g) + 2 H_2(g) \rightleftharpoons CH_3OH(g)$$

A reaction mixture at 780 °C initially contains [CO] = 0.500 M and [H₂] = 1.00 M. At equilibrium, the CO concentration is found to be 0.15 M. What is the value of the equilibrium constant?

EXAMPLE 14.6

Finding Equilibrium Constants from Experimental Concentration Measurements

Consider the following reaction:

$$2 CH_4(g) \rightleftharpoons C_2H_2(g) + 3 H_2(g)$$

A reaction mixture at 1700 °C initially contains [CH₄] = 0.115 M. At equilibrium, the mixture contains [C₂H₂] = 0.035 M. What is the value of the equilibrium constant?

---

1. Using the balanced equation as a guide, prepare an ICE table showing the known initial concentrations and equilibrium concentrations of the reactants and products. Leave space in the middle of the table for determining the changes in concentration that occur during the reaction.

$$CO(g) + 2 H_2(g) \rightleftharpoons CH_3OH(g)$$

	[CO]	[H₂]	[CH₃OH]
Initial	0.500	1.00	0.00
Change			
Equil	0.15		

$$2 CH_4(g) \rightleftharpoons C_2H_2(g) + 3 H_2(g)$$

	[CH₄]	[C₂H₂]	[H₂]
Initial	0.115	0.00	0.00
Change			
Equil		0.035	

---

2. For the reactant or product whose concentration is known both initially and at equilibrium, calculate the change in concentration that occurs.

$$CO(g) + 2 H_2(g) \rightleftharpoons CH_3OH(g)$$

	[CO]	[H₂]	[CH₃OH]
Initial	0.500	1.00	0.00
Change	−0.35		
Equil	0.15		

$$2 CH_4(g) \rightleftharpoons C_2H_2(g) + 3 H_2(g)$$

	[CH₄]	[C₂H₂]	[H₂]
Initial	0.115	0.00	0.00
Change		+0.035	
Equil		0.035	

---

3. Use the change calculated in step 2 and the stoichiometric relationships from the balanced chemical equation to determine the changes in concentration of all other reactants and products. Since reactants are consumed during the reaction, the changes in their concentrations are negative. Since products are formed, the changes in their concentrations are positive.

$$CO(g) + 2 H_2(g) \rightleftharpoons CH_3OH(g)$$

	[CO]	[H₂]	[CH₃OH]
Initial	0.500	1.00	0.00
Change	−0.35	−0.70	+0.35
Equil	0.15		

$$2 CH_4(g) \rightleftharpoons C_2H_2(g) + 3 H_2(g)$$

	[CH₄]	[C₂H₂]	[H₂]
Initial	0.115	0.00	0.00
Change	−0.070	+0.035	+0.105
Equil		0.035	

---

4. Sum each column for each reactant and product to determine the equilibrium concentrations.

	[CO]	[H₂]	[CH₃OH]
Initial	0.500	1.00	0.00
Change	−0.35	−0.70	+0.35
Equil	0.15	0.30	0.35

	[CH₄]	[C₂H₂]	[H₂]
Initial	0.115	0.00	0.00
Change	−0.070	+0.035	+0.105
Equil	0.045	0.035	0.105

---

5. Use the balanced equation to write an expression for the equilibrium constant and substitute the equilibrium concentrations to calculate K.

$$K_c = \frac{[CH_3OH]}{[CO][H_2]^2}$$

$$= \frac{0.35}{(0.15)(0.30)^2}$$

$$= 26$$

$$K_c = \frac{[C_2H_2][H_2]^3}{[CH_4]^2}$$

$$= \frac{(0.035)(0.105)^3}{(0.045)^2}$$

$$= 0.020$$

FOR PRACTICE 14.5

The reaction in Example 14.5 between CO and H_2 is carried out at a different temperature with initial concentrations of $[CO] = 0.27$ M and $[H_2] = 0.49$ M. At equilibrium, the concentration of CH_3OH is 0.11 M. Find the equilibrium constant at this temperature.

FOR PRACTICE 14.6

The reaction of CH_4 in Example 14.6 is carried out at a different temperature with an initial concentration of $[CH_4] = 0.087$ M. At equilibrium, the concentration of H_2 is 0.012 M. Find the equilibrium constant at this temperature.

14.7 The Reaction Quotient: Predicting the Direction of Change

When the reactants of a chemical reaction mix, they generally react to form products—we say that the reaction proceeds to the right (toward the products). The amount of products formed when equilibrium is reached depends on the magnitude of the equilibrium constant, as we have seen. However, what if a reaction mixture not at equilibrium contains both reactants *and products*? Can we predict the direction of change for such a mixture?

To gauge the progress of a reaction relative to equilibrium, we use a quantity called the *reaction quotient*. The definition of the reaction quotient takes the same form as the definition of the equilibrium constant, except that the reaction need not be at equilibrium. So, for the general reaction:

$$aA + bB \rightleftharpoons cC + dD$$

we define the **reaction quotient** (Q_c) as the ratio—at any point in the reaction—of the concentrations of the products raised to their stoichiometric coefficients divided by the concentrations of the reactants raised to their stoichiometric coefficients. For gases with amounts measured in atmospheres, the reaction quotient uses the partial pressures in place of concentrations and is called Q_p:

$$Q_c = \frac{[C]^c[D]^d}{[A]^a[B]^b} \qquad Q_p = \frac{P_C^c P_D^d}{P_A^a P_B^b}$$

The difference between the reaction quotient and the equilibrium constant is that, at a given temperature, the equilibrium constant has only one value and it specifies the relative amounts of reactants and products *at equilibrium*. The reaction quotient, by contrast, depends on the current state of the reaction and has many different values as the reaction proceeds. For example, in a reaction mixture containing only reactants, the reaction quotient is zero $(Q_c = 0)$:

$$Q_c = \frac{[0]^c[0]^d}{[A]^a[B]^b} = 0$$

In a reaction mixture containing only products, the reaction quotient is infinite $(Q_c = \infty)$:

$$Q_c = \frac{[C]^c[D]^d}{[0]^a[0]^b} = \infty$$

In a reaction mixture containing both reactants and products, each at a concentration of 1 M, the reaction quotient is one $(Q_c = 1)$:

$$Q_c = \frac{(1)^c(1)^d}{(1)^a(1)^b} = 1$$

The reaction quotient is useful because *the value of Q relative to K is a measure of the progress of the reaction toward equilibrium. At equilibrium, the reaction quotient*

Q, K, and the Direction of a Reaction

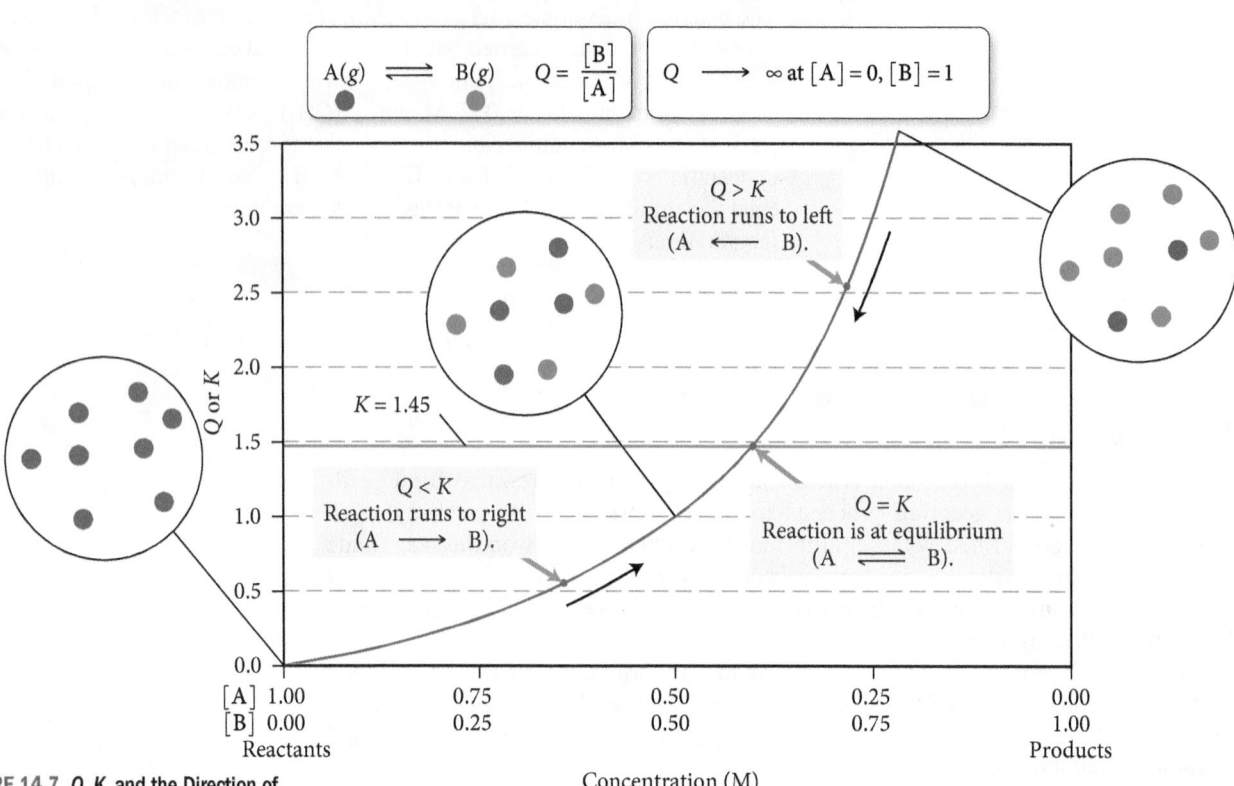

▲ FIGURE 14.7 *Q, K,* and the Direction of a Reaction   The graph shows a plot of Q as a function of the concentrations of the reactants and products in a simple reaction A $\rightleftharpoons$ B, in which $K = 1.45$ and the sum of the reactant and product concentrations is 1 M. The far left of the graph represents pure reactant and the far right represents pure product. The midpoint of the graph represents an equal mixture of A and B. When Q is less than K, the reaction moves in the forward direction (A $\longrightarrow$ B). When Q is greater than K, the reaction moves in the reverse direction (A $\longleftarrow$ B). When Q is equal to K, the reaction is at equilibrium.

is equal to the equilibrium constant. Figure 14.7 ▲ shows a plot of Q as a function of the concentrations of A and B for the simple reaction A(g) $\rightleftharpoons$ B(g), which has an equilibrium constant of $K = 1.45$. The following points are representative of three possible conditions:

Q	K	Predicted Direction of Reaction
0.55	1.45	To the right (toward products)
2.55	1.45	To the left (toward reactants)
1.45	1.45	No change (at equilibrium)

For the first set of values in the table, Q is less than K and must therefore get larger as the reaction proceeds toward equilibrium. Q becomes larger as the reactant concentration decreases and the product concentration increases—the reaction proceeds to the right. For the second set of values, Q is greater than K and must therefore get smaller as the reaction proceeds toward equilibrium. Q gets smaller as the reactant concentration increases and the product concentration decreases—the reaction proceeds to the left. In the third set of values, $Q = K$, implying that the reaction is at equilibrium—the reaction will not proceed in either direction.

Summarizing Direction of Change Predictions:
The reaction quotient (Q) relative to the equilibrium constant (K) is a measure of the progress of a reaction toward equilibrium.

▶ $Q < K$ Reaction goes to the right (toward products).

▶ $Q > K$ Reaction goes to the left (toward reactants).

▶ $Q = K$ Reaction is at equilibrium.

EXAMPLE 14.7   Predicting the Direction of a Reaction
                              by Comparing Q and K

Consider the reaction and its equilibrium constant:

$$I_2(g) + Cl_2(g) \rightleftharpoons 2\ ICl(g) \qquad K_p = 81.9$$

A reaction mixture contains $P_{I_2} = 0.114$ atm, $P_{Cl_2} = 0.102$ atm, and $P_{ICl} = 0.355$ atm. Is the reaction mixture at equilibrium? If not, in which direction will the reaction proceed?

SOLUTION

To determine the progress of the reaction relative to the equilibrium state, first calculate Q.	$Q_p = \left(\dfrac{P_{ICl}^2}{P_{I_2} P_{Cl_2}} \right)$ $= \dfrac{(0.355)^2}{(0.114)(0.102)}$ $= 10.8$
Compare Q to K.	$Q_p = 10.8;\ K_p = 81.9$ Since $Q_p < K_p$, the reaction is not at equilibrium and will proceed to the right.

FOR PRACTICE 14.7

Consider the reaction and its equilibrium constant:

$$N_2O_4(g) \rightleftharpoons 2\ NO_2(g) \qquad K_c = 5.85 \times 10^{-3} \text{ (at some temperature)}$$

A reaction mixture contains $[NO_2] = 0.0255$ M and $[N_2O_4] = 0.0331$ M. Calculate Q_c and determine the direction in which the reaction will proceed.

Conceptual Connection 14.5 Q and K

For the reaction $N_2O_4(g) \rightleftharpoons 2\ NO_2(g)$, a reaction mixture at a certain temperature initially contains both N_2O_4 and NO_2 in their standard states (see the definition of standard state in Section 6.9). If $K_p = 0.15$, which statement is true of the reaction mixture before any reaction occurs?

(a) $Q = K$; the reaction is at equilibrium.
(b) $Q < K$; the reaction will proceed to the right.
(c) $Q > K$; the reaction will proceed to the left.

14.8 Finding Equilibrium Concentrations

In Section 14.6, we discussed how to calculate an equilibrium constant from the equilibrium concentrations of the reactants and products. Just as commonly we will want to calculate equilibrium concentrations of reactants or products from the equilibrium constant. These kinds of calculations are important because they allow us to calculate the amount of a reactant or product at equilibrium. For example, in a synthesis reaction, we might want to know how much of the product forms when the reaction reaches equilibrium. Or for the hemoglobin–oxygen equilibrium discussed in Section 14.1, we might want to know the concentration of oxygenated hemoglobin present under certain oxygen concentrations within the lungs or muscles.

We can divide these types of problems into two categories: (1) finding equilibrium concentrations when we know the equilibrium constant and all but one of the equilibrium concentrations of the reactants and products, and (2) finding equilibrium concentrations when we know the equilibrium constant and only initial concentrations. The second category of problem is more difficult than the first. Let's examine each separately.

Finding Equilibrium Concentrations from the Equilibrium Constant and All but One of the Equilibrium Concentrations of the Reactants and Products

We can use the equilibrium constant to calculate the equilibrium concentration of one of the reactants or products, given the equilibrium concentrations of the others. To solve this type of problem, we can follow our general problem-solving procedure.

EXAMPLE 14.8 Finding Equilibrium Concentrations When You Know the Equilibrium Constant and All but One of the Equilibrium Concentrations of the Reactants and Products

Consider the following reaction:

$$2\ COF_2(g) \rightleftharpoons CO_2(g) + CF_4(g) \qquad K_c = 2.00 \text{ at } 1000\ °C$$

In an equilibrium mixture, the concentration of COF_2 is 0.255 M and the concentration of CF_4 is 0.118 M. What is the equilibrium concentration of CO_2?

SORT You are given the equilibrium constant of a chemical reaction, together with the equilibrium concentrations of the reactant and one product. You are asked to find the equilibrium concentration of the other product.	**GIVEN:** $[COF_2] = 0.255$ M $[CF_4] = 0.118$ M $K_c = 2.00$ **FIND:** $[CO_2]$
STRATEGIZE You can calculate the concentration of the product using the given quantities and the expression for K_c.	**CONCEPTUAL PLAN** 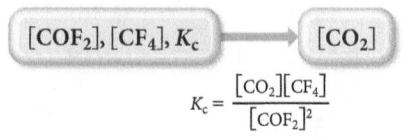 $K_c = \dfrac{[CO_2][CF_4]}{[COF_2]^2}$
SOLVE Solve the equilibrium expression for $[CO_2]$ and then substitute in the appropriate values to calculate it.	**SOLUTION** $[CO_2] = K_c \dfrac{[COF_2]^2}{[CF_4]}$ $[CO_2] = 2.00\left(\dfrac{(0.255)^2}{0.118}\right) = 1.10$ M

CHECK Check your answer by mentally substituting the given values of $[COF_2]$ and $[CF_4]$ as well as your calculated value for CO_2 back into the equilibrium expression.

$$K_c = \frac{[CO_2][CF_4]}{[COF_2]^2}$$

$[CO_2]$ was found to be roughly equal to 1. $[COF_2]^2 \approx 0.06$ and $[CF_4] \approx 0.12$. Therefore K_c is approximately 2, as given in the problem.

FOR PRACTICE 14.8

Diatomic iodine $[I_2]$ decomposes at high temperature to form I atoms according to the reaction:

$$I_2(g) \rightleftharpoons 2\ I(g) \qquad K_c = 0.011 \text{ at } 1200\ °C$$

In an equilibrium mixture, the concentration of I_2 is 0.10 M. What is the equilibrium concentration of I?

Finding Equilibrium Concentrations from the Equilibrium Constant and Initial Concentrations or Pressures

More commonly, we know the equilibrium constant and only initial concentrations of reactants and need to find the *equilibrium concentrations* of the reactants or products. These kinds of problems are generally more involved than those we just examined and require a specific procedure to solve them. The procedure has some similarities to the one used in Example 14.5 and 14.6 in that we set up an ICE table showing the initial conditions, the changes, and the equilibrium conditions. However, unlike Example 14.5 and 14.6, here the changes in concentration are not known and are represented with the variable x. For example, consider again the simple reaction:

$$A(g) \rightleftharpoons 2B(g)$$

Suppose that, as before (see Section 14.6), we have a reaction mixture in which the initial concentration of A is 1.0 M and the initial concentration of B is 0.00 M. However, now we know the equilibrium constant, $K = 0.33$, and want to find the equilibrium concentrations. We set up the ICE table with the given initial concentrations and then *represent the unknown change in [A] with the variable x* as follows:

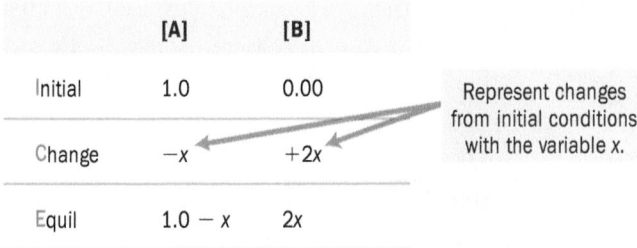

	[A]	[B]	
Initial	1.0	0.00	Represent changes from initial conditions with the variable x.
Change	$-x$	$+2x$	
Equil	$1.0 - x$	$2x$	

Notice that, due to the stoichiometry of the reaction, the change in [B] must be $+2x$. As before, each *equilibrium* concentration is the sum of the two entries above it in the ICE table. In order to find the equilibrium concentrations of A and B, we must find the value of the variable x. Since we know the value of the equilibrium constant, we can use the equilibrium constant expression to set up an equation in which x is the only variable:

$$K = \frac{[B]^2}{[A]} = \frac{(2x)^2}{1.0 - x} = 0.33$$

or more simply:

$$\frac{4x^2}{1.0 - x} = 0.33$$

This equation is a *quadratic* equation—it contains the variable x raised to the second power. In general, we can solve quadratic equations with the quadratic formula (see Appendix IC), which we introduce in Example 14.10. If the quadratic equation is a perfect square, however, we can solve it by simpler means, as shown in Example 14.9. For both of these examples, we give the general procedure in the left column and apply the procedure to the two different example problems in the center and right columns. Later in this section, we see that quadratic equations can often be simplified by making some approximations based on our chemical knowledge.

PROCEDURE FOR...	EXAMPLE 14.9	EXAMPLE 14.10
Finding Equilibrium Concentrations from Initial Concentrations and the Equilibrium Constant	**Finding Equilibrium Concentrations from Initial Concentrations and the Equilibrium Constant**	**Finding Equilibrium Concentrations from Initial Concentrations and the Equilibrium Constant**
To solve these types of problems, follow the given procedure.	Consider the reaction:	Consider the reaction:

EXAMPLE 14.9

Consider the reaction:

$$N_2(g) + O_2(g) \rightleftharpoons 2\,NO(g)$$
$$K_c = 0.10 \text{ (at 2000 °C)}$$

A reaction mixture at 2000 °C initially contains $[N_2] = 0.200$ M and $[O_2] = 0.200$ M. Find the equilibrium concentrations of the reactants and product at this temperature.

EXAMPLE 14.10

Consider the reaction:

$$N_2O_4(g) \rightleftharpoons 2\,NO_2(g)$$
$$K_c = 0.36 \text{ (at 100 °C)}$$

A reaction mixture at 100 °C initially contains $[NO_2] = 0.100$ M. Find the equilibrium concentrations of NO_2 and N_2O_4 at this temperature.

---

1. Using the balanced equation as a guide, prepare a table showing the known initial concentrations of the reactants and products. Leave room in the table for the changes in concentrations and for the equilibrium concentrations.

$$N_2(g) + O_2(g) \rightleftharpoons 2\,NO(g)$$

	$[N_2]$	$[O_2]$	$[NO]$
Initial	0.200	0.200	0.00
Change			
Equil			

$$N_2O_4(g) \rightleftharpoons 2\,NO_2(g)$$

	$[N_2O_4]$	$[NO_2]$
Initial	0.00	0.100
Change		
Equil		

---

2. Use the initial concentrations to calculate the reaction quotient (Q) for the initial concentrations. Compare Q to K to predict the direction in which the reaction will proceed.

$$Q_c = \frac{[NO]^2}{[N_2][O_2]} = \frac{(0.00)^2}{(0.200)(0.200)}$$
$$= 0$$

$Q < K$; therefore, the reaction will proceed to the right.

$$Q_c = \frac{[NO_2]^2}{[N_2O_4]} = \frac{(0.100)^2}{0.00}$$
$$= \infty$$

$Q > K$; therefore, the reaction will proceed to the left.

---

3. Represent the change in the concentration of one of the reactants or products with the variable x. Define the changes in the concentrations of the other reactants or products in terms of x. It is usually most convenient to let x represent the change in concentration of the reactant or product with the smallest stoichiometric coefficient.

$$N_2(g) + O_2(g) \rightleftharpoons 2\,NO(g)$$

	$[N_2]$	$[O_2]$	$[NO]$
Initial	0.200	0.200	0.00
Change	$-x$	$-x$	$+2x$
Equil			

$$N_2O_4(g) \rightleftharpoons 2\,NO_2(g)$$

	$[N_2O_4]$	$[NO_2]$
Initial	0.00	0.100
Change	$+x$	$-2x$
Equil		

---

4. Sum each column for each reactant and each product to determine the equilibrium concentrations in terms of the initial concentrations and the variable x.

$$N_2(g) + O_2(g) \rightleftharpoons 2\,NO(g)$$

	$[N_2]$	$[O_2]$	$[NO]$
Initial	0.200	0.200	0.00
Change	$-x$	$-x$	$+2x$
Equil	$0.200-x$	$0.200-x$	$2x$

$$N_2O_4(g) \rightleftharpoons 2\,NO_2(g)$$

	$[N_2O_4]$	$[NO_2]$
Initial	0.00	0.100
Change	$+x$	$-2x$
Equil	x	$0.100 - 2x$

5. Substitute the expressions for the equilibrium concentrations (from step 4) into the expression for the equilibrium constant. Using the given value of the equilibrium constant, solve the expression for the variable x. In some cases, such as Example 14.9, you can take the square root of both sides of the expression to solve for x. In other cases, such as Example 14.10, you must solve a quadratic equation to find x. Remember the quadratic formula: $ax^2 + bx + c = 0$ $x = \dfrac{-b \pm \sqrt{b^2 - 4ac}}{2a}$	$K_c = \dfrac{[NO]^2}{[N_2][O_2]}$ $= \dfrac{(2x)^2}{(0.200 - x)(0.200 - x)}$ $0.10 = \dfrac{(2x)^2}{(0.200 - x)^2}$ $\sqrt{0.10} = \dfrac{2x}{0.200 - x}$ $\sqrt{0.10}\,(0.200 - x) = 2x$ $\sqrt{0.10}\,(0.200) - \sqrt{0.10}\,x$ $= 2x$ $0.063 = 2x + \sqrt{0.10}\,x$ $0.063 = 2.3x$ $x = 0.027$	$K_c = \dfrac{[NO_2]^2}{[N_2O_4]}$ $= \dfrac{(0.100 - 2x)^2}{x}$ $0.36 = \dfrac{0.0100 - 0.400x + 4x^2}{x}$ $0.36x = 0.0100 - 0.400x + 4x^2$ $4x^2 - 0.76x + 0.0100 = 0$ (*quadratic*) $x = \dfrac{-b \pm \sqrt{b^2 - 4ac}}{2a}$ $= \dfrac{-(-0.76) \pm \sqrt{(-0.76)^2 - 4(4)(0.0100)}}{2(4)}$ $= \dfrac{0.76 \pm 0.65}{8}$ $x = 0.176$ or $x = 0.014$
6. Substitute x into the expressions for the equilibrium concentrations of the reactants and products (from step 4) and calculate the concentrations. In cases where you solved a quadratic and have two values for x, choose the value for x that gives a physically realistic answer. For example, reject the value of x that results in any negative concentrations.	$[N_2] = 0.200 - 0.027$ $= 0.173$ M $[O_2] = 0.200 - 0.027$ $= 0.173$ M $[NO] = 2(0.027)$ $= 0.054$ M	We reject the root $x = 0.176$ because it gives a negative concentration for NO_2. Using $x = 0.014$, we get the following concentrations: $[NO_2] = 0.100 - 2x$ $= 0.100 - 2(0.014) = 0.072$ M $[N_2O_4] = x$ $= 0.014$ M
7. Check your answer by substituting the calculated equilibrium values into the equilibrium expression. The calculated value of K should match the given value of K. Note that rounding errors could cause a difference in the least significant digit when comparing values of the equilibrium constant.	$K_c = \dfrac{[NO]^2}{[N_2][O_2]}$ $= \dfrac{(0.054)^2}{(0.173)(0.173)} = 0.097$ Since the calculated value of K_c matches the given value (to within one digit in the least significant figure), the answer is valid.	$K_c = \dfrac{[NO_2]^2}{[N_2O_4]} = \dfrac{(0.072)^2}{0.014}$ $= 0.37$ Since the calculated value of K_c matches the given value (to within one digit in the least significant figure), the answer is valid.
	FOR PRACTICE 14.9 The reaction in Example 14.9 is carried out at a different temperature at which $K_c = 0.055$. This time, however, the reaction mixture starts with only the product, $[NO] = 0.0100$ M, and no reactants. Find the equilibrium concentrations of N_2, O_2, and NO at equilibrium.	**FOR PRACTICE 14.10** The reaction in Example 14.10 is carried out at the same temperature, but this time the reaction mixture initially contains only the reactant, $[N_2O_4] = 0.0250$ M, and no NO_2. Find the equilibrium concentrations of N_2O_4 and NO_2.

When the initial conditions are given in terms of partial pressures (instead of concentrations) and the equilibrium constant is given as K_p instead of K_c, use the same procedure, but substitute partial pressures for concentrations, as shown in Example 14.11.

EXAMPLE 14.11 Finding Equilibrium Partial Pressures When You Are Given the Equilibrium Constant and Initial Partial Pressures

Consider the reaction:

$$I_2(g) + Cl_2(g) \rightleftharpoons 2\,ICl(g) \qquad K_p = 81.9 \text{ (at 25 °C)}$$

A reaction mixture at 25 °C initially contains $P_{I_2} = 0.100$ atm, $P_{Cl_2} = 0.100$ atm, and $P_{ICl} = 0.100$ atm. Find the equilibrium partial pressures of I_2, Cl_2, and ICl at this temperature.

SOLUTION

Follow the procedure used in Example 14.5 and 14.6 (using partial pressures in place of concentrations) to solve the problem.

1. Using the balanced equation as a guide, prepare a table showing the known initial partial pressures of the reactants and products.	$I_2(g) + Cl_2(g) \rightleftharpoons 2\,ICl(g)$ 	

	P_{I_2} (atm)	P_{Cl_2} (atm)	P_{ICl} (atm)
Initial	0.100	0.100	0.100
Change			
Equil			

2. Use the initial partial pressures to calculate the reaction quotient (Q). Compare Q to K to predict the direction in which the reaction will proceed.	$Q_p = \dfrac{(P_{ICl})^2}{P_{I_2}P_{Cl_2}} = \dfrac{(0.100)^2}{(0.100)(0.100)} = 1$ $K_p = 81.9$ (given) $Q < K$; therefore, the reaction will proceed to the right.

3. Represent the change in the partial pressure of one of the reactants or products with the variable x. Define the changes in the partial pressures of the other reactants or products in terms of x.	$I_2(g) + Cl_2(g) \rightleftharpoons 2\,ICl(g)$

	P_{I_2} (atm)	P_{Cl_2} (atm)	P_{ICl} (atm)
Initial	0.100	0.100	0.100
Change	$-x$	$-x$	$+2x$
Equil			

4. Sum each column for each reactant and product to determine the equilibrium partial pressures in terms of the initial partial pressures and the variable x.	$I_2(g) + Cl_2(g) \rightleftharpoons 2\,ICl(g)$

	P_{I_2} (atm)	P_{Cl_2} (atm)	P_{ICl} (atm)
Initial	0.100	0.100	0.100
Change	$-x$	$-x$	$+2x$
Equil	$0.100 - x$	$0.100 - x$	$0.100 + 2x$

5. Substitute the expressions for the equilibrium partial pressures (from step 4) into the expression for the equilibrium constant. Use the given value of the equilibrium constant to solve the expression for the variable x.	$K_p = \dfrac{(P_{ICl})^2}{P_{I_2}P_{Cl_2}} = \dfrac{(0.100 + 2x)^2}{(0.100 - x)(0.100 - x)}$ $81.9 = \dfrac{(0.100 + 2x)^2}{(0.100 - x)^2}$ (perfect square) $\sqrt{81.9} = \dfrac{(0.100 + 2x)}{(0.100 - x)}$ $\sqrt{81.9}\,(0.100 - x) = 0.100 + 2x$ $\sqrt{81.9}\,(0.100) - \sqrt{81.9}\,x = 0.100 + 2x$ $\sqrt{81.9}\,(0.100) - 0.100 = 2x + \sqrt{81.9}\,x$ $0.805 = 11.05x$ $x = 0.0729$

6. Substitute x into the expressions for the equilibrium partial pressures of the reactants and products (from step 4) and calculate the partial pressures.	$P_{I_2} = 0.100 - 0.0729 = 0.027$ atm $P_{Cl_2} = 0.100 - 0.0729 = 0.027$ atm $P_{ICl} = 0.100 + 2(0.0729) = 0.246$ atm

7. Check your answer by substituting the calculated equilibrium partial pressures into the equilibrium expression. The calculated value of K should match the given value of K.

$$K_p = \frac{(P_{ICl})^2}{P_{I_2}P_{Cl_2}} = \frac{(0.246)^2}{(0.027)(0.027)} = 83$$

Since the calculated value of K_p matches the given value (within the uncertainty indicated by the significant figures), the answer is valid.

FOR PRACTICE 14.11

The reaction between I_2 and Cl_2 in Example 14.11 is carried out at the same temperature, but with these initial partial pressures: $P_{I_2} = 0.150$ atm, $P_{Cl_2} = 0.150$ atm, $P_{ICl} = 0.00$ atm. Find the equilibrium partial pressures of all three substances.

Simplifying Approximations in Working Equilibrium Problems

For some equilibrium problems of the type shown in Example 14.9, 14.10, and 14.11, we can make an approximation that simplifies the calculations without any significant loss of accuracy. For example, if the equilibrium constant is relatively small, the reaction will not proceed very far to the right. Therefore, if the initial reactant concentration is relatively large, we can make the assumption that x is small relative to the initial concentration of reactant. To see how this approximation works, consider again the simple reaction $A \rightleftharpoons 2\,B$. Suppose that, as before, we have a reaction mixture in which the initial concentration of A is 1.0 M and the initial concentration of B is 0.0 M and that we want to find the equilibrium concentrations. However, suppose that in this case the equilibrium constant is much smaller, say $K = 3.3 \times 10^{-5}$. The ICE table is identical to the one we set up previously:

	[A]	[B]
Initial	1.0	0.0
Change	$-x$	$+2x$
Equil	$1.0 - x$	$2x$

Except for the value of K, we end up with the exact quadratic equation that we had before:

$$K = \frac{[B]^2}{[A]} = \frac{(2x)^2}{1.0 - x} = 3.3 \times 10^{-5}$$

or more simply:

$$\frac{4x^2}{1.0 - x} = 3.3 \times 10^{-5}$$

We can rearrange this quadratic equation into standard form and solve it using the quadratic formula. But since K is small, the reaction will not proceed very far toward products and, therefore, x will also be small. If x is much smaller than 1.0, then $(1.0 - x)$ (the quantity in the denominator) can be approximated by (1.0):

$$\frac{4x^2}{(1.0 - \cancel{x})} = 3.3 \times 10^{-5}$$

This approximation greatly simplifies the equation, which we can then solve for x as follows:

$$\frac{4x^2}{1.0} = 3.3 \times 10^{-5}$$

$$4x^2 = 3.3 \times 10^{-5}$$

$$x = \sqrt{\frac{3.3 \times 10^{-5}}{4}} = 0.0029$$

We can check the validity of this approximation by comparing the calculated value of x to the number it was subtracted from. The ratio of x to the number it is subtracted from should be less than 0.05 (or 5%) for the approximation to be valid. In this case, x was subtracted from 1.0, and therefore the ratio of the value of x to 1.0 is calculated as follows:

$$\frac{0.0029}{1.0} \times 100\% = 0.29\%$$

The approximation is therefore valid. In Example 14.12 and 14.13, we treat two nearly identical problems—the only difference is the initial concentration of the reactant. In Example 14.12, the initial concentration of the reactant is relatively large, the equilibrium constant is small, and the *x is small* approximation works well. In Example 14.13, however, the initial concentration of the reactant is much smaller, and even though the equilibrium constant is the same, the *x is small* approximation does not work (because the initial concentration is also small). In cases such as this, we have a couple of options to solve the problem. We can either solve the equation exactly (using the quadratic formula, for example), or we can use the *method of successive approximations*, which is introduced in Example 14.13. In this method, we essentially solve for *x* as if it were small, and then substitute the value obtained back into the equation (where *x* was initially neglected) to solve for *x* again. This can be repeated until the calculated value of *x* stops changing with each iteration, an indication that we have arrived at an acceptable value for *x*.

Note that the *x is small* approximation does not imply that *x is zero*. If that were the case, the reactant and product concentrations would not change from their initial values. The *x is small* approximation just means that when *x* is added or subtracted to another number, it does not change that number by very much. For example, we can calculate the value of the difference $1.0 - x$ when $x = 3.0 \times 10^{-4}$:

$$1.0 - x = 1.0 - 3.0 \times 10^{-4} = 0.9997 = 1.0$$

Since the value of 1.0 is known only to two significant figures, subtracting the small *x* does not change the value at all. This situation is similar to weighing yourself on a bathroom scale with and without a penny in your pocket. Unless your scale is unusually precise, removing the penny from your pocket will not change the reading on the scale. This does not imply that the penny is weightless, only that its weight is small when compared to your body weight. You can neglect the weight of the penny in reading your weight with no detectable loss in accuracy.

PROCEDURE FOR...	EXAMPLE 14.12	EXAMPLE 14.13
Finding Equilibrium Concentrations from Initial Concentrations in Cases with a Small Equilibrium Constant	**Finding Equilibrium Concentrations from Initial Concentrations in Cases with a Small Equilibrium Constant**	**Finding Equilibrium Concentrations from Initial Concentrations in Cases with a Small Equilibrium Constant**
To solve these types of problems, follow the given procedure.	Consider the reaction for the decomposition of hydrogen disulfide: $2\,H_2S(g) \rightleftharpoons 2\,H_2(g) + S_2(g)$ $K_c = 1.67 \times 10^{-7}$ at 800 °C A 0.500 L reaction vessel initially contains 0.0125 mol of H_2S at 800 °C. Find the equilibrium concentrations of H_2 and S_2.	Consider the reaction for the decomposition of hydrogen disulfide: $2\,H_2S(g) \rightleftharpoons 2\,H_2(g) + S_2(g)$ $K_c = 1.67 \times 10^{-7}$ at 800 °C A 0.500 L reaction vessel initially contains 1.25×10^{-4} mol of H_2S at 800 °C. Find the equilibrium concentrations of H_2 and S_2.

1. Using the balanced equation as a guide, prepare a table showing the known initial concentrations of the reactants and products. (In these examples, you must first calculate the concentration of H_2S from the given number of moles and volume.)

Example 14.12:

$$[H_2S] = \frac{0.0125 \text{ mol}}{0.500 \text{ L}} = 0.0250 \text{ M}$$

$2\,H_2S(g) \rightleftharpoons 2\,H_2(g) + S_2(g)$

	$[H_2S]$	$[H_2]$	$[S_2]$
Initial	0.0250	0.00	0.00
Change			
Equil			

Example 14.13:

$$[H_2S] = \frac{1.25 \times 10^{-4} \text{ mol}}{0.500 \text{ L}}$$
$$= 2.50 \times 10^{-4} \text{ M}$$

$2\,H_2S(g) \rightleftharpoons 2\,H_2(g) + S_2(g)$

	$[H_2S]$	$[H_2]$	$[S_2]$
Initial	2.50×10^{-4}	0.00	0.00
Change			
Equil			

2. Use the initial concentrations to calculate the reaction quotient (Q). Compare Q to K to predict the direction in which the reaction will proceed.	By inspection, $Q = 0$; the reaction will proceed to the right.	By inspection, $Q = 0$; the reaction will proceed to the right.

3. Represent the change in the concentration of one of the reactants or products with the variable x. Define the changes in the concentrations of the other reactants or products with respect to x.

$$2\,H_2S(g) \rightleftharpoons 2\,H_2(g) + S_2(g)$$

	[H₂S]	[H₂]	[S₂]
Initial	0.0250	0.00	0.00
Change	$-2x$	$+2x$	$+x$
Equil			

$$2\,H_2S(g) \rightleftharpoons 2\,H_2(g) + S_2(g)$$

	[H₂S]	[H₂]	[S₂]
Initial	2.50×10^{-4}	0.00	0.00
Change	$-2x$	$+2x$	$+x$
Equil			

4. Sum each column for each reactant and product to determine the equilibrium concentrations in terms of the initial concentrations and the variable x.

$$2\,H_2S(g) \rightleftharpoons 2\,H_2(g) + S_2(g)$$

	[H₂S]	[H₂]	[S₂]
Initial	0.0250	0.00	0.00
Change	$-2x$	$+2x$	$+x$
Equil	$0.0250 - 2x$	$2x$	x

$$2\,H_2S(g) \rightleftharpoons 2\,H_2(g) + S_2(g)$$

	[H₂S]	[H₂]	[S₂]
Initial	2.50×10^{-4}	0.00	0.00
Change	$-2x$	$+2x$	$+x$
Equil	$2.50 \times 10^{-4} - 2x$	$2x$	x

5. Substitute the expressions for the equilibrium concentrations (from step 4) into the expression for the equilibrium constant. Use the given value of the equilibrium constant to solve the resulting equation for the variable x.

In this case, the resulting equation is cubic in x. Although cubic equations can be solved, the solutions are not usually simple. However, since the equilibrium constant is small, we know that the reaction does not proceed very far to the right. Therefore, x will be a small number and can be dropped from any quantities in which it is added to or subtracted from another number (as long as the number itself is not too small).

$$K_c = \frac{[H_2]^2[S_2]}{[H_2S]^2}$$

$$= \frac{(2x)^2 x}{(0.0250 - 2x)^2}$$

$$1.67 \times 10^{-7} = \frac{4x^3}{(0.0250 - 2x)^2}$$

x is small.

$$1.67 \times 10^{-7} = \frac{4x^3}{(0.0250 - \cancel{2x})^2}$$

$$1.67 \times 10^{-7} = \frac{4x^3}{6.25 \times 10^{-4}}$$

$$6.25 \times 10^{-4}(1.67 \times 10^{-7}) = 4x^3$$

$$x^3 = \frac{6.25 \times 10^{-4}(1.67 \times 10^{-7})}{4}$$

$$x = 2.97 \times 10^{-4}$$

$$K_c = \frac{[H_2]^2[S_2]}{[H_2S]^2}$$

$$= \frac{(2x)^2 x}{(2.50 \times 10^{-4} - 2x)^2}$$

$$1.67 \times 10^{-7} = \frac{4x^3}{(2.50 \times 10^{-4} - 2x)^2}$$

x is small.

$$1.67 \times 10^{-7} = \frac{4x^3}{(2.50 \times 10^{-4} - \cancel{2x})^2}$$

$$1.67 \times 10^{-7} = \frac{4x^3}{6.25 \times 10^{-8}}$$

$$6.25 \times 10^{-8}(1.67 \times 10^{-7}) = 4x^3$$

$$x^3 = \frac{6.25 \times 10^{-8}(1.67 \times 10^{-7})}{4}$$

$$x = 1.38 \times 10^{-5}$$

Check whether your approximation was valid by comparing the calculated value of x to the number it was added to or subtracted from. The ratio of the two numbers should be less than 0.05 (or 5%) for the approximation to be valid. If approximation is not valid, proceed to step 5a.

Checking the *x is small* approximation:

$$\frac{2.97 \times 10^{-4}}{0.0250} \times 100\% = 1.19\%$$

The *x is small* approximation is valid, proceed to step 6.

Checking the *x is small* approximation:

$$\frac{1.38 \times 10^{-5}}{2.50 \times 10^{-4}} \times 100\% = 5.52\%$$

The approximation does not satisfy the <5% rule (although it is close).

5a. If the approximation is not valid, you can either solve the equation exactly (by hand or with your calculator), or use the method of successive approximations. In this case, we use the method of successive approximations.

$$1.67 \times 10^{-7} = \frac{4x^3}{(2.50 \times 10^{-4} - 2x)^2}$$

$$x = 1.38 \times 10^{-5}$$

$$1.67 \times 10^{-7} = \frac{4x^3}{(2.50 \times 10^{-4} - 2.76 \times 10^{-5})^2}$$

$$x = 1.27 \times 10^{-5}$$

Substitute the value obtained for x in step 5 back into the original cubic equation, but only at the exact spot where x was assumed to be negligible, and then solve the equation for x again. Continue this procedure until the value of x obtained from solving the equation is the same as the one that is substituted into the equation.

If we substitute this value of x back into the cubic equation and solve it, we get $x = 1.28 \times 10^{-5}$, which is nearly identical to 1.27×10^{-5}. Therefore, we have arrived at the best approximation for x.

6. Substitute x into the expressions for the equilibrium concentrations of the reactants and products (from step 4) and calculate the concentrations.

$[H_2S] = 0.0250 - 2(2.97 \times 10^{-4})$
  $= 0.0244$ M
$[H_2] = 2(2.97 \times 10^{-4})$
  $= 5.94 \times 10^{-4}$ M
$[S_2] = 2.97 \times 10^{-4}$ M

$[H_2S] = 2.50 \times 10^{-4} - 2(1.28 \times 10^{-5})$
  $= 2.24 \times 10^{-4}$ M
$[H_2] = 2(1.28 \times 10^{-5})$
  $= 2.56 \times 10^{-5}$ M
$[S_2] = 1.28 \times 10^{-5}$ M

7. Check your answer by substituting the calculated equilibrium values into the equilibrium expression. The calculated value of K should match the given value of K. Note that the approximation method and rounding errors could cause a difference of up to about 5% when comparing values of the equilibrium constant.

$$K_c = \frac{(5.94 \times 10^{-4})^2 (2.97 \times 10^{-4})}{(0.0244)^2}$$

$$= 1.76 \times 10^{-7}$$

The calculated value of K is close enough to the given value when we consider the uncertainty introduced by the approximation. Therefore the answer is valid.

$$K_c = \frac{(2.56 \times 10^{-5})^2 (1.28 \times 10^{-5})}{(2.24 \times 10^{-4})^2}$$

$$= 1.67 \times 10^{-7}$$

The calculated value of K is equal to the given value. Therefore the answer is valid.

FOR PRACTICE 14.12

The reaction in Example 14.12 is carried out at the same temperature with the following initial concentrations: $[H_2S] = 0.100$ M, $[H_2] = 0.100$ M, and $[S_2] = 0.00$ M. Find the equilibrium concentration of $[S_2]$.

FOR PRACTICE 14.13

The reaction in Example 14.13 is carried out at the same temperature with the following initial concentrations: $[H_2S] = 1.00 \times 10^{-4}$ M, $[H_2] = 0.00$ M, and $[S_2] = 0.00$ M. Find the equilibrium concentration of $[S_2]$.

Conceptual Connection 14.6 The *x is small* Approximation

For the generic reaction, A(g) $\rightleftharpoons$ B(g), consider each value of K and initial concentration of A. For which set will the *x is small* approximation most likely apply?

(a) $K = 1.0 \times 10^{-5}$; $[A] = 0.250$ M
(b) $K = 1.0 \times 10^{-2}$; $[A] = 0.250$ M
(c) $K = 1.0 \times 10^{-5}$; $[A] = 0.00250$ M
(d) $K = 1.0 \times 10^{-2}$; $[A] = 0.00250$ M

14.9 Le Châtelier's Principle: How a System at Equilibrium Responds to Disturbances

We have seen that a chemical system not in equilibrium tends to progress toward equilibrium and that the relative concentrations of the reactants and products at equilibrium are characterized by the equilibrium constant, K. What happens, however, when a chemical system already at equilibrium is disturbed? **Le Châtelier's principle** states that the chemical system responds to minimize the disturbance.

| Pronounced "Le-sha-te-lyay"

> **Le Châtelier's principle: When a chemical system at equilibrium is disturbed, the system shifts in a direction that minimizes the disturbance.**

In other words, a system at equilibrium tends to maintain that equilibrium—it bounces back when disturbed.

We can understand Le Châtelier's principle by returning to our two neighboring countries analogy. Suppose the populations of Country A and Country B are at equilibrium. This means that the rate of people moving out of Country A and into Country B is equal to the rate of people moving into Country A and out of Country B, and the populations of the two countries are stable.

$$\text{Country A} \rightleftharpoons \text{Country B}$$

Now imagine disturbing the balance (Figure 14.8 ▼). Suppose there is a notable increase in the birthrate in Country B. What happens? After Country B becomes more crowded, the rate of people leaving Country B increases. The net flow of people is out of Country B and into Country A. Equilibrium is disturbed by the addition of more people to Country B, and people leave Country B in response. In effect, the system responded by shifting in the direction that minimized the disturbance.

On the other hand, what happens if there is a baby boom in Country A instead? As Country A gets more crowded, the rate of people leaving Country A increases. The net flow of people is out of Country A and into Country B. The number of people in Country A initially increases and the system responds; people move out of Country A. Chemical systems behave similarly: when their equilibrium is disturbed, they react to

The two-country analogy should help you see the effects of disturbing a system in equilibrium—it should not be taken as an exact parallel.

Le Châtelier's Principle: An Analogy

◄ FIGURE 14.8 A Population Analogy for Le Châtelier's Principle   A baby boom in Country B shifts the equilibrium to the left. People leave Country B (because it has become too crowded) and migrate to Country A until equilibrium is reestablished.

counter the disturbance. We can disturb a system in chemical equilibrium in several different ways, including changing the concentration of a reactant or product, changing the volume or pressure, and changing the temperature. We consider each of these separately.

The Effect of a Concentration Change on Equilibrium

Consider the following reaction in chemical equilibrium:

$$N_2O_4(g) \rightleftharpoons 2\,NO_2(g)$$

Suppose we disturb the equilibrium by adding NO_2 to the equilibrium mixture (Figure 14.9 ▼). In other words, we increase the concentration of NO_2, the product. What happens? According to Le Châtelier's principle, the system shifts in a direction to minimize the disturbance. The reaction goes to the left (it proceeds in the reverse direction), consuming some of the added NO_2 and thus bringing its concentration back down, as shown graphically in Figure 14.10a ▶.

The reaction shifts to the left because the value of Q changes as follows:

- Before addition of NO_2: $Q = K$.
- Immediately after addition of NO_2: $Q > K$.
- Reaction shifts to left to reestablish equilibrium.

Le Châtelier's Principle: Changing Concentration

▲ **FIGURE 14.9 Le Châtelier's Principle: The Effect of a Concentration Change**   Adding NO_2 causes the reaction to shift left, consuming some of the added NO_2 and forming more N_2O_4.

Le Châtelier's Principle: Graphical Representation

On the other hand, what happens if we add extra N_2O_4 (the reactant), increasing its concentration? In this case, the reaction shifts to the right, consuming some of the added N_2O_4 and bringing *its* concentration back down, as shown graphically in Figure 14.10b ▲.

▲ FIGURE 14.10 Le Châtelier's Principle: Changing Concentration The graph shows the concentrations of NO_2 and N_2O_4 for the reaction $N_2O_4(g) \longrightarrow 2\,NO_2(g)$ as a function of time in three distinct stages of the reaction: initially at equilibrium (left), upon disturbance of the equilibrium by addition of more NO_2 **(a)** or N_2O_4 **(b)** to the reaction mixture (center), and upon reestablishment of equilibrium (right).

The reaction shifts to the right because the value of Q changes as follows:

- Before addition of N_2O_4: $Q = K$.
- Immediately after addition of N_2O_4: $Q < K$.
- Reaction shifts to right to reestablish equilibrium.

In both of these cases, the system shifts in a direction that minimizes the disturbance. Lowering the concentration of a reactant (which makes $Q > K$) causes the system to shift in the direction of the reactants to minimize the disturbance. Lowering the concentration of a product (which makes $Q < K$) causes the system to shift in the direction of products.

Summarizing the Effect of a Concentration Change on Equilibrium:
If a chemical system is at equilibrium:

▶ *Increasing* the concentration of one or more of the *reactants* (which makes $Q < K$) causes the reaction to *shift to the right* (in the direction of the products).

▶ *Increasing* the concentration of one or more of the *products* (which makes $Q > K$) causes the reaction to *shift to the left* (in the direction of the reactants).

▶ *Decreasing* the concentration of one or more of the *reactants* (which makes $Q > K$) causes the reaction to *shift to the left* (in the direction of the reactants).

▶ *Decreasing* the concentration of one or more of the *products* (which makes $Q < K$) causes the reaction to *shift to the right* (in the direction of the products).

EXAMPLE 14.14   The Effect of a Concentration Change on Equilibrium

Consider the following reaction at equilibrium:

$$CaCO_3(s) \rightleftharpoons CaO(s) + CO_2(g)$$

What is the effect of adding additional CO_2 to the reaction mixture? What is the effect of adding additional $CaCO_3$?

SOLUTION

Adding additional CO_2 increases the concentration of CO_2 and causes the reaction to shift to the left. Adding additional $CaCO_3$, however, does *not* increase the concentration of $CaCO_3$ because $CaCO_3$ is a solid and therefore has a constant concentration. Thus, adding additional $CaCO_3$ has no effect on the position of the equilibrium. (Note that, as we saw in Section 14.5, solids are not included in the equilibrium expression.)

FOR PRACTICE 14.14

Consider the following reaction in chemical equilibrium:

$$2\,BrNO(g) \rightleftharpoons 2\,NO(g) + Br_2(g)$$

What is the effect of adding additional Br_2 to the reaction mixture? What is the effect of adding additional BrNO?

The Effect of a Volume (or Pressure) Change on Equilibrium

How does a system in chemical equilibrium respond to a volume change? Recall from Chapter 5 that changing the volume of a gas (or a gas mixture) results in a change in pressure. Remember also that pressure and volume are inversely related: a *decrease* in volume causes an *increase* in pressure, and an *increase* in volume causes a *decrease* in pressure. So, if the volume of a reaction mixture at chemical equilibrium is changed, the pressure changes and the system shifts in a direction to minimize that change. For example, consider the following reaction at equilibrium in a cylinder equipped with a moveable piston:

In considering the effect of a change in volume, we are assuming that the change in volume is carried out at constant temperature.

$$N_2(g) + 3\,H_2(g) \rightleftharpoons 2\,NH_3(g)$$

What happens if we push down on the piston, lowering the volume and raising the pressure (Figure 14.11 ▶)? How can the chemical system respond to bring the pressure back down? Look carefully at the reaction coefficients. If the reaction shifts to the right, 4 mol of gas particles are converted to 2 mol of gas particles. From the ideal gas law ($PV = nRT$), we know that decreasing the number of moles of a gas (n) results in a lower pressure (P). Therefore, the system shifts to the right, decreasing the number of gas molecules and bringing the pressure back down, minimizing the disturbance.

Consider the same reaction mixture at equilibrium again. What happens if, this time, we pull *up* on the piston, *increasing* the volume (Figure 14.11b)? The higher volume results in a lower pressure and the system responds to bring the pressure back up. It does this by shifting to the left, converting every 2 mol of gas particles into 4 mol of gas particles, increasing the pressure and minimizing the disturbance.

Consider again the same reaction mixture at equilibrium. What happens if, this time, we keep the volume the same but increase the pressure *by adding an inert gas* to the mixture? Although the overall pressure of the mixture increases, the partial pressures of the reactants and products do not change. Consequently, there is no effect and the reaction does not shift in either direction.

Summarizing the Effect of Volume Change on Equilibrium:

If a chemical system is at equilibrium:

▶ *Decreasing* the volume causes the reaction to shift in the direction that has *the fewer moles of gas particles*.

▶ *Increasing* the volume causes the reaction to shift in the direction that has *the greater number of moles of gas particles*.

Le Châtelier's Principle: Changing Pressure

$N_2(g) + 3 H_2(g) \rightleftharpoons 2 NH_3(g)$

4 mol of gas   2 mol of gas

Reaction shifts right
(toward side with fewer
moles of gas particles).

(a)

$N_2(g) + 3 H_2(g) \rightleftharpoons 2 NH_3(g)$

4 mol of gas   2 mol of gas

Reaction shifts left
(toward side with more
moles of gas particles).

(b)

◄ FIGURE 14.11 Le Châtelier's Principle: The Effect of a Pressure Change (a) Decreasing the volume increases the pressure, causing the reaction to shift to the right (fewer moles of gas, lower pressure). (b) Increasing the volume reduces the pressure, causing the reaction to shift to the left (more moles of gas, higher pressure).

▶ If a reaction has an equal number of moles of gas on both sides of the chemical equation, then a change in volume produces no effect on the equilibrium.

▶ Adding an inert gas to the mixture at a fixed volume has no effect on the equilibrium.

EXAMPLE 14.15 The Effect of a Volume Change on Equilibrium

Consider the following reaction at chemical equilibrium:
$$2 KClO_3(s) \rightleftharpoons 2 KCl(s) + 3 O_2(g)$$
What is the effect of decreasing the volume of the reaction mixture? Increasing the volume of the reaction mixture? Adding an inert gas at constant volume?

SOLUTION

The chemical equation has 3 mol of gas on the right and zero moles of gas on the left. Decreasing the volume of the reaction mixture increases the pressure and causes the reaction to shift to the left (toward the side with fewer moles of gas particles). Increasing the volume of the reaction mixture decreases the pressure and causes the reaction to shift to the right (toward the side with more moles of gas particles.) Adding an inert gas has no effect.

FOR PRACTICE 14.15

Consider the following reaction at chemical equilibrium:
$$2 SO_2(g) + O_2(g) \rightleftharpoons 2 SO_3(g)$$
What is the effect of decreasing the volume of the reaction mixture? Increasing the volume of the reaction mixture?

The Effect of a Temperature Change on Equilibrium

According to Le Châtelier's principle, if the temperature of a system at equilibrium is changed, the system will shift in a direction to counter that change. So, if the temperature is increased, the reaction will shift in the direction that tends to decrease the temperature and vice versa. Recall from Chapter 6 that an exothermic reaction (negative ΔH) emits heat:

$$\text{Exothermic reaction: A + B} \rightleftharpoons \text{C + D + heat}$$

We can think of heat as a product in an exothermic reaction. In an endothermic reaction (positive ΔH), the reaction absorbs heat.

$$\text{Endothermic reaction: A + B + heat} \rightleftharpoons \text{C + D}$$

We can think of heat as a reactant in an endothermic reaction.

At constant pressure, raising the temperature of an *exothermic* reaction—think of this as adding heat—is similar to adding more product, causing the reaction to shift left. For example, the reaction of nitrogen with hydrogen to form ammonia is exothermic:

Add heat

$$N_2(g) + 3\,H_2(g) \rightleftharpoons 2\,NH_3(g) + \text{heat}$$

Reaction shifts left.
Smaller K

Raising the temperature of an equilibrium mixture of these three gases causes the reaction to shift left, absorbing some of the added heat and forming less products and more reactants. Note that, unlike adding additional NH_3 to the reaction mixture (which does *not* change the value of the equilibrium constant), *changing the temperature does change the value of the equilibrium constant*. The new equilibrium mixture will have more reactants and fewer products and therefore a smaller value of K.

Conversely, lowering the temperature causes the reaction to shift right, releasing heat and producing more products because the value of K has increased:

Remove heat

$$N_2(g) + 3\,H_2(g) \rightleftharpoons 2NH_3(g) + \text{heat}$$

Reaction shifts right.
Larger K

In contrast, for an *endothermic* reaction, raising the temperature (adding heat) causes the reaction to shift right to absorb the added heat. For example, the following reaction is endothermic:

Add heat

$$\underset{\text{colorless}}{N_2O_4(g)} + \text{heat} \rightleftharpoons \underset{\text{brown}}{2\,NO_2(g)}$$

Reaction shifts right.
Larger K

Le Châtelier's Principle: Changing Temperature

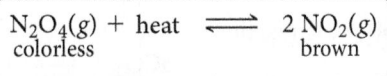

$$N_2O_4(g) + \text{heat} \rightleftharpoons 2\,NO_2(g)$$
colorless   brown

Lower temperature: N_2O_4 favored

Higher temperature: NO_2 favored

▲ **FIGURE 14.12 Le Châtelier's Principle: The Effect of a Temperature Change** Because the reaction is endothermic, raising the temperature causes a shift to the right, toward the formation of brown NO_2.

Raising the temperature of an equilibrium mixture of these two gases causes the reaction to shift right, absorbing some of the added heat and producing more products because the value of K has increased. Since N_2O_4 is colorless and NO_2 is brown, the effects of changing the temperature of this reaction are easily seen (Figure 14.12 ▲). On the other hand, lowering the temperature (removing heat) of a reaction mixture of these two gases causes the reaction to shift left, releasing heat, forming less products, and lowering the value of K:

Remove heat

$$N_2O_4(g) + \text{heat} \rightleftharpoons 2\,NO_2(g)$$
colorless   brown

Reaction shifts left. Smaller K

Summarizing the Effect of a Temperature Change on Equilibrium:

In an *exothermic* chemical reaction, heat is a product.

▶ *Increasing* the temperature causes an exothermic reaction to *shift left* (in the direction of the reactants); the value of the equilibrium constant decreases.

▶ *Decreasing* the temperature causes an exothermic reaction to *shift right* (in the direction of the products); the value of the equilibrium constant increases.

In an *endothermic* chemical reaction, heat is a reactant.

▶ *Increasing* the temperature causes an endothermic reaction to *shift right* (in the direction of the products); the equilibrium constant increases.

▶ *Decreasing* the temperature causes an endothermic reaction to *shift left* (in the direction of the reactants); the equilibrium constant decreases.

Adding heat favors the endothermic direction. Removing heat favors the exothermic direction.

EXAMPLE 14.16 The Effect of a Temperature Change on Equilibrium

The following reaction is endothermic:

$$CaCO_3(s) \rightleftharpoons CaO(s) + CO_2(g)$$

What is the effect of increasing the temperature of the reaction mixture? Decreasing the temperature?

SOLUTION

Since the reaction is endothermic, we can think of heat as a reactant:

$$Heat + CaCO_3(s) \rightleftharpoons CaO(s) + CO_2(g)$$

Raising the temperature is equivalent to adding a reactant, causing the reaction to shift to the right. Lowering the temperature is equivalent to removing a reactant, causing the reaction to shift to the left.

FOR PRACTICE 14.16

The following reaction is exothermic:

$$2 SO_2(g) + O_2(g) \rightleftharpoons 2 SO_3(g)$$

What is the effect of increasing the temperature of the reaction mixture? Decreasing the temperature?

CHAPTER IN REVIEW

Self Assessment Quiz

Q1. What is the correct expression for the equilibrium constant (K_c) for the reaction between carbon and hydrogen gas to form methane shown here?

$$C(s) + 2 H_2(g) \rightleftharpoons CH_4(g)$$

a) $K_c = \dfrac{[CH_4]}{[H_2]}$

b) $K_c = \dfrac{[CH_4]}{[C][H_2]}$

c) $K_c = \dfrac{[CH_4]}{[C][H_2]^2}$

d) $K_c = \dfrac{[CH_4]}{[H_2]^2}$

Q2. The equilibrium constant for the reaction shown here is $K_c = 1.0 \times 10^3$. A reaction mixture at equilibrium contains $[A] = 1.0 \times 10^{-3}$ M. What is the concentration of B in the mixture?

$$A(g) \rightleftharpoons B(g)$$

a) 1.0×10^{-3} M
b) 1.0 M
c) 2.0 M
d) 1.0×10^3 M

Q3. Use the data below to find the equilibrium constant (K_c) for the reaction $A(g) \rightleftharpoons 2 B(g) + C(g)$.

$$A(g) \rightleftharpoons 2 X(g) + C(g) \qquad K_c = 1.55$$
$$B(g) \rightleftharpoons X(g) \qquad K_c = 25.2$$

a) 984
b) 26.8
c) 6.10×10^{-4}
d) 2.44×10^{-3}

Q4. The reaction shown here has a $K_p = 4.5 \times 10^2$ at 825 K. Find K_c for the reaction at this temperature.

$$CH_4(g) + CO_2(g) \rightleftharpoons 2 CO(g) + 2 H_2(g)$$

a) 0.098
b) 2.1×10^6
c) 6.6
d) 4.5×10^{-2}

Q5. Consider the reaction between NO and Cl_2 to form NOCl:

$$2 NO(g) + Cl_2(g) \rightleftharpoons 2 NOCl(g)$$

A reaction mixture at a certain temperature initially contains only [NO] = 0.50 M and [Cl_2] = 0.50 M. After the reaction comes to equilibrium, the concentration of NOCl is 0.30 M. Find the value of the equilibrium constant (K_c) at this temperature.

a) 11
b) 4.3
c) 6.4
d) 0.22

Q6. For the reaction $2 A(g) \rightleftharpoons B(g)$, the equilibrium constant is $K_p = 0.76$. A reaction mixture initially contains 2.0 atm of each gas ($P_A = 2.0$ atm and $P_B = 2.0$ atm). Which statement is true of the reaction mixture?

a) The reaction mixture is at equilibrium.
b) The reaction mixture will proceed toward products.
c) The reaction mixture will proceed toward reactants.
d) It is not possible to determine from the information given the future direction of the reaction mixture.

Q7. Consider the reaction between iodine gas and chlorine gas to form iodine monochloride:

$$I_2(g) + Cl_2(g) \rightleftharpoons 2 ICl(g) \qquad K_p = 81.9 \text{ (at 298 K)}$$

A reaction mixture at 298 K initially contains $P_{I_2} = 0.25$ atm and $P_{Cl_2} = 0.25$ atm. What is the partial pressure of iodine monochloride when the reaction reaches equilibrium?

a) 0.17 atm
b) 0.64 atm
c) 0.41 atm
d) 2.3 atm

Q8. Consider the reaction of A to form B:

$$2\,A(g) \rightleftharpoons B(g) \qquad K_c = 1.8 \times 10^{-5} \text{ (at 298 K)}$$

A reaction mixture at 298 K initially contains [A] = 0.50 M. What is the concentration of B when the reaction reaches equilibrium?

a) 9.0×10^{-6} M   b) 0.060 M

c) 0.030 M   d) 4.5×10^{-6} M

Q9. The decomposition of NH_4HS is endothermic:

$$NH_4HS(s) \rightleftharpoons NH_3(g) + H_2S(g)$$

Which change to an equilibrium mixture of this reaction results in the formation of more H_2S?

a) a decrease in the volume of the reaction vessel (at constant temperature)

b) an increase in the amount of NH_4HS in the reaction vessel

c) an increase in temperature

d) all of the above

Q10. The solid XY decomposes into gaseous X and Y:

$$XY(s) \rightleftharpoons X(g) + Y(g) \qquad K_p = 4.1 \text{ (at 0 °C)}$$

If the reaction is carried out in a 22.4 L container, which initial amounts of X and Y will result in the formation of solid XY?

a) 5 mol X; 0.5 mol Y

b) 2.0 mol X; 2.0 mol Y

c) 1 mol X; 1 mol Y

d) none of the above

Q11. What is the effect of adding helium gas (at constant volume) to an equilibrium mixture of the reaction:

$$CO(g) + Cl_2(g) \rightleftharpoons COCl_2(g)$$

a) The reaction shifts toward the products.

b) The reaction shifts toward the reactants.

c) The reaction does not shift in either direction.

d) The reaction slows down.

Q12. The reaction $X_2(g) \rightleftharpoons 2\,X(g)$ occurs in a closed reaction vessel at constant volume and temperature. Initially, the vessel contains only X_2 at a pressure of 1.55 atm. After the reaction reaches equilibrium, the total pressure is 2.85 atm. What is the value of the equilibrium constant, K_p, for the reaction?

a) 27

b) 10

c) 5.2

d) 32

Answers: 1. (d) 2. (b) 3. (d) 4. (a) 5. (c) 6. (b) 7. (c) 8. (d) 9. (c) 10. (d) 11. (c) 12. (a)

Key Terms

Section 14.2
reversible (651)
dynamic equilibrium (651)

Section 14.3
equilibrium constant (K) (654)
law of mass action (654)

Section 14.7
reaction quotient (Q) (665)

Section 14.9
Le Châtelier's principle (677)

Key Concepts

The Equilibrium Constant (14.1)

▶ The relative concentrations of the reactants and the products at equilibrium are expressed by the equilibrium constant, K.

▶ The equilibrium constant measures how far a reaction proceeds toward products: a large K (much greater than 1) indicates a high concentration of products at equilibrium, and a small K (less than 1) indicates a low concentration of products at equilibrium.

Dynamic Equilibrium (14.2)

▶ Most chemical reactions are reversible; they can proceed in either the forward or the reverse direction.

▶ When a chemical reaction is in dynamic equilibrium, the rate of the forward reaction equals the rate of the reverse reaction, so the net concentrations of reactants and products do not change. However, this does *not* imply that the concentrations of the reactants and the products are equal at equilibrium.

The Equilibrium Constant Expression (14.3)

▶ The equilibrium constant expression is given by the law of mass action and is equal to the concentrations of the products, raised to their stoichiometric coefficients, divided by the concentrations of the reactants, raised to their stoichiometric coefficients.

▶ When the equation for a chemical reaction is reversed, multiplied, or added to another equation, K must be modified accordingly.

The Equilibrium Constant, K (14.4)

▶ The equilibrium constant can be expressed in terms of concentrations (K_c) or in terms of partial pressures (K_p). These two constants are related by Equation 14.2. Concentration must always be expressed in units of molarity for K_c. Partial pressures must always be expressed in units of atmospheres for K_p.

States of Matter and the Equilibrium Constant (14.5)

▶ The equilibrium constant expression contains only partial pressures or concentrations of reactants and products that exist as gases or solutes dissolved in solution. Pure liquids and solids are not included in the expression for the equilibrium constant.

Calculating K (14.6)

▶ We can calculate the equilibrium constant from equilibrium concentrations or partial pressures by substituting measured values into the expression for the equilibrium constant (as obtained from the law of mass action).

▶ In most cases, we can calculate the equilibrium concentrations of the reactants and products—and therefore the value of the equilibrium constant—from the initial concentrations of the reactants and products and the equilibrium concentration of *just one* reactant or product.

The Reaction Quotient, Q (14.7)

▶ The reaction quotient, Q, is the ratio of the concentrations (or partial pressures) of products raised to their stoichiometric coefficients to the concentrations of reactants raised to their stoichiometric coefficients *at any point in the reaction*.

▶ Like K, Q can be expressed in terms of concentrations (Q_c) or partial pressures (Q_p).

▶ At equilibrium, Q is equal to K; therefore, the direction in which a reaction proceeds can be determined by comparing Q to K. If $Q < K$, the reaction moves in the direction of the products; if $Q > K$, the reaction moves in the reverse direction.

Finding Equilibrium Concentrations (14.8)

▶ There are two general types of problems in which K is given and one (or more) equilibrium concentrations can be found:
 (1) K and all but one equilibrium concentration are given.
 (2) K and *only* initial concentrations are given.

▶ We solve the first type by rearranging the law of mass action and substituting the given values.

▶ We solve the second type by creating an ICE table and using a variable x to represent the change in concentration.

Le Châtelier's Principle (14.9)

▶ When a system at equilibrium is disturbed—by a change in the amount of a reactant or product, a change in volume, or a change in temperature—the system shifts in the direction that minimizes the disturbance.

Key Equations and Relationships

Expression for the Equilibrium Constant, K_c (14.3)

$$aA + bB \rightleftharpoons cC + dD$$

$$K = \frac{[C]^c[D]^d}{[A]^a[B]^b} \quad \text{(equilibrium concentrations only)}$$

Relationship between the Equilibrium Constant and the Chemical Equation (14.3)

1. If you reverse the equation, invert the equilibrium constant.
2. If you multiply the coefficients in the equation by a factor, raise the equilibrium constant to the same factor.
3. If you add two or more individual chemical equations to obtain an overall equation, multiply the corresponding equilibrium constants by each other to obtain the overall equilibrium constant.

Expression for the Equilibrium Constant, K_p (14.4)

$$aA + bB \rightleftharpoons cC + dD$$

$$K_p = \frac{P_C^c P_D^d}{P_A^a P_B^b} \quad \text{(equilibrium partial pressures only)}$$

Relationship between the Equilibrium Constants, K_c and K_p (14.4)

$$K_p = K_c(RT)^{\Delta n}$$

The Reaction Quotient, Q_c (14.7)

$$aA + bB \rightleftharpoons cC + dD$$

$$Q_c = \frac{[C]^c[D]^d}{[A]^a[B]^b} \quad \text{(concentrations at any point in the reaction)}$$

The Reaction Quotient, Q_p (14.7)

$$aA + bB \rightleftharpoons cC + dD$$

$$Q_P = \frac{P_C^c P_D^d}{P_A^a P_B^b} \quad \text{(partial pressures at any point in the reaction)}$$

Relationship of Q to the Direction of the Reaction (14.7)

$$Q < K \quad \text{Reaction goes to the right.}$$

$$Q > K \quad \text{Reaction goes to the left.}$$

$$Q = K \quad \text{Reaction is at equilibrium.}$$

Key Learning Outcomes

Chapter Objectives		Assessment
Expressing Equilibrium Constants for Chemical Equations (14.3)	**Law of Mass Action** $$K = \frac{[C]^c[D]^d}{[A]^a[B]^b}$$ Products / Reactants	Example 14.1 For Practice 14.1 Exercises 21, 22

Key Learning Outcomes, *continued*

Manipulating the Equilibrium Constant to Reflect Changes in the Chemical Equation (**14.3**)	Example 14.2 For Practice 14.2 For More Practice 14.2 Exercises 27–30
Relating K_p and K_c (**14.4**)	Example 14.3 For Practice 14.3 Exercises 31, 32
Writing Equilibrium Expressions for Reactions Involving a Solid or a Liquid (**14.5**)	Example 14.4 For Practice 14.4 Exercises 33, 34
Finding Equilibrium Constants from Experimental Concentration Measurements (**14.6**)	Examples 14.5, 14.6 For Practice 14.5, 14.6 Exercises 35, 36, 43, 44
Predicting the Direction of a Reaction by Comparing Q and K (**14.7**)	Example 14.7 For Practice 14.7 Exercises 47–50
Calculating Equilibrium Concentrations from the Equilibrium Constant and One or More Equilibrium Concentrations (**14.8**)	Example 14.8 For Practice 14.8 Exercises 37–46
Finding Equilibrium Concentrations from Initial Concentrations and the Equilibrium Constant (**14.8**)	Examples 14.9, 14.10 For Practice 14.9, 14.10 Exercises 53–58
Calculating Equilibrium Partial Pressures from the Equilibrium Constant and Initial Partial Pressures (**14.8**)	Example 14.11 For Practice 14.11 Exercises 59, 60
Finding Equilibrium Concentrations from Initial Concentrations in Cases with a Small Equilibrium Constant (**14.8**)	Examples 14.12, 14.13 For Practice 14.12, 14.13 Exercises 61, 62
Determining the Effect of a Concentration Change on Equilibrium (**14.9**)	Example 14.14 For Practice 14.14 Exercises 63–66
Determining the Effect of a Volume Change on Equilibrium (**14.9**)	Example 14.15 For Practice 14.15 Exercises 67, 68
Determining the Effect of a Temperature Change on Equilibrium (**14.9**)	Example 14.16 For Practice 14.16 Exercises 69, 70

Add heat

$$N_2(g) + 3 H_2(g) \rightleftharpoons 2 NH_3(g) + heat$$

Reaction shifts left.
Smaller K

EXERCISES

Review Questions

1. How does a developing fetus get oxygen in the womb?

2. What is dynamic equilibrium? Why is it called *dynamic*?

3. Give the general expression for the equilibrium constant of the following generic reaction:

$$aA + bB \rightleftharpoons cC + dD$$

4. What is the significance of the equilibrium constant? What does a large equilibrium constant tell us about a reaction? A small one?

5. What happens to the value of the equilibrium constant for a reaction if the reaction equation is reversed? Multiplied by a constant?

6. If two reactions sum to an overall reaction, and the equilibrium constants for the two reactions are K_1 and K_2, what is the equilibrium constant for the overall reaction?

7. Explain the difference between K_c and K_p. For a given reaction, how are the two constants related?

8. What units should be used when expressing concentrations or partial pressures in the equilibrium constant? What are the units of K_p and K_c? Explain.

9. Why are the concentrations of solids and liquids omitted from equilibrium expressions?

10. Does the value of the equilibrium constant depend on the initial concentrations of the reactants and products? Do the equilibrium concentrations of the reactants and products depend on their initial concentrations? Explain.

11. Explain how you might deduce the equilibrium constant for a reaction in which you know the initial concentrations of the reactants and products and the equilibrium concentration of only one reactant or product.

12. What is the definition of the reaction quotient (Q) for a reaction? What does Q measure?

13. What is the value of Q when each reactant and product is in its standard state? (See Section 6.9 for the definition of standard states.)

14. In what direction will a reaction proceed for each condition: (a) $Q < K$; (b) $Q > K$; and (c) $Q = K$?

15. Many equilibrium calculations involve finding the equilibrium concentrations of reactants and products given their initial concentrations and the equilibrium constant. Outline the general procedure used in solving these kinds of problems.

16. In equilibrium problems involving equilibrium constants that are small relative to the initial concentrations of reactants, we can often assume that the quantity x (which represents how far the reaction proceeds toward products) is small. When this assumption is made, we can ignore the quantity x when it is subtracted from a large number but not when it is multiplied by a large number. In other words, $2.5 - x \approx 2.5$, but $2.5x \neq 2.5$. Explain why we can ignore a small x in the first case, but not in the second.

17. What happens to a chemical system at equilibrium when that equilibrium is disturbed?

18. What is the effect of a change in concentration of a reactant or product on a chemical reaction initially at equilibrium?

19. What is the effect of a change in volume on a chemical reaction (that includes gaseous reactants or products) initially at equilibrium?

20. What is the effect of a temperature change on a chemical reaction initially at equilibrium? How does the effect differ for an exothermic reaction compared to an endothermic one?

Problems by Topic

Equilibrium and the Equilibrium Constant Expression

21. Write an expression for the equilibrium constant of each chemical equation.
    a. $SbCl_5(g) \rightleftharpoons SbCl_3(g) + Cl_2(g)$
    b. $2\,BrNO(g) \rightleftharpoons 2\,NO(g) + Br_2(g)$
    c. $CH_4(g) + 2\,H_2S(g) \rightleftharpoons CS_2(g) + 4\,H_2(g)$
    d. $2\,CO(g) + O_2(g) \rightleftharpoons 2\,CO_2(g)$

22. Find and fix each mistake in the equilibrium constant expressions.
    a. $2\,H_2S(g) \rightleftharpoons 2\,H_2(g) + S_2(g)$ $K = \dfrac{[H_2][S_2]}{[H_2S]}$

    b. $CO(g) + Cl_2(g) \rightleftharpoons COCl_2(g)$ $K = \dfrac{[CO][Cl_2]}{[COCl_2]}$

23. When this reaction comes to equilibrium, will the concentrations of the reactants or products be greater? Does the answer to this question depend on the initial concentrations of the reactants and products?

$$A(g) + B(g) \rightleftharpoons 2\,C(g)   K_c = 1.4 \times 10^{-5}$$

24. Ethene (C_2H_4) can be halogenated by this reaction:

$$C_2H_4(g) + X_2(g) \rightleftharpoons C_2H_4X_2(g)$$

where X_2 can be Cl_2 (green), Br_2 (brown), or I_2 (purple). Examine the three figures representing equilibrium concentrations in this reaction at the same temperature for the three different halogens. Rank the equilibrium constants for the three reactions from largest to smallest.

(a)   (b)

(c)

25. H$_2$ and I$_2$ are combined in a flask and allowed to react according to the reaction:

$$H_2(g) + I_2(g) \rightleftharpoons 2\,HI(g)$$

Examine the figures (sequential in time) and answer the questions:

a. Which figure represents the point at which equilibrium is reached?

b. How would the series of figures change in the presence of a catalyst?

c. Would there be different amounts of reactants and products in the final figure (vi) in the presence of a catalyst?

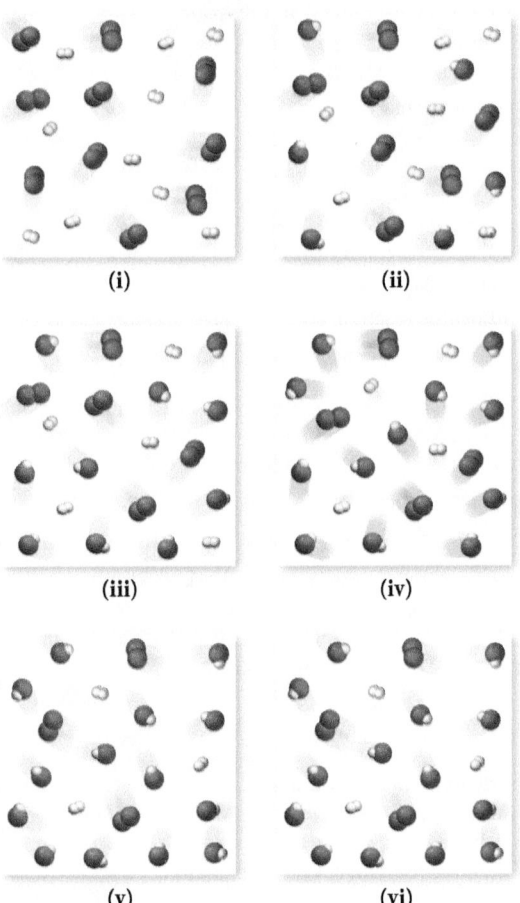

(i)   (ii)

(iii)   (iv)

(v)   (vi)

26. A chemist trying to synthesize a particular compound attempts two different synthesis reactions. The equilibrium constants for the two reactions are 23.3 and 2.2 × 10^4 at room temperature. However, upon carrying out both reactions for 15 minutes, the chemist finds that the reaction with the smaller equilibrium constant produces more of the desired product. Explain how this might be possible.

27. This reaction has an equilibrium constant of $K_p = 2.26 \times 10^4$ at 298 K.

$$CO(g) + 2\,H_2(g) \rightleftharpoons CH_3OH(g)$$

Calculate K_p for each reaction and predict whether reactants or products will be favored at equilibrium.

a. $CH_3OH(g) \rightleftharpoons CO(g) + 2\,H_2(g)$

b. $\frac{1}{2}CO(g) + H_2(g) \rightleftharpoons \frac{1}{2}CH_3OH(g)$

c. $2\,CH_3OH(g) \rightleftharpoons 2\,CO(g) + 4\,H_2(g)$

28. This reaction has an equilibrium constant of $K_p = 2.2 \times 10^6$ at 298 K.

$$2\,COF_2(g) \rightleftharpoons CO_2(g) + CF_4(g)$$

Calculate K_p for each reaction and predict whether reactants or products will be favored at equilibrium.

a. $COF_2(g) \rightleftharpoons \frac{1}{2}CO_2(g) + \frac{1}{2}CF_4(g)$

b. $6\,COF_2(g) \rightleftharpoons 3\,CO_2(g) + 3\,CF_4(g)$

c. $2\,CO_2(g) + 2\,CF_4(g) \rightleftharpoons 4\,COF_2(g)$

29. Consider the reactions and their respective equilibrium constants:

$$NO(g) + \frac{1}{2}Br_2(g) \rightleftharpoons NOBr(g) \qquad K_p = 5.3$$

$$2\,NO(g) \rightleftharpoons N_2(g) + O_2(g) \qquad K_p = 2.1 \times 10^{30}$$

Use these reactions and their equilibrium constants to predict the equilibrium constant for the following reaction:

$$N_2(g) + O_2(g) + Br_2(g) \rightleftharpoons 2\,NOBr(g)$$

30. Use the following reactions and their equilibrium constants to predict the equilibrium constant for the reaction $2\,A(s) \rightleftharpoons 3\,D(g)$.

$$A(s) \rightleftharpoons \frac{1}{2}B(g) + C(g) \qquad K_1 = 0.0334$$

$$3\,D(g) \rightleftharpoons B(g) + 2\,C(g) \qquad K_2 = 2.35$$

K_p, K_c, and Heterogeneous Equilibria

31. Calculate K_c for each reaction:

a. $I_2(g) \rightleftharpoons 2\,I(g)$ $K_p = 6.26 \times 10^{-22}$ (at 298 K)

b. $CH_4(g) + H_2O(g) \rightleftharpoons CO(g) + 3\,H_2(g)$
$$K_p = 7.7 \times 10^{24} \text{ (at 298 K)}$$

c. $I_2(g) + Cl_2(g) \rightleftharpoons 2\,ICl(g)$ $K_p = 81.9$ (at 298 K)

32. Calculate K_p for each reaction:

a. $N_2O_4(g) \rightleftharpoons 2\,NO_2(g)$ $K_c = 5.9 \times 10^{-3}$ (at 298 K)

b. $N_2(g) + 3\,H_2(g) \rightleftharpoons 2\,NH_3(g)$
$$K_c = 3.7 \times 10^8 \text{ (at 298 K)}$$

c. $N_2(g) + O_2(g) \rightleftharpoons 2\,NO(g)$
$$K_c = 4.10 \times 10^{-31} \text{ (at 298 K)}$$

33. Write an equilibrium expression for each chemical equation involving one or more solid or liquid reactants or products.
    a. $CO_3^{2-}(aq) + H_2O(l) \rightleftharpoons HCO_3^-(aq) + OH^-(aq)$
    b. $2\ KClO_3(s) \rightleftharpoons 2\ KCl(s) + 3\ O_2(g)$
    c. $HF(aq) + H_2O(l) \rightleftharpoons H_3O^+(aq) + F^-(aq)$
    d. $NH_3(aq) + H_2O(l) \rightleftharpoons NH_4^+(aq) + OH^-(aq)$

34. Find and fix the mistake in the equilibrium expression.

$$PCl_5(g) \rightleftharpoons PCl_3(l) + Cl_2(g)$$

$$K_c = \frac{[PCl_3][Cl_2]}{[PCl_5]}$$

Relating the Equilibrium Constant to Equilibrium Concentrations and Equilibrium Partial Pressures

35. Consider the reaction:

$$CO(g) + 2\ H_2(g) \rightleftharpoons CH_3OH(g)$$

An equilibrium mixture of this reaction at a certain temperature has $[CO] = 0.105$ M, $[H_2] = 0.114$ M, and $[CH_3OH] = 0.185$ M. What is the value of the equilibrium constant (K_c) at this temperature?

36. Consider the reaction:

$$NH_4HS(s) \rightleftharpoons NH_3(g) + H_2S(g)$$

An equilibrium mixture of this reaction at a certain temperature has $[NH_3] = 0.278$ M and $[H_2S] = 0.355$ M. What is the value of the equilibrium constant (K_c) at this temperature?

37. Consider the reaction:

$$N_2(g) + 3\ H_2(g) \rightleftharpoons 2\ NH_3(g)$$

Complete the table. Assume that all concentrations are equilibrium concentrations in M.

T (K)	[N₂]	[H₂]	[NH₃]	Kc
500	0.115	0.105	0.439	_____
575	0.110	_____	0.128	9.6
775	0.120	0.140	_____	0.0584

38. Consider the following reaction:

$$H_2(g) + I_2(g) \rightleftharpoons 2\ HI(g)$$

Complete the table. Assume that all concentrations are equilibrium concentrations in M.

T (°C)	[H₂]	[I₂]	[HI]	Kc
25	0.0355	0.0388	0.922	_____
340	_____	0.0455	0.387	9.6
445	0.0485	0.0468	_____	50.2

39. Consider the reaction:

$$2\ NO(g) + Br_2(g) \rightleftharpoons 2\ NOBr(g)$$
$$K_p = 28.4 \text{ at } 298\ K$$

In a reaction mixture at equilibrium, the partial pressure of NO is 108 torr and that of Br_2 is 126 torr. What is the partial pressure of NOBr in this mixture?

40. Consider the reaction:

$$SO_2Cl_2(g) \rightleftharpoons SO_2(g) + Cl_2(g)$$
$$K_p = 2.91 \times 10^3 \text{ at } 298\ K$$

In a reaction at equilibrium, the partial pressure of SO_2 is 137 torr and that of Cl_2 is 285 torr. What is the partial pressure of SO_2Cl_2 in this mixture?

41. For the reaction $A(g) \rightleftharpoons 2\ B(g)$, a reaction vessel initially contains only A at a pressure of $P_A = 1.32$ atm. At equilibrium, $P_A = 0.25$ atm. Calculate the value of K_p. (Assume no changes in volume or temperature.)

42. For the reaction $2\ A(g) \rightleftharpoons B(g) + 2\ C(g)$, a reaction vessel initially contains only A at a pressure of $P_A = 255$ mmHg. At equilibrium, $P_A = 55$ mmHg. Calculate the value of K_p. (Assume no changes in volume or temperature.)

43. Consider the reaction:

$$Fe^{3+}(aq) + SCN^-(aq) \rightleftharpoons FeSCN^{2+}(aq)$$

A solution is made containing an initial $[Fe^{3+}]$ of 1.0×10^{-3} M and an initial $[SCN^-]$ of 8.0×10^{-4} M. At equilibrium, $[FeSCN^{2+}] = 1.7 \times 10^{-4}$ M. Calculate the value of the equilibrium constant (K_c).

44. Consider the reaction:

$$SO_2Cl_2(g) \rightleftharpoons SO_2(g) + Cl_2(g)$$

A reaction mixture is made containing an initial $[SO_2Cl_2]$ of 0.020 M. At equilibrium, $[Cl_2] = 1.2 \times 10^{-2}$ M. Calculate the value of the equilibrium constant (K_c).

45. Consider the reaction:

$$H_2(g) + I_2(g) \rightleftharpoons 2\ HI(g)$$

A reaction mixture in a 3.67 L flask at a certain temperature initially contains 0.763 g H_2 and 96.9 g I_2. At equilibrium, the flask contains 90.4 g HI. Calculate the equilibrium constant (K_c) for the reaction at this temperature.

46. Consider the reaction:

$$CO(g) + 2\ H_2(g) \rightleftharpoons CH_3OH(g)$$

A reaction mixture in a 5.19 L flask at a certain temperature contains 26.9 g CO and 2.34 g H_2. At equilibrium, the flask contains 8.65 g CH_3OH. Calculate the equilibrium constant (K_c) for the reaction at this temperature.

The Reaction Quotient and Reaction Direction

47. Consider the reaction:

$$NH_4HS(s) \rightleftharpoons NH_3(g) + H_2S(g)$$

At a certain temperature, $K_c = 8.5 \times 10^{-3}$. A reaction mixture at this temperature containing solid NH_4HS has $[NH_3] = 0.166$ M and $[H_2S] = 0.166$ M. Will more of the solid form or will some of the existing solid decompose as equilibrium is reached?

48. Consider the reaction:

$$2\ H_2S(g) \rightleftharpoons 2\ H_2(g) + S_2(g)$$
$$K_p = 2.4 \times 10^{-4} \text{ at } 1073\ K$$

A reaction mixture contains 0.112 atm of H_2, 0.055 atm of S_2, and 0.445 atm of H_2S. Is the reaction mixture at equilibrium? If not, in what direction will the reaction proceed?

49. Silver sulfate dissolves in water according to the reaction:

$$Ag_2SO_4(s) \rightleftharpoons 2\, Ag^+(aq) + SO_4^{2-}(aq)$$
$$K_c = 1.1 \times 10^{-5} \text{ at } 298 \text{ K}$$

A 1.5 L solution contains 6.55 g of dissolved silver sulfate. If additional solid silver sulfate is added to the solution, will it dissolve?

50. Nitrogen dioxide dimerizes according to the reaction:

$$2\, NO_2(g) \rightleftharpoons N_2O_4(g)$$
$$K_p = 6.7 \text{ at } 298 \text{ K}$$

A 2.25 L container contains 0.055 mol of NO_2 and 0.082 mol of N_2O_4 at 298 K. Is the reaction at equilibrium? If not, in what direction will the reaction proceed?

Finding Equilibrium Concentrations from Initial Concentrations and the Equilibrium Constant

51. Consider the reaction and the associated equilibrium constant:

$$aA(g) \rightleftharpoons bB(g) \qquad K_c = 4.0$$

Find the equilibrium concentrations of A and B for each value of a and b. Assume that the initial concentration of A in each case is 1.0 M and that no B is present at the beginning of the reaction.
a. $a = 1$; $b = 1$
b. $a = 2$; $b = 2$
c. $a = 1$; $b = 2$

52. Consider the reaction and the associated equilibrium constant:

$$aA(g) + bB(g) \rightleftharpoons cC(g) \qquad K_c = 5.0$$

Find the equilibrium concentrations of A, B, and C for each value of a, b, and c. Assume that the initial concentrations of A and B are each 1.0 M and that no product is present at the beginning of the reaction.
a. $a = 1$; $b = 1$; $c = 2$
b. $a = 1$; $b = 1$; $c = 1$
c. $a = 2$; $b = 1$; $c = 1$ (set up equation for x; don't solve)

53. For the reaction, $K_c = 0.513$ at 500 K.

$$N_2O_4(g) \rightleftharpoons 2\, NO_2(g)$$

If a reaction vessel initially contains an N_2O_4 concentration of 0.0500 M at 500 K, what are the equilibrium concentrations of N_2O_4 and NO_2 at 500 K?

54. For the reaction, $K_c = 255$ at 1000 K.

$$CO(g) + Cl_2(g) \rightleftharpoons COCl_2(g)$$

If a reaction mixture initially contains a CO concentration of 0.1500 M and a Cl_2 concentration of 0.175 M at 1000 K, what are the equilibrium concentrations of CO, Cl_2, and $COCl_2$ at 1000 K?

55. Consider the reaction:

$$NiO(s) + CO(g) \rightleftharpoons Ni(s) + CO_2(g)$$
$$K_c = 4.0 \times 10^3 \text{ at } 1500 \text{ K}$$

If a mixture of solid nickel(II) oxide and 0.20 M carbon monoxide comes to equilibrium at 1500 K, what is the equilibrium concentration of CO_2?

56. Consider the reaction:

$$CO(g) + H_2O(g) \rightleftharpoons CO_2(g) + H_2(g)$$
$$K_c = 102 \text{ at } 500 \text{ K}$$

If a reaction mixture initially contains 0.110 M CO and 0.110 M H_2O, what will the equilibrium concentration of each of the reactants and products be?

57. Consider the reaction:

$$HC_2H_3O_2(aq) + H_2O(l) \rightleftharpoons H_3O^+(aq) + C_2H_3O_2^-(aq)$$
$$K_c = 1.8 \times 10^{-5} \text{ at } 25\,^\circ C$$

If a solution initially contains 0.210 M $HC_2H_3O_2$, what is the equilibrium concentration of H_3O^+ at 25 °C?

58. Consider the reaction:

$$SO_2Cl_2(g) \rightleftharpoons SO_2(g) + Cl_2(g)$$
$$K_c = 2.99 \times 10^{-7} \text{ at } 227\,^\circ C$$

If a reaction mixture initially contains 0.175 M SO_2Cl_2, what is the equilibrium concentration of Cl_2 at 227 °C?

59. Consider the reaction:

$$Br_2(g) + Cl_2(g) \rightleftharpoons 2\, BrCl(g)$$
$$K_p = 1.11 \times 10^{-4} \text{ at } 150 \text{ K}$$

A reaction mixture initially contains a Br_2 partial pressure of 755 torr and a Cl_2 partial pressure of 735 torr at 150 K. Calculate the equilibrium partial pressure of BrCl.

60. Consider the reaction:

$$CO(g) + H_2O(g) \rightleftharpoons CO_2(g) + H_2(g)$$
$$K_p = 0.0611 \text{ at } 2000 \text{ K}$$

A reaction mixture initially contains a CO partial pressure of 1344 torr and a H_2O partial pressure of 1766 torr at 2000 K. Calculate the equilibrium partial pressures of each of the products.

61. Consider the reaction:

$$A(g) \rightleftharpoons B(g) + C(g)$$

Find the equilibrium concentrations of A, B, and C for each value of K_c. Assume that the initial concentration of A in each case is 1.0 M and that the reaction mixture initially contains no products. Make any appropriate simplifying assumptions.
a. $K_c = 1.0$
b. $K_c = 0.010$
c. $K_c = 1.0 \times 10^{-5}$

62. Consider the reaction:

$$A(g) \rightleftharpoons 2\, B(g)$$

Find the equilibrium partial pressures of A and B for each value of K. Assume that the initial partial pressure of B in each case is 1.0 atm and that the initial partial pressure of A is 0.0 atm. Make any appropriate simplifying assumptions.
a. $K_c = 1.0$
b. $K_c = 1.0 \times 10^{-4}$
c. $K_c = 1.0 \times 10^5$

Le Châtelier's Principle

63. Consider this reaction at equilibrium:

$$CO(g) + Cl_2(g) \rightleftharpoons COCl_2(g)$$

Predict whether the reaction will shift left, shift right, or remain unchanged after each disturbance:
a. $COCl_2$ is added to the reaction mixture.
b. Cl_2 is added to the reaction mixture.
c. $COCl_2$ is removed from the reaction mixture.

64. Consider this reaction at equilibrium:

$$2\,BrNO(g) \rightleftharpoons 2\,NO(g) + Br_2(g)$$

Predict whether the reaction will shift left, shift right, or remain unchanged after each disturbance.
a. NO is added to the reaction mixture.
b. BrNO is added to the reaction mixture.
c. Br_2 is removed from the reaction mixture.

65. Consider this reaction at equilibrium:

$$2\,KClO_3(s) \rightleftharpoons 2\,KCl(s) + 3\,O_2(g)$$

Predict whether the reaction will shift left, shift right, or remain unchanged after each disturbance.
a. O_2 is removed from the reaction mixture.
b. KCl is added to the reaction mixture.
c. $KClO_3$ is added to the reaction mixture.
d. O_2 is added to the reaction mixture.

66. Consider this reaction at equilibrium:

$$C(s) + H_2O(g) \rightleftharpoons CO(g) + H_2(g)$$

Predict whether the reaction will shift left, shift right, or remain unchanged after each disturbance.
a. C is added to the reaction mixture.
b. H_2O is condensed and removed from the reaction mixture.
c. CO is added to the reaction mixture.
d. H_2 is removed from the reaction mixture.

67. Each reaction is allowed to come to equilibrium and then the volume is changed as indicated. Predict the effect (shift right, shift left, or no effect) of the indicated volume change.
a. $I_2(g) \rightleftharpoons 2\,I(g)$ (volume is increased)
b. $2\,H_2S(g) \rightleftharpoons 2\,H_2(g) + S_2(g)$ (volume is decreased)
c. $I_2(g) + Cl_2(g) \rightleftharpoons 2\,ICl(g)$ (volume is decreased)

68. Each reaction is allowed to come to equilibrium and then the volume is changed as indicated. Predict the effect (shift right, shift left, or no effect) of the indicated volume change.
a. $CO(g) + H_2O(g) \rightleftharpoons CO_2(g) + H_2(g)$ (volume is decreased)
b. $PCl_3(g) + Cl_2(g) \rightleftharpoons PCl_5(g)$ (volume is increased)
c. $CaCO_3(s) \rightleftharpoons CaO(s) + CO_2(g)$ (volume is increased)

69. This reaction is endothermic.

$$C(s) + CO_2(g) \rightleftharpoons 2\,CO(g)$$

Predict the effect (shift right, shift left, or no effect) of increasing and decreasing the reaction temperature. How does the value of the equilibrium constant depend on temperature?

70. This reaction is exothermic.

$$C_6H_{12}O_6(s) + 6\,O_2(g) \rightleftharpoons 6\,CO_2(g) + 6\,H_2O(g)$$

Predict the effect (shift right, shift left, or no effect) of increasing and decreasing the reaction temperature. How does the value of the equilibrium constant depend on temperature?

71. Coal, which is primarily carbon, can be converted to natural gas, primarily CH_4, by the exothermic reaction:

$$C(s) + 2\,H_2(g) \rightleftharpoons CH_4(g)$$

Which disturbance will favor CH_4 at equilibrium?
a. adding more C to the reaction mixture
b. adding more H_2 to the reaction mixture
c. raising the temperature of the reaction mixture
d. lowering the volume of the reaction mixture
e. adding a catalyst to the reaction mixture
f. adding neon gas to the reaction mixture

72. Coal can be used to generate hydrogen gas (a potential fuel) by the endothermic reaction:

$$C(s) + H_2O(g) \rightleftharpoons CO(g) + H_2(g)$$

If this reaction mixture is at equilibrium, predict whether each disturbance will result in the formation of additional hydrogen gas, the formation of less hydrogen gas, or have no effect on the quantity of hydrogen gas.
a. adding more C to the reaction mixture
b. adding more H_2O to the reaction mixture
c. raising the temperature of the reaction mixture
d. increasing the volume of the reaction mixture
e. adding a catalyst to the reaction mixture
f. adding an inert gas to the reaction mixture

Cumulative Problems

73. Carbon monoxide replaces oxygen in oxygenated hemoglobin according to the reaction:

$$HbO_2(aq) + CO(aq) \rightleftharpoons HbCO(aq) + O_2(aq)$$

a. Use the reactions and associated equilibrium constants at body temperature to find the equilibrium constant for the reaction just shown.

$$Hb(aq) + O_2(aq) \rightleftharpoons HbO_2(aq) \quad K_c = 1.8$$
$$Hb(aq) + CO(aq) \rightleftharpoons HbCO(aq) \quad K_c = 306$$

b. Suppose that an air mixture becomes polluted with carbon monoxide at a level of 0.10%. Assuming the air contains 20.0% oxygen, and that the oxygen and carbon monoxide ratios that dissolve in the blood are identical to the ratios in the air, what is the ratio of HbCO to HbO_2 in the blood stream? Comment on the toxicity of carbon monoxide.

74. Nitrogen oxide is a pollutant in the lower atmosphere that irritates the eyes and lungs and leads to the formation of acid rain. Nitrogen oxide forms naturally in atmosphere according to the endothermic reaction:

$$N_2(g) + O_2(g) \rightleftharpoons 2\,NO(g) \quad K_p = 4.1 \times 10^{-31} \text{ at } 298 \text{ K}$$

Use the ideal gas law to calculate the concentrations of nitrogen and oxygen present in air at a pressure of 1.0 atm and a temperature of 298 K. Assume that nitrogen composes 78% of air by volume and that oxygen composes 21% of air. Find the "natural" equilibrium concentration of NO in air in units of molecules/cm³. How would you expect this concentration to change in an automobile engine in which combustion is occurring?

75. The reaction $CO_2(g) + C(s) \rightleftharpoons 2\,CO(g)$ has $K_p = 5.78$ at 1200 K.
    a. Calculate the total pressure at equilibrium when 4.45 g of CO_2 is introduced into a 10.0 L container and heated to 1200 K in the presence of 2.00 g of graphite.
    b. Repeat the calculation of part a in the presence of 0.50 g of graphite.

76. A mixture of water and graphite is heated to 600 K. When the system comes to equilibrium it contains 0.13 mol of H_2, 0.13 mol of CO, 0.43 mol of H_2O, and some graphite. Some O_2 is added to the system and a spark is applied so that the H_2 reacts completely with the O_2. Find the amount of CO in the flask when the system returns to equilibrium.

77. At 650 K, the reaction $MgCO_3(s) \rightleftharpoons MgO(s) + CO_2(g)$ has $K_p = 0.026$. A 10.0 L container at 650 K has 1.0 g of MgO(s) and CO_2 at P = 0.0260 atm. The container is then compressed to a volume of 0.100 L. Find the mass of $MgCO_3$ that is formed.

78. A system at equilibrium contains $I_2(g)$ at a pressure of 0.21 atm and I(g) at a pressure of 0.23 atm. The system is then compressed to half its volume. Find the pressure of each gas when the system returns to equilibrium.

79. Consider the exothermic reaction:
    $$C_2H_4(g) + Cl_2(g) \rightleftharpoons C_2H_4Cl_2(g)$$
    If you were trying to maximize the amount of $C_2H_4Cl_2$ produced, which tactic might you try? Assume that the reaction mixture reaches equilibrium.
    a. increasing the reaction volume
    b. removing $C_2H_4Cl_2$ from the reaction mixture as it forms
    c. lowering the reaction temperature
    d. adding Cl_2

80. Consider the endothermic reaction:
    $$C_2H_4(g) + I_2(g) \rightleftharpoons C_2H_4I_2(g)$$
    If you were trying to maximize the amount of $C_2H_4I_2$ produced, which tactic might you try? Assume that the reaction mixture reaches equilibrium.
    a. decreasing the reaction volume
    b. removing I_2 from the reaction mixture
    c. raising the reaction temperature
    d. adding C_2H_4 to the reaction mixture

81. Consider the reaction:
    $$H_2(g) + I_2(g) \rightleftharpoons 2\,HI(g)$$
    A reaction mixture at equilibrium at 175 K contains $P_{H_2} = 0.958$ atm, $P_{I_2} = 0.877$ atm, and $P_{HI} = 0.020$ atm. A second reaction mixture, also at 175 K, contains $P_{H_2} = P_{I_2} = 0.621$ atm and $P_{HI} = 0.101$ atm. Is the second reaction at equilibrium? If not, what will be the partial pressure of HI when the reaction reaches equilibrium at 175 K?

82. Consider the reaction:
    $$2\,H_2S(g) + SO_2(g) \rightleftharpoons 3\,S(s) + 2\,H_2O(g)$$
    A reaction mixture initially containing 0.500 M H_2S and 0.500 M SO_2 contains 0.0011 M H_2O at a certain temperature. A second reaction mixture at the same temperature initially contains $[H_2S] = 0.250\,M$ and $[SO_2] = 0.325\,M$. Calculate the equilibrium concentration of H_2O in the second mixture at this temperature.

83. Ammonia can be synthesized according to the reaction:
    $$N_2(g) + 3\,H_2(g) \rightleftharpoons 2\,NH_3(g)$$
    $$K_p = 5.3 \times 10^{-5} \text{ at 725 K}$$
    A 200.0 L reaction container initially contains 1.27 kg of N_2 and 0.310 kg of H_2 at 725 K. Assuming ideal gas behavior, calculate the mass of NH_3 (in g) present in the reaction mixture at equilibrium. What is the percent yield of the reaction under these conditions?

84. Hydrogen can be extracted from natural gas according to the reaction:
    $$CH_4(g) + CO_2(g) \rightleftharpoons 2\,CO(g) + 2\,H_2(g)$$
    $$K_p = 4.5 \times 10^2 \text{ at 825 K}$$
    An 85.0 L reaction container initially contains 22.3 kg of CH_4 and 55.4 kg of CO_2 at 825 K. Assuming ideal gas behavior, calculate the mass of H_2 (in g) present in the reaction mixture at equilibrium. What is the percent yield of the reaction under these conditions?

85. The system described by the reaction: $CO(g) + Cl_2(g) \rightleftharpoons COCl_2(g)$ is at equilibrium at a given temperature when $P_{CO} = 0.30$ atm, $P_{Cl_2} = 0.10$ atm, and $P_{COCl_2} = 0.60$ atm. An additional pressure of $Cl_2(g) = 0.40$ atm is added. Find the pressure of CO when the system returns to equilibrium.

86. A reaction vessel at 27 °C contains a mixture of SO_2 (P = 3.00 atm) and O_2 (P = 1.00 atm). When a catalyst is added, this reaction takes place: $2\,SO_2(g) + O_2(g) \rightleftharpoons 2\,SO_3(g)$. At equilibrium, the total pressure is 3.75 atm. Find the value of K_c.

87. At 70 K, CCl_4 decomposes to carbon and chlorine. The K_p for the decomposition is 0.76. Find the starting pressure of CCl_4 at this temperature that will produce a total pressure of 1.0 atm at equilibrium.

88. The equilibrium constant for the reaction $SO_2(g) + NO_2(g) \rightleftharpoons SO_3(g) + NO(g)$ is 3.0. Find the amount of NO_2 that must be added to 2.4 mol of SO_2 in order to form 1.2 mol of SO_3 at equilibrium.

89. A sample of $CaCO_3(s)$ is introduced into a sealed container of volume 0.654 L and heated to 1000 K until equilibrium is reached. The K_p for the reaction $CaCO_3(s) \rightleftharpoons CaO(s) + CO_2(g)$ is 3.9×10^{-2} at this temperature. Calculate the mass of CaO(s) that is present at equilibrium.

90. An equilibrium mixture contains N_2O_4, (P = 0.28 atm) and NO_2 (P = 1.1 atm) at 350 K. The volume of the container is doubled at constant temperature. Calculate the equilibrium pressures of the two gases when the system reaches a new equilibrium.

91. Carbon monoxide and chlorine gas react to form phosgene:
    $$CO(g) + Cl_2(g) \rightleftharpoons COCl_2(g) \quad K_p = 3.10 \text{ at 700 K}$$
    If a reaction mixture initially contains 215 torr of CO and 245 torr of Cl_2, what is the mole fraction of $COCl_2$ when equilibrium is reached?

92. Solid carbon can react with gaseous water to form carbon monoxide gas and hydrogen gas. The equilibrium constant for the reaction at 700.0 K is $K_p = 1.60 \times 10^{-3}$. If a 1.55 L reaction vessel initially contains 145 torr of water at 700.0 K in contact with excess solid carbon, find the percent by mass of hydrogen gas of the gaseous reaction mixture at equilibrium.

Challenge Problems

93. Consider the reaction:

$$2\,NO(g) + O_2(g) \rightleftharpoons 2\,NO_2(g)$$

a. A reaction mixture at 175 K initially contains 522 torr of NO and 421 torr of O_2. At equilibrium, the total pressure in the reaction mixture is 748 torr. Calculate K_p at this temperature.

b. A second reaction mixture at 175 K initially contains 255 torr of NO and 185 torr of O_2. What is the equilibrium partial pressure of NO_2 in this mixture?

94. Consider the reaction:

$$2\,SO_2(g) + O_2(g) \rightleftharpoons 2\,SO_3(g)$$
$$K_p = 0.355 \text{ at } 950 \text{ K}$$

A 2.75 L reaction vessel at 950 K initially contains 0.100 mol of SO_2 and 0.100 mol of O_2. Calculate the total pressure (in atmospheres) in the reaction vessel when equilibrium is reached.

95. Nitric oxide reacts with chlorine gas according to the reaction:

$$2\,NO(g) + Cl_2(g) \rightleftharpoons 2\,NOCl(g)$$
$$K_p = 0.27 \text{ at } 700 \text{ K}$$

A reaction mixture initially contains equal partial pressures of NO and Cl_2. At equilibrium, the partial pressure of NOCl is 115 torr. What were the initial partial pressures of NO and Cl_2?

96. At a given temperature, a system containing $O_2(g)$ and some oxides of nitrogen can be described by these reactions:

$$2\,NO(g) + O_2(g) \rightleftharpoons 2\,NO_2(g) \quad K_p = 10^4$$
$$2\,NO_2(g) \rightleftharpoons N_2O_4(g) \quad K_p = 0.10$$

A pressure of 1 atm of $N_2O_4(g)$ is placed in a container at this temperature. Predict which, if any, component (other than N_2O_4) will be present at a pressure greater than 0.2 atm at equilibrium.

97. A sample of pure NO_2 is heated to 337 °C, at which temperature it partially dissociates according to the equation:

$$2\,NO_2(g) \rightleftharpoons 2\,NO(g) + O_2(g)$$

At equilibrium the density of the gas mixture is 0.520 g/L at 0.750 atm. Calculate K_c for the reaction.

98. When $N_2O_5(g)$ is heated it dissociates into $N_2O_3(g)$ and $O_2(g)$ according to the reaction:

$$N_2O_5(g) \rightleftharpoons N_2O_3(g) + O_2(g)$$
$$K_c = 7.75 \text{ at a given temperature}$$

The $N_2O_3(g)$ dissociates to give $N_2O(g)$ and $O_2(g)$ according the reaction:

$$N_2O_3(g) \rightleftharpoons N_2O(g) + O_2(g)$$
$$K_c = 4.00 \text{ at the same temperature}$$

When 4.00 mol of $N_2O_5(g)$ is heated in a 1.00 L reaction vessel to this temperature, the concentration of $O_2(g)$ at equilibrium is 4.50 mol/L. Find the concentrations of all the other species in the equilibrium system.

99. A sample of SO_3 is introduced into an evacuated sealed container and heated to 600 K. The following equilibrium is established:

$$2\,SO_3(g) \rightleftharpoons 2\,SO_2(g) + O_2(g)$$

The total pressure in the system is 3.0 atm and the mole fraction of O_2 is 0.12. Find K_p.

Conceptual Problems

100. A reaction $A(g) \rightleftharpoons B(g)$ has an equilibrium constant of 1.0×10^{-4}. For which of the initial reaction mixtures is the x is *small* approximation most likely to apply?
a. [A] = 0.0010 M; [B] = 0.00 M
b. [A] = 0.00 M; [B] = 0.10 M
c. [A] = 0.10 M; [B] = 0.10 M
d. [A] = 0.10 M; [B] = 0.00 M

101. The reaction $A(g) \rightleftharpoons 2\,B(g)$ has an equilibrium constant of $K_c = 1.0$ at a given temperature. If a reaction vessel contains equal initial amounts (in moles) of A and B, will the direction in which the reaction proceeds depend on the volume of the reaction vessel? Explain.

102. A particular reaction has an equilibrium constant of $K_p = 0.50$. A reaction mixture is prepared in which all the reactants and products are in their standard states. In which direction will the reaction proceed?

103. Consider the reaction:

$$aA(g) \rightleftharpoons bB(g)$$

Each of the entries in the following table represents equilibrium partial pressures of A and B under different initial conditions. What are the values of a and b in the reaction?

P_A (atm)	P_B (atm)
4.0	2.0
2.0	1.4
1.0	1.0
0.50	0.71
0.25	0.50

104. Consider the simple one-step reaction:

$$A(g) \rightleftharpoons B(g)$$

Since the reaction occurs in a single step, the forward reaction has a rate of $k_{for}[A]$ and the reverse reaction has a rate of $k_{rev}[B]$. What happens to the rate of the forward reaction when we increase the concentration of A? How does this explain the reason behind Le Châtelier's principle?

Answers to Conceptual Connections

Equilibrium Constants

14.1 **(b)** The reaction mixture will contain [A] = 0.1 M and [B] = 1.0 M so that [B]/[A] = 10.

The Equilibrium Constant and the Chemical Equation

14.2 **(b)** The reaction is reversed and divided through by two. Therefore, you invert the equilibrium constant and take the square root of the result. $K = (1/0.010)^{1/2} = 10$.

The Relationship between K_p and K_c

14.3 **(a)** When $a + b = c + d$, the quantity Δn is zero so that $K_p = K_c (RT)^0$. Since $(RT)^0$ is equal to 1, $K_p = K_c$.

Heterogeneous Equilibria, K_p, and K_c

14.4 **(b)** Since Δn for gaseous reactants and products is zero, K_p equals K_c.

Q and K

14.5 **(c)** Because N_2O_4 and NO_2 are both in their standard states, they each have a partial pressure of 1.0 atm. Consequently, $Q_p = 1$. Since $K_p = 0.15$, $Q_p > K_p$, and the reaction proceeds to the left.

The x Is *Small* Approximation

14.6 **(a)** The *x is small* approximation is most likely to apply to a reaction with a small equilibrium constant and an initial concentration of reactant that is not too small. The bigger the equilibrium constant and the smaller the initial concentration of reactant, the less likely that the *x is small* approximation will apply.

15 Acids and Bases

The differences between the various acid–base concepts are not concerned with which is right, but which is most convenient to use in a particular situation.

—James E. Huheey (1935–)

N THIS CHAPTER, we apply the equilibrium concepts learned in the previous chapter to acid–base phenomena. Acids are common in many foods, such as limes, lemons, and vinegar, and in a number of consumer products, such as toilet cleaners and batteries. Bases are less common in foods but are key ingredients in consumer products such as drain openers and antacids. We will examine three different models for acid–base behavior, all of which define that behavior differently. In spite of their differences, the three models coexist, each being useful at explaining a particular range of acid–base phenomena. We also examine how to calculate the acidity or basicity of solutions and define a useful scale, called the pH scale, to quantify acidity and basicity. These types of calculations often involve solving the kind of equilibrium problems that we explored in Chapter 14.

Milk of magnesia contains a base that can neutralize stomach acid and relieve heartburn.

15.1 Heartburn

Heartburn is a painful burning sensation in the esophagus (the tube that joins the throat to the stomach) just below the chest. The pain is caused by hydrochloric acid (HCl), which the stomach excretes to kill microorganisms and to activate enzymes that break down food. Hydrochloric acid sometimes backs up out of the stomach and into the esophagus, a phenomenon called *acid reflux*. Recall from Section 4.8 that acids are substances that—by one definition that we elaborate on shortly—produce H^+ ions in solution. When hydrochloric acid from the stomach comes in contact with the lining of the esophagus, the H^+ ions irritate the tissues, resulting in the burning sensation. Some of the acid can work its way into the lower throat and even the mouth, producing pain in the throat and a sour taste (characteristic of acids) in the mouth. Almost everyone experiences heartburn at some time, most commonly after a large meal when the stomach is full. Strenuous activity or lying in a horizontal position after a large meal increases the likelihood of stomach acid reflux and the resulting heartburn.

| Bases were first defined in Section 4.8.

The simplest way to relieve mild heartburn is to swallow repeatedly. Saliva contains the bicarbonate ion (HCO_3^-), which acts as a base and, when swallowed, neutralizes some of the acid in the esophagus. Later in this chapter, we will see how bicarbonate acts as a base. You can also treat heartburn with antacids such as Tums, milk of magnesia, or Mylanta. These over-the-counter medications contain more base than saliva and therefore are effective at neutralizing esophageal acid. We look at the bases in these medicines more carefully later (see the *Chemistry and Medicine* box in Section 15.7).

For some people, heartburn becomes a chronic problem. Gastroesophageal reflux disease (GERD) is the medical condition associated with chronic heartburn. In patients with GERD, the band of muscles (called the esophageal sphincter) at the bottom of the esophagus just above the stomach does not close tightly enough, allowing the stomach contents to leak back into the esophagus on a regular basis. Medical researchers have developed a wireless sensor to help diagnose and evaluate treatment of GERD. Using a tube that goes down through the throat, a physician attaches the sensor to tissues in the patient's esophagus. The sensor reads pH—a measure of acidity that we discuss in Section 15.5—and transmits the readings to a recorder worn on the patient's body. The patient goes about his or her normal business for the next few days while the recorder monitors esophageal pH. The physician then reads the record of esophageal pH to make a diagnosis or evaluate treatment.

| The concentration of stomach acid, [H_3O^+], varies from about 0.01 to 0.1 M.

In this chapter, we examine acid and base behavior. Acids and bases are not only important to our health (as we have just seen), but are also found in many household products, foods, medicines, and of course in nearly every chemistry laboratory. Acid–base chemistry is central to much of biochemistry and molecular biology. The building blocks of proteins, for example, are acids (called amino acids) and the molecules that carry the genetic code in DNA are bases.

15.2 The Nature of Acids and Bases

| For a review of acid naming, see Section 3.6.

Acids have the following general properties: a sour taste, the ability to dissolve many metals, the ability to turn blue litmus paper red, and the ability to neutralize bases. Table 15.1 lists some common acids.

| Litmus paper contains certain dyes that change color in the presence of acids and bases.

You can find hydrochloric acid in most chemistry laboratories. In industry, it is used to clean metals, to prepare and process some foods, and to refine metal ores. As we just discussed in Section 15.1, hydrochloric acid is also the main component of stomach acid.

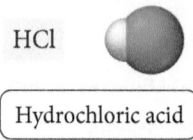

HCl

Hydrochloric acid

| The formula for acetic acid can also be written as CH_3COOH.

TABLE 15.1   Some Common Acids

Name	Occurrence/Uses
Hydrochloric acid (HCl)	Metal cleaning; food preparation; ore refining; primary component of stomach acid
Sulfuric acid (H_2SO_4)	Fertilizer and explosives manufacturing; dye and glue production; automobile batteries; electroplating of copper
Nitric acid (HNO_3)	Fertilizer and explosives manufacturing; dye and glue production
Acetic acid ($HC_2H_3O_2$)	Plastic and rubber manufacturing; food preservative; active component of vinegar
Citric acid ($H_3C_6H_5O_7$)	Present in citrus fruits such as lemons and limes; used to adjust pH in foods and beverages
Carbonic acid (H_2CO_3)	Found in carbonated beverages due to the reaction of carbon dioxide with water
Hydrofluoric acid (HF)	Metal cleaning; glass frosting and etching
Phosphoric acid (H_3PO_4)	Fertilizer manufacture; biological buffering; preservative in beverages

Sulfuric acid and nitric acid are also common in the laboratory. They play major roles in the manufacture of fertilizers, explosives, dyes, and glues. Sulfuric acid, produced in larger quantities than any other industrial chemical, is contained in most automobile batteries.

H_2SO_4

Sulfuric Acid

HNO_3

Nitric Acid

You can probably find acetic acid in your home—it is the active component of vinegar. It is also produced in improperly stored wines. The word *vinegar* originates from the French words *vin aigre*, which means "sour wine". Wine experts consider the presence of vinegar in wines a serious fault, since it makes the wine taste like salad dressing.

$HC_2H_3O_2$

Acetic acid

Acetic acid is a **carboxylic acid**, an acid that contains the following grouping of atoms:

Carboxylic acid group

Carboxylic acids are often found in substances derived from living organisms. Other examples of carboxylic acids are citric acid, the main acid in lemons and limes, and malic acid, found in apples, grapes, and wine.

▲ Acetic acid makes vinegar taste sour.

$H_3C_6H_5O_7$

Citric acid

$H_2C_4H_4O_5$

Malic acid

◀ Citrus fruits, apples, and grapes all contain acids.

▲ Many common household products and remedies contain bases.

Coffee is acidic overall, but bases present in coffee—such as caffeine—and other compounds impart a bitter flavor.

TABLE 15.2 Common Bases

Name	Occurrence/Uses
Sodium hydroxide (NaOH)	Petroleum processing; soap and plastic manufacturing
Potassium hydroxide (KOH)	Cotton processing; electroplating; soap production; batteries
Sodium bicarbonate (NaHCO$_3$)	Antacid; ingredient of baking soda; source of CO$_2$
Sodium carbonate (Na$_2$CO$_3$)	Manufacture of glass and soap; general cleanser; water softener
Ammonia (NH$_3$)	Detergent; fertilizer and explosives manufacturing; synthetic fiber production

Bases have the following general properties: a bitter taste, a slippery feel, the ability to turn red litmus paper blue, and the ability to neutralize acids. Because of their bitterness, bases are less common in foods than are acids. Our aversion to the taste of bases is probably an evolutionary adaptation to warn us against **alkaloids**, organic bases found in plants that are often poisonous. (For example, the active component of hemlock—the poisonous plant that killed the Greek philosopher Socrates—is the alkaloid coniine.) Nonetheless, some foods, such as coffee and chocolate (especially dark chocolate), contain bitter flavors. Many people enjoy the bitterness, but only after acquiring the taste over time.

Bases feel slippery because they react with oils on the skin to form soap-like substances. Some household cleaning solutions, such as ammonia, are basic and have the characteristic slippery feel of a base. Bases turn red litmus paper blue; in the laboratory, litmus paper is routinely used to test the basicity of solutions.

Some common bases are listed in Table 15.2. You can find sodium hydroxide and potassium hydroxide in most chemistry laboratories. They are used in petroleum and cotton processing and in soap and plastic manufacturing. Sodium hydroxide is the active ingredient in products such as Drāno that unclog drains. In many homes, you can find sodium bicarbonate in the medicine cabinet (it is an active ingredient in some antacids) as well as in the kitchen (labeled as baking soda).

15.3 Definitions of Acids and Bases

What are the main characteristics of the molecules and ions that exhibit acid and base behavior? In this chapter, we examine three different definitions: the Arrhenius definition, the Brønsted–Lowry definition, and the Lewis definition. Why three definitions, and which one is correct? As Huheey noted in the quotation that opens this chapter, no single definition is "correct." Rather, each definition is useful in a given instance. We discuss the Lewis definition of acids and bases in Section 15.11; here we discuss the other two.

The Arrhenius Definition

In the 1880s, Swedish chemist Svante Arrhenius proposed the following molecular definitions of acids and bases:

Acid: A substance that produces H$^+$ ions in aqueous solution.

Base: A substance that produces OH$^-$ ions in aqueous solution.

According to the **Arrhenius definition**, HCl is an acid because it produces H$^+$ ions in solution (Figure 15.1 ◄):

$$\text{HCl}(aq) \longrightarrow \text{H}^+(aq) + \text{Cl}^-(aq)$$

Hydrogen chloride (HCl) is a covalent compound and does not contain ions. However, in water it *ionizes* completely to form H$^+$(aq) ions and Cl$^-$(aq) ions. The H$^+$ ions are highly reactive. In aqueous solution, the ions bond to water to form H$_3$O$^+$:

$$\text{H}^+ + \overset{\cdot\cdot}{\underset{\cdot\cdot}{\text{O}}}\text{:H} \longrightarrow \left[\text{H:}\overset{\text{H}}{\underset{\cdot\cdot}{\text{O}}}\text{:H} \right]^+$$

Arrhenius Acid

HCl

HCl(aq) ⟶ H$^+$(aq) + Cl$^-$(aq)

▲ **FIGURE 15.1 Arrhenius Acid**
An Arrhenius acid produces H$^+$ ions in solution.

The H_3O^+ ion is called the **hydronium ion**. In water, H^+ ions *always* associate with H_2O molecules to form hydronium ions and other associated species with the general formula $H(H_2O)_n^+$. For example, an H^+ ion can associate with two water molecules to form $H(H_2O)_2^+$, with three to form $H(H_2O)_3^+$, and so on. Chemists often use $H^+(aq)$ and $H_3O^+(aq)$ interchangeably to mean the same thing—an H^+ ion that has been solvated (or dissolved) in water.

According to the Arrhenius definition, NaOH is a base because it produces OH^- ions in solution (Figure 15.2 ▶):

$$NaOH(aq) \longrightarrow Na^+(aq) + OH^-(aq)$$

NaOH is an ionic compound and therefore contains Na^+ and OH^- ions. When NaOH is added to water, it *dissociates* or breaks apart into its component ions.

Under the Arrhenius definition, acids and bases combine to form water, neutralizing each other in the process:

$$H^+(aq) + OH^-(aq) \longrightarrow H_2O(l)$$

Arrhenius Base

NaOH

$$NaOH(aq) \longrightarrow Na^+(aq) + OH^-(aq)$$

▲ FIGURE 15.2 **Arrhenius Base** An Arrhenius base produces OH^- ions in solution.

The Brønsted–Lowry Definition

A second, more widely applicable definition of acids and bases, called the **Brønsted–Lowry definition**, was introduced in 1923. This definition focuses on the *transfer of H^+ ions* in an acid–base reaction. Since an H^+ ion is a proton—a hydrogen atom without its electron—this definition focuses on the idea of a proton donor and a proton acceptor:

Acid: proton (H^+ ion) *donor*

Base: proton (H^+ ion) *acceptor*

According to this definition, HCl is an acid because, in solution, it donates a proton to water:

$$HCl(aq) + H_2O(l) \longrightarrow H_3O^+(aq) + Cl^-(aq)$$

This definition clearly describes what happens to the H^+ ion from an acid—it associates with a water molecule to form H_3O^+ (a hydronium ion). The Brønsted–Lowry definition also applies nicely to bases (such as NH_3) that do not inherently contain OH^- ions but still produce OH^- ions in solution. According to the Brønsted–Lowry definition, NH_3 is a base because it accepts a proton from water:

$$NH_3(aq) + H_2O(l) \rightleftharpoons NH_4^+(aq) + OH^-(aq)$$

According to the Brønsted–Lowry definition, acids (proton donors) and bases (proton acceptors) always occur together in an acid–base reaction. In the reaction between HCl and H_2O, HCl is the proton donor (acid) and H_2O is the proton acceptor (base).

$$\underset{\substack{\text{acid} \\ \text{(proton donor)}}}{HCl(aq)} + \underset{\substack{\text{base} \\ \text{(proton acceptor)}}}{H_2O(l)} \longrightarrow H_3O^+(aq) + Cl^-(aq)$$

In the reaction between NH_3 and H_2O, H_2O is the proton donor (acid) and NH_3 is the proton acceptor (base).

$$\underset{\substack{\text{base} \\ \text{(proton acceptor)}}}{NH_3(aq)} + \underset{\substack{\text{acid} \\ \text{(proton donor)}}}{H_2O(l)} \rightleftharpoons NH_4^+(aq) + OH^-(aq)$$

According to the Brønsted–Lowry definition, some substances—such as water in the previous two equations—can act as acids *or* bases. Substances that can act as acids or bases are **amphoteric**. Notice what happens when we reverse an equation representing a Brønsted–Lowry acid–base reaction.

$$\underset{\substack{\text{acid} \\ \text{(proton donor)}}}{NH_4^+(aq)} + \underset{\substack{\text{base} \\ \text{(proton acceptor)}}}{OH^-(aq)} \rightleftharpoons NH_3(aq) + H_2O(l)$$

All Arrhenius acids and bases are acids and bases under the Brønsted-Lowry definition. However, some Brønsted-Lowry acids and bases cannot be classified as Arrhenius acids and bases.

▶ **FIGURE 15.3 Conjugate Acid-Base Pairs**   A conjugate acid–base pair consists of two substances related to each other by the transfer of a proton.

Conjugate acid–base pair

Conjugate acid–base pair

In this reaction, NH_4^+ is the proton donor (acid) and OH^- is the proton acceptor (base). The substance that was the base (NH_3) has become the acid (NH_4^+) and vice versa. NH_4^+ and NH_3 are often referred to as a **conjugate acid–base pair**, two substances related to each other by the transfer of a proton (Figure 15.3 ▲). A **conjugate acid** is any base to which a proton has been added, and a **conjugate base** is any acid from which a proton has been removed. Going back to the original forward reaction, we can identify the conjugate acid–base pairs:

$$NH_3(aq) + H_2O(l) \rightleftharpoons NH_4^+(aq) + OH^-(aq)$$

Base   Acid   Conjugate acid   Conjugate base

Summarizing the Brønsted–Lowry Definition of Acids and Bases:

▶ A base accepts a proton and becomes a conjugate acid.

▶ An acid donates a proton and becomes a conjugate base.

EXAMPLE 15.1   Identifying Brønsted–Lowry Acids and Bases and Their Conjugates

In each reaction, identify the Brønsted–Lowry acid, the Brønsted–Lowry base, the conjugate acid, and the conjugate base.

(a) $H_2SO_4(aq) + H_2O(l) \longrightarrow HSO_4^-(aq) + H_3O^+(aq)$

(b) $HCO_3^-(aq) + H_2O(l) \rightleftharpoons H_2CO_3(aq) + OH^-(aq)$

SOLUTION

(a) Because H_2SO_4 donates a proton to H_2O in this reaction, it is the acid (proton donor). After H_2SO_4 donates the proton, it becomes HSO_4^-, the conjugate base. Because H_2O accepts a proton, it is the base (proton acceptor). After H_2O accepts the proton, it becomes H_3O^+, the conjugate acid.	$H_2SO_4(aq) + H_2O(l) \longrightarrow HSO_4^-(aq) + H_3O^+(aq)$ $H_2SO_4(aq) + H_2O(l) \longrightarrow HSO_4^-(aq) + H_3O^+(aq)$ Acid Base Conjugate base Conjugate acid
(b) Because H_2O donates a proton to HCO_3^- in this reaction, it is the acid (proton donor). After H_2O donates the proton, it becomes OH^-, the conjugate base. Because HCO_3^- accepts a proton, it is the base (proton acceptor). After HCO_3^- accepts the proton, it becomes H_2CO_3, the conjugate acid.	$HCO_3^-(aq) + H_2O(l) \rightleftharpoons H_2CO_3(aq) + OH^-(aq)$ $HCO_3^-(aq) + H_2O(l) \rightleftharpoons H_2CO_3(aq) + OH^-(aq)$ Base Acid Conjugate acid Conjugate base

FOR PRACTICE 15.1

In each reaction, identify the Brønsted–Lowry acid, the Brønsted–Lowry base, the conjugate acid, and the conjugate base.

(a) $C_5H_5N(aq) + H_2O(l) \rightleftharpoons C_5H_5NH^+(aq) + OH^-(aq)$

(b) $HNO_3(aq) + H_2O(l) \rightleftharpoons H_3O^+(aq) + NO_3^-(aq)$

Conceptual Connection 15.1 Conjugate Acid–Base Pairs

Which pair is not a conjugate acid–base pair?

(a) $(CH_3)_3\,N; (CH_3)_3\,NH^+$ **(b)** $H_2SO_4; H_2SO_3$ **(c)** $HNO_2; NO_2^-$

15.4 Acid Strength and the Acid Ionization Constant (K_a)

The strength of an electrolyte, first discussed in Section 4.5, depends on the extent of its dissociation into its component ions in solution. A *strong electrolyte* completely dissociates into ions in solution, whereas a *weak electrolyte* only partially dissociates. We define strong and weak acids accordingly. A **strong acid** completely ionizes in solution, whereas a **weak acid** only partially ionizes. In other words, the strength of an acid depends on the equilibrium:

$$HA(aq) + H_2O(l) \rightleftharpoons H_3O^+(aq) + A^-(aq)$$

In the preceding equation, HA is a generic formula for an acid. If the equilibrium lies far to the right, the acid is strong—it completely ionizes. If the equilibrium lies to the left, the acid is weak—only a small percentage of the acid molecules ionize. Of course, the range of acid strength is continuous, but for most purposes, the categories of strong and weak are useful.

Strong Acids

Hydrochloric acid (HCl) is an example of a strong acid.

Single arrow indicates complete ionization.

$$HCl(aq) + H_2O(l) \longrightarrow H_3O^+(aq) + Cl^-(aq)$$

An HCl solution contains virtually no intact HCl; the HCl has essentially all ionized to form $H_3O^+(aq)$ and $Cl^-(aq)$ (Figure 15.4 ▼). A 1.0 M HCl solution has an H_3O^+ concentration of 1.0 M. Abbreviating the concentration of H_3O^+ as $[H_3O^+]$, we say that a 1.0 M HCl solution has $[H_3O^+] = 1.0$ M.

Table 15.3 lists the six important strong acids. The first five acids in the table are **monoprotic acids**, acids containing only one ionizable proton. Sulfuric acid is an example of a **diprotic acid**, an acid containing two ionizable protons.

An ionizable proton is one that ionizes in solution. We discuss polyprotic acids in more detail in Section 15.9.

TABLE 15.3 Strong Acids

Hydrochloric acid (HCl)	Nitric acid (HNO$_3$)
Hydrobromic acid (HBr)	Perchloric acid (HClO$_4$)
Hydriodic acid (HI)	Sulfuric acid (H$_2$SO$_4$) (*diprotic*)

A Strong Acid

When HCl dissolves in water, it ionizes completely.

◀ **FIGURE 15.4 Ionization of a Strong Acid**   When HCl dissolves in water, it completely ionizes to form H_3O^+ and Cl^-. The solution contains virtually no intact HCl.

A Weak Acid

When HF dissolves in water, only a fraction of the molecules ionize.

▲ **FIGURE 15.5 Ionization of a Weak Acid**   When HF dissolves in water, only a fraction of the dissolved molecules ionize to form H_3O^+ and F^-. The solution contains many intact HF molecules.

Weak Acids

In contrast to HCl, HF is a weak acid, one that does not completely ionize in solution.

Equilibrium arrow indicates partial ionization.

$$HF(aq) + H_2O(l) \rightleftharpoons H_3O^+(aq) + F^-(aq)$$

An HF solution contains a large number of intact (or un-ionized) HF molecules; it also contains some $H_3O^+(aq)$ and $F^-(aq)$ (Figure 15.5 ▲). In other words, a 1.0 M HF solution has an $[H_3O^+]$ that is much less than 1.0 M because only some of the HF molecules ionize to form H_3O^+.

The degree to which an acid is strong or weak depends on the attraction between the anion of the acid (the conjugate base) and the hydrogen ion, relative to the attractions of these ions to water. Recall that HA is a generic formula for an acid. The degree to which the following reaction proceeds in the forward direction depends on the strength of the attraction between H^+ and A^-:

$$\underset{\text{acid}}{HA(aq)} + H_2O(l) \rightleftharpoons H_3O^+(aq) + \underset{\text{conjugate base}}{A^-(aq)}$$

If the attraction between H^+ and A^- is *weak*, then the reaction favors the forward direction and the acid is *strong*. If the attraction between H^+ and A^- is *strong*, then the reaction favors the reverse direction and the acid is *weak*, as shown in Figure 15.6 ◄.

For example, in HCl, the conjugate base (Cl^-) has a relatively weak attraction to H^+—the reverse reaction does not occur to any significant extent. In HF, on the other hand, the conjugate base (F^-) has a greater attraction to H^+—the reverse reaction occurs to a significant degree. *In general, the stronger the acid, the weaker the conjugate base and vice versa.* If the forward reaction (that of the acid) has a high tendency to occur, then the reverse reaction (that of the conjugate base) has a low tendency to occur. Table 15.4 lists some common weak acids.

Notice that two of the weak acids in Table 15.4 are diprotic, meaning that they have two ionizable protons, and one is **triprotic** (three ionizable protons). We discuss polyprotic acids in more detail in Section 15.9.

The terms strong and weak acids are often confused with the terms concentrated and dilute acids. Can you articulate the difference between these terms?

Strong acid

Weak attraction
Complete ionization

Weak acid

Strong attraction
Partial ionization

▲ **FIGURE 15.6 Ionic Attraction and Acid Strength**   In a strong acid, the attraction between H^+ and A^- is weak, resulting in complete ionization. In a weak acid, the attraction between H^+ and A^- is strong, resulting in only partial ionization.

We can also write the formulas for acetic acid and formic acid as CH_3COOH and $HCOOH$, respectively, to indicate that in these compounds the only H that ionizes is the one attached to an oxygen atom.

TABLE 15.4 Some Weak Acids	
Hydrofluoric acid (HF)	Sulfurous acid (H_2SO_3) (*diprotic*)
Acetic acid ($HC_2H_3O_2$)	Carbonic acid (H_2CO_3) (*diprotic*)
Formic acid ($HCHO_2$)	Phosphoric acid (H_3PO_4) (*triprotic*)

The Acid Ionization Constant (K_a)

We quantify the relative strength of a weak acid with the **acid ionization constant (K_a)**, which is the equilibrium constant for the ionization reaction of the weak acid. As we saw in Section 14.3, for the two equivalent reactions:

> Sometimes K_a is also referred to as the acid dissociation constant.

$$HA(aq) + H_2O(l) \rightleftharpoons H_3O^+(aq) + A^-(aq)$$
$$HA(aq) \rightleftharpoons H^+(aq) + A^-(aq)$$

the equilibrium constant is:

$$K_a = \frac{[H_3O^+][A^-]}{[HA]} = \frac{[H^+][A^-]}{[HA]}$$

> Recall from Chapter 14 that the concentrations of pure solids or pure liquids are not included in the expression for K_c; therefore, $H_2O(l)$ is not included in the expression for K_a.

Since $[H_3O^+]$ is equivalent to $[H^+]$, both forms of the expression are equal. Although the ionization constants for all weak acids are relatively small (otherwise the acid would not be a weak acid), they do vary in magnitude. The smaller the constant, the less the acid ionizes, and the weaker the acid. Table 15.5 lists the acid ionization constants for a number of common weak acids in order of decreasing acid strength.

TABLE 15.5 Acid Ionization Constants (K_a) for Some Monoprotic Weak Acids at 25 °C

Acid	Formula	Structural Formula	Ionization Reaction	K_a
Chlorous acid	$HClO_2$	H—O—Cl=O	$HClO_2(aq) + H_2O(l) \rightleftharpoons$ $H_3O^+(aq) + ClO_2^-(aq)$	1.1×10^{-2}
Nitrous acid	HNO_2	H—O—N=O	$HNO_2(aq) + H_2O(l) \rightleftharpoons$ $H_3O^+(aq) + NO_2^-(aq)$	4.6×10^{-4}
Hydrofluoric acid	HF	H—F	$HF(aq) + H_2O(l) \rightleftharpoons$ $H_3O^+(aq) + F^-(aq)$	3.5×10^{-4}
Formic acid	$HCHO_2$	H—O—C(=O)—H	$HCHO_2(aq) + H_2O(l) \rightleftharpoons$ $H_3O^+(aq) + CHO_2^-(aq)$	1.8×10^{-4}
Benzoic acid	$HC_7H_5O_2$	H—O—C(=O)—C (benzene ring)	$HC_7H_5O_2(aq) + H_2O(l) \rightleftharpoons$ $H_3O^+(aq) + C_7H_5O_2^-(aq)$	6.5×10^{-5}
Acetic acid	$HC_2H_3O_2$	H—O—C(=O)—CH₃	$HC_2H_3O_2(aq) + H_2O(l) \rightleftharpoons$ $H_3O^+(aq) + C_2H_3O_2^-(aq)$	1.8×10^{-5}
Hypochlorous acid	$HClO$	H—O—Cl	$HClO(aq) + H_2O(l) \rightleftharpoons$ $H_3O^+(aq) + ClO^-(aq)$	2.9×10^{-8}
Hydrocyanic acid	HCN	H—C≡N	$HCN(aq) + H_2O(l) \rightleftharpoons$ $H_3O^+(aq) + CN^-(aq)$	4.9×10^{-10}
Phenol	HC_6H_5O	HO—C (benzene ring)	$HC_6H_5O(aq) + H_2O(l) \rightleftharpoons$ $H_3O^+(aq) + C_6H_5O^-(aq)$	1.3×10^{-10}

Conceptual Connection 15.2 Relative Strengths of Weak Acids

Consider these two acids and their K_a values:

$$HF \qquad K_a = 3.5 \times 10^{-4}$$
$$HClO \qquad K_a = 2.9 \times 10^{-8}$$

Which acid is stronger?

15.5 Autoionization of Water and pH

We saw previously that water acts as a base when it reacts with HCl and as an acid when it reacts with NH_3:

$$HCl(aq) + H_2O(l) \longrightarrow H_3O^+(aq) + Cl^-(aq)$$

Acid   **Base**
(proton donor)   (proton acceptor)

$$NH_3(aq) + H_2O(l) \rightleftharpoons NH_4^+(aq) + OH^-(aq)$$

Base   **Acid**
(proton acceptor)   (proton donor)

Water is *amphoteric*; it can act as either an acid or a base. Even when pure, water acts as an acid and a base with itself, a process called **autoionization**:

$$H_2O(l) + H_2O(l) \rightleftharpoons H_3O^+(aq) + OH^-(aq)$$

Acid   **Base**
(proton donor)   (proton acceptor)

We can write the autoionization reaction as:

$$H_2O(l) \rightleftharpoons H^+(aq) + OH^-(aq)$$

The equilibrium constant for this reaction is the product of the concentration of the two ions:

$$K_w = [H_3O^+][OH^-] = [H^+][OH^-]$$

This equilibrium constant is called the **ion product constant for water (K_w)** (sometimes called the *dissociation constant for water*). At 25 °C, $K_w = 1.0 \times 10^{-14}$. In pure water, since H_2O is the only source of these ions, the concentrations of H_3O^+ and OH^- are equal, and the solution is **neutral**. Since the concentrations are equal, we can easily calculate them from K_w.

$$[H_3O^+] = [OH^-] = \sqrt{K_w} = 1.0 \times 10^{-7} \quad \text{(in pure water at 25 °C)}$$

As you can see, in pure water, the concentrations of H_3O^+ and OH^- are *very small* (1.0×10^{-7} M) at room temperature.

An **acidic solution** contains an acid that creates additional H_3O^+ ions, causing $[H_3O^+]$ to increase. However, the *ion product constant still applies*:

$$[H_3O^+][OH^-] = K_w = 1.0 \times 10^{-14}$$

The concentration of H_3O^+ times the concentration of OH^- is always 1.0×10^{-14} at 25 °C. If $[H_3O^+]$ increases, then $[OH^-]$ must decrease for the ion product constant to remain 1.0×10^{-14}. For example, if $[H_3O^+] = 1.0 \times 10^{-3}$, then we can find $[OH^-]$ by solving the ion product constant expression for $[OH^-]$:

$$(1.0 \times 10^{-3})[OH^-] = 1.0 \times 10^{-14}$$

$$[OH^-] = \frac{1.0 \times 10^{-14}}{1.0 \times 10^{-3}} = 1.0 \times 10^{-11} \text{ M}$$

In an acidic solution $[H_3O^+] > [OH^-]$.

A **basic solution** contains a base that creates additional OH^- ions, causing $[OH^-]$ to increase and $[H_3O^+]$ to decrease, but again the *ion product constant still applies*. Suppose $[OH^-] = 1.0 \times 10^{-2}$; then we can find $[H_3O^+]$ by solving the ion product constant expression for $[H_3O^+]$:

$$[H_3O^+](1.0 \times 10^{-2}) = 1.0 \times 10^{-14}$$

$$[H_3O^+] = \frac{1.0 \times 10^{-14}}{1.0 \times 10^{-2}} = 1.0 \times 10^{-12} \text{ M}$$

In a basic solution $[OH^-] > [H_3O^+]$.

Notice that changing $[H_3O^+]$ in an aqueous solution produces an inverse change in $[OH^-]$ and vice versa.

Summarizing K_w:

▶ A *neutral solution* contains $[H_3O^+] = [OH^-] = 1.0 \times 10^{-7}$ M (at 25 °C).

▶ An *acidic solution* contains $[H_3O^+] > [OH^-]$.

▶ A *basic solution* contains $[OH^-] > [H_3O^+]$.

▶ In *all aqueous solutions* both H_3O^+ and OH^- are present, with $[H_3O^+][OH^-] = K_w = 1.0 \times 10^{-14}$ (at 25 °C).

The ion product constant K_w depends on temperature. For all calcuations in this book, assume 25 °C unless otherwise noted.

EXAMPLE 15.2 Using K_w in Calculations

Calculate $[OH^-]$ at 25 °C for each solution and determine if the solution is acidic, basic, or neutral.

(a) $[H_3O^+] = 7.5 \times 10^{-5}$ M   **(b)** $[H_3O^+] = 1.5 \times 10^{-9}$ M

(c) $[H_3O^+] = 1.0 \times 10^{-7}$ M

SOLUTION

(a) To find $[OH^-]$ use the ion product constant. Substitute the given value for $[H_3O^+]$ and solve the equation for $[OH^-]$. Since $[H_3O^+] > [OH^-]$, the solution is acidic.	$[H_3O^+][OH^-] = K_w = 1.0 \times 10^{-14}$ $(7.5 \times 10^{-5})[OH^-] = 1.0 \times 10^{-14}$ $[OH^-] = \dfrac{1.0 \times 10^{-14}}{7.5 \times 10^{-5}} = 1.3 \times 10^{-10}$ M Acidic solution
(b) Substitute the given value for $[H_3O^+]$ and solve the acid ionization equation for $[OH^-]$. Since $[H_3O^+] < [OH^-]$, the solution is basic.	$(1.5 \times 10^{-9})[OH^-] = 1.0 \times 10^{-14}$ $[OH^-] = \dfrac{1.0 \times 10^{-14}}{1.5 \times 10^{-9}} = 6.7 \times 10^{-6}$ M Basic solution
(c) Substitute the given value for $[H_3O^+]$ and solve the acid ionization equation for $[OH^-]$. Since $[H_3O^+] = 1.0 \times 10^{-7}$ and $[OH^-] = 1.0 \times 10^{-7}$, the solution is neutral.	$(1.0 \times 10^{-7})[OH^-] = 1.0 \times 10^{-14}$ $[OH^-] = \dfrac{1.0 \times 10^{-14}}{1.0 \times 10^{-7}} = 1.0 \times 10^{-7}$ M Neutral solution

FOR PRACTICE 15.2

Calculate $[H_3O^+]$ at 25 °C for each solution and determine if the solution is acidic, basic, or neutral.

(a) $[OH^-] = 1.5 \times 10^{-2}$ M   **(b)** $[OH^-] = 1.0 \times 10^{-7}$ M

(c) $[OH^-] = 8.2 \times 10^{-10}$ M

The pH Scale: A Way to Quantify Acidity and Basicity

The log of a number is the exponent to which 10 must be raised to obtain that number. Thus, $\log 10^1 = 1$; $\log 10^2 = 2$; $\log 10^{-1} = -1$; $\log 10^{-2} = -2$, etc. (see Appendix I).

The pH scale is a compact way to specify the acidity of a solution. We define **pH** as the negative of the log of the hydronium ion concentration:

$$pH = -\log[H_3O^+]$$

A solution with $[H_3O^+] = 1.0 \times 10^{-3}$ M (acidic) has a pH of:

$$
\begin{aligned}
pH &= -\log[H_3O^+] \\
&= -\log(1.0 \times 10^{-3}) \\
&= -(-3.00) \\
&= 3.00
\end{aligned}
$$

When you take the log of a quantity, the result should have the same number of decimal places as the number of significant figures in the original quantity.

Notice that we report the pH to two *decimal places* here. This is because only the numbers to the right of the decimal point are significant in a logarithm. Because our original value for the concentration had two significant figures, the log of that number has two decimal places.

Concentrated acid solutions can have negative pH. For example, if $[H_3O^+] = 2.0$ M, the pH is -0.30.

2 significant digits   2 decimal places

$$\log(1.0) \times 10^{-3} = 3.00$$

If the original number had three significant digits, the log would be reported to three decimal places.

3 significant digits   3 decimal places

$$\log(1.00) \times 10^{-3} = 3.000$$

A solution with $[H_3O^+] = 1.0 \times 10^{-7}$ M (neutral at 25 °C) has a pH of:

$$
\begin{aligned}
pH &= -\log[H_3O^+] \\
&= -\log(1.0 \times 10^{-7}) \\
&= -(-7.00) \\
&= 7.00
\end{aligned}
$$

In general, at 25 °C:

- pH < 7   The solution is *acidic*.
- pH > 7   The solution is *basic*.
- pH = 7   The solution is *neutral*.

Table 15.6 lists the pH of some common substances. As we discussed in Section 15.2, many foods, especially fruits, are acidic and have low pH values. Relatively few foods are basic. The foods with the lowest pH values are limes and lemons, and they are among the sourest. Because the pH scale is a *logarithmic scale*, a change of 1 pH unit corresponds to a 10-fold change in H_3O^+ concentration (Figure 15.7 ▼). For example, a lime with a pH of

TABLE 15.6 The pH of Some Common Substances

Substance	pH
Gastric juice (human stomach)	1.0–3.0
Limes	1.8–2.0
Lemons	2.2–2.4
Soft drinks	2.0–4.0
Plums	2.8–3.0
Wines	2.8–3.8
Apples	2.9–3.3
Peaches	3.4–3.6
Cherries	3.2–4.0
Beers	4.0–5.0
Rainwater (unpolluted)	5.6
Human blood	7.3–7.4
Egg whites	7.6–8.0
Milk of magnesia	10.5
Household ammonia	10.5–11.5
4% NaOH solution	14

The pH Scale

0	1	2	3	4	5	6	7	8	9	10	11	12	13	14

Acidic   pH   Basic

10^{-0}	10^{-1}	10^{-2}	10^{-3}	10^{-4}	10^{-5}	10^{-6}	10^{-7}	10^{-8}	10^{-9}	10^{-10}	10^{-11}	10^{-12}	10^{-13}	10^{-14}

$[H^+]$

▲ FIGURE 15.7 **The pH Scale**   An increase of 1 on the pH scale corresponds to a factor of 10 decrease in $[H_3O^+]$.

2.0 is 10 times more acidic than a plum with a pH of 3.0 and 100 times more acidic than a cherry with a pH of 4.0.

EXAMPLE 15.3 Calculating pH from $[H_3O^+]$ or $[OH^-]$

Calculate the pH of each solution at 25 °C and indicate whether the solution is acidic or basic.

(a) $[H_3O^+] = 1.8 \times 10^{-4}$ M   **(b)** $[OH^-] = 1.3 \times 10^{-2}$ M

SOLUTION

(a) To calculate pH, substitute the given $[H_3O^+]$ into the pH equation. Since pH < 7, this solution is acidic.	$\begin{aligned} pH &= -\log[H_3O^+] \\ &= -\log(1.8 \times 10^{-4}) \\ &= -(-3.74) \\ &= 3.74 \text{ (acidic)} \end{aligned}$
(b) First use K_w to find $[H_3O^+]$ from $[OH^-]$.	$[H_3O^+][OH^-] = K_w = 1.0 \times 10^{-14}$ $[H_3O^+](1.3 \times 10^{-2}) = 1.0 \times 10^{-14}$ $[H_3O^+] = \dfrac{1.0 \times 10^{-14}}{1.3 \times 10^{-2}} = 7.7 \times 10^{-13}$ M
Then substitute $[H_3O^+]$ into the pH expression to find pH.	$\begin{aligned} pH &= -\log[H_3O^+] \\ &= -\log(7.7 \times 10^{-13}) \\ &= -(-12.11) \\ &= 12.11 \text{ (basic)} \end{aligned}$
Since pH > 7, this solution is basic.	

FOR PRACTICE 15.3

Calculate the pH of each solution and indicate whether the solution is acidic or basic.

(a) $[H_3O^+] = 9.5 \times 10^{-9}$ M   **(b)** $[OH^-] = 7.1 \times 10^{-3}$ M

EXAMPLE 15.4 Calculating $[H_3O^+]$ from pH

Calculate the $[H_3O^+]$ for a solution with a pH of 4.80.

SOLUTION

To find the $[H_3O^+]$ from pH, start with the equation that defines pH. Substitute the given value of pH and then solve for $[H_3O^+]$. Since the given pH value was reported to two decimal places, the $[H_3O^+]$ is written to two significant figures. (Remember that $10^{\log x} = x$ (see Appendix I). Some calculators use an inv log key to represent this function.)	$\begin{aligned} pH &= -\log[H_3O^+] \\ 4.80 &= -\log[H_3O^+] \\ -4.80 &= \log[H_3O^+] \\ 10^{-4.80} &= 10^{\log[H_3O^+]} \\ 10^{-4.80} &= [H_3O^+] \\ [H_3O^+] &= 1.6 \times 10^{-5} \text{ M} \end{aligned}$

FOR PRACTICE 15.4

Calculate the $[H_3O^+]$ for a solution with a pH of 8.37.

---

pOH and Other p Scales

The pOH scale is analogous to the pH scale but is defined with respect to $[OH^-]$ instead of $[H_3O^+]$.

$$pOH = -\log[OH^-]$$

A solution with an $[OH^-]$ of 1.0×10^{-3} M (basic) has a pOH of 3.00. On the pOH scale, a pOH less than 7 is basic and a pOH greater than 7 is acidic. A pOH of 7 is neutral

Notice that p is the mathematical operator $-\log$; thus, $pX = -\log X$.

0.0	1.0	2.0	3.0	4.0	5.0	6.0	7.0	8.0	9.0	10.0	11.0	12.0	13.0	14.0

Acidic   pH   Basic

14.0	13.0	12.0	11.0	10.0	9.0	8.0	7.0	6.0	5.0	4.0	3.0	2.0	1.0	0.0

pOH

▲ FIGURE 15.8 pH and pOH

(Figure 15.8 ▲). We can derive a relationship between pH and pOH at 25 °C from the expression for K_w:

$$[H_3O^+][OH^-] = 1.0 \times 10^{-14}$$

Taking the log of both sides, we get:

$$\log([H_3O^+][OH^-]) = \log(1.0 \times 10^{-14})$$
$$\log[H_3O^+] + \log[OH^-] = -14.00$$
$$-\log[H_3O^+] - \log[OH^-] = 14.00$$
$$pH + pOH = 14.00$$

The sum of pH and pOH is always equal to 14.00 at 25 °C. Therefore, a solution with a pH of 3 has a pOH of 11.

Another common p scale is the pK_a scale defined as:

$$pK_a = -\log K_a$$

The pK_a of a weak acid is another way to quantify its strength. The smaller the pK_a, the stronger the acid. For example, chlorous acid, with a K_a of 1.1×10^{-2}, has a pK_a of 1.96; and formic acid, with a K_a of 1.8×10^{-4}, has a pK_a of 3.74.

Chemistry and Medicine

Ulcers

An ulcer is a lesion on the wall of the stomach or small intestine. Under normal circumstances, a thick layer of mucus lines the stomach wall and protects it from the hydrochloric acid and other gastric juices in the stomach. If that mucous layer is damaged, however, stomach juices come in direct contact with the stomach wall and begin to digest it, creating an ulcer. The main symptom of an ulcer is a burning or gnawing pain in the stomach.

Acidic drugs, such as aspirin, and acidic foods, such as citrus fruits and pickling fluids, irritate ulcers. When consumed, these substances increase the acidity of the stomach juices, exacerbating the irritation to the stomach wall. On the other hand, antacids—which contain bases—relieve ulcers. Common antacids include Tums and milk of magnesia.

The causes of ulcers are manifold. For many years, a stressful lifestyle and a rich diet were blamed. More recent research, however, has shown that a bacterial infection of the stomach lining is responsible for many ulcers. (The 2005 Nobel Prize in Physiology or Medicine was awarded to Australians Barry J. Marshall and J. Robin Warren, for their discovery of the bacterial cause of ulcers.) Long-term use of some over-the-counter pain relievers, such as aspirin, is also believed to produce ulcers.

Question

Which dessert would be less likely to irritate an ulcer, key lime pie or meringue (made of egg whites)?

◀ An ulcer is a lesion in the stomach wall.

15.6 Finding the [H_3O^+] and pH of Strong and Weak Acid Solutions

A solution containing a strong or weak acid has two potential sources of H_3O^+: the ionization of the acid itself and the autoionization of water. If we let HA be a strong or weak acid, the ionization equations are:

$$HA(aq) + H_2O(l) \rightleftharpoons H_3O^+(aq) + A^-(aq) \qquad \text{Strong or Weak Acid}$$
$$H_2O(l) + H_2O(l) \rightleftharpoons H_3O^+(aq) + OH^-(aq) \qquad K_w = 1.0 \times 10^{-14}$$

Except in extremely dilute acid solutions, the autoionization of water contributes a negligibly small amount of H_3O^+ compared to the ionization of the strong or weak acid. Recall from Section 15.5 that autoionization in pure water at 25 °C produces an H_3O^+ concentration of 1.0×10^{-7} M. In a strong or weak acid solution, the additional H_3O^+ from the acid causes the autoionization of water equilibrium to shift left (as described by Le Châtelier's principle). Consequently, in most strong or weak acid solutions, the autoionization of water produces even less H_3O^+ than in pure water and can be ignored. Therefore we can focus exclusively on the amount of H_3O^+ produced by the acid.

> The only exceptions would be extremely dilute ($<10^{-5}$ M) strong acid solutions.

Strong Acids

Because strong acids, by definition, completely ionize in solution, and because we can (in nearly all cases) ignore the contribution of the autoionization of water, *the concentration of H_3O^+ in a strong acid solution is equal to the concentration of the strong acid*. For example, a 0.10 M HCl solution has an H_3O^+ concentration of 0.10 M and a pH of 1.00.

$$0.10 \text{ M HCl} \Rightarrow [H_3O^+] = 0.10 \text{ M} \Rightarrow pH = -\log(0.10) = 1.00$$

Weak Acids

Finding the pH of a weak acid solution is more complicated because the concentration of H_3O^+ is *not equal* to the concentration of the weak acid. For example, if we make solutions of 0.10 M HCl (a strong acid) and 0.10 M acetic acid (a weak acid) in the laboratory and measure the pH of each, we get the following results:

0.10 M HCl	pH = 1.00
0.10 M $HC_2H_3O_2$	pH = 2.87

The pH of the acetic acid solution is higher (it is less acidic) because acetic acid only partially ionizes. Calculating the [H_3O^+] formed by the ionization of a weak acid requires solving an equilibrium problem similar to those in Chapter 14. Consider, for example, a 0.10 M solution of the generic weak acid HA with an acid ionization constant K_a. Since we can ignore the contribution of the autoionization of water, we only have to determine the concentration of H_3O^+ formed by the following equilibrium:

$$HA(aq) + H_2O(l) \rightleftharpoons H_3O^+(aq) + A^-(aq) \qquad K_a$$

We can summarize the initial conditions, the changes, and the equilibrium conditions in the following ICE table:

> ICE tables were first introduced in Section 14.6. The reactant $H_2O(l)$ is a pure liquid and is therefore not included in the equilibrium constant nor in the ICE table (see Section 14.5).

	[HA]	[H_3O^+]	[A^-]
Initial	0.10	≈ 0.00	0.00
Change	−x	+x	+x
Equilibrium	0.10 − x	x	x

The initial H_3O^+ concentration is listed as *approximately* zero because of the negligibly small contribution of H_3O^+ due to the autoionization of water (discussed previously). The variable x represents the amount of HA that ionizes. As discussed in Chapter 14, each *equilibrium* concentration is the sum of the two entries above it in the ICE table.

In order to find the equilibrium concentration of H_3O^+, we must find the value of the variable x. We can use the equilibrium expression to set up an equation in which x is the only variable:

$$K_a = \frac{[H_3O^+][A^-]}{[HA]}$$

$$= \frac{x^2}{0.10 - x}$$

As is often the case with equilibrium problems, we arrive at a quadratic equation in x, which we can solve using the quadratic formula (see Appendix IC). However, in many cases we can apply the *x is small* approximation (first discussed in Section 14.8). In Examples 15.5 and 15.6, we examine the general procedure for solving weak acid equilibrium problems. In both of these examples, the *x is small* approximation works well. In Example 15.7, we solve a problem in which the *x is small* approximation does not work. In such cases, we can solve the quadratic equation explicitly, or apply the method of successive approximations (also discussed in Section 14.8). Finally, in Example 15.8, we work a problem in which we find the equilibrium constant of a weak acid from its pH.

PROCEDURE FOR...	EXAMPLE 15.5	EXAMPLE 15.6
Finding the pH (or $[H_3O^+]$) of a Weak Acid Solution	**Finding the $[H_3O^+]$ of a Weak Acid Solution**	**Finding the pH of a Weak Acid Solution**
To solve these types of problems, follow the outlined procedure.	Find the $[H_3O^+]$ of a 0.100 M HCN solution.	Find the pH of a 0.200 M HNO_2 solution.

1. **Write the balanced equation for the ionization of the acid and use it as a guide to prepare an ICE table showing the given concentration of the weak acid as its initial concentration.** Leave room in the table for the changes in concentrations and for the equilibrium concentrations.

   (Note that the $[H_3O^+]$ is listed as approximately zero because the autoionization of water produces a negligibly small amount of H_3O^+).

   $HCN(aq) + H_2O(l) \rightleftharpoons H_3O^+(aq) + CN^-(aq)$

	[HCN]	[H₃O⁺]	[CN⁻]
Initial	0.100	≈ 0.00	0.00
Change			
Equil			

   $HNO_2(aq) + H_2O(l) \rightleftharpoons H_3O^+(aq) + NO_2^-(aq)$

	[HNO₂]	[H₃O⁺]	[NO₂⁻]
Initial	0.200	≈ 0.00	0.00
Change			
Equil			

2. **Represent the change in the concentration of H_3O^+ with the variable x. Define the changes in the concentrations of the other reactants and products in terms of x. Always keep in mind the stoichiometry of the reaction.**

   $HCN(aq) + H_2O(l) \rightleftharpoons H_3O^+(aq) + CN^-(aq)$

	[HCN]	[H₃O⁺]	[CN⁻]
Initial	0.100	≈ 0.00	0.00
Change	$-x$	$+x$	$+x$
Equil			

   $HNO_2(aq) + H_2O(l) \rightleftharpoons H_3O^+(aq) + NO_2^-(aq)$

	[HNO₂]	[H₃O⁺]	[NO₂⁻]
Initial	0.200	≈ 0.00	0.00
Change	$-x$	$+x$	$+x$
Equil			

3. **Sum each column to determine the equilibrium concentrations in terms of the initial concentrations and the variable x.**

   $HCN(aq) + H_2O(l) \rightleftharpoons H_3O^+(aq) + CN^-(aq)$

	[HCN]	[H₃O⁺]	[CN⁻]
Initial	0.100	≈ 0.00	0.00
Change	$-x$	$+x$	$+x$
Equil	$0.100 - x$	x	x

   $HNO_2(aq) + H_2O(l) \rightleftharpoons H_3O^+(aq) + NO_2^-(aq)$

	[HNO₂]	[H₃O⁺]	[NO₂⁻]
Initial	0.200	≈ 0.00	0.00
Change	$-x$	$+x$	$+x$
Equil	$0.200 - x$	x	x

4. Substitute the expressions for the equilibrium concentrations (from step 3) into the expression for the acid ionization constant (K_a). In many cases, you can make the approximation that *x is small* (as discussed in Section 14.8). **Substitute the value of the acid ionization constant (from Table 15.5) into the K_a expression and solve for x.** Confirm that the *x is small* approximation is valid by calculating the ratio of x to the number it was subtracted from in the approximation. The ratio should be less than 0.05 (or 5%).	$K_a = \dfrac{[H_3O^+][CN^-]}{[HCN]}$ $= \dfrac{x^2}{0.100 - x}$ (*x is small*) $4.9 \times 10^{-10} = \dfrac{x^2}{0.100}$ $\sqrt{4.9 \times 10^{-10}} = \sqrt{\dfrac{x^2}{0.100}}$ $x = \sqrt{(0.100)(4.9 \times 10^{-10})}$ $= 7.0 \times 10^{-6}$ $\dfrac{7.0 \times 10^{-6}}{0.100} \times 100\% = 7.0 \times 10^{-3}\%$ Therefore the approximation is valid.	$K_a = \dfrac{[H_3O^+][NO_2^-]}{[HNO_2]}$ $= \dfrac{x^2}{0.200 - x}$ (*x is small*) $4.6 \times 10^{-4} = \dfrac{x^2}{0.200}$ $\sqrt{4.6 \times 10^{-4}} = \sqrt{\dfrac{x^2}{0.200}}$ $x = \sqrt{(0.200)(4.6 \times 10^{-4})}$ $= 9.6 \times 10^{-3}$ $\dfrac{9.6 \times 10^{-3}}{0.200} \times 100\% = 4.8\%$ Therefore the approximation is valid (but barely so).
5. Determine the [H₃O⁺] from the calculated value of x and calculate the pH if necessary.	$[H_3O^+] = 7.0 \times 10^{-6}\,M$ (pH was not asked for in this problem.)	$[H_3O^+] = 9.6 \times 10^{-3}\,M$ $pH = -\log[H_3O^+]$ $\quad = -\log(9.6 \times 10^{-3})$ $\quad = 2.02$
6. Check your answer by substituting the computed equilibrium values into the acid ionization expression. The calculated value of K_a should match the given value of K_a. Note that rounding errors and the *x is small* approximation could result in a difference in the least significant digit when comparing values of K_a.	$K_a = \dfrac{[H_3O^+][CN^-]}{[HCN]} = \dfrac{(7.0 \times 10^{-6})^2}{0.100}$ $= 4.9 \times 10^{-10}$ Since the calculated value of K_a matches the given value, the answer is valid.	$K_a = \dfrac{[H_3O^+][NO_2^-]}{[HNO_2]} = \dfrac{(9.6 \times 10^{-3})^2}{0.200}$ $= 4.6 \times 10^{-4}$ Since the calculated value of K_a matches the given value, the answer is valid.
	FOR PRACTICE 15.5 Find the H_3O^+ concentration of a 0.250 M hydrofluoric acid solution.	**FOR PRACTICE 15.6** Find the pH of a 0.0150 M acetic acid solution.

EXAMPLE 15.7 Finding the pH of a Weak Acid Solution in Cases Where the *x is small* Approximation Does Not Work

Find the pH of a 0.100 M HClO₂ solution.

SOLUTION

1. Write the balanced equation for the ionization of the acid and use it as a guide to prepare an ICE table showing the given concentration of the weak acid as its initial concentration. (Note that the H₃O⁺ concentration is listed as approximately zero. Although a little H₃O⁺ is present from the autoionization of water, this amount is negligibly small compared to the amount of HClO₂ or H₃O⁺ formed by the acid.)	$HClO_2(aq) + H_2O(l) \rightleftharpoons H_3O^+(aq) + ClO_2^-(aq)$ <table><tr><th></th><th>[HClO₂]</th><th>[H₃O⁺]</th><th>[ClO₂⁻]</th></tr><tr><td>Initial</td><td>0.100</td><td>≈0.00</td><td>0.00</td></tr><tr><td>Change</td><td></td><td></td><td></td></tr><tr><td>Equil</td><td></td><td></td><td></td></tr></table>
2. Represent the change in [H₃O⁺] with the variable x. Define the changes in the concentrations of the other reactants and products in terms of x.	$HClO_2(aq) + H_2O(l) \rightleftharpoons H_3O^+(aq) + ClO_2^-(aq)$ <table><tr><th></th><th>[HClO₂]</th><th>[H₃O⁺]</th><th>[ClO₂⁻]</th></tr><tr><td>Initial</td><td>0.100</td><td>≈0.00</td><td>0.00</td></tr><tr><td>Change</td><td>−x</td><td>+x</td><td>+x</td></tr><tr><td>Equil</td><td></td><td></td><td></td></tr></table>

3. Sum each column to determine the equilibrium concentrations in terms of the initial concentrations and the variable x.	$HClO_2(aq) + H_2O(l) \rightleftharpoons H_3O^+(aq) + ClO_2^-(aq)$

	[HClO$_2$]	[H$_3$O$^+$]	[ClO$_2^-$]
Initial	0.100	≈ 0.00	0.00
Change	$-x$	$+x$	$+x$
Equil	$0.100 - x$	x	x

4. Substitute the expressions for the equilibrium concentrations (from step 3) into the expression for the acid ionization constant (K_a). Make the *x is small* approximation and substitute the value of the acid ionization constant (from Table 15.5) into the K_a expression. Solve for x.	$K_a = \dfrac{[H_3O^+][ClO_2^-]}{[HNO_2]}$ $= \dfrac{x^2}{0.100 - \cancel{x}}$ (*x is small*) $0.011 = \dfrac{x^2}{0.100}$ $\sqrt{0.011} = \sqrt{\dfrac{x^2}{0.100}}$ $x = \sqrt{(0.100)(0.011)}$ $= 0.033$

Check to see if the *x is small* approximation is valid by calculating the ratio of x to the number it was subtracted from in the approximation. The ratio should be less than 0.05 (or 5%).	$\dfrac{0.033}{0.100} \times 100\% = 33\%$ Therefore, the *x is small* approximation is *not valid*.

4a. If the *x is small* approximation is not valid, solve the quadratic equation explicitly or use the method of successive approximations to find x. In this case, we solve the quadratic equation.	$0.011 = \dfrac{x^2}{0.100 - x}$ $0.011(0.100 - x) = x^2$ $0.0011 - 0.011x = x^2$ $x^2 + 0.011x - 0.0011 = 0$ $x = \dfrac{-b \pm \sqrt{b^2 - 4ac}}{2a}$ $= \dfrac{-(0.011) \pm \sqrt{(0.011)^2 - 4(1)(-0.0011)}}{2(1)}$ $= \dfrac{-0.011 \pm 0.0672}{2}$ $x = -0.039$ *or* $x = 0.028$ Since x represents the concentration of H_3O^+, and since concentrations cannot be negative, we reject the negative root. $x = 0.028$

5. Determine the H_3O^+ concentration from the calculated value of x and calculate the pH (if necessary).	$[H_3O^+] = 0.028$ M $pH = -\log[H_3O^+]$ $= -\log 0.028$ $= 1.55$

6. Check your answer by substituting the calculated equilibrium values into the acid ionization expression. The calculated value of K_a should match the given value of K_a. Note that rounding errors could result in a difference in the least significant digit when comparing values of K_a.	$K_a = \dfrac{[H_3O^+][ClO_2^-]}{[HClO_2]} = \dfrac{0.028^2}{0.100 - 0.028}$ $= 0.011$ Since the calculated value of K_a matches the given value, the answer is valid.

FOR PRACTICE 15.7

Find the pH of a 0.010 M HNO_2 solution.

EXAMPLE 15.8 Finding the Equilibrium Constant from pH

A 0.100 M weak acid (HA) solution has a pH of 4.25. Find K_a for the acid.

SOLUTION

Use the given pH to find the equilibrium concentration of $[H_3O^+]$. Then write the balanced equation for the ionization of the acid and use it as a guide to prepare an ICE table showing all known concentrations.	$pH = -\log[H_3O^+]$ $4.25 = -\log[H_3O^+]$ $[H_3O^+] = 5.6 \times 10^{-5}\,M$ $HA(aq) + H_2O(l) \rightleftharpoons H_3O^+(aq) + A^-(aq)$

	[HA]	[H₃O⁺]	[A⁻]
Initial	0.100	≈ 0.00	0.00
Change			
Equil		5.6 × 10⁻⁵	

Use the equilibrium concentration of H_3O^+ and the stoichiometry of the reaction to predict the changes and equilibrium concentration for all species. For most weak acids, the initial and equilibrium concentrations of the weak acid (HA) are effectively equal because the amount that ionizes is usually very small compared to the initial concentration.	$HA(aq) + H_2O(l) \rightleftharpoons H_3O^+(aq) + A^-(aq)$

	[HA]	[H₃O⁺]	[A⁻]
Initial	0.100	≈ 0.00	0.00
Change	−5.6 × 10⁻⁵	+5.6 × 10⁻⁵	+5.6 × 10⁻⁵
Equil	(0.100 − 5.6 × 10⁻⁵) ≈ 0.100	5.6 × 10⁻⁵	5.6 × 10⁻⁵

Substitute the equilibrium concentrations into the expression for K_a and calculate its value.	$K_a = \dfrac{[H_3O^+][A^-]}{[HA]}$ $= \dfrac{(5.6 \times 10^{-5})(5.6 \times 10^{-5})}{0.100}$ $= 3.1 \times 10^{-8}$

FOR PRACTICE 15.8

A 0.175 M weak acid solution has a pH of 3.25. Find K_a for the acid.

Conceptual Connection 15.3 The *x is small* Approximation

The initial concentration and K_a's of several weak acid (HA) solutions are listed here. For which of these is the *x is small* approximation *least* likely to work in finding the pH of the solution?

(a) initial [HA] = 0.100 M; $K_a = 1.0 \times 10^{-5}$
(b) initial [HA] = 1.00 M; $K_a = 1.0 \times 10^{-6}$
(c) initial [HA] = 0.0100 M; $K_a = 1.0 \times 10^{-3}$
(d) initial [HA] = 1.0 M; $K_a = 1.5 \times 10^{-3}$

Conceptual Connection 15.4 Strong and Weak Acids

Which solution is most acidic (that is, which one has the lowest pH)?

(a) 0.10 M HCl
(b) 0.10 M HF
(c) 0.20 M HF

Percent Ionization of a Weak Acid

We can quantify the ionization of a weak acid according to the percentage of acid molecules that actually ionizes. We define the **percent ionization** of a weak acid as the ratio of the ionized acid concentration to the initial acid concentration, multiplied by 100%:

$$\text{Percent ionization} = \frac{\text{concentration of ionized acid}}{\text{initial concentration of acid}} \times 100\% = \frac{[H_3O^+]_{\text{equil}}}{[HA]_{\text{init}}} \times 100\%$$

Since the concentration of ionized acid is equal to the H_3O^+ concentration at equilibrium (for a monoprotic acid), we can use $[H_3O^+]_{\text{equil}}$ and $[HA]_{\text{init}}$ in the formula to calculate the percent ionization. For example, in Example 15.6, we found that a 0.200 M HNO_2 solution contains 9.6×10^{-3} M H_3O^+. The 0.200 M HNO_2 solution therefore has the following percent ionization:

$$\% \text{ ionization} = \frac{[H_3O^+]_{\text{equil}}}{[HA]_{\text{init}}} \times 100\%$$

$$= \frac{9.6 \times 10^{-3} \text{ M}}{0.200 \text{ M}} \times 100\%$$

$$= 4.8\%$$

As you can see, the percent ionization is relatively small. In this case, even though HNO_2 has the second largest K_a in Table 15.5, fewer than 5 molecules out of 100 ionize. For most other weak acids (with smaller K_a values) the percent ionization is even less.

In Example 15.9, we calculate the percent ionization of a more concentrated HNO_2 solution. In the example, notice that the calculated H_3O^+ concentration is much greater (as we would expect for a more concentrated solution), but the *percent ionization* is actually smaller.

EXAMPLE 15.9   Finding the Percent Ionization of a Weak Acid

Find the percent ionization of a 2.5 M HNO_2 solution.

SOLUTION

To find the percent ionization, you must find the equilibrium concentration of H_3O^+. Follow the procedure in Example 15.5, shown in condensed form here.	$HNO_2(aq) + H_2O(l) \rightleftharpoons H_3O^+(aq) + NO_2^-(aq)$

	[HNO₂]	**[H₃O⁺]**	**[NO₂⁻]**
Initial	2.5	≈ 0.00	0.00
Change	$-x$	$+x$	$+x$
Equil	$2.5 - x$	x	x

$$K_a = \frac{[H_3O^+][NO_2^-]}{[HNO_2]} = \frac{x^2}{2.5 - \cancel{x}} \quad (x \text{ is small})$$

$$4.6 \times 10^{-4} = \frac{x^2}{2.5}$$

$$x = 0.034$$

Therefore, $[H_3O^+] = 0.034$ M.

Use the definition of percent ionization to calculate it. (Since the percent ionization is less than 5%, the *x is small* approximation is valid.)	$\% \text{ ionization} = \dfrac{[H_3O^+]_{\text{equil}}}{[HA]_{\text{init}}} \times 100\%$ $= \dfrac{0.034 \text{ M}}{2.5 \text{ M}} \times 100\%$ $= 1.4\%$

FOR PRACTICE 15.9

Find the percent ionization of a 0.250 M $HC_2H_3O_2$ solution at 25 °C.

We can summarize the results of Examples 15.6 and 15.9:

[HNO$_2$]	[H$_3$O$^+$]	Percent Dissociation
0.200	0.0096	4.8%
2.5	0.034	1.4%

The trend you can see in the table applies to all weak acids.

- The *equilibrium H$_3$O$^+$ concentration* of a weak acid *increases* with increasing initial concentration of the acid.
- The *percent ionization* of a weak acid *decreases* with increasing concentration of the acid.

In other words, as the concentration of a weak acid solution increases, the concentration of the hydronium ion also increases, but the increase is not linear. The H$_3$O$^+$ concentration increases more slowly than the concentration of the acid because as the acid concentration increases, a smaller fraction of weak acid molecules ionize.

We can understand this behavior by analogy with Le Châtelier's principle. Consider the following weak acid ionization equilibrium:

$$HA(aq) \rightleftharpoons H^+(aq) + A^-(aq)$$

1 mol dissolved particles   2 mol dissolved particles

If we dilute a weak acid solution initially at equilibrium, the system (according to Le Châtelier's principle) responds to minimize the disturbance. The equilibrium shifts to the right because the right side of the equation contains more particles in solution (2 mol versus 1 mol) than the left side. If the system shifts to the right, the percent ionization is greater in the more dilute solution, which is what we observe.

Conceptual Connection 15.5 Percent Ionization

Which of these weak acid solutions has the greatest percent ionization? Which solution has the lowest (most acidic) pH?

(a) 0.100 M HC$_2$H$_3$O$_2$

(b) 0.500 M HC$_2$H$_3$O$_2$

(c) 0.0100 M HC$_2$H$_3$O$_2$

Mixtures of Acids

Finding the pH of a mixture of acids may seem difficult at first. However, in many cases, the relative strengths of the acids in the mixture allow us to neglect the weaker acid and focus only on the stronger one. Here, we consider two possible acid mixtures: a strong acid with a weak acid, and a weak acid with another weak acid.

A Strong Acid and a Weak Acid Consider a mixture that is 0.10 M in HCl and 0.10 M in HCHO$_2$. There are three sources of H$_3$O$^+$ ions: the strong acid (HCl), the weak acid (HCHO$_2$), and the autoionization of water.

$$HCl(aq) + H_2O(l) \longrightarrow H_3O^+(aq) + Cl^-(aq) \qquad \text{Strong}$$
$$HCHO_2(aq) + H_2O(l) \rightleftharpoons H_3O^+(aq) + CHO_2^-(aq) \qquad K_a = 1.8 \times 10^{-4}$$
$$H_2O(l) + H_2O(l) \rightleftharpoons H_3O^+(aq) + OH^-(aq) \qquad K_w = 1.0 \times 10^{-14}$$

Since HCl is strong, we know that it completely ionizes to produce a significant concentration of H$_3$O$^+$(0.10 M). The H$_3$O$^+$ formed by HCl then *suppresses* the formation of additional H$_3$O$^+$ formed by the ionization of HCHO$_2$ or the autoionization of water. In other words, according to Le Châtelier's principle, the formation of H$_3$O$^+$ by the strong acid causes the weak acid to ionize even less than it would in the absence of the strong acid. To see this clearly, let us calculate [H$_3$O$^+$] and [CHO$_2^-$] in this solution.

In an initial estimate of $[H_3O^+]$, we can neglect the contribution of $HCHO_2$ and H_2O. The concentration of H_3O^+ is then equal to the initial concentration of HCl.

$$[H_3O^+] = [HCl] = 0.10 \text{ M}$$

To find $[CHO_2^-]$ we must solve an equilibrium problem. However, the initial concentration of H_3O^+ in this case is not negligible (as it has been in all the other weak acid equilibrium problems that we have worked so far) because HCl has formed a significant amount of H_3O^+. The concentration of H_3O^+ formed by HCl becomes the *initial* concentration of H_3O^+ in the ICE table for $HCHO_2$ as shown here:

$$HCHO_2(aq) + H_2O(l) \rightleftharpoons H_3O^+(aq) + CHO_2^-(aq)$$

	[HCHO$_2$]	[H$_3$O$^+$]	[CHO$_2^-$]
Initial	0.10	0.10	0.00
Change	$-x$	$+x$	$+x$
Equil	$0.10 - x$	$0.10 + x$	x

We then use the equilibrium expression to set up an equation in which x is the only variable:

$$K_a = \frac{[H_3O^+][CHO_2^-]}{[HCHO_2]}$$

$$= \frac{(0.10 + x)x}{0.10 - x}$$

Since the equilibrium constant is small relative to the initial concentration of the acid, we can make the *x is small* approximation:

$$K_a = \frac{(0.10 + x)x}{0.10 - \cancel{x}}$$

$$1.8 \times 10^{-4} = \frac{(0.10)x}{0.10}$$

$$x = 1.8 \times 10^{-4}$$

Checking the *x is small* approximation:

$$\frac{1.8 \times 10^{-4}}{0.10} \times 100\% = 0.18\%$$

We find that the approximation is valid. Therefore, $[CHO_2^-] = 1.8 \times 10^{-4}$ M. We can now see that we can completely ignore the ionization of the weak acid ($HCHO_2$) in calculating $[H_3O^+]$ for the mixture. The contribution to the concentration of H_3O^+ by the weak acid must necessarily be equal to the concentration of CHO_2^- that we just calculated (because of the stoichiometry of the ionization reaction). Therefore, we have the following contributions to $[H_3O^+]$:

HCl contributes 0.10 M

$HCHO_2$ contributes 1.8×10^{-4} M or 0.00018 M

Total $[H_3O^+] = 0.10 \text{ M} + 0.00018 \text{ M} = 0.10 \text{ M}$

As we can see, since the significant figure rules for addition limit the answer to two decimal places, the amount of H_3O^+ contributed by $HCHO_2$ is completely negligible. The amount of H_3O^+ contributed by the autoionization of water is even smaller and therefore similarly negligible.

A Mixture of Two Weak Acids When two weak acids are mixed, we again have three potential sources of H_3O^+ to consider: each of the two weak acids and the autoionization of water. However, if the K_a's of the two weak acids are sufficiently different in magnitude (if they differ by more than a factor of several hundred), then as long as the concentrations of the two acids are similar in magnitude (or the concentration of the stronger one is greater than that of the weaker), we can assume that the weaker acid will not make a significant contribution to the concentration of H_3O^+. We make this assumption for the same reason that we made a similar assumption for a mixture of a strong acid and a weak one: the H_3O^+ formed by the stronger acid suppresses the ionization of the weaker one, in accordance with Le Châtelier's principle. Example 15.10 shows how to calculate the concentration of H_3O^+ in a mixture of two weak acids.

EXAMPLE 15.10 Mixtures of Weak Acids

Find the pH of a mixture that is 0.150 M in HF and 0.100 M in HClO.

SOLUTION

The three possible sources of H_3O^+ ions are HF, HClO, and H_2O. Write the ionization equations for the three sources and their corresponding equilibrium constants. Since the equilibrium constant for the ionization of HF is about 12,000 times larger than that for the ionization of HClO, the contribution of HF to $[H_3O^+]$ is by far the greatest. You can therefore just calculate the $[H_3O^+]$ formed by HF and neglect the other two potential sources of H_3O^+.	$HF(aq) + H_2O(l) \rightleftharpoons H_3O^+(aq) + F^-(aq)$ $K_a = 3.5 \times 10^{-4}$ $HClO(aq) + H_2O(l) \rightleftharpoons H_3O^+(aq) + ClO^-(aq)$ $K_a = 2.9 \times 10^{-8}$ $H_2O(l) + H_2O(l) \rightleftharpoons H_3O^+(aq) + OH^-(aq)$ $K_w = 1.0 \times 10^{-14}$

Write the balanced equation for the ionization of HF and use it as a guide to prepare an ICE table.

$HF(aq) + H_2O(l) \rightleftharpoons H_3O^+(aq) + F^-(aq)$

	[HF]	$[H_3O^+]$	$[F^-]$
Initial	0.150	≈ 0.00	0.00
Change	$-x$	$+x$	$+x$
Equil	$0.150 - x$	x	x

Substitute the expressions for the equilibrium concentrations into the expression for the acid ionization constant (K_a). Since the equilibrium constant is small relative to the initial concentration of HF, you can make the *x is small* approximation. Substitute the value of the acid ionization constant (from Table 15.5) into the K_a expression and solve for x.	$K_a = \dfrac{[H_3O^+][F^-]}{[HF]} = \dfrac{x^2}{0.150 - x}$ (*x is small*) $3.5 \times 10^{-4} = \dfrac{x^2}{0.150}$ $\sqrt{(0.150)(3.5 \times 10^{-4})} = \sqrt{x^2}$
Confirm that the *x is small* approximation is valid by calculating the ratio of x to the number it was subtracted from in the approximation. The ratio should be less than 0.05 (or 5%).	$x = 7.2 \times 10^{-3}$ $\dfrac{7.2 \times 10^{-3}}{0.150} \times 100\% = 4.8\%$ Therefore, the approximation is valid (though barely so).
Determine the H_3O^+ concentration from the calculated value of x and find the pH.	$[H_3O^+] = 7.2 \times 10^{-3}$ M $pH = -\log(7.2 \times 10^{-3}) = 2.14$

FOR PRACTICE 15.10

Find the ClO^- concentration of the above mixture of HF and HClO.

Conceptual Connection 15.6 Judging Relative pH

Which solution is most acidic (that is, has the lowest pH)?

(a) 1.0 M HCl   (b) 2.0 M HF

(c) A solution that is 1.0 M in HF and 1.0 M in HClO

15.7 Base Solutions

Strong Bases

Just as we define a strong acid as one that completely ionizes in solution, analogously we define a **strong base** as a base that completely dissociates in solution. NaOH, for example, is a strong base:

$$NaOH(aq) \longrightarrow Na^+(aq) + OH^-(aq)$$

An NaOH solution contains no intact NaOH—it has all dissociated to form $Na^+(aq)$ and $OH^-(aq)$ (Figure 15.9 ▼). In other words, a 1.0 M NaOH solution has $[OH^-] = 1.0$ M and $[Na^+] = 1.0$ M. Table 15.7 lists the common strong bases.

As you can see, most strong bases are group 1A or group 2A metal hydroxides. The group 1A metal hydroxides are highly soluble in water and can form concentrated base solutions. The group 2A metal hydroxides, however, are only slightly soluble, a useful property for some applications (see the *Chemistry and Medicine* box in this section). Notice that the general formula for the group 2A metal hydroxides is $M(OH)_2$. When they dissolve in water, they produce 2 mol of OH^- per mole of the base. For example, $Sr(OH)_2$ dissociates as follows:

$$Sr(OH)_2(aq) \longrightarrow Sr^{2+}(aq) + 2\,OH^-(aq)$$

Unlike diprotic acids, which ionize in two steps, bases containing two OH^- ions dissociate in one step.

A Strong Base

▲ **FIGURE 15.9 Ionization of a Strong Base** When NaOH dissolves in water, it dissociates completely into Na^+ and OH^-. The solution contains virtually no intact NaOH.

TABLE 15.7 Strong Bases	
Lithium hydroxide (LiOH)	Strontium hydroxide [$Sr(OH)_2$]
Sodium hydroxide (NaOH)	Calcium hydroxide [$Ca(OH)_2$]
Potassium hydroxide (KOH)	Barium hydroxide [$Ba(OH)_2$]

Weak Bases

A **weak base** is analogous to a weak acid. Unlike strong bases that contain OH^- and *dissociate* in water, the most common weak bases produce OH^- by accepting a proton from water, ionizing water to form OH^- according to the general equation:

$$B(aq) + H_2O(l) \rightleftharpoons BH^+(aq) + OH^-(aq)$$

In this equation, B is a generic symbol for a weak base. Ammonia, for example, ionizes water as follows:

$$NH_3(aq) + H_2O(l) \rightleftharpoons NH_4^+(aq) + OH^-(aq)$$

The double arrow indicates that the ionization is not complete. An NH_3 solution contains mostly NH_3 with only some NH_4^+ and OH^- (Figure 15.10 ▶). A 1.0 M NH_3 solution will have $[OH^-] < 1.0$ M.

A Weak Base

▲ **FIGURE 15.10 Ionization of a Weak Base** When NH_3 dissolves in water, it partially ionizes water to form NH_4^+ and OH^-. Most of the NH_3 molecules in solution remain as NH_3.

The extent of ionization of a weak base is quantified with the **base ionization constant**, K_b. For the general reaction in which a weak base ionizes water, we define K_b as follows:

$$B(aq) + H_2O(l) \rightleftharpoons BH^+(aq) + OH^-(aq) \qquad K_b = \frac{[BH^+][OH^-]}{[B]}$$

By analogy with K_a, the smaller the value of K_b, the weaker the base. Table 15.8 lists some common weak bases, their ionization reactions, and values for K_b. The "p" scale can also be applied to K_b, so that $pK_b = -\log K_b$.

All but two of the weak bases listed in Table 15.8 are either ammonia or an amine, which we can think of as ammonia with one or more hydrocarbon groups substituted for one or more hydrogen atoms. All of these bases have a nitrogen atom with a lone pair (Figure 15.11 ▶). This lone pair acts as the proton acceptor that makes the substance a base, as shown in the reactions for ammonia and methylamine:

$$H-\overset{\cdot\cdot}{\underset{\underset{H}{|}}{N}}-H(aq) + H-\overset{\cdot\cdot}{\underset{\cdot\cdot}{O}}-H(l) \rightleftharpoons H-\overset{H}{\underset{\underset{H}{|}}{\overset{|}{N^+}}}-H(aq) + :\overset{\cdot\cdot}{\underset{\cdot\cdot}{O}}{=}H$$

$$H-\overset{H}{\underset{\underset{H}{|}}{\overset{|}{C}}}-\overset{\cdot\cdot}{\underset{\underset{H}{|}}{N}}-H(aq) + H-\overset{\cdot\cdot}{\underset{\cdot\cdot}{O}}-H(l) \rightleftharpoons H-\overset{H}{\underset{\underset{H}{|}}{\overset{|}{C}}}-\overset{H}{\underset{\underset{H}{|}}{\overset{|}{N^+}}}-H(aq) + :\overset{\cdot\cdot}{\underset{\cdot\cdot}{O}}{=}H$$

TABLE 15.8 Some Common Weak Bases

Weak Base	Ionization Reaction	K_b (at 25 °C)
Carbonate ion (CO_3^{2-})*	$CO_3^{2-}(aq) + H_2O(l) \rightleftharpoons HCO_3^-(aq) + OH^-(aq)$	1.8×10^{-4}
Methylamine (CH_3NH_2)	$CH_3NH_2(aq) + H_2O(l) \rightleftharpoons CH_3NH_3^+(aq) + OH^-(aq)$	4.4×10^{-4}
Ethylamine ($C_2H_5NH_2$)	$C_2H_5NH_2(aq) + H_2O(l) \rightleftharpoons C_2H_5NH_3^+(aq) + OH^-(aq)$	5.6×10^{-4}
Ammonia (NH_3)	$NH_3(aq) + H_2O(l) \rightleftharpoons NH_4^+(aq) + OH^-(aq)$	1.76×10^{-5}
Bicarbonate ion (HCO_3^-)* (or hydrogen carbonate)	$HCO_3^-(aq) + H_2O(l) \rightleftharpoons H_2CO_3(aq) + OH^-(aq)$	2.3×10^{-8}
Pyridine (C_5H_5N)	$C_5H_5N(aq) + H_2O(l) \rightleftharpoons C_5H_5NH^+(aq) + OH^-(aq)$	1.7×10^{-9}
Aniline ($C_6H_5NH_2$)	$C_6H_5NH_2(aq) + H_2O(l) \rightleftharpoons C_6H_5NH_3^+(aq) + OH^-(aq)$	3.9×10^{-10}

*The carbonate and bicarbonate ions must occur with a positively charged ion such as Na^+ that serves to balance the charge but does not have any part in the ionization reaction. For example, it is the bicarbonate ion that makes sodium bicarbonate ($NaHCO_3$) basic. We look more closely at ionic bases in Section 15.8.

▶ **FIGURE 15.11 Lone Pairs in Weak Bases** Many weak bases have a nitrogen atom with a lone pair that acts as the proton acceptor.

Ammonia   Methylamine   Pyridine

Finding the [OH⁻] and pH of Basic Solutions

Finding the [OH⁻] and pH of a strong base solution is relatively straightforward, as shown in Example 15.11. As we did in calculating the [H₃O⁺] in strong acid solutions, we can neglect the contribution of the autoionization of water to the [OH⁻] and focus solely on the strong base itself.

EXAMPLE 15.11 Finding the [OH⁻] and pH of a Strong Base Solution

What is the OH⁻ concentration and pH in each solution?

(a) 0.225 M KOH   **(b)** 0.0015 M Sr(OH)₂

SOLUTION

(a) Since KOH is a strong base, it completely dissociates into K⁺ and OH⁻ in solution. The concentration of OH⁻ will therefore be the same as the given concentration of KOH. Use this concentration and K_w to find [H₃O⁺].	$KOH(aq) \longrightarrow K^+(aq) + OH^-(aq)$ $[OH^-] = 0.225$ M $[H_3O^+][OH^-] = K_w = 1.0 \times 10^{-14}$ $[H_3O^+](0.225) = 1.0 \times 10^{-14}$ $[H_3O^+] = 4.44 \times 10^{-14}$ M
Then substitute [H₃O⁺] into the pH expression to find the pH.	$pH = -\log[H_3O^+]$ $\quad = -\log(4.44 \times 10^{-14})$ $\quad = 13.35$
(b) Since Sr(OH)₂ is a strong base, it completely dissociates into 1 mol of Sr²⁺ and 2 mol of OH⁻ in solution. The concentration of OH⁻ will therefore be twice the given concentration of Sr(OH)₂.	$Sr(OH)_2(aq) \longrightarrow Sr^{2+}(aq) + 2\,OH^-(aq)$ $[OH^-] = 2(0.0015)$ M $\quad\quad = 0.0030$ M
Use this concentration and K_w to find [H₃O⁺].	$[H_3O^+][OH^-] = K_w = 1.0 \times 10^{-14}$ $[H_3O^+](0.0030) = 1.0 \times 10^{-14}$ $[H_3O^+] = 3.3 \times 10^{-12}$ M
Substitute [H₃O⁺] into the pH expression to find the pH.	$pH = -\log[H_3O^+]$ $\quad = -\log(3.3 \times 10^{-12})$ $\quad = 11.48$

FOR PRACTICE 15.11

Find the [OH⁻] and pH of a 0.010 M Ba(OH)₂ solution.

Finding the [OH⁻] and pH of a *weak base* solution is analogous to finding the [H₃O⁺] and pH of a weak acid. Similarly, we can neglect the contribution of the autoionization of water to the [OH⁻] and focus solely on the weak base itself. We find the contribution of the weak base by preparing an ICE table showing the relevant concentrations of all species and then use the base ionization constant expression to find the [OH⁻]. Example 15.12 shows how to find the [OH⁻] and pH of a weak base solution.

EXAMPLE 15.12 Finding the [OH⁻] and pH of a Weak Base Solution

Find the $[OH^-]$ and pH of a 0.100 M NH_3 solution.

SOLUTION

1. Write the balanced equation for the ionization of water by the base and use it as a guide to prepare an ICE table showing the given concentration of the weak base as its initial concentration. Leave room in the table for the changes in concentrations and for the equilibrium concentrations. (Note that you should list the OH^- concentration as approximately zero. Although a little OH^- is present from the autoionization of water, this amount is negligibly small compared to the amount of OH^- formed by the base.)

$$NH_3(aq) + H_2O(l) \rightleftharpoons NH_4^+(aq) + OH^-(aq)$$

	$[NH_3]$	$[NH_4^+]$	$[OH^-]$
Initial	0.100	0.00	≈ 0.00
Change			
Equil			

2. Represent the change in the concentration of OH^- with the variable x. Define the changes in the concentrations of the other reactants and products in terms of x.

$$NH_3(aq) + H_2O(l) \rightleftharpoons NH_4^+(aq) + OH^-(aq)$$

	$[NH_3]$	$[NH_4^+]$	$[OH^-]$
Initial	0.100	0.00	≈ 0.00
Change	$-x$	$+x$	$+x$
Equil			

3. Sum each column to determine the equilibrium concentrations in terms of the initial concentrations and the variable x.

$$NH_3(aq) + H_2O(l) \rightleftharpoons NH_4^+(aq) + OH^-(aq)$$

	$[NH_3]$	$[NH_4^+]$	$[OH^-]$
Initial	0.100	0.00	≈ 0.00
Change	$-x$	$+x$	$+x$
Equil	$0.100 - x$	x	x

4. Substitute the expressions for the equilibrium concentrations (from step 3) into the expression for the base ionization constant.

In many cases, you can make the approximation that x is small (as discussed in Chapter 14).

Substitute the value of the base ionization constant (from Table 15.8) into the K_b expression and solve for x.

$$K_b = \frac{[NH_4^+][OH^-]}{[NH_3]}$$
$$= \frac{x^2}{0.100 - \cancel{x}} \quad (x \text{ is small})$$
$$1.76 \times 10^{-5} = \frac{x^2}{0.100}$$
$$\sqrt{1.76 \times 10^{-5}} = \sqrt{\frac{x^2}{0.100}}$$
$$x = \sqrt{(0.100)(1.76 \times 10^{-5})}$$
$$= 1.33 \times 10^{-3}$$

Confirm that the x is small approximation is valid by calculating the ratio of x to the number it was subtracted from in the approximation. The ratio should be less than 0.05 (or 5%).

$$\frac{1.33 \times 10^{-3}}{0.100} \times 100\% = 1.33\%$$

Therefore, the approximation is valid.

5. Determine the OH^- concentration from the calculated value of x.

Use the expression for K_w to find $[H_3O^+]$.

$$[OH^-] = 1.33 \times 10^{-3} \text{ M}$$
$$[H_3O^+][OH^-] = K_w = 1.00 \times 10^{-14}$$
$$[H_3O^+](1.33 \times 10^{-3}) = 1.00 \times 10^{-14}$$
$$[H_3O^+] = 7.52 \times 10^{-12} \text{ M}$$

Substitute $[H_3O^+]$ into the pH equation to find pH.

$$pH = -\log[H_3O^+]$$
$$= -\log(7.52 \times 10^{-12})$$
$$= 11.124$$

FOR PRACTICE 15.12

Find the $[OH^-]$ and pH of a 0.33 M methylamine solution.

Chemistry and Medicine

What's in My Antacid?

In the opening section of this chapter, we discussed heartburn and its treatment with antacids. Some common antacids and their active ingredients include the following:

Amphogel	$Al(OH)_3$
Milk of magnesia	$Mg(OH)_2$
Maalox	$Mg(OH)_2$ and $Al(OH)_3$
Mylanta	$Mg(OH)_2$ and $Al(OH)_3$
Tums	$CaCO_3$

We categorize antacids into three main groups: calcium-based, magnesium-based, and aluminum-based. Calcium-based antacids may cause acid rebound—which means that, although they initially relieve heartburn, they can also cause the stomach to produce more acid, resulting in a quick return of the symptoms. Aluminum- and magnesium-based antacids do not cause acid rebound but have downsides of their own. Aluminum-based antacids tend to cause constipation, and magnesium-based ones tend to cause diarrhea. (In fact, milk of magnesia is sometimes used as a laxative.) A person who takes repeated doses of these antacids should alternate between the two or choose a product that contains both.

Notice the absence of group 1A metal hydroxides, such as KOH or NaOH, in the list of antacids. Why are those substances—which are completely soluble and act as strong bases—not used in antacids? Because a solution containing sufficient KOH or NaOH to neutralize stomach acid would also burn the mouth and throat. In contrast, $Mg(OH)_2$ and $Al(OH)_3$

are only slightly soluble. Therefore liquid antacids containing these are actually *suspensions* of $Mg(OH)_2$ and $Al(OH)_3$—they are heterogeneous mixtures in which the solid is finely divided into the liquid. As a result, the concentration of OH^- in these suspensions is relatively small compared to what it would be with a group 1A metal hydroxide.

▶ Antacids contain a variety of bases that effectively neutralize excess stomach acid.

Initially, it might seem as though the relatively lower OH^- concentration would make the antacid much less effective. However, the solid $Mg(OH)_2$ or $Al(OH)_3$ continues to dissolve as the OH^- neutralizes stomach acid. For example, a suspension of magnesium hydroxide contains solid $Mg(OH)_2$ in equilibrium with dissolved Mg^{2+} and OH^- ions:

$$Mg(OH)_2(s) \rightleftharpoons Mg^{2+}(aq) + 2\,OH^-(aq)$$

As stomach acid is neutralized, OH^- is used up, and the equilibrium shifts to the right providing additional OH^- ions. In this way, a suspension of $Mg(OH)_2$ provides a steady concentration of dissolved OH^- ions to neutralize stomach acid.

Question

Write chemical equations showing the reactions of each of the bases in the antacids discussed here with stomach acid (HCl).

15.8 The Acid–Base Properties of Ions and Salts

We have already seen that some ions act as bases. For example, the bicarbonate ion acts as a base according to the following equation:

$$HCO_3^-(aq) + H_2O(l) \rightleftharpoons H_2CO_3(aq) + OH^-(aq)$$

The bicarbonate ion, like any ion, does not exist by itself—in order to be charge neutral, it must pair with a counter ion (in this case a cation) to form an ionic compound, called a *salt*. For example, the sodium salt of bicarbonate is sodium bicarbonate. Like all soluble salts, sodium bicarbonate dissociates in solution to form a sodium cation and bicarbonate anion:

$$NaHCO_3(s) \rightleftharpoons Na^+(aq) + HCO_3^-(aq)$$

The sodium ion has neither acidic nor basic properties (it does not ionize water), as we will see shortly. The bicarbonate ion, by contrast, acts as a weak base, ionizing water as just shown to form a basic solution. Consequently, the pH of a sodium bicarbonate solution is above 7 (the solution is basic). In this section, we consider some of the acid–base properties of salts and the ions they contain. Some salts are pH-neutral when put into water, others are acidic, and still others are basic, depending on their constituent anions and cations. In general, anions tend to form either *basic* or neutral solutions, while cations tend to form either *acidic* or neutral solutions.

Anions as Weak Bases

We can think of any anion as the conjugate base of an acid. Consider the following anions and their corresponding acids:

This anion	is the conjugate base of	this acid
Cl^-		HCl
F^-		HF
NO_3^-		HNO_3
$C_2H_3O_2^-$		$HC_2H_3O_2$

In general, the anion A^- is the conjugate base of the acid HA. Since every anion can be regarded as the conjugate base of an acid, every anion itself can potentially act as a base. However, *not every anion does act as a base*—it depends on the strength of the corresponding acid. In general:

- An anion that is the conjugate base of a *weak acid* is itself a *weak base*.
- An anion that is the conjugate base of a *strong acid* is pH-*neutral* (forms solutions that are neither acidic nor basic).

For example, the Cl^- anion is the conjugate base of HCl, a strong acid. Therefore the Cl^- anion is pH-neutral (neither acidic nor basic). The F^- anion, however, is the conjugate base of HF, a weak acid. Therefore the F^- ion is itself a weak base and ionizes water according to the reaction:

$$F^-(aq) + H_2O(l) \rightleftharpoons OH^-(aq) + HF(aq)$$

We can understand why the conjugate base of a weak acid is basic by asking ourselves why an acid is weak to begin with. Hydrofluoric acid is a weak acid because the following reaction lies to the left:

$$HF(aq) + H_2O(l) \rightleftharpoons H_3O^+(aq) + F^-(aq)$$

The equilibrium lies to the left because the F^- ion has a significant affinity for H^+ ions. Consequently, when F^- is put into water, its affinity for H^+ ions allows it to remove H^+ ions from water molecules, thus acting as a weak base. In general, as shown in Figure 15.12 ▾,

Acid Strength		Acid	Base		Base Strength
	Strong	HCl	Cl^-	Neutral	
		H_2SO_4	HSO_4^-		
		HNO_3	NO_3^-		
		H_3O^+	H_2O		
		HSO_4^-	SO_4^{2-}		
		H_2SO_3	HSO_3^-		
		H_3PO_4	$H_2PO_4^-$		
		HF	F^-		
		$HC_2H_3O_2$	$C_2H_3O_2^-$	Weak	
		H_2CO_3	HCO_3^-		
	Weak	H_2S	HS^-		
		HSO_3^-	SO_3^{2-}		
		$H_2PO_4^-$	HPO_4^{2-}		
		HCN	CN^-		
		NH_4^+	NH_3		
		HCO_3^-	CO_3^{2-}		
		HPO_4^{2-}	PO_4^{3-}		
		H_2O	OH^-		
	Negligible	HS^-	S^{2-}	Strong	
		OH^-	O^{2-}		

◀ FIGURE 15.12 **Strength of Conjugate Acid–Base Pairs** The stronger an acid, the weaker its conjugate base.

the weaker the acid, the stronger the conjugate base (as we saw in Section 15.4). In contrast, the conjugate base of a strong acid, such as Cl^-, does not act as a base because this reaction lies far to the right:

$$HCl(aq) + H_2O(l) \longrightarrow H_3O^+(aq) + Cl^-(aq)$$

The reaction lies far to the right because the Cl^- ion has a low affinity for H^+ ions. Consequently, when Cl^- is put into water, it does not remove H^+ ions from water molecules.

EXAMPLE 15.13 Determining Whether an Anion Is Basic or pH-Neutral

Classify each anion as a weak base or pH-neutral:

(a) NO_3^- (b) NO_2^- (c) $C_2H_3O_2^-$

SOLUTION

(a) From Table 15.3, we can see that NO_3^- is the conjugate base of a *strong* acid (HNO_3) and is therefore pH-neutral.

(b) From Table 15.5 (or from its absence in Table 15.3), we know that NO_2^- is the conjugate base of a weak acid (HNO_2) and is therefore a weak base.

(c) From Table 15.5 (or from its absence in Table 15.3), we know that $C_2H_3O_2^-$ is the conjugate base of a weak acid ($HC_2H_3O_2$) and is therefore a weak base.

FOR PRACTICE 15.13

Classify each anion as a weak base or pH-neutral:

(a) CHO_2^- (b) ClO_4^-

We can determine the pH of a solution containing an anion that acts as a weak base in a manner similar to how we determine the pH of any weak base solution. However, we need to know K_b for the anion acting as a base, which we can readily determine from K_a of the corresponding acid. Recall from Section 15.4 the expression for K_a for a generic acid HA:

$$HA(aq) + H_2O(l) \rightleftharpoons H_3O^+(aq) + A^-(aq)$$

$$K_a = \frac{[H_3O^+][A^-]}{[HA]}$$

Similarly, the expression for K_b for the conjugate base (A^-) is:

$$A^-(aq) + H_2O(l) \rightleftharpoons OH^-(aq) + HA(aq)$$

$$K_b = \frac{[OH^-][HA]}{[A^-]}$$

If we multiply the expressions for K_a and K_b we get K_w:

$$K_a \times K_b = \frac{[H_3O^+][\cancel{A^-}][OH^-][\cancel{HA}]}{[\cancel{HA}][\cancel{A^-}]} = [H_3O^+][OH^-] = K_w$$

Or simply,

$$K_a \times K_b = K_w$$

The product of K_a for an acid and K_b for its conjugate base is K_w (1.0×10^{-14} at 25 °C). Consequently, we can find K_b for an anion acting as a base from the value of K_a for the corresponding acid. For example, for acetic acid ($HC_2H_3O_2$), $K_a = 1.8 \times 10^{-5}$. We calculate K_b for the conjugate base ($C_2H_3O_2^-$) by substituting into the equation:

$$K_a \times K_b = K_w$$

$$K_b = \frac{K_w}{K_a} = \frac{1.0 \times 10^{-14}}{1.8 \times 10^{-5}} = 5.6 \times 10^{-10}$$

Knowing K_b, we can find the pH of a solution containing an anion acting as a base, as demonstrated in Example 15.14.

EXAMPLE 15.14   Determining the pH of a Solution Containing an Anion Acting as a Base

Find the pH of a 0.100 M $NaCHO_2$ solution. The salt completely dissociates into $Na^+(aq)$ and $CHO_2^-(aq)$, and the Na^+ ion has no acid or base properties.

SOLUTION

1. Since the Na^+ ion does not have any acidic or basic properties, you can ignore it. Write the balanced equation for the ionization of water by the basic anion and use it as a guide to prepare an ICE table showing the given concentration of the weak base as its initial concentration.	$CHO_2^-(aq) + H_2O(l) \rightleftharpoons HCHO_2(aq) + OH^-(aq)$

	$[CHO_2^-]$	$[HCHO_2]$	$[OH^-]$
Initial	0.100	0.00	≈ 0.00
Change			
Equil			

2. Represent the change in the concentration of OH^- with the variable x. Define the changes in the concentrations of the other reactants and products in terms of x.	$CHO_2^-(aq) + H_2O(l) \rightleftharpoons HCHO_2(aq) + OH^-(aq)$

	$[CHO_2^-]$	$[HCHO_2]$	$[OH^-]$
Initial	0.100	0.00	≈ 0.00
Change	$-x$	$+x$	$+x$
Equil			

3. Sum each column to determine the equilibrium concentrations in terms of the initial concentrations and the variable x.	$CHO_2^-(aq) + H_2O(l) \rightleftharpoons HCHO_2(aq) + OH^-(aq)$

	$[CHO_2^-]$	$[HCHO_2]$	$[OH^-]$
Initial	0.100	0.00	≈ 0.00
Change	$-x$	$+x$	$+x$
Equil	$0.100 - x$	x	x

4. Find K_b from K_a (for the conjugate acid). Substitute the expressions for the equilibrium concentrations (from step 3) into the expression for K_b. In many cases, you can make the approximation that x is small. Substitute the value of K_b into the K_b expression and solve for x. Confirm that the x is small approximation is valid by calculating the ratio of x to the number it was subtracted from in the approximation. The ratio should be less than 0.05 (or 5%).	$K_a \times K_b = K_w$ $K_b = \dfrac{K_w}{K_a} = \dfrac{1.0 \times 10^{-14}}{1.8 \times 10^{-4}} = 5.6 \times 10^{-11}$ $K_b = \dfrac{[HCHO_2][OH^-]}{[CHO_2^-]}$ $= \dfrac{x^2}{0.100 - \cancel{x}}$ $5.6 \times 10^{-11} = \dfrac{x^2}{0.100}$ $x = 2.4 \times 10^{-6}$ $\dfrac{2.4 \times 10^{-6}}{0.100} \times 100\% = 0.0024\%$ Therefore, the approximation is valid.

5. Determine the OH^- concentration from the calculated value of x. Use the expression for K_w to find $[H_3O^+]$. Substitute $[H_3O^+]$ into the pH equation to find pH.	$[OH^-] = 2.4 \times 10^{-6} \, M$ $[H_3O^+][OH^-] = K_w = 1.0 \times 10^{-14}$ $[H_3O^+](2.4 \times 10^{-6}) = 1.0 \times 10^{-14}$ $[H_3O^+] = 4.2 \times 10^{-9} \, M$ $pH = -\log[H_3O^+]$ $\quad = -\log(4.2 \times 10^{-9})$ $\quad = 8.38$

FOR PRACTICE 15.14
Find the pH of a 0.250 M $NaC_2H_3O_2$ solution.

We can also express the relationship between K_a and K_b in terms of pK_a and pK_b. By taking the log of both sides of $K_a \times K_b = K_w$, we get:

$$\log (K_a \times K_b) = \log K_w$$
$$\log K_a + \log K_b = \log K_w$$

Since $K_w = 10^{-14}$, we can rearrange the equation to get:

$$\log K_a + \log K_b = \log 10^{-14} = -14$$

Rearranging further:

$$-\log K_a - \log K_b = 14$$

Since $-\log K = pK$, we get:

$$pK_a + pK_b = 14$$

Cations as Weak Acids

In contrast to anions, which in some cases act as weak bases, cations can in some cases act as *weak acids*. We can generally divide cations into three categories: cations that are the counterions of strong bases; cations that are the conjugate acids of *weak* bases; and cations that are small, highly charged metals. We examine each individually.

Cations That Are the Counterions of Strong Bases Strong bases such as NaOH or $Ca(OH)_2$ generally contain hydroxide ions and a counterion. In solution, a strong base completely dissociates to form $OH^-(aq)$ and the solvated (in solution) counterion. Although these counterions interact with water molecules via ion–dipole forces, they do not ionize water and they do not contribute to the acidity or basicity of the solution. In general *cations that are the counterions of strong bases are themselves pH-neutral* (they form solutions that are neither acidic nor basic). For example, Na^+, K^+, and Ca^{2+} are the counterions of the strong bases NaOH, KOH, and $Ca(OH)_2$ and are therefore themselves pH-neutral.

Cations That Are the Conjugate Acids of Weak Bases A cation can be formed from any nonionic weak base by adding a proton (H^+) to its formula. The cation will be the conjugate acid of the base. Consider the following cations and their corresponding weak bases:

This cation	is the conjugate acid of	this weak base
NH_4^+		NH_3
$C_2H_5NH_3^+$		$C_2H_5NH_2$
$CH_3NH_3^+$		CH_3NH_2

Any of these cations, with the general formula BH^+, will act as a weak acid according to the equation:

$$BH^+(aq) + H_2O(aq) \rightleftharpoons H_3O^+(aq) + B(aq)$$

In general, *a cation that is the conjugate acid of a weak base is a weak acid.*

We can calculate the pH of a solution containing the conjugate acid of a weak base just like that of any other weakly acidic solution. However, the value of K_a for the acid must be derived from K_b using the previously derived relationship: $K_a \times K_b = K_w$.

Cations That Are Small, Highly Charged Metals *Small, highly charged metal cations such as Al^{3+} and Fe^{3+} form weakly acidic solutions.* For example, when Al^{3+} is dissolved in water, it becomes hydrated according to the equation:

$$Al^{3+}(aq) + 6\,H_2O(l) \longrightarrow Al(H_2O)_6^{3+}(aq)$$

The hydrated form of the ion then acts as a Brønsted–Lowry acid:

$$Al(H_2O)_6^{3+}(aq) \quad + \quad H_2O(aq) \quad \rightleftharpoons \quad Al(H_2O)_5(OH)^{2+}(aq) + H_3O^+(aq)$$

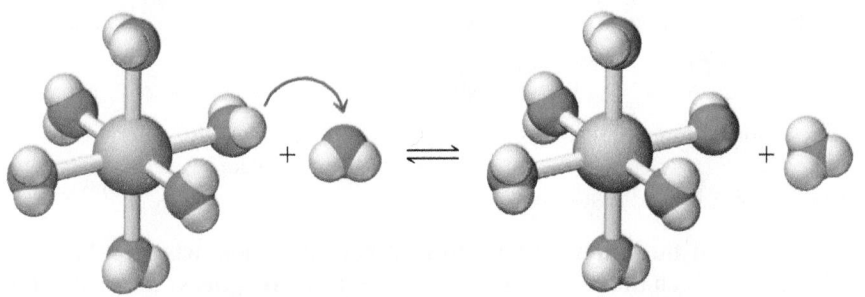

In effect, the binding of a water molecule to the cation makes the water more acidic. See Section 15.10.

Neither the alkali metal cations nor the alkaline earth metal cations ionize water in this way, but the cations of many other metals do. The smaller and more highly charged the cation, the more acidic its behavior.

EXAMPLE 15.15 Determining Whether a Cation Is Acidic or pH-Neutral

Classify each cation as a weak acid or pH-neutral.

(a) $C_5H_5NH^+$ (b) Ca^{2+} (c) Cr^{3+}

SOLUTION

(a) The $C_5H_5NH^+$ cation is the conjugate acid of a weak base and is therefore a weak acid.

(b) The Ca^{2+} cation is the counterion of a strong base and is therefore pH-neutral (neither acidic nor basic).

(c) The Cr^{3+} cation is a small, highly charged metal cation and is therefore a weak acid.

FOR PRACTICE 15.15

Classify each cation as a weak acid or pH-neutral.

(a) Li^+ (b) $CH_3NH_3^+$ (c) Fe^{3+}

Classifying Salt Solutions as Acidic, Basic, or Neutral

Since salts contain both a cation and an anion, they can form acidic, basic, or neutral solutions when dissolved in water. The pH of the solution depends on the specific cation and anion involved. We examine the four possibilities individually.

1. **Salts in which neither the cation nor the anion acts as an acid or a base form pH-neutral solutions**. A salt in which the cation is the counterion of a strong base and in which the anion is the conjugate base of strong acid form *neutral* solutions. Some salts in this category include:

   NaCl Ca(NO$_3$)$_2$ KBr
   sodium chloride calcium nitrate potassium bromide

   Cations are pH–neutral   Anions are conjugate bases of strong acids.

2. **Salts in which the cation does not act as an acid and the anion acts as a base form basic solutions**. A salt in which the cation is the counterion of a strong base and in which the anion is the conjugate base of *weak* acid form *basic* solutions. Salts in this category include:

   NaF Ca(C$_2$H$_3$O$_2$)$_2$ KNO$_2$
   sodium fluoride calcium acetate potassium nitrite

   Cations are pH–neutral   Anions are conjugate bases of weak acids.

3. **Salts in which the cation acts as an acid and the anion does not act as a base form acidic solutions.** A salt in which the cation is either the conjugate acid of a weak base or a small, highly charged metal ion and in which the anion is the conjugate base of *strong* acid form *acidic* solutions. Salts in this category include:

$$FeCl_3 \qquad Al(NO_3)_3 \qquad NH_4Br$$
iron(III) chloride · aluminum nitrate · ammonium bromide

Cations are conjugate acids of *weak* bases or small, highly charged metal ions.

Anions are conjugate bases of *strong* acids.

4. **Salts in which the cation acts as an acid and the anion acts as a base form solutions in which the pH depends on the relative strengths of the acid and the base.** A salt in which the cation is either the conjugate acid of a weak base or a small, highly charged metal ion and in which the anion is the conjugate base of a *weak* acid form a solution in which the pH depends on the relative strengths of the acid and base. Salts in this category include:

$$FeF_3 \qquad Al(C_2H_3O_2)_3 \qquad NH_4NO_2$$
iron(III) fluoride · aluminum acetate · ammonium nitrate

Cations are conjugate acids of *weak* bases or small, highly charged metal ions.

Anions are conjugate bases of *weak* acids.

We can determine the overall pH of a solution containing one of these salts by comparing the K_a of the acid to the K_b of the base—the ion with the higher value of K dominates and determines whether the solution will be acidic or basic, as shown in part (e) of Example 15.16. Table 15.9 summarizes all of these possibilities.

TABLE 15.9   pH of Salt Solutions

		ANION	
		Conjugate base of strong acid	Conjugate base of weak acid
CATION	**Conjugate acid of weak base**	*Acidic*	*Depends on relative strengths*
	Small, highly charged metal ion	*Acidic*	*Depends on relative strengths*
	Counterion of strong base	*Neutral*	*Basic*

EXAMPLE 15.16   Determining the Overall Acidity or Basicity of Salt Solutions

Determine if the solution formed by each salt is acidic, basic, or neutral.

(a) $SrCl_2$
(b) $AlBr_3$
(c) $CH_3NH_3NO_3$
(d) $NaCHO_2$
(e) NH_4F

SOLUTION

(a) The Sr^{2+} cation is the counterion of a strong base ($Sr(OH)_2$) and is pH-neutral. The Cl^- anion is the conjugate base of a strong acid (HCl) and is pH-neutral as well. The $SrCl_2$ solution is therefore pH-neutral (neither acidic nor basic).

$SrCl_2$

pH-neutral cation · pH-neutral anion

Neutral solution

(b) The Al^{3+} cation is a small, highly charged metal ion (that is not an alkali metal or an alkaline earth metal) and is a weak acid. The Br^- anion is the conjugate base of a strong acid (HBr) and is pH-neutral. The $AlBr_3$ solution is therefore acidic.

$AlBr_3$

acidic cation   pH-neutral anion

Acidic solution

(c) The $CH_3NH_3^+$ ion is the conjugate acid of a weak base (CH_3NH_2) and is acidic. The NO_3^- anion is the conjugate base of a strong acid (HNO_3) and is pH-neutral. The $CH_3NH_3NO_3$ solution is therefore acidic.

$CH_3NH_3NO_3$

acidic cation   pH-neutral anion

Acidic solution

(d) The Na^+ cation is the counterion of a strong base and is pH-neutral. The CHO_2^- anion is the conjugate base of a weak acid and is basic. The $NaCHO_2$ solution is therefore basic.

$NaCHO_2$

pH-neutral cation   basic anion

Basic solution

(e) The NH_4^+ ion is the conjugate acid of a weak base (NH_3) and is acidic. The F^- ion is the conjugate base of a weak acid and is basic. To determine the overall acidity or basicity of the solution, compare the values of K_a for the acidic cation and K_b for the basic anion. Obtain each value of K from the conjugate by using $K_a \times K_b = K_w$.

NH_4F

acidic cation   basic anion

$$K_a(NH_4^+) = \frac{K_w}{K_b(NH_3)} = \frac{1.0 \times 10^{-14}}{1.76 \times 10^{-5}}$$

$$= 5.68 \times 10^{-10}$$

$$K_b(F^-) = \frac{K_w}{K_a(HF)} = \frac{1.0 \times 10^{-14}}{3.5 \times 10^{-4}}$$

$$= 2.9 \times 10^{-11}$$

Since K_a is greater than K_b, the solution is acidic.

$K_a > K_b$ Acidic solution

FOR PRACTICE 15.16
Determine if the solution formed by each salt is acidic, basic, or neutral.
(a) $NaHCO_3$ **(b)** $CH_3CH_2NH_3Cl$ **(c)** KNO_3 **(d)** $Fe(NO_3)_3$

15.9 Polyprotic Acids

In Section 15.4, we discussed that some acids, called polyprotic acids, contain two or more ionizable protons. Recall that sulfurous acid (H_2SO_3) is a diprotic acid containing two ionizable protons and phosphoric acid (H_3PO_4) is a triprotic acid containing three ionizable protons. Typically, a **polyprotic acid** ionizes in successive steps, each with its own K_a. For example, sulfurous acid ionizes in two steps:

$$H_2SO_3(aq) \rightleftharpoons H^+(aq) + HSO_3^-(aq) \qquad K_{a_1} = 1.6 \times 10^{-2}$$

$$HSO_3^-(aq) \rightleftharpoons H^+(aq) + SO_3^{2-}(aq) \qquad K_{a_2} = 6.4 \times 10^{-8}$$

K_{a_1} is the acid ionization constant for the first step and K_{a_2} is the acid ionization constant for the second step. Notice that K_{a_2} is smaller than K_{a_1}. This is true for all polyprotic acids and makes sense because the first proton separates from a neutral molecule while the second must separate from an anion. The negatively charged anion holds the positively charged proton more tightly, making the proton more difficult to remove and resulting in a smaller value of K_a. Table 15.10 lists some common polyprotic acids and their acid ionization constants. Notice that in all cases, the value of K_a for each step becomes successively smaller. The value of K_{a_1} for sulfuric acid is listed as strong because sulfuric acid is strong in the first step and weak in the second.

TABLE 15.10 Common Polyprotic Acids and Ionization Constants at 25 °C

Name (Formula)	Structure	Space-filling model	K_{a_1}	K_{a_2}	K_{a_3}
Sulfuric Acid (H_2SO_4)			Strong	1.2×10^{-2}	
Oxalic Acid ($H_2C_2O_4$)			6.0×10^{-2}	6.1×10^{-5}	
Sulfurous Acid (H_2SO_3)			1.6×10^{-2}	6.4×10^{-8}	
Phosphoric Acid (H_3PO_4)			7.5×10^{-3}	6.2×10^{-8}	4.2×10^{-13}
Citric Acid ($H_3C_6H_5O_7$)			7.4×10^{-4}	1.7×10^{-5}	4.0×10^{-7}
Ascorbic Acid ($H_2C_6H_6O_6$)			8.0×10^{-5}	1.6×10^{-12}	
Carbonic Acid (H_2CO_3)			4.3×10^{-7}	5.6×10^{-11}	

Finding the pH of Polyprotic Acid Solutions

Finding the pH of a polyprotic acid solution is less difficult than we might first imagine because, for most polyprotic acids, K_{a_1} is much larger than K_{a_2} (or K_{a_3} for triprotic acids). Therefore the amount of H_3O^+ formed by the first ionization step is much larger than that formed by the second or third ionization step. In addition, the formation of H_3O^+ in the first step inhibits the formation of additional H_3O^+ in the second step (because of Le Châtelier's principle). Consequently, we treat most polyprotic acid solutions as if the first step were the only one that contributes to the H_3O^+ concentration, as shown in Example 15.17. A major exception is a dilute solution of sulfuric acid, which we examine in Example 15.18.

EXAMPLE 15.17   Finding the pH of a Polyprotic Acid Solution

Find the pH of a 0.100 M ascorbic acid ($H_2C_6H_6O_6$) solution.

SOLUTION

To find the pH, you must find the equilibrium concentration of H_3O^+. Treat the problem as a weak acid pH problem with a single ionizable proton. The second proton contributes a negligible amount to the concentration of H_3O^+ and can be ignored. Follow the procedure from Example 15.6, shown in condensed form here. Use K_{a_1} for ascorbic acid from Table 15.10.

$$H_2C_6H_6O_6(aq) + H_2O(l) \rightleftharpoons H_3O^+(aq) + HC_6H_6O_6^-(aq)$$

	$[H_2C_6H_6O_6]$	$[H_3O^+]$	$[HC_6H_6O_6^-]$
Initial	0.100	≈ 0.00	0.000
Change	$-x$	$+x$	$+x$
Equil	$0.100 - x$	x	x

$$K_{a_1} = \frac{[H_3O^+][HC_6H_6O_6^-]}{[H_2C_6H_6O_6]}$$

$$= \frac{x^2}{0.100 - \cancel{x}} \quad (x \text{ is small})$$

$$8.0 \times 10^{-5} = \frac{x^2}{0.100}$$

$$x = 2.8 \times 10^{-3}$$

Confirm that the *x is small* approximation is valid by calculating the ratio of x to the number it was subtracted from in the approximation. The ratio should be less than 0.05 (or 5%).

$$\frac{2.8 \times 10^{-3}}{0.100} \times 100\% = 2.8\%$$

The approximation is valid. Therefore,

Calculate the pH from H_3O^+ concentration.

$$[H_3O^+] = 2.8 \times 10^{-3} \text{M}.$$

$$pH = -\log(2.8 \times 10^{-3}) = 2.55$$

FOR PRACTICE 15.17
Find the pH of a 0.050 M H_2CO_3 solution.

EXAMPLE 15.18   Dilute H_2SO_4 Solutions

Find the pH of a 0.0100 M sulfuric acid (H_2SO_4) solution.

SOLUTION

Sulfuric acid is strong in its first ionization step and weak in its second. Begin by writing the equations for the two steps. As the concentration of an H_2SO_4 solution becomes smaller, the second ionization step becomes more significant because the percent ionization increases (as discussed in Section 15.6). Therefore, for a concentration of 0.0100 M, you can't neglect the H_3O^+ contribution from the second step, as you can for other polyprotic acids. You must calculate the H_3O^+ contributions from both steps.

$$H_2SO_4(aq) + H_2O(l) \longrightarrow H_3O^+(aq) + HSO_4^-(aq) \quad \text{Strong}$$

$$HSO_4^-(aq) + H_2O(l) \rightleftharpoons H_3O^+(aq) + SO_4^{2-}(aq) \quad K_{a_2} = 0.012$$

The $[H_3O^+]$ that results from the first ionization step is 0.0100 M (because the first step is strong). To determine the $[H_3O^+]$ formed by the second step, prepare an ICE table for the second step in which the initial concentration of H_3O^+ is 0.0100 M. The initial concentration of HSO_4^- must also be 0.0100 M (due to the stoichiometry of the ionization reaction).

	$[HSO_4^-]$	$[H_3O^+]$	$[SO_4^{2-}]$
Initial	0.0100	≈ 0.0100	0.000
Change	$-x$	$+x$	$+x$
Equil	$0.0100 - x$	$0.0100 + x$	x

Substitute the expressions for the equilibrium concentrations (from the table just shown) into the expression for K_{a_2}. In this case, you cannot make the *x is small* approximation because the equilibrium constant (0.012) *is not small* relative to the initial concentration (0.0100).

Substitute the value of K_{a_2} and multiply out the expression to arrive at the standard quadratic form.

$$K_{a_2} = \frac{[H_3O^+][SO_4^{2-}]}{[HSO_4^-]}$$
$$= \frac{(0.0100 + x)x}{0.0100 - x}$$
$$0.012 = \frac{0.0100x + x^2}{0.0100 - x}$$
$$0.012(0.0100 - x) = 0.0100x + x^2$$
$$0.00012 - 0.012x = 0.0100x + x^2$$
$$x^2 + 0.022x - 0.00012 = 0$$

Solve the quadratic equation using the quadratic formula.

$$x = \frac{-b \pm \sqrt{b^2 - 4ac}}{2a}$$
$$= \frac{-(0.022) \pm \sqrt{(0.022)^2 - 4(1)(-0.00012)}}{2(1)}$$
$$= \frac{-0.022 \pm 0.031}{2}$$

$x = -0.027$ or $x = 0.0045$

Since x represents a concentration, and since concentrations cannot be negative, we reject the negative root.
$x = 0.0045$

Determine the H_3O^+ concentration from the calculated value of x and calculate the pH. Notice that the second step produces almost half as much H_3O^+ as the first step—an amount that must not be neglected. This will always be the case with dilute H_2SO_4 solutions.

$$[H_3O^+] = 0.0100 + x$$
$$= 0.0100 + 0.0045$$
$$= 0.0145 \text{ M}$$
$$pH = -\log[H_3O^+]$$
$$= -\log(0.0145)$$
$$= 1.84$$

FOR PRACTICE 15.18
Find the pH and $[SO_4^{2-}]$ of a 0.0075 M sulfuric acid solution.

Finding the Concentration of the Anions for a Weak Diprotic Acid Solution

In some cases, we may want to know the concentrations of the anions formed by a polyprotic acid. Consider the following generic polyprotic acid H_2X and its ionization steps:

$$H_2X(aq) + H_2O(l) \rightleftharpoons H_3O^+(aq) + HX^-(aq) \qquad K_{a_1}$$
$$HX^-(aq) + H_2O(l) \rightleftharpoons H_3O^+(aq) + X^{2-}(aq) \qquad K_{a_2}$$

In Examples 15.17 and 15.18, we illustrated how to find the concentration of H_3O^+ for such a solution, which is equal to the concentration of HX^-. What if instead we needed to find the concentration of X^{2-}? To find the concentration of X^{2-}, we use the concentration of HX^- and H_3O^+ (from the first ionization step) as the initial concentrations for the second ionization step. We then solve a second equilibrium problem using the second ionization equation and K_{a_2}, as shown in Example 15.19.

EXAMPLE 15.19 Finding the Concentration of the Anions for a Weak Diprotic Acid Solution

Find the $[C_6H_6O_6^{2-}]$ of the 0.100 M ascorbic acid ($H_2C_6H_6O_6$) solution in Example 15.17.

SOLUTION

To find the $[C_6H_6O_6^{2-}]$, use the concentrations of $[HC_6H_6O_6^-]$ and H_3O^+ produced by the first ionization step (as calculated in Example 15.17) as the initial concentrations for the second step. Because of the 1:1 stoichiometry, $[HC_6H_6O_6^-]$ = $[H_3O^+]$. Then solve an equilibrium problem for the second step similar to that of Example 15.6, shown in condensed form here. Use K_{a_2} for ascorbic acid from Table 15.10.

$$HC_6H_6O_6^-(aq) + H_2O(l) \rightleftharpoons H_3O^+(aq) + C_6H_6O_6^{2-}(aq)$$

	$[HC_6H_6O_6^-]$	$[H_3O^+]$	$[C_6H_6O_6^{2-}]$
Initial	2.8×10^{-3}	2.8×10^{-3}	0.000
Change	$-x$	$+x$	$+x$
Equil	$2.8 \times 10^{-3} - x$	$2.8 \times 10^{-3} + x$	x

$$K_{a_2} = \frac{[H_3O^+][C_6H_6O_6^{2-}]}{[HC_6H_6O_6^-]}$$

$$= \frac{(2.8 \times 10^{-3} + \cancel{x})x}{2.8 \times 10^{-3} - \cancel{x}} \quad (x \text{ is small})$$

$$= \frac{(\cancel{2.8 \times 10^{-3}})x}{\cancel{2.8 \times 10^{-3}}}$$

$$x = K_{a_2} = 1.6 \times 10^{-12}$$

Since x is much smaller than 2.8×10^{-3}, the x *is small* approximation is valid. Therefore,

$$[C_6H_6O_6^{2-}] = 1.6 \times 10^{-12} \text{ M}.$$

FOR PRACTICE 15.19

Find the $[CO_3^{2-}]$ of the 0.050 M carbonic acid (H_2CO_3) solution in For Practice 15.17.

Notice from the results of Example 15.19 that the concentration of X^{2-} for a weak diprotic acid H_2X is equal to K_{a_2}. This general result applies to all diprotic acids in which the x *is small* approximation is valid. Notice also that the concentration of H_3O^+ produced by the second ionization step of a diprotic acid is very small compared to the concentration produced by the first step, as shown in Figure 15.13 ▼.

Dissociation of a Polyprotic Acid

$$H_2C_6H_6O_6(aq) + H_2O(l) \rightleftharpoons H_3O^+(aq) + HC_6H_6O_6^-(aq)$$

$$\left[H_3O^+\right] = 2.8 \times 10^{-3} \text{ M}$$

$$HC_6H_6O_6^-(aq) + H_2O(l) \rightleftharpoons H_3O^+(aq) + C_6H_6O_6^{2-}(aq)$$

$$\left[H_3O^+\right] = 1.6 \times 10^{-12} \text{ M}$$

0.100 M $H_2C_6H_6O_6$

$$\text{Total} \left[H_3O^+\right] = 2.8 \times 10^{-3} \text{ M} + 1.6 \times 10^{-12} \text{ M}$$

$$= 2.8 \times 10^{-3} \text{ M}$$

◀ **FIGURE 15.13 Dissociation of a Polyprotic Acid** A 0.100 M $H_2C_6H_6O_6$ solution contains an H_3O^+ concentration of 2.8×10^{-3} M from the first step. The amount of H_3O^+ contributed by the second step is only 1.6×10^{-12} M, which is insignificant compared to the amount produced by the first step.

15.10 Acid Strength and Molecular Structure

We have learned that a Brønsted–Lowry acid is a proton (H^+) donor. However, we have not explored why some hydrogen-containing molecules act as acids while others do not, or why some acids are strong and others weak. For example, why is H_2S acidic while CH_4 is not? Or why is HF a weak acid while HCl is a strong acid? We will divide our discussion about these issues into two categories: binary acids (those containing hydrogen and only one other element) and oxyacids (those containing hydrogen bonded to an oxygen atom that is bonded to another element).

Binary Acids

Consider the bond between a hydrogen atom and some other generic element (which we will call Y):

$$H—Y$$

The factors affecting the ease with which this hydrogen is donated (and therefore be acidic) are the *polarity* of the bond and the *strength* of the bond.

Bond Polarity Using the notation introduced in Chapter 9, the H—Y bond must be polarized with the hydrogen atom as the positive pole in order for HY to be acidic:

$$\delta^+H—Y^{\delta-}$$

This requirement makes physical sense because the hydrogen atom must be lost as a positively charged ion (H^+). A partial positive charge on the hydrogen atom facilitates its loss. Consider the following three bonds and their corresponding dipole moments:

$$H—Li \qquad H—C \qquad H—F$$

Not acidic   Not acidic   Acidic

LiH is ionic with *the negative charge on the hydrogen atom*; therefore, LiH is not acidic. The C—H bond is virtually nonpolar because the electronegativities of carbon and hydrogen are similar; therefore C—H is not acidic. In contrast, the H—F bond is polar with the positive charge on the hydrogen atom. As we know from this chapter, HF is an acid. This is because the partial positive charge on the hydrogen atom makes it easier for the hydrogen to be lost as an H^+ ion.

Bond Strength The strength of the H—Y bond also affects the strength of the corresponding acid. As you might expect, the stronger the bond, the weaker the acid—the more tightly the hydrogen atom is held, the less likely it is to come off. We can see the effect of bond strength by comparing the bond strengths and acidities of the hydrogen halides:

Acid	Bond Energy (kJ/mol)	Type of Acid
H—F	565	Weak
H—Cl	431	Strong
H—Br	364	Strong

HCl and HBr have weaker bonds and are both strong acids. HF, however, has a stronger bond and is therefore a weak acid, despite the greater bond polarity of HF.

The Combined Effect of Bond Polarity and Bond Strength We can see the combined effect of bond polarity and bond strength by examining the trends in acidity of the group 6A and 7A hydrides as shown in Figure 15.14 ◄. The hydrides become more acidic from left to right as the H—Y bond becomes more polar. The hydrides also become more acidic from top to bottom as the H—Y bond becomes weaker.

Increasing electronegativity
Increasing acidity

Decreasing bond strength
Increasing acidity

6A	7A
H_2O	HF
H_2S	HCl
H_2Se	HBr
H_2Te	HI

▲ FIGURE 15.14 **Acidity of the Group 6A and 7A Hydrides** From left to right, the hydrides become more acidic because the H—Y bond becomes more polar. From top to bottom, these hydrides become more acidic because the H—Y bond becomes weaker.

Oxyacids

Oxyacids contain a hydrogen atom bonded to an oxygen atom. The oxygen atom is in turn bonded to another atom (which we will call Y):

| Oxyacids are sometimes called oxoacids.

$$H-O-Y-\blacktriangleleft$$

Y may or may not be bonded to yet other atoms. The factors affecting the ease with which the hydrogen in an oxyacid will be donated (and therefore be acidic) are the *electronegativity of the element Y* and the *number of oxygen atoms attached to the element Y*.

The Electronegativity of Y The more electronegative the element Y, the more it weakens and polarizes the H—O bond and the more acidic the oxyacid is. We can see this effect by comparing the electronegativity of Y and the acid ionization constants of the following oxyacids:

Acid	Electronegativity of Y	K_a
H—O—I	2.5	2.3×10^{-11}
H—O—Br	2.8	2.0×10^{-9}
H—O—Cl	3.0	2.9×10^{-8}

Chlorine is the most electronegative of the three elements and the corresponding acid has the greatest K_a.

The Number of Oxygen Atoms Bonded to Y Oxyacids may contain additional oxygen atoms bonded to the element Y. Because these additional oxygen atoms are electronegative, they draw electron density away from Y, which in turn draws electron density away from the H—O bond, further weakening and polarizing it, and leading to increasing acidity. We can see this effect by comparing the following series of acid ionization constants:

Acid	Structure	K_a
$HClO_4$	H—O—Cl(=O)(=O)=O	Strong
$HClO_3$	H—O—Cl(=O)=O	1
$HClO_2$	H—O—Cl=O	1.1×10^{-2}
$HClO$	H—O—Cl	2.9×10^{-8}

The greater the number of oxygen atoms bonded to Y, the stronger the acid. On this basis we would predict that H_2SO_4 is a stronger acid than H_2SO_3 and that HNO_3 is stronger than HNO_2. As we have seen in this chapter, both H_2SO_4 and HNO_3 are strong acids, while H_2SO_3 and HNO_2 are weak acids, as predicted.

Conceptual Connection 15.7 Acid Strength and Molecular Structure

Which of the protons shown in red is more acidic?

$$H-C(=O)-O-H \qquad H-C(H)(H)-O-H$$

(a)   (b)

15.11 Lewis Acids and Bases

We began our definitions of acids and bases with the Arrhenius model. We then saw how the Brønsted–Lowry model, by introducing the concept of a proton donor and proton acceptor, expanded the range of substances that we consider acids and bases. We now introduce a third model, which further broadens the range of substances that we can consider acids. This third model is the *Lewis model*, named after G. N. Lewis, the American chemist who devised the electron-dot representation of chemical bonding (Section 9.1). While the Brønsted–Lowry model focuses on the transfer of a proton, the Lewis model focuses on the transfer of an electron pair. Consider the simple acid–base reaction between the H^+ ion and NH_3, shown here with Lewis structures:

$$H^+ \ + \ :NH_3 \longrightarrow \left[H{:}NH_3\right]^+$$

Brønsted–Lowry model focuses on the proton

Lewis model focuses on the electron pair

According to the Brønsted–Lowry model, the ammonia accepts a proton, thus acting as a base. According to the Lewis model, the ammonia acts as a base by *donating an electron pair*. The general definitions of acids and bases according to the Lewis model focus on the electron pair.

Lewis acid: electron pair acceptor

Lewis base: electron pair donor

According to the Lewis definition, H^+ in the reaction just shown is acting as an acid because it is accepting an electron pair from NH_3. NH_3 is acting as a Lewis base because it is donating an electron pair to H^+.

Although the Lewis model does not significantly expand the substances that can be considered a base—because all proton acceptors must have an electron pair to bind the proton—it does significantly expand the substances that can be considered an acid. According to the Lewis model, a substance need not even contain hydrogen to be an acid. For example, consider the gas-phase reaction between boron trifluoride and ammonia shown here:

$$BF_3 \ + \ :NH_3 \longrightarrow F_3B{:}NH_3$$

Lewis acid   Lewis base   adduct

Boron trifluoride has an empty orbital that can accept the electron pair from ammonia and form the product (the product of a Lewis acid–base reaction is sometimes called an *adduct*). The reaction just shown demonstrates an important property of Lewis acids:

A Lewis acid has an empty orbital (or can rearrange electrons to create an empty orbital) that can accept an electron pair.

Consequently, the Lewis definition subsumes a whole new class of acids. Next we examine a few examples.

Molecules That Act as Lewis Acids

Since molecules with incomplete octets have empty orbitals, they can serve as Lewis acids. For example, both $AlCl_3$ and BCl_3 have incomplete octets:

These both act as Lewis acids, as shown in the following reactions:

$$:\ddot{C}l-Al \begin{smallmatrix} :\ddot{C}l: \\ | \\ | \\ :\ddot{C}l: \end{smallmatrix} + :N \begin{smallmatrix} H \\ | \\ | \\ H \end{smallmatrix}-H \longrightarrow :\ddot{C}l-Al:N \begin{smallmatrix} :\ddot{C}l: \\ | \\ | \\ :\ddot{C}l: \end{smallmatrix} \begin{smallmatrix} H \\ | \\ | \\ H \end{smallmatrix}-H$$

$$:\ddot{C}l-B \begin{smallmatrix} :\ddot{C}l: \\ | \\ | \\ :\ddot{C}l: \end{smallmatrix} + H_3C \overset{\ddot{O}:}{\underset{C}{\underset{H_2}{}}} \underset{H_2}{\overset{}{C}} CH_3 \longrightarrow H_3C \overset{:\ddot{C}l:}{\underset{C}{\underset{H_2}{}}} \overset{:\ddot{C}l-B-\ddot{C}l:}{\underset{C}{\underset{H_2}{}}} CH_3$$

Some molecules that may not initially contain empty orbitals can rearrange their electrons to act as Lewis acids. Consider the reaction between carbon dioxide and water:

$$\underset{\substack{\text{Water} \\ \textbf{Lewis base}}}{H \overset{H}{\underset{H}{\ddot{O}:}} + \overset{\ddot{O}:}{\underset{:O:}{C}}} \underset{\substack{\text{Carbon dioxide} \\ \textbf{Lewis acid}}}{\overset{\ddot{O}:}{\underset{:O:}{}}} \longrightarrow H-\overset{}{\underset{:O:}{O}}-C \longrightarrow \underset{\substack{\text{Carbonic acid}}}{H-\ddot{O}-\overset{H-\ddot{O}:}{\underset{:O:}{C}}}$$

Water   Carbon dioxide   Carbonic acid
Lewis base   Lewis acid

The electrons in the double bond on carbon move to the terminal oxygen atom, allowing carbon dioxide to act as a Lewis acid by accepting an electron pair from water. The molecule then undergoes a rearrangement in which the hydrogen atom shown in red bonds with the terminal oxygen atom instead of the internal one.

Cations That Act as Lewis Acids

Some cations, since they are positively charged and have lost some electrons, have empty orbitals that allow them to also act as Lewis acids. Consider the hydration process of the Al^{3+} ion discussed in Section 15.8 shown here:

$$\underset{\substack{\text{Lewis} \\ \text{acid}}}{Al^{3+}(aq)} + 6 \underset{\substack{\text{Lewis} \\ \text{base}}}{\left[\begin{smallmatrix} H \\ | \\ :O: \\ | \\ H \end{smallmatrix} \right](l)} \longrightarrow Al \left[\begin{smallmatrix} H \\ | \\ :O: \\ | \\ H \end{smallmatrix} \right]_6^{3+}(aq)$$

The aluminum ion acts as a Lewis acid, accepting lone pairs from six water molecules to form the hydrated ion. Many other small, highly charged metal ions also act as Lewis acids in this way.

15.12 Acid Rain

About 83% of U.S. energy comes from the combustion of fossil fuels, including petroleum, natural gas, and coal (Figure 15.15 ▶). Some fossil fuels, especially coal, contain small amounts of sulfur impurities. During combustion, these impurities react with oxygen to form SO_2. In addition, during combustion of any fossil fuel, nitrogen from the air reacts with oxygen to form NO_2. SO_2 and NO_2 react with water and O_2 in the atmosphere to form sulfuric acid and nitric acid:

$$2\,SO_2 + O_2 + 2\,H_2O \longrightarrow 2\,H_2SO_4$$
$$4\,NO_2 + O_2 + 2\,H_2O \longrightarrow 4\,HNO_3$$

U.S. Energy Consumption by Source, 2010

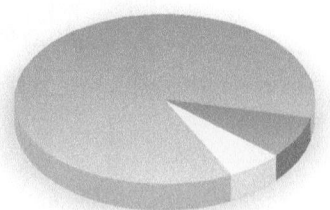

■ Fossil Fuels: 83%
■ Nuclear: 9%
▨ Renewable Energy: 8%

▲ **FIGURE 15.15 Sources of U.S. Energy** About 83% of U.S. energy comes from fossil fuel combustion.
Source: U.S EIA Annual Energy Review 2011

▶ FIGURE 15.16 **Acid Rain** Acid rain is a significant problem in the northeastern United States. The map shows the pH of rain that falls across the United States.
Source: National Atmospheric Deposition Program, National Trends Network

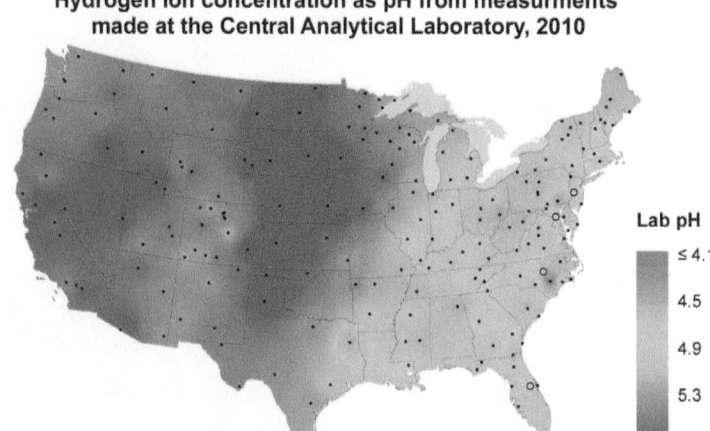

Hydrogen ion concentration as pH from measurments made at the Central Analytical Laboratory, 2010

Lab pH
≤ 4.1
4.5
4.9
5.3
≥ 5.7

These acids combine with rain to form *acid rain*. The problem is greatest in the northeastern portion of the United States, where the rain is significantly acidic because the sulfur and nitrogen oxides produced by coal combustion in the Midwest are carried toward the Northeast by natural air currents.

Even in relatively unpolluted areas, rain is naturally somewhat acidic because of atmospheric carbon dioxide. Carbon dioxide combines with rainwater to form carbonic acid:

$$CO_2 + H_2O \longrightarrow H_2CO_3$$

However, carbonic acid is a relatively weak acid. Rain that is saturated with CO_2 has a pH of about 5.6, which is only mildly acidic. When nitric acid and sulfuric acid mix with rain, the pH of the rain can fall below 4.3 (Figure 15.16 ▲). Remember that because of the logarithmic nature of the pH scale, rain with a pH of 4.3 has an $[H_3O^+]$ that is 20 times greater than rain with a pH of 5.6. Rain that is this acidic has a harmful impact.

▼ FIGURE 15.17 **The Effects of Acid Rain** (a) Buildings, gravestones, and statues damaged by acid rain are a common sight in the northeastern United States and in many other industrialized nations. (b) Some species of trees are highly susceptible to the effects of acid rain.

Effects of Acid Rain

Acids dissolve metals and acid rain degrades metal structures. Bridges, railroads, and even automobiles can be damaged by acid rain. Since acids react with carbonates, acid rain also harms building materials that contain carbonates (CO_3^{2-}), including marble, cement, and limestone. Statues, buildings, and pathways in the Northeast show significant signs of acid rain damage (Figure 15.17a ▼).

(a)

(b)

Acid rain also accumulates in lakes and rivers and affects aquatic life. Many lakes, especially those whose surrounding land contains significant amounts of limestone ($CaCO_3$), have the ability to neutralize acidic rain. In the Midwest, for example, limestone-rich soils prevent most lakes from becoming acidified. In the northeastern United States, however, the lack of limestone makes lakes more susceptible, and over 2000 lakes and streams have increased acidity levels due to acid rain. Aquatic plants, frogs, salamanders, and some species of fish are sensitive to acid levels and cannot survive in the acidified water. Trees can also be affected by acid rain because the acid removes nutrients from the soil, making survival difficult (Figure 15.17b ◀).

Acid Rain Legislation

In 1990, the U.S. Congress passed amendments to the Clean Air Act specifically targeted at reducing acid rain. These amendments force electrical utilities—which are the most significant source of SO_2—to lower their SO_2 emissions gradually over time. The result has been a 75% decrease in SO_2 pollutant levels in the United States since 1990 (Figure 15.18 ▼). The acidity of rain over the northeastern United States has begun to decrease, and lakes are beginning to recover. In the early 1990s, scientists categorized 30% of the lakes in the Northeast as being of *acute concern*, which means that a complete loss of fish population is expected. Today, the fraction of lakes in this category has been reduced to less than 18%. The acid rain program has been a dramatic success, and today's environmental legislation—such as legislation aimed at global warming—is using the acid rain legislation as a model for what can work.

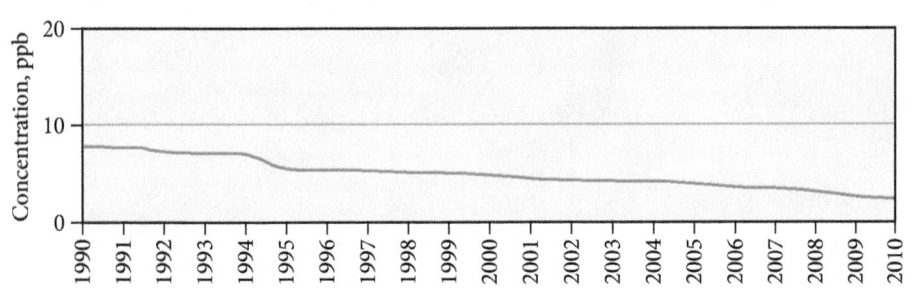

SO₂ AIR QUALITY, 1990-2010

◀ **FIGURE 15.18 U.S. Sulfur Dioxide Pollutant Levels** As a result of amendments to the Clean Air Act passed in 1990, SO_2 levels have been decreasing and will continue to decrease in the coming years.
Source: U.S. EPA Air Trends, 2011

CHAPTER IN REVIEW

Self Assessment Quiz

Q1. Identify the conjugate base in the reaction shown here:

$$HClO_2(aq) + H_2O(aq) \rightleftharpoons H_3O^+(aq) + ClO_2^-(aq)$$

a) $HClO_2$
b) H_2O
c) H_3O^+
d) ClO_2^-

Q2. Which pair is a Brønsted–Lowry conjugate acid–base pair?
a) NH_3; NH_4^+
b) H_3O^+; OH^-
c) HCl; HBr
d) ClO_4^-; ClO_3^-

Q3. Consider the given acid ionization constants. Identify the strongest conjugate base.

Acid	K_a
$HNO_2(aq)$	4.6×10^{-4}
$HCHO_2(aq)$	1.8×10^{-4}
$HClO(aq)$	2.9×10^{-8}
$HCN(aq)$	4.9×10^{-10}

a) $NO_2^-(aq)$
b) $CHO_2^-(aq)$
c) $ClO^-(aq)$
d) $CN^-(aq)$

Q4. What is the OH^- concentration in an aqueous solution at 25 °C in which $[H_3O^+] = 1.9 \times 10^{-9}$ M?
a) 1.9×10^{-9} M
b) 5.3×10^{-6} M
c) 5.3×10^6 M
d) 1.9×10^{-23} M

Q5. An $HNO_3(aq)$ solution has a pH of 1.75. What is the molar concentration of the $HNO_3(aq)$ solution?
a) 1.75 M
b) 5.6×10^{-13} M
c) 56 M
d) 0.018 M

Q6. Find the pH of a 0.350 M aqueous benzoic acid solution. For benzoic acid, $K_a = 6.5 \times 10^{-5}$.
a) 4.64
b) 4.19
c) 2.32
d) 11.68

Q7. Find the pH of a 0.155 M $HClO_2(aq)$ solution. For $HClO_2$, $K_a = 0.011$.
a) 0.92
b) 1.44
c) 1.39
d) 0.69

Q8. Calculate the percent ionization of 1.45 M aqueous acetic acid solution. For acetic acid, $K_a = 1.8 \times 10^{-5}$.
a) 0.35%
b) 0.0018%
c) 0.29%
d) 0.0051%

Q9. Consider two aqueous solutions of nitrous acid (HNO_2). Solution A has a concentration of $[HNO_2] = 0.55$ M and solution B has a concentration of $[HNO_2] = 1.25$ M. Which statement about the two solutions is true?
a) Solution A has the higher percent ionization and the higher pH.
b) Solution B has the higher percent ionization and the higher pH.
c) Solution A has the higher percent ionization and solution B has the higher pH.
d) Solution B has the higher percent ionization and solution A has the higher pH.

Q10. Find the $[OH^-]$ in a 0.200 M solution of ethylamine ($C_2H_5NH_2$). For ethylamine, $K_b = 5.6 \times 10^{-4}$.
a) 11.52 M
b) 2.48 M
c) 0.033 M
d) 0.011 M

Q11. Which ion will form a basic solution when dissolved in water?
a) Br^-
b) NO_3^-
c) HSO_4^-
d) SO_3^{2-}

Q12. Which compound will form an acidic solution when dissolved in water?
a) NH_4Cl
b) $NaCl$
c) KNO_2
d) $Ca(NO_3)_2$

Q13. Find the pH of 0.175 M NaCN solution. For HCN, $K_a = 4.9 \times 10^{-10}$.
a) 5.03
b) 11.28
c) 2.31
d) 8.97

Q14. What is the concentration of X^{2-} in a 0.150 M solution of the diprotic acid H_2X? For H_2X, $K_{a_1} = 4.5 \times 10^{-6}$ and $K_{a_2} = 1.2 \times 10^{-11}$.
a) 9.9×10^{-8} M
b) 2.0×10^{-9} M
c) 8.2×10^{-4} M
d) 1.2×10^{-11} M

Q15. Which acid has the largest K_a: $HClO_2(aq)$, $HBrO_2(aq)$, or $HIO_2(aq)$?
a) $HClO_2(aq)$
b) $HBrO_2(aq)$
c) $HIO_2(aq)$
d) All three acids have the same K_a.

Answers: 1. (d) 2. (a) 3. (d) 4. (b) 5. (d) 6. (c) 7. (b) 8. (a) 9. (a) 10. (d) 11. (d) 12. (a) 13. (b) 14. (a) 15. (a)

Key Terms

Section 15.2
carboxylic acid (699)
alkaloid (700)

Section 15.3
Arrhenius definitions (of acids and bases) (700)
hydronium ion (701)
Brønsted–Lowry definitions (of acids and bases) (701)

amphoteric (701)
conjugate acid–base pair (702)
conjugate acid (702)
conjugate base (702)

Section 15.4
strong acid (703)
weak acid (703)
monoprotic acid (703)
diprotic acid (703)

triprotic acid (704)
acid ionization constant (K_a) (705)

Section 15.5
autoionization (706)
ion product constant for water (K_w) (706)
neutral (706)
acidic solution (706)

basic solution (707)
pH (708)

Section 15.6
percent ionization (716)

Section 15.7
strong base (720)
weak base (720)
base ionization constant
  (K_b) (721)

Section 15.9
polyprotic acid (731)

Section 15.11
Lewis acid (738)
Lewis base (738)

Key Concepts

Heartburn (15.1)
▶ Hydrochloric acid from the stomach sometimes comes in contact with the esophageal lining, resulting in irritation, called heartburn. Heartburn is treated with antacids, bases that neutralize stomach acid.

The Nature of Acids and Bases (15.2)
▶ Acids generally taste sour, dissolve metals, turn blue litmus paper red, and neutralize bases. Common acids are hydrochloric, sulfuric, nitric, and carboxylic acids.
▶ Bases generally taste bitter, feel slippery, turn red litmus paper blue, and neutralize acids. Common bases are sodium hydroxide, sodium bicarbonate, and potassium hydroxide.

Definitions of Acids and Bases (15.3)
▶ The Arrhenius definition of acids and bases states that in an aqueous solution, an acid produces hydrogen ions and a base produces hydroxide ions.
▶ The Brønsted–Lowry definition states that an acid is a proton (hydrogen ion) donor and a base is a proton acceptor. According to the Brønsted–Lowry definition, two substances related by the transfer of a proton are a conjugate acid–base pair.

Acid Strength and the Acid Dissociation Constant, K_a (15.4)
▶ In a solution, a strong acid completely ionizes but a weak acid only partially ionizes.
▶ Generally, the stronger the acid, the weaker the conjugate base, and vice versa.
▶ The extent of dissociation of a weak acid is quantified by the acid dissociation constant, K_a, which is the equilibrium constant for the ionization of the weak acid.

Autoionization of Water and pH (15.5)
▶ In an acidic solution, the concentration of hydrogen ions is always greater than the concentration of hydroxide ions. $[H_3O^+]$ multiplied by $[OH^-]$ is always constant at a constant temperature.
▶ There are two types of logarithmic acid–base scales: pH and pOH. At 25 °C, the sum of the pH and pOH is always 14.

Finding the $[H_3O^+]$ and pH of Strong and Weak Acid Solutions (15.6)
▶ In a strong acid solution, the hydrogen ion concentration equals the initial concentration of the acid.
▶ In a weak acid solution, the hydrogen ion concentration—which can be determined by solving an equilibrium problem—is lower than the initial acid concentration.
▶ The percent ionization of weak acids decreases as the acid (and hydrogen ion) concentration increases.

▶ In mixtures of two acids with large K_a differences, the concentration of hydrogen ions can usually be determined by considering only the stronger of the two acids.

Base Solutions (15.7)
▶ A strong base dissociates completely; a weak base does not.
▶ Most weak bases produce hydroxide ions through the ionization of water. The base ionization constant, K_b, indicates the extent of ionization.

Ions as Acids and Bases (15.8)
▶ A cation is a weak acid if it is the conjugate acid of a weak base; it is neutral if it is the conjugate acid of a strong base.
▶ An anion is a weak base if it is the conjugate base of a weak acid; it is neutral if it is the conjugate base of a strong acid.
▶ To calculate the pH of an acidic cation or basic anion, we determine K_a or K_b from the equation $K_a \times K_b = K_w$.

Polyprotic Acids (15.9)
▶ Polyprotic acids contain two or more ionizable protons.
▶ Generally, polyprotic acids ionize in successive steps, with the value of K_a becoming smaller for each step.
▶ In many cases, we can determine the $[H_3O^+]$ of a polyprotic acid solution by considering only the first ionization step; then, the concentration of the acid anion formed in the second ionization step is equivalent to the value of K_{a_2}.

Acid Strength and Molecular Structure (15.10)
▶ For binary acids, acid strength decreases with increasing bond energy and increases with increasing bond polarity.
▶ For oxyacids, acid strength increases with the electronegativity of the atoms bonded to the oxygen atom and also increases with the number of oxygen atoms in the molecule.

Lewis Acids and Bases (15.11)
▶ A third model of acids and bases, the Lewis model, defines a base as an electron pair donor and an acid as an electron pair acceptor; therefore, according to this definition, an acid does not have to contain hydrogen. According to this definition an acid can be a compound with an empty orbital—or one that will rearrange to make an empty orbital—or a cation.

Acid Rain (15.12)
▶ The combustion of fossil fuels produces oxides of sulfur and nitrogen, which react with oxygen and water to form sulfuric and nitric acids. These acids then combine with rain to form acid rain.
▶ Acid rain corrodes man-made structures and damages aquatic environments and forests. Environmental legislation has helped stabilize the amount of acid rain being produced.

Key Equations and Relationships

Note: In all of these equations [H$^+$] is interchangeable with [H$_3$O$^+$].

Expression for the Acid Ionization Constant, K_a (15.4)

$$K_a = \frac{[H_3O^+][A^-]}{[HA]}$$

The Ion Product Constant for Water, K_w (15.5)

$$K_w = [H_3O^+][OH^-] = 1.0 \times 10^{-14}\,(\text{at } 25\,°C)$$

Expression for the pH Scale (15.5)

$$pH = -\log[H_3O^+]$$

Expression for the pOH Scale (15.5)

$$pOH = -\log[OH^-]$$

Relationship between pH and pOH (15.5)

$$pH + pOH = 14.00$$

Expression for the pK_a Scale (15.5)

$$pK_a = -\log K_a$$

Expression for Percent Ionization (15.6)

$$\text{Percent ionization} = \frac{\text{concentration of ionized acid}}{\text{initial concentration of acid}} \times 100\%$$

$$= \frac{[H_3O^+]_{equil}}{[HA]_{init}} \times 100\%$$

Relationship between K_a, K_b, and K_w (15.8)

$$K_a \times K_b = K_w$$

Key Learning Outcomes

Chapter Objectives	Assessment
Identifying Brønsted–Lowry Acids and Bases and Their Conjugates (15.3)	Example 15.1 For Practice 15.1 Exercises 35, 36
Using K_w in Calculations (15.5)	Example 15.2 For Practice 15.2 Exercises 47, 48
Calculating pH from [H$_3$O$^+$] or [OH$^-$] (15.5)	Examples 15.3, 15.4 For Practice 15.3, 15.4 Exercises 49–52
Finding the pH of a Weak Acid Solution (15.6)	Examples 15.5, 15.6, 15.7 For Practice 15.5, 15.6, 15.7 Exercises 63–68
Finding the Acid Ionization Constant from pH (15.6)	Example 15.8 For Practice 15.8 Exercises 69, 70
Finding the Percent Ionization of a Weak Acid (15.6)	Example 15.9 For Practice 15.9 Exercises 71–74
Mixtures of Weak Acids (15.6)	Example 15.10 For Practice 15.10 Exercises 79, 80
Finding the [OH$^-$] and pH of a Strong Base Solution (15.7)	Example 15.11 For Practice 15.11 Exercises 81, 82
Finding the [OH$^-$] and pH of a Weak Base Solution (15.7)	Example 15.12 For Practice 15.12 Exercises 89, 90
Determining Whether an Anion Is Basic or Neutral (15.8)	Example 15.13 For Practice 15.13 Exercises 95, 96
Determining the pH of a Solution Containing an Anion Acting as a Base (15.8)	Example 15.14 For Practice 15.14 Exercises 97, 98
Determining Whether a Cation Is Acidic or Neutral (15.8)	Example 15.15 For Practice 15.15 Exercises 99, 100
Determining the Overall Acidity or Basicity of Salt Solutions (15.8)	Example 15.16 For Practice 15.16 Exercises 101, 102

In the objectives table, the molecular models shown are Ammonia, Methylamine, and Pyridine.

Key Learning Outcome example in objectives:

$$H_2SO_4(aq) + H_2O(l) \longrightarrow HSO_4^-(aq) + H_3O^+(aq)$$

Acid · Base · Conjugate base · Conjugate acid

Key Learning Outcomes, *continued*

Finding the pH of a Polyprotic Acid Solution (15.9)	Example 15.17 For Practice 15.17 Exercises 111, 112
Finding the [H_3O^+] in Dilute H_2SO_4 Solutions (15.9)	Example 15.18 For Practice 15.18 Exercise 115
Finding the Concentration of the Anions for a Weak Diprotic Acid Solution (15.9)	Example 15.19 For Practice 15.19 Exercises 113, 114

EXERCISES

Review Questions

1. What causes heartburn? What are some possible ways to alleviate heartburn?

2. What are the general physical and chemical properties of acids? Of bases?

3. What is a carboxylic acid? Give an example.

4. What is the Arrhenius definition of an acid? Of a base?

5. What is a hydronium ion? Does H^+ exist in solution by itself?

6. What is the Brønsted–Lowry definition of an acid? Of a base?

7. Why is there more than one definition of acid–base behavior? Which definition is the right one?

8. Describe amphoteric behavior and give an example.

9. What is a conjugate acid–base pair? Provide an example.

10. Explain the difference between a strong acid and a weak acid and list one example of each.

11. What are diprotic and triprotic acids? List an example of each.

12. Define the acid ionization constant and explain its significance.

13. Write an equation for the autoionization of water and an expression for the ion product constant for water (K_w). What is the value of K_w at 25 °C?

14. What happens to the [OH^-] of a solution when the [H_3O^+] is increased? Decreased?

15. Define pH. What pH range is considered acidic? Basic? Neutral?

16. Define pOH. What pOH range is considered acidic? Basic? Neutral?

17. In most solutions containing a strong or weak acid, the autoionization of water can be neglected when calculating [H_3O^+]. Explain why this statement is valid.

18. When calculating [H_3O^+] for weak acid solutions, we can often use the *x is small* approximation. Explain the nature of this approximation and why it is valid.

19. What is the percent ionization of an acid? Explain what happens to the percent ionization of a weak acid as a function of the concentration of the weak acid solution.

20. In calculating [H_3O^+] for a mixture of a strong acid and weak acid, the weak acid can often be neglected. Explain why this statement is valid.

21. Write a generic equation showing how a weak base ionizes water.

22. How can you determine if an anion will act as a weak base? Write a generic equation showing the reaction by which an anion, A^-, acts as a weak base.

23. What is the relationship between the acid ionization constant for a weak acid (K_a) and the base ionization constant for its conjugate base (K_b)?

24. What kinds of cations act as weak acids? List some examples.

25. When calculating the [H_3O^+] for a polyprotic acid, the second ionization step can often be neglected. Explain why this statement is valid.

26. For a weak diprotic acid H_2X, what is the relationship between [X^{2-}] and K_{a_2}? Under what conditions does this relationship exist?

27. For a binary acid, $H{-}Y$, which factors affect the relative ease with which the acid ionizes?

28. Which factors affect the relative acidity of an oxyacid?

29. What is the Lewis definition of an acid? Of a base?

30. What is a general characteristic of a Lewis acid? Of a Lewis base?

31. What is acid rain? What causes it and where is the problem the greatest?

32. What are the main detrimental effects of acid rain? What is being done to address the problem of acid rain?

Problems by Topic

The Nature and Definitions of Acids and Base

33. Identify each substance as an acid or a base and write a chemical equation showing how it is an acid or a base according to the Arrhenius definition.
    a. $HNO_3(aq)$ b. $NH_4^+(aq)$
    c. $KOH(aq)$ d. $HC_2H_3O_2(aq)$

34. Identify each substance as an acid or a base and write a chemical equation showing how it is an acid or a base in aqueous solution according to the Arrhenius definition.
    a. $NaOH(aq)$
    b. $H_2SO_4(aq)$
    c. $HBr(aq)$
    d. $Sr(OH)_2(aq)$

35. In each reaction, identify the Brønsted–Lowry acid, the Brønsted–Lowry base, the conjugate acid, and the conjugate base.
 a. $H_2CO_3(aq) + H_2O(l) \rightleftharpoons H_3O^+(aq) + HCO_3^-(aq)$
 b. $NH_3(aq) + H_2O(l) \rightleftharpoons NH_4^+(aq) + OH^-(aq)$
 c. $HNO_3(aq) + H_2O(l) \longrightarrow H_3O^+(aq) + NO_3^-(aq)$
 d. $C_5H_5N(aq) + H_2O(l) \rightleftharpoons C_5H_5NH^+(aq) + OH^-(aq)$

36. In each reaction, identify the Brønsted–Lowry acid, the Brønsted–Lowry base, the conjugate acid, and the conjugate base.
 a. $HI(aq) + H_2O(l) \longrightarrow H_3O^+(aq) + I^-(aq)$
 b. $CH_3NH_2(aq) + H_2O(l) \rightleftharpoons CH_3NH_3^+(aq) + OH^-(aq)$
 c. $CO_3^{2-}(aq) + H_2O(l) \rightleftharpoons HCO_3^-(aq) + OH^-(aq)$
 d. $HBr(aq) + H_2O(l) \longrightarrow H_3O^+(aq) + Br^-(aq)$

37. Write the formula for the conjugate base of each acid.
 a. HCl   **b.** H_2SO_3 **c.** $HCHO_2$ **d.** HF

38. Write the formula for the conjugate acid of each base.
 a. NH_3 **b.** ClO_4^- **c.** HSO_4^- **d.** CO_3^{2-}

39. Both H_2O and $H_2PO_4^-$ are amphoteric. Write an equation to show how each substance can act as an acid and another equation to show how each can act as a base.

40. Both HCO_3^- and HS^- are amphoteric. Write an equation to show how each substance can act as an acid and another equation to show how each can act as a base.

Acid Strength and K_a

41. Classify each acid as strong or weak. If the acid is weak, write an expression for the acid ionization constant (K_a).
 a. HNO_3 **b.** HCl   **c.** HBr   **d.** H_2SO_3

42. Classify each acid as strong or weak. If the acid is weak, write an expression for the acid ionization constant (K_a).
 a. HF   **b.** $HCHO_2$ **c.** H_2SO_4 **d.** H_2CO_3

43. The three diagrams represent three different solutions of the binary acid HA. Water molecules have been omitted for clarity and hydronium ions (H_3O^+) are represented by hydrogen ions (H^+). Rank the acids in order of decreasing acid strength.

| (a) | (b) | (c) |

44. Rank the solutions in order of decreasing $[H_3O^+]$: 0.10 M HCl; 0.10 M HF; 0.10 M HClO; 0.10 M HC_6H_5O.

45. Pick the stronger base from each pair.
 a. F^- or Cl^- **b.** NO_2^- or NO_3^- **c.** F^- or ClO^-

46. Pick the stronger base from each pair.
 a. ClO_4^- or ClO_2^- **b.** Cl^- or H_2O **c.** CN^- or ClO^-

Autoionization of Water and pH

47. Calculate $[OH^-]$ in each aqueous solution at 25 °C, and classify the solution as acidic or basic.
 a. $[H_3O^+] = 1.2 \times 10^{-8}$ M
 b. $[H_3O^+] = 8.5 \times 10^{-5}$ M
 c. $[H_3O^+] = 3.5 \times 10^{-2}$ M

48. Calculate $[H_3O^+]$ in each aqueous solution at 25 °C, and classify each solution as acidic or basic.
 a. $[OH^-] = 1.1 \times 10^{-9}$ M
 b. $[OH^-] = 2.9 \times 10^{-2}$ M
 c. $[OH^-] = 6.9 \times 10^{-12}$ M

49. Calculate the pH and pOH of each solution.
 a. $[H_3O^+] = 1.7 \times 10^{-8}$ M
 b. $[H_3O^+] = 1.0 \times 10^{-7}$ M
 c. $[H_3O^+] = 2.2 \times 10^{-6}$ M

50. Calculate $[H_3O^+]$ and $[OH^-]$ for each solution.
 a. pH = 8.55   **b.** pH = 11.23   **c.** pH = 2.87

51. Complete the table. (All solutions are at 25 °C.)

$[H_3O^+]$	$[OH^-]$	pH	Acidic or Basic
____	____	3.15	____
3.7×10^{-9}	____	____	____
____	____	11.1	____
____	1.6×10^{-11}	____	____

52. Complete the table. (All solutions are at 25 °C.)

$[H_3O^+]$	$[OH^-]$	pH	Acidic or Basic
3.5×10^{-3}	____	____	____
____	3.8×10^{-7}	____	____
1.8×10^{-9}	____	____	____
____	____	7.15	____

53. Like all equilibrium constants, the value of K_w depends on temperature. At body temperature (37 °C), $K_w = 2.4 \times 10^{-14}$. What are the $[H_3O^+]$ and pH of pure water at body temperature?

54. The value of K_w increases with increasing temperature. Is the autoionization of water endothermic or exothermic?

55. Calculate the pH of each acid solution. Explain how the resulting pH values demonstrate that the pH of an acid solution should carry as many digits to the right of the decimal place as the number of significant figures in the concentration of the solution.
 $[H_3O^+] = 0.044$ M
 $[H_3O^+] = 0.045$ M
 $[H_3O^+] = 0.046$ M

56. Determine the concentration of H_3O^+ to the correct number of significant figures in a solution with each pH. Describe how these calculations show the relationship between the number of digits to the right of the decimal place in pH and the number of significant figures in concentration.
 pH = 2.50
 pH = 2.51
 pH = 2.52

Acid Solutions

57. For each strong acid solution, determine $[H_3O^+]$, $[OH^-]$, and pH.
 a. 0.25 M HCl
 b. 0.015 M HNO_3
 c. a solution that is 0.052 M in HBr and 0.020 M in HNO_3
 d. a solution that is 0.655% HNO_3 by mass (assume a density of 1.01 g/mL for the solution)

58. Determine the pH of each solution.
  a. 0.048 M HI
  b. 0.0895 M HClO₄
  c. a solution that is 0.045 M in HClO₄ and 0.048 M in HCl
  d. a solution that is 1.09% HCl by mass (assume a density of 1.01 g/mL for the solution)

59. What mass of HI should be present in 0.250 L of solution to obtain a solution with each pH value?
  a. pH = 1.25   **b.** pH = 1.75   **c.** pH = 2.85

60. What mass of HClO₄ should be present in 0.500 L of solution to obtain a solution with each pH value?
  a. pH = 2.50   **b.** pH = 1.50   **c.** pH = 0.50

61. What is the pH of a solution in which 224 mL of HCl(g), measured at 27.2 °C and 1.02 atm, is dissolved in 1.5 L of aqueous solution?

62. What volume of a concentrated HCl solution, which is 36.0% HCl by mass and has a density of 1.179 g/mL, should be used to make 5.00 L of an HCl solution with a pH of 1.8?

63. Determine the [H₃O⁺] and pH of a 0.100 M solution of benzoic acid.

64. Determine the [H₃O⁺] and pH of a 0.200 M solution of formic acid.

65. Determine the pH of an HNO₂ solution of each concentration. In which cases can you *not* make the simplifying assumption that x is small?
  a. 0.500 M   **b.** 0.100 M   **c.** 0.0100 M

66. Determine the pH of an HF solution of each concentration. In which cases can you *not* make the simplifying assumption that x is small?
  a. 0.250 M   **b.** 0.0500 M   **c.** 0.0250 M

67. If 15.0 mL of glacial acetic acid (pure HC₂H₃O₂) is diluted to 1.50 L with water, what is the pH of the resulting solution? The density of glacial acetic acid is 1.05 g/mL.

68. Calculate the pH of a formic acid solution that contains 1.35% formic acid by mass. (Assume a density of 1.01 g/mL for the solution.)

69. A 0.185 M solution of a weak acid (HA) has a pH of 2.95. Calculate the acid ionization constant (K_a) for the acid.

70. A 0.115 M solution of a weak acid (HA) has a pH of 3.29. Calculate the acid ionization constant (K_a) for the acid.

71. Determine the percent ionization of a 0.125 M HCN solution.

72. Determine the percent ionization of a 0.225 M solution of benzoic acid.

73. Calculate the percent ionization of an acetic acid solution having the given concentration.
  a. 1.00 M   **b.** 0.500 M   **c.** 0.100 M   **d.** 0.0500 M

74. Calculate the percent ionization of a formic acid solution having the given concentration.
  a. 1.00 M   **b.** 0.500 M   **c.** 0.100 M   **d.** 0.0500 M

75. A 0.148 M solution of a monoprotic acid has a percent ionization of 1.55%. Determine the acid ionization constant (K_a) for the acid.

76. A 0.085 M solution of a monoprotic acid has a percent ionization of 0.59%. Determine the acid ionization constant (K_a) for the acid.

77. Find the pH and percent ionization of each HF solution.
  a. 0.250 M HF   **b.** 0.100 M HF   **c.** 0.050 M HF

78. Find the pH and percent ionization of a 0.100 M solution of a weak monoprotic acid having the given K_a values.
  a. $K_a = 1.0 \times 10^{-5}$ **b.** $K_a = 1.0 \times 10^{-3}$
  c. $K_a = 1.0 \times 10^{-1}$

79. Find the pH of each mixture of acids.
  a. 0.115 M in HBr and 0.125 M in HCHO₂
  b. 0.150 M in HNO₂ and 0.085 M in HNO₃
  c. 0.185 M in HCHO₂ and 0.225 M in HC₂H₃O₂
  d. 0.050 M in acetic acid and 0.050 M in hydrocyanic acid

80. Find the pH of each mixture of acids.
  a. 0.075 M in HNO₃ and 0.175 M in HC₇H₅O₂
  b. 0.020 M in HBr and 0.015 M in HClO₄
  c. 0.095 M in HF and 0.225 M in HC₆H₅O
  d. 0.100 M in formic acid and 0.050 M in hypochlorous acid

Base Solutions

81. For each strong base solution, determine [OH⁻], [H₃O⁺], pH, and pOH.
  a. 0.15 M NaOH   **b.** 1.5×10^{-3} M Ca(OH)₂
  c. 4.8×10^{-4} M Sr(OH)₂   **d.** 8.7×10^{-5} M KOH

82. For each strong base solution, determine [OH⁻], [H₃O⁺], pH, and pOH.
  a. 8.77×10^{-3} M LiOH   **b.** 0.0112 M Ba(OH)₂
  c. 1.9×10^{-4} M KOH   **d.** 5.0×10^{-4} M Ca(OH)₂

83. Determine the pH of a solution that is 3.85% KOH by mass. Assume that the solution has density of 1.01 g/mL.

84. Determine the pH of a solution that is 1.55% NaOH by mass. Assume that the solution has density of 1.01 g/mL.

85. What volume of 0.855 M KOH solution is required to make 3.55 L of a solution with pH of 12.4?

86. What volume of a 15.0% by mass NaOH solution, which has a density of 1.116 g/mL, should be used to make 5.00 L of an NaOH solution with a pH of 10.8?

87. Write equations showing how each weak base ionizes water to form OH⁻. Also write the corresponding expression for K_b.
  a. NH₃   **b.** HCO₃⁻   **c.** CH₃NH₂

88. Write equations showing how each weak base ionizes water to form OH⁻. Also write the corresponding expression for K_b.
  a. CO₃²⁻   **b.** C₆H₅NH₂   **c.** C₂H₅NH₂

89. Determine the [OH⁻], pH, and pOH of a 0.15 M ammonia solution.

90. Determine the [OH⁻], pH, and pOH of a solution that is 0.125 M in CO₃²⁻.

91. Caffeine (C₈H₁₀N₄O₂) is a weak base with a pK_b of 10.4. Calculate the pH of a solution containing a caffeine concentration of 455 mg/L.

92. Amphetamine (C₉H₁₃N) is a weak base with a pK_b of 4.2. Calculate the pH of a solution containing an amphetamine concentration of 225 mg/L.

93. Morphine is a weak base. A 0.150 M solution of morphine has a pH of 10.5. What is K_b for morphine?

94. A 0.135 M solution of a weak base has a pH of 11.23. Determine K_b for the base.

Acid–Base Properties of Ions and Salts

95. Determine if each anion acts as a weak base in solution. For those anions that are basic, write an equation that shows how the anion acts as a base.
  a. Br⁻   **b.** ClO⁻   **c.** CN⁻   **d.** Cl⁻

96. Determine whether each anion is basic or neutral. For those anions that are basic, write an equation that shows how the anion acts as a base.
  a. C₇H₅O₂⁻   **b.** I⁻   **c.** NO₃⁻   **d.** F⁻

97. Determine the $[OH^-]$ and pH of a solution that is 0.140 M in F^-.

98. Determine the $[OH^-]$ and pH of a solution that is 0.250 M in HCO_3^-.

99. Determine whether each cation is acidic or pH-neutral. For those cations that are acidic, write an equation that shows how the cation acts as an acid.
   a. NH_4^+
   b. Na^+
   c. Co^{3+}
   d. $CH_2NH_3^+$

100. Determine whether each cation is acidic or pH-neutral. For those cations that are acidic, write an equation that shows how the cation acts as an acid.
   a. Sr^{2+}
   b. Mn^{3+}
   c. $C_5H_5NH^+$
   d. Li^+

101. Determine if each salt will form a solution that is acidic, basic, or pH-neutral.
   a. $FeCl_3$
   b. NaF
   c. $CaBr_2$
   d. NH_4Br
   e. $C_6H_5NH_3NO_2$

102. Determine if each salt will form a solution that is acidic, basic, or pH-neutral.
   a. $Al(NO_3)_3$
   b. $C_2H_5NH_3NO_3$
   c. K_2CO_3
   d. RbI
   e. NH_4ClO

103. Arrange the solutions in order of increasing acidity.
   $$NaCl, NH_4Cl, NaHCO_3, NH_4ClO_2, NaOH$$

104. Arrange the solutions in order of increasing basicity.
   $$CH_3NH_3Br, KOH, KBr, KCN, C_5H_5NHNO_2$$

105. Determine the pH of each solution.
   a. 0.10 M NH_4Cl
   b. 0.10 M $NaC_2H_3O_2$
   c. 0.10 M $NaCl$

106. Determine the pH of each solution.
   a. 0.20 M $KCHO_2$
   b. 0.20 M CH_3NH_3I
   c. 0.20 M KI

107. Calculate the concentration of all species in a 0.15 M KF solution.

108. Calculate the concentration of all species in a 0.225 M $C_6H_5NH_3Cl$ solution.

Polyprotic Acids

109. Write chemical equations and corresponding equilibrium expressions for each of the three ionization steps of phosphoric acid.

110. Write chemical equations and corresponding equilibrium expressions for each of the two ionization steps of carbonic acid.

111. Calculate the $[H_3O^+]$ and pH of each polyprotic acid solution.
   a. 0.350 M H_3PO_4
   b. 0.350 M $H_2C_2O_4$

112. Calculate the $[H_3O^+]$ and pH of each polyprotic acid solution.
   a. 0.125 M H_2CO_3
   b. 0.125 M $H_3C_6H_5O_7$

113. Calculate the concentration of all species in a 0.500 M solution of H_2SO_3.

114. Calculate the concentration of all species in a 0.155 M solution of H_2CO_3.

115. Calculate the $[H_3O^+]$ and pH of each H_2SO_4 solution. At approximately what concentration does the *x is small* approximation break down?
   a. 0.50 M
   b. 0.10 M
   c. 0.050 M

116. Consider a 0.10 M solution of a weak polyprotic acid (H_2A) with the possible values of K_{a_1} and K_{a_2} given here.
   a. $K_{a_1} = 1.0 \times 10^{-4}$; $K_{a_2} = 5.0 \times 10^{-5}$
   b. $K_{a_1} = 1.0 \times 10^{-4}$; $K_{a_2} = 1.0 \times 10^{-5}$
   c. $K_{a_1} = 1.0 \times 10^{-4}$; $K_{a_2} = 1.0 \times 10^{-6}$

   Calculate the contributions to $[H_3O^+]$ from each ionization step. At what point can the contribution of the second step be neglected?

Molecular Structure and Acid Strength

117. Based on their molecular structure, pick the stronger acid from each pair of binary acids. Explain your choice.
   a. HF and HCl
   b. H_2O or HF
   c. H_2Se or H_2S

118. Based on molecular structure, arrange the binary compounds in order of increasing acid strength. Explain your choice.
   $$H_2Te, HI, H_2S, NaH$$

119. Based on their molecular structure, pick the stronger acid from each pair of oxyacids. Explain your choice.
   a. H_2SO_4 or H_2SO_3
   b. $HClO_2$ or $HClO$
   c. HClO or HBrO
   d. CCl_3COOH or CH_3COOH

120. Based on molecular structure, arrange the oxyacids in order of increasing acid strength. Explain your choice.
   $$HClO_3, HIO_3, HBrO_3$$

121. Which is a stronger base, S^{2-} or Se^{2-}? Explain.

122. Which is a stronger base, PO_4^{3-} or AsO_4^{3-}? Explain.

Lewis Acids and Bases

123. Classify each species as either a Lewis acid or a Lewis base.
   a. Fe^{3+}
   b. BH_3
   c. NH_3
   d. F^-

124. Classify each species as either a Lewis acid or a Lewis base.
   a. $BeCl_2$
   b. OH^-
   c. $B(OH)_3$
   d. CN^-

125. Identify the Lewis acid and Lewis base from among the reactants in each equation.
   a. $Fe^{3+}(aq) + 6\,H_2O(l) \rightleftharpoons Fe(H_2O)_6^{3+}(aq)$
   b. $Zn^{2+}(aq) + 4\,NH_3(aq) \rightleftharpoons Zn(NH_3)_4^{2+}(aq)$
   c. $(CH_3)_3N(g) + BF_3(g) \rightleftharpoons (CH_3)_3NBF_3(s)$

126. Identify the Lewis acid and Lewis base from among the reactants in each equation.
   a. $Ag^+(aq) + 2\,NH_3(aq) \rightleftharpoons Ag(NH_3)_2^+(aq)$
   b. $AlBr_3 + NH_3 \rightleftharpoons H_3NAlBr_3$
   c. $F^-(aq) + BF_3(aq) \rightleftharpoons BF_4^-(aq)$

Cumulative Problems

127. Based on these molecular views, determine whether each pictured acid is weak or strong.

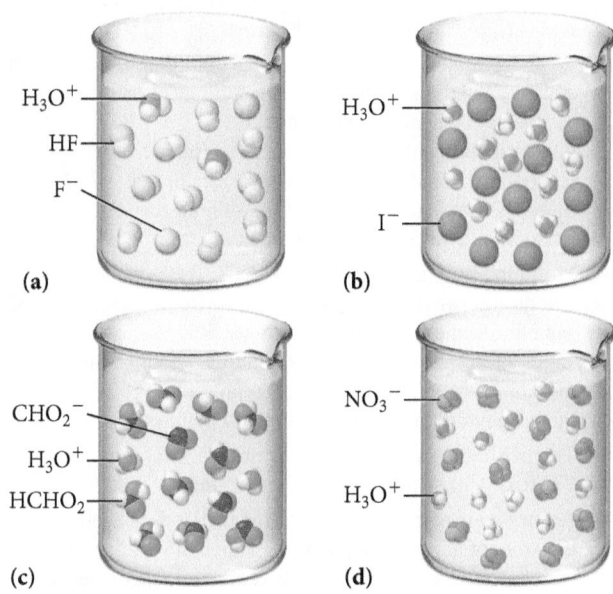

(a) **(b)**

(c) **(d)**

128. Based on these molecular views, determine whether each pictured base is weak or strong.

(a) **(b)**

(c) **(d)**

129. The binding of oxygen by hemoglobin in the blood involves the equilibrium reaction:

$$HbH^+(aq) + O_2(aq) \rightleftharpoons HbO_2(aq) + H^+(aq)$$

In this equation, Hb is hemoglobin. The pH of normal human blood is highly controlled within a range of 7.35 to 7.45. Given the above equilibrium, why is this important? What would happen to the oxygen-carrying capacity of hemoglobin if blood became too acidic (a dangerous condition known as acidosis)?

130. Carbon dioxide dissolves in water according to the equations:

$$CO_2(g) + H_2O(l) \rightleftharpoons H_2CO_3(aq)$$
$$H_2CO_3(aq) + H_2O(l) \rightleftharpoons HCO_3^-(aq) + H_3O^+(aq)$$

Carbon dioxide levels in the atmosphere have increased about 20% over the last century. Given that Earth's oceans are exposed to atmospheric carbon dioxide, what effect might the increased CO_2 have on the pH of the world's oceans? What effect might this change have on the limestone structures (primarily $CaCO_3$) of coral reefs and marine shells?

131. People often take milk of magnesia to reduce the discomfort associated with acid stomach or heartburn. The recommended dose is 1 teaspoon, which contains 4.00×10^2 mg of $Mg(OH)_2$. What volume of an HCl solution with a pH of 1.3 can be neutralized by one dose of milk of magnesia? If the stomach contains 2.00×10^2 mL of pH 1.3 solution, will all the acid be neutralized? If not, what fraction will be neutralized?

132. Lakes that have been acidified by acid rain can be neutralized by liming, the addition of limestone ($CaCO_3$). How much limestone (in kg) is required to completely neutralize a 4.3 billion liter lake with a pH of 5.5?

▲ Liming a lake.

133. Acid rain over the Great Lakes has a pH of about 4.5. Calculate the $[H_3O^+]$ of this rain and compare that value to the $[H_3O^+]$ of rain over the West Coast that has a pH of 5.4. How many times more concentrated is the acid in rain over the Great Lakes?

134. White wines tend to be more acidic than red wines. Find the $[H_3O^+]$ in a Sauvignon Blanc with a pH of 3.23 and a Cabernet Sauvignon with a pH of 3.64. How many times more acidic is the Sauvignon Blanc?

135. Common aspirin is acetylsalicylic acid, which has the structure shown here and a pK_a of 3.5.

Calculate the pH of a solution in which one normal adult dose of aspirin (6.5×10^2 mg) is dissolved in 8.0 ounces of water.

136. The AIDS drug zalcitabine (also known as ddC) is a weak base with the structure shown here and a pK_b of 9.8.

What percentage of the base is protonated in an aqueous zalcitabine solution containing 565 mg/L?

137. Determine the pH of each solution.
   a. 0.0100 M $HClO_4$ **b.** 0.115 M $HClO_2$
   c. 0.045 M $Sr(OH)_2$ **d.** 0.0852 M KCN
   e. 0.155 M NH_4Cl

138. Determine the pH of each solution.
   a. 0.0650 M HNO_3 **b.** 0.150 M HNO_2
   c. 0.0195 M KOH   **d.** 0.245 M CH_3NH_3I
   e. 0.318 M KC_6H_5O

139. Determine the pH of each two-component solution.
   a. 0.0550 M in HI and 0.00850 M in HF
   b. 0.112 M in NaCl and 0.0953 M in KF
   c. 0.132 M in NH_4Cl and 0.150 M HNO_3
   d. 0.0887 M in sodium benzoate and 0.225 M in potassium bromide
   e. 0.0450 M in HCl and 0.0225 M in HNO_3

140. Determine the pH of each two-component solution.
   a. 0.050 M KOH and 0.015 M $Ba(OH)_2$
   b. 0.265 M NH_4NO_3 and 0.102 M HCN
   c. 0.075 M RbOH and 0.100 M $NaHCO_3$
   d. 0.088 M $HClO_4$ and 0.022 M KOH
   e. 0.115 M NaClO and 0.0500 M KI

141. Write net ionic equations for the reactions that take place when aqueous solutions of the following substances are mixed:
   a. sodium cyanide and nitric acid
   b. ammonium chloride and sodium hydroxide
   c. sodium cyanide and ammonium bromide
   d. potassium hydrogen sulfate and lithium acetate
   e. sodium hypochlorite and ammonia

142. Morphine has the formula $C_{17}H_{19}NO_3$. It is a base and accepts one proton per molecule. It is isolated from opium. A 0.682 g sample of opium is found to require 8.92 mL of a 0.0116 M solution of sulfuric acid for neutralization. Assuming that morphine is the only acid or base present in opium, calculate the percent morphine in the sample of opium.

143. The pH of a 1.00 M solution of urea, a weak organic base, is 7.050. Calculate the K_a of protonated urea.

144. A solution is prepared by dissolving 0.10 mol of acetic acid and 0.10 mol of ammonium chloride in enough water to make 1.0 L of solution. Find the concentration of ammonia in the solution.

145. Lactic acid is a weak acid found in milk. Its calcium salt is a source of calcium for growing animals. A saturated solution of this salt, which we can represent as $Ca(Lact)_2$ has a $[Ca^{2+}] = 0.26$ M and a pH = 8.40. Assuming the salt is completely dissociated, calculate the K_a of lactic acid.

146. A solution of 0.23 mol of the chloride salt of protonated quinine (QH^+), a weak organic base, in 1.0 L of solution has pH = 4.58. Find the K_b of quinine (Q).

Challenge Problems

147. A student mistakenly calculates the pH of a 1.0×10^{-7} M HI solution to be 7.0. Explain why the student is incorrect and calculate the correct pH.

148. When 2.55 g of an unknown weak acid (HA) with a molar mass of 85.0 g/mol is dissolved in 250.0 g of water, the freezing point of the resulting solution is $-0.257 \,°C$. Calculate K_a for the unknown weak acid.

149. Calculate the pH of a solution that is 0.00115 M in HCl and 0.0100 M in $HClO_2$.

150. To what volume should you dilute 1 L of a solution of a weak acid HA to reduce the $[H^+]$ to one-half of that in the original solution?

151. HA, a weak acid, with $K_a = 1.0 \times 10^{-8}$, also forms the ion HA_2^-. The reaction is $HA(aq) + A^-(aq) \rightleftharpoons HA_2^-(aq)$ and its $K = 4.0$. Calculate the $[H^+]$, $[A^-]$, and $[HA_2^-]$ in a 1.0 M solution of HA.

152. Basicity in the gas phase can be defined as the proton affinity of the base, for example, $CH_3NH_2(g) + H^+(g) \rightleftharpoons CH_3NH_3^+(g)$. In the gas phase, $(CH_3)_3N$ is more basic than CH_3NH_2 while in solution the reverse is true. Explain this observation.

153. Calculate the pH of a solution prepared from 0.200 mol of NH_4CN and enough water to make 1.00 L of solution.

154. To 1.0 L of a 0.30 M solution of $HClO_2$ is added 0.20 mol of NaF. Calculate the $[HClO_2]$ at equilibrium.

155. A mixture of Na_2CO_3 and $NaHCO_3$ has a mass of 82.2 g. It is dissolved in 1.00 L of water and the pH is found to be 9.95. Find the mass of $NaHCO_3$ in the mixture.

156. A mixture of NaCN and $NaHSO_4$ consists of a total of 0.60 mol. When the mixture is dissolved in 1.0 L of water and comes to equilibrium the pH is found to be 9.9. Find the amount of NaCN in the mixture.

Conceptual Problems

157. Without doing any calculations, determine which solution in each pair is more acidic.
    a. 0.0100 M in HCl and 0.0100 M in KOH
    b. 0.0100 M in HF and 0.0100 M in KBr
    c. 0.0100 M in NH_4Cl and 0.0100 M in CH_3NH_3Br
    d. 0.100 M in NaCN and 0.100 M in $CaCl_2$

158. Without doing any calculations, determine which solution in each pair is more basic.
    a. 0.100 M in NaClO and 0.100 M in NaF
    b. 0.0100 M in KCl and 0.0100 M in $KClO_2$

    c. 0.0100 M in HNO_3 and 0.0100 M in NaOH
    d. 0.0100 M in NH_4Cl and 0.0100 M in HCN

159. Rank the acids in order of increasing acid strength.

$$CH_3COOH \quad CH_2ClCOOH \quad CHCl_2COOH \quad CCl_3COOH$$

Answers to Conceptual Connections

Conjugate Acid–Base Pairs

15.1 (b) H_2SO_4 and H_2SO_3 are both acids; this is not a conjugate acid–base pair.

Relative Strengths of Weak Acids

15.2 HF is stronger because it has a larger acid ionization constant.

The x is *small* Approximation

15.3 (c) The validity of the *x is small* approximation depends on both the value of the equilibrium constant and the initial concentration—the closer that these are to one another, the less likely the approximation will be valid.

Strong and Weak Acids

15.4 (a) A weak acid solution will usually be less than 5% dissociated. Since HCl is a strong acid, the 0.10 M solution is much more acidic than either a weak acid with the same concentration or even a weak acid that is twice as concentrated.

Percent Ionization

15.5 Solution (c) has the greatest percent ionization because percent ionization increases with decreasing weak acid concentration. Solution (b) has the lowest pH because the equilibrium H_3O^+ concentration increases with increasing weak acid concentration.

Judging Relative pH

15.6 (a) A weak acid solution will usually be less than 5% dissociated. Therefore, since HCl is the only strong acid, the 1.0 M solution is much more acidic than either a weak acid that is twice as concentrated or a combination of two weak acids with the same concentrations.

Acid Strength and Molecular Structure

15.7 (a) Since the carbon atom in (a) is bonded to another oxygen atom, which draws electron density away from the $O-H$ bond (weakening and polarizing it), and the carbon atom in (b) is bonded only to other hydrogen atoms, the proton in structure (a) is more acidic.

16 Aqueous Ionic Equilibrium

In the strictly scientific sense of the word, insolubility does not exist, and even those substances characterized by the most obstinate resistance to the solvent action of water may properly be designated as extraordinarily difficult of solution, not as insoluble.

—Otto N. Witt (1853–1915)

W E HAVE ALREADY seen the importance of aqueous solutions, first in Chapters 4, 12, and 14, and most recently in Chapter 15 on acids and bases. We now turn our attention to two additional topics involving aqueous solutions: buffers (solutions that resist pH change) and solubility equilibria (the extent to which slightly soluble ionic compounds dissolve in water). Buffers are tremendously important in biology because nearly all physiological processes must occur within a narrow pH range. Solubility equilibria are related to the solubility rules that we discussed in Chapter 4. In this chapter, we find a more complicated picture: solids that we considered insoluble under the simple "solubility rules" are actually better described as being only very slightly soluble, as the chapter-opening quotation from Otto Witt suggests. Solubility equilibria are important in predicting not only solubility, but also precipitation reactions that might occur when aqueous solutions are mixed.

Neutral

6   7   8   9   10   Alkali
                                                                    1

Human blood is held at nearly constant pH by the action of buffers, a main topic of this chapter.

16.1 The Danger of Antifreeze

Every year, thousands of dogs and cats die from consuming a common household product: antifreeze that was improperly stored or that leaked out of a car radiator. Most types of antifreeze used in cars are aqueous solutions of ethylene glycol:

Some brands of antifreeze use propylene-glycol, which is less toxic than ethylene glycol.

HOCH$_2$CH$_2$OH

Ethylene glycol has a somewhat sweet taste that can attract curious dogs and cats—and sometimes even young children, who are also vulnerable to this toxic compound. The first stage of ethylene glycol poisoning is a state resembling drunkenness. Since the compound is an alcohol, it affects the brain much as an alcoholic beverage would. Once ethylene glycol starts to be metabolized, however, a second and more deadly stage commences.

In the liver, ethylene glycol is oxidized to glycolic acid ($HOCH_2COOH$), which enters the bloodstream. The acidity of blood is critically important and tightly regulated because many proteins only function in a narrow pH range. In human blood, for example, pH is held between 7.36 and 7.42. This nearly constant blood pH is maintained by *buffers*. We discuss buffers more carefully later in this chapter, but for now know that a buffer is a chemical system that resists pH changes by neutralizing added acid or base. An important buffer in blood is a mixture of carbonic acid (H_2CO_3) and the bicarbonate ion (HCO_3^-). The carbonic acid neutralizes added base:

$$H_2CO_3(aq) + \underset{\text{added base}}{OH^-(aq)} \longrightarrow H_2O(l) + HCO_3^-(aq)$$

The bicarbonate ion neutralizes added acid:

$$HCO_3^-(aq) + \underset{\text{added acid}}{H^+(aq)} \longrightarrow H_2CO_3(aq)$$

In this way, the carbonic acid and bicarbonate ion buffering system keeps blood pH nearly constant.

When the glycolic acid generated by antifreeze consumption first enters the bloodstream, the acid's tendency to lower blood pH is countered by the buffering action of the bicarbonate ion. However, if the quantities of consumed antifreeze are large enough, the glycolic acid overwhelms the capacity of the buffer (we discuss buffer capacity in Section 16.3), causing blood pH to drop to dangerously low levels.

Low blood pH results in *acidosis*, a condition in which the acid affects the equilibrium between hemoglobin (Hb) and oxygen:

$$\overset{\text{Excess } H^+}{\underset{\text{Shift left}}{HbH^+(aq) + O_2(g) \rightleftharpoons HbO_2(aq) + H^+(aq)}}$$

The excess acid causes the equilibrium to shift to the left, reducing the blood's ability to carry oxygen. At this point, the cat or dog may begin hyperventilating in an effort to overcome the acidic blood's lowered oxygen-carrying capacity. If no treatment is administered, the animal will eventually go into a coma and die.

One treatment for ethylene glycol poisoning is the administration of ethyl alcohol (the alcohol found in alcoholic beverages). The two molecules are similar enough that the liver enzyme that catalyzes the metabolism of ethylene glycol also acts on ethyl alcohol, but the enzyme has a higher affinity for ethyl alcohol than for ethylene glycol. Consequently, the enzyme preferentially metabolizes ethyl alcohol, allowing the unmetabolized ethylene glycol to escape through the urine. If administered early, this treatment can save the life of a dog or cat that has consumed ethylene glycol.

16.2 Buffers: Solutions That Resist pH Change

Most solutions significantly change pH when an acid or base is added to them. As we have just learned, however, a **buffer** resists pH change by neutralizing added acid or added base. A buffer contains either:

1. significant amounts of a weak acid and its conjugate base or
2. significant amounts of a weak base and its conjugate acid.

For example, the buffer in blood is composed of carbonic acid (H_2CO_3) and its conjugate base, the bicarbonate ion (HCO_3^-). When additional base is added to a buffer, the weak acid reacts with the base, neutralizing it. When additional acid is added to a buffer, the conjugate base reacts with the acid, neutralizing it. In this way, a buffer can maintain a nearly constant pH.

A weak acid by itself, even though it partially ionizes to form some of its conjugate base, does not contain sufficient base to be a buffer. Similarly, a weak base by itself, even though it partially ionizes water to form some of its conjugate acid, does not contain

Formation of a Buffer

sufficient acid to be a buffer. *A buffer must contain significant amounts of both a weak
acid and its conjugate base (or vice versa).* Consider the simple buffer made by dissolving acetic acid ($HC_2H_3O_2$) and sodium acetate ($NaC_2H_3O_2$) in water (Figure 16.1▲).

| $C_2H_3O_2^-$ is the conjugate base of $HC_2H_3O_2$.

Suppose that we add a strong base, such as NaOH, to this solution. The acetic acid
neutralizes the base:

$$NaOH(aq) + HC_2H_3O_2(aq) \longrightarrow H_2O(l) + NaC_2H_3O_2(aq)$$

As long as the amount of added NaOH is less than the amount of $HC_2H_3O_2$ in solution,
the buffer neutralizes the added NaOH and the resulting pH change is small. Suppose, on
the other hand, that we add a strong acid, such as HCl, to the solution. In this case, the
conjugate base, $NaC_2H_3O_2$, neutralizes the added HCl:

$$HCl(aq) + NaC_2H_3O_2(aq) \longrightarrow HC_2H_3O_2(aq) + NaCl(aq)$$

As long as the amount of added HCl is less than the amount of $NaC_2H_3O_2$ in solution,
the buffer neutralizes the added HCl and the resulting pH change is small.

Summarizing Buffer Characteristics:

▶ Buffers resist pH change.

▶ A buffer contains significant amounts of either 1) a weak acid and its conjugate
base, or 2) a weak base and its conjugate acid.

▶ The weak acid neutralizes added base.

▶ The base neutralizes added acid.

Conceptual Connection 16.1 Buffers

Which solution is a buffer?

(a) a solution that is 0.100 M in HNO_2 and 0.100 M in HCl

(b) a solution that is 0.100 M in HNO_3 and 0.100 M in $NaNO_3$

(c) a solution that is 0.100 M in HNO_2 and 0.100 M in NaCl

(d) a solution that is 0.100 M in HNO_2 and 0.100 M in $NaNO_2$

► **FIGURE 16.2 The Common Ion Effect** The pH of a 0.100 M acetic acid solution is 2.9. The pH of a 0.100 M sodium acetate solution is 8.9. The pH of a solution that is 0.100 M in acetic acid and 0.100 M in sodium acetate is 4.7.

pH = 2.9

pH = 8.9

pH = 4.7

0.100 M
$HC_2H_3O_2$

0.100 M
$NaC_2H_3O_2$

0.100 M $HC_2H_3O_2$
0.100 M $NaC_2H_3O_2$

Calculating the pH of a Buffer Solution

In Chapter 15, we learned how to calculate the pH of a solution containing either a weak acid or its conjugate base, but not both. How do we calculate the pH of a buffer—a solution containing both? Consider a solution that initially contains $HC_2H_3O_2$ and $NaC_2H_3O_2$, each at a concentration of 0.100 M. The acetic acid ionizes according to the reaction:

$$HC_2H_3O_2(aq) + H_2O(l) \rightleftharpoons H_3O^+(aq) + C_2H_3O_2^-(aq)$$

Initial concentration: 0.100 M   0.100 M

Le Châtelier's principle is discussed in Section 14.9.

However, the ionization of $HC_2H_3O_2$ in the solution is suppressed compared to its ionization in a solution that does not initially contain any $C_2H_3O_2^-$, because the presence of $C_2H_3O_2^-$ *shifts the equilibrium to the left* (as we would expect from Le Châtelier's principle). In other words, the presence of the $C_2H_3O_2^-(aq)$ ion causes the acid to ionize even less than it normally would (Figure 16.2 ▲), resulting in a less acidic solution (higher pH). This effect is known as the **common ion effect**, so named because the solution contains two substances ($HC_2H_3O_2$ and $NaC_2H_3O_2$) that share a common ion ($C_2H_3O_2^-$). To find the pH of a buffer solution containing common ions, we work an equilibrium problem in which the initial concentrations include both the acid and its conjugate base, as shown in Example 16.1.

EXAMPLE 16.1   Calculating the pH of a Buffer Solution

Calculate the pH of a buffer solution that is 0.100 M in $HC_2H_3O_2$ and 0.100 M in $NaC_2H_3O_2$

SOLUTION

1. Write the balanced equation for the ionization of the acid and use it as a guide to prepare an ICE table showing the given concentrations of the acid and its conjugate base as the initial concentrations. Leave room in the table for the changes in concentrations and for the equilibrium concentrations.	$HC_2H_3O_2(aq) + H_2O(l) \rightleftharpoons H_3O^+(aq) + C_2H_3O_2^-(aq)$		

	[HC₂H₃O₂]	**[H₃O⁺]**	**[C₂H₃O₂⁻]**
Initial	0.100	≈ 0.00	0.100
Change			
Equil			

2. Represent the change in the concentration of H_3O^+ with the variable x. Express the changes in the concentrations of the other reactants and products in terms of x.	$HC_2H_3O_2(aq) + H_2O(l) \rightleftharpoons H_3O^+(aq) + C_2H_3O_2^-(aq)$		

	[HC₂H₃O₂]	**[H₃O⁺]**	**[C₂H₃O₂⁻]**
Initial	0.100	≈ 0.00	0.100
Change	$-x$	$+x$	$+x$
Equil			

3. Sum each column to determine the equilibrium concentrations in terms of the initial concentrations and the variable x.				

$$HC_2H_3O_2(aq) + H_2O(l) \rightleftharpoons H_3O^+(aq) + C_2H_3O_2^-(aq)$$

	$[HC_2H_3O_2]$	$[H_3O^+]$	$[C_2H_3O_2^-]$
Initial	0.100	≈ 0.00	0.100
Change	$-x$	$+x$	$+x$
Equil	$0.100 - x$	x	$0.100 + x$

4. Substitute the expressions for the equilibrium concentrations (from step 3) into the expression for the acid ionization constant.
In most cases, you can make the approximation that x *is small*. (See Sections 14.8 and 15.6 to review the x *is small* approximation.)

$$K_a = \frac{[H_3O^+][C_2H_3O^-]}{[HC_2H_3O_2]}$$

$$= \frac{x(0.100 + x)}{0.100 - x} \quad (x \text{ is small})$$

Substitute the value of the acid ionization constant (from Table 15.5) into the K_a expression and solve for x.

$$1.8 \times 10^{-5} = \frac{x(0.100)}{0.100}$$

$$x = 1.8 \times 10^{-5}$$

Confirm that x *is small* by calculating the ratio of x and the number it was subtracted from in the approximation. The ratio should be less than 0.05 (or 5%).

$$\frac{1.8 \times 10^{-5}}{0.100} \times 100\% = 0.018\%$$

Therefore the approximation is valid.

5. Determine the H_3O^+ concentration from the calculated value of x and substitute into the pH equation to find pH.

$$[H_3O^+] = x = 1.8 \times 10^{-5} \, M$$

$$pH = -\log[H_3O^+]$$
$$= -\log(1.8 \times 10^{-5})$$
$$= 4.74$$

FOR PRACTICE 16.1

Calculate the pH of a buffer solution that is 0.200 M in $HC_2H_3O_2$ and 0.100 M in $NaC_2H_3O_2$.

FOR MORE PRACTICE 16.1

Calculate the pH of the buffer that results from mixing 60.0 mL of 0.250 M $HCHO_2$ and 15.0 mL of 0.500 M $NaCHO_2$.

The Henderson–Hasselbalch Equation

We can derive an equation that relates the pH of a buffer solution to the initial concentration of the buffer components, thus simplifying the calculation of the pH of a buffer solution. Consider a buffer containing the generic weak acid HA and its conjugate base A^-. The acid ionizes as follows:

$$HA(aq) + H_2O(l) \rightleftharpoons H_3O^+(aq) + A^-(aq)$$

We derive an expression for the concentration of H_3O^+ from the acid ionization equilibrium expression by solving the expression for $[H_3O^+]$:

$$K_a = \frac{[H_3O^+][A^-]}{[HA]}$$

$$[H_3O^+] = K_a \frac{[HA]}{[A^-]} \qquad [16.1]$$

If we make the same x *is small* approximation that we make for weak acid or weak base equilibrium problems, *we can consider the equilibrium concentrations of HA and A^- to be essentially identical to the initial concentrations of HA and A^-* (see step 4 of Example 16.1). Therefore, to determine $[H_3O^+]$ for any buffer solution, we multiply K_a by the ratio of the

> Recall that the variable x in a weak acid equilibrium problem represents the change in the initial acid concentration. The x *is small* approximation is valid because so little of the weak acid ionizes compared to its initial concentration.

concentrations of the acid and the conjugate base. To find the $[H_3O^+]$ of the buffer in Example 16.1 (a solution that is 0.100 M in $HC_2H_3O_2$ and 0.100 M in $NaC_2H_3O_2$), we substitute the concentrations of $HC_2H_3O_2$ and $C_2H_3O_2^-$ into Equation 16.1:

$$[H_3O^+] = K_a \frac{[HC_2H_3O_2]}{[C_2H_3O_2^-]}$$

$$= K_a \frac{0.100}{0.100}$$

$$= K_a$$

In this buffer solution, as in any in which the acid and conjugate base concentrations are equal, $[H_3O^+]$ is equal to K_a.

We can derive an equation for the pH of a buffer by taking the negative logarithm of both sides of Equation 16.1:

$$[H_3O^+] = K_a \frac{[HA]}{[A^-]}$$

| Recall that log AB = log A + log B, so −log AB = −log A − log B.

$$-\log[H_3O^+] = -\log(K_a \frac{[HA]}{[A^-]})$$

$$-\log[H_3O^+] = -\log K_a - \log\frac{[HA]}{[A^-]} \qquad [16.2]$$

We can rearrange Equation 16.2 to get:

| Recall that log (A/B) = −log (B/A), so −log (A/B) = log (B/A).

$$-\log[H_3O^+] = -\log K_a + \log\frac{[A^-]}{[HA]}$$

Since $pH = -\log[H_3O^+]$ and since $pK_a = -\log K_a$, we obtain the result:

$$pH = pK_a + \log\frac{[A^-]}{[HA]}$$

Since A^- is a weak base and HA is a weak acid, we can generalize the equation:

| Note that, as expected, the pH of a buffer increases with an increase in the amount of base relative to the amount of acid.

$$pH = pK_a + \log\frac{[base]}{[acid]} \qquad [16.3]$$

where the base is the conjugate base of the acid or the acid is the conjugate acid of the base. This equation, known as the **Henderson–Hasselbalch equation**, allows us to quickly calculate the pH of a buffer solution from the initial concentrations of the buffer components *as long as the x is small approximation is valid.* In Example 16.2, we show how to find the pH of a buffer in two ways: in the left column we solve a common ion effect equilibrium problem using a method similar to the one we used in Example 16.1; in the right column we use the Henderson–Hasselbalch equation.

EXAMPLE 16.2 Calculating the pH of a Buffer Solution as an Equilibrium Problem and with the Henderson–Hasselbalch Equation

Calculate the pH of a buffer solution that is 0.050 M in benzoic acid ($HC_7H_5O_2$) and 0.150 M in sodium benzoate ($NaC_7H_5O_2$). For benzoic acid, $K_a = 6.5 \times 10^{-5}$.

SOLUTION

Equilibrium Approach	**Henderson–Hasselbalch Approach**
Write the balanced equation for the ionization of the acid and use it as a guide to prepare an ICE table.	To find the pH of this solution, determine which component is the acid and which is the base and substitute their concentrations into the Henderson–Hasselbalch equation to calculate pH.

$$HC_7H_5O_2(aq) + H_2O(l) \rightleftharpoons H_3O^+(aq) + C_7H_5O_2^-(aq)$$

	[HC$_7$H$_5$O$_2$]	[H$_3$O$^+$]	[C$_7$H$_5$O$_2^-$]
Initial	0.050	≈ 0.00	0.150
Change	$-x$	$+x$	$+x$
Equil	$0.050 - x$	x	$0.150 + x$

Substitute the expressions for the equilibrium concentrations into the expression for the acid ionization constant. Make the *x is small* approximation and solve for *x*.

$$K_a = \frac{[H_3O^+][C_7H_5O_2^-]}{[HC_7H_5O_2]}$$

$$= \frac{x(0.150 + \cancel{x})}{0.050 - \cancel{x}} \qquad (x \text{ is small})$$

$$6.5 \times 10^{-5} = \frac{x(0.150)}{0.050}$$

$$x = 2.2 \times 10^{-5}$$

Since $[H_3O^+] = x$, we calculate pH as follows:

$$pH = -\log[H_3O^+]$$

$$= -\log(2.2 \times 10^{-5})$$

$$= 4.66$$

HC$_7$H$_5$O$_2$ is the acid and NaC$_7$H$_5$O$_2$ is the base. Therefore, we calculate the pH as follows:

$$pH = pK_a + \log\frac{[base]}{[acid]}$$

$$= -\log(6.5 \times 10^{-5}) + \log\frac{0.150}{0.050}$$

$$= 4.1\underline{8}7 + 0.4\underline{7}7$$

$$= 4.66$$

Confirm that the *x is small* approximation is valid by calculating the ratio of *x* to the number it was subtracted from in the approximation. The ratio should be less than 0.05 (or 5%). (See Sections 14.8 and 15.6 to review the *x is small* approximation.)

$$\frac{2.2 \times 10^{-5}}{0.050} \times 100\% = 0.044\%$$

The approximation is valid.

Confirm that the *x is small* approximation is valid by calculating the $[H_3O^+]$ from the pH. Since $[H_3O^+]$ is formed by ionization of the acid, the calculated $[H_3O^+]$ has to be less than 0.05 (or 5%) of the initial concentration of the acid in order for the *x is small* approximation to be valid.

$$pH = 4.66 = -\log[H_3O^+]$$

$$[H_3O^+] = 10^{-4.66} = 2.2 \times 10^{-5} \text{ M}$$

$$\frac{2.2 \times 10^{-5}}{0.050} \times 100\% = 0.044\%$$

The approximation is valid.

FOR PRACTICE 16.2

Calculate the pH of a buffer solution that is 0.250 M in HCN and 0.170 M in KCN. For HCN, $K_a = 4.9 \times 10^{-10}$ ($pK_a = 9.31$). Use both the equilibrium approach and the Henderson–Hasselbalch approach.

You may be wondering how to decide whether to use the equilibrium approach or the Henderson–Hasselbalch equation when calculating the pH of buffer solutions. The answer depends on the specific problem. In cases where you can make the *x is small* approximation, the Henderson–Hasselbalch equation is adequate. However, as you can see from Example 16.2, checking the *x is small* approximation is not as convenient with the Henderson–Hasselbalch equation (because the approximation is implicit). Thus, the equilibrium approach, although lengthier, gives you a better sense of the important quantities in the problem and the nature of the approximation. When first working buffer problems, use the equilibrium approach until you get a good sense for when the *x is small* approximation is adequate. Then, you can switch to the more streamlined approach in cases where the approximation applies (and only in those cases). In general, remember that the *x is small* approximation applies to problems in which both of the following are true: (a) the initial concentrations of acids (and/or bases) are not too dilute; and (b) the equilibrium constant is fairly small. Although the exact values depend on the details of the problem, for many buffer problems this means that the initial concentrations of acids and conjugate bases should be at least 10^2–10^3 times greater than the equilibrium constant (depending on the required accuracy).

Conceptual Connection 16.2 pH of Buffer Solutions

A buffer contains the weak acid HA and its conjugate base A⁻. The weak acid has a pK_a of 4.82 and the buffer has a pH of 4.25. Which statement is true of the relative concentrations of the weak acid and conjugate base in the buffer?

(a) [HA] > [A⁻]   (b) [HA] < [A⁻]   (c) [HA] = [A⁻]

Which buffer component would you add to change the pH of the buffer to 4.72?

Calculating pH Changes in a Buffer Solution

When we add acid or base to a buffer, the buffer resists a pH change. Nonetheless, the pH does change by a small amount. Calculating the pH change requires breaking up the problem into two parts:

1. **The stoichiometry calculation** in which we calculate how the addition changes the relative amounts of acid and conjugate base.
2. **The equilibrium calculation** in which we calculate the pH based on the new amounts of acid and conjugate base.

We demonstrate this calculation with a 1.0 L buffer solution that is 0.100 M in the generic acid HA and 0.100 M in its conjugate base A⁻. Since the concentrations of the weak acid and the conjugate base are equal, the pH of the buffer is equal to pK_a. Let's calculate the pH of the solution after we add 0.025 mol of strong acid (H⁺) (assuming that the change in volume from adding the acid is negligible).

The Stoichiometry Calculation As the added acid is neutralized, it converts a stoichiometric amount of the base into its conjugate acid through the neutralization reaction (Figure 16.3a on p. 762):

$$H^+(aq) + A^-(aq) \longrightarrow HA(aq)$$
added acid   weak base in buffer

Neutralizing 0.025 mol of the strong acid (H⁺) requires 0.025 mol of the weak base (A⁻). Consequently, the amount of A⁻ *decreases* by 0.025 mol and the amount of HA *increases* by 0.025 mol (because of the 1:1:1 stoichiometry of the neutralization reaction). We can track these changes in tabular form as follows:

It is best to work with amounts in moles instead of concentrations when tracking these changes, as explained later.

	H⁺(aq)	+	A⁻(aq)	⟶	HA(aq)
Before addition	≈0.00 mol		0.100 mol		0.100 mol
Addition	+0.025 mol		—		—
After addition	≈0.00 mol		0.075 mol		0.125 mol

Notice that this table is not an ICE table. This table simply tracks the stoichiometric changes that occur during the neutralization of the added acid. We write ≈0.00 mol for the amount of H⁺ because the amount is so small compared to the amounts of A⁻ and HA. (Remember that weak acids ionize only to a small extent and that the presence of the common ion further suppresses the ionization.) The amount of H⁺, of course, is not *exactly* zero, as we can see by completing the equilibrium part of the calculation.

The Equilibrium Calculation We have just seen that adding a small amount of acid to a buffer is equivalent to changing the initial concentrations of the acid and conjugate base present in the buffer (in this case, since the volume is 1.0 L, [HA] increased from 0.100 M to 0.125 M and [A⁻] decreased from 0.100 M to 0.075 M). Knowing these new initial concentrations, we can calculate the new pH in the same way that we calculate the pH of any buffer: either by working a full equilibrium problem or by using the Henderson–Hasselbalch equation (see Examples 16.1 and 16.2). In this case, we work the full equilibrium problem. We begin by writing the balanced equation for the ionization of the acid and using it as a guide to prepare an ICE table. The initial concentrations for the ICE table are those that we calculated in the stoichiometry part of the calculation:

$$HA(aq) + H_2O(l) \rightleftharpoons H_3O^+(aq) + A^-(aq)$$

	[HA]	[H₃O⁺]	[A⁻]	
Initial	0.125 ←	≈0.00	0.075 ←	From stoichiometry calculation
Change	−x	+x	+x	
Equil	0.125 − x	x	0.075 + x	

We then substitute the expressions for the equilibrium concentrations into the expression for the acid ionization constant. As long as K_a is sufficiently small relative to the initial concentrations, we can make the *x is small* approximation and solve for x, which is equal to $[H_3O^+]$.

$$K_a = \frac{[H_3O^+][A^-]}{[HA]}$$

$$= \frac{x(0.075 + \cancel{x})}{0.125 - \cancel{x}} \quad (x \text{ is small})$$

$$K_a = \frac{x(0.075)}{0.125}$$

$$x = [H_3O^+] = K_a \frac{0.125}{0.075}$$

Once we calculate $[H_3O^+]$, we can calculate the pH with the equation $pH = -\log[H_3O^+]$.

Notice that, since the expression for x contains a *ratio* of concentrations $[HA]/[A^-]$, the *amounts of acid and base in moles* may be substituted in place of concentration because, in a single buffer solution, the volume is the same for both the acid and the base. Therefore, the volumes cancel:

$$[HA]/[A^-] = \frac{\dfrac{n_{HA}}{\cancel{V}}}{\dfrac{n_{A^-}}{\cancel{V}}} = n_{HA}/n_{A^-}$$

The effect of adding a small amount of strong base to the buffer is exactly the opposite of adding acid. The added base converts a stoichiometric amount of the acid into its conjugate base through the neutralization reaction (Figure 16.3b ▶):

$$\underset{\text{added base} \quad \text{weak acid in buffer}}{OH^-(aq) + HA(aq)} \longrightarrow H_2O(l) + A^-(aq)$$

If we add 0.025 mol of OH^-, the amount of A^- goes *up* by 0.025 mol and the amount of HA goes *down* by 0.025 mol as shown in the following table:

	OH⁻(aq)	+	HA(aq)	⟶	H₂O(l)	+	A⁻(aq)
Before addition	≈ 0.00 mol		0.100 mol				0.100 mol
Addition	+0.025 mol		—				—
After addition	≈ 0.00 mol		0.075 mol				0.125 mol

When you calculate the pH of a buffer after adding small amounts of acid or base, remember the following:

▶ Adding a small amount of strong acid to a buffer converts a stoichiometric amount of the base to the conjugate acid and decreases the pH of the buffer (adding acid decreases pH just as we would expect).

▶ Adding a small amount of strong base to a buffer converts a stoichiometric amount of the acid to the conjugate base and increases the pH of the buffer (adding base increases the pH just as we would expect).

The easiest way to remember these changes is relatively simple: adding acid creates more acid; adding base creates more base.

▶ FIGURE 16.3 **Buffering Action**
(a) When an acid is added to a buffer, a stoichiometric amount of the weak base is converted to the conjugate acid.
(b) When a base is added to a buffer, a stoichiometric amount of the weak acid is converted to the conjugate base.

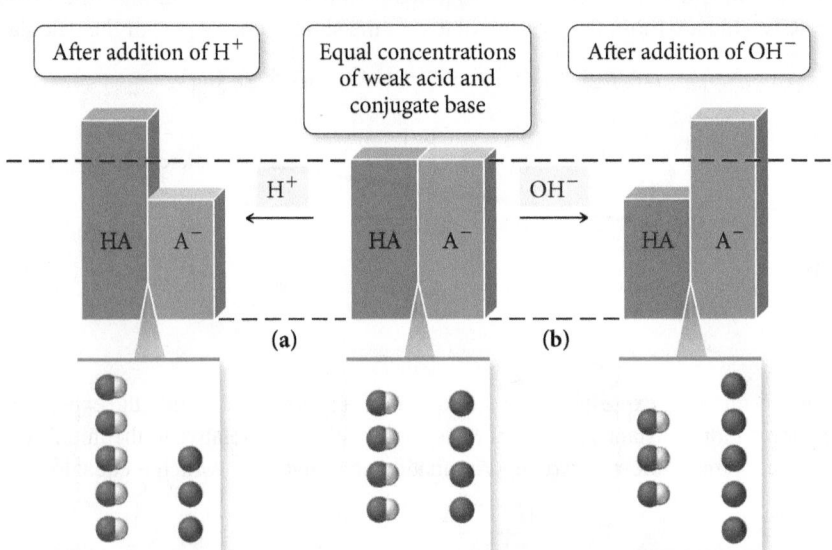

Action of a Buffer

Example 16.3 and the For Practice Problems that follow it involve calculating pH changes in a buffer solution after small amounts of strong acid or strong base are added. As we have seen, these problems generally have two parts:

- Part I. Stoichiometry—use the stoichiometry of the neutralization equation to calculate the changes in the amounts (in moles) of the buffer components upon addition of the acid or base.

- Part II. Equilibrium—use the new amounts of buffer components to work an equilibrium problem to find pH. (For most buffers, this can also be done with the Henderson–Hasselbalch equation.)

EXAMPLE 16.3 Calculating the pH Change in a Buffer Solution after the Addition of a Small Amount of Strong Acid or Base

A 1.0 L buffer solution contains 0.100 mol $HC_2H_3O_2$ and 0.100 mol $NaC_2H_3O_2$. The value of K_a for $HC_2H_3O_2$ is 1.8×10^{-5}. Because the initial amounts of acid and conjugate base are equal, the pH of the buffer is equal to $pK_a = -\log(1.8 \times 10^{-5}) = 4.74$. Calculate the new pH after adding 0.010 mol of solid NaOH to the buffer. For comparison, calculate the pH after adding 0.010 mol of solid NaOH to 1.0 L of pure water. (Ignore any small changes in volume that might occur upon addition of the base.)

SOLUTION

Part I: Stoichiometry. The addition of the base converts a stoichiometric amount of acid to the conjugate base (adding base creates more base). Write an equation showing the neutralization reaction and then set up a table to track the changes.

	$OH^-(aq)$	$+$ $HC_2H_3O_2(aq)$	$\longrightarrow H_2O(l) + C_2H_3O_2^-(aq)$
Before addition	≈0.00 mol	0.100 mol	0.100 mol
Addition	0.010 mol	—	—
After addition	≈0.00 mol	0.090 mol	0.110 mol

Part II: Equilibrium. Write the balanced equation for the ionization of the acid and use it as a guide to prepare an ICE table. Use the amounts of acid and conjugate base from part I as the initial amounts of acid and conjugate base in the ICE table.

$HC_2H_3O_2(aq) + H_2O(l) \rightleftharpoons H_3O^+(aq) + C_2H_3O_2^-(aq)$

	$[HC_2H_3O_2]$	$[H_3O^+]$	$[C_2H_3O_2^-]$
Initial	0.090	≈0.00	0.110
Change	$-x$	$+x$	$+x$
Equil	$0.090 - x$	x	$0.110 + x$

Substitute the expressions for the equilibrium concentrations of acid and conjugate base into the expression for the acid ionization constant. Make the *x is small* approximation and solve for *x*. Calculate the pH from the value of *x*, which is equal to $[H_3O^+]$.	$$K_a = \frac{[H_3O^+][C_2H_3O_2^-]}{[HC_2H_3O_2]}$$ $$= \frac{x(0.110 + \cancel{x})}{0.090 - \cancel{x}} \qquad (x \text{ is small})$$ $$1.8 \times 10^{-5} = \frac{x(0.110)}{0.090}$$ $$x = [H_3O^+] = 1.\underline{47} \times 10^{-5}\,M$$ $$pH = -\log[H_3O^+]$$ $$= -\log(1.\underline{47} \times 10^{-5})$$ $$= 4.83$$
Confirm that the *x is small* approximation is valid by calculating the ratio of *x* to the smallest number it was subtracted from in the approximation. The ratio should be less than 0.05 (or 5%).	$$\frac{1.\underline{47} \times 10^{-5}}{0.090} \times 100\% = 0.016\%$$ The approximation is valid.
Part II: Equilibrium Alternative (using the Henderson–Hasselbalch equation). As long as the *x is small* approximation is valid, you can substitute the quantities of acid and conjugate base after the addition (from part I) into the Henderson–Hasselbalch equation and calculate the new pH.	$$pH = pK_a + \log\frac{[\text{base}]}{[\text{acid}]}$$ $$= -\log(1.8 \times 10^{-5}) + \log\frac{0.110}{0.090}$$ $$= 4.74 + 0.087$$ $$= 4.83$$
The pH of 1.0 L of water after adding 0.010 mol of NaOH is calculated from the $[OH^-]$. For a strong base, $[OH^-]$ is simply the number of moles of OH^- divided by the number of liters of solution.	$$[OH^-] = \frac{0.010\ \text{mol}}{1.0\ \text{L}} = 0.010\ M$$ $$pOH = -\log[OH^-] = -\log(0.010)$$ $$= 2.00$$ $$pOH + pH = 14.00$$ $$pH = 14.00 - pOH$$ $$= 14.00 - 2.00$$ $$= 12.00$$

CHECK Notice that the buffer solution changed from pH = 4.74 to pH = 4.83 upon addition of the base (a small fraction of a single pH unit). In contrast, the pure water changed from pH = 7.00 to pH = 12.00, five whole pH units (a factor of 10^5). Notice also that even the buffer solution got slightly more basic upon addition of a base, as we would expect. To check your answer, always make sure the pH goes in the direction you expect: adding base should make the solution more basic (higher pH); adding acid should make the solution more acidic (lower pH).

FOR PRACTICE 16.3
Calculate the pH of the solution in Example 16.3 upon addition of 0.015 mol of NaOH to the original buffer.

FOR MORE PRACTICE 16.3
Calculate the pH of the solution in Example 16.3 upon addition of 10.0 mL of 1.00 M HCl to the original buffer in Example 16.3.

Conceptual Connection 16.3 Adding Acid or Base to a Buffer

A buffer contains equal amounts of a weak acid and its conjugate base and has a pH of 5.25. Which would be a reasonable value of buffer pH after the addition of a small amount of acid?

(a) 4.15

(b) 5.15

(c) 5.35

(d) 6.35

Buffers Containing a Base and Its Conjugate Acid

So far, we have seen examples of buffers composed of an acid and its conjugate base (where the conjugate base is an ion). A buffer can also be composed of a base and its conjugate acid (where the conjugate acid is an ion). For example, a solution containing significant amounts of both NH_3 and NH_4Cl will act as a buffer (Figure 16.4 ▼). The NH_3 is a weak base that neutralizes small amounts of added acid, and the NH_4^+ ion is the conjugate acid that neutralizes small amounts of added base. We calculate the pH of a solution like this in the same way that we calculated the pH of a buffer containing a weak acid and its conjugate base. When using the Henderson–Hasselbalch equation, however, we must first calculate pK_a for the conjugate acid of the weak base. Recall from Section 15.8 that for a conjugate acid–base pair, $K_a \times K_b = K_w$ and $pK_a + pK_b = 14$. Consequently, we can find pK_a of the conjugate acid by subtracting pK_b of the weak base from 14. Example 16.4 illustrates the procedure for calculating the pH of a buffer composed of a weak base and its conjugate acid.

Formation of a Buffer

Weak base

Conjugate acid

Buffer solution

Ammonia
NH_3

Ammonium chloride
NH_4Cl

NH_3

NH_4^+ Cl^- H_3O^+

▲ **FIGURE 16.4 Buffer Containing a Base** A buffer can also consist of a weak base and its conjugate acid.

EXAMPLE 16.4 Using the Henderson–Hasselbalch Equation to Calculate the pH of a Buffer Solution Composed of a Weak Base and Its Conjugate Acid

Use the Henderson–Hasselbalch equation to calculate the pH of a buffer solution that is 0.50 M in NH_3 and 0.20 M in NH_4Cl. For ammonia, $pK_b = 4.75$.

SOLUTION

Since K_b for NH_3 (1.8×10^{-5}) is much smaller than the initial concentrations in this problem, you can use the Henderson–Hasselbalch equation to calculate the pH of the buffer. First calculate pK_a from pK_b.	$pK_a + pK_b = 14$ $pK_a = 14 - pK_b$ $\quad = 14 - 4.75$ $\quad = 9.25$
Then substitute the given quantities into the Henderson–Hasselbalch equation and calculate pH.	$pH = pK_a + \log \dfrac{[\text{base}]}{[\text{acid}]}$ $\quad = 9.25 + \log \dfrac{0.50}{0.20}$ $\quad = 9.25 + 0.40$ $\quad = 9.65$

FOR PRACTICE 16.4

Calculate the pH of 1.0 L of the solution in Example 16.4 upon addition of 0.010 mol of solid NaOH to the original buffer solution.

FOR MORE PRACTICE 16.4

Calculate the pH of 1.0 L of the solution in Example 16.4 upon addition of 30.0 mL of 1.0 M HCl to the original buffer solution.

16.3 Buffer Effectiveness: Buffer Range and Buffer Capacity

An effective buffer neutralizes small to moderate amounts of added acid or base. Recall from the opening section of this chapter, however, that a buffer can be destroyed by the addition of too much acid or too much base. What factors influence the effectiveness of a buffer? In this section, we examine two such factors: *the relative amounts of the acid and conjugate base* and *the absolute concentrations of the acid and conjugate base*. We then define the *capacity of a buffer* (how much added acid or base it can effectively neutralize) and the *range of a buffer* (the pH range over which a particular acid and its conjugate base can be effective).

Relative Amounts of Acid and Base

A buffer is most effective (most resistant to pH changes) when the concentrations of acid and conjugate base are equal. Let's explore this idea by considering the behavior of a generic buffer composed of HA and A^- for which $pK_a = 5.00$ and calculating the percent change in pH upon addition of 0.010 mol of NaOH for two different 1.0-liter solutions of this buffer system. Both solutions have 0.20 mol of *total* acid and conjugate base. However, solution I has equal amounts of acid and conjugate base (0.10 mol of each), while solution II has much more acid than conjugate base (0.18 mol HA and 0.020 mol A^-). We can calculate the initial pH values of each solution using the Henderson–Hasselbalch equation. Solution I has an initial pH of 5.00 and solution II has an initial pH of 4.05.

Solution I: 0.10 mol HA and 0.10 mol A⁻; initial pH = 5.00

	$OH^-(aq)$ + HA(aq) ⟶ $H_2O(l)$ + $A^-(aq)$		
Before addition	≈ 0.00 mol	0.100 mol	0.100 mol
Addition	0.010 mol	—	—
After addition	≈ 0.00 mol	0.090 mol	0.110 mol

$$\text{pH} = \text{p}K_a + \log\frac{[\text{base}]}{[\text{acid}]}$$

$$= 5.00 + \log\frac{0.110}{0.090}$$

$$= 5.09$$

$$\% \text{ change} = \frac{5.09 - 5.00}{5.00} \times 100\%$$

$$= 1.8\%$$

Solution II: 0.18 mol HA and 0.020 mol A⁻; initial pH = 4.05

	$OH^-(aq)$ + HA(aq) ⟶ $H_2O(l)$ + $A^-(aq)$		
Before addition	≈ 0.00 mol	0.18 mol	0.020 mol
Addition	0.010 mol	—	—
After addition	≈ 0.00 mol	0.17 mol	0.030 mol

$$\text{pH} = \text{p}K_a + \log\frac{[\text{base}]}{[\text{acid}]}$$

$$= 5.00 + \log\frac{0.030}{0.17}$$

$$= 4.25$$

$$\% \text{ change} = \frac{4.25 - 4.05}{4.05} \times 100\%$$

$$= 5.0\%$$

As you can see, the buffer with equal amounts of acid and conjugate base is more resistant to pH change and is therefore the more effective buffer. A buffer becomes less effective as the difference in the relative amounts of acid and conjugate base increases. As a guideline, we can say that an effective buffer must have a [base]/[acid] ratio in the range of 0.10 to 10. *In order for a buffer to be reasonably effective, the relative concentrations of acid and conjugate base should not differ by more than a factor of 10.*

Absolute Concentrations of the Acid and Conjugate Base

A buffer is most effective (most resistant to pH changes) when the concentrations of acid and conjugate base are high. Let's explore this idea by again considering a generic buffer composed of HA and A⁻ and a pK_a of 5.00 and calculating the percent change in pH upon addition of 0.010 mol of NaOH for two 1.0-liter solutions of this buffer system. In this case, both the acid and the base in solution I are ten times more concentrated than the acid and base in solution II. Both solutions have equal relative amounts of acid and conjugate base and therefore have the same initial pH of 5.00.

Solution I: 0.50 mol HA and 0.50 mol A⁻; initial pH = 5.00

	$OH^-(aq)$ + HA(aq) ⟶ $H_2O(l)$ + $A^-(aq)$		
Before addition	≈ 0.00 mol	0.50 mol	0.50 mol
Addition	0.010 mol	—	—
After addition	≈ 0.00 mol	0.49 mol	0.51 mol

$$\text{pH} = \text{p}K_a + \log\frac{[\text{base}]}{[\text{acid}]}$$

$$= 5.00 + \log\frac{0.51}{0.49}$$

$$= 5.02$$

$$\% \text{ change} = \frac{5.02 - 5.00}{5.00} \times 100\%$$

$$= 0.4\%$$

Solution II: 0.050 mol HA and 0.050 mol A⁻; initial pH = 5.00

	$OH^-(aq)$ + HA(aq) ⟶ $H_2O(l)$ + $A^-(aq)$		
Before addition	≈ 0.00 mol	0.050 mol	0.050 mol
Addition	0.010 mol	—	—
After Addition	≈ 0.00 mol	0.040 mol	0.060 mol

$$\text{pH} = \text{p}K_a + \log\frac{[\text{base}]}{[\text{acid}]}$$

$$= 5.00 + \log\frac{0.060}{0.040}$$

$$= 5.18$$

$$\% \text{ change} = \frac{5.18 - 5.00}{5.00} \times 100\%$$

$$= 3.6\%$$

As you can see, the buffer with greater amounts of acid and conjugate base is more resistant to pH changes and therefore the more effective buffer. The more dilute the buffer components, the less effective the buffer.

Buffer Range

In light of the guideline that the relative concentrations of acid and conjugate base should not differ by more than a factor of 10 in order for a buffer to be reasonably effective, we can calculate the pH range over which a particular acid and its conjugate base make an effective buffer. Since the pH of a buffer is given by the Henderson–Hasselbalch equation, we can calculate the outermost points of the effective range as follows:

▲ A concentrated buffer contains more of the weak acid and its conjugate base than a weak buffer does. It can therefore neutralize more added acid or added base.

Lowest pH for effective buffer occurs when the base is one-tenth as concentrated as the acid.

$$pH = pK_a + \log\frac{[base]}{[acid]}$$
$$= pK_a + \log 0.10$$
$$= pK_a - 1$$

Highest pH for effective buffer occurs when the base is ten times as concentrated as the acid.

$$pH = pK_a + \log\frac{[base]}{[acid]}$$
$$= pK_a + \log 10$$
$$= pK_a + 1$$

The effective range for a buffering system is one pH unit on either side of pK_a. For example, we can use a weak acid with a pK_a of 5.0 (and its conjugate base) to prepare a buffer in the range of 4.0–6.0. We can adjust the relative amounts of acid and conjugate base to achieve any pH within this range. As we noted earlier, however, the buffer would be most effective at pH 5.0 because the buffer components would be exactly equal at that pH. Example 16.5 demonstrates how to pick an acid/conjugate base system for a buffer and how to calculate the relative amounts of acid and conjugate base required for a desired pH.

EXAMPLE 16.5 Preparing a Buffer

Which acid would you choose to combine with its sodium salt to make a solution buffered at pH 4.25? For the best choice, calculate the ratio of the conjugate base to the acid required to attain the desired pH.

chlorous acid ($HClO_2$) $pK_a = 1.95$ formic acid ($HCHO_2$) $pK_a = 3.74$
nitrous acid (HNO_2) $pK_a = 3.34$ hypochlorous acid ($HClO$) $pK_a = 7.54$

SOLUTION

The best choice is formic acid because its pK_a lies closest to the desired pH. You can calculate the ratio of conjugate base (CHO_2^-) to acid ($HCHO_2$) required by using the Henderson–Hasselbalch equation as follows:

$$pH = pK_a + \log\frac{[base]}{[acid]}$$
$$4.25 = 3.74 + \log\frac{[base]}{[acid]}$$
$$\log\frac{[base]}{[acid]} = 4.25 - 3.74$$
$$= 0.51$$
$$\frac{[base]}{[acid]} = 10^{0.51}$$
$$= 3.24$$

FOR PRACTICE 16.5

Which acid in Example 16.5 would you choose to create a buffer with pH = 7.35? If you have 500.0 mL of a 0.10 M solution of the acid, what mass of the corresponding sodium salt of the conjugate base do you need to make the buffer?

Chemistry and Medicine

Buffer Effectiveness in Human Blood

As we discussed in the opening section of this chapter, blood contains several buffering systems, the most important of which consists of carbonic acid and the carbonate ion. The concentrations of these buffer components in normal blood plasma are $[HCO_3^-] = 0.024$ M and $[H_2CO_3] = 0.0012$ M. The pK_a for carbonic acid at body temperature is 6.1. If we substitute these quantities into the Henderson–Hasselbalch equation, we can calculate the normal pH of blood:

$$pH = pK_a + \log\frac{[\text{base}]}{[\text{acid}]}$$

$$= 6.1 + \log\frac{[HCO_3^-]}{[H_2CO_3]}$$

$$= 6.1 + \log\frac{0.024\ M}{0.0012\ M}$$

$$= 7.4$$

Normal blood has a pH of 7.4. Notice that the concentration of the bicarbonate ion is 20 times higher than the concentration of carbonic acid and the pH of the buffer is more than one pH unit away from pK_a. Why?

The higher bicarbonate ion concentration in blood makes the buffer capacity of blood greater for acid than for base, which is necessary because the products of metabolism that enter blood are mostly acidic. For example, when we exercise, our bodies produce lactic acid ($HC_3H_5O_3$). The lactic acid enters the bloodstream and must be neutralized.

The bicarbonate ion neutralizes the lactic acid according to the equation:

$$HCO_3^-(aq) + HC_3H_5O_3(aq) \longrightarrow$$
$$H_2CO_3(aq) + C_3H_5O_3^-(aq)$$

An enzyme called carbonic anhydrase then catalyzes the conversion of carbonic acid into carbon dioxide and water:

$$H_2CO_3(aq) \rightleftharpoons CO_2(g) + H_2O(l)$$

We eliminate the carbon dioxide from our blood when we breathe. When large amounts of lactic acid are produced, we must breathe faster to keep up with the need to eliminate carbon dioxide. This is why we pant when we exert ourselves.

Question

A 70 kg person has a total blood volume of about 5.0 L. Given the carbonic acid and bicarbonate concentrations stated, what volume (in mL) of 6.0 M HCl can be neutralized by blood without the blood pH dropping below 7.0 (which would result in death)?

▶ Normal blood has a pH of 7.4.

Buffer Capacity

Buffer capacity is the amount of acid or base that you can add to a buffer without causing a large change in pH. Given what we just learned about the absolute concentrations of acid and conjugate base in an effective buffer, we can conclude that the *buffer capacity increases with increasing absolute concentrations of the buffer components*. The more concentrated the weak acid and conjugate base that compose the buffer, the higher the buffer capacity. In addition, *overall buffer capacity increases as the relative concentrations of the buffer components become more similar to each other.* As the ratio of the buffer components gets closer to 1, the *overall* capacity of the buffer (the ability to neutralize added acid *and* added base) becomes greater. In some cases, however, a buffer that must neutralize primarily added acid (or primarily added base) may be overweighted in one of the buffer components, as shown in the *Chemistry and Medicine* box in this section.

Conceptual 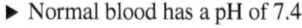 Connection 16.4 Buffer Capacity

A 1.0 L buffer solution is 0.10 M in HF and 0.050 M in NaF. Which action destroys the buffer?

(a) adding 0.050 mol of HCl   (b) adding 0.050 mol of NaOH

(c) adding 0.050 mol of NaF   (d) none of the above

16.4 Titrations and pH Curves

We first examined acid–base titrations in Section 4.8. In an **acid–base titration**, a basic (or acidic) solution of unknown concentration reacts with an acidic (or basic) solution of known concentration. The known solution is slowly added to the unknown one while the pH is monitored with either a pH meter or an **indicator** (a substance whose color depends on the pH). As the acid and base combine, they neutralize each other. At the **equivalence point**—the point in the titration when the number of moles of base is stoichiometrically equal to the number of moles of acid—the titration is complete. When the equivalence point is reached, neither reactant is in excess and the number of moles of the reactants are related by the reaction stoichiometry (Figure 16.5 ▼).

In this section, we examine acid–base titrations more closely, concentrating on the pH changes that occur during the titration. A plot of the pH of the solution during a titration is known as a *titration curve* or *pH curve*. Figure 16.6 ▼ is a pH curve for the titration of HCl with NaOH. Before any base is added to the solution, the pH is low (as expected for a solution of HCl). As the NaOH is added, the solution becomes less acidic because the NaOH begins to neutralize the HCl. The point of inflection in the middle of the curve is the equivalence point. Notice that the pH changes very quickly near the

> The equivalence point is so named because the number of moles of acid and base are stoichiometrically equivalent at this point.

▲ FIGURE 16.5 **Acid–Base Titration**   As OH⁻ is added in a titration, it neutralizes the H⁺, forming water. At the equivalence point, the titration is complete.

▲ FIGURE 16.6 **Titration Curve: Strong Acid + Strong Base**   This curve represents the titration of 50.0 mL of 0.100 M HCl with 0.100 M NaOH.

equivalence point (small amounts of added base cause large changes in pH). Beyond the equivalence point, the solution is basic because the HCl has been completely neutralized and excess base is being added to the solution. The exact shape of the pH curve depends on several factors, including the strength of the acid or base being titrated. Let's consider several combinations individually.

The Titration of a Strong Acid with a Strong Base

Consider the titration of 25.0 mL of 0.100 M HCl with 0.100 M NaOH. We begin by calculating the volume of base required to reach the equivalence point, and then the pH at several points during the titration.

Volume of NaOH Required to Reach the Equivalence Point   During the titration, the added sodium hydroxide neutralizes the hydrochloric acid:

$$HCl(aq) + NaOH(aq) \longrightarrow H_2O(l) + NaCl(aq)$$

The equivalence point is reached when the number of moles of base added equals the number of moles of acid initially in solution. We calculate the amount of acid initially in solution from its volume and its concentration:

$$\text{Initial mol HCl} = 0.0250 \, \cancel{L} \times \frac{0.100 \, \text{mol}}{1 \, \cancel{L}} = 0.00250 \, \text{mol HCl}$$

The amount of NaOH that must be added is 0.00250 mol NaOH. We calculate the volume of NaOH required from its concentration:

$$\text{Volume NaOH solution} = 0.00250 \, \cancel{mol} \times \frac{1 \, L}{0.100 \, \cancel{mol}} = 0.0250 \, L$$

The equivalence point is reached when 25.0 mL of NaOH has been added. In this case, the concentrations of both solutions are identical, so the volume of NaOH solution required to reach the equivalence point is equal to the volume of the HCl solution that is being titrated.

Initial pH (before Adding Any Base)   The initial pH of the solution is simply the pH of a 0.100 M HCl solution. Since HCl is a strong acid, the concentration of H_3O^+ is also 0.100 M and the pH is 1.00:

$$pH = -\log[H_3O^+]$$
$$= -\log(0.100)$$
$$= 1.00$$

pH after Adding 5.00 mL NaOH   As NaOH is added to the solution, it neutralizes H_3O^+:

$$OH^-(aq) + H_3O^+(aq) \longrightarrow 2 \, H_2O(l)$$

We calculate the amount of H_3O^+ at any given point (before the equivalence point) by using the reaction stoichiometry—1 mol of NaOH neutralizes 1 mol of H_3O^+. The initial number of moles of H_3O^+ (as just calculated) is 0.00250 mol. We calculate the number of moles of NaOH added at 5.00 mL by multiplying the added volume (in L) by the concentration of the NaOH solution:

$$\text{mol NaOH added} = 0.00500 \, \cancel{L} \times \frac{0.100 \, \text{mol}}{1 \, \cancel{L}} = 0.000500 \, \text{mol NaOH}$$

The addition of OH^- causes the amount of H^+ to decrease as shown in the following table:

	$OH^-(aq)$	+	$H_3O^+(aq) \longrightarrow 2 \, H_2O(l)$
Before addition	≈ 0.00 mol		0.00250 mol
Addition	0.000500 mol		—
After addition	≈ 0.00 mol		0.00200 mol

We calculate the H_3O^+ concentration by dividing the number of moles of H_3O^+ remaining by the *total volume* (initial volume plus added volume):

$$[H_3O^+] = \frac{0.00200 \text{ mol } H_3O^+}{\underbrace{0.0250 \text{ L}}_{\text{Initial volume}} + \underbrace{0.00500 \text{ L}}_{\text{Added volume}}} = 0.0667 \text{ M}$$

The pH is therefore 1.18:

$$pH = -\log 0.0667$$
$$= 1.18$$

pH's after Adding 10.0, 15.0, and 20.0 mL NaOH As more NaOH is added, it further neutralizes the H_3O^+ in the solution. We calculate the pH at each of these points in the same way that we calculated the pH at the 5.00 mL point. The results are tabulated as follows:

Volume (mL)	pH
10.0	1.37
15.0	1.60
20.0	1.95

pH after Adding 25.0 mL NaOH (Equivalence Point) The pH at the equivalence point of a strong acid–strong base titration will always be 7.00 (at 25 °C). At the equivalence point, the strong base has completely neutralized the strong acid. The only source of hydronium ions then is the ionization of water. The $[H_3O^+]$ at 25 °C from the ionization of water is 1.00×10^{-7} M and the pH is 7.00.

pH after Adding 30.00 mL NaOH As NaOH is added beyond the equivalence point, it becomes the excess reagent. We calculate the amount of OH^- at any given point (past the equivalence point) by subtracting the initial amount of H_3O^+ from the amount of OH^- added. The number of moles of OH^- added at 30.00 mL is:

$$\text{mol } OH^- \text{ added} = 0.0300 \text{ L} \times \frac{0.100 \text{ mol}}{1 \text{ L}} = 0.00300 \text{ mol } OH^-$$

The number of moles of OH^- remaining after neutralization is shown in the following table:

	$OH^-(aq)$	+	$H_3O^+(aq) \longrightarrow 2\,H_2O(l)$
Before addition	≈ 0.00 mol		0.00250 mol
Addition	0.00300 mol		—
After addition	0.00050 mol		≈ 0.00 mol

We calculate the OH^- concentration by dividing the number of moles of OH^- remaining by the *total volume* (initial volume plus added volume):

$$[OH^-] = \frac{0.000500 \text{ mol } OH^-}{0.0250 \text{ L} + 0.0300 \text{ L}} = 0.00909 \text{ M}$$

We can then calculate the $[H_3O^+]$ and pH:

$$[H_3O^+][OH^-] = 10^{-14}$$
$$[H_3O^+] = \frac{10^{-14}}{[OH^-]} = \frac{10^{-14}}{0.00909}$$
$$= 1.10 \times 10^{-12} \text{ M}$$
$$pH = -\log(1.10 \times 10^{-12})$$
$$= 11.96$$

Volume of NaOH added (mL)

pH's after Adding 35.0, 40.0, and 50.0 mL NaOH   As more NaOH is added, it further increases the basicity of the solution. We calculate the pH at each of these points in the same way that we calculated the pH at the 30.00 mL point. The results are tabulated as follows:

Volume (mL)	pH
35.0	12.22
40.0	12.36
50.0	12.52

The Overall pH Curve   The overall pH curve for the titration of a strong acid with a strong base has the characteristic S-shape we just plotted. The overall curve is as follows:

Summarizing the Titration of a Strong Acid with a Strong Base:

▶ The initial pH is simply the pH of the strong acid solution to be titrated.

▶ Before the equivalence point, H_3O^+ is in excess. Calculate the $[H_3O^+]$ by subtracting the number of moles of added OH^- from the initial number of moles of H_3O^+ and dividing by the *total* volume.

▶ At the equivalence point, neither reactant is in excess and the pH = 7.00.

▶ Beyond the equivalence point, OH^- is in excess. Calculate the $[OH^-]$ by subtracting the initial number of moles of H_3O^+ from the number of moles of added OH^- and dividing by the *total* volume.

The pH curve for the titration of a strong base with a strong acid is shown in Figure 16.7 ▼. Calculating the points along this curve is very similar to calculating the points along the pH curve for the titration of a strong acid with a strong base. The main difference is that the curve starts basic and then becomes acidic after the equivalence point (instead of vice versa).

▶ FIGURE 16.7 **Titration Curve: Strong Base + Strong Acid**   This curve represents the titration of 25.0 mL of 0.100 M NaOH with 0.100 M HCl.

EXAMPLE 16.6 Strong Acid–Strong Base Titration pH Curve

A 50.0 mL sample of 0.200 M sodium hydroxide is titrated with 0.200 M nitric acid. Calculate pH:

(a)   after adding 30.00 mL of HNO_3 **(b)**   at the equivalence point

SOLUTION

(a) Begin by calculating the initial amount of NaOH (in moles) from the volume and molarity of the NaOH solution. Because NaOH is a strong base, it dissociates completely, so the amount of OH^- is equal to the amount of NaOH.	$\text{moles NaOH} = 0.0500 \text{ L} \times \dfrac{0.200 \text{ mol}}{1 \text{ L}}$ $= 0.0100 \text{ mol}$ $\text{moles OH}^- = 0.0100 \text{ mol}$
Calculate the amount of HNO_3 (in moles) added at 30.0 mL from the molarity of the HNO_3 solution.	$\text{mol HNO}_3 \text{ added} = 0.0300 \text{ L} \times \dfrac{0.200 \text{ mol}}{1 \text{ L}}$ $= 0.00600 \text{ mol HNO}_3$

As HNO_3 is added to the solution, it neutralizes some of the OH^-. Calculate the number of moles of OH^- remaining by setting up a table based on the neutralization reaction that shows the amount of OH^- before the addition, the amount of H_3O^+ added, and the amounts left after the addition.

	$OH^-(aq)$	$+$	$H_3O^+(aq)$	$\longrightarrow$	$2 H_2O(l)$
Before addition	0.0100 mol		≈ 0.00 mol		
Addition	—		0.00600 mol		
After addition	0.0040 mol		0.00 mol		

Calculate the OH^- concentration by dividing the amount of OH^- remaining by the *total volume* (initial volume plus added volume).	$[OH^-] = \dfrac{0.0040 \text{ mol}}{0.0500 \text{ L} + 0.0300 \text{ L}}$ $= 0.0500 \text{ M}$
Calculate the pOH from $[OH^-]$.	$pOH = -\log(0.0500)$ $= 1.30$
Calculate the pH from the pOH using the equation $pH + pOH = 14$.	$pH = 14 - pOH$ $= 14 - 1.30$ $= 12.70$
(b) At the equivalence point, the strong base has completely neutralized the strong acid. The $[H_3O^+]$ at 25 °C from the ionization of water is 1.00×10^{-7} M and the pH is therefore 7.00.	$pH = 7.00$

FOR PRACTICE 16.6

Calculate the pH in the titration in Example 16.6 after the addition of 60.0 mL of 0.200 M HNO_3.

Conceptual Connection 16.5 Titration Equivalence Point

The amount of acid in the flask at right is to be titrated by a strong base. Which mark on the burette next to the flask indicates the amount of base required to reach the equivalence point?

(a) A   **(b)** B   **(c)** C   **(d)** D

The Titration of a Weak Acid with a Strong Base

Consider the titration of 25.0 mL of 0.100 M $HCHO_2$ with 0.100 M NaOH.

$$NaOH(aq) + HCHO_2(aq) \longrightarrow H_2O(l) + NaCHO_2(aq)$$

The concentrations and the volumes here are identical to those in our previous titration, in which we calculated the pH curve for the titration of a *strong* acid with a strong base. The only difference is that $HCHO_2$ is a *weak* acid rather than a strong one. We begin by calculating the volume required to reach the equivalence point of the titration.

Volume of NaOH Required to Reach the Equivalence Point From the stoichiometry of the equation, we can see that the equivalence point occurs when the amount (in moles) of added base equals the amount (in moles) of acid initially in solution.

$$\text{Initial mol HCHO}_2 = 0.0250 \ \cancel{L} \times \frac{0.100 \text{ mol}}{1 \ \cancel{L}} = 0.00250 \text{ mol HCHO}_2$$

The amount of NaOH that must be added is 0.00250 mol NaOH. The volume of NaOH required is therefore:

$$\text{Volume NaOH solution} = 0.00250 \ \cancel{\text{mol}} \times \frac{1 \text{ L}}{0.100 \ \cancel{\text{mol}}} = 0.0250 \text{ L NaOH solution}$$

The equivalence point occurs when 25.0 mL of base has been added. Notice that the volume of NaOH required to reach the equivalence point for this weak acid is identical to that required for a strong acid. *The volume at the equivalence point in an acid–base titration does not depend on whether the acid being titrated is a strong acid or a weak acid; it depends only on the amount (in moles) of acid present in solution before the titration begins and on the concentration of the added base.*

Initial pH (before Adding Any Base) The initial pH of the solution is the pH of a 0.100 M $HCHO_2$ solution. Since $HCHO_2$ is a weak acid, we calculate the concentration of H_3O^+ and the pH by doing an equilibrium problem for the ionization of $HCHO_2$. The procedure for solving weak acid ionization problems is given in Examples 15.5 and 15.6. We show a highly condensed calculation here (K_a for $HCHO_2$ is 1.8×10^{-4}).

$$HCHO_2(aq) + H_2O(l) \rightleftharpoons H_3O^+(aq) + CHO_2^-(aq)$$

	$[HCHO_2]$	$[H_3O^+]$	$[CHO_2^-]$
Initial	0.100	≈ 0.00	0.00
Change	$-x$	$+x$	$+x$
Equil	$0.100 - x$	x	x

$$K_a = \frac{[H_3O^+][CHO_2^-]}{[HCHO_2]}$$

$$= \frac{x^2}{0.100 - \cancel{x}} \quad (x \text{ is small})$$

$$1.8 \times 10^{-4} = \frac{x^2}{0.100}$$

$$x = 4.24 \times 10^{-3}$$

Therefore, $[H_3O^+] = 4.24 \times 10^{-3} \text{ M}.$

$$pH = -\log(4.24 \times 10^{-3})$$
$$= 2.37$$

Notice that the pH is initially at a higher value (less acidic) than it is for a strong acid of the same concentration, as we would expect because the acid is weak.

pH after Adding 5.00 mL NaOH When titrating a *weak acid* with a strong base, the added NaOH *converts a stoichiometric amount of the acid into its conjugate base.* As we calculated previously, 5.00 mL of the 0.100 M NaOH solution contains 0.000500 mol OH^-. When the 0.000500 mol OH^- is added to the weak acid solution, the OH^- reacts stoichiometrically with $HCHO_2$ causing the amount of $HCHO_2$ to *decrease* by 0.000500 mol and the amount of CHO_2^- to *increase* by 0.000500 mol. This is very similar to what happens when you add strong base to a buffer, and it is summarized in the following table:

	$OH^-(aq)$ +	$HCHO_2(aq)$ $\longrightarrow$	$H_2O(l)$ +	$CHO_2^-(aq)$
Before addition	≈ 0.00 mol	0.00250 mol	—	0.00 mol
Addition	0.000500 mol	—	—	—
After addition	≈ 0.00 mol	0.00200 mol	—	0.000500 mol

The x-axis of the graph reads: Volume of NaOH added (mL); the y-axis reads: pH.

Notice that, after the addition, the solution contains significant amounts of both an acid ($HCHO_2$) and its conjugate base (CHO_2^-) —*the solution is now a buffer.* To calculate the pH of a buffer (when the *x is small* approximation applies as it does here), we can use the Henderson–Hasselbalch equation and pK_a for $HCHO_2$ (which is 3.74):

$$pH = pK_a + \log\frac{[base]}{[acid]}$$

$$= 3.74 + \log\frac{0.000500}{0.00200}$$

$$= 3.74 - 0.60$$

$$= 3.14$$

pH's after Adding 10.0, 12.5, 15.0, and 20.0 mL NaOH As more NaOH is added, it converts more $HCHO_2$ into CHO_2^-. We calculate the relative amounts of $HCHO_2$ and CHO_2^- at each of these volumes using the reaction stoichiometry and then calculate the pH of the resulting buffer using the Henderson–Hasselbalch equation (as we did for the pH at 5.00 mL). The amounts of $HCHO_2$ and CHO_2^- (after addition of the OH^-) at each volume and the corresponding pH's are tabulated as follows:

Half-equivalence point ($pH = pK_a$)

Volume (mL)	mol $HCHO_2$	mol CHO_2^-	pH
10.0	0.00150	0.00100	3.56
12.5	0.00125	0.00125	3.74
15.0	0.00100	0.00150	3.92
20.0	0.00050	0.00200	4.34

As the titration proceeds, more of the $HCHO_2$ is converted to the conjugate base (CHO_2^-). Notice that an added NaOH volume of 12.5 mL corresponds to one-half of the equivalence point. At this volume, one-half of the initial amount of $HCHO_2$ has been converted to CHO_2^-, resulting in *equal amounts of weak acid and conjugate base.* For any buffer in which the amounts of weak acid and conjugate base are equal, the pH = pK_a:

$$pH = pK_a + \log\frac{[base]}{[acid]}$$

If [base] = [acid], then [base]/[acid] = 1.

$$pH = pK_a + \log 1$$

$$= pK_a + 0$$

$$= pK_a$$

Since pH = pK_a halfway to the equivalence point, titrations can be used to measure the pK_a of an acid.

pH after Adding 25.0 mL NaOH (Equivalence Point) At the equivalence point, 0.000250 mol of OH^- have been added and therefore all of the $HCHO_2$ has been converted into its conjugate base (CHO_2^-) as summarized in the following table:

	$OH^-(aq)$	$+$	$HCHO_2(aq)$	$\longrightarrow$	$H_2O(l)$	$+$	$CHO_2^-(aq)$
Before addition	≈ 0.00 mol		0.00250 mol		—		0.00 mol
Addition	0.00250 mol		—		—		—
After addition	≈ 0.00 mol		0.00 mol		—		0.00250 mol

The solution is no longer a buffer (it no longer contains significant amounts of both a weak acid and its conjugate base). Instead, the solution contains an ion (CHO_2^-) acting as a weak base. You learned how to calculate the pH of solutions such as this in Section 15.8 (see Example 15.14) by solving an equilibrium problem involving the ionization of water by the weak base (CHO_2^-):

$$CHO_2^-(aq) + H_2O(l) \rightleftharpoons HCHO_2(aq) + OH^-(aq)$$

We calculate the initial concentration of CHO_2^- for the equilibrium problem by dividing the number of moles of CHO_2^- (0.00250 mol) by the *total* volume at the equivalence point (initial volume plus added volume):

Moles CHO_2^- at equivalence point

$$[CHO_2^-] = \frac{0.00250\ \text{mol}}{0.0250\ \text{L} + 0.0250\ \text{L}} = 0.0500\ \text{M}$$

Initial volume   Added volume at equivalence point

We then proceed to solve the equilibrium problem as shown in condensed form as follows:

$$CHO_2^-(aq) + H_2O(l) \rightleftharpoons HCHO_2(aq) + OH^-(aq)$$

	$[CHO_2^-]$	$[HCHO_2]$	$[OH^-]$
Initial	0.0500	0.00	≈ 0.00
Change	$-x$	$+x$	$+x$
Equil	$0.0500 - x$	x	x

Before substituting into the expression for K_b, we find the value of K_b from K_a for formic acid ($K_a = 1.8 \times 10^{-4}$) and K_w:

$$K_a \times K_b = K_w$$

$$K_b = \frac{K_w}{K_a} = \frac{1.0 \times 10^{-14}}{1.8 \times 10^{-4}} = 5.6 \times 10^{-11}$$

Then we substitute the equilibrium concentrations from the previous table into the expression for K_b:

$$K_b = \frac{[HCHO_2][OH^-]}{[CHO_2^-]}$$

$$= \frac{x^2}{0.0500 - \cancel{x}} \qquad (x\ is\ small)$$

$$5.6 \times 10^{-11} = \frac{x^2}{0.0500}$$

$$x = 1.7 \times 10^{-6}$$

Remember that x represents the concentration of the hydroxide ion. We calculate $[H_3O^+]$ and pH:

$$[OH^-] = 1.7 \times 10^{-6}\,M$$

$$[H_3O^+][OH^-] = K_w = 1.0 \times 10^{-14}$$

$$[H_3O^+](1.7 \times 10^{-6}) = 1.0 \times 10^{-14}$$

$$[H_3O^+] = 5.9 \times 10^{-9}\,M$$

$$pH = -\log[H_3O^+]$$

$$= -\log(5.9 \times 10^{-9})$$

$$= 8.23$$

Volume of NaOH added (mL)

Notice that the pH at the equivalence point is *not* neutral but basic. *The titration of a weak acid by a strong base always has a basic equivalence point* because, at the equivalence point, all of the acid has been converted into its conjugate base, resulting in a weakly basic solution.

pH after Adding 30.00 mL NaOH At this point in the titration, 0.00300 mol of OH^- have been added. NaOH has thus become the excess reagent as shown in the following table:

	$OH^-(aq)$	+	$HCHO_2(aq)$	$\longrightarrow$	$H_2O(l)$	+	$CHO_2^-(aq)$
Before addition	≈ 0.00 mol		0.00250 mol		—		0.00 mol
Addition	0.00300 mol		—		—		—
After addition	0.00050 mol		≈ 0.00 mol		—		0.00250 mol

The solution is now a mixture of a strong base (NaOH) and a weak base (CHO_2^-). The strong base completely overwhelms the weak base and we can calculate the pH by considering the strong base alone (as we did for the titration of a strong acid and a strong base). We calculate the OH^- concentration by dividing the amount of OH^- remaining by the *total volume* (initial volume plus added volume):

$$[OH^-] = \frac{0.00050 \text{ mol } OH^-}{0.0250 \text{ L} + 0.0300 \text{ L}} = 0.0091 \text{ M}$$

We can then calculate the $[H_3O^+]$ and pH:

$$[H_3O^+][OH^-] = 10^{-14}$$

$$[H_3O^+] = \frac{10^{-14}}{[OH^-]} = \frac{10^{-14}}{0.0091} = 1.10 \times 10^{-12} \text{ M}$$

$$pH = -\log(1.10 \times 10^{-12})$$

$$= 11.96$$

pH's after Adding 35.0, 40.0, and 50.0 mL NaOH As more NaOH is added, the basicity of the solution increases further. We calculate the pH at each of these volumes in the same way we calculated the pH at 30.00 mL of added NaOH. The results are tabulated as follows:

Volume (mL)	pH
35.0	12.22
40.0	12.36
50.0	12.52

The Overall pH Curve The overall pH curve for the titration of a weak acid with a strong base has a characteristic S-shape similar to that for the titration of a strong acid with a strong base. The main difference is that the equivalence point pH is basic (not neutral). Notice that calculating the pH in different regions throughout the titration involves working different kinds of acid–base problems, all of which we have encountered before.

Summarizing Titration of a Weak Acid with a Strong Base:

▶ The initial pH is that of the weak acid solution to be titrated. Calculate the pH by working an equilibrium problem (similar to Examples 15.5 and 15.6) using the concentration of the weak acid as the initial concentration.

▶ Between the initial pH and the equivalence point, the solution becomes a buffer. Use the reaction stoichiometry to calculate the amounts of each buffer component and then use the Henderson–Hasselbalch equation to calculate the pH (as in Example 16.3).

▶ Halfway to the equivalence point, the buffer components are exactly equal and $pH = pK_a$.

▶ At the equivalence point, the acid has all been converted into its conjugate base. Calculate the pH by working an equilibrium problem for the ionization of water by the ion acting as a weak base (similar to Example 15.14). (Calculate the concentration of the ion acting as a weak base by dividing the number of moles of the ion by the total volume at the equivalence point.)

▶ Beyond the equivalence point, OH^- is in excess. Ignore the weak base and calculate the $[OH^-]$ by subtracting the initial number of moles of the weak acid from the number of moles of added OH^- and dividing by the *total* volume.

EXAMPLE 16.7 Weak Acid–Strong Base Titration pH Curve

A 40.0 mL sample of 0.100 M HNO_2 is titrated with 0.200 M KOH. Calculate:

(a) the volume required to reach the equivalence point

(b) the pH after adding 5.00 mL of KOH

(c) the pH at one-half the equivalence point

SOLUTION

(a) The equivalence point occurs when the amount (in moles) of added base equals the amount (in moles) of acid initially in the solution. Begin by calculating the amount (in moles) of acid initially in the solution. The amount (in moles) of KOH that must be added is equal to the amount of the weak acid.

$$\text{mol } HNO_2 = 0.0400 \text{ L} \times \frac{0.100 \text{ mol}}{\text{L}}$$
$$= 4.00 \times 10^{-3} \text{ mol}$$
$$\text{mol KOH required} = 4.00 \times 10^{-3} \text{ mol}$$

Calculate the volume of KOH required from the number of moles of KOH and the molarity.

$$\text{volume KOH solution} = 4.00 \times 10^{-3} \text{ mol} \times \frac{1 \text{ L}}{0.200 \text{ mol}}$$
$$= 0.0200 \text{ L KOH solution}$$
$$= 20.0 \text{ mL KOH solution}$$

(b) Use the concentration of the KOH solution to calculate the amount (in moles) of OH^- in 5.00 mL of the solution.

$$\text{mol } OH^- = 5.00 \times 10^{-3} \text{ L} \times \frac{0.200 \text{ mol}}{1 \text{ L}}$$
$$= 1.00 \times 10^{-3} \text{ mol } OH^-$$

Prepare a table showing the amounts of HNO_2 and NO_2^- before and after the addition of 5.00 mL KOH. The addition of the KOH stoichiometrically reduces the concentration of HNO_2 and increases the concentration of NO_2^-.

	$OH^-(aq)$	+	$HNO_2(aq)$	⟶	$H_2O(l)$	+	$NO_2^-(aq)$
Before addition	≈0.00 mol		4.00×10^{-3} mol		—		0.00 mol
Addition	1.00×10^{-3} mol		—		—		—
After addition	≈0.00 mol		3.00×10^{-3} mol		—		1.00×10^{-3} mol

Since the solution now contains significant amounts of a weak acid and its conjugate base, use the Henderson–Hasselbalch equation and pK_a for HNO_2 (which is 3.34) to calculate the pH of the solution.

$$pH = pK_a + \log\frac{[\text{base}]}{[\text{acid}]}$$
$$= 3.34 + \log\frac{1.00 \times 10^{-3}}{3.00 \times 10^{-3}}$$
$$= 3.34 - 0.48 = 2.86$$

(c) At one-half the equivalence point, the amount of added base is exactly one-half the initial amount of acid. The base converts exactly half of the HNO_2 into NO_2^-, resulting in equal amounts of the weak acid and its conjugate base. The pH is therefore equal to pK_a.

	$OH^-(aq)$	$+$	$HNO_2(aq)$	$\longrightarrow$	$H_2O(l)$	$+$	$NO_2^-(aq)$
Before addition	≈ 0.00 mol		4.00×10^{-3} mol		—		0.00 mol
Addition	2.00×10^{-3} mol		—		—		—
After addition	≈ 0.00 mol		2.00×10^{-3} mol		—		2.00×10^{-3} mol

$$pH = pK_a + \log\frac{[base]}{[acid]}$$

$$= 3.34 + \log\frac{2.00 \times 10^{-3}}{2.00 \times 10^{-3}}$$

$$= 3.34 + 0 = 3.34$$

FOR PRACTICE 16.7
Determine the pH at the equivalence point for the titration of HNO_2 and KOH in Example 16.7.

The Titration of a Weak Base with a Strong Acid

The pH curve for the titration of a weak base with a strong acid is shown in Figure 16.8 ▼. Calculating the points along this curve is very similar to calculating the points along the pH curve for the titration of a weak acid with a strong base (which we just did). The main differences are that the curve starts basic and has an acidic equivalence point. We calculate the pH in the buffer region using $pH = pK_a + \log\frac{[base]}{[acid]}$ where the pK_a corresponds to the conjugate acid of the base being titrated.

Conceptual Connection 16.6 The Half-Equivalence Point

What is the pH at the half-equivalence point in the titration of a weak base with a strong acid? The pK_b of the weak base is 8.75.

(a) 8.75   **(b)** 7.0   **(c)** 5.25   **(d)** 4.37

The Titration of a Polyprotic Acid

When a diprotic acid is titrated with a strong base, if K_{a_1} and K_{a_2} are sufficiently different, the pH curve will have two equivalence points. For example, Figure 16.9 ▼ shows the

▲ **FIGURE 16.8 Titration Curve: Weak Base with Strong Acid**
This curve represents the titration of 0.100 M NH_3 with 0.100 M HCl.

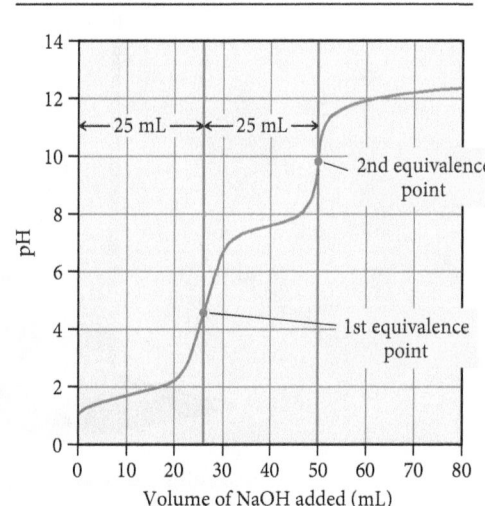

▲ **FIGURE 16.9 Titration Curve: Diprotic Acid with Strong Base** This curve represents the titration of 25.0 mL of 0.100 M H_2SO_3 with 0.100 M NaOH.

pH curve for the titration of sulfurous acid (H_2SO_3) with sodium hydroxide. Recall from Section 15.9 that sulfurous acid ionizes in two steps as follows:

$$H_2SO_3(aq) \rightleftharpoons H^+(aq) + HSO_3^-(aq) \quad K_{a_1} = 1.6 \times 10^{-2}$$
$$HSO_3^-(aq) \rightleftharpoons H^+(aq) + SO_3^{2-}(aq) \quad K_{a_2} = 6.4 \times 10^{-8}$$

The first equivalence point in the titration curve represents the titration of the first proton while the second equivalence point represents the titration of the second proton. Notice that the volume required to reach the first equivalence point is identical to the volume required to the reach the second one because the number of moles of H_2SO_3 in the first step determines the number of moles of HSO_3^- in the second step.

Conceptual Connection 16.7 Acid–Base Titrations

Consider these three titrations:

(i) the titration of 25.0 mL of a 0.100 M monoprotic weak acid with 0.100 M NaOH
(ii) the titration of 25.0 mL of a 0.100 M diprotic weak acid with 0.100 M NaOH
(iii) the titration of 25.0 mL of a 0.100 M strong acid with 0.100 M NaOH

Which statement is most likely to be true?

(a) All three titrations have the same the initial pH.
(b) All three titrations have the same pH at their first equivalence point.
(c) All three titrations require the same volume of NaOH to reach their first equivalence point.

Indicators: pH-Dependent Colors

We can monitor the pH of a titration with either a pH meter or an indicator. The direct monitoring of pH with a meter yields data like the pH curves we have examined previously, allowing determination of the equivalence point from the pH curve itself, as shown in Figure 16.10 ▼. With an indicator, we rely on the point where the indicator changes color—called the **endpoint**—to determine the equivalence point, as shown in

NaOH(aq)

HCl(aq)

▲ FIGURE 16.10 **Monitoring the pH during a Titration** A pH meter monitors pH during titration. The inflection point in the resulting pH curve signifies the equivalence point.

Using an Indicator

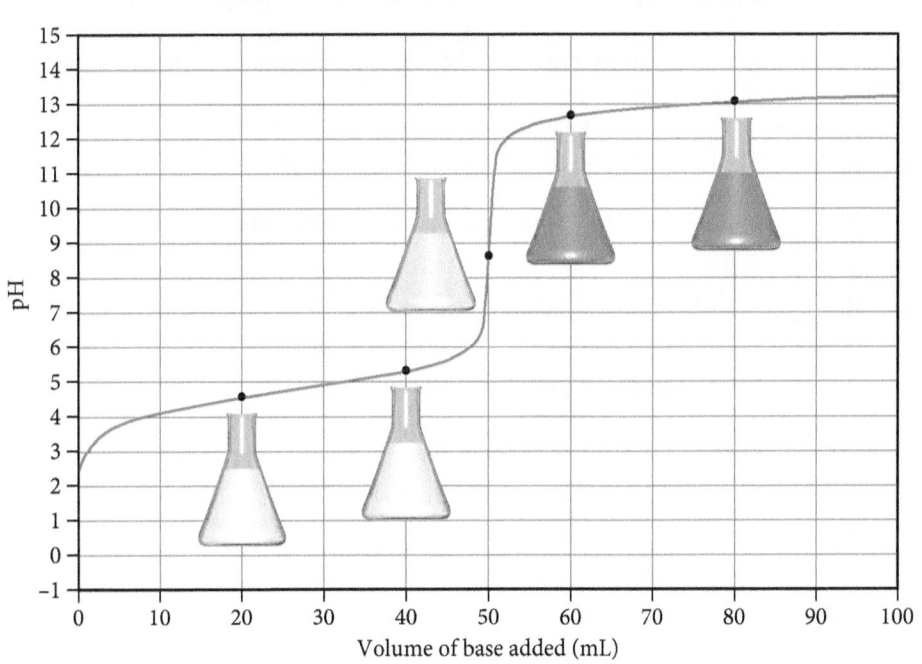

◀ FIGURE 16.11 Monitoring the Color Change during a Titration Titration of 0.100 M HC₂H₃O₂ with 0.100 M NaOH. The endpoint of a titration is signaled by a color change in an appropriate indicator (in this case, phenolphthalein).

Figure 16.11 ▲. With the correct indicator, the endpoint of the titration (indicated by the color change) occurs at the equivalence point (when the amount of acid equals the amount of base).

An indicator is itself a weak organic acid that is a different color than its conjugate base. For example, phenolphthalein (whose structure is shown in Figure 16.12 ▼) is a common indicator whose acid form is colorless and conjugate base form is pink. If we let HIn represent the acid form of a generic indicator and In⁻ the conjugate base form, we have the following equilibrium:

$$\underset{\text{color 1}}{\text{HIn}(aq)} + \text{H}_2\text{O}(l) \rightleftharpoons \text{H}_3\text{O}^+(aq) + \underset{\text{color 2}}{\text{In}^-(aq)}$$

Because its color is intense, only a small amount of indicator is required—an amount that will not affect the pH of the solution or the equivalence point of the neutralization reaction. When the [H₃O⁺] changes during the titration, the equilibrium shifts in response. At low pH, the [H₃O⁺] is high and the equilibrium lies far to the left, resulting in a solution of color 1. As the titration proceeds, the [H₃O⁺] decreases, shifting the equilibrium to the

Phenolphthalein, a Common Indicator

+2 OH⁻ ⇌ +2 H⁺

Acidic - Colorless   Basic - Pink

▲ FIGURE 16.12 Phenolphthalein Phenolphthalein, a weakly acidic compound, is colorless. Its conjugate base is pink.

right. Since the pH change is large near the equivalence point of the titration, there is a large change in $[H_3O^+]$ near the equivalence point. Provided that the correct indicator is chosen, there will also be a correspondingly significant change in color. For the titration of a strong acid with a strong base, one drop of the base near the endpoint is usually enough to change the indicator from color 1 to color 2.

The color of a solution containing an indicator depends on the relative concentrations of HIn and In^-. As a useful guideline, we can assume the following:

If $\dfrac{[In^-]}{[HIn]} = 1$, the indicator solution will be intermediate in color.

If $\dfrac{[In^-]}{[HIn]} > 10$, the indicator solution will be the color of In^-.

If $\dfrac{[In^-]}{[HIn]} < 0.1$, the indicator solution will be the color of HIn.

From the Henderson–Hasselbalch equation, we can derive an expression for the ratio of $[In^-]/[HIn]$:

$$pH = pK_a + \log \frac{[base]}{[acid]}$$

$$= pK_a + \log \frac{[In^-]}{[HIn]}$$

$$\log \frac{[In^-]}{[HIn]} = pH - pK_a$$

$$\frac{[In^-]}{[HIn]} = 10^{(pH - pK_a)}$$

Consider the following three pH values relative to pK_a and the corresponding colors of the indicator solution:

pH (relative to pK_a)	$[In^-]/[HIn]$ ratio	Color of Indicator Solution
$pH = pK_a$	$\dfrac{[In^-]}{[HIn]} = 10^0 = 1$	Intermediate color
$pH = pK_a + 1$	$\dfrac{[In^-]}{[HIn]} = 10^1 = 10$	Color of In^-
$pH = pK_a - 1$	$\dfrac{[In^-]}{[HIn]} = 10^{-1} = 0.10$	Color of HIn

Indicator Color Change: Methyl Red

When the pH of the solution equals the pK_a of the indicator, the solution will have an intermediate color. When the pH is 1 unit (or more) above pK_a, the indicator will be the color of In^-, and when the pH is 1 unit (or more) below pK_a, the indicator will be the color of HIn. As you can see, the indicator changes color within a range of two pH units centered at pK_a (Figure 16.13 ◄). Table 16.1 shows various indicators and their colors as a function of pH.

◄ FIGURE 16.13 Indicator Color Change
An indicator (in this case, methyl red) generally changes color within a range of two pH units. (The pH for each solution is marked on its test tube.)

TABLE 16.1   Ranges of Color Changes for Several Acid–Base Indicators

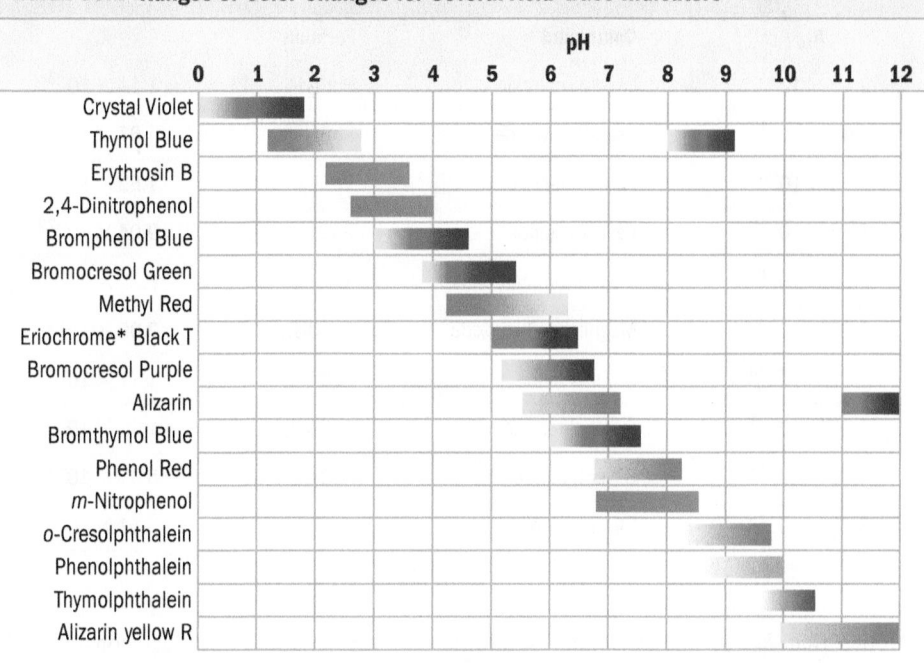

*Trademark of CIBA GEIGY CORP.

16.5 Solubility Equilibria and the Solubility Product Constant

Recall from Chapter 4 that a compound is considered *soluble* if it dissolves in water and *insoluble* if it does not. Recall also that, with the *solubility rules* in Table 4.1, we were able to classify ionic compounds simply as soluble or insoluble. Now we have the tools to examine *degrees* of solubility.

We can better understand the solubility of an ionic compound by applying the concept of equilibrium to the process of dissolution. For example, we can represent the dissolution of calcium fluoride in water as an equilibrium:

$$CaF_2(s) \rightleftharpoons Ca^{2+}(aq) + 2\,F^-(aq)$$

The equilibrium constant for a chemical equation representing the dissolution of an ionic compound is the **solubility product constant** (K_{sp}). For CaF_2, the expression of the solubility product constant is:

$$K_{sp} = [Ca^{2+}][F^-]^2$$

Notice that, as we discussed in Section 14.5, solids are omitted from the equilibrium expression because the concentration of a solid is constant (it is determined by its density and does not change when more solid is added).

The value of K_{sp} is a measure of the solubility of a compound. Table 16.2 lists the values of K_{sp} for a number of ionic compounds. A more complete list can be found in Appendix IIC.

K_{sp} and Molar Solubility

Recall from Section 12.2 that the *solubility* of a compound is the quantity of the compound that dissolves in a certain amount of liquid. The **molar solubility** is the solubility in units of moles per liter (mol/L). We can calculate the molar solubility of a compound directly from K_{sp}. Consider silver chloride:

$$AgCl(s) \rightleftharpoons Ag^+(aq) + Cl^-(aq) \qquad K_{sp} = 1.77 \times 10^{-10}$$

TABLE 16.2 Selected Solubility Product Constants (K_{sp}) at 25 °C

Compound	Formula	K_{sp}	Compound	Formula	K_{sp}
Barium fluoride	BaF_2	2.45×10^{-5}	Lead(II) chloride	$PbCl_2$	1.17×10^{-5}
Barium sulfate	$BaSO_4$	1.07×10^{-10}	Lead(II) bromide	$PbBr_2$	4.67×10^{-6}
Calcium carbonate	$CaCO_3$	4.96×10^{-9}	Lead(II) sulfate	$PbSO_4$	1.82×10^{-8}
Calcium fluoride	CaF_2	1.46×10^{-10}	Lead(II) sulfide*	PbS	9.04×10^{-29}
Calcium hydroxide	$Ca(OH)_2$	4.68×10^{-6}	Magnesium carbonate	$MgCO_3$	6.82×10^{-6}
Calcium sulfate	$CaSO_4$	7.10×10^{-5}	Magnesium hydroxide	$Mg(OH)_2$	2.06×10^{-13}
Copper(II) sulfide*	CuS	1.27×10^{-36}	Silver chloride	$AgCl$	1.77×10^{-10}
Iron(II) carbonate	$FeCO_3$	3.07×10^{-11}	Silver chromate	Ag_2CrO_4	1.12×10^{-12}
Iron(II) hydroxide	$Fe(OH)_2$	4.87×10^{-17}	Silver bromide	$AgBr$	5.35×10^{-13}
Iron(II) sulfide*	FeS	3.72×10^{-19}	Silver iodide	AgI	8.51×10^{-17}

*Sulfide equilibrium is of the type: $MS(s) + H_2O(l) \rightleftharpoons M^{2+}(aq) + HS^-(aq) + OH^-(aq)$

Notice that K_{sp} is *not* the molar solubility, but the solubility product constant. The solubility product constant has only one value at a given temperature. The solubility, however, can have different values in different kinds of solutions. For example, due to the common ion effect, the solubility of AgCl in pure water is different from its solubility in an NaCl solution, even though the solubility product constant is the same for both solutions. Notice also that the solubility of AgCl is directly related (by the reaction stoichiometry) to the amount of Ag^+ or Cl^- present in solution when equilibrium is reached. Consequently, finding molar solubility from K_{sp} involves solving an equilibrium problem. For AgCl, we set up an ICE table for the dissolution of AgCl into its ions in pure water:

$$AgCl(s) \rightleftharpoons Ag^+(aq) + Cl^-(aq)$$

	[Ag⁺]	[Cl⁻]
Initial	0.00	0.00
Change	+S	+S
Equil	S	S

Alternatively, the variable x can be used in place of S, as it was for other equilibrium calculations.

We let S represent the concentration of AgCl that dissolves (which is the molar solubility) and then represent the concentrations of the ions formed in terms of S. In this case, for every 1 mol of AgCl that dissolves, 1 mol of Ag^+ and 1 mol of Cl^- are produced. Therefore, the concentrations of Ag^+ or Cl^- present in solution are equal to S. Substituting the equilibrium concentrations of Ag^+ and Cl^- into the expression for the solubility product constant, we get:

$$K_{sp} = [Ag^+][Cl^-]$$
$$= S \times S$$
$$= S^2$$

Therefore,

$$S = \sqrt{K_{sp}}$$
$$= \sqrt{1.77 \times 10^{-10}}$$
$$= 1.33 \times 10^{-5} \text{ M}$$

The molar solubility of AgCl is 1.33×10^{-5} mol per liter.

EXAMPLE 16.8 Calculating Molar Solubility from K_{sp}

Calculate the molar solubility of $PbCl_2$ in pure water.

SOLUTION

Begin by writing the reaction by which solid $PbCl_2$ dissolves into its constituent aqueous ions and write the corresponding expression for K_{sp}.	$PbCl_2(s) \rightleftharpoons Pb^{2+}(aq) + 2\,Cl^-(aq)$ $K_{sp} = [Pb^{2+}][Cl^-]^2$
Refer to the stoichiometry of the reaction and prepare an ICE table, showing the equilibrium concentrations of Pb^{2+} and Cl^- relative to S, the amount of $PbCl_2$ that dissolves.	$PbCl_2(s) \rightleftharpoons Pb^{2+}(aq) + 2\,Cl^-(aq)$

	$[Pb^{2+}]$	$[Cl^-]$
Initial	0.00	0.00
Change	$+S$	$+2S$
Equil	S	$2S$

Substitute the equilibrium expressions for $[Pb^{2+}]$ and $[Cl^-]$ from the previous step into the expression for K_{sp}.	$K_{sp} = [Pb^{2+}][Cl^-]^2$ $\quad = S(2S)^2 = 4S^3$
Solve for S and substitute the numerical value of K_{sp} (from Table 16.2) to calculate S.	$S = \sqrt[3]{\dfrac{K_{sp}}{4}}$ $S = \sqrt[3]{\dfrac{1.17 \times 10^{-5}}{4}} = 1.43 \times 10^{-2}\,M$

FOR PRACTICE 16.8

Calculate the molar solubility of $Fe(OH)_2$ in pure water.

Chemistry in Your Day

Hard Water

In many parts of the United States, significant concentrations of $CaCO_3$ and $MgCO_3$ dissolve into rainwater runoff as it flows through soils rich in these compounds. Water containing dissolved calcium and magnesium ions is known as hard water. Hard water is not a health hazard because both calcium and magnesium are part of a healthy diet. However, their presence in water can be a nuisance. Because of their relatively low solubility, the water becomes saturated with $CaCO_3$ and $MgCO_3$ as it evaporates. If evaporation continues, some dissolved ions precipitate out as salts. These precipitates show up as scaly deposits on faucets, sinks, or cookware. Washing cars or dishes with hard water leaves spots of $CaCO_3$ and $MgCO_3$.

Water can be softened with water softeners. These devices replace the Ca^{2+} and Mg^{2+} ions present in hard water with ions such as K^+ or Na^+.

Since potassium and sodium salts are soluble, they do not form scaly deposits in the way that Ca^{2+} and Mg^{2+} ions do. However, when sodium is used to soften drinking water, the resulting water is high in sodium content, a disadvantage to those who must control their sodium intake due to high blood pressure.

Question

Use the K_{sp} values from Table 16.2 to calculate the molar solubility of $CaCO_3$ and $MgCO_3$. What mass of $CaCO_3$ (in grams) is in 5 L of water that is saturated with $CaCO_3$?

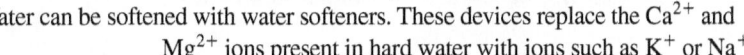

▲ The water in reservoirs where the soil is rich in limestone (calcium carbonate) contains Ca^{2+} ions. This so-called "hard water" contains dissolved $CaCO_3$ and $MgCO_3$. When hard water evaporates, it can leave deposits of these salts on the shores of lakes and reservoirs (left) and on plumbing fixtures (such as the pipe shown here).

EXAMPLE 16.9 Calculating K_{sp} from Molar Solubility

The molar solubility of Ag_2SO_4 in pure water is 1.2×10^{-5} M. Calculate K_{sp}.

SOLUTION

Begin by writing the reaction by which solid Ag_2SO_4 dissolves into its constituent aqueous ions, then write the corresponding expression for K_{sp}.	$Ag_2SO_4(s) \rightleftharpoons 2\,Ag^+(aq) + SO_4^{2-}(aq)$ $K_{sp} = [Ag^+]^2[SO_4^{2-}]$
Use an ICE table to define $[Ag^+]$ and $[SO_4^{2-}]$ in terms of S, the amount of Ag_2SO_4 that dissolves.	$Ag_2SO_4(s) \rightleftharpoons 2\,Ag^+(aq) + SO_4^{2-}(aq)$

	$[Ag^+]$	$[SO_4^{2-}]$
Initial	0.00	0.00
Change	$+2S$	$+S$
Equil	$2S$	S

Substitute the expressions for $[Ag^+]$ and $[SO_4^{2-}]$ from the previous step into the expression for K_{sp}. Substitute the given value *of the molar solubility for S and calculate* K_{sp}.	$\begin{aligned} K_{sp} &= [Ag^+]^2[SO_4^{2-}] \\ &= (2S)^2 S \\ &= 4S^3 \\ &= 4(1.2 \times 10^{-5})^3 \\ &= 6.9 \times 10^{-15} \end{aligned}$

FOR PRACTICE 16.9

The molar solubility of AgBr in pure water is 7.3×10^{-7} M. Calculate K_{sp}.

K_{sp} and Relative Solubility

As we have just seen, molar solubility and K_{sp} are related, and each can be calculated from the other; however, you cannot generally use the K_{sp} values of two different compounds to directly compare their relative solubilities. For example, consider the following compounds, their K_{sp} values, and their molar solubilities:

Compound	K_{sp}	Solubility
$Mg(OH)_2$	2.06×10^{-13}	3.72×10^{-5} M
$FeCO_3$	3.07×10^{-11}	5.54×10^{-6} M

Magnesium hydroxide has a smaller K_{sp} than iron(II) carbonate, but a higher molar solubility. Why? The relationship between K_{sp} and molar solubility depends on the stoichiometry of the dissociation reaction. Consequently, any direct comparison of K_{sp} values for different compounds can only be made if the compounds have the same dissociation stoichiometry. Consider the following compounds with the same dissociation stoichiometry, their K_{sp} values, and their molar solubilities:

Compound	K_{sp}	Solubility
$Mg(OH)_2$	2.06×10^{-13}	3.72×10^{-5} M
CaF_2	1.46×10^{-10}	3.32×10^{-4} M

In this case, magnesium hydroxide and calcium fluoride have the same dissociation stoichiometry (1 mol of each compound produces 3 mol of dissolved ions); therefore, the K_{sp} values can be directly compared as a measure of relative solubility.

The Effect of a Common Ion on Solubility

How is the solubility of an ionic compound affected when the compound is dissolved in a solution that already contains one of its ions? For example, what is the solubility of CaF_2 in a solution that is 0.100 M in NaF? We can determine the change in solubility by considering the common ion effect, which we first encountered in Section 16.2. We represent the dissociation of CaF_2 in a 0.100 M NaF solution as shown at right.

In accordance with Le Châtelier's principle, the presence of the F^- ion in solution causes the equilibrium to shift to the left (compared to its position in pure water), which means that less CaF_2 dissolves—that is, its solubility is decreased.

Common ion
0.100 M $F^-(aq)$

$\downarrow$

$$CaF_2(s) \rightleftharpoons Ca^{2+}(aq) + 2\,F^-(aq)$$

$\longleftarrow$

Equilibrium shifts left

In general, the solubility of an ionic compound is lower in a solution containing a common ion than in pure water.

We can calculate the exact value of the solubility by working an equilibrium problem in which the concentration of the common ion is accounted for in the initial conditions, as shown in Example 16.10.

EXAMPLE 16.10 Calculating Molar Solubility in the Presence of a Common Ion

What is the molar solubility of CaF_2 in a solution containing 0.100 M NaF?

SOLUTION

Begin by writing the reaction by which solid CaF_2 dissolves into its constituent aqueous ions. Write the corresponding expression for K_{sp}.	$CaF_2(s) \rightleftharpoons Ca^{2+}(aq) + 2\,F^-(aq)$ $K_{sp} = [Ca^{2+}][F^-]^2$
Use the stoichiometry of the reaction to prepare an ICE table showing the initial concentration of the common ion. Fill in the equilibrium concentrations of Ca^{2+} and F^- relative to S, the amount of CaF_2 that dissolves.	$CaF_2(s) \rightleftharpoons Ca^{2+}(aq) + 2\,F^-(aq)$ <table><tr><td></td><td>$[Ca^{2+}]$</td><td>$[F^-]$</td></tr><tr><td>Initial</td><td>0.00</td><td>0.100</td></tr><tr><td>Change</td><td>+S</td><td>+2S</td></tr><tr><td>Equil</td><td>S</td><td>0.100 + 2S</td></tr></table>
Substitute the equilibrium expressions for $[Ca^{2+}]$ and $[F^-]$ from the previous step into the expression for K_{sp}. Since K_{sp} is small, you can make the approximation that 2S is much less than 0.100 and will therefore be insignificant when added to 0.100 (this is similar to the *x is small* approximation in equilibrium problems).	$K_{sp} = [Ca^{2+}][F^-]^2$ $= S(0.100 + 2S)^2$ *(S is small)* $= S(0.100)^2$
Solve for S and substitute the numerical value of K_{sp} (from Table 16.2) to calculate S. Note that the calculated value of S is indeed small compared to 0.100; our approximation is valid.	$K_{sp} = S(0.100)^2$ $S = \dfrac{K_{sp}}{0.0100} = \dfrac{1.46 \times 10^{-10}}{0.0100} = 1.46 \times 10^{-8}\,M$

For comparison, the molar solubility of CaF_2 in pure water is 3.32×10^{-4} M, which means CaF_2 is over 20,000 times more soluble in water than in the NaF solution. (Confirm this for yourself by calculating its solubility in pure water from the value of K_{sp}).

FOR PRACTICE 16.10
Calculate the molar solubility of CaF_2 in a solution containing 0.250 M $Ca(NO_3)_2$.

Conceptual Connection 16.8 Common Ion Effect

In which solution is $BaSO_4$ most soluble?

(a) in a solution that is 0.10 M in $BaNO_3$
(b) in a solution that is 0.10 M in Na_2SO_4
(c) in a solution that is 0.10 M in $NaNO_3$

The Effect of pH on Solubility

The pH of a solution can affect the solubility of a compound in that solution. For example, consider the dissociation of $Mg(OH)_2$, the active ingredient in milk of magnesia:

$$Mg(OH)_2(s) \rightleftharpoons Mg^{2+}(aq) + 2\,OH^-(aq)$$

The solubility of this compound is highly dependent on the pH of the solution into which it dissolves. If the pH is high, then the concentration of OH^- in the solution is high. In accordance with the common ion effect, this shifts the equilibrium to the left, lowering the solubility:

$$\text{High}\,[OH^-]$$

$$Mg(OH)_2(s) \rightleftharpoons Mg^{2+}(aq) + 2\,OH^-(aq)$$

Equilibrium shifts left

If the pH is low, then the concentration of $H_3O^+(aq)$ in the solution is high. As the $Mg(OH)_2$ dissolves, these H_3O^+ ions neutralize the newly dissolved OH^- ions, driving the reaction to the right:

$$H_3O^+ \text{ reacts with } OH^-$$

$$Mg(OH)_2(s) \rightleftharpoons Mg^{2+}(aq) + 2\,OH^-(aq)$$

Equilibrium shifts right

Consequently, the solubility of $Mg(OH)_2$ in an acidic solution is higher than in a pH-neutral or basic solution.

> **In general, the solubility of an ionic compound with a strongly basic or weakly basic anion increases with increasing acidity (decreasing pH).**

Common basic anions include OH^-, S^{2-}, and CO_3^{2-}. Therefore, hydroxides, sulfides, and carbonates are more soluble in acidic water than in pure water. Since rainwater is naturally acidic due to dissolved carbon dioxide, it can dissolve rocks high in limestone ($CaCO_3$) as it flows through the ground, sometimes resulting in huge underground caverns such as those at Carlsbad Caverns National Park in New Mexico. Dripping water saturated in $CaCO_3$ within the cave creates the dramatic mineral formations known as stalagmites and stalactites.

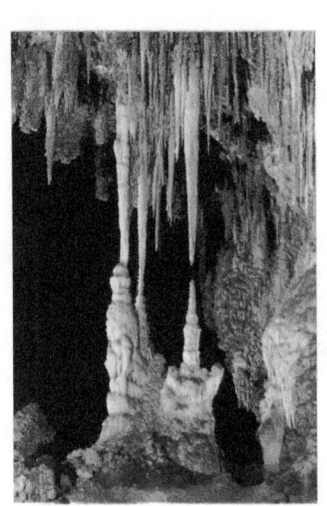

▲ Stalactites (which hang from the ceiling) and stalagmites (which grow up from the ground) form as calcium carbonate precipitates out of the water evaporating in underground caves.

EXAMPLE 16.11 The Effect of pH on Solubility

Determine whether each compound is more soluble in an acidic solution than in a neutral solution.

(a) BaF_2 **(b)** AgI **(c)** $Ca(OH)_2$

SOLUTION

(a)   The solubility of BaF_2 is greater in acidic solution because the F^- ion is a weak base. (F^- is the conjugate base of the weak acid HF and is therefore a weak base.)

(b)   The solubility of AgI is not greater in acidic solution because the I^- is *not* a base. (I^- is the conjugate base of the *strong* acid HI and is therefore pH-neutral.)

(c)   The solubility of $Ca(OH)_2$ is greater in acidic solution because the OH^- ion is a strong base.

FOR PRACTICE 16.11

Which compound, $FeCO_3$ or $PbBr_2$, is more soluble in acid than in base? Why?

16.6 Precipitation

In Chapter 4, we learned that a precipitation reaction can occur upon the mixing of two solutions containing ionic compounds when one of the possible cross products—the combination of a cation from one solution and the anion from the other—is insoluble. In this chapter, however, we have seen that the terms *soluble* and *insoluble* are extremes in a continuous range of solubility—many compounds are slightly soluble and even those that we categorized as insoluble in Chapter 4 actually have some limited degree of solubility (they have very small solubility product constants).

We can better understand precipitation reactions by revisiting a concept from Chapter 14—the reaction quotient (Q). The reaction quotient for the reaction by which an ionic compound dissolves is the product of the concentrations of the ionic components raised to their stoichiometric coefficients. For example, consider the reaction by which CaF_2 dissolves:

$$CaF_2(s) \rightleftharpoons Ca^{2+}(aq) + 2\,F^-(aq)$$

The reaction quotient for this reaction is:

$$Q = [Ca^{2+}][F^-]^2$$

The difference between Q and K_{sp} is that K_{sp} is the value of this product *at equilibrium only*, whereas Q is the value of the product under any conditions. We can therefore use the value of Q to compare a solution containing any concentrations of the component ions to a solution that is at equilibrium.

Consider a solution of calcium fluoride in which Q is less than K_{sp}. Recall from Chapter 14 that if Q is less than K_{sp}, the reaction will proceed to the right (toward products). Consequently, if the solution contains any solid CaF_2, the CaF_2 will continue to dissolve. If all of the solid has already dissolved, the solution will simply remain as it is, containing less than the equilibrium amount of the dissolved ions. Such a solution is an *unsaturated solution*. If more solid is added to an unsaturated solution, it will dissolve, as long as Q remains less than K_{sp}.

Now consider a solution in which Q is exactly equal to K_{sp}. In this case, the reaction is at equilibrium and will not make progress in either direction. Such a solution most likely contains at least a small amount of the solid in equilibrium with its component ions. However, the amount of solid may be too small to be visible. Such a solution is a *saturated solution*.

Finally, consider a solution in which Q is greater than K_{sp}. In this case, the reaction will proceed to the left (toward the reactants) and solid calcium fluoride will form from the dissolved calcium and fluoride ions. In other words, the solid normally precipitates out of a solution in which Q is greater than K_{sp}. Under certain circumstances, however, Q can remain greater than K_{sp} for an unlimited period of time. Such a solution, called a *supersaturated solution*, is unstable and will form a precipitate when sufficiently disturbed. Figure 16.14 ► shows a supersaturated solution of sodium acetate. When a small seed crystal of solid sodium acetate is dropped into the solution, it triggers the precipitation reaction.

— Na$_2$CrO$_4$

— AgNO$_3$
— Ag$_2$CrO$_4$

▼ **FIGURE 16.14 Precipitation from a Supersaturated Solution** The excess solute in a supersaturated solution of sodium acetate precipitates out if a small sodium acetate crystal is added.

Summarizing the Relationship of Q and K_{sp} in Solutions Containing an Ionic Compound:

▶ If $Q < K_{sp}$, the solution is unsaturated and more of the solid ionic compound can dissolve in the solution.

▶ If $Q = K_{sp}$, the solution is saturated. The solution is holding the equilibrium amount of the dissolved ions and additional solid does not dissolve in the solution.

▶ If $Q > K_{sp}$, the solution is supersaturated. Under most circumstances, the excess solid precipitates out of a supersaturated solution.

Seed crystal

Supersaturated solution of sodium acetate

Solid sodium acetate forming

We can use Q to predict whether a precipitation reaction will occur upon the mixing of two solutions containing dissolved ionic compounds. For example, consider mixing a silver nitrate solution with a potassium iodide solution to form a mixture that is 0.010 M in $AgNO_3$ and 0.015 M in KI. Will a precipitate form in the newly mixed solution? From Chapter 4 we know that one of the cross products, KNO_3, is soluble and will therefore not precipitate. The other cross product, AgI, *may* precipitate if the concentrations of Ag^+ and I^- are high enough in the newly mixed solution: we can compare Q to K_{sp} to determine if a precipitate will form. For AgI, $K_{sp} = 8.51 \times 10^{-17}$. For the newly mixed solution, $[Ag^+] = 0.010\,M$ and $[I^-] = 0.015\,M$. We calculate Q as follows:

$$Q = [Ag^+][I^-] = (0.010)(0.015) = 1.5 \times 10^{-4}$$

The value of Q is much greater than K_{sp}; therefore, AgI should precipitate out of the newly mixed solution.

EXAMPLE 16.12 Predicting Precipitation Reactions by Comparing Q and K_{sp}

A solution containing lead(II) nitrate is mixed with one containing sodium bromide to form a solution that is 0.0150 M in $Pb(NO_3)_2$ and 0.00350 M in NaBr. Does a precipitate form in the newly mixed solution?

SOLUTION

First, determine the possible cross products and their K_{sp} values (Table 16.2). Any cross products that are soluble will *not* precipitate (see Table 4.1).	Possible cross products: $NaNO_3$ soluble $PbBr_2$ $K_{sp} = 4.67 \times 10^{-6}$
Calculate Q and compare it to K_{sp}. A precipitate will only form if $Q > K_{sp}$.	$Q = [Pb^{2+}][Br^-]^2$ $\quad = (0.0150)(0.00350)^2$ $\quad = 1.84 \times 10^{-7}$ $Q < K_{sp}$; therefore no precipitate forms.

FOR PRACTICE 16.12

If the original solutions in Example 16.12 are concentrated through evaporation and mixed again to form a solution that is 0.0600 M in $Pb(NO_3)_2$ and 0.0158 M in NaBr, will a precipitate form in this newly mixed solution?

Selective Precipitation

A solution may contain several different dissolved metal cations that can often be separated by **selective precipitation**, a process involving the addition of a reagent that forms a precipitate with one of the dissolved cations but not the others. For example, seawater contains dissolved magnesium and calcium cations with the concentrations $[Mg^{2+}] = 0.059$ M and $[Ca^{2+}] = 0.011$ M. We can separate these ions by adding a reagent that will precipitate one of the ions but not the other. From Table 16.2, we find that $Mg(OH)_2$ has a K_{sp} of 2.06×10^{-13} and that $Ca(OH)_2$ has a K_{sp} of 4.68×10^{-6}, indicating that the hydroxide ion forms a precipitate with magnesium at a much lower concentration than it does with calcium. Consequently, a soluble hydroxide—such as KOH or NaOH—is a good choice for the precipitating reagent. When we add an appropriate amount of KOH or NaOH to seawater, the hydroxide ion causes the precipitation of $Mg(OH)_2$ (the compound with the lowest K_{sp}) but not $Ca(OH)_2$. Calculations for this selective precipitation are shown in Examples 16.13 and 16.14. In these calculations, you compare Q to K_{sp} to determine the concentration that triggers precipitation.

The difference in K_{sp} values required for selective precipitation is a factor of at least 10^3.

EXAMPLE 16.13 Finding the Minimum Required Reagent Concentration for Selective Precipitation

The magnesium and calcium ions present in seawater ($[Mg^{2+}] = 0.059\,M$ and $[Ca^{2+}] = 0.011\,M$) can be separated by selective precipitation with KOH. What minimum $[OH^-]$ triggers the precipitation of the Mg^{2+} ion?

SOLUTION

The precipitation commences when the value of Q for the precipitating compound just equals the value of K_{sp}. Set the expression for Q for magnesium hydroxide equal to the value of K_{sp}, and solve for $[OH^-]$. This is the concentration above which $Mg(OH)_2$ precipitates.	$Q = [Mg^{2+}][OH^-]^2$ $\quad = (0.059)[OH^-]^2$ When $Q = K_{sp}$, $(0.059)[OH^-]^2 = K_{sp} = 2.06 \times 10^{-13}$ $[OH^-]^2 = \dfrac{2.06 \times 10^{-13}}{0.059}$ $[OH^-] = 1.9 \times 10^{-6}\,M$

FOR PRACTICE 16.13

If the concentration of Mg^{2+} in the previous solution was 0.025 M, what minimum $[OH^-]$ triggers precipitation of the Mg^{2+} ion?

EXAMPLE 16.14 Finding the Concentrations of Ions Left in Solution after Selective Precipitation

You add potassium hydroxide to the solution in Example 16.13. When the $[OH^-]$ reaches $1.9 \times 10^{-6}\,M$ (as you just calculated), magnesium hydroxide begins to precipitate out of solution. As you continue to add KOH, the magnesium hydroxide continues to precipitate. However, at some point, the $[OH^-]$ becomes high enough to begin to precipitate the calcium ions as well. What is the concentration of Mg^{2+} when Ca^{2+} begins to precipitate?

SOLUTION

First, find the OH^- concentration at which Ca^{2+} begins to precipitate by writing the expression for Q for calcium hydroxide and substituting the concentration of Ca^{2+} from Example 16.13.	$Q = [Ca^{2+}][OH^-]^2$ $\quad = (0.011)[OH^-]^2$
Set the expression for Q equal to the value of K_{sp} for calcium hydroxide and solve for $[OH^-]$. This is the concentration above which $Ca(OH)_2$ precipitates.	When $Q = K_{sp}$, $(0.011)[OH^-]^2 = K_{sp} = 4.68 \times 10^{-6}$ $[OH^-]^2 = \dfrac{4.68 \times 10^{-6}}{0.011}$ $[OH^-] = 2.0\underline{6} \times 10^{-2}\,M$
Find the concentration of Mg^{2+} when OH^- reaches the concentration you just calculated by writing the expression for Q *for magnesium hydroxide* and substituting the concentration of OH^- that you just calculated. Then set the expression for Q equal to the value of K_{sp} for magnesium hydroxide and solve for $[Mg^{2+}]$. This is the concentration of Mg^{2+} that remains when $Ca(OH)_2$ begins to precipitate.	$Q = [Mg^{2+}][OH^-]^2$ $\quad = [Mg^{2+}](2.0\underline{6} \times 10^{-2})^2$ When $Q = K_{sp}$, $[Mg^{2+}](2.0\underline{6} \times 10^{-2})^2 = K_{sp} = 2.06 \times 10^{-13}$ $[Mg^{2+}] = \dfrac{2.06 \times 10^{-13}}{(2.0\underline{6} \times 10^{-2})^2}$ $[Mg^{2+}] = 4.9 \times 10^{-10}\,M$

As you can see from the results, the selective precipitation worked very well. The concentration of Mg^{2+} dropped from 0.059 M to 4.9×10^{-10} M before any calcium began to precipitate, which means that we separated 99.99% of the magnesium out of the solution.

FOR PRACTICE 16.14

A solution is 0.085 M in Pb^{2+} and 0.025 M in Ag^+. (a) If selective precipitation is to be achieved using NaCl, what minimum concentration of NaCl do you need to begin to precipitate the ion that precipitates first? (b) What is the concentration of each ion left in solution at the point where the second ion begins to precipitate?

16.7 Qualitative Chemical Analysis

Selective precipitation as discussed in Section 16.6 can be used in a systematic way to determine which metal ions are present in an unknown solution. This method is known as **qualitative analysis**. The word *qualitative* means *involving quality or kind*. Qualitative analysis involves finding the *kind* of ions present in the solution. This stands in contrast to **quantitative analysis**, which is concerned with quantity, or the amounts of substances in a solution or mixture.

In the past, qualitative analysis by selective precipitation was used extensively to determine the metals present in a sample. This process—dubbed *wet chemistry* because it involves the mixing of many aqueous solutions in the lab—has been replaced by more precise and less time-intensive instrumental techniques. Nonetheless, both for the sake of history and also because of the importance of the principles involved, we now examine a traditional qualitative analysis scheme. You may use such a scheme in your general chemistry laboratory as an exercise in qualitative analysis.

The basic idea behind qualitative analysis is straightforward. A sample containing a mixture of metal cations is subjected to the addition of several precipitating agents. At each step, some of the metal cations—those that form insoluble compounds with the precipitating agent—precipitate from the mixture and are separated out as solids. The remaining aqueous mixture is then subjected to the next precipitating agent, and so on (Figure 16.15 ▼).

▲ FIGURE 16.15 **Qualitative Analysis** In qualitative analysis, specific ions are precipitated successively by the addition of appropriate reagents.

Figure 16.16 ▼ is a diagram of a general qualitative analysis scheme. The scheme involves separating a mixture of the common ions into five groups by sequentially adding five different precipitating agents. After each precipitating agent is added, the mixture is put into a centrifuge to separate the solid from the liquid. The liquid is decanted for the next step, and the solid is set aside for subsequent analysis. We examine each group separately.

Group 1: Insoluble Chlorides

In the first step, the aqueous mixture containing the metal cations is treated with 6 M HCl. Since most chlorides are soluble, the chloride ions *do not form* a precipitate with the majority of the cations in the mixture. However, Ag^+, Pb^{2+}, and Hg_2^{2+} *do form* insoluble chlorides. So, if any of those metal cations are present, they precipitate out. The absence of a precipitate constitutes a negative test for Ag^+, Pb^{2+}, and Hg_2^{2+}. If a precipitate forms, one or more of these ions is present. After the solid is separated from the liquid, the solution is ready for the next step.

Group 2: Acid-Insoluble Sulfides

In the second step, the acidic aqueous mixture containing the remaining metal cations is treated with H_2S, a weak diprotic acid that dissociates in two steps:

$$H_2S \rightleftharpoons H^+ + HS^-$$
$$HS^- \rightleftharpoons H^+ + S^{2-}$$

The concentration of S^{2-} ions in an H_2S solution is pH-dependent. At low pH (high H^+ concentration) the equilibria shift left, minimizing the amount of available S^{2-}. At high pH (low H^+ concentration) the equilbria shift right, maximizing the amount of available S^{2-}.

▼ FIGURE 16.16 A General Qualitative Analysis Scheme

$(NH_4)_2S$ CdS Sb_2S_3 PbS

At this stage, the solution is acidic (from the addition of HCl in the previous step), and the concentration of S^{2-} in solution is relatively low. Only the most insoluble metal sulfides (those with the smallest K_{sp} values) precipitate under these conditions. These include Hg^{2+}, Cd^{2+}, Bi^{3+}, Cu^{2+}, Sn^{4+}, As^{3+}, Pb^{2+}, and Sb^{3+}. If any of these metal cations are present, they precipitate out as sulfides. After the solid is separated from the liquid, the solution is ready for the next step.

Group 3: Base-Insoluble Sulfides and Hydroxides

In the third step, additional base and H_2S are added to the acidic aqueous mixture containing the remaining metal cations. The added base reacts with acid, shifting the H_2S ionization equilibria to the right and creating a higher S^{2-} concentration. This causes the precipitation of those sulfides that were too soluble to precipitate out in the previous step but not soluble enough to prevent precipitation with the higher sulfide ion concentration. The ions that precipitate as sulfides at this point (if they are present) are Fe^{2+}, Co^{2+}, Zn^{2+}, Mn^{2+}, and Ni^{2+}. In addition, the additional base causes Cr^{3+}, Fe^{3+}, and Al^{3+} to precipitate as hydroxides. After the solid is separated from the liquid, the solution is ready for the next step.

Group 4: Insoluble Phosphates

At this stage, all of the cations have precipitated except those belonging to the alkali metal family (group 1A in the periodic table) and the alkaline earth metal family (group 2A in the periodic table). The alkaline earth metal cations can be precipitated by adding $(NH_4)_2HPO_4$ to the solution, causing Mg^{2+}, Ca^{2+}, and Ba^{2+} to precipitate as metal phosphates, which are separated from the liquid.

Group 5: Alkali Metals and NH_4^+

The only dissolved ions that the liquid decanted from the previous step can now contain are Na^+, K^+, and NH_4^+. These cations do not form insoluble compounds with any anions and cannot be precipitated from the solution. Their presence can be determined, however, by other means. Sodium and potassium ions, for example, are usually identified through flame tests. The sodium ion produces a yellow-orange flame and the potassium ion produces a violet flame, as shown in Figure 16.17 ▼.

By applying this procedure, nearly two dozen metal cations can be separated from a solution initially containing all of them. Each of the groups can be further analyzed to determine which specific ions are present. The specific procedures for these steps are found in many general chemistry laboratory manuals.

▶ FIGURE 16.17 **Flame Tests** The sodium ion produces a yellow-orange flame. The potassium ion produces a violet flame.

Sodium   Potassium

16.8 Complex Ion Equilibria

We have discussed several different types of equilibria so far, including acid–base equilibria and solubility equilibria. We now turn to equilibria of another type, which primarily involve transition metal ions in solution. Transition metal ions tend to be good electron acceptors (good Lewis acids). In aqueous solutions, water molecules can act as electron donors (Lewis bases) to hydrate transition metal ions. For example, silver ions are hydrated by water in solution to form $Ag(H_2O)_2^+(aq)$. Chemists often write $Ag^+(aq)$ as a shorthand notation for the hydrated silver ion, but the bare ion does not really exist by itself in solution.

Species such as $Ag(H_2O)_2^{2+}$ are known as *complex ions*. A **complex ion** contains a central metal ion bound to one or more *ligands*. A **ligand** is a neutral molecule or ion that acts as a Lewis base with the central metal ion. In $Ag(H_2O)_2^+$, water is the ligand. If a stronger Lewis base is put into a solution containing $Ag(H_2O)_2^+$, the stronger Lewis base displaces the water in the complex ion. For example, ammonia reacts with $Ag(H_2O)_2^+$ according to the following reaction:

$$Ag(H_2O)_2^+(aq) + 2\ NH_3(aq) \rightleftharpoons Ag(NH_3)_2^+(aq) + 2\ H_2O(l)$$

For simplicity, we often leave water out of the equation:

$$Ag^+(aq) + 2\ NH_3(aq) \rightleftharpoons Ag(NH_3)_2^+(aq) \quad K_f = 1.7 \times 10^7$$

The equilibrium constant associated with the reaction for the formation of a complex ion, such as the one just shown, is called the **formation constant** (K_f). The expression for K_f is determined by the law of mass action, like any equilibrium constant. For $Ag(NH_3)_2^+$, the expression for K_f is:

$$K_f = \frac{[Ag(NH_3)_2^+]}{[Ag^+][NH_3]^2}$$

Notice that the value of K_f for $Ag(NH_3)_2^+$ is large, indicating that the formation of the complex ion is highly favored. Table 16.3 lists the formation constants for a number of common complex ions. You can see that, in general, values of K_f are very large, indicating that the formation of complex ions is highly favored in each case. Example 16.15 illustrates how to use K_f in calculations.

> We cover complex ions in more detail in Chapter 24. Here, we focus on the equilibria associated with their formation.

TABLE 16.3 Formation Constants of Selected Complex Ions in Water at 25 °C

Complex Ion	K_f	Complex Ion	K_f
$Ag(CN)_2^-$	1×10^{21}	$Cu(NH_3)_4^{2+}$	1.7×10^{13}
$Ag(NH_3)_2^+$	1.7×10^7	$Fe(CN)_6^{4-}$	1.5×10^{35}
$Ag(S_2O_3)_2^{3-}$	2.8×10^{13}	$Fe(CN)_6^{3-}$	2×10^{43}
AlF_6^{3-}	7×10^{19}	$Hg(CN)_4^{2-}$	1.8×10^{41}
$Al(OH)_4^-$	3×10^{33}	$HgCl_4^{2-}$	1.1×10^{16}
$CdBr_4^{2-}$	5.5×10^3	HgI_4^{2-}	2×10^{30}
CdI_4^{2-}	2×10^6	$Ni(NH_3)_6^{2+}$	2.0×10^8
$Cd(CN)_4^{2-}$	3×10^{18}	$Pb(OH)_3^-$	8×10^{13}
$Co(NH_3)_6^{3+}$	2.3×10^{33}	$Sn(OH)_3^-$	3×10^{25}
$Co(OH)_4^{2-}$	5×10^9	$Zn(CN)_4^{2-}$	2.1×10^{19}
$Co(SCN)_4^{2-}$	1×10^3	$Zn(NH_3)_4^{2+}$	2.8×10^9
$Cr(OH)_4^-$	8.0×10^{29}	$Zn(OH)_4^{2-}$	2×10^{15}
$Cu(CN)_4^{2-}$	1.0×10^{25}		

EXAMPLE 16.15 Complex Ion Equilibria

You mix a 200.0 mL sample of a solution that is 1.5×10^{-3} M in $Cu(NO_3)_2$ with a 250.0 mL sample of a solution that is 0.20 M in NH_3. After the solution reaches equilibrium, what concentration of $Cu^{2+}(aq)$ remains?

SOLUTION

Write the balanced equation for the complex ion equilibrium that occurs and look up the value of K_f in Table 16.3. Since this is an equilibrium problem, you have to create an ICE table, which requires the initial concentrations of Cu^{2+} and NH_3. Calculate those concentrations from the given values.	$Cu^{2+}(aq) + 4\,NH_3(aq) \rightleftharpoons Cu(NH_3)_4{}^{2+}(aq)$ $K_f = 1.7 \times 10^{13}$ $[Cu^{2+}]_{initial} = \dfrac{0.200\,\cancel{L} \times \dfrac{1.5 \times 10^{-3}\,mol}{\cancel{L}}}{0.200\,L + 0.250\,L} = 6.7 \times 10^{-4}\,M$ $[NH_3]_{initial} = \dfrac{0.250\,\cancel{L} \times \dfrac{0.20\,mol}{1\,\cancel{L}}}{0.200\,L + 0.250\,L} = 0.11\,M$

Construct an ICE table for the reaction and write down the initial concentrations of each species.

$Cu^{2+}(aq) + 4\,NH_3(aq) \rightleftharpoons Cu(NH_3)_4{}^{2+}(aq)$

	$[Cu^{2+}]$	$[NH_3]$	$[Cu(NH_3)_4{}^{2+}]$
Initial	6.7×10^{-4}	0.11	0.0
Change			
Equil			

Since the equilibrium constant is large and the concentration of ammonia is much larger than the concentration of Cu^{2+}, you can assume that the reaction will be driven to the right so that most of the Cu^{2+} is consumed. Unlike previous ICE tables, where you let x represent the change in concentration in going to equilibrium, here you let x represent the small amount of Cu^{2+} that remains when equilibrium is reached.

$Cu^{2+}(aq) + 4\,NH_3(aq) \rightleftharpoons Cu(NH_3)_4{}^{2+}(aq)$

	$[Cu^{2+}]$	$[NH_3]$	$[Cu(NH_3)_4{}^{2+}]$
Initial	6.7×10^{-4}	0.11	0.0
Change	$\approx (-6.7 \times 10^{-4})$	$\approx 4(-6.7 \times 10^{-4})$	$\approx (+6.7 \times 10^{-4})$
Equil	x	0.11	6.7×10^{-4}

Substitute the expressions for the equilibrium concentrations into the expression for K_f and solve for x.	$K_f = \dfrac{[Cu(NH_3)_4{}^{2+}]}{[Cu^{2+}][NH_3]^4}$ $= \dfrac{6.7 \times 10^{-4}}{x(0.11)^4}$ $x = \dfrac{6.7 \times 10^{-4}}{K_f(0.11)^4}$ $= \dfrac{6.7 \times 10^{-4}}{1.7 \times 10^{13}(0.11)^4}$ $= 2.7 \times 10^{-13}$
Confirm that x is indeed small compared to the initial concentration of the metal cation.	Since $x = 2.7 \times 10^{-13} \ll 6.7 \times 10^{-4}$, the approximation is valid. The remaining $[Cu^{2+}] = 2.7 \times 10^{-13}$ M.
The remaining Cu^{2+} is very small because the formation constant is very large.	

FOR PRACTICE 16.15

You mix a 125.0 mL sample of a solution that is 0.0117 M in $NiCl_2$ with a 175.0 mL sample of a solution that is 0.250 M in NH_3. After the solution reaches equilibrium, what concentration of $Ni^{2+}(aq)$ remains?

The Effect of Complex Ion Equilibria on Solubility

Recall from Section 16.5 that the solubility of an ionic compound with a basic anion increases with increasing acidity because the acid reacts with the anion and drives the reaction to the right. Similarly, *the solubility of an ionic compound containing a metal cation that forms complex ions increases in the presence of Lewis bases that complex with the cation.* The most common Lewis bases that increase the solubility of metal cations are NH_3, CN^-, and OH^-. For example, silver chloride is only slightly soluble in pure water:

$$AgCl(s) \rightleftharpoons Ag^+(aq) + Cl^-(aq) \qquad K_{sp} = 1.77 \times 10^{-10}$$

However, adding ammonia increases its solubility dramatically because, as we saw previously in this section, the ammonia forms a complex ion with the silver cations:

$$Ag^+(aq) + 2\,NH_3(aq) \rightleftharpoons Ag(NH_3)_2^+(aq) \qquad K_f = 1.7 \times 10^7$$

The large value of K_f significantly lowers the concentration of $Ag^+(aq)$ in solution and therefore drives the dissolution of $AgCl(s)$. The two previous reactions can be added together:

$$AgCl(s) \rightleftharpoons Ag^+(aq) + Cl^-(aq) \qquad K_{sp} = 1.77 \times 10^{-10}$$
$$\underline{Ag^+(aq) + 2\,NH_3(aq) \rightleftharpoons Ag(NH_3)_2^+(aq) \qquad\qquad K_f = 1.7 \times 10^7}$$
$$AgCl(s) + 2\,NH_3(aq) \rightleftharpoons Ag(NH_3)_2^+(aq) + Cl^-(aq) \qquad K = K_{sp} \times K_f = 3.0 \times 10^{-3}$$

As we learned in Section 14.3, the equilibrium constant for a reaction that is the sum of two other reactions is the product of the equilibrium constants for the two other reactions. Adding ammonia changes the equilibrium constant for the dissolution of $AgCl(s)$ by a factor of $3.0 \times 10^{-3}/1.77 \times 10^{-10} = 1.7 \times 10^7$ (17 million), which makes the otherwise relatively insoluble $AgCl(s)$ quite soluble, as shown in Figure 16.18 ▼.

Complex Ion Formation

$$2\,NH_3(aq) + AgCl(s) \rightleftharpoons Ag(NH_3)_2^+(aq) + Cl^-(aq)$$

◀ **FIGURE 16.18 Complex Ion Formation** Normally insoluble AgCl is made soluble by the addition of NH_3, which forms a complex ion with Ag^+ and dissolves the AgCl.

Conceptual Connection 16.9 Solubility and Complex Ion Equilibria

Which compound, when added to water, is most likely to increase the solubility of CuS?

(a) NaCl   (b) KNO_3 (c) NaCN   (d) $MgBr_2$

The Solubility of Amphoteric Metal Hydroxides

Many metal hydroxides are insoluble or only very slightly soluble in pH-neutral water. For example, $Al(OH)_3$ has $K_{sp} = 2 \times 10^{-32}$, which means that if you put $Al(OH)_3$ in water, the vast majority of it will settle to the bottom as an undissolved solid. All metal hydroxides, however, have a basic anion (OH^-) and therefore become more soluble in acidic solutions (see the previous subsection and Section 16.5). The metal hydroxides become more soluble because they can act as a base and react with $H_3O^+(aq)$. For example, $Al(OH)_3$ dissolves in acid according to the reaction:

$$Al(OH)_3(s) + 3 H_3O^+(aq) \longrightarrow Al^{3+}(aq) + 6 H_2O(l)$$

$Al(OH)_3$ acts as a base in this reaction.

> Recall from Section 15.3 that a substance that can act as either an acid or a base is said to be amphoteric.

Interestingly, some metal hydroxides can also act as acids—they are *amphoteric*. The ability of an amphoteric metal hydroxide to act as an acid increases its solubility in basic solution. For example, $Al(OH)_3(s)$ dissolves in basic solution according to the reaction:

$$Al(OH)_3(s) + OH^-(aq) \longrightarrow Al(OH)_4^-(aq)$$

$Al(OH)_3$ acts as an acid in this reaction.

$Al(OH)_3$ is soluble at high pH and soluble at low pH but *insoluble* in a pH-neutral solution.

We can observe the whole range of the pH-dependent solubility behavior of Al^{3+} by considering a hydrated aluminum ion in solution, beginning at an acidic pH. We know from Section 15.8 that Al^{3+} in solution is inherently acidic because it complexes with water to form $Al(H_2O)_6^{3+}(aq)$. The complex ion then acts as an acid by losing a proton from one of the complexed water molecules according to the reaction:

$$Al(H_2O)_6^{3+}(aq) + H_2O(l) \rightleftharpoons Al(H_2O)_5(OH)^{2+}(aq) + H_3O^+(l)$$

Addition of base to the solution drives the reaction to the right and continues to remove protons from complexed water molecules:

$$Al(H_2O)_5(OH)^{2+}(aq) + OH^-(aq) \rightleftharpoons Al(H_2O)_4(OH)_2^+(aq) + H_2O(l)$$

$$Al(H_2O)_4(OH)_2^+(aq) + OH^-(aq) \rightleftharpoons Al(H_2O)_3(OH)_3(s) + H_2O(l)$$
equivalent to $Al(OH)_3(s)$

The result of removing three protons from $Al(H_2O)_6^{3+}$ is the solid white precipitate $Al(H_2O)_3(OH)_3(s)$, which is more commonly written as $Al(OH)_3(s)$. The solution is now pH-neutral and the hydroxide is insoluble. Addition of more OH^- makes the solution basic and dissolves the solid precipitate:

$$Al(H_2O)_3(OH)_3(s) + OH^-(aq) \rightleftharpoons Al(H_2O)_2(OH)_4^-(aq) + H_2O(l)$$

As the solution goes from acidic to neutral to basic, the solubility of Al^{3+} changes accordingly, as illustrated in Figure 16.19 ▸.

The extent to which a metal hydroxide dissolves in both acid and base depends on the degree to which it is amphoteric. Cations that form amphoteric hydroxides include Al^{3+}, Cr^{3+}, Zn^{2+}, Pb^{2+}, and Sn^{2+}. Other metal hydroxides, such as those of Ca^{2+}, Fe^{2+}, and Fe^{3+}, are not amphoteric—they become soluble in acidic solutions, but not in basic ones.

pH-Dependent Solubility of an Amphoteric Hydroxide

$Al(H_2O)_6^{3+}(aq)$

$Al(H_2O)_3(OH)_3(s)$
or $Al(OH)_3(s)$

$Al(H_2O)_2(OH)_4^{+}(aq)$

▲ **FIGURE 16.19 Solubility of an Amphoteric Hydroxide** Because aluminum hydroxide is amphoteric, its solubility is pH-dependent. At low pH, the formation of $Al(H_2O)_6^{3+}$ drives the dissolution. At neutral pH, insoluble $Al(OH)_3$ precipitates out of solution. At high pH, the formation of $Al(H_2O)_2(OH)_4^-$ drives the dissolution.

CHAPTER IN REVIEW

Self Assessment Quiz

Q1. A buffer is 0.100 M in NH_4Cl and 0.100 M in NH_3. When a small amount of hydrobromic acid is added to this buffer, which buffer component neutralizes the added acid?
a) NH_4^+
b) Cl^-
c) NH_3
d) None of the above (hydrobromic acid will not be neutralized by this buffer).

Q2. What is the pH of a buffer that is 0.120 M in formic acid ($HCHO_2$) and 0.080 M in potassium formate ($KCHO_2$)? For formic acid, $K_a = 1.8 \times 10^{-4}$.
a) 2.33   b) 3.57   c) 3.74   d) 3.91

Q3. A buffer with a pH of 9.85 contains CH_3NH_2 and CH_3NH_3Cl in water. What can you conclude about the relative concentrations of CH_3NH_2 and CH_3NH_3Cl in this buffer? For CH_3NH_2, $pK_b = 3.36$.
a) $CH_3NH_2 > CH_3NH_3Cl$
b) $CH_3NH_2 < CH_3NH_3Cl$
c) $CH_3NH_2 = CH_3NH_3Cl$
d) Nothing can be concluded about the relative concentrations of CH_3NH_2 and CH_3NH_3Cl.

Q4. A 500.0 mL buffer solution is 0.10 M in benzoic acid and 0.10 M in sodium benzoate and has an initial pH of 4.19. What is the pH of the buffer upon addition of 0.010 mol of NaOH?
a) 1.70
b) 4.01
c) 4.29
d) 4.37

Q5. Consider a buffer composed of the weak acid HA and its conjugate base A^-. Which pair of concentrations results in the most effective buffer?
a) 0.10 M HA; 0.10 M A^-
b) 0.50 M HA; 0.50 M A^-
c) 0.90 M HA; 0.10 M A^-
d) 0.10 M HA; 0.90 M A^-

Q6. Which combination is the best choice to prepare a buffer with a pH of 9.0?
a) NH_3; NH_4Cl (pK_b for NH_3 is 4.75)
b) C_5H_5N; C_5H_5NHCl (pK_b for C_5H_5N is 8.76)
c) HNO_2; $NaNO_2$ (pK_a for HNO_2 is 3.33)
d) $HCHO_2$; $NaCHO_2$ (pK_a for $HCHO_2$ is 3.74)

Q7. A 25.0 mL sample of an unknown HBr solution is titrated with 0.100 M NaOH. The equivalence point is reached upon the addition of 18.88 mL of the base. What is the concentration of the HBr solution?
a) 0.0755 M
b) 0.0376 M
c) 0.100 M
d) 0.00188 M

Q8. A 10.0 mL sample of 0.200 M hydrocyanic acid (HCN) is titrated with 0.0998 M NaOH. What is the pH at the equivalence point? For hydrocyanic acid, $pK_a = 9.31$.
a) 7.00
b) 8.76
c) 9.31
d) 11.07

Q9. A 20.0 mL sample of 0.150 M ethylamine is titrated with 0.0981 M HCl. What is the pH after the addition of 5.0 mL of HCl? For ethylamine, $pK_b = 3.25$.
a) 10.75
b) 11.04
c) 2.96
d) 11.46

Q10. Three 15.0 mL acid samples—0.10 M HA, 0.10 M HB, and 0.10 M H_2C—are all titrated with 0.100 M NaOH. If HA is a weak acid, HB is a strong acid, and H_2C is a diprotic acid, which statement is true of all three titrations?
a) All three titrations have the same pH at the first equivalence point.
b) All three titrations have the same initial pH.
c) All three titrations have the same final pH.
d) All three titrations require the same volume of NaOH to reach the first equivalence point.

Q11. A weak unknown monoprotic acid is titrated with a strong base. The titration curve is shown below. Find K_a for the unknown acid.

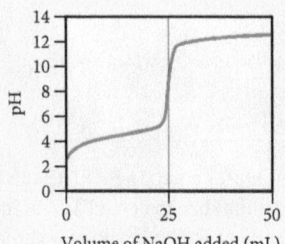

a) 2.5×10^{-3} b) 3.2×10^{-5}
c) 3.2×10^{-7} d) 2.5×10^{-9}

Q12. Calculate the molar solubility of lead(II) bromide ($PbBr_2$). For lead(II) bromide, $K_{sp} = 4.67 \times 10^{-6}$.
a) 0.00153 M
b) 0.0105 M
c) 0.0167 M
d) 0.0211 M

Q13. Calculate the molar solubility of magnesium fluoride (MgF_2) in a solution that is 0.250 M in NaF. For magnesium fluoride, $K_{sp} = 5.16 \times 10^{-11}$.
a) 2.35×10^{-4} M
b) 2.06×10^{-10} M
c) 2.87×10^{-5} M
d) 8.26×10^{-10} M

Q14. A solution is 0.025 M in Pb^{2+}. What minimum concentration of Cl^- is required to begin to precipitate $PbCl_2$? For $PbCl_2$, $K_{sp} = 1.17 \times 10^{-5}$.
a) 1.17×10^{-5} M
b) 0.0108 M
c) 0.0216 M
d) 5.41×10^{-4} M

Q15. Which compound is more soluble in an acidic solution than in a neutral solution?
a) $PbBr_2$
b) $CuCl$
c) AgI
d) BaF_2

Answers: 1. (c) 2. (b) 3. (b) 4. (d) 5. (b) 6. (a) 7. (a) 8. (d) 9. (d) 10. (d) 11. (b) 12. (b) 13. (d) 14. (c) 15. (d)

Key Terms

Section 16.2
buffer (754)
common ion effect (756)
Henderson–Hasselbalch
    equation (758)

Section 16.3
buffer capacity (768)

Section 16.4
acid–base titration (769)
indicator (769)
equivalence point (769)
endpoint (780)

Section 16.5
solubility product constant
    (K_{sp}) (783)
molar solubility (783)

Section 16.6
selective precipitation (790)

Section 16.7
qualitative analysis (792)
quantitative analysis (792)

Section 16.8
complex ion (795)
ligand (795)
formation constant (K_f) (795)

Key Concepts

The Dangers of Antifreeze (16.1)
▶ Although buffers closely regulate the pH of mammalian blood, the capacity of these buffers to neutralize can be overwhelmed.
▶ Ethylene glycol, the main component of antifreeze, is metabolized by the liver into glycolic acid. The resulting acidity can exceed the buffering capacity of blood and cause acidosis, a serious condition that results in oxygen deprivation.

Buffers: Solutions That Resist pH Change (16.2)
▶ Buffers contain significant amounts of both a weak acid and its conjugate base (or a weak base and its conjugate acid), enabling the buffer to neutralize added acid or added base.
▶ Adding a small amount of acid to a buffer converts a stoichiometric amount of base to the conjugate acid. Adding a small amount of base to a buffer converts a stoichiometric amount of the acid to the conjugate base.
▶ We can determine the pH of a buffer solution by solving an equilibrium problem, focusing on the common ion effect, or by using the Henderson–Hasselbalch equation.

Buffer Range and Buffer Capacity (16.3)
▶ A buffer works best when the amounts of acid and conjugate base it contains are large and approximately equal.
▶ If the relative amounts of acid and base in a buffer differ by more than a factor of 10, the ability of the buffer to neutralize added acid and added base diminishes. The maximum pH range at which a buffer is effective is one pH unit on either side of the acid's pK_a.

Titrations and pH Curves (16.4)
▶ A titration curve is a graph of the change in pH versus added volume of acid or base during a titration.
▶ This chapter examines three types of titration curves, representing three types of acid–base reactions: a strong acid with a strong base, a weak acid with a strong base (or vice versa), and a polyprotic acid with a base.
▶ The equivalence point of a titration can be made visible by an indicator, a compound that changes color over a specific pH range.

Solubility Equilibria and the Solubility Product Constant (16.5)
▶ The solubility product constant (K_{sp}) is an equilibrium constant for the dissolution of an ionic compound in water.
▶ We can determine the molar solubility of an ionic compound from K_{sp} and vice versa. Although the value of K_{sp} is constant at a given temperature, the solubility of an ionic substance can depend on other factors such as the presence of common ions and the pH of the solution.

Precipitation (16.6)
▶ We can compare the magnitude of K_{sp} to the reaction quotient, Q, in order to determine the relative saturation of a solution.
▶ Substances with cations that have sufficiently different values of K_{sp} can be separated by selective precipitation, in which an added reagent forms a precipitate with one of the dissolved cations but not others.

Qualitative Chemical Analysis (16.7)
▶ Qualitative analysis operates on the principle that a mixture of cations can be separated and analyzed based on the differences in the solubilities of their salts.
▶ In a classic qualitative analysis scheme, an unknown mixture of cations is sequentially treated with different reagents, each of which precipitates a known subgroup of cations.

Complex Ion Equilibria (16.8)
▶ A complex ion contains a central metal ion coordinated to two or more ligands.
▶ The equilibrium constant for the formation of a complex ion is called a formation constant and is usually quite large.
▶ The solubility of an ionic compound containing a metal cation that forms complex ions increases in the presence of Lewis bases that complex with the cation because the formation of the complex ion drives the dissolution reaction to the right.
▶ All metal hydroxides become more soluble in the presence of acids, but amphoteric metal hydroxides also become more soluble in the presence of bases.

Key Equations and Relationships

The Henderson–Hasselbalch Equation (16.2)

$$pH = pK_a + \log\frac{[\text{base}]}{[\text{acid}]}$$

Effective Buffer Range (16.3)

$$pH \text{ range} = pK_a \pm 1$$

The Relation between Q and K_{sp} (16.3)

If $Q < K_{sp}$, the solution is unsaturated. More of the solid ionic compound can dissolve in the solution.

If $Q = K_{sp}$, the solution is saturated. The solution is holding the equilibrium amount of the dissolved ions, and additional solid will not dissolve in the solution.

If $Q > K_{sp}$, the solution is supersaturated. Under most circumstances, the solid will precipitate out of a supersaturated solution.

Key Learning Outcomes

Chapter Objectives	Assessment
Calculating the pH of a Buffer Solution (16.2)	Example 16.1 For Practice 16.1 For More Practice 16.1 Exercises 29, 30, 33, 34
Using the Henderson–Hasselbalch Equation to Calculate the pH of a Buffer Solution (16.2)	Example 16.2 For Practice 16.2 Exercises 37–42

Key Learning Outcomes, *continued*

Calculating the pH Change in a Buffer Solution after the Addition of a Small Amount of Strong Acid or Base (**16.2**)	Example 16.3　For Practice 16.3　For More Practice 16.3　Exercises 47–50
Using the Henderson–Hasselbalch Equation to Calculate the pH of a Buffer Solution Composed of a Weak Base and Its Conjugate Acid (**16.2**)	Example 16.4　For Practice 16.4　For More Practice 16.4　Exercises 37–40
Determining Buffer Range (**16.3**)	Example 16.5　For Practice 16.5　Exercises 57–58
Strong Acid–Strong Base Titration pH Curve (**16.4**)	Example 16.6　For Practice 16.6　Exercises 67–70

Weak Acid–Strong Base Titration pH Curve (**16.4**)	Example 16.7　For Practice 16.7　Exercises 65–66, 71–72, 75, 77–80
Calculating Molar Solubility from K_{sp} (**16.5**)	Example 16.8　For Practice 16.8　Exercises 87–88
Calculating K_{sp} from Molar Solubility (**16.5**)	Example 16.9　For Practice 16.9　Exercises 89–90, 92, 94
Calculating Molar Solubility in the Presence of a Common Ion (**16.5**)	Example 16.10　For Practice 16.10　Exercises 95–96
Determining the Effect of pH on Solubility (**16.5**)	Example 16.11　For Practice 16.11　Exercises 97–100
Predicting Precipitation Reactions by Comparing Q and K_{sp} (**16.6**)	Example 16.12　For Practice 16.12　Exercises 101–104
Finding the Minimum Required Reagent Concentration for Selective Precipitation (**16.6**)	Example 16.13　For Practice 16.13　Exercises 105–106
Finding the Concentrations of Ions Left in Solution after Selective Precipitation (**16.6**)	Example 16.14　For Practice 16.14　Exercises 107–108
Working with Complex Ion Equilibria (**16.8**)	Example 16.15　For Practice 16.15　Exercises 109–112

EXERCISES

Review Questions

1. What is the pH range of human blood? How is human blood maintained in this pH range?

2. What is a buffer? How does a buffer work? How does it neutralize added acid? Added base?

3. What is the common ion effect?

4. What is the Henderson–Hasselbalch equation and why is it useful?

5. What is the pH of a buffer solution when the concentrations of both buffer components (the weak acid and its conjugate base) are equal? What happens to the pH when the buffer contains more of the weak acid than the conjugate base? More of the conjugate base than the weak acid?

6. Suppose that a buffer contains equal amounts of a weak acid and its conjugate base. What happens to the relative amounts of the weak acid and conjugate base when a small amount of strong acid is added to the buffer? What happens when a small amount of strong base is added?

7. How do you use the Henderson–Hasselbalch equation to calculate the pH of a buffer containing a base and its conjugate acid? Specifically, how do you determine the correct value for pK_a?

8. What factors influence the effectiveness of a buffer? What are the characteristics of an effective buffer?

9. What is the effective pH range of a buffer (relative to the pK_a of the weak acid component)?

10. Describe acid–base titration. What is the equivalence point?

11. The pH at the equivalence point of the titration of a strong acid with a strong base is 7.0. However, the pH at the equivalence point of the titration of a *weak* acid with a strong base is above 7.0. Explain.

12. The volume required to reach the equivalence point of an acid–base titration depends on the volume and concentration of the acid or base to be titrated and on the concentration of the acid or base used to do the titration. It does not, however, depend on the whether or not the acid or base being titrated is strong or weak. Explain.

13. In the titration of a strong acid with a strong base, how would you calculate these quantities?
    a. initial pH
    b. pH before the equivalence point
    c. pH at the equivalence point
    d. pH beyond the equivalence point

14. In the titration of a weak acid with a strong base, how would you calculate these quantities?
    a. initial pH
    b. pH before the equivalence point
    c. pH at one-half the equivalence point
    d. pH at the equivalence point
    e. pH beyond the equivalence point

15. The titration of a polyprotic acid with sufficiently different pK_a's displays two equivalence points. Why?

16. In the titration of a polyprotic acid, the volume required to reach the first equivalence point is identical to the volume required to reach the second one. Why?

17. What is the difference between the endpoint and the equivalence point in a titration?

18. What is an indicator? How can an indicator signal the equivalence point of a titration?

19. What is the solubility product constant? Write a general expression for the solubility constant of a compound with the general formula A_mX_n.

20. What is molar solubility? How can you obtain the molar solubility of a compound from K_{sp}?

21. How does a common ion affect the solubility of a compound? More specifically, how is the solubility of a compound with the general formula AX different in a solution containing one of the common ions (A^+ or X^-) than it is in pure water? Explain.

22. How is the solubility of an ionic compound with a basic anion affected by pH? Explain.

23. For a given solution containing an ionic compound, what is the relationship between Q, K_{sp}, and the relative saturation of the solution?

24. What is selective precipitation? Under which conditions does selective precipitation occur?

25. What is qualitative analysis? How does *qualitative* analysis differ from *quantitative* analysis?

26. What are the main groups in the general qualitative analysis scheme described in this chapter? Describe the steps and reagents necessary to identify each group.

Problems by Topic

The Common Ion Effect and Buffers

27. In which of these solutions will HNO_2 ionize less than it does in pure water?
    a. 0.10 M NaCl
    b. 0.10 M KNO_3
    c. 0.10 M NaOH
    d. 0.10 M $NaNO_2$

28. A formic acid solution has a pH of 3.25. Which of these substances will raise the pH of the solution upon addition? Explain your answer.
    a. HCl
    b. NaBr
    c. $NaCHO_2$
    d. KCl

29. Solve an equilibrium problem (using an ICE table) to calculate the pH of each solution.
    a. a solution that is 0.20 M in $HCHO_2$ and 0.15 M in $NaCHO_2$
    b. a solution that is 0.16 M in NH_3 and 0.22 M in NH_4Cl

30. Solve an equilibrium problem (using an ICE table) to calculate the pH of each solution.
    a. a solution that is 0.195 M in $HC_2H_3O_2$ and 0.125 M in $KC_2H_3O_2$
    b. a solution that is 0.255 M in CH_3NH_2 and 0.135 M in CH_3NH_3Br

31. Calculate the percent ionization of a 0.15 M benzoic acid solution in pure water and in a solution containing 0.10 M sodium benzoate. Why does the percent ionization differ significantly in the two solutions?

32. Calculate the percent ionization of a 0.13 M formic acid solution in pure water and also in a solution containing 0.11 M potassium formate. Explain the difference in percent ionization in the two solutions.

33. Solve an equilibrium problem (using an ICE table) to calculate the pH of each solution.
    a. 0.15 M HF   b. 0.15 M NaF
    c. a mixture that is 0.15 M in HF and 0.15 M in NaF

34. Solve an equilibrium problem (using an ICE table) to calculate the pH of each solution.
    a. 0.18 M CH_3NH_2 b. 0.18 M CH_3NH_3Cl
    c. a mixture that is 0.18 M in CH_3NH_2 and 0.18 M in CH_3NH_3Cl

35. A buffer contains significant amounts of acetic acid and sodium acetate. Write equations showing how this buffer neutralizes added acid and added base.

36. A buffer contains significant amounts of ammonia and ammonium chloride. Write equations showing how this buffer neutralizes added acid and added base.

37. Use the Henderson–Hasselbalch equation to calculate the pH of each solution in Problem 29.

38. Use the Henderson–Hasselbalch equation to calculate the pH of each solution in Problem 30.

39. Use the Henderson–Hasselbalch equation to calculate the pH of each solution.
    a. a solution that is 0.135 M in HClO and 0.155 M in KClO
    b. a solution that contains 1.05% $C_2H_5NH_2$ by mass and 1.10% $C_2H_5NH_3Br$ by mass
    c. a solution that contains 10.0 g of $HC_2H_3O_2$ and 10.0 g of $NaC_2H_3O_2$ in 150.0 mL of solution

40. Use the Henderson–Hasselbalch equation to calculate the pH of each solution.
    a. a solution that is 0.145 M in propanoic acid and 0.115 M in potassium propanoate
    b. a solution that contains 0.785% C_5H_5N by mass and 0.985% C_5H_5NHCl by mass
    c. a solution that contains 15.0 g of HF and 25.0 g of NaF in 125 mL of solution

41. Calculate the pH of the solution that results from each mixture.
    a. 50.0 mL of 0.15 M $HCHO_2$ with 75.0 mL of 0.13 M $NaCHO_2$
    b. 125.0 mL of 0.10 M NH_3 with 250.0 mL of 0.10 M NH_4Cl

42. Calculate the pH of the solution that results from each mixture.
    a. 150.0 mL of 0.25 M HF with 225.0 mL of 0.30 M NaF
    b. 175.0 mL of 0.10 M $C_2H_5NH_2$ with 275.0 mL of 0.20 M $C_2H_5NH_3Cl$

43. Calculate the ratio of NaF to HF required to create a buffer with pH = 4.00.

44. Calculate the ratio of CH_3NH_2 to CH_3NH_3Cl concentration required to create a buffer with pH = 10.24.

45. What mass of sodium benzoate should you add to 150.0 mL of a 0.15 M benzoic acid solution to obtain a buffer with a pH of 4.25? (Assume no volume change.)

46. What mass of ammonium chloride should you add to 2.55 L of a 0.155 M NH_3 to obtain a buffer with a pH of 9.55? (Assume no volume change.)

47. A 250.0 mL buffer solution is 0.250 M in acetic acid and 0.250 M in sodium acetate.
    a. What is the initial pH of this solution?
    b. What is the pH after addition of 0.0050 mol of HCl?
    c. What is the pH after addition of 0.0050 mol of NaOH?

48. A 100.0 mL buffer solution is 0.175 M in HClO and 0.150 M in NaClO.
    a. What is the initial pH of this solution?
    b. What is the pH after addition of 150.0 mg of HBr?
    c. What is the pH after addition of 85.0 mg of NaOH?

49. For each solution, calculate the initial and final pH after adding 0.010 mol of HCl.
    a. 500.0 mL of pure water
    b. 500.0 mL of a buffer solution that is 0.125 M in $HC_2H_3O_2$ and 0.115 M in $NaC_2H_3O_2$
    c. 500.0 mL of a buffer solution that is 0.155 M in $C_2H_5NH_2$ and 0.145 M in $C_2H_5NH_3Cl$

50. For each solution, calculate the initial and final pH after adding 0.010 mol of NaOH.
    a. 250.0 mL of pure water
    b. 250.0 mL of a buffer solution that is 0.195 M in $HCHO_2$ and 0.275 M in $KCHO_2$
    c. 250.0 mL of a buffer solution that is 0.255 M in $CH_3CH_2NH_2$ and 0.235 M in $CH_3CH_2NH_3Cl$

51. A 350.0 mL buffer solution is 0.150 M in HF and 0.150 M in NaF. What mass of NaOH can this buffer neutralize before the pH rises above 4.00? If the same volume of the buffer was 0.350 M in HF and 0.350 M in NaF, what mass of NaOH could be handled before the pH rises above 4.00?

52. A 100.0 mL buffer solution is 0.100 M in NH_3 and 0.125 M in NH_4Br. What mass of HCl can this buffer neutralize before the pH falls below 9.00? If the same volume of the buffer were 0.250 M in NH_3 and 0.400 M in NH_4Br, what mass of HCl could be handled before the pH fell below 9.00?

53. Determine whether or not the mixing of each pair of solutions results in a buffer.
    a. 100.0 mL of 0.10 M NH_3; 100.0 mL of 0.15 M NH_4Cl
    b. 50.0 mL of 0.10 M HCl; 35.0 mL of 0.150 M NaOH
    c. 50.0 mL of 0.15 M HF; 20.0 mL of 0.15 M NaOH
    d. 175.0 mL of 0.10 M NH_3; 150.0 mL of 0.12 M NaOH
    e. 125.0 mL of 0.15 M NH_3; 150.0 mL of 0.20 M NaOH

54. Determine whether or not the mixing of each pair of solutions results in a buffer.
    a. 75.0 mL of 0.10 M HF; 55.0 mL of 0.15 M NaF
    b. 150.0 mL of 0.10 M HF; 135.0 mL of 0.175 M HCl
    c. 165.0 mL of 0.10 M HF; 135.0 mL of 0.050 M KOH
    d. 125.0 mL of 0.15 M CH_3NH_2; 120.0 mL of 0.25 M CH_3NH_3Cl
    e. 105.0 mL of 0.15 M CH_3NH_2; 95.0 mL of 0.10 M HCl

55. Blood is buffered by carbonic acid and the bicarbonate ion. Normal blood plasma is 0.024 M in HCO_3^- and 0.0012 M H_2CO_3 (pK_{a_1} for H_2CO_3 at body temperature is 6.1).
    a. What is the pH of blood plasma?
    b. If the volume of blood in a normal adult is 5.0 L, what mass of HCl can be neutralized by the buffering system in blood before the pH falls below 7.0 (which would result in death)?
    c. Given the volume from part (b), what mass of NaOH can be neutralized before the pH rises above 7.8?

56. The fluids within cells are buffered by $H_2PO_4^-$ and HPO_4^{2-}.
    a. Calculate the ratio of HPO_4^{2-} to $H_2PO_4^-$ required to maintain a pH of 7.1 within a cell.
    b. Could a buffer system employing H_3PO_4 as the weak acid and $H_2PO_4^-$ as the weak base be used as a buffer system within cells? Explain.

57. Which buffer system is the best choice to create a buffer with pH = 7.20? For the best system, calculate the ratio of the masses of the buffer components required to make the buffer.

    $HC_2H_3O_2/KC_2H_3O_2$ $HClO_2/KClO_2$
    NH_3/NH_4Cl $HClO/KClO$

58. Which buffer system is the best choice to create a buffer with pH = 9.00? For the best system, calculate the ratio of the masses of the buffer components required to make the buffer.

    HF/KF HNO_2/KNO_2
    NH_3/NH_4Cl $HClO/KClO$

59. A 500.0 mL buffer solution is 0.100 M in HNO_2 and 0.150 M in KNO_2. Determine if each addition would exceed the capacity of the buffer to neutralize it.
    a. 250 mg NaOH   b. 350 mg KOH
    c. 1.25 g HBr   d. 1.35 g HI

60. A 1.0 L buffer solution is 0.125 M in HNO_2 and 0.145 M in $NaNO_2$. Determine the concentrations of HNO_2 and $NaNO_2$ after the addition of each substance:
    a. 1.5 g HCl   b. 1.5 g NaOH
    c. 1.5 g HI

Titrations, pH Curves, and Indicators

61. The graphs labeled (a) and (b) show the titration curves for two equal-volume samples of monoprotic acids, one weak and one strong. Both titrations were carried out with the same concentration of strong base.

(a)

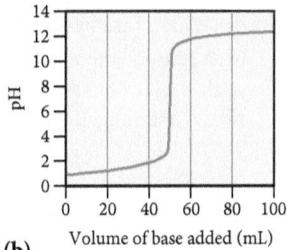
(b)

    (i) What is the approximate pH at the equivalence point of each curve?
    (ii) Which graph corresponds to the titration of the strong acid and which one to the titration of the weak acid?

62. Two 25.0 mL samples, one 0.100 M HCl and the other 0.100 M HF, are titrated with 0.200 M KOH.
    a. What is the volume of added base at the equivalence point for each titration?
    b. Is the pH at the equivalence point for each titration acidic, basic, or neutral?
    c. Which titration curve has the lower initial pH?
    d. Sketch each titration curve.

63. Two 20.0 mL samples, one 0.200 M KOH and the other 0.200 M CH_3NH_2 are titrated with 0.100 M HI.
    a. What is the volume of added acid at the equivalence point for each titration?
    b. Is the pH at the equivalence point for each titration acidic, basic, or neutral?
    c. Which titration curve has the lower initial pH?
    d. Sketch each titration curve.

64. The graphs labeled (a) and (b) show the titration curves for two equal-volume samples of bases, one weak and one strong. Both titrations were carried out with the same concentration of strong acid.

(a)

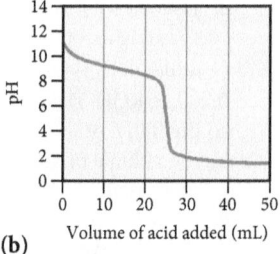
(b)

    (i) What is the approximate pH at the equivalence point of each curve?
    (ii) Which graph corresponds to the titration of the strong base and which one to the weak base?

65. Consider the curve shown here for the titration of a weak monoprotic acid with a strong base and answer each question.

    a. What is the pH and what is the volume of added base at the equivalence point?
    b. At what volume of added base is the pH calculated by working an equilibrium problem based on the initial concentration and K_a of the weak acid?
    c. At what volume of added base does pH = pK_a?
    d. At what volume of added base is the pH calculated by working an equilibrium problem based on the concentration and K_b of the conjugate base?
    e. Beyond what volume of added base is the pH calculated by focusing on the amount of excess strong base added?

66. Consider the curve shown here for the titration of a weak base with a strong acid and answer each question.

a. What is the pH and what is the volume of added acid at the equivalence point?

b. At what volume of added acid is the pH calculated by working an equilibrium problem based on the initial concentration and K_b of the weak base?

c. At what volume of added acid does pH $= 14 - pK_b$?

d. At what volume of added acid is the pH calculated by working an equilibrium problem based on the concentration and K_a of the conjugate acid?

e. Beyond what volume of added acid is the pH calculated by focusing on the amount of excess strong acid added?

67. Consider the titration of a 35.0 mL sample of 0.175 M HBr with 0.200 M KOH. Determine each quantity.

a. the initial pH

b. the volume of added base required to reach the equivalence point

c. the pH at 10.0 mL of added base

d. the pH at the equivalence point

e. the pH after adding 5.0 mL of base beyond the equivalence point

68. A 20.0 mL sample of 0.125 M HNO_3 is titrated with 0.150 M NaOH. Calculate the pH for at least five different points throughout the titration curve and sketch the curve. Indicate the volume at the equivalence point on your graph.

69. Consider the titration of a 25.0 mL sample of 0.115 M RbOH with 0.100 M HCl. Determine each quantity.

a. the initial pH

b. the volume of added acid required to reach the equivalence point

c. the pH at 5.0 mL of added acid

d. the pH at the equivalence point

e. the pH after adding 5.0 mL of acid beyond the equivalence point

70. A 15.0 mL sample of 0.100 M $Ba(OH)_2$ is titrated with 0.125 M HCl. Calculate the pH for at least five different points throughout the titration curve and sketch the curve. Indicate the volume at the equivalence point on your graph.

71. Consider the titration of a 20.0 mL sample of 0.105 M $HC_2H_3O_2$ with 0.125 M NaOH. Determine each quantity.

a. the initial pH

b. the volume of added base required to reach the equivalence point

c. the pH at 5.0 mL of added base

d. the pH at one-half of the equivalence point

e. the pH at the equivalence point

f. the pH after adding 5.0 mL of base beyond the equivalence point

72. A 30.0 mL sample of 0.165 M propanoic acid is titrated with 0.300 M KOH. Calculate the pH at each volume of added base: 0 mL, 5 mL, 10 mL, equivalence point, one-half equivalence point, 20 mL, 25 mL. Sketch the titration curve.

73. Consider the titration of a 25.0 mL sample of 0.175 M CH_3NH_2 with 0.150 M HBr. Determine each quantity.

a. the initial pH

b. the volume of added acid required to reach the equivalence point

c. the pH at 5.0 mL of added acid

d. the pH at one-half of the equivalence point

e. the pH at the equivalence point

f. the pH after adding 5.0 mL of acid beyond the equivalence point

74. A 25.0 mL sample of 0.125 M pyridine is titrated with 0.100 M HCl. Calculate the pH at each volume of added acid: 0 mL, 10 mL, 20 mL, equivalence point, one-half equivalence point, 40 mL, 50 mL. Sketch the titration curve.

75. Consider the titration curves (labeled a and b) for two weak acids, both titrated with 0.100 M NaOH.

(a)

(b)

(i) Which acid solution is more concentrated?

(ii) Which acid has the larger K_a?

76. Consider the titration curves (labeled a and b) for two weak bases, both titrated with 0.100 M HCl.

(a)

(b)

(i) Which base solution is more concentrated?

(ii) Which base has the larger K_b?

77. A 0.229 g sample of an unknown monoprotic acid is titrated with 0.112 M NaOH. The resulting titration curve is shown here. Determine the molar mass and pK_a of the acid.

78. A 0.446 g sample of an unknown monoprotic acid is titrated with 0.105 M KOH. The resulting titration curve is shown here. Determine the molar mass and pK_a of the acid.

79. A 20.0 mL sample of 0.115 M sulfurous acid (H_2SO_3) solution is titrated with 0.1014 M KOH. At what added volume of base solution does each equivalence point occur?

80. A 20.0 mL sample of a 0.125 M diprotic acid (H_2A) solution is titrated with 0.1019 M KOH. The acid ionization constants for the acid are $K_{a_1} = 5.2 \times 10^{-5}$ and $K_{a_2} = 3.4 \times 10^{-10}$. At what added volume of base does each equivalence point occur?

81. Methyl red has a pK_a of 5.0 and is red in its acid form and yellow in its basic form. If several drops of this indicator are placed in a 25.0 mL sample of 0.100 M HCl, what color will the solution appear? If 0.100 M NaOH is slowly added to the HCl sample, in what pH range will the indicator change color?

82. Phenolphthalein has a pK_a of 9.7. It is colorless in its acid form and pink in its basic form. For each of the pH's, calculate $[In^-]/[HIn]$ and predict the color of a phenolphthalein solution.
  a. pH = 2.0
  b. pH = 5.0
  c. pH = 8.0
  d. pH = 11.0

83. Referring to Table 16.1, pick an indicator for use in the titration of each acid with a strong base.
  a. HF
  b. HCl
  c. HCN

84. Referring to Table 16.1, pick an indicator for use in the titration of each base with a strong acid.
  a. CH_3NH_2
  b. NaOH
  c. $C_6H_5NH_2$

Solubility Equilibria

85. Write balanced equations and expressions for K_{sp} for the dissolution of each ionic compound.
  a. $BaSO_4$
  b. $PbBr_2$
  c. Ag_2CrO_4

86. Write balanced equations and expressions for K_{sp} for the dissolution of each ionic compound.
  a. $CaCO_3$
  b. $PbCl_2$
  c. AgI

87. Refer to the K_{sp} values in Table 16.2 to calculate the molar solubility of each compound in pure water.
  a. AgBr
  b. $Mg(OH)_2$
  c. CaF_2

88. Refer to the K_{sp} values in Table 16.2 to calculate the molar solubility of each compound in pure water.
  a. MX ($K_{sp} = 1.27 \times 10^{-36}$)
  b. Ag_2CrO_4
  c. $Ca(OH)_2$

89. Use the given molar solubilities in pure water to calculate K_{sp} for each compound.
  a. MX; molar solubility = 3.27×10^{-11} M
  b. PbF_2; molar solubility = 5.63×10^{-3} M
  c. MgF_2; molar solubility = 2.65×10^{-4} M

90. Use the given molar solubilities in pure water to calculate K_{sp} for each compound.
  a. $BaCrO_4$; molar solubility = 1.08×10^{-5} M
  b. Ag_2SO_3; molar solubility = 1.55×10^{-5} M
  c. $Pd(SCN)_2$; molar solubility = 2.22×10^{-8} M

91. Two compounds with general formulas AX and AX_2 have $K_{sp} = 1.5 \times 10^{-5}$. Which of the two compounds has the higher molar solubility?

92. Consider the compounds with the generic formulas listed and their corresponding molar solubilities in pure water. Which compound has the smallest value of K_{sp}?
  a. AX; molar solubility = 1.35×10^{-4} M
  b. AX_2; molar solubility = 2.25×10^{-4} M
  c. A_2X; molar solubility = 1.75×10^{-4} M

93. Refer to the K_{sp} value from Table 16.2 to calculate the solubility of iron(II) hydroxide in pure water in grams per 100.0 mL of solution.

94. The solubility of copper(I) chloride is 3.91 mg per 100.0 mL of solution. Calculate K_{sp} for CuCl.

95. Calculate the molar solubility of barium fluoride in each liquid or solution.
  a. pure water
  b. 0.10 M $Ba(NO_3)_2$
  c. 0.15 M NaF

96. Calculate the molar solubility of MX ($K_{sp} = 1.27 \times 10^{-36}$) in each liquid or solution.
  a. pure water
  b. 0.25 M MCl_2
  c. 0.20 M Na_2X

97. Calculate the molar solubility of calcium hydroxide in a solution buffered at each pH.
  a. pH = 4
  b. pH = 7
  c. pH = 9

98. Calculate the solubility (in grams per 1.00×10^2 mL of solution) of magnesium hydroxide in a solution buffered at pH = 10. How does this compare to the solubility of $Mg(OH)_2$ in pure water?

99. Determine if each compound is more soluble in acidic solution than in pure water. Explain.
  a. $BaCO_3$
  b. CuS
  c. AgCl
  d. PbI_2

100. Determine if each compound is more soluble in acidic solution than in pure water. Explain.
a. Hg_2Br_2
b. $Mg(OH)_2$
c. $CaCO_3$
d. AgI

Precipitation and Qualitative Analysis

101. A solution containing sodium fluoride is mixed with one containing calcium nitrate to form a solution that is 0.015 M in NaF and 0.010 M in $Ca(NO_3)_2$. Does a precipitate form in the mixed solution? If so, identify the precipitate.

102. A solution containing potassium bromide is mixed with one containing lead acetate to form a solution that is 0.013 M in KBr and 0.0035 M in $Pb(C_2H_3O_2)_2$. Does a precipitate form in the mixed solution? If so, identify the precipitate.

103. Predict whether a precipitate will form if you mix 75.0 mL of a NaOH solution with pOH = 2.58 with 125.0 mL of a 0.018 M $MgCl_2$ solution. Identify the precipitate, if any.

104. Predict whether a precipitate will form if you mix 175.0 mL of a 0.0055 M KCl solution with 145.0 mL of a 0.0015 M $AgNO_3$ solution. Identify the precipitate, if any.

105. Potassium hydroxide is used to precipitate each of the cations from their respective solution. Determine the minimum concentration of KOH required for precipitation to begin in each case.
a. 0.015 M $CaCl_2$
b. 0.0025 M $Fe(NO_3)_2$
c. 0.0018 M $MgBr_2$

106. Determine the minimum concentration of the precipitating agent on the right to cause precipitation of the cation from the solution on the left.
a. 0.035 M $BaNO_3$; NaF
b. 0.085 M CaI_2; K_2SO_4
c. 0.0018 M $AgNO_3$; RbCl

107. A solution is 0.010 M in Ba^{2+} and 0.020 M in Ca^{2+}.
a. If sodium sulfate is used to selectively precipitate one of the cations while leaving the other cation in solution, which cation will precipitate first? What minimum concentration of Na_2SO_4 will trigger the precipitation of the cation that precipitates first?
b. What is the remaining concentration of the cation that precipitates first, when the other cation begins to precipitate?

108. A solution is 0.022 M in Fe^{2+} and 0.014 M in Mg^{2+}.
a. If potassium carbonate is used to selectively precipitate one of the cations while leaving the other cation in solution, which cation will precipitate first? What minimum concentration of K_2CO_3 will trigger the precipitation of the cation that precipitates first?
b. What is the remaining concentration of the cation that precipitates first, when the other cation begins to precipitate?

Complex Ion Equilibria

109. A solution is made 1.1×10^{-3} M in $Zn(NO_3)_2$ and 0.150 M in NH_3. After the solution reaches equilibrium, what concentration of $Zn^{2+}(aq)$ remains?

110. A 120.0 mL sample of a solution that is 2.8×10^{-3} M in $AgNO_3$ is mixed with a 225.0 mL sample of a solution that is 0.10 M in NaCN. After the solution reaches equilibrium, what concentration of $Ag^+(aq)$ remains?

111. Use the appropriate values of K_{sp} and K_f to find the equilibrium constant for the reaction.

$$FeS(s) + 6\,CN^-(aq) \rightleftharpoons Fe(CN)_6{}^{4-}(aq) + S^{2-}(aq)$$

112. Use the appropriate values of K_{sp} and K_f to find the equilibrium constant for the reaction.

$$PbCl_2(s) + 3\,OH^-(aq) \rightleftharpoons Pb(OH)_3{}^-(aq) + 2\,Cl^-(aq)$$

Cumulative Problems

113. A 150.0 mL solution contains 2.05 g of sodium benzoate and 2.47 g of benzoic acid. Calculate the pH of the solution.

114. A solution is made by combining 10.0 mL of 17.5 M acetic acid with 5.54 g of sodium acetate and diluting to a total volume of 1.50 L. Calculate the pH of the solution.

115. A buffer is created by combining 150.0 mL of 0.25 M $HCHO_2$ with 75.0 mL of 0.20 M NaOH. Determine the pH of the buffer.

116. A buffer is created by combining 3.55 g of NH_3 with 4.78 g of HCl and diluting to a total volume of 750.0 mL. Determine the pH of the buffer.

117. A 1.0 L buffer solution initially contains 0.25 mol of NH_3 and 0.25 mol of NH_4Cl. In order to adjust the buffer pH to 8.75, should you add NaOH or HCl to the buffer mixture? What mass of the correct reagent should you add?

118. A 250.0 mL buffer solution initially contains 0.025 mol of $HCHO_2$ and 0.025 mol of $NaCHO_2$. In order to adjust the buffer pH to 4.10, should you add NaOH or HCl to the buffer mixture? What mass of the correct reagent should you add?

119. In analytical chemistry, bases used for titrations must often be standardized; that is, their concentration must be precisely determined. Standardization of sodium hydroxide solutions can be accomplished by titrating potassium hydrogen phthalate ($KHC_8H_4O_4$) also known as KHP, with the NaOH solution to be standardized.
a. Write an equation for the reaction between NaOH and KHP.
b. The titration of 0.5527 g of KHP required 25.87 mL of an NaOH solution to reach the equivalence point. What is the concentration of the NaOH solution?

120. A 0.5224 g sample of an unknown monoprotic acid was titrated with 0.0998 M NaOH. The equivalence point of the titration occurs at 23.82 mL. Determine the molar mass of the unknown acid.

121. A 0.25 mol sample of a weak acid with an unknown pK_a was combined with 10.0 mL of 3.00 M KOH, and the resulting solution was diluted to 1.500 L. The measured pH of the solution was 3.85. What is the pK_a of the weak acid?

122. A 5.55 g sample of a weak acid with $K_a = 1.3 \times 10^{-4}$ was combined with 5.00 mL of 6.00 M NaOH, and the resulting solution was diluted to 750 mL. The measured pH of the solution was 4.25. What is the molar mass of the weak acid?

123. A 0.552 g sample of ascorbic acid (vitamin C) was dissolved in water to a total volume of 20.0 mL and titrated with 0.1103 M KOH. The equivalence point occurred at 28.42 mL. The pH of the solution at 10.0 mL of added base was 3.72. From this data, determine the molar mass and K_a for vitamin C.

124. Sketch the titration curve from Problem 123 by calculating the pH at the beginning of the titration, at one-half of the equivalence point, at the equivalence point, and at 5.0 mL beyond the equivalence point. Pick a suitable indicator for this titration from Table 16.1.

125. One of the main components of hard water is $CaCO_3$. When hard water evaporates, some of the $CaCO_3$ is left behind as a white mineral deposit. If a hard water solution is saturated with calcium carbonate, what volume of the solution has to evaporate to deposit 1.00×10^2 mg of $CaCO_3$?

126. Gout—a condition that results in joint swelling and pain—is caused by the formation of sodium urate ($NaC_5H_3N_4$) crystals within tendons, cartilage, and ligaments. Sodium urate precipitates out of blood plasma when uric acid levels become abnormally high. This sometimes happens as a result of eating too many rich foods and consuming too much alcohol, which is why gout is sometimes referred to as the "disease of kings." If the sodium concentration in blood plasma is 0.140 M, and K_{sp} for sodium urate is 5.76×10^{-8}, what minimum concentration of urate would result in precipitation?

127. Pseudogout, a condition with symptoms similar to those of gout (see Problem 126), is caused by the formation of calcium diphosphate ($Ca_2P_2O_7$) crystals within tendons, cartilage, and ligaments. Calcium diphosphate will precipitate out of blood plasma when diphosphate levels become abnormally high. If the calcium concentration in blood plasma is 9.2 mg/dL, and K_{sp} for calcium diphosphate is 8.64×10^{-13}, what minimum concentration of diphosphate results in precipitation?

128. Calculate the solubility of silver chloride in a solution that is 0.100 M in NH_3.

129. Calculate the solubility of CuX in a solution that is 0.150 M in NaCN. K_{sp} for CuX is 1.27×10^{-36}.

130. Aniline, abbreviated ϕNH_2, where ϕ is C_6H_5, is an important organic base used in the manufacture of dyes. It has $K_b = 4.3 \times 10^{-10}$. In a certain manufacturing process it is necessary to keep the concentration of ϕNH_3^+ (aniline's conjugate acid, the anilinium ion) below 1.0×10^{-9} M in a solution that is 0.10 M in aniline. Find the concentration of NaOH required for this process.

131. The K_b of hydroxylamine, NH_2OH, is 1.10×10^{-8}. A buffer solution is prepared by mixing 100.0 mL of a 0.36 M hydroxyl amine solution with 50.0 mL of a 0.26 M HCl solution. Determine the pH of the resulting solution.

132. A 0.867 g sample of an unknown acid requires 32.2 mL of a 0.182 M barium hydroxide solution for neutralization. Assuming the acid is diprotic, calculate the molar mass of the acid.

133. A 25.0 mL volume of a sodium hydroxide solution requires 19.6 mL of a 0.189 M hydrochloric acid for neutralization. A 10.0 mL volume of a phosphoric acid solution requires 34.9 mL of the sodium hydroxide solution for complete neutralization. Calculate the concentration of the phosphoric acid solution.

134. Find the mass of sodium formate that must be dissolved in 250.0 cm^3 of a 1.4 M solution of formic acid to prepare a buffer solution with pH $= 3.36$.

135. What relative masses of dimethyl amine and dimethyl ammonium chloride do you need to prepare a buffer solution of pH $= 10.43$?

136. You are asked to prepare 2.0 L of a HCN/NaCN buffer that has a pH of 9.8 and an osmotic pressure of 1.35 atm at 298 K. What masses of HCN and NaCN should you use to prepare the buffer? (Assume complete dissociation of NaCN.)

137. What should the molar concentrations of benzoic acid and sodium benzoate be in a solution that is buffered at a pH of 4.55 and has a freezing point of $-2.0\,°C$? (Assume complete dissociation of sodium benzoate and a density of 1.01 g/mL for the solution.)

Challenge Problems

138. Derive an equation similar to the Henderson–Hasselbalch equation for a buffer composed of a weak base and its conjugate acid. Instead of relating pH to pK_a and the relative concentrations of an acid and its conjugate base (as the Henderson–Hasselbalch equation does), the equation should relate pOH to pK_b and the relative concentrations of a base and its conjugate acid.

139. Since soap and detergent action is hindered by hard water, laundry formulations usually include water softeners—called builders—designed to remove hard water ions (especially Ca^{2+} and Mg^{2+}) from the water. A common builder used in North America is sodium carbonate. Suppose that the hard water used to do laundry contains 75 ppm $CaCO_3$ and 55 ppm $MgCO_3$ (by mass). What mass of Na_2CO_3 is required to remove 90.0% of these ions from 10.0 L of laundry water?

140. A 0.558 g sample of a diprotic acid with a molar mass of 255.8 g/mol is dissolved in water to a total volume of 25.0 mL. The solution is then titrated with a saturated calcium hydroxide solution.
 a. Assuming that the pK_a values for each ionization step are sufficiently different to see two equivalence points, determine the volume of added base for the first and second equivalence points.
 b. The pH after adding 25.0 mL of the base is 3.82. Find the value of K_{a_1}.
 c. The pH after adding 20.0 mL past the first equivalence point is 8.25. Find the value of K_{a_2}.

141. When excess solid $Mg(OH)_2$ is shaken with 1.00 L of 1.0 M NH_4Cl solution, the resulting saturated solution has pH $= 9.00$. Calculate the K_{sp} of $Mg(OH)_2$.

142. What amount of solid NaOH must be added to 1.0 L of a 0.10 M H_2CO_3 solution to produce a solution with $[H^+] = 3.2 \times 10^{-11}$ M? There is no significant volume change as the result of the addition of the solid.

143. Calculate the solubility of $Au(OH)_3$ in (a) water and (b) 1.0 M nitric acid solution. ($K_{sp} = 5.5 \times 10^{-46}$).

144. Calculate the concentration of I^- in a solution obtained by shaking 0.10 M KI with an excess of $AgCl(s)$.

145. What volume of 0.100 M sodium carbonate solution is required to precipitate 99% of the Mg from 1.00 L of 0.100 M magnesium nitrate solution?

146. Find the solubility of CuI in 0.40 M HCN solution. The K_{sp} of CuI is 1.1×10^{-12} and the K_f for the $Cu(CN)_2^-$ complex ion is 1×10^{24}.

147. Find the pH of a solution prepared from 1.0 L of a 0.10 M solution of $Ba(OH)_2$ and excess $Zn(OH)_2(s)$. The K_{sp} of $Zn(OH)_2$ is 3×10^{-15} and the K_f of $Zn(OH)_4^{2-}$ is 2×10^{15}.

148. What amount of HCl gas must be added to 1.00 L of a buffer solution that contains [acetic acid] = 2.0 M and [acetate] = 1.0 M in order to produce a solution with pH = 4.00?

Conceptual Problems

149. Without doing any calculations, determine if $pH = pK_a$, $pH > pK_a$, or $pH < pK_a$. Assume that HA is a weak monoprotic acid.
    a. 0.10 mol HA and 0.050 mol of A^- in 1.0 L of solution
    b. 0.10 mol HA and 0.150 mol of A^- in 1.0 L of solution
    c. 0.10 mol HA and 0.050 mol of OH^- in 1.0 L of solution
    d. 0.10 mol HA and 0.075 mol of OH^- in 1.0 L of solution

150. A buffer contains 0.10 mol of a weak acid and 0.20 mol of its conjugate base in 1.0 L of solution. Determine whether or not each addition exceeds the capacity of the buffer.
    a. adding 0.020 mol of NaOH
    b. adding 0.020 mol of HCl
    c. adding 0.10 mol of NaOH
    d. adding 0.010 mol of HCl

151. Consider three solutions:
    i.   0.10 M solution of a weak monoprotic acid
    ii 0.10 M solution of strong monoprotic acid
    iii 0.10 M solution of a weak diprotic acid

    Each solution is titrated with 0.15 M NaOH. Which quantity is the same for all three solutions?
    a. the volume required to reach the final equivalence point
    b. the volume required to reach the first equivalence point
    c. the pH at the first equivalence point
    d. the pH at one-half the first equivalence point

152. Two monoprotic acid solutions (A and B) are titrated with identical NaOH solutions. The volume to reach the equivalence point for solution A is twice the volume required to reach the equivalence point for solution B, and the pH at the equivalence point of solution A is higher than the pH at the equivalence point for solution B. Which statement is true?
    a. The acid in solution A is more concentrated than in solution B and is also a stronger acid than that in solution B.
    b. The acid in solution A is less concentrated than in solution B and is also a weaker acid than that in solution B.
    c. The acid in solution A is more concentrated than in solution B and is also a weaker acid than that in solution B.
    d. The acid in solution A is less concentrated than in solution B and is also a stronger acid than that in solution B.

153. Describe the solubility of CaF_2 in each solution compared to its solubility in water.
    a. in a 0.10 M NaCl solution
    b. in a 0.10 M NaF solution
    c. in a 0.10 M HCl solution

Answers to Conceptual Connections

Buffers

16.1 (d) Only this solution contains significant amounts of a weak acid and its conjugate base. (Remember that HNO_3 is a strong acid, but HNO_2 is a weak acid.)

pH of Buffer Solutions

16.2 (a) Since the pH of the buffer is less than the pK_a of the acid, the buffer must contain more acid than base ($[HA] > [A^-]$). In order to raise the pH of the buffer from 4.25 to 4.72, you must add more of the weak base (adding a base will make the buffer solution more basic).

Adding Acid or Base to a Buffer

16.3 (b) Since acid is added to the buffer, the pH will become slightly lower (slightly more acidic). Answer (a) reflects too large a change in pH for a buffer, and answers (c) and (d) have the pH changing in the wrong direction.

Buffer Capacity

16.4 (a) Adding 0.050 mol of HCl destroys the buffer because it will react with all of the NaF, leaving no conjugate base in the buffer mixture.

Titration Equivalence Point

16.5 (d) Because the flask contains 7 H^+ ions, the equivalence point is reached when 7 OH^- ions have been added.

The Half-Equivalence Point

16.6 (c) The pH at the half-equivalence point is the pK_a of the conjugate acid, which is equal to $14.00 - 8.75 = 5.25$.

Acid–Base Titrations

16.7 (c) Since the volumes and concentrations of all three acids are the same, the volume of NaOH required to reach the first equivalence point (and the only equivalence point for titrations i and iii) is the same for all three titrations.

Common Ion Effect

16.8 (c) The sodium nitrate solution is the only one that has no common ion with barium sulfate. The other two solutions have common ions with barium sulfate; therefore, the solubility of barium sulfate is lower in these solutions.

Solubility and Complex Ion Equilibria

16.9 (c) Only NaCN contains an anion (CN^-) that forms a complex ion with Cu^{2+} [from Table 16.3 we can see that $K_f = 1.0 \times 10^{25}$ for $Cu(CN)_4^{2-}$]. Therefore, the presence of CN^- will drive the dissolution reaction of CuS.

17

Free Energy and Thermodynamics

Die Energie der Welt ist konstant. Die Entropie der Welt strebt einem Maximum zu. (The energy of the world is constant. The entropy of the world tends towards a maximum.)

—Rudolf Clausius (1822–1888)

THROUGHOUT THIS BOOK, we have examined and learned about chemical and physical changes. We have studied how fast chemical changes occur (kinetics) and how to predict how far they will go (through the use of equilibrium constants). We have learned that acids neutralize bases and that gases expand to fill their containers. We now turn to the following question: why do these changes occur in the first place? What ultimately drives physical and chemical changes in matter? The answer may surprise you. The driving force behind chemical and physical change in the universe is a quantity called *entropy,* which is related to the dispersion (or spreading out) of energy. Nature tends toward that state in which energy is spread out to the greatest extent possible. Although it does not seem obvious at first glance, the freezing of water below 0 °C, the dissolving of a solid into a solution, the neutralization of an acid by a base, and even the development of a person from an embryo all increase the entropy in the universe (they all result in greater energy dispersion). In our universe, entropy always increases.

In this clever illusion, it seems that the water can perpetually flow through the canal. However, perpetual motion is forbidden under the laws of thermodynamics.

17.1 Nature's Heat Tax: You Can't Win and You Can't Break Even

Energy transactions are like gambling—you walk into the casino with your pockets full of cash and (if you keep gambling long enough) you walk out empty-handed. In the long run, you lose money in gambling because the casino takes a cut on each transaction. So it is with energy. Nature takes a cut—sometimes called nature's heat tax—on every energy transaction so that, in the end, energy is dissipated.

Recall from Chapter 6 that, according to the first law of thermodynamics, energy is conserved in chemical processes. When we burn gasoline to run a car, for example, the amount of energy produced by the chemical reaction does not vanish, nor does any

▲ A rechargeable battery always requires more energy to charge than the energy available for work during discharging because some energy is always lost to the surroundings during the charging/discharging cycle.

See the box entitled *Redheffer's Perpetual Motion Machine* in Section 6.3.

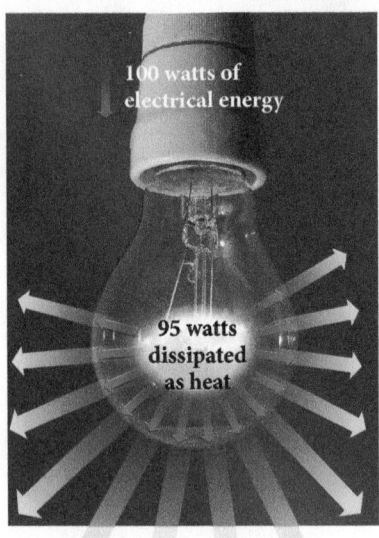

100 watts of electrical energy

95 watts dissipated as heat

5 watts emitted as light

▲ FIGURE 17.1 Energy Loss In most energy transactions, some energy is lost to the surroundings, so each transaction is only fractionally efficient.

new energy appear that was not present as potential energy (within the gasoline) before the combustion. Some of the energy from the combustion reaction goes toward driving the car forward (about 20%), and the rest is dissipated into the surroundings as heat (feel your engine after a drive if you doubt this). The total energy given off by the combustion reaction exactly equals the sum of the amount of energy that goes to propel the car and the amount dissipated as heat—energy is conserved. In other words, when it comes to energy, you can't win; you cannot create energy that was not there to begin with.

The picture becomes more interesting, however, when we consider the second law of thermodynamics. The second law—which we examine in more detail throughout this chapter—implies that not only can we not win in an energy transaction, we cannot even break even. For example, consider a rechargeable battery. Suppose that when we use the fully charged battery for some application, the energy from the battery does 100 kJ of work. Recharging the battery to its original state will *necessarily* (according to the second law of thermodynamics) require *more than* 100 kJ of energy. Energy is not destroyed during the cycle of discharging and recharging the battery, but some energy must be lost to the surroundings in order for the process to occur at all. Nature imposes a *heat tax,* an unavoidable cut of every energy transaction. The implications of the second law for energy use are significant. First of all, according to the second law, we cannot create a perpetual motion machine (a machine that perpetually moves *without any energy input).* If the machine is to be in motion, it must pay the heat tax with each cycle of its motion—over time, it will therefore run down and stop moving.

Secondly, in most energy transactions, not only is the "heat tax" lost to the surroundings, but additional energy is also lost as heat because real-world processes do not achieve the theoretically possible maximum efficiency (Figure 17.1 ◄). Consequently, the most efficient use of energy generally occurs with the smallest number of transactions. For example, heating your home with natural gas is generally cheaper and more efficient than heating it with electricity (Figure 17.2 ►). When you heat your home with natural gas, there is only one energy transaction—you burn the gas and the heat from the reaction warms the house. When you heat your home with electricity, several transactions occur. Most electricity is generated from the combustion of fossil fuels; the heat from the burning fuel boils water to create steam. The steam then turns a turbine on a generator to create electricity. The electricity travels from the power plant to your home, and some of the energy is lost as heat during the trip. Finally, the electricity runs the heater that generates heat. With each transaction, energy is lost to the surroundings, resulting in a less efficient use of energy than if you had burned natural gas directly.

Conceptual Connection 17.1 Nature's Heat Tax and Diet

Advocates of a vegetarian diet argue that the amount of cropland required for one person to maintain a meat-based diet is about 6–10 times greater than the amount required for the same person to maintain a vegetarian diet. Apply the concept of nature's heat tax to explain this assertion.

17.2 Spontaneous and Nonspontaneous Processes

A fundamental goal of thermodynamics is to predict *spontaneity.* For example, will rust spontaneously form when iron comes into contact with oxygen? Will water spontaneously decompose into hydrogen and oxygen? A **spontaneous process** is one that occurs *without ongoing outside intervention* (such as the performance of work by some external force). For example, when you drop a book in a gravitational field, it spontaneously drops to the floor. When you place a ball on a slope, it spontaneously rolls down the slope. For simple mechanical systems, such as the

Heating with Natural Gas

Heating with Electricity

▲ **FIGURE 17.2 Heating with Gas versus Heating with Electricity**   When natural gas heats a home, only a single energy transaction is involved, so the heat tax is minimized. When electricity is used to heat a home, a number of energy transactions are required, each of which involves some loss. The result is a much lower efficiency.

dropping of a book or the rolling of a ball, predicting spontaneity is fairly intuitive. A mechanical system tends toward lowest potential energy, which is usually easy to see (at least in *simple* mechanical systems). However, the prediction of spontaneity for chemical systems is not so intuitively obvious. To make these predictions, we need to develop a criterion for the spontaneity of chemical systems. In other words, we need to develop a *chemical potential* that predicts the direction of a chemical system, much as mechanical potential energy predicts the direction of a mechanical system (Figure 17.3 ▶).

We must not confuse the *spontaneity* of a chemical reaction with the *speed* of a chemical reaction. In thermodynamics, we study the *spontaneity* of a reaction—the direction in which and extent to which a chemical reaction proceeds. In kinetics, we

◀ Iron spontaneously rusts when it comes in contact with oxygen.

The Concept of Chemical Potential

Solid NaCl

Dissolved ions

(a)   (b)

▲ **FIGURE 17.3 Mechanical Potential Energy and Chemical Potential** **(a)** Mechanical potential energy predicts the direction in which a mechanical system will spontaneously move. **(b)** We seek a chemical potential that predicts the direction in which a chemical system will spontaneously move.

study the *speed* of the reaction—how fast a reaction takes place (Figure 17.4 ▶). A reaction may be thermodynamically spontaneous but kinetically slow at a given temperature. For example, the conversion of diamond to graphite is thermodynamically spontaneous. But your diamonds will not become worthless anytime soon, because the process is extremely slow kinetically. Although the rate of a spontaneous process can be increased by the use of a catalyst, a nonspontaneous process cannot be made spontaneous by the use of a catalyst. Catalysts affect only the rate of a reaction, not the spontaneity.

Spontaneous

Slow rate

▶ Even though graphite is thermodynamically more stable than diamond, the conversion of diamond to graphite is kinetically so slow that it does not occur at any measurable rate.

Diamond   Graphite

One last word about nonspontaneity—a nonspontaneous process is not *impossible*. For example, the extraction of iron metal from iron ore is a nonspontaneous process; it does not happen if the iron ore is left to itself, but that does not mean it is impossible. As we will see later in this chapter, a nonspontaneous process can be made spontaneous by coupling it to another process that is spontaneous or by supplying energy from an external source. Iron can be separated from its ore if external energy is supplied, usually by means of another reaction (that is itself highly spontaneous).

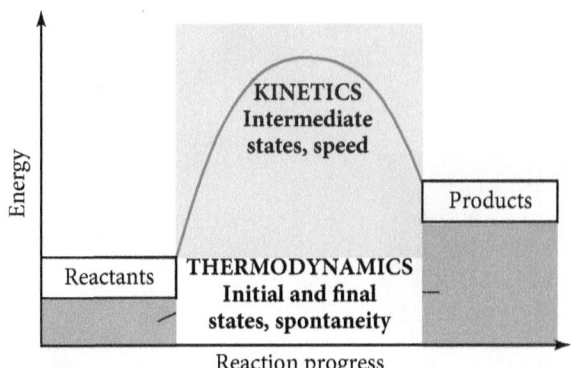

◀ **FIGURE 17.4 Thermodynamics and Kinetics** Thermodynamics deals with the relative chemical potentials of the reactants and products. It enables us to predict whether a reaction will be spontaneous and to calculate how much work it can do. Kinetics deals with the chemical potential of intermediate states and enables us to determine why a reaction is slow or fast.

17.3 Entropy and the Second Law of Thermodynamics

The first candidate in our search for a chemical potential might be enthalpy, which we defined in Chapter 6. Perhaps, just as a mechanical system proceeds in the direction of lowest potential energy, so a chemical system might proceed in the direction of lowest enthalpy. If this were the case, all exothermic reactions would be spontaneous and all endothermic reactions would not. However, although *most* spontaneous processes are exothermic, some spontaneous processes are *endothermic*. For example, above 0 °C, ice spontaneously melts (an endothermic process). So enthalpy must not be the sole criterion for spontaneity.

See Section 6.6 for the definition of enthalpy.

We can learn more about the driving force behind chemical reactions by considering several processes (like ice melting) that involve an increase in enthalpy. The processes listed here are energetically uphill (they are endothermic), yet they occur spontaneously. What drives them?

- the melting of ice above 0 °C
- the evaporation of liquid water to gaseous water
- the dissolution of sodium chloride in water

Each of these processes is endothermic *and* spontaneous. Do they have anything in common? Notice that, in each process, disorder or randomness increases. In the melting of ice, the arrangement of the water molecules changes from a highly ordered one (in ice) to a somewhat disorderly one (in liquid water).

The use of the word *disorder* here is analogous to our macroscopic notions of disorder. The definition of molecular disorder, which is covered shortly, is very specific.

$H_2O(s)$

Increasing entropy

$H_2O(l)$

◀ When ice melts, the arrangement of water molecules changes from orderly to more disorderly.

During the evaporation of a liquid to a gas, the arrangement changes from a *somewhat* disorderly one (atoms or molecules in the liquid) to a *highly* disorderly one (atoms or molecules in the gas).

▶ When water evaporates, the arrangement of water molecules becomes still more disorderly.

$H_2O(g)$

Increasing entropy

$H_2O(l)$

In the dissolution of a salt into water, the arrangement again changes from an orderly one (in which the ions in the salt occupy regular positions in the crystal lattice) to a more disorderly one (in which the ions are randomly dispersed throughout the liquid water).

$NaCl(aq)$

Increasing entropy

▶ When salt dissolves in water, the arrangement of the molecules and ions becomes more disorderly.

$NaCl(s)$

In all three of these processes, a quantity called *entropy*—related to disorder or randomness at the molecular level—increases.

Entropy

We have now hit upon the criterion for spontaneity in chemical systems: entropy. Informally, we can think of entropy as disorder or randomness. But the concept of disorder or randomness on the macroscopic scale—such as the messiness of a drawer—is only *analogous* to the concept of disorder or randomness on the molecular scale. Formally, **entropy**, abbreviated by the symbol S, has the following definition:

> **Entropy (S) is a thermodynamic function that increases with the number of *energetically equivalent* ways to arrange the components of a system to achieve a particular state.**

This definition was expressed mathematically by Ludwig Boltzmann in the 1870s as:

$$S = k \ln W$$

where k is the Boltzmann constant (the gas constant divided by Avogadro's number, $R/N_A = 1.38 \times 10^{-23}$ J/K) and W is the number of energetically equivalent ways to arrange the components of the system. Since W is unitless (it is simply a number), the units of entropy are joules per kelvin (J/K). We talk about the significance of the units shortly. As you can see from the equation, as W increases, entropy increases.

The key to understanding entropy is the quantity W. What does W—the number of energetically equivalent ways to arrange the components of the system—signify? Imagine a system of particles such as a fixed amount of an ideal gas. A given set of conditions (P, V, and T) defines the *state* (or *macrostate*) of the system. As long as these conditions remain constant, the energy of the system also remains constant. However, exactly where that energy is at any given instant is anything but constant.

At any one instant, a particular gas particle may have lots of kinetic energy. However, after a very short period of time, that particle may have only a little kinetic energy (because it lost its energy through collisions with other particles). The exact internal energy distribution among the particles at any one instant is sometimes referred to as a *microstate*. You can think of a microstate as a snapshot of the system at a given instant in time. The next instant, the snapshot (the microstate) changes. However, the *macrostate*—defined by P, V, and T—remains constant. A given macrostate can exist as a result of a large number of different microstates. In other words, the snapshot (or microstate) of a given macrostate is generally different from one moment to the next as the energy of the system is constantly redistributing itself among the particles of the system.

We can conceive of W in terms of microstates. The quantity, W, is the number of *possible* microstates that can result in a given macrostate. For example, suppose we have two systems (call them System A and System B), and that each is composed of two particles (one blue and one red). Both systems have a total energy of 4 joules, but System A has only one energy level and System B has two:

▲ Boltzmann's equation is engraved on his tombstone.

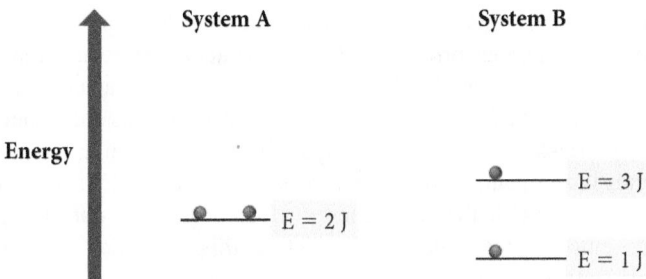

Each system has the same total energy (4 J), but System A has only one possible microstate (the red and the blue particle both occupying the 2 J energy level) while System B has a second possible microstate:

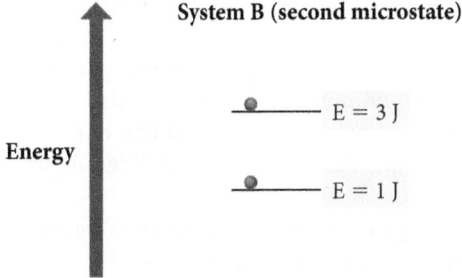

In this second microstate for System B, the blue particle has 3 J and the red one has 1 J (as opposed to System B's first microstate, where the energy of the particles is switched). This second microstate is not possible for System A because it has only one energy level. For System A, $W = 1$, but for System B, $W = 2$. In other words, System B has more microstates that result in the same 4 J macrostate. Since W is larger for System B than for

System A, System B has greater *entropy*; it has more *energetically equivalent ways to arrange the components of the system.*

We can understand an important aspect of entropy by turning our attention to energy for a moment. The entropy of a state increases with the number of *energetically equivalent* ways to arrange the components of the system to achieve that particular state. This implies that *the state with the highest entropy also has the greatest dispersal of energy.* Returning to our previous example, the energy of System B is dispersed over two energy levels instead of being confined to just one. At the heart of entropy is the concept of energy dispersal or energy randomization. *A state in which a given amount of energy is more highly dispersed (or more highly randomized) has more entropy than a state in which the same energy is more highly concentrated.*

Although we have already alluded to the **second law of thermodynamics**, we can now formally define it:

For any spontaneous process, the entropy of the *universe* increases ($\Delta S_{univ} > 0$).

The criterion for spontaneity is the entropy of the universe. Processes that increase the entropy of the universe—those that result in greater dispersal or randomization of energy—occur spontaneously. Processes that decrease the entropy of the universe do not occur spontaneously.

See the discussion of state functions in Section 6.3.

Entropy, like enthalpy, is a *state function*—its value depends only on the state of the system, not on how the system arrived at that state. Therefore, for any process, *the change in entropy is the entropy of the final state minus the entropy of the initial state.*

$$\Delta S = S_{final} - S_{initial}$$

Entropy determines the direction of chemical and physical change. *A chemical system proceeds in a direction that increases the entropy of the universe*—it proceeds in a direction that has the largest number of *energetically equivalent* ways to arrange its components.

See the discussion of work done by an expanding gas in Section 6.4.

To better understand this tendency, let us examine the expansion of an ideal gas into a vacuum (a spontaneous process with no associated change in enthalpy). Consider a flask containing an ideal gas that is connected to another, evacuated, flask by a tube equipped with a stopcock. When the stopcock is opened, the gas spontaneously expands into the evacuated flask. Since the gas is expanding into a vacuum, the pressure against which it expands is zero, and therefore the work ($w = -P_{ext}\Delta V$) is also zero.

However, even though the total energy of the gas does not change during the expansion, the entropy does change. To picture this, consider a simplified system containing only four gas atoms.

When the stopcock is opened, several possible energetically equivalent final states may result, each with the four atoms distributed in a different way. For example, there could be three atoms in the flask on the left and one in the flask on the right, or vice versa. For simplicity, we consider only the possibilities shown at left: state A, state B, and state C.

Since the energy of any one atom is the same in either flask, and since the atoms do not interact, states A, B, and C are energetically equivalent.

Now we ask the following question for each state: how many microstates give rise to the same macrostate? To keep track of the microstates we label the atoms 1–4. Although they have different numbered labels, since the atoms are all the same, there is externally no difference between them. For states A and B, only one microstate results in the specified macrostate—atoms 1–4 on the left side or the right side, respectively.

Macrostate   **Microstates**

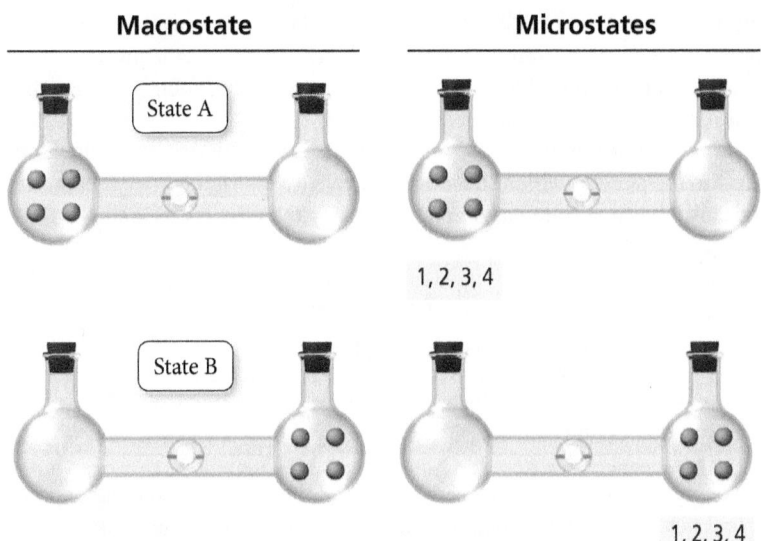

1, 2, 3, 4

1, 2, 3, 4

For state C, however, six different possible microstates all result in the same macrostate (two atoms on each side).

Macrostate   **Microstates**

This means that if the atoms are just randomly moving between the two flasks, the statistical probability of finding the atoms in state C is six times greater than the probability of finding the atoms in state A or state B. Consequently, even for a simple system consisting of only four atoms, the atoms are most likely to be found in state C. State C has the greatest entropy—it has the greatest number of energetically equivalent ways to distribute its components.

As the number of atoms increases, the number of microstates that leads to the atoms being equally distributed between the two flasks increases dramatically. For example, with 10 atoms, the number of microstates leading to an equal distribution of atoms between two flasks is 252 and with 20 atoms the number of microstates is 184,756. Yet, the number of microstates that leads to all of the atoms being only in the left flask

In these drawings, the exact location of an atom within a flask is insignificant. The significant aspect is whether the atom is in the left flask or the right flask.

For n particles, the number of ways to put r particles in one flask and $n-r$ particles in the other flask is $n!/[(n-r)!r!]$. For 10 atoms, $n = 10$ and $r = 5$.

(or all only in the right flask) does not increase—it is always only 1. In other words, the arrangement in which the atoms are equally distributed between the two flasks has a much larger number of possible microstates and therefore much greater entropy. The system thus tends toward that state.

The *change in entropy* in transitioning from a state in which all of the atoms are in the left flask to the state in which the atoms are evenly distributed between both flasks is *positive* because the final state has a greater entropy than the initial state:

$$\Delta S = S_{\text{final}} - S_{\text{initial}}$$

Entropy of state in which atoms are distributed between both flasks

Entropy of state in which atoms are all in one flask

Since S_{final} is greater than S_{initial}, ΔS is positive and the process is spontaneous according to the second law. Notice that when the atoms are confined to one flask, their energy is also confined to that one flask; however, when the atoms are evenly distributed between both flasks, their energy is spread out over a greater volume. As the gas expands into the empty flask, energy is dispersed.

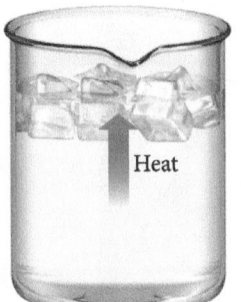

Heat

The second law explains many phenomena not explained by the first law. In Chapter 6, we learned that heat travels from a substance at higher temperature to one at lower temperature. For example, if we drop an ice cube into water, heat travels from the water to the ice cube—the water cools and the ice warms (and eventually melts). Why? The first law would not prohibit some heat from flowing the other way—from the ice to the water. The ice could lose 10 J of heat (cooling even more) and the water could gain 10 J of heat (warming even more). The first law of thermodynamics would not be violated by such a heat transfer. Imagine putting ice into water only to have the water get warmer as it absorbed thermal energy from the ice! It will never happen because heat transfer from cold to hot violates the second law of thermodynamics. According to the second law, energy is dispersed, not concentrated. The transfer of heat from a substance of higher temperature to one of lower temperature results in greater energy randomization—the energy that was concentrated in the hot substance becomes dispersed between the two substances. The second law accounts for this pervasive tendency.

Conceptual Connection 17.2 Entropy

Consider these three changes in the possible distributions of six gaseous particles within three interconnected boxes. Which change has a positive ΔS?

The Entropy Change Associated with a Change in State

The entropy of a sample of matter *increases* as it changes state from a solid to a liquid or from a liquid to a gas (Figure 17.5 ▶). We can informally think of this increase in entropy by analogy with macroscopic disorder. The gaseous state is more disorderly than

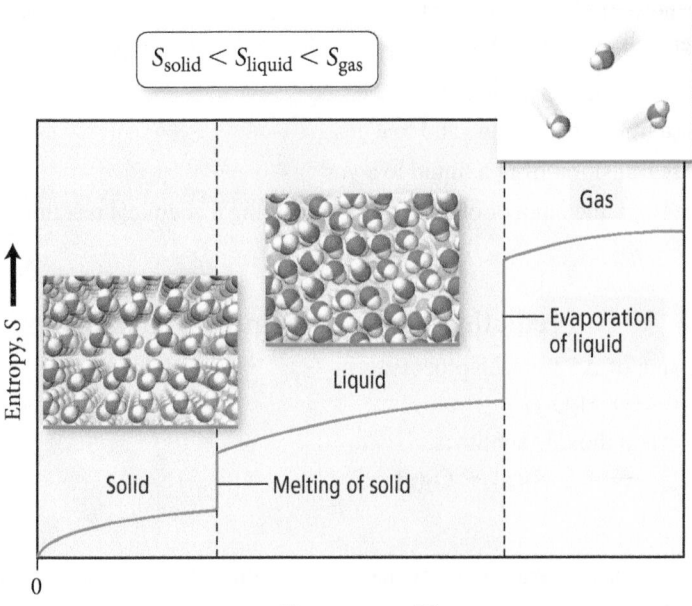

$$S_{\text{solid}} < S_{\text{liquid}} < S_{\text{gas}}$$

◀ **FIGURE 17.5 Entropy and State Change** Entropy increases when matter changes from a solid to a liquid and from a liquid to a gas.

the liquid state, which is in turn more disorderly than the solid state. More formally, however, the differences in entropy are related to the number of energetically equivalent ways of arranging the particles in each state—there are more in the gas than in the liquid, and more in the liquid than in the solid.

A gas has more energetically equivalent configurations because it has more ways to distribute its energy than a solid. The energy in a molecular solid consists largely of the vibrations between its molecules. If the same substance is vaporized, however, the energy can take the form of straight-line motions of the molecules (called translational energy) and rotations of the molecules (called rotational energy). In other words, when a solid vaporizes into a gas, there are new "places" to put energy (Figure 17.6 ▼). The gas thus has more possible microstates (more energetically equivalent configurations) than the solid and therefore a greater entropy.

Additional "Places" for Energy

▲ **FIGURE 17.6 "Places" for Energy** In the solid state, energy is contained largely in the vibrations between molecules. In the gas state, energy can be contained in both the straight-line motion of molecules (translational energy) and the rotation of molecules (rotational energy).

We can now predict the sign of ΔS for processes involving changes of state (or phase). In general, entropy increases ($\Delta S > 0$) for each of the following:

- the phase transition from a solid to a liquid
- the phase transition from a solid to a gas
- the phase transition from a liquid to a gas
- an increase in the number of moles of a gas during a chemical reaction

EXAMPLE 17.1   Predicting the Sign of Entropy Change

Predict the sign of ΔS for each process:

(a) $H_2O(g) \longrightarrow H_2O(l)$

(b) Solid carbon dioxide sublimes.

(c) $2\ N_2O(g) \longrightarrow 2\ N_2(g) + O_2(g)$

SOLUTION

(a) Since a gas has a greater entropy than a liquid, the entropy decreases and ΔS is negative.

(b) Since a solid has a lower entropy than a gas, the entropy increases and ΔS is positive.

(c) Since the number of moles of gas increases, the entropy increases and ΔS is positive.

FOR PRACTICE 17.1

Predict the sign of ΔS for each process:

(a) the boiling of water

(b) $I_2(g) \longrightarrow I_2(s)$

(c) $CaCO_3(s) \longrightarrow CaO(s) + CO_2(g)$

17.4 Heat Transfer and Changes in the Entropy of the Surroundings

We have now seen that the criterion for spontaneity is an increase in the entropy of the universe. However, you can probably think of several spontaneous processes in which entropy seems to decrease. For example, when water freezes at temperatures below 0 °C, the entropy of the water decreases, yet the process is spontaneous. Similarly, when water vapor in air condenses into fog on a cold night, the entropy of the water also decreases. Why are these processes spontaneous?

To answer this question, we must return to the second law: for any spontaneous process, the entropy *of the universe* increases ($\Delta S_{univ} > 0$). Even though the entropy *of the water* decreases during freezing and condensation, the entropy *of the universe* must somehow increase in order for these processes to be spontaneous. In Chapter 6, we distinguished between a thermodynamic system and its surroundings. The same distinction is useful in our discussion of entropy. For the freezing of water, let us consider the system to be the water. The surroundings are then the rest of the universe. Accordingly, ΔS_{sys} is the entropy change for the water itself, ΔS_{surr} is the entropy change for the surroundings, and ΔS_{univ} is the entropy change for the universe. The entropy change for the universe is the sum of the entropy changes for the system and the surroundings:

$$\Delta S_{univ} = \Delta S_{sys} + \Delta S_{surr}$$

The second law states that the entropy of the universe must increase ($\Delta S_{univ} > 0$) for a process to be spontaneous. The entropy of the *system* can decrease ($\Delta S_{sys} < 0$) as long as the entropy of the *surroundings* increases by a greater amount ($\Delta S_{surr} > -\Delta S_{sys}$), so that the overall entropy of the *universe* undergoes a net increase.

For liquid water freezing or water vapor condensing, we know that the change in entropy for the system (ΔS_{sys}) is negative because the water becomes more orderly in both cases.

For ΔS_{univ} to be positive, therefore, ΔS_{surr} must be positive and greater in absolute value (or magnitude) than ΔS_{sys} as shown graphically here:

$$\Delta S_{univ} = \Delta S_{sys} + \Delta S_{surr}$$

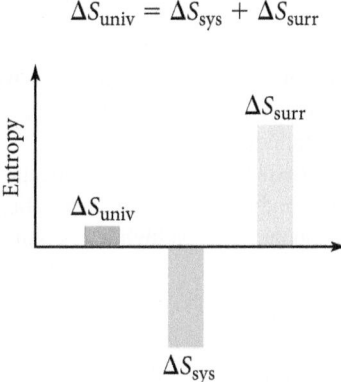

But why does the freezing of ice or the condensation of water increase the entropy of the surroundings? Because both processes are *exothermic:* they give off heat to the surroundings. Because we think of entropy as the dispersal or randomization of energy, *the release of heat energy by the system disperses that energy into the surroundings, increasing the entropy of the surroundings.* The freezing of water below 0 °C and the condensation of water vapor on a cold night both increase the entropy of the universe because the heat given off to the surroundings increases the entropy of the surroundings to a sufficient degree to overcome the entropy decrease in the water.

Even though (as we saw earlier) enthalpy by itself cannot determine spontaneity, the increase in the entropy of the surroundings caused by the release of heat explains why exothermic processes are so *often* spontaneous.

Summarizing Entropy Changes in the Surroundings:

▶ An exothermic process increases the entropy of the surroundings.

▶ An endothermic process decreases the entropy of the surroundings.

The Temperature Dependence of ΔS_{surr}

We have just seen how the freezing of water increases the entropy of the surroundings by dispersing heat energy into the surroundings. Yet we know that the freezing of water is not spontaneous at all temperatures. The freezing of water becomes *nonspontaneous* above 0 °C. Why? Because the magnitude of the increase in the entropy of the surroundings due to the dispersal of energy into the surroundings is *temperature dependent.*

The greater the temperature, the smaller the increase in entropy for a given amount of energy dispersed into the surroundings. Recall that the units of entropy are joules per kelvin: energy units divided by temperature units. *Entropy is a measure of energy dispersal (joules) per unit temperature (kelvins).* The higher the temperature, the lower the amount of entropy for a given amount of energy dispersed. We can understand the temperature dependence of entropy changes due to heat flow with a simple analogy. Imagine that you have $1000 to give away. If you gave the $1000 to a rich man, the impact on his net worth would be negligible (because he already has so much money). If you gave the same $1000 to a poor man, however, his net worth would change substantially (because he has so little money). Similarly, if you disperse 1000 J of energy into surroundings that are hot, the entropy increase is small (because the impact of the 1000 J is small on surroundings that already contain a lot of energy). If you disperse the same 1000 J of energy into surroundings that are cold, however, the entropy increase is large (because the impact of the 1000 J is great on surroundings that contain little energy). For this same reason, the impact of the heat released to the surroundings by the freezing of water depends on the temperature of the surroundings—the higher the temperature, the smaller the impact.

We can now understand why water spontaneously freezes at low temperature but not at high temperature. For the freezing of liquid water into ice, the change in entropy of the system is negative at all temperatures:

$$\Delta S_{\text{univ}} = \Delta S_{\text{sys}} + \Delta S_{\text{surr}}$$

Negative   Positive and large at low temperature
Positive and small at high temperature

At low temperatures, the decrease in entropy of the system is overcome by the large increase in the entropy of the surroundings (a positive quantity), resulting in a positive ΔS_{univ} and a spontaneous process. At high temperatures, on the other hand, the decrease in entropy of the system is not overcome by the increase in entropy of the surroundings (because the magnitude of the positive ΔS_{surr} is smaller at higher temperatures), resulting in a negative ΔS_{univ}; therefore, the freezing of water is not spontaneous at high temperature as shown graphically here:

$$\Delta S_{\text{univ}} = \Delta S_{\text{sys}} + \Delta S_{\text{surr}} \quad \text{(for water freezing)}$$

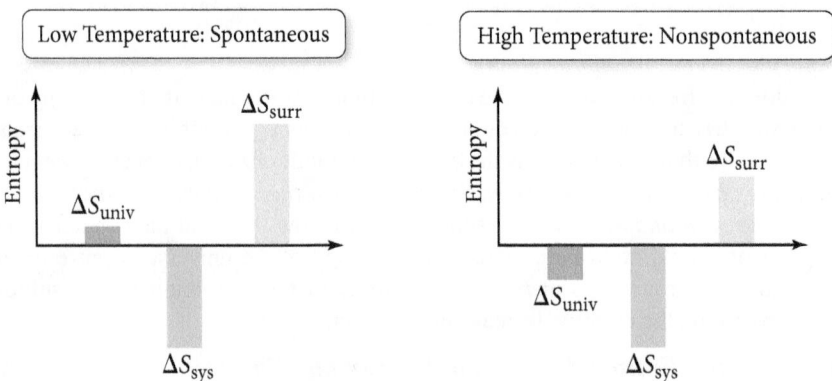

Quantifying Entropy Changes in the Surroundings

We have seen that when a system exchanges heat with the surroundings, it changes the entropy of the surroundings. At constant pressure, we can use q_{sys} to quantify the change in *entropy* for the surroundings (ΔS_{surr}). In general,

- a process that emits heat into the surroundings (q_{sys} negative) *increases* the entropy of the surroundings (positive ΔS_{surr}).
- a process that absorbs heat from the surroundings (q_{sys} positive) *decreases* the entropy of the surroundings (negative ΔS_{surr}).
- the magnitude of the change in entropy of the surroundings is proportional to the magnitude of q_{sys}.

We can summarize these three points with the proportionality:

$$\Delta S_{\text{surr}} \propto -q_{\text{sys}} \qquad [17.1]$$

We have also seen that, for a given amount of heat exchanged with the surroundings, the magnitude of ΔS_{surr} is inversely proportional to the temperature. In general, the higher the temperature, the lower the magnitude of ΔS_{surr} for a given amount of heat exchanged:

$$\Delta S_{\text{surr}} \propto \frac{1}{T} \qquad [17.2]$$

Combining the proportionalities in Equations 17.1 and 17.2, we get the following general expression at constant temperature:

$$\Delta S_{\text{surr}} = \frac{-q_{\text{sys}}}{T}$$

For any chemical or physical process occurring at constant temperature and pressure, the entropy change of the surroundings is equal to the energy dispersed into the surroundings ($-q_{\text{sys}}$) divided by the temperature of the surroundings in kelvins.

This equation provides insight into why exothermic processes have a tendency to be spontaneous at low temperatures—they increase the entropy of the surroundings. As temperature increases, however, a given negative q produces a smaller positive ΔS_{surr}; thus, exothermicity becomes less of a determining factor for spontaneity as temperature increases.

Under conditions of constant pressure $q_{sys} = \Delta H_{sys}$; therefore,

$$\Delta S_{surr} = \frac{-\Delta H_{sys}}{T} \qquad \text{(constant } P, T) \qquad [17.3]$$

EXAMPLE 17.2 Calculating Entropy Changes in the Surroundings

Consider the combustion of propane gas:

$$C_3H_8(g) + 5\,O_2(g) \longrightarrow 3\,CO_2(g) + 4\,H_2O(g) \qquad \Delta H_{rxn} = -2044 \text{ kJ}$$

(a) Calculate the entropy change in the surroundings associated with this reaction occurring at 25 °C.

(b) Determine the sign of the entropy change for the system.

(c) Determine the sign of the entropy change for the universe. Will the reaction be spontaneous?

SOLUTION

(a) The entropy change of the surroundings is given by Equation 17.3. Substitute the value of ΔH_{rxn} and the temperature in kelvins and calculate ΔS_{surr}.	$T = 273 + 25 = 298$ K $\Delta S_{surr} = \dfrac{-\Delta H_{rxn}}{T}$ $= \dfrac{-(-2044 \text{ kJ})}{298 \text{ K}}$ $= +6.86 \text{ kJ/K}$ $= +6.86 \times 10^3 \text{ J/K}$
(b) Determine the number of moles of gas on each side of the reaction. An increase in the number of moles of gas implies a positive ΔS_{sys}.	$C_3H_8(g) + 5\,O_2(g) \longrightarrow 3\,CO_2(g) + 4\,H_2O(g)$ 6 mol gas 7 mol gas ΔS_{sys} is positive.
(c) The change in entropy of the universe is the sum of the entropy changes of the system and the surroundings. If the entropy changes of the system and surroundings are both the same sign, the entropy change for the universe also has the same sign.	$\Delta S_{univ} = \Delta S_{sys} + \Delta S_{surr}$ Positive Positive Therefore, ΔS_{univ} is positive and the reaction is spontaneous.

FOR PRACTICE 17.2

Consider the reaction between nitrogen and oxygen gas to form dinitrogen monoxide:

$$2\,N_2(g) + O_2(g) \longrightarrow 2\,N_2O(g) \qquad \Delta H_{rxn} = +163.2 \text{ kJ}$$

(a) Calculate the entropy change in the surroundings associated with this reaction occurring at 25 °C.

(b) Determine the sign of the entropy change for the system.

(c) Determine the sign of the entropy change for the universe. Will the reaction be spontaneous?

FOR MORE PRACTICE 17.2

A reaction has $\Delta H_{rxn} = -107$ kJ and $\Delta S_{rxn} = 285$ J/K. At what temperature is the change in entropy for the reaction equal to the change in entropy for the surroundings?

Conceptual Connection 17.3 Entropy and Biological Systems

Do biological systems contradict the second law of thermodynamics? By taking energy from their surroundings and synthesizing large, complex biological molecules, plants and animals tend to concentrate energy, not disperse it. How can this be so?

17.5 Gibbs Free Energy

Equation 17.3 establishes a relationship between the enthalpy change in a system and the entropy change in the surroundings. Recall that for any process the entropy change of the universe is the sum of the entropy change of the system and the entropy change of the surroundings:

$$\Delta S_{univ} = \Delta S_{sys} + \Delta S_{surr} \qquad [17.4]$$

Combining Equation 17.4 with Equation 17.3 gives us the following relationship at constant temperature and pressure:

$$\Delta S_{univ} = \Delta S_{sys} - \frac{\Delta H_{sys}}{T} \qquad [17.5]$$

Using Equation 17.5, we can calculate ΔS_{univ} while focusing only on the *system*. If we multiply Equation 17.5 by $-T$, we arrive at the expression:

$$-T\Delta S_{univ} = -T\Delta S_{sys} + T\frac{\Delta H_{sys}}{T}$$

$$= \Delta H_{sys} - T\Delta S_{sys} \qquad [17.6]$$

If we drop the subscript *sys*—from now on ΔH and ΔS without subscripts mean ΔH_{sys} and ΔS_{sys}—we get the expression:

$$-T\Delta S_{univ} = \Delta H - T\Delta S \qquad [17.7]$$

The right hand side of Equation 17.7 represents the change in a thermodynamic function called *Gibbs free energy*. The formal definition of **Gibbs free energy (G)** is:

$$G = H - TS \qquad [17.8]$$

where H is enthalpy, T is the temperature in kelvins, and S is entropy. The *change* in Gibbs free energy, symbolized by ΔG, is expressed as follows (at constant temperature):

$$\Delta G = \Delta H - T\Delta S \qquad [17.9]$$

If we combine Equations 17.7 and 17.9, we have an equation that makes clear the significance of ΔG:

$$\Delta G = -T\Delta S_{univ} \quad \text{(constant } T, P) \qquad [17.10]$$

The change in Gibbs free energy for a process occurring at constant temperature and pressure is proportional to the negative of ΔS_{univ}. Since ΔS_{univ} is a criterion for spontaneity, ΔG is also a criterion for spontaneity (although opposite in sign). In fact, Gibbs free energy is also called *chemical potential* because it is analogous to mechanical potential energy discussed earlier. Just as mechanical systems tend toward lower potential energy, so chemical systems tend toward lower Gibbs free energy (toward lower chemical potential) (Figure 17.7 ▶).

Summarizing Gibbs Free Energy (at Constant Temperature and Pressure):

▶ ΔG is proportional to the negative of ΔS_{univ}.

▶ A decrease in Gibbs free energy ($\Delta G < 0$) corresponds to a spontaneous process.

▶ An increase in Gibbs free energy ($\Delta G > 0$) corresponds to a nonspontaneous process.

**Gibbs Free Energy Determines the
Direction of Spontaneous Change**

$$N_2(g) + 3\,H_2(g) \;\rightleftharpoons\; 2\,NH_3(g)$$

Pure
$N_2 + H_2$

Free energy

Spontaneous   Spontaneous

Pure NH_3

$Q < K$ $Q > K$

Equilibrium
mixture
$(Q = K)$

◀ FIGURE 17.7 **Gibbs Free
Energy**   Gibbs free energy is also
called chemical potential because
it determines the direction of
spontaneous change for
chemical systems.

Notice that we can calculate changes in Gibbs free energy solely with reference to the system. So, to determine whether a process is spontaneous, we only have to find the change in *entropy* for the system (ΔS) and the change in *enthalpy* for the system (ΔH). We can then predict the spontaneity of the process at any temperature. In Chapter 6, we learned how to calculate changes in enthalpy (ΔH) for chemical reactions. In Section 17.6, we learn how to calculate changes in entropy (ΔS) for chemical reactions. We can then use those two quantities to calculate changes in free energy (ΔG) for chemical reactions and predict their spontaneity (Section 17.7). Before we move on to these matters, however, let us examine some examples that demonstrate how ΔH, ΔS, and T affect the spontaneity of chemical processes.

The Effect of ΔH, ΔS, and T on Spontaneity

Case 1: ΔH Negative, ΔS Positive If a reaction is exothermic ($\Delta H < 0$), and if the change in entropy for the reaction is positive ($\Delta S > 0$), then the change in free energy is negative at all temperatures and the reaction is spontaneous at all temperatures.

$$\Delta G = \Delta H - T\,\Delta S$$

Negative at   Negative   Positive
all temperatures

As an example, consider the dissociation of N_2O:

$$2\,N_2O(g) \longrightarrow 2\,N_2(g) + O_2(g) \qquad \Delta H^{\circ}_{rxn} = -163.2\ \text{kJ}$$

2 mol gas   3 mol gas

The change in *enthalpy* is negative—heat is emitted, increasing the entropy of the surroundings. The change in *entropy* for the reaction is positive, which means that the entropy of the system increases. (We can see that the change in entropy is positive from the balanced equation—the number of moles of gas increases.) Since the entropy of both the system and the surroundings increases, the entropy of the universe must also increase, making the reaction spontaneous at all temperatures.

Recall from Chapter 6 that ΔH° represents the standard enthalpy change. The definition of the standard state was first given in Section 6.9 and is summarized in Section 17.6.

Case 2: ΔH Positive, ΔS Negative If a reaction is endothermic ($\Delta H > 0$), and if the change in entropy for the reaction is negative ($\Delta S < 0$), then the change in free energy is positive at all temperatures and the reaction is nonspontaneous at all temperatures.

$$\Delta G = \Delta H - T\,\Delta S$$

| Positive at all temperatures | Positive | Negative |

As an example, consider the formation of ozone from oxygen:

$$3\ O_2(g) \longrightarrow 2\ O_3(g) \quad \Delta H^\circ_{rxn} = +285.4\ \text{kJ}$$
$$\text{3 mol gas} \qquad\quad \text{2 mol gas}$$

The change in *enthalpy* is positive—heat is therefore absorbed, *decreasing* the entropy of the surroundings. The change in *entropy* is negative, which means that the entropy of the system decreases. (We can see that the change in entropy is negative from the balanced equation—the number of moles of gas decreases.) Since the entropy of both the system and the surroundings decreases, the entropy of the universe must also decrease, making the reaction nonspontaneous at all temperatures.

Case 3: ΔH Negative, ΔS Negative If a reaction is exothermic ($\Delta H < 0$), and if the change in entropy for the reaction is negative ($\Delta S < 0$), then the sign of the change in free energy depends on temperature. The reaction is spontaneous at low temperature, but nonspontaneous at high temperature.

$$\Delta G = \Delta H - T\,\Delta S$$

| Negative at low temperatures Positive at high temperatures | Negative | Negative |

As an example, consider the freezing of liquid water to form ice:

$$H_2O(l) \longrightarrow H_2O(s) \qquad \Delta H^\circ = -6.01\ \text{kJ}$$

The change in *enthalpy* is negative—heat is emitted, increasing the entropy of the surroundings. The change in *entropy* is negative, which means that the entropy of the system decreases. (We can see that the change in entropy is negative from the balanced equation—a liquid turns into a solid.)

Unlike the two previous cases, where the changes in *entropy* of the system and of the surroundings had the same sign, the changes here are opposite in sign. Therefore, the sign of the change in free energy depends on the relative magnitudes of the two changes. At a low enough temperature, the heat emitted into the surroundings causes a large entropy change in the surroundings, making the process spontaneous. At high temperature, the same amount of heat is dispersed into warmer surroundings, so the positive entropy change in the surroundings is smaller, resulting in a nonspontaneous process.

Case 4: ΔH Positive, ΔS Positive If a reaction is endothermic ($\Delta H > 0$), and if the change in entropy for the reaction is positive ($\Delta S > 0$), then the sign of the change in free energy again depends on temperature. The reaction is nonspontaneous at low temperature but spontaneous at high temperature.

$$\Delta G = \Delta H - T\,\Delta S$$

| Positive at low temperatures Negative at high temperatures | Positive | Positive |

As an example, consider the vaporizing of liquid water to gaseous water:

$$H_2O(l) \longrightarrow H_2O(g) \qquad \Delta H^\circ = +40.7\ \text{kJ (at 100 °C)}$$

The change in *enthalpy* is positive—heat is absorbed from the surroundings, so the entropy of the surroundings decreases. The change in *entropy* is positive, which means that the entropy of the system increases. (We can see that the change in entropy is

TABLE 17.1 The Effect of ΔH, ΔS, and T on Spontaneity

ΔH	ΔS	Low Temperature	High Temperature	Example
−	+	Spontaneous ($\Delta G < 0$)	Spontaneous ($\Delta G < 0$)	$2\,N_2O(g) \longrightarrow 2\,N_2(g) + O_2(g)$
+	−	Nonspontaneous ($\Delta G > 0$)	Nonspontaneous ($\Delta G > 0$)	$3\,O_2(g) \longrightarrow 2\,O_3(g)$
−	−	Spontaneous ($\Delta G < 0$)	Nonspontaneous ($\Delta G > 0$)	$H_2O(l) \longrightarrow H_2O(s)$
+	+	Nonspontaneous ($\Delta G > 0$)	Spontaneous ($\Delta G < 0$)	$H_2O(l) \longrightarrow H_2O(g)$

positive from the balanced equation—a liquid turns into a gas.) The changes in entropy of the system and the surroundings again have opposite signs, only this time the entropy of the surroundings decreases while the entropy of the system increases. In cases such as this, high temperature favors spontaneity because the absorption of heat from the surroundings has less effect on the entropy of the surroundings as temperature increases.

The results of this section are summarized in Table 17.1. Notice that when ΔH and ΔS have opposite signs, the spontaneity of the reaction does not depend on temperature. *When ΔH and ΔS have the same sign, however, the spontaneity does depend on temperature.* The temperature at which the reaction changes from being spontaneous to being nonspontaneous (or vice versa) is the temperature at which ΔG changes sign, which can be found by setting $\Delta G = 0$ and solving for T, as shown in part b of Example 17.3.

EXAMPLE 17.3 Computing Gibbs Free Energy Changes and Predicting Spontaneity from ΔH and ΔS

Consider the reaction for the decomposition of carbon tetrachloride gas:

$$CCl_4(g) \longrightarrow C(s, \text{graphite}) + 2\,Cl_2(g) \qquad \Delta H = +95.7\ kJ;\ \Delta S = +142.2\ J/K$$

(a) Calculate ΔG at 25 °C and determine whether the reaction is spontaneous.

(b) If the reaction is not spontaneous at 25 °C, determine at what temperature (if any) the reaction becomes spontaneous.

SOLUTION

(a) Use Equation 17.9 to calculate ΔG from the given values of ΔH and ΔS. The temperature must be in kelvins. *Be sure to express both ΔH and ΔS in the same units (usually joules).*

$$T = 273 + 25 = 298\ K$$
$$\Delta G = \Delta H - T\Delta S$$
$$= 95.7 \times 10^3\ J - (298\ K)142.2\ J/K$$
$$= 95.7 \times 10^3\ J - 42.4 \times 10^3\ J$$
$$= +53.3 \times 10^3\ J$$

The reaction is not spontaneous.

(b) Since ΔS is positive, ΔG becomes more negative with increasing temperature. To determine the temperature at which the reaction becomes spontaneous, use Equation 17.9 to find the temperature at which ΔG changes from positive to negative (set $\Delta G = 0$ and solve for T). The reaction is spontaneous above this temperature.

$$\Delta G = \Delta H - T\,\Delta S$$
$$0 = 95.7 \times 10^3\ J - (T)142.2\ J/K$$
$$T = \frac{95.7 \times 10^3\ J}{142.2\ J/K}$$
$$= 673\ K$$

FOR PRACTICE 17.3

Consider the reaction:

$$C_2H_4(g) + H_2(g) \longrightarrow C_2H_6(g) \qquad \Delta H = -137.5\ kJ;\ \Delta S = -120.5\ J/K$$

Calculate ΔG at 25 °C and determine whether the reaction is spontaneous. Does ΔG become more negative or more positive as the temperature increases?

Conceptual Connection 17.4 ΔH, ΔS, and ΔG

Which statement is true regarding the sublimation of dry ice (solid CO_2)?

(a) ΔH is positive, ΔS is positive, and ΔG is positive at low temperature and negative at high temperature.

(b) ΔH is negative, ΔS is negative, and ΔG is negative at low temperature and positive at high temperature.

(c) ΔH is negative, ΔS is positive, and ΔG is negative at all temperatures.

(d) ΔH is positive, ΔS is negative, and ΔG is positive at all temperatures.

17.6 Entropy Changes in Chemical Reactions: Calculating ΔS°_{rxn}

In Chapter 6, we learned how to calculate standard changes in enthalpy (ΔH°_{rxn}) for chemical reactions. We now turn to calculating standard changes in *entropy* for chemical reactions. Recall from Section 6.9 that the standard enthalpy change for a reaction (ΔH°_{rxn}) is the change in enthalpy for a process in which all reactants and products are in their standard states. Recall also the definition of the standard state:

- *For a Gas:* The standard state for a gas is the pure gas at a pressure of exactly 1 atm.

- *For a Liquid or Solid:* The standard state for a liquid or solid is the pure substance in its most stable form at a pressure of 1 atm and at the temperature of interest (often taken to be 25 °C).

- *For a Substance in Solution:* The standard state for a substance in solution is a concentration of 1 M.

> The standard state has recently been changed to a pressure of 1 bar, which is very close to 1 atm (1 atm = 1.013 bar). Both standards are now in common use.

We now define the **standard entropy change for a reaction (ΔS°_{rxn})** as the change in *entropy* for a process in which all reactants and products are in their standard states. Since entropy is a function of state, the standard change in entropy is therefore the standard entropy of the products minus the standard entropy of the reactants:

$$\Delta S^\circ_{rxn} = S^\circ_{products} - S^\circ_{reactants}$$

But how do we find the standard entropies of the reactants and products? Recall from Chapter 6 that we defined *standard molar enthalpies of formation (ΔH°_f)* to use in calculating ΔH°_{rxn}. We now need to define **standard molar entropies (S°)** to use in calculating ΔS°_{rxn}.

Standard Molar Entropies (S°) and the Third Law of Thermodynamics

In Chapter 6, we defined a *relative* zero for enthalpy. To do this, we assigned a value of zero to the standard enthalpy of formation for an element in its standard state. This was necessary because absolute values of enthalpy cannot be determined. In other words, for enthalpy, there is no absolute zero against which to measure all other values; therefore, we always have to rely on enthalpy changes from an arbitrarily assigned standard (the elements in their standard states and most stable forms). For entropy, however, *there is an absolute zero*. The absolute zero of entropy is established by the **third law of thermodynamics**, which states:

The entropy of a perfect crystal at absolute zero (0 K) is zero.

A perfect crystal at a temperature of absolute zero has only one possible way ($W = 1$) to arrange its components (Figure 17.8 ◄). Based on Boltzmann's definition of entropy ($S = k \ln W$), its entropy is zero ($S = k \ln 1 = 0$).

We can measure all entropy values against the absolute zero of entropy as defined by the third law. Table 17.2 lists values of standard entropies at 25 °C for selected substances. A more complete list can be found in Appendix IIB. Standard entropy values are listed in units of joules per mole per kelvin (J/mol·K). The units of mole in the

Perfect crystal at 0 K
$W = 1$ $S = 0$

▲ FIGURE 17.8 Zero Entropy
A perfect crystal at 0 K has only one possible way to arrange its components.

TABLE 17.2 Standard Molar Entropy Values (S°) for Selected Substances at 298 K

Substance	S°(J/mol·K)	Substance	S°(J/mol·K)	Substance	S°(J/mol·K)
Gases		**Liquids**		**Solids**	
$H_2(g)$	130.7	$H_2O(l)$	70.0	$MgO(s)$	27.0
$Ar(g)$	154.8	$CH_3OH(l)$	126.8	$Fe(s)$	27.3
$CH_4(g)$	186.3	$Br_2(l)$	152.2	$Li(s)$	29.1
$H_2O(g)$	188.8	$C_6H_6(l)$	173.4	$Cu(s)$	33.2
$N_2(g)$	191.6			$Na(s)$	51.3
$NH_3(g)$	192.8			$K(s)$	64.7
$F_2(g)$	202.8			$NaCl(s)$	72.1
$O_2(g)$	205.2			$CaCO_3(s)$	91.7
$Cl_2(g)$	223.1			$FeCl_3(s)$	142.3
$C_2H_4(g)$	219.3				

denominator is required because *entropy is an extensive property*—it depends on the amount of the substance.

At 25 °C, the standard entropy of any substance is the energy dispersed into one mole of that substance at 25 °C, which depends on the number of "places" to put energy within the substance. The factors that affect the number of "places" to put energy—and therefore the standard entropy—include the state of the substance, the molar mass of the substance, the particular allotrope, its molecular complexity, and its extent of dissolution. Let's examine each of these separately.

Some elements exist in two or more forms, called *allotropes*, within the same state.

Relative Standard Entropies: Gases, Liquids, and Solids As we saw in Section 17.3, the entropy of a gas is generally greater than the entropy of a liquid, which is in turn greater than the entropy of a solid. We can see these trends in the tabulated values of standard entropies. For example, consider the relative standard entropies of liquid water and gaseous water at 25 °C:

	S°(J/mol·K)
$H_2O(l)$	70.0
$H_2O(g)$	188.8

Gaseous water has a much greater standard entropy because, as we discussed in Section 17.3, it has more energetically equivalent ways to arrange its components, which in turn results in greater energy dispersal at 25 °C.

Relative Standard Entropies: Molar Mass Consider the standard entropies of the noble gases at 25 °C:

	S° (J/mol·K)	
$He(g)$	126.2	
$Ne(g)$	146.1	
$Ar(g)$	154.8	
$Kr(g)$	163.8	
$Xe(g)$	169.4	

The more massive the noble gas, the greater its entropy at 25 °C. A complete explanation of why entropy increases with increasing molar mass is beyond the scope of this book. Briefly, the energy states associated with the motion of heavy atoms are more closely spaced than those of lighter atoms. The more closely spaced energy states allow for greater dispersal of energy at a given temperature and therefore greater entropy. This trend holds only for elements in the same state. (The effect of a state change—from a liquid to a gas, for example—is far greater than the effect of molar mass.)

Relative Standard Entropies: Allotropes As mentioned previously, some elements can exist in two or more forms—called *allotropes*—in the same state of matter. For example, the allotropes of carbon include diamond and graphite—both solid forms of carbon. Since the arrangement of atoms within these forms is different, their standard molar entropies are different:

	$S°$ (J/mol·K)	
C(s, diamond)	2.4	
C(s, graphite)	5.7	

In diamond the atoms are constrained by chemical bonds in a highly restricted three-dimensional crystal structure. In graphite the atoms bond together in sheets, but the sheets have freedom to slide past each other. The less constrained structure of graphite results in more "places" to put energy and therefore greater entropy compared to diamond.

Relative Standard Entropies: Molecular Complexity For a given state of matter, entropy generally increases with increasing molecular complexity. For example, consider the standard entropies of the argon and nitrogen monoxide gas:

	Molar Mass (g/mol)	$S°$(J/mol·K)
Ar(g)	39.948	154.8
NO(g)	30.006	210.8

Ar has a greater molar mass than NO, yet it has less entropy at 25 °C. Why? Molecules generally have more "places" to put energy than do atoms. In a gaseous sample of argon, the only form that energy can take is the translational motion of the atoms. In a gaseous sample of NO, on the other hand, energy can take the form of translational motion, rotational motion, and (at high enough temperatures) vibrational motions of the molecules (Figure 17.9 ▶). Therefore, for a given state, molecules will generally have a greater entropy than free atoms. Similarly, more complex molecules will generally have more entropy than simpler ones. For example, consider the standard entropies of carbon monoxide and ethene gas:

	Molar Mass (g/mol)	$S°$(J/mol·K)
CO(g)	28.01	197.7
C_2H_4(g)	28.05	219.3

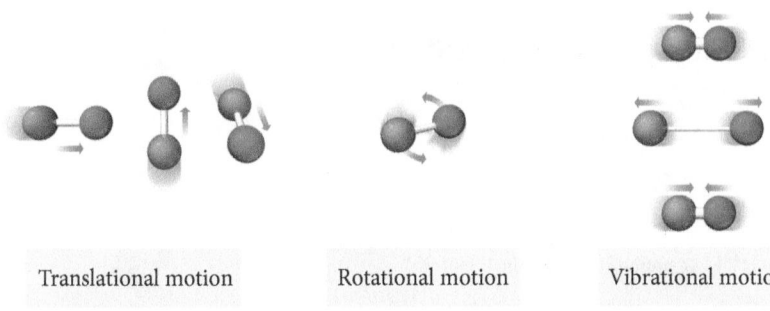

◀ FIGURE 17.9 "Places" for Energy in
Gaseous NO Energy can be contained
in translational motion, rotational
motion, and (at high enough
temperatures) vibrational motion.

Translational motion   Rotational motion   Vibrational motion

These two substances have nearly the same molar mass, but the greater complexity of C_2H_4 results in a greater molar entropy. When molecular complexity and molar mass both increase (as is often the case), molar entropy also increases, as demonstrated by the oxides of nitrogen:

	S°(J/mol·K)
$NO(g)$	210.8
$NO_2(g)$	240.1
$N_2O_4(g)$	304.4

The increasing molecular complexity as you move down this list, as well as the increasing molar mass, results in more "places" to put energy and therefore greater entropy.

Relative Standard Entropies: Dissolution The dissolution of a crystalline solid into solution usually results in an increase in entropy. For example, consider the standard entropies of solid and aqueous potassium chlorate:

The standard entropies for aqueous solutions are for the solution in its standard state, which is defined as having a concentration of 1 M.

	S°(J/mol·K)
$KClO_3(s)$	143.1
$KClO_3(aq)$	265.7

When solid potassium chlorate dissolves in water, the energy that was concentrated within the crystal becomes dispersed throughout the entire solution. The greater energy dispersal results in greater entropy.

Conceptual Connection 17.5 Standard Entropies

Arrange these gases in order of increasing standard molar entropy: SO_3, Kr, Cl_2.

Calculating the Standard Entropy Change (ΔS°_{rxn}) for a Reaction Since entropy is a state function, and since standard entropies for many common substances are tabulated, we can calculate the standard entropy change for a chemical reaction by calculating the difference in entropy between the products and the reactants. More specifically,

To calculate ΔS°_{rxn}, subtract the standard entropies of the reactants multiplied by their stoichiometric coefficients from the standard entropies of the products multiplied by their stoichiometric coefficients. In the form of an equation:

$$\Delta S^\circ_{rxn} = \sum n_p S^\circ(\text{products}) - \sum n_r S^\circ(\text{reactants}) \qquad [17.11]$$

In Equation 17.11, n_p represents the stoichiometric coefficients of the products, n_r represents the stoichiometric coefficients of the reactants, and S° represents the standard entropies. Keep in mind when using this equation that, *unlike enthalpies of formation, which are zero for elements in their standard states, standard entropies are always nonzero at 25 °C*. Example 17.4 demonstrates the application of Equation 17.11.

EXAMPLE 17.4 Calculating Standard Entropy Changes (ΔS°_{rxn})

Calculate ΔS°_{rxn} for the balanced chemical equation:

$$4\ NH_3(g) + 5\ O_2(g) \longrightarrow 4\ NO(g) + 6\ H_2O(g)$$

SOLUTION

Begin by looking up the standard entropy for each reactant and product in Appendix IIB. Always note the correct state—(g), (l), (aq), or (s)—for each reactant and product.	**Reactant or product**	**S° (in J/mol·K)**
	$NH_3(g)$	192.8
	$O_2(g)$	205.2
	$NO\ (g)$	210.8
	$H_2O(g)$	188.8

Calculate ΔS°_{rxn} by substituting the appropriate values into Equation 17.11. Remember to include the stoichiometric coefficients in your calculation.

$$\Delta S^\circ_{rxn} = \sum n_p S^\circ(\text{products}) - \sum n_r S^\circ(\text{reactants})$$

$$= [4(S^\circ_{NO(g)}) + 6(S^\circ_{H_2O(g)})] - [4(S^\circ_{NH_3(g)}) + 5(S^\circ_{O_2(g)})]$$

$$= [4(210.8\ \text{J/K}) + 6(188.8\ \text{J/K})] - [4(192.8\ \text{J/K}) + 5(205.2\ \text{J/K})]$$

$$= 1976.0\ \text{J/K} - 1797.2\ \text{J/K}$$

$$= 178.8\ \text{J/K}$$

CHECK Notice that ΔS°_{rxn} is positive, as you would expect for a reaction in which the number of moles of gas increases.

FOR PRACTICE 17.4

Calculate ΔS°_{rxn} for the balanced chemical equation:

$$2\ H_2S(g) + 3\ O_2(g) \longrightarrow 2\ H_2O(g) + 2\ SO_2(g)$$

17.7 Free Energy Changes in Chemical Reactions: Calculating ΔG°_{rxn}

In the previous section, we learned how to calculate the standard change in entropy for a chemical reaction (ΔS°_{rxn}). However, the criterion for spontaneity at standard conditions is the **standard change in free energy (ΔG°_{rnx})**. In this section, we examine three methods to calculate the standard change in free energy for a reaction (ΔG°_{rxn}). In the first method, we calculate ΔH°_{rxn} and ΔS°_{rxn} from tabulated values of ΔH°_f and S°, and then use the relationship $\Delta G^\circ_{rxn} = \Delta H^\circ_{rxn} - T\Delta S^\circ_{rxn}$ to calculate ΔG°_{rxn}. In the second method, we use tabulated values of free energies of formation to calculate ΔG°_{rxn} directly. In the third method, we determine the free energy change for a stepwise reaction from the free energy changes of each of the steps. At the end of this section, we discuss what is "free" about free energy. Remember that ΔG°_{rxn} is extremely useful because it tells us about the spontaneity of a process at standard conditions. The more negative ΔG°_{rxn} is, the more spontaneous the process (the further it will go toward products to reach equilibrium).

Calculating Standard Free Energy Changes with $\Delta G^\circ_{rxn} = \Delta H^\circ_{rxn} - T\Delta S^\circ_{rxn}$

In Chapter 6 (Section 6.9), we learned how to use tabulated values of standard enthalpies of formation to calculate ΔH°_{rxn}. In the previous section, we learned how to use tabulated values of standard entropies to calculate ΔS°_{rxn}. We can use these calculated values of

ΔH°_{rxn} and ΔS°_{rxn} to determine the standard free energy change for a reaction by using the equation:

$$\Delta G^\circ_{rxn} = \Delta H^\circ_{rxn} - T\Delta S^\circ_{rxn} \qquad [17.12]$$

Since tabulated values of standard enthalpies of formation (ΔH°_f) and standard entropies (S°) are usually applicable at 25 °C, the equation should (strictly speaking) be valid only when $T = 298$ K (25 °C). However, the changes in ΔH°_{rxn} and ΔS°_{rxn} over a limited temperature range are small when compared to the changes in the value of the temperature itself. Therefore, we can use Equation 17.12 to estimate changes in free energy at temperatures other than 25 °C.

EXAMPLE 17.5 **Calculating the Standard Change in Free Energy for a Reaction Using $\Delta G^\circ_{rxn} = \Delta H^\circ_{rxn} - T\Delta S^\circ_{rxn}$**

One of the possible initial steps in the formation of acid rain is the oxidation of the pollutant SO_2 to SO_3 by the reaction:

$$SO_2(g) + \tfrac{1}{2}O_2(g) \longrightarrow SO_3(g)$$

Calculate ΔG°_{rxn} at 25 °C and determine whether the reaction is spontaneous.

SOLUTION

Begin by looking up (in Appendix IIB) the standard enthalpy of formation and the standard entropy for each reactant and product.	**Reactant or product**	**ΔH°_f (kJ/mol)**	**S° (J/mol · K)**
	$SO_2(g)$	−296.8	248.2
	$O_2(g)$	0	205.2
	$SO_3(g)$	−395.7	256.8

Calculate ΔH°_{rxn} using Equation 6.15.

$$\Delta H^\circ_{rxn} = \sum n_p \Delta H^\circ_f(\text{products}) - \sum n_r \Delta H^\circ_f(\text{reactants})$$
$$= [\Delta H^\circ_{f,\,SO_3(g)}] - [\Delta H^\circ_{f,\,SO_2(g)} + \tfrac{1}{2}(\Delta H^\circ_{f,\,O_2(g)})]$$
$$= -395.7 \text{ kJ} - (-296.8 \text{ kJ} + 0.0 \text{ kJ})$$
$$= -98.9 \text{ kJ}$$

Calculate ΔS°_{rxn} using Equation 17.11.

$$\Delta S^\circ_{rxn} = \sum n_p S^\circ(\text{products}) - \sum n_r S^\circ(\text{reactants})$$
$$= [S^\circ_{SO_3(g)}] - [S^\circ_{SO_2(g)} + \tfrac{1}{2}(S^\circ_{O_2(g)})]$$
$$= 256.8 \text{ J/K} - [248.2 \text{ J/K} + \tfrac{1}{2}(205.2 \text{ J/K})]$$
$$= -94.0 \text{ J/K}$$

Calculate ΔG°_{rxn} using the calculated values of ΔH°_{rxn} and ΔS°_{rxn} and Equation 17.12. Convert the temperature to kelvins.

$$T = 25 + 273 = 298 \text{ K}$$
$$\Delta G^\circ_{rxn} = \Delta H^\circ_{rxn} - T\Delta S^\circ_{rxn}$$
$$= -98.9 \times 10^3 \text{ J} - 298 \text{ K} (-94.0 \text{ J/K})$$
$$= -70.9 \times 10^3 \text{ J}$$
$$= -70.9 \text{ kJ}$$

The reaction is spontaneous at this temperature because ΔG°_{rxn} is negative.

FOR PRACTICE 17.5

Consider the oxidation of NO to NO_2:

$$NO(g) + \tfrac{1}{2}O_2(g) \longrightarrow NO_2(g)$$

Calculate ΔG°_{rxn} at 25 °C and determine whether the reaction is spontaneous at standard conditions.

EXAMPLE 17.6 **Estimating the Standard Change in Free Energy for a Reaction at a Temperature Other than 25 °C Using $\Delta G^\circ_{rxn} = \Delta H^\circ_{rxn} - T\,\Delta S^\circ_{rxn}$**

For the reaction in Example 17.5, estimate the value of ΔG°_{rxn} at 125 °C. Is the reaction more or less spontaneous at this elevated temperature; that is, is the value of ΔG°_{rxn} more negative (more spontaneous) or more positive (less spontaneous)?

SOLUTION

Estimate ΔG°_{rxn} at the new temperature using the calculated values of ΔH°_{rxn} and ΔS°_{rxn} from Example 17.5. For T, convert the given temperature to kelvins. Make sure to use the same units for ΔH°_{rxn} and ΔS°_{rxn} (usually joules).	$T = 125 + 273 = 398$ K $\\ \Delta G^\circ_{rxn} = \Delta H^\circ_{rxn} - T\Delta S^\circ_{rxn} \\ \quad = -98.9 \times 10^3 \text{ J} - 398 \text{ K}(-94.0 \text{ J/K}) \\ \quad = -61.5 \times 10^3 \text{ J} \\ \quad = -61.5 \text{ kJ}$

Since the value of ΔG°_{rxn} at this elevated temperature is less negative (or more positive) than the value of ΔG°_{rxn} at 25 °C (which is −70.9 kJ), the reaction is less spontaneous.

FOR PRACTICE 17.6

For the reaction in For Practice 17.5, calculate the value of ΔG°_{rxn} at −55 °C. Is the reaction more spontaneous (more negative ΔG°_{rxn}) or less spontaneous (more positive ΔG°_{rxn}) at the lower temperature?

Calculating ΔG°_{rxn} with Tabulated Values of Free Energies of Formation

Because ΔG°_{rxn} is the *change* in free energy for a chemical reaction—the difference in free energy between the products and the reactants—and because free energy is a state function, we can calculate ΔG°_{rxn} by subtracting the free energies of the reactants of the reaction from the free energies of the products of the reaction. Also, since we are interested only in *changes* in free energy (and not in absolute values of free energy), we are free to define the *zero* of free energy as conveniently as possible. By analogy with our definition of enthalpies of formation, we define the **free energy of formation (ΔG°_f)** as follows:

> The free energy of formation (ΔG°_f) is the change in free energy when 1 mol of a compound in its standard state forms from its constituent elements in their standard states. The free energy of formation of pure elements in their standard states is zero.

We can measure all changes in free energy relative to pure elements in their standard states. To calculate ΔG°_{rxn}, we subtract the free energies of formation of the reactants multiplied by their stoichiometric coefficients from the free energies of formation of the products multiplied by their stoichiometric coefficients. In the form of an equation:

$$\Delta G^\circ_{rxn} = \sum n_p \Delta G^\circ_f (\text{products}) - \sum n_r \Delta G^\circ_f (\text{reactants}) \qquad [17.13]$$

In Equation 17.13, n_p represents the stoichiometric coefficients of the products, n_r represents the stoichiometric coefficients of the reactants, and ΔG°_f represents the standard free energies of formation. Table 17.3 lists ΔG°_f values for selected substances. You can find a more complete list in Appendix IIB. Notice that, by definition, *elements* have standard free energies of formation of zero. Notice also that most *compounds* have negative standard free energies of formation. This means that those compounds spontaneously form from their elements in their standard states. Compounds with positive free energies of formation do not spontaneously form from their elements and are therefore less common.

Example 17.7 demonstrates the calculation of ΔG°_{rxn} from ΔG°_f values. This method of calculating ΔG°_{rxn} works only at the temperature for which the free energies of

TABLE 17.3 Standard Molar Free Energies of Formation (ΔG°_{f}) for Selected Substances at 298 K

Substance	ΔG°_{f} (kJ/mol)	Substance	ΔG°_{f} (kJ/mol)
$H_2(g)$	0	$CH_4(g)$	−50.5
$O_2(g)$	0	$H_2O(g)$	−228.6
$N_2(g)$	0	$H_2O(l)$	−237.1
C(s, graphite)	0	$NH_3(g)$	−16.4
C(s, diamond)	2.900	$NO(g)$	+87.6
$CO(g)$	−137.2	$NO_2(g)$	+51.3
$CO_2(g)$	−394.4	$NaCl(s)$	−384.1

formation are tabulated, namely, 25 °C. To estimate ΔG°_{rxn} at other temperatures we must use $\Delta G^{\circ}_{rxn} = \Delta H^{\circ}_{rxn} - T\Delta S^{\circ}_{rxn}$, as demonstrated previously.

EXAMPLE 17.7 Calculating ΔG°_{rxn} from Standard Free Energies of Formation

Ozone in the lower atmosphere is a pollutant that can form by the following reaction involving the oxidation of unburned hydrocarbons:

$$CH_4(g) + 8\ O_2(g) \longrightarrow CO_2(g) + 2\ H_2O(g) + 4\ O_3(g)$$

Use the standard free energies of formation to determine ΔG°_{rxn} for this reaction at 25 °C.

SOLUTION

Begin by looking up (in Appendix IIB) the standard free energies of formation for each reactant and product. Remember that the standard free energy of formation of a pure element in its standard state is zero.

Reactant/product	ΔG°_{f} (in kJ/mol)
$CH_4(g)$	−50.5
$O_2(g)$	0.0
$CO_2(g)$	−394.4
$H_2O(g)$	−228.6
$O_3(g)$	163.2

Calculate ΔG°_{rxn} by substituting into Equation 17.13.

$$\Delta G^{\circ}_{rxn} = \sum n_p\ \Delta G^{\circ}_{f}(\text{products}) - \sum n_r\ \Delta G^{\circ}_{f}(\text{reactants})$$

$$= [\Delta G^{\circ}_{f,\ CO_2(g)} + 2(\Delta G^{\circ}_{f,\ H_2O(g)}) + 4(\Delta G^{\circ}_{f,\ O_3(g)})] - [\Delta G^{\circ}_{f,\ CH_4(g)} + 8(\Delta G^{\circ}_{f,\ O_2(g)})]$$

$$= [-394.4\ \text{kJ} + 2(-228.6\ \text{kJ}) + 4(163.2\ \text{kJ})] - [-50.5\ \text{kJ} + 8(0.0\ \text{kJ})]$$

$$= -198.8\ \text{kJ} + 50.5\ \text{kJ}$$

$$= -148.3\ \text{kJ}$$

FOR PRACTICE 17.7

One of the reactions that occurs within a catalytic converter in the exhaust pipe of a car is the simultaneous oxidation of carbon monoxide and reduction of NO (both of which are harmful pollutants).

$$2\ CO(g) + 2\ NO(g) \longrightarrow 2\ CO_2(g) + N_2(g)$$

Use standard free energies of formation to determine ΔG°_{rxn} for this reaction at 25 °C. Is the reaction spontaneous at standard conditions?

FOR MORE PRACTICE 17.7

In For Practice 17.7, you calculated ΔG°_{rxn} for the simultaneous oxidation of carbon monoxide and reduction of NO using standard free energies of formation. Calculate ΔG°_{rxn} for that reaction again at 25 °C, only this time use $\Delta G^{\circ}_{rxn} = \Delta H^{\circ}_{rxn} - T\Delta S^{\circ}_{rxn}$. How do the two values compare? Use your results to calculate ΔG°_{rxn} at 500.0 K and explain why you could not calculate ΔG°_{rxn} at 500.0 K using tabulated standard free energies of formation.

Chemistry in Your Day

Making a Nonspontaneous Process Spontaneous

A process that is nonspontaneous can be made spontaneous by coupling it with another process that is highly spontaneous. For example, hydrogen gas is a potential future fuel because it can be used in a fuel cell (a type of battery in which the reactants are constantly supplied—see Chapter 18) to generate electricity. The main problem with switching to hydrogen is securing a source. Where can we get the huge amounts of hydrogen gas that would be needed to meet our world's energy needs? Earth's oceans and lakes, of course, contain vast amounts of hydrogen. But that hydrogen is locked up in water molecules, and the decomposition of water into hydrogen and oxygen has a positive ΔG_{rxn}° and is therefore nonspontaneous:

$$H_2O(g) \longrightarrow H_2(g) + \tfrac{1}{2} O_2(g) \qquad \Delta G_{rxn}^{\circ} = +228.6 \text{ kJ}$$

To obtain hydrogen from water, we need to find another reaction with a highly negative ΔG_{rxn}° that can couple with the decomposition reaction to give an overall reaction with a negative ΔG_{rxn}°. For example, the oxidation of carbon monoxide to carbon dioxide has a large negative ΔG_{rxn}° and is highly spontaneous:

$$CO(g) + \tfrac{1}{2} O_2(g) \longrightarrow CO_2(g) \qquad \Delta G_{rxn}^{\circ} = -257.2 \text{ kJ}$$

If we add the two reactions together, we get a negative ΔG_{rxn}°:

Nonspontaneous

$$H_2O(g) \longrightarrow H_2(g) + \tfrac{1}{2} O_2(g) \qquad \Delta G_{rxn}^{\circ} = +228.6 \text{ kJ}$$
$$CO(g) + \tfrac{1}{2} O_2(g) \longrightarrow CO_2(g) \qquad \Delta G_{rxn}^{\circ} = -257.2 \text{ kJ}$$
$$\overline{H_2O(g) + CO(g) \longrightarrow H_2(g) + CO_2(g) \qquad \Delta G_{rxn}^{\circ} = -28.6 \text{ kJ}}$$

Spontaneous

The reaction between water and carbon monoxide is thus a spontaneous way to generate hydrogen gas.

The coupling of nonspontaneous reactions with highly spontaneous ones is also important in biological systems. The synthesis reactions that create the complex biological molecules (such as proteins and DNA) needed by living organisms, for example, are themselves nonspontaneous. Living systems grow and reproduce by coupling these nonspontaneous reactions to highly spontaneous ones. The main spontaneous reaction that ultimately drives the nonspontaneous ones is the metabolism of food. The oxidation of glucose, for example, is highly spontaneous:

$$C_6H_{12}O_6(s) + 6\ O_2(g) \longrightarrow 6\ CO_2(g) + 6\ H_2O(l)$$
$$\Delta G_{rxn}^{\circ} = -2880 \text{ kJ}$$

Spontaneous reactions such as these ultimately drive the nonspontaneous reactions necessary to sustain life.

Calculating ΔG_{rxn}° for a Stepwise Reaction from the Changes in Free Energy for Each of the Steps

Recall from Section 6.8 that since enthalpy is a state function, we can calculate ΔH_{rxn}° for a stepwise reaction from the sum of the changes in enthalpy for each step (according to Hess's law). Since free energy is also a state function, the same relationships that we covered in Chapter 6 for enthalpy also apply to free energy:

1. If a chemical equation is multiplied by some factor, then ΔG_{rxn} is also multiplied by the same factor.
2. If a chemical equation is reversed, then ΔG_{rxn} changes sign.
3. If a chemical equation can be expressed as the sum of a series of steps, then ΔG_{rxn} for the overall equation is the sum of the free energies of reactions for each step.

The following example illustrates the use of these relationships to calculate ΔG_{rxn}° for a stepwise reaction.

EXAMPLE 17.8 Calculating ΔG_{rxn}° for a Stepwise Reaction

Find ΔG_{rxn}° for the reaction.

$$3\ C(s) + 4\ H_2(g) \longrightarrow C_3H_8(g)$$

Use the following reactions with known ΔG's:

$$C_3H_8(g) + 5\ O_2(g) \longrightarrow 3\ CO_2(g) + 4\ H_2O(g) \qquad \Delta G_{rxn}^{\circ} = -2074 \text{ kJ}$$
$$C(s) + O_2(g) \longrightarrow CO_2(g) \qquad \Delta G_{rxn}^{\circ} = -394.4 \text{ kJ}$$
$$2\ H_2(g) + O_2(g) \longrightarrow 2\ H_2O(g) \qquad \Delta G_{rxn}^{\circ} = -457.1 \text{ kJ}$$

SOLUTION

To work this problem, manipulate the reactions with known ΔG_{rxn}°'s in such a way as to get the reactants of interest on the left, the products of interest on the right, and other species to cancel.

Since the first reaction has C_3H_8 as a reactant, and the reaction of interest has C_3H_8 as a product, reverse the first reaction and change the sign of ΔG°_{rxn}.	$3\ CO_2(g) + 4\ H_2O(g) \longrightarrow C_3H_8(g) + 5\ O_2(g)$	$\Delta G^\circ_{rxn} = +2074\ kJ$
The second reaction has C as a reactant and CO_2 as a product, as required in the reaction of interest. However, the coefficient for C is 1, and in the reaction of interest, the coefficient for C is 3. Therefore, multiply this equation and its ΔG°_{rxn} by 3.	$3 \times [C(s) + O_2(g) \longrightarrow CO_2(g)]$	$\Delta G^\circ_{rxn} = 3 \times (-394.4\ kJ)$ $= -1183\ kJ$
The third reaction has $H_2(g)$ as a reactant, as required. However, the coefficient for H_2 is 2, and in the reaction of interest, the coefficient for H_2 is 4. Multiply this reaction and its ΔG°_{rxn} by 2.	$2 \times [2\ H_2(g) + O_2(g) \longrightarrow 2\ H_2O(g)]$	$\Delta G^\circ_{rxn} = 2 \times (-457.1\ kJ)$ $= -914.2$
Lastly, rewrite the three reactions after multiplying through by the indicated factors and show how they sum to the reaction of interest. ΔG°_{rxn} for the reaction of interest is then the sum of the ΔG's for the steps.	$3\ \cancel{CO_2}(g) + 4\ \cancel{H_2O}(g) \longrightarrow C_3H_8(g) + 5\ \cancel{O_2}(g)$ $3\ C(s) + 3\ \cancel{O_2}(g) \longrightarrow 3\ \cancel{CO_2}(g)$ $4\ H_2(g) + 2\ \cancel{O_2}(g) \longrightarrow 4\ \cancel{H_2O}(g)$ _____ $3\ C(s) + 4\ H_2(g) \longrightarrow C_3H_8(g)$	$\Delta G^\circ_{rxn} = +2074\ kJ$ $\Delta G^\circ_{rxn} = -1183\ kJ$ $\Delta G^\circ_{rxn} = -914.2\ kJ$ _____ $\Delta G^\circ_{rxn} = -23\ kJ$

FOR PRACTICE 17.8

Find ΔG°_{rxn} for the reaction:

$$N_2O(g) + NO_2(g) \longrightarrow 3\ NO(g)$$

Use the following reactions with known ΔG values:

$$2\ NO(g) + O_2(g) \longrightarrow 2\ NO_2(g) \qquad \Delta G^\circ_{rxn} = -71.2\ kJ$$
$$N_2(g) + O_2(g) \longrightarrow 2\ NO(g) \qquad \Delta G^\circ_{rxn} = +175.2\ kJ$$
$$2\ N_2O(g) \longrightarrow 2\ N_2(g) + O_2(g) \qquad \Delta G^\circ_{rxn} = -207.4\ kJ$$

Why Free Energy Is "Free"

We often want to use the energy released by a chemical reaction to do work. For example, in an automobile, we use the energy released by the combustion of gasoline to move the car forward. The change in free energy of a chemical reaction represents the maximum amount of energy available, or *free*, to do work (if ΔG°_{rxn} is negative). For many reactions, the amount of free energy change is less than the change in enthalpy for the reaction. Consider the reaction between carbon and hydrogen occurring at 25 °C:

$$C(s, graphite) + 2\ H_2(g) \longrightarrow CH_4(g)$$
$$\Delta H^\circ_{rxn} = -74.6\ kJ$$
$$\Delta S^\circ_{rxn} = -80.8\ J/K$$
$$\Delta G^\circ_{rxn} = -50.5\ kJ$$

The reaction is exothermic and gives off 74.6 kJ of heat energy. However, the maximum amount of energy available for useful work is only 50.5 kJ (Figure 17.10 ▶). Why? We can see that the change in entropy of the *system* is negative. Nevertheless, the reaction is spontaneous. This is possible only if some of the emitted heat goes to increase the entropy of the surroundings by an amount sufficient to make the change in entropy of the *universe* positive. The amount of energy available to do work (the free energy) is what remains after accounting for the heat that must be lost to the surroundings.

The change in free energy for a chemical reaction represents a *theoretical limit* as to how much work can be done by the reaction. In a *real* reaction, the amount of energy available to do work is even *less* than ΔG°_{rxn} because additional energy is lost to the

Maximum work = 50.5 kJ

$C(s, graphite) + 2\ H_2(g)$

$CH_4(g)$
$\Delta H^\circ_{rxn} = -74.6\ kJ$

Minimum heat lost to surroundings = 24.1 kJ

▲ **FIGURE 17.10 Free Energy** Although the reaction produces 74.6 kJ of heat, only a maximum of 50.5 kJ is available to do work. The rest of the energy is lost to the surroundings.

Reversible Process

Weight of sand exactly matches pressure at each increment.

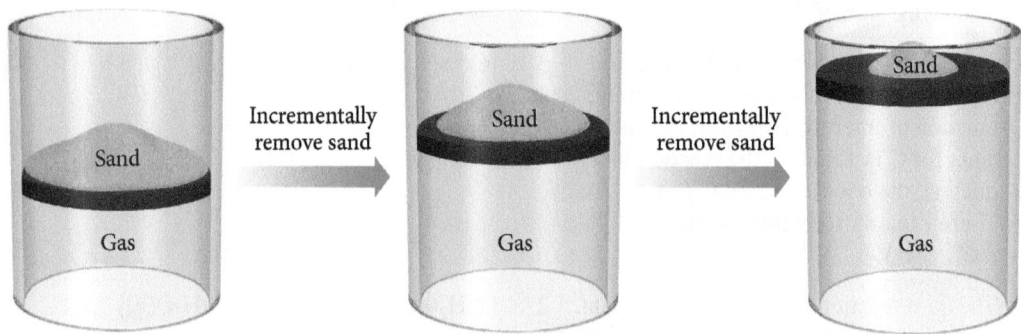

▲ FIGURE 17.11 **A Reversible Process** In a reversible process, the free energy is drawn out in infinitesimally small increments that exactly match the amount of energy that the process is producing in that increment. In this case, grains of sand are removed one at a time, resulting in a series of small expansions in which the weight of sand almost exactly matches the pressure of the expanding gas. This process is close to reversible—each sand grain would need to have an infinitesimally small mass for the process to be fully reversible.

More formally, *a reversible reaction is one that will change direction upon an infinitesimally small change in a variable (such as temperature or pressure) related to the reaction.*

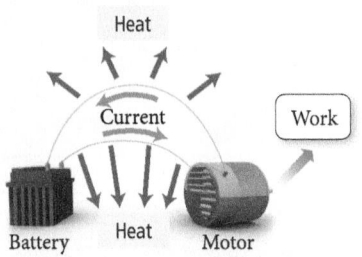

▲ FIGURE 17.12 **Energy Loss in a Battery** When current is drawn from a battery to do work, some energy is lost as heat due to resistance in the wire. Consequently, the quantity of energy required to recharge the battery will be more than the quantity of work done.

surroundings as heat. A reaction that achieves the theoretical limit with respect to free energy is called a **reversible reaction**. A reversible reaction occurs infinitesimally slowly, and the free energy can only be drawn out in infinitesimally small increments that exactly match the amount of energy that the reaction is producing during that increment (Figure 17.11 ▲).

All real reactions are **irreversible reactions** and therefore do not achieve the theoretical limit of available free energy. Let's return to our discharging battery from the opening section of this chapter as an example of this concept. A battery contains chemical reactants configured in such a way that, upon spontaneous reaction, they produce an electrical current. The free energy released by the reaction is then harnessed to do work. For example, an electric motor can be wired to the battery. Flowing electrical current makes the motor turn (Figure 17.12 ◄). Owing to resistance in the wire, the flowing electrical current will also produce some heat, which is lost to the surroundings and is not available to do work. The amount of free energy lost as heat can be lowered by slowing down the rate of current flow. The slower the rate of current flow, the less free energy is lost as heat and the more is available to do work. However, only in the theoretical case of infinitesimally slow current flow will the maximum amount of work (equal to ΔG_{rxn}°) be done. Any real rate of current flow will result in some loss of energy as heat. This lost energy is the "heat tax" that we discussed in the opening section of this chapter. Recharging the battery will necessarily require more energy than was obtained as work because some of the energy was lost as heat.

If the change in free energy of a chemical reaction is positive, then ΔG_{rxn}° represents *the minimum amount of energy required to make the reaction occur*. Again, ΔG_{rxn}° represents a theoretical limit. Making a real nonspontaneous reaction occur always requires more energy than the theoretical limit.

17.8 Free Energy Changes for Nonstandard States: The Relationship between ΔG_{rxn}° and ΔG_{rxn}

We have learned how to calculate the *standard* free energy change for a reaction (ΔG_{rxn}°). However, the standard free energy change applies only to a very narrow set of conditions, namely, those conditions in which the reactants and products are in their standard states. Consider the standard free energy change for the evaporation of liquid water to gaseous water:

$$H_2O(l) \rightleftharpoons H_2O(g) \qquad \Delta G_{rxn}^{\circ} = +8.59 \text{ kJ/mol}$$

The standard free energy change for this process is positive, so the process is nonspontaneous. But you know that if you spill water onto the floor under ordinary conditions, it spontaneously evaporates. Why? *Because ordinary conditions are not standard conditions* and ΔG°_{rxn} applies only to standard conditions. For a gas (such as the water vapor in the reaction just given), standard conditions are those in which the pure gas is present at a partial pressure of 1 atmosphere. In a flask containing liquid water and water vapor under standard conditions ($P_{H_2O} = 1$ atm) at 25 °C the water would not vaporize. In fact, since ΔG°_{rxn} is negative for the reverse reaction, the reaction would spontaneously occur in reverse—water vapor would condense.

In open air under ordinary circumstances, the partial pressure of water vapor is much less than 1 atm. The conditions are not standard, and therefore the value of ΔG°_{rxn} does not apply. For nonstandard conditions, we must calculate ΔG_{rxn} (as opposed to ΔG°_{rxn}) to predict spontaneity.

The Free Energy Change of a Reaction under Nonstandard Conditions

We can calculate the **free energy change of a reaction under nonstandard conditions** (ΔG_{rxn}) from ΔG°_{rxn} using the relationship:

$$\Delta G_{rxn} = \Delta G^\circ_{rxn} + RT \ln Q \qquad [17.14]$$

where Q is the reaction quotient (defined in Section 14.7), T is the temperature in kelvins, and R is the gas constant in the appropriate units (8.314 J/mol·K). In Equation 17.14 and all subsequent thermodynamic equations, use Q_p for reactions involving gases, and use Q_c for reactions involving substances dissolved in solution. We can demonstrate the use of this equation by applying it to the liquid–vapor water equilibrium under several different conditions, as shown in Figure 17.13 ▼. Note that by the law of mass action, for this equilibrium, $Q = P_{H_2O}$ (where the pressure is expressed in atmospheres):

$$H_2O(l) \longrightarrow H_2O(g) \qquad Q = P_{H_2O}$$

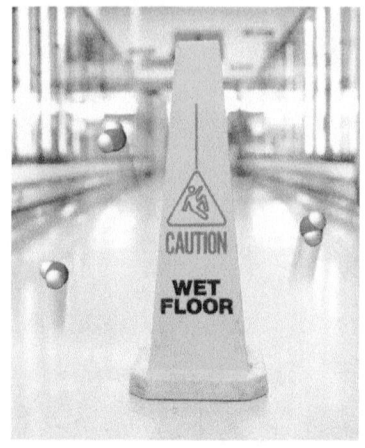

▲ Spilled water spontaneously evaporates even though ΔG° for the vaporization of water is positive. Why?

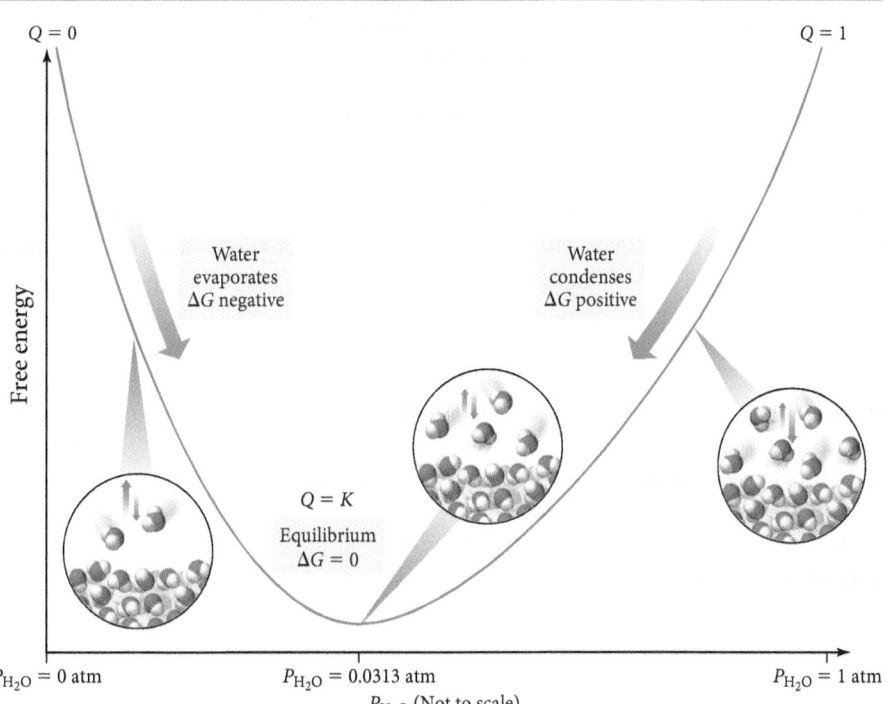

▲ **FIGURE 17.13 Free Energy versus Pressure for Water** The free energy change for the vaporization of water is a function of pressure.

Standard Conditions Under standard conditions, $P_{H_2O} = 1$ atm and therefore $Q = 1$. Substituting, we get the expression:

$$\Delta G_{rxn} = \Delta G^\circ_{rxn} + RT \ln Q$$
$$= +8.59 \text{ kJ/mol} + RT \ln(1)$$
$$= +8.59 \text{ kJ/mol}$$

Under standard conditions, Q will always be equal to 1, and since $\ln(1) = 0$, the value of ΔG_{rxn} will therefore be equal to ΔG°_{rxn}, as expected. For the liquid–vapor water equilibrium, because $\Delta G^\circ_{rxn} > 0$, the reaction is not spontaneous in the forward direction but is spontaneous in the reverse direction. As stated previously, under standard conditions water vapor condenses into liquid water.

Equilibrium Conditions At 25.00 °C, liquid water is in equilibrium with water vapor at a pressure of 0.0313 atm; therefore, $Q = K_p = 0.0313$. Substituting:

$$\Delta G_{rxn} = \Delta G^\circ_{rxn} + RT \ln(0.0313)$$
$$= +8.59 \text{ kJ/mol} + 8.314\frac{J}{mol \cdot K}(298.15K) \ln(0.0313)$$
$$= +8.59 \text{ kJ/mol} + (-8.59 \times 10^3 \text{ J/mol})$$
$$= +8.59 \text{ kJ/mol} - 8.59 \text{ kJ/mol}$$
$$= 0$$

Under equilibrium conditions, the value of $RT \ln Q$ is always equal in magnitude but opposite in sign to the value of ΔG°_{rxn}. Therefore, the value of ΔG_{rxn} is zero. Because $\Delta G_{rxn} = 0$, the reaction is not spontaneous in either direction, as expected for a reaction at equilibrium.

A water partial pressure of 5.00×10^{-3} atm corresponds to a relative humidity of 16% at 25 °C.

Other Nonstandard Conditions To calculate the value of ΔG_{rxn} under any other set of nonstandard conditions, calculate Q and substitute the value into Equation 17.14. For example, the partial pressure of water vapor in the air on a dry (nonhumid) day might be 5.00×10^{-3} atm, so $Q = 5.00 \times 10^{-3}$. Substituting:

$$\Delta G_{rxn} = \Delta G^\circ_{rxn} + RT \ln(5.00 \times 10^{-3})$$
$$= +8.59 \text{ kJ/mol} + 8.314\frac{J}{mol \cdot K}(298 \text{ K}) \ln(5.00 \times 10^{-3})$$
$$= +8.59 \text{ kJ/mol} + (-13.1 \times 10^3 \text{ J/mol})$$
$$= +8.59 \text{ kJ/mol} - 13.1 \text{ kJ/mol}$$
$$= -4.5 \text{ kJ/mol}$$

Under these conditions, the value of $\Delta G_{rxn} < 0$, so the reaction is spontaneous in the forward direction, consistent with our experience of water evaporating when spilled on the floor.

EXAMPLE 17.9   Calculating ΔG_{rxn} under Nonstandard Conditions

Consider the reaction at 298 K:

$$2 \text{ NO}(g) + O_2(g) \longrightarrow 2 \text{ NO}_2(g) \qquad \Delta G^\circ_{rxn} = -71.2 \text{ kJ}$$

Calculate ΔG_{rxn} under these conditions:

$$P_{NO} = 0.100 \text{ atm}; \qquad P_{O_2} = 0.100 \text{ atm}; \qquad P_{NO_2} = 2.00 \text{ atm}$$

Is the reaction more or less spontaneous under these conditions than under standard conditions?

SOLUTION

Use the law of mass action to calculate Q.	$Q = \dfrac{P^2_{NO_2}}{P^2_{NO}P_{O_2}} = \dfrac{(2.00)^2}{(0.100)^2(0.100)} = 4.00 \times 10^3$

Substitute Q, T, and ΔG°_{rxn} into Equation 17.14 to calculate ΔG_{rxn}. (Since the units of R include joules, write ΔG°_{rxn} in joules.)	$\Delta G_{rxn} = \Delta G^\circ_{rxn} + RT \ln Q$ $= -71.2 \times 10^3 \, \text{J} + 8.314 \dfrac{\text{J}}{\text{mol} \cdot \text{K}} (298 \text{ K}) \ln(4.00 \times 10^3)$ $= -71.2 \times 10^3 \, \text{J} + 20.5 \times 10^3 \, \text{J}$ $= -50.7 \times 10^3 \, \text{J}$ $= -50.7 \, \text{kJ}$ The reaction is spontaneous under these conditions, but less spontaneous than it would be under standard conditions (because ΔG_{rxn} is less negative than ΔG°_{rxn}).

CHECK The calculated result is consistent with what you would expect based on Le Châtelier's principle; increasing the concentration of the products and decreasing the concentration of the reactants relative to standard conditions should make the reaction less spontaneous than it was under standard conditions.

FOR PRACTICE 17.9

Consider the reaction at 298 K:

$$2 \, H_2S(g) + SO_2(g) \longrightarrow 3 \, S(s, \text{rhombic}) + 2 \, H_2O(g) \qquad \Delta G^\circ_{rxn} = -102 \, \text{kJ}$$

Calculate ΔG_{rxn} under these conditions:

$$P_{H_2S} = 2.00 \text{ atm}; \quad P_{SO_2} = 1.50 \text{ atm}; \quad P_{H_2O} = 0.0100 \text{ atm}$$

Is the reaction more or less spontaneous under these conditions than under standard conditions?

Conceptual Connection 17.6 Free Energy Changes and Le Châtelier's Principle

According to Le Châtelier's principle and the dependence of free energy on reactant and product concentrations, which statement is true? (Assume that both the reactants and products are gaseous.)

(a) A high concentration of reactants relative to products results in a more spontaneous reaction than one in which the reactants and products are in their standard states.

(b) A high concentration of products relative to reactants results in a more spontaneous reaction than one in which the reactants and products are in their standard states.

(c) A reaction in which the reactants are in standard states, but in which no products have formed, has a ΔG_{rxn} that is more positive than ΔG°_{rxn}.

17.9 Free Energy and Equilibrium: Relating ΔG°_{rxn} to the Equilibrium Constant (K)

We have discussed throughout this chapter that ΔG°_{rxn} determines the spontaneity of a reaction when the reactants and products are in their standard states. In Chapter 14, we learned that the equilibrium constant (K) determines how far a reaction goes toward products, a measure of spontaneity. Therefore, as you might expect, the standard free energy change of a reaction and the equilibrium constant are related—the equilibrium constant becomes larger as the standard free energy change becomes more negative. In other words, if the reactants in a particular reaction undergo a large *negative* free energy change as they become products, then the reaction has a large equilibrium constant, with products strongly favored at equilibrium. If, on the other hand, the reactants in a particular reaction undergo a large *positive* free energy change as they become products, then the reaction has a small equilibrium constant, with reactants strongly favored at equilibrium. We can derive a relationship between $\Delta G°_{rxn}$ and K from Equation 17.14. We know that at equilibrium $Q = K$ and $\Delta G_{rxn} = 0$. Making these substitutions:

$$\Delta G_{rxn} = \Delta G°_{rxn} + RT \ln Q$$

$$0 = \Delta G°_{rxn} + RT \ln K$$

$$\Delta G°_{rxn} = -RT \ln K \qquad\qquad [17.15]$$

The relationship between $\Delta G°_{rxn}$ and K is logarithmic—small changes in $\Delta G°_{rxn}$ have a large effect on K.

In Equation 17.15 and all subsequent thermodynamic equations, use K_p for reactions involving gases, and use K_c for reactions involving substances dissolved in solution.

We can better understand the relationship between $\Delta G°_{rxn}$ and K by considering the following ranges of values for K, as summarized in Figure 17.14 ▼.

- When $K < 1$, $\ln K$ is negative and $\Delta G°_{rxn}$ is positive. Under standard conditions (when $Q = 1$) the reaction is spontaneous in the reverse direction.

- When $K > 1$, $\ln K$ is positive and $\Delta G°_{rxn}$ is negative. Under standard conditions (when $Q = 1$) the reaction is spontaneous in the forward direction.

- When $K = 1$, $\ln K$ is zero and $\Delta G°_{rxn}$ is zero. The reaction happens to be at equilibrium under standard conditions.

Free Energy and the Equilibrium Constant

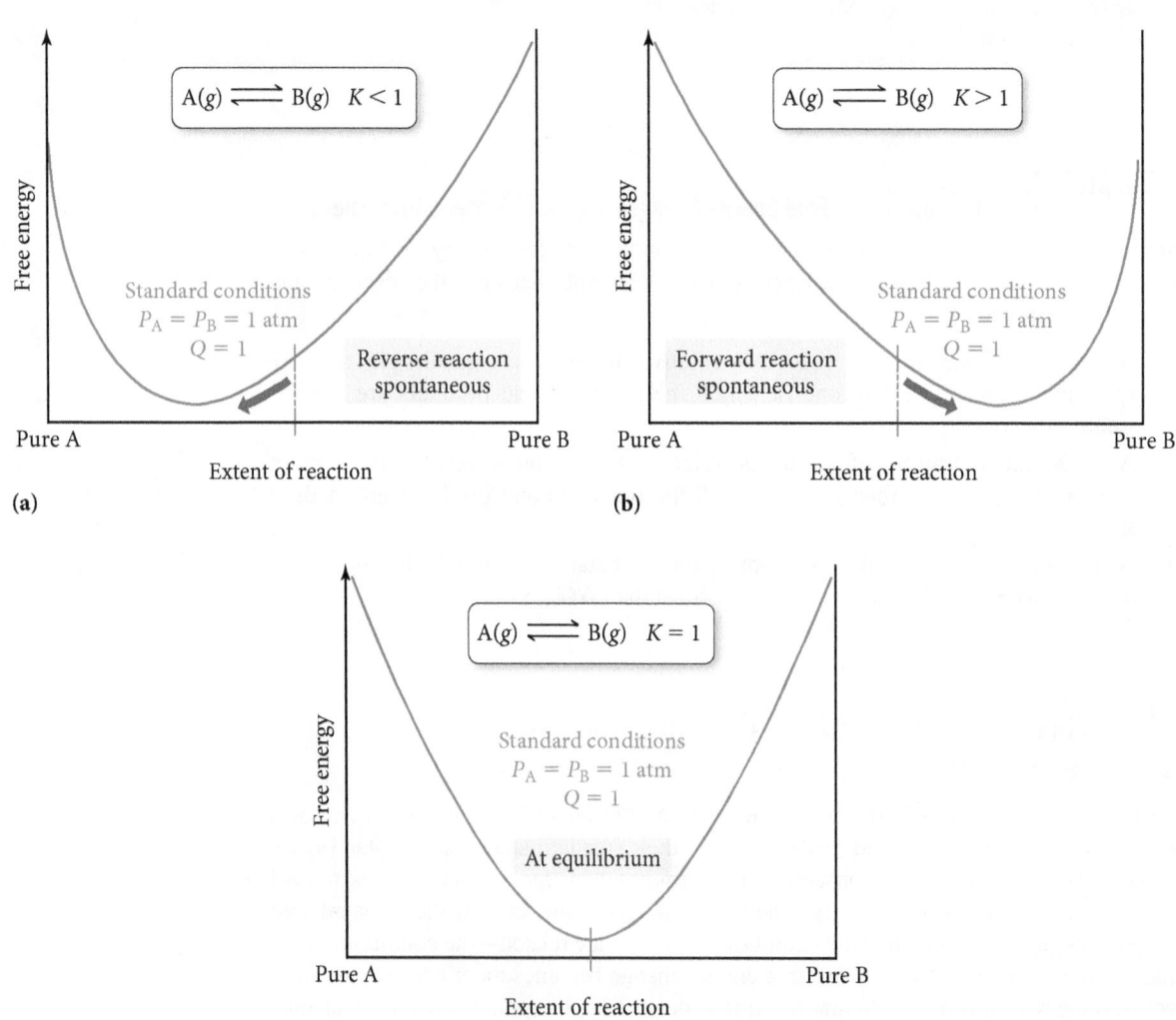

▲ FIGURE 17.14 Free Energy and the Equilibrium Constant   (a) Free energy curve for a reaction with a small equilibrium constant. (b) Free energy curve for a reaction with a large equilibrium constant. (c) Free energy curve for a reaction in which $K = 1$.

EXAMPLE 17.10   The Equilibrium Constant and ΔG°_{rxn}

Use tabulated free energies of formation to calculate the equilibrium constant for the reaction at 298 K:

$$N_2O_4(g) \rightleftharpoons 2 \; NO_2(g)$$

SOLUTION

Look up (in Appendix IIB) the standard free energies of formation for each reactant and product.	

Reactant or product	ΔG°_f (in kJ/mol)
$N_2O_4(g)$	99.8
$NO_2(g)$	51.3

Calculate ΔG°_{rxn} by substituting into Equation 17.13.	$\begin{aligned}\Delta G^\circ_{rxn} &= \sum n_p \Delta G^\circ_f(\text{products}) - \sum n_r \Delta G^\circ_f(\text{reactants}) \\ &= 2[\Delta G^\circ_{f,\,NO_2(g)}] - \Delta G^\circ_{f,\,N_2O_4(g)} \\ &= 2(51.3 \text{ kJ}) - 99.8 \text{ kJ} \\ &= 2.8 \text{ kJ}\end{aligned}$
Calculate K from ΔG°_{rxn} by solving Equation 17.15 for K and substituting the values of ΔG°_{rxn} and temperature.	$\begin{aligned}\Delta G^\circ_{rxn} &= -RT \ln K \\ \ln K &= \frac{-\Delta G^\circ_{rxn}}{RT} \\ &= \frac{-2.8 \times 10^3 \text{ J/mol}}{8.314\dfrac{\text{J}}{\text{mol} \cdot \text{K}}(298 \text{ K})} \\ &= -1.13 \\ K &= e^{-1.13} \\ &= 0.32\end{aligned}$

FOR PRACTICE 17.10

Calculate ΔG°_{rxn} at 298 K for the reaction:

$$I_2(g) + Cl_2(g) \rightleftharpoons 2 \; ICl(g) \qquad K_p = 81.9$$

Conceptual Connection 17.7 K and ΔG°_{rxn}

The reaction $A(g) \rightleftharpoons B(g)$ has an equilibrium constant that is less than one. What can you conclude about ΔG°_{rxn} for the reaction?

(a) $\Delta G^\circ_{rxn} = 0$ **(b)** $\Delta G^\circ_{rxn} < 0$ **(c)** $\Delta G^\circ_{rxn} > 0$

The Temperature Dependence of the Equilibrium Constant

We now have an equation that relates the standard free energy change for a reaction (ΔG°_{rxn}) to the equilibrium constant for a reaction (K):

$$\Delta G^\circ_{rxn} = -RT \ln K \qquad\qquad [17.16]$$

We also have an equation for how the free energy change for a reaction (ΔG°_{rxn}) depends on temperature (T):

$$\Delta G^\circ_{rxn} = \Delta H^\circ_{rxn} - T \; \Delta S^\circ_{rxn} \qquad\qquad [17.17]$$

We can combine these two equations to obtain an equation for how the equilibrium constant depends on temperature. Combining Equations 17.16 and 17.17, we get:

$$-RT \ln K = \Delta H^\circ_{rxn} - T \; \Delta S^\circ_{rxn} \qquad\qquad [17.18]$$

We can then divide both sides of Equation 17.18 by the quantity RT:

$$-\ln K = \frac{\Delta H^{\circ}_{rxn}}{RT} - \frac{T\,\Delta S^{\circ}_{rxn}}{RT}$$

Canceling and rearranging, we get this important result:

$$\ln K = -\frac{\Delta H^{\circ}_{rxn}}{R}\left(\frac{1}{T}\right) + \frac{\Delta S^{\circ}_{rxn}}{R} \qquad [17.19]$$

$$y = mx + b$$

Equation 17.19 is in the form of a straight line. A plot of the natural log of the equilibrium constant ($\ln K$) versus the inverse of the temperature in kelvins ($1/T$) yields a straight line with a slope of $-\Delta H^{\circ}_{rxn}/R$ and a y-intercept of $\Delta S^{\circ}_{rxn}/R$. Such a plot is useful for obtaining thermodynamic data (namely, ΔH°_{rxn} and ΔS°_{rxn}) from measurements of K as a function of temperature. However, since ΔH°_{rxn} and ΔS°_{rxn} can themselves be slightly temperature dependent, this analysis works only over a relatively limited temperature range. The equation can also be expressed in a two-point form:

$$\ln \frac{K_2}{K_1} = -\frac{\Delta H^{\circ}_{rxn}}{R}\left(\frac{1}{T_2} - \frac{1}{T_1}\right) \qquad [17.20]$$

We can use this equation to find ΔH°_{rxn} from a measurement of the equilibrium constant at two different temperatures or to find the equilibrium constant at some other temperature if we know the equilibrium constant at a given temperature and ΔH°_{rxn}.

CHAPTER IN REVIEW

Self Assessment Quiz

Q1. Which reaction is most likely to have a positive ΔS_{sys}?
a) $SiO_2(s) + 3\,C(s) \rightarrow SiC(s) + 2\,CO(g)$
b) $6\,CO_2(g) + 6\,H_2O(g) \rightarrow C_6H_{12}O_6(s) + 6\,O_2(g)$
c) $CO(g) + Cl_2(g) \rightarrow COCl_2(g)$
d) $3\,NO_2(g) + H_2O(l) \rightarrow 2\,HNO_3(l) + NO(g)$

Q2. The sign of ΔH_{rxn} and ΔS_{rxn} for several different reactions are given. In which case is the reaction spontaneous at all temperatures?
a) $\Delta H_{rxn} < 0;\ \Delta S_{rxn} < 0$
b) $\Delta H_{rxn} > 0;\ \Delta S_{rxn} > 0$
c) $\Delta H_{rxn} < 0;\ \Delta S_{rxn} > 0$
d) $\Delta H_{rxn} > 0;\ \Delta S_{rxn} < 0$

Q3. Arrange the gases—F_2, Ar, and CH_3F—in order of increasing standard entropy (S°) at 298 K.
a) $F_2 < Ar < CH_3F$
b) $CH_3F < F_2 < Ar$
c) $CH_3F < Ar < F_2$
d) $Ar < F_2 < CH_3F$

Q4. A reaction has a $\Delta H_{rxn} = 54.2$ kJ. Calculate the change in entropy for the surroundings (ΔS_{surr}) for the reaction at 25.0 °C. (Assume constant pressure and temperature.)
a) 2.17×10^3 J/K
b) -2.17×10^3 J/K
c) -182 J/K
d) 182 J/K

Q5. A reaction has $\Delta H^{\circ}_{rxn} = -255$ kJ and $\Delta S^{\circ}_{rxn} = 211$ J/K. Calculate ΔG°_{rxn} at 55 °C.
a) 11.9×10^3 kJ
b) 69.5×10^3 kJ
c) -267 kJ
d) -324 kJ

Q6. Use standard entropies to calculate ΔS°_{rxn} for the balanced chemical equation:

$$2\,PCl_3(l) + O_2(g) \rightarrow 2\,POCl_3(l)$$

Substance	S° (J/mol·K)
$POCl_3(l)$	222.5
$POCl_3(g)$	325.5
$PCl_3(l)$	217.1
$PCl_3(g)$	311.8
$O_2(g)$	205.2

a) -194.4 J/K
b) -199.8 J/K
c) 10.8 J/K
d) 1084.4 J/K

Q7. Use standard free energies of formation to calculate ΔG°_{rxn} for the balanced chemical equation:

$$Mg(s) + N_2O(g) \rightarrow MgO(s) + N_2(g)$$

Substance	ΔG°_{rxn}(kJ/mol)
$N_2O(g)$	103.7
$MgO(s)$	−569.3

a) 673.0 kJ
b) −673.0 kJ
c) −465.6 kJ
d) 465.6 kJ

Q8. Find ΔG°_{rxn} for the reaction $2\,A + B \rightarrow 2\,C$ from the given data.

$$A \rightarrow B \quad \Delta G^{\circ}_{rxn} = 128 \text{ kJ}$$
$$C \rightarrow 2\,B \quad \Delta G^{\circ}_{rxn} = 455 \text{ kJ}$$
$$A \rightarrow C \quad \Delta G^{\circ}_{rxn} = -182 \text{ kJ}$$

a) −401 kJ
b) 509 kJ
c) 401 kJ
d) −509 kJ

Q9. The following reaction has a $\Delta G^{\circ}_{rxn} = 9.4$ kJ at 25 °C. Find ΔG_{rxn} when $P_{NO_2} = 0.115$ atm and $P_{NO} = 9.7$ atm at 25 °C.

$$3\,NO_2(g) + H_2O(l) \rightarrow 2\,HNO_3(l) + NO(g)$$

a) −12.3 kJ
b) 21.7×10^3 kJ
c) 31.1 kJ
d) 18.8 kJ

Q10. The reaction $A(g) \rightleftharpoons B(g)$ has an equilibrium constant of $K_p = 2.3 \times 10^{-5}$. What can you conclude about the sign of ΔG°_{rxn} for the reaction?

a) $\Delta G^{\circ}_{rxn} = 0$
b) ΔG°_{rxn} is negative
c) ΔG°_{rxn} is positive
d) Nothing can be concluded about the sign of ΔG°_{rxn} for the reaction.

Q11. A reaction has an equilibrium constant of $K_p = 0.018$ at 25 °C. Find ΔG°_{rxn} for the reaction at this temperature.

a) −835 J
b) −4.32 kJ
c) −9.95 kJ
d) 9.96 kJ

Q12. Which distribution of six particles into three interconnected boxes has the highest entropy?

a)

b)

c)

d)

Q13. Which process results in the increase in entropy of the universe?

a) the cooling of a hot cup of coffee in room temperature air
b) the evaporation of water from a desk at room temperature
c) the melting of snow above 0 °C
d) all of the above

Q14. Under which set of conditions is ΔG_{rxn} for the reaction $A(g) \rightarrow B(g)$ most likely to be negative?

a) $P_A = 10.0$ atm; $P_B = 10.0$ atm
b) $P_A = 10.0$ atm; $P_B = 0.010$ atm
c) $P_A = 0.010$ atm; $P_B = 10.0$ atm
d) $P_A = 0.010$ atm; $P_B = 0.010$ atm

Q15. Which statement is true for the freezing of liquid water below 0 °C?

a) ΔH is positive; ΔS is negative; ΔG is negative
b) ΔH is negative; ΔS is negative; ΔG is negative
c) ΔH is positive; ΔS is positive; ΔG is positive
d) ΔH is positive; ΔS is negative; ΔG is positive

Answers: 1. (a) 2. (c) 3. (d) 4. (c) 5. (d) 6. (a) 7. (b) 8. (d) 9. (c) 10. (c) 11. (d) 12. (b) 13. (d) 14. (b) 15. (b)

Key Terms

Section 17.2
spontaneous process (814)

Section 17.3
entropy (S) (818)
second law of thermodynamics (820)

Section 17.5
Gibbs free energy (G) (828)

Section 17.6
standard entropy change for a reaction (ΔS°_{rxn}) (832)
standard molar entropies (S°) (832)
third law of thermodynamics (832)

Section 17.7
standard free energy change (ΔG°_{rxn}) (836)
free energy of formation (ΔG°_f) (838)

reversible reaction (842)
irreversible reaction (842)

Section 17.8
free energy change of a reaction under nonstandard conditions (ΔG_{rxn}) (843)

Key Concepts

Nature's Heat Tax: You Can't Win and You Can't Break Even (17.1)

▶ The first law of thermodynamics states that energy can be neither created nor destroyed.

▶ The second law implies that for every energy transaction, some energy is lost to the surroundings; this lost energy is nature's heat tax.

Spontaneous and Nonspontaneous Processes (17.2)

▶ Both spontaneous and nonspontaneous processes can occur, but only spontaneous processes can take place without outside intervention.

▶ Thermodynamics is the study of the *spontaneity* of reactions, *not* to be confused with kinetics, the study of the *rate* of reactions.

Entropy and the Second Law of Thermodynamics (17.3)

▶ The second law of thermodynamics states that for *any* spontaneous process, the entropy of the universe increases.

▶ Entropy (S) is proportional to the number of energetically equivalent ways in which the components of a system can be arranged and is a measure of energy dispersal per unit temperature.

Heat Transfer and Changes in the Entropy of the Surroundings (17.4)

▶ For a process to be spontaneous, the total entropy of the universe (system plus surroundings) must increase.

▶ The entropy of the surroundings increases when the change in *enthalpy* of the system (ΔH_{sys}) is negative (i.e., for exothermic reactions).

▶ The change in entropy of the surroundings for a given ΔH_{sys} depends inversely on temperature—the greater the temperature, the lower the magnitude of ΔS_{surr}.

Gibbs Free Energy (17.5)

▶ Gibbs free energy, G, is a thermodynamic function that is proportional to the negative of the change in the entropy of the universe. A negative ΔG represents a spontaneous reaction and a positive ΔG represents a nonspontaneous reaction.

▶ We can calculate the value of ΔG for a reaction from the values of ΔH and ΔS for the *system* using the equation $\Delta G = \Delta H - T\Delta S$.

Entropy Changes in Chemical Reactions: Calculating ΔS°_{rxn} (17.6)

▶ We calculate the standard change in entropy for a reaction similarly to the way we calculate the standard change in enthalpy for a reaction: by subtracting the sum of the standard entropies of the reactants multiplied by their stoichiometric coefficients from the sum of the standard entropies of the products multiplied by their stoichiometric coefficients.

▶ Standard entropies are *absolute*: an entropy of zero is established by the third law of thermodynamics as the entropy of a perfect crystal at absolute zero.

▶ The entropy of a substance at a given temperature depends on factors that affect the number of energetically equivalent arrangements of the substance; these include the state, size, and molecular complexity of the substance.

Free Energy Changes in Chemical Reactions: Calculating ΔG°_{rxn} (17.7)

▶ There are three ways to calculate ΔG°_{rxn}: (1) from ΔH° and ΔS°, (2) from free energies of formations (only at 25 °C), and (3) from the ΔG°'s of reactions that sum to the reaction of interest.

▶ The magnitude of a negative ΔG°_{rxn} represents the theoretical amount of energy available to do work, while a positive ΔG°_{rxn} represents the minimum amount of energy required to make a nonspontaneous process occur.

Free Energy Changes for Nonstandard States: The Relationship between ΔG°_{rxn} and ΔG_{rxn} (17.8)

▶ The value of ΔG°_{rxn} applies only to standard conditions, and most real conditions are not standard.

▶ Under nonstandard conditions, we can calculate ΔG_{rxn} from the equation $\Delta G_{rxn} = \Delta G^{\circ}_{rxn} + RT \ln Q$.

Free Energy and Equilibrium: Relating ΔG°_{rxn} to the Equilibrium Constant (K) (17.9)

▶ Under standard conditions, the free energy change for a reaction is directly proportional to the negative of the natural log of the equilibrium constant, K; the more negative the free energy change (i.e., the more spontaneous the reaction), the larger the equilibrium constant.

▶ We can use the temperature dependence of ΔG°_{rxn}, as given by $\Delta G^{\circ} = \Delta H^{\circ} - T\Delta S^{\circ}$, to derive an expression for the temperature dependence of the equilibrium constant.

Key Equations and Relationships

The Definition of Entropy (17.3)

$$S = k \ln W \quad k = 1.38 \times 10^{-23} \text{ J/K}$$

Change in Entropy (17.3)

$$\Delta S = S_{final} - S_{initial}$$

Change in the Entropy of the Universe (17.4)

$$\Delta S_{univ} = \Delta S_{sys} + \Delta S_{surr}$$

Change in the Entropy of the Surroundings (17.4)

$$\Delta S_{surr} = \frac{-\Delta H_{sys}}{T} \text{ (constant } T, P)$$

Change in Gibbs Free Energy (17.5)

$$\Delta G = \Delta H - T\Delta S$$

The Relationship between Spontaneity and ΔH, ΔS, and T (17.5)

ΔH	ΔS	Low Temperature	High Temperature
−	+	Spontaneous	Spontaneous
+	−	Nonspontaneous	Nonspontaneous
−	−	Spontaneous	Nonspontaneous
+	+	Nonspontaneous	Spontaneous

Standard Change in Entropy (**17.6**)

$$\Delta S^\circ_{rxn} = \sum n_p S^\circ(\text{products}) - \sum n_r S^\circ(\text{reactants})$$

Methods for Calculating the Free Energy of Formation (ΔG°_{rxn}) (**17.7**)

1. $\Delta G^\circ_{rxn} = \Delta H^\circ_{rxn} - T\,\Delta S^\circ_{rxn}$
2.

$$\Delta G^\circ_{rxn} = \sum n_p\,\Delta G^\circ_f(\text{products}) - \sum n_r\,\Delta G^\circ_f(\text{reactants})$$

3. $\Delta G^\circ_{rxn(overall)} = \Delta G^\circ_{rxn(step\ 1)} + \Delta G^\circ_{rxn(step\ 2)} + \Delta G^\circ_{rxn(step\ 3)} + \ldots$

The Relationship between ΔG°_{rxn} and ΔG_{rxn} (**17.8**)

$$\Delta G_{rxn} = \Delta G^\circ_{rxn} + RT \ln Q \qquad R = 8.314 \text{ J/mol} \cdot \text{K}$$

The Relationship between ΔG°_{rxn} and K (**17.9**)

$$\Delta G^\circ_{rxn} = -RT \ln K$$

The Temperature Dependence of the Equilibrium Constant (**17.9**)

$$\ln K = -\frac{\Delta H^\circ_{rxn}}{R}\left(\frac{1}{T}\right) + \frac{\Delta S^\circ_{rxn}}{R}$$

$$\ln \frac{K_2}{K_1} = -\frac{\Delta H^\circ_{rxn}}{R}\left(\frac{1}{T_2} - \frac{1}{T_1}\right)$$

Key Learning Outcomes

Chapter Objectives	Assessment
Predicting the Sign of Entropy Change (**17.3**)	Example 17.1 For Practice 17.1 Exercises 27–28, 31–34, 37–38
Calculating Entropy Changes in the Surroundings (**17.4**) $\quad \Delta S_{univ} = \Delta S_{sys} + \Delta S_{surr}$ Positive Positive	Example 17.2 For Practice 17.2 For More Practice 17.2 Exercises 33–36
Computing Gibbs Free Energy Changes and Predicting Spontaneity from ΔH and ΔS (**17.5**)	Example 17.3 For Practice 17.3 Exercises 39–44
Computing Standard Entropy Changes (ΔS°_{rxn}) (**17.6**) Perfect crystal at 0 K $W = 1$ $S = 0$	Example 17.4 For Practice 17.4 Exercises 51–52
Calculating the Standard Change in Free Energy for a Reaction using $\Delta G^\circ_{rxn} = \Delta H^\circ_{rxn} - T\,\Delta S^\circ_{rxn}$ (**17.7**)	Examples 17.5, 17.6 For Practice 17.5, 17.6 Exercises 55–58, 61–62
Calculating ΔG°_{rxn} from Standard Free Energies of Formation (**17.7**)	Example 17.7 For Practice 17.7 For More Practice 17.7 Exercises 59–60
Determining ΔG°_{rxn} for a Stepwise Reaction (**17.7**)	Example 17.8 For Practice 17.8 Exercises 63–64
Calculating ΔG_{rxn} under Nonstandard Conditions (**17.8**)	Example 17.9 For Practice 17.9 Exercises 65–72
Relating the Equilibrium Constant and ΔG°_{rxn} (**17.9**)	Example 17.10 For Practice 17.10 Exercises 73–76

EXERCISES

Review Questions

1. What is the first law of thermodynamics and how does it relate to energy use?

2. What is nature's "heat tax" and how does it relate to energy use?

3. What is a perpetual motion machine? Can such a machine exist given the laws of thermodynamics?

4. Is it more efficient to heat your home with a natural gas furnace or an electric furnace? Explain.

5. What is a spontaneous process? Provide an example.

6. Explain the difference between the spontaneity of a reaction (which depends on thermodynamics) and the speed at which the reaction occurs (which depends on kinetics). Can a catalyst make a nonspontaneous reaction spontaneous?

7. What is the precise definition of entropy? What is the significance of entropy being a state function?

8. Why does the entropy of a gas increase when it expands into a vacuum?

9. Explain the difference between macrostates (external arrangements of particles) and microstates (internal arrangements of particles).

10. Based on its fundamental definition, explain why entropy is a measure of energy dispersion.

11. Provide the definition of the second law of thermodynamics. How does the second law explain why heat travels from a substance at higher temperature to one at lower temperature?

12. What happens to the entropy of a sample of matter when it changes state from a solid to a liquid? From a liquid to a gas?

13. Explain why water spontaneously freezes to form ice below 0 °C even though the entropy of the water decreases during the state transition. Why is the freezing of water not spontaneous above 0 °C?

14. Why do exothermic processes tend to be spontaneous at low temperatures? Why does their tendency toward spontaneity decrease with increasing temperature?

15. What is the significance of the change in Gibbs free energy (ΔG) for a reaction?

16. Predict the spontaneity of a reaction (and the temperature dependence of the spontaneity) for each possible combination of signs for ΔH and ΔS (for the system).
    a. ΔH negative, ΔS positive
    b. ΔH positive, ΔS negative
    c. ΔH negative, ΔS negative
    d. ΔH positive, ΔS positive

17. State the third law of thermodynamics and explain its significance.

18. Why is the standard entropy of a substance in the gas state greater than its standard entropy in the liquid state?

19. How does the standard entropy of a substance depend on its molar mass? On its molecular complexity?

20. How can you calculate the standard entropy change for a reaction from tables of standard entropies?

21. What are three different methods to calculate $\Delta G°$ for a reaction? Which method would you choose to calculate $\Delta G°$ for a reaction at a temperature other than 25 °C?

22. Why is free energy "free"?

23. Explain the difference between $\Delta G°$ and ΔG.

24. Why does water spilled on the floor evaporate even though $\Delta G°$ for the evaporation process is positive at room temperature?

25. How do you calculate the change in free energy for a reaction under nonstandard conditions?

26. How does the value of $\Delta G°$ for a reaction relate to the equilibrium constant for the reaction? What does a negative $\Delta G°$ for a reaction imply about K for the reaction? A positive $\Delta G°$?

Problems by Topic

Entropy, the Second Law of Thermodynamics, and the Direction of Spontaneous Change

27. Which of these processes is spontaneous?
    a. the combustion of natural gas
    b. the extraction of iron metal from iron ore
    c. a hot drink cooling to room temperature
    d. drawing heat energy from the ocean's surface to power a ship

28. Which of these processes are nonspontaneous? Are the nonspontaneous processes impossible?
    a. a bike going up a hill
    b. a meteor falling to Earth
    c. obtaining hydrogen gas from liquid water
    d. a ball rolling down a hill

29. Suppose that two systems, each composed of two particles represented by circles, have 20 J of total energy. Which system, A or B, has the greatest entropy? Why?

System A

10 J ———— • •

System B

12 J ———— •

8 J ———— •

30. Suppose two systems, each composed of three particles represented by circles, have 30 J of total energy. How many energetically equivalent ways can you distribute the particles in each system? Which system has greater entropy?

System A

10 J ———● ● ●———

System B

12 J ———●———

10 J ———●———

8 J ———●———

31. Without doing any calculations, determine the sign of ΔS_{sys} for each chemical reaction.
   a. $2\ KClO_3(s) \longrightarrow 2\ KCl(s) + 3\ O_2(g)$
   b. $CH_2{=}CH_2(g) + H_2(g) \longrightarrow CH_3CH_3(g)$
   c. $Na(s) + 1/2\ Cl_2(g) \longrightarrow NaCl(s)$
   d. $N_2(g) + 3\ H_2(g) \longrightarrow 2\ NH_3(g)$

32. Without doing any calculations, determine the sign of ΔS_{sys} for each chemical reaction.
   a. $Mg(s) + Cl_2(g) \longrightarrow MgCl_2(s)$
   b. $2\ H_2S(g) + 3\ O_2(g) \longrightarrow 2\ H_2O(g) + 2\ SO_2(g)$
   c. $2\ O_3(g) \longrightarrow 3\ O_2(g)$
   d. $HCl(g) + NH_3(g) \longrightarrow NH_4Cl(s)$

33. Without doing any calculations, determine the sign of ΔS_{sys} and ΔS_{surr} for each chemical reaction. In addition, predict under what temperatures (all temperatures, low temperatures, or high temperatures), if any, the reaction is spontaneous.
   a. $C_3H_8(g) + 5\ O_2(g) \longrightarrow 3\ CO_2(g) + 4\ H_2O(g)$
$$\Delta H^\circ_{rxn} = -2044\ kJ$$
   b. $N_2(g) + O_2(g) \longrightarrow 2\ NO(g)\quad \Delta H^\circ_{rxn} = +182.6\ kJ$
   c. $2\ N_2(g) + O_2(g) \longrightarrow 2\ N_2O(g)\quad \Delta H^\circ_{rxn} = +163.2\ kJ$
   d. $4\ NH_3(g) + 5\ O_2(g) \longrightarrow 4\ NO(g) + 6\ H_2O(g)$
$$\Delta H^\circ_{rxn} = -906\ kJ$$

34. Without doing any calculations, determine the sign of ΔS_{sys} and ΔS_{surr} for each chemical reaction. In addition, predict under what temperatures (all temperatures, low temperatures, or high temperatures), if any, the reaction is spontaneous.
   a. $2\ CO(g) + O_2(g) \longrightarrow 2\ CO_2(g)\quad \Delta H^\circ_{rxn} = -566.0\ kJ$
   b. $2\ NO_2(g) \longrightarrow 2\ NO(g) + O_2(g)\quad \Delta H^\circ_{rxn} = +113.1\ kJ$
   c. $2\ H_2(g) + O_2(g) \longrightarrow 2\ H_2O(g)\quad \Delta H^\circ_{rxn} = -483.6\ kJ$
   d. $CO_2(g) \longrightarrow C(s) + O_2(g)\quad \Delta H^\circ_{rxn} = +393.5\ kJ$

35. Calculate ΔS_{surr} at the indicated temperature for each reaction.
   a. $\Delta H^\circ_{rxn} = -385\ kJ;\ 298\ K$ **b.** $\Delta H^\circ_{rxn} = -385\ kJ;\ 77\ K$
   c. $\Delta H^\circ_{rxn} = +114\ kJ;\ 298\ K$ **d.** $\Delta H^\circ_{rxn} = +114\ kJ;\ 77\ K$

36. A reaction has $\Delta H^\circ_{rxn} = -112\ kJ$ and $\Delta S^\circ_{rxn} = 354\ J/K$. At what temperature is the change in entropy for the reaction equal to the change in entropy for the surroundings?

37. Given the values of ΔH°_{rxn}, ΔS°_{rxn}, and T, determine ΔS_{univ} and predict whether or not each reaction is spontaneous.
   a. $\Delta H^\circ_{rxn} = +115\ kJ;\ \Delta S^\circ_{rxn} = -263\ J/K;\ T = 298\ K$
   b. $\Delta H^\circ_{rxn} = -115\ kJ;\ \Delta S^\circ_{rxn} = +263\ J/K;\ T = 298\ K$
   c. $\Delta H^\circ_{rxn} = -115\ kJ;\ \Delta S^\circ_{rxn} = -263\ J/K;\ T = 298\ K$
   d. $\Delta H^\circ_{rxn} = -115\ kJ;\ \Delta S^\circ_{rxn} = -263\ J/K;\ T = 615\ K$

38. Given the values of ΔH_{rxn}, ΔS_{rxn}, and T, determine ΔS_{univ} and predict whether or not each reaction is spontaneous.
   a. $\Delta H^\circ_{rxn} = -95\ kJ;\ \Delta S^\circ_{rxn} = -157\ J/K;\ T = 298\ K$
   b. $\Delta H^\circ_{rxn} = -95\ kJ;\ \Delta S^\circ_{rxn} = -157\ J/K;\ T = 855\ K$
   c. $\Delta H^\circ_{rxn} = +95\ kJ;\ \Delta S^\circ_{rxn} = -157\ J/K;\ T = 298\ K$
   d. $\Delta H^\circ_{rxn} = -95\ kJ;\ \Delta S^\circ_{rxn} = +157\ J/K;\ T = 398\ K$

Standard Entropy Changes and Gibbs Free Energy

39. Calculate the change in Gibbs free energy for each of the sets of ΔH_{rxn}, ΔS_{rxn}, and T given in Problem 37. Predict whether or not each reaction is spontaneous at the temperature indicated.

40. Calculate the change in Gibbs free energy for each of the sets of ΔH_{rxn}, ΔS_{rxn}, and T given in Problem 38. Predict whether or not each reaction is spontaneous at the temperature indicated.

41. Calculate the free energy change for this reaction at 25 °C. Is the reaction spontaneous?
$$C_3H_8(g) + 5\ O_2(g) \longrightarrow 3\ CO_2(g) + 4\ H_2O(g)$$
$$\Delta H^\circ_{rxn} = -2217\ kJ;\ \Delta S^\circ_{rxn} = 101.1\ J/K$$

42. Calculate the free energy change for this reaction at 25 °C. Is the reaction spontaneous?
$$2\ Ca(s) + O_2(g) \longrightarrow 2\ CaO(s)$$
$$\Delta H^\circ_{rxn} = -1269.8\ kJ;\ \Delta S^\circ_{rxn} = -364.6\ J/K$$

43. Fill in the blanks in the table. Both ΔH and ΔS refer to the system.

ΔH	ΔS	ΔG	Low Temperature	High Temperature
−	+	−	Spontaneous	_____
−	−	Temperature dependent	_____	_____
+	+	_____	_____	Spontaneous
_____	−	_____	Nonspontaneous	Nonspontaneous

44. Predict the conditions (high temperature, low temperature, all temperatures, or no temperatures) under which each reaction is spontaneous.
   a. $H_2O(g) \longrightarrow H_2O(l)$
   b. $CO_2(s) \longrightarrow CO_2(g)$
   c. $H_2(g) \longrightarrow 2\ H(g)$
   d. $2\ NO_2(g) \longrightarrow 2\ NO(g) + O_2(g)$ (endothermic)

45. How does the molar entropy of a substance change with increasing temperature?

46. What is the molar entropy of a pure crystal at 0 K? What is the significance of the answer to this question?

47. For each pair of substances, choose the one that you expect to have the higher standard molar entropy (S°) at 25 °C. Explain the reasons for your choices.
   a. $CO(g)$; $CO_2(g)$ **b.** $CH_3OH(l)$; $CH_3OH(g)$
   c. $Ar(g)$; $CO_2(g)$ **d.** $CH_4(g)$; $SiH_4(g)$
   e. $NO_2(g)$; $CH_3CH_2CH_3(g)$ **f.** $NaBr(s)$; $NaBr(aq)$

48. For each pair of substances, choose the one that you expect to have the higher standard molar entropy (S°) at 25 °C. Explain the reasons for your choices.
   a. $NaNO_3(s)$; $NaNO_3(aq)$ **b.** $CH_4(g)$; $CH_3CH_3(g)$
   c. $Br_2(l)$; $Br_2(g)$ **d.** $Br_2(g)$; $F_2(g)$
   e. $PCl_3(g)$; $PCl_5(g)$
   f. $CH_3CH_2CH_2CH_3(g)$; $SO_2(g)$

49. Rank each set of substances in order of increasing standard molar entropy ($S°$). Explain your reasoning.
    a. $NH_3(g)$; $Ne(g)$; $SO_2(g)$; $CH_3CH_2OH(g)$; $He(g)$
    b. $H_2O(s)$; $H_2O(l)$; $H_2O(g)$
    c. $CH_4(g)$; $CF_4(g)$; $CCl_4(g)$

50. Rank each set of substances in order of increasing standard molar entropy ($S°$). Explain your reasoning.
    a. $I_2(g)$; $F_2(g)$; $Br_2(g)$; $Cl_2(g)$
    b. $H_2O(g)$; $H_2O_2(g)$; $H_2S(g)$
    c. $C(s, graphite)$; $C(s, diamond)$; $C(s, amorphous)$

51. Use data from Appendix IIB to calculate $\Delta S°_{rxn}$ for each of the reactions. In each case, try to rationalize the sign of $\Delta S°_{rxn}$.
    a. $C_2H_4(g) + H_2(g) \longrightarrow C_2H_6(g)$
    b. $C(s) + H_2O(g) \longrightarrow CO(g) + H_2(g)$
    c. $CO(g) + H_2O(g) \longrightarrow H_2(g) + CO_2(g)$
    d. $2 H_2S(g) + 3 O_2(g) \longrightarrow 2 H_2O(l) + 2 SO_2(g)$

52. Use data from Appendix IIB to calculate $\Delta S°_{rxn}$ for each of the reactions. In each case, try to rationalize the sign of $\Delta S°_{rxn}$.
    a. $3 NO_2(g) + H_2O(l) \longrightarrow 2 HNO_3(aq) + NO(g)$
    b. $Cr_2O_3(s) + 3 CO(g) \longrightarrow 2 Cr(s) + 3 CO_2(g)$
    c. $SO_2(g) + \frac{1}{2}O_2(g) \longrightarrow SO_3(g)$
    d. $N_2O_4(g) + 4 H_2(g) \longrightarrow N_2(g) + 4 H_2O(g)$

53. Find $\Delta S°$ for the formation of $CH_2Cl_2(g)$ from its gaseous elements in their standard states. Rationalize the sign of $\Delta S°$.

54. Find $\Delta S°$ for the reaction between nitrogen gas and fluorine gas to form nitrogen trifluoride gas. Rationalize the sign of $\Delta S°$.

55. Methanol burns in oxygen to form carbon dioxide and water. Write a balanced equation for the combustion of liquid methanol and calculate $\Delta H°_{rxn}$, $\Delta S°_{rxn}$, and $\Delta G°_{rxn}$ at 25 °C. Is the combustion of methanol spontaneous?

56. In photosynthesis, plants form glucose ($C_6H_{12}O_6$) and oxygen from carbon dioxide and water. Write a balanced equation for photosynthesis and calculate $\Delta H°_{rxn}$, $\Delta S°_{rxn}$, and $\Delta G°_{rxn}$ at 25 °C. Is photosynthesis spontaneous?

57. For each reaction, calculate $\Delta H°_{rxn}$, $\Delta S°_{rxn}$, and $\Delta G°_{rxn}$ at 25 °C and state whether or not the reaction is spontaneous. If the reaction is not spontaneous, would a change in temperature make it spontaneous? If so, should the temperature be raised or lowered from 25 °C?
    a. $N_2O_4(g) \longrightarrow 2 NO_2(g)$
    b. $NH_4Cl(s) \longrightarrow HCl(g) + NH_3(g)$
    c. $3 H_2(g) + Fe_2O_3(s) \longrightarrow 2 Fe(s) + 3 H_2O(g)$
    d. $N_2(g) + 3 H_2(g) \longrightarrow 2 NH_3(g)$

58. For each reaction, calculate $\Delta H°_{rxn}$, $\Delta S°_{rxn}$, and $\Delta G°_{rxn}$ at 25 °C and state whether or not the reaction is spontaneous. If the reaction is not spontaneous, would a change in temperature make it spontaneous? If so, should the temperature be raised or lowered from 25 °C?
    a. $2 CH_4(g) \longrightarrow C_2H_6(g) + H_2(g)$
    b. $2 NH_3(g) \longrightarrow N_2H_4(g) + H_2(g)$
    c. $N_2(g) + O_2(g) \longrightarrow 2 NO(g)$
    d. $2 KClO_3(s) \longrightarrow 2 KCl(s) + 3 O_2(g)$

59. Use standard free energies of formation to calculate $\Delta G°$ at 25 °C for each reaction in Problem 57. How do the values of $\Delta G°$ calculated this way compare to those calculated from $\Delta H°$ and $\Delta S°$? Which of the two methods could be used to determine how $\Delta G°$ changes with temperature?

60. Use standard free energies of formation to calculate $\Delta G°$ at 25 °C for each reaction in Problem 58. How well do the values of $\Delta G°$ calculated this way compare to those calculated from

$\Delta H°$ and $\Delta S°$? Which of the two methods could be used to determine how $\Delta G°$ changes with temperature?

61. Consider the reaction:
    $$2 NO(g) + O_2(g) \longrightarrow 2 NO_2(g)$$
    Estimate $\Delta G°$ for this reaction at each temperature and predict whether or not the reaction is spontaneous. (Assume that $\Delta H°$ and $\Delta S°$ do not change too much within the given temperature range.)
    a. 298 K   b. 715 K   c. 855 K

62. Consider the reaction:
    $$CaCO_3(s) \longrightarrow CaO(s) + CO_2(g)$$
    Estimate $\Delta G°$ for this reaction at each temperature and predict whether or not the reaction is spontaneous. (Assume that $\Delta H°$ and $\Delta S°$ do not change too much within the given temperature range.)
    a. 298 K   b. 1055 K   c. 1455 K

63. Determine $\Delta G°$ for the reaction:
    $$Fe_2O_3(s) + 3 CO(g) \longrightarrow 2 Fe(s) + 3 CO_2(g)$$
    Use the following reactions with known $\Delta G°_{rxn}$ values:
    $2 Fe(s) + \frac{3}{2}O_2(g) \longrightarrow Fe_2O_3(s)$ $\Delta G°_{rxn} = -742.2$ kJ
    $CO(g) + \frac{1}{2}O_2(g) \longrightarrow CO_2(g)$ $\Delta G°_{rxn} = -257.2$ kJ

64. Calculate $\Delta G°_{rxn}$ for the reaction:
    $$CaCO_3(s) \longrightarrow CaO(s) + CO_2(g)$$
    Use the following reactions and given $\Delta G°_{rxn}$ values:
    $Ca(s) + CO_2(g) + \frac{1}{2}O_2(g) \longrightarrow CaCO_3(s)$ $\Delta G°_{rxn} = -734.4$ kJ
    $2 Ca(s) + O_2(g) \longrightarrow 2 CaO(s)$ $\Delta G°_{rxn} = -1206.6$ kJ

Free Energy Changes, Nonstandard Conditions, and the Equilibrium Constant

65. Consider the sublimation of iodine at 25.0 °C:
    $$I_2(s) \longrightarrow I_2(g)$$
    a. Find $\Delta G°_{rxn}$ at 25.0 °C.
    b. Find ΔG_{rxn} at 25.0 °C under the following nonstandard conditions:
       i $P_{I_2} = 1.00$ mmHg
       ii $P_{I_2} = 0.100$ mmHg
    c. Explain why iodine spontaneously sublimes in open air at 25.0 °C.

66. Consider the evaporation of methanol at 25.0 °C:
    $$CH_3OH(l) \longrightarrow CH_3OH(g)$$
    a. Find $\Delta G_r°$ at 25.0 °C.
    b. Find ΔG_r at 25.0 °C under the following nonstandard conditions:
       i $P_{CH_3OH} = 150.0$ mmHg
       ii $P_{CH_3OH} = 100.0$ mmHg
       iii $P_{CH_3OH} = 10.0$ mmHg
    c. Explain why methanol spontaneously evaporates in open air at 25.0 °C.

67. Consider the reaction:
    $$CH_3OH(g) \rightleftharpoons CO(g) + 2 H_2(g)$$
    Calculate ΔG for this reaction at 25 °C under the following conditions:
    $P_{CH_3OH} = 0.855$ atm
    $P_{CO} = 0.125$ atm
    $P_{H_2} = 0.183$ atm

68. Consider the reaction:

$$CO_2(g) + CCl_4(g) \rightleftharpoons 2\ COCl_2(g)$$

Calculate ΔG for this reaction at 25 °C under the following conditions:

$P_{CO_2} = 0.112$ atm

$P_{CCl_4} = 0.174$ atm

$P_{COCl_2} = 0.744$ atm

69. Use data from Appendix IIB to calculate the equilibrium constants at 25 °C for each reaction.
a. $2\ CO(g) + O_2(g) \rightleftharpoons 2\ CO_2(g)$
b. $2\ H_2S(g) \rightleftharpoons 2\ H_2(g) + S_2(g)$

70. Use data from Appendix IIB to calculate the equilibrium constants at 25 °C for each reaction. ΔG_f° for $BrCl(g)$ is -1.0 kJ/mol.
a. $2\ NO_2(g) \rightleftharpoons N_2O_4(g)$
b. $Br_2(g) + Cl_2(g) \rightleftharpoons 2\ BrCl(g)$

71. Consider the reaction:

$$CO(g) + 2\ H_2(g) \rightleftharpoons CH_3OH(g)$$
$$K_p = 2.26 \times 10^4 \text{ at } 25\ ^\circ C$$

Calculate ΔG_{rxn} for the reaction at 25 °C under each of the following conditions:
a. standard conditions
b. at equilibrium
c. $P_{CH_3OH} = 1.0$ atm; $P_{CO} = P_{H_2} = 0.010$ atm

72. Consider the reaction:

$$I_2(g) + Cl_2(g) \rightleftharpoons 2\ ICl(g)$$
$$K_p = 81.9 \text{ at } 25\ ^\circ C$$

Calculate ΔG_{rxn} for the reaction at 25 °C under each of the following conditions:
a. standard conditions
b. at equilibrium
c. $P_{ICl} = 2.55$ atm; $P_{I_2} = 0.325$ atm; $P_{Cl_2} = 0.221$ atm

73. Estimate the value of the equilibrium constant at 525 K for each reaction in Problem 69.

74. Estimate the value of the equilibrium constant at 655 K for each reaction in Problem 70. (ΔH_f° for BrCl is 14.6 kJ/mol.)

75. Consider the reaction:

$$H_2(g) + I_2(g) \rightleftharpoons 2\ HI(g)$$

The following data show the equilibrium constant for this reaction measured at several different temperatures. Use the data to find ΔH_{rxn}° and ΔS_{rxn}° for the reaction.

Temperature	K_p
150 K	1.4×10^{-6}
175 K	4.6×10^{-4}
200 K	3.6×10^{-2}
225 K	1.1
250 K	15.5

76. Consider the reaction:

$$2\ NO(g) + O_2(g) \rightleftharpoons 2\ NO_2(g)$$

The following data show the equilibrium constant for this reaction measured at several different temperatures. Use the data to find ΔH_{rxn}° and ΔS_{rxn}° for the reaction.

Temperature	K_p
170 K	3.8×10^{-3}
180 K	0.34
190 K	18.4
200 K	681

77. The change in enthalpy (ΔH_{rxn}°) for a reaction is -25.8 kJ/mol. The equilibrium constant for the reaction is 1.4×10^3 at 298 K. What is the equilibrium constant for the reaction at 655 K?

78. A reaction has an equilibrium constant of 8.5×10^3 at 298 K. At 755 K, the equilibrium constant is 0.65. Find ΔH_{rxn}° for the reaction.

Cumulative Problems

79. Determine the sign of ΔS_{sys} for each process:
a. water boiling
b. water freezing
c.

80. Determine the sign of ΔS_{sys} for each process:
a. dry ice subliming
b. dew forming
c.

81. Our atmosphere is composed primarily of nitrogen and oxygen, which coexist at 25 °C without reacting to any significant extent. However, the two gases can react to form nitrogen monoxide according to the reaction:

$$N_2(g) + O_2(g) \rightleftharpoons 2\ NO(g)$$

a. Calculate ΔG° and K_p for this reaction at 298 K. Is the reaction spontaneous?
b. Estimate ΔG° at 2000 K. Does the reaction become more spontaneous as temperature increases?

82. Nitrogen dioxide, a pollutant in the atmosphere, can combine with water to form nitric acid. One of the possible reactions is shown here. Calculate ΔG° and K_p for this reaction at 25 °C and comment on the spontaneity of the reaction.

$$3\ NO_2(g) + H_2O(l) \longrightarrow 2\ HNO_3(aq) + NO(g)$$

83. Ethene (C_2H_4) can be halogenated by the reaction:

$$C_2H_4(g) + X_2(g) \rightleftharpoons C_2H_4X_2(g)$$

where X_2 can be Cl_2, Br_2, or I_2. Use the thermodynamic data given to calculate $\Delta H°$, $\Delta S°$, $\Delta G°$, and K_p for the halogenation reaction by each of the three halogens at 25 °C. Which reaction is most spontaneous? Least spontaneous? What is the main factor responsible for the difference in the spontaneity of the three reactions? Does higher temperature make the reactions more spontaneous or less spontaneous?

Compound	$\Delta H°_f$ (kJ/mol)	$S°$(J/mol·K)
$C_2H_4Cl_2(g)$	−129.7	308.0
$C_2H_4Br_2(g)$	+38.3	330.6
$C_2H_4I_2(g)$	+66.5	347.8

84. H_2 reacts with the halogens (X_2) according to the reaction:

$$H_2(g) + X_2(g) \rightleftharpoons 2\ HX(g)$$

where X_2 can be Cl_2, Br_2, or I_2. Use the thermodynamic data in Appendix IIB to calculate $\Delta H°$, $\Delta S°$, $\Delta G°$, and K_p for the reaction between hydrogen and each of the three halogens. Which reaction is most spontaneous? Least spontaneous? What is the main factor responsible for the difference in the spontaneity of the three reactions? Does higher temperature make the reactions more spontaneous or less spontaneous?

85. Consider this reaction occurring at 298 K:

$$N_2O(g) + NO_2(g) \rightleftharpoons 3\ NO(g)$$

   a. Show that the reaction is not spontaneous under standard conditions by calculating $\Delta G°_{rxn}$.
   b. If a reaction mixture contains only N_2O and NO_2 at partial pressures of 1.0 atm each, the reaction will be spontaneous until some NO forms in the mixture. What maximum partial pressure of NO builds up before the reaction ceases to be spontaneous?
   c. Can the reaction be made more spontaneous by an increase or decrease in temperature? If so, what temperature is required to make the reaction spontaneous under standard conditions?

86. Consider this reaction occurring at 298 K:

$$BaCO_3(s) \rightleftharpoons BaO(s) + CO_2(g)$$

   a. Show that the reaction is not spontaneous under standard conditions by calculating $\Delta G°_{rxn}$.
   b. If $BaCO_3$ is placed in an evacuated flask, what is the partial pressure of CO_2 when the reaction reaches equilibrium?
   c. Can the reaction be made more spontaneous by an increase or decrease in temperature? If so, at what temperature is the partial pressure of carbon dioxide 1.0 atm?

87. Living organisms use energy from the metabolism of food to create an energy-rich molecule called adenosine triphosphate (ATP). The ATP then acts as an energy source for a variety of reactions that the living organism must carry out to survive. ATP provides energy through its hydrolysis, which can be symbolized as follows:

$$ATP(aq) + H_2O(l) \longrightarrow ADP(aq) + P_i(aq) \quad \Delta G°_{rxn} = -30.5\ kJ$$

where ADP represents adenosine diphosphate and P_i represents an inorganic phosphate group (such as HPO_4^{2-}).

   a. Calculate the equilibrium constant, K, for the given reaction at 298 K.
   b. The free energy obtained from the oxidation (reaction with oxygen) of glucose ($C_6H_{12}O_6$) to form carbon dioxide and water can be used to re-form ATP by driving the given reaction in reverse. Calculate the standard free energy change for the oxidation of glucose and estimate the maximum number of moles of ATP that can be formed by the oxidation of one mole of glucose.

88. The standard free energy change for the hydrolysis of ATP was given in Problem 87. In a particular cell, the concentrations of ATP, ADP, and P_i are 0.0031 M, 0.0014 M, and 0.0048 M, respectively. Calculate the free energy change for the hydrolysis of ATP under these conditions. (Assume a temperature of 298 K.)

89. These reactions are important in catalytic converters in automobiles. Calculate $\Delta G°$ for each at 298 K. Predict the effect of increasing temperature on the magnitude of $\Delta G°$.
   a. $2\ CO(g) + 2\ NO(g) \longrightarrow N_2(g) + 2\ CO_2(g)$
   b. $5\ H_2(g) + 2\ NO(g) \longrightarrow 2\ NH_3(g) + 2\ H_2O(g)$
   c. $2\ H_2(g) + 2\ NO(g) \longrightarrow N_2(g) + 2\ H_2O(g)$
   d. $2\ NH_3(g) + 2\ O_2(g) \longrightarrow N_2O(g) + 3\ H_2O(g)$

90. Calculate $\Delta G°$ at 298 K for these reactions and predict the effect on $\Delta G°$ of lowering the temperature.
   a. $NH_3(g) + HBr(g) \longrightarrow NH_4Br(s)$
   b. $CaCO_3(s) \longrightarrow CaO(s) + CO_2(g)$
   c. $CH_4(g) + 3\ Cl_2(g) \longrightarrow CHCl_3(g) + 3\ HCl(g)$
   ($\Delta G°_f$ for $CHCl_3(g)$ is −70.4 kJ/mol.)

91. All the oxides of nitrogen have positive values of $\Delta G°_f$ at 298 K, but only one common oxide of nitrogen has a positive $\Delta S°_f$. Identify that oxide of nitrogen without reference to thermodynamic data and explain.

92. The values of $\Delta G°_f$ for the hydrogen halides become less negative with increasing atomic number. The $\Delta G°_f$ of HI is slightly positive. On the other hand, the trend in $\Delta S°_f$ is to become more positive with increasing atomic number. Explain.

93. Consider the reaction $X_2(g) \longrightarrow 2\ X(g)$. When a vessel initially containing 755 torr of X_2 comes to equilibrium at 298 K, the equilibrium partial pressure of X is 103 torr. The same reaction is repeated with an initial partial pressure of 748 torr of X_2 at 755 K; the equilibrium partial pressure of X is 532 torr. Find $\Delta H°$ for the reaction.

94. Dinitrogen tetroxide decomposes to nitrogen dioxide:

$$N_2O_4(g) \longrightarrow 2\ NO_2(g) \quad \Delta H°_{rxn} = 55.3\ kJ$$

At 298 K, a reaction vessel initially contains 0.100 atm of N_2O_4. When equilibrium is reached, 58% of the N_2O_4 has decomposed to NO_2. What percentage of N_2O_4 decomposes at 388 K? Assume that the initial pressure of N_2O_4 is the same (0.100 atm).

95. Indicate and explain the sign of ΔS_{univ} for each process.
   a. $2\ H_2(g) + O_2(g) \longrightarrow 2\ H_2O(l)$ at 298 K
   b. the electrolysis of $H_2O(l)$ to $H_2(g)$ and $O_2(g)$ at 298 K
   c. the growth of an oak tree from a little acorn

96. The Haber process is very important for agriculture because it converts $N_2(g)$ from the atmosphere into bound nitrogen, which can be taken up and used by plants. The Haber process reaction is $N_2(g) + 3\ H_2(g) \rightleftharpoons 2\ NH_3(g)$. The reaction is exothermic but is carried out at relatively high temperatures. Why?

97. A metal salt with the formula MCl_2 crystallizes from water to form a solid with the composition $MCl_2 \cdot 6\,H_2O$. The equilibrium vapor pressure of water above this solid at 298 K is 18.3 mmHg. What is the value of ΔG for the reaction $MCl_2 \cdot 6\,H_2O(s) \rightleftharpoons MCl_2(s) + 6\,H_2O(g)$ when the pressure of water vapor is 18.3 mmHg? When the pressure of water vapor is 760 mmHg?

98. The solubility of $AgCl(s)$ in water at 25 °C is 1.33×10^{-5} mol/L and its $\Delta H°$ of solution is 65.7 kJ/mol. What is its solubility at 50.0 °C?

Challenge Problems

99. Review the box in this chapter entitled *Chemistry in Your Day: Making a Nonspontaneous Process Spontaneous.* The hydrolysis of ATP, shown in Problem 87, is often used to drive nonspontaneous processes—such as muscle contraction and protein synthesis—in living organisms. The nonspontaneous process to be driven must be coupled to the ATP hydrolysis reaction. For example, suppose the nonspontaneous process is A + B $\longrightarrow$ AB ($\Delta G°$ positive). The coupling of a nonspontaneous reaction such as this one to the hydrolysis of ATP is often accomplished by the mechanism:

$$\text{A + ATP + H}_2\text{O} \longrightarrow \text{A—P}_i + \text{ADP}$$
$$\underline{\text{A—P}_i + \text{B} \longrightarrow \text{AB + P}_i}$$
$$\text{A + B + ATP + H}_2\text{O} \longrightarrow \text{AB + ADP + P}_i$$

As long as ΔG_{rxn} for the nonspontaneous reaction is less than 30.5 kJ, the reaction can be made spontaneous by coupling in this way to the hydrolysis of ATP. Suppose that ATP is to drive the reaction between glutamate and ammonia to form glutamine:

a. Calculate K for the reaction between glutamate and ammonia. (The standard free energy change for the reaction is +14.2 kJ/mol. Assume a temperature of 298 K.)

b. Write a set of reactions such as those given showing how the glutamate and ammonia reaction can couple with the hydrolysis of ATP. What is $\Delta G_{rxn}°$ and K for the coupled reaction?

100. Calculate the entropy of each state and rank the states in order of increasing entropy.

(a)

(b)

(c)

101. Suppose we redefine the standard state as $P = 2$ atm. Find the new standard $\Delta G_f°$ values of each substance.
a. $HCl(g)$
b. $N_2O(g)$
c. $H(g)$
Explain the results in terms of the relative entropies of reactants and products of each reaction.

102. The ΔG for the freezing of $H_2O(l)$ at −10 °C is −210 J/mol, and the heat of fusion of ice at this temperature is 5610 J/mol. Find the entropy change of the universe when 1 mol of water freezes at −10 °C.

103. Consider the reaction that occurs during the Haber process:

$$N_2(g) + 3\,H_2(g) \longrightarrow 2\,NH_3(g)$$

The equilibrium constant is 3.9×10^5 at 300 K and 1.2×10^{-1} at 500 K. Calculate $\Delta H_{rxn}°$ and $\Delta S_{rxn}°$ for this reaction.

104. The salt ammonium nitrate can follow three modes of decomposition: (a) to $HNO_3(g)$ and $NH_3(g)$, (b) to $N_2O(g)$ and $H_2O(g)$, and (c) to $N_2(g)$, $O_2(g)$, and $H_2O(g)$. Calculate $\Delta G_{rxn}°$ for each mode of decomposition at 298 K. Explain in light of these results how it is still possible to use ammonium nitrate as a fertilizer and the precautions that should be taken when it is used.

105. Given the data, calculate ΔS_{vap} for each of the first four liquids. ($\Delta S_{vap} = \Delta H_{vap}/T$, where T is in K)

Compound	Name	BP (°C)	ΔH_{vap}(kJ/mol) at BP
$C_4H_{10}O$	Diethyl ether	34.6	26.5
C_3H_6O	Acetone	56.1	29.1
C_6H_6O	Benzene	79.8	30.8
$CHCl_3$	Chloroform	60.8	29.4
C_2H_5OH	Ethanol	77.8	38.6
H_2O	Water	100	40.7

All four values should be close to each other. Predict whether the last two liquids in the table have ΔS_{vap} in this same range. If not, predict whether it is larger or smaller and explain. Verify your prediction.

Conceptual Problems

106. Which is more efficient, a butane lighter or an electric lighter (such as can be found in most automobiles)? Explain.

107. Which statement is true?
   a. A spontaneous reaction is always a fast reaction.
   b. A spontaneous reaction is always a slow reaction.
   c. The spontaneity of a reaction is not necessarily related to the speed of a reaction.

108. Which process is necessarily driven by an increase in the entropy of the surroundings?
   a. the condensation of water
   b. the sublimation of dry ice
   c. the freezing of water

109. Consider the changes in the distribution of nine particles into three interconnected boxes shown here. Which has the most negative ΔS?

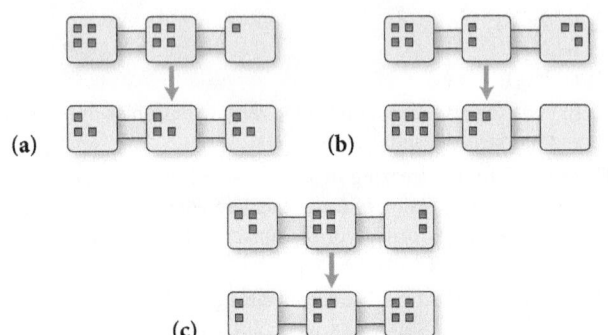

(a)   (b)

(c)

110. Which statement is true?
   a. A reaction in which the entropy of the system increases can be spontaneous only if it is exothermic.
   b. A reaction in which the entropy of the system increases can be spontaneous only if it is endothermic.
   c. A reaction in which the entropy of the system decreases can be spontaneous only if it is exothermic.

111. Which process is spontaneous at 298 K?
   a. $H_2O(l) \longrightarrow H_2O(g, 1\ atm)$
   b. $H_2O(l) \longrightarrow H_2O(g, 0.10\ atm)$
   c. $H_2O(l) \longrightarrow H_2O(g, 0.010\ atm)$

112. The free energy change of the reaction $A(g) \longrightarrow B(g)$ is zero under certain conditions. The *standard* free energy change of the reaction is -42.5 kJ. Which statement must be true about the reaction?
   a. The concentration of the product is greater than the concentration of the reactant.
   b. The reaction is at equilibrium.
   c. The concentration of the reactant is greater than the concentration of the product.

113. The reaction $A(g) \rightleftharpoons B(g)$ has an equilibrium constant of 5.8 and under certain conditions has Q = 336. What can you conclude about the sign of ΔG_{rxn}° and ΔG_{rxn} for this reaction under these conditions?

Answers to Conceptual Connections

Nature's Heat Tax and Diet

17.1 A person subsisting on a vegetarian diet eats fruits and vegetables, metabolizing the energy-containing molecules of these foods directly. A person subsisting on a meat-based diet eats the meat of animals such as cows and metabolizes energy-containing molecules that were part of the animals. A cow synthesized its energy-containing molecules from compounds that it obtained by eating and digesting plants. Since breaking down and resynthesizing biological molecules requires energy—and since the cow also needs to extract some of the energy in its food to live—a meat-based diet necessitates additional energy transactions in the overall process of obtaining energy for life. Due to nature's heat tax, the meat-based diet is less efficient than the vegetarian diet.

Entropy

17.2 **(a)** The more spread out the particles are between the three boxes, the greater the entropy. Therefore, the entropy change is positive only in scheme **(a)**.

Entropy and Biological Systems

17.3 Biological systems do not violate the second law of thermodynamics. The key to understanding this concept is realizing that entropy changes in the system can be negative as long as the entropy change of the universe is positive. Biological systems can decrease their own entropy, but only at the expense of creating more entropy in the surroundings (which they do primarily by emitting the heat they generate by their metabolic processes). Thus, for any biological process, ΔS_{univ} is positive.

ΔH, ΔS, and ΔG

17.4 **(a)** Sublimation is endothermic (it requires energy to overcome the intermolecular forces that hold solid carbon dioxide together), so ΔH is positive. The number of moles of gas increases when the solid turns into a gas, so the entropy of the carbon dioxide increases and ΔS is positive. Since $\Delta G = \Delta H - T\Delta S$, ΔG is positive at low temperature and negative at high temperature.

Standard Entropies

17.5 $Kr < Cl_2 < SO_3$. Because Krypton is a monoatomic gas, it has the least entropy. Because SO_3 is the most complex molecule, it has the most entropy. The molar masses of the three gases vary slightly, but not enough to overcome the differences in molecular complexity.

Free Energy Changes and Le Châtelier's Principle

17.6 **(a)** A high concentration of reactants relative to products will lead to $Q < 1$, making the term $RT \ln Q$ in Equation 17.14 negative. ΔG_{rxn} is more negative than ΔG_{rxn}° and the reaction is more spontaneous.

K and ΔG_{rxn}°

17.7 **(c)** Since the equilibrium constant is less than 1, the reaction proceeds toward reactants under standard conditions (when $Q = 1$). Therefore, ΔG_{rxn}° is positive.

18

Electrochemistry

One day sir, you may tax it.

—Michael Faraday (1791–1867)

[In response to Mr. Gladstone, the British chancellor of the exchequer, when asked about the practical worth of electricity.]

THIS CHAPTER'S OPENING QUOTE FROM MICHAEL FARADAY illustrates an important aspect of basic research (research for the sake of understanding how nature works). The chancellor of the exchequer (the British cabinet minister responsible for all financial matters) wanted to know how Michael Faraday's apparently esoteric investigations of electricity would ever be useful to the empire. Faraday responded in a way that the chancellor would understand—he pointed out the eventual financial payoff. Today, of course, electricity is a fundamental form of energy, powering our entire economy. Although basic research does not always lead to useful applications, much of the technology our society relies on has grown out of basic research. The history of modern science shows that you must first understand nature (the goal of basic research) before you can harness its power. In this chapter, we discuss oxidation–reduction reactions (first introduced in Chapter 4) and how we can exploit them to generate electricity. The applications range from the batteries that power flashlights to the fuel cells that may one day power our homes and automobiles.

The equations shown in the image:

Anode reaction:
$$2 H_2(g) + 4 OH^-(aq) \rightarrow 4 H_2O(l) + 4 e^-$$

Cathode reaction:
$$O_2(g) + 2 H_2O(l) + 4 e^- \rightarrow 4 OH^-(aq)$$

Overall reaction:
$$2 H_2(g) + O_2(g) \rightarrow 2 \ldots$$

18.1 Pulling the Plug on the Power Grid

The power grid distributes centrally generated electricity throughout the country to homes and businesses. When you turn on a light or electrical appliance, electricity flows from the grid, through the wires in your home, to the light or appliance. The electrical energy is converted into light within the lightbulb or into work within the appliance. The average U.S. household consumes about 1000 kilowatt-hours (kWh) of electricity per month. The local electrical utility, of course, monitors your electricity use and bills you for it.

In the future, you may have the option of disconnecting from the power grid. Several innovative companies are developing small, fuel-cell power plants—each no bigger than a refrigerator—to sit next to homes and quietly generate enough electricity to meet each household's power needs. The heat produced by a fuel cell's operation can be recaptured and used to heat water or the space within the home, eliminating the need for a hot-water

The smartphone shown here is powered by a hydrogen–oxygen fuel cell, a device that generates electricity from the reaction between hydrogen and oxygen to form water.

The kilowatt-hour is a unit of energy first introduced in Section 6.2.

▲ The energy produced by this fuel cell can power an entire house.

▲ The B-Class F-Cell vehicle from Mercedes Benz is a four passenger sedan that accelerates from 0 to 60 mph in about 9 seconds. The car runs on hydrogen and its only emission is water.

| Review Section 4.9 on assigning oxidation states.

heater or a furnace. Similar fuel cells can also power cars. Fuel cells are highly efficient and, although some obstacles to their development and use must yet be overcome, one day they may supply a majority of our power while producing less pollution than fossil fuel combustion.

Fuel cells are based on oxidation–reduction reactions (see Section 4.9). The most common type of fuel cell—called the hydrogen–oxygen fuel cell—is based on the reaction between hydrogen and oxygen:

$$2 \, H_2(g) + O_2(g) \longrightarrow 2 \, H_2O(l)$$

In this reaction, hydrogen and oxygen form covalent bonds with one another. Recall that, according to Lewis theory, a single covalent bond is a shared electron pair. However, since oxygen is more electronegative than hydrogen, the electron pair in a hydrogen–oxygen bond is not *equally* shared: oxygen gets the larger portion (see Section 9.6). In effect, oxygen has more electrons in H_2O than it does in elemental O_2—it has gained electrons in the reaction and has therefore been reduced.

In a reaction between hydrogen and oxygen, oxygen atoms gain electrons directly from hydrogen atoms. In a hydrogen–oxygen fuel cell, this same redox reaction occurs, but the hydrogen and oxygen are separated, forcing electrons to travel through an external wire to get from hydrogen to oxygen. The moving electrons constitute an electrical current. In this way, fuel cells employ the electron-gaining tendency of oxygen and the electron-losing tendency of hydrogen to force electrons to move through a wire to create the electricity that can provide power for a home or an electric automobile. Smaller fuel cells can also replace batteries and be used to power consumer electronics such as laptop computers, smart phones, and MP3 players. The generation of electricity from spontaneous redox reactions (such as those that occur in a fuel cell) and the use of electricity to drive nonspontaneous redox reactions (such as those that occur in gold or silver plating) are examples of electrochemistry, the subject of this chapter.

18.2 Balancing Oxidation–Reduction Equations

Recall from Section 4.9 that *oxidation* is the loss of electrons, and *reduction* is the gain of electrons. Recall also that we can identify oxidation–reduction reactions through changes in oxidation states: *oxidation corresponds to an increase in oxidation state and reduction corresponds to a decrease in oxidation state.* For example, consider the following reaction between calcium and water:

$$\underset{0}{Ca(s)} + \underset{+1 \; -2}{2 \, H_2O(l)} \longrightarrow \underset{+2 \; -2 +1}{Ca(OH)_2(aq)} + \underset{0}{H_2(g)}$$

Because calcium increases in oxidation state from 0 to +2, it is oxidized. Because hydrogen decreases in oxidation state from +1 to 0, it is reduced.

Balancing redox reactions can be more complicated than balancing other types of reactions because both the mass (or number of each type of atom) and the *charge* must be balanced. We can balance redox reactions occurring in aqueous solutions with a special procedure called the *half-reaction method of balancing*. In this procedure, we break down the overall equation into two half-reactions: one for oxidation and one for reduction. We then balance the half-reactions individually and add them together. The steps differ slightly for reactions occurring in acidic and in basic solution. Examples 18.1 and 18.2 demonstrate the method for an acidic solution, and Example 18.3 demonstrates the method for a basic solution.

PROCEDURE FOR...	**EXAMPLE 18.1**	**EXAMPLE 18.2**
Half-Reaction Method of Balancing Aqueous Redox Equations in Acidic Solution	**Half-Reaction Method of Balancing Aqueous Redox Equations in Acidic Solution**	**Half-Reaction Method of Balancing Aqueous Redox Equations in Acidic Solution**
GENERAL PROCEDURE	Balance the redox equation: $Al(s) + Cu^{2+}(aq) \longrightarrow Al^{3+}(aq) + Cu(s)$	Balance the redox equation: $Fe^{2+}(aq) + MnO_4^-(aq) \longrightarrow$ $Fe^{3+}(aq) + Mn^{2+}(aq)$
Step 1 *Assign oxidation states* to all atoms and identify the substances being oxidized and reduced.	$Al(s) + Cu^{2+}(aq) \longrightarrow Al^{3+}(aq) + Cu(s)$ 0 +2 +3 0 Reduction Oxidation	$Fe^{2+}(aq) + MnO_4^-(aq) \longrightarrow Fe^{3+}(aq) + Mn^{2+}(aq)$ +2 +7 −2 +3 +2 Reduction Oxidation
Step 2 *Separate the overall reaction into two half-reactions*: one for oxidation and one for reduction.	***Oxidation:*** $Al(s) \longrightarrow Al^{3+}(aq)$ ***Reduction:*** $Cu^{2+}(aq) \longrightarrow Cu(s)$	***Oxidation:*** $Fe^{2+}(aq) \longrightarrow Fe^{3+}(aq)$ ***Reduction:*** $MnO_4^-(aq) \longrightarrow Mn^{2+}(aq)$
Step 3 *Balance each half-reaction with respect to mass* in the following order: • Balance all elements other than H and O. • Balance O by adding H_2O. • Balance H by adding H^+.	All elements are balanced, so proceed to the next step.	All elements other than H and O are balanced so proceed to balance H and O. $Fe^{2+}(aq) \longrightarrow Fe^{3+}(aq)$ $MnO_4^-(aq) \longrightarrow Mn^{2+}(aq) + 4\,H_2O(l)$ $8\,H^+(aq) + MnO_4^-(aq) \longrightarrow$ $Mn^{2+}(aq) + 4\,H_2O(l)$
Step 4 *Balance each half-reaction with respect to charge* by adding electrons. (Make the sum of the charges on both sides of the equation equal by adding as many electrons as necessary.)	$Al(s) \longrightarrow Al^{3+}(aq) + 3\,e^-$ $2\,e^- + Cu^{2+}(aq) \longrightarrow Cu(s)$	$Fe^{2+}(aq) \longrightarrow Fe^{3+}(aq) + 1e^-$ $5e^- + 8\,H^+(aq) + MnO_4^-(aq) \longrightarrow$ $Mn^{2+}(aq) + 4\,H_2O(l)$
Step 5 *Make the number of electrons in both half-reactions equal* by multiplying one or both half-reactions by a small whole number.	$2[Al(s) \longrightarrow Al^{3+}(aq) + 3\,e^-]$ $2\,Al(s) \longrightarrow 2\,Al^{3+}(aq) + 6\,e^-$ $3[2\,e^- + Cu^{2+}(aq) \longrightarrow Cu(s)]$ $6\,e^- + 3\,Cu^{2+}(aq) \longrightarrow 3\,Cu(s)$	$5[Fe^{2+}(aq) \longrightarrow Fe^{3+}(aq) + 1\,e^-]$ $5\,Fe^{2+}(aq) \longrightarrow 5\,Fe^{3+}(aq) + 5\,e^-$ $5\,e^- + 8\,H^+(aq) + MnO_4^-(aq) \longrightarrow$ $Mn^{2+}(aq) + 4\,H_2O(l)$
Step 6 *Add the two half-reactions together*, canceling electrons and other species as necessary.	$2\,Al(s) \longrightarrow 2\,Al^{3+}(aq) + 6\,e^-$ $6\,e^- + 3\,Cu^{2+}(aq) \longrightarrow 3\,Cu(s)$ ――――――――――――― $2\,Al(s) + 3\,Cu^{2+}(aq) \longrightarrow$ $2\,Al^{3+}(aq) + 3\,Cu(s)$	$5\,Fe^{2+}(aq) \longrightarrow 5\,Fe^{3+}(aq) + 5\,e^-$ $5\,e^- + 8\,H^+(aq) + MnO_4^-(aq) \longrightarrow$ $Mn^{2+}(aq) + 4\,H_2O(l)$ ――――――――――――― $5\,Fe^{2+}(aq) + 8\,H^+(aq) + MnO_4^-(aq) \longrightarrow$ $5\,Fe^{3+}(aq) + Mn^{2+}(aq) + 4\,H_2O(l)$

Step 7	*Verify that the reaction is balanced both with respect to mass and with respect to charge.*

Reactants	Products
2 Al	2 Al
3 Cu	3 Cu
+6 charge	+6 charge

Reactants	Products
5 Fe	5 Fe
8 H	8 H
1 Mn	1 Mn
4 O	4 O
+17 charge	+17 charge

FOR PRACTICE 18.1

Balance the redox reaction in acidic solution:

$$H^+(aq) + Cr(s) \longrightarrow H_2(g) + Cr^{2+}(aq)$$

FOR PRACTICE 18.2

Balance the redox reaction in acidic solution:

$$Cu(s) + NO_3^-(aq) \longrightarrow Cu^{2+}(aq) + NO_2(g)$$

When a redox reaction occurs in basic solution, we balance the reaction in a similar manner, except that we add an additional step to neutralize any H^+ with OH^-. The H^+ and the OH^- combine to form H_2O as shown in Example 18.3.

EXAMPLE 18.3 Balancing Redox Reactions Occurring in Basic Solution

Balance the equation occurring in basic solution:

$$I^-(aq) + MnO_4^-(aq) \longrightarrow I_2(aq) + MnO_2(s)$$

SOLUTION

To balance redox reactions occurring in basic solution, follow the half-reaction method outlined in Examples 18.1 and 18.2, but add an extra step to neutralize the acid with OH^- as shown in step 3.

1. Assign oxidation states.	$$\underset{-1}{I^-}(aq) + \underset{+7\ -2}{MnO_4^-}(aq) \longrightarrow \underset{0}{I_2}(aq) + \underset{+4\ -2}{MnO_2}(s)$$ Reduction / Oxidation
2. Separate the overall reaction into two half-reactions.	*Oxidation:* $I^-(aq) \longrightarrow I_2(aq)$ *Reduction:* $MnO_4^-(aq) \longrightarrow MnO_2(s)$
3. Balance each half-reaction with respect to mass. • Balance all elements other than H and O. • Balance O by adding H_2O. • Balance H by adding H^+. • Neutralize H^+ by adding enough OH^- to neutralize each H^+. Add the same number of OH^- ions to each side of the equation.	$\begin{cases} 2\,I^-(aq) \longrightarrow I_2(aq) \\ MnO_4^-(aq) \longrightarrow MnO_2(s) \end{cases}$ $\begin{cases} 2\,I^-(aq) \longrightarrow I_2(aq) \\ MnO_4^-(aq) \longrightarrow MnO_2(s) + 2\,H_2O(l) \end{cases}$ $\begin{cases} 2\,I^-(aq) \longrightarrow I_2(aq) \\ 4\,H^+(aq) + MnO_4^-(aq) \longrightarrow MnO_2(s) + 2\,H_2O(l) \end{cases}$ $\begin{cases} 2\,I^-(aq) \longrightarrow I_2(aq) \\ 4\,H^+(aq) + 4\,OH^-(aq) + MnO_4^-(aq) \longrightarrow MnO_2(s) + 2\,H_2O(l) + 4\,OH^-(aq) \end{cases}$ $\underbrace{\qquad\qquad}_{4\,H_2O(l)}$

4. Balance each half-reaction with respect to charge.	$2\,I^-(aq) \longrightarrow I_2(aq) + 2\,e^-$ $4\,H_2O(l) + MnO_4^-(aq) + 3\,e^- \longrightarrow MnO_2(s) + 2\,H_2O(l) + 4\,OH^-(aq)$
5. Make the number of electrons in both half-reactions equal.	$3[2\,I^-(aq) \longrightarrow I_2(aq) + 2\,e^-]$ $6\,I^-(aq) \longrightarrow 3\,I_2(aq) + 6\,e^-$ $2[4\,H_2O(l) + MnO_4^-(aq) + 3\,e^- \longrightarrow MnO_2(s) + 2\,H_2O(l) + 4\,OH^-(aq)]$ $8\,H_2O(l) + 2\,MnO_4^-(aq) + 6\,e^- \longrightarrow 2\,MnO_2(s) + 4\,H_2O(l) + 8\,OH^-(aq)$
6. Add the half-reactions together.	$6\,I^-(aq) \longrightarrow 3\,I_2(aq) + \cancel{6\,e^-}$ $\cancel{4}8\,H_2O(l) + 2\,MnO_4^-(aq) + \cancel{6\,e^-} \longrightarrow 2\,MnO_2(s) + \cancel{4\,H_2O(l)} + 8\,OH^-(aq)$ ——————————————————————————————— $6\,I^-(aq) + 4\,H_2O(l) + 2\,MnO_4^-(aq) \longrightarrow 3\,I_2(aq) + 2\,MnO_2(s) + 8\,OH^-(aq)$

7. Verify that the reaction is balanced.

Reactants	Products
6 I	6 I
8 H	8 H
2 Mn	2 Mn
12 O	12 O
−8 charge	−8 charge

FOR PRACTICE 18.3

Balance the following redox reaction occurring in basic solution.

$$ClO^-(aq) + Cr(OH)_4^-(aq) \longrightarrow CrO_4^{2-}(aq) + Cl^-(aq)$$

18.3 Voltaic (or Galvanic) Cells: Generating Electricity from Spontaneous Chemical Reactions

Electrical current is the flow of electric charge. Electrons flowing through a wire or ions flowing through a solution both constitute electrical current. Since redox reactions involve the transfer of electrons from one substance to another, they have the potential to generate electrical current as we discussed in Section 18.1. For example, consider the spontaneous redox reaction:

$$Zn(s) + Cu^{2+}(aq) \longrightarrow Zn^{2+}(aq) + Cu(s)$$

When Zn metal is placed in a Cu^{2+} solution, the greater tendency of zinc to lose electrons results in Zn being oxidized and Cu^{2+} being reduced. Electrons are transferred directly from the Zn to the Cu^{2+} (Figure 18.1 ▶). Although the actual process is more complicated, we can imagine that—on the atomic scale—a zinc atom within the zinc metal transfers two electrons to a copper ion in solution. The zinc atom then becomes a zinc ion dissolved in the solution. The copper ion accepts the two electrons and is deposited on the zinc as solid copper.

Suppose we could separate the zinc atoms and copper ions and force the electron transfer to occur another way—not directly from the zinc atom to the copper ion, but through a wire connecting the two half-reactions. The flowing electrons would constitute an electrical current and could be used to do electrical work.

▶ **FIGURE 18.1 A Spontaneous Oxidation–Reduction Reaction** When zinc is immersed in a solution containing copper ions, the zinc atoms transfer electrons to the copper ions. The zinc atoms are oxidized and dissolve in the solution. The copper ions are reduced and are deposited on the electrode.

A Spontaneous Redox Reaction: Zn + Cu²⁺

Zinc strip

Copper (II) sulfate solution

Zn atoms (solid)

Cu²⁺ ions in solution

e⁻

Zn²⁺ ion

Cu atom

$$\text{Zn}(s) + \text{Cu}^{2+}(aq) \longrightarrow \text{Zn}^{2+}(aq) + \text{Cu}(s)$$

The generation of electricity through redox reactions is normally carried out in a device called an **electrochemical cell**. A **voltaic (or galvanic) cell**, is an electrochemical cell that *produces* electrical current from a *spontaneous* chemical reaction. A second type of electrochemical cell, called an **electrolytic cell**, *consumes* electrical current to drive a *nonspontaneous* chemical reaction. We discuss voltaic cells in this section and electrolytic cells in Section 18.8.

In the voltaic cell in Figure 18.2 ▶, a solid strip of zinc is placed in a $\text{Zn(NO}_3\text{)}_2$ solution to form a **half-cell**. A solid strip of copper placed in a $\text{Cu(NO}_3\text{)}_2$ solution forms a second half-cell. The strips act as **electrodes**, conductive surfaces through which electrons can enter or leave the half-cells. Each metal strip reaches equilibrium with its ions in solution according to these half-reactions:

$$\text{Zn}(s) \rightleftharpoons \text{Zn}^{2+}(aq) + 2\,\text{e}^-$$
$$\text{Cu}(s) \rightleftharpoons \text{Cu}^{2+}(aq) + 2\,\text{e}^-$$

The *continual* flow of electrical current in a voltaic cell requires a pathway by which counterions can flow to neutralize charge build-up; this is discussed later.

However, the position of these equilibria is not the same for both metals. As we have just seen, the zinc has a greater tendency to ionize than the copper, so the zinc half-reaction lies further to the right. As a result, the zinc electrode becomes negatively charged relative to the copper electrode.

The idea that one electrode in a voltaic cell becomes more negatively charged relative to the other electrode due to differences in ionization tendencies is central to understanding how a voltaic cell works.

If the two half-cells are connected by a wire running from the zinc—through a lightbulb or other electrical device—to the copper, electrons spontaneously flow from the zinc electrode (which is more negatively charged and therefore repels electrons) to the copper electrode. As the electrons flow away from the zinc electrode, the Zn/Zn^{2+} equilibrium shifts to the right (according to Le Châtelier's principle) and oxidation occurs. As electrons flow to the copper electrode, the Cu/Cu^{2+} equilibrium shifts to the left, and reduction occurs. The flowing electrons constitute an electrical current that lights the bulb.

A Voltaic Cell

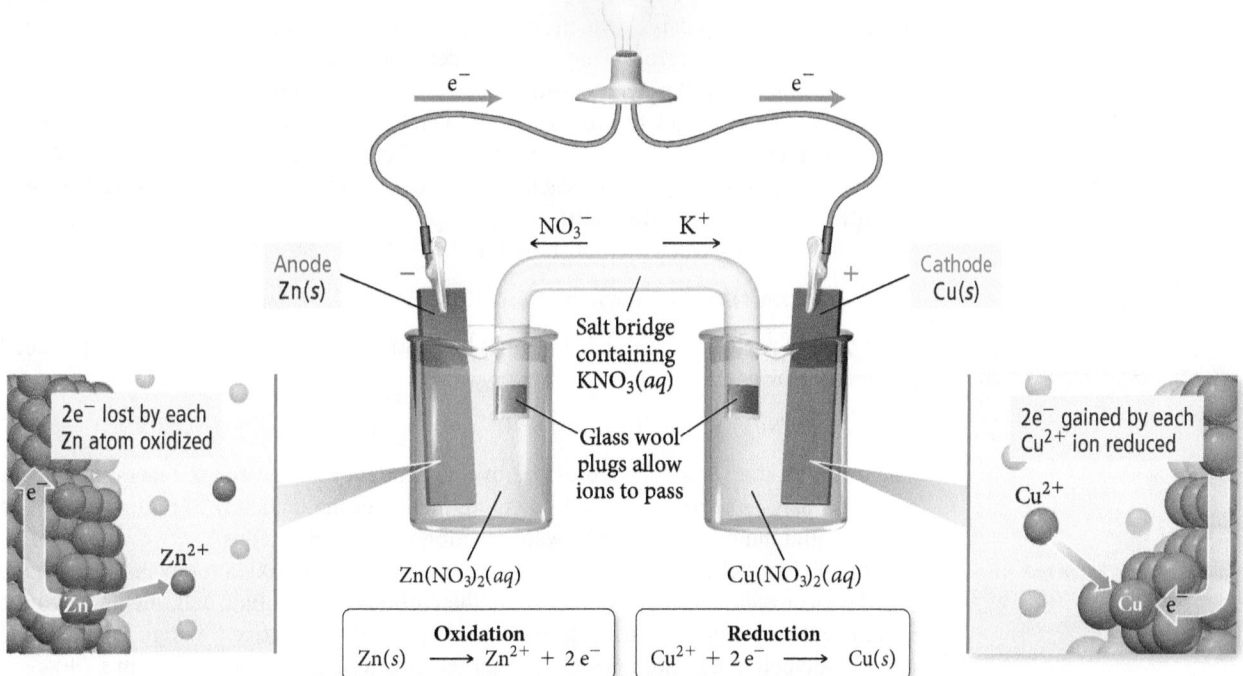

▲ FIGURE 18.2 **A Voltaic Cell** The tendency of zinc to transfer electrons to copper results in a flow of electrons through the wire that lights the bulb. The movement of electrons from the zinc anode to the copper cathode creates a positive charge buildup at the zinc half-cell and a negative charge buildup at the copper half-cell. The flow of ions within the salt bridge neutralizes this charge buildup, allowing the reaction to continue.

We can understand electrical current and why it flows by analogy with water current in a stream (Figure 18.3 ▶). The *rate of electrons flowing* through a wire is analogous to the *rate of water moving* through a stream. Electrical current is measured in units of **amperes (A)**, also called *amps*. One ampere represents the flow of one coulomb (a measure of electrical charge) per second.

$$1\,A = 1\,C/s$$

Because an electron has a charge of 1.602×10^{-19} C, 1 A corresponds to the flow of 6.242×10^{18} electrons per second.

The *driving force* for electrical current is analogous to the driving force for water current. Water current is driven by a difference in gravitational potential energy (caused by a gravitational field). Streams flow downhill, from higher to lower potential energy. Electrical current is also driven by a difference in potential energy (caused by an electric field resulting from the charge difference on the two electrodes) called **potential difference**. *Potential difference is a measure of the difference in potential energy (usually in joules) per unit of charge (coulombs)*. The SI unit of potential difference is the **volt (V)**, which is equal to one joule per coulomb.

$$1\,V = 1\,J/C$$

In other words, a potential difference of one volt indicates that a charge of one coulomb experiences an energy difference of one joule between the two electrodes.

A large potential difference corresponds to a large difference in charge between the two electrodes and therefore a strong tendency for electron flow (analogous to a steeply descending streambed). Potential difference, since it gives rise to the force that results in the motion of electrons, is also referred to as **electromotive force (emf)**.

| The ampere is often abbreviated as *amp*.

▲ FIGURE 18.3 **An Analogy for Electrical Current** Just as water flows downhill in response to a difference in gravitational potential energy, electrons flow through a conductor in response to an electrical potential difference, creating an electrical current.

In a voltaic cell, the potential difference between the two electrodes is the **cell potential (E_{cell})** or **cell emf**. The cell potential depends on the relative tendencies of the reactants to undergo oxidation and reduction. Combining the oxidation of a substance with a strong tendency to undergo oxidation and the reduction of a substance with a strong tendency to undergo reduction produces a large difference in charge between the two electrodes and therefore a high positive cell potential.

In general, the cell potential also depends on the concentrations of the reactants and products in the cell and the temperature (which we will assume to be 25 °C unless otherwise noted). Under standard conditions (1 M concentration for reactants in solution and 1 atm pressure for gaseous reactants), the cell potential is called the **standard cell potential (E°_{cell})** or **standard emf**. For example, the standard cell potential in the zinc and copper cell described previously is 1.10 volts.

$$Zn(s) + Cu^{2+}(aq) \longrightarrow Zn^{2+}(aq) + Cu(s) \quad E^{\circ}_{cell} = +1.10 \text{ V}$$

If the zinc is replaced with nickel (which has a lower tendency to be oxidized) the cell potential is lower.

$$Ni(s) + Cu^{2+}(aq) \longrightarrow Ni^{2+}(aq) + Cu(s) \quad E^{\circ}_{cell} = +0.62 \text{ V}$$

The cell potential is a measure of the overall tendency of the redox reaction to occur spontaneously—the lower the cell potential, the lower the tendency to occur. A negative cell potential indicates that the forward reaction is not spontaneous.

In all electrochemical cells, we call the electrode where oxidation occurs the **anode** and the electrode where reduction occurs the **cathode**. In a voltaic cell, the anode is the more negatively charged electrode and we label it with a negative (−) sign. The cathode of a voltaic cell is the more positively charged electrode and we label it with a (+) sign. Electrons flow from the anode to the cathode (from negative to positive) through the wires connecting the electrodes.

As electrons flow out of the anode, positive ions (Zn^{2+} in the preceding example) form in the oxidation half-cell, resulting in a buildup of *positive charge* in the *solution*. As electrons flow into the cathode, positive ions (Cu^{2+} in the preceding example) are reduced at the reduction half-cell, resulting in a buildup of *negative charge* in the *solution*.

If the movement of electrons from anode to cathode were the only flow of charge, the build up of the opposite charge in the solution would stop electron flow almost immediately. The cell needs a pathway by which counterions can flow between the half-cells without the solutions in the half-cells totally mixing. One such pathway is a **salt bridge**, an inverted, U-shaped tube that contains a strong electrolyte such as KNO_3 and connects the two half-cells (see Figure 18.2). The electrolyte is usually suspended in a gel and held within the tube by permeable stoppers. The salt bridge allows a flow of ions that neutralizes the charge buildup in the solution. *The negative ions within the salt bridge flow to neutralize the accumulation of positive charge at the anode, and the positive ions flow to neutralize the accumulation of negative charge at the cathode.* In other words, the salt bridge completes the circuit, allowing electrical current to flow.

Conceptual Connection 18.1 **Voltaic Cells**

In a voltaic cell, electrons flow

(a) from the more negatively charged electrode to the more positively charged electrode.

(b) from the more positively charged electrode to the more negatively charged electrode.

(c) from lower potential energy to higher potential energy.

Electrochemical Cell Notation

We can represent electrochemical cells with a compact notation called a *cell diagram* or *line notation*. For example, we can represent the electrochemical cell discussed previously in which Zn is oxidized to Zn^{2+} and Cu^{2+} is reduced to Cu as follows:

$$Zn(s)\,|\,Zn^{2+}(aq)\,||\,Cu^{2+}(aq)\,|\,Cu(s)$$

In this representation,

- we write the oxidation half-reaction on the left and the reduction on the right. A double vertical line, indicating the salt bridge, separates the two half-reactions.

- substances in different phases are separated by a single vertical line, which represents the boundary between the phases.

- for some redox reactions, the reactants and products of one or both of the half-reactions may be in the same phase. In these cases (which are explained further next), we separate the reactants and products from each other with a comma in the line diagram. Such cells use an inert electrode, such as platinum (Pt) or graphite, as the anode or cathode (or both).

Consider the redox reaction in which Fe(s) is oxidized and $MnO_4^-(aq)$ is reduced:

$$5\,Fe(s) + 2\,MnO_4^-(aq) + 16\,H^+(aq) \longrightarrow 5\,Fe^{2+}(aq) + 2\,Mn^{2+}(aq) + 8\,H_2O(l)$$

The half-reactions for this overall reaction are:

Oxidation: $Fe(s) \longrightarrow Fe^{2+}(aq) + 2\,e^-$

Reduction: $MnO_4^-(aq) + 5\,e^- + 8\,H^+(aq) \longrightarrow Mn^{2+}(aq) + 4\,H_2O(l)$

Notice that in the reduction half-reaction the principal species are all in the aqueous phase. In this case, the electron transfer needs an electrode on which to occur. An inert platinum electrode is employed, and the electron transfer takes place at its surface. Using line notation, we represent the electrochemical cell corresponding to the above reaction as:

$$Fe(s)\,|\,Fe^{2+}(aq)\,||\,MnO_4^-(aq),\,H^+(aq),\,Mn^{2+}(aq)\,|\,Pt(s)$$

The Pt(s) on the far right indicates that an inert platinum electrode acts as the cathode in this reaction, as depicted in Figure 18.4 ▼.

Inert Platinum Electrode

Oxidation
$Fe(s) \longrightarrow Fe^{2+}(aq) + 2\,e^-$

Reduction
$MnO_4^-(aq) + 5\,e^- + 8\,H^+(aq) \longrightarrow Mn^{2+}(aq) + 4\,H_2O(l)$

◀ **FIGURE 18.4 Inert Platinum Electrode** When the participants in a half-reaction are all in the aqueous phase, a conductive surface is needed for electron transfer to take place. In such cases an inert electrode of graphite or platinum is often used. In this electrochemical cell, an iron strip acts as the anode and a platinum strip acts as the cathode. Iron is oxidized at the anode and MnO_4^- is reduced at the cathode.

High
potential
energy

Low
potential
energy

Direction of
spontaneous
flow

▲ **FIGURE 18.5 An Analogy for Electrode Potential**

18.4 Standard Electrode Potentials

As we have just seen, the standard cell potential (E°_{cell}) for an electrochemical cell depends on the specific half-reactions occurring in the half-cells and is a measure of the potential energy difference (per unit charge) between the two electrodes. We can think of the electrode in each half-cell as having its own individual potential, called the **standard electrode potential**. The overall standard cell potential (E°_{cell}) is the difference between the two standard electrode potentials.

We can better understand this idea with an analogy. Consider two water tanks with different water levels connected by a common pipe, as shown in Figure 18.5 ◀. The water in each tank has its own level and corresponding potential energy. When the tanks are connected, water flows from the tank with the higher level (higher potential energy) to the tank with a lower water level (lower potential energy). Similarly, each half-cell in an electrochemical cell has its own charge and corresponding electrode potential. *When the cells are connected, electrons flow from the electrode with more negative charge (greater potential energy) to the electrode with more positive charge (less potential energy).*

One limitation to this analogy is that, unlike the water level in a tank, we cannot measure the electrode potential in a half-cell directly—we can only measure the overall potential that occurs when two half-cells are combined in a whole cell. However, we can arbitrarily assign a potential of zero to the electrode in a *particular* type of half-cell and then measure all other electrode potentials relative to that zero.

The half-cell electrode that is normally chosen to have a potential of zero is the **standard hydrogen electrode (SHE)**. This half-cell consists of an inert platinum electrode immersed in 1 M HCl with hydrogen gas at 1 atm bubbling through the solution, as shown in Figure 18.6 ▼. When the SHE acts as the cathode, the following half-reaction occurs:

$$2\,H^+(aq) + 2\,e^- \longrightarrow H_2(g) \quad E^\circ_{cathode} = 0.00\ V$$

If we connect the standard hydrogen electrode to an electrode in another half-cell of interest, we can measure the potential difference (or voltage) between the two electrodes. Since we assigned the standard hydrogen electrode zero voltage, we can now determine the electrode potential of the other half-cell.

For example, consider the electrochemical cell shown in Figure 18.7 ▶. In this electrochemical cell, Zn is oxidized to Zn^{2+} and H^+ is reduced to H_2 under standard conditions (all solutions are 1 M in concentration and all gases are 1 atm in pressure) and

Standard Hydrogen Electrode (SHE)

$H_2(g)$
1 atm

Pt

$H^+(aq)$, 1 M

▶ **FIGURE 18.6 The Standard Hydrogen Electrode** The standard hydrogen electrode (SHE) is arbitrarily assigned an electrode potential of zero. All other electrode potentials are then measured relative to the SHE.

Measuring Half-Cell Potential with the SHE

▲ FIGURE 18.7 **Measuring Electrode Potential** Because the electrode potential of the SHE is zero, the electrode potential for the oxidation of Zn is equal to the cell potential.

at 25 °C. Electrons travel from the anode (where oxidation occurs) to the cathode (where reduction occurs), so we define $E°_{cell}$ as *the difference in voltage between the cathode (final state) and the anode (initial state).*

$$E°_{cell} = E°_{final} - E°_{initial}$$
$$= E°_{cathode} - E°_{anode}$$

The measured cell potential for this cell is +0.76 V. The anode (in this case, Zn/Zn^{2+}) is at a more negative voltage (higher potential energy) than the cathode (in this case, the SHE). Therefore, electrons spontaneously flow from the anode to the cathode. We can diagram the potential energy and the voltage as follows:

Referring back to our water tank analogy, the zinc half-cell is like the water tank with the higher water level, and electrons therefore flow from the zinc electrode to the standard hydrogen electrode.

Because we assigned the SHE a potential of zero (0.00 V), we can determine the electrode potential for the Zn/Zn^{2+} half-cell (the anode) from the measured cell potential ($E°_{cell}$).

$$E°_{cell} = E°_{cathode} - E°_{anode}$$
$$0.76 \text{ V} = 0.00 \text{ V} - E°_{anode}$$
$$E°_{anode} = -0.76 \text{ V}$$

The potential for the Zn/Zn^{2+} electrode is *negative*. The negative potential indicates that an electron at the Zn/Zn^{2+} electrode has greater potential energy than it does at the SHE. *Remember that the more negative the electrode potential is, the greater the potential energy of an electron at that electrode (because negative charge repels electrons).*

What would happen if we connected an electrode in which the electron has *more positive* potential (than the standard hydrogen electrode) to the standard hydrogen electrode? That electrode would then have a more *positive* voltage (lower potential energy for an electron).

For example, suppose we connect the standard hydrogen electrode to a Cu electrode immersed in a 1 M Cu^{2+} solution. The measured cell potential for this cell is -0.34 V. The anode (defined as Cu/Cu^{2+}) is at a more positive voltage (lower potential energy) than the cathode (the SHE). Therefore, electrons will *not* spontaneously flow from the anode to the cathode. We can diagram the potential energy and the voltage of this cell as follows:

The copper half-cell is like the water tank with the lower water level and electrons *do not* spontaneously flow from the copper electrode to the standard hydrogen electrode.

We can again determine the electrode potential for the Cu/Cu^{2+} half-cell (the anode) from the measured cell potential.

$$E^{\circ}_{cell} = E^{\circ}_{cathode} - E^{\circ}_{anode}$$

$$-0.34 \text{ V} = 0.00 \text{ V} - E^{\circ}_{anode}$$

$$E^{\circ}_{anode} = +0.34 \text{ V}$$

The potential for the Cu/Cu^{2+} electrode is *positive*. The positive potential indicates that an electron at the Cu/Cu^{2+} electrode has *lower* potential energy than it does at the SHE. The more positive the electrode potential, the lower the potential energy of an electron at that electrode (because positive charge attracts electrons).

By convention, standard electrode potentials are written for *reduction* half-reactions. We write the standard electrode potentials for the two half-reactions just discussed as:

$$Cu^{2+}(aq) + 2\,e^- \longrightarrow Cu(s) \quad E^{\circ} = +0.34 \text{ V}$$

$$Zn^{2+}(aq) + 2\,e^- \longrightarrow Zn(s) \quad E^{\circ} = -0.76 \text{ V}$$

We can see that the Cu/Cu^{2+} electrode is positive relative to the SHE (and will therefore tend to draw electrons *away* from the SHE), and that the Zn/Zn^{2+} electrode is negative relative to the SHE (and will therefore tend to repel electrons towards the SHE). The standard electrode potentials for a number of common half-reactions are listed in Table 18.1.

Summarizing Standard Electrode Potentials:

▶ The electrode potential of the standard hydrogen electrode (SHE) is exactly zero.

▶ The electrode in any half-cell with a greater tendency to undergo reduction is positively charged relative to the SHE and therefore has a positive E°.

▶ The electrode in any half-cell with a lesser tendency to undergo reduction (or greater tendency to undergo oxidation) is negatively charged relative to the SHE and therefore has a negative E°.

▶ The cell potential of any electrochemical cell (E°_{cell}) is the difference between the electrode potentials of the cathode and the anode ($E^{\circ}_{cell} = E^{\circ}_{cat} - E^{\circ}_{an}$).

▶ E°_{cell} is positive for spontaneous reactions and negative for nonspontaneous reactions.

TABLE 18.1 Standard Electrode Potentials at 25 °C

Reduction Half-Reaction		$E°$(V)
$F_2(g) + 2\,e^-$	$\longrightarrow 2\,F^-(aq)$	2.87
$H_2O_2(aq) + 2\,H^+(aq) + 2\,e^-$	$\longrightarrow 2\,H_2O(l)$	1.78
$PbO_2(s) + 4\,H^+(aq) + SO_4{}^{2-}(aq) + 2\,e^-$	$\longrightarrow PbSO_4(s) + 2\,H_2O(l)$	1.69
$MnO_4{}^-(aq) + 4\,H^+(aq) + 3\,e^-$	$\longrightarrow MnO_2(s) + 2\,H_2O(l)$	1.68
$MnO_4{}^-(aq) + 8\,H^+(aq) + 5\,e^-$	$\longrightarrow Mn^{2+}(aq) + 4\,H_2O(l)$	1.51
$Au^{3+}(aq) + 3\,e^-$	$\longrightarrow Au(s)$	1.50
$PbO_2(s) + 4\,H^+(aq) + 2\,e^-$	$\longrightarrow Pb^{2+}(aq) + 2\,H_2O(l)$	1.46
$Cl_2(g) + 2\,e^-$	$\longrightarrow 2\,Cl^-(aq)$	1.36
$Cr_2O_7{}^{2-}(aq) + 14\,H^+(aq) + 6\,e^-$	$\longrightarrow 2\,Cr^{3+}(aq) + 7\,H_2O(l)$	1.33
$O_2(g) + 4\,H^+(aq) + 4\,e^-$	$\longrightarrow 2\,H_2O(l)$	1.23
$MnO_2(s) + 4\,H^+(aq) + 2\,e^-$	$\longrightarrow Mn^{2+}(aq) + 2\,H_2O(l)$	1.21
$IO_3{}^-(aq) + 6\,H^+(aq) + 5\,e^-$	$\longrightarrow \frac{1}{2}I_2(aq) + 3\,H_2O(l)$	1.20
$Br_2(l) + 2\,e^-$	$\longrightarrow 2\,Br^-(aq)$	1.09
$VO_2{}^+(aq) + 2\,H^+(aq) + e^-$	$\longrightarrow VO^{2+}(aq) + H_2O(l)$	1.00
$NO_3{}^-(aq) + 4\,H^+(aq) + 3\,e^-$	$\longrightarrow NO(g) + 2\,H_2O(l)$	0.96
$ClO_2(g) + e^-$	$\longrightarrow ClO_2{}^-(aq)$	0.95
$Ag^+(aq) + e^-$	$\longrightarrow Ag(s)$	0.80
$Fe^{3+}(aq) + e^-$	$\longrightarrow Fe^{2+}(aq)$	0.77
$O_2(g) + 2\,H^+(aq) + 2\,e^-$	$\longrightarrow H_2O_2(aq)$	0.70
$MnO_4{}^-(aq) + e^-$	$\longrightarrow MnO_4{}^{2-}(aq)$	0.56
$I_2(s) + 2\,e^-$	$\longrightarrow 2\,I^-(aq)$	0.54
$Cu^+(aq) + e^-$	$\longrightarrow Cu(s)$	0.52
$O_2(g) + 2\,H_2O(l) + 4\,e^-$	$\longrightarrow 4\,OH^-(aq)$	0.40
$Cu^{2+}(aq) + 2\,e^-$	$\longrightarrow Cu(s)$	0.34
$SO_4{}^{2-}(aq) + 4\,H^+(aq) + 2\,e^-$	$\longrightarrow H_2SO_3(aq) + H_2O(l)$	0.20
$Cu^{2+}(aq) + e^-$	$\longrightarrow Cu^+(aq)$	0.16
$Sn^{4+}(aq) + 2\,e^-$	$\longrightarrow Sn^{2+}(aq)$	0.15
$2\,H^+(aq) + 2\,e^-$	$\longrightarrow H_2(g)$	0
$Fe^{3+}(aq) + 3\,e^-$	$\longrightarrow Fe(s)$	−0.036
$Pb^{2+}(aq) + 2\,e^-$	$\longrightarrow Pb(s)$	−0.13
$Sn^{2+}(aq) + 2\,e^-$	$\longrightarrow Sn(s)$	−0.14
$Ni^{2+}(aq) + 2\,e^-$	$\longrightarrow Ni(s)$	−0.23
$Cd^{2+}(aq) + 2\,e^-$	$\longrightarrow Cd(s)$	−0.40
$Fe^{2+}(aq) + 2\,e^-$	$\longrightarrow Fe(s)$	−0.45
$Cr^{3+}(aq) + e^-$	$\longrightarrow Cr^{2+}(aq)$	−0.50
$Cr^{3+}(aq) + 3\,e^-$	$\longrightarrow Cr(s)$	−0.73
$Zn^{2+}(aq) + 2\,e^-$	$\longrightarrow Zn(s)$	−0.76
$2\,H_2O(l) + 2\,e^-$	$\longrightarrow H_2(g) + 2\,OH^-(aq)$	−0.83
$Mn^{2+}(aq) + 2\,e^-$	$\longrightarrow Mn(s)$	−1.18
$Al^{3+}(aq) + 3\,e^-$	$\longrightarrow Al(s)$	−1.66
$Mg^{2+}(aq) + 2\,e^-$	$\longrightarrow Mg(s)$	−2.37
$Na^+(aq) + e^-$	$\longrightarrow Na(s)$	−2.71
$Ca^{2+}(aq) + 2\,e^-$	$\longrightarrow Ca(s)$	−2.76
$Ba^{2+}(aq) + 2\,e^-$	$\longrightarrow Ba(s)$	−2.90
$K^+(aq) + e^-$	$\longrightarrow K(s)$	−2.92
$Li^+(aq) + e^-$	$\longrightarrow Li(s)$	−3.04

Stronger oxidizing agent ↑

Weaker oxidizing agent

Weaker reducing agent ↓

Stronger reducing agent

Example 18.4 shows how to calculate the potential of an electrochemical cell from the standard electrode potentials of the half-reactions.

EXAMPLE 18.4 Calculating Standard Potentials for Electrochemical Cells from Standard Electrode Potentials of the Half-Reactions

Use tabulated standard electrode potentials to calculate the standard cell potential for the following reaction occurring in an electrochemical cell at 25 °C. (The equation is balanced.)

$$Al(s) + NO_3^-(aq) + 4\,H^+(aq) \longrightarrow Al^{3+}(aq) + NO(g) + 2\,H_2O(l)$$

SOLUTION

Begin by separating the reaction into oxidation and reduction half-reactions. (In this case, you can readily see that Al(s) is oxidized. In cases where it is not so apparent, you many want to assign oxidation states to determine the correct half-reactions.)	*Oxidation:* $Al(s) \longrightarrow Al^{3+}(aq) + 3\ e^-$ *Reduction:* $NO_3^-(aq) + 4\,H^+(aq) + 3\ e^- \longrightarrow NO(g) + 2\,H_2O(l)$
Look up the standard electrode potentials for each half-reaction in Table 18.1. Add the half-cell reactions together to obtain the overall redox equation. Calculate the standard cell potential by subtracting the electrode potential of the anode from the electrode potential of the cathode.	*Oxidation (Anode):* $\qquad\qquad\qquad Al(s) \longrightarrow Al^{3+}(aq) + 3\,e^- \qquad E° = -1.66\ V$ *Reduction (Cathode):* $\quad \dfrac{NO_3^-(aq) + 4\,H^+(aq) + 3\,e^- \longrightarrow NO(g) + 2\,H_2O(l) \quad E° = 0.96\ V}{Al(s) + NO_3^-(aq) + 4\,H^+(aq) \longrightarrow Al^{3+}(aq) + NO(g) + 2\,H_2O(l)}$ $E°_{cell} = E°_{cat} - E°_{an}$ $\qquad\ = 0.96\ V - (-1.66\ V)$ $\qquad\ = 2.62\ V$

FOR PRACTICE 18.4

Use tabulated standard electrode potentials to calculate the standard cell potential for the following reaction occurring in an electrochemical cell at 25 °C. (The equation is balanced.)

$$3\,Pb^{2+}(aq) + 2\,Cr(s) \longrightarrow 3\,Pb(s) + 2\,Cr^{3+}(aq)$$

Conceptual Connection 18.2 Standard Electrode Potentials

An electrode has a negative electrode potential. Which statement is correct regarding the potential energy of an electron at this electrode?

(a) An electron at this electrode has a lower potential energy than it has at a standard hydrogen electrode.

(b) An electron at this electrode has a higher potential energy than it has at a standard hydrogen electrode.

(c) An electron at this electrode has the same potential energy as it has at a standard hydrogen electrode.

Predicting the Spontaneous Direction of an Oxidation–Reduction Reaction

To determine the spontaneous direction of an oxidation–reduction reaction, examine the electrode potentials of the two relevant half-reactions in Table 18.1. The half-reaction with the more *negative* electrode potential tends to lose electrons and therefore undergo oxidation. (Remember that negative charge repels electrons.) The half-reaction having the more *positive* electrode potential tends to gain electrons and therefore undergo reduction. (Remember that positive charge attracts electrons.)

For example, consider the two reduction half-reactions:

$$Ni^{2+}(aq) + 2\,e^- \longrightarrow Ni(s) \qquad E° = -0.23\ \text{V}$$
$$Mn^{2+}(aq) + 2\,e^- \longrightarrow Mn(s) \qquad E° = -1.18\ \text{V}$$

Because the manganese half-reaction has a more negative electrode potential, it repels electrons and proceeds in the reverse direction (oxidation). Because the nickel half-reaction has the more positive (or least negative) electrode potential, it attracts electrons and proceeds in the forward direction.

We can confirm this by calculating the standard electrode potential for manganese acting as the anode (oxidation) and nickel acting as the cathode (reduction).

Oxidation *(Anode):* $\qquad\qquad\qquad Mn(s) \longrightarrow Mn^{2+}(aq) + 2\,e^- \qquad E° = -1.18\ \text{V}$

Reduction *(Cathode):* $\dfrac{Ni^{2+}(aq) + 2\,e^- \longrightarrow Ni(s)}{Ni^{2+}(aq) + Mn(s) \longrightarrow Ni(s) + Mn^{2+}(aq)} \quad \begin{aligned} E° &= -0.23\ \text{V} \\ E°_{cell} = E°_{cat} - E°_{an} \\ &= -0.23\ \text{V} - (-1.18\ \text{V}) \\ &= 0.95\ \text{V} \end{aligned}$

The overall cell potential is positive, indicating a spontaneous reaction. Consider the electrochemical cell corresponding to this spontaneous redox reaction in Figure 18.8 ▼. We draw the manganese half-cell on the left as the anode and the nickel half-cell on the right as the cathode. Electrons flow from the anode to the cathode.

Another way to predict the spontaneity of a redox reaction is to note the relative positions of the two half-reactions in Table 18.1. Since the table lists half-reactions in order of *decreasing* electrode potential, the half-reactions near the top of the table—those having large *positive* electrode potentials—attract electrons and therefore tend to occur in the forward direction. Half-reactions near the bottom of the table—those having large *negative* electrode potentials—repel electrons and therefore tend to occur in the reverse direction. In other words, as you move down Table 18.1, the half-reactions become less likely to occur in the forward direction and more likely to occur in the reverse direction. As a result, *any reduction half-reaction listed is spontaneous when paired with the reverse of a half-reaction that appears below it in Table 18.1.*

For example, if we return to our two previous half-reactions involving manganese and nickel we can see that the manganese half-reaction is listed below the nickel half-reaction in Table 18.1.

$$Ni^{2+}(aq) + 2\,e^- \longrightarrow Ni(s) \qquad E° = -0.23\ \text{V}$$
$$Mn^{2+}(aq) + 2\,e^- \longrightarrow Mn(s) \qquad E° = -1.18\ \text{V}$$

Therefore, the nickel reaction occurs in the forward direction (reduction) and the manganese reaction occurs in the reverse direction (oxidation).

The following mnemonics (NIO and PIR) can help you predict the spontaneous direction of redox reactions:
N.I.O.–More Negative Is Oxidation
P.I.R.–More Positive Is Reduction

◀ **FIGURE 18.8** **Mn/Ni^{2+} Electrochemical Cell** Since the reduction of Mn^{2+} is listed below the reduction of Ni^{2+} in Table 18.1, the reduction of Ni^{2+} is spontaneous when paired with the oxidation of Mn.

Recall from Section 4.9 that an *oxidizing agent* causes the oxidation of another substance (and is itself reduced) and that a *reducing agent* causes the reduction of another substance (and is itself oxidized).

Summarizing the Prediction of Spontaneous Direction for Redox Reactions:

▶ The half-reaction with the more *positive* electrode potential attracts electrons more strongly and will undergo reduction. (Substances listed at the top of Table 18.1 tend to undergo reduction; they are good oxidizing agents.)

▶ The half-reaction with the more *negative* electrode potential repels electrons more strongly and will undergo oxidation. (Substances listed near the bottom of Table 18.1 tend to undergo oxidation; they are good reducing agents.)

▶ Any reduction reaction in Table 18.1 is spontaneous when paired with the *reverse* of any of the reactions listed below it on the table.

EXAMPLE 18.5 Predicting Spontaneous Redox Reactions and Sketching Electrochemical Cells

Without calculating $E°_{cell}$, predict whether each of the following redox reactions is spontaneous. If the reaction is spontaneous as written, make a sketch of the electrochemical cell in which the reaction could occur. If the reaction is not spontaneous as written, write an equation for the spontaneous direction in which the reaction would occur and sketch the electrochemical cell in which the spontaneous reaction would occur. In your sketches, make sure to label the anode (which should be drawn on the left), the cathode, and the direction of electron flow.

(a) $Fe(s) + Mg^{2+}(aq) \longrightarrow Fe^{2+}(aq) + Mg(s)$

(b) $Fe(s) + Pb^{2+}(aq) \longrightarrow Fe^{2+}(aq) + Pb(s)$

SOLUTION

(a) $Fe(s) + Mg^{2+}(aq) \longrightarrow Fe^{2+}(aq) + Mg(s)$

This reaction involves the reduction of Mg^{2+}:

$$Mg^{2+}(aq) + 2 e^- \longrightarrow Mg(s) \qquad E° = -2.37\,V$$

and the oxidation of Fe:

$$Fe(s) \longrightarrow Fe^{2+}(aq) + 2 e^- \qquad E° = -0.45\,V$$

However, the magnesium half-reaction has the more negative electrode potential and therefore repels electrons more strongly and undergoes oxidation. The iron half-reaction has the more positive electrode potential and therefore attracts electrons more strongly and undergoes reduction. So the reaction as written is *not* spontaneous. (The reaction pairs the reduction of Mg^{2+} with the reverse of a half-reaction *above it* in Table 18.1—such pairings are not spontaneous.)

However, the reverse reaction is spontaneous.

$$Fe^{2+}(aq) + Mg(s) \longrightarrow Fe(s) + Mg^{2+}(aq)$$

The corresponding electrochemical cell is shown in Figure 18.9 ◀.

(b) $Fe(s) + Pb^{2+}(aq) \longrightarrow Fe^{2+}(aq) + Pb(s)$

This reaction involves the reduction of Pb^{2+}:

$$Pb^{2+}(aq) + 2 e^- \longrightarrow Pb(s) \qquad E° = -0.13\,V$$

and the oxidation of iron:

$$Fe(s) \longrightarrow Fe^{2+}(aq) + 2 e^- \qquad E° = -0.45\,V$$

The iron half-reaction has the more negative electrode potential and therefore repels electrons and undergoes oxidation. The lead half-reaction has the more positive electrode potential and therefore attracts electrons and undergoes reduction. Therefore, the reaction *is* spontaneous as written. (The reaction pairs the reduction of Pb^{2+} with the reverse of a half-reaction *below it* in Table 18.1—such pairings are always spontaneous.) The corresponding electrochemical cell is shown in Figure 18.10 ◀.

▲ FIGURE 18.9 Mg/Fe^{2+} Electrochemical Cell

▲ FIGURE 18.10 Fe/Pb^{2+} Electrochemical Cell

FOR PRACTICE 18.5

Are the following redox reactions spontaneous under standard conditions?

(a) $Zn(s) + Ni^{2+}(aq) \longrightarrow Zn^{2+}(aq) + Ni(s)$

(b) $Zn(s) + Ca^{2+}(aq) \longrightarrow Zn^{2+}(aq) + Ca(s)$

Connection 18.3 Selective Oxidation

A solution contains both NaI and NaBr. Which oxidizing agent could you add to the solution to selectively oxidize $I^-(aq)$ but not $Br^-(aq)$?

(a) Cl_2 **(b)** H_2O_2 **(c)** $CuCl_2$ **(d)** HNO_3

Predicting Whether a Metal Will Dissolve in Acid

In Chapter 15, we learned that acids dissolve metals. Most acids dissolve metals by the reduction of H^+ ions to hydrogen gas and the corresponding oxidation of the metal to its ion. For example, if solid Zn is dropped into hydrochloric acid, the following reaction occurs:

$$2\,H^+(aq) + 2\,e^- \longrightarrow H_2(g)$$
$$\underline{\,Zn(s) \longrightarrow Zn^{2+}(aq) + 2\,e^-}$$
$$Zn(s) + 2\,H^+(aq) \longrightarrow Zn^{2+}(aq) + H_2(g)$$

We observe the reaction as the dissolving of the zinc and the bubbling of hydrogen gas. The zinc is oxidized and the H^+ ions are reduced. Notice that this reaction involves the pairing of a reduction half-reaction (the reduction of H^+) with the reverse of a half-reaction that falls below it in Table 18.1. Therefore, this reaction is spontaneous. What happens, however, if we pair the reduction of H^+ with the oxidation of Cu? The reaction is not spontaneous, because it involves pairing the reduction of H^+ with the reverse of a half-reaction that is listed *above it* in the table. Consequently, copper does not react with H^+ and does not dissolve in acids such as HCl. In general, *metals whose reduction half-reactions are listed below the reduction of H^+ to H_2 in Table 18.1 dissolve in acids, while metals listed above it do not.*

An important exception to this rule is nitric acid (HNO_3), which can oxidize metals through the reduction half-reaction:

$$NO_3^-(aq) + 4\,H^+(aq) + 3\,e^- \longrightarrow NO(g) + 2\,H_2O(l)\quad E^\circ = 0.96\text{ V}$$

Since this half-reaction is above the reduction of H^+ in Table 18.1, HNO_3 can oxidize metals (such as copper) that can't be oxidized by HCl.

$$Zn(s) + 2\,H^+(aq) \longrightarrow$$
$$Zn^{2+}(aq) + H_2(g)$$

▲ When zinc is immersed in hydrochloric acid, the zinc is oxidized, forming ions that become solvated in the solution. Hydrogen ions are reduced, forming bubbles of hydrogen gas.

Connection 18.4 Metals Dissolving in Acids

Which metal dissolves in HNO_3 but not in HCl?

(a) Fe   **(b)** Au   **(c)** Ag

18.5 Cell Potential, Free Energy, and the Equilibrium Constant

We have seen that a positive standard cell potential (E°_{cell}) corresponds to a spontaneous oxidation–reduction reaction. And we know (from Chapter 17) that the spontaneity of a reaction is determined by the sign of ΔG°. Therefore, E°_{cell} and ΔG° must be related. We also know from Section 17.9 that ΔG° for a reaction is related to the equilibrium constant (K) for the reaction. Since E°_{cell} and ΔG° are related, then E°_{cell} and K must also be related.

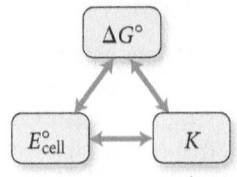

Before we look at the nature of each of these relationships in detail, let's consider the following generalizations.

For a spontaneous redox reaction (one that will proceed in the forward direction when all reactants and products are in their standard states):

- $\Delta G°$ is negative (<0)
- $E°_{cell}$ is positive (>0)
- $K > 1$

For a nonspontaneous reaction (one that will proceed in the reverse direction when all reactants and products are in their standard states):

- $\Delta G°$ is positive (>0)
- $E°_{cell}$ is negative (<0)
- $K < 1$

The Relationship between $\Delta G°$ and $E°_{cell}$

We can derive a relationship between $\Delta G°$ and $E°_{cell}$ by briefly returning to the definition of potential difference from Section 18.3—a potential difference is a measure of the difference of potential energy per unit charge (q):

$$E = \frac{\text{potential energy difference (in J)}}{\text{charge (in C)}}$$

Since the potential energy difference represents the maximum amount of work that can be done by the system on the surroundings, we can write:

$$w_{max} = -qE°_{cell} \qquad [18.1]$$

The negative sign follows the convention used throughout this book that work done by the system on the surroundings is negative.

We can quantify the charge (q) that flows in an electrochemical reaction by using **Faraday's constant (F)**, which represents the charge in coulombs of 1 mol of electrons.

$$F = \frac{96{,}485 \text{ C}}{\text{mol e}^-}$$

The total charge is $q = nF$, where n is the number of moles of electrons from the balanced chemical equation and F is Faraday's constant. Substituting $q = nF$ into Equation 18.1:

$$w_{max} = -qE°_{cell}$$
$$= -nFE°_{cell} \qquad [18.2]$$

Finally, recall from Chapter 17 that the standard change in free energy for a chemical reaction ($\Delta G°$) represents the maximum amount of work that can be done by the reaction. Therefore, $w_{max} = \Delta G°$. Making this substitution into Equation 18.2, we arrive at the following important result:

$$\Delta G° = -nFE°_{cell} \qquad [18.3]$$

where $\Delta G°$ is the standard change in free energy for an electrochemical reaction, n is the number of moles of electrons transferred in the balanced equation, F is Faraday's constant, and $E°_{cell}$ is the standard cell potential. Example 18.6 shows how to apply this equation to calculate the standard free energy change for an electrochemical cell.

EXAMPLE 18.6   Relating ΔG° and E°_{cell}

Use the tabulated electrode potentials to calculate ΔG° for the reaction.

$$I_2(s) + 2\,Br^-(aq) \longrightarrow 2\,I^-(aq) + Br_2(l)$$

Is the reaction spontaneous?

SORT You are given a redox reaction and asked to find ΔG°.	**GIVEN:** $I_2(s) + 2\,Br^-(aq) \longrightarrow 2\,I^-(aq) + Br_2(l)$ **FIND:** ΔG°
STRATEGIZE Refer to the values of electrode potentials in Table 18.1 to calculate E°_{cell}. Then use Equation 18.3 to calculate ΔG° from E°_{cell}.	**CONCEPTUAL PLAN** 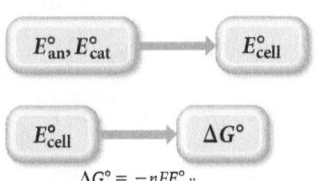

SOLVE Separate the reaction into oxidation and reduction half-reactions and find the standard electrode potentials for each. Determine E°_{cell} by subtracting E_{an} from E_{cat}.

SOLUTION

Oxidation (Anode):	$2\,Br^-(aq) \longrightarrow Br_2(l) + 2\,e^-$	$E^\circ = 1.09\ V$
Reduction (Cathode):	$I_2(s) + 2\,e^- \longrightarrow 2\,I^-(aq)$	$E^\circ = 0.54\ V$

$$I_2(s) + 2\,Br^-(aq) \longrightarrow 2\,I^-(aq) + Br_2(l) \qquad E^\circ_{cell} = E^\circ_{cat} - E^\circ_{an}$$
$$= -0.55\ V$$

Calculate ΔG° from E°_{cell}. The value of n (the number of moles of electrons) corresponds to the number of electrons that are canceled in the half-reactions. Remember that $1\ V = 1\ J/C$.

$$\Delta G^\circ = -nFE^\circ_{cell}$$
$$= -2\,mol\,e^- \left(\frac{96{,}485\ C}{mol\,e^-} \right)\left(-0.55\frac{J}{C} \right)$$
$$= +1.1 \times 10^5\ J$$

Since ΔG° is positive, the reaction is not spontaneous under standard conditions.

CHECK The answer is in the correct units (joules) and seems reasonable in magnitude (≈ 110 kJ). You have seen (in Chapter 17) that values of ΔG° typically range from plus or minus tens to hundreds of kilojoules. The sign is positive, as expected for a reaction in which E°_{cell} is negative.

FOR PRACTICE 18.6

Use tabulated electrode potentials to calculate ΔG° for the reaction.

$$2\,Na(s) + 2\,H_2O(l) \longrightarrow H_2(g) + 2\,OH^-(aq) + 2\,Na^+(aq)$$

Is the reaction spontaneous?

Conceptual Connection 18.5   Periodic Trends and the Direction of Spontaneity for Redox Reactions

Consider the result of Example 18.6. The calculation revealed that the reaction is not spontaneous. Based on conceptual reasoning, which of the following best explains why I_2 does not oxidize Br^-?

(a) Br is more electronegative than I; therefore, we do not expect Br^- to give up an electron to I_2.

(b) I is more electronegative than Br; therefore, we do not expect I_2 to give up an electron to Br^-.

(c) Br^- is in solution and I_2 is a solid. Solids do not gain electrons from substances in solution.

The Relationship between $E°_{cell}$ and K

We can derive a relationship between the standard cell potential ($E°_{cell}$) and the equilibrium constant for the redox reaction occurring in the cell (K) by returning to the relationship between $\Delta G°$ and K that we learned in Chapter 17. Recall from Section 17.9 that:

$$\Delta G° = -RT \ln K \qquad [18.4]$$

By setting Equations 18.3 and 18.4 equal to each other, we get:

$$-nFE°_{cell} = -RT \ln K$$

$$E°_{cell} = \frac{RT}{nF} \ln K \qquad [18.5]$$

Equation 18.5 is usually simplified for use at 25 °C by making the following substitutions:

$$R = 8.314 \frac{J}{mol \cdot K}; T = 298.15 \text{ K}; F = \left(\frac{96,485 \text{ C}}{mol \text{ } e^-}\right); \text{ and } \ln K = 2.303 \log K$$

Substituting into Equation 18.5, we get the following important result:

$$E°_{cell} = \frac{0.0592 \text{ V}}{n} \log K \qquad [18.6]$$

where $E°_{cell}$ is the standard cell potential, n is the number of moles of electrons transferred in the redox reaction, and K is the equilibrium constant for the balanced redox reaction at 25 °C. Example 18.7 demonstrates how to use Equation 18.6.

EXAMPLE 18.7 Relating $E°_{cell}$ and K

Use the tabulated electrode potentials to calculate K for the oxidation of copper by H^+ (at 25 °C).

$$Cu(s) + 2 H^+(aq) \longrightarrow Cu^{2+}(aq) + H_2(g)$$

SORT You are given a redox reaction and asked to find K.	**GIVEN:** $Cu(s) + 2 H^+(aq) \longrightarrow Cu^{2+}(aq) + H_2(g)$ **FIND:** K
STRATEGIZE Refer to the values of electrode potentials in Table 18.1 to calculate $E°_{cell}$. Then use Equation 18.6 to calculate K from $E°_{cell}$.	**CONCEPTUAL PLAN** $E°_{cell} = \frac{0.0592 \text{ V}}{n} \log K$
SOLVE Separate the reaction into oxidation and reduction half-reactions and find the standard electrode potentials for each. Find $E°_{cell}$ by subtracting E_{an} from E_{cat}.	**SOLUTION** ***Oxidation*** *(Anode):* $\qquad Cu(s) \longrightarrow Cu^{2+}(aq) + 2 e^- \qquad E° = 0.34$ V ***Reduction*** *(Cathode):* $\quad 2 H^+(aq) + 2 e^- \longrightarrow H_2(g) \qquad E° = 0.00$ V $\overline{\qquad Cu(s) + 2 H^+(aq) \longrightarrow Cu^{2+}(aq) + H_2(g) \quad E°_{cell} = E°_{cat} - E°_{an}}$ $\qquad\qquad\qquad\qquad\qquad\qquad\qquad\qquad\qquad\qquad\qquad = -0.34$ V
Calculate K from $E°_{cell}$. The value of n (the number of moles of electrons) corresponds to the number of electrons that are canceled in the half-reactions.	$E°_{cell} = \frac{0.0592 \text{ V}}{n} \log K$ $\log K = E°_{cell} \frac{n}{0.0592 \text{ V}}$ $\log K = -0.34 \text{ V} \frac{2}{0.0592 \text{ V}} = -11.48$ $K = 10^{-11.48} = 3.3 \times 10^{-12}$

CHECK The answer has no units, as expected for an equilibrium constant. The magnitude of the answer is small, indicating that the reaction lies far to the left at equilibrium, as expected for a reaction in which E°_{cell} is negative.

FOR PRACTICE 18.7

Use the tabulated electrode potentials to calculate K for the oxidation of iron by H^+ (at 25 °C).

$$2\,Fe(s) + 6\,H^+(aq) \longrightarrow 2\,Fe^{3+}(aq) + 3\,H_2(g)$$

Notice that the fundamental quantity in the given relationships is the standard change in free energy for a chemical reaction (ΔG°_{rxn}). From that quantity, we can calculate both E°_{cell} and K. The relationships between these three quantities is summarized with the following diagram:

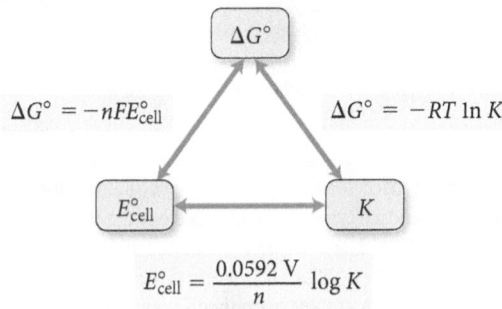

$$E^\circ_{cell} = \frac{0.0592\ V}{n}\ \log K$$

Conceptual Connection 18.6 Relating K, ΔG°_{rxn}, and E°_{cell}

A redox reaction has an equilibrium constant of $K = 1.2 \times 10^3$. Which statement is true regarding ΔG°_{rxn} and E°_{cell} for this reaction?

(a) E°_{cell} is positive and ΔG°_{rxn} is positive.

(b) E°_{cell} is negative and ΔG°_{rxn} is negative.

(c) E°_{cell} is positive and ΔG°_{rxn} is negative.

(d) E°_{cell} is negative and ΔG°_{rxn} is positive.

18.6 Cell Potential and Concentration

We have learned how to find E°_{cell} under standard conditions. For example, we know that when $[Cu^{2+}] = 1\ M$ and $[Zn^{2+}] = 1\ M$, the following reaction produces a potential of 1.10 V.

$$Zn(s) + Cu^{2+}(aq, 1\,M) \longrightarrow Zn^{2+}(aq, 1\,M) + Cu(s) \quad E^\circ_{cell} = 1.10\ V$$

However, what if $[Cu^{2+}] > 1\,M$ and $[Zn^{2+}] < 1\,M$? For example, how would the cell potential for the following conditions be different from the potential under standard conditions?

$$Zn(s) + Cu^{2+}(aq, 2\,M) \longrightarrow Zn^{2+}(aq, 0.010\,M) + Cu(s) \quad E_{cell} = ?$$

Since the concentration of a reactant is greater than standard conditions, and since the concentration of product is less than standard conditions, we can use Le Châtelier's principle to predict that the reaction has an even stronger tendency to occur in the forward direction and that E_{cell} is therefore greater than +1.10 V (Figure 18.11 ▶).

▲ FIGURE 18.11 **Cell Potential and Concentration**   This figure compares the Zn/Cu^{2+} electrochemical cell under standard and nonstandard conditions. In this case, the nonstandard conditions consist of a higher Cu^{2+} concentration ($[Cu^{2+}] > 1\,M$) at the cathode and a lower Zn^{2+} concentration at the anode ($[Zn^{2+}] < 1\,M$). According to Le Châtelier's principle, the forward reaction has a greater tendency to occur, resulting in a greater overall cell potential than the potential under standard conditions.

We can derive an exact relationship between E_{cell} (under nonstandard conditions) and E_{cell}° by considering the relationship between the change in free energy (ΔG) and the *standard* change in free energy (ΔG°) from Section 17.8:

$$\Delta G = \Delta G^{\circ} + RT \ \ln Q \qquad [18.7]$$

where R is the gas constant (8.314 J/mol · K), T is the temperature in kelvins, and Q is the reaction quotient corresponding to the nonstandard conditions. Since we know the relationship between ΔG and E_{cell} (Equation 18.3), we can substitute into Equation 18.7:

$$\Delta G = \Delta G^{\circ} + RT \ \ln Q$$
$$-nFE_{cell} = -nFE_{cell}^{\circ} + RT \ \ln Q$$

We can then divide each side by $-nF$ to arrive at:

$$E_{cell} = E_{cell}^{\circ} - \frac{RT}{nF} \ \ln Q \qquad [18.8]$$

As we have seen, R and F are constants; at $T = 25\ ^{\circ}C$, $\dfrac{RT}{nF} \ln Q = \dfrac{0.0592\ \text{V}}{n} \log Q$.

Substituting into Equation 18.8, we arrive at the **Nernst equation**:

$$E_{cell} = E_{cell}^{\circ} - \frac{0.0592\,\text{V}}{n} \log Q \qquad [18.9]$$

where E_{cell} is the cell potential in volts, E_{cell}° is the *standard* cell potential in volts, n is the number of moles of electrons transferred in the redox reaction, and Q is the reaction quotient. Notice that, under standard conditions, $Q = 1$, and (since $\log 1 = 0$) $E_{cell} = E_{cell}^{\circ}$, as expected. Example 18.8 shows how to calculate the cell potential under nonstandard conditions.

EXAMPLE 18.8 Calculating E_{cell} under Nonstandard Conditions

Determine the cell potential for an electrochemical cell based on the following two half-reactions:

Oxidation: $Cu(s) \longrightarrow Cu^{2+}(aq, 0.010\ M) + 2\ e^-$
Reduction: $MnO_4^-(aq, 2.0\ M) + 4\ H^+(aq, 1.0\ M) + 3\ e^- \longrightarrow MnO_2(s) + 2\ H_2O(l)$

SORT You are given the half-reactions for a redox reaction and the concentrations of the aqueous reactants and products. You are asked to find the cell potential.	**GIVEN:** $[MnO_4^-] = 2.0\ M;\ [H^+] = 1.0\ M;\ [Cu^{2+}] = 0.010\ M$ **FIND:** E_{cell}
STRATEGIZE Use the tabulated values of electrode potentials to calculate E°_{cell}. Then use Equation 18.9 to calculate E_{cell}.	**CONCEPTUAL PLAN** 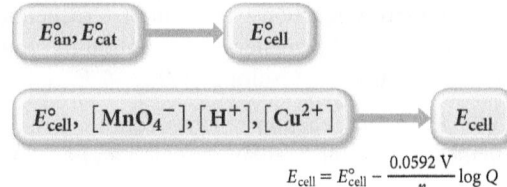 $$E_{cell} = E^\circ_{cell} - \frac{0.0592\ V}{n} \log Q$$
SOLVE Write the oxidation and reduction half-reactions, multiplying by the appropriate coefficients to cancel the electrons. Find the standard electrode potentials for each. Find E°_{cell}.	**SOLUTION** *Oxidation (Anode):* $\quad 3[Cu(s) \longrightarrow Cu^{2+}(aq) + 2e^-] \quad E^\circ = 0.34\ V$ *Reduction (Cathode):* $\quad 2[MnO_4^-(aq) + 4\ H^+(aq) + 3e^- \longrightarrow MnO_2(s) + 2\ H_2O(l)] \quad E^\circ = 1.68\ V$ $\overline{3\ Cu(s) + 2\ MnO_4^-(aq) + 8\ H^+(aq) \longrightarrow 3\ Cu^{2+}(aq) + 2\ MnO_2(s) + 4\ H_2O(l)}$ $E^\circ_{cell} = E^\circ_{cat} - E^\circ_{an} = 1.34\ V$
Calculate E_{cell} from E°_{cell}. The value of n (the number of moles of electrons) corresponds to the number of electrons (6 in this case) canceled in the half-reactions. Determine Q based on the overall balanced equation and the given concentrations of the reactants and products. (Note that pure liquid water, solid MnO_2, and solid copper are omitted from the expression for Q.)	$E_{cell} = E^\circ_{cell} - \dfrac{0.0592\ V}{n} \log Q$ $= E^\circ_{cell} - \dfrac{0.0592\ V}{n} \log \dfrac{[Cu^{2+}]^3}{[MnO_4^-]^2[H^+]^8}$ $= 1.34\ V - \dfrac{0.0592\ V}{6} \log \dfrac{(0.010)^3}{(2.0)^2(1.0)^8}$ $= 1.34\ V - (-0.065\ V)$ $= 1.41\ V$

CHECK The answer has the correct units (V). The value of E_{cell} is larger than E°_{cell}, as expected based on Le Châtelier's principle because one of the aqueous reactants has a concentration greater than standard conditions and the one aqueous product has a concentration less than standard conditions. Therefore, the reaction has a greater tendency to proceed toward products and has a greater cell potential.

FOR PRACTICE 18.8
Determine the cell potential of an electrochemical cell based on the following two half-reactions:

Oxidation: $Ni(s) \longrightarrow Ni^{2+}(aq, 2.0\ M) + 2\ e^-$

Reduction:
$VO_2^+(aq, 0.010\ M) + 2\ H^+(aq, 1.0\ M) + e^- \longrightarrow VO^{2+}(aq, 2.0\ M) + H_2O(l)$

From Equation 18.9, we can conclude the following:

- When a redox reaction within a voltaic cell occurs under standard conditions $Q = 1$; therefore, $E_{cell} = E°_{cell}$.

$$E_{cell} = E°_{cell} - \frac{0.0592\ V}{n} \log Q$$

$$= E°_{cell} - \frac{0.0592\ V}{n} \log 1 \quad \longleftarrow \log 1 = 0$$

$$= E°_{cell}$$

- When a redox reaction within a voltaic cell occurs under conditions in which $Q < 1$, the greater concentration of reactants relative to products drives the reaction to the right, resulting in $E_{cell} > E°_{cell}$.

- When a redox reaction within an electrochemical cell occurs under conditions in which $Q > 1$, the greater concentration of products relative to reactants drives the reaction to the left, resulting in $E_{cell} < E°_{cell}$.

- When a redox reaction reaches equilibrium, $Q = K$. The redox reaction has no tendency to occur in either direction and $E_{cell} = 0$.

$$E_{cell} = E°_{cell} - \frac{0.0592\ V}{n} \log Q \quad \longleftarrow E°_{cell} \quad (\text{see Equation 18.6})$$

$$= E°_{cell} - \frac{0.0592\ V}{n} \log K$$

$$= E°_{cell} - E°_{cell}$$

$$= 0$$

This last point explains why batteries do not last forever—as the reactants are depleted, the reaction proceeds toward equilibrium and the potential tends toward zero.

Conceptual Connection 18.7   Relating Q, K, E_{cell}, and $E°_{cell}$

In an electrochemical cell, $Q = 0.0010$ and $K = 0.10$. What can you conclude about E_{cell} and $E°_{cell}$?

(a) E_{cell} is positive and $E°_{cell}$ is negative.
(b) E_{cell} is negative and $E°_{cell}$ is positive.
(c) Both E_{cell} and $E°_{cell}$ are positive.
(d) Both E_{cell} and $E°_{cell}$ are negative.

Concentration Cells

Since cell potential depends not only on the half-reactions occurring in the cell, but also on the *concentrations* of the reactants and products in those half-reactions, we can construct a voltaic cell in which both half-reactions are the same, but in which *a difference in concentration drives the current flow*. For example, consider the electrochemical cell shown in Figure 18.12 ▶, in which copper is oxidized at the anode and copper ions are reduced at the cathode. The second part of Figure 18.12 depicts this cell under nonstandard conditions, with $[Cu^{2+}] = 2.0$ M in one half-cell and $[Cu^{2+}] = 0.010$ M in the other:

$$Cu(s) + Cu^{2+}(aq, 2.0\ M) \longrightarrow Cu^{2+}(aq, 0.010\ M) + Cu(s)$$

A Concentration Cell

▲ FIGURE 18.12 Cu/Cu²⁺ Concentration Cell If two half-cells have the same Cu^{2+} concentration, the cell potential is zero. If one half-cell has a greater Cu^{2+} concentration than the other, a spontaneous reaction occurs. In the reaction, Cu^{2+} ions in the more concentrated cell are reduced (to solid copper), while Cu^{2+} ions in the more dilute cell are formed (from solid copper). The concentration of copper ions in the two half-cells tends toward equality.

The half-reactions are identical and the *standard* cell potential is therefore zero.

Reduction *(Cathode):* $Cu^{2+}(aq) + 2e^- \longrightarrow Cu(s)$ $\qquad\qquad E° = 0.34$ V

Oxidation *(Anode):* $\qquad\qquad Cu(s) \longrightarrow Cu^{2+}(aq) + 2e^-$ $\quad E° = 0.34$ V

$$Cu^{2+}(aq) + Cu(s) \longrightarrow Cu(s) + Cu^{2+}(aq) \quad E°_{cell} = E°_{cat} - E°_{an}$$
$$= +0.00 \text{ V}$$

Because of the different concentrations in the two half-cells, the cell potential must be calculated using the Nernst equation.

$$E_{cell} = E°_{cell} - \frac{0.0592 \text{ V}}{2} \log \frac{0.010}{2.0}$$
$$= 0.000 \text{ V} + 0.068 \text{ V}$$
$$= 0.068 \text{ V}$$

The cell produces a potential of 0.068 V. *Electrons spontaneously flow from the half-cell with the lower copper ion concentration to the half-cell with the higher copper ion concentration.* You can imagine a concentration cell in the same way you think about any concentration gradient. If you mix a concentrated solution of Cu^{2+} with a dilute solution, the Cu^{2+} ions flow from the concentrated solution to the dilute one. Similarly, in a concentration cell, the transfer of electrons *from* the dilute half-cell results in the formation of Cu^{2+} ions in the dilute half-cell. The electrons flow to the concentrated cell, where they react with Cu^{2+} ions and reduce them to Cu(s). Therefore, *the flow of electrons has the effect of increasing the concentration of Cu^{2+} in the dilute cell and decreasing the concentration of Cu^{2+} in the concentrated half-cell.*

Chemistry and Medicine

Concentration Cells in Human Nerve Cells

Recall from Section 8.1 that tiny pumps in the membranes of human nerve cells pump ions—especially sodium (Na^+) and potassium (K^+)—through those membranes, establishing a concentration gradient for each type of ion: the concentration of sodium ions is higher outside the cell than within, while exactly the opposite is true for potassium ions. These concentration gradients result in an electrical potential across the cell membrane, called the resting potential, of about -70 mV. (The interior of the cell is negative with respect to the exterior.)

When the nerve cell is stimulated, certain channels in the membrane open, allowing Na^+ ions to rush into the cell and causing the potential to temporarily rise to about $+30$ mV (Figure 18.13 ▼). Other channels that allow K^+ ions to rush out of the cell open in turn, bringing the potential back down to near its resting potential. The result is a spike in the electrochemical potential across the membrane, which provides the

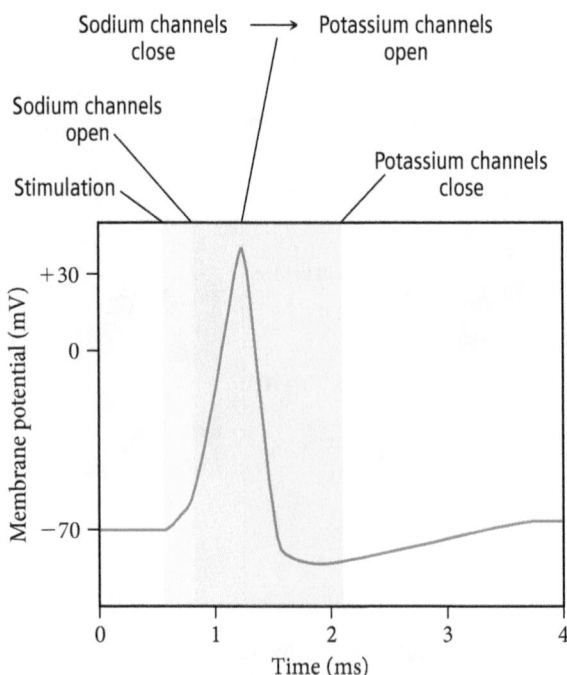

▲ **FIGURE 18.14 Potential Changes across the Nerve Cell Membrane** The changes in ion concentrations that take place when a nerve cell is stimulated result in a spike in the electrochemical potential across the membrane.

▲ **FIGURE 18.13 Concentration Changes in Nerve Cells**

stimulus for a similar spike in the neighboring segment of the membrane (Figure 18.14 ▶). In this way, an electrical signal moves down the length of a nerve cell.

In a nerve cell at rest, the concentration of sodium ions is higher outside the cell than inside. The reverse is true for potassium ions. When a nerve cell is stimulated, sodium channels open and Na^+ ions flood into the cell. A fraction of a second later, the sodium channels close and potassium channels open, allowing K^+ ions to leave the cell.

When the electrical signal reaches the end of the nerve cell, it triggers the release of a chemical neurotransmitter, which travels to the neighboring nerve cell and stimulates the same kind of electrochemical spike. In this way, neural signals travel throughout the brain and nervous system.

18.7 Batteries: Using Chemistry to Generate Electricity

We have seen that we can combine the electron-losing tendency of one substance with the electron-gaining tendency of another to create electrical current in a voltaic cell. Batteries are voltaic cells conveniently packaged to act as portable sources of electricity. The actual oxidation and reduction reactions depend on the particular type of battery. In this section, we examine several different types.

Dry-Cell Batteries

Common batteries, such as the kind you find in a flashlight, are called **dry-cell batteries** because they do not contain large amounts of liquid water. There are several familiar types of dry-cell batteries. The most inexpensive are composed of a zinc case that acts as the anode (Figure 18.15(a) ▶). The zinc is oxidized according to the reaction:

Oxidation *(Anode):* $Zn(s) \longrightarrow Zn^{2+}(aq) + 2 e^-$

The cathode is a carbon rod immersed in a moist paste of MnO_2 that also contains NH_4Cl. The MnO_2 is reduced to Mn_2O_3 according to the reaction:

Reduction *(Cathode):* $2 MnO_2(s) + 2 NH_4^+(aq) + 2 e^- \longrightarrow$
$$Mn_2O_3(s) + 2 NH_3(g) + H_2O(l)$$

These two half-reactions produce a voltage of about 1.5 V. Two or more of these batteries can be connected in series (cathode-to-anode connection) to produce higher voltages.

The more common **alkaline batteries** (Figure 18.15(b)) employ slightly different half-reactions in a basic medium (therefore the name alkaline). In an alkaline battery, the zinc is oxidized in a basic environment:

Oxidation *(Anode):* $Zn(s) + 2 OH^-(aq) \longrightarrow Zn(OH)_2(s) + 2 e^-$
Reduction *(Cathode):* $2 MnO_2(s) + 2 H_2O(l) + 2 e^- \longrightarrow$
$$2 MnO(OH)(s) + 2 OH^-(aq)$$

Overall reaction: $Zn(s) + 2 MnO_2(s) + 2 H_2O(l) \longrightarrow$
$$Zn(OH)_2(s) + 2 MnO(OH)(s)$$

Alkaline batteries have a longer working life and a longer shelf life than their nonalkaline counterparts.

Lead–Acid Storage Batteries

The batteries in most automobiles are **lead–acid storage batteries**. These batteries consist of six electrochemical cells wired in series (Figure 18.16 ▼). Each cell produces 2 V for a total of 12 V. Each cell contains a porous lead anode where oxidation occurs and a lead(IV) oxide cathode where reduction occurs according to the reactions:

Oxidation *(Anode):* $Pb(s) + HSO_4^-(aq) \longrightarrow PbSO_4(s) + H^+(aq) + 2 e^-$
Reduction *(Cathode):* $PbO_2(s) + HSO_4^-(aq) + 2 3H^+(aq) + 2 e^- \longrightarrow$
$$PbSO_4(s) + 2 H_2O(l)$$

Overall reaction: $Pb(s) + PbO_2(s) + 2 HSO_4^-(aq) + 2 H^+(aq) \longrightarrow$
$$2 PbSO_4(s) + 2 H_2O(l)$$

Both the anode and the cathode are immersed in sulfuric acid (H_2SO_4). As electrical current is drawn from the battery, both electrodes become coated with $PbSO_4(s)$. If the battery is run for a long time without recharging, too much $PbSO_4(s)$ develops on the surface of the electrodes and the battery goes dead. The lead–acid storage battery can be recharged by an electrical current (which must come from an external source such as an alternator in a car). The current causes the preceding reaction to occur in reverse, converting the $PbSO_4(s)$ back to $Pb(s)$ and $PbO_2(s)$.

▲ **FIGURE 18.15 Dry-Cell Battery**
(a) In a common dry-cell battery, the zinc case acts as the anode and a graphite rod immersed in a moist, slightly acidic paste of MnO_2 and NH_4Cl acts as the cathode. (b) The longer-lived alkaline batteries employ a graphite cathode immersed in a paste of MnO_2 and a base.

Terminals

Anode (−):
Lead grid packed with finely divided spongy lead

Electrolyte: 30% solution of H_2SO_4

Cathode (+):
Lead grid packed with PbO_2

◀ **FIGURE 18.16 Lead–Acid Storage Battery** A lead–acid storage battery consists of six cells wired in series. Each cell contains a porous lead anode and a lead oxide cathode, both immersed in sulfuric acid.

Other Rechargeable Batteries

The ubiquity of power electronic products such as laptops, cell phones, and digital cameras, as well as the growth in popularity of hybrid electric vehicles, drive the need for efficient, long-lasting, rechargeable batteries. The most common types include the **nickel–cadmium (NiCad) battery**, the **nickel–metal hydride (NiMH) battery**, and the **lithium ion battery**.

The Nickel-Cadmium (NiCad) Battery Nickel–cadmium batteries consist of an anode composed of solid cadmium and a cathode composed of $NiO(OH)(s)$. The electrolyte is usually $KOH(aq)$. During operation, the cadmium is oxidized and the $NiO(OH)$ is reduced according to the equations:

Oxidation *(Anode):* $Cd(s) + 2\,OH^-(aq) \longrightarrow Cd(OH)_2(s) + 2\,e^-$

Reduction *(Cathode):* $2\,NiO(OH)(s) + 2\,H_2O(l) + 2\,e^- \longrightarrow$
$$2\,Ni(OH)_2(s) + 2\,OH^-(aq)$$

The overall reaction produces about 1.30 V. As current is drawn from the NiCad battery, solid cadmium hydroxide accumulates on the anode and solid nickel(II) hydroxide accumulates on the cathode. But by running current in the opposite direction, the reactants can be regenerated from the products. A common problem in recharging NiCad and other rechargeable batteries is knowing when to stop. Once all of the products of the reaction are converted back to reactants, the charging process should ideally terminate—otherwise the electrical current will drive other, usually unwanted, reactions such as the electrolysis of water to form hydrogen and oxygen gas. These reactions typically damage the battery and may sometimes even cause an explosion. Consequently, most commercial battery chargers have sensors that measure when the charging is complete. These sensors rely on the small changes in voltage or increases in temperature that occur once the products have all been converted back to reactants.

▲ Several types of batteries, including NiCad, NiMH, and lithium ion batteries, are recharged by chargers that use household current.

The Nickel-Metal Hydride (NiMH) Battery Although NiCad batteries were the standard rechargeable battery for many years, they are being replaced by other types of rechargeable batteries, in part because of the toxicity of cadmium and the resulting disposal problems. One of these replacements is the nickel–metal hydride or NiMH battery. The NiMH battery employs the same cathode reaction as the NiCad battery but a different anode reaction. In the anode of a NiMH battery, hydrogen atoms held in a metal alloy are oxidized. If we let M represent the metal alloy, we can write the half-reactions as follows:

Oxidation *(Anode):* $M \cdot H(s) + OH^-(aq) \longrightarrow M(s) + H_2O(l) + e^-$

Reduction *(Cathode):* $NiO(OH)(s) + H_2O(l) + e^- \longrightarrow Ni(OH)_2(s) + OH^-(aq)$

In addition to being more environmentally friendly than NiCad batteries, NiMH batteries also have a greater energy density (energy content per unit battery mass), as we can see in Table 18.2. In some cases, a NiMH battery can carry twice the energy of a NiCad battery of the same mass, making NiMH batteries the most common choice for hybrid electric vehicles.

The Lithium Ion Battery The newest and most expensive common type of rechargeable battery is the lithium ion battery. Since lithium is the least dense metal (0.53 g/cm^3), lithium batteries have high energy densities (see Table 18.2). The lithium battery works differently than the other batteries we have examined so far, and the details of its operation are beyond the scope

TABLE 18.2 Energy Density and Overcharge Tolerance of Several Rechargeable Batteries

Battery Type	Energy Density (W · h/kg)	Overcharge Tolerance
NiCad	45–80	Moderate
NiMH	60–120	Low
Li ion	110–160	Low
Pb storage	30–50	High

of our current discussion. Briefly, you can think of the operation of the lithium battery as being due primarily to the motion of lithium ions from the anode to the cathode. The anode is composed of graphite into which lithium ions are incorporated between layers of carbon atoms. Upon discharge, the lithium ions spontaneously migrate to the cathode, which consists of a lithium transition metal oxide such as $LiCoO_2$ or $LiMn_2O_4$. The transition metal is reduced during this process. Upon recharging, the transition metal is oxidized, forcing the lithium to migrate back into the graphite (Figure 18.17 ▶). The flow of lithium ions from the anode to the cathode causes a corresponding flow of electrons in the external circuit. Lithium ion batteries are commonly used in applications where light weight and high energy density are important. These include cell phones, laptop computers, and digital cameras.

Fuel Cells

We discussed the potential for *fuel cells* in the opening section of this chapter. Fuel cells may one day replace—or at least work in combination with—centralized power grid electricity. In addition, vehicles powered by fuel cells may one day usurp vehicles powered by internal combustion engines. Fuel cells are like batteries; the key difference is that a battery is self-contained, while in a fuel cell the reactants need to be constantly replenished from an external source. With use, normal batteries lose their ability to generate voltage because the reactants become depleted as electrical current is drawn from the battery. In a **fuel cell**, the reactants—the fuel provided from an external source—constantly flow through the battery, generating electrical current as they undergo a redox reaction.

The most common fuel cell is the hydrogen–oxygen fuel cell (Figure 18.18 ▼). In this cell, hydrogen gas flows past the anode (a screen coated with platinum catalyst) and undergoes oxidation.

Oxidation *(Anode):* $2 H_2(g) + 4 OH^-(aq) \longrightarrow 4 H_2O(l) + 4 e^-$

Graphite   Lithium-transition metal oxide

Lithium ions

Charge ⟵ Li^+ ⟶ Discharge

▲ **FIGURE 18.17 Lithium Ion Battery** In the lithium ion battery, the spontaneous flow of lithium ions from the graphite anode to the lithium transition metal oxide cathode causes a corresponding flow of electrons in the external circuit.

Hydrogen–Oxygen Fuel Cell

- Electron
- Proton
- Oxygen atom

Electric circuit

Anode   Cathode

Hydrogen inlet

H_2 H^+ OH^- Oxygen inlet

H_2O O_2

Electrolyte

Oxidation	Reduction
$2 H_2(g) + 4 OH^-(aq)$ $\longrightarrow 4 H_2O(l) + 4 e^-$	$O_2(g) + 2 H_2O(l) + 4 e^-$ $\longrightarrow 4 OH^-(aq)$

◀ **FIGURE 18.18 Hydrogen–Oxygen Fuel Cell** In this fuel cell, hydrogen and oxygen combine to form water.

Chemistry in Your Day

The Fuel-Cell Breathalyzer

Police often use a device called a breathalyzer to measure the amount of ethyl alcohol (C_2H_6O) in the bloodstream of a person suspected of driving under the influence of alcohol (Figure 18.19 ▼). Breathalyzers work because the quantity of ethyl alcohol in the breath is proportional to the quantity of ethyl alcohol in the bloodstream. One type of breathalyzer employs a fuel cell to measure the quantity of alcohol in the breath. When a suspect blows into the breathalyzer, ethyl alcohol is oxidized to acetic acid at the anode:

$$\textit{Oxidation (Anode):}\quad CH_3CH_2OH(g) + 4\,OH^-(aq) \longrightarrow$$
ethyl alcohol

$$HC_2H_3O_2(g) + 3\,H_2O(l) + 4\,e^-$$
acetic acid

At the cathode, oxygen is reduced:

$$\textit{Reduction (Cathode):}\quad O_2(g) + 2\,H_2O(l) + 4\,e^- \longrightarrow$$
$$4\,OH^-(aq)$$

The overall reaction is the oxidation of ethyl alcohol to acetic acid and water:

$$\textit{Overall:}\quad CH_3CH_2OH(g) + O_2(g) \longrightarrow$$
$$HC_2H_3O_2(g) + H_2O(l)$$

The magnitude of electrical current produced depends on the quantity of alcohol in the breath. A higher current results from a higher blood alcohol level. When calibrated correctly, the fuel-cell breathalyzer can precisely measure the blood alcohol level of a suspected drunk driver.

▲ **FIGURE 18.19 Fuel-Cell Breathalyzer** The fuel-cell breathalyzer works by oxidizing ethyl alcohol in the breath to acetic acid. The electrical current that is produced is proportional to the concentration of ethyl alcohol in the breath.

Oxygen gas flows past the cathode (a similar screen) and undergoes reduction:

$$\textit{Reduction (Cathode):}\ O_2(g) + 2\,H_2O(l) + 4\,e^- \longrightarrow 4\,OH^-(aq)$$

The half-reactions sum to the following overall reaction:

$$\textit{Overall reaction:}\ 2\,H_2(g) + O_2(g) \longrightarrow 2\,H_2O(l)$$

Notice that the only product is water. In the space shuttle program, hydrogen–oxygen fuel cells consume hydrogen to provide electricity and astronauts drink the water that is produced by the reaction. In order for hydrogen-powered fuel cells to become more widely used, a more readily available source of hydrogen must be developed.

18.8 Electrolysis: Driving Nonspontaneous Chemical Reactions with Electricity

In a voltaic cell, a spontaneous redox reaction produces electrical current. In an *electrolytic cell*, electrical current drives an otherwise nonspontaneous redox reaction through a process called **electrolysis**. We have seen that the reaction of hydrogen with

Electrolysis of Water

Anode	Cathode
$2 H_2O(l) \longrightarrow$ $O_2(g) + 4 H^+(aq) + 4 e^-$	$2 H_2O(l) + 2 e^- \longrightarrow$ $H_2(g) + 2 OH^-(aq)$

◄ FIGURE 18.20 Electrolysis of Water Electrical current can decompose water into hydrogen and oxygen gas.

oxygen to form water is spontaneous and can be used to produce an electrical current in a fuel cell. Conversely, by *supplying* electrical current, we can cause the reverse reaction to occur, separating water into hydrogen and oxygen (Figure 18.20 ▲).

$2 H_2(g) + O_2(g) \longrightarrow 2 H_2O(l)$ (spontaneous—produces electrical current; occurs in a voltaic cell)

$2 H_2O(l) \longrightarrow 2 H_2(g) + O_2(g)$ (nonspontaneous—consumes electrical current; occurs in an electrolytic cell)

Recall from the previous section that one of the problems associated with the widespread adoption of hydrogen fuel cells is the scarcity of hydrogen. Where will the hydrogen to power these fuel cells come from? One possible answer is to obtain hydrogen from water through solar-powered electrolysis. A solar-powered electrolytic cell can produce hydrogen from water when the sun is shining. The hydrogen made in this way could be converted back to water to generate electricity and could also be used to power fuel-cell vehicles.

Electrolysis also has numerous other applications. For example, most metals are found in Earth's crust as metal oxides. Converting an oxide to a pure metal requires that the metal be reduced, a nonspontaneous process. Electrolysis can be used to produce these metals. Thus, sodium is produced by the electrolysis of molten sodium chloride (discussed in the following subsection). Electrolysis is also used to plate metals onto other metals. For example, silver can be plated onto a less expensive metal using the electrolytic cell shown in Figure 18.21 ►. In this cell, a silver electrode is placed in a solution containing silver ions. An electrical current causes the oxidation of silver at the anode (replenishing the silver ions in solution) and the reduction of silver ions at the cathode (coating the less expensive metal with solid silver).

Oxidation (Anode): $Ag(s) \longrightarrow Ag^+(aq) + e^-$
Reduction (Cathode): $Ag^+(aq) + e^- \longrightarrow Ag(s)$

▼ FIGURE 18.21 Silver Plating Silver can be plated from a solution of silver ions onto metallic objects in an electrolytic cell.

Electrolytic Cell for Silver Plating

Anode	Cathode
$Ag(s) \longrightarrow$ $Ag^+(aq) + e^-$	$Ag^+(aq) + e^-$ $\longrightarrow Ag(s)$

▲ **FIGURE 18.22 Voltaic versus Electrolytic Cells** In a Zn/Cu^{2+} voltaic cell, the reaction proceeds in the spontaneous direction. In a Zn^{2+}/Cu electrolytic cell, electrical current drives the reaction in the nonspontaneous direction.

Since the standard cell potential of the reaction is zero, the reaction is not spontaneous under standard conditions. An external power source can be used to drive current flow and cause the reaction to occur.

The voltage required to cause electrolysis depends on the specific half-reactions. For example, we have seen that the oxidation of zinc and the reduction of Cu^{2+} produces a voltage of 1.10 V under standard conditions.

Reduction (Cathode): $\quad Cu^{2+}(aq) + 2e^- \longrightarrow Cu(s) \qquad\qquad E° = 0.34\ V$

Oxidation (Anode): $\qquad\qquad\quad Zn(s) \longrightarrow Zn^{2+}(aq) + 2e^- \quad E° = -0.76\ V$

$$Cu^{2+}(aq) + Zn(s) \longrightarrow Cu(s) + Zn^{2+}(aq) \quad E°_{cell} = E°_{cat} - E°_{an}$$

$$= +1.10\ V$$

If a power source producing *more than 1.10 V* is inserted into the Zn/Cu^{2+} voltaic cell, electrons can be forced to flow in the opposite direction, causing the reduction of Zn^{2+} and the oxidation of Cu, as shown in Figure 18.22 ▲. Notice that in the electrolytic cell, the anode has become the cathode (oxidation always occurs at the anode) and the cathode has become the anode.

In a *voltaic cell*, the anode is the source of electrons and is therefore labeled with a negative charge. The cathode draws electrons and is therefore labeled with a positive charge. In an *electrolytic cell*, however, the source of the electrons is the external power source. The external power source must *draw electrons away* from the anode; thus, the anode must be connected to the positive terminal of the battery (as shown in Figure 18.22). Similarly, the power source drives electrons toward the cathode (where they will be used in reduction), so the cathode must be connected to the *negative* terminal of the battery. The charge labels (+ and −) on an electrolytic cell are opposite of what they are in a voltaic cell.

Summarizing Characteristics of Electrochemical Cell Types:

In all electrochemical cells:

▶ Oxidation occurs at the anode.

▶ Reduction occurs at the cathode.

In voltaic cells:

▶ The anode is the source of electrons and has a negative charge (anode −).

▶ The cathode draws electrons and has a positive charge (cathode +).

In electrolytic cells:

▶ Electrons are drawn away from the anode, which must be connected to the positive terminal of the external power source (anode +).

▶ Electrons are forced to the cathode, which must be connected to the negative terminal of the power source (cathode −).

Predicting the Products of Electrolysis

Predicting the products of an electrolysis reaction is in some cases relatively straightforward and in other cases more complex. We cover the simpler cases first and follow with the more complex ones.

Pure Molten Salts Consider the electrolysis of a molten salt such as sodium chloride, shown in Figure 18.23 ▶. Na^+ and Cl^- are the only species present in the cell. The chloride ion cannot be further reduced (−1 is its lowest oxidation state), so it must be oxidized. The sodium ion cannot be further oxidized (+1 is its highest oxidation state), so it must be reduced. Thus, we can write the half-reactions:

Oxidation (Anode): $\qquad\qquad\qquad 2\,Cl^-(l) \longrightarrow Cl_2(g) + 2\,e^-$

Reduction (Cathode): $\qquad 2\,Na^+(l) + 2\,e^- \longrightarrow 2\,Na(s)$

Overall: $\qquad\qquad\qquad 2\,Na^+(l) + 2\,Cl^-(l) \longrightarrow 2\,Na(s) + Cl_2(g)$

Although the reaction as written is not spontaneous, it can be driven to occur in an electrolytic cell by an external power source. We can generalize as follows:

• In the electrolysis of a pure molten salt, the anion is oxidized and the cation is reduced.

Mixtures of Cations or Anions What if a molten salt contains more than one anion or cation? For example, suppose our electrolysis cell contained both NaCl and KCl. Which of the two cations would be reduced at the cathode? In order to answer this question, we must determine which of the two cations is more easily reduced. Although the values of electrode potentials for aqueous solutions given in Table 18.1 do not apply to molten salts, the relative ordering of the electrode potentials does reflect the relative ease with which the metal cations are reduced. We can see from the table that the reduction of Na^+ is listed *above* the reduction of K^+; that is, Na^+ has a more positive electrode potential.

$$Na^+(aq) + e^- \longrightarrow Na(s) \qquad E° = -2.71\ V \quad \text{(for aqueous solution)}$$
$$K^+(aq) + e^- \longrightarrow K(s) \qquad E° = -2.92\ V \quad \text{(for aqueous solution)}$$

Therefore, Na^+ is easier to reduce than K^+. Consequently, in a mixture of NaCl and KCl, Na^+ has a greater tendency to be reduced at the cathode.

Similarly, what if a mixture of molten salts contained more than one anion? For example, in a mixture of NaBr and NaCl, which of the two anions is oxidized at the cathode? The answer is similar: the anion that is more easily oxidized (the one with the more negative electrode potential).

$$2\,Cl^-(aq) \longrightarrow Cl_2(g) + 2\,e^- \qquad E° = 1.36\ V \quad \text{(for aqueous solution)}$$
$$2\,Br^-(aq) \longrightarrow Br_2(l) + 2\,e^- \qquad E° = 1.09\ V \quad \text{(for aqueous solution)}$$

Since the electrode potential for the bromine half-reaction is more negative, electrons are more easily extracted from it. The bromide ion is therefore oxidized at the anode.

We can generalize as follows:

• The cation that is most easily reduced (the one with the more positive electrode potential) is reduced first.

• The anion that is most easily oxidized (the one with the more negative electrode potential) is oxidized first.

Electrolysis of a Molten Salt

▲ FIGURE 18.23 **Electrolysis of Molten NaCl** In the electrolysis of a pure molten salt, the anion (in this case Cl^-) is oxidized and the cation (in this case Na^+) is reduced.

Throughout this discussion "more positive" means the same thing as "less negative."

Throughout this discussion "more negative" means the same thing as "less positive."

Remember NIO and PIR:
N.I.O.—More Negative Is Oxidation
P.I.R.—More Positive Is Reduction

Aqueous Solutions Electrolysis in an aqueous solution is complicated by the possibility of the electrolysis of water itself. Recall that water can be either oxidized or reduced according to the following half-reactions:

Oxidation (Anode): $2 H_2O(l) \longrightarrow O_2(g) + 4 H^+(aq) + 4 e^-$ $E° = 1.23$ V (standard conditions)

$$E = 0.82 \text{ V}([H^+] = 10^{-7} \text{ M})$$

Reduction (Cathode): $2 H_2O(l) + 2 e^- \longrightarrow H_2(g) + 2 OH^-(aq)$ $E° = -0.83$ V (standard conditions)

$$E = -0.41 \text{ V}([OH^-] = 10^{-7} \text{ M})$$

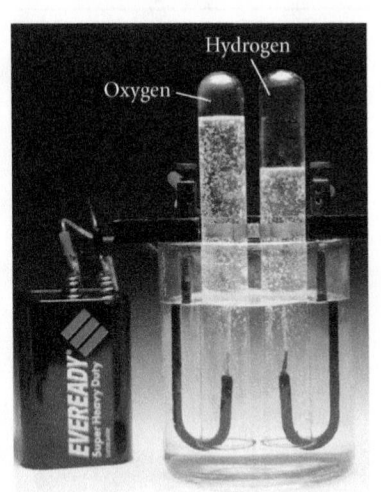

Hydrogen

Oxygen

▲ Pure water is a poor conductor of electrical current, but the addition of an electrolyte allows electrolysis to take place, producing hydrogen and oxygen gas in a stoichiometric ratio.

The electrode potentials under standard conditions are shown to the right of each half-reaction. However, in pure water at room temperature, the concentrations of H^+ and OH^- are not standard. The electrode potentials for $[H^+] = 10^{-7}$ M and $[OH^-] = 10^{-7}$ M are shown in blue. Using those electrode potentials, we can calculate E_{cell} for the electrolysis of water as follows:

$$E_{cell} = E_{cat} - E_{an} = -0.41 \text{ V} - 0.82 \text{ V} = -1.23 \text{ V}$$

When a battery with a potential of several volts is connected to an electrolysis cell containing pure water, no reaction occurs, because the concentration of ions in pure water is too low to conduct any significant electrical current. When an electrolyte such as Na_2SO_4 is added to the water, however, electrolysis occurs readily.

In any aqueous solution in which electrolysis is to take place, the electrolysis of water is also possible. For example, consider the electrolysis of a sodium iodide solution, as shown in Figure 18.24 ▼. For the electrolysis of *molten* NaI, we can readily predict that I^- is oxidized at the anode and that Na^+ is reduced at the cathode. In an aqueous solution, however, two different oxidation half-reactions are possible at the anode, the oxidation of I^- and the oxidation of water:

Oxidation: $2 I^-(aq) \longrightarrow I_2(aq) + 2 e^-$ $E° = 0.54$ V
Oxidation: $2 H_2O(l) \longrightarrow O_2(g) + 4 H^+(aq) + 4 e^-$

$$E = 0.82 \text{ V } ([H^+] = 10^{-7} \text{ M})$$

Similarly, two different reduction half-reactions are possible at the cathode, the reduction of Na^+ and the reduction of water:

Reduction: $2 Na^+(aq) + 2 e^- \longrightarrow 2 Na(s)$ $E° = -2.71$ V

Reduction: $2 H_2O(l) + 2 e^- \longrightarrow H_2(g) + 2 OH^-(aq)$

$$E = -0.41 \text{ V } ([OH^-] = 10^{-7} \text{ M})$$

Electrolysis of an Aqueous Salt Solution

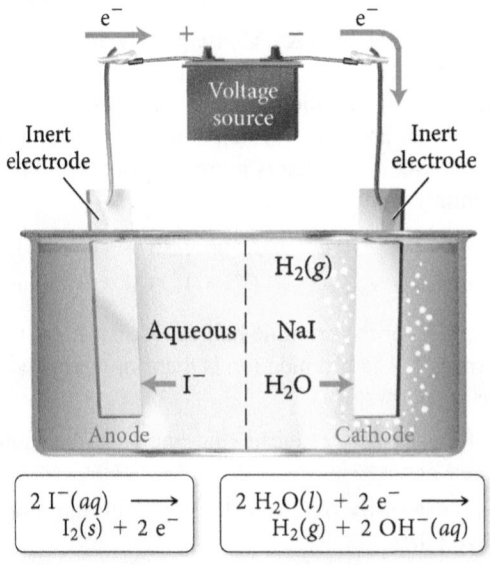

▶ **FIGURE 18.24 Electrolysis of Aqueous NaI** In this cell, I^- is oxidized to I_2 at the anode and H_2O is reduced to H_2 at the cathode. Sodium ions are not reduced, because their electrode potential is more negative than the electrode potential of water.

e^- +   − e^-

Voltage source

Inert electrode

Inert electrode

$H_2(g)$

Aqueous   NaI

← I^- H_2O →

Anode   Cathode

$2 I^-(aq) \longrightarrow I_2(s) + 2 e^-$

$2 H_2O(l) + 2 e^- \longrightarrow H_2(g) + 2 OH^-(aq)$

How do we know which reactions actually occur? In both cases, the answer is the same: *the half-reaction that occurs the easiest.* For oxidation, the half-reaction with the more negative electrode potential is the easier one from which to extract electrons. In this case, therefore, the iodide ion is oxidized at the anode. For reduction, the half-reaction with the more positive electrode potential is the easiest one to get to accept electrons. In this case, therefore, water is reduced at the cathode. Notice that Na^+ cannot be reduced in an aqueous solution—water is reduced before Na^+. We can make the following generalization:

- The cations of active metals—those that are not easily reduced, such as Li^+, K^+, Na^+, Mg^{2+}, Ca^{2+}, and Al^{3+}—cannot be reduced from aqueous solutions by electrolysis because water is reduced at a lower voltage.

The Electrolysis of Aqueous Sodium Chloride and Overvoltage An additional complication that we must consider when predicting the products of electrolysis is *overvoltage*—an additional voltage that must be applied in order to get some nonspontaneous reactions to occur. We can demonstrate this concept by considering the electrolysis of a sodium chloride solution, shown in Figure 18.25 ▼. In order to predict the product of the electrolysis, we consider the two possible oxidation half-reactions:

$$\textit{Oxidation: } 2\,Cl^-(aq) \longrightarrow Cl_2(g) + 2\,e^- \qquad E° = 1.36\,V$$

$$\textit{Oxidation: } 2\,H_2O(l) \longrightarrow O_2(g) + 4\,H^+(aq) + 4\,e^-$$

$$E = 0.82\,V\,([H^+] = 10^{-7}\,M)$$

and the two possible reduction half-reactions:

$$\textit{Reduction: } 2\,Na^+(aq) + 2\,e^- \longrightarrow 2\,Na(s) \qquad E° = -2.71\,V$$

$$\textit{Reduction: } 2\,H_2O(l) + 2\,e^- \longrightarrow H_2(g) + 2\,OH^-(aq)$$

$$E = -0.41\,V\,([OH^-] = 10^{-7}\,M)$$

Since the oxidation of water has a more negative electrode potential than the oxidation of Cl^-, we would initially predict that it would be easier to remove electrons from water, and thus water should be oxidized at the anode. Similarly, since the reduction of water has a more positive electrode potential than the reduction of Na^+, we would expect that it would be easier to get water to accept electrons, so water should be reduced at the cathode. In other words, we initially predict that a sodium chloride solution would simply result in the electrolysis of water, producing oxygen gas at the anode and hydrogen gas at the cathode. If we construct such a cell, however, we find that, although hydrogen gas is indeed formed at the cathode (as predicted), oxygen gas is *not* formed at the anode— chlorine gas is formed instead. Why? The answer is that even though the electrode potential for the oxidation of water is 0.82 V, the reaction actually requires a voltage greater

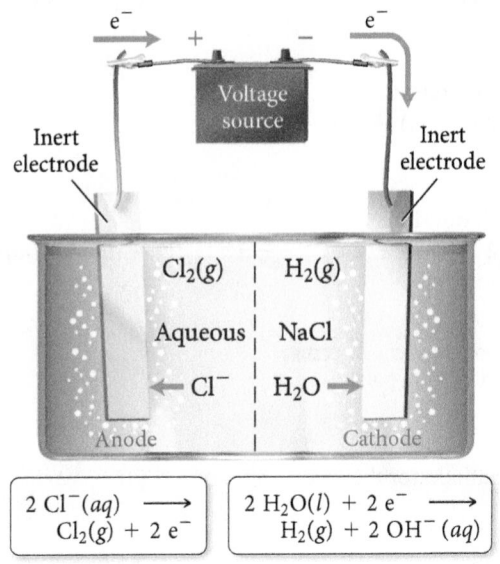

◄ FIGURE 18.25 **Electrolysis of Aqueous NaCl: The Effect of Overvoltage** Because of overvoltage, the anode reaction of this cell is the oxidation of Cl^- to Cl_2 gas rather than the oxidation of water to H^+ and O_2 gas.

than 0.82 V in order to occur. (The reasons for this behavior are related to kinetic factors that are beyond the scope of our current discussion.) This additional voltage, the *overvoltage*, increases the voltage required for the oxidation of water to about 1.4 V. The result is that the chloride ion oxidizes more easily than water and $Cl_2(g)$ is observed at the anode.

EXAMPLE 18.9 Predicting the Products of Electrolysis Reactions

Predict the half-reaction occurring at the anode and the cathode for electrolysis for each reaction.

(a) a mixture of molten $AlBr_3$ and $MgBr_2$

(b) an aqueous solution of LiI

SOLUTION

(a) In the electrolysis of a molten salt, the anion is oxidized and the cation is reduced. However, this mixture contains two cations. Start by writing the possible oxidation and reduction half-reactions that might occur.

Since Br^- is the only anion, write the equation for its oxidation, which occurs at the anode.

At the cathode, both the reduction of Al^{3+} and the reduction of Mg^{2+} are possible. The one that actually occurs is the one that occurs most easily. Since the reduction of Al^{3+} has a more positive electrode potential in aqueous solution, this ion is more easily reduced. Therefore, the reduction of Al^{3+} occurs at the cathode.

Oxidation: $2\,Br^-(l) \longrightarrow Br_2(g) + 2\,e^-$

Reduction: $Al^{3+}(l) + 3\,e^- \longrightarrow Al(s)$ $E° = -1.66$ V (for aqueous solution)

Reduction that actually occurs (more positive potential)

$Mg^{2+}(l) + 2\,e^- \longrightarrow Mg(s)$ $E° = -2.37$ V (for aqueous solution)

(b) Since LiI is in an aqueous solution, two different oxidation half-reactions are possible at the anode, the oxidation of I^- and the oxidation of water. Write half-reactions for each including the electrode potential. Remember to use the electrode potential of water under conditions in which $[H^+] = 10^{-7}$ M. Since the oxidation of I^- has the more negative electrode potential, it will be the half-reaction to occur at the anode.

Similarly, write half-reactions for the two possible reduction half-reactions that might occur at the cathode, the reduction of Li^+ and the reduction of water. Since the reduction of water has the more positive electrode potential (even when considering overvoltage, which would raise the necessary voltage by about 0.4–0.6 V), it will be the half reaction to occur at the cathode.

Oxidation that actually occurs (more negative potential)

Oxidation:
$2\,I^-(aq) \longrightarrow I_2(l) + 2\,e^-$
$E° = 0.54$ V

Oxidation:
$2\,H_2O(l) \longrightarrow O_2(g) + 4\,H^+(aq) + 4\,e^-$
$E° = 0.82$ V ($[H^+] = 10^{-7}$ M)

Reduction:
$2\,Li^+(aq) + 2\,e^- \longrightarrow 2\,Li(s)$
$E° = -3.04$ V

Reduction:
$2\,H_2O(l) + 2\,e^- \longrightarrow H_2(g) + 2\,OH^-(aq)$
$E = -0.41$ V ($[OH^-] = 10^{-7}$ M)

Reduction that actually occurs (more positive potential)

FOR PRACTICE 18.9

Predict the half-reactions occurring at the anode and the cathode for the electrolysis of aqueous Na_2SO_4.

Stoichiometry of Electrolysis

In an electrolytic cell, electrical current is used to drive a particular chemical reaction. In a sense, the electrons act as a reactant and therefore have a stoichiometric relationship with the other reactants and products. Unlike ordinary reactants, for which we usually measure quantity as mass, for electrons we measure quantity as charge. For example, consider an electrolytic cell used to coat copper onto metals, as shown in Figure 18.26 ▼. The half-reaction by which copper is deposited onto the metal is:

$$Cu^{2+}(aq) + 2\,e^- \longrightarrow Cu(s)$$

For every 2 mol of electrons that flow through the cell, 1 mol of solid copper is plated. We can write the stoichiometric relationship:

$$2\ mol\ e^- : 1\ mol\ Cu(s)$$

We can determine the number of moles of electrons that have flowed in a given electrolysis cell by measuring the total charge that has flowed through the cell, which in turn depends on the *magnitude* of the current and on the *time* that the current runs. Recall from Section 18.3 that the unit of current is the ampere.

$$1\,A = 1\frac{C}{s}$$

If we multiply the amount of current (in A) flowing through the cell by the time (in s) that the current flowed, we find the total charge that passed through the cell in that time:

$$Current\left(\frac{C}{s}\right) \times time\ (s) = charge\ (C)$$

The relationship between charge and the number of moles of electrons is given by Faraday's constant, which, as we saw previously, corresponds to the charge in coulombs of 1 mol of electrons.

$$F = \frac{96{,}485\ C}{mol\ e^-}$$

These relationships can be used to solve problems involving the stoichiometry of electrolytic cells, as shown in Example 18.10.

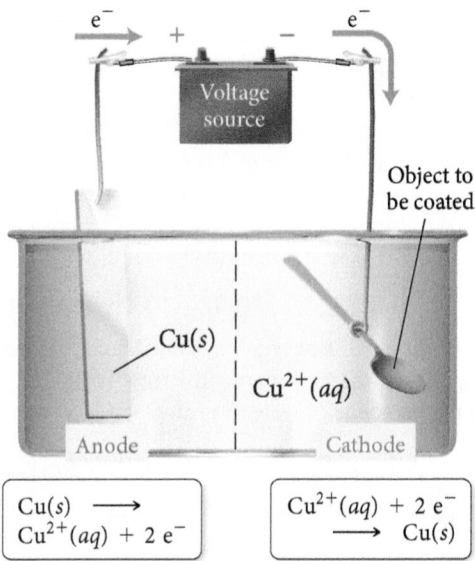

▲ **FIGURE 18.26 Electrolytic Cell for Copper Plating** In this cell, copper ions are plated onto other metals. It takes two moles of electrons to plate one mole of copper atoms.

EXAMPLE 18.10   Stoichiometry of Electrolysis

Gold can be plated out of a solution containing Au^{3+} according to the half-reaction:

$$Au^{3+}(aq) + 3\ e^- \longrightarrow Au(s)$$

What mass of gold (in grams) is plated by a 25-minute flow of 5.5 A current?

SORT You are given the half-reaction for the plating of gold, which shows the stoichiometric relationship between moles of electrons and moles of gold. You are also given the current and duration. You must find the mass of gold that will be deposited in that time.	**GIVEN:** 3 mol e^- : 1 mol Au
	      5.5 amps
	      25 min
	
	FIND: g Au

STRATEGIZE You need to find the amount of gold, which is related stoichiometrically to the number of electrons that have flowed through the cell. Begin with time in minutes and convert to seconds. Then, since current is a measure of charge per unit time, use the given current and the time to find the number of coulombs. You can use Faraday's constant to calculate the number of moles of electrons and the stoichiometry of the reaction to find the number of moles of gold. Finally, use the molar mass of gold to convert to mass of gold.	**CONCEPTUAL PLAN** 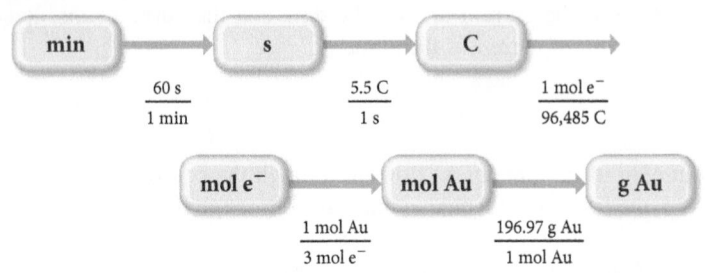
SOLVE Follow the conceptual plan to solve the problem, canceling units to arrive at the mass of gold.	**SOLUTION** $$25\ \cancel{min} \times \frac{60\ \cancel{s}}{1\ \cancel{min}} \times \frac{5.5\ \cancel{C}}{1\ \cancel{s}} \times \frac{1\ \cancel{mol\ e^-}}{96{,}485\ \cancel{C}} \times \frac{1\ \cancel{mol\ Au}}{3\ \cancel{mol\ e^-}} \times \frac{196.97\ g\ Au}{1\ \cancel{mol\ Au}} = 5.6\ g\ Au$$

CHECK The answer has the correct units (g Au). The magnitude of the answer is reasonable if we consider that 10 amps of current for 1 hour is the equivalent of about 1/3 mol of electrons (check for yourself), which would produce 1/9 mol (or about 20 g) of gold.

FOR PRACTICE 18.10

Silver can be plated out of a solution containing Ag^+ according to the half-reaction:

$$Ag^+(aq) + e^- \longrightarrow Ag(s)$$

How much time (in minutes) would it take to plate 12 g of silver using a current of 3.0 A?

18.9 Corrosion: Undesirable Redox Reactions

Corrosion is the (usually) gradual, nearly always undesired, oxidation of metals that are exposed to oxidizing agents in the environment. From Table 18.1, we can see that the reduction of oxygen in the presence of water has an electrode potential of +0.40 V.

$$O_2(g) + 2\ H_2O(l) + 4\ e^- \longrightarrow 4\ OH^-(aq) \qquad E° = +0.40\ V$$

In the presence of acid, the reduction of oxygen has an even more positive electrode potential of +1.23 V.

$$O_2(g) + 4\ H^+(aq) + 4\ e^- \longrightarrow 2\ H_2O(l) \qquad E° = +1.23\ V$$

▲ A metal must usually be reduced to extract it from its ore. In corrosion, the metal is oxidized back to its more natural state.

The reduction of oxygen, therefore, has a strong tendency to occur and can bring about the oxidation of other substances, especially metals. Notice that the half-reactions for the reduction of most metal ions are listed *below* the half-reactions for the reduction of oxygen in Table 18.1. Consequently, the oxidation (or corrosion) of those metals is spontaneous when paired with the reduction of oxygen. Corrosion is the opposite of the process by which metals are extracted from their ores. In extraction, the free metal is reduced out from its ore. In corrosion, the metal is oxidized.

Given the ease with which metals oxidize in the presence of oxygen, acid, and water, why are metals used so frequently as building materials in the first place? Many metals form oxides that coat the surface of the metal and prevent further corrosion. For example, bare aluminum metal, with an electrode potential of -1.66 V, is quickly oxidized in the presence of oxygen. However, the oxide that forms at the surface of aluminum is Al_2O_3. In its crystalline form, Al_2O_3 is sapphire, a highly inert and structurally solid substance. The Al_2O_3 coating acts to protect the underlying aluminum metal, preventing further corrosion.

The oxides of iron, however, are not structurally stable, and they tend to flake away from the underlying metal, exposing it to further corrosion. A significant part of the iron produced each year is used to replace rusted iron. Rusting is a redox reaction in which iron is oxidized according to the following half-reaction:

$$Fe(s) \longrightarrow Fe^{2+}(aq) + 2\,e^{-} \quad E° = -0.45\ V$$

This oxidation reaction tends to occur at defects on the surface of the iron—known as *anodic regions* because oxidation is occurring at these locations—as shown in Figure 18.27 ▼. The electrons produced at the anodic region travel through the metal to areas called *cathodic regions* where they react with oxygen and H^+ ions dissolved in moisture. (The H^+ ions come from carbonic acid, which naturally forms in water from carbon dioxide in air.)

$$O_2(g) + 4\,H^+(aq) + 4\,e^{-} \longrightarrow 2\,H_2O(l) \quad E° = +1.23\ V$$

The overall reaction has a cell potential of $+1.68$ V and is highly spontaneous.

$$2\,Fe(s) + O_2(g) + 4\,H^+(aq) \longrightarrow 2\,H_2O(l) + 2\,Fe^{2+}(aq) \quad E°_{cell} = +1.68\ V$$

The Fe^{2+} ions formed in the anodic regions can migrate through moisture on the surface of the iron to cathodic regions, where they are further oxidized by reaction with more oxygen.

$$4\,Fe^{2+}(aq) + O_2(g) + (4 + 2n)\,H_2O(l) \longrightarrow 2\,Fe_2O_3 \cdot nH_2O(s) + 8\,H^+(aq)$$
rust

Rust is a hydrated form of iron(III) oxide whose exact composition depends on the conditions under which it forms.

Consider each of the following important components in the formation of rust:

- *Moisture must be present for rusting to occur.* The presence of water is necessary because water is a reactant in the last reaction and because charge (either electrons or ions) must be free to flow between the anodic and cathodic regions.

- *Additional electrolytes promote rusting.* The presence of an electrolyte (such as sodium chloride) on the surface of iron promotes rusting because it enhances current flow. This is why cars rust so quickly in cold climates where roads are salted, or in coastal areas where salt water mist is present.

- *The presence of acids promotes rusting.* Since H^+ ions are involved in the reduction of oxygen, lower pH enhances the cathodic reaction and leads to faster rusting.

▲ Aluminum is stable because its oxide forms a protective film over the underlying metal, preventing further oxidation.

▼ FIGURE 18.27 **Corrosion of Iron: Rusting** The oxidation of iron occurs at anodic regions on the metal surface. The iron ions migrate to cathodic regions, where they react with oxygen and water to form rust.

The Rusting of Iron

▲ A scratch in paint often allows the underlying iron to rust.

▲ If a metal more active than iron, such as magnesium or aluminum, is in electrical contact with iron, the metal rather than the iron will be oxidized. This principle underlies the use of sacrificial electrodes to prevent the corrosion of iron.

Preventing Corrosion

Preventing the rusting of iron is a major industry. The most obvious way to prevent rust is to keep iron dry. Without water, the redox reaction cannot occur. Another way to prevent rust is to coat iron with a substance that is impervious to water. Cars, for example, are painted and sealed to prevent rust. A scratch in the paint can lead to rusting of the underlying iron.

Rust can also be prevented by placing a *sacrificial electrode* in electrical contact with the iron. The sacrificial electrode must be composed of a metal that oxidizes more easily than iron (that is, it must be below iron in Table 18.1). The sacrificial electrode oxidizes in place of the iron (just as the more easily oxidizable species in a mixture is the one to oxidize), protecting the iron from oxidation. A related way to protect iron from rusting is to coat it with a metal that oxidizes more easily than iron. Galvanized nails, for example, are coated with a thin layer of zinc. Since zinc has a more negative electrode potential than iron, it will oxidize in place of the underlying iron (just as a sacrificial electrode does). The oxide of zinc is not crumbly and remains on the nail as a protective coating.

▲ In galvanized nails, a layer of zinc prevents the underlying iron from rusting. The zinc oxidizes in place of the iron, forming a protective layer of zinc oxide.

Conceptual Connection 18.8 Sacrificial Electrodes

Which of these metals does not act as a sacrificial electrode for iron?

Zn, Mg, Mn, Cu

CHAPTER IN REVIEW

Self Assessment Quiz

Q1. Balance the redox reaction equation (occurring in acidic solution) and choose the correct coefficients for each reactant and product.

$$\_VO_2^+(aq) + \_Sn(s) + \_H^+(aq) \rightarrow \_VO^{2+}(aq) + \_Sn^{2+}(aq) + \_H_2O(l)$$

a) $2,1,4 \rightarrow 2,1,2$ b) $1,1,2 \rightarrow 1,1,1$
c) $2,1,2 \rightarrow 2,1,1$ d) $2,1,2 \rightarrow 2,1,2$

Q2. Which statement is true for voltaic cells?
a) Electrons flow from the anode to the cathode.
b) Electrons flow from the more negatively charged electrode to the more positively charged electrode.
c) Electrons flow from higher potential energy to lower potential energy.
d) All of the above

Q3. Use data from Table 18.1 to calculate E_{cell}° for the reaction.
$$2\,ClO_2(g) + Pb(s) \rightarrow 2\,ClO_2^-(aq) + Pb^{2+}(aq)$$
a) 1.77 V
b) 2.03 V
c) 0.82 V
d) 1.08 V

Q4. Use data from Table 18.1 to determine which statement is true of the voltaic cell picture here.

Sn(s)   Ag(s)

Salt bridge

1 M Ag$^+$

1 M Sn^{2+}

a) Sn is the anode; Ag is the cathode; electrons flow from left to right
b) Sn is the cathode; Ag is the anode; electrons flow from left to right
c) Sn is the anode; Ag is the cathode; electrons flow from right to left
d) Sn is the cathode; Ag is the anode; electrons flow from right to left

Q5. Use data from Table 18.1 to determine which metal *does not* dissolve in hydrochloric acid (HCl).
a) Zn   b) Cd   c) Cu   d) Fe

Q6. The Zn/Zn^{2+} electrode has a standard electrode potential of $E° = -0.76$ V. How does the relative potential energy of an electron at the Zn/Zn^{2+} electrode compare to the potential energy of an electron at the standard hydrogen electrode?
a) An electron at the Zn/Zn^{2+} electrode has a higher potential energy than an electron at the standard hydrogen electrode.
b) An electron at the Zn/Zn^{2+} electrode has a lower potential energy than an electron at the standard hydrogen electrode.
c) An electron at the Zn/Zn^{2+} electrode has the same potential energy as an electron at the standard hydrogen electrode.
d) Nothing can be concluded about the relative potential energy of an electron at the standard electrode potential.

Q7. Use data from Table 18.1 to calculate $\Delta G°$ for the reaction.
$$2\,MnO_4^-(aq) + Cd(s) \rightarrow 2\,MnO_4^{2-}(aq) + Cd^{2+}(aq)$$
a) +30.9 kJ   b) −30.9 kJ   c) −185 kJ   d) +185 kJ

Q8. A redox reaction has an $E°_{cell} = -0.56$ V. What can you conclude about the equilibrium constant (K) for the reaction?
a) $K < 1$
b) $K > 1$
c) $K = 0$
d) Nothing can be concluded about K from $E°_{cell}$.

Q9. Find E_{cell} for an electrochemical cell based on the following reaction with $[MnO_4^-] = 2.0$ M, $[H^+] = 1.0$ M, and $[Ag^+] = 0.010$ M. $E°_{cell}$ for the reaction is $+0.88$ V.
$$MnO_4^-(aq) + 4\,H^+(aq) + 3\,Ag(s) \rightarrow MnO_2(s)$$
$$+ 2\,H_2O(l) + 3\,Ag^+(aq)$$
a) 0.83 V   b) 1.00 V   c) 0.76 V   d) 0.93 V

Q10. In an electrochemical cell, $Q = 0.010$ and $K = 855$. What can you conclude about E_{cell} and $E°_{cell}$?
a) E_{cell} is positive and $E°_{cell}$ is negative.
b) E_{cell} is negative and $E°_{cell}$ is positive.
c) E_{cell} and $E°_{cell}$ are both negative.
d) E_{cell} and $E°_{cell}$ are both positive.

Q11. Which reaction occurs at the *anode* of a lead storage battery?
a) $Zn(s) + 2\,OH^-(aq) \rightarrow Zn(OH)_2(s) + 2\,e^-$
b) $PbO_2(s) + HSO_4^-(aq) + 3\,H^+(aq) + 2\,e^- \rightarrow$
$$PbSO_4(s) + 2\,H_2O(l)$$
c) $Pb(s) + HSO_4^-(aq) \rightarrow PbSO_4(s) + H^+(aq) + 2\,e^-$
d) $O_2(g) + 2\,H_2O(l) + 4\,e^- \rightarrow 4\,OH^-(aq)$

Q12. Which reaction could be used to generate electricity in a voltaic electrochemical cell?
a) $Pb^{2+}(aq) + Mg(s) \rightarrow Mg^{2+}(aq) + Pb(s)$
b) $Zn^{2+}(aq) + Sn(s) \rightarrow Sn^{2+}(aq) + Zn(s)$
c) $NaCl(aq) + AgNO_3(aq) \rightarrow AgCl(s) + NaNO_3(aq)$
d) None of the above

Q13. Which reaction occurs at the cathode of an electrolytic cell containing a mixture of molten KCl and ZnCl$_2$?
a) $K(s) \rightarrow K^+(l) + e^-$ b) $K^+(l) + e^- \rightarrow K(s)$
c) $Zn^{2+}(l) + 2\,e^- \rightarrow Zn(s)$ d) $2\,Cl^-(l) \rightarrow Cl_2(g) + 2\,e^-$

Q14. Copper is plated onto the cathode of an electrolytic cell containing CuCl$_2$(aq). How long does it take to plate 111 mg of copper with a current of 3.8 A?
a) 1.3×10^3 s b) 44 s   c) 89 s   d) 22 s

Q15. Which metal can be used as a sacrificial electrode to prevent the rusting of an iron pipe?
a) Au   b) Ag   c) Cu   d) Mn

Answers: 1. (a) **2.** (d) **3.** (d) **4.** (a) **5.** (c) **6.** (a) **7.** (c) **8.** (a) **9.** (b) **10.** (d) **11.** (c) **12.** (a) **13.** (c) **14.** (c) **15.** (d)

Key Terms

Section 18.3
electrical current (865)
electrochemical cell (866)
voltaic (galvanic) cell (866)
electrolytic cell (866)
half-cell (866)
electrode (866)
ampere (A) (867)
potential difference (867)
volt (V) (867)
electromotive force (emf) (867)
cell potential (cell emf) (E_{cell}) (868)
standard cell potential
    (standard emf) ($E°_{cell}$) (868)

anode (868)
cathode (868)
salt bridge (868)

Section 18.4
standard electrode potential (870)
standard hydrogen electrode
    (SHE) (870)

Section 18.5
Faraday's constant (F) (878)

Section 18.6
Nernst equation (882)

Section 18.7
dry-cell battery (886)
alkaline battery (887)
lead–acid storage battery (887)
nickel–cadmium (NiCad) battery (888)
nickel–metal hydride (NiMH) battery (888)
lithium ion battery (888)
fuel cell (889)

Section 18.8
electrolysis (890)

Section 18.9
corrosion (898)

Key Concepts

Pulling the Plug on the Power Grid (18.1)

▶ Oxidation–reduction reactions are reactions in which electrons are transferred from one reactant to another

▶ In the most common form of fuel cell, an electrical current is created as hydrogen is oxidized and oxygen is reduced; water is the only product.

Balancing Oxidation–Reduction Equations (18.2)

▶ Oxidation is the loss of electrons and corresponds to an increase in oxidation state; reduction is the gain of electrons and corresponds to a decrease in oxidation state.

▶ We can balance redox reactions using the half-reaction method, in which the oxidation and reduction reactions are balanced separately and then added. This method differs slightly for redox reactions in acidic and in basic solutions.

Voltaic (or Galvanic) Cells: Generating Electricity from Spontaneous Chemical Reactions (18.3)

▶ A voltaic electrochemical cell separates the reactants of a spontaneous redox reaction into two half-cells that are connected by a wire and a means to exchange ions so that electricity is generated.

▶ In an electrochemical cell, the electrode where oxidation occurs is the anode and the electrode where reduction occurs is the cathode; electrons flow from the anode to the cathode.

▶ The rate of electrons flowing through a wire is measured in amperes (A), and the cell potential is measured in volts (V).

▶ A salt bridge is commonly used to allow ions to flow between the half-cell solutions and prevent the build up of charge.

▶ Cell diagram or line notation is a technique for symbolizing electrochemical cells concisely by separating the components of the reaction using lines or commas.

Standard Electrode Potentials (18.4)

▶ The electrode potentials of half-cells are measured in relation to that of a standard hydrogen electrode, which is assigned an electrode potential of zero under standard conditions (solution concentrations of 1 M, gas pressures of 1 atm, and a temperature of 25 °C).

▶ A species with a highly positive $E°$ has a strong tendency to attract electrons and undergo reduction (and is therefore an excellent oxidizing agent).

▶ A species with a highly negative $E°$ has a strong tendency to repel electrons and undergo oxidation (and is therefore an excellent reducing agent).

Cell Potential, Free Energy, and the Equilibrium Constant (18.5)

▶ In a spontaneous reaction, $E°_{cell}$ is positive, the change in free energy ($\Delta G°$) is negative, and the equilibrium constant (K) is greater than 1.

▶ In a nonspontaneous reaction, $E°_{cell}$ is negative, $\Delta G°$ is positive, and K is less than 1.

▶ Because $E°_{cell}$, $\Delta G°$, and K all relate to spontaneity, we can derive equations relating all three quantities.

Cell Potential and Concentration (18.6)

▶ The standard cell potential ($E°_{cell}$) is related to the cell potential (E_{cell}) by the Nernst equation, $E_{cell} = E°_{cell} - (0.0592 \text{ V}/n) \log Q$.

▶ As shown by the Nernst equation, E_{cell} is related to the reaction quotient (Q); E_{cell} equals zero when Q equals K.

▶ In a concentration cell, the reactions at both electrodes are identical and electrons flow because of a difference in concentration. Nerve cells are a biological example of concentration cells.

Batteries: Using Chemistry to Generate Electricity (18.7)

▶ Batteries are packaged voltaic cells.

▶ Dry-cell batteries, including alkaline batteries, do not contain large amounts of water.

▶ The reactions in rechargeable batteries, such as lead–acid storage, nickel–cadmium, nickel–metal hydride, and lithium ion batteries, can be reversed.

▶ Fuel cells are similar to batteries except that fuel-cell reactants must be continually replenished from an external source.

Electrolysis: Driving Nonspontaneous Chemical Reactions with Electricity (18.8)

▶ An electrolytic electrochemical cell differs from a voltaic cell in that (1) an electrical charge is used to drive the reaction, and (2) although the anode is still the site of oxidation and the cathode the site of reduction, they are represented with signs opposite those of a voltaic cell (anode +, cathode −).

▶ In electrolysis reactions, the anion is oxidized; if there is more than one anion, the anion with the more negative $E°$ is oxidized.

▶ We can use stoichiometry to calculate the quantity of reactants consumed or products produced in an electrolytic cell.

Corrosion: Undesirable Redox Reactions (18.9)

▶ Corrosion is the undesired oxidation of metal by environmental oxidizing agents.

▶ When some metals, such as aluminum, oxidize they form a stable compound that prevents further oxidation. Iron, however, does not form a structurally stable compound when oxidized and therefore rust flakes off and exposes more iron to corrosion.

▶ Iron corrosion can be prevented by preventing water contact, minimizing the presence of electrolytes and acids, or using a sacrificial electrode.

Key Equations and Relationships

Definition of an Ampere (18.3)

$$1 \text{ A} = 1 \text{ C/s}$$

Definition of a Volt (18.3)

$$1 \text{ V} = 1 \text{ J/C}$$

Standard Hydrogen Electrode (18.4)

$$2 \text{ H}^+(aq) + 2 \text{ e}^- \longrightarrow \text{H}_2(g) \quad E° = 0.00 \text{ V}$$

Equation for Cell Potential (18.4)

$$E°_{cell} = E°_{cathode} - E°_{anode}$$

Relating $\Delta G°$ and $E°_{cell}$ (**18.5**)

$$\Delta G° = -nF E°_{cell} \qquad F = \frac{96,485 \text{ C}}{\text{mol e}^-}$$

Relating $E°_{cell}$ and K (**18.5**)

$$E°_{cell} = \frac{0.0592 \text{ V}}{n} \log K \qquad \text{(at 25 °C)}$$

The Nernst Equation (**18.6**)

$$E_{cell} = E°_{cell} - \frac{0.0592 \text{ V}}{n} \log Q \qquad \text{(at 25 °C)}$$

Key Learning Outcomes

Chapter Objectives	Assessment
Half-Reaction Method of Balancing Aqueous Redox Equations in Acidic Solution (**18.2**)	Examples 18.1, 18.2 For Practice 18.1, 18.2 Exercises 37–40
Balancing Redox Reactions Occurring in Basic Solution (**18.2**)	Example 18.3 For Practice 18.3 Exercises 41, 42
Calculating Standard Potentials for Electrochemical Cells from Standard Electrode Potentials of the Half-Reactions (**18.4**)	Example 18.4 For Practice 18.4 Exercises 45, 46, 61, 62
Predicting Spontaneous Redox Reactions and Sketching Electrochemical Cells (**18.4**)	Example 18.5 For Practice 18.5 Exercises 43, 44, 47, 48, 51–54
Relating $\Delta G°$ and $E°_{cell}$ (**18.5**)	Example 18.6 For Practice 18.6 Exercises 65, 66
Relating $E°_{cell}$ and K (**18.5**)	Example 18.7 For Practice 18.7 Exercises 67–72
Calculating E_{cell} under Nonstandard Conditions (**18.6**)	Example 18.8 For Practice 18.8 Exercises 73–78
Predicting the Products of Electrolysis Reactions (**18.8**)	Example 18.9 For Practice 18.9 Exercises 91–96
Stoichiometry of Electrolysis (**18.8**)	Example 18.10 For Practice 18.10 Exercises 99–102

In the "Calculating Standard Potentials" row, a figure appears:

High potential energy → Low potential energy

Direction of spontaneous flow

In the "Relating $E°_{cell}$ and K" row, a figure appears:

$\Delta G°$ ↔ $E°_{cell}$ ↔ K

EXERCISES

Review Questions

1. In electrochemistry, spontaneous redox reactions are used for what purpose?

2. In electrochemistry, what kind of reaction can be driven by electricity?

3. Give the basic definitions of oxidation and reduction and explain the basic procedure for balancing redox reactions.

4. Explain the difference between a voltaic (or galvanic) electrochemical cell and an electrolytic one.

5. What reaction (oxidation or reduction) occurs at the anode of a voltaic cell? What is the sign of the anode? Do electrons flow toward or away from the anode?

6. What reaction (oxidation or reduction) occurs at the cathode of a voltaic cell? What is the sign of the cathode? Do electrons flow toward or away from the cathode?

7. Explain the purpose of a salt bridge in an electrochemical cell.

8. What unit is used to measure the magnitude of electrical current? What unit is used to measure the magnitude of a potential difference? Explain how electrical current and potential difference differ.

9. What is the definition of the standard cell potential (E_{cell}°)? What does a large positive standard cell potential imply about the spontaneity of the redox reaction occurring in the cell? What does a negative standard cell potential imply about the reaction?

10. Describe the basic features of a cell diagram (or line notation) for an electrochemical cell.

11. Why do some electrochemical cells employ inert electrodes such as platinum?

12. Describe the standard hydrogen electrode (SHE) and explain its use in determining standard electrode potentials.

13. How is the cell potential of an electrochemical cell (E_{cell}°) related to the potentials of the half-cells?

14. Does a large positive electrode potential indicate a strong oxidizing agent or a strong reducing agent? What about a large negative electrode potential?

15. Is a spontaneous redox reaction obtained by pairing any reduction half-reaction with one listed above it or with one listed below it in Table 18.1?

16. How can Table 18.1 be used to predict whether or not a metal will dissolve in HCl? In HNO_3?

17. Explain why E_{cell}°, ΔG_{rxn}°, and K are all interrelated.

18. Does a redox reaction with a small equilibrium constant ($K < 1$) have a positive or a negative E_{cell}°? Does it have a positive or a negative ΔG_{rxn}°?

19. How does E_{cell} depend on the concentrations of the reactants and products in the redox reaction occurring in the cell? What effect does increasing the concentration of a reactant have on E_{cell}? Increasing the concentration of a product?

20. Use the Nernst equation to show that $E_{cell} = E_{cell}^{\circ}$ under standard conditions.

21. What is a concentration electrochemical cell?

22. What are the anode and cathode reactions in a common dry-cell battery? In an alkaline battery?

23. What are the anode and cathode reactions in a lead–acid storage battery? What happens when the battery is recharged?

24. What are the three common types of portable rechargeable batteries and how does each one work?

25. What is a fuel cell? What is the most common type of fuel cell and what reactions occur at its anode and cathode?

26. Explain how a fuel-cell breathalyzer works.

27. List some applications of electrolysis.

28. The anode of an electrolytic cell must be connected to which terminal—positive or negative—of the power source?

29. What species is oxidized and what species is reduced in the electrolysis of a pure molten salt?

30. If an electrolytic cell contains a mixture of species that can be oxidized, how do you determine which species will actually be oxidized? If it contains a mixture of species that can be reduced, how do you determine which one will actually be reduced?

31. Why does the electrolysis of an aqueous sodium chloride solution produce hydrogen gas at the cathode?

32. What is overvoltage in an electrochemical cell? Why is it important?

33. How is the amount of current flowing through an electrolytic cell related to the amount of product produced in the redox reaction?

34. What is corrosion? Why is corrosion only a problem for some metals (such as iron)?

35. Explain the role of each of the following in promoting corrosion: moisture, electrolytes, and acids.

36. How can the corrosion of iron be prevented?

Problems by Topic

Balancing Redox Reactions

37. Balance each redox reaction occurring in acidic aqueous solution.
    a. $K(s) + Cr^{3+}(aq) \longrightarrow Cr(s) + K^+(aq)$
    b. $Al(s) + Fe^{2+}(aq) \longrightarrow Al^{3+}(aq) + Fe(s)$
    c. $BrO_3^-(aq) + N_2H_4(g) \longrightarrow Br^-(aq) + N_2(g)$

38. Balance each redox reaction occurring in acidic aqueous solution.
    a. $Zn(s) + Sn^{2+}(aq) \longrightarrow Zn^{2+}(aq) + Sn(s)$
    b. $Mg(s) + Cr^{3+}(aq) \longrightarrow Mg^{2+}(aq) + Cr(s)$
    c. $MnO_4^-(aq) + Al(s) \longrightarrow Mn^{2+}(aq) + Al^{3+}(aq)$

39. Balance each redox reaction occurring in acidic aqueous solution.
    a. $PbO_2(s) + I^-(aq) \longrightarrow Pb^{2+}(aq) + I_2(s)$
    b. $SO_3^{2-}(aq) + MnO_4^-(aq) \longrightarrow SO_4^{2-}(aq) + Mn^{2+}(aq)$
    c. $S_2O_3^{2-}(aq) + Cl_2(g) \longrightarrow SO_4^{2-}(aq) + Cl^-(aq)$

40. Balance each redox reaction occurring in acidic aqueous solution.
    a. $I^-(aq) + NO_2^-(aq) \longrightarrow I_2(s) + NO(g)$
    b. $ClO_4^-(aq) + Cl^-(aq) \longrightarrow ClO_3^-(aq) + Cl_2(g)$
    c. $NO_3^-(aq) + Sn^{2+}(aq) \longrightarrow Sn^{4+}(aq) + NO(g)$

41. Balance each redox reaction occurring in basic aqueous solution.
    a. $H_2O_2(aq) + ClO_2(aq) \longrightarrow ClO_2^-(aq) + O_2(g)$
    b. $Al(s) + MnO_4^-(aq) \longrightarrow MnO_2(s) + Al(OH)_4^-(aq)$
    c. $Cl_2(g) \longrightarrow Cl^-(aq) + ClO^-(aq)$

42. Balance each redox reaction occurring in basic aqueous solution.
    a. $MnO_4^-(aq) + Br^-(aq) \longrightarrow MnO_2(s) + BrO_3^-(aq)$
    b. $Ag(s) + CN^-(aq) + O_2(g) \longrightarrow Ag(CN)_2^-(aq)$
    c. $NO_2^-(aq) + Al(s) \longrightarrow NH_3(g) + AlO_2^-(aq)$

Voltaic Cells, Standard Cell Potentials, and Direction of Spontaneity

43. Sketch a voltaic cell for each redox reaction. Label the anode and cathode and indicate the half-reaction that occurs at each electrode and the species present in each solution. Also indicate the direction of electron flow.
    a. $2 Ag^+(aq) + Pb(s) \longrightarrow 2 Ag(s) + Pb^{2+}(aq)$
    b. $2 ClO_2(g) + 2 I^-(aq) \longrightarrow 2 ClO_2^-(aq) + I_2(s)$
    c. $O_2(g) + 4 H^+(aq) + 2 Zn(s) \longrightarrow 2 H_2O(l) + 2 Zn^{2+}(aq)$

44. Sketch a voltaic cell for each redox reaction. Label the anode and cathode and indicate the half-reaction that occurs at each electrode and the species present in each solution. Also indicate the direction of electron flow.
  a. $Ni^{2+}(aq) + Mg(s) \longrightarrow Ni(s) + Mg^{2+}(aq)$
  b. $2\,H^+(aq) + Fe(s) \longrightarrow H_2(g) + Fe^{2+}(aq)$
  c. $2\,NO_3^-(aq) + 8\,H^+(aq) + 3\,Cu(s) \longrightarrow$
$$2\,NO(g) + 4\,H_2O(l) + 3\,Cu^{2+}(aq)$$

45. Calculate the standard cell potential for each of the electrochemical cells in Problem 43.

46. Calculate the standard cell potential for each of the electrochemical cells in Problem 44.

47. Consider the voltaic cell:

Fe(s)   Cr(s)

Salt bridge containing $KNO_3(aq)$

1 M Fe^{3+}

1 M Cr^{3+}

  a. Determine the direction of electron flow and label the anode and the cathode.
  b. Write a balanced equation for the overall reaction and calculate E°_{cell}.
  c. Label each electrode as negative or positive.
  d. Indicate the direction of anion and cation flow in the salt bridge.

48. Consider the voltaic cell:

Pb(s) $Cl_2(g)$

Salt bridge containing $NaNO_3(aq)$

1 M Pb^{2+}

1 M Cl^+

  a. Determine the direction of electron flow and label the anode and the cathode.
  b. Write a balanced equation for the overall reaction and calculate E°_{cell}.
  c. Label each electrode as negative or positive.
  d. Indicate the direction of anion and cation flow in the salt bridge.

49. Use line notation to represent each electrochemical cell in Problem 43.

50. Use line notation to represent each electrochemical cell in Problem 44.

51. Make a sketch of the voltaic cell represented by the line notation. Write the overall balanced equation for the reaction and calculate E°_{cell}.

$$Sn(s)\,|\,Sn^{2+}(aq)\,\|\,NO(g)\,|\,NO_3^-(aq),\,H^+(aq)\,|\,Pt(s)$$

52. Make a sketch of the voltaic cell represented by the line notation. Write the overall balanced equation for the reaction and calculate E°_{cell}.

$$Mn(s)\,|\,Mn^{2+}(aq)\,\|\,ClO_2^-(aq)\,|\,ClO_2(g)\,|\,Pt(s)$$

53. Determine whether or not each redox reaction occurs spontaneously in the forward direction.
  a. $Ni(s) + Zn^{2+}(aq) \longrightarrow Ni^{2+}(aq) + Zn(s)$
  b. $Ni(s) + Pb^{2+}(aq) \longrightarrow Ni^{2+}(aq) + Pb(s)$
  c. $Al(s) + 3\,Ag^+(aq) \longrightarrow Al^{3+}(aq) + 3\,Ag(s)$
  d. $Pb(s) + Mn^{2+}(aq) \longrightarrow Pb^{2+}(aq) + Mn(s)$

54. Determine whether or not each redox reaction occurs spontaneously in the forward direction.
  a. $Ca^{2+}(aq) + Zn(s) \longrightarrow Ca(s) + Zn^{2+}(aq)$
  b. $2\,Ag^+(aq) + Ni(s) \longrightarrow 2\,Ag(s) + Ni^{2+}(aq)$
  c. $Fe(s) + Mn^{2+}(aq) \longrightarrow Fe^{2+}(aq) + Mn(s)$
  d. $2\,Al(s) + 3\,Pb^{2+}(aq) \longrightarrow 2\,Al^{3+}(aq) + 3\,Pb(s)$

55. Which metal could you use to reduce Mn^{2+} ions but not Mg^{2+} ions?

56. Which metal can be oxidized with an Sn^{2+} solution but not with an Fe^{2+} solution?

57. Determine whether or not each metal dissolves in 1 M HCl. For those metals that do dissolve, write a balanced redox reaction showing what happens when the metal dissolves.
  a. Al   **b.** Ag   **c.** Pb

58. Determine whether or not each metal dissolves in 1 M HCl. For those metals that do dissolve, write a balanced redox reaction showing what happens when the metal dissolves.
  a. Cu   **b.** Fe   **c.** Au

59. Determine whether or not each metal dissolves in 1 M HNO_3. For those metals that do dissolve, write a balanced redox reaction showing what happens when the metal dissolves.
  a. Cu   **b.** Au

60. Determine whether or not each metal dissolves in 1 M HIO_3. For those metals that do dissolve, write a balanced redox equation for the reaction that occurs.
  a. Au   **b.** Cr

61. Calculate E°_{cell} for each balanced redox reaction and determine if the reaction is spontaneous as written.
  a. $2\,Cu(s) + Mn^{2+}(aq) \longrightarrow 2\,Cu^+(aq) + Mn(s)$
  b. $MnO_2(s) + 4\,H^+(aq) + Zn(s) \longrightarrow$
$$Mn^{2+}(aq) + 2\,H_2O(l) + Zn^{2+}(aq)$$
  c. $Cl_2(g) + 2\,F^-(aq) \longrightarrow F_2(g) + 2\,Cl^-(aq)$

62. Calculate E°_{cell} for each balanced redox reaction and determine if the reaction is spontaneous as written.
  a. $O_2(g) + 2\,H_2O(l) + 4\,Ag(s) \longrightarrow 4\,OH^-(aq) + 4\,Ag^+(aq)$
  b. $Br_2(l) + 2\,I^-(aq) \longrightarrow 2\,Br^-(aq) + I_2(s)$
  c. $PbO_2(s) + 4\,H^+(aq) + Sn(s) \longrightarrow$
$$Pb^{2+}(aq) + 2\,H_2O(l) + Sn^{2+}(aq)$$

63. Which metal cation is the best oxidizing agent?
  a. Pb^{2+} **b.** Cr^{3+} **c.** Fe^{2+} **d.** Sn^{2+}

64. Which metal is the best reducing agent?
  a. Mn   **b.** Al   **c.** Ni   **d.** Cr

Cell Potential, Free Energy, and the Equilibrium Constant

65. Use tabulated electrode potentials to calculate ΔG°_{rxn} for each reaction at 25 °C.
    a. $Pb^{2+}(aq) + Mg(s) \longrightarrow Pb(s) + Mg^{2+}(aq)$
    b. $Br_2(l) + 2\,Cl^-(aq) \longrightarrow 2\,Br^-(aq) + Cl_2(g)$
    c. $MnO_2(s) + 4\,H^+(aq) + Cu(s) \longrightarrow$
       $$Mn^{2+}(aq) + 2\,H_2O(l) + Cu^{2+}(aq)$$

66. Use tabulated electrode potentials to calculate ΔG°_{rxn} for each reaction at 25 °C.
    a. $2\,Fe^{3+}(aq) + 3\,Sn(s) \longrightarrow 2\,Fe(s) + 3\,Sn^{2+}(aq)$
    b. $O_2(g) + 2\,H_2O(l) + 2\,Cu(s) \longrightarrow$
       $$4\,OH^-(aq) + 2\,Cu^{2+}(aq)$$
    c. $Br_2(l) + 2\,I^-(aq) \longrightarrow 2\,Br^-(aq) + I_2(s)$

67. Calculate the equilibrium constant for each of the reactions in Problem 65.

68. Calculate the equilibrium constant for each of the reactions in Problem 66.

69. Calculate the equilibrium constant for the reaction between $Ni^{2+}(aq)$ and $Cd(s)$ (at 25 °C).

70. Calculate the equilibrium constant for the reaction between $Fe^{2+}(aq)$ and $Zn(s)$ (at 25 °C).

71. Calculate ΔG°_{rxn} and E°_{cell} for a redox reaction with $n = 2$ that has an equilibrium constant of $K = 25$ (at 25 °C).

72. Calculate ΔG°_{rxn} and E°_{cell} for a redox reaction with $n = 3$ that has an equilibrium constant of $K = 0.050$ (at 25 °C).

Nonstandard Conditions and the Nernst Equation

73. A voltaic cell employs the following redox reaction:
    $$Sn^{2+}(aq) + Mn(s) \longrightarrow Sn(s) + Mn^{2+}(aq)$$
    Calculate the cell potential at 25 °C under each set of conditions.
    a. standard conditions
    b. $[Sn^{2+}] = 0.0100\ M;\ [Mn^{2+}] = 2.00\ M$
    c. $[Sn^{2+}] = 2.00\ M;\ [Mn^{2+}] = 0.0100\ M$

74. A voltaic cell employs the redox reaction:
    $$2\,Fe^{3+}(aq) + 3\,Mg(s) \longrightarrow 2\,Fe(s) + 3\,Mg^{2+}(aq)$$
    Calculate the cell potential at 25 °C under each set of conditions.
    a. standard conditions
    b. $[Fe^{3+}] = 1.0 \times 10^{-3}\ M;\ [Mg^{2+}] = 2.50\ M$
    c. $[Fe^{3+}] = 2.00\ M;\ [Mg^{2+}] = 1.5 \times 10^{-3}\ M$

75. An electrochemical cell is based on these two half-reactions:
    $$Ox:\ Pb(s) \longrightarrow Pb^{2+}(aq,\ 0.10\ M) + 2\,e^-$$
    $$Red:\ MnO_4^-(aq, 1.50\ M) + 4\,H^+(aq, 2.0\ M) + 3\,e^- \longrightarrow$$
    $$MnO_2(s) + 2\,H_2O(l)$$
    Calculate the cell potential at 25 °C.

76. An electrochemical cell is based on these two half-reactions:
    $$Ox:\ Sn(s) \longrightarrow Sn^{2+}(aq,\ 2.00\ M) + 2\,e^-$$
    $$Red:\ ClO_2(g,\ 0.100\ atm) + e^- \longrightarrow ClO_2^-(aq,\ 2.00\ M)$$
    Calculate the cell potential at 25 °C.

77. A voltaic cell consists of a Zn/Zn^{2+} half-cell and a Ni/Ni^{2+} half-cell at 25 °C. The initial concentrations of Ni^{2+} and Zn^{2+} are 1.50 M and 0.100 M, respectively.
    a. What is the initial cell potential?
    b. What is the cell potential when the concentration of Ni^{2+} has fallen to 0.500 M?
    c. What are the concentrations of Ni^{2+} and Zn^{2+} when the cell potential falls to 0.45 V?

78. A voltaic cell consists of a Pb/Pb^{2+} half-cell and a Cu/Cu^{2+} half-cell at 25 °C. The initial concentrations of Pb^{2+} and Cu^{2+} are 0.0500 M and 1.50 M, respectively.
    a. What is the initial cell potential?
    b. What is the cell potential when the concentration of Cu^{2+} has fallen to 0.200 M?
    c. What are the concentrations of Pb^{2+} and Cu^{2+} when the cell potential falls to 0.35 V?

79. Make a sketch of a concentration cell employing two Zn/Zn^{2+} half-cells. The concentration of Zn^{2+} in one of the half-cells is 2.0 M and the concentration in the other half-cell is 1.0×10^{-3} M. Label the anode and the cathode and indicate the half-reaction occurring at each electrode. Also indicate the direction of electron flow.

80. Consider the concentration cell:

Pb(s)   Pb(s)

Salt bridge containing $NaNO_3(aq)$

2.5 M Pb^{2+}

$5.0 \times 10^{-3}\ M\ Pb^{2+}$

    a. Label the anode and cathode.
    b. Indicate the direction of electron flow.
    c. Indicate what happens to the concentration of Pb^{2+} in each half-cell.

81. A concentration cell consists of two Sn/Sn^{2+} half-cells. The cell has a potential of 0.10 V at 25 °C. What is the ratio of the Sn^{2+} concentrations in the two half-cells?

82. A Cu/Cu^{2+} concentration cell has a voltage of 0.22 V at 25 °C. The concentration of Cu^{2+} in one of the half-cells is 1.5×10^{-3} M. What is the concentration of Cu^{2+} in the other half-cell? (Assume the concentration in the unknown cell to be the *lower* of the two concentrations.)

Batteries, Fuel Cells, and Corrosion

83. Determine the optimum mass ratio of Zn to MnO_2 in an alkaline battery.

84. What mass of lead sulfate is formed in a lead–acid storage battery when 1.00 g of Pb undergoes oxidation?

85. Refer to the tabulated values of ΔG°_f in Appendix IIB to calculate E°_{cell} for a fuel cell that employs the reaction between methane gas (CH_4) and oxygen to form carbon dioxide and gaseous water.

86. Refer to the tabulated values of ΔG°_f in Appendix IIB to calculate E°_{cell} for the fuel cell breathalyzer, which employs the following reaction. (ΔG°_f for $HC_2H_3O_2(g) = -374.2$ kJ/mol.)
    $$CH_3CH_2OH(g) + O_2(g) \longrightarrow HC_2H_3O_2(g) + H_2O(g)$$

87. Determine whether or not each metal, if coated onto iron, would prevent the corrosion of iron.
    a. Zn   b. Sn   c. Mn

88. Determine whether or not each metal, if coated onto iron, would prevent the corrosion of iron.
a. Mg   **b.** Cr   **c.** Cu

Electrolytic Cells and Electrolysis

89. Consider the electrolytic cell:

a. Label the anode and the cathode and indicate the half-reactions occurring at each.
b. Indicate the direction of electron flow.
c. Label the terminals on the battery as positive or negative and calculate the minimum voltage necessary to drive the reaction.

90. Draw an electrolytic cell in which Mn^{2+} is reduced to Mn and Sn is oxidized to Sn^{2+}. Label the anode and cathode, indicate the direction of electron flow, and write an equation for the half-reaction occurring at each electrode. What minimum voltage is necessary to drive the reaction?

91. Write equations for the half-reactions that occur in the electrolysis of molten potassium bromide.

92. What products are obtained in the electrolysis of molten NaI?

93. Write equations for the half-reactions that occur in the electrolysis of a mixture of molten potassium bromide and molten lithium bromide.

94. What products are obtained in the electrolysis of a molten mixture of KI and KBr?

95. Write equations for the half-reactions that occur at the anode and cathode for the electrolysis of each aqueous solution:
a. $NaBr(aq)$ **b.** $PbI_2(aq)$ **c.** $Na_2SO_4(aq)$

96. Write equations for the half-reactions that occur at the anode and cathode for the electrolysis of each aqueous solution:
a. $Ni(NO_3)_2(aq)$ **b.** $KCl(aq)$ **c.** $CuBr_2(aq)$

97. Make a sketch of an electrolysis cell that electroplates copper onto other metal surfaces. Label the anode and the cathode and indicate the reactions that occur at each.

98. Make a sketch of an electrolysis cell that electroplates nickel onto other metal surfaces. Label the anode and the cathode and indicate the reactions that occur at each.

99. Copper can be electroplated at the cathode of an electrolysis cell by the half-reaction:

$$Cu^{2+}(aq) + 2\,e^- \longrightarrow Cu(s)$$

How much time would it take for 325 mg of copper to be plated at a current of 5.6 A?

100. Silver can be electroplated at the cathode of an electrolysis cell by the half-reaction:

$$Ag^+(aq) + e^- \longrightarrow Ag(s)$$

What mass of silver would plate onto the cathode if a current of 6.8 A flowed through the cell for 72 min?

101. A major source of sodium metal is the electrolysis of molten sodium chloride. What magnitude of current produces 1.0 kg of sodium metal in 1 hour?

102. What mass of aluminum metal can be produced per hour in the electrolysis of a molten aluminum salt by a current of 25 A?

Cumulative Problems

103. Consider the unbalanced redox reaction:

$$MnO_4^-(aq) + Zn(s) \longrightarrow Mn^{2+}(aq) + Zn^{2+}(aq)$$

Balance the equation and determine the volume of a 0.500 M $KMnO_4$ solution required to completely react with 2.85 g of Zn.

104. Consider the unbalanced redox reaction:

$$Cr_2O_7^{2-}(aq) + Cu(s) \longrightarrow Cr^{3+}(aq) + Cu^{2+}(aq)$$

Balance the equation and determine the volume of a 0.850 M $K_2Cr_2O_7$ solution required to completely react with 5.25 g of Cu.

105. Consider the molecular views of an Al strip and Cu^{2+} solution. Draw a similar sketch showing what happens to the atoms and ions after the Al strip is submerged in the solution for a few minutes.

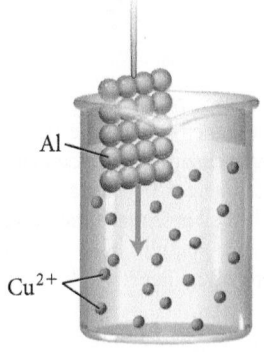

106. Consider the molecular view of an electrochemical cell involving the overall reaction:

$$Zn(s) + Ni^{2+}(aq) \longrightarrow Zn^{2+}(aq) + Ni(s)$$

Draw a similar sketch of the cell after it has generated a substantial amount of electrical current.

107. Determine whether HI can dissolve each metal sample. If it can, write a balanced chemical reaction showing how the metal dissolves in HI and determine the minimum volume of 3.5 M HI required to completely dissolve the sample.
    a. 2.15 g Al   b. 4.85 g Cu   c. 2.42 g Ag

108. Determine if HNO_3 can dissolve each metal sample. If it can, write a balanced chemical reaction showing how the metal dissolves in HNO_3 and determine the minimum volume of 6.0 M HNO_3 required to completely dissolve the sample.
    a. 5.90 g Au   b. 2.55 g Cu   c. 4.83 g Sn

109. The cell potential of this electrochemical cell depends on the pH of the solution in the anode half-cell.

    $$Pt(s)\,|\,H_2(g, 1\ atm)\,|\,H^+(aq, ?\ M)\,||\,Cu^{2+}(aq, 1.0\ M)\,|\,Cu(s)$$

    What is the pH of the solution if E_{cell} is 355 mV?

110. The cell potential of this electrochemical cell depends on the gold concentration in the cathode half-cell.

    $$Pt(s)\,|\,H_2(g, 1.0\ atm)\,|\,H^+(aq, 1.0\ M)\,||\,Au^{3+}(aq, ?\ M)\,|\,Au(s)$$

    What is the concentration of Au^{3+} in the solution if E_{cell} is 1.22 V?

111. A friend wants you to invest in a new battery she has designed that produces 24 V in a single voltaic cell. Why should you be wary of investing in such a battery?

112. What voltage can theoretically be achieved in a battery in which lithium metal is oxidized and fluorine gas is reduced? Why might such a battery be difficult to produce?

113. A battery relies on the oxidation of magnesium and the reduction of Cu^{2+}. The initial concentrations of Mg^{2+} and Cu^{2+} are 1.0×10^{-4} M and 1.5 M, respectively, in 1.0-liter half-cells.
    a. What is the initial voltage of the battery?
    b. What is the voltage of the battery after delivering 5.0 A for 8.0 h?
    c. How long can the battery deliver 5.0 A before going dead?

114. A rechargeable battery is constructed based on a concentration cell constructed of two Ag/Ag^+ half-cells. The volume of each half-cell is 2.0 L and the concentrations of Ag^+ in the half-cells are 1.25 M and 1.0×10^{-3} M.
    a. How long can this battery deliver 2.5 A of current before it goes dead?
    b. What mass of silver is plated onto the cathode by running at 3.5 A for 5.5 h?
    c. Upon recharging, how long would it take to redissolve 1.00×10^2 g of silver at a charging current of 10.0 amps?

115. If a water electrolysis cell operates at a current of 7.8 A, how long will it take to generate 25.0 L of hydrogen gas at a pressure of 25.0 atm and a temperature of 25 °C?

116. When a suspected drunk driver blows 188 mL of his breath through the fuel-cell breathalyzer described in Section 18.7, the breathalyzer produces an average of 324 mA of current for 10 s. Assuming a pressure of 1.0 atm and a temperature of 25 °C, what percent (by volume) of the driver's breath is ethanol?

117. The K_{sp} of CuI is 1.1×10^{-12}. Find E_{cell} for the cell:

    $$Cu(s)\,|\,CuI(s)\,|\,I^-(aq)(1.0\ M)\,||\,Cu^+(aq)(1.0\ M)\,|\,Cu(s)$$

118. The K_{sp} of $Zn(OH)_2$ is 1.8×10^{-14}. Find E_{cell} for the half-reaction:

    $$Zn(OH)_2(s) + 2\,e^- \rightleftharpoons Zn(s) + 2\,OH^-(aq)$$

119. Calculate ΔG°_{rxn} and K for each reaction.
    a. The disproportionation of $Mn^{2+}(aq)$ to $Mn(s)$ and $MnO_2(s)$ in acid solution at 25 °C.
    b. The disproportionation of $MnO_2(s)$ to $Mn^{2+}(aq)$ and $MnO_4^-(aq)$ in acid solution at 25 °C.

120. Calculate ΔG°_{rxn} and K for each reaction.
    a. The reaction of $Cr^{2+}(aq)$ with $Cr_2O_7^{2-}(aq)$ in acid solution to form $Cr^{3+}(aq)$.
    b. The reaction of $Cr^{3+}(aq)$ and $Cr(s)$ to form $Cr^{2+}(aq)$. [The electrode potential of $Cr^{2+}(aq)$ to $Cr(s)$ is −0.91 V.]

121. The molar mass of a metal (M) is 50.9 g/mol; it forms a chloride of unknown composition. Electrolysis of a sample of the molten chloride with a current of 6.42 A for 23.6 minutes produces 1.20 g of M at the cathode. Determine the empirical formula of the chloride.

122. A metal forms the fluoride MF_3. Electrolysis of the molten fluoride by a current of 3.86 A for 16.2 minutes deposits 1.25 g of the metal. Calculate the molar mass of the metal.

123. A sample of impure tin of mass 0.535 g is dissolved in strong acid to give a solution of Sn^{2+}. The solution is then titrated with a 0.0448 M solution of NO_3^-, which is reduced to $NO(g)$. The equivalence point is reached upon the addition of 0.0344 L of the NO_3^- solution. Find the percent by mass of tin in the original sample, assuming that it contains no other reducing agents.

124. A 0.0251 L sample of a solution of Cu^+ requires 0.0322 L of 0.129 M $KMnO_4$ solution to reach the equivalence point. The products of the reaction are Cu^{2+} and Mn^{2+}. What is the concentration of the Cu^{2+} solution?

125. A current of 11.3 A is applied to 1.25 L of a solution of 0.552 M HBr converting some of the H^+ to $H_2(g)$, which bubbles out of solution. What is the pH of the solution after 73 minutes?

126. A 215 mL sample of a 0.500 M NaCl solution with an initial pH of 7.00 is subjected to electrolysis. After 15.0 minutes, a 10.0 mL portion (or aliquot) of the solution was removed from the cell and titrated with 0.100 M HCl solution. The endpoint in the titration was reached upon addition of 22.8 mL of HCl. Assuming constant current, what was the current (in A) running through the cell?

127. An $MnO_2(s)/Mn^{2+}(aq)$ electrode in which the pH is 10.24 is prepared. Find the $[Mn^{2+}]$ necessary to lower the potential of the half-cell to 0.00 V (at 25 °C).

128. To what pH should you adjust a standard hydrogen electrode to get an electrode potential of −0.122 V? (Assume that the partial pressure of hydrogen gas remains at 1 atm.)

Challenge Problems

129. Suppose a hydrogen–oxygen fuel-cell generator produces electricity for a house. Use the balanced redox reactions and the standard cell potential to predict the volume of hydrogen gas (at STP) required each month to generate the electricity. Assume the home uses 1.2×10^3 kWh of electricity per month.

130. A voltaic cell designed to measure $[Cu^{2+}]$ is constructed of a standard hydrogen electrode and a copper metal electrode in the Cu^{2+} solution of interest. If you want to construct a calibration curve for how the cell potential varies with the concentration of copper(II), what do you plot in order to obtain a straight line? What is the slope of the line?

131. The surface area of an object to be gold plated is 49.8 cm^2 and the density of gold is 19.3 g/cm^3. A current of 3.25 A is applied to a solution that contains gold in the +3 oxidation state. Calculate the time required to deposit an even layer of gold 1.00×10^{-3} cm thick on the object.

132. To electrodeposit all the Cu and Cd from a solution of CuSO$_4$ and CdSO$_4$ required 1.20 F of electricity (1 F = 1 mol e$^-$). The mixture of Cu and Cd that was deposited had a mass of 50.36 g. What mass of CuSO$_4$ was present in the original mixture?

133. Sodium oxalate, Na$_2$C$_2$O$_4$, in solution is oxidized to CO$_2(g)$ by MnO$_4^-$, which is reduced to Mn^{2+}. A 50.1 mL volume of a solution of MnO$_4^-$ is required to titrate a 0.339 g sample of sodium oxalate. This solution of MnO$_4^-$ is used to analyze uranium-containing samples. A 4.62 g sample of a uranium-containing material requires 32.5 mL of the solution for titration. The oxidation of the uranium can be represented by the change UO^{2+} $\longrightarrow$ UO$_2^{2+}$. Calculate the percentage of uranium in the sample.

134. Three electrolytic cells are connected in a series. The electrolytes in the cells are aqueous copper(II) sulfate, gold(III) sulfate, and silver nitrate. A current of 2.33 A is applied, and after some time 1.74 g Cu is deposited. How long was the current applied? What mass of gold and silver were deposited?

135. The cell Pt(s) | Cu$^+$(1 M), Cu^{2+}(1 M) || Cu$^+$(1 M) | Cu(s) has $E^\circ = 0.364$ V. The cell Cu(s) | Cu^{2+}(1 M) || Cu$^+$(1 M) | Cu(s) has $E^\circ = 0.182$ V. Write the cell reaction for each cell and explain the differences in E°. Calculate ΔG° for each cell reaction to help explain these differences.

Conceptual Problems

136. An electrochemical cell has a positive standard cell potential but a negative cell potential. Which statement is true for the cell?
   a. $K > 1; Q > K$ b. $K < 1; Q > K$
   c. $K > 1; Q < K$ d. $K < 1; Q < K$

137. Which oxidizing agent will oxidize Br$^-$ but not Cl$^-$?
   a. K$_2$Cr$_2$O$_7$ (in acid)   b. KMnO$_4$ (in acid)   c. HNO$_3$

138. A redox reaction employed in an electrochemical cell has a negative $\Delta G^\circ_{\text{rxn}}$. Which statement is true?
   a. E°_{cell} is positive; $K < 1$ b. E°_{cell} is positive; $K > 1$
   c. E°_{cell} is negative; $K > 1$ d. E°_{cell} is negative; $K < 1$

139. A redox reaction has an equilibrium constant of $K = 0.055$. What is true of $\Delta G^\circ_{\text{rxn}}$ and E°_{cell} for this reaction?

Answers to Conceptual Problems

Voltaic Cells

18.1 (a) Electrons are negatively charged and therefore flow away from the more negatively charged electrode and toward the more positively charged electrode.

Standard Electrode Potentials

18.2 (b) A negative electrode potential indicates that an electron at that electrode has greater potential energy than it has at a standard hydrogen electrode.

Selective Oxidation

18.3 (d) The reduction of HNO$_3$ is listed below the reduction of Br$_2$ and above the reduction of I$_2$ in Table 18.1. Since any reduction half-reaction is spontaneous when paired with the reverse of a half-reaction below it in the table, the reduction of HNO$_3$ is spontaneous when paired with the oxidation of I$^-$ but is not spontaneous when paired with the oxidation of Br$^-$.

Metals Dissolving in Acids

18.4 (c) Ag falls *above* the half-reaction for the reduction of H$^+$ but *below* the half-reaction for the reduction of NO$_3^-$ in Table 18.1.

Periodic Trends and the Direction of Spontaneity for Redox Reactions

18.5 (a) Br is more electronegative than I. If the two atoms were in competition for the electron, the electron would go to the more electronegative atom (Br). Therefore, I$_2$ does not spontaneously gain electrons from Br$^-$.

Relating K, $\Delta G^\circ_{\text{rxn}}$, and E°_{cell}

18.6 (c) Since $K > 1$, the reaction is spontaneous under standard conditions (when $Q = 1$, the reaction proceeds toward the products). Therefore, E°_{cell} is positive and $\Delta G^\circ_{\text{rxn}}$ is negative.

Relating Q, K, E_{cell}, and E°_{cell}

18.7 (a) Since $K < 1$, E°_{cell} is negative (under standard conditions, the reaction is not spontaneous). Since $Q < K$, E_{cell} is positive (the reaction is spontaneous under the nonstandard conditions of the cell).

Sacrificial Electrodes

18.8 Cu. The electrode potential for Fe is more negative than that of Cu. Therefore, Fe will oxidize more easily than Cu.

19 Radioactivity and Nuclear Chemistry

I am among those who think that science has great beauty. A scientist in his laboratory is not only a technician; he is also a child placed before natural phenomena which impress him like a fairy tale.

—Marie Curie (1867–1934)

I N THIS CHAPTER, WE EXAMINE RADIOACTIVITY and nuclear chemistry, both of which involve changes within the *nuclei* of atoms. Unlike ordinary chemical processes, in which elements retain their identity, nuclear processes often result in one element changing into another, frequently emitting tremendous amounts of energy. Radioactivity has numerous applications, including the diagnosis and treatment of medical conditions such as cancer, thyroid disease, abnormal kidney and bladder function, and heart disease. Naturally occurring radioactivity allows us to estimate the age of fossils, rocks, and ancient artifacts. And radioactivity, perhaps most famously, led to the discovery of nuclear fission, used for electricity generation and nuclear weapons. In this chapter, we discuss radioactivity—how it was discovered, what it is, and how we use it.

19.1 Diagnosing Appendicitis

Antibodies labeled with radioactive atoms can be used to diagnose an infected appendix.

One morning a few years ago I awoke with a dull pain on the lower right side of my abdomen that was worse by early afternoon. Since pain in this area can indicate appendicitis (inflammation of the appendix), and since I know that appendicitis can be dangerous if left untreated, I went to the hospital emergency room. The doctor who examined me recommended a simple blood test to determine my white blood cell count. Patients with appendicitis usually have a high white blood cell count because the body is trying to fight the infection. In my case, the test was negative—I had a normal white blood cell count.

Although my symptoms were consistent with appendicitis, the negative blood test clouded the diagnosis. The doctor said that I could elect to have my appendix removed anyway (even though it might be healthy) or I could submit to another test that might confirm the appendicitis. I chose the additional test, which involved *nuclear medicine*, an area of medical practice that employs *radioactivity* to diagnose and treat disease. **Radioactivity** is the emission of subatomic particles or high-energy electromagnetic radiation by the nuclei of certain atoms. Such atoms are said to be **radioactive**. Most radioactive emissions can pass through many types of matter (such as skin and muscle, in this case).

During the test, antibodies—naturally occurring molecules that fight infection—were labeled with radioactive atoms and then injected into my bloodstream. Since antibodies attack infection, they migrate to areas of the body where infection is present. If my appendix was indeed infected, the antibodies would accumulate there. I waited about an hour, and then the technician took me to a room and laid me on a table. She inserted a photographic film in a panel above me and removed the covering that prevents exposure of the film. Radioactivity is invisible to the eye, but it exposes photographic film. If my appendix had been infected, it would have (by then) contained a high concentration of the radioactively labeled antibodies. The antibodies would emit radiation and expose the film. The test, however, was negative. No radioactivity was emanating from my appendix. After several hours, the pain in my abdomen subsided and I went home. I never did find out what caused the pain.

19.2 The Discovery of Radioactivity

Radioactivity was discovered in 1896 by a French scientist named Antoine-Henri Becquerel (1852–1908). Becquerel was interested in the newly discovered X-rays (see Chapter 7), which were a hot topic of physics research in his time. He hypothesized that X-rays were emitted in conjunction with **phosphorescence**, the long-lived *emission* of light that sometimes follows the absorption of light by certain atoms and molecules. Phosphorescence is probably most familiar to you as the *glow* in glow-in-the-dark products (such as toys or stickers). After such a product is exposed to light, it reemits some of that light, usually at slightly longer wavelengths. If you turn off the room lights or put the glow-in-the-dark product in the dark, you see the greenish glow of the emitted light. Becquerel hypothesized that this visible greenish glow was associated with the emission of X-rays (which are invisible).

To test his hypothesis, Becquerel placed crystals—composed of potassium uranyl sulfate, a compound known to phosphoresce—on top of a photographic plate wrapped in black cloth. He then exposed the crystals to sunlight. He knew the crystals had phosphoresced because he could see the emitted light when he brought them back into the dark. If the crystals had also emitted X-rays, the X-rays would have passed through the black cloth and exposed the underlying photographic plate. Becquerel performed the experiment several times and always got the same result—the photographic plate showed a dark exposure spot where the crystals had been (Figure 19.1 ▾). Becquerel believed his hypothesis was correct and presented the results—that phosphorescence and X-rays were linked—to the French Academy of Sciences.

Becquerel later retracted his results, however, when he discovered that a photographic plate with the same crystals showed a dark exposure spot even when the plate and the crystals were stored in a drawer and not exposed to sunlight. Becquerel realized

▲ The greenish light emitted from glow-in-the-dark toys is phosphorescence.

▶ FIGURE 19.1 **The Discovery of Radioactivity** This photographic plate (with Becquerel's original comments at top) played a key role in the discovery of radioactivity. Becquerel placed a uranium-containing compound on the plate (which was wrapped in black cloth to shield it from visible light). He found that the plate was darkened by some unknown form of penetrating radiation that was produced continuously, independently of phosphorescence.

that the crystals themselves were constantly emitting something that exposed the photographic plate, regardless of whether or not they phosphoresced. Becquerel concluded that it was the uranium within the crystals that was the source of the emissions, and he named the emissions *uranic rays*.

Soon after Becquerel's discovery, a young graduate student named Marie Sklodowska Curie (1867–1934) (one of the first women in France to pursue doctoral work) decided to study uranic rays for her doctoral thesis. Her first task was to determine whether any other substances besides uranium (the heaviest known element at the time) emitted these rays. In her search, Curie discovered two new elements, both of which also emitted uranic rays. Curie named one of her newly discovered elements polonium, after her home country of Poland. The other element she named radium, because of its high level of radioactivity. Radium is so radioactive that it gently glows in the dark and emits significant amounts of heat. Since it was clear that these rays were not unique to uranium, Curie changed the name of uranic rays to radioactivity. In 1903, Curie and her husband, Pierre Curie, as well as Becquerel were all awarded the Nobel Prize in physics for the discovery of radioactivity. In 1911, Curie received a second Nobel Prize, this time in chemistry, for her discovery of the two new elements.

▲ Marie Curie, one of the first women in France to pursue a doctoral degree, was twice awarded the Nobel Prize, in 1903 and 1911. She is seen here with her daughters, in about 1905. Irène (left) became a distinguished nuclear physicist in her own right, winning a Nobel Prize in 1935. Eve (right) wrote a highly acclaimed biography of her mother.

Element 96 is named curium in honor of Marie Curie and her contributions to our understanding of radioactivity.

19.3 Types of Radioactivity

While Curie focused her work on discovering the different kinds of radioactive elements, Ernest Rutherford and others focused on characterizing the radioactivity itself. These scientists found that the emissions are produced by the nuclei of radioactive atoms. Such nuclei are unstable and spontaneously decompose, emitting small pieces of themselves to gain stability. These fragments are the radioactivity that Becquerel and Curie detected. Natural radioactivity can be categorized into several different types, including *alpha (α) decay, beta (β) decay, gamma (γ) ray emission*, and *positron emission*. In addition, some unstable atomic nuclei can attain greater stability by absorbing an electron from one of the atom's own orbitals, a process called *electron capture*.

In order to understand these different types of radioactivity, we must briefly review the notation for symbolizing isotopes from Section 2.6. Recall that we can represent any isotope with the following notation:

▲ Radium, discovered by Marie Curie, is so radioactive that it glows visibly and emits heat.

Mass number ⟶ $^{A}_{Z}X$ ⟵ Chemical symbol
Atomic number ⟶

Mass number (A) = the sum of the number of protons and number of neutrons in the nucleus

Atomic number (Z) = the number of protons in the nucleus

Since A represents the sum of the number of protons and neutrons, and since Z represents the number of protons, the number of neutrons in the nucleus (N) is $A - Z$.

$$N = A - Z$$
↑
Number of neutrons

For example, the symbol $^{21}_{10}Ne$ represents the neon isotope containing 10 protons and 11 neutrons. The symbol $^{20}_{10}Ne$ represents the neon isotope containing 10 protons and 10 neutrons. Remember that most elements have several different isotopes. When we are discussing nuclear properties, we often refer to a particular isotope (or species) of an element as a **nuclide**.

We represent the main subatomic particles—protons, neutrons, and electrons—with similar notation.

Proton symbol $^{1}_{1}p$ Neutron symbol $^{1}_{0}n$ Electron symbol $^{0}_{-1}e$

Alpha Decay

▲ **FIGURE 19.2 Alpha Decay** In alpha decay, a nucleus emits a particle composed of two protons and two neutrons (a helium-4 nucleus).

As we will discuss in Section 19.4, nuclei are unstable when they are too large or when they contain an unbalanced ratio of neutrons to protons.

In nuclear chemistry, we are primarily interested in changes within the nucleus; therefore, the 2+ charge that we would normally write for a helium nucleus is omitted for an alpha particle.

The 1 in the lower left of the proton symbol represents 1 proton, and the 0 in the lower left corner of the neutron symbol represents 0 protons. The −1 in the lower left corner of the electron symbol is a bit different from the other atomic numbers, but it will make sense when we see it in the context of nuclear decay a bit later in this section.

Alpha (α) Decay

Alpha (α) decay occurs when an unstable nucleus emits a particle composed of two protons and two neutrons (Figure 19.2 ◄). Since two protons and two neutrons combined are identical to a helium-4 nucleus, the symbol for alpha radiation is the symbol for helium-4:

$$\textbf{Alpha } (\alpha) \textbf{ particle} \quad {}^{4}_{2}\text{He} \quad$$

When an element emits an alpha particle, the number of protons in its nucleus changes, transforming the element into a different element. We symbolize this phenomenon with a **nuclear equation**, an equation that represents nuclear processes such as radioactivity. For example, the nuclear equation for the alpha decay of uranium-238 is:

Parent nuclide   Daughter nuclide

$${}^{238}_{92}\text{U} \longrightarrow {}^{234}_{90}\text{Th} + {}^{4}_{2}\text{He}$$

The original atom is called the *parent nuclide*, and the product of the decay is called the *daughter nuclide*. In this case, uranium-238 (the parent nuclide) becomes thorium-234 (the daughter nuclide). Unlike a chemical reaction, in which elements retain their identities, in a nuclear reaction elements often change their identities. Like a chemical equation, however, a nuclear equation must be balanced. *The sum of the atomic numbers on both sides of a nuclear equation must be equal, and the sum of the mass numbers on both sides must also be equal.*

$${}^{238}_{92}\text{U} \longrightarrow {}^{234}_{90}\text{Th} + {}^{4}_{2}\text{He}$$

Reactants	Products
Sum of mass numbers = 238	Sum of mass numbers = 234 + 4 = 238
Sum of atomic numbers = 92	Sum of atomic numbers = 90 + 2 = 92

We can deduce the identity and symbol of the daughter nuclide in any alpha decay from the mass and atomic number of the parent nuclide. During alpha decay, the mass number decreases by 4 and the atomic number decreases by 2, as shown in Example 19.1.

EXAMPLE 19.1 Writing Nuclear Equations for Alpha Decay

Write the nuclear equation for the alpha decay of Ra-224.

SOLUTION

Begin with the symbol for Ra-224 on the left side of the equation and the symbol for an alpha particle on the right side.	${}^{224}_{88}\text{Ra} \longrightarrow {}^{?}_{?}? + {}^{4}_{2}\text{He}$
Equalize the sum of the mass numbers and the sum of the atomic numbers on both sides of the equation by writing the appropriate mass number and atomic number for the unknown daughter nuclide.	${}^{224}_{88}\text{Ra} \longrightarrow {}^{220}_{86}? + {}^{4}_{2}\text{He}$
Refer to the periodic table to deduce the identity of the unknown daughter nuclide from its atomic number and write its symbol. Since the atomic number is 86, the daughter nuclide is radon (Rn).	${}^{224}_{88}\text{Ra} \longrightarrow {}^{220}_{86}\text{Rn} + {}^{4}_{2}\text{He}$

FOR PRACTICE 19.1

Write the nuclear equation for the alpha decay of Po-216.

Alpha radiation is the 18-wheeler truck of radioactivity. The alpha particle is by far the most massive of all particles emitted by radioactive nuclei. Consequently, alpha radiation has the most potential to interact with and damage other molecules, including biological ones. Highly energetic radiation interacts with other molecules and atoms by ionizing them. When radiation ionizes molecules within the cells of living organisms, those molecules may undergo damaging chemical reactions, and the cells can die or begin to reproduce abnormally. The ability of radiation to ionize other molecules and atoms is called its **ionizing power**. Of all types of radioactivity, alpha radiation has the highest ionizing power.

However, alpha particles, because of their large size, have the lowest **penetrating power**—the ability to penetrate matter. (Imagine a semitruck trying to get through a traffic jam.) In order for radiation to damage important molecules within living cells, it must penetrate into the cell. Alpha radiation does not easily penetrate into cells because it can be stopped by a sheet of paper, by clothing, or even by air. Consequently, a low-level alpha emitter that remains outside the body is relatively safe. If an alpha emitter is ingested, however, it becomes very dangerous because the alpha particles then have direct access to the molecules that compose organs and tissues.

Beta (β) Decay

Beta (β) decay occurs when an unstable nucleus emits an electron (Figure 19.3 ►). How does a nucleus, which contains only protons and neutrons, emit an electron? In some unstable nuclei, a neutron changes into a proton and emits an electron.

$$\textbf{Beta decay} \qquad \text{Neutron} \longrightarrow \text{proton} + \text{emitted electron}$$

The symbol for a beta (β) particle in a nuclear equation is:

$$\textbf{Beta } (\boldsymbol{\beta}) \textbf{ particle} \qquad _{-1}^{0}e \qquad \bullet$$

We can represent beta decay with this nuclear equation:

$$_{0}^{1}\text{n} \longrightarrow _{1}^{1}\text{p} + _{-1}^{0}e$$

The -1 reflects the charge of the electron, which is equivalent to an atomic number of -1 in a nuclear equation. When an atom emits a beta particle, its atomic number increases by 1 because it now has an additional proton. For example, the nuclear equation for the beta decay of radium-228 is:

$$_{88}^{228}\text{Ra} \longrightarrow _{89}^{228}\text{Ac} + _{-1}^{0}e$$

Notice that the nuclear equation is balanced—the sum of the mass numbers on both sides is equal and the sum of the atomic numbers on both sides is equal.

Beta radiation is the four-door sedan of radioactivity. Beta particles are much less massive than alpha particles and consequently have a lower ionizing power. However, because of their smaller size, beta particles have a higher penetrating power and only something as substantive as a sheet of metal or a thick piece of wood will stop them. Consequently, a beta emitter outside of the body poses a higher risk than an alpha emitter. If ingested, however, the beta emitter does less damage than an alpha emitter.

Gamma (γ) Ray Emission

Gamma (γ) ray emission is significantly different from alpha or beta radiation. Gamma radiation is a form of *electromagnetic* radiation (see Section 7.2). Gamma rays are high-energy (short-wavelength) photons. The symbol for a gamma ray is:

$$\textbf{Gamma } (\boldsymbol{\gamma}) \textbf{ ray} \qquad _{0}^{0}\gamma \qquad \text{〜〜〜〜〜➔}$$

A gamma ray has no charge and no mass. When a gamma-ray photon is emitted from a radioactive atom, it does not change the mass number or the atomic number of the element. Gamma rays, however, are usually emitted in conjunction with other types of radiation. For example, the alpha emission of U-238 (discussed previously) is also accompanied by the emission of a gamma ray.

$$_{92}^{238}\text{U} \longrightarrow _{90}^{234}\text{Th} + _{2}^{4}\text{He} + _{0}^{0}\gamma$$

Beta Decay

Electron (β particle) is emitted from nucleus

Neutron becomes a proton

Neutron

$_{-1}^{0}e$

$_{6}^{14}\text{C}$ nucleus $\qquad _{7}^{14}\text{N}$ nucleus

▲ FIGURE 19.3 **Beta Decay** In beta decay, a neutron emits an electron and becomes a proton.

This kind of beta radiation is also called beta minus (β^-) radiation due to its negative charge.

See Section 7.2 for a review of electromagnetic radiation.

Gamma rays are the motorbikes of radioactivity. They have the lowest ionizing power, but the highest penetrating power. (Imagine a motorbike zipping through a traffic jam.) Stopping gamma rays requires several inches of lead shielding or thick slabs of concrete.

Positron Emission

Positron emission occurs when an unstable nucleus emits a positron (Figure 19.4 ◄). A **positron** is the *antiparticle* of the electron; it has the same mass as an electron, but the opposite charge. If a positron collides with an electron, the two particles annihilate each other, releasing energy in the form of gamma rays. In positron emission, a proton is converted into a neutron and emits a positron.

Positron Emission

Positron is emitted from nucleus

Proton becomes a neutron

$_{+1}^{0}e$

Proton

$_{6}^{10}C$ nucleus $_{5}^{10}B$ nucleus

▲ **FIGURE 19.4 Positron Emission** In positron emission, a proton emits a positron and becomes a neutron.

> Positron emission can be thought of as a type of beta emission and is sometimes referred to as beta plus emission (β^+).

$$\text{Positron emission} \qquad \text{Proton} \longrightarrow \text{neutron} + \text{emitted positron}$$

The symbol for a positron in a nuclear equation is:

$$\text{Positron} \qquad _{+1}^{0}e \quad \bullet$$

We can represent positron emission with this nuclear equation:

$$_{1}^{1}p \longrightarrow _{0}^{1}n + _{+1}^{0}e$$

When an atom emits a positron, its atomic number *decreases* by 1 because it has one less proton after emission. Consider the nuclear equation for the positron emission of phosphorus-30 as an example:

$$_{15}^{30}P \longrightarrow _{14}^{30}Si + _{+1}^{0}e$$

We can determine the identity and symbol of the daughter nuclide in any positron emission in a manner similar to that used for alpha and beta decay, as shown in Example 19.2. Positrons are similar to beta particles in their ionizing and penetrating power.

Electron Capture

Unlike the forms of radioactive decay that we have discussed so far, electron capture involves a particle being *absorbed by* instead of *emitted from* an unstable nucleus. **Electron capture** occurs when a nucleus assimilates an electron from an inner orbital of its electron cloud. Like positron emission, the net effect of electron capture is the conversion of a proton into a neutron.

$$\text{Electron capture} \qquad \text{Proton} + \text{electron} \longrightarrow \text{neutron}$$

We can represent electron capture with this nuclear equation:

$$_{1}^{1}p + _{-1}^{0}e \longrightarrow _{0}^{1}n$$

When an atom undergoes electron capture, its atomic number decreases by 1 because it has one less proton. For example, when Ru-92 undergoes electron capture, its atomic number changes from 44 to 43:

$$_{44}^{92}Ru + _{-1}^{0}e \longrightarrow _{43}^{92}Tc$$

Table 19.1 summarizes the different kinds of radiation.

EXAMPLE 19.2 Writing Nuclear Equations for Beta Decay, Positron Emission, and Electron Capture

Write the nuclear equation for each type of decay.

(a) beta decay in Bk-249

(b) positron emission in O-15

(c) electron capture in I-111

SOLUTION

(a) In beta decay, the atomic number *increases* by 1 and the mass number remains unchanged. The daughter nuclide is element number 98, californium.	$_{97}^{249}Bk \longrightarrow _{98}^{249}? + _{-1}^{0}e$ $_{97}^{249}Bk \longrightarrow _{98}^{249}Cf + _{-1}^{0}e$

(b) In positron emission, the atomic number *decreases* by 1 and the mass number remains unchanged. The daughter nuclide is element number 7, nitrogen.	$^{15}_{8}O \longrightarrow {}^{15}_{7}? + {}^{0}_{+1}e$ $^{15}_{8}O \longrightarrow {}^{15}_{7}N + {}^{0}_{+1}e$
(c) In electron capture, the atomic number also *decreases* by 1 and the mass number remains unchanged. The daughter nuclide is element number 52, tellurium.	$^{111}_{53}I + {}^{0}_{-1}e \longrightarrow {}^{111}_{52}?$ $^{111}_{53}I + {}^{0}_{-1}e \longrightarrow {}^{111}_{52}Te$

FOR PRACTICE 19.2

(a) Write three nuclear equations to represent the nuclear decay sequence that begins with the alpha decay of U-235 followed by a beta decay of the daughter nuclide and then another alpha decay.

(b) Write the nuclear equation for the positron emission of Na-22.

(c) Write the nuclear equation for electron capture in Kr-76.

FOR MORE PRACTICE 19.2

Potassium-40 decays to produce Ar-40. What is the method of decay? Write the nuclear equation for this decay.

TABLE 19.1 Modes of Radioactive Decay

Decay Mode	Process	A	Change in: Z	N/Z*	Example
α	Parent nuclide → Daughter nuclide + $^{4}_{2}$He (α particle)	−4	−2	Increase	$^{238}_{92}U \longrightarrow {}^{234}_{90}Th + {}^{4}_{2}He$
β	Neutron → Neutron becomes a proton; Parent nuclide → Daughter nuclide + $^{0}_{-1}e$ (β particle)	0	+1	Decrease	$^{228}_{88}Ra \longrightarrow {}^{228}_{89}Ac + {}^{0}_{-1}e$
γ	Excited nuclide → Stable nuclide + $^{0}_{0}\gamma$ (Photon)	0	0	None	$^{234}_{90}Th \longrightarrow {}^{234}_{90}Th + {}^{0}_{0}\gamma$
Positron emission	Proton → Proton becomes a neutron; Parent nuclide → Daughter nuclide + $^{0}_{+1}e$ (Positron)	0	−1	Increase	$^{30}_{15}P \longrightarrow {}^{30}_{14}Si + {}^{0}_{+1}e$
Electron capture	Proton → Proton becomes a neutron; Parent nuclide + $^{0}_{-1}e$ → Daughter nuclide	0	−1	Increase	$^{92}_{44}Ru + {}^{0}_{-1}e \longrightarrow {}^{92}_{43}Tc$

* Neutron-to-proton ratio

Conceptual Connection 19.1 Alpha and Beta Decay

Consider the graphical representation of a series of decays shown here.

The arrow labeled x and the arrow labeled y each correspond to what kind of decay?

(a) x corresponds to alpha decay and y corresponds to positron emission.

(b) x corresponds to positron emission and y corresponds to alpha decay.

(c) x corresponds to alpha decay and y corresponds to beta decay.

(d) x corresponds to beta decay and y corresponds to alpha decay.

19.4 The Valley of Stability: Predicting the Type of Radioactivity

So far, we have described various different types of radioactivity. But what causes a particular nuclide to be radioactive in the first place? And why do some nuclides decay via alpha decay, while others decay via beta decay or positron emission? The answers to these questions are not simple, but we can get a basic idea of the factors that influence the stability of the nucleus and the nature of its decay.

A nucleus is a collection of protons (positively charged) and neutrons (uncharged). We know that positively charged particles such as protons repel one another. So what binds the nucleus together? The binding is provided by a fundamental force of physics known as the **strong force**. All **nucleons**—protons and neutrons—are attracted to one another by the strong force. However, the strong force acts only at very short distances. We can think of the stability of a nucleus as a balance between the *repulsive* coloumbic force among protons and the *attractive* strong force among all nucleons. The neutrons in a nucleus, therefore, play an important role in stabilizing the nucleus because they attract other nucleons (through the strong force) but lack the repulsive force associated with positive charge. (It might seem that adding more neutrons would *always* lead to greater stability, so that the more neutrons the better. This is not the case, however, because protons and neutrons occupy energy levels in a nucleus that are similar to those occupied by electrons in an atom. As you add more neutrons, they must occupy increasingly higher energy levels within the nucleus. At some point, the energy payback from the strong force is not enough to compensate for the high energy state that the neutrons must occupy.)

An important number in determining nuclear stability is the *ratio* of neutrons to protons (N/Z). Figure 19.5 ◄ shows a plot of the number of neutrons versus the number of protons for all known stable nuclei. The green dots along the diagonal of the graph represent stable nuclei; this region is known as the *valley* (or *island*) *of stability*. Notice that for the lighter elements, the N/Z ratio of stable isotopes is about one (equal numbers of neutrons and protons). For example, the most abundant isotope of carbon ($Z = 6$) is carbon-12, which contains six protons and six neutrons. However, beyond about $Z = 20$, the N/Z ratio of stable nuclei begins to get larger. For example, at $Z = 40$, stable nuclei have an N/Z ratio of about 1.25 and at $Z = 80$, the N/Z ratio reaches about 1.5. Above $Z = 83$, stable nuclei do not exist—bismuth ($Z = 83$) is the heaviest element with stable (nonradioactive) isotopes.

The type of radioactivity emitted by a nuclide depends in part on the N/Z ratio.

***N/Z* too high:** Nuclides that lie above the valley of stability have too many neutrons and tend to convert neutrons to protons via beta decay. The process of undergoing beta decay moves the nuclide down in the plot in Figure 19.5 and closer to (or into) the valley of stability.

▼ FIGURE 19.5 Stable and Unstable Nuclei A plot of N (the number of neutrons) versus Z (the number of protons) for all known stable nuclei—represented by green dots on this graph—shows that these nuclei cluster together in a region known as the valley (or island) of stability. Nuclei with an N/Z ratio that is too high tend to undergo beta decay. Nuclei with an N/Z ratio that is too low tend to undergo positron emission or electron capture.

The Valley of Stability

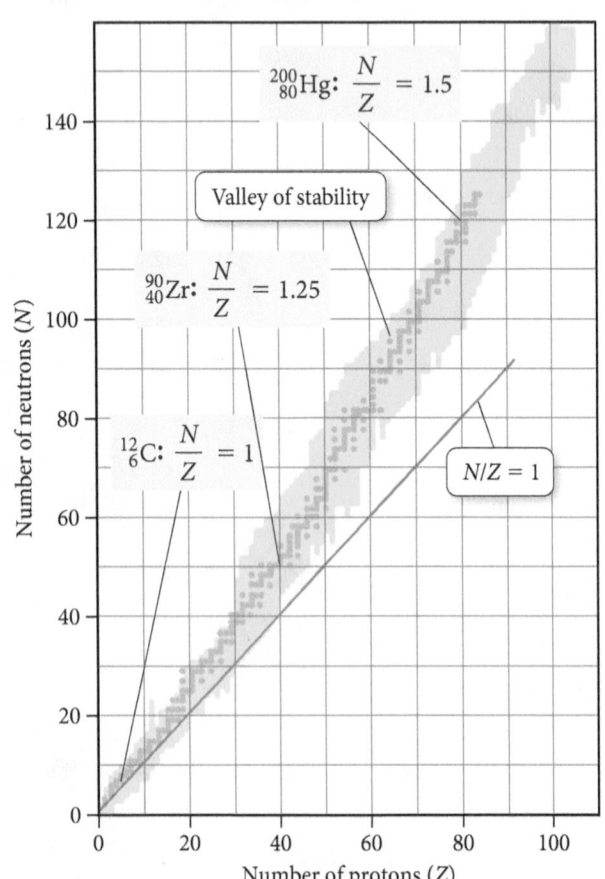

N/Z **too low:** Nuclides that lie below the valley of stability have too many protons and tend to convert protons to neutrons via positron emission or electron capture. This moves the nuclide up in the plot in Figure 19.5 and closer to (or into) the valley of stability. (Alpha decay also raises the *N/Z* ratio for nuclides in which *N/Z* > 1, but the effect is smaller than for positron emission or electron capture.)

One way to decide whether a particular nuclide has an *N/Z* that is too high, too low, or about right is to consult Figure 19.5. Those nuclides that lie within the valley of stability are stable. Alternatively, we can also compare the mass number of the nuclide to the atomic mass listed in the periodic table for the corresponding element. The atomic mass is an average of the masses of the stable nuclides for an element and thus represents an *N/Z* that is about right. For example, suppose we want to evaluate *N/Z* for Ru-112. Ruthenium has an atomic mass of 101.07 so we know that the nuclide with a mass number of 112 must contain too many neutrons and therefore have an *N/Z* that is too high. The following example shows how to apply these considerations in predicting the mode of decay for a nucleus.

EXAMPLE 19.3 Predicting the Type of Radioactive Decay

Predict whether each nuclide is more likely to decay via beta decay or positron emission.
(a) Mg-28   **(b)** Mg-22   **(c)** Mo-102

SOLUTION

(a) Magnesium-28 has 16 neutrons and 12 protons, so *N/Z* = 1.33. However, for *Z* = 12, you can see from Figure 19.5 that stable nuclei should have an *N/Z* of about 1. Alternatively, you can see from the periodic table that the atomic mass of magnesium is 24.31. Therefore, a nuclide with a mass number of 28 is too heavy to be stable because the *N/Z* ratio is too high and Mg-28 undergoes *beta decay*, resulting in the conversion of a neutron to a proton.

(b) Magnesium-22 has 10 neutrons and 12 protons, so *N/Z* = 0.83 (too low). Alternatively you can see from the periodic table that the atomic mass of magnesium is 24.31. A nuclide with a mass number of 22 is too light; the *N/Z* ratio is too low. Therefore, Mg-22 undergoes *positron emission*, resulting in the conversion of a proton to a neutron. (Electron capture would accomplish the same thing as positron emission, but in Mg-22, positron emission is the only decay mode observed.)

(c) Molybdenum-102 has 60 neutrons and 42 protons, so *N/Z* = 1.43. However, for *Z* = 42, you can see from Figure 19.5 that stable nuclei should have an *N/Z* ratio of about 1.3. Alternatively you can see from the periodic table that the atomic mass of molybdenum is 95.94. A nuclide with a mass number of 102 is too heavy to be stable; the *N/Z* ratio is too high. Therefore, Mo-102 undergoes *beta decay*, resulting in the conversion of a neutron to a proton.

FOR PRACTICE 19.3
Predict whether each nuclide is more likely to decay via beta decay or positron emission.
(a) Pb-192   **(b)** Pb-212   **(c)** Xe-114

Magic Numbers

In addition to the *N/Z* ratio, the *actual number* of protons and neutrons also affects the stability of the nucleus. Table 19.2 shows the number of nuclei with different possible combinations of even or odd nucleons. Notice that a large number of stable nuclides have both an even number of protons and an even number of neutrons. Only five stable nuclides have an odd and odd combination.

The reason for this is that nucleons occupy energy levels within the nucleus much as electrons occupy energy levels within an atom. Just as atoms with certain numbers of electrons are uniquely stable (in particular, the number of electrons associated with the

TABLE 19.2 Number of Stable Nuclides with Even and Odd Numbers of Nucleons

Z	N	Number of Nuclides
Even	Even	157
Even	Odd	53
Odd	Even	50
Odd	Odd	5

A Decay Series

▲ **FIGURE 19.6 The Uranium-238 Radioactive Decay Series** Uranium-238 decays via a series of steps ending in Pb-206, a stable element. Each diagonal line to the left represents an alpha decay and each diagonal line to the right represents a beta decay.

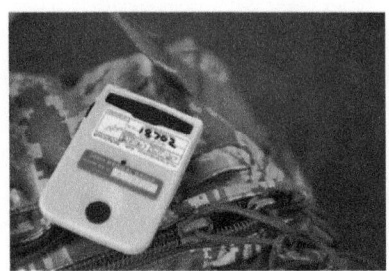

▲ **FIGURE 19.7 Film-Badge Dosimeter** A film-badge dosimeter consists of a piece of photographic film in a light-resistant container. The film's exposure in a given time is proportional to the amount of radiation it receives.

noble gases: 2, 10, 18, 36, 54, etc.), so atoms with certain numbers of nucleons (N or Z = 2, 8, 20, 28, 50, 82, and N = 126) are uniquely stable. These numbers are often referred to as **magic numbers**. Nuclei containing a magic number of protons or neutrons are particularly stable. Since the magic numbers are even, this accounts in part for the abundance of stable nuclides with even numbers of nucleons. Moreover, nucleons also have a tendency to pair together (much as electrons pair together). This tendency and the resulting stability of paired nucleons also contribute to the abundance of stable nuclides with even numbers of nucleons.

Radioactive Decay Series

Atoms with $Z > 83$ are radioactive and decay in one or more steps involving primarily alpha and beta decay (with some gamma decay to carry away excess energy). For example, uranium (atomic number 92) is the heaviest naturally occurring element. Its most common isotope is U-238, an alpha emitter that decays to Th-234.

$$^{238}_{92}\text{U} \longrightarrow {}^{234}_{90}\text{Th} + {}^{4}_{2}\text{He}$$

The daughter nuclide, Th-234, is itself radioactive—it is a beta emitter that decays to Pa-234.

$$^{234}_{90}\text{Th} \longrightarrow {}^{234}_{91}\text{Pa} + {}^{0}_{-1}\text{e}$$

Protactinium-234 is also radioactive, decaying to U-234 via beta emission. Radioactive decay continues until a stable nuclide, Pb-206, is reached. Figure 19.6 ◄ illustrates the entire uranium-238 decay series.

19.5 Detecting Radioactivity

The particles emitted by radioactive nuclei have a lot of energy and can therefore be readily detected. In a radiation detector, the particles are detected through their interactions with atoms or molecules. The simplest radiation detectors are pieces of photographic film that become exposed when radiation passes through them. **Film-badge dosimeters**—which consist of photographic film held in a small case that is pinned to clothing—are issued to most people working with or near radioactive substances (Figure 19.7 ◄). These badges are collected and processed (or developed) regularly as a way to monitor a person's exposure. The more exposed the film has become in a given period of time, the more radioactivity the person has been exposed to during that period.

Radioactivity can be instantly detected with devices such as a **Geiger-Müller counter** (Figure 19.8 ▶). In this instrument (commonly referred to as a Geiger counter), particles emitted by radioactive nuclei pass through an argon-filled chamber. The energetic particles create a trail of ionized argon atoms. High voltage applied between a wire within the chamber and the chamber itself causes these newly formed ions to produce an electrical signal that can be displayed on a meter or turned into an audible click. Each click corresponds to a radioactive particle passing through the argon gas chamber. This clicking is the stereotypical sound most people associate with a radiation detector.

A second type of device commonly used to detect radiation instantly is a **scintillation counter**. In a scintillation counter, radioactive emissions pass through a material (such as NaI or CsI) that emits ultraviolet or visible light in response to excitation by energetic particles. The radioactivity excites the atoms to a higher energy state. The atoms release this energy as light, which is detected and turned into an electrical signal that can be read on a meter.

▲ FIGURE 19.8 **Geiger-Müller Counter** When ionizing radiation passes through the argon-filled chamber, it ionizes the argon atoms, giving rise to a brief, tiny pulse of electrical current that is transduced onto a meter or into an audible click.

19.6 The Kinetics of Radioactive Decay and Radiometric Dating

Radioactivity is a natural component of our environment. The ground beneath you most likely contains radioactive atoms that emit radiation. The food you eat contains a residual quantity of radioactive atoms that are absorbed into your body fluids and incorporated into tissues. Small amounts of radiation from space make it through our atmosphere to constantly bombard Earth. Humans and other living organisms have evolved in this environment and have adapted to survive in it.

One reason for the radioactivity in our environment is the instability of all atomic nuclei beyond atomic number 83 (bismuth). Every element with more than 83 protons in its nucleus is unstable and therefore radioactive. In addition, some isotopes of elements with fewer than 83 protons are also unstable and radioactive. Radioactive nuclides *persist* in our environment because new ones are constantly being formed, and because many of the existing ones decay away only very slowly.

All radioactive nuclei decay via first-order kinetics, so the rate of decay in a particular sample is directly proportional to the number of nuclei present as indicated in the equation:

$$\text{Rate} = kN$$

You may find it useful to review the discussion of first-order kinetics in Section 13.3.

where N is the number of radioactive nuclei and k is the rate constant. Different radioactive nuclides decay into their daughter nuclides with different rate constants. Some nuclides decay quickly (large rate constant) while others decay slowly (small rate constant).

The time it takes for one-half of the parent nuclides in a radioactive sample to decay to the daughter nuclides is the *half-life*, and is identical to the concept of half-life for chemical reactions that we discussed in Chapter 13. Thus, the relationship between the half-life of a nuclide and its rate constant is given by the same expression (Equation 13.19) that we derived for a first-order reaction in Section 13.4:

$$t_{1/2} = \frac{0.693}{k} \qquad\qquad [19.1]$$

Nuclides that decay quickly have short half-lives and large rate constants—they are considered very active (many decay events per unit time). Nuclides that decay slowly have long half-lives and are less active (fewer decay events per unit time). For example, thorium-232 is an alpha emitter with a half-life of 1.4×10^{10} years, or 14 billion years.

▶ FIGURE 19.9 **The Decay of Radon-220** Radon-220 decays with a half-life of approximately 1 minute.

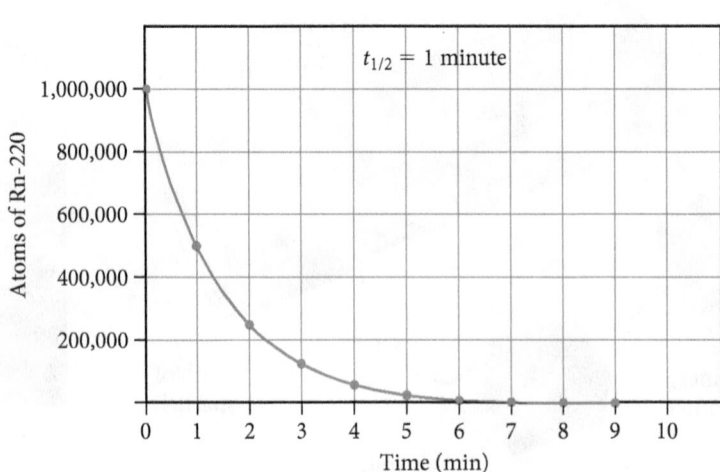

Decay of Radon-220

A sample of Th-232 containing 1 million atoms decays to $\frac{1}{2}$ million atoms in 14 billion years and then to $\frac{1}{4}$ million in another 14 billion years and so on. Notice that a radioactive sample does *not* decay to *zero* atoms in two half-lives—you can't add two half-lives together to get a "whole" life. The amount that remains after one half-life is always one-half of what was present at the start. The amount that remains after two half-lives is one-quarter of what was present at the start, and so on.

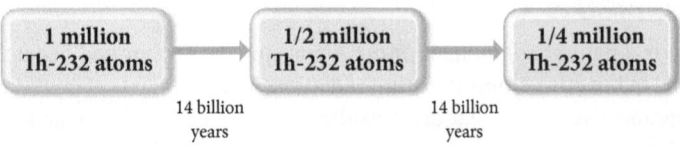

Some nuclides have very short half-lives. For example, radon-220 has a half-life of approximately 1 minute (Figure 19.9 ▲). A 1-million-atom sample of radon-220, decays to $\frac{1}{4}$ million radon-220 atoms in just 2 minutes and to approximately 1000 atoms in 10 minutes. Table 19.3 lists several nuclides and their half-lives.

TABLE 19.3 Selected Nuclides and Their Half-Lives

Nuclide	Half-Life	Type of Decay
$^{232}_{90}$Th	1.4×10^{10} yr	Alpha
$^{238}_{92}$U	4.5×10^{9} yr	Alpha
$^{14}_{6}$C	5730 yr	Beta
$^{220}_{86}$Rn	55.6 s	Alpha
$^{219}_{90}$Th	1.05×10^{-6} s	Alpha

Conceptual Connection 19.2 Half-Life

Consider this graph representing the decay of a radioactive nuclide.

What is the half-life of the nuclide?

(a) 625 years   **(b)** 1250 years   **(c)** 2500 years   **(d)** 3125 years

The Integrated Rate Law

Recall from Chapter 13 that for first-order chemical reactions, the concentration of a reactant as a function of time is given by the integrated rate law.

$$\ln\frac{[A]_t}{[A]_0} = -kt \qquad\qquad [19.2]$$

Since nuclear decay follows first-order kinetics, we can substitute the number of nuclei for concentration to arrive at the equation:

$$\ln\frac{N_t}{N_0} = -kt \qquad\qquad [19.3]$$

where N_t is the number of radioactive nuclei at time t and N_0 is the initial number of radioactive nuclei. Example 19.4 demonstrates the use of this equation.

EXAMPLE 19.4 Radioactive Decay Kinetics

Plutonium-236 is an alpha emitter with a half-life of 2.86 years. If a sample initially contains 1.35 mg of Pu-236, what mass of Pu-236 is present after 5.00 years?

SORT You are given the initial mass of Pu-236 in a sample and asked to find the mass after 5.00 years.	**GIVEN:** $m_{Pu\text{-}236}(\text{initial}) = 1.35\,\text{mg}$; $\qquad t = 5.00\,\text{yr}$; $t_{1/2} = 2.86\,\text{yr}$ **FIND:** $m_{Pu\text{-}236}$ (final)
STRATEGIZE Use the integrated rate law (Equation 19.3) to solve this problem. You must determine the value of the rate constant (k) from the half-life expression (Equation 19.1).	**CONCEPTUAL PLAN**
Use the value of the rate constant, the initial mass of Pu-236, and the time along with integrated rate law to find the final mass of Pu-236. Since the mass of the Pu-236 ($m_{Pu\text{-}236}$) is directly proportional to the number of atoms (N), and since the integrated rate law contains the ratio (N_t/N_0), the initial and final masses can be substituted for the initial and final number of atoms.	
SOLVE Follow your plan. Begin by determining the rate constant from the half-life.	**SOLUTION** $t_{1/2} = \dfrac{0.693}{k}$ $k = \dfrac{0.693}{t_{1/2}} = \dfrac{0.693}{2.86\,\text{yr}}$ $\quad = 0.24\underline{2}3/\text{yr}$
Solve the integrated rate law for N_t and substitute the values of the rate constant, the initial mass of Pu-236, and the time into the solved equation. Calculate the final mass of Pu-236.	$\ln\dfrac{N_t}{N_0} = -kt$ $\dfrac{N_t}{N_0} = e^{-kt}$ $N_t = N_0 e^{-kt}$ $N_t = 1.35\,\text{mg}\left[e^{-(0.24\underline{2}3/\text{yr})(5.00\,\text{yr})}\right]$ $N_t = 0.402\,\text{mg}$

CHECK The units of the answer (mg) are correct. The magnitude of the answer (0.402 mg) is about one-third of the original mass (1.35 mg), which seems reasonable given that the amount of time is between one and two half-lives. (One half-life would result in one-half of the original mass and two half-lives would result in one-fourth of the original mass.)

FOR PRACTICE 19.4
How long will it take for the 1.35 mg sample of Pu-236 in Example 19.4 to decay to 0.100 mg?

Since radioactivity is a first-order process, the rate of decay is linearly proportional to the number of nuclei in the sample. Therefore, the initial rate of decay ($rate_0$) and the rate of decay at time t ($rate_t$) can also be used in the integrated rate law.

$$Rate_t = kN_t \qquad Rate_0 = kN_0$$

$$\frac{N_t}{N_0} = \frac{rate_t/k}{rate_0/k} = \frac{rate_t}{rate_0}$$

Substituting into Equation 19.3, we get the following result:

$$\ln \frac{rate_t}{rate_0} = -kt \qquad\qquad [19.4]$$

We can use Equation 19.4 to predict how the rate of decay of a radioactive sample will change with time or how much time has passed based on how the rate has changed (see examples later in this section).

The radioactive isotopes in our environment and their predictable decay with time can therefore be used to estimate the age of rocks or artifacts containing those isotopes. The technique is known as **radiometric dating**, and we examine two different types individually.

Conceptual Connection 19.3 Half-Life and the Amount of Radioactive Sample

A sample initially contains 1.6 moles of a radioactive isotope. How much of the sample remains after four half-lives?

(a) 0.0 mol   **(b)** 0.10 mol   **(c)** 0.20 mol   **(d)** 0.40 mol

Radiocarbon Dating: Using Radioactivity to Measure the Age of Fossils and Artifacts

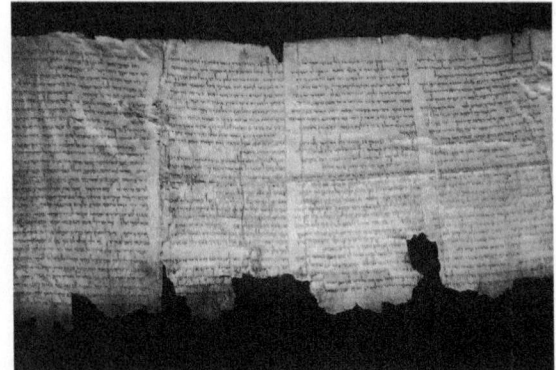

▲ The Dead Sea Scrolls are 2000-year-old biblical manuscripts. Their age was determined by radiocarbon dating.

Archeologists, geologists, anthropologists, and other scientists use **radiocarbon dating**, a technique devised in 1949 by Willard Libby at the University of Chicago, to estimate the ages of fossils and artifacts. For example, in 1947, young shepherds searching for a stray goat near the Dead Sea (east of Jerusalem) entered a cave and discovered ancient scrolls that had been stuffed into jars. These scrolls—now named the Dead Sea Scrolls—are 2000-year-old texts of the Hebrew Bible, predating other previously discovered manuscripts by almost a thousand years.

The Dead Sea Scrolls, like other ancient artifacts, contain a radioactive signature that reveals their age. This signature results from the presence of carbon-14 (which is radioactive) in the environment. Carbon-14 is constantly formed in the upper atmosphere by the neutron bombardment of nitrogen.

$$^{14}_{7}N + ^{1}_{0}n \longrightarrow ^{14}_{6}C + ^{1}_{1}H$$

After it forms, carbon-14 decays back to nitrogen by beta emission with a half-life of 5730 years.

Libby received the Nobel Prize in 1960 for the development of radiocarbon dating.

$$^{14}_{6}C \longrightarrow ^{14}_{7}N + ^{0}_{-1}e \qquad t_{1/2} = 5730 \text{ yr}$$

The continuous formation of carbon-14 in the atmosphere and its continuous decay to nitrogen-14 produce a nearly constant equilibrium amount of atmospheric carbon-14. The atmospheric carbon-14 is oxidized to carbon dioxide and incorporated into plants by photosynthesis. The C-14 then makes its way up the food chain and ultimately into all living organisms. As a result, the tissues in all living plants, animals, and humans contain the same ratio of carbon-14 to carbon-12 ($^{14}C : ^{12}C$) as that found in the atmosphere. When a living organism dies, however, it stops incorporating new carbon-14 into its tissues. The $^{14}C : ^{12}C$ ratio then begins to decrease with a half-life of 5730 years. Since many artifacts, including the Dead Sea Scrolls, are made from materials that were once living—such as papyrus, wood, or other plant and animal derivatives—the $^{14}C : ^{12}C$ ratio in these artifacts indicates their age. For example, suppose an ancient artifact has a $^{14}C : ^{12}C$ ratio that is 25% of that found in living organisms. How old is the artifact? Since it contains one-quarter as much carbon-14 as a living organism, it must be two half-lives or 11,460 years old. The maximum age that can be estimated from carbon-14 dating is about 50,000 years—beyond that, the amount of carbon-14 becomes too low to measure accurately.

The accuracy of carbon-14 dating can be checked against objects whose ages are known from historical sources. These kinds of comparisons reveal that ages obtained from C-14 dating may deviate from the actual ages by up to about 5%. For a 6000-year-old object, that would result in an error of about 300 years. The reason for the deviations is the variance of atmospheric C-14 levels over time.

In order to make C-14 dating more accurate, scientists have studied the carbon-14 content of western bristlecone pine trees, which can live up to 5000 years. Each tree trunk contains growth rings corresponding to each year of the tree's life, and the wood laid down in each ring incorporates carbon derived from the carbon dioxide in the atmosphere at that time. The rings thus provide a record of the historical atmospheric carbon-14 content. In addition, the rings of living trees can be correlated with the rings of dead trees (if part of the lifetimes of the trees overlapped), allowing the record to be extended back about 11,000 years. Using the data from the bristlecone pine, the 5% deviations from historical dates can be corrected. In this way, the known ages of bristlecone pine trees are used to calibrate C-14 dating, resulting in more accurate results.

▲ Western bristlecone pine trees can live up to 5000 years; scientists can precisely determine the age of a tree by counting the annual rings in its trunk. The trees can therefore be used to calibrate the timescale for radiocarbon dating.

EXAMPLE 19.5 Radiocarbon Dating

A skull believed to belong to an ancient human being has a carbon-14 decay rate of 4.50 disintegrations per minute per gram of carbon (4.50 dis/min · g C). If living organisms have a decay rate of 15.3 dis/min · g C, how old is the skull? (The decay rate is directly proportional to the amount of carbon-14 present.)

SORT You are given the current rate of decay for the skull and the assumed initial rate. You are asked to find the age of the skull, which is the time that passed in order for the rate to have reached its current value.	**GIVEN:** $\text{rate}_t = 4.50$ dis/min · g C; $\quad\quad\quad\text{rate}_0 = 15.3$ dis/min · g C; **FIND:** t
STRATEGIZE Use the expression for half-life (Equation 19.1) to find the rate constant (k) from the half-life for C-14, which is 5730 yr (Table 19.3).	**CONCEPTUAL PLAN** $t_{1/2} \longrightarrow k$ $t_{1/2} = \dfrac{0.693}{k}$
Use the value of the rate constant and the initial and current rates to find t from the integrated rate law (Equation 19.4).	$k, \text{rate}_t, \text{rate}_0 \longrightarrow t$ $\ln \dfrac{\text{rate}_t}{\text{rate}_0} = -kt$

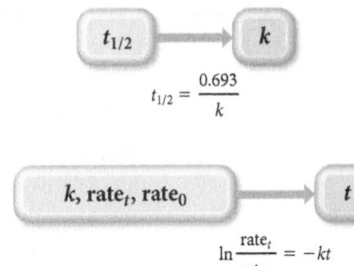

SOLVE Follow your plan. Begin by finding the rate constant from the half-life.	**SOLUTION** $$t_{1/2} = \frac{0.693}{k}$$ $$k = \frac{0.693}{t_{1/2}} = \frac{0.693}{5730 \text{ yr}}$$ $$= 1.209 \times 10^{-4}/\text{yr}$$
Substitute the rate constant and the initial and current rates into the integrated rate law and solve for t.	$$\ln \frac{rate_t}{rate_0} = -kt$$ $$t = -\frac{\ln \dfrac{rate_t}{rate_0}}{k} = -\frac{\ln \dfrac{4.50 \text{ dis/min} \cdot \text{g C}}{15.3 \text{ dis/min} \cdot \text{g C}}}{1.209 \times 10^{-4}/\text{yr}}$$ $$= 1.0 \times 10^4 \text{ yr}$$

CHECK The units of the answer (yr) are correct. The magnitude of the answer is about 10,000 years, which is a little less than two half-lives. This value is reasonable given that two half-lives would result in a decay rate of about 3.8 dis/min·g C.

FOR PRACTICE 19.5

A researcher claims that an ancient scroll originated from Greek scholars in about 500 B.C. A measure of its carbon-14 decay rate gives a value that is 89% of that found in living organisms. How old is the scroll and could it be authentic?

 ## Chemistry in Your Day

Radiocarbon Dating and the Shroud of Turin

The Shroud of Turin—kept in the cathedral of Turin in Italy—is an old linen cloth that bears a mysterious image. Many people have interpreted the image as that of a man who appears to have been crucified. The image becomes clearer if the shroud is photographed and viewed as a negative. Some claim that the shroud is the original burial cloth of Jesus, miraculously imprinted with his image. In 1988, the Roman Catholic Church chose three independent laboratories to perform radiocarbon dating on the shroud. The laboratories took samples of the cloth and measured the carbon-14 content. The three independent laboratories all arrived at similar results—the shroud was made from linen originating in about A.D. 1325. Although some have disputed the results (and continue to do so), and although no scientific test is 100% reliable, newspapers around the world announced that the Shroud did not date back to biblical times.

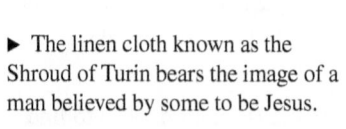
▶ The linen cloth known as the Shroud of Turin bears the image of a man believed by some to be Jesus.

Uranium/Lead Dating

Radiocarbon dating can only measure the ages of objects that were once living and that are relatively young (<50,000 years). Other radiometric dating techniques can measure the ages of prehistoric objects that were never alive. The most dependable technique relies on the ratio of uranium-238 to lead-206 within igneous rocks (rocks of volcanic origin). This technique measures the time that has passed since the rock solidified (at which point the "radiometric clock" was reset).

Since U-238 decays into Pb-206 with a half-life of 4.5×10^9 years, the relative amounts of U-238 and Pb-206 in a uranium-containing rock reveal its age. For example, if a rock originally contained U-238 and currently contains equal amounts of U-238 and Pb-206, it would be 4.5 billion years old, assuming that the rock did not contain any Pb-206 when it was formed. The latter assumption can be tested because the lead that results from the decay of uranium has a different isotopic composition than the lead that was deposited in rocks at the time of their formation. Example 19.6 shows how the relative amounts of Pb-206 and U-238 in a rock can be used to estimate its age.

EXAMPLE 19.6 Using Uranium/Lead Dating to Estimate the Age of a Rock

A meteor contains 0.556 g of Pb-206 to every 1.00 g of U-238. Assuming that the meteor did not contain any Pb-206 at the time of its formation, determine the age of the meteor. Uranium-238 decays to lead-206 with a half-life of 4.5 billion years.

SORT You are given the current masses of Pb-206 and U-238 in a rock and asked to find its age. You are also given the half-life of U-238.	**GIVEN:** $m_{\text{U-238}} = 1.00$ g; $m_{\text{Pb-206}} = 0.556$ g; $t_{1/2} = 4.5 \times 10^9$ yr **FIND:** t

STRATEGIZE Use the integrated rate law (Equation 19.3) to solve this problem. To do so, you must first determine the value of the rate constant (k) from the half-life expression (Equation 19.1). Before substituting into the integrated rate law, you also need the ratio of the current amount of U-238 to the original amount (N_t/N_0). The current mass of uranium is simply 1.00 g. The initial mass includes the current mass (1.00 g) plus the mass that has decayed into lead-206, which can be determined from the current mass of Pb-206. Use the value of the rate constant and the initial and current amounts of U-238 along with the integrated rate law to find t.	**CONCEPTUAL PLAN** $t_{1/2} \longrightarrow k$ $t_{1/2} = \dfrac{0.693}{k}$ g Pb-206 $\longrightarrow$ mol Pb-206 $\longrightarrow$ mol U-238 $\longrightarrow$ g U-238 $\dfrac{1 \text{ mol Pb}}{206 \text{ g Pb}}$ $\dfrac{1 \text{ mol U}}{1 \text{ mol Pb}}$ $\dfrac{238 \text{ g U}}{1 \text{ mol U}}$ $k, N_t, N_0 \longrightarrow t$ $\ln \dfrac{N_t}{N_0} = -kt$

SOLVE Follow your plan. Begin by finding the rate constant from the half-life.	**SOLUTION** $t_{1/2} = \dfrac{0.693}{k}$ $k = \dfrac{0.693}{t_{1/2}} = \dfrac{0.693}{4.5 \times 10^9 \text{ yr}}$ $= 1.5\underline{4} \times 10^{-10}/\text{yr}$

Determine the mass in grams of U-238 that is required to form the given mass of Pb-206.	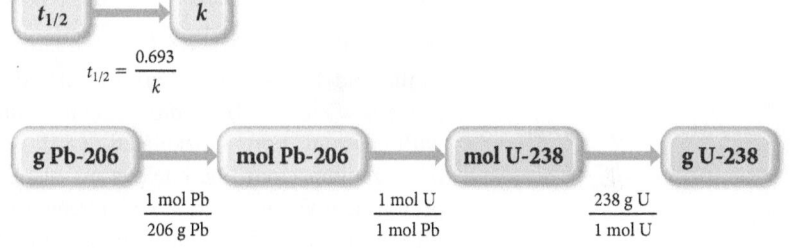 $= 0.642\underline{4}$ g U-238

Substitute the rate constant and the initial and current masses of U-238 into the integrated rate law and solve for t. (The initial mass of U-238 is the sum of the current mass and the mass that is required to form the given mass of Pb-206.)	$\ln \dfrac{N_t}{N_0} = -kt$ $t = -\dfrac{\ln \dfrac{N_t}{N_0}}{k} = -\dfrac{\ln \dfrac{1.00 \text{ g}}{1.00 \text{ g} + 0.642\underline{4} \text{ g}}}{1.5\underline{4} \times 10^{-10}/\text{yr}}$ $= 3.2 \times 10^9$ yr

CHECK The units of the answer (yr) are correct. The magnitude of the answer is about 3.2 billion years, which is less than one half-life. This value is reasonable given that less than half of the uranium in the meteor has decayed into lead.

FOR PRACTICE 19.6
A rock contains a Pb-206 to U-238 mass ratio of 0.145 : 1.00. Assuming that the rock did not contain any Pb-206 at the time of its formation, determine its age.

The age of the universe is estimated from its expansion rate, which can be measured by examining changes in the wavelength of light from distant galaxies.

The Age of Earth The uranium/lead radiometric dating technique as well as other radiometric dating techniques (such as the decay of potassium-40 to argon-40) have been widely used to measure the ages of rocks on Earth and have produced highly consistent results. Rocks with ages greater than 3.5 billion years have been found on every continent. The oldest rocks have an age of approximately 4.0 billion years, establishing a lower limit for Earth's age (Earth must be at least as old as its oldest rocks). The ages of about 70 meteorites that have struck Earth have also been extensively studied and have been found to be about 4.5 billion years old. Since the meteorites were formed at the same time as our solar system (which includes Earth), the best estimate for Earth's age is therefore about 4.5 billion years. That age is consistent with the estimated age of our universe—about 13.7 billion years.

19.7 The Discovery of Fission: The Atomic Bomb and Nuclear Power

The element with atomic number 100 is named fermium in honor of Enrico Fermi.

In the mid-1930s Enrico Fermi (1901–1954), an Italian physicist, attempted to synthesize a new element by bombarding uranium—the heaviest known element at that time—with neutrons. Fermi speculated that if a neutron could be incorporated into the nucleus of a uranium atom, the nucleus might undergo beta decay, converting a neutron into a proton. If that happened, a new element, with atomic number 93, would be synthesized for the first time. The nuclear equation for the process is shown here.

$$^{238}_{92}\text{U} + ^{1}_{0}\text{n} \longrightarrow ^{239}_{92}\text{U} \longrightarrow ^{239}_{93}\text{X} + ^{0}_{-1}\text{e}$$

Neutron — Newly synthesized element

Fermi performed the experiment and detected the emission of beta particles. However, his results were inconclusive. Had he synthesized a new element? Fermi never chemically examined the products to determine their composition and therefore could not say with certainty that he had.

The element with atomic number 109 is named meitnerium in honor of Lise Meitner.

Three researchers in Germany—Lise Meitner (1878–1968), Fritz Strassmann (1902–1980), and Otto Hahn (1879–1968)—repeated Fermi's experiments, and then performed careful chemical analysis of the products. What they found in the products—several elements *lighter* than uranium—would change the world forever. On January 6, 1939, Meitner, Strassmann, and Hahn reported that the neutron bombardment of uranium resulted in **nuclear fission**—the splitting of the uranium atom. The nucleus of the neutron-bombarded uranium atom had been split into barium, krypton, and other smaller products. They also determined that the process emits enormous amounts of energy. A nuclear equation for a fission reaction, showing how uranium breaks apart into the daughter nuclides, is shown here.

$$^{235}_{92}\text{U} + ^{1}_{0}\text{n} \longrightarrow ^{140}_{56}\text{Ba} + ^{93}_{36}\text{Kr} + 3\,^{1}_{0}\text{n} + \text{energy}$$

Fission Chain Reaction

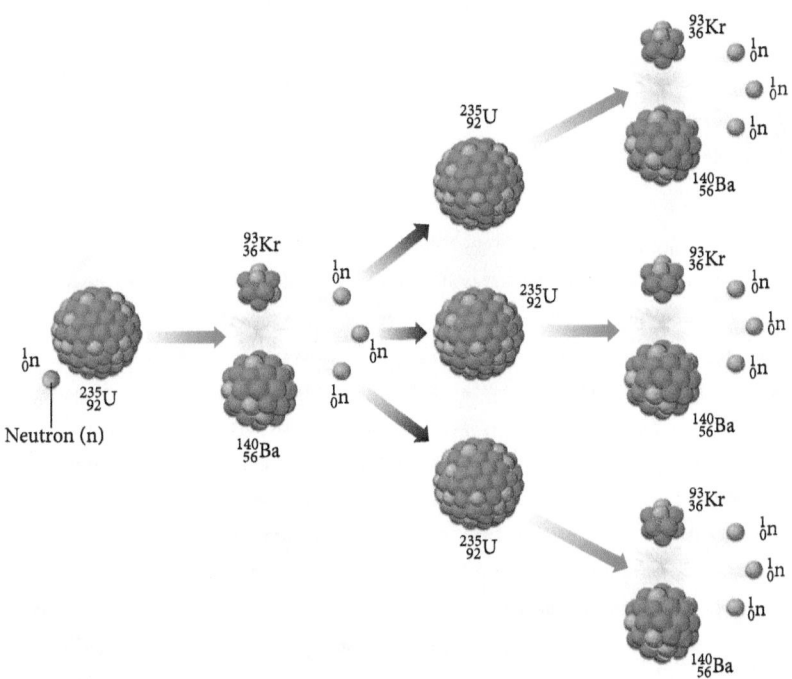

▲ **FIGURE 19.10 A Self-Amplifying Chain Reaction**   The fission of one U-235 nucleus emits neutrons that can then initiate fission in other U-235 nuclei, resulting in a chain reaction that releases enormous amounts of energy.

Notice that the initial uranium atom is the U-235 isotope, which constitutes less than 1% of all naturally occurring uranium. U-238, the most abundant uranium isotope, does not undergo fission. Notice also that the process produces three neutrons, which have the potential to initiate fission in three other U-235 atoms.

Scientists quickly realized that a sample rich in U-235 could undergo a **chain reaction** in which neutrons produced by the fission of one uranium nucleus would induce fission in other uranium nuclei (Figure 19.10 ▲). This self-amplifying reaction is capable of producing an enormous amount of energy. This is the energy that is harnessed in an atomic bomb. However, to make a bomb, a **critical mass** of U-235—enough U-235 to produce a self-sustaining reaction—is necessary. Fearing that Nazi Germany would develop such a bomb, several U.S. scientists persuaded Albert Einstein, the most famous scientist of the time, to write a letter to President Franklin Roosevelt warning of this possibility. Einstein wrote, ". . . and it is conceivable—though much less certain— that extremely powerful bombs of a new type may thus be constructed. A single bomb of this type, carried by boat and exploded in a port, might very well destroy the whole port together with some of the surrounding territory."

Einstein's letter convinced Roosevelt, and in 1941 he assembled the resources to begin the costliest scientific project ever attempted. The top-secret endeavor was called the *Manhattan Project* and its main goal was to build an atomic bomb before the Germans did. The project was led by physicist J. R. Oppenheimer (1904–1967) at a high-security research facility in Los Alamos, New Mexico. Four years later, on July 16, 1945, the world's first nuclear weapon was successfully detonated at a test site in New Mexico. The first atomic bomb exploded with a force equivalent to 18,000 tons of dynamite. Ironically, the Germans—who had *not* made a successful nuclear bomb— had already been defeated by this time. Instead, the United States used the atomic bomb on Japan. One bomb was dropped on Hiroshima and a second bomb was dropped on Nagasaki. Together, the bombs killed approximately 200,000 people and led to Japan's surrender.

▲ Lise Meitner in Otto Hahn's Berlin laboratory. Together with Hahn and Fritz Strassmann, Meitner determined that U-235 could undergo nuclear fission.

▲ On July 16, 1945, in the New Mexico desert, the world's first atomic bomb was detonated. It had the power of 18,000 tons of dynamite.

```
                                               Albert Einstein
                                               Old Grove Rd.
                                               Nassau Point
                                               Peconic, Long Island

                                               August 2nd, 1939

        F.D. Roosevelt,
        President of the United States,
        White House
        Washington, D.C.


        Sir:

             Some recent work by E.Fermi and L. Szilard, which has been com-
        municated to me in manuscript, leads me to expect that the element uran-
        ium may be turned into a new and important source of energy in the im-
        mediate future. Certain aspects of the situation which has arisen seem
        to call for watchfulness and, if necessary, quick action on the part
        of the Administration. I believe therefore that it is my duty to bring
        to your attention the following facts and recommendations:

             In the course of the last four months it has been made probable -
        through the work of Joliot in France as well as Fermi and Szilard in
        America - that it may become possible to set up a nuclear chain reaction
        in a large mass of uranium,by which vast amounts of power and large quant-
        ities of new radium-like elements would be generated. Now it appears
        almost certain that this could be achieved in the immediate future.

             This new phenomenon would also lead to the construction of bombs,
        and it is conceivable - though much less certain - that extremely power-
        ful bombs of a new type may thus be constructed. A single bomb of this
        type, carried by boat and exploded in a port, might very well destroy
        the whole port together with some of the surrounding territory. However,
        such bombs might very well prove to be too heavy for transportation by
        air.
```

▲ Einstein's letter (part of which is shown here) helped persuade Franklin Roosevelt to begin research into the building of a fission bomb.

Nuclear Power: Using Fission to Generate Electricity

Nuclear reactions, such as fission, generate enormous amounts of energy. In a nuclear bomb, the energy is released all at once. The energy can also be released more slowly and used for peaceful purposes such as electricity generation. In the United States, nuclear fission generates about 20% of electricity. In some other countries, nuclear fission generates as much as 70% of electricity. To get an idea of the amount of energy released during fission, imagine a hypothetical nuclear-powered car. Suppose the fuel for such a car was a uranium cylinder about the size of a pencil. How often would you have to refuel the car? The energy content of the uranium cylinder is equivalent to about 1000 twenty-gallon tanks of gasoline. If you refuel your gasoline-powered car once a week, your nuclear-powered car could go 1000 weeks—almost 20 years— before refueling.

Similarly, a nuclear-powered electricity generation plant can produce a lot of electricity from a small amount of fuel. Such plants exploit the heat created by fission, using it to boil water and make steam, which then turns the turbine on a generator to produce electricity (Figure 19.11 ▶). The fission reaction occurs in the nuclear core of the power plant. The core consists of uranium fuel rods—enriched to about 3.5% U-235— interspersed between retractable neutron-absorbing control rods. When the control rods

Nuclear Reactor

◄ FIGURE 19.11 A Nuclear Reactor
The fission of U-235 in the core of a nuclear power plant generates heat that creates steam and turns a turbine on an electrical generator. Control rods are raised or lowered to control the fission reaction. (Note that the water carrying heat away from the reactor core is contained within its own pipes and does not come into direct contact with the steam that drives the turbines.)

are fully retracted from the fuel rod assembly, the chain reaction can occur. When the control rods are fully inserted into the fuel assembly, however, they absorb the neutrons that would otherwise induce fission, shutting down the chain reaction. By retracting or inserting the control rods, the operator can increase or decrease the rate of fission. In this way, the fission reaction is controlled to produce the right amount of heat needed for electricity generation. In case of a power failure, the control rods automatically drop into the fuel rod assembly, shutting down the fission reaction.

A typical nuclear power plant generates enough electricity for a city of about 1 million people and uses about 50 kg of fuel per day. In contrast, a coal-burning power plant uses about 2,000,000 kg of fuel to generate the same amount of electricity. Furthermore, a nuclear power plant generates no air pollution and no greenhouse gases. A coal-burning power plant emits pollutants such as carbon monoxide, nitrogen oxides, and sulfur oxides. Coal-burning power plants also emit carbon dioxide, a greenhouse gas.

Nuclear power generation, however, is not without problems. Foremost among them is the danger of nuclear accidents. In spite of safety precautions, the fission reaction occurring in a nuclear power plant can overheat. The most famous examples of this occurred in Chernobyl, in the former Soviet Union, on April 26, 1986, and at the Fukushima Daiichi Nuclear Power Plant in Japan in March of 2011.

In the Chernobyl incident, operators of the plant were performing an experiment designed to reduce maintenance costs. In order to perform the experiment they had to disable many of the safety features of the reactor core. The experiment failed with disastrous results. The nuclear core, composed partly of graphite, overheated and began to burn. The accident caused 31 immediate deaths and produced a fire that scattered radioactive debris into the atmosphere, making much of the surrounding land (within about a 32-kilometer radius) uninhabitable. As bad as the accident was, however, it was a not a nuclear detonation. A nuclear power plant *cannot* become a nuclear bomb. The uranium fuel used in electricity generation is not sufficiently enriched in U-235 to produce a nuclear detonation. U.S. nuclear power plants have additional safety features designed to prevent similar accidents. For example, U.S. nuclear power plants have large containment structures to contain radioactive debris in the event of an accident.

▲ In 1986, the reactor core at Chernobyl (in what is now Ukraine) overheated, exploded, and destroyed part of the containment structure. The release of radioactive nuclides into the environment forced the government to relocate over 335,000 people. It is estimated that there may eventually be several thousand additional cancer deaths among the exposed populations.

Reactor cores in the United States are not made of graphite and cannot burn in the way that the Chernobyl core did.

In the 2011 Japanese accident, a 9.0 magnitude earthquake triggered a tsunami that flooded the coastal plant and caused the cooling system pumps to fail. Several of the nuclear cores within the plant dramatically overheated and at least one of the cores experienced a partial meltdown (in which the fuel gets so hot that it melts). The accident was intensified by the loss of water in the fuel storage ponds (pools of water used to keep spent fuel as well as future fuel cool), which caused the fuel stored in the ponds to also overheat. The release of radiation into the environment, however, while significant, was lower in Japan than at Chernobyl. As of press time, no radioactivity-related deaths have been reported at the Fukushima plant or the surrounding area. The cleanup of the site, however, will continue for many years.

A second problem associated with nuclear power is waste disposal. Although the amount of nuclear fuel used in electricity generation is small compared to other fuels, the products of the reaction are radioactive and have long half-lives. What do we do with this waste? Currently, in the United States, nuclear waste is stored on site at the nuclear power plants. A single permanent disposal site was being developed in Yucca Mountain, Nevada to store U.S. waste. However, in the Spring of 2010, the Obama administration halted the development of this project and formed the Blue Ribbon Commission on America's Nuclear Future to explore alternatives.

19.8 Converting Mass to Energy: Mass Defect and Nuclear Binding Energy

Nuclear fission produces large amounts of energy. But where does the energy come from? We can answer this question by carefully examining the masses of the reactants and products in the fission equation from Section 19.7.

$$^{235}_{92}\text{U} + ^{1}_{0}\text{n} \longrightarrow ^{140}_{56}\text{Ba} + ^{93}_{36}\text{Kr} + 3^{1}_{0}\text{n}$$

Mass Reactants		Mass Products	
$^{235}_{92}$U	235.04392 amu	$^{140}_{56}$Ba	139.910581 amu
$^{1}_{0}$n	1.00866 amu	$^{93}_{36}$Kr	92.931130 amu
		3^{1}_{0}n	3(1.00866) amu
Total	**236.05258 amu**		**235.86769 amu**

In a chemical reaction, there are also mass changes associated with the emission or absorption of energy. Because the energy involved in chemical reactions is so much smaller than that of nuclear reactions, however, these mass changes are completely negligible.

Notice that the products of the nuclear reaction have *less mass* than the reactants. The missing mass is converted to energy. In Chapter 1, we learned that matter is conserved in chemical reactions. In nuclear reactions matter can be converted to energy. The relationship between the amount of matter that is lost and the amount of energy formed is given by Einstein's famous equation relating the two quantities:

$$E = mc^2$$

where E is the energy produced, m is the mass lost, and c is the speed of light. For example, in the fission reaction just shown, we calculate the quantity of energy produced as follows:

$$\text{Mass lost } (m) = 236.05258 \text{ amu} - 235.86769 \text{ amu}$$
$$= 0.18489 \text{ amu} \times \frac{1.66054 \times 10^{-27} \text{ kg}}{1 \text{ amu}}$$
$$= 3.0702 \times 10^{-28} \text{ kg}$$

$$\text{Energy produced } (E) = mc^2$$
$$= 3.0702 \times 10^{-28} \text{ kg } (2.9979 \times 10^8 \text{ m/s})^2$$
$$= 2.7593 \times 10^{-11} \text{ J}$$

The result (2.7593×10^{-11} J) is the energy produced when one nucleus of U-235 undergoes fission. This may not seem like much energy, but it is only the energy produced by the fission of a *single* nucleus. Let's calculate the energy produced *per mole* of U-235 to compare it to a chemical reaction.

$$2.7593 \times 10^{-11} \frac{J}{U\text{-}235 \text{ atoms}} \times \frac{6.0221 \times 10^{23} \text{ U-235 atoms}}{1 \text{ mol U-235}}$$

$$= 1.6617 \times 10^{13} \text{ J/mol U-235}$$

The energy produced by the fission of 1 mol of U-235 is about 17 billion kJ. In contrast, a highly exothermic chemical reaction produces 1000 kJ per mole of reactant. Fission produces over a million times more energy per mole than chemical processes.

Mass Defect

We can examine the formation of a stable nucleus from its component particles as a nuclear reaction in which mass is converted to energy. For example, consider the formation of helium-4 from its components:

$$2\,{}^{1}_{1}H + 2\,{}^{1}_{0}n \longrightarrow {}^{4}_{2}He$$

Mass Reactants		Mass Products	
$2\,{}^{1}_{1}H$	2(1.00783) amu	${}^{4}_{2}He$	4.00260 amu
$2\,{}^{1}_{0}n$	2(1.00866) amu		
Total	**4.03298 amu**	**4.00260 amu**	

> The electrons are contained on the left side in the two ${}^{1}_{1}H$, and on the right side in ${}^{4}_{2}He$. If you write the equation using only two protons on the left (${}^{1}_{1}p$), you must also add two electrons to the left.

A helium-4 atom has less mass than the sum of the masses of its separate components. This difference in mass, known as the **mass defect**, exists in all stable nuclei. The energy corresponding to the mass defect—obtained by substituting the mass defect into the equation $E = mc^2$—is known as the **nuclear binding energy**, the amount of energy required to break apart the nucleus into its component nucleons.

Although chemists typically report energies in joules, nuclear physicists often use the electron volt (eV) or megaelectron volt (MeV): 1 MeV $= 1.602 \times 10^{-13}$ J. Unlike energy in joules, which is usually reported per mole, energy in electron volts is usually reported per nucleus. A particularly useful conversion for calculating and reporting nuclear binding energies is the relationship between amu (mass units) and MeV (energy units).

> An electron volt is defined as the kinetic energy of an electron that has been accelerated through a potential difference of 1 V.

$$1 \text{ amu} = 931.5 \text{ MeV}$$

A mass defect of 1 amu, when substituted into the equation $E = mc^2$, gives an energy of 931.5 MeV. Using this conversion factor, we can readily calculate the binding energy of the helium nucleus.

$$\text{Mass defect} = 4.03298 \text{ amu} - 4.00260 \text{ amu}$$
$$= 0.03038 \text{ amu}$$

$$\text{Nuclear binding energy} = 0.03038 \text{ amu} \times \frac{931.5 \text{ MeV}}{1 \text{ amu}}$$
$$= 28.30 \text{ MeV}$$

So the binding energy of the helium nucleus is 28.30 MeV. In order to compare the binding energy of one nucleus to that of another, we calculate the *binding energy per nucleon*, which is the nuclear binding energy of a nuclide divided by the number of nucleons in the nuclide. For helium-4, we calculate the binding energy per nucleon as follows:

$$\text{Binding energy per nucleon} = \frac{28.30 \text{ MeV}}{4 \text{ nucleons}}$$
$$= 7.075 \text{ MeV per nucleon}$$

We can calculate the binding energy per nucleon for other nuclides in the same way. For example, the nuclear binding energy of carbon-12 is 7.680 MeV per nucleon. Since the binding energy per nucleon of carbon-12 is greater than that of helium-4, we conclude the carbon-12 nuclide is more *stable* (it has lower potential energy).

EXAMPLE 19.7 Mass Defect and Nuclear Binding Energy

Calculate the mass defect and nuclear binding energy per nucleon (in MeV) for C-16, a radioactive isotope of carbon with a mass of 16.014701 amu.

SOLUTION

Calculate the mass defect as the difference between the mass of one C-16 atom and the sum of the masses of 6 hydrogen atoms and 10 neutrons.	Mass defect $= 6(\text{mass } {}_{1}^{1}\text{H}) + 10(\text{mass } {}_{0}^{1}\text{n}) - \text{mass } {}_{6}^{16}\text{C}$ $= 6(1.00783 \text{ amu}) + 10(1.00866 \text{ amu}) - 16.014701 \text{ amu}$ $= 0.118879 \text{ amu}$
Calculate the nuclear binding energy by converting the mass defect (in amu) into MeV. (Use 1 amu = 931.5 MeV.)	$0.118879 \text{ amu} \times \dfrac{931.5 \text{ MeV}}{\text{amu}} = 110.74 \text{ MeV}$
Determine the nuclear binding energy per nucleon by dividing by the number of nucleons in the nucleus.	Nuclear binding energy per nucleon $= \dfrac{110.74 \text{ MeV}}{16 \text{ nucleons}}$ $= 6.921 \text{ MeV/nucleon}$

FOR PRACTICE 19.7

Calculate the mass defect and nuclear binding energy per nucleon (in MeV) for U-238, which has a mass of 238.050784 amu.

Figure 19.12 ▼ shows the binding energy per nucleon plotted as a function of mass number (*A*). The binding energy per nucleon is relatively low for small mass numbers and increases until about *A* = 60, where it reaches a maximum. Nuclides with mass numbers of about 60, therefore, are among the most stable. Beyond *A* = 60, the binding energy per nucleon decreases again. Figure 19.12 illustrates why nuclear fission is a highly exothermic process. When a heavy nucleus, such as U-235, breaks up into smaller nuclei, such as Ba-140 and Kr-93, the binding energy per nucleon increases. This is analogous to a chemical reaction in which weak bonds break and strong bonds form. In both cases, the

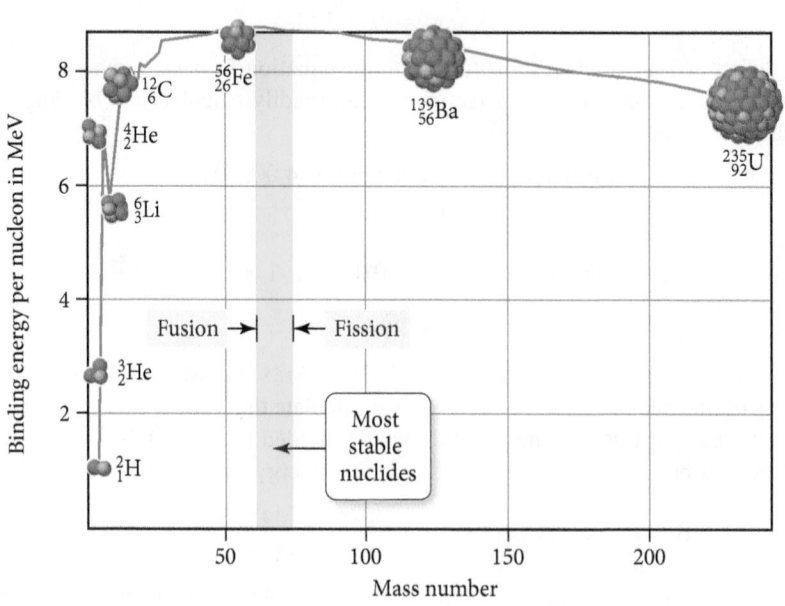

The Curve of Binding Energy

▲ **FIGURE 19.12 Nuclear Binding Energy per Nucleon**   The nuclear binding energy per nucleon (a measure of the stability of a nucleus) reaches a maximum at Fe-56. Energy can be obtained either by breaking a heavy nucleus up into lighter ones (fission) or by combining lighter nuclei into heavier ones (fusion).

process is exothermic. Figure 19.12 also reveals that the *combining* of two lighter nuclei (below $A = 60$) to form a heavier nucleus should be exothermic as well. This process is called *nuclear fusion*, which we discuss in the next section of this chapter.

19.9 Nuclear Fusion: The Power of the Sun

Nuclear fission is the *splitting* of a heavy nucleus to form two or more lighter ones. **Nuclear fusion**, by contrast, is the *combination* of two light nuclei to form a heavier one. Both fusion and fission emit large amounts of energy because, as we have just seen, they both form daughter nuclides with greater binding energies per nucleon than the parent nuclides. Nuclear fusion is the energy source of stars, including our sun. In stars, hydrogen atoms fuse together to form helium atoms, emitting energy in the process.

Nuclear fusion is also the basis of modern nuclear weapons called hydrogen bombs. A modern hydrogen bomb has up to 1000 times the explosive force of the first atomic bombs. These bombs employ the fusion reaction shown here:

$$^2_1\text{H} + {}^3_1\text{H} \longrightarrow {}^4_2\text{He} + {}^1_0\text{n}$$

In this reaction, deuterium (the isotope of hydrogen with one neutron) and tritium (the isotope of hydrogen with two neutrons) combine to form helium-4 and a neutron (Figure 19.13 ▶). Because fusion reactions require two positively charged nuclei (which repel each other) to fuse together, extremely high temperatures are required. In a hydrogen bomb, a small fission bomb is detonated first, creating temperatures high enough for fusion to proceed.

Nuclear fusion has been intensely investigated as a way to produce electricity. Because of the higher energy density—fusion provides about 10 times more energy per gram of fuel than does fission—and because the products of the reaction are less problematic than those of fission, fusion holds promise as a future energy source. However, despite concerted efforts, the generation of electricity by fusion remains elusive. One of the main problems is the high temperature required for fusion to occur—no material can withstand those temperatures. Using powerful magnetic fields or laser beams, scientists have succeeded in compressing and heating nuclei to the point where fusion has been initiated and even sustained for brief periods of time (Figure 19.14 ▼). To date, however, the amount of energy generated by fusion reactions has been less than the amount required to get it to occur. After years of spending billions of dollars on fusion research, the U.S. Congress has reduced funding for these projects. Whether fusion will ever be a viable energy source remains uncertain.

Deuterium-Tritium Fusion Reaction

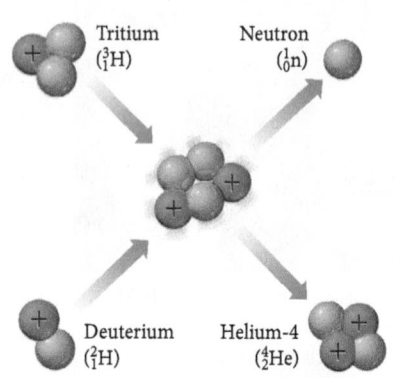

▲ **FIGURE 19.13 A Nuclear Fusion Reaction**   In this reaction, two heavy isotopes of hydrogen, deuterium (hydrogen-2) and tritium (hydrogen-3), fuse to form helium-4 and a neutron.

Tokamak Fusion Reactor

Coils generate magnetic fields to contain fusing nuclei

Plasma

◀ **FIGURE 19.14 Tokamak Fusion Reactor**   A tokamak uses powerful magnetic fields to confine nuclear fuel at the enormous temperatures needed for fusion. The high temperatures produce a plasma, a state of matter in which some fraction of the atoms are ionized.

19.10 Nuclear Transmutation and Transuranium Elements

One of the goals of the early chemists of the Middle Ages, who were known as *alchemists*, was the transformation of ordinary metals into gold. Many alchemists hoped to turn low-cost metals, such as lead or tin, into precious metals, and in this way become wealthy. These alchemists were never successful because their attempts were merely chemical— they mixed different metals together or tried to get them to react with other substances in order to turn them into gold. In a chemical reaction, an element retains its identity, so a less valuable metal—such as lead—always remains lead, even when it forms a compound with another element.

Nuclear reactions, by contrast, result in the transformation of one element into another, a process known as **transmutation**. We have already seen how this occurs in radioactive decay, in fission, and in fusion. In addition, other nuclear reactions that transmute elements are possible. For example, in 1919 Ernest Rutherford bombarded nitrogen-17 with alpha particles to form oxygen:

$$^{14}_{7}\text{N} + {}^{4}_{2}\text{He} \longrightarrow {}^{17}_{8}\text{O} + {}^{1}_{1}\text{H}$$

Irène Joliot-Curie (daughter of Marie Curie) and her husband Frédéric bombarded aluminum-27 with alpha particles to form phosphorus:

$$^{27}_{13}\text{Al} + {}^{4}_{2}\text{He} \longrightarrow {}^{30}_{15}\text{P} + {}^{1}_{0}\text{n}$$

▲ The Joliot-Curies won the 1935 Nobel Prize in Chemistry for their work on nuclear transmutation.

In the 1930s, scientists began building devices that accelerate particles to high velocities, opening the door to even more possibilities. These devices are generally of two types, the **linear accelerator** and the **cyclotron**.

In a single-stage linear accelerator, a charged particle such as a proton is accelerated in an evacuated tube. The accelerating force is provided by a potential difference (or voltage) between the ends of the tube. In multistage linear accelerators, such as the Stanford Linear Accelerator (SLAC) at Stanford University, a series of tubes of increasing length are connected to a source of alternating voltage, as shown in Figure 19.15 ▼. The voltage alternates in such a way that, as a positively charged particle leaves a particular tube, that tube becomes positively charged, repelling the particle to the next tube. At the same time, the tube that the particle is now approaching becomes negatively charged, pulling the particle toward it. This continues throughout the linear accelerator, allowing the particle to be accelerated to velocities up to 90% of the speed of light. When particles of this speed collide with a target, they produce a shower of subatomic particles that can be studied. For example, researchers using the Stanford Linear Accelerator were awarded the 1990 Nobel Prize in physics for discovering evidence that protons and neutrons were composed of still smaller subatomic particles called quarks.

In a cyclotron, a similarly alternating voltage is used to accelerate a charged particle, only this time the alternating voltage is applied between the two semicircular halves of the cyclotron (Figure 19.16 ▶). A charged particle originally in the middle of the two semicircles is accelerated back and forth between them. Additional magnets cause the particle to move in a spiral path. As the charged particle spirals out from the center, it gains speed and eventually exits the cyclotron aimed at the target.

▶ **FIGURE 19.15 The Linear Accelerator** In a multistage linear accelerator, the charge on successive tubes is rapidly alternated in such a way that as a positively charged particle leaves a particular tube, that tube becomes positively charged, repelling the particle toward the next tube. At the same time, the tube that the particle is now approaching becomes negatively charged, pulling the particle toward it. This process repeats through a number of tubes until the particle has been accelerated to a high velocity.

▲ **FIGURE 19.16 The Cyclotron** In a cyclotron, two semicircular D-shaped structures are subjected to an alternating voltage. A charged particle, starting from a point between the two, is accelerated back and forth between them, while additional magnets cause the particle to move in a spiral path.

▲ The Stanford Linear Accelerator (top) is located at Stanford University in California. The Fermi National Accelerator Laboratory complex in Batavia, Illinois (bottom), includes two cyclotrons in a figure-8 configuration.

With linear accelerators or cyclotrons, all sorts of nuclear transmutations can be achieved. In this way, scientists have made nuclides that don't normally exist in nature. For example, uranium-238 can be made to collide with carbon-12 to form an element with atomic number 98:

$$\ce{^{238}_{92}U} + \ce{^{12}_{6}C} \longrightarrow \ce{^{244}_{98}Cf} + 6\ce{^{1}_{0}n}$$

This element was named californium (Cf) because it was first produced (by a slightly different nuclear reaction) at the University of California at Berkeley. Many other nuclides with atomic numbers larger than that of uranium have been synthesized since the 1940s. These synthetic elements—called transuranium elements—have been added to the periodic table.

Most synthetic elements are unstable and have very short half-lives. Some exist for only fractions of a second after they are made.

Conceptual Connection 19.4 Nuclear Transformations

Californium-252 is bombarded with a boron-10 nucleus to produce another nuclide and six neutrons. What nuclide forms?

19.11 The Effects of Radiation on Life

As we discussed in Section 19.2, the energy associated with radioactivity can ionize molecules. When radiation ionizes important molecules in living cells, problems can develop. The ingestion of radioactive materials—especially alpha and beta emitters—is particularly dangerous because the radioactivity once inside the body can do even more damage. The effects of radiation can be divided into three different types: acute radiation damage, increased cancer risk, and genetic effects.

Acute Radiation Damage

Acute radiation damage results from exposure to large amounts of radiation in a short period of time. The main sources of this kind of exposure are nuclear bombs and exposed nuclear reactor cores. These high levels of radiation kill large numbers of cells. Rapidly dividing cells, such as those in the immune system and the intestinal lining, are most susceptible. Consequently, people exposed to high levels of radiation have weakened immune systems and a lowered ability to absorb nutrients from food. In milder cases, recovery is possible with time. In more extreme cases, death results, often from infection.

Increased Cancer Risk

Lower doses of radiation over extended periods of time can increase cancer risk. Radiation increases cancer risk because it can damage DNA, the molecules in cells that carry instructions for cell growth and replication. When the DNA within a cell is damaged, the cell normally dies. Occasionally, however, changes in DNA cause cells to grow abnormally and to become cancerous. These cancerous cells grow into tumors that can spread and, in some cases, cause death. Cancer risk increases with increasing radiation exposure. However, cancer is so prevalent and has so many convoluted causes that determining an exact threshold for increased cancer risk from radiation exposure is difficult.

| We explain DNA in more detail in Chapter 21.

Genetic Defects

Another possible effect of radiation exposure is genetic defects in future generations. If radiation damages the DNA of reproductive cells—such as eggs or sperm—then the offspring that develop from those cells may have genetic abnormalities. Genetic defects of this type have been observed in laboratory animals exposed to high levels of radiation. However, such genetic defects—with a clear causal connection to radiation exposure—have yet to be verified in humans, even in studies of Hiroshima survivors.

Measuring Radiation Exposure

We can measure radiation exposure in a number of different ways. One method is to measure the number of decay events to which a person is exposed. The unit used for this type of exposure measurement is the *curie* (Ci), defined as 3.7×10^{10} decay events per second. A person exposed to a curie of radiation from an alpha emitter is bombarded by 3.7×10^{10} alpha particles per second. However, we already know that different kinds of radiation produce different effects. For example, we know that alpha radiation has a much greater ionizing power than beta radiation. Consequently, a certain number of alpha decays occurring within a person's body (due to the ingestion of an alpha emitter) would do more damage than the same number of beta decays. If the alpha emitter and beta emitter were external to the body, however, the radiation from the alpha emitter would largely be stopped by clothing or the skin (due to the low penetrating power of alpha radiation), while the radiation from the beta emitter could penetrate the skin and cause more damage. Consequently, the curie is not an effective measure of how much biological tissue damage the radiation actually does.

A better way to assess radiation exposure is to measure the amount of energy actually absorbed by body tissue. The units used for this type of exposure measurement are the *gray* (Gy), which corresponds to 1 J of energy absorbed per kilogram of body tissue, and the *rad* (for *r*adiation *a*bsorbed *d*ose), which corresponds to 0.01 Gy.

$$\text{1 gray (Gy)} = \text{1 J/kg body tissue}$$
$$\text{1 rad} = \text{0.01 J/kg body tissue}$$

Although these units measure the actual energy absorbed by bodily tissues, they still do not account for the amount of damage to biological molecules caused by that energy absorption, which differs from one type of radiation to another and from one type of biological tissue to another. For example, when a gamma ray passes through biological tissue, the energy absorbed is spread out over the long distance that the radiation travels through the body, resulting in a low ionization density within the tissue. When an alpha particle passes through biological tissue, in contrast, the energy is absorbed over a much shorter distance, resulting in a much higher ionization density. The higher ionization density results in greater damage, even though the amount of energy absorbed by the tissue might be the same.

| A *roentgen* is defined as the amount of radiation that produces 2.58×10^{-1} C of charge per kg of air.

Consequently, a correction factor, called the **biological effectiveness factor**, or **RBE** (for *R*elative *B*iological *E*ffectiveness), is usually multiplied by the dose in rads to obtain the dose in a unit called the **rem** for *r*oentgen *e*quivalent *m*an.

$$\text{Dose in rads} \times \text{biological effectiveness factor} = \text{dose in rems}$$

The biological effectiveness factor for alpha radiation, for example, is much higher than that for gamma radiation.

TABLE 19.4 Exposure by Source for Persons Living in the United States

Source	Dose
Natural Radiation	
A 5-hour jet airplane ride	2.5 mrem/trip (0.5 mrem/hr at 39,000 feet) (whole body dose)
Cosmic radiation from outer space	27 mrem/yr (whole body dose)
Terrestrial radiation	28 mrem/yr (whole body dose)
Natural radionuclides in the body	35 mrem/yr (whole body dose)
Radon gas	200 mrem/yr (lung dose)
Diagnostic Medical Procedures	
Chest X-ray	8 mrem (whole body dose)
Dental X-rays (panoramic)	30 mrem (skin dose)
Dental X-rays (two bitewings)	80 mrem (skin dose)
Mammogram	138 mrem per image
Barium enema (X-ray portion only)	406 mrem (bone marrow dose)
Upper gastrointestinal tract test	244 mrem (X-ray portion only) (bone marrow dose)
Thallium heart scan	500 mrem (whole body dose)
Consumer Products	
Building materials	3.5 mrem/year (whole body dose)
Luminous watches (H-3 and Pm-147)	0.04–0.1 mrem/year (whole body dose)
Tobacco products (to smokers of 30 cigarettes per day)	16,000 mrem/year (bronchial epithelial dose)

Source: Department of Health and Human Services, National Institutes of Health.

On average, each of us is exposed to approximately 310 mrem of radiation per year from natural sources shown in Table 19.4. The majority of this exposure comes from radon, one of the products in the uranium decay series. As you can see from Table 19.4, however, some medical procedures also involve exposure levels similar to those received from natural sources. The increased use of computed tomography (CT) scans over the last decade—which have associated exposures of 200–1600 mrem—has raised some concerns about the overuse of that technology in medicine.

It takes much more than the average natural radiation dose or the dose from a medical diagnostic procedure to produce significant health effects in humans. The first measurable effect, a decreased white blood cell count, occurs at instantaneous exposures of approximately 20 rem (Table 19.5). Exposures of 100 rem produce a definite increase in cancer risk, and exposures of over 500 rem often result in death.

> The SI unit that corresponds to the rem is the sievert (Sv). However, the rem is still commonly used in the United States. The conversion factor is 1 rem = 0.01 Sv.

TABLE 19.5 Effects of Instantaneous Radiation Exposure

Approximate Dose (rem)	Probable Outcome
20–100	Decreased white blood cell count; possible increase in cancer risk
100–400	Radiation sickness including vomiting and diarrhea; skin lesions; increase in cancer risk
500	Death (often within 2 months)
1000	Death (often within 2 weeks)
2000	Death (within hours)

Conceptual Connection 19.5 Radiation Exposure

Suppose a person ingests equal amounts of two nuclides, both of which are beta emitters (of roughly equal energy). Nuclide A has a half-life of 8.5 hours and Nuclide B has a half-life of 15.0 hours. Both nuclides are eliminated from the body within 24 hours of ingestion. Which of the two nuclides produces the greater radiation exposure?

19.12 Radioactivity in Medicine and Other Applications

Radioactivity is often perceived as dangerous; however, it is also immensely useful to physicians in the diagnosis and treatment of disease and has numerous other valuable applications. The use of radioactivity in medicine can be broadly divided into *diagnostic techniques* (which diagnose disease) and *therapeutic techniques* (which treat disease).

Diagnosis in Medicine

The use of radioactivity in diagnosis usually involves a **radiotracer**, a radioactive nuclide attached to a compound or introduced into a mixture in order to track the movement of the compound or mixture within the body. Tracers are useful in the diagnosis of disease because of two main factors: (1) the sensitivity with which radioactivity can be detected, and (2) the identical chemical behavior of a radioactive nucleus and its nonradioactive counterpart. For example, the thyroid gland naturally concentrates iodine. When a patient is given small amounts of iodine-131 (a radioactive isotope of iodine), the radioactive iodine accumulates in the thyroid, just as nonradioactive iodine does. However, the radioactive iodine emits radiation, which can then be detected with great sensitivity and used to measure the rate of iodine uptake by the thyroid, and thus to image the gland.

Since different elements are taken up preferentially by different organs or tissues, various radiotracers are used to monitor metabolic activity and image a variety of organs and structures, including the kidneys, heart, brain, gallbladder, bones, and arteries, as shown in Table 19.6. Radiotracers can also be employed to locate infections or cancers within the body. To locate an infection, antibodies are labeled (or tagged) with a radioactive nuclide, such as technetium-99m (where "m" means metastable), and administered to the patient. The tagged antibodies aggregate at the infected site, as described in Section 19.1. Cancerous tumors can be detected because they naturally concentrate phosphorus. When a patient is given phosphorus-32 (a radioactive isotope of phosphorus) or a phosphate compound incorporating another radioactive isotope such as Tc-99m, the tumors concentrate the radioactive substance and become sources of radioactivity that can be detected (Figure 19.17 ◄).

bones for lab

▲ FIGURE 19.17 **A Bone Scan** These images, front and rear views of the human body, were created by the gamma ray emissions of Tc-99m. Such scans are often used to locate cancer that has metastasized (spread) to the bones from a primary tumor elsewhere.

A specialized imaging technique known as **positron emission tomography (PET)** employs positron-emitting nuclides, such as fluorine-18, synthesized in cyclotrons. The fluorine-18 is attached to a metabolically active substance such as glucose and administered to the patient. As the glucose travels through the bloodstream and to the heart and brain, it carries the radioactive fluorine, which decays with a half-life of just under 2 hours. When a fluorine-18 nuclide decays, it emits a positron that immediately combines with any

TABLE 19.6 Common Radiotracers

Nuclide	Type of Emission	Half-Life	Part of Body Studied
Technetium-99m	Gamma (primarily)	6.01 hours	Various organs, bones
Iodine-131	Beta	8.0 days	Thyroid
Iron-59	Beta	44.5 days	Blood, spleen
Thallium-201	Electron capture	3.05 days	Heart
Fluorine-18	Positron emission	1.83 hours	PET studies of heart, brain
Phosphorus-32	Beta	14.3 days	Tumors in various organs

nearby electrons. Since a positron and an electron are antiparticles, they annihilate one other, producing two gamma rays that travel in exactly opposing directions. The gamma rays can be detected by an array of detectors that can locate the point of origin of the rays with great accuracy. The result is a set of highly detailed images that show both the rate of glucose metabolism and structural features of the imaged organ (Figure 19.18 ▶).

▲ **FIGURE 19.18 A PET Scan** The colored areas indicate regions of high metabolic activity in the brain of a schizophrenic patient experiencing hallucinations.

Radiotherapy in Medicine

Because radiation kills cells and is particularly effective at killing rapidly dividing cells, it is often used as a therapy for cancer (cancer cells reproduce much faster than normal cells). Gamma rays are focused on internal tumors to kill them. The gamma ray beam is usually moved in a circular path around the tumor (Figure 19.19 ▼), maximizing the exposure of the tumor while minimizing the exposure of the surrounding healthy tissue. Nonetheless, cancer patients receiving such treatment usually develop the symptoms of radiation sickness, which include vomiting, skin burns, and hair loss.

You may wonder why radiation—which is known to cause cancer—is also used to treat cancer. The answer lies in risk analysis. A cancer patient is normally exposed to radiation doses of about 100 rem. Such a dose increases cancer risk by about 1%. However, if the patient has a 100% chance of dying from the cancer that he already has, such a risk becomes acceptable, especially since there is a significant chance of curing the cancer.

Other Applications

Radioactivity is often used to kill microorganisms. For example, physicians use radiation to sterilize medical devices that are to be surgically implanted. The radiation kills bacteria that might otherwise lead to infection. Similarly, radiation is used to kill bacteria and parasites in foods. Like the pasteurization of milk, the irradiation of foods makes them safer to consume and gives them a longer shelf life (Figure 19.20 ▶). The irradiation of raw meat and poultry kills *E. coli* and *Salmonella*, bacteria that can lead to serious illness and even death when consumed. The

▲ **FIGURE 19.19 Radiotherapy for Cancer** This treatment involves exposing a malignant tumor to gamma rays generated by nuclides such as cobalt-60. The beam is moved in a circular pattern around the tumor to maximize exposure of the tumor to radiation while minimizing the exposure of healthy tissues.

irradiation of food does not, however, make the food itself radioactive, nor does it decrease the nutritional value of the food. In the United States, the irradiation of many different types of foods—including beef, poultry, potatoes, flour, and fruit—has been approved by the U.S. Food and Drug Administration (FDA) and the U.S. Department of Agriculture (USDA).

Radioactivity is also used to control the populations of harmful insects. For example, fruit flies can be raised in large numbers in captivity and sterilized with radiation. When these fruit flies are released, they mate with wild fruit flies but do not produce offspring. The efforts of the wild fruit flies, which might otherwise lead to reproduction, are wasted and the next generation of flies is smaller than it would otherwise have been. Similar strategies have been employed to control the populations of disease-carrying mosquitoes.

◀ **FIGURE 19.20 Irradiation of Food** Irradiation kills microbes that cause food to decay, allowing for longer and safer storage. The food is not made radioactive and its properties are unchanged in the process. These strawberries were picked at the same time, but those on the bottom were irradiated before storage.

CHAPTER IN REVIEW

Self Assessment Quiz

Q1. What daughter nuclide forms when polonium-214 undergoes alpha decay?

a) $^{218}_{86}Rn$ b) $^{214}_{85}At$ c) $^{214}_{83}Bi$ d) $^{210}_{82}Pb$

Q2. Which nuclear equation accurately represents the beta decay of Xe-133?

a) $^{133}_{54}Xe \rightarrow ^{133}_{55}Cs + ^{0}_{-1}e$

b) $^{133}_{54}Xe \rightarrow ^{133}_{53}I + ^{0}_{-1}e$

c) $^{133}_{54}Xe + ^{0}_{-1}e \rightarrow ^{133}_{53}I$

d) $^{133}_{54}Xe \rightarrow ^{129}_{52}Cs + ^{4}_{2}He$

Q3. Which nuclide is most likely to undergo beta decay?

a) Si-22   b) Rb-91

c) Ar-35   d) Co-52

Q4. Which form of radioactive decay would you be most likely to detect if it were happening in the room next to the one you are currently in?

a) alpha   b) beta

c) gamma   d) positron emission

Q5. The chart below shows the mass of a decaying nuclide versus time. What is the half-life of the decay?

a) 15 min   b) 25 min
c) 35 min   d) 70 min

Q6. Iron-59 is a beta emitter with a half-life of 44.5 days. If a sample initially contains 132 mg of iron-59, how much iron-59 is left in the sample after 265 days?

a) 0.00 mg   b) 2.13 mg
c) 33.2 mg   d) 66.0 mg

Q7. An artifact has a carbon-14 decay rate of 8.55 disintegrations per minute per gram of carbon (8.55 dis/min · g C). Living organisms have carbon-14 decay rate of 15.3 dis/min · g C. How old is the artifact? (The half-life of carbon-14 is 5730 yr.)

a) 4.81×10^3 yr   b) 2.10×10^3 yr
c) 3.20×10^3 yr   d) 1.21×10^{-4} yr

Q8. An igneous rock contains a Pb-206/U-238 mass ratio of 0.372. How old is the rock? (U-238 decays into Pb-206 with a half-life of 4.5×10^9 yr.)

a) 4.50×10^9 yr   b) 6.42×10^9 yr
c) 2.05×10^9 yr   d) 2.32×10^9 yr

Q9. Calculate the nuclear binding energy per nucleon for cobalt-59, the only stable isotope of cobalt. The mass of cobalt-59 is 58.933198 amu. (The mass of H^1_1 is 1.00783 amu, and the mass of a neutron is 1.00866 amu.)

a) 517.3 MeV   b) 8.768 MeV
c) 19.16 MeV   d) 1.011×10^{-5} MeV

Q10. Which problem is not associated with nuclear power generation?

a) danger of overheated nuclear core

b) waste disposal

c) global warming

d) none of the above (All of the above are problems associated with nuclear power generation.)

Answers: 1. (d) 2. (a) 3. (b) 4. (c) 5. (c) 6. (b) 7. (a) 8. (d) 9. (b) 10. (c)

Key Terms

Section 19.1
radioactivity (911)
radioactive (912)

Section 19.2
phosphorescence (912)

Section 19.3
nuclide (913)
alpha (α) decay (914)

alpha (α) particle (914)
nuclear equation (914)
ionizing power (915)
penetrating power (915)
beta (β) decay (915)
beta (β) particle (915)
gamma (γ) ray emission (915)
gamma (γ) ray (915)
positron emission (916)

positron (916)
electron capture (916)

Section 19.4
strong force (918)
nucleons (918)
magic numbers (920)

Section 19.5
film-badge dosimeter (920)

Key Concepts

Diagnosing Appendicitis (19.1)

▶ Radioactivity is the emission of subatomic particles or energetic electromagnetic radiation by the nuclei of certain atoms.

▶ Because some of these emissions can pass through matter, radioactivity is useful in medicine and many other areas of study.

The Discovery of Radioactivity (19.2)

▶ Radioactivity was discovered by Antoine-Henri Becquerel when he found that uranium causes a photographic exposure in the absence of light.

▶ Marie Sklodowska Curie later determined that this phenomenon was not unique to uranium, and she began calling the rays that produced the exposure radioactivity. Curie also discovered two new elements, polonium and radium.

Types of Radioactivity (19.3)

▶ The major types of natural radioactivity are alpha (α) decay, beta (β) decay, gamma (γ) ray emission, and positron emission.

▶ Alpha radiation is helium nuclei. Beta particles are electrons. Gamma rays are electromagnetic radiation of very high energy. Positrons are the antiparticles of electrons.

▶ A nucleus may absorb one of its orbital electrons in a process called electron capture.

▶ We can represent each radioactive process with a nuclear equation that illustrates how the parent nuclide changes into the daughter nuclide. In a nuclear equation, although the specific types of atoms may not balance, the atomic numbers and mass numbers must.

▶ Each type of radioactivity has a different ionizing and penetrating power. These values are inversely related; a particle with a higher ionizing power has a lower penetrating power. Alpha particles are the most massive and they have the highest ionizing power, followed by beta particles and positrons, which are equivalent in their ionizing power. Gamma rays have the lowest ionizing power.

The Valley of Stability: Predicting the Type of Radioactivity (19.4)

▶ The stability of a nucleus, and therefore the probability that it will undergo radioactive decay, depends largely on two factors. The first is the ratio of neutrons to protons (N/Z), because neutrons provide a strong force that overcomes the electromagnetic repulsions between the positive protons. This ratio is one for smaller elements, but becomes greater than one for larger elements. The second factor related to nuclei stability is a concept known as magic numbers; certain numbers of nucleons are more stable than others.

Detecting Radioactivity (19.5)

▶ Radiation detectors are used to determine the quantity of radioactivity in an area or sample.

▶ Film-badge dosimeters utilize photographic film for that purpose; such detectors do not provide an instantaneous response.

▶ Two detectors that instantly register the amount of radiation are the Geiger-Müller counter, which uses the ionization of argon by radiation to produce an electrical signal, and the scintillation counter, which uses the emission of light induced by radiation.

The Kinetics of Radioactive Decay and Radiometric Dating (19.6)

▶ All radioactive elements decay according to first-order kinetics (Chapter 13); the half-life equation and the integrated rate law for radioactive decay are derived from the first-order rate laws.

▶ The kinetics of radioactive decay is used to date objects and artifacts. The age of materials that were once part of living organisms is measured by carbon-14 dating. The age of ancient rocks and even Earth itself is determined by uranium/lead dating.

The Discovery of Fission: The Atomic Bomb and Nuclear Power (19.7)

▶ Fission is the splitting of an atom, such as uranium-235, into two atoms of lesser atomic weight.

▶ Because the fission of one uranium-235 atom releases enormous amounts of energy and produces neutrons that can split other uranium-235 atoms, the energy from these collective reactions can be harnessed in an atomic bomb or nuclear reactor.

▶ Nuclear power produces no air pollution and requires little mass to release lots of energy; however, there is always a danger of accidents, and it is difficult to dispose of nuclear waste.

Converting Mass to Energy: Mass Defect and Nuclear Binding Energy (19.8)

▶ In a nuclear fission reaction, mass is converted into energy.

▶ The difference in mass between a nuclide and the individual protons and neutrons that compose it is called the mass defect, and the corresponding energy, calculated from Einstein's equation $E = mc^2$, is the nuclear binding energy.

▶ The stability of a nucleus is determined by the binding energy per nucleon, which increases up to mass number 60 and then decreases.

Nuclear Fusion: The Power of the Sun (19.9)

▶ Stars produce their energy by a process that is the opposite of fission: nuclear fusion, the combination of two light nuclei to form a heavier one.

▶ Modern nuclear weapons employ fusion. Although fusion has been examined as a possible method to produce electricity, experiments with hydrogen fusion have been more costly than productive.

Nuclear Transmutation and Transuranium Elements (19.10)

▶ Nuclear transmutation, the changing of one element to another element, has been used to create the transuranium elements, elements with atomic numbers greater than that of uranium.

▶ Two devices are most commonly used to accelerate particles to the high speeds necessary for transmutation reactions: the linear accelerator and the cyclotron. Both use alternating voltage to propel particles by electromagnetic forces.

The Effects of Radiation on Life (19.11)

▶ The effects of radiation can be grouped into three categories. Acute radiation damage is caused by a large exposure to radiation for a short period of time. Lower radiation exposures may result

in increased cancer risk because of damage to DNA. Genetic defects are caused by damage to the DNA of reproductive cells.

▶ The most effective unit of measurement for the amount of radiation absorbed is the rem, which takes into account the different penetrating and ionizing powers of the various types of radiation.

Radioactivity in Medicine (19.12)

▶ Radioactivity is central to the diagnosis of medical problems by means of radiotracers and positron emission tomography (PET). Both of these techniques can provide data about the appearance and metabolic activity of an organ, or help locate a tumor.

▶ Radiation is also used to treat cancer because it kills cells. Radiation can also be used to kill bacteria in foods and to control harmful insect populations.

Key Equations and Relationships

The First-Order Rate Law (19.6)

$$\text{Rate} = kN$$

The Half-Life Equation (19.6)

$$t_{1/2} = \frac{0.693}{k} \quad k = \text{rate constant}$$

The Integrated Rate Law (19.6)

$$\ln \frac{N_t}{N_0} = -kt \quad N_t = \text{number of radioactive nuclei at time } t$$

$$N_0 = \text{initial number of radioactive nuclei}$$

Einstein's Energy–Mass Equation (19.8)

$$E = mc^2$$

Key Learning Outcomes

Chapter Objectives	Assessment
Writing Nuclear Equations for Alpha Decay (19.3)	Example 19.1 For Practice 19.1 Exercises 31–36
Writing Nuclear Equations for Beta Decay, Positron Emission, and Electron Capture (19.3)	Example 19.2 For Practice 19.2 For More Practice 19.2 Exercises 31–36
Predicting the Type of Radioactive Decay (19.4)	Example 19.3 For Practice 19.3 Exercises 41, 42
Using Radioactive Decay Kinetics (19.6)	Example 19.4 For Practice 19.4 Exercises 45–52
Using Radiocarbon Dating (19.6) 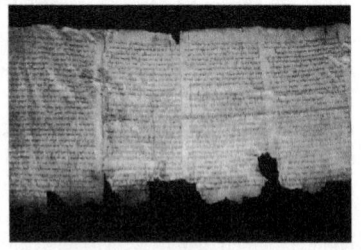	Example 19.5 For Practice 19.5 Exercises 53, 54
Using Uranium/Lead Dating to Estimate the Age of a Rock (19.6)	Example 19.6 For Practice 19.6 Exercises 55, 56
Determining the Mass Defect and Nuclear Binding Energy (19.8)	Example 19.7 For Practice 19.7 Exercises 65–72

EXERCISES

Review Questions

1. What is radioactivity? Who discovered it? How was it discovered?
2. Explain Marie Curie's role in the discovery of radioactivity.
3. Define A, Z, and X in the following notation used to specify a nuclide: $_{Z}^{A}X$.
4. Use the notation from Question 3 to write symbols for a proton, a neutron, and an electron.
5. What is an alpha particle? What happens to the mass number and atomic number of a nuclide that emits an alpha particle?
6. What is a beta particle? What happens to the mass number and atomic number of a nuclide that emits a beta particle?
7. What is a gamma ray? What happens to the mass number and atomic number of a nuclide that emits a gamma ray?
8. What is a positron? What happens to the mass number and atomic number of a nuclide that emits a positron?
9. Describe the process of electron capture. What happens to the mass number and atomic number of a nuclide that undergoes electron capture?
10. Rank alpha particles, beta particles, positrons, and gamma rays in terms of: (a) increasing ionizing power; (b) increasing penetrating power.
11. Explain why the ratio of neutrons to protons (N/Z) is important in determining nuclear stability. How can you use the N/Z ratio of a nuclide to predict the kind of radioactive decay that it might undergo?
12. What are magic numbers? How are they important in determining the stability of a nuclide?
13. Describe the basic way that each device detects radioactivity: (a) film-badge dosimeter; (b) Geiger-Müller counter; and (c) scintillation counter.
14. Explain the concept of half-life with respect to radioactive nuclides. What rate law is characteristic of radioactivity?
15. Explain the main concepts behind the technique of radiocarbon dating. How can radiocarbon dating be corrected for changes in atmospheric concentrations of C-14? What range of ages can be reliably determined by C-14 dating?
16. How is the uranium to lead ratio in a rock used to estimate its age? How does this dating technique provide an estimate for Earth's age? How old is Earth according to this dating method?
17. Describe fission. Include the concepts of chain reaction and critical mass in your description. How and by whom was fission discovered? Explain how fission can be used to generate electricity.
18. What was the Manhattan Project? Briefly describe its development and culmination.
19. Describe the advantages and disadvantages of using fission to generate electricity.
20. The products of a nuclear reaction usually have a different mass than the reactants. Why?
21. Explain the concepts of mass defect and nuclear binding energy. At what mass number does the nuclear binding energy per nucleon peak? What is the significance of this?
22. What is fusion? Why can fusion and fission both produce energy? Explain.
23. What are some of the problems associated with using fusion to generate electricity?
24. Explain transmutation and provide one or two examples.
25. How does a linear accelerator work? For what purpose is it used?
26. Explain the basic principles of cyclotron function.
27. How does radiation affect living organisms?
28. Explain why different kinds of radiation affect biological tissues differently, even though the amount of radiation exposure may be the same.
29. Explain the significance of the biological effectiveness factor in measuring radiation exposure. What types of radiation would you expect to have the highest biological effectiveness factor?
30. Describe some of the medical uses, both in diagnosis and in treatment of disease, of radioactivity.

Problems by Topic

Radioactive Decay and Nuclide Stability

31. Write a nuclear equation for the indicated decay of each nuclide:
    a. U-234 (alpha)
    b. Th-230 (alpha)
    c. Pb-214 (beta)
    d. N-13 (positron emission)
    e. Cr-51 (electron capture)
32. Write a nuclear equation for the indicated decay of each nuclide:
    a. Po-210 (alpha)
    b. Ac-227 (beta)
    c. Tl-207 (beta)
    d. O-15 (positron emission)
    e. Pd-103 (electron capture)
33. Write a partial decay series for Th-232 undergoing the sequential decays: α, β, β, α.

34. Write a partial decay series for Rn-220 undergoing the sequential decays: α, β, β, α.
35. Fill in the missing particles in each nuclear equation.
    a. $\underline{\hspace{1cm}} \longrightarrow {}_{85}^{217}\text{At} + {}_{2}^{4}\text{He}$
    b. ${}_{94}^{241}\text{Pu} \longrightarrow {}_{95}^{241}\text{Am} + \underline{\hspace{1cm}}$
    c. ${}_{11}^{19}\text{Na} \longrightarrow {}_{10}^{19}\text{Ne} + \underline{\hspace{1cm}}$
    d. ${}_{34}^{75}\text{Se} + \underline{\hspace{1cm}} \longrightarrow {}_{33}^{75}\text{As}$
36. Fill in the missing particles in each nuclear equation.
    a. ${}_{95}^{241}\text{Am} \longrightarrow {}_{93}^{237}\text{Np} + \underline{\hspace{1cm}}$
    b. $\underline{\hspace{1cm}} \longrightarrow {}_{92}^{233}\text{U} + {}_{-1}^{0}\text{e}$
    c. ${}_{93}^{237}\text{Np} \longrightarrow \underline{\hspace{1cm}} + {}_{2}^{4}\text{He}$
    d. ${}_{35}^{75}\text{Br} \longrightarrow \underline{\hspace{1cm}} + {}_{+1}^{0}\text{e}$

37. Determine whether or not each nuclide is likely to be stable. State your reasons.
    a. Mg-26
    b. Ne-25
    c. Co-51
    d. Te-124

38. Determine whether or not each nuclide is likely to be stable. State your reasons.
    a. Ti-48
    b. Cr-63
    c. Sn-102
    d. Y-88

39. The first six elements of the first transition series have the following number of stable isotopes:

Element	Number of Stable Isotopes
Sc	1
Ti	5
V	1
Cr	3
Mn	1
Fe	4

Explain why Sc, V, and Mn each has only one stable isotope while the other elements have several.

40. Neon and magnesium each has three stable isotopes while sodium and aluminum each has only one. Explain why this might be so.

41. Predict a likely mode of decay for each unstable nuclide.
    a. Mo-109
    b. Ru-90
    c. P-27
    d. Rn-196

42. Predict a likely mode of decay for each unstable nuclide.
    a. Sb-132
    b. Te-139
    c. Fr-202
    d. Ba-123

43. Which one of each pair of nuclides would you expect to have the longer half-life?
    a. Cs-113 or Cs-125
    b. Fe-62 or Fe-70

44. Which one of each pair of nuclides would you expect to have the longer half-life?
    a. Cs-149 or Cs-139
    b. Fe-45 or Fe-52

The Kinetics of Radioactive Decay and Radiometric Dating

45. One of the nuclides in spent nuclear fuel is U-235, an alpha emitter with a half-life of 703 million years. How long will take for the amount of U-235 to reach 10.0% of its initial amount?

46. A patient is given 0.050 mg of technetium-99m, a radioactive isotope with a half-life of about 6.0 hours. How long does it take for the radioactive isotope to decay to 1.0×10^{-3} mg? (Assume no excretion of the nuclide from the body.)

47. A radioactive sample contains 1.55 g of an isotope with a half-life of 3.8 days. What mass of the isotope remains after 5.5 days? (Assume no excretion of the nuclide from the body.)

48. At 8:00 A.M., a patient receives a 58 mg dose of I-131 to obtain an image of her thyroid. If the nuclide has a half-life of 8 days, what mass of the nuclide remains in the patient at 5:00 P.M. the next day?

49. A sample of F-18 has an initial decay rate of 1.5×10^5/s. How long will it take for the decay rate to fall to 2.5×10^3/s? (F-18 has a half-life of 1.83 hours.)

50. A sample of Tl-201 has an initial decay rate of 5.88×10^4/s. How long will it take for the decay rate to fall to 287/s? (Tl-201 has a half-life of 3.042 days.)

51. A wooden boat discovered just south of the Great Pyramid in Egypt has a carbon-14/carbon-12 ratio that is 72.5% of that found in living organisms. How old is the boat?

52. A layer of peat beneath the glacial sediments of the last ice age has a carbon-14/carbon-12 ratio that is 22.8% of that found in living organisms. How long ago was this ice age?

53. An ancient skull has a carbon-14 decay rate of 0.85 disintegrations per minute per gram of carbon (0.85 dis/min · g C). How old is the skull? (Assume that living organisms have a carbon-14 decay rate of 15.3 dis/min · g C and that carbon-14 has a half-life of 5730 yr.)

54. A mammoth skeleton has a carbon-14 decay rate of 0.48 disintegrations per minute per gram of carbon (0.48 dis/min · g C). When did the mammoth live? (Assume that living organisms have a carbon-14 decay rate of 15.3 dis/min · g C and that carbon-14 has a half-life of 5730 yr.)

55. A rock from Australia contains 0.438 g of Pb-206 to every 1.00 g of U-238. Assuming that the rock did not contain any Pb-206 at the time of its formation, how old is the rock?

56. A meteor has a Pb-206:U-238 mass ratio of 0.855:1.00. What is the age of the meteor? (Assume that the meteor did not contain any Pb-206 at the time of its formation.)

Fission, Fusion, and Transmutation

57. Write the nuclear reaction for the neutron-induced fission of U-235 to form Xe-144 and Sr-90. How many neutrons are produced in the reaction?

58. Write the nuclear reaction for the neutron-induced fission of U-235 to produce Te-137 and Zr-97. How many neutrons are produced in the reaction?

59. Write the nuclear equation for the fusion of two H-2 atoms to form He-3 and one neutron.

60. Write the nuclear equation for the fusion of H-3 with H-1 to form He-4.

61. A breeder nuclear reactor is a reactor in which nonfissionable (nonfissile) U-238 is converted into fissionable (fissile) Pu-239. The process involves bombardment of U-238 by neutrons to form U-239, which then undergoes two sequential beta decays. Write nuclear equations for this process.

62. Write the series of nuclear equations to represent the bombardment of Al-27 with a neutron to form a product that subsequently undergoes an alpha decay followed by a beta decay.

63. Rutherfordium-257 was synthesized by bombarding Cf-249 with C-12. Write the nuclear equation for this reaction.

64. Element 107, now named bohrium, was synthesized by German researchers by colliding bismuth-209 with chromium-54 to form a bohrium isotope and one neutron. Write the nuclear equation to represent this reaction.

Energetics of Nuclear Reactions, Mass Defect, and Nuclear Binding Energy

65. If 1.0 g of matter is converted to energy, how much energy is formed?

66. A typical home uses approximately 1.0×10^3 kWh of energy per month. If the energy came from a nuclear reaction, what mass would have to be converted to energy per year to meet the energy needs of the home?

67. Calculate the mass defect and nuclear binding energy per nucleon of each nuclide.
    a. O-16 (atomic mass = 15.994915 amu)
    b. Ni-58 (atomic mass = 57.935346 amu)
    c. Xe-129 (atomic mass = 128.904780 amu)

68. Calculate the mass defect and nuclear binding energy per nucleon of each nuclide.
    a. Li-7 (atomic mass = 7.016003 amu)
    b. Ti-48 (atomic mass = 47.947947 amu)
    c. Ag-107 (atomic mass = 106.905092 amu)

69. Calculate the quantity of energy produced per gram of U-235 (atomic mass = 235.043922 amu) for the neutron-induced fission of U-235 to form Xe-144 (atomic mass = 143.9385 amu) and Sr-90 (atomic mass = 89.907738 amu) (discussed in Problem 57).

70. Calculate the quantity of energy produced per mole of U-235 (atomic mass = 235.043922 amu) for the neutron-induced fission of U-235 to produce Te-137 (atomic mass = 136.9253 amu) and Zr-97 (atomic mass = 96.910950 amu) (discussed in Problem 58).

71. Calculate the quantity of energy produced per gram of reactant for the fusion of two H-2 (atomic mass = 2.014102 amu) atoms to form He-3 (atomic mass = 3.016029 amu) and one neutron (discussed in Problem 59).

72. Calculate the quantity of energy produced per gram of reactant for the fusion of H-3 (atomic mass = 3.016049 amu) with H-1 (atomic mass = 1.007825 amu) to form He-4 (atomic mass = 4.002603 amu) (discussed in Problem 60).

Effects and Applications of Radioactivity

73. A 75 kg human is exposed to 32.8 rad of radiation. How much energy is absorbed by the person's body? Compare this energy to the amount of energy absorbed by the person's body if they jumped from a chair to the floor (assume that the chair is 0.50 m from the ground and that all of the energy from the fall is absorbed by the person).

74. If a 55-gram laboratory mouse is exposed to 20.5 rad of radiation, how much energy is absorbed by the mouse's body?

75. PET studies require fluorine-18, which is produced in a cyclotron and decays with a half-life of 1.83 hours. Assuming that the F-18 can be transported at 60.0 miles/hour, how close must the hospital be to the cyclotron if 65% of the F-18 produced makes it to the hospital?

76. Suppose a patient is given 155 mg of I-131, a beta emitter with a half-life of 8.0 days. Assuming that none of the I-131 is eliminated from the person's body in the first 4.0 hours of treatment, what is the exposure (in Ci) during those first four hours?

Cumulative Problems

77. Complete each nuclear equation and calculate the energy change (in J/mol of reactant) associated with each. (Be-9 = 9.012182 amu, Bi-209 = 208.980384 amu, He-4 = 4.002603 amu, Li-6 = 6.015122 amu, Ni-64 = 63.927969 amu, Rg-272 = 272.1535 amu, Ta-179 = 178.94593 amu, and W-179 = 178.94707 amu).
    a. _____ + $^{9}_{4}Be \longrightarrow ^{6}_{3}Li + ^{4}_{2}He$
    b. $^{209}_{83}Bi + ^{64}_{28}Ni \longrightarrow ^{272}_{111}Rg + $ _____
    c. $^{179}_{74}W + $ _____ $\longrightarrow ^{179}_{73}Ta$

78. Complete each nuclear equation and calculate the energy change (in J/mol of reactant) associated with each. (Al-27 = 26.981538 amu, Am-241 = 241.056822 amu, He-4 = 4.002603 amu, Np-237 = 237.048166 amu, P-30 = 29.981801 amu, S-32 = 31.972071 amu, and Si-29 = 28.976495 amu).
    a. $^{27}_{13}Al + ^{4}_{2}He \longrightarrow ^{30}_{15}P + $ _____
    b. $^{32}_{16}S + $ _____ $\longrightarrow ^{29}_{14}Si + ^{4}_{2}He$
    c. $^{241}_{95}Am \longrightarrow ^{237}_{93}Np + $ _____

79. Write the nuclear equation for the most likely mode of decay for each unstable nuclide:
    a. Ru-114
    b. Ra-216
    c. Zn-58
    d. Ne-31

80. Write the nuclear equation for the most likely mode of decay for each unstable nuclide:
    a. Kr-74
    b. Th-221
    c. Ar-44
    d. Nb-85

81. Bismuth-210 is a beta emitter with a half-life of 5.0 days. If a sample contains 1.2 g of Bi-210 (atomic mass = 209.984105 amu), how many beta emissions occur in 13.5 days? If a person's body intercepts 5.5% of those emissions, to what dose of radiation (in Ci) is the person exposed?

82. Polonium-218 is an alpha emitter with a half-life of 3.0 minutes. If a sample contains 55 mg of Po-218 (atomic mass = 218.008965 amu), how many alpha emissions occur in 25.0 minutes? If the polonium is ingested by a person, to what dose of radiation (in Ci) is the person exposed?

83. Radium-226 (atomic mass = 226.025402 amu) decays to radon-224 (a radioactive gas) with a half-life of 1.6×10^3 years. What volume of radon gas (at 25.0 °C and 1.0 atm) does 25.0 g of radium produce in 5.0 days? (Report your answer to two significant digits.)

84. In one of the neutron-induced fission reactions of U-235 (atomic mass = 235.043922 amu), the products are Ba-140 and Kr-93 (a radioactive gas). What volume of Kr-93 (at 25.0 °C and 1.0 atm) is produced when 1.00 g of U-235 undergoes this fission reaction?

85. When a positron and an electron annihilate one another, the resulting mass is completely converted to energy. Calculate the energy associated with this process in kJ/mol.

86. A typical nuclear reactor produces about 1.0 MW of power per day. What is the minimum rate of mass loss required to produce this much energy?

87. Find the binding energy in an atom of ^{3}He, which has a mass of 3.016030 amu.

88. The overall hydrogen burning reaction in stars can be represented as the conversion of four protons to one α particle. Use the data for the mass of H-1 and He-4 to calculate the energy released by this process.

89. The nuclide ^{247}Es can be made by bombardment of ^{238}U in a reaction that emits five neutrons. Identify the bombarding particle.

90. The nuclide ^{6}Li reacts with ^{2}H to form two identical particles. Identify the particles.

91. The half-life of ^{238}U is 4.5×10^9 yr. A sample of rock of mass 1.6 g produces 29 dis/s. Assuming all the radioactivity is due to ^{238}U, find the percent by mass of ^{238}U in the rock.

92. The half-life of ^{232}Th is 1.4×10^{10} yr. Find the number of disintegrations per hour emitted by 1.0 mol of ^{232}Th in 1 minute.

93. A 1.50 L gas sample at 745 mm Hg and 25.0 °C contains 3.55% radon-220 by volume. Radon-220 is an alpha-emitter with a half-life of 55.6 s. How many alpha particles are emitted by the gas sample in 5.00 minutes?

94. A 228 mL sample of an aqueous solution contains 2.35% MgCl$_2$ by mass. Exactly one-half of the magnesium ions are Mg-28, a beta emitter with a half-life of 21 hours. What is the decay rate of Mg-28 in the solution after 4.00 days? (Assume a density of 1.02 g/mL for the solution.)

95. When a positron and an electron collide and annihilate each other, two photons of equal energy are produced. Find the wavelength of these photons.

96. The half-life of ^{235}U, an alpha emitter, is 7.1×10^8 yr. Calculate the number of alpha particles emitted by 1.0 mg of this nuclide in 1.0 minute.

97. Given that the energy released in the fusion of two deuterons to a ^{3}He and a neutron is 3.3 MeV, and in the fusion to tritium and a proton it is 4.0 MeV, calculate the energy change for the process ^{3}He + ^{1}n $\longrightarrow$ ^{3}H + ^{1}p. Suggest an explanation for why this process occurs at much lower temperatures than either of the first two.

98. The nuclide ^{18}F decays by both electron capture and β^+ decay. Find the difference in the energy released by these two processes. The atomic masses are ^{18}F = 18.000950 and ^{18}O = 17.9991598.

Challenge Problems

99. The space shuttle carries about 72,500 kg of solid aluminum fuel, which is oxidized with ammonium perchlorate according to the reaction shown here:

$$10 \, \text{Al}(s) + 6 \, \text{NH}_4\text{ClO}_4(s) \longrightarrow$$
$$4 \, \text{Al}_2\text{O}_3(s) + 2 \, \text{AlCl}_3(s) + 12 \, \text{H}_2\text{O}(g) + 3 \, \text{N}_2(g)$$

The space shuttle also carries about 608,000 kg of oxygen (which reacts with hydrogen to form gaseous water).
a. Assuming that aluminum and oxygen are the limiting reactants, determine the total energy produced by these fuels. (ΔH_f° for solid ammonium perchlorate is -295 kJ/mol.)
b. Suppose that a future space shuttle is powered by matter–antimatter annihilation. The matter could be normal hydrogen (containing a proton and an electron) and the antimatter could be antihydrogen (containing an antiproton and a positron). What mass of antimatter is required to produce the energy equivalent of the aluminum and oxygen fuel currently carried on the space shuttle?

100. Suppose that an 85.0-gram laboratory animal ingests 10.0 mg of a substance that contained 2.55% by mass Pu-239, an alpha emitter with a half-life of 24,110 years.
a. What is the animal's initial radiation exposure in curies?
b. If all of the energy from the emitted alpha particles is absorbed by the animal's tissues, and if the energy of each emission is 7.77×10^{-12} J, what is the dose in rads to the animal in the first 4.0 hours following the ingestion of the radioactive material? Assuming a biological effectiveness factor of 20, what is the 4.0-hour dose in rems?

101. In addition to the natural radioactive decay series that begins with U-238 and ends with Pb-206, there are natural radioactive decay series that begin with U-235 and Th-232. Both of these series end with nuclides of Pb. Predict the likely end product of each series and the number of α decay steps that occur.

102. The hydride of an unstable nuclide of a Group IIA metal, MH$_2$(s), decays by α-emission. A 0.025 mol sample of the hydride is placed in an evacuated 2.0 L container at 298 K. After 82 minutes, the pressure in the container is 0.55 atm. Find the half-life of the nuclide.

103. The nuclide ^{38}Cl decays by beta emission with a half-life of 40.0 min. A sample of 0.40 mol of H^{38}Cl is placed in a 6.24 L container. After 80.0 min the pressure is 1650 mmHg. What is the temperature of the container?

104. When BF$_3$ is bombarded with neutrons, the boron undergoes an α decay, but the F is unaffected. A 0.20 mol sample of BF$_3$ contained in a 3.0 L container at 298 K is bombarded with neutrons until half of the BF$_3$ has reacted. What is the pressure in the container at 298 K?

Conceptual Problems

105. Closely examine the diagram representing the beta decay of fluorine-21 and draw in the missing nucleus.

$$^{21}_{9}\text{F} \longrightarrow \; ? \; + \; ^{0}_{-1}\text{e}$$

106. Approximately how many half-lives must pass for the amount of radioactivity in a substance to decrease to below 1% of its initial level?

107. A person is exposed for 3 days to identical amounts of two different nuclides that emit positrons of roughly equal energy. The half-life of nuclide A is 18.5 days and the half-life of nuclide B is 255 days. Which of the two nuclides poses the greater health risk?

108. Identical amounts of two different nuclides, an alpha emitter and a gamma emitter, with roughly equal half-lives are spilled in a building adjacent to your bedroom. Which of the two nuclides poses the greater health threat to you while you sleep in your bed? If you accidentally wander into the building and ingest equal amounts of the two nuclides, which one poses the greater health threat?

109. Drugstores in many areas now carry tablets, under such trade names as Iosat and NoRad, designed to be taken in the event of an accident at a nuclear power plant or a terrorist attack that releases radioactive material. These tablets contain potassium iodide (KI). Can you explain the nature of the protection that they provide? (*Hint:* see the label in the photo.)

Answers to Conceptual Connections

Alpha and Beta Decay

19.1 (c) The arrow labeled x represents a decrease of two neutrons and two protons, indicative of alpha decay. The arrow labeled y represents a decrease of one neutron and an increase of one proton, indicative of beta decay.

Half-Life

19.2 (b) The half-life is the time it takes for the number of nuclei to decay to one-half of their original number.

Half-Life and the Amount of Radioactive Sample

19.3 (b) 0.10 mol. The sample loses one-half of the number of moles per half-life; so over the course of four half-lives, the amount falls to 0.10 mol.

Nuclear Transformations

19.4 Lawrencium-256

Radiation Exposure

19.5 Nuclide A. Because nuclide A has a shorter half-life, more of the nuclides will decay, and therefore produce radiation, before they exit the body.

20 Organic Chemistry

Organic chemistry just now is enough to drive one mad. It gives one the impression of a primeval, tropical forest full of the most remarkable things....

—Friedrich Wöhler (1800–1882)

O RGANIC CHEMISTRY IS THE STUDY of carbon-containing compounds. Carbon is unique in the sheer number of compounds that it forms. Millions of organic compounds are known, and researchers discover new ones every day. Carbon is also unique in the diversity of compounds that it forms. In most cases, a fixed number of carbon atoms can combine with a fixed number of atoms of another element to form many different compounds. For example, 10 carbon atoms and 22 hydrogen atoms can form 75 distinctly different compounds. With carbon as the backbone, nature can take the same combination of atoms and bond them together in slightly different ways to produce a huge variety of substances. It is not surprising that life is based on the chemistry of carbon because life needs diversity to exist, and organic chemistry is nothing if not diverse. In this chapter, we peer into Friedrich Wöhler's "primeval tropical forest" (see chapter-opening quotation) and discover the most remarkable things.

20.1 Fragrances and Odors

Have you ever ridden an elevator with someone wearing too much perfume? Or found yourself too close to a skunk? Or caught a whiff of rotting fish? What causes these fragrances and odors? When we inhale certain molecules called odorants, they bind with olfactory receptors in our noses. This interaction sends a nerve signal to the brain that we experience as a smell. Some smells, such as that of perfume, are pleasant (when not overdone). Other smells, such as that of the skunk or rotting fish, are unpleasant. Our sense of smell helps us identify food, people, and other organisms, and it alerts us to dangers such as polluted air or spoiled food. Smell (olfaction) is one way we probe the environment around us.

Odorants, if they are to reach our noses, must be volatile. However, many volatile substances have no scent at all. Nitrogen, oxygen, water, and carbon dioxide molecules, for example, are constantly passing through our noses, yet they produce no smell because

About half of all men's colognes contain at least some patchouli alcohol ($C_{15}H_{26}O$), an organic compound (pictured here) derived from the patchouli plant. Patchouli alcohol has a pungent, musty, earthy fragrance.

$CH_3CH=CHCH_2SH$

2-Butene-1-thiol

CH_3
|
$CH_3CHCH_2CH_2SH$

3-Methyl-1-butanethiol

▲ The smell of skunk is due primarily to the molecules shown here.

they do not bind to olfactory receptors. Most common smells are caused by **organic molecules**, molecules containing carbon combined with several other elements such as hydrogen, nitrogen, oxygen, and sulfur. Organic molecules are responsible for the smells of roses, vanilla, cinnamon, almond, jasmine, body odor, and rotting fish. When you wander into a rose garden, you experience the sweet smell caused in part by geraniol, an organic compound emitted by roses. Men's colognes often contain patchouli alcohol, an earthy-smelling organic compound extracted from the patchouli plant. If you have been in the vicinity of skunk spray (or have been unfortunate enough to be sprayed yourself), you are familiar with the unpleasant smell of 2-butene-1-thiol and 3-methyl-1-butanethiol, two particularly odoriferous compounds present in the secretion that skunks use to defend themselves.

The study of compounds containing carbon combined with one or more of the elements mentioned previously (hydrogen, nitrogen, oxygen, and sulfur), including their properties and their reactions, is known as **organic chemistry**. Besides composing much of what we smell, organic compounds are prevalent in foods, drugs, petroleum products, and pesticides. Organic chemistry is also the basis for living organisms. Life has evolved based on carbon-containing compounds, making organic chemistry of utmost importance to any person interested in understanding living organisms.

20.2 Carbon: Why It Is Unique

Why did life evolve based on the chemistry of carbon? Why is life not based on some other element? The answer may not be simple, but we know that life—in order to exist—must entail complexity, and carbon chemistry is clearly complex. The number of compounds containing carbon is greater than the number of compounds containing all of the other elements combined. The reasons for carbon's unique and versatile behavior include its ability to form four covalent bonds, its ability to form double and triple bonds, and its tendency to *catenate* (that is, to form chains).

Carbon's Tendency to Form Four Covalent Bonds Carbon—with its four valence electrons—forms four covalent bonds. Consider the Lewis structure and space-filling models of two simple carbon compounds, methane and ethane:

The geometry about a carbon atom forming four single bonds is tetrahedral, as shown in the figure for methane. Carbon's ability to form four bonds, and to form those bonds with a number of different elements, results in the potential to form many different compounds. As you learn to draw structures for organic compounds, always remember to draw carbon with four bonds.

Carbon's Ability to Form Double and Triple Bonds Carbon atoms also form double bonds (trigonal planar geometry) and triple bonds (linear geometry), adding even more diversity to the number of compounds that carbon forms.

In contrast, silicon (the element in the periodic table with properties closest to that of carbon) does not readily form double or triple bonds because the greater size of silicon atoms results in a Si—Si bond that is too long for much overlap between nonhybridized *p* orbitals.

Chemistry in Your Day

Vitalism and the Perceived Difference between Organic and Inorganic

By the end of the eighteenth century, chemists had learned that compounds could be broadly categorized as either organic or inorganic. Organic compounds come from living things while inorganic compounds come from the nonliving things on Earth. Sugar—obtained from sugarcane or the sugar beet—is a common example of an organic compound. Salt—mined from the ground or extracted from ocean water—is a common example of an inorganic compound.

Organic and inorganic compounds are different, not only in their origin, but also in their properties. Organic compounds are easily decomposed. Sugar, for example, readily decomposes into carbon and water when heated. (Think of the last time you burned something sugary in a pan or in the oven.) Inorganic compounds are more difficult to decompose. Salt decomposes only when heated to very high temperatures. Even more curious to these early chemists was their inability to synthesize a single organic compound in the laboratory. Although they were able to synthesize many inorganic compounds, despite concerted efforts, they were not able to synthesize any organic compounds.

The origin and properties of organic compounds led early chemists to postulate that organic compounds were unique to living organisms. They hypothesized that living organisms contained a *vital force*—a mystical or supernatural power—that allowed them to produce organic compounds. They thought that producing an organic compound outside of a living organism was impossible because the vital force was not present. This belief—which became known as *vitalism*—explained why no chemist had succeeded in synthesizing an organic compound in the laboratory.

An experiment performed in 1828 by German chemist Friedrich Wöhler (1800–1882) marked the beginning of the end of vitalism. Wöhler heated ammonium cyanate (an inorganic compound) and formed urea (an organic compound).

$$NH_4OCN \xrightarrow{\text{heat}} H_2NCONH_2$$
$$\text{ammonium cyanate} \qquad\qquad \text{urea}$$

Urea was a known organic compound that had previously been isolated only from urine. Although it was not realized at the time, Wöhler's simple experiment was a key step in opening all of life to scientific investigation. He showed that the compounds composing living organisms—like all compounds—follow scientific laws and can be studied and understood. Today, known organic compounds number in the millions, and modern organic chemistry is a vast field that produces substances as diverse as drugs, petroleum products, and plastics.

Freidrich Wöhler

▶ The synthesis of urea in 1828 by German chemist Friedrich Wöhler marked the beginning of the end for vitalism.

Urea

Carbon's Tendency to Catenate Carbon, more than any other element, can bond to itself to form chain, branched, and ring structures.

Propane

Isobutane

Cyclohexane

Although other elements can form chains, none surpasses carbon at this ability. Silicon, for example, can form chains with itself. However, silicon's affinity for oxygen (the Si—O bond is stronger than the Si—Si bond) coupled with the prevalence of oxygen in our atmosphere means that silicon–silicon chains are readily oxidized to form silicates (the silicon–oxygen compounds that compose a significant proportion of minerals). By contrast, the C—C bond (347 kJ/mol) and the C—O bond (359 kJ/mol) are nearly the same strength, allowing carbon chains to exist relatively peacefully in an oxygen-rich environment. Silicon's affinity for oxygen robs it of the rich diversity that catenation provides to carbon.

20.3 Hydrocarbons: Compounds Containing Only Carbon and Hydrogen

Hydrocarbons—compounds that contain only carbon and hydrogen—are the simplest organic compounds. However, because of the uniqueness of carbon, many different kinds of hydrocarbons exist. We use hydrocarbons as fuels. Candle wax, oil, gasoline, LP gas, and natural gas are all composed of hydrocarbons. Hydrocarbons are also the starting materials in the synthesis of many different consumer products including fabrics, soaps, dyes, cosmetics, drugs, plastic, and rubber.

As shown in Figure 20.1 ▼, we can classify hydrocarbons into four different types: **alkanes, alkenes, alkynes**, and **aromatic hydrocarbons**. Alkanes, alkenes, and alkynes—also called **aliphatic hydrocarbons**—are differentiated based on the kinds of bonds between carbon atoms. (We discuss aromatic hydrocarbons in detail in Section 20.7.) As shown in Table 20.1, alkanes have only single bonds between carbon atoms, alkenes have a double bond, and alkynes have a triple bond.

▶ **FIGURE 20.1 Four Types of Hydrocarbons**

TABLE 20.1 Alkanes, Alkenes, Alkynes

Type of Hydrocarbon	Type of Bonds	Generic Formula*	Example
Alkane	All single	C_nH_{2n+2}	Ethane
Alkenes	One (or more) double	C_nH_{2n}	Ethene
Alkynes	One (or more) triple	C_nH_{2n-2}	$H-C\equiv C-H$ Ethyne

* n is the number of carbon atoms. These formulas apply only to noncyclic structures containing no more than one multiple bond.

Drawing Hydrocarbon Structures

Throughout this book, we have relied primarily on molecular formulas as the simplest way to represent compounds. In organic chemistry, however, molecular formulas are insufficient because, as we have already discussed, the same atoms can bond together in different ways to form different compounds. For example, consider an alkane with 4 carbon atoms and 10 hydrogen atoms. Two different structures, named butane and isobutane, are possible:

Butane   Isobutane

Butane and isobutane are **structural isomers**, molecules with the same molecular formula but different structures. Because of their different structures, they have different properties—indeed they are different compounds. Isomerism is ubiquitous in organic chemistry. Butane has 2 structural isomers. Pentane (C_5H_{12}) has 3, hexane (C_6H_{14}) has 5, and decane ($C_{10}H_{22}$) has 75!

We represent the structure of a particular hydrocarbon with a **structural formula**, a formula that shows not only the numbers of each kind of atoms, but also how the atoms are bonded together. Organic chemists use several different kinds of structural formulas. For example, we can represent butane and isobutane in each of the following ways:

	Structural formula	Condensed structural formula	Carbon skeleton formula	Ball-and-stick model	Space-filling model
Butane		$CH_3-CH_2-CH_2-CH_3$			
Isobutane		$CH_3-CH-CH_3$ with CH_3 above			

The structural formula shows all of the carbon and hydrogen atoms in the molecule and how they are bonded together. The *condensed structural formula* groups the hydrogen atoms with the carbon atom to which they are bonded. Condensed structural formulas may show some of the bonds (as the previous examples do) or none at all. The condensed structural formula for butane can also be written as $CH_3CH_2CH_2CH_3$. The *carbon skeleton formula* (also called a line formula) shows the carbon–carbon bonds only as lines. Each end or bend of a line represents a carbon atom bonded to as many hydrogen atoms as necessary to form a total of four bonds. Carbon skeleton formulas allow us to draw complex structures quickly.

Note that structural formulas are generally not three-dimensional representations of the molecule—as space-filling or ball-and-stick models are—but rather two-dimensional representations that show how atoms are bonded together. As such, the most important feature of a structural formula is the *connectivity* of the atoms, not the exact way the formula is drawn. For example, consider the two condensed structural formulas for butane and the corresponding space-filling models below them:

A carbon skeleton formula is called a *line* formula because it uses lines to represent a molecule.

$$CH_3-CH_2-CH_2-CH_3 \quad CH_3-CH_2-CH_2$$
$$|$$
$$CH_3$$

Same molecule

Since rotation about single bonds is relatively unhindered at room temperature, the two structural formulas are identical, even though they are drawn differently.

We represent double and triple bonds in structural formulas with double or triple lines. For example, we draw the structural formulas for C_3H_6 (propene) and C_3H_4 (propyne) as follows:

Structural formula	Condensed structural formula	Carbon skeleton formula	Ball-and-stick model	Space-filling model

The kind of structural formula we use depends on how much information we want to portray. Example 20.1 illustrates how to write structural formulas for a compound.

EXAMPLE 20.1 Writing Structural Formulas for Hydrocarbons

Write the structural formulas and carbon skeleton formulas for the five isomers of C_6H_{14} (hexane).

SOLUTION

To start, draw the carbon backbone of the straight-chain isomer.	C—C—C—C—C—C
Next, determine the carbon backbone structure of the other isomers by arranging the carbon atoms in four other unique ways.	
Fill in all the hydrogen atoms so that each carbon forms four bonds.	

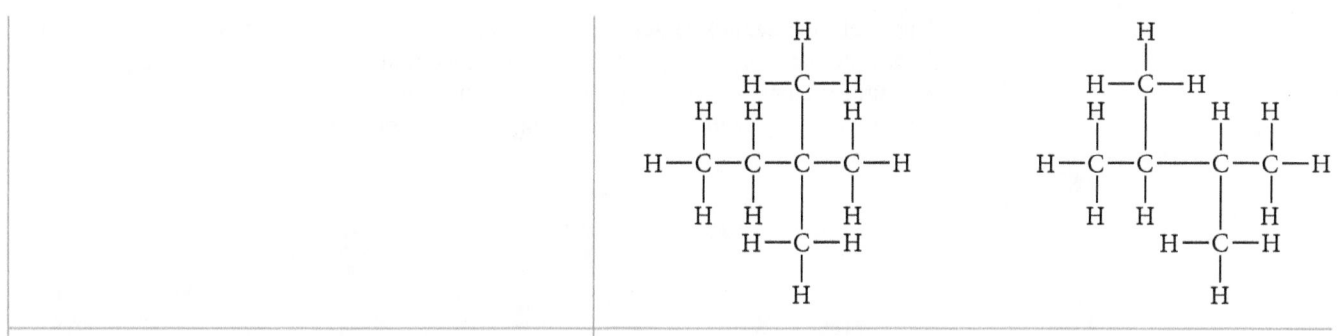

Write the carbon skeleton formulas by using lines to represent each carbon–carbon bond. Remember that each end or bend represents a carbon atom.	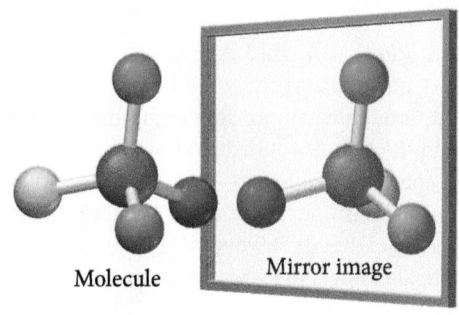

FOR PRACTICE 20.1

Write the structural formulas and carbon skeleton formulas for the three isomers of C_5H_{12} (pentane).

Conceptual Connection 20.1 Organic Structures

Which structure is an *isomer* of $CH_3-CH-CH_2-CH-CH_3$ (and not just the same structure)?

with CH_3 above the second carbon and CH_3 below the fourth carbon.

(a) $CH_3-CH-CH_2-CH-CH_3$ with CH_3 below the second carbon and CH_3 below the fourth carbon.

(b) $CH_3-CH-CH_2-CH$ with CH_3 below the second carbon, CH_3 above the fourth carbon, and CH_3 below the fourth carbon.

(c) $CH-CH_2-CH$ with CH_3 above and below the first carbon and CH_3 above and below the third carbon.

(d) $CH_3-CH-CH_2-CH_2-CH_2$ with CH_3 below the second carbon and CH_3 below the fifth carbon.

Stereoisomerism and Optical Isomerism

Stereoisomers are molecules in which the atoms have the same connectivity but a different spatial arrangement. We can categorize stereoisomers into two types: geometric (or cis–trans) isomers and optical isomers. We discuss geometric isomers in Section 20.5. **Optical isomers** are two molecules that are nonsuperimposable mirror images of one another. Consider the molecule shown here with its mirror image.

Molecule   Mirror image

The molecule cannot be superimposed onto its mirror image. If we swing the mirror image around to try to superimpose the two, we find that there is no way to get all four substituent atoms to align together. (A substituent is an atom or group of atoms that is substituted for a hydrogen atom in an organic compound.)

The mirror image is not superimposable on original molecule.

Molecule   Mirror image

▲ **FIGURE 20.2 Mirror Images** The left and right hand are nonsuperimposable mirror images, just as are optical isomers.

Optical isomers are similar to your right and left hands (Figure 20.2 ◄). The two are mirror images of one another, but you cannot superimpose one on the other. For this reason, a right-handed glove does not fit on your left hand and vice versa.

Any carbon atom with four different substituents in a tetrahedral arrangement exhibits optical isomerism. Consider 3-methylhexane:

Chiral center

Optical isomers of 3-methylhexane

The molecules shown here are nonsuperimposable mirror images and are optical isomers of one other. Optical isomers are also called **enantiomers**. Any molecule, such as 3-methylhexane, that exhibits optical isomerism is said to be **chiral**, from the Greek word *cheir*, which means "hand." Optical isomerism is important, not only to organic chemistry, but also to biology and biochemistry. Most biological molecules are chiral and usually only one or the other enantiomer is active in biological systems. For example, glucose, the primary fuel of cells, is chiral. Only one of the enantiomers of glucose has that familiar sweet taste and only that enantiomer can fuel our cellular functioning; the other enantiomer is not even metabolized by the body.

Some of the physical and chemical properties of enantiomers are indistinguishable from one another. For example, both of the optical isomers of 3-methylhexane have identical freezing points, melting points, and densities. However, the properties of enantiomers differ from one another in two important ways: (1) in the direction in which they rotate polarized light and (2) in their chemical behavior in a chiral environment.

Rotation of Polarized Light *Plane-polarized light* is light that is made up of electric field waves that oscillate in only one plane as shown in Figure 20.3 ►. When a beam of plane-polarized light is directed through a sample containing only one of two optical isomers, the plane of polarization of the light is rotated as shown in Figure 20.4 ►. One of the two optical isomers rotates the polarization of the light clockwise and is called the **dextrorotatory** isomer (or the *d* isomer). The other isomer rotates the polarization of the light counterclockwise and is called the **levorotatory** isomer (or the *l* isomer). An equimolar mixture of both optical isomers does not rotate the polarization of light at all and is called a **racemic mixture**.

Dextrorotatory means turning clockwise or to the right. *Levorotatory* means turning counterclockwise or to the left.

◀ FIGURE 20.3 **Plane-Polarized Light** The electric field of plane-polarized light oscillates in one plane.

▲ FIGURE 20.4 **Rotation of Plane-Polarized Light** Plane-polarized light rotates as it passes through a sample containing only one of two optical isomers.

Chemical Behavior in a Chiral Environment Optical isomers also exhibit different chemical behavior when they are in a chiral environment (a chiral environment is one that is not superimposable on its mirror image). Enzymes are large biological molecules that catalyze reactions in living organisms and provide chiral environments. Consider the following simplified picture of two enantiomers in a chiral environment:

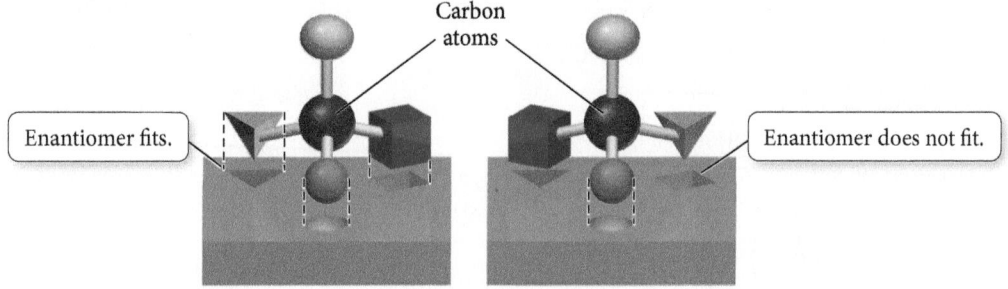

One of the enantiomers fits the template, but the other does not, no matter how it is rotated. In this way, an enzyme is able to catalyze the reaction of one enantiomer because that particular enantiomer fits the "template." As we have already seen, most biological molecules are chiral and usually only one or the other enantiomer is active in biological systems.

Conceptual Connection 20.2 Optical Isomers

Which molecule exhibits optical isomerism?

(a)
$$
\begin{array}{c}
\text{H} \\
| \\
\text{H}-\text{C}-\text{Cl} \\
| \\
\text{Br}
\end{array}
$$

(b)
$$
\begin{array}{c}
\text{H}\quad\text{H} \\
|\quad\ | \\
\text{Br}-\text{C}-\text{C}-\text{H} \\
|\quad\ | \\
\text{Cl}\quad\text{H}
\end{array}
$$

(c)
$$
\begin{array}{c}
\text{H}\quad\text{H} \\
|\quad\ | \\
\text{Br}-\text{C}-\text{C}-\text{Cl} \\
|\quad\ | \\
\text{H}\quad\text{H}
\end{array}
$$

(d)
$$
\begin{array}{c}
\text{H}\quad\text{Cl} \\
|\quad\ | \\
\text{Br}-\text{C}-\text{C}-\text{Cl} \\
|\quad\ | \\
\text{H}\quad\text{H}
\end{array}
$$

20.4 Alkanes: Saturated Hydrocarbons

Alkanes (hydrocarbons containing only single bonds) are often referred to as **saturated hydrocarbons** because they are saturated (loaded to capacity) with hydrogen. The simplest hydrocarbons are methane (CH_4), the main component of natural gas; ethane (C_2H_6), a minority component in natural gas; and propane (C_3H_8), the main component of liquid petroleum (LP) gas.

Methane   Ethane   Propane

TABLE 20.2 n-Alkane Boiling Points

n-Alkane	Boiling Point (°C)
Methane	−161.5
Ethane	−88.6
Propane	−42.1
n-Butane	−0.5
n-Pentane	36.0
n-Hexane	68.7
n-Heptane	98.5
n-Octane	125.6

Alkanes containing four or more carbon atoms may be straight or branched (as we have already seen). The straight-chain isomers are often called normal alkanes, or n-alkanes. As the number of carbon atoms increases in the n-alkanes, so does their boiling point (as shown in Table 20.2). The increase is due to the increasing dispersion force with increasing molar mass (see Section 11.3). Methane, ethane, propane, and n-butane are all gases at room temperature, but the next n-alkane in the series, pentane, is a liquid at room temperature. Pentane is a component of gasoline. Table 20.3 summarizes the n-alkanes through decane, which contains ten carbon atoms. Like pentane, hexane through decane are all components of gasoline. Table 20.4 summarizes the uses of hydrocarbons.

TABLE 20.3 n-Alkanes

n	Name	Molecular Formula C_nH_{2n+2}	Structural Formula	Condensed Structural Formula
1	Methane	CH_4		CH_4
2	Ethane	C_2H_6		CH_3CH_3
3	Propane	C_3H_8		$CH_3CH_2CH_3$
4	n-Butane	C_4H_{10}		$CH_3CH_2CH_2CH_3$
5	n-Pentane	C_5H_{12}		$CH_3CH_2CH_2CH_2CH_3$

(Continued)

TABLE 20.3 n-Alkanes (Continued)

6	n-Hexane	C_6H_{14}		$CH_3CH_2CH_2CH_2CH_2CH_3$
7	n-Heptane	C_7H_{16}		$CH_3CH_2CH_2CH_2CH_2CH_2CH_3$
8	n-Octane	C_8H_{18}		$CH_3CH_2CH_2CH_2CH_2CH_2CH_2CH_3$
9	n-Nonane	C_9H_{20}		$CH_3CH_2CH_2CH_2CH_2CH_2CH_2CH_2CH_3$
10	n-Decane	$C_{10}H_{22}$		$CH_3CH_2CH_2CH_2CH_2CH_2CH_2CH_2CH_2CH_3$

TABLE 20.4 Uses of Hydrocarbons

Number of Carbon Atoms	State	Major Uses
1–4	Gas	Heating fuel, cooking fuel
5–7	Low-boiling liquids	Solvents, gasoline
6–18	Liquids	Gasoline
12–24	Liquids	Jet fuel, portable-stove fuel
18–50	High-boiling liquids	Diesel fuel, lubricants, heating oil
50+	Solids	Petroleum jelly, paraffin wax

Naming Alkanes

Many organic compounds have common names that we can learn only through familiarity. Because of the sheer number of organic compounds, however, we need a systematic method of nomenclature. In this book, we adopt the nomenclature system recommended by the IUPAC (International Union of Pure and Applied Chemistry), which is used throughout the world. In this system, the longest continuous chain of carbon atoms—called the base chain—determines the base name of the compound. The root of the base name depends on the number of carbon atoms in the base chain, as shown in Table 20.5. Base names for alkanes always have the ending -ane. Groups of carbon atoms branching off the base chain are alkyl groups and are named as substituents. Remember that a substituent is an atom or group of atoms that has been substituted for a hydrogen atom in an organic compound. Common alkyl groups are shown in Table 20.6.

TABLE 20.5 Prefixes for Base Names of Alkane Chains

Number of Carbon Atoms	Prefix
1	meth-
2	eth-
3	prop-
4	but-
5	pent-
6	hex-
7	hept-
8	oct-
9	non-
10	dec-

TABLE 20.6 Common Alkyl Groups

Condensed Structural Formula	Name	Condensed Structural Formula	Name
$-CH_3$	Methyl	$-CHCH_3$ $\quad\ \vert$ $\quad\ CH_3$	Isopropyl
$-CH_2CH_3$	Ethyl	$-CH_2CHCH_3$ $\qquad\ \vert$ $\qquad\ CH_3$	Isobutyl
$-CH_2CH_2CH_3$	Propyl	$-CHCH_2CH_3$ $\quad\ \vert$ $\quad\ CH_3$	sec-Butyl
$-CH_2CH_2CH_2CH_3$	Butyl	$\qquad CH_3$ $\qquad\ \vert$ $-CCH_3$ $\qquad\ \vert$ $\qquad CH_3$	tert-Butyl

The procedure in Examples 20.2 and 20.3 will allow you to systematically name many alkanes. The procedure is presented in the left column and two examples of applying the procedure are shown in the center and right columns.

PROCEDURE FOR...	EXAMPLE 20.2	EXAMPLE 20.3
Naming Alkanes	**Naming Alkanes** Name this alkane. $CH_3-CH_2-CH-CH_2-CH_3$ $\qquad\qquad\quad \vert$ $\qquad\qquad\ CH_2$ $\qquad\qquad\quad \vert$ $\qquad\qquad\ CH_3$	**Naming Alkanes** Name this alkane. $CH_3-CH-CH_2-CH-CH_2-CH_2-CH-CH_3$ $\qquad\ \vert \qquad\qquad\ \vert \qquad\qquad\qquad\ \vert$ $\qquad CH_3 \qquad\quad CH_2 \qquad\qquad CH_3$ $\qquad\qquad\qquad\quad \vert$ $\qquad\qquad\qquad CH_3$
1. Count the number of carbon atoms in the longest continuous carbon chain to determine the base name of the compound. Locate the prefix corresponding to this number of atoms in Table 20.5 and add the ending -ane to form the base name.	**SOLUTION** This compound has five carbon atoms in its longest continuous chain. $CH_3-CH_2-CH-CH_2-CH_3$ $\qquad\qquad\quad \vert$ $\qquad\qquad\ CH_2$ $\qquad\qquad\quad \vert$ $\qquad\qquad\ CH_3$ The correct prefix from Table 20.5 is *pent-*. The base name is pentane.	**SOLUTION** This compound has eight carbon atoms in its longest continuous chain. $CH_3-CH-CH_2-CH-CH_2-CH_2-CH-CH_3$ $\qquad\ \vert \qquad\qquad\ \vert \qquad\qquad\qquad\ \vert$ $\qquad CH_3 \qquad\quad CH_2 \qquad\qquad CH_3$ $\qquad\qquad\qquad\quad \vert$ $\qquad\qquad\qquad CH_3$ The correct prefix from Table 20.5 is *oct-*. The base name is octane.

2. Consider every branch from the base chain to be a substituent. Name each substituent according to Table 20.6.	This compound has one substituent named *ethyl*. $CH_3-CH_2-CH-CH_2-CH_3$ $\qquad\qquad\quad\; \mid$ $\qquad\qquad\quad CH_2$ $\qquad\qquad\quad\; \mid$ ethyl → CH_3	This compound has one substituent named *ethyl* and two named *methyl*. $CH_3-CH-CH_2-CH-CH_2-CH_2-CH-CH_3$ $\qquad\quad\; \mid \qquad\qquad\; \mid \qquad\qquad\qquad\quad \mid$ $\qquad\quad CH_3 \qquad\quad CH_2 \; ←\; ethyl \qquad CH_3$ $\qquad\qquad\qquad\qquad\quad\; \mid$ $\qquad\qquad\qquad\qquad\; CH_3$ $\qquad\qquad\qquad\qquad\qquad methyl$
3. Beginning with the end closest to the branching, number the base chain and assign a number to each substituent. (If two substituents occur at equal distances from each end, go to the next substituent to determine from which end to start numbering.)	Number the base chain as follows: $\overset{1}{C}H_3-\overset{2}{C}H_2-\overset{3}{C}H-\overset{4}{C}H_2-\overset{5}{C}H_3$ $\qquad\qquad\qquad\; \mid$ $\qquad\qquad\quad\; CH_2$ $\qquad\qquad\qquad\; \mid$ $\qquad\qquad\quad\; CH_3$ Assign the number 3 to the ethyl substituent.	Number the base chain as follows: $\overset{1}{C}H_3-\overset{2}{C}H-\overset{3}{C}H_2-\overset{4}{C}H-\overset{5}{C}H_2-\overset{6}{C}H_2-\overset{7}{C}H-\overset{8}{C}H_3$ $\qquad\quad\; \mid \qquad\qquad\; \mid \qquad\qquad\qquad\quad \mid$ $\qquad\quad CH_3 \qquad\quad CH_2 \qquad\qquad\quad CH_3$ $\qquad\qquad\qquad\qquad\quad\; \mid$ $\qquad\qquad\qquad\qquad\; CH_3$ Assign the number 4 to the ethyl substituent and the numbers 2 and 7 to the two methyl substituents.
4. Write the name of the compound in the following format: (substituent number)-(substituent name)(base name) If there are two or more substituents, give each one a number and list them alphabetically with hyphens between words and numbers.	The name of the compound is: 3-ethylpentane	The basic form of the name of the compound is: 4-ethyl-2,7-methyloctane List ethyl before methyl because substituents are listed in alphabetical order.
5. If a compound has two or more identical substituents, indicate the number of identical substituents with the prefix *di-* (2), *tri-* (3), or *tetra-* (4) before the substituent's name. Separate the numbers indicating the positions of the substituents relative to each other with a comma. Do not take the prefixes into account when alphabetizing.	Does not apply to this compound.	This compound has two methyl substituents; therefore, the name of the compound is: 4-ethyl-2,7-dimethyloctane
	FOR PRACTICE 20.2 Name this alkane. $CH_3-CH_2-CH-CH_2-CH_2-CH_3$ $\qquad\qquad\qquad\; \mid$ $\qquad\qquad\quad\; CH_3$	**FOR PRACTICE 20.3** Name this alkane. $CH_3-CH_2-CH-CH_2-CH-CH_2-CH_3$ $\qquad\qquad\qquad\; \mid \qquad\quad\; \mid$ $\qquad\qquad\quad\; CH_3 \qquad\; CH_3$

EXAMPLE 20.4 Naming Alkanes

Name this alkane. $CH_3-CH-CH_2-CH-CH_3$
$\qquad\qquad\qquad\ \ \ |\qquad\qquad\ \ \ |$
$\qquad\qquad\qquad\ CH_3\qquad\quad\ CH_3$

SOLUTION

1. The longest continuous carbon chain has five atoms. Therefore, the base name is pentane.	$CH_3-CH-CH_2-CH-CH_3$ $\vert$ $\vert$ CH_3 CH_3
2. This compound has two substituents, both of which are named methyl.	$CH_3-CH-CH_2-CH-CH_3$ $\vert$ $\vert$ CH_3 CH_3 methyl
3. Since both substituents are equidistant from the ends, it does not matter from which end you start numbering.	$\overset{1}{C}H_3-\overset{2}{C}H-\overset{3}{C}H_2-\overset{4}{C}H-\overset{5}{C}H_3$ $\vert$ $\vert$ CH_3 CH_3
4, 5. Use the general form for the name: (substituent number)-(substituent name)(base name) Because this compound contains two identical substituents, step 5 from the naming procedure applies and you use the prefix *di-*. Indicate the position of each substituent with a number separated by a comma.	2,4-dimethylpentane

FOR PRACTICE 20.4

Name this alkane. $CH_3-CH-CH_2-CH-CH-CH_3$
$\qquad\qquad\qquad\ \ \ |\qquad\qquad\ \ \ |\quad\ \ |$
$\qquad\qquad\qquad\ CH_3\qquad\quad\ CH_3\ CH_3$

20.5 Alkenes and Alkynes

Alkenes are hydrocarbons containing at least one double bond between carbon atoms. Alkynes contain at least one triple bond. Because of the double or triple bond, alkenes and alkynes have fewer hydrogen atoms than the corresponding alkanes and are therefore called **unsaturated hydrocarbons** because they are not loaded to capacity with hydrogen. Recall that noncyclic alkenes have the formula C_nH_{2n} and noncyclic alkynes have the formula C_nH_{2n-2}. The simplest alkene is ethene (C_2H_4), also called ethylene.

The general formulas shown here for alkenes and alkynes assume only one multiple bond.

Ethene or ethylene C_2H_4

$\begin{array}{cc} H & H \\ \diagdown & \diagup \\ C{=}C \\ \diagup & \diagdown \\ H & H \end{array}$

Formula   Structural formula   Space-filling model

The geometry about each carbon atom in ethene is trigonal planar (see Example 10.8 for the valence bond model of ethene), making ethene a flat, rigid molecule. Ethene is a ripening agent in fruit such as bananas. When a banana within a cluster of bananas begins to ripen, it emits ethene. The ethene then causes other bananas in the cluster to ripen. Banana farmers usually pick bananas green for ease of shipping. When the bananas arrive at their destination, they are often "gassed" with ethene to initiate ripening. Table 20.7 lists the names and structures of several other alkenes. Most of them do not have familiar uses except their presence as minority components in fuels.

TABLE 20.7 Alkenes

n	Name	Molecular Formula C_nH_{2n}	Structural Formula	Condensed Structural Formula
2	Ethene	C_2H_4		$CH_2 \!=\! CH_2$
3	Propene	C_3H_6		$CH_2 \!=\! CHCH_3$
4	1-Butene*	C_4H_8		$CH_2 \!=\! CHCH_2CH_3$
5	1-Pentene*	C_5H_{10}		$CH_2 \!=\! CHCH_2CH_2CH_3$
6	1-Hexene*	C_6H_{12}		$CH_2 \!=\! CHCH_2CH_2CH_2CH_3$

* These alkenes have one or more isomers depending on the position of the double bond. The isomers shown here have the double bond in the 1 position, meaning the first carbon–carbon bond of the chain.

The simplest alkyne is ethyne, C_2H_2, also known as acetylene.

Ethyne or acetylene C_2H_2 $H\!-\!C\!\equiv\!C\!-\!H$

Formula   Structural formula   Space-filling model

The geometry about each carbon atom in ethyne is linear, making ethyne a linear molecule. Ethyne (or acetylene) is commonly used as fuel for welding torches. The names and structures of several other alkynes are shown in Table 20.8. Like alkenes, the alkynes do not have familiar uses other than their presence as minority components of gasoline.

Naming Alkenes and Alkynes

We name alkenes and alkynes in the same way we name alkanes with the following exceptions:

- The base chain is the longest continuous carbon chain *that contains the double or triple bond.*
- The base name has the ending *-ene* for alkenes and *-yne* for alkynes.
- We number the base chain to give the double or triple bond the lowest possible number.
- We insert a number indicating the position of the double or triple bond (lowest possible number) just before the base name.

For example, the alkene and alkyne shown here are 2-methyl-2-pentene and 1-butyne:

$$CH_3CH_2CH\!=\!CCH_3$$
$$|$$
$$CH_3$$

2-Methyl-2-pentene

$$CH\!\equiv\!CCH_2CH_3$$

1-butyne

▲ Welding torches burn ethyne in pure oxygen to produce the very hot flame needed for melting metals.

TABLE 20.8 Alkynes

n	Name	Molecular Formula C_nH_{2n-2}	Structural Formula	Condensed Structural Formula
2	Ethyne	C_2H_2	$H-C\equiv C-H$	$CH\equiv CH$
3	Propyne	C_3H_4	$H-C\equiv C-\overset{\displaystyle H}{\underset{\displaystyle H}{C}}-H$	$CH\equiv CCH_3$
4	1-Butyne*	C_4H_6	$H-C\equiv C-\overset{H}{\underset{H}{C}}-\overset{H}{\underset{H}{C}}-H$	$CH\equiv CCH_2CH_3$
5	1-Pentyne*	C_5H_8	$H-C\equiv C-\overset{H}{\underset{H}{C}}-\overset{H}{\underset{H}{C}}-\overset{H}{\underset{H}{C}}-H$	$CH\equiv CCH_2CH_2CH_3$
6	1-Hexyne*	C_6H_{10}	$H-C\equiv C-\overset{H}{\underset{H}{C}}-\overset{H}{\underset{H}{C}}-\overset{H}{\underset{H}{C}}-\overset{H}{\underset{H}{C}}-H$	$CH\equiv CCH_2CH_2CH_2CH_3$

* These alkynes have one or more isomers depending on the position of the triple bond. The isomers shown here have the triple bond in the 1 position, meaning the first carbon–carbon bond of the chain.

EXAMPLE 20.5 Naming Alkenes and Alkynes

Name each compound.

(a) $CH_3-\underset{\underset{\displaystyle CH_3}{\overset{\displaystyle |}{\underset{\displaystyle |}{CH_2}}}}{\overset{\displaystyle CH_3}{\overset{\displaystyle |}{C}}}=C-CH_2-CH_3$

(b) $CH_3-\overset{\overset{\displaystyle CH_3}{\displaystyle |}}{\underset{\underset{\displaystyle CH_3}{\displaystyle |}}{CH}}-CH-C\equiv CH$

SOLUTION

(a) 1. The longest continuous carbon chain containing the double bond has six carbon atoms. The base name is therefore *hexene*.

$CH_3-\overset{\overset{\displaystyle CH_3}{\displaystyle |}}{\underset{\underset{\displaystyle CH_3}{\displaystyle |}}{C}}=C-CH_2-CH_3$ (with CH_2, CH_3 branch)

2. The two substituents are both methyl.

3. One of the exceptions listed previously states that, in naming alkenes, you should number the chain so that the *double bond* has the lowest number. In this case, the double bond is equidistant from the ends. Assign the double bond the number 3. The two methyl groups are then at positions 3 and 4.	$$CH_3-\underset{3}{\overset{\overset{\displaystyle CH_3}{\displaystyle \vert}}{C}}=\underset{4}{C}-\underset{5}{CH_2}-\underset{6}{CH_3}$$ with $\underset{2}{CH_2}$ and $\underset{1}{CH_3}$ branching below
4, 5. Use the general form for the name: (substituent number)-(substituent name)(base name) Because this compound contains two identical substituents, step 5 of the naming procedure applies. Use the prefix *di-*. In addition, indicate the position of each substituent with a number separated by a comma. Because this compound is an alkene, specify the position of the double bond, isolated by hyphens, just before the base name.	3,4-dimethyl-3-hexene
(b) 1. The longest continuous carbon chain containing the triple bond is five carbon atoms long; therefore, the base name is *pentyne*.	$$CH_3-CH-CH-C\equiv CH$$ with CH_3-CH (bearing CH_3) above and CH_3 below
2. There are two substituents; one is a methyl group and the other an isopropyl group.	isopropyl → CH_3-CH (bearing CH_3) above; $CH_3-CH-CH-C\equiv CH$ with CH_3 ← methyl below
3. Number the base chain, giving the triple bond the lowest number (1). Assign the isopropyl and methyl groups the numbers 3 and 4, respectively.	$$\underset{5}{CH_3}-\underset{4}{CH}-\underset{3}{CH}-\underset{2}{C}\equiv\underset{1}{CH}$$ with CH_3-CH (bearing CH_3) above position 4 and CH_3 below position 4
4. Use the general form for the name: (substituent number)-(substituent name)(base name) Since there are two substituents, list both of them in alphabetical order. Since this compound is an alkyne, specify the position of the triple bond with a number isolated by hyphens just before the base name.	3-isopropyl-4-methyl-1-pentyne

FOR PRACTICE 20.5

Name each compound.

(a) $CH_3-C\equiv C-\underset{\underset{\displaystyle CH_3}{\vert}}{\overset{\overset{\displaystyle CH_3}{\vert}}{C}}-CH_3$

(b) $CH_3-\underset{\underset{\displaystyle CH_3}{\vert}}{CH}-CH_2-\underset{\underset{\displaystyle CH_3}{\vert}}{CH}-\underset{\underset{\displaystyle CH_2}{\vert}\,(CH_3)}{CH}-CH=CH_2$

Geometric (Cis–Trans) Isomerism in Alkenes

A major difference between a single bond and a double bond is the degree to which rotation occurs about the bond. As discussed in Section 10.7, rotation about a double bond is highly restricted due to the overlap between unhybridized p orbitals on the adjacent carbon atoms. Consider the difference between 1,2-dichloroethane and 1,2-dichloroethene:

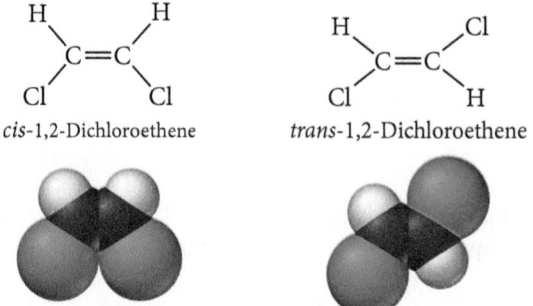

1, 2-Dichloroethane   1, 2-Dichloroethene

The hybridization of the carbon atoms in 1,2-dichloroethane is sp^3, resulting in relatively free rotation about the sigma single bond. Consequently, the two structures are identical at room temperature because they quickly interconvert.

In contrast, rotation about the double bond (sigma + pi) in 1,2-dichloroethene is restricted, so at room temperature, 1,2-dichloroethene exists in two isomeric forms.

cis-1,2-Dichloroethene   *trans*-1,2-Dichloroethene

These two forms of 1,2-dichloroethene are different compounds with different properties as shown in Table 20.9. This kind of isomerism is a type of stereoisomerism (see Section 20.3) called **geometric** (or **cis–trans**) **isomerism**. We distinguish between the two isomers with the designations *cis* (meaning "same side") and *trans* (meaning "opposite sides"). Cis–trans isomerism is common in alkenes. As another example,

---

TABLE 20.9   **Physical Properties of *cis*- and *trans*-1,2-Dichloroethene**

Name	Structure	Space-filling Model	Density (g/mL)	Melting Point (°C)	Boiling Point (°C)
cis-1,2-Dichloroethene			1.284	−80.5	60.1
trans-1,2-Dichloroethene			1.257	−49.4	47.5

consider *cis*- and *trans*-2-butene. Like the two isomers of 1,2-dichloroethene, these two isomers have different physical properties. For example, *cis*-2-butene boils at 3.7 °C, and *trans*-2-butene boils at 0.9 °C.

cis-2-Butene   *trans*-2-Butene

20.6 Hydrocarbon Reactions

One of the most common hydrocarbon reactions is combustion, the burning of hydrocarbons in the presence of oxygen. Hydrocarbon combustion reactions are highly exothermic and are commonly used to warm homes and buildings, to generate electricity, and to power the engines of cars, ships, and airplanes. It is not an exaggeration to say that hydrocarbon combustion makes our current way of life possible. Approximately 90% of energy produced in the United States is generated by hydrocarbon combustion. Alkanes, alkenes, and alkynes all undergo combustion. In a combustion reaction, the hydrocarbon reacts with oxygen to form carbon dioxide and water.

$$CH_3CH_2CH_3(g) + 5\,O_2(g) \longrightarrow 3\,CO_2(g) + 4\,H_2O(g) \qquad \text{Alkane combustion}$$

$$CH_2{=}CHCH_2CH_3(g) + 6\,O_2(g) \longrightarrow 4\,CO_2(g) + 4\,H_2O(g) \qquad \text{Alkene combustion}$$

$$CH{\equiv}CCH_3(g) + 4\,O_2(g) \longrightarrow 3\,CO_2(g) + 2\,H_2O(g) \qquad \text{Alkyne combustion}$$

Reactions of Alkanes

In addition to combustion reactions, alkanes also undergo *substitution* reactions, in which one or more hydrogen atoms on an alkane are replaced by one or more other atoms. The most common substitution reaction is halogen substitution (also referred to as halogenation). For example, methane can react with chlorine gas in the presence of heat or light to form chloromethane.

$$CH_4(g) + Cl_2(g) \xrightarrow{\text{heat or light}} CH_3Cl(g) + HCl(g)$$
Methane   Chlorine   Chloromethane

Ethane reacts with chlorine gas to form chloroethane.

$$CH_3CH_3(g) + Cl_2(g) \xrightarrow{\text{heat or light}} CH_3CH_2Cl(g) + HCl(g)$$
Ethane   Chlorine   Chloromethane

Multiple halogenation reactions can occur because halogens can replace more than one of the hydrogen atoms on an alkane. For example, chloromethane can react with chlorine and the product of that reaction can react again (and so on).

$$CH_3Cl(g) + Cl_2(g) \xrightarrow{\text{heat or light}} CH_2Cl_2(g) + HCl(g)$$
Chloromethane   Chlorine   Dichloromethane
                                            (also known as
                                            methylene chloride)

$$CH_2Cl_2(g) + Cl_2(g) \xrightarrow{\text{heat or light}} CHCl_3(g) + HCl(g)$$
Dichloromethane   Chlorine   Trichloromethane
                                            (also known as
                                            chloroform)

$$CHCl_3(g) + Cl_2(g) \xrightarrow{\text{heat of light}} CCl_4(g) + HCl(g)$$
Trichloromethane   Chlorine   Tetrachloromethane
                                            (also known as
                                            carbon tetrachloride)

The general form for halogen substitution reactions is:

$$R-H + \underset{\text{Alkane}}{}\ \underset{\text{Halogen}}{X_2} \xrightarrow{\text{heat or light}} \underset{\text{Haloalkane}}{R-X} + \underset{\substack{\text{Hydrogen} \\ \text{halide}}}{HX}$$

Notice that the halogenation of hydrocarbons requires initiation with heat or light, which causes the chlorine–chlorine bond to break.

$$Cl-Cl \xrightarrow{\text{heat or light}} Cl\cdot\ +\ Cl\cdot$$

The resulting chlorine atoms are *free radicals* (see Section 9.9), as the dot that represents each chlorine atom's unpaired electron indicates. Chlorine radicals are highly reactive and attack the C—H bond in hydrocarbons. The subsequent reaction proceeds by this mechanism:

$$Cl\cdot\ +\ R-H \longrightarrow R\cdot\ +\ HCl$$

$$R\cdot\ +\ Cl_2 \longrightarrow R-Cl + Cl\cdot$$

Notice that a chlorine free radical is produced as a product of the last step. This free radical can go on to react again, unless it encounters another chlorine free radical, in which case it reacts with it to re-form Cl_2.

Reactions of Alkenes and Alkynes

Alkenes and alkynes undergo addition reactions in which molecules add across (on either side of) the multiple bond. For example, ethene reacts with chlorine gas to form dichloroethane.

The addition of chlorine converts the carbon–carbon double bond into a single bond because each carbon atom bonds to a chlorine atom. Alkenes and alkynes can also add hydrogen in hydrogenation reactions. For example, in the presence of an appropriate catalyst, propene reacts with hydrogen gas to form propane.

We often indicate the presence of a catalyst by adding a label over the reaction arrow.

Hydrogenation reactions convert unsaturated hydrocarbons into saturated hydrocarbons. For example, hydrogenation reactions convert unsaturated vegetable oils into saturated fats. Most vegetable oils are unsaturated because their carbon chains contain double bonds. The double bonds put bends into the carbon chains that result in less efficient packing of molecules; thus vegetable oils are liquids at room temperature while saturated fats are solids at room temperature. When food manufacturers add hydrogen to the double bonds of vegetable oil, the unsaturated fat is converted into a saturated fat, turning the liquid oil into a solid at room temperature. The words "partially hydrogenated vegetable oil" on a label indicate a food product that contains saturated fats made via hydrogenation reactions.

Alkenes can also add unsymmetrical reagents across the double bond. For example, ethene reacts with hydrogen chloride to form chloroethane.

Chloroethane

▲ Partially hydrogenated vegetable oil is a saturated fat that is made by hydrogenating unsaturated fats.

If the alkene itself is also unsymmetrical, then the addition of an unsymmetrical reagent leads to the potential for two different products. For example, when HCl reacts with propene, two products are possible:

$$CH_3-\underset{\underset{H}{|}}{\overset{\overset{H}{|}}{C}}-\underset{\underset{Cl}{|}}{\overset{\overset{H}{|}}{C}}-H \quad \text{1-chloropropane (not observed)}$$

$$\underset{H}{\overset{CH_3}{\diagdown}}C=C\underset{H}{\overset{H}{\diagup}} + HCl$$

$$CH_3-\underset{\underset{Cl}{|}}{\overset{\overset{H}{|}}{C}}-\underset{\underset{H}{|}}{\overset{\overset{H}{|}}{C}}-H \quad \text{2-chloropropane}$$

When this reaction is carried out in the lab, however, only the 2-chloropropane forms. We can predict the product of the addition of an unsymmetrical reagent to an unsymmetrical alkene with Markovnikov's rule, which states the following:

> **When a polar reagent is added to an unsymmetrical alkene, the positive end (the least electronegative part) of the reagent adds to the carbon atom that has the most hydrogen atoms.**

In most reactions of this type, the positive end of the reagent is hydrogen; therefore, the hydrogen atom bonds to the carbon atom that already contains the most hydrogen atoms.

EXAMPLE 20.6 Alkene Addition Reactions

Determine the products of the reactions.

(a) $CH_3CH_2CH=CH_2 + Br_2 \longrightarrow$

(b) $CH_3CH_2CH=CH_2 + HBr \longrightarrow$

SOLUTION

(a) The reaction of 1-butene with bromine is an example of a symmetric addition. The bromine adds across the double bond and each carbon forms a single bond to a bromine atom.

(b) The reaction of 1-butene with hydrogen bromide is an example of an unsymmetrical addition. Apply Markovnikov's rule to determine which carbon the hydrogen bonds with and which carbon the bromine atom bonds with. Markovnikov's rule predicts that the hydrogen bonds to the end carbon in this case.

FOR PRACTICE 20.6
Determine the products of the reactions.

(a) $CH_3-\underset{\underset{H}{|}}{\overset{\overset{CH_3}{|}}{C}}-\underset{\underset{H}{|}}{C}=CH_2 + H_2 \xrightarrow{\text{catalyst}}$

(b) $CH_3-\underset{\underset{H}{|}}{\overset{\overset{CH_3}{|}}{C}}-\underset{\underset{H}{|}}{C}=CH_2 + HCl \longrightarrow$

20.7 Aromatic Hydrocarbons

As you might imagine, determining the structure of organic compounds has not always been easy. During the mid-1800s chemists were working to determine the structure of a particularly stable organic compound named benzene (C_6H_6). In 1865, Friedrich August Kekulé (1829–1896) had a dream in which he envisioned chains of carbon atoms as snakes. The snakes danced before him, and one of them twisted around and bit its tail. Based on that vision, Kekulé proposed the following structure for benzene:

This structure has alternating single and double bonds. When we examine the carbon–carbon bond lengths in benzene, however, we find that all the bonds are the same length, which indicates that the following resonance structures are a more accurate representation of benzene:

Recall from Section 9.8 that the actual structure of a molecule represented by resonance structures is intermediate between the two resonance structures and is called a *resonance hybrid*.

The true structure of benzene is a hybrid of the two resonance structures. We often represent benzene with the following carbon skeletal formula (or line formula):

The ring represents the delocalized π electrons that occupy the molecular orbital shown superimposed on the ball-and-stick model. When drawing benzene rings, either by themselves or as parts of other compounds, organic chemists use either this diagram or just one of the resonance structures with alternating double bonds. Both representations indicate the same thing—a benzene ring.

The benzene ring structure occurs in many organic compounds. An atom or group of atoms can be substituted for one or more of the six hydrogen atoms on the ring to form compounds referred to as substituted benzenes, such as chlorobenzene and phenol.

Chlorobenzene   Phenol

Because many compounds containing benzene rings have pleasant aromas, benzene rings are also called *aromatic rings*, and compounds containing them are called *aromatic compounds*. Aromatic compounds are responsible for the pleasant smells of cinnamon, vanilla, and jasmine.

Naming Aromatic Hydrocarbons

Monosubstituted benzenes—benzenes in which only one of the hydrogen atoms has been substituted—are often named as derivatives of benzene.

Ethylbenzene   Bromobenzene

These names take the general form:

(name of substituent)benzene

However, many monosubstituted benzenes have names that can only be learned through familiarity. Some common ones are shown here.

Some substituted benzenes, especially those with large substituents, are named by treating the benzene ring as the substituent. In these cases, the benzene substituent is referred to as a **phenyl group**.

Disubstituted benzenes—benzenes in which two hydrogen atoms have been substituted—are numbered and the substituents are listed alphabetically. We determine the order of numbering on the ring by the alphabetical order of the substituents.

When the two substituents are identical, we use the prefix *di-*.

Also in common use, in place of numbering, are the prefixes ortho (1,2 disubstituted), meta (1,3 disubstituted), and para (1,4 disubstituted).

Compounds containing fused aromatic rings are called polycyclic aromatic hydrocarbons. Some common examples (shown in Figure 20.5 ▶) include naphthalene, the substance that composes mothballs, and pyrene, a carcinogen found in cigarette smoke.

▶ FIGURE 20.5 **Polycyclic aromatic compounds** The structures of some common polycyclic aromatic compounds contain fused rings.

Naphthalene

Anthracene

Pyrene

Tetracene

Reactions of Aromatic Compounds

We might expect benzene to react similarly to the alkenes, readily undergoing addition reactions across its double bonds. However, because of electron delocalization around the ring and the resulting greater stability, benzene does not typically undergo addition reactions. Instead, benzene undergoes substitution reactions in which the hydrogen atoms are replaced by other atoms or groups of atoms as shown in the following examples:

The substances shown over the arrows are catalysts needed to increase the rate of the reaction.

Chlorobenzene

ethylbenzene

20.8 Functional Groups

Most other families of organic compounds are hydrocarbons with a *functional group*—a characteristic atom or group of atoms—inserted into the hydrocarbon. A group of organic compounds that all have the same functional group is a *family*. For example, the members of the family of alcohols each have an —OH functional group and the general formula R—OH, where R represents a hydrocarbon group. (That is, we refer to the hydrocarbon group as an "R group.") Some specific examples include methanol and isopropyl alcohol (also known as rubbing alcohol).

Methanol   Isopropyl alcohol

The presence of a functional group in a hydrocarbon alters the properties of the compound significantly. For example, methane is a nonpolar gas. By contrast, methanol—methane with an —OH group substituted for one of the hydrogen atoms—is a polar, hydrogen-bonded liquid at room temperature. Although each member of a family is unique and different, their common functional group causes some similarities in both their physical and chemical properties. Table 20.10 lists some common functional groups, their general formulas, and an example of each.

TABLE 20.10 Some Common Functional Groups

Family	General Formula*	Condensed General Formula	Example	Name
Alcohols	R — OH	ROH	CH_3CH_2OH	Ethanol (ethyl alcohol)
Ethers	R — O — R	ROR	CH_3OCH_3	Dimethyl ether
Aldehydes	R — C(=O) — H	RCHO	CH_3 — C(=O) — H	Ethanal (acetaldehyde)
Ketones	R — C(=O) — R	RCOR	CH_3 — C(=O) — CH_3	Propanone (acetone)
Carboxylic acids	R — C(=O) — OH	RCOOH	CH_3 — C(=O) — OH	Ethanoic acid (acetic acid)
Esters	R — C(=O) — OR	RCOOR	CH_3 — C(=O) — OCH_3	Methyl acetate
Amines	R — N(R) — R	R_3N	CH_3CH_2 — N(H) — H	Ethylamine

*In ethers, ketones, esters, and amines, the R groups may be the same or different.

20.9 Alcohols

As we discussed in Section 20.8, **alcohols** are organic compounds containing the $-OH$ functional group, or **hydroxyl group**, and they have the general formula $R-OH$. In addition to methanol and isopropyl alcohol, ethanol and 1-butanol (shown here) are also common alcohols.

$$CH_3-CH_2-OH$$
Ethanol

$$CH_3-CH_2-CH_2-CH_2-OH$$
1-Butanol

Naming Alcohols

The names of alcohols are like the names of alkanes with the following differences:

- The base chain is the longest continuous carbon chain that contains the $-OH$ functional group.

- The base name has the ending *-ol*.

- We number the base chain to assign the $-OH$ group the lowest possible number.

- We insert a number indicating the position of the $-OH$ group just before the base name. For example:

$$CH_3CH_2CH_2\underset{\underset{OH}{|}}{CH}CH_3$$
2-Pentanol

$$\underset{\underset{OH}{|}}{CH_2}-CH_2-\underset{\underset{CH_3}{|}}{CH}-CH_3$$
3-Methyl-1-butanol

About Alcohols

The familiar alcohol in alcoholic beverages, ethanol, is most commonly formed by the yeast fermentation of sugars, such as glucose, from fruits and grains.

$$\underset{\text{Glucose}}{C_6H_{12}O_6} \xrightarrow{\text{yeast}} 2\ \underset{\text{Ethanol}}{CH_3CH_2OH} + 2\ CO_2$$

Alcoholic beverages contain ethanol, water, and a few other components that impart flavor and color. Beer usually contains 3–6% ethanol. Wine contains about 12–14% ethanol, and spirits—beverages like whiskey, rum, or tequila—range from 40% to 80% ethanol, depending on their *proof*. The proof of an alcoholic beverage is twice the percentage of its ethanol content, so an 80-proof whiskey contains 40% ethanol. Ethanol is used as a gasoline additive because it increases the octane rating of gasoline and fosters its complete combustion, reducing the levels of certain pollutants such as carbon monoxide and the precursors of ozone.

Isopropyl alcohol (or 2-propanol) is available at any drug store under the name of rubbing alcohol. It is commonly used as a disinfectant for wounds and to sterilize medical instruments. Isopropyl alcohol should never be consumed internally, as it is highly toxic. Four ounces of isopropyl alcohol can cause death. A third common alcohol is methanol, also called wood alcohol. Methanol is commonly used as a laboratory solvent and as a fuel additive. Like isopropyl alcohol, methanol is toxic and should never be consumed.

Alcohol Reactions

Alcohols undergo a number of reactions including substitution, elimination (or dehydration), and oxidation. Alcohols also react with active metals to form strong bases.

Substitution Alcohols react with acids such as HBr to form halogenated hydrocarbons:

$$ROH + HBr \longrightarrow R{-}Br + H_2O$$

In these reactions, the halogen replaces the hydroxyl group on the alcohol. For example, ethanol reacts with hydrobromic acid to form bromoethane and water:

$$CH_3CH_2OH + HBr \longrightarrow CH_3CH_2Br + H_2O$$

Elimination (or Dehydration) In the presence of concentrated acids such as H_2SO_4, alcohols react and eliminate water, forming an alkene. For example, ethanol eliminates water to form ethene according to the reaction:

$$\underset{\overset{|}{H} \quad \overset{|}{OH}}{CH_2{-}CH_2} \xrightarrow{H_2SO_4} CH_2{=}CH_2 + H_2O$$

Oxidation In organic chemistry, we think of oxidation and reduction in terms of the changes to the carbon atoms in the molecule. Thus, oxidation is the gaining of oxygen or the losing of hydrogen by a carbon atom. Reduction is the loss of oxygen or the gaining of hydrogen by a carbon atom. We can draw a series showing relative states of oxidation:

Oxidation

$$CH_3{-}CH_3 \xrightarrow[\text{gain O}]{} CH_3{-}CH_2{-}OH \xrightarrow[\text{lose H}]{} \underset{}{CH_3{-}\overset{\overset{\displaystyle O}{\|}}{C}{-}H} \xrightarrow[\text{gain O}]{} \underset{}{CH_3{-}\overset{\overset{\displaystyle O}{\|}}{C}{-}OH}$$

| Alkane | Alcohol | Aldehyde | Carboxylic acid |

Reduction

In this view, an alcohol is a partially oxidized hydrocarbon; it can be further oxidized to form an aldehyde or carboxylic acid, or it can be reduced to form a hydrocarbon (but this is rare). For example, ethanol can be oxidized to acetic acid according to the reaction:

$$CH_3CH_2OH \xrightarrow[H_2SO_4]{Na_2Cr_2O_7} CH_3CHOOH$$

Reaction with Active Metals Alcohols react with active metals, such as sodium, much as water does. For example, methanol reacts with sodium to form *sodium methoxide* and hydrogen gas:

$$CH_3OH + Na \longrightarrow \underset{\text{Sodium methoxide}}{CH_3ONa} + \tfrac{1}{2}H_2$$

The reaction of *water* with sodium produces *sodium hydroxide* and hydrogen gas:

$$H_2O + Na \longrightarrow NaOH + \tfrac{1}{2}H_2$$

In both cases, a strong base forms (OH^- for water and CH_3O^- for methanol).

EXAMPLE 20.7 Alcohol Reactions

Determine the type of reaction (substitution, dehydration, oxidation, or reaction with an active metal) that occurs in each case, and write formulas for the products.

(a)
$$
\begin{array}{c}
\quad\quad\ \text{CH}_3 \\
\quad\quad\ | \\
\text{CH}_3\text{—CH—CH}_2\text{—CH}_2\text{—OH} + \text{HBr} \longrightarrow
\end{array}
$$

(b)
$$
\begin{array}{c}
\quad\quad\ \text{CH}_3 \\
\quad\quad\ | \\
\text{CH}_3\text{—CH—CH}_2\text{—CH}_2\text{—OH} \xrightarrow[\text{H}_2\text{SO}_4]{\text{Na}_2\text{Cr}_2\text{O}_7}
\end{array}
$$

SOLUTION

(a) An alcohol reacting with an acid is an example of a *substitution reaction*. The product of the substitution reaction is a halogenated hydrocarbon and water.	$\begin{array}{c} \text{CH}_3 \\ \| \\ \text{CH}_3\text{—CH—CH}_2\text{—CH}_2\text{—OH} + \text{HBr} \longrightarrow \\[1em] \text{CH}_3 \\ \| \\ \text{CH}_3\text{—CH—CH}_2\text{—CH}_2\text{—Br} + \text{H}_2\text{O} \end{array}$
(b) An alcohol in solution with sodium dichromate and acid undergoes an *oxidation reaction*. The product of the oxidation reaction is a carboxylic acid functional group. (We discuss carboxylic acid functional groups in detail in Section 20.11.)	$\begin{array}{c} \text{CH}_3 \\ \| \\ \text{CH}_3\text{—CH—CH}_2\text{—CH}_2\text{—OH} \xrightarrow[\text{H}_2\text{SO}_4]{\text{Na}_2\text{Cr}_2\text{O}_7} \\[1em] \text{CH}_3 \quad\quad\ \text{O} \\ \| \quad\quad\quad \| \\ \text{CH}_3\text{—CH—CH}_2\text{—C—OH} \end{array}$

FOR PRACTICE 20.7

Determine the type of reaction (substitution, dehydration, oxidation, or reaction with an active metal) that occurs in each case, and write formulas for the products.

(a) $\text{CH}_3\text{CH}_2\text{OH} + \text{Na} \longrightarrow$

(b)
$$
\begin{array}{c}
\quad\quad\ \text{CH}_3 \\
\quad\quad\ | \\
\text{CH}_3\text{—CH—CH}_2\text{—OH} \xrightarrow{\text{H}_2\text{SO}_4}
\end{array}
$$

20.10 Aldehydes and Ketones

Aldehydes and **ketones** have the following general formulas:

$$
\begin{array}{cc}
\quad \text{O} & \quad \text{O} \\
\quad \| & \quad \| \\
\text{R—C—H} & \text{R—C—R} \\
\text{Aldehyde} & \text{Ketone}
\end{array}
$$

The functional group for both aldehydes and ketones is the **carbonyl group**:

$$
\begin{array}{c}
\text{O} \\
\| \\
\diagup \text{C} \diagdown
\end{array}
$$

> The condensed structural formula for aldehydes is RCHO and that for ketones is RCOR.

Ketones have an R group attached to both sides of the carbonyl, while aldehydes have one R group and a hydrogen atom. (An exception is formaldehyde, which is an aldehyde with two H atoms bonded to the carbonyl group.)

$$
\begin{array}{c}
\quad\ \text{O} \\
\quad\ \| \\
\quad\ \text{C} \\
\diagup \quad \diagdown \\
\text{H} \quad\quad \text{H}
\end{array}
$$

Formaldehyde or methanal

▲ FIGURE 20.6 Common Aldehydes and Ketones

Other common aldehydes and ketones are shown in Figure 20.6 ▲.

Naming Aldehydes and Ketones

Many aldehydes and ketones have common names that we can learn only by becoming familiar with them, but we can systematically name simple aldehydes according to the number of carbon atoms in the longest continuous carbon chain that contains the carbonyl group. We form the base name from the name of the corresponding alkane by dropping the -*e* and adding the ending -*al*.

$$CH_3-CH_2-CH_2-\overset{\displaystyle O}{\overset{\|}{C}}-H \qquad CH_3-CH_2-CH_2-CH_2-\overset{\displaystyle O}{\overset{\|}{C}}-H$$

Butanal   Pentanal

We name simple ketones according to the longest continuous carbon chain containing the carbonyl group, forming the base name from the name of the corresponding alkane by dropping the letter -*e* and adding the ending -*one*. For ketones, we number the chain to give the carbonyl group the lowest possible number.

$$CH_3-CH_2-CH_2-\overset{\displaystyle O}{\overset{\|}{C}}-CH_3 \qquad CH_3-CH_2-CH_2-\overset{\displaystyle O}{\overset{\|}{C}}-CH_2-CH_3$$

2-Pentanone   3-Hexanone

About Aldehydes and Ketones

The most familiar aldehyde is probably formaldehyde, shown earlier in this section. Formaldehyde is a gas with a pungent odor. It is often mixed with water to make formalin, a preservative and disinfectant. Formaldehyde is also found in wood smoke, which is one reason that smoking is an effective method of food preservation—the formaldehyde kills bacteria. Aromatic aldehydes, those that also contain an aromatic ring, have pleasant aromas. For example, vanillin causes the smell of vanilla, cinnamaldehyde is the sweet-smelling component of cinnamon, and benzaldehyde accounts for the smell of almonds (Figure 20.7 ▼).

▲ FIGURE 20.7 The Nutty Aroma of Almonds   Benzaldehyde is partly responsible for the smell of almonds.

Ionone

▲ **FIGURE 20.8 The Fragrance of Raspberries** Ionone is partly responsible for the smell of raspberries.

The most familiar ketone is acetone, the main component of nail polish remover. Other ketones have more pleasant aromas. For example, carvone is largely responsible for the smell of spearmint, 2-heptanone (among other compounds) for the smell of cloves, and ionone for the smell of raspberries (Figure 20.8 ▲).

Carvone

$CH_3—CH_2—CH_2—CH_2—CH_2—\overset{\overset{O}{\|}}{C}—CH_3$

2-Heptanone

Aldehyde and Ketone Reactions

Aldehydes and ketones can be formed by the *oxidation* of alcohols. For example, ethanol can be oxidized to ethanal, and 2-propanol can be oxidized to 2-propanone (or acetone).

Ethanol $\xrightarrow{\text{oxidation}}$ Ethanal

2-Propanol $\xrightarrow{\text{oxidation}}$ 2-Propanone

In the reverse reaction, an aldehyde or ketone is reduced to an alcohol. For example, 2-butanone can be reduced to 2-butanol in the presence of a reducing agent.

2-Butanone $\xrightarrow{\text{reduction}}$ 2-Butanol

The carbonyl group in aldehydes and ketones is unsaturated, much like the double bond in an alkene. Because of this feature, the most common reactions of aldehydes and ketones are **addition reactions**. However, in contrast to the carbon–carbon double bond in alkenes, which is nonpolar, the double bond in the carbonyl group is highly polar (Figure 20.9 ▶). Consequently, additions across the double bond result in the more electronegative part of the reagent bonding to the carbon atom and the less electronegative part (often hydrogen) bonding to the oxygen atom. For example, HCN adds across the carbonyl double bond in formaldehyde.

Formaldehyde

Acetaldehyde

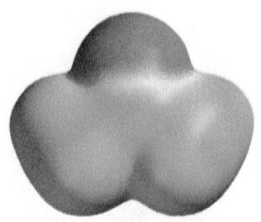
Acetone

◀ FIGURE 20.9 **Charge Density Plots of the Carbonyl Group** The carbonyl group is highly polar, as shown in these plots of electrostatic potential.

20.11 Carboxylic Acids and Esters

Carboxylic acids and **esters** have the general formulas:

$$\underset{\text{Carboxylic acid}}{R-\overset{\overset{\displaystyle O}{\|}}{C}-OH} \qquad \underset{\text{Ester}}{R-\overset{\overset{\displaystyle O}{\|}}{C}-OR}$$

Figure 20.10 ▶ shows the structures of some common carboxylic acids and esters.

> The condensed structural formula for carboxylic acids is RCOOH; for esters it is RCOOR.

Naming Carboxylic Acids and Esters

We systematically name carboxylic acids according to the number of carbon atoms in the longest chain containing the —COOH functional group. We form the base name by dropping the *-e* from the name of the corresponding alkane and adding the ending *-oic acid*.

$$\underset{\text{Propanoic acid}}{CH_3-CH_2-\overset{\overset{\displaystyle O}{\|}}{C}-OH} \qquad \underset{\text{Pentanoic acid}}{CH_3-CH_2-CH_2-CH_2-\overset{\overset{\displaystyle O}{\|}}{C}-OH}$$

We name esters as if they were derived from a carboxylic acid by replacing the H on the OH with an alkyl group. The R group from the parent acid forms the base name of the compound. We change the *-ic* on the name of the corresponding carboxylic acid to *-ate*, and drop *acid*, naming the R group that replaced the H on the carboxylic acid as an alkyl group with the ending *-yl*, as shown in the following examples:

$$\underset{\text{Propanoic acid}}{CH_3-CH_2-\overset{\overset{\displaystyle O}{\|}}{C}-OH} \qquad \underset{\text{Pentanoic acid}}{CH_3-CH_2-CH_2-CH_2-\overset{\overset{\displaystyle O}{\|}}{C}-OH}$$

$$\underset{\text{Methyl propanoate}}{CH_3-CH_2-\overset{\overset{\displaystyle O}{\|}}{C}-OCH_3} \qquad \underset{\text{Ethyl pentanoate}}{CH_3-CH_2-CH_2-CH_2-\overset{\overset{\displaystyle O}{\|}}{C}-OCH_2CH_3}$$

$$\underset{\text{Ethanoic acid or acetic acid}}{CH_3-\overset{\overset{\displaystyle O}{\|}}{C}-OH}$$

$$\underset{\text{Butanoic acid}}{CH_3-CH_2-CH_2-\overset{\overset{\displaystyle O}{\|}}{C}-OH}$$

$$\underset{\text{Methyl butanoate}}{CH_3-CH_2-CH_2-\overset{\overset{\displaystyle O}{\|}}{C}-O-CH_3}$$

$$\underset{\text{Ethyl propanoate}}{CH_3-CH_2-\overset{\overset{\displaystyle O}{\|}}{C}-O-CH_2-CH_3}$$

▲ FIGURE 20.10 **Common Carboxylic Acids and Esters**

About Carboxylic Acids and Esters

Like all acids, carboxylic acids taste sour. The most familiar carboxylic acid is ethanoic acid, better known by its common name, acetic acid. Acetic acid is the active ingredient in vinegar. It can form by the oxidation of ethanol, which is why wines left open to air become sour. Some yeasts and bacteria also form acetic acid when they metabolize sugars in bread dough. These are added to bread dough to make sourdough bread. Other common carboxylic acids include methanoic acid (formic acid), present in bee stings and

Citric acid

▲ FIGURE 20.11 **The Tart Taste of Limes** Citric acid is partly responsible for the sour taste of limes.

ant bites; lactic acid, which collects in muscles after intense exercise causing soreness; and citric acid, found in limes, lemons, and oranges (Figure 20.11 ▲).

Formic or methanoic acid

Lactic acid

Esters are best known for their sweet smells. Methyl butanoate is largely responsible for the smell and taste of apples, and ethyl butanoate is largely responsible for the smell and taste of pineapples (see Figure 20.12 ▼).

$$CH_3-CH_2-CH_2-\overset{\overset{\displaystyle O}{\|}}{C}-O-CH_3$$
Methyl butanoate

$$CH_3-CH_2-CH_2-\overset{\overset{\displaystyle O}{\|}}{C}-O-CH_2-CH_3$$
Ethyl butanoate

▲ FIGURE 20.12 **The Aroma of Pineapple** Ethyl butanoate is partly responsible for the aroma of pineapples.

Carboxylic Acid and Ester Reactions

Carboxylic acids act as weak acids in solution.

$$RCOOH(aq) + H_2O(l) \rightleftharpoons H_3O^+(aq) + RCOO^-(aq)$$

Like all acids, carboxylic acids react with strong bases via neutralization reactions. For example, propanoic acid reacts with sodium hydroxide to form sodium propanoate and water.

$$CH_3CH_2COOH(aq) + NaOH(aq) \longrightarrow CH_3CH_2COO^-Na^+(aq) + HOH(l)$$

A carboxylic acid reacts with an alcohol to form an ester via a **condensation reaction**, a reaction in which two (or more) organic compounds join, often with the loss of water (or some other small molecule).

$$\underset{\text{Acid}}{R-\overset{\overset{\displaystyle O}{\|}}{C}-OH} + \underset{\text{Alcohol}}{HO-R'} \xrightarrow{H_2SO_4} \underset{\text{Ester}}{R-\overset{\overset{\displaystyle O}{\|}}{C}-O-R'} + \underset{\text{Water}}{H_2O}$$

An important example of this reaction is the formation of acetylsalicylic acid (aspirin) from ethanoic acid (acetic acid) and salicylic acid (originally obtained from the bark of the willow tree).

If we subject a carboxylic acid to high temperatures, it undergoes a condensation reaction with itself to form an acid anhydride (anhydride means "without water").

$$RCOOH(aq) + HOOCR(aq) \longrightarrow RCOOOCR(aq) + HOH(aq)$$
Acid anhydride

We can add water to an acid anhydride to reverse the reaction just shown and regenerate the carboxylic acid molecules.

Conceptual Connection 20.3 Oxidation

Arrange the compounds from least oxidized to most oxidized.

20.12 Ethers

Ethers are organic compounds with the general formula ROR. The two R groups may be identical or they may be different. Some common ethers are shown in Figure 20.13 ▾.

Naming Ethers
Common names for ethers have the format:

(R group 1) (R group 2) ether

▲ FIGURE 20.13 **Ethers**

If the two R groups differ, we use each of their names in alphabetical order. If the two R groups are the same, we use the prefix *di-*. Some examples include:

$$H_3C-CH_2-CH_2-O-CH_2-CH_2-CH_3$$
Dipropyl ether

$$H_3C-CH_2-O-CH_2-CH_2-CH_3$$
Ethyl propyl ether

About Ethers

The most common ether is diethyl ether. Diethyl ether is a useful laboratory solvent because it can dissolve many organic compounds and it has a low boiling point (34.6 °C). The low boiling point allows for easy removal of the solvent. Diethyl ether was used as a general anesthetic for many years. When inhaled, diethyl ether depresses the central nervous system, causing unconsciousness and insensitivity to pain. Its use as an anesthetic, however, has decreased in recent years because other compounds have the same anesthetic effect with fewer side effects (such as nausea).

20.13 Amines

The simplest nitrogen-containing compound is ammonia (NH_3). **Amines** are organic compounds containing nitrogen that are derived from ammonia with one or more of the hydrogen atoms replaced by alkyl groups. Like ammonia, amines are weak bases. We systematically name amines according to the hydrocarbon groups attached to the nitrogen and assign the ending *-amine*.

$$CH_3-CH_2-\underset{\underset{H}{|}}{N}-H$$
Ethylamine

$$CH_3-CH_2-\underset{\underset{CH_3}{|}}{N}-H$$
Ethylmethylamine

Amines are most commonly known for their awful odors. When a living organism dies, the bacteria that feast on its proteins emit amines. For example, trimethylamine causes the smell of rotten fish, and cadaverine causes the smell of decaying animal flesh.

$$CH_3-\underset{\underset{CH_3}{|}}{\overset{\overset{CH_3}{|}}{N}}-CH_3$$
Trimethylamine

$$NH_2-CH_2-CH_2-CH_2-CH_2-CH_2-NH_2$$
Cadaverine

Amine Reactions

Just as carboxylic acids act as weak acids, so amines act as weak bases:

$$RNH_2(aq) + H_2O(l) \rightleftharpoons RNH_3^+(aq) + OH^-(aq)$$

Like all bases, amines react with strong acids to form salts called ammonium salts. For example, methylamine reacts with hydrochloric acid to form methylammonium chloride:

$$CH_3NH_2(aq) + HCl(aq) \longrightarrow CH_3NH_3^+Cl^-(aq)$$
Methylammonium chloride

An important amine reaction that we will see again in Chapter 21 is the condensation reaction between a carboxylic acid and an amine.

$$CH_3COOH(aq) + HNHR(aq) \longrightarrow CH_3CONHR(aq) + HOH(l)$$

This reaction is responsible for the formation of proteins from amino acids (see Section 21.4).

20.14 Polymers

Polymers are long, chainlike molecules composed of repeating units called **monomers**. In Chapter 21, we will learn about natural polymers such as starches, proteins, and DNA, which play important roles in living organisms. In this section, we learn about synthetic polymers, which we encounter daily in plastic products such as PVC tubing, styrofoam coffee cups, nylon rope, and plexiglass windows. Polymer materials are common in our everyday lives, found in everything from computers to toys to packaging materials. Most polymers are durable, partly because of the length of their molecules. In general, the longer the length of a molecule, the greater the intermolecular forces between molecules, and the higher the melting point and boiling point of the substance. Since breaking or tearing a polymeric material involves either overcoming the intermolecular forces between chains, or actually breaking the covalent bonds between monomers, polymers tend to be durable materials.

One of the simplest synthetic polymers is polyethylene. The polyethylene monomer is ethene (also called ethylene).

$$H_2C=CH_2$$ Monomer

Ethene or ethylene

Ethene monomers can react with each other, breaking the double bond between carbons and bonding together to form a long polymer chain.

$$\cdots CH_2-CH_2-CH_2-CH_2-CH_2-CH_2-CH_2-CH_2-CH_2\cdots$$

Polymer

Polyethylene

Polyethylene is the plastic that is used for soda bottles, juice containers, and garbage bags (Figure 20.14 ▼). It is an example of an **addition polymer**, a polymer in which the monomers link together without the elimination of any atoms.

Substituted polyethylenes make up an entire class of polymers. For example, polyvinyl chloride (PVC)—the plastic used to make certain kinds of pipes and plumbing fixtures—is composed of monomers in which a chlorine atom has been substituted for one of the hydrogen atoms in ethene (Figure 20.15 ▼). These monomers (shown here) react to form PVC:

$$\cdots CH-CH_2-CH-CH_2-CH-CH_2-CH-CH_2-CH\cdots$$
$$\qquad | \qquad\qquad | \qquad\qquad | \qquad\qquad | \qquad\qquad |$$
$$\qquad Cl \qquad\quad Cl \qquad\quad Cl \qquad\quad Cl \qquad\quad Cl$$

Polymer

$$HC=CH_2$$
$$|$$
$$Cl$$
Monomer

Chloroethene

Polyvinyl chloride (PVC)

▲ **FIGURE 20.14 Polyethylene** Soda and juice bottles are made from polyethylene.

▶ **FIGURE 20.15 Polyvinyl Chloride** Polyvinyl chloride is used for many plastic plumbing supplies, such as pipes and connectors.

TABLE 20.11 Polymers of Commercial Importance

Polymer	Structure	Uses
Addition Polymers		
Polyethylene	$-(CH_2 - CH_2)_n$	Films, packaging, bottles
Polypropylene	$\left[CH_2 - \underset{\underset{CH_3}{\mid}}{CH_2} \right]_n$	Kitchenware, fibers, appliances
Polystyrene	$\left[CH_2 - CH(C_6H_5) \right]_n$	Packaging, disposable food containers, insulation
Polyvinyl chloride	$\left[CH_2 - \underset{\underset{Cl}{\mid}}{CH} \right]_n$	Pipe fittings, clear film for meat packaging
Condensation Polymers		
Polyurethane	$\left[\underset{\underset{O}{\parallel}}{C} - NH - R - NH - \underset{\underset{O}{\parallel}}{C} - O - R' - O \right]_n$ $R, R' = -CH_2 - CH_2 -$ (for example)	"Foam" furniture stuffing, spray-on insulation, automotive parts, footwear, water-protective coatings
Polyethylene terephthalate (a polyester)	$\left[O - CH_2 - CH_2 - O - \underset{\underset{O}{\parallel}}{C} - C_6H_4 - \underset{\underset{O}{\parallel}}{C} \right]_n$	Tire cord, magnetic tape, apparel, soda bottles
Nylon 6,6	$\left[NH - (CH_2)_6 - NH - \underset{\underset{O}{\parallel}}{C} - (CH_2)_4 - \underset{\underset{O}{\parallel}}{C} \right]_n$	Home furnishings, apparel, carpet fibers, fish line, polymer blends

Table 20.11 lists several other substituted polyethylene polymers.

Some polymers—called copolymers—consist of two different kinds of monomers. For example, the monomers that compose nylon 6,6 are hexamethylenediamine and adipic acid. These two monomers add together via a condensation reaction as follows:

Monomers

Hexamethylenediamine   Adipic acid

Dimer

The product that forms between the reaction of two monomers is called a **dimer**. The polymer (nylon 6,6) forms as the dimer continues to add more monomers. Polymers that eliminate an atom or a small group of atoms during polymerization are called **condensation polymers**. Nylon 6,6 and other similar nylons can be drawn into fibers and used to make consumer products such as panty hose, carpet fibers, and fishing line. Table 20.11 shows other condensation polymers.

CHAPTER IN REVIEW

Self Assessment Quiz

Q1. Which property of carbon is related to its ability to form a large number of compounds?
 a) its tendency to form four covalent bonds
 b) its ability to form double and triple bonds
 c) its tendency to catenate
 d) all of the above

Q2. What is the correct formula for the alkane (noncyclical) containing eight carbon atoms?
 a) C_8H_{16} b) C_8H_{18}
 c) C_8H_{14} d) C_8H_8

Q3. Which structure is not an isomer of $CH_3CH_2CH_2CH_2CH_3$?

 a) CH_3 CH_3
        | |
        CH_2—CH_2—CH_2

 b) CH_3—CH—CH_2—CH_3
              |
              CH_3

 c) CH_3—$\overset{\displaystyle CH_3}{\underset{\displaystyle CH_3}{C}}$—$CH_3$

 d) None of the above (all are isomers).

Q4. Which structure can exhibit optical isomerism?

 a)   H   H
        | |
    H—C—C—Cl
        | |
        H   H

 b)   H   H   Cl
        | | |
    H—C—C—C—H
        | | |
        Cl H   H

 c)   Br Br H
        | | |
    H—C—C—C—H
        | | |
        H   H   H

 d)   Br H   Br
        | | |
    H—C—C—C—Br
        | | |
        Br H   Br

Q5. Name the compound.

$$CH_3{-}CH_2{-}CH_2{-}CH{-}\overset{\displaystyle CH_3}{\underset{\displaystyle \underset{\displaystyle CH_3}{|}\;CH_2}{CH}}{-}CH_3$$

 a) 4-ethyl-5-methylhexane
 b) 3-ethyl-2-methylhexane
 c) 3-ethyl-2-methylnonane
 d) 4-methyl-5ethylhexane

Q6. Name the compound.

$$CH_3{-}C{\equiv}C{-}CH{-}CH_3$$
$$\underset{\displaystyle CH_3}{|}$$

 a) 4-methyl-2-pentyne
 b) 2-methyl-3-pentyne
 c) 2-methyl-3-hexyne
 d) 4-methyl-2-hexyne

Q7. Determine the product of the reaction.

$$CH_3{-}CH{=}\overset{\displaystyle CH_3}{\underset{\displaystyle |}{C}}{-}CH_3 + HBr \longrightarrow$$

 a) $CH_2Br{-}CH{=}\overset{\displaystyle CH_3}{\underset{\displaystyle |}{C}}{-}CH_3$

 b) $CH_3{-}CH_2{-}\overset{\displaystyle CH_3}{\underset{\displaystyle |}{CH}}{-}CH_3$

 c) $CH_3{-}CH{-}\overset{\displaystyle CH_3}{\underset{\displaystyle |}{CH}}{-}CH_3$
     $\underset{\displaystyle Br}{|}$

 d) $CH_3{-}CH_2{-}\overset{\displaystyle CH_3}{\underset{\displaystyle \underset{\displaystyle Br}{|}}{C}}{-}CH_3$

Q8. Determine the product of the reaction.

$$CH_3-CH-CH_2-OH + HCl \longrightarrow$$
$$\quad\quad\;\; | $$
$$\quad\quad\; CH_3$$

a) $CH_3-CH-CH_3$
$$\quad\quad | $$
$$\quad\quad Cl$$

b) $CH_3-CH-CH_3$
$$\quad\quad\quad | $$
$$\quad\quad\; CH_3$$

c) $CH_3-\underset{\underset{CH_3}{|}}{\overset{\overset{Cl}{|}}{C}}-CH_2-OH$

d) $CH_3-CH-CH_2-Cl$
$$\quad\quad\quad | $$
$$\quad\quad\;\; CH_3$$

Q9. Which compound is an ester?

a) $CH_3-CH_2-O-CH_3$

b) $CH_3-CH_2-\overset{\overset{O}{||}}{C}-OH$

c) $CH_3-\overset{\overset{O}{||}}{C}-CH_3$

d) $CH_3-\overset{\overset{O}{||}}{C}-O-CH_2CH_3$

Q10. Which compound is most likely to have a foul odor?

a) $CH_3-\overset{\overset{O}{||}}{C}-O-CH_3$

b) $CH_3-CH_2-NH_2$

c) $CH_3-CH_2-O-CH_3$

d) $CH_3-CH_2-CH_2-HO$

Answers: 1. (d) **2.** (b) **3.** (a) **4.** (c) **5.** (b) **6.** (a) **7.** (d) **8.** (d) **9.** (d) **10.** (b)

Key Terms

Section 20.1
organic molecule (952)
organic chemistry (952)

Section 20.3
alkane (954)
alkene (954)
alkyne (954)
aromatic hydrocarbon (954)
aliphatic hydrocarbon (954)
structural isomers (955)
structural formula (955)
stereoisomers (957)
optical isomers (957)
enantiomers (958)

chiral (958)
dextrorotatory (958)
levorotatory (958)
racemic mixture (958)

Section 20.4
saturated hydrocarbon (960)

Section 20.5
unsaturated hydrocarbon (964)
geometric (cis–trans)
    isomerism (968)

Section 20.7
phenyl group (973)
disubstituted benzene (973)

Section 20.9
alcohol (976)
hydroxyl group (976)

Section 20.10
aldehyde (978)
ketone (978)
carbonyl group (978)
addition reaction (980)

Section 20.11
carboxylic acid (981)
esters (981)
condensation reaction (982)

Section 20.12
ether (983)

Section 20.13
amine (984)

Section 20.14
polymer (985)
monomer (985)
addition polymer (985)
dimer (987)
condensation polymer (987)

Key Concepts

Fragrances and Odors (20.1)
▶ Organic chemistry is the study of organic compounds, which contain carbon (and other elements including hydrogen, oxygen, and nitrogen).

Carbon (20.2)
▶ Carbon forms more compounds than all the other elements combined for several reasons.

▶ Carbon's four valence electrons (in conjunction with its size) allow carbon to form four bonds (in the form of single, double, or triple bonds).
▶ Carbon also has the capacity to catenate, to form long chains, because of the strength of the carbon–carbon bond.

Hydrocarbons (20.3)

▶ Organic compounds containing only carbon and hydrogen are called hydrocarbons, the key components of our world's fuels.

▶ Hydrocarbons can be divided into four different types: alkanes, alkenes, alkynes, and aromatic hydrocarbons.

▶ Stereoisomers are molecules that feature the same atoms bonded in the same order but arranged differently in space. Optical isomerism, a type of stereoisomerism, occurs when two molecules are nonsuperimposable mirror images of one another.

Alkanes (20.4)

▶ Alkanes are saturated hydrocarbons—they contain only single bonds and are therefore represented by the generic formula C_nH_{2n+2}. Alkane names always end in -ane.

Alkenes and Alkynes (20.5)

▶ Alkenes and alkynes are unsaturated hydrocarbons—they contain double bonds (alkenes) or triple bonds (alkynes) and are represented by the generic formulas C_nH_{2n} and C_nH_{2n-2}, respectively.

▶ Alkene names end in -ene and alkynes end in -yne.

▶ Because rotation about a double bond is severely restricted, geometric (or cis–trans) isomerism occurs in alkenes.

Hydrocarbon Reactions (20.6)

▶ The most common hydrocarbon reaction is probably combustion, in which hydrocarbons react with oxygen to form carbon dioxide and water; this reaction is exothermic and is used to provide most of our society's energy.

▶ Alkanes can also undergo substitution reactions, where heat or light causes another atom, commonly a halogen such as bromine, to be substituted for a hydrogen atom.

▶ Unsaturated hydrocarbons undergo addition reactions. If the addition reaction is between two unsymmetrical molecules, Markovnikov's rule predicts that the positive end of the polar reagent adds to the carbon with the most hydrogen atoms.

Aromatic Hydrocarbons (20.7)

▶ Aromatic hydrocarbons contain six-membered benzene rings represented with alternating single and double bonds that become equivalent through resonance. These compounds are called aromatic because they often produce pleasant fragrances.

▶ Because of the stability of the aromatic ring, benzene is more stable than a straight-chain alkene, and it undergoes substitution rather than addition reactions.

Functional Groups (20.8)

▶ Characteristic groups of atoms, such as hydroxyl (—OH), are called functional groups. Molecules that contain the same functional group have similar chemical and physical properties, and they are referred to as families.

Alcohols (20.9)

▶ The family of alcohols contains the —OH group and is named with the suffix -ol.

▶ Alcohols are commonly used in gasoline, in alcoholic beverages, and in sterilization procedures.

▶ Alcohols undergo substitution reactions, in which a substituent such as a halogen replaces the hydroxyl group.

▶ Alcohols undergo elimination reactions, in which water is eliminated across a bond to form an alkene, and oxidation or reduction reactions.

▶ Alcohols also react with active metals to form alkoxide ions and hydrogen gas.

Aldehydes and Ketones (20.10)

▶ Aldehydes and ketones both contain a carbonyl group (a carbon atom double-bonded to oxygen).

▶ In aldehydes, the carbonyl group is at the end of a carbon chain, while in ketones it is between two other carbon atoms.

▶ Aldehydes are named with the suffix -al and ketones with the suffix -one.

▶ A carbonyl can be formed by the oxidation of an alcohol or reverted to an alcohol by reduction.

▶ Like alkenes, carbonyls undergo addition reactions; however, because the carbon–oxygen bond is highly polar, the electronegative component of the reagent always adds to the carbon atom, and the less electronegative part adds to the oxygen.

Carboxylic Acids and Esters (20.11)

▶ Carboxylic acids contain a carbonyl group and a hydroxide on the same carbon and are named with the suffix -oic acid.

▶ Esters contain a carbonyl group bonded to an oxygen atom that is in turn bonded to an R group; they are named with the suffix -oate.

▶ Carboxylic acids taste sour, such as acetic acid in vinegar, while esters smell sweet.

▶ Carboxylic acids react as weak acids but can also form esters through condensation reactions with alcohols.

Ethers (20.12)

▶ The family of ethers contains an oxygen atom between two R groups.

▶ Ethers are named with the ending -yl ether.

Amines (20.13)

▶ Amines are organic compounds that contain nitrogen and are named with the suffix -amine.

▶ They are known for their terrible odors; the smell of decaying animal flesh is produced by cadaverine.

▶ Amines act as weak bases and produce a salt when mixed with a strong acid.

▶ The combination of an amine with a carboxylic acid leads to a condensation reaction; this reaction is used by our bodies to produce proteins from amino acids.

Polymers (20.14)

▶ Polymers are long, chainlike molecules that consist of repeating units called monomers. They can be natural or synthetic.

▶ Polyethylene is an addition polymer, a polymer formed without the elimination of any atoms.

▶ Condensation polymers, such as nylon, are formed by the elimination of small groups of atoms.

Key Equations and Relationships

Halogen Substitution Reactions in Alkanes (20.6)

$$R-H \ + \ X_2 \ \xrightarrow{\text{heat or light}} \ R-X \ + \ HX$$

alkane   halogen   haloalkane hydrogen halide

Common Functional Groups (20.8)

Family	General Formula	Condensed General Formula	Example	Name
Alcohols	R — OH	ROH	CH_3CH_2OH	Ethanol (ethyl alcohol)
Ethers	R — O — R	ROR	CH_3OCH_3	Dimethyl ether
Aldehydes	R—C(=O)—H	RCHO	H_3C—C(=O)—H	Ethanal (acetaldehyde)
Ketones	R—C(=O)—R	RCOR	H_3C—C(=O)—CH_3	Propanone (acetone)
Carboxylic acids	R—C(=O)—OH	RCOOH	H_3C—C(=O)—OH	Acetic acid
Esters	R—C(=O)—OR	RCOOR	H_3C—C(=O)—OCH_3	Methyl acetate
Amines	R—N(R)—R	R_3N	H_3CH_2C—N(H)—H	Ethylamine

Alcohol Reactions (20.9)

Substitution $ROH + HBr \longrightarrow R{-}Br + H_2O$

Oxidation

$$R{-}CH_2{-}CH_2 \underset{\text{OH}}{} \xrightarrow[\text{H}_2\text{SO}_4]{\text{Na}_2\text{Cr}_2\text{O}_7} R{-}CH_2{-}C{-}OH$$

Alcohol   Aldehyde

Elimination $R{-}CH_2{-}CH_2 \underset{\text{OH}}{} \xrightarrow{\text{H}_2\text{SO}_4} R{-}CH{=}CH_2 + H_2O$

Carboxylic Acid Condensation Reactions (20.11)

$$\underset{\text{Acid}}{R{-}C({=}O){-}OH} + \underset{\text{Alcohol}}{HO{-}R'} \xrightarrow{\text{H}_2\text{SO}_4} \underset{\text{Ester}}{R{-}C({=}O){-}O{-}R'} + \underset{\text{Water}}{H_2O}$$

Amine Acid–Base Reactions (20.13)

$$RNH_2(aq) + H_2O(l) \longrightarrow RNH_3^+(aq) + OH^-(aq)$$

Amine–Carboxylic Acid Condensation Reactions (20.13)

$$CH_3COOH(aq) + HNHR(aq) \longrightarrow CH_3CONHR(aq) + H_2O(l)$$

Key Learning Outcomes

Chapter Objectives	Assessment
Writing Structural Formulas for Hydrocarbons (20.3)	Example 20.1 For Practice 20.1 Exercises 37, 38
Naming Alkanes (20.4)	Examples 20.2, 20.3, 20.4 For Practice 20.2, 20.3, 20.4 Exercises 43, 44
Naming Alkenes and Alkynes (20.5)	Example 20.5 For Practice 20.5 Exercises 53–56

Key Learning Outcomes, *continued*

Writing Reactions: Addition Reactions (**20.6**)	Example 20.6 For Practice 20.6 Exercises 59–62
Writing Reactions: Alcohols (**20.9**) CH$_3$−CH$_2$−OH Ethanol	Example 20.7 For Practice 20.7 Exercises 75, 76

EXERCISES

Review Questions

1. What kinds of molecules often trigger our sense of smell?

2. What is organic chemistry?

3. What is unique about carbon and carbon-based compounds? Why did life evolve around carbon?

4. Why does carbon form such a large diversity of compounds?

5. Why does silicon exhibit less diversity of compounds than carbon does?

6. Describe the geometry and hybridization about a carbon atom that forms
   a. four single bonds.
   b. two single bonds and one double bond.
   c. one single bond and one triple bond.

7. What are hydrocarbons? What are their main uses?

8. What are the main classifications of hydrocarbons? What are their generic molecular formulas?

9. Explain the differences between a structural formula, a condensed structural formula, a carbon skeleton formula, a ball-and-stick model, and a space-filling model.

10. What are structural isomers? How do the properties of structural isomers differ from one another?

11. What are optical isomers? How do the properties of optical isomers differ from one another?

12. Define each term related to optical isomerism: enantiomers, chiral, dextrorotatory, levorotatory, racemic mixture.

13. What is the difference between saturated and unsaturated hydrocarbons?

14. What are the key differences in the way that alkanes, alkenes, and alkynes are named?

15. Explain geometric isomerism in alkenes. How do the properties of geometric isomers differ from one another?

16. Describe and provide an example of a hydrocarbon combustion reaction.

17. What kinds of reactions are common to alkanes? List an example of each.

18. Describe each kind of reaction.
   a. substitution reaction   b. addition reaction
   c. elimination reaction

19. What kinds of reactions are common to alkenes? Give an example of each.

20. Explain Markovnikov's rule and give an example of a reaction to which it applies.

21. What is the structure of benzene? What are the different ways in which this structure is represented?

22. What kinds of reactions are common to aromatic compounds? Provide an example of each.

23. What is a functional group? List some examples.

24. What is the generic structure of alcohols? Write the structures of two specific alcohols.

25. Explain oxidation and reduction with respect to organic compounds.

26. What kinds of reactions are common to alcohols? Provide an example of each.

27. What are the generic structures for aldehydes and ketones? Write a structure for a specific aldehyde and ketone.

28. What kind of reactions are common to aldehydes and ketones? List an example of each.

29. What are the generic structures for carboxylic acids and esters? Write a structure for a specific carboxylic acid and ester.

30. What kind of reactions are common to carboxylic acids and esters? Provide an example of each.

31. What is the generic structure of ethers? Write the structures of two specific ethers.

32. What is the generic structure of amines? Write the structures of two specific amines.

33. What is a polymer? What is the difference between a polymer and a copolymer?

34. How do an addition polymer and a condensation polymer differ from each other?

Problems by Topic

Hydrocarbons

35. Based on the molecular formula, determine whether each compound is an alkane, alkene, or alkyne. (Assume that the hydrocarbons are noncyclical and there is no more than one multiple bond.)
    a. C_5H_{12}
    b. C_3H_6
    c. C_7H_{12}
    d. $C_{11}H_{22}$

36. Based on the molecular formula, determine whether each compound is an alkane, alkene, or alkyne. (Assume that the hydrocarbons are noncyclical and there is no more than one multiple bond.)
    a. C_8H_{16}
    b. C_4H_6
    c. C_7H_{16}
    d. C_2H_2

37. Write structural formulas for each of the nine structural isomers of heptane.

38. Write structural formulas for any 6 of the 18 structural isomers of octane.

39. Determine whether each compound exhibits optical isomerism.
    a. CCl_4
    b. $CH_3-CH_2-CH-CH_2-CH_2-CH_2-CH_3$
       $\quad\quad\quad\quad\quad\quad |$
       $\quad\quad\quad\quad\quad\quad CH_3$
    c. $CH_3-\overset{\overset{\displaystyle H}{|}}{\underset{\underset{\displaystyle NH_2}{|}}{C}}-Cl$
    d. $CH_3CHClCH_3$

40. Determine whether each compound exhibits optical isomerism.
    a. $CH_3CH_2CHClCH_3$
    b. $CH_3CCl_2CH_3$
    c.
    d. $CH_3-\overset{\overset{\displaystyle CH_3}{|}}{\underset{\underset{\displaystyle CH}{\underset{\|}{\underset{\displaystyle CH_2}{}}}}{\underset{|}{\underset{\displaystyle CH_2}{C}}}}-\overset{\overset{\displaystyle O}{\|}}{C}-OH$

41. Determine whether the molecules in each pair are the same or enantiomers.
    a.
    b.
    c.

42. Determine whether the molecules in each pair are the same or enantiomers.
    a.
    b.
    c.

Alkanes

43. Name each alkane.
    a. $CH_3-CH_2-CH_2-CH_2-CH_3$
    b. $CH_3-CH_2-\overset{\overset{\displaystyle }{|}}{\underset{\underset{\displaystyle CH_3}{|}}{CH}}-CH_3$
    c. $CH_3-\overset{\overset{\displaystyle CH_3}{|}}{CH}-CH_2-\overset{\overset{\displaystyle CH-CH_3}{\overset{|}{\displaystyle CH_3}}}{CH}-CH_2-CH_2-CH_3$
    d. $CH_3-\overset{\overset{\displaystyle }{|}}{\underset{\underset{\displaystyle CH_3}{|}}{CH}}-CH_2-\overset{\overset{\displaystyle }{|}}{\underset{\underset{\displaystyle CH_2-CH_3}{|}}{CH}}-CH_2-CH_3$

44. Name each alkane.
    a. $CH_3-\overset{\overset{\displaystyle }{|}}{\underset{\underset{\displaystyle CH_3}{|}}{CH}}-CH_3$
    b. $CH_3-\overset{\overset{\displaystyle CH_3}{|}}{CH}-CH_2-\overset{\overset{\displaystyle CH_3}{|}}{\underset{\underset{\displaystyle CH_3}{|}}{CH}}-CH_2$
    c. $CH_3-\overset{\overset{\displaystyle CH_3\,CH_3}{|\quad|}}{\underset{\underset{\displaystyle CH_3\,CH_3}{|\quad|}}{C-C}}-CH_3$
    d. $CH_3-\overset{\overset{\displaystyle CH_3}{|}}{CH}-CH_2-\overset{\overset{\displaystyle }{|}}{\underset{\underset{\displaystyle CH_3}{|}}{CH}}-\overset{\overset{\displaystyle CH_3}{\overset{|}{\displaystyle CH_2}}}{CH}-CH_2-CH_2-CH_3$

45. Draw a structure for each alkane.
  a. 3-ethylhexane
  b. 3-ethyl-3-methylpentane
  c. 2,3-dimethylbutane
  d. 4,7-diethyl-2,2-dimethylnonane

46. Draw a structure for each alkane.
  a. 2,2-dimethylpentane
  b. 3-isopropylheptane
  c. 4-ethyl-2,2-dimethylhexane
  d. 4,4-diethyloctane

47. Complete and balance each hydrocarbon combustion reaction.
  a. $CH_3CH_2CH_3 + O_2 \longrightarrow$
  b. $CH_3CH_2CH{=}CH_2 + O_2 \longrightarrow$
  c. $CH{\equiv}CH + O_2 \longrightarrow$

48. Complete and balance each hydrocarbon combustion reaction.
  a. $CH_3CH_2CH_2CH_3 + O_2 \longrightarrow$
  b. $CH_2{=}CHCH_3 + O_2 \longrightarrow$
  c. $CH{\equiv}CCH_2CH_3 + O_2 \longrightarrow$

49. List all the possible products for each alkane substitution reaction. (Assume monosubstitution.)
  a. $CH_3CH_3 + Br_2 \longrightarrow$
  b. $CH_3CH_2CH_3 + Cl_2 \longrightarrow$
  c. $CH_2Cl_2 + Br_2 \longrightarrow$
  d. $CH_3{-}CH{-}CH_3 + Cl_2 \longrightarrow$
        $\quad\quad\ \ |$
        $\quad\quad\ CH_3$

50. List all the possible products for each alkane substitution reaction. (Assume monosubstitution.)
  a. $CH_4 + Cl_2 \longrightarrow$
  b. $CH_3CH_2Br + Br_2 \longrightarrow$
  c. $CH_3CH_2CH_2CH_3 + Cl_2 \longrightarrow$
  d. $CH_3CHBr_2 + Br_2 \longrightarrow$

Alkenes and Alkynes

51. Write structural formulas for each of the possible isomers of *n*-hexene that are formed by moving the position of the double bond.

52. Write structural formulas for each of the possible isomers of *n*-pentyne that are formed by moving the position of the triple bond.

53. Name each alkene.
  a. $CH_2{=}CH{-}CH_2{-}CH_3$

  b.
$$CH_3{-}\overset{\overset{\displaystyle CH_3}{|}}{CH}{-}\overset{\overset{\displaystyle CH_3}{|}}{C}{=}CH{-}CH_3$$

  c.
$$CH_2{=}HC{-}\underset{\underset{\displaystyle CH_3}{\underset{\displaystyle |}{CH_3{-}CH}}}{CH}{-}CH_2{-}CH_2{-}CH_3$$

  d.
$$CH_3{-}\overset{\overset{\displaystyle CH_3}{|}}{CH}{-}CH{=}\underset{\underset{\displaystyle CH_2{-}CH_3}{|}}{C}{-}CH_3$$

54. Name each alkene.
  a. $CH_3{-}CH_2{-}CH{=}CH{-}CH_2{-}CH_3$

  b.
$$CH_3{-}\underset{\underset{\displaystyle CH_3}{|}}{CH}{-}CH{=}CH{-}CH_3$$

  c.
$$CH_3{-}\underset{\underset{\displaystyle CH_3}{|}}{CH}{-}CH{=}\overset{\overset{\displaystyle CH_3}{\overset{\displaystyle |}{\overset{\displaystyle CH_2}{|}}}}{C}{-}\underset{\underset{\displaystyle CH_3}{|}}{CH}{-}CH_3$$

  d.
$$CH_3{-}\overset{\overset{\displaystyle CH_3}{|}}{\underset{\underset{\displaystyle CH_3}{|}}{C}}{-}CH{=}\overset{\overset{\displaystyle CH_3}{|}}{C}{-}CH_2{-}CH_3$$

55. Name each alkyne.
  a. $CH_3{-}C{\equiv}C{-}CH_3$

  b.
$$CH_3{-}C{\equiv}C{-}\overset{\overset{\displaystyle CH_3}{|}}{\underset{\underset{\displaystyle CH_3}{|}}{C}}{-}CH_2{-}CH_3$$

  c.
$$CH{\equiv}C{-}\underset{\underset{\underset{\displaystyle CH_3}{|}}{\underset{\displaystyle CH{-}CH_3}{|}}}{CH}{-}CH_2{-}CH_2{-}CH_3$$

  d.
$$CH_3{-}\underset{\underset{\underset{\displaystyle CH_3}{|}}{\underset{\displaystyle CH_2}{|}}}{CH}{-}C{\equiv}C{-}\overset{\overset{\displaystyle CH_3}{|}}{\underset{\underset{\underset{\displaystyle CH_3}{|}}{\underset{\displaystyle CH_2}{|}}}{CH}}{-}CH_2$$

56. Name each alkyne.
  a.
$$CH{\equiv}C{-}\underset{\underset{\displaystyle CH_3}{|}}{CH}{-}CH_3$$

  b.
$$CH_3{-}C{\equiv}C{-}CH{-}\underset{\underset{\displaystyle CH_3}{|}}{CH}{-}CH_2{-}CH_3$$

(where the CH bears a CH_3 above)

  c.
$$CH{\equiv}C{-}\overset{\overset{\displaystyle CH_3}{|}}{\underset{\underset{\underset{\displaystyle CH_3}{|}}{\underset{\displaystyle CH_2}{|}}}{C}}{-}CH_2{-}CH_3$$

  d.
$$CH_3{-}C{\equiv}C{-}CH{-}\overset{\overset{\displaystyle CH_3}{|}}{\underset{\underset{\underset{\displaystyle CH_3}{|}}{\underset{\displaystyle CH_2}{|}}}{C}}{-}CH_3$$

57. Draw the correct structure for each compound.
   a. 4-octyne
   b. 3-nonene
   c. 3,3-dimethyl-1-pentyne
   d. 5-ethyl-3,6-dimethyl-2-heptene

58. Draw the correct structure for each compound.
   a. 2-hexene
   b. 1-heptyne
   c. 4,4-dimethyl-2-hexene
   d. 3-ethyl-4-methyl-2-pentene

59. List the products of each alkene addition reaction.

   a. $CH_3-CH=CH-CH_3 + Cl_2 \longrightarrow$

   b. $CH_3-\underset{\underset{CH_3}{|}}{CH}-CH=CH-CH_3 + HBr \longrightarrow$

   c. $CH_3-CH_2-CH=CH-CH_3 + Br_2 \longrightarrow$

   d. $CH_3-\underset{\underset{CH_3}{|}}{CH}-CH=\underset{\overset{CH_3}{|}}{C}-CH_3 + HCl \longrightarrow$

60. What are the products of each alkene addition reaction?

   a. $CH_3-\underset{\underset{CH_3}{|}}{CH}-CH=CH_2 + Br_2 \longrightarrow$

   b. $CH_2=CH-CH_3 + Cl_2 \longrightarrow$

   c. $CH_3-\underset{\underset{CH_3}{|}}{\overset{\overset{CH_3}{|}}{C}}-CH=CH_2 + HCl \longrightarrow$

   d. $CH_3-\underset{\underset{CH_2-CH_3}{|}}{CH}-CH=\underset{\overset{CH_3}{|}}{C}-CH_3 + HBr \longrightarrow$

61. Complete each hydrogenation reaction.

   a. $CH_2=CH-CH_3 + H_2 \xrightarrow{\text{catalyst}}$

   b. $CH_3-\underset{\underset{CH_3}{|}}{CH}-CH=CH_2 + H_2 \xrightarrow{\text{catalyst}}$

   c. $CH_3-\underset{\underset{CH_3}{|}}{CH}-\underset{\underset{CH_3}{|}}{C}=CH_2 + H_2 \xrightarrow{\text{catalyst}}$

62. Complete each hydrogenation reaction.

   a. $CH_3-CH_2-CH=CH_2 + H_2 \xrightarrow{\text{catalyst}}$

   b. $CH_3-CH_2-\underset{\underset{CH_3}{|}}{\overset{\overset{CH_3}{|}}{C}}=\overset{\overset{CH_3}{|}}{C}-CH_3 + H_2 \xrightarrow{\text{catalyst}}$

   c. $CH_3-CH_2-\underset{\underset{CH_3}{|}}{C}=CH_2 + H_2 \xrightarrow{\text{Catalyst}}$

Aromatic Hydrocarbons

63. Name each monosubstituted benzene.

   a.   b. c.

64. Name each monosubstituted benzene.

   a. H_2C-CH_3 b. F c. $H_3C-\underset{|}{\overset{\overset{CH_3}{|}}{C}}-CH_3$

65. Name each compound in which the benzene ring is best treated as a substituent.

   a. $CH_3-\underset{\underset{CH_2-CH_3}{|}}{CH}-CH_2-\underset{\overset{CH_3}{|}}{CH}-CH_2-CH-CH_2-CH_3$

   b. $CH_3-CH-CH=CH-CH_2-CH_2-CH_2-CH_3$

   c. $CH_3-C\equiv C-CH-\underset{\underset{CH_3}{|}}{CH}-\underset{\underset{CH_3}{|}}{CH}-CH_2-CH_3$

66. Name each compound in which the benzene ring is best treated as a substituent.

   a. $H_3C-CH_2-CH-\underset{\underset{H_3C}{|}}{CH}-CH_2-CH_3$

   b. $CH_2-CH_2-CH_2-CH_2-C\equiv C-CH_3$

   c. $CH_3-CH-\underset{\underset{CH_3}{|}}{CH}-\underset{\overset{CH_3}{|}}{C}=CH-CH-CH_2-CH_3$

67. Name each disubstituted benzene.

   a. b. CH_2-CH_3 c. F, Cl

68. Name each disubstituted benzene.

a. [structure: benzene with Br and Cl]
b. [structure: benzene with Cl and CH₂—CH₃]
c. [structure: benzene with two I groups]

69. Draw the structure for each compound.
    a. isopropylbenzene   b. *meta*-dibromobenzene
    c. 1-chloro-4-methylbenzene

70. Draw the structure for each compound.
    a. ethylbenzene   b. 1-iodo-2-methylbenzene
    c. *para*-diethylbenzene

71. What are the products of each aromatic substitution reaction?

a. [benzene structure] $+ Br_2 \xrightarrow{FeBr_3}$

b. [benzene] $+ CH_3-\underset{CH_3}{CH}-Cl \xrightarrow{AlCl_3}$

72. What are the products of each aromatic substitution reaction?

a. [benzene structure] $+ Cl_2 \xrightarrow{FeCl_3}$

b. [benzene] $+ CH_3-\underset{\underset{CH_3}{|}}{\overset{\overset{CH_3}{|}}{C}}-Cl \xrightarrow{AlCl_3}$

Alcohols

73. Name each alcohol.
a. $CH_3-CH_2-CH_2-OH$

b. $CH_3-\underset{\underset{OH}{|}}{\overset{\overset{CH_2-CH_3}{|}}{CH}}-CH_2-CH-CH_3$

c. $CH_3-\underset{\underset{CH_3}{|}}{CH}-CH_2-\underset{\underset{OH}{|}}{CH}-CH_2-\overset{\overset{CH_3}{|}}{CH}-CH_3$

d. $H_3C-CH_2-\underset{\underset{H_3C}{|}}{\overset{\overset{HO}{|}}{C}}-CH_2-CH_3$

74. Draw the structure for each alcohol.
    a. 2-butanol   b. 2-methyl-1-propanol
    c. 3-ethyl-1-hexanol   d. 2-methyl-3-pentanol

75. List the products of each alcohol reaction.
a. $CH_3-CH_2-CH_2-OH + HBr \longrightarrow$

b. $CH_3-\underset{\underset{CH_3}{|}}{CH}-CH_2-OH \xrightarrow{H_2SO_4}$

c. $CH_3-CH_2-OH + Na \longrightarrow$

d. $CH_3-\underset{\underset{CH_3}{|}}{\overset{\overset{CH_3}{|}}{C}}-CH_2-CH_2-OH \xrightarrow[H_2SO_4]{Na_2Cr_2O_7}$

76. List the products of each alcohol reaction.

a. $CH_3-\underset{\underset{CH_3}{|}}{\overset{\overset{CH_3}{|}}{C}}-OH \xrightarrow{H_2SO_4}$

b. $CH_3-\underset{\underset{CH_3}{|}}{CH}-CH_2-CH_2-OH \xrightarrow[H_2SO_4]{Na_2Cr_2O_7}$

c. $CH_3-CH_2-OH + HCl \longrightarrow$

d. $CH_3-\underset{\underset{CH_3}{|}}{CH}-CH_2-OH + Na \longrightarrow$

Aldehydes and Ketones

77. Name each aldehyde or ketone.

a. $CH_3-\overset{\overset{O}{||}}{C}-CH_2-CH_3$

b. $CH_3-CH_2-CH_2-CH_2-\overset{\overset{O}{||}}{CH}$

c. $CH_3-\underset{\underset{CH_3}{|}}{\overset{\overset{CH_3}{|}}{C}}-CH_2-\overset{\overset{CH_3}{|}}{CH}-CH_2-\overset{\overset{O}{||}}{C}-H$

d. $CH_3-\underset{\underset{CH_2-CH_3}{|}}{CH}-CH_2-\overset{\overset{O}{||}}{C}-CH_3$

78. Draw the structure of each aldehyde or ketone.
    a. hexanal   b. 2-pentanone
    c. 2-methylbutanal   d. 4-heptanone

79. Determine the product of the addition reaction.

$CH_3-CH_2-CH_2-\overset{\overset{O}{||}}{CH} + H-C\equiv N \xrightarrow{NaCN}$

80. Determine the product of the addition reaction.

$CH_3-\overset{\overset{O}{||}}{C}-CH_2-CH_3 + HCN \xrightarrow{NaCN}$

Carboxylic Acids and Esters

81. Name each carboxylic acid or ester.

a. $CH_3-CH_2-CH_2-\overset{\overset{\displaystyle O}{\|}}{C}-O-CH_3$

b. $CH_3-CH_2-\overset{\overset{\displaystyle O}{\|}}{C}-OH$

c. $CH_3-\underset{\underset{\displaystyle CH_3}{|}}{CH}-CH_2-CH_2-CH_2-\overset{\overset{\displaystyle O}{\|}}{C}-OH$

d. $CH_3-CH_2-CH_2-CH_2-\overset{\overset{\displaystyle O}{\|}}{C}-O-CH_2-CH_3$

82. Draw the structure of each carboxylic acid or ester.
    a. pentanoic acid
    b. methyl hexanoate
    c. 3-ethylheptanoic acid
    d. butyl ethanoate

83. Determine the products of each carboxylic acid reaction.

a. $CH_3-CH_2-CH_2-CH_2-\overset{\overset{\displaystyle O}{\|}}{C}-OH +$
   $CH_3-CH_2-OH \xrightarrow{H_2SO_4}$

b. $\xrightarrow{\text{Heat}}$

84. Determine the products of each carboxylic acid reaction.

a. $CH_3-CH_2-\overset{\overset{\displaystyle O}{\|}}{C}-OH + NaOH \longrightarrow$

b. $CH_3-CH_2-CH_2-\overset{\overset{\displaystyle O}{\|}}{C}-OH +$
   $CH_3-CH_2-CH_2-OH \xrightarrow{H_2SO_4}$

Ethers

85. Name each ether.
    a. $CH_3-CH_2-CH_2-O-CH_2-CH_3$
    b. $CH_3-CH_2-CH_2-CH_2-CH_2-O-CH_2-CH_3$
    c. $CH_3-CH_2-CH_2-O-CH_2-CH_2-CH_3$
    d. $CH_3-CH_2-O-CH_2-CH_2-CH_2-CH_3$

86. Draw the structure for each ether.
    a. ethyl propyl ether
    b. dibutyl ether
    c. methyl hexyl ether
    d. dipentyl ether

Amines

87. Name each amine.

a. $CH_3-CH_2-\underset{\underset{\displaystyle H}{|}}{N}-CH_2-CH_3$

b. $CH_3-CH_2-CH_2-\underset{\underset{\displaystyle H}{|}}{N}-CH_3$

c. $CH_3-CH_2-CH_2-\underset{\underset{\displaystyle CH_3}{|}}{N}-CH_2-CH_2-CH_2-CH_3$

88. Draw the structure for each amine.
    a. isopropylamine
    b. triethylamine
    c. butylethylamine

89. Classify each amine reaction as acid–base or condensation and list its products.
    a. $CH_3NHCH_3 + HCl \longrightarrow$
    b. $CH_3CH_2NH_2 + CH_3CH_2COOH \longrightarrow$
    c. $CH_3NH_2 + H_2SO_4 \longrightarrow$

90. List the products of each amine reaction.
    a. $N(CH_2CH_3)_3 + HNO_3 \longrightarrow$

b. $CH_3-\overset{\overset{\displaystyle H}{|}}{N}-\underset{\underset{\displaystyle CH_3}{|}}{CH}-CH_3 + HCN \longrightarrow$

c. $CH_3-\overset{\overset{\displaystyle H}{|}}{N}-\underset{\underset{\displaystyle CH_3}{|}}{CH}-CH_3 +$
   $CH_3-\underset{\underset{\displaystyle CH_3}{|}}{CH}-CH_2-\overset{\overset{\displaystyle O}{\|}}{C}-OH \longrightarrow$

Polymers

91. Teflon is an addition polymer formed from the monomer shown here. Draw the structure of the polymer.

92. Saran, the polymer used to make saran wrap, is an addition polymer formed from two monomers—vinylidene chloride and vinyl chloride. Draw the structure of the polymer. (Hint: The monomers alternate.)

Vinylidene chloride   Vinyl chloride

93. One kind of polyester is a condensation copolymer formed from terephthalic acid and ethylene glycol. Draw the structure of the dimer and circle the ester functional group. [Hint: Water (circled) is eliminated when the bond between the monomers forms.]

Terephthalic acid   Ethylene glycol

94. Nomex, a condensation copolymer used by firefighters because of its flame-resistant properties, forms from isophthalic acid and *m*-aminoaniline. Draw the structure of the dimer. (Hint: Water is eliminated when the bond between the monomers forms.)

Isophthalic acid   *m*-Aminoaniline

Cumulative Problems

95. Identify each organic compound as an alkane, alkene, alkyne, aromatic hydrocarbon, alcohol, ether, aldehyde, ketone, carboxylic acid, ester, or amine, and provide a name for the compound.

a. $H_3C-HC-CH_2-\overset{\overset{\displaystyle O}{\|}}{C}-O-CH_3$
      $\quad\quad\;\;|$
      $\quad\quad\;CH_3$

b. $\quad\quad\quad\quad\overset{\displaystyle CH_3}{|}$
      $CH_3-CH_2-CH-CH_2-O-CH_2-CH_3$

c. H_2C-CH_3

(benzene ring with CH_3 substituent)

d. $\quad\quad\quad\quad\quad\overset{\displaystyle CH_2-CH_3}{|}$
      $CH_3-C\equiv C-CH-CH-CH_2-CH_3$
      $\quad\quad\quad\quad\;\;\overset{\displaystyle |}{CH_3}$

e. $H_3C-CH_2-CH_2-\overset{\overset{\displaystyle O}{\|}}{C}H$

f. $\quad\quad\quad\quad\overset{\displaystyle OH}{|}$
      $H_3C-CH-CH_2$
      $\quad\;\;\overset{\displaystyle |}{H_3C}$

96. Identify each organic compound as an alkane, alkene, alkyne, aromatic hydrocarbon, alcohol, ether, aldehyde, ketone, carboxylic acid, ester, or amine, and provide a name for the compound.

a. $\quad\quad\quad\quad\overset{\displaystyle H_3C}{|}$
      $H_3C-HC-C=C-CH_3$
      $\quad\quad\overset{\displaystyle |}{CH_3}\;\;\overset{\displaystyle |}{CH_3}$

b. $\quad\quad\;\overset{\displaystyle CH_3}{|}\quad\quad\overset{\displaystyle CH_3}{|}$
      $CH_3-C-CH_2-CH-CH_2-CH_3$
      $\quad\quad\;\overset{\displaystyle |}{CH_3}$

c. $\quad\quad\quad\quad\quad\overset{\displaystyle CH_3}{|}\quad\quad\overset{\overset{\displaystyle O}{\|}}{}$
      $CH_3-CH_2-CH-CH_2-C-OH$

d. $\quad\quad\quad\quad\overset{\displaystyle H}{|}$
      $CH_3-CH-N-CH_2-CH_2-CH_2-CH_3$
      $\quad\quad\overset{\displaystyle |}{CH_3}$

e. $\quad\quad\quad\quad\quad\quad\overset{\displaystyle CH_2-OH}{|}$
      $CH_3-CH-CH_2-CH-CH_3$
      $\quad\quad\overset{\displaystyle |}{CH_2-CH_3}$

f. $\quad\quad\quad\quad\quad\quad\overset{\overset{\displaystyle O}{\|}}{}$
      $CH_3-CH_2-CH_2-C-CH-CH_3$
      $\quad\quad\quad\quad\quad\quad\overset{\displaystyle |}{CH_3}$

97. Name each compound.

a. $\quad\quad\quad\quad\overset{\displaystyle CH_3}{|}$
      $CH_3-CH_2-CH-CH_2-CH-CH_2-CH_2-CH_2-CH_3$
      $\quad\quad\quad\quad\quad\quad\quad\overset{\displaystyle HC-CH_3}{|}$
      $\quad\quad\quad\quad\quad\quad\quad\quad\overset{\displaystyle CH_2}{|}$
      $\quad\quad\quad\quad\quad\quad\quad\quad\overset{\displaystyle CH_3}{}$

b. $\quad\quad\quad\quad\quad\quad\overset{\overset{\displaystyle O}{\|}}{}$
      $CH_3-CH-CH_2-C-CH_2-CH_3$
      $\quad\quad\overset{\displaystyle |}{CH_3}$

c. $\quad\quad\quad\quad\overset{\displaystyle OH}{|}$
      $CH_3-CH-CH-CH_3$
      $\quad\quad\quad\quad\overset{\displaystyle |}{CH_3}$

d. $\quad\quad\quad\quad\quad\quad\overset{\displaystyle CH_3}{|}$
      $\quad\quad\quad\quad\quad\overset{\displaystyle CH_2}{|}\;\overset{\displaystyle CH_3}{|}$
      $CH_3-CH-CH-CH-C\equiv C-H$
      $\quad\quad\quad\quad\overset{\displaystyle |}{CH_3}$

98. Name each compound.

a. $\quad\quad\quad\quad\quad\quad\overset{\displaystyle CH_3}{|}\;\overset{\displaystyle CH_3}{|}$
      $CH_3-CH=CH-C-CH-CH_2-CH_3$
      $\quad\quad\quad\quad\quad\quad\overset{\displaystyle CH_2}{|}$
      $\quad\quad\quad\quad\quad\quad\overset{\displaystyle CH_3}{}$

b.

(benzene ring with Br and CH_2-CH_3)

c. $\quad\quad\quad\quad\quad\quad\overset{\displaystyle CH_3}{|}\quad\overset{\overset{\displaystyle O}{\|}}{}\quad\overset{\displaystyle CH_3}{|}$
      $CH_3-CH_2-CH-CH_2-C-O-CH-CH_3$

d. $\quad\quad\quad\quad\quad\quad\quad\overset{\overset{\displaystyle O}{\|}}{}$
      $CH_3-CH-CH_2-CH$
      $\quad\quad\overset{\displaystyle |}{CH_3}$

99. Determine whether the two structures are isomers or the same molecule drawn in two different ways.

a. $CH_3-CH_2-\overset{\overset{\displaystyle O}{\|}}{C}-O-CH_3$

      $CH_3-\overset{\overset{\displaystyle O}{\|}}{C}-O-CH_2-CH_3$

b.

(benzene ring with I at positions 1,2) and (benzene ring with I at positions 1,3)

c. $CH_3-HC-CH-CH_3$
      $\quad\quad\;\overset{\displaystyle |}{CH_3}\overset{\displaystyle |}{CH_3}$

      $\quad\quad\quad\quad\overset{\displaystyle CH_3}{|}$
      $CH_3-HC-CH-CH_3$
      $\quad\quad\quad\quad\overset{\displaystyle |}{CH_3}$

100. Determine whether the two structures are isomers or the same molecule drawn two different ways.

a. $CH_3-CH_2-CH-CH_2-CH_3$
$\quad\quad\quad\quad\quad | $
$\quad\quad\quad\quad\quad CH_3$

$\quad\quad CH_3$
$\quad\quad |$
$\quad\quad CH_2$
$\quad\quad |$
$CH_3-CH_2-CH-CH_3$

b. $\quad CH_3$
$\quad\quad |$
$CH_3-CH-CH_2-O-CH_2-CH_3$

$\quad\quad\quad\quad\quad\quad\quad\quad CH_3$
$\quad\quad\quad\quad\quad\quad\quad\quad |$
$CH_3-CH_2-CH_2-O-CH_2-CH_2$

c. $\quad CH_3\quad\quad O$
$\quad\quad |\quad\quad\quad ||$
$CH_3-CH-CH_2-C-CH_2-CH_3$

$\quad\quad\quad\quad\quad\quad O$
$\quad\quad\quad\quad\quad\quad ||$
$CH_3-CH-CH_2-C-CH_2$
$\quad\quad |\quad\quad\quad\quad\quad |$
$\quad\quad CH_3\quad\quad\quad\quad CH_3$

101. What minimum amount of hydrogen gas, in grams, is required to completely hydrogenate 15.5 kg of 2-butene?

102. How many kilograms of CO_2 does the complete combustion of 3.8 kg of *n*-octane produce?

103. Classify each organic reaction as combustion, alkane substitution, alkene addition or hydrogenation, aromatic substitution, or alcohol substitution, elimination, or oxidation.

a. $2\,CH_3CH{=}CH_2 + 9\,O_2 \longrightarrow 6\,CO_2 + 6\,H_2O$

b. $CH_3CH_2CH_3 + Cl_2 \longrightarrow CH_3CH_2CH_2Cl + HCl$

c. $CH_3-CH_2-CH-CH_2-OH \xrightarrow{H_2SO_4}$
$\quad\quad\quad\quad\quad |$
$\quad\quad\quad\quad\quad CH_3$
$\quad\quad\quad\quad\quad\quad\quad\quad CH_3-CH_2-C{=}CH_2$
$\quad\quad\quad\quad\quad\quad\quad\quad\quad\quad\quad\quad |$
$\quad\quad\quad\quad\quad\quad\quad\quad\quad\quad\quad\quad CH_3$

d. (benzene) $+ I_2 \xrightarrow{FeI_3}$ (iodobenzene) $+ HI$

104. Determine the products of each reaction.

a. $CH_3-CH_2-C{=}CH_2 + H_2 \longrightarrow$
$\quad\quad\quad\quad\quad\quad |$
$\quad\quad\quad\quad\quad\quad CH_3$

b. $CH_3-CH_2-CH_2-CH_2-OH + HCl \longrightarrow$

c. $\quad\quad\quad\quad CH_3\quad\quad O$
$\quad\quad\quad\quad\quad |\quad\quad\quad ||$
$CH_3-CH_2-CH-CH_2-C-OH +$
$\quad\quad\quad\quad\quad\quad\quad\quad CH_3CH_2OH \longrightarrow$

d. $\quad\quad\quad\quad\quad\quad H$
$\quad\quad\quad\quad\quad\quad |$
$CH_3-CH_2-N-CH_2-CH_3 + HCl \longrightarrow$

105. Draw the structure that corresponds to each name and indicate which structures can exist as stereoisomers.
a. 3-methyl-1-pentene
b. 3,5-dimethyl-2-hexene
c. 3-propyl-2-hexene

106. Identify the two compounds that display stereoisomerism and draw their structures.
a. 3-methyl-3-pentanol
b. 2-methyl-2-pentanol
c. 3-methyl-2-pentanol
d. 2-methyl-3-pentanol
e. 2,4-dimethyl-3-pentanol

107. There are 11 structures (ignoring stereoisomerism) with the formula C_4H_8O that have no carbon branches. Draw the structures and identify the functional groups in each.

108. There are eight structures with the formula C_3H_7NO in which the O is part of a carbonyl group. Draw the structures and identify the functional groups in each.

109. Explain why carboxylic acids are much stronger acids than alcohols.

110. The hydrogen at C-1 of 1-butyne is much more acidic than the one at C-1 in 1-butene. Explain.

Challenge Problems

111. Determine the one or two steps it takes to get from the starting material to the product using the reactions found in this chapter.

112. Given the following synthesis of ethyl 3-chloro-3-methylbutanoate, fill in the missing intermediates or reactants.

113. For the chlorination of propane, the two isomers shown here are possible.

$$CH_3CH_2CH_3 + Cl_2 \longrightarrow$$

$$CH_3-CH_2-CH_2-Cl + CH_3-\overset{\overset{\displaystyle Cl}{|}}{CH}-CH_3$$

1-chloropropane   2-chloropropane

Propane has six hydrogen atoms on terminal carbon atoms—called primary (1°) hydrogen atoms—and two hydrogen atoms on the interior carbon atom—called secondary (2°) hydrogen atoms.

a. If the two different types of hydrogen atoms were equally reactive, what ratio of 1-chloropropane to 2-chloropropane would we expect as monochlorination products?

b. The result of a reaction yields 55% 2-chloropropane and 45% 1-chloropropane. What can we conclude about the relative reactivity of the two different kinds of hydrogen atoms? Determine a ratio of the reactivity of one type of hydrogen atom to the other.

114. There are two isomers of C_4H_{10}. Suppose that each isomer is treated with Cl_2 and the products that have the composition $C_4H_8Cl_2$ are isolated. Find the number of different products that form from each of the original C_4H_{10} compounds. Do not consider optical isomerism.

115. Identify the compounds formed in the previous problem that are chiral.

116. Nitromethane has the formula CH_3NO_2, with the N bonded to the C and without O—O bonds. Draw its two most important contributing structures.

a. What is the hybridization of the C and how many hybrid orbitals are in the molecule?

b. What is the shortest bond?

c. Between which two atoms is the strongest bond found?

d. Predict whether the HCH bond angles are greater or less than 109.5° and justify your prediction.

117. Free radical fluorination of methane is uncontrollably violent and free radical iodination of methane is a very poor reaction. Explain these observations in light of bond energies.

118. There are two compounds with the formula, C_3H_6, one of which does not have a multiple bond. Draw its structure and explain why it is much less stable than the isomer with the double bond.

119. Consider molecules that have two carbons and two chlorines. Draw the structures of three of these with no dipole moment and two with a dipole moment.

Conceptual Problems

120. Pick the more oxidized structure from each pair.

a. $CH_3-\overset{\overset{\displaystyle O}{||}}{CH}$ or CH_3-CH_2-OH

b. CH_3-CH_2-OH or CH_3-CH_3

c. $CH_3-CH_2-\overset{\overset{\displaystyle O}{||}}{CH}$ or $CH_3-CH_2-\overset{\overset{\displaystyle O}{||}}{C}-OH$

121. Draw the structure and name a compound with the formula C_8H_{18} that forms only one product with the formula $C_8H_{17}Br$ when it is treated with Br_2.

122. Determine whether each structure is chiral.

a. $\overset{\overset{\displaystyle Cl}{|}}{\underset{\underset{\displaystyle CH_3}{|}}{HC}}-CH_3$

b. $CH_3-CH-\underset{\underset{\displaystyle CH_3}{|}}{CH}-CH_3$ with Cl on the first CH

$CH_3-\underset{\underset{\displaystyle Cl}{|}}{CH}-\underset{\underset{\displaystyle CH_3}{|}}{CH}-CH_3$

c. CH_3-CH_2-OH

d. $\overset{\overset{\displaystyle Cl}{|}}{\underset{\underset{\displaystyle CH_3}{|}}{HC}}-\underset{\underset{\displaystyle Br}{|}}{CH_2}$

Answers to Conceptual Connections

Organic Structures

20.1 **(d)** The others are simply the same structure drawn in slightly different ways.

Optical Isomers

20.2 **(b)** This structure is the only one that contains a carbon atom (the one on the left) with four different substituent groups attached (a Br atom, a Cl atom, an H atom, and a CH_3 group).

Oxidation

20.3 **(c, d, a, b)** Oxidation includes the gain of oxygen or the loss of hydrogen.

23

Metals and Metallurgy

The metals are not presented immediately to the hand of man . . . but they are, for the most part, buried in darkness, in the bowels of the earth, where they are so much disguised, by combination and mixture with other substances, that they often appear entirely unlike themselves.

—William Henry (1774–1836)

I F YOU LOOK AROUND YOUR HOUSE, classroom, or neighborhood, much of what you see is made of metal or at least has some metal parts. Can you imagine life without metals? Without metals, we would have no skyscrapers, which need the rigid framework of steel beams; no automobiles, which need metal engines and bodies; and no electricity, which needs copper and aluminum wire for transmission. Metallurgy is both a very old and a very new science. We find the roots of metallurgy in the distant past, when our primitive ancestors began to search for and process metals. Of the three prehistoric ages of humankind—the Stone Age, the Bronze Age, and the Iron Age—two are named after our quest for metals. But we do not commonly find metals as elements on Earth; instead we find them in compounds, often scattered within other compounds. The mining, separating, and refining of the vast array of metals is a fairly new science. Many modern metals were not available even as recently as 200 years ago. In the middle of the nineteenth century, gold was cheaper than aluminum because aluminum was so difficult to refine, and titanium, which is important in the aerospace industry, could not even be manufactured. In this chapter, we cover the area of chemistry known as metallurgy.

Oil is sometimes contaminated with vanadium, which is thought to have been the metal used for oxygen transport by some ancient life forms.

23.1 Vanadium: A Problem and an Opportunity

Recently, some members of a university's chemistry and engineering departments met with representatives of an oil company to discuss how the faculty and students could cooperate on industrial research. One major topic they discussed was vanadium contamination in oil, a serious problem of continuing concern. Because vanadium is toxic, the U.S. government regulates the quantity of vanadium that can be emitted by industrial processes and oil companies have to figure out environmentally acceptable ways to remove vanadium from oil.

Vanadium is a rare element, making up only about 0.015% of Earth's crust (by mass). It is a soft white metal with high ductility and malleability, which means that it can be easily drawn into narrow wires or rolled into thin sheets. Because of the high reactivity of pure vanadium, this element occurs naturally within compounds (not in its elemental form). However, vanadium compounds are not normally found in the rocks or soils near oil fields, so why does this rare, reactive metal occur in oil? The answer lies in the biology of ancient life-forms. Most modern animals use iron in hemoglobin to transport oxygen through their bloodstreams (see Sections 1.1 and 14.1), and a few (such as lobsters) use copper for this function. It appears that some extinct animals used vanadium. Even today,

▲ Vanadium is a soft white metal.

one group of simple marine organisms, the tunicates or sea squirts, are believed to employ vanadium compounds for oxygen transport. The source of vanadium in some crude oil may be the very animals from which the oil was formed.

During refining, crude oil is heated to carry out the reactions that form the different petroleum products. If some of the vanadium-containing oil burns during heating, the vanadium forms vanadate compounds, ionic compounds with vanadium oxide polyatomic ions such as VO_4^{3-} and VO_3^-. These compounds, which have low melting points, can dissolve the protective oxide coatings on stainless steel containers, causing the steel to corrode and ruining the containers in which the oil is stored. If the vanadium compounds are not removed from the oil before storage, the customer inherits the problem. In addition, vanadium and many of its compounds are toxic, so oil companies cannot simply dump the extracted vanadium compounds into the environment.

The presence of vanadium in crude oil may, however, turn out to be profitable for the oil companies. If vanadium can be economically recovered from oil, then oil could become a major source of vanadium, a valuable metal with several important industrial uses, including the production of iron alloys and sulfuric acid.

The recovery of vanadium from oil involves metallurgy, the topic of this chapter. **Metallurgy** includes all the processes associated with mining, separating, and refining metals and the subsequent production of pure metals and mixtures of metals called *alloys* (which we define in Section 23.4). In this chapter we explore the general properties and natural distribution of metals; several different categories of metallurgical processes, including pyrometallurgy, hydrometallurgy, electrometallurgy, and powder metallurgy; the structures and alloys formed by metals; and the metallic products and applications for several selected materials.

23.2 The General Properties and Natural Distribution of Metals

Metals share several common properties. All metals are opaque (we cannot see through them), and they are good conductors of heat and electricity. They generally have high malleability (the ability to be bent or hammered into desired forms) and ductility (the ability to be drawn into wires). We can explain these properties by the bonding theories that we have already examined for metals: the electron sea model and band theory. In the electron sea model, discussed in Section 9.11, each metal atom within a metal sample donates one or more electrons to an *electron sea*, which flows within the metal. In band theory, discussed in Section 11.13, the atomic orbitals of the metal atoms are combined, forming *bands* that are delocalized over the entire crystalline solid; electrons move freely within these bands. The mobile electrons in both of these models endow metals with many of their shared properties.

Each metal, however, is also unique, and even their shared properties may vary within a range. For example, some metals, such as copper, silver, and aluminum, have much higher thermal and electrical conductivities than do other metals. Table 23.1 lists the thermal conductivity and electrical resistivity (a low resistivity corresponds to a high conductivity) of a few metals. Notice that both properties can vary by factors of 10 or more. Most metals are very strong, malleable, and ductile. But lead is a soft, weak metal, and chromium is a brittle metal that will not bend without breaking. When we think about the shared properties of metals, we must allow for a range of properties as well as some unique ones.

Over 75% of the elements in the periodic table are metals, yet metals make up only about 25% of the mass of Earth's crust (see Figure 22.2 for the composition of Earth's crust). Earth's core is thought to be composed of iron and nickel, but because the core

TABLE 23.1 Thermal Conductivity and Electrical Resistivity of Several Metals

Metal	Thermal Conductivity (W/cm · K)	Electrical Resistivity ($\mu\Omega$ · cm)
Ag, silver	4.29	1.59
Cu, copper	4.01	1.67
Fe, iron	0.804	9.71
V, vanadium	0.307	24.8

is so far from the surface, these metals are not accessible. The most abundant metal on Earth is aluminum, a main-group metal. Several alkali and alkaline earth metals (calcium, sodium, potassium, and magnesium) make up more than 1% of Earth's crust. Iron, which makes up about 5% of the crust, is the only transition metal that accounts for more than 0.1% of the crust. Of the first-row transition metals, titanium, chromium, iron, nickel, copper, and zinc are all plentiful enough to be important industrial materials.

Only a few metals occur naturally as elements, including nickel, copper, palladium, silver, platinum, and gold. Because of their low reactivity, these metals are often called the *noble metals*. They are usually concentrated within mountainous or volcanic regions in small, isolated veins within a rock matrix.

▲ Gold is one of the few metals that can be found as an element in nature, often in veins like the one shown here.

Most of the rest of the metals occur naturally in positive oxidation states within mineral deposits. **Minerals** (as we saw in Chapter 22) are homogeneous, naturally occurring, crystalline inorganic solids. A rock that contains a high concentration of a specific mineral is called an **ore**. Metallurgical processes separate useful minerals from other, unusable material in the ore.

The main sources for the alkali metals are chloride minerals, such as halite (sodium chloride) and sylvite (potassium chloride). Halite occurs in large deposits in sites that were once ancient oceans, or it can be precipitated by evaporating ocean water. The main source for some other metals are oxide minerals, such as hematite (Fe_2O_3), rutile (TiO_2), and cassiterite (SnO_2). The ores containing these minerals are unevenly distributed throughout the earth. For example, North America has large deposits of hematite, but no substantial deposits of cassiterite. Sulfides are the most important minerals for many metals, such as galena (PbS), cinnabar (HgS), sphalerite (ZnS), and molybdenite (MoS_2).

The main mineral source for some other metals can be complex. For example, the primary *mineral* sources for vanadium are vanadinite [$Pb_5(VO_4)_3Cl$] and carnotite [$K_2(UO_2)_2(VO_4)_2 \cdot 3\,H_2O$], which is also a main mineral source for uranium. Vanadium, as we have seen, is also found in crude oil. No specific minerals contain the metal radium. Yet radium sometime substitutes for uranium within uranium-containing minerals. The small amount of radium that replaces uranium in carnotite is also the major source of radium. Tantalum and niobium, named after the Greek god Tantalus and his daughter Niobe, always occur together in mixed deposits of columbite [$Fe(NbO_3)_2$] and tantalite [$Fe(TaO_3)_2$]. The minerals are mined together and the elements are later separated by recrystallization (see Section 12.4).

▲ Most NaCl salt is produced by trapping ocean water in shallow basins and letting the water evaporate.

23.3 Metallurgical Processes

Mined ores are first physically *separated* into their metal-containing and nonmetal-containing components. Then, the elemental metal is extracted from the compounds in which it is found, a process called **extractive metallurgy**. In this section, we look at several metallurgical processes, including pyrometallurgy, hydrometallurgy, electrometallurgy, and powder metallurgy. After separation and extraction, the metal is **refined**; refining is the process in which the crude material is purified.

Separation

The first step in processing metal-containing ores is crushing the ore into smaller particles. The particles that contain the minerals are then separated from the undesired material, called **gangue** (pronounced "gang"), usually by physical methods. For example, in some cases, a cyclone of wind is used to lift the gangue away from the metal-containing particles, as shown in Figure 23.1 ▶. If the minerals are magnetic, magnets can separate the minerals. Electrostatic forces are also used to separate polar minerals from nonpolar gangue.

▲ FIGURE 23.1 **Separation by Air** An industrial cyclone separates the crushed light particles of gangue from the heavier metal-bearing particles.

► **FIGURE 23.2 Separation by Using a Solution** A wetting agent helps the minerals attach to the froth in a bubbled solution. The minerals in the froth are separated from the gangue remaining in the solution.

Water/ore/oil/detergent mixture

Stirrer

Compressed air

Froth separation

Oil and detergent recycle

Desired product

Gangue
(rock, sand)

Sometimes solutions are used to separate the minerals from the gangue, as shown in Figure 23.2 ▲. A *wetting agent* (or detergent) that preferentially attaches to the mineral surfaces is added to a mixture of the mined material and water. Air is then blown through the mixture, forming bubbles and a froth. Because they are attached to the wetting agent, the minerals segregate into the froth, where they can be collected. The gangue separates into the solution.

Pyrometallurgy

Pyrometallurgy contains the Greek stem *pyro*, meaning fire or heat.

Once the mineral is separated from the gangue, the elemental metal is extracted from the mineral. Several different techniques can achieve this separation. In **pyrometallurgy**, heat is employed to extract a metal from its mineral. Different heating conditions have different effects on the mineral.

Calcination is the heating of an ore in order to decompose it and drive off a volatile product. For example, when carbonate minerals are heated, carbon dioxide is driven off, as shown in these examples:

$$PbCO_3(s) \xrightarrow{heat} PbO(s) + CO_2(g)$$

$$4\,FeCO_3(s) + O_2(g) \xrightarrow{heat} 2\,Fe_2O_3(s) + 4\,CO_2(g)$$

Hydrated compounds are discussed in Section 3.5.

Many minerals occur in a hydrated form (that is, they contain water). Calcination can also drive off water.

$$Fe_2O_3 \cdot 2\,Fe(OH)_3(s) \xrightarrow{heat} 2\,Fe_2O_3(s) + 3\,H_2O(g)$$

Heating that causes a chemical reaction between the furnace atmosphere (the gases in the furnace) and the mineral is called **roasting**. Roasting is particularly important in processing sulfide ores. The ores are heated in the presence of oxygen, converting the sulfide into an oxide and emitting sulfur dioxide. For example, the roasting of lead(II) sulfide occurs by the reaction:

$$2\,PbS(s) + 3\,O_2(g) \xrightarrow{heat} 2\,PbO(s) + 2\,SO_2(g)$$

In some cases, especially with the less active metals such as mercury, roasting the sulfide produces the pure metal.

$$HgS(s) + O_2(g) \xrightarrow{heat} Hg(g) + SO_2(g)$$

When roasting forms a liquid product, which makes separation easier, it is called **smelting**. Consider, for example, the smelting of zinc oxide:

$$ZnO(s) + C(s) \xrightarrow{\text{heat}} Zn(l) + CO(g)$$

The gaseous carbon monoxide separates from the liquid zinc, allowing the metal to be readily recovered. In some cases, a flux must be added to the mixture during smelting to help separate the two materials. The **flux** is a material that will react with the gangue to form a substance with a low melting point. For example, oxides of silicon within gangue can be liquefied by reaction with calcium carbonate according to the reaction:

$$\underset{\text{gangue}}{SiO_2(s)} + \underset{\text{flux}}{CaCO_3(s)} \longrightarrow CO_2(g) + \underset{\text{slag}}{CaSiO_3(l)}$$

The waste liquid solution that forms from the flux and gangue is usually a silicate material called a **slag**. The liquid metal and the liquid slag have different densities and therefore separate. Holes tapped at different heights into the side of the container holding the liquid metal and slag allow the more dense liquid to flow out of the lower tap holes and the less dense liquid to flow out of the higher tap holes.

Hydrometallurgy

The use of an aqueous solution to extract metals from their ores is known as **hydrometallurgy**. One early example of hydrometallurgy is a process used to obtain gold. Gold occurs in its elemental state, but often as very small particles mixed with other substances. The gold can be separated out of the mixture by selectively dissolving it into solution, a process called **leaching**. In this process, solid gold reacts with sodium cyanide to form a soluble gold complex.

$$4\,Au(s) + 8\,CN^-(aq) + O_2(g) + 2\,H_2O(l) \longrightarrow 4\,Au(CN)_2^-(aq) + 4\,OH^-(aq)$$

The impurities are filtered out of the solution and the gold is reduced back to elemental gold with a reactive metal such as zinc.

$$2\,Au(CN)_2^-(aq) + Zn(s) \longrightarrow Zn(CN)_4^{2-}(aq) + 2\,Au(s)$$

Leaching has been practiced for many years and often results in the contamination of streams and rivers with cyanide. New alternatives, using the thiosulfate ion ($S_2O_3^-$), are being investigated to replace it.

   Different acid, base, and salt solutions are sometimes used to selectively separate out metal-bearing minerals. For example, sulfuric acid is used to separate the copper and iron from the mineral chalcopyrite, $CuFeS_2$, and a sodium chloride solution is used to separate the lead from the insoluble mineral anglesite, $PbSO_4$.

$$2\,CuFeS_2(s) + H_2SO_4(aq) + 4\,O_2(g) \longrightarrow 2\,CuSO_4(aq) + Fe_2O_3(s) + 3\,S(s) + H_2O(l)$$
$$PbSO_4(s) + 4\,NaCl(aq) \longrightarrow Na_2[PbCl_4](aq) + Na_2SO_4(aq)$$

Hydrometallurgy is often more economical than pyrometallurgy, due to the high energy costs associated with the elevated temperatures needed for calcination and roasting.

Electrometallurgy

In **electrometallurgy**, electrolysis is used to produce metals from their compounds. For example, the *Hall process* is an electrometallurgical process crucial to aluminum production. The main source of aluminum is bauxite, $Al_2O_3 \cdot n\,H_2O$. A hydrometallurgical process, the *Bayer process*, separates bauxite from the iron and silicon dioxide with which it is usually found. In this process, the bauxite is heated in a concentrated aqueous NaOH solution under high pressure. The aluminum oxide dissolves, leaving the other oxides behind in solid form.

See Section 18.8 for a description of electrolysis.

$$Al_2O_3 \cdot n\,H_2O(s) + 2\,OH^-(aq) + 2\,H_2O(l) \longrightarrow 2\,Al(OH)_4^-(aq)$$

▶ **FIGURE 23.3 The Hall Process**   The Hall process produces aluminum metal by reducing the aluminum ions in alumina. Graphite electrodes act as reducing agents. Dissolved oxygen ions in the molten cryolite oxidize the carbon in the graphite electrodes to form carbon dioxide.

The basic aluminum solution is separated from the oxide solids, and then the aluminum oxide is precipitated out of solution by neutralizing it (recall the pH dependence of the solubility of $Al(OH)_3$ from Section 16.8). Calcination of the precipitate at temperatures greater than 1000 °C yields anhydrous alumina (Al_2O_3). Electrolysis is then used to reduce the aluminum out of the aluminum oxide. Because Al_2O_3 melts at such a high temperature (greater than 2000 °C), however, the electrolysis is not carried out on molten Al_2O_3. Instead, in the Hall process the Al_2O_3 is dissolved into molten cryolite (Na_3AlF_6), and graphite rods are used as electrodes to carry out the electrolysis in the liquid mixture (Figure 23.3 ▲). The carbon that composes the graphite electrodes is oxidized by the dissolved oxygen ions in the molten salt and converted to carbon dioxide. The aluminum ions dissolved in the molten salt reduce to molten aluminum, which sinks down to the bottom of the cell and is removed.

Oxidation: $C(s) + 2\,O^{2-}(\text{dissolved}) \longrightarrow CO_2(g) + 4\,e^-$

Reduction: $3\,e^- + Al^{3+}(\text{dissolved}) \longrightarrow Al(l)$

$Cu^{2+} + 2e^- \longrightarrow Cu$
Cathode
$-$

$Cu \longrightarrow Cu^{2+} + 2e^-$
Anode
$+$

Thin sheet   Anode $CuSO_4, H_2SO_4$ Slab of
of pure   sludge   solution   impure
copper   copper

▲ **FIGURE 23.4 Copper Electrolysis Cell**
Copper is refined by electrolysis. The impure copper is oxidized at the anode and then reduced to form pure metal on the cathode. Many precious metals collect in the sludge at the bottom of the electrolysis cell.

Another important example of metallurgy is the refinement of copper. The most abundant copper source is the mineral chalcopyrite, $CuFeS_2$. First, the chalcopyrite is converted to CuS by roasting. During this process, the iron also forms oxides and sulfides. Silica is added to form an iron silicate slag, which is then removed. The remaining copper(II) sulfide is reacted with oxygen to form sulfur dioxide gas and copper metal, but the metal is not very pure. Electrolysis is employed to refine the copper.

In the electrolysis cell used to refine copper, both the anode and the cathode are made of copper (Figure 23.4 ◀). The anode is the impure copper (that needs to be refined) and the cathode is a thin sheet of pure copper. As the current flows through the cell, the copper from the anode oxidizes and dissolves in a copper sulfate solution. It then plates out as pure copper on the cathode. The impurities in the copper anode separate from the copper during electrolysis because, even though the more active metals also oxidize from the anode, they stay in solution and do not plate out on the cathode. The less active metals do not oxidize at all and simply fall to the bottom of the cell as the copper is dissolved from the anode. The sludge at the bottom of the electrolysis cell contains many precious metals, including gold and silver. About one-quarter of the silver produced in the United States is from the impurities recovered from the refinement of copper.

Powder Metallurgy

Powder metallurgy, first developed in the 1920s, is used to make metallic components from powdered metal. In powder metallurgy, micron-sized metal particles are pressed together under high pressures to form the desired component. The component is then heated (*sintered*). The sintering process occurs below the melting point of the powder but at a temperature high enough to cause the metal particles to fuse together, strengthening the metal and increasing its density.

Originally, iron powder from mill scrap was used in powder metallurgy. The scrap was primarily iron oxide that would fall off the steel as it was being milled. The iron oxide dust was heated in a hydrogen atmosphere to reduce the oxide to iron particles. Manufacturers called the powdered metal *iron sponge* because numerous holes form in the particles when the oxygen escapes.

In the 1960s the A. O. Smith Company in the United States introduced a new method for the development of powdered metal, called water atomization. In this method, the pure metal is melted and a small stream of the liquid is allowed to flow from the bottom of the container of molten metal. A high-pressure blast of cold water hits the stream of metal, breaking it into small droplets that quickly solidify. Powdered metal particles made in this way are more smooth and dense than the sponge powder particles from oxide scrap. In addition to powdered iron metal, many copper, bronze, carbide, and brass parts are made through powder metallurgical processes.

Powder metallurgy offers several advantages over traditional casting or milling of metal. For example, waste is almost eliminated because the part can be pressed directly into the desired shape. Intricate teeth on gears and multiple holes can be designed into the press and therefore do not have to be machined after production. Making cast metal objects from metals with high melting points, such as molybdenum and tungsten, can be difficult because of the high temperatures necessary to melt the metal. Using the powder avoids the need for high temperatures.

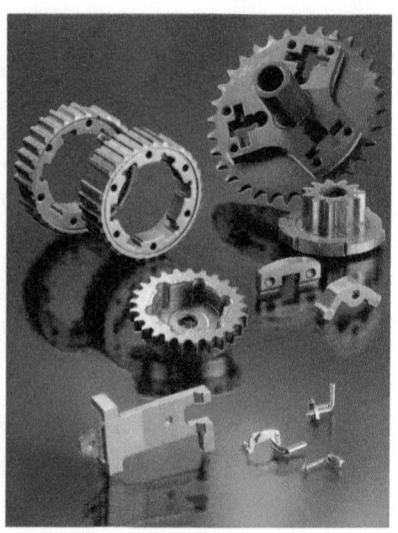

▲ These metal products were all made by powder metallurgy.

23.4 Metal Structures and Alloys

We can describe the structures of metals as the closest packing of spheres, first discussed in Section 11.11. Elemental metals generally crystallize in one of the basic types of crystal lattices, including face-centered cubic, body-centered cubic, and hexagonal closest packed. The crystal structure of a metal may change, however, as a function of temperature and pressure. Table 23.2 lists the crystal structures for the 3*d* transition metals at atmospheric pressure.

TABLE 23.2 The Crystal Structures of the 3*d* Elements

Metal	Natural Crystal Structure at Room Temperature	Other Crystal Structures at Different Temperatures and Pressures
Sc	Hexagonal closest packed	Face-centered cubic, body-centered cubic
Ti	Hexagonal closest packed	Body-centered cubic above 882 °C
V	Body-centered cubic	
Cr	Body-centered cubic	Hexagonal closest packed
Mn	Alpha complex body-centered cubic form	Beta simple cubic form above 727 °C
		Face-centered cubic above 1095 °C
		Body-centered cubic above 1133 °C
Fe	Body-centered cubic	Face-centered cubic above 909 °C
		Body-centered cubic above 1403 °C
Co	Hexagonal closest packed	Face-centered cubic above 420 °C
Ni	Face-centered cubic	
Cu	Face-centered cubic	
Zn	Hexagonal closest packed	

Alloys

An **alloy** is a metallic material that contains more than one element. Some alloys are simply solid solutions, while others are specific compounds with definite ratios of the component elements. Alloys have metallic properties, but they can consist of either two or more metals or a metal and a nonmetal. We broadly classify alloys as substitutional or interstitial. In a **substitutional alloy**, one metal atom substitutes for another in the crystal structure. The crystal structure may either stay the same upon the substitution, or it may change to accommodate the differences between the atoms. In an **interstitial alloy**, small, usually nonmetallic atoms fit in between the metallic atoms of a crystal. The alloy maintains its metallic properties with these interstitial atoms in the structure.

Substitutional Alloys

For two metals to form a substitutional alloy, the radii of the two metal atoms must be similar, usually within 15% of each other. For example, the atomic radii of copper and nickel are both 135 pm, and both of the elements form the face-centered cubic structure. Therefore, either metal can easily replace the other in the metal crystal structure.

▲ Copper crystallizes in the face-centered structure shown here.

▲ In a nickel and copper alloy, nickel atoms substitute for some of the copper atoms.

Figure 23.5 ▼ is a phase diagram for a copper and nickel alloy. This phase diagram, called a *binary* phase diagram, is different from the diagrams that we discussed in Section 11.8, which show the phases of a pure substance at different pressures and temperatures. This diagram shows the different phases for a mixture at different *compositions* and temperatures. The *x*-axis indicates the composition (in this case, the mole percent of nickel in the alloy, with the left side representing pure copper and the right side representing pure nickel). The *y*-axis indicates the temperature.

Pure copper melts at 1084 °C, as indicated by the change from solid to liquid at 0% nickel. Pure nickel melts at 1455 °C, as indicated by the change from solid to liquid at 100% nickel. The area on the diagram above the line connecting the melting points of copper and nickel represents a liquid solution of the two metals. The area below that line represents a solid solution of the two metals. Any ratios of copper and nickel can form the face-centered cubic structure.

▶ FIGURE 23.5 **Cu-Ni Phase Diagram** Because copper and nickel have similar crystal structures and similar size, they can form a solid solution. A solution forms at all compositions from pure copper to pure nickel.

GUIDELINES FOR...	EXAMPLE 23.1	EXAMPLE 23.2
Interpreting a Binary Phase Diagram	**Determining Alloy Compositions from a Phase Diagram**	**Determining Alloy Compositions from a Phase Diagram**
	Determine the composition and phase present at point A on Figure 23.5.	Determine the composition and phase present at point B on Figure 23.5.
Locate the temperature and composition of the alloy on the binary phase diagram.	Point A represents 30 mol % Ni at 1300 °C.	Point B represents 75 mol % Ni at 1100 °C.
Identify the phase.	The point is above the melting point line, so the phase is liquid.	The point is below the melting point line, so the phase is solid.
Identify the amount of copper and nickel in the phase.	This liquid phase is made up of 30 mol % Ni, so it is 70 mol % Cu.	This solid phase is made up of 75 mol % Ni, so it is 25 mol % Cu.
	FOR PRACTICE 23.1 Determine the composition and phase present at point C on Figure 23.5.	**FOR PRACTICE 23.2** Determine the composition and phase present at point D on Figure 23.5.

The phase diagrams of some alloys are more complex. Consider the phase diagram for Cr and V, shown in Figure 23.6 ▶. Both Cr and V form the body-centered cubic crystal, and the atoms are close in size. Yet this phase diagram reveals an important difference between this alloy and the Cu and Ni alloy: the melting temperature does not vary in a uniform way from the lower melting point of Cr to the higher melting point of V. Instead we see that the alloys with intermediate compositions melt at lower temperatures than either pure metal. The lowest melting point is 1750 °C at a composition of 30 mol % vanadium. Solid compositions that melt at temperatures lower than either of the pure metals, as well as compositions that melt at temperatures higher than either of the two metals, are common in these types of alloys.

▲ FIGURE 23.6 **Cr–V Phase Diagram** In a binary phase diagram of two metals that form a solid solution, an intermediate composition can have either the highest or lowest melting point. In the chromium and vanadium phase diagram an intermediate composition has the lowest melting point.

Alloys with Limited Solubility

Some alloys are composed of metals that have different crystal structures. For example, nickel crystallizes in the face-centered cubic structure and chromium in the body-centered cubic structure. Because of their different structures, these two metals do not form a miscible solid solution at all compositions. At some intermediate composition, the structure has to change from that of one of the metals to that of the other. Figure 23.7 ▼ shows the nickel and chromium phase diagram from 700 °C to 1900 °C. Notice that the diagram has two different solid phases: face-centered cubic and body-centered cubic. From pure nickel (0 mol % chromium) to about 40–50 mol % chromium, the structure is face-centered cubic. In this structure, Cr atoms substitute for Ni atoms in the face-centered cubic structure of nickel. However, beyond a certain percentage of chromium (which depends on temperature), that structure is no longer stable. At 700 °C about 40 mol % Cr can fit in the crystal and at 1200 °C about 50 mol % Cr can fit in. Adding additional Cr beyond these points results in a different phase.

▶ FIGURE 23.7 **Cr–Ni Phase Diagram** Because chromium and nickel form solids with crystal structures that differ from each other, an alloy mixture of the two metals does not form a solid solution at all compositions. A two-phase region exists at compositions between the possible compositions of the two different structures. In the two-phase region, both crystal structures coexist in equilibrium.

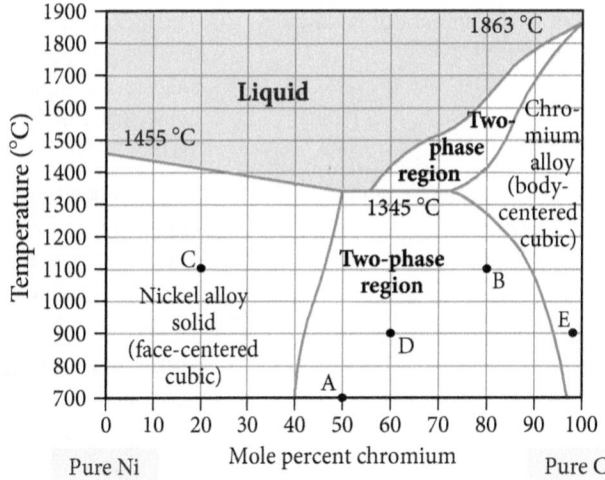

At the other end of the diagram (nearly pure chromium) and at 700 °C, only a small amount of nickel can be substituted into the body-centered cubic structure of the chromium. As the temperature rises to 1300 °C, however, about 20 mol % nickel can be accommodated into the chromium structure. The region in between the two phases is called a **two-phase region**. At these compositions, the two phases (nickel-rich face-centered cubic and chromium-rich body-centered cubic) exist together. The amount of each phase depends upon the composition of the alloy.

We can determine the composition and relative amounts of the two different phases that coexist in a two-phase region from a phase diagram. Point A on Figure 23.7 in the Cr–Ni phase diagram represents 50% composition at 700 °C, and both phases are present. Some of the Cr atoms have substituted into the nickel-rich face-centered cubic structure, but there is too much Cr to all fit into the crystal. The leftover Cr atoms form the chromium-rich body-centered cubic structure with a small number of Ni atoms in the crystal.

The two crystals that exist at point A are (1) the nickel-rich face-centered cubic structure with 40 mol % Cr; and (2) the chromium-rich body-centered cubic structure with 5 mol % Ni. The 50% composition on the phase diagram has just slightly more Cr atoms than can fit into the nickel structure. Thus most of the crystals in the two-phase region are the nickel-rich face-centered cubic structure with only a small amount of the chromium-rich body-centered cubic structure, as determined by a method called the *lever rule*. The **lever rule** tells us that in a two-phase region, whichever phase is closest to the composition of the alloy is the more abundant phase. In this example, the 50 mol % Cr composition on the phase diagram is closer to the 40 mol % Cr composition of the nickel-rich face-centered cubic phase than the 95 mol % Cr composition of the chromium-body-centered cubic phase, so more face-centered cubic crystals are present than body-centered cubic crystals.

GUIDELINES FOR...	EXAMPLE 23.3	EXAMPLE 23.4
Interpreting the Phases and Compositions in a Binary Phase Diagram as Described by the Lever Rule	**Alloy Compositions in a Solid Solution with Limited Solubility** Determine the composition, relative amounts, and phases present at point B on Figure 23.7.	**Alloy Compositions in a Solid Solution with Limited Solubility** Determine the composition, relative amounts, and phases present at point C on Figure 23.7.
Locate the temperature and composition of the alloy on the binary phase diagram.	Point B represents 80 mol % Cr at 1100 °C.	Point C represents 20 mol % Cr at 1100 °C.
Identify the phases(s).	Point B is located in the two-phase region, consisting of the nickel-rich face-centered cubic structure and the chromium-rich body-centered cubic structure.	Point C is located in the one-phase region of the nickel-rich face-centered cubic structure.
Identify the amount of Ni and Cr in the phases.	The nickel-rich face-centered cubic structure has 45 mol % Cr and 55 mol % Ni, and the chromium rich body-centered cubic structure has 90 mol % Cr and 10 mol % Ni.	The nickel-rich face-centered cubic structure at this point has 20 mol % Cr and 80 mol % Ni.
Identify the relative amounts of the phases.	At a composition of 80 mol % Cr, the composition is closer to the Cr-rich body-centered cubic phase, so there is more of this phase than there is of the Ni-rich face-centered cubic phase.	There is only one phase. It is 100 mol % of the Ni face-centered cubic phase.
	FOR PRACTICE 23.3 Determine the composition, relative amounts, and phases present at point D on Figure 23.7.	**FOR PRACTICE 23.4** Determine the composition, relative amounts, and phases present at point E on Figure 23.7.

Interstitial Alloys

Recall that in contrast to substitutional alloys, where one metal atom substitutes for another in the lattice, interstitial alloys contain atoms of one kind that fit into the holes, or interstitial sites, of the crystal structure of the other. In metals with the interstitial elements hydrogen, boron, nitrogen, or carbon, the alloy that results retains its metallic properties.

Closest-packed crystal structures have two different types of holes between the atoms in the crystalline lattice. An **octahedral hole**, shown in Figure 23.8 ▶, exists in the middle of six atoms on two adjacent closest-packed sheets of metal atoms. The hole is located directly above the center of three closest-packed metal atoms in one sheet and below the three metal atoms in the adjacent sheet. This configuration of metal atoms is identical to a regular octahedral configuration that consists of four atoms in a square plane with one atom above and one atom below the square. We can calculate the size of an octahedral hole by determining the size of a hole on a square of four atoms in a plane (Figure 23.9 ▶). Any of the four corners of the square is the 90° angle of a right triangle formed from the adjacent two sides and the diagonal line that runs across the center of the square. According to the Pythagorean theorem, the length of the diagonal line (c) is related to the length of the sides (a and b) as follows:

$$c^2 = a^2 + b^2 \qquad [23.1]$$

If we let r_m equal the metal atom radius, the lengths of the sides are $2r_m$. We can then substitute $2r_m$ for both a and b.

$$c^2 = (2r_m)^2 + (2r_m)^2$$
$$c^2 = 8r_m^2$$
$$c = 2.828r_m \qquad [23.2]$$

We can see from Figure 23.9 that the length of the diagonal (c) is twice the radius of the atoms plus twice the radius of the hole.

$$c = 2r_m + 2r_{hole} \qquad [23.3]$$

Combining Equations 23.2 and 23.3, we get the important result:

$$2.828r_m = 2r_m + 2r_{hole}$$
$$0.828r_m = 2r_{hole}$$
$$r_{hole} = 0.414r_m \qquad [23.4]$$

The octahedral hole, surrounded by six metal atoms, has a radius that is 41.4% of the metal atom radius. By contrast, the hole in the center of a cube in the *simple cubic* structure has a radius that is 73% of the metal atom radius. The *number* of octahedral holes in a closest-packed structure is equal to the number of metal atoms.

The second type of interstitial hole in a closest-packed structure is a **tetrahedral hole** (first introduced in Section 11.12), which forms directly above the center point of three closest-packed metal atoms in one plane and below a fourth metal atom located directly above the center point in the adjacent plane (Figure 23.10 ▼). The number of tetrahedral holes in a closest-packed structure is equal to *twice* the number of metal atoms.

Octahedral hole

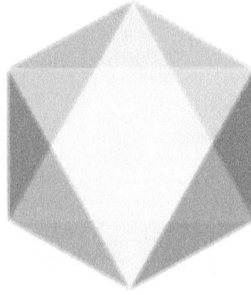

▲ **FIGURE 23.8 Octahedral Holes in Closest-Packed Crystals** Octahedral holes are found in a closest-packed structure. The octahedral hole is surrounded by six of the atoms in the closest-packed structure.

Largest atom that fits in hole

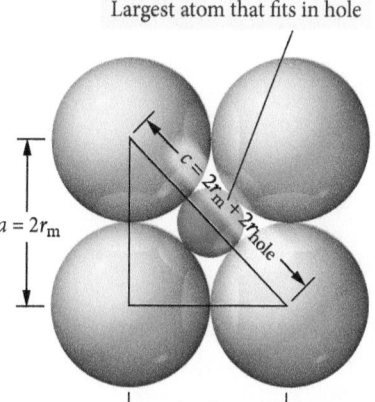

▲ **FIGURE 23.9 A Different View of an Octahedral Hole** An octahedral hole can be viewed as the area in the middle of a square plane of atoms, with one additional atom above the hole and one additional atom below the hole, accounting for the six close atoms. The diagonal of the square is equal to the radius of the two corner atoms plus the diameter of the hole. The length of the diagonal is related to the lengths of the sides of the square by the Pythagorean theorem.

Tetrahedral hole

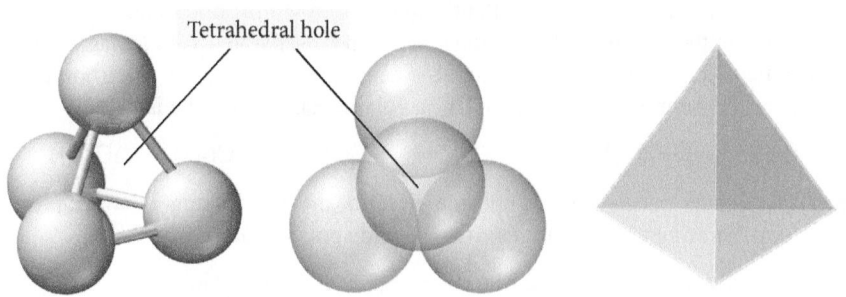

◀ **FIGURE 23.10 A Tetrahedral Hole in a Closest-Packed Crystal** Tetrahedral holes are found in a closest-packed structure. The tetrahedral hole is surrounded by four of the atoms in the closest-packed structure.

TABLE 23.3 Formulas of Several Interstitial Alloys

Compound	Type of Interstitial Hole Occupied	Fraction of Holes Occupied	Formula
Titanium carbide	Octahedral	All	TiC
Molybdenum nitride	Octahedral	One-half	Mo_2N
Tungsten nitride	Octahedral	One-half	W_2N
Manganese nitride	Octahedral	One-quarter	Mn_4N
Palladium hydride	Tetrahedral	One-quarter	Pd_2H
Titanium hydride	Tetrahedral	All	TiH_2

Because this hole is surrounded by only four atoms, the hole is smaller than the octahedral interstitial hole. We can apply geometric considerations similar to those used previously for the octahedral hole to determine that the tetrahedral hole has a radius that is 23% of the metal atom radius.

Interstitial alloys form when small nonmetallic atoms fit within the octahedral or tetrahedral holes of the crystalline lattice of the metal. The formulas for these alloys depend both on the type of hole occupied by the nonmetallic atom and on the fraction of holes occupied. For example, titanium and carbon form an alloy with a closest-packed structure for titanium in which all of the octahedral holes are filled with carbon atoms. Since the number of octahedral holes in a closest-packed structure is equal to the number of atoms in the structure, the ratio of carbon atoms to titanium atoms must be 1:1 and the corresponding formula is TiC. In the compound formed between molybdenum and nitrogen, by contrast, only one-half of the octahedral holes in the closest-packed structure of Mo are filled with N. Therefore, the formula for this compound is Mo_2N. Table 23.3 lists the formulas and relative number of holes filled for several different interstitial alloys.

Conceptual Connection 23.1 Interstitial Alloys

An interstitial alloy contains a nonmetal (X) that occupies one-eighth of the tetrahedral holes of the closest-packed structure of the metal (M). What is its formula?

23.5 Sources, Properties, and Products of Some of the 3d Transition Metals

In this section we examine major sources, interesting properties, and important products of several of the 3d transition metals, specifically, titanium, chromium, manganese, cobalt, copper, nickel, and zinc. We also survey the different metallurgical methods used to separate and refine them. The variety of uses for these metals reflects their varied properties.

Titanium

Titanium is the ninth most abundant element in Earth's crust, and the fourth most abundant metal. Titanium was discovered in 1791, but the pure metal was not isolated until 1910. The principal minerals of titanium are rutile (TiO_2) and ilmenite ($FeTiO_3$). Another source of titanium is coal ash, the residue from burned coal. Black shiny ilmenite is found in granite deposits along the North Atlantic coast, often within silica sand. The mineral is magnetic due to the presence of Fe^{2+} ions, so it can be separated with a magnet from the nonmagnetic silica. The separated mineral is heated in the presence of carbon under an atmosphere of chlorine gas, forming $TiCl_4$, a volatile gas that can be isolated.

$$FeTiO_3(s) + 3\,Cl_2(g) + 3\,C(s) \longrightarrow 3\,CO(g) + FeCl_2(s) + TiCl_4(g)$$

The $TiCl_4$ gas is reacted with hot magnesium metal turnings (shaved pieces of magnesium), forming elemental titanium—a solid sponge material.

$$TiCl_4(g) + 2\,Mg(s) \longrightarrow 2\,MgCl_2(l) + Ti(s)$$

Titanium is very reactive, readily oxidizing in the presence of oxygen and even nitrogen. Consequently, the elemental titanium is **arc-melted**—a method in which the solid metal is melted with an arc (an electrical discharge) from a high-voltage electric source in a controlled atmosphere to prevent oxidation—and then collected in a water-cooled copper pot. Because of titanium's high reactivity, any further processing must be done in a protective atmosphere of an inert gas, such as Ar, to prevent oxidation.

Despite its reactivity, solid titanium is highly resistant to corrosion in air, acid, and seawater because it quickly reacts with oxygen to form an oxide that coats the surface, preventing further oxidation of the underlying metal. Consequently, titanium is often used in the production of ship components such as propeller shafts and rigging. Titanium is also very strong and light; it is stronger than steel and less than half as dense. It is denser than aluminum but twice as strong. For these reasons, titanium is used in the airline industry for the production of jet engine parts. When titanium is alloyed with 5% aluminum and trace amounts of Fe, Cr, and Mo, the resulting metal retains its strength under higher temperature.

The most common use of titanium, however, is as titanium(IV) oxide (TiO_2), which forms a clear crystal but a brilliant white powder. Most white paints include TiO_2, which is far less toxic than PbO_2, which was used in older paints. Titanium(IV) oxide is made by reacting sulfuric acid with ilmenite, which dissolves the titanium into solution.

$$FeTiO_3(s) + 3\,H_2SO_4(l) \longrightarrow FeSO_4(aq) + Ti(SO_4)_2(aq) + 3\,H_2O(l)$$

Neutralizing the solution with strong base forms titanium(IV) oxide.

$$Ti^{4+}(aq) + 4\,OH^-(aq) \longrightarrow TiO_2(s) + 2\,H_2O(l)$$

Calcination of the oxide dries it to form TiO_2 rutile crystals. Large rutile crystals are sometimes used as gems because they resemble diamonds.

Chromium

The name *chromium* comes from the Greek root *chroma*, which means color. The different compounds of chromium are brightly colored (Table 23.4; Figure 23.11 ▶). The main ore source of chromium is chromite, $FeCr_2O_4$. No appreciable sources of chromium ores exist in the United States. Chromium metal is produced by reducing chromium ore with aluminum.

$$3\,FeCr_2O_4(s) + 8\,Al(s) \longrightarrow 4\,Al_2O_3(s) + 6\,Cr(s) + 3\,Fe(s)$$

Metallic chromium is a white, hard, lustrous, and brittle metal. The metal readily dissolves in acids such as hydrochloric acid and sulfuric acid, but it does not dissolve in concentrated nitric acid (because nitric acid forms an oxide on the surface of the chromium that resists further reaction). The primary use of chromium is in the production of steel alloys called *stainless steels*. Reducing chromite with carbon produces ferrochrome, an alloy that is added to steel.

$$FeCr_2O_4(s) + 4\,C(s) \xrightarrow{\text{heat}} Fe_xCr_y(s) + 4\,CO(g)$$

▼ FIGURE 23.11 **Chromium Compounds** Chromium compounds tend to be brightly colored.

TABLE 23.4 The Colors of Various Chromium Compounds

Compound	Color
Chromates (CrO_4^{2-})	Yellow
Chromium(II) iodide	Red-brown
Chromium(III) iodide	Green-black
Chromium(II) chloride	White
Chromium(III) chloride	Violet
Dichromates ($Cr_2O_7^{2-}$)	Orange
Chromium(III) oxide	Deep green
Chrome alum	Purple
Chromium(VI) oxychloride (CrO_2Cl_2)	Dark red
Chromium(II) acetate	Red

The chromium reacts with any oxygen in the steel to protect the iron from rusting. Chromium compounds were also used extensively in metal coatings such as paints, because the chromium helps to rustproof the underlying metal, and in wood preservatives, because these compounds kill many of the bacteria and molds that rot wood. Chromium compounds are finding less use today, however, because of their toxicity and potential carcinogenicity. Nonetheless, because of their great corrosion resistance, chromate coatings are still used on large outdoor steel structures such as bridges, and chromate paints are used to mark streets (on the pavement) and on street signs.

Because chromium has the electron configuration $[Ar] 4s^1 3d^5$, with six orbitals available for bonding, it can have oxidation states from $+1$ to $+6$. Low-oxidation-state chromium exists primarily as the *cation* in salt compounds such as $Cr(NO_3)_3$ and $CrCl_3$. High-oxidation-state chromium occurs within the polyatomic *anions* of salts. The most important compounds with chromium in the $+6$ oxidation state are the chromates and dichromates. In an acidic solution (below pH 6), the orange-red dichromate ion $Cr_2O_7^{2-}$ is more stable. In more basic solutions (above pH 6), the yellow chromate ion CrO_4^{2-} dominates. Adding acid to a solution containing the chromate ion produces the dichromate ion.

$$2 H^+(aq) + 2 CrO_4^{2-}(aq) \longrightarrow Cr_2O_7^{2-}(aq) + H_2O(l)$$

The chromate ion has a tetrahedral arrangement of oxygen atoms around a chromium atom. The dichromate ion has one bridging oxygen between the two tetrahedrons surrounding the chromium ions.

Chromate (CrO_4^{2-})

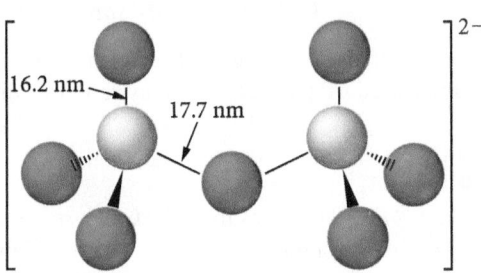

Dichromate ($Cr_2O_7^{2-}$)

The high-oxidation-state chromates and dichromates are very strong oxidizing agents (that is, they are easily reduced). Consequently, they are used as coatings on other metal surfaces to prevent oxidation. The chromates react with the atoms on the surface of the other metals, forming a strongly bonded gel-like film. The film is non-metallic and bonds very effectively with paint and resins that are applied over the film. We can see evidence of the oxidizing power of dichromate in the ability of ammonium dichromate to sustain combustion without any additional oxygen. Once ignited, ammonium dichromate burns with visible flames, giving off a smoke of green chromium oxide dust.

$$(NH_4)_2Cr_2O_7(s) \xrightarrow{\text{heat}} 4 H_2O(g) + N_2(g) + Cr_2O_3(s)$$

▲ Ammonium dichromate does not require additional oxygen to burn.

Manganese

Manganese, with the electron configuration $[Ar] 4s^2 3d^5$, exhibits the widest range of oxidation states, from $+1$ to $+7$. The most common natural sources of manganese are pyrolusite (MnO_2), hausmannite (Mn_3O_4), and rhodochrosite ($MnCO_3$) minerals. Calcination of rhodochrosite produces manganese (IV) oxide.

$$MnCO_3(s) + \tfrac{1}{2}O_2(g) \xrightarrow{\text{heat}} MnO_2(s) + CO_2(g)$$

The manganese (IV) oxide or pyrolusite minerals can react with active metals such as Al or Na to produce the elemental metal.

$$3 MnO_2(s) + 4 Al(s) \longrightarrow 3 Mn(s) + 2 Al_2O_3(s)$$

Pyrolusite, however, is often found as an impure mineral, containing mixtures of MnO and Fe_2O_3. Heating the mineral in the presence of carbon can reduce the mineral, forming an alloy of manganese and iron called ferromanganese.

$$MnO_2(s) + MnO(s) + Fe_2O_3(s) + n\ C(s) \longrightarrow Mn_xFe_yC_z(s) + n\ CO(g)$$

Ferromanganese generally contains about 5–6% carbon and is used as an alloying material in steel production. Manganese is added to steel alloys to change the physical properties of the steel. For example, manganese makes the steel easier to deform at high temperatures. Adding manganese to steel helps the rolling and forging steps of steel production. Steel alloys containing about 12% manganese are used in military armor and industrial applications such as bulldozer blades. Manganese also strengthens copper, aluminum, and magnesium alloys.

Manganese is a reactive metal that dissolves in most acids. When heated in the presence of air, it forms the various manganese oxides, including MnO, Mn_3O_4, and MnO_2. When heated in pure oxygen, the high-oxidation-state oxide Mn_2O_7 also forms. At high oxidation states, the manganese compounds are good oxidizing agents. Dissolving MnO_2 into a solution of hydrochloric acid oxidizes the chloride and produces chlorine gas.

$$MnO_2(s) + 4\ HCl(aq) \longrightarrow Cl_2(g) + 2\ H_2O(l) + MnCl_2(aq)$$

The permanganate ion (MnO_4^-) has an oxidation state of +7 for Mn and is also an important oxidizing agent. The permanganate ion can even oxidize hydrogen peroxide, which is itself used as an oxidizing agent.

$$2\ MnO_4^-(aq) + 3\ H_2O_2(aq) + 2\ H^+(aq) \longrightarrow 2\ MnO_2(s) + 3\ O_2(g) + 4\ H_2O(g)$$

The compound MnO_2 is a glass additive. By itself, MnO_2 is either a brown or black crystal, depending on the degree of hydration. Yet, when added to a silica glass, it imparts a pink color to the glass. The pink color is useful because it counteracts the green color often seen in glass, which is due to small concentrations of impure iron oxides. In other words, MnO_2 is added to glass to "decolorize" it. Old manganese-containing glass that has been exposed to UV light for over 100 years develops a slight purple tint. This purple color is due to the oxidation of MnO_2 to Mn(VII) oxides.

Cobalt

Cobalt ore is often found within the ores of other metals, such as iron, nickel, lead, and silver. Cobalt's most common ores are sulfide minerals, such as cobaltite (CoAsS), which is collected as a by-product in the extraction processes of the other metal ores. No large deposits of cobalt ores occur in the United States, but surveys indicated that there are cobalt-rich deposits in the Pacific Ocean near the Hawaiian Islands.

Cobalt, like iron and nickel, is **ferromagnetic** and is important in the production of magnets. Like in the paramagnetic materials described in Section 8.7, the atoms in ferromagnetic materials contain unpaired electrons. In ferromagnetic materials, however, these electrons can all align with their spins oriented in the same direction, creating a permanent magnetic field.

Magnets are increasingly important in industrial and military applications. In the United States, concerns have arisen over the lack of domestic sources of cobalt for these applications. New and stronger magnetic materials that do not require cobalt have been developed, but these require neodymium, which is found mostly in China.

Cobalt is also an important additive for high-strength steels. Carbaloy, a mixture composed primarily of cobalt metal with grains of tungsten carbide, is a very tough material. The strength of the cobalt and hardness of the carbides make this a good material for industrial cutting and abrasion. In addition, cobalt forms many compounds with brilliant blue colors and is used in making pigments and inks. Cobalt compounds are also essential for health, because cobalt is the metal in vitamin B_{12}, which prevents anemia.

Copper

Copper, which can be found in its elemental form, was one of the first elements to be isolated and used by humans—copper products have been known for over 10,000 years. Ancient civilizations used copper to form tools. The earliest known artifacts produced

▲ Copper wiring is used to conduct electricity in wires.

▲ Copper is used in a variety of applications.

by the smelting of copper are at a site in Tepe Yahya, Iran, dating from about 3800 B.C. The discovery of **bronze**, a copper and tin alloy, improved tool making because copper's bronze alloys are stronger, and they resist wear and corrosion better than pure copper.

The most important copper ores are chalcopyrite ($CuFeS_2$) and malachite [$Cu_2(OH)_2CO_3$]. Copper ores often occur near deposits of elemental copper, providing early humans with an easy way to locate copper ores. The electrometallurgical production of pure copper from chalcopyrite is described in Section 23.3.

The high natural abundance and generally high concentration of copper and copper ores makes copper an economical choice for many industrial applications. Today over 40% of copper products are made from recycled copper. The ease and low cost of recycling copper has allowed copper to remain an important industrial metal.

The high conductivity of copper is second only to that of silver, making copper the most important metal for electrical wires. Along with iron in steel, copper is now among the most widely-used metals; it is used in electrical motors and devices, the electrical wiring that snakes though the walls of houses, and the electrical transmission network linking power sources to homes and industries all over the world. Because of its high heat conductivity, copper is also used as a heat exchange material—for example, in car radiators. In addition, copper is used to make pipes for water distribution. Copper pipes can be readily connected to each other with watertight seals by soldering. Copper displaced lead for use as water pipes because of the toxicity of lead. Today, because of its lower price and lighter weight, plastic is used for many water pipes.

Copper has a distinctive reddish color that can be polished to a beautiful metallic luster; it has been used in architecture, as a decorative metal in jewelry, and as a material for sculpture. Copper composes the decorative sheathings on many domes and roof-top art works. When exposed to the atmosphere and rain, copper can oxidize, forming a number of different compounds, such as malachite and brochanite ($Cu_4SO_4(OH)_6$), that have beautiful blue or green colors. Copper roofing shingles can be purchased as polished copper sheets or as sheets that have already been oxidized and exhibit a beautiful weathered *patina* (a coating that comes with age and use). Chemical compounds speed up the aging process and produce the desired patina, which takes 20 or more years to develop naturally.

Even though copper has many useful properties, it is not a very strong metal; therefore, alloys of copper with improved strength have been developed. Bronze was one of the first alloys ever produced. This alloy of copper and tin has been used for thousands of years because it could be made even in the low heat of a Stone Age campfire. **Brass**, another widely used alloy, contains copper and zinc. Many brass and bronze alloys also contain other metals to achieve certain physical properties. Some of the most important applications of bronze and brass are for plumbing fixtures, bearings, and art decorations. In addition, the tendency of brass and bronze alloys (unlike those of iron) not to spark when struck make them useful in applications where sparks could be dangerous.

Nickel

Most of the world's nickel comes from deposits in Ontario, Canada. These deposits are believed to have formed from a meteorite impact (most meteorites have high nickel content). The nickel occurs as a sulfide compound mixed with copper and iron sulfides. To produce nickel, the sulfides are roasted in air to form metal oxides, and then they are reduced to the elemental metals with carbon. The metal mixture is heated in the presence of carbon monoxide, forming nickel carbonyl, which has a boiling point of 43 °C and can be collected as a gas.

$$Ni(s) + 4\,CO(g) \xrightarrow{\text{heat}} Ni(CO)_4(g)$$

When the nickel carbonyl is heated past 200 °C, it decomposes back to nickel metal and carbon monoxide. This method of refining nickel is called the *Mond process*.

Nickel metal is fairly unreactive and resistant to corrosion, characteristics that it shares with platinum and palladium. Consequently, nickel is used as an alloying metal in the production of stainless steels. Many nickel alloys are used for applications where corrosion resistance is important. For example, the alloy Monel contains 72% Ni,

25% Cu, and 3% Fe and is resistant to reaction with most chemicals. Monel does not react even with fluorine gas at room temperature. Nickel–steel alloys are used for armor plates, and elemental nickel is often plated onto other metals as a protective coating.

Zinc

Elemental zinc was officially discovered in Europe in 1746 when calamine (zinc silicate) was reduced with charcoal to produce the metal. However, zinc had been used for many hundreds of years before this discovery because zinc ores and copper ores were used to form copper–zinc brass alloys. The main sources of zinc are ores composed of sphalerite (ZnS), smithsonite ($ZnCO_3$), and an oxide mixture of zinc, iron, and manganese called franklinite. These ores are roasted to form the oxides of the metals and then reduced with carbon to produce the elemental metals. Zinc combines with many different metals to form useful alloys. As we have seen, the combination of zinc and copper produces the brass family of alloys. The combination of zinc and nickel with copper produces alloys with a silver color called *German* or *silver brass*. Zinc is also used in solder alloys with low melting points.

Galvanizing a steel object (such as a nail) involves dipping the object into a molten bath of zinc. The zinc, which is more reactive than the iron in steel, preferentially oxidizes, forming a tough protective coating. Zinc compounds are also used to coat steel before applying other coatings. The zinc compounds, such as zinc phosphate, adhere strongly to the steel surface, forming rough crystals onto which other coatings, such as paint, adhere very well. If a painted steel surface is scratched, the underlying exposed metal is susceptible to rust, but the added zinc ions prevent this by migrating toward the defect and forming a protective zinc oxide coating.

Zinc and zinc compounds have generally been considered safe. Zinc additives in coatings have replaced many of the chromium and lead additives (both of which are toxic) that were previously used. Today, however, even zinc additives in coatings are being studied for environmental hazards. In Europe, all substances that contain zinc compounds must be labeled as potential polluters of environmental water. More environmentally safe organic compounds have been developed to replace the metallic anticorrosion additives, but these compounds are more expensive to produce. Opportunities abound for chemists to develop needed products that are both environmentally safe and economically viable.

▲ Zinc phosphate adheres strongly to steel surfaces, forming rough crystals onto which other coatings, such as paint, can be applied.

CHAPTER IN REVIEW

Self Assessment Quiz

Q1. Which metal is naturally found in its elemental state?
a) gold
b) titanium
c) chromium
d) iron

Q2. Which reaction is an example of pyrometallurgy?
a) $Ti^{4+}(aq) + 4\,OH^-(aq) \longrightarrow TiO_2(s) + 2\,H_2O(l)$
b) $2\,MnCO_3(s) + O_2(g) \xrightarrow{heat} 2\,MnO_2(s) + 2\,CO_2(g)$
c) $Ni(s) + 4\,CO(g) \longrightarrow Ni(CO)_4(g)$
d) $3\,MnO_2(s) + 4\,Al(s) \longrightarrow 3\,Mn(s) + 2\,Al_2O_3(s)$

Q3. Based on the data in the table, which pair of metals is likely to form a substitutional alloy?

Metal	Atomic Radius	Crystal Structure
Sc	162 pm	Hexagonal closet packed
W	135 pm	Body-centered cubic
Cu	128 pm	Face-centered cubic
Cr	128 pm	Body-centered cubic

a) Sc and W
b) Cu and Cr
c) Cu and Sc
d) Cr and W

Q4. Two metals, A and B, form a substitutional alloy with the binary phase diagram shown here. What is the melting point of the alloy at a composition that is 75% A and 25% B?

a) 1000 °C
b) 1300 °C
c) 1450 °C
d) 2000 °C

Q5. Two metals, A and B, form a substitutional alloy with the binary phase diagram shown here. Determine the composition and relative amounts of the two phases present at 50% composition and 1500 °C.

a) The A-rich bcc phase is 80% A and 20% B; the B-rich fcc phase is 37% A and 63% B; the mixture contains more of the A-rich fcc phase.
b) The A-rich bcc phase is 20% A and 80% B; the B-rich fcc phase is 63% A and 37% B; the mixture contains more of the B-rich fcc phase.
c) The A-rich bcc phase is 50% A and 50% B; the B-rich fcc phase is 50% A and 50% B; the mixture contains equal amounts of both phases.
d) The A-rich bcc phase is 80% A and 20% B; the B-rich fcc phase is 37% A and 63% B; the mixture contains more of the B-rich fcc phase.

Q6. An interstitial alloy contains a nonmetal (X) that occupies one-fourth of the octahedral holes in the closet-packed lattice of the metal (M). What is the formula for the alloy?
a) M_4X
b) MX_4
c) M_2X
d) MX_2

Q7. Which metal is commonly used to make electrical wires?
a) zinc
b) cobalt
c) manganese
d) copper

Q8. Which metal is commonly used to make parts for aircraft engines?
a) zinc
b) titanium
c) nickel
d) silver

Q9. Calculate the mass percent of chromium in the mineral chromite ($FeCr_2O_4$).
a) 83.97%
b) 46.46%
c) 86.78%
d) 36.13%

Q10. What is a common use for zinc?
a) galvanization of steel
b) lightweight aircraft parts
c) paint pigments
d) production of magnets

Key Terms

Key Concepts

General Properties (23.2)

▶ Metals have many common physical properties, such as high conductivity of electricity and heat and high malleability and ductility. These properties vary among the different metals.

Natural Distribution of Metals (23.2)

▶ Metals are unevenly distributed throughout Earth's crust. All the metals together compose about 25% of the mass of Earth's crust, but just a few key metals are abundant enough to each individually compose more than 1% of the crust.

▶ Few metals exist naturally in their elemental state; most are found in ores, rocks that contain a high concentration of metal-containing minerals.

▶ Most metal-containing minerals are oxides, sulfides, chlorides, carbonates, or more complex compounds.

Metallurgical Processes (23.3)

▶ To be useful, metals have to be separated from the gangue, the unusable part of the ores, reduced to the elemental metals, and refined to be more pure.

▶ Extractive metallurgy is the general term for the processes such as pyrometallurgy, hydrometallurgy, and electrometallurgy that separate metal from ore.

▶ A new method of forming metal components from micron-sized metal particles is powder metallurgy.

Phase Diagrams (23.4)

▶ Elemental metals tend to crystallize in three main crystalline structures: face-centered cubic, body centered cubic, and hexagonal closest packed.

▶ When two types of metal atoms bond together, they form an alloy.

▶ A binary phase diagram is a graphical representation of the phases and crystal types of alloys present at different compositions and temperatures.

▶ If the two metals in an alloy are similar in size and have the same crystal structure, they tend to form a miscible solid solution, which means that they can form an alloy at any composition ratio. If the two metals are dissimilar in size or crystal structure, the solubility of one atom in the other's crystal structure is often limited. At certain compositions two different crystals can coexist in equilibrium; this is called a two-phase region. The lever rule determines which phase is present in a greater proportion.

Types of Alloys (23.4)

▶ There are two different types of alloys, substitutional and interstitial.

▶ A substitutional alloy is a mixture in which one type of metal atom replaces another type of metal atom in the crystal structure.

▶ In an interstitial alloy, one type of atom (either a metal or non-metal) fits into the holes within the crystal structure of the metal. Interstitial alloys can be made with different atoms filling different fractions of the different types of holes.

Key Equations and Relationships

Lever Rule (23.4)

In a two-phase region on a phase diagram, two different crystal structures coexist in equilibrium. Whichever phase has a composition closer to the overall composition of the alloy is the phase present in the larger relative amount.

Key Learning Outcomes

Chapter Objectives	Assessment
Using a Phase Diagram to Determine the Composition, Relative Amounts, and Phases Present (**23.4**)	Examples 23.1, 23.2, 23.3, 23.4 For Practice 23.1, 23.2, 23.3, 23.4 Exercises 35–38
Determining the Composition of an Interstitial Alloy from the Occupancy of the Interstitial Holes (**23.4**)	Exercises 41, 42

EXERCISES

Review Questions

1. Why is vanadium present in oil from some sources?

2. List three categories of metallurgical processes.

3. Why is Ni not considered a common metal even though it composes over 2% of the total mass of Earth and only Fe and Mg have a higher percent composition of Earth's total mass?

4. Metal elements are found in both minerals and ores. Describe the difference between a mineral and an ore.

5. Ores contain minerals and gangue. Describe the difference between a mineral and gangue.

6. Calcination, roasting, and smelting are three pyrometallurgical processes. Compare and contrast the processes.

7. What compound has been historically used to leach gold from gold ores? Why is this process being discontinued?

8. Name three advantages of making metal components from the powder metallurgical process.

9. Describe the difference between body-centered cubic and face-centered cubic structures.

10. Describe the difference between a substitutional alloy and an interstitial alloy.

11. Why was copper one of the first metals that humans used?

12. Describe why bronze was one of the first alloys that humans used.

13. Both brass and bronze contain copper. Describe the difference between these two alloys.

14. List the properties of copper that make it appropriate for electric wires and the properties that make it appropriate for water pipes.

Problems by Topic

The General Properties and Natural Distribution of Metals

15. Describe three typical properties of metals.

16. Describe whether each property is generally higher or lower for metals compared to nonmetals.
    a. thermal conductivity
    b. electrical resistivity
    c. transparency
    d. ductility

17. List four metal elements that each individually compose more than 1% of Earth's crust.

18. List four metals that occur as elements in their natural state.

19. List the name and formula of one important mineral source for each of these metals: Fe, Hg, V, and Nb.

20. List the name and formula of one important mineral source for each of these metals: Ti, Zn, U, and Ta.

Metallurgical Processes

21. Two ores of magnesium are $MgCO_3$ and $Mg(OH)_2$. Write balanced equations for the calcination of these two minerals to form MgO.

22. Two ores of copper are CuO and CuS. Write balanced equations for the roasting of CuO with C to form Cu metal and the roasting of CuS with O_2 to form CuO.

23. Give the definition of a flux and identify the flux in the reaction.

$$SiO(s) + MgO(s) \longrightarrow MgSiO_3(l)$$

24. Give the definition of a slag and identify the slag in the reaction.

$$SiO_2(s) + MgO(s) \longrightarrow MgSiO_3(l)$$

25. Provide a general description of how hydrometallurgy is used to extract metals from ores.

26. Provide a general description of how electrometallurgy is used to extract metals from ores.

27. How is Al_2O_3 separated from other oxides using the Bayer process? What soluble form of aluminum forms from Al_2O_3 during the Bayer process?

28. When copper is purified using an electrochemical cell, which electrode has the pure copper and which electrode has the impure copper? Explain how gold is obtained from this process.

29. Describe the difference between sponge powdered iron and water-atomized powdered iron.

30. Describe the difference in the processing of sponge powdered iron and water-atomized powdered iron.

Metal Structures and Alloys

31. Determine the composition of each vanadium alloy.
  a. One-half of the V atoms are replaced by Cr atoms.
  b. One-fourth of the V atoms are replaced by Fe atoms.
  c. One-fourth of the V atoms are replaced by Cr atoms, and one-fourth of the V atoms are replaced by Fe atoms.

32. Determine the composition of each cobalt alloy.
  a. One-third of the Co atoms are replaced by Zn atoms.
  b. One-eighth of the Co atoms are replaced by Ti atoms.
  c. One-third of the Co atoms are replaced by Zn atoms, and one-sixth of the Co atoms are replaced by Ti atoms.

33. Referring to Table 23.2, explain why you might expect Cr and Fe to form miscible alloys.

34. Referring to Table 23.2, explain why you might expect Co and Cu to not form miscible alloys.

35. Determine the composition and phases present at points A and B on the Cr–Fe phase diagram.

36. Determine the composition and phase present at points C and D on the Cr–Fe phase diagram (see previous problem for diagram).

37. Determine the composition, relative amounts, and phases present at points A and B on the Co–Cu phase diagram.

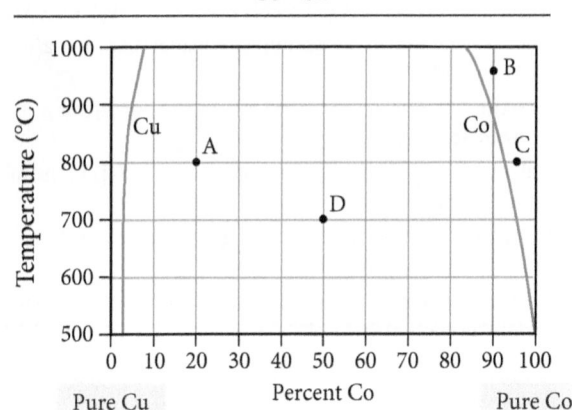

38. Determine the composition, relative amounts and phases present at points C and D on the Co–Cu phase diagram (see previous problem for phase diagram).

39. The elements Mn and Si are added to steel to improve its properties in electric motors, and some C is often found as a detrimental impurity. Which of these elements fills interstitial holes in the Fe lattice and which substitutes for the Fe in the lattice?

40. The elements Si and P are added to steel to improve its properties in electric motors, and some N is often found as a detrimental impurity. Which of these elements fills interstitial holes in the Fe lattice and which substitutes for the Fe in the lattice?

41. Determine the formula for each interstitial alloy.
  a. Nitrogen occupies one-half of the octahedral sites of a closest-packed Mo structure.
  b. Hydrogen occupies all of the tetrahedral sites of a Cr closest-packed structure.

42. Determine the formula for each interstitial alloy.
  a. Nitrogen occupies one-fourth of the octahedral sites of a closest-packed Fe structure.
  b. Hydrogen occupies one-half of the tetrahedral sites of a Ti closest-packed structure.

Sources, Properties, and Products of Some of the 3d Transition Metals

43. Identify the metal found in each mineral.
  a. sphalerite
  b. malachite
  c. hausmannite

44. Name at least one important mineral that is a source for each metal.
  a. Fe   **b.** Co   **c.** Cr

45. Calculate the heat of reaction (ΔH°_{rxn}) for the calcination of rhodochrosite. (ΔH°_f for rhodochrosite is -894.1 kJ/mol.)

46. The extraction of Mn from pyrolusite with aluminum produces pure Mn metal and Al_2O_3. Calculate the heat of reaction (ΔH°_{rxn}).

47. Describe the effects of adding Cr to steel and give a use for chromium–steel alloys.

48. Describe the effects of adding Mn to steel and give a use for manganese–steel alloys.

49. Calculate the mole percent and mass percent of Ti in the minerals rutile and ilmenite.

50. Calculate the mole percent and mass percent of Mn in the minerals pyrolusite and rhodochrosite.

51. Why is it important to use an inert atmosphere to surround the metal when arc-melting titanium?

52. Titanium is a very reactive metal. Explain why titanium has a high corrosion resistance to seawater and can be used for the production of ship components.

53. Which compound of Ti is the most important industrial product of titanium metal? Describe an application for this compound.

54. Describe how Zn is used to protect the surface of steel products. What is the name of this process?

55. Describe the Bayer process.

56. Describe the Mond process.

57. Which metals are found in carbaloy steel?

58. Which metals are found in Monel steel?

Cumulative Problems

59. After 2.0×10^4 kg of an ore that contains 0.051% ilmenite is mined, the percent yield from extracting and refining the metals from the mineral is 87% for the iron and 63% for the titanium. Calculate the mass of iron and titanium produced from the ore.

60. Calculate the mass of aluminum metal that is needed to produce Cr metal from 5.00×10^2 g of chromite. Calculate how many grams of Cr metal are produced from 5.00×10^2 g of chromite.

61. How many lattice atoms surround a tetrahedral hole and an octahedral hole in a closest-packed structure? Describe which hole site is larger and explain why.

62. Explain why the crystal structure and atomic size of the two elements are important factors in a two-component phase diagram.

63. Why does Mn form compounds with higher oxidation states than Cr?

64. Why is MnO_2 added to silica glass?

65. Co, Fe, and Ni are ferromagnetic. What is the difference between ferromagnetic and paramagnetic?

66. Is the chromate ion or dichromate ion more stable in an acidic solution? Which ion has a higher Cr : O ratio? Which ion has a higher oxidation state for Cr?

67. The first ionization energies of iron, cobalt, nickel, and the first three platinum metals are all about the same, but the first ionization energies of osmium, iridium, and platinum are substantially greater. Suggest an explanation for this observation.

68. Although both the Group IA and IB metals have a half-filled s subshell, the IB metals have markedly higher first ionization energies, densities, and melting points, and markedly lower second and third ionization energies than the corresponding IA metals. Explain these observations.

Challenge Problems

69. Iron powder is placed into a tall cylinder-shaped die and pressed from the top and bottom to make a cylinder-shaped pressed part with a height of 5.62 cm and radius of 4.00 cm. The density of the iron powder before it was pressed was 2.41 g/mL. The density of a pressed iron part is 6.85 g/mL. The density of pure solid iron is 7.78 g/mL.

a. Calculate the original height of the powder before it was pressed.

b. Calculate the theoretical height of the pressed component if it could be pressed to the same density of pure iron.

c. What percentage of the component is composed of voids between the iron particles?

70. When a part is made by pressing together powdered metal, no metal is wasted. In contrast, metal is typically scrapped after a metal part is cut from a solid metal plate. If a circular part with a diameter of 10.0 cm is made from an original shape of a square with a side length of 10.0 cm, calculate the percentage of the metal that is thrown away as scrap. If the circular shape also has a circular hole with a diameter of 6.0 cm, calculate the percentage of the metal that is thrown away as scrap.

71. Hydrogen can be in both the octahedral and tetrahedral holes for lanthanum. Determine the percentage of the holes that are filled if the formula is $LaH_{2.76}$.

72. Tin exists in two allotropic forms. Gray tin has a diamond structure and white tin has a close-packed structure. Predict which allotrope is (a) denser, (b) a conductor of electricity. Predict the valence electronic configuration of tin in each allotrope.

73. Find the equilibrium constant at 298 K for the reaction.

$$[Ag(CN)_2]^-(aq) + Cu(s) \rightleftharpoons [Cu(CN)_2]^-(aq) + Ag(s)$$

The K_f for $[Cu(CN)_2]^- = 1.0 \times 10^{24}$ and the rest of the data needed are in Appendix II.

74. Find the equilibrium constant at 298 K for the reaction.

$$2 [Cu(NH_3)_2]^+(aq) \rightleftharpoons [Cu(NH_3)_4]^{2+}(aq) + Cu(s)$$

The K_f for $[Cu(NH_3)_2]^+ = 6.3 \times 10^{10}$ and the rest of the data needed are in Appendix II.

75. Propose a chemical procedure to extract cobalt from the mineral cobaltite, CoAsS. What are some of the hazards of such a procedure?

Conceptual Problems

76. Why are metals such as Ni and Co economical to mine and use in industrial processes even though they have a very low natural abundance in Earth's crust?

77. Explain why metals such as Au and Ag are found in their elemental states in nature, but metals like Na and Ca are always found in compounds in nature.

78. What allows some pairs of metals to form alloys that have the same structure at any composition, while other pairs of metals form alloys with structures that depend on the relative composition of the two metals?

Answers to Conceptual Connections

Interstitial Alloys

23.1 M_4X. Since there are twice as many tetrahedral holes as metal atoms in a closest-packed structure, and since one-eighth of them are occupied by nonmetal atoms, there must be one-quarter as many nonmetal atoms as metal atoms.

24

Transition Metals and Coordination Compounds

"Chemistry must become the astronomy of the molecular world."

—Alfred Werner (1866–1919)

I N THIS CHAPTER, WE EXAMINE the chemistry of the transition metals and an important class of their compounds called coordination compounds. We will see that coordination compounds form all of the types of isomers that we have studied so far, as well as some new types. In our examination of the transition metals, we draw on much of what we learned in Chapters 7 and 8 about electronic structure and periodicity. We also briefly revisit valence bond theory to explain bonding in coordination compounds, but we quickly shift to a different theory—called crystal field theory—that better explains many of the properties of these compounds. Transition metals and coordination compounds are important, not only because of their interesting chemistry, but because of their numerous applications. Coordination compounds are the basis for a number of therapeutic drugs, chemical sensors, and coloring agents. In addition, many biological molecules contain transition metals that bond in ways that are similar to coordination compounds. For example, the oxygen-carrying site on hemoglobin is an iron ion bonded partly to an amino acid in the hemoglobin molecule and partly to a flat molecule called a porphyrin. An oxygen molecule reversibly bonds to the iron and is transported throughout the body by blood flow.

The color of ruby is caused by a splitting of the d-orbital energy levels in Cr^{3+} by the host crystal.

24.1 The Colors of Rubies and Emeralds

Rubies are deep red and emeralds are brilliant green, yet the color of both gemstones is caused by the same ion, Cr^{3+}. The difference lies in the crystal that hosts the ion. Rubies are crystals of aluminum oxide (Al_2O_3) in which about 1% of the Al^{3+} ions are replaced by Cr^{3+} ions. Emeralds, by contrast, are crystals of beryllium aluminum silicate [$Be_3Al_2(SiO_3)_6$] in which a similar percentage of the Al^{3+} ions are replaced by Cr^{3+}. The imbedded Cr^{3+} ion is red in the aluminum oxide crystal but green in the beryllium aluminum silicate crystal. Why?

The answer to this question lies in the effect that the host crystal has on the energies of the atomic orbitals in Cr^{3+}. Atoms in the crystal create a field around the ion—sometimes called the *crystal field*—that splits the five normally degenerate d orbitals into two or more levels. The color of the gemstone is caused by electron transitions between these levels. In rubies, the crystal field is stronger (and the corresponding splitting of the d orbitals greater) than it is in emeralds. Recall from Chapter 7 that the color of a substance depends on the colors *absorbed* by that substance, which in turn depends on the energy differences between the orbitals involved in the absorption. The greater splitting in ruby results in a greater energy difference between the d orbitals of Cr^{3+}, and consequently the absorption of a different color of light than in emerald.

▲ **Ruby and Emerald** The red color of ruby and the green color of emerald are both caused by Cr^{3+}.

The colors of several other gemstones are also caused by the splitting of the d orbitals in transition metal ions imbedded within host crystals. For example, the red in garnet, which has $Mg_3Al_2(SiO_4)_3$ as a host crystal, and the yellow-green of peridot, which has Mg_2SiO_4 as a host crystal are both caused by electron transitions between d orbitals in Fe^{2+}. Similarly, the blue in turquoise, which has $[Al_6(PO_4)_4(OH)_8 \cdot 4\,H_2O]^{2-}$ as a host crystal, is caused by transitions between the d orbitals in Cu^{2+}.

In this chapter, we examine the properties of the transition metals and their ions more closely. We also examine the properties of coordination compounds in some detail. We first discussed this common type of transition metal compound in Chapter 16 (see Section 16.8). In a coordination compound, bonds to a central metal ion split the d orbitals much as they are split in the crystals of gemstones. The theory that explains these splittings and the corresponding colors is **crystal field theory**, which we also explore in this chapter.

▲ **Garnet, Peridot, and Turquoise** The red in garnet and the yellow-green of peridot are both caused by Fe^{2+}. The blue of turquoise is caused by Cu^{2+}.

24.2 Properties of Transition Metals

Transition metals, the elements in the d block of the periodic table, are a study in similarities and differences. When we compare their properties with the varied properties of the main-group elements, they seem markedly similar. For example, almost all transition metals have moderate to high densities, good electrical conductivity, high melting points, and moderate to extreme hardness. Their similar properties are related to their similar electron configurations: they all have electrons in d orbitals that can be involved in metallic bonding. In spite of their similarities, however, each element is also unique, and they exhibit a wide variety of chemical behavior. Before we examine some of the periodic properties of the transition metals, let's review the electron configurations of these elements, first discussed in Chapter 8.

Electron Configurations

Recall from Section 8.4 that, as we move to the right across a row of transition elements, electrons are added to $(n-1)d$ orbitals (where n is the row number in the periodic table and also the quantum number of the highest occupied principal level). For example, as we move across the fourth-period transition metals, electrons are added to the $3d$ orbitals, as shown in Table 24.1.

In general, the ground state electron configuration for the first two rows of transition elements is [noble gas] $ns^2(n-1)d^x$ and for the third and fourth rows is [noble gas] $ns^2(n-2)f^{14}(n-1)d^x$, where x ranges from 1 to 10. Recall from Section 8.4, however, that because the ns and $(n-1)d$ sublevels are close in energy, many exceptions occur. For example, in the first transition series of the d block, the outer configuration is $4s^23d^x$ with two exceptions: Cr is $4s^13d^5$ and Cu is $4s^13d^{10}$. This behavior is related to the closely spaced $3d$ and $4s$ energy levels and the stability associated with a half-filled or completely filled d sublevel.

Recall from Section 8.7 that the transition metals form ions by losing electrons from the ns orbital *before* losing electrons from the $(n-1)d$ orbitals. For example, Fe^{2+} has an electron configuration of [Ar] $3d^6$, because it has lost both of the $4s$ electrons to form the 2+ charge. Examples 24.1 and 24.2 review the steps in writing electron configurations for transition metals and their ions.

TABLE 24.1 First-Row Transition Metal Orbital Occupancy

	4s	3d				
Sc	↑↓	↑				
Ti	↑↓	↑	↑			
V	↑↓	↑	↑	↑		
Cr	↑	↑	↑	↑	↑	↑
Mn	↑↓	↑	↑	↑	↑	↑
Fe	↑↓	↑↓	↑	↑	↑	↑
Co	↑↓	↑↓	↑↓	↑	↑	↑
Ni	↑↓	↑↓	↑↓	↑↓	↑	↑
Cu	↑	↑↓	↑↓	↑↓	↑↓	↑↓
Zn	↑↓	↑↓	↑↓	↑↓	↑↓	↑↓

PROCEDURE FOR... **Writing Electron Configurations**	EXAMPLE 24.1 **Writing Electron Configurations for Transition Metals** Write the ground state electron configuration for Zr.	EXAMPLE 24.2 **Writing Electron Configurations for Transition Metals** Write the ground state electron configuration for Co^{3+}.
Identify the noble gas that precedes the element and write it in square brackets.	SOLUTION $[Kr]$	SOLUTION $[Ar]$
Count down the periods to determine the outer principal quantum level—this is the quantum level for the *s* orbital. Subtract one to obtain the quantum level for the *d* orbital. If the element is in the third or fourth transition series, include $(n - 2)f^{14}$ electrons in the configuration.	Zr is in the fifth period so the orbitals used are $[Kr]\, 5s4d$	Co is in the fourth period so the orbitals used are $[Ar]\, 4s3d$
Count across the row to see how many electrons are in the neutral atom and fill the orbitals accordingly.	Zr has four more electrons than Kr. $[Kr]\, 5s^2 4d^2$	Co has nine more electrons than Ar. $[Ar]\, 4s^2 3d^7$
For an ion, remove the required number of electrons, first from the *s* and then from the *d* orbitals.		Co^{3+} has lost three electrons relative to the Co atom. $[Ar]\, 4s^0 3d^6$ or $[Ar]\, 3d^6$
	FOR PRACTICE 24.1 Write the ground state electron configuration for Os.	FOR PRACTICE 24.2 Write the ground state electron configuration for Nb^{2+}.

▶ FIGURE 24.1 **Trends in Atomic Radius** With the exception of a decrease in radius from the first to the second element, there is only a small variation in atomic radius across a row. There is a small and expected increase in radius from the first to the second transition row but virtually no difference in radius from the second to the third.

Atomic Size

As we discussed in Section 8.6, for main-group elements, the size of atoms decreases across a period and increases down a column. For transition metals, however, there is little variation in size across a row (other than for the first two elements in each transition metal row, such as Sc and Ti in the first row), as shown in Figure 24.1 ▲. The reason for the difference is that, across a row of transition elements, the number of electrons in the outermost principal energy level (highest n value) is nearly constant. As another proton is added to the nucleus with each successive element, another electron is added as well, but the electron goes into an $n - 1$ orbital. The number of outermost electrons thus stays the same, and the electrons experience a roughly constant effective nuclear charge as we move across the row, keeping the radii approximately constant.

Looking down a group, we see a small but expected increase in size from the first transition metal row to the second, but the size of elements in the third row is about the same as it is for those in the second row. This pattern is also different from that of the main-group elements, especially when we consider that in any given column, the third transition row has 32 more electrons than the second row. The reason that the third transition row elements are not larger is because 14 of the 32 electrons are in a $(n - 2)f$ sublevel, and while electrons in f orbitals are in lower principal quantum levels, they are not very effective at shielding the outer electrons from nuclear charge. Consequently, the outer electrons are held more tightly by the nucleus, offsetting the typical increase in size between the periods—an effect called the **lanthanide contraction**.

Conceptual Connection 24.1 Atomic Size

Which element has the larger atomic radius, Fe or W?

Ionization Energy

The first ionization energies of transition elements follow the expected main-group periodic trend and slowly increase across a row (Figure 24.2 ▶), but the increase is smaller than for main-group elements. As we move down a group, we see that the third transition row generally has a higher ionization energy than do the first two rows, a trend counter to that observed in the main-group elements. In the transition elements the charge of the nucleus increases substantially from one row to the next, but there is only a small increase in atomic size between the first and second rows, and no increase in size between the second and third row. The outer electrons are therefore held more tightly in the third transition row than in the first two rows.

◀ FIGURE 24.2 **Trends in First Ionization Energy** First ionization energy generally increases across a row, following the main-group trend. However, in contrast to the main-group trend, the third transition row has a greater ionization energy than the first and second rows.

Electronegativity

The electronegativity values of the transition metals, like their ionization energies, follow the main-group trend and slowly increase across a row, as shown in Figure 24.3 ▶. The increase is smaller than the increase that occurs in the main-group elements, but we would expect that given the similarity in the sizes of the atoms. The trend in electronegativity values down a group (or column) is another example of the transition metals behaving differently from the main-group elements. The electronegativity values generally increase from the first transition row to the second, but there is no further increase for the third row. In the main-group elements, by contrast, we see a *decrease* in electronegativity down a group. The difference is again caused by the relatively small change in atomic size as we move down a column for the transition elements, accompanied by a large increase in nuclear charge. One of the heaviest metals, gold (Au), is also the most electronegative metal. Its electronegativity value (EN = 2.4) is even higher than that of some nonmetals (EN of P is 2.1), and compounds of an Au^- ion have been observed.

▲ FIGURE 24.3 **Trends in Electronegativity** The electronegativity of the transition elements generally increases across a row, following the main-group trend. However, in contrast to the main-group trend, electronegativity increases from the first transition row to the second. There is little electronegativity difference between the second and third transition rows.

Oxidation States

Unlike main-group metals, which tend to exhibit only one oxidation state, the transition metals often exhibit a variety of oxidation states (Figure 24.4 ▼). The highest oxidation state for a transition metal is +7 for manganese (Mn). The electron configuration of

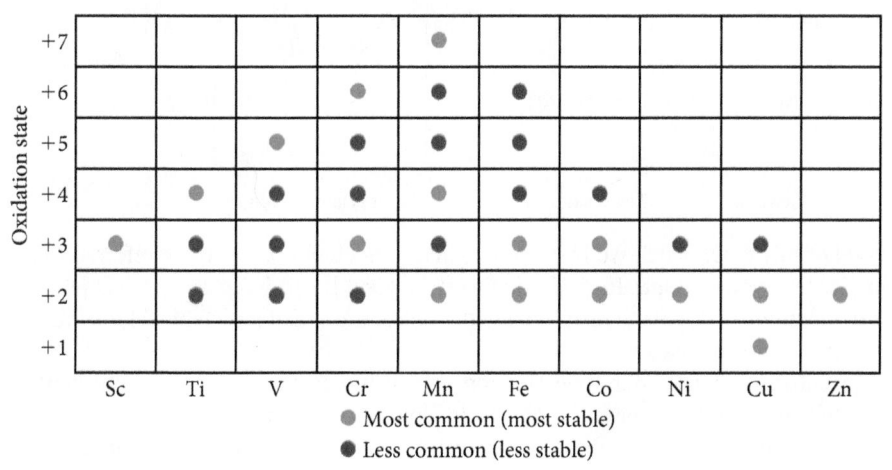

- Most common (most stable)
- Less common (less stable)

◀ FIGURE 24.4 **First-Row Transition Metal Oxidation States** The transition metals exhibit many more oxidation states than the main-group elements. These oxidation states range from +7 to +1.

Metals in high oxidation states, such as +7, exist only when the metal is bound to a highly electronegative element such as oxygen; they do not exist as bare ions.

manganese in this oxidation state corresponds to the loss of all the electrons in the $4s$ and $3d$ orbitals, leaving a noble gas electron configuration ([Ar]). This is the same configuration we see for all of the highest oxidation states of the elements to the left of Mn. To the right of manganese, the oxidation states are all lower, mostly +2 or +3. A +2 oxidation state for a transition metal is not surprising, since $4s$ electrons are readily lost.

24.3 Coordination Compounds

We discussed at the end of Chapter 16 that transition metals tend to form *complex ions*. A **complex ion** contains a central metal ion bound to one or more *ligands*. A **ligand** is a Lewis base (or electron donor) that forms a bond with the metal. When a complex ion combines with one or more *counterions* (ions of opposite charge that are not acting as ligands), the resulting neutral compound is a **coordination compound**. The first coordination compounds were discovered in the early eighteenth century, but their nature was not understood until nearly 200 years later. Swiss chemist Alfred Werner studied coordination compounds extensively—especially a series of cobalt(III) compounds with ammonia, whose formulas were then written as $CoCl_3 \cdot 6\,NH_3$, $CoCl_3 \cdot 5\,NH_3$ and, $CoCl_3 \cdot 4\,NH_3$. In 1893, he proposed that the central metal ion has two types of interactions that he named **primary valence** and **secondary valence**. The primary valence is the oxidation state on the central metal atom, and the secondary valence is the number of molecules or ions directly bound to the metal atom, called the **coordination number**. In $CoCl_3 \cdot 6\,NH_3$ the primary valence is +3, and it was discovered that the ammonia molecules are directly bound to the central cobalt, giving a coordination number of 6. Today we write the formula of this compound as $[Co(NH_3)_6]Cl_3$ to better represent the coordination compound as the combination of a complex ion, $Co(NH_3)_6{}^{3+}$, and three Cl^- counterions.

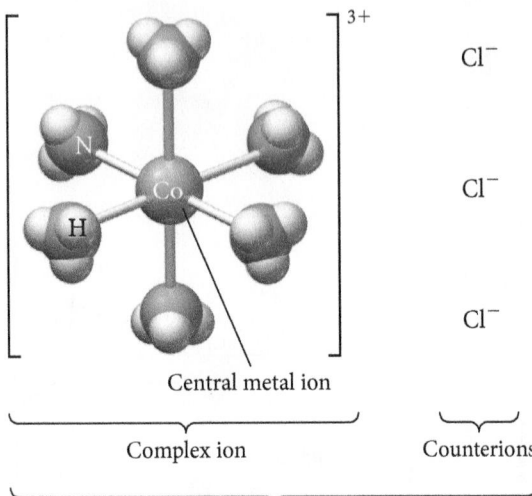

Central metal ion

Complex ion

Counterions

Coordination compound

▲ **Complex Ion and Coordination Compound** A coordination compound contains a complex ion and corresponding counterions. The complex ion contains a central metal atom coordinated to several ligands. The compound shown here is $[Co(NH_3)_6]Cl_3$.

We write the formulas of the other cobalt(III) compounds studied by Werner as $[Co(NH_3)_5Cl]Cl_2$ and $[Co(NH_3)_4Cl_2]Cl$. In these two cases, the complex ions are $Co(NH_3)_5Cl^{2+}$ (with two Cl^- counterions) and $Co(NH_3)_4Cl_2{}^+$ (with one Cl^- counterion), respectively. With this series of compounds, Werner demonstrated that the Cl^- can replace NH_3 in the secondary valence. In other words, Cl^- can act as a counterion, or it can bond directly to the metal as part of the complex ion.

The complex ion itself contains the metal ion in the center and the ligands—which can be neutral molecules or ions—arranged around it. We can think of the metal–ligand complex as a Lewis acid–base adduct (see Section 15.11) because the bond is formed when the ligand donates a pair of electrons to an empty orbital on the metal. For example, consider the reaction between the silver ion and ammonia:

Lewis acid   Lewis base   Lewis acid–base adduct

A bond of this type, which we first encountered in Section 10.6, is often referred to as a **coordinate covalent bond**. Ligands are therefore good Lewis bases and have at least one pair of electrons to donate to, and bond with, the central metal ion. Table 24.2 contains a number of common ligands.

Ligands that donate only one electron pair to the central metal are **monodentate**. Some ligands, however, have the ability to donate two pairs of electrons (from two different atoms) to the metal; these are **bidentate**. Examples of bidentate ligands include

TABLE 24.2 Common Ligands

Name	Lewis diagram
Water	$H-\overset{\cdot\cdot}{\underset{}{O}}\,\!\cdot-H$
Ammonia	$H-\overset{\cdot\cdot}{\underset{\underset{H}{\mid}}{N}}-H$
Chloride ion	$\left[:\overset{\cdot\cdot}{\underset{\cdot\cdot}{Cl}}:\right]^{-}$
Carbon monoxide	$:C\equiv O:$
Cyanide ion	$\left[:C\equiv N:\right]^{-}$
Thiocyanate ion	$\left[:\overset{\cdot\cdot}{\underset{\cdot\cdot}{S}}=C=\overset{\cdot\cdot}{N}:\right]^{-}$
Oxalate ion (ox)	$\left[\begin{array}{c} \overset{\cdot\cdot}{\underset{}{O}}\quad\quad\overset{\cdot\cdot}{\underset{}{O}} \\ \parallel\quad\quad\parallel \\ C-C \\ \overset{}{\underset{\cdot\cdot}{O}}\quad\quad\overset{}{\underset{\cdot\cdot}{O}} \end{array}\right]^{2-}$
Ethylenediamine (en)	$H-\overset{\cdot\cdot}{\underset{\underset{H}{\mid}}{N}}-\overset{\overset{H}{\mid}}{\underset{\underset{H}{\mid}}{C}}-\overset{\overset{H}{\mid}}{\underset{\underset{H}{\mid}}{C}}-\overset{\cdot\cdot}{\underset{\underset{H}{\mid}}{N}}-H$
Ethylenediaminetetraacetate (EDTA)	

the oxalate ion (abbreviated ox) and the ethylenediamine molecule (abbreviated en) shown here in the right margin. The ethylenediamine ligand bonded to Co^{3+} is shown in Figure 24.5(a) ▶ (on the next page).

Some ligands, called **polydentate** ligands, can donate even more than two electron pairs (from more than two atoms) to the metal. The most common polydentate ligand is the ethylenediaminetetraacetate ion ($EDTA^{4-}$) shown below.

Ethylenediamine

$EDTA^{4-}$

▶ FIGURE 24.5 **Bidentate and Polydentate Ligands Coordinated to Co(III)** **(a)** Ethylenediamine is a bidentate ligand; **(b)** EDTA is a hexadentate ligand.

Bidentate and Polydentate Ligands Coordinated to Co(III)

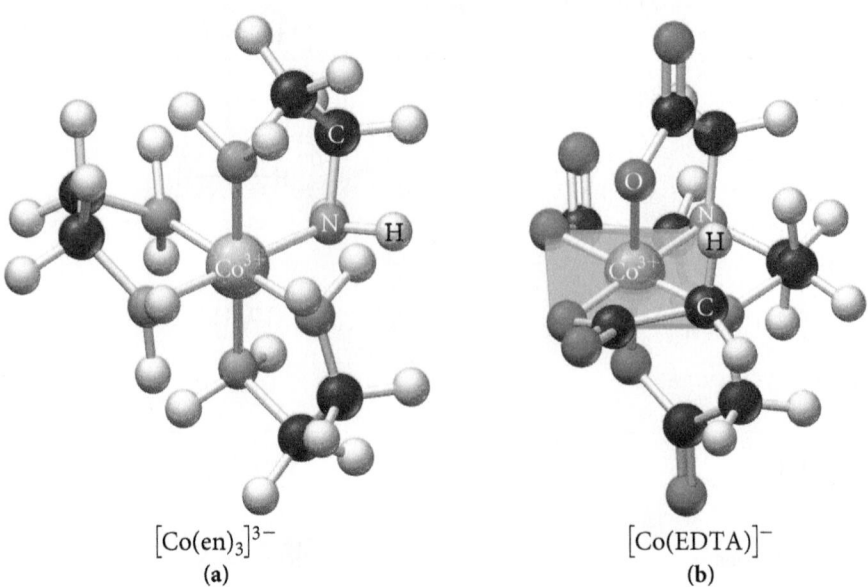

$[Co(en)_3]^{3-}$
(a)

$[Co(EDTA)]^-$
(b)

The EDTA ligand wraps itself completely around the metal, donating up to six pairs of electrons (Figure 24.5b ▲). A complex ion that contains either a bidentate or polydentate ligand is a **chelate** (pronounced "key-late"), and the coordinating ligand is known as a **chelating agent**.

A survey of many coordination compounds shows that coordination numbers can vary from as low as 2 to as high as 12. The most common coordination numbers are 6, as occurs in $[Co(NH_3)_6]^{3+}$, and 4, as occurs in $[PdCl_4]^{2-}$. Coordination numbers greater than 6 are rarely observed for the first-row transition metals. Typically, only 1+ metal ions have a coordination number as low as 2, as occurs in $[Ag(NH_3)_2]^+$. Odd coordination numbers exist, but they are rare.

The common geometries of complex ions, shown in Table 24.3, depend in part on their coordination number. A coordination number of 2 results in a linear geometry, and a coordination number of 6 results in an octahedral geometry. A coordination number of 4

TABLE 24.3 Common Geometries of Complex Ions

Coordination Number	Shape	Model	Example
2	Linear		$[Ag(NH_3)_2]^+$
4	Square planar		$[PdCl_4]^{2-}$
4	Tetrahedral		$[Zn(NH_3)_4]^{2+}$
6	Octahedral		$[Fe(H_2O)_6]^{3+}$

can have either a tetrahedral geometry or a square planar geometry, depending on the number of d electrons in the metal ion. Metal ions with a d^8 electron configuration (such as $[PdCl_4]^{2-}$) exhibit square planar geometry, and metal ions with a d^{10} electron configuration (such as $[Zn(NH_3)_4]^{2+}$) exhibit tetrahedral geometry.

Naming Coordination Compounds

To name coordination compounds, you follow a series of general rules based on the system originally proposed by Werner. As with all salts (see Section 3.5), the name of the cation goes before the name of the anion.

Guidelines for Naming Complex Ions	Examples
1. Name the ligands.	
• Name neutral ligands as molecules with the following notable exceptions.	$NH_2CH_2CH_2NH_2$ is ethylenediamine.
$\quad$ H_2O (aqua)	H_2O is aqua.
$\quad$ NH_3 (ammine)	
$\quad$ CO (carbonyl)	
• Name anionic ligands with the name of the ion plus an ending modified as follows:	
$\quad$ *-ide* becomes -o	Cl^- is chloro.
$\quad$ *-ate* becomes -ato	SO_4^{2-} is sulfato.
$\quad$ *-ite* becomes -ito	SO_3^{2-} is sulfito.
Table 24.4 lists the names of some common ligands.	
2. List the names of the ligands in alphabetical order before the name of the metal cation.	Ammine (NH_3) is listed before chloro (Cl^-), which is listed before nitrito (NO_2^-).
3. Use a prefix to indicate the number of ligands (when there is more than one of a particular type): *di-* (2), *tri-* (3), *tetra-* (4), *penta-* (5), or *hexa-* (6).	Trichloro indicates three Cl^- ligands. Tetraammine indicates four NH_3 ligands.
$\quad$ If the name of the ligand already contains a prefix, such as ethylenediamine, place parentheses around the ligand name and use *bis-* (2), *tris-* (3), or *tetrakis-* (4) to indicate the number.	Tris(ethylenediamine) indicates three ethylenediamine ligands.
$\quad$ Prefixes do not affect the order in which you list the ligands.	
4. Name the metal.	In cations:
$\quad$ **a.** When the complex ion is a cation, use the name of the metal followed by the oxidation state written with a roman numeral.	Co^{3+} is cobalt(III). Pt^{2+} is platinum(II). Cu^+ is copper(I).
	In anions:
$\quad$ **b.** If the complex ion is an anion, drop the ending of the metal and add *–ate* followed by the oxidation state written with a Roman numeral. Some metals use the Latin root with the *-ate* ending. Table 24.5 lists the names for some common metals in anionic complexes.	Co^{3+} is cobaltate(III). Pt^{2+} is platinate(II). Cu^+ is cuprate(I).
5. Write the entire name of the complex ion by listing the ligands first followed by the metal.	$[Pt(NH_3)_2Cl_4]^{2-}$ is diamminetetrachloroplatinate(II). $[Co(NH_3)_6]^{3+}$ is hexaamminecobalt(III).

TABLE 24.4 Names and Formulas of Common Ligands

Ligand	Name in Complex Ion
Anions	
Bromide, Br^-	Bromo
Chloride, Cl^-	Chloro
Hydroxide, OH^-	Hydroxo
Cyanide, CN^-	Cyano
Nitrite, NO_2^-	Nitro
Oxalate, $C_2O_4^{2-}$ (ox)	Oxalato
Ethylenediaminetetraacetate ($EDTA^{4-}$)	Ethylenediaminetetraacetato
Neutral molecules	
Water, H_2O	Aqua
Ammonia, NH_3	Ammine
Carbon monoxide, CO	Carbonyl
Ethylenediamine (en)	Ethylenediamine

TABLE 24.5 Names of Common Metals when Found in Anionic Complex Ions

Metal	Name in Anionic Complex
Chromium	Chromate
Cobalt	Cobaltate
Copper	Cuprate
Gold	Aurate
Iron	Ferrate
Lead	Plumbate
Manganese	Manganate
Molybdenum	Molybdate
Nickel	Nickelate
Platinum	Platinate
Silver	Argentate
Tin	Stannate
Zinc	Zincate

When you write the *formula* of a complex ion, write the symbol for the metal first, followed by neutral molecules and then anions. If there is more than one anion or neutral molecule acting as a ligand, list them in alphabetical order based on the chemical symbol.

PROCEDURE FOR... **Naming Coordination Compounds**	**EXAMPLE 24.3** **Naming Coordination Compounds** Name the following compound: $[Cr(H_2O)_5Cl]Cl_2$.	**EXAMPLE 24.4** **Naming Coordination Compounds** Name the following compound: $K_3[Fe(CN)_6]$.
Identify the cation and anion and first name the simple ion (i.e., not the complex one).	**SOLUTION** $[Cr(H_2O)_5Cl]^{2+}$ is a complex cation. Cl^- is chloride.	**SOLUTION** K^+ is potassium. $[Fe(CN)_6]^{3-}$ is a complex anion.
Give each ligand a name and list them in alphabetical order.	H_2O is aqua. Cl^- is chloro.	CN^- is cyano.
Name the metal ion.	Cr^{3+} is chromium(III).	Fe^{3+} is ferrate(III) because the complex is anionic.
Name the complex ion by adding prefixes to indicate the number of each ligand followed by the name of each ligand followed by the name of the metal ion.	$[Cr(H_2O)_5Cl]^{2+}$ is pentaaquachlorochromium(III).	$[Fe(CN)_6]^{3-}$ is hexacyanoferrate(III).
Name the compound by writing the name of the cation before the anion. The only space is between ion names.	$[Cr(H_2O)_5Cl]Cl_2$ is pentaaquachloro-chromium(III) chloride.	$K_3[Fe(CN)_6]$ is potassium hexacyanoferrate(III).
	FOR PRACTICE 24.3 Name the following compound: $[Mn(CO)(NH_3)_5]SO_4$.	**FOR PRACTICE 24.4** Name the following compound: $Na_2[PtCl_4]$.

24.4 Structure and Isomerization

Isomerism is common in coordination compounds. We broadly divide the isomerism observed in coordination compounds into two categories, each with subcategories, as shown in Figure 24.6 ▾. In **structural isomers**, atoms are connected to one another in different ways, whereas in **stereoisomers**, atoms are connected in the same way but the ligands have a different spatial arrangement about the metal atom.

▲ FIGURE 24.6 Types of Isomers

Structural Isomerism

We can subdivide the broad category of structural isomers into two types: coordination isomers and linkage isomers. **Coordination isomers** occur when a coordinated ligand exchanges places with the uncoordinated counterion. For example, two different compounds have the general formula $Co(NH_3)_5 BrCl$. In one of them, the bromine coordinates to the metal and chloride is a counterion, pentaamminebromocobalt(II) chloride, $[Co(NH_3)_5Br]Cl$; in the other one, the chlorine coordinates to the metal and bromide is the counterion, pentaamminechlorocobalt(II) bromide, $[Co(NH_3)_5Cl]Br$.

Linkage isomers have ligands that can coordinate to the metal in different orientations. For example, the nitrite ion (NO_2^-) has a lone pair on the N atom as well as lone pairs on the O atoms—either of the two atoms can form coordinate covalent bonds with the metal. When the nitrite ion coordinates through the N atom it is a *nitro* ligand and is represented as NO_2^-, but when it coordinates through the O atom, it is a *nitrito* ligand and is usually represented as ONO^-. An example of linkage isomerization can be seen in the yellow-orange complex ion pentaamminenitrocobalt(III), $[Co(NH_3)_5NO_2]^{2+}$, which contrasts with the red-orange complex ion pentaamminenitritocobalt(III), $[Co(NH_3)_5ONO]^{2+}$, as shown in Figure 24.7 ▸. Other ligands capable of linkage isomerization are listed in Table 24.6.

▶ FIGURE 24.7 **Linkage Isomers**
In $[Co(NH_3)_5NO_2]^{2+}$, the NO_2 ligand
bonds to the central metal atom
through the nitrogen atom. In
$[Co(NH_3)_5ONO]^{2+}$, the NO_2 ligand
bonds through the oxygen atoms. The
different isomers have different colors.

N-bond and O-bond NO_2^- ligand

Nitro isomer   Nitrito isomer

Stereoisomerism

We can also subdivide the broad category of stereoisomers into two types: geometric
isomers and optical isomers. **Geometric isomers** result when the ligands bonding to
the metal have a different spatial arrangement. One type of geometric isomerism, as we
saw in Section 20.5, is cis–trans isomerism, which in complex ions occurs in square
planar complexes of the general formula MA_2B_2 or octahedral complexes of the general
formula MA_4B_2. For example, cis–trans isomerism occurs in the square planar complex
$Pt(NH_3)_2Cl_2$. Figure 24.8(a) ▶ shows the two distinct ways in which the ligands can be
oriented around the metal. In one complex, the Cl^- ligands are next to each other on one
side of the molecule—this is the cis isomer. In the other complex, the Cl^- ligands are on
opposite sides of the molecule—this is the trans isomer. Geometric isomerism also exists
in the octahedral complex ion $[Co(NH_3)_4Cl_2]^+$. As shown in Figure 24.8(b) ▶, the ligands
arrange themselves around the metal in two ways, one with the Cl^- ligands on the same

---

TABLE 24.6   Ligands Capable of Linkage Isomerization

nitro
$$\left[\ddot{\text{O}} - \dot{\text{N}} = \ddot{\text{O}} \right]^-$$
nitrito

cyano
$$\left[\ddot{\text{C}} \equiv \text{N} \ddot{} \right]^-$$
isocyano

isocyanato
$$\left[\ddot{\text{O}} = \text{C} = \dot{\text{N}} \ddot{} \right]^-$$
cyanato

isothiocyanato
$$\left[\ddot{\text{S}} = \text{C} = \dot{\text{N}} \ddot{} \right]^-$$
thiocyanato

Cis   Trans

$Pt(NH_3)_2Cl_2$
(a)

Cis   Trans

$\left[Co(NH_3)_4Cl_2\right]^+$
(b)

▲ **FIGURE 24.8 Cis-trans Isomerism** (a) Cis–trans isomerism in square planar $Pt(NH_3)_2Cl_2$. In the cis isomer, the Cl^- ligands are next to each other on one side of the molecule. In the trans isomer, the Cl^- ligands are on opposite sides of the molecule. (b) Cis–trans isomerism in octahedral $[Co(NH_3)_4Cl_2]^+$. In the cis isomer, the Cl^- ligands are on the same side. In the trans isomer, the Cl^- ligands are on opposite sides.

side (the cis isomer) and another with the Cl^- ligands on opposite sides of the metal (the trans isomer). Note that cis–trans isomerism does not occur in tetrahedral complexes because all bond angles around the metal are 109.5°, and each corner of a tetrahedron is considered to be adjacent to all three other corners.

Another type of geometric isomerism is fac–mer isomerism, which occurs in octahedral complexes of the general formula MA_3B_3. For example, in $Co(NH_3)_3Cl_3$, the ligands arrange themselves around the metal in two ways (Figure 24.9 ▼). In the fac isomer the three Cl^- ligands are all on one side of the molecule and make up one face of the octahedron (fac is short for facial). In the mer isomer the three ligands form an arc around the middle of the octahedron (mer is short for meridian).

Fac   Mer

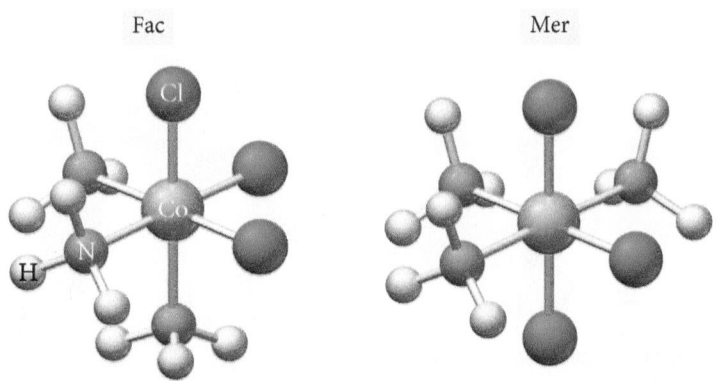

◄ **FIGURE 24.9 Fac-Mer Isomerism in** $CO(NH_3)_3Cl_3$ In the fac isomer, the three Cl^- ligands are all on one side of the molecule and make up one face of the octahedron. In the mer isomer, the three ligands inscribe an arc around the middle (or meridian) of the octahedron.

PROCEDURE FOR...	EXAMPLE 24.5	EXAMPLE 24.6
Identifying and Drawing Geometric Isomers	**Identifying and Drawing Geometric Isomers**	**Identifying and Drawing Geometric Isomers**
	Draw the structures and label the type of all the isomers of $[Co(en)_2Cl_2]^+$.	Draw the structures and label the type for of the isomers of $[Ni(CN)_2Cl_2]^{2-}$.
	SOLUTION	**SOLUTION**
Identify the coordination number and the geometry around the metal.	The ethylenediamine (en) ligand is bidentate so each occupies two coordination sites. Each Cl^- is monodentate, occupying one site. The total coordination number is 6, so this must be an octahedral complex.	All the ligands are monodentate, so the total coordination number is 4. Ni^{2+} is a d^8 electronic configuration, so we expect a square planar complex.
Identify if this is cis–trans or fac–mer isomerism.	With ethylenediamine occupying four sites and Cl^- occupying two sites, it fits the general formula MA_4B_2, leading to cis–trans isomers.	Square planar complexes can only have cis–trans isomers.
Draw and label the two isomers.	*Cis* *Trans*	*Cis* *Trans*
	FOR PRACTICE 24.5	**FOR PRACTICE 24.6**
	Draw the structures and label the type of all the isomers of $[Cr(H_2O)_3Cl_3]^+$.	Draw the structures and label the type of all the isomers of $[Co(NH_3)_2Cl_2(ox)]^-$.

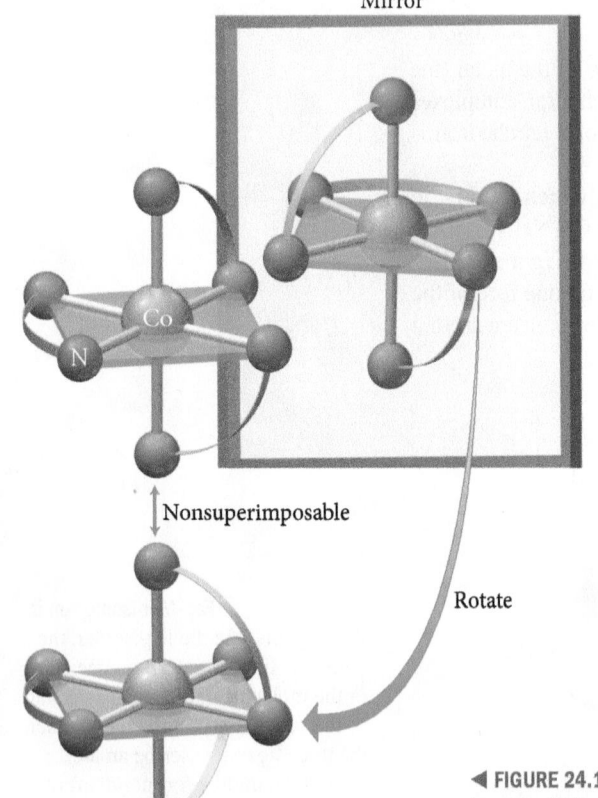

Mirror

Nonsuperimposable

Rotate

◀ **FIGURE 24.10 Optical Isomerism in $[Co(en)_3]^{3+}$** The mirror images of $[Co(en)_3]^{3+}$ are not superimposable. (The connected nitrogen atoms represent the ethylenediamine ligand.)

The second category of stereoisomerism is optical isomerism. Recall from Section 20.3 that **optical isomers** are nonsuperimposable mirror images of one another. If you hold your right hand up to a mirror, the image in the mirror looks like your left hand. No matter how you rotate or flip your left hand, you cannot superimpose it on your right hand. Molecules or ions that exhibit this quality are *chiral*. The isomers are *enantiomers*, and they exhibit the property of optical activity (the rotation of polarized light). The complex ion $[Co(en)_3]^{3+}$ is nonsuperimposable on its mirror image, so it is a chiral complex (Figure 24.10 ◀).

EXAMPLE 24.7 Recognizing and Drawing Optical Isomers

Determine whether the cis or trans isomers in Example 24.5 are optically active (demonstrate optical isomerism).

SOLUTION

Draw the trans isomer of $[Co(en)_2Cl_2]^+$ and its mirror image. Check to see if they are superimposable by rotating one isomer 180°.

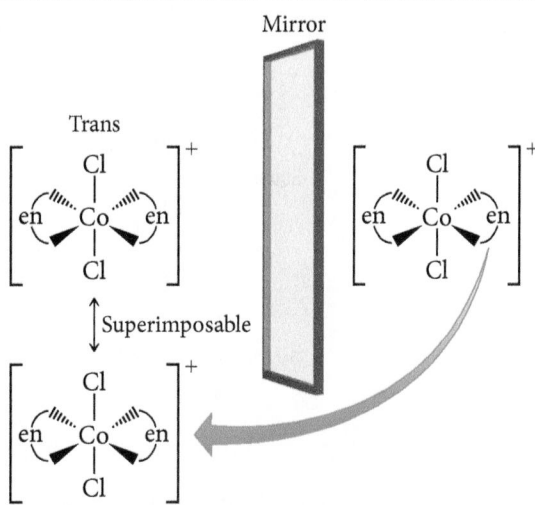

In this case the two are identical, so there is no optical activity.

Draw the cis isomer and its mirror image. Check to see if they are superimposable by rotating one isomer 180°.

In this case the two structures are not superimposable, so the cis isomer does exhibit optical activity.

FOR PRACTICE 24.7

Determine whether the fac or mer isomers of $[Cr(H_2O)_3Cl_3]^+$ are optically active.

The previous examples demonstrate optical isomerism in octahedral complexes. Tetrahedral complexes can also exhibit optical isomerism, but only if all four coordination sites are occupied by different ligands. Square planar complexes do not normally exhibit optical isomerism as they are superimposable on their mirror images.

24.5 Bonding in Coordination Compounds

Valence Bond Theory

The bonding in complex ions, particularly the geometries of the ions, can be described by one of our previous bonding models, valence bond theory. Recall from Section 10.6 that in valence bond theory, a coordinate covalent bond is the overlap between a completely

Geometry	Hybridization	Orbitals
Linear	sp	
Tetrahedral	sp^3	
Square planar	dsp^2	
Octahedral	d^2sp^3	

filled atomic orbital and an empty atomic orbital. In complex ions, the filled orbital is on the ligand, and the empty orbital is on the metal ion. The metal ion orbitals are hybridized according to the geometry of the complex ion. The common hybridization schemes are shown in Figure 24.11 ▲. An octahedral complex ion requires six empty orbitals in an octahedral arrangement on the metal ion. A full set of d^2sp^3 hybrid orbitals results in the exact orbitals needed for this geometry. A set of sp^3 hybrid orbitals results in a tetrahedral arrangement of orbitals, a set of dsp^2 hybrid orbitals results in a square planar arrangement, and a set of sp hybrid orbitals results in a linear arrangement of orbitals. In each case, the coordinate covalent bond is formed by the overlap between the orbitals on the ligands and the hybridized orbitals on the metal ion.

Crystal Field Theory

Valence bond theory, while useful for describing the geometries of the complex ions, cannot explain other properties such as color and magnetism. Crystal field theory (CFT), a bonding model for transition metal complexes, accounts for these properties. To illustrate the basic principles of CFT, we examine the central metal atom's d orbitals in an octahedral complex.

Octahedral Complexes

The basic premise of CFT is that complex ions form because of attractions between the electrons on the ligands and the positive charge on the metal ion. However, the electrons on the ligands also repel the electrons in the *unhybridized* metal d orbitals. CFT focuses on these repulsions. Figure 24.12 ► shows how the ligand positions superimpose on the d orbitals in an octahedral complex. Notice that the ligands in an octahedral complex are located in the same space as the lobes of the $d_{x^2-y^2}$ and d_{z^2} orbitals. The repulsions *between* electron pairs in the ligands and any potential electrons in the d orbitals result in an increase in the energies of these orbitals. In contrast, the d_{xy}, d_{xz}, and d_{yz} orbitals lie *between* the axes and have nodes directly on the axes, which results in less repulsion and lower energies for these three orbitals. In other words, the d orbitals—which are degenerate in the bare metal ion—are split into higher and lower energy levels because of the spatial arrangement of the ligands (Figure 24.13 ►). The difference in energy between these split d orbitals is known as the crystal field splitting energy (Δ). The magnitude of the splitting depends on the particular complex. In **strong-field complexes**, the splitting is large; and in **weak-field complexes**, the splitting is small.

Ligands overlap with orbital lobes, resulting in strong repulsions.

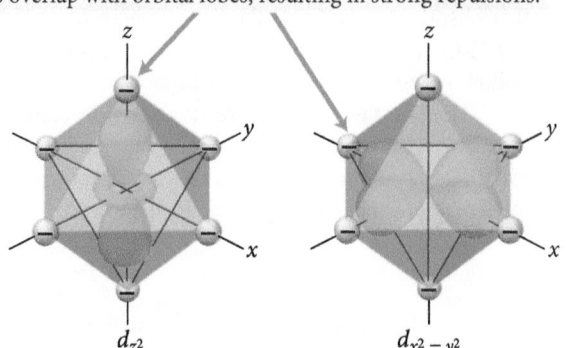

d_{z^2}

$d_{x^2-y^2}$

Ligands come in between orbital lobes, resulting in weak repulsions.

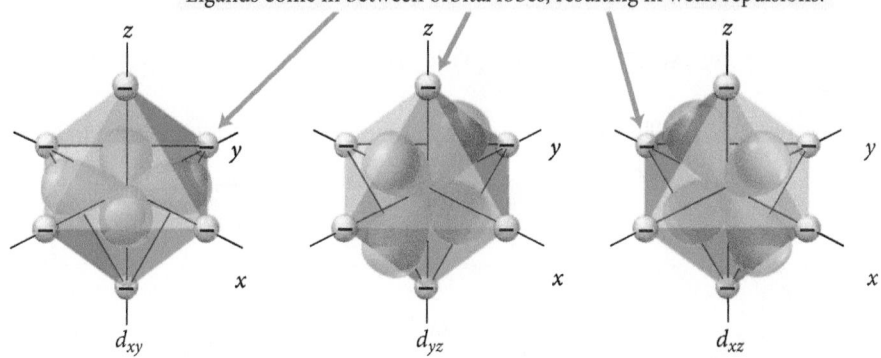

d_{xy} d_{yz} d_{xz}

▼ FIGURE 24.13 *d* Orbital Splitting in an Octahedral Field The otherwise degenerate *d* orbitals are split into two energy levels by the ligands in an octahedral complex ion.

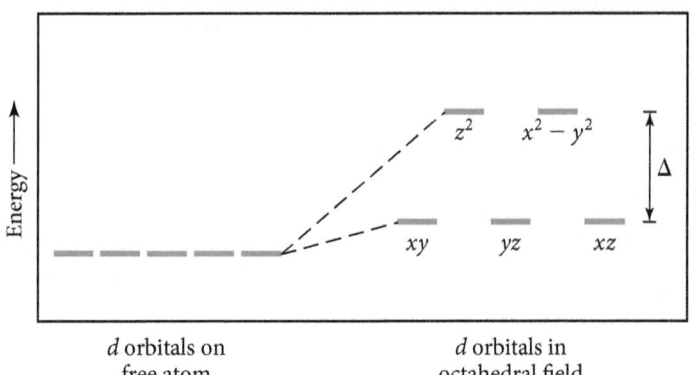

d orbitals on free atom

d orbitals in octahedral field

The Color of Complex Ions and Crystal Field Strength

We discussed in the opening section of this chapter that transition metals in host crystals often show brilliant colors because of the crystal field splitting of their *d* orbitals. Solutions of complex ions display brilliant colors because of similar splittings. For example, an $[Fe(CN)_6]^{3-}$ solution is deep red, and an $[Ni(NH_3)_6]^{2+}$ solution is blue (Figure 24.14 ▶). Recall from Chapter 7 that the color of an object is related to the absorption of light energy by its electrons. If a substance absorbs all of the visible wavelengths, it appears black. If it transmits (or reflects) all the wavelengths (absorbs no light), it appears colorless. A substance appears to be a particular color if it absorbs some visible light but also transmits (or reflects) the wavelengths associated with that color. A substance also appears to be a given color if it transmits (or reflects) most wavelengths but absorbs the

(a)   (b)

▲ FIGURE 24.14 Colors of Complex Ions (a) The complex ion $[Fe(CN)_6]^{3-}$ forms a deep red solution, and (b) $[Ni(NH_3)_6]^{2+}$ is blue.

▲ **FIGURE 24.15 The Color Wheel** Colors across from one another on the color wheel are said to be complementary. A substance that absorbs a color on the wheel will appear to be its complementary color.

complementary color on a color wheel (Figure 24.15 ◄). For example, a substance that absorbs green light (the complement of red) will appear red. A solution of $[Ti(H_2O)_6]^{3+}$ is purple because it absorbs strongly between 490 and 580 nm, the yellow-green region of the visible spectrum (Figure 24.16a ▼).

The easiest way to measure the energy difference between the *d* orbitals in a complex ion is to use spectroscopy to determine the wavelength of light absorbed when an electron makes a transition from the lower energy *d* orbitals to the higher energy ones. With that information we can calculate the crystal field splitting energy, Δ:

$$E_{\text{photon}} = h\nu = \frac{hc}{\lambda} = \Delta$$

Consider the $[Ti(H_2O)_6]^{3+}$ absorption spectrum shown in Figure 24.16b. The maximum absorbance is at 498 nm. Using this wavelength, we calculate Δ:

$$\Delta = hc/\lambda = (6.626 \times 10^{-34}\ \text{J} \cdot \text{s})(3.00 \times 10^{8}\ \text{m/s})/(498\ \text{nm} \times 1 \times 10^{-9}\ \text{m/nm})$$

$$\Delta = 3.99 \times 10^{-19}\ \text{J}$$

This energy corresponds to a single $[Ti(H_2O)_6]^{3+}$ ion. We can convert to kilojoules per mole:

$$\Delta = (3.99 \times 10^{-19}\ \text{J/ion})(6.02 \times 10^{23}\ \text{ion/mol})(1\ \text{kJ/1000 J}) = 240\ \text{kJ/mol}$$

► **FIGURE 24.16 The Color and Absorption Spectrum of $[Ti(H_2O)_6]^{3+}$** (**a**) A solution containing $[Ti(H_2O)_6]^{3+}$ is purple. (**b**) The absorption spectrum of $[Ti(H_2O)_6]^{3+}$ extends across the green-yellow region of the spectrum.

EXAMPLE 24.8 Crystal Field Splitting Energy

The complex ion $[Cu(NH_3)_6]^{2+}$ is blue in aqueous solution. Estimate the crystal field splitting energy (in kJ/mol) for this ion.

SOLUTION

Begin by consulting the color wheel to determine approximately what wavelength is being absorbed.	Since the solution is blue, you can deduce that orange light is absorbed since orange is the complementary color to blue.
Estimate the absorbed wavelength.	The color orange ranges from 580 to 650 nm, so you can estimate the average wavelength as 615 nm.
Calculate the energy corresponding to this wavelength, using $E = hc/\lambda$. This energy corresponds to Δ.	$E = \dfrac{(6.626 \times 10^{-34}\ \text{J} \cdot \text{s})(3.00 \times 10^{8}\ \text{m/s})}{(615\ \text{nm})(1 \times 10^{-9}\ \text{m/nm})}$ $E = 3.23 \times 10^{-19}\ \text{J} = \Delta$
Convert J/ion into kJ/mol.	$\Delta = \dfrac{(3.23 \times 10^{-19}\ \text{J/ion})(6.02 \times 10^{23}\ \text{ion/mol})}{(1000\ \text{J/kJ})}$ $\Delta = 195\ \text{kJ/mol}$

FOR PRACTICE 24.8

The complex ion $[Co(NH_3)_5NO_2]^{2+}$ is yellow. Estimate the crystal field splitting energy (in kJ/mol) for this ion.

The magnitude of the crystal field splitting in a complex ion—and, therefore whether it is a strong-field or a weak-field complex—depends in large part on the ligands attached to the central metal ion. Spectroscopic studies of various ligands attached to the same metal allow us to arrange different ligands in order of their ability to split the *d* orbitals. This list is known as the *spectrochemical series* and is arranged from ligands that result in the largest Δ to those that result in the smallest:

$$CN^- > NO_2^- > en > NH_3 > H_2O > OH^- > F^- > Cl^- > Br^- > I^-$$

large Δ small Δ

typically strong-field ligands   typically weak-field ligands

Ligands that produce large values of Δ are *strong-field ligands* and those that give small values of Δ are *weak-field ligands*.

The metal ion also has an effect on the magnitude of Δ. If we examine different metal ions with the same ligand, we find that Δ increases as the charge on the metal ion increases. The greater charge on the metal draws the ligands closer, causing greater repulsion with the *d* orbitals and therefore a larger Δ. An example of this behavior occurs in the complex ions between NH_3 (a ligand in the middle of the spectrochemical series) and the +2 or +3 oxidation states of cobalt. Hexaamminecobalt(II) ion, $[Co(NH_3)_6]^{2+}$, has a weak crystal field (small Δ) and hexaamminecobalt(III) ion, $[Co(NH_3)_6]^{3+}$, has a strong field (large Δ).

Conceptual Connection 24.2   Weak- and Strong-Field Ligands

Two ligands, A and B, both form complexes with a particular metal ion. When the metal ion complexes with ligand A, the resulting solution is red. When the metal ion complexes with ligand B, the resulting solution is yellow. Which of the two ligands produces the larger Δ?

Magnetic Properties

The strength of the crystal field can affect the magnetic properties of a transition metal complex. Recall that, according to Hund's rule, electrons occupy degenerate orbitals singly as long as an empty orbital is available. When the energies of the *d* orbitals are split by ligands, the lower energy orbitals fill first. Once they are half-filled, the next electron can either (1) pair with an electron in one of the lower energy half-filled orbitals by overcoming the electron–electron repulsion associated with having two electrons in the same orbital or (2) go into an empty orbital of higher energy by overcoming the energy difference between the orbitals—in this case, the crystal field splitting energy, Δ. The magnitude of Δ compared to the electron–electron repulsions determines which of these two actually occurs.

We can compare two iron(II) complexes to see the difference in behavior under strong- and weak-field conditions. $[Fe(CN)_6]^{4-}$ is known to be diamagnetic and $[Fe(H_2O)_6]^{2+}$ is known to be paramagnetic. Both of these complexes contain Fe^{2+}, which has an electron configuration of [Ar] $3d^6$. In the case of $[Fe(CN)_6]^{4-}$, CN^- is a strong-field ligand that generates a large Δ, so it takes more energy to occupy the higher energy level than it does to pair the electrons in the lower energy level. The result is that all six electrons are paired and the compound is diamagnetic, as shown in the accompanying figure.

In $[Fe(H_2O)_6]^{2+}$, H_2O is a weak-field ligand that generates a small Δ, so the electron pairing energy is greater than Δ. Consequently, the first five electrons occupy the five *d* orbitals singly and only the sixth pairs up, resulting in a paramagnetic compound with four unpaired electrons, as shown in the accompanying figure.

In general, complexes with strong-field ligands have fewer unpaired electrons relative to the free metal ion and are therefore called **low-spin complexes**. Complexes with weak-field ligands, by contrast, have the same number of unpaired electrons as the free metal ion and are called **high-spin complexes**.

Recall from Section 8.7 that a paramagnetic species contains unpaired electrons and a diamagnetic one does not.

$[Fe(CN_6)]^{4-}$

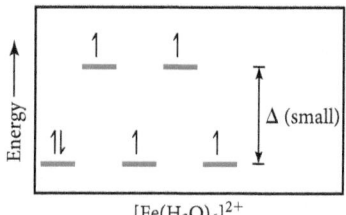

$[Fe(H_2O)_6]^{2+}$

When we examine the orbital diagrams of the d^1 through d^{10} metal ions in octahedral complexes, we find that only d^4, d^5, d^6, and d^7 metal ions have low- and high-spin possibilities. Since there are three lower energy d orbitals, the d^1, d^2, and d^3 metal ions always have unpaired electrons, independent of Δ. In the d^8, d^9, and d^{10} metal ions, the three lower energy orbitals are completely filled, so the remaining electrons fill the two higher orbitals (as expected according to Hund's rule), also independent of Δ.

PROCEDURE FOR... Determining the Number of Unpaired Electrons in Octahedral Complexes	EXAMPLE 24.9 High- and Low-Spin Octahedral Complexes How many unpaired electrons are there in the complex ion $[CoF_6]^{3-}$?	EXAMPLE 24.10 High- and Low-Spin Octahedral Complexes How many unpaired electrons are there in the complex ion $[Co(NH_3)_5NO_2]^{2+}$?
Begin by determining the charge and number of d electrons on the metal.	**SOLUTION** The metal is Co^{3+} and has a d^6 electronic configuration.	**SOLUTION** The metal is Co^{3+} and has a d^6 electronic configuration.
Look at the spectrochemical series to determine whether the ligand is a strong-field or a weak-field ligand.	F^- is a weak-field ligand, so Δ is relatively small.	NH_3 and NO_2^- are both strong-field ligands, so Δ is relatively large.
Decide if the complex is high- or low-spin and draw the electron configuration.	Weak-field ligands yield high-spin configurations.	Strong-field ligands yield low-spin configurations.
Count the unpaired electrons.	This configuration has four unpaired electrons.	This configuration has no unpaired electrons.
	FOR PRACTICE 24.9 How many unpaired electrons are there in the complex ion $[FeCl_6]^{3-}$?	**FOR PRACTICE 24.10** How many unpaired electrons are there in the complex ion $[Co(CN)_6]^{4-}$?

Tetrahedral and Square Planar Complexes

So far, we have examined the d orbital energy changes only for octahedral complexes, but transition metal complexes can have other geometries, such as tetrahedral and square planar. We use crystal field theory to determine the d orbital splitting pattern for these geometries as well. For a tetrahedral complex, the d orbital splitting pattern is the opposite of the octahedral splitting pattern: three d orbitals (d_{xy}, d_{xz}, and d_{yz}) are higher in energy, and two d orbitals ($d_{x^2-y^2}$ and d_{z^2}) are lower in energy (Figure 24.17 ▶). Almost all tetrahedral complexes are high-spin because of reduced ligand–metal interactions. The d orbitals in a tetrahedral complex interact with only four ligands, as opposed to six in the octahedral complex, so the value of Δ is generally smaller.

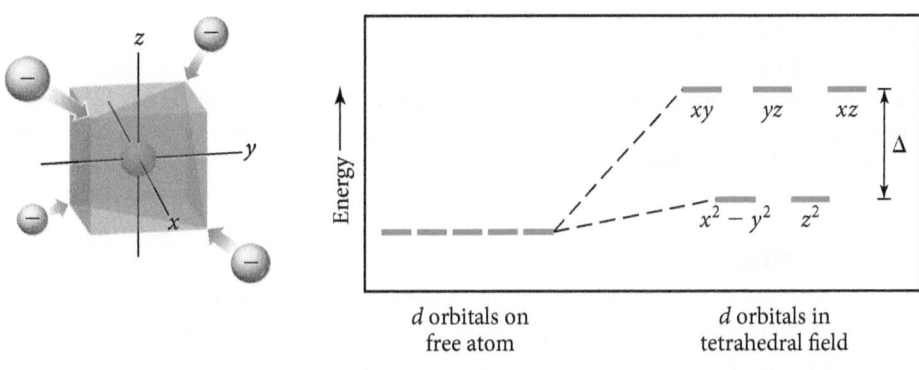

◀ **FIGURE 24.17 Splitting of d Orbitals by a Tetrahedral Ligand Geometry** In tetrahedral complexes, the splitting of the d orbitals has a pattern that is the opposite of the octahedral splitting pattern. The d_{xy}, d_{yz}, and d_{xz} orbitals are higher in energy than the d_{z^2} and $d_{x^2-y^2}$ orbitals.

A square planar complex gives us the most complex splitting pattern of the three geometries (Figure 24.18 ▼). As we discussed previously, square planar complexes occur in d^8 metal ions, such as Pt^{2+}, Pd^{2+}, Ir^+, or Au^{3+}, and in nearly all cases they are low-spin.

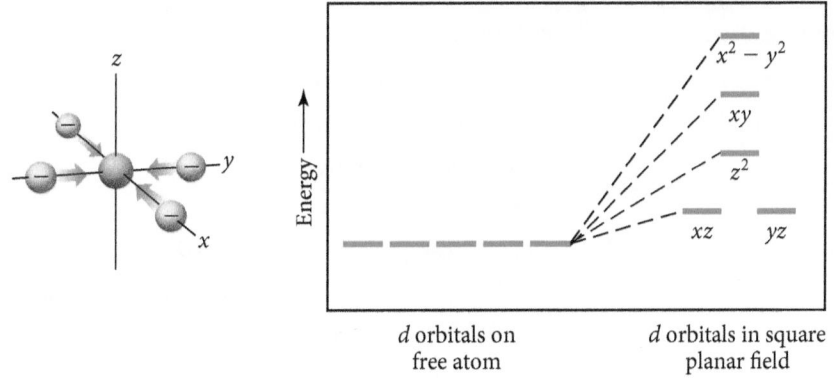

◀ **FIGURE 24.18 Splitting of d Orbitals by a Square Planar Ligand Geometry** Square planar complexes produce the d orbital energy pattern shown here.

24.6 Applications of Coordination Compounds

Coordination compounds are found in living systems, in industry, and even in household products. Recall from Chapter 23 how both silver and gold metals are extracted from their respective ores using cyanide complexes and how nickel metal is extracted by forming the gaseous carbonyl complex, $Ni(CO)_4$. In this section we describe a few additional applications of coordination compounds.

Chelating Agents

In Section 24.3, we introduced the chelating agent ethylenediaminetetraacetate ion ($EDTA^{4-}$). This ligand has lone pairs on six different donor atoms that can interact with a metal ion to form very stable metal complexes. EDTA is used to treat the victims of heavy metal poisoning such as lead poisoning. The patient is given $[Ca(EDTA)]^{2-}$ and since the lead complex ($K_f = 2 \times 10^{18}$) is more stable than the calcium complex ($K_f = 4 \times 10^{10}$), the lead displaces the calcium. The body excretes the lead complex and leaves behind the calcium, which is nontoxic (and is in fact a nutrient).

Chemical Analysis

Some ligands are selective in their binding, preferring specific metal ions; these ligands can be used in chemical analysis. For example, dimethylglyoxime (dmg) is used to chemically analyze a sample for Ni^{2+} or Pd^{2+}. In the presence of Ni^{2+}, an insoluble red precipitate forms, and in the presence of Pd^{2+}, an insoluble yellow precipitate forms. Similarly, the SCN^- ligand is used to test for Co^{2+} or Fe^{3+}. In the presence of Co^{2+} a blue solution forms, and in the presence of Fe^{3+} a deep red solution forms (Figure 24.19 ▶).

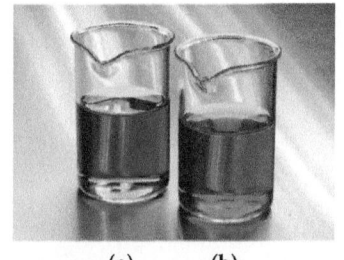

(a)   (b)

▲ **FIGURE 24.19 Chemical Analysis with SCN⁻** (a) Blue indicates Co^{2+}. (b) Red indicates Fe^{3+}.

Coloring Agents

Because of the wide variety of colors found in coordination complexes, they are often used as coloring agents. For example, a commercially available agent, iron blue, is a mixture of the hexacyano complexes of iron(II) and iron(III). Iron blue is used in ink, paint, cosmetics (eye shadow), and blueprints.

Biomolecules

Living systems contain many molecules based on metal complexes. Hemoglobin (involved in oxygen transport), cytochrome c (involved in electron transport), carbonic anhydrase (involved in respiration), and chlorophyll (involved in photosynthesis) all have coordinated metal ions that are critical to their structure and function. Table 24.7 summarizes the biological significance of many of the other first-row transition metals.

TABLE 24.7 Transition Metals and Some of Their Functions in the Human Body

Transition Metal	Biological Function
Chromium	Works with insulin to control utilization of glucose
Manganese	Fat and carbohydrate synthesis
Molybdenum	Involved in hemoglobin synthesis
Iron	Oxygen transport
Copper	Involved in hemoglobin synthesis
Zinc	Involved in cell reproduction and tissue growth; part of more than 70 enzymes; assists in the utilization of carbohydrate, protein, and fat

Hemoglobin and Cytochrome C In hemoglobin and in cytochrome c, an iron complex called a heme is connected to a protein, as shown in the figure below. A heme is an iron ion coordinated to a flat, polydentate ligand called a porphyrin (Figure 24.20 ▶). The porphyrin ligand has a planar ring structure with four nitrogen atoms that can coordinate to the metal ion. Different porphyrins have different substituent groups connected around the outside of the ring.

Cytochrome c   Heme (H atoms omitted for clarity)

Hemoglobin is discussed in Sections 1.1 and 14.1.

In hemoglobin, the iron complex is octahedral, with the four nitrogen atoms of the porphyrin in a square planar arrangement around the metal. A nitrogen atom from a nearby amino acid of the protein occupies the fifth coordination site, and either O_2 or H_2O occupies the last coordination site (Figure 24.21 ▶). In the lungs, where the oxygen content is high, the hemoglobin coordinates to an O_2 molecule. The oxygen-rich

◀ FIGURE 24.20 **Porphyrin** A porphyrin has four nitrogen atoms that can coordinate to a central metal atom.

◀ FIGURE 24.21 **Hemoglobin** In hemoglobin, the iron complex is octahedral, with the four nitrogen atoms of the porphyrin in a square planar arrangement around the metal. A nitrogen atom from a nearby amino acid of the protein occupies the fifth coordination site, and either O_2 or H_2O occupies the last coordination site.

Hemoglobin

Heme structure

hemoglobin is carried by the bloodstream to areas throughout the body that are depleted in oxygen, where oxygen is released and replaced by a water molecule. The hemoglobin then travels back to the lungs to repeat the cycle.

Chlorophyll Chlorophyll, shown in Figure 24.22 ▶, is another porphyrin-based biomolecule, but in chlorophyll the porphyrin is not surrounded by a protein, and the coordinated metal is magnesium (which is not a transition metal). Chlorophyll is essential for photosynthesis process performed by plants, in which light energy from the sun is converted to chemical energy to fuel the plant's growth.

Carbonic Anhydrase In carbonic anhydrase, the zinc ion is bound in a tetrahedral complex, with three of the coordination sites occupied by nitrogen atoms from surrounding amino acids and the fourth site available to bind a water molecule (Figure 24.23 ▶). Carbonic anhydrase catalyzes the reaction between water and CO_2 in respiration.

$$H_2O(l) + CO_2(g) \rightleftharpoons H^+(aq) + HCO_3^-(aq)$$

A water molecule alone is not acidic enough to react with a CO_2 molecule at a sufficient rate. When the water molecule is bound to the zinc ion in carbonic anhydrase, the positive charge on the metal draws electron density from the O—H bond and the H_2O becomes more acidic—sufficiently so to readily lose a proton. The resulting bound OH^- easily reacts with a CO_2 molecule, and the reaction is much faster than the uncatalyzed version.

▲ FIGURE 24.22 **Chlorophyll** Chlorophyll, involved in photosynthesis in plants, contains magnesium coordinated to a porphyrin.

▶ FIGURE 24.23 **Carbonic Anhydrase** Carbonic anhydrase contains a zinc ion that is bound in a tetrahedral complex, with three of the coordination sites occupied by nitrogen atoms from surrounding amino acids. The fourth site is available to bind a water molecule.

▲ FIGURE 24.24 **Cisplatin** Cisplatin is an effective anticancer agent.

Drugs and Therapeutic Agents In the mid-1960s researchers found that the platinum(II) complex *cis*-[Pt(NH$_3$)$_2$Cl$_2$], known as cisplatin, is an effective anticancer agent (Figure 24.24 ◀). Interestingly, the closely related geometric isomer *trans*-[Pt(NH$_3$)$_2$Cl$_2$] has little or no effect on cancer tumors. Cisplatin is believed to function by attaching itself to the cancer cell's DNA and replacing the Cl$^-$ ligands with donor atoms from the DNA strands. The cis arrangement of the Cl$^-$ ligands corresponds to the geometry required to bind to the DNA strands. The trans isomer, although closely related, cannot bind properly due to the arrangement of the Cl$^-$ ligands and is therefore not an effective agent. Cisplatin and other closely related platinum(II) complexes are still used today in chemotherapy for certain types of cancer and are among the most effective anticancer agents available for these cases.

CHAPTER IN REVIEW

Self Assessment Quiz

Q1. What is the electron configuration of the Cu$^+$ ion?
a) [Ar]$4s^2 3d^9$
b) [Ar]$4s^2 3d^8$
c) [Ar]$4s^1 3d^9$
d) [Ar]$4s^0 3d^{10}$

Q2. Which metal has the highest first ionization energy?
a) Ti
b) Mn
c) Ru
d) Au

Q3. What is the name of the compound [CoCl(NH$_3$)$_5$]Cl$_2$?
a) pentaaminetrichlorocobalt(III) chloride
b) pentaaminechlorocobalt(III) chloride
c) pentaaminechlorocobalt(II) chloride
d) pentaaminetrichlorocobalt(II) chloride

Q4. What is the formula of hexaaquamanganese(II) sulfate?
a) [Mn(OH)$_6$]SO$_4$
b) [Mn(H$_2$O)$_6$]SO$_4$
c) [Mn(H$_2$O)$_6$]$_2$SO$_4$
d) [Mn$_2$(H$_2$O)$_6$]SO$_4$

Q5. Which complex ion can exhibit geometric isomerism? Assume that M is the metal ion, A and B are ligands, and the geometry is octahedral.
a) [MA$_6$]$^{2+}$
b) [MA$_5$B]$^{2+}$
c) [MA$_4$B$_2$]$^{2+}$
d) [MA$_3$B$_3$]$^{2+}$

Q6. Pick the optical isomer of the complex ion represented here:

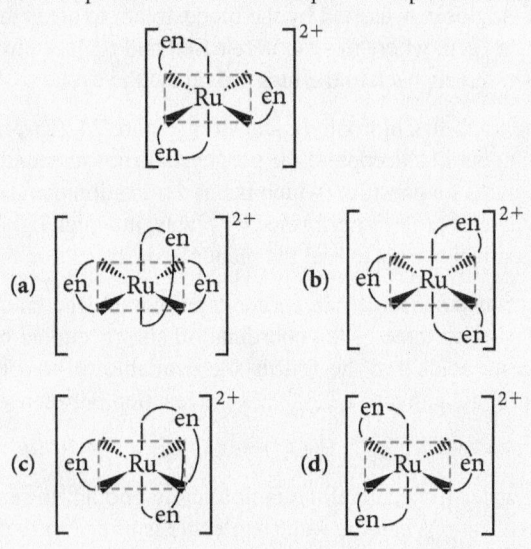

Q7. According to valence bond theory, what is the hybridization of the central metal ion in an octahedral complex ion?
a) sp
b) sp^3
c) dsp^2
d) d^2sp^3

Q8. Estimate the crystal field splitting energy (in kJ/mol) for a complex ion that is red in solution.
a) 228 kJ/mol
b) 171 kJ/mol
c) 2.84×10^{-19} kJ/mol
d) 3.79×10^{-19} kJ/mol

Q9. Use crystal field theory to determine the number of unpaired electrons in the complex ion $[Fe(CN)_6]^{4-}$.
a) 0
b) 2
c) 3
d) 4

Q10. Which complex ion is diamagnetic?
a) $[Cr(H_2O)_4Cl_2]^+$
b) $[Fe(H_2O)_6]^{2+}$
c) $[Co(NH_3)_6]^{3+}$
d) $[CoCl_6]^{3-}$

Answers: 1. (d) 2. (d) 3. (b) 4. (b) 5. (c) 6. (b) 7. (d) 8. (a) 9. (a) 10. (c)

Key Terms

Section 24.1
crystal field theory (1100)

Section 24.2
lanthanide contraction (1102)

Section 24.3
complex ion (1104)
ligand (1104)
coordination compound (1104)

primary valence (1104)
secondary valence (1104)
coordination number (1104)
coordinate covalent bond (1104)
monodentate (1104)
bidentate (1104)
polydentate (1105)
chelate (1106)

chelating agent (1106)

Section 24.4
structural isomers (1109)
stereoisomers (1109)
coordination isomers (1109)
linkage isomers (1109)
geometric isomers (1110)
optical isomers (1112)

Section 24.5
strong-field complex (1114)
weak-field complex (1114)
low-spin complex (1117)
high-spin complex (1117)

Key Concepts

Electron Configurations (24.2)

▶ As we move across a row of transition elements, we add electrons to the $(n-1)d$ orbitals, resulting in a general electron configuration for first- and second-row transition elements of [noble gas] $ns^2(n-1)d^x$ and for the third and fourth rows of [noble gas] $ns^2(n-2)f^{14}(n-1)d^x$, where x ranges from 1 to 10.

▶ A transition element forms a cation by losing electrons from the ns orbitals before losing electrons from the $(n-1)d$ orbitals.

Periodic Trends (24.2)

▶ The variations in atomic size, ionization energy, and electronegativity across a row in the periodic table are similar to those of main-group elements (although the trends are less pronounced and less regular). As we move down a group, however, atomic size increases from the first row to the second but stays roughly constant from the second row to the third because of the lanthanide contraction. This contraction results in ionization energy and electronegativity trends as we move down a column that are opposite of the main group elements.

Composition and Naming of Coordination Compounds (24.3)

▶ A coordination compound is composed of a complex ion and a counterion.

▶ A complex ion contains a central metal ion bound to one or more ligands. The number of ligands directly bound to the metal ion is called the coordination number.

▶ The ligand forms a coordinate covalent bond to the metal ion by donating a pair of electrons to an empty orbital on the metal.

▶ Ligands that donate a single pair of electrons are monodentate. A ligand that donates two pairs of electrons is bidentate, and a ligand that donates more than two pairs is polydentate.

▶ In naming coordination compounds, we use the name of the cation followed by the name of the anion. To name a complex ion we use the guidelines outlined in Section 24.3.

Types of Isomers (24.4)

▶ We broadly divide the isomerism observed in coordination compounds into two categories: structural isomers, in which atoms are connected differently to one another, and stereoisomers, in which atoms are connected in the same way but the ligands have a different spatial arrangement about the metal atom.

▶ Structural isomers are either coordination isomers (a coordinated ligand exchanges places with an uncoordinated counterion) or linkage isomers (a particular ligand has the ability to coordinate to the metal in different ways).

▶ Stereoisomers are either geometric isomers (the ligands bonded to the metal have a different spatial arrangement relative to each other, leading to cis–trans or fac–mer isomers) or optical isomers (nonsuperimposable mirror images of one another).

Crystal Field Theory (24.5)

▶ Crystal field theory is a bonding model for transition metal complex ions. The model describes how the degeneracy of the d orbitals is broken by the repulsive forces between the electrons on the ligands around the metal ion and the d orbitals in the metal ion.

▶ The energy difference between the split d orbitals is the crystal field splitting energy (Δ). The magnitude of Δ depends in large part on the ligands bound to the metal.

▶ Octahedral complexes with a d^4, d^5, d^6, or d^7 metal ion can have two possible electronic configurations with different numbers of

unpaired electrons. The first, called high-spin, has the same number of unpaired electrons as the free metal ion and is usually the result of a weak crystal field. The second, called low-spin, has fewer unpaired electrons than the free metal ion and is usually the result of a strong crystal field.

Key Equations and Relationships

Crystal Field Splitting Energy (**24.5**)

$$\Delta = hc/\lambda \text{ (where } \lambda \text{ is the wavelength of maximum absorption)}$$

Key Learning Outcomes

Chapter Objectives	Assessment
Writing Electronic Configurations for Transition Metals and Their Ions (**24.2**)	Examples 24.1, 24.2 For Practice 24.1, 24.2 Exercises 19–20, 57, 58
Naming Coordination Compounds (**24.3**)	Examples 24.3, 24.4 For Practice 24.3, 24.4 Exercises 23–28
Recognizing and Drawing Geometric Isomers (**24.4**)	Examples 24.5, 24.6 For Practice 24.5, 24.6 Exercises 5–40, 61–62
Recognizing and Drawing Optical Isomers (**24.4**)	Example 24.7 For Practice 24.7 Exercises 39–40, 61–62
Calculating Crystal Field Splitting Energy (**24.5**)	Example 24.8 For Practice 24.8 Exercises 43–46
Recognizing and Predicting High-Spin and Low-Spin Octahedral Complex Ions (**24.5**)	Examples 24.9, 24.10 For Practice 24.9, 24.10 Exercises 49–52, 65

EXERCISES

Review Questions

1. When a transition metal atom forms an ion, which electrons are lost first?

2. Explain why transition metals exhibit multiple oxidation states instead of a single oxidation state (like most of the main-group metals).

3. Why is the +2 oxidation state so common for transition metals?

4. Explain why atomic radii of elements in the third row of the transition metals are no larger than those of elements in the second row.

5. Gold is the most electronegative transition metal. Explain.

6. Briefly define each term.
   a. coordination number   b. ligand
   c. bidentate and polydentate d. complex ion
   e. chelating agent

7. Using the Lewis acid–base definition, how would you categorize a ligand? How would you categorize a transition metal ion?

8. Explain the differences between each pair of isomer types.
   a. structural isomer and stereoisomer
   b. linkage isomer and coordination isomer
   c. geometric isomer and optical isomer

9. Which complex ion geometry has the potential to exhibit cis–trans isomerism: linear, tetrahedral, square planar, octahedral?

10. How can you tell whether a complex ion is optically active?

11. Explain the differences between weak-field and strong-field metal complexes.

12. Explain why compounds of Sc^{3+} are colorless, but compounds of Ti^{3+} are colored.

13. Explain why compounds of Zn^{2+} are white, but compounds of Cu^{2+} are often blue or green.

14. Explain the differences between high-spin and low-spin metal complexes.

15. Why are almost all tetrahedral complexes high-spin?

16. Many transition metal compounds are colored. How does crystal field theory account for this?

Problems by Topic

Properties of Transition Metals

17. Write the ground state electron configuration for each atom and ion pair.
    a. Ni, Ni^{2+}
    b. Mn, Mn^{4+}
    c. Y, Y^{+}
    d. Ta, Ta^{2+}

18. Write the ground state electron configuration for each atom and ion pair.
    a. Zr, Zr^{2+}
    b. Co, Co^{2+}
    c. Tc, Tc^{3+}
    d. Os, Os^{4+}

19. Determine the highest possible oxidation state for each element.
    a. V
    b. Re
    c. Pd

20. Which first-row transition metal(s) has the following highest possible oxidation state?
    a. +3
    b. +7
    c. +4

Coordination Compounds

21. Determine the oxidation state and coordination number of the metal ion in each complex ion.
    a. $[Cr(H_2O)_6]^{3+}$
    b. $[Co(NH_3)_3Cl_3]^-$
    c. $[Cu(CN)_4]^{2-}$
    d. $[Ag(NH_3)_2]^+$

22. Determine the oxidation state and coordination number of the metal ion in each complex ion.
    a. $[Co(NH_3)_5Br]^{2+}$
    b. $[Fe(CN)_6]^{4-}$
    c. $[Co(ox)_3]^{4-}$
    d. $[PdCl_4]^{2-}$

23. Name each complex ion or coordination compound.
    a. $[Cr(H_2O)_6]^{3+}$
    b. $[Cu(CN)_4]^{2-}$
    c. $[Fe(NH_3)_5Br]SO_4$
    d. $[Co(H_2O)_4(NH_3)(OH)]Cl_2$

24. Name each complex ion or coordination compound.
    a. $[Cu(en)_2]^{2+}$
    b. $[Mn(CO)_3(NO_2)_3]^{2+}$
    c. $Na[Cr(H_2O)_2(ox)_2]$
    d. $[Co(en)_3][Fe(CN)_6]$

25. Write the formula for each complex ion or coordination compound.
    a. hexaamminechromium(III)
    b. potassium hexacyanoferrate(III)
    c. ethylenediaminedithiocyanatocopper(II)
    d. tetraaquaplatinum(II) hexachloroplatinate(IV)

26. Write the formula for each complex ion or coordination compound.
    a. hexaaquanickel(II) chloride
    b. pentacarbonylchloromanganese(I)
    c. ammonium diaquatetrabromovanadate(III)
    d. tris(ethylenediamine)cobalt(III) trioxalatoferrate(III)

27. Write the formula and the name of each complex ion.
    a. a complex ion with Co^{3+} as the central ion and three NH_3 molecules and three CN^- ions as ligands
    b. a complex ion with Cr^{3+} as the central ion and a coordination number of 6 with ethylenediamine ligands

28. Write the formula and the name of each complex ion or coordination compound.
    a. a complex ion with four water molecules and two ONO^- ions connected to an Fe(III) ion
    b. a coordination compound made of two complex ions: one a complex of V(III) with two ethylenediamine molecules and two Cl^- ions as ligands and the other a complex of Ni(II) having a coordination number of 4 with Cl^- ions as ligands

Structure and Isomerism

29. Draw two linkage isomers of $[Mn(NH_3)_5(NO_2)]^{2+}$.

30. Draw two linkage isomers of $[PtCl_3(SCN)]^{2-}$.

31. Write the formulas and names for the coordination isomers of $[Fe(H_2O)_6]Cl_2$.

32. Write the formulas and names for the coordination isomers of $[Co(en)_3][Cr(ox)_3]$.

33. Which complexes exhibit geometric isomerism?
    a. $[Cr(NH_3)_5(OH)]^{2+}$ **b.** $[Cr(en)_2Cl_2]^+$
    c. $[Cr(H_2O)(NH_3)_3Cl_2]^+$ **d.** $[Pt(NH_3)Cl_3]^-$
    e. $[Pt(H_2O)_2(CN)_2]$

34. Which complexes exhibit geometric isomerism?
 a. $[Co(H_2O)_2(ox)_2]^-$ **b.** $[Co(en)_3]^{3+}$
 c. $[Co(H_2O)_2(NH_3)_2(ox)]^+$ **d.** $[Ni(NH_3)_2(en)]^{2+}$
 e. $[Ni(CO)_2Cl_2]$

35. If W, X, Y, and Z are different monodentate ligands, how many geometric isomers are there for each ion?
 a. square planar $[NiWXYZ]^{2+}$
 b. tetrahedral $[ZnWXYZ]^{2+}$

36. How many geometric isomers are there for each species?
 a. $[Fe(CO)_3Cl_3]$
 b. $[Mn(CO)_2Cl_2Br_2]^+$

37. Draw the structures and label the type for all the isomers of each ion.
 a. $[Cr(CO)_3(NH_3)_3]^{3+}$
 b. $[Pd(CO)_2(H_2O)Cl]^+$

38. Draw the structures and label the type for all the isomers of each species.
 a. $[Fe(CO)_4Cl_2]^+$
 b. $[Pt(en)Cl_2]$

39. Determine if either isomer of $[Cr(NH_3)_2(ox)_2]^-$ is optically active.

40. Determine if either isomer of $[Fe(CO)_3Cl_3]$ is optically active.

Bonding in Coordination Compounds

41. Draw the octahedral crystal field splitting diagram for each metal ion.
 a. Zn^{2+}
 b. Fe^{3+} (high- and low-spin)
 c. V^{3+}
 d. Co^{2+} (high-spin)

42. Draw the octahedral crystal field splitting diagram for each metal ion.
 a. Cr^{3+}
 b. Cu^{2+}
 c. Mn^{3+} (high- and low-spin)
 d. Fe^{2+} (low-spin)

43. The $[CrCl_6]^{3-}$ ion has a maximum in its absorption spectrum at 735 nm. Calculate the crystal field splitting energy (in kJ/mol) for this ion.

44. The absorption spectrum of the complex ion $[Rh(NH_3)_6]^{3+}$ has maximum absorbance at 295 nm. Calculate the crystal field splitting energy (in kJ/mol) for this ion.

45. Three complex ions of cobalt(III), $[Co(CN)_6]^{3-}$, $[Co(NH_3)_6]^{3+}$, and $[CoF_6]^{3-}$, absorb light at wavelengths of (in no particular order) 290 nm, 440 nm, and 770 nm. Match each complex ion to the appropriate wavelength absorbed. What color would you expect each solution to be?

46. Three bottles of aqueous solutions are discovered in an abandoned lab. The solutions are green, yellow, and purple. It is known that three complex ions of chromium(III) were commonly used in that lab: $[Cr(H_2O)_6]^{3+}$, $[Cr(NH_3)_6]^{3+}$, and $[Cr(H_2O)_4Cl_2]^+$. Determine the likely identity of each of the colored solutions.

47. The $[Mn(NH_3)_6]^{2+}$ ion is paramagnetic with five unpaired electrons. The NH_3 ligand is usually a strong field ligand. Is NH_3 acting as a strong field ligand in this case?

48. The complex $[Fe(H_2O)_6]^{2+}$ is paramagnetic. Is the H_2O ligand inducing a strong or weak field?

49. How many unpaired electrons would you expect for each complex ion?
 a. $[RhCl_6]^{3-}$ **b.** $[Co(OH)_6]^{4-}$ **c.** *cis*-$[Fe(en)_2(NO_2)_2]^+$

50. How many unpaired electrons would you expect for each complex ion?
 a. $[Cr(CN)_6]^{4-}$ **b.** $[MnF_6]^{4-}$ **c.** $[Ru(en)_3]^{2+}$

51. How many unpaired electrons would you expect for the complex ion $[CoCl_4]^{2-}$ if it is a tetrahedral shape?

52. The complex ion $[PdCl_4]^{2-}$ is known to be diamagnetic. Use this information to determine if it is a tetrahedral or square planar structure.

Applications of Coordination Compounds

53. What structural feature do hemoglobin, cytochrome c, and chlorophyll have in common?

54. Identify the central metal atom in each complex.
 a. hemoglobin   **b.** carbonic anhydrase
 c. chlorophyll   **d.** iron blue

55. Hemoglobin exists in two predominant forms in our bodies. One form, known as oxyhemoglobin, has O_2 bound to the iron and the other, known as deoxyhemoglobin, has a water molecule bound instead. Oxyhemoglobin is a low-spin complex that gives arterial blood its red color, and deoxyhemoglobin is a high-spin complex that gives venous blood its darker color. Explain these observations in terms of crystal field splitting. Would you categorize O_2 as a strong- or weak-field ligand?

56. Carbon monoxide and the cyanide ion are both toxic because they bind more strongly than oxygen to the iron in hemoglobin (Hb).

$$Hb + O_2 \rightleftharpoons HbO_2 \qquad K = 2 \times 10^{12}$$
$$Hb + CO \rightleftharpoons HbCO \qquad K = 1 \times 10^{14}$$

Calculate the equilibrium constant value for this reaction:

$$HbO_2 + CO \rightleftharpoons HbCO + O_2$$

Does the equilibrium favor reactants or products?

Cumulative Problems

57. Recall from Chapter 8 that Cr and Cu are exceptions to the normal orbital filling, resulting in a $[Ar]4s^1 3d^x$ configuration. Write the ground state electron configuration for each species.
 a. Cr, Cr^+, Cr^{2+}, Cr^{3+}
 b. Cu, Cu^+, Cu^{2+}

58. Most of the second row transition metals do not follow the normal orbital filling pattern. Five of them—Nb, Mo, Ru, Rh, and Ag—have a $[Kr]5s^1 4d^x$ configuration and Pd has a $[Kr]4d^{10}$ configuration. Write the ground state electron configuration for each species.
 a. Mo, Mo^+, Ag, Ag^+ **b.** Ru, Ru^{3+}
 c. Rh, Rh^{2+} **d.** Pd, Pd^+, Pd^{2+}

59. Draw the Lewis diagrams for each ligand. Indicate the lone pair(s) that may be donated to the metal. Indicate any you expect to be bidentate or polydentate.
    a. NH_3 b. SCN^- c. H_2O

60. Draw the Lewis diagrams for each ligand. Indicate the lone pair(s) that may be donated to the metal. Indicate any you expect to be bidentate or polydentate.
    a. CN^-
    b. bipyridyl (bipy), which has the following structure:

    c. NO_2^-

61. List all the different formulas for an octahedral complex made from a metal (M) and three different ligands (A, B, and C). Describe any isomers for each complex.

62. Amino acids, such as glycine (gly), form complexes with the trace metal ions found in the bloodstream. Glycine, whose structure is shown here, acts as a bidentate ligand coordinating with the nitrogen atom and one of the oxygen atoms.

    Draw all the possible isomers of:
    a. square planar $[Ni(gly)_2]$
    b. tetrahedral $[Zn(gly)_2]$
    c. octahedral $[Fe(gly)_3]$

63. Oxalic acid solutions remove rust stains. Draw a complex ion that is likely responsible for this effect. Does it have any isomers?

64. W, X, Y, and Z are different monodentate ligands.
    a. Is the square planar $[NiWXYZ]^{2+}$ optically active?
    b. Is the tetrahedral $[ZnWXYZ]^{2+}$ optically active?

65. Hexacyanomanganate(III) ion is a low-spin complex. Draw the crystal field splitting diagram with electrons filled in appropriately. Is this complex paramagnetic or diamagnetic?

66. Determine the color and approximate wavelength absorbed most strongly by each solution.
    a. blue solution
    b. red solution
    c. yellow solution

67. Draw the structures of all the geometric isomers of $[Ru(H_2O)_2(NH_3)_2Cl_2]^+$. Draw the mirror images of any that are chiral.

68. A 0.32 mol amount of NH_3 is dissolved in 0.47 L of a 0.38 M silver nitrate solution. Calculate the equilibrium concentrations of all species in the solution.

Challenge Problems

69. When a solution of $PtCl_2$ reacts with the ligand trimethylphosphine, $P(CH_3)_3$, two compounds are produced. The compounds share the same elemental analysis: 46.7% Pt; 17.0% Cl; 14.8% P; 17.2% C; 4.34% H. Determine the formula, draw the structure, and give the systematic name for each compound.

70. Draw a crystal field splitting diagram for a trigonal planar complex ion. Assume the plane of the molecule is perpendicular to the z axis.

71. Draw a crystal field splitting diagram for a trigonal bipyramidal complex ion. Assume the axial positions are on the z axis.

72. Explain why $[Ni(NH_3)_4]^{2+}$ is paramagnetic, while $[Ni(CN)_4]^{2-}$ is diamagnetic.

73. Sulfide (S^{2-}) salts are notoriously insoluble in aqueous solution.
    a. Calculate the molar solubility of nickel(II) sulfide in water. $K_{sp}(NiS) = 3 \times 10^{-16}$
    b. Nickel(II) ions form a complex ion in the presence of ammonia with a formation constant (K_f) of 2.0×10^8: $Ni^{2+} + 6 NH_3 \rightleftharpoons [Ni(NH_3)_6]^{2+}$. Calculate the molar solubility of NiS in 3.0 M NH_3.
    c. Explain any differences between the answers to parts **a** and **b**.

74. Calculate the solubility of $Zn(OH)_2(s)$ in 2.0 M NaOH solution. (Hint: you must take into account the formation of $Zn(OH)_4^{2-}$, which has a $K_f = 2 \times 10^{15}$.)

75. Halide complexes of metal M of the form $[MX_6]^{3-}$ are found to be stable in aqueous solution. But it is possible that they undergo rapid ligand exchange with water (or other ligands) that is not detectable because the complexes are less stable. This property is referred to as their *lability*. Suggest an experiment to measure the lability of these complexes that does not employ radioactive labels.

76. The K_f for $[Cu(en)_2]^{2+}$ is much larger than the one for $[Cu(NH_3)_4]^{2+}$. This difference is primarily an entropy effect. Explain why and calculate the difference between the $\Delta S°$ values at 298 K for the complete dissociation of the two complex ions. (Hint: the value of ΔH is about the same for both systems.)

77. When solid $Cd(OH)_2$ is added to a solution of 0.10 M NaI some of it dissolves. Calculate the pH of the solution at equilibrium.

Conceptual Problems

78. Two ligands, A and B, both form complexes with a particular metal ion. When the metal ion complexes with ligand A, the solution is green. When the metal ion complexes with ligand B, the solution is violet. Which of the two ligands results in the largest Δ?

79. Which element has the higher ionization energy, Cu or Au?

80. The complexes of Fe^{3+} have magnetic properties that depend on whether the ligands are strong or weak field. Explain why this observation supports the idea that electrons are lost from the 4s orbital before the 3d orbitals in the transition metals.

Answers to Conceptual Connections

Atomic Size

24.1 The element W has the larger radius because it is in the third transition row and Fe is in the first. Atomic radii increase from the first to the second transition row and stay roughly constant from the second to the third.

Weak- and Strong-Field Ligands

24.2 Ligand B forms a yellow solution, which means that the complex absorbs in the violet region. Ligand A forms a red solution, which means that the complex absorbs in the green. Since the violet region of the electromagnetic spectrum is of shorter wavelength (higher energy) than the green region, ligand B produces a higher Δ.

Appendix I:
Common Mathematical Operations in Chemistry

A. Scientific Notation

A number written in scientific notation consists of a **decimal part**, a number that is usually between 1 and 10, and an **exponential part**, 10 raised to an **exponent**, n.

Each of the following numbers is written in both scientific and decimal notation:

$$1.0 \times 10^5 = 100{,}000 \qquad 1.0 \times 10^{-5} = 0.000001$$

$$6.7 \times 10^3 = 6700 \qquad 6.7 \times 10^{-3} = 0.0067$$

A positive exponent means 1 multiplied by 10 n times.

$$10^0 = 1$$

$$10^1 = 1 \times 10$$

$$10^2 = 1 \times 10 \times 10 = 100$$

$$10^3 = 1 \times 10 \times 10 \times 10 = 1000$$

A negative exponent ($-n$) means 1 divided by 10 n times.

$$10^{-1} = \frac{1}{10} = 0.1$$

$$10^{-2} = \frac{1}{10 \times 10} = 0.01$$

$$10^{-3} = \frac{1}{10 \times 10 \times 10} = 0.001$$

To convert a number to scientific notation, we move the decimal point to obtain a number between 1 and 10 and then multiply by 10 raised to the appropriate power. For example, to write 5983 in scientific notation, we move the decimal point to the left three places to get 5.983 (a number between 1 and 10) and then multiply by 1000 to make up for moving the decimal point.

$$5983 = 5.983 \times 1000$$

Since 1000 is 10^3, we write:

$$5983 = 5.983 \times 10^3$$

We can do this in one step by counting how many places we move the decimal point to obtain a number between 1 and 10 and then writing the decimal part multiplied by 10 raised to the number of places we moved the decimal point.

$$5983 = 5.983 \times 10^3$$

If the decimal point is moved to the left, as in the previous example, the exponent is positive. If the decimal is moved to the right, the exponent is negative.

$$0.00034 = 3.4 \times 10^{-4}$$

To express a number in scientific notation:

1. **Move the decimal point to obtain a number between 1 and 10.**
2. **Write the result from step 1 multiplied by 10 raised to the number of places you moved the decimal point.**

- *The exponent is positive if you moved the decimal point to the left.*

- *The exponent is negative if you moved the decimal point to the right.*

Consider the following additional examples:

$$290{,}809{,}000 \qquad = 2.90809 \times 10^8$$

$$0.000000000070 \, \text{m} = 7.0 \times 10^{-11} \, \text{m}$$

Multiplication and Division

To multiply numbers expressed in scientific notation, multiply the decimal parts and add the exponents.

$$(A \times 10^m)(B \times 10^n) = (A \times B) \times 10^{m+n}$$

To divide numbers expressed in scientific notation, divide the decimal parts and subtract the exponent in the denominator from the exponent in the numerator.

$$\frac{(A \times 10^m)}{(B \times 10^n)} = \left(\frac{A}{B}\right) \times 10^{m-n}$$

Consider the following example involving multiplication:

$$(3.5 \times 10^4)(1.8 \times 10^6) = (3.5 \times 1.8) \times 10^{4+6}$$

$$= 6.3 \times 10^{10}$$

Consider the following example involving division:

$$\frac{(5.6 \times 10^7)}{(1.4 \times 10^3)} = \left(\frac{5.6}{1.4}\right) \times 10^{7-3}$$

$$= 4.0 \times 10^4$$

Addition and Subtraction

To add or subtract numbers expressed in scientific notation, rewrite all the numbers so that they have the same exponent, then add or subtract the decimal parts of the numbers. The exponents remained unchanged.

$$A \times 10^n$$
$$\pm B \times 10^n$$
$$\overline{(A \pm B) \times 10^n}$$

Notice that the numbers *must have* the same exponent. Consider the following example involving addition:

$$4.82 \times 10^7$$
$$+3.4 \times 10^6$$

First, express both numbers with the same exponent. In this case, we rewrite the lower number and perform the addition as follows:

$$4.82 \times 10^7$$
$$+0.34 \times 10^7$$
$$\overline{5.16 \times 10^7}$$

Consider the following example involving subtraction:

$$7.33 \times 10^5$$
$$-1.9 \times 10^4$$

First, express both numbers with the same exponent. In this case, we rewrite the lower number and perform the subtraction as follows:

$$7.33 \times 10^5$$
$$-0.19 \times 10^5$$
$$\overline{7.14 \times 10^5}$$

Powers and Roots

To raise a number written in scientific notation to a power, raise the decimal part to the power and multiply the exponent by the power:

$$(4.0 \times 10^6)^2 = 4.0^2 \times 10^{6\times2}$$
$$= 16 \times 10^{12}$$
$$= 1.6 \times 10^{13}$$

To take the nth root of a number written in scientific notation, take the nth root of the decimal part and divide the exponent by the root:

$$(4.0 \times 10^6)^{1/3} = 4.0^{1/3} \times 10^{6/3}$$
$$= 1.6 \times 10^2$$

B. Logarithms

Common (or Base 10) Logarithms

The common or base 10 logarithm (abbreviated log) of a number is the exponent to which 10 must be raised to obtain

that number. For example, the log of 100 is 2 because 10 must be raised to the second power to get 100. Similarly, the log of 1000 is 3 because 10 must be raised to the third power to get 1000. The logs of several multiples of 10 are shown below:

$$\log 10 = 1$$
$$\log 100 = 2$$
$$\log 1000 = 3$$
$$\log 10,000 = 4$$

Because $10^0 = 1$ by definition, $\log 1 = 0$.

The log of a number smaller than one is negative because 10 must be raised to a negative exponent to get a number smaller than one. For example, the log of 0.01 is -2 because 10 must be raised to -2 to get 0.01. Similarly, the log of 0.001 is -3 because 10 must be raised to -3 to get 0.001. The logs of several fractional numbers are shown below:

$$\log 0.1 = -1$$
$$\log 0.01 = -2$$
$$\log 0.001 = -3$$
$$\log 0.0001 = -4$$

The logs of numbers that are not multiples of 10 can be computed on your calculator. See your calculator manual for specific instructions.

Inverse Logarithms

The inverse logarithm or invlog function is exactly the opposite of the log function. For example, the log of 100 is 2 and the inverse log of 2 is 100. The log function and the invlog function undo one another.

$$\log 100 = 2$$
$$\text{invlog } 2 = 100$$
$$\text{invlog} (\log 100) = 100$$

The inverse log of a number is 10 rasied to that number.

$$\text{invlog } x = 10^x$$
$$\text{invlog } 3 = 10^3 = 1000$$

The inverse logs of numbers can be computed on your calculator. See your calculator manual for specific instructions.

Natural (or Base e) Logarithms

The natural (or base e) logarithm (abbreviated ln) of a number is the exponent to which e (which has the value of 2.71828...) must be raised to obtain that number. For example, the ln of 100 is 4.605 because e must be raised to 4.605 to get 100. Similarly, the ln of 10.0 is 2.303 because e must be raised to 2.303 to get 10.0.

The inverse natural logarithm or invln function is exactly the opposite of the ln function. For example, the ln of 100 is

4.605 and the inverse ln of 4.605 is 100. The inverse ln of a number is simply e raised to that number.

$$\text{invln } x = e^x$$

$$\text{invln } 3 = e^3 = 20.1$$

The invln of a number can be computed on your calculator. See your calculator manual for specific instructions.

Mathematical Operations Using Logarithms

Because logarithms are exponents, mathematical operations involving logarithms are similar to those involving exponents as follows:

$$\log(a \times b) = \log a + \log b \qquad \ln(a \times b) = \ln a + \ln b$$

$$\log \frac{a}{b} = \log a - \log b \qquad \ln \frac{a}{b} = \ln a - \ln b$$

$$\log a^n = n \log a \qquad \ln a^n = n \ln a$$

C. Quadratic Equations

A quadratic equation contains at least one term in which the variable x is raised to the second power (and no terms in which x is raised to a higher power). A quadratic equation has the following general form:

$$ax^2 + bx + c = 0$$

A quadratic equation can be solved for x using the quadratic formula:

$$x = \frac{-b \pm \sqrt{b^2 - 4ac}}{2a}$$

Quadratic equations are often encountered when solving equilibrium problems. Below we show how to use the quadratic formula to solve a quadratic equation for x.

$$3x^2 - 5x + 1 = 0 \quad (\textit{quadratic equation})$$

$$x = \frac{-b \pm \sqrt{b^2 - 4ac}}{2a}$$

$$= \frac{-(-5) \pm \sqrt{(-5)^2 - 4(3)(1)}}{2(3)}$$

$$= \frac{5 \pm 3.6}{6}$$

$$x = 1.43 \quad \text{or} \quad x = 0.233$$

As you can see, the solution to a quadratic equation usually has two values. In any real chemical system, one of the values can be eliminated because it has no physical significance. (For example, it may correspond to a negative concentration, which does not exist.)

D. Graphs

Graphs are often used to visually show the relationship between two variables. For example, in Chapter 5 we show

the following relationship between the volume of a gas and its pressure:

▲ **Volume versus Pressure** A plot of the volume of a gas sample—as measured in a J-tube—versus pressure. The plot shows that volume and pressure are inversely related.

The horizontal axis is the x-axis and is normally used to show the independent variable. The vertical axis is the y-axis and is normally used to show how the other variable (called the dependent variable) varies with a change in the independent variable. In this case, the graph shows that as the pressure of a gas sample increases, its volume decreases.

Many relationships in chemistry are *linear*, which means that if you change one variable by a factor of n the other variable will also change by a factor of n. For example, the volume of a gas is linearly related to the number of moles of gas. When two quantities are linearly related, a graph of one versus the other produces a straight line. For example, the graph below shows how the volume of an ideal gas sample depends on the number of moles of gas in the sample:

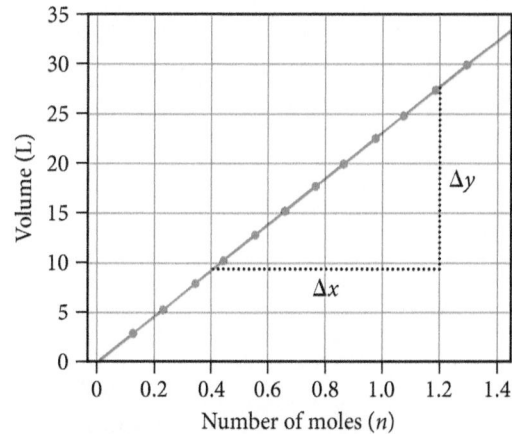

▲ **Volume versus Number of Moles** The volume of a gas sample increases linearly with the number of moles of gas in the sample.

A linear relationship between any two variables x and y can be expressed by the following equation:

$$y = mx + b$$

where m is the slope of the line and b is the y-intercept. The slope is the change in y divided by the change in x.

$$m = \frac{\Delta y}{\Delta x}$$

For the graph above, we can estimate the slope by simply estimating the changes in y and x for a given interval. For example, between $x = 0.4$ mol and 1.2 mol, $\Delta x = 0.80$ mol and we can estimate that $\Delta y = 18$ L. Therefore the slope is

$$m = \frac{\Delta y}{\Delta x} = \frac{18\,\text{L}}{0.80\,\text{mol}} = 23\,\text{mol/L}$$

In several places in this book, logarithmic relationships between variables can be plotted in order to obtain a linear relationship. For example, the variables $[A]_t$ and t in the following equation are not linearly related, but the natural logarithm of $[A]_t$ and t are linearly related.

$$\ln[A]_t = -kt + \ln[A]_0$$

$$y = mx + b$$

A plot of $\ln[A]_t$ versus t will therefore produce a straight line with slope $= -k$ and y-intercept $= \ln[A]_0$.

Appendix II:
Useful Data

A. Atomic Colors

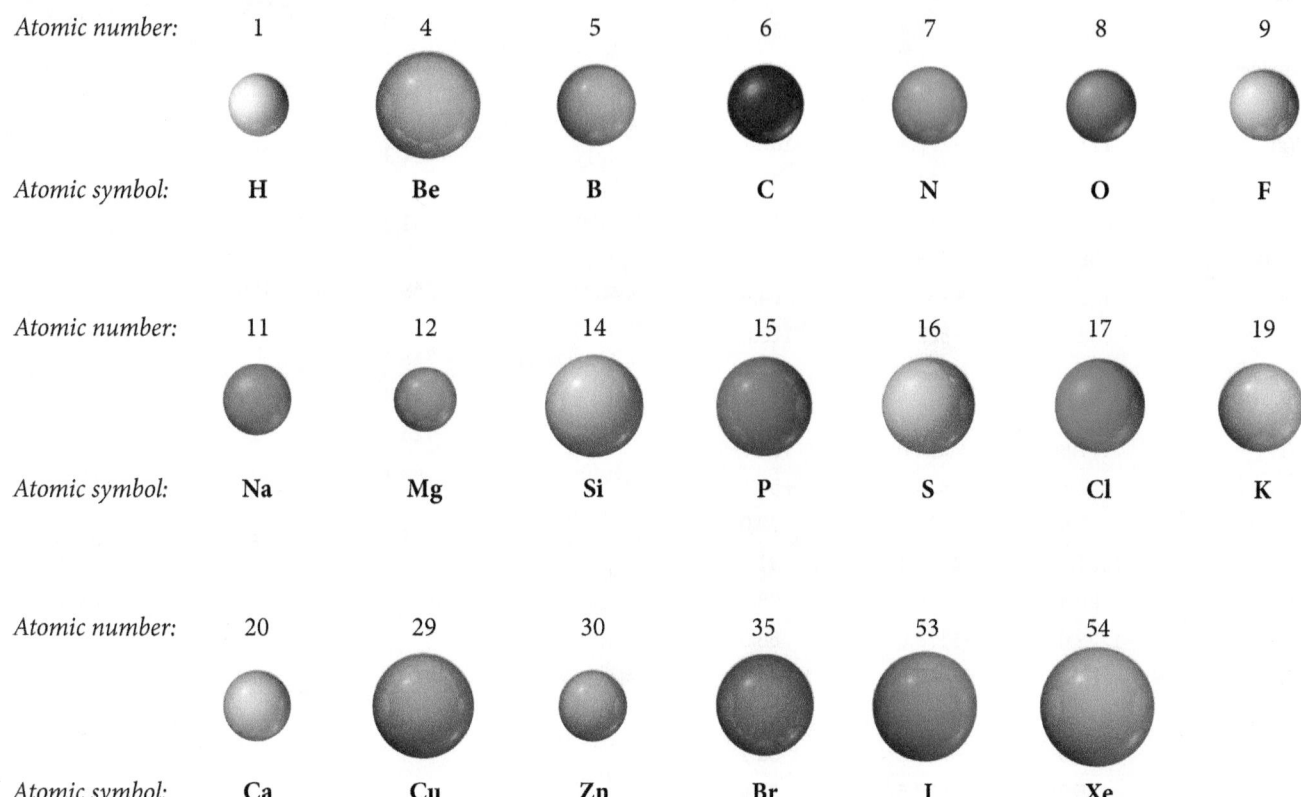

Atomic number:	1	4	5	6	7	8	9
Atomic symbol:	H	Be	B	C	N	O	F

Atomic number:	11	12	14	15	16	17	19
Atomic symbol:	Na	Mg	Si	P	S	Cl	K

Atomic number:	20	29	30	35	53	54
Atomic symbol:	Ca	Cu	Zn	Br	I	Xe

B. Standard Thermodynamic Quantities for Selected Substances at 25 °C

Substance	ΔH_f° (kJ/mol)	ΔG_f° (kJ/mol)	S° (J/mol·K)	Substance	ΔH_f° (kJ/mol)	ΔG_f° (kJ/mol)	S° (J/mol·K)
Aluminum				**Beryllium**			
Al(s)	0	0	28.32	Be(s)	0	0	9.5
Al(g)	330.0	289.4	164.6	BeO(s)	−609.4	−580.1	13.8
Al^{3+}(aq)	−538.4	−483	−325	Be(OH)$_2$(s)	−902.5	−815.0	45.5
AlCl$_3$(s)	−704.2	−628.8	109.3	**Bismuth**			
Al$_2$O$_3$(s)	−1675.7	−1582.3	50.9	Bi(s)	0	0	56.7
Barium				BiCl$_3$(s)	−379.1	−315.0	177.0
Ba(s)	0	0	62.5	Bi$_2$O$_3$(s)	−573.9	−493.7	151.5
Ba(g)	180.0	146.0	170.2	Bi$_2$S$_3$(s)	−143.1	−140.6	200.4
Ba^{2+}(aq)	−537.6	−560.8	9.6	**Boron**			
BaCO$_3$(s)	−1213.0	−1134.4	112.1	B(s)	0	0	5.9
BaCl$_2$(s)	−855.0	−806.7	123.7	B(g)	565.0	521.0	153.4
BaO(s)	−548.0	−520.3	72.1	BCl$_3$(g)	−403.8	−388.7	290.1
Ba(OH)$_2$(s)	−944.7			BF$_3$(g)	−1136.0	−1119.4	254.4
BaSO$_4$(s)	−1473.2	−1362.2	132.2	B$_2$H$_6$(g)	36.4	87.6	232.1

(continued on the next page)

Substance	ΔH_f°(kJ/mol)	ΔG_f°(kJ/mol)	S°(J/mol · K)
$B_2O_3(s)$	−1273.5	−1194.3	54.0
$H_3BO_3(s)$	−1094.3	−968.9	90.0
Bromine			
$Br(g)$	111.9	82.4	175.0
$Br_2(l)$	0	0	152.2
$Br_2(g)$	30.9	3.1	245.5
$Br^-(aq)$	−121.4	−102.8	80.71
$HBr(g)$	−36.3	−53.4	198.7
Cadmium			
$Cd(s)$	0	0	51.8
$Cd(g)$	111.8	77.3	167.7
$Cd^{2+}(aq)$	−75.9	−77.6	−73.2
$CdCl_2(s)$	−391.5	−343.9	115.3
$CdO(s)$	−258.4	−228.7	54.8
$CdS(s)$	−161.9	−156.5	64.9
$CdSO_4(s)$	−933.3	−822.7	123.0
Calcium			
$Ca(s)$	0	0	41.6
$Ca(g)$	177.8	144.0	154.9
$Ca^{2+}(aq)$	−542.8	−553.6	−53.1
$CaC_2(s)$	−59.8	−64.9	70.0
$CaCO_3(s)$	−1207.6	−1129.1	91.7
$CaCl_2(s)$	−795.4	−748.8	108.4
$CaF_2(s)$	−1228.0	−1175.6	68.5
$CaH_2(s)$	−181.5	−142.5	41.4
$Ca(NO_3)_2(s)$	−938.2	−742.8	193.2
$CaO(s)$	−634.9	−603.3	38.1
$Ca(OH)_2(s)$	−985.2	−897.5	83.4
$CaSO_4(s)$	−1434.5	−1322.0	106.5
$Ca_3(PO_4)_2(s)$	−4120.8	−3884.7	236.0
Carbon			
$C(s, graphite)$	0	0	5.7
$C(s, diamond)$	1.88	2.9	2.4
$C(g)$	716.7	671.3	158.1
$CH_4(g)$	−74.6	−50.5	186.3
$CH_3Cl(g)$	−81.9	−60.2	234.6
$CH_2Cl_2(g)$	−95.4		270.2
$CH_2Cl_2(l)$	−124.2	−63.2	177.8
$CHCl_3(l)$	−134.1	−73.7	201.7
$CCl_4(g)$	−95.7	−62.3	309.7
$CCl_4(l)$	−128.2	−66.4	216.4
$CH_2O(g)$	−108.6	−102.5	218.8
CH_2O_2 (l, formic acid)	−425.0	−361.4	129.0
CH_3NH_2 (g, methylamine)	−22.5	32.7	242.9
$CH_3OH(l)$	−238.6	−166.6	126.8
$CH_3OH(g)$	−201.0	−162.3	239.9

Substance	ΔH_f°(kJ/mol)	ΔG_f°(kJ/mol)	S°(J/mol · K)
$C_2H_2(g)$	227.4	209.9	200.9
$C_2H_4(g)$	52.4	68.4	219.3
$C_2H_6(g)$	−84.68	−32.0	229.2
$C_2H_5OH(l)$	−277.6	−174.8	160.7
$C_2H_5OH(g)$	−234.8	−167.9	281.6
C_2H_3Cl (g, vinyl chloride)	37.2	53.6	264.0
$C_2H_4Cl_2$ (l, dichloroethane)	−166.8	−79.6	208.5
C_2H_4O (g, acetaldehyde)	−166.2	−133.0	263.8
$C_2H_4O_2$ (l, acetic acid)	−484.3	−389.9	159.8
$C_3H_8(g)$	−103.85	−23.4	270.3
C_3H_6O (l, acetone)	−248.4	−155.6	199.8
C_3H_7OH (l, isopropanol)	−318.1		181.1
$C_4H_{10}(l)$	−147.3	−15.0	231.0
$C_4H_{10}(g)$	−125.7	−15.71	310.0
$C_6H_6(l)$	49.1	124.5	173.4
$C_6H_5NH_2$ (l, aniline)	31.6	149.2	191.9
C_6H_5OH (s, phenol)	−165.1	−50.4	144.0
$C_6H_{12}O_6$ (s, glucose)	−1273.3	−910.4	212.1
$C_{10}H_8$ (s, naphthalene)	78.5	201.6	167.4
$C_{12}H_{22}O_{11}$ (s, sucrose)	−2226.1	−1544.3	360.24
$CO(g)$	−110.5	−137.2	197.7
$CO_2(g)$	−393.5	−394.4	213.8
$CO_2(aq)$	−413.8	−386.0	117.6
$CO_3^{2-}(aq)$	−677.1	−527.8	−56.9
$HCO_3^-(aq)$	−692.0	−586.8	91.2
$H_2CO_3(aq)$	−699.7	−623.2	187.4
$CN^-(aq)$	151	166	118
$HCN(l)$	108.9	125.0	112.8
$HCN(g)$	135.1	124.7	201.8
$CS_2(l)$	89.0	64.6	151.3
$CS_2(g)$	116.7	67.1	237.8
$COCl_2(g)$	−219.1	−204.9	283.5
$C_{60}(s)$	2327.0	2302.0	426.0
Cesium			
$Cs(s)$	0	0	85.2
$Cs(g)$	76.5	49.6	175.6
$Cs^+(aq)$	−258.0	−292.0	132.1
$CsBr(s)$	−400	−387	117
$CsCl(s)$	−438	−414	101.2

Substance	ΔH_f°(kJ/mol)	ΔG_f°(kJ/mol)	S°(J/mol · K)
CsF(s)	−553.5	−525.5	92.8
CsI(s)	−342	−337	127
Chlorine			
Cl(g)	121.3	105.3	165.2
Cl$_2$(g)	0	0	223.1
Cl$^-$(aq)	−167.1	−131.2	56.6
HCl(g)	−92.3	−95.3	186.9
HCl(aq)	−167.2	−131.2	56.5
ClO$_2$(g)	102.5	120.5	256.8
Cl$_2$O(g)	80.3	97.9	266.2
Chromium			
Cr(s)	0	0	23.8
Cr(g)	396.6	351.8	174.5
Cr^{3+}(aq)	−1971		
CrO$_4{}^{2-}$(aq)	−872.2	−717.1	44
Cr$_2$O$_3$(s)	−1139.7	−1058.1	81.2
Cr$_2$O$_7{}^{2-}$(aq)	−1476	−1279	238
Cobalt			
Co(s)	0	0	30.0
Co(g)	424.7	380.3	179.5
CoO(s)	−237.9	−214.2	53.0
Co(OH)$_2$(s)	−539.7	−454.3	79.0
Copper			
Cu(s)	0	0	33.2
Cu(g)	337.4	297.7	166.4
Cu$^+$(aq)	51.9	50.2	−26
Cu^{2+}(aq)	64.9	65.5	−98
CuCl(s)	−137.2	−119.9	86.2
CuCl$_2$(s)	−220.1	−175.7	108.1
CuO(s)	−157.3	−129.7	42.6
CuS(s)	−53.1	−53.6	66.5
CuSO$_4$(s)	−771.4	−662.2	109.2
Cu$_2$O(s)	−168.6	−146.0	93.1
Cu$_2$S(s)	−79.5	−86.2	120.9
Fluorine			
F(g)	79.38	62.3	158.75
F$_2$(g)	0	0	202.79
F$^-$(aq)	−335.35	−278.8	−13.8
HF(g)	−273.3	−275.4	173.8
Gold			
Au(s)	0	0	47.4
Au(g)	366.1	326.3	180.5
Helium			
He(g)	0	0	126.2
Hydrogen			
H(g)	218.0	203.3	114.7
H$^+$(aq)	0	0	0

Substance	ΔH_f°(kJ/mol)	ΔG_f°(kJ/mol)	S°(J/mol · K)
H$^+$(g)	1536.3	1517.1	108.9
H$_2$(g)	0	0	130.7
Iodine			
I(g)	106.76	70.2	180.79
I$_2$(s)	0	0	116.14
I$_2$(g)	62.42	19.3	260.69
I$^-$(aq)	−56.78	−51.57	106.45
HI(g)	26.5	1.7	206.6
Iron			
Fe(s)	0	0	27.3
Fe(g)	416.3	370.7	180.5
Fe^{2+}(aq)	−87.9	−84.94	113.4
Fe^{3+}(aq)	−47.69	−10.54	293.3
FeCO$_3$(s)	−740.6	−666.7	92.9
FeCl$_2$(s)	−341.8	−302.3	118.0
FeCl$_3$(s)	−399.5	−334.0	142.3
FeO(s)	−272.0	−255.2	60.75
Fe(OH)$_3$(s)	−823.0	−696.5	106.7
FeS$_2$(s)	−178.2	−166.9	52.9
Fe$_2$O$_3$(s)	−824.2	−742.2	87.4
Fe$_3$O$_4$(s)	−1118.4	−1015.4	146.4
Lead			
Pb(s)	0	0	64.8
Pb(g)	195.2	162.2	175.4
Pb^{2+}(aq)	0.92	−24.4	18.5
PbBr$_2$(s)	−278.7	−261.9	161.5
PbCO$_3$(s)	−699.1	−625.5	131.0
PbCl$_2$(s)	−359.4	−314.1	136.0
PbI$_2$(s)	−175.5	−173.6	174.9
Pb(NO$_3$)$_2$(s)	−451.9		
PbO(s)	−217.3	−187.9	68.7
PbO$_2$(s)	−277.4	−217.3	68.6
PbS(s)	−100.4	−98.7	91.2
PbSO$_4$(s)	−920.0	−813.0	148.5
Lithium			
Li(s)	0	0	29.1
Li(g)	159.3	126.6	138.8
Li$^+$(aq)	−278.47	−293.3	12.24
LiBr(s)	−351.2	−342.0	74.3
LiCl(s)	−408.6	−384.4	59.3
LiF(s)	−616.0	−587.7	35.7
LiI(s)	−270.4	−270.3	86.8
LiNO$_3$(s)	−483.1	−381.1	90.0
LiOH(s)	−487.5	−441.5	42.8
Li$_2$O(s)	−597.9	−561.2	37.6

(continued on the next page)

Substance	ΔH_f° (kJ/mol)	ΔG_f° (kJ/mol)	S° (J/mol · K)
Magnesium			
Mg(s)	0	0	32.7
Mg(g)	147.1	112.5	148.6
Mg^{2+}(aq)	−467.0	−455.4	−137
$MgCl_2$(s)	−641.3	−591.8	89.6
$MgCO_3$(s)	−1095.8	−1012.1	65.7
MgF_2(s)	−1124.2	−1071.1	57.2
MgO(s)	−601.6	−569.3	27.0
$Mg(OH)_2$(s)	−924.5	−833.5	63.2
$MgSO_4$(s)	−1284.9	−1170.6	91.6
Mg_3N_2(s)	−461	−401	88
Manganese			
Mn(s)	0	0	32.0
Mn(g)	280.7	238.5	173.7
Mn^{2+}(aq)	−219.4	−225.6	−78.8
MnO(s)	−385.2	−362.9	59.7
MnO_2(s)	−520.0	−465.1	53.1
MnO_4^-(aq)	−529.9	−436.2	190.6
Mercury			
Hg(l)	0	0	75.9
Hg(g)	61.4	31.8	175.0
Hg^{2+}(aq)	170.21	164.4	−36.19
Hg_2^{2+}(aq)	166.87	153.5	65.74
$HgCl_2$(s)	−224.3	−178.6	146.0
HgO(s)	−90.8	−58.5	70.3
HgS(s)	−58.2	−50.6	82.4
Hg_2Cl_2(s)	−265.4	−210.7	191.6
Nickel			
Ni(s)	0	0	29.9
Ni(g)	429.7	384.5	182.2
$NiCl_2$(s)	−305.3	−259.0	97.7
NiO(s)	−239.7	−211.7	37.99
NiS(s)	−82.0	−79.5	53.0
Nitrogen			
N(g)	472.7	455.5	153.3
N_2(g)	0	0	191.6
NF_3(g)	−132.1	−90.6	260.8
NH_3(g)	−45.9	−16.4	192.8
NH_3(aq)	−80.29	−26.50	111.3
NH_4^+(aq)	−133.26	−79.31	111.17
NH_4Br(s)	−270.8	−175.2	113.0
NH_4Cl(s)	−314.4	−202.9	94.6
NH_4CN(s)	0.4		
NH_4F(s)	−464.0	−348.7	72.0
NH_4HCO_3(s)	−849.4	−665.9	120.9
NH_4I(s)	−201.4	−112.5	117.0
NH_4NO_3(s)	−365.6	−183.9	151.1
NH_4NO_3(aq)	−339.9	−190.6	259.8

Substance	ΔH_f° (kJ/mol)	ΔG_f° (kJ/mol)	S° (J/mol · K)
HNO_3(g)	−133.9	−73.5	266.9
HNO_3(aq)	−207	−110.9	146
NO(g)	91.3	87.6	210.8
NO_2(g)	33.2	51.3	240.1
NO_3^-(aq)	−206.85	−110.2	146.70
NOBr(g)	82.2	82.4	273.7
NOCl(g)	51.7	66.1	261.7
N_2H_4(l)	50.6	149.3	121.2
N_2H_4(g)	95.4	159.4	238.5
N_2O(g)	81.6	103.7	220.0
N_2O_4(l)	−19.5	97.5	209.2
N_2O_4(g)	9.16	99.8	304.4
N_2O_5(s)	−43.1	113.9	178.2
N_2O_5(g)	13.3	117.1	355.7
Oxygen			
O(g)	249.2	231.7	161.1
O_2(g)	0	0	205.2
O_3(g)	142.7	163.2	238.9
OH^-(aq)	−230.02	−157.3	−10.90
H_2O(l)	−285.8	−237.1	70.0
H_2O(g)	−241.8	−228.6	188.8
H_2O_2(l)	−187.8	−120.4	109.6
H_2O_2(g)	−136.3	−105.6	232.7
Phosphorus			
P(s, white)	0	0	41.1
P(s, red)	−17.6	−12.1	22.8
P(g)	316.5	280.1	163.2
P_2(g)	144.0	103.5	218.1
P_4(g)	58.9	24.4	280.0
PCl_3(l)	−319.7	−272.3	217.1
PCl_3(g)	−287.0	−267.8	311.8
PCl_5(s)	−443.5		
PCl_5(g)	−374.9	−305.0	364.6
PF_5(g)	−1594.4	−1520.7	300.8
PH_3(g)	5.4	13.5	210.2
$POCl_3$(l)	−597.1	−520.8	222.5
$POCl_3$(g)	−558.5	−512.9	325.5
PO_4^{3-}(aq)	−1277.4	−1018.7	−220.5
HPO_4^{2-}(aq)	−1292.1	−1089.2	−33.5
$H_2PO_4^-$(aq)	−1296.3	−1130.2	90.4
H_3PO_4(s)	−1284.4	−1124.3	110.5
H_3PO_4(aq)	−1288.3	−1142.6	158.2
P_4O_6(s)	−1640.1		
P_4O_{10}(s)	−2984	−2698	228.9
Platinum			
Pt(s)	0	0	41.6
Pt(g)	565.3	520.5	192.4

Substance	ΔH_f°(kJ/mol)	ΔG_f°(kJ/mol)	S°(J/mol · K)
Potassium			
K(s)	0	0	64.7
K(g)	89.0	60.5	160.3
K^+(aq)	−252.14	−283.3	101.2
KBr(s)	−393.8	−380.7	95.9
KCN(s)	−113.0	−101.9	128.5
KCl(s)	−436.5	−408.5	82.6
$KClO_3$(s)	−397.7	−296.3	143.1
$KClO_4$(s)	−432.8	−303.1	151.0
KF(s)	−567.3	−537.8	66.6
KI(s)	−327.9	−324.9	106.3
KNO_3(s)	−494.6	−394.9	133.1
KOH(s)	−424.6	−379.4	81.2
KOH(aq)	−482.4	−440.5	91.6
KO_2(s)	−284.9	−239.4	116.7
K_2CO_3(s)	−1151.0	−1063.5	155.5
K_2O(s)	−361.5	−322.1	94.14
K_2O_2(s)	−494.1	−425.1	102.1
K_2SO_4(s)	−1437.8	−1321.4	175.6
Rubidium			
Rb(s)	0	0	76.8
Rb(g)	80.9	53.1	170.1
Rb^+(aq)	−251.12	−283.1	121.75
RbBr(s)	−394.6	−381.8	110.0
RbCl(s)	−435.4	−407.8	95.9
$RbClO_3$(s)	−392.4	−292.0	152
RbF(s)	−557.7		
RbI(s)	−333.8	−328.9	118.4
Scandium			
Sc(s)	0	0	34.6
Sc(g)	377.8	336.0	174.8
Selenium			
Se(s, gray)	0	0	42.4
Se(g)	227.1	187.0	176.7
H_2Se(g)	29.7	15.9	219.0
Silicon			
Si(s)	0	0	18.8
Si(g)	450.0	405.5	168.0
$SiCl_4$(l)	−687.0	−619.8	239.7
SiF_4(g)	−1615.0	−1572.8	282.8
SiH_4(g)	34.3	56.9	204.6
SiO_2(s, quartz)	−910.7	−856.3	41.5
Si_2H_6(g)	80.3	127.3	272.7
Silver			
Ag(s)	0	0	42.6
Ag(g)	284.9	246.0	173.0
Ag^+(aq)	105.79	77.11	73.45

Substance	ΔH_f°(kJ/mol)	ΔG_f°(kJ/mol)	S°(J/mol · K)
AgBr(s)	−100.4	−96.9	107.1
AgCl(s)	−127.0	−109.8	96.3
AgF(s)	−204.6	−185	84
AgI(s)	−61.8	−66.2	115.5
$AgNO_3$(s)	−124.4	−33.4	140.9
Ag_2O(s)	−31.1	−11.2	121.3
Ag_2S(s)	−32.6	−40.7	144.0
Ag_2SO_4(s)	−715.9	−618.4	200.4
Sodium			
Na(s)	0	0	51.3
Na(g)	107.5	77.0	153.7
Na^+(aq)	−240.34	−261.9	58.45
NaBr(s)	−361.1	−349.0	86.8
NaCl(s)	−411.2	−384.1	72.1
NaCl(aq)	−407.2	−393.1	115.5
$NaClO_3$(s)	−365.8	−262.3	123.4
NaF(s)	−576.6	−546.3	51.1
$NaHCO_3$(s)	−950.8	−851.0	101.7
$NaHSO_4$(s)	−1125.5	−992.8	113.0
NaI(s)	−287.8	−286.1	98.5
$NaNO_3$(s)	−467.9	−367.0	116.5
$NaNO_3$(aq)	−447.5	−373.2	205.4
NaOH(s)	−425.8	−379.7	64.4
NaOH(aq)	−470.1	−419.2	48.2
NaO_2(s)	−260.2	−218.4	115.9
Na_2CO_3(s)	−1130.7	−1044.4	135.0
Na_2O(s)	−414.2	−375.5	75.1
Na_2O_2(s)	−510.9	−447.7	95.0
Na_2SO_4(s)	−1387.1	−1270.2	149.6
Na_3PO_4(s)	−1917	−1789	173.8
Strontium			
Sr(s)	0	0	55.0
Sr(g)	164.4	130.9	164.6
Sr^{2+}(aq)	−545.51	−557.3	−39
$SrCl_2$(s)	−828.9	−781.1	114.9
$SrCO_3$(s)	−1220.1	−1140.1	97.1
SrO(s)	−592.0	−561.9	54.4
$SrSO_4$(s)	−1453.1	−1340.9	117.0
Sulfur			
S(s, rhombic)	0	0	32.1
S(s, monoclinic)	0.3	0.096	32.6
S(g)	277.2	236.7	167.8
S_2(g)	128.6	79.7	228.2
S_8(g)	102.3	49.7	430.9
S^{2-}(aq)	41.8	83.7	22
SF_6(g)	−1220.5	−1116.5	291.5
HS^-(aq)	−17.7	12.4	62.0

(continued on the next page)

Substance	ΔH_f° (kJ/mol)	ΔG_f° (kJ/mol)	S° (J/mol · K)
$H_2S(g)$	−20.6	−33.4	205.8
$H_2S(aq)$	−39.4	−27.7	122
$SOCl_2(l)$	−245.6		
$SO_2(g)$	−296.8	−300.1	248.2
$SO_3(g)$	−395.7	−371.1	256.8
$SO_4^{2-}(aq)$	−909.3	−744.6	18.5
$HSO_4^-(aq)$	−886.5	−754.4	129.5
$H_2SO_4(l)$	−814.0	−690.0	156.9
$H_2SO_4(aq)$	−909.3	−744.6	18.5
$S_2O_3^{2-}(aq)$	−648.5	−522.5	67
Tin			
$Sn(s, white)$	0	0	51.2
$Sn(s, gray)$	−2.1	0.1	44.1
$Sn(g)$	301.2	266.2	168.5
$SnCl_4(l)$	−511.3	−440.1	258.6
$SnCl_4(g)$	−471.5	−432.2	365.8
$SnO(s)$	−280.7	−251.9	57.2
$SnO_2(s)$	−577.6	−515.8	49.0
Titanium			
$Ti(s)$	0	0	30.7
$Ti(g)$	473.0	428.4	180.3
$TiCl_4(l)$	−804.2	−737.2	252.3
$TiCl_4(g)$	−763.2	−726.3	353.2

Substance	ΔH_f° (kJ/mol)	ΔG_f° (kJ/mol)	S° (J/mol · K)
$TiO_2(s)$	−944.0	−888.8	50.6
Tungsten			
$W(s)$	0	0	32.6
$W(g)$	849.4	807.1	174.0
$WO_3(s)$	−842.9	−764.0	75.9
Uranium			
$U(s)$	0	0	50.2
$U(g)$	533.0	488.4	199.8
$UF_6(s)$	−2197.0	−2068.5	227.6
$UF_6(g)$	−2147.4	−2063.7	377.9
$UO_2(s)$	−1085.0	−1031.8	77.0
Vanadium			
$V(s)$	0	0	28.9
$V(g)$	514.2	754.4	182.3
Zinc			
$Zn(s)$	0	0	41.6
$Zn(g)$	130.4	94.8	161.0
$Zn^{2+}(aq)$	−153.39	−147.1	−109.8
$ZnCl_2(s)$	−415.1	−369.4	111.5
$ZnO(s)$	−350.5	−320.5	43.7
ZnS (s, zinc blende)	−206.0	−201.3	57.7
$ZnSO_4(s)$	−982.8	−871.5	110.5

C. Aqueous Equilibrium Constants

1. Dissociation Constants for Acids at 25 °C

Name	Formula	K_{a_1}	K_{a_2}	K_{a_3}
Acetic	$HC_2H_3O_2$	1.8×10^{-5}		
Acetylsalicylic	$HC_9H_7O_4$	3.3×10^{-4}		
Adipic	$H_2C_6H_8O_4$	3.9×10^{-5}	3.9×10^{-6}	
Arsenic	H_3AsO_4	5.5×10^{-3}	1.7×10^{-7}	5.1×10^{-12}
Arsenous	H_3AsO_3	5.1×10^{-10}		
Ascorbic	$H_2C_6H_6O_6$	8.0×10^{-5}	1.6×10^{-12}	
Benzoic	$HC_7H_5O_2$	6.5×10^{-5}		
Boric	H_3BO_3	5.4×10^{-10}		
Butanoic	$HC_4H_7O_2$	1.5×10^{-5}		
Carbonic	H_2CO_3	4.3×10^{-7}	5.6×10^{-11}	
Chloroacetic	$HC_2H_2O_2Cl$	1.4×10^{-3}		
Chlorous	$HClO_2$	1.1×10^{-2}		
Citric	$H_3C_6H_5O_7$	7.4×10^{-4}	1.7×10^{-5}	4.0×10^{-7}
Cyanic	HCNO	2×10^{-4}		
Formic	$HCHO_2$	1.8×10^{-4}		
Hydrazoic	HN_3	2.5×10^{-5}		

Name	Formula	K_{a_1}	K_{a_2}	K_{a_3}
Hydrocyanic	HCN	4.9×10^{-10}		
Hydrofluoric	HF	3.5×10^{-4}		
Hydrogen chromate ion	$HCrO_4^-$	3.0×10^{-7}		
Hydrogen peroxide	H_2O_2	2.4×10^{-12}		
Hydrogen selenate ion	$HSeO_4^-$	2.2×10^{-2}		
Hydrosulfuric	H_2S	8.9×10^{-8}	1×10^{-19}	
Hydrotelluric	H_2Te	2.3×10^{23}	1.6×10^{-11}	
Hypobromous	HBrO	2.8×10^{-9}		
Hypochlorous	HClO	2.9×10^{-8}		
Hypoiodous	HIO	2.3×10^{-11}		
Iodic	HIO_3	1.7×10^{-1}		
Lactic	$HC_3H_5O_3$	1.4×10^{-4}		
Maleic	$H_2C_4H_2O_4$	1.2×10^{-2}	5.9×10^{-7}	
Malonic	$H_2C_3H_2O_4$	1.5×10^{-3}	2.0×10^{-6}	

Name	Formula	K_{a_1}	K_{a_2}	K_{a_3}
Nitrous	HNO_2	4.6×10^{-4}		
Oxalic	$H_2C_2O_4$	6.0×10^{-2}	6.1×10^{-5}	
Paraperiodic	H_5IO_6	2.8×10^{-2}	5.3×10^{-9}	
Phenol	HC_6H_5O	1.3×10^{-10}		
Phosphoric	H_3PO_4	7.5×10^{-3}	6.2×10^{-8}	4.2×10^{-13}
Phosphorous	H_3PO_3	5×10^{-2}	2.0×10^{-7}	
Propanoic	$HC_3H_5O_2$	1.3×10^{-5}		
Pyruvic	$HC_3H_3O_3$	4.1×10^{-3}		
Pyrophosphoric	$H_4P_2O_7$	1.2×10^{-1}	7.9×10^{-3}	2.0×10^{-7}

Name	Formula	K_{a_1}	K_{a_2}	K_{a_3}
Selenous	H_2SeO_3	2.4×10^{-3}	4.8×10^{-9}	
Succinic	$H_2C_4H_4O_4$	6.2×10^{-5}	2.3×10^{-6}	
Sulfuric	H_2SO_4	Strong acid	1.2×10^{-2}	
Sulfurous	H_2SO_3	1.6×10^{-2}	6.4×10^{-8}	
Tartaric	$H_2C_4H_4O_6$	1.0×10^{-3}	4.6×10^{-5}	
Trichloroacetic	$HC_2Cl_3O_2$	2.2×10^{-1}		
Trifluoroacetic acid	$HC_2F_3O_2$	3.0×10^{-1}		

2. Dissociation Constants for Hydrated Metal Ions at 25 °C

Cation	Hydrated Ion	K_a
Al^{3+}	$Al(H_2O)_6^{3+}$	1.4×10^{-5}
Be^{2+}	$Be(H_2O)_6^{2+}$	3×10^{-7}
Co^{2+}	$Co(H_2O)_6^{2+}$	1.3×10^{-9}
Cr^{3+}	$Cr(H_2O)_6^{3+}$	1.6×10^{-4}
Cu^{2+}	$Cu(H_2O)_6^{2+}$	3×10^{-8}
Fe^{2+}	$Fe(H_2O)_6^{2+}$	3.2×10^{-10}

Cation	Hydrated Ion	K_a
Fe^{3+}	$Fe(H_2O)_6^{3+}$	6.3×10^{-3}
Ni^{2+}	$Ni(H_2O)_6^{2+}$	2.5×10^{-11}
Pb^{2+}	$Pb(H_2O)_6^{2+}$	3×10^{-8}
Sn^{2+}	$Sn(H_2O)_6^{2+}$	4×10^{-4}
Zn^{2+}	$Zn(H_2O)_6^{2+}$	2.5×10^{-10}

3. Dissociation Constants for Bases at 25 °C

Name	Formula	K_b
Ammonia	NH_3	1.76×10^{-5}
Aniline	$C_6H_5NH_2$	3.9×10^{-10}
Bicarbonate ion	HCO_3^-	2.3×10^{-8}
Carbonate ion	CO_3^{2-}	1.8×10^{-4}
Codeine	$C_{18}H_{21}NO_3$	1.6×10^{-6}
Diethylamine	$(C_2H_5)_2NH$	6.9×10^{-4}
Dimethylamine	$(CH_3)_2NH$	5.4×10^{-4}
Ethylamine	$C_2H_5NH_2$	5.6×10^{-4}
Ethylenediamine	$C_2H_8N_2$	8.3×10^{-5}
Hydrazine	H_2NNH_2	1.3×10^{-6}
Hydroxylamine	$HONH_2$	1.1×10^{-8}

Name	Formula	K_b
Ketamine	$C_{13}H_{16}ClNO$	3×10^{-7}
Methylamine	CH_3NH_2	4.4×10^{-4}
Morphine	$C_{17}H_{19}NO_3$	1.6×10^{-6}
Nicotine	$C_{10}H_{14}N_2$	1.0×10^{-6}
Piperidine	$C_5H_{10}NH$	1.33×10^{-3}
Propylamine	$C_3H_7NH_2$	3.5×10^{-4}
Pyridine	C_5H_5N	1.7×10^{-9}
Strychnine	$C_{21}H_{22}N_2O_2$	1.8×10^{-6}
Triethylamine	$(C_2H_5)_3N$	5.6×10^{-4}
Trimethylamine	$(CH_3)_3N$	6.4×10^{-5}

4. Solubility Product Constants for Compounds at 25 °C

Compound	Formula	K_{sp}
Aluminum hydroxide	$Al(OH)_3$	1.3×10^{-33}
Aluminum phosphate	$AlPO_4$	9.84×10^{-21}
Barium carbonate	$BaCO_3$	2.58×10^{-9}
Barium chromate	$BaCrO_4$	1.17×10^{-10}
Barium fluoride	BaF_2	2.45×10^{-5}
Barium hydroxide	$Ba(OH)_2$	5.0×10^{-3}
Barium oxalate	BaC_2O_4	1.6×10^{-6}
Barium phosphate	$Ba_3(PO_4)_2$	6×10^{-39}
Barium sulfate	$BaSO_4$	1.07×10^{-10}

Compound	Formula	K_{sp}
Cadmium carbonate	$CdCO_3$	1.0×10^{-12}
Cadmium hydroxide	$Cd(OH)_2$	7.2×10^{-15}
Cadmium sulfide	CdS	8×10^{-28}
Calcium carbonate	$CaCO_3$	4.96×10^{-9}
Calcium chromate	$CaCrO_4$	7.1×10^{-4}
Calcium fluoride	CaF_2	1.46×10^{-10}
Calcium hydroxide	$Ca(OH)_2$	4.68×10^{-6}
Calcium hydrogen phosphate	$CaHPO_4$	1×10^{-7}

(continued on the next page)

Compound	Formula	K_{sp}
Calcium oxalate	CaC_2O_4	2.32×10^{-9}
Calcium phosphate	$Ca_3(PO_4)_2$	2.07×10^{-33}
Calcium sulfate	$CaSO_4$	7.10×10^{-5}
Chromium(III) hydroxide	$Cr(OH)_3$	6.3×10^{-31}
Cobalt(II) carbonate	$CoCO_3$	1.0×10^{-10}
Cobalt(II) hydroxide	$Co(OH)_2$	5.92×10^{-15}
Cobalt(II) sulfide	CoS	5×10^{-22}
Copper(I) bromide	$CuBr$	6.27×10^{-9}
Copper(I) chloride	$CuCl$	1.72×10^{-7}
Copper(I) cyanide	$CuCN$	3.47×10^{-20}
Copper(II) carbonate	$CuCO_3$	2.4×10^{-10}
Copper(II) hydroxide	$Cu(OH)_2$	2.2×10^{-20}
Copper(II) phosphate	$Cu_3(PO_4)_2$	1.40×10^{-37}
Copper(II) sulfide	CuS	1.27×10^{-36}
Iron(II) carbonate	$FeCO_3$	3.07×10^{-11}
Iron(II) hydroxide	$Fe(OH)_2$	4.87×10^{-17}
Iron(II) sulfide	FeS	3.72×10^{-19}
Iron(III) hydroxide	$Fe(OH)_3$	2.79×10^{-39}
Lanthanum fluoride	LaF_3	2×10^{-19}
Lanthanum iodate	$La(IO_3)_3$	7.50×10^{-12}
Lead(II) bromide	$PbBr_2$	4.67×10^{-6}
Lead(II) carbonate	$PbCO_3$	7.40×10^{-14}
Lead(II) chloride	$PbCl_2$	1.17×10^{-5}
Lead(II) chromate	$PbCrO_4$	2.8×10^{-13}
Lead(II) fluoride	PbF_2	3.3×10^{-8}
Lead(II) hydroxide	$Pb(OH)_2$	1.43×10^{-20}
Lead(II) iodide	PbI_2	9.8×10^{-9}
Lead(II) phosphate	$Pb_3(PO_4)_2$	1×10^{-54}
Lead(II) sulfate	$PbSO_4$	1.82×10^{-8}
Lead(II) sulfide	PbS	9.04×10^{-29}
Magnesium carbonate	$MgCO_3$	6.82×10^{-6}
Magnesium fluoride	MgF_2	5.16×10^{-11}
Magnesium hydroxide	$Mg(OH)_2$	2.06×10^{-13}
Magnesium oxalate	MgC_2O_4	4.83×10^{-6}

Compound	Formula	K_{sp}
Manganese(II) carbonate	$MnCO_3$	2.24×10^{-11}
Manganese(II) hydroxide	$Mn(OH)_2$	1.6×10^{-13}
Manganese(II) sulfide	MnS	2.3×10^{-13}
Mercury(I) bromide	Hg_2Br_2	6.40×10^{-23}
Mercury(I) carbonate	Hg_2CO_3	3.6×10^{-17}
Mercury(I) chloride	Hg_2Cl_2	1.43×10^{-18}
Mercury(I) chromate	Hg_2CrO_4	2×10^{-9}
Mercury(I) cyanide	$Hg_2(CN)_2$	5×10^{-40}
Mercury(I) iodide	Hg_2I_2	5.2×10^{-29}
Mercury(II) hydroxide	$Hg(OH)_2$	3.1×10^{-26}
Mercury(II) sulfide	HgS	1.6×10^{-54}
Nickel(II) carbonate	$NiCO_3$	1.42×10^{-7}
Nickel(II) hydroxide	$Ni(OH)_2$	5.48×10^{-16}
Nickel(II) sulfide	NiS	3×10^{-20}
Silver bromate	$AgBrO_3$	5.38×10^{-5}
Silver bromide	$AgBr$	5.35×10^{-13}
Silver carbonate	Ag_2CO_3	8.46×10^{-12}
Silver chloride	$AgCl$	1.77×10^{-10}
Silver chromate	Ag_2CrO_4	1.12×10^{-12}
Silver cyanide	$AgCN$	5.97×10^{-17}
Silver iodide	AgI	8.51×10^{-17}
Silver phosphate	Ag_3PO_4	8.89×10^{-17}
Silver sulfate	Ag_2SO_4	1.20×10^{-5}
Silver sulfide	Ag_2S	6×10^{-51}
Strontium carbonate	$SrCO_3$	5.60×10^{-10}
Strontium chromate	$SrCrO_4$	3.6×10^{-5}
Strontium phosphate	$Sr_3(PO_4)_2$	1×10^{-31}
Strontium sulfate	$SrSO_4$	3.44×10^{-7}
Tin(II) hydroxide	$Sn(OH)_2$	5.45×10^{-27}
Tin(II) sulfide	SnS	1×10^{-26}
Zinc carbonate	$ZnCO_3$	1.46×10^{-10}
Zinc hydroxide	$Zn(OH)_2$	3×10^{-17}
Zinc oxalate	ZnC_2O_4	2.7×10^{-8}
Zinc sulfide	ZnS	2×10^{-25}

5. Complex Ion Formation Constants in Water at 25 °C

Complex Ion	K_f
$[Ag(CN)_2]^-$	1×10^{21}
$[Ag(EDTA)]^{3-}$	2.1×10^{7}
$[Ag(en)_2]^+$	5.0×10^{7}
$[Ag(NH_3)_2]^+$	1.7×10^{7}
$[Ag(SCN)_4]^{3-}$	1.2×10^{10}
$[Ag(S_2O_3)_2]^-$	2.8×10^{13}
$[Al(EDTA)]^-$	1.3×10^{16}
$[AlF_6]^{3-}$	7×10^{19}

Complex Ion	K_f
$[Al(OH)_4]^-$	3×10^{33}
$[Al(ox)_3]^{3-}$	2×10^{16}
$[CdBr_4]^{2-}$	5.5×10^{3}
$[Cd(CN)_4]^{2-}$	3×10^{18}
$[CdCl_4]^{2-}$	6.3×10^{2}
$[Cd(en)_3]^{2+}$	1.2×10^{12}
$[CdI_4]^{2-}$	2×10^{6}
$[Co(EDTA)]^{2-}$	2.0×10^{16}

Complex Ion	K_f
$[Co(EDTA)]^-$	1×10^{36}
$[Co(en)_3]^{2+}$	8.7×10^{13}
$[Co(en)_3]^{3+}$	4.9×10^{48}
$[Co(NH_3)_6]^{2+}$	1.3×10^5
$[Co(NH_3)_6]^{3+}$	2.3×10^{33}
$[Co(OH)_4]^{2-}$	5×10^9
$[Co(ox)_3]^{4-}$	5×10^9
$[Co(ox)_3]^{3-}$	1×10^{20}
$[Co(SCN)_4]^{2-}$	1×10^3
$[Cr(EDTA)]^-$	1×10^{23}
$[Cr(OH)_4]^-$	8.0×10^{29}
$[CuCl_3]^{2-}$	5×10^5
$[Cu(CN)_4]^{2-}$	1.0×10^{25}
$[Cu(EDTA)]^{2-}$	5×10^{18}
$[Cu(en)_2]^{2+}$	1×10^{20}
$[Cu(NH_3)_4]^{2+}$	1.7×10^{13}
$[Cu(ox)_2]^{2-}$	3×10^8
$[Fe(CN)_6]^{4-}$	1.5×10^{35}
$[Fe(CN)_6]^{3-}$	2×10^{43}
$[Fe(EDTA)]^{2-}$	2.1×10^{14}
$[Fe(EDTA)]^-$	1.7×10^{24}
$[Fe(en)_3]^{2+}$	5.0×10^9
$[Fe(ox)_3]^{4-}$	1.7×10^5
$[Fe(ox)_3]^{3-}$	2×10^{20}
$[Fe(SCN)]^{2+}$	8.9×10^2
$[Hg(CN)_4]^{2-}$	1.8×10^{41}

Complex Ion	K_f
$[HgCl_4]^{2-}$	1.1×10^{16}
$[Hg(EDTA)]^{2-}$	6.3×10^{21}
$[Hg(en)_2]^{2+}$	2×10^{23}
$[HgI_4]^{2-}$	2×10^{30}
$[Hg(ox)_2]^{2-}$	9.5×10^6
$[Ni(CN)_4]^{2-}$	2×10^{31}
$[Ni(EDTA)]^{2-}$	3.6×10^{18}
$[Ni(en)_3]^{2+}$	2.1×10^{18}
$[Ni(NH_3)_6]^{2+}$	2.0×10^8
$[Ni(ox)_3]^{4-}$	3×10^8
$[PbCl_3]^-$	2.4×10^1
$[Pb(EDTA)]^{2-}$	2×10^{18}
$[PbI_4]^{2-}$	3.0×10^4
$[Pb(OH)_3]^-$	8×10^{13}
$[Pb(ox)_2]^{2-}$	3.5×10^6
$[Pb(S_2O_3)_3]^{4-}$	2.2×10^6
$[PtCl_4]^{2-}$	1×10^{16}
$[Pt(NH_3)_6]^{2+}$	2×10^{35}
$[Sn(OH)_3]^-$	3×10^{25}
$[Zn(CN)_4]^{2-}$	2.1×10^{19}
$[Zn(EDTA)]^{2-}$	3×10^{16}
$[Zn(en)_3]^{2+}$	1.3×10^{14}
$[Zn(NH_3)_4]^{2+}$	2.8×10^9
$[Zn(OH)_4]^{2-}$	2×10^{15}
$[Zn(ox)_3]^{4-}$	1.4×10^8

D. Standard Electrode Potentials at 25 °C

Half-Reaction	$E°$(V)
$F_2(g) + 2\,e^- \longrightarrow 2\,F^-(aq)$	2.87
$O_3(g) + 2\,H^+(aq) + 2\,e^- \longrightarrow O_2(g) + H_2(l)$	2.08
$Ag^{2+}(aq) + e^- \longrightarrow Ag^+(aq)$	1.98
$Co^{3+}(aq) + e^- \longrightarrow Co^{2+}(aq)$	1.82
$H_2O_2(aq) + 2\,H^+(aq) + 2\,e^- \longrightarrow 2\,H_2O(l)$	1.78
$PbO_2(s) + 4\,H^+(aq) + SO_4^{2-}(aq) + 2\,e^- \longrightarrow$ $PbSO_4(s) + 2\,H_2O(l)$	1.69
$MnO_4^-(aq) + 4\,H^+(aq) + 3\,e^- \longrightarrow MnO_2(s) + 2\,H_2O(l)$	1.68
$2\,HClO(aq) + 2\,H^+(aq) + 2\,e^- \longrightarrow Cl_2(g) + 2\,H_2O(l)$	1.61
$MnO_4^-(aq) + 8\,H^+(aq) + 5\,e^- \longrightarrow Mn^{2+}(aq) + 4\,H_2O(l)$	1.51
$Au^{3+}(aq) + 3\,e^- \longrightarrow Au(s)$	1.50
$2\,BrO_3^-(aq) + 12\,H^+(aq) + 10e^- \longrightarrow Br_2(l) + 6\,H_2O(l)$	1.48
$PbO_2(s) + 4\,H^+(aq) + 2\,e^- \longrightarrow Pb^{2+}(aq) + 2\,H_2O(l)$	1.46

Half-Reaction	$E°$(V)
$Cl_2(g) + 2\,e^- \longrightarrow 2\,Cl^-(aq)$	1.36
$Cr_2O_7^{2-}(aq) + 14\,H^+(aq) + 6\,e^- \longrightarrow$ $2\,Cr^{3+}(aq) + 7\,H_2O(l)$	1.33
$O_2(g) + 4\,H^+(aq) + 4\,e^- \longrightarrow 2\,H_2O(l)$	1.23
$MnO_2(s) + 4\,H^+(aq) + 2\,e^- \longrightarrow Mn^{2+}(aq) + 2\,H_2O(l)$	1.21
$IO_3^-(aq) + 6\,H^+(aq) + 5\,e^- \longrightarrow \frac{1}{2}I_2(aq) + 3\,H_2O(l)$	1.20
$Br_2(l) + 2\,e^- \longrightarrow 2\,Br^-(aq)$	1.09
$AuCl_4^-(aq) + 3\,e^- \longrightarrow Au(s) + 4\,Cl^-(aq)$	1.00
$VO_2^+(aq) + 2\,H^+(aq) + e^- \longrightarrow VO^{2+}(aq) + H_2O(l)$	1.00
$HNO_2(aq) + H^+(aq) + e^- \longrightarrow NO(g) + 2\,H_2O(l)$	0.98
$NO_3^-(aq) + 4\,H^+(aq) + 3\,e^- \longrightarrow NO(g) + 2\,H_2O(l)$	0.96
$ClO_2(g) + e^- \longrightarrow ClO_2^-(aq)$	0.95
$2\,Hg^{2+}(aq) + 2\,e^- \longrightarrow 2\,Hg_2^{2+}(aq)$	0.92

(continued on the next page)

Half-Reaction	$E°(V)$
$Ag^+(aq) + e^- \longrightarrow Ag(s)$	0.80
$Hg_2^{2+}(aq) + 2\,e^- \longrightarrow 2\,Hg(l)$	0.80
$Fe^{3+}(aq) + e^- \longrightarrow Fe^{2+}(aq)$	0.77
$PtCl_4^{2-}(aq) + 2\,e^- \longrightarrow Pt(s) + 4\,Cl^-(aq)$	0.76
$O_2(g) + 2\,H^+(aq) + 2\,e^- \longrightarrow H_2O_2(aq)$	0.70
$MnO_4^-(aq) + e^- \longrightarrow MnO_4^{2-}(aq)$	0.56
$I_2(s) + 2\,e^- \longrightarrow 2\,I^-(aq)$	0.54
$Cu^+(aq) + e^- \longrightarrow Cu(s)$	0.52
$O_2(g) + 2\,H_2O(l) + 4\,e^- \longrightarrow 4\,OH^-(aq)$	0.40
$Cu^{2+}(aq) + 2\,e^- \longrightarrow Cu(s)$	0.34
$BiO^+(aq) + 2\,H^+(aq) + 3\,e^- \longrightarrow Bi(s) + H_2O(l)$	0.32
$Hg_2Cl_2(s) + 2\,e^- \longrightarrow 2\,Hg(l) + 2\,Cl^-(aq)$	0.27
$AgCl(s) + e^- \longrightarrow Ag(s) + Cl^-(aq)$	0.22
$SO_4^{2-}(aq) + 4\,H^+(aq) + 2\,e^- \longrightarrow H_2SO_3(aq) + H_2O(l)$	0.20
$Cu^{2+}(aq) + e^- \longrightarrow Cu^+(aq)$	0.16
$Sn^{4+}(aq) + 2\,e^- \longrightarrow Sn^{2+}(aq)$	0.15
$S(s) + 2\,H^+(aq) + 2\,e^- \longrightarrow H_2S(g)$	0.14
$AgBr(s) + e^- \longrightarrow Ag(s) + Br^-(aq)$	0.071
$2\,H^+(aq) + 2\,e^- \longrightarrow H_2(g)$	0.00
$Fe^{3+}(aq) + 3\,e^- \longrightarrow Fe(s)$	-0.036
$Pb^{2+}(aq) + 2\,e^- \longrightarrow Pb(s)$	-0.13
$Sn^{2+}(aq) + 2\,e^- \longrightarrow Sn(s)$	-0.14

Half-Reaction	$E°(V)$
$AgI(s) + e^- \longrightarrow Ag(s) + I^-(aq)$	-0.15
$N_2(g) + 5\,H^+(aq) + 4\,e^- \longrightarrow N_2H_5^+(aq)$	-0.23
$Ni^{2+}(aq) + 2\,e^- \longrightarrow Ni(s)$	-0.23
$Co^{2+}(aq) + 2\,e^- \longrightarrow Co(s)$	-0.28
$PbSO_4(s) + 2\,e^- \longrightarrow Pb(s) + SO_4^{2-}(aq)$	-0.36
$Cd^{2+}(aq) + 2\,e^- \longrightarrow Cd(s)$	-0.40
$Fe^{2+}(aq) + 2\,e^- \longrightarrow Fe(s)$	-0.45
$2\,CO_2(g) + 2\,H^+(aq) + 2\,e^- \longrightarrow H_2C_2O_4(aq)$	-0.49
$Cr^{3+}(aq) + e^- \longrightarrow Cr^{2+}(aq)$	-0.50
$Cr^{3+}(aq) + 3\,e^- \longrightarrow Cr(s)$	-0.73
$Zn^{2+}(aq) + 2\,e^- \longrightarrow Zn(s)$	-0.76
$2\,H_2O(l) + 2\,e^- \longrightarrow H_2(g) + 2\,OH^-(aq)$	-0.83
$Mn^{2+}(aq) + 2\,e^- \longrightarrow Mn(s)$	-1.18
$Al^{3+}(aq) + 3\,e^- \longrightarrow Al(s)$	-1.66
$H_2(g) + 2\,e^- \longrightarrow 2\,H^-(aq)$	-2.23
$Mg^{2+}(aq) + 2\,e^- \longrightarrow Mg(s)$	-2.37
$La^{3+}(aq) + 3\,e^- \longrightarrow La(s)$	-2.38
$Na^+(aq) + e^- \longrightarrow Na(s)$	-2.71
$Ca^{2+}(aq) + 2\,e^- \longrightarrow Ca(s)$	-2.76
$Ba^{2+}(aq) + 2\,e^- \longrightarrow Ba(s)$	-2.90
$K^+(aq) + e^- \longrightarrow K(s)$	-2.92
$Li^+(aq) + e^- \longrightarrow Li(s)$	-3.04

E. Vapor Pressure of Water at Various Temperatures

T (°C)	P (torr)	T (°C)	P (torr)	T (°C)	P (torr)	T (°C)	P (torr)
0	4.58	21	18.65	35	42.2	92	567.0
5	6.54	22	19.83	40	55.3	94	610.9
10	9.21	23	21.07	45	71.9	96	657.6
12	10.52	24	22.38	50	92.5	98	707.3
14	11.99	25	23.76	55	118.0	100	760.0
16	13.63	26	25.21	60	149.4	102	815.9
17	14.53	27	26.74	65	187.5	104	875.1
18	15.48	28	28.35	70	233.7	106	937.9
19	16.48	29	30.04	80	355.1	108	1004.4
20	17.54	30	31.82	90	525.8	110	1074.6

Appendix III:
Answers to Selected Exercises

Chapter 1

33. a. theory   **b.** observation
c. law   **d.** observation
35. Several answers possible.
37. a. mixture, homogeneous
b. pure substance, compound
c. pure substance, element
d. mixture, heterogeneous

39.

Substance	Pure or Mixture	Type
Aluminum	Pure	Element
Apple juice	Mixture	Homogeneous
Hydrogen peroxide	Pure	Compound
Chicken soup	Mixture	Heterogeneous

41. a. pure substance, compound
b. mixture, heterogeneous
c. mixture, homogeneous
d. pure substance, element
43. physical, chemical, physical, physical, physical
45. a. chemical   **b.** physical
c. physical   **d.** chemical
47. a. chemical   **b.** physical
c. chemical   **d.** chemical
49. a. physical   **b.** chemical   **c.** physical
51. a. 0 °C   **b.** −321 °F
c. −78.3 °F   **d.** 310.2 K
53. −62.2 °C, 210.9 K
55. a. 1.2 nm   **b.** 22 fs
c. 1.5 Gg   **d.** 3.5 ML
57. a. 4.5×10^{-9} s   **b.** 1.8×10^{-14} s
c. 1.28×10^{-10} m   **d.** 3.5×10^{-5} m

59.

1245 kg	1.245×10^6 g	1.245×10^9 mg
515 km	5.15×10^6 dm	5.15×10^7 cm
122.355 s	1.22355×10^5 ms	0.122355 ks
3.345 kJ	3.345×10^3 J	3.345×10^6 mJ

61. a. 254.998 km   **b.** 2.54998×10^{-1} Mm
c. 254998×10^3 mm   **d.** 254998×10^2 cm
63. 10,000 1 cm squares
65. no
67. 1.26 g/cm^3
69. a. 463 g   **b.** 3.7 L
71. $201. \times 10^3$ g
73. a. 73.7 mL   **b.** 88.3 °C   **c.** 647 mL
75. a. 1,050,501   **b.** 0.00$\underline{2}$0
c. 0.0000000000000$\underline{2}$ **d.** 0.001$\underline{0}$90
77. a. 3   **b.** ambiguous, without more information
       assume three significant figures
c. 3   **d.** 5
e. ambiguous, without more information assume one significant figure

79. a. not exact   **b.** exact
c. not exact   **d.** exact
81. a. 156.9   **b.** 156.8
c. 156.8   **d.** 156.9
83. a. 1.84   **b.** 0.033
c. 0.500   **d.** 34
85. a. 41.4   **b.** 133.5
c. 73.0   **d.** 0.42
87. a. 391.3   **b.** 1.1×10^4
c. 5.96   **d.** 5.93×10^4
89. a. 2.78×10^4 cm^3 **b.** 1.898×10^{-3} kg
c. 1.98×10^7 cm
91. a. 60.6 in   **b.** 3.14×10^3 g
c. 3.7 qt   **d.** 4.29 in
93. 5.0×10^1 min
95. 4.0×10^1 mi/gal
97. a. 1.95×10^{-4} km^2 **b.** 1.95×10^4 dm^2
c. 1.95×10^6 cm^2
99. 0.680 mi^2
101. 0.95 mL
103. 3.1557×10^7 s/solar year
105. a. extensive   **b.** intensive
c. intensive   **d.** intensive
e. extensive
107. −34 °F
109. $F = \text{kg}(\text{m/s}^2) = $ N (for newton), kN, pN
111. a. 2.2×10^{-6}
b. 0.0159
c. 6.9×10^4
113. a. mass of can of gold $= 1.9 \times 10^4$ g
      mass of can of sand $= 3.0 \times 10^3$ g
b. Yes, the thief sets off the trap because the can of sand is lighter than the gold cylinder.
115. 22 in^3
117. 7.6 g/cm^3
119. 3.11×10^5 lb
121. 3.3×10^2 km
123. 6.8×10^{-15}
125. 2.4×10^{19} km
127. 488 grams
129. 0.661 Ω
131. 0.492
133. 18.2 atm
135. 1 J = 1 kg m^2/s^2
     $m = $ kg, $v^2 = $ (m/s)^2 $mv = $ kg m^2/s^2
     $P = $ N/m$^2 = $ kg m/s^2/m$^2 = $ kg/m s^2
     $V = $ m^3 $PV = $ kg m^3/m s$^2 = $ kg m^2/s^2
137. 9.0×10^1 mg CO
139. 13% increase

141. No. Since the container is sealed the atoms and molecules can move around, but they cannot leave. If no atoms or molecules can leave, the mass must be constant.

143. 343 1 cm cubes

145. a. the dark block   **b.** the light-colored block
c. cannot tell

147. a. law   **b.** theory
c. observation   **d.** law

Chapter 2

29. 13.5 g

31. These results are not consistent with the law of definite proportions because sample 1 is composed of 11.5 parts Cl to 1 part C and sample 2 is composed of 9.05 parts Cl to 1 part C. The law of definite proportions states that a given compound always contains exactly the same proportion of elements by mass.

33. 23.8 g

35. For the law of multiple proportions to hold, the ratio of the masses of O combining with 1 g of O's in the compound should be a small whole number.
$0.3369/0.168 = 2.00$

37. Sample 1: 1.00 g $O_2/1.00$ g S;
Sample 2: 1.50 g $O_2/1.00$ g S
Sample 2/sample 1 $= 1.50/1.00 = 1.50$
3 O atoms/2 O atoms $= 1.5$

39. a. not consistent
b. consistent: Dalton's atomic theory states that the atoms of a given element are identical.
c. consistent: Dalton's atomic theory states that atoms combine in simple whole-number ratios to form compounds.
d. not consistent

41. a. consistent: Rutherford's nuclear model states that the atom is largely empty space.
b. consistent: Rutherford's nuclear model states that most of the atom's mass is concentrated in a tiny region called the nucleus.
c. not consistent   **d.** not consistent

43. -2.3×10^{-19} C

45. 9.4×10^{13} excess electrons, 8.5×10^{-17} kg

47. a, b, c

49. 1.83×10^3 e$^-$

51. a. Ag-107   **b.** Ag-109
c. U-238   **d.** H-2

53. a. 7 $^1_1$p and 7 $^0_1$n   **b.** 11 $^1_1$p and 12 $^0_1$n
c. 86 $^1_1$p and 136 $^0_1$n   **d.** 82 $^1_1$p and 126 $^0_1$n

55. 6 $^1_1$p and 8 $^1_0$n, $^{14}_6$C

57. a. 28 $^1_1$p and 26 e$^-$ **b.** 16 $^1_1$p and 18 e$^-$
c. 35 $^1_1$p and 36 e$^-$ **d.** 24 $^1_1$p and 21 e$^-$

59. a. 2$-$ **b.** 1+
c. 3+   **d.** 1+

61.

Symbol	Ion Formed	Number of Electrons in Ion	Number of Protons in Ion
Ca	Ca^{2+}	18	20
Be	Be^{2+}	2	4
Se	Se^{2-}	36	34
In	In^{3+}	46	49

63. a. potassium, metal   **b.** barium, metal
c. iodine, nonmetal   **d.** oxygen, nonmetal
e. antimony, metalloid

65. a and **b** are main group elements.

67. a. alkali metal   **b.** halogen
c. alkaline earth metal   **d.** alkaline earth metal
e. noble gas

69. Cl and F because they are in the same group or family. Elements in the same group or family have similar chemical properties.

71.

73. The fluorine-19 isotope must have a large percent abundance, which would make fluorine produce a large peak at this mass. Chlorine has two isotopes (Cl-35 and Cl-37). The atomic mass is simply the weighted average of these two, which means that there is no chlorine isotope with a mass of 35.45 amu.

75. 121.8 amu, Sb

77. Br-79 78.92, amu 50.96%

79. 152 amu

81. 3.32×10^{24} atoms

83. a. 0.295 mol Ar   **b.** 0.0543 mol Zn
c. 0.144 mol Ta   **d.** 0.0304 mol Li

85. 2.11×10^{22} atoms

87. a. 1.01×10^{23} atoms   **b.** 6.78×10^{21} atoms
c. 5.39×10^{21} atoms   **d.** 5.6×10^{20} atoms

89. a. 36 grams   **b.** 0.187 grams
c. 62 grams   **d.** 3.1 grams

91. 2.6×10^{21} atoms

93. 3.239×10^{-22} g

95. 1.50 g

97. C_2O_3

99. 4.82241×10^7 C/kg

101. 207 amu

103. ^{237}Pa, ^{238}U, ^{239}Np, ^{240}Pu, ^{235}Ac, ^{234}Ra, etc.

105.

Symbol	Z	A	#p	#e$^-$	#n	Charge
O	8	16	8	10	8	2$-$
Ca^{2+}	20	40	20	18	20	2+
Mg^{2+}	12	25	12	10	13	2+
N^{3-}	7	14	7	10	7	3$-$

107. $V_n = 8.2 \times 10^{-8}$ pm^3, $V_a = 1.4 \times 10^6$ pm^3, 5.9×10^{-12}%

109. 6.022×10^{21} dollars total, 9.3×10^{11} dollars per person, billionaires

111. 15.985 amu

113. 4.76×10^{24} atoms

115. Li$-6 = 7.494$%, Li$-7 = 92.506$%

117. 75.0% gold

119. 106.91 amu

121. 1.66×10^{22} gold atoms

123. 1×10^{78} atoms/universe

125. 0.423

127. 63.67 g/mol

129. 25.06 g/mol

131.   Li-6   Li-7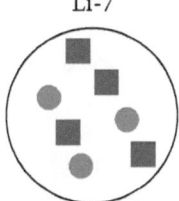

133. If the amu and mole were not based on the same isotope, the numerical values obtained for an atom of material and a mole of material would not be the same. If, for example, the mole was based on the number of particles in C-12 but the amu was changed to a fraction of the mass of an atom of Ne-20, the number of particles and the number of amu that make up one mole of material would no longer be the same. We would no longer have the relationship in which the mass of an atom in amu is numerically equal to the mass of a mole of those atoms in grams.

135. The different isotopes of the same element have the same number of protons and electrons, so the attractive forces between the nucleus and the electrons are constant and there is no difference in the radii of the isotopes. Ions, on the other hand, have a different number of electrons than the parent atom from which they are derived. Cations have fewer electrons than the parent atom. The attractive forces are greater because there is a larger positive charge in the nucleus than the negative charge in the electron cloud. So, cations are smaller than the atom they are derived from. Anions have more electrons than the parent. The electron cloud has a greater negative charge than the nucleus, so the anions have larger radii than the parent.

Chapter 3

23. a. 3 Mg, 2 P, 8 O   **b.** 1 Ba, 2 Cl
c. 1 Fe, 2 N, 4 O   **d.** 1 Ca, 2 O, 2 H

25. a. NH$_3$ **b.** C$_2$H$_6$ **c.** SO$_3$

27. a. atomic   **b.** molecular
c. atomic   **d.** molecular

29. a. molecular   **b.** ionic
c. ionic   **d.** molecular

31. a. molecular element   **b.** molecular compound
c. atomic element

33. a. CaO   **b.** ZnS
c. RbBr   **d.** Al$_2$O$_3$

35. a. Ca(OH)$_2$ **b.** CaCrO$_4$
c. Ca$_3$(PO$_4$)$_2$ **d.** Ca(CN)$_2$

37. a. magnesium nitride   **b.** potassium fluoride
c. sodium oxide   **d.** lithium sulfide
e. cesium fluoride   **f.** potassium iodide

39. a. tin(II) oxide   **b.** chromium(III) sulfide
c. rubidium iodide   **d.** barium bromide

41. a. copper(I) nitrite   **b.** magnesium acetate
c. barium nitrate   **d.** lead(II) acetate

43. a. NaHSO$_3$ **b.** LiMnO$_4$
c. AgNO$_3$ **d.** K$_2$SO$_4$
e. RbHSO$_4$ **f.** KHCO$_3$

45. a. cobalt(II) sulfate heptahydrate
b. IrBr$_3 \cdot 4$ H$_2$O
c. Magnesium bromate hexahydrate
d. K$_2$CO$_3 \cdot 2$ H$_2$O

47. a. carbon monoxide   **b.** nitrogen triiodide
c. silicon tetrachloride   **d.** tetranitrogen tetraselenide

49. a. PCl$_3$ **b.** ClO
c. S$_2$F$_4$ **d.** PF$_5$

51. a. hydroiodic acid   **b.** nitric acid
c. carbonic acid

53. a. HF   **b.** HBr   **c.** H$_2$SO$_3$

55. a. strontium chloride
b. tin(IV) oxide
c. diphosphorus pentasulfide
d. acetic acid

57. a. potassium chlorate   **b.** diiodine pentoxide
c. lead(II) sulfate

59. a. 46.01 amu   **b.** 58.12 amu
c. 180.16 amu   **d.** 238.03 amu

61. a. 0.471 mol   **b.** 0.0362 mol
c. 968 mol   **d.** 0.279 mol

63. a. 0.554 mol   **b.** 28.4 mol
c. 0.378 mol   **d.** 1093 mol

65. a. 2.2×10^{23} molecules
b. 7.06×10^{23} molecules
c. 4.16×10^{23} molecules
d. 1.09×10^{23} molecules

67. a. 0.0790 g   **b.** 0.84 g   **c.** 2.992×10^{-22} g

69. 0.10 mg

71. a. 74.87% C   **b.** 79.88% C
c. 92.24% C   **d.** 37.23% C

73. NH$_3$: 82.27% N
CO(NH$_2$)$_2$: 46.65% N
NH$_4$NO$_3$: 35.00% N
(NH$_4$)$_2$SO$_4$: 21.20% N
NH$_3$ has the highest N content

75. 20.8 g F

77. 196 μg KI

79. a. 2 : 1   **b.** 4 : 1   **c.** 6 : 2 : 1

81. a. 0.885 mol H   **b.** 5.2 mol H
c. 29 mol H   **d.** 33.7 mol H

83. a. 3.3 g Na   **b.** 3.6 g Na
c. 1.4 g Na   **d.** 1.7 g Na

85. a. Ag$_2$O   **b.** Co$_3$As$_2$O$_8$ **c.** SeBr$_4$

87. a. C_5H_7N **b.** $C_4H_5N_2O$

89. $C_{13}H_{18}O_2$

91. NCl_3

93. a. $C_{12}H_{14}N_2$ **b.** $C_6H_3Cl_3$
     c. $C_{10}H_{20}N_2S_4$

95. CH_2

97. C_2H_4O

99. $2\ SO_2(g) + O_2(g) + 2\ H_2O(l) \longrightarrow 2\ H_2SO_4(aq)$

101. $2\ Na(s) + 2\ H_2O(l) \longrightarrow H_2(g) + 2\ NaOH(aq)$

103. $C_{12}H_{22}O_{11}(s) + H_2O(l) \longrightarrow 4\ C_2H_5OH(aq) + 4\ CO_2(g)$

105. a. $PbS(s) + 2\ HBr(aq) \longrightarrow PbBr_2(s) + H_2S(g)$
     b. $CO(g) + 3\ H_2(g) \longrightarrow CH_4(g) + H_2O(l)$
     c. $4\ HCl(aq) + MnO_2(s) \longrightarrow$
                   $MnCl_2(aq) + 2\ H_2O(l) + Cl_2(g)$
     d. $C_5H_{12}(l) + 8\ O_2(g) \longrightarrow 5\ CO_2(g) + 6\ H_2O(g)$

107. $Na_2CO_3(aq) + CuCl_2(aq) \longrightarrow CuCO_3(s) + 2\ NaCl(aq)$

109. a. $2\ CO_2(g) + CaSiO_3(s) + H_2O(l) \longrightarrow$
                   $SiO_2(s) + Ca(HCO_3)_2(aq)$
     b. $2\ Co(NO_3)_3(aq) + 3\ (NH_4)_2S(aq) \longrightarrow$
                   $Co_2S_3(s) + 6\ NH_4NO_3(aq)$
     c. $Cu_2O(s) + C(s) \longrightarrow 2\ Cu(s) + CO(g)$
     d. $H_2(g) + Cl_2(g) \longrightarrow 2\ HCl(g)$

111. a. inorganic   **b.** organic
     c. organic   **d.** inorganic

113. a. alkene   **b.** alkane
     c. alkyne   **d.** alkane

115. a. $CH_3CH_2CH_3$ **b.** propane
     c. $CH_3CH_2CH_2CH_2CH_2CH_2CH_2CH_3$
     d. pentane

117. a. functionalized hydrocarbon, alcohol
     b. hydrocarbon
     c. functionalized hydrocarbon, ketone
     d. functionalized hydrocarbon, amine

119. 1.50×10^{24} molecules EtOH

121. a. K_2CrO_4, 40.27% K, 26.78% Cr, 32.95% O
     b. $Pb_3(PO_4)_2$, 76.60% Pb, 7.63% P, 15.77% O
     c. H_2SO_3, 2.46% H, 39.07% S, 58.47% O
     d. $CoBr_2$, 26.94% Co, 73.06% Br

123. 1.80×10^2 g Cl_2./yr

125. M = Fe

127. estradiol = $C_{18}H_{24}O_2$

129. $C_{18}H_{20}O_2$

131. $7\ H_2O$

133. C_6H_9BrO

135. 1.87×10^{21} atoms

137. 92.93 amu

139. $x = 1, y = 2$

141. 41.7 mg

143. 0.224 g

145. 22.0% by mass

147. 1.6×10^7 kg Cl

149. 7.8×10^3 kg rock

151. $C_5H_{10}SI$

153. X_2Y_3

155. The sphere in the molecular models represents the electron cloud of the atom. On this scale, the nucleus would be too small to see.

157. The statement is incorrect because a chemical formula is based on the ratio of atoms combined, not the ratio of grams combined. The statement should read, "The chemical formula for ammonia (NH_3) indicates that ammonia contains three hydrogen atoms to each nitrogen atom."

159. O, S, H

Chapter 4

25. $2\ C_6H_{14}(g) + 19\ O_2(g) \longrightarrow$
                   $12\ CO_2(g) + 14\ H_2O(g)$, 68 mol O_2

27. a. 5.0 mol NO_2
     b. 14. mol NO_2
     c. 0.281 mol NO_2
     d. 53.1 mol NO_2

29.

mol SiO_2	mol C	mol SiC	mol CO
3	9	3	6
2	6	2	4
5	15	5	10
2.8	8.4	2.8	5.6
0.517	1.55	0.517	1.03

31. a. 9.3 g HBr, 0.12 g H_2

33. a. 5.56 g $BaCl_2$ **b.** 6.55 g $CaCO_3$
     c. 6.09 g MgO   **d.** 6.93 g Al_2O_3

35. a. 4.42 g HCl   **b.** 8.25 g HNO_3
     c. 4.24 g H_2SO_4

37. a. Na   **b.** Na
     c. Br_2 **d.** Na

39. 3 molecules Cl_2

41. a. 2 mol   **b.** 7 mol   **c.** 9.40 mol

43. 0.5 mol O_2

45. a. 2.5 g   **b.** 31.1 g   **c.** 1.16 g

47. 2.91 grams CO_2 remaining

49. limiting reactant: Pb^{2+}, theoretical yield: 34.5 g $PbCl_2$, percent yield: 85.3%

51. limiting reactant: NH_3, theoretical yield: 240.5 kg CH_4N_2O, percent yield: 70.01%

53. a. 1.17 M LiCl   **b.** 0.123 M $C_6H_{12}O_6$
     c. 0.00453 M NaCl

55. a. 0.150 M NO_3^- **b.** 0.300 M NO_3^-
     c. 0.450 M NO_3^-

57. a. 1.3 mol   **b.** 1.5 mol   **c.** 0.211 mol

59. 37 g

61. 0.27 M

63. 6.0 L

65. 37.1 mL

67. 2.1 L

69. barium nitrate, 2.81g $Ba(NO_3)_2$, 87.1%

71. a. yes   **b.** no
     c. yes   **d.** no

73. a. soluble Ag^+, NO_3^- **b.** soluble Pb^{2+}, $C_2H_3O_2^-$
     c. soluble K^+, NO_3^- **d.** soluble NH_4^+, S^{2-}

75. a. NO REACTION   **b.** NO REACTION
     c. $CrBr_2(aq) + Na_2CO_3(aq) \longrightarrow CrCO_3(s) + 2\ NaBr(aq)$
     d. $3\ NaOH(aq) + FeCl_3(aq) \longrightarrow Fe(OH)_3(s) + 3\ NaCl(aq)$

77. a. $K_2CO_3(aq) + Pb(NO_3)_2(aq) \longrightarrow$
$$PbCO_3(s) + 2 KNO_3(aq)$$
b. $Li_2SO_4(aq) + Pb(C_2H_3O_2)_2(aq) \longrightarrow$
$$PbSO_4(s) + 2 LiC_2H_3O_2(aq)$$
c. $Cu(NO_3)_2(aq) + MgS(aq) \longrightarrow$
$$CuS(s) + Mg(NO_3)_2(aq)$$
d. NO REACTION

79. a. Complete:
$H^+(aq) + Cl^-(aq) + Li^+(aq) + OH^-(aq) \longrightarrow$
$$H_2O(l) + Li^+(aq) + Cl^-(aq)$$
Net: $H^+(aq) + OH^-(aq) \longrightarrow H_2O(l)$
b. Complete:
$Mg^{2+}(aq) + S^{2-}(aq) + Cu^{2+}(aq) + 2 Cl^-(aq) \longrightarrow$
$$CuS(s) + Mg^{2+}(aq) + 2 Cl^-(aq)$$
Net: $Cu^{2+}(aq) + S^{2-}(aq) \longrightarrow CuS(s)$
c. Complete:
$Na^+(aq) + OH^-(aq) + HC_2H_3O_2(aq) \longrightarrow$
$$H_2O(l) + Na^+(aq) + C_2H_3O_2^-(aq)$$
Net: $OH^-(aq) + HC_2H_3O_2(aq) \longrightarrow$
$$H_2O(l) + C_2H_3O_2^-(aq)$$
d. Complete:
$6 Na^+(aq) + 2 PO_4^{3-}(aq) + 3 Ni^{2+}(aq) + 6 Cl^-(aq) \longrightarrow$
$$Ni_3(PO_4)_2(s) + 6 Na^+(aq) + 6 Cl^-(aq)$$
Net: $3 Ni^{2+}(aq) + 2 PO_4^{3-}(aq) \longrightarrow Ni_3(PO_4)_2(s)$

81. Complete:
$Hg_2^{2+}(aq) + 2 NO_3^-(aq) + 2 Na^+(aq) + 2 Cl^-(aq) \longrightarrow$
$$Hg_2Cl_2(s) + 2 Na^+(aq) + 2 NO_3^-(aq)$$
Net: $Hg_2^{2+}(aq) + 2 Cl^-(aq) \longrightarrow Hg_2Cl_2(s)$

83. Molecular:
$HBr(aq) + KOH(aq) \longrightarrow H_2O(l) + KBr(aq)$
Net ionic: $H^+(aq) + OH^-(aq) \longrightarrow H_2O(l)$

85. a. $H_2SO_4(aq) + Ca(OH)_2(aq) \longrightarrow 2 H_2O(l) + CaSO_4(s)$
b. $HClO_4(aq) + KOH(aq) \longrightarrow H_2O(l) + KClO_4(aq)$
c. $H_2SO_4(aq) + 2 NaOH(aq) \longrightarrow$
$$2 H_2O(l) + Na_2SO_4(aq)$$

87. 0.1810 M $HClO_4$

89. a. $2 HBr(aq) + NiS(s) \longrightarrow H_2S(g) + NiBr_2(aq)$
b. $NH_4I(aq) + NaOH(aq) \longrightarrow$
$$H_2O(l) + NH_3(g) + NaI(aq)$$
c. $2 HBr(aq) + Na_2S(aq) \longrightarrow H_2S(g) + 2 NaBr(aq)$
d. $2 HClO_4(aq) + Li_2CO_3(aq) \longrightarrow$
$$H_2O(l) + CO_2(g) + 2 LiClO_4(aq)$$

91. a. Ag: 0 **b.** Ag: +1
c. Ca: +2, F: −1 **d.** H: +1, S: −2
e. C: +4, O: −2 **f.** Cr: +6, O: −2

93. a. +2 **b.** +6 **c.** +3

95. a. redox reaction, oxidizing agent: O_2, reducing agent: Li
b. redox reaction, oxidizing agent: Fe^{2+}, reducing agent: Mg
c. not a redox reaction **d.** not a redox reaction

97. a. $S(s) + O_2(g) \longrightarrow SO_2(g)$
b. $2 C_3H_6(g) + 9 O_2(g) \longrightarrow 6 CO_2(g) + 6 H_2O(g)$
c. $2 Ca(s) + O_2(g) \longrightarrow 2 CaO(g)$
d. $C_5H_{12}S(l) + 9 O_2(g) \longrightarrow$
$$5 CO_2(g) + SO_2(g) + 6 H_2O(g)$$

99. 3.32 M
101. 1.1 g
103. 3.1 kg

105. limiting reactant: $C_7H_6O_3$, theoretical yield: 1.63 g $C_9H_8O_4$, percent yield: 74.8%
107. b
109. a. $2 HCl(aq) + Hg_2(NO_3)_2(aq) \longrightarrow$
$$Hg_2Cl_2(s) + 2 HNO_3(aq)$$
b. $KHSO_3(aq) + HNO_3(aq) \longrightarrow$
$$H_2O(l) + SO_2(g) + KNO_3(aq)$$
c. $2 NH_4Cl(aq) + Pb(NO_3)_2(aq) \longrightarrow$
$$PbCl_2(s) + 2 NH_4NO_3(aq)$$
d. $2 NH_4Cl(aq) + Ca(OH)_2(aq) \longrightarrow$
$$2 NH_3(g) + 2 H_2O(g) + CaCl_2(aq)$$

111. 22 g
113. 6.9 g
115. $NaNO_3$ is more economical.
117. Br is the oxidizing agent, Au is the reducing agent, 38.8 g $KAuF_4$
119. Ca^{2+} and Cu^{2+} present in the original solution. Net ionic for first precipitate:
$$Ca^{2+}(aq) + SO_4^{2-}(aq) \longrightarrow CaSO_4(s)$$
Net ionic for second precipitate:
$$Cu^{2+}(aq) + CO_3^{2-}(aq) \longrightarrow CuCO_3(s)$$
121. 0.333 g PH_3
123. 30.8 kg CO_2
125. 1.6 g C_2H_2
127. 11.8 g AgI
129. 5.5% by mass
131. 14 g KO_2. In designing the unit you would need to consider the theoretical yield and % yield of the reaction, how changing the limiting reactant would affect the reaction, and the stoichiometry between KO_2 and O_2 to determine the mass of KO_2 required to produce enough O_2 for 10 minutes. You might also consider the speed of the reaction and whether or not the reaction produced heat. Additionally, because your body does not use 100% of the oxygen taken in with each breath, the apparatus would only need to replenish the oxygen used. The percentage of oxygen in air is about 20% and the percentage in exhaled air is about 16%, so we will assume that 4% of the air would need to be replenished with oxygen.
133. 37.9 g B_5H_9
135. a. Since the mol ratio of H_2 to NO is 5:2, the 10 mol of H_2 will require 4 mole NO, and H_2 is the limiting reactant. This eliminates answers b and c. Since there is excess NO, this eliminates d, leaving answer a.
137. a

Chapter 5

25. a. 0.832 atm **b.** 632 mmHg
c. 12.2 psi **d.** 8.43×10^4 Pa
27. a. 809.0 mmHg **b.** 1.064 atm
c. 809.0 torr **d.** 107.9 kPa
29. a. 832 mmHg **b.** 718 mmHg
31. 4.4×10^2 mmHg
33. 58.9 mL
35. 4.22 L
37. 3.0 L The volume would not be different if the gas was argon.

39. 1.16 atm
41. 2.1 mol
43. Yes, the final gauge pressure is 43.5 psi, which exceeds the maximum rating.
45. 16.2 L
47. 286 atm, 17.5 bottles purged
49. b
51. 4.76 atm
53. 37.3 L
55. 9.43 g/L
57. 44.0 g/mol
59. 4.00 g/mol
61. $P_{tot} = 434$ torr, $mass_{N_2} = 0.437$ g, $mass_{O_2} = 0.237$ g, $mass_{He} = 0.0340$ g
63. 1.84 atm
65. $\chi_{N_2} = 0.627$, $\chi_{O_2} = 0.373$, $P_{N_2} = 0.687$ atm, $P_{O_2} = 0.409$ atm
67. $P_{H_2} = 0.921$ atm, $mass_{H_2} = 0.0539$ g
69. 7.47×10^{-2} g
71. 38 L
73. $V_{H_2} = 48.2$ L, $V_{CO} = 24.1$ L
75. 22.8 g NaN_3
77. 60.4%
79. F_2, 2.84 g ClF_3
81. a. yes   **b.** no
c. No. Even though the argon atoms are more massive than the helium atoms, both have the same kinetic energy at a given temperature. The argon atoms therefore move more slowly and so exert the same pressure as the helium atoms.
d. He
83. F_2: $u_{rms} = 442$ m/s, $KE_{avg} = 3.72 \times 10^3$ J; Cl_2: $u_{rms} = 324$ m/s, $KE_{avg} = 3.72 \times 10^3$ J; Br_2: $u_{rms} = 216$ m/s, $KE_{avg} = 3.72 \times 10^3$ J; rankings: u_{rms}: $Br_2 < Cl_2 < F_2$, KE_{avg}: $Br_2 = Cl_2 = F_2$, rate of effusion: $Br_2 < Cl_2 < F_2$
85. rate $^{238}UF_6$/rate $^{235}UF_6 = 0.99574$
87. krypton
89. A has the higher molar mass, B has the higher rate of effusion.
91. That the volume of gas particles is small compared to the space between them breaks down under conditions of high pressure. At high pressure the particles themselves occupy a significant portion of the total gas volume.
93. 0.05826 L (ideal); 0.0708 L (V.D.W.); Difference because of high pressure, at which Ne no longer acts ideally.
95. 97.8%
97. 27.8 g/mol
99. C_4H_{10}
101. 4.70 L
103. 2 HCl(aq) + $K_2S(s)$ $\longrightarrow$
      $H_2S(g)$ + 2 KCl(aq), 0.191 g $K_2S(s)$
105. 11.7 L
107. $mass_{air} = 8.56$ g, $mass_{He} = 1.20$ g, mass difference = 7.36 g

109. 4.76 L/s
111. total force = 6.15×10^3 pounds; no, the can cannot withstand this force.
113. 5.8×10^3 balloons
115. 4.0 cm
117. 77.7%
119. 0.32 grams
121. 311 K
123. 5.0 g
125. C_3H_8
127. 0.39 g Ar
129. 74.0 mmHg
131. 25% N_2H_4
133. 25%
135. $P_{CH_4} = 7.30 \times 10^{-2}$ atm, $P_{O_2} = 4.20 \times 10^{-1}$ atm, $P_{NO} = 2.79 \times 10^{-3}$ atm, $P_{CO_2} = 5.03 \times 10^{-3}$ atm, $P_{H_2O} = 5.03 \times 10^{-3}$ atm, $P_{NO_2} = 2.51 \times 10^{-2}$ atm, $P_{OH} = 1.01 \times 10^{-2}$ atm, $P_{tot} = 0.542$ atm
137. 0.42 atm
139. Because helium is less dense than air, the balloon moves in a direction opposite the direction the air inside the car is moving due to the acceleration and deceleration of the car.
141. -29%
143. a. false   **b.** false
c. false   **d.** true
145. four times the intial pressure
147. Although the velocity "tails" have different lengths, the average length of the tails on the helium atoms is longer than the average length of the tails on the neon atoms, which is in turn longer than the average length of the tails on the krypton atoms. The lighter the atom, the faster the tails must move on average to have the same kinetic energy.

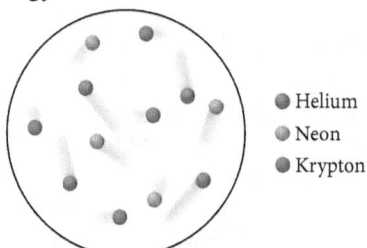

● Helium
● Neon
● Krypton

Chapter 6

33. a. 1.92×10^9 J   **b.** 5.14×10^4 cal
c. 2.37×10^6 J   **d.** 0.681 Cal
35. a. 9.987×10^6 J   **b.** 9.987×10^3 kJ
c. 2.78 kWh
37. d
39. a. heat, +   **b.** work, $-$ **c.** heat, +
41. -7.27×10^2 kJ
43. 311 kJ
45. The drinks that went into cooler B had more thermal energy than the refrigerated drinks that went into cooler A. The temperature difference between the drinks in cooler B and the ice was greater than the

difference between the drinks and the ice in cooler A. More thermal energy was exchanged between the drinks and the ice in cooler B, which resulted in more melting.

47. 4.7×10^5 J

49. a. 7.6×10^2 °C   **b.** 4.3×10^2 °C
    c. 1.3×10^2 °C   **d.** 49 °C

51. -2.8×10^2 J

53. 489 J

55. $\Delta E = -3463$ J, $\Delta H = -3452$ kJ

57. a. exothermic, $-$ **b.** endothermic, $+$
    c. exothermic, $-$

59. -4.30×10^3 kJ

61. 6.46×10^4 kJ

63. 9.5×10^2 g CO_2

65. mass of silver 77.1 grams

67. final temperature 28.4 °C

69. specific heat capacity of substance A 1.10 J/g · °C

71. Measurement B corresponds to conditions of constant pressure. Measurement A corresponds to conditions of constant volume. When a fuel is burned under constant pressure some of the energy released does work on the atmosphere by expanding against it. Less energy is manifest as heat due to this work. When a fuel is burned under constant volume, all of the energy released by the combustion reaction is evolved as heat.

73. -6.3×10^3 kJ/mol

75. -1.6×10^5 J

77. a. $-\Delta H_1$
    b. $2 \, \Delta H_1$
    c. $-\frac{1}{2}\Delta H_1$

79. -23.9 kJ

81. -173.2 kJ

83. a. $N_2(g) + 3 \, H_2(g) \longrightarrow$
            $2 \, NH_3(g)$, $\Delta H_f^\circ = -45.9$ kJ/mol
    b. $C(s, \text{graphite}) + O_2(g) \longrightarrow$
            $CO_2(g)$, $\Delta H_f^\circ = -393.5$ kJ/mol
    c. $2 \, Fe(s) + 3/2 \, O_2(g) \longrightarrow$
            $Fe_2O_3(s)$, $\Delta H_f^\circ = -824.2$ kJ/mol
    d. $C(s, \text{graphite}) + 2 \, H_2(g) \longrightarrow$
            $CH_4(g)$, $\Delta H_f^\circ = -74.6$ kJ/mol

85. -382.1 kJ/mol

87. a. -137.1 kJ
    b. -41.2 kJ
    c. -137 kJ
    d. 290.7 kJ

89. $6 \, CO_2(g) + 6 \, H_2O(l) \longrightarrow$
        $C_6H_{12}O_6(s) + 6 \, O_2(g)$, $\Delta H_{rxn}^\circ = 2803$ kJ

91. -113.0 kJ/mol

93. a. 5.49 g CO_2
    b. 6.46 g CO_2
    c. 6.94 g CO_2
    Natural gas, $CH_4(g)$, contributes the least to global warming by producing the least $CO_2(g)$ per kJ of heat produced.

95. 2×10^{13} kg CO_2 produced per year, 150 years

97. $\Delta E = -1.7$ J, $q = -0.5$ J, $w = -1.2$ J

99. 78 g

101. $\Delta H = 6.0$ kJ/mol, 1.1×10^2 g

103. 26.1 °C

105. palmitic acid: 9.9378 Cal/g, sucrose: 3.938 Cal/g, fat contains more Cal/g than sugar

107. $\Delta H = \Delta E + nR\Delta T$

109. 5.7 Cal/g

111. $\Delta E = 0$, $\Delta H = 0$, $q = -w = 3.0 \times 10^3$ J

113. -294 kJ/mol

115. 94.0 kJ

117. 23.9 °C

119. 7.3×10^3 g H_2SO_4

121. 7.2×10^2 g

123. 78.2 °C

125. $C_v = \frac{3}{2}R$, $C_p = \frac{5}{2}R$

127. $q = 1030$ kJ, $\Delta H = 1030$ kJ, $\Delta E = 952$ kJ, $w = -78$ kJ

129. -1292 kJ

131. d

133. a. At constant pressure, heat can be added and work can be done on the system. $\Delta E = q + w$; therefore, $q = \Delta E - w$.

135. The aluminum is cooler because it has a lower heat capacity (specific heat).

137. $q = -2418$ J, $w = -5$ kJ, $\Delta H = -2418$ J/mol, $\Delta E = -2423$ J/mol

139. b. $\Delta H > \Delta E$

Chapter 7

35. 499 s

37. (i) d, c, b, a   **(ii) a, b, c, d**

39. a. 4.74×10^{14} Hz   **b.** 5.96×10^{14} Hz
    c. 5.8×10^{18} Hz

41. a. 3.14×10^{-19} J   **b.** 3.95×10^{-19} J
    c. 3.8×10^{-15} J

43. 1.03×10^{16} photons

45. a. 79.8 kJ/mol   **b.** 239 kJ/mol
    c. 798 kJ/mol

47.

49. 3.6×10^6 m/s

51. 5.39 nm

53. 1.1×10^{-34} m. The wavelength of a baseball is negligible with respect to its size.

55. $\Delta v = 1.04 \times 10^5$ m/s

57. $2s$

59. a. $l = 0$ **b.** $l = 0, 1$
    c. $l = 0, 1, 2$ **d.** $l = 0, 1, 2, 3$

61. c

63. See Figures 7.25 and 7.26. The $2s$ and $3p$ orbitals would, on average, be farther from the nucleus and have more nodes than the $1s$ and $2p$ orbitals.

65. $n = 1$

67. $2p \longrightarrow 1s$

69. a. 122 nm, UV   **b.** 103 nm, UV
    c. 486 nm, visible   **d.** 434 nm, visible

71. $n = 2$

73. 344 nm

75. 6.4×10^{17} photons/s

77. 0.0547 nm

79. 91.2 nm

81. a. 4   **b.** 9   **c.** 16

83. $n = 4 \longrightarrow n = 3$, $n = 5 \longrightarrow n = 3$,
$n = 6 \longrightarrow n = 3$, respectively

85. 4.84×10^{14} s^{-1}

87. 11 m

89. 6.78×10^{-3} J

91. 632 nm

93. a. $E_1 = 2.51 \times 10^{-18}$ J, $E_2 = 1.00 \times 10^{-17}$ J,
$E_3 = 2.26 \times 10^{-17}$ J

b. 26.5 nm, UV; 15.8 nm, UV

95.

The plot for the 2s wave function extends below the
x-axis. The x-intercept represents the radial node of
the orbital.

97. 7.39×10^5 m/s

99. $\Delta E = 1.1 \times 10^{-20}$ J, 7.0×10^2 nm

101. 11 m

103. In the Bohr model, electrons exist in specific orbits
encircling the atom. In the quantum mechanical model,
electrons exist in orbitals that are really probability
density maps of where the electron is likely to be
found. The Bohr model is inconsistent with
Heisenberg's uncertainty principle.

105. a. yes   **b.** no
     c. yes   **d.** no

Chapter 8

41. a. $1s^2 2s^2 2p^6 3s^2 3p^2$
     b. $1s^2 2s^2 2p^4$
     c. $1s^2 2s^2 2p^6 3s^2 3p^6 4s^1$
     d. $1s^2 2s^2 2p^6$

43. a.

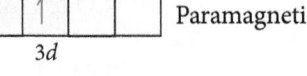

b.

c.

d.

45. a. [Ne] $3s^2 3p^3$ **b.** [Ar] $4s^2 3d^{10} 4p^2$
     c. [Kr] $5s^2 4d^2$ **d.** [Kr] $5s^2 4d^{10} 5p^5$

47. a. 1   **b.** 10   **c.** 5   **d.** 2

49. a. V, As   **b.** Se   **c.** V   **d.** Kr

51. a. 2   **b.** 1   **c.** 10   **d.** 6

53. reactive metal: **a**, reactive nonmetal: **c**

55. c

57. The valence electrons of nitrogen will experience a
greater effective nuclear charge. The valence electrons
of both atoms are screened by two core electrons, but
N has a greater number of protons and therefore a
greater net nuclear charge.

59. a. 1+   **b.** 2+   **c.** 6+   **d.** 4+

61. a. In   **b.** Si   **c.** Pb   **d.** C

63. F, S, Si, Ge, Ca, Rb

65. a. [Ne]   **b.** [Kr]   **c.** [Kr]   **d.** [Ar] $3d^6$
     e. [Ar] $3d^9$

67. a. [Ar] Diamagnetic

b. [Ar]

Paramagnetic

c. [Ar]

Paramagnetic

d. [Ar]

Paramagnetic

69. a. Li   **b.** I$^-$ **c.** Cr   **d.** O^{2-}

71. O^{2-}, F$^-$, Ne, Na$^+$, Mg^{2+}

73. a. Br
     b. Na
     c. Cannot tell based on periodic trends.
     d. P

75. In, Si, N, F

77. a. second and third   **b.** fifth and sixth
     c. sixth and seventh   **d.** first and second

79. a. Na   **b.** S   **c.** C   **d.** F

81. a. Sr   **b.** Bi
    c. Cannot tell based on periodic trends.
    d. As
83. S, Se, Sb, In, Ba, Fr
85. $Sr(s) + I_2(g) \longrightarrow SrI_2(s)$
87. $2\ Li(s) + 2\ H_2O(l) \longrightarrow$
                             $2\ Li^+(aq) + 2\ OH^-(aq) + H_2(g)$
89. $H_2(g) + Br_2(g) \longrightarrow 2\ HBr(g)$
91. Br: $1s^2 2s^2 2p^6 3s^2 3p^6 4s^2 3d^{10} 4p^5$
    Kr: $1s^2 2s^2 2p^6 3s^2 3p^6 4s^2 3d^{10} 4p^6$
    Krypton's outer electron shell is filled, giving it chemical stability. Bromine is missing an electron from its outer shell and subsequently has a high electron affinity. Bromine tends to be easily reduced by gaining an electron, giving the bromide ion stability due to the filled p subshell that corresponds to krypton's chemically stable electron configuration.
93. V: $[Ar]\ 4s^2 3d^3$
    V^{3+}: $[Ar]\ 3d^2$
    Both V and V^{3+} contain unpaired electrons in their $3d$ orbitals.
95. A substitute for K^+ would need to exhibit a $1+$ electric charge and have similar mass and atomic radius. Na^+ and Rb^+ would not be good substitutes because their radii are significantly smaller and larger, respectively. Based on mass, Ca^+ and Ar^+ are the closest to K^+. Because the first ionization energy of Ca^+ is closest to that of K^+, Ca^+ is the best choice for a substitute. The difficulty lies in Ca's low second ionization energy, making it easily oxidized.
97. Si, Ge
99. a. N: $[He]\ 2s^2 2p^3$, Mg: $[Ne]\ 3s^2$, O: $[He]\ 2s^2 2p^4$, F: $[He]\ 2s^2 2p^5$, Al: $[Ne]\ 3s^2 3p^1$
    b. Mg, Al, O, F, N   **c.** Al, Mg, O, N, F
    d. Aluminum's first ionization energy is lower than Mg because its $3p$ electron is shielded by the $3s$ orbital. Oxygen's first ionization energy is lower than that of N because its fourth $2p$ electron experiences electron–electron repulsion by the other electron in its orbital.
101. For main-group elements, atomic radii decrease across a period because the addition of a proton in the nucleus and an electron in the outermost energy level increases Z_{eff}. This does not happen in the transition metals because the electrons are added to the $n_{highest-1}$ orbital and the Z_{eff} stays roughly the same.
103. Noble gases are exceptionally unreactive due to the stability of their completely filled outer quantum levels and their high ionization energies. The ionization energies of Kr, Xe, and Rn are low enough to form some compounds.
105. 6A: $ns^2 np^4$, 7A: $ns^2 np^5$, group 7A elements require only one electron to achieve a noble gas configuration. Since group 6A elements require two electrons, their affinity for one electron is less negative, because one electron will merely give them an np^5 configuration.
107. 85
109. a. One If By Land (O, Ne, I, F, B, Y, La, Nd)
    b. Atoms are Fun (N, U, Fe, Ra, S, Mo, Ta backward)

111. 1.390×10^3 kJ/mol, 86.14 nm
113. a. $d_{Ar} \approx 2$ g/L, $d_{Xe} \approx 6.5$ g/L
    b. $d_{118} \approx 13$ g/L
    c. mass = 3.35×10^{-23} g/Ne atom, density of Ne atom = 2.3×10^4 g/L. The separation of Ne atoms relative to their size is immense.
    d. Kr: 2.69×10^{22} atoms/L, Ne: 2.69×10^{22} atoms/L. It seems Ar will also have 2.69×10^{22} atoms/L. $d_{Ar} = 1.78$ g/L. This corresponds to accepted values.
115. Density increases to the right, because, though electrons are added successively across the period, they are added to the $3d$ subshell, which is not a part of the outermost principal energy level. As a result, the atomic radius does not increase significantly across the period, while mass does.
117. Longest λ:

Next longest λ:

Next longest λ:

119. 168, noble gas
121. A relatively high effective nuclear charge is found in gallium with its completed $3d$ subshell and in thallium with its completed $4f$ subshell, accounting for the relatively high first ionization energies of these elements.
123. The second electron affinity requires the addition of an electron to something that is already negatively charged. The monoanions of both of these elements have relatively high electron density in a relatively small volume. As we shall see in Chapter 9 the dianions of these elements do exist in many compounds because they are stabilized by chemical bonding.
125. 120, 170
127. Fr, $[Rn]\ 7s^1$, > 265, < 376, > 1.879, < 29
    a. $Fr^+(aq)$, $OH^-(aq)$, $H_2(g)$ **b.** $Fr_2O(s)$ **c.** $FrCl(s)$
129. a. any group 6A element
    b. any group 5A element
    c. any group 1A element
131. a. true   **b.** true   **c.** false   **d.** true
133. Since Ca has valence electrons of $4s^2$, it has a relatively low ionization energy to lose two electrons. F has a highly exothermic electron affinity when gaining one electron but not a second electron because of its $2s^2 2p^5$ valence electrons. Therefore, calcium and fluoride combine in a 2:1 ratio.

Chapter 9

35. $1s^2 \underline{2s^2 2p^3}$ ·N̈:

37. a. ·Äl·   **b.** Na^+
    c. :C̈l: **d.** $\left[:\ddot{C}l: \right]^-$

39. a. $Na^+\left[:\ddot{F}:\right]^-$ **b.** $Ca^{2+}\left[:\ddot{O}:\right]^{2-}$

c. $Sr^{2+}\,2\left[:\ddot{B}r:\right]^-$ **d.** $2\,K^+\left[:\ddot{O}:\right]^{2-}$

41. a. SrSe
  b. $BaCl_2$
  c. Na_2S
  d. Al_2O_3

43. As the size of the alkaline earth metal ions increases, so does the distance between the metal cations and oxygen anions. Therefore, the magnitude of the lattice energy decreases accordingly because the potential energy decreases as the distance increases.

45. One factor of lattice energy is the product of the charges of the two ions. The product of the ion charges for CsF is -1 while that for BaO is -4. Because this product is four times greater, the lattice energy is also four times greater.

47. -708 kJ/mol

49. a. H:H, filled duets, 0 formal charge on both atoms
  b. $:\ddot{C}l:\ddot{C}l:$, filled octets, 0 formal charge on both atoms
  c. $\ddot{O}=\ddot{O}$, filled octets, 0 formal charge on both atoms
  d. $:N\equiv N:$, filled octets, 0 formal charge on both atoms

51. a. H—P—H with H below
  b. $:\ddot{S}—\ddot{C}l:$ with :Cl: below
  c. H—Ï:
  d. H—C—H with H above and below

53. a. $:\ddot{F}—\ddot{S}—\ddot{F}:$
  b. H—Si—H (with H above and below)
  c. $:\ddot{O}=C—\ddot{O}:$ with H below
  d. H—C—$\ddot{S}$—H

55. a. pure covalent   **b.** polar covalent
  c. pure covalent   **d.** ionic bond

57. $:C=O:$, 25%

59. a. $:\ddot{I}—C—\ddot{I}:$ with :I: above and below
  b. $:N\equiv N—\ddot{O}:$
  c. H—Si—H
  d. $:\ddot{C}l—C—\ddot{C}l:$ with :O: above

61. a. $H—\ddot{N}=\ddot{N}—H$ **b.** $H—\ddot{N}—\ddot{N}—H$ with H below each N
  c. $H—C\equiv C—H$ **d.** $H—C=C—H$ with H below each C

63. a. $:\ddot{O}—\ddot{S}e=O:$ ⟷ $:O=\ddot{S}e—\ddot{O}:$
  b. carbonate resonance structures
  c. $\left[:\ddot{C}l—\ddot{O}:\right]^-$
  d. $\left[:\ddot{O}=N—\ddot{O}:\right]^- ⟷ \left[:\ddot{O}—N=\ddot{O}:\right]^-$

65. $H—C=\ddot{S}$ $H—\ddot{S}=\ddot{C}$ H_2CS is the better structure

67. $:O\equiv C—\ddot{O}:$
  does not provide a significant contribution to the resonance hybrid as it has a $+1$ formal charge on a very electronegative atom (oxygen).

69. resonance structures

71. N has a formal charge of $+1$; O has a formal charge of -1.

73. a. BCl3   **b.** $\ddot{O}=N—\ddot{O}: ⟷ :\ddot{O}—N=\ddot{O}$ **c.** BH3

75. a. (resonance structures of PO_4^{3-})

b. $\left[:C\equiv N:\right]^-$

c. (resonance structures of SO_3^{2-})

d. $\left[:\ddot{O}-\overset{..}{Cl}-\ddot{O}:\right]^-$

77. a. PF_5 structure

b. $\left[:\ddot{I}\cdots\ddot{I}\cdots\ddot{I}:\right]^-$ (I₃⁻)

c. SF_4 structure

d. GeF_4 structure

79. H_3CCH_3, H_2CCH_2, HCCH

81. -128 kJ

83. -614 kJ

85. a. BI_3 structure

b. $2\,K^+\left[:\ddot{S}:\right]^{2-}$

c. $H-\overset{..}{C}-\ddot{F}:$ (with O double bond)

d. $:\ddot{Br}-\overset{..}{P}-\ddot{Br}:$ (with Br)

87. a. Ba^{2+} (resonance structures of CO_3^{2-})

b. $Ca^{2+}\,2\left[:\ddot{O}-H\right]^-$

c. K^+ (resonance structures of NO_3^-)

d. $Li^+\left[:\ddot{I}-\ddot{O}:\right]^-$

89. a. (structure of C₄H₁₀)

b. (cyclobutadiene resonance structures)

c. (cyclohexane structure)

d. (benzene resonance structures)

91. CH_2O_2,
$$H-\overset{\displaystyle :O:}{\overset{\|}{C}}-\overset{..}{\underset{..}{O}}-H$$

93. The reaction is exothermic due to the energy released when the Al_2O_3 lattice forms.

95.
$$H-\overset{..}{\underset{..}{O}}-\overset{:O:^0}{\underset{}{N}}-\overset{..}{\underset{..}{O}}: \longleftrightarrow H-\overset{..}{\underset{..}{O}}-N=\overset{:O:^{-1}}{\underset{}{O}} \longleftrightarrow$$
$$\quad\; 0 \quad\; 0 \;\; +1 \;\; -1 \qquad\qquad 0 \quad\; 0 \;\; +1 \quad 0$$

Most important

$$H-\overset{..}{O}=\overset{:O:^{-1}}{\underset{}{N}}-\overset{..}{\underset{..}{O}}:$$
$$\quad 0 \;\; +1 \;\; +1 \;\; -1$$

97.
$$\left[\overset{..}{\underset{}{C}}=N=\overset{..}{\underset{..}{O}}\right]^- \longleftrightarrow \left[:C\equiv \overset{..}{N}-\overset{..}{\underset{..}{O}}:\right]^-$$
$$\;\; -2 \;\; +1 \;\; 0 \qquad\qquad -1 \;\; +1 \;\; -1$$

The fulminate ion is less stable because nitrogen is more electronegative than carbon and should therefore be terminal to accomodate the negative formal charge.

99. a.
$$H-\overset{\displaystyle H}{\underset{\displaystyle H}{C}}=C-H$$
b.
$$H-\overset{\displaystyle H}{\underset{\displaystyle H}{C}}-\overset{\displaystyle H}{\underset{\displaystyle H}{N}}-H$$

c.
$$H-\overset{:O:}{\overset{\|}{C}}-H$$
d.
$$H-\overset{\displaystyle H}{\underset{\displaystyle H}{C}}-\overset{\displaystyle H}{\underset{\displaystyle H}{C}}-\overset{..}{\underset{..}{O}}-H$$

e.
$$H-\overset{:O:}{\overset{\|}{C}}-\overset{..}{\underset{..}{O}}-H$$

101.
Nonpolar — $:S:$ H — Polar
$$H-\overset{\|}{\underset{}{C}}-\overset{..}{\underset{}{N}}-H$$
Nonpolar   Polar

103. a. $\left[\overset{..}{\underset{..}{O}}=\overset{..}{\underset{.}{O}}\right]^-$ **b.** $\left[:\overset{..}{\underset{..}{O}}:\right]^-$

c. $:\overset{.}{\underset{..}{O}}-H$ **d.**
$$H-\overset{\displaystyle H}{\underset{\displaystyle H}{C}}-\overset{..}{\underset{..}{O}}-\overset{..}{\underset{..}{O}}\cdot$$

105. $\Delta H_{rxn(H_2)} = -243$ kJ/mol $= -121$ kJ/g
$\Delta H_{rxn(CH_4)} = -802$ kJ/mol $= -50.0$ kJ/g
CH_4 yields more energy per mole while H_2 yields more energy per gram.

107. a. $\overset{..}{O}=\overset{:O:}{\overset{\|}{Cl}}-\overset{..}{\underset{..}{O}}-\overset{:O:}{\overset{\|}{Cl}}=\overset{..}{O}$ **b.**
$$H-\overset{\displaystyle :O:}{\overset{\displaystyle \|}{\underset{\displaystyle :O:}{\underset{\displaystyle |}{\underset{\displaystyle H}{P}}}}}-\overset{..}{\underset{..}{O}}-H$$

c.
$$H-\overset{..}{\underset{..}{O}}-\overset{:O:}{\overset{\displaystyle \|}{\underset{\displaystyle :O:}{\underset{\displaystyle |}{\underset{\displaystyle H}{As}}}}}-\overset{..}{\underset{..}{O}}-H$$

109. Na^+F^-, Na^+O^{2-}, $Mg^{2+}F^-$, $Mg^{2+}O^{2-}$, $Al^{3+}O^{2-}$

111. 333 kJ/mol

113. $H-C\equiv C-H$

115.
$$\overset{..}{O}=\overset{..}{S}=\overset{..}{O} + :\overset{..}{O}-H \longrightarrow H-\overset{..}{\underset{..}{O}}-\overset{:O:}{\overset{\displaystyle \|}{S}}-\overset{..}{\underset{..}{O}}:$$

$$H-\overset{..}{\underset{..}{O}}-\overset{:O:}{\overset{\displaystyle \|}{\underset{\displaystyle :O:}{\underset{\displaystyle |}{S}}}}-\overset{..}{\underset{..}{O}}: + \overset{..}{O}=\overset{..}{O} \longrightarrow$$

$$:\overset{..}{\underset{..}{O}}-\overset{:O:}{\overset{\displaystyle \|}{\underset{\displaystyle |}{S}}}-\overset{..}{\underset{..}{O}}: + H-\overset{..}{\underset{..}{O}}-\overset{..}{\underset{}{O}}\cdot$$

$$:\overset{..}{\underset{..}{O}}-\overset{:O:}{\overset{\displaystyle \|}{S}}-\overset{..}{\underset{..}{O}}: + H-\overset{..}{\underset{..}{O}}-H \longrightarrow :\overset{..}{\underset{}{O}}-\overset{\displaystyle H \;\; :\overset{..}{O}}{\overset{\displaystyle |}{\underset{\displaystyle |}{\underset{\displaystyle H-\overset{..}{\underset{..}{O}}:}{S}}}}=\overset{..}{O}:$$

$\Delta H_{rxn} = -172$ kJ

117. $r_{HCl} = 113$ pm
$r_{HF} = 84$ pm
These values are close to the accepted values.

119.

121. 126 kJ/mol

123. The oxidation number of the S atoms bonded directly to hydrogen atoms is -1. The oxidation number of interior S atoms is 0.

125. 536 kJ

127. The compounds are energy rich because a great deal of energy is released when these compounds undergo a reaction that breaks weak bonds and forms strong ones.

129. The theory is successful because it allows us to predict and account for many chemical observations. The theory is limited because electrons cannot be treated as localized "dots."

Chapter 10

31. 4

33. a. 4 e⁻ groups, 4 bonding groups, 0 lone pairs
b. 5 e⁻ groups, 3 bonding groups, 2 lone pairs
c. 6 e⁻ groups, 5 bonding groups, 1 lone pair

35. a. e⁻ geometry: tetrahedral molecular geometry: trigonal pyramidal idealized bond angle: 109.5°, deviation
b. e⁻ geometry: tetrahedral molecular geometry: bent idealized bond angle: 109.5°, deviation
c. e⁻ geometry: tetrahedral molecular geometry: tetrahedral idealized bond angle: 109.5°, deviation (due to large size of Cl compared to H)
d. e⁻ geometry: linear molecular geometry: linear idealized bond angle: 180°

37. H_2O has a smaller bond angle due to lone pair–lone pair repulsions, the strongest electron group repulsion.

39. a. seesaw,

b. T-shape, Cl—F

c. linear, F—I—F

d. square planar,

41. a. linear, H—C≡C—H

b. Trigonal planar, $\begin{array}{c} H \\ \diagdown \\ C=C \\ \diagup \\ H \end{array} \begin{array}{c} H \\ \diagup \\ \\ \diagdown \\ H \end{array}$

c. tetrahedral, H‖‖‖C—C‖‖‖H

43. a. The lone pair will cause lone pair–bonding pair repulsions, pushing the three bonding pairs out of the same plane. The correct molecular geometry is trigonal pyramidal.

b. The lone pair should take an equatorial position to minimize 90° bonding pair interactions. The correct molecular geometry is seesaw.

c. The lone pairs should take positions on opposite sides of the central atom to reduce lone pair–lone pair interactions. The correct molecular geometry is square planar.

45. a. C: tetrahedral   O: bent

$\begin{array}{c} O\text{‖‖‖}H \\ | \\ H\text{‖‖‖}C \\ | \\ H \end{array}$ $\begin{array}{c} H & O & H \\ \diagdown | \diagup \\ H\text{—}C\quad C\text{‖‖‖}H \\ | \quad\quad | \\ H \quad\quad H \end{array}$

b. C's: tetrahedral
O: bent

c. O's: bent $\begin{array}{c} H \\ \diagdown \\ O\text{—}O \\ \diagup \\ H \end{array}$

47. The vectors of the polar bonds in both CO_2 and CCl_4 oppose each other with equal magnitude and sum to 0.

49. PF_3, polar
SBr_2, nonpolar
$CHCl_3$, polar
CS_2, nonpolar

51. a. polar
b. polar
c. polar
d. nonpolar

53. a. 0
b. 3
c. 1

55. P:

H$_1$: 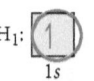   Expected bond angle = 90°

Valence bond theory is compatible with experimentally determined bond angle of 93.3° without hybrid orbitals.

H$_2$:

H$_3$:

57.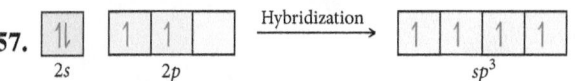

59. sp^2

61. a. sp^3

b. sp^3

c. sp^3

d. sp

63. a. sp^2

$\sigma: C(sp^2) - O(p)$

$\sigma: Cl(p) - C(sp^2)$

$\pi: C(p) - O(p)$

b. sp^3d^2

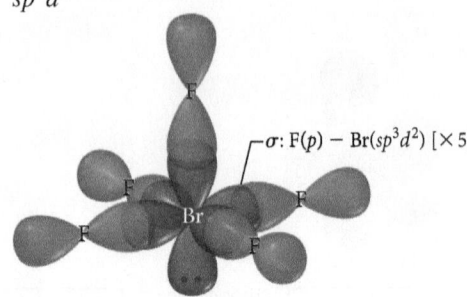

$\sigma: F(p) - Br(sp^3d^2) \, [\times 5]$

c. sp^3d

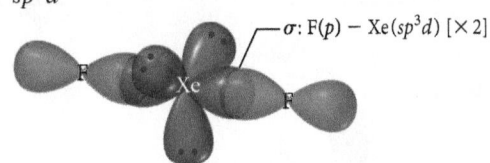

$\sigma: F(p) - Xe(sp^3d) \, [\times 2]$

d. sp^3d

$\sigma: I(p) - I(sp^3d) \, [\times 2]$

65. a. N's: sp^2

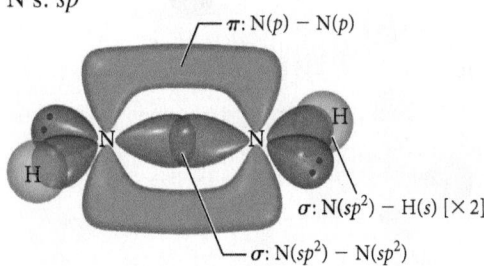

$\pi: N(p) - N(p)$

$\sigma: N(sp^2) - H(s) \, [\times 2]$

$\sigma: N(sp^2) - N(sp^2)$

b. N's: sp^3

$\sigma: H(s) - N(sp^3) \, [\times 4]$

$\sigma: N(sp^3) - N(sp^3)$

c. C: sp^3
   N: sp^3

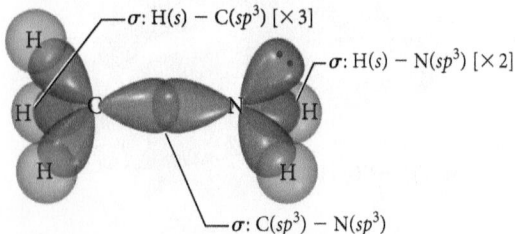

$\sigma: H(s) - C(sp^3) \, [\times 3]$

$\sigma: H(s) - N(sp^3) \, [\times 2]$

$\sigma: C(sp^3) - N(sp^3)$

67.

sp^3

sp^3

sp^2

69.

Constructive interference

71. Be_2^+ $\underline{1} \sigma_{2s}^*$ Be_2^-

$\underline{\uparrow\downarrow} \sigma_{2s}$

$\underline{\uparrow\downarrow} \sigma_{2s}$

$\underline{1} \sigma_{2p}$

$\underline{\uparrow\downarrow} \sigma_{2s}^*$

$\underline{\uparrow\downarrow} \sigma_{2s}$

bond order $Be_2^+ = 1/2$
bond order $Be_2^- = 1/2$
Both will exist in gas phase.

73.   Bonding

Antibonding

75. a.

$\underline{} \sigma_{2p}^*$

$\underline{} \ \underline{} \pi_{2p}^*$

$\underline{} \sigma_{2p}$

$\underline{} \ \underline{} \pi_{2p}$

$\underline{\uparrow\downarrow} \sigma_{2s}^*$

$\underline{\uparrow\downarrow} \sigma_{2s}$

bond order $= 0$
diamagnetic

b.

$\underline{} \sigma_{2p}^*$

$\underline{} \ \underline{} \pi_{2p}^*$

$\underline{} \sigma_{2p}$

$\underline{1} \ \underline{1} \pi_{2p}$

$\underline{\uparrow\downarrow} \sigma_{2s}^*$

$\underline{\uparrow\downarrow} \sigma_{2s}$

bond order $= 1$
paramagnetic

c.

$\underline{} \sigma_{2p}^*$

$\underline{} \ \underline{} \pi_{2p}^*$

$\underline{} \sigma_{2p}$

$\underline{\uparrow\downarrow} \ \underline{\uparrow\downarrow} \pi_{2p}$

$\underline{\uparrow\downarrow} \sigma_{2s}^*$

$\underline{\uparrow\downarrow} \sigma_{2s}$

bond order $= 2$
diamagnetic

d.

$\underline{} \sigma_{2p}^*$

$\underline{} \ \underline{} \pi_{2p}^*$

$\underline{1} \sigma_{2p}$

$\underline{\uparrow\downarrow} \ \underline{\uparrow\downarrow} \pi_{2p}$

$\underline{\uparrow\downarrow} \sigma_{2s}^*$

$\underline{\uparrow\downarrow} \sigma_{2s}$

bond order $= 2.5$
paramagnetic

77. a. not stable
b. not stable
c. stable
d. not stable
79. C_2^- has the highest bond order, the highest bond energy, and the shortest bond length.

81.

——	σ_{2p}^*
—— ——	π_{2p}^*
⇅ ⇅	π_{2p}
⇅	σ_{2p}
⇅	σ_{2s}^*
⇅	σ_{2s}

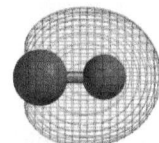

bond order = 3

83. a. :F—C—F: (with =O: on top)
trigonal planar
polar
C: sp^2

b. :Cl—S—S—Cl:
bent polar
S's: sp^3

c. :F—S—F: (with :F: top and :F: bottom)
seesaw polar
S: sp^3d

85. a.

sp^3, Bent sp^3, Tetrahedral
:O—C—C—C—O—H (H's attached; :O: double bond; N—H below)
sp^3, Tetrahedral
sp^3, bent
sp^2, Trigonal planar
sp^3, Trigonal pyramidal

(serine: H, OH, H_2N, O, OH)

b.

sp^3, Trigonal pyramidal
sp^3, Tetrahedral sp^3, Tetrahedral
sp^2, Trigonal planar
:N—C—C—C—C—O—H
sp^3, Bent
sp^2, Trigonal planar
sp^3, Trigonal pyramidal

(asparagine: H_2N, O, H_2N, O, OH)

c.

sp^3, Bent sp^3, Tetrahedral
sp^3, Bent
:S—C—C—C—O—H
sp^3, Tetrahedral sp^2, Trigonal planar
sp^3, Trigonal pyramidal

(cysteine: SH, H, N, H, O, OH)

87. σ bonds: 25
π bonds: 4
lone pairs: on O's and N (without methyl group):
  sp^2 orbitals
  on N's (with methyl group): sp^3 orbitals
89. a. water soluble
b. fat soluble
c. water soluble
d. fat soluble

91.

——	σ_p^*
⇅ ⇅	π_p^*
⇅ ⇅	π_p
⇅	σ_p
⇅	σ_s^*
⇅	σ_s

bond order = 1
93. BrF, unhybridized, linear

:Br—F:

BrF_2^- has two bonds and three lone pairs on the central atom. The hybridization is sp^3d. The electron geometry is trigonal bipyramidal with the three lone pairs equatorial. The molecular geometry is linear.

$$\left[:F—Br—F: \right]^-$$

BrF_3 has three bonds and two lone pairs on the central atom. The hybridization is sp^3d. The electron geometry is trigonal bipyramidal with the two lone pairs equatorial. The molecular geometry is T-shaped.

$$\left[:F—Br—F: \atop :F: \right]^-$$

BrF_4^- has four bonds and two lone pairs on the central atom. The hybridization is sp^3d^2. The electron geometry is octahedral with the two lone pairs on the same axis. The molecular geometry is square planar.

$$\left[:F—Br—F: \atop :F: \right]^-$$

BrF_5 has five bonds and one lone pair on the central atom. The hybridization is sp^3d^2. The electron geometry is octahedral. The molecular geometry is square pyramidal.

:F—Br—F: (with :F: top and :F: :F: bottom)

95. The moments of the two Cl's cancel.

97. a. 10   **b.** 14   **c.** 2

99. According to valence bond theory, CH_4, NH_3, and H_2O are all sp^3 hybridized. This hybridization results in a tetrahedral electron group configuration with a 109.5° bond angle. NH_3 and H_2O deviate from this idealized bond angle because their lone electron pairs exist in their own sp^3 orbitals. The presence of lone pairs lowers the tendency for the central atom's orbitals to hybridize. As a result, as lone pairs are added, the bond angle moves further from the 109.5° hybrid angle and closer to the 90° unhybridized angle.

101. NH_3 is stable due to its bond order of 3.

103. In NO_2^+, the central N has two electron groups, so the hybridization is sp and the ONO angle is 180°. In NO_2^- the central N has three electron groups, two bonds and one lone pair. The ideal hybridization is sp^2 but the ONO bond angle should close down a bit because of the lone pair. A bond angle around 115° is a good guess. In NO_2 there are three electron groups, but one group is a single electron. Again the ideal hybridization would be sp^2, but since one unpaired electron must be much smaller than a lone pair or even a bonding pair, we predict that the ONO bond angle will spread and be greater than 120°. As a guess the angle is probably significantly greater than 120°.

105. In addition to the $2s$ and the three $2p$ orbitals one more orbital is required to make five hybrid orbitals. The closest in energy is the $3s$ orbital. So the hybridization is s^2p^3. VSEPR predicts trigonal bipyramidal geometry for five identical substituents.

107.

Lewis Structure   Resonance Structure

Terminal carbon is tetrahedral, central carbon is trigonal planar, nitrogen is trigonal pyramidal (but resonance structure is trigonal planar).

109. a. This is the best.
  b. This statement is similar to **a** but leaves out non-bonding lone-pair electron groups.
  c. Molecular geometries are not determined by overlapping orbitals but rather by the number and type of electron groups around each central atom.

111. Lewis theory defines a single bond, double bond, and triple bond as a sharing of two electrons, four electrons, and six electrons, respectively, between two atoms. Valence bond theory defines a single bond as a sigma overlap of two orbitals, a double bond as a single sigma bond combined with a pi bond, and a triple bond as a double bond with an additional pi bond. Molecular orbital theory defines a single bond, double bond, and triple bond as a bond order of 1, 2, or 3, respectively, between two atoms.

Chapter 11

49. a. dispersion
  b. dispersion, dipole–dipole, hydrogen bonding
  c. dispersion, dipole–dipole
  d. dispersion

51. a. dispersion, dipole–dipole
  b. dispersion, dipole–dipole, hydrogen bonding
  c. dispersion
  d. dispersion

53. a, b, c, d, Boiling point increases with increasing intermolecular forces. The molecules increase in their intermolecular forces as follows: **a,** dispersion forces; **b,** stronger dispersion forces (broader electron cloud); **c,** dispersion forces and dipole–dipole interactions; **d,** dispersion forces, dipole–dipole interactions, and hydrogen bonding.

55. a. CH_3OH, hydrogen bonding
  b. CH_3CH_2OH, hydrogen bonding
  c. CH_3CH_3, greater mass, broader electron cloud causes greater dispersion forces

57. a. Br_2, smaller mass results in weaker dispersion forces
  b. H_2S, lacks hydrogen bonding
  c. PH_3, lacks hydrogen bonding

59. a. not homogeneous
  b. homogeneous, dispersion, dipole–dipole, hydrogen bonding, ion–dipole
  c. homogeneous, dispersion
  d. homogeneous, dispersion, dipole–dipole, hydrogen bonding

61. Water. Surface tension increases with increasing intermolecular forces, and water can hydrogen bond while acetone cannot.

63. compound A

65. When the tube is clean, water experiences adhesive forces with glass that are stronger than its cohesive forces, causing it to climb the surface of a glass tube. Water does not experience strong intermolecular forces with oil, so if the tube is coated in oil, the water's cohesive forces will be greater and it will not be attracted to the surface of the tube.

67. The water in the 12 cm dish will evaporate more quickly. The vapor pressure does not change but the surface area does. The water in the dish evaporates more quickly because the greater surface area allows for more molecules to obtain enough energy at the surface and break free.

69. Water is more volatile than vegetable oil. When the water evaporates, the endothermic process results in cooling.

71. 0.405 L

73. 91 °C

75. $\Delta H_{vap} = 24.7$ kJ/mol, bp = 239 K

77. 41 torr

79. 22.0 kJ

81. 2.7 °C

83. 30.5 kJ

85. **a.** solid   **b.** liquid
    c. gas   **d.** supercritical fluid
    e. solid/liquid   **f.** liquid/gas
    g. solid/liquid/gas

87. N_2 has a stable liquid phase at 1 atm.

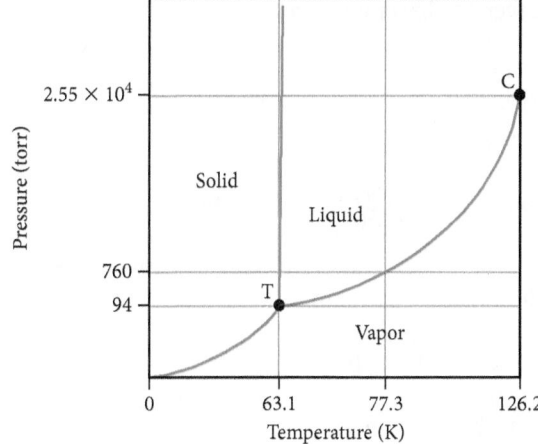

89. **a.** 0.027 mmHg   **b.** rhombic

91. Water has strong intermolecular forces. It is polar and experiences hydrogen bonding.

93. Water's exceptionally high specific heat capacity has a moderating effect on Earth's climate. Also, its high ΔH_{vap} causes water evaporation and condensation to have a strong effect on temperature.

95. 162 pm

97. **a.** 1   **b.** 2   **c.** 4

99. $l = 393$ pm, $d = 21.3$ g/cm^3

101. 134.5 pm

103. 6.0×10^{23} atoms/mol

105. **a.** atomic   **b.** molecular
    c. ionic   **d.** atomic

107. LiCl(s). The other three solids are held together by intermolecular forces while LiCl is held together by stronger coulombic interactions between the cations and anions of the crystal lattice.

109. **a.** $TiO_2(s)$, ionic solid
    b. $SiCl_4(s)$, larger, stronger dispersion forces
    c. Xe(s), larger, stronger dispersion forces
    d. CaO, ions have greater charge, and therefore stronger coulombic forces

111. TiO_2

113. Cs: 1(1) = 1
    Cl: 8(1/8) = 1
    1 : 1
    CsCl
    Ba: 8(1/8) + 6(1/2) = 4
    Cl: 8(1) = 8
    4 : 8 = 1 : 2
    $BaCl_2$

115. a

117. **a.** p-type   **b.** n-type

119. The general trend is that melting point increases with increasing mass. This is due to the fact that the electrons of the larger molecules are held more loosely and a stronger dipole moment can be induced more easily. HF is the exception to the rule. It has a relatively high melting point due to hydrogen bonding.

121. yes, 1.22 g

123. gas $\longrightarrow$ liquid $\longrightarrow$ solid

125. 26 °C

127.

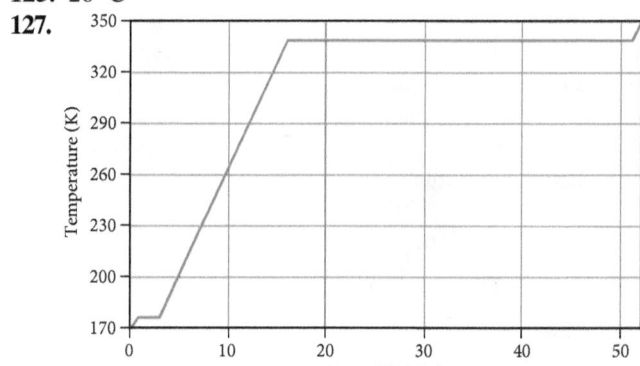

129. 3.4×10^3 g H_2O

131. CsCl has a higher melting point than AgI because of its higher coordination number. In CsCl, one anion bonds to eight cations (and vice versa) while in AgI, one anion bonds to only four cations.

133. **a.** $4r$
    b. $c^2 = a^2 + b^2$ $c = 4r, a = l, b = l$
    $(4r)^2 = l^2 + l^2$
    $16r^2 = 2l^2$
    $8r^2 = l^2$
    $l = \sqrt[3]{8r^2}$
    $l = 2\sqrt{2}r$

135. 8 atoms/unit

137. a. $CO_2(s) \longrightarrow CO_2(g)$ at 195 K
    b. $CO_2(s) \longrightarrow$ triple point at 216 K $\longrightarrow CO_2(g)$ just above 216 K
    c. $CO_2(s) \longrightarrow CO_2(l)$ at somewhat above 216 K $\longrightarrow CO_2(g)$ at around 250 K
    d. $CO_2(s) \longrightarrow CO_2(g) \longrightarrow$ supercritical fluid

139. 55.843 g/mol

141. 2.00 g/cm^3

143. Decreasing the pressure will decrease the temperature of liquid nitrogen. Because the nitrogen is boiling, its temperature must be constant at a given pressure. As the pressure decreases, the boiling point decreases, and therefore so does the temperature. If the pressure drops below the pressure of the triple point, the phase change will shift from vaporization to sublimation and the liquid nitrogen will become solid.

145. body diagonal = $\sqrt{6}r$,
radius = $(\sqrt{3} - \sqrt{2})r/\sqrt{2} = 0.2247r$

147. 70.7 L

149. 0.48 atm

151. The water within a container with a larger surface area will evaporate more quickly because there is more surface area for the molecules to evaporate from. Vapor pressure is the pressure of the gas when it is in dynamic equilibrium with the liquid. The vapor pressure is dependent only on the substance and the temperature. The larger the surface area, the more quickly it will reach the dynamic state.

153. The triple point will be at a lower temperature since the fusion equilibrium line has a positive slope. This means that we will be increasing both temperature and pressure as we travel from the triple point to the normal melting point.

155. The liquid segment will have the least steep slope because it takes the most kJ/mol to raise the temperature of the phase.

157. There are substantial intermolecular attractions in the liquid, but virtually none in the gas.

159.

Chapter 12

29. a. hexane, toluene, or CCl_4; dispersion forces
    b. water, methanol; dispersion, dipole–dipole, hydrogen bonding
    c. hexane, toluene, or CCl_4; dispersion forces
    d. water, acetone, methanol, ethanol; dispersion, ion–dipole

31. $HOCH_2CH_2CH_2OH$

33. a. water; dispersion, dipole–dipole, hydrogen bonding
    b. hexane; dispersion
    c. water; dispersion, dipole–dipole
    d. water; dispersion, dipole–dipole, hydrogen bonding

35. a. endothermic
    b. The lattice energy is greater in magnitude than the heat of hydration.
    c.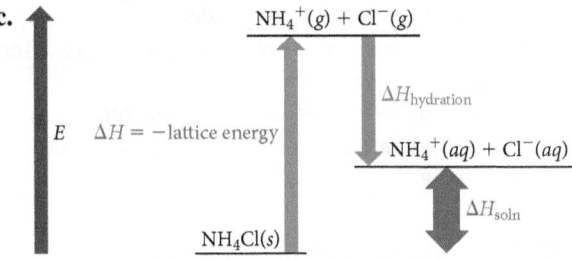
    d. The solution forms because chemical systems tend toward greater entropy.

37. −797 kJ/mol

39. $\Delta H_{soln} = -6 \times 10^1$ kJ/mol, −7 kJ of energy evolved

41. unsaturated

43. About 31 g will precipitate.

45. Boiling water releases any O_2 dissolved in it. The solubility of gases decreases with increasing temperature.

47. As pressure increases, nitrogen will more easily dissolve in blood. To reverse this process, divers should ascend to lower pressures.

49. 1.1 g

51. 1.92 M, 2.0 m, 10.4%

53. 0.340 L

55. 1.6×10^2 g

57. 1.4×10^4 g

59. Add water to 7.31 mL of concentrated solution until a total volume of 1.15 L is acquired.

61. a. Add water to 3.73 g KCl to a volume of 100 mL.
    b. Add 3.59 g KCl to 96.41 g H_2O.
    c. Add 5.0 g KCl to 95 g H_2O.

63. a. 0.417 M   **b.** 0.444 m   **c.** 7.41% by mass
    d. 0.00794   **e.** 0.794% by mole

65. 0.89 M

67. 15 m, 0.22

69. The level has decreased more in the beaker filled with pure water. The dissolved salt in the seawater decreases the vapor pressure and subsequently lowers the rate of vaporization.

71. 30.7 torr

73. a. $P_{hep} = 24.4$ torr, $P_{oct} = 5.09$ torr
    b. 29.5 torr
    c. 80.8% heptane by mass, 19.2% octane by mass
    d. The vapor is richer in the more volatile component.

75. $P_{chl} = 51.9$ torr, $P_{ace} = 274$ torr, $P_{tot} = 326$ torr. The solution is not ideal. The chloroform–acetone interactions are stronger than the chloroform–chloroform and acetone–acetone interactions.

77. freezing point (fp) = −1.27 °C, bp = 100.349 °C

79. freezing point (fp) = 1.0 °C, boiling point (bp) = 82.4 °C

81. 1.8×10^2 g/mol

83. 26.1 atm

85. 6.36×10^3 g/mol

87. a. fp = −0.558 °C, bp = 100.154 °C
    b. fp = −1.98 °C, bp = 100.546 °C
    c. fp = −2.5 °C, bp = 100.70 °C

89. 157 g

91. a. −0.632 °C
  b. 5.4 atm
  c. 100.18 °C
93. 2.3
95. 3.4
97. 23.0 torr
99. Chloroform is polar and has stronger solute–solvent interactions than nonpolar carbon tetrachloride.
101. $\Delta H_{soln} = 51$ kJ/mol, −8.7 °C
103. 2.2×10^{-3} M/atm
105. 1.3×10^4 L
107. 0.24 g
109. −24 °C
111. a. 1.1% by mass/V
  b. 1.6% by mass/V
  c. 5.3% by mass/V
113. 2.484
115. 0.229 atm
117. χ_{CHCl_3}(original) = 0.657, P_{CHCl_3}(condensed) = 0.346 atm
119. 1.74 M
121. $C_6H_{14}O_2$
123. 12 grams
125. 6.4×10^{-3} L
127. 22.4% glucose by mass, 77.6% sucrose by mass
129. $P_{iso} = 0.131$ atm, $P_{pro} = 0.068$ atm. The major intermolecular attractions are between the OH groups. The OH group at the end of the chain in propyl alcohol is more accessible than the one in the middle of the chain in isopropyl alcohol. In addition, the molecular shape of propyl alcohol is a straight chain of carbon atoms, while that of isopropyl alcohol is a branched chain and is more like a ball. The contact area between two ball-like objects is smaller than that of two chain-like objects. The smaller contact area in isopropyl alcohol means the molecules don't attract each other as strongly as do those of propyl alcohol. As a result of both of these factors, the vapor pressure of isopropyl alcohol is higher.
131. 0.0097 m
133. Na_2CO_3 0.050 M, $NaHCO_3$ 0.075 M
135. The water should not be immediately cycled back into the river. As the water was warmed, dissolved oxygen would have been released, since the amount of a gas able to be dissolved into a liquid decreases as the temperature of the liquid increases. As such, the water returned to the river would lack dissolved oxygen if it was still hot. To preserve the dissolved oxygen necessary for the survival of fish and other aquatic life, the water must first be cooled.
137. b. NaCl

Chapter 13

25. a. Rate $= -\dfrac{1}{2}\dfrac{\Delta[HBr]}{\Delta t} = \dfrac{\Delta[H_2]}{\Delta t} = \dfrac{\Delta[Br_2]}{\Delta t}$
  b. 1.8×10^{-3} M/s
  c. 0.040 mol Br_2

27. a. Rate $= -\dfrac{1}{2}\dfrac{\Delta[A]}{\Delta t} = -\dfrac{\Delta[B]}{\Delta t} = \dfrac{1}{3}\dfrac{\Delta[C]}{\Delta t}$
  b. $\dfrac{\Delta[B]}{\Delta t} = -0.0500$ M/s, $\dfrac{\Delta[C]}{\Delta t} = 0.150$ M/s

29.

$\Delta[Cl_2]/\Delta t$	$\Delta[F_2]/\Delta t$	$\Delta[ClF_3]/\Delta t$	Rate
−0.012 M/s	−0.036 M/s	0.024 M/s	0.012 M/s

31. a. 0 $\longrightarrow$ 10 s: Rate $= 8.7 \times 10^{-3}$ M/s
  40 $\longrightarrow$ 50 s: Rate $= 6.0 \times 10^{-3}$ M/s
  b. 1.4×10^{-2} M/s
33. a. (i) 1.0×10^{-2} M/s
  (ii) 8.5×10^{-3} M/s
  (iii) 0.013 M/s
  b.

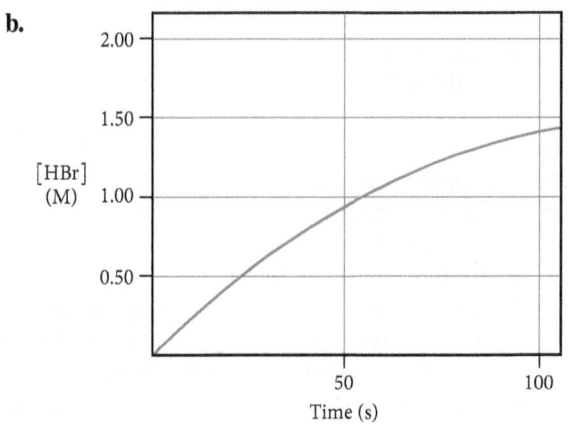

35. a. first order
  b.

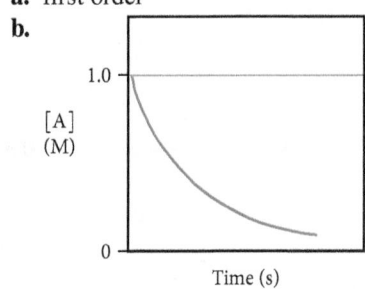

  c. Rate $= k[A]^1$, $k = 0.010$ s^{-1}
37. a. s^{-1} **b.** M^{-1}s^{-1} **c.** M·s^{-1}
39. a. Rate $= k[A][B]^2$ **b.** third order
  c. 2   **d.** 4
  e. 1   **f.** 8
41. second order, Rate $= 5.25$ M^{-1} s$^{-1}[A]^2$
43. Rate $= k[NO_2][F_2]$, $k = 2.57$ M^{-1} s^{-1}, second order
45. a. zero order
  b. first order
  c. second order
47. second order, $k = 2.25 \times 10^{-2}$ M^{-1} s^{-1}, [AB] at 25 s = 0.619 M
49. first order, $k = 1.12 \times 10^{-2}$ s^{-1}, Rate $= 2.8 \times 10^{-3}$ M/s
51. a. 4.5×10^{-3} s^{-1} **b.** Rate $= 4.5 \times 10^{-3}$ s$^{-1}[A]$
  c. 1.5×10^2 s   **d.** [A] = 0.0908 M
53. a. 4.88×10^3 s   **b.** 9.8×10^3 s
  c. 1.7×10^3 s   **d.** 0.146 M at 200 s, 0.140 M at 500 s
55. 6.8×10^8 yrs; 1.8×10^{17} atoms

57.

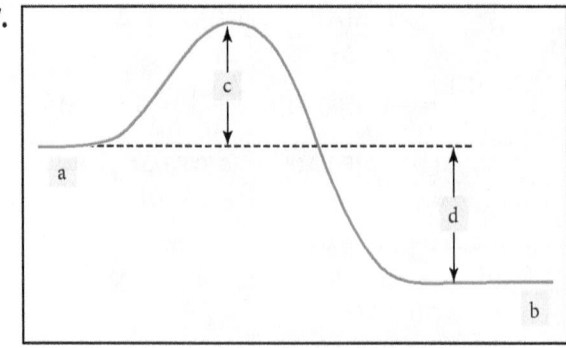

59. 17 s^{-1}

61. 61.90 kJ/mol

63. $E_a = 251$ kJ/mol, $A = 7.93 \times 10^{11} \text{ s}^{-1}$

65. $E_a = 23.0$ kJ/mol, $A = 8.05 \times 10^{10} \text{ s}^{-1}$

67. a. 122 kJ/mol

    b. 0.101 s^{-1}

69. 47.85 kJ/mol

71. a

73. The mechanism is valid.

75. a. $Cl_2(g) + CHCl_3(g) \longrightarrow HCl(g) + CCl_4(g)$

    b. $Cl(g)$, $CCl_3(g)$

    c. Rate $= k[Cl_2]^{1/2}[CHCl_3]$

77. Heterogeneous catalysts require a large surface area because catalysis can only happen at the surface. A greater surface area means greater opportunity for the substrate to react, which results in a faster reaction.

79. 10^{12}

81. a. first order, $k = 0.0462 \text{ hr}^{-1}$

    b. 15 hr

    c. 5.0×10^1 hr

83. 0.0531 M/s

85. rate $= 4.5 \times 10^{-4} [CH_3CHO]^2$, $k = 4.5 \times 10^{-4}$, 0.37 atm

87. 219 torr

89. 1×10^{-7} s

91. 1.6×10^2 seconds

93. a. 2

    b.

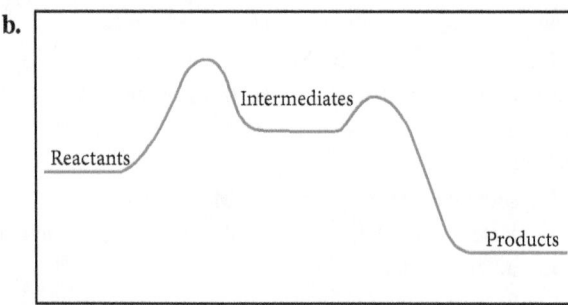

    c. first step   **d.** exothermic

95. a. 5.41 s

    b. 2.2 s for 25%, 5.4 s for 50%

    c. 0.28 at 10 s, 0.077 at 20 s

97. a. $E_a = 89.5$ kJ/mol, $A = 4.22 \times 10^{11} \text{ s}^{-1}$

    b. $2.5 \times 10^{-5} \text{ M}^{-1} \text{ s}^{-1}$

    c. 6.0×10^{-4} M/s

99. a. No

    b. No bond is broken, and the two radicals attract each other.

    c. Formation of diatomic gases from atomic gases.

101. 1.35×10^4 years

103. a. Both are valid. For both, all steps sum to overall reaction and the predicted rate law is consistent with experimental data.

    b. Buildup of $I(g)$

105. rate $= k_2[(k_1/k_{-1})[Br_2]]^{1/2}[H_2]$

    The rate law is 3/2 order overall.

107. a. 0%

    b. 25%

    c. 33%

109. 174 kJ

111. a. second order

    b. $CH_3NC + CH_3NC \underset{k_2}{\overset{k_1}{\rightleftharpoons}} CH_3NC^* + CH_3NC$ (fast)

    $CH_3NC^* \xrightarrow{k_3} CH_3CN$ (slow)

    Rate $= k_3[CH_3NC^*]$

    $k_1[CH_3NC]^2 = k_2[CH_3NC^*][CH_3NC]$

    $[CH_3NC^*] = \dfrac{k_1}{k_2}[CH_3NC]$

    Rate $= k_3 \times \dfrac{k_1}{k_2}[CH_3NC]$

    Rate $= k[CH_3NC]$

113. Rate $= k[A]^2$

$$Rate = -\frac{d[A]}{dt}$$

$$\frac{d[A]}{dt} = -k[A]^2$$

$$-\frac{d[A]}{[A]^2} = k \, dt$$

$$\int_{[A]_0}^{[A]} -\frac{1}{[A]^2} d[A] = \int_0^t k \, dt$$

$$\left[\frac{1}{[A]} \right]_{[A]_0}^{[A]} = k \, [t]_0^t$$

$$\frac{1}{[A]} - \frac{1}{[A]_0} = kt$$

$$\frac{1}{[A]} = kt + \frac{1}{[A]_0}$$

115. Rate $= k [CO][Cl_2]^{\frac{3}{2}}$

117. $[Cl_2] = 0.0084$ mol/L, $[NO] = 0.017$ mol/L

119. B is first order and A is second order.
B will be linear if you plot $\ln[B]$ versus time; A will be linear if you plot $1/[A]$ versus time.

Chapter 14

21. a. $K = \dfrac{[SbCl_3][Cl_2]}{[SbCl_5]}$ **b.** $K = \dfrac{[NO]^2[Br_2]}{[BrNO]^2}$

    c. $K = \dfrac{[CS_2][H_2]^4}{[CH_4][H_2S]^2}$ **d.** $K = \dfrac{[CO_2]^2}{[CO]^2[O_2]}$

23. The concentration of the reactants will be greater. No, this is not dependent on initial concentrations; it is dependent on the value of K_c.

25. a. figure v
  b. The change in the decrease of reactants and increase of products would be faster.
  c. No, catalysts affect kinetics, not equilibrium.
27. a. 4.42×10^{-5}, reactants favored
  b. 1.50×10^2, products favored
  c. 1.96×10^{-9}, reactants favored
29. 1.3×10^{-29}
31. a. 2.56×10^{-23}
  b. 1.3×10^{22}
  c. 81.9
33. a. $K_c = \dfrac{[HCO_3^-][OH^-]}{[CO_3^{2-}]}$

  b. $K_c = [O_2]^3$

  c. $K_c = \dfrac{[H_3O^+][F^-]}{[HF]}$

  d. $K_c = \dfrac{[NH_4^+][OH^-]}{[NH_3]}$

35. 136
37.

T (K)	[N₂]	[H₂]	[NH₃]	Kc
500	0.115	0.105	0.439	1.45×10^{-3}
575	0.110	0.249	0.128	9.6
775	0.120	0.140	4.39×10^{-3}	0.0584

39. 234 torr
41. 18
43. 3.3×10^2
45. 764
47. More solid will form.
49. Additional solid will not dissolve.
51. a. [A] = 0.20 M, [B] = 0.80 M
  b. [A] = 0.33 M, [B] = 0.67 M
  c. [A] = 0.38 M, [B] = 1.2 M
53. $[N_2O_4]$ = 0.0115 M, $[NO_2]$ = 0.0770 M
55. 0.199 M
57. 1.9×10^{-3} M
59. 7.84 torr
61. a. [A] = 0.38 M, [B] = 0.62 M, [C] = 0.62 M
  b. [A] = 0.90 M, [B] = 0.095 M, [C] = 0.095 M
  c. [A] = 1.0 M, [B] = 3.2×10^{-3} M,
     [C] = 3.2×10^{-3} M
63. a. shift left **b.** shift right
  c. shift right
65. a. shift right **b.** no effect
  c. no effect **d.** shift left
67. a. shift right **b.** shift left
  c. no effect
69. Increase temperature ⟶ shift right, decrease temperature ⟶ shift left. Increasing the temperature will increase the equilibrium constant.
71. b, d
73. a. 1.7×10^2
  b. $\dfrac{[Hb-CO]}{[Hb-O_2]}$ = 0.85 or 17/20

CO is highly toxic, as it blocks O_2 uptake by hemoglobin. CO at a level of 0.1% will replace nearly half of the O_2 in blood.

75. a. 1.68 atm
  b. 1.41 atm
77. 0.406 g
79. b, c, d
81. 0.0144 atm
83. 3.1×10^2 g, 20% yield
85. 0.12 atm
87. 0.72 atm
89. 0.017 g
91. 0.226
93. a. 29.3
  b. 86.3 torr
95. $P_{NO} = P_{Cl_2}$ = 429 torr
97. 1.27×10^{-2}
99. $K_P = 5.1 \times 10^{-2}$
101. Yes, because the volume affects Q.
103. a = 1, b = 2

Chapter 15

33. a. acid, $HNO_3(aq) \longrightarrow H^+(aq) + NO_3^-(aq)$
  b. acid, $NH_4^+(aq) \rightleftharpoons H^+(aq) + NH_3(aq)$
  c. base, $KOH(aq) \longrightarrow K^+(aq) + OH^-(aq)$
  d. acid, $HC_2H_3O_2(aq) \rightleftharpoons H^+(aq) + C_2H_3O_2^-(aq)$
35. a. $H_2CO_3(aq) + H_2O(l) \rightleftharpoons H_3O^+(aq) + HCO_3^-(aq)$
     acid   base   conj. acid   conj. base
  b. $NH_3(aq) + H_2O(l) \rightleftharpoons NH_4^+(aq) + OH^-(aq)$
     acid   base   conj. acid   conj. base
  c. $HNO_3(aq) + H_2O(l) \rightleftharpoons H_3O^+(aq) + NO_3^-(aq)$
     acid   base   conj. acid   conj. base
  d. $C_5H_5N(aq) + H_2O(l) \rightleftharpoons C_5H_5NH^+(aq) + OH^-(aq)$
     acid   base   conj. acid   conj. base
37. a. Cl^- **b.** HSO_3^- **c.** CHO_2^- **d.** F^-
39. $H_2PO_4^-(aq) + H_2O(l) \rightleftharpoons HPO_4^{2-}(aq) + H_3O^+(aq)$
  $H_2PO_4^-(aq) + H_2O(l) \rightleftharpoons H_3PO_4(aq) + OH^-(aq)$
41. a. strong   **b.** strong
  c. strong   **d.** weak, $K_a = \dfrac{[H_3O^+][HSO_3^-]}{[H_2SO_3]}$
43. a, b, c
45. a. F^- **b.** NO_2^- **c.** ClO^-
47. a. 8.3×10^{-7}, basic
  b. 1.2×10^{-10}, acidic
  c. 2.9×10^{-13}, acidic
49. a. pH = 7.77, pOH = 6.23
  b. pH = 7.00, pOH = 7.00
  c. pH = 5.66, pOH = 8.34
51.

[H₃O⁺]	[OH⁻]	pH	Acidic or Basic
7.1×10^{-4}	1.4×10^{-11}	3.15	Acidic
3.7×10^{-9}	2.7×10^{-6}	8.43	Basic
7.9×10^{-12}	1.3×10^{-3}	11.1	Basic
6.3×10^{-4}	1.6×10^{-11}	3.20	Acidic

53. $[H_3O^+] = 1.5 \times 10^{-7}$ M, pH = 6.81
55. pH = 1.36, 1.35, 1.34. A difference of 1 in the second significant digit in a concentration value produces a difference of 0.01 in pH. Therefore, the second significant digit in value of the concentration corresponds to the hundredths place in a pH value.

A-36   Appendix III: Answers to Selected Exercises

57. a. $[H_3O^+] = 0.25$ M, $[OH^-] = 4.0 \times 10^{-14}$ M, pH = 0.60
   b. $[H_3O^+] = 0.015$ M, $[OH^-] = 6.7 \times 10^{-13}$ M, pH = 1.82
   c. $[H_3O^+] = 0.072$ M, $[OH^-] = 1.4 \times 10^{-13}$ M, pH = 1.14
   d. $[H_3O^+] = 0.105$ M, $[OH^-] = 9.5 \times 10^{-14}$ M, pH = 0.979

59. a. 1.8 g **b.** 0.57 g **c.** 0.045 g

61. 2.21

63. $[H_3O^+] = 2.5 \times 10^{-3}$ M, pH = 2.59

65. a. 1.82 (approximation valid)
   b. 2.18 (approximation breaks down)
   c. 2.72 (approximation breaks down)

67. 2.75

69. 6.8×10^{-6}

71. 0.0063%

73. a. 0.42% **b.** 0.60% **c.** 1.3% **d.** 1.9%

75. 3.61×10^{-5}

77. a. pH = 2.03, percent ionization = 3.7%
   b. pH = 2.24, percent ionization = 5.7%
   c. pH = 2.40, percent ionization = 8.0%

79. a. 0.939 **b.** 1.07 **c.** 2.19 **d.** 3.02

81. a. $[OH^-] = 0.15$ M, $[H_3O^+] = 6.7 \times 10^{-14}$ M,
      pH = 13.17, pOH = 0.83
   b. $[OH^+] = 0.003$ M, $[H_3O^+] = 3.3 \times 10^{-12}$ M,
      pH = 11.48, pOH = 2.52
   c. $[OH^-] = 9.6 \times 10^{-4}$ M, $[H_3O^+] = 1.0 \times 10^{-11}$ M,
      pH = 10.98, pOH = 3.02
   d. $[OH^-] = 8.7 \times 10^{-5}$ M, $[H_3O^+] = 1.1 \times 10^{-10}$ M,
      pH = 9.93, pOH = 4.07

83. 13.842

85. 0.104 L

87. a. $NH_3(aq) + H_2O(l) \rightleftharpoons NH_4^+(aq) + OH^-(aq)$,
$$K_b = \frac{[NH_4^+][OH^-]}{[NH_3]}$$
   b. $HCO_3^-(aq) + H_2O(l) \rightleftharpoons$
      $H_2CO_3(aq) + OH^-(aq)$, $K_b = \dfrac{[H_2CO_3][OH^-]}{[HCO_3^-]}$
   c. $CH_3NH_2(aq) + H_2O(l) \rightleftharpoons$
      $CH_3NH_3^+(aq) + OH^-(aq)$, $K_b = \dfrac{[CH_3NH_3^+][OH^-]}{[CH_3NH_2]}$

89. $[OH^-] = 1.6 \times 10^{-3}$ M, pOH = 2.79, pH = 11.21

91. 7.48

93. 6.7×10^{-7}

95. a. neutral
   b. basic,
      $ClO^-(aq) + H_2O(l) \rightleftharpoons HClO(aq) + OH^-(aq)$
   c. basic,
      $CN^-(aq) + H_2O(l) \rightleftharpoons HCN(aq) + OH^-(aq)$
   d. neutral

97. $[OH^-] = 2.0 \times 10^{-6}$ M, pH = 8.30

99. a. acidic,
      $NH_4^+(aq) + H_2O(l) \rightleftharpoons NH_3(aq) + H_3O^+(aq)$
   b. neutral
   c. acidic, $Co(H_2O)_6^{3+}(aq) + H_2O(l) \rightleftharpoons$
      $Co(H_2O)_5(OH)^{2+}(aq) + H_3O^+(aq)$
   d. acidic, $CH_2NH_3^+(aq) + H_2O(l) \rightleftharpoons$
      $CH_2NH_2(aq) + H_3O^+(aq)$

101. a. acidic **b.** basic **c.** neutral
   d. acidic **e.** acidic

103. NaOH, NaHCO₃, NaCl, NH₄ClO₂, NH₄Cl

105. a. 5.13 **b.** 8.87 **c.** 7.0

107. $[K^+] = 0.15$ M, $[F^-] = 0.15$ M, $[HF] = 2.1 \times 10^{-6}$ M,
   $[OH^-] = 2.1 \times 10^{-6}$ M; $[H_3O^+] = 4.8 \times 10^{-9}$ M

109. $H_3PO_4(aq) + H_2O(l) \rightleftharpoons H_2PO_4^-(aq) + H_3O^+(aq)$,
$$K_{a_1} = \frac{[H_3O^+][H_2PO_4^-]}{[H_3PO_4]}$$
   $H_2PO_4^-(aq) + H_2O(l) \rightleftharpoons HPO_4^{2-}(aq) + H_3O^+(aq)$,
$$K_{a_2} = \frac{[H_3O^+][HPO_4^{2-}]}{[H_2PO_4^-]}$$
   $HPO_4^{2-}(aq) + H_2O(l) \rightleftharpoons PO_4^{3-}(aq) + H_3O^+(aq)$,
$$K_{a_3} = \frac{[H_3O^+][PO_4^{3-}]}{[HPO_4^{2-}]}$$

111. a. $[H_3O^+] = 0.048$ M, pH = 1.32
   b. $[H_3O^+] = 0.12$ M, pH = 0.92

113. $[H_2SO_3] = 0.418$ M
   $[HSO_3^-] = 0.082$ M
   $[SO_3^{2-}] = 6.4 \times 10^{-8}$ M
   $[H_3O^+] = 0.082$ M

115. a. $[H_3O^+] = 0.50$ M, pH = 0.30
   b. $[H_3O^+] = 0.11$ M, pH = 0.96 (*x is small*
      approximation breaks down)
   c. $[H_3O^+] = 0.059$ M, pH = 1.23

117. a. HCl, weaker bond
   b. HF, bond polarity
   c. H₂Se, weaker bond

119. a. H₂SO₄, more oxygen atoms bonded to S
   b. HClO₂, more oxygen atoms bonded to Cl
   c. HClO, Cl has higher electronegativity
   d. CCl₃COOH, Cl has higher electronegativity

121. S^{2-}, its conjugate acid (H₂S), is a weaker acid than H₂S

123. a. Lewis acid **b.** Lewis acid
   c. Lewis base **d.** Lewis base

125. a. acid: Fe^{3+}, base: H_2O
   b. acid: Zn^{2+}, base: NH_3
   c. acid: BF_3, base: $(CH_3)_3N$

127. a. weak **b.** strong
   c. weak **d.** strong

129. If blood became acidic, the H^+ concentration would
   increase. According to Le Châtelier's principle, equilibrium would be shifted to the left and the concentration
   of oxygenated Hb would decrease.

131. All acid will be neutralized.

133. $[H_3O^+]$(Great Lakes) = 3×10^{-5} M,
   $[H_3O^+]$(West Coast) = 4×10^{-6} M. The rain over the
   Great Lakes is about eight times more concentrated.

135. 2.7

137. a. 2.000 **b.** 1.52 **c.** 12.95
   d. 11.12 **e.** 5.03

139. a. 1.260   **b.** 8.22   **c.** 0.824
    d. 8.57   **e.** 1.171

141. a. $CN^-(aq) + H^+(aq) \rightleftharpoons HCN(aq)$
    b. $NH_4^+(aq) + OH^-(aq) \rightleftharpoons NH_3(aq) + H_2O(l)$
    c. $CN^-(aq) + NH_4^+(aq) \rightleftharpoons HCN(aq) + NH_3(aq)$
    d. $HSO_4^-(aq) + C_2H_3O_2^-(aq) \rightleftharpoons$
                    $SO_4^{2-}(aq) + HC_2H_3O_2(aq)$
    e. no reaction between the major species

143. 0.794

145. $K_a = 8.3 \times 10^{-4}$

147. 6.79

149. 2.14

151. $[A^-] = 4.5 \times 10^{-5}$ M
    $[H^+] = 2.2 \times 10^{-4}$ M
    $[HA_2^-] = 1.8 \times 10^{-4}$ M

153. 9.28

155. 50.1 g $NaHCO_3$

157. b

159. $CH_3COOH < CH_2ClCOOH < CHCl_2COOH < CCl_3COOH$

Chapter 16

27. d

29. a. 3.62
    b. 9.11

31. pure water: 2.1%, in $NaC_7H_5O_2$: 0.065%. The percent ionization in the sodium benzoate solution is much smaller because the presence of the benzoate ion shifts the equilibrium to the left.

33. a. 2.14   **b.** 8.32   **c.** 3.46

35. $HCl + NaC_2H_3O_2 \longrightarrow HC_2H_3O_2 + NaCl$
    $NaOH + HC_2H_3O_2 \longrightarrow NaC_2H_3O_2 + H_2O$

37. a. 3.62   **b.** 9.11

39. a. 7.60   **b.** 11.18   **c.** 4.61

41. a. 3.86   **b.** 8.95

43. 3.5

45. 3.7 g

47. a. 4.74   **b.** 4.68   **c.** 4.81

49. a. initial 7.00   after 1.70
    b. initial 4.71   after 4.56
    c. initial 10.78   after 10.66

51. 1.2 g; 2.7 g

53. a. yes   **b.** no
    c. yes   **d.** no
    e. no

55. a. 7.4   **b.** 0.3 g   **c.** 0.14 g

57. $KClO/HClO = 0.79$

59. a. does not exceed capacity
    b. does not exceed capacity
    c. does not exceed capacity
    d. does not exceed capacity

61. i. (a) pH = 8, (b) pH = 7
    ii. (a) weak acid, (b) strong acid

63. a. 40.0 mL HI for both
    b. KOH: neutral, CH_3NH_2: acidic
    c. CH_3NH_2

d. Titration of KOH with HI:

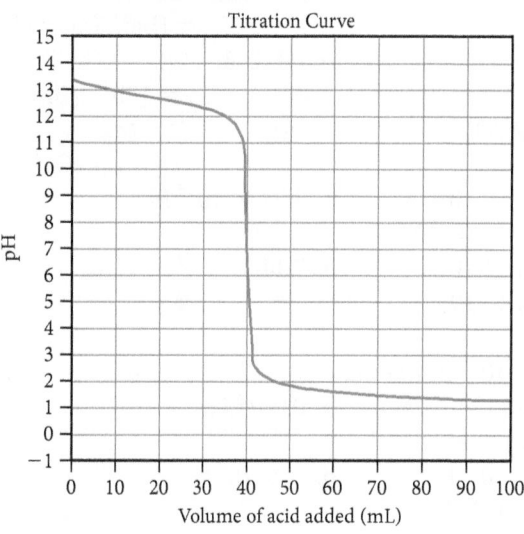

Titration of CH_3NH_2 with HI:

65. a. pH = 9, added base = 30 mL
    b. 0 mL   **c.** 15 mL
    d. 30 mL   **e** 30 mL

67. a. 0.757   **b.** 30.6 mL   **c.** 1.038
    d. 7   **e** 12.15

69. a. 13.06   **b.** 28.8 mL   **c.** 12.90
    d. 7   **e.** 2.07

71. a. 2.86   **b.** 16.8 mL   **c.** 4.37
    d. 4.74   **e.** 8.75   **f.** 12.17

73. a. 11.94   **b.** 29.2 mL   **c.** 11.33
    d. 10.64   **e.** 5.87   **f.** 1.90

75. i. (a)   **ii.** (b)

77. $pK_a = 3$, 82 g/mol

79. First equivalence: 22.7 mL
    Second equivalence: 45.4 mL

81. The indicator will appear red. The pH range is 4 to 6.

83. a. phenol red, *m*-nitrophenol
    b. alizarin, bromothymol blue, phenol red
    c. alizarin yellow R

85. a. $BaSO_4(s) \rightleftharpoons Ba^{2+}(aq) + SO_4^{2-}(aq)$,
$$K_{sp} = [Ba^{2+}][SO_4^{2-}]$$
   b. $PbBr_2(s) \rightleftharpoons Pb^{2+}(aq) + 2\ Br^-(aq)$,
$$K_{sp} = [Pb^{2+}][Br^-]^2$$
   c. $Ag_2CrO_4(s) \rightleftharpoons 2\ Ag^+(aq) + CrO_4^{2-}(aq)$,
$$K_{sp} = [Ag^+]^2[CrO_4^{2-}]$$

87. a. 7.31×10^{-7} M   **b.** 3.72×10^{-5} M
   c. 3.32×10^{-4} M
89. a. 1.07×10^{-21} **b.** 7.14×10^{-7}
   c. 7.44×10^{-11}
91. AX_2
93. 2.07×10^{-5} g/100 mL
95. a. 0.0183 M   **b.** 0.00755 M
   c. 0.00109 M
97. a. 5×10^{14} M   **b.** 5×10^8 M
   c. 5×10^4 M
99. a. more soluble, CO_3^{2-} is basic
   b. more soluble, S^{2-} is basic
   c. not, neutral
   d. not, neutral
101. precipitate will form, CaF_2
103. precipitate will form, $Mg(OH)_2$
105. a. 0.018 M   **b.** 1.4×10^{-7} M
   c. 1.1×10^{-5} M
107. a. $BaSO_4$, 1.1×10^{-8} M
   b. 3.0×10^{-8} M
109. 8.7×10^{-10} M
111. 5.6×10^{16}
113. 4.03
115. 3.57
117. HCl, 4.7 g
119. a. $NaOH(aq) + KHC_8H_4O_4(aq) \longrightarrow Na^+(aq) +$
$$K^+(aq) + C_8H_4O_4^{2-}(aq) + H_2O(l)$$
   b. 0.1046 M
121. 4.73
123. 176 g/mol; 1.0×10^{-4}
125. 14.2 L
127. 1.6×10^{-7} M
129. 8.0×10^{-8} M
131. 6.29
133. 0.172 M
135. The ratio by mass of dimethyl ammonium chloride to dimethyl amine needed is 3.6.
137. 0.18 M benzoic acid, 0.41 M sodium benzoate
139. 51.6 g
141. 1.8×10^{-11} (based on this data)
143. a. 5.5×10^{-25} M   **b.** 5.5×10^{-4} M
145. 1.38 L
147. 12.97
149. a. pH < pK_a **b.** pH > pK_a
   c. pH = pK_a **d.** pH > pK_a
151. b
153. a. no difference   **b.** less soluble
   c. more soluble

Chapter 17

27. a, c
29. System B has the greatest entropy. There is only one energetically equivalent arrangement for System A. However, the particles of System B may exchange positions for a second energetically equivalent arrangement.
31. a. $\Delta S > 0$ **b.** $\Delta S < 0$
   c. $\Delta S < 0$ **d.** $\Delta S < 0$
33. a. $\Delta S_{sys} > 0$, $\Delta S_{surr} > 0$, spontaneous at all temperatures
   b. $\Delta S_{sys} < 0$, $\Delta S_{surr} < 0$, nonspontaneous at all temperatures
   c. $\Delta S_{sys} < 0$, $\Delta S_{surr} < 0$, nonspontaneous at all temperatures
   d. $\Delta S_{sys} > 0$, $\Delta S_{surr} > 0$, spontaneous at all temperatures
35. a. 1.29×10^3 J/K   **b.** 5.00×10^3 J/K
   c. -3.83×10^2 J/K   **d.** -1.48×10^3 J/K
37. a. -649 J/K, nonspontaneous
   b. 649 J/K, spontaneous
   c. 123 J/K, spontaneous
   d. -76 J/K, nonspontaneous
39. a. 1.93×10^5 J, nonspontaneous
   b. -1.93×10^5 J, spontaneous
   c. -3.7×10^4 J, spontaneous
   d. 4.7×10^4 J, nonspontaneous
41. -2.247×10^6 J, spontaneous
43.

ΔH	ΔS	ΔG	Low Temperature	High Temperature
−	+	−	Spontaneous	Spontaneous
−	−	Temperature dependent	Spontaneous	Nonspontaneous
+	+	Temperature dependent	Nonspontaneous	Spontaneous
+	−	+	Nonspontaneous	Nonspontaneous

45. It increases.
47. a. $CO_2(g)$, greater molar mass and complexity
   b. $CH_3OH(g)$, gas phase
   c. $CO_2(g)$, greater molar mass and complexity
   d. $SiH_4(g)$, greater molar mass
   e. $CH_3CH_2CH_3(g)$, greater molar mass and complexity
   f. $NaBr(aq)$, aqueous
49. a. He, Ne, SO_2, NH_3, CH_3CH_2OH. From He to Ne there is an increase in molar mass; beyond that, the molecules increase in complexity.
   b. $H_2O(s)$, $H_2O(l)$, $H_2O(g)$; increase in entropy in going from solid to liquid to gas phase.
   c. CH_4, CF_4, CCl_4; increasing entropy with increasing molar mass.
51. a. -120.8 J/K, decrease in moles of gas
   b. 133.9 J/K, increase in moles of gas
   c. -42.0 J/K, small change because moles of gas stay constant
   d. -390.8 J/K, decrease in moles of gas

53. -89.3 J/K, decrease in moles of gas
55. $\Delta H^\circ_{rxn} = -1277$ kJ, $\Delta S^\circ_{rxn} = 313.6$ J/K,
$\Delta G^\circ_{rxn} = -1.370 \times 10^3$ kJ; yes
57. a. $\Delta H^\circ_{rxn} = 57.2$ kJ, $\Delta S^\circ_{rxn} = 175.8$ J/K,
$\Delta G^\circ_{rxn} = 4.8 \times 10^3$ J/mol; nonspontaneous, becomes spontaneous at high temperatures
b. $\Delta H^\circ_{rxn} = 176.2$ kJ, $\Delta S^\circ_{rxn} = 285.1$ J/K,
$\Delta G^\circ_{rxn} = 91.2$ kJ; nonspontaneous, becomes spontaneous at high temperatures
c. $\Delta H^\circ_{rxn} = 98.8$ kJ, $\Delta S^\circ_{rxn} = 141.5$ J/K,
$\Delta G^\circ_{rxn} = 56.6$ kJ; nonspontaneous, becomes spontaneous at high temperatures
d. $\Delta H^\circ_{rxn} = -91.8$ kJ, $\Delta S^\circ_{rxn} = -198.1$ J/K,
$\Delta G^\circ_{rxn} = -32.8$ kJ; spontaneous
59. a. 2.8 kJ
b. 91.2 kJ
c. 56.4 kJ
d. -32.8 kJ
Values are comparable. The method using ΔH° and ΔS° can be used to determine how ΔG° changes with temperature.
61. a. -72.5 kJ, spontaneous
b. -11.4 kJ, spontaneous
c. 9.1 kJ, nonspontaneous
63. -29.4 kJ
65. a. 19.3 kJ
b. (i) 2.9 kJ   (ii) -2.9 kJ
c. The partial pressure of iodine is very low.
67. 11.9 kJ
69. a. 1.48×10^{90} **b.** 2.09×10^{-26}
71. a. -24.8 kJ   **b.** 0   **c.** 9.4 kJ
73. a. 1.90×10^{47} **b.** 1.51×10^{-13}
75. $\Delta H^\circ = 50.6$ kJ
$\Delta S^\circ = 226$ J$\cdot$K
77. 4.8
79. a. $+$ **b.** $-$ **c.** $-$
81. a. $\Delta G^\circ = 175.2$ kJ, $K = 1.95 \times 10^{-31}$, nonspontaneous
b. 133 kJ, yes
83. Cl_2: $\Delta H^\circ_{rxn} = -182.1$ kJ, $\Delta S^\circ_{rxn} = -134.4$ J/K,
$\Delta G^\circ_{rxn} = -142.0$ kJ $K = 7.94 \times 10^{24}$
Br_2: $\Delta H^\circ_{rxn} = -121.6$ kJ, $\Delta S^\circ_{rxn} = -134.2$ J/K,
$\Delta G^\circ_{rxn} = -81.6$ kJ $K = 2.02 \times 10^{14}$
I_2: $\Delta H^\circ_{rxn} = -48.3$ kJ, $\Delta S^\circ_{rxn} = -132.2$ J/K,
$\Delta G^\circ_{rxn} = -8.9$ kJ $K = 37$
Cl_2 is the most spontaneous, I_2 is the least. Spontaneity is determined by the standard enthalpy of formation of the dihalogenated ethane. Higher temperatures make the reactions less spontaneous.
85. a. 107.8 kJ   **b.** 5.0×10^{-7} atm
c. spontaneous at higher temperatures, $T = 923.4$ K
87. a. 2.22×10^5 **b.** 94.4 mol

89. a. $\Delta G^\circ = -689.6$ kJ, ΔG° becomes less negative
b. $\Delta G^\circ = -665.2$ kJ, ΔG° becomes less negative
c. $\Delta G^\circ = -632.4$ kJ, ΔG° becomes less negative
d. $\Delta G^\circ = -549.3$ kJ, ΔG° becomes less negative
91. With one exception, the formation of any oxide of nitrogen at 298 K requires more moles of gas as reactants than are formed as products. For example, 1 mol of N_2O requires 0.5 mol of O_2 and 1 mol of N_2, 1 mol of N_2O_3 requires 1 mol of N_2 and 1.5 mol of O_2, and so on. The exception is NO, where 1 mol of NO requires 0.5 mol of O_2 and 0.5 mol of N_2:
$$\frac{1}{2}N_2(g) + \frac{1}{2}O_2(g) \longrightarrow NO(g)$$
This reaction has a positive ΔS because what is essentially mixing of the N and O has taken place in the product.
93. 15.0 kJ
95. a. Positive, the process is spontaneous. It is slow unless a spark is applied.
b. Positive, although the change in the system is not spontaneous; the overall change, which includes such processes as combustion or water flow to generate electricity, is spontaneous.
c. Positive, the acorn-oak tree system is becoming more ordered, so the processes associated with growth are not spontaneous. But they are driven by spontaneous processes such as the generation of heat by the sun and the reactions that produce energy in the cell.
97. At 18.3 mmHg $\Delta G = 0$, at 760 mmHg
$\Delta G^\circ = 55.4$ kJ
99. a. 3.24×10^{-3}
b. $NH_3 + ATP + H_2O \longrightarrow NH_3{-}P_i + ADP$
$NH_3{-}P_i + C_5H_8O_4N^- \longrightarrow C_5H_9O_3N_2 + P_i + H_2O$
$NH_3 + C_5H_8O_4N^- + ATP \longrightarrow C_5H_9O_3N_2 + ADP + P_i$
$\Delta G^\circ = -16.3$ kJ, $K = 7.20 \times 10^2$
101. a. -95.3 kJ/mol. Since the number of moles of reactants and products are the same, the decrease in volume affects the entropy of both equally, so there is no change in ΔG.
b. 102.8 kJ/mol. The entropy of the reactants (1.5 mol) is decreased more than the entropy of the product (1 mol). Since the product is relatively more favored at lower volume, ΔG is less positive.
c. 204.2 kJ/mol. The entropy of the product (1 mol) is decreased more than the entropy of the reactant (0.5 mol). Since the product is relatively less favored, ΔG is more positive.
103. $\Delta H^\circ = -93$ kJ, $\Delta S^\circ = -2.0 \times 10^2$ J/K
105. ΔS_{vap} diethyl ether $= 86.1$ J/mol K,
ΔS_{vap} acetone $= 88.4$ J/mol K,
ΔS_{vap} benzene $= 87.3$ J/mol K,
ΔS_{vap} chloroform $= 88.0$ J/mol K
Because water and ethanol hydrogen bond they are more ordered in the liquid and we expect ΔS_{vap} to be more positive. Ethanol $38600/351.0 = 110$ J/mol K, $H_2O = 40700/373.2 = 109$ J/mol K

107. c
109. b
111. c
113. $\Delta G^\circ_{\text{rxn}}$ is negative and ΔG_{rxn} is positive.

Chapter 18

37. a. $3 \text{ K}(s) + \text{Cr}^{3+}(aq) \longrightarrow \text{Cr}(s) + 3 \text{ K}^+(aq)$
  b. $2 \text{ Al}(s) + 3 \text{ Fe}^{2+}(aq) \longrightarrow 2 \text{ Al}^{3+}(aq) + 3 \text{ Fe}(s)$
  c. $2 \text{ BrO}_3^-(aq) + 3 \text{ N}_2\text{H}_4(g) \longrightarrow$
       $2 \text{ Br}^-(aq) + 3 \text{ N}_2(g) + 6 \text{ H}_2\text{O}(l)$
39. a. $\text{PbO}_2(s) + 2 \text{ I}^-(aq) + 4 \text{ H}^+(aq) \longrightarrow$
       $\text{Pb}^{2+}(aq) + \text{I}_2(s) + 2 \text{ H}_2\text{O}(l)$
  b. $5 \text{ SO}_3^{2-}(aq) + 2 \text{ MnO}_4^-(aq) + 6 \text{ H}^+(aq) \longrightarrow$
       $5 \text{ SO}_4^{2-}(aq) + 2 \text{ Mn}^{2+}(aq) + 3 \text{ H}_2\text{O}(l)$
  c. $\text{S}_2\text{O}_3^{2-}(aq) + 4 \text{ Cl}_2(g) + 5 \text{ H}_2\text{O}(l) \longrightarrow$
       $2 \text{ SO}_4^{2-}(aq) + 8 \text{ Cl}^-(aq) + 10 \text{ H}^+(aq)$
41. a. $\text{H}_2\text{O}_2(aq) + 2 \text{ ClO}_2(aq) + 2 \text{ OH}^-(aq) \longrightarrow$
       $\text{O}_2(g) + 2 \text{ ClO}_2^-(aq) + 2 \text{ H}_2\text{O}(l)$
  b. $\text{Al}(s) + \text{MnO}_4^-(aq) + 2 \text{ H}_2\text{O}(l) \longrightarrow$
       $\text{Al(OH)}_4^-(aq) + \text{MnO}_2(s)$
  c. $\text{Cl}_2(g) + 2 \text{ OH}^-(aq) \longrightarrow$
       $\text{Cl}^-(aq) + \text{ClO}^-(aq) + \text{H}_2\text{O}(l)$

43. a.

b.

c.

$\begin{array}{l}\text{Zn}(s) \longrightarrow \\ \text{Zn}^{2+}(aq) + 2 \text{ e}^-\end{array}$ $\begin{array}{l}\text{O}_2(g) + 4 \text{ H}^+(aq) + 2 \text{ e}^- \longrightarrow \\ \qquad\qquad\qquad 2 \text{ H}_2\text{O}(l)\end{array}$

45. a. 0.93 V   **b.** 0.41 V   **c.** 1.99 V
47. a, c, d

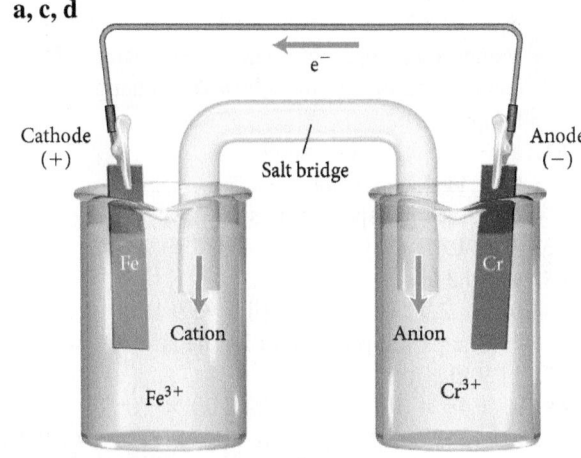

  b. $\text{Cr}(s) + \text{Fe}^{3+}(aq) \longrightarrow \text{Cr}^{3+}(aq) + \text{Fe}(s)$, $E^\circ_{\text{cell}} = 0.69$ V
49. a. $\text{Pb}(s)\,|\,\text{Pb}^{2+}(aq)\,\|\,\text{Ag}^+(aq)\,|\,\text{Ag}(s)$
  b. $\text{Pt}(s),\,\text{I}_2(s)\,|\,\text{I}^-(aq)\,\|\,\text{ClO}_2^-(aq)\,|\,\text{ClO}_2(g)\,|\,\text{Pt}(s)$
  c. $\text{Zn}(s)\,|\,\text{Zn}^{2+}(aq)\,\|\,\text{H}_2\text{O}(l)\,|\,\text{H}^+(aq)\,|\,\text{O}_2(g)\,|\,\text{Pt}(s)$

51.

$3 \text{ Sn}(s) + 2 \text{ NO}_3^-(aq) + 8 \text{ H}^+(aq) \longrightarrow$
$3 \text{ Sn}^{2+}(aq) + 2 \text{ NO}(g) + 4 \text{ H}_2\text{O}(l)$, $E^\circ_{\text{cell}} = 1.10$ V
53. b, c occur spontaneously in the forward direction
55. aluminum

57. a. yes, $2\ Al(s) + 6\ H^+(aq) \longrightarrow 2\ Al^{3+}(aq) + 3\ H_2(g)$
 b. no
 c. yes, $Pb(s) + 2\ H^+(aq) \longrightarrow Pb^{2+}(aq) + H_2(g)$
59. a. yes, $3\ Cu(s) + 2\ NO_3^-(aq) + 8\ H^+(aq) \longrightarrow$
$$3\ Cu^{2+}(aq) + 2\ NO(g) + 4\ H_2O(l)$$
 b. no
61. a. -1.70 V, nonspontaneous **b.** 1.97 V, spontaneous
 c. -1.51 V, nonspontaneous
63. a
65. a. -432 kJ   **b.** 52 kJ   **c.** -1.7×10^2 kJ
67. a. 5.31×10^{75} **b.** 7.7×10^{-10} **c.** 6.3×10^{29}
69. 5.6×10^5
71. $\Delta G° = -7.97$ kJ, $E°_{cell} = 0.041$ V
73. a. 1.04 V   **b.** 0.97 V   **c.** 1.11 V
75. 1.87 V
77. a. 0.56 V   **b.** 0.52 V
 c. $[Ni^{2+}] = 0.003$ M, $[Zn^{2+}] = 1.60$ M

79.

81. $\dfrac{[Sn^{2+}](ox)}{[Sn^{2+}](red)} = 4.2 \times 10^{-4}$

83. 0.3762
85. 1.038 V
87. a, c would prevent the corrosion of iron
89.

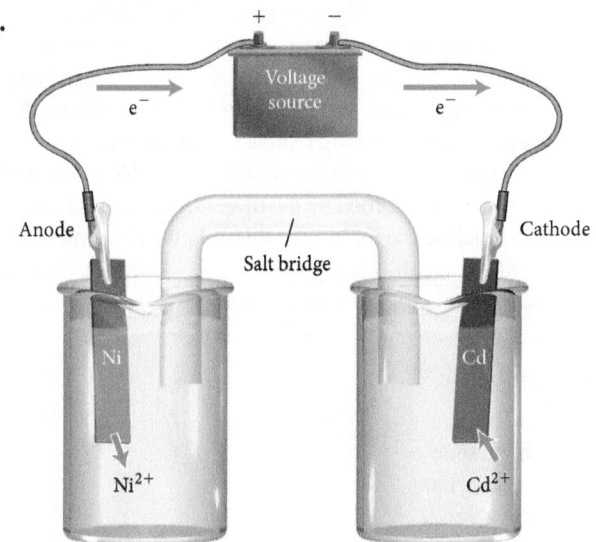

minimum voltage $= 0.17$ V

91. oxidation: $2\ Br^-(l) \longrightarrow Br_2(g) + 2\ e^-$
 reduction: $K^+(l) + e^- \longrightarrow K(l)$
93. oxidation: $2\ Br^-(l) \longrightarrow Br_2(g) + 2\ e^-$
 reduction: $K^+(l) + e^- \longrightarrow K(l)$
95. a. anode: $2\ Br^- \longrightarrow Br_2(l) + 2\ e^-$
 cathode: $2\ H_2O(l) + 2\ e^- \longrightarrow H_2(g) + 2\ OH^-(aq)$
 b. anode: $2\ I^-(aq) \longrightarrow I_2(s) + 2\ e^-$
 cathode: $Pb^{2+}(aq) + 2\ e^- \longrightarrow Pb(s)$
 c. anode: $2\ H_2O(l) \longrightarrow O_2(g) + 4\ H^+(aq) + 4\ e^-$
 cathode: $2\ H_2O(l) + 2\ e^- \longrightarrow H_2(g) + 2\ OH^-(aq)$

97.

99. 1.8×10^2 s
101. 1.2×10^3 A
103. $2\ MnO_4^-(aq) + 5\ Zn(s) + 16\ H^+(aq) \longrightarrow$
$$2\ Mn^{2+}(aq) + 5\ Zn^{2+}(aq) + 8\ H_2O(l)$$
 34.9 mL
105. The drawing should show that several Al atoms
 dissolve into solution as Al^{3+} ions and that several
 Cu^{2+} ions are deposited on the Al surface as solid Cu.
107. a. 68.3 mL
 b. cannot be dissolved
 c. cannot be dissolved
109. 0.25
111. There are no paired reactions that produce more than
 about 5 or 6 V.
113. a. 2.83 V
 b. 2.71 V
 c. 16 hr
115. 176 hr
117. 0.71 V
119. a. $\Delta G° = 461$ kJ, $K = 1.4 \times 10^{-81}$
 b. $\Delta G° = 2.7 \times 10^2$ kJ, $K = 2.0 \times 10^{-48}$
121. MCl_4
123. 51.3%
125. $pH = 0.85$
127. 0.83 M
129. 4.1×10^5 L
131. 435 s

133. 8.39% U

135. The overall cell reaction for both cells is
$2\,Cu^+(aq) \longrightarrow Cu^{2+}(aq) + Cu(s)$. The difference in
$E°$ is because n = 1 for the first cell and n = 2 for the
second cell. For both cells, $\Delta G° = -35.1$ kJ.

137. a

139. $\Delta G°_{rxn}$ is positive and $E°_{cell}$ is negative.

Chapter 19

31. a. $^{234}_{92}U \longrightarrow {}^{4}_{2}He + {}^{230}_{90}Th$

  b. $^{230}_{90}Th \longrightarrow {}^{4}_{2}He + {}^{226}_{88}Ra$

  c. $^{214}_{82}Pb \longrightarrow {}^{0}_{-1}e + {}^{214}_{83}Bi$

  d. $^{13}_{7}N \longrightarrow {}^{0}_{+1}e + {}^{13}_{6}C$

  e. $^{51}_{24}Cr + {}^{0}_{-1}e \longrightarrow {}^{51}_{23}V$

33. $^{232}_{90}Th \longrightarrow {}^{4}_{2}He + {}^{228}_{88}Ra$

  $^{228}_{88}Ra \longrightarrow {}^{0}_{-1}e + {}^{228}_{89}Ac$

  $^{228}_{89}Ac \longrightarrow {}^{0}_{-1}e + {}^{228}_{90}Th$

  $^{228}_{90}Th \longrightarrow {}^{4}_{2}He + {}^{224}_{88}Ra$

35. a. $^{221}_{87}Fr$

  b. $^{0}_{-1}e$

  c. $^{0}_{+1}e$

  d. $^{0}_{-1}e$

37. a. stable, N/Z ratio is close to 1, acceptable for low
   Z atoms

  b. not stable, N/Z ratio is much too high for low
   Z atom

  c. not stable, N/Z ratio is less than 1, much too low

  d. stable, N/Z ratio is acceptable for this Z

39. Sc, V, and Mn, each have odd numbers of protons.
   Atoms with an odd number of protons typically have
   less stable isotopes than those with an even number
   of protons.

41. a. beta decay

  b. positron emission

  c. positron emission

  d. positron emission

43. a. Cs-125

  b. Fe-62

45. 2.34×10^9 years

47. 0.57 g

49. 10.8 hrs

51. 2.66×10^3 yr

53. 2.4×10^4 yr

55. 2.7×10^9 yr

57. $^{235}_{92}U + {}^{1}_{0}n \longrightarrow {}^{144}_{54}Xe + {}^{90}_{38}Sr + 2\,{}^{1}_{0}n$

59. $^{2}_{1}H + {}^{2}_{1}H \longrightarrow {}^{3}_{2}He + {}^{1}_{0}n$

61. $^{238}_{92}U + {}^{1}_{0}n \longrightarrow {}^{239}_{92}U$

  $^{239}_{92}U \longrightarrow {}^{239}_{93}Np + {}^{0}_{-1}e$

  $^{239}_{93}Np \longrightarrow {}^{239}_{94}Pu + {}^{0}_{-1}e$

63. $^{249}_{98}Cf + {}^{12}_{6}C \longrightarrow {}^{257}_{104}Rf + 4\,{}^{1}_{0}n$

65. 9.0×10^{13} J

67. a. mass defect = 0.13701 amu
   binding energy = 7.976 MeV/nucleon

  b. mass defect = 0.54369 amu
   binding energy = 8.732 MeV/nucleon

  c. mass defect = 1.16754 amu
   binding energy = 8.431 MeV/nucleon

69. 7.228×10^{10} J/g U-235

71. 7.84×10^{10} J/g H-2

73. radiation: 25 J, fall: 370 J

75. 68 mi

77. a. $^{1}_{1}p + {}^{9}_{4}Be \longrightarrow {}^{6}_{3}Li + {}^{4}_{2}He$
   1.03×10^{11} J/mol

  b. $^{209}_{83}Bi + {}^{64}_{28}Ni \longrightarrow {}^{272}_{111}Rg + {}^{1}_{0}n$
   1.141×10^{13} J/mol

  c. $^{179}_{74}W + {}^{0}_{-1}e \longrightarrow {}^{179}_{73}Ta$
   7.59×10^{10} J/mol

79. a. $^{114}_{44}Ru \longrightarrow {}^{0}_{-1}e + {}^{114}_{45}Rh$

  b. $^{216}_{88}Ra \longrightarrow {}^{0}_{+1}e + {}^{216}_{87}Fr$

  c. $^{58}_{30}Zn \longrightarrow {}^{0}_{+1}e + {}^{58}_{29}Cu$

  d. $^{31}_{10}Ne \longrightarrow {}^{0}_{-1}e + {}^{31}_{11}Na$

81. 2.9×10^{21} beta emissions, 3700 Ci

83. 1.6×10^{-5} L

85. 4.94×10^7 kJ/mol

87. 7.72 MeV

89. ^{14}N

91. 0.15%

93. 1.24×10^{21} atoms

95. 2.42×10^{-12} m

97. −0.7 MeV, there is no coulombic barrier for collision
   with a neutron.

99. a. 1.164×10^{10} kJ

  b. 0.1299 g

101. U-235 forms Pb-207 in seven α-decays and four
   β-decays and Th-232 forms Pb-208 in six α-decays and
   four β-decays.

103. 3.0×10^2 K

105. $^{21}_{9}F \longrightarrow {}^{21}_{10}Ne + {}^{0}_{-1}e$

107. Nuclide A is more dangerous because the half-life is
   shorter (18.5 days) and so it decays faster.

109. Iodine is used by the thyroid gland to make hormones.
   Normally we ingest iodine in foods, especially iodized
   salt. The thyroid gland cannot tell the difference between
   stable and radioactive iodine and will absorb both. KI tablets work by blocking radioactive iodine from entering the
   thyroid. When a person takes KI, the stable iodine in the
   tablet gets absorbed by the thyroid. Because KI contains
   so much stable iodine, the thyroid gland becomes "full"
   and cannot absorb any more iodine—either stable or radioactive—for the next 24 hours.

Chapter 20

35. a. alkane

  b. alkene

  c. alkyne

  d. alkene

37. $CH_3-CH_2-CH_2-CH_2-CH_2-CH_2-CH_3$

$CH_3-CH-CH_2-CH_2-CH_2-CH_3$
$\quad\quad\;\; |$
$\quad\quad\; CH_3$

$CH_3-CH_2-CH-CH_2-CH_2-CH_3$
$\quad\quad\quad\quad\;\; |$
$\quad\quad\quad\quad CH_3$

$\quad\quad\; CH_3$
$\quad\quad\quad |$
$CH_3-CH-CH-CH_2-CH_3$
$\quad\quad\quad\quad |$
$\quad\quad\quad\; CH_3$

$\quad\quad\quad\; CH_3$
$\quad\quad\quad\quad |$
$CH_3-CH_2-C-CH_2-CH_3$
$\quad\quad\quad\quad |$
$\quad\quad\quad\; CH_3$

$\quad\quad\;\; CH_3$
$\quad\quad\quad\; |$
$H_3C-C-CH_2-CH_2-CH_3$
$\quad\quad\quad |$
$\quad\quad\; CH_3$

$H_3C-CH-CH_2-CH-CH_3$
$\quad\quad\;\; |\quad\quad\quad\; |$
$\quad\quad\; CH_3\quad\quad\; CH_3$

$\quad\quad\quad\; CH_3$
$\quad\quad\quad\quad |$
$H_3C-C-CH-CH_3$
$\quad\quad\quad |\quad\; |$
$\quad\quad\; CH_3\; CH_3$

$H_3C-CH_2-CH-CH_2-CH_3$
$\quad\quad\quad\quad |$
$\quad\quad\quad\; CH_2$
$\quad\quad\quad\quad |$
$\quad\quad\quad\; CH_3$

39. a. no **b.** yes **c.** yes **d.** no
41. a. enantiomers **b.** same
c. enantiomers
43. a. pentane **b.** 2-methylbutane
c. 4-isopropyl-2-methylheptane
d. 4-ethyl-2-methylhexane
45. a. $CH_3-CH_2-CH-CH_2-CH_2-CH_3$
$\quad\quad\quad\quad\quad |$
$\quad\quad\quad\quad\; CH_2-CH_3$

b. $CH_3-CH_2-\underset{\underset{CH_2-CH_3}{|}}{\overset{\overset{CH_3}{|}}{C}}-CH_2-CH_3$

c. $CH_3-CH-CH-CH_3$
$\quad\quad\;\; |\quad\;\; |$
$\quad\quad\; CH_3\; CH_3$

d. $CH_3-\underset{\underset{CH_3}{|}}{\overset{\overset{CH_3}{|}}{C}}-CH_2-\underset{\underset{CH_2-CH_3}{|}}{CH}-CH_2-CH_2-\overset{\overset{CH_2-CH_3}{|}}{CH}-CH_2-CH_3$

47. a. $CH_3CH_2CH_3 + 5\,O_2 \longrightarrow 3\,CO_2 + 4\,H_2O$
b. $CH_3CH_2CH{=}CH_2 + 6\,O_2 \longrightarrow 4\,CO_2 + 4\,H_2O$
c. $2\,CH{\equiv}CH + 5\,O_2 \longrightarrow 4\,CO_2 + 2\,H_2O$
49. a. CH_3CH_2Br
b. $CH_3CH_2CH_2Cl,\; CH_3CHClCH_3$
c. $CHCl_2Br$
d.
$\quad\quad\quad\; H$
$\quad\quad\quad\, |$
CH_3-C-CH_2-Cl
$\quad\quad\quad |$
$\quad\quad\; CH_3$

$\quad\quad\quad\; Cl$
$\quad\quad\quad\, |$
CH_3-C-CH_3
$\quad\quad\quad |$
$\quad\quad\; CH_3$

51. $CH_2{=}CH-CH_2-CH_2-CH_2-CH_3$
$CH_3-CH{=}CH-CH_2-CH_2-CH_3$
$CH_3-CH_2-CH{=}CH-CH_2-CH_3$
53. a. 1-butene **b.** 3,4-dimethyl-2-pentene
c. 3-isopropyl-1-hexene **d.** 2,4-dimethyl-3-hexene
55. a. 2-butyne **b.** 4,4-dimethyl-2-hexyne
c. 3-isopropyl-1-hexyne **d.** 3,6-dimethyl-4-nonyne
57. a. $CH_3-CH_2-CH-C{\equiv}C-CH_2-CH_2-CH_3$
b. CH_3-CH_2-CH
$\quad\quad\quad\quad\quad\;\; \|$
$\quad\quad\quad\quad\quad\; CH-CH_2-CH_2-CH_2-CH_2-CH_3$

c. $CH{\equiv}C-\underset{\underset{CH_3}{|}}{\overset{\overset{CH_3}{|}}{C}}H_2-CH_2-CH_3$

d. $CH_3-CH{=}\overset{\overset{CH_3}{|}}{C}-CH_2-\underset{\underset{CH_2-CH_3}{|}}{CH}-\overset{\overset{CH_3}{|}}{CH}-CH_3$

59. a. $CH_3-\underset{\underset{Cl}{|}}{CH}-\underset{\underset{Cl}{|}}{CH}-CH_3$

b. $CH_3-\underset{\underset{CH_3}{|}}{CH}-CH_2-\underset{\underset{Br}{|}}{CH}-CH_3 +$
$\quad\quad\quad\quad\quad\; CH_3-\underset{\underset{CH_3}{|}}{CH}-\underset{\underset{Br}{|}}{CH}-CH_2-CH_3$

c. $CH_3-CH_2-\underset{\underset{Br}{|}}{CH}-\underset{\underset{Br}{|}}{CH}-CH_3$

d. $CH_3-\underset{\underset{CH_3}{|}}{CH}-CH_2-\underset{\underset{Cl}{|}}{\overset{\overset{CH_3}{|}}{C}}-CH_3$

61. a. $CH_2{=}CH-CH_3 + H_2 \longrightarrow CH_3-CH_2-CH_3$
b. $CH_3-\underset{\underset{CH_3}{|}}{CH}-CH{=}CH_2 + H_2 \longrightarrow$
$\quad\quad\quad\quad\quad\; CH_3-\underset{\underset{CH_3}{|}}{CH}-CH_2-CH_3$

c. $CH_3-\underset{\underset{CH_3}{|}}{CH}-\underset{\underset{CH_3}{|}}{C}{=}CH_2 + H_2 \longrightarrow$
$\quad\quad\quad\quad\quad\; CH_3-\underset{\underset{CH_3}{|}}{CH}-\underset{\underset{CH_3}{|}}{CH}-CH_3$

63. a. methylbenzene or toluene
   b. bromobenzene
   c. chlorobenzene
65. a. 3,5-dimethyl-7-phenylnonane
   b. 2-phenyl-3-octene
   c. 4,5-dimethyl-6-phenyl-2-octyne
67. a. 1,4-dibromobenzene or *p*-dibromobenzene
   b. 1,3-diethylbenzene or *m*-diethylbenzene
   c. 1-chloro-2-fluorobenzene or *o*-chlorofluorobenzene

69. a. $CH_3—CH—CH_3$ **b.** Br

(phenyl ring structures) **c.** Cl

CH_3

71. a. (bromobenzene structure with H's) $+ HBr$ **b.** (benzene with isopropyl group $CH_3—CH—CH_3$) $+ HCl$

73. a. 1-propanol   **b.** 4-methyl-2-hexanol
   c. 2,6-dimethyl-4-heptanol   **d.** 3-methyl-3-pentanol
75. a. $CH_3CH_2CH_2Br + H_2O$ **b.** $CH_3—C=CH_2 + H_2O$ with CH_3
   c. $CH_3CH_2ONa + \frac{1}{2} H_2$ **d.** $CH_3—C—CH_2—C—OH$ with CH_3 and O
77. a. butanone   **b.** pentanal
   c. 3,5,5-trimethylhexanal   **d.** 4-methyl-2-hexanone

79. $CH_3—CH_2—CH_2—\underset{H}{\overset{OH}{C}}—C\equiv N$

81. a. methylbutanoate   **b.** propanoic acid
   c. 5-methylhexanoic acid   **d.** ethylpentanoate

83. a. $CH_3—CH_2—CH_2—CH_2—\overset{O}{C}—O—CH_2—CH_3 + H_2O$
   b. (cyclic anhydride structure with H_2C, CH_2, CH_2) $+ H_2O$

85. a. ethyl propyl ether   **b.** ethyl pentyl ether
   c. dipropyl ether   **d.** butyl ethyl ether
87. a. diethylamine   **b.** methylpropylamine
   c. butylmethylpropylamine
89. a. acid–base, $(CH_3)_2NH_2^+(aq) + Cl^-(aq)$
   b. condensation, $CH_3CH_2CONHCH_2CH_3(aq) + H_2O$
   c. acid–base, $CH_3NH_3^+(aq) + HSO_4^-(aq)$

91. ... (fluorocarbon chain structure) ...

93. $HO—\overset{O}{C}—$(benzene ring)$—\overset{O}{C}—O—CH_2—CH_2—OH$

95. a. ester, methyl 3-methylbutanoate
   b. ether, ethyl 2-methylbutyl ether
   c. aromatic, 1-ethyl-3-methylbenzene or *m*-ethylmethylbenzene
   d. alkyne, 5-ethyl-4-methyl-2-heptyne
   e. aldehyde, butanal
   f. alcohol, 2-methyl-1-propanol
97. a. 5-isobutyl-3-methylnonane
   b. 5-methyl-3-hexanone
   c. 3-methyl-2-butanol
   d. 4-ethyl-3,5-dimethyl-1-hexyne
99. a. isomers   **b.** isomers   **c.** same
101. 558 g
103. a. combustion   **b.** alkane substitution
   c. alcohol elimination   **d.** aromatic substitution
105. a. $CH_3—CH_2—CH—CH=CH_2$ with CH_3
   Can exist as a stereoisomer
   b. $CH_3—CH=C—CH_2—CH—CH_3$ with CH_3 and CH_3
   Can exist as a stereoisomer
   c. $H_3C—CH=C—CH_2—CH_2—CH_3$ with $CH_2CH_2CH_3$
   Can exist as a stereoisomer

107. 1. $H_3C—CH_2—CH_2—\overset{O}{CH}$
   Aldehyde
2. $H_3C—\overset{O}{C}—CH_2—CH_3$
   Ketone
3. $H_3C—CH=CH—O—CH_3$
   Alkene, ether
4. $H_2C=CH—O—CH_2—CH_3$
   Alkene, ether
5. $H_2C=CH—CH_2—O—CH_3$
   Alkene, ether
6. $H_3C—CH=CH—CH_2—OH$
   Alkene, alcohol
7. $H_3C—\underset{OH}{C}=CH—CH_3$
   Alkene, alcohol
8. $H_3C—CH_2—CH=\underset{OH}{CH}$
   Alkene, alcohol
9. $H_3C—CH_2—\underset{OH}{C}=CH_2$
   Alkene, alcohol
10. $H_2C=CH—\underset{OH}{CH}—CH_3$
   Alkene, alcohol
11. $H_2C=CH—CH_2—CH_2—OH$
   Alkene, alcohol

109. In the acid form of the carboxylic acid, electron withdrawal by the $C=O$ enhances acidity. The conjugate base, the carboxylate anion, is stabilized by resonance so the two O atoms are equivalent and bear the negative charge equally.

111. a.

b.

c. $CH_3-CH_2-C=CH_2 + HBr \longrightarrow CH_3-CH_2-\overset{Br}{\underset{CH_3}{C}}-CH_3$

with CH_3 below the C on left

113. a. 3 : 1
   b. 2° hydrogen atoms are more reactive. The reactivity of 2° hydrogens to 1° hydrogens is 11 : 3.

115.

117. The first propagation step for F is very rapid and exothermic because of the strength of the $H-F$ bond that forms. For I the first propagation step is endothermic and slow because the $H-I$ bond that forms is relatively weak.

119.

121.

2,2,3,3-tetramethylbutane

Chapter 21

31. c. saturated fatty acid;   **d.** steroid
33. a. saturated fatty acid   **b.** not a fatty acid
   c. not a fatty acid
   d. monounsaturated fatty acid

35.

Triglyceride is expected to be an oil.

37. a. monosaccharide;
   c. disaccharide
39. a. aldose, hexose
   b. aldose, pentose
   c. ketose, tetrose
   d. aldose, tetrose
41. a. 5   **b.** 3
   c. 1   **d.** 3

43.

45.

47.

Glucose   Fructose

49. a.

$$H_3N^+-CH-\overset{\displaystyle O}{\overset{\|}{C}}-O^-$$
$$HO-CH$$
$$CH_3$$

b.

$$H_3N^+-CH-\overset{\displaystyle O}{\overset{\|}{C}}-O^-$$
$$CH_3$$

c.

$$H_3N^+-CH-\overset{\displaystyle O}{\overset{\|}{C}}-O^-$$
$$CH_2$$
$$H_3C-CH$$
$$CH_3$$

d.

$$H_3N^+-CH-\overset{\displaystyle O}{\overset{\|}{C}}-O^-$$
$$CH_2$$
$$CH_2$$
$$CH_2$$
$$CH_2$$
$$NH_2$$

51.

$$\overset{H_2N}{\underset{H_3C}{\diagdown}}\overset{\displaystyle H}{\overset{|}{C}}-\overset{\displaystyle O}{\overset{\|}{C}}-OH \qquad \overset{H_3C}{\underset{H_2N}{\diagdown}}\overset{\displaystyle H}{\overset{|}{C}}-\overset{\displaystyle O}{\overset{\|}{C}}-OH$$

53. 6, Ser-Gly-Cys, Ser-Cys-Gly, Gly-Ser-Cys, Gly-Cys-Ser, Cys-Ser-Gly, Cys-Gly-Ser

55.

$$H_2N-\overset{\displaystyle H}{\overset{|}{C}}-\overset{\displaystyle O}{\overset{\|}{C}}-OH + H_2N-\overset{\displaystyle H}{\overset{|}{C}}-\overset{\displaystyle O}{\overset{\|}{C}}-OH \longrightarrow$$
$$CH_2 \qquad\qquad CH_2$$
$$OH$$

(with phenol ring and OH)

$$H_2N-\overset{\displaystyle H}{\overset{|}{C}}-\overset{\displaystyle O}{\overset{\|}{C}}-NH-\overset{\displaystyle H}{\overset{|}{C}}-\overset{\displaystyle O}{\overset{\|}{C}}-OH$$
$$CH_2 \qquad\qquad CH_2$$
$$OH$$

(with phenol ring and OH)

$$+ H_2O$$

57. a.

$$H_2N-\overset{\overset{\displaystyle H}{|}}{C}-\overset{\overset{\displaystyle O}{\|}}{C}-NH-\overset{\overset{\displaystyle H}{|}}{C}-\overset{\overset{\displaystyle O}{\|}}{C}-NH-\overset{\overset{\displaystyle H}{|}}{C}-\overset{\overset{\displaystyle O}{\|}}{C}-OH$$
$$CH_2 \qquad\qquad CH_2 \qquad\qquad CH_2$$
$$CH_2 \qquad\qquad CH_2 \qquad\qquad SH$$
$$C=O \qquad\qquad S$$
$$NH_2 \qquad\qquad CH_3$$

b.

$$H_2N-\overset{\overset{\displaystyle H}{|}}{C}-\overset{\overset{\displaystyle O}{\|}}{C}-NH-\overset{\overset{\displaystyle H}{|}}{C}-\overset{\overset{\displaystyle O}{\|}}{C}-NH-\overset{\overset{\displaystyle H}{|}}{C}-\overset{\overset{\displaystyle O}{\|}}{C}-OH$$
$$CH_2 \qquad\qquad CH_2 \qquad\qquad CH_2$$
$$OH \qquad H_3C-CH \qquad SH$$
$$CH_3$$

c.

$$H_2N-\overset{\overset{\displaystyle H}{|}}{C}-\overset{\overset{\displaystyle O}{\|}}{C}-NH-\overset{\overset{\displaystyle H}{|}}{C}-\overset{\overset{\displaystyle O}{\|}}{C}-NH-\overset{\overset{\displaystyle H}{|}}{C}-\overset{\overset{\displaystyle O}{\|}}{C}-OH$$
$$CH_2 \qquad\qquad CH_2 \qquad\qquad CH_2$$
$$SH \qquad H_3C-CH \qquad OH$$
$$CH_3$$

59. tertiary
61. primary
63. a. A;
　　c. T

65.

67. A C A T G C G
69. 154 codons, 462 nucleotides
71. a. protein
　　b. carbohydrate
　　c. lipid
73. A codon is composed of three nucleotides. A codon codes for a specific amino acid while a gene codes for an entire protein.

75.

$$H-N-\overset{\overset{\displaystyle H}{|}}{C}-\overset{\overset{\displaystyle O}{\|}}{C}-OH$$
$$CH_3$$

Trigonal planar, Bent, Tetrahedral, Trigonal planar (labels)

77. valine, leucine, isoleucine, phenylalanine
79. Gly-Arg-Ala-Leu-Phe-Gly-Asn-Lys-Trp-Glu-Cys

81.

a.

b.

83. As the temperature increases the favorable entropy for uncoiling a chain becomes dominant. On cooling the favorable enthalpy of forming hydrogen bonds between paired bases is dominant.

85. When the fake thymine nucleotide is added to the replicating DNA, the chain cannot continue to form, because the $-N{=}N^+{=}NH$ group on the sugar prevents future phosphate linkages.

87. $V_{max} = 47.6$, $K_t = 1.68$

89. $H_3N^+CH_2COO^- + H^+ \rightleftharpoons$
$\qquad\qquad (H_3N^+CH_2COOH\ [HA]/[A^-] = 2,$
$H_3N^+CH_2COO^- \rightleftharpoons$
$\qquad H_2NCH_2COO^- + H^+\ [HA]/[A^-]\ = 0.4, pH = 6.0$

91. A three-base codon codes for a single amino acid. If there are only three bases, there could be 27 different three-base codon arrangements. Therefore, you could theoretically code for the 20 different amino acids needed.

Chapter 22

17. a. +4 **b.** +4 **c.** +4

19. $Ca_3Al_2(SiO_4)_3$

21. 4

23. tetrahedrons stand alone, orthosilicates

25. amphibole or double-chain structure;
$Ca^{2+}, Mg^{2+}, Fe^{2+}, Al^{3+}$

27. 950 g

29. NCl_3 has a lone pair that BCl_3 lacks, giving it a trigonal pyramidal shape, as opposed to BCl_3's trigonal planar shape.

31. a. 6 vertices, 8 faces **b.** 12 vertices, 20 faces

33. *closo*-Boranes have the formula $B_nH_n{}^{2-}$ and form fully closed polyhedra, *nido*-boranes have the formula B_nH_{n+4} and consist of a cage missing a corner, and *arachno*-boranes have the formula B_nH_{n+6} and consist of a cage missing two or three corners.

35. Graphite consists of covalently bonded sheets that are held to each other by weak interactions, allowing them to slip past each other. Diamond is not a good lubricant, because it is an extremely strong network covalent solid, where all of the carbon atoms are covalently bonded.

37. Activated charcoal consists of fine particles, rather than a lump of charcoal, and subsequently has a much higher surface area.

39. Ionic carbides are composed of carbon, generally in the form of the carbide ion, $C_2{}^{2-}$, and low-electronegativity metals, such as the alkali and alkaline earth metals. Covalent carbides are composed of carbon and low-electronegativity nonmetals or metalloids, such as silicon.

41. a. solid $\longrightarrow$ gas
b. gas $\longrightarrow$ liquid $\longrightarrow$ solid
c. solid $\longrightarrow$ gas

43. a. $CO(g) + CuO(s) \longrightarrow CO_2(g) + Cu(s)$
b. $SiO_2(s) + 3\ C(s) \longrightarrow SiC(s) + 2\ CO(g)$
c. $S(s) + CO(g) \longrightarrow COS(g)$

45. a. +2 **b.** +4 **c.** +4/3

47. Fixing nitrogen refers to converting N_2 to a nitrogen-containing compound.

49. White phosphorus consists of P_4 molecules in a tetrahedral shape with the atoms at the corners of the tetrahedron. This allotrope is unstable because of the strain from the bond angles. Red phosphorus is much more stable because one bond of the tetrahedron is broken, allowing the phosphorus atoms to make chains with bond angles that are less strained.

51. saltpeter: 13.86% N by mass
Chile saltpeter: 16.48% N by mass

53. HN_3 has a positive ΔG_f°, meaning that it spontaneously decomposes into H_2 and N_2 at room temperature. There are no temperatures at which HN_3 will be stable. ΔH_f is positive and ΔS_f is negative, so ΔG_f will always be negative.

55. a. $NH_4NO_3(aq) + heat \longrightarrow N_2O(g) + 2\ H_2O(l)$
b. $3\ NO_2(g) + H_2O(l) \longrightarrow 2\ HNO_3(l) + NO(g)$
c. $2\ PCl_3(l) + O_2(g) \longrightarrow 2\ POCl_3(l)$

57. $NO_3^-, NO_2^-, N_3^-, N_2H_5^+, NH_4^+$

59.

Trigonal pyramidal   Trigonal bipyramidal

61. $CO(NH_2)_2 + 2\ H_2O \longrightarrow (NH_4)_2CO_3$
14 g

63. P_4O_6 forms if there is only a limited amount of oxygen available, while P_4O_{10} will form with greater amounts of oxygen.

65. The major source of oxygen is the fractionation of air by which air is cooled and liquefied and oxygen is separated from the other components.

67. a. superoxide **b.** oxide **c.** peroxide

69. Initially, liquid sulfur becomes less viscous when heated because the S_8 rings have greater thermal energy, which overcomes intermolecular forces. Above 150 °C the rings break and the broken rings entangle one another, causing greater viscosity.

71. a. 4×10^{-22} g   **b.** 4.0×10^{-19} g

73. $2 FeS_2(s) \xrightarrow{heat} 2 FeS(s) + S_2(g)$
510 L

75. a. +2, linear   **b.** +6, octahedral
c. +6, square pyramidal

77. $Cl_2(g) + 2 Br^-(aq) \longrightarrow 2 Cl^-(aq) + Br_2(l)$
Oxidizing agent: Cl_2
Reducing agent: Br^-

79. No, there is not enough HF to dissolve all of the SiO_2. HF is the limiting reagent. 1.6 g SiO_2.

81. 8 kg from lignite, 40 kg from bituminous

83. Chlorine is much more electronegative than iodine, allowing it to withdraw an electron and ionize in solution much more easily.

85. a. $rate_{HCl}/rate_{Cl_2} = 1.395$
b. $rate_{HCl}/rate_{HF} = 0.7407$
c. $rate_{HCl}/rate_{HI} = 1.873$

87. $4 Na_2O_2 + 3 Fe \longrightarrow 4 Na_2O + Fe_3O_4$

89. The bond length of the O_2 species increases as electrons are added because they are added to the π^* antibonding orbital. O_2^{2-} is diamagnetic.

91. 2.0 mol of C—C bonds, 715 kJ/mol, 6.9×10^2 kJ/mol, This value calculated from the bond energy is too low because it doesn't include van der Waals attractions between C atoms not directly bonded to each other.

93. -50 kJ/mol

95. a. -13.6 kJ/mol   **b.** -11.0 kJ/mol
c. -24.8 kJ/mol
Fe_2O_3 is the most exothermic because it has the highest oxidation state and is therefore able to oxidize the most CO per mol Fe.

97. a. $\ddot{O}{=}C{=}C{=}C{=}\ddot{O}$ **b.** sp
c. -92 kJ/mol

99. a. 7.6×10^{-22} **b.** 1.2×10^{-8}
c. $[N_2H_4] = 0.009$ M, $[N_2H_5^+] = 0.0025$ M,
$[N_2H_6^{2+}] = 7.0 \times 10^{-13}$ M

101. The acid is

a. $HO{-}\overset{\displaystyle ..}{N}{=}\underset{\displaystyle ..}{N}{-}OH$

and the base is

b. $H_2N{-}\overset{\displaystyle \overset{O}{\|}}{\underset{}{N^+}}{-}O^-$

The acid is weaker than nitrous acid because of electron donation by resonance in contributing structures such as

c. $HO{-}\overset{\displaystyle \overset{\ominus}{..}}{\underset{\displaystyle ..}{N}}{-}N{=}\overset{\displaystyle \oplus}{\underset{\displaystyle ..}{O}}H$

The base is weaker than ammonia because of electron withdrawal by the electronegative nitro group.

103. The triple bond in nitrogen is much stronger than the double bond in oxygen, so it is much harder to break. This makes it less likely that the bond in nitrogen will be broken.

105. Sodium dinitrogen phosphate (NaH_2PO_4) can act as a weak base or a weak acid. A buffer can be made by mixing it with either Na_2HPO_4 or with Na_3PO_4, depending on the desired pH of the buffer solution.

107. F is extremely small and so there is a huge driving force to fill the octet by adding an electron, giving a -1 oxidation state. Other halogens have access to d orbitals, which allows for more hybridization and oxidation state options.

109. SO_3 cannot be a reducing agent, because the oxidation state of S is +6, the highest possible oxidation state for S. Reducing agents need to be able to be oxidized. SO_2 can be a reducing agent or an oxidizing agent, because the oxidation state of S is +4.

Chapter 23

15. Metals are typically opaque, are good conductors of heat and electricity, and are ductile and malleable, meaning they can be drawn into wires and flattened into sheets.

17. aluminum, iron, calcium, magnesium, sodium, potassium

19. Fe: hematite (Fe_2O_3), magnetite (Fe_3O_4)
Hg: cinnabar (HgS)
V: vanadite $[Pb_5(VO_4)Cl]$, carnotite
$[K_2(UO_2)_2(VO_4)_2 \cdot 3 H_2O]$
Nb: columbite $[Fe(NbO_3)_2]$

21. $MgCO_3(s) + heat \longrightarrow MgO(s) + CO_2(g)$
$Mg(OH)_2(s) + heat \longrightarrow MgO(s) + H_2O(g)$

23. The flux is a material that will react with the gangue to form a substance with a low melting point. MgO is the flux.

25. Hydrometallurgy is used to separate metals from ores by selectively dissolving the metal in a solution, filtering out impurities, and then reducing the metal to its elemental form.

27. The Bayer process is a hydrometallurgical process by which Al_2O_3 is selectively dissolved, leaving other oxides as solids. The soluble form of aluminum is $Al(OH)_4^-$.

29. Sponge powdered iron contains many small holes in the iron particles due to the escaping of the oxygen when the iron is reduced. Water atomized powdered iron has much smoother and denser particles as the powder is formed from molten iron.

31. a. 50% Cr, 50% V by moles; 50.5% Cr, 49.5% V by mass
b. 25% Fe, 75% V by moles; 26.8% Fe, 73.2% V by mass
c. 25% Cr, 25% Fe, 50% V by moles; 24.8% Cr, 26.6% Fe, 48.6% V by mass

33. Cr and Fe are very close to each other in mass, so their respective atomic radii are probably close enough to form an alloy. Also, they both form body-centered cubic structures.

35. A: solid, 20% Cr, 80% Fe
B: liquid, 50% Cr, 50% Fe

37. A: solid (20% Co and 80% Cu overall. Two phases; one is the Cu structure with 4% Co, and the other is the Co structure with 7% Cu. There will be more of the Cu structure).
B: solid (Co structure), 90% Co, 10% Cu

39. C would fill interstitial holes; Mn and Si would substitute for Fe.

41. a. Mo_2N **b.** CrH_2

43. a. zinc   **b.** copper

     c. manganese

45. -19.4 kJ/mol

47. When Cr is added to steel it reacts with oxygen in steel to prevent it from rusting. A Cr steel alloy would be used in any situation where the steel might be easily oxidized, such as when it comes in contact with water.

49. rutile: 33.3% Ti by moles, 59.9% Ti by mass
ilmenite: 20.0% Ti by moles, 31.6% Ti by mass

51. Titanium must be arc-melted in an inert atmosphere because the high temperature and flow of electrons would cause the metal to oxidize in a normal atmosphere.

53. TiO_2 is the most important industrial product of titanium and it is often used as a pigment in white paint.

55. The Bayer process is a hydrometallurgical process used to separate Al_2O_3 from other oxides. The Al_2O_3 is selectively dissolved by hot, concentrated NaOH. The other oxides are removed as solids and the Al_2O_3 precipitates out of solution when the solution is neutralized.

57. cobalt and tungsten

59. 3.3 kg Fe, 2.0 kg Ti

61. Four atoms surround a tetrahedral hole and six atoms surround an octahedral hole. The octahedral hole is larger because it is surrounded by a greater number of atoms.

63. Mn has one more electron orbital available for bonding than does chromium.

65. Ferromagnetic atoms, like paramagnetic ones, have unpaired electrons. However, in ferromagnetic atoms, these electrons align with their spin oriented in the same direction, resulting in a permanent magnetic field.

67. The nuclear charge of the last three is relatively high because of the lanthanide series in which the $4f$ subshell falls between them and the other six metals of the group.

69. a. 16.0 cm   **b.** 4.95 cm   **c.** 14%

71. 92%

73. 5.4×10^7

75. First, roast to form the oxide.
$$4\,CoAsS(s) + 9\,O_2(g) \longrightarrow$$
$$4\,CoO(s) + 4\,SO_2(g) + As_4O_6(s)$$
Then reduce the oxide with coke.
$$CoO(s) + C(s) \longrightarrow Co(s) + CO(g)$$
The oxides of arsenic are relatively volatile and can be separated, but they are poisonous.

77. Au and Ag are found in elemental form because of their low reactivity. Na and Ca are group 1 and group 2 metals, respectively, and are highly reactive as they readily lose their valence electrons to obtain octets.

Chapter 24

17. a. [Ar] $4s^2 3d^8$, [Ar] $3d^8$
     b. [Ar] $4s^2 3d^5$, [Ar] $3d^3$
     c. [Kr] $5s^2 4d^1$, [Kr] $5s^1 4d^1$
     d. [Xe] $6s^2 4f^{14} 5d^3$, [Xe] $4f^{14} 5d^3$

19. a. $+5$ **b.** $+7$ **c.** $+4$

21. a. $+3, 6$ **b.** $+2, 6$
     c. $+2, 4$ **d.** $+1, 2$

23. a. hexaaquachromium(III)
     b. tetracyanocuprate(II)
     c. pentaaminebromoiron(III) sulfate
     d. aminetetraaquahydroxycobalt(III) chloride

25. a. $[Cr(NH_3)_6]^{3+}$
     b. $K_3[Fe(CN)_6]$
     c. $[Cu(en)(SCN)_2]$
     d. $[Pt(H_2O)_4][PtCl_6]$

27. a. $[Co(NH_3)_3(CN)_3]$, triaminetricyanocobalt(III)
     b. $[Cr(en)_3]^{3+}$, tris(ethylenediamine)chromium(III)

29.

31. $[Fe(H_2O)_5Cl]Cl \cdot H_2O$, pentaaquachloroiron(II) chloride monohydrate
$[Fe(H_2O)_4Cl_2] \cdot 2\,H_2O$, tetraaquadichloroiron(II) dihydrate

33. b, c, e

35. a. 3   **b.** No geometric isomers.

37. a.

Fac   Mer

     b.

Cis   Trans

39. *cis* isomer is optically active

41. a.

     b.

     c.

     d.

43. 163 kJ/mol
45. $[Co(CN)_6]^{3-}$ ⟶ 290 nm, colorless
$[Co(NH_3)_6]^{3+}$ ⟶ 440 nm, yellow
$[CoF_6]^{3-}$ ⟶ 770 nm, green
47. weak
49. **a.** 4
  b. 3
  c. 1
51. 3
53. porphyrin
55. Water is a weak field ligand that forms a high-spin complex with hemoglobin. Because deoxyhemoglobin is weak field it absorbs large wavelength light and appears blue. Oxyhemoglobin is a low-spin complex and absorbs small wavelength light, so O_2 must be a strong field ligand.
57. **a.** [Ar] $4s^1 3d^5$, [Ar] $3d^5$, [Ar] $3d^4$, [Ar] $3d^3$
  b. [Ar] $4s^1 3d^{10}$, [Ar] $3d^{10}$, [Ar] $3d^9$
59. **a.** H—N̈—H   **b.** [S̈=C=N̈]   **c.** (water structure)
          |
          H
61. $[MA_2B_2C_2]$ all cis; A trans and B and C cis; B trans and A and C cis; C trans and A and B cis; all trans.
$[MA_2B_3C]$ will have fac–mer isomers.
$[MAB_2C_3]$ will have fac–mer isomers.
$[MAB_3C_2]$ will have fac–mer isomers.
$[MA_3B_2C]$ will have fac–mer isomers.
$[MA_2BC_3]$ will have fac–mer isomers.
$[MA_3BC_2]$ will have fac–mer isomers.
$[MABC_2]$ will have AB cis–trans isomers.
$[MAB_4C]$ will have AC cis–trans isomers.
$[MA_4BC]$ will have BC cis–trans isomers.
$[MABC_4]$ will have AB cis–trans isomers.
63. , optical isomers
65. ⟮↿⇂ ↿ ↿⟯, paramagnetic

67.

Only structure 3. is chiral. This is its mirror image.

69.
cis-dichlorobis (trimethyl phosphine) platinum(II)

trans-dichlorobis (trimethyl phosphine) platinum(II)

71. ____ d_{z^2}
  ____ ____ $d_{x^2-y^2}$ and d_{xy}
  ____ ____ d_{xz} and d_{yz}
73. **a.** 2×10^{-8} M
  b. 6.6×10^{-3} M
  c. NiS will dissolve more easily in the ammonia solution because the formation of the complex ion is favorable, removing Ni^{2+} ions from the solution and allowing more NiS to dissolve.
75. Prepare a solution that contains both $[MCl_6]^{3-}$ and $[MBr_6]^{3-}$ and see if any complex ions that contain both Cl and Br form. If they do it would demonstrate that these complexes are labile.
77. pH = 10.1
79. Au

Appendix IV:
Answers to In-Chapter Practice Problems

Chapter 1

1.1. a. The composition of the copper is not changing; thus, being hammered flat is a physical change that signifies a physical property.
  b. The dissolution and color change of the nickel indicate that it is undergoing a chemical change and exhibiting a chemical property.
  c. Sublimation is a physical change indicative of a physical property.
  d. When a match ignites, a chemical change begins as the match reacts with oxygen to form carbon dioxide and water. Flammability is a chemical property.
1.2. a. 29.8 °C
  b. 302.9 K
1.3. 21.4 g/cm^3. This matches the density of platinum.
1.3. *For More Practice* 4.50 g/cm^3 The metal is titanium.
1.4. The thermometer shown has markings every 1 °F; thus, the first digit of uncertainty is 0.1. The answer is 103.1 °F.
1.5. a. Each figure in this number is significant by rule 1: three significant figures.
  b. This is a defined quantity that has an unlimited number of significant figures.
  c. Both 1's are significant (rule 1) and the interior zero is significant as well (rule 2): three significant figures.
  d. Only the two 9's are significant, the leading zeroes are not (rule 3): two significant figures.
  e. There are five significant figures because the 1, 4, and 5 are nonzero (rule 1) and the trailing zeroes are after a decimal point so they are significant as well (rule 4).
  f. The number of significant figures is ambiguous because the trailing zeroes occur before an implied decimal point (rule 4). Assume two significant figures.
1.6. a. 0.381
  b. 121.0
  c. 1.174
  d. 8
1.7. 3.15 yd
1.8. 2.446 gal
1.9. 1.61×10^6 cm^3
1.9. *For More Practice* 3.23×10^3 kg
1.10. 1.03 kg
1.10. *For More Practice* 2.9×10^{-2} cm^3
1.11. 0.855 cm
1.12. 2.70 g/cm^3

Chapter 2

2.1. For the first sample:
$$\frac{\text{mass of oxygen}}{\text{mass of carbon}} = \frac{17.2 \text{ g O}}{12.9 \text{ g C}} = 1.33 \text{ or } 1.33 : 1$$
For the second sample:
$$\frac{\text{mass of oxygen}}{\text{mass of carbon}} = \frac{10.5 \text{ g O}}{7.88 \text{ g C}} = 1.33 \text{ or } 1.33 : 1$$
The ratios of oxygen to carbon are the same in the two samples of carbon monoxide, so these results are consistent with the law of definite proportions.

2.2. $\dfrac{\text{mass of hydrogen to 1 g of oxygen in hydrogen peroxide}}{\text{mass of hydrogen to 1 g of oxygen in water}}$
$$= \frac{0.250}{0.125} = 2.00$$
The ratio of the mass of hydrogen from one compound to the mass of hydrogen in the other is equal to 2. This is a simple whole number and therefore consistent with the law of multiple proportions.

2.3. a. $Z = 6$, $A = 13$, $^{13}_{6}\text{C}$
  b. 19 protons, 20 neutrons
2.4. a. N^{3-} **b.** Rb^+
2.5. 24.31 amu
2.5. *For More Practice* 70.92 amu
2.6. 4.65×10^{-2} mol Ag
2.7. 0.563 mol Cu
2.7. *For More Practice* 22.6 g Ti
2.8. 1.3×10^{22} C atoms
2.8. *For More Practice* 6.87 g W
2.9. $l = 1.72$ cm
2.9. *For More Practice* 2.90×10^{24} Cu atoms

Chapter 3

3.1. a. C_5H_{12}
  b. HgCl
  c. CH_2O
3.2. a. molecular element
  b. molecular compound
  c. atomic element
  d. ionic compound
  e. ionic compound
3.3. K_2S
3.4. AlN
3.5. silver nitride
3.5. *For More Practice* Rb_2S

3.6. iron(II) sulfide

3.6. *For More Practice* RuO_2

3.7. tin(II) chlorate

3.7. *For More Practice* $Co_3(PO_4)_2$

3.8. dinitrogen pentoxide

3.8. *For More Practice* PBr_3

3.9. hydrofluoric acid

3.10. nitrous acid

3.10. *For More Practice* $HClO_4$

3.11. sulfurous acid

3.12. 164.10 amu

3.13. 5.839×10^{20} $C_{13}H_{18}O_2$ molecules

3.13. *For More Practice* 1.06 g H_2O

3.14. 53.29%

3.14. *For More Practice* 74.19% Na

3.15. 83.9 g Fe_2O_3

3.15. *For More Practice* 8.6 g Na

3.16. 4.0 g O

3.16. *For More Practice* 3.60 g C

3.17. CH_2O

3.18. $C_{13}H_{18}O_2$

3.19. C_6H_6

3.19. *For More Practice* $C_2H_8N_2$

3.20. C_2H_5

3.21. C_2H_4O

3.22. $SiO_2(s) + 3\,C(s) \longrightarrow SiC(s) + 2\,CO(g)$

3.23. $2\,C_2H_6(g) + 7\,O_2(g) \longrightarrow 4\,CO_2(g) + 6\,H_2O(g)$

3.24. $Pb(NO_3)_2(aq) + 2\,KCl(aq) \longrightarrow$
$$PbCl_2(s) + 2\,KNO_3(aq)$$

Chapter 4

4.1. 4.08 g HCl

4.2. 22 kg HNO_3

4.3. H_2 is the limiting reagent, since it produces the least amount of NH_3. Therefore, 29.4 kg NH_3 is the theoretical yield.

4.4. CO is the limiting reagent, since it only produces 114 g Fe. Therefore, 114 g Fe is the theoretical yield: percentage yield = 63.4% yield

4.5. 0.214 M $NaNO_3$

4.5. *For More Practice* 44.6 g KBr

4.6. 402 g $C_{12}H_{22}O_{11}$

4.6. *For More Practice* 221 mL of KCl solution

4.7. 667 mL

4.7. *For More Practice* 0.105 L

4.8. 51.4 mL HNO_3 solution

4.8. *For More Practice* 0.170 g CO_2

4.9. a. insoluble
   b. insoluble
   c. soluble
   d. soluble

4.10. $NH_4Cl(aq) + Fe(NO_3)_3(aq) \longrightarrow$ NO REACTION

4.11. $2\,NaOH(aq) + CuBr_2(aq) \longrightarrow$
$$Cu(OH)_2(s) + 2\,NaBr(aq)$$

4.12. $2\,H^+(aq) + 2\,I^-(aq) + Ba^{2+}(aq) + 2\,OH^-(aq) \longrightarrow$
$$2\,H_2O(l) + Ba^{2+}(aq) + 2\,I^-(aq)$$
$$H^+(aq) + OH^-(aq) \longrightarrow H_2O(l)$$

4.13. $H_2SO_4(aq) + 2\,LiOH(aq) \longrightarrow 2\,H_2O(l) + Li_2SO_4(aq)$
$$H^+(aq) + OH^-(aq) \longrightarrow H_2O(aq)$$

4.14. 9.03×10^{-2} M H_2SO_4

4.14. *For More Practice* 24.5 mL NaOH solution

4.15. $2\,HBr(aq) + K_2SO_3(aq) \longrightarrow$
$$H_2O(l) + SO_2(g) + 2\,KBr(aq)$$

4.15. *For More Practice* $2\,H^+(aq) + S^{2-}(aq) \longrightarrow H_2S(g)$

4.16. a. Cr = 0
   b. Cr^{3+} = +3
   c. Cl^- = −1, C = +4
   d. Br = −1, Sr = +2
   e. O = −2, S = +6
   f. O = −2, N = +5

4.17. Sn is oxidized and N is reduced.

4.17. *For More Practice* **b.** Reaction b is the only redeox reaction. Al is oxidized and O is reduced.

4.18. a. This is a redox reaction in which Li is the reducing agent (it is oxidized) and Cl_2 is the oxidizing reagent (it is reduced).
   b. This is a redox reaction in which Al is the reducing agent and Sn^{2+} is the oxidizing agent.
   c. This is not a redox reaction because no oxidation states change.
   d. This is a redox reaction in which C is the reducing agent and O_2 is the oxidizing agent.

4.19. $2\,C_2H_5SH(l) + 9\,O_2(g) \longrightarrow$
$$4\,CO_2(g) + 2\,SO_2(g) + 6\,H_2O(g)$$

Chapter 5

5.1. 15.0 psi

5.1. *For More Practice* 80.6 kPa

5.2. 2.1 atm at a depth of approximately 11 m.

5.3. 123 mL

5.4. 11.3 L

5.5. 1.63 atm, 23.9 psi

5.6. 16.1 L

5.6. *For More Practice* 976 mmHg

5.7. $d = 4.91$ g/L

5.7. *For More Practice* 44.0 g/mol

5.8. 70.7 g/mol

5.9. 0.0610 mol H_2

5.10. 4.2 atm

5.11. 12.0 mg H_2

5.12. 82.3 g Ag_2O

5.12. *For More Practice* 7.10 g Ag_2O

5.13. 6.53 L O_2

5.14. $u_{rms} = 238$ m/s

5.15. $\dfrac{rate_{H_2}}{rate_{Kr}} = 6.44$

Chapter 6

6.1. $\Delta E = 71$ J

6.2. $C_s = 0.38\dfrac{\text{J}}{\text{g} \cdot {}^\circ\text{C}}$

The specific heat capacity of gold is 0.128 J/g $\cdot$ °C; therefore, the rock cannot be pure gold.

6.2. *For More Practice* $T_f = 42.1$ °C

6.3. 37.8 grams Cu

6.4. -122 J

6.4. *For More Practice* $\Delta E = -998$ J

6.5. $\Delta E_{\text{reaction}} = -3.91 \times 10^3$ kJ/mol C_6H_{14}

6.5. *For More Practice* $C_{\text{cal}} = 4.55\dfrac{\text{kJ}}{{}^\circ\text{C}}$

6.6. a. endothermic, positive ΔH
b. endothermic, positive ΔH
c. exothermic, negative ΔH

6.7. -2.06×10^3 kJ

6.7. *For More Practice* 33 g C_4H_{10}
99 g CO_2

6.8. $\Delta H_{\text{rxn}} = -68$ kJ

6.9. $N_2O(g) + NO_2(g) \longrightarrow 3\ NO(g),\ \Delta H_{\text{rxn}} = +157.6$ kJ

6.9. *For More Practice*
$3\ H_2(g) + O_3(g) \longrightarrow 3\ H_2O(g),\ \Delta H_{\text{rxn}} = -868.1$ kJ

6.10. a. $Na(s) + \dfrac{1}{2}Cl_2(g) \longrightarrow$
$NaCl(s),\ \Delta H_f^\circ = -411.2$ kJ/mol
b. $Pb(s) + N_2(g) + 3\ O_2(g) \longrightarrow$
$Pb(NO_3)_2(s),\ \Delta H_f^\circ = -451.9$ kJ/mol

6.11. $\Delta H_{\text{rxn}}^\circ = -851.5$ kJ

6.12. $\Delta H_{\text{rxn}}^\circ = -1648.4$ kJ
111 kJ emitted (-111 kJ)

6.13. 1.2×10^2 kg CO_2

Chapter 7

7.1. $5.83 \times 10^{14}\,\text{s}^{-1}$

7.2. 2.64×10^{20} photons

7.2. *For More Practice* 435 nm

7.3. a. blue < green < red
b. red < green < blue
c. red < green < blue

7.4. 6.1×10^6 m/s

7.5. For the 5*d* orbitals:
$n = 5$
$l = 2$
$m_l = -2, -1, 0, 1, 2$
The 5 integer values for m_l signify that there are five 5*d* orbitals.

7.6. a. *l* cannot equal 3 if $n = 3$. $l = 2$
b. m_l cannot equal -2 if $l = -1$. Possible values for $m_l = -1, 0,$ or 1
c. *l* cannot be 1 if $n = 1$. $l = 0$

7.7. 397 nm

7.7. *For More Practice* $n = 1$

Chapter 8

8.1. a. Cl $1s^2 2s^2 2p^6 3s^2 3p^5$ or [Ne] $3s^2 3p^5$
b. Si $1s^2 2s^2 2p^6 3s^2 3p^2$ or [Ne] $3s^2 3p^2$
c. Sr $1s^2 2s^2 2p^6 3s^2 3p^6 4s^2 3d^{10} 4p^6 5s^2$ or [Kr] $5s^2$
d. O $1s^2 2s^2 2p^4$ or [He] $2s^2 p^4$

8.2. There are no unpaired electrons.

8.3. $1s^2 2s^2 2p^6 3s^2 3p^3$ or [Ne] $3s^2 3p^3$. The 5 electrons in the $3s^2 3p^3$ orbitals are the valence electrons, while the 10 electrons in the $1s^2 2s^2 2p^6$ orbitals belong to the core.

8.4. [Xe] $6s^2 4f^{14} 5d^{10} 6p^3$

8.4. *For More Practice* [Kr] $5s^2 4d^{10} 5p^5$

8.5. a. Sn
b. cannot predict
c. W
d. Se

8.5. *For More Practice* Rb > Ca > Si > S > F

8.6. a. [Ar] $4s^0 3d^7$. Co^{2+} is paramagnetic.

Co^{2+} [Ar]   ⟦ ⟧ ⟦↿⇂│↿⇂│↿│↿│↿⟧
4s   3d

b. [He] $2s^2 2p^6$. N^{3-} is diamagnetic.

N^{3-} [He]   ⟦↿⇂⟧ ⟦↿⇂│↿⇂│↿⇂⟧
2s   2p

c. [Ne] $3s^2 3p^6$. Ca^{2+} is diamagnetic.

Ca^{2+} [Ne]   ⟦↿⇂⟧ ⟦↿⇂│↿⇂│↿⇂⟧
3s   3p

8.7. a. K   **b.** F^- **c.** Cl^-

8.7. *For More Practice* $Cl^- > Ar > Ca^{2+}$

8.8. a. I   **b.** Ca
c. cannot predict   **d.** F

8.8. *For More Practice* F > S > Si > Ca > Rb

8.9. a. Sn
b. cannot predict based on simple trends (Po is larger)
c. Bi
d. B

8.9. *For More Practice* Cl < Si < Na < Rb

8.10. a. $2\ Al(s) + 3\ Cl_2(g) \longrightarrow 2\ AlCl_3(s)$
b. $2\ Li(s) + 2\ H_2O(l) \longrightarrow$
$2\ Li^+(aq) + 2\ OH^-(aq) + H_2(g)$
c. $H_2(g) + Br_2(l) \longrightarrow 2\ HBr(g)$

Chapter 9

9.1. Mg_3N_2

9.2. KI < LiBr < CaO

9.2. *For More Practice* $MgCl_2$

9.3. **a.** pure covalent
b. ionic
c. polar covalent

9.4. $:C \equiv O:$

9.5.
$$H - \overset{\overset{\displaystyle :O:}{\|}}{C} - H$$

9.6. $\left[:\ddot{C}l:\ddot{O}: \right]^{-}$

9.7. $\left[:\ddot{O}=\ddot{N}-\ddot{O}: \right]^{-} \longleftrightarrow \left[:\ddot{O}-\ddot{N}=\ddot{O}: \right]^{-}$

9.8.

Structure	A			B			C		
	$:\ddot{N}=N=\ddot{O}:$			$:N\equiv N-\ddot{O}:$			$:\ddot{N}-N\equiv O:$		
number of valence e⁻	5	5	6	5	5	6	5	5	6
number of nonbonding e⁻	−4	−0	−4	−2	−0	−6	−6	−0	−2
1/2(number of bonding e⁻)	−2	−4	−2	−3	−4	−1	−1	−4	−3
Formal charge	**−1**	**+1**	**0**	**0**	**+1**	**−1**	**−2**	**+1**	**+1**

Structure B contributes the most to the correct overall structure of N_2O.

9.8. *For More Practice* The nitrogen is +1, the singly bonded oxygen atoms are −1, and the double-bonded oxygen atom has no formal charge.

9.9.
$$H - \overset{\overset{\displaystyle H}{|}}{\underset{}{C}} \overset{-1}{-} \overset{+1}{N} \equiv N: \longleftrightarrow H - \overset{\overset{\displaystyle H}{|}}{\underset{}{C}} = \overset{+1}{N} = \ddot{N}:^{-1}$$

9.10.
$$:\ddot{F} - \overset{\overset{\displaystyle :\ddot{F}:}{|}}{\underset{\underset{\displaystyle :\ddot{F}:}{|}}{Xe}} - \ddot{F}:$$

9.10. *For More Practice*
$$H - \ddot{O} - \overset{\overset{\displaystyle :O:}{|}}{\underset{\underset{\displaystyle :O:^{0}}{\|}}{P^{0}}} - \ddot{O} - H$$

9.11. $CH_3OH(g) + \dfrac{3}{2} O_2(g) \longrightarrow CO_2(g) + 2\,H_2O(g)$

$\Delta H_{rxn} = -641$ kJ

9.11. *For More Practice* $\Delta H_{rxn} = -8.0 \times 10^1$ kJ

Chapter 10

10.1. tetrahedral
$$:\ddot{C}l - \overset{\overset{\displaystyle :\ddot{C}l:}{|}}{\underset{\underset{\displaystyle :\ddot{C}l:}{|}}{C}} - \ddot{C}l:$$

10.2. bent
10.3. linear

10.4.

Atom	Number of Electron Groups	Number of Lone Pairs	Molecular Geometry
Carbon (left)	4	0	Tetrahedral
Carbon (right)	3	0	Trigonal planar
Oxygen	4	2	Bent

10.5. The molecule is nonpolar.

10.6. The xenon atom has six electron groups and therefore has an octahedral electron geometry. An octahedral electron geometry corresponds to sp^3d^2 hybridization (refer to Table 10.3).

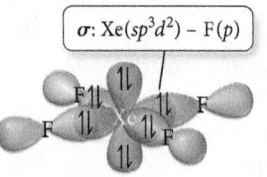
σ: Xe(sp^3d^2) – F(p)

10.7. Since there are only two electron groups around the central atom (C), the electron geometry is linear. According to Table 10.3, the corresponding hybridization on the carbon atom is sp.

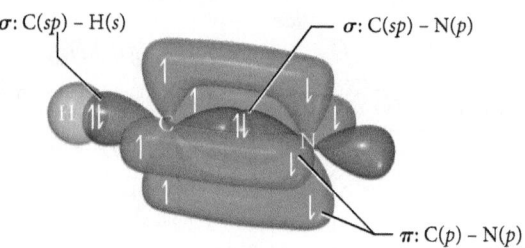
σ: C(sp) – H(s) σ: C(sp) – N(p)
π: C(p) – N(p)

10.8. Since there are only two electron groups about the central atom (C), the electron geometry is linear. The hybridization on C is sp (refer to Table 10.3).

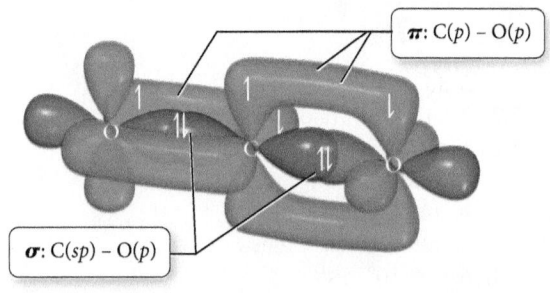
π: C(p) – O(p)
σ: C(sp) – O(p)

10.8. *For More Practice* There are five electron groups about the central atom (I); therefore, the electron geometry is trigonal bipyramidal and the corresponding hybridization of I is sp^3d (refer to Table 10.3).

10.9. H_2^+ bond order $= +\dfrac{1}{2}$

Since the bond order is positive, the H_2^+ ion should be stable; however, the bond order of H_2^+ is lower than the bond order of H_2 (bond order $=1$). Therefore, the bond in H_2^+ is weaker than in H_2.

10.10. The bond order of N_2^+ is 2.5, which is lower than that of the N_2 molecule (bond order $=3$); therefore, the bond is weaker. The MO diagram shows that the N_2^+ ion has one unpaired electron and is therefore paramagnetic.

10.10. *For More Practice* The bond order of Ne_2 is 0, which indicates that dineon does not exist.

10.11. The bond order of NO is $+2.5$. The MO diagram shows that the ion has one unpaired electron and is therefore paramagnetic.

Chapter 11

11.1. **b, c**

11.2. HF has a higher boiling point than HCl because, unlike HCl, HF is able to form hydrogen bonds. The hydrogen bond is the strongest of the intermolecular forces and requires more energy to break.

11.3. 5.83×10^3 kJ

11.3. *For More Practice* 49 °C

11.4. 33.8 KJ/mol

11.5. 7.04×10^3 torr

11.6. $29.4°$

11.7. $7.18 \dfrac{g}{cm^3}$

Chapter 12

12.1. **a.** not soluble
b. soluble
c. not soluble
d. not soluble

12.2. 2.7×10^{-4} M

12.3. 42.5 g $C_{12}H_{22}O_{11}$

12.3. *For More Practice* 3.3×10^4 L

12.4. **a.** $M = 0.415$ M
b. $m = 0.443$ m
c. % by mass $= 13.2\%$
d. $\chi C_{12}H_{22}O_{11} = 0.00793$
e. mole percent $= 0.793\%$

12.5. 0.600 M

12.5. *For More Practice* 0.651 m

12.6. 22.5 torr

12.6. *For More Practice* 0.144

12.7. **a.** $P_{benzene} = 26.6$ torr
$P_{toluene} = 20.4$ torr
b. 47.0 torr
c. 52.5% benzene; 47.5% toluene
The vapor will be richer in the more volatile component, which in this case is benzene.

12.8. $T_f = -4.8$ °C

12.9. 101.84 °C

12.10. 11.8 atm

12.11. -0.60 °C

12.12. 0.014 mol NaCl

Chapter 13

13.1. $\dfrac{\Delta[H_2O_2]}{\Delta t} = -4.40 \times 10^{-3}$ M/s

$\dfrac{\Delta[I_3^-]}{\Delta t} = 4.40 \times 10^{-3}$ M/s

13.2. **a.** Rate $= k[CHCl_3][Cl_2]^{1/2}$. (Fractional-order reactions are not common but are occasionally observed.)
b. $3.5 \ M^{-1/2} \cdot s^{-1}$

13.3. 5.78×10^{-2} M

13.4. 0.0277 M

13.5. 1.64×10^{-3} M

13.6. 79.2 s

13.7. $2.07 \times 10^{-5} \dfrac{L}{mol \cdot s}$

13.8. $6.13 \times 10^{-4} \dfrac{L}{mol \cdot s}$

13.9. $2 A + B \longrightarrow A_2B$
Rate $= k[A]^2$

Chapter 14

14.1. $K = \dfrac{[CO_2]^3[H_2O]^4}{[C_3H_8][O_2]^5}$

14.2. 2.1×10^{-13}

14.2. *For More Practice* 1.4×10^2

14.3. 6.2×10^2

14.4. $K_c = \dfrac{[Cl_2]^2}{[HCl]^4[O_2]}$

14.5. 9.4

14.6. 1.1×10^{-6}

14.7. $Q_c = 0.0196$
Reaction proceeds to the left.

14.8. 0.033 M

14.9. $[N_2] = 4.45 \times 10^{-3}$ M
$[O_2] = 4.45 \times 10^{-3}$ M
$[NO] = 1.1 \times 10^{-3}$ M

14.10. $[N_2O_4] = 0.005$ M
$[NO_2] = 0.041$ M

14.11. $P_{I_2} = 0.0027$ atm
$P_{Cl_2} = 0.0027$ atm
$P_{ICl_2} = 0.246$ atm

14.12. 1.67×10^{-7} M

14.13. 6.78×10^{-6} M

14.14. Adding Br_2 increases the concentration of Br_2, causing a shift to the left (away from the Br_2). Adding BrNO increases the concentration of BrNO, causing a shift to the right.

14.15. Decreasing the volume causes the reaction to shift right. Increasing the volume causes the reaction to shift left.

14.16. If we increase the temperature, the reaction shifts to the left. If we decrease the temperature, the reaction shifts to the right.

Chapter 15

15.1. a. H_2O donates a proton to C_5H_5N, making it the acid. The conjugate base is therefore OH^-. Since C_5H_5N accepts the proton, it is the base and becomes the conjugate acid $C_5H_5NH^+$.
  b. Since HNO_3 donates a proton to H_2O, it is the acid, making NO_3^- the conjugate base. Since H_2O is the proton acceptor, it is the base and becomes the conjugate acid, H_3O^+.

15.2. a. Since $[H_3O^+] < [OH^-]$ the solution is basic.
  b. $[H_3O^+] = 1.0 \times 10^{-7}$ M
    Neutral solution.
  c. $[H_3O^+] = 1.2 \times 10^{-5}$ M
    Since $[H_3O^+] > [OH^-]$ the solution is acidic.

15.3. a. 8.02 (basic)
  b. 11.85 (basic)

15.4. 4.3×10^{-9} M

15.5. 9.4×10^{-3} M

15.6. 3.28

15.7. 2.72

15.8. 1.8×10^{-6}

15.9. 0.85%

15.10. 4.0×10^{-7} M

15.11. $[OH^-] = 0.020$ M
pH = 12.30

15.12. $[OH^-] = 1.2 \times 10^{-2}$ M
pH = 12.08

15.13. a. weak base   **b.** pH-neutral

15.14. 9.07

15.15. a. pH-neutral   **b.** weak acid
  c. weak acid

15.16. a. basic   **b.** acidic
  c. pH-neutral   **d.** acidic

15.17. 3.83

15.18. $[SO_4^{2-}] = 0.00386$ M
pH = 1.945

15.19. 5.6×10^{-11} M

Chapter 16

16.1. 4.44

16.1. *For More Practice* 3.44

16.2. 9.14

16.3. 4.87

16.3. *For More Practice* 4.65

16.4. 9.68

16.4. *For More Practice* 9.56

16.5. hypochlorous acid (HClO); 2.4 g NaClO

16.6. 1.74

16.7. 18.08

16.8. 2.30×10^{-6} M

16.9. 5.3×10^{-13}

16.10. 1.21×10^{-5} M

16.11. $FeCO_3$ will be more soluble in an acidic solution than $PbBr_2$ because the CO_3^{2-} ion is a basic anion, whereas Br^- is the conjugate base of a strong acid (HBr) and is therefore pH-neutral.

16.12. $Q > K_{sp}$; therefore, a precipitate forms.

16.13. 2.9×10^{-6} M

16.14. a. AgCl precipitates first; $[NaCl] = 7.1 \times 10^{-9}$ M
  b. $[Ag^+]$ is 1.5×10^{-8} M when $PbCl_2$ begins to precipitate, and $[Pb^{2+}]$ is 0.085 M.

16.15. 9.6×10^{-6} M

Chapter 17

17.1. a. positive
  b. negative
  c. positive

17.2. a. -548 J/K
  b. ΔS_{sys} is negative.
  c. ΔS_{univ} is negative, and the reaction is not spontaneous.

17.2. *For More Practice* 375 K

17.3. $\Delta G = -101.6 \times 10^3$ J
  Therefore, the reaction is spontaneous. Since both ΔH and ΔS are negative, as the temperature increases ΔG will become more positive.

17.4. -153.2 J/K

17.5. $\Delta G^\circ_{rxn} = -36.3$ kJ
  Since ΔG°_{rxn} is negative, the reaction is spontaneous at this temperature.

17.6. $\Delta G^\circ_{rxn} = -42.1$ kJ
  Since the value of ΔG°_{rxn} at the lowered temperature is more negative (or less positive) (which is -36.3 kJ), the reaction is more spontaneous.

17.7. $\Delta G^\circ_{rxn} = -689.6$ kJ
  Since ΔG°_{rxn} is negative, the reaction is spontaneous at this temperature.

17.7. *For More Practice* $\Delta G^\circ_{rxn} = -689.7$ kJ (at 25°)
  The value calculated for ΔG°_{rxn} from the tabulated values (-689.6 kJ) is the same, to within 1 in the

least significant digit, as the value calculated using the equation for ΔG°_{rxn}.

$\Delta G^\circ_{rxn} = -649.7$ kJ (at 500.0 K)

You could not calculate ΔG°_{rxn} at 500.0 K using tabulated ΔG°_f values because the tabulated values of free energy are calculated at a standard temperature of 298 K, much lower than 500 K.

17.8. $+107.1$ kJ

17.9. $\Delta G_{rxn} = -129$ kJ

The reaction is more spontaneous under these conditions than under standard conditions because ΔG_{rxn} is more negative than ΔG°_{rxn}.

17.10. -10.9 kJ

Chapter 18

18.1. $2\ Cr(s) + 4\ H^+(aq) \longrightarrow 2\ Cr^{2+}(aq) + 2\ H_2(g)$

18.2. $Cu(s) + 4\ H^+(aq) + 2\ NO_3^-(aq) \longrightarrow$
$Cu^{2+}(aq) + 2\ NO_2(g) + 2\ H_2O(l)$

18.3. $3\ ClO^-(aq) + 2\ Cr(OH)_4^-(aq) + 2\ OH^-(aq) \longrightarrow$
$3\ Cl^-(aq) + 2\ CrO_4^{2-}(aq) + 5\ H_2O(l)$

18.4. $+0.60$ V

18.5. **a.** The reaction *will* be spontaneous as written.
b. The reaction *will not* be spontaneous as written.

18.6. $\Delta G^\circ = -3.63 \times 10^5$ J
Since ΔG° is negative, the reaction is spontaneous.

18.7. 4.5×10^3

18.8. 1.08 V

18.9. *Anode:* $2\ H_2O(l) \longrightarrow O_2(g) + 4\ H^+(aq) + 4\ e^-$
Cathode: $2\ H_2O(l) + 2\ e^- \longrightarrow H_2(g) + 2\ OH^-(aq)$

18.10. 6.0×10^1 min

Chapter 19

19.1. $^{216}_{84}Po \longrightarrow {}^{212}_{82}Pb + {}^4_2He$

19.2. a. $^{235}_{92}U \longrightarrow {}^{231}_{90}Th + {}^4_2He$
$^{231}_{90}Th \longrightarrow {}^{231}_{91}Pa + {}^0_{-1}e$
$^{231}_{91}Pa \longrightarrow {}^{227}_{89}Ac + {}^4_2He$
b. $^{22}_{11}Na \longrightarrow {}^{22}_{10}Ne + {}^0_{+1}e$
c. $^{76}_{36}Kr + {}^0_{-1}e \longrightarrow {}^{76}_{35}Br$

19.2. *For More Practice* Positron emission
$(^{40}_{19}K \longrightarrow {}^{40}_{18}Ar + {}^0_{+1}e)$ or electron capture
$(^{40}_{19}K + {}^0_{+1}e \longrightarrow {}^{40}_{18}Ar)$

19.3. a. positron emission
b. beta decay
c. positron emission

19.4. 10.7 yr

19.5. $t = 964$ yr
No, the C-14 content suggests that the scroll is from about A.D. 1000, not 500 B.C.

19.6. 1.0×10^9 yr

19.7. Mass defect $= 1.934$ amu
Nuclear binding energy $= 7.569$ MeV/nucleon

Chapter 20

20.1.

or

20.2. 3-methylhexane

20.3. 3,5-dimethylheptane

20.4. 2,3,5-trimethylhexane

20.5. a. 4,4-dimethyl-2-pentyne
b. 3-ethyl-4,6-dimethyl-1-heptene

20.6. a. 2-methylbutane

b. 2-chloro-3-methylbutane

20.7. a. Alcohol reacting with an active metal.

$CH_3CH_2OH + Na \longrightarrow CH_3CH_2ONa + \dfrac{1}{2}H_2$

b. dehydration reaction

Chapter 21

21.1. Fructose exhibits optical isomerism. It contains three chiral carbons.

21.2.

Chapter 22

22.1. $KAlSi_3O_8$

22.2. $x = 2$

22.3. Orthosilicate (or neosilicate): each of the two Be ions has a charge of 2+ for a total of 4+, and the SiO_4 unit has a charge of 4−.

22.4. Inosilicate (or pyroxene): Ca and Mg each have a charge of 2+ for a total of 4+, and the Si_2O_6 unit has a charge of 4− (two SiO_3^{2-} units).

22.5. $2\,H_2S(g) + 3\,O_2(g) \longrightarrow 2\,H_2O(g) + SO_2(g)$
S changes from the −2 to +4 oxidation state.

22.6. The oxidation state for Cl is +7 in ClO_4^- and −1 in Cl^-.

22.7. $I_2(s) + 5\,F_2(g) \longrightarrow 2\,IF_5(g)$

22.8. The electron geometry is tetrahedral and the shape is bent for ICl_2^+.

22.9. The electron geometry is octahedral for BrF_5, and the molecular geometry is square pyramidal.

22.10. The oxidation number changes from −1 to 0 for the oxidation of the Cl in HCl to Cl_2 and from +5 to +4 for the reduction of the Cl in $NaClO_3$ to ClO_2. The oxidizing agent is $NaClO_3$, and the reducing agent is HCl.

Chapter 23

23.1. At 50 mol % Ni and 1000 °C this is a solid phase with half of the atoms each Ni and Cu.

23.2. At 50 mol % Ni and 1400 °C this is a liquid phase with half of the atoms each Ni and Cu.

23.3. At 900 °C and 60 mol % Cr this is a two-phase region with more Ni-rich face-centered cubic crystals than Cr-rich body-centered cubic crystals. The Ni-rich phase is about 42 mol % Cr and 58 mol % Ni. The Cr-rich phase is about 94 mol % Cr and 6 mol % Ni.

23.4. At 900 °C and 98 mol % Cr this is a single-phase region with 100 mol % of the Cr-rich body-centered cubic crystals that contains 2% Ni.

Chapter 24

24.1. $[Xe]\,6s^2 4f^{14} 5d^6$

24.2. $[Kr]\,5s^0 4d^3$ or $[Kr]\,4d^3$

24.3. pentaamminecarbonylmanganese(II) sulfate

24.4. sodium tetrachloroplatinate(II)

24.5. The complex ion $[Cr(H_2O)_3Cl_3]^+$ fits the general formula MA_3B_3, which results in fac and mer isomers.

Fac   Mer

24.6. The oxalate ligand is a small bidentate ligand, so it will have to occupy two adjacent (cis) positions of the octahedron. There are three ways to arrange the two NH_3 and two Cl^- ligands in the four remaining positions. One has both NH_3 and both Cl^- in cis positions (cis isomer). Another has the NH_3 ligands in a trans arrangement with both Cl^- in cis positions (*trans*-ammine isomer). The third has both NH_3 ligands cis and the Cl^- ligands trans (*trans*-chloro isomer).

Cis isomer

Trans (in NH_3)   Trans (in Cl^-)

24.7. Both the fac and mer isomers are superimposable (by rotating 180°) on their mirror images, so neither one is optically active.

24.8. 288 kJ/mol

24.9. five unpaired electrons

24.10. one unpaired electron

Glossary

accuracy   A term that refers to how close a measured value is to the actual value. (1.7)

acid   A molecular compound that is able to donate an H^+ ion (proton) when dissolved in water, thereby increasing the concentration of H^+. (3.6)

acid ionization constant (K_a)   The equilibrium constant for the ionization reaction of a weak acid; used to compare the relative strengths of weak acids. (15.4)

acid–base reaction (neutralization reaction)   A reaction in which an acid reacts with a base and the two neutralize each other, producing water. (4.8)

acid–base titration   A laboratory procedure in which a basic (or acidic) solution of unknown concentration is reacted with an acidic (or basic) solution of known concentration, in order to determine the concentration of the unknown. (16.4)

acidic solution   A solution containing an acid that creates additional H_3O^+ ions, causing $[H_3O^+]$ to increase. (15.4)

activated carbon   Very fine carbon particles with high surface area. (22.5)

activated complex (transition state)   A high-energy intermediate state between reactant and product. (13.5)

activation energy   An energy barrier in a chemical reaction that must be overcome for the reactants to be converted into products. (13.5)

active site   The specific area of an enzyme at which catalysis occurs. (13.7)

actual yield   The amount of product actually produced by a chemical reaction. (4.3)

addition polymer   A polymer in which the monomers simply link together without the elimination of any atoms. (20.14)

addition reaction   A type of organic reaction in which two substituents are added across a double bond. (20.10)

alcohol   A member of the family of organic compounds that contain a hydroxyl functional group (—OH). (3.11, 20.9)

aldehyde   A member of the family of organic compounds that contain a carbonyl functional group (C=O) bonded to two R groups, one of which is a hydrogen atom. (20.10)

aldose   A sugar that is an aldehyde. (21.3)

aliphatic hydrocarbons   Organic compounds in which carbon atoms are joined in straight or branched chains. (20.3)

alkali metals   Highly reactive metals in group 1A of the periodic table. (2.7)

alkaline battery   A dry-cell battery that employs slightly different half-reactions in a basic medium. (18.7)

alkaline earth metals   Fairly reactive metals in group 2A of the periodic table. (2.7)

alkaloid   Organic bases found in plants; they are often poisonous. (15.2)

alkane   A hydrocarbon containing only single bonds. (3.11)

alkene   A hydrocarbon containing one or more carbon–carbon double bonds. (3.11)

alkyne   A hydrocarbon containing one or more carbon–carbon triple bonds. (3.11)

alloy   A metallic material that contains more than one element. (23.4)

alpha (α) decay   The form of radioactive decay that occurs when an unstable nucleus emits a particle composed of two protons and two neutrons. (19.3)

alpha (α) particle   A low-energy particle released during alpha decay; equivalent to a He-4 nucleus. (19.3)

α-helix   A pattern in the secondary structure of a protein that occurs when the amino acid chain is wrapped tightly in a coil with the side chains extending outward. (21.5)

aluminosilicates   Members of a family of compounds in which aluminum atoms substitute for silicon atoms in some of the silicon lattice sites of the silica structure. (22.3)

amino acids   Organic compounds that contain a carbon atom, called the α-carbon, bonded to four different groups: an amine group, an R group, a carboxylic acid group, and a hydrogen atom. (21.4)

ammonia NH_3, the strong smelling compound in which nitrogen displays its lowest oxidation state (-3). (22.6)

amorphous solid   A solid in which atoms or molecules do not have any long-range order. (1.3, 11.2)

ampere (A)   The SI unit for electrical current; $1\ A = 1\ C/s$. (18.3)

amphoteric   Able to act as either an acid or a base. (15.3)

amplitude   The vertical height of a crest (or depth of a trough) of a wave; a measure of wave intensity. (7.2)

angular momentum quantum number (l)   An integer that determines the shape of an orbital. (7.5)

anion   A negatively charged ion. (2.6)

anode   The electrode in an electrochemical cell where oxidation occurs; electrons flow away from the anode. (18.3)

antibonding orbital   A molecular orbital that is higher in energy than any of the atomic orbitals from which it was formed. (10.8)

aqueous solution   A solution in which water acts as the solvent. (4.4, 12.2)

***arachno*-boranes**   Boranes with the formula B_nH_{n+6}, consisting of a cage of boron atoms that is missing two or three corners. (22.4)

arc-melting   A method in which the solid metal is melted with an arc from a high-voltage electric source in a controlled atmosphere to prevent oxidation. (23.5)

Arrhenius definitions (of acids and bases)   The definitions of an acid as a substance that produces H^+ ions in aqueous solution and a base as a substance that produces OH^- ions in aqueous solution. (4.8, 15.3)

Arrhenius equation   An equation that relates the rate constant of a reaction to the temperature, the activation energy, and the frequency factor; $k = Ae^{\frac{-E_a}{RT}}$. (13.5)

Arrhenius plot   A plot of the natural log of the rate constant ($\ln k$) versus the inverse of the temperature in kelvins ($1/T$) that yields a straight line with a slope of $-E_a/R$ and a y-intercept of $\ln A$. (13.5)

atmosphere (atm)   A unit of pressure based on the average pressure of air at sea level; $1\ atm = 101{,}325\ Pa$. (5.2)

atom   A submicroscopic particle that constitutes the fundamental building block of ordinary matter; the smallest identifiable unit of an element. (1.1)

atomic element   Those elements that exist in nature with single atoms as their basic units. (3.4)

atomic mass (atomic weight)   The average mass in amu of the atoms of a particular element based on the relative abundance of the various isotopes; it is numerically equivalent to the mass in grams of one mole of the element. (2.8)

atomic mass unit (amu)   A unit used to express the masses of atoms and subatomic particles, defined as 1/12 the mass of a carbon atom containing 6 protons and 6 neutrons. (2.6)

atomic number (Z)   The number of protons in an atom; the atomic number defines the element. (2.6)

atomic solids   Solids whose composite units are atoms; they include nonbonding atomic solids, metallic atomic solids, and network covalent solids. (11.12)

atomic theory   The theory that each element is composed of tiny indestructible particles called atoms, that all atoms of a given element have the same mass and other properties, and that atoms combine in simple, whole-number ratios to form compounds. (1.2, 2.3)

aufbau principle   The principle that indicates the pattern of orbital filling in an atom. (8.3)

autoionization   The process by which water acts as an acid and a base with itself. (15.4)

Avogadro's law   The law that states that the volume of a gas is directly proportional to its amount in moles ($V \propto n$). (5.3)

Avogadro's number   The number of ^{12}C atoms in exactly 12 g of ^{12}C; equal to 6.0221421×10^{23}. (2.9)

balanced   see *chemical equation* (3.10)

ball-and-stick model   A representation of the arrangement of atoms in a molecule that shows how the atoms are bonded to each other and the overall shape of the molecule. (3.3)

band gap   An energy gap that exists between the valence band and conduction band of semiconductors and insulators. (11.13)

band theory   A model for bonding in atomic solids that comes from molecular orbital theory in which atomic orbitals combine and become delocalized over the entire crystal. (11.13)

barometer   An instrument used to measure atmospheric pressure. (5.2)

base ionization constant (K_b)   The equilibrium constant for the ionization reaction of a weak base; used to compare the relative strengths of weak bases. (15.7)

basic solution   A solution containing a base that creates additional OH^- ions, causing the $[OH^-]$ to increase. (15.4)

beta (β) decay   The form of radioactive decay that occurs when an unstable nucleus emits an electron. (19.3)

beta (β) particle   A medium-energy particle released during beta decay; equivalent to an electron. (19.3)

β-pleated sheet   A pattern in the secondary structure of a protein that occurs when the amino acid chain is extended and forms a zigzag pattern. (21.5)

bidentate   Describes ligands that donate two electron pairs to the central metal. (24.3)

bimolecular   An elementary step in a reaction that involves two particles, either the same species or different, that collide and go on to form products. (13.6)

binary acid   An acid composed of hydrogen and a nonmetal. (3.6)

binary compound   A compound that contains only two different elements. (3.5)

biochemistry   The study of the chemistry occurring in living organisms. (21.1)

biological effectiveness factor (RBE)   A correction factor multiplied by the dose of radiation exposure in rad to obtain the dose in rem. (19.11)

black phosphorus   An allotrope of phosphorus with a structure similar to that of graphite; the most thermodynamically stable form. (22.6)

body-centered cubic   A unit cell that consists of a cube with one atom at each corner and one atom at the center of the cube. (11.11)

boiling point   The temperature at which the vapor pressure of a liquid equals the external pressure. (11.5)

boiling point elevation   The effect of a solute that causes a solution to have a higher boiling point than the pure solvent. (12.7)

bomb calorimeter   A piece of equipment designed to measure ΔE_{rxn} for combustion reactions at constant volume. (6.4)

bond energy   The energy required to break 1 mol of the bond in the gas phase. (9.10)

bond length   The average length of a bond between two particular atoms in a variety of compounds. (9.10)

bond order   For a molecule, the number of electrons in bonding orbitals minus the number of electrons in nonbonding orbitals divided by two; a positive bond order implies that the molecule is stable. (10.8)

bonding orbital   A molecular orbital that is lower in energy than any of the atomic orbitals from which it was formed. (10.8)

bonding pair   A pair of electrons shared between two atoms. (9.5)

boranes   Compounds composed of boron and hydrogen. (22.4)

Born–Haber cycle   A hypothetical series of steps based on Hess's law that represents the formation of an ionic compound from its constituent elements. (9.4)

Boyle's law   The law that states that volume of a gas is inversely proportional to its pressure $\left(V \propto \dfrac{1}{P} \right)$. (5.3)

brass   A widely used alloy that contains copper and zinc. (23.5)

Brønsted-Lowry definitions (of acids and bases)   The definitions of an acid as a proton (H^+ ion) donor and a base as a proton acceptor. (15.3)

bronze   An alloy of copper and tin that has been used for thousands of years. (23.5)

buffer   A solution containing significant amounts of both a weak acid and its conjugate base (or a weak base and its conjugate acid) that resists pH change by neutralizing added acid or added base. (16.2)

buffer capacity   The amount of acid or base that can be added to a buffer without destroying its effectiveness. (16.3)

calcination   The heating of an ore in order to decompose it and drive off a volatile product. (23.3)

calorie (cal)   A unit of energy defined as the amount of energy required to raise one gram of water 1 °C; equal to 4.184 J. (6.1)

Calorie (Cal)   Shorthand notation for the kilocalorie (kcal), or 1000 calories; also called the nutritional calorie, the unit of energy used on nutritional labels. (6.1)

calorimetry   The experimental procedure used to measure the heat evolved in a chemical reaction. (6.4)

capillary action   The ability of a liquid to flow against gravity up a narrow tube due to adhesive and cohesive forces. (11.4)

carbohydrate   A polyhydroxyl aldehyde or ketone. (21.3)

carbon black   A fine powdered form of carbon. (22.5)

carbonyl group   A functional group consisting of a carbon atom double-bonded to an oxygen atom ($C{=}O$). (20.10)

carboxylic acid An organic acid containing the functional group —COOH. (15.2, 20.11)

catalyst A substance that is not consumed in a chemical reaction but increases the rate of the reaction by providing an alternate mechanism in which the rate-determining step has a smaller activation energy. (13.7)

cathode The electrode in an electrochemical cell where reduction occurs; electrons flow toward the cathode. (18.3)

cathode rays A stream of electrons produced when a high electrical voltage is applied between two electrodes within a partially evacuated tube. (2.4)

cation A positively charged ion. (2.6)

cell potential (cell emf) (E_{cell}) The potential difference between the cathode and the anode in an electrochemical cell. (18.3)

cellulose A polysaccharide that consists of glucose units bonded together by β-glycosidic linkages; the main structural component of plants, and the most abundant organic substance on Earth. (21.3)

Celsius (°C) scale The temperature scale most often used by scientists (and by most countries other than the United States), on which pure water freezes at 0 °C and boils at 100 °C (at atmospheric pressure). (1.6)

chain reaction A series of reactions in which previous reactions cause future ones; in a fission bomb, neutrons produced by the fission of one uranium nucleus induce fission in other uranium nuclei. (19.7)

charcoal A fuel similar to coal made by heating wood in the absence of air. (22.5)

Charles's law The law that states that the volume of a gas is directly proportional to its temperature ($V \propto T$). (5.3)

chelate A complex ion that contains either a bi- or polydentate ligand. (24.3)

chelating agent The coordinating ligand of a chelate. (24.3)

chemical bond The sharing or transfer of electrons to attain stable electron configurations for the bonding atoms. (9.3)

chemical change A change that alters the molecular composition of a substance; see also *chemical reaction*. (1.4)

chemical energy The energy associated with the relative positions of electrons and nuclei in atoms and molecules. (6.1)

chemical equation A symbolic representation of a chemical reaction; a balanced equation contains equal numbers of the atoms of each element on both sides of the equation. (3.10)

chemical formula A symbolic representation of a compound that indicates the elements present in the compound and the relative number of atoms of each. (3.3)

chemical property A property that a substance displays only by changing its composition via a chemical change. (1.4)

chemical reaction A process by which one or more substances are converted to one or more different substances; see also *chemical change*. (3.10)

chemical symbol A one- or two-letter abbreviation for an element that is listed directly below its atomic number on the periodic table. (2.6)

chemistry The science that seeks to understand the behavior of matter by studying the behavior of atoms and molecules. (1.1)

chiral molecule A molecule that is not superimposable on its mirror image and thus exhibits optical isomerism. (20.3)

chromosome The DNA-containing structures that occur in the nuclei of living cells. (21.6)

cis–trans isomerism Another term for geometric isomerism; cis-isomers have the same functional group on the same side of a bond and trans-isomers have the same functional group on opposite sides of a bond. (20.5)

Claus process An industrial process for obtaining sulfur through the oxidation of hydrogen sulfide. (22.8)

Clausius–Clapeyron equation An equation that displays the exponential relationship between vapor pressure and temperature; $\ln(P_{vap}) = \dfrac{-\Delta H_{vap}}{R}\left(\dfrac{1}{T}\right) + \ln \beta$. (11.5)

***closo*-boranes** Boranes that have the formula $B_{12}H_{12}{}^{2-}$ and form the full icosohedral shape. (22.4)

coal A solid, black fuel with high carbon content, the product of the decomposition of ancient plant material. (22.5)

codon A sequence of three bases in a nucleic acid that codes for one amino acid. (21.6)

coffee-cup calorimeter A piece of equipment designed to measure ΔH_{rxn} for reactions at constant pressure. (6.5)

coke A solid formed by heating coal in the absence of air that consists primarily of carbon and ash. (22.5)

colligative property A property that depends on the amount of a solute but not on the type. (12.7)

collision model A model of chemical reactions in which a reaction occurs after a sufficiently energetic collision between two reactant molecules. (13.5)

colloidal dispersion (colloid) A mixture in which a dispersed substance is finely dived but not truly dissolved in a dispersing medium. (12.8)

combustion analysis A method of obtaining empirical formulas for unknown compounds, especially those containing carbon and hydrogen, by burning a sample of the compound in pure oxygen and analyzing the products of the combustion reaction. (3.9)

combustion reaction A type of chemical reaction in which a substance combines with oxygen to form one or more oxygen-containing compounds; the reaction often causes the evolution of heat and light in the form of a flame. (3.10)

common ion effect The tendency for a common ion to decrease the solubility of an ionic compound or to decrease the ionization of a weak acid or weak base. (16.2)

common name A traditional name of a compound that gives little or no information about its chemical structure; for example, the common name of $NaHCO_3$ is "baking soda." (3.5)

complementary Capable of precise pairing; in particular, the bases of nucleic acids. (21.6)

complementary properties Those properties that exclude one another, that is, the more you know about one, the less you know about the other. For example, the wave nature and particle nature of the electron are complementary. (7.4)

complete ionic equation An equation that lists individually all of the ions present as either reactants or products in a chemical reaction. (4.7)

complex carbohydrate Another term for a polysaccharide based on the fact that it is made up of many simple sugars. (21.3)

complex ion An ion that contains a central metal ion bound to one or more ligands. (16.8, 24.3)

compound A substance composed of two or more elements in fixed, definite proportions. (1.3)

concentrated solution A solution that contains a large amount of solute relative to the amount of solvent. (4.4, 12.5)

condensation The phase transition from gas to liquid. (11.5)

condensation polymer A polymer formed by elimination of an atom or small group of atoms (usually water) between pairs of monomers during polymerization. (20.14)

condensation reaction A reaction in which two or more organic compounds are joined, often with the loss of water or some other small molecule. (20.11)

conjugate acid–base pair Two substances related to each other by the transfer of a proton. (15.3)

constructive interference The interaction of waves from two sources that align with overlapping crests, resulting in a wave of greater amplitude. (7.2)

contact process An industrial method for the production of sulfuric acid. (22.8)

conversion factor A factor used to convert between two different units; a conversion factor can be constructed from any two quantities known to be equivalent. (1.8)

coordinate covalent bond The bond formed when a ligand donates electrons to an empty orbital of a metal in a complex ion. (24.3)

coordination compound A neutral compound made when a complex ion combines with one or more counterions. (24.3)

coordination isomers Isomers of complex ions that occur when a coordinated ligand exchanges places with the uncoordinated counter-ion. (24.4)

coordination number (secondary valence) The number of molecules or ions directly bound to the metal atom in a complex ion. (24.3)

coordination number The number of atoms with which each atom in a crystal lattice is in direct contact. (11.11)

core electrons Those electrons in a complete principal energy level and those in complete d and f sublevels. (8.4)

corrosion The gradual, nearly always undesired oxidation of metals that occurs when they are exposed to oxidizing agents in the environment. (18.9)

covalent bond A chemical bond in which two atoms share electrons that interact with the nuclei of both atoms, lowering the potential energy of each through electrostatic interactions. (3.2, 9.2)

covalent carbides Binary compounds composed of carbon combined with low-electronegativity nonmetals or metalloids. (22.5)

covalent radius (bonding atomic radius) Defined in nonmetals as one-half the distance between two atoms bonded together, and in metals as one-half the distance between two adjacent atoms in a crystal of the metal. (8.6)

critical mass The necessary amount of a radioactive isotope required to produce a self-sustaining fission reaction. (19.7)

critical point The temperature and pressure above which a supercritical fluid exists. (11.8)

critical pressure The pressure required to bring about a transition to a liquid at the critical temperature. (11.5)

critical temperature The temperature above which a liquid cannot exist, regardless of pressure. (11.5)

crystalline lattice The regular arrangement of atoms in a crystalline solid. (11.11)

crystalline solid (crystal) A solid in which atoms, molecules, or ions are arranged in patterns with long-range, repeating order. (1.3, 11.2)

cubic closest packing A closest-packed arrangement in which the third layer of atoms is offset from the first; the same structure as the face-centered cubic. (11.11)

cyclotron A particle accelerator in which a charged particle is accelerated in an evacuated ring-shaped tube by an alternating voltage applied to each semi-circular half of the ring. (19.10)

Dalton's law of partial pressures The law stating that the sum of the partial pressures of the components in a gas mixture must equal the total pressure. (5.6)

de Broglie relation The observation that the wavelength of a particle is inversely proportional to its momentum $\lambda = \dfrac{h}{mv}$. (7.4)

decanting A method of separating immiscible liquids by pouring the top layer into another container. (1.3)

degenerate A term describing two or more electron orbitals with the same value of n that have the same energy. (8.3)

density (d) The ratio of an object's mass to its volume. (1.6)

deposition The phase transition from gas to solid. (11.6)

derived unit A unit that is a combination of other base units. For example, the SI unit for speed is meters per second (m/s), a derived unit. (1.6)

destructive interference The interaction of waves from two sources aligned so that the crest of one overlaps the trough of the other, resulting in cancellation. (7.2)

deterministic A characteristic of the classical laws of motion, which imply that present circumstances determine future events. (7.4)

dextrorotatory Capable of rotating the plane of polarization of light clockwise. (20.3)

diamagnetic The state of an atom or ion that contains only paired electrons and is, therefore, slightly repelled by an external magnetic field. (8.7, 10.8)

diamond An elemental form of carbon with a crystal structure that consists of carbon atoms connected to four other carbon atoms at the corners of a tetrahedron, creating a strong network covalent solid. (22.5)

diffraction The phenomena by which a wave emerging from an aperture spreads out to form a new wave front. (7.2)

diffusion The process by which a gas spreads through a space occupied by another gas. (5.9)

dilute solution A solution that contains a very small amount of solute relative to the amount of solvent. (4.4, 12.5)

dimensional analysis The use of units as a guide to solving problems. (1.8)

dimer The product that forms from the reaction of two monomers. (20.14)

diode A device that allows the flow of electrical current in only one direction. (11.13)

dipeptide Two amino acids linked together. (21.4)

dipole moment A measure of the separation of positive and negative charge in a molecule. (9.6)

dipole–dipole force An intermolecular force exhibited by polar molecules that results from the uneven charge distribution. (11.3)

diprotic acid An acid that contains two ionizable protons. (4.8, 15.4)

disaccharide A carbohydrate composed of two monosaccharides. (21.3)

dispersion force (London force) An intermolecular force exhibited by all atoms and molecules that results from fluctuations in the electron distribution. (11.3)

distillation The process by which mixtures of miscible liquids are separated by heating the mixture to boil off the more volatile liquid. The vaporized component is then recondensed and collected in a separate flask. (1.3)

disubstituted benzene A benzene in which two hydrogen atoms have been replaced by other atoms. (20.7)

double bond The bond that forms when two electrons are shared between two atoms. (9.5)

dry-cell battery A battery that does not contain a large amount of liquid water, often using the oxidation of zinc and the reduction of MnO_2 to provide the electrical current. (18.7)

duet A Lewis structure with two dots, signifying a filled outer electron shell for the elements H and He. (9.3)

dynamic equilibrium The point at which the rate of the reverse reaction or process equals the rate of the forward reaction or process. (11.5, 12.4, 14.2)

effective nuclear charge (Z_{eff}) The actual nuclear charge experienced by an electron, defined as the charge of the nucleus plus the charge of the shielding electrons. (8.3)

effusion The process by which a gas escapes from a container into a vacuum through a small hole. (5.9)

electrical charge A fundamental property of certain particles that causes them to experience a force in the presence of electric fields. (2.4)

electrical current The flow of electric charge. (18.3)

electrochemical cell A device in which a chemical reaction either produces or is carried out by an electrical current. (18.3)

electrolysis The process by which electrical current is used to drive an otherwise nonspontaneous redox reaction. (18.8)

electrolyte A substance that dissolves in water to form solutions that conduct electricity. (4.5)

electrolytic cell An electrochemical cell that uses electrical current to drive a nonspontaneous chemical reaction. (18.3)

electromagnetic radiation A form of energy embodied in oscillating electric and magnetic fields. (7.2)

electromagnetic spectrum The range of the wavelengths of all possible electromagnetic radiation. (7.2)

electrometallurgy The use of electrolysis to produce metals from their compounds. (23.3)

electromotive force (emf) The force that results in the motion of electrons due to a difference in potential. (18.3)

electron A negatively charged, low-mass particle found outside the nucleus of all atoms that occupies most of the atom's volume but contributes almost none of its mass. (2.4)

electron affinity (EA) The energy change associated with the gaining of an electron by an atom in its gaseous state. (8.7)

electron capture The form of radioactive decay that occurs when a nucleus assimilates an electron from an inner orbital. (19.3)

electron configuration A notation that shows the particular orbitals that are occupied by electrons in an atom. (8.3)

electron geometry The geometrical arrangement of electron groups in a molecule. (10.3)

electron groups A general term for lone pairs, single bonds, multiple bonds, or lone electrons in a molecule. (10.2)

electron spin A fundamental property of electrons; spin can have a value of $\pm \frac{1}{2}$. (7.5)

electronegativity The ability of an atom to attract electrons to itself in a covalent bond. (9.6)

element A substance that cannot be chemically broken down into simpler substances. (1.3)

elementary step An individual step in a reaction mechanism. (13.6)

emission spectrum The range of wavelengths emitted by a particular element; used to identify the element. (7.3)

empirical formula A chemical formula that shows the simplest whole number ratio of atoms in the compound. (3.3)

empirical formula molar mass The sum of the masses of all the atoms in an empirical formula. (3.9)

enantiomers (optical isomers) Two molecules that are nonsuperimposable mirror images of one another. (20.3, 24.4)

endothermic reaction A chemical reaction that absorbs heat from its surroundings; for an endothermic reaction, $\Delta H > 0$. (6.5)

endpoint The point of pH change where an indicator changes color. (16.4)

energy The capacity to do work. (1.5, 6.1)

English system The system of units used in the United States and various other countries in which the inch is the unit of length, the pound is the unit of force, and the ounce is the unit of mass. (1.6)

enthalpy (H) The sum of the internal energy of a system and the product of its pressure and volume; the energy associated with the breaking and forming of bonds in a chemical reaction. (6.5)

entropy A thermodynamic function that is proportional to the number of energetically equivalent ways to arrange the components of a system to achieve a particular state; a measure of the energy randomization or energy dispersal in a system. (12.2, 17.3)

enzyme A biochemical catalyst made of protein that increases the rates of biochemical reactions. (13.7, 21.4)

equilibrium constant (K) The ratio, at equilibrium, of the concentrations of the products of a reaction raised to their stoichiometric coefficients to the concentrations of the reactants raised to their stoichiometric coefficients. (14.3)

equivalence point The point in a titration at which the added solute completely reacts with the solute present in the solution; for acid–base titrations, the point at which the amount of acid is stoichiometrically equal to the amount of base in solution. (4.8, 16.4)

ester A family of organic compounds with the general structure R—COO—R. (20.11)

ester linkage The bonds that form between a carboxylic acid and an alcohol to form an ester, such as those in triglycerides. (21.2)

ether A member of the family of organic compounds of the form R—O—R'. (20.12)

exact numbers Numbers that have no uncertainty and thus do not limit the number of significant figures in any calculation. (1.7)

exothermic reaction A chemical reaction that releases heat to its surroundings; for an exothermic reaction, $\Delta H < 0$. (6.5)

experiment A highly controlled procedure designed to generate observations that may support a hypothesis or prove it wrong. (1.2)

exponential factor A number between zero and one that represents the fraction of molecules that have enough energy to make it over the activation barrier on a given approach. (13.5)

extensive property A property that depends on the amount of a given substance, such as mass. (1.6)

extractive metallurgy The process by which an elemental metal must be extracted from the compounds in which it is found. (23.3)

face-centered cubic A crystal structure whose unit cell consists of a cube with one atom at each corner and one atom in the center of every face. (11.11)

Fahrenheit (°F) scale The temperature scale that is most familiar in the United States, on which pure water freezes at 32 °F and boils at 212 °F. (1.6)

---

family A group of organic compounds with the same functional group. (3.11)

family (group) Columns within the main group elements in the periodic table that contain elements that exhibit similar chemical properties. (2.7)

Faraday's constant (F) The charge in coulombs of 1 mol of electrons: $F = \dfrac{96{,}485\ \text{C}}{\text{mol e}^-}$. (18.5)

fatty acid A carboxylic acid with a long hydrocarbon tail. (21.2)

ferromagnetic The state of an atom or ion that is very strongly attracted by an external magnetic field. (23.5)

fertilizer A material containing large amounts of nitrogen or phosphorus that is used to increase plant growth. (22.6)

fibrous protein A protein with a relatively linear structure; fibrous proteins tend to be insoluble in aqueous solutions. (21.5)

film-badge dosimeter A device for monitoring exposure to radiation consisting of photographic film held in a small case that is pinned to clothing. (19.5)

filtration A procedure used to separate a mixture composed of an insoluble solid and a liquid by pouring it through filter paper or some other porous membrane or layer. (1.3)

first law of thermodynamics The law stating that the total energy of the universe is constant. (6.2)

flux In pyrometallurgy, material that will react with the gangue to form a substance with a low melting point. (23.3)

formal charge The charge that an atom in a Lewis structure would have if all the bonding electrons were shared equally between the bonded atoms. (9.8)

formation constant (K_f) The equilibrium constant associated with reactions for the formation of complex ions. (16.8)

formula mass The average mass of a molecule of a compound in amu. (3.7)

formula unit The smallest, electrically neutral collection of ions in an ionic compound. (3.4)

Frasch process An industrial process for the recovery of sulfur that uses superheated water to liquefy sulfur deposits in Earth's crust and bring the molten sulfur to the surface. (22.8)

free energy of formation (ΔG_f°) The change in free energy when 1 mol of a compound forms from its constituent elements in their standard states. (17.7)

free radical A molecule or ion with an odd number of electrons in its Lewis structure. (9.9)

freezing The phase transition from liquid to solid. (11.6)

freezing point depression The effect of a solute that causes a solution to have a lower melting point than the pure solvent. (12.7)

frequency (ν) For waves, the number of cycles (or complete wavelengths) that pass through a stationary point in one second. (7.2)

frequency factor The number of times that reactants approach the activation energy per unit time. (13.5)

fuel cell A voltaic cell that uses the oxidation of hydrogen and the reduction of oxygen, forming water, to provide electrical current. (18.7)

fullerenes Carbon clusters, such as C_{60}, bonded in roughly spherical shapes containing from 36 to over 100 carbon atoms. (22.5)

functional group A characteristic atom or group of atoms that imparts certain chemical properties to an organic compound. (3.11)

gamma (γ) rays The form of electromagnetic radiation with the shortest wavelength and highest energy. (7.2, 19.3)

gamma (γ) ray emission The form of radioactive decay that occurs when an unstable nucleus emits extremely high frequency electromagnetic radiation. (19.3)

gangue The undesirable minerals that are separated from specific ores. (23.3)

gas A state of matter in which atoms or molecules have a great deal of space between them and are free to move relative to one another; lacking a definite shape or volume, a gas conforms to those of its container. (1.3)

gas-evolution reaction A reaction in which two aqueous solutions are mixed and a gas forms, resulting in bubbling. (4.8)

Geiger-Müller counter A device used to detect radioactivity that uses argon atoms that become ionized in the presence of energetic particles to produce an electrical signal. (19.5)

gene A sequence of codons within a DNA molecule that codes for a single protein. (21.6)

geometric isomerism A form of stereoisomerism involving the orientation of functional groups in a molecule that contains bonds incapable of rotating. (20.5)

geometric isomers For complex ions, isomers that result when the ligands bonded to the metal have a different spatial arrangement. (24.4)

Gibbs free energy (G) A thermodynamic state function related to enthalpy and entropy by the equation $G = H - TS$; chemical systems tend toward lower Gibbs free energy, also called the *chemical potential*. (17.5)

globular protein A protein that folds into a roughly spherical shape so that its polar side chains are oriented outward and its nonpolar side chains toward the interior; globular proteins tend to be soluble in water. (21.5)

glycogen A highly branched form of starch. (21.3)

glycolipid A triglyceride composed of a fatty acid, a hydrocarbon chain, and a sugar molecule as the polar section. (21.2)

glycosidic linkage A bond between carbohydrates that results from a dehydration reaction. (21.3)

graphite An elemental form of carbon consisting of flat sheets of carbon atoms, bonded together as interconnected hexagonal rings held together by intermolecular forces, that can easily slide past each other. (22.5)

Haber-Bosch process The industrial process for producing ammonia from nitrogen gas and hydrogen gas. (22.6)

half-cell One half of an electrochemical cell where either oxidation or reduction occurs. (18.3)

half-life ($t_{1/2}$) The time required for the concentration of a reactant or the amount of a radioactive isotope to fall to one-half of its initial value. (13.4)

halogens Highly reactive nonmetals in group 7A of the periodic table. (2.7)

heat (q) The flow of energy caused by a temperature difference. (6.1)

heat capacity (C) The quantity of heat required to change a system's temperature by 1 °C. (6.3)

heat of fusion (ΔH_{fus}) The amount of heat required to melt 1 mole of a solid. (11.6)

heat of hydration ($\Delta H_{hydration}$) The enthalpy change that occurs when 1 mole of gaseous solute ions are dissolved in water. (12.3)

heat of reaction (ΔH_{rxn}) The enthalpy change for a chemical reaction. (6.5)

heat of vaporization (ΔH_{vap}) The amount of heat required to vaporize one mole of a liquid to a gas. (11.5)

Heisenberg's uncertainty principle The principle stating that due to the wave-particle duality, it is fundamentally impossible to precisely determine both the position and velocity of a particle at a given moment in time. (7.4)

Henderson-Hasselbalch equation An equation used to easily calculate the pH of a buffer solution from the initial concentrations of the buffer components, assuming that the "*x is small*" approximation is valid: $pH = pK_a + \log\frac{[base]}{[acid]}$. (16.2)

Henry's law An equation that expresses the relationship between solubility of a gas and pressure: $S_{gas} = k_H P_{gas}$. (12.4)

Hess's law The law stating that if a chemical equation can be expressed as the sum of a series of steps, then ΔH_{rxn} for the overall equation is the sum of the heats of reactions for each step. (6.7)

heterogeneous catalysis Catalysis in which the catalyst and the reactants exist in different phases. (13.7)

heterogeneous mixture A mixture in which the composition varies from one region to another. (1.3)

hexagonal closest packing A closest-packed arrangement in which the atoms of the third layer align exactly over those in the first layer. (11.11)

hexose A six-carbon sugar. (21.3)

high-spin complex A complex ion with weak field ligands that have the same number of unpaired electrons as the free metal ion. (24.5)

homogeneous catalysis Catalysis in which the catalyst exists in the same phase as the reactants. (13.7)

homogeneous mixture A mixture with the same composition throughout. (1.3)

Hund's rule The principle stating that when electrons fill degenerate orbitals, they first fill them singly with parallel spins. (8.3)

hybrid orbitals Orbitals formed from the combination of standard atomic orbitals that correspond more closely to the actual distribution of electrons in a chemically bonded atom. (10.7)

hybridization A mathematical procedure in which standard atomic orbitals are combined to form new, hybrid orbitals. (10.7)

hydrate An ionic compound that contains a specific number of water molecules associated with each formula unit. (3.5)

hydrazine N_2H_4, a nitrogen and hydrogen compound in which nitrogen has a negative oxidation state (-2). (22.6)

hydrocarbon An organic compound that contains only carbon and hydrogen. (3.11)

hydrogen azide A nitrogen and hydrogen compound with a higher hydrogen-to-nitrogen ratio than ammonia or hydrazine. (22.6)

hydrogen bond A strong dipole–dipole attractive force between a hydrogen bonded to O, N, or F and one of these electronegative atoms on a neighboring molecule. (11.3)

hydrogenation The catalyzed addition of hydrogen to alkene double bonds to make single bonds. (13.7)

hydrolysis The splitting of a chemical bond with water, resulting in the addition of H and OH to the products. (21.3)

hydrometallurgy The use of an aqueous solution to extract metals from their ores. (23.3)

hydronium ion H_3O^+, the ion formed from the association of a water molecule with an H^+ ion donated by an acid. (4.8, 15.3)

hypothesis A tentative interpretation or explanation of an observation. A good hypothesis is *falsifiable*. (1.2)

hypoxia A physiological condition caused by low levels of oxygen, marked by dizziness, headache, shortness of breath, and eventually unconsciousness or even death in severe cases. (5.6)

ideal gas constant The proportionality constant of the ideal gas law, R, equal to 8.314 J/mol · K or 0.08206 L · atm/mol · K. (5.4)

ideal gas law The law that combines the relationships of Boyle's, Charles's, and Avogadro's laws into one comprehensive equation of state with the proportionality constant R in the form $PV = nRT$. (5.4)

ideal solution A solution that follows Raoult's law at all concentrations for both solute and solvent. (12.6)

indeterminacy The principle that present circumstances do not necessarily determine future evens in the quantum-mechanical realm. (7.4)

indicator A dye whose color depends on the pH of the solution it is dissolved in; often used to detect the endpoint of a titration. (4.8, 16.4)

infrared (IR) radiation Electromagnetic radiation emitted from warm objects, with wavelengths slightly larger than those of visible light. (7.2)

insoluble Incapable of dissolving in water or being extremely difficult of solution. (4.5)

integrated rate law A relationship between the concentrations of the reactants in a chemical reaction and time. (13.4)

intensive property A property such as density that is independent of the amount of a given substance. (1.6)

interference The superposition of two or more waves overlapping in space, resulting in either an increase in amplitude (constructive interference) or a decrease in amplitude (destructive interference). (7.2)

interhalogen compounds A class of covalent compounds that contain two different halogens. (22.9)

internal energy (E) The sum of the kinetic and potential energies of all of the particles that compose a system. (6.2)

International System of Units (SI) The standard unit system used by scientists, based on the metric system. (1.6)

interstitial alloy An alloy in which small, usually nonmetallic atoms fit between the metallic atoms of a crystal. (23.4)

ion An atom or molecule with a net charge caused by the loss or gain of electrons. (2.6)

ion product constant for water (K_w) The equilibrium constant for the autoionization of water. (15.5)

ion–dipole force An intermolecular force between an ion and the oppositely charged end of a polar molecule. (11.3)

ionic bond A chemical bond formed between two oppositely charged ions, generally a metallic cation and a nonmetallic anion, that are attracted to one another by electrostatic forces. (3.2, 9.2)

ionic carbides Binary compounds composed of carbon combined with low-electronegativity metals. (22.5)

ionic compound A compound composed of cations and anions bound together by electrostatic attraction. (3.4)

ionic solids Solids whose composite units are ions; they generally have high melting points. (11.12)

ionization energy (IE) The energy required to remove an electron from an atom or ion in its gaseous state. (8.7)

ionizing power The ability of radiation to ionize other molecules and atoms. (19.3)

irreversible reaction A reaction that does not achieve the theoretical limit of available free energy. (17.7)

isotopes Atoms of the same element with the same number of protons but different numbers of neutrons and consequently different masses. (2.6)

joule (J) The SI unit for energy: equal to $1 \text{ kg} \cdot \text{m}^2/\text{s}^2$. (6.1)

kelvin (K) The SI standard unit of temperature. (1.6)

Kelvin scale The temperature scale that assigns 0 K ($-273\ °C$ or $-459\ °F$) to the coldest temperature possible, absolute zero, which is the temperature at which molecular motion virtually stops: $1\ K = 1\ °C$. (1.6)

ketone A member of the family of organic compounds that contain a carbonyl functional group $(C = O)$ bonded to two R groups, neither of which is a hydrogen atom. (20.10)

ketose A sugar that is a ketone. (21.3)

kilogram (kg) The SI standard unit of mass defined as the mass of a block of metal kept at the International Bureau of Weights and Measures at Sèvres, France. (1.6)

kilowatt-hour (kWh) An energy unit used primarily to express large amounts of energy produced by the flow of electricity; equal to 3.60×10^6 J. (6.1)

kinetic energy The energy associated with motion of an object. (1.5, 6.1)

kinetic molecular theory A model of an ideal gas as a collection of point particles in constant motion undergoing completely elastic collisions. (5.8)

lanthanide contraction The trend toward leveling off in size of the atoms in the third and fourth transition rows due to the ineffective shielding of the f sublevel electrons. (24.2)

lattice energy The energy associated with forming a crystalline lattice from gaseous ions. (9.4)

law see *scientific law*

law of conservation of energy A law stating that energy can neither be created nor destroyed, only converted from one form to another. (1.5, 6.1)

law of conservation of mass A law stating that matter is neither created nor destroyed in a chemical reaction. (1.2)

law of definite proportions A law stating that all samples of a given compound have the same proportions of their constituent elements. (2.3)

law of mass action The relationship between the balanced chemical equation and the expression of the equilibrium constant. (14.3)

law of multiple proportions A law stating that when two elements (A and B) form two different compounds, the masses of element B that combine with one gram of element A can be expressed as a ratio of small whole numbers. (2.3)

Le Châtelier's principle The principle stating that when a chemical system at equilibrium is disturbed, the system shifts in a direction that minimizes the disturbance. (14.9)

leaching The process by which a metal is separated out of a mixture by selectively dissolving it into solution. (23.3)

lead–acid storage battery A battery that uses the oxidation of lead and the reduction of lead(IV) oxide in sulfuric acid to provide electrical current. (18.7)

lever rule The rule that states that in a two-phase region, whichever phase is closest to the composition of the alloy is the more abundant phase. (23.4)

levorotatory Capable of rotating the polarization of light counterclockwise. (20.3)

Lewis acid An atom, ion, or molecule that is an electron pair acceptor. (15.11)

Lewis base An atom, ion, or molecule that is an electron pair donor. (15.11)

Lewis electron-dot structures (Lewis structures) A drawing that represents chemical bonds between atoms as shared or transferred electrons; the valence electrons of atoms are represented as dots. (9.1)

Lewis theory A simple model of chemical bonding using diagrams that represent bonds between atoms as lines or pairs of dots. In this theory, atoms bond together to obtain stable octets (eight valence electrons). (9.1)

ligand A neutral molecule or an ion that acts as a Lewis base with the central metal ion in a complex ion. (16.8, 24.3)

limiting reactant The reactant that has the smallest stoichiometric amount in a reactant mixture and consequently limits the amount of product in a chemical reaction. (4.3)

linear accelerator A particle accelerator in which a charged particle is accelerated in an evacuated tube by a potential difference between the ends of the tube or by alternating charges in sections of the tube. (19.10)

linear geometry The molecular geometry of three atoms with a $180°$ bond angle due to the repulsion of two electron groups. (10.2)

linkage isomers Isomers of complex ions that occur when some ligands coordinate to the metal in different ways. (24.4)

lipid A member of the class of biochemical compounds that are insoluble in water but soluble in nonpolar solvents, including fatty acids, triglycerides, and steroids. (21.2)

lipid bilayer A double-layered structure made of phospholipids or glycolipids, in which the polar heads of the molecules interact with the environment and the nonpolar tails interact with each other; a component of many cellular membranes. (21.2)

liquid A state of matter in which atoms or molecules pack about as closely as they do in solid matter but are free to move relative to each other, giving a fixed volume but not a fixed shape. (1.3)

liter (L) A unit of volume equal to 1000 cm^3 or 1.057 qt. (1.6)

lithium ion battery A battery that produces electrical current in the form of motion of lithium ions from the anode to the cathode. (18.7)

lone pair A pair of electrons associated with only one atom. (9.5)

low-spin complex A complex ion with strong field ligands that have fewer unpaired electrons than the free metal ion. (24.5)

magic numbers Certain numbers of nucleons (N or Z = 2, 8, 20, 28, 50, 82, and $N = 126$) that confer unique stability. (19.4)

magnetic quantum number (m_l) An integer that specifies the orientation of an orbital. (7.5)

main-group elements Those elements found in the s or p blocks of the periodic table, whose properties tend to be predictable based on their position in the table. (2.7, 22.2)

manometer An instrument used to determine the pressure of a gaseous sample, consisting of a liquid-filled U-shaped tube with one end exposed to the ambient pressure and the other end connected to the sample. (5.2)

mass A measure of the quantity of matter making up an object. (1.6)

mass defect The difference in mass between the nucleus of an atom and the sum of the separated particles that make up that nucleus. (19.8)

mass number (A) The sum of the number of protons and neutrons in an atom. (2.6)

mass percent composition (mass percent) An element's percentage of the total mass of a compound containing the element. (3.8)

mass spectrometry   An experimental method of determining the precise mass and relative abundance of isotopes in a given sample using an instrument called a *mass spectrometer*. (2.8)

matter   Anything that occupies space and has mass. (1.3)

mean free path   The average distance that a molecule in a gas travels between collisions. (5.9)

melting (fusion)   The phase transition from solid to liquid. (11.6)

melting point   The temperature at which the molecules of a solid have enough thermal energy to overcome intermolecular forces and become a liquid. (11.6)

metals   A large class of elements that are generally good conductors of heat and electricity, malleable, ductile, lustrous, and tend to lose electrons during chemical changes. (2.7)

metallic atomic solids   Atomic solids held together by metallic bonds; they have variable melting points. (11.12)

metallic bonding   The type of bonding that occurs in metal crystals, in which metal atoms donate their electrons to an electron sea, delocalized over the entire crystal lattice. (9.2)

metallic carbides   Binary compounds composed of carbon combined with metals that have a metallic lattice with holes small enough to fit carbon atoms. (22.5)

metalloids   A category of elements found on the boundary between the metals and nonmetals of the periodic table, with properties intermediate between those of both groups; also called *semimetals*. (2.7)

metallurgy   The part of chemistry that includes all the processes associated with mining, separating, and refining metals and the subsequent production of pure metals and mixtures of metals called alloys. (23.1)

meter (m)   The SI standard unit of length; equivalent to 39.37 inches. (1.6)

metric system   The system of measurements used in most countries in which the meter is the unit of length, the kilogram is the unit of mass, and the second is the unit of time. (1.6)

microwaves   Electromagnetic radiation with wavelengths slightly longer than those of infrared radiation; used for radar and in microwave ovens. (7.2)

milliliter (mL)   A unit of volume equal to 10^{-3} L or 1 cm^3. (1.6)

millimeter of mercury (mmHg)   A common unit of pressure referring to the air pressure required to push a column of mercury to a height of 1 mm in a barometer; 760 mmHg = 1 atm. (5.2)

mineral   A homogenous, naturally occurring, crystalline inorganic solid. (22.2)

miscibility   The ability to mix without separating into two phases. (11.3)

miscible   The ability of two or more substances to be soluble in each other in all proportions. (12.2)

mixture   A substance composed of two or more different types of atoms or molecules that can be combined in variable proportions. (1.3)

molality (m)   A means of expressing solution concentration as the number of moles of solute per kilogram of solvent. (12.5)

molar heat capacity   The amount of heat required to raise the temperature of one mole of a substance by 1 °C. (6.3)

molar mass   The mass in grams of one mole of atoms of an element; numerically equivalent to the atomic mass of the element in amu. (2.9)

molar solubility   The solubility of a compound in units of moles per liter. (16.5)

molar volume   The volume occupied by one mole of a gas; the molar volume of an ideal gas at STP is 22.4 L. (5.5)

molarity (M)   A means of expressing solution concentration as the number of moles of solute per liter of solution. (4.4, 12.5)

mole (mol)   A unit defined as the amount of material containing 6.0221421×10^{23} (Avogadro's number) particles. (2.9)

mole fraction (χ_A)   The number of moles of a component in a mixture divided by the total number of moles in the mixture. (5.6)

mole fraction (χ_{solute})   A means of expressing solution concentration as the number of moles of solute per moles of solution. (12.5)

mole percent   A means of expressing solution concentration as the mole fraction multiplied by 100%. (12.5)

molecular compound   Compounds composed of two or more covalently bonded nonmetals. (3.4)

molecular element   Those elements that exist in nature with diatomic or polyatomic molecules as their basic unit. (3.4)

molecular equation   An equation showing the complete neutral formula for each compound in a reaction. (4.7)

molecular formula   A chemical formula that shows the actual number of atoms of each element in a molecule of a compound. (3.3)

molecular geometry   The geometrical arrangement of atoms in a molecule. (10.3)

molecular orbital theory   An advanced model of chemical bonding in which electrons reside in molecular orbitals delocalized over the entire molecule. In the simplest version, the molecular orbitals are simply linear combinations of atomic orbitals. (10.8)

molecular solids   Solids whose composite units are molecules; they generally have low melting points. (11.12)

molecularity   The number of reactant particles involved in an elementary step. (13.6)

molecule   Two or more atoms joined chemically in a specific geometrical arrangement. (1.1)

monodentate   Describes ligands that donate only one electron pair to the central metal. (24.3)

monoprotic acid   An acid that contains only one ionizable proton. (15.4)

monosaccharide   The simplest carbohydrates, with three to eight carbon atoms and only one aldehyde or ketone group. (21.3)

nanotubes   Long, tubular structures consisting of interconnected C_6 rings. (22.5)

natural abundance   The relative percentage of a particular isotope in a naturally occurring sample with respect to other isotopes of the same element. (2.6)

Nernst equation   The equation relating the cell potential of an electrochemical cell to the standard cell potential and the reaction quotient; $E_{cell} = E_{cell}^{\circ} - \dfrac{0.0592 \text{ V}}{n} \log Q$. (18.6)

net ionic equation   An equation that shows only the species that actually change during the reaction. (4.7)

network covalent atomic solids   Atomic solids held together by covalent bonds; they have high melting points. (11.12)

neutral   The state of a solution where the concentrations of H_3O^+ and OH^- are equal. (15.4)

neutron   An electrically neutral subatomic particle found in the nucleus of an atom, with a mass almost equal to that of a proton. (2.5)

nickel–cadmium (NiCad) battery A battery that consists of an anode composed of solid cadmium and a cathode composed of $NiO(OH)(s)$ in a KOH solution. (18.7)

nickel–metal hydride (NiMH) battery A battery that uses the same cathode reaction as the NiCad battery but a different anode reaction, the oxidation of hydrogens in a metal alloy. (18.7)

nido-**boranes** Boranes that have the formula B_nH_{n+4} and consist of a cage of boron atoms missing one corner. (22.4)

nitrogen narcosis A physiological condition caused by an increased partial pressure of nitrogen, resulting in symptoms similar to those of intoxication. (5.6)

noble gases The group 8A elements, which are largely unreactive (inert) due to their stable filled p orbitals. (2.7)

node A point where the wave function (ψ), and therefore the probability density (ψ^2) and radial distribution function, all go through zero (7.6)

nonbonding atomic solids Atomic solids held together by dispersion forces; they have low melting points. (11.12)

nonbonding orbital An orbital whose electrons remain localized on an atom. (10.8)

nonelectrolyte A compound that does not dissociate into ions when dissolved in water. (4.5)

nonmetal A class of elements that tend to be poor conductors of heat and electricity and usually gain electrons during chemical reactions. (2.7)

nonvolatile Not easily vaporized. (11.5)

normal boiling point The temperature at which the vapor pressure of a liquid equals 1 atm. (11.5)

n-type semiconductor A semiconductor that employs negatively charged electrons in the conduction band as the charge carriers. (11.13)

nuclear binding energy The amount of energy that would be required to break apart the nucleus into its component nucleons. (19.8)

nuclear equation An equation that represents nuclear processes such as radioactivity. (19.3)

nuclear fission The splitting of the nucleus of an atom, resulting in a tremendous release of energy. (19.7)

nuclear fusion The combination of two light nuclei to form a heavier one. (19.9)

nuclear theory The theory that most of the atom's mass and all of its positive charge is contained in a small, dense nucleus. (2.5)

nucleons The particles that compose the nucleus and that are protons and neutrons. (19.4)

nucleotides The individual units composing nucleic acids; each consists of a phosphate group, a sugar, and a nitrogenous base. (21.6)

nucleus The very small, dense core of the atom that contains most of the atom's mass and all of its positive charge; it is composed of protons and neutrons. (2.5)

nuclide A particular isotope of an atom. (19.3)

octahedral arrangement The molecular geometry of seven atoms with 90° bond angles. (10.2)

octahedral hole A space that exists in the middle of six atoms on two adjacent close-packed sheets of atoms in a crystal lattice. (23.4)

octet A Lewis structure with eight dots, signifying a filled outer electron shell for s and p block elements. (9.3)

octet rule The tendency for most bonded atoms to possess or share eight electrons in their outer shell to obtain stable electron configurations and lower their potential energy. (9.3)

optical isomers Two molecules that are nonsuperimposable mirror images of one another. (20.3, 24.4)

orbital A probability distribution map, based on the quantum mechanical model of the atom, used to describe the likely position of an electron in an atom; also an allowed energy state for an electron. (7.5)

orbital diagram A diagram that gives information similar to an electron configuration but symbolizes an electron as an arrow in a box representing an orbital, with the arrow's direction denoting the electron's spin. (8.3)

ore A rock that contains a high concentration of a specific mineral. (23.2)

organic chemistry The study of carbon-based compounds. (20.1)

organic molecule A molecule containing carbon combined with several other elements including hydrogen, nitrogen, oxygen, or sulfur. (20.1)

orthosilicates Silicates in which tetrahedral SO_4^{4-} ions stand alone. (22.3)

osmosis The flow of solvent from a solution of lower solute concentration to one of higher solute concentration. (12.7)

osmotic pressure The pressure required to stop osmotic flow. (12.7)

Ostwald process An industrial process used for commercial preparation of nitric acid. (22.6)

overall order The sum of the orders of all reactants in a chemical reaction. (13.3)

oxidation The loss of one or more electrons; also the gaining of oxygen or the loss of hydrogen. (4.9)

oxidation state (oxidation number) A positive or negative whole number that represents the "charge" an atom in a compound would have if all shared electrons were assigned to the atom with a greater attraction for those electrons. (4.9)

oxidation–reduction (redox) reaction Reactions in which electrons are transferred from one reactant to another and the oxidation states of certain atoms are changed. (4.9)

oxidizing agent A substance that causes the oxidation of another substance; an oxidizing agent gains electrons and is reduced. (4.9)

oxyacid An acid composed of hydrogen and an oxyanion. (3.6)

oxyanion A polyatomic anion containing a nonmetal covalently bonded to one or more oxygen atoms. (3.5)

oxygen toxicity A physiological condition caused by an increased level of oxygen in the blood, resulting in muscle twitching, tunnel vision, and convulsions. (5.6)

ozone O_3, an allotrope of oxygen that is a toxic blue diamagnetic gas with a strong odor. (22.7)

packing efficiency The percentage of volume of a unit cell occupied by the atoms, assumed to be spherical. (11.11)

paramagnetic The state of an atom or ion that contains unpaired electrons and is, therefore, attracted by an external magnetic field. (8.7, 10.8)

partial pressure (P_n) The pressure due to any individual component in a gas mixture. (5.6)

parts by mass A unit for expressing solution concentration as the mass of the solute divided by the mass of the solution multiplied by a multiplication factor. (12.5)

parts by volume A unit for expressing solution concentration as the volume of the solute divided by the volume of the solution multiplied by a multiplication factor. (12.5)

parts per billion (ppb) A unit for expressing solution concentration in parts by mass where the multiplication factor is 10^9. (12.5)

parts per million (ppm) A unit for expressing solution concentration in parts by mass where the multiplication factor is 10^6. (12.5)

pascal (Pa) The SI unit of pressure, defined as 1 N/m^2. (5.2)

Pauli exclusion principle The principle that no two electrons in an atom can have the same four quantum numbers. (8.3)

penetrating power The ability of radiation to penetrate matter. (19.3)

penetration The phenomenon of some higher-level atomic orbitals having significant amounts of probability within the space occupied by orbitals of lower energy level. For example, the $2s$ orbital penetrates into the $1s$ orbital. (8.3)

peptide bond The bond that forms between the amine end of one amino acid and the carboxylic end of another. (21.4)

percent by mass A unit for expressing solution concentration in parts by mass with a multiplication factor of 100%. (12.5)

percent ionic character The ratio of a bond's actual dipole moment to the dipole moment it would have if the electron were transferred completely from one atom to the other, multiplied by 100%. (9.6)

percent ionization The concentration of ionized acid in a solution divided by the initial concentration of acid multiplied by 100%. (15.6)

percent yield The percentage of the theoretical yield of a chemical reaction that is actually produced; the ratio of the actual yield to the theoretical yield multiplied by 100%. (4.3)

periodic law A law based on the observation that when the elements are arranged in order of increasing mass, certain sets of properties recur periodically. (2.7)

periodic property A property of an element that is predictable based on an element's position in the periodic table. (8.1)

permanent dipole A permanent separation of charge; a molecule with a permanent dipole always has a slightly negative charge at one end and a slightly positive charge at the other. (11.3)

pH The negative log of the concentration of H_3O^+ in a solution; the pH scale is a compact way to specify the acidity of a solution. (15.4)

phase With regard to waves and orbitals, the phase is the sign of the amplitude of the wave, which can be positive or negative. (7.6)

phase diagram A map of the phase of a substance as a function of pressure and temperature. (11.8)

phenyl group A benzene ring treated as a substituent. (20.7)

phosphine PH_3, a colorless, poisonous gas that smells like decaying fish and has an oxidation state of -3 for phosphorus. (22.6)

phospholipid Compound similar in structure to a triglyceride but with one fatty acid replaced by a phosphate group. (21.2)

phosphorescence The long-lived emission of light that sometimes follows the absorption of light by certain atoms and molecules. (19.2)

photoelectric effect The observation that many metals emit electrons when light falls upon them. (7.2)

photon (quantum) The smallest possible packet of electromagnetic radiation with an energy equal to $h\nu$. (7.2)

physical change A change that alters only the state or appearance of a substance but not its chemical composition. (1.4)

physical property A property that a substance displays without changing its chemical composition. (1.4)

pi (π) bond The bond that forms between two p orbitals that overlap side to side. (10.7)

p–n junctions Tiny areas in electronic circuits that have p-type semiconductors on one side and n-type on the other. (11.13)

polar covalent bond A covalent bond between two atoms with significantly different electronegativities, resulting in an uneven distribution of electron density. (9.6)

polyatomic ion An ion composed of two or more atoms. (3.5)

polydentate Describes ligands that donate more than one electron pair to the central metal. (24.3)

polypeptide A chain of amino acids joined together by peptide bonds. (21.4)

polyprotic acid An acid that contains more than one ionizable proton and releases them sequentially. (4.8, 15.9)

polysaccharide A long, chainlike molecule composed of many monosaccharide units bonded together. (21.3)

positron The particle released in positron emission; equal in mass to an electron but opposite in charge. (19.3)

positron emission The form of radioactive decay that occurs when an unstable nucleus emits a positron. (19.3)

positron emission tomography (PET) A specialized imaging technique that employs positron-emitting nuclides, such as fluorine-18, as a radiotracer. (19.12)

potential difference A measure of the difference in potential energy (usually in joules) per unit of charge (coulombs). (18.3)

potential energy The energy associated with the position or composition of an object. (1.5, 6.1)

powder metallurgy A process by which metallic components are made from powdered metal. (23.3)

precipitate A solid, insoluble ionic compound that forms in, and separates from, a solution. (4.6)

precipitation reaction A reaction in which a solid, insoluble product forms upon mixing two solutions. (4.6)

precision A term that refers to how close a series of measurements are to one another or how reproducible they are. (1.7)

prefix multipliers Multipliers that change the value of the unit by powers of ten. (1.6)

pressure A measure of force exerted per unit area; in chemistry, most commonly the force exerted by gas molecules as they strike the surfaces around them. (5.1)

pressure–volume work The work that occurs when a volume change takes place against an external pressure. (6.3)

primary structure The sequence of amino acids in a protein chain. (21.5)

primary valence The oxidation state on the central metal atom in a complex ion. (24.3)

principal level (shell) The group of orbitals with the same value of n. (7.5)

principal quantum number (n) An integer that specifies the overall size and energy of an orbital. The higher the quantum number n, the greater the average distance between the electron and the nucleus and the higher its energy. (7.5)

probability density The probability (per unit volume) of finding the electron at a point in space as expressed by a three-dimensional plot of the wave function squared (ψ^2). (7.6)

products The substances produced in a chemical reaction; they appear on the right-hand side of a chemical equation. (3.10)

proton   A positively charged subatomic particle found in the nucleus of an atom. (2.5)

p-type semiconductor   A semiconductor that employs positively charged "holes" in the valence band as the charge carriers. (11.13)

pure substance   A substance composed of only one type of atom or molecule. (1.3)

pyrometallurgy   A technique of extractive metallurgy in which heat is used to extract a metal from its mineral. (23.3)

pyrosilicates   Silicates in which two SO_4^{4-} tetrahedral ions share a corner. (22.3)

pyroxenes   Silicates in which SO_4^{4-} tetrahedral ions bond together to form chains. (22.3)

qualitative analysis   A systematic way to determine the ions present in an unknown solution. (16.7)

quantitative analysis   A systematic way to determine the amounts of substances in a solution or mixture. (16.7)

quantum number   One of four interrelated numbers that determine the shape and energy of orbitals, as specified by a solution of the Schrödinger equation. (7.5)

quantum-mechanical model   A model that explains the behavior of absolutely small particles such as electrons and photons. (7.1)

quartz   A silicate crystal that has a formula unit of SiO_2. (22.3)

quaternary structure   The way that subunits fit together in a multimeric protein. (21.5)

racemic mixture   An equimolar mixture of two optical isomers that does not rotate the plane of polarization of light at all. (20.3)

radio waves   The form of electromagnetic radiation with the longest wavelengths and smallest energy. (7.2)

radioactive   The state of those unstable atoms that emit subatomic particles or high-energy electromagnetic radiation. (19.1)

radioactivity   The emission of subatomic particles or high-energy electromagnetic radiation by the unstable nuclei of certain atoms. (2.5, 19.1)

radiocarbon dating   A form of radiometric dating based on the C-14 isotope. (19.6)

radiometric dating   A technique used to estimate the age of rocks, fossils, or artifacts that depends on the presence of radioactive isotopes and their predictable decay with time. (19.6)

radiotracer   A radioactive nuclide that has been attached to a compound or introduced into a mixture in order to track the movement of the compound or mixture within the body. (19.12)

random coils   Sections of a protein's secondary structure that have less-regular patterns than α-helixes or β-pleated sheets. (21.5)

random error   Error that has equal probability of being too high or too low. (1.7)

Raoult's law   An equation used to determine the vapor pressure of a solution; $P_{soln} = X_{solv}P_{solv}^{\circ}$. (12.6)

rate constant (k)   A constant of proportionality in the rate law. (13.3)

rate law   A relationship between the rate of a reaction and the concentration of the reactants. (13.3)

rate-determining step   The step in a reaction mechanism that occurs much more slowly than any of the other steps. (13.6)

reactants   The starting substances of a chemical reaction; they appear on the left-hand side of a chemical equation. (3.10)

reaction intermediates   Species that are formed in one step of a reaction mechanism and consumed in another. (13.6)

reaction mechanism   A series of individual chemical steps by which an overall chemical reaction occurs. (13.6)

reaction order (n)   A value in the rate law that determines how the rate depends on the concentration of the reactants. (13.3)

reaction quotient (Q_c)   The ratio, at any point in the reaction, of the concentrations of the products of a reaction raised to their stoichiometric coefficients to the concentrations of the reactants raised to their stoichiometric coefficients. (14.7)

recrystallization   A technique used to purify solids in which the solid is put into hot solvent until the solution is saturated; when the solution cools, the purified solute comes out of solution. (12.4)

red phosphorus   An allotrope of phosphorus similar in structure to white phosphorus but with one of the bonds between two phosphorus atoms in the tetrahedron broken; red phosphorus is more stable than white. (22.6)

reducing agent   A substance that causes the reduction of another substance; a reducing agent loses electrons and is oxidized. (4.9)

reduction   The gaining of one or more electrons; also the gaining of hydrogen or the loss of oxygen. (4.9)

refine   To purify, particularly a metal. (23.3)

refining   A process in which the crude material is purified. (23.3)

rem   A unit of the dose of radiation exposure that stands for roentgen equivalent man, where a roentgen is defined as the amount of radiation that produces 2.58×10^{-4} C of charge per kg of air. (19.11)

resonance hybrid   The actual structure of a molecule that is intermediate between two or more resonance structures. (9.8)

resonance structures   Two or more valid Lewis structures that are shown with double-headed arrows between them to indicate that the actual structure of the molecule is intermediate between them. (9.8)

reversible   As applied to a reaction, the ability to proceed in either the forward or the reverse direction. (14.2)

reversible reaction   A reaction that achieves the theoretical limit with respect to free energy and will change direction upon an infinitesimally small change in a variable (such as temperature or pressure) related to the reaction. (17.7)

roasting   Heating that causes a chemical reaction between a furnace atmosphere and a mineral in order to process ores. (23.3)

salt   An ionic compound formed in a neutralization reaction by the replacement of an H^+ ion from the acid with a cation from the base. (4.8)

salt bridge   An inverted, U-shaped tube containing a strong electrolyte such as KNO_3 that connects the two half-cells, allowing a flow of ions that neutralizes the charge build-up. (18.3)

saturated fat   A triglyceride with no double bonds in the hydrocarbon chain; saturated fats tend to be solid at room temperature. (21.2)

saturated hydrocarbon   A hydrocarbon containing no double bonds in the carbon chain. (20.4)

saturated solution   A solution in which the dissolved solute is in dynamic equilibrium with any undissolved solute; any added solute will not dissolve. (12.4)

scientific law   A brief statement or equation that summarizes past observations and predicts future ones. (1.2)

scientific method   An approach to acquiring knowledge about the natural world that begins with observations and leads to the formation of testable hypotheses. (1.2)

scintillation counter   A device for the detection of radioactivity using a material that emits ultraviolet or visible light in response to excitation by energetic particles. (19.5)

second (s)   The SI standard unit of time, defined as the duration of 9,192,631,770 periods of the radiation emitted from a certain transition in a cesium-133 atom. (1.6)

second law of thermodynamics   A law stating that for any spontaneous process, the entropy of the universe increases ($\Delta S_{univ} > 0$). (17.3)

secondary structure   The regular periodic or repeating patterns in the arrangement of protein chains. (21.5)

secondary valence   The number of molecules or ions directly bound to the metal atom in a complex ion; also called the *coordination number*. (24.3)

seesaw   The molecular geometry of a molecule with trigonal bipyramidal electron geometry and one lone pair in an axial position. (10.3)

selective precipitation   A process involving the addition of a reagent to a solution that forms a precipitate with one of the dissolved ions but not the others. (16.6)

semiconductor   A material with intermediate electrical conductivity that can be changed and controlled. (2.7)

semipermeable membrane   A membrane that selectively allows some substances to pass through but not others. (12.7)

shielding   The effect on an electron of repulsion by electrons in lower-energy orbitals that screen it from the full effects of nuclear charge. (8.3)

sigma (σ) bond   The resulting bond that forms between a combination of any two *s*, *p*, or hybridized orbitals that overlap end to end. (10.7)

significant figures (significant digits)   In any reported measurement, the non-place-holding digits that indicate the precision of the measured quantity. (1.7)

silica   A silicate crystal that has a formula unit of SiO_2, also called *quartz*. (22.3)

silicates   Covalent atomic solids that contain silicon, oxygen, and various metal atoms. (22.3)

simple cubic   A unit cell that consists of a cube with one atom at each corner. (11.11)

slag   In pyrometallurgy, the waste liquid solution that is formed between the flux and gangue; usually a silicate material. (23.3)

smelting   A form of roasting in which the product is liquefied, which aids in the separation. (23.3)

solid   A state of matter in which atoms or molecules are packed close to one another in fixed locations with definite volume. (1.3)

solubility   The amount of a substance that will dissolve in a given amount of solvent. (12.2)

solubility product constant (K_{sp})   The equilibrium expression for a chemical equation representing the dissolution of a slightly to moderately soluble ionic compound. (16.5)

soluble   Able to dissolve to a significant extent, usually in water. (4.5)

solute   The minority component of a solution. (4.4, 12.1)

solution   A homogenous mixture of two substances. (4.4, 12.1)

solvent   The majority component of a solution. (4.4, 12.1)

space-filling molecular model   A representation of a molecule that shows how the atoms fill the space between them. (3.3)

specific heat capacity (C_s)   The amount of heat required to raise the temperature of 1 g of a substance by 1 °C. (6.3)

spectator ion   Ions in a complete ionic equation that do not participate in the reaction and therefore remain in solution. (4.7)

spin quantum number (m_s)   The fourth quantum number, which denotes the electron's spin as either $\frac{1}{2}$ (up arrow) or $-\frac{1}{2}$ (down arrow). (8.3)

spontaneous process   A process that occurs without ongoing outside intervention. (17.2)

square planar   The molecular geometry of a molecule with octahedral electron geometry and two lone pairs. (10.3)

square pyramidal   The molecular geometry of a molecule with octahedral electron geometry and one lone pair. (10.3)

standard cell potential (standard emf) (E_{cell}°)   The cell potential for a system in standard states (solute concentration of 1 M and gaseous reactant partial pressure of 1 atm). (18.3)

standard change in free energy (ΔG_{rxn}°)   The change in free energy for a process when all reactants and products are in their standard states. (17.7)

standard enthalpy change ($\Delta H°$)   The change in enthalpy for a process when all reactants and products are in their standard states. (6.8)

standard enthalpy of formation (ΔH_f°)   The change in enthalpy when 1 mol of a compound forms from its constituent elements in their standard states. (6.8)

standard entropy change (ΔS_{rxn})   The change in entropy for a process when all reactants and products are in their standard states. (17.6)

standard entropy change for a reaction (ΔS_{rxn}°)   The change in entropy for a process in which all reactants and products are in their standard states. (17.6)

Standard Hydrogen Electrode (SHE)   The half-cell consisting of an inert platinum electrode immersed in 1 M HCl with hydrogen gas at 1 atm bubbling through the solution; used as the standard of a cell potential of zero. (18.4)

standard molar entropy ($S°$)   A measure of the energy dispersed into one mole of a substance at a particular temperature. (17.6)

standard state   For a gas the standard state is the pure gas at a pressure of exactly 1 atm; for a liquid or solid the standard state is the pure substance in its most stable form at a pressure of 1 atm and the temperature of interest (often taken to be 25 °C); for a substance in solution the standard state is a concentration of exactly 1 M. (6.8)

standard temperature and pressure (STP)   The conditions of $T = 0 °C$ (273 K) and $P = 1$ atm; used primarily in reference to a gas. (5.5)

starch   A polysaccharide that consists of glucose units bonded together by α-glycosidic linkages; the main energy storage medium for plants. (21.3)

state   A classification of the form of matter as a solid, liquid, or gas. (1.3)

state function   A function whose value depends only on the state of the system, not on how the system got to that state. (6.2)

stereoisomers   Molecules in which the atoms are bonded in the same order but have a different spatial arrangement. (20.3, 24.4)

steroid   A lipid composed of four fused hydrocarbon rings. (21.2)

stock solution   A highly concentrated form of a solution used in laboratories to make less concentrated solutions via dilution. (4.4)

stoichiometry   The numerical relationships between amounts of reactants and products in a balanced chemical equation. (4.2)

strong acid   An acid that completely ionizes in solution. (4.5, 15.4)

strong base   A base that completely dissociates in solution. (15.7)

strong electrolyte   A substance that completely dissociates into ions when dissolved in water. (4.5)

strong force   Of the four fundamental forces of physics, the one that is the strongest but acts over the shortest distance; the strong force is responsible for holding the protons and neutrons together in the nucleus of an atom. (19.4)

strong-field complex   A complex ion in which the crystal field splitting is large. (24.5)

structural formula A molecular formula that shows how the atoms in a molecule are connected or bonded to each other. (3.3, 20.3)

structural isomers Molecules with the same molecular formula but different structures. (20.3, 24.4)

sublevel (subshell) Those orbitals in the same principle level with the same value of n and l. (7.5)

sublimation The phase transition from solid to gas. (11.6)

substitutional alloy An alloy in which one metal atom substitutes for another in the crystal structure. (23.4)

substrate The reactant molecule of a biochemical reaction that binds to an enzyme at the active site. (13.7)

supersaturated solution An unstable solution in which more than the equilibrium amount of solute is dissolved. (12.4)

surface tension The energy required to increase the surface area of a liquid by a unit amount; responsible for the tendency of liquids to minimize their surface area, giving rise to a membrane-like surface. (11.4)

surroundings In thermodynamics, everything in the universe that exists outside the system under investigation. (6.1)

system In thermodynamics, the portion of the universe that is singled out for investigation. (6.1)

systematic error Error that tends toward being consistently either too high or too low. (1.7)

systematic name An official name for a compound, based on well-established rules, that can be determined by examining its chemical structure. (3.5)

temperature A measure of the average kinetic energy of the atoms or molecules that compose a sample of matter. (1.6)

termolecular An elementary step of a reaction in which three particles collide and go on to form products. (13.6)

tertiary structure The large-scale bends and folds produced by interactions between the R groups of amino acids that are separated by large distances in the linear sequence of a protein chain. (21.5)

tetrahedral geometry The molecular geometry of five atoms with 109.5° bond angles. (10.2)

tetrahedral hole A space that exists directly above the center point of three closest-packed metal atoms in one plane and a fourth metal located directly above the center point in the adjacent plane in a crystal lattice. (23.4)

theoretical yield The greatest possible amount of product that can be made in a chemical reaction based on the amount of limiting reactant. (4.3)

theory A proposed explanation for observations and laws, based on well-established and tested hypotheses, that presents a model of the way nature works and predicts behavior beyond the observations and laws on which it was based. (1.2)

thermal energy A type of kinetic energy associated with the temperature of an object, arising from the motion of individual atoms or molecules in the object; see also *heat*. (1.5, 6.1)

thermal equilibrium The point at which there is no additional net transfer of heat between a system and its surroundings. (6.3)

thermochemistry The study of the relationship between chemistry and energy. (6.1)

thermodynamics The general study of energy and its interconversions. (6.2)

third law of thermodynamics The law stating that the entropy of a perfect crystal at absolute zero (0 K) is zero. (17.6)

titration A laboratory procedure in which a substance in a solution of known concentration is reacted with another substance in a solution of unknown concentration in order to determine the unknown concentration; see also *acid–base titration*. (4.8)

transition elements (transition metals) Those elements found in the d block of the periodic table whose properties tend to be less predictable based simply on their position in the table. (2.7)

transmutation The transformation of one element into another as a result of nuclear reactions. (19.10)

triglyceride Triesters composed of glycerol with three fatty acids attached. (21.2)

trigonal bipyramidal The molecular geometry of six atoms with 120° bond angles between the three equatorial electron groups and 90° bond angles between the two axial electron groups and the trigonal plane. (10.2)

trigonal planar geometry The molecular geometry of four atoms with 120° bond angles in a plane. (10.2)

trigonal pyramidal The molecular geometry of a molecule with tetrahedral electron geometry and one lone pair. (10.3)

triple bond The bond that forms when three electron pairs are shared between two atoms. (9.5)

triple point The unique set of conditions at which all three phases of a substance are equally stable and in equilibrium. (11.8)

triprotic acid An acid that contains three ionizable protons. (15.4)

T-shaped The molecular geometry of a molecule with trigonal bipyramidal electron geometry and two lone pairs in axial positions. (10.3)

two-phase region The region between the two phases in a metal alloy phase diagram, where the amount of each phase depends upon the composition of the alloy. (23.4)

Tyndall effect The scattering of light by a colloidal dispersion. (12.8)

ultraviolet (UV) radiation Electromagnetic radiation with slightly smaller wavelengths than visible light. (7.2)

unimolecular Describes a reaction that involves only one particle that goes on to form products. (13.6)

unit cell The smallest divisible unit of a crystal that, when repeated in three dimensions, reproduces the entire crystal lattice. (11.11)

units Standard quantities used to specify measurements. (1.6)

unsaturated fat A triglyceride with one or more double bonds in the hydrocarbon chain; unsaturated fats tend to be liquid at room temperature. (21.2)

unsaturated hydrocarbon A hydrocarbon that includes one or more double or triple bonds. (20.5)

unsaturated solution A solution containing less than the equilibrium amount of solute; any added solute will dissolve until equilibrium is reached. (12.4)

valence bond theory An advanced model of chemical bonding in which electrons reside in quantum-mechanical orbitals localized on individual atoms that are a hybridized blend of standard atomic orbitals; chemical bonds result from an overlap of these orbitals. (10.6)

valence electrons Those electrons that are important in chemical bonding. For main-group elements, the valence electrons are those in the outermost principal energy level. (8.4)

valence shell electron pair repulsion (VSEPR) theory A theory that allows prediction of the shapes of molecules based on the idea that electrons—either as lone pairs or as bonding pairs—repel one another. (10.2)

van der Waals equation   The extrapolation of the ideal gas law that considers the effects of intermolecular forces and particle volume in a nonideal gas: $P + a\left(\dfrac{n}{V}\right)^2 \times (V - nb) = nRT$. (5.9)

van der Waals radius (nonbonding atomic radius)   Defined as one-half the distance between the centers of adjacent, nonbonding atoms in a crystal. (8.6)

van't Hoff factor (i)   The ratio of moles of particles in a solution to moles of formula units dissolved. (12.7)

vapor pressure   The partial pressure of a vapor in dynamic equilibrium with its liquid. (5.6, 11.5)

vaporization   The phase transition from liquid to gas. (11.5)

viscosity   A measure of the resistance of a liquid to flow. (11.4)

visible light   Those frequencies of electromagnetic radiation that can be detected by the human eye. (7.2)

volatile   Tending to vaporize easily. (1.3, 11.5)

voltaic (galvanic) cell   An electrochemical cell that produces electrical current from a spontaneous chemical reaction. (18.3)

volume (V)   A measure of space. Any unit of length, when cubed (raised to the third power), becomes a unit of volume. (1.6)

washing soda   The hydrated crystal of sodium carbonate, $Na_2CO_3 \cdot 10\ H_2O$. (22.5)

wave function (ψ)   A mathematical function that describes the wavelike nature of the electron. (7.5)

wavelength (λ)   The distance between adjacent crests of a wave. (7.2)

weak acid   An acid that does not completely ionize in water. (4.5, 15.4)

weak base   A base that only partially ionizes in water. (15.7)

weak electrolyte   A substance that does not completely ionize in water and only weakly conducts electricity in solution. (4.5)

weak-field complex   A complex ion in which the crystal field splitting is small. (24.5)

white phosphorus   An unstable allotrope of phosphorus consisting of P_4 molecules in a tetrahedral shape, with the phosphorus atoms at the corners of the tetrahedron. (22.6)

work (w)   The result of a force acting through a distance. (1.5, 6.1)

X-rays   Electromagnetic radiation with wavelengths slightly longer than those of gamma rays; used to image bones and internal organs. (7.2)

X-ray diffraction   A powerful laboratory technique that allows for the determination of the arrangement of atoms in a crystal and the measuring of the distance between them. (11.10)

Photo and Text Credits

Chapter 1 Page xxxviii: Albert Einstein (1879–1955). Page 3 center right: Tomas Abab/ Alamy. Page 3: Lavoisier, A. Traité élémentaire de chimie, présenté dans un ordre nouveau et d'aprés les découvertes modernes, 2 vols. Paris: Chez Cuchet, 1789. Reprinted Bruxelles: Cultures et Civilisations, 1965. Page 5: Thomas Kuhn, The Structure of Scientific Revolutions, University of Chicago Press, 1965. Page 6 center left: oneo/Fotolia. Page 7 left: tomprout/iStockphoto. Page 7 center left: Fotolia. Page 7 center right: YinYang/ iStockphoto. Page 7 right: DenisLarkin/iStockphoto. Page 9 bottom left: zoom-zoom/ iStockphoto.com. Page 9 bottom right: Siede Preis/Getty Images. Page 10 top: Charles D. Winters/Photo Researchers, Inc. Page 10 center: Renn Sminkey/Pearson Education. Page 10 bottom: Clark Brennan/Alamy. Page 13: NASAs metric confusion caused Mars orbiter loss, CNN Tech. Page 13 bottom: NASA. Page 14: The International Bureau of Weights and Measures. Page 14 top left: Dorling Kindersley Media Library. Page 14 center left: Icon Sports Media 465/Newscom. Page 14 center: Siede Preis/Getty Images. Page 14 bottom left: Richard Megna/Fundamental Photographs. Page 16 left: Marty Honig/Getty Images. Page 16 center left: teekaygee/iStockphoto. Page 16 center right: AndrazG /iStockphoto. Page 16 right: Byron W Moore/Shutterstock. Page 20: National Osteoporosis Foundation. Page 20 top right: ETH Zurich/IBM Research Division. Page 20 center right: Kristiana007/Dreamstime. Page 20 bottom: (Long Beach Site 060374002) Environmental Protection Agency. Page 21 top right: Richard Megna/Fundamental Photographs. Page 21 center right: Richard Megna/Fundamental Photographs. Page 21 top right: Richard Megna/ Fundamental Photographs. Page 21 center right: Pearson Education/Stacey Stambaugh. Page 21 bottom right: Richard Megna/Fundamental Photographs. Page 36 center: ETH Zurich/IBM Research Division. Page 39 top: Richard Megna/Fundamental Photographs. Page 39 center: zoom-zoom/iStockphoto. Page 39 bottom: Pearson Education/Stacey Stambaugh. Page 40 top left: Pearson Education/Stacey Stambaugh. Page 40 top center: Warren Rosenberg/Fundamental Photographs. Page 40 top right: Warren Rosenberg/ Fundamental Photographs. Page 41 Question 126: Science 2.0: http://www.science20.com/ news_articles/how_fast_can_human_run_100_meter_sprint. Page 41 Question 127: U.S. Food and Drug Administration. Page 42 Question 136: A New Class of Black Holes? NASA Science News, NASA. Page 42 center: NASA. **Chapter 2** Page 44: John Dalton, A New System of Chemical Philosophy. 3 vols. Manchester, 1808, 1810, 1827. Page 45: G. Binnig, H. Rohrer (1986). "Scanning tunneling microscopy". IBM Journal of Research and Development 30. Page 46 bottom left: Veeco Instruments, Inc. Page 46 bottom right: IBM Research Division. Page 47: Democritus (460–370 B.C.). Page 48: Joseph Proust (1754– 1826). Page 48 bottom left: Charles D. Winters/Photo Researchers, Inc. Page 48 bottom center: Charles D Winters/Photo Researchers, Inc. Page 48 bottom right: Joseph Calev/ Shutterstock. Page 51: Feynman, Richard (1964). The Feynman Lectures on Physics; Volume 1. U.S.A: Addison Wesley. Page 51 bottom right: Richard Megna/Fundamental Photographs. Page 53 top: Adapted from Millikan, R.A. 1913, On the Elementary Electric charge and the Avogadro Constant. Page 54: Adapted from The Scattering of a and β Particles by Matter and the Structure of the Atom. Page 56 top left: Richard Megna/ Fundamental Photographs, NYC. Page 56 bottom right: Jeremy Woodhouse/Getty Images. Page 57 top left: Steve Cole/Getty Images. Page 57 top right: Pearson Education. Page 58 bottom left: Library of Congress. Page 60: NASA. Page 62 center: noonika/iStockphoto. com. Page 63 left: Matthias Zepper/Wikimedia Commons. Page 63 2nd from left: Charles D. Winters/Photo Researchers, Inc. Page 63 3rd from left: Steffen Foerster Photography/ Shutterstock. Page 63 4th from left: Clive Streeter/Dorling Kindersley Publishing. Page 63 5th from left: Pearson Education. Page 63 6th from left: Enricoros. Page 63 7th from left: Harry Taylor/Dorling Kindersley. Page 63 8th from left: Gary Ombler/Dorling Kindersley. Page 63 top right: iStockphoto. Page 63 center right: Charles D. Winters/Photo Researchers, Inc. Page 63 bottom right: Perennou Nuridsany/Photo Researchers, Inc. Page 64 top left: Richard Megna/Fundamental Photographs. Page 64 2nd from top left: Martyn F. Chillmaid/ Photo Researchers, Inc. Page 64 3rd from top left: Charles D. Winters/Photo Researchers, Inc. Page 64 bottom left: Charles D. Winters/Photo Researchers, Inc. Page 69: Pure Appl. Chem. 83(2) p. 359–396, 2011. Page 69 bottom: Copyright © 2012 International Union of Pure and Applied Chemistry. Page 70 top: Pearson Education/Stacey Stambaugh. Page 70 bottom: Pearson Education/Stacey Stambaugh. Page 78 top: Jeremy Woodhouse/Getty Images. Page 78 center: Charles D. Winters/Photo Researchers, Inc. Page 78 bottom: Pearson Education/Stacey Stambaugh. Page 81 Copyright 1993–2012 Mark Winter [The University of Sheffield and WebElements Ltd, UK]. All rights reserved. Page 82 Copyright 1993–2012 Mark Winter [The University of Sheffield and WebElements Ltd, UK]. All rights reserved. Page 82 top right: IBM Corporation. **Chapter 3** Page 86 top: Francis Harry Compton Crick, What Mad Pursuit: A personal View of Scientific Discovery (1988) p. 61, Basic Books. Page 88: malerapaso/iStockphoto.Page 89 bottom left: Richard Megna/ Fundamental Photographs. Page 89 bottom center: Charles Falco/Photo Researchers, Inc. Page 89 bottom right: Charles D. Winters/Photo Researchers, Inc. Page 93 center right: Charles D. Winters/Photo Researchers, Inc. Page 94 top: Charles Falco/Photo Researchers, Inc. Page 94 bottom left: Pearson Education.Page 95 bottom: Pearson Education/Renn Sminkey. Page 96 top left: Sydney Moulds/Photo Researchers, Inc. Page 96 top right: Basement Stock/Alamy. Page 100 bottom left: Richard Megna/Fundamental Photographs. Page 102 bottom left: Shutterstock. Page 103 top: Richard Megna/Fundamental Photographs. Page 104: Clean Air Act, Environmental Protection Agency. Page 104 bottom left: Andre Jenny Stock Connection Worldwide/Newscom. Page 104 bottom right: Richard Megna/Fundamental Photographs. Page 109 center right: NASA. Page 111 bottom right: Richard Megna/Fundamental Photographs. Page 114: U.S. Food and Drug Administration. Page 114 top right: David R. Frazier Photolibrary, Inc./Alamy. Page 123 center left:

Sinelyov/Shutterstock. Page 124 center left: Lightpoet/Fotolia. Page 125 bottom right: Renn Sminkey/CDV LLC, Creative Digital Visions/Pearson Education. Page 129 center: Pearson Education/Renn Sminkey. Page 129 bottom: Shutterstock. **Chapter 4** Page 140 bottom left: NCDC/NESDIS/NOAA. Page 140 bottom right: NCDC/NESDIS/National Oceanic and Atmospheric Administration (NOAA). Page 142: Gerlach, T. M., Present-day emissions from volcanoes; Eos, Transactions, American Geophysical Union, Vol. 72, No. 23, June 4, 1991, pp. 249 and 254–255. Page 151: U.S. Environmental Protection Agency. Page 151 bottom right: Robert W. Ginn/PhotoEdit. Page 160 bottom left: Richard Megna/ Fundamental Photographs. Page 161: Richard Megna/Fundamental Photographs. Page 162: Martyn F. Chillmaid/Photo Researchers, Inc. Page 163: Dorling Kindersley Publishing. Page 164: Richard Megna/Fundamental Photographs. Page 168: Chip Clark/Fundamental Photographs. Page 169 center right: Eric Schrader/Pearson Education. Page 169 bottom right: Eric Schrader/Pearson Education. Page 170: Richard Megna/Fundamental Photographs. Page 172: Richard Megna/Fundamental Photographs. Page 174: Richard Megna/Fundamental Photographs. Page 176 top left: Tom Bochsler/Pearson Education. Page 176 top right: Charles D. Winters/Photo Researchers, Inc. Page 177: Richard Megna/ Fundamental Photographs. Page 181: ImageShop/Corbis. Page 185 2nd from bottom: Chip Clark/Fundamental Photographs. Page 185 bottom: Charles D. Winters/Photo Researchers, Inc. **Chapter 5** Page 194: In W.D. Niven (ed.) 'Illustrations of the Dynamical Theory of Gases,' The Scientific Papers of James Clerk Maxwell, Vol 1, 377. Page 199: Patrick Watson/Pearson Education. Page 203: Hanna-Barbera Productions, Inc, CBS, 1960-1966. Page 204 top left: Carlos Caetano/Shutterstock. Page 204 bottom left: Dorling Kindersley. Page 207 bottom right: Renn Sminkey/Pearson Education. Page 237 2nd from top: Renn Sminkey/Pearson Education. Page 242 bottom: Tom Bochsler/Pearson Education. **Chapter 6** Page 251: The Franklin Institute. Page 257 bottom: Larry Brownstein/Getty Images. Page 266 top left: Tom Bochsler/Pearson Education. Page 266 top right: Stan Fellerman/ Corbis. Page 277 bottom: Richard Megna/Fundamental Photographs. Page 280 top: U.S. Energy Information Administration, Annual Energy Report, 2010. Page 281 top right: Source: EPA's 2010 National Air Quality and Emissions Trends Report. Page 282 bottom: American Honda Motor Co. Page 283 center left: National Geophysical Data Center. Page 283 center: Sandia National Laboratories. Page 283 center right: Randy Montoya/ Sandia National Laboratories. Page 283 top right: Getty Images. Page 286 bottom: Tom Bochsler/Pearson Education. Page 290: iStockphoto. Page 291: md8speed/Shutterstock. **Chapter 7** Page 297 center: YegorPiaskovsky/iStockphoto. Page 298 bottom left: Comstock Stock Photography. Page 298 bottom right: Uluc Ceylani/Shutterstock. Page 300 top: Poznyakov/Shutterstock. Page 300 center: Person Education. Page 300 bottom: iStockphoto. Page 301 top right: Bob Richards/Sierra Pacific Innovations Corporation. Page 301 center right: Bonita R. Cheshier/Shutterstock. Page 306 top: Karin Hildebrand Lau/ Shutterstock. Page 306 bottom: Tom Bochsler/Pearson Education. Page 307 top: Richard Megna/Fundamental Photographs. Page 307 center: Wabash Instrument Corp/Fundamental Photographs. Page 308 center: American National Standards Institute/Pearson Education. Page 308 top left: mjs1973/iStockphoto. Page 308 top right: Jerry Mason/Photo Researchers, Inc. Page 309 top 2nd from left: Andrew Lambert Photography/Photo Researchers, Inc. Page 309 top 3rd from left: Andrew Lambert Photography/Photo Researchers, Inc. Page 309 top right: Andrew Lambert Photography/Photo Researchers, Inc. Page 309 bottom: American National Standards Institute/Pearson Education. Page 313 top: Segre Collection/AIP/Photo Researchers, Inc. Page 314 center: Stephen Dunn/Getty Images. Page 314 bottom: Reuters/ Tim Sharp. Page 329: Bob Richards/Sierra Pacific Innovations Corporation. **Chapter 8** Page 336 bottom: Ilya Yefimovich Repin. Page 337 top left: Charles D Winters/Photo Researchers, Inc. Page 337 top right: Richard Megna/Fundamental Photographs. Page 365 2nd from left: Richard Megna/Fundamental Photographs. Page 365 3rd from left: http:// images-of-elements.com/aluminium.php. Page 365 5th from left: Charles D Winters/Photo Researchers, Inc. Page 365 6th from left: Dorling Kindersley Publishing. Page 365 7th from left: Charles D Winters/Photo Researchers, Inc. Page 365 1st from top: Dorling Kindersley. Page 365 2nd from top: Charles D Winters/Photo Researchers, Inc. Page 365 3rd from top: Dorling Kindersley. Page 365 4th from top: Manamana/Shutterstock. Page 365 5th from top: Charles D Winters/Photo Researchers, Inc. Page 367 bottom: Andrew Lambert Photography/SPL/Photo Researchers, Inc. Page 368 top: Richard Megna/Fundamental Photographs. Page 369 top: Richard Megna/Fundamental Photographs. Page 370 top: Nukepills.com. Page 370 bottom: Glenn Grant/National Science Foundation and US Antarctic Program. **Chapter 9** Page 382 top: The Bancroft Library/Photo Researchers, Inc. Page 383 top left: Madlen/Shutterstock. Page 383 top right: John A Rizzo/Getty Images. Page 383 center: Dorling Kindersley. Page 390 bottom: Richard Megna/Fundamental Photographs. Page 391 top: Allies Interactive Services Pvt. Ltd./Shutterstock. Page 407 top: Chubykin Arkady/Shutterstock. Page 407 bottom: Syda Productions/Shutterstock. Page 414 bottom: robeo/iStockphoto. **Chapter 10** Page 428 top: Renn Sminkey/Pearson Education. Page 428 center: Renn Sminkey/Pearson Education. Page 429 top right: Renn Sminkey/ Pearson Education. Page 429 bottom right: Renn Sminkey/Pearson Education. Page 442 top center: Kip Peticolas/Fundamental Photographs. Page 442 top right: Richard Megna/ Fundamental Photographs. Page 442 center right: blueee/Fotolia. Page 467 center: Richard Megna/Fundamental Photographs. **Chapter 11** Page 483 top: Eric Isselee/iStockphoto. Page 483 bottom: Andrew Syred/Photo Researchers, Inc. Page 491 bottom: Richard Megna/ Fundamental Photographs. Page 497 top right: Douglas Allen/iStockphoto. Page 497 bottom right: Kuzmik/Shutterstock. Page 498 top left: NASA Johnson Space Center. Page 499 bottom right: Pearson Education. Page 499 top right: Iris Sample Processing. Page 499 center right: Richard Megna/Fundamental Photographs. Page 499 bottom right:

Index

Caproic acid, 1003
Carbaloy, 1089
Carbides, 1047–1048
Carbohydrates, 1006–1010
  complex, 1009–1010
  simple, 1007–1009
  structure of, 1006
Carbon, 57, 63, 1044–1050. *See also* Hydrocarbons; Organic chemistry
  ability to form double and triple bonds, 952
  chemistry of life and, 66
  electron configuration for, 342
  elemental, 1044–1047
  hybridization in, 446–447
  Lewis structure of, 384
  molar entropies of allotropes of, 834
  orbital diagram for, 342, 466
  organic compounds, 123–124
  reactions of
    with oxygen, 252–253
    with sulfur, 179
    with water, 272
  tendency to catenate, 953
  tendency to form four covalent bonds, 952
  uniqueness of, 950, 952–953
λ-Carbon, 1010–1011
Carbon-14 dating, 924–925
Carbonate(s), 99, 740, 1049–1050
  in gas-evolution reactions, 175
  solubilities of, 788
Carbonate ion, 721, 768
  solubility and, 162
Carbon black, 1046
Carbon dioxide, 2, 49–50, 1048
  atmospheric, 213, 281–282
  chemical formula for, 90
  formula mass of, 107
  from fossil fuel combustion, 139–141, 281–282
  as greenhouse gas, 139, 140
  molar mass of, 107
  molecular geometry of, 427, 439
  phase diagrams of, 515
  reaction between water and, 740, 1121
  solid (dry ice), 291, 509, 527, 1048
    sublimation of, 10
  solubility of, 1049
  supercritical, 509
  van der Waals constants for, 232
  from volcanoes, 140, 142
  in water, Henry's law constants for, 558
Carbonic acid, 698, 704, 740, 754, 768, 1049
  ionization constants for, 732
Carbonic anhydrase, 768, 1121–1122
Carbonization, 1045
Carbon monoxide, 1–2, 20–21, 49–50, 628, 629, 1049
  reaction between hydroxyl radical and, 407
  reaction between nitrogen dioxide and, 624–625
Carbon monoxide ligand, 1105
Carbon nanotubes, 1035–1036
Carbon oxides, 1048–1049
Carbon tetrachloride, 550
  chemical formula for, 90
  freezing point depression and boiling point elevation constants for, 575
  van der Waals constants for, 232
Carbonyl chloride (phosgene), 1049
Carbonyl group in aldehydes and ketones, 978, 981
  charge density plots of, 981
Carbonyl sulfide, 1049

Carboxylic acids, 699, 981–983
  functional group of, 975
  general formula for, 126
  naming, 981
  reactions of, 982–983
Carlsbad Caverns National Park, 788
Carnotite, 1077
Cars, hybrid, 251
Carvone, 980
Cassiterite, 1077
Catalysis, 627–632
  enzymes, 631–632
  homogeneous and heterogeneous, 629–631
Catalytic converter, 628–629
Cataracts, 300
Catenation of carbon, 953
Cathode, 867–868
  in electrolytic cell, 891–893
  in voltaic cell, 867–868
Cathode rays, 51–52
Cathode ray tube, 51–52
Cathode reaction in batteries, 887–890
Cathodic regions, 899
Cation(s), 61, 89
  as conjugate acids of weak bases, 728
  as counterions of strong bases, 728
  electrolysis of mixture of anions and, 893
  electron configuration and, 349, 355
  as Lewis acids, 739
  metal, 728–729
  periodic table and, 64
  radii of, 357
  in salts, 729–730
  as weak acids, 728–729
Cell diagram, 867
Cell potential (E_{cell}) or cell emf, 868
  concentration and, 881–886
Cells, taste, 426
Cellular fluids, 546
Cellulose, 1009–1010
Celsius (°C) scale, 15–16
Cementite, 1048
Centipoise (cP), 498
Centi prefix, 17
Cesium
  charge of, 97
  properties of, 357
Cesium chloride, 1.498
CFCs. *See* Chlorofluorocarbons
Chadwick, James, 55
Chain reaction in fission of uranium-235, 928–929
Chalcopyrite, 1090
  extracting copper from, 1080
Champagne, 195
Charcoal, 1045–1046
  density of, 19
Charles, J. A. C., 203
Charles's law, 202–205, 222
  kinetic molecular theory and, 224
Chelate, 1106
Chelating agents, 1106, 1119
Chemical analysis, coordination compounds used in, 1119
Chemical bonds. *See* Bond(s); Bonding
Chemical changes, 9–11. *See also* Reaction(s)
Chemical energy, 13, 248
Chemical equations. *See* Equation(s)
Chemical formula(s), 90–92
  composition of compounds from, 112–113
  conversion factors from, 112–113

determining from experimental data, 114–119
    combustion analysis, 117–119
    for compounds, 116–117
  elemental composition and, 113
  for ionic compounds, 96–97
  from mass percent composition, 110–111
Chemical gradient, 335
Chemical kinetics. *See* Reaction rate(s)
Chemical potential, 815–816
  Gibbs free energy, 828–832
Chemical property, 9
Chemical quantities, 138–151
Chemical reactions. *See* Reaction(s)
Chemical symbol, 56–57
Chemistry, defined, 3
Chernobyl nuclear accident (1986), 370, 931
Cherries, pH of, 708, 709
Chiral, 1112
Chiral complex, 1112
Chiral environment, chemical behavior in, 959
Chiral molecule, 958
Chlorate, 99
Chlordane, 564
Chloride ion, 1105
Chloride minerals, 1077
Chlorides, 98
  insoluble, 793
Chlorine, 57, 58, 64, 396
  catalytic ozone destruction and, 628–629
  dipole moment of, 397
  electron affinity of, 363
  electron configuration of, 347, 358
  electron configuration of anion, 358
  elemental, 1064
  ionization energies of, 360, 363
  Lewis structure of, 392
  mass spectrum of, 68
  properties of, 88, 368, 1062
  reactions of
    with chloromethane, 969
    with ethene, 970
    with hydrogen, 176
    with iron, 368
    with ozone, 241
    with potassium, 384–385
    with sodium, 48, 176, 386
  van der Waals constants for, 232
Chlorine dioxide, 1066
Chlorine fluoride, dipole moment of, 397
Chlorine oxides, 1066
Chlorite, 99
Chlorobenzene, 972
Chloroethane, 969, 970
Chloroethene, 985
1-Chloro-3-ethylbenzene, 973
Chlorofluorocarbons (CFCs), 109, 607–608, 629, 1058
Chloroform, 548
  freezing point depression and boiling point elevation constants for, 575
Chloromethane, 969
  reaction between chlorine and, 969
Chlorophyll, 1121
1-Chloropropane, 971
2-Chloropropane, 971
Chlorous acid, 705
Cholesterol, 1005–1006
Chromate, 99
Chromate compounds, 1088
Chromate ion, 1088
Chromite, 1087–1088